DR. JAMES BECKETT

TWENTY-FIFTH EDITION

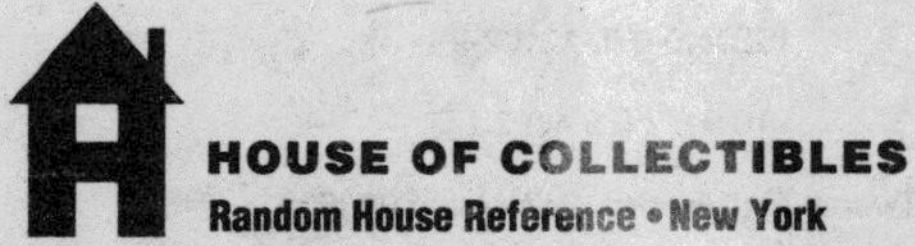

Important Notice: All of the information, including valuations, in this book has been compiled from the most reliable sources, and every effort has been made to eliminate errors and questionable data. Nevertheless, the possibility of error, in a work of such immense scope, always exists. The publisher will not be held responsible for losses that may occur in the purchase, sale, or other transaction of items because of information contained herein. Readers who feel they have discovered errors are invited to *write* and inform us, so they may be corrected in subsequent editions. Those seeking further information on the topics covered in this book are advised to refer to the complete line of *Official Price Guides* published by the House of Collectibles.

House of Collectibles and colophon
are trademarks of Random House, Inc.

www.houseofcollectibles.com

Published by:
House of Collectibles
Random House Reference
New York, New York

Distributed by The Random House Information Group,
a division of Random House, Inc.,
New York, and simultaneously in Canada by
Random House of Canada Limited, Toronto.
Random House is a registered trademark of Random House, Inc.

www.randomhouse.com

Manufactured in the United States of America

ISSN: 0748-1365

ISBN: 0-375-72102-9

10 9 8 7 6 5 4 3 2 1

Twenty-Fifth Edition: September 2005

Table of Contents

About the Author xi
How to Use This Book xi
Prices in This Guide xii
Acknowledgments xii
Introduction xii
How to Collect 1
Obtaining Cards 1
Preserving Your Cards 2
Collecting vs. Investing 2
Terminology 3
Glossary/Legend 3
Understanding Card Values 7
Determining Value 7
Regional Variation 8
Set Prices 8
Scarce Series 9
Grading Your Cards 9
Centering 9
Corner Wear 10
Creases 10
Alterations 10
Categorization of Defects 11
Condition Guide 11
Selling Your Cards 12
Interesting Notes 14
History of Football Cards 14
Additional Reading 18

2000 Absolute 19
2000 Absolute Boss Hogg Autographs 20
2001 Absolute Memorabilia 20
2002 Absolute Memorabilia 21
2003 Absolute Memorabilia 22
2004 Absolute Memorabilia 22
2004 Absolute Memorabilia Retail 23
2000 Aurora 23
2004 Bazooka 24
1948 Bowman 25
1950 Bowman 26
1951 Bowman 26
1952 Bowman Large 27
1952 Bowman Small 28
1953 Bowman 28
1954 Bowman 29
1955 Bowman 29
1993 Bowman 30
1994 Bowman 32
1995 Bowman 34
1999 Bowman 35
2000 Bowman 36
2001 Bowman 37
2002 Bowman 38
2003 Bowman 39
2004 Bowman 41
1998 Bowman Chrome 42
1998 Bowman Chrome Golden Anniversary 43
1998 Bowman Chrome Interstate Refractors 43
1998 Bowman Chrome Refractors 43
2000 Bowman Chrome 43
2000 Bowman Chrome Refractors 44
2000 Bowman Chrome Rookie Autographs 44
2001 Bowman Chrome 44
2001 Bowman Chrome Gold Refractors 45
2001 Bowman Chrome Xfractors 45
2002 Bowman Chrome 45
2002 Bowman Chrome Refractors 46
2002 Bowman Chrome Refractors Gold 46
2002 Bowman Chrome Xfractors 46
2003 Bowman Chrome 46
2003 Bowman Chrome Refractors 47
2003 Bowman Chrome Uncircluated Blue Refractors 47
2003 Bowman Chrome Gold Refractors 48
2003 Bowman Chrome Red Refractors 48
2003 Bowman Chrome Xfractors 48
2004 Bowman Chrome 48
2004 Bowman Chrome Gold Refractors 49
2004 Bowman Chrome Red Refractors 49
2004 Bowman Chrome Refractors 49
2004 Bowman Chrome Uncirculated White Refractors 49
2004 Bowman Chrome Xfractors 49
2000 Bowman Reserve 49
1995 Bowman's Best 50
1995 Bowman's Best Refractors 51
1996 Bowman's Best 51
1996 Bowman's Best Atomic Refractors 51
1996 Bowman's Best Refractors 51
1997 Bowman's Best 51
1997 Bowman's Best Atomic Refractors 52
1997 Bowman's Best Refractors 52
1999 Bowman's Best 52
2000 Bowman's Best 53
2000 Bowman's Best Acetate Parallel 53
2001 Bowman's Best 53
2002 Bowman's Best 54
2002 Bowman's Best Blue 55
2002 Bowman's Best Gold 55
2002 Bowman's Best Red 55
2003 Bowman's Best 55
2003 Bowman's Best Blue 56
2003 Bowman's Best Red 56
2004 Bowman's Best 56
2004 Bowman's Best Green 57
2004 Bowman's Best Red 57
1996 Collector's Edge Cowboybilia Autographs 57
1999 Collector's Edge Advantage 57
2000 Collector's Edge EG 58
1998 Collector's Edge First Place 59
1999 Collector's Edge First Place 60
1999 Collector's Edge Fury 61
1998 Collector's Edge Masters 61
1999 Collector's Edge Masters 62
2000 Collector's Edge Masters 63
1999 Collector's Edge Odyssey 64
2000 Collector's Edge Odyssey 65
1999 Collector's Edge Supreme 66
2000 Collector's Edge Supreme 67
2000 Collector's Edge T3 68
1999 Collector's Edge Triumph 69
1996 Crown Royale 70
1996 Crown Royale Blue 70
1996 Crown Royale Silver 70
1997 Crown Royale 70
1997 Crown Royale Blue Holofoil 71
1997 Crown Royale Gold Holofoil 71
1997 Crown Royale Silver 71
1999 Crown Royale 71
2000 Crown Royale 72
2001 Crown Royale 72
2002 Crown Royale 73
2000 Dominion 74
1999 Donruss 75
2000 Donruss 76
2000 Donruss Rookie Gridiron Kings Studio Autographs 77
2002 Donruss 77
2001 Donruss Classics 79
2002 Donruss Classics 80
2002 Donruss Classics Timeless Tributes 80
2003 Donruss Classics 80
2003 Donruss Classics Timeless Tributes 82
2004 Donruss Classics 82
2004 Donruss Classics Timeless Tributes Green 83
2004 Donruss Classics Timeless Tributes Red 83
1999 Donruss Elite 83
2000 Donruss Elite 84

Table of Contents

2000 Donruss Elite Rookie Die Cuts 85
2001 Donruss Elite 85
2001 Donruss Elite Aspirations 85
2001 Donruss Elite Status 86
2002 Donruss Elite 86
2002 Donruss Elite Aspirations 86
2002 Donruss Elite Status 87
2003 Donruss Elite 87
2003 Donruss Elite Aspirations 87
2003 Donruss Elite Status 88
2004 Donruss Elite 88
2004 Donruss Elite Aspirations 88
2004 Donruss Elite Status 88
1997 E-X2000 89
1997 E-X2000 Essential Credentials 89
1998 E-X2001 89
1998 E-X2001 Essential Credentials Future 89
1999 E-X Century 89
1999 E-X Century Essential Credentials Future 90
1999 E-X Century Essential Credentials Now 90
1999 E-X Century Authen-Kicks 90
2000 E-X 90
2000 E-X Essential Credentials 91
2001 E-X 91
2001 E-X Essential Credentials 91
1995 Finest 91
1995 Finest Refractors 93
1996 Finest 93
1996 Finest Refractors 94
1997 Finest 94
1997 Finest Embossed 96
1997 Finest Embossed Refractors 96
1997 Finest Refractors 96
1998 Finest 96
1998 Finest No-Protectors 97
1998 Finest No-Protectors Refractors 97
1998 Finest Refractors 97
1999 Finest 97
1999 Finest Gold Refractors 98
1999 Finest Refractors 98
2000 Finest 98
2000 Finest Gold/Refractors 99
2001 Finest 99
2002 Finest 100
2002 Finest Refractors 100
2002 Finest Refractors Gold 100
2003 Finest 100
2003 Finest Refractors 101
2003 Finest Refractors Gold 101
2003 Finest Xfractors 101
2004 Finest 101
2004 Finest Refractors 102
2004 Finest Refractors Gold 102
2004 Finest Uncirculated Gold Xfractors 102
2002 Flair 102
2003 Flair 103
2004 Flair 103
2004 Flair Collection Row 1 104
1999 Flair Showcase 104
1999 Flair Showcase Legacy Collection 104
1960 Fleer 104
1961 Fleer 105
1962 Fleer 106
1963 Fleer 106
1990 Fleer Update 107
2000 Fleer Focus 107
2001 Fleer Focus 109
2002 Fleer Focus JE 109
2003 Fleer Focus 110
2003 Fleer Focus Anniversary Gold 111
2003 Fleer Focus Numbers Century 111
2001 Fleer Genuine 111
2002 Fleer Genuine 112
2004 Fleer Genuine 112
2001 Fleer Hot Prospects 113
2002 Fleer Hot Prospects 113
2003 Fleer Hot Prospects 114
2004 Fleer Hot Prospects 114
2004 Fleer Inscribed 115
2004 Fleer Inscribed Black Border Gold 115
2004 Fleer Inscribed Autographs Purple 115
2001 Fleer Legacy 116
2001 Fleer Legacy Ultimate Legacy 116
1999 Fleer Mystique 116
2000 Fleer Mystique 117
2000 Fleer Mystique Gold 117
2002 Fleer Platinum 117
2002 Fleer Platinum Finish 119
2003 Fleer Platinum 119
2003 Fleer Platinum Finish 120
2004 Fleer Platinum 120
2004 Fleer Platinum Finish 121
2001 Fleer Premium 121
2001 Fleer Premium Star Ruby 122
2002 Fleer Premium 122
2000 Fleer Showcase 123
2001 Fleer Showcase 123
2001 Fleer Showcase Legacy 124
2002 Fleer Showcase 124
2002 Fleer Showcase Legacy 125
2003 Fleer Showcase 125
2003 Fleer Showcase Legacy 125
2004 Fleer Showcase 125
2004 Fleer Showcase Legacy 126
2004 Fleer Sweet Sigs 126
2004 Fleer Sweet Sigs Black 127
2004 Fleer Sweet Sigs Gold 127
2002 Fleer Throwbacks 127
1999 Fleer Tradition 127
2000 Fleer Tradition 129
2001 Fleer Tradition 130
2001 Fleer Tradition Glossy 132
2002 Fleer Tradition 134
2003 Fleer Tradition 135
2004 Fleer Tradition 137
2004 Fleer Tradition Blue 139
2004 Fleer Tradition Crystal 139
2004 Fleer Tradition Draft Day 139
2004 Fleer Tradition Green 139
2000 Greats of the Game 139
2004 Greats of the Game 140
2004 Greats of the Game Green/Red 140
2002 Gridiron Kings 140
2003 Gridiron Kings 141
2003 Gridiron Kings Bronze 142
2003 Gridiron Kings Gold 142
2003 Gridiron Kings Silver 142
2000 Impact 142
1948 Leaf 143
1949 Leaf 143
1999 Leaf Certified 144
2000 Leaf Certified 145
2000 Leaf Certified Mirror Gold 146
2000 Leaf Certified Mirror Red 146
2000 Leaf Certified Rookie Die Cuts 146
2001 Leaf Certified Materials 146
2001 Leaf Certified Materials Mirror Gold 146
2001 Leaf Certified Materials Mirror Red 146
2002 Leaf Certified 147
2002 Leaf Certified Mirror Red 147
2003 Leaf Certified Materials 147
2003 Leaf Certified Materials Mirror Red 148
2004 Leaf Certified Materials 148
2004 Leaf Certified Materials Mirror Blue 149
2004 Leaf Certified Materials Mirror Gold 149
2004 Leaf Certified Materials Mirror Red 149
2004 Leaf Certified Materials Mirror White 149
2000 Leaf Limited 149
2000 Leaf Limited Limited Series 151
2003 Leaf Limited 151
2003 Leaf Limited Bronze Spotlight 152
2003 Leaf Limited Gold Spotlight 152
2003 Leaf Limited Silver Spotlight 152
2004 Leaf Limited 152
2004 Leaf Limited Bronze Spotlight 153
2004 Leaf Limited Gold Spotlight 153
2004 Leaf Limited Silver Spotlight 153
1998 Leaf Rookies and Stars 153
1998 Leaf Rookies and Stars Longevity 155
1998 Leaf Rookies and Stars True Blue 155
1999 Leaf Rookies and Stars 155
1999 Leaf Rookies and Stars Longevity 156
2000 Leaf Rookies and Stars 156
2000 Leaf Rookies and Stars Longevity 157

Table of Contents

2000 Leaf Rookies and Stars Autographs 157
2001 Leaf Rookies and Stars 158
2001 Leaf Rookies and Stars Longevity 159
2002 Leaf Rookies and Stars 159
2002 Leaf Rookies and Stars Longevity 160
2003 Leaf Rookies and Stars 160
2003 Leaf Rookies and Stars Longevity 161
2004 Leaf Rookies and Stars 161
2004 Leaf Rookies and Stars Longevity Parallel 163
2004 Leaf Rookies and Stars Longevity Holofoil Parallel 163
2004 Leaf Rookies and Stars Longevity True Blue Parallel 163
2004 Leaf Rookies and Stars Longevity Black 163
2004 Leaf Rookies and Stars Longevity Emerald 163
2004 Leaf Rookies and Stars Longevity Gold 163
2004 Leaf Rookies and Stars Longevity Ruby 163
2004 Leaf Rookies and Stars Longevity Sapphire 163
1999 Metal Universe 163
2000 Metal 164
1991 Pacific 166
1999 Pacific 169
1999 Pacific Copper 171
1999 Pacific Gold 171
1999 Pacific Opening Day 171
1999 Pacific Platinum Blue 171
1999 Pacific Red 171
2000 Pacific 171
2001 Pacific 173
2002 Pacific 175
2002 Pacific Adrenaline 177
2001 Pacific Dynagon 179
2001 Pacific Dynagon Retail 179
2002 Pacific Exclusive 179
2002 Pacific Heads Up 180
2001 Pacific Impressions 181
2001 Pacific Invincible 182
2001 Pacific Invincible Blue 183
2001 Pacific Invincible Premiere Date 183
2001 Pacific Invincible Red 183
1999 Pacific Omega 184
2000 Pacific Omega 185
1997 Pacific Philadelphia 186
1995 Pacific Prisms 187
1999 Pacific Prisms 188
2001 Pacific Prism Atomic 189
2001 Pacific Prism Atomic Blue 190
2001 Pacific Prism Atomic Gold 190
2001 Pacific Prism Atomic Red 190
2000 Pacific Prism Prospects 190
1998 Paramount 191
1999 Paramount 192
2000 Paramount 193
1964 Philadelphia 194
1965 Philadelphia 195
1966 Philadelphia 196
1967 Philadelphia 197
1993 Pinnacle Rookies 198
1997 Pinnacle Totally Certified Platinum Red 198
1997 Pinnacle Totally Certified Platinum Blue 199
1997 Pinnacle Totally Certified Platinum Gold 199
1993 Playoff 199
1998 Playoff Contenders Ticket 200
1998 Playoff Contenders Ticket Red 201
1999 Playoff Contenders SSD 201
1999 Playoff Contenders SSD Finesse Gold 202
1999 Playoff Contenders SSD Power Blue 202
1999 Playoff Contenders SSD Speed Red 202
2000 Playoff Contenders 202
2000 Playoff Contenders Championship Ticket 203
2001 Playoff Contenders 204
2001 Playoff Contenders Championship Ticket 205
2001 Playoff Contenders Legendary Contenders Autographs 205
2002 Playoff Contenders 205
2002 Playoff Contenders Championship Ticket 206
2003 Playoff Contenders 207
2003 Playoff Contenders Playoff Ticket 208
2004 Playoff Contenders 208
2004 Playoff Contenders Playoff Ticket 209
2004 Playoff Contenders Legendary Contenders Orange 209
2003 Playoff Hogg Heaven 210
2003 Playoff Hogg Heaven Hogg Wild 211
2004 Playoff Hogg Heaven 211
2004 Playoff Hogg Heaven Hogg Wild 211
2001 Playoff Honors 212
2002 Playoff Honors 213
2002 Playoff Honors O's 214
2002 Playoff Honors X's 214
2003 Playoff Honors 214
2003 Playoff Honors X's 215
2004 Playoff Honors 215
2004 Playoff Honors X's 216
1998 Playoff Momentum Hobby 216
1998 Playoff Momentum Hobby Gold 217
1999 Playoff Momentum SSD 217
2000 Playoff Momentum 218
2000 Playoff Momentum O's 219
2000 Playoff Momentum X's 219
2001 Playoff Preferred 219
2001 Playoff Preferred Signatures Bronze 220
2001 Playoff Preferred Signatures Silver 221
1999 Playoff Prestige EXP 221
1999 Playoff Prestige SSD 222
2000 Playoff Prestige 223
2002 Playoff Prestige 224
2002 Playoff Prestige Stars of the NFL Autographs 225
2003 Playoff Prestige 225
2003 Playoff Prestige Xtra Points Green 226
2003 Playoff Prestige Xtra Points Purple 226
2004 Playoff Prestige 226
2004 Playoff Prestige Xtra Points Black 227
2004 Playoff Prestige Xtra Points Green 227
2004 Playoff Prestige Xtra Points Purple 227
2004 Playoff Prestige Xtra Points Red 227
2005 Playoff Prestige 227
2005 Playoff Prestige Xtra Points Black 228
2005 Playoff Prestige Xtra Points Green 228
2005 Playoff Prestige Xtra Points Purple 228
2005 Playoff Prestige Xtra Points Red 228
2005 Playoff Prestige Changing Stripes 228
2005 Playoff Prestige Draft Picks 229
2005 Playoff Prestige Draft Picks Rights Autographs 229
2005 Playoff Prestige Fans of the Game 229
2005 Playoff Prestige Fans of the Game Autographs 229
2005 Playoff Prestige Game Day Jerseys 229
2005 Playoff Prestige Gridiron Heritage 229
2005 Playoff Prestige Gridiron Heritage Jerseys 229
2005 Playoff Prestige League Leaders 229
2005 Playoff Prestige League Leaders Jerseys 230
2005 Playoff Prestige Prestigious Pros Orange 230
2005 Playoff Prestige Prestigious Pros Gold Jerseys 231
2005 Playoff Prestige Stars of the NFL 231
2005 Playoff Prestige Stars of the NFL Jersey 231
2005 Playoff Prestige Super Bowl Heroes 231
2005 Playoff Prestige Super Bowl Heroes Holofoil 231
2005 Playoff Prestige Turning Pro Jerseys 231
2002 Playoff Prime Signatures 231
2004 Playoff Prime Signatures 232
2004 Playoff Prime Signatures Bronze Proofs 233
2004 Playoff Prime Signatures Gold Proofs 233
2004 Playoff Prime Signatures Silver Proofs 233
1993 Power Update Prospects 233
2000 Private Stock 233
2001 Private Stock 234
2001 Private Stock Blue Framed 235
2001 Private Stock Gold Framed 235
2001 Private Stock Premiere Date 235
2001 Private Stock Retail 235
2001 Private Stock Silver Framed 235
2002 Private Stock 235
1991 Pro Line Portraits Autographs 236
1992 Pro Line Portraits Autographs 237
1992 Pro Line Profiles Autographs 238
1993 Pro Line Live Autographs 238
1993 Pro Line Portraits Autographs 238
1993 Pro Line Profiles Autographs 239
1994 Pro Line Live Autographs 239
1995 Pro Line Autographs 239
1995 Pro Line Autograph Printer's Proofs 240
1996 Pro Line Autographs Gold 240
1996 Pro Line Autographs Blue 241

Table of Contents

1997 Pro Line Autographs 241
1997 Pro Line Autographs Emerald 241
1996 Pro Line Memorabilia Rookie Autographs 241
1989 Pro Set 241
1990 Pro Set 244
1991 Pro Set 249
2000 Quantum Leaf 254
2001 Quantum Leaf 255
2001 Quantum Leaf Infinity Green 257
2001 Quantum Leaf Infinity Purple 257
2001 Quantum Leaf Infinity Red 257
2004 Reflections 257
2004 Reflections Green 258
2004 Reflections Red 258
1999 Revolution 258
2000 Revolution 259
1989 Score 260
1989 Score Supplemental 261
1990 Score Supplemental 262
1991 Score 262
1999 Score 265
1999 Score Supplemental 267
2000 Score 267
2001 Score 268
2002 Score 270
2003 Score 271
2003 Score Scorecard 273
2004 Score 273
2004 Score Glossy 275
2004 Score Scorecard 275
2004 Score Inscriptions 275
2001 Score Select 275
1993 Select 276
1994 Select 277
1995 Select Certified 278
1995 Select Certified Mirror Gold 279
1996 Select Certified 279
1996 Select Certified Artist's Proofs 279
1996 Select Certified Blue 279
1996 Select Certified Mirror Blue 279
1996 Select Certified Mirror Gold 279
1996 Select Certified Mirror Red 279
1996 Select Certified Mirror Red Premium Stock 279
1996 Select Certified Premium Stock 279
1996 Select Certified Red 279
2000 SkyBox 279
1999 SkyBox Dominion 281
2003 SkyBox LE 282
2003 SkyBox LE Artist Proofs 283
2003 SkyBox LE Gold Proofs 283
2004 SkyBox LE 283
2004 SkyBox LE Black Border Red 283
2004 SkyBox LE Gold 283
2004 SkyBox LE Black Border Platinum 283
1999 SkyBox Molten Metal 283
1998 SkyBox Premium 284
1998 SkyBox Premium Star Rubies 285
1999 SkyBox Premium 285
1993 SP 287
1994 SP 288
1994 SP Die Cuts 289
1995 SP 289
1996 SP 290
1997 SP Authentic 290
1998 SP Authentic 291
1998 SP Authentic Die Cuts 292
1999 SP Authentic 292
1999 SP Authentic Excitement 293
1999 SP Authentic Excitement Gold 293
1999 SP Authentic Player's Ink Purple 293
2000 SP Authentic 293
2001 SP Authentic 294
2001 SP Authentic Rookie Gold 100 295
2002 SP Authentic 295
2002 SP Authentic Gold 296
2003 SP Authentic 296
2003 SP Authentic Gold 297
2004 SP Authentic 298
2004 SP Authentic Gold 298
2001 SP Game Used Edition 299
2003 SP Game Used Edition 299
2003 SP Game Used Edition Gold Rookies 300
2004 SP Game Used Edition 300
2004 SP Game Used Edition Gold 301
2002 SP Legendary Cuts 301
2002 SP Legendary Cuts Autographs 302
1999 SP Signature 302
1999 SP Signature Autographs 303
1999 SP Signature Autographs Gold 304
2003 SP Signature 304
2003 SP Signature Autographs Black Ink 305
2003 SP Signature Autographs Blue Ink 305
2003 SP Signature Autographs Blue Ink Numbered 305
2003 SP Signature Autographs Green Ink 305
2003 SP Signature Autographs Red Ink 305
2003 SP Signature Dual Autographs 306
1999 Sports Illustrated 306
1999 Sports Illustrated Autographs 306
1996 SPx 307
1998 SPx Finite 307
1998 SPx Finite Radiance 309
1999 SPx 309
1999 SPx Radiance 309
2000 SPx 310
2000 SPx Spectrum 310
2000 SPx Winning Materials Autographs 311
2001 SPx 311
2001 SPx Winning Materials 312
2002 SPx 313
2002 SPx Supreme Signatures 314
2003 SPx 314
2003 SPx Spectrum 315
2003 SPx Supreme Signatures 315
2003 SPx Supreme Signatures Spectrum 315
2003 SPx Winning Materials Patches Autographs 315
2003 SPx Winning Materials Team Logos 315
2003 SPx Winning Materials Team Logos Spectrum 315
2004 SPx 316
2004 SPx Spectrum Gold 317
2004 SPx Rookie Swatch Supremacy 317
2004 SPx Rookie Winning Materials 317
2004 SPx Super Scripts Autographs 317
2004 SPx Super Scripts Triple Autographs 317
2004 SPx Swatch Supremacy 318
2004 SPx Swatch Supremacy Autographs 318
2004 SPx Winning Materials 318
2004 SPx Winning Materials Autographs 318
1991 Stadium Club 319
1992 Stadium Club 321
1993 Stadium Club 324
1997 Stadium Club Co-Signers 327
1998 Stadium Club Co-Signers 328
1999 Stadium Club 328
1999 Stadium Club Co-Signers 329
1999 Stadium Club Lone Star Autographs 329
2000 Stadium Club 329
2000 Stadium Club Co-Signers 330
2000 Stadium Club Lone Star Signatures 330
2000 Stadium Club Pro Bowl Jerseys Autographs 330
2001 Stadium Club Common Threads Autographs 330
2001 Stadium Club Co-Signers 330
2001 Stadium Club Lone Star Signatures 330
2001 Stadium Club Pro Bowl Jerseys Autographs 331
2002 Stadium Club Co-Signers 331
2002 Stadium Club Lone Star Signatures 331
1999 Stadium Club Chrome 331
2002 Sweet Spot 332
2003 Sweet Spot 332
2003 Sweet Spot Gold 333
2003 Sweet Spot Jerseys 334
2003 Sweet Spot Signatures 334
2004 Sweet Spot 334
2004 Sweet Spot Gold 335
2004 Sweet Spot Silver 335
2004 Sweet Spot Gold Rookie Autographs 335
2004 Sweet Spot Signatures 336
2004 Sweet Spot Sweet Panel Signatures 336
2004 Sweet Spot Sweet Swatches 336
2001 Titanium 336
2001 Titanium Retail 337
2002 Titanium 338
1950 Topps Felt Backs 339
1951 Topps Magic 339
1955 Topps All-American 340

Table of Contents

1956 Topps 340
1957 Topps 341
1958 Topps 342
1959 Topps 343
1960 Topps 344
1961 Topps 345
1962 Topps 346
1963 Topps 347
1964 Topps 348
1965 Topps 349
1966 Topps 349
1967 Topps 350
1968 Topps 351
1969 Topps 352
1970 Topps 353
1971 Topps 354
1972 Topps 356
1973 Topps 357
1974 Topps 360
1975 Topps 362
1976 Topps 365
1977 Topps 367
1978 Topps 370
1979 Topps 373
1980 Topps 376
1981 Topps 379
1982 Topps 382
1983 Topps 385
1984 Topps 387
1984 Topps USFL 389
1985 Topps 390
1985 Topps USFL 392
1986 Topps 393
1987 Topps 395
1988 Topps 397
1989 Topps 399
1989 Topps Traded 401
1990 Topps Traded 401
1997 Topps Hall of Fame Class Autographs 402
1998 Topps Autographs 402
1999 Topps 402
1999 Topps Autographs 404
1999 Topps Hall of Fame Autographs 404
2000 Topps 404
2000 Topps Autographs 406
2000 Topps Hall of Fame Autographs 406
2000 Topps Unitas Reprints Autographs 406
2000 Topps Rookie Premier Autographs 406
2001 Topps 406
2001 Topps Autographs 408
2001 Topps Hall of Fame Autographs 408
2001 Topps King of Kings 408
2001 Topps King of Kings Golden Edition 408
2001 Topps Pro Bowl Jerseys 408
2001 Topps Pro Bowl Jerseys Autographs 408
2001 Topps Rookie Premier Autographs 409
2001 Topps Rookie Reprint Jerseys 409
2001 Topps Team Topps Legends Autographs 409
2002 Topps 409
2002 Topps Autographs 411
2002 Topps King of Kings Super Bowl MVP's 411
2002 Topps Ring of Honor Autographs 411
2002 Topps Rookie Premier Autographs 411
2002 Topps Super Bowl Goal Posts 411
2003 Topps 412
2003 Topps Black 413
2003 Topps Collection 413
2003 Topps First Edition 413
2003 Topps Gold 413
2003 Topps Autographs 413
2003 Topps Pro Bowl Jerseys 413
2003 Topps Record Breakers Autographs 414
2003 Topps Record Breakers Autographs Duals 414
2003 Topps Record Breakers Jerseys 414
2003 Topps Record Breakers Jerseys Duals 414
2003 Topps Rookie Premiere Autographs 414
2003 Topps Split the Uprights 414
2003 Topps Super Tix 414
2004 Topps 415
2004 Topps Black 416
2004 Topps Collection 416
2004 Topps First Edition 416
2004 Topps Gold 416
2004 Topps Autographs 416
2004 Topps Game Breakers Relics 417
2004 Topps Hall of Fame Autographs 417
2004 Topps Hobby Masters 417
2004 Topps League Leaders Relics 417
2004 Topps Own the Game 417
2004 Topps Premiere Prospects 417
2004 Topps Premiere Prospects Autographs 417
2004 Topps Pro Bowl Jerseys 418
2004 Topps Ring of Honor Coaches' Cuts 418
2004 Topps Rookie Premiere Autographs 418
2004 Topps Super Tix 418
2003 Topps All American 418
2003 Topps All American Foil 419
2003 Topps All American Foil Gold 419
2003 Topps All American Autographs 419
2003 Topps All American Campus Connection Autographs 419
2003 Topps All American Conference Call Autographs 419
2001 Topps Archives 419
2001 Topps Archives Rookie Reprint Autographs 420
2001 Topps Archives Reserve Rookie Reprint Autographs 420
1996 Topps Chrome 421
1996 Topps Chrome Refractors 421
1997 Topps Chrome 421
1997 Topps Chrome Refractors 422
1998 Topps Chrome 422
1998 Topps Chrome Refractors 423
1999 Topps Chrome 423
1999 Topps Chrome Refractors 424
2000 Topps Chrome 424
2000 Topps Chrome Refractors 425
2001 Topps Chrome 425
2001 Topps Chrome Refractors 426
2001 Topps Chrome King of Kings 426
2001 Topps Chrome Rookie Reprint Jerseys 427
2002 Topps Chrome 427
2002 Topps Chrome Refractors 428
2002 Topps Chrome King of Kings Super Bowl MVP's 428
2002 Topps Chrome Super Bowl Goal Posts 428
2003 Topps Chrome 428
2003 Topps Chrome Black Refractors 429
2003 Topps Chrome Gold Xfractors 429
2003 Topps Chrome Gridiron Badges 429
2003 Topps Chrome Pro Bowl Jerseys 429
2003 Topps Chrome Record Breakers Jerseys 430
2004 Topps Chrome 430
2004 Topps Chrome Black Refractors 431
2004 Topps Chrome Gold Xfractors 431
2004 Topps Chrome Refractors 431
2004 Topps Chrome Gridiron Badges 431
2004 Topps Chrome Premiere Prospects 431
2004 Topps Chrome Premium Performers Autographed Jerseys 431
2004 Topps Chrome Pro Bowl Jerseys 432
2001 Topps Debut 432
2002 Topps Debut 432
2002 Topps Debut Red 433
2003 Topps Draft Picks and Prospects 433
2003 Topps Draft Picks and Prospects Chrome 434
2003 Topps Draft Picks and Prospects Chrome Gold Refractors 434
2003 Topps Draft Picks and Prospects Class Marks Autographs 434
2003 Topps Draft Picks and Prospects Classmate Cuts 434
2003 Topps Draft Picks and Prospects Collegiate Cuts 435
2003 Topps Draft Picks and Prospects Pen Pals Autographs 435
2004 Topps Draft Picks and Prospects 435
2004 Topps Draft Picks and Prospects Chrome 436
2004 Topps Draft Picks and Prospects Gold Chrome ..436
2004 Topps Draft Picks and Prospects Big Dog Relics 436
2004 Topps Draft Picks and Prospects Class Marks Autographs 436
2004 Topps Draft Picks and Prospects Class Marks Autographs Silver 436
2004 Topps Draft Picks and Prospects Old School Dual Relics 436
2004 Topps Draft Picks and Prospects Quarterback Legacy Autographs 437

Table of Contents

2004 Topps Fan Favorites 437
2004 Topps Fan Favorites Chrome 437
2004 Topps Fan Favorites Chrome Refractors 437
2004 Topps Fan Favorites Autographs 437
2004 Topps Fan Favorites Co-Signers 438
2004 Topps Fan Favorites Jumbos 438
2000 Topps Gallery 438
2001 Topps Gallery 439
2001 Topps Gallery Autographs 440
2001 Topps Gallery Originals Relics 440
2002 Topps Gallery 440
2002 Topps Gallery Autographs 441
1999 Topps Gold Label Class 1 441
2000 Topps Gold Label Rookie Autographs 441
2001 Topps Heritage 442
2001 Topps Heritage Retrofractor 442
2001 Topps Heritage Classic Renditions 442
2001 Topps Heritage Real One Autographs 442
2002 Topps Heritage 443
2002 Topps Heritage Hall of Fame Autographs 443
2002 Topps Heritage Real One Autographs 443
2002 Topps Pristine 444
2002 Topps Pristine Gold Refractors 444
2002 Topps Pristine Refractors 444
2002 Topps Pristine Autographs 445
2002 Topps Pristine Patches 445
2003 Topps Pristine 445
2003 Topps Pristine Gold Refractors 446
2003 Topps Pristine Refractors 446
2003 Topps Pristine All-Star Jersey Autographs 446
2003 Topps Pristine Autographs 446
2003 Topps Pristine Gems Relics 446
2003 Topps Pristine Igniters Relics 446
2003 Topps Pristine Performance 446
2004 Topps Pristine 446
2004 Topps Pristine Gold Refractors 447
2004 Topps Pristine Refractors 447
2004 Topps Pristine All-Pro Endorsement Jersey Autographs 447
2004 Topps Pristine Clutch Performers Jersey 447
2004 Topps Pristine Fantasy Favorites Jersey 447
2004 Topps Pristine Minis 447
2004 Topps Pristine Minis Jersey 448
2004 Topps Pristine Personal Endorsement Autographs ..448
2004 Topps Pristine Personal Endorsement Autographs Gold 448
2004 Topps Pristine Pristine Gems Jersey 448
2004 Topps Pristine Real Deal Jersey 448
2004 Topps Pristine Rookie Revolution Jersey 448
2001 Topps Reserve 448
2001 Topps Reserve Autographs 449
2002 Topps Reserve Autographs 449
2002 Topps Reserve Jerseys 449
1999 Topps Season Opener 450
2000 Topps Season Opener 450
2000 Topps Season Opener Autographs 451
2004 Topps Signature 451
2004 Topps Signature Blue 452
2004 Topps Signature Autographs Green 452
2004 Topps Signature Buy Back Autographs 452
2004 Topps Signature Canton Cuts Autographs 452
1997 Topps Stars Rookie Reprints Autographs 452
1998 Topps Stars Rookie Reprints Autographs 453
1999 Topps Stars 453
1999 Topps Stars Rookie Reprints Autographs 453
2000 Topps Stars 453
2000 Topps Stars Autographs 454
2003 Topps Total 454
2003 Topps Total Silver 457
2003 Topps Total Signatures 457
2004 Topps Total 457
2004 Topps Total First Edition 460
2004 Topps Total Silver 460
2004 Topps Total Award Winners 460
2004 Topps Total Signatures 460
2004 Topps Total Team Checklists 460
2004 Topps Total Total Production 460
2004 Topps Total Total Topps 460
1997 UD3 Signature Performers 461
2002 UD Authentics 461
2002 UD Authentics Gold 25 461
2002 UD Authentics American Authentics Level 1 461
2004 UD Diamond All-Star 462
2004 UD Diamond All-Star Gold Honors 462
2004 UD Diamond All-Star Silver Honors 462
2004 UD Diamond All-Star Dean's List Jersey 462
2004 UD Diamond All-Star Future Gems Jersey 462
2004 UD Diamond All-Star Premium Stars 462
2004 UD Diamond All-Star Promo 463
2004 UD Diamond All-Star Stars of 2004 Autographs 463
2004 UD Diamond Pro Sigs 463
2004 UD Diamond Pro Sigs Rookie Gold 464
2004 UD Diamond Pro Sigs Signature Collection 464
2001 UD Game Gear 464
2001 UD Game Gear Rookie Jerseys 465
2001 UD Game Gear Autographs 465
2000 UD Graded 465
2000 UD Graded Jerseys 466
2001 UD Graded 466
2001 UD Graded Rookie Autographs 467
2001 UD Graded Rookie Jerseys 467
2002 UD Graded 467
2002 UD Graded Gold 468
2002 UD Graded Dual Game Jerseys 468
2002 UD Graded Jerseys 468
2002 UD Graded Rookie Jerseys 469
1999 UD Ionix 469
1999 UD Ionix UD Authentics 469
2000 UD Ionix 469
2000 UD Ionix UD Authentics 470
2000 UD Ionix UD Authentics Green 470
2003 UD Patch Collection 470
2003 UD Patch Collection Gold Patches 471
2003 UD Patch Collection Signature Patches 471
2002 UD Piece of History 471
2003 Ultimate Collection 472
2003 Ultimate Collection Gold 472
2003 Ultimate Collection Buy Back Autographs 472
2003 Ultimate Collection Game Jerseys 473
2003 Ultimate Collection Game Jersey Autographs 473
2003 Ultimate Collection Game Jersey Duals 473
2003 Ultimate Collection Game Jersey Duals Autographs ..473
2003 Ultimate Collection Game Jersey Patches 473
2003 Ultimate Collection Ultimate Signatures 474
2003 Ultimate Collection Ultimate Signatures Duals ..474
2003 Ultimate Collection Ultimate Signatures Duals Gold 474
2004 Ultimate Collection 474
2004 Ultimate Collection Gold 475
2004 Ultimate Collection HoloGold 475
2004 Ultimate Collection Buy Back Autographs 475
2004 Ultimate Collection Game Jerseys 475
2004 Ultimate Collection Game Jersey Autographs 476
2004 Ultimate Collection Game Jersey Duals 476
2004 Ultimate Collection Game Jersey Dual Patches ..476
2004 Ultimate Collection Game Jersey Patches 476
2004 Ultimate Collection Game Jersey Super Patches 476
2004 Ultimate Collection Rookie Jerseys 477
2004 Ultimate Collection Ultimate Signatures 477
2004 Ultimate Collection Ultimate Signatures Duals ..477
1991 Ultra 477
1991 Ultra Update 479
1997 Ultra 479
1997 Ultra Gold Medallion 481
1997 Ultra Platinum Medallion 481
1998 Ultra 481
1998 Ultra Gold Medallion 482
1998 Ultra Platinum Medallion 482
1999 Ultra 483
2000 Ultra 484
2000 Ultra Gold Medallion 485
2000 Ultra Platinum Medallion 485
2001 Ultra 485
2001 Ultra Gold Medallion 486
2001 Ultra Platinum Medallion 486
2001 Ultra College Greats Previews Autographs 486
2002 Ultra 486
2002 Ultra Gold Medallion 487
2003 Ultra 488
2003 Ultra Gold Medallion 488
2003 Ultra Platinum Medallion 488
2003 Ultra Autographs 488
2003 Ultra Award Winners Memorabilia 489

Table of Contents

2003 Ultra Award Winners Memorabilia UltraSwatch ..489
2003 Ultra Touchdown Kings Memorabilia 489
2003 Ultra Touchdown Kings Memorabilia Career 489
2003 Ultra Touchdown Kings Memorabilia UltraSwatch ..489
2004 Ultra 489
2004 Ultra Gold Medallion 490
2004 Ultra Platinum Medallion 490
2004 Ultra Gridiron Producers 490
2004 Ultra Gridiron Producers Game Used Copper 490
2004 Ultra Gridiron Producers Game Used UltraSwatch 491
2004 Ultra Hummer H2 In Package 491
2004 Ultra Passing Kings 491
2004 Ultra Performers 491
2004 Ultra Performers Game Used Copper 491
2004 Ultra Performers Game Used UltraSwatch 491
2004 Ultra Receiving Kings 491
2004 Ultra Rushing Kings 491
2004 Ultra Season Crowns Autographs 492
2004 Ultra Season Crowns Autographs Gold 492
2004 Ultra Season Crowns Game Used Copper 492
2004 Ultra Three Kings Game Used 492
1991 Upper Deck 492
1991 Upper Deck Joe Montana Heroes 495
1991 Upper Deck Joe Namath Heroes 495
1992 Upper Deck Dan Marino Heroes 496
1992 Upper Deck Walter Payton Heroes 496
1996 Upper Deck Game Jerseys 496
1997 Upper Deck Game Jerseys 496
1998 Upper Deck 496
1998 Upper Deck Bronze 497
1998 Upper Deck Game Jerseys 497
1999 Upper Deck 497
1999 Upper Deck Game Jersey 499
1999 Upper Deck Game Jersey Patch 499
2000 Upper Deck 499
2000 Upper Deck Exclusives Gold 500
2000 Upper Deck Exclusives Silver 500
2000 Upper Deck Game Jersey 500
2000 Upper Deck Game Jersey Autographs 500
2000 Upper Deck Game Jersey Autographs Numbered 500
2000 Upper Deck Game Jersey Greats Autographs 501
2000 Upper Deck Game Jersey Patch 501
2000 Upper Deck Game Jersey Patch Autographs 501
2001 Upper Deck 501
2001 Upper Deck Gold 502
2001 Upper Deck e-Card Prizes 502
2001 Upper Deck Game Jersey Autographs 502
2002 Upper Deck 502
2003 Upper Deck 504
2003 Upper Deck Gold 505
2003 Upper Deck Game Jerseys 505
2003 Upper Deck Game Jerseys Autographs 505
2003 Upper Deck Game Jerseys Duals 505
2003 Upper Deck Rookie Future Jerseys 506
2003 Upper Deck Rookie Future Jerseys Autographs ..506
2004 Upper Deck 506
2004 Upper Deck UD Exclusive 507
2004 Upper Deck Game Jersey Duals 507
2004 Upper Deck Game Jersey Patch Logos 507
2004 Upper Deck Game Jersey Patch Names 507
2004 Upper Deck Game Jersey Patch Numbers 508
2004 Upper Deck Game Jerseys 508
2004 Upper Deck Rewind to 1997 Jerseys 508
2004 Upper Deck Rookie Futures Jerseys 508
2004 Upper Deck Rookie Prospects 508
2004 Upper Deck Rookie Review Jerseys 508
2004 Upper Deck Signature Sensations 509
2004 Upper Deck Rookie Premiere 509
2004 Upper Deck Rookie Premiere Gold 509
2004 Upper Deck Rookie Premiere Autographs 509
2005 Upper Deck AFL 509
2005 Upper Deck AFL Gold 510
2005 Upper Deck AFL Arena Action 510
2005 Upper Deck AFL ArenaBowl Archives 510
2005 Upper Deck AFL Arenagraphs 510
2005 Upper Deck AFL Arenagraphs Duals 510
2005 Upper Deck AFL Dance Team Stars 510
2005 Upper Deck AFL Jerseys 511
2005 Upper Deck AFL League Luminaries 511
2005 Upper Deck AFL Timeline 511
1999 Upper Deck Century Legends Epic Signatures 511
1999 Upper Deck Century Legends Epic Signatures Century Gold 511
1999 Upper Deck Century Legends Jerseys of the Century ..511
1998 Upper Deck Encore UD Authentics 511
1999 Upper Deck Encore 512
1999 Upper Deck Encore Game Used Helmets 512
1999 Upper Deck Encore UD Authentics 513
2000 Upper Deck Encore 513
2000 Upper Deck Encore UD Authentics 514
2003 Upper Deck Finite 514
2003 Upper Deck Finite Gold 515
2003 Upper Deck Finite Autographs 515
2003 Upper Deck Finite Autographs Gold 516
2004 Upper Deck Finite HG 516
2004 Upper Deck Finite HG Fabrics 517
2004 Upper Deck Finite HG Fabrics Duals 517
2004 Upper Deck Finite HG Fabrics Triples 518
2004 Upper Deck Finite HG Rookie Fabrics 518
2004 Upper Deck Finite HG Signatures 518
2004 Upper Deck Finite HG Signatures Radiance 518
2004 Upper Deck Foundations 518
2004 Upper Deck Foundations Exclusive Gold 520
2004 Upper Deck Foundations Dual Endorsements 520
2004 Upper Deck Foundations Patches 520
2004 Upper Deck Foundations Rookie Foundations Patch 520
2004 Upper Deck Foundations Signature Foundations 520
2000 Upper Deck Gold Reserve UD Authentics 521
1999 Upper Deck HoloGrFX 521
1999 Upper Deck HoloGrFX UD Authentics 521
2002 Upper Deck Honor Roll 521
2002 Upper Deck Honor Roll Letterman Autographs ..522
2003 Upper Deck Honor Roll 522
2003 Upper Deck Honor Roll Silver 523
2003 Upper Deck Honor Roll Dean's List 523
2003 Upper Deck Honor Roll Letterman Autographs ..524
1997 Upper Deck Legends Autographs 524
1997 Upper Deck Legends Sign of the Times 525
2000 Upper Deck Legends 525
2000 Upper Deck Legends Autographs 525
2000 Upper Deck Legends Legendary Jerseys 526
2001 Upper Deck Legends 526
2001 Upper Deck Legends Autographs 527
2001 Upper Deck Legends Legendary Cuts 527
2001 Upper Deck Legends Memorable Materials 527
2004 Upper Deck Legends 527
2004 Upper Deck Legends Gold 528
2004 Upper Deck Legends Future Legends Jersey 528
2004 Upper Deck Legends Future Legends Throwback Jersey 528
2004 Upper Deck Legends Immortal Inscriptions 528
2004 Upper Deck Legends Legendary Jerseys 529
2004 Upper Deck Legends Legendary Lines of Defense 529
2004 Upper Deck Legends Legendary Signatures 529
2004 Upper Deck Legends Link to the Future 529
2004 Upper Deck Legends Link to the Past 530
1999 Upper Deck MVP 530
1999 Upper Deck MVP ProSign 531
2000 Upper Deck MVP 531
2000 Upper Deck MVP Game Used Souvenirs Autographs 532
2000 Upper Deck MVP ProSign 532
2000 Upper Deck MVP ProSign Gold 532
2001 Upper Deck MVP 532
2001 Upper Deck MVP Campus Classics Game Jersey Autographs 534
2002 Upper Deck MVP 534
2002 Upper Deck MVP ProSign 535
2003 Upper Deck MVP 535
2003 Upper Deck MVP Silver 537
2003 Upper Deck MVP ProSign 537
1999 Upper Deck Ovation 537
1999 Upper Deck Ovation Super Signatures Silver 538
2000 Upper Deck Ovation 538
2000 Upper Deck Ovation Super Signatures Silver 538
2001 Upper Deck Ovation 538
2001 Upper Deck Ovation Rookie Autographs 539
2004 Upper Deck Power Up 539
2004 Upper Deck Power Up Blue 540
2004 Upper Deck Power Up Green 540
2004 Upper Deck Power Up Orange 540
2004 Upper Deck Power Up Red 540
2004 Upper Deck Power Up Shining Through 540

Table of Contents

2004 Upper Deck Power Up Stickers 540
2000 Upper Deck Pros and Prospects 540
2000 Upper Deck Pros and Prospects Signature Piece 1 541
2000 Upper Deck Pros and Prospects Signature Piece 2 541
2001 Upper Deck Pros and Prospects 541
2001 Upper Deck Pros and Prospects A Piece of History Autographs 542
2003 Upper Deck Pros and Prospects 542
2003 Upper Deck Pros and Prospects Game Day Jerseys 543
2003 Upper Deck Pros and Prospects Game Day Jersey Duals 543
1999 Upper Deck Retro 544
1999 Upper Deck Retro Inkredible 544
1999 Upper Deck Retro Inkredible Gold 545
2001 Upper Deck Rookie F/X 545
2001 Upper Deck Rookie F/X Legendary Cuts 547
2003 Upper Deck Standing O Signatures 547
2001 Upper Deck Top Tier 547
2000 Upper Deck Ultimate Victory 549
1999 Upper Deck Victory 549
2000 Upper Deck Victory 551
2001 Upper Deck Victory 552
2001 Upper Deck Vintage 554
2001 Upper Deck Vintage Signatures 556
2001 Upper Deck Vintage Threads Autographs 556
2001 Upper Deck Vintage Threads Combos 556
2002 Upper Deck XL 556
2001 Vanguard 559
1992 Wild Card 559
1992 Wild Card 1000 Stripe 561
1996 Press Pass Autographs 561
1996 Press Pass Paydirt Autographs 561
1997 Press Pass Autographs 562
1998 Press Pass Autographs 562
1998 Press Pass Game Jerseys 562
1999 Press Pass 562
1999 Press Pass Autographs 562
1999 Press Pass Game Jerseys 563
2000 Press Pass 563
2000 Press Pass Autographs 563
2001 Press Pass 563
2001 Press Pass Autographs 564
2001 Press Pass Autograph Power Picks 564
2002 Press Pass 564
2002 Press Pass Autographs 564
2002 Press Pass Autograph Power Picks 565
2003 Press Pass 565
2003 Press Pass Gold Zone 565
2003 Press Pass Reflectors 565
2003 Press Pass Autographs Bronze 565
2003 Press Pass Autograph Power Picks 565
2003 Press Pass Game Used Jerseys Gold 566
2004 Press Pass 566
2004 Press Pass Blue 566
2004 Press Pass Gold 566
2004 Press Pass Reflectors 566
2004 Press Pass Reflectors Proof 566
2004 Press Pass Autographs Bronze 566
2004 Press Pass Autographs Blue 566
2004 Press Pass Autographs Gold 567
2004 Press Pass Autographs Silver 567
2004 Press Pass Big Numbers 567
2004 Press Pass Game Used Jerseys Silver 567
2004 Press Pass Paydirt 567
2004 Press Pass Showbound 567
2005 Press Pass 568
2005 Press Pass Blue 568
2005 Press Pass Reflectors 568
2005 Press Pass Reflectors Proof 568
2005 Press Pass Autograph Power Picks 568
2005 Press Pass Autographs Bronze 568
2005 Press Pass Autographs Blue 569
2005 Press Pass Autographs Gold 569
2005 Press Pass Autographs Silver 569
2005 Press Pass Big Numbers 569
2005 Press Pass Game Used Jerseys Silver 569
2005 Press Pass Paydirt 570
2005 Press Pass Showbound 570
2002 Press Pass JE 570
2002 Press Pass JE Autographs 570
2002 Press Pass JE Class of 2002 Autographs 570
2003 Press Pass JE 570
2003 Press Pass JE Class of 2003 Autographs 571
2003 Press Pass JE Game Used Jerseys Autographs 571
2003 Press Pass JE Game Used Jerseys Gold 571
2003 Press Pass JE Game Used Jerseys Holofoil 571
2003 Press Pass JE Game Used Jerseys Silver 571
2001 Press Pass SE 571
2001 Press Pass SE Autographs Bronze 572
2001 Press Pass SE Autographs Silver 572
2001 Press Pass SE Class of 2001 Autographs 572
2001 Press Pass SE Game Jersey Autographs 572
2004 Press Pass SE 572
2004 Press Pass SE First Down Gold 572
2004 Press Pass SE Class of 2004 572
2004 Press Pass SE Class of 2004 Autographs 573
2004 Press Pass SE Game Used Jerseys Autographs 573
2004 Press Pass SE Game Used Jerseys Bronze 573
2004 Press Pass SE Old School 573
2004 Press Pass SE Up Close 573
2005 Press Pass SE 573
2005 Press Pass SE Class of 2005 574
2005 Press Pass SE Class of 2005 Autographs 574
2005 Press Pass SE Game Used Jerseys Silver 574
2005 Press Pass SE Game Used Jerseys Autographs 574
2005 Press Pass SE Old School 574
2005 Press Pass SE Up Close 574
1999 SAGE 574
1999 SAGE Autographs Red 575
2000 SAGE 575
2000 SAGE Autographs Red 575
2001 SAGE 576
2001 SAGE Autographs Red 576
2002 SAGE 576
2002 SAGE Autographs Red 576
2003 SAGE 577
2003 SAGE Autographs Red 577
2003 SAGE Jerseys Red 577
2004 SAGE 578
2004 SAGE Autographs Red 578
2004 SAGE Jerseys Red 578
2000 SAGE HIT 578
2000 SAGE HIT Autographs Emerald 579
2001 SAGE HIT 579
2001 SAGE HIT Autographs 579
2002 SAGE HIT 580
2002 SAGE HIT Autographs Emerald 580
2003 SAGE HIT 580
2003 SAGE HIT Autographs Emerald 580
2003 SAGE HIT Class of 2003 Autographs 581
2003 SAGE HIT Jerseys 581
2003 SAGE HIT Write Stuff Autographs 581
2004 SAGE HIT 581
2004 SAGE HIT Autographs Emerald 581
2004 SAGE HIT Autographs Gold 582
2004 SAGE HIT Autographs Silver 582
2004 SAGE HIT Inside the Numbers 582
2004 SAGE HIT Jerseys 582
2004 SAGE HIT Ohio State Autographs 582
2004 SAGE HIT Q&A Autographs 582
2004 SAGE HIT Q&A Emerald 583
2004 SAGE HIT SEC Autographs 583
2004 SAGE HIT Write Stuff 583
2004 SAGE HIT Write Stuff Autographs 583
2004 SAGE Jersey Update 584
2004 SAGE Jersey Update Roethlisberger 584
2005 SAGE HIT 584
2005 SAGE HIT ACC Autographs 584
2005 SAGE HIT Autographs Blue 584
2005 SAGE HIT Ben Roethlisberger 584
2005 SAGE HIT Jerseys 584
2005 SAGE HIT MAC Autographs 585
2005 SAGE HIT Reflect Blue 585
2005 SAGE HIT Reflect Silver 585
2005 SAGE HIT Reflect Gold Autographs 585
2005 SAGE HIT SEC Autographs 585
2005 SAGE HIT Write Stuff 585
2005 SAGE HIT Write Stuff Autographs 585

Acknowledgments 585

About the Author

Jim Beckett, the leading authority on sports card values in the United States, maintains a wide range of activities in the world of sports. He possesses one of the finest collections of sportscards and autographs in the world, has made numerous appearances on radio and television, and has been frequently cited in many national publications. He was awarded the first "Special Achievement Award for Contributions to the Hobby" by the National Sports Collectors Convention in 1980, the "Jock-Jaspersen Award for Hobby Dedication" in 1983, and the "Buck Barker, Spirit of the Hobby Award" in 1991.

Dr. Beckett is the author of *Beckett Baseball Card Price Guide, The Official Price Guide to Baseball Cards, The Sport Americana Price Guide to Baseball Collectibles, Beckett Almanac of Baseball Cards and Collectibles, The Sport Americana Baseball Memorabilia and Autograph Price Guide, Beckett Football Card Price Guide, The Official Price Guide to Football Cards, Beckett Hockey Card Price Guide and Alphabetical Checklist, Beckett Basketball Card Price Guide, The Official Price Guide to Basketball Cards,* and *Beckett Baseball Card Alphabetical Checklist.* In addition, he is the founder, and publisher, of sports collectible magazines: *Beckett Baseball, Beckett Basketball, Beckett Football, Beckett Hockey,* and *Beckett.*

Jim Beckett received his Ph.D. in Statistics from Southern Methodist University in 1975. Prior to starting Beckett Publications in 1984, Dr. Beckett served as an Associate Professor of Statistics at Bowling Green State University and as a Vice President of a consulting firm in Dallas, Texas. He currently resides in Dallas.

How to Use This Book

Isn't it great? Every year this book gets better with all the new sets coming out. But even more exciting is that every year there are more attractive choices and, subsequently, more interest in the cards we love so much. This edition has been enhanced and expanded from the previous edition. The cards you collect —who appears on them, what they look like, where they are from, and (most important to most of you) what their current values are—are enumerated within. Many of the features contained in the other *Beckett Price Guides* have been incorporated into this volume since condition-grading, terminology, and many other aspects of collecting are common to the card hobby in general. We hope you find the book both interesting and useful in your collecting pursuits.

The Beckett Guide has been successful where other attempts have failed because it is complete, current, and valid. This price guide contains not just one, but two prices by condition for all the football cards listed. These account for most of the football cards in existence. The prices were added to the card lists just prior to printing and reflect not the author's opinions or desires but the going retail prices for each card, based on the marketplace (sports memorabilia conventions and shows, sportscard shops, hobby papers, current mail-order catalogs, Internet sales, auction results, and other firsthand reporting of actually realized prices).

What is the best price guide available on the market today? Of course card sellers will prefer the price guide with the highest prices, while card buyers will naturally prefer the one with the lowest prices. Accuracy, however, is the true test. Use the price guide used by more collectors and dealers than all the others combined. Look for the Beckett name. I won't put my name on anything I won't stake my reputation on. Not the lowest and not the highest—but the most accurate, with integrity.

To facilitate your use of this book, read the complete introductory section on the following pages before going to the pricing pages. Every collectible field has its own terminology; we've tried to capture most of these terms and definitions in our glossary. Please read carefully the section on grading and the condition of your cards, as you will not be able to determine which price column is appropriate for a given card without first knowing its condition.

Prices in This Guide

Prices found in this guide reflect current retail rates just prior to the printing of this book. They do not reflect the for-sale prices of the author, the publisher, the distributors, the advertisers, or any card dealers associated with this guide. No one is obligated in any way to buy, sell, or trade his or her cards based on these prices. The price listings were compiled by the author from actual buy/sell transactions at sports conventions, sportscard shops, buy/sell advertisements in the hobby papers, for-sale prices from dealer catalogs and price lists, and discussions with leading hobbyists in the U.S. and Canada. All prices are in U.S. dollars.

Acknowledgments

A great deal of diligence, hard work, and dedicated effort went into this year's volume. The high standards to which we hold ourselves, however, could not have been met without the expert input and generous amount of time contributed by many people. Our sincere thanks are extended to each and every one of you.

A complete list of these invaluable contributors appears after the Price Guide section.

Introduction

Welcome to the exciting world of sportscard collecting, one of America's most popular avocations. You have made a good choice in buying this book, since it will open up to you the entire panorama of this field in the simplest, most concise way.

The growth of *Beckett Baseball, Beckett Basketball, Beckett Football, Beckett Hockey,* and *Beckett Racing* is an indication of the unprecedented popularity of sportscards. Founded in 1984 by Dr. James Beckett, *Beckett Baseball* contains the most extensive and accepted monthly price guide, collectible glossy superstar covers, colorful feature articles, "Hot List," Convention Calendar, tips for beginners, "Readers Write" letters to and responses from the editor, information on errors and varieties, autograph collecting tips, and profiles of the sport's hottest stars. Published every month, Beckett Baseball is the hobby's largest paid circulation periodical. The other five magazines were built on the success of Baseball.

So collecting sportscards—while still pursued as a hobby with youthful exuberance by kids in the neighborhood—has also taken on the trappings of an industry, with thousands of full- and part-time card dealers, as well as vendors of supplies, clubs, and conventions. In fact, each year since 1980 thousands of hobbyists have assembled for a National Sports Collectors Convention, at which hundreds of dealers have displayed their wares, seminars have been conducted, autographs penned by sports notables, and millions of cards changed hands. The Beckett Guide is the best annual guide available to the exciting world of football cards. Read it and use it. May your enjoyment and your card collection increase in the coming months and years.

How to Collect

Each collection is personal and reflects the individuality of its owner. There are no set rules on how to collect cards. Since card collecting is a hobby or leisure pastime, what you collect, how much you collect, and how much time and money you spend collecting are entirely up to you. The funds you have available for collecting and your own personal taste should determine how you collect. The information and ideas presented here are intended to help you get the most enjoyment from this hobby.

It is impossible to collect every card ever produced. Therefore, beginners as well as intermediate and advanced collectors usually specialize in some way. One of the reasons this hobby is popular is that individual collectors can define and tailor their collecting methods to match their own tastes. To give you some ideas of the various approaches to collecting, we will list some of the more popular areas of specialization.

Many collectors select complete sets from particular years. For example, they may concentrate on assembling complete sets from all the years since their birth or since they became avid sports fans. They may try to collect a card for every player during that specified period of time. Many others wish to acquire only certain players. Usually such players are the superstars of the sport, but occasionally collectors will specialize in all the cards of players who attended a particular college or came from a certain town. Some collectors are only interested in the first cards or Rookie Cards of certain players.

Another fun way to collect cards is by team. Most fans have a favorite team, and it is natural for that loyalty to be translated into a desire for cards of the players on that favorite team. For most of the recent years, team sets (all the cards from a given team for that year) are readily available at a reasonable price. See Beckett.com for searchable player checklists.

Obtaining Cards

Several avenues are open to card collectors. Cards still can be purchased in the traditional way: by the pack at the local discount, grocery, or convenience stores. But there are also thousands of card shops across the country that specialize in selling cards individually or by the pack, box, or set. Another alternative is the thousands of card shows held each month around the country, which feature anywhere from five to 800 tables of sports cards and memorabilia for sale.

For many years, it has been possible to purchase complete sets of cards through mail-order advertisers found in traditional sports media publications, such as *The Sporting News, Football Digest, Street & Smith* yearbooks, and others. These sets also are advertised in the card collecting periodicals. Many collectors will begin by subscribing to at least one of the hobby periodicals, all with good up-to-date information. Another way of obtaining cards and information is through Beckett's Web site, www.beckett.com.

Most serious card collectors obtain old (and new) cards from one or more of several main sources: (1) trading or buying from other collectors or dealers; (2) responding to sale or auction ads in the hobby publications; (3) buying at a local hobby store; (4) attending sports collectibles shows or conventions; and/or (5) purchasing cards over the Internet.

We advise that you try all four methods since each has its own distinct advantages: (1) trading is a great way to make new friends; (2) hobby periodicals help you keep up with what's going on in the hobby (including when and where the conventions are happening); (3) stores provide the opportunity to enjoy personalized service and consider a great diversity of material in a relaxed sports-oriented atmosphere; (4) shows allow you to choose from multiple dealers and thousands of cards under one roof in a competitive situation; and (5) the Internet allows you to purchase cards in a convenient manner from almost anywhere in the world.

Preserving Your Cards

Cards are fragile. They must be handled properly in order to retain their value. Careless handling can easily result in creased or bent cards. It is, however, not recommended that tweezers or tongs be used to pick up your cards since such utensils might mar or indent card surfaces and thus reduce those cards' conditions and values. In general, your cards should be handled directly as little as possible. This is sometimes easier to say than to do.

Although there are still many who use custom boxes, storage trays, or even shoe boxes, plastic sheets are the preferred method of many collectors for storing cards. A collection stored in plastic pages in a three-ring album allows you to view your collection at any time without the need to touch the card itself. Cards can also be kept in single holders (of various types and thicknesses) designed for the enjoyment of each card individually. For a large collection, some collectors may use a combination of the above methods. When purchasing plastic sheets for your cards, be sure that you find the pocket size that fits the cards snugly. Don't put your 1951 Bowman in a sheet designed to fit 1981 Topps.

Most hobby and collectibles shops and virtually all collectors' conventions will have these plastic pages available in quantity for the various sizes offered, or you can purchase them directly from the advertisers in this book. Also, remember that pocket size isn't the only factor to consider when looking for plastic sheets. Other factors such as safety, economy, appearance, availability, or personal preference also may indicate which types of sheets a collector may want to buy.

Damp, sunny, and/or hot conditions. No, this is not a weather forecast, but rather three elements to avoid in extremes if you are interested in preserving your collection. Too much (or too little) humidity can cause gradual deterioration of a card. Direct, bright sun (or fluorescent light) over time will bleach out the color of a card. Extreme heat accelerates the decomposition of the card. On the other hand, many cards have lasted more than 50 years without much scientific intervention. So be cautious, even if the above factors typically present a problem only when present in the extreme. It never hurts to be prudent.

Collecting vs. Investing

Collecting individual players and collecting complete sets are both popular vehicles for investment and speculation. Most investors and speculators stock up on complete sets or on quantities of players they think have good investment potential.

There is obviously no guarantee in this book, or anywhere else for that matter, that cards will outperform the stock market or other investment alternatives in the future. After all, football cards do not pay quarterly dividends and cards cannot be sold at their "current values" as easily as stocks or bonds.

Nevertheless, investors have noticed a favorable long-term trend in the past performance of sports collectibles, and certain cards and sets have outperformed just about any other investment in some years. Many hobbyists maintain that the best investment is and always will be the building of a collection, which traditionally has held up better than outright speculation.

Some of the obvious questions are Which cards? When to buy? When to sell? The best investment you can make is in your own education. The more you know about your collection and the hobby, the more informed decisions you will be able to make. We're not selling investment tips. We're selling information about the current value of football cards. It's up to you to use that information to your best advantage.

Terminology

Each hobby has its own language to describe its area of interest. The terminology traditionally used for trading cards is derived from the American Card Catalog, published in 1960 by Nostalgia Press. That catalog, written by Jefferson Burdick (who is called the "Father of Card Collecting" for his pioneering work), uses letter and number designations for each separate set of cards. The letter used in the ACC designation refers to the generic type of card. While both sport and non-sport issues are classified in the ACC, we shall confine ourselves to the sport issues. The following list defines the letters and their meanings as used by the American Card Catalog, as applied to football cards:

(none) or **N** - 19th Century U.S. Tobacco
F - Food Inserts
H - Advertising
M - Periodicals
N - 19th Century U.S. Tobacco
PC - Postcards
R - Recent Candy and Gum Cards, 1930 to Present
UO - Gas and Oil Inserts
V - Canadian Candy
W - Exhibits, Strip Cards, Team Cards

Following the letter prefix and an optional hyphen are one-, two-, or three-digit numbers, R(-)999. These typically represent the company or entity issuing the cards. In several cases, the ACC number is extended by an additional hyphen and another one- or two-digit numerical suffix. For example, the 1957 Topps regular-series football card issue carries an ACC designation of R415-5. The "R" indicates a Candy or Gum card produced since 1930. The "415" is the ACC designation for the 1957 regular issue (Topps fifth football set).

Like other traditional methods of identification, this system provides order to the process of cataloging cards; however, most serious collectors learn the ACC designation of the popular sets by repetition and familiarity, rather than by attempting to "figure out" what they might or should be. From 1948 forward, collectors and dealers commonly refer to all sets by their year, maker, type of issue, and any other distinguishing characteristic. For example, such a characteristic could be an unusual issue or one of several regular issues put out by a specific maker in a single year. Regional issues are usually referred to by year, maker, and sometimes by title or theme of the set.

Glossary/Legend

Our glossary defines terms frequently used in the card collecting hobby. Many of these terms are also common to other types of sports memorabilia collecting. Some terms may have several meanings depending on use and context.

ACC - Acronym for American Card Catalog.

ACETATE - A transparent plastic.

AFC - American Football Conference.

AFL - American Football League.

AS - All-Star.

ATG - All Time Great card.

AU(TO) - An autographed card.

BRICK - A group or "lot" or cards, usually 50 or more having common characteristics, that is intended to be bought, sold, or traded as a unit.

C - Center.

CB - Cornerback.

CFL - Canadian Football League.

CL - Checklist card. A card that lists in order the cards and players in the set or series. Older checklist cards in mint condition that have not been checked off are very desirable and command large premiums.

CO - Coach card.

COLLECTOR ISSUE - A set produced for the sake of the card itself, with no product or service sponsor. It derives its name from the fact that most of these sets are produced for sale directly to the hobby market.

COMBINATION CARD - A single card depicting two or more players (not including team cards).

COMMON CARD - The typical card of any set; it has no premium value accruing from subject matter, numerical scarcity, popular demand, or anomaly.

CONVENTION - A large gathering of dealers and collectors at a single location for the purpose of buying, selling, and sometimes trading sports memorabilia items. Conventions are open to the public and sometimes also feature autograph guests, door prizes, films, contests, etc. More commonly called "shows."

COR - Corrected card. A version of an error card that was fixed by the manufacturer.

DB - Defensive back.

DIE-CUT - A card with its stock partially cut. In some cases, after removal or appropriate folding, the remaining part of the card can be made to stand up.

DISC - A circular-shaped card.

DISPLAY SHEET - A clear, plastic page that is punched for insertion into a binder (with standard three-ring spacing) containing pockets for displaying cards. Many different styles of sheets exist with pockets of varying sizes to hold the many differing card formats. The vast majority of current cards measure 2-1/2 by 3-1/2 inches and fit in nine-pocket sheets.

DP - Double Print. A card that was printed in approximately double the quantity compared to other cards in the same series, or draft pick card.

DT - Defensive tackle or Dream Team.

DUFEX - A method of card manufacturing technology patented by Pinnacle Brands, Inc. It involves a refractive quality to a card with a foil coating.

EMBOSSED - A raised surface; features of a card that are projected from a flat background.

ERR - Error card. A card with erroneous information, spelling, or depiction on either side of the card. Most errors are never corrected by the producing card company.

ETCHED - Impressions within the surface of a card.

EXHIBIT - The generic name given to thick-stock, postcard-size cards with single-color, obverse pictures. The name is derived from the Exhibit Supply Co. of Chicago, the principal manufacturer of this type of card. These are also known as Arcade cards since they were found in many arcades.

FB - Fullback.

FDP - First (round) draft pick.

FG - Field goal.

FOIL - A special type of sticker with a metallic-looking surface.

FULL-BLEED - A borderless card; a card containing a photo that encompasses the entire card.

FULL SHEET - A complete sheet of cards that has not been cut into individual cards by the manufacturer. Also called an uncut sheet.

G - Guard.

GLOSS - A card with luster; a shiny finish as in a card with UV coating.

HIGH NUMBER - The cards in the last series of number, in a year in which such higher-numbered cards were printed or distributed in significantly lesser amount than the lower-numbered cards. The high-number designation refers to a scarcity of the high-numbered cards.

HL - Highlight card, for example from the 1978 Topps subset.

HOF - Hall of Fame, or Hall of Famer (also abbreviated HOFer).

HOLOGRAM - A three-dimensional photographic image.

HOR - Horizontal pose on a card as opposed to the standard vertical orientation found on most cards.

IA - In Action card. A special type of card depicting a player in an action photo, such as the 1982 Topps cards.

IL - Inside linebacker.

INSERT - A card of a different type, e.g., a poster, or any other sports collectible contained and sold in the same package along with a card or cards of a major set.

INTERACTIVE - A concept that involves collector participation.

K - Kicker.

KARAT - A unit of measure for the fineness of gold; i.e., 24K.

KP - Kid Picture card.

LAYERING - The separation or peeling of one or more layers of the card stock, usually at the corner of the card. Also see the Condition Guide.

LB - Linebacker.

LID - A circular-shaped card (possibly with tab) that forms the top of the container for the product being promoted.

LL - League leader card. A card depicting the leader or leaders in a specific statistical category from the previous season. Not to be confused with team leader (TL).

LOGO - NFLPA logo on card.

MAJOR SET - A set produced by a national manufacturer of cards, containing a large number of cards. Usually 100 or more different cards comprise a major set.

MEM - Memorial.

METALLIC - A glossy design that enhances card features.

MINI - A small card or stamp (specifically the 1969 Topps Four-in-One football inserts or the 1987 Topps mini football set issued for the United Kingdom).

MVP - Most Valuable Player.

NFLPA - National Football League Players Association.

NO LOGO - No NFLPA logo on card.

NO TR - No trade reference on card.

NPO - No position.

NT - Nose tackle.

OFF - Officials cards.

O-ROY - Offensive Rookie of the Year.

OT - Offensive tackle.

P - Punter.

P1 - First Printing.

P2 - Second Printing.

PACKS - A means with which cards are issued in terms of pack type (wax, cello, foil, rack, etc.) and channels of distribution (hobby, retail, etc.).

PANEL - An extended card that is composed of multiple individual cards.

PARALLEL - A card that is similar in design to its counterpart from a basic set, but offers a distinguishing quality.

PB - Pro Bowl.

PLATINUM - A metallic element used in the process of creating a glossy card.

POY - Player of the Year.

PREMIUM - A card, sometimes on photographic stock, that is purchased or obtained in conjunction with (or redeemed for) another card or product. This term applies mainly to older products, as newer cards distributed in this manner are generally lumped together as peripheral sets.

PREMIUM CARDS - A class of products introduced recently, intended to have higher quality card stock and photography than regular cards, but more limited production and higher cost. Defining what is and isn't a premium card is somewhat subjective.

PRISMATIC/PRISM - A glossy or bright design that refracts or disperses light.

PROMOTIONAL SET - A set, usually containing a small number of cards, issued by a national card producer and distributed in limited quantities or to a select group of people, such as major show attendees or dealers with wholesale accounts. Presumably, the purpose of a promo set is to stir up demand for an upcoming set. Also called a preview, prototype, or test set.

QB - Quarterback.

RARE - A card or series of cards of very limited availability. Unfortunately, "rare" is a subjective term sometimes used indiscriminately. Using the strict definitions, rare cards are harder to obtain than scarce cards.

RB - Record Breaker card or running back.

RC - Rookie Card. A player's first appearance on a regular issue card from one of the major card companies. With a few exceptions, each player has only one RC in any given set. A Rookie Card typically cannot be an All-Star, Highlight, In Action, league leader, Super Action, or team leader card. It can, however, be a coach card or draft pick card.

REDEMPTION - A program established by manufacturers that allows collectors to mail in a special card (usually a random insert) in return for special cards, sets, or other prizes not available through conventional channels.

REFRACTORS - A card that features a design element which enhances (distorts) its color/appearance through deflecting light.

REGIONAL - A card issued and distributed only in a limited geographical area of the country. The producer may or may not be a major, national producer of trading cards. The key is whether the set was distributed nationally in any form or not.

REPLICA - An identical copy or reproduction.

RET - Retired.

REV NEG - Reversed or flopped photo side of the card. This is a major type of error card, but only some are corrected.

ROY - Rookie of the Year.

S - Safety.

SB - Super Bowl.

SCARCE - A card or series of cards of limited availability. This subjective term is sometimes used indiscriminately to promote or hype value. Using strict definitions, scarce cards are easier to obtain than rare cards.

SEMI-HIGH - A card from the next-to-last series of a sequentially issued set. It has more value than an average card and generally less value than a high number. A card is not called a semi-high unless its next-to-last series has an additional premium attached to it.

SERIES - The entire set of cards issued by a particular producer in a particular year, e.g., the 1978 Topps series. Also, within a particular set, series can refer to a group of (consecutively numbered) cards printed at the same time, e.g., the first series of the 1948 Leaf set (#1 through #49).

SET - One each of an entire run of cards of the same type, produced by a particular manufacturer during a single season. In other words, if you have a complete set of 1975 Topps football cards, then you have every card from #1 up to and including #528; i.e., all the different cards that were produced.

SHEEN - Brightness or luster emitted by a card.

SKIP-NUMBERED - A set that has many unissued card numbers between the lowest number in the set and the highest number in the set, e.g., the 1949 Leaf football set contains 49 cards skip-numbered from number 1 to number 144. A major set in which a few numbers were not printed is not considered to be skip-numbered.

SP - Single or Short Print. A card which was printed in lesser quantity compared to the other cards in the same series (also see DP). This term can only be used in a relative sense and in reference to one particular set. For instance, the 1989 Pro Set Pete Rozelle SP is less common than the other cards in that set, but it isn't necessarily scarcer than regular cards of any other set.

SPECIAL CARD - A card that portrays something other than a single player or team; for example, the 1990 Fleer Joe Montana/Jerry Rice Super Bowl

MVPs card #397.

SR - Super Rookie.

STAMP - Adhesive-backed papers depicting a player. The stamp may be individual or in a sheet of many stamps. Moisture must be applied to the adhesive in order for the stamp to be attached to another surface.

STAR CARD - A card that portrays a player of some repute, usually determined by his ability, but sometimes referring to sheer popularity.

STICKER - A card-like item with a removable layer that can be affixed to another surface. Example: 1983 Topps inserts.

STOCK - The cardboard or paper on which the card is printed.

SUPERIMPOSED - To be affixed on top of something, i.e., a player photo over a solid background.

SUPERSTAR CARD - A card that portrays a superstar, e.g., a Hall of Fame member or a player whose current performance may eventually warrant serious Hall of Fame consideration.

TAB - A card portion set off from the rest of the card, usually with perforations, that may be removed without damaging the central character or event depicted by the card.

TC - Team card or team checklist card.

TEAM CARD - A card that depicts an entire team.

THREE-DIMENSIONAL (3D) - A visual image that provides an illusion of depth and perspective.

TL - Team leader card or Top Leader.

TOPICAL - A subset or group of cards that have a common theme, i.e., MVP award winners.

TR - Trade reference on card.

TRANSPARENT - Clear, see-through.

TRIMMED - A card cut down from its original size. Trimmed cards are undesirable to most collectors, and are therefore less valuable than otherwise identical, untrimmed cards. Also see the Condition Guide.

UER - Uncorrected error card.

USFL - United States Football League.

UV - Ultraviolet, a glossy coating used in producing cards.

VAR - Variation card. One of two or more cards from the same series, with the same card number (or player with identical pose, if the series is unnumbered) differing from one another in some aspect, from the printing, stock, or other feature of the card. This is often caused when the manufacturer of the cards notices an error, in a particular card, corrects the error and then resumes the print run. In this case there will be two versions or variations of the same card. Sometimes one of the variations is relatively scarce. Variations also can result from accidental or deliberate design changes, information updates, photo substitutions, etc.

VERT - Vertical pose on a card.

WFL - World Football League.

WLAF - World League of American Football.

WR - Wide receiver.

XRC - Extended Rookie Card. A player's first appearance on a card, but issued in a set that was not distributed nationally or in packs. In football sets, this term generally refers to the 1984 and 1985 Topps USFL sets.

Understanding Card Values

Determining Value

Why are some cards more valuable than others? Obviously, the economic laws of supply and demand are applicable to card collecting just as they are to any other field where a commodity is bought, sold, or traded in a free, unregulated market.

Supply (the number of cards available on the market) is less than the total number of cards originally produced since attrition diminishes that original quantity. Each year a percentage of cards is typically thrown away, destroyed, or otherwise lost to collectors. This percentage is much, much smaller today than it was in the past because more and more people have become increasingly aware of the value of their cards.

For those who collect only mint condition cards, the supply of older cards can be quite small indeed. Until recently, collectors were not so conscious of the need to preserve the condition of their cards. For this reason, it is difficult to know exactly how many 1962 Topps are currently available, mint or otherwise. It is generally accepted that there are fewer 1962 Topps available than 1972, 1982, or 1992 Topps cards. If demand were equal for each of these sets, the law of supply and demand would increase the price for the least available sets.

Demand, however, is never equal for all sets, so price correlations can be complicated. The demand for a card is influenced by many factors. These include: (1) the age of the card; (2) the number of cards printed; (3) the player(s) portrayed on the card; (4) the attractiveness and popularity of the set; and (5) the physical condition of the card.

In general, (1) the older the card, (2) the fewer the number of the cards printed, (3) the more famous, popular, and talented the player, (4) the more attractive and popular the set, and (5) the better the condition of the card, the higher the value of the card will be. There are exceptions to all but one of these factors: the condition of the card. Given two cards similar in all respects except condition, the one in the better condition will always be valued higher.

While those guidelines help to establish the value of a card, the countless exceptions and peculiarities make any simple, direct mathematical formula to determine card values impossible.

Regional Variation

Since the market varies from region to region, card prices of local players may be higher. This is known as a regional premium. How significant the premium is—and if there is any premium at all—depends on the local popularity of the team and the player.

The largest regional premiums usually do not apply to superstars, who often are so well known nationwide that the prices of their key cards are too high for local dealers to realize a premium.

Lesser stars often command the strongest premiums. Their popularity is concentrated in their home region, creating local demand that greatly exceeds overall demand.

Regional premiums can apply to popular retired players and sometimes can be found in the areas where the players grew up or starred in college.

A regional discount is the converse of a regional premium. Regional discounts occur when a player has been so popular in his region for so long that local collectors and dealers have accumulated quantities of his cards. The abundant supply may make the cards available in that area at the lowest prices anywhere.

Set Prices

A somewhat paradoxical situation exists in the price of a complete set vs. the combined cost of the individual cards in the set. In nearly every case, the sum of the prices for the individual cards is higher than the cost for the complete set. This is prevalent especially in the cards of the past few years. The reasons for this apparent anomaly stem from the habits of collectors and from the carrying costs to dealers. Today, each card in a set normally is produced in the same quantity as all others in its set.

Many collectors pick up only stars, superstars, and particular teams. As a result, the dealer is left with a shortage of certain player cards and an abundance of others. He therefore incurs an expense in simply "carrying" these less desirable cards in stock. On the other hand, if he sells a complete set, he gets rid of large numbers of cards at one time. For this reason, he generally is willing to receive less money for a complete set. By doing this, he recovers all of his costs and also makes a profit.

Set prices do not include rare card varieties, unless specifically stated. Of course, the prices for sets do include one example of each type for the given set, but this is the least expensive variety.

Scarce Series

Scarce series occur because cards issued before 1973 were made available to the public each year in several series of finite numbers of cards, rather than all cards of the set being available for purchase at one time. At some point during the season, interest in current year cards waned. Consequently, the manufacturers produced smaller numbers of these later-series cards. Nearly all nationwide issues from post World War II manufacturers (1948 to 1972) exhibit these series variations.

In the past, Topps, for example, may have issued series consisting of many different numbers of cards, including 55, 66, 80, 88, 110, and others. However, after 1968, the sheet size generally has been 132. Despite Topps' standardization of the sheet size, the company double-printed one sheet in 1983 and possibly in 1984 and 1985, too. This was apparently an effort to induce collectors to buy more packs.

We are always looking for information or photographs of printing sheets of cards for research. Each year, we try to update the hobby's knowledge of distribution anomalies. Please let us know at the address in this book if you have firsthand knowledge that would be helpful in this pursuit.

Grading Your Cards

Each hobby has its own grading terminology—stamps, coins, comic books, record collecting, etc. Collectors of sports cards are no exception. The one invariable criterion for determining the value of a card is its condition: the better the condition of the card, the more valuable it is. Condition grading, however, is subjective. Individual card dealers and collectors differ in the strictness of their grading, but the stated condition of a card should be determined without regard to whether it is being bought or sold.

No allowance is made for age. A 1952 card is judged by the same standards as a 1992 card. But there are specific sets and cards that are condition-sensitive because of their border color, consistently poor centering, etc. Such cards and sets sometimes command premiums above the listed percentages in mint condition.

Centering

Current centering terminology uses numbers representing the percentage of border on either side of the main design. Obviously, centering is diminished in importance for borderless cards such as Stadium Club.

Slightly Off-Center (60/40) - A slightly off-center card is one that upon close inspection is found to have one border bigger than the opposite border.

This degree once was offensive only to purists, but now some hobbyists try to avoid cards that are anything other than perfectly centered.

Off-Center (70/30) - An off-center card has one border that is noticeably more than twice as wide as the opposite border.

Badly Off-Center (80/20 or worse) - A badly off-center card has virtually no border on one side of the card.

Miscut - A miscut card actually shows part of the adjacent card in its larger border and consequently a corresponding amount of its card is cut off.

Corner Wear

Corner wear is the most scrutinized grading criteria in the hobby. These are the major categories of corner wear:

Corner with a slight touch of wear - The corner still is sharp, but there is a slight touch of wear showing. On a dark-bordered card, this shows as a dot of white.

Fuzzy corner - The corner still comes to a point, but the point has just begun to fray. A slightly "dinged" corner is considered the same as a fuzzy corner.

Slightly rounded corner - The fraying of the corner has increased to where there is only a hint of a point. Mild layering may be evident. A "dinged" corner is considered the same as a slightly rounded corner.

Rounded corner - The point is completely gone. Some layering is noticeable.

Badly rounded corner - The corner is completely round and rough. Severe layering is evident.

Creases

A third common defect is the crease. The degree of creasing in a card is difficult to show in a drawing or picture. On giving the specific condition of an expensive card for sale, the seller should note any creases additionally. Creases can be categorized as to severity according to the following scale.

Light Crease - A light crease is a crease that is barely noticeable upon close inspection. In fact, when cards are in plastic sheets or holders, a light crease may not be seen (until the card is taken out of the holder). A light crease on the front is much more serious than a light crease on the card back only.

Medium Crease - A medium crease is noticeable when held and studied at arm's length by the naked eye, but does not overly detract from the appearance of the card. It is an obvious crease, but not one that breaks the picture surface of the card.

Heavy Crease - A heavy crease is one that has torn or broken through the card's picture surface, e.g., puts a tear in the photo surface.

Alterations

Deceptive Trimming - This occurs when someone alters the card in order (1) to shave off edge wear, (2) to improve the sharpness of the corners, or (3) to improve centering. Obviously their objective is to falsely increase the perceived value of the card to an unsuspecting buyer. The shrinkage usually is evident only if the trimmed card is compared to an adjacent full-sized card or if the trimmed card is itself measured.

Obvious Trimming - Obvious trimming is noticeable and unfortunate. It is usually performed by non-collectors who give no thought to the present or future value of their cards.

Deceptively Retouched Borders - This occurs when the borders (especially on those cards with dark borders) are touched up on the edges and corners with magic marker or crayons of appropriate color in order to make the card appear to be mint.

Categorization of Defects

Miscellaneous Flaws

The following are common minor flaws that, depending on severity, lower a card's condition by one to four grades and often render it no better than excellent-mint: bubbles (lumps in surface), gum and wax stains, diamond cutting (slanted borders), notching, off-centered backs, paper wrinkles, scratched-off cartoons or puzzles on back, rubber band marks, scratches, surface impressions, and warping.

The following are common serious flaws that, depending on severity, lower a card's condition at least four grades and often render it no better than good: chemical or sun fading, erasure marks, mildew, miscutting (severe off-centering), holes, bleached or retouched borders, tape marks, tears, trimming, water or coffee stains, and writing.

Condition Guide

Grades

Mint (Mt) - A card with no flaws or wear. The card has four perfect corners, 55/45 or better centering from top to bottom and from left to right, original gloss, smooth edges, and original color borders. A mint card does not have print spots, color, or focus imperfections.

Near Mint-Mint (NrMt-Mt) - A card with one minor flaw. Any one of the following would lower a mint card to near mint-mint: one corner with a slight touch of wear, barely noticeable print spots, color or focus imperfections. The card must have 60/40 or better centering in both directions, original gloss, smooth edges, and original color borders.

Near Mint (NrMt) - A card with one minor flaw. Any one of the following would lower a mint card to near mint: one fuzzy corner or two to four corners with slight touches of wear, 70/30 to 60/40 centering, slightly rough edges, minor print spots, color or focus imperfections. The card must have original gloss and original color borders.

Excellent-Mint (ExMt) - A card with two or three fuzzy, but not rounded, corners and centering no worse than 80/20. The card may have no more than two of the following: slightly rough edges, very slightly discolored borders, minor print spots, color or focus imperfections. The card must have original gloss.

Excellent (Ex) - A card with four fuzzy but definitely not rounded corners and centering no worse than 80/20. The card may have a small amount of original gloss lost, rough edges, slightly discolored borders and minor print spots, color or focus imperfections.

Very Good (Vg) - A card that has been handled but not abused: slightly rounded corners with slight layering, slight notching on edges, a significant amount of gloss lost from the surface but no scuffing and moderate discoloration of borders. The card may have a few light creases.

Good (G), Fair (F), Poor (P) - A well-worn, mishandled, or abused card: badly rounded and layered corners, scuffing, most or all original gloss missing, seriously discolored borders, moderate or heavy creases, and one or more serious flaws. The grade of good, fair, or poor depends on the severity of wear and flaws. Good, fair, and poor cards generally are used only as fillers.

The most widely used grades are defined above. Obviously, many cards will not perfectly fit one of the definitions.

Therefore, categories between the major grades known as in-between grades are used, such as good to very good (G-Vg), very good to excellent (VgEx), and excellent-mint to near nint (ExMt-NrMt). Such grades indicate a card with all qualities of the lower category but with at least a few qualities of the higher category.

The Beckett Guide lists each card and set in three grades, with the middle grade valued at about 40%–45% of the top grade, and the bottom grade valued at about 10%–15% of the top grade.

The value of cards that fall between the listed columns can also be calculated using a percentage of the top grade. For example, a card that falls between the top and middle grades (Ex, ExMt, or NrMt in most cases) will generally be valued at anywhere from 50% to 90% of the top grade.

Similarly, a card that falls between the middle and bottom grades (G-Vg, Vg, or VgEx in most cases) will generally be valued at anywhere from 20% to 40% of the top grade.

There are also cases where cards are in better condition than the top grade or worse than the bottom grade. Cards that grade worse than the lowest grade are generally valued at 5%–10% of the top grade.

When a card exceeds the top grade by one—such as NrMt-Mt when the top grade is NrMt, or Mint when the top grade is NrMt-Mt—a premium of up to 50% is possible, with 10%–20% the usual norm.

When a card exceeds the top grade by two—such as Mint when the top grade is NrMt, or NrMt-Mt when the top grade is ExMt—a premium of 25%–50% is the usual norm. But certain condition-sensitive cards or sets, particularly those from the pre-war era, can bring premiums of up to 100% or even more.

Unopened packs, boxes, and factory-collated sets are considered mint in their unknown (and presumed perfect) state. Once opened, however, each card can be graded (and valued) in its own right by taking into account any defects that may be present in spite of the fact that the card has never been handled.

Selling Your Cards

Just about every collector sells cards or will sell cards eventually. Someday you may be interested in selling your duplicates or maybe even your whole collection. You may sell to other collectors, friends, or dealers. You may even sell cards you purchased from a certain dealer back to that same dealer. In any event, it helps to know some of the mechanics of the typical transaction between buyer and seller.

Dealers will buy cards in order to resell them to other collectors who are interested in the cards. Dealers will always pay a higher percentage for items that (in their opinion) can be resold quickly, and a much lower percentage for those items that are perceived as having low demand and hence are slow moving. In either case, dealers must buy at a price that allows for the expense of doing business and a margin for profit.

If you have cards for sale, the best advice we can give is that you get several offers for your cards—either from card shops or at a card show—and take the best offer, all things considered. Note, the "best" offer may not be the one for the highest amount. And remember, if a dealer really wants your cards, he won't let you get away without making his best competitive offer. Another alternative is to place your cards in an auction as one or several lots.

Many people think nothing of going into a department store and paying $15 for an item of clothing for which the store paid $5. But if you were selling your $15 card to a dealer and he offered you $5 for it, you might think his markup unreasonable. To complete the analogy, most department stores (and card dealers) that consistently pay $10 for $15 items eventually go out of business.

Centering

Well-Centered

Slightly Off-Centered

Off-Centered

Badly Off-Centered

Miscut

An exception is when the dealer has lined up a willing buyer for the item(s) you are attempting to sell, or if the cards are so hot that it's likely he'll have to hold the cards for only a short period of time.

In those cases, an offer of up to 75% of book value still will allow the dealer to make a reasonable profit considering the short time he will need to hold the merchandise. In general, however, most cards and collections will bring offers in the range of 25% to 50% of retail price. Also consider that most material from the past five to 20 years is plentiful. If that's what you're selling, don't be surprised if your best offer is well below that range.

Interesting Notes

The first card numerically of an issue is the single card most likely to obtain excessive wear. Consequently, you typically will find the price on the #1 card (in NrMt or mint condition) somewhat higher than might otherwise be the case. Similarly, but to a lesser extent (because normally the less important, reverse side of the card is the one exposed), the last card numerically in an issue also is prone to abnormal wear. This extra wear and tear occurs because the first and last cards are exposed to the elements (human element included) more than any other cards. They are generally end cards in any brick formations, rubber bandings, stackings on wet surfaces, and like activities.

Sports cards have no intrinsic value. The value of a card, like the value of other collectibles, can be determined only by you and your enjoyment in viewing and possessing these cardboard treasures.

Remember, the buyer ultimately determines the price of each card. You are the determining price factor because you have the ability to say "No" to the price of any card by not exchanging your hard-earned money for a given card. When the cost of a trading card exceeds the enjoyment you will receive from it, your answer should be "No." We assess and report the prices. You set them!

We are always interested in receiving the price input of collectors and dealers from around the country. We happily credit major contributors. We welcome your opinions, since your contributions assist us in ensuring a better guide each year. If you would like to join our survey list for the next editions of this book and others authored by Dr. Beckett, please send your name and address to Dr. James Beckett, 15850 Dallas Parkway, Dallas, TX 75248.

History of Football Cards

Until the 1930s, the only set devoted exclusively to football players was the Mayo N302 set. The first bubblegum issue dedicated entirely to football players did not appear until the National Chicle issue of 1935. Before this, athletes from several sports were pictured in the multi-sport Goudey Sport Kings issue of 1933. In that set, football was represented by three legends whose fame has not diminished through the years: Red Grange, Knute Rockne, and Jim Thorpe.

But it was not until 1948, and the post-war bubblegum boom, that the next football issues appeared. Bowman and Leaf Gum companies both issued football card sets in that year. From this point on, football cards have been issued annually by one company or another up to the present time, with Topps being the only major card producer until 1989, when Pro Set and Score debuted and sparked a football card boom.

Football cards depicting players from the Canadian Football League (CFL) did not appear until Parkhurst issued a 100-card set in 1952. Four years later, Parkhurst issued another CFL set with 50 small cards this time. Topps began issuing CFL sets in 1958 and continued annually until 1965, although from 1961 to 1965 these cards were printed in Canada by O-Pee-Chee. Post

Corner Wear

The partial cards here have been photographed at 300%. This was done in order to magnify each card's corner wear to such a degree that differences could be shown on a printed page.

This 1985 Topps Fred Quillan card has a fuzzy corner. Notice the extremely slight fraying on the corner.

This 1985 Topps Fred Smerlas card has a slightly rounded corner. Notice that there is no longer a sharp corner but heavy wear.

This 1985 Topps Daryl Turner card has a rounded corner evident by the lack of a sharp point and heavy wear on both edges.

This 1985 Topps Kim Bokamper card displays a badly rounded corner. Notice a large portion of missing cardboard accompanied by heavy wear and excessive fraying.

This 1985 Topps Neil O'Donaghue card displays creases of varying degrees. Light creases (left side of the card) may not break the card's surface, while heavy creases (right side) will.

Cereal issued two CFL sets in 1962 and 1963; these cards formed the backs of boxes of Post Cereals distributed in Canada. The O-Pee-Chee company, which has maintained a working relationship with the Topps Gum Company, issued four CFL sets in the years 1968, 1970, 1971, and 1972. Since 1981, the JOGO Novelties Company has been producing a number of CFL sets depicting past and present players.

Returning to American football issues, Bowman resumed its football cards (by then with full-color fronts) from 1950 to 1955. The company twice increased the size of its card during that period. Bowman was unopposed during most of the early 1950s as the sole producer of cards featuring pro football players.

Topps issued its first football card set in 1950 with a group of very small, felt-back cards. In 1951 Topps issued what is referred to as the "Magic Football Card" set. This set of 75 has a scratch-off section on the back which answers a football quiz. Topps did not issue another football set until 1955 when its All-American Football set paid tribute to past college football greats. In January 1956, Topps Gum Company (of Brooklyn) purchased the Bowman Company (of Philadelphia).

After the purchase, Topps issued sets of National Football League (NFL) players up until 1963. The 1961 Topps football set also included American Football League (AFL) players in the high-number series (133–198). Topps sets from 1964 to 1967 contained AFL players only. From 1968 to the present, Topps has issued a major set of football cards each year.

When the AFL was founded in 1960, Fleer produced a 132-card set of AFL players and coaches. In 1961, Fleer issued a 220-card set (even larger than the Topps issue of that year) featuring players from both the NFL and AFL. Apparently, for that one year, Topps and Fleer tested a reciprocal arrangement, trading the card printing rights to each other's contracted players. The 1962 and 1963 Fleer sets feature only AFL players. Both sets are relatively small at 88 cards each.

Post Cereal issued a 200-card set of National League football players in 1962 which contains numerous scarcities, namely those players appearing on unpopular varieties of Post Cereal. From 1964 to 1967, the Philadelphia Gum company issued four 198-card NFL player sets.

In 1984 and 1985, Topps produced a set for the now defunct United States Football League, in addition to its annual NFL set. The 1984 set in particular is quite scarce, due to both low distribution and the high demand for the extended Rookie Cards of current NFL superstars Jim Kelly and Reggie White, among others.

In 1986, McDonald's Restaurants generated the most excitement in football cards in many years. McDonald's created a nationwide football card promotion in which customers could receive a card or two per food purchase, upon request. However, the cards distributed were only of the local team, or of the "McDonald's All-Stars" for areas not near NFL cities. Also, each set was produced with four possible color tabs: blue, black, gold, and green. The tab color distributed depended on the week of the promotion. In general, cards with blue tabs are the scarcest, although for some teams the cards with black tabs are the hardest to find. The tabs were intended to be scratched off and removed by customers to be redeemed for food and other prizes, but among collectors, cards with scratched or removed tabs are categorized as having a major defect, and therefore are valued considerably less.

The entire set, including four color tabs for all 29 subsets, totals over 2,800 different cards. The hoopla over the McDonald's cards fell off precipitously after 1988 as collector interest shifted to the new 1989 Score and Pro

Set issues.

The popularity of football cards has continued to grow since 1986. Topps introduced "Super Rookie" cards in 1987. Card companies other than Topps noticed the burgeoning interest in football cards, resulting in the two landmark 1989 football sets: a 330-card Score issue, and a 440-card Pro Set release. Score later produced a self-contained 110-card supplemental set, while Pro Set printed 100 Series II cards and a 21-card "Final Update" set. Topps, Pro Set, and Score all improved card quality and increased the size of their sets for 1990. That season also marked Fleer's return to football cards and Action Packed's first major set.

In 1991, Pacific, Pro Line, Upper Deck, and Wild Card joined a market that is now at least as competitive as the baseball card market. And the premium card trend that began in baseball cards spilled over to the gridiron in the form of Fleer Ultra, Pro Set Platinum, Score Pinnacle, and Topps Stadium Club sets.

The year 1992 brought even more growth with the debuts of All World, Collectors Edge, GameDay, Playoff, Pro Set Power, SkyBox Impact, and SkyBox Primetime.

The football card market stabilized somewhat in 1993 thanks to an agreement between the long-feuding NFL licensing bodies, NFL Properties and the NFL Players Association. Also helping the stabilization was the emergence of several promising rookies, including Drew Bledsoe, Jerome Bettis, and Rick Mirer. Limited production became the industry buzzword in sports cards, and football was no exception. The result was the success of three new product lines: 1993 Playoff Contenders, 1993 Select, and 1993 SP.

The year 1994 brought further stabilization and limited production. Pro Set and Wild Card dropped out, while no new card companies joined the ranks. However, several new NFL sets were added to the mix by existing manufacturers: Classic NFL Experience, Collector's Choice, Excalibur, Finest, and Sportflics. The new trend centered around multi-level parallel sets and interactive game inserts with parallel prizes. Another strong rookie crop and reported production cutbacks contributed to strong football card sales throughout 1994.

The football card market continued to grow between 1995 and 1998. Many new sets were released by the major manufacturers and a few new players entered the hobby. Companies continued to push the limits of printing technology with issues printed on plastic, leather, cloth, and various metals. Rookie Cards once more came into vogue and the "1-of-1" insert card was born. There are more choices than ever before for the football card collector; most like it that way. In the last couple of years, more changes have occurred in the football card market. The Rookie Card popularity continued but with a twist. Since 1998, many Rookie Cards have been sequentially numbered and/or printed to a shorter supply than other cards in the set they are in.

Also, many companies have begun to issue "game-worn jerseys" or certified autographed cards of leading players, both active and retired.

In addition, graded cards, old and new, have revitalized the card market. Many collectors and dealers have been able to trade over Internet services such as eBay or the many different ways cards are available on beckett.com.

The trend towards short printed Rookie Cards as well as a growing use of memorablia on card continued through the 2001 seasons.

Many of the key Rookie Cards are now issued with some combination of either an autograph, uniform swatch or even both. In addition, the print run of many of these is smaller each and every year.

In addition, a significant amount of the autographs are no longer actually signed on the cards but are signed on stickers which are then affixed to a card.

One after-effect of all this emphasis on Rookie and Memorabilia cards is that many supposed "second-tier" players just do not have many cards issued. The most notable example for 2001 card season was that Tom Brady (who quarterbacked the Patriots to a Super Bowl championship) had less than five cards issued in more than 50 sets.

The 2002 football card season saw an increase in the number of memorabilia cards being issued, and a slight decrease in the number of certified autograph cards being released. Michael Vick was at the forefront of a strong collecting season, as he and several other young players look to establish themselves in the market, as many of the NFL's superstars grow older and near retirement.

While some collectors are frustrated by the changing hobby, others are thrilled because there are more choices than ever for the football card collector—and many of the collectors like it that way.

Additional Reading

Each year Beckett Publications produces comprehensive annual price guides for each of the four major sports: *Beckett Baseball Card Price Guide, Beckett Football Card Price Guide, Beckett Basketball Card Price Guide*, and *Beckett Hockey Card Price Guide*. The aim of these annual guides is to provide information and accurate pricing on a wide array of sports cards, ranging from main issues by the major card manufacturers to various regional, promotional, and food issues. Also other alphabetical checklists, such as *The Beckett Baseball Card Alphabetical, The Beckett Football Card Alphabetical, The Beckett Basketball Card Alphabetical,* and *The Beckett Hockey Card Price Guide and Alphabetical*, are published to assist the collector in identifying all the cards of any particular player. Our Web site Beckett.com was created to allow our readers with Internet access an avenue for buying and selling cards as well as participating in online auctions and interactive price guides. The seasoned collector will find these tools valuable sources of information that will enable him to pursue his hobby interests.

In addition, abridged editions of the Beckett Price Guides have been published for each of the three major sports as part of the House of Collectibles series: *The Official Price Guide to Baseball Cards, The Official Price Guide to Football Cards,* and *The Official Price Guide to Basketball Cards*. Published in a convenient mass-market paperback format, these price guides provide information and accurate pricing on all the important issues by the major card manufacturers.

2000 Absolute

	Nm-Mt	Ex-Mt
COMPLETE SET (250)	250.00	110.00
COMP.SET w/o SP's (150)	20.00	9.00
❑ 1 Frank Sanders	.50	.23
❑ 2 Rob Moore	.50	.23
❑ 3 Jake Plummer	.50	.23
❑ 4 David Boston	.75	.35
❑ 5 Chris Chandler	.50	.23
❑ 6 Tim Dwight	.75	.35
❑ 7 Terance Mathis	.50	.23
❑ 8 Jamal Anderson	.75	.35
❑ 9 Priest Holmes	1.00	.45
❑ 10 Tony Banks	.50	.23
❑ 11 Jermaine Lewis	.30	.14
❑ 12 Qadry Ismail	.50	.23
❑ 13 Brandon Stokley	.50	.23
❑ 14 Shannon Sharpe	.50	.23
❑ 15 Trent Dilfer	.50	.23
❑ 16 Eric Moulds	.75	.35
❑ 17 Doug Flutie	.75	.35
❑ 18 Antowain Smith	.50	.23
❑ 19 Jonathan Linton	.30	.14
❑ 20 Peerless Price	.75	.35
❑ 21 Rob Johnson	.50	.23
❑ 22 Muhsin Muhammad	.50	.23
❑ 23 Wesley Walls	.30	.14
❑ 24 Tim Biakabutuka	.50	.23
❑ 25 Steve Beuerlein	.50	.23
❑ 26 Patrick Jeffers	.75	.35
❑ 27 Natrone Means	.30	.14
❑ 28 Curtis Enis	.30	.14
❑ 29 Bobby Engram	.50	.23
❑ 30 Marcus Robinson	.75	.35
❑ 31 Marty Booker	.50	.23
❑ 32 Cade McNown	.30	.14
❑ 33 Darnay Scott	.50	.23
❑ 34 Carl Pickens	.50	.23
❑ 35 Corey Dillon	.75	.35
❑ 36 Akili Smith	.30	.14
❑ 37 Michael Basnight	.30	.14
❑ 38 Karim Abdul-Jabbar	.50	.23
❑ 39 Tim Couch	.50	.23
❑ 40 Kevin Johnson	.75	.35
❑ 41 Darrin Chiaverini	.30	.14
❑ 42 Errict Rhett	.50	.23
❑ 43 Emmitt Smith	1.50	.70
❑ 44 Michael Irvin	.50	.23
❑ 45 Rocket Ismail	.50	.23
❑ 46 Troy Aikman	1.50	.70
❑ 47 Jason Tucker	.30	.14
❑ 48 Randall Cunningham	.75	.35
❑ 49 Joey Galloway	.50	.23
❑ 50 Ed McCaffrey	.75	.35
❑ 51 Rod Smith	.50	.23
❑ 52 Brian Griese	.75	.35
❑ 53 John Elway	2.50	1.10
❑ 54 Terrell Davis	.75	.35
❑ 55 Olandis Gary	.75	.35
❑ 56 Johnnie Morton	.50	.23
❑ 57 Charlie Batch	.75	.35
❑ 58 Barry Sanders	2.00	.90
❑ 59 Germane Crowell	.30	.14
❑ 60 Herman Moore	.50	.23
❑ 61 James Stewart	.50	.23
❑ 62 Corey Bradford	.30	.14
❑ 63 Dorsey Levens	.50	.23
❑ 64 Antonio Freeman	.75	.35
❑ 65 Brett Favre	2.50	1.10
❑ 66 Bill Schroeder	.50	.23
❑ 67 Marvin Harrison	.75	.35
❑ 68 Peyton Manning	1.50	.70
❑ 69 Terrence Wilkins	.30	.14
❑ 70 Edgerrin James	1.25	.55
❑ 71 Keenan McCardell	.50	.23
❑ 72 Mark Brunell	.75	.35
❑ 73 Fred Taylor	.75	.35
❑ 74 Jimmy Smith	.50	.23
❑ 75 Elvis Grbac	.50	.23
❑ 76 Tony Gonzalez	.50	.23
❑ 77 Donnell Bennett	.30	.14
❑ 78 Warren Moon	.75	.35
❑ 79 Kimble Anders	.30	.14
❑ 80 Dan Marino	2.50	1.10
❑ 81 O.J. McDuffie	.50	.23
❑ 82 Tony Martin	.50	.23
❑ 83 James Johnson	.30	.14
❑ 84 Thurman Thomas	.50	.23
❑ 85 Randy Moss	1.25	.55
❑ 86 Cris Carter	.75	.35
❑ 87 Robert Smith	.75	.35
❑ 88 Daunte Culpepper	1.00	.45
❑ 89 Terry Glenn	.50	.23
❑ 90 Drew Bledsoe	1.00	.45
❑ 91 Kevin Faulk	.50	.23
❑ 92 Ricky Williams	.75	.35
❑ 93 Jeff Blake	.50	.23
❑ 94 Jake Reed	.50	.23
❑ 95 Amani Toomer	.50	.23
❑ 96 Kerry Collins	.50	.23
❑ 97 Tiki Barber	.50	.23
❑ 98 Ike Hilliard	.50	.23
❑ 99 Curtis Martin	.75	.35
❑ 100 Vinny Testaverde	.50	.23
❑ 101 Wayne Chrebet	.50	.23
❑ 102 Ray Lucas	.50	.23
❑ 103 Tyrone Wheatley	.50	.23
❑ 104 Napoleon Kaufman	.50	.23
❑ 105 Tim Brown	.75	.35
❑ 106 Rich Gannon	.75	.35
❑ 107 Duce Staley	.75	.35
❑ 108 Donovan McNabb	1.25	.55
❑ 109 Kordell Stewart	.50	.23
❑ 110 Jerome Bettis	.75	.35
❑ 111 Troy Edwards	.30	.14
❑ 112 Junior Seau	.75	.35
❑ 113 Jim Harbaugh	.50	.23
❑ 114 Ryan Leaf	.50	.23
❑ 115 Jermaine Fazande	.30	.14
❑ 116 Curtis Conway	.50	.23
❑ 117 Terrell Owens	.75	.35
❑ 118 Charlie Garner	.50	.23
❑ 119 Jerry Rice	1.50	.70
❑ 120 Steve Young	1.00	.45
❑ 121 Jeff Garcia	.75	.35
❑ 122 Derrick Mayes	.50	.23
❑ 123 Ricky Watters	.50	.23
❑ 124 Jon Kitna	.75	.35
❑ 125 Sean Dawkins	.30	.14
❑ 126 Az-Zahir Hakim	.50	.23
❑ 127 Isaac Bruce	.75	.35
❑ 128 Marshall Faulk	1.00	.45
❑ 129 Trent Green	.75	.35
❑ 130 Kurt Warner	1.50	.70
❑ 131 Torry Holt	.75	.35
❑ 132 Jacquez Green	.30	.14
❑ 133 Warren Sapp	.50	.23
❑ 134 Mike Alstott	.75	.35
❑ 135 Warrick Dunn	.75	.35
❑ 136 Shaun King	.30	.14
❑ 137 Keyshawn Johnson	.75	.35
❑ 138 Eddie George	.75	.35
❑ 139 Yancey Thigpen	.30	.14
❑ 140 Steve McNair	.75	.35
❑ 141 Kevin Dyson	.50	.23
❑ 142 Frank Wycheck	.30	.14
❑ 143 Jevon Kearse	.75	.35
❑ 144 Stephen Davis	.75	.35
❑ 145 Brad Johnson	.75	.35
❑ 146 Michael Westbrook	.50	.23
❑ 147 Albert Connell	.30	.14
❑ 148 Bruce Smith	.50	.23
❑ 149 Jeff George	.50	.23
❑ 150 Deion Sanders	.75	.35
❑ 151 Peter Warrick RC	4.00	1.80
❑ 152 Courtney Brown RC	4.00	1.80
❑ 153 Plaxico Burress RC	8.00	3.60
❑ 154 Corey Simon RC	4.00	1.80
❑ 155 Thomas Jones RC	6.00	2.70
❑ 156 Travis Taylor RC	4.00	1.80
❑ 157 Shaun Alexander RC	10.00	4.50
❑ 158 Chris Redman RC	3.00	1.35
❑ 159 Chad Pennington RC	15.00	6.75
❑ 160 Jamal Lewis RC	10.00	4.50
❑ 161 Brian Urlacher RC	15.00	6.75
❑ 162 Bubba Franks RC	4.00	1.80
❑ 163 Dez White RC	4.00	1.80
❑ 164 Ahmed Plummer RC	4.00	1.80
❑ 165 Ron Dayne RC	4.00	1.80
❑ 166 Shaun Ellis RC	4.00	1.80
❑ 167 Sylvester Morris RC	.50	.23
❑ 168 Deltha O'Neal RC	4.00	1.80
❑ 169 R.Jay Soward RC	3.00	1.35
❑ 170 Sherrod Gideon RC	2.00	.90
❑ 171 John Abraham RC	4.00	1.80
❑ 172 Travis Prentice RC	3.00	1.35
❑ 173 Darrell Jackson RC	8.00	3.60
❑ 174 Giovanni Carmazzi RC	3.00	1.35
❑ 175 Anthony Lucas RC	2.00	.90
❑ 176 Danny Farmer RC	3.00	1.35
❑ 177 Dennis Northcutt RC	4.00	1.80
❑ 178 Troy Walters RC	4.00	1.80
❑ 179 Laveranues Coles RC	5.00	2.20
❑ 180 Kwame Cavil RC	2.00	.90
❑ 181 Tee Martin RC	4.00	1.80
❑ 182 J.R. Redmond RC	3.00	1.35
❑ 183 Tim Rattay RC	8.00	3.60
❑ 184 Jerry Porter RC	5.00	2.20
❑ 185 Sebastian Janikowski RC	4.00	1.80
❑ 186 Michael Wiley RC	3.00	1.35
❑ 187 Reuben Droughns RC	5.00	2.20
❑ 188 Trung Canidate RC	3.00	1.35
❑ 189 Shyrone Stith RC	3.00	1.35
❑ 190 Ian Gold RC	3.00	1.35
❑ 191 Hank Poteat RC	3.00	1.35
❑ 192 Darren Howard RC	3.00	1.35
❑ 193 Rob Morris RC	3.00	1.35
❑ 194 Marc Bulger RC	8.00	3.60
❑ 195 Tom Brady RC	40.00	18.00
❑ 196 Doug Johnson RC	4.00	1.80
❑ 197 Todd Husak RC	4.00	1.80
❑ 198 Gari Scott RC	2.00	.90
❑ 199 Erron Kinney RC	4.00	1.80
❑ 200 Nate Webster RC	2.00	.90
❑ 201 Anthony Becht RC	4.00	1.80
❑ 202 Sammy Morris RC	3.00	1.35
❑ 203 Rondell Mealey RC	2.00	.90
❑ 204 Doug Chapman RC	3.00	1.35
❑ 205 Rogers Beckett RC	3.00	1.35
❑ 206 Ron Dugans RC	2.00	.90
❑ 207 Deon Dyer RC	3.00	1.35
❑ 208 Marcus Knight RC	3.00	1.35
❑ 209 Thomas Hamner RC	2.00	.90
❑ 210 Joe Hamilton RC	3.00	1.35
❑ 211 Todd Pinkston RC	4.00	1.80
❑ 212 Chris Cole RC	3.00	1.35
❑ 213 Ron Dixon RC	3.00	1.35
❑ 214 JaJuan Dawson RC	2.00	.90
❑ 215 Terrelle Smith RC	3.00	1.35
❑ 216 Curtis Keaton RC	3.00	1.35
❑ 217 Keith Bulluck RC	4.00	1.80
❑ 218 John Engelberger RC	3.00	1.35
❑ 219 Raynoch Thompson RC	3.00	1.35
❑ 220 Cornelius Griffin RC	3.00	1.35
❑ 221 William Bartee RC	3.00	1.35
❑ 222 Fred Robbins RC	2.00	.90
❑ 223 Dwayne Goodrich RC	2.00	.90
❑ 224 Deon Grant RC	3.00	1.35
❑ 225 Jacoby Shepherd RC	3.00	1.35
❑ 226 Ben Kelly RC	2.00	.90
❑ 227 Corey Moore RC	2.00	.90
❑ 228 Aaron Shea RC	3.00	1.35
❑ 229 Trevor Gaylor RC	3.00	1.35
❑ 230 Frank Moreau RC	3.00	1.35
❑ 231 Avion Black RC	3.00	1.35

❑ 232 Paul Smith RC	3.00	1.35
❑ 233 Dante Hall RC	8.00	3.60
❑ 234 Muneer Moore RC	2.00	.90
❑ 235 James Whalen RC	2.00	.90
❑ 236 Chad Morton RC	4.00	1.80
❑ 237 Frank Murphy RC	2.00	.90
❑ 238 Mareno Philyaw RC	2.00	.90
❑ 239 James Williams RC	3.00	1.35
❑ 240 Mike Anderson RC	4.00	1.80
❑ 241 Jarious Jackson RC	3.00	1.35
❑ 242 Demario Brown RC	2.00	.90
❑ 243 Chris Coleman RC	4.00	1.80
❑ 244 Rashard Anderson RC	3.00	1.35
❑ 245 John Jones RC	3.00	1.35
❑ 246 Erik Flowers RC	3.00	1.35
❑ 247 JaJuan Seider RC	2.00	.90
❑ 248 Leon Murray RC	2.00	.90
❑ 249 Bashir Yamini RC	2.00	.90
❑ 250 Na'il Diggs RC	3.00	1.35

2000 Absolute Boss Hogg Autographs

	Nm-Mt	Ex-Mt
❑ BH1 Eric Moulds	20.00	9.00
❑ BH2 Cade McNown	20.00	9.00
❑ BH3 Tim Couch	20.00	9.00
❑ BH4 Terrell Davis	30.00	13.50
❑ BH5 Barry Sanders	100.00	45.00
❑ BH6 Peyton Manning	80.00	36.00
❑ BH7 Edgerrin James	50.00	22.00
❑ BH8 Marvin Harrison	30.00	13.50
❑ BH9 Mark Brunell	25.00	11.00
❑ BH10 Fred Taylor EXCH		
❑ BH11 Dan Marino	150.00	70.00
❑ BH12 Cris Carter	30.00	13.50
❑ BH13 Drew Bledsoe	30.00	13.50
❑ BH14 Ricky Williams	40.00	18.00
❑ BH15 Curtis Martin EXCH		
❑ BH16 Kurt Warner	40.00	18.00
❑ BH17 Isaac Bruce	30.00	13.50
❑ BH18 Eddie George	25.00	11.00
❑ BH19 Steve McNair	30.00	13.50
❑ BH20 Brad Johnson	25.00	11.00

2001 Absolute Memorabilia

	Nm-Mt	Ex-Mt
COMP.SET w/o SP's (100)	30.00	9.00
❑ 1 David Boston	1.25	.35
❑ 2 Jake Plummer	.75	.23
❑ 3 Thomas Jones	.75	.23
❑ 4 Jamal Anderson	1.25	.35
❑ 5 Chris Redman	.50	.15
❑ 6 Jamal Lewis	2.00	.60
❑ 7 Qadry Ismail	.75	.23
❑ 8 Ray Lewis	1.25	.35
❑ 9 Shannon Sharpe	.75	.23
❑ 10 Travis Taylor	.75	.23
❑ 11 Trent Dilfer	.75	.23
❑ 12 Elvis Grbac	.75	.23
❑ 13 Eric Moulds	.75	.23
❑ 14 Rob Johnson	.75	.23
❑ 15 Muhsin Muhammad	.75	.23
❑ 16 Brian Urlacher	2.00	.60
❑ 17 Cade McNown	.50	.15
❑ 18 Marcus Robinson	1.25	.35
❑ 19 Akili Smith	.50	.15
❑ 20 Corey Dillon	1.25	.35
❑ 21 Peter Warrick	1.25	.35
❑ 22 Courtney Brown	.75	.23
❑ 23 Tim Couch	.75	.23
❑ 24 Emmitt Smith	2.50	.75
❑ 25 Troy Aikman	2.00	.60
❑ 26 Brian Griese	1.25	.35
❑ 27 Ed McCaffrey	1.25	.35
❑ 28 John Elway	4.00	1.20
❑ 29 Mike Anderson	1.25	.35
❑ 30 Rod Smith	.75	.23
❑ 31 Terrell Davis	1.25	.35
❑ 32 Barry Sanders	2.50	.75
❑ 33 James Stewart	.75	.23
❑ 34 Ahman Green	1.25	.35
❑ 35 Antonio Freeman	1.25	.35
❑ 36 Brett Favre	4.00	1.20
❑ 37 Edgerrin James	1.50	.45
❑ 38 Marvin Harrison	1.25	.35
❑ 39 Peyton Manning	3.00	.90
❑ 40 Fred Taylor	1.25	.35
❑ 41 Jimmy Smith	.75	.23
❑ 42 Keenan McCardell	.50	.15
❑ 43 Mark Brunell	1.25	.35
❑ 44 Sylvester Morris	.50	.15
❑ 45 Tony Gonzalez	.75	.23
❑ 46 Dan Marino	4.00	1.20
❑ 47 Jay Fiedler	1.25	.35
❑ 48 Lamar Smith	.75	.23
❑ 49 Cris Carter	1.25	.35
❑ 50 Daunte Culpepper	1.25	.35
❑ 51 Randy Moss	2.50	.75
❑ 52 Drew Bledsoe	1.50	.45
❑ 53 Terry Glenn	.75	.23
❑ 54 Aaron Brooks	1.25	.35
❑ 55 Joe Horn	.75	.23
❑ 56 Ricky Williams	1.25	.35
❑ 57 Amani Toomer	.75	.23
❑ 58 Ike Hilliard	.75	.23
❑ 59 Kerry Collins	.75	.23
❑ 60 Ron Dayne	1.25	.35
❑ 61 Tiki Barber	.75	.23
❑ 62 Chad Pennington	2.00	.60
❑ 63 Curtis Martin	1.25	.35
❑ 64 Laveranues Coles	1.25	.35
❑ 65 Vinny Testaverde	.75	.23
❑ 66 Wayne Chrebet	.75	.23
❑ 67 Charles Woodson	.75	.23
❑ 68 Rich Gannon	1.25	.35
❑ 69 Tim Brown	1.25	.35
❑ 70 Tyrone Wheatley	.75	.23
❑ 71 Corey Simon	.75	.23
❑ 72 Donovan McNabb	1.50	.45
❑ 73 Duce Staley	1.25	.35
❑ 74 Jerome Bettis	1.25	.35
❑ 75 Plaxico Burress	1.25	.35
❑ 76 Doug Flutie	1.25	.35
❑ 77 Junior Seau	1.25	.35
❑ 78 Charlie Garner	.75	.23
❑ 79 Jeff Garcia	1.25	.35
❑ 80 Jerry Rice	2.50	.75
❑ 81 Steve Young	1.25	.35
❑ 82 Terrell Owens	1.25	.35
❑ 83 Darrell Jackson	1.25	.35
❑ 84 Ricky Watters	.50	.15
❑ 85 Shaun Alexander	1.50	.45
❑ 86 Isaac Bruce	1.25	.35
❑ 87 Kurt Warner	2.50	.75
❑ 88 Marshall Faulk	1.50	.45
❑ 89 Torry Holt	1.25	.35
❑ 90 Brad Johnson	1.25	.35
❑ 91 Keyshawn Johnson	1.25	.35
❑ 92 Mike Alstott	1.25	.35
❑ 93 Shaun King	.50	.15
❑ 94 Warren Sapp	.75	.23
❑ 95 Warrick Dunn	1.25	.35
❑ 96 Eddie George	1.25	.35
❑ 97 Jevon Kearse	.75	.23
❑ 98 Steve McNair	1.25	.35
❑ 99 Jeff George	.75	.23
❑ 100 Stephen Davis	1.25	.35
❑ 101 Jason McKinley RC	4.00	1.20
❑ 102 Bobby Newcombe RC	4.00	1.20
❑ 103 Cedrick Wilson RC	6.00	1.80
❑ 104 Ken-Yon Rambo RC	4.00	1.20
❑ 105 Kevin Kasper RC	6.00	1.80
❑ 106 Jamal Reynolds RC	6.00	1.80
❑ 107 Scotty Anderson RC	4.00	1.20
❑ 108 T.J. Houshmandzadeh RC	6.00	1.80
❑ 109 Chris Taylor RC	4.00	1.20
❑ 110 Vinny Sutherland RC	4.00	1.20
❑ 111 Jabari Holloway RC	4.00	1.20
❑ 112 Shad Meier RC	4.00	1.20
❑ 113 Correll Buckhalter RC	8.00	2.40
❑ 114 Dan Alexander RC	6.00	1.80
❑ 115 David Allen RC	4.00	1.20
❑ 116 LaMont Jordan RC	8.00	2.40
❑ 117 Nate Clements RC	6.00	1.80
❑ 118 Reggie White RC	4.00	1.20
❑ 119 Javon Green RC	4.00	1.20
❑ 120 Shaun Rogers RC	6.00	1.80
❑ 121 Heath Evans RC	4.00	1.20
❑ 122 Moran Norris RC	2.50	.75
❑ 123 Ben Leard RC	4.00	1.20
❑ 124 David Rivers RC	4.00	1.20
❑ 125 A.J. Feeley RC	6.00	1.80
❑ 126 Boo Williams RC	4.00	1.20
❑ 127 Ronney Daniels RC	2.50	.75
❑ 128 Alge Crumpler RC	8.00	2.40
❑ 129 Todd Heap RC	6.00	1.80
❑ 130 Tim Hasselbeck RC	6.00	1.80
❑ 131 Josh Booty RC	6.00	1.80
❑ 132 Jamie Winborn RC	4.00	1.20
❑ 133 Brian Allen RC	2.50	.75
❑ 134 Sedrick Hodge RC	2.50	.75
❑ 135 Tommy Polley RC	6.00	1.80
❑ 136 Torrance Marshall RC	6.00	1.80
❑ 137 Damione Lewis RC	4.00	1.20
❑ 138 Marcus Stroud RC	6.00	1.80
❑ 139 Aaron Schobel RC	6.00	1.80
❑ 140 DeLawrence Grant RC	2.50	.75
❑ 141 Fred Smoot RC	6.00	1.80
❑ 142 Jamar Fletcher RC	4.00	1.20
❑ 143 Ken Lucas RC	4.00	1.20
❑ 144 Will Allen RC	4.00	1.20
❑ 145 Adam Archuleta RC	6.00	1.80
❑ 146 Derrick Gibson RC	4.00	1.20
❑ 147 Jarrod Cooper RC	6.00	1.80
❑ 148 Eddie Berlin RC	4.00	1.20
❑ 149 Steve Smith RC	8.00	2.40
❑ 150 Willie Middlebrooks RC	4.00	1.20
❑ 151 Michael Vick RPM RC	80.00	24.00
❑ 152 Drew Brees RPM RC	30.00	9.00
❑ 153 Chris Weinke RPM RC	15.00	4.50
❑ 154 M.Tuiasosopo RPM RC	15.00	4.50
❑ 155 Mike McMahon RPM RC	15.00	4.50
❑ 156 D.McAllister RPM RC	30.00	9.00
❑ 157 Leonard Davis RPM RC	10.00	3.00
❑ 158 L.Tomlinson RPM RC	40.00	12.00
❑ 159 A.Thomas RPM RC	25.00	7.50
❑ 160 Travis Henry RPM RC	20.00	6.00
❑ 161 James Jackson RPM RC	15.00	4.50
❑ 162 Michael Bennett RPM RC	30.00	9.00
❑ 163 Kevan Barlow RPM RC	15.00	4.50
❑ 164 Travis Minor RPM RC	10.00	3.00
❑ 165 David Terrell RPM RC	15.00	4.50
❑ 166 Santana Moss RPM RC	25.00	7.50
❑ 167 Rod Gardner RPM RC	15.00	4.50
❑ 168 Quincy Morgan RPM RC	15.00	4.50
❑ 169 Freddie Mitchell RPM RC	15.00	4.50
❑ 170 Reggie Wayne RPM RC	25.00	7.50
❑ 171 Koren Robinson RPM RC	15.00	4.50

❑ 172 Chad Johnson RPM RC	25.00	7.50
❑ 173 Chris Chambers RPM RC	20.00	6.00
❑ 174 Josh Heupel RPM RC	15.00	4.50
❑ 175 Andre Carter RPM RC	15.00	4.50
❑ 176 Justin Smith RPM RC	15.00	4.50
❑ 177 R.Seymour RPM RC	15.00	4.50
❑ 178 Dan Morgan RPM RC	15.00	4.50
❑ 179 Gerard Warren RPM RC	15.00	4.50
❑ 180 R.Ferguson RPM RC	15.00	4.50
❑ 181 Sage Rosenfels RPM RC	15.00	4.50
❑ 182 Rudi Johnson RPM RC	30.00	9.00
❑ 183 Snoop Minnis RPM RC	10.00	3.00
❑ 184 Jesse Palmer RPM RC	15.00	4.50
❑ 185 Quincy Carter RPM RC	15.00	4.50

2002 Absolute Memorabilia

	Nm-Mt	Ex-Mt
COMP.SET w/o SP's (150)	30.00	9.00
❑ 1 Aaron Brooks	1.25	.35
❑ 2 Ahman Green	1.25	.35
❑ 3 Alge Crumpler	.75	.23
❑ 4 Amani Toomer	.75	.23
❑ 5 Andre Carter	.50	.15
❑ 6 Anthony Thomas	1.25	.35
❑ 7 Antonio Freeman	1.25	.35
❑ 8 Antowain Smith	.75	.23
❑ 9 Az-Zahir Hakim	.50	.15
❑ 10 Bill Schroeder	.75	.23
❑ 11 Brad Johnson	.75	.23
❑ 12 Brett Favre	3.00	.90
❑ 13 Brian Griese	1.25	.35
❑ 14 Brian Urlacher	2.00	.60
❑ 15 Chad Johnson	1.25	.35
❑ 16 Chad Pennington	1.50	.45
❑ 17 Champ Bailey	.75	.23
❑ 18 Charles Woodson	.75	.23
❑ 19 Charlie Batch	.75	.23
❑ 20 Charlie Garner	.75	.23
❑ 21 Chris Chambers	1.25	.35
❑ 22 Chris Redman	.50	.15
❑ 23 Chris Weinke	.75	.23
❑ 24 Corey Dillon	.75	.23
❑ 25 Correll Buckhalter	.75	.23
❑ 26 Cris Carter	1.25	.35
❑ 27 Curtis Martin	1.25	.35
❑ 28 Darnay Scott	.75	.23
❑ 29 Darrell Jackson	.75	.23
❑ 30 Daunte Culpepper	1.25	.35
❑ 31 David Boston	1.25	.35
❑ 32 David Terrell	1.25	.35
❑ 33 Derrick Alexander	.75	.23
❑ 34 Derrick Mason	.75	.23
❑ 35 Deuce McAllister	1.50	.45
❑ 36 Dominic Rhodes	.75	.23
❑ 37 Donald Hayes	.50	.15
❑ 38 Donovan McNabb	1.50	.45
❑ 39 Doug Flutie	1.25	.35
❑ 40 Drew Bledsoe	1.50	.45
❑ 41 Drew Brees	1.25	.35
❑ 42 Duce Staley	1.25	.35
❑ 43 Ed McCaffrey	1.25	.35
❑ 44 Eddie George	1.25	.35
❑ 45 Edgerrin James	1.50	.45
❑ 46 Elvis Joseph	.50	.15
❑ 47 Emmitt Smith	3.00	.90
❑ 48 Eric Moulds	.75	.23
❑ 49 Frank Sanders	.50	.15
❑ 50 Fred Taylor	1.25	.35
❑ 51 Freddie Mitchell	.75	.23
❑ 52 Garrison Hearst	.75	.23
❑ 53 Gerard Warren	.50	.15
❑ 54 Germane Crowell	.50	.15
❑ 55 Isaac Bruce	1.25	.35
❑ 56 Jake Plummer	.75	.23
❑ 57 Jamal Anderson	.75	.23
❑ 58 Jamal Lewis	1.25	.35
❑ 59 James Allen	.75	.23
❑ 60 James Jackson	.50	.15
❑ 61 James Stewart	.75	.23
❑ 62 Jason Brookins	.50	.15
❑ 63 Jay Fiedler	.75	.23
❑ 64 Jeff Garcia	1.25	.35
❑ 65 Jerome Bettis	1.25	.35
❑ 66 Jerry Rice	2.50	.75
❑ 67 Jevon Kearse	.75	.23
❑ 68 Jim Miller	.50	.15
❑ 69 Jimmy Smith	.75	.23
❑ 70 Joe Horn	.75	.23
❑ 71 Joey Galloway	.75	.23
❑ 72 Jon Kitna	.75	.23
❑ 73 Junior Seau	1.25	.35
❑ 74 Keenan McCardell	.50	.15
❑ 75 Kendrell Bell	1.25	.35
❑ 76 Kerry Collins	.75	.23
❑ 77 Kevan Barlow	.75	.23
❑ 78 Kevin Dyson	.75	.23
❑ 79 Kevin Johnson	.75	.23
❑ 80 Kevin Kasper	.50	.15
❑ 81 Keyshawn Johnson	1.25	.35
❑ 82 Kordell Stewart	.75	.23
❑ 83 Koren Robinson	.75	.23
❑ 84 Kurt Warner	1.25	.35
❑ 85 LaDainian Tomlinson	2.00	.60
❑ 86 Lamar Smith	.75	.23
❑ 87 Laveranues Coles	.75	.23
❑ 88 MarTay Jenkins	.50	.15
❑ 89 Mark Brunell	1.25	.35
❑ 90 Marshall Faulk	1.25	.35
❑ 91 Marty Booker	.75	.23
❑ 92 Marvin Harrison	1.25	.35
❑ 93 Snoop Minnis	.50	.15
❑ 94 Michael Bennett	.75	.23
❑ 95 Michael Strahan	.75	.23
❑ 96 Michael Vick	4.00	1.20
❑ 97 Mike Alstott	1.25	.35
❑ 98 Mike Anderson	1.25	.35
❑ 99 Mike McMahon	1.25	.35
❑ 100 Muhsin Muhammad	.75	.23
❑ 101 Nate Clements	.50	.15
❑ 102 Oronde Gadsden	.75	.23
❑ 103 Peter Warrick	.75	.23
❑ 104 Peyton Manning	2.50	.75
❑ 105 Plaxico Burress	.75	.23
❑ 106 Priest Holmes	1.50	.45
❑ 107 Quincy Carter	.75	.23
❑ 108 Quincy Morgan	.75	.23
❑ 109 Rocket Ismail	.75	.23
❑ 110 Randy Moss	2.50	.75
❑ 111 Ray Lewis	1.25	.35
❑ 112 Reggie Wayne	.75	.23
❑ 113 Rich Gannon	1.25	.35
❑ 114 Rickey Dudley	.50	.15
❑ 115 Ricky Watters	.75	.23
❑ 116 Ricky Williams	1.25	.35
❑ 117 Rod Gardner	.75	.23
❑ 118 Rod Smith	.75	.23
❑ 119 Robert Ferguson	.50	.15
❑ 120 Santana Moss	1.25	.35
❑ 121 Shaun Alexander	1.25	.35
❑ 122 Stephen Davis	.75	.23
❑ 123 Steve McNair	1.25	.35
❑ 124 Steve Smith	.75	.23
❑ 125 Terrell Davis	1.25	.35
❑ 126 Terrell Owens	1.25	.35
❑ 127 Terry Glenn	.75	.23
❑ 128 Thomas Jones	.75	.23
❑ 129 Tiki Barber	.75	.23
❑ 130 Tim Brown	1.25	.35
❑ 131 Tim Couch	.75	.23
❑ 132 Todd Heap	.75	.23
❑ 133 Todd Pinkston	.75	.23
❑ 134 Tom Brady	3.00	.90
❑ 135 Tony Boselli	.50	.15
❑ 136 Tony Gonzalez	.75	.23
❑ 137 Torry Holt	1.25	.35
❑ 138 Travis Henry	1.25	.35
❑ 139 Travis Taylor	.75	.23
❑ 140 Trent Dilfer	.75	.23
❑ 141 Trent Green	.75	.23
❑ 142 Troy Brown	.75	.23
❑ 143 Troy Hambrick	.50	.15
❑ 144 Trung Canidate	.75	.23
❑ 145 Vinny Testaverde	.75	.23
❑ 146 Warren Sapp	.75	.23
❑ 147 Warrick Dunn	1.25	.35
❑ 148 Wayne Chrebet	.75	.23
❑ 149 Wesley Walls	.50	.15
❑ 150 Zach Thomas	1.25	.35
❑ 151 Quentin Jammer RC	6.00	1.80
❑ 152 Randy Fasani RC	5.00	1.50
❑ 153 Kurt Kittner RC	5.00	1.50
❑ 154 Chad Hutchinson RC	6.00	1.80
❑ 155 Major Applewhite RC	6.00	1.80
❑ 156 Wes Pate RC	3.00	.90
❑ 157 J.T. O'Sullivan RC	5.00	1.50
❑ 158 Ryan Denney RC	3.00	.90
❑ 159 Ronald Curry RC	6.00	1.80
❑ 160 Lamar Gordon RC	6.00	1.80
❑ 161 Brian Westbrook RC	10.00	3.00
❑ 162 Jonathan Wells RC	6.00	1.80
❑ 163 Ricky Williams RC	5.00	1.50
❑ 164 Verron Haynes RC	6.00	1.80
❑ 165 Josh Scobey RC	6.00	1.80
❑ 166 Larry Ned RC	5.00	1.50
❑ 167 Adrian Peterson RC	6.00	1.80
❑ 168 Chester Taylor RC	6.00	1.80
❑ 169 Luke Staley RC	5.00	1.50
❑ 170 Damien Anderson RC	5.00	1.50
❑ 171 Lee Mays RC	5.00	1.50
❑ 172 Deion Branch RC	12.00	3.60
❑ 173 Terry Charles RC	5.00	1.50
❑ 174 Woody Dantzler RC	6.00	1.80
❑ 175 Jason McAddley RC	5.00	1.50
❑ 176 Kelly Campbell RC	5.00	1.50
❑ 177 Freddie Milons RC	5.00	1.50
❑ 178 Kahlil Hill RC	5.00	1.50
❑ 179 Brian Poli-Dixon RC	5.00	1.50
❑ 180 Mike Echols RC	3.00	.90
❑ 181 Pete Rebstock RC	3.00	.90
❑ 182 Dwight Freeney RC	8.00	2.40
❑ 183 Bryan Thomas RC	5.00	1.50
❑ 184 Charles Grant RC	6.00	1.80
❑ 185 Kalimba Edwards RC	6.00	1.80
❑ 186 Ryan Sims RC	6.00	1.80
❑ 187 John Henderson RC	6.00	1.80
❑ 188 Wendell Bryant RC	6.00	1.80
❑ 189 Albert Haynesworth RC	5.00	1.50
❑ 190 Larry Tripplett RC	3.00	.90
❑ 191 Phillip Buchanon RC	6.00	1.80
❑ 192 Lito Sheppard RC	6.00	1.80
❑ 193 Mike Rumph RC	6.00	1.80
❑ 194 Levar Fisher RC	3.00	.90
❑ 195 Ed Reed RC	10.00	3.00
❑ 196 Rocky Calmus RC	6.00	1.80
❑ 197 Michael Lewis RC	6.00	1.80
❑ 198 Napoleon Harris RC	6.00	1.80
❑ 199 Robert Thomas RC	6.00	1.80
❑ 200 Anthony Weaver RC	5.00	1.50
❑ 201 Ladell Betts RPM RC	12.00	3.60
❑ 202 Antonio Bryant RPM RC	12.00	3.60
❑ 203 Reche Caldwell RPM RC	12.00	3.60
❑ 204 David Carr RPM RC	30.00	9.00
❑ 205 Tim Carter RPM RC	6.00	1.80
❑ 206 Eric Crouch RPM RC	20.00	6.00
❑ 207 Rohan Davey RPM RC	12.00	3.60
❑ 208 Andre Davis RPM RC	12.00	3.60
❑ 209 T.J. Duckett RPM RC	20.00	6.00
❑ 210 DeShaun Foster RPM RC	12.00	3.60
❑ 211 Jabar Gaffney RPM RC	12.00	3.60
❑ 212 Daniel Graham RPM RC	12.00	3.60
❑ 213 William Green RPM RC	20.00	6.00
❑ 214 Joey Harrington RPM RC	30.00	9.00
❑ 215 David Garrard RPM RC	6.00	1.80
❑ 216 Ron Johnson RPM RC	6.00	1.80
❑ 217 Ashley Lelie RPM RC	25.00	7.50
❑ 218 Josh McCown RPM RC	15.00	4.50

❑ 219 Maurice Morris RPM RC 12.00 3.60
❑ 220 Julius Peppers RPM RC 25.00 7.50
❑ 221 Clinton Portis RPM RC 30.00 9.00
❑ 222 Patrick Ramsey RPM RC 25.00 7.50
❑ 223 Antwaan Randle El RPM RC 15.004.50
❑ 224 Josh Reed RPM RC 12.00 3.60
❑ 225 Cliff Russell RPM RC 6.00 1.80
❑ 226 Jeremy Shockey RPM RC 30.00 9.00
❑ 227 Donte Stallworth RPM RC 25.00 7.50
❑ 228 Travis Stephens RPM RC 6.00 1.80
❑ 229 Javon Walker RPM RC 25.00 7.50
❑ 230 Marquise Walker RPM RC 6.00 1.80
❑ 231 Roy Williams RPM RC 30.00 9.00
❑ 232 Mike Williams RPM RC 6.00 1.80

2003 Absolute Memorabilia

	MINT	NRMT
COMP.SET w/o SP's (100)	25.00	11.00
❑ 1 Jamal Lewis	1.25	.55
❑ 2 Ray Lewis	1.25	.55
❑ 3 Todd Heap	.75	.35
❑ 4 Drew Bledsoe	1.25	.55
❑ 5 Travis Henry	.75	.35
❑ 6 Peerless Price	.75	.35
❑ 7 Corey Dillon	.75	.35
❑ 8 Chad Johnson	.75	.35
❑ 9 Tim Couch	.50	.23
❑ 10 William Green	.75	.35
❑ 11 Andre Davis	.50	.23
❑ 12 Brian Griese	1.25	.55
❑ 13 Ashley Lelie	1.25	.55
❑ 14 Clinton Portis	2.00	.90
❑ 15 Rod Smith	.75	.35
❑ 16 David Carr	2.00	.90
❑ 17 Corey Bradford	.50	.23
❑ 18 Jonathan Wells	.50	.23
❑ 19 Peyton Manning	2.00	.90
❑ 20 Edgerrin James	1.25	.55
❑ 21 Marvin Harrison	1.25	.55
❑ 22 Mark Brunell	.75	.35
❑ 23 Fred Taylor	1.25	.55
❑ 24 Jimmy Smith	.75	.35
❑ 25 Trent Green	.75	.35
❑ 26 Priest Holmes	1.50	.70
❑ 27 Tony Gonzalez	.75	.35
❑ 28 Jay Fiedler	.75	.35
❑ 29 Ricky Williams	1.25	.55
❑ 30 Chris Chambers	1.25	.55
❑ 31 Zach Thomas	1.25	.55
❑ 32 Tom Brady	2.00	.90
❑ 33 Troy Brown	.75	.35
❑ 34 Antowain Smith	.75	.35
❑ 35 Chad Pennington	1.50	.70
❑ 36 Curtis Martin	1.25	.55
❑ 37 Laveranues Coles	.75	.35
❑ 38 Rich Gannon	.75	.35
❑ 39 Charlie Garner	.50	.23
❑ 40 Jerry Rice	2.50	1.10
❑ 41 Tim Brown	1.25	.55
❑ 42 Tommy Maddox	1.25	.55
❑ 43 Jerome Bettis	1.25	.55
❑ 44 Plaxico Burress	.75	.35
❑ 45 Hines Ward	1.25	.55
❑ 46 Drew Brees	1.25	.55
❑ 47 LaDainian Tomlinson	1.25	.55
❑ 48 Junior Seau	1.25	.55
❑ 49 Steve McNair	1.25	.55
❑ 50 Eddie George	.75	.35
❑ 51 Jevon Kearse	.75	.35
❑ 52 Jake Plummer	.75	.35
❑ 53 David Boston	.75	.35
❑ 54 Marcel Shipp	.75	.35
❑ 55 Michael Vick	3.00	1.35
❑ 56 T.J. Duckett	.75	.35
❑ 57 Warrick Dunn	.75	.35
❑ 58 Muhsin Muhammad	.75	.35
❑ 59 Julius Peppers	1.25	.55
❑ 60 Steve Smith	.75	.35
❑ 61 Anthony Thomas	1.25	.55
❑ 62 Brian Urlacher	2.00	.90
❑ 63 Marty Booker	.75	.35
❑ 64 Antonio Bryant	.75	.35
❑ 65 Chad Hutchinson	.75	.35
❑ 66 Roy Williams	1.25	.55
❑ 67 Emmitt Smith	3.00	1.35
❑ 68 Joey Harrington	2.00	.90
❑ 69 James Stewart	.75	.35
❑ 70 Az-Zahir Hakim	.50	.23
❑ 71 Brett Favre	3.00	1.35
❑ 72 Ahman Green	1.25	.55
❑ 73 Donald Driver	.75	.35
❑ 74 Daunte Culpepper	1.25	.55
❑ 75 Randy Moss	2.00	.90
❑ 76 Michael Bennett	.75	.35
❑ 77 Aaron Brooks	1.25	.55
❑ 78 Deuce McAllister	1.25	.55
❑ 79 Donte Stallworth	1.25	.55
❑ 80 Tiki Barber	.75	.35
❑ 81 Kerry Collins	.75	.35
❑ 82 Jeremy Shockey	2.00	.90
❑ 83 Donovan McNabb	1.50	.70
❑ 84 Duce Staley	.75	.35
❑ 85 Antonio Freeman	.75	.35
❑ 86 Jeff Garcia	1.25	.55
❑ 87 Terrell Owens	1.25	.55
❑ 88 Garrison Hearst	.75	.35
❑ 89 Matt Hasselbeck	.75	.35
❑ 90 Koren Robinson	.75	.35
❑ 91 Shaun Alexander	1.25	.55
❑ 92 Kurt Warner	1.25	.55
❑ 93 Marshall Faulk	1.25	.55
❑ 94 Isaac Bruce	1.25	.55
❑ 95 Brad Johnson	.75	.35
❑ 96 Keyshawn Johnson	1.25	.55
❑ 97 Warren Sapp	.75	.35
❑ 98 Patrick Ramsey	1.25	.55
❑ 99 Rod Gardner	.75	.35
❑ 100 Stephen Davis	.75	.35
❑ 101 Jason Gesser RC	6.00	2.70
❑ 102 Brandon Lloyd RC	8.00	3.60
❑ 103 Ken Dorsey RC	10.00	4.50
❑ 104 Avon Cobourne RC	3.00	1.35
❑ 105 Cecil Sapp RC	5.00	2.20
❑ 106 Derek Watson RC	5.00	2.20
❑ 107 Dwone Hicks RC	3.00	1.35
❑ 108 Earnest Graham RC	5.00	2.20
❑ 109 LaBrandon Toefield RC	6.00	2.70
❑ 110 Quentin Griffin RC	15.00	6.75
❑ 111 Sultan McCullough RC	5.00	2.20
❑ 112 Lee Suggs RC	12.00	5.50
❑ 113 Talman Gardner RC	6.00	2.70
❑ 114 Arnaz Battle RC	6.00	2.70
❑ 115 Billy McMullen RC	5.00	2.20
❑ 116 Doug Gabriel RC	6.00	2.70
❑ 117 Justin Gage RC	6.00	2.70
❑ 118 Kareem Kelly RC	5.00	2.20
❑ 119 Paul Arnold RC	5.00	2.20
❑ 120 Sam Aiken RC	5.00	2.20
❑ 121 Shaun McDonald RC	6.00	2.70
❑ 122 Terrence Edwards	5.00	2.20
❑ 123 Walter Young RC	3.00	1.35
❑ 124 Ryan Hoag RC	3.00	1.35
❑ 125 Jason Witten RC	12.00	5.50
❑ 126 Bennie Joppru RC	6.00	2.70
❑ 127 George Wrighster RC	5.00	2.20
❑ 128 L.J. Smith RC	6.00	2.70
❑ 129 Robert Johnson RC	3.00	1.35
❑ 130 Chris Kelsay RC	6.00	2.70
❑ 131 Cory Redding RC	5.00	2.20
❑ 132 DeWayne White RC	5.00	2.20
❑ 133 Kenny Peterson RC	5.00	2.20
❑ 134 Jerome McDougle RC	6.00	2.70
❑ 135 Michael Haynes RC	6.00	2.70
❑ 136 Jimmy Kennedy RC	6.00	2.70
❑ 137 Kevin Williams RC	6.00	2.70
❑ 138 Johnathan Sullivan RC	5.00	2.20
❑ 139 Rien Long RC	3.00	1.35
❑ 140 Ty Warren RC	6.00	2.70
❑ 141 William Joseph RC	6.00	2.70
❑ 142 E.J. Henderson RC	6.00	2.70
❑ 143 Boss Bailey RC	8.00	3.60
❑ 144 Dennis Weathersby RC	3.00	1.35
❑ 145 Chris Simms RC	12.00	5.50
❑ 146 Rashean Mathis RC	5.00	2.20
❑ 147 Charles Rogers RC	8.00	3.60
❑ 148 Andre Woolfolk RC	6.00	2.70
❑ 149 Troy Polamalu RC	6.00	2.70
❑ 150 Mike Doss RC	6.00	2.70
❑ 151 Carson Palmer RPM RC	30.00	13.50
❑ 152 Byron Leftwich RPM RC	40.00	18.00
❑ 153 Kyle Boller RPM RC	25.00	11.00
❑ 154 Rex Grossman RPM RC	25.00	11.00
❑ 155 Dave Ragone RPM RC	12.00	5.50
❑ 156 Kliff Kingsbury RPM RC	10.00	4.50
❑ 157 Seneca Wallace RPM RC	12.00	5.50
❑ 158 Larry Johnson RPM RC	25.00	11.00
❑ 159 Willis McGahee RPM RC	25.00	11.00
❑ 160 Justin Fargas RPM RC	12.00	5.50
❑ 161 Onterrio Smith RPM RC	15.00	6.75
❑ 162 Chris Brown RPM RC	25.00	11.00
❑ 163 Musa Smith RPM RC	12.00	5.50
❑ 164 Artose Pinner RPM RC	12.00	5.50
❑ 165 Andre Johnson RPM RC	25.00	11.00
❑ 166 Kelley Washington RPM RC	12.005.50	
❑ 167 Taylor Jacobs RPM RC	12.00	5.50
❑ 168 Bryant Johnson RPM RC	12.00	5.50
❑ 169 Tyrone Calico RPM RC	15.00	6.75
❑ 170 Anquan Boldin RPM RC	25.00	11.00
❑ 171 Bethel Johnson RPM RC	20.00	9.00
❑ 172 Nate Burleson RPM RC	20.00	9.00
❑ 173 Kevin Curtis RPM RC	12.00	5.50
❑ 174 Dallas Clark RPM RC	12.00	5.50
❑ 175 Teyo Johnson RPM RC	12.00	5.50
❑ 176 Terrell Suggs RPM RC	20.00	9.00
❑ 177 DeWayne Robertson RPM RC	12.00	5.50
❑ 178 Brian St.Pierre RPM RC	12.00	5.50
❑ 179 Terence Newman RPM RC	20.00	9.00
❑ 180 Marcus Trufant RPM RC	12.00	5.50

2004 Absolute Memorabilia

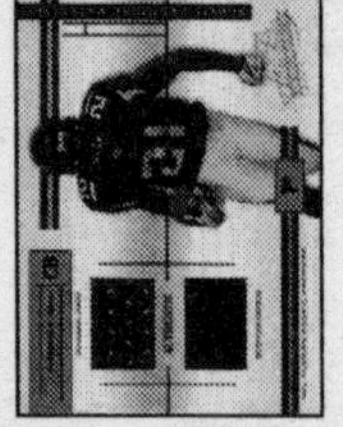

	Nm-Mt	Ex-Mt
COMP.SET w/o SP's (150)	80.00	24.00

1-150 PRINT RUN 1150 SER.#'d SETS
151-233 PRINT RUN 750 SER.#'d SETS
UNPRICED SPECTRUM PLATINUM #'d TO 1

	Nm-Mt	Ex-Mt
❑ 1 Anquan Boldin	3.00	.90
❑ 2 Emmitt Smith	6.00	1.80
❑ 3 Josh McCown	2.00	.60
❑ 4 Marcel Shipp	2.00	.60
❑ 5 Michael Vick	6.00	1.80
❑ 6 Peerless Price	2.00	.60
❑ 7 T.J. Duckett	2.00	.60
❑ 8 Warrick Dunn	2.00	.60
❑ 9 Jamal Lewis	3.00	.90
❑ 10 Kyle Boller	3.00	.90
❑ 11 Ray Lewis	3.00	.90
❑ 12 Terrell Suggs	2.00	.60
❑ 13 Drew Bledsoe	3.00	.90
❑ 14 Eric Moulds	2.00	.60

❑ 15 Josh Reed 1.25 .35
❑ 16 Travis Henry 2.00 .60
❑ 17 DeShaun Foster 2.00 .60
❑ 18 Jake Delhomme 3.00 .90
❑ 19 Julius Peppers 3.00 .90
❑ 20 Muhsin Muhammad 2.00 .60
❑ 21 Stephen Davis 2.00 .60
❑ 22 Steve Smith 2.00 .60
❑ 23 Anthony Thomas 2.00 .60
❑ 24 Brian Urlacher 4.00 1.20
❑ 25 Marty Booker 2.00 .60
❑ 26 Rex Grossman 3.00 .90
❑ 27 Carson Palmer 4.00 1.20
❑ 28 Chad Johnson 2.00 .60
❑ 29 Corey Dillon 2.00 .60
❑ 30 Peter Warrick 2.00 .60
❑ 31 Rudi Johnson 2.00 .60
❑ 32 Andre Davis 1.25 .35
❑ 33 Dennis Northcutt 1.25 .35
❑ 34 Lee Suggs 3.00 .90
❑ 35 Tim Couch 1.25 .35
❑ 36 Jeff Garcia 3.00 .90
❑ 37 William Green 2.00 .60
❑ 38 Antonio Bryant 2.00 .60
❑ 39 Quincy Carter 2.00 .60
❑ 40 Roy Williams S 2.00 .60
❑ 41 Terence Newman 2.00 .60
❑ 42 Keyshawn Johnson 2.00 .60
❑ 43 Garrison Hearst 2.00 .60
❑ 44 Champ Bailey 2.00 .60
❑ 45 Ashley Lelie 2.00 .60
❑ 46 Jake Plummer 2.00 .60
❑ 47 Rod Smith 2.00 .60
❑ 48 Shannon Sharpe 2.00 .60
❑ 49 Charles Rogers 2.00 .60
❑ 50 Joey Harrington 3.00 .90
❑ 51 Ahman Green 3.00 .90
❑ 52 Brett Favre 8.00 2.40
❑ 53 Donald Driver 2.00 .60
❑ 54 Javon Walker 2.00 .60
❑ 55 Robert Ferguson 1.25 .35
❑ 56 Andre Johnson 3.00 .90
❑ 57 David Carr 3.00 .90
❑ 58 Domanick Davis 3.00 .90
❑ 59 Edgerrin James 3.00 .90
❑ 60 Marvin Harrison 3.00 .90
❑ 61 Peyton Manning 5.00 1.50
❑ 62 Reggie Wayne 2.00 .60
❑ 63 Byron Leftwich 5.00 1.50
❑ 64 Fred Taylor 2.00 .60
❑ 65 Jimmy Smith 2.00 .60
❑ 66 Dante Hall 3.00 .90
❑ 67 Priest Holmes 4.00 1.20
❑ 68 Tony Gonzalez 2.00 .60
❑ 69 Trent Green 2.00 .60
❑ 70 Chris Chambers 2.00 .60
❑ 71 Jay Fiedler 1.25 .35
❑ 72 David Boston 2.00 .60
❑ 73 Ricky Williams 3.00 .90
❑ 74 Zach Thomas 3.00 .90
❑ 75 Daunte Culpepper 3.00 .90
❑ 76 Michael Bennett 2.00 .60
❑ 77 Moe Williams 1.25 .35
❑ 78 Randy Moss 4.00 1.20
❑ 79 David Givens 2.00 .60
❑ 80 Deion Branch 3.00 .90
❑ 81 Kevin Faulk 1.25 .35
❑ 82 Richard Seymour 1.25 .35
❑ 83 Tom Brady 5.00 1.50
❑ 84 Troy Brown 2.00 .60
❑ 85 Ty Law 2.00 .60
❑ 86 Aaron Brooks 2.00 .60
❑ 87 Deuce McAllister 3.00 .90
❑ 88 Donte Stallworth 2.00 .60
❑ 89 Joe Horn 2.00 .60
❑ 90 Amani Toomer 2.00 .60
❑ 91 Jeremy Shockey 3.00 .90
❑ 92 Kerry Collins 2.00 .60
❑ 93 Michael Strahan 2.00 .60
❑ 94 Tiki Barber 2.00 .60
❑ 95 Chad Pennington 4.00 1.20
❑ 96 Curtis Martin 3.00 .90
❑ 97 Santana Moss 2.00 .60
❑ 98 Wayne Chrebet 2.00 .60
❑ 99 Justin McCareins 1.25 .35
❑ 100 Charles Woodson 2.00 .60
❑ 101 Jerry Porter 2.00 .60
❑ 102 Jerry Rice 6.00 1.80
❑ 103 Rich Gannon 2.00 .60
❑ 104 Tim Brown 3.00 .90
❑ 105 Warren Sapp 2.00 .60
❑ 106 A.J. Feeley 3.00 .90
❑ 107 Brian Westbrook 2.00 .60
❑ 108 Correll Buckhalter 2.00 .60
❑ 109 Donovan McNabb 4.00 1.20
❑ 110 Freddie Mitchell 2.00 .60
❑ 111 Terrell Owens 3.00 .90
❑ 112 Jevon Kearse 2.00 .60
❑ 113 Todd Pinkston 1.25 .35
❑ 114 Antwaan Randle El 2.00 .60
❑ 115 Hines Ward 3.00 .90
❑ 116 Jerome Bettis 3.00 .90
❑ 117 Kendrell Bell 2.00 .60
❑ 118 Plaxico Burress 2.00 .60
❑ 119 Tommy Maddox 2.00 .60
❑ 120 Duce Staley 2.00 .60
❑ 121 Drew Brees 3.00 .90
❑ 122 LaDainian Tomlinson 3.00 .90
❑ 123 Kevan Barlow 2.00 .60
❑ 124 Tai Streets 1.25 .35
❑ 125 Tim Rattay 2.00 .60
❑ 126 Darrell Jackson 2.00 .60
❑ 127 Koren Robinson 2.00 .60
❑ 128 Matt Hasselbeck 2.00 .60
❑ 129 Shaun Alexander 3.00 .90
❑ 130 Isaac Bruce 2.00 .60
❑ 131 Kurt Warner 3.00 .90
❑ 132 Marc Bulger 3.00 .90
❑ 133 Marshall Faulk 3.00 .90
❑ 134 Torry Holt 3.00 .90
❑ 135 Derrick Brooks 2.00 .60
❑ 136 Keenan McCardell 1.25 .35
❑ 137 Mike Alstott 2.00 .60
❑ 138 Thomas Jones 2.00 .60
❑ 139 Charlie Garner 2.00 .60
❑ 140 Derrick Mason 2.00 .60
❑ 141 Drew Bennett 2.00 .60
❑ 142 Eddie George 2.00 .60
❑ 143 Keith Bulluck 1.25 .35
❑ 144 Steve McNair 3.00 .90
❑ 145 LaVar Arrington 6.00 1.80
❑ 146 Laveranues Coles 2.00 .60
❑ 147 Patrick Ramsey 2.00 .60
❑ 148 Rod Gardner 2.00 .60
❑ 149 Clinton Portis 3.00 .90
❑ 150 Mark Brunell 2.00 .60
❑ 151 Craig Krenzel AU RC EXCH 15.004.50
❑ 152 Andy Hall AU RC EXCH 12.00 3.60
❑ 153 Josh Harris RC 6.00 1.80
❑ 154 Jim Sorgi AU RC 15.00 4.50
❑ 155 Jeff Smoker AU RC 20.00 6.00
❑ 156 John Navarre AU RC EXCH 15.004.50
❑ 157 Jared Lorenzen AU RC 12.00 3.60
❑ 158 Cody Pickett AU RC 15.00 4.50
❑ 159 Casey Bramlet RC 5.00 1.50
❑ 160 Matt Mauck AU RC 15.00 4.50
❑ 161 B.J. Symons AU RC 15.00 4.50
❑ 162 Bradlee Van Pelt RC 6.00 1.80
❑ 163 Ryan Dinwiddie RC 5.00 1.50
❑ 164 Michael Turner RC 5.00 1.50
❑ 165 Drew Henson RC 15.00 4.50
❑ 166 Troy Fleming RC 5.00 1.50
❑ 167 Adimchinobe Echemandu RC 5.001.50
❑ 168 Quincy Wilson RC 5.00 1.50
❑ 169 Derrick Ward RC 3.00 .90
❑ 170 Bruce Perry RC 5.00 1.50
❑ 171 Brandon Miree RC 5.00 1.50
❑ 172 Jarrett Payton AU RC EXCH 15.004.50
❑ 173 Ran Carthon RC 5.00 1.50
❑ 174 Carlos Francis AU RC EXCH 12.003.60
❑ 175 Samie Parker RC 6.00 1.80
❑ 176 Jerricho Cotchery RC 6.00 1.80
❑ 177 Ernest Wilford RC 6.00 1.80
❑ 178 Johnnie Morant RC 6.00 1.80
❑ 179 Maurice Mann AU RC 15.00 4.50
❑ 180 D.J. Hackett RC 5.00 1.50
❑ 181 Drew Carter RC 6.00 1.80
❑ 182 P.K. Sam RC 5.00 1.50
❑ 183 Jamaar Taylor RC 6.00 1.80
❑ 184 Ryan Krause RC 5.00 1.50
❑ 185 Triandos Luke RC 6.00 1.80
❑ 186 Jeris McIntyre RC 5.00 1.50
❑ 187 Clarence Moore AU RC 15.00 4.50
❑ 188 Mark Jones RC 5.00 1.50
❑ 189 Sloan Thomas AU RC 12.00 3.60
❑ 190 Sean Taylor RC 8.00 2.40
❑ 191 Derek Abney RC 6.00 1.80
❑ 192 Jonathan Vilma RC 6.00 1.80
❑ 193 Tommie Harris RC 8.00 2.40
❑ 194 D.J. Williams RC 8.00 2.40
❑ 195 Will Smith RC 6.00 1.80
❑ 196 Kenechi Udeze RC 6.00 1.80
❑ 197 Vince Wilfork RC 8.00 2.40
❑ 198 Ahmad Carroll RC 8.00 2.40
❑ 199 Jason Babin RC 6.00 1.80
❑ 200 Chris Gamble RC 8.00 2.40
❑ 201 Larry Fitzgerald RPM RC 30.00 9.00
❑ 202 DeAngelo Hall RPM RC 12.00 3.60
❑ 203 Matt Schaub RPM RC 15.00 4.50
❑ 204 Michael Jenkins RPM AU RC 25.007.50
❑ 205 Devard Darling RPM AU RC 25.007.50
❑ 206 J.P. Losman RPM RC 25.00 7.50
❑ 207 Lee Evans RPM RC 15.00 4.50
❑ 208 Keary Colbert RPM AU RC 30.00 9.00
❑ 209 Bernard Berrian RPM AU RC 25.007.50
❑ 210 Chris Perry RPM RC 20.00 6.00
❑ 211 Kellen Winslow RPM RC 25.00 7.50
❑ 212 Luke McCown RPM RC 10.00 3.00
❑ 213 Julius Jones RPM RC 40.00 12.00
❑ 214 Darius Watts RPM RC 12.00 3.60
❑ 215 Tatum Bell RPM AU RC EXCH 40.00
12.00
❑ 216 Kevin Jones RPM RC 30.00 9.00
❑ 217 Roy Williams RPM RC 30.00 9.00
❑ 218 Dunta Robinson RPM RC 10.00 3.00
❑ 219 Greg Jones RPM AU RC 25.00 7.50
❑ 220 Reggie Williams RPM RC 12.00 3.60
❑ 221 Mewelde Moore RPM RC 12.00 3.60
❑ 222 Ben Watson RPM RC 10.00 3.00
❑ 223 Cedric Cobbs RPM RC 15.00 4.50
❑ 224 Devery Henderson RPM AU RC 25.00 7.50
❑ 225 Eli Manning RPM RC 50.00 15.00
❑ 226 Robert Gallery RPM RC 15.00 4.50
❑ 227 Ben Roethlisberger RPM RC 80.00
24.00
❑ 228 Philip Rivers RPM RC 30.00 9.00
❑ 229 Derrick Hamilton RPM RC 8.00 2.40
❑ 230 Rashaun Woods RPM RC 15.00 4.50
❑ 231 Steven Jackson RPM RC 30.00 9.00
❑ 232 Michael Clayton RPM RC 25.00 7.50
❑ 233 Ben Troupe RPM RC 10.00 3.00

2004 Absolute Memorabilia Retail

Nm-Mt Ex-Mt

*RETAIL VETERANS: .1X TO .3X HOBBY
RETAIL CARDS NOT SERIAL NUMBERED

2000 Aurora

Nm-Mt Ex-Mt

COMPLETE SET (150) 30.00 13.50
❑ 1 David Boston .60 .25
❑ 2 Thomas Jones RC 1.50 .70
❑ 3 Rob Moore .40 .18

❑ 4 Jake Plummer .40 .18
❑ 5 Frank Sanders .40 .18
❑ 6 Jamal Anderson .60 .25
❑ 7 Chris Chandler .40 .18
❑ 8 Tim Dwight .60 .25
❑ 9 Doug Johnson RC 1.00 .45
❑ 10 Tony Banks .40 .18
❑ 11 Qadry Ismail .40 .18
❑ 12 Jamal Lewis RC 2.50 1.10
❑ 13 Chris Redman RC .75 .35
❑ 14 Travis Taylor RC 1.00 .45
❑ 15 Doug Flutie .60 .25
❑ 16 Rob Johnson .40 .18
❑ 17 Eric Moulds .60 .25
❑ 18 Peerless Price .60 .25
❑ 19 Antowain Smith .40 .18
❑ 20 Steve Beuerlein .40 .18
❑ 21 Tim Biakabutuka .40 .18
❑ 22 Patrick Jeffers .60 .25
❑ 23 Muhsin Muhammad .40 .18
❑ 24 Curtis Enis .25 .11
❑ 25 Cade McNown .25 .11
❑ 26 Marcus Robinson .60 .25
❑ 27 Dez White RC 1.00 .45
❑ 28 Corey Dillon .60 .25
❑ 29 Ron Dugans RC .75 .35
❑ 30 Darnay Scott .40 .18
❑ 31 Akili Smith .25 .11
❑ 32 Peter Warrick RC 1.00 .45
❑ 33 Tim Couch .40 .18
❑ 34 JaJuan Dawson RC .75 .35
❑ 35 Kevin Johnson .60 .25
❑ 36 Dennis Northcutt RC 1.00 .45
❑ 37 Travis Prentice RC 1.00 .45
❑ 38 Troy Aikman 1.25 .55
❑ 39 Rocket Ismail .40 .18
❑ 40 Emmitt Smith 1.25 .55
❑ 41 Jason Tucker .25 .11
❑ 42 Terrell Davis .60 .25
❑ 43 Olandis Gary .60 .25
❑ 44 Brian Griese .60 .25
❑ 45 Ed McCaffrey .60 .25
❑ 46 Rod Smith .40 .18
❑ 47 Charlie Batch .60 .25
❑ 48 Germane Crowell .25 .11
❑ 49 Reuben Droughns RC 1.25 .55
❑ 50 Herman Moore .40 .18
❑ 51 Barry Sanders 1.50 .70
❑ 52 Brett Favre 2.00 .90
❑ 53 Bubba Franks RC 1.00 .45
❑ 54 Antonio Freeman .60 .25
❑ 55 Dorsey Levens .40 .18
❑ 56 Bill Schroeder .40 .18
❑ 57 Marvin Harrison .60 .25
❑ 58 Edgerrin James 1.00 .45
❑ 59 Peyton Manning 1.50 .70
❑ 60 Terrence Wilkins .25 .11
❑ 61 Mark Brunell .60 .25
❑ 62 Keenan McCardell .40 .18
❑ 63 Jimmy Smith .40 .18
❑ 64 R.Jay Soward RC .75 .35
❑ 65 Shyrone Stith RC 1.00 .45
❑ 66 Fred Taylor .60 .25
❑ 67 Derrick Alexander .40 .18
❑ 68 Donnell Bennett .25 .11
❑ 69 Tony Gonzalez .40 .18
❑ 70 Elvis Grbac .40 .18
❑ 71 Sylvester Morris RC .75 .35
❑ 72 Damon Huard .60 .25
❑ 73 James Johnson .25 .11
❑ 74 Dan Marino 2.00 .90
❑ 75 Tony Martin .40 .18
❑ 76 O.J. McDuffie .40 .18
❑ 77 Quinton Spotwood RC .75 .35
❑ 78 Cris Carter .60 .25
❑ 79 Daunte Culpepper .75 .35
❑ 80 Randy Moss 1.25 .55
❑ 81 Robert Smith .60 .25
❑ 82 Troy Walters RC 1.00 .45
❑ 83 Drew Bledsoe .75 .35
❑ 84 Tom Brady RC 15.00 6.75
❑ 85 Kevin Faulk .40 .18
❑ 86 Terry Glenn .40 .18
❑ 87 J.R. Redmond RC .75 .35
❑ 88 Marc Bulger RC 2.00 .90
❑ 89 Sherrod Gideon RC .75 .35
❑ 90 Keith Poole .25 .11
❑ 91 Ricky Williams .60 .25
❑ 92 Kerry Collins .40 .18
❑ 93 Ron Dayne RC 1.00 .45
❑ 94 Ike Hilliard .40 .18
❑ 95 Amani Toomer .25 .11
❑ 96 Wayne Chrebet .40 .18
❑ 97 Laveranues Coles RC 1.25 .55
❑ 98 Curtis Martin .60 .25
❑ 99 Chad Pennington RC 4.00 1.80
❑ 100 Vinny Testaverde .40 .18
❑ 101 Tim Brown .60 .25
❑ 102 Rich Gannon .60 .25
❑ 103 Napoleon Kaufman .40 .18
❑ 104 Jerry Porter RC 1.25 .55
❑ 105 Tyrone Wheatley .40 .18
❑ 106 Charles Johnson .40 .18
❑ 107 Donovan McNabb 1.00 .45
❑ 108 Todd Pinkston RC 1.00 .45
❑ 109 Duce Staley .60 .25
❑ 110 Jerome Bettis .60 .25
❑ 111 Plaxico Burress RC 2.00 .90
❑ 112 Troy Edwards .25 .11
❑ 113 Richard Huntley .25 .11
❑ 114 Tee Martin RC 1.00 .45
❑ 115 Kordell Stewart .40 .18
❑ 116 Isaac Bruce .60 .25
❑ 117 Trung Canidate RC .75 .35
❑ 118 Marshall Faulk .75 .35
❑ 119 Torry Holt .60 .25
❑ 120 Kurt Warner 1.25 .55
❑ 121 Jermaine Fazande .25 .11
❑ 122 Trevor Gaylor RC .75 .35
❑ 123 Jim Harbaugh .40 .18
❑ 124 Junior Seau .60 .25
❑ 125 Giovanni Carmazzi RC .75 .35
❑ 126 Charlie Garner .40 .18
❑ 127 Terrell Owens .60 .25
❑ 128 Jerry Rice 1.25 .55
❑ 129 J.J. Stokes .40 .18
❑ 130 Steve Young .75 .35
❑ 131 Shaun Alexander RC 2.50 1.10
❑ 132 Christian Fauria .25 .11
❑ 133 Jon Kitna .60 .25
❑ 134 Derrick Mayes .40 .18
❑ 135 Ricky Watters .40 .18
❑ 136 Mike Alstott .60 .25
❑ 137 Warrick Dunn .60 .25
❑ 138 Jacquez Green .25 .11
❑ 139 Joe Hamilton RC .75 .35
❑ 140 Shaun King .25 .11
❑ 141 Eddie George .60 .25
❑ 142 Jevon Kearse .60 .25
❑ 143 Steve McNair .60 .25
❑ 144 Yancey Thigpen .25 .11
❑ 145 Frank Wycheck .25 .11
❑ 146 Albert Connell .25 .11
❑ 147 Stephen Davis .60 .25
❑ 148 Todd Husak RC 1.00 .45
❑ 149 Brad Johnson .60 .25
❑ 150 Michael Westbrook .40 .18
❑ S1 Jon Kitna Sample 1.00 .45

2004 Bazooka

	Nm-Mt	Ex-Mt
COMPLETE SET (220)	50.00	15.00

❑ 1 Peyton Manning 1.50 .45
❑ 2 Rod Gardner .60 .18
❑ 3 Marc Bulger 1.00 .30
❑ 4 Champ Bailey .60 .18
❑ 5 Moe Williams .40 .12
❑ 6 Andre' Davis .40 .12
❑ 7 Corey Dillon .60 .18
❑ 8 Trent Green .60 .18
❑ 9 Daunte Culpepper 1.00 .30
❑ 10 Chad Pennington 1.25 .35
❑ 11 Hines Ward 1.00 .30
❑ 12 Tim Brown 1.00 .30
❑ 13 Jerome Pathon .40 .12
❑ 14 Drew Brees 1.00 .30
❑ 15 Eddie George .60 .18
❑ 16 Duce Staley .60 .18
❑ 17 Marques Tuiasosopo .60 .18
❑ 18 Willis McGahee 1.00 .30
❑ 19 T.J. Duckett .60 .18
❑ 20 Brian Urlacher 1.25 .35
❑ 21 Ashley Lelie .60 .18
❑ 22 Robert Ferguson .40 .12
❑ 23 Tai Streets .40 .12
❑ 24 Junior Seau 1.00 .30
❑ 25 Priest Holmes 1.25 .35
❑ 26 Ty Law .60 .18
❑ 27 Correll Buckhalter .60 .18
❑ 28 Plaxico Burress .60 .18
❑ 29 Brad Johnson .60 .18
❑ 30 Shaun Alexander 1.00 .30
❑ 31 Mark Brunell .60 .18
❑ 32 Julian Peterson .40 .12
❑ 33 Marcel Shipp .60 .18
❑ 34 Kyle Boller 1.00 .30
❑ 35 Rudi Johnson .60 .18
❑ 36 Quincy Carter .60 .18
❑ 37 Jabar Gaffney .60 .18
❑ 38 Reggie Wayne .60 .18
❑ 39 Deion Branch 1.00 .30
❑ 40 Terrell Owens 1.00 .30
❑ 41 Chris Brown 1.00 .30
❑ 42 Bobby Engram .40 .12
❑ 43 Josh Reed .40 .12
❑ 44 Thomas Jones .60 .18
❑ 45 Stephen Davis .60 .18
❑ 46 Mike Anderson .60 .18
❑ 47 Javon Walker .60 .18
❑ 48 Edgerrin James 1.00 .30
❑ 49 Randy McMichael .40 .12
❑ 50 Deuce McAllister 1.00 .30
❑ 51 Nate Burleson 1.00 .30
❑ 52 Jevon Kearse .60 .18
❑ 53 Jay Fiedler .40 .12
❑ 54 Patrick Ramsey .60 .18
❑ 55 Brian Westbrook .60 .18
❑ 56 Tyrone Calico .60 .18
❑ 57 Alge Crumpler .60 .18
❑ 58 Josh McCown .60 .18
❑ 59 Quincy Morgan .60 .18
❑ 60 Jeff Garcia 1.00 .30
❑ 61 Garrison Hearst .60 .18
❑ 62 Chad Johnson .60 .18
❑ 63 Byron Leftwich 1.50 .45
❑ 64 Donald Driver .60 .18
❑ 65 Ricky Williams 1.00 .30
❑ 66 Todd Pinkston .40 .12
❑ 67 Amani Toomer .60 .18
❑ 68 David Givens .60 .18
❑ 69 Jerome Bettis 1.00 .30
❑ 70 Derrick Mason .60 .18
❑ 71 Darrell Jackson .60 .18
❑ 72 Kassim Osgood .40 .12
❑ 73 Todd Heap .60 .18
❑ 74 Warrick Dunn .60 .18
❑ 75 Brett Favre 2.50 .75
❑ 76 Chris Chambers .60 .18
❑ 77 Fred Taylor .60 .18
❑ 78 Charles Rogers .60 .18
❑ 79 Onterrio Smith .60 .18
❑ 80 Joe Horn .60 .18
❑ 81 Justin McCareins .40 .12
❑ 82 Ike Hilliard .40 .12
❑ 83 Kevan Barlow .60 .18
❑ 84 Charlie Garner .60 .18

❑ 85 Anquan Boldin 1.00 .30
❑ 86 Anthony Thomas .60 .18
❑ 87 Julius Peppers 1.00 .30
❑ 88 Dat Nguyen .40 .12
❑ 89 Peerless Price .60 .18
❑ 90 Randy Moss 1.25 .35
❑ 91 Jamie Sharper .40 .12
❑ 92 Travis Henry .60 .18
❑ 93 Terrell Suggs .60 .18
❑ 94 Joey Galloway .60 .18
❑ 95 Torry Holt 1.00 .30
❑ 96 Freddie Mitchell .60 .18
❑ 97 Jerry Porter .60 .18
❑ 98 Dwight Freeney .40 .12
❑ 99 Joey Harrington 1.00 .30
❑ 100 Michael Vick 2.00 .60
❑ 101 Kelley Washington .40 .12
❑ 102 Marty Booker .60 .18
❑ 103 Tim Rattay .60 .18
❑ 104 Derrick Brooks .60 .18
❑ 105 Laveranues Coles .60 .18
❑ 106 Ray Lewis 1.00 .30
❑ 107 Jon Kitna .60 .18
❑ 108 Terry Glenn .40 .12
❑ 109 Steve Smith .60 .18
❑ 110 Ahman Green 1.00 .30
❑ 111 Andre Johnson 1.00 .30
❑ 112 Dallas Clark .60 .18
❑ 113 Kevin Faulk .40 .12
❑ 114 Michael Bennett .60 .18
❑ 115 Tony Gonzalez .60 .18
❑ 116 Michael Strahan .60 .18
❑ 117 Tommy Maddox .60 .18
❑ 118 Isaac Bruce .60 .18
❑ 119 Brandon Lloyd .60 .18
❑ 120 Steve McNair 1.00 .30
❑ 121 Keith Brooking .40 .12
❑ 122 Drew Bledsoe 1.00 .30
❑ 123 Peter Warrick .60 .18
❑ 124 Antonio Bryant .60 .18
❑ 125 Clinton Portis 1.00 .30
❑ 126 Kelly Holcomb .60 .18
❑ 127 Jake Delhomme 1.00 .30
❑ 128 Rod Smith .60 .18
❑ 129 Lee Suggs 1.00 .30
❑ 130 Domanick Davis 1.00 .30
❑ 131 Carson Palmer 1.25 .35
❑ 132 Kerry Collins .60 .18
❑ 133 Teyo Johnson .40 .12
❑ 134 Curtis Martin 1.00 .30
❑ 135 Matt Hasselbeck .60 .18
❑ 136 Cedrick Wilson .40 .12
❑ 137 Eric Moulds .60 .18
❑ 138 Keyshawn Johnson .60 .18
❑ 139 Dante Hall 1.00 .30
❑ 140 Jamal Lewis 1.00 .30
❑ 141 Kelly Campbell .40 .12
❑ 142 Jeremy Shockey 1.00 .30
❑ 143 Jerry Rice 2.00 .60
❑ 144 Kurt Warner 1.00 .30
❑ 145 Jake Plummer .60 .18
❑ 146 Keenan McCardell .40 .12
❑ 147 Jimmy Smith .60 .18
❑ 148 Zach Thomas 1.00 .30
❑ 149 Eddie Kennison .40 .12
❑ 150 Tom Brady 1.50 .45
❑ 151 Donte' Stallworth .60 .18
❑ 152 John Abraham .40 .12
❑ 153 Koren Robinson .60 .18
❑ 154 Rex Grossman 1.00 .30
❑ 155 Donovan McNabb 1.25 .35
❑ 156 David Carr 1.00 .30
❑ 157 David Boston .60 .18
❑ 158 Tiki Barber .60 .18
❑ 159 Santana Moss .60 .18
❑ 160 LaDainian Tomlinson 1.00 .30
❑ 161 Justin Fargas .60 .18
❑ 162 Troy Brown .60 .18
❑ 163 Marshall Faulk 1.00 .30
❑ 164 Aaron Brooks .60 .18
❑ 165 Marvin Harrison 1.00 .30
❑ 166 Kevin Jones RC 5.00 1.50
❑ 167 Michael Clayton RC 4.00 1.20
❑ 168 Bernard Berrian RC 1.50 .45
❑ 169 Ben Watson RC 1.50 .45
❑ 170 Philip Rivers RC 5.00 1.50
❑ 171 Vince Wilfork RC 2.00 .60
❑ 172 Jason Babin RC 1.50 .45
❑ 173 Marcus Tubbs RC 1.50 .45
❑ 174 Sean Taylor RC 2.00 .60
❑ 175 Larry Fitzgerald RC 5.00 1.50
❑ 176 Craig Krenzel RC 1.50 .45
❑ 177 Cedric Cobbs RC 1.50 .45
❑ 178 Lee Evans RC 2.50 .75
❑ 179 Johnnie Morant RC 1.50 .45
❑ 180 Kellen Winslow RC 4.00 1.20
❑ 181 Mewelde Moore RC 2.00 .60
❑ 182 Carlos Francis RC 1.25 .35
❑ 183 Josh Harris RC 1.50 .45
❑ 184 Julius Jones RC 6.00 1.80
❑ 185 Reggie Williams RC 2.00 .60
❑ 186 DeAngelo Hall RC 2.00 .60
❑ 187 D.J. Williams RC 2.00 .60
❑ 188 Cody Pickett RC 1.50 .45
❑ 189 Dunta Robinson RC 1.50 .45
❑ 190 J.P. Losman RC 4.00 1.20
❑ 191 Jonathan Vilma RC 1.50 .45
❑ 192 Jerricho Cotchery RC 1.50 .45
❑ 193 Keary Colbert RC 2.00 .60
❑ 194 Ben Troupe RC 1.50 .45
❑ 195 Drew Henson RC 4.00 1.20
❑ 196 Chris Gamble RC 2.00 .60
❑ 197 Samie Parker RC 1.50 .45
❑ 198 Tatum Bell RC 2.50 .75
❑ 199 Robert Gallery RC 2.50 .75
❑ 200 Eli Manning RC 8.00 2.40
❑ 201 Ahmad Carroll RC 2.00 .60
❑ 202 Devery Henderson RC 1.25 .35
❑ 203 Matt Schaub RC 2.50 .75
❑ 204 Greg Jones RC 1.50 .45
❑ 205 Roy Williams RC 5.00 1.50
❑ 206 Tommie Harris RC 2.00 .60
❑ 207 Jeff Smoker RC 2.50 .75
❑ 208 Kenechi Udeze RC 1.50 .45
❑ 209 Derrick Hamilton RC 1.25 .35
❑ 210 Ben Roethlisberger RC 15.00 4.50
❑ 211 Darius Watts RC 2.00 .60
❑ 212 John Navarre RC 1.50 .45
❑ 213 Ernest Wilford RC 1.50 .45
❑ 214 Rashaun Woods RC 2.00 .60
❑ 215 Steven Jackson RC 5.00 1.50
❑ 216 Michael Jenkins RC 1.50 .45
❑ 217 Will Smith RC 1.50 .45
❑ 218 Devard Darling RC 1.50 .45
❑ 219 Chris Perry RC 3.00 .90
❑ 220 Luke McCown RC 1.50 .45

1948 Bowman

	ExMt	VgEx
COMPLETE SET (108)	6000.00	2700.00
COMMON 1/4/7/-/-/-	20.00	9.00
COMMON 2/5/8/-/-/-	25.00	11.00
COMMON SP 3/6/9 /-/-/-	100.00	45.00
WRAPPER (1-CENT)	250.00	110.00

❑ 1 Joe Tereshinski RC 150.00 38.00
❑ 2 Larry Olsonoski 25.00 11.00
❑ 3 John Lujack SP RC 350.00 160.00
❑ 4 Ray Poole 20.00 9.00
❑ 5 Bill DeCorrevont 25.00 11.00
❑ 6 Paul Briggs SP 100.00 45.00
❑ 7 Steve Van Buren RC 200.00 80.00
❑ 8 Kenny Washington RC 60.00 27.00
❑ 9 Nolan Luhn SP 100.00 45.00
❑ 10 Chris Iversen 20.00 9.00
❑ 11 Jack Wiley 25.00 11.00
❑ 12 Charley Conerly RC SP 350.00 160.00
❑ 13 Hugh Taylor RC 25.00 11.00
❑ 14 Frank Seno 25.00 11.00
❑ 15 Gil Bouley SP 100.00 45.00
❑ 16 Tommy Thompson RC 35.00 16.00
❑ 17 Charley Trippi RC 100.00 45.00
❑ 18 Vince Banonis SP 100.00 45.00
❑ 19 Art Faircloth 20.00 9.00
❑ 20 Clyde Goodnight 25.00 11.00
❑ 21 Bill Chipley SP 100.00 45.00
❑ 22 Sammy Baugh RC 500.00 220.00
❑ 23 Don Kindt 25.00 11.00
❑ 24 John Koniszewski SP 100.00 45.00
❑ 25 Pat McHugh 20.00 9.00
❑ 26 Bob Waterfield RC 200.00 90.00
❑ 27 Tony Compagno SP 100.00 45.00
❑ 28 Paul Governali RC 25.00 11.00
❑ 29 Pat Harder RC 60.00 27.00
❑ 30 Vic Lindskog SP 100.00 45.00
❑ 31 Salvatore Rosato 20.00 9.00
❑ 32 John Mastrangelo 25.00 11.00
❑ 33 Fred Gehrke SP 100.00 45.00
❑ 34 Bosh Pritchard 20.00 9.00
❑ 35 Mike Micka 25.00 11.00
❑ 36 Bulldog Turner RC SP 250.00 110.00
❑ 37 Len Younce 20.00 9.00
❑ 38 Pat West 25.00 11.00
❑ 39 Russ Thomas SP 100.00 45.00
❑ 40 James Peebles 20.00 9.00
❑ 41 Bob Skoglund 25.00 11.00
❑ 42 Walt Stickle SP 100.00 45.00
❑ 43 Whitey Wistert RC 25.00 11.00
❑ 44 Paul Christman RC 60.00 27.00
❑ 45 Jay Rhodemyre SP 100.00 45.00
❑ 46 Tony Minisi 20.00 9.00
❑ 47 Bob Mann 25.00 11.00
❑ 48 Mal Kutner RC SP 110.00 50.00
❑ 49 Dick Poillon 20.00 9.00
❑ 50 Charles Cherundolo 25.00 11.00
❑ 51 Gerald Cowhig SP 100.00 45.00
❑ 52 Neill Armstrong RC 25.00 11.00
❑ 53 Frank Maznicki 25.00 11.00
❑ 54 John Sanchez SP 100.00 45.00
❑ 55 Frank Reagan 20.00 9.00
❑ 56 Jim Hardy 25.00 11.00
❑ 57 John Badaczewski SP 100.00 45.00
❑ 58 Robert Nussbaumer 20.00 9.00
❑ 59 Marvin Pregulman 25.00 11.00
❑ 60 Elbert Nickel RC SP 125.00 55.00
❑ 61 Alex Wojciechowicz RC 150.00 70.00
❑ 62 Walt Schlinkman 25.00 11.00
❑ 63 Pete Pihos RC SP 225.00 100.00
❑ 64 Joseph Sulaitis 20.00 9.00
❑ 65 Mike Holovak RC 50.00 22.00
❑ 66 Cecil Souders SP 100.00 45.00
❑ 67 Paul McKee 20.00 9.00
❑ 68 Bill Moore 25.00 11.00
❑ 69 Frank Minini SP 100.00 45.00
❑ 70 Jack Ferrante 20.00 9.00
❑ 71 Les Horvath RC 50.00 22.00
❑ 72 Ted Fritsch Sr. RC SP 110.00 50.00
❑ 73 Tex Coulter RC 25.00 11.00
❑ 74 Boley Dancewicz 25.00 11.00
❑ 75 Dante Mangani SP 100.00 45.00
❑ 76 James Hefti 20.00 9.00
❑ 77 Paul Sarringhaus 25.00 11.00
❑ 78 Joe Scott SP 100.00 45.00
❑ 79 Bucko Kilroy RC 25.00 11.00
❑ 80 Bill Dudley RC 125.00 55.00
❑ 81 Marshall Goldberg RC SP 110.00 50.00
❑ 82 John Cannady 20.00 9.00
❑ 83 Perry Moss 25.00 11.00
❑ 84 Harold Crisler RC SP 110.00 50.00
❑ 85 Bill Gray 20.00 9.00
❑ 86 John Clement 25.00 11.00
❑ 87 Dan Sandifer SP 100.00 45.00
❑ 88 Ben Kish 20.00 9.00
❑ 89 Herbert Banta 25.00 11.00
❑ 90 Bill Garnaas SP 100.00 45.00
❑ 91 Jim White 20.00 9.00
❑ 92 Frank Barzilauskas 25.00 11.00
❑ 93 Vic Sears SP 100.00 45.00
❑ 94 John Adams 20.00 9.00

Card	ExMt	VgEx
❑ 95 George McAfee RC	150.00	55.00
❑ 96 Ralph Heywood SP	100.00	45.00
❑ 97 Joe Muha	20.00	9.00
❑ 98 Fred Enke	25.00	11.00
❑ 99 Harry Gilmer RC SP	175.00	80.00
❑ 100 Bill Miklich	20.00	9.00
❑ 101 Joe Gottlieb	25.00	11.00
❑ 102 Bud Angsman SP RC	110.00	50.00
❑ 103 Tom Farmer	20.00	9.00
❑ 104 Bruce Smith RC	75.00	34.00
❑ 105 Bob Cifers SP	100.00	45.00
❑ 106 Ernie Steele	20.00	9.00
❑ 107 Sid Luckman RC	300.00	110.00
❑ 108 Buford Ray SP RC	400.00	100.00

1950 Bowman

	ExMt	VgEx
COMPLETE SET (144)	4000.00	1800.00
WRAPPER (5-CENT)	175.00	80.00
❑ 1 Doak Walker	250.00	60.00
❑ 2 John Greene	25.00	11.00
❑ 3 Bob Nowasky	25.00	11.00
❑ 4 Jonathan Jenkins	25.00	11.00
❑ 5 Y.A. Tittle RC	250.00	110.00
❑ 6 Lou Groza RC	175.00	80.00
❑ 7 Alex Agase RC	30.00	13.50
❑ 8 Mac Speedie RC	50.00	22.00
❑ 9 Tony Canadeo RC	90.00	40.00
❑ 10 Larry Craig	30.00	13.50
❑ 11 Ted Fritsch Sr.	30.00	13.50
❑ 12 Joe Goldring	25.00	11.00
❑ 13 Martin Ruby	25.00	11.00
❑ 14 George Taliaferro	30.00	13.50
❑ 15 Tank Younger RC	50.00	22.00
❑ 16 Glenn Davis RC	125.00	55.00
❑ 17 Bob Waterfield	125.00	55.00
❑ 18 Val Jansante	25.00	11.00
❑ 19 Joe Geri	25.00	11.00
❑ 20 Jerry Nuzum	25.00	11.00
❑ 21 Elmer Bud Angsman	25.00	11.00
❑ 22 Billy Dewell	25.00	11.00
❑ 23 Steve Van Buren	90.00	40.00
❑ 24 Cliff Patton	25.00	11.00
❑ 25 Bosh Pritchard	25.00	11.00
❑ 26 John Lujack	80.00	36.00
❑ 27 Sid Luckman	125.00	55.00
❑ 28 Bulldog Turner	60.00	27.00
❑ 29 Bill Dudley	60.00	27.00
❑ 30 Hugh Taylor	30.00	13.50
❑ 31 George Thomas	25.00	11.00
❑ 32 Ray Poole	25.00	11.00
❑ 33 Travis Tidwell	25.00	11.00
❑ 34 Gail Bruce	25.00	11.00
❑ 35 Joe Perry RC	200.00	90.00
❑ 36 Frankie Albert RC	40.00	18.00
❑ 37 Bobby Layne	200.00	90.00
❑ 38 Leon Hart	40.00	18.00
❑ 39 Bob Hoernschemeyer RC	30.00	13.50
❑ 40 Dick Barwegan RC	25.00	11.00
❑ 41 Adrian Burk RC	30.00	13.50
❑ 42 Barry French	25.00	11.00
❑ 43 Marion Motley RC	250.00	110.00
❑ 44 Jim Martin	30.00	13.50
❑ 45 Otto Graham RC	450.00	200.00
❑ 46 Al Baldwin	25.00	11.00
❑ 47 Larry Coutre	30.00	13.50
❑ 48 John Rauch	25.00	11.00
❑ 49 Sam Tamburo	25.00	11.00
❑ 50 Mike Swistowicz	25.00	11.00
❑ 51 Tom Fears RC	150.00	70.00
❑ 52 Elroy Hirsch RC	225.00	100.00
❑ 53 Dick Huffman	25.00	11.00
❑ 54 Bob Gage	25.00	11.00
❑ 55 Buddy Tinsley	25.00	11.00
❑ 56 Bill Blackburn	25.00	11.00
❑ 57 John Cochran	25.00	11.00
❑ 58 Bill Fischer	25.00	11.00
❑ 59 Whitey Wistert	30.00	13.50
❑ 60 Clyde Scott	25.00	11.00
❑ 61 Walter Barnes	25.00	11.00
❑ 62 Bob Perina	25.00	11.00
❑ 63 Bill Wightkin	25.00	11.00
❑ 64 Bob Goode	25.00	11.00
❑ 65 Al Demao	25.00	11.00
❑ 66 Harry Gilmer	30.00	13.50
❑ 67 Bill Austin	25.00	11.00
❑ 68 Joe Scott	25.00	11.00
❑ 69 Tex Coulter	30.00	13.50
❑ 70 Paul Salata	25.00	11.00
❑ 71 Emil Sitko RC	30.00	13.50
❑ 72 Bill Johnson	25.00	11.00
❑ 73 Don Doll RC	25.00	11.00
❑ 74 Dan Sandifer	25.00	11.00
❑ 75 John Panelli	25.00	11.00
❑ 76 Bill Leonard	25.00	11.00
❑ 77 Bob Kelly	25.00	11.00
❑ 78 Dante Lavelli RC	150.00	70.00
❑ 79 Tony Adamle	30.00	13.50
❑ 80 Dick Wildung	25.00	11.00
❑ 81 Tobin Rote RC	50.00	22.00
❑ 82 Paul Burris	25.00	11.00
❑ 83 Lowell Tew	25.00	11.00
❑ 84 Barney Poole	25.00	11.00
❑ 85 Fred Naumetz	25.00	11.00
❑ 86 Dick Hoerner	25.00	11.00
❑ 87 Bob Reinhard	25.00	11.00
❑ 88 Howard Hartley RC	25.00	11.00
❑ 89 Darrell Hogan RC	25.00	11.00
❑ 90 Jerry Shipkey	25.00	11.00
❑ 91 Frank Tripucka	30.00	13.50
❑ 92 Garrard Ramsey RC	25.00	11.00
❑ 93 Pat Harder	30.00	13.50
❑ 94 Vic Sears	25.00	11.00
❑ 95 Tommy Thompson	30.00	13.50
❑ 96 Bucko Kilroy	30.00	13.50
❑ 97 George Connor	50.00	22.00
❑ 98 Fred Morrison	25.00	11.00
❑ 99 Jim Keane	25.00	11.00
❑ 100 Sammy Baugh	250.00	110.00
❑ 101 Harry Ulinski	25.00	11.00
❑ 102 Frank Spaniel	25.00	11.00
❑ 103 Charley Conerly	90.00	40.00
❑ 104 Dick Hensley	25.00	11.00
❑ 105 Eddie Price	25.00	11.00
❑ 106 Ed Carr	25.00	11.00
❑ 107 Leo Nomellini	75.00	34.00
❑ 108 Verl Lillywhite	25.00	11.00
❑ 109 Wallace Triplett	25.00	11.00
❑ 110 Joe Watson	25.00	11.00
❑ 111 Cloyce Box RC	30.00	13.50
❑ 112 Billy Stone	25.00	11.00
❑ 113 Earl Murray	25.00	11.00
❑ 114 Chet Mutryn RC	30.00	13.50
❑ 115 Ken Carpenter	30.00	13.50
❑ 116 Lou Rymkus RC	30.00	13.50
❑ 117 Dub Jones RC	30.00	13.50
❑ 118 Clayton Tonnemaker	25.00	11.00
❑ 119 Walt Schlinkman	25.00	11.00
❑ 120 Billy Grimes	25.00	11.00
❑ 121 George Ratterman RC	30.00	13.50
❑ 122 Bob Mann	25.00	11.00
❑ 123 Buddy Young RC	40.00	18.00
❑ 124 Jack Zilly	25.00	11.00
❑ 125 Tom Kalmanir	25.00	11.00
❑ 126 Frank Sinkovitz	25.00	11.00
❑ 127 Elbert Nickel	30.00	13.50
❑ 128 Jim Finks RC	75.00	34.00
❑ 129 Charley Trippi	60.00	27.00
❑ 130 Tom Wham	25.00	11.00
❑ 131 Ventan Yablonski	25.00	11.00
❑ 132 Chuck Bednarik	125.00	55.00
❑ 133 Joe Muha	25.00	11.00
❑ 134 Pete Pihos	80.00	36.00
❑ 135 Washington Serini	25.00	11.00
❑ 136 George Gulyanics	25.00	11.00
❑ 137 Ken Kavanaugh	30.00	13.50
❑ 138 Howie Livingston	25.00	11.00
❑ 139 Joe Tereshinski	25.00	11.00
❑ 140 Jim White	25.00	11.00
❑ 141 Gene Roberts	25.00	11.00
❑ 142 Bill Swiacki	30.00	13.50
❑ 143 Norm Standlee	25.00	11.00
❑ 144 Knox Ramsey RC	100.00	25.00

1951 Bowman

	ExMt	VgEx
COMPLETE SET (144)	3500.00	1600.00
WRAPPER (1-CENT)	250.00	110.00
WRAPPER (5-CENT)	300.00	135.00
❑ 1 Weldon Humble RC	80.00	20.00
❑ 2 Otto Graham	200.00	90.00
❑ 3 Mac Speedie	35.00	16.00
❑ 4 Norm Van Brocklin RC	300.00	135.00
❑ 5 Woodley Lewis RC	25.00	11.00
❑ 6 Tom Fears	50.00	22.00
❑ 7 George Musacco	20.00	9.00
❑ 8 George Taliaferro	25.00	11.00
❑ 9 Barney Poole	20.00	9.00
❑ 10 Steve Van Buren	60.00	27.00
❑ 11 Whitey Wistert	25.00	11.00
❑ 12 Chuck Bednarik	80.00	36.00
❑ 13 Bulldog Turner	50.00	22.00
❑ 14 Bob Williams	20.00	9.00
❑ 15 John Lujack	60.00	27.00
❑ 16 Roy Rebel Steiner	20.00	9.00
❑ 17 Jug Girard	25.00	11.00
❑ 18 Bill Neal	20.00	9.00
❑ 19 Travis Tidwell	20.00	9.00
❑ 20 Tom Landry RC	500.00	220.00
❑ 21 Arnie Weinmeister RC	60.00	27.00
❑ 22 Joe Geri	20.00	9.00
❑ 23 Bill Walsh RC	25.00	11.00
❑ 24 Fran Rogel	20.00	9.00
❑ 25 Doak Walker	60.00	27.00
❑ 26 Leon Hart	35.00	16.00
❑ 27 Thurman McGraw	20.00	9.00
❑ 28 Buster Ramsey	20.00	9.00
❑ 29 Frank Tripucka	35.00	16.00
❑ 30 Don Paul	20.00	9.00
❑ 31 Alex Loyd	20.00	9.00
❑ 32 Y.A. Tittle	135.00	60.00
❑ 33 Verl Lillywhite	20.00	9.00
❑ 34 Sammy Baugh	175.00	80.00
❑ 35 Chuck Drazenovich	20.00	9.00
❑ 36 Bob Goode	20.00	9.00
❑ 37 Horace Gillom	25.00	11.00
❑ 38 Lou Rymkus	25.00	11.00
❑ 39 Ken Carpenter	20.00	9.00
❑ 40 Bob Waterfield	75.00	34.00
❑ 41 Vitamin Smith RC	25.00	11.00
❑ 42 Glenn Davis	60.00	27.00
❑ 43 Dan Edwards	20.00	9.00
❑ 44 John Rauch	20.00	9.00
❑ 45 Zollie Toth	20.00	9.00
❑ 46 Pete Pihos	60.00	27.00
❑ 47 Russ Craft	20.00	9.00
❑ 48 Walter Barnes	20.00	9.00
❑ 49 Fred Morrison	20.00	9.00
❑ 50 Ray Bray	20.00	9.00
❑ 51 Ed Sprinkle RC	25.00	11.00
❑ 52 Floyd Reid	20.00	9.00
❑ 53 Billy Grimes	20.00	9.00

❑ 54 Ted Fritsch Sr.	25.00	11.00
❑ 55 Al DeRogatis	25.00	11.00
❑ 56 Charley Conerly	75.00	34.00
❑ 57 Jon Baker	20.00	9.00
❑ 58 Tom McWilliams	20.00	9.00
❑ 59 Jerry Shipkey	20.00	9.00
❑ 60 Lynn Chandnois RC	25.00	11.00
❑ 61 Don Doll	20.00	9.00
❑ 62 Lou Creekmur	50.00	22.00
❑ 63 Bob Hoernschemeyer	25.00	11.00
❑ 64 Tom Wham	20.00	9.00
❑ 65 Bill Fischer	20.00	9.00
❑ 66 Robert Nussbaumer	20.00	9.00
❑ 67 Gordy Soltau RC	20.00	9.00
❑ 68 Visco Grgich	20.00	9.00
❑ 69 John Strzykalski RC	20.00	9.00
❑ 70 Pete Stout	20.00	9.00
❑ 71 Paul Lipscomb	20.00	9.00
❑ 72 Harry Gilmer	35.00	16.00
❑ 73 Dante Lavelli	50.00	22.00
❑ 74 Dub Jones	25.00	11.00
❑ 75 Lou Groza	75.00	34.00
❑ 76 Elroy Hirsch	75.00	34.00
❑ 77 Tom Kalmanir	20.00	9.00
❑ 78 Jack Zilly	20.00	9.00
❑ 79 Bruce Alford	20.00	9.00
❑ 80 Art Weiner	20.00	9.00
❑ 81 Brad Ecklund	20.00	9.00
❑ 82 Bosh Pritchard	20.00	9.00
❑ 83 John Green	20.00	9.00
❑ 84 Ebert Van Buren	20.00	9.00
❑ 85 Julie Rykovich	20.00	9.00
❑ 86 Fred Davis	20.00	9.00
❑ 87 John Hoffman RC	20.00	9.00
❑ 88 Tobin Rote	25.00	11.00
❑ 89 Paul Burris	20.00	9.00
❑ 90 Tony Canadeo	50.00	22.00
❑ 91 Emlen Tunnell RC	100.00	45.00
❑ 92 Otto Schnellbacher RC	20.00	9.00
❑ 93 Ray Poole	20.00	9.00
❑ 94 Darrell Hogan	20.00	9.00
❑ 95 Frank Sinkovitz	20.00	9.00
❑ 96 Ernie Stautner	75.00	34.00
❑ 97 Elmer Bud Angsman	20.00	9.00
❑ 98 Jack Jennings	20.00	9.00
❑ 99 Jerry Groom	20.00	9.00
❑ 100 John Prchlik	20.00	9.00
❑ 101 J. Robert Smith	20.00	9.00
❑ 102 Bobby Layne	135.00	60.00
❑ 103 Frankie Albert	35.00	16.00
❑ 104 Gail Bruce	20.00	9.00
❑ 105 Joe Perry	75.00	34.00
❑ 106 Leon Heath	20.00	9.00
❑ 107 Ed Quirk	20.00	9.00
❑ 108 Hugh Taylor	25.00	11.00
❑ 109 Marion Motley	100.00	45.00
❑ 110 Tony Adamle	20.00	9.00
❑ 111 Alex Agase	25.00	11.00
❑ 112 Tank Younger	35.00	16.00
❑ 113 Bob Boyd	20.00	9.00
❑ 114 Jerry Williams	20.00	9.00
❑ 115 Joe Golding	20.00	9.00
❑ 116 Sherman Howard	20.00	9.00
❑ 117 John Wozniak	20.00	9.00
❑ 118 Frank Reagan	20.00	9.00
❑ 119 Vic Sears	20.00	9.00
❑ 120 Clyde Scott	20.00	9.00
❑ 121 George Gulyanics	20.00	9.00
❑ 122 Bill Wightkin	20.00	9.00
❑ 123 Chuck Hunsinger	20.00	9.00
❑ 124 Jack Cloud	20.00	9.00
❑ 125 Abner Wimberly	20.00	9.00
❑ 126 Dick Wildung	20.00	9.00
❑ 127 Eddie Price	20.00	9.00
❑ 128 Joe Scott	20.00	9.00
❑ 129 Jerry Nuzum	20.00	9.00
❑ 130 Jim Finks	35.00	16.00
❑ 131 Bob Gage	20.00	9.00
❑ 132 Bill Swiacki	25.00	11.00
❑ 133 Joe Watson	20.00	9.00
❑ 134 Ollie Cline	20.00	9.00
❑ 135 Jack Lininger	20.00	9.00
❑ 136 Fran Polsfoot	20.00	9.00
❑ 137 Charley Trippi	50.00	22.00
❑ 138 Ventan Yablonski	20.00	9.00
❑ 139 Emil Sitko	20.00	9.00
❑ 140 Leo Nomellini	60.00	27.00
❑ 141 Norm Standlee	20.00	9.00
❑ 142 Eddie Saenz	20.00	9.00
❑ 143 Al Demao	20.00	9.00
❑ 144 Bill Dudley	150.00	38.00
❑ NNO Johnny Lujack Proof	300.00	135.00
❑ NNO Bob Gage Proof	125.00	55.00
❑ NNO Darrell Hogan Proof	125.00	55.00

1952 Bowman Large

	ExMt	VgEx
COMPLETE SET (144)	12500.00	5600.00
COMMON CARD (1-72)	35.00	16.00
COMMON CARD (73-144)	40.00	18.00
WRAPPER (5-CENT)	60.00	27.00
❑ 1 Norm Van Brocklin	500.00	125.00
❑ 2 Otto Graham	300.00	135.00
❑ 3 Doak Walker	100.00	45.00
❑ 4 Steve Owen CO RC	75.00	34.00
❑ 5 Frankie Albert	50.00	22.00
❑ 6 Laurie Niemi	35.00	16.00
❑ 7 Chuck Hunsinger	35.00	16.00
❑ 8 Ed Modzelewski	50.00	22.00
❑ 9 Joe Spencer SP	75.00	34.00
❑ 10 Chuck Bednarik SP	300.00	135.00
❑ 11 Barney Poole	35.00	16.00
❑ 12 Charley Trippi	75.00	34.00
❑ 13 Tom Fears	75.00	34.00
❑ 14 Paul Brown CO RC	250.00	110.00
❑ 15 Leon Hart	50.00	22.00
❑ 16 Frank Gifford RC	500.00	220.00
❑ 17 Y.A. Tittle	300.00	135.00
❑ 18 Charlie Justice SP	175.00	80.00
❑ 19 George Connor SP	175.00	80.00
❑ 20 Lynn Chandnois	35.00	16.00
❑ 21 Billy Howton RC	50.00	22.00
❑ 22 Kenneth Snyder	35.00	16.00
❑ 23 Gino Marchetti RC	250.00	110.00
❑ 24 John Karras	35.00	16.00
❑ 25 Tank Younger	50.00	22.00
❑ 26 Tommy Thompson LB	35.00	16.00
❑ 27 Bob Miller SP RC	300.00	135.00
❑ 28 Kyle Rote RC SP	175.00	80.00
❑ 29 Hugh McElhenny RC	250.00	110.00
❑ 30 Sammy Baugh	350.00	160.00
❑ 31 Jim Dooley RC	45.00	20.00
❑ 32 Ray Mathews	35.00	16.00
❑ 33 Fred Cone	35.00	16.00
❑ 34 Al Pollard	35.00	16.00
❑ 35 Brad Ecklund	35.00	16.00
❑ 36 John Lee Hancock SP RC	350.00	160.00
❑ 37 Elroy Hirsch SP	200.00	90.00
❑ 38 Keever Jankovich	35.00	16.00
❑ 39 Emlen Tunnell	125.00	55.00
❑ 40 Steve Dowden	35.00	16.00
❑ 41 Claude Hipps	35.00	16.00
❑ 42 Norm Standlee	35.00	16.00
❑ 43 Dick Todd CO	35.00	16.00
❑ 44 Babe Parilli	50.00	22.00
❑ 45 Steve Van Buren SP	300.00	135.00
❑ 46 Art Donovan RC SP	350.00	160.00
❑ 47 Bill Fischer	35.00	16.00
❑ 48 George Halas CO RC	275.00	125.00
❑ 49 Jerrell Price	35.00	16.00
❑ 50 John Sandusky RC	35.00	16.00
❑ 51 Ray Beck	35.00	16.00
❑ 52 Jim Martin	45.00	20.00
❑ 53 Joe Bach CO UER (Misspelled Back)	35.00	16.00
❑ 54 Glen Christian SP	75.00	34.00
❑ 55 Andy Davis SP	75.00	34.00
❑ 56 Tobin Rote	45.00	20.00
❑ 57 Wayne Millner CO RC	90.00	40.00
❑ 58 Zollie Toth	35.00	16.00
❑ 59 Jack Jennings	35.00	16.00
❑ 60 Bill McColl	35.00	16.00
❑ 61 Les Richter RC	45.00	20.00
❑ 62 Walt Michaels RC	45.00	20.00
❑ 63 Charley Conerly SP	700.00	325.00
❑ 64 Howard Hartley SP	75.00	34.00
❑ 65 Jerome Smith	35.00	16.00
❑ 66 James Clark	35.00	16.00
❑ 67 Dick Logan	35.00	16.00
❑ 68 Wayne Robinson	35.00	16.00
❑ 69 James Hammond	35.00	16.00
❑ 70 Gene Schroeder	35.00	16.00
❑ 71 Tex Coulter	45.00	20.00
❑ 72 John Schweder SP RC	600.00	275.00
❑ 73 Vitamin Smith SP	150.00	70.00
❑ 74 Joe Campanella RC	40.00	18.00
❑ 75 Joe Kuharich CO RC	50.00	22.00
❑ 76 Herman Clark	40.00	18.00
❑ 77 Dan Edwards	40.00	18.00
❑ 78 Bobby Layne	300.00	110.00
❑ 79 Bob Hoernschemeyer	50.00	22.00
❑ 80 John Carr Blount	40.00	18.00
❑ 81 John Kastan RC SP	150.00	70.00
❑ 82 Harry Minarik RC SP	150.00	70.00
❑ 83 Joe Perry	100.00	45.00
❑ 84 Ray(Buddy) Parker CO RC	50.00	22.00
❑ 85 Andy Robustelli RC	200.00	90.00
❑ 86 Dub Jones	50.00	22.00
❑ 87 Mal Cook	40.00	18.00
❑ 88 Billy Stone	40.00	18.00
❑ 89 George Taliaferro	50.00	22.00
❑ 90 Thomas Johnson RC SP	150.00	70.00
❑ 91 Leon Heath SP	100.00	45.00
❑ 92 Pete Pihos	100.00	45.00
❑ 93 Fred Benners	40.00	18.00
❑ 94 George Tarasovic	40.00	18.00
❑ 95 Lawr. (Buck) Shaw CO RC	40.00	18.00
❑ 96 Bill Wightkin	40.00	18.00
❑ 97 John Wozniak	40.00	18.00
❑ 98 Bobby Dillon RC	50.00	22.00
❑ 99 Joe Stydahar CO SP RC	650.00	300.00
❑ 100 Dick Alban RC SP	150.00	70.00
❑ 101 Arnie Weinmeister	60.00	27.00
❑ 102 Bobby Cross	40.00	18.00
❑ 103 Don Paul	40.00	18.00
❑ 104 Buddy Young	60.00	27.00
❑ 105 Lou Groza	125.00	55.00
❑ 106 Ray Pelfrey	40.00	18.00
❑ 107 Maurice Nipp	40.00	18.00
❑ 108 Hubert Johnston SP RC	650.00	300.00
❑ 109 Volney Quinlan RC SP	100.00	45.00
❑ 110 Jack Simmons	40.00	18.00
❑ 111 George Ratterman	50.00	22.00
❑ 112 John Badaczewski	40.00	18.00
❑ 113 Bill Reichardt	40.00	18.00
❑ 114 Art Weiner	40.00	18.00
❑ 115 Keith Flowers	40.00	18.00
❑ 116 Russ Craft	40.00	18.00
❑ 117 Jim O'Donahue RC SP	150.00	70.00
❑ 118 Darrell Hogan SP	100.00	45.00
❑ 119 Frank Ziegler	40.00	18.00
❑ 120 Deacon Dan Towler	60.00	27.00
❑ 121 Fred Williams	40.00	18.00
❑ 122 Jimmy Phelan CO	40.00	18.00
❑ 123 Eddie Price	40.00	18.00
❑ 124 Chet Ostrowski	40.00	18.00
❑ 125 Leo Nomellini	100.00	45.00
❑ 126 Steve Romanik SP RC	300.00	135.00
❑ 127 Ollie Matson RC SP	300.00	135.00
❑ 128 Dante Lavelli	90.00	40.00
❑ 129 Jack Christiansen RC	175.00	80.00
❑ 130 Dom Moselle	40.00	18.00
❑ 131 John Rapacz	40.00	18.00
❑ 132 Chuck Ortmann UER (Avg. gain 9.4, should be 4.8)	40.00	18.00

❑ 133 Bob Williams	40.00	18.00
❑ 134 Chuck Ulrich	40.00	18.00
❑ 135 Gene Ronzani CO SP RC	650.00	300.00
❑ 136 Bert Rechichar SP	100.00	45.00
❑ 137 Bob Waterfield	125.00	55.00
❑ 138 Bobby Walston RC	50.00	22.00
❑ 139 Jerry Shipkey	40.00	18.00
❑ 140 Yale Lary RC	175.00	80.00
❑ 141 Gordy Soltau	40.00	18.00
❑ 142 Tom Landry	600.00	275.00
❑ 143 John Papit	40.00	18.00
❑ 144 Jim Lansford SP RC	3000.00	750.00

1952 Bowman Small

	ExMt	VgEx
COMPLETE SET (144)	5000.00	2200.00
COMMON CARD (1-72)	25.00	11.00
COMMON CARD (73-144)	30.00	13.50
WRAPPER (1-CENT)	60.00	27.00
❑ 1 Norm Van Brocklin	350.00	90.00
❑ 2 Otto Graham	200.00	90.00
❑ 3 Doak Walker	60.00	27.00
❑ 4 Steve Owen CO RC	60.00	27.00
❑ 5 Frankie Albert	35.00	16.00
❑ 6 Laurie Niemi	25.00	11.00
❑ 7 Chuck Hunsinger	25.00	11.00
❑ 8 Ed Modzelewski	35.00	16.00
❑ 9 Joe Spencer	25.00	11.00
❑ 10 Chuck Bednarik	75.00	34.00
❑ 11 Barney Poole	25.00	11.00
❑ 12 Charley Trippi	60.00	27.00
❑ 13 Tom Fears	60.00	27.00
❑ 14 Paul Brown CO RC	150.00	70.00
❑ 15 Leon Hart	35.00	16.00
❑ 16 Frank Gifford RC	400.00	180.00
❑ 17 Y.A. Tittle	125.00	55.00
❑ 18 Charlie Justice	45.00	20.00
❑ 19 George Connor	35.00	16.00
❑ 20 Lynn Chandnois	25.00	11.00
❑ 21 Billy Howton RC	40.00	18.00
❑ 22 Kenneth Snyder	25.00	11.00
❑ 23 Gino Marchetti RC	125.00	55.00
❑ 24 John Karras	25.00	11.00
❑ 25 Tank Younger	35.00	16.00
❑ 26 Tommy Thompson	25.00	11.00
❑ 27 Bob Miller RC	25.00	11.00
❑ 28 Kyle Rote RC	50.00	22.00
❑ 29 Hugh McElhenny RC	175.00	80.00
❑ 30 Sammy Baugh	250.00	110.00
❑ 31 Jim Dooley RC	30.00	13.50
❑ 32 Ray Mathews	25.00	11.00
❑ 33 Fred Cone	25.00	11.00
❑ 34 Al Pollard	25.00	11.00
❑ 35 Brad Ecklund	25.00	11.00
❑ 36 John Lee Hancock	25.00	11.00
❑ 37 Elroy Hirsch	60.00	27.00
❑ 38 Keever Jankovich	25.00	11.00
❑ 39 Emlen Tunnell	50.00	22.00
❑ 40 Steve Dowden	25.00	11.00
❑ 41 Claude Hipps	25.00	11.00
❑ 42 Norm Standlee	25.00	11.00
❑ 43 Dick Todd CO	25.00	11.00
❑ 44 Babe Parilli	35.00	16.00
❑ 45 Steve Van Buren	75.00	34.00
❑ 46 Art Donovan RC	200.00	90.00
❑ 47 Bill Fischer	25.00	11.00
❑ 48 George Halas CO RC	250.00	110.00
❑ 49 Jerrell Price	25.00	11.00
❑ 50 John Sandusky RC	25.00	11.00
❑ 51 Ray Beck	25.00	11.00
❑ 52 Jim Martin	30.00	13.50
❑ 53 Joe Bach CO UER (Misspelled Back)	25.00	11.00
❑ 54 Glen Christian	25.00	11.00
❑ 55 Andy Davis	25.00	11.00
❑ 56 Tobin Rote	30.00	13.50
❑ 57 Wayne Millner CO RC	50.00	22.00
❑ 58 Zollie Toth	25.00	11.00
❑ 59 Jack Jennings	25.00	11.00
❑ 60 Bill McColl	25.00	11.00
❑ 61 Les Richter RC	30.00	13.50
❑ 62 Walt Michaels RC	30.00	13.50
❑ 63 Charley Conerly	75.00	34.00
❑ 64 Howard Hartley	25.00	11.00
❑ 65 Jerome Smith	25.00	11.00
❑ 66 James Clark	25.00	11.00
❑ 67 Dick Logan	25.00	11.00
❑ 68 Wayne Robinson	25.00	11.00
❑ 69 James Hammond	25.00	11.00
❑ 70 Gene Schroeder	25.00	11.00
❑ 71 Tex Coulter	30.00	13.50
❑ 72 John Schweder	25.00	11.00
❑ 73 Vitamin Smith	35.00	16.00
❑ 74 Joe Campanella RC	30.00	13.50
❑ 75 Joe Kuharich CO RC	35.00	16.00
❑ 76 Herman Clark	30.00	13.50
❑ 77 Dan Edwards	30.00	13.50
❑ 78 Bobby Layne	150.00	70.00
❑ 79 Bob Hoernschemeyer	35.00	16.00
❑ 80 John Carr Blount	30.00	13.50
❑ 81 John Kastan RC	30.00	13.50
❑ 82 Harry Minarik	30.00	13.50
❑ 83 Joe Perry	75.00	34.00
❑ 84 Ray(Buddy) Parker CO RC	35.00	16.00
❑ 85 Andy Robustelli RC	125.00	55.00
❑ 86 Dub Jones	35.00	16.00
❑ 87 Mal Cook	30.00	13.50
❑ 88 Billy Stone	30.00	13.50
❑ 89 George Taliaferro	35.00	16.00
❑ 90 Thomas Johnson RC	30.00	13.50
❑ 91 Leon Heath	30.00	13.50
❑ 92 Pete Pihos	50.00	22.00
❑ 93 Fred Benners	30.00	13.50
❑ 94 George Tarasovic	30.00	13.50
❑ 95 Lawr. (Buck) Shaw CO RC	30.00	13.50
❑ 96 Bill Wightkin	30.00	13.50
❑ 97 John Wozniak	30.00	13.50
❑ 98 Bobby Dillon RC	35.00	16.00
❑ 99 Joe Stydahar CO RC	45.00	20.00
❑ 100 Dick Alban RC	30.00	13.50
❑ 101 Arnie Weinmeister	40.00	18.00
❑ 102 Bobby Cross	30.00	13.50
❑ 103 Don Paul	30.00	13.50
❑ 104 Buddy Young	40.00	18.00
❑ 105 Lou Groza	75.00	34.00
❑ 106 Ray Pelfrey	30.00	13.50
❑ 107 Maurice Nipp	30.00	13.50
❑ 108 Hubert Johnston	30.00	13.50
❑ 109 Volney Quinlan RC	30.00	13.50
❑ 110 Jack Simmons	30.00	13.50
❑ 111 George Ratterman	35.00	16.00
❑ 112 John Badaczewski	30.00	13.50
❑ 113 Bill Reichardt	30.00	13.50
❑ 114 Art Weiner	30.00	13.50
❑ 115 Keith Flowers	30.00	13.50
❑ 116 Russ Craft	30.00	13.50
❑ 117 Jim O'Donahue RC	30.00	13.50
❑ 118 Darrell Hogan	30.00	13.50
❑ 119 Frank Ziegler	30.00	13.50
❑ 120 Deacon Dan Towler	40.00	18.00
❑ 121 Fred Williams	30.00	13.50
❑ 122 Jimmy Phelan CO	30.00	13.50
❑ 123 Eddie Price	30.00	13.50
❑ 124 Chet Ostrowski	30.00	13.50
❑ 125 Leo Nomellini	75.00	34.00
❑ 126 Steve Romanik	30.00	13.50
❑ 127 Ollie Matson RC	125.00	55.00
❑ 128 Dante Lavelli	60.00	27.00
❑ 129 Jack Christiansen RC	80.00	36.00
❑ 130 Dom Moselle	30.00	13.50
❑ 131 John Rapacz	30.00	13.50
❑ 132 Chuck Ortmann UER (Avg. gain 9.4, should be 4.8)	30.00	13.50
❑ 133 Bob Williams	30.00	13.50
❑ 134 Chuck Ulrich	30.00	13.50
❑ 135 Gene Ronzani CO RC	30.00	13.50
❑ 136 Bert Rechichar	35.00	16.00
❑ 137 Bob Waterfield	75.00	34.00
❑ 138 Bobby Walston RC	35.00	16.00
❑ 139 Jerry Shipkey	30.00	13.50
❑ 140 Yale Lary RC	80.00	36.00
❑ 141 Gordy Soltau	30.00	13.50
❑ 142 Tom Landry	400.00	180.00
❑ 143 John Papit	30.00	13.50
❑ 144 Jim Lansford RC	175.00	45.00

1953 Bowman

	ExMt	VgEx
COMPLETE SET (96)	3400.00	1500.00
WRAPPER (5-CENT)	150.00	70.00
❑ 1 Eddie LeBaron RC	125.00	31.00
❑ 2 John Dottley	30.00	13.50
❑ 3 Babe Parilli	35.00	16.00
❑ 4 Bucko Kilroy	35.00	16.00
❑ 5 Joe Tereshinski	30.00	13.50
❑ 6 Doak Walker	75.00	34.00
❑ 7 Fran Polsfoot	30.00	13.50
❑ 8 Sisto Averno	30.00	13.50
❑ 9 Marion Motley	75.00	34.00
❑ 10 Pat Brady	30.00	13.50
❑ 11 Norm Van Brocklin	125.00	55.00
❑ 12 Bill McColl	30.00	13.50
❑ 13 Jerry Groom	30.00	13.50
❑ 14 Al Pollard	30.00	13.50
❑ 15 Dante Lavelli	50.00	22.00
❑ 16 Eddie Price	30.00	13.50
❑ 17 Charley Trippi	50.00	22.00
❑ 18 Elbert Nickel	35.00	16.00
❑ 19 George Taliaferro	35.00	16.00
❑ 20 Charley Conerly	80.00	36.00
❑ 21 Bobby Layne	125.00	55.00
❑ 22 Elroy Hirsch	100.00	45.00
❑ 23 Jim Finks	40.00	18.00
❑ 24 Chuck Bednarik	75.00	34.00
❑ 25 Kyle Rote	40.00	18.00
❑ 26 Otto Graham	175.00	80.00
❑ 27 Harry Gilmer	35.00	16.00
❑ 28 Tobin Rote	35.00	16.00
❑ 29 Billy Stone	30.00	13.50
❑ 30 Buddy Young	40.00	18.00
❑ 31 Leon Hart	40.00	18.00
❑ 32 Hugh McElhenny	75.00	34.00
❑ 33 Dale Samuels	30.00	13.50
❑ 34 Lou Creekmur	50.00	22.00
❑ 35 Tom Catlin	30.00	13.50
❑ 36 Tom Fears	60.00	27.00
❑ 37 George Connor	40.00	18.00
❑ 38 Bill Walsh C	30.00	13.50
❑ 39 Leo Sanford SP	45.00	20.00
❑ 40 Horace Gillom	35.00	16.00
❑ 41 John Schweder SP	45.00	20.00
❑ 42 Tom O'Connell	30.00	13.50
❑ 43 Frank Gifford SP	300.00	200.00
❑ 44 Frank Continetti SP	45.00	20.00
❑ 45 John Olszewski SP	45.00	20.00
❑ 46 Dub Jones	35.00	16.00
❑ 47 Don Paul SP	45.00	20.00
❑ 48 Gerald Weatherly	30.00	13.50
❑ 49 Fred Bruney SP	45.00	20.00

Card	NM	Ex
❑ 50 Jack Scarbath	30.00	13.50
❑ 51 John Karras	30.00	13.50
❑ 52 Al Conway	30.00	13.50
❑ 53 Emlen Tunnell SP	125.00	55.00
❑ 54 Gern Nagler SP	45.00	20.00
❑ 55 Kenneth Snyder SP	45.00	20.00
❑ 56 Y.A. Tittle	150.00	70.00
❑ 57 John Rapacz SP	45.00	20.00
❑ 58 Harley Sewell SP	45.00	20.00
❑ 59 Don Bingham	30.00	13.50
❑ 60 Darrell Hogan	30.00	13.50
❑ 61 Tony Curcillo	30.00	13.50
❑ 62 Ray Renfro RC SP	50.00	22.00
❑ 63 Leon Heath	30.00	13.50
❑ 64 Tex Coulter SP	45.00	20.00
❑ 65 Dewayne Douglas	30.00	13.50
❑ 66 J. Robert Smith SP	45.00	20.00
❑ 67 Bob McChesney SP	45.00	20.00
❑ 68 Dick Alban SP	45.00	20.00
❑ 69 Andy Kozar	30.00	13.50
❑ 70 Merwin Hodel SP	45.00	20.00
❑ 71 Thurman McGraw	30.00	13.50
❑ 72 Cliff Anderson	30.00	13.50
❑ 73 Pete Pihos	60.00	27.00
❑ 74 Julie Rykovich	30.00	13.50
❑ 75 John Kreamcheck SP	45.00	20.00
❑ 76 Lynn Chandnois	30.00	13.50
❑ 77 Cloyce Box SP	45.00	20.00
❑ 78 Ray Mathews	30.00	13.50
❑ 79 Bobby Walston	35.00	16.00
❑ 80 Jim Dooley	30.00	13.50
❑ 81 Pat Harder SP	45.00	20.00
❑ 82 Jerry Shipkey	30.00	13.50
❑ 83 Bobby Thomason RC	30.00	13.50
❑ 84 Hugh Taylor	35.00	16.00
❑ 85 George Ratterman	35.00	16.00
❑ 86 Don Stonesifer	30.00	13.50
❑ 87 John Williams SP RC	45.00	20.00
❑ 88 Leo Nomellini	50.00	22.00
❑ 89 Frank Ziegler	30.00	13.50
❑ 90 Don Paul UER (19th in punt returns& should be 9th) Chicago Cardinals	30.00	13.50
❑ 91 Tom Dublinski	30.00	13.50
❑ 92 Ken Carpenter	30.00	13.50
❑ 93 Ted Marchibroda RC	40.00	18.00
❑ 94 Chuck Drazenovich	30.00	13.50
❑ 95 Lou Groza SP	125.00	55.00
❑ 96 William Cross SP RC	100.00	25.00

1954 Bowman

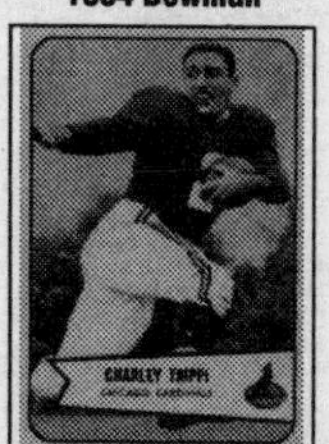

	NM	Ex
COMPLETE SET (128)	1800.00	800.00
COMMON CARD (1-64)	5.00	2.20
COMMON SP (65-96)	25.00	11.00
COMMON CARD (97-128)	5.00	2.20
WRAPPER (1-CENT)	15.00	6.75
WRAPPER (5-CENT)	30.00	13.50
❑ 1 Ray Mathews	30.00	7.50
❑ 2 John Huzvar	5.00	2.20
❑ 3 Jack Scarbath	5.00	2.20
❑ 4 Doug Atkins RC	50.00	22.00
❑ 5 Bill Stits	5.00	2.20
❑ 6 Joe Perry	30.00	13.50
❑ 7 Kyle Rote	15.00	6.75
❑ 8 Norm Van Brocklin	50.00	22.00
❑ 9 Pete Pihos	20.00	9.00
❑ 10 Babe Parilli	8.00	3.60
❑ 11 Zeke Bratkowski RC	25.00	11.00
❑ 12 Ollie Matson	25.00	11.00
❑ 13 Pat Brady	5.00	2.20
❑ 14 Fred Enke	5.00	2.20
❑ 15 Harry Ulinski	5.00	2.20
❑ 16 Bob Garrett	5.00	2.20
❑ 17 Bill Bowman	5.00	2.20
❑ 18 Leo Rucka	5.00	2.20
❑ 19 John Cannady	5.00	2.20
❑ 20 Tom Fears	25.00	11.00
❑ 21 Norm Willey	5.00	2.20
❑ 22 Floyd Reid	5.00	2.20
❑ 23 George Blanda RC	175.00	80.00
❑ 24 Don Doheney	5.00	2.20
❑ 25 John Schweder	5.00	2.20
❑ 26 Bert Rechichar	5.00	2.20
❑ 27 Harry Dowda	5.00	2.20
❑ 28 John Sandusky	5.00	2.20
❑ 29 Les Bingaman RC	15.00	6.75
❑ 30 Joe Arenas	5.00	2.20
❑ 31 Ray Wietecha RC	5.00	2.20
❑ 32 Elroy Hirsch	30.00	13.50
❑ 33 Harold Giancanelli	5.00	2.20
❑ 34 Billy Howton	8.00	3.60
❑ 35 Fred Morrison	5.00	2.20
❑ 36 Bobby Cavazos	5.00	2.20
❑ 37 Darrell Hogan	5.00	2.20
❑ 38 Buddy Young	8.00	3.60
❑ 39 Charlie Justice	20.00	9.00
❑ 40 Otto Graham	80.00	34.00
❑ 41 Doak Walker	35.00	16.00
❑ 42 Y.A. Tittle	60.00	27.00
❑ 43 Buford Long	5.00	2.20
❑ 44 Volney Quinlan	5.00	2.20
❑ 45 Bobby Thomason	5.00	2.20
❑ 46 Fred Cone	5.00	2.20
❑ 47 Gerald Weatherly	5.00	2.20
❑ 48 Don Stonesifer	5.00	2.20
❑ 49A Lynn Chandnois ERR Name spelled Chadnois on back	5.00	2.20
❑ 49B Lynn Chandnois COR	5.00	2.50
❑ 50 George Taliaferro	5.00	2.20
❑ 51 Dick Alban	5.00	2.20
❑ 52 Lou Groza	35.00	16.00
❑ 53 Bobby Layne	60.00	27.00
❑ 54 Hugh McElhenny	40.00	18.00
❑ 55 Frank Gifford UER (Avg. gain 7.83& should be 3.1)	100.00	45.00
❑ 56 Leon McLaughlin	5.00	2.20
❑ 57 Chuck Bednarik	40.00	18.00
❑ 58 Art Hunter	5.00	2.20
❑ 59 Bill McColl	5.00	2.20
❑ 60 Charley Trippi	25.00	11.00
❑ 61 Jim Finks	15.00	6.75
❑ 62 Bill Lange	5.00	2.20
❑ 63 Laurie Niemi	5.00	2.20
❑ 64 Ray Renfro	8.00	3.60
❑ 65 Dick Chapman	25.00	11.00
❑ 66 Bob Hantla	25.00	11.00
❑ 67 Ralph Starkey	25.00	11.00
❑ 68 Don Paul	25.00	11.00
❑ 69 Kenneth Snyder	25.00	11.00
❑ 70 Tobin Rote	30.00	13.50
❑ 71 Art DeCarlo	25.00	11.00
❑ 72 Tom Keane	25.00	11.00
❑ 73 Hugh Taylor	30.00	13.50
❑ 74 Warren Lahr RC	25.00	11.00
❑ 75 Jim Neal	25.00	11.00
❑ 76 Leo Nomellini	60.00	27.00
❑ 77 Dick Yelvington	25.00	11.00
❑ 78 Les Richter	30.00	13.50
❑ 79 Bucko Kilroy	30.00	13.50
❑ 80 John Martinkovic	25.00	11.00
❑ 81 Dale Dodrill RC	25.00	11.00
❑ 82 Ken Jackson	25.00	11.00
❑ 83 Paul Lipscomb	25.00	11.00
❑ 84 John Bauer	25.00	11.00
❑ 85 Lou Creekmur	50.00	22.00
❑ 86 Eddie Price	25.00	11.00
❑ 87 Kenneth Farragut	25.00	11.00
❑ 88 Dave Hanner RC	30.00	13.50
❑ 89 Don Boll	25.00	11.00
❑ 90 Chet Hanulak	25.00	11.00
❑ 91 Thurman McGraw	25.00	11.00
❑ 92 Don Heinrich RC	30.00	13.50
❑ 93 Dan McKown	25.00	11.00
❑ 94 Bob Fleck	25.00	11.00
❑ 95 Jerry Hilgenberg	25.00	11.00
❑ 96 Bill Walsh	25.00	11.00
❑ 97A Tom Finnin ERR	60.00	27.00
❑ 97B Tom Finnan COR	8.00	3.60
❑ 98 Paul Barry	5.00	2.20
❑ 99 Chick Jagade	5.00	2.20
❑ 100 Jack Christiansen	20.00	9.00
❑ 101 Gordy Soltau	5.00	2.20
❑ 102A Emlen Tunnel ERR	20.00	10.00
❑ 102B Emlen Tunnell COR two L's almost touching	20.00	9.00
❑ 102C Emlen Tunnell COR Two L's normally spaced	20.00	10.00
❑ 103 Stan West	5.00	2.20
❑ 104 Jerry Williams	5.00	2.20
❑ 105 Veryl Switzer	5.00	2.20
❑ 106 Billy Stone	5.00	2.20
❑ 107 Jerry Watford	5.00	2.20
❑ 108 Elbert Nickel	8.00	3.60
❑ 109 Ed Sharkey	5.00	2.20
❑ 110 Steve Meilinger	5.00	2.20
❑ 111 Dante Lavelli	20.00	9.00
❑ 112 Leon Hart	15.00	6.75
❑ 113 Charley Conerly	30.00	13.50
❑ 114 Richard Lemmon	5.00	2.20
❑ 115 Al Carmichael	5.00	2.20
❑ 116 George Connor	20.00	9.00
❑ 117 John Olszewski	5.00	2.20
❑ 118 Ernie Stautner	25.00	11.00
❑ 119 Ray Smith	5.00	2.20
❑ 120 Neil Worden	5.00	2.20
❑ 121 Jim Dooley	5.00	2.20
❑ 122 Arnold Galiffa	5.00	2.20
❑ 123 Kline Gilbert	5.00	2.20
❑ 124 Bob Hoernschemeyer	8.00	3.60
❑ 125 Wilford Whizzer White RC (not the Supreme Court Justice)	15.00	6.75
❑ 126 Art Spinney	5.00	2.20
❑ 127 Joe Koch	5.00	2.20
❑ 128 John Lattner RC	80.00	20.00

1955 Bowman

	NM	Ex
COMPLETE SET (160)	1600.00	700.00
COMMON CARD (1-64)	5.00	2.20
COMMON CARD (65-160)	8.00	3.60
WRAPPER (1-CENT)	225.00	100.00
WRAPPER (5-CENT)	100.00	45.00
❑ 1 Doak Walker	75.00	19.00
❑ 2 Mike McCormack RC	30.00	13.50
❑ 3 John Olszewski	5.00	2.20
❑ 4 Dorne Dibble	5.00	2.20
❑ 5 Lindon Crow	5.00	2.20
❑ 6 Hugh Taylor UER (First word in bio should be Bones)	8.00	3.60
❑ 7 Frank Gifford	75.00	34.00
❑ 8 Alan Ameche RC	40.00	18.00
❑ 9 Don Stonesifer	5.00	2.20
❑ 10 Pete Pihos	15.00	6.75
❑ 11 Bill Austin	5.00	2.20
❑ 12 Dick Alban	5.00	2.20
❑ 13 Bobby Walston	8.00	3.60

❑ 14 Len Ford RC	40.00	18.00
❑ 15 Jug Girard	5.00	2.20
❑ 16 Charley Conerly	25.00	11.00
❑ 17 Volney Peters	5.00	2.20
❑ 18 Max Boydston	5.00	2.20
❑ 19 Leon Hart	12.00	5.50
❑ 20 Bert Rechichar	5.00	2.20
❑ 21 Lee Riley	5.00	2.20
❑ 22 Johnny Carson	5.00	2.20
❑ 23 Harry Thompson	5.00	2.20
❑ 24 Ray Wietecha	5.00	2.20
❑ 25 Ollie Matson	25.00	11.00
❑ 26 Eddie LeBaron	15.00	6.75
❑ 27 Jack Simmons	5.00	2.20
❑ 28 Jack Christiansen	15.00	6.75
❑ 29 Bucko Kilroy	8.00	3.60
❑ 30 Tom Keane	5.00	2.20
❑ 31 Dave Leggett	5.00	2.20
❑ 32 Norm Van Brocklin	40.00	18.00
❑ 33 Harlon Hill RC	8.00	3.60
❑ 34 Robert Haner	5.00	2.20
❑ 35 Veryl Switzer	5.00	2.20
❑ 36 Dick Stanfel RC	12.00	5.50
❑ 37 Lou Groza	25.00	11.00
❑ 38 Tank Younger	12.00	5.50
❑ 39 Dick Flanagan	5.00	2.20
❑ 40 Jim Dooley	5.00	2.20
❑ 41 Ray Collins	5.00	2.20
❑ 42 John Henry Johnson RC	40.00	18.00
❑ 43 Tom Fears	15.00	6.75
❑ 44 Joe Perry	30.00	13.50
❑ 45 Gene Brito RC	5.00	2.20
❑ 46 Bill Johnson	5.00	2.20
❑ 47 Deacon Dan Towler	12.00	5.50
❑ 48 Dick Moegle	8.00	3.60
❑ 49 Kline Gilbert	5.00	2.20
❑ 50 Les Gobel	5.00	2.20
❑ 51 Ray Krouse RC	5.00	2.20
❑ 52 Pat Summerall RC	70.00	32.00
❑ 53 Ed Brown RC	12.00	5.50
❑ 54 Lynn Chandnois	5.00	2.20
❑ 55 Joe Heap	5.00	2.20
❑ 56 John Hoffman	5.00	2.20
❑ 57 Howard Ferguson	5.00	2.20
❑ 58 Bobby Watkins	5.00	2.20
❑ 59 Charlie Ane RC	5.00	2.20
❑ 60 Ken MacAfee E RC	8.00	3.60
❑ 61 Ralph Guglielmi RC	8.00	3.60
❑ 62 George Blanda	60.00	27.00
❑ 63 Kenneth Snyder	5.00	2.20
❑ 64 Chet Ostrowski	5.00	2.20
❑ 65 Buddy Young	15.00	6.75
❑ 66 Gordy Soltau	8.00	3.60
❑ 67 Eddie Bell	8.00	3.60
❑ 68 Ben Agajanian RC	12.00	5.50
❑ 69 Tom Dahms	8.00	3.60
❑ 70 Jim Ringo RC	50.00	22.00
❑ 71 Bobby Layne	75.00	34.00
❑ 72 Y.A. Tittle	75.00	34.00
❑ 73 Bob Gaona	8.00	3.60
❑ 74 Tobin Rote	12.00	5.50
❑ 75 Hugh McElhenny	30.00	13.50
❑ 76 John Kreamcheck	8.00	3.60
❑ 77 Al Dorow	12.00	5.50
❑ 78 Bill Wade	15.00	6.75
❑ 79 Dale Dodrill	8.00	3.60
❑ 80 Chuck Drazenovich	8.00	3.60
❑ 81 Billy Wilson RC	12.00	5.50
❑ 82 Les Richter	12.00	5.50
❑ 83 Pat Brady	8.00	3.60
❑ 84 Bob Hoernschemeyer	12.00	5.50
❑ 85 Joe Arenas	8.00	3.60
❑ 86 Len Szafaryn UER (Listed as Ben on front)	8.00	3.60
❑ 87 Rick Casares RC	20.00	9.00
❑ 88 Leon McLaughlin	8.00	3.60
❑ 89 Charley Toogood	8.00	3.60
❑ 90 Tom Bettis	8.00	3.60
❑ 91 John Sandusky	8.00	3.60
❑ 92 Bill Wightkin	8.00	3.60
❑ 93 Darrel Brewster	8.00	3.60
❑ 94 Marion Campbell	15.00	6.75
❑ 95 Floyd Reid	8.00	3.60
❑ 96 Chick Jagade	8.00	3.60
❑ 97 George Taliaferro	8.00	3.60
❑ 98 Carlton Massey	8.00	3.60
❑ 99 Fran Rogel	8.00	3.60
❑ 100 Alex Sandusky	8.00	3.60
❑ 101 Bob St. Clair RC	35.00	16.00
❑ 102 Al Carmichael	8.00	3.60
❑ 103 Carl Taseff RC	8.00	3.60
❑ 104 Leo Nomellini	25.00	11.00
❑ 105 Tom Scott	8.00	3.60
❑ 106 Ted Marchibroda	15.00	6.75
❑ 107 Art Spinney	8.00	3.60
❑ 108 Wayne Robinson	8.00	3.60
❑ 109 Jim Ricca	8.00	3.60
❑ 110 Lou Ferry	8.00	3.60
❑ 111 Roger Zatkoff	8.00	3.60
❑ 112 Lou Creekmur	15.00	6.75
❑ 113 Kenny Konz	8.00	3.60
❑ 114 Doug Eggers	8.00	3.60
❑ 115 Bobby Thomason	8.00	3.60
❑ 116 Bill McPeak	8.00	3.60
❑ 117 William Brown	8.00	3.60
❑ 118 Royce Womble	8.00	3.60
❑ 119 Frank Gatski RC	35.00	16.00
❑ 120 Jim Finks	15.00	6.75
❑ 121 Andy Robustelli	25.00	11.00
❑ 122 Bobby Dillon	8.00	3.60
❑ 123 Leo Sanford	8.00	3.60
❑ 124 Elbert Nickel	12.00	5.50
❑ 125 Wayne Hansen	8.00	3.60
❑ 126 Buck Lansford RC	8.00	3.60
❑ 127 Gern Nagler	8.00	3.60
❑ 128 Jim Salsbury	8.00	3.60
❑ 129 Dale Atkeson RC	8.00	3.60
❑ 130 John Schweder	8.00	3.60
❑ 131 Dave Hanner	12.00	5.50
❑ 132 Eddie Price	8.00	3.60
❑ 133 Vic Janowicz	30.00	9.00
❑ 134 Ernie Stautner	25.00	11.00
❑ 135 James Parmer	8.00	3.60
❑ 136 Emlen Tunnell UER (Misspelled Tunnel on card front)	20.00	9.00
❑ 137 Kyle Rote UER (Longest gain 1.8 yards& should be 18 yards)	15.00	6.75
❑ 138 Norm Willey	8.00	3.60
❑ 139 Charley Trippi	20.00	9.00
❑ 140 Billy Howton	12.00	5.50
❑ 141 Bobby Clatterbuck	8.00	3.60
❑ 142 Bob Boyd	8.00	3.60
❑ 143 Bob Toneff RC UER (name misspelled Toneoff)	12.00	5.50
❑ 144 Jerry Helluin	8.00	3.60
❑ 145 Adrian Burk	8.00	3.60
❑ 146 Walt Michaels	12.00	5.50
❑ 147 Zollie Toth	8.00	3.60
❑ 148 Frank Varrichione RC	8.00	3.60
❑ 149 Dick Bielski	8.00	3.60
❑ 150 George Ratterman	12.00	5.50
❑ 151 Mike Jarmoluk	8.00	3.60
❑ 152 Tom Landry	200.00	90.00
❑ 153 Ray Renfro	12.00	5.50
❑ 154 Zeke Bratkowski	12.00	5.50
❑ 155 Jerry Norton	8.00	3.60
❑ 156 Maurice Bassett	8.00	3.60
❑ 157 Volney Quinlan	8.00	3.60
❑ 158 Chuck Bednarik	30.00	13.50
❑ 159 Don Colo	8.00	3.60
❑ 160 L.G. Dupre RC	40.00	10.00

1993 Bowman

	Nm-Mt	Ex-Mt
COMPLETE SET (423)	25.00	11.00
❑ 1 Troy Aikman FOIL	3.00	1.35
❑ 2 John Parrella RC	.20	.09
❑ 3 Dana Stubblefield RC	.75	.35
❑ 4 Mark Higgs	.20	.09
❑ 5 Tom Carter RC	.40	.18
❑ 6 Nate Lewis	.20	.09
❑ 7 Vaughn Hebron RC	.20	.09
❑ 8 Ernest Givins	.40	.18
❑ 9 Vince Buck	.20	.09
❑ 10 Levon Kirkland	.20	.09
❑ 11 J.J. Birden	.20	.09
❑ 12 Steve Jordan	.20	.09
❑ 13 Simon Fletcher	.20	.09
❑ 14 Willie Green	.20	.09
❑ 15 Pepper Johnson	.20	.09
❑ 16 Roger Harper RC	.20	.09
❑ 17 Rob Moore	.40	.18
❑ 18 David Lang	.20	.09
❑ 19 David Klingler	.20	.09
❑ 20 Garrison Hearst FOIL RC	2.00	.90
❑ 21 Anthony Johnson	.40	.18
❑ 22 Eric Curry FOIL RC	.40	.18
❑ 23 Nolan Harrison	.20	.09
❑ 24 Earl Dotson RC	.20	.09
❑ 25 Leonard Russell	.40	.18
❑ 26 Doug Riesenberg	.20	.09
❑ 27 Dwayne Harper	.20	.09
❑ 28 Richard Dent	.40	.18
❑ 29 Victor Bailey RC	.20	.09
❑ 30 Junior Seau	.75	.35
❑ 31 Steve Tasker	.40	.18
❑ 32 Kurt Gouveia	.20	.09
❑ 33 Renaldo Turnbull UER (Listed as wide receiver)	.20	.09
❑ 34 Dale Carter	.20	.09
❑ 35 Russell Maryland	.20	.09
❑ 36 Dana Hall	.20	.09
❑ 37 Marco Coleman	.20	.09
❑ 38 Greg Montgomery	.20	.09
❑ 39 Deon Figures RC	.20	.09
❑ 40 Troy Drayton RC	.40	.18
❑ 41 Eric Metcalf	.40	.18
❑ 42 Michael Husted RC	.20	.09
❑ 43 Harry Newsome	.20	.09
❑ 44 Kelvin Pritchett	.20	.09
❑ 45 Andre Rison FOIL	.75	.35
❑ 46 John Copeland RC	.40	.18
❑ 47 Greg Biekert RC	.20	.09
❑ 48 Johnny Johnson	.20	.09
❑ 49 Chuck Cecil	.20	.09
❑ 50 Rick Mirer FOIL RC	1.50	.70
❑ 51 Rod Bernstine	.20	.09
❑ 52 Steve McMichael	.40	.18
❑ 53 Roosevelt Potts RC	.20	.09
❑ 54 Mike Sherrard	.20	.09
❑ 55 Terrell Buckley	.20	.09
❑ 56 Eugene Chung	.20	.09
❑ 57 Kimble Anders RC	.75	.35
❑ 58 Daryl Johnston	.75	.35
❑ 59 Harris Barton	.20	.09
❑ 60 Thurman Thomas FOIL	1.50	.70
❑ 61 Eric Martin	.20	.09
❑ 62 Reggie Brooks FOIL RC	.40	.18
❑ 63 Eric Bieniemy	.20	.09
❑ 64 John Offerdahl	.20	.09
❑ 65 Wilber Marshall	.20	.09
❑ 66 Mark Carrier WR	.40	.18
❑ 67 Merril Hoge	.20	.09
❑ 68 Cris Carter	.75	.35
❑ 69 Marty Thompson RC	.20	.09
❑ 70 Randall Cunningham FOIL	1.50	.70
❑ 71 Winston Moss	.20	.09
❑ 72 Doug Pelfrey RC	.20	.09
❑ 73 Jackie Slater	.20	.09
❑ 74 Pierce Holt	.20	.09
❑ 75 Hardy Nickerson	.40	.18
❑ 76 Chris Burkett	.20	.09
❑ 77 Michael Brandon	.20	.09
❑ 78 Tom Waddle	.20	.09

❑ 79 Walter Reeves .20 .09
❑ 80 Lawrence Taylor FOIL .75 .35
❑ 81 Wayne Simmons RC .20 .09
❑ 82 Brent Williams .20 .09
❑ 83 Shannon Sharpe .75 .35
❑ 84 Robert Blackmon .20 .09
❑ 85 Keith Jackson .40 .18
❑ 86 A.J. Johnson .20 .09
❑ 87 Ryan McNeil RC .75 .35
❑ 88 Michael Dean Perry .40 .18
❑ 89 Russell Copeland RC .40 .18
❑ 90 Sam Mills .20 .09
❑ 91 Courtney Hall .20 .09
❑ 92 Gino Torretta RC .40 .18
❑ 93 Artie Smith RC .20 .09
❑ 94 David Whitmore .20 .09
❑ 95 Charles Haley .40 .18
❑ 96 Rod Woodson .75 .35
❑ 97 Lorenzo White .20 .09
❑ 98 Tom Scott RC .20 .09
❑ 99 Tyji Armstrong .20 .09
❑ 100 Boomer Esiason .40 .18
❑ 101 Rocket Ismail FOIL .75 .35
❑ 102 Mark Carrier DB .20 .09
❑ 103 Broderick Thompson .20 .09
❑ 104 Bob Whitfield .20 .09
❑ 105 Ben Coleman RC .20 .09
❑ 106 Jon Vaughn .20 .09
❑ 107 Marcus Buckley RC .20 .09
❑ 108 Cleveland Gary .20 .09
❑ 109 Ashley Ambrose .20 .09
❑ 110 Reggie White FOIL 1.50 .70
❑ 111 Arthur Marshall RC .20 .09
❑ 112 Greg McMurtry .20 .09
❑ 113 Mike Johnson .20 .09
❑ 114 Tim McGee .20 .09
❑ 115 John Carney .20 .09
❑ 116 Neil Smith .75 .35
❑ 117 Mark Stepnoski .20 .09
❑ 118 Don Beebe .20 .09
❑ 119 Scott Mitchell .75 .35
❑ 120 Randall McDaniel .20 .09
❑ 121 Chidi Ahanotu RC .20 .09
❑ 122 Ray Childress .20 .09
❑ 123 Tony McGee RC .40 .18
❑ 124 Marc Boutte .20 .09
❑ 125 Ronnie Lott .40 .18
❑ 126 Jason Elam RC .75 .35
❑ 127 Martin Harrison RC .20 .09
❑ 128 Leonard Renfro RC .20 .09
❑ 129 Jessie Armstead RC .40 .18
❑ 130 Quentin Coryatt .40 .18
❑ 131 Luis Sharpe .20 .09
❑ 132 Bill Maas .20 .09
❑ 133 Jesse Solomon .20 .09
❑ 134 Kevin Greene .40 .18
❑ 135 Derek Brown RBK RC .40 .18
❑ 136 Greg Townsend .20 .09
❑ 137 Neal Anderson .20 .09
❑ 138 John L. Williams .20 .09
❑ 139 Vincent Brisby RC .75 .35
❑ 140 Barry Sanders FOIL 5.00 2.20
❑ 141 Charles Mann .20 .09
❑ 142 Ken Norton .40 .18
❑ 143 Eric Moten .20 .09
❑ 144 John Alt .20 .09
❑ 145 Dan Footman RC .20 .09
❑ 146 Bill Brooks .20 .09
❑ 147 James Thornton .20 .09
❑ 148 Martin Mayhew .20 .09
❑ 149 Andy Harmon .40 .18
❑ 150 Dan Marino FOIL 6.00 2.70
❑ 151 Micheal Barrow RC .75 .35
❑ 152 Flipper Anderson .20 .09
❑ 153 Jackie Harris .20 .09
❑ 154 Todd Kelly RC .20 .09
❑ 155 Dan Williams RC .20 .09
❑ 156 Harold Green .20 .09
❑ 157 David Treadwell .20 .09
❑ 158 Chris Doleman .20 .09
❑ 159 Eric Hill .20 .09
❑ 160 Lincoln Kennedy RC .20 .09
❑ 161 Devon McDonald RC .20 .09
❑ 162 Natrone Means RC .75 .35
❑ 163 Rick Hamilton RC .20 .09
❑ 164 Kelvin Martin .20 .09
❑ 165 Jeff Hostetler .40 .18
❑ 166 Mark Brunell RC 4.00 1.80
❑ 167 Tim Barnett .20 .09
❑ 168 Ray Crockett .20 .09
❑ 169 William Perry .40 .18
❑ 170 Michael Irvin .75 .35
❑ 171 Marvin Washington .20 .09
❑ 172 Irving Fryar .40 .18
❑ 173 Scott Sisson RC .20 .09
❑ 174 Gary Anderson K .20 .09
❑ 175 Bruce Smith .75 .35
❑ 176 Clyde Simmons .20 .09
❑ 177 Russell White RC .40 .18
❑ 178 Irv Smith RC .20 .09
❑ 179 Mark Wheeler .20 .09
❑ 180 Warren Moon .75 .35
❑ 181 Del Speer RC .20 .09
❑ 182 Henry Thomas .20 .09
❑ 183 Keith Kartz .20 .09
❑ 184 Ricky Ervins .20 .09
❑ 185 Phil Simms .40 .18
❑ 186 Tim Brown .75 .35
❑ 187 Willis Peguese .20 .09
❑ 188 Rich Moran .20 .09
❑ 189 Robert Jones .20 .09
❑ 190 Craig Heyward .40 .18
❑ 191 Ricky Watters .75 .35
❑ 192 Stan Humphries .40 .18
❑ 193 Larry Webster .20 .09
❑ 194 Brad Baxter .20 .09
❑ 195 Randal Hill .20 .09
❑ 196 Robert Porcher .20 .09
❑ 197 Patrick Robinson RC .20 .09
❑ 198 Ferrell Edmunds .20 .09
❑ 199 Melvin Jenkins .20 .09
❑ 200 Joe Montana FOIL 6.00 2.70
❑ 201 Marv Cook .20 .09
❑ 202 Henry Ellard .40 .18
❑ 203 Calvin Williams .40 .18
❑ 204 Craig Erickson .40 .18
❑ 205 Steve Atwater .20 .09
❑ 206 Najee Mustafaa .20 .09
❑ 207 Darryl Talley .20 .09
❑ 208 Jarrod Bunch .20 .09
❑ 209 Tim McDonald .20 .09
❑ 210 Patrick Bates RC .20 .09
❑ 211 Sean Jones .20 .09
❑ 212 Leslie O'Neal .40 .18
❑ 213 Mike Golic .20 .09
❑ 214 Mark Clayton .20 .09
❑ 215 Leonard Marshall .20 .09
❑ 216 Curtis Conway RC 1.50 .70
❑ 217 Andre Hastings RC .40 .18
❑ 218 Barry Word .20 .09
❑ 219 Will Wolford .20 .09
❑ 220 Desmond Howard .40 .18
❑ 221 Rickey Jackson .20 .09
❑ 222 Alvin Harper .40 .18
❑ 223 William White .20 .09
❑ 224 Steve Broussard .20 .09
❑ 225 Aeneas Williams .20 .09
❑ 226 Michael Brooks .20 .09
❑ 227 Reggie Cobb .20 .09
❑ 228 Derrick Walker .20 .09
❑ 229 Marcus Allen .75 .35
❑ 230 Jerry Ball .20 .09
❑ 231 J.B. Brown .20 .09
❑ 232 Terry McDaniel .20 .09
❑ 233 LeRoy Butler .20 .09
❑ 234 Kyle Clifton .20 .09
❑ 235 Henry Jones .20 .09
❑ 236 Shane Conlan .20 .09
❑ 237 Michael Bates RC .20 .09
❑ 238 Vincent Brown .20 .09
❑ 239 William Fuller .20 .09
❑ 240 Ricardo McDonald .20 .09
❑ 241 Gary Zimmerman .20 .09
❑ 242 Fred Barnett .40 .18
❑ 243 Elvis Grbac RC 4.00 1.80
❑ 244 Myron Baker RC .20 .09
❑ 245 Steve Emtman .20 .09
❑ 246 Mike Compton RC .75 .35
❑ 247 Mark Jackson .20 .09
❑ 248 Santo Stephens RC .20 .09
❑ 249 Tommie Agee .20 .09
❑ 250 Broderick Thomas .20 .09
❑ 251 Fred Baxter RC .20 .09
❑ 252 Andre Collins .20 .09
❑ 253 Ernest Dye RC .20 .09
❑ 254 Raylee Johnson RC .40 .18
❑ 255 Rickey Dixon .20 .09
❑ 256 Ron Heller .20 .09
❑ 257 Joel Steed .20 .09
❑ 258 Everett Lindsay RC .20 .09
❑ 259 Tony Smith .20 .09
❑ 260 Sterling Sharpe UER .75 .35
(Edgar Bennett is pictured on front)
❑ 261 Tommy Vardell .20 .09
❑ 262 Morten Andersen .20 .09
❑ 263 Eddie Robinson .20 .09
❑ 264 Jerome Bettis RC 5.00 2.20
❑ 265 Alonzo Spellman .20 .09
❑ 266 Harvey Williams .40 .18
❑ 267 Jason Belser RC .20 .09
❑ 268 Derek Russell .20 .09
❑ 269 Derrick Lassic RC .20 .09
❑ 270 Steve Young FOIL 3.00 1.35
❑ 271 Adrian Murrell RC .75 .35
❑ 272 Lewis Tillman .20 .09
❑ 273 O.J. McDuffie RC .75 .35
❑ 274 Marty Carter .20 .09
❑ 275 Ray Seals .20 .09
❑ 276 Earnest Byner .20 .09
❑ 277 Marion Butts .20 .09
❑ 278 Chris Spielman .40 .18
❑ 279 Carl Pickens .40 .18
❑ 280 Drew Bledsoe FOIL RC 6.00 2.70
❑ 281 Mark Kelso .20 .09
❑ 282 Eugene Robinson .20 .09
❑ 283 Eric Allen .20 .09
❑ 284 Ethan Horton .20 .09
❑ 285 Greg Lloyd .40 .18
❑ 286 Anthony Carter .40 .18
❑ 287 Edgar Bennett .75 .35
❑ 288 Bobby Hebert .20 .09
❑ 289 Haywood Jeffires .40 .18
❑ 290 Glyn Milburn RC .75 .35
❑ 291 Bernie Kosar .40 .18
❑ 292 Jumbo Elliott .20 .09
❑ 293 Jessie Hester .20 .09
❑ 294 Brent Jones .40 .18
❑ 295 Carl Banks .20 .09
❑ 296 Brian Washington .20 .09
❑ 297 Steve Beuerlein .40 .18
❑ 298 John Lynch RC 2.00 .90
❑ 299 Troy Vincent .20 .09
❑ 300 Emmitt Smith FOIL 5.00 2.20
❑ 301 Chris Zorich .20 .09
❑ 302 Wade Wilson .20 .09
❑ 303 Darrien Gordon RC .20 .09
❑ 304 Fred Stokes .20 .09
❑ 305 Nick Lowery .20 .09
❑ 306 Rodney Peete .20 .09
❑ 307 Chris Warren .40 .18
❑ 308 Herschel Walker .40 .18
❑ 309 Audray Bruce .20 .09
❑ 310 Barry Foster FOIL .40 .18
❑ 311 George Teague RC .40 .18
❑ 312 Darryl Williams .20 .09
❑ 313 Thomas Smith RC .40 .18
❑ 314 Dennis Brown .20 .09
❑ 315 Marvin Jones FOIL RC .40 .18
❑ 316 Andre Tippett .20 .09
❑ 317 Demetrius DuBose RC .20 .09
❑ 318 Kirk Lowdermilk .20 .09
❑ 319 Shane Dronett .20 .09
❑ 320 Terry Kirby RC .75 .35
❑ 321 Qadry Ismail RC .75 .35
❑ 322 Lorenzo Lynch .20 .09
❑ 323 Willie Drewrey .20 .09
❑ 324 Jessie Tuggle .20 .09
❑ 325 Leroy Hoard .40 .18
❑ 326 Mark Collins .20 .09
❑ 327 Darrell Green .20 .09
❑ 328 Anthony Miller .40 .18
❑ 329 Brad Muster .20 .09

Card	Nm-Mt	Ex-Mt
❑ 330 Jim Kelly FOIL	1.50	.70
❑ 331 Sean Gilbert	.40	.18
❑ 332 Tim McKyer	.20	.09
❑ 333 Scott Mersereau	.20	.09
❑ 334 Willie Davis	.75	.35
❑ 335 Brett Favre FOIL	6.00	2.70
❑ 336 Kevin Gogan	.20	.09
❑ 337 Jim Harbaugh	.75	.35
❑ 338 James Trapp RC	.20	.09
❑ 339 Pete Stoyanovich	.20	.09
❑ 340 Jerry Rice FOIL	3.00	1.35
❑ 341 Gary Anderson RB	.20	.09
❑ 342 Carlton Gray RC	.20	.09
❑ 343 Dermontti Dawson	.20	.09
❑ 344 Ray Buchanan RC	.75	.35
❑ 345 Derrick Fenner	.20	.09
❑ 346 Dennis Smith	.20	.09
❑ 347 Todd Rucci RC	.20	.09
❑ 348 Seth Joyner	.20	.09
❑ 349 Jim McMahon	.40	.18
❑ 350 Rodney Hampton	.40	.18
❑ 351 Al Smith	.20	.09
❑ 352 Steve Everitt RC	.20	.09
❑ 353 Vinnie Clark	.20	.09
❑ 354 Eric Swann	.40	.18
❑ 355 Brian Mitchell	.40	.18
❑ 356 Will Shields RC	.75	.35
❑ 357 Cornelius Bennett	.40	.18
❑ 358 Darrin Smith RC	.40	.18
❑ 359 Chris Mims	.20	.09
❑ 360 Blair Thomas	.20	.09
❑ 361 Dennis Gibson	.20	.09
❑ 362 Santana Dotson	.40	.18
❑ 363 Mark Ingram	.20	.09
❑ 364 Don Mosebar	.20	.09
❑ 365 Ty Detmer	.75	.35
❑ 366 Bob Christian RC	.20	.09
❑ 367 Adrian Hardy	.20	.09
❑ 368 Vaughan Johnson	.20	.09
❑ 369 Jim Everett	.40	.18
❑ 370 Ricky Sanders	.20	.09
❑ 371 Jonathan Hayes	.20	.09
❑ 372 Bruce Matthews	.20	.09
❑ 373 Darren Drozdov RC	.75	.35
❑ 374 Scott Brumfield RC	.20	.09
❑ 375 Cortez Kennedy	.40	.18
❑ 376 Tim Harris	.20	.09
❑ 377 Neil O'Donnell	.75	.35
❑ 378 Robert Smith RC	3.00	1.35
❑ 379 Mike Caldwell RC	.20	.09
❑ 380 Burt Grossman	.20	.09
❑ 381 Corey Miller	.20	.09
❑ 382 Kevin Williams FOIL RC	.40	.18
❑ 383 Ken Harvey	.20	.09
❑ 384 Greg Robinson RC	.20	.09
❑ 385 Harold Alexander RC	.20	.09
❑ 386 Andre Reed	.40	.18
❑ 387 Reggie Langhorne	.20	.09
❑ 388 Courtney Hawkins	.20	.09
❑ 389 James Hasty	.20	.09
❑ 390 Pat Swilling	.20	.09
❑ 391 Chris Slade RC	.40	.18
❑ 392 Keith Byars	.20	.09
❑ 393 Dalton Hilliard	.20	.09
❑ 394 David Williams	.20	.09
❑ 395 Terry Obee RC	.20	.09
❑ 396 Heath Sherman	.20	.09
❑ 397 John Taylor	.40	.18
❑ 398 Irv Eatman	.20	.09
❑ 399 Johnny Holland	.20	.09
❑ 400 John Elway FOIL	6.00	2.70
❑ 401 Clay Matthews	.40	.18
❑ 402 Dave Meggett	.20	.09
❑ 403 Eric Green	.20	.09
❑ 404 Bryan Cox	.20	.09
❑ 405 Jay Novacek	.40	.18
❑ 406 Kenneth Davis	.20	.09
❑ 407 Lamar Thomas RC	.20	.09
❑ 408 Lance Gunn RC	.20	.09
❑ 409 Audray McMillian	.20	.09
❑ 410 Derrick Thomas FOIL	1.50	.70
❑ 411 Rufus Porter	.20	.09
❑ 412 Coleman Rudolph RC	.20	.09
❑ 413 Mark Rypien	.20	.09
❑ 414 Duane Bickett	.20	.09
❑ 415 Chris Singleton	.20	.09
❑ 416 Mitch Lyons RC	.20	.09
❑ 417 Bill Fralic	.20	.09
❑ 418 Gary Plummer	.20	.09
❑ 419 Ricky Proehl	.20	.09
❑ 420 Howie Long	.75	.35
❑ 421 Willie Roaf FOIL RC	.75	.35
❑ 422 Checklist 1-212	.20	.09
❑ 423 Checklist 213-423	.20	.09

1994 Bowman

	Nm-Mt	Ex-Mt
COMPLETE SET (390)	50.00	22.00
❑ 1 Dan Wilkinson RC	.40	.18
❑ 2 Marshall Faulk RC	15.00	6.75
❑ 3 Heath Shuler RC	.75	.35
❑ 4 Willie McGinest RC	.75	.35
❑ 5 Trent Dilfer RC	3.00	1.35
❑ 6 Brent Jones	.40	.18
❑ 7 Sam Adams RC	.40	.18
❑ 8 Randy Baldwin	.20	.09
❑ 9 Jamir Miller RC	.40	.18
❑ 10 John Thierry RC	.20	.09
❑ 11 Aaron Glenn RC	.75	.35
❑ 12 Joe Johnson RC	.20	.09
❑ 13 Bernard Williams RC	.20	.09
❑ 14 Wayne Gandy RC	.20	.09
❑ 15 Aaron Taylor RC	.20	.09
❑ 16 Charles Johnson RC	.75	.35
❑ 17 Dewayne Washington RC	.40	.18
❑ 18 Bernie Kosar	.40	.18
❑ 19 Johnnie Morton RC	2.50	1.10
❑ 20 Rob Fredrickson RC	.40	.18
❑ 21 Shante Carver RC	.20	.09
❑ 22 Thomas Lewis RC	.40	.18
❑ 23 Greg Hill RC	.75	.35
❑ 24 Cris Dishman	.20	.09
❑ 25 Jeff Burris RC	.40	.18
❑ 26 Isaac Davis RC	.20	.09
❑ 27 Bert Emanuel RC	.75	.35
❑ 28 Allen Aldridge RC	.20	.09
❑ 29 Kevin Lee RC	.20	.09
❑ 30 Chris Brantley RC	.20	.09
❑ 31 Rich Braham RC	.20	.09
❑ 32 Ricky Watters	.40	.18
❑ 33 Quentin Coryatt	.20	.09
❑ 34 Hardy Nickerson	.40	.18
❑ 35 Johnny Johnson	.20	.09
❑ 36 Ken Harvey	.20	.09
❑ 37 Chris Zorich	.20	.09
❑ 38 Chris Warren	.40	.18
❑ 39 David Palmer RC	.75	.35
❑ 40 Chris Miller	.20	.09
❑ 41 Ken Ruettgers	.20	.09
❑ 42 Joe Panos RC	.20	.09
❑ 43 Mario Bates RC	.75	.35
❑ 44 Harry Colon	.20	.09
❑ 45 Barry Foster	.20	.09
❑ 46 Steve Tasker	.40	.18
❑ 47 Richmond Webb	.20	.09
❑ 48 James Folston RC	.20	.09
❑ 49 Erik Williams	.20	.09
❑ 50 Rodney Hampton	.40	.18
❑ 51 Derek Russell	.20	.09
❑ 52 Greg Montgomery	.20	.09
❑ 53 Anthony Phillips	.20	.09
❑ 54 Andre Coleman RC	.20	.09
❑ 55 Gary Brown	.20	.09
❑ 56 Neil Smith	.40	.18
❑ 57 Myron Baker	.20	.09
❑ 58 Sean Dawkins RC	.75	.35
❑ 59 Marvin Washington	.20	.09
❑ 60 Steve Beuerlein	.40	.18
❑ 61 Brenston Buckner RC	.20	.09
❑ 62 William Gaines RC	.20	.09
❑ 63 LeShon Johnson RC	.40	.18
❑ 64 Errict Rhett RC	.75	.35
❑ 65 Jim Everett	.40	.18
❑ 66 Desmond Howard	.40	.18
❑ 67 Jack Del Rio	.20	.09
❑ 68 Isaac Bruce RC	12.00	5.50
❑ 69 Van Malone RC	.20	.09
❑ 70 Jim Kelly	.75	.35
❑ 71 Leon Lett	.20	.09
❑ 72 Greg Robinson	.20	.09
❑ 73 Ryan Yarborough RC	.20	.09
❑ 74 Terry Wooden	.20	.09
❑ 75 Eric Allen	.20	.09
❑ 76 Ernest Givins	.40	.18
❑ 77 Marcus Spears RC	.20	.09
❑ 78 Thomas Randolph RC	.20	.09
❑ 79 Willie Clark RC	.20	.09
❑ 80 John Elway	4.00	1.80
❑ 81 Aubrey Beavers RC	.20	.09
❑ 82 Jeff Cothran RC	.20	.09
❑ 83 Norm Johnson	.20	.09
❑ 84 Donnell Bennett RC	.75	.35
❑ 85 Phillippi Sparks	.20	.09
❑ 86 Scott Mitchell	.40	.18
❑ 87 Bucky Brooks RC	.20	.09
❑ 88 Courtney Hawkins	.20	.09
❑ 89 Kevin Greene	.40	.18
❑ 90 Doug Nussmeier RC	.20	.09
❑ 91 Floyd Turner	.20	.09
❑ 92 Anthony Newman	.20	.09
❑ 93 Vinny Testaverde	.40	.18
❑ 94 Ronnie Lott	.40	.18
❑ 95 Troy Aikman	2.00	.90
❑ 96 John Taylor	.40	.18
❑ 97 Henry Ellard	.40	.18
❑ 98 Carl Lee	.20	.09
❑ 99 Terry McDaniel	.20	.09
❑ 100 Joe Montana	4.00	1.80
❑ 101 David Klingler	.20	.09
❑ 102 Bruce Walker RC	.20	.09
❑ 103 Rick Cunningham RC	.20	.09
❑ 104 Robert Delpino	.20	.09
❑ 105 Mark Ingram	.20	.09
❑ 106 Leslie O'Neal	.20	.09
❑ 107 Darrell Thompson	.20	.09
❑ 108 Dave Meggett	.20	.09
❑ 109 Chris Gardocki	.20	.09
❑ 110 Andre Rison	.40	.18
❑ 111 Kelvin Martin	.20	.09
❑ 112 Marcus Robertson	.20	.09
❑ 113 Jason Gildon RC	3.00	1.35
❑ 114 Mel Gray	.20	.09
❑ 115 Tommy Vardell	.20	.09
❑ 116 Dexter Carter	.20	.09
❑ 117 Scottie Graham RC	.40	.18
❑ 118 Horace Copeland	.20	.09
❑ 119 Cornelius Bennett	.40	.18
❑ 120 Chris Maumalanga RC	.20	.09
❑ 121 Mo Lewis	.20	.09
❑ 122 Toby Wright RC	.20	.09
❑ 123 George Hegamin RC	.20	.09
❑ 124 Chip Lohmiller	.20	.09
❑ 125 Calvin Jones RC	.20	.09
❑ 126 Steve Shine	.20	.09
❑ 127 Chuck Levy RC	.20	.09
❑ 128 Sam Mills	.20	.09
❑ 129 Terance Mathis	.40	.18
❑ 130 Randall Cunningham	.75	.35
❑ 131 John Fina	.20	.09
❑ 132 Reggie White	.75	.35
❑ 133 Tom Waddle	.20	.09
❑ 134 Chris Calloway	.20	.09
❑ 135 Kevin Mawae RC	.75	.35
❑ 136 Lake Dawson RC	.40	.18
❑ 137 Alai Kalaniubalu	.20	.09
❑ 138 Tom Nalen RC	.75	.35

❑	139	Cody Carlson	.20	.09
❑	140	Dan Marino	4.00	1.80
❑	141	Harris Barton	.20	.09
❑	142	Don Mosebar	.20	.09
❑	143	Romeo Bandison	.20	.09
❑	144	Bruce Smith	.75	.35
❑	145	Warren Moon	.75	.35
❑	146	David Lutz	.20	.09
❑	147	Dermontti Dawson	.20	.09
❑	148	Ricky Proehl	.20	.09
❑	149	Lou Benfatti RC	.20	.09
❑	150	Craig Erickson	.20	.09
❑	151	Sean Gilbert	.20	.09
❑	152	Zefross Moss	.20	.09
❑	153	Darnay Scott RC	1.25	.55
❑	154	Courtney Hall	.20	.09
❑	155	Brian Mitchell	.20	.09
❑	156	Joe Burch RC UER	.20	.09
❑	157	Terry Mickens	.20	.09
❑	158	Jay Novacek	.40	.18
❑	159	Chris Gedney	.20	.09
❑	160	Bruce Matthews	.20	.09
❑	161	Mario Perry RC	.20	.09
❑	162	Vince Buck	.20	.09
❑	163	Michael Bates	.20	.09
❑	164	Willie Davis	.40	.18
❑	165	Mike Pritchard	.20	.09
❑	166	Doug Riesenberg	.20	.09
❑	167	Herschel Walker	.40	.18
❑	168	Tim Ruddy RC	.20	.09
❑	169	William Floyd RC	.75	.35
❑	170	John Randle	.40	.18
❑	171	Winston Moss	.20	.09
❑	172	Thurman Thomas	.75	.35
❑	173	Eric England RC	.20	.09
❑	174	Vincent Brisby	.40	.18
❑	175	Greg Lloyd	.40	.18
❑	176	Paul Gruber	.20	.09
❑	177	Brad Ottis RC	.20	.09
❑	178	George Teague	.20	.09
❑	179	Willie Jackson RC	.75	.35
❑	180	Barry Sanders	3.00	1.35
❑	181	Brian Washington	.20	.09
❑	182	Michael Jackson	.40	.18
❑	183	Jason Mathews RC	.20	.09
❑	184	Chester McGlockton	.20	.09
❑	185	Tydus Winans RC	.20	.09
❑	186	Michael Haynes	.40	.18
❑	187	Erik Kramer	.40	.18
❑	188	Chris Doleman	.20	.09
❑	189	Haywood Jeffires	.40	.18
❑	190	Larry Whigham RC	.20	.09
❑	191	Shawn Jefferson	.20	.09
❑	192	Pete Stoyanovich	.20	.09
❑	193	Rod Bernstine	.20	.09
❑	194	William Thomas	.20	.09
❑	195	Marcus Allen	.75	.35
❑	196	Dave Brown	.40	.18
❑	197	Harold Bishop RC	.20	.09
❑	198	Lorenzo Lynch	.20	.09
❑	199	Dwight Stone	.20	.09
❑	200	Jerry Rice	2.00	.90
❑	201	Rocket Ismail	.40	.18
❑	202	LeRoy Butler	.20	.09
❑	203	Glenn Parker	.20	.09
❑	204	Bruce Armstrong	.20	.09
❑	205	Shane Conlan	.20	.09
❑	206	Russell Maryland	.20	.09
❑	207	Herman Moore	.75	.35
❑	208	Eric Martin	.20	.09
❑	209	John Friesz	.40	.18
❑	210	Boomer Esiason	.40	.18
❑	211	Jim Harbaugh	.75	.35
❑	212	Harold Green	.20	.09
❑	213	Perry Klein RC	.20	.09
❑	214	Eric Metcalf	.40	.18
❑	215	Steve Everitt	.20	.09
❑	216	Victor Bailey	.20	.09
❑	217	Lincoln Kennedy	.20	.09
❑	218	Glyn Milburn	.40	.18
❑	219	John Copeland	.20	.09
❑	220	Drew Bledsoe	2.00	.90
❑	221	Kevin Williams	.40	.18
❑	222	Roosevelt Potts	.20	.09
❑	223	Troy Drayton	.20	.09
❑	224	Terry Kirby	.75	.35
❑	225	Ronald Moore	.20	.09
❑	226	Tyrone Hughes	.40	.18
❑	227	Wayne Simmons	.20	.09
❑	228	Tony McGee	.20	.09
❑	229	Derek Brown RBK	.20	.09
❑	230	Jason Elam	.40	.18
❑	231	Qadry Ismail	.75	.35
❑	232	O.J. McDuffie	.75	.35
❑	233	Mike Caldwell	.20	.09
❑	234	Reggie Brooks	.40	.18
❑	235	Rick Mirer	.75	.35
❑	236	Steve Tovar	.20	.09
❑	237	Patrick Robinson	.20	.09
❑	238	Tom Carter	.20	.09
❑	239	Ben Coates	.40	.18
❑	240	Jerome Bettis	1.25	.55
❑	241	Garrison Hearst	.75	.35
❑	242	Natrone Means	.75	.35
❑	243	Dana Stubblefield	.40	.18
❑	244	Willie Roaf	.20	.09
❑	245	Cortez Kennedy	.40	.18
❑	246	Todd Steussie RC	.40	.18
❑	247	Pat Coleman	.20	.09
❑	248	David Wyman	.20	.09
❑	249	Jeremy Lincoln	.20	.09
❑	250	Carlester Crumpler	.20	.09
❑	251	Dale Carter	.20	.09
❑	252	Corey Raymond RC	.20	.09
❑	253	Bryan Cox	.20	.09
❑	254	Charlie Garner RC	3.00	1.35
❑	255	Jeff Hostetler	.40	.18
❑	256	Shane Bonham RC	.20	.09
❑	257	Thomas Everett	.20	.09
❑	258	John Jackson	.20	.09
❑	259	Terry Irving RC	.20	.09
❑	260	Corey Sawyer	.20	.09
❑	261	Rob Waldrop	.20	.09
❑	262	Curtis Conway	.75	.35
❑	263	Winfred Tubbs RC	.40	.18
❑	264	Sean Jones	.20	.09
❑	265	James Washington	.20	.09
❑	266	Lonnie Johnson RC	.20	.09
❑	267	Rob Moore	.40	.18
❑	268	Flipper Anderson	.20	.09
❑	269	Jon Hand	.20	.09
❑	270	Joe Patton RC	.20	.09
❑	271	Howard Ballard	.20	.09
❑	272	Fernando Smith RC	.20	.09
❑	273	Jessie Tuggle	.20	.09
❑	274	John Alt	.20	.09
❑	275	Corey Miller	.20	.09
❑	276	Gus Frerotte RC	.75	.35
❑	277	Jeff Cross	.20	.09
❑	278	Kevin Smith	.20	.09
❑	279	Corey Louchiey RC	.20	.09
❑	280	Micheal Barrow	.20	.09
❑	281	Jim Flanigan RC	.40	.18
❑	282	Calvin Williams	.40	.18
❑	283	Jeff Jaeger	.20	.09
❑	284	John Reece RC	.20	.09
❑	285	Jason Hanson	.20	.09
❑	286	Kurt Haws RC	.20	.09
❑	287	Eric Davis	.20	.09
❑	288	Maurice Hurst	.20	.09
❑	289	Kirk Lowdermilk	.20	.09
❑	290	Rod Woodson	.40	.18
❑	291	Andre Reed	.40	.18
❑	292	Vince Workman	.20	.09
❑	293	Wayne Martin	.20	.09
❑	294	Keith Lyle RC	.20	.09
❑	295	Brett Favre	4.00	1.80
❑	296	Doug Brien RC	.20	.09
❑	297	Junior Seau	.75	.35
❑	298	Randall McDaniel	.20	.09
❑	299	Johnny Mitchell	.20	.09
❑	300	Emmitt Smith	3.00	1.35
❑	301	Michael Brooks	.20	.09
❑	302	Steve Jackson	.20	.09
❑	303	Jeff George	.75	.35
❑	304	Irving Fryar	.40	.18
❑	305	Derrick Thomas	.75	.35
❑	306	Dante Jones	.20	.09
❑	307	Darrell Green	.20	.09
❑	308	Mark Bavaro	.20	.09
❑	309	Eugene Robinson	.20	.09
❑	310	Shannon Sharpe	.40	.18
❑	311	Michael Timpson	.20	.09
❑	312	Kevin Mitchell RC	.20	.09
❑	313	Stevon Moore	.20	.09
❑	314	Eric Swann	.40	.18
❑	315	James Bostic RC	.75	.35
❑	316	Robert Brooks	.75	.35
❑	317	Pete Pierson RC	.20	.09
❑	318	Jim Sweeney	.20	.09
❑	319	Anthony Smith	.20	.09
❑	320	Rohn Stark	.20	.09
❑	321	Gary Anderson K	.20	.09
❑	322	Robert Porcher	.20	.09
❑	323	Darryl Talley	.20	.09
❑	324	Stan Humphries	.40	.18
❑	325	Shelly Hammonds RC	.20	.09
❑	326	Jim McMahon	.40	.18
❑	327	Lamont Warren RC	.20	.09
❑	328	Chris Penn RC	.20	.09
❑	329	Tony Woods	.20	.09
❑	330	Raymont Harris RC	.75	.35
❑	331	Mitch Davis RC	.20	.09
❑	332	Michael Irvin	.75	.35
❑	333	Kent Graham	.40	.18
❑	334	Brian Blades	.40	.18
❑	335	Lomas Brown	.20	.09
❑	336	Willie Drewrey	.20	.09
❑	337	Russell Freeman	.20	.09
❑	338	Eric Zomalt RC	.20	.09
❑	339	Santana Dotson	.40	.18
❑	340	Sterling Sharpe	.40	.18
❑	341	Ray Crittenden RC	.20	.09
❑	342	Perry Carter RC	.20	.09
❑	343	Austin Robbins	.20	.09
❑	344	Mike Wells RC	.20	.09
❑	345	Toddrick McIntosh RC	.20	.09
❑	346	Mark Carrier WR	.40	.18
❑	347	Eugene Daniel	.20	.09
❑	348	Tre Johnson RC	.20	.09
❑	349	D.J. Johnson	.20	.09
❑	350	Steve Young	1.50	.70
❑	351	Jim Pyne RC	.20	.09
❑	352	Jocelyn Borgella RC	.20	.09
❑	353	Pat Carter	.20	.09
❑	354	Sam Rogers RC	.20	.09
❑	355	Jason Sehorn RC	1.25	.55
❑	356	Darren Carrington	.20	.09
❑	357	Lamar Smith RC	4.00	1.80
❑	358	James Burton RC	.20	.09
❑	359	Darrin Smith	.20	.09
❑	360	Marco Coleman	.20	.09
❑	361	Webster Slaughter	.20	.09
❑	362	Lewis Tillman	.20	.09
❑	363	David Alexander	.20	.09
❑	364	Bradford Banta RC	.20	.09
❑	365	Erric Pegram	.20	.09
❑	366	Mike Fox	.20	.09
❑	367	Jeff Lageman	.20	.09
❑	368	Kurt Gouveia	.20	.09
❑	369	Tim Brown	.75	.35
❑	370	Seth Joyner	.20	.09
❑	371	Irv Eatman	.20	.09
❑	372	Dorsey Levens RC	4.00	1.80
❑	373	Anthony Pleasant	.20	.09
❑	374	Henry Jones	.20	.09
❑	375	Cris Carter	1.00	.45
❑	376	Morten Andersen	.20	.09
❑	377	Neil O'Donnell	.75	.35
❑	378	Tyronne Drakeford RC	.20	.09
❑	379	John Carney	.20	.09
❑	380	Vincent Brown	.20	.09
❑	381	J.J. Birden	.20	.09
❑	382	Chris Spielman	.40	.18
❑	383	Mark Bortz	.20	.09
❑	384	Ray Childress	.20	.09
❑	385	Carlton Bailey	.20	.09
❑	386	Charles Haley	.40	.18
❑	387	Shane Dronett	.20	.09
❑	388	Jon Vaughn	.20	.09
❑	389	Checklist 1-195	.20	.09
❑	390	Checklist 196-390	.20	.09

1995 Bowman

	Nm-Mt	Ex-Mt
COMPLETE SET (357)	60.00	27.00
❑ 1 Ki-Jana Carter RC	.75	.35
❑ 2 Tony Boselli RC	.75	.35
❑ 3 Steve McNair RC	8.00	3.60
❑ 4 Michael Westbrook RC	.60	.25
❑ 5 Kerry Collins RC	4.00	1.80
❑ 6 Kevin Carter RC	.75	.35
❑ 7 Mike Mamula RC	.20	.09
❑ 8 Joey Galloway RC	4.00	1.80
❑ 9 Kyle Brady RC	.75	.35
❑ 10 J.J. Stokes RC	.75	.35
❑ 11 Derrick Alexander DE RC	.20	.09
❑ 12 Warren Sapp RC	4.00	1.80
❑ 13 Mark Fields RC	.75	.35
❑ 14 Ruben Brown RC	.75	.35
❑ 15 Ellis Johnson RC	.20	.09
❑ 16 Hugh Douglas RC	.75	.35
❑ 17 Mike Pelton RC	.20	.09
❑ 18 Napoleon Kaufman RC	3.00	1.35
❑ 19 James O. Stewart RC	2.50	1.10
❑ 20 Luther Elliss RC	.20	.09
❑ 21 Rashaan Salaam RC	.40	.18
❑ 22 Tyrone Poole RC	.75	.35
❑ 23 Ty Law RC	3.00	1.35
❑ 24 Korey Stringer RC	.40	.18
❑ 25 Billy Milner RC	.20	.09
❑ 26 Devin Bush RC	.20	.09
❑ 27 Mark Bruener RC	.40	.18
❑ 28 Derrick Brooks RC	4.00	1.80
❑ 29 Blake Brockermeyer RC	.20	.09
❑ 30 Alundis Brice RC	.20	.09
❑ 31 Trezelle Jenkins RC	.20	.09
❑ 32 Craig Newsome RC	.20	.09
❑ 33 Fred Barnett	.30	.14
❑ 34 Ray Childress	.15	.07
❑ 35 Chris Miller	.15	.07
❑ 36 Charles Haley	.30	.14
❑ 37 Ray Crittenden	.15	.07
❑ 38 Gus Frerotte	.30	.14
❑ 39 Jeff George	.30	.14
❑ 40 Dan Marino	3.00	1.35
❑ 41 Shawn Lee	.15	.07
❑ 42 Herman Moore	.60	.25
❑ 43 Chris Calloway	.15	.07
❑ 44 Jeff Graham	.15	.07
❑ 45 Ray Buchanan	.15	.07
❑ 46 Doug Pelfrey	.15	.07
❑ 47 Lake Dawson	.30	.14
❑ 48 Glenn Parker	.15	.07
❑ 49 Terry McDaniel	.15	.07
❑ 50 Rod Woodson	.30	.14
❑ 51 Santana Dotson	.15	.07
❑ 52 Anthony Miller	.30	.14
❑ 53 Bo Orlando	.15	.07
❑ 54 David Palmer	.30	.14
❑ 55 William Floyd	.30	.14
❑ 56 Edgar Bennett	.30	.14
❑ 57 Jeff Blake RC	2.50	1.10
❑ 58 Anthony Pleasant	.15	.07
❑ 59 Quinn Early	.30	.14
❑ 60 Bobby Houston	.15	.07
❑ 61 Terrell Fletcher RC	.20	.09
❑ 62 Gary Brown	.15	.07
❑ 63 Dwayne Sabb	.15	.07
❑ 64 Roman Phifer	.15	.07
❑ 65 Sherman Williams RC	.20	.09
❑ 66 Roosevelt Potts	.15	.07
❑ 67 Darnay Scott	.30	.14
❑ 68 Charlie Garner	.60	.25
❑ 69 Bert Emanuel	.60	.25
❑ 70 Herschel Walker	.30	.14
❑ 71 Lorenzo Styles RC	.20	.09
❑ 72 Andre Coleman	.15	.07
❑ 73 Tyronne Drakeford	.15	.07
❑ 74 Jay Novacek	.30	.14
❑ 75 Raymont Harris	.15	.07
❑ 76 Tamarick Vanover RC	.75	.35
❑ 77 Tom Carter	.15	.07
❑ 78 Eric Green	.15	.07
❑ 79 Patrick Hunter	.15	.07
❑ 80 Jeff Hostetler	.30	.14
❑ 81 Robert Blackmon	.15	.07
❑ 82 Anthony Cook RC	.20	.09
❑ 83 Craig Erickson	.15	.07
❑ 84 Glyn Milburn	.15	.07
❑ 85 Greg Lloyd	.30	.14
❑ 86 Brent Jones	.15	.07
❑ 87 Barrett Brooks RC	.20	.09
❑ 88 Alvin Harper	.15	.07
❑ 89 Sean Jones	.15	.07
❑ 90 Cris Carter	.60	.25
❑ 91 Russell Copeland	.15	.07
❑ 92 Frank Sanders RC	.75	.35
❑ 93 Mo Lewis	.15	.07
❑ 94 Michael Haynes	.30	.14
❑ 95 Andre Rison	.30	.14
❑ 96 Jesse James RC	.20	.09
❑ 97 Stan Humphries	.30	.14
❑ 98 James Hasty	.15	.07
❑ 99 Ricardo McDonald	.15	.07
❑ 100 Jerry Rice	1.50	.70
❑ 101 Chris Hudson RC	.20	.09
❑ 102 Dave Meggett	.15	.07
❑ 103 Brian Mitchell	.15	.07
❑ 104 Mike Johnson	.15	.07
❑ 105 Kordell Stewart RC	4.00	1.80
❑ 106 Michael Brooks	.15	.07
❑ 107 Steve Walsh	.15	.07
❑ 108 Eric Metcalf	.30	.14
❑ 109 Ricky Watters	.30	.14
❑ 110 Brett Favre	3.00	1.35
❑ 111 Aubrey Beavers	.15	.07
❑ 112 Brian Williams LB RC	.20	.09
❑ 113 Eugene Robinson	.15	.07
❑ 114 Matt O'Dwyer RC	.20	.09
❑ 115 Micheal Barrow	.15	.07
❑ 116 Rocket Ismail	.30	.14
❑ 117 Scott Gragg RC	.20	.09
❑ 118 Leon Lett	.15	.07
❑ 119 Reggie Roby	.15	.07
❑ 120 Marshall Faulk	2.00	.90
❑ 121 Jack Jackson RC	.20	.09
❑ 122 Keith Byars	.15	.07
❑ 123 Eric Hill	.15	.07
❑ 124 Todd Sauerbrun RC	.20	.09
❑ 125 Dexter Carter	.15	.07
❑ 126 Vinny Testaverde	.30	.14
❑ 127 Shane Conlan	.15	.07
❑ 128 Terrance Shaw RC	.20	.09
❑ 129 Willie Roaf	.15	.07
❑ 130 Jim Kelly	.60	.25
❑ 131 Neil O'Donnell	.30	.14
❑ 132 Ray McElroy RC	.20	.09
❑ 133 Ed McDaniel	.15	.07
❑ 134 Brian Gelzheiser RC	.20	.09
❑ 135 Marcus Allen	.60	.25
❑ 136 Carl Pickens	.30	.14
❑ 137 Mike Verstegen RC	.20	.09
❑ 138 Chris Mims	.15	.07
❑ 139 Darryl Pounds RC	.20	.09
❑ 140 Emmitt Smith	2.50	1.10
❑ 141 Mike Frederick RC	.20	.09
❑ 142 Henry Ellard	.30	.14
❑ 143 Willie McGinest	.30	.14
❑ 144 Michael Roan RC	.20	.09
❑ 145 Chris Spielman	.30	.14
❑ 146 Darryl Talley	.15	.07
❑ 147 Randall Cunningham	.60	.25
❑ 148 Andrew Greene RC	.20	.09
❑ 149 George Teague	.15	.07
❑ 150 Tyrone Hughes	.30	.14
❑ 151 Ron Davis RC	.20	.09
❑ 152 Stevon Moore	.15	.07
❑ 153 Merton Hanks	.15	.07
❑ 154 Darren Perry	.15	.07
❑ 155 Dave Brown	.30	.14
❑ 156 Mike Morton RC	.20	.09
❑ 157 Seth Joyner	.15	.07
❑ 158 Bryan Cox	.15	.07
❑ 159 Corey Fuller RC	.20	.09
❑ 160 John Elway	3.00	1.35
❑ 161 Dewayne Washington	.30	.14
❑ 162 Chris Warren	.30	.14
❑ 163 Jeff Kopp RC	.20	.09
❑ 164 Sean Dawkins	.30	.14
❑ 165 Mark Carrier DB	.15	.07
❑ 166 Andre Hastings	.30	.14
❑ 167 Derek West RC	.20	.09
❑ 168 Glenn Montgomery	.15	.07
❑ 169 Trent Dilfer	.60	.25
❑ 170 Rob Johnson RC	2.50	1.10
❑ 171 Todd Scott	.15	.07
❑ 172 Charles Johnson	.30	.14
❑ 173 Kez McCorvey RC	.20	.09
❑ 174 Rob Fredrickson	.15	.07
❑ 175 Corey Sawyer	.15	.07
❑ 176 Brett Perriman	.30	.14
❑ 177 Ken Dilger RC	.75	.35
❑ 178 Dana Stubblefield	.30	.14
❑ 179 Eric Allen	.15	.07
❑ 180 Drew Bledsoe	1.00	.45
❑ 181 Tyrone Davis RC	.20	.09
❑ 182 Reggie Brooks	.30	.14
❑ 183 Dale Carter	.30	.14
❑ 184 William Henderson RC	3.00	1.35
❑ 185 Reggie White	.60	.25
❑ 186 Lorenzo White	.15	.07
❑ 187 Leslie O'Neal	.30	.14
❑ 188 Stoney Case RC	.20	.09
❑ 189 Jeff Burris	.15	.07
❑ 190 Leroy Hoard	.15	.07
❑ 191 Thomas Randolph	.15	.07
❑ 192 Rodney Thomas RC	.40	.18
❑ 193 Quentin Coryatt	.30	.14
❑ 194 Terry Wooden	.15	.07
❑ 195 David Sloan RC	.20	.09
❑ 196 Bernie Parmalee	.30	.14
❑ 197 Zack Crockett RC	.40	.18
❑ 198 Troy Aikman	1.50	.70
❑ 199 Bruce Smith	.60	.25
❑ 200 Eric Zeier RC	.75	.35
❑ 201 Anthony Smith	.15	.07
❑ 202 Jake Reed	.30	.14
❑ 203 Hardy Nickerson	.15	.07
❑ 204 Patrick Riley RC	.20	.09
❑ 205 Bruce Matthews	.15	.07
❑ 206 Larry Centers	.30	.14
❑ 207 Troy Drayton	.15	.07
❑ 208 John Burrough RC	.20	.09
❑ 209 Jason Elam	.30	.14
❑ 210 Donnell Woolford	.15	.07
❑ 211 Sam Shade RC	.20	.09
❑ 212 Kevin Greene	.30	.14
❑ 213 Ronald Moore	.15	.07
❑ 214 Shane Hannah RC	.20	.09
❑ 215 Jim Everett	.15	.07
❑ 216 Scott Mitchell	.30	.14
❑ 217 Antonio Freeman RC	3.00	1.35
❑ 218 Tony McGee	.15	.07
❑ 219 Clay Matthews	.30	.14
❑ 220 Neil Smith	.30	.14
❑ 221 Mark Williams FOIL	.40	.18
❑ 222 Derrick Graham FOIL	.40	.18
❑ 223 Mike Hollis FOIL	.40	.18
❑ 224 Darion Conner FOIL	.40	.18
❑ 225 Steve Beuerlein FOIL	.40	.18
❑ 226 Rod Smith DB FOIL	.40	.18
❑ 227 James Williams FOIL	.40	.18
❑ 228 Bob Christian FOIL	.40	.18
❑ 229 Jeff Lageman FOIL	.40	.18
❑ 230 Frank Reich FOIL	.40	.18
❑ 231 Harry Colon FOIL	.40	.18
❑ 232 Carlton Bailey FOIL	.40	.18

❑ 233 Mickey Washington FOIL	.40	.18
❑ 234 Shawn Bouwens FOIL	.40	.18
❑ 235 Don Beebe FOIL	.40	.18
❑ 236 Kelvin Pritchett FOIL	.40	.18
❑ 237 Tommy Barnhardt FOIL	.40	.18
❑ 238 Mike Dumas FOIL	.40	.18
❑ 239 Brett Maxie FOIL	.40	.18
❑ 240 Desmond Howard FOIL	.40	.18
❑ 241 Sam Mills FOIL	.40	.18
❑ 242 Keith Goganious FOIL	.40	.18
❑ 243 Bubba McDowell FOIL	.40	.18
❑ 244 Vinnie Clark FOIL	.40	.18
❑ 245 Lamar Lathon FOIL	.40	.18
❑ 246 Bryan Barker FOIL	.40	.18
❑ 247 Darren Carrington FOIL	.40	.18
❑ 248 Jay Barker RC	.20	.09
❑ 249 Eric Davis	.15	.07
❑ 250 Heath Shuler	.30	.14
❑ 251 Donta Jones RC	.20	.09
❑ 252 LeRoy Butler	.15	.07
❑ 253 Michael Zordich	.15	.07
❑ 254 Cortez Kennedy	.30	.14
❑ 255 Brian DeMarco RC	.20	.09
❑ 256 Randal Hill	.15	.07
❑ 257 Michael Irvin	.60	.25
❑ 258 Natrone Means	.30	.14
❑ 259 Linc Harden RC	.20	.09
❑ 260 Jerome Bettis	.60	.25
❑ 261 Tony Bennett	.15	.07
❑ 262 Dameian Jeffries RC	.20	.09
❑ 263 Cornelius Bennett	.30	.14
❑ 264 Chris Zorich	.15	.07
❑ 265 Bobby Taylor RC	.75	.35
❑ 266 Terrell Buckley	.15	.07
❑ 267 Troy Dumas RC	.20	.09
❑ 268 Rodney Hampton	.30	.14
❑ 269 Steve Everitt	.15	.07
❑ 270 Mel Gray	.15	.07
❑ 271 Antonio Armstrong RC	.20	.09
❑ 272 Jim Harbaugh	.30	.14
❑ 273 Gary Clark	.15	.07
❑ 274 Tau Pupua RC	.20	.09
❑ 275 Warren Moon	.30	.14
❑ 276 Corey Croom	.15	.07
❑ 277 Tony Berti RC	.20	.09
❑ 278 Shannon Sharpe	.30	.14
❑ 279 Boomer Esiason	.30	.14
❑ 280 Aeneas Williams	.15	.07
❑ 281 Lethon Flowers RC	.20	.09
❑ 282 Derek Brown TE	.15	.07
❑ 283 Charlie Williams RC	.20	.09
❑ 284 Dan Wilkinson	.30	.14
❑ 285 Mike Sherrard	.15	.07
❑ 286 Evan Pilgrim RC	.20	.09
❑ 287 Kimble Anders	.30	.14
❑ 288 Greg Jefferson RC	.20	.09
❑ 289 Ken Norton	.30	.14
❑ 290 Terance Mathis	.30	.14
❑ 291 Torey Hunter RC	.20	.09
❑ 292 Ken Harvey	.15	.07
❑ 293 Irving Fryar	.30	.14
❑ 294 Michael Reed RC	.20	.09
❑ 295 Andre Reed	.30	.14
❑ 296 Vencie Glenn	.15	.07
❑ 297 Corey Swinson	.15	.07
❑ 298 Harvey Williams	.15	.07
❑ 299 Willie Davis	.30	.14
❑ 300 Barry Sanders	2.50	1.10
❑ 301 Curtis Martin RC	8.00	3.60
❑ 302 Johnny Mitchell	.15	.07
❑ 303 Daryl Johnston	.30	.14
❑ 304 Lorenzo Lynch	.15	.07
❑ 305 Christian Fauria RC	.40	.18
❑ 306 Sean Gilbert	.30	.14
❑ 307 Ray Zellars RC	.40	.18
❑ 308 William Strong RC	.20	.09
❑ 309 Jack Del Rio	.15	.07
❑ 310 Junior Seau	.60	.25
❑ 311 Justin Armour RC	.20	.09
❑ 312 Eric Bjornson RC	.20	.09
❑ 313 Vincent Brown	.15	.07
❑ 314 Darius Holland RC	.20	.09
❑ 315 Chad May RC	.20	.09
❑ 316 Simon Fletcher	.15	.07
❑ 317 Roell Preston RC	.30	.14
❑ 318 John Thierry	.15	.07
❑ 319 Orlando Thomas RC	.20	.09
❑ 320 Zach Wiegert RC	.20	.09
❑ 321 Derrick Alexander WR	.60	.25
❑ 322 Chris Cowart RC	.20	.09
❑ 323 Chris Sanders RC	.40	.18
❑ 324 Robert Brooks	.60	.25
❑ 325 Todd Collins RC	.40	.18
❑ 326 Ken Irvin RC	.20	.09
❑ 327 Erric Pegram	.30	.14
❑ 328 Damien Covington RC	.20	.09
❑ 329 Brendan Stai RC	.20	.09
❑ 330 James A.Stewart RC	.20	.09
❑ 331 Jessie Tuggle	.15	.07
❑ 332 Marco Coleman	.15	.07
❑ 333 Steve Young	1.25	.55
❑ 334 Greg Hill	.30	.14
❑ 335 Darryl Williams	.15	.07
❑ 336 Calvin Williams	.30	.14
❑ 337 Cris Dishman	.15	.07
❑ 338 Anthony Morgan	.15	.07
❑ 339 Renaldo Turnbull	.15	.07
❑ 340 Rick Mirer	.30	.14
❑ 341 Tim Brown	.60	.25
❑ 342 Dennis Gibson	.15	.07
❑ 343 Brad Baxter	.15	.07
❑ 344 Henry Jones	.15	.07
❑ 345 Johnny Bailey	.15	.07
❑ 346 Rocket Ismail	.30	.14
❑ 347 Richmond Webb	.15	.07
❑ 348 Robert Jones	.15	.07
❑ 349 Garrison Hearst	.60	.25
❑ 350 Errict Rhett	.30	.14
❑ 351 Steve Atwater	.15	.07
❑ 352 Joe Cain	.15	.07
❑ 353 Ben Coates	.30	.14
❑ 354 Aaron Glenn	.15	.07
❑ 355 Antonio Langham	.15	.07
❑ 356 Eugene Daniel	.15	.07
❑ 357 Tim Bowens	.15	.07

1999 Bowman

	Nm-Mt	Ex-Mt
COMPLETE SET (220)	40.00	18.00
❑ 1 Dan Marino	2.50	1.10
❑ 2 Michael Westbrook	.50	.23
❑ 3 Yancey Thigpen	.30	.14
❑ 4 Tony Martin	.50	.23
❑ 5 Michael Strahan	.50	.23
❑ 6 Dedric Ward	.30	.14
❑ 7 Joey Galloway	.50	.23
❑ 8 Bobby Engram	.50	.23
❑ 9 Frank Sanders	.50	.23
❑ 10 Jake Plummer	.50	.23
❑ 11 Eddie Kennison	.50	.23
❑ 12 Curtis Martin	.75	.35
❑ 13 Chris Spielman	.30	.14
❑ 14 Trent Dilfer	.50	.23
❑ 15 Tim Biakabutuka	.50	.23
❑ 16 Elvis Grbac	.50	.23
❑ 17 Charlie Batch	.75	.35
❑ 18 Takeo Spikes	.30	.14
❑ 19 Tony Banks	.50	.23
❑ 20 Doug Flutie	.75	.35
❑ 21 Ty Law	.50	.23
❑ 22 Isaac Bruce	.75	.35
❑ 23 James Jett	.50	.23
❑ 24 Kent Graham	.30	.14
❑ 25 Derrick Mayes	.30	.14
❑ 26 Amani Toomer	.30	.14
❑ 27 Ray Lewis	.75	.35
❑ 28 Shawn Springs	.30	.14
❑ 29 Warren Sapp	.30	.14
❑ 30 Jamal Anderson	.75	.35
❑ 31 Byron Bam Morris	.30	.14
❑ 32 Johnnie Morton	.30	.14
❑ 33 Terance Mathis	.30	.14
❑ 34 Terrell Davis	.75	.35
❑ 35 John Randle	.50	.23
❑ 36 Vinny Testaverde	.30	.14
❑ 37 Junior Seau	.75	.35
❑ 38 Reidel Anthony	.50	.23
❑ 39 Brad Johnson	.30	.14
❑ 40 Emmitt Smith	1.50	.70
❑ 41 Mo Lewis	.30	.14
❑ 42 Terry Glenn	.75	.35
❑ 43 Dorsey Levens	.75	.35
❑ 44 Thurman Thomas	.50	.23
❑ 45 Rob Moore	.50	.23
❑ 46 Corey Dillon	.75	.35
❑ 47 Jessie Armstead	.30	.14
❑ 48 Marshall Faulk	1.00	.45
❑ 49 Charles Woodson	.30	.14
❑ 50 John Elway	2.50	1.10
❑ 51 Kevin Dyson	.50	.23
❑ 52 Tony Simmons	.30	.14
❑ 53 Keenan McCardell	.50	.23
❑ 54 O.J. Santiago	.30	.14
❑ 55 Jermaine Lewis	.50	.23
❑ 56 Herman Moore	.50	.23
❑ 57 Gary Brown	.30	.14
❑ 58 Jim Harbaugh	.50	.23
❑ 59 Mike Alstott	.75	.35
❑ 60 Brett Favre	2.50	1.10
❑ 61 Tim Brown	.75	.35
❑ 62 Steve McNair	.75	.35
❑ 63 Ben Coates	.50	.23
❑ 64 Jerome Pathon	.30	.14
❑ 65 Ray Buchanan	.30	.14
❑ 66 Troy Aikman	1.50	.70
❑ 67 Andre Reed	.50	.23
❑ 68 Bubby Brister	.30	.14
❑ 69 Karim Abdul-Jabbar	.50	.23
❑ 70 Peyton Manning	2.50	1.10
❑ 71 Charles Johnson	.30	.14
❑ 72 Natrone Means	.50	.23
❑ 73 Michael Sinclair	.30	.14
❑ 74 Skip Hicks	.30	.14
❑ 75 Derrick Alexander	.50	.23
❑ 76 Wayne Chrebet	.50	.23
❑ 77 Rod Smith	.50	.23
❑ 78 Carl Pickens	.50	.23
❑ 79 Adrian Murrell	.50	.23
❑ 80 Fred Taylor	.75	.35
❑ 81 Eric Moulds	.75	.35
❑ 82 Lawrence Phillips	.50	.23
❑ 83 Marvin Harrison	.75	.35
❑ 84 Cris Carter	.75	.35
❑ 85 Ike Hilliard	.30	.14
❑ 86 Hines Ward	.75	.35
❑ 87 Terrell Owens	.75	.35
❑ 88 Ricky Proehl	.30	.14
❑ 89 Bert Emanuel	.50	.23
❑ 90 Randy Moss	2.00	.90
❑ 91 Aaron Glenn	.30	.14
❑ 92 Robert Smith	.75	.35
❑ 93 Andre Hastings	.30	.14
❑ 94 Jake Reed	.50	.23
❑ 95 Curtis Enis	.30	.14
❑ 96 Andre Wadsworth	.30	.14
❑ 97 Ed McCaffrey	.50	.23
❑ 98 Zach Thomas	.75	.35
❑ 99 Kerry Collins	.50	.23
❑ 100 Drew Bledsoe	1.00	.45
❑ 101 Germane Crowell	.30	.14
❑ 102 Bryan Still	.30	.14
❑ 103 Chad Brown	.30	.14
❑ 104 Jacquez Green	.30	.14
❑ 105 Garrison Hearst	.50	.23
❑ 106 Napoleon Kaufman	.75	.35
❑ 107 Ricky Watters	.50	.23

❑	108 O.J. McDuffie	.50	.23
❑	109 Keyshawn Johnson	.75	.35
❑	110 Jerome Bettis	.75	.35
❑	111 Duce Staley	.75	.35
❑	112 Curtis Conway	.50	.23
❑	113 Chris Chandler	.50	.23
❑	114 Marcus Nash	.30	.14
❑	115 Stephen Alexander	.30	.14
❑	116 Darnay Scott	.30	.14
❑	117 Bruce Smith	.50	.23
❑	118 Priest Holmes	1.25	.55
❑	119 Mark Brunell	.75	.35
❑	120 Jerry Rice	1.50	.70
❑	121 Randall Cunningham	.75	.35
❑	122 Scott Mitchell	.30	.14
❑	123 Antonio Freeman	.75	.35
❑	124 Kordell Stewart	.50	.23
❑	125 Jon Kitna	.75	.35
❑	126 Ahman Green	.75	.35
❑	127 Warrick Dunn	.75	.35
❑	128 Robert Brooks	.50	.23
❑	129 Derrick Thomas	.50	.23
❑	130 Steve Young	1.00	.45
❑	131 Peter Boulware	.30	.14
❑	132 Michael Irvin	.50	.23
❑	133 Shannon Sharpe	.30	.14
❑	134 Jimmy Smith	.50	.23
❑	135 John Avery	.30	.14
❑	136 Fred Lane	.30	.14
❑	137 Trent Green	.75	.35
❑	138 Andre Rison	.50	.23
❑	139 Antowain Smith	.30	.14
❑	140 Eddie George	.75	.35
❑	141 Jeff Blake	.50	.23
❑	142 Rocket Ismail	.50	.23
❑	143 Rickey Dudley	.30	.14
❑	144 Courtney Hawkins	.30	.14
❑	145 Mikhael Ricks	.30	.14
❑	146 J.J. Stokes	.50	.23
❑	147 Levon Kirkland	.30	.14
❑	148 Deion Sanders	.75	.35
❑	149 Barry Sanders	2.50	1.10
❑	150 Tiki Barber	.50	.23
❑	151 David Boston RC	2.00	.90
❑	152 Chris McAlister RC	1.50	.70
❑	153 Peerless Price RC	3.00	1.35
❑	154 D'Wayne Bates RC	1.50	.70
❑	155 Cade McNown RC	1.50	.70
❑	156 Akili Smith RC	1.50	.70
❑	157 Kevin Johnson RC	2.00	.90
❑	158 Tim Couch RC	2.00	.90
❑	159 Sedrick Irvin RC	.75	.35
❑	160 Chris Claiborne RC	.75	.35
❑	161 Edgerrin James RC	8.00	3.60
❑	162 Mike Cloud RC	1.50	.70
❑	163 Cecil Collins RC	.75	.35
❑	164 James Johnson RC	1.50	.70
❑	165 Rob Konrad RC	2.00	.90
❑	166 Daunte Culpepper RC	8.00	3.60
❑	167 Kevin Faulk RC	2.00	.90
❑	168 Donovan McNabb RC	10.00	4.50
❑	169 Troy Edwards RC	1.50	.70
❑	170 Amos Zereoue RC	2.00	.90
❑	171 Karsten Bailey RC	1.50	.70
❑	172 Brock Huard RC	2.00	.90
❑	173 Joe Germaine RC	1.50	.70
❑	174 Torry Holt RC	5.00	2.20
❑	175 Shaun King RC	1.50	.70
❑	176 Jevon Kearse RC	3.00	1.35
❑	177 Champ Bailey RC	2.50	1.10
❑	178 Ebenezer Ekuban RC	1.50	.70
❑	179 Andy Katzenmoyer	1.50	.70
❑	180 Antoine Winfield RC	1.50	.70
❑	181 Jermaine Fazande RC	1.50	.70
❑	182 Ricky Williams RC	5.00	2.20
❑	183 Joel Makovicka RC	2.00	.90
❑	184 Reginald Kelly RC	.75	.35
❑	185 Brandon Stokley RC	2.50	1.10
❑	186 L.C. Stevens RC	.75	.35
❑	187 Marty Booker RC	2.00	.90
❑	188 Jerry Azumah	2.00	.90
❑	189 Ted White RC	.75	.35
❑	190 Scott Covington RC	2.00	.90
❑	191 Tim Alexander RC	.75	.35
❑	192 Darrin Chiaverini RC	1.50	.70
❑	193 Dat Nguyen RC	2.00	.90
❑	194 Wane McGarity RC	.75	.35
❑	195 Al Wilson RC	2.00	.90
❑	196 Travis McGriff RC	.75	.35
❑	197 Stacey Mack RC	2.00	.90
❑	198 Antuan Edwards RC	.75	.35
❑	199 Aaron Brooks RC	6.00	2.70
❑	200 De'Mond Parker RC	.75	.35
❑	201 Jed Weaver RC	.75	.35
❑	202 Madre Hill RC	.75	.35
❑	203 Jim Kleinsasser RC	2.00	.90
❑	204 Michael Bishop RC	2.00	.90
❑	205 Michael Basnight RC	.75	.35
❑	206 Sean Bennett RC	.75	.35
❑	207 Dameane Douglas RC	1.50	.70
❑	208 Na Brown RC	1.50	.70
❑	209 Patrick Kerney RC	2.00	.90
❑	210 Malcolm Johnson RC	.75	.35
❑	211 Dre Bly RC	2.00	.90
❑	212 Terry Jackson RC	1.50	.70
❑	213 Eugene Baker RC	.75	.35
❑	214 Autry Denson RC	1.50	.70
❑	215 Darnell McDonald RC	1.50	.70
❑	216 Charlie Rogers RC	1.50	.70
❑	217 Joe Montgomery RC	1.50	.70
❑	218 Cecil Martin RC	1.50	.70
❑	219 Larry Parker RC	2.00	.90
❑	220 Mike Peterson RC	2.00	.90

2000 Bowman

		Nm-Mt	Ex-Mt
	COMPLETE SET (240)	40.00	18.00
❑	1 Eddie George	.60	.25
❑	2 Ike Hilliard	.40	.18
❑	3 Terrell Owens	.60	.25
❑	4 James Stewart	.40	.18
❑	5 Joey Galloway	.40	.18
❑	6 Jake Reed	.40	.18
❑	7 Derrick Alexander	.40	.18
❑	8 Jeff George	.40	.18
❑	9 Kerry Collins	.40	.18
❑	10 Tony Gonzalez	.40	.18
❑	11 Marcus Robinson	.60	.25
❑	12 Charles Woodson	.40	.18
❑	13 Germane Crowell	.25	.11
❑	14 Yancey Thigpen	.25	.11
❑	15 Tony Martin	.40	.18
❑	16 Frank Sanders	.40	.18
❑	17 Napoleon Kaufman	.40	.18
❑	18 Jay Fiedler	.60	.25
❑	19 Patrick Jeffers	.60	.25
❑	20 Steve McNair	.60	.25
❑	21 Herman Moore	.40	.18
❑	22 Tim Brown	.60	.25
❑	23 Olandis Gary	.60	.25
❑	24 Corey Dillon	.60	.25
❑	25 Warren Sapp	.40	.18
❑	26 Curtis Enis	.25	.11
❑	27 Vinny Testaverde	.40	.18
❑	28 Tim Biakabutuka	.40	.18
❑	29 Kevin Johnson	.60	.25
❑	30 Charlie Batch	.60	.25
❑	31 Jermaine Fazande	.25	.11
❑	32 Shaun King	.25	.11
❑	33 Errict Rhett	.40	.18
❑	34 O.J. McDuffie	.40	.18
❑	35 Bruce Smith	.40	.18
❑	36 Antonio Freeman	.60	.25
❑	37 Tim Couch	.40	.18
❑	38 Duce Staley	.60	.25
❑	39 Jeff Blake	.40	.18
❑	40 Jim Harbaugh	.40	.18
❑	41 Jeff Graham	.25	.11
❑	42 Drew Bledsoe	.75	.35
❑	43 Mike Alstott	.60	.25
❑	44 Terance Mathis	.40	.18
❑	45 Antowain Smith	.40	.18
❑	46 Johnnie Morton	.40	.18
❑	47 Chris Chandler	.40	.18
❑	48 Keith Poole	.40	.18
❑	49 Ricky Watters	.40	.18
❑	50 Darnay Scott	.40	.18
❑	51 Damon Huard	.60	.25
❑	52 Peerless Price	.60	.25
❑	53 Brian Griese	.60	.25
❑	54 Frank Wycheck	.25	.11
❑	55 Kevin Dyson	.40	.18
❑	56 Junior Seau	.60	.25
❑	57 Curtis Conway	.40	.18
❑	58 Jamal Anderson	.60	.25
❑	59 Jim Miller	.25	.11
❑	60 Rob Johnson	.25	.11
❑	61 Mark Brunell	.60	.25
❑	62 Wayne Chrebet	.40	.18
❑	63 James Johnson	.25	.11
❑	64 Sean Dawkins	.25	.11
❑	65 Stephen Davis	.60	.25
❑	66 Daunte Culpepper	.75	.35
❑	67 Doug Flutie	.60	.25
❑	68 Pete Mitchell	.25	.11
❑	69 Bill Schroeder	.40	.18
❑	70 Terrence Wilkins	.25	.11
❑	71 Cade McNown	.25	.11
❑	72 Muhsin Muhammad	.40	.18
❑	73 E.G. Green	.25	.11
❑	74 Edgerrin James	1.00	.45
❑	75 Troy Edwards	.25	.11
❑	76 Terry Glenn	.40	.18
❑	77 Tony Banks	.40	.18
❑	78 Derrick Mayes	.40	.18
❑	79 Curtis Martin	.60	.25
❑	80 Kordell Stewart	.40	.18
❑	81 Amani Toomer	.40	.18
❑	82 Dorsey Levens	.40	.18
❑	83 Brad Johnson	.60	.25
❑	84 Ed McCaffrey	.60	.25
❑	85 Charlie Garner	.40	.18
❑	86 Brett Favre	2.00	.90
❑	87 J.J. Stokes	.40	.18
❑	88 Steve Young	.75	.35
❑	89 Jonathan Linton	.25	.11
❑	90 Isaac Bruce	.60	.25
❑	91 Shawn Jefferson	.25	.11
❑	92 Rod Smith	.40	.18
❑	93 Champ Bailey	.40	.18
❑	94 Ricky Williams	.60	.25
❑	95 Priest Holmes	.75	.35
❑	96 Corey Bradford	.40	.18
❑	97 Eric Moulds	.60	.25
❑	98 Warrick Dunn	.60	.25
❑	99 Jevon Kearse	.60	.25
❑	100 Albert Connell	.25	.11
❑	101 Az-Zahir Hakim	.25	.11
❑	102 Marvin Harrison	.60	.25
❑	103 Qadry Ismail	.40	.18
❑	104 Oronde Gadsden	.40	.18
❑	105 Rob Moore	.40	.18
❑	106 Marshall Faulk	.75	.35
❑	107 Steve Beuerlein	.25	.11
❑	108 Torry Holt	.60	.25
❑	109 Donovan McNabb	1.00	.45
❑	110 Rich Gannon	.60	.25
❑	111 Jerome Bettis	.60	.25
❑	112 Peyton Manning	1.50	.70
❑	113 Cris Carter	.60	.25
❑	114 Jake Plummer	.40	.18
❑	115 Kent Graham	.25	.11
❑	116 Keenan McCardell	.40	.18
❑	117 Tim Dwight	.60	.25
❑	118 Fred Taylor	.60	.25
❑	119 Jerry Rice	1.25	.55

❑ 120 Michael Westbrook	.40	.18
❑ 121 Kurt Warner	1.25	.55
❑ 122 Jimmy Smith	.40	.18
❑ 123 Emmitt Smith	1.25	.55
❑ 124 Terrell Davis	.60	.25
❑ 125 Randy Moss	1.25	.55
❑ 126 Akili Smith	.25	.11
❑ 127 Rocket Ismail	.40	.18
❑ 128 Jon Kitna	.60	.25
❑ 129 Elvis Grbac	.40	.18
❑ 130 Wesley Walls	.25	.11
❑ 131 Torrance Small	.25	.11
❑ 132 Tyrone Wheatley	.40	.18
❑ 133 Carl Pickens	.40	.18
❑ 134 Zach Thomas	.60	.25
❑ 135 Jacquez Green	.25	.11
❑ 136 Robert Smith	.60	.25
❑ 137 Keyshawn Johnson	.60	.25
❑ 138 Matthew Hatchette	.25	.11
❑ 139 Troy Aikman	1.25	.55
❑ 140 Charles Johnson	.40	.18
❑ 141 Terry Battle EP	.30	.14
❑ 142 Pepe Pearson EP RC	.75	.35
❑ 143 Cory Sauter EP	.30	.14
❑ 144 Brian Shay EP	.30	.14
❑ 145 Marcus Crandell EP RC	.50	.23
❑ 146 Danny Wuerffel EP	.50	.23
❑ 147 L.C. Stevens EP	.30	.14
❑ 148 Ted White EP	.30	.14
❑ 149 Matt Lytle EP RC	.50	.23
❑ 150 Vershan Jackson EP RC	.30	.14
❑ 151 Mario Bailey EP	.30	.14
❑ 152 Darryl Daniel EP RC	.50	.23
❑ 153 Sean Morey EP RC	.50	.23
❑ 154 Jim Kubiak EP RC	.50	.23
❑ 155 Aaron Stecker EP RC	.75	.35
❑ 156 Damon Dunn EP RC	.50	.23
❑ 157 Kevin Daft EP	.30	.14
❑ 158 Corey Thomas EP	.30	.14
❑ 159 Deon Mitchell EP RC	.50	.23
❑ 160 Todd Floyd EP RC	.30	.14
❑ 161 Norman Miller EP RC	.30	.14
❑ 162 Jeremaine Copeland EP	.30	.14
❑ 163 Michael Blair EP	.30	.14
❑ 164 Ron Powlus EP RC	.75	.35
❑ 165 Pat Barnes EP	.50	.23
❑ 166 Dez White RC	1.00	.45
❑ 167 Trung Canidate RC	.75	.35
❑ 168 Thomas Jones RC	1.50	.70
❑ 169 Courtney Brown RC	1.00	.45
❑ 170 Jamal Lewis RC	2.50	1.10
❑ 171 Chris Redman RC	.75	.35
❑ 172 Ron Dayne RC	1.00	.45
❑ 173 Chad Pennington RC	4.00	1.80
❑ 174 Plaxico Burress RC	2.00	.90
❑ 175 R.Jay Soward RC	.75	.35
❑ 176 Travis Taylor RC	1.00	.45
❑ 177 Shaun Alexander RC	2.50	1.10
❑ 178 Brian Urlacher RC	4.00	1.80
❑ 179 Danny Farmer RC	.75	.35
❑ 180 Tee Martin RC	1.00	.45
❑ 181 Sylvester Morris RC	.75	.35
❑ 182 Curtis Keaton RC	.75	.35
❑ 183 Peter Warrick RC	1.00	.45
❑ 184 Anthony Becht RC	1.00	.45
❑ 185 Travis Prentice RC	1.00	.45
❑ 186 J.R. Redmond RC	.75	.35
❑ 187 Bubba Franks RC	1.00	.45
❑ 188 Ron Dugans RC	.50	.23
❑ 189 Reuben Droughns RC	1.25	.55
❑ 190 Corey Simon RC	1.00	.45
❑ 191 Joe Hamilton RC	.75	.35
❑ 192 Laveranues Coles RC	1.25	.55
❑ 193 Todd Pinkston RC	1.00	.45
❑ 194 Jerry Porter RC	1.25	.55
❑ 195 Dennis Northcutt RC	1.00	.45
❑ 196 Tim Rattay RC	2.00	.90
❑ 197 Giovanni Carmazzi RC	.75	.35
❑ 198 Mareno Philyaw RC	.50	.23
❑ 199 Avion Black RC	.75	.35
❑ 200 Chafie Fields RC	.50	.23
❑ 201 Rondell Mealey RC	.50	.23
❑ 202 Troy Walters RC	1.00	.45
❑ 203 Frank Moreau RC	.75	.35
❑ 204 Vaughn Sanders RC	.50	.23
❑ 205 Sherrod Gideon RC	.50	.23
❑ 206 Doug Chapman RC	.75	.35
❑ 207 Marcus Knight RC	.75	.35
❑ 208 Jamel White RC	.75	.35
❑ 209 Windrell Hayes RC	.75	.35
❑ 210 Reggie Jones RC	.50	.23
❑ 211 Jarious Jackson RC	.75	.35
❑ 212 Ronney Jenkins RC	.75	.35
❑ 213 Quinton Spotwood RC	.50	.23
❑ 214 Rob Morris RC	.75	.35
❑ 215 Gari Scott RC	.50	.23
❑ 216 Kevin Thompson RC	.50	.23
❑ 217 Trevor Insley RC	.50	.23
❑ 218 Frank Murphy RC	.50	.23
❑ 219 Patrick Pass RC	.75	.35
❑ 220 Mike Anderson RC	1.00	.45
❑ 221 Derrius Thompson RC	1.00	.45
❑ 222 John Abraham RC	1.00	.45
❑ 223 Dante Hall RC	2.00	.90
❑ 224 Chad Morton RC	1.00	.45
❑ 225 Ahmed Plummer RC	1.00	.45
❑ 226 Julian Peterson RC	1.00	.45
❑ 227 Mike Green RC	.75	.35
❑ 228 Michael Wiley RC	.75	.35
❑ 229 Spergon Wynn RC	.75	.35
❑ 230 Trevor Gaylor RC	.75	.35
❑ 231 Doug Johnson RC	1.00	.45
❑ 232 Marc Bulger RC	2.00	.90
❑ 233 Ron Dixon RC	.75	.35
❑ 234 Aaron Shea RC	.75	.35
❑ 235 Thomas Hamner RC	.50	.23
❑ 236 Tom Brady RC	25.00	11.00
❑ 237 Deltha O'Neal RC	1.00	.45
❑ 238 Todd Husak RC	1.00	.45
❑ 239 Erron Kinney RC	1.00	.45
❑ 240 JaJuan Dawson RC	.50	.23

2001 Bowman

	Nm-Mt	Ex-Mt
COMPLETE SET (275)	60.00	18.00
❑ 1 Emmitt Smith	1.25	.35
❑ 2 James Stewart	.40	.12
❑ 3 Jeff Graham	.25	.07
❑ 4 Keyshawn Johnson	.60	.18
❑ 5 Stephen Davis	.60	.18
❑ 6 Chad Lewis	.25	.07
❑ 7 Drew Bledsoe	.75	.23
❑ 8 Fred Taylor	.60	.18
❑ 9 Mike Anderson	.60	.18
❑ 10 Tony Gonzalez	.40	.12
❑ 11 Aaron Brooks	.60	.18
❑ 12 Vinny Testaverde	.40	.12
❑ 13 Jerome Bettis	.60	.18
❑ 14 Marshall Faulk	.75	.23
❑ 15 Jeff Garcia	.60	.18
❑ 16 Terry Glenn	.40	.12
❑ 17 Jay Fiedler	.60	.18
❑ 18 Ahman Green	.60	.18
❑ 19 Cade McNown	.25	.07
❑ 20 Rob Johnson	.40	.12
❑ 21 Jamal Anderson	.60	.18
❑ 22 Corey Dillon	.60	.18
❑ 23 Jake Plummer	.40	.12
❑ 24 Rod Smith	.40	.12
❑ 25 Trent Green	.60	.18
❑ 26 Ricky Williams	.60	.18
❑ 27 Charlie Garner	.40	.12
❑ 28 Shaun Alexander	.75	.23
❑ 29 Jeff George	.40	.12
❑ 30 Torry Holt	.60	.18
❑ 31 James Thrash	.40	.12
❑ 32 Rich Gannon	.60	.18
❑ 33 Ron Dayne	.60	.18
❑ 34 Dedric Ward	.25	.07
❑ 35 Edgerrin James	.75	.23
❑ 36 Cris Carter	.60	.18
❑ 37 Derrick Mason	.40	.12
❑ 38 Brad Johnson	.60	.18
❑ 39 Charlie Batch	.60	.18
❑ 40 Joey Galloway	.40	.12
❑ 41 James Allen	.40	.12
❑ 42 Tim Biakabutuka	.40	.12
❑ 43 Ray Lewis	.60	.18
❑ 44 David Boston	.60	.18
❑ 45 Kevin Johnson	.40	.12
❑ 46 Jimmy Smith	.40	.12
❑ 47 Joe Horn	.40	.12
❑ 48 Terrell Owens	.60	.18
❑ 49 Eddie George	.60	.18
❑ 50 Brett Favre	2.00	.60
❑ 51 Wayne Chrebet	.40	.12
❑ 52 Hines Ward	.60	.18
❑ 53 Warrick Dunn	.60	.18
❑ 54 Matt Hasselbeck	.40	.12
❑ 55 Tiki Barber	.40	.12
❑ 56 Lamar Smith	.40	.12
❑ 57 Tim Couch	.40	.12
❑ 58 Eric Moulds	.40	.12
❑ 59 Shawn Jefferson	.25	.07
❑ 60 Donald Hayes	.25	.07
❑ 61 Brian Urlacher	1.00	.30
❑ 62 Steve McNair	.60	.18
❑ 63 Kurt Warner	1.25	.35
❑ 64 Tim Brown	.60	.18
❑ 65 Troy Brown	.40	.12
❑ 66 Albert Connell	.25	.07
❑ 67 Peyton Manning	1.50	.45
❑ 68 Peter Warrick	.60	.18
❑ 69 Elvis Grbac	.40	.12
❑ 70 Chris Chandler	.40	.12
❑ 71 Akili Smith	.25	.07
❑ 72 Keenan McCardell	.25	.07
❑ 73 Kerry Collins	.40	.12
❑ 74 Junior Seau	.60	.18
❑ 75 Donovan McNabb	.75	.23
❑ 76 Tony Banks	.40	.12
❑ 77 Steve Beuerlein	.25	.07
❑ 78 Daunte Culpepper	.60	.18
❑ 79 Darrell Jackson	.60	.18
❑ 80 Isaac Bruce	.60	.18
❑ 81 Tyrone Wheatley	.40	.12
❑ 82 Derrick Alexander	.40	.12
❑ 83 Germane Crowell	.25	.07
❑ 84 Jon Kitna	.40	.12
❑ 85 Jamal Lewis	1.00	.30
❑ 86 Ed McCaffrey	.60	.18
❑ 87 Mark Brunell	.60	.18
❑ 88 Jeff Blake	.40	.12
❑ 89 Duce Staley	.60	.18
❑ 90 Doug Flutie	.60	.18
❑ 91 Kordell Stewart	.40	.12
❑ 92 Randy Moss	1.25	.35
❑ 93 Marvin Harrison	.60	.18
❑ 94 Muhsin Muhammad	.40	.12
❑ 95 Brian Griese	.60	.18
❑ 96 Antonio Freeman	.60	.18
❑ 97 Amani Toomer	.40	.12
❑ 98 Oronde Gadsden	.40	.12
❑ 99 Curtis Martin	.60	.18
❑ 100 Jerry Rice	1.25	.35
❑ 101 Michael Pittman	.25	.07
❑ 102 Shannon Sharpe	.40	.12
❑ 103 Peerless Price	.40	.12
❑ 104 Bill Schroeder	.40	.12
❑ 105 Ike Hilliard	.40	.12
❑ 106 Freddie Jones	.25	.07
❑ 107 Tai Streets	.25	.07
❑ 108 Ricky Watters	.40	.12
❑ 109 Az-Zahir Hakim	.25	.07
❑ 110 Jacquez Green	.25	.07
❑ 111 Bobby Shaw	.25	.07

❑ 112 Johnnie Morton .40 .12
❑ 113 Laveranues Coles .60 .18
❑ 114 Chad Pennington 1.00 .30
❑ 115 Champ Bailey .40 .12
❑ 116 Charles Woodson .40 .12
❑ 117 Curtis Conway .40 .12
❑ 118 Marcus Robinson .60 .18
❑ 119 Michael Westbrook .40 .12
❑ 120 Mike Alstott .60 .18
❑ 121 Priest Holmes .75 .23
❑ 122 Qadry Ismail .40 .12
❑ 123 Rocket Ismail .40 .12
❑ 124 Shawn Bryson .25 .07
❑ 125 Jeff Lewis .25 .07
❑ 126 Jeremy Mcdaniel .25 .07
❑ 127 Terance Mathis .25 .07
❑ 128 Travis Prentice .25 .07
❑ 129 Warren Sapp .40 .12
❑ 130 Jevon Kearse .40 .12
❑ 131 George Layne RC .75 .23
❑ 132 Correll Buckhalter RC 1.50 .45
❑ 133 Tony Stewart RC 1.25 .35
❑ 134 Chris Barnes RC .75 .23
❑ 135 A.J. Feeley RC 1.25 .35
❑ 136 Margin Hooks RC .50 .15
❑ 137 Anthony Henry RC 1.25 .35
❑ 138 Dwight Smith RC .50 .15
❑ 139 Torrance Marshall RC 1.25 .35
❑ 140 Gary Baxter RC .75 .23
❑ 141 Derek Combs RC .75 .23
❑ 142 Marcus Bell DT RC .75 .23
❑ 143 Delawrence Grant RC .50 .15
❑ 144 Jameel Cook RC .75 .23
❑ 145 Eric Downing RC .50 .15
❑ 146 Marlon McCree RC .50 .15
❑ 147 Tay Cody RC .50 .15
❑ 148 Mario Monds RC .50 .15
❑ 149 Kenny Smith RC .75 .23
❑ 150 Sedrick Hodge RC .50 .15
❑ 151 Marcus Stroud RC 1.25 .35
❑ 152 Steve Smith RC 1.50 .45
❑ 153 Tyrone Robertson RC .50 .15
❑ 154 James Reed RC .50 .15
❑ 155 Kris Kocurek RC .50 .15
❑ 156 Dan O'Leary RC .75 .23
❑ 157 Harold Blackmon RC .50 .15
❑ 158 Fred Smoot RC 1.25 .35
❑ 159 Billy Baber RC .50 .15
❑ 160 Jarrod Cooper RC 1.25 .35
❑ 161 Travis Henry RC 1.50 .45
❑ 162 David Terrell RC 1.25 .35
❑ 163 Josh Heupel RC 1.25 .35
❑ 164 Drew Brees RC 2.50 .75
❑ 165 T.J. Houshmandzadeh RC 1.25 .35
❑ 166 Rod Gardner RC 1.25 .35
❑ 167 Richard Seymour RC 1.25 .35
❑ 168 Koren Robinson RC 1.25 .35
❑ 169 Scotty Anderson RC .75 .23
❑ 170 Marques Tuiasosopo RC 1.25 .35
❑ 171 John Capel RC .75 .23
❑ 172 LaMont Jordan RC 1.50 .45
❑ 173 James Jackson RC 1.25 .35
❑ 174 Bobby Newcombe RC 1.25 .35
❑ 175 Anthony Thomas RC 2.00 .60
❑ 176 Dan Alexander RC 1.25 .35
❑ 177 Quincy Carter RC 1.25 .35
❑ 178 Morlon Greenwood RC .75 .23
❑ 179 Robert Ferguson RC 1.25 .35
❑ 180 Sage Rosenfels RC 1.25 .35
❑ 181 Michael Stone RC .50 .15
❑ 182 Chris Weinke RC 1.25 .35
❑ 183 Travis Minor RC .75 .23
❑ 184 Gerard Warren RC 1.25 .35
❑ 185 Jamar Fletcher RC .75 .23
❑ 186 Andre Carter RC 1.25 .35
❑ 187 Deuce McAllister RC 2.50 .75
❑ 188 Dan Morgan RC 1.25 .35
❑ 189 Todd Heap RC 1.25 .35
❑ 190 Snoop Minnis RC .75 .23
❑ 191 Will Allen RC .75 .23
❑ 192 Freddie Mitchell RC 1.25 .35
❑ 193 Rudi Johnson RC 2.50 .75
❑ 194 Kevan Barlow RC 1.25 .35
❑ 195 Jamie Winborn RC .75 .23
❑ 196 Onomo Ojo RC .75 .23
❑ 197 Leonard Davis RC .75 .23
❑ 198 Santana Moss RC 2.00 .60
❑ 199 Chris Chambers RC 1.50 .45
❑ 200 Michael Vick RC 8.00 2.40
❑ 201 Michael Bennett RC 2.50 .75
❑ 202 Mike McMahon RC 1.25 .35
❑ 203 Jonathan Carter RC .75 .23
❑ 204 Jamal Reynolds RC 1.25 .35
❑ 205 Justin Smith RC 1.25 .35
❑ 206 Quincy Morgan RC 1.25 .35
❑ 207 Chad Johnson RC 2.50 .75
❑ 208 Jesse Palmer RC 1.25 .35
❑ 209 Reggie Wayne RC 2.00 .60
❑ 210 LaDainian Tomlinson RC 4.00 1.20
❑ 211 Andre King RC .75 .23
❑ 212 Richmond Flowers RC .75 .23
❑ 213 Derrick Blaylock RC 1.25 .35
❑ 214 Cedrick Wilson RC 1.25 .35
❑ 215 Zeke Moreno RC 1.25 .35
❑ 216 Tommy Polley RC 1.25 .35
❑ 217 Damione Lewis RC .75 .23
❑ 218 Aaron Schobel RC 1.25 .35
❑ 219 Alge Crumpler RC 1.50 .45
❑ 220 Nate Clements RC 1.25 .35
❑ 221 Quentin McCord RC .75 .23
❑ 222 Ken-Yon Rambo RC .75 .23
❑ 223 Milton Wynn RC .75 .23
❑ 224 Derrick Gibson RC .75 .23
❑ 225 Chris Taylor RC .75 .23
❑ 226 Corey Hall RC .50 .15
❑ 227 Vinny Sutherland RC .75 .23
❑ 228 Kendrell Bell RC 3.00 .90
❑ 229 Casey Hampton RC .75 .23
❑ 230 Demetric Evans RC .50 .15
❑ 231 Brian Allen RC .50 .15
❑ 232 Rodney Bailey RC .50 .15
❑ 233 Otis Leverette RC .50 .15
❑ 234 Ron Edwards RC .50 .15
❑ 235 Michael Jameson RC .50 .15
❑ 236 Markus Steele RC .75 .23
❑ 237 Jimmy Williams RC .50 .15
❑ 238 Roger Knight RC .50 .15
❑ 239 Randy Garner RC .50 .15
❑ 240 Raymond Perryman RC .50 .15
❑ 241 Karon Riley RC .50 .15
❑ 242 Adam Archuleta RC 1.25 .35
❑ 243 Arnold Jackson RC .75 .23
❑ 244 Ryan Pickett RC .50 .15
❑ 245 Shad Meier RC .75 .23
❑ 246 Reggie Germany RC .75 .23
❑ 247 Justin McCareins RC 1.25 .35
❑ 248 Idrees Bashir RC .50 .15
❑ 249 Josh Booty RC 1.25 .35
❑ 250 Eddie Berlin RC .75 .23
❑ 251 Heath Evans RC .75 .23
❑ 252 Alex Bannister RC .75 .23
❑ 253 Corey Alston RC .50 .15
❑ 254 Reggie White RC .75 .23
❑ 255 Orlando Huff RC .50 .15
❑ 256 Ken Lucas RC .75 .23
❑ 257 Matt Stewart RC .50 .15
❑ 258 Cedric Scott RC .75 .23
❑ 259 Ronney Daniels RC .50 .15
❑ 260 Kevin Kasper RC 1.25 .35
❑ 261 Tony Driver RC .75 .23
❑ 262 Kyle Vanden Bosch RC 1.25 .35
❑ 263 T.J. Turner RC .50 .15
❑ 264 Eric Westmoreland RC .75 .23
❑ 265 Ronald Flemons RC .50 .15
❑ 266 Eric Kelly RC .50 .15
❑ 267 Moran Norris RC .50 .15
❑ 268 Damerien McCants RC .75 .23
❑ 269 James Boyd RC .50 .15
❑ 270 Keith Adams RC .50 .15
❑ 271 B.Manumaleuna RC .75 .23
❑ 272 Dee Brown RC 1.25 .35
❑ 273 Ross Kolodziej RC .50 .15
❑ 274 Boo Williams RC .75 .23
❑ 275 Patrick Chukwurah RC .50 .15

2002 Bowman

	Nm-Mt	Ex-Mt
COMPLETE SET (275)	50.00	15.00

❑ 1 Emmitt Smith 1.50 .45
❑ 2 Drew Brees .60 .18
❑ 3 Duce Staley .60 .18
❑ 4 Curtis Martin .60 .18
❑ 5 Isaac Bruce .60 .18
❑ 6 Stephen Davis .40 .12
❑ 7 Darrell Jackson .40 .12
❑ 8 James Stewart .40 .12
❑ 9 Tim Couch .40 .12
❑ 10 Travis Henry .60 .18
❑ 11 Thomas Jones .40 .12
❑ 12 Jamal Lewis .60 .18
❑ 13 Chris Chambers .60 .18
❑ 14 Jeff Blake .40 .12
❑ 15 Plaxico Burress .60 .18
❑ 16 Michael Pittman .25 .07
❑ 17 Jeff Garcia .60 .18
❑ 18 Tim Brown .60 .18
❑ 19 Kent Graham .25 .07
❑ 20 Shannon Sharpe .40 .12
❑ 21 Corey Dillon .40 .12
❑ 22 Muhsin Muhammad .40 .12
❑ 23 Tony Gonzalez .40 .12
❑ 24 Qadry Ismail .40 .12
❑ 25 Mike McMahon .60 .18
❑ 26 Edgerrin James .75 .23
❑ 27 Daunte Culpepper .60 .18
❑ 28 Deuce McAllister .75 .23
❑ 29 Kerry Collins .40 .12
❑ 30 Eddie George .60 .18
❑ 31 Torry Holt .60 .18
❑ 32 Todd Pinkston .40 .12
❑ 33 Quincy Carter .40 .12
❑ 34 Rod Smith .40 .12
❑ 35 Michael Vick 2.00 .60
❑ 36 Jim Miller .25 .07
❑ 37 Troy Brown .40 .12
❑ 38 Wayne Chrebet .40 .12
❑ 39 Curtis Conway .25 .07
❑ 40 Reidel Anthony .25 .07
❑ 41 Mark Brunell .60 .18
❑ 42 Chris Weinke .40 .12
❑ 43 Eric Moulds .40 .12
❑ 44 Ike Hilliard .25 .07
❑ 45 Jay Fiedler .40 .12
❑ 46 Keyshawn Johnson .60 .18
❑ 47 Rod Gardner .40 .12
❑ 48 Chris Redman .25 .07
❑ 49 James Allen .40 .12
❑ 50 Kordell Stewart .40 .12
❑ 51 Priest Holmes .75 .23
❑ 52 Anthony Thomas .60 .18
❑ 53 Peter Warrick .40 .12
❑ 54 Jake Plummer .40 .12
❑ 55 Jerry Rice 1.25 .35
❑ 56 Joe Horn .40 .12
❑ 57 Derrick Mason .40 .12
❑ 58 Kurt Warner .60 .18
❑ 59 Antowain Smith .40 .12
❑ 60 Randy Moss 1.25 .35
❑ 61 Warrick Dunn .60 .18
❑ 62 Laveranues Coles .40 .12
❑ 63 LaDainian Tomlinson 1.00 .30
❑ 64 Michael Westbrook .25 .07
❑ 65 Travis Taylor .25 .07
❑ 66 Brian Griese .60 .18
❑ 67 Bill Schroeder .40 .12
❑ 68 Ahman Green .60 .18

Card	MINT	NRMT
❑ 69 Jimmy Smith	.40	.12
❑ 70 Charlie Garner	.40	.12
❑ 71 Terrell Owens	.60	.18
❑ 72 Brad Johnson	.40	.12
❑ 73 James Thrash	.40	.12
❑ 74 Marvin Harrison	.60	.18
❑ 75 Brett Favre	1.50	.45
❑ 76 Rocket Ismail	.40	.12
❑ 77 David Boston	.60	.18
❑ 78 Jermaine Lewis	.25	.07
❑ 79 Aaron Brooks	.60	.18
❑ 80 Shaun Alexander	.60	.18
❑ 81 Steve McNair	.60	.18
❑ 82 Marshall Faulk	.60	.18
❑ 83 Terrell Davis	.60	.18
❑ 84 Corey Bradford	.25	.07
❑ 85 David Terrell	.60	.18
❑ 86 Kevin Johnson	.40	.12
❑ 87 Jon Kitna	.40	.12
❑ 88 Az-Zahir Hakim	.25	.07
❑ 89 Drew Bledsoe	.75	.23
❑ 90 Garrison Hearst	.40	.12
❑ 91 Doug Flutie	.60	.18
❑ 92 Jerome Bettis	.60	.18
❑ 93 Vinny Testaverde	.40	.12
❑ 94 Tiki Barber	.40	.12
❑ 95 Johnnie Morton	.40	.12
❑ 96 Lamar Smith	.40	.12
❑ 97 Marcus Robinson	.40	.12
❑ 98 Fred Taylor	.60	.18
❑ 99 Tom Brady	1.50	.45
❑ 100 Peyton Manning	1.25	.35
❑ 101 Donovan McNabb	.75	.23
❑ 102 Rich Gannon	.60	.18
❑ 103 Hines Ward	.60	.18
❑ 104 Michael Bennett	.60	.18
❑ 105 Ricky Williams	.60	.18
❑ 106 Germane Crowell	.25	.07
❑ 107 Joey Galloway	.40	.12
❑ 108 Amani Toomer	.40	.12
❑ 109 Trent Green	.40	.12
❑ 110 Terry Glenn	.40	.12
❑ 111 Donte Stallworth RC	3.00	.90
❑ 112 Mike Williams RC	1.25	.35
❑ 113 Kurt Kittner RC	1.25	.35
❑ 114 Josh Reed RC	1.50	.45
❑ 115 Raonall Smith RC	1.25	.35
❑ 116 David Garrard RC	1.50	.45
❑ 117 Eric Crouch RC	2.50	.75
❑ 118 Bryan Thomas RC	1.25	.35
❑ 119 Levi Jones RC	1.25	.35
❑ 120 Andre Davis RC	1.50	.45
❑ 121 Herb Haygood RC	.75	.23
❑ 122 Josh McCown RC	2.00	.60
❑ 123 Quentin Jammer RC	1.50	.45
❑ 124 Cliff Russell RC	1.25	.35
❑ 125 Jeremy Shockey RC	5.00	1.50
❑ 126 Jamin Elliott RC	.75	.23
❑ 127 Roy Williams RC	4.00	1.20
❑ 128 Marquise Walker RC	1.25	.35
❑ 129 Kalimba Edwards RC	1.50	.45
❑ 130 Daniel Graham RC	1.50	.45
❑ 131 Freddie Milons RC	1.25	.35
❑ 132 Anthony Weaver RC	1.25	.35
❑ 133 Jake Schifino RC	1.25	.35
❑ 134 Antonio Bryant RC	1.50	.45
❑ 135 DeShaun Foster RC	1.50	.45
❑ 136 Antwaan Randle El RC	2.00	.60
❑ 137 William Green RC	2.50	.75
❑ 138 Ed Reed RC	2.50	.75
❑ 139 Maurice Morris RC	1.50	.45
❑ 140 Joey Harrington RC	5.00	1.50
❑ 141 T.J. Duckett RC	2.50	.75
❑ 142 Javon Walker RC	3.00	.90
❑ 143 Albert Haynesworth RC	1.25	.35
❑ 144 Julius Peppers RC	3.00	.90
❑ 145 Clinton Portis RC	5.00	1.50
❑ 146 Craig Nall RC	1.50	.45
❑ 147 Ashley Lelie RC	3.00	.90
❑ 148 Reche Caldwell RC	1.50	.45
❑ 149 Rohan Davey RC	1.50	.45
❑ 150 Patrick Ramsey RC	3.00	.90
❑ 151 Jabar Gaffney RC	1.50	.45
❑ 152 Tank Williams RC	1.25	.35
❑ 153 Ron Johnson RC	1.25	.35
❑ 154 Ladell Betts RC	1.50	.45
❑ 155 Brian Westbrook RC	2.50	.75
❑ 156 Jamar Martin RC	1.25	.35
❑ 157 Travis Stephens RC	1.25	.35
❑ 158 Tim Carter RC	1.25	.35
❑ 159 Darrell Hill RC	1.50	.45
❑ 160 Luke Staley RC	1.25	.35
❑ 161 Randy Fasani RC	1.25	.35
❑ 162 Matt Schobel RC	1.25	.35
❑ 163 Jon McGraw RC	.75	.23
❑ 164 Dwight Freeney RC	2.00	.60
❑ 165 Chad Hutchinson RC	1.50	.45
❑ 166 Adrian Peterson RC	1.50	.45
❑ 167 Josh Scobey RC	1.50	.45
❑ 168 Jonathan Wells RC	1.50	.45
❑ 169 Sam Simmons RC	.75	.23
❑ 170 Jerramy Stevens RC	1.50	.45
❑ 171 Jason McAddley RC	1.25	.35
❑ 172 Ken Simonton RC	.75	.23
❑ 173 Chester Taylor RC	1.50	.45
❑ 174 Brandon Doman RC	1.50	.45
❑ 175 Javin Hunter RC	.75	.23
❑ 176 Eddie Drummond RC	1.25	.35
❑ 177 Andre Lott RC	1.50	.45
❑ 178 Travis Fisher RC	1.50	.45
❑ 179 Jarvis Green RC	1.25	.35
❑ 180 Ross Tucker RC	.75	.23
❑ 181 Lamont Brightful RC	.75	.23
❑ 182 Rocky Calmus RC	1.50	.45
❑ 183 Wes Pate RC	.75	.23
❑ 184 Lamar Gordon RC	1.50	.45
❑ 185 Terry Jones RC	1.25	.35
❑ 186 Kyle Johnson RC	.75	.23
❑ 187 Daryl Jones RC	1.25	.35
❑ 188 Tellis Redmon RC	1.25	.35
❑ 189 Howard Green RC	.75	.23
❑ 190 Jarrod Baxter RC	1.25	.35
❑ 191 Delvon Flowers RC	1.25	.35
❑ 192 Kevin Curtis RC	.75	.23
❑ 193 Kelly Campbell RC	1.25	.35
❑ 194 Eddie Freeman RC	.75	.23
❑ 195 Atrews Bell RC	.75	.23
❑ 196 Omar Easy RC	1.50	.45
❑ 197 Jeremy Allen RC	1.50	.45
❑ 198 Andra Davis RC	1.25	.35
❑ 199 Jack Brewer RC	1.25	.35
❑ 200 Mike Rumph RC	1.50	.45
❑ 201 Seth Burford RC	1.25	.35
❑ 202 Marquand Manuel RC	.75	.23
❑ 203 Marques Anderson RC	1.50	.45
❑ 204 Ben Leber RC	1.50	.45
❑ 205 Ryan Denney RC	.75	.23
❑ 206 Justin Peelle RC	.75	.23
❑ 207 Lito Sheppard RC	1.50	.45
❑ 208 Damien Anderson RC	1.25	.35
❑ 209 Lamont Thompson RC	1.25	.35
❑ 210 David Priestley RC	1.25	.35
❑ 211 Michael Lewis RC	1.50	.45
❑ 212 Lee Mays RC	1.25	.35
❑ 213 Alan Harper RC	.75	.23
❑ 214 Verron Haynes RC	1.50	.45
❑ 215 Chris Hope RC	1.25	.35
❑ 216 David Thornton RC	.75	.23
❑ 217 Derek Ross RC	1.25	.35
❑ 218 Brett Keisel RC	1.50	.45
❑ 219 Joseph Jefferson RC	1.25	.35
❑ 220 Andre Goodman RC	1.50	.45
❑ 221 Robert Royal RC	1.50	.45
❑ 222 Sheldon Brown RC	1.50	.45
❑ 223 DeVeren Johnson RC	1.25	.35
❑ 224 Rock Cartwright RC	2.00	.60
❑ 225 Quincy Monk RC	.75	.23
❑ 226 Nick Rogers RC	1.25	.35
❑ 227 Kendall Simmons RC	1.25	.35
❑ 228 Joe Burns RC	1.50	.45
❑ 229 Wesly Mallard RC	1.25	.35
❑ 230 Chris Cash RC	1.25	.35
❑ 231 David Givens RC	5.00	1.50
❑ 232 John Owens RC	1.25	.35
❑ 233 Jarrett Ferguson RC	1.25	.35
❑ 234 Randy McMichael RC	2.50	.75
❑ 235 Chris Baker RC	1.25	.35
❑ 236 Rashad Bauman RC	1.25	.35
❑ 237 Matt Murphy RC	1.25	.35
❑ 238 LaVar Glover RC	.75	.23
❑ 239 Steve Bellisari RC	1.50	.45
❑ 240 Chad Williams RC	1.25	.35
❑ 241 Kevin Thomas RC	1.50	.45
❑ 242 Carlos Hall RC	1.50	.45
❑ 243 Nick Greisen RC	.75	.23
❑ 244 Justin Bannan RC	1.25	.35
❑ 245 Charles Hill RC	.75	.23
❑ 246 Mark Anelli RC	.75	.23
❑ 247 Coy Wire RC	1.50	.45
❑ 248 Darnell Sanders RC	1.25	.35
❑ 249 Larry Foote RC	1.50	.45
❑ 250 David Carr RC	5.00	1.50
❑ 251 Ricky Williams RC	1.25	.35
❑ 252 Napoleon Harris RC	1.50	.45
❑ 253 Ennis Haywood RC	1.25	.35
❑ 254 Keyuo Craver RC	1.25	.35
❑ 255 Kahlil Hill RC	1.25	.35
❑ 256 J.T. O'Sullivan RC	1.25	.35
❑ 257 Woody Dantzler RC	1.50	.45
❑ 258 Phillip Buchanon RC	1.50	.45
❑ 259 Charles Grant RC	1.50	.45
❑ 260 Dusty Bonner RC	.75	.23
❑ 261 James Allen RC	.75	.23
❑ 262 Ronald Curry RC	1.50	.45
❑ 263 Deion Branch RC	3.00	.90
❑ 264 Larry Ned RC	1.25	.35
❑ 265 Mel Mitchell RC	1.25	.35
❑ 266 Kendall Newson RC	.75	.23
❑ 267 Shaun Hill RC	1.50	.45
❑ 268 David Pugh RC	.75	.23
❑ 269 Dante Wesley RC	.75	.23
❑ 270 Josh Mallard RC	.75	.23
❑ 271 Akin Ayodele RC	.75	.23
❑ 272 Pete Hunter RC	1.25	.35
❑ 273 Kevin McCadam RC	1.25	.35
❑ 274 Jeff Kelly RC	1.25	.35
❑ 275 John Henderson RC	1.50	.45

2003 Bowman

	MINT	NRMT
COMPLETE SET (273)	60.00	27.00
❑ 1 Brett Favre	2.00	.90
❑ 2 Jeremy Shockey	1.25	.55
❑ 3 Fred Taylor	.75	.35
❑ 4 Rich Gannon	.50	.23
❑ 5 Joey Galloway	.50	.23
❑ 6 Ray Lewis	.75	.35
❑ 7 Jeff Blake	.30	.14
❑ 8 Stacey Mack	.30	.14
❑ 9 Matt Hasselbeck	.50	.23
❑ 10 Laveranues Coles	.50	.23
❑ 11 Brad Johnson	.50	.23
❑ 12 Tommy Maddox	.75	.35
❑ 13 Curtis Martin	.75	.35
❑ 14 Tom Brady	1.25	.55
❑ 15 Ricky Williams	.75	.35
❑ 16 Stephen Davis	.50	.23
❑ 17 Chad Johnson	.50	.23
❑ 18 Joey Harrington	1.25	.55
❑ 19 Tony Gonzalez	.50	.23
❑ 20 Peerless Price	.50	.23
❑ 21 LaDainian Tomlinson	.75	.35
❑ 22 James Thrash	.30	.14
❑ 23 Charlie Garner	.50	.23
❑ 24 Eddie George	.50	.23
❑ 25 Terrell Owens	.75	.35

❑ 26 Brian Urlacher	1.25	.55
❑ 27 Eric Moulds	.50	.23
❑ 28 Emmitt Smith	2.00	.90
❑ 29 Tim Couch	.30	.14
❑ 30 Jake Plummer	.50	.23
❑ 31 Marvin Harrison	.75	.35
❑ 32 Chris Chambers	.75	.35
❑ 33 Tiki Barber	.50	.23
❑ 34 Kurt Warner	.75	.35
❑ 35 Michael Pittman	.30	.14
❑ 36 Kevin Dyson	.50	.23
❑ 37 Clinton Portis	1.25	.55
❑ 38 Peyton Manning	1.25	.55
❑ 39 Travis Taylor	.50	.23
❑ 40 Jeff Garcia	.75	.35
❑ 41 Patrick Ramsey	.75	.35
❑ 42 Shaun Alexander	.75	.35
❑ 43 Joe Horn	.50	.23
❑ 44 Daunte Culpepper	.75	.35
❑ 45 Travis Henry	.50	.23
❑ 46 Brian Finneran	.30	.14
❑ 47 William Green	.50	.23
❑ 48 Kordell Stewart	.50	.23
❑ 49 Reggie Wayne	.50	.23
❑ 50 Priest Holmes	1.00	.45
❑ 51 Jay Fiedler	.50	.23
❑ 52 Corey Dillon	.50	.23
❑ 53 Jamal Lewis	.75	.35
❑ 54 Mark Brunell	.50	.23
❑ 55 Santana Moss	.50	.23
❑ 56 Duce Staley	.50	.23
❑ 57 Torry Holt	.75	.35
❑ 58 Rod Gardner	.50	.23
❑ 59 Kerry Collins	.50	.23
❑ 60 Randy Moss	1.25	.55
❑ 61 Jerry Porter	.50	.23
❑ 62 Plaxico Burress	.50	.23
❑ 63 Steve McNair	.75	.35
❑ 64 Muhsin Muhammad	.50	.23
❑ 65 Drew Bledsoe	.75	.35
❑ 66 T.J. Duckett	.50	.23
❑ 67 Ahman Green	.75	.35
❑ 68 Rod Smith	.50	.23
❑ 69 Jimmy Smith	.50	.23
❑ 70 Trent Green	.50	.23
❑ 71 Tim Brown	.75	.35
❑ 72 Jerome Bettis	.75	.35
❑ 73 Isaac Bruce	.75	.35
❑ 74 Derrick Mason	.50	.23
❑ 75 Donovan McNabb	1.00	.45
❑ 76 Deuce McAllister	.75	.35
❑ 77 Zach Thomas	.75	.35
❑ 78 Garrison Hearst	.50	.23
❑ 79 Koren Robinson	.50	.23
❑ 80 Marshall Faulk	.75	.35
❑ 81 Keyshawn Johnson	.75	.35
❑ 82 Jake Delhomme	.75	.35
❑ 83 Marty Booker	.50	.23
❑ 84 James Stewart	.50	.23
❑ 85 Corey Bradford	.30	.14
❑ 86 Derrius Thompson	.30	.14
❑ 87 Edgerrin James	.75	.35
❑ 88 Darrell Jackson	.50	.23
❑ 89 Hines Ward	.75	.35
❑ 90 David Boston	.50	.23
❑ 91 Curtis Conway	.50	.23
❑ 92 David Patten	.30	.14
❑ 93 Michael Bennett	.50	.23
❑ 94 Todd Pinkston	.50	.23
❑ 95 Jerry Rice	1.50	.70
❑ 96 Jon Kitna	.50	.23
❑ 97 Ed McCaffrey	.75	.35
❑ 98 Donald Driver	.50	.23
❑ 99 Anthony Thomas	.75	.35
❑ 100 Michael Vick	2.00	.90
❑ 101 Terry Glenn	.30	.14
❑ 102 Quincy Morgan	.50	.23
❑ 103 David Carr	1.25	.55
❑ 104 Troy Brown	.50	.23
❑ 105 Aaron Brooks	.75	.35
❑ 106 Amani Toomer	.50	.23
❑ 107 Drew Brees	.75	.35
❑ 108 Chad Hutchinson	.50	.23
❑ 109 Warrick Dunn	.50	.23

❑ 110 Chad Pennington	1.00	.45
❑ 111 Carson Palmer RC	5.00	2.20
❑ 112 Brian St.Pierre RC	1.50	.70
❑ 113 Keenan Howry RC	1.50	.70
❑ 114 Sultan McCullough RC	1.25	.55
❑ 115 Terence Newman RC	3.00	1.35
❑ 116 Kelley Washington RC	1.50	.70
❑ 117 Musa Smith RC	1.50	.70
❑ 118 Kevin Williams RC	1.50	.70
❑ 119 Jordan Gross RC	1.25	.55
❑ 120 Lance Briggs RC	1.50	.70
❑ 121 Victor Hobson RC	1.50	.70
❑ 122 Bryant Johnson RC	1.50	.70
❑ 123 Travis Anglin RC	.75	.35
❑ 124 Artose Pinner RC	1.50	.70
❑ 125 Willis McGahee RC	4.00	1.80
❑ 126 Rashean Mathis RC	1.25	.55
❑ 127 B.J. Askew RC	1.50	.70
❑ 128 DeWayne White RC	1.25	.55
❑ 129 Kevin Curtis RC	1.50	.70
❑ 130 Tyrone Calico RC	2.00	.90
❑ 131 Julian Battle RC	1.25	.55
❑ 132 Ricky Manning RC	1.50	.70
❑ 133 Cory Redding RC	1.25	.55
❑ 134 Michael Haynes RC	1.50	.70
❑ 135 Dallas Clark RC	1.50	.70
❑ 136 Shaun McDonald RC	1.50	.70
❑ 137 Marcus Trufant RC	1.50	.70
❑ 138 Kareem Kelly RC	1.25	.55
❑ 139 Sam Aiken RC	1.25	.55
❑ 140 Terrell Suggs RC	2.50	1.10
❑ 141 Gibran Hamdan RC	.75	.35
❑ 142 Bobby Wade RC	1.50	.70
❑ 143 Aaron Walker RC	1.25	.55
❑ 144 Calvin Pace RC	1.25	.55
❑ 145 Quentin Griffin RC	4.00	1.80
❑ 146 Ken Dorsey RC	2.50	1.10
❑ 147 Jerome McDougle RC	1.50	.70
❑ 148 Earnest Graham RC	1.25	.55
❑ 149 Rashad Moore RC	1.25	.55
❑ 150 Charles Rogers RC	2.00	.90
❑ 151 Cecil Sapp RC	1.25	.55
❑ 152 Cato June RC	1.25	.55
❑ 153 Ahmaad Galloway RC	1.25	.55
❑ 154 William Joseph RC	1.50	.70
❑ 155 Anquan Boldin RC	4.00	1.80
❑ 156 L.J. Smith RC	1.50	.70
❑ 157 Antwoine Sanders RC	.75	.35
❑ 158 Justin Griffith RC	1.25	.55
❑ 159 Kevin Garrett RC	.75	.35
❑ 160 Teyo Johnson RC	1.50	.70
❑ 161 Chris Crocker RC	1.50	.70
❑ 162 Brad Banks RC	1.25	.55
❑ 163 Justin Gage RC	1.50	.70
❑ 164 Doug Gabriel RC	1.50	.70
❑ 165 Terry Pierce RC	1.25	.55
❑ 166 Bradie James RC	1.50	.70
❑ 167 Bennie Joppru RC	1.50	.70
❑ 168 Malaefou Mackenzie RC	.75	.35
❑ 169 Terrence Edwards RC	1.25	.55
❑ 170 E.J. Henderson RC	1.50	.70
❑ 171 Tony Romo RC	1.50	.70
❑ 172 DeWayne Robertson RC	1.50	.70
❑ 173 Dwone Hicks RC	.75	.35
❑ 174 Carl Ford RC	.75	.35
❑ 175 Byron Leftwich RC	6.00	2.70
❑ 176 Ken Hamlin RC	1.50	.70
❑ 177 Domanick Davis RC	3.00	1.35
❑ 178 Adrian Madise RC	1.25	.55
❑ 179 Siddeeq Shabazz RC	.75	.35
❑ 180 Dave Ragone RC	1.50	.70
❑ 181 Mike Seidman RC	.75	.35
❑ 182 Brooks Bollinger RC	1.50	.70
❑ 183 DeAndrew Rubin RC	.75	.35
❑ 184 Mike Pinkard RC	.75	.35
❑ 185 Nate Burleson RC	2.50	1.10
❑ 186 LaBrandon Toefield RC	1.50	.70
❑ 187 Angelo Crowell RC	1.25	.55
❑ 188 J.R. Tolver RC	1.25	.55
❑ 189 Osi Umenyiora RC	1.50	.70
❑ 190 Larry Johnson RC	2.50	1.10
❑ 191 Nick Barnett RC	2.50	1.10
❑ 192 Brandon Drumm RC	.75	.35
❑ 193 Rien Long RC	.75	.35

❑ 194 Zuriel Smith RC	.75	.35
❑ 195 Onterrio Smith RC	2.00	.90
❑ 196 Ronald Bellamy RC	1.25	.55
❑ 197 Kenny Peterson RC	1.25	.55
❑ 198 Charles Tillman RC	2.50	1.10
❑ 199 Chaun Thompson RC	.75	.35
❑ 200 Andre Johnson RC	5.00	2.20
❑ 201 Gerald Hayes RC	.75	.35
❑ 202 Terrence Holt RC	1.25	.55
❑ 203 Ovie Mughelli RC	.75	.35
❑ 204 Talman Gardner RC	1.50	.70
❑ 205 Bethel Johnson RC	2.50	1.10
❑ 206 Avon Cobourne RC	.75	.35
❑ 207 Brandon Lloyd RC	2.00	.90
❑ 208 Andre Woolfolk RC	1.50	.70
❑ 209 George Wrighster RC	1.25	.55
❑ 210 Justin Fargas RC	1.50	.70
❑ 211 Jimmy Kennedy RC	1.50	.70
❑ 212 Arnaz Battle RC	1.50	.70
❑ 213 Marquel Blackwell RC	.75	.35
❑ 214 Walter Young RC	.75	.35
❑ 215 Kliff Kingsbury RC	1.25	.55
❑ 216 Kawika Mitchell RC	1.50	.70
❑ 217 Drayton Florence RC	.75	.35
❑ 218 Jeremi Johnson RC	1.25	.55
❑ 219 Billy McMullen RC	1.25	.55
❑ 220 Lee Suggs RC	3.00	1.35
❑ 221 David Kircus RC	1.25	.55
❑ 222 Rod Babers RC	1.25	.55
❑ 223 Jon Olinger RC	.75	.35
❑ 224 Ty Warren RC	1.50	.70
❑ 225 Kyle Boller RC	4.00	1.80
❑ 226 Danny Curley RC	.75	.35
❑ 227 Andrew Pinnock RC	1.25	.55
❑ 228 Kirk Farmer RC	.75	.35
❑ 229 Tully Banta-Cain RC	1.25	.55
❑ 230 Alonzo Jackson RC	1.25	.55
❑ 231 Anthony Adams RC	1.25	.55
❑ 232 Trent Smith RC	1.50	.70
❑ 233 Seneca Wallace RC	1.50	.70
❑ 234 Shane Walton RC	.75	.35
❑ 235 Chris Brown RC	3.00	1.35
❑ 236 Dahrran Diedrick RC	1.50	.70
❑ 237 Juston Wood RC	.75	.35
❑ 238 Mike Doss RC	1.50	.70
❑ 239 Visanthe Shiancoe RC	1.25	.55
❑ 240 Rex Grossman RC	4.00	1.80
❑ 241 David Young RC	.75	.35
❑ 242 Jimmy Wilkerson RC	1.25	.55
❑ 243 Jason Witten RC	2.50	1.10
❑ 244 Dennis Weathersby RC	.75	.35
❑ 245 Taylor Jacobs RC	1.50	.70
❑ 246 Chris Davis RC	1.25	.55
❑ 247 LaTarence Dunbar RC	1.25	.55
❑ 248 Eugene Wilson RC	1.25	.55
❑ 249 Ryan Hoag RC	.75	.35
❑ 250 Chris Simms RC	3.00	1.35
❑ 251 Ivan Taylor RC	.75	.35
❑ 252 Brock Forsey RC	1.50	.70
❑ 253 Curt Anes RC	.75	.35
❑ 254 Taco Wallace RC	1.25	.55
❑ 255 Johnathan Sullivan RC	1.25	.55
❑ 256 David Tyree RC	1.25	.55
❑ 257 Troy Polamalu RC	1.50	.70
❑ 258 Nate Hybl RC	1.50	.70
❑ 259 Spencer Nead RC	1.25	.55
❑ 260 Boss Bailey RC	2.00	.90
❑ 261 LaMarcus McDonald RC	.75	.35
❑ 262 Casey Moore RC	1.25	.55
❑ 263 Pisa Tinoisamoa RC	2.50	1.10
❑ 264 Willie Ponder RC	.75	.35
❑ 265 Donald Lee RC	1.25	.55
❑ 266 Nnamdi Asomugha RC	1.25	.55
❑ 267 Sammy Davis RC	1.50	.70
❑ 268 Joffrey Reynolds RC	.75	.35
❑ 269 Eddie Moore RC	1.25	.55
❑ 270 Tony Hollings RC	1.50	.70
❑ 271 Nick Maddox RC	.75	.35
❑ 272 Kevin Walter RC	1.25	.55
❑ 273 Dan Klecko RC	1.50	.70
❑ 274 Antwan Peek RC	1.25	.55
❑ 275 Tyler Brayton RC	1.50	.70

2004 Bowman

		Nm-Mt	Ex-Mt
COMPLETE SET (275)		60.00	18.00
❑ 1	Brett Favre	2.00	.60
❑ 2	Jay Fiedler	.30	.09
❑ 3	Andre Davis	.30	.09
❑ 4	Travis Henry	.50	.15
❑ 5	Jimmy Smith	.50	.15
❑ 6	Santana Moss	.50	.15
❑ 7	Correll Buckhalter	.50	.15
❑ 8	Randy Moss	1.00	.30
❑ 9	Edgerrin James	.75	.23
❑ 10	Marc Bulger	.75	.23
❑ 11	Derrick Mason	.50	.15
❑ 12	Mark Brunell	.50	.15
❑ 13	Donte' Stallworth	.50	.15
❑ 14	Deion Branch	.75	.23
❑ 15	Jake Plummer	.50	.15
❑ 16	Steve Smith	.50	.15
❑ 17	Jon Kitna	.50	.15
❑ 18	Andre Johnson	.75	.23
❑ 19	A.J. Feeley	.75	.23
❑ 20	Drew Bledsoe	.75	.23
❑ 21	Antonio Bryant	.50	.15
❑ 22	Reggie Wayne	.50	.15
❑ 23	Thomas Jones	.50	.15
❑ 24	Alge Crumpler	.50	.15
❑ 25	Anquan Boldin	.75	.23
❑ 26	Tim Rattay	.50	.15
❑ 27	Charlie Garner	.50	.15
❑ 28	James Thrash	.30	.09
❑ 29	Koren Robinson	.50	.15
❑ 30	Terrell Owens	.75	.23
❑ 31	Amani Toomer	.50	.15
❑ 32	Kelly Campbell	.30	.09
❑ 33	Patrick Ramsey	.50	.15
❑ 34	Plaxico Burress	.50	.15
❑ 35	Chad Pennington	1.00	.30
❑ 36	Fred Taylor	.50	.15
❑ 37	Domanick Davis	.75	.23
❑ 38	DeShaun Foster	.50	.15
❑ 39	T.J. Duckett	.50	.15
❑ 40	Ahman Green	.75	.23
❑ 41	Lee Suggs	.75	.23
❑ 42	Tony Gonzalez	.50	.15
❑ 43	Rich Gannon	.50	.15
❑ 44	Kevan Barlow	.50	.15
❑ 45	Torry Holt	.75	.23
❑ 46	Aaron Brooks	.50	.15
❑ 47	Tyrone Calico	.50	.15
❑ 48	Keenan McCardell	.30	.09
❑ 49	Hines Ward	.75	.23
❑ 50	LaDainian Tomlinson	.75	.23
❑ 51	Dante Hall	.75	.23
❑ 52	Marcus Pollard	.30	.09
❑ 53	Corey Dillon	.50	.15
❑ 54	Justin McCareins	.30	.09
❑ 55	Stephen Davis	.50	.15
❑ 56	Jeff Garcia	.75	.23
❑ 57	Ashley Lelie	.50	.15
❑ 58	Javon Walker	.50	.15
❑ 59	Kyle Boller	.75	.23
❑ 60	Chad Johnson	.50	.15
❑ 61	Anthony Thomas	.50	.15
❑ 62	Byron Leftwich	1.25	.35
❑ 63	David Boston	.50	.15
❑ 64	Onterrio Smith	.50	.15
❑ 65	Deuce McAllister	.75	.23
❑ 66	Antwaan Randle El	.50	.15
❑ 67	Justin Fargas	.50	.15
❑ 68	Laveranues Coles	.50	.15
❑ 69	Quincy Morgan	.50	.15
❑ 70	Priest Holmes	1.00	.30
❑ 71	Robert Ferguson	.30	.09
❑ 72	Charles Rogers	.50	.15
❑ 73	Drew Brees	.75	.23
❑ 74	Matt Hasselbeck	.50	.15
❑ 75	Peyton Manning	1.25	.35
❑ 76	Rudi Johnson	.50	.15
❑ 77	Jake Delhomme	.75	.23
❑ 78	Tiki Barber	.50	.15
❑ 79	Brad Johnson	.50	.15
❑ 80	Steve McNair	.75	.23
❑ 81	Willis McGahee	.75	.23
❑ 82	Josh McCown	.50	.15
❑ 83	Garrison Hearst	.50	.15
❑ 84	Quincy Carter	.50	.15
❑ 85	Ricky Williams	.75	.23
❑ 86	Trent Green	.50	.15
❑ 87	Curtis Martin	.75	.23
❑ 88	Jerry Porter	.50	.15
❑ 89	Brian Westbrook	.50	.15
❑ 90	Clinton Portis	.75	.23
❑ 91	Eric Moulds	.50	.15
❑ 92	Marcel Shipp	.50	.15
❑ 93	Joey Harrington	.75	.23
❑ 94	David Carr	.75	.23
❑ 95	Marvin Harrison	.75	.23
❑ 96	Joe Horn	.50	.15
❑ 97	Chris Chambers	.50	.15
❑ 98	Darrell Jackson	.50	.15
❑ 99	Eddie George	.50	.15
❑ 100	Donovan McNabb	1.00	.30
❑ 101	Marshall Faulk	.75	.23
❑ 102	Rex Grossman	.75	.23
❑ 103	Tai Streets	.30	.09
❑ 104	Jeremy Shockey	.75	.23
❑ 105	Jamal Lewis	.75	.23
❑ 106	Tom Brady	1.25	.35
❑ 107	Shaun Alexander	.75	.23
❑ 108	Carson Palmer	1.00	.30
❑ 109	Daunte Culpepper	.75	.23
❑ 110	Michael Vick	1.50	.45
❑ 111	Eli Manning RC	8.00	2.40
❑ 112	Kevin Jones RC	5.00	1.50
❑ 113	Philip Rivers RC	5.00	1.50
❑ 114	Ben Roethlisberger RC	15.00	4.50
❑ 115	Roy Williams RC	5.00	1.50
❑ 116	Tommie Harris RC	2.00	.60
❑ 117	Vontez Duff RC	1.25	.35
❑ 118	Karlos Dansby RC	1.50	.45
❑ 119	Thomas Tapeh RC	1.25	.35
❑ 120	Matt Schaub RC	2.50	.75
❑ 121	Dexter Reid RC	.75	.23
❑ 122	Jonathan Smith RC	1.25	.35
❑ 123	Ricardo Colclough RC	1.50	.45
❑ 124	Jeff Dugan RC	.75	.23
❑ 125	Larry Fitzgerald RC	5.00	1.50
❑ 126	Gibril Wilson RC	1.50	.45
❑ 127	Sean Taylor RC	2.00	.60
❑ 128	Marquise Hill RC	1.25	.35
❑ 129	Ernest Wilford RC	1.50	.45
❑ 130	Cedric Cobbs RC	1.50	.45
❑ 131	Rich Gardner RC	1.25	.35
❑ 132	Chris Cooley RC	1.50	.45
❑ 133	Kenechi Udeze RC	1.50	.45
❑ 134	John Navarre RC	1.50	.45
❑ 135	Ben Troupe RC	1.50	.45
❑ 136	Dave Ball RC	.75	.23
❑ 137	Antwan Odom RC	1.50	.45
❑ 138	Stuart Schweigert RC	1.50	.45
❑ 139	Derek Abney RC	1.50	.45
❑ 140	Keary Colbert RC	2.00	.60
❑ 141	Jeris McIntyre RC	1.25	.35
❑ 142	Matt Kranchick RC	1.50	.45
❑ 143	Rodney Leisle RC	.75	.23
❑ 144	Vince Wilfork RC	2.00	.60
❑ 145	Lee Evans RC	2.50	.75
❑ 146	Darnell Dockett RC	1.25	.35
❑ 147	Jeremy LeSueur RC	1.25	.35
❑ 148	Gilbert Gardner RC	1.25	.35
❑ 149	Amon Gordon RC	.75	.23
❑ 150	Darius Watts RC	2.00	.60
❑ 151	Junior Siavii RC	1.50	.45
❑ 152	Igor Olshansky RC	1.50	.45
❑ 153	Courtney Watson RC	1.50	.45
❑ 154	D.J. Williams RC	2.00	.60
❑ 155	Mewelde Moore RC	2.00	.60
❑ 156	Teddy Lehman RC	1.50	.45
❑ 157	Nathan Vasher RC	1.50	.45
❑ 158	Randy Starks RC	1.25	.35
❑ 159	Isaac Sopoaga RC	.75	.23
❑ 160	Drew Henson RC	4.00	1.20
❑ 161	Erik Coleman RC	1.50	.45
❑ 162	Robert Kent RC	.75	.23
❑ 163	Jammal Lord RC	1.50	.45
❑ 164	Richard Seigler RC	1.25	.35
❑ 165	Jeff Smoker RC	2.50	.75
❑ 166	Niko Koutouvides RC	1.25	.35
❑ 167	Adimchinobe Echemandu RC	1.25	.35
❑ 168	Matt Mauck RC	1.50	.45
❑ 169	Brandon Miree RC	1.25	.35
❑ 170	Dunta Robinson RC	1.50	.45
❑ 171	B.J. Symons RC	1.50	.45
❑ 172	Courtney Anderson RC	1.25	.35
❑ 173	Bruce Perry RC	1.25	.35
❑ 174	Shaun Phillips RC	1.25	.35
❑ 175	Greg Jones RC	1.50	.45
❑ 176	Ryan Krause RC	1.25	.35
❑ 177	Charlie Anderson RC	.75	.23
❑ 178	Tank Johnson RC	1.25	.35
❑ 179	Dwan Edwards RC	.75	.23
❑ 180	Julius Jones RC	6.00	1.80
❑ 181	Chad Lavalais RC	1.25	.35
❑ 182	Tim Anderson RC	1.50	.45
❑ 183	Jarrett Payton RC	1.50	.45
❑ 184	Matt Ware RC	1.50	.45
❑ 185	DeAngelo Hall RC	2.00	.60
❑ 186	Ben Hartsock RC	1.50	.45
❑ 187	Bradlee Van Pelt RC	1.50	.45
❑ 188	Michael Boulware RC	1.50	.45
❑ 189	Keith Smith RC	1.25	.35
❑ 190	Michael Jenkins RC	1.50	.45
❑ 191	Quincy Wilson RC	1.25	.35
❑ 192	Dontarrious Thomas RC	1.50	.45
❑ 193	Sloan Thomas RC	1.25	.35
❑ 194	Tony Hargrove RC	1.25	.35
❑ 195	Ben Watson RC	1.50	.45
❑ 196	Craig Krenzel RC	1.50	.45
❑ 197	Jason Babin RC	1.50	.45
❑ 198	Jim Sorgi RC	1.50	.45
❑ 199	Triandos Luke RC	1.50	.45
❑ 200	Kellen Winslow RC	4.00	1.20
❑ 201	Patrick Crayton RC	1.50	.45
❑ 202	Michael Waddell RC	.75	.23
❑ 203	Chris Gamble RC	2.00	.60
❑ 204	Josh Harris RC	1.50	.45
❑ 205	Devard Darling RC	1.50	.45
❑ 206	Shawntae Spencer RC	1.50	.45
❑ 207	Will Smith RC	1.50	.45
❑ 208	Samie Parker RC	1.50	.45
❑ 209	Darrion Scott RC	1.50	.45
❑ 210	Chris Perry RC	3.00	.90
❑ 211	P.K. Sam RC	1.25	.35
❑ 212	Wes Welker RC	1.50	.45
❑ 213	Ryan Dinwiddie RC	1.25	.35
❑ 214	Rod Davis RC	.75	.23
❑ 215	Casey Clausen RC	2.00	.60
❑ 216	Clarence Moore RC	1.50	.45
❑ 217	D.J. Hackett RC	1.25	.35
❑ 218	Casey Bramlet RC	1.25	.35
❑ 219	Jared Lorenzen RC	1.25	.35
❑ 220	Devery Henderson RC	1.25	.35
❑ 221	Sean Jones RC	1.25	.35
❑ 222	Maurice Mann RC	1.25	.35
❑ 223	Jared Allen RC	1.50	.45
❑ 224	Bruce Thornton RC	.75	.23
❑ 225	Tatum Bell RC	2.50	.75
❑ 226	Leon Joe RC	.75	.23
❑ 227	Tim Euhus RC	1.50	.45
❑ 228	John Standeford RC	1.25	.35
❑ 229	Reggie Torbor RC	1.25	.35
❑ 230	Rashaun Woods RC	2.00	.60
❑ 231	Jason Shivers RC	.75	.23
❑ 232	Jason Peters RC	1.50	.45

❑ 233 Ahmad Carroll RC	2.00	.60
❑ 234 Jason David RC	1.50	.45
❑ 235 Keyaron Fox RC	1.25	.35
❑ 236 Corey Williams RC	.75	.23
❑ 237 Raheem Orr RC	.75	.23
❑ 238 Carlos Francis RC	1.25	.35
❑ 239 Von Hutchins RC	1.25	.35
❑ 240 Marcus Tubbs RC	1.50	.45
❑ 241 Daryl Smith RC	1.50	.45
❑ 242 Robert Gallery RC	2.50	.75
❑ 243 Sean Tufts RC	1.25	.35
❑ 244 Marquis Cooper RC	1.25	.35
❑ 245 Bernard Berrian RC	1.50	.45
❑ 246 Derrick Strait RC	1.50	.45
❑ 247 Travis LaBoy RC	1.50	.45
❑ 248 Johnnie Morant RC	1.50	.45
❑ 249 Caleb Miller RC	1.25	.35
❑ 250 Michael Clayton RC	4.00	1.20
❑ 251 Will Poole RC	1.50	.45
❑ 252 Andy Hall RC	1.25	.35
❑ 253 Demorrio Williams RC	1.50	.45
❑ 254 Chris Thompson RC	.75	.23
❑ 255 Derrick Hamilton RC	1.25	.35
❑ 256 Glenn Earl RC	1.25	.35
❑ 257 Jonathan Vilma RC	1.50	.45
❑ 258 Donnell Washington RC	1.50	.45
❑ 259 Drew Carter RC	1.50	.45
❑ 260 Steven Jackson RC	5.00	1.50
❑ 261 Jamaar Taylor RC	1.50	.45
❑ 262 Nate Lawrie RC	1.25	.35
❑ 263 Cody Pickett RC	1.50	.45
❑ 264 Keiwan Ratliff RC	1.25	.35
❑ 265 Luke McCown RC	1.50	.45
❑ 266 Jerricho Cotchery RC	1.50	.45
❑ 267 Joey Thomas RC	1.50	.45
❑ 268 Shawn Andrews RC	1.50	.45
❑ 269 Derrick Ward RC	.75	.23
❑ 270 Reggie Williams RC	2.00	.60
❑ 271 Rod Rutherford RC	1.25	.35
❑ 272 Michael Turner RC	1.25	.35
❑ 273 Michael Gaines RC	1.25	.35
❑ 274 Will Allen RC	1.50	.45
❑ 275 J.P. Losman RC	4.00	1.20

1998 Bowman Chrome

	Nm-Mt	Ex-Mt
COMPLETE SET (220)	100.00	45.00
❑ 1 Peyton Manning RC	40.00	18.00
❑ 2 Keith Brooking RC	4.00	1.80
❑ 3 Duane Starks RC	2.00	.90
❑ 4 Takeo Spikes RC	4.00	1.80
❑ 5 Andre Wadsworth RC	3.00	1.35
❑ 6 Greg Ellis RC	2.00	.90
❑ 7 Brian Griese RC	8.00	3.60
❑ 8 Germane Crowell RC	3.00	1.35
❑ 9 Jerome Pathon RC	4.00	1.80
❑ 10 Ryan Leaf RC	4.00	1.80
❑ 11 Fred Taylor RC	6.00	2.70
❑ 12 Robert Edwards RC	3.00	1.35
❑ 13 Grant Wistrom RC	3.00	1.35
❑ 14 Robert Holcombe RC	3.00	1.35
❑ 15 Tim Dwight RC	4.00	1.80
❑ 16 Jacquez Green RC	3.00	1.35
❑ 17 Marcus Nash RC	2.00	.90
❑ 18 Jason Peter RC	2.00	.90
❑ 19 Anthony Simmons RC	3.00	1.35
❑ 20 Curtis Enis RC	2.00	.90
❑ 21 John Avery RC	3.00	1.35
❑ 22 Pat Johnson RC	3.00	1.35
❑ 23 Joe Jurevicius RC	4.00	1.80
❑ 24 Brian Simmons RC	3.00	1.35
❑ 25 Kevin Dyson RC	4.00	1.80
❑ 26 Skip Hicks RC	3.00	1.35
❑ 27 Hines Ward RC	10.00	4.50
❑ 28 Tavian Banks RC	3.00	1.35
❑ 29 Ahman Green RC	20.00	9.00
❑ 30 Tony Simmons RC	3.00	1.35
❑ 31 Charles Johnson	.50	.23
❑ 32 Freddie Jones	.50	.23
❑ 33 Joey Galloway	.75	.35
❑ 34 Tony Banks	.75	.35
❑ 35 Jake Plummer	1.25	.55
❑ 36 Reidel Anthony	.75	.35
❑ 37 Steve McNair	1.25	.55
❑ 38 Michael Westbrook	.75	.35
❑ 39 Chris Sanders	.50	.23
❑ 40 Isaac Bruce	.50	.23
❑ 41 Charlie Garner	.75	.35
❑ 42 Wayne Chrebet	1.25	.55
❑ 43 Michael Strahan	.75	.35
❑ 44 Brad Johnson	1.25	.55
❑ 45 Mike Alstott	.50	.23
❑ 46 Tony Gonzalez	1.25	.55
❑ 47 Johnnie Morton	.75	.35
❑ 48 Darnay Scott	.75	.35
❑ 49 Rae Carruth	.50	.23
❑ 50 Terrell Davis	1.25	.55
❑ 51 Jermaine Lewis	.75	.35
❑ 52 Frank Sanders	.75	.35
❑ 53 Byron Hanspard	.50	.23
❑ 54 Gus Frerotte	.50	.23
❑ 55 Terry Glenn	1.25	.55
❑ 56 J.J. Stokes	.75	.35
❑ 57 Will Blackwell	.50	.23
❑ 58 Keyshawn Johnson	1.25	.55
❑ 59 Tiki Barber	1.25	.55
❑ 60 Dorsey Levens	1.25	.55
❑ 61 Zach Thomas	1.25	.55
❑ 62 Corey Dillon	1.25	.55
❑ 63 Antowain Smith	1.25	.55
❑ 64 Michael Sinclair	.50	.23
❑ 65 Rod Smith	.75	.35
❑ 66 Trent Dilfer	1.25	.55
❑ 67 Warren Sapp	.75	.35
❑ 68 Charles Way	.50	.23
❑ 69 Tamarick Vanover	.50	.23
❑ 70 Drew Bledsoe	2.00	.90
❑ 71 John Mobley	.50	.23
❑ 72 Kerry Collins	.75	.35
❑ 73 Peter Boulware	.50	.23
❑ 74 Simeon Rice	.75	.35
❑ 75 Eddie George	1.25	.55
❑ 76 Fred Lane	.50	.23
❑ 77 Jamal Anderson	1.25	.55
❑ 78 Antonio Freeman	1.25	.55
❑ 79 Jason Sehorn	.75	.35
❑ 80 Curtis Martin	1.25	.55
❑ 81 Bobby Hoying	.75	.35
❑ 82 Garrison Hearst	1.25	.55
❑ 83 Glenn Foley	.75	.35
❑ 84 Danny Kanell	.75	.35
❑ 85 Kordell Stewart	1.25	.55
❑ 86 O.J. McDuffie	.75	.35
❑ 87 Marvin Harrison	1.25	.55
❑ 88 Bobby Engram	.75	.35
❑ 89 Chris Slade	.50	.23
❑ 90 Warrick Dunn	1.25	.55
❑ 91 Ricky Watters	.75	.35
❑ 92 Rickey Dudley	.50	.23
❑ 93 Terrell Owens	1.25	.55
❑ 94 Karim Abdul-Jabbar	1.25	.55
❑ 95 Napoleon Kaufman	1.25	.55
❑ 96 Darrell Green	.75	.35
❑ 97 Levon Kirkland	.50	.23
❑ 98 Jeff George	.75	.35
❑ 99 Andre Hastings	.50	.23
❑ 100 John Elway	5.00	2.20
❑ 101 John Randle	.75	.35
❑ 102 Andre Rison	.75	.35
❑ 103 Keenan McCardell	.75	.35
❑ 104 Marshall Faulk	1.50	.70
❑ 105 Emmitt Smith	4.00	1.80
❑ 106 Robert Brooks	.75	.35
❑ 107 Scott Mitchell	.75	.35
❑ 108 Shannon Sharpe	.75	.35
❑ 109 Deion Sanders	1.25	.55
❑ 110 Jerry Rice	2.50	1.10
❑ 111 Erik Kramer	.50	.23
❑ 112 Michael Jackson	.50	.23
❑ 113 Aeneas Williams	.50	.23
❑ 114 Terry Allen	1.25	.55
❑ 115 Steve Young	1.50	.70
❑ 116 Warren Moon	1.25	.55
❑ 117 Junior Seau	1.25	.55
❑ 118 Jerome Bettis	1.25	.55
❑ 119 Irving Fryar	.75	.35
❑ 120 Barry Sanders	4.00	1.80
❑ 121 Tim Brown	.50	.23
❑ 122 Chad Brown	.50	.23
❑ 123 Ben Coates	.75	.35
❑ 124 Robert Smith	1.25	.55
❑ 125 Brett Favre	5.00	2.20
❑ 126 Derrick Thomas	.75	.35
❑ 127 Reggie White	1.25	.55
❑ 128 Troy Aikman	2.50	1.10
❑ 129 Jeff Blake	.75	.35
❑ 130 Mark Brunell	1.25	.55
❑ 131 Curtis Conway	.75	.35
❑ 132 Wesley Walls	.75	.35
❑ 133 Thurman Thomas	1.25	.55
❑ 134 Chris Chandler	.75	.35
❑ 135 Dan Marino	5.00	2.20
❑ 136 Larry Centers	.50	.23
❑ 137 Shawn Jefferson	.50	.23
❑ 138 Andre Reed	.75	.35
❑ 139 Jake Reed	.75	.35
❑ 140 Cris Carter	1.25	.55
❑ 141 Elvis Grbac	.75	.35
❑ 142 Mark Chmura	.75	.35
❑ 143 Michael Irvin	1.25	.55
❑ 144 Carl Pickens	.75	.35
❑ 145 Herman Moore	.75	.35
❑ 146 Marvin Jones	.50	.23
❑ 147 Terance Mathis	.75	.35
❑ 148 Rob Moore	.75	.35
❑ 149 Bruce Smith	.75	.35
❑ 150 Rob Johnson CL	.50	.23
❑ 151 Leslie Shepherd	.50	.23
❑ 152 Chris Spielman	.50	.23
❑ 153 Tony McGee	.50	.23
❑ 154 Kevin Smith	.50	.23
❑ 155 Bill Romanowski	.50	.23
❑ 156 Stephen Boyd	.50	.23
❑ 157 James Stewart	.75	.35
❑ 158 Jason Taylor	.75	.35
❑ 159 Troy Drayton	.50	.23
❑ 160 Mark Fields	.50	.23
❑ 161 Jessie Armstead	.50	.23
❑ 162 James Jett	.75	.35
❑ 163 Bobby Taylor	.50	.23
❑ 164 Kimble Anders	.75	.35
❑ 165 Jimmy Smith	.75	.35
❑ 166 Quentin Coryatt	.50	.23
❑ 167 Bryant Westbrook	.50	.23
❑ 168 Neil Smith	.75	.35
❑ 169 Darren Woodson	.50	.23
❑ 170 Ray Buchanan	.50	.23
❑ 171 Earl Holmes	.50	.23
❑ 172 Ray Lewis	1.25	.55
❑ 173 Steve Broussard	.50	.23
❑ 174 Derrick Brooks	1.25	.55
❑ 175 Ken Harvey	.50	.23
❑ 176 Darryll Lewis	.50	.23
❑ 177 Derrick Rodgers	.50	.23
❑ 178 James McKnight	1.25	.55
❑ 179 Cris Dishman	.50	.23
❑ 180 Hardy Nickerson	.50	.23
❑ 181 Charles Woodson RC	5.00	2.20
❑ 182 Randy Moss RC	20.00	9.00
❑ 183 Stephen Alexander RC	3.00	1.35
❑ 184 Samari Rolle RC	2.00	.90
❑ 185 Jamie Duncan RC	2.00	.90
❑ 186 Lance Schulters RC	2.00	.90
❑ 187 Tony Parrish RC	4.00	1.80
❑ 188 Corey Chavous RC	4.00	1.80
❑ 189 Jammi German RC	2.00	.90

❑ 190 Sam Cowart RC	3.00	1.35
❑ 191 Donald Hayes RC	3.00	1.35
❑ 192 R.W. McQuarters RC	3.00	1.35
❑ 193 Az-Zahir Hakim RC	4.00	1.80
❑ 194 C.Fuamatu-Ma'afala RC	3.00	1.35
❑ 195 Allen Rossum RC	2.00	.90
❑ 196 Jon Ritchie RC	3.00	1.35
❑ 197 Blake Spence RC	2.00	.90
❑ 198 Brian Alford RC	2.00	.90
❑ 199 Fred Weary RC	2.00	.90
❑ 200 Rod Rutledge RC	2.00	.90
❑ 201 Michael Myers RC	2.00	.90
❑ 202 Rashaan Shehee RC	3.00	1.35
❑ 203 Donovin Darius RC	3.00	1.35
❑ 204 E.G. Green RC	3.00	1.35
❑ 205 Vonnie Holliday RC	3.00	1.35
❑ 206 Charlie Batch RC	4.00	1.80
❑ 207 Michael Pittman RC	4.00	1.80
❑ 208 Artrell Hawkins RC	2.00	.90
❑ 209 Jonathan Quinn RC	4.00	1.80
❑ 210 Kailee Wong RC	2.00	.90
❑ 211 Deshea Townsend RC	2.00	.90
❑ 212 Patrick Surtain RC	4.00	1.80
❑ 213 Brian Kelly RC	3.00	1.35
❑ 214 Tebucky Jones RC	2.00	.90
❑ 215 Pete Gonzalez RC	2.00	.90
❑ 216 Shaun Williams RC	3.00	1.35
❑ 217 Scott Frost RC	2.00	.90
❑ 218 Leonard Little RC	4.00	1.80
❑ 219 Alonzo Mayes RC	2.00	.90
❑ 220 Cordell Taylor RC	2.00	.90

1998 Bowman Chrome Golden Anniversary

Nm-Mt Ex-Mt

*GOLD.ANN.STARS: 15X TO 40X
*GOLD.ANN.RCs: 2X TO 5X

1998 Bowman Chrome Interstate Refractors

Nm-Mt Ex-Mt

*INTERSTATE REF.STARS: 3X TO 8X BASIC CARDS
*INTERSTATE REF.RCs: 1.5X TO 4X BASIC CARDS

1998 Bowman Chrome Refractors

	Nm-Mt	Ex-Mt
COMPLETE SET (220)	1200.00	550.00

*REFRACTOR STARS: 2X TO 5X BASIC CARDS
*REFRACTOR RCs: 1X TO 2.5X BASIC CARDS

2000 Bowman Chrome

	Nm-Mt	Ex-Mt
❑ 1 Eddie George	1.00	.45
❑ 2 Ike Hilliard	.60	.25
❑ 3 Terrell Owens	1.00	.45
❑ 4 James Stewart	.60	.25
❑ 5 Joey Galloway	.60	.25
❑ 6 Jake Reed	.40	.18
❑ 7 Derrick Alexander	.60	.25
❑ 8 Jeff George	.60	.25
❑ 9 Kerry Collins	.60	.25
❑ 10 Tony Gonzalez	.60	.25
❑ 11 Marcus Robinson	1.00	.45
❑ 12 Charles Woodson	.60	.25
❑ 13 Germane Crowell	.40	.18
❑ 14 Yancey Thigpen	.40	.18
❑ 15 Tony Martin	.40	.18
❑ 16 Frank Sanders	.60	.25
❑ 17 Napoleon Kaufman	.60	.25
❑ 18 Jay Fiedler	1.00	.45
❑ 19 Patrick Jeffers	1.00	.45
❑ 20 Steve McNair	1.00	.45
❑ 21 Herman Moore	.60	.25
❑ 22 Tim Brown	1.00	.45
❑ 23 Olandis Gary	1.00	.45
❑ 24 Corey Dillon	1.00	.45
❑ 25 Warren Sapp	.60	.25
❑ 26 Curtis Enis	.40	.18
❑ 27 Vinny Testaverde	.60	.25
❑ 28 Tim Biakabutuka	.60	.25
❑ 29 Kevin Johnson	1.00	.45
❑ 30 Charlie Batch	1.00	.45
❑ 31 Jermaine Fazande	.60	.25
❑ 32 Shaun King	.40	.18
❑ 33 Errict Rhett	.60	.25
❑ 34 O.J. McDuffie	.60	.25
❑ 35 Bruce Smith	.60	.25
❑ 36 Antonio Freeman	1.00	.45
❑ 37 Tim Couch	.60	.25
❑ 38 Duce Staley	1.00	.45
❑ 39 Jeff Blake	.60	.25
❑ 40 Jim Harbaugh	.60	.25
❑ 41 Jeff Graham	.40	.18
❑ 42 Drew Bledsoe	1.25	.55
❑ 43 Mike Alstott	1.00	.45
❑ 44 Terance Mathis	.60	.25
❑ 45 Antowain Smith	.60	.25
❑ 46 Johnnie Morton	.60	.25
❑ 47 Chris Chandler	.60	.25
❑ 48 Keith Poole	.40	.18
❑ 49 Ricky Watters	.60	.25
❑ 50 Darnay Scott	.40	.18
❑ 51 Damon Huard	.60	.25
❑ 52 Peerless Price	1.00	.45
❑ 53 Brian Griese	1.00	.45
❑ 54 Frank Wycheck	.60	.25
❑ 55 Kevin Dyson	.60	.25
❑ 56 Junior Seau	1.00	.45
❑ 57 Curtis Conway	.60	.25
❑ 58 Jamal Anderson	1.00	.45
❑ 59 Jim Miller	.40	.18
❑ 60 Rob Johnson	.60	.25
❑ 61 Mark Brunell	1.00	.45
❑ 62 Wayne Chrebet	.60	.25
❑ 63 James Johnson	.40	.18
❑ 64 Sean Dawkins	.40	.18
❑ 65 Stephen Davis	1.00	.45
❑ 66 Daunte Culpepper	1.25	.55
❑ 67 Doug Flutie	1.00	.45
❑ 68 Pete Mitchell	.40	.18
❑ 69 Bill Schroeder	.40	.18
❑ 70 Terrence Wilkins	.40	.18
❑ 71 Cade McNown	.40	.18
❑ 72 Muhsin Muhammad	.60	.25
❑ 73 E.G. Green	.40	.18
❑ 74 Edgerrin James	1.50	.70
❑ 75 Troy Edwards	.40	.18
❑ 76 Terry Glenn	.60	.25
❑ 77 Tony Banks	.60	.25
❑ 78 Derrick Mayes	.60	.25
❑ 79 Curtis Martin	1.00	.45
❑ 80 Kordell Stewart	.60	.25
❑ 81 Amani Toomer	.60	.25
❑ 82 Dorsey Levens	.60	.25
❑ 83 Brad Johnson	1.00	.45
❑ 84 Ed McCaffrey	1.00	.45
❑ 85 Charlie Garner	.60	.25
❑ 86 Brett Favre	3.00	1.35
❑ 87 J.J. Stokes	.60	.25
❑ 88 Steve Young	1.25	.55
❑ 89 Jonathan Linton	.40	.18
❑ 90 Isaac Bruce	1.00	.45
❑ 91 Shawn Jefferson	.40	.18
❑ 92 Rod Smith	.60	.25
❑ 93 Champ Bailey	.60	.25
❑ 94 Ricky Williams	1.00	.45
❑ 95 Priest Holmes	1.25	.55
❑ 96 Corey Bradford	.60	.25
❑ 97 Eric Moulds	1.00	.45
❑ 98 Warrick Dunn	1.00	.45
❑ 99 Jevon Kearse	1.00	.45
❑ 100 Albert Connell	.40	.18
❑ 101 Az-Zahir Hakim	.40	.18
❑ 102 Marvin Harrison	1.00	.45
❑ 103 Qadry Ismail	.60	.25
❑ 104 Oronde Gadsden	.60	.25
❑ 105 Rob Moore	.60	.25
❑ 106 Marshall Faulk	1.50	.70
❑ 107 Steve Beuerlein	.60	.25
❑ 108 Torry Holt	1.00	.45
❑ 109 Donovan McNabb	1.50	.70
❑ 110 Rich Gannon	1.00	.45
❑ 111 Jerome Bettis	1.00	.45
❑ 112 Peyton Manning	2.50	1.10
❑ 113 Cris Carter	1.00	.45
❑ 114 Jake Plummer	.60	.25
❑ 115 Kent Graham	.40	.18
❑ 116 Keenan McCardell	.60	.25
❑ 117 Tim Dwight	1.00	.45
❑ 118 Fred Taylor	1.00	.45
❑ 119 Jerry Rice	2.00	.90
❑ 120 Michael Westbrook	.60	.25
❑ 121 Kurt Warner	2.00	.90
❑ 122 Jimmy Smith	.60	.25
❑ 123 Emmitt Smith	2.00	.90
❑ 124 Terrell Davis	1.00	.45
❑ 125 Randy Moss	2.00	.90
❑ 126 Akili Smith	.40	.18
❑ 127 Rocket Ismail	.60	.25
❑ 128 Jon Kitna	1.00	.45
❑ 129 Elvis Grbac	.60	.25
❑ 130 Wesley Walls	.40	.18
❑ 131 Torrance Small	.40	.18
❑ 132 Tyrone Wheatley	.60	.25
❑ 133 Carl Pickens	.40	.18
❑ 134 Zach Thomas	1.00	.45
❑ 135 Jacquez Green	.40	.18
❑ 136 Robert Smith	1.00	.45
❑ 137 Keyshawn Johnson	1.00	.45
❑ 138 Matthew Hatchette	.40	.18
❑ 139 Troy Aikman	2.00	.90
❑ 140 Charles Johnson	.60	.25
❑ 141 Terry Battle EP	1.00	.45
❑ 142 Pepe Pearson EP RC	2.00	.90
❑ 143 Cory Sauter EP	1.00	.45
❑ 144 Brian Shay EP	1.00	.45
❑ 145 Marcus Crandell EP RC	1.50	.70
❑ 146 Danny Wuerffel EP	1.50	.70
❑ 147 L.C. Stevens EP	1.00	.45
❑ 148 Ted White EP	1.00	.45
❑ 149 Matt Lytle EP RC	1.50	.70
❑ 150 Vershan Jackson EP RC	1.00	.45
❑ 151 Mario Bailey EP	1.00	.45
❑ 152 Darryl Daniel EP RC	1.50	.70
❑ 153 Sean Morey EP RC	1.50	.70
❑ 154 Jim Kubiak EP RC	1.50	.70
❑ 155 Aaron Stecker EP RC	2.00	.90
❑ 156 Damon Dunn EP RC	1.50	.70
❑ 157 Kevin Daft EP	1.00	.45
❑ 158 Corey Thomas EP	1.00	.45
❑ 159 Deon Mitchell EP RC	1.50	.70
❑ 160 Todd Floyd EP RC	1.00	.45
❑ 161 Norman Miller EP RC	1.00	.45
❑ 162 Jeremaine Copeland EP	1.00	.45
❑ 163 Michael Blair EP	1.00	.45
❑ 164 Ron Powlus EP RC	2.00	.90
❑ 165 Pat Barnes EP	1.50	.70
❑ 166 Dez White RC	4.00	1.80
❑ 167 Trung Canidate SP RC	25.00	11.00
❑ 168 Thomas Jones SP RC	50.00	22.00
❑ 169 Courtney Brown SP RC	30.00	13.50
❑ 170 Jamal Lewis SP RC	50.00	22.00
❑ 171 Chris Redman SP RC	25.00	11.00
❑ 172 Ron Dayne SP RC	30.00	13.50
❑ 173 Chad Pennington SP RC	80.00	36.00
❑ 174 Plaxico Burress SP RC	60.00	27.00
❑ 175 R.Jay Soward SP RC	25.00	11.00
❑ 176 Travis Taylor SP RC	30.00	13.50
❑ 177 Shaun Alexander SP RC	60.00	27.00
❑ 178 Brian Urlacher RC	20.00	9.00

Card	Nm-Mt	Ex-Mt
❑ 179 Danny Farmer RC	3.00	1.35
❑ 180 Tee Martin SP RC	30.00	13.50
❑ 181 Sylvester Morris SP RC	25.00	11.00
❑ 182 Curtis Keaton RC	3.00	1.35
❑ 183 Peter Warrick SP RC	30.00	13.50
❑ 184 Anthony Becht RC	4.00	1.80
❑ 185 Travis Prentice SP RC	30.00	13.50
❑ 186 J.R. Redmond SP RC	25.00	11.00
❑ 187 Bubba Franks SP RC	30.00	13.50
❑ 188 Ron Dugans SP RC	20.00	9.00
❑ 189 Reuben Droughns RC	5.00	2.20
❑ 190 Corey Simon RC	2.00	.90
❑ 191 Joe Hamilton RC	3.00	1.35
❑ 192 Laveranues Coles RC	5.00	2.20
❑ 193 Todd Pinkston SP RC	30.00	13.50
❑ 194 Jerry Porter SP RC	50.00	22.00
❑ 195 Dennis Northcutt RC	4.00	1.80
❑ 196 Tim Rattay RC	8.00	3.60
❑ 197 Giovanni Carmazzi RC	3.00	1.35
❑ 198 Mareno Philyaw RC	2.00	.90
❑ 199 Avion Black RC	3.00	1.35
❑ 200 Chafie Fields RC	2.00	.90
❑ 201 Rondell Mealey RC	2.00	.90
❑ 202 Troy Walters RC	4.00	1.80
❑ 203 Frank Moreau RC	3.00	1.35
❑ 204 Vaughn Sanders RC	2.00	.90
❑ 205 Sherrod Gideon RC	2.00	.90
❑ 206 Doug Chapman RC	3.00	1.35
❑ 207 Marcus Knight RC	3.00	1.35
❑ 208 Jamel White RC	3.00	1.35
❑ 209 Windrell Hayes RC	3.00	1.35
❑ 210 Reggie Jones RC	2.00	.90
❑ 211 Jarious Jackson RC	3.00	1.35
❑ 212 Ronney Jenkins RC	3.00	1.35
❑ 213 Quinton Spotwood RC	2.00	.90
❑ 214 Rob Morris RC	3.00	1.35
❑ 215 Gari Scott RC	2.00	.90
❑ 216 Kevin Thompson RC	2.00	.90
❑ 217 Trevor Insley RC	2.00	.90
❑ 218 Frank Murphy RC	2.00	.90
❑ 219 Patrick Pass RC	3.00	1.35
❑ 220 Mike Anderson RC	2.00	.90
❑ 221 Derrius Thompson RC	4.00	1.80
❑ 222 John Abraham RC	6.00	2.70
❑ 223 Dante Hall RC	8.00	3.60
❑ 224 Chad Morton RC	4.00	1.80
❑ 225 Ahmed Plummer RC	4.00	1.80
❑ 226 Julian Peterson RC	4.00	1.80
❑ 227 Mike Green RC	3.00	1.35
❑ 228 Michael Wiley RC	3.00	1.35
❑ 229 Spergon Wynn RC	3.00	1.35
❑ 230 Trevor Gaylor RC	3.00	1.35
❑ 231 Doug Johnson RC	4.00	1.80
❑ 232 Marc Bulger RC	8.00	3.60
❑ 233 Ron Dixon RC	3.00	1.35
❑ 234 Aaron Shea RC	1.50	.70
❑ 235 Thomas Hamner RC	2.00	.90
❑ 236 Tom Brady RC	60.00	27.00
❑ 237 Deltha O'Neal RC	4.00	1.80
❑ 238 Todd Husak RC	4.00	1.80
❑ 239 Erron Kinney RC	4.00	1.80
❑ 240 JaJuan Dawson RC	2.00	.90
❑ 241 Nick Williams	1.00	.45
❑ 242 Deon Grant RC	3.00	1.35
❑ 243 Brad Hoover RC	3.00	1.35
❑ 244 Kamil Loud	.40	.18
❑ 245 Rashard Anderson RC	3.00	1.35
❑ 246 Clint Stoerner RC	1.50	.70
❑ 247 Antwan Harris RC	2.00	.90
❑ 248 Jason Webster RC	2.00	.90
❑ 249 Kevin McDougal RC	3.00	1.35
❑ 250 Tony Scott RC	2.00	.90
❑ 251 Thabiti Davis RC	2.00	.90
❑ 252 Ian Gold RC	3.00	1.35
❑ 253 Sammy Morris RC	3.00	1.35
❑ 254 Raynoch Thompson RC	3.00	1.35
❑ 255 Jeremy McDaniel	1.00	.45
❑ 256 Terrelle Smith RC	3.00	1.35
❑ 257 Deon Dyer RC	3.00	1.35
❑ 258 Na'il Diggs RC	3.00	1.35
❑ 259 Brandon Short RC	3.00	1.35
❑ 260 Mike Brown RC	8.00	3.60
❑ 261 John Engelberger RC	3.00	1.35
❑ 262 Rogers Beckett RC	3.00	1.35
❑ 263 JaJuan Seider RC	2.00	.90
❑ 264 Desmond Kitchings RC	3.00	1.35
❑ 265 Reggie Davis RC	3.00	1.35
❑ 266 Corey Moore RC	2.00	.90
❑ 267 Cornelius Griffin RC	3.00	1.35
❑ 268 Stockar McDougle RC	2.00	.90
❑ 269 James Williams RC	3.00	1.35
❑ 270 Darrell Jackson RC	6.00	2.70

2000 Bowman Chrome Refractors

	Nm-Mt	Ex-Mt
*REF.STARS: 1.5X TO 4X BASIC CARDS		
*EP.REF.STARS: 1.2X TO 3X BASIC CARDS		
*REF.RCs: 1.5X TO 4X BASIC CARDS		
*REF.RC SP's: .5X TO 1.2X BASIC CARDS		
❑ 236 Tom Brady	200.00	90.00

2000 Bowman Chrome Rookie Autographs

Card	Nm-Mt	Ex-Mt
❑ 168 Thomas Jones	150.00	70.00
❑ 170 Jamal Lewis	300.00	135.00
❑ 172 Ron Dayne	120.00	55.00
❑ 173 Chad Pennington	300.00	135.00
❑ 174 Plaxico Burress	200.00	90.00
❑ 175 R.Jay Soward	60.00	27.00
❑ 177 Shaun Alexander	250.00	110.00
❑ 181 Sylvester Morris	80.00	36.00
❑ 183 Peter Warrick	175.00	80.00
❑ 185 Travis Prentice	80.00	36.00

2001 Bowman Chrome

Card	Nm-Mt	Ex-Mt
COMP.SET w/o SP's (110)	25.00	7.50
❑ 1 Emmitt Smith	2.00	.60
❑ 2 James Stewart	.60	.18
❑ 3 Jeff Graham	.40	.12
❑ 4 Keyshawn Johnson	1.00	.30
❑ 5 Stephen Davis	1.00	.30
❑ 6 Chad Lewis	.40	.12
❑ 7 Drew Bledsoe	1.25	.35
❑ 8 Fred Taylor	1.00	.30
❑ 9 Mike Anderson	1.00	.30
❑ 10 Tony Gonzalez	.60	.18
❑ 11 Aaron Brooks	1.00	.30
❑ 12 Vinny Testaverde	.60	.18
❑ 13 Jerome Bettis	1.00	.30
❑ 14 Marshall Faulk	1.25	.35
❑ 15 Jeff Garcia	1.00	.30
❑ 16 Terry Glenn	.60	.18
❑ 17 Jay Fiedler	1.00	.30
❑ 18 Ahman Green	1.00	.30
❑ 19 Cade McNown	.40	.12
❑ 20 Rob Johnson	.60	.18
❑ 21 Jamal Anderson	1.00	.30
❑ 22 Corey Dillon	1.00	.30
❑ 23 Jake Plummer	.60	.18
❑ 24 Rod Smith	.60	.18
❑ 25 Trent Green	1.00	.30
❑ 26 Ricky Williams	1.00	.30
❑ 27 Charlie Garner	.60	.18
❑ 28 Shaun Alexander	1.25	.35
❑ 29 Jeff George	.60	.18
❑ 30 Torry Holt	1.00	.30
❑ 31 James Thrash	.60	.18
❑ 32 Rich Gannon	1.00	.30
❑ 33 Ron Dayne	1.00	.30
❑ 34 Dedric Ward	.40	.12
❑ 35 Edgerrin James	1.25	.35
❑ 36 Cris Carter	1.00	.30
❑ 37 Derrick Mason	.60	.18
❑ 38 Brad Johnson	1.00	.30
❑ 39 Charlie Batch	1.00	.30
❑ 40 Joey Galloway	.60	.18
❑ 41 James Allen	.60	.18
❑ 42 Tim Biakabutuka	.60	.18
❑ 43 Ray Lewis	1.00	.30
❑ 44 David Boston	1.00	.30
❑ 45 Kevin Johnson	.60	.18
❑ 46 Jimmy Smith	.60	.18
❑ 47 Joe Horn	.60	.18
❑ 48 Terrell Owens	1.00	.30
❑ 49 Eddie George	1.00	.30
❑ 50 Brett Favre	3.00	.90
❑ 51 Wayne Chrebet	.60	.18
❑ 52 Hines Ward	1.00	.30
❑ 53 Warrick Dunn	1.00	.30
❑ 54 Matt Hasselbeck	.60	.18
❑ 55 Tiki Barber	.60	.18
❑ 56 Lamar Smith	.60	.18
❑ 57 Tim Couch	.60	.18
❑ 58 Eric Moulds	.60	.18
❑ 59 Shawn Jefferson	.40	.12
❑ 60 Donald Hayes	.40	.12
❑ 61 Brian Urlacher	1.50	.45
❑ 62 Steve McNair	1.00	.30
❑ 63 Kurt Warner	2.00	.60
❑ 64 Tim Brown	1.00	.30
❑ 65 Troy Brown	.60	.18
❑ 66 Albert Connell	.40	.12
❑ 67 Peyton Manning	2.50	.75
❑ 68 Peter Warrick	1.00	.30
❑ 69 Elvis Grbac	.60	.18
❑ 70 Chris Chandler	.60	.18
❑ 71 Akili Smith	.40	.12
❑ 72 Keenan McCardell	.40	.12
❑ 73 Kerry Collins	.60	.18
❑ 74 Junior Seau	1.00	.30
❑ 75 Donovan McNabb	1.25	.35
❑ 76 Tony Banks	.60	.18
❑ 77 Steve Beuerlein	.60	.18
❑ 78 Daunte Culpepper	1.00	.30
❑ 79 Darrell Jackson	1.00	.30
❑ 80 Isaac Bruce	1.00	.30
❑ 81 Tyrone Wheatley	.60	.18
❑ 82 Derrick Alexander	.60	.18
❑ 83 Germane Crowell	.40	.12
❑ 84 Jon Kitna	.60	.18
❑ 85 Jamal Lewis	1.50	.45
❑ 86 Ed McCaffrey	1.00	.30
❑ 87 Mark Brunell	1.00	.30
❑ 88 Jeff Blake	.60	.18
❑ 89 Duce Staley	1.00	.30
❑ 90 Doug Flutie	1.00	.30
❑ 91 Kordell Stewart	.60	.18
❑ 92 Randy Moss	2.00	.60
❑ 93 Marvin Harrison	1.00	.30
❑ 94 Muhsin Muhammad	.60	.18
❑ 95 Brian Griese	1.00	.30
❑ 96 Antonio Freeman	1.00	.30
❑ 97 Amani Toomer	.60	.18
❑ 98 Oronde Gadsden	.60	.18
❑ 99 Curtis Martin	1.00	.30
❑ 100 Jerry Rice	2.00	.60
❑ 101 Michael Pittman	.40	.12
❑ 102 Shannon Sharpe	.60	.18
❑ 103 Peerless Price	.60	.18
❑ 104 Bill Schroeder	.60	.18
❑ 105 Ike Hilliard	.60	.18
❑ 106 Freddie Jones	.40	.12
❑ 107 Tai Streets	.40	.12
❑ 108 Ricky Watters	.60	.18
❑ 109 Az-Zahir Hakim	.40	.12
❑ 110 Jacquez Green	.40	.12
❑ 111 George Layne RC	5.00	1.50
❑ 112 Correll Buckhalter RC	10.00	3.00
❑ 113 Tony Stewart RC	8.00	2.40
❑ 114 Chris Barnes RC	5.00	1.50
❑ 115 A.J. Feeley RC	8.00	2.40

	Nm-Mt	Ex-Mt
❑ 116 Margin Hooks RC	3.00	.90
❑ 117 Anthony Henry RC	8.00	2.40
❑ 118 Dwight Smith RC	3.00	.90
❑ 119 Torrance Marshall RC	8.00	2.40
❑ 120 Gary Baxter RC	5.00	1.50
❑ 121 Derek Combs RC	5.00	1.50
❑ 122 Marcus Bell RC	5.00	1.50
❑ 123 DeLawrence Grant RC	3.00	.90
❑ 124 Jameel Cook RC	5.00	1.50
❑ 125 Eric Downing RC	3.00	.90
❑ 126 Marlon McCree RC	3.00	.90
❑ 127 Tay Cody RC	3.00	.90
❑ 128 Mario Monds RC	3.00	.90
❑ 129 Kenny Smith RC	5.00	1.50
❑ 130 Sedrick Hodge RC	3.00	.90
❑ 131 Marcus Stroud RC	8.00	2.40
❑ 132 Steve Smith RC	10.00	3.00
❑ 133 Tyrone Robertson RC	3.00	.90
❑ 134 James Reed RC	3.00	.90
❑ 135 Kris Kocurek RC	3.00	.90
❑ 136 Dan O'Leary RC	5.00	1.50
❑ 137 Harold Blackmon RC	3.00	.90
❑ 138 Fred Smoot RC	8.00	2.40
❑ 139 Billy Baber RC	3.00	.90
❑ 140 Jarrod Cooper RC	8.00	2.40
❑ 141 Travis Henry RC	10.00	3.00
❑ 142 David Terrell RC	8.00	2.40
❑ 143 Josh Heupel RC	8.00	2.40
❑ 144 Drew Brees RC	15.00	4.50
❑ 145 T.J. Houshmandzadeh RC	8.00	2.40
❑ 146 Rod Gardner RC	8.00	2.40
❑ 147 Richard Seymour RC	8.00	2.40
❑ 148 Koren Robinson RC	8.00	2.40
❑ 149 Scotty Anderson RC	5.00	1.50
❑ 150 Marques Tuiasosopo RC	8.00	2.40
❑ 151 John Capel RC	5.00	1.50
❑ 152 LaMont Jordan RC	12.00	3.60
❑ 153 James Jackson RC	8.00	2.40
❑ 154 Bobby Newcombe RC	5.00	1.50
❑ 155 Anthony Thomas RC	12.00	3.60
❑ 156 Dan Alexander RC	8.00	2.40
❑ 157 Quincy Carter RC	8.00	2.40
❑ 158 Morlon Greenwood RC	5.00	1.50
❑ 159 Robert Ferguson RC	8.00	2.40
❑ 160 Sage Rosenfels RC	8.00	2.40
❑ 161 Michael Stone RC	3.00	.90
❑ 162 Chris Weinke RC	8.00	2.40
❑ 163 Travis Minor RC	5.00	1.50
❑ 164 Gerard Warren RC	8.00	2.40
❑ 165 Jamar Fletcher RC	5.00	1.50
❑ 166 Andre Carter RC	8.00	2.40
❑ 167 Deuce McAllister RC	20.00	6.00
❑ 168 Dan Morgan RC	8.00	2.40
❑ 169 Todd Heap RC	8.00	2.40
❑ 170 Snoop Minnis RC	5.00	1.50
❑ 171 Will Allen RC	5.00	1.50
❑ 172 Freddie Mitchell RC	8.00	2.40
❑ 173 Rudi Johnson RC	15.00	4.50
❑ 174 Kevan Barlow RC	8.00	2.40
❑ 175 Jamie Winborn RC	5.00	1.50
❑ 176 Onome Ojo RC	5.00	1.50
❑ 177 Leonard Davis RC	5.00	1.50
❑ 178 Santana Moss RC	12.00	3.60
❑ 179 Chris Chambers RC	10.00	3.00
❑ 180 Michael Vick RC	80.00	24.00
❑ 181 Michael Bennett RC	15.00	4.50
❑ 182 Mike McMahon RC	8.00	2.40
❑ 183 Jonathan Carter RC	5.00	1.50
❑ 184 Jamal Reynolds RC	8.00	2.40
❑ 185 Justin Smith RC	8.00	2.40
❑ 186 Quincy Morgan RC	8.00	2.40
❑ 187 Chad Johnson RC	15.00	4.50
❑ 188 Jesse Palmer RC	8.00	2.40
❑ 189 Reggie Wayne RC	12.00	3.60
❑ 190 LaDainian Tomlinson RC	40.00	12.00
❑ 191 Andre King RC	5.00	1.50
❑ 192 Richmond Flowers RC	5.00	1.50
❑ 193 Derrick Blaylock RC	8.00	2.40
❑ 194 Cedrick Wilson RC	8.00	2.40
❑ 195 Zeke Moreno RC	8.00	2.40
❑ 196 Tommy Polley RC	8.00	2.40
❑ 197 Damione Lewis RC	5.00	1.50
❑ 198 Aaron Schobel RC	8.00	2.40
❑ 199 Alge Crumpler RC	10.00	3.00
❑ 200 Nate Clements RC	8.00	2.40
❑ 201 Quentin McCord RC	5.00	1.50
❑ 202 Ken-Yon Rambo RC	5.00	1.50
❑ 203 Milton Wynn RC	5.00	1.50
❑ 204 Derrick Gibson RC	5.00	1.50
❑ 205 Chris Taylor RC	5.00	1.50
❑ 206 Corey Hall RC	3.00	.90
❑ 207 Vinny Sutherland RC	5.00	1.50
❑ 208 Kendrell Bell RC	20.00	6.00
❑ 209 Casey Hampton RC	5.00	1.50
❑ 210 Demetric Evans RC	3.00	.90
❑ 211 Brian Allen RC	3.00	.90
❑ 212 Rodney Bailey RC	3.00	.90
❑ 213 Otis Leverette RC	3.00	.90
❑ 214 Ron Edwards RC	3.00	.90
❑ 215 Michael Jameson RC	3.00	.90
❑ 216 Markus Steele RC	5.00	1.50
❑ 217 Jimmy Williams RC	3.00	.90
❑ 218 Roger Knight RC	3.00	.90
❑ 219 Randy Garner RC	3.00	.90
❑ 220 Raymond Perryman RC	3.00	.90
❑ 221 Karon Riley RC	3.00	.90
❑ 222 Adam Archuleta RC	8.00	2.40
❑ 223 Arnold Jackson RC	5.00	1.50
❑ 224 Ryan Pickett RC	3.00	.90
❑ 225 Shad Meier RC	5.00	1.50
❑ 226 Reggie Germany RC	5.00	1.50
❑ 227 Justin McCareins RC	8.00	2.40
❑ 228 Idrees Bashir RC	3.00	.90
❑ 229 Josh Booty RC	8.00	2.40
❑ 230 Eddie Berlin RC	5.00	1.50
❑ 231 Heath Evans RC	5.00	1.50
❑ 232 Alex Bannister RC	5.00	1.50
❑ 233 Corey Alston RC	3.00	.90
❑ 234 Reggie White RC	5.00	1.50
❑ 235 Orlando Huff RC	3.00	.90
❑ 236 Ken Lucas RC	5.00	1.50
❑ 237 Matt Stewart RC	3.00	.90
❑ 238 Cedric Scott RC	5.00	1.50
❑ 239 Ronney Daniels RC	3.00	.90
❑ 240 Kevin Kasper RC	8.00	2.40
❑ 241 Tony Driver RC	5.00	1.50
❑ 242 Kyle Vanden Bosch RC	8.00	2.40
❑ 243 T.J. Turner RC	3.00	.90
❑ 244 Eric Westmoreland RC	5.00	1.50
❑ 245 Ronald Flemons RC	3.00	.90
❑ 246 Eric Kelly RC	3.00	.90
❑ 247 Moran Norris RC	3.00	.90
❑ 248 Damerien McCants RC	5.00	1.50
❑ 249 James Boyd RC	3.00	.90
❑ 250 Keith Adams RC	3.00	.90
❑ 251 B.Manumaleuna RC	5.00	1.50
❑ 252 Dee Brown RC	8.00	2.40
❑ 253 Ross Kolodziej RC	3.00	.90
❑ 254 Boo Williams RC	5.00	1.50
❑ 255 Patrick Chukwurah RC	3.00	.90

2001 Bowman Chrome Gold Refractors

	Nm-Mt	Ex-Mt
*STARS: 5X TO 12X BASIC CARDS		
*ROOKIES: 1.2X TO 3X BASIC CARDS		
❑ 180 Michael Vick	300.00	90.00

2001 Bowman Chrome Xfractors

	Nm-Mt	Ex-Mt
*STARS: 2.5X TO 6X BASIC CARDS		
*ROOKIES: .8X TO 2X BASIC CARDS		
❑ 180 Michael Vick	200.00	60.00

2002 Bowman Chrome

	Nm-Mt	Ex-Mt
COMP.SET w/o SP's (110)	25.00	7.50
❑ 1 Emmitt Smith	2.50	.75
❑ 2 Drew Brees	1.00	.30
❑ 3 Duce Staley	1.00	.30
❑ 4 Curtis Martin	1.00	.30
❑ 5 Isaac Bruce	1.00	.30
❑ 6 Stephen Davis	.60	.18
❑ 7 Darrell Jackson	.60	.18
❑ 8 James Stewart	.60	.18

	Nm-Mt	Ex-Mt
❑ 9 Tim Couch	.60	.18
❑ 10 Travis Henry	1.00	.30
❑ 11 Thomas Jones	.60	.18
❑ 12 Jamal Lewis	1.00	.30
❑ 13 Chris Chambers	1.00	.30
❑ 14 Jeff Blake	.60	.18
❑ 15 Plaxico Burress	.60	.18
❑ 16 Michael Pittman	.40	.12
❑ 17 Jeff Garcia	1.00	.30
❑ 18 Tim Brown	1.00	.30
❑ 19 Kent Graham	.40	.12
❑ 20 Shannon Sharpe	.60	.18
❑ 21 Corey Dillon	.60	.18
❑ 22 Muhsin Muhammad	.60	.18
❑ 23 Tony Gonzalez	.60	.18
❑ 24 Qadry Ismail	.60	.18
❑ 25 Mike McMahon	1.00	.30
❑ 26 Edgerrin James	1.25	.35
❑ 27 Daunte Culpepper	1.00	.30
❑ 28 Deuce McAllister	1.25	.35
❑ 29 Kerry Collins	.60	.18
❑ 30 Eddie George	1.00	.30
❑ 31 Torry Holt	1.00	.30
❑ 32 Todd Pinkston	.60	.18
❑ 33 Quincy Carter	.60	.18
❑ 34 Rod Smith	.60	.18
❑ 35 Michael Vick	3.00	.90
❑ 36 Jim Miller	.60	.18
❑ 37 Troy Brown	.60	.18
❑ 38 Wayne Chrebet	.60	.18
❑ 39 Curtis Conway	.40	.12
❑ 40 Reidel Anthony	.40	.12
❑ 41 Mark Brunell	1.00	.30
❑ 42 Chris Weinke	.60	.18
❑ 43 Eric Moulds	.60	.18
❑ 44 Ike Hilliard	.60	.18
❑ 45 Jay Fiedler	.60	.18
❑ 46 Keyshawn Johnson	1.00	.30
❑ 47 Rod Gardner	.60	.18
❑ 48 Chris Redman	.40	.12
❑ 49 James Allen	.60	.18
❑ 50 Kordell Stewart	.60	.18
❑ 51 Priest Holmes	1.25	.35
❑ 52 Anthony Thomas	1.00	.30
❑ 53 Peter Warrick	.60	.18
❑ 54 Jake Plummer	.60	.18
❑ 55 Jerry Rice	2.00	.60
❑ 56 Joe Horn	.60	.18
❑ 57 Derrick Mason	.60	.18
❑ 58 Kurt Warner	1.00	.30
❑ 59 Antowain Smith	.60	.18
❑ 60 Randy Moss	2.00	.60
❑ 61 Warrick Dunn	1.00	.30
❑ 62 Laveranues Coles	.60	.18
❑ 63 LaDainian Tomlinson	1.50	.45
❑ 64 Michael Westbrook	.60	.18
❑ 65 Travis Taylor	.60	.18
❑ 66 Brian Griese	1.00	.30
❑ 67 Bill Schroeder	.60	.18
❑ 68 Ahman Green	1.00	.30
❑ 69 Jimmy Smith	.60	.18
❑ 70 Charlie Garner	.60	.18
❑ 71 Terrell Owens	1.00	.30
❑ 72 Brad Johnson	.60	.18
❑ 73 James Thrash	.60	.18
❑ 74 Marvin Harrison	1.00	.30
❑ 75 Brett Favre	2.50	.75
❑ 76 Rocket Ismail	.60	.18

❑ 77 David Boston 1.00 .30
❑ 78 Jermaine Lewis .40 .12
❑ 79 Aaron Brooks 1.00 .30
❑ 80 Shaun Alexander 1.00 .30
❑ 81 Steve McNair 1.00 .30
❑ 82 Marshall Faulk 1.00 .30
❑ 83 Terrell Davis 1.00 .30
❑ 84 Corey Bradford .40 .12
❑ 85 David Terrell 1.00 .30
❑ 86 Kevin Johnson .60 .18
❑ 87 Jon Kitna .60 .18
❑ 88 Az-Zahir Hakim .40 .12
❑ 89 Drew Bledsoe 1.25 .35
❑ 90 Garrison Hearst .60 .18
❑ 91 Doug Flutie 1.00 .30
❑ 92 Jerome Bettis 1.00 .30
❑ 93 Vinny Testaverde .60 .18
❑ 94 Tiki Barber .60 .18
❑ 95 Johnnie Morton .60 .18
❑ 96 Lamar Smith .60 .18
❑ 97 Marcus Robinson .60 .18
❑ 98 Fred Taylor 1.00 .30
❑ 99 Tom Brady 2.50 .75
❑ 100 Peyton Manning 2.00 .60
❑ 101 Donovan McNabb 1.25 .35
❑ 102 Rich Gannon 1.00 .30
❑ 103 Hines Ward 1.00 .30
❑ 104 Michael Bennett .60 .18
❑ 105 Ricky Williams 1.00 .30
❑ 106 Germane Crowell .40 .12
❑ 107 Joey Galloway .60 .18
❑ 108 Amani Toomer .60 .18
❑ 109 Trent Green .60 .18
❑ 110 Terry Glenn .60 .18
❑ 111 Donte Stallworth RC 10.00 3.00
❑ 112 Mike Williams RC 4.00 1.20
❑ 113 Kurt Kittner RC 4.00 1.20
❑ 114 Josh Reed RC 5.00 1.50
❑ 115 Raonall Smith RC 4.00 1.20
❑ 116 David Garrard RC 5.00 1.50
❑ 117 Eric Crouch RC 8.00 2.40
❑ 118 Levi Jones RC 4.00 1.20
❑ 119 Quentin Jammer RC 5.00 1.50
❑ 120 Cliff Russell RC 4.00 1.20
❑ 121 Jamin Elliott RC 2.50 .75
❑ 122 Roy Williams RC 12.00 3.60
❑ 123 Marquise Walker RC 4.00 1.20
❑ 124 Kalimba Edwards RC 5.00 1.50
❑ 125 Daniel Graham RC 5.00 1.50
❑ 126 Anthony Weaver RC 4.00 1.20
❑ 127 Antonio Bryant RC 5.00 1.50
❑ 128 DeShaun Foster RC 5.00 1.50
❑ 129 Antwaan Randle El RC 6.00 1.80
❑ 130 William Green RC 8.00 2.40
❑ 131 Joey Harrington RC 15.00 4.50
❑ 132 T.J. Duckett RC 8.00 2.40
❑ 133 Javon Walker RC 10.00 3.00
❑ 134 Albert Haynesworth RC 4.00 1.20
❑ 135 Julius Peppers RC 10.00 3.00
❑ 136 Clinton Portis RC 15.00 4.50
❑ 137 Ashley Lelie RC 10.00 3.00
❑ 138 Reche Caldwell RC 5.00 1.50
❑ 139 Rohan Davey RC 5.00 1.50
❑ 140 Patrick Ramsey RC 10.00 3.00
❑ 141 Ron Johnson RC 4.00 1.20
❑ 142 Jamar Martin RC 4.00 1.20
❑ 143 Travis Stephens RC 4.00 1.20
❑ 143AU Travis Stephens AU 12.00 3.60
❑ 144 Darrell Hill RC 4.00 1.20
❑ 145 Jon McGraw RC 2.50 .75
❑ 146 Javin Hunter RC 2.50 .75
❑ 146AU Javin Hunter AU 10.00 3.00
❑ 147 Eddie Drummond RC 4.00 1.20
❑ 148 Andre Lott RC 5.00 1.50
❑ 149 Travis Fisher RC 5.00 1.50
❑ 150 Lamont Brightful RC 2.50 .75
❑ 151 Rocky Calmus RC 5.00 1.50
❑ 152 Wes Pate RC 2.50 .75
❑ 152AU Wes Pate AU 10.00 3.00
❑ 153 Lamar Gordon RC 5.00 1.50
❑ 154 Terry Jones RC 4.00 1.20
❑ 155 Kyle Johnson RC 2.50 .75
❑ 155AU Kyle Johnson AU 10.00 3.00
❑ 156 Daryl Jones RC 4.00 1.20
❑ 157 Tellis Redmon RC 4.00 1.20
❑ 158 Jarrod Baxter RC 4.00 1.20
❑ 159 Delvon Flowers RC 4.00 1.20
❑ 160 Kelly Campbell RC 4.00 1.20
❑ 161 Eddie Freeman RC 2.50 .75
❑ 162 Atrews Bell RC 2.50 .75
❑ 163 Omar Easy RC 5.00 1.50
❑ 164 Jeremy Allen RC 5.00 1.50
❑ 165 Andra Davis RC 4.00 1.20
❑ 166 Mike Rumph RC 5.00 1.50
❑ 167 Seth Burford RC 4.00 1.20
❑ 168 Marquand Manuel RC 2.50 .75
❑ 169 Marques Anderson RC 5.00 1.50
❑ 170 Ben Leber RC 5.00 1.50
❑ 171 Ryan Denney RC 2.50 .75
❑ 172 Justin Peelle RC 2.50 .75
❑ 173 Lito Sheppard RC 5.00 1.50
❑ 174 Damien Anderson RC 4.00 1.20
❑ 175 Lamont Thompson RC 4.00 1.20
❑ 176 David Priestley RC 4.00 1.20
❑ 177 Michael Lewis RC 5.00 1.50
❑ 178 Lee Mays RC 4.00 1.20
❑ 179 Alan Harper RC 2.50 .75
❑ 180 Verron Haynes RC 5.00 1.50
❑ 181 Chris Hope RC 4.00 1.20
❑ 182 Derek Ross RC 4.00 1.20
❑ 183 Joseph Jefferson RC 4.00 1.20
❑ 184 Carlos Hall RC 5.00 1.50
❑ 185 Robert Royal RC 5.00 1.50
❑ 186 Sheldon Brown RC 5.00 1.50
❑ 187 DeVeren Johnson RC 4.00 1.20
❑ 188 Rock Cartwright RC 6.00 1.80
❑ 189 Kendall Simmons RC 4.00 1.20
❑ 190 Joe Burns RC 5.00 1.50
❑ 191 David Givens RC 15.00 4.50
❑ 192 John Owens RC 4.00 1.20
❑ 193 Jarrett Ferguson RC 4.00 1.20
❑ 194 Randy McMichael RC 8.00 2.40
❑ 195 Chris Baker RC 4.00 1.20
❑ 196 Rashad Bauman RC 4.00 1.20
❑ 197 Matt Murphy RC 4.00 1.20
❑ 198 Steve Bellisari RC 5.00 1.50
❑ 199 Jeff Kelly RC 4.00 1.20
❑ 200 Mark Anelli RC 2.50 .75
❑ 201 Darnell Sanders RC 4.00 1.20
❑ 202 Coy Wire RC 5.00 1.50
❑ 203 Ricky Williams RC 4.00 1.20
❑ 204 Napoleon Harris RC 5.00 1.50
❑ 205 Ennis Haywood RC 4.00 1.20
❑ 206 Keyuo Craver RC 4.00 1.20
❑ 207 Kahlil Hill RC 4.00 1.20
❑ 208 J.T. O'Sullivan RC 4.00 1.20
❑ 209 Woody Dantzler RC 5.00 1.50
❑ 210 Phillip Buchanon RC 5.00 1.50
❑ 211 Charles Grant RC 5.00 1.50
❑ 212 Dusty Bonner RC 2.50 .75
❑ 213 James Allen RC 2.50 .75
❑ 214 Ronald Curry RC 5.00 1.50
❑ 215 Deion Branch RC 10.00 3.00
❑ 216 Larry Ned RC 4.00 1.20
❑ 217 Kendall Newson RC 2.50 .75
❑ 218 Shaun Hill RC 5.00 1.50
❑ 219 Akin Ayodele RC 2.50 .75
❑ 220 John Henderson RC 5.00 1.50
❑ 221 Andre Davis AU A RC 20.00 6.00
❑ 222 Bryan Thomas AU A RC 20.00 6.00
❑ 223 Brian Westbrook AU C RC 60.00 18.00
❑ 224 Chad Hutchinson AU C RC 20.00 6.00
❑ 225 Craig Nall AU D RC 20.00 6.00
❑ 226 David Carr AU A RC 100.00 30.00
❑ 227 Dwight Freeney AU D RC 30.00 9.00
❑ 228 Adrian Peterson AU A RC 25.00 7.50
❑ 229 Randy Fasani AU E RC 12.00 3.60
❑ 230 Ed Reed AU A RC 30.00 9.00
❑ 231 Freddie Milons AU B RC 12.00 3.60
❑ 232 Herb Haygood AU E RC 10.00 3.00
❑ 233 Jabar Gaffney AU A RC 20.00 6.00
❑ 234 Josh McCown AU A RC 30.00 9.00
❑ 235 Jeremy Shockey AU A RC 80.00 24.00
❑ 236 Jake Schifino AU F RC 12.00 3.60
❑ 237 Josh Scobey AU E RC 20.00 6.00
❑ 238 Jonathan Wells AU D RC 20.00 6.00
❑ 239 Ladell Betts AU A RC 30.00 9.00
❑ 240 Luke Staley AU E RC 12.00 3.60
❑ 241 Maurice Morris AU B RC 20.00 6.00
❑ 242 Matt Schobel AU D RC 12.00 3.60
❑ 243 Sam Simmons AU C RC 10.00 3.00
❑ 244 Tim Carter AU A RC 12.00 3.60
❑ 245 Tank Williams AU E RC 12.00 3.60
❑ 246 Jerramy Stevens AU A RC 20.00 6.00
❑ 247 Jason McAddley AU C RC 12.00 3.60
❑ 248 Ken Simonton AU D RC 10.00 3.00
❑ 249 Chester Taylor AU F RC 15.00 4.50
❑ 250 Brandon Doman AU C RC 20.00 6.00

2002 Bowman Chrome Refractors

Nm-Mt Ex-Mt

*STARS: 1.5X TO 4X HI COL.
*ROOKIES: 1.2X TO 2.5X

2002 Bowman Chrome Refractors Gold

Nm-Mt Ex-Mt

*STARS: 5X TO 12X BASIC CARDS
*ROOKIES: 2X TO 5X

2002 Bowman Chrome Xfractors

Nm-Mt Ex-Mt

*STARS: 2.5X TO 6X BASIC CARDS
*ROOKIES 111-220: 2X TO 5X
*ROOKIE AU 221-250: 1X TO 2.5X

❑ 226 David Carr AU 250.00 75.00
❑ 235 Jeremy Shockey AU 250.00 75.00

2003 Bowman Chrome

MINT NRMT

COMP.SET w/o SP's (110) 25.00 11.00
❑ 1 Brett Favre 2.50 1.10
❑ 2 Jeremy Shockey 1.50 .70
❑ 3 Fred Taylor 1.00 .45
❑ 4 Rich Gannon .60 .25
❑ 5 Joey Galloway .60 .25
❑ 6 Ray Lewis 1.00 .45
❑ 7 Jeff Blake .40 .18
❑ 8 Stacey Mack .40 .18
❑ 9 Matt Hasselbeck .60 .25
❑ 10 Laveranues Coles .60 .25
❑ 11 Brad Johnson .60 .25
❑ 12 Tommy Maddox 1.00 .45
❑ 13 Curtis Martin 1.00 .45
❑ 14 Tom Brady 1.50 .70
❑ 15 Ricky Williams 1.00 .45
❑ 16 Stephen Davis .60 .25
❑ 17 Chad Johnson .60 .25
❑ 18 Joey Harrington 1.50 .70
❑ 19 Tony Gonzalez .60 .25
❑ 20 Peerless Price .60 .25
❑ 21 LaDainian Tomlinson 1.00 .45
❑ 22 James Thrash .60 .25
❑ 23 Charlie Garner .60 .25
❑ 24 Eddie George .60 .25
❑ 25 Terrell Owens 1.00 .45
❑ 26 Brian Urlacher 1.50 .70
❑ 27 Eric Moulds .60 .25
❑ 28 Emmitt Smith 2.50 1.10
❑ 29 Tim Couch .40 .18
❑ 30 Jake Plummer .60 .25

	No.	Player	Mint	NrMt
❑	31	Marvin Harrison	1.00	.45
❑	32	Chris Chambers	1.00	.45
❑	33	Tiki Barber	.60	.25
❑	34	Kurt Warner	1.00	.45
❑	35	Michael Pittman	.40	.18
❑	36	Kevin Dyson	.60	.25
❑	37	Clinton Portis	1.50	.70
❑	38	Peyton Manning	1.50	.70
❑	39	Travis Taylor	.60	.25
❑	40	Jeff Garcia	1.00	.45
❑	41	Patrick Ramsey	1.00	.45
❑	42	Shaun Alexander	1.00	.45
❑	43	Joe Horn	.60	.25
❑	44	Daunte Culpepper	1.00	.45
❑	45	Travis Henry	.60	.25
❑	46	Brian Finneran	.40	.18
❑	47	William Green	.60	.25
❑	48	Kordell Stewart	.60	.25
❑	49	Reggie Wayne	.60	.25
❑	50	Priest Holmes	1.25	.55
❑	51	Jay Fiedler	.60	.25
❑	52	Corey Dillon	.60	.25
❑	53	Jamal Lewis	1.00	.45
❑	54	Mark Brunell	.60	.25
❑	55	Santana Moss	.60	.25
❑	56	Duce Staley	.60	.25
❑	57	Torry Holt	1.00	.45
❑	58	Rod Gardner	.60	.25
❑	59	Kerry Collins	.60	.25
❑	60	Randy Moss	1.50	.70
❑	61	Jerry Porter	.60	.25
❑	62	Plaxico Burress	.60	.25
❑	63	Steve McNair	1.00	.45
❑	64	Muhsin Muhammad	.60	.25
❑	65	Drew Bledsoe	1.00	.45
❑	66	T.J. Duckett	.60	.25
❑	67	Ahman Green	1.00	.45
❑	68	Rod Smith	.60	.25
❑	69	Jimmy Smith	.60	.25
❑	70	Trent Green	.60	.25
❑	71	Tim Brown	1.00	.45
❑	72	Jerome Bettis	1.00	.45
❑	73	Isaac Bruce	1.00	.45
❑	74	Derrick Mason	.60	.25
❑	75	Donovan McNabb	1.25	.55
❑	76	Deuce McAllister	1.00	.45
❑	77	Zach Thomas	1.00	.45
❑	78	Garrison Hearst	.60	.25
❑	79	Koren Robinson	.60	.25
❑	80	Marshall Faulk	1.00	.45
❑	81	Keyshawn Johnson	1.00	.45
❑	82	Jake Delhomme	1.00	.45
❑	83	Marty Booker	.60	.25
❑	84	James Stewart	.60	.25
❑	85	Corey Bradford	.40	.18
❑	86	Derrius Thompson	.40	.18
❑	87	Edgerrin James	1.00	.45
❑	88	Darrell Jackson	.60	.25
❑	89	Hines Ward	1.00	.45
❑	90	David Boston	.60	.25
❑	91	Curtis Conway	.40	.18
❑	92	David Patten	.40	.18
❑	93	Michael Bennett	.60	.25
❑	94	Todd Pinkston	.60	.25
❑	95	Jerry Rice	2.00	.90
❑	96	Jon Kitna	.60	.25
❑	97	Ed McCaffrey	1.00	.45
❑	98	Donald Driver	.60	.25
❑	99	Anthony Thomas	1.00	.45
❑	100	Michael Vick	2.50	1.10
❑	101	Terry Glenn	.40	.18
❑	102	Quincy Morgan	.60	.25
❑	103	David Carr	1.50	.70
❑	104	Troy Brown	.60	.25
❑	105	Aaron Brooks	1.00	.45
❑	106	Amani Toomer	.60	.25
❑	107	Drew Brees	1.00	.45
❑	108	Chad Hutchinson	.60	.25
❑	109	Warrick Dunn	.60	.25
❑	110	Chad Pennington	1.25	.55
❑	111	Brian St.Pierre RC	5.00	2.20
❑	112	Keenan Howry RC	5.00	2.20
❑	113	Sultan McCullough RC	4.00	1.80
❑	114	Terence Newman RC	10.00	4.50
❑	115	Kelley Washington RC	5.00	2.20
❑	116	Musa Smith RC	5.00	2.20
❑	117	Victor Hobson RC	5.00	2.20
❑	118	Travis Anglin RC	2.50	1.10
❑	119	Artose Pinner RC	5.00	2.20
❑	120	Rashean Mathis RC	4.00	1.80
❑	121	DeWayne White RC	4.00	1.80
❑	122	Kevin Curtis RC	5.00	2.20
❑	123	Tyrone Calico RC	6.00	2.70
❑	124	Ricky Manning RC	5.00	2.20
❑	125	Cory Redding RC	4.00	1.80
❑	126	Dallas Clark RC	5.00	2.20
❑	127	Marcus Trufant RC	5.00	2.20
❑	128	Terrell Suggs RC	8.00	3.60
❑	129	Aaron Walker RC	4.00	1.80
❑	130	Calvin Pace RC	4.00	1.80
❑	131	Ken Dorsey RC	8.00	3.60
❑	132	Earnest Graham RC	4.00	1.80
❑	133	Cecil Sapp RC	4.00	1.80
❑	134	William Joseph RC	5.00	2.20
❑	135	Anquan Boldin RC	12.00	5.50
❑	136	Justin Griffith RC	4.00	1.80
❑	137	Teyo Johnson RC	5.00	2.20
❑	138	Chris Crocker RC	2.50	1.10
❑	139	Doug Gabriel RC	6.00	2.70
❑	140	Terry Pierce RC	4.00	1.80
❑	141	Bradie James RC	5.00	2.20
❑	142	Terrence Edwards RC	4.00	1.80
❑	143	E.J. Henderson RC	5.00	2.20
❑	144	Tony Romo RC	5.00	2.20
❑	145	DeWayne Robertson RC	5.00	2.20
❑	146	Dwone Hicks RC	2.50	1.10
❑	147	Carl Ford RC	2.50	1.10
❑	148	Ken Hamlin RC	5.00	2.20
❑	149	Adrian Madise RC	4.00	1.80
❑	150	Siddeeq Shabazz RC	2.50	1.10
❑	151	Dave Ragone RC	5.00	2.20
❑	152	Mike Seidman RC	2.50	1.10
❑	153	DeAndrew Rubin RC	2.50	1.10
❑	154	Mike Pinkard RC	2.50	1.10
❑	155	Nate Burleson RC	8.00	3.60
❑	156	Angelo Crowell RC	4.00	1.80
❑	157	J.R. Tolver RC	4.00	1.80
❑	158	Osi Umenyiora RC	5.00	2.20
❑	159	Nick Barnett RC	8.00	3.60
❑	160	Brandon Drumm RC	2.50	1.10
❑	161	Rien Long RC	2.50	1.10
❑	162	Zuriel Smith RC	2.50	1.10
❑	163	Onterrio Smith RC	6.00	2.70
❑	164	Kenny Peterson RC	4.00	1.80
❑	165	Chaun Thompson RC	2.50	1.10
❑	166	Terrence Holt RC	4.00	1.80
❑	167	Ovie Mughelli RC	2.50	1.10
❑	168	Bethel Johnson RC	8.00	3.60
❑	169	Avon Cobourne RC	2.50	1.10
❑	170	Andre Woolfolk RC	5.00	2.20
❑	171	George Wrighster RC	4.00	1.80
❑	172	Justin Fargas RC	5.00	2.20
❑	173	Marquel Blackwell RC	2.50	1.10
❑	174	Walter Young RC	2.50	1.10
❑	175	Kawika Mitchell RC	5.00	2.20
❑	176	Drayton Florence RC	2.50	1.10
❑	177	Jeremi Johnson RC	4.00	1.80
❑	178	Lee Suggs RC	10.00	4.50
❑	179	David Kircus RC	4.00	1.80
❑	180	Rex Grossman RC	15.00	6.75
❑	180AU	Rex Grossman AU B	60.00	27.00
❑	181	Jon Olinger RC	2.50	1.10
❑	182	Dan Curley RC	2.50	1.10
❑	183	Andrew Pinnock RC	4.00	1.80
❑	184	Kirk Farmer RC	2.50	1.10
❑	185	Charles Rogers RC	6.00	2.70
❑	186	Alonzo Jackson RC	4.00	1.80
❑	187	Trent Smith RC	4.00	1.80
❑	188	Seneca Wallace RC	5.00	2.20
❑	189	Shane Walton RC	2.50	1.10
❑	190	Chris Brown RC	10.00	4.50
❑	191	Dahrran Diedrick RC	5.00	2.20
❑	192	Juston Wood RC	2.50	1.10
❑	193	Mike Doss RC	5.00	2.20
❑	194	Visanthe Shiancoe RC	4.00	1.80
❑	195	Andre Johnson RC	15.00	6.75
❑	196	Dennis Weathersby RC	2.50	1.10
❑	197	Chris Davis RC	4.00	1.80
❑	198	LaTarence Dunbar RC	4.00	1.80
❑	199	Eugene Wilson RC	4.00	1.80
❑	200	Ryan Hoag RC	2.50	1.10
❑	201	Chris Simms RC	10.00	4.50
❑	202	Curt Anes RC	2.50	1.10
❑	203	Taco Wallace RC	4.00	1.80
❑	204	David Tyree RC	4.00	1.80
❑	205	Nate Hybl RC	5.00	2.20
❑	206	Willis McGahee RC	12.00	5.50
❑	207	Casey Moore RC	4.00	1.80
❑	208	Pisa Tinoisamoa RC	8.00	3.60
❑	209	Willie Ponder RC	2.50	1.10
❑	210	Donald Lee RC	4.00	1.80
❑	211	Nnamdi Asomugha RC	4.00	1.80
❑	212	Sammy Davis RC	5.00	2.20
❑	213	Joffrey Reynolds RC	2.50	1.10
❑	214	Eddie Moore RC	4.00	1.80
❑	215	Tony Hollings RC	5.00	2.20
❑	216	Nick Maddox RC	2.50	1.10
❑	217	Kevin Walter RC	4.00	1.80
❑	218	Dan Klecko RC	5.00	2.20
❑	219	Antwan Peek RC	4.00	1.80
❑	220	Tyler Brayton RC	5.00	2.20
❑	221	Byron Leftwich AU B RC	120.00	55.00
❑	222	Bobby Wade AU D RC	15.00	6.75
❑	223	Jerome McDougle AU C RC	12.00	5.50
❑	224	Michael Haynes AU D RC	12.00	5.50
❑	225	Taylor Jacobs AU C RC	20.00	9.00
❑	226	Shaun McDonald AU D RC	12.00	5.50
❑	227	Bryant Johnson AU B RC EXCH	25.00	11.00
❑	228	Taman Gardner AU D RC EXCH	12.00	5.50
❑	229	Domanick Davis AU D RC	40.00	18.00
❑	230	Jason Witten AU D RC	25.00	11.00
❑	231	Kyle Boller AU B RC	60.00	27.00
❑	232	L.J. Smith AU C RC	20.00	9.00
❑	233	Boss Bailey AU C RC	15.00	6.75
❑	234	Billy McMullen AU D RC	10.00	4.50
❑	235	Larry Johnson AU B RC	50.00	22.00
❑	236	Kareem Kelly AU E RC	10.00	4.50
❑	237	Carson Palmer AU A RC	250.00	110.00
❑	238	Quentin Griffin AU D RC	40.00	18.00
❑	239	Kevin Garrett AU E RC	12.00	5.50
❑	240	Charles Tillman AU E RC	25.00	11.00
❑	241	Arnaz Battle AU D RC	15.00	6.75
❑	242	Brooks Bollinger AU E RC	12.00	5.50
❑	243	LaBrandon Toefield AU D RC	12.00	5.50
❑	244	Sam Aiken AU D RC	10.00	4.50
❑	245	Justin Gage AU D RC	12.00	5.50
❑	246	Gibran Hamdan AU D RC	10.00	4.50

2003 Bowman Chrome Refractors

MINT NRMT

*STARS: 2X TO 5X BASIC CARDS
*ROOKIES: .8X TO 2X

2003 Bowman Chrome Uncircluated Blue Refractors

MINT NRMT

STATED PRINT RUN 235 SETS

2003 Bowman Chrome Gold Refractors

	MINT	NRMT
*STARS: 6X TO 15X BASIC CARDS		
*ROOKIES 111-220: 2.5X TO 6X		
1-220 STATED ODDS 1:67		
*ROOKIES 221-246: 1.5X TO 4X		
❑ 180 Rex Grossman	60.00	27.00
❑ 180AU Rex Grossman AU	150.00	70.00
❑ 221 Byron Leftwich AU	300.00	135.00
❑ 229 Domanick Davis AU	120.00	55.00
❑ 231 Kyle Boller AU	250.00	110.00
❑ 235 Larry Johnson AU	200.00	90.00
❑ 237 Carson Palmer AU	300.00	135.00
❑ 238 Quentin Griffin AU	120.00	55.00

2003 Bowman Chrome Red Refractors

	MINT	NRMT
*ROOKIES 111-220: 1.2X TO 3X BASIC CARDS		

2003 Bowman Chrome Xfractors

	MINT	NRMT
*STARS: 2.5X TO 6X BASIC CARDS		
*ROOKIES: 1X TO 2.5X		

2004 Bowman Chrome

	Nm-Mt	Ex-Mt
COMP.SET w/o SP's (220)	175.00	52.50
COMP.SET w/o RC's (110)	30.00	9.00
ONE ROOKIE CARD PER PACK		
ROOKIE AU/199 GROUP A ODDS 1:603		
ROOKIE AU GROUP B ODDS 1:1293		
ROOKIE AU GROUP C ODDS 1:359		
ROOKIE AU GROUP D ODDS 1:21		
❑ 1 Brett Favre	2.50	.75
❑ 2 Jay Fiedler	.40	.12
❑ 3 Andre Davis	.40	.12
❑ 4 Travis Henry	.60	.18
❑ 5 Jimmy Smith	.60	.18
❑ 6 Santana Moss	.60	.18
❑ 7 Correll Buckhalter	.60	.18
❑ 8 Randy Moss	1.25	.35
❑ 9 Edgerrin James	1.00	.30
❑ 10 Marc Bulger	1.00	.30
❑ 11 Derrick Mason	.60	.18
❑ 12 Mark Brunell	.60	.18
❑ 13 Donte Stallworth	.60	.18
❑ 14 Deion Branch	1.00	.30
❑ 15 Jake Plummer	.60	.18
❑ 16 Steve Smith	.60	.18
❑ 17 Jon Kitna	.60	.18
❑ 18 Andre Johnson	1.00	.30
❑ 19 A.J. Feeley	1.00	.30
❑ 20 Drew Bledsoe	1.00	.30
❑ 21 Antonio Bryant	.60	.18
❑ 22 Reggie Wayne	.60	.18
❑ 23 Thomas Jones	.60	.18
❑ 24 Alge Crumpler	.60	.18
❑ 25 Anquan Boldin	1.00	.30
❑ 26 Tim Rattay	.60	.18
❑ 27 Charlie Garner	.60	.18
❑ 28 James Thrash	.40	.12
❑ 29 Koren Robinson	.60	.18
❑ 30 Terrell Owens	1.00	.30
❑ 31 Amani Toomer	.60	.18
❑ 32 Kelly Campbell	.40	.12
❑ 33 Patrick Ramsey	.60	.18
❑ 34 Plaxico Burress	.60	.18
❑ 35 Chad Pennington	1.25	.35
❑ 36 Fred Taylor	.60	.18
❑ 37 Domanick Davis	1.00	.30
❑ 38 DeShaun Foster	.60	.18
❑ 39 T.J. Duckett	.60	.18
❑ 40 Ahman Green	1.00	.30
❑ 41 Lee Suggs	1.00	.30
❑ 42 Tony Gonzalez	.60	.18
❑ 43 Rich Gannon	.60	.18
❑ 44 Kevan Barlow	.60	.18
❑ 45 Torry Holt	1.00	.30
❑ 46 Aaron Brooks	.60	.18
❑ 47 Tyrone Calico	.60	.18
❑ 48 Keenan McCardell	.40	.12
❑ 49 Hines Ward	1.00	.30
❑ 50 LaDainian Tomlinson	1.00	.30
❑ 51 Dante Hall	1.00	.30
❑ 52 Marcus Pollard	.40	.12
❑ 53 Corey Dillon	.60	.18
❑ 54 Justin McCareins	.40	.12
❑ 55 Stephen Davis	.60	.18
❑ 56 Jeff Garcia	1.00	.30
❑ 57 Ashley Lelie	.60	.18
❑ 58 Javon Walker	.60	.18
❑ 59 Kyle Boller	1.00	.30
❑ 60 Chad Johnson	.60	.18
❑ 61 Anthony Thomas	.60	.18
❑ 62 Byron Leftwich	1.50	.45
❑ 63 David Boston	.60	.18
❑ 64 Onterrio Smith	.60	.18
❑ 65 Deuce McAllister	1.00	.30
❑ 66 Antwaan Randle El	.60	.18
❑ 67 Justin Fargas	.60	.18
❑ 68 Laveranues Coles	.60	.18
❑ 69 Quincy Morgan	.60	.18
❑ 70 Priest Holmes	1.25	.35
❑ 71 Robert Ferguson	.40	.12
❑ 72 Charles Rogers	.60	.18
❑ 73 Drew Brees	1.00	.30
❑ 74 Matt Hasselbeck	.60	.18
❑ 75 Peyton Manning	1.50	.45
❑ 76 Rudi Johnson	.60	.18
❑ 77 Jake Delhomme	1.00	.30
❑ 78 Tiki Barber	.60	.18
❑ 79 Brad Johnson	.60	.18
❑ 80 Steve McNair	1.00	.30
❑ 81 Willis McGahee	1.00	.30
❑ 82 Josh McCown	.60	.18
❑ 83 Garrison Hearst	.60	.18
❑ 84 Quincy Carter	.60	.18
❑ 85 Ricky Williams	1.00	.30
❑ 86 Trent Green	.60	.18
❑ 87 Curtis Martin	1.00	.30
❑ 88 Jerry Porter	.60	.18
❑ 89 Brian Westbrook	.60	.18
❑ 90 Clinton Portis	1.00	.30
❑ 91 Eric Moulds	.60	.18
❑ 92 Marcel Shipp	.60	.18
❑ 93 Joey Harrington	1.00	.30
❑ 94 David Carr	1.00	.30
❑ 95 Marvin Harrison	1.00	.30
❑ 96 Joe Horn	.60	.18
❑ 97 Chris Chambers	.60	.18
❑ 98 Darrell Jackson	.60	.18
❑ 99 Eddie George	.60	.18
❑ 100 Donovan McNabb	1.25	.35
❑ 101 Marshall Faulk	1.00	.30
❑ 102 Rex Grossman	1.00	.30
❑ 103 Tai Streets	.40	.12
❑ 104 Jeremy Shockey	1.00	.30
❑ 105 Jamal Lewis	1.00	.30
❑ 106 Tom Brady	1.50	.45
❑ 107 Shaun Alexander	1.00	.30
❑ 108 Carson Palmer	1.25	.35
❑ 109 Daunte Culpepper	1.00	.30
❑ 110 Michael Vick	2.00	.60
❑ 111 Ben Roethlisberger AU/199 RC	400.00	120.00
❑ 112 Tommie Harris RC	5.00	1.50
❑ 113 Thomas Tapeh RC	3.00	.90
❑ 114 Matt Schaub RC	6.00	1.80
❑ 115 Jonathan Smith RC	3.00	.90
❑ 116 Ricardo Colclough RC	4.00	1.20
❑ 117 Jeff Dugan RC	2.00	.60
❑ 118 Larry Fitzgerald RC	12.00	3.60
❑ 119 Gibril Wilson RC	4.00	1.20
❑ 120 Sean Taylor RC	5.00	1.50
❑ 121 Marquise Hill RC	3.00	.90
❑ 122 Cedric Cobbs RC	4.00	1.20
❑ 123 Rich Gardner RC	3.00	.90
❑ 124 Chris Cooley RC	4.00	1.20
❑ 125 Ben Troupe RC	4.00	1.20
❑ 126 Antwan Odom RC	4.00	1.20
❑ 127 Stuart Schweigert RC	4.00	1.20
❑ 128 Derek Abney RC	4.00	1.20
❑ 129 Keary Colbert RC	5.00	1.50
❑ 130 Jeris McIntyre RC	3.00	.90
❑ 131 Matt Kranchick RC	4.00	1.20
❑ 132 Rodney Leisle RC	2.00	.60
❑ 133 Vince Wilfork RC	5.00	1.50
❑ 134 Darnell Dockett RC	3.00	.90
❑ 135 Jeremy LeSueur RC	3.00	.90
❑ 136 Gilbert Gardner RC	3.00	.90
❑ 137 Amon Gordon RC	2.00	.60
❑ 138 Darius Watts RC	5.00	1.50
❑ 139 Junior Siavii RC	4.00	1.20
❑ 140 Igor Olshansky RC	4.00	1.20
❑ 141 Mewelde Moore RC	5.00	1.50
❑ 142 Nathan Vasher RC	4.00	1.20
❑ 143 Randy Starks RC	3.00	.90
❑ 144 Isaac Sopoaga RC	2.00	.60
❑ 145 Drew Henson RC	10.00	3.00
❑ 146 Erik Coleman RC	4.00	1.20
❑ 147 Robert Kent RC	2.00	.60
❑ 148 Jammal Lord RC	4.00	1.20
❑ 149 Richard Seigler RC	3.00	.90
❑ 150 Niko Koutouvides RC	3.00	.90
❑ 151 Brandon Miree RC	3.00	.90
❑ 152 Dunta Robinson RC	4.00	1.20
❑ 153 Courtney Anderson RC	3.00	.90
❑ 154 Bruce Perry RC	3.00	.90
❑ 155 Shaun Phillips RC	3.00	.90
❑ 156 Greg Jones RC	4.00	1.20
❑ 157 Tank Johnson RC	3.00	.90
❑ 158 Dwan Edwards RC	2.00	.60
❑ 159 Julius Jones RC	15.00	4.50
❑ 160 Chad Lavalais RC	3.00	.90
❑ 161 Tim Anderson RC	4.00	1.20
❑ 162 Jarrett Payton RC	4.00	1.20
❑ 163 Matt Ware RC	4.00	1.20
❑ 164 DeAngelo Hall RC	5.00	1.50
❑ 165 Ben Hartsock RC	4.00	1.20
❑ 166 Keith Smith RC	3.00	.90
❑ 167 Michael Jenkins RC	4.00	1.20
❑ 168 Quincy Wilson RC	3.00	.90
❑ 169 Dontarrious Thomas RC	4.00	1.20
❑ 170 Tony Hargrove RC	3.00	.90
❑ 171 Ben Watson RC	4.00	1.20
❑ 172 Triandos Luke RC	4.00	1.20
❑ 173 Kellen Winslow RC	10.00	3.00
❑ 174 Patrick Crayton RC	4.00	1.20
❑ 175 Devard Darling RC	4.00	1.20
❑ 176 Shawntae Spencer RC	4.00	1.20
❑ 177 Will Smith RC	4.00	1.20
❑ 178 Darrion Scott RC	4.00	1.20
❑ 179 Wes Welker RC	4.00	1.20
❑ 180 Ryan Dinwiddie RC	3.00	.90
❑ 181 Rod Davis RC	2.00	.60
❑ 182 Casey Clausen RC	5.00	1.50
❑ 183 Clarence Moore RC	4.00	1.20
❑ 184 D.J. Hackett RC	3.00	.90
❑ 185 Devery Henderson RC	3.00	.90
❑ 186 Sean Jones RC	3.00	.90
❑ 187 Bruce Thornton RC	2.00	.60
❑ 188 Tatum Bell RC	6.00	1.80
❑ 189 Tim Euhus RC	4.00	1.20
❑ 190 John Standeford RC	3.00	.90
❑ 191 Reggie Torbor RC	3.00	.90
❑ 192 Rashaun Woods RC	5.00	1.50
❑ 193 Jason Shivers RC	2.00	.60
❑ 194 Ahmad Carroll RC	5.00	1.50
❑ 195 Keyaron Fox RC	3.00	.90
❑ 196 Von Hutchins RC	3.00	.90

		Nm-Mt	Ex-Mt
❑ 197	Marcus Tubbs RC	4.00	1.20
❑ 198	Daryl Smith RC	4.00	1.20
❑ 199	Robert Gallery RC	6.00	1.80
❑ 200	Marquis Cooper RC	3.00	.90
❑ 201	Bernard Berrian RC	4.00	1.20
❑ 202	Derrick Strait RC	4.00	1.20
❑ 203	Travis LaBoy RC	4.00	1.20
❑ 204	Caleb Miller RC	3.00	.90
❑ 205	Michael Clayton RC	10.00	3.00
❑ 206	Will Poole RC	4.00	1.20
❑ 207	Derrick Hamilton RC	3.00	.90
❑ 208	Glenn Earl RC	3.00	.90
❑ 209	Donnell Washington RC	4.00	1.20
❑ 210	Nate Lawrie RC	3.00	.90
❑ 211	Keiwan Ratliff RC	3.00	.90
❑ 212	Luke McCown RC	4.00	1.20
❑ 213	Joey Thomas RC	4.00	1.20
❑ 214	Shawn Andrews RC	4.00	1.20
❑ 215	Derrick Ward RC	2.00	.60
❑ 216	Reggie Williams RC	5.00	1.50
❑ 217	Rod Rutherford RC	3.00	.90
❑ 218	Michael Gaines RC	3.00	.90
❑ 219	Will Allen RC	4.00	1.20
❑ 220	J.P. Losman RC	10.00	3.00
❑ 221	Roy Williams AU/199 RC	120.00	36.00
❑ 222	Kevin Jones AU/199 RC	150.00	45.00
❑ 223	Philip Rivers AU/199 RC	120.00	36.00
❑ 224	Steven Jackson AU/199 RC	150.00	45.00
❑ 225	Eli Manning AU/199 RC	225.00	70.00
❑ 226	Cody Pickett AU D RC	20.00	6.00
❑ 227	P.K. Sam AU D RC	15.00	4.50
❑ 228	Maurice Mann AU D RC	15.00	4.50
❑ 229	Andy Hall AU D RC	15.00	4.50
❑ 230	Chris Perry AU D RC	25.00	7.50
❑ 231	Ernest Wilford AU C RC	20.00	6.00
❑ 232	Kenechi Udeze AU D RC	20.00	6.00
❑ 233	Michael Boulware AU D RC	20.00	6.00
❑ 234	B.J. Symons AU D RC	20.00	6.00
❑ 235	Jared Lorenzen AU D RC	15.00	4.50
❑ 236	Matt Mauck AU D RC	20.00	6.00
❑ 237	Carlos Francis AU D RC	15.00	4.50
❑ 238	Michael Turner AU D RC	15.00	4.50
❑ 239	Lee Evans AU B RC	40.00	12.00
❑ 240	Jerricho Cotchery AU D RC	20.00	6.00
❑ 241	John Navarre AU D RC	20.00	6.00
❑ 242	Jonathan Vilma AU D RC	25.00	7.50
❑ 243	Josh Harris AU D RC	20.00	6.00
❑ 244	Jeff Smoker AU C RC	25.00	7.50
❑ 245	Jamaar Taylor AU D RC	20.00	6.00

2004 Bowman Chrome Gold Refractors

Nm-Mt Ex-Mt

*STARS: 6X TO 15X BASE CARD HI
*ROOKIES: 4X TO 10X BASE CARD HI
1-220 STATED ODDS 1:59
*ROOKIE AUTOS: 1X TO 2.5X BASE CARD HI
ROOKIE AUTO STATED ODDS 1:646
STATED PRINT RUN 50 SER.#'d SETS

2004 Bowman Chrome Red Refractors

Nm-Mt Ex-Mt

*ROOKIES 112-220: 2X TO 5X
112-220 PRINT RUN 210 SER.#'d SETS
UNPRICED 111/221-245 AU PRINT RUN 10
ONE RED REFRACTOR PER HOBBY BOX

		Nm-Mt	Ex-Mt
❑ NNO	EXCH Card	12.00	3.60

2004 Bowman Chrome Refractors

Nm-Mt Ex-Mt

*STARS: 2X TO 5X BASE CARD HI
*ROOKIES: .8X TO 2X BASE CARD HI
STATED ODDS 1:6
STATED PRINT RUN 500 SER.#'d SETS

2004 Bowman Chrome Uncirculated White Refractors

Nm-Mt Ex-Mt

*ROOKIES 112-220: 2X TO 5X
CARDS ISSUED VIA EXCH AT THEPIT.COM
STATED PRINT RUN 210 SETS

2004 Bowman Chrome Xfractors

Nm-Mt Ex-Mt

*STARS: 2.5X TO 6X BASE CARD HI
*ROOKIES: 1.2X TO 3X BASE CARD HI
STATED ODDS 1:12
STATED PRINT RUN 250 SER.#'d SETS

2000 Bowman Reserve

		Nm-Mt	Ex-Mt
COMP.SET w/o SP's (100)		40.00	18.00
❑ 1	Chad Pennington RC	50.00	22.00
❑ 2	Shaun Alexander RC	40.00	18.00

		Nm-Mt	Ex-Mt
❑ 3	Thomas Jones RC	25.00	11.00
❑ 4	Courtney Brown RC	15.00	6.75
❑ 5	Curtis Keaton RC	12.00	5.50
❑ 6	Jerry Porter RC	20.00	9.00
❑ 7	Jamal Lewis RC	40.00	18.00
❑ 8	Ron Dayne RC	15.00	6.75
❑ 9	R.Jay Soward RC	12.00	5.50
❑ 10	Tee Martin RC	15.00	6.75
❑ 11	Travis Taylor RC	15.00	6.75
❑ 12	Plaxico Burress RC	30.00	13.50
❑ 13	Giovanni Carmazzi RC	12.00	5.50
❑ 14	Sylvester Morris RC	12.00	5.50
❑ 15	Chris Redman RC	12.00	5.50
❑ 16	Trung Canidate RC	12.00	5.50
❑ 17	J.R. Redmond RC	12.00	5.50
❑ 18	Bubba Franks RC	15.00	6.75
❑ 19	Travis Prentice RC	12.00	5.50
❑ 20	Peter Warrick RC	15.00	6.75
❑ 21	Frank Sanders	.75	.35
❑ 22	Edgerrin James	2.00	.90
❑ 23	Marcus Robinson	1.25	.55
❑ 24	Mike Alstott	1.25	.55
❑ 25	Jerry Rice	2.50	1.10
❑ 26	Marshall Faulk	1.50	.70
❑ 27	Brad Johnson	1.25	.55
❑ 28	Elvis Grbac	.75	.35
❑ 29	Wayne Chrebet	.75	.35
❑ 30	Akili Smith	.50	.23
❑ 31	Rob Johnson	.75	.35
❑ 32	Brett Favre	4.00	1.80
❑ 33	Ricky Williams	1.25	.55
❑ 34	Donovan McNabb	2.00	.90
❑ 35	Cris Carter	1.25	.55
❑ 36	Ricky Watters	.75	.35
❑ 37	Steve McNair	2.00	.90
❑ 38	Stephen Davis	1.25	.55
❑ 39	Fred Taylor	1.25	.55
❑ 40	Rocket Ismail	.75	.35
❑ 41	Terry Glenn	.75	.35
❑ 42	Ed McCaffrey	1.25	.55
❑ 43	Patrick Jeffers	1.25	.55
❑ 44	Jake Plummer	.75	.35
❑ 45	Doug Flutie	1.25	.55
❑ 46	Terrell Davis	1.25	.55
❑ 47	Marvin Harrison	1.25	.55
❑ 48	Amani Toomer	.75	.35
❑ 49	Tyrone Wheatley	.75	.35
❑ 50	Charlie Garner	.75	.35
❑ 51	Jevon Kearse	1.25	.55
❑ 52	Michael Westbrook	.75	.35
❑ 53	Eddie George	1.25	.55
❑ 54	Robert Smith	1.25	.55
❑ 55	Keyshawn Johnson	1.25	.55
❑ 56	Torry Holt	1.25	.55
❑ 57	Jon Kitna	1.25	.55
❑ 58	Curtis Conway	.75	.35
❑ 59	Jeff Garcia	1.25	.55
❑ 60	Randy Moss	2.50	1.10
❑ 61	Jimmy Smith	.75	.35
❑ 62	James Stewart	.75	.35
❑ 63	Troy Aikman	2.50	1.10
❑ 64	Cade McNown	.50	.23
❑ 65	Natrone Means	.75	.35
❑ 66	Jamal Anderson	1.25	.55
❑ 67	Warrick Dunn	1.25	.55
❑ 68	Kordell Stewart	.75	.35
❑ 69	Duce Staley	1.25	.55
❑ 70	Rich Gannon	1.25	.55

❑ 71 Curtis Martin 1.25 .55
❑ 72 Kerry Collins .75 .35
❑ 73 Jeff Blake .75 .35
❑ 74 Drew Bledsoe 1.50 .70
❑ 75 Kevin Dyson .75 .35
❑ 76 Tony Gonzalez .75 .35
❑ 77 Mark Brunell 1.25 .55
❑ 78 Peyton Manning 3.00 1.35
❑ 79 Dorsey Levens .75 .35
❑ 80 Germane Crowell .50 .23
❑ 81 Brian Griese 1.25 .55
❑ 82 Steve Beuerlein .75 .35
❑ 83 Eric Moulds 1.25 .55
❑ 84 Tony Banks .75 .35
❑ 85 Chris Chandler .75 .35
❑ 86 Isaac Bruce 1.25 .55
❑ 87 Terrell Owens 1.25 .55
❑ 88 Jerome Bettis 1.25 .55
❑ 89 Daunte Culpepper 1.50 .70
❑ 90 Emmitt Smith 2.50 1.10
❑ 91 Curtis Enis .50 .23
❑ 92 Shaun King .50 .23
❑ 93 Tim Brown 1.25 .55
❑ 94 Antonio Freeman 1.25 .55
❑ 95 Charlie Batch 1.25 .55
❑ 96 Tim Couch .75 .35
❑ 97 Corey Dillon 1.25 .55
❑ 98 Muhsin Muhammad .75 .35
❑ 99 Joey Galloway .75 .35
❑ 100 Kurt Warner 2.50 1.10
❑ 101 David Boston 1.25 .55
❑ 102 Rod Smith .50 .23
❑ 103 Derrick Mayes .75 .35
❑ 104 Tony Martin .75 .35
❑ 105 Darnay Scott .75 .35
❑ 106 Joe Horn .75 .35
❑ 107 Troy Edwards .50 .23
❑ 108 James Johnson .50 .23
❑ 109 Vinny Testaverde .75 .35
❑ 110 Qadry Ismail .75 .35
❑ 111 Andre Reed .75 .35
❑ 112 Zach Thomas 1.25 .55
❑ 113 Ike Hilliard .75 .35
❑ 114 Herman Moore .75 .35
❑ 115 Kevin Johnson 1.25 .55
❑ 116 Shawn Jefferson .50 .23
❑ 117 Terance Mathis .75 .35
❑ 118 Peerless Price 1.25 .55
❑ 119 Bert Emanuel .50 .23
❑ 120 Terrence Wilkins .50 .23
❑ 121 Mike Anderson RC 15.00 6.75
❑ 122 Dez White RC 15.00 6.75
❑ 123 Todd Pinkston RC 15.00 6.75
❑ 124 Reuben Droughns RC 20.00 9.00
❑ 125 Danny Farmer RC 12.00 5.50

1995 Bowman's Best

	Nm-Mt	Ex-Mt
COMPLETE SET (180)	100.00	45.00

❑ R1 Ki-Jana Carter RC 1.50 .70
❑ R2 Tony Boselli RC 1.50 .70
❑ R3 Steve McNair RC 15.00 6.75
❑ R4 Michael Westbrook RC 1.50 .70
❑ R5 Kerry Collins RC 6.00 2.70
❑ R6 Kevin Carter RC 1.50 .70
❑ R7 Mike Mamula RC .40 .18
❑ R8 Joey Galloway RC 6.00 2.70
❑ R9 Kyle Brady RC 1.50 .70
❑ R10 Ray McElroy RC .40 .18
❑ R11 Derrick Alexander DE RC .40 .18
❑ R12 Warren Sapp RC 6.00 2.70
❑ R13 Mark Fields RC 1.50 .70
❑ R14 Ruben Brown RC 1.50 .70
❑ R15 Ellis Johnson RC .40 .18
❑ R16 Hugh Douglas RC 1.50 .70
❑ R17 Alundis Brice RC .40 .18
❑ R18 Napoleon Kaufman RC 5.00 2.20
❑ R19 James O. Stewart RC 3.00 1.35
❑ R20 Luther Elliss RC .40 .18
❑ R21 Rashaan Salaam RC .75 .35
❑ R22 Tyrone Poole RC 1.50 .70
❑ R23 Ty Law RC 4.00 1.80
❑ R24 Korey Stringer RC .75 .35
❑ R25 Billy Milner RC .40 .18
❑ R26 Roell Preston RC .75 .35
❑ R27 Mark Bruener RC .75 .35
❑ R28 Derrick Brooks RC 6.00 2.70
❑ R29 Blake Brockermeyer RC .40 .18
❑ R30 Mike Frederick RC .40 .18
❑ R31 Trezelle Jenkins RC .40 .18
❑ R32 Craig Newsome RC .40 .18
❑ R33 Matt O'Dwyer RC .40 .18
❑ R34 Terrance Shaw RC .40 .18
❑ R35 Anthony Cook RC .40 .18
❑ R36 Darick Holmes RC .75 .35
❑ R37 Cory Raymer RC .40 .18
❑ R38 Zach Wiegert RC .40 .18
❑ R39 Sam Shade RC .40 .18
❑ R40 Brian DeMarco RC .40 .18
❑ R41 Ron Davis RC .40 .18
❑ R42 Orlando Thomas RC .40 .18
❑ R43 Derek West RC .40 .18
❑ R44 Ray Zellars RC .75 .35
❑ R45 Todd Collins RC .75 .35
❑ R46 Linc Harden RC .40 .18
❑ R47 Frank Sanders RC 1.50 .70
❑ R48 Ken Dilger RC 1.50 .70
❑ R49 Barrett Robbins RC .40 .18
❑ R50 Bobby Taylor RC 2.50 1.10
❑ R51 Terrell Fletcher RC .40 .18
❑ R52 Jack Jackson RC .40 .18
❑ R53 Jeff Kopp RC .40 .18
❑ R54 Brendan Stai RC .40 .18
❑ R55 Corey Fuller RC .40 .18
❑ R56 Todd Sauerbrun RC .40 .18
❑ R57 Dameian Jeffries RC .40 .18
❑ R58 Troy Dumas RC .40 .18
❑ R59 Charlie Williams RC .40 .18
❑ R60 Kordell Stewart RC 6.00 2.70
❑ R61 Jay Barker RC .40 .18
❑ R62 Jesse James RC .40 .18
❑ R63 Shane Hannah RC .40 .18
❑ R64 Rob Johnson RC 4.00 1.80
❑ R65 Darius Holland RC .40 .18
❑ R66 William Henderson RC 5.00 2.20
❑ R67 Chris Sanders RC .75 .35
❑ R68 Darryl Pounds RC .40 .18
❑ R69 Melvin Tuten RC .40 .18
❑ R70 David Sloan RC .40 .18
❑ R71 Chris Hudson RC .40 .18
❑ R72 William Strong RC .40 .18
❑ R73 Brian Williams LB RC .40 .18
❑ R74 Curtis Martin RC 15.00 6.75
❑ R75 Mike Verstegen RC .40 .18
❑ R76 Justin Armour RC .40 .18
❑ R77 Lorenzo Styles RC .40 .18
❑ R78 Oliver Gibson RC .40 .18
❑ R79 Zack Crockett RC .75 .35
❑ R80 Tau Pupua RC .40 .18
❑ R81 Tamarick Vanover RC 1.50 .70
❑ R82 Steve McLaughlin RC .40 .18
❑ R83 Sean Harris RC .40 .18
❑ R84 Eric Zeier RC 1.50 .70
❑ R85 Rodney Young RC .40 .18
❑ R86 Chad May RC .40 .18
❑ R87 Evan Pilgrim RC .40 .18
❑ R88 James A.Stewart RC .40 .18
❑ R89 Torey Hunter RC .40 .18
❑ R90 Antonio Freeman RC 4.00 1.80
❑ V1 Rob Moore .60 .25
❑ V2 Craig Heyward .60 .25
❑ V3 Jim Kelly 1.25 .55
❑ V4 John Kasay .30 .14
❑ V5 Jeff Graham .30 .14
❑ V6 Jeff Blake RC 2.50 1.10
❑ V7 Antonio Langham .30 .14
❑ V8 Troy Aikman 3.00 1.35
❑ V9 Simon Fletcher .30 .14
❑ V10 Barry Sanders 5.00 2.20
❑ V11 Edgar Bennett .60 .25
❑ V12 Ray Childress .30 .14
❑ V13 Ray Buchanan .30 .14
❑ V14 Desmond Howard .60 .25
❑ V15 Dale Carter .60 .25
❑ V16 Troy Vincent .30 .14
❑ V17 David Palmer .60 .25
❑ V18 Ben Coates .60 .25
❑ V19 Derek Brown TE .30 .14
❑ V20 Dave Brown .60 .25
❑ V21 Mo Lewis .30 .14
❑ V22 Harvey Williams .30 .14
❑ V23 Randall Cunningham 1.25 .55
❑ V24 Kevin Greene .60 .25
❑ V25 Junior Seau 1.25 .55
❑ V26 Merton Hanks .30 .14
❑ V27 Cortez Kennedy .60 .25
❑ V28 Troy Drayton .30 .14
❑ V29 Hardy Nickerson .30 .14
❑ V30 Brian Mitchell .30 .14
❑ V31 Raymont Harris .30 .14
❑ V32 Keith Goganious .30 .14
❑ V33 Andre Reed .60 .25
❑ V34 Terance Mathis .60 .25
❑ V35 Garrison Hearst 1.25 .55
❑ V36 Glyn Milburn .30 .14
❑ V37 Emmitt Smith 5.00 2.20
❑ V38 Vinny Testaverde .60 .25
❑ V39 Darnay Scott .60 .25
❑ V40 Mickey Washington .30 .14
❑ V41 Craig Erickson .30 .14
❑ V42 Chris Chandler 1.25 .55
❑ V43 Brett Favre 6.00 2.70
❑ V44 Scott Mitchell .60 .25
❑ V45 Chris Slade .30 .14
❑ V46 Warren Moon .60 .25
❑ V47 Dan Marino 6.00 2.70
❑ V48 Greg Hill .60 .25
❑ V49 Rocket Ismail .60 .25
❑ V50 Bobby Houston .30 .14
❑ V51 Rodney Hampton .60 .25
❑ V52 Jim Everett .30 .14
❑ V53 Rick Mirer .60 .25
❑ V54 Steve Young 2.50 1.10
❑ V55 Dennis Gibson .30 .14
❑ V56 Rod Woodson .60 .25
❑ V57 Calvin Williams .60 .25
❑ V58 Tom Carter .30 .14
❑ V59 Trent Dilfer 1.25 .55
❑ V60 Shane Conlan .30 .14
❑ V61 Cornelius Bennett .60 .25
❑ V62 Eric Metcalf .60 .25
❑ V63 Frank Reich .30 .14
❑ V64 Eric Hill .30 .14
❑ V65 Erik Kramer .30 .14
❑ V66 Michael Irvin 1.25 .55
❑ V67 Tony McGee .30 .14
❑ V68 Andre Rison .60 .25
❑ V69 Shannon Sharpe .60 .25
❑ V70 Quentin Coryatt .60 .25
❑ V71 Robert Brooks 1.25 .55
❑ V72 Steve Beuerlein .60 .25
❑ V73 Herman Moore 1.25 .55
❑ V74 Jack Del Rio .30 .14
❑ V75 Dave Meggett .30 .14
❑ V76 Pete Stoyanovich .30 .14
❑ V77 Neil Smith .60 .25
❑ V78 Corey Miller .30 .14
❑ V79 Tim Brown 1.25 .55
❑ V80 Tyrone Hughes .60 .25
❑ V81 Boomer Esiason .60 .25
❑ V82 Natrone Means .60 .25
❑ V83 Chris Warren .60 .25
❑ V84 Byron Bam Morris .30 .14
❑ V85 Jerry Rice 3.00 1.35
❑ V86 Michael Zordich .30 .14
❑ V87 Errict Rhett .60 .25

		Nm-Mt	Ex-Mt
❑ V88	Henry Ellard	.60	.25
❑ V89	Chris Miller	.30	.14
❑ V90	John Elway	6.00	2.70

1995 Bowman's Best Refractors

	Nm-Mt	Ex-Mt
COMPLETE SET (180)	500.00	220.00

*STARS: 1.2X TO 3X BASIC CARDS
*ROOKIES: 1X TO 2.5X BASIC CARDS

1996 Bowman's Best

		Nm-Mt	Ex-Mt
COMPLETE SET (180)		80.00	36.00
❑ 1	Emmitt Smith	3.00	1.35
❑ 2	Kordell Stewart	.75	.35
❑ 3	Mark Chmura	.40	.18
❑ 4	Sean Dawkins	.20	.09
❑ 5	Steve Young	1.50	.70
❑ 6	Tamarick Vanover	.40	.18
❑ 7	Scott Mitchell	.40	.18
❑ 8	Aaron Hayden	.20	.09
❑ 9	William Thomas	.20	.09
❑ 10	Dan Marino	4.00	1.80
❑ 11	Curtis Conway	.75	.35
❑ 12	Steve Atwater	.20	.09
❑ 13	Derrick Brooks	.75	.35
❑ 14	Rick Mirer	.40	.18
❑ 15	Mark Brunell	1.00	.45
❑ 16	Garrison Hearst	.40	.18
❑ 17	Eric Turner	.20	.09
❑ 18	Mark Carrier WR	.20	.09
❑ 19	Darnay Scott	.40	.18
❑ 20	Steve McNair	1.50	.70
❑ 21	Jim Everett	.20	.09
❑ 22	Wayne Chrebet	1.00	.45
❑ 23	Ben Coates	.40	.18
❑ 24	Harvey Williams	.20	.09
❑ 25	Michael Westbrook	.75	.35
❑ 26	Kevin Carter	.20	.09
❑ 27	Dave Brown	.20	.09
❑ 28	Jake Reed	.40	.18
❑ 29	Thurman Thomas	.75	.35
❑ 30	Jeff George	.40	.18
❑ 31	Carnell Lake	.20	.09
❑ 32	J.J. Stokes	.75	.35
❑ 33	Jay Novacek	.20	.09
❑ 34	Brett Perriman	.20	.09
❑ 35	Robert Brooks	.75	.35
❑ 36	Neil Smith	.40	.18
❑ 37	Chris Zorich	.20	.09
❑ 38	Micheal Barrow	.20	.09
❑ 39	Quentin Coryatt	.20	.09
❑ 40	Kerry Collins	.75	.35
❑ 41	Aeneas Williams	.20	.09
❑ 42	James O.Stewart	.40	.18
❑ 43	Warren Moon	.40	.18
❑ 44	Willie McGinest	.20	.09
❑ 45	Rodney Hampton	.40	.18
❑ 46	Jeff Hostetler	.20	.09
❑ 47	Darrell Green	.20	.09
❑ 48	Warren Sapp	.20	.09
❑ 49	Troy Drayton	.20	.09
❑ 50	Junior Seau	.75	.35
❑ 51	Mike Mamula	.20	.09
❑ 52	Antonio Langham	.20	.09
❑ 53	Eric Metcalf	.20	.09
❑ 54	Adrian Murrell	.40	.18
❑ 55	Joey Galloway	.75	.35
❑ 56	Anthony Miller	.40	.18
❑ 57	Carl Pickens	.40	.18
❑ 58	Bruce Smith	.40	.18
❑ 59	Merton Hanks	.20	.09
❑ 60	Troy Aikman	2.00	.90
❑ 61	Erik Kramer	.20	.09
❑ 62	Tyrone Poole	.20	.09
❑ 63	Michael Jackson	.40	.18
❑ 64	Rob Moore	.40	.18
❑ 65	Marcus Allen	.75	.35
❑ 66	Orlando Thomas	.20	.09
❑ 67	Dave Meggett	.20	.09
❑ 68	Trent Dilfer	.75	.35
❑ 69	Herman Moore	.40	.18
❑ 70	Brett Favre	4.00	1.80
❑ 71	Blaine Bishop	.20	.09
❑ 72	Eric Allen	.20	.09
❑ 73	Bernie Parmalee	.20	.09
❑ 74	Kyle Brady	.20	.09
❑ 75	Terry McDaniel	.20	.09
❑ 76	Rodney Peete	.20	.09
❑ 77	Yancey Thigpen	.40	.18
❑ 78	Stan Humphries	.40	.18
❑ 79	Craig Heyward	.20	.09
❑ 80	Rashaan Salaam	.40	.18
❑ 81	Shannon Sharpe	.40	.18
❑ 82	Jim Harbaugh	.40	.18
❑ 83	Vinnie Clark	.20	.09
❑ 84	Steve Bono	.20	.09
❑ 85	Drew Bledsoe	1.00	.45
❑ 86	Ken Norton	.20	.09
❑ 87	Brian Mitchell	.20	.09
❑ 88	Hardy Nickerson	.20	.09
❑ 89	Todd Lyght	.20	.09
❑ 90	Barry Sanders	3.00	1.35
❑ 91	Robert Blackmon	.20	.09
❑ 92	Larry Centers	.40	.18
❑ 93	Jim Kelly	.75	.35
❑ 94	Lamar Lathon	.20	.09
❑ 95	Cris Carter	.75	.35
❑ 96	Hugh Douglas	.40	.18
❑ 97	Michael Strahan	.40	.18
❑ 98	Lee Woodall	.20	.09
❑ 99	Michael Irvin	.75	.35
❑ 100	Marshall Faulk	1.00	.45
❑ 101	Terance Mathis	.20	.09
❑ 102	Eric Zeier	.20	.09
❑ 103	Marty Carter	.20	.09
❑ 104	Steve Tovar	.20	.09
❑ 105	Isaac Bruce	.75	.35
❑ 106	Tony Martin	.40	.18
❑ 107	Dale Carter	.20	.09
❑ 108	Terry Kirby	.40	.18
❑ 109	Tyrone Hughes	.20	.09
❑ 110	Bryce Paup	.20	.09
❑ 111	Errict Rhett	.40	.18
❑ 112	Ricky Watters	.40	.18
❑ 113	Chris Chandler	.40	.18
❑ 114	Edgar Bennett	.40	.18
❑ 115	John Elway	4.00	1.80
❑ 116	Sam Mills	.20	.09
❑ 117	Seth Joyner	.20	.09
❑ 118	Jeff Lageman	.20	.09
❑ 119	Chris Calloway	.20	.09
❑ 120	Curtis Martin	1.50	.70
❑ 121	Ken Harvey	.20	.09
❑ 122	Eugene Daniel	.20	.09
❑ 123	Tim Brown	.75	.35
❑ 124	Mo Lewis	.20	.09
❑ 125	Jeff Blake	.75	.35
❑ 126	Jessie Tuggle	.20	.09
❑ 127	Vinny Testaverde	.40	.18
❑ 128	Chris Warren	.40	.18
❑ 129	Terrell Davis	1.50	.70
❑ 130	Greg Lloyd	.40	.18
❑ 131	Deion Sanders	1.00	.45
❑ 132	Derrick Thomas	.40	.18
❑ 133	Darryll Lewis UER back Daryl Lewis	.20	.09
❑ 134	Reggie White	.75	.35
❑ 135	Jerry Rice	2.00	.90
❑ 136	Tony Banks RC	1.00	.45
❑ 137	Derrick Mayes RC	1.00	.45
❑ 138	Leeland McElroy RC	.50	.23
❑ 139	Bryan Still RC	.50	.23
❑ 140	Tim Biakabutuka RC	1.00	.45
❑ 141	Rickey Dudley RC	1.00	.45
❑ 142	Tory James RC	.50	.23
❑ 143	Lawyer Milloy RC	1.25	.55
❑ 144	Mike Ulufale RC	.25	.11
❑ 145	Bobby Engram RC	1.00	.45
❑ 146	Willie Anderson RC	.25	.11
❑ 147	Terrell Owens RC	15.00	6.75
❑ 148	Jonathan Ogden RC	1.00	.45
❑ 149	Darrius Johnson RC	.25	.11
❑ 150	Kevin Hardy RC	1.00	.45
❑ 151	Simeon Rice RC	2.50	1.10
❑ 152	Alex Molden RC	.25	.11
❑ 153	Cedric Jones RC	.25	.11
❑ 154	Duane Clemons RC	.25	.11
❑ 155	Karim Abdul-Jabbar RC	1.00	.45
❑ 156	Dedric Mathis RC	.25	.11
❑ 157	John Michels RC	.25	.11
❑ 158	Winslow Oliver RC	.25	.11
❑ 159	Stepfret Williams RC	.25	.11
❑ 160	Eddie Kennison RC	1.00	.45
❑ 161	Marcus Coleman RC	.25	.11
❑ 162	Tedy Bruschi RC	25.00	11.00
❑ 163	Detron Smith RC	.25	.11
❑ 164	Ray Lewis RC	30.00	13.50
❑ 165	Marvin Harrison RC	12.00	5.50
❑ 166	Je'rod Cherry RC	.25	.11
❑ 167	Jerris McPhail RC	.25	.11
❑ 168	Eric Moulds RC	8.00	3.60
❑ 169	Walt Harris RC	.25	.11
❑ 170	Eddie George RC	8.00	3.60
❑ 171	Jermaine Lewis RC	1.00	.45
❑ 172	Jeff Lewis RC	.50	.23
❑ 173	Ray Mickens RC	.25	.11
❑ 174	Amani Toomer RC	5.00	2.20
❑ 175	Zach Thomas RC	3.00	1.35
❑ 176	Lawrence Phillips RC	.50	.23
❑ 177	John Mobley RC	.25	.11
❑ 178	Anthony Dorsett RC	.25	.11
❑ 179	DeRon Jenkins	.20	.09
❑ 180	Keyshawn Johnson RC	6.00	2.70

1996 Bowman's Best Atomic Refractors

		Nm-Mt	Ex-Mt
COMP.ATOMIC REF. (180)		500.00	220.00

*ATOMIC REF.STARS: 3X TO 8X
*ATOMIC REF.RCs: 1.2X TO 3X

❑ 162	Tedy Bruschi	120.00	55.00
❑ 164	Ray Lewis	200.00	90.00

1996 Bowman's Best Refractors

		Nm-Mt	Ex-Mt
COMP.REF.SET (180)		250.00	110.00

*REF.STARS: 1.2X TO 3X BASE CARDS
*REFRACTOR RCs: .8X TO 2X

❑ 162	Tedy Bruschi	60.00	27.00
❑ 164	Ray Lewis	80.00	36.00

1997 Bowman's Best

	Nm-Mt	Ex-Mt
COMPLETE SET (125)	30.00	13.50

Card	Nm-Mt	Ex-Mt
❑ 1 Brett Favre	4.00	1.80
❑ 2 Larry Centers	.60	.25
❑ 3 Trent Dilfer	1.00	.45
❑ 4 Rodney Hampton	.60	.25
❑ 5 Wesley Walls	.60	.25
❑ 6 Jerome Bettis	1.00	.45
❑ 7 Keyshawn Johnson	1.00	.45
❑ 8 Keenan McCardell	.60	.25
❑ 9 Terry Allen	1.00	.45
❑ 10 Troy Aikman	2.00	.90
❑ 11 Tony Banks	.60	.25
❑ 12 Ty Detmer	.60	.25
❑ 13 Chris Chandler	.60	.25
❑ 14 Marshall Faulk	1.25	.55
❑ 15 Heath Shuler	.40	.18
❑ 16 Stan Humphries	.60	.25
❑ 17 Bryan Cox	.40	.18
❑ 18 Chris Spielman	.40	.18
❑ 19 Derrick Thomas	.60	.25
❑ 20 Steve Young	1.25	.55
❑ 21 Desmond Howard	.60	.25
❑ 22 Jeff Blake	.60	.25
❑ 23 Michael Jackson	.60	.25
❑ 24 Cris Carter	1.00	.45
❑ 25 Joey Galloway	.60	.25
❑ 26 Simeon Rice	.60	.25
❑ 27 Reggie White	1.00	.45
❑ 28 Dave Brown	.40	.18
❑ 29 Mike Alstott	1.00	.45
❑ 30 Emmitt Smith	3.00	1.35
❑ 31 Anthony Johnson	.40	.18
❑ 32 Mark Brunell	1.25	.55
❑ 33 Ricky Watters	.60	.25
❑ 34 Terrell Davis	1.25	.55
❑ 35 Ben Coates	.60	.25
❑ 36 Gus Frerotte	.40	.18
❑ 37 Andre Reed	.60	.25
❑ 38 Isaac Bruce	1.00	.45
❑ 39 Junior Seau	1.00	.45
❑ 40 Eddie George	1.00	.45
❑ 41 Adrian Murrell	.60	.25
❑ 42 Jake Reed	.60	.25
❑ 43 Karim Abdul-Jabbar	.60	.25
❑ 44 Scott Mitchell	.60	.25
❑ 45 Ki-Jana Carter	.40	.18
❑ 46 Curtis Conway	.60	.25
❑ 47 Jim Harbaugh	.60	.25
❑ 48 Tim Brown	1.00	.45
❑ 49 Mario Bates	.40	.18
❑ 50 Jerry Rice	2.00	.90
❑ 51 Byron Bam Morris	.40	.18
❑ 52 Marcus Allen	1.00	.45
❑ 53 Errict Rhett	.40	.18
❑ 54 Steve McNair	1.25	.55
❑ 55 Kerry Collins	1.00	.45
❑ 56 Bert Emanuel	.60	.25
❑ 57 Curtis Martin	1.25	.55
❑ 58 Bryce Paup	.40	.18
❑ 59 Brad Johnson	1.00	.45
❑ 60 John Elway	4.00	1.80
❑ 61 Natrone Means	.60	.25
❑ 62 Deion Sanders	1.00	.45
❑ 63 Tony Martin	.60	.25
❑ 64 Michael Westbrook	.60	.25
❑ 65 Chris Calloway	.40	.18
❑ 66 Antonio Freeman	1.00	.45
❑ 67 Rob Johnson	1.00	.45
❑ 68 Kent Graham	.40	.18
❑ 69 O.J. McDuffie	.60	.25
❑ 70 Barry Sanders	3.00	1.35
❑ 71 Chris Warren	.60	.25
❑ 72 Kordell Stewart	1.00	.45
❑ 73 Thurman Thomas	1.00	.45
❑ 74 Marvin Harrison	1.00	.45
❑ 75 Carl Pickens	.60	.25
❑ 76 Brent Jones	.40	.18
❑ 77 Irving Fryar	.60	.25
❑ 78 Neil O'Donnell	.60	.25
❑ 79 Elvis Grbac	.60	.25
❑ 80 Drew Bledsoe	1.25	.55
❑ 81 Shannon Sharpe	.60	.25
❑ 82 Vinny Testaverde	.60	.25
❑ 83 Chris Sanders	.40	.18
❑ 84 Herman Moore	.60	.25
❑ 85 Jeff George	.60	.25
❑ 86 Bruce Smith	.60	.25
❑ 87 Robert Smith	.60	.25
❑ 88 Kevin Hardy	.40	.18
❑ 89 Kevin Greene	.60	.25
❑ 90 Dan Marino	4.00	1.80
❑ 91 Michael Irvin	1.00	.45
❑ 92 Garrison Hearst	.60	.25
❑ 93 Lake Dawson	.40	.18
❑ 94 Lawrence Phillips	.40	.18
❑ 95 Terry Glenn	1.00	.45
❑ 96 Jake Plummer RC	6.00	2.70
❑ 97 Byron Hanspard RC	.60	.25
❑ 98 Bryant Westbrook RC	.40	.18
❑ 99 Troy Davis RC	.60	.25
❑ 100 Danny Wuerffel RC	1.00	.45
❑ 101 Tony Gonzalez RC	4.00	1.80
❑ 102 Jim Druckenmiller RC	.60	.25
❑ 103 Kevin Lockett RC	.60	.25
❑ 104 Renaldo Wynn RC	.40	.18
❑ 105 James Farrior RC	1.00	.45
❑ 106 Rae Carruth RC	.40	.18
❑ 107 Tom Knight RC	.40	.18
❑ 108 Corey Dillon RC	8.00	3.60
❑ 109 Kenny Holmes RC	1.00	.45
❑ 110 Orlando Pace RC	1.00	.45
❑ 111 Reidel Anthony RC	1.00	.45
❑ 112 Chad Scott RC	.60	.25
❑ 113 Antowain Smith RC	3.00	1.35
❑ 114 David LaFleur RC	.40	.18
❑ 115 Yatil Green RC	.60	.25
❑ 116 Darrell Russell RC	.40	.18
❑ 117 Joey Kent RC	1.00	.45
❑ 118 Darnell Autry RC	.60	.25
❑ 119 Peter Boulware RC	1.00	.45
❑ 120 Shawn Springs RC	.60	.25
❑ 121 Ike Hilliard RC	1.50	.70
❑ 122 Dwayne Rudd RC	1.00	.45
❑ 123 Reinard Wilson RC	.60	.25
❑ 124 Michael Booker RC	.40	.18
❑ 125 Warrick Dunn RC	3.00	1.35

1997 Bowman's Best Atomic Refractors

	Nm-Mt	Ex-Mt
COMPLETE SET (125)	600.00	275.00

*ATOMIC REF.STARS: 3X TO 8X BASIC CARDS
*ATOMIC REF.RCs: 1.5X TO 4X BASIC CARDS

1997 Bowman's Best Refractors

	Nm-Mt	Ex-Mt
COMPLETE SET (125)	400.00	180.00

*REFRACTOR STARS: 2X TO 5X BASIC CARDS
*REFRACTOR RCs: 1.25X TO 3X

1999 Bowman's Best

	Nm-Mt	Ex-Mt
COMPLETE SET (133)	80.00	36.00
❑ 1 Randy Moss	2.50	1.10
❑ 2 Skip Hicks	.40	.18
❑ 3 Robert Smith	1.00	.45
❑ 4 Drew Bledsoe	1.25	.55
❑ 5 Tim Brown	1.00	.45
❑ 6 Marshall Faulk	1.25	.55
❑ 7 Terance Mathis	.60	.25
❑ 8 Sean Dawkins	.40	.18
❑ 9 Ed McCaffrey	.60	.25
❑ 10 Jamal Anderson	1.00	.45
❑ 11 Antonio Freeman	1.00	.45
❑ 12 Terry Kirby	.60	.25
❑ 13 Vinny Testaverde	.60	.25
❑ 14 Eddie George	1.00	.45
❑ 15 Ricky Watters	.60	.25
❑ 16 Johnnie Morton	.60	.25
❑ 17 Natrone Means	.60	.25
❑ 18 Terry Glenn	1.00	.45
❑ 19 Michael Westbrook	.60	.25
❑ 20 Doug Flutie	1.00	.45
❑ 21 Jake Plummer	.60	.25
❑ 22 Darnay Scott	.60	.25
❑ 23 Andre Rison	.60	.25
❑ 24 Jon Kitna	1.00	.45
❑ 25 Dan Marino	3.00	1.35
❑ 26 Ike Hilliard	.60	.25
❑ 27 Warrick Dunn	1.00	.45
❑ 28 Jerome Bettis	1.00	.45
❑ 29 Curtis Conway	.60	.25
❑ 30 Emmitt Smith	2.00	.90
❑ 31 Jimmy Smith	.60	.25
❑ 32 Isaac Bruce	1.00	.45
❑ 33 Jerry Rice	2.00	.90
❑ 34 Curtis Martin	1.00	.45
❑ 35 Steve McNair	1.00	.45
❑ 36 Jeff Blake	.60	.25
❑ 37 Rob Moore	.60	.25
❑ 38 Dorsey Levens	1.00	.45
❑ 39 Terrell Davis	1.00	.45
❑ 40 John Elway	3.00	1.35
❑ 41 Trent Dilfer	.60	.25
❑ 42 Joey Galloway	.60	.25
❑ 43 Keyshawn Johnson	1.00	.45
❑ 44 O.J. McDuffie	.60	.25
❑ 45 Fred Taylor	1.00	.45
❑ 46 Andre Reed	.60	.25
❑ 47 Frank Sanders	.60	.25
❑ 48 Keenan McCardell	.60	.25
❑ 49 Elvis Grbac	.60	.25
❑ 50 Barry Sanders	3.00	1.35
❑ 51 Terrell Owens	1.00	.45
❑ 52 Trent Green	1.00	.45
❑ 53 Brad Johnson	1.00	.45
❑ 54 Rich Gannon	1.00	.45
❑ 55 Randall Cunningham	1.00	.45
❑ 56 Tony Martin	.60	.25
❑ 57 Rod Smith	.60	.25
❑ 58 Eric Moulds	1.00	.45
❑ 59 Yancey Thigpen	.40	.18
❑ 60 Brett Favre	3.00	1.35
❑ 61 Cris Carter	1.00	.45
❑ 62 Marvin Harrison	1.00	.45
❑ 63 Chris Chandler	.60	.25
❑ 64 Antowain Smith	1.00	.45
❑ 65 Carl Pickens	.60	.25
❑ 66 Shannon Sharpe	.60	.25
❑ 67 Mike Alstott	1.00	.45
❑ 68 J.J. Stokes	.60	.25
❑ 69 Ben Coates	.60	.25
❑ 70 Peyton Manning	3.00	1.35
❑ 71 Duce Staley	1.00	.45
❑ 72 Michael Irvin	.60	.25
❑ 73 Tim Biakabutuka	.60	.25
❑ 74 Priest Holmes	1.50	.70
❑ 75 Steve Young	1.25	.55
❑ 76 Jerome Pathon	.60	.25
❑ 77 Wayne Chrebet	1.00	.45
❑ 78 Bert Emanuel	.40	.18
❑ 79 Curtis Enis	.40	.18
❑ 80 Mark Brunell	1.00	.45
❑ 81 Herman Moore	.60	.25
❑ 82 Corey Dillon	1.00	.45
❑ 83 Jim Harbaugh	.60	.25
❑ 84 Gary Brown	.40	.18
❑ 85 Kordell Stewart	.60	.25
❑ 86 Garrison Hearst	.60	.25
❑ 87 Rocket Ismail	.60	.25
❑ 88 Charlie Batch	1.00	.45
❑ 89 Napoleon Kaufman	1.00	.45

Card	Nm-Mt	Ex-Mt
❑ 90 Troy Aikman	2.00	.90
❑ 91 Brett Favre BP	1.50	.70
❑ 92 Randy Moss BP	1.25	.55
❑ 93 Terrell Davis BP	1.00	.45
❑ 94 Barry Sanders BP	1.50	.70
❑ 95 Peyton Manning BP	1.50	.70
❑ 96 Troy Edwards BP	.60	.25
❑ 97 Cade McNown BP	.60	.25
❑ 98 Edgerrin James BP	2.50	1.10
❑ 99 Torry Holt BP	1.00	.45
❑ 100 Tim Couch BP	1.00	.45
❑ 101 Chris Claiborne RC	1.00	.45
❑ 102 Brock Huard RC	2.00	.90
❑ 103 Amos Zereoue RC	2.00	.90
❑ 104 Sedrick Irvin RC	1.00	.45
❑ 105 Kevin Faulk RC	2.00	.90
❑ 106 Ebenezer Ekuban RC	1.00	.45
❑ 107 Daunte Culpepper RC	8.00	3.60
❑ 108 Rob Konrad RC	1.50	.70
❑ 109 James Johnson RC	1.50	.70
❑ 110 Kurt Warner RC	10.00	4.50
❑ 111 Mike Cloud RC	1.50	.70
❑ 112 Andy Katzenmoyer RC	1.50	.70
❑ 113 Jevon Kearse RC	3.00	1.35
❑ 114 Akili Smith RC	1.50	.70
❑ 115 Edgerrin James RC	8.00	3.60
❑ 116 Cecil Collins RC	1.00	.45
❑ 117 Chris McAlister RC	1.50	.70
❑ 118 Donovan McNabb RC	10.00	4.50
❑ 119 Kevin Johnson RC	2.00	.90
❑ 120 Torry Holt RC	5.00	2.20
❑ 121 Antoine Winfield RC	1.00	.45
❑ 122 Michael Bishop RC	2.00	.90
❑ 123 Joe Germaine RC	1.50	.70
❑ 124 David Boston RC	2.00	.90
❑ 125 D'Wayne Bates RC	1.50	.70
❑ 126 Champ Bailey RC	2.50	1.10
❑ 127 Cade McNown RC	1.50	.70
❑ 128 Shaun King RC	1.50	.70
❑ 129 Peerless Price RC	3.00	1.35
❑ 130 Troy Edwards RC	1.50	.70
❑ 131 Karsten Bailey RC	1.50	.70
❑ 132 Tim Couch RC	2.00	.90
❑ 133 Ricky Williams RC	4.00	1.80
❑ C1 Rookie Class Photo	8.00	3.60

2000 Bowman's Best

	Nm-Mt	Ex-Mt
COMPLETE SET (150)	500.00	220.00
❑ 1 Troy Edwards	.30	.14
❑ 2 Kurt Warner	1.50	.70
❑ 3 Steve McNair	.75	.35
❑ 4 Terry Glenn	.50	.23
❑ 5 Charlie Batch	.75	.35
❑ 6 Patrick Jeffers	.75	.35
❑ 7 Jake Plummer	.50	.23
❑ 8 Derrick Alexander	.50	.23
❑ 9 Joey Galloway	.50	.23
❑ 10 Tony Banks	.50	.23
❑ 11 Robert Smith	.75	.35
❑ 12 Jerry Rice	1.50	.70
❑ 13 Jeff Garcia	.75	.35
❑ 14 Michael Westbrook	.50	.23
❑ 15 Curtis Conway	.50	.23
❑ 16 Brian Griese	.75	.35
❑ 17 Peyton Manning	2.00	.90
❑ 18 Daunte Culpepper	1.00	.45
❑ 19 Frank Sanders	.50	.23
❑ 20 Muhsin Muhammad	.50	.23
❑ 21 Corey Dillon	.75	.35
❑ 22 Brett Favre	2.50	1.10
❑ 23 Warrick Dunn	.75	.35
❑ 24 Tim Brown	.75	.35
❑ 25 Kerry Collins	.50	.23
❑ 26 Brad Johnson	.75	.35
❑ 27 Rocket Ismail	.50	.23
❑ 28 Jamal Anderson	.75	.35
❑ 29 Jimmy Smith	.50	.23
❑ 30 Torry Holt	.75	.35
❑ 31 Duce Staley	.75	.35
❑ 32 Drew Bledsoe	1.00	.45
❑ 33 Jerome Bettis	.75	.35
❑ 34 Keyshawn Johnson	.75	.35
❑ 35 Fred Taylor	.75	.35
❑ 36 Akili Smith	.30	.14
❑ 37 Rob Johnson	.50	.23
❑ 38 Elvis Grbac	.50	.23
❑ 39 Antonio Freeman	.75	.35
❑ 40 Curtis Enis	.30	.14
❑ 41 Terance Mathis	.50	.23
❑ 42 Terrell Davis	.75	.35
❑ 43 Randy Moss	1.50	.70
❑ 44 Jon Kitna	.75	.35
❑ 45 Curtis Martin	.75	.35
❑ 46 Terrell Owens	.75	.35
❑ 47 Robert Smith	.75	.35
❑ 48 Albert Connell	.30	.14
❑ 49 Edgerrin James	1.25	.55
❑ 50 Tony Gonzalez	.50	.23
❑ 51 Eric Moulds	.75	.35
❑ 52 Natrone Means	.50	.23
❑ 53 Carl Pickens	.50	.23
❑ 54 Mark Brunell	.75	.35
❑ 55 Rob Moore	.50	.23
❑ 56 Marshall Faulk	1.00	.45
❑ 57 Stephen Davis	.75	.35
❑ 58 Rich Gannon	.75	.35
❑ 59 Ricky Williams	.75	.35
❑ 60 Emmitt Smith	1.50	.70
❑ 61 Germane Crowell	.30	.14
❑ 62 Doug Flutie	.75	.35
❑ 63 O.J. McDuffie	.50	.23
❑ 64 Chris Chandler	.50	.23
❑ 65 Qadry Ismail	.50	.23
❑ 66 Tim Couch	.50	.23
❑ 67 James Stewart	.50	.23
❑ 68 Marvin Harrison	.75	.35
❑ 69 Cris Carter	.75	.35
❑ 70 Cade McNown	.30	.14
❑ 71 Marcus Robinson	.75	.35
❑ 72 Steve Beuerlein	.50	.23
❑ 73 Jevon Kearse	.75	.35
❑ 74 Eddie George	.75	.35
❑ 75 Donovan McNabb	1.25	.55
❑ 76 Jeff Blake	.50	.23
❑ 77 Wayne Chrebet	.50	.23
❑ 78 Kordell Stewart	.50	.23
❑ 79 Steve Young	1.00	.45
❑ 80 Mike Alstott	.75	.35
❑ 81 Ricky Watters	.50	.23
❑ 82 Charlie Garner	.50	.23
❑ 83 Troy Aikman	1.50	.70
❑ 84 Dorsey Levens	.50	.23
❑ 85 Ike Hilliard	.50	.23
❑ 86 Shaun King	.30	.14
❑ 87 Isaac Bruce	.75	.35
❑ 88 Tyrone Wheatley	.50	.23
❑ 89 Amani Toomer	.50	.23
❑ 90 Ed McCaffrey	.75	.35
❑ 91 Edgerrin James Marshall Faulk	.75	.35
❑ 92 Drew Bledsoe Brad Johnson	.75	.35
❑ 93 Jimmy Smith Randy Moss	1.00	.45
❑ 94 Eddie George Stephen Davis	.50	.23
❑ 95 Mark Brunell Troy Aikman	1.00	.45
❑ 96 Marvin Harrison Cris Carter	.75	.35
❑ 97 Curtis Martin Emmitt Smith	1.00	.45
❑ 98 Tim Brown Isaac Bruce	.50	.23
❑ 99 Fred Taylor Ricky Williams	.75	.35
❑ 100 Kurt Warner Peyton Manning	1.00	.45
❑ 101 Shaun Alexander RC	20.00	9.00
❑ 102 Thomas Jones RC	12.00	5.50
❑ 103 Courtney Brown RC	8.00	3.60
❑ 104 Curtis Keaton RC	6.00	2.70
❑ 105 Jerry Porter RC	10.00	4.50
❑ 106 Corey Simon RC	8.00	3.60
❑ 107 Dez White RC	8.00	3.60
❑ 108 Jamal Lewis RC	20.00	9.00
❑ 109 Ron Dayne RC	8.00	3.60
❑ 110 R.Jay Soward RC	6.00	2.70
❑ 111 Tee Martin RC	8.00	3.60
❑ 112 Brian Urlacher RC	25.00	11.00
❑ 113 Reuben Droughns RC	10.00	4.50
❑ 114 Travis Taylor RC	8.00	3.60
❑ 115 Plaxico Burress RC	15.00	6.75
❑ 116 Chad Pennington RC	25.00	11.00
❑ 117 Sylvester Morris RC	6.00	2.70
❑ 118 Ron Dugans RC	4.00	1.80
❑ 119 Joe Hamilton RC	6.00	2.70
❑ 120 Chris Redman RC	6.00	2.70
❑ 121 Trung Canidate RC	6.00	2.70
❑ 122 J.R. Redmond RC	6.00	2.70
❑ 123 Danny Farmer RC	6.00	2.70
❑ 124 Todd Pinkston RC	8.00	3.60
❑ 125 Dennis Northcutt RC	8.00	3.60
❑ 126 Laveranues Coles RC	10.00	4.50
❑ 127 Bubba Franks RC	8.00	3.60
❑ 128 Travis Prentice RC	6.00	2.70
❑ 129 Peter Warrick RC	8.00	3.60
❑ 130 Anthony Becht RC	8.00	3.60
❑ 131 Ike Charlton RC	4.00	1.80
❑ 132 Shaun Ellis RC	8.00	3.60
❑ 133 Sean Morey RC	6.00	2.70
❑ 134 Sebastian Janikowski RC	8.00	3.60
❑ 135 Aaron Stecker RC	8.00	3.60
❑ 136 Ronney Jenkins RC	6.00	2.70
❑ 137 Jamel White RC	6.00	2.70
❑ 138 Nick Williams	4.00	1.80
❑ 139 Andy McCullough	4.00	1.80
❑ 140 Kevin Daft	4.00	1.80
❑ 141 Thomas Hamner RC	4.00	1.80
❑ 142 Tim Rattay RC	15.00	6.75
❑ 143 Spergon Wynn RC	6.00	2.70
❑ 144 Brandon Short RC	6.00	2.70
❑ 145 Chad Morton RC	8.00	3.60
❑ 146 Gari Scott RC	4.00	1.80
❑ 147 Frank Murphy RC	4.00	1.80
❑ 148 James Williams RC	6.00	2.70
❑ 149 Windrell Hayes RC	6.00	2.70
❑ 150 Doug Johnson RC	8.00	3.60

2000 Bowman's Best Acetate Parallel

Nm-Mt Ex-Mt

*STARS: 3X TO 8X HI COL.
*PARALLEL BP's: 5X TO 12X
*PARALLEL RC's: .5X TO 1.2X HI COL.

2001 Bowman's Best

	Nm-Mt	Ex-Mt
COMP.SET w/o SP's (100)	20.00	6.00
❑ 1 Jerry Rice	1.50	.45
❑ 2 Doug Flutie	.75	.23
❑ 3 Drew Bledsoe	1.00	.30
❑ 4 Edgerrin James	1.00	.30
❑ 5 Muhsin Muhammad	.50	.15
❑ 6 Charlie Batch	.75	.23
❑ 7 Marshall Faulk	1.00	.30
❑ 8 Trent Green	.75	.23
❑ 9 Rich Gannon	.75	.23
❑ 10 Emmitt Smith	1.50	.45
❑ 11 Steve McNair	.75	.23
❑ 12 Darrell Jackson	.75	.23
❑ 13 Amani Toomer	.50	.15
❑ 14 Jimmy Smith	.50	.15
❑ 15 Kevin Johnson	.50	.15
❑ 16 Ray Lewis	.75	.23
❑ 17 Peter Warrick	.75	.23
❑ 18 Cris Carter	.75	.23
❑ 19 Jerome Bettis	.75	.23
❑ 20 Keyshawn Johnson	.75	.23
❑ 21 Joey Galloway	.50	.15
❑ 22 Chris Chandler	.50	.15
❑ 23 Brett Favre	2.50	.75
❑ 24 Aaron Brooks	.75	.23
❑ 25 Kurt Warner	1.50	.45
❑ 26 Jeff Graham	.30	.09
❑ 27 Curtis Martin	.75	.23
❑ 28 Mike Anderson	.75	.23
❑ 29 Eric Moulds	.50	.15
❑ 30 David Boston	.75	.23
❑ 31 Elvis Grbac	.50	.15
❑ 32 James Stewart	.50	.15
❑ 33 Randy Moss	1.50	.45
❑ 34 Donovan McNabb	1.00	.30
❑ 35 Matt Hasselbeck	.50	.15
❑ 36 Stephen Davis	.75	.23
❑ 37 Brad Johnson	.75	.23
❑ 38 Jamal Anderson	.75	.23
❑ 39 Tim Biakabutuka	.50	.15
❑ 40 Antonio Freeman	.75	.23
❑ 41 Mark Brunell	.75	.23
❑ 42 Tiki Barber	.50	.15
❑ 43 Charlie Garner	.50	.15
❑ 44 Eddie George	.75	.23
❑ 45 Ricky Williams	.75	.23
❑ 46 Rob Johnson	.50	.15
❑ 47 Jake Plummer	.50	.15
❑ 48 Peyton Manning	2.00	.60
❑ 49 Lamar Smith	.50	.15
❑ 50 Corey Dillon	.75	.23
❑ 51 Derrick Alexander	.50	.15
❑ 52 Troy Brown	.50	.15
❑ 53 Wayne Chrebet	.50	.15
❑ 54 Shaun Alexander	1.00	.30
❑ 55 Jeff George	.50	.15
❑ 56 Tim Brown	.75	.23
❑ 57 Brian Griese	.75	.23
❑ 58 Cade McNown	.30	.09
❑ 59 Jamal Lewis	1.25	.35
❑ 60 Germane Crowell	.30	.09
❑ 61 Junior Seau	.75	.23
❑ 62 Warrick Dunn	.75	.23
❑ 63 Isaac Bruce	.75	.23
❑ 64 Terry Glenn	.50	.15
❑ 65 Fred Taylor	.75	.23
❑ 66 Tim Couch	.50	.15
❑ 67 Akili Smith	.30	.09
❑ 68 Tony Gonzalez	.50	.15
❑ 69 Kerry Collins	.50	.15
❑ 70 James Thrash	.50	.15
❑ 71 Terrell Owens	.75	.23
❑ 72 Derrick Mason	.50	.15
❑ 73 Tyrone Wheatley	.50	.15
❑ 74 Oronde Gadsden	.50	.15
❑ 75 Ahman Green	.75	.23
❑ 76 Jon Kitna	.50	.15
❑ 77 Tony Banks	.50	.15
❑ 78 Marvin Harrison	.75	.23
❑ 79 Daunte Culpepper	.75	.23
❑ 80 Vinny Testaverde	.50	.15
❑ 81 Chad Lewis	.30	.09
❑ 82 Torry Holt	.75	.23
❑ 83 Jeff Garcia	.75	.23
❑ 84 Rod Smith	.50	.15
❑ 85 Marcus Robinson	.75	.23
❑ 86 Keenan McCardell	.30	.09
❑ 87 Joe Horn	.50	.15
❑ 88 Kordell Stewart	.50	.15
❑ 89 Jay Fiedler	.75	.23
❑ 90 Ed McCaffrey	.75	.23
❑ 91 Eddie George Stephen Davis	.50	.15
❑ 92 Peyton Manning Jeff Garcia	1.50	.45
❑ 93 Rod Smith Torry Holt	.75	.23
❑ 94 Edgerrin James Marshall Faulk	1.50	.45
❑ 95 Elvis Grbac Daunte Culpepper	.75	.23
❑ 96 Marvin Harrison Randy Moss	1.25	.35
❑ 97 Mike Anderson Emmitt Smith	.75	.23
❑ 98 Brian Griese Kurt Warner	1.00	.30
❑ 99 Muhsin Muhammad Ed McCaffrey	.75	.23
❑ 100 Eric Moulds Terrell Owens	.75	.23
❑ 101 David Terrell JSY RC	8.00	2.40
❑ 102 Kevan Barlow JSY RC	8.00	2.40
❑ 103 Quincy Morgan JSY RC	8.00	2.40
❑ 104 Chris Weinke JSY RC	8.00	2.40
❑ 105 Josh Heupel JSY RC	8.00	2.40
❑ 106 Chris Chambers JSY RC	12.00	3.60
❑ 107 Reggie Wayne JSY RC	15.00	4.50
❑ 108 Gerard Warren JSY RC	8.00	2.40
❑ 109 Freddie Mitchell JSY RC	8.00	2.40
❑ 110 Anthony Thomas JSY RC	15.00	4.50
❑ 111 Robert Ferguson JSY RC	8.00	2.40
❑ 112 Deuce McAllister JSY RC	25.00	7.50
❑ 113 Travis Henry JSY RC	12.00	3.60
❑ 114 Rod Gardner JSY RC	8.00	2.40
❑ 115 Michael Bennett JSY RC	20.00	6.00
❑ 116 Santana Moss JSY RC	15.00	4.50
❑ 117 Chad Johnson JSY RC	20.00	6.00
❑ 118 Jesse Palmer JSY RC	8.00	2.40
❑ 119 James Jackson JSY RC	8.00	2.40
❑ 120 Dan Morgan JSY RC	8.00	2.40
❑ 121 Drew Brees RC	12.00	3.60
❑ 122 Travis Minor RC	4.00	1.20
❑ 123 Quincy Carter RC	6.00	1.80
❑ 124 LaDainian Tomlinson RC	20.00	6.00
❑ 125 Michael Vick RC	40.00	12.00
❑ 126 Ryan Pickett RC	2.50	.75
❑ 127 Mike McMahon RC	6.00	1.80
❑ 128 Alex Bannister RC	4.00	1.20
❑ 129 A.J. Feeley RC	6.00	1.80
❑ 130 Shad Meier RC	4.00	1.20
❑ 131 Jamie Winborn RC	4.00	1.20
❑ 132 Fred Smoot RC	6.00	1.80
❑ 133 Milton Wynn RC	4.00	1.20
❑ 134 Onome Ojo RC	4.00	1.20
❑ 135 Jonathan Carter RC	4.00	1.20
❑ 136 Todd Heap RC	6.00	1.80
❑ 137 Bobby Newcombe RC	4.00	1.20
❑ 138 Tony Stewart RC	6.00	1.80
❑ 139 Torrance Marshall RC	6.00	1.80
❑ 140 Jamal Reynolds RC	6.00	1.80
❑ 141 Jamar Fletcher RC	4.00	1.20
❑ 142 Richard Seymour RC	6.00	1.80
❑ 143 Tay Cody RC	2.50	.75
❑ 144 Koren Robinson RC	6.00	1.80
❑ 145 Eddie Berlin RC	4.00	1.20
❑ 146 Damione Lewis RC	4.00	1.20
❑ 147 Marques Tuiasosopo RC	8.00	2.40
❑ 148 Snoop Minnis RC	4.00	1.20
❑ 149 Chris Barnes RC	4.00	1.20
❑ 150 Leonard Davis RC	4.00	1.20
❑ 151 Vinny Sutherland RC	4.00	1.20
❑ 152 Rudi Johnson RC	12.00	3.60
❑ 153 Derrick Gibson RC	4.00	1.20
❑ 154 Dan Alexander RC	6.00	1.80
❑ 155 Damerien McCants RC	4.00	1.20
❑ 156 Adam Archuleta RC	6.00	1.80
❑ 157 Correll Buckhalter RC	8.00	2.40
❑ 158 LaMont Jordan RC	8.00	2.40
❑ 159 Quentin McCord RC	4.00	1.20
❑ 160 Justin Smith RC	6.00	1.80
❑ 161 Nate Clements RC	6.00	1.80
❑ 162 Alge Crumpler RC	8.00	2.40
❑ 163 Dan O'Leary RC	4.00	1.20
❑ 164 Sage Rosenfels RC	8.00	2.40
❑ 165 Andre Carter RC	6.00	1.80
❑ 166 Marcus Stroud RC	6.00	1.80
❑ 167 Will Allen RC	4.00	1.20
❑ 168 Tommy Polley RC	6.00	1.80
❑ 169 Justin McCareins RC	6.00	1.80
❑ 170 Josh Booty RC	6.00	1.80

2002 Bowman's Best

	Nm-Mt	Ex-Mt
COMP.SET w/o SP's (90)	40.00	12.00
❑ 1 Peyton Manning	3.00	.90
❑ 2 Chris Weinke	1.00	.30
❑ 3 Daunte Culpepper	1.50	.45
❑ 4 Deuce McAllister	2.00	.60
❑ 5 Duce Staley	1.50	.45
❑ 6 Koren Robinson	1.00	.30
❑ 7 Emmitt Smith	4.00	1.20
❑ 8 Jamal Lewis	1.50	.45
❑ 9 Jake Plummer	1.00	.30
❑ 10 Tim Brown	1.50	.45
❑ 11 LaDainian Tomlinson	2.50	.75
❑ 12 Derrick Mason	1.00	.30
❑ 13 Keyshawn Johnson	1.50	.45
❑ 14 Priest Holmes	2.00	.60
❑ 15 Marcus Robinson	1.00	.30
❑ 16 Drew Bledsoe	2.00	.60
❑ 17 Troy Brown	1.00	.30
❑ 18 Ahman Green	1.50	.45
❑ 19 Edgerrin James	2.00	.60
❑ 20 Hines Ward	1.50	.45
❑ 21 Marshall Faulk	1.50	.45
❑ 22 Rod Gardner	1.00	.30
❑ 23 Amani Toomer	1.00	.30
❑ 24 Ricky Williams	1.50	.45
❑ 25 Peter Warrick	1.00	.30
❑ 26 Ray Lewis	1.50	.45
❑ 27 Warrick Dunn	1.50	.45
❑ 28 Jermaine Lewis	1.00	.30
❑ 29 Mark Brunell	1.50	.45
❑ 30 Randy Moss	3.00	.90
❑ 31 Laveranues Coles	1.00	.30
❑ 32 Kordell Stewart	1.00	.30
❑ 33 Darrell Jackson	1.00	.30
❑ 34 Jeff Garcia	1.50	.45
❑ 35 Eddie George	1.50	.45
❑ 36 Tim Dwight	1.00	.30
❑ 37 Trent Green	1.00	.30
❑ 38 Quincy Carter	1.00	.30
❑ 39 Mike McMahon	1.50	.45
❑ 40 Corey Dillon	1.00	.30
❑ 41 Corey Bradford	.60	.18
❑ 42 Aaron Brooks	1.50	.45
❑ 43 Todd Pinkston	1.00	.30
❑ 44 Isaac Bruce	1.50	.45
❑ 45 Shane Matthews	1.00	.30
❑ 46 Eric Moulds	1.00	.30
❑ 47 Anthony Thomas	1.50	.45
❑ 48 David Boston	1.50	.45
❑ 49 Kevin Johnson	1.00	.30
❑ 50 Brett Favre	4.00	1.20

❑ 51 Ron Dayne 1.00 .30
❑ 52 Donovan McNabb 2.00 .60
❑ 53 Brad Johnson 1.00 .30
❑ 54 Garrison Hearst 1.00 .30
❑ 55 Jimmy Smith 1.00 .30
❑ 56 Muhsin Muhammad 1.00 .30
❑ 57 Michael Vick 5.00 1.50
❑ 58 Kerry Collins 1.00 .30
❑ 59 Jerome Bettis 1.50 .45
❑ 60 Trent Dilfer 1.00 .30
❑ 61 Torry Holt 1.50 .45
❑ 62 Stephen Davis 1.00 .30
❑ 63 Steve McNair 1.50 .45
❑ 64 Marvin Harrison 1.50 .45
❑ 65 Zach Thomas 1.50 .45
❑ 66 Antowain Smith 1.00 .30
❑ 67 Joe Horn 1.00 .30
❑ 68 Jim Miller 1.00 .30
❑ 69 Travis Taylor 1.00 .30
❑ 70 James Allen 1.00 .30
❑ 71 Tom Brady 4.00 1.20
❑ 72 Tiki Barber 1.00 .30
❑ 73 Doug Flutie 1.50 .45
❑ 74 Rich Gannon 1.50 .45
❑ 75 Kurt Warner 1.50 .45
❑ 76 Michael Pittman .60 .18
❑ 77 Curtis Martin 1.50 .45
❑ 78 Plaxico Burress 1.50 .45
❑ 79 Terrell Owens 1.50 .45
❑ 80 Tony Gonzalez 1.00 .30
❑ 81 Michael Bennett 1.50 .45
❑ 82 Brian Griese 1.50 .45
❑ 83 Tim Couch 1.00 .30
❑ 84 Shaun Alexander 1.50 .45
❑ 85 Drew Brees 1.50 .45
❑ 86 Vinny Testaverde 1.00 .30
❑ 87 Chris Chambers 1.50 .45
❑ 88 David Terrell 1.50 .45
❑ 89 Rod Smith 1.00 .30
❑ 90 Jerry Rice 3.00 .90
❑ 91 David Carr JSY RC 25.00 7.50
❑ 92 Joey Harrington JSY RC 25.00 7.50
❑ 93 Marquise Walker JSY RC 6.00 1.80
❑ 94 Ladell Betts JSY RC 8.00 2.40
❑ 95 David Garrard JSY RC 8.00 2.40
❑ 96 Antwaan Randle El JSY RC 12.00 3.60
❑ 97 Antonio Bryant JSY RC 8.00 2.40
❑ 98 Eric Crouch JSY RC 12.00 3.60
❑ 99 Tim Carter JSY RC 6.00 1.80
❑ 100 William Green JSY RC 12.00 3.60
❑ 101 Rohan Davey JSY RC 8.00 2.40
❑ 102 Julius Peppers JSY RC 15.00 4.50
❑ 103 Donte Stallworth JSY RC 15.00 4.50
❑ 104 Ashley Lelie JSY RC 15.00 4.50
❑ 105 Jeremy Shockey JSY RC 25.00 7.50
❑ 106 Javon Walker JSY RC 15.00 4.50
❑ 107 Patrick Ramsey JSY RC 15.00 4.50
❑ 108 Roy Williams JSY RC 20.00 6.00
❑ 109 T.J. Duckett JSY RC 12.00 3.60
❑ 110 Jabar Gaffney JSY RC 8.00 2.40
❑ 111 Andre Davis JSY RC 8.00 2.40
❑ 112 Reche Caldwell JSY RC 8.00 2.40
❑ 113 Josh McCown JSY RC 10.00 3.00
❑ 114 Maurice Morris JSY RC 8.00 2.40
❑ 115 Ron Johnson JSY RC 6.00 1.80
❑ 116 DeShaun Foster JSY RC 8.00 2.40
❑ 117 Clinton Portis JSY RC 25.00 7.50
❑ 118 Aaron Lockett AU RC 6.00 1.80
❑ 119 Robert Thomas AU RC 12.00 3.60
❑ 121 Atrews Bell AU RC 6.00 1.80
❑ 122 Brandon Doman AU RC 12.00 3.60
❑ 124 Bryan Thomas AU RC 10.00 3.00
❑ 125 Bryant McKinnie AU RC 10.00 3.00
❑ 126 Chad Hutchinson AU RC 20.00 6.00
❑ 127 Charles Grant AU RC 12.00 3.60
❑ 128 Chester Taylor AU RC 12.00 3.60
❑ 129 Craig Nall AU RC 12.00 3.60
❑ 130 Deion Branch AU RC 40.00 12.00
❑ 131 Doug Jolley AU RC 12.00 3.60
❑ 132 Dwight Freeney AU RC 20.00 6.00
❑ 133 Ed Reed AU RC 40.00 12.00
❑ 134 Freddie Milons AU RC 10.00 3.00
❑ 135 Herb Haygood AU RC 6.00 1.80
❑ 136 J.T. O'Sullivan AU RC 10.00 3.00
❑ 137 Jake Schifino AU RC 10.00 3.00
❑ 138 Jason McAddley AU RC 10.00 3.00
❑ 139 Jeff Kelly AU RC 10.00 3.00
❑ 140 Jerramy Stevens AU RC 12.00 3.60
❑ 141 John Henderson AU RC 12.00 3.60
❑ 142 Jonathan Wells AU RC 12.00 3.60
❑ 143 Josh Scobey AU RC 12.00 3.60
❑ 144 Kelly Campbell AU RC 10.00 3.00
❑ 145 Kahlil Hill AU RC 10.00 3.00
❑ 146 Kalimba Edwards AU RC 12.00 3.60
❑ 147 Ken Simonton AU RC 6.00 1.80
❑ 148 Kurt Kittner AU RC 10.00 3.00
❑ 149 Lamar Gordon AU RC 12.00 3.60
❑ 150 Leonard Henry AU RC 10.00 3.00
❑ 151 Lito Sheppard AU RC 12.00 3.60
❑ 152 Luke Staley AU RC 10.00 3.00
❑ 153 Matt Schobel AU RC 10.00 3.00
❑ 154 Mike Rumph AU RC 12.00 3.60
❑ 155 Najeh Davenport AU RC 12.00 3.60
❑ 156 Napoleon Harris AU RC 12.00 3.60
❑ 158 Quentin Jammer AU RC 12.00 3.60
❑ 159 Randy Fasani AU RC 10.00 3.00
❑ 160 Ronald Curry AU RC 12.00 3.60
❑ 161 Ryan Sims AU RC 12.00 3.60
❑ 162 Sam Simmons AU RC 6.00 1.80
❑ 163 Seth Burford AU RC 10.00 3.00
❑ 164 Tellis Redmon AU RC 10.00 3.00
❑ 165 Terry Charles AU RC 10.00 3.00
❑ 166 Tracey Wistrom AU RC 10.00 3.00
❑ 167 Verron Haynes AU RC 12.00 3.60
❑ 168 Wes Pate AU RC 6.00 1.80
❑ 169 Wendell Bryant AU RC 12.00 3.60
❑ 170 Damien Anderson AU RC 10.00 3.00

2002 Bowman's Best Blue

Nm-Mt Ex-Mt

*STARS: 2X TO 5X BASIC CARDS
*ROOKIE JSY 91-117: .5X TO 1.2X
*ROOKIE AU 118-170: .5X TO 1.2X

2002 Bowman's Best Gold

Nm-Mt Ex-Mt

*STARS: 10X TO 25X BASIC CARDS
1-90 PRINT RUN 25 SER.#'d SETS
1-90 STATED ODDS 1:62
*ROOKIE JSY 91-117: 1.5X TO 3X
*ROOKIE AU 118-170: 1X TO 2.5X

2002 Bowman's Best Red

Nm-Mt Ex-Mt

*STARS: 2.5X TO 6X BASIC CARDS
*ROOKIE JSY 91-117: 1X TO 2X
*ROOKIE AU 118-170: .8X TO 1.5X

2003 Bowman's Best

MINT NRMT

COMP.SET w/o SP's (80) 30.00 13.50
ROOKIE AU STATED ODDS 1:136
CARDS 170, 175 NOT RELEASED

❑ 1 Terrell Owens 1.50 .70
❑ 2 Peerless Price 1.00 .45
❑ 3 Joey Harrington 2.50 1.10
❑ 4 Ricky Williams 1.50 .70
❑ 5 David Boston 1.00 .45
❑ 6 Troy Brown 1.00 .45
❑ 7 Deuce McAllister 1.50 .70
❑ 8 Marvin Harrison 1.50 .70
❑ 9 Ahman Green 1.50 .70
❑ 10 Emmitt Smith 4.00 1.80
❑ 11 Brian Urlacher 2.50 1.10
❑ 12 Jamal Lewis 1.50 .70
❑ 13 Keyshawn Johnson 1.50 .70
❑ 14 Kurt Warner 1.50 .70
❑ 15 Rod Gardner 1.00 .45
❑ 16 Plaxico Burress 1.00 .45
❑ 17 Chad Pennington 2.00 .90
❑ 18 Jeremy Shockey 2.50 1.10
❑ 19 Donovan McNabb 2.00 .90
❑ 20 T.J. Duckett 1.00 .45
❑ 21 Fred Taylor 1.50 .70
❑ 22 Daunte Culpepper 1.50 .70
❑ 23 Tiki Barber 1.00 .45
❑ 24 Brian Griese 1.50 .70
❑ 25 Chad Johnson 1.00 .45
❑ 26 Julius Peppers 1.50 .70
❑ 27 Chad Hutchinson 1.00 .45
❑ 28 Eddie George 1.00 .45
❑ 29 Torry Holt 1.50 .70
❑ 30 Drew Brees 1.50 .70
❑ 31 Rich Gannon 1.00 .45
❑ 32 Trent Green 1.00 .45
❑ 33 Clinton Portis 2.50 1.10
❑ 34 Tom Brady 2.50 1.10
❑ 35 Aaron Brooks 1.50 .70
❑ 36 Ray Lewis 1.50 .70
❑ 37 David Carr 2.50 1.10
❑ 38 Chris Chambers 1.50 .70
❑ 39 Brad Johnson 1.00 .45
❑ 40 Tommy Maddox 1.50 .70
❑ 41 Curtis Martin 1.50 .70
❑ 42 Travis Henry 1.00 .45
❑ 43 Brett Favre 4.00 1.80
❑ 44 Randy Moss 2.50 1.10
❑ 45 Jimmy Smith 1.00 .45
❑ 46 Joey Galloway 1.00 .45
❑ 47 Derrick Mason 1.00 .45
❑ 48 Darrell Jackson 1.00 .45
❑ 49 Curtis Conway .60 .25
❑ 50 Michael Vick 4.00 1.80
❑ 51 Rod Smith 1.00 .45
❑ 52 Muhsin Muhammad 1.00 .45
❑ 53 Drew Bledsoe 1.50 .70
❑ 54 Michael Bennett 1.00 .45
❑ 55 Joe Horn 1.00 .45
❑ 56 Stephen Davis 1.00 .45
❑ 57 Isaac Bruce 1.50 .70
❑ 58 Shaun Alexander 1.50 .70
❑ 59 Jerry Rice 3.00 1.35
❑ 60 Peyton Manning 2.50 1.10
❑ 61 Tony Gonzalez 1.00 .45
❑ 62 Jake Plummer 1.00 .45
❑ 63 Tim Couch .60 .25
❑ 64 Marty Booker 1.00 .45
❑ 65 Corey Dillon 1.00 .45
❑ 66 Steve McNair 1.50 .70
❑ 67 Jeff Garcia 1.50 .70
❑ 68 Hines Ward 1.50 .70
❑ 69 Laveranues Coles 1.00 .45
❑ 70 Amani Toomer 1.00 .45
❑ 71 Eric Moulds 1.00 .45
❑ 72 Donald Driver 1.00 .45
❑ 73 Jay Fiedler 1.00 .45
❑ 74 Charlie Garner 1.00 .45
❑ 75 Priest Holmes 2.00 .90
❑ 76 Edgerrin James 1.50 .70
❑ 77 Kerry Collins 1.00 .45
❑ 78 LaDainian Tomlinson 1.50 .70
❑ 79 Mark Brunell 1.00 .45
❑ 80 Marshall Faulk 1.50 .70
❑ 81 Lee Suggs RC 8.00 3.60
❑ 82 William Joseph RC 4.00 1.80
❑ 83 Brandon Lloyd RC 5.00 2.20
❑ 84 Nick Barnett RC 6.00 2.70
❑ 85 Andre Woolfolk RC 4.00 1.80
❑ 86 Jimmy Kennedy RC 4.00 1.80
❑ 87 Kliff Kingsbury RC 4.00 1.80
❑ 88 Andrew Williams RC 4.00 1.80
❑ 89 Mike Doss RC 4.00 1.80
❑ 90 Troy Polamalu RC 4.00 1.80
❑ 91 Bryant Johnson JSY RC 6.00 2.70
❑ 92 Justin Fargas JSY RC 6.00 2.70

❑ 93 Terence Newman JSY RC 12.00 5.50
❑ 94 Brian St.Pierre JSY RC 6.00 2.70
❑ 95 DeWayne Robertson JSY RC 6.00 2.70
❑ 96 Dave Ragone JSY RC 6.00 2.70
❑ 97 Teyo Johnson JSY RC 6.00 2.70
❑ 98 Bethel Johnson JSY RC 10.00 4.50
❑ 99 Tyrone Calico JSY RC 8.00 3.60
❑ 100 Carson Palmer JSY RC 20.00 9.00
❑ 101 Marcus Trufant JSY RC 6.00 2.70
❑ 102 Nate Burleson JSY RC 10.00 4.50
❑ 103 Musa Smith JSY RC 6.00 2.70
❑ 104 Anquan Boldin JSY RC 15.00 6.75
❑ 105 Chris Simms JSY RC 12.00 5.50
❑ 106 Taylor Jacobs JSY RC 6.00 2.70
❑ 107 Dallas Clark JSY RC 6.00 2.70
❑ 108 Seneca Wallace JSY RC 6.00 2.70
❑ 109 Ken Dorsey JSY RC 10.00 4.50
❑ 110 Willis McGahee JSY RC 15.00 6.75
❑ 111 Chris Brown JSY RC 12.00 5.50
❑ 112 Terrell Suggs JSY RC 10.00 4.50
❑ 113 Kelley Washington JSY RC 6.00 2.70
❑ 114 Onterrio Smith JSY RC 8.00 3.60
❑ 115 Rex Grossman JSY RC 15.00 6.75
❑ 116 LaBrandon Toefield AU RC 12.00 5.50
❑ 117 Sam Aiken AU RC 10.00 4.50
❑ 118 Malaefou Mackenzie AU RC 8.00 3.60
❑ 119 David Tyree AU RC 10.00 4.50
❑ 120 Jerome McDougle AU RC 12.00 5.50
❑ 121 DeWayne White AU RC 10.00 4.50
❑ 122 Zuriel Smith AU RC 8.00 3.60
❑ 123 Shaun McDonald AU RC 12.00 5.50
❑ 124 Andre Johnson AU/199 RC 80.00 36.00
❑ 125 Ahmaad Galloway AU RC 10.00 4.50
❑ 126 Keenan Howry AU RC 12.00 5.50
❑ 127 Kareem Kelly AU RC 10.00 4.50
❑ 128 Brooks Bollinger AU RC 12.00 5.50
❑ 129 Arnaz Battle AU RC 15.00 6.75
❑ 130 Adrian Madise AU RC 10.00 4.50
❑ 131 LaTarence Dunbar AU RC 10.00 4.50
❑ 132 L.J. Smith AU RC 12.00 5.50
❑ 133 B.J. Askew AU RC 12.00 5.50
❑ 134 Michael Haynes AU RC 12.00 5.50
❑ 135 David Kircus AU RC 10.00 4.50
❑ 136 Kyle Boller AU/199 RC 75.00 34.00
❑ 137 Domanick Davis AU RC 50.00 22.00
❑ 138 Osi Umenyiora AU RC 12.00 5.50
❑ 139 Bobby Wade AU RC 12.00 5.50
❑ 140 Boss Bailey AU RC 15.00 6.75
❑ 141 Billy McMullen AU RC 10.00 4.50
❑ 142 Doug Gabriel AU RC 12.00 5.50
❑ 143 J.R. Tolver AU RC 10.00 4.50
❑ 144 Gibran Hamdan AU RC 8.00 3.60
❑ 145 Walter Young AU RC 8.00 3.60
❑ 146 Carl Ford AU RC 8.00 3.60
❑ 147 Andrew Pinnock AU RC 10.00 4.50
❑ 148 Byron Leftwich AU/199 RC 150.00 70.00
❑ 149 Ty Warren AU RC 12.00 5.50
❑ 150 Visanthe Shiancoe AU RC 10.00 4.50
❑ 151 Justin Gage AU RC 12.00 5.50
❑ 152 Brock Forsey AU RC 12.00 5.50
❑ 153 Casey Moore AU RC 10.00 4.50
❑ 154 Juston Wood AU RC 8.00 3.60
❑ 155 Aaron Walker AU RC 10.00 4.50
❑ 156 Trent Smith AU RC 12.00 5.50
❑ 157 Travis Anglin AU RC 8.00 3.60
❑ 158 Jeremi Johnson AU RC 10.00 4.50
❑ 159 Justin Griffith AU RC 10.00 4.50
❑ 160 Chris Davis AU RC 10.00 4.50
❑ 161 J.T. Wall AU RC 8.00 3.60
❑ 162 Larry Johnson AU/199 RC 50.00 22.00
❑ 163 Jon Olinger AU RC 10.00 4.50
❑ 164 Donald Lee AU RC 10.00 4.50
❑ 165 Taco Wallace AU RC 10.00 4.50
❑ 166 DeAndrew Rubin AU RC 8.00 3.60
❑ 167 Ryan Hoag AU RC 8.00 3.60
❑ 168 Kevin Williams AU RC 12.00 5.50
❑ 169 Ovie Mughelli AU RC 8.00 3.60
❑ 171 Brandon Drumm AU RC 10.00 4.50
❑ 172 Brad Banks AU RC 10.00 4.50
❑ 173 Talman Gardner AU RC 12.00 5.50
❑ 174 Jason Witten AU RC 25.00 11.00

2003 Bowman's Best Blue

MINT NRMT

*STARS: 1X TO 2.5X BASE CARD HI
*ROOKIES: .8X TO 2X BASE CARD HI
*ROOKIE JSYs: .5X TO 1.2X BASE CARD HI
*ROOKIE AU/50: .6X TO 1.5X BASE AU/199
*ROOKIE AUs: .5X TO 1.2X BASE CARD HI
CARDS 170, 175 NOT RELEASED

2003 Bowman's Best Red

MINT NRMT

*STARS: 3X TO 8X BASE CARD HI
*ROOKIES: 2.5X TO 6X BASE CARD HI
*ROOKIE JSY's: 1X TO 2.5X BASE CARD HI
*ROOKIE AU/25: 1X TO 2.5X BASE AU/199
*ROOKIE AU/50: 1X TO 2.5X BASE AU RC
RED PRINT RUN 50 SER.#'d SETS
CARDS 170, 175 NOT RELEASED

2004 Bowman's Best

Nm-Mt Ex-Mt

COMP.SET w/o SP's (100) 50.00 15.00
RC JSY GROUP A ODDS 1:130
RC JSY GROUP B ODDS 1:236
RC JSY GROUP C ODDS 1:86
RC JSY GROUP D ODDS 1:38
RC JSY GROUP E ODDS 1:31
RC JSY GROUP F ODDS 1:27
RC JSY GROUP G ODDS 1:50
RC JSY GROUP H ODDS 1:89
RC JSY GROUP I ODDS 1:29
RC AU/199 STATED ODDS 1:311
RC AU STATED ODDS 1:3

❑ 1 Brett Favre 4.00 1.20
❑ 2 Chris Chambers 1.00 .30
❑ 3 Kyle Boller 1.50 .45
❑ 4 Brian Urlacher 2.00 .60
❑ 5 Marvin Harrison 1.50 .45
❑ 6 Matt Hasselbeck 1.00 .30
❑ 7 Aaron Brooks 1.00 .30
❑ 8 Curtis Martin 1.50 .45
❑ 9 Keenan McCardell .60 .18
❑ 10 Terrell Owens 1.50 .45
❑ 11 Jimmy Smith 1.00 .30
❑ 12 Garrison Hearst 1.00 .30
❑ 13 Joe Horn 1.00 .30
❑ 14 David Carr 1.50 .45
❑ 15 Tom Brady 2.50 .75
❑ 16 Shaun Alexander 1.50 .45
❑ 17 Tommy Maddox 1.00 .30
❑ 18 Tiki Barber 1.00 .30
❑ 19 Trent Green 1.00 .30
❑ 20 Anquan Boldin 1.50 .45
❑ 21 Peerless Price 1.00 .30
❑ 22 Jake Delhomme 1.50 .45
❑ 23 Eric Moulds 1.00 .30
❑ 24 Quincy Carter 1.00 .30
❑ 25 Steve McNair 1.50 .45
❑ 26 Tim Rattay 1.00 .30
❑ 27 Laveranues Coles 1.00 .30
❑ 28 Corey Dillon 1.00 .30
❑ 29 Byron Leftwich 2.50 .75
❑ 30 Chad Pennington 2.00 .60
❑ 31 Koren Robinson 1.00 .30
❑ 32 Plaxico Burress 1.00 .30
❑ 33 Steve Smith 1.00 .30
❑ 34 Warrick Dunn 1.00 .30
❑ 35 Jamal Lewis 1.50 .45
❑ 36 Charles Rogers 1.00 .30
❑ 37 Tony Gonzalez 1.00 .30
❑ 38 Jake Plummer 1.00 .30
❑ 39 Chad Johnson 1.00 .30
❑ 40 Peyton Manning 2.50 .75
❑ 41 Daunte Culpepper 1.50 .45
❑ 42 Fred Taylor 1.00 .30
❑ 43 Amani Toomer 1.00 .30
❑ 44 Santana Moss 1.00 .30
❑ 45 Deuce McAllister 1.50 .45
❑ 46 Rex Grossman 1.50 .45
❑ 47 Ray Lewis 1.50 .45
❑ 48 Hines Ward 1.50 .45
❑ 49 Darrell Jackson 1.00 .30
❑ 50 Randy Moss 2.00 .60
❑ 51 Carson Palmer 2.00 .60
❑ 52 Rod Smith 1.00 .30
❑ 53 Drew Bledsoe 1.50 .45
❑ 54 Brad Johnson 1.00 .30
❑ 55 Travis Henry 1.00 .30
❑ 56 Joey Harrington 1.50 .45
❑ 57 Edgerrin James 1.50 .45
❑ 58 Kurt Warner 1.50 .45
❑ 59 Josh McCown 1.00 .30
❑ 60 Clinton Portis 1.50 .45
❑ 61 Brian Westbrook 1.00 .30
❑ 62 Marc Bulger 1.50 .45
❑ 63 Charlie Garner 1.00 .30
❑ 64 Torry Holt 1.50 .45
❑ 65 LaDainian Tomlinson 1.50 .45
❑ 66 Mark Brunell 1.00 .30
❑ 67 Derrick Mason 1.00 .30
❑ 68 Andre Johnson 1.50 .45
❑ 69 Keyshawn Johnson 1.00 .30
❑ 70 Ahman Green 1.50 .45
❑ 71 Rudi Johnson 1.00 .30
❑ 72 Stephen Davis 1.00 .30
❑ 73 Jeff Garcia 1.50 .45
❑ 74 Michael Strahan 1.00 .30
❑ 75 Michael Vick 3.00 .90
❑ 76 Ricky Williams 1.50 .45
❑ 77 Domanick Davis 1.50 .45
❑ 78 Priest Holmes 2.00 .60
❑ 79 Marshall Faulk 1.50 .45
❑ 80 Donovan McNabb 2.00 .60
❑ 81 Dunta Robinson RC 4.00 1.20
❑ 82 Robert Gallery RC 6.00 1.80
❑ 83 Ben Troupe RC 4.00 1.20
❑ 84 Antwan Odom RC 4.00 1.20
❑ 85 Brandon Miree RC 3.00 .90
❑ 86 Darnell Dockett RC 3.00 .90
❑ 87 Vince Wilfork RC 5.00 1.50
❑ 88 Randy Starks RC 3.00 .90
❑ 89 Chris Cooley RC 4.00 1.20
❑ 90 Dwan Edwards RC 2.00 .60
❑ 91 Patrick Crayton RC 4.00 1.20
❑ 92 Sean Jones RC 3.00 .90
❑ 93 Sean Ryan RC 3.00 .90
❑ 94 Chris Gamble RC 5.00 1.50
❑ 95 Will Smith RC 4.00 1.20
❑ 96 Sloan Thomas RC 3.00 .90
❑ 97 Tim Euhus RC 4.00 1.20
❑ 98 Tommie Harris RC 5.00 1.50
❑ 99 Will Poole RC 4.00 1.20
❑ 100 Karlos Dansby RC 4.00 1.20
❑ 101 Bernard Berrian JSY RC D 6.00 1.80
❑ 102 DeAngelo Hall JSY RC A 8.00 2.40
❑ 103 Mewelde Moore JSY RC G 8.00 2.40
❑ 104 Rashaun Woods JSY RC G 8.00 2.40
❑ 105 Reggie Williams JSY RC 8.00 2.40
❑ 106 Derrick Hamilton JSY RC F 5.00 1.50
❑ 107 Kellen Winslow JSY RC C 15.00 4.50
❑ 108 Devard Darling JSY RC D 6.00 1.80
❑ 109 Michael Clayton JSY RC B 15.00 4.50
❑ 110 Larry Fitzgerald JSY RC E 20.00 6.00
❑ 111 Greg Jones JSY RC E 6.00 1.80
❑ 112 Chris Perry JSY RC H 12.00 3.60
❑ 113 Lee Evans JSY RC F 10.00 3.00
❑ 114 Tatum Bell JSY RC E 10.00 3.00
❑ 115 Steven Jackson JSY RC I 20.00 6.00
❑ 116 Matt Schaub JSY RC A 10.00 3.00
❑ 117 Ben Troupe JSY 6.00 1.80

Card	Nm-Mt	Ex-Mt
❑ 118 Devery Henderson JSY RC F	5.00	1.50
❑ 119 Ben Watson JSY RC E	6.00	1.80
❑ 120 J.P. Losman JSY RC I	15.00	4.50
❑ 121 Keary Colbert JSY RC F	8.00	2.40
❑ 122 Darius Watts JSY RC C	8.00	2.40
❑ 123 Cedric Cobbs JSY RC D	6.00	1.80
❑ 124 Luke McCown JSY RC A	6.00	1.80
❑ 125 Michael Jenkins JSY RC A	6.00	1.80
❑ 126 Eli Manning AU/199 RC	150.00	45.00
❑ 127 Roy Williams AU/199 RC	80.00	24.00
❑ 128 Kevin Jones AU/199 RC	120.00	36.00
❑ 129 Philip Rivers AU/199 RC	80.00	24.00
❑ 130 Ben Roethlisberger AU/199 RC	350.00	105.00
❑ 131 Carlos Francis AU RC	10.00	3.00
❑ 132 Bradlee Van Pelt AU RC	12.00	3.60
❑ 133 Michael Turner AU RC	10.00	3.00
❑ 134 Kenechi Udeze AU RC	12.00	3.60
❑ 135 Jeff Smoker AU RC	15.00	4.50
❑ 136 Josh Harris AU RC	12.00	3.60
❑ 137 Derrick Strait AU RC	12.00	3.60
❑ 138 Jonathan Vilma AU RC	12.00	3.60
❑ 139 Triandos Luke AU RC	12.00	3.60
❑ 140 Jim Sorgi AU RC	12.00	3.60
❑ 141 Ryan Krause AU RC	10.00	3.00
❑ 142 Julius Jones AU RC	75.00	22.00
❑ 143 Mark Jones AU RC	10.00	3.00
❑ 144 P.K. Sam AU RC	10.00	3.00
❑ 145 B.J. Symons AU RC	12.00	3.60
❑ 146 Adimchinobe Echemandu AU RC	10.00	3.00
❑ 147 Casey Bramlet AU RC	10.00	3.00
❑ 148 Clarence Moore AU RC	12.00	3.60
❑ 149 D.J. Williams AU RC	12.00	3.60
❑ 150 Jeris McIntyre AU RC	10.00	3.00
❑ 151 Jerricho Cotchery AU RC	12.00	3.60
❑ 152 Andy Hall AU RC	10.00	3.00
❑ 153 Samie Parker AU RC	12.00	3.60
❑ 154 Maurice Mann AU RC	10.00	3.00
❑ 155 Jonathan Smith AU RC	10.00	3.00
❑ 156 Derrick Ward AU RC	8.00	2.40
❑ 157 D.J. Hackett AU RC	10.00	3.00
❑ 158 Craig Krenzel AU RC	12.00	3.60
❑ 159 Jared Lorenzen AU RC	10.00	3.00
❑ 160 Cody Pickett AU RC	12.00	3.60
❑ 161 Jamaar Taylor AU RC	12.00	3.60
❑ 162 Michael Boulware AU RC	12.00	3.60
❑ 163 Matt Mauck AU RC	12.00	3.60
❑ 164 John Navarre AU RC	12.00	3.60
❑ 165 Ahmad Carroll AU RC	15.00	4.50
❑ 166 Bruce Perry AU RC	10.00	3.00
❑ 167 Erik Jensen AU RC	10.00	3.00
❑ 168 Matt Kranchick AU RC	12.00	3.60
❑ 169 Courtney Anderson AU RC	10.00	3.00
❑ 170 Nate Lawrie AU RC	10.00	3.00
❑ 171 Thomas Tapeh AU RC	10.00	3.00
❑ 172 Courtney Watson AU RC	12.00	3.60
❑ 173 Drew Carter AU RC	12.00	3.60
❑ 174 Ricardo Colclough AU RC	12.00	3.60
❑ 175 Dontarrious Thomas AU RC	12.00	3.60
❑ 176 Ernest Wilford AU RC	12.00	3.60
❑ 177 Quincy Wilson AU RC	10.00	3.00
❑ 178 Derek Abney AU RC	12.00	3.60
❑ 179 Jeff Dugan AU RC	8.00	2.40
❑ 180 Ben Hartsock AU RC	12.00	3.60
❑ 181 Matt Kegel AU RC	12.00	3.60
❑ 182 Derrick Knight AU RC	10.00	3.00
❑ 183 Teddy Lehman AU RC	12.00	3.60
❑ 184 Johnnie Morant AU RC	12.00	3.60
❑ 185 Bob Sanders AU RC	12.00	3.60
❑ 186 Michael Gaines AU RC	10.00	3.00
❑ 187 Daryl Smith AU RC	12.00	3.60
❑ 188 Jason Babin AU RC	6.00	1.80

2004 Bowman's Best Green

Nm-Mt Ex-Mt

*STARS: .8X TO 2X BASIC CARDS
*ROOKIES 81-100: .8X TO 2X BASIC CARDS
1-100 GREEN STATED ODDS 1:3
*ROOKIE JSYs 101-125: .5X TO 1.2X
*ROOKIE AUs 126-188: .5X TO 1.2X
GREEN AU STATED ODDS 1:5
GREEN PRINT RUN 499 SER.#'d SETS

2004 Bowman's Best Red

Nm-Mt Ex-Mt

*STARS: 2.5X TO 6X BASIC CARDS
*ROOKIES 81-100: 2X TO 5X BASIC CARDS
*ROOKIE JSYs 101-125: 1X TO 2.5X
*ROOKIE AUs 126-188: 1X TO 2.5X
RED STATED ODDS 1:26
RED AU STATED ODDS 1:46
RED PRINT RUN 50 SER.#'d SETS

1996 Collector's Edge Cowboybilia Autographs

Card	Nm-Mt	Ex-Mt
COMPLETE SET (25)	500.00	220.00
❑ DCA1 Chris Boniol/4000	12.00	5.50
❑ DCA2 John Jett/4000	12.00	5.50
❑ DCA3 Sherman Williams/4000	12.00	5.50
❑ DCA4 Chad Hennings/4000	12.00	5.50
❑ DCA5 Larry Allen/4000	20.00	9.00
❑ DCA6 Jason Garrett/4000	12.00	5.50
❑ DCA7 Tony Tolbert/4000	12.00	5.50
❑ DCA8 Kevin Williams/4000	12.00	5.50
❑ DCA9 Mark Tuinei/4000	25.00	11.00
❑ DCA10 Larry Brown/4000 MVP gold foil	12.00	5.50
❑ DCA11 Kevin Smith/4000	20.00	9.00
❑ DCA12 Darrin Smith/4000	12.00	5.50
❑ DCA13 Robert Jones/4000	12.00	5.50
❑ DCA14 Nate Newton/4000	12.00	5.50
❑ DCA15 D.Woodson/4000	25.00	11.00
❑ DCA16 Leon Lett/4000	20.00	9.00
❑ DCA17 R.Maryland/4000	12.00	5.50
❑ DCA18 Erik Williams/4000	20.00	9.00
❑ DCA19 Bill Bates/4000	25.00	11.00
❑ DCA20 Daryl Johnston/2300	25.00	11.00
❑ DCA21 Jay Novacek/2300	30.00	13.50
❑ DCA22 Charles Haley/2300	25.00	11.00
❑ DCA23 Troy Aikman/600 all cards unsigned	80.00	36.00
❑ DCA24 Michael Irvin/500	150.00	70.00
❑ DCA25 Emmitt Smith/500	225.00	100.00
❑ NNO Roger Staubach Drew Pearson Hail Mary Pass numbered of 1000	120.00	55.00

1999 Collector's Edge Advantage

Card	Nm-Mt	Ex-Mt
COMPLETE SET (190)	50.00	22.00
❑ 1 Larry Centers	.30	.14
❑ 2 Rob Moore	.50	.23
❑ 3 Adrian Murrell	.50	.23
❑ 4 Jake Plummer	.50	.23
❑ 5 Frank Sanders	.50	.23
❑ 6 Jamal Anderson	.75	.35
❑ 7 Chris Chandler	.50	.23
❑ 8 Tim Dwight	.75	.35
❑ 9 Tony Martin	.50	.23
❑ 10 Terance Mathis	.50	.23
❑ 11 O.J. Santiago	.30	.14
❑ 12 Jim Harbaugh	.50	.23
❑ 13 Priest Holmes	1.25	.55
❑ 14 Jermaine Lewis	.50	.23
❑ 15 Rod Woodson	.50	.23
❑ 16 Eric Zeier	.50	.23
❑ 17 Doug Flutie	.75	.35
❑ 18 Sam Gash	.30	.14
❑ 19 Rob Johnson	.50	.23
❑ 20 Eric Moulds	.75	.35
❑ 21 Andre Reed	.50	.23
❑ 22 Antowain Smith	.75	.35
❑ 23 Bruce Smith	.50	.23
❑ 24 Thurman Thomas	.50	.23
❑ 25 Steve Beuerlein	.50	.23
❑ 26 Kevin Greene	.50	.23
❑ 27 Rocket Ismail	.50	.23
❑ 28 Fred Lane	.30	.14
❑ 29 Muhsin Muhammad	.50	.23
❑ 30 Edgar Bennett	.30	.14
❑ 31 Curtis Conway	.50	.23
❑ 32 Bobby Engram	.50	.23
❑ 33 Curtis Enis	.30	.14
❑ 34 Erik Kramer	.50	.23
❑ 35 Jeff Blake	.50	.23
❑ 36 Corey Dillon	.75	.35
❑ 37 Neil O'Donnell	.50	.23
❑ 38 Carl Pickens	.50	.23
❑ 39 Takeo Spikes	.30	.14
❑ 40 Troy Aikman	1.50	.70
❑ 41 Billy Davis	.30	.14
❑ 42 Michael Irvin	.50	.23
❑ 43 Deion Sanders	.75	.35
❑ 44 Emmitt Smith	1.50	.70
❑ 45 Darren Woodson	.30	.14
❑ 46 Bubby Brister	.50	.23
❑ 47 Terrell Davis	.75	.35
❑ 48 John Elway	2.50	1.10
❑ 49 Ed McCaffrey	.50	.23
❑ 50 Bill Romanowski	.30	.14
❑ 51 Shannon Sharpe	.50	.23
❑ 52 Rod Smith	.50	.23
❑ 53 Charlie Batch	.75	.35
❑ 54 Germane Crowell	.30	.14
❑ 55 Herman Moore	.50	.23
❑ 56 Johnnie Morton	.50	.23
❑ 57 Barry Sanders	2.50	1.10
❑ 58 Robert Brooks	.50	.23
❑ 59 Brett Favre	2.50	1.10
❑ 60 Antonio Freeman	.75	.35
❑ 61 Darick Holmes	.30	.14
❑ 62 Dorsey Levens	.75	.35
❑ 63 Roell Preston	.30	.14
❑ 64 Marshall Faulk	1.00	.45
❑ 65 E.G.Green	.30	.14
❑ 66 Marvin Harrison	.75	.35
❑ 67 Peyton Manning	2.50	1.10
❑ 68 Jerome Pathon	.30	.14
❑ 69 Mark Brunell	.75	.35
❑ 70 Kevin Hardy	.30	.14
❑ 71 Keenan McCardell	.50	.23
❑ 72 Jimmy Smith	.50	.23
❑ 73 Fred Taylor	.75	.35
❑ 74 Alvis Whitted	.30	.14
❑ 75 Kimble Anders	.50	.23
❑ 76 Donnell Bennett	.30	.14
❑ 77 Rich Gannon	.75	.35
❑ 78 Elvis Grbac	.50	.23
❑ 79 Byron Bam Morris	.30	.14
❑ 80 Andre Rison	.50	.23
❑ 81 Karim Abdul-Jabbar	.50	.23
❑ 82 John Avery	.30	.14

❑ 83 Oronde Gadsden	.50	.23
❑ 84 Sam Madison	.30	.14
❑ 85 Dan Marino	2.50	1.10
❑ 86 O.J. McDuffie	.50	.23
❑ 87 Zach Thomas	.75	.35
❑ 88 Cris Carter	.75	.35
❑ 89 Randall Cunningham	.75	.35
❑ 90 Brad Johnson	.75	.35
❑ 91 Randy Moss	2.00	.90
❑ 92 John Randle	.50	.23
❑ 93 Jake Reed	.50	.23
❑ 94 Robert Smith	.75	.35
❑ 95 Drew Bledsoe	1.00	.45
❑ 96 Ben Coates	.50	.23
❑ 97 Robert Edwards	.30	.14
❑ 98 Terry Glenn	.75	.35
❑ 99 Ty Law	.50	.23
❑ 100 Cam Cleeland	.30	.14
❑ 101 Kerry Collins	.50	.23
❑ 102 Gary Brown	.30	.14
❑ 103 Kent Graham	.30	.14
❑ 104 Ike Hilliard	.50	.23
❑ 105 Joe Jurevicius	.50	.23
❑ 106 Danny Kanell	.30	.14
❑ 107 Wayne Chrebet	.50	.23
❑ 108 Aaron Glenn	.30	.14
❑ 109 Keyshawn Johnson	.75	.35
❑ 110 Curtis Martin	.75	.35
❑ 111 Vinny Testaverde	.50	.23
❑ 112 Tim Brown	.75	.35
❑ 113 Jeff George	.50	.23
❑ 114 James Jett	.50	.23
❑ 115 Napoleon Kaufman	.75	.35
❑ 116 Charles Woodson	.75	.35
❑ 117 Koy Detmer	.30	.14
❑ 118 Duce Staley	.75	.35
❑ 119 Jerome Bettis	.75	.35
❑ 120 Charles Johnson	.50	.23
❑ 121 Kordell Stewart	.50	.23
❑ 122 Tony Banks	.50	.23
❑ 123 Isaac Bruce	.75	.35
❑ 124 June Henley RC	.30	.14
❑ 125 Ryan Leaf	.75	.35
❑ 126 Natrone Means	.50	.23
❑ 127 Mikhael Ricks	.30	.14
❑ 128 Craig Whelihan	.30	.14
❑ 129 Garrison Hearst	.50	.23
❑ 130 Terrell Owens	.75	.35
❑ 131 Jerry Rice	1.50	.70
❑ 132 J.J.Stokes	.50	.23
❑ 133 Steve Young	1.00	.45
❑ 134 Joey Galloway	.50	.23
❑ 135 Ahman Green	.75	.35
❑ 136 Jon Kitna	.75	.35
❑ 137 Ricky Watters	.50	.23
❑ 138 Mike Alstott	.75	.35
❑ 139 Reidel Anthony	.50	.23
❑ 140 Trent Dilfer	.50	.23
❑ 141 Warrick Dunn	.75	.35
❑ 142 Jacquez Green	.30	.14
❑ 143 Kevin Dyson	.50	.23
❑ 144 Eddie George	.75	.35
❑ 145 Steve McNair	.75	.35
❑ 146 Yancey Thigpen	.30	.14
❑ 147 Terry Allen	.50	.23
❑ 148 Trent Green	.75	.35
❑ 149 Skip Hicks	.30	.14
❑ 150 Michael Westbrook	.50	.23
❑ 151 Rahim Abdullah RC	1.25	.55
❑ 152 Champ Bailey RC	2.00	.90
❑ 153 Marlon Barnes RC	.75	.35
❑ 154 D'Wayne Bates RC	1.25	.55
❑ 155 Michael Bishop RC	1.50	.70
❑ 156 Dre' Bly RC	1.50	.70
❑ 157 David Boston RC	1.50	.70
❑ 158 Chris Claiborne RC	.75	.35
❑ 159 Tim Couch RC	1.50	.70
❑ 160 Daunte Culpepper RC	6.00	2.70
❑ 161 Autry Denson RC	1.25	.55
❑ 162 Jared DeVries RC	1.25	.55
❑ 163 Troy Edwards RC	1.25	.55
❑ 164 Kris Farris RC	.75	.35
❑ 165 Kevin Faulk RC	1.50	.70
❑ 166 Martin Gramatica RC	.75	.35
❑ 167 Torry Holt RC	4.00	1.80
❑ 168 Brock Huard RC	1.50	.70
❑ 169 Sedrick Irvin RC	.75	.35
❑ 170 Edgerrin James RC	6.00	2.70
❑ 171 James Johnson RC	1.25	.55
❑ 172 Kevin Johnson RC	1.50	.70
❑ 173 Andy Katzenmoyer RC	1.25	.55
❑ 174 Jevon Kearse RC	2.50	1.10
❑ 175 Shaun King RC	1.25	.55
❑ 176 Rob Konrad RC	1.25	.55
❑ 177 Chris McAlister RC	1.25	.55
❑ 178 Darnell McDonald RC	1.25	.55
❑ 179 Donovan McNabb RC	8.00	3.60
❑ 180 Cade McNown RC	1.25	.55
❑ 181 Dat Nguyen RC	1.50	.70
❑ 182 Peerless Price RC	2.50	1.10
❑ 183 Akili Smith RC	1.25	.55
❑ 184 Tai Streets RC	1.50	.70
❑ 185 Cuncho Brown RC UER (Photo is actually Courtney Brown)	.75	.35
❑ 186 Ricky Williams RC	3.00	1.35
❑ 187 Craig Yeast RC	1.25	.55
❑ 188 Amos Zereoue RC	1.50	.70
❑ 189 Checklist	.30	.14
❑ 190 Checklist	.30	.14

2000 Collector's Edge EG

	Nm-Mt	Ex-Mt
COMPLETE SET (148)	120.00	55.00
❑ 1 Marcus Robinson	1.25	.55
❑ 2 Adrian Murrell	.75	.35
❑ 3 Qadry Ismail	.75	.35
❑ 4 Tim Biakabutuka	.75	.35
❑ 5 Jamal Anderson	1.25	.55
❑ 6 Dorsey Levens	.75	.35
❑ 7 Robert Smith	1.25	.55
❑ 8 Tony Banks	.75	.35
❑ 9 Yancey Thigpen	.50	.23
❑ 10 Elvis Grbac	.75	.35
❑ 11 Sedrick Irvin	.50	.23
❑ 12 Rob Johnson	.75	.35
❑ 13 Frank Sanders	.75	.35
❑ 14 Rich Gannon	1.25	.55
❑ 15 Steve Beuerlein	.75	.35
❑ 16 James Stewart	.75	.35
❑ 17 Ricky Watters	.75	.35
❑ 18 Curtis Enis	.50	.23
❑ 19 Eddie Kennison	.50	.23
❑ 20 Kerry Collins	.75	.35
❑ 21 Ray Lucas	.75	.35
❑ 22 Carl Pickens	.75	.35
❑ 23 Natrone Means	.50	.23
❑ 24 Daunte Culpepper	1.50	.70
❑ 25 Karim Abdul-Jabbar	.75	.35
❑ 26 David Boston	1.25	.55
❑ 27 Rocket Ismail	.75	.35
❑ 28 Jacquez Green	.50	.23
❑ 29 Kevin Dyson	.75	.35
❑ 30 Chris Chandler	.75	.35
❑ 31 Brian Griese	1.25	.55
❑ 32 Charlie Garner	.75	.35
❑ 33 Wayne Chrebet	.75	.35
❑ 34 Mike Alstott	1.25	.55
❑ 35 Germane Crowell	.50	.23
❑ 36 Michael Cloud	.50	.23
❑ 37 Antowain Smith	.75	.35
❑ 38 Jeff George	.75	.35
❑ 39 Antonio Freeman	1.25	.55
❑ 40 Champ Bailey	.75	.35
❑ 41 Terrence Wilkins	.50	.23
❑ 42 Junior Seau	1.25	.55
❑ 43 Jimmy Smith	.75	.35
❑ 44 Greg Hill	.50	.23
❑ 45 Tyrone Wheatley	.75	.35
❑ 46 Tony Gonzalez	.75	.35
❑ 47 Rod Smith	.75	.35
❑ 48 Damon Huard	1.25	.55
❑ 49 Jerome Bettis	1.25	.55
❑ 50 Cris Carter	1.25	.55
❑ 51 Darnay Scott	.75	.35
❑ 52 Ike Hilliard	.75	.35
❑ 53 Errict Rhett	.75	.35
❑ 54 Tim Brown	1.25	.55
❑ 55 Terry Glenn	.75	.35
❑ 56 Jeff Blake	.75	.35
❑ 57 Terance Mathis	.75	.35
❑ 58 Duce Staley	1.25	.55
❑ 59 Amani Toomer	.50	.23
❑ 60 Terry Allen	.75	.35
❑ 61 Corey Dillon	1.25	.55
❑ 62 Kordell Stewart	.75	.35
❑ 63 Az-Zahir Hakim	.75	.35
❑ 64 Jim Harbaugh	.75	.35
❑ 65 Bill Schroeder	.75	.35
❑ 66 O.J. McDuffie	.75	.35
❑ 67 Keenan McCardell	.75	.35
❑ 68 Terrell Owens	1.25	.55
❑ 69 Joey Galloway	.75	.35
❑ 70 Derrick Alexander	.75	.35
❑ 71 Ed McCaffrey	1.25	.55
❑ 72 Reidel Anthony	.50	.23
❑ 73 Michael Irvin	.75	.35
❑ 74 Herman Moore	.75	.35
❑ 75 Joe Montgomery	.50	.23
❑ 76 Muhsin Muhammad	.75	.35
❑ 77 Charles Johnson	.75	.35
❑ 78 Michael Westbrook	.75	.35
❑ 79 Jevon Kearse	1.25	.55
❑ 80 Courtney Brown RC	2.00	.90
❑ 81 Shaun Alexander RC	5.00	2.20
❑ 82 R.Jay Soward RC	1.50	.70
❑ 83 Sylvester Morris RC	1.50	.70
❑ 84 Giovanni Carmazzi RC	1.50	.70
❑ 85 J.R. Redmond RC	1.50	.70
❑ 86 Sherrod Gideon RC	1.50	.70
❑ 87 Tee Martin RC	2.00	.90
❑ 88 Dennis Northcutt RC	2.00	.90
❑ 89 Troy Walters RC	2.00	.90
❑ 90 Joe Hamilton RC	1.50	.70
❑ 91 Reuben Droughns RC	2.50	1.10
❑ 92 Trung Canidate RC	1.50	.70
❑ 93A Bill Burke		
❑ 93B Bill Burke Red		
❑ 94 Tim Rattay RC	4.00	1.80
❑ 95 Jerry Porter RC	2.50	1.10
❑ 96 Michael Wiley RC	1.50	.70
❑ 97 Anthony Lucas RC	1.50	.70
❑ 98 Danny Farmer RC	1.50	.70
❑ 99 Travis Prentice RC	1.50	.70
❑ 100 Dez White RC	2.00	.90
❑ 101 Chad Pennington RC	8.00	3.60
❑ 102 Chris Redman RC	1.50	.70
❑ 103 Thomas Jones RC	3.00	1.35
❑ 104 Ron Dayne RC	2.00	.90
❑ 105 Jamal Lewis RC	5.00	2.20
❑ 106 Shyrone Stith RC	2.00	.90
❑ 107 Peter Warrick RC	2.00	.90
❑ 108 Plaxico Burress RC	4.00	1.80
❑ 109 Travis Taylor RC	2.00	.90
❑ 110A LaVar Arrington RC	80.00	36.00
❑ 110B LaVar Arrington RC Red	40.00	18.00
❑ 111 Terrell Davis	1.25	.55
❑ 112 Dan Marino	4.00	1.80
❑ 113 Brad Johnson	1.25	.55
❑ 114 Isaac Bruce	1.25	.55
❑ 115 Eric Moulds	1.25	.55
❑ 116 Olandis Gary	1.25	.55
❑ 117 Drew Bledsoe	1.50	.70
❑ 118 Steve Young	1.50	.70
❑ 119 Keyshawn Johnson	1.25	.55
❑ 120 Emmitt Smith	2.50	1.10
❑ 121 Warrick Dunn	1.25	.55

❑ 122 Doug Flutie	1.25	.55
❑ 123 Troy Edwards	.50	.23
❑ 124 Brett Favre	4.00	1.80
❑ 125 Charlie Batch	1.25	.55
❑ 126 Curtis Martin	1.25	.55
❑ 127 Stephen Davis	1.25	.55
❑ 128 Troy Aikman	2.50	1.10
❑ 129 Fred Taylor	1.25	.55
❑ 130 Jerry Rice	2.50	1.10
❑ 131 Jon Kitna	1.25	.55
❑ 132 Steve McNair	1.25	.55
❑ 133 Jake Plummer	.75	.35
❑ 134 Donovan McNabb	2.00	.90
❑ 135 Ricky Williams	1.25	.55
❑ 136 Torry Holt	1.25	.55
❑ 137 James Johnson	.50	.23
❑ 138 Kevin Johnson	1.25	.55
❑ 139 Akili Smith	.50	.23
❑ 140 Cade McNown	.50	.23
❑ 141 Eddie George	1.25	.55
❑ 142 Shaun King	.50	.23
❑ 143 Marshall Faulk	1.50	.70
❑ 144 Kurt Warner	2.50	1.10
❑ 145 Randy Moss	2.50	1.10
❑ 146 Mark Brunell	1.25	.55
❑ 147 Marvin Harrison	1.25	.55
❑ 148 Edgerrin James	2.00	.90
❑ 149 Tim Couch	.75	.35
❑ 150 Peyton Manning	3.00	1.35

1998 Collector's Edge First Place

	Nm-Mt	Ex-Mt
COMPLETE SET (250)	60.00	27.00
❑ 1 Karim Abdul-Jabbar	.75	.35
❑ 2 Flozell Adams RC	.60	.25
❑ 3 Troy Aikman	1.50	.70
❑ 4 Robert Smith	.75	.35
❑ 5 Stephen Alexander RC	.75	.35
❑ 6 Harold Shaw RC	.60	.25
❑ 7 Marcus Allen	.75	.35
❑ 8 Terry Allen	.75	.35
❑ 9 Mike Alstott	.75	.35
❑ 10 Jamal Anderson	.75	.35
❑ 11 Reidel Anthony	.50	.23
❑ 12 Jamie Asher	.30	.14
❑ 13 Darnell Autry	.30	.14
❑ 14 Phil Savoy RC	.75	.35
❑ 15 Jon Ritchie RC	.75	.35
❑ 16 Tony Banks	.50	.23
❑ 17 Tiki Barber	.75	.35
❑ 18 Pat Barnes	.30	.14
❑ 19 Charlie Batch RC	1.25	.55
❑ 20 Mikhael Ricks RC	.75	.35
❑ 21 Jerome Bettis	.75	.35
❑ 22 Tim Biakabutuka	.50	.23
❑ 23 Roosevelt Blackmon RC	.60	.25
❑ 24 Jeff Blake	.50	.23
❑ 25 Drew Bledsoe	1.25	.55
❑ 26 Tony Boselli	.30	.14
❑ 27 Peter Boulware	.30	.14
❑ 28 Tony Brackens	.30	.14
❑ 29 Corey Bradford RC	1.25	.55
❑ 30 Michael Pittman RC	1.50	.70
❑ 31 Keith Brooking RC	1.25	.55
❑ 32 Robert Brooks	.50	.23
❑ 33 Derrick Brooks	.75	.35
❑ 34 Ken Oxendine RC	.60	.25
❑ 35 R.W. McQuarters RC	.75	.35
❑ 36 Tim Brown	.75	.35
❑ 37 Chad Brown	.30	.14
❑ 38 Isaac Bruce	.75	.35
❑ 39 Mark Brunell	.75	.35
❑ 40 Chris Canty	.30	.14
❑ 41 Mark Carrier	.30	.14
❑ 42 Rae Carruth	.30	.14
❑ 43 Ki-Jana Carter	.30	.14
❑ 44 Cris Carter	.75	.35
❑ 45 Larry Centers	.30	.14
❑ 46 Corey Chavous RC	1.25	.55
❑ 47 Mark Chmura	.50	.23
❑ 48 Cameron Cleeland RC	.60	.25
❑ 49 Dexter Coakley	.30	.14
❑ 50 Ben Coates	.50	.23
❑ 51 Jonathan Linton RC	.75	.35
❑ 52 Todd Collins	.30	.14
❑ 53 Kerry Collins	.50	.23
❑ 54 Tebucky Jones RC	.60	.25
❑ 55 Curtis Conway	.50	.23
❑ 56 Sam Cowart RC	.75	.35
❑ 57 Bryan Cox	.30	.14
❑ 58 Randall Cunningham	.75	.35
❑ 59 Terrell Davis	.75	.35
❑ 60 Troy Davis	.30	.14
❑ 61 Pat Johnson RC	.75	.35
❑ 62 Trent Dilfer	.75	.35
❑ 63 Vonnie Holliday RC	.75	.35
❑ 64 Corey Dillon	.75	.35
❑ 65 Hugh Douglas	.30	.14
❑ 66 Jim Druckenmiller	.30	.14
❑ 67 Warrick Dunn	.75	.35
❑ 68 Robert Edwards RC	.75	.35
❑ 69 Greg Ellis RC	.60	.25
❑ 70 John Elway	3.00	1.35
❑ 71 Bert Emanuel	.50	.23
❑ 72 Bobby Engram	.50	.23
❑ 73 Curtis Enis RC	.60	.25
❑ 74 Marshall Faulk	1.00	.45
❑ 75 Brett Favre	3.00	1.35
❑ 76 Doug Flutie	.75	.35
❑ 77 Glenn Foley	.50	.23
❑ 78 Antonio Freeman	.75	.35
❑ 79 Gus Frerotte	.30	.14
❑ 80 John Friesz	.30	.14
❑ 81 Irving Fryar	.50	.23
❑ 82 Joey Galloway	.50	.23
❑ 83 Rich Gannon	.75	.35
❑ 84 Charlie Garner	.50	.23
❑ 85 Jeff George	.50	.23
❑ 86 Eddie George	.75	.35
❑ 87 Sean Gilbert	.30	.14
❑ 88 Terry Glenn	.75	.35
❑ 89 Aaron Glenn	.30	.14
❑ 90 Tony Gonzalez	.75	.35
❑ 91 Jeff Graham	.30	.14
❑ 92 Elvis Grbac	.50	.23
❑ 93 Jacquez Green RC	.75	.35
❑ 94 Kevin Greene	.50	.23
❑ 95 Brian Griese RC UER	2.50	1.10
❑ 96 Byron Hanspard	.30	.14
❑ 97 Jim Harbaugh	.50	.23
❑ 98 Kevin Hardy	.30	.14
❑ 99 Walt Harris	.30	.14
❑ 100 Marvin Harrison	.75	.35
❑ 101 Rodney Harrison	.50	.23
❑ 102 Jeff Hartings	.50	.23
❑ 103 Ken Harvey	.30	.14
❑ 104 Garrison Hearst	.75	.35
❑ 105 Ike Hilliard	.50	.23
❑ 106 Jeff Hostetler	.30	.14
❑ 107 Bobby Hoying	.50	.23
❑ 108 Michael Jackson	.30	.14
❑ 109 Anthony Johnson	.30	.14
❑ 110 Brad Johnson	.75	.35
❑ 111 Keyshawn Johnson	.75	.35
❑ 112 Charles Johnson	.30	.14
❑ 113 Daryl Johnston	.50	.23
❑ 114 Chris Jones	.30	.14
❑ 115 George Jones	.30	.14
❑ 116 Donald Hayes RC	.75	.35
❑ 117 Danny Kanell	.50	.23
❑ 118 Napoleon Kaufman	.75	.35
❑ 119 Cortez Kennedy	.30	.14
❑ 120 Eddie Kennison	.50	.23
❑ 121 Levon Kirkland	.30	.14
❑ 122 Jon Kitna	.75	.35
❑ 123 Erik Kramer	.30	.14
❑ 124 David LaFleur	.30	.14
❑ 125 Lamar Lathon	.30	.14
❑ 126 Ty Law	.50	.23
❑ 127 Ryan Leaf RC	1.25	.55
❑ 128 Dorsey Levens	.75	.35
❑ 129 Ray Lewis	.75	.35
❑ 130 Darryll Lewis	.30	.14
❑ 131 Matt Hasselbeck RC	25.00	11.00
❑ 132 Greg Lloyd	.30	.14
❑ 133 Kevin Lockett	.30	.14
❑ 134 Keith Lyle	.30	.14
❑ 135 Peyton Manning RC	12.00	5.50
❑ 136 Dan Marino	3.00	1.35
❑ 137 Wayne Martin	.30	.14
❑ 138 Ahman Green RC	6.00	2.70
❑ 139 Tony Martin	.50	.23
❑ 140 E.G. Green RC	.75	.35
❑ 141 Derrick Mayes	.50	.23
❑ 142 Ed McCaffrey	.50	.23
❑ 143 Keenan McCardell	.50	.23
❑ 144 O.J. McDuffie	.50	.23
❑ 145 Leeland McElroy	.30	.14
❑ 146 Willie McGinest	.30	.14
❑ 147 Chester McGlockton	.30	.14
❑ 148 Steve McNair	.75	.35
❑ 149 Natrone Means	.50	.23
❑ 150 Eric Metcalf	.30	.14
❑ 151 Anthony Miller	.30	.14
❑ 152 Rick Mirer	.30	.14
❑ 153 Scott Mitchell	.50	.23
❑ 154 John Mobley	.30	.14
❑ 155 Warren Moon	.75	.35
❑ 156 Herman Moore	.50	.23
❑ 157 Randy Moss RC	6.00	2.70
❑ 158 Eric Moulds	.75	.35
❑ 159 Muhsin Muhammad	.50	.23
❑ 160 Adrian Murrell	.50	.23
❑ 161 Marcus Nash RC	.60	.25
❑ 162 Hardy Nickerson	.30	.14
❑ 163 Ken Norton	.30	.14
❑ 164 Neil O'Donnell	.50	.23
❑ 165 Terrell Owens	.75	.35
❑ 166 Orlando Pace	.30	.14
❑ 167 Jammi German RC	.60	.25
❑ 168 Erric Pegram	.30	.14
❑ 169 Jason Peter RC	.60	.25
❑ 170 Carl Pickens	.50	.23
❑ 171 Jake Plummer	.75	.35
❑ 172 John Randle	.50	.23
❑ 173 Andre Reed	.50	.23
❑ 174 Jake Reed	.50	.23
❑ 175 Errict Rhett	.50	.23
❑ 176 Simeon Rice	.50	.23
❑ 177 Jerry Rice	1.50	.70
❑ 178 Andre Rison	.50	.23
❑ 179 Darrell Russell	.30	.14
❑ 180 Rashaan Salaam	.30	.14
❑ 181 Deion Sanders	.75	.35
❑ 182 Barry Sanders	2.50	1.10
❑ 183 Chris Sanders	.30	.14
❑ 184 Warren Sapp	.50	.23
❑ 185 Junior Seau	.75	.35
❑ 186 Jason Sehorn	.50	.23
❑ 187 Shannon Sharpe	.50	.23
❑ 188 Sedrick Shaw	.30	.14
❑ 189 Heath Shuler	.30	.14
❑ 190 Chris Floyd RC	.60	.25
❑ 191 Terry Fair RC	.75	.35
❑ 192 Kevin Dyson RC	1.25	.55
❑ 193 Torrance Small	.30	.14
❑ 194 Antowain Smith	.75	.35
❑ 195 Bruce Smith	.50	.23
❑ 196 Tarik Smith RC	.75	.35
❑ 197 Emmitt Smith	2.50	1.10
❑ 198 Neil Smith	.50	.23
❑ 199 Jimmy Smith	.50	.23
❑ 200 Chris Spielman	.30	.14
❑ 201 Danny Wuerffel	.50	.23

❑ 202 Irving Spikes	.30	.14
❑ 203 Shawn Springs	.30	.14
❑ 204 Duane Starks RC	.60	.25
❑ 205 Kordell Stewart	.75	.35
❑ 206 J.J. Stokes	.50	.23
❑ 207 Eric Swann	.30	.14
❑ 208 Steve Tasker	.30	.14
❑ 209 Tim Dwight RC	1.25	.55
❑ 210 Jason Taylor	.50	.23
❑ 211 Vinny Testaverde	.50	.23
❑ 212 Thurman Thomas	.75	.35
❑ 213 Broderick Thomas	.30	.14
❑ 214 Derrick Thomas	.50	.23
❑ 215 Zach Thomas	.75	.35
❑ 216 Germane Crowell RC	.75	.35
❑ 217 Amani Toomer	.50	.23
❑ 218 Tamarick Vanover	.30	.14
❑ 219 Ross Verba	.30	.14
❑ 220 Andre Wadsworth RC	.75	.35
❑ 221 Ray Zellars	.30	.14
❑ 222 Chris Warren	.50	.23
❑ 223 Steve Young	1.00	.45
❑ 224 Tyrone Wheatley	.50	.23
❑ 225 Reggie White	.75	.35
❑ 226 John Avery RC	.75	.35
❑ 227 Charles Woodson RC	1.50	.70
❑ 228 Takeo Spikes RC	1.25	.55
❑ 229 Bryant Young	.30	.14
❑ 230 Tavian Banks RC	.50	.23
❑ 231 Fred Beasley RC	.60	.25
❑ 232 Chris Ruhman RC	.60	.25
❑ CK1A Broncos Logo CL	.10	.05
❑ CK1B Steelers Logo CL	.10	.05
❑ CK2A 49ers Logo CL	.10	.05
❑ CK2B Panthers Logo CL	.10	.05
❑ CK3A Giants Logo CL	.10	.05
❑ CK3B Packers Logo CL	.10	.05
❑ CK4A Colts Logo CL	.10	.05
❑ CK4B Dolphins Logo CL	.10	.05
❑ CK5A Chargers Logo CL	.10	.05
❑ CK5B Vikings Logo Cl	.10	.05
❑ CK6A Patriots Logo Cl	.10	.05
❑ CK6B Raiders Logo CL	.10	.05
❑ CK7A Buccaneers Logo CL	.10	.05
❑ CK7B Cowboys Logo CL	.10	.05
❑ CK8A Bills Logo CL	.10	.05
❑ CK8B Lions Logo CL	.10	.05
❑ CK9A Chiefs Logo CL	.10	.05
❑ CK9B Seahawks Logo CL	.10	.05

1999 Collector's Edge First Place

	Nm-Mt	Ex-Mt
COMPLETE SET (200)	50.00	22.00
❑ 1 Adrian Murrell	.50	.23
❑ 2 Rob Moore	.50	.23
❑ 3 Jake Plummer	.50	.23
❑ 4 Simeon Rice	.50	.23
❑ 5 Frank Sanders	.50	.23
❑ 6 Jamal Anderson	.75	.35
❑ 7 Chris Calloway	.30	.14
❑ 8 Chris Chandler	.50	.23
❑ 9 Tim Dwight	.75	.35
❑ 10 Terance Mathis	.50	.23
❑ 11 Jessie Tuggle	.30	.14
❑ 12 Tony Banks	.50	.23
❑ 13 Priest Holmes	1.25	.55
❑ 14 Jermaine Lewis	.50	.23
❑ 15 Scott Mitchell	.30	.14
❑ 16 Doug Flutie	.75	.35
❑ 17 Eric Moulds	.75	.35
❑ 18 Andre Reed	.50	.23
❑ 19 Antowain Smith	.75	.35
❑ 20 Bruce Smith	.50	.23
❑ 21 Thurman Thomas	.50	.23
❑ 22 Steve Beuerlein	.50	.23
❑ 23 Tim Biakabutuka	.50	.23
❑ 24 Kevin Greene	.30	.14
❑ 25 Muhsin Muhammad	.50	.23
❑ 26 Edgar Bennett	.30	.14
❑ 27 Curtis Conway	.50	.23
❑ 28 Bobby Engram	.50	.23
❑ 29 Curtis Enis	.30	.14
❑ 30 Erik Kramer	.30	.14
❑ 31 Jeff Blake	.50	.23
❑ 32 Corey Dillon	.75	.35
❑ 33 Carl Pickens	.50	.23
❑ 34 Darnay Scott	.30	.14
❑ 35 Takeo Spikes	.30	.14
❑ 36 Ty Detmer	.30	.14
❑ 37 Terry Kirby	.30	.14
❑ 38 Leslie Shepherd	.30	.14
❑ 39 Chris Spielman	.30	.14
❑ 40 Troy Aikman	1.50	.70
❑ 41 Michael Irvin	.50	.23
❑ 42 Rocket Ismail	.50	.23
❑ 43 Ernie Mills	.30	.14
❑ 44 Deion Sanders	.75	.35
❑ 45 Emmitt Smith	1.50	.70
❑ 46 Chris Warren	.30	.14
❑ 47 Bubba Brister	.30	.14
❑ 48 Terrell Davis	.75	.35
❑ 49 Brian Griese	.75	.35
❑ 50 Ed McCaffrey	.50	.23
❑ 51 Shannon Sharpe	.50	.23
❑ 52 Rod Smith	.50	.23
❑ 53 Charlie Batch	.75	.35
❑ 54 Terry Fair	.30	.14
❑ 55 Herman Moore	.50	.23
❑ 56 Johnnie Morton	.50	.23
❑ 57 Barry Sanders	2.50	1.10
❑ 58 Santana Dotson	.30	.14
❑ 59 Brett Favre	2.50	1.10
❑ 60 Mark Chmura	.30	.14
❑ 61 Antonio Freeman	.75	.35
❑ 62 Dorsey Levens	.75	.35
❑ 63 Derrick Mayes	.50	.23
❑ 64 Marvin Harrison	.75	.35
❑ 65 Peyton Manning	2.50	1.10
❑ 66 Jerome Pathon	.30	.14
❑ 67 Mark Brunell	.75	.35
❑ 68 Keenan McCardell	.50	.23
❑ 69 Jimmy Smith	.50	.23
❑ 70 Fred Taylor	.75	.35
❑ 71 Derrick Alexander WR	.50	.23
❑ 72 Kimble Anders	.50	.23
❑ 73 Elvis Grbac	.50	.23
❑ 74 Warren Moon	.75	.35
❑ 75 Byron Bam Morris	.30	.14
❑ 76 Andre Rison	.50	.23
❑ 77 Karim Abdul-Jabbar	.50	.23
❑ 78 Dan Marino	2.50	1.10
❑ 79 Tony Martin	.50	.23
❑ 80 O.J. McDuffie	.50	.23
❑ 81 Zach Thomas	.75	.35
❑ 82 Cris Carter	.75	.35
❑ 83 Randall Cunningham	.75	.35
❑ 84 Jeff George	.50	.23
❑ 85 Randy Moss	2.00	.90
❑ 86 Jake Reed	.50	.23
❑ 87 Robert Smith	.75	.35
❑ 88 Drew Bledsoe	1.00	.45
❑ 89 Ben Coates	.50	.23
❑ 90 Terry Glenn	.75	.35
❑ 91 Ty Law	.50	.23
❑ 92 Shawn Jefferson	.30	.14
❑ 93 Cameron Cleeland	.30	.14
❑ 94 Andre Hastings	.30	.14
❑ 95 Billy Joe Hobert	.30	.14
❑ 96 Eddie Kennison	.50	.23
❑ 97 Gary Brown	.30	.14
❑ 98 Kerry Collins	.50	.23
❑ 99 Kent Graham	.30	.14
❑ 100 Ike Hilliard	.30	.14
❑ 101 Joe Jurevicius	.50	.23
❑ 102 Wayne Chrebet	.50	.23
❑ 103 Aaron Glenn	.30	.14
❑ 104 Keyshawn Johnson	.75	.35
❑ 105 Mo Lewis	.30	.14
❑ 106 Curtis Martin	.75	.35
❑ 107 Vinny Testaverde	.50	.23
❑ 108 Tim Brown	.75	.35
❑ 109 Rich Gannon	.75	.35
❑ 110 James Jett	.50	.23
❑ 111 Napoleon Kaufman	.75	.35
❑ 112 Charles Woodson	.75	.35
❑ 113 Koy Detmer	.30	.14
❑ 114 Charles Johnson	.30	.14
❑ 115 Duce Staley	.75	.35
❑ 116 Jerome Bettis	.75	.35
❑ 117 Courtney Hawkins	.30	.14
❑ 118 Levon Kirkland	.30	.14
❑ 119 Kordell Stewart	.50	.23
❑ 120 Isaac Bruce	.75	.35
❑ 121 Marshall Faulk	1.00	.45
❑ 122 Trent Green	.75	.35
❑ 123 Amp Lee	.30	.14
❑ 124 Jim Harbaugh	.50	.23
❑ 125 Bryan Still	.30	.14
❑ 126 Freddie Jones	.30	.14
❑ 127 Mikhael Ricks	.30	.14
❑ 128 Natrone Means	.50	.23
❑ 129 Junior Seau	.75	.35
❑ 130 Lawrence Phillips	.50	.23
❑ 131 Terrell Owens	.75	.35
❑ 132 Jerry Rice	1.50	.70
❑ 133 J.J. Stokes	.50	.23
❑ 134 Steve Young	1.00	.45
❑ 135 Joey Galloway	.50	.23
❑ 136 Jon Kitna	.75	.35
❑ 137 Ricky Watters	.50	.23
❑ 138 Mike Alstott	.75	.35
❑ 139 Reidel Anthony	.50	.23
❑ 140 Trent Dilfer	.50	.23
❑ 141 Warrick Dunn	.75	.35
❑ 142 Kevin Dyson	.50	.23
❑ 143 Eddie George	.75	.35
❑ 144 Steve McNair	.75	.35
❑ 145 Frank Wycheck	.30	.14
❑ 146 Skip Hicks	.30	.14
❑ 147 Brad Johnson	.75	.35
❑ 148 Michael Westbrook	.50	.23
❑ 149 Checklist Card	.30	.14
❑ 150 Checklist Card	.30	.14
❑ 151 David Boston RC	1.25	.55
❑ 152 Patrick Kerney RC	1.25	.55
❑ 153 Chris McAlister RC	1.00	.45
❑ 154 Peerless Price RC	2.00	.90
❑ 155 Antoine Winfield RC	1.00	.45
❑ 156 D'Wayne Bates RC	1.00	.45
❑ 157 Cade McNown RC	1.00	.45
❑ 158 Akili Smith RC	1.00	.45
❑ 159 Rahim Abdullah RC	1.00	.45
❑ 160 Tim Couch RC	1.25	.55
❑ 161 Kevin Johnson RC	1.25	.55
❑ 162 Ebenezer Ekuban RC	1.00	.45
❑ 163 Dat Nguyen RC	1.25	.55
❑ 164 Al Wilson RC	1.00	.45
❑ 165 Chris Claiborne RC	.60	.25
❑ 166 Sedrick Irvin RC	.60	.25
❑ 167 Antuan Edwards RC	1.00	.45
❑ 168 Aaron Brooks RC	4.00	1.80
❑ 169 De'Mond Parker RC	.60	.25
❑ 170 Edgerrin James RC	5.00	2.20
❑ 171 Fernando Bryant RC	1.00	.45
❑ 172 Mike Cloud RC	1.00	.45
❑ 173 John Tait RC	.60	.25
❑ 174 Cecil Collins RC	.60	.25
❑ 175 James Johnson RC	1.00	.45
❑ 176 Rob Konrad RC	1.25	.55
❑ 177 Daunte Culpepper RC	5.00	2.20
❑ 178 Jim Kleinsasser RC	1.25	.55
❑ 179 Brock Huard RC	1.25	.55
❑ 180 Michael Bishop RC	1.25	.55
❑ 181 Kevin Faulk RC	1.25	.55

Card	Nm-Mt	Ex-Mt
❑ 182 Andy Katzenmoyer RC	1.00	.45
❑ 183 Ricky Williams RC	2.50	1.10
❑ 184 Joe Montgomery RC	1.00	.45
❑ 185 Donovan McNabb RC	6.00	2.70
❑ 186 Troy Edwards RC	1.00	.45
❑ 187 Amos Zereoue RC	1.25	.55
❑ 188 Joe Germaine RC	1.00	.45
❑ 189 Torry Holt RC	3.00	1.35
❑ 190 Jermaine Fazande RC	1.00	.45
❑ 191 Reggie McGrew RC	1.00	.45
❑ 192 Karsten Bailey RC	1.00	.45
❑ 193 Lamar King RC	.60	.25
❑ 194 Autry Denson RC	1.00	.45
❑ 195 Martin Gramatica RC	.60	.25
❑ 196 Shaun King RC	1.00	.45
❑ 197 Darnell McDonald RC	1.00	.45
❑ 198 Anthony McFarland RC	1.25	.55
❑ 199 Jevon Kearse RC	2.00	.90
❑ 200 Champ Bailey RC	1.50	.70
❑ 201 Kurt Warner RC/500	100.00	45.00
❑ 201PG Kurt Warner Promo Gold foil on front	12.00	5.50
❑ 201PS Kurt Warner Promo Silver foil on front	12.00	3.60

1999 Collector's Edge Fury

	Nm-Mt	Ex-Mt
COMPLETE SET (200)	40.00	18.00
❑ 1 Checklist Card 1	.30	.14
❑ 2 Checklist Card 2	.30	.14
❑ 3 Karim Abdul-Jabbar	.50	.23
❑ 4 Troy Aikman	1.50	.70
❑ 5 Derrick Alexander WR	.50	.23
❑ 6 Mike Alstott	.75	.35
❑ 7 Jamal Anderson	.75	.35
❑ 8 Reidel Anthony	.50	.23
❑ 9 Tiki Barber	.50	.23
❑ 10 Charlie Batch	.75	.35
❑ 11 Edgar Bennett	.30	.14
❑ 12 Jerome Bettis	.75	.35
❑ 13 Steve Beuerlein	.50	.23
❑ 14 Tim Biakabutuka	.50	.23
❑ 15 Jeff Blake	.50	.23
❑ 16 Drew Bledsoe	1.00	.45
❑ 17 Bubby Brister	.30	.14
❑ 18 Robert Brooks	.50	.23
❑ 19 Gary Brown	.30	.14
❑ 20 Tim Brown	.75	.35
❑ 21 Isaac Bruce	.75	.35
❑ 22 Mark Brunell	.75	.35
❑ 23 Chris Calloway	.30	.14
❑ 24 Cris Carter	.75	.35
❑ 25 Larry Centers	.30	.14
❑ 26 Chris Chandler	.50	.23
❑ 27 Wayne Chrebet	.50	.23
❑ 28 Cam Cleeland	.30	.14
❑ 29 Kerry Collins	.50	.23
❑ 30 Curtis Conway	.50	.23
❑ 31 Germane Crowell	.30	.14
❑ 32 Randall Cunningham	.75	.35
❑ 33 Terrell Davis	.75	.35
❑ 34 Koy Detmer	.30	.14
❑ 35 Ty Detmer	.50	.23
❑ 36 Trent Dilfer	.50	.23
❑ 37 Corey Dillon	.75	.35
❑ 38 Warrick Dunn	.75	.35
❑ 39 Tim Dwight	.75	.35
❑ 40 Kevin Dyson	.50	.23
❑ 41 John Elway	2.50	1.10
❑ 42 Bobby Engram	.50	.23
❑ 43 Curtis Enis	.30	.14
❑ 44 Terry Fair	.30	.14
❑ 45 Marshall Faulk	1.00	.45
❑ 46 Brett Favre	2.50	1.10
❑ 47 Doug Flutie	.75	.35
❑ 48 Antonio Freeman	.75	.35
❑ 49 Joey Galloway	.50	.23
❑ 50 Rich Gannon	.75	.35
❑ 51 Eddie George	.75	.35
❑ 52 Jeff George	.50	.23
❑ 53 Terry Glenn	.75	.35
❑ 54 Elvis Grbac	.50	.23
❑ 55 Ahman Green	.75	.35
❑ 56 Jacquez Green	.30	.14
❑ 57 Trent Green	.75	.35
❑ 58 Kevin Greene	.30	.14
❑ 59 Brian Griese	.75	.35
❑ 60 Az-Zahir Hakim	.30	.14
❑ 61 Jim Harbaugh	.50	.23
❑ 62 Marvin Harrison	.75	.35
❑ 63 Courtney Hawkins	.30	.14
❑ 64 Garrison Hearst	.50	.23
❑ 65 Ike Hilliard	.30	.14
❑ 66 Billy Joe Hobert	.30	.14
❑ 67 Priest Holmes	1.25	.55
❑ 68 Michael Irvin	.50	.23
❑ 69 Rocket Ismail	.50	.23
❑ 70 Shawn Jefferson	.30	.14
❑ 71 James Jett	.50	.23
❑ 72 Brad Johnson	.75	.35
❑ 73 Charles Johnson	.30	.14
❑ 74 Keyshawn Johnson	.75	.35
❑ 75 Pat Johnson	.30	.14
❑ 76 Joe Jurevicius	.50	.23
❑ 77 Napoleon Kaufman	.75	.35
❑ 78 Eddie Kennison	.50	.23
❑ 79 Terry Kirby	.30	.14
❑ 80 Jon Kitna	.75	.35
❑ 81 Erik Kramer	.30	.14
❑ 82 Fred Lane	.30	.14
❑ 83 Ty Law	.50	.23
❑ 84 Ryan Leaf	.75	.35
❑ 85 Amp Lee	.30	.14
❑ 86 Dorsey Levens	.75	.35
❑ 87 Jermaine Lewis	.50	.23
❑ 88 Sam Madison	.30	.14
❑ 89 Peyton Manning	2.50	1.10
❑ 90 Dan Marino	2.50	1.10
❑ 91 Curtis Martin	.75	.35
❑ 92 Tony Martin	.50	.23
❑ 93 Terance Mathis	.50	.23
❑ 94 Ed McCaffrey	.50	.23
❑ 95 Keenan McCardell	.50	.23
❑ 96 O.J. McDuffie	.50	.23
❑ 97 Steve McNair	.75	.35
❑ 98 Natrone Means	.50	.23
❑ 99 Herman Moore	.50	.23
❑ 100 Rob Moore	.50	.23
❑ 101 Byron Bam Morris	.30	.14
❑ 102 Johnnie Morton	.30	.14
❑ 103 Randy Moss	2.00	.90
❑ 104 Eric Moulds	.75	.35
❑ 105 Muhsin Muhammad	.50	.23
❑ 106 Adrian Murrell	.50	.23
❑ 107 Terrell Owens	.75	.35
❑ 108 Jerome Pathon	.30	.14
❑ 109 Carl Pickens	.50	.23
❑ 110 Jake Plummer	.50	.23
❑ 111 Andre Reed	.50	.23
❑ 112 Jake Reed	.50	.23
❑ 113 Jerry Rice	1.50	.70
❑ 114 Mikhael Ricks	.30	.14
❑ 115 Andre Rison	.50	.23
❑ 116 Barry Sanders	2.50	1.10
❑ 117 Deion Sanders	.75	.35
❑ 118 Frank Sanders	.50	.23
❑ 119 O.J. Santiago	.30	.14
❑ 120 Darnay Scott	.30	.14
❑ 121 Junior Seau	.75	.35
❑ 122 Shannon Sharpe	.50	.23
❑ 123 Leslie Shepherd UER Back lists him with wrong team	.30	.14
❑ 124 Antowain Smith	.75	.35
❑ 125 Bruce Smith	.50	.23
❑ 126 Emmitt Smith	1.50	.70
❑ 127 Jimmy Smith	.50	.23
❑ 128 Robert Smith	.75	.35
❑ 129 Rod Smith	.50	.23
❑ 130 Chris Spielman	.30	.14
❑ 131 Takeo Spikes	.30	.14
❑ 132 Duce Staley	.75	.35
❑ 133 Kordell Stewart	.50	.23
❑ 134 Bryan Still	.30	.14
❑ 135 J.J. Stokes	.50	.23
❑ 136 Fred Taylor	.75	.35
❑ 137 Vinny Testaverde	.50	.23
❑ 138 Yancey Thigpen	.30	.14
❑ 139 Thurman Thomas	.50	.23
❑ 140 Zach Thomas	.75	.35
❑ 141 Amani Toomer	.30	.14
❑ 142 Hines Ward	.75	.35
❑ 143 Chris Warren	.30	.14
❑ 144 Ricky Watters	.50	.23
❑ 145 Michael Westbrook	.50	.23
❑ 146 Alvis Whitted	.30	.14
❑ 147 Charles Woodson	.75	.35
❑ 148 Rod Woodson	.50	.23
❑ 149 Frank Wycheck	.30	.14
❑ 150 Steve Young	1.00	.45
❑ 151 Rahim Abdullah RC	1.00	.45
❑ 152 Champ Bailey RC	2.00	.90
❑ 153 D'Wayne Bates RC	1.00	.45
❑ 154 Michael Bishop RC	1.50	.70
❑ 155 Dre' Bly RC	1.50	.70
❑ 156 David Boston RC	1.50	.70
❑ 157 Fernando Bryant RC	1.00	.45
❑ 158 Chris Claiborne RC	.50	.23
❑ 159 Mike Cloud RC	1.00	.45
❑ 160 Cecil Colliins RC	.50	.23
❑ 161 Tim Couch RC	1.50	.70
❑ 162 Daunte Culpepper RC	6.00	2.70
❑ 163 Antuan Edwards RC	.50	.23
❑ 164 Troy Edwards RC	1.00	.45
❑ 165 Ebenezer Ekuban RC	1.00	.45
❑ 166 Kevin Faulk RC	1.50	.70
❑ 167 Joe Germaine RC	1.00	.45
❑ 168 Aaron Gibson RC	.50	.23
❑ 169 Martin Gramatica RC	.50	.23
❑ 170 Torry Holt RC	4.00	1.80
❑ 171 Brock Huard RC	1.50	.70
❑ 172 Sedrick Irvin RC	.50	.23
❑ 173 Edgerrin James RC	6.00	2.70
❑ 174 James Johnson RC	1.00	.45
❑ 175 Kevin Johnson RC	1.50	.70
❑ 176 Andy Katzenmoyer RC	1.00	.45
❑ 177 Jevon Kearse RC	2.50	1.10
❑ 178 Patrick Kerney RC	1.50	.70
❑ 179 Lamar King RC	.50	.23
❑ 180 Shaun King RC	1.00	.45
❑ 181 Jim Kleinsasser RC	1.50	.70
❑ 182 Rob Konrad RC	1.00	.45
❑ 183 Chris McAlister RC	1.00	.45
❑ 184 Anthony McFarland RC	1.50	.70
❑ 185 Karsten Bailey RC	1.00	.45
❑ 186 Donovan McNabb RC	8.00	3.60
❑ 187 Cade McNown RC	1.00	.45
❑ 188 Joe Montgomery RC	1.00	.45
❑ 189 Dat Nguyen RC	1.50	.70
❑ 190 Luke Petitgout RC	.50	.23
❑ 191 Peerless Price RC	2.50	1.10
❑ 192 Akili Smith RC	1.00	.45
❑ 193 Matt Stinchcomb RC	.50	.23
❑ 194 John Tait RC	.50	.23
❑ 195 Jermaine Fazande RC	1.00	.45
❑ 196 Ricky Williams RC	3.00	1.35
❑ 197 Al Wilson RC	1.00	.45
❑ 198 Antoine Winfield RC	1.00	.45
❑ 199 Damien Woody RC	.50	.23
❑ 200 Amos Zereoue RC	1.50	.70

1998 Collector's Edge Masters

	Nm-Mt	Ex-Mt
COMPLETE SET (199)	200.00	90.00
❑ 1 Rob Moore	1.00	.45
❑ 2 Adrian Murrell	1.00	.45

❑ 3 Jake Plummer 1.50 .70
❑ 4 Michael Pittman RC 3.00 1.35
❑ 5 Frank Sanders 1.00 .45
❑ 6 Andre Wadsworth RC 2.00 .90
❑ 7 Jamal Anderson 1.50 .70
❑ 8 Chris Chandler 1.00 .45
❑ 9 Tim Dwight RC 2.50 1.10
❑ 10 Tony Martin 1.00 .45
❑ 11 Terance Mathis 1.00 .45
❑ 12 Ken Oxendine RC 1.25 .55
❑ 13 Jim Harbaugh 1.00 .45
❑ 14 Priest Holmes RC 25.00 11.00
❑ 15 Michael Jackson .60 .25
❑ 16 Pat Johnson RC 2.00 .90
❑ 17 Jermaine Lewis 1.00 .45
❑ 18 Eric Zeier 1.00 .45
❑ 19 Doug Flutie 1.50 .70
❑ 20 Rob Johnson 1.00 .45
❑ 21 Eric Moulds 1.50 .70
❑ 22 Andre Reed 1.00 .45
❑ 23 Antowain Smith 1.50 .70
❑ 24 Bruce Smith 1.00 .45
❑ 25 Thurman Thomas 1.50 .70
❑ 26 Steve Beuerlein 1.00 .45
❑ 27 Kevin Greene 1.00 .45
❑ 29 Rocket Ismail .60 .25
❑ 30 Fred Lane .60 .25
❑ 31 Muhsin Muhammad 1.00 .45
❑ 32 Edgar Bennett .60 .25
❑ 33 Curtis Conway 1.00 .45
❑ 34 Bobby Engram 1.00 .45
❑ 35 Curtis Enis RC 1.25 .55
❑ 36 Erik Kramer .60 .25
❑ 37 Chris Penn .60 .25
❑ 38 Jeff Blake 1.00 .45
❑ 39 Corey Dillon 1.50 .70
❑ 40 Neil O'Donnell 1.00 .45
❑ 41 Carl Pickens 1.00 .45
❑ 42 Darnay Scott 1.00 .45
❑ 43 Damon Gibson RC 1.25 .55
❑ 44 Troy Aikman 3.00 1.35
❑ 45 Billy Davis .60 .25
❑ 46 Michael Irvin 1.50 .70
❑ 47 Ernie Mills .60 .25
❑ 48 Deion Sanders 1.50 .70
❑ 49 Emmitt Smith 5.00 2.20
❑ 50 Chris Warren 1.00 .45
❑ 51 Bubby Brister .60 .25
❑ 52 Terrell Davis 1.50 .70
❑ 53 John Elway 6.00 2.70
❑ 54 Brian Griese RC 5.00 2.20
❑ 55 Ed McCaffrey 1.00 .45
❑ 56 Marcus Nash RC 1.25 .55
❑ 57 Shannon Sharpe 1.00 .45
❑ 58 Rod Smith 1.00 .45
❑ 59 Charlie Batch RC 2.50 1.10
❑ 60 Germane Crowell RC 2.00 .90
❑ 61 Scott Mitchell 1.00 .45
❑ 62 Johnnie Morton 1.00 .45
❑ 63 Herman Moore 1.00 .45
❑ 64 Barry Sanders 5.00 2.20
❑ 65 Robert Brooks 1.00 .45
❑ 66 Brett Favre 6.00 2.70
❑ 67 Antonio Freeman 1.50 .70
❑ 68 Raymont Harris .60 .25
❑ 69 Dorsey Levens 1.50 .70
❑ 70 Reggie White 1.50 .70
❑ 71 Marshall Faulk 2.00 .90
❑ 72 Marvin Harrison 1.50 .70
❑ 73 Peyton Manning RC 25.00 11.00
❑ 74 Jerome Pathon RC 2.50 1.10
❑ 75 Tavian Banks RC 2.00 .90
❑ 76 Mark Brunell 1.50 .70
❑ 77 Keenan McCardell 1.00 .45
❑ 78 Jimmy Smith 1.00 .45
❑ 79 Fred Taylor RC 4.00 1.80
❑ 80 Derrick Alexander 1.00 .45
❑ 81 Donnell Bennett .60 .25
❑ 82 Rich Gannon 1.50 .70
❑ 83 Elvis Grbac 1.00 .45
❑ 84 Andre Rison 1.00 .45
❑ 85 Rashaan Shehee RC 2.00 .90
❑ 86 Karim Abdul-Jabbar 1.50 .70
❑ 87 John Avery RC 2.00 .90
❑ 88 Oronde Gadsden RC 2.50 1.10
❑ 89 Dan Marino 6.00 2.70
❑ 90 O.J. McDuffie 1.00 .45
❑ 91 Zach Thomas 1.50 .70
❑ 92 Cris Carter 1.50 .70
❑ 93 Randall Cunningham 1.50 .70
❑ 94 Brad Johnson 1.50 .70
❑ 95 Randy Moss RC 12.00 5.50
❑ 96 Jake Reed 1.00 .45
❑ 97 Robert Smith 1.50 .70
❑ 98 Drew Bledsoe 2.50 1.10
❑ 99 Ben Coates 1.00 .45
❑ 100 Robert Edwards RC 2.00 .90
❑ 101 Terry Glenn 1.50 .70
❑ 102 Shawn Jefferson .60 .25
❑ 103 Ty Law 1.00 .45
❑ 104 Cameron Cleeland RC 1.25 .55
❑ 105 Kerry Collins 1.00 .45
❑ 106 Sean Dawkins .60 .25
❑ 107 Andre Hastings .60 .25
❑ 108 Lamar Smith 1.00 .45
❑ 109 Danny Wuerffel 1.00 .45
❑ 110 Gary Brown .60 .25
❑ 111 Chris Calloway .60 .25
❑ 112 Ike Hilliard 1.00 .45
❑ 113 Joe Jurevicius RC 2.50 1.10
❑ 114 Danny Kanell 1.00 .45
❑ 115 Wayne Chrebet 1.50 .70
❑ 116 Glenn Foley 1.00 .45
❑ 117 Keyshawn Johnson 1.50 .70
❑ 118 Leon Johnson .60 .25
❑ 119 Curtis Martin 1.50 .70
❑ 120 Vinny Testaverde 1.00 .45
❑ 121 Tim Brown 1.50 .70
❑ 122 Jeff George 1.00 .45
❑ 123 James Jett 1.00 .45
❑ 124 Napoleon Kaufman 1.50 .70
❑ 125 Charles Woodson RC 3.00 1.35
❑ 126 Irving Fryar 1.00 .45
❑ 127 Jeff Graham .60 .25
❑ 128 Bobby Hoying 1.00 .45
❑ 129 Duce Staley 2.00 .90
❑ 130 Jerome Bettis 1.50 .70
❑ 131 C.Fuamatu-Ma'afala RC 2.00 .90
❑ 132 Courtney Hawkins .60 .25
❑ 133 Charles Johnson .60 .25
❑ 134 Kordell Stewart 1.50 .70
❑ 135 Hines Ward RC 6.00 2.70
❑ 136 Tony Banks 1.00 .45
❑ 137 Isaac Bruce 1.50 .70
❑ 138 Robert Holcombe RC 2.00 .90
❑ 139 Eddie Kennison 1.00 .45
❑ 140 Ryan Leaf RC 2.50 1.10
❑ 141 Natrone Means 1.00 .45
❑ 142 Mikhael Ricks RC 2.00 .90
❑ 143 Junior Seau 1.50 .70
❑ 144 Bryan Still .60 .25
❑ 145 Garrison Hearst 1.50 .70
❑ 146 R.W. McQuarters RC 2.00 .90
❑ 147 Terrell Owens 1.50 .70
❑ 148 Jerry Rice 3.00 1.35
❑ 149 J.J. Stokes 1.00 .45
❑ 150 Steve Young 2.00 .90
❑ 151 Joey Galloway 1.00 .45
❑ 152 Ahman Green RC 12.00 5.50
❑ 153 Warren Moon 1.50 .70
❑ 154 Shawn Springs .60 .25
❑ 155 Ricky Watters 1.00 .45
❑ 156 Mike Alstott 1.50 .70
❑ 157 Reidel Anthony 1.00 .45
❑ 158 Trent Dilfer 1.50 .70
❑ 159 Warrick Dunn 1.50 .70
❑ 160 Jacquez Green RC 2.00 .90
❑ 161 Kevin Dyson RC 2.50 1.10
❑ 162 Eddie George 1.50 .70
❑ 163 Steve McNair 1.50 .70
❑ 164 Yancey Thigpen .60 .25
❑ 165 Frank Wycheck .60 .25
❑ 166 Terry Allen 1.50 .70
❑ 167 Gus Frerotte .60 .25
❑ 168 Trent Green 1.50 .70
❑ 169 Skip Hicks RC 2.00 .90
❑ 170 Michael Westbrook 1.00 .45
❑ 171 Jamal Anderson SM 1.50 .70
❑ 172 Carl Pickens SM 1.00 .45
❑ 173 Deion Sanders SM 1.50 .70
❑ 174 Emmitt Smith SM 3.00 1.35
❑ 175 Terrell Davis SM 1.50 .70
❑ 176 John Elway SM 4.00 1.80
❑ 177 Charlie Batch SM 2.50 1.10
❑ 178 Herman Moore SM 1.00 .45
❑ 179 Barry Sanders SM 3.00 1.35
❑ 180 Brett Favre SM 4.00 1.80
❑ 181 Antonio Freeman SM 1.00 .45
❑ 182 Marshall Faulk SM 2.00 .90
❑ 183 Peyton Manning SM 20.00 9.00
❑ 184 Mark Brunell SM 1.50 .70
❑ 185 Dan Marino SM 4.00 1.80
❑ 186 Randy Moss SM 10.00 4.50
❑ 187 Drew Bledsoe SM 1.50 .70
❑ 188 Robert Edwards SM 1.00 .45
❑ 189 Curtis Martin SM 1.50 .70
❑ 190 Charles Woodson SM 2.50 1.10
❑ 191 Jerome Bettis SM 1.50 .70
❑ 192 Robert Holcombe SM 1.00 .45
❑ 193 Ryan Leaf SM 2.50 1.10
❑ 194 Natrone Means SM 1.00 .45
❑ 195 Jerry Rice SM 2.00 .90
❑ 196 Steve Young SM 1.50 .70
❑ 197 Warrick Dunn SM 1.50 .70
❑ 198 Eddie George SM 1.00 .45
❑ 199 Peyton Manning CL 10.00 4.50
❑ 200 Ryan Leaf CL 1.50 .70

1999 Collector's Edge Masters

	Nm-Mt	Ex-Mt
COMPLETE SET (200)	500.00	220.00
❑ 1 David Boston RC	5.00	2.20
❑ 2 Mac Cody RC	2.50	1.10
❑ 3 Chris Greisen RC	4.00	1.80
❑ 4 Joel Makovicka RC	5.00	2.20
❑ 5 Adrian Murrell	.75	.35
❑ 6 Jake Plummer	.75	.35
❑ 7 Frank Sanders	.75	.35
❑ 8 Jamal Anderson	1.25	.55
❑ 9 Chris Chandler	.75	.35
❑ 10 Reginald Kelly RC	4.00	1.80
❑ 11 Patrick Kerney RC	5.00	2.20
❑ 12 Terance Mathis	.75	.35
❑ 13 Jeff Paulk RC	2.50	1.10
❑ 14 Stoney Case	.50	.23
❑ 15 Qadry Ismail	.75	.35
❑ 16 Chris McAlister RC	4.00	1.80
❑ 17 Errict Rhett	.50	.23

❑ 18 Brandon Stokley RC 6.00 2.70
❑ 19 Doug Flutie 1.25 .55
❑ 20 Kamil Loud RC 2.50 1.10
❑ 21 Eric Moulds 1.25 .55
❑ 22 Peerless Price RC 8.00 3.60
❑ 23 Andre Reed .75 .35
❑ 24 Antowain Smith 1.25 .55
❑ 25 Antoine Winfield RC 4.00 1.80
❑ 26 Steve Beuerlein .75 .35
❑ 27 Tim Biakabutuka .75 .35
❑ 28 Dameyune Craig RC 5.00 2.20
❑ 29 Patrick Jeffers RC 15.00 6.75
❑ 30 Muhsin Muhammad .75 .35
❑ 31 D'Wayne Bates RC 4.00 1.80
❑ 32 Marty Booker RC 5.00 2.20
❑ 33 Bobby Engram .50 .23
❑ 34 Curtis Enis .50 .23
❑ 35 Ty Hallock RC 2.50 1.10
❑ 36 Shane Matthews 1.25 .55
❑ 37 Cade McNown RC 4.00 1.80
❑ 38 Marcus Robinson 2.00 .90
❑ 39 Scott Covington RC 5.00 2.20
❑ 40 Corey Dillon 1.25 .55
❑ 41 Damon Griffin RC 4.00 1.80
❑ 42 Carl Pickens .75 .35
❑ 43 Darnay Scott .75 .35
❑ 44 Akili Smith RC 4.00 1.80
❑ 45 Craig Yeast RC 4.00 1.80
❑ 46 Darrin Chiaverini RC 4.00 1.80
❑ 47 Tim Couch RC 5.00 2.20
❑ 48 Phil Dawson RC 4.00 1.80
❑ 49 Kevin Johnson RC 5.00 2.20
❑ 50 Terry Kirby .50 .23
❑ 51 Wali Rainer RC 4.00 1.80
❑ 52 Troy Aikman 2.50 1.10
❑ 53 Ebenezer Ekuban RC 4.00 1.80
❑ 54 Michael Irvin .75 .35
❑ 55 Rocket Ismail .75 .35
❑ 56 Wane McGarity RC 2.50 1.10
❑ 57 Dat Nguyen RC 5.00 2.20
❑ 58 Deion Sanders 1.25 .55
❑ 59 Emmitt Smith 2.50 1.10
❑ 60 Byron Chamberlain RC .75 .35
❑ 61 Andre Cooper RC 2.50 1.10
❑ 62 Terrell Davis 1.25 .55
❑ 63 Olandis Gary RC 5.00 2.20
❑ 64 Brian Griese 1.25 .55
❑ 65 Ed McCaffrey .75 .35
❑ 66 Travis McGriff RC 2.50 1.10
❑ 67 Shannon Sharpe .75 .35
❑ 68 Rod Smith .75 .35
❑ 69 Al Wilson RC 5.00 2.20
❑ 70 Charlie Batch 1.25 .55
❑ 71 Chris Claiborne RC 2.50 1.10
❑ 72 Germane Crowell .50 .23
❑ 73 Greg Hill .50 .23
❑ 74 Sedrick Irvin RC 2.50 1.10
❑ 75 Herman Moore .75 .35
❑ 76 Johnnie Morton .75 .35
❑ 77 Barry Sanders 4.00 1.80
❑ 78 Aaron Brooks RC 15.00 6.75
❑ 79 Antuan Edwards RC 4.00 1.80
❑ 80 Brett Favre 4.00 1.80
❑ 81 Antonio Freeman 1.25 .55
❑ 82 Dorsey Levens 1.25 .55
❑ 83 Bill Schroeder 1.25 .55
❑ 84 E.G. Green .50 .23
❑ 85 Marvin Harrison 1.25 .55
❑ 86 Edgerrin James RC 15.00 6.75
❑ 87 Peyton Manning 4.00 1.80
❑ 88 Mark Brunell 1.25 .55
❑ 89 Jay Fiedler RC 8.00 3.60
❑ 90 Keenan McCardell .75 .35
❑ 91 Jimmy Smith .75 .35
❑ 92 James Stewart .75 .35
❑ 93 Fred Taylor 1.25 .55
❑ 94 Derrick Alexander WR .75 .35
❑ 95 Mike Cloud RC 4.00 1.80
❑ 96 Elvis Grbac .75 .35
❑ 97 Byron Bam Morris .50 .23
❑ 98 Andre Rison .75 .35
❑ 99 Cecil Collins RC 2.50 1.10
❑ 100 Damon Huard 2.50 1.10
❑ 101 James Johnson RC 4.00 1.80
❑ 102 Rob Konrad RC 5.00 2.20
❑ 103 Dan Marino 4.00 1.80
❑ 104 O.J. McDuffie .75 .35
❑ 105 Cris Carter 1.25 .55
❑ 106 Daunte Culpepper RC 15.00 6.75
❑ 107 Randall Cunningham 1.25 .55
❑ 108 Jeff George .75 .35
❑ 109 Jim Kleinsasser RC 5.00 2.20
❑ 110 Randy Moss 3.00 1.35
❑ 111 Robert Smith 1.25 .55
❑ 112 Terry Allen .75 .35
❑ 113 Michael Bishop RC 5.00 2.20
❑ 114 Drew Bledsoe 1.50 .70
❑ 115 Kevin Faulk RC 5.00 2.20
❑ 116 Terry Glenn 1.25 .55
❑ 117 Andy Katzenmoyer RC 4.00 1.80
❑ 118 Billy Joe Hobert .50 .23
❑ 119 Eddie Kennison .75 .35
❑ 120 Ricky Williams RC 8.00 3.60
❑ 121 Tiki Barber .75 .35
❑ 122 Sean Bennett RC 2.50 1.10
❑ 123 Gary Brown .50 .23
❑ 124 Kent Graham .50 .23
❑ 125 Ike Hilliard .50 .23
❑ 126 Joe Montgomery RC 4.00 1.80
❑ 127 Amani Toomer .50 .23
❑ 128 Wayne Chrebet 1.25 .55
❑ 129 Keyshawn Johnson 1.25 .55
❑ 130 Curtis Martin 1.25 .55
❑ 131 Ray Lucas RC 3.00 1.35
❑ 132 Vinny Testaverde .75 .35
❑ 133 Tim Brown 1.25 .55
❑ 134 Tony Bryant RC 4.00 1.80
❑ 135 Scott Dreisbach RC 4.00 1.80
❑ 136 Rich Gannon 1.25 .55
❑ 137 Tyrone Wheatley 1.25 .55
❑ 138 Charles Woodson 1.25 .55
❑ 139 Na Brown RC 4.00 1.80
❑ 140 Charles Johnson .50 .23
❑ 141 Cecil Martin RC 4.00 1.80
❑ 142 Donovan McNabb RC 20.00 9.00
❑ 143 Doug Pederson .50 .23
❑ 144 Duce Staley 1.25 .55
❑ 145 Jerome Bettis 1.25 .55
❑ 146 Kris Brown RC 4.00 1.80
❑ 147 Troy Edwards RC 4.00 1.80
❑ 148 Kordell Stewart .75 .35
❑ 149 Hines Ward 1.25 .55
❑ 150 Amos Zereoue RC 5.00 2.20
❑ 151 Dre' Bly RC 5.00 2.20
❑ 152 Isaac Bruce 1.25 .55
❑ 153 Marshall Faulk 1.50 .70
❑ 154 Joe Germaine RC 4.00 1.80
❑ 155 Az-Zahir Hakim .50 .23
❑ 156 Torry Holt RC 12.00 5.50
❑ 157 Kurt Warner RC 30.00 13.50
❑ 158 Justin Watson RC 2.50 1.10
❑ 159 Jermaine Fazande RC 4.00 1.80
❑ 160 Jeff Graham .50 .23
❑ 161 Jim Harbaugh .75 .35
❑ 162 Steve Heiden RC 2.50 1.10
❑ 163 Erik Kramer .50 .23
❑ 164 Natrone Means .75 .35
❑ 165 Mikhael Ricks .50 .23
❑ 166 Junior Seau 1.25 .55
❑ 167 Jeff Garcia RC 25.00 11.00
❑ 168 Charlie Garner .75 .35
❑ 169 Terry Jackson RC 4.00 1.80
❑ 170 Terrell Owens 1.25 .55
❑ 171 Jerry Rice 2.50 1.10
❑ 172 Steve Young 1.50 .70
❑ 173 Karsten Bailey RC 4.00 1.80
❑ 174 Joey Galloway .75 .35
❑ 175 Brock Huard RC 5.00 2.20
❑ 176 Jon Kitna 1.25 .55
❑ 177 Derrick Mayes .75 .35
❑ 178 Charlie Rogers RC 4.00 1.80
❑ 179 Ricky Watters .75 .35
❑ 180 Rabih Abdullah RC 4.00 1.80
❑ 181 Mike Alstott 1.25 .55
❑ 182 Reidel Anthony .75 .35
❑ 183 Trent Dilfer .75 .35
❑ 184 Warrick Dunn 1.25 .55
❑ 185 Martin Gramatica RC 2.50 1.10
❑ 186 Shaun King RC 4.00 1.80
❑ 187 Darnell McDonald RC 4.00 1.80
❑ 188 Yo Murphy RC 4.00 1.80
❑ 189 Kevin Daft RC 4.00 1.80
❑ 190 Kevin Dyson .75 .35
❑ 191 Eddie George 1.25 .55
❑ 192 Jevon Kearse RC 8.00 3.60
❑ 193 Steve McNair 1.25 .55
❑ 194 Yancey Thigpen .50 .23
❑ 195 Champ Bailey RC 6.00 2.70
❑ 196 Albert Connell .50 .23
❑ 197 Stephen Davis 1.25 .55
❑ 198 Skip Hicks .50 .23
❑ 199 Brad Johnson 1.25 .55
❑ 200 Michael Westbrook .75 .35

2000 Collector's Edge Masters

	Nm-Mt	Ex-Mt
COMP.SET w/o SP's (200)	25.00	11.00

❑ 1 David Boston 2.00 .90
❑ 2 Michael Pittman .75 .35
❑ 3 Jake Plummer 1.25 .55
❑ 4 Frank Sanders 1.25 .55
❑ 5 Jamal Anderson 2.00 .90
❑ 6 Chris Chandler 1.25 .55
❑ 7 Tim Dwight 2.00 .90
❑ 8 Shawn Jefferson .75 .35
❑ 9 Terance Mathis 1.25 .55
❑ 10 Tony Banks 1.25 .55
❑ 11 Trent Dilfer 1.25 .55
❑ 12 Priest Holmes 2.50 1.10
❑ 13 Qadry Ismail 1.25 .55
❑ 14 Jermaine Lewis 1.25 .55
❑ 15 Shannon Sharpe 1.25 .55
❑ 16 Doug Flutie 2.00 .90
❑ 17 Rob Johnson 1.25 .55
❑ 18 Jeremy McDaniel 1.25 .55
❑ 19 Eric Moulds 2.00 .90
❑ 20 Peerless Price 1.25 .55
❑ 21 Antowain Smith 1.25 .55
❑ 22 Steve Beuerlein 1.25 .55
❑ 23 Tim Biakabutuka 1.25 .55
❑ 24 Dialleo Burks RC .75 .35
❑ 25 Dameyune Craig .75 .35
❑ 26 Donald Hayes .75 .35
❑ 27 Patrick Jeffers 2.00 .90
❑ 28 Muhsin Muhammad 1.25 .55
❑ 29 Reggie White 2.00 .90
❑ 30 Bobby Engram 1.25 .55
❑ 31 Curtis Enis .75 .35
❑ 32 Eddie Kennison .75 .35
❑ 33 Cade McNown .75 .35
❑ 34 Marcus Robinson 2.00 .90
❑ 35 Corey Dillon 2.00 .90
❑ 36 James Hundon .75 .35
❑ 37 Scott Mitchell .75 .35
❑ 38 Tony McGee .75 .35
❑ 39 Akili Smith .75 .35
❑ 40 Craig Yeast .75 .35
❑ 41 Darrin Chiaverini .75 .35
❑ 42 Tim Couch 1.25 .55
❑ 43 Kevin Johnson 2.00 .90
❑ 44 Errict Rhett 1.25 .55
❑ 45 Troy Aikman 4.00 1.80
❑ 46 Randall Cunningham 2.00 .90
❑ 47 Joey Galloway 1.25 .55

❑ 48 Rocket Ismail	1.25	.55
❑ 49 James McKnight	1.25	.55
❑ 50 Dat Nguyen	.75	.35
❑ 51 Emmitt Smith	4.00	1.80
❑ 52 Chris Warren	.75	.35
❑ 53 Robert Brooks	1.25	.55
❑ 54 Terrell Davis	2.00	.90
❑ 55 Gus Frerotte	.75	.35
❑ 56 Olandis Gary	2.00	.90
❑ 57 Brian Griese	2.00	.90
❑ 58 Ed McCaffrey	2.00	.90
❑ 59 Rod Smith	1.25	.55
❑ 60 Charlie Batch	2.00	.90
❑ 61 Germane Crowell	.75	.35
❑ 62 Sedrick Irvin	.75	.35
❑ 63 Herman Moore	1.25	.55
❑ 64 Johnnie Morton	1.25	.55
❑ 65 James Stewart	1.25	.55
❑ 66 Corey Bradford	1.25	.55
❑ 67 Brett Favre	6.00	2.70
❑ 68 Antonio Freeman	2.00	.90
❑ 69 Matt Hasselbeck	1.25	.55
❑ 70 Dorsey Levens	1.25	.55
❑ 71 Bill Schroeder	1.25	.55
❑ 72 Ken Dilger	.75	.35
❑ 73 E.G. Green	.75	.35
❑ 74 Marvin Harrison	2.00	.90
❑ 75 Edgerrin James	3.00	1.35
❑ 76 Peyton Manning	5.00	2.20
❑ 77 Jerome Pathon	1.25	.55
❑ 78 Terrence Wilkins	.75	.35
❑ 79 Kyle Brady	.75	.35
❑ 80 Mark Brunell	2.00	.90
❑ 81 Kevin Hardy	.75	.35
❑ 82 Stacey Mack	1.25	.55
❑ 83 Keenan McCardell	1.25	.55
❑ 84 Jimmy Smith	1.25	.55
❑ 85 Fred Taylor	2.00	.90
❑ 86 Derrick Alexander	1.25	.55
❑ 87 Mike Cloud	.75	.35
❑ 88 Tony Gonzalez	1.25	.55
❑ 89 Elvis Grbac	1.25	.55
❑ 90 Kevin Lockett	.75	.35
❑ 91 Tony Richardson RC	.75	.35
❑ 92 Jay Fiedler	2.00	.90
❑ 93 Oronde Gadsden	1.25	.55
❑ 94 Damon Huard	1.25	.55
❑ 95 Rob Konrad	.75	.35
❑ 96 James Johnson	.75	.35
❑ 97 Tony Martin	1.25	.55
❑ 98 O.J. McDuffie	1.25	.55
❑ 99 Lamar Smith	1.25	.55
❑ 100 Thurman Thomas	1.25	.55
❑ 101 Todd Bouman	2.00	.90
❑ 102 Bubby Brister	.75	.35
❑ 103 Cris Carter	2.00	.90
❑ 104 Daunte Culpepper	2.50	1.10
❑ 105 Matthew Hatchette	.75	.35
❑ 106 Randy Moss	4.00	1.80
❑ 107 Robert Smith	2.00	.90
❑ 108 Moe Williams	1.25	.55
❑ 109 Michael Bishop	1.25	.55
❑ 110 Drew Bledsoe	2.50	1.10
❑ 111 Troy Brown	1.25	.55
❑ 112 Kevin Faulk	1.25	.55
❑ 113 Terry Glenn	1.25	.55
❑ 114 Andy Katzenmoyer	.75	.35
❑ 115 Tony Simmons	.75	.35
❑ 116 Jeff Blake	1.25	.55
❑ 117 Aaron Brooks	2.00	.90
❑ 118 Jake Delhomme RC	8.00	3.60
❑ 119 Joe Horn	1.25	.55
❑ 120 Jake Reed	1.25	.55
❑ 121 Ricky Williams	2.00	.90
❑ 122 Tiki Barber	1.25	.55
❑ 123 Kerry Collins	1.25	.55
❑ 124 Ike Hilliard	1.25	.55
❑ 125 Amani Toomer	1.25	.55
❑ 126 Wayne Chrebet	1.25	.55
❑ 127 Ray Lucas	1.25	.55
❑ 128 Curtis Martin	2.00	.90
❑ 129 Vinny Testaverde	1.25	.55
❑ 130 Dedric Ward	.75	.35
❑ 131 Tim Brown	2.00	.90
❑ 132 Rickey Dudley	.75	.35
❑ 133 Rich Gannon	2.00	.90
❑ 134 James Jett	.75	.35
❑ 135 Napoleon Kaufman	1.25	.55
❑ 136 Tyrone Wheatley	1.25	.55
❑ 137 Charles Woodson	1.25	.55
❑ 138 Charles Johnson	1.25	.55
❑ 139 Donovan McNabb	3.00	1.35
❑ 140 Torrance Small	.75	.35
❑ 141 Duce Staley	2.00	.90
❑ 142 Jerome Bettis	2.00	.90
❑ 143 Troy Edwards	.75	.35
❑ 144 Kent Graham	.75	.35
❑ 145 Richard Huntley	.75	.35
❑ 146 Kordell Stewart	1.25	.55
❑ 147 Amos Zereoue	2.00	.90
❑ 148 Isaac Bruce	2.00	.90
❑ 149 Kevin Carter	.75	.35
❑ 150 Marshall Faulk	2.50	1.10
❑ 151 Trent Green	2.00	.90
❑ 152 Az-Zahir Hakim	.75	.35
❑ 153 Robert Holcombe	.75	.35
❑ 154 Torry Holt	2.00	.90
❑ 155 Kurt Warner	4.00	1.80
❑ 156 Kenny Bynum	.75	.35
❑ 157 Robert Chancey	.75	.35
❑ 158 Curtis Conway	1.25	.55
❑ 159 Jermaine Fazande	.75	.35
❑ 160 Jeff Graham	.75	.35
❑ 161 Jim Harbaugh	1.25	.55
❑ 162 Ryan Leaf	1.25	.55
❑ 163 Junior Seau	2.00	.90
❑ 164 Jeff Garcia	2.00	.90
❑ 165 Charlie Garner	1.25	.55
❑ 166 Terrell Owens	2.00	.90
❑ 167 Jerry Rice	4.00	1.80
❑ 168 J.J. Stokes	1.25	.55
❑ 169 Karsten Bailey	.75	.35
❑ 170 Sean Dawkins	.75	.35
❑ 171 Brock Huard	1.25	.55
❑ 172 Jon Kitna	2.00	.90
❑ 173 Derrick Mayes	1.25	.55
❑ 174 Ricky Watters	1.25	.55
❑ 175 Rabih Abdullah	.75	.35
❑ 176 Mike Alstott	2.00	.90
❑ 177 Reidel Anthony	.75	.35
❑ 178 Warrick Dunn	2.00	.90
❑ 179 Jacquez Green	.75	.35
❑ 180 Keyshawn Johnson	2.00	.90
❑ 181 Shaun King	.75	.35
❑ 182 Warren Sapp	1.25	.55
❑ 183 Kevin Dyson	1.25	.55
❑ 184 Eddie George	2.00	.90
❑ 185 Jevon Kearse	2.00	.90
❑ 186 Steve McNair	2.00	.90
❑ 187 Neil O'Donnell	.75	.35
❑ 188 Carl Pickens	1.25	.55
❑ 189 Yancey Thigpen	.75	.35
❑ 190 Frank Wycheck	.75	.35
❑ 191 Champ Bailey	1.25	.55
❑ 192 Larry Centers	.75	.35
❑ 193 Albert Connell	.75	.35
❑ 194 Stephen Davis	2.00	.90
❑ 195 Jeff George	1.25	.55
❑ 196 Brad Johnson	2.00	.90
❑ 197 Deion Sanders	2.00	.90
❑ 198 Bruce Smith	1.25	.55
❑ 199 James Thrash	2.00	.90
❑ 200 Michael Westbrook	1.25	.55
❑ 201 Thomas Jones RC	10.00	4.50
❑ 202 Jamal Lewis RC	15.00	6.75
❑ 203 Chris Redman RC	5.00	2.20
❑ 204 Travis Taylor RC	6.00	2.70
❑ 205 Avion Black RC	5.00	2.20
❑ 206 Kwame Cavil RC	3.00	1.35
❑ 207 Sammy Morris RC	5.00	2.20
❑ 208 Brian Urlacher RC	25.00	11.00
❑ 209 Dez White RC	6.00	2.70
❑ 210 Ron Dugans RC	3.00	1.35
❑ 211 Danny Farmer RC	5.00	2.20
❑ 212 Curtis Keaton RC	5.00	2.20
❑ 213 Peter Warrick RC	6.00	2.70
❑ 214 Courtney Brown RC	6.00	2.70
❑ 215 JaJuan Dawson RC	3.00	1.35
❑ 216 Dennis Northcutt RC	6.00	2.70
❑ 217 Travis Prentice RC	5.00	2.20
❑ 218 Spergon Wynn RC	5.00	2.20
❑ 219 Michael Wiley RC	5.00	2.20
❑ 220 Mike Anderson RC	6.00	2.70
❑ 221 Chris Cole RC	5.00	2.20
❑ 222 Deltha O'Neal RC	6.00	2.70
❑ 223 Reuben Droughns RC	8.00	3.60
❑ 224 Bubba Franks RC	6.00	2.70
❑ 225 Charles Lee RC	3.00	1.35
❑ 226 Rob Morris RC	5.00	2.20
❑ 227 R.Jay Soward RC	5.00	2.20
❑ 228 Shyrone Stith RC	5.00	2.20
❑ 229 Frank Moreau RC	5.00	2.20
❑ 230 Sylvester Morris RC	5.00	2.20
❑ 231 J.R. Redmond RC	5.00	2.20
❑ 232 Chad Morton RC	6.00	2.70
❑ 233 Ron Dayne RC	6.00	2.70
❑ 234 Ron Dixon RC	5.00	2.20
❑ 235 Anthony Becht RC	6.00	2.70
❑ 236 Laveranues Coles RC	8.00	3.60
❑ 237 Chad Pennington RC	25.00	11.00
❑ 238 Sebastian Janikowski RC	6.00	2.70
❑ 239 Jerry Porter RC	8.00	3.60
❑ 240 Todd Pinkston RC	6.00	2.70
❑ 241 Gari Scott RC	3.00	1.35
❑ 242 Corey Simon RC	6.00	2.70
❑ 243 Plaxico Burress RC	12.00	5.50
❑ 244 Tee Martin RC	6.00	2.70
❑ 245 Trung Canidate RC	5.00	2.20
❑ 246 Trevor Gaylor RC	5.00	2.20
❑ 247 Giovanni Carmazzi RC	5.00	2.20
❑ 248 Tim Rattay RC	12.00	5.50
❑ 249 Shaun Alexander RC	15.00	6.75
❑ 250 Joe Hamilton RC	5.00	2.20

1999 Collector's Edge Odyssey

	Nm-Mt	Ex-Mt
COMPLETE SET (193)	120.00	55.00
COMP.SET w/o SP's (148)	40.00	18.00
❑ 1 Checklist Card	.30	.14
❑ 2 Checklist Card	.30	.14
❑ 3 David Boston RC	1.00	.45
❑ 4 Rob Moore	.50	.23
❑ 5 Adrian Murrell	.50	.23
❑ 6 Jake Plummer	.50	.23
❑ 7 Frank Sanders	.50	.23
❑ 8 Jamal Anderson	.75	.35
❑ 9 Chris Calloway	.30	.14
❑ 10 Chris Chandler	.50	.23
❑ 11 Tim Dwight	.75	.35
❑ 12 Terance Mathis	.50	.23
❑ 13 Tony Banks	.50	.23
❑ 14 Priest Holmes	1.25	.55
❑ 15 Jermaine Lewis	.50	.23
❑ 16 Chris McAlister RC	.75	.35
❑ 17 Scott Mitchell	.50	.23
❑ 18 Doug Flutie	.75	.35
❑ 19 Eric Moulds	.75	.35
❑ 20 Peerless Price RC	1.50	.70
❑ 21 Antowain Smith (on front) Andre Reed (on back) (was pulled from packout, has embossed player image on front)	80.00	36.00
❑ 22 Antowain Smith	.75	.35
❑ 23 Antoine Winfield RC	.50	.23

❑ 24 Steve Beuerlein .50 .23
❑ 25 Tim Biakabutuka .50 .23
❑ 26 Rae Carruth .30 .14
❑ 27 Muhsin Muhammad .50 .23
❑ 28 D'Wayne Bates RC .75 .35
❑ 29 Bobby Engram .50 .23
❑ 30 Curtis Enis .30 .14
❑ 31 Shane Matthews .75 .35
❑ 32 Cade McNown RC .75 .35
❑ 33 Jeff Blake .50 .23
❑ 34 Corey Dillon .75 .35
❑ 35 Carl Pickens .50 .23
❑ 36 Darnay Scott .50 .23
❑ 37 Akili Smith RC .75 .35
❑ 38 Tim Couch RC 1.00 .45
❑ 39 Kevin Johnson RC 1.00 .45
❑ 40 Terry Kirby .50 .23
❑ 41 Leslie Shepherd .30 .14
❑ 42 Troy Aikman 1.50 .70
❑ 43 Michael Irvin .50 .23
❑ 44 Rocket Ismail .50 .23
❑ 45 Deion Sanders .75 .35
❑ 46 Emmitt Smith 1.50 .70
❑ 47 Bubby Brister .50 .23
❑ 48 Terrell Davis .75 .35
❑ 49 Brian Griese .75 .35
❑ 50 Ed McCaffrey .50 .23
❑ 51 Shannon Sharpe .50 .23
❑ 52 Rod Smith .50 .23
❑ 53 Charlie Batch .75 .35
❑ 54 Chris Claiborne RC .75 .35
❑ 56 Herman Moore .50 .23
❑ 57 Johnnie Morton .50 .23
❑ 58 Ron Rivers .30 .14
❑ 59 Brett Favre 2.50 1.10
❑ 60 Mark Chmura .50 .23
❑ 61 Antonio Freeman .75 .35
❑ 62 Dorsey Levens .75 .35
❑ 63 E.G. Green .30 .14
❑ 64 Marvin Harrison .75 .35
❑ 65 Edgerrin James RC 4.00 1.80
❑ 66 Peyton Manning 2.50 1.10
❑ 67 Mark Brunell .75 .35
❑ 68 Keenan McCardell .50 .23
❑ 69 Jimmy Smith .50 .23
❑ 70 Fred Taylor .75 .35
❑ 71 Derrick Alexander WR .50 .23
❑ 72 Kimble Anders .50 .23
❑ 73 Mike Cloud RC .75 .35
❑ 74 Elvis Grbac .50 .23
❑ 75 Andre Rison .50 .23
❑ 76 Karim Abdul-Jabbar .50 .23
❑ 77 Cecil Collins RC .50 .23
❑ 78 James Johnson RC .75 .35
❑ 79 Rob Konrad RC 1.00 .45
❑ 80 Dan Marino 2.50 1.10
❑ 81 O.J. McDuffie .50 .23
❑ 82 Cris Carter .75 .35
❑ 83 Daunte Culpepper RC 4.00 1.80
❑ 84 Randall Cunningham .75 .35
❑ 85 Randy Moss 2.00 .90
❑ 86 Jake Reed .50 .23
❑ 87 Robert Smith .75 .35
❑ 88 Terry Allen .50 .23
❑ 89 Drew Bledsoe 1.00 .45
❑ 90 Ben Coates .30 .14
❑ 91 Kevin Faulk RC 1.00 .45
❑ 92 Terry Glenn .75 .35
❑ 93 Andy Katzenmoyer RC .75 .35
❑ 94 Cameron Cleeland .30 .14
❑ 95 Billy Joe Hobert .30 .14
❑ 96 Eddie Kennison .50 .23
❑ 97 Ricky Williams RC 2.00 .90
❑ 98 Sean Bennett RC .50 .23
❑ 99 Gary Brown .30 .14
❑ 100 Kerry Collins .50 .23
❑ 101 Kent Graham .30 .14
❑ 102 Ike Hilliard .50 .23
❑ 103 Wayne Chrebet .75 .35
❑ 104 Keyshawn Johnson .75 .35
❑ 105 Curtis Martin .75 .35
❑ 106 Rick Mirer .30 .14
❑ 107 Tim Brown .75 .35
❑ 108 Rich Gannon .75 .35
❑ 109 Napoleon Kaufman .75 .35
❑ 110 Charles Woodson .75 .35
❑ 111 Charles Johnson .30 .14
❑ 112 Donovan McNabb RC 5.00 2.20
❑ 113 Doug Pederson .50 .23
❑ 114 Duce Staley .75 .35
❑ 115 Jerome Bettis .75 .35
❑ 116 Troy Edwards RC .75 .35
❑ 117 Kordell Stewart .50 .23
❑ 118 Amos Zereoue RC 1.00 .45
❑ 119 Isaac Bruce .75 .35
❑ 120 Marshall Faulk 1.00 .45
❑ 121 Joe Germaine RC .75 .35
❑ 122 Torry Holt RC 2.50 1.10
❑ 123 Kurt Warner RC 10.00 4.50
❑ 124 Jim Harbaugh .50 .23
❑ 125 Erik Kramer .30 .14
❑ 126 Natrone Means .50 .23
❑ 127 Junior Seau .75 .35
❑ 128 Terrell Owens .75 .35
❑ 129 Lawrence Phillips .50 .23
❑ 130 Jerry Rice 1.50 .70
❑ 131 J.J. Stokes .50 .23
❑ 132 Steve Young 1.00 .45
❑ 133 Karsten Bailey RC .75 .35
❑ 134 Joey Galloway .50 .23
❑ 135 Brock Huard RC 1.00 .45
❑ 136 Jon Kitna .75 .35
❑ 137 Ricky Watters .50 .23
❑ 138 Reidel Anthony .30 .14
❑ 139 Trent Dilfer .50 .23
❑ 140 Warrick Dunn .75 .35
❑ 141 Shaun King RC .75 .35
❑ 142 Jevon Kearse RC 1.50 .70
❑ 143 Kevin Dyson .50 .23
❑ 144 Eddie George .75 .35
❑ 145 Steve McNair .75 .35
❑ 146 Champ Bailey RC 1.25 .55
❑ 147 Stephen Davis .75 .35
❑ 148 Skip Hicks .30 .14
❑ 149 Brad Johnson .75 .35
❑ 150 Michael Westbrook .50 .23
❑ 151 Chris McAlister 2Q 1.00 .45
❑ 152 Peerless Price 2Q 2.00 .90
❑ 153 Antoine Winfield 2Q 1.00 .45
❑ 154 D'Wayne Bates 2Q 1.00 .45
❑ 155 Kevin Johnson 2Q 1.25 .55
❑ 156 Chris Claiborne 2Q 1.00 .45
❑ 157 Sedrick Irvin 2Q 1.00 .45
❑ 158 Mike Cloud 2Q 1.25 .55
❑ 159 Cecil Collins 2Q 1.00 .45
❑ 160 James Johnson 2Q 1.25 .55
❑ 161 Rob Konrad 2Q 1.25 .55
❑ 162 Daunte Culpepper 2Q 3.00 1.35
❑ 163 Andy Katzenmoyer 2Q 1.25 .55
❑ 164 Amos Zereoue 2Q 1.25 .55
❑ 165 Joe Germaine 2Q 1.25 .55
❑ 166 Karsten Bailey 2Q 1.25 .55
❑ 167 Brock Huard 2Q 1.25 .55
❑ 168 Shaun King 2Q 1.25 .55
❑ 169 Jevon Kearse 2Q 2.00 .90
❑ 170 Champ Bailey 2Q 1.50 .70
❑ 171 Jake Plummer 3Q 2.00 .90
❑ 172 Doug Flutie 3Q .75 .35
❑ 173 Troy Aikman 3Q 5.00 2.20
❑ 174 Emmitt Smith 3Q 5.00 2.20
❑ 175 Terrell Davis 3Q 2.50 1.10
❑ 176 Barry Sanders 3Q 8.00 3.60
❑ 177 Brett Favre 3Q 8.00 3.60
❑ 178 Peyton Manning 3Q 8.00 3.60
❑ 179 Mark Brunell 3Q .75 .35
❑ 180 Fred Taylor 3Q 2.50 1.10
❑ 181 Dan Marino 3Q 8.00 3.60
❑ 182 Randy Moss 3Q 6.00 2.70
❑ 183 Drew Bledsoe 3Q 3.00 1.35
❑ 184 Jerry Rice 3Q 5.00 2.20
❑ 185 Steve Young 3Q 3.00 1.35
❑ 186 David Boston 4Q 5.00 2.20
❑ 187 Cade McNown 4Q 5.00 2.20
❑ 188 Akili Smith 4Q 5.00 2.20
❑ 189 Tim Couch 4Q 5.00 2.20
❑ 190 Edgerrin James 4Q 12.00 5.50
❑ 191 Kevin Faulk 4Q 5.00 2.20
❑ 192 Ricky Williams 4Q 6.00 2.70
❑ 193 Donovan McNabb 4Q 15.00 6.75
❑ 194 Troy Edwards 4Q 5.00 2.20
❑ 195 Torry Holt 4Q 10.00 4.50

2000 Collector's Edge Odyssey

	Nm-Mt	Ex-Mt
COMPLETE SET (190)	400.00	180.00
COMP.SET w/o SP's (100)	15.00	6.75

❑ 1 David Boston .75 .35
❑ 2 Jake Plummer .50 .23
❑ 3 Frank Sanders .50 .23
❑ 4 Jamal Anderson .75 .35
❑ 5 Chris Chandler .50 .23
❑ 6 Terance Mathis .50 .23
❑ 7 Tony Banks .50 .23
❑ 8 Qadry Ismail .50 .23
❑ 9 Doug Flutie .75 .35
❑ 10 Rob Johnson .50 .23
❑ 11 Eric Moulds .75 .35
❑ 12 Peerless Price .75 .35
❑ 13 Antowain Smith .50 .23
❑ 14 Steve Beuerlein .30 .14
❑ 15 Tim Biakabutuka .50 .23
❑ 16 Muhsin Muhammad .50 .23
❑ 17 Curtis Enis .30 .14
❑ 18 Cade McNown .30 .14
❑ 19 Marcus Robinson .75 .35
❑ 20 Corey Dillon .75 .35
❑ 21 Akili Smith .30 .14
❑ 22 Tim Couch .50 .23
❑ 23 Kevin Johnson .75 .35
❑ 24 Errict Rhett .50 .23
❑ 25 Troy Aikman 1.50 .70
❑ 26 Joey Galloway .50 .23
❑ 27 Rocket Ismail .50 .23
❑ 28 Emmitt Smith 1.50 .70
❑ 29 Terrell Davis .75 .35
❑ 30 Olandis Gary .75 .35
❑ 31 Brian Griese .75 .35
❑ 32 Ed McCaffrey .75 .35
❑ 33 Charlie Batch .75 .35
❑ 34 Germane Crowell .30 .14
❑ 35 Herman Moore .50 .23
❑ 36 James Stewart .50 .23
❑ 37 Brett Favre 2.50 1.10
❑ 38 Antonio Freeman .75 .35
❑ 39 Dorsey Levens .50 .23
❑ 40 Marvin Harrison .75 .35
❑ 41 Edgerrin James 1.25 .55
❑ 42 Peyton Manning 2.00 .90
❑ 43 Terrence Wilkins .30 .14
❑ 44 Mark Brunell .75 .35
❑ 45 Keenan McCardell .50 .23
❑ 46 Jimmy Smith .50 .23
❑ 47 Fred Taylor .75 .35
❑ 48 Mike Cloud .30 .14
❑ 49 Tony Gonzalez .50 .23
❑ 50 Elvis Grbac .50 .23
❑ 51 Damon Huard .75 .35
❑ 52 James Johnson .30 .14
❑ 53 Tony Martin .50 .23
❑ 54 Cris Carter .75 .35
❑ 55 Daunte Culpepper 1.00 .45
❑ 56 Randy Moss 1.50 .70
❑ 57 Robert Smith .75 .35
❑ 58 Drew Bledsoe 1.00 .45

❑ 59 Terry Glenn	.50	.23
❑ 60 Jeff Blake	.50	.23
❑ 61 Ricky Williams	.75	.35
❑ 62 Kerry Collins	.50	.23
❑ 63 Ike Hilliard	.50	.23
❑ 64 Amani Toomer	.50	.23
❑ 65 Wayne Chrebet	.50	.23
❑ 66 Curtis Martin	.75	.35
❑ 67 Vinny Testaverde	.50	.23
❑ 68 Tim Brown	.75	.35
❑ 69 Rich Gannon	.75	.35
❑ 70 Donovan McNabb	1.25	.55
❑ 71 Duce Staley	.75	.35
❑ 72 Jerome Bettis	.75	.35
❑ 73 Troy Edwards	.30	.14
❑ 74 Kordell Stewart	.50	.23
❑ 75 Isaac Bruce	.75	.35
❑ 76 Marshall Faulk	1.00	.45
❑ 77 Torry Holt	.75	.35
❑ 78 Kurt Warner	1.50	.70
❑ 79 Jermaine Fazande	.30	.14
❑ 80 Jim Harbaugh	.50	.23
❑ 81 Jeff Garcia	.75	.35
❑ 82 Charlie Garner	.50	.23
❑ 83 Terrell Owens	.75	.35
❑ 84 Jerry Rice	1.50	.70
❑ 85 Jon Kitna	.75	.35
❑ 86 Derrick Mayes	.50	.23
❑ 87 Ricky Watters	.50	.23
❑ 88 Mike Alstott	.75	.35
❑ 89 Warrick Dunn	.75	.35
❑ 90 Keyshawn Johnson	.75	.35
❑ 91 Shaun King	.30	.14
❑ 92 Kevin Dyson	.50	.23
❑ 93 Eddie George	.75	.35
❑ 94 Jevon Kearse	.75	.35
❑ 95 Steve McNair	.75	.35
❑ 96 Carl Pickens	.50	.23
❑ 97 Champ Bailey	.50	.23
❑ 98 Stephen Davis	.75	.35
❑ 99 Brad Johnson	.75	.35
❑ 100 Michael Westbrook	.50	.23
❑ 101 Thomas Jones RC	12.00	5.50
❑ 102 Doug Johnson RC	8.00	3.60
❑ 103 Mareno Philyaw RC	4.00	1.80
❑ 104 Jamal Lewis RC	20.00	9.00
❑ 105 Chris Redman RC	6.00	2.70
❑ 106 Travis Taylor RC	8.00	3.60
❑ 107 Kwame Cavil RC	4.00	1.80
❑ 108 Sammy Morris RC	6.00	2.70
❑ 109 Frank Murphy RC	4.00	1.80
❑ 110 Brian Urlacher RC	30.00	13.50
❑ 111 Dez White RC	8.00	3.60
❑ 112 Ron Dugans RC	4.00	1.80
❑ 113 Curtis Keaton RC	6.00	2.70
❑ 114 Peter Warrick RC	8.00	3.60
❑ 115 Courtney Brown RC	8.00	3.60
❑ 116 JaJuan Dawson RC	4.00	1.80
❑ 117 Dennis Northcutt RC	8.00	3.60
❑ 118 Travis Prentice RC	6.00	2.70
❑ 119 Michael Wiley RC	6.00	2.70
❑ 120 Mike Anderson RC	8.00	3.60
❑ 121 Chris Cole RC	6.00	2.70
❑ 122 Jarious Jackson RC	6.00	2.70
❑ 123 Deltha O'Neal RC	8.00	3.60
❑ 124 Reuben Droughns RC	10.00	4.50
❑ 125 Bubba Franks RC	8.00	3.60
❑ 126 Anthony Lucas RC	4.00	1.80
❑ 127 Rondell Mealey RC	4.00	1.80
❑ 128 Rob Morris RC	6.00	2.70
❑ 129 R.Jay Soward RC	6.00	2.70
❑ 130 Shyrone Stith RC	6.00	2.70
❑ 131 Frank Moreau RC	6.00	2.70
❑ 132 Sylvester Morris RC	6.00	2.70
❑ 133 Doug Chapman RC	6.00	2.70
❑ 134 J.R. Redmond RC	6.00	2.70
❑ 135 Marc Bulger RC	15.00	6.75
❑ 136 Sherrod Gideon RC	4.00	1.80
❑ 137 Terrelle Smith RC	6.00	2.70
❑ 138 Ron Dayne RC	8.00	3.60
❑ 139 Anthony Becht RC	8.00	3.60
❑ 140 Laveranues Coles RC	10.00	4.50
❑ 141 Shaun Ellis RC	8.00	3.60
❑ 142 Chad Pennington RC	30.00	13.50
❑ 143 Sebastian Janikowski RC	8.00	3.60
❑ 144 Jerry Porter RC	10.00	4.50
❑ 145 Todd Pinkston RC	8.00	3.60
❑ 146 Gari Scott RC	4.00	1.80
❑ 147 Corey Simon RC	8.00	3.60
❑ 148 Plaxico Burress RC	15.00	6.75
❑ 149 Danny Farmer RC	6.00	2.70
❑ 150 Tee Martin RC	8.00	3.60
❑ 151 Trung Canidate RC	6.00	2.70
❑ 152 Trevor Gaylor RC	6.00	2.70
❑ 153 Giovanni Carmazzi RC	6.00	2.70
❑ 154 John Engelberger RC	6.00	2.70
❑ 155 Ahmed Plummer RC	8.00	3.60
❑ 156 Tim Rattay RC	15.00	6.75
❑ 157 Shaun Alexander RC	20.00	9.00
❑ 158 Joe Hamilton RC	6.00	2.70
❑ 159 Keith Bulluck RC	8.00	3.60
❑ 160 Todd Husak RC	8.00	3.60
❑ 161 Cade McNown SV	4.00	1.80
❑ 162 Tim Couch SV	1.50	.70
❑ 163 Terrell Davis SV	1.50	.70
❑ 164 Brett Favre SV	6.00	2.70
❑ 165 Edgerrin James SV	3.00	1.35
❑ 166 Peyton Manning SV	5.00	2.20
❑ 167 Daunte Culpepper SV	2.50	1.10
❑ 168 Randy Moss SV	4.00	1.80
❑ 169 Ricky Williams SV	1.50	.70
❑ 170 Kurt Warner SV	4.00	1.80
❑ 171 Cade McNown LV	1.50	.70
❑ 172 Akili Smith LV	1.50	.70
❑ 173 Tim Couch LV	1.50	.70
❑ 174 Troy Aikman LV	4.00	1.80
❑ 175 Emmitt Smith LV	4.00	1.80
❑ 176 Terrell Davis LV	1.50	.70
❑ 177 Brett Favre LV	6.00	2.70
❑ 178 Edgerrin James LV	3.00	1.35
❑ 179 Peyton Manning LV	5.00	2.20
❑ 180 Mark Brunell LV	1.50	.70
❑ 181 Daunte Culpepper LV	2.50	1.10
❑ 182 Randy Moss LV	4.00	1.80
❑ 183 Drew Bledsoe LV	2.50	1.10
❑ 184 Ricky Williams LV	1.50	.70
❑ 185 Donovan McNabb LV	3.00	1.35
❑ 186 Torry Holt LV	1.50	.70
❑ 187 Kurt Warner LV	4.00	1.80
❑ 188 Shaun King LV	1.50	.70
❑ 189 Eddie George LV	1.50	.70
❑ 190 Steve McNair LV	1.50	.70

1999 Collector's Edge Supreme

	Nm-Mt	Ex-Mt
COMPLETE SET (170)	250.00	110.00
COMP.SET w/o #166 (169)	100.00	45.00
❑ 1 Randy Moss CL	1.00	.45
❑ 2 Peyton Manning CL	.75	.35
❑ 3 Rob Moore	.50	.23
❑ 4 Adrian Murrell	.50	.23
❑ 5 Jake Plummer	.50	.23
❑ 6 Andre Wadsworth	.30	.14
❑ 7 Jamal Anderson	.75	.35
❑ 8 Chris Chandler	.50	.23
❑ 9 Tony Martin	.50	.23
❑ 10 Terance Mathis	.50	.23
❑ 11 Jim Harbaugh	.50	.23
❑ 12 Priest Holmes	1.25	.55
❑ 13 Jermaine Lewis	.50	.23
❑ 14 Eric Zeier	.30	.14
❑ 15 Doug Flutie	.75	.35
❑ 16 Eric Moulds	.75	.35
❑ 17 Andre Reed	.50	.23
❑ 18 Antowain Smith	.75	.35
❑ 19 Steve Beuerlein	.30	.14
❑ 20 Kevin Greene	.30	.14
❑ 21 Rocket Ismail	.50	.23
❑ 22 Fred Lane	.30	.14
❑ 23 Edgar Bennett	.30	.14
❑ 24 Curtis Conway	.50	.23
❑ 25 Curtis Enis	.30	.14
❑ 26 Erik Kramer	.30	.14
❑ 27 Corey Dillon	.75	.35
❑ 28 Neil O'Donnell	.30	.14
❑ 29 Carl Pickens	.50	.23
❑ 30 Darnay Scott	.30	.14
❑ 31 Troy Aikman	1.50	.70
❑ 32 Michael Irvin	.50	.23
❑ 33 Deion Sanders	.75	.35
❑ 34 Emmitt Smith	1.50	.70
❑ 35 Chris Warren	.30	.14
❑ 36 Terrell Davis	.75	.35
❑ 37 John Elway	2.50	1.10
❑ 38 Ed McCaffrey	.50	.23
❑ 39 Shannon Sharpe	.50	.23
❑ 40 Rod Smith	.50	.23
❑ 41 Charlie Batch	.75	.35
❑ 42 Herman Moore	.50	.23
❑ 43 Johnnie Morton	.30	.14
❑ 44 Barry Sanders	2.50	1.10
❑ 45 Robert Brooks	.50	.23
❑ 46 Brett Favre	2.50	1.10
❑ 47 Antonio Freeman	.75	.35
❑ 48 Darick Holmes	.30	.14
❑ 49 Dorsey Levens	.75	.35
❑ 50 Reggie White	.30	.14
❑ 51 Marshall Faulk	1.00	.45
❑ 52 Marvin Harrison	.75	.35
❑ 53 Peyton Manning	2.50	1.10
❑ 54 Jerome Pathon	.30	.14
❑ 55 Tavian Banks	.30	.14
❑ 56 Mark Brunell	.75	.35
❑ 57 Keenan McCardell	.50	.23
❑ 58 Fred Taylor	.75	.35
❑ 59 Derrick Alexander	.30	.14
❑ 60 Donnell Bennett	.30	.14
❑ 61 Rich Gannon	.75	.35
❑ 62 Andre Rison	.50	.23
❑ 63 Karim Abdul-Jabbar	.50	.23
❑ 64 John Avery	.30	.14
❑ 65 Oronde Gadsden	.50	.23
❑ 66 Dan Marino	2.50	1.10
❑ 67 O.J. McDuffie	.50	.23
❑ 68 Cris Carter	.75	.35
❑ 69 Randall Cunningham	.75	.35
❑ 70 Brad Johnson	.75	.35
❑ 71 Randy Moss	2.50	1.10
❑ 72 Jake Reed	.50	.23
❑ 73 Robert Smith	.75	.35
❑ 74 Drew Bledsoe	1.00	.45
❑ 75 Ben Coates	.50	.23
❑ 76 Robert Edwards	.30	.14
❑ 77 Terry Glenn	.75	.35
❑ 78 Cameron Cleeland	.30	.14
❑ 79 Kerry Collins	.50	.23
❑ 80 Sean Dawkins	.30	.14
❑ 81 Lamar Smith	.50	.23
❑ 82 Gary Brown	.30	.14
❑ 83 Chris Calloway	.30	.14
❑ 84 Danny Kanell	.30	.14
❑ 85 Ike Hilliard	.30	.14
❑ 86 Wayne Chrebet	.50	.23
❑ 87 Keyshawn Johnson	.75	.35
❑ 88 Curtis Martin	.75	.35
❑ 89 Vinny Testaverde	.50	.23
❑ 90 Tim Brown	.75	.35
❑ 91 Jeff George	.50	.23
❑ 92 Napoleon Kaufman	.75	.35
❑ 93 Charles Woodson	.75	.35
❑ 94 Irving Fryar	.50	.23
❑ 95 Bobby Hoying	.50	.23
❑ 96 Duce Staley	.75	.35
❑ 97 Jerome Bettis	.75	.35

❑ 98 Courtney Hawkins .30 .14
❑ 99 Charles Johnson .30 .14
❑ 100 Kordell Stewart .50 .23
❑ 101 Hines Ward .75 .35
❑ 102 Tony Banks .50 .23
❑ 103 Isaac Bruce .75 .35
❑ 104 Robert Holcombe .30 .14
❑ 105 Ryan Leaf .75 .35
❑ 106 Natrone Means .50 .23
❑ 107 Mikhael Ricks .30 .14
❑ 108 Junior Seau .75 .35
❑ 109 Garrison Hearst .50 .23
❑ 110 Terrell Owens .75 .35
❑ 111 Jerry Rice 1.50 .70
❑ 112 J.J. Stokes .50 .23
❑ 113 Steve Young 1.00 .45
❑ 114 Joey Galloway .50 .23
❑ 115 Jon Kitna .75 .35
❑ 116 Warren Moon .75 .35
❑ 117 Ricky Watters .50 .23
❑ 118 Mike Alstott .75 .35
❑ 119 Reidel Anthony .50 .23
❑ 120 Warrick Dunn .75 .35
❑ 121 Trent Dilfer .50 .23
❑ 122 Jacquez Green .30 .14
❑ 123 Kevin Dyson .50 .23
❑ 124 Eddie George .75 .35
❑ 125 Steve McNair .75 .35
❑ 126 Frank Wycheck .30 .14
❑ 127 Terry Allen .50 .23
❑ 128 Trent Green .75 .35
❑ 129 Skip Hicks .30 .14
❑ 130 Michael Westbrook .50 .23
❑ 131 Rahim Abdullah RC 1.00 .45
❑ 132 Champ Bailey RC 2.00 .90
❑ 133 Marlon Barnes RC .60 .25
❑ 134 D'Wayne Bates RC 1.00 .45
❑ 135 Michael Bishop RC 1.50 .70
❑ 136 Dre' Bly RC 1.50 .70
❑ 137 David Boston RC 1.50 .70
❑ 138 Cuncho Brown RC UER .60 .25
(Photo is actually Courtney Brown)
❑ 139 Na Brown RC 1.00 .45
❑ 140 Tony Bryant RC 1.00 .45
❑ 141 Tim Couch RC ERR 50.00 22.00
(text on back reads "already sent")
❑ 141TC Tim Couch RC COR 6.00 2.70
(card number reads "TC")
❑ 142 Chris Claiborne RC .60 .25
❑ 143 Daunte Culpepper RC 5.00 2.20
❑ 144 Jared DeVries RC 1.00 .45
❑ 145 Troy Edwards RC UER 1.00 .45
❑ 146 Kris Farris RC .60 .25
❑ 147 Kevin Faulk RC 1.50 .70
❑ 148 Joe Germaine RC 1.00 .45
❑ 149 Aaron Gibson RC .60 .25
❑ 150 Torry Holt RC 3.00 1.35
❑ 151 Brock Huard RC 1.50 .70
❑ 152 Sedrick Irvin RC .60 .25
❑ 153 James Johnson RC 1.00 .45
❑ 154 Kevin Johnson RC 1.50 .70
❑ 155 Andy Katzenmoyer RC 1.00 .45
❑ 156 Jevon Kearse RC 2.50 1.10
❑ 157 Shaun King RC 1.00 .45
❑ 158 Rob Konrad RC 1.00 .45
❑ 159 Chris McAlister RC 1.00 .45
❑ 160 Darnell McDonald RC 1.00 .45
❑ 161 Donovan McNabb RC 6.00 2.70
❑ 162 Cade McNown RC 1.00 .45
❑ 163 Peerless Price RC 2.50 1.10
❑ 164 Akili Smith RC 1.00 .45
❑ 165 Matt Stinchcomb RC .60 .25
❑ 166A Michael Wiley 80.00 36.00
(pink tint on cardfront)
❑ 166B Edgerrin James RC 25.00 11.00
(issue via mail redemption)
❑ 167 Ricky Williams RC 3.00 1.35
❑ 168 Antoine Winfield RC 1.00 .45
❑ 169 Craig Yeast RC 1.00 .45
❑ 170 Amos Zereoue RC 1.50 .70

2000 Collector's Edge Supreme

	Nm-Mt	Ex-Mt
COMPLETE SET (190)	80.00	36.00
COMP.FACT.SET (190)	40.00	18.00
COMP.SET w/o SP's (150)	20.00	9.00

❑ 1 David Boston .60 .25
❑ 2 Adrian Murrell .40 .18
❑ 3 Michael Pittman .25 .11
❑ 4 Jake Plummer .40 .18
❑ 5 Frank Sanders .40 .18
❑ 6 Jamal Anderson .60 .25
❑ 7 Chris Chandler .40 .18
❑ 8 Terance Mathis .40 .18
❑ 9 Justin Armour .25 .11
❑ 10 Tony Banks .40 .18
❑ 11 Qadry Ismail .40 .18
❑ 12 Errict Rhett .40 .18
❑ 13 Doug Flutie .60 .25
❑ 14 Eric Moulds .60 .25
❑ 15 Peerless Price .60 .25
❑ 16 Andre Reed .40 .18
❑ 17 Antowain Smith .40 .18
❑ 18 Steve Beuerlein .40 .18
❑ 19 Tim Biakabutuka .40 .18
❑ 20 Muhsin Muhammad .40 .18
❑ 21 Wesley Walls .25 .11
❑ 22 Bobby Engram .25 .11
❑ 23 Curtis Enis .25 .11
❑ 24 Shane Matthews .40 .18
❑ 25 Cade McNown .25 .11
❑ 26 Jim Miller .25 .11
❑ 27 Marcus Robinson .60 .25
❑ 28 Corey Dillon .60 .25
❑ 29 Carl Pickens .40 .18
❑ 30 Darnay Scott .40 .18
❑ 31 Akili Smith .25 .11
❑ 32 Karim Abdul-Jabbar .40 .18
❑ 33 Tim Couch .40 .18
❑ 34 Kevin Johnson .60 .25
❑ 35 Troy Aikman 1.25 .55
❑ 36 Michael Irvin .40 .18
❑ 37 Rocket Ismail .40 .18
❑ 38 Deion Sanders .60 .25
❑ 39 Emmitt Smith 1.25 .55
❑ 40 Terrell Davis .60 .25
❑ 41 Olandis Gary .60 .25
❑ 42 Brian Griese .60 .25
❑ 43 Ed McCaffrey .60 .25
❑ 44 Rod Smith .40 .18
❑ 45 Charlie Batch .60 .25
❑ 46 Germane Crowell .25 .11
❑ 47 Greg Hill .25 .11
❑ 48 Sedrick Irvin .25 .11
❑ 49 Herman Moore .40 .18
❑ 50 Johnnie Morton .40 .18
❑ 51 Corey Bradford .40 .18
❑ 52 Brett Favre 2.00 .90
❑ 53 Antonio Freeman .60 .25
❑ 54 Dorsey Levens .40 .18
❑ 55 Bill Schroeder .40 .18
❑ 56 E.G. Green .25 .11
❑ 57 Marvin Harrison .60 .25
❑ 58 Edgerrin James 1.00 .45
❑ 59 Peyton Manning 1.50 .70
❑ 60 Terrence Wilkins .25 .11
❑ 61 Mark Brunell .60 .25
❑ 62 Keenan McCardell .40 .18
❑ 63 Jimmy Smith .40 .18
❑ 64 James Stewart .40 .18
❑ 65 Fred Taylor .60 .25
❑ 66 Derrick Alexander .40 .18
❑ 67 Donnell Bennett .25 .11
❑ 68 Mike Cloud .25 .11
❑ 69 Tony Gonzalez .40 .18
❑ 70 Elvis Grbac .40 .18
❑ 71 Damon Huard .60 .25
❑ 72 James Johnson .25 .11
❑ 73 Rob Konrad .25 .11
❑ 74 Dan Marino 2.00 .90
❑ 75 Tony Martin .40 .18
❑ 76 O.J. McDuffie .40 .18
❑ 77 Cris Carter .60 .25
❑ 78 Daunte Culpepper .75 .35
❑ 79 Jeff George .40 .18
❑ 80 Randy Moss 1.25 .55
❑ 81 Robert Smith .60 .25
❑ 82 Terry Allen .40 .18
❑ 83 Drew Bledsoe .75 .35
❑ 84 Kevin Faulk .40 .18
❑ 85 Terry Glenn .40 .18
❑ 86 Shawn Jefferson .25 .11
❑ 87 Billy Joe Hobert .25 .11
❑ 88 Eddie Kennison .40 .18
❑ 89 Billy Joe Tolliver .25 .11
❑ 90 Ricky Williams .60 .25
❑ 91 Tiki Barber .40 .18
❑ 92 Gary Brown .25 .11
❑ 93 Kent Graham .25 .11
❑ 94 Ike Hilliard .40 .18
❑ 95 Amani Toomer .25 .11
❑ 96 Wayne Chrebet .40 .18
❑ 97 Keyshawn Johnson .60 .25
❑ 98 Ray Lucas .40 .18
❑ 99 Curtis Martin .60 .25
❑ 100 Vinny Testaverde .40 .18
❑ 101 Tim Brown .60 .25
❑ 102 Rich Gannon .60 .25
❑ 103 James Jett .25 .11
❑ 104 Napoleon Kaufman .40 .18
❑ 105 Tyrone Wheatley .40 .18
❑ 106 Charles Johnson .40 .18
❑ 107 Donovan McNabb 1.00 .45
❑ 108 Duce Staley .60 .25
❑ 109 Jerome Bettis .60 .25
❑ 110 Troy Edwards .25 .11
❑ 111 Kordell Stewart .40 .18
❑ 112 Hines Ward .60 .25
❑ 113 Isaac Bruce .60 .25
❑ 114 Marshall Faulk .75 .35
❑ 115 Az-Zahir Hakim .40 .18
❑ 116 Torry Holt .60 .25
❑ 117 Kurt Warner 1.25 .55
❑ 118 Jeff Graham .25 .11
❑ 119 Jim Harbaugh .40 .18
❑ 120 Freddie Jones .25 .11
❑ 121 Natrone Means .25 .11
❑ 122 Junior Seau .60 .25
❑ 123 Jeff Garcia .60 .25
❑ 124 Charlie Garner .40 .18
❑ 125 Terrell Owens .60 .25
❑ 126 Jerry Rice 1.25 .55
❑ 127 Steve Young .75 .35
❑ 128 Sean Dawkins .25 .11
❑ 129 Joey Galloway .40 .18
❑ 130 Jon Kitna .60 .25
❑ 131 Derrick Mayes .40 .18
❑ 132 Ricky Watters .40 .18
❑ 133 Mike Alstott .60 .25
❑ 134 Reidel Anthony .25 .11
❑ 135 Trent Dilfer .40 .18
❑ 136 Warrick Dunn .60 .25
❑ 137 Jacquez Green .25 .11
❑ 138 Shaun King .25 .11
❑ 139 Kevin Dyson .40 .18
❑ 140 Eddie George .60 .25
❑ 141 Jevon Kearse .60 .25
❑ 142 Steve McNair .60 .25
❑ 143 Yancey Thigpen .25 .11
❑ 144 Champ Bailey .40 .18

❑ 145 Albert Connell	.25	.11
❑ 146 Stephen Davis	.60	.25
❑ 147 Brad Johnson	.60	.25
❑ 148 Michael Westbrook	.40	.18
❑ 149 Checklist	.25	.11
❑ 150 Checklist	.25	.11
❑ 151 Sylvester Morris RC (issued via redemption)	5.00	2.20
❑ 151B LaVar Arrington SP	200.00	60.00
❑ 152 Peter Warrick RC	6.00	2.70
❑ 153 Chad Pennington RC	25.00	11.00
❑ 154 Courtney Brown RC	6.00	2.70
❑ 155 Thomas Jones RC	10.00	4.50
❑ 156 Chris Redman RC	5.00	2.20
❑ 157 R.Jay Soward RC	5.00	2.20
❑ 158 Jamal Lewis RC	15.00	6.75
❑ 159 Shaun Alexander RC	15.00	6.75
❑ 160 Travis Taylor RC	6.00	2.70
❑ 161 Ron Dayne RC	6.00	2.70
❑ 162 Travis Prentice RC	5.00	2.20
❑ 163 Plaxico Burress RC	12.00	5.50
❑ 164 J.R. Redmond RC	5.00	2.20
❑ 165 Sherrod Gideon RC	4.00	1.80
❑ 166 Dez White RC	6.00	2.70
❑ 167 Chafie Fields RC	4.00	1.80
❑ 168 Brandon Short RC (issued via redemption)	6.00	2.70
❑ 169 Reuben Droughns RC	8.00	3.60
❑ 170 Trung Canidate RC	5.00	2.20
❑ 171 Keith Bulluck RC (issued via redemption)	6.00	2.70
❑ 172 Doug Johnson RC (issued via redemption)	6.00	2.70
❑ 173 Shyrone Stith RC	6.00	2.70
❑ 174 Michael Wiley RC	5.00	2.20
❑ 175 Bubba Franks RC	6.00	2.70
❑ 176 Tom Brady RC	50.00	22.00
❑ 177 Anthony Lucas RC	6.00	2.70
❑ 178 Danny Farmer RC	5.00	2.20
❑ 179 Rob Morris RC	6.00	2.70
❑ 180 Dennis Northcutt RC	6.00	2.70
❑ 181 Troy Walters RC	6.00	2.70
❑ 182 Giovanni Carmazzi RC	5.00	2.20
❑ 183 Tee Martin RC	6.00	2.70
❑ 184 Joe Hamilton RC	5.00	2.20
❑ 185 Tim Rattay RC	12.00	5.50
❑ 186 Sebastian Janikowski RC	6.00	2.70
❑ 187 Na'il Diggs RC	5.00	2.20
❑ 188 Todd Husak RC (issued via redemption)	6.00	2.70
❑ 189 Jerry Porter RC	8.00	3.60
❑ 190 Brian Urlacher RC (issued via redemption)	25.00	11.00
❑ 59A P.Manning AUTO/300	70.00	32.00

2000 Collector's Edge T3

	Nm-Mt	Ex-Mt
COMP.SET w/o SP's (150)	30.00	13.50
❑ 1 David Boston	.75	.35
❑ 2 Rob Moore	.50	.23
❑ 3 Michael Pittman	.30	.14
❑ 4 Jake Plummer	.50	.23
❑ 5 Frank Sanders	.50	.23
❑ 6 Jamal Anderson	.75	.35
❑ 7 Chris Chandler	.50	.23
❑ 8 Tim Dwight	.75	.35
❑ 9 Shawn Jefferson	.30	.14
❑ 10 Terance Mathis	.50	.23
❑ 11 Tony Banks	.50	.23
❑ 12 Priest Holmes	1.00	.45
❑ 13 Qadry Ismail	.50	.23
❑ 14 Shannon Sharpe	.50	.23
❑ 15 Doug Flutie	.75	.35
❑ 16 Rob Johnson	.50	.23
❑ 17 Eric Moulds	.75	.35
❑ 18 Peerless Price	.75	.35
❑ 19 Antowain Smith	.50	.23
❑ 20 Steve Beuerlein	.50	.23
❑ 21 Tim Biakabutuka	.50	.23
❑ 22 Muhsin Muhammad	.50	.23
❑ 23 Patrick Jeffers	.75	.35
❑ 24 Wesley Walls	.30	.14
❑ 25 Bobby Engram	.30	.14
❑ 26 Curtis Enis	.30	.14
❑ 27 Cade McNown	.30	.14
❑ 28 Marcus Robinson	.75	.35
❑ 29 Corey Dillon	.75	.35
❑ 30 Carl Pickens	.50	.23
❑ 31 Darnay Scott	.50	.23
❑ 32 Akili Smith	.30	.14
❑ 33 Tim Couch	.50	.23
❑ 34 Kevin Johnson	.75	.35
❑ 35 Errict Rhett	.50	.23
❑ 36 Troy Aikman	1.50	.70
❑ 37 Joey Galloway	.50	.23
❑ 38 Rocket Ismail	.50	.23
❑ 39 Emmitt Smith	1.50	.70
❑ 40 Chris Warren	.30	.14
❑ 41 Terrell Davis	.75	.35
❑ 42 Olandis Gary	.75	.35
❑ 43 Brian Griese	.75	.35
❑ 44 Ed McCaffrey	.75	.35
❑ 45 Rod Smith	.50	.23
❑ 46 Charlie Batch	.75	.35
❑ 47 Germane Crowell	.30	.14
❑ 48 Sedrick Irvin	.30	.14
❑ 49 Herman Moore	.50	.23
❑ 50 Johnnie Morton	.50	.23
❑ 51 James Stewart	.50	.23
❑ 52 Brett Favre	2.50	1.10
❑ 53 Antonio Freeman	.75	.35
❑ 54 Dorsey Levens	.50	.23
❑ 55 Bill Schroeder	.50	.23
❑ 56 Ken Dilger	.30	.14
❑ 57 Marvin Harrison	.75	.35
❑ 58 Edgerrin James	1.25	.55
❑ 59 Peyton Manning	2.00	.90
❑ 60 Terrence Wilkins	.30	.14
❑ 61 Mark Brunell	.75	.35
❑ 62 Keenan McCardell	.50	.23
❑ 63 Jimmy Smith	.50	.23
❑ 64 Fred Taylor	.75	.35
❑ 65 Derrick Alexander	.50	.23
❑ 66 Donnell Bennett	.30	.14
❑ 67 Mike Cloud	.30	.14
❑ 68 Tony Gonzalez	.50	.23
❑ 69 Elvis Grbac	.50	.23
❑ 70 Tony Richardson RC	.50	.23
❑ 71 Damon Huard	.75	.35
❑ 72 James Johnson	.30	.14
❑ 73 Rob Konrad	.30	.14
❑ 74 Tony Martin	.50	.23
❑ 75 O.J. McDuffie	.50	.23
❑ 76 Cris Carter	.75	.35
❑ 77 Daunte Culpepper	1.00	.45
❑ 78 Randy Moss	1.50	.70
❑ 79 Robert Smith	.75	.35
❑ 80 Drew Bledsoe	1.00	.45
❑ 81 Kevin Faulk	.50	.23
❑ 82 Terry Glenn	.50	.23
❑ 83 Willie McGinest	.30	.14
❑ 84 Tony Simmons	.30	.14
❑ 85 Jeff Blake	.50	.23
❑ 86 Jake Reed	.50	.23
❑ 87 Ricky Williams	.75	.35
❑ 88 Kerry Collins	.50	.23
❑ 89 Ike Hilliard	.50	.23
❑ 90 Joe Montgomery	.30	.14
❑ 91 Amani Toomer	.30	.14
❑ 92 Wayne Chrebet	.50	.23
❑ 93 Ray Lucas	.50	.23
❑ 94 Curtis Martin	.75	.35
❑ 95 Vinny Testaverde	.50	.23
❑ 96 Tim Brown	.75	.35
❑ 97 Rich Gannon	.75	.35
❑ 98 James Jett	.30	.14
❑ 99 Napoleon Kaufman	.50	.23
❑ 100 Tyrone Wheatley	.50	.23
❑ 101 Charles Woodson	.50	.23
❑ 102 Charles Johnson	.50	.23
❑ 103 Donovan McNabb	1.25	.55
❑ 104 Duce Staley	.75	.35
❑ 105 Jerome Bettis	.75	.35
❑ 106 Troy Edwards	.30	.14
❑ 107 Kent Graham	.30	.14
❑ 108 Kordell Stewart	.50	.23
❑ 109 Hines Ward	.75	.35
❑ 110 Isaac Bruce	.75	.35
❑ 111 Kevin Carter	.30	.14
❑ 112 Marshall Faulk	1.00	.45
❑ 113 Trent Green	.75	.35
❑ 114 Az-Zahir Hakim	.50	.23
❑ 115 Torry Holt	.75	.35
❑ 116 Kurt Warner	1.50	.70
❑ 117 Curtis Conway	.50	.23
❑ 118 Jermaine Fazande	.30	.14
❑ 119 Jeff Graham	.30	.14
❑ 120 Jim Harbaugh	.50	.23
❑ 121 Junior Seau	.75	.35
❑ 122 Jeff Garcia	.75	.35
❑ 123 Charlie Garner	.50	.23
❑ 124 Garrison Hearst	.50	.23
❑ 125 Terrell Owens	.75	.35
❑ 126 Jerry Rice	1.50	.70
❑ 127 Steve Young	1.00	.45
❑ 128 Sean Dawkins	.30	.14
❑ 129 Jon Kitna	.75	.35
❑ 130 Derrick Mayes	.50	.23
❑ 131 Ricky Watters	.50	.23
❑ 132 Mike Alstott	.75	.35
❑ 133 Warrick Dunn	.75	.35
❑ 134 Jacquez Green	.30	.14
❑ 135 Keyshawn Johnson	.75	.35
❑ 136 Shaun King	.30	.14
❑ 137 Warren Sapp	.50	.23
❑ 138 Kevin Dyson	.50	.23
❑ 139 Eddie George	.75	.35
❑ 140 Jevon Kearse	.75	.35
❑ 141 Steve McNair	.75	.35
❑ 142 Yancey Thigpen	.30	.14
❑ 143 Frank Wycheck	.30	.14
❑ 144 Champ Bailey	.50	.23
❑ 145 Larry Centers	.30	.14
❑ 146 Albert Connell	.30	.14
❑ 147 Stephen Davis	.75	.35
❑ 148 Jeff George	.50	.23
❑ 149 Brad Johnson	.75	.35
❑ 150 Michael Westbrook	.50	.23
❑ 151 Thomas Jones RC	12.00	5.50
❑ 152 Doug Johnson RC	8.00	3.60
❑ 153 Mareno Philyaw RC	4.00	1.80
❑ 154 Jamal Lewis RC	20.00	9.00
❑ 155 Chris Redman RC	6.00	2.70
❑ 156 Travis Taylor RC	8.00	3.60
❑ 157 Kwame Cavil RC	4.00	1.80
❑ 158 Sammy Morris RC	6.00	2.70
❑ 159 Deon Grant RC	6.00	2.70
❑ 160 Frank Murphy RC	4.00	1.80
❑ 161 Brian Urlacher RC	30.00	13.50
❑ 162 Dez White RC	8.00	3.60
❑ 163 Ron Dugans RC	4.00	1.80
❑ 164 Curtis Keaton RC	6.00	2.70
❑ 165 Peter Warrick RC	8.00	3.60
❑ 166 Courtney Brown RC	8.00	3.60
❑ 167 JaJuan Dawson RC	4.00	1.80
❑ 168 Dennis Northcutt RC	8.00	3.60
❑ 169 Travis Prentice RC	6.00	2.70
❑ 170 Michael Wiley RC	6.00	2.70
❑ 171 Mike Anderson RC	8.00	3.60
❑ 172 Chris Cole RC	6.00	2.70
❑ 173 Jarious Jackson RC	6.00	2.70
❑ 174 Deltha O'Neal RC	8.00	3.60
❑ 175 Reuben Droughns RC	10.00	4.50
❑ 176 Na'il Diggs RC	6.00	2.70
❑ 177 Bubba Franks RC	8.00	3.60
❑ 178 Anthony Lucas RC	4.00	1.80

❑ 179 Rondell Mealey RC 4.00 1.80
❑ 180 Dan Kendra RC 4.00 1.80
❑ 181 Rob Morris RC 8.00 3.60
❑ 182 R.Jay Soward RC 6.00 2.70
❑ 183 Shyrone Stith RC 8.00 3.60
❑ 184 William Bartee RC 6.00 2.70
❑ 185 Frank Moreau RC 6.00 2.70
❑ 186 Sylvester Morris RC 6.00 2.70
❑ 187 Deon Dyer RC 6.00 2.70
❑ 188 Quinton Spotwood RC 4.00 1.80
❑ 189 Doug Chapman RC 6.00 2.70
❑ 190 Troy Walters RC 8.00 3.60
❑ 191 J.R. Redmond RC 6.00 2.70
❑ 192 Marc Bulger RC 15.00 6.75
❑ 193 Sherrod Gideon RC 4.00 1.80
❑ 194 Darren Howard RC 6.00 2.70
❑ 195 Chad Morton RC 8.00 3.60
❑ 196 Terrelle Smith RC 6.00 2.70
❑ 197 Ron Dayne RC 8.00 3.60
❑ 198 John Abraham RC 8.00 3.60
❑ 199 Anthony Becht RC 8.00 3.60
❑ 200 Laveranues Coles RC 10.00 4.50
❑ 201 Shaun Ellis RC 8.00 3.60
❑ 202 Chad Pennington RC 30.00 13.50
❑ 203 Sebastian Janikowski RC 8.00 3.60
❑ 204 Jerry Porter RC 10.00 4.50
❑ 205 Todd Pinkston RC 8.00 3.60
❑ 206 Corey Simon RC 8.00 3.60
❑ 207 Plaxico Burress RC 15.00 6.75
❑ 208 Danny Farmer RC 6.00 2.70
❑ 209 Tee Martin RC 8.00 3.60
❑ 210 Hank Poteat RC 6.00 2.70
❑ 211 Trung Canidate RC 6.00 2.70
❑ 212 Jacoby Shepherd RC 6.00 2.70
❑ 213 Trevor Gaylor RC 6.00 2.70
❑ 214 Giovanni Carmazzi RC 6.00 2.70
❑ 215 John Engelberger RC 6.00 2.70
❑ 216 Chafie Fields RC 4.00 1.80
❑ 217 Julian Peterson RC 8.00 3.60
❑ 218 Ahmed Plummer RC 8.00 3.60
❑ 219 Tim Rattay RC 15.00 6.75
❑ 220 Shaun Alexander RC 20.00 9.00
❑ 221 Joe Hamilton RC 6.00 2.70
❑ 222 Keith Bulluck RC 8.00 3.60
❑ 223 Erron Kinney RC 8.00 3.60
❑ 224 Todd Husak RC 8.00 3.60
❑ 225 Chris Samuels RC 6.00 2.70

1999 Collector's Edge Triumph

	Nm-Mt	Ex-Mt
COMPLETE SET (180)	50.00	22.00
❑ 1 Jamal Anderson	.75	.35
❑ 2 Jerome Bettis	.75	.35
❑ 3 Terrell Davis	.75	.35
❑ 4 Corey Dillon	.75	.35
❑ 5 Warrick Dunn	.75	.35
❑ 6 Marshall Faulk	1.00	.45
❑ 7 Eddie George	.75	.35
❑ 8 Garrison Hearst	.50	.23
❑ 9 Skip Hicks	.30	.14
❑ 10 Napoleon Kaufman	.75	.35
❑ 11 Dorsey Levens	.75	.35
❑ 12 Curtis Martin	.75	.35
❑ 13 Natrone Means	.50	.23
❑ 14 Adrian Murrell	.50	.23
❑ 15 Barry Sanders	2.50	1.10
❑ 16 Antowain Smith	.75	.35
❑ 17 Emmitt Smith	1.50	.70
❑ 18 Robert Smith	.75	.35
❑ 19 Fred Taylor	.75	.35
❑ 20 Ricky Watters	.50	.23
❑ 21 Cameron Cleeland	.30	.14
❑ 22 Ben Coates	.50	.23
❑ 23 Shannon Sharpe	.50	.23
❑ 24 Frank Wycheck	.30	.14
❑ 25 Derrick Alexander WR	.50	.23
❑ 26 Reidel Anthony	.50	.23
❑ 27 Robert Brooks	.50	.23
❑ 28 Tim Brown	.75	.35
❑ 29 Cris Carter	.75	.35
❑ 30 Wayne Chrebet	.50	.23
❑ 31 Curtis Conway	.50	.23
❑ 32 Tim Dwight	.75	.35
❑ 33 Kevin Dyson	.50	.23
❑ 34 Antonio Freeman	.75	.35
❑ 35 Joey Galloway	.50	.23
❑ 36 Terry Glenn	.75	.35
❑ 37 Marvin Harrison	.75	.35
❑ 38 Ike Hilliard	.30	.14
❑ 39 Michael Irvin	.50	.23
❑ 40 Keyshawn Johnson	.75	.35
❑ 41 Jermaine Lewis	.50	.23
❑ 42 Terance Mathis	.50	.23
❑ 43 Ed McCaffrey	.50	.23
❑ 44 Keenan McCardell	.50	.23
❑ 45 O.J. McDuffie	.50	.23
❑ 46 Herman Moore	.50	.23
❑ 47 Rob Moore	.50	.23
❑ 48 Randy Moss	2.00	.90
❑ 49 Eric Moulds	.75	.35
❑ 50 Muhsin Muhammad	.50	.23
❑ 51 Terrell Owens	.75	.35
❑ 52 Jerome Pathon	.30	.14
❑ 53 Carl Pickens	.50	.23
❑ 54 Andre Reed	.50	.23
❑ 55 Jake Reed	.50	.23
❑ 56 Jerry Rice	1.50	.70
❑ 57 Andre Rison	.50	.23
❑ 58 Jimmy Smith	.50	.23
❑ 59 Rod Smith WR	.50	.23
❑ 60 Michael Westbrook	.50	.23
❑ 61 Morten Andersen	.30	.14
❑ 62 Gary Anderson	.30	.14
❑ 63 Doug Brien	.30	.14
❑ 64 Chris Boniol	.30	.14
❑ 65 John Carney	.30	.14
❑ 66 Steve Christie	.30	.14
❑ 67 Richie Cunningham	.30	.14
❑ 68 Brad Daluiso	.30	.14
❑ 69 AL Del Greco	.30	.14
❑ 70 Jason Elam	.30	.14
❑ 71 John Hall	.30	.14
❑ 72 Jason Hanson	.30	.14
❑ 73 Mike Hollis	.30	.14
❑ 74 Norm Johnson	.30	.14
❑ 75 Olindo Mare	.30	.14
❑ 76 Doug Pelfrey	.30	.14
❑ 77 Wade Richey	.30	.14
❑ 78 Pete Stoyanovich	.30	.14
❑ 79 Mike Vanderjagt	.30	.14
❑ 80 Adam Vinatieri	.75	.35
❑ 81 Ray Buchanan	.30	.14
❑ 82 Jim Flanigan	.30	.14
❑ 83 Darrell Green	.30	.14
❑ 84 Kevin Greene	.30	.14
❑ 85 Ty Law	.50	.23
❑ 86 Ken Norton Jr.	.30	.14
❑ 87 John Randle	.50	.23
❑ 88 Bill Romanowski	.30	.14
❑ 89 Deion Sanders	.75	.35
❑ 90 Junior Seau	.75	.35
❑ 91 Michael Sinclair	.30	.14
❑ 92 Bruce Smith	.50	.23
❑ 93 Takeo Spikes	.30	.14
❑ 94 Michael Strahan	.50	.23
❑ 95 Derrick Thomas	.50	.23
❑ 96 Zach Thomas	.75	.35
❑ 97 Andre Wadsworth	.30	.14
❑ 98 Charles Woodson	.75	.35
❑ 99 Checklist Card	.30	.14
❑ 100 Checklist Card	.30	.14
❑ 101 Troy Aikman	1.50	.70
❑ 102 Tony Banks	.50	.23
❑ 103 Charlie Batch	.75	.35
❑ 104 Steve Beuerlein	.30	.14
❑ 105 Jeff Blake	.50	.23
❑ 106 Drew Bledsoe	1.00	.45
❑ 107 Bubby Brister	.30	.14
❑ 108 Mark Brunell	.75	.35
❑ 109 Chris Chandler	.50	.23
❑ 110 Kerry Collins	.50	.23
❑ 111 Randall Cunningham	.75	.35
❑ 112 Koy Detmer	.30	.14
❑ 113 Ty Detmer	.30	.14
❑ 114 Trent Dilfer	.50	.23
❑ 115 John Elway	2.50	1.10
❑ 116 Brett Favre	2.50	1.10
❑ 117 Doug Flutie	.75	.35
❑ 118 Rich Gannon	.75	.35
❑ 119 Jeff Garcia RC	8.00	3.60
❑ 120 Jeff George	.50	.23
❑ 121 Jon Kitna	.75	.35
❑ 122 Elvis Grbac	.50	.23
❑ 123 Brian Griese	.75	.35
❑ 124 Trent Green	.75	.35
❑ 125 Jim Harbaugh	.50	.23
❑ 126 Billy Joe Hobert	.30	.14
❑ 127 Brad Johnson	.75	.35
❑ 128 Rob Johnson	.50	.23
❑ 129 Jon Kitna	.75	.35
❑ 130 Erik Kramer	.30	.14
❑ 131 Ryan Leaf	.75	.35
❑ 132 Peyton Manning	2.50	1.10
❑ 133 Dan Marino	2.50	1.10
❑ 134 Steve McNair	.75	.35
❑ 135 Scott Mitchell	.30	.14
❑ 136 Warren Moon	.75	.35
❑ 137 Jake Plummer	.50	.23
❑ 138 Kordell Stewart	.50	.23
❑ 139 Vinny Testaverde	.50	.23
❑ 140 Steve Young	1.00	.45
❑ 141 Champ Bailey RC	2.00	.90
❑ 142 Karsten Bailey RC	1.00	.45
❑ 143 D'Wayne Bates RC	1.00	.45
❑ 144 David Boston RC	1.50	.70
❑ 145 Cuncho Brown RC	.50	.23
❑ 146 Dat Nguyen RC	1.50	.70
❑ 147 Chris Claiborne RC	.50	.23
❑ 148 Mike Cloud RC	1.00	.45
❑ 149 Cecil Collins RC	.50	.23
❑ 150 Tim Couch RC	1.50	.70
❑ 151 Daunte Culpepper RC	6.00	2.70
❑ 152 Autry Denson RC	1.00	.45
❑ 153 Troy Edwards RC	1.00	.45
❑ 154 Ebenezer Ekuban RC	1.00	.45
❑ 155 Kevin Faulk RC	1.50	.70
❑ 156 Jermaine Fazande RC	1.00	.45
❑ 157 Joe Germaine RC	1.00	.45
❑ 158 Martin Gramatica RC	.50	.23
❑ 159 Torry Holt RC	4.00	1.80
❑ 160 Brock Huard RC	1.50	.70
❑ 161 Sedrick Irvin RC	.50	.23
❑ 162 Edgerrin James RC	6.00	2.70
❑ 163 James Johnson RC	1.00	.45
❑ 164 Kevin Johnson RC	1.50	.70
❑ 165 Andy Katzenmoyer RC	1.00	.45
❑ 166 Jevon Kearse RC	2.50	1.10
❑ 167 Patrick Kerney RC	1.50	.70
❑ 168 Shaun King RC	1.00	.45
❑ 169 Jim Kleinsasser RC	1.50	.70
❑ 170 Rob Konrad RC	1.50	.70
❑ 171 Chris McAlister RC	1.00	.45
❑ 172 Donovan McNabb RC	8.00	3.60
❑ 173 Cade McNown RC	1.00	.45
❑ 174 Joe Montgomery RC	1.00	.45
❑ 175 Peerless Price RC	2.50	1.10
❑ 176 Akili Smith RC	1.00	.45
❑ 177 Ricky Williams RC	3.00	1.35
❑ 178 Larry Parker RC	1.50	.70
❑ 179 Antoine Winfield RC	1.00	.45
❑ 180 Amos Zereoue RC	1.50	.70

1996 Crown Royale

	Nm-Mt	Ex-Mt
COMPLETE SET (144)	50.00	22.00
❑ 1 Dan Marino	6.00	2.70
❑ 2 Frank Sanders	.60	.25
❑ 3 Bobby Engram RC	1.25	.55
❑ 4 Cornelius Bennett	.40	.18
❑ 5 Steve Bono	.40	.18
❑ 6 Aaron Hayden RC	.40	.18
❑ 7 Leroy Hoard	.40	.18
❑ 8 Brett Perriman	.40	.18
❑ 9 Irv Smith	.40	.18
❑ 10 Jim Kelly	1.25	.55
❑ 11 Rodney Thomas	.40	.18
❑ 12 Eric Bieniemy	.40	.18
❑ 13 Darnay Scott	.60	.25
❑ 14 Ki-Jana Carter	.60	.25
❑ 15 Kerry Collins	1.25	.55
❑ 16 Shannon Sharpe	.60	.25
❑ 17 Michael Westbrook	1.25	.55
❑ 18 Steve McNair	2.50	1.10
❑ 19 Tony Banks RC	2.00	.90
❑ 20 Rashaan Salaam	.60	.25
❑ 21 Terrell Fletcher	.40	.18
❑ 22 Michael Timpson	.40	.18
❑ 23 Bobby Hoying RC	1.25	.55
❑ 24 Quinn Early	.40	.18
❑ 25 Warren Moon	.60	.25
❑ 26 Tommy Vardell	.40	.18
❑ 27 Marvin Harrison RC	12.00	5.50
❑ 28 Lake Dawson	.40	.18
❑ 29 Karim Abdul-Jabbar RC	2.00	.90
❑ 30 Chris Warren	.60	.25
❑ 31 Heath Shuler	.60	.25
❑ 32 Bert Emanuel	.60	.25
❑ 33 Howard Griffith RC	.60	.25
❑ 34 Alex Van Dyke RC	.60	.25
❑ 35 Isaac Bruce	1.25	.55
❑ 36 Mark Brunell	2.00	.90
❑ 37 Winslow Oliver RC	.60	.25
❑ 38 O.J. McDuffie	.60	.25
❑ 39 Terrell Owens RC	12.00	5.50
❑ 40 Jerry Rice	3.00	1.35
❑ 41 Henry Ellard	.40	.18
❑ 42 Chris Sanders	.60	.25
❑ 43 Craig Heyward	.40	.18
❑ 44 Eddie Kennison RC	2.00	.90
❑ 45 Terrell Davis	2.50	1.10
❑ 46 Rodney Hampton	.60	.25
❑ 47 Bryan Still RC	.60	.25
❑ 48 Tim Brown	1.25	.55
❑ 49 Keyshawn Johnson RC	6.00	2.70
❑ 50 Barry Sanders	5.00	2.20
❑ 51 Terry Allen	.60	.25
❑ 52 Sean Dawkins	.40	.18
❑ 53 Bryce Paup	.40	.18
❑ 54 Brett Favre	6.00	2.70
❑ 55 Deion Sanders	2.00	.90
❑ 56 Kevin Hardy RC	2.00	.90
❑ 57 Kevin Williams	.40	.18
❑ 58 Jeff George	.60	.25
❑ 59 Tim Biakabutuka RC	2.00	.90
❑ 60 Drew Bledsoe	2.00	.90
❑ 61 Michael Jackson	.60	.25
❑ 62 James O. Stewart	.60	.25
❑ 63 Mario Bates	.60	.25
❑ 64 Daryl Johnston	.60	.25
❑ 65 Herman Moore	.60	.25
❑ 66 Ben Coates	.60	.25
❑ 67 Terry Glenn RC	6.00	2.70
❑ 68 Robert Smith	.60	.25
❑ 69 Irving Fryar	.60	.25
❑ 70 Napoleon Kaufman	1.25	.55
❑ 71 Rickey Dudley RC	2.00	.90
❑ 72 Bernie Parmalee	.40	.18
❑ 73 Kyle Brady	.40	.18
❑ 74 Neil O'Donnell	.60	.25
❑ 75 Lawrence Phillips RC	2.00	.90
❑ 76 Hardy Nickerson	.40	.18
❑ 77 John Elway	6.00	2.70
❑ 78 Pete Mitchell	.60	.25
❑ 79 Jason Dunn RC	1.25	.55
❑ 80 Reggie White	1.25	.55
❑ 81 J.J. Stokes	1.25	.55
❑ 82 Jake Reed	.60	.25
❑ 83 Yancey Thigpen	.60	.25
❑ 84 Jonathan Ogden RC	2.00	.90
❑ 85 Larry Centers	.60	.25
❑ 86 Scott Mitchell	.60	.25
❑ 87 Eric Zeier	.40	.18
❑ 88 Anthony Miller	.60	.25
❑ 89 Brian Blades	.40	.18
❑ 90 Cris Carter	1.25	.55
❑ 91 Kordell Stewart	1.25	.55
❑ 92 Charles Way RC	1.25	.55
❑ 93 Jeff Hostetler	.40	.18
❑ 94 Brad Johnson	2.50	1.10
❑ 95 Marcus Allen	1.25	.55
❑ 96 Errict Rhett	.60	.25
❑ 97 Stan Humphries	.60	.25
❑ 98 Michael Haynes	.40	.18
❑ 99 Curtis Martin	2.50	1.10
❑ 100 Troy Aikman	3.00	1.35
❑ 101 Earnest Byner	.40	.18
❑ 102 Vincent Brisby	.40	.18
❑ 103 Zack Crockett	.40	.18
❑ 104 Haywood Jeffires	.40	.18
❑ 105 Joey Galloway	1.25	.55
❑ 106 Carl Pickens	.60	.25
❑ 107 Leeland McElroy RC	1.25	.55
❑ 108 Adrian Murrell	.60	.25
❑ 109 Joe Horn RC/C	10.00	4.50
❑ 110 Steve Young	2.50	1.10
❑ 111 Andre Rison	.60	.25
❑ 112 Jim Everett	.40	.18
❑ 113 Jamie Asher RC	1.25	.55
❑ 114 Steve Walsh	.40	.18
❑ 115 Robert Brooks	1.25	.55
❑ 116 Eric Moulds RC	8.00	3.60
❑ 117 Edgar Bennett	.60	.25
❑ 118 Greg Lloyd	.60	.25
❑ 119 Jerris McPhail RC	.60	.25
❑ 120 Marshall Faulk	2.00	.90
❑ 121 Dave Brown	.40	.18
❑ 122 Harvey Williams	.40	.18
❑ 123 Trent Dilfer	1.25	.55
❑ 124 Eddie George RC	8.00	3.60
❑ 125 Jeff Blake	1.25	.55
❑ 126 Mark Chmura	.60	.25
❑ 127 Boomer Esiason	.60	.25
❑ 128 Jim Harbaugh	.60	.25
❑ 129 Bryan Cox	.40	.18
❑ 130 Ricky Watters	.60	.25
❑ 131 Amani Toomer RC	6.00	2.70
❑ 132 Jim Miller	1.25	.55
❑ 133 Cortez Kennedy	.40	.18
❑ 134 Courtney Hawkins	.40	.18
❑ 135 Junior Seau	1.25	.55
❑ 136 Tamarick Vanover	.60	.25
❑ 137 Jerome Bettis	1.25	.55
❑ 138 Chris Calloway	.40	.18
❑ 139 Rick Mirer	.60	.25
❑ 140 Thurman Thomas	1.25	.55
❑ 141 Sheddrick Wilson RC	.60	.25
❑ 142 Charlie Garner	.60	.25
❑ 143 Erik Kramer	.40	.18
❑ 144 Emmitt Smith	5.00	2.20

1996 Crown Royale Blue

	Nm-Mt	Ex-Mt
COMPLETE SET (144)	400.00	180.00

*STARS: 1.5X TO 4X BASIC CARDS
*RCs: 1X TO 2.5X BASIC CARDS

1996 Crown Royale Silver

	Nm-Mt	Ex-Mt
COMPLETE SET (144)	500.00	220.00

*STARS: 2X TO 5X BASIC CARDS
*RCs: 1.2X TO 3X BASIC CARDS

1997 Crown Royale

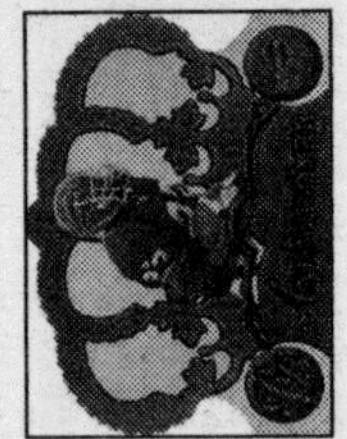

	Nm-Mt	Ex-Mt
COMPLETE SET (144)	100.00	45.00
❑ 1 Larry Centers	1.25	.55
❑ 2 Kent Graham	.75	.35
❑ 3 LeShon Johnson	.75	.35
❑ 4 Leeland McElroy	.75	.35
❑ 5 Jake Plummer RC	12.00	5.50
❑ 6 Jamal Anderson	2.00	.90
❑ 7 Chris Chandler	1.25	.55
❑ 8 Byron Hanspard RC	1.25	.55
❑ 9 O.J. Santiago RC	1.25	.55
❑ 10 Derrick Alexander WR	1.25	.55
❑ 11 Jay Graham RC	1.25	.55
❑ 12 Michael Jackson	1.25	.55
❑ 13 Vinny Testaverde	1.25	.55
❑ 14 Todd Collins	.75	.35
❑ 15 Jay Riemersma RC	.75	.35
❑ 16 Antowain Smith RC	6.00	2.70
❑ 17 Steve Tasker	.75	.35
❑ 18 Thurman Thomas	2.00	.90
❑ 19 Rae Carruth RC	.75	.35
❑ 20 Kerry Collins	2.00	.90
❑ 21 Anthony Johnson	.75	.35
❑ 22 Fred Lane RC	1.25	.55
❑ 23 Muhsin Muhammad	1.25	.55
❑ 24 Wesley Walls	1.25	.55
❑ 25 Darnell Autry RC	1.25	.55
❑ 26 Raymont Harris	.75	.35
❑ 27 Erik Kramer	.75	.35
❑ 28 Rick Mirer	.75	.35
❑ 29 Rashaan Salaam	.75	.35
❑ 30 Jeff Blake	1.25	.55
❑ 31 Ki-Jana Carter	.75	.35
❑ 32 Corey Dillon RC	15.00	6.75
❑ 33 Carl Pickens	1.25	.55
❑ 34 Troy Aikman	4.00	1.80
❑ 35 Michael Irvin	2.00	.90
❑ 36 Daryl Johnston	1.25	.55
❑ 37 David LaFleur RC	2.00	.90
❑ 38 Deion Sanders	2.00	.90
❑ 39 Emmitt Smith	6.00	2.70
❑ 40 Terrell Davis	2.50	1.10
❑ 41 John Elway	8.00	3.60
❑ 42 Ed McCaffrey	1.25	.55
❑ 43 Shannon Sharpe	1.25	.55
❑ 44 Neil Smith	1.25	.55
❑ 45 Scott Mitchell	1.25	.55
❑ 46 Herman Moore	1.25	.55
❑ 47 Johnnie Morton	1.25	.55
❑ 48 Barry Sanders	6.00	2.70
❑ 49 Robert Brooks	1.25	.55
❑ 50 Mark Chmura	1.25	.55
❑ 51 Brett Favre	8.00	3.60
❑ 52 Antonio Freeman	2.00	.90
❑ 53 Dorsey Levens	2.00	.90
❑ 54 Reggie White	2.00	.90
❑ 55 Ken Dilger	.75	.35

❑ 56 Marshall Faulk	2.50	1.10
❑ 57 Jim Harbaugh	1.25	.55
❑ 58 Marvin Harrison	2.00	.90
❑ 59 Mark Brunell	2.50	1.10
❑ 60 Rob Johnson	2.00	.90
❑ 61 Keenan McCardell	1.25	.55
❑ 62 Natrone Means	1.25	.55
❑ 63 Jimmy Smith	1.25	.55
❑ 64 Marcus Allen	2.00	.90
❑ 65 Tony Gonzalez RC	8.00	3.60
❑ 66 Elvis Grbac	1.25	.55
❑ 67 Greg Hill	.75	.35
❑ 68 Tamarick Vanover	1.25	.55
❑ 69 Karim Abdul-Jabbar	1.25	.55
❑ 70 Fred Barnett	.75	.35
❑ 71 Dan Marino	8.00	3.60
❑ 72 O.J. McDuffie	1.25	.55
❑ 73 Jerris McPhail	.75	.35
❑ 74 Cris Carter	2.00	.90
❑ 75 Randall Cunningham	2.00	.90
❑ 76 Brad Johnson	2.00	.90
❑ 77 Jake Reed	1.25	.55
❑ 78 Robert Smith	1.25	.55
❑ 79 Drew Bledsoe	2.50	1.10
❑ 80 Ben Coates	1.25	.55
❑ 81 Terry Glenn	2.00	.90
❑ 82 Curtis Martin	2.50	1.10
❑ 83 Troy Davis RC	1.25	.55
❑ 84 Heath Shuler	.75	.35
❑ 85 Irv Smith	.75	.35
❑ 86 Danny Wuerffel RC	2.00	.90
❑ 87 Tiki Barber RC	10.00	4.50
❑ 88 Dave Brown	.75	.35
❑ 89 Rodney Hampton	1.25	.55
❑ 90 Ike Hilliard RC	4.00	1.80
❑ 91 Amani Toomer	1.25	.55
❑ 92 Wayne Chrebet	2.00	.90
❑ 93 Keyshawn Johnson	2.00	.90
❑ 94 Adrian Murrell	1.25	.55
❑ 95 Neil O'Donnell	1.25	.55
❑ 96 Dedric Ward RC	1.25	.55
❑ 97 Tim Brown	2.00	.90
❑ 98 Jeff George	1.25	.55
❑ 99 Desmond Howard	1.25	.55
❑ 100 Napoleon Kaufman	2.00	.90
❑ 101 Ty Detmer	1.25	.55
❑ 102 Irving Fryar	1.25	.55
❑ 103 Bobby Hoying	1.25	.55
❑ 104 Ricky Watters	1.25	.55
❑ 105 Jerome Bettis	2.00	.90
❑ 106 Will Blackwell RC	1.25	.55
❑ 107 Charles Johnson	1.25	.55
❑ 108 George Jones RC	1.25	.55
❑ 109 Kordell Stewart	2.00	.90
❑ 110 Tony Banks	1.25	.55
❑ 111 Isaac Bruce	2.00	.90
❑ 112 Eddie Kennison	1.25	.55
❑ 113 Lawrence Phillips	.75	.35
❑ 114 Jim Everett	.75	.35
❑ 115 Stan Humphries	1.25	.55
❑ 116 Freddie Jones	1.25	.55
❑ 117 Tony Martin	1.25	.55
❑ 118 Junior Seau	2.00	.90
❑ 119 Jim Druckenmiller RC	1.25	.55
❑ 120 Garrison Hearst	1.25	.55
❑ 121 Brent Jones	.75	.35
❑ 122 Terrell Owens	2.50	1.10
❑ 123 Jerry Rice	4.00	1.80
❑ 124 Steve Young	2.50	1.10
❑ 125 Chad Brown	.75	.35
❑ 126 Joey Galloway	1.25	.55
❑ 127 Jon Kitna RC	10.00	4.50
❑ 128 Warren Moon	2.00	.90
❑ 129 Chris Warren	1.25	.55
❑ 130 Mike Alstott	2.00	.90
❑ 131 Reidel Anthony RC	2.00	.90
❑ 132 Trent Dilfer	2.00	.90
❑ 133 Warrick Dunn RC	6.00	2.70
❑ 134 Karl Williams RC	1.25	.55
❑ 135 Willie Davis	.75	.35
❑ 136 Eddie George	2.00	.90
❑ 137 Joey Kent RC	2.00	.90
❑ 138 Steve McNair	2.50	1.10
❑ 139 Chris Sanders	.75	.35
❑ 140 Terry Allen	2.00	.90
❑ 141 Jamie Asher	.75	.35
❑ 142 Stephen Davis	2.00	.90
❑ 143 Henry Ellard	.75	.35
❑ 144 Gus Frerotte	.75	.35
❑ S1 Mark Brunell Sample	1.00	.45

1997 Crown Royale Blue Holofoil

	Nm-Mt	Ex-Mt

*BLUE HOLO.STARS: 6X TO 15X BASIC CARDS
*BLUE HOLO.RCs: 2.5X TO 6X BASIC CARDS

1997 Crown Royale Gold Holofoil

	Nm-Mt	Ex-Mt

*GOLD HOLO.STARS: 2X TO 5X BASIC CARDS
*ROOKIES: 1X TO 2.5X BASIC CARDS

1997 Crown Royale Silver

	Nm-Mt	Ex-Mt

*SILVER STARS: 2X TO 4X HI COL.
*SILVER RCs: 1X TO 2X
SILVERS INSERTED IN SPECIAL RETAIL

1999 Crown Royale

	Nm-Mt	Ex-Mt
COMPLETE SET (144)	120.00	55.00
❑ 1 David Boston RC	3.00	1.35
❑ 2 Chris Greisen RC	2.50	1.10
❑ 3 Rob Moore	1.25	.55
❑ 4 Jake Plummer	1.25	.55
❑ 5 Frank Sanders	1.25	.55
❑ 6 Jamal Anderson	2.00	.90
❑ 7 Chris Chandler	1.25	.55
❑ 8 Tim Dwight	2.00	.90
❑ 9 Byron Hanspard	.75	.35
❑ 10 Stoney Case	.75	.35
❑ 11 Priest Holmes	3.00	1.35
❑ 12 Jermaine Lewis	1.25	.55
❑ 13 Chris McAlister RC	2.50	1.10
❑ 14 Brandon Stokley RC	4.00	1.80
❑ 15 Doug Flutie	2.00	.90
❑ 16 Eric Moulds	2.00	.90
❑ 17 Peerless Price RC	5.00	2.20
❑ 18 Antowain Smith	2.00	.90
❑ 19 Steve Beuerlein	.75	.35
❑ 20 Tim Biakabutuka	1.25	.55
❑ 21 Muhsin Muhammad	1.25	.55
❑ 22 Curtis Conway	1.25	.55
❑ 23 Curtis Enis	.75	.35
❑ 24 Shane Matthews	1.25	.55
❑ 25 Cade McNown RC	2.50	1.10
❑ 26 Marcus Robinson	3.00	1.35
❑ 27 Jeff Blake	1.25	.55
❑ 28 Scott Covington RC	3.00	1.35
❑ 29 Corey Dillon	2.00	.90
❑ 30 Damon Griffin RC	2.50	1.10
❑ 31 Carl Pickens	1.25	.55
❑ 32 Akili Smith RC	2.50	1.10
❑ 33 Tim Couch RC	3.00	1.35
❑ 34 Kevin Johnson RC	3.00	1.35
❑ 35 Terry Kirby	.75	.35
❑ 36 Leslie Shepherd	.75	.35
❑ 37 Troy Aikman	4.00	1.80
❑ 38 Rocket Ismail	.75	.35
❑ 39 Wane McGarity RC	1.50	.70
❑ 40 Deion Sanders	2.00	.90
❑ 41 Emmitt Smith	4.00	1.80
❑ 42 Terrell Davis	2.00	.90
❑ 43 Brian Griese	2.00	.90
❑ 44 Ed McCaffrey	1.25	.55
❑ 45 Shannon Sharpe	1.25	.55
❑ 46 Rod Smith	1.25	.55
❑ 47 Charlie Batch	2.00	.90
❑ 48 Germane Crowell	.75	.35
❑ 49 Sedrick Irvin RC	1.50	.70
❑ 50 Herman Moore	1.25	.55
❑ 51 Barry Sanders	6.00	2.70
❑ 52 Brett Favre	6.00	2.70
❑ 53 Antonio Freeman	2.00	.90
❑ 54 Matt Hasselbeck	3.00	1.35
❑ 55 Dorsey Levens	2.00	.90
❑ 56 Basil Mitchell RC	1.50	.70
❑ 57 E.G. Green	.75	.35
❑ 58 Marvin Harrison	2.00	.90
❑ 59 Edgerrin James RC	10.00	4.50
❑ 60 Peyton Manning	6.00	2.70
❑ 61 Terrence Wilkins RC	2.50	1.10
❑ 62 Mark Brunell	2.00	.90
❑ 63 Keenan McCardell	1.25	.55
❑ 64 Jimmy Smith	1.25	.55
❑ 65 Fred Taylor	2.00	.90
❑ 66 Derrick Alexander WR	1.25	.55
❑ 67 Elvis Grbac	1.25	.55
❑ 68 Warren Moon	.75	.35
❑ 69 Larry Parker RC	3.00	1.35
❑ 70 Andre Rison	1.25	.55
❑ 71 Cecil Collins RC	1.50	.70
❑ 72 Damon Huard	4.00	1.80
❑ 73 James Johnson RC	2.50	1.10
❑ 74 Rob Konrad RC	2.50	1.10
❑ 75 Dan Marino	6.00	2.70
❑ 76 O.J. McDuffie	1.25	.55
❑ 77 Cris Carter	2.00	.90
❑ 78 Daunte Culpepper RC	10.00	4.50
❑ 79 Randall Cunningham	2.00	.90
❑ 80 Randy Moss UER (card actually #81)	5.00	2.20
❑ 81 Robert Smith	.75	.35
❑ 82 Michael Bishop RC	3.00	1.35
❑ 83 Drew Bledsoe	2.50	1.10
❑ 84 Ben Coates	1.25	.55
❑ 85 Kevin Faulk RC	3.00	1.35
❑ 86 Terry Glenn	2.00	.90
❑ 87 Billy Joe Hobert	.75	.35
❑ 88 Eddie Kennison	1.25	.55
❑ 89 Keith Poole	.75	.35
❑ 90 Ricky Williams RC	5.00	2.20
❑ 91 Sean Bennett RC	1.50	.70
❑ 92 Kerry Collins	1.25	.55
❑ 93 Pete Mitchell	.75	.35
❑ 94 Amani Toomer	.75	.35
❑ 95 Wayne Chrebet	1.25	.55
❑ 96 Keyshawn Johnson	2.00	.90
❑ 97 Curtis Martin	2.00	.90
❑ 98 Tim Brown	2.00	.90
❑ 99 Scott Dreisbach RC	2.50	1.10
❑ 100 Rich Gannon	2.00	.90
❑ 101 Napoleon Kaufman	2.00	.90
❑ 102 Tyrone Wheatley	1.25	.55
❑ 103 Duce Staley	2.00	.90
❑ 104 Charles Johnson	.75	.35
❑ 105 Donovan McNabb RC	12.00	5.50
❑ 106 Torrance Small	.75	.35
❑ 107 Jed Weaver RC	1.50	.70
❑ 108 Jerome Bettis	2.00	.90
❑ 109 Troy Edwards RC	2.50	1.10
❑ 110 Kordell Stewart	1.25	.55
❑ 111 Amos Zereoue RC	3.00	1.35
❑ 112 Isaac Bruce	2.00	.90
❑ 113 Marshall Faulk	2.50	1.10
❑ 114 Joe Germaine RC	2.50	1.10
❑ 115 Torry Holt RC	8.00	3.60
❑ 116 Kurt Warner RC	15.00	6.75
❑ 117 Jim Harbaugh	1.25	.55
❑ 118 Erik Kramer	.75	.35
❑ 119 Natrone Means	1.25	.55

Card	Nm-Mt	Ex-Mt
❑ 120 Junior Seau	2.00	.90
❑ 121 Jeff Garcia RC	15.00	6.75
❑ 122 Terrell Owens	2.00	.90
❑ 123 Jerry Rice	4.00	1.80
❑ 124 J.J. Stokes	1.25	.55
❑ 125 Steve Young	2.50	1.10
❑ 126 Sean Dawkins	.75	.35
❑ 127 Brock Huard RC	3.00	1.35
❑ 128 Jon Kitna	2.00	.90
❑ 129 Derrick Mayes	1.25	.55
❑ 130 Charlie Rogers RC	1.50	.70
❑ 131 Ricky Watters	1.25	.55
❑ 132 Mike Alstott	2.00	.90
❑ 133 Trent Dilfer	1.25	.55
❑ 134 Warrick Dunn	2.00	.90
❑ 135 Eric Zeier	1.25	.55
❑ 136 Kevin Daft RC	2.50	1.10
❑ 137 Kevin Dyson	1.25	.55
❑ 138 Eddie George	2.00	.90
❑ 139 Steve McNair	2.00	.90
❑ 140 Neil O'Donnell	1.25	.55
❑ 141 Champ Bailey RC	4.00	1.80
❑ 142 Albert Connell	.75	.35
❑ 143 Stephen Davis	2.00	.90
❑ 144 Brad Johnson	2.00	.90

2000 Crown Royale

	Nm-Mt	Ex-Mt
COMPLETE SET (144)	120.00	55.00
❑ 1 Rob Moore	.60	.25
❑ 2 Jake Plummer	.60	.25
❑ 3 Frank Sanders	.60	.25
❑ 4 Jamal Anderson	1.00	.45
❑ 5 Chris Chandler	.60	.25
❑ 6 Tim Dwight	1.00	.45
❑ 7 Tony Banks	.60	.25
❑ 8 Priest Holmes	1.25	.55
❑ 9 Qadry Ismail	.60	.25
❑ 10 Doug Flutie	1.00	.45
❑ 11 Rob Johnson	.60	.25
❑ 12 Eric Moulds	1.00	.45
❑ 13 Peerless Price	1.00	.45
❑ 14 Steve Beuerlein	.60	.25
❑ 15 Patrick Jeffers	1.00	.45
❑ 16 Muhsin Muhammad	.60	.25
❑ 17 Curtis Enis	.40	.18
❑ 18 Cade McNown	.40	.18
❑ 19 Marcus Robinson	1.00	.45
❑ 20 Corey Dillon	1.00	.45
❑ 21 Darnay Scott	.60	.25
❑ 22 Akili Smith	.40	.18
❑ 23 Karim Abdul-Jabbar	.60	.25
❑ 24 Tim Couch	.60	.25
❑ 25 Kevin Johnson	1.00	.45
❑ 26 Troy Aikman	2.00	.90
❑ 27 Joey Galloway	.60	.25
❑ 28 Emmitt Smith	2.00	.90
❑ 29 Terrell Davis	1.00	.45
❑ 30 Olandis Gary	1.00	.45
❑ 31 Brian Griese	1.00	.45
❑ 32 Ed McCaffrey	1.00	.45
❑ 33 Charlie Batch	1.00	.45
❑ 34 Herman Moore	.60	.25
❑ 35 Barry Sanders	2.50	1.10
❑ 36 James Stewart	.60	.25
❑ 37 Brett Favre	3.00	1.35
❑ 38 Antonio Freeman	1.00	.45
❑ 39 Dorsey Levens	.60	.25
❑ 40 Marvin Harrison	1.00	.45
❑ 41 Edgerrin James	1.50	.70
❑ 42 Peyton Manning	2.50	1.10
❑ 43 Mark Brunell	1.00	.45
❑ 44 Keenan McCardell	.60	.25
❑ 45 Jimmy Smith	.60	.25
❑ 46 Fred Taylor	1.00	.45
❑ 47 Derrick Alexander	.60	.25
❑ 48 Tony Gonzalez	.60	.25
❑ 49 Elvis Grbac	.60	.25
❑ 50 Damon Huard	1.00	.45
❑ 51 James Johnson	.40	.18
❑ 52 Dan Marino	3.00	1.35
❑ 53 O.J. McDuffie	.60	.25
❑ 54 Cris Carter	1.00	.45
❑ 55 Daunte Culpepper	1.25	.55
❑ 56 Jeff George	.60	.25
❑ 57 Randy Moss	2.00	.90
❑ 58 Robert Smith	1.00	.45
❑ 59 Drew Bledsoe	1.25	.55
❑ 60 Terry Glenn	.60	.25
❑ 61 Lawyer Milloy	.60	.25
❑ 62 Jeff Blake	.60	.25
❑ 63 Keith Poole	.40	.18
❑ 64 Ricky Williams	1.00	.45
❑ 65 Kerry Collins	.60	.25
❑ 66 Ike Hilliard	.60	.25
❑ 67 Amani Toomer	.40	.18
❑ 68 Wayne Chrebet	.60	.25
❑ 69 Keyshawn Johnson	1.00	.45
❑ 70 Ray Lucas	.60	.25
❑ 71 Curtis Martin	1.00	.45
❑ 72 Vinny Testaverde	.60	.25
❑ 73 Tim Brown	1.00	.45
❑ 74 Rich Gannon	1.00	.45
❑ 75 Napoleon Kaufman	.60	.25
❑ 76 Tyrone Wheatley	.60	.25
❑ 77 Donovan McNabb	1.50	.70
❑ 78 Torrance Small	.40	.18
❑ 79 Duce Staley	1.00	.45
❑ 80 Jerome Bettis	1.00	.45
❑ 81 Troy Edwards	.40	.18
❑ 82 Kordell Stewart	.60	.25
❑ 83 Isaac Bruce	1.00	.45
❑ 84 Marshall Faulk	1.25	.55
❑ 85 Torry Holt	1.00	.45
❑ 86 Kurt Warner	2.00	.90
❑ 87 Jim Harbaugh	.60	.25
❑ 88 Jermaine Fazande	.40	.18
❑ 89 Junior Seau	1.00	.45
❑ 90 Charlie Garner	.60	.25
❑ 91 Terrell Owens	1.00	.45
❑ 92 Jerry Rice	2.00	.90
❑ 93 Steve Young	1.25	.55
❑ 94 Sean Dawkins	.40	.18
❑ 95 Jon Kitna	1.00	.45
❑ 96 Derrick Mayes	.60	.25
❑ 97 Ricky Watters	.60	.25
❑ 98 Mike Alstott	1.00	.45
❑ 99 Warrick Dunn	1.00	.45
❑ 100 Jacquez Green	.40	.18
❑ 101 Shaun King	.40	.18
❑ 102 Kevin Dyson	.60	.25
❑ 103 Eddie George	1.00	.45
❑ 104 Jevon Kearse	1.00	.45
❑ 105 Steve McNair	1.00	.45
❑ 106 Stephen Davis	1.00	.45
❑ 107 Brad Johnson	1.00	.45
❑ 108 Michael Westbrook	.60	.25
❑ 109 Shaun Alexander RC	6.00	2.70
❑ 110 Tom Brady RC	30.00	13.50
❑ 111 Marc Bulger RC	5.00	2.20
❑ 112 Plaxico Burress RC	4.00	1.80
❑ 113 Giovanni Carmazzi RC	2.00	.90
❑ 114 Kwame Cavil RC	1.25	.55
❑ 115 Chris Cole RC	2.00	.90
❑ 116 Chris Coleman RC	2.50	1.10
❑ 117 Laveranues Coles RC	2.50	1.10
❑ 118 Ron Dayne RC	2.50	1.10
❑ 119 Reuben Droughns RC	3.00	1.35
❑ 120 Ron Dugans RC	1.25	.55
❑ 121 Danny Farmer RC	2.00	.90
❑ 122 Chafie Fields RC	1.25	.55
❑ 123 Joe Hamilton RC	2.00	.90
❑ 124 Todd Husak RC	2.50	1.10
❑ 125 Darrell Jackson RC	4.00	1.80
❑ 126 Thomas Jones RC	4.00	1.80
❑ 127 Jamal Lewis RC	6.00	2.70
❑ 128 Tee Martin RC	2.50	1.10
❑ 129 Rondell Mealey RC	1.25	.55
❑ 130 Sylvester Morris RC	2.00	.90
❑ 131 Chad Morton RC	2.50	1.10
❑ 132 Dennis Northcutt RC	2.50	1.10
❑ 133 Chad Pennington RC	10.00	4.50
❑ 134 Travis Prentice RC	2.00	.90
❑ 135 Tim Rattay RC	4.00	1.80
❑ 136 Chris Redman RC	2.00	.90
❑ 137 J.R. Redmond RC	2.00	.90
❑ 138 R.Jay Soward RC	2.00	.90
❑ 139 Shyrone Stith RC	2.50	1.10
❑ 140 Travis Taylor RC	2.50	1.10
❑ 141 Troy Walters RC	2.50	1.10
❑ 142 Peter Warrick RC	2.50	1.10
❑ 143 Dez White RC	2.50	1.10
❑ 144 Michael Wiley RC	2.00	.90
❑ S1 Jon Kitna Sample	2.00	.90

2001 Crown Royale

	Nm-Mt	Ex-Mt
COMP.SET w/o SP's (144)	25.00	7.50
❑ 1 David Boston	1.00	.30
❑ 2 Thomas Jones	.60	.18
❑ 3 Rob Moore	.60	.18
❑ 4 Michael Pittman	.40	.12
❑ 5 Jake Plummer	.60	.18
❑ 6 Jamal Anderson	1.00	.30
❑ 7 Chris Chandler	.60	.18
❑ 8 Tim Dwight	1.00	.30
❑ 9 Shawn Jefferson	.40	.12
❑ 10 Doug Johnson	.40	.12
❑ 11 Terance Mathis	.60	.18
❑ 12 Tony Banks	.60	.18
❑ 13 Trent Dilfer	.60	.18
❑ 14 Elvis Grbac	.60	.18
❑ 15 Priest Holmes	1.25	.35
❑ 16 Qadry Ismail	.60	.18
❑ 17 Jamal Lewis	1.50	.45
❑ 18 Ray Lewis	1.00	.30
❑ 19 Shannon Sharpe	.60	.18
❑ 20 Shawn Bryson	.40	.12
❑ 21 Rob Johnson	.60	.18
❑ 22 Eric Moulds	.60	.18
❑ 23 Peerless Price	.60	.18
❑ 24 Antowain Smith	.60	.18
❑ 25 Steve Beuerlein	.60	.18
❑ 26 Tim Biakabutuka	.60	.18
❑ 27 Patrick Jeffers	.60	.18
❑ 28 Muhsin Muhammad	.60	.18
❑ 29 James Allen	.60	.18
❑ 30 Bobby Engram	.40	.12
❑ 31 Cade McNown	.40	.12
❑ 32 Marcus Robinson	1.00	.30
❑ 33 Brian Urlacher	1.50	.45
❑ 34 Corey Dillon	1.00	.30
❑ 35 Jon Kitna	.60	.18
❑ 36 Akili Smith	.40	.12
❑ 37 Peter Warrick	1.00	.30
❑ 38 Tim Couch	.60	.18
❑ 39 Kevin Johnson	.60	.18
❑ 40 Travis Prentice	.40	.12
❑ 41 Troy Aikman	1.50	.45
❑ 42 Rocket Ismail	.60	.18

❑ 43 Emmitt Smith 2.00 .60
❑ 44 Mike Anderson 1.00 .30
❑ 45 Terrell Davis 1.00 .30
❑ 46 Olandis Gary .60 .18
❑ 47 Brian Griese 1.00 .30
❑ 48 Ed McCaffrey 1.00 .30
❑ 49 Rod Smith .60 .18
❑ 50 Charlie Batch 1.00 .30
❑ 51 Herman Moore .60 .18
❑ 52 Johnnie Morton .60 .18
❑ 53 James Stewart .60 .18
❑ 54 Brett Favre 3.00 .90
❑ 55 Antonio Freeman 1.00 .30
❑ 56 Ahman Green 1.00 .30
❑ 57 Dorsey Levens .60 .18
❑ 58 Bill Schroeder .60 .18
❑ 59 Marvin Harrison 1.00 .30
❑ 60 Edgerrin James 1.25 .35
❑ 61 Peyton Manning 2.50 .75
❑ 62 Jerome Pathon .60 .18
❑ 63 Mark Brunell 1.00 .30
❑ 64 Keenan McCardell .40 .12
❑ 65 Jimmy Smith .60 .18
❑ 66 Fred Taylor 1.00 .30
❑ 67 Derrick Alexander .60 .18
❑ 68 Tony Gonzalez .60 .18
❑ 69 Sylvester Morris .40 .12
❑ 70 Tony Richardson .40 .12
❑ 71 Jay Fiedler 1.00 .30
❑ 72 Oronde Gadsden .60 .18
❑ 73 Tony Martin .60 .18
❑ 74 James McKnight .60 .18
❑ 75 Lamar Smith .60 .18
❑ 76 Cris Carter 1.00 .30
❑ 77 Daunte Culpepper 1.00 .30
❑ 78 Randy Moss 2.00 .60
❑ 79 Robert Smith .60 .18
❑ 80 Drew Bledsoe 1.25 .35
❑ 81 Troy Brown .60 .18
❑ 82 Kevin Faulk .60 .18
❑ 83 Terry Glenn .60 .18
❑ 84 J.R. Redmond .40 .12
❑ 85 Jeff Blake .60 .18
❑ 86 Aaron Brooks .40 .12
❑ 87 Joe Horn .60 .18
❑ 88 Ricky Williams 1.00 .30
❑ 89 Tiki Barber .60 .18
❑ 90 Kerry Collins .60 .18
❑ 91 Ron Dayne 1.00 .30
❑ 92 Ike Hilliard .60 .18
❑ 93 Amani Toomer .40 .12
❑ 94 Wayne Chrebet .60 .18
❑ 95 Curtis Martin 1.00 .30
❑ 96 Chad Pennington 1.50 .45
❑ 97 Vinny Testaverde .60 .18
❑ 98 Dedric Ward .40 .12
❑ 99 Tim Brown 1.00 .30
❑ 100 Rich Gannon 1.00 .30
❑ 101 Napoleon Kaufman .60 .18
❑ 102 Andre Rison .60 .18
❑ 103 Tyrone Wheatley .60 .18
❑ 104 Charles Johnson .40 .12
❑ 105 Donovan McNabb 1.25 .35
❑ 106 Torrance Small .40 .12
❑ 107 Duce Staley 1.00 .30
❑ 108 Jerome Bettis 1.00 .30
❑ 109 Plaxico Burress 1.00 .30
❑ 110 Kordell Stewart .60 .18
❑ 111 Hines Ward 1.00 .30
❑ 112 Isaac Bruce 1.00 .30
❑ 113 Marshall Faulk 1.25 .35
❑ 114 Trent Green 1.00 .30
❑ 115 Az-Zahir Hakim .40 .12
❑ 116 Torry Holt 1.00 .30
❑ 117 Kurt Warner 2.00 .60
❑ 118 Curtis Conway .60 .18
❑ 119 Doug Flutie 1.00 .30
❑ 120 Jeff Graham .40 .12
❑ 121 Junior Seau 1.00 .30
❑ 122 Jeff Garcia 1.00 .30
❑ 123 Charlie Garner .60 .18
❑ 124 Terrell Owens 1.00 .30
❑ 125 Jerry Rice 2.00 .60
❑ 126 Shaun Alexander 1.25 .35
❑ 127 Darrell Jackson 1.00 .30
❑ 128 Ricky Watters .60 .18
❑ 129 Mike Alstott 1.00 .30
❑ 130 Warrick Dunn 1.00 .30
❑ 131 Brad Johnson 1.00 .30
❑ 132 Keyshawn Johnson 1.00 .30
❑ 133 Shaun King .40 .12
❑ 134 Ryan Leaf .60 .18
❑ 135 Warren Sapp .60 .18
❑ 136 Kevin Dyson .60 .18
❑ 137 Eddie George 1.00 .30
❑ 138 Jevon Kearse .60 .18
❑ 139 Derrick Mason .60 .18
❑ 140 Steve McNair 1.00 .30
❑ 141 Stephen Davis 1.00 .30
❑ 142 Jeff George .60 .18
❑ 143 Deion Sanders 1.00 .30
❑ 144 Michael Westbrook .60 .18
❑ 145 Anthony Thomas AUTO RC/250 50.00 15.00
❑ 146 Michael Vick AUTO RC/250 200.00 60.00
❑ 147 Chris Chambers AUTO RC/250 50.00 15.00
❑ 148 Michael Bennett AUTO RC/250 60.00 18.00
❑ 149 Chris Weinke AUTO RC/250 25.00 7.50
❑ 150 Drew Brees AUTO RC/250 60.00 18.00
❑ 151 LaDanianTomlinson AUTO RC/250 120.00 36.00
❑ 152 Marques Tuiasosopo AUTO RC/250 40.00 12.00
❑ 153 David Terrell AUTO RC/250 30.00 9.00
❑ 154 Rod Gardner AUTO RC/250 40.00 12.00
❑ 155 Dan Alexander/1750 RC 10.00 3.00
❑ 156 Brian Allen/1750 RC 6.00 1.80
❑ 157 David Allen/750 RC 12.00 3.60
❑ 158 Will Allen/1750 RC 6.00 1.80
❑ 159 Scotty Anderson RC/1000 8.00 2.40
❑ 160 Adam Archuleta/1750 RC 10.00 3.00
❑ 161 Jeff Backus/1750 RC 6.00 1.80
❑ 162 Alex Bannister/1000 RC 8.00 2.40
❑ 163 Kevan Barlow/750 RC 12.00 3.60
❑ 164 Gary Baxter/1750 RC 6.00 1.80
❑ 165 Josh Booty/500 RC 20.00 6.00
❑ 166 Larry Casher/1750 RC 6.00 1.80
❑ 167 Tay Cody/1750 RC 5.00 1.50
❑ 168 Jarrod Cooper/1750 RC 10.00 3.00
❑ 169 Ennis Davis/1750 RC 5.00 1.50
❑ 170 Leonard Davis/1750 RC 6.00 1.80
❑ 171 Tony Dixon/1750 RC 8.00 2.40
❑ 172 Tony Driver/1750 RC 10.00 3.00
❑ 173 Heath Evans/1750 RC 6.00 1.80
❑ 174 Jamar Fletcher/1750 RC 6.00 1.80
❑ 175 Derrick Gibson/1750 RC 6.00 1.80
❑ 176 Morlon Greenwood/1750 RC 6.00 1.80
❑ 177 Edgerton Hartwell/1750 RC 5.00 1.50
❑ 178 Tim Hasselbeck/500 RC 20.00 6.00
❑ 179 Todd Heap/1750 RC 10.00 3.00
❑ 180 Travis Henry/750 RC 20.00 6.00
❑ 181 Josh Heupel/500 RC 20.00 6.00
❑ 182 Sedrick Hodge/1750 RC 5.00 1.50
❑ 183 Jabari Holloway/1750 RC 6.00 1.80
❑ 184 Willie Howard/1750 RC 6.00 1.80
❑ 185 Steve Hutchinson/1750 RC 6.00 1.80
❑ 186 James Jackson/750 RC 12.00 3.60
❑ 187 Chad Johnson/1000 RC 25.00 7.50
❑ 188 Rudi Johnson/750 RC 25.00 7.50
❑ 189 LaMont Jordan/750 RC 15.00 4.50
❑ 190 Ben Leard/500 RC 12.00 3.60
❑ 191 Alex Lincoln/1750 RC 6.00 1.80
❑ 192 Torrance Marshall/1750 RC 10.00 3.00
❑ 193 Deuce McAllister RC/750 40.00 12.00
❑ 194 Jason McKinley/500 RC 12.00 3.60
❑ 195 Mike McMahon/500 RC 20.00 6.00
❑ 196 Snoop Minnis/1000 RC 8.00 2.40
❑ 197 Travis Minor/750 RC 12.00 3.60
❑ 198 Freddie Mitchell 12.00 3.60
RC/1000
❑ 199 Zeke Moreno/1750 RC 10.00 3.00
❑ 200 Quincy Morgan/1000 RC 12.00 3.60
❑ 201 Santana Moss/1000 RC 20.00 6.00
❑ 202 Bobby Newcombe RC/1000 8.00 2.40
❑ 203 Moran Norris/1750 RC 5.00 1.50
❑ 204 Tommy Polley/1750 RC 10.00 3.00
❑ 205 Ken-Yon Rambo RC/1000 8.00 2.40
❑ 206 Koren Robinson RC/1000 12.00 3.60
❑ 207 Sage Rosenfels/500 RC 20.00 6.00
❑ 208 John Schlech/1750t RC 5.00 1.50
❑ 209 Brandon Spoon/1750 RC 10.00 3.00
❑ 210 Michael Stone/1750 RC 5.00 1.50
❑ 211 Marcus Stroud/1750 RC 10.00 3.00
❑ 212 Vinny Sutherland RC/1000 8.00 2.40
❑ 213 Joe Tafoya/1750 RC 5.00 1.50
❑ 214 Clevan Thomas/1750 RC 5.00 1.50
❑ 215 Ja'Mar Toombs/1750 RC 6.00 1.80
❑ 216 Fred Wakefield/1750 RC 6.00 1.80
❑ 217 Reggie Wayne/1000 RC 20.00 6.00
❑ 218 Reggie White/750 RC 12.00 3.60

2002 Crown Royale

	Nm-Mt	Ex-Mt
COMPLETE SET (216)	200.00	60.00
COMP.SET w/o SP's (144)	50.00	15.00

❑ 1 David Boston 1.25 .35
❑ 2 Thomas Jones .75 .23
❑ 3 Jake Plummer .75 .23
❑ 4 Frank Sanders .50 .15
❑ 5 Jamal Anderson .75 .23
❑ 6 Warrick Dunn 1.25 .35
❑ 7 Brian Finneran .50 .15
❑ 8 Shawn Jefferson .50 .15
❑ 9 Michael Vick 4.00 1.20
❑ 10 Jeff Blake .75 .23
❑ 11 Jamal Lewis 1.25 .35
❑ 12 Ray Lewis 1.25 .35
❑ 13 Chris Redman .50 .15
❑ 14 Travis Taylor .75 .23
❑ 15 Drew Bledsoe 1.50 .45
❑ 16 Travis Henry 1.25 .35
❑ 17 Eric Moulds .75 .23
❑ 18 Peerless Price .75 .23
❑ 19 Isaac Byrd .50 .15
❑ 20 Muhsin Muhammad .75 .23
❑ 21 Lamar Smith .75 .23
❑ 22 Chris Weinke .75 .23
❑ 23 Marty Booker .50 .15
❑ 24 Jim Miller .50 .15
❑ 25 Marcus Robinson .75 .23
❑ 26 Anthony Thomas 1.25 .35
❑ 27 Brian Urlacher 2.00 .60
❑ 28 Corey Dillon .75 .23
❑ 29 Gus Frerotte .50 .15
❑ 30 Jon Kitna .75 .23
❑ 31 Darnay Scott .50 .15
❑ 32 Peter Warrick .75 .23
❑ 33 Tim Couch .75 .23
❑ 34 James Jackson .50 .15
❑ 35 Kevin Johnson .75 .23
❑ 36 Quincy Morgan .50 .15
❑ 37 Quincy Carter .75 .23
❑ 38 Joey Galloway .75 .23

- ❑ 39 Rocket Ismail .75 .23
- ❑ 40 Emmitt Smith 3.00 .90
- ❑ 41 Mike Anderson 1.25 .35
- ❑ 42 Terrell Davis 1.25 .35
- ❑ 43 Brian Griese 1.25 .35
- ❑ 44 Ed McCaffrey 1.25 .35
- ❑ 45 Rod Smith .75 .23
- ❑ 46 Germane Crowell .50 .15
- ❑ 47 Az-Zahir Hakim .50 .15
- ❑ 48 Mike McMahon 1.25 .35
- ❑ 49 Bill Schroeder .75 .23
- ❑ 50 Brett Favre 3.00 .90
- ❑ 51 Bubba Franks .75 .23
- ❑ 52 Antonio Freeman 1.25 .35
- ❑ 53 Terry Glenn .75 .23
- ❑ 54 Ahman Green 1.25 .35
- ❑ 55 James Allen .75 .23
- ❑ 56 Corey Bradford .50 .15
- ❑ 57 Kent Graham .50 .15
- ❑ 58 Jermaine Lewis .50 .15
- ❑ 59 Marvin Harrison 1.25 .35
- ❑ 60 Edgerrin James 1.50 .45
- ❑ 61 Peyton Manning 2.50 .75
- ❑ 62 Dominic Rhodes .75 .23
- ❑ 63 Reggie Wayne .75 .23
- ❑ 64 Mark Brunell 1.25 .35
- ❑ 65 Patrick Johnson .50 .15
- ❑ 66 Jimmy Smith .75 .23
- ❑ 67 Fred Taylor 1.25 .35
- ❑ 68 Tony Gonzalez .75 .23
- ❑ 69 Trent Green .75 .23
- ❑ 70 Priest Holmes 1.50 .45
- ❑ 71 Johnnie Morton .75 .23
- ❑ 72 Chris Chambers 1.25 .35
- ❑ 73 Jay Fiedler .75 .23
- ❑ 74 James McKnight .50 .15
- ❑ 75 Ricky Williams 1.25 .35
- ❑ 76 Derrick Alexander .75 .23
- ❑ 77 Michael Bennett .75 .23
- ❑ 78 Daunte Culpepper 1.25 .35
- ❑ 79 Randy Moss 2.50 .75
- ❑ 80 Tom Brady 3.00 .90
- ❑ 81 Troy Brown .75 .23
- ❑ 82 Kevin Faulk .75 .23
- ❑ 83 David Patten .50 .15
- ❑ 84 Antowain Smith .75 .23
- ❑ 85 Aaron Brooks 1.25 .35
- ❑ 86 Joe Horn .75 .23
- ❑ 87 Deuce McAllister 1.50 .45
- ❑ 88 Jerome Pathon .50 .15
- ❑ 89 Tiki Barber .75 .23
- ❑ 90 Kerry Collins .75 .23
- ❑ 91 Ron Dayne .75 .23
- ❑ 92 Ike Hilliard .75 .23
- ❑ 93 Michael Strahan .75 .23
- ❑ 94 Amani Toomer .75 .23
- ❑ 95 Wayne Chrebet .75 .23
- ❑ 96 Laveranues Coles .75 .23
- ❑ 97 Curtis Martin 1.25 .35
- ❑ 98 Vinny Testaverde .75 .23
- ❑ 99 Tim Brown 1.25 .35
- ❑ 100 Rich Gannon 1.25 .35
- ❑ 101 Charlie Garner .75 .23
- ❑ 102 Jerry Rice 2.50 .75
- ❑ 103 Tyrone Wheatley .75 .23
- ❑ 104 Charles Woodson .75 .23
- ❑ 105 Donovan McNabb 1.50 .45
- ❑ 106 Todd Pinkston .75 .23
- ❑ 107 Duce Staley 1.25 .35
- ❑ 108 James Thrash .75 .23
- ❑ 109 Jerome Bettis 1.25 .35
- ❑ 110 Plaxico Burress .75 .23
- ❑ 111 Kordell Stewart .75 .23
- ❑ 112 Hines Ward 1.25 .35
- ❑ 113 Isaac Bruce 1.25 .35
- ❑ 114 Marshall Faulk 1.25 .35
- ❑ 115 Torry Holt 1.25 .35
- ❑ 116 Kurt Warner 1.25 .35
- ❑ 117 Drew Brees 1.25 .35
- ❑ 118 Curtis Conway .50 .15
- ❑ 119 Tim Dwight .75 .23
- ❑ 120 Doug Flutie 1.25 .35
- ❑ 121 Junior Seau 1.25 .35
- ❑ 122 LaDainian Tomlinson 2.00 .60
- ❑ 123 Jeff Garcia 1.25 .35
- ❑ 124 Garrison Hearst .75 .23
- ❑ 125 Terrell Owens 1.25 .35
- ❑ 126 J.J. Stokes .50 .15
- ❑ 127 Shaun Alexander 1.25 .35
- ❑ 128 Trent Dilfer .75 .23
- ❑ 129 Darrell Jackson .75 .23
- ❑ 130 Koren Robinson .75 .23
- ❑ 131 Mike Alstott 1.25 .35
- ❑ 132 Brad Johnson .75 .23
- ❑ 133 Keyshawn Johnson 1.25 .35
- ❑ 134 Keenan McCardell .50 .15
- ❑ 135 Michael Pittman .50 .15
- ❑ 136 Warren Sapp .75 .23
- ❑ 137 Kevin Dyson .75 .23
- ❑ 138 Eddie George 1.25 .35
- ❑ 139 Derrick Mason .75 .23
- ❑ 140 Steve McNair 1.25 .35
- ❑ 141 Stephen Davis .75 .23
- ❑ 142 Rod Gardner .75 .23
- ❑ 143 Jacquez Green .50 .15
- ❑ 144 Shane Matthews .50 .15
- ❑ 145 Jason McAddley RC 2.50 .75
- ❑ 146 Josh McCown RC 4.00 1.20
- ❑ 147 Josh Scobey RC 3.00 .90
- ❑ 148 T.J. Duckett RC 5.00 1.50
- ❑ 149 Kahlil Hill RC 2.50 .75
- ❑ 150 Kurt Kittner RC 2.50 .75
- ❑ 151 Ron Johnson RC 2.50 .75
- ❑ 152 Tellis Redmon RC 2.50 .75
- ❑ 153 Chester Taylor RC 3.00 .90
- ❑ 154 Josh Reed RC 3.00 .90
- ❑ 155 Randy Fasani RC 2.50 .75
- ❑ 156 DeShaun Foster RC 3.00 .90
- ❑ 157 Julius Peppers RC 6.00 1.80
- ❑ 158 Adrian Peterson RC 3.00 .90
- ❑ 159 Andre Davis RC 3.00 .90
- ❑ 160 William Green RC 5.00 1.50
- ❑ 161 Antonio Bryant RC 3.00 .90
- ❑ 162 Woody Dantzler RC 3.00 .90
- ❑ 163 Ennis Haywood RC 2.50 .75
- ❑ 164 Chad Hutchinson RC 3.00 .90
- ❑ 165 Jamar Martin RC 2.50 .75
- ❑ 166 Roy Williams RC 8.00 2.40
- ❑ 167 Herb Haygood RC 1.50 .45
- ❑ 168 Ashley Lelie RC 6.00 1.80
- ❑ 169 Clinton Portis RC 10.00 3.00
- ❑ 170 Eddie Drummond RC 2.50 .75
- ❑ 171 Joey Harrington RC 10.00 3.00
- ❑ 172 Luke Staley RC 2.50 .75
- ❑ 173 Craig Nall RC 3.00 .90
- ❑ 174 Javon Walker RC 6.00 1.80
- ❑ 175 Jarrod Baxter RC 2.50 .75
- ❑ 176 David Carr RC 10.00 3.00
- ❑ 177 Delvon Flowers RC 2.50 .75
- ❑ 178 Jabar Gaffney RC 3.00 .90
- ❑ 179 Jonathan Wells RC 3.00 .90
- ❑ 180 David Garrard RC 3.00 .90
- ❑ 181 John Henderson RC 3.00 .90
- ❑ 182 Omar Easy RC 3.00 .90
- ❑ 183 Leonard Henry RC 2.50 .75
- ❑ 184 Atrews Bell RC 1.50 .45
- ❑ 185 Deion Branch RC 6.00 1.80
- ❑ 186 Rohan Davey RC 3.00 .90
- ❑ 187 Daniel Graham RC 3.00 .90
- ❑ 188 Antwoine Womack RC 2.50 .75
- ❑ 189 J.T. O'Sullivan RC 2.50 .75
- ❑ 190 Donte Stallworth RC 6.00 1.80
- ❑ 191 Tim Carter RC 2.50 .75
- ❑ 192 Daryl Jones RC 2.50 .75
- ❑ 193 Jeremy Shockey RC 10.00 3.00
- ❑ 194 Ronald Curry RC 3.00 .90
- ❑ 195 Napoleon Harris RC 3.00 .90
- ❑ 196 Larry Ned RC 2.50 .75
- ❑ 197 Freddie Milons RC 2.50 .75
- ❑ 198 Lito Sheppard RC 3.00 .90
- ❑ 199 Brian Westbrook RC 5.00 1.50
- ❑ 200 Lee Mays RC 2.50 .75
- ❑ 201 Antwaan Randle El RC 4.00 1.20
- ❑ 202 Eric Crouch RC 5.00 1.50
- ❑ 203 Lamar Gordon RC 3.00 .90
- ❑ 204 Robert Thomas RC 3.00 .90
- ❑ 205 Seth Burford RC 2.50 .75
- ❑ 206 Reche Caldwell RC 3.00 .90
- ❑ 207 Quentin Jammer RC 3.00 .90
- ❑ 208 Brandon Doman RC 3.00 .90
- ❑ 209 Maurice Morris RC 3.00 .90
- ❑ 210 Jerramy Stevens RC 3.00 .90
- ❑ 211 Travis Stephens RC 2.50 .75
- ❑ 212 Marquise Walker RC 2.50 .75
- ❑ 213 Jake Schifino RC 2.50 .75
- ❑ 214 Ladell Betts RC 3.00 .90
- ❑ 215 Patrick Ramsey RC 6.00 1.80
- ❑ 216 Cliff Russell RC 2.50 .75

2000 Dominion

	Nm-Mt	Ex-Mt
COMPLETE SET (243)	30.00	13.50
❑ 1 Tim Couch	.30	.14
❑ 2 Byron Hanspard	.20	.09
❑ 3 Jay Riemersma	.20	.09
❑ 4 Cade McNown	.20	.09
❑ 5 Darnay Scott	.30	.14
❑ 6 Emmitt Smith	1.00	.45
❑ 7 Rod Smith	.30	.14
❑ 8 James Stewart	.30	.14
❑ 9 Marvin Harrison	.50	.23
❑ 10 Keenan McCardell	.30	.14
❑ 11 Andre Rison	.30	.14
❑ 12 Jeff George	.30	.14
❑ 13 Terry Glenn	.30	.14
❑ 14 Cam Cleeland	.20	.09
❑ 15 Curtis Martin	.50	.23
❑ 16 Troy Edwards	.20	.09
❑ 17 Mikhael Ricks	.20	.09
❑ 18 Joey Galloway	.30	.14
❑ 19 Az-Zahir Hakim	.30	.14
❑ 20 Mike Alstott	.50	.23
❑ 21 Samari Rolle	.20	.09
❑ 22 Michael Pittman	.20	.09
❑ 23 Tony Banks	.30	.14
❑ 24 Bruce Smith	.30	.14
❑ 25 Curtis Enis	.20	.09
❑ 26 Jake Plummer	.30	.14
❑ 27 Darren Woodson	.20	.09
❑ 28 Bill Romanowski	.20	.09
❑ 29 Antonio Freeman	.50	.23
❑ 30 Terrence Wilkins	.20	.09
❑ 31 Kevin Hardy	.20	.09
❑ 32 Peerless Price	.50	.23
❑ 33 Cris Carter	.50	.23
❑ 34 Willie McGinest	.20	.09
❑ 35 Kerry Collins	.30	.14
❑ 36 Bryan Cox	.20	.09
❑ 37 Tyrone Wheatley	.30	.14
❑ 38 Jason Sehorn	.20	.09
❑ 39 Jerry Rice	1.00	.45
❑ 40 Christian Fauria	.20	.09
❑ 41 Kevin Carter	.20	.09
❑ 42 John Lynch	.30	.14
❑ 43 Brad Johnson	.50	.23
❑ 44 David Boston	.50	.23
❑ 45 Peter Boulware	.20	.09
❑ 46 Muhsin Muhammad	.30	.14
❑ 47 Bobby Engram	.30	.14
❑ 48 Kevin Johnson	.50	.23
❑ 49 Charlie Batch	.50	.23
❑ 50 Dorsey Levens	.30	.14
❑ 51 Cornelius Bennett	.20	.09
❑ 52 Kyle Brady	.20	.09
❑ 53 Damon Huard	.50	.23
❑ 54 Robert Smith	.50	.23

No.	Player	Nm-Mt	Ex-Mt
55	Ty Law	.30	.14
56	Amani Toomer	.30	.14
57	Aaron Glenn	.20	.09
58	Donovan McNabb	.75	.35
59	Levon Kirkland	.20	.09
60	Terrell Owens	.50	.23
61	Sam Adams	.20	.09
62	London Fletcher RC	.30	.14
63	Steve McNair	.50	.23
64	Stephen Davis	.50	.23
65	Daunte Culpepper	.60	.25
66	Andre Wadsworth	.20	.09
67	Priest Holmes	.60	.25
68	Patrick Jeffers	.50	.23
69	Walt Harris	.20	.09
70	Darrin Chiaverini	.20	.09
71	Dat Nguyen	.20	.09
72	Robert Porcher	.20	.09
73	Bill Schroeder	.30	.14
74	Tyrone Poole	.20	.09
75	Bryce Paup	.20	.09
76	O.J. McDuffie	.30	.14
77	Jake Reed	.30	.14
78	Ike Hilliard	.30	.14
79	Victor Green	.20	.09
80	Duce Staley	.50	.23
81	Amos Zereoue	.50	.23
82	Charlie Garner	.30	.14
83	Shawn Springs	.20	.09
84	Shaun King	.20	.09
85	Eddie George	.50	.23
86	Michael Westbrook	.30	.14
87	Ricky Williams	.50	.23
88	Chris Chandler	.30	.14
89	Chris McAlister	.20	.09
90	Steve Beuerlein	.30	.14
91	Marty Booker	.30	.14
92	Karim Abdul-Jabbar	.30	.14
93	Brian Griese	.50	.23
94	Germane Crowell	.20	.09
95	Mark Chmura	.20	.09
96	E.G. Green	.20	.09
97	Elvis Grbac	.30	.14
98	Tony Martin	.30	.14
99	John Randle	.30	.14
100	Michael Strahan	.30	.14
101	Tim Brown	.50	.23
102	Torrance Small	.20	.09
103	Junior Seau	.50	.23
104	Bryant Young	.20	.09
105	Kurt Warner	1.00	.45
106	Trent Dilfer	.30	.14
107	Kevin Dyson	.30	.14
108	Stephen Alexander	.20	.09
109	Tim Dwight	.50	.23
110	Rob Johnson	.30	.14
111	Tim Biakabutuka	.30	.14
112	Akili Smith	.20	.09
113	Terry Kirby	.20	.09
114	Terrell Davis	.50	.23
115	Herman Moore	.30	.14
116	Vonnie Holliday	.20	.09
117	Mark Brunell	.50	.23
118	Derrick Alexander	.30	.14
119	Oronde Gadsden	.30	.14
120	Ed McDaniel	.20	.09
121	Eddie Kennison	.30	.14
122	Jessie Armstead	.20	.09
123	Charles Woodson	.30	.14
124	Troy Vincent	.20	.09
125	Jeff Garcia	.50	.23
126	Marshall Faulk	.60	.25
127	Jacquez Green	.20	.09
128	Frank Wycheck	.20	.09
129	Champ Bailey	.30	.14
130	Natrone Means	.20	.09
131	Jamal Anderson	.50	.23
132	Doug Flutie	.50	.23
133	Michael Bates	.20	.09
134	Corey Dillon	.50	.23
135	Corey Fuller	.20	.09
136	Olandis Gary	.50	.23
137	Johnnie Morton	.30	.14
138	Peyton Manning	1.25	.55
139	Fred Taylor	.50	.23
140	Tony Gonzalez	.30	.14
141	Zach Thomas	.50	.23
142	Drew Bledsoe	.60	.25
143	Keith Poole	.20	.09
144	Vinny Testaverde	.30	.14
145	Rich Gannon	.50	.23
146	Jeremiah Trotter RC	1.50	.70
147	Freddie Jones	.20	.09
148	Jon Kitna	.50	.23
149	Isaac Bruce	.50	.23
150	Warrick Dunn	.50	.23
151	Yancey Thigpen	.20	.09
152	Darrell Green	.20	.09
153	Terance Mathis	.30	.14
154	Eric Moulds	.50	.23
155	Wesley Walls	.20	.09
156	Carl Pickens	.30	.14
157	Troy Aikman	1.00	.45
158	Dwayne Carswell	.20	.09
159	David Sloan	.20	.09
160	Edgerrin James	.75	.35
161	Jimmy Smith	.30	.14
162	Tamarick Vanover	.20	.09
163	Sam Madison	.20	.09
164	Tony Simmons	.20	.09
165	Andre Hastings	.20	.09
166	Keyshawn Johnson	.50	.23
167	Napoleon Kaufman	.30	.14
168	Hines Ward	.50	.23
169	Jeff Graham	.20	.09
170	Derrick Mayes	.30	.14
171	Torry Holt	.50	.23
172	Blaine Bishop	.20	.09
173	Rob Moore	.30	.14
174	Pat Johnson	.20	.09
175	Antowain Smith	.30	.14
176	Marcus Robinson	.50	.23
177	Takeo Spikes	.20	.09
178	Rocket Ismail	.30	.14
179	Ed McCaffrey	.50	.23
180	Brett Favre	1.50	.70
181	Ken Dilger	.20	.09
182	Carnell Lake	.20	.09
183	Cris Dishman	.20	.09
184	Randy Moss	1.00	.45
185	Lawyer Milloy	.30	.14
186	Jake Delhomme RC	2.50	1.10
187	Wayne Chrebet	.30	.14
188	Darrell Russell	.20	.09
189	Jerome Bettis	.50	.23
190	Steve Young	.60	.25
191	Ricky Watters	.30	.14
192	Grant Wistrom	.20	.09
193	Warren Sapp	.30	.14
194	Jevon Kearse	.50	.23
195	James Jett	.20	.09
196	Courtney Brown RC	.60	.25
197	Peter Warrick RC	.60	.25
198	Thomas Jones RC	1.00	.45
199	Sylvester Morris RC	.40	.18
200	Chad Pennington RC	2.50	1.10
201	Ron Dayne RC	.60	.25
202	Todd Pinkston RC	.60	.25
203	Deon Dyer RC	.40	.18
204	Chris Redman RC	.40	.18
205	Jerry Porter RC	.75	.35
206	Michael Wiley RC	.40	.18
207	J.R. Redmond RC	.40	.18
208	Dennis Northcutt RC	.60	.25
209	Gari Scott RC	.40	.18
210	Anthony Lucas RC	.40	.18
211	Danny Farmer RC	.40	.18
212	Marcus Knight RC	.40	.18
213	Plaxico Burress RC	1.25	.55
215	Bubba Franks RC	.60	.25
216	Shaun Alexander RC	1.50	.70
217	Dez White RC	.60	.25
218	Mareno Philyaw RC	.40	.18
219	Travis Taylor RC	.60	.25
220	Kwame Cavil RC	.40	.18
221	Jamal Lewis RC	1.50	.70
222	Sebastian Janikowski RC	.60	.25
223	Shyrone Stith RC	.60	.25
224	Ron Dugans RC	.40	.18
225	Darrell Jackson RC	1.25	.55
227	Tee Martin RC	.60	.25
228	Tim Rattay RC	1.25	.55
229	Marc Bulger RC	1.25	.55
230	Doug Johnson RC	.60	.25
231	Joe Hamilton RC Todd Husak RC	.60	.25
232	Travis Prentice RC R.Jay Soward RC	.40	.18
233	Trung Canidate RC Reuben Droughns RC	.75	.35
234	Tom Brady RC Giovanni Carmazzi RC	10.00	4.50
235	Laveranues Coles RC Chafie Fields RC	.75	.35
236	Jarious Jackson RC Sherrod Gideon RC	.40	.18
237	Troy Walters RC Erron Kinney RC	.60	.25
238	Ronell Mealey RC Joey Goodspeed RC	.40	.18
239	Anthony Becht RC Quinton Spotwood RC	.60	.25
240	Deltha O'Neal RC Na'il Diggs RC	.40	.18
241	Corey Simon RC Chris Hovan RC	.60	.25
242	Brian Urlacher RC Corey Moore RC	2.50	1.10
243	Keith Bulluck RC Rob Morris RC	.60	.25
244	Raynoch Thompson RC Deon Grant RC	.40	.18
245	John Abraham RC Shaun Ellis RC	.60	.25
P1	Tim Couch Promo	1.00	.45

1999 Donruss

		Nm-Mt	Ex-Mt
COMPLETE SET (200)		100.00	45.00
COMP.SET w/o SP's (150)		20.00	9.00
1	Jake Plummer	.40	.18
2	Rob Moore	.40	.18
3	Adrian Murrell	.40	.18
4	Frank Sanders	.40	.18
5	Jamal Anderson	.60	.25
6	Tim Dwight	.40	.18
7	Terance Mathis	.40	.18
8	Chris Chandler	.40	.18
9	Byron Hanspard	.25	.11
10	Priest Holmes	1.00	.45
11	Jermaine Lewis	.40	.18
12	Errict Rhett	.40	.18
13	Doug Flutie	.60	.25
14	Eric Moulds	.60	.25
15	Antowain Smith	.60	.25
16	Thurman Thomas	.40	.18
17	Andre Reed	.40	.18
18	Bruce Smith	.40	.18
19	Tim Biakabutuka	.40	.18
20	Rae Carruth	.25	.11
21	Muhsin Muhammad	.40	.18
22	Curtis Enis	.25	.11
23	Curtis Conway	.40	.18
24	Bobby Engram	.40	.18
25	Corey Dillon	.60	.25
26	Carl Pickens	.40	.18

❑ 27 Jeff Blake	.40	.18
❑ 28 Darnay Scott	.40	.18
❑ 29 Ty Detmer	.40	.18
❑ 30 Leslie Shepherd	.25	.11
❑ 31 Emmitt Smith	1.25	.55
❑ 32 Troy Aikman	1.25	.55
❑ 33 Michael Irvin	.40	.18
❑ 34 Deion Sanders	.60	.25
❑ 35 Rocket Ismail	.40	.18
❑ 36 John Elway	2.00	.90
❑ 37 Terrell Davis	.60	.25
❑ 38 Ed McCaffrey	.40	.18
❑ 39 Shannon Sharpe	.40	.18
❑ 40 Rod Smith	.40	.18
❑ 41 Bubby Brister	.25	.11
❑ 42 Brian Griese	.60	.25
❑ 43 Barry Sanders	2.00	.90
❑ 44 Charlie Batch	.60	.25
❑ 45 Herman Moore	.40	.18
❑ 46 Germane Crowell	.25	.11
❑ 47 Johnnie Morton	.40	.18
❑ 48 Ron Rivers	.25	.11
❑ 49 Brett Favre	2.00	.90
❑ 50 Antonio Freeman	.60	.25
❑ 51 Dorsey Levens	.60	.25
❑ 52 Mark Chmura	.25	.11
❑ 53 Corey Bradford	.60	.25
❑ 54 Bill Schroeder	.60	.25
❑ 55 Peyton Manning	2.00	.90
❑ 56 Marvin Harrison	.60	.25
❑ 57 E.G. Green	.25	.11
❑ 58 Fred Taylor	.60	.25
❑ 59 Mark Brunell	.60	.25
❑ 60 Tavian Banks	.25	.11
❑ 61 Jimmy Smith	.40	.18
❑ 62 Keenan McCardell	.40	.18
❑ 63 Warren Moon	.60	.25
❑ 64 Derrick Alexander WR	.40	.18
❑ 65 Byron Bam Morris	.25	.11
❑ 66 Elvis Grbac	.40	.18
❑ 67 Andre Rison	.40	.18
❑ 68 Dan Marino	2.00	.90
❑ 69 Karim Abdul-Jabbar	.40	.18
❑ 70 O.J. McDuffie	.40	.18
❑ 71 Tony Martin	.25	.11
❑ 72 Randy Moss	1.50	.70
❑ 73 Cris Carter	.60	.25
❑ 74 Randall Cunningham	.60	.25
❑ 75 Robert Smith	.60	.25
❑ 76 Jeff George	.40	.18
❑ 77 Jake Reed	.40	.18
❑ 78 Terry Allen	.40	.18
❑ 79 Drew Bledsoe	.75	.35
❑ 80 Terry Glenn	.60	.25
❑ 81 Ben Coates	.40	.18
❑ 82 Tony Simmons	.25	.11
❑ 83 Cam Cleeland	.25	.11
❑ 84 Eddie Kennison	.40	.18
❑ 85 Kerry Collins	.25	.11
❑ 86 Ike Hilliard	.25	.11
❑ 87 Gary Brown	.25	.11
❑ 88 Joe Jurevicius	.40	.18
❑ 89 Kent Graham	.25	.11
❑ 90 Wayne Chrebet	.40	.18
❑ 91 Keyshawn Johnson	.60	.25
❑ 92 Curtis Martin	.60	.25
❑ 93 Vinny Testaverde	.40	.18
❑ 94 Tim Brown	.60	.25
❑ 95 Napoleon Kaufman	.60	.25
❑ 96 Charles Woodson	.60	.25
❑ 97 Tyrone Wheatley	.40	.18
❑ 98 Rich Gannon	.60	.25
❑ 99 Charles Johnson	.25	.11
❑ 100 Duce Staley	.60	.25
❑ 101 Kordell Stewart	.40	.18
❑ 102 Jerome Bettis	.60	.25
❑ 103 Hines Ward	.60	.25
❑ 104 Ryan Leaf	.60	.25
❑ 105 Natrone Means	.40	.18
❑ 106 Jim Harbaugh	.40	.18
❑ 107 Junior Seau	.60	.25
❑ 108 Mikhael Ricks	.25	.11
❑ 109 Jerry Rice	1.25	.55
❑ 110 Steve Young	.75	.35
❑ 111 Garrison Hearst	.40	.18
❑ 112 Terrell Owens	.60	.25
❑ 113 Lawrence Phillips	.40	.18
❑ 114 J.J. Stokes	.40	.18
❑ 115 Sean Dawkins	.25	.11
❑ 116 Derrick Mayes	.25	.11
❑ 117 Joey Galloway	.40	.18
❑ 118 Jon Kitna	.60	.25
❑ 119 Ahman Green	.60	.25
❑ 120 Ricky Watters	.40	.18
❑ 121 Isaac Bruce	.60	.25
❑ 122 Marshall Faulk	.75	.35
❑ 123 Az-Zahir Hakim	.25	.11
❑ 124 Warrick Dunn	.60	.25
❑ 125 Mike Alstott	.60	.25
❑ 126 Trent Dilfer	.40	.18
❑ 127 Reidel Anthony	.40	.18
❑ 128 Jacquez Green	.25	.11
❑ 129 Warren Sapp	.40	.18
❑ 130 Eddie George	.60	.25
❑ 131 Steve McNair	.60	.25
❑ 132 Kevin Dyson	.40	.18
❑ 133 Yancey Thigpen	.25	.11
❑ 134 Frank Wycheck	.25	.11
❑ 135 Stephen Davis	.60	.25
❑ 136 Brad Johnson	.60	.25
❑ 137 Skip Hicks	.25	.11
❑ 138 Michael Westbrook	.40	.18
❑ 139 Darrell Green	.25	.11
❑ 140 Albert Connell	.25	.11
❑ 141 Tim Couch RC	2.00	.90
❑ 142 Donovan McNabb RC	8.00	3.60
❑ 143 Akili Smith RC	1.50	.70
❑ 144 Edgerrin James RC	6.00	2.70
❑ 145 Ricky Williams RC	3.00	1.35
❑ 146 Torry Holt RC	4.00	1.80
❑ 147 Champ Bailey RC	2.50	1.10
❑ 148 David Boston RC	2.00	.90
❑ 149 Andy Katzenmoyer RC	1.50	.70
❑ 150 Chris McAlister RC	1.50	.70
❑ 151 Daunte Culpepper RC	6.00	2.70
❑ 152 Cade McNown RC	1.50	.70
❑ 153 Troy Edwards RC	1.50	.70
❑ 154 Kevin Johnson RC	2.00	.90
❑ 155 James Johnson RC	1.50	.70
❑ 156 Rob Konrad RC	1.50	.70
❑ 157 Jim Kleinsasser RC	2.00	.90
❑ 158 Kevin Faulk RC	2.00	.90
❑ 159 Joe Montgomery RC	1.50	.70
❑ 160 Shaun King RC	1.50	.70
❑ 161 Peerless Price RC	3.00	1.35
❑ 162 Mike Cloud RC	1.50	.70
❑ 163 Jermaine Fazande RC	1.50	.70
❑ 164 D'Wayne Bates RC	1.50	.70
❑ 165 Brock Huard RC	2.00	.90
❑ 166 Marty Booker RC	2.00	.90
❑ 167 Karsten Bailey RC	1.50	.70
❑ 168 Shawn Bryson RC	2.00	.90
❑ 169 Jeff Paulk RC	1.00	.45
❑ 170 Travis McGriff RC	1.00	.45
❑ 171 Amos Zereoue RC	2.00	.90
❑ 172 Craig Yeast RC	1.50	.70
❑ 173 Joe Germaine RC	1.50	.70
❑ 174 Dameane Douglas RC	1.50	.70
❑ 175 Brandon Stokley RC	2.50	1.10
❑ 176 Larry Parker RC	2.00	.90
❑ 177 Joel Makovicka RC	2.00	.90
❑ 178 Wane McGarity RC	1.00	.45
❑ 179 Na Brown RC	1.50	.70
❑ 180 Cecil Collins RC	1.00	.45
❑ 181 Nick Williams RC	1.50	.70
❑ 182 Charlie Rogers RC	1.50	.70
❑ 183 Darrin Chiaverini RC	1.50	.70
❑ 184 Terry Jackson RC	1.50	.70
❑ 185 De'Mond Parker RC	1.00	.45
❑ 186 Sedrick Irvin RC	1.00	.45
❑ 187 MarTay Jenkins RC	2.00	.90
❑ 188 Kurt Warner RC	12.00	5.50
❑ 189 Michael Bishop RC	2.00	.90
❑ 190 Sean Bennett RC	1.00	.45
❑ 191 Jamal Anderson CL	.25	.11
❑ 192 Eric Moulds CL	.25	.11
❑ 193 Terrell Davis CL	.60	.25
❑ 194 John Elway CL	.75	.35
❑ 195 Barry Sanders CL	.75	.35
❑ 196 Peyton Manning CL	.75	.35
❑ 197 Fred Taylor CL	.60	.25
❑ 198 Dan Marino CL	.75	.35
❑ 199 Randy Moss CL	.60	.25
❑ 200 Terrell Owens CL	.40	.18

2000 Donruss

	Nm-Mt	Ex-Mt
COMPLETE SET (250)	400.00	180.00
❑ 1 Jake Plummer	.30	.14
❑ 2 Frank Sanders	.30	.14
❑ 3 Rob Moore	.30	.14
❑ 4 David Boston	.50	.23
❑ 5 Tim Dwight	.50	.23
❑ 6 Jamal Anderson	.50	.23
❑ 7 Chris Chandler	.30	.14
❑ 8 Terance Mathis	.30	.14
❑ 9 Tony Banks	.30	.14
❑ 10 Jermaine Lewis	.30	.14
❑ 11 Shannon Sharpe	.30	.14
❑ 12 Trent Dilfer	.30	.14
❑ 13 Qadry Ismail	.30	.14
❑ 14 Eric Moulds	.50	.23
❑ 15 Doug Flutie	.50	.23
❑ 16 Antowain Smith	.30	.14
❑ 17 Jonathan Linton	.20	.09
❑ 18 Peerless Price	.50	.23
❑ 19 Rob Johnson	.30	.14
❑ 20 Natrone Means	.30	.14
❑ 21 Muhsin Muhammad	.30	.14
❑ 22 Wesley Walls	.30	.14
❑ 23 Tim Biakabutuka	.30	.14
❑ 24 Steve Beuerlein	.30	.14
❑ 25 Patrick Jeffers	.50	.23
❑ 26 Curtis Enis	.20	.09
❑ 27 Cade McNown	.20	.09
❑ 28 Bobby Engram	.30	.14
❑ 29 Marcus Robinson	.50	.23
❑ 30 Marty Booker	.30	.14
❑ 31 Corey Dillon	.50	.23
❑ 32 Darnay Scott	.30	.14
❑ 33 Carl Pickens	.30	.14
❑ 34 Akili Smith	.20	.09
❑ 35 Michael Basnight	.20	.09
❑ 36 Tim Couch	.30	.14
❑ 37 Kevin Johnson	.50	.23
❑ 38 Karim Abdul-Jabbar	.30	.14
❑ 39 Errict Rhett	.30	.14
❑ 40 Darrin Chiaverini	.20	.09
❑ 41 Emmitt Smith	1.00	.45
❑ 42 Troy Aikman	1.00	.45
❑ 43 Joey Galloway	.30	.14
❑ 44 Randall Cunningham	.50	.23
❑ 45 Michael Irvin	.30	.14
❑ 46 Rocket Ismail	.30	.14
❑ 47 Jason Tucker	.20	.09
❑ 48 Terrell Davis	.50	.23
❑ 49 John Elway	1.50	.70
❑ 50 Olandis Gary	.30	.14
❑ 51 Ed McCaffrey	.50	.23
❑ 52 Rod Smith	.30	.14
❑ 53 Brian Griese	.50	.23
❑ 54 Charlie Batch	.50	.23
❑ 55 Barry Sanders	1.25	.55
❑ 56 Herman Moore	.30	.14
❑ 57 Johnnie Morton	.30	.14
❑ 58 Germane Crowell	.20	.09

❑ 59 James Stewart	.30	.14
❑ 60 Brett Favre	1.50	.70
❑ 61 Dorsey Levens	.30	.14
❑ 62 Antonio Freeman	.50	.23
❑ 63 Corey Bradford	.30	.14
❑ 64 Bill Schroeder	.30	.14
❑ 65 E.G. Green	.20	.09
❑ 66 Peyton Manning	1.25	.55
❑ 67 Edgerrin James	.75	.35
❑ 68 Marvin Harrison	.50	.23
❑ 69 Terrence Wilkins	.20	.09
❑ 70 Mark Brunell	.50	.23
❑ 71 Fred Taylor	.50	.23
❑ 72 Keenan McCardell	.30	.14
❑ 73 Jimmy Smith	.30	.14
❑ 74 Warren Moon	.50	.23
❑ 75 Elvis Grbac	.30	.14
❑ 76 Tony Gonzalez	.30	.14
❑ 77 Dan Marino	1.50	.70
❑ 78 O.J. McDuffie	.30	.14
❑ 79 Tony Martin	.30	.14
❑ 80 James Johnson	.20	.09
❑ 81 Thurman Thomas	.30	.14
❑ 82 Randy Moss	1.00	.45
❑ 83 Daunte Culpepper	.60	.25
❑ 84 Cris Carter	.50	.23
❑ 85 Robert Smith	.50	.23
❑ 86 John Randle	.30	.14
❑ 87 Drew Bledsoe	.60	.25
❑ 88 Terry Glenn	.30	.14
❑ 89 Kevin Faulk	.30	.14
❑ 90 Ricky Williams	.50	.23
❑ 91 Jeff Blake	.30	.14
❑ 92 Jake Reed	.30	.14
❑ 93 Amani Toomer	.30	.14
❑ 94 Kerry Collins	.30	.14
❑ 95 Tiki Barber	.30	.14
❑ 96 Ike Hilliard	.30	.14
❑ 97 Curtis Martin	.50	.23
❑ 98 Vinny Testaverde	.30	.14
❑ 99 Wayne Chrebet	.30	.14
❑ 100 Ray Lucas	.30	.14
❑ 101 Charles Woodson	.30	.14
❑ 102 Napoleon Kaufman	.30	.14
❑ 103 Tim Brown	.50	.23
❑ 104 Tyrone Wheatley	.30	.14
❑ 105 Rich Gannon	.50	.23
❑ 106 Duce Staley	.50	.23
❑ 107 Donovan McNabb	.75	.35
❑ 108 Amos Zereoue	.50	.23
❑ 109 Kordell Stewart	.30	.14
❑ 110 Jerome Bettis	.50	.23
❑ 111 Troy Edwards	.20	.09
❑ 112 Ryan Leaf	.30	.14
❑ 113 Junior Seau	.50	.23
❑ 114 Jim Harbaugh	.30	.14
❑ 115 Jermaine Fazande	.20	.09
❑ 116 Curtis Conway	.30	.14
❑ 117 Steve Young	.60	.25
❑ 118 Jerry Rice	1.00	.45
❑ 119 Terrell Owens	.50	.23
❑ 120 Charlie Garner	.30	.14
❑ 121 Jeff Garcia	.50	.23
❑ 122 Jon Kitna	.50	.23
❑ 123 Derrick Mayes	.30	.14
❑ 124 Ricky Watters	.30	.14
❑ 125 Kurt Warner	1.00	.45
❑ 126 Marshall Faulk	.60	.25
❑ 127 Torry Holt	.50	.23
❑ 128 Az-Zahir Hakim	.30	.14
❑ 129 Isaac Bruce	.50	.23
❑ 130 Mike Alstott	.50	.23
❑ 131 Warrick Dunn	.50	.23
❑ 132 Shaun King	.20	.09
❑ 133 Keyshawn Johnson	.50	.23
❑ 134 Jacquez Green	.20	.09
❑ 135 Reidel Anthony	.30	.14
❑ 136 Warren Sapp	.30	.14
❑ 137 Eddie George	.50	.23
❑ 138 Steve McNair	.50	.23
❑ 139 Yancey Thigpen	.20	.09
❑ 140 Kevin Dyson	.30	.14
❑ 141 Frank Wycheck	.30	.14
❑ 142 Jevon Kearse	.50	.23
❑ 143 Stephen Davis	.50	.23
❑ 144 Skip Hicks	.20	.09
❑ 145 Brad Johnson	.50	.23
❑ 146 Bruce Smith	.30	.14
❑ 147 Michael Westbrook	.30	.14
❑ 148 Albert Connell	.20	.09
❑ 149 Jeff George	.30	.14
❑ 150 Deion Sanders	.50	.23
❑ 151 Courtney Brown RC	6.00	2.70
❑ 152 Corey Simon RC	6.00	2.70
❑ 153 Brian Urlacher RC	25.00	11.00
❑ 154 Shaun Ellis RC	6.00	2.70
❑ 155 John Abraham RC	6.00	2.70
❑ 156 Deltha O'Neal RC	6.00	2.70
❑ 157 Ahmed Plummer RC	6.00	2.70
❑ 158 Chris Hovan RC	5.00	2.20
❑ 159 Rob Morris RC	5.00	2.20
❑ 160 Keith Bulluck RC	6.00	2.70
❑ 161 Darren Howard RC	5.00	2.20
❑ 162 John Engelberger RC	5.00	2.20
❑ 163 Raynoch Thompson RC	5.00	2.20
❑ 164 Cornelius Griffin RC	5.00	2.20
❑ 165 William Bartee RC	5.00	2.20
❑ 166 Fred Robbins RC	3.00	1.35
❑ 167 Micheal Boireau RC	3.00	1.35
❑ 168 Brandon Short RC	5.00	2.20
❑ 169 Jacoby Shepherd RC	3.00	1.35
❑ 170 Peter Warrick RC	6.00	2.70
❑ 171 Jamal Lewis RC	15.00	6.75
❑ 172 Thomas Jones RC	10.00	4.50
❑ 173 Plaxico Burress RC	12.00	5.50
❑ 174 Travis Taylor RC	6.00	2.70
❑ 175 Ron Dayne RC	6.00	2.70
❑ 176 Bubba Franks RC	6.00	2.70
❑ 177 Sebastian Janikowski RC	6.00	2.70
❑ 178 Chad Pennington RC	25.00	11.00
❑ 179 Shaun Alexander RC	15.00	6.75
❑ 180 Sylvester Morris RC	5.00	2.20
❑ 181 Anthony Becht RC	6.00	2.70
❑ 182 R.Jay Soward RC	5.00	2.20
❑ 183 Trung Canidate RC	5.00	2.20
❑ 184 Dennis Northcutt RC	6.00	2.70
❑ 185 Todd Pinkston RC	6.00	2.70
❑ 186 Jerry Porter RC	8.00	3.60
❑ 187 Travis Prentice RC	5.00	2.20
❑ 188 Giovanni Carmazzi RC	5.00	2.20
❑ 189 Ron Dugans RC	3.00	1.35
❑ 190 Erron Kinney RC	6.00	2.70
❑ 191 Dez White RC	6.00	2.70
❑ 192 Chris Cole RC	5.00	2.20
❑ 193 Ron Dixon RC	5.00	2.20
❑ 194 Chris Redman RC	5.00	2.20
❑ 195 J.R. Redmond RC	5.00	2.20
❑ 196 Laveranues Coles RC	8.00	3.60
❑ 197 JaJuan Dawson RC	3.00	1.35
❑ 198 Darrell Jackson RC	12.00	5.50
❑ 199 Reuben Droughns RC	8.00	3.60
❑ 200 Doug Chapman RC	5.00	2.20
❑ 201 Terrelle Smith RC	5.00	2.20
❑ 202 Curtis Keaton RC	5.00	2.20
❑ 203 Gari Scott RC	3.00	1.35
❑ 204 Danny Farmer RC	5.00	2.20
❑ 205 Hank Poteat RC	5.00	2.20
❑ 206 Ben Kelly RC	3.00	1.35
❑ 207 Corey Moore RC	3.00	1.35
❑ 208 Na'il Diggs RC	5.00	2.20
❑ 209 Aaron Shea RC	5.00	2.20
❑ 210 Trevor Gaylor RC	5.00	2.20
❑ 211 Julian Peterson RC	6.00	2.70
❑ 212 Frank Moreau RC	5.00	2.20
❑ 213 Deon Dyer RC	5.00	2.20
❑ 214 Avion Black RC	5.00	2.20
❑ 215 Paul Smith RC	5.00	2.20
❑ 216 Michael Wiley RC	5.00	2.20
❑ 217 Dante Hall RC	12.00	5.50
❑ 218 Mike Brown RC	10.00	4.50
❑ 219 Sammy Morris RC	5.00	2.20
❑ 220 Billy Volek RC	10.00	4.50
❑ 221 Tee Martin RC	6.00	2.70
❑ 222 Troy Walters RC	6.00	2.70
❑ 223 Chad Morton RC	6.00	2.70
❑ 224 Erik Flowers RC	5.00	2.20
❑ 225 Ronney Jenkins RC	5.00	2.20
❑ 226 Thomas Hamner RC	3.00	1.35
❑ 227 Mareno Philyaw RC	3.00	1.35
❑ 228 James Williams RC	5.00	2.20
❑ 229 Mike Anderson RC		
❑ 230 Tom Brady RC	80.00	36.00
❑ 231 Mike Green RC	5.00	2.20
❑ 232 Todd Husak RC	6.00	2.70
❑ 233 Tim Rattay RC	12.00	5.50
❑ 234 Jarious Jackson RC	5.00	2.20
❑ 235 Joe Hamilton RC	5.00	2.20
❑ 236 Shyrone Stith RC	5.00	2.20
❑ 237 Rondell Mealey RC	3.00	1.35
❑ 238 Demario Brown RC	3.00	1.35
❑ 239 Chris Coleman RC	6.00	2.70
❑ 240 Dwayne Goodrich RC	3.00	1.35
❑ 241 Drew Haddad RC	3.00	1.35
❑ 242 Doug Johnson RC	6.00	2.70
❑ 243 Windrell Hayes RC	5.00	2.20
❑ 244 Charles Lee RC	3.00	1.35
❑ 245 Kevin McDougal RC	5.00	2.20
❑ 246 Spergon Wynn RC	5.00	2.20
❑ 247 Shockmain Davis RC	3.00	1.35
❑ 248 Jamel White RC	5.00	2.20
❑ 249 Bashir Yamini RC	3.00	1.35
❑ 250 Kwame Cavil RC	3.00	1.35

2000 Donruss Rookie Gridiron Kings Studio Autographs

	Nm-Mt	Ex-Mt
❑ 1 Peter Warrick	40.00	18.00
❑ 2 Jamal Lewis	80.00	36.00
❑ 3 Thomas Jones	40.00	18.00
❑ 4 Plaxico Burress	60.00	27.00
❑ 5 Travis Taylor	40.00	18.00
❑ 6 Ron Dayne	40.00	18.00
❑ 7 Chad Pennington	120.00	55.00
❑ 8 Shaun Alexander EXCH		
❑ 9 Sylvester Morris EXCH		
❑ 10 Chris Redman	30.00	13.50

2002 Donruss

	Nm-Mt	Ex-Mt
COMPLETE SET (300)	150.00	45.00
COMP.SET w/o SP's (100)	20.00	6.00
❑ 1 Jake Plummer	.30	.09
❑ 2 David Boston	.50	.15
❑ 3 MarTay Jenkins	.20	.06
❑ 4 Thomas Jones	.30	.09
❑ 5 Frank Sanders	.20	.06
❑ 6 Shawn Jefferson	.20	.06

❑ 7 Alge Crumpler .30 .09
❑ 8 Michael Vick 1.50 .45
❑ 9 Jamal Anderson .30 .09
❑ 10 Warrick Dunn .50 .15
❑ 11 Peter Boulware .20 .06
❑ 12 Jamal Lewis .50 .15
❑ 13 Jeff Blake .20 .06
❑ 14 Travis Taylor .30 .09
❑ 15 Ray Lewis .50 .15
❑ 16 Todd Heap .20 .06
❑ 17 Nate Clements .20 .06
❑ 18 Alex Van Pelt .20 .06
❑ 19 Reggie Germany .20 .06
❑ 20 Larry Centers .20 .06
❑ 21 Eric Moulds .30 .09
❑ 22 Travis Henry .50 .15
❑ 23 Wesley Walls .20 .06
❑ 24 Steve Smith .30 .09
❑ 25 Lamar Smith .30 .09
❑ 26 Patrick Jeffers .20 .06
❑ 27 Chris Weinke .30 .09
❑ 28 Muhsin Muhammad .30 .09
❑ 29 Marcus Robinson .30 .09
❑ 30 Jim Miller .20 .06
❑ 31 Anthony Thomas .50 .15
❑ 32 David Terrell .50 .15
❑ 33 Brian Urlacher .75 .23
❑ 34 Marty Booker .20 .06
❑ 35 Darnay Scott .20 .06
❑ 36 Jon Kitna .30 .09
❑ 37 Chad Johnson .50 .15
❑ 38 T.J. Houshmandzadeh .30 .09
❑ 39 Corey Dillon .30 .09
❑ 40 Peter Warrick .30 .09
❑ 41 Gerard Warren .20 .06
❑ 42 Anthony Henry .20 .06
❑ 43 Quincy Morgan .20 .06
❑ 44 JaJuan Dawson .20 .06
❑ 45 Tim Couch .30 .09
❑ 46 Kevin Johnson .30 .09
❑ 47 James Jackson .20 .06
❑ 48 La'Roi Glover .20 .06
❑ 49 Anthony Wright .20 .06
❑ 50 Rocket Ismail .30 .09
❑ 51 Troy Hambrick .20 .06
❑ 52 Emmitt Smith 1.25 .35
❑ 53 Quincy Carter .30 .09
❑ 54 Joey Galloway .30 .09
❑ 55 Shannon Sharpe .30 .09
❑ 56 Kevin Kasper .20 .06
❑ 57 Olandis Gary .30 .09
❑ 58 Brian Griese .50 .15
❑ 59 Rod Smith .30 .09
❑ 60 Terrell Davis .50 .15
❑ 61 Ed McCaffrey .50 .15
❑ 62 Mike Anderson .50 .15
❑ 63 Bill Schroeder .30 .09
❑ 64 Scotty Anderson .20 .06
❑ 65 Mike McMahon .50 .15
❑ 66 James Stewart .30 .09
❑ 67 Az-Zahir Hakim .20 .06
❑ 68 Germane Crowell .20 .06
❑ 69 Kabeer Gbaja-Biamila .20 .06
❑ 70 LeRoy Butler .20 .06
❑ 71 Antonio Freeman .50 .15
❑ 72 Bubba Franks .30 .09
❑ 73 Brett Favre 1.25 .35
❑ 74 Ahman Green .50 .15
❑ 75 Terry Glenn .30 .09
❑ 76 Jamie Sharper .20 .06
❑ 77 Tony Simmons .20 .06
❑ 78 James Allen .30 .09
❑ 79 Terrence Wilkins .20 .06
❑ 80 Dominic Rhodes .30 .09
❑ 81 Qadry Ismail .30 .09
❑ 82 Peyton Manning 1.00 .30
❑ 83 Edgerrin James .60 .18
❑ 84 Marvin Harrison .50 .15
❑ 85 Reggie Wayne .30 .09
❑ 86 Fred Taylor .50 .15
❑ 87 Elvis Joseph .20 .06
❑ 88 Mark Brunell .50 .15
❑ 89 Keenan McCardell .20 .06
❑ 90 Jimmy Smith .30 .09
❑ 91 Kyle Brady .20 .06
❑ 92 Derrick Alexander .30 .09
❑ 93 Johnnie Morton .30 .09
❑ 94 Trent Green .30 .09
❑ 95 Priest Holmes .60 .18
❑ 96 Tony Gonzalez .30 .09
❑ 97 Snoop Minnis .20 .06
❑ 98 Travis Minor .20 .06
❑ 99 Oronde Gadsden .30 .09
❑ 100 Jay Fiedler .30 .09
❑ 101 Chris Chambers .50 .15
❑ 102 Ricky Williams .50 .15
❑ 103 Zach Thomas .50 .15
❑ 104 Byron Chamberlain .20 .06
❑ 105 Todd Bouman .20 .06
❑ 106 Daunte Culpepper .50 .15
❑ 107 Michael Bennett .30 .09
❑ 108 Randy Moss 1.00 .30
❑ 109 Cris Carter .50 .15
❑ 110 David Patten .20 .06
❑ 111 Donald Hayes .20 .06
❑ 112 Tom Brady 1.25 .35
❑ 113 Antowain Smith .30 .09
❑ 114 Troy Brown .30 .09
❑ 115 Drew Bledsoe .60 .18
❑ 116 Bryan Cox .20 .06
❑ 117 Boo Williams .20 .06
❑ 118 Aaron Brooks .50 .15
❑ 119 Deuce McAllister .60 .18
❑ 120 Joe Horn .30 .09
❑ 121 Amani Toomer .30 .09
❑ 122 Ron Dayne .30 .09
❑ 123 Kerry Collins .30 .09
❑ 124 Ike Hilliard .30 .09
❑ 125 Tiki Barber .30 .09
❑ 126 Michael Strahan .30 .09
❑ 127 Chad Pennington .60 .18
❑ 128 Santana Moss .50 .15
❑ 129 LaMont Jordan .50 .15
❑ 130 Curtis Martin .50 .15
❑ 131 Wayne Chrebet .30 .09
❑ 132 Laveranues Coles .30 .09
❑ 133 Vinny Testaverde .30 .09
❑ 134 Charles Woodson .30 .09
❑ 135 Tyrone Wheatley .30 .09
❑ 136 Jerry Porter .20 .06
❑ 137 Rich Gannon .50 .15
❑ 138 Charlie Garner .30 .09
❑ 139 Tim Brown .50 .15
❑ 140 Jerry Rice 1.00 .30
❑ 141 James Thrash .30 .09
❑ 142 Todd Pinkston .30 .09
❑ 143 A.J. Feeley .50 .15
❑ 144 Donovan McNabb .60 .18
❑ 145 Duce Staley .50 .15
❑ 146 Freddie Mitchell .30 .09
❑ 147 Correll Buckhalter .30 .09
❑ 148 Casey Hampton .20 .06
❑ 149 Hines Ward .50 .15
❑ 150 Chris Fuamatu-Ma'afala .20 .06
❑ 151 Jerome Bettis .50 .15
❑ 152 Kordell Stewart .30 .09
❑ 153 Plaxico Burress .30 .09
❑ 154 Kendrell Bell .50 .15
❑ 155 Trevor Gaylor .20 .06
❑ 156 Curtis Conway .20 .06
❑ 157 Doug Flutie .50 .15
❑ 158 Drew Brees .50 .15
❑ 159 LaDainian Tomlinson .75 .23
❑ 160 Junior Seau .50 .15
❑ 161 Bryant Young .20 .06
❑ 162 Andre Carter .20 .06
❑ 163 Eric Johnson .20 .06
❑ 164 Jeff Garcia .50 .15
❑ 165 Garrison Hearst .30 .09
❑ 166 Terrell Owens .50 .15
❑ 167 Kevan Barlow .30 .09
❑ 168 Levon Kirkland .20 .06
❑ 169 Ricky Watters .20 .06
❑ 170 Trent Dilfer .30 .09
❑ 171 Shaun Alexander .50 .15
❑ 172 Koren Robinson .30 .09
❑ 173 Darrell Jackson .30 .09
❑ 174 Adam Archuleta .20 .06
❑ 175 Aeneas Williams .20 .06
❑ 176 Trung Canidate .30 .09
❑ 177 Kurt Warner .50 .15
❑ 178 Marshall Faulk .50 .15
❑ 179 Torry Holt .50 .15
❑ 180 Isaac Bruce .50 .15
❑ 181 John Lynch .30 .09
❑ 182 Joe Jurevicius .20 .06
❑ 183 Brad Johnson .30 .09
❑ 184 Rob Johnson .30 .09
❑ 185 Keyshawn Johnson .50 .15
❑ 186 Mike Alstott .50 .15
❑ 187 Warren Sapp .30 .09
❑ 188 Drew Bennett .50 .15
❑ 189 Frank Wycheck .20 .06
❑ 190 Kevin Dyson .30 .09
❑ 191 Steve McNair .50 .15
❑ 192 Eddie George .50 .15
❑ 193 Jevon Kearse .30 .09
❑ 194 Derrick Mason .30 .09
❑ 195 Champ Bailey .30 .09
❑ 196 Darrell Green .20 .06
❑ 197 Bruce Smith .20 .06
❑ 198 Jacquez Green .20 .06
❑ 199 Stephen Davis .30 .09
❑ 200 Rod Gardner .30 .09
❑ 201 David Carr RC 10.00 3.00
❑ 202 Joey Harrington RC 10.00 3.00
❑ 203 Patrick Ramsey RC 6.00 1.80
❑ 204 Kurt Kittner RC 2.50 .75
❑ 205 Rohan Davey RC 3.00 .90
❑ 206 Josh McCown RC 4.00 1.20
❑ 207 David Garrard RC 3.00 .90
❑ 208 Randy Fasani RC 2.50 .75
❑ 209 Atrews Bell RC 1.50 .45
❑ 210 Brandon Doman RC 3.00 .90
❑ 211 Eric Crouch RC 5.00 1.50
❑ 212 Woody Dantzler RC 3.00 .90
❑ 213 Chad Hutchinson RC 3.00 .90
❑ 214 Zak Kustok RC 3.00 .90
❑ 215 Ronald Curry RC 3.00 .90
❑ 216 William Green RC 5.00 1.50
❑ 217 T.J. Duckett RC 5.00 1.50
❑ 218 Clinton Portis RC 10.00 3.00
❑ 219 DeShaun Foster RC 3.00 .90
❑ 220 Lamar Gordon RC 3.00 .90
❑ 221 Jonathan Wells RC 3.00 .90
❑ 222 Adrian Peterson RC 3.00 .90
❑ 223 Ladell Betts RC 3.00 .90
❑ 224 Maurice Morris RC 3.00 .90
❑ 225 Brian Westbrook RC 5.00 1.50
❑ 226 Luke Staley RC 2.50 .75
❑ 227 Travis Stephens RC 2.50 .75
❑ 228 Craig Nall RC 3.00 .90
❑ 229 Chester Taylor RC 3.00 .90
❑ 230 Ken Simonton RC 1.50 .45
❑ 231 Verron Haynes RC 3.00 .90
❑ 232 Tellis Redmon RC 2.50 .75
❑ 233 J.T. O'Sullivan RC 2.50 .75
❑ 234 Major Applewhite RC 3.00 .90
❑ 235 Ricky Williams RC 2.50 .75
❑ 236 James Mungro RC 3.00 .90
❑ 237 Josh Scobey RC 3.00 .90
❑ 238 Najeh Davenport RC 3.00 .90
❑ 239 Dicenzo Miller RC 1.50 .45
❑ 240 Ennis Haywood RC 2.50 .75
❑ 241 Jabar Gaffney RC 3.00 .90
❑ 242 Antonio Bryant RC 3.00 .90
❑ 243 Donte Stallworth RC 6.00 1.80
❑ 244 Josh Reed RC 3.00 .90
❑ 245 Ashley Lelie RC 6.00 1.80
❑ 246 Reche Caldwell RC 3.00 .90
❑ 247 Marquise Walker RC 2.50 .75
❑ 248 Javon Walker RC 6.00 1.80
❑ 249 Andre Davis RC 3.00 .90
❑ 250 Antwaan Randle El RC 4.00 1.20
❑ 251 Kelly Campbell RC 2.50 .75
❑ 252 Cliff Russell RC 2.50 .75
❑ 253 Kahlil Hill RC 2.50 .75
❑ 254 Ron Johnson RC 2.50 .75
❑ 255 Deion Branch RC 6.00 1.80
❑ 256 Brian Poli-Dixon RC 2.50 .75
❑ 257 Freddie Milons RC 2.50 .75
❑ 258 Lee Mays RC 2.50 .75

No.	Player	Nm-Mt	Ex-Mt
259	Tim Carter RC	2.50	.75
260	Terry Charles RC	2.50	.75
261	Jamar Martin RC	2.50	.75
262	Jason McAddley RC	2.50	.75
263	Chris Hope RC	2.50	.75
264	Howard Green RC	1.50	.45
265	Jeremy Shockey RC	10.00	3.00
266	Daniel Graham RC	3.00	.90
267	Eddie Freeman RC	1.50	.45
268	Julius Peppers RC	6.00	1.80
269	Kalimba Edwards RC	3.00	.90
270	Dwight Freeney RC	4.00	1.20
271	Dennis Johnson RC	1.50	.45
272	Alex Brown RC	3.00	.90
273	Bryan Thomas RC	2.50	.75
274	Bryan Fletcher RC	1.50	.45
275	Will Overstreet RC	1.50	.45
276	Ryan Denney RC	1.50	.45
277	Charles Grant RC	3.00	.90
278	John Henderson RC	3.00	.90
279	Albert Haynesworth RC	2.50	.75
280	Wendell Bryant RC	3.00	.90
281	Ryan Sims RC	3.00	.90
282	Anthony Weaver RC	2.50	.75
283	Larry Tripplett RC	1.50	.45
284	Alan Harper RC	1.50	.45
285	Napoleon Harris RC	3.00	.90
286	Robert Thomas RC	3.00	.90
287	Levar Fisher RC	1.50	.45
288	Andra Davis RC	2.50	.75
289	Quentin Jammer RC	3.00	.90
290	Phillip Buchanon RC	3.00	.90
291	Keyuo Craver RC	2.50	.75
292	Lito Sheppard RC	3.00	.90
293	Rocky Calmus RC	3.00	.90
294	Mike Rumph RC	3.00	.90
295	Mike Echols RC	1.50	.45
296	Joseph Jefferson RC	2.50	.75
297	Roy Williams RC	8.00	2.40
298	Ed Reed RC	5.00	1.50
299	Michael Lewis RC	3.00	.90
300	Eddie Drummond RC	2.50	.75

2001 Donruss Classics

No.	Player	Nm-Mt	Ex-Mt
	COMP.SET w/o SPs (100)	20.00	6.00
1	David Boston	.75	.23
2	Jake Plummer	.50	.15
3	Thomas Jones	.50	.15
4	Jamal Anderson	.75	.23
5	Chris Redman	.30	.09
6	Elvis Grbac	.50	.15
7	Jamal Lewis	1.25	.35
8	Qadry Ismail	.50	.15
9	Ray Lewis	.75	.23
10	Shannon Sharpe	.50	.15
11	Travis Taylor	.50	.15
12	Eric Moulds	.50	.15
13	Rob Johnson	.50	.15
14	Muhsin Muhammad	.50	.15
15	Brian Urlacher	1.25	.35
16	Cade McNown	.30	.09
17	Marcus Robinson	.75	.23
18	Akili Smith	.30	.09
19	Corey Dillon	.75	.23
20	Peter Warrick	.75	.23
21	Courtney Brown	.50	.15
22	Tim Couch	.50	.15
23	Emmitt Smith	1.50	.45
24	Brian Griese	.75	.23
25	Ed McCaffery	.75	.23
26	Olandis Gary	.50	.15
27	Mike Anderson	.75	.23
28	Rod Smith	.50	.15
29	Terrell Davis	.75	.23
30	Charlie Batch	.75	.23
31	James Stewart	.50	.15
32	Ahman Green	.75	.23
33	Antonio Freeman	.75	.23
34	Brett Favre	2.50	.75
35	Edgerrin James	1.00	.30
36	Marvin Harrison	.75	.23
37	Peyton Manning	2.00	.60
38	Fred Taylor	.75	.23
39	Jimmy Smith	.50	.15
40	Keenan McCardell	.30	.09
41	Mark Brunell	.75	.23
42	Sylvester Morris	.30	.09
43	Tony Gonzalez	.50	.15
44	Zach Thomas	.75	.23
45	Jay Fiedler	.75	.23
46	Lamar Smith	.50	.15
47	Cris Carter	.75	.23
48	Daunte Culpepper	.75	.23
49	Randy Moss	1.50	.45
50	Drew Bledsoe	1.00	.30
51	Terry Glenn	.50	.15
52	Aaron Brooks	.75	.23
53	Joe Horn	.50	.15
54	Ricky Williams	.75	.23
55	Amani Toomer	.50	.15
56	Ike Hilliard	.50	.15
57	Kerry Collins	.50	.15
58	Ron Dayne	.75	.23
59	Tiki Barber	.50	.15
60	Chad Pennington	1.25	.35
61	Curtis Martin	.75	.23
62	Laveranues Coles	.75	.23
63	Vinny Testaverde	.50	.15
64	Wayne Chrebet	.50	.15
65	Charles Woodson	.50	.15
66	Rich Gannon	.75	.23
67	Tim Brown	.75	.23
68	Tyrone Wheatley	.50	.15
69	Corey Simon	.50	.15
70	Donovan McNabb	1.00	.30
71	Duce Staley	.75	.23
72	Jerome Bettis	.75	.23
73	Plaxico Burress	.75	.23
74	Doug Flutie	.75	.23
75	Junior Seau	.75	.23
76	Jeff Garcia	.75	.23
77	Jerry Rice	1.50	.45
78	Giovanni Carmazzi	.30	.09
79	Terrell Owens	.75	.23
80	Darrell Jackson	.75	.23
81	Ricky Watters	.50	.15
82	Shaun Alexander	1.00	.30
83	Isaac Bruce	.75	.23
84	Kurt Warner	2.50	.75
85	Marshall Faulk	1.00	.30
86	Torry Holt	.75	.23
87	Brad Johnson	.75	.23
88	Keyshawn Johnson	.75	.23
89	Mike Alstott	.75	.23
90	Shaun King	.30	.09
91	Warren Sapp	.50	.15
92	Warrick Dunn	.75	.23
93	Eddie George	.75	.23
94	Jevon Kearse	.50	.15
95	Steve McNair	.75	.23
96	Jeff George	.50	.15
97	Stephen Davis	.75	.23
98	Charlie Garner	.50	.15
99	Trent Dilfer	.50	.15
100	Troy Aikman	1.25	.35
101	Michael Vick RC	60.00	18.00
102	Drew Brees RC	20.00	6.00
103	Chris Weinke RC	10.00	3.00
104	Mike McMahon RC	10.00	3.00
105	Jesse Palmer RC	10.00	3.00
106	Quincy Carter RC	10.00	3.00
107	Josh Heupel RC	10.00	3.00
108	Tim Hasselbeck RC	10.00	3.00
109	LaDainian Tomlinson RC	30.00	9.00
110	Deuce McAllister RC	25.00	7.50
111	Michael Bennett RC	20.00	6.00
112	Anthony Thomas RC	15.00	4.50
113	LaMont Jordan RC	12.00	3.60
114	Travis Henry RC	12.00	3.60
115	Kevan Barlow RC	10.00	3.00
116	Travis Minor RC	6.00	1.80
117	Rudi Johnson RC	20.00	6.00
118	David Allen RC	6.00	1.80
119	Heath Evans RC	6.00	1.80
120	Moran Norris RC	4.00	1.20
121	David Terrell RC	10.00	3.00
122	Koren Robinson RC	10.00	3.00
123	Rod Gardner RC	10.00	3.00
124	Santana Moss RC	15.00	4.50
125	Freddie Mitchell RC	10.00	3.00
126	Reggie Wayne RC	15.00	4.50
127	Quincy Morgan RC	10.00	3.00
128	Chad Johnson RC	20.00	6.00
129	Robert Ferguson RC	10.00	3.00
130	Chris Chambers RC	12.00	3.60
131	Snoop Minnis RC	6.00	1.80
132	Eddie Berlin RC	6.00	1.80
133	Alex Bannister RC	6.00	1.80
134	Todd Heap RC	10.00	3.00
135	Alge Crumpler RC	12.00	3.60
136	Justin Smith RC	10.00	3.00
137	Andre Carter RC	10.00	3.00
138	Jamal Reynolds RC	10.00	3.00
139	Richard Seymour RC	10.00	3.00
140	Marcus Stroud RC	10.00	3.00
141	Casey Hampton RC	6.00	1.80
142	Gerard Warren RC	10.00	3.00
143	Torrance Marshall RC	10.00	3.00
144	Brian Allen RC	4.00	1.20
145	Morlon Greenwood RC	6.00	1.80
146	Keith Adams RC	4.00	1.20
147	Will Allen RC	6.00	1.80
148	Nate Clements RC	10.00	3.00
149	Adam Archuleta RC	10.00	3.00
150	Hakim Akbar RC	4.00	1.20
151	James Lofton	1.00	.30
152	Jim Kelly	2.50	.75
153	Gale Sayers	2.50	.75
154	Mike Singletary	2.00	.60
155	Boomer Esiason	1.50	.45
156	Charlie Joiner	1.00	.30
157	Ken Anderson	1.50	.45
158	Y.A. Tittle	2.00	.60
159	Jim Brown	3.00	.90
160	Otto Graham	1.50	.45
161	Ozzie Newsome	1.00	.30
162	Drew Pearson	1.50	.45
163	Lance Alworth	1.50	.45
164	Roger Staubach	4.00	1.20
165	Tony Dorsett	2.00	.60
166	John Elway	5.00	1.50
167	Barry Sanders	3.00	.90
168	Bart Starr	4.00	1.20
169	Paul Hornung	2.00	.60
170	Earl Campbell	2.00	.60
171	Warren Moon	2.00	.60
172	Johnny Unitas	3.00	.90
173	Deacon Jones	1.50	.45
174	Eric Dickerson	1.50	.45
175	Bob Griese	2.00	.60
176	Dan Marino	5.00	1.50
177	Larry Csonka	2.00	.60
178	Paul Warfield	2.00	.60
179	Fran Tarkenton	2.50	.75
180	Archie Manning	1.50	.45
181	Frank Gifford	2.00	.60
182	Lawrence Taylor	2.00	.60
183	Dan Fouts	2.00	.60
184	Don Maynard	1.50	.45
185	Joe Namath	4.00	1.20
186	Fred Biletnikoff	2.00	.60
187	Marcus Allen	2.50	.75
188	Jim Plunkett	1.50	.45
189	Franco Harris	2.50	.75
190	Terry Bradshaw	4.00	1.20

❑ 191 Joe Montana	10.00	3.00
❑ 192 Roger Craig	1.50	.45
❑ 193 Steve Young	2.50	.75
❑ 194 Dwight Clark	1.50	.45
❑ 195 Steve Largent	2.00	.60
❑ 196 Art Monk	1.50	.45
❑ 197 Charley Taylor	1.50	.45
❑ 198 Joe Theismann	2.00	.60
❑ 199 Sammy Baugh	2.00	.60
❑ 200 Sonny Jurgensen	2.00	.60

2002 Donruss Classics

	Nm-Mt	Ex-Mt
COMP.SET w/o SP's (100)	20.00	6.00
❑ 1 David Boston	.75	.23
❑ 2 Jake Plummer	.50	.15
❑ 3 Jamal Anderson	.50	.15
❑ 4 Michael Vick	2.50	.75
❑ 5 Chris Weinke	.50	.15
❑ 6 Muhsin Muhammad	.50	.15
❑ 7 Steve Smith	.50	.15
❑ 8 Anthony Thomas	.75	.23
❑ 9 David Terrell	.75	.23
❑ 10 Brian Urlacher	1.25	.35
❑ 11 Marty Booker	.50	.15
❑ 12 Quincy Carter	.50	.15
❑ 13 Emmitt Smith	2.00	.60
❑ 14 Mike McMahon	.75	.23
❑ 15 James Stewart	.50	.15
❑ 16 Brett Favre	2.00	.60
❑ 17 Ahman Green	.75	.23
❑ 18 Antonio Freeman	.75	.23
❑ 19 Michael Bennett	.50	.15
❑ 20 Randy Moss	1.50	.45
❑ 21 Cris Carter	.75	.23
❑ 22 Daunte Culpepper	.75	.23
❑ 23 Aaron Brooks	.75	.23
❑ 24 Ricky Williams	.75	.23
❑ 25 Deuce McAllister	1.00	.30
❑ 26 Kerry Collins	.50	.15
❑ 27 Michael Strahan	.50	.15
❑ 28 Donovan McNabb	1.00	.30
❑ 29 Duce Staley	.75	.23
❑ 30 Freddie Mitchell	.50	.15
❑ 31 Correll Buckhalter	.50	.15
❑ 32 Jeff Garcia	.75	.23
❑ 33 Terrell Owens	.75	.23
❑ 34 Garrison Hearst	.50	.15
❑ 35 Marshall Faulk	.75	.23
❑ 36 Isaac Bruce	.75	.23
❑ 37 Kurt Warner	.75	.23
❑ 38 Torry Holt	.75	.23
❑ 39 Brad Johnson	.50	.15
❑ 40 Keyshawn Johnson	.75	.23
❑ 41 Mike Alstott	.75	.23
❑ 42 Warrick Dunn	.75	.23
❑ 43 Stephen Davis	.50	.15
❑ 44 Rod Gardner	.50	.15
❑ 45 Bruce Smith	.30	.09
❑ 46 Elvis Grbac	.50	.15
❑ 47 Ray Lewis	.75	.23
❑ 48 Jamal Lewis	.75	.23
❑ 49 Rob Johnson	.50	.15
❑ 50 Eric Moulds	.50	.15
❑ 51 Travis Henry	.75	.23
❑ 52 Corey Dillon	.50	.15
❑ 53 Peter Warrick	.50	.15
❑ 54 Tim Couch	.50	.15
❑ 55 James Jackson	.30	.09
❑ 56 Kevin Johnson	.50	.15
❑ 57 Brian Griese	.75	.23
❑ 58 Terrell Davis	.75	.23
❑ 59 Rod Smith	.50	.15
❑ 60 Mike Anderson	.75	.23
❑ 61 Peyton Manning	1.50	.45
❑ 62 Marvin Harrison	.75	.23
❑ 63 Edgerrin James	1.00	.30
❑ 64 Dominic Rhodes	.50	.15
❑ 65 Mark Brunell	.75	.23
❑ 66 Fred Taylor	.75	.23
❑ 67 Jimmy Smith	.50	.15
❑ 68 Tony Gonzalez	.50	.15
❑ 69 Trent Green	.50	.15
❑ 70 Priest Holmes	1.00	.30
❑ 71 Snoop Minnis	.30	.09
❑ 72 Jay Fiedler	.50	.15
❑ 73 Lamar Smith	.50	.15
❑ 74 Chris Chambers	.75	.23
❑ 75 Tom Brady	2.00	.60
❑ 76 Drew Bledsoe	1.00	.30
❑ 77 Antowain Smith	.50	.15
❑ 78 Troy Brown	.50	.15
❑ 79 Vinny Testaverde	.50	.15
❑ 80 Curtis Martin	.75	.23
❑ 81 Wayne Chrebet	.50	.15
❑ 82 Laveranues Coles	.50	.15
❑ 83 Tim Brown	.75	.23
❑ 84 Jerry Rice	1.50	.45
❑ 85 Rich Gannon	.75	.23
❑ 86 Charlie Garner	.50	.15
❑ 87 Kordell Stewart	.50	.15
❑ 88 Jerome Bettis	.75	.23
❑ 89 Kendrell Bell	.75	.23
❑ 90 Plaxico Burress	.50	.15
❑ 91 Drew Brees	.75	.23
❑ 92 LaDainian Tomlinson	1.25	.35
❑ 93 Doug Flutie	.75	.23
❑ 94 Shaun Alexander	.75	.23
❑ 95 Matt Hasselbeck	.50	.15
❑ 96 Koren Robinson	.50	.15
❑ 97 Steve McNair	.75	.23
❑ 98 Eddie George	.75	.23
❑ 99 Derrick Mason	.50	.15
❑ 100 Jevon Kearse	.50	.15
❑ 101 Joe Montana	12.00	3.60
❑ 102 Joe Namath	5.00	1.50
❑ 103 Warren Moon	3.00	.90
❑ 104 Dan Marino	10.00	3.00
❑ 105 Steve Bartkowski	2.50	.75
❑ 106 John Elway	10.00	3.00
❑ 107 Troy Aikman	5.00	1.50
❑ 108 Steve Young	3.00	.90
❑ 109 Terry Bradshaw	5.00	1.50
❑ 110 Bart Starr	6.00	1.80
❑ 111 Bert Jones	1.50	.45
❑ 112 Craig Morton	2.50	.75
❑ 113 Bob Griese	3.00	.90
❑ 114 Dan Fouts	3.00	.90
❑ 115 Phil Simms	2.50	.75
❑ 116 Jim McMahon	4.00	1.20
❑ 117 Joe Theismann	3.00	.90
❑ 118 Ken Stabler	5.00	1.50
❑ 119 Johnny Unitas	5.00	1.50
❑ 120 Roger Staubach	5.00	1.50
❑ 121 Len Dawson	3.00	.90
❑ 122 Tony Dorsett	4.00	1.20
❑ 123 Gale Sayers	5.00	1.50
❑ 124 Jim Kelly	4.00	1.20
❑ 125 Herschel Walker	2.50	.75
❑ 126 John Riggins	4.00	1.20
❑ 127 Eric Dickerson	2.50	.75
❑ 128 Franco Harris	4.00	1.20
❑ 129 Earl Campbell	3.00	.90
❑ 130 Thurman Thomas	2.50	.75
❑ 131 Barry Sanders	5.00	1.50
❑ 132 Marcus Allen	4.00	1.20
❑ 134 Natrone Means	1.50	.45
❑ 135 Steve Largent	3.00	.90
❑ 136 Don Maynard	2.50	.75
❑ 137 Henry Ellard	2.50	.75
❑ 138 Sterling Sharpe	3.00	.90
❑ 139 Art Monk	2.50	.75
❑ 140 Andre Reed	2.50	.75
❑ 141 Raymond Berry	2.50	.75
❑ 142 Ozzie Newsome	2.50	.75
❑ 143 William Perry	2.50	.75
❑ 144 Deacon Jones	2.50	.75
❑ 145 Howie Long	4.00	1.20
❑ 146 L.C. Greenwood	2.50	.75
❑ 147 Ronnie Lott	2.50	.75
❑ 148 Dick Butkus	5.00	1.50
❑ 149 Fran Tarkenton	4.00	1.20
❑ 150 Mike Singletary	3.00	.90
❑ 151 David Carr RC	20.00	6.00
❑ 152 Joey Harrington RC	20.00	6.00
❑ 153 Patrick Ramsey RC	12.00	3.60
❑ 154 Kurt Kittner RC	5.00	1.50
❑ 155 DeShaun Foster RC	6.00	1.80
❑ 156 William Green RC	10.00	3.00
❑ 157 Clinton Portis RC	20.00	6.00
❑ 158 T.J. Duckett RC	10.00	3.00
❑ 159 Cliff Russell RC	5.00	1.50
❑ 160 Antonio Bryant RC	6.00	1.80
❑ 161 Donte Stallworth RC	12.00	3.60
❑ 162 Reche Caldwell RC	6.00	1.80
❑ 163 Jabar Gaffney RC	6.00	1.80
❑ 164 Ashley Lelie RC	12.00	3.60
❑ 165 Andre Davis RC	6.00	1.80
❑ 166 Josh Reed RC	6.00	1.80
❑ 167 Ron Johnson RC	5.00	1.50
❑ 168 Kelly Campbell RC	5.00	1.50
❑ 169 Javon Walker RC	12.00	3.60
❑ 170 Antwaan Randle El RC	8.00	2.40
❑ 171 Marquise Walker RC	5.00	1.50
❑ 172 Jeremy Shockey RC	20.00	6.00
❑ 173 Jerramy Stevens RC	6.00	1.80
❑ 174 Daniel Graham RC	6.00	1.80
❑ 175 Julius Peppers RC	12.00	3.60
❑ 176 Kalimba Edwards RC	6.00	1.80
❑ 177 Alex Brown RC	6.00	1.80
❑ 178 Will Overstreet RC	5.00	1.50
❑ 179 Dwight Freeney RC	8.00	2.40
❑ 180 John Henderson RC	6.00	1.80
❑ 181 Ryan Sims RC	6.00	1.80
❑ 182 Albert Haynesworth RC	5.00	1.50
❑ 183 Wendell Bryant RC	6.00	1.80
❑ 184 Anthony Weaver RC	5.00	1.50
❑ 185 Napoleon Harris RC	6.00	1.80
❑ 186 Robert Thomas RC	6.00	1.80
❑ 187 Quentin Jammer RC	6.00	1.80
❑ 188 Ed Reed RC	10.00	3.00
❑ 189 Roy Williams RC	15.00	4.50
❑ 190 Phillip Buchanon RC	6.00	1.80
❑ 191 Lito Sheppard RC	6.00	1.80
❑ 192 Mike Rumph RC	6.00	1.80
❑ 193 Keyuo Craver RC	5.00	1.50
❑ 194 Randy Fasani RC	5.00	1.50
❑ 195 Rohan Davey RC	6.00	1.80
❑ 196 Chad Hutchinson RC	6.00	1.80
❑ 197 Eric Crouch RC	10.00	3.00
❑ 198 Lamar Gordon RC	6.00	1.80
❑ 199 Brian Westbrook RC	10.00	3.00
❑ 200 Adrian Peterson RC	6.00	1.80

2002 Donruss Classics Timeless Tributes

Nm-Mt Ex-Mt

*STARS 1-100: 4X TO 10X BASIC CARDS
*RETIRED 101-150: 2X TO 5X
*ROOKIES 151-200: .8X TO 2X

2003 Donruss Classics

	MINT	NRMT
COMP.SET w/o SP's (100)	20.00	9.00
❑ 1 Jake Plummer	.50	.23
❑ 2 Marcel Shipp	.50	.23
❑ 3 David Boston	.50	.23
❑ 4 Michael Vick	2.00	.90
❑ 5 T.J. Duckett	.50	.23
❑ 6 Warrick Dunn	.50	.23
❑ 7 Ray Lewis	.75	.35
❑ 8 Jamal Lewis	.75	.35
❑ 9 Todd Heap	.50	.23
❑ 10 Drew Bledsoe	.75	.35
❑ 11 Travis Henry	.50	.23

Card	Hi	Lo
❑ 12 Peerless Price	.50	.23
❑ 13 Eric Moulds	.50	.23
❑ 14 Julius Peppers	.75	.35
❑ 15 Steve Smith	.30	.14
❑ 16 Lamar Smith	.30	.14
❑ 17 Anthony Thomas	.75	.35
❑ 18 Marty Booker	.50	.23
❑ 19 Brian Urlacher	1.25	.55
❑ 20 Corey Dillon	.50	.23
❑ 21 Chad Johnson	.50	.23
❑ 22 Tim Couch	.30	.14
❑ 23 William Green	.50	.23
❑ 24 Quincy Morgan	.50	.23
❑ 25 Chad Hutchinson	.50	.23
❑ 26 Emmitt Smith	2.00	.90
❑ 27 Antonio Bryant	.50	.23
❑ 28 Roy Williams	.75	.35
❑ 29 Brian Griese	.75	.35
❑ 30 Clinton Portis	1.25	.55
❑ 31 Rod Smith	.50	.23
❑ 32 Ashley Lelie	.75	.35
❑ 33 Joey Harrington	1.25	.55
❑ 34 James Stewart	.50	.23
❑ 35 Bill Schroeder	.50	.23
❑ 36 Brett Favre	2.00	.90
❑ 37 Ahman Green	.75	.35
❑ 38 Donald Driver	.50	.23
❑ 39 David Carr	1.25	.55
❑ 40 Jonathan Wells	.30	.14
❑ 41 Corey Bradford	.30	.14
❑ 42 Peyton Manning	1.25	.55
❑ 43 Edgerrin James	.75	.35
❑ 44 Marvin Harrison	.75	.35
❑ 45 Mark Brunell	.50	.23
❑ 46 Fred Taylor	.75	.35
❑ 47 Jimmy Smith	.50	.23
❑ 48 Trent Green	.50	.23
❑ 49 Priest Holmes	1.00	.45
❑ 50 Tony Gonzalez	.50	.23
❑ 51 Ricky Williams	.75	.35
❑ 52 Chris Chambers	.75	.35
❑ 53 Zach Thomas	.75	.35
❑ 54 Daunte Culpepper	.75	.35
❑ 55 Michael Bennett	.50	.23
❑ 56 Randy Moss	1.25	.55
❑ 57 Tom Brady	1.25	.55
❑ 58 Antowain Smith	.50	.23
❑ 59 Troy Brown	.50	.23
❑ 60 Aaron Brooks	.75	.35
❑ 61 Deuce McAllister	.75	.35
❑ 62 Donte Stallworth	.75	.35
❑ 63 Kerry Collins	.50	.23
❑ 64 Jeremy Shockey	1.25	.55
❑ 65 Amani Toomer	.50	.23
❑ 66 Chad Pennington	1.00	.45
❑ 67 Curtis Martin	.75	.35
❑ 68 Laveranues Coles	.50	.23
❑ 69 Rich Gannon	.50	.23
❑ 70 Charlie Garner	.50	.23
❑ 71 Jerry Rice	1.50	.70
❑ 72 Tim Brown	.75	.35
❑ 73 Donovan McNabb	1.00	.45
❑ 74 Duce Staley	.50	.23
❑ 75 Todd Pinkston	.50	.23
❑ 76 Tommy Maddox	.75	.35
❑ 77 Jerome Bettis	.75	.35
❑ 78 Plaxico Burress	.50	.23
❑ 79 Hines Ward	.75	.35
❑ 80 Drew Brees	.75	.35
❑ 81 LaDainian Tomlinson	.75	.35
❑ 82 Junior Seau	.75	.35
❑ 83 Jeff Garcia	.75	.35
❑ 84 Garrison Hearst	.50	.23
❑ 85 Terrell Owens	.75	.35
❑ 86 Matt Hasselbeck	.50	.23
❑ 87 Shaun Alexander	.75	.35
❑ 88 Koren Robinson	.50	.23
❑ 89 Kurt Warner	.75	.35
❑ 90 Marshall Faulk	.75	.35
❑ 91 Isaac Bruce	.75	.35
❑ 92 Brad Johnson	.50	.23
❑ 93 Mike Alstott	.75	.35
❑ 94 Keyshawn Johnson	.75	.35
❑ 95 Steve McNair	.75	.35
❑ 96 Eddie George	.50	.23
❑ 97 Derrick Mason	.50	.23
❑ 98 Patrick Ramsey	.75	.35
❑ 99 Stephen Davis	.50	.23
❑ 100 Rod Gardner	.50	.23
❑ 101 Archie Manning	3.00	1.35
❑ 102 Bo Jackson	6.00	2.70
❑ 103 Bob Griese	3.00	1.35
❑ 104 Bob Lilly	2.50	1.10
❑ 105 Craig James	2.50	1.10
❑ 106 Cliff Branch	2.50	1.10
❑ 107 Dan Fouts	3.00	1.35
❑ 108 Daryl Johnston	3.00	1.35
❑ 109 Daryle Lamonica	1.50	.70
❑ 110 Dick Butkus	5.00	2.20
❑ 111 Don Maynard	2.50	1.10
❑ 112 Ed Too Tall Jones	2.50	1.10
❑ 113 Franco Harris	4.00	1.80
❑ 114 Frank Gifford	3.00	1.35
❑ 115 Fred Biletnikoff	3.00	1.35
❑ 116 Gale Sayers	5.00	2.20
❑ 117 George Blanda	3.00	1.35
❑ 118 Herman Edwards	2.50	1.10
❑ 119 Herschel Walker	2.50	1.10
❑ 120 Jack Ham	2.50	1.10
❑ 121 Jack Tatum	1.50	.70
❑ 122 Jack Youngblood	1.50	.70
❑ 123 James Lofton	1.50	.70
❑ 124 Jay Novacek	1.50	.70
❑ 125 Jim Brown	6.00	2.70
❑ 126 Jim McMahon/100	40.00	18.00
❑ 127 Jim Plunkett	2.50	1.10
❑ 128 Jimmy Johnson/100 EXCH		
❑ 129 Joe Greene	3.00	1.35
❑ 130 Joe Montana	12.00	5.50
❑ 131 John Riggins	4.00	1.80
❑ 132 John Stallworth	2.50	1.10
❑ 133 John Taylor/100	3.00	1.35
❑ 134 Ken Stabler	5.00	2.20
❑ 135 L.C. Greenwood	2.50	1.10
❑ 136 Lance Alworth	2.50	1.10
❑ 137 Mel Blount	2.50	1.10
❑ 138 Mike Ditka/100	5.00	2.20
❑ 139 Paul Hornung	3.00	1.35
❑ 140 Randy White	2.50	1.10
❑ 141 Raymond Berry	2.50	1.10
❑ 142 Roger Craig	2.50	1.10
❑ 143 Roger Staubach	5.00	2.20
❑ 144 Ron Jaworski	1.50	.70
❑ 145 Sammy Baugh	3.00	1.35
❑ 146 Sonny Jurgenson	3.00	1.35
❑ 147 Steve Young	3.00	1.35
❑ 148 Ted Hendricks	1.50	.70
❑ 149 Thurman Thomas	2.50	1.10
❑ 150 Tom Jackson/100	3.00	1.35
❑ 151 Brian St.Pierre RC	6.00	2.70
❑ 152 Byron Leftwich RC	25.00	11.00
❑ 153 Carson Palmer RC	20.00	9.00
❑ 154 Chris Simms RC	12.00	5.50
❑ 155 Dave Ragone RC	6.00	2.70
❑ 156 Ken Dorsey RC	10.00	4.50
❑ 157 Kliff Kingsbury RC	5.00	2.20
❑ 158 Kyle Boller RC	15.00	6.75
❑ 159 Rex Grossman RC	15.00	6.75
❑ 160 Seneca Wallace RC	6.00	2.70
❑ 161 Jason Gesser RC	6.00	2.70
❑ 162 Artose Pinner RC	6.00	2.70
❑ 163 Avon Cobourne RC	3.00	1.35
❑ 164 Cecil Sapp RC	5.00	2.20
❑ 165 Chris Brown RC	12.00	5.50
❑ 166 Derek Watson RC	5.00	2.20
❑ 167 Domanick Davis RC	12.00	5.50
❑ 168 Dwone Hicks RC	3.00	1.35
❑ 169 Earnest Graham RC	5.00	2.20
❑ 170 Justin Fargas RC	6.00	2.70
❑ 171 Larry Johnson RC	12.00	5.50
❑ 172 Lee Suggs RC	12.00	5.50
❑ 173 Musa Smith RC	6.00	2.70
❑ 174 Onterrio Smith RC	8.00	3.60
❑ 175 Quentin Griffin RC	15.00	6.75
❑ 176 Willis McGahee RC	15.00	6.75
❑ 177 Sultan McCullough RC	5.00	2.20
❑ 178 LaBrandon Toefield RC	6.00	2.70
❑ 179 B.J. Askew RC	6.00	2.70
❑ 180 Andre Johnson RC	15.00	6.75
❑ 181 Anquan Boldin RC	15.00	6.75
❑ 182 Arnaz Battle RC	6.00	2.70
❑ 183 Bethel Johnson RC	10.00	4.50
❑ 184 Billy McMullen RC	5.00	2.20
❑ 185 Bobby Wade RC	6.00	2.70
❑ 186 Brandon Lloyd RC	8.00	3.60
❑ 187 Bryant Johnson RC	6.00	2.70
❑ 188 Charles Rogers RC	8.00	3.60
❑ 189 Doug Gabriel RC	6.00	2.70
❑ 190 Justin Gage RC	6.00	2.70
❑ 191 Kareem Kelly RC	5.00	2.20
❑ 192 Kelley Washington RC	6.00	2.70
❑ 193 Kevin Curtis RC	6.00	2.70
❑ 194 Nate Burleson RC	10.00	4.50
❑ 195 Sam Aiken RC	5.00	2.20
❑ 196 Shaun McDonald RC	6.00	2.70
❑ 197 Talman Gardner RC	6.00	2.70
❑ 198 Taylor Jacobs RC	6.00	2.70
❑ 199 Terrence Edwards RC	5.00	2.20
❑ 200 Tyrone Calico RC	8.00	3.60
❑ 201 Walter Young RC	3.00	1.35
❑ 202 Ryan Hoag/100 RC	12.00	5.50
❑ 203 Paul Arnold RC	5.00	2.20
❑ 204 Bennie Joppru RC	6.00	2.70
❑ 205 Dallas Clark RC	6.00	2.70
❑ 206 George Wrighster RC	5.00	2.20
❑ 207 Jason Witten RC	10.00	4.50
❑ 208 Mike Pinkard RC	3.00	1.35
❑ 209 Robert Johnson RC	3.00	1.35
❑ 210 Teyo Johnson RC	6.00	2.70
❑ 211 Calvin Pace RC	5.00	2.20
❑ 212 Chris Kelsay RC	6.00	2.70
❑ 213 Cory Redding RC	5.00	2.20
❑ 214 DeWayne Robertson RC	6.00	2.70
❑ 215 DeWayne White RC	5.00	2.20
❑ 216 Jerome McDougle RC	6.00	2.70
❑ 217 Kenny Peterson RC	5.00	2.20
❑ 218 Kindal Moorehead RC	5.00	2.20
❑ 219 Michael Haynes RC	6.00	2.70
❑ 220 Terrell Suggs RC	10.00	4.50
❑ 221 Tully Banta-Cain RC	5.00	2.20
❑ 222 Jimmy Kennedy RC	6.00	2.70
❑ 223 Johnathan Sullivan RC	5.00	2.20
❑ 224 Kevin Williams RC	6.00	2.70
❑ 225 Nick Eason/100 RC	12.00	5.50
❑ 226 Rien Long RC	3.00	1.35
❑ 227 Ty Warren RC	6.00	2.70
❑ 228 William Joseph RC	6.00	2.70
❑ 229 Boss Bailey RC	8.00	3.60
❑ 230 Bradie James RC	6.00	2.70
❑ 231 Victor Hobson RC	6.00	2.70
❑ 232 Clifton Smith RC	3.00	1.35
❑ 233 E.J. Henderson/100 RC	12.00	5.50
❑ 234 Gerald Hayes/100 RC	12.00	5.50
❑ 235 LaMarcus McDonald RC	3.00	1.35
❑ 236 Nick Barnett RC	10.00	4.50
❑ 237 Terry Pierce RC	5.00	2.20
❑ 238 Andre Woolfolk RC	6.00	2.70
❑ 239 Dennis Weathersby RC	3.00	1.35
❑ 240 Drayton Florence RC	3.00	1.35
❑ 241 Eugene Wilson RC	5.00	2.20
❑ 242 Marcus Trufant RC	6.00	2.70
❑ 243 Rashean Mathis RC	5.00	2.20
❑ 244 Ricky Manning RC	6.00	2.70
❑ 245 Sammy Davis/100 RC	12.00	5.50
❑ 246 Terence Newman RC	12.00	5.50
❑ 247 Julian Battle RC	5.00	2.20

❑ 248 Ken Hamlin RC	6.00	2.70
❑ 249 Mike Doss RC	6.00	2.70
❑ 250 Troy Polamalu RC	6.00	2.70

2003 Donruss Classics Timeless Tributes

MINT NRMT

*STARS 1-100: 4X TO 10X BASIC CARDS
*STARS 101-150: 1.5X TO 4X BASIC CARDS
*ROOKIES 151-250: .8X TO 2X BASIC CARDS

2004 Donruss Classics

	Nm-Mt	Ex-Mt
COMP.SET w/o SP's (100)	20.00	6.00

101-150 LEG PRINT RUN 2000 SER.#'d SETS
151-175 RC PRINT RUN 1850 SER.#'d SETS
176-200 RC PRINT RUN 1250 SER.#'d SETS
201-225 RC PRINT RUN 925 SER.#'d SETS
226-250 RC PRINT RUN 500 SER.#'d SETS

❑ 1 Anquan Boldin	.75	.23
❑ 2 Emmitt Smith	1.50	.45
❑ 3 Michael Vick	1.50	.45
❑ 4 Peerless Price	.50	.15
❑ 5 Warrick Dunn	.50	.15
❑ 6 Jamal Lewis	.75	.23
❑ 7 Kyle Boller	.75	.23
❑ 8 Terrell Suggs	.50	.15
❑ 9 Todd Heap	.50	.15
❑ 10 Drew Bledsoe	.75	.23
❑ 11 Travis Henry	.50	.15
❑ 12 DeShaun Foster	.50	.15
❑ 13 Jake Delhomme	.75	.23
❑ 14 Stephen Davis	.50	.15
❑ 15 Steve Smith	.50	.15
❑ 16 Anthony Thomas	.50	.15
❑ 17 Brian Urlacher	1.00	.30
❑ 18 Rex Grossman	.75	.23
❑ 19 Chad Johnson	.50	.15
❑ 20 Carson Palmer	1.00	.30
❑ 21 Rudi Johnson	.50	.15
❑ 22 Andre Davis	.30	.09
❑ 23 Lee Suggs	.75	.23
❑ 24 Quincy Carter	.50	.15
❑ 25 Roy Williams S	.50	.15
❑ 26 Clinton Portis	.75	.23
❑ 27 Jake Plummer	.50	.15
❑ 28 Rod Smith	.50	.15
❑ 29 Charles Rogers	.50	.15
❑ 30 Joey Harrington	.75	.23
❑ 31 Ahman Green	.75	.23
❑ 32 Brett Favre	2.00	.60
❑ 33 Javon Walker	.50	.15
❑ 34 Andre Johnson	.75	.23
❑ 35 David Carr	.75	.23
❑ 36 Domanick Davis	.75	.23
❑ 37 Edgerrin James	.75	.23
❑ 38 Marvin Harrison	.75	.23
❑ 39 Peyton Manning	1.25	.35
❑ 40 Reggie Wayne	.50	.15
❑ 41 Byron Leftwich	1.25	.35
❑ 42 Fred Taylor	.50	.15
❑ 43 Jimmy Smith	.50	.15
❑ 44 Priest Holmes	1.00	.30
❑ 45 Dante Hall	.75	.23
❑ 46 Tony Gonzalez	.50	.15
❑ 47 Trent Green	.50	.15
❑ 48 Chris Chambers	.50	.15
❑ 49 Ricky Williams	.75	.23
❑ 50 Zach Thomas	.75	.23
❑ 51 Daunte Culpepper	.75	.23
❑ 52 Michael Bennett	.50	.15
❑ 53 Randy Moss	1.00	.30
❑ 54 Deion Branch	.75	.23
❑ 55 Adam Vinatieri	.75	.23
❑ 56 Tedy Bruschi	.50	.15
❑ 57 Tom Brady	1.25	.35
❑ 58 Aaron Brooks	.50	.15
❑ 59 Deuce McAllister	.75	.23
❑ 60 Donte' Stallworth	.50	.15
❑ 61 Joe Horn	.50	.15
❑ 62 Jeremy Shockey	.75	.23
❑ 63 Kerry Collins	.50	.15
❑ 64 Michael Strahan	.50	.15
❑ 65 Tiki Barber	.50	.15
❑ 66 Chad Pennington	1.00	.30
❑ 67 Curtis Martin	.75	.23
❑ 68 Santana Moss	.50	.15
❑ 69 Jerry Rice	1.50	.45
❑ 70 Charles Woodson	.50	.15
❑ 71 Rod Woodson	.50	.15
❑ 72 Tim Brown	.75	.23
❑ 73 Brian Westbrook	.50	.15
❑ 74 Correll Buckhalter	.50	.15
❑ 75 Donovan McNabb	1.00	.30
❑ 76 Antwaan Randle El	.50	.15
❑ 77 Hines Ward	.75	.23
❑ 78 Kendrell Bell	.50	.15
❑ 79 David Boston	.50	.15
❑ 80 Drew Brees	.75	.23
❑ 81 LaDainian Tomlinson	.75	.23
❑ 82 Jeff Garcia	.75	.23
❑ 83 Kevan Barlow	.50	.15
❑ 84 Terrell Owens	.75	.23
❑ 85 Koren Robinson	.50	.15
❑ 86 Matt Hasselbeck	.50	.15
❑ 87 Shaun Alexander	.75	.23
❑ 88 Isaac Bruce	.50	.15
❑ 89 Marc Bulger	.75	.23
❑ 90 Marshall Faulk	.75	.23
❑ 91 Torry Holt	.75	.23
❑ 92 Brad Johnson	.50	.15
❑ 93 Keenan McCardell	.30	.09
❑ 94 Keyshawn Johnson	.50	.15
❑ 95 Derrick Mason	.50	.15
❑ 96 Eddie George	.50	.15
❑ 97 Steve McNair	.75	.23
❑ 98 LaVar Arrington	1.50	.45
❑ 99 Laveranues Coles	.50	.15
❑ 100 Patrick Ramsey	.50	.15
❑ 101 Archie Manning	2.00	.60
❑ 102 Bart Starr	5.00	1.50
❑ 103 Bo Jackson	4.00	1.20
❑ 104 Bob Griese	2.00	.60
❑ 105 Christian Okoye	1.00	.30
❑ 106 Daryl Johnston	2.00	.60
❑ 107 Deacon Jones	1.50	.45
❑ 108 Deion Sanders	3.00	.90
❑ 109 Dick Butkus	3.00	.90
❑ 110 Lynn Swann	2.50	.75
❑ 111 Don Maynard	1.50	.45
❑ 112 Don Shula	2.00	.60
❑ 113 Franco Harris	2.50	.75
❑ 114 Fred Biletnikoff	2.00	.60
❑ 115 Gale Sayers	2.50	.75
❑ 116 George Blanda	2.00	.60
❑ 117 Herman Edwards	1.50	.45
❑ 118 Herschel Walker	1.50	.45
❑ 119 Jack Lambert	3.00	.90
❑ 120 James Lofton	1.00	.30
❑ 121 Jim Plunkett	1.50	.45
❑ 122 Jim Thorpe	2.00	.60
❑ 123 Joe Greene	2.00	.60
❑ 124 John Riggins	2.50	.75
❑ 125 L.C. Greenwood	1.50	.45
❑ 126 Larry Csonka	2.00	.60
❑ 127 Leroy Kelly	1.50	.45
❑ 128 Walter Payton	8.00	2.40
❑ 129 Marcus Allen	2.00	.60
❑ 130 Mark Bavaro	1.00	.30
❑ 131 Mel Blount	1.50	.45
❑ 132 Michael Irvin	2.00	.60
❑ 133 Mike Ditka	2.00	.60
❑ 134 Mike Singletary	2.00	.60
❑ 135 Ozzie Newsome	1.50	.45
❑ 136 Paul Hornung	2.00	.60
❑ 137 Paul Warfield	1.50	.45
❑ 138 Randall Cunningham	1.50	.45
❑ 139 Ray Nitschke	2.00	.60
❑ 140 Reggie White	2.00	.60
❑ 141 Richard Dent	1.00	.30
❑ 142 Sammy Baugh	2.00	.60
❑ 143 Sonny Jurgensen	1.50	.45
❑ 144 Sterling Sharpe	1.50	.45
❑ 145 Steve Largent	2.00	.60
❑ 146 Terrell Davis	2.00	.60
❑ 147 Terry Bradshaw	4.00	1.20
❑ 148 Thurman Thomas	1.50	.45
❑ 149 Tony Dorsett	2.00	.60
❑ 150 Warren Moon	1.50	.45
❑ 151 John Navarre RC	5.00	1.50
❑ 152 Derek Abney RC	5.00	1.50
❑ 153 Ryan Dinwiddie RC	4.00	1.20
❑ 154 Bruce Perry/100 RC	20.00	6.00
❑ 155 Adimchinobe Echemandu RC	4.00	1.20
❑ 156 Troy Fleming RC	4.00	1.20
❑ 157 Brandon Miree RC	4.00	1.20
❑ 158 Jarrett Payton RC	5.00	1.50
❑ 159 Ben Hartsock RC	5.00	1.50
❑ 160 Chris Cooley RC	5.00	1.50
❑ 161 Derrick Ward RC	2.50	.75
❑ 162 Triandos Luke RC	5.00	1.50
❑ 163 Clarence Moore RC	5.00	1.50
❑ 164 D.J. Hackett RC	4.00	1.20
❑ 165 Mark Jones RC	4.00	1.20
❑ 166 Sloan Thomas RC	4.00	1.20
❑ 167 Jamaar Taylor RC	5.00	1.50
❑ 168 Casey Bramlet RC	4.00	1.20
❑ 169 Drew Carter RC	5.00	1.50
❑ 170 Antwan Odom RC	5.00	1.50
❑ 171 Marquise Hill RC	4.00	1.20
❑ 172 Ricardo Colclough RC	5.00	1.50
❑ 173 Keith Smith RC	4.00	1.20
❑ 174 Joey Thomas RC	5.00	1.50
❑ 175 Stuart Schweigert RC	5.00	1.50
❑ 176 Cody Pickett RC	6.00	1.80
❑ 177 B.J. Symons RC	6.00	1.80
❑ 178 Matt Mauck RC	6.00	1.80
❑ 179 Bradlee Van Pelt RC	8.00	2.40
❑ 180 Jim Sorgi RC	6.00	1.80
❑ 181 Ernest Wilford RC	6.00	1.80
❑ 182 Bernard Berrian RC	6.00	1.80
❑ 183 Darius Watts RC	8.00	2.40
❑ 184 Derrick Hamilton RC	5.00	1.50
❑ 185 Jerricho Cotchery RC	6.00	1.80
❑ 186 Jeris McIntyre RC	5.00	1.50
❑ 187 Carlos Francis RC	5.00	1.50
❑ 188 Maurice Mann RC	5.00	1.50
❑ 189 Randy Starks RC	5.00	1.50
❑ 190 Darnell Dockett RC	5.00	1.50
❑ 191 Marcus Tubbs RC	6.00	1.80
❑ 192 Daryl Smith RC	6.00	1.80
❑ 193 Karlos Dansby RC	6.00	1.80
❑ 194 Michael Boulware RC	6.00	1.80
❑ 195 Teddy Lehman RC	6.00	1.80
❑ 196 Will Poole RC	6.00	1.80
❑ 197 Derrick Strait RC	8.00	2.40
❑ 198 Ahmad Carroll RC	8.00	2.40
❑ 199 Jeremy LeSueur RC	5.00	1.50
❑ 200 Bob Sanders RC	6.00	1.80
❑ 201 J.P. Losman RC	15.00	4.50
❑ 202 Matt Schaub RC	10.00	3.00
❑ 203 Josh Harris RC	6.00	1.80
❑ 204 Luke McCown RC	6.00	1.80
❑ 205 Quincy Wilson RC	5.00	1.50
❑ 206 Michael Turner RC	5.00	1.50
❑ 207 Mewelde Moore RC	8.00	2.40
❑ 208 Cedric Cobbs RC	6.00	1.80
❑ 209 Ben Watson RC	6.00	1.80
❑ 210 Michael Jenkins RC	6.00	1.80
❑ 211 Devery Henderson RC	5.00	1.50
❑ 212 Johnnie Morant RC	6.00	1.80
❑ 213 Keary Colbert RC	8.00	2.40
❑ 214 Devard Darling RC	6.00	1.80
❑ 215 P.K. Sam RC	5.00	1.50
❑ 216 Samie Parker RC	6.00	1.80

❑	217 Jason Babin RC	6.00	1.80
❑	218 Tommie Harris RC	8.00	2.40
❑	219 Vince Wilfork RC	8.00	2.40
❑	220 Jonathan Vilma RC	6.00	1.80
❑	221 D.J. Williams RC	8.00	2.40
❑	222 Chris Gamble RC	8.00	2.40
❑	223 Matt Ware RC	6.00	1.80
❑	224 Shawntae Spencer RC	6.00	1.80
❑	225 Sean Jones RC	5.00	1.50
❑	226 Drew Henson RC	20.00	6.00
❑	227 Ben Roethlisberger RC	60.00	18.00
❑	228 Eli Manning RC	40.00	12.00
❑	229 Philip Rivers RC	25.00	7.50
❑	230 Steven Jackson RC	25.00	7.50
❑	231 Kevin Jones RC	25.00	7.50
❑	232 Chris Perry RC	15.00	4.50
❑	233 Greg Jones RC	8.00	2.40
❑	234 Tatum Bell RC	12.00	3.60
❑	235 Jeff Smoker RC	12.00	3.60
❑	236 Julius Jones RC	30.00	9.00
❑	237 Kellen Winslow RC	20.00	6.00
❑	238 Ben Troupe RC	8.00	2.40
❑	239 Larry Fitzgerald RC	25.00	7.50
❑	240 Craig Krenzel RC	8.00	2.40
❑	241 Roy Williams RC	25.00	7.50
❑	242 Reggie Williams RC	10.00	3.00
❑	243 Michael Clayton RC	20.00	6.00
❑	244 Lee Evans RC	12.00	3.60
❑	245 Rashaun Woods RC	10.00	3.00
❑	246 Kenechi Udeze RC	8.00	2.40
❑	247 Will Smith RC	8.00	2.40
❑	248 DeAngelo Hall RC	10.00	3.00
❑	249 Dunta Robinson RC	8.00	2.40
❑	250 Sean Taylor RC	10.00	3.00

2004 Donruss Classics Timeless Tributes Green

Nm-Mt Ex-Mt

*STARS 1-100: 8X TO 20X BASIC CARDS
*LEGENDS 101-150: 2.5X TO 6X BASIC CARDS
*ROOKIES 151-175: 1.2X TO 3X BASIC CARDS
*ROOKIES 176-200: 1X TO 2.5X BASIC CARDS
*ROOKIES 201-225: 1X TO 2.5X BASIC CARDS
*ROOKIES 226-250: .8X TO 2X BASIC CARDS
STATED PRINT RUN 75 SER.#'d SETS
UNPRICED PLATINUM PRINT RUN 1 SET

2004 Donruss Classics Timeless Tributes Red

Nm-Mt Ex-Mt

*STARS 1-100: 4X TO 10X BASIC CARDS
*LEGENDS 101-150: 1.2X TO 3X BASIC CARDS
*ROOKIES 151-175: .8X TO 2X BASIC CARDS
*ROOKIES 176-200: .6X TO 1.5X BASIC CARDS
*ROOKIES 201-225: .6X TO 1.5X BASIC CARDS
*ROOKIES 226-250: .5X TO 1.2X BASIC CARDS
STATED PRINT RUN 100 SER.#'d SETS

1999 Donruss Elite

	Nm-Mt	Ex-Mt
COMPLETE SET (200)	150.00	70.00
COMP.SET w/o SP's (160)	30.00	13.50

❑	1 Warren Moon	1.25	.55
❑	2 Terry Allen	.75	.35
❑	3 Jeff George	.75	.35
❑	4 Brett Favre	4.00	1.80
❑	5 Rob Moore	.75	.35
❑	6 Bubby Brister	.50	.23
❑	7 John Elway	4.00	1.80
❑	8 Troy Aikman	2.50	1.10
❑	9 Steve McNair	1.25	.55
❑	10 Charlie Batch	1.25	.55
❑	11 Elvis Grbac	.75	.35
❑	12 Trent Dilfer	.75	.35
❑	13 Kerry Collins	.75	.35
❑	14 Neil O'Donnell	.50	.23
❑	15 Tony Simmons	.50	.23
❑	16 Ryan Leaf	1.25	.55
❑	17 Bobby Hoying	.75	.35
❑	18 Marvin Harrison	1.25	.55
❑	19 Keyshawn Johnson	1.25	.55
❑	20 Cris Carter	1.25	.55
❑	21 Deion Sanders	1.25	.55
❑	22 Emmitt Smith	2.50	1.10
❑	23 Antowain Smith	1.25	.55
❑	24 Terry Fair	.50	.23
❑	25 Robert Holcombe	.50	.23
❑	26 Napoleon Kaufman	1.25	.55
❑	27 Eddie George	1.25	.55
❑	28 Corey Dillon	1.25	.55
❑	29 Adrian Murrell	.75	.35
❑	30 Charles Way	.50	.23
❑	31 Amp Lee	.50	.23
❑	32 Ricky Watters	.75	.35
❑	33 Gary Brown	.50	.23
❑	34 Thurman Thomas	.75	.35
❑	35 Pat Johnson	.50	.23
❑	36 Jerome Bettis	1.25	.55
❑	37 Muhsin Muhammad	.75	.35
❑	38 Kimble Anders	.75	.35
❑	39 Curtis Enis	.50	.23
❑	40 Mike Alstott	1.25	.55
❑	41 Charles Johnson	.50	.23
❑	42 Chris Warren	.50	.23
❑	43 Tony Banks	.75	.35
❑	44 Leroy Hoard	.50	.23
❑	45 Chris Fuamatu-Ma'afala	.50	.23
❑	46 Michael Irvin	1.25	.55
❑	47 Robert Edwards	.50	.23
❑	48 Hines Ward	1.25	.55
❑	49 Trent Green	1.25	.55
❑	50 Eric Zeier	.50	.23
❑	51 Sean Dawkins	.50	.23
❑	52 Yancey Thigpen	.50	.23
❑	53 Jacquez Green	.50	.23
❑	54 Zach Thomas	1.25	.55
❑	55 Junior Seau	1.25	.55
❑	56 Darnay Scott	.50	.23
❑	57 Kent Graham	.50	.23
❑	58 O.J. Santiago	.50	.23
❑	59 Tony Gonzalez	1.25	.55
❑	60 Ty Detmer	.50	.23
❑	61 Albert Connell	.50	.23
❑	62 James Jett	.75	.35
❑	63 Bert Emanuel	.75	.35
❑	64 Derrick Alexander WR	.75	.35
❑	65 Wesley Walls	.75	.35
❑	66 Jake Reed	.75	.35
❑	67 Randall Cunningham	1.25	.55
❑	68 Leslie Shepherd	.50	.23
❑	69 Mark Chmura	.50	.23
❑	70 Bobby Engram	.75	.35
❑	71 Rickey Dudley	.50	.23
❑	72 Darick Holmes	.50	.23
❑	73 Andre Reed	.75	.35
❑	74 Az-Zahir Hakim	.50	.23
❑	75 Cameron Cleeland	.50	.23
❑	76 Lamar Thomas	.50	.23
❑	77 Oronde Gadsden	.75	.35
❑	78 Ben Coates	.75	.35
❑	79 Bruce Smith	.75	.35
❑	80 Jerry Rice	2.50	1.10
❑	81 Tim Brown	1.25	.55
❑	82 Michael Westbrook	.75	.35
❑	83 J.J. Stokes	.75	.35
❑	84 Shannon Sharpe	.75	.35
❑	85 Reidel Anthony	.75	.35
❑	86 Antonio Freeman	1.25	.55
❑	87 Keenan McCardell	.75	.35
❑	88 Terry Glenn	1.25	.55
❑	89 Andre Rison	.75	.35
❑	90 Neil Smith	.75	.35
❑	91 Terrance Mathis	.75	.35
❑	92 Rocket Ismail	.75	.35
❑	93 Byron Bam Morris	.50	.23
❑	94 Ike Hilliard	.50	.23
❑	95 Eddie Kennison	.75	.35
❑	96 Tavian Banks	.50	.23
❑	97 Yatil Green	.50	.23
❑	98 Frank Wycheck	.50	.23
❑	99 Warren Sapp	.50	.23
❑	100 Germane Crowell	.50	.23
❑	101 Curtis Martin	2.50	1.10
❑	102 John Avery	1.00	.45
❑	103 Eric Moulds	2.50	1.10
❑	104 Randy Moss	8.00	3.60
❑	105 Terrell Owens	2.50	1.10
❑	106 Vinny Testaverde	1.50	.70
❑	107 Doug Flutie	1.25	.55
❑	108 Mark Brunell	1.25	.55
❑	109 Isaac Bruce	2.50	1.10
❑	110 Kordell Stewart	1.50	.70
❑	111 Drew Bledsoe	3.00	1.35
❑	112 Chris Chandler	1.50	.70
❑	113 Dan Marino	8.00	3.60
❑	114 Brian Griese	2.50	1.10
❑	115 Carl Pickens	1.50	.70
❑	116 Jake Plummer	1.50	.70
❑	117 Natrone Means	1.50	.70
❑	118 Peyton Manning	10.00	4.50
❑	119 Garrison Hearst	2.50	1.10
❑	120 Barry Sanders	8.00	3.60
❑	121 Steve Young	3.00	1.35
❑	122 Rashaan Shehee	1.00	.45
❑	123 Ed McCaffrey	1.50	.70
❑	124 Charles Woodson	2.50	1.10
❑	125 Dorsey Levens	2.50	1.10
❑	126 Robert Smith	2.50	1.10
❑	127 Greg Hill	1.00	.45
❑	128 Fred Taylor	2.50	1.10
❑	129 Marcus Nash	1.00	.45
❑	130 Terrell Davis	2.50	1.10
❑	131 Ahman Green	2.50	1.10
❑	132 Jamal Anderson	2.50	1.10
❑	133 Karim Abdul-Jabbar	1.50	.70
❑	134 Jermaine Lewis	1.50	.70
❑	135 Jerome Pathon	1.50	.70
❑	136 Brad Johnson	2.50	1.10
❑	137 Herman Moore	1.50	.70
❑	138 Tim Dwight	2.50	1.10
❑	139 Johnnie Morton	1.00	.45
❑	140 Marshall Faulk	3.00	1.35
❑	141 Frank Sanders	1.50	.70
❑	142 Kevin Dyson	1.50	.70
❑	143 Curtis Conway	1.50	.70
❑	144 Derrick Mayes	1.00	.45
❑	145 O.J. McDuffie	1.50	.70
❑	146 Joe Jurevicius	1.50	.70
❑	147 Jon Kitna	2.50	1.10
❑	148 Joey Galloway	1.50	.70
❑	149 Jimmy Smith	1.50	.70
❑	150 Skip Hicks	1.00	.45
❑	151 Rod Smith	1.50	.70
❑	152 Duce Staley	2.50	1.10

❑ 153 James Stewart 1.00 .45
❑ 154 Rob Johnson 1.50 .70
❑ 155 Mikhael Ricks 1.00 .45
❑ 156 Wayne Chrebet 1.50 .70
❑ 157 Robert Brooks 1.50 .70
❑ 158 Tim Biakabutuka 1.50 .70
❑ 159 Priest Holmes 4.00 1.80
❑ 160 Warrick Dunn 2.50 1.10
❑ 161 Champ Bailey RC 5.00 2.20
❑ 162 D'Wayne Bates RC 2.50 1.10
❑ 163 Michael Bishop RC 3.00 1.35
❑ 164 David Boston RC 3.00 1.35
❑ 165 Na Brown RC 2.50 1.10
❑ 166 Chris Claiborne RC 1.50 .70
❑ 167 Joe Montgomery RC 2.50 1.10
❑ 168 Mike Cloud RC 2.50 1.10
❑ 169 Travis McGriff RC 1.50 .70
❑ 170 Tim Couch RC 3.00 1.35
❑ 171 Daunte Culpepper RC 12.00 5.50
❑ 172 Autry Denson RC 2.50 1.10
❑ 173 Jermaine Fazande RC 2.50 1.10
❑ 174 Troy Edwards RC 2.50 1.10
❑ 175 Kevin Faulk RC 3.00 1.35
❑ 176 Dee Miller RC 1.50 .70
❑ 177 Brock Huard RC 3.00 1.35
❑ 178 Torry Holt RC 8.00 3.60
❑ 179 Sedrick Irvin RC 1.50 .70
❑ 180 Edgerrin James RC 12.00 5.50
❑ 181 Joe Germaine RC 2.50 1.10
❑ 182 James Johnson RC 2.50 1.10
❑ 183 Kevin Johnson RC 2.50 1.10
❑ 184 Andy Katzenmoyer RC 2.50 1.10
❑ 185 Jevon Kearse RC 6.00 2.70
❑ 186 Shaun King RC 2.50 1.10
❑ 187 Rob Konrad RC 3.00 1.35
❑ 188 Jim Kleinsasser RC 3.00 1.35
❑ 189 Chris McAlister RC 2.50 1.10
❑ 190 Donovan McNabb RC 15.00 6.75
❑ 191 Cade McNown RC 2.50 1.10
❑ 192 De'Mond Parker RC 1.00 .45
❑ 193 Craig Yeast RC 2.50 1.10
❑ 194 Shawn Bryson RC 3.00 1.35
❑ 195 Peerless Price RC 6.00 2.70
❑ 196 Darnell McDonald RC 2.50 1.10
❑ 197 Akili Smith RC 1.50 .70
❑ 198 Tai Streets RC 3.00 1.35
❑ 199 Ricky Williams RC 6.00 2.70
❑ 200 Amos Zereoue RC 2.50 1.10

2000 Donruss Elite

	Nm-Mt	Ex-Mt
COMPLETE SET (200)	500.00	220.00
❑ 1 Jake Plummer	.50	.23
❑ 2 David Boston	.75	.35
❑ 3 Rob Moore	.50	.23
❑ 4 Chris Chandler	.50	.23
❑ 5 Tim Dwight	.75	.35
❑ 6 Terance Mathis	.50	.23
❑ 7 Jamal Anderson	.75	.35
❑ 8 Priest Holmes	1.00	.45
❑ 9 Tony Banks	.50	.23
❑ 10 Shannon Sharpe	.50	.23
❑ 11 Qadry Ismail	.50	.23
❑ 12 Eric Moulds	.75	.35
❑ 13 Doug Flutie	.75	.35
❑ 14 Antowain Smith	.50	.23
❑ 15 Peerless Price	.75	.35
❑ 16 Muhsin Muhammad	.50	.23
❑ 17 Tim Biakabutuka	.50	.23
❑ 18 Patrick Jeffers	.75	.35
❑ 19 Steve Beuerlein	.50	.23
❑ 20 Wesley Walls	.30	.14
❑ 21 Curtis Enis	.30	.14
❑ 22 Marcus Robinson	.75	.35
❑ 23 Carl Pickens	.50	.23
❑ 24 Corey Dillon	.75	.35
❑ 25 Akili Smith	.30	.14
❑ 26 Darnay Scott	.50	.23
❑ 27 Kevin Johnson	.75	.35
❑ 28 Errict Rhett	.50	.23
❑ 29 Emmitt Smith	1.50	.70
❑ 30 Deion Sanders	.75	.35
❑ 31 Troy Aikman	1.50	.70
❑ 32 Joey Galloway	.50	.23
❑ 33 Michael Irvin	.50	.23
❑ 34 Rocket Ismail	.50	.23
❑ 35 Jason Tucker	.30	.14
❑ 36 Ed McCaffrey	.75	.35
❑ 37 Rod Smith	.50	.23
❑ 38 Brian Griese	.75	.35
❑ 39 Terrell Davis	.75	.35
❑ 40 Olandis Gary	.75	.35
❑ 41 Charlie Batch	.75	.35
❑ 42 Johnnie Morton	.50	.23
❑ 43 Herman Moore	.50	.23
❑ 44 James Stewart	.50	.23
❑ 45 Dorsey Levens	.50	.23
❑ 46 Antonio Freeman	.75	.35
❑ 47 Brett Favre	2.50	1.10
❑ 48 Bill Schroeder	.50	.23
❑ 49 Peyton Manning	2.00	.90
❑ 50 Keenan McCardell	.50	.23
❑ 51 Fred Taylor	.75	.35
❑ 52 Jimmy Smith	.50	.23
❑ 53 Elvis Grbac	.50	.23
❑ 54 Tony Gonzalez	.50	.23
❑ 55 Derrick Alexander	.50	.23
❑ 56 Dan Marino	2.50	1.10
❑ 57 Tony Martin	.50	.23
❑ 58 James Johnson	.30	.14
❑ 59 Damon Huard	.75	.35
❑ 60 Thurman Thomas	.50	.23
❑ 61 Robert Smith	.75	.35
❑ 62 Randall Cunningham	.75	.35
❑ 63 Jeff George	.50	.23
❑ 64 Terry Glenn	.50	.23
❑ 65 Drew Bledsoe	1.00	.45
❑ 66 Jeff Blake	.50	.23
❑ 67 Amani Toomer	.50	.23
❑ 68 Kerry Collins	.50	.23
❑ 69 Joe Montgomery	.30	.14
❑ 70 Vinny Testaverde	.50	.23
❑ 71 Ray Lucas	.50	.23
❑ 72 Keyshawn Johnson	.75	.35
❑ 73 Wayne Chrebet	.50	.23
❑ 74 Napoleon Kaufman	.50	.23
❑ 75 Tim Brown	.75	.35
❑ 76 Rich Gannon	.75	.35
❑ 77 Duce Staley	.75	.35
❑ 78 Kordell Stewart	.50	.23
❑ 79 Jerome Bettis	.75	.35
❑ 80 Troy Edwards	.30	.14
❑ 81 Natrone Means	.30	.14
❑ 82 Curtis Conway	.50	.23
❑ 83 Jim Harbaugh	.50	.23
❑ 84 Junior Seau	.75	.35
❑ 85 Jermaine Fazande	.30	.14
❑ 86 Terrell Owens	.75	.35
❑ 87 Charlie Garner	.50	.23
❑ 88 Steve Young	1.00	.45
❑ 89 Jeff Garcia	.75	.35
❑ 90 Derrick Mayes	.50	.23
❑ 91 Ricky Watters	.50	.23
❑ 92 Az-Zahir Hakim	.50	.23
❑ 93 Torry Holt	.75	.35
❑ 94 Warren Sapp	.50	.23
❑ 95 Mike Alstott	.75	.35
❑ 96 Warrick Dunn	.75	.35
❑ 97 Kevin Dyson	.50	.23
❑ 98 Bruce Smith	.50	.23
❑ 99 Albert Connell	.30	.14
❑ 100 Michael Westbrook	.50	.23
❑ 101 Cade McNown	.30	.14
❑ 102 Tim Couch	2.00	.90
❑ 103 John Elway	6.00	2.70
❑ 104 Barry Sanders	5.00	2.20
❑ 105 Germane Crowell	1.25	.55
❑ 106 Marvin Harrison	2.00	.90
❑ 107 Edgerrin James	3.00	1.35
❑ 108 Mark Brunell	2.00	.90
❑ 109 Randy Moss	4.00	1.80
❑ 110 Cris Carter	2.00	.90
❑ 111 Daunte Culpepper	2.50	1.10
❑ 112 Ricky Williams	.75	.35
❑ 113 Curtis Martin	2.00	.90
❑ 114 Donovan McNabb	3.00	1.35
❑ 115 Jerry Rice	4.00	1.80
❑ 116 Jon Kitna	2.00	.90
❑ 117 Isaac Bruce	2.00	.90
❑ 118 Marshall Faulk	2.50	1.10
❑ 119 Kurt Warner	4.00	1.80
❑ 120 Shaun King	.30	.14
❑ 121 Eddie George	2.00	.90
❑ 122 Steve McNair	2.00	.90
❑ 123 Jevon Kearse	2.00	.90
❑ 124 Stephen Davis	2.00	.90
❑ 125 Brad Johnson	2.00	.90
❑ 126 Mike Anderson RC	2.00	.90
❑ 127 Peter Warrick RC	5.00	2.20
❑ 128 Courtney Brown RC	2.00	.90
❑ 129 Plaxico Burress RC	10.00	4.50
❑ 130 Corey Simon RC	5.00	2.20
❑ 131 Thomas Jones RC	8.00	3.60
❑ 132 Travis Taylor RC	2.00	.90
❑ 133 Shaun Alexander RC	12.00	5.50
❑ 134 Deon Grant RC	4.00	1.80
❑ 135 Chris Redman RC	4.00	1.80
❑ 136 Chad Pennington RC	20.00	9.00
❑ 137 Jamal Lewis RC	12.00	5.50
❑ 138 Brian Urlacher RC	20.00	9.00
❑ 139 Keith Bulluck RC	5.00	2.20
❑ 140 Bubba Franks RC	5.00	2.20
❑ 141 Dez White RC	5.00	2.20
❑ 142 Na'il Diggs RC	4.00	1.80
❑ 143 Ahmed Plummer RC	5.00	2.20
❑ 144 Ron Dayne RC	5.00	2.20
❑ 145 Shaun Ellis RC	5.00	2.20
❑ 146 Sylvester Morris RC	4.00	1.80
❑ 147 Deltha O'Neal RC	5.00	2.20
❑ 148 Raynoch Thompson RC	4.00	1.80
❑ 149 R.Jay Soward RC	4.00	1.80
❑ 150 Mario Edwards RC	4.00	1.80
❑ 151 John Engelberger RC	4.00	1.80
❑ 152 D.Goodrich RC	5.00	2.20
❑ 153 Sherrod Gideon RC	2.50	1.10
❑ 154 John Abraham RC	5.00	2.20
❑ 155 Ben Kelly RC	5.00	2.20
❑ 156 Travis Prentice RC	4.00	1.80
❑ 157 Darrell Jackson RC	10.00	4.50
❑ 158 Giovanni Carmazzi RC	4.00	1.80
❑ 159 Anthony Lucas RC	2.50	1.10
❑ 160 Danny Farmer RC	4.00	1.80
❑ 161 Dennis Northcutt RC	5.00	2.20
❑ 162 Troy Walters RC	5.00	2.20
❑ 163 Laveranues Coles RC	6.00	2.70
❑ 164 Tee Martin RC	5.00	2.20
❑ 165 J.R. Redmond RC	4.00	1.80
❑ 166 Tim Rattay RC	4.00	1.80
❑ 167 Jerry Porter RC	6.00	2.70
❑ 168 Sebastian Janikowski RC	5.00	2.20
❑ 169 Michael Wiley RC	4.00	1.80
❑ 170 Reuben Droughns RC	6.00	2.70
❑ 171 Trung Canidate RC	4.00	1.80
❑ 172 Shyrone Stith RC	5.00	2.20
❑ 173 Chris Hovan RC	4.00	1.80
❑ 174 Brandon Short RC	5.00	2.20
❑ 175 Mark Roman RC	5.00	2.20
❑ 176 Trevor Gaylor RC	4.00	1.80
❑ 177 Chris Cole RC	4.00	1.80
❑ 178 Hank Poteat RC	4.00	1.80
❑ 179 Darren Howard RC	4.00	1.80
❑ 180 Rob Morris RC	5.00	2.20
❑ 181 Spergon Wynn RC	4.00	1.80
❑ 182 Marc Bulger RC	10.00	4.50
❑ 183 Tom Brady RC	60.00	27.00
❑ 184 Todd Husak RC	5.00	2.20

❑ 185 Gari Scott RC	2.50	1.10
❑ 186 Erron Kinney RC	4.00	1.80
❑ 187 Julian Peterson RC	5.00	2.20
❑ 188 Sammy Morris RC	4.00	1.80
❑ 189 Rondell Mealey RC	2.50	1.10
❑ 190 Doug Chapman RC	4.00	1.80
❑ 191 Ron Dugans RC	2.50	1.10
❑ 192 Deon Dyer RC	4.00	1.80
❑ 193 Fred Robbins RC	2.50	1.10
❑ 194 Ike Charlton RC	5.00	2.20
❑ 195 Mareno Philyaw RC	2.50	1.10
❑ 196 Thomas Hamner RC	2.50	1.10
❑ 197 Jarious Jackson RC	4.00	1.80
❑ 198 Anthony Becht RC	5.00	2.20
❑ 199 Joe Hamilton RC	4.00	1.80
❑ 200 Todd Pinkston RC	5.00	2.20

2000 Donruss Elite Rookie Die Cuts

	Nm-Mt	Ex-Mt

*DIE CUTS: .6X TO 1.5X BASE ROOKIE CARD

2001 Donruss Elite

	Nm-Mt	Ex-Mt
COMP.SET w/o SP's (100)	20.00	6.00
❑ 1 David Boston	.60	.18
❑ 2 Jake Plummer	.40	.12
❑ 3 Thomas Jones	.40	.12
❑ 4 Jamal Anderson	.60	.18
❑ 5 Chris Redman	.25	.07
❑ 6 Jamal Lewis	1.00	.30
❑ 7 Shannon Sharpe	.40	.12
❑ 8 Travis Taylor	.40	.12
❑ 9 Trent Dilfer	.40	.12
❑ 10 Doug Flutie	.60	.18
❑ 11 Eric Moulds	.40	.12
❑ 12 Rob Johnson	.40	.12
❑ 13 Muhsin Muhammad	.40	.12
❑ 14 Steve Beuerlein	.25	.07
❑ 15 Brian Urlacher	1.00	.30
❑ 16 Cade McNown	.25	.07
❑ 17 Marcus Robinson	.60	.18
❑ 18 Akili Smith	.25	.07
❑ 19 Corey Dillon	.60	.18
❑ 20 Peter Warrick	.60	.18
❑ 21 Kevin Johnson	.40	.12
❑ 22 Tim Couch	.40	.12
❑ 23 Emmitt Smith	1.25	.35
❑ 24 Troy Aikman	1.00	.30
❑ 25 Brian Griese	.60	.18
❑ 26 John Elway	2.00	.60
❑ 27 Mike Anderson	.60	.18
❑ 28 Rod Smith	.40	.12
❑ 29 Terrell Davis	.60	.18
❑ 30 Barry Sanders	1.25	.35
❑ 31 Charlie Batch	.60	.18
❑ 32 James Stewart	.40	.12
❑ 33 Ahman Green	.60	.18
❑ 34 Antonio Freeman	.60	.18
❑ 35 Brett Favre	2.00	.60
❑ 36 Edgerrin James	.75	.23
❑ 37 Marvin Harrison	.60	.18
❑ 38 Peyton Manning	1.50	.45
❑ 39 Fred Taylor	.60	.18
❑ 40 Jimmy Smith	.40	.12
❑ 41 Keenan McCardell	.25	.07
❑ 42 Mark Brunell	.60	.18
❑ 43 Derrick Alexander	.40	.12
❑ 44 Elvis Grbac	.40	.12
❑ 45 Sylvester Morris	.25	.07
❑ 46 Tony Gonzalez	.40	.12
❑ 47 Dan Marino	2.00	.60
❑ 48 Jay Fiedler	.60	.18
❑ 49 Lamar Smith	.40	.12
❑ 50 Oronde Gadsden	.40	.12
❑ 51 Cris Carter	.60	.18
❑ 52 Daunte Culpepper	.60	.18
❑ 53 Randy Moss	1.25	.35
❑ 54 Robert Smith	.40	.12
❑ 55 Drew Bledsoe	.75	.23
❑ 56 Terry Glenn	.25	.07
❑ 57 Aaron Brooks	.60	.18
❑ 58 Joe Horn	.40	.12
❑ 59 Ricky Williams	.60	.18
❑ 60 Amani Toomer	.25	.07
❑ 61 Ike Hilliard	.40	.12
❑ 62 Kerry Collins	.40	.12
❑ 63 Ron Dayne	.60	.18
❑ 64 Tiki Barber	.40	.12
❑ 65 Chad Pennington	1.00	.30
❑ 66 Curtis Martin	.60	.18
❑ 67 Vinny Testaverde	.40	.12
❑ 68 Wayne Chrebet	.40	.12
❑ 69 Rich Gannon	.60	.18
❑ 70 Tim Brown	.60	.18
❑ 71 Tyrone Wheatley	.40	.12
❑ 72 Donovan McNabb	.75	.23
❑ 73 Jerome Bettis	.60	.18
❑ 74 Plaxico Burress	.60	.18
❑ 75 Junior Seau	.60	.18
❑ 76 Charlie Garner	.40	.12
❑ 77 Jeff Garcia	.60	.18
❑ 78 Jerry Rice	1.25	.35
❑ 79 Terrell Owens	.60	.18
❑ 80 Darrell Jackson	.60	.18
❑ 81 Ricky Watters	.40	.12
❑ 82 Shaun Alexander	.75	.23
❑ 83 Isaac Bruce	.60	.18
❑ 84 Kurt Warner	1.25	.35
❑ 85 Marshall Faulk	.75	.23
❑ 86 Torry Holt	.60	.18
❑ 87 Trent Green	.60	.18
❑ 88 Keyshawn Johnson	.60	.18
❑ 89 Shaun King	.25	.07
❑ 90 Warren Sapp	.40	.12
❑ 91 Warrick Dunn	.60	.18
❑ 92 Eddie George	.60	.18
❑ 93 Jevon Kearse	.40	.12
❑ 94 Steve McNair	.60	.18
❑ 95 Albert Connell	.25	.07
❑ 96 Jeff George	.40	.12
❑ 97 Brad Johnson	.60	.18
❑ 98 Bruce Smith	.25	.07
❑ 99 Michael Westbrook	.40	.12
❑ 100 Stephen Davis	.60	.18
❑ 101 Michael Vick RC	80.00	24.00
❑ 102 Drew Brees RC	20.00	6.00
❑ 103 Chris Weinke RC	10.00	3.00
❑ 104 Quincy Carter RC	10.00	3.00
❑ 105 Sage Rosenfels RC	10.00	3.00
❑ 106 Josh Heupel RC	10.00	3.00
❑ 107 Tony Driver RC	6.00	1.80
❑ 108 Ben Leard RC	6.00	1.80
❑ 109 Marques Tuiasosopo RC	10.00	3.00
❑ 110 Tim Hasselbeck RC	10.00	3.00
❑ 111 Mike McMahon RC	10.00	3.00
❑ 112 Deuce McAllister RC	25.00	7.50
❑ 113 LaMont Jordan RC	12.00	3.60
❑ 114 LaDainian Tomlinson RC	40.00	12.00
❑ 115 James Jackson RC	10.00	3.00
❑ 116 Anthony Thomas RC	15.00	4.50
❑ 117 Travis Henry RC	12.00	3.60
❑ 118 DeAngelo Evans RC	6.00	1.80
❑ 119 Travis Minor RC	6.00	1.80
❑ 120 Rudi Johnson RC	20.00	6.00
❑ 121 Michael Bennett RC	20.00	6.00
❑ 122 Kevan Barlow RC	10.00	3.00
❑ 123 Dan Alexander RC	10.00	3.00
❑ 124 David Allen RC	6.00	1.80
❑ 125 Correll Buckhalter RC	12.00	3.60
❑ 126 David Rivers RC	6.00	1.80
❑ 127 Reggie White RC	6.00	1.80
❑ 128 Moran Norris RC	4.00	1.20
❑ 129 Ja'Mar Toombs RC	6.00	1.80
❑ 130 Jason McKinley RC	6.00	1.80
❑ 131 Scotty Anderson RC	6.00	1.80
❑ 132 Dustin McClintock RC	10.00	3.00
❑ 133 Heath Evans RC	6.00	1.80
❑ 134 David Terrell RC	10.00	3.00
❑ 135 Santana Moss RC	15.00	4.50
❑ 136 Rod Gardner RC	10.00	3.00
❑ 137 Quincy Morgan RC	10.00	3.00
❑ 138 Freddie Mitchell RC	10.00	3.00
❑ 139 Boo Williams RC	6.00	1.80
❑ 140 Reggie Wayne RC	15.00	4.50
❑ 141 Ronney Daniels RC	4.00	1.20
❑ 142 Bobby Newcombe RC	6.00	1.80
❑ 143 Reggie Germany/250 RC	12.00	3.60
❑ 144 Jesse Palmer RC	10.00	3.00
❑ 145 Robert Ferguson RC	10.00	3.00
❑ 146 Ken-Yon Rambo RC	6.00	1.80
❑ 147 Alex Bannister RC	6.00	1.80
❑ 148 Koren Robinson RC	12.00	3.60
❑ 149 Chad Johnson RC	20.00	6.00
❑ 150 Chris Chambers RC	12.00	3.60
❑ 151 Javon Green RC	6.00	1.80
❑ 152 Snoop Minnis RC	6.00	1.80
❑ 153 Vinny Sutherland RC	6.00	1.80
❑ 154 Cedrick Wilson RC	10.00	3.00
❑ 155 John Capel/250 RC	12.00	3.60
❑ 156 T.J. Houshmandzadeh RC	10.00	3.00
❑ 157 Todd Heap RC	10.00	3.00
❑ 158 Alge Crumpler RC	12.00	3.60
❑ 159 Jabari Holloway RC	6.00	1.80
❑ 160 Marcellus Rivers RC	6.00	1.80
❑ 161 Rashon Burns RC	4.00	1.20
❑ 162 Tony Stewart RC	10.00	3.00
❑ 163 Jevaris Johnson RC	4.00	1.20
❑ 164 Jamal Reynolds RC	10.00	3.00
❑ 165 Andre Carter RC	10.00	3.00
❑ 166 David Warren RC	4.00	1.20
❑ 167 Justin Smith RC	10.00	3.00
❑ 168 Josh Booty RC	10.00	3.00
❑ 169 Karon Riley RC	4.00	1.20
❑ 170 Cedric Scott RC	4.00	1.20
❑ 171 Kenny Smith RC	6.00	1.80
❑ 172 Richard Seymour RC	10.00	3.00
❑ 173 Willie Howard RC	6.00	1.80
❑ 174 Markus Steele RC	6.00	1.80
❑ 175 Marcus Stroud RC	10.00	3.00
❑ 176 Damione Lewis RC	6.00	1.80
❑ 177 Casey Hampton RC	6.00	1.80
❑ 178 Ennis Davis RC	4.00	1.20
❑ 179 Gerard Warren RC	.60	.18
❑ 180 Tommy Polley RC	10.00	3.00
❑ 181 Kendrell Bell/250 RC	60.00	18.00
❑ 182 Dan Morgan RC	10.00	3.00
❑ 183 Morlon Greenwood RC	6.00	1.80
❑ 184 Quinton Caver/250	10.00	3.00
❑ 185 Keith Adams RC	4.00	1.20
❑ 186 Brian Allen RC	4.00	1.20
❑ 187 Carlos Polk RC	4.00	1.20
❑ 188 Torrance Marshall RC	10.00	3.00
❑ 189 Jamie Winborn RC	6.00	1.80
❑ 190 Jamar Fletcher RC	6.00	1.80
❑ 191 Ken Lucas RC	6.00	1.80
❑ 192 Fred Smoot RC	10.00	3.00
❑ 193 Nate Clements RC	10.00	3.00
❑ 194 Will Allen RC	6.00	1.80
❑ 195 W.Middlebrooks RC/250	10.00	3.00
❑ 196 Gary Baxter RC	6.00	1.80
❑ 197 Derrick Gibson RC	6.00	1.80
❑ 198 Robert Carswell/250 RC	10.00	3.00
❑ 199 Hakim Akbar RC	4.00	1.20
❑ 200 Adam Archuleta RC	10.00	3.00

2001 Donruss Elite Aspirations

	Nm-Mt	Ex-Mt

*STARS/70-99: 10X TO 25X BASIC CARDS
*ROOKIES/70-99: .25X TO .6X BASIC CARDS
*STARS/45-69: 15X TO 40X BASIC CARDS
*ROOKIES/45-69: .4X TO 1X BASIC CARDS
*ROOKIES/30-44: .5X TO 1.2X BASIC CARDS
*STARS/20-29: 40X TO 100X BASIC CARDS

*ROOKIES/20-29: 1X TO 2.5X BASIC CARDS
*STARS/10-19: 50X TO 120X BASIC CARDS
*ROOKIES/10-19: 1.2X TO 3X BASIC CARDS

❑ 143 Reggie Germany/20	30.00	9.00
❑ 155 John Capel/90	8.00	2.40
❑ 181 Kendrell Bell/63	120.00	36.00
❑ 184 Quinton Caver/47	10.00	3.00
❑ 195 Willie Middlebrooks/58	10.00	3.00
❑ 198 Robert Carswell/91	6.00	1.80

2001 Donruss Elite Status

Nm-Mt Ex-Mt

*STARS/70-99: 10X TO 25X BASIC CARDS
*ROOKIES/70-99: .25X TO .6X BASIC CARDS
*STARS/45-69: 15X TO 40X BASIC CARDS
*ROOKIES/45-69: .4X TO 1X BASIC CARDS
*STARS/30-44: 20X TO 50X BASIC CARDS
*ROOKIES/30-44: .5X TO 1.2X BASIC CARDS
*STARS/20-29: 40X TO 100X BASIC CARDS
*ROOKIES/20-29: 1X TO 2.5X BASIC CARDS

	Nm-Mt	Ex-Mt
❑ 181 Kendrell Bell/37	80.00	24.00
❑ 195 Willie Middlebrooks/42	12.00	3.60
❑ 198 Robert Carswell/9		

2002 Donruss Elite

	Nm-Mt	Ex-Mt
COMP.SET w/o SP's (100)	20.00	6.00
❑ 1 Elvis Grbac	.30	.09
❑ 2 Jamal Lewis	.50	.15
❑ 3 Ray Lewis	.50	.15
❑ 4 Travis Henry	.50	.15
❑ 5 Eric Moulds	.30	.09
❑ 6 Corey Dillon	.30	.09
❑ 7 Peter Warrick	.30	.09
❑ 8 Tim Couch	.30	.09
❑ 9 James Jackson	.20	.06
❑ 10 Kevin Johnson	.30	.09
❑ 11 Mike Anderson	.50	.15
❑ 12 Terrell Davis	.50	.15
❑ 13 Brian Griese	.50	.15
❑ 14 Rod Smith	.30	.09
❑ 15 Marvin Harrison	.50	.15
❑ 16 Reggie Wayne	.30	.09
❑ 17 Dominic Rhodes	.30	.09
❑ 18 Edgerrin James	.60	.18
❑ 19 Mark Brunell	.50	.15
❑ 20 Keenan McCardell	.20	.06
❑ 21 Jimmy Smith	.30	.09
❑ 22 Tony Gonzalez	.30	.09
❑ 23 Trent Green	.30	.09
❑ 24 Priest Holmes	.60	.18
❑ 25 Snoop Minnis	.20	.06
❑ 26 Chris Chambers	.50	.15
❑ 27 Jay Fiedler	.30	.09
❑ 28 Travis Minor	.20	.06
❑ 29 Lamar Smith	.30	.09
❑ 30 Tom Brady	1.25	.35
❑ 31 Troy Brown	.30	.09
❑ 32 Antowain Smith	.30	.09
❑ 33 Laveranues Coles	.30	.09
❑ 34 Curtis Martin	.50	.15
❑ 35 Vinny Testaverde	.30	.09
❑ 36 Wayne Chrebet	.30	.09
❑ 37 Tim Brown	.50	.15
❑ 38 Rich Gannon	.50	.15
❑ 39 Jerry Rice	1.00	.30
❑ 40 Charlie Garner	.30	.09
❑ 41 Jerome Bettis	.50	.15
❑ 42 Plaxico Burress	.30	.09
❑ 43 Kordell Stewart	.30	.09
❑ 44 Kendrell Bell	.50	.15
❑ 45 Doug Flutie	.50	.15
❑ 46 LaDainian Tomlinson	.75	.23
❑ 47 Junior Seau	.50	.15
❑ 48 Drew Brees	.50	.15
❑ 49 Shaun Alexander	.50	.15
❑ 50 Koren Robinson	.30	.09
❑ 51 Ricky Watters	.30	.09
❑ 52 Eddie George	.50	.15
❑ 53 Derrick Mason	.30	.09
❑ 54 Steve McNair	.50	.15
❑ 55 David Boston	.50	.15
❑ 56 Jake Plummer	.30	.09
❑ 57 Chris Chandler	.30	.09
❑ 58 Jamal Anderson	.30	.09
❑ 59 Michael Vick	1.50	.45
❑ 60 Wesley Walls	.20	.06
❑ 61 Chris Weinke	.30	.09
❑ 62 David Terrell	.50	.15
❑ 63 Anthony Thomas	.50	.15
❑ 64 Brian Urlacher	.75	.23
❑ 65 Quincy Carter	.30	.09
❑ 66 Rocket Ismail	.30	.09
❑ 67 Emmitt Smith	1.25	.35
❑ 68 James Stewart	.30	.09
❑ 69 Germane Crowell	.20	.06
❑ 70 Mike McMahon	.50	.15
❑ 71 Brett Favre	1.25	.35
❑ 72 Ahman Green	.50	.15
❑ 73 Antonio Freeman	.50	.15
❑ 74 Michael Bennett	.30	.09
❑ 75 Cris Carter	.50	.15
❑ 76 Daunte Culpepper	.50	.15
❑ 77 Randy Moss	1.00	.30
❑ 78 Aaron Brooks	.50	.15
❑ 79 Deuce McAllister	.60	.18
❑ 80 Ricky Williams	.50	.15
❑ 81 Kerry Collins	.30	.09
❑ 82 Ron Dayne	.30	.09
❑ 83 Amani Toomer	.30	.09
❑ 84 Correll Buckhalter	.30	.09
❑ 85 James Thrash	.30	.09
❑ 86 Freddie Mitchell	.30	.09
❑ 87 Duce Staley	.50	.15
❑ 88 Jeff Garcia	.50	.15
❑ 89 Garrison Hearst	.30	.09
❑ 90 Terrell Owens	.50	.15
❑ 91 Isaac Bruce	.50	.15
❑ 92 Marshall Faulk	.50	.15
❑ 93 Torry Holt	.50	.15
❑ 94 Kurt Warner	.50	.15
❑ 95 Mike Alstott	.50	.15
❑ 96 Brad Johnson	.30	.09
❑ 97 Keyshawn Johnson	.50	.15
❑ 98 Stephen Davis	.30	.09
❑ 99 Rod Gardner	.30	.09
❑ 100 Tony Banks	.20	.06
❑ 101 David Carr RC	50.00	15.00
❑ 102 Joey Harrington RC	50.00	15.00
❑ 103 Rohan Davey RC	15.00	4.50
❑ 104 Chad Hutchinson RC	15.00	4.50
❑ 105 Patrick Ramsey RC	25.00	7.50
❑ 106 Kurt Kittner RC	12.00	3.60
❑ 107 Eric Crouch RC	25.00	7.50
❑ 108 David Garrard RC	15.00	4.50
❑ 109 Ronald Curry RC	15.00	4.50
❑ 110 Zak Kustok RC	15.00	4.50
❑ 111 Woody Dantzler RC	15.00	4.50
❑ 112 Wes Pate RC	6.00	1.80
❑ 113 Brian Westbrook RC	25.00	7.50
❑ 114 Josh McCown RC	20.00	6.00
❑ 115 Travis Stephens RC	12.00	3.60
❑ 116 Luke Staley RC	12.00	3.60
❑ 117 William Green RC	25.00	7.50
❑ 118 Clinton Portis RC	50.00	15.00
❑ 119 DeShaun Foster RC	15.00	4.50
❑ 120 Verron Haynes RC	15.00	4.50
❑ 121 T.J. Duckett RC	25.00	7.50
❑ 122 Antwoine Womack RC	12.00	3.60
❑ 123 Leonard Henry RC	12.00	3.60
❑ 124 Lamar Gordon RC	15.00	4.50
❑ 125 Adrian Peterson RC	15.00	4.50
❑ 126 Chester Taylor RC	15.00	4.50
❑ 127 Damien Anderson RC	12.00	3.60
❑ 128 Maurice Morris RC	15.00	4.50
❑ 129 Ricky Williams RC	12.00	3.60
❑ 130 Terry Charles RC	12.00	3.60
❑ 131 Demontray Carter RC	6.00	1.80
❑ 132 Jason McAddley RC	12.00	3.60
❑ 133 Ladell Betts RC	15.00	4.50
❑ 134 Cortlen Johnson RC	6.00	1.80
❑ 135 James Mungro RC	15.00	4.50
❑ 136 Atrews Bell RC	6.00	1.80
❑ 137 Josh Scobey RC	15.00	4.50
❑ 138 Justin Peelle RC	6.00	1.80
❑ 139 Najeh Davenport RC	15.00	4.50
❑ 140 Josh Reed RC	15.00	4.50
❑ 141 Marquise Walker RC	12.00	3.60
❑ 142 Jabar Gaffney RC	15.00	4.50
❑ 143 Antwaan Randle El RC	20.00	6.00
❑ 144 Ashley Lelie RC	30.00	9.00
❑ 145 Tavon Mason RC	6.00	1.80
❑ 146 Antonio Bryant RC	15.00	4.50
❑ 147 Javon Walker RC	30.00	9.00
❑ 148 Kelly Campbell RC	12.00	3.60
❑ 149 Ron Johnson RC	12.00	3.60
❑ 150 Andre Davis RC	15.00	4.50
❑ 151 Cliff Russell RC	12.00	3.60
❑ 152 Reche Caldwell RC	15.00	4.50
❑ 153 Kyle Johnson RC	6.00	1.80
❑ 154 Freddie Milons RC	12.00	3.60
❑ 155 Brian Poli-Dixon RC	12.00	3.60
❑ 156 David Thornton RC	6.00	1.80
❑ 157 Bryan Thomas RC	12.00	3.60
❑ 158 Kahlil Hill RC	12.00	3.60
❑ 159 Deion Branch RC	25.00	7.50
❑ 160 Akin Ayodele RC	6.00	1.80
❑ 161 Donte Stallworth RC	30.00	9.00
❑ 162 Tim Carter RC	12.00	3.60
❑ 163 Kenyon Coleman RC	6.00	1.80
❑ 164 Jeremy Shockey RC	50.00	15.00
❑ 165 Eddie Freeman RC	6.00	1.80
❑ 166 Tracey Wistrom RC	12.00	3.60
❑ 167 Daniel Graham RC	15.00	4.50
❑ 168 Julius Peppers RC	30.00	9.00
❑ 169 Alex Brown RC	15.00	4.50
❑ 170 Dwight Freeney RC	20.00	6.00
❑ 171 Kalimba Edwards RC	15.00	4.50
❑ 172 Dennis Johnson RC	6.00	1.80
❑ 173 Travis Fisher RC	15.00	4.50
❑ 174 John Henderson RC	15.00	4.50
❑ 175 Anthony Weaver RC	12.00	3.60
❑ 176 Ryan Sims RC	15.00	4.50
❑ 177 Alan Harper RC	6.00	1.80
❑ 178 Larry Tripplett RC	6.00	1.80
❑ 179 Wendell Bryant RC	15.00	4.50
❑ 180 Albert Haynesworth RC	12.00	3.60
❑ 181 Levar Fisher RC	6.00	1.80
❑ 182 Andra Davis RC	12.00	3.60
❑ 183 Joseph Jefferson RC	12.00	3.60
❑ 184 Lamont Thompson RC	12.00	3.60
❑ 185 Robert Thomas RC	15.00	4.50
❑ 186 Michael Lewis RC	15.00	4.50
❑ 187 Rocky Calmus RC	15.00	4.50
❑ 188 Napoleon Harris RC	15.00	4.50
❑ 189 Lito Sheppard RC	15.00	4.50
❑ 190 Quentin Jammer RC	15.00	4.50
❑ 191 Roy Williams RC	40.00	12.00
❑ 192 Marques Anderson RC	15.00	4.50
❑ 193 Chris Hope RC	12.00	3.60
❑ 194 Raonall Smith RC	12.00	3.60
❑ 195 Mike Rumph RC	15.00	4.50
❑ 196 James Allen RC	6.00	1.80
❑ 197 Ed Reed RC	25.00	7.50
❑ 198 Mike Williams RC	12.00	3.60
❑ 199 Phillip Buchanon RC	15.00	4.50
❑ 200 Bryant McKinnie RC	12.00	3.60

2002 Donruss Elite Aspirations

Nm-Mt Ex-Mt

*STARS/70-99: 8X TO 20X BASIC CARDS
*ROOKIES/70-99: .5X TO 1.2X
*STARS/45-69: 10X TO 25X
*ROOKIES/45-69: .5X TO 1.2X

*STARS/30-44: 15X TO 40X
*ROOKIES/30-44: .6X TO 1.5X
*STARS/20-29: 25X TO 60X
*ROOKIES/20-29: 1.2X TO 3X
CARDS #'d/19 OR LESS NOT PRICED DUE TO SCARCITY

2002 Donruss Elite Status

Nm-Mt Ex-Mt

*STARS/70-99: 6X TO 15X BASIC CARDS
*ROOKIES/70-99: .4X TO 1X
*STARS/45-69: 10X TO 25X
*ROOKIES/45-69: .5X TO 1.2X
*ROOKIES/30-44: .6X TO 1.5X
*STARS/20-29: 25X TO 60X
*ROOKIES/20-29: 1.2X TO 3X
CARDS #'d/19 OR LESS NOT PRICED DUE TO SCARCITY

2003 Donruss Elite

	Nm-Mt	Ex-Mt
COMP.SET w/o SP's (100)	20.00	6.00
❑ 1 Jamal Lewis	.50	.15
❑ 2 Ray Lewis	.50	.15
❑ 3 Todd Heap	.30	.09
❑ 4 Drew Bledsoe	.50	.15
❑ 5 Travis Henry	.30	.09
❑ 6 Eric Moulds	.30	.09
❑ 7 Peerless Price	.30	.09
❑ 8 Jon Kitna	.30	.09
❑ 9 Corey Dillon	.30	.09
❑ 10 Chad Johnson	.30	.09
❑ 11 Tim Couch	.20	.06
❑ 12 William Green	.30	.09
❑ 13 Andre Davis	.20	.06
❑ 14 Brian Griese	.50	.15
❑ 15 Ashley Lelie	.50	.15
❑ 16 Clinton Portis	.75	.23
❑ 17 Rod Smith	.30	.09
❑ 18 David Carr	.75	.23
❑ 19 Jonathan Wells	.20	.06
❑ 20 Jabar Gaffney	.30	.09
❑ 21 Peyton Manning	.75	.23
❑ 22 Edgerrin James	.50	.15
❑ 23 Marvin Harrison	.50	.15
❑ 24 Mark Brunell	.30	.09
❑ 25 Jimmy Smith	.30	.09
❑ 26 Fred Taylor	.50	.15
❑ 27 Priest Holmes	.60	.18
❑ 28 Trent Green	.30	.09
❑ 29 Tony Gonzalez	.30	.09
❑ 30 Chris Chambers	.50	.15
❑ 31 Zach Thomas	.30	.09
❑ 32 Ricky Williams	.50	.15
❑ 33 Tom Brady	.75	.23
❑ 34 Antowain Smith	.30	.09
❑ 35 Troy Brown	.30	.09
❑ 36 Chad Pennington	.60	.18
❑ 37 Curtis Martin	.50	.15
❑ 38 Laveranues Coles	.30	.09
❑ 39 Tim Brown	.50	.15
❑ 40 Rich Gannon	.30	.09
❑ 41 Jerry Rice	1.00	.30
❑ 42 Charlie Garner	.30	.09
❑ 43 Antwaan Randle El	.50	.15
❑ 44 Plaxico Burress	.30	.09
❑ 45 Tommy Maddox	.50	.15
❑ 46 Jerome Bettis	.50	.15
❑ 47 Drew Brees	.50	.15
❑ 48 LaDainian Tomlinson	.50	.15
❑ 49 Junior Seau	.50	.15
❑ 50 Eddie George	.30	.09
❑ 51 Steve McNair	.50	.15
❑ 52 Derrick Mason	.30	.09
❑ 53 David Boston	.30	.09
❑ 54 Jake Plummer	.30	.09
❑ 55 Marcel Shipp	.30	.09
❑ 56 Michael Vick	1.25	.35
❑ 57 T.J. Duckett	.30	.09
❑ 58 Warrick Dunn	.30	.09
❑ 59 Julius Peppers	.50	.15
❑ 60 Steve Smith	.20	.06
❑ 61 Muhsin Muhammad	.30	.09
❑ 62 Anthony Thomas	.50	.15
❑ 63 Brian Urlacher	.75	.23
❑ 64 Marty Booker	.30	.09
❑ 65 Chad Hutchinson	.30	.09
❑ 66 Antonio Bryant	.30	.09
❑ 67 Emmitt Smith	1.25	.35
❑ 68 Joey Harrington	.75	.23
❑ 69 Germane Crowell	.20	.06
❑ 70 James Stewart	.30	.09
❑ 71 Brett Favre	1.25	.35
❑ 72 Donald Driver	.30	.09
❑ 73 Ahman Green	.50	.15
❑ 74 Randy Moss	.75	.23
❑ 75 Michael Bennett	.30	.09
❑ 76 Daunte Culpepper	.50	.15
❑ 77 Aaron Brooks	.50	.15
❑ 78 Deuce McAllister	.50	.15
❑ 79 Donte Stallworth	.50	.15
❑ 80 Tiki Barber	.30	.09
❑ 81 Jeremy Shockey	.75	.23
❑ 82 Kerry Collins	.30	.09
❑ 83 Donovan McNabb	.60	.18
❑ 84 James Thrash	.20	.06
❑ 85 Duce Staley	.30	.09
❑ 86 Jeff Garcia	.50	.15
❑ 87 Terrell Owens	.50	.15
❑ 88 Garrison Hearst	.30	.09
❑ 89 Shaun Alexander	.50	.15
❑ 90 Darrell Jackson	.30	.09
❑ 91 Koren Robinson	.20	.06
❑ 92 Marshall Faulk	.50	.15
❑ 93 Kurt Warner	.50	.15
❑ 94 Isaac Bruce	.50	.15
❑ 95 Keyshawn Johnson	.50	.15
❑ 96 Brad Johnson	.30	.09
❑ 97 Warren Sapp	.30	.09
❑ 98 Patrick Ramsey	.50	.15
❑ 99 Rod Gardner	.30	.09
❑ 100 Stephen Davis	.30	.09
❑ 101 Brian St.Pierre RC	12.00	3.60
❑ 102 Byron Leftwich RC	40.00	12.00
❑ 103 Carson Palmer RC	30.00	9.00
❑ 104 Chris Simms RC	25.00	7.50
❑ 105 Dave Ragone RC	12.00	3.60
❑ 106 Ken Dorsey RC	20.00	6.00
❑ 107 Kliff Kingsbury RC	10.00	3.00
❑ 108 Kyle Boller RC	30.00	9.00
❑ 109 Rex Grossman RC	30.00	9.00
❑ 110 Seneca Wallace RC	12.00	3.60
❑ 111 Jason Gesser RC	12.00	3.60
❑ 112 Artose Pinner RC	12.00	3.60
❑ 113 Avon Cobourne RC	6.00	1.80
❑ 114 Cecil Sapp RC	10.00	3.00
❑ 115 Chris Brown RC	25.00	7.50
❑ 116 Derek Watson RC	10.00	3.00
❑ 117 Domanick Davis RC	25.00	7.50
❑ 118 Dwone Hicks/100 RC	30.00	9.00
❑ 119 Earnest Graham RC	10.00	3.00
❑ 120 Justin Fargas RC	12.00	3.60
❑ 121 Larry Johnson RC	25.00	7.50
❑ 122 Lee Suggs RC	25.00	7.50
❑ 123 Musa Smith RC	12.00	3.60
❑ 124 Onterrio Smith RC	15.00	4.50
❑ 125 Quentin Griffin RC	30.00	9.00
❑ 126 Willis McGahee RC	30.00	9.00
❑ 127 Sultan McCullough RC	10.00	3.00
❑ 128 LaBrandon Toefield RC	12.00	3.60
❑ 129 B.J. Askew RC	12.00	3.60
❑ 130 Andre Johnson RC	30.00	9.00
❑ 131 Anquan Boldin RC	30.00	9.00
❑ 132 Amaz Battle RC	12.00	3.60
❑ 133 Bethel Johnson RC	20.00	6.00
❑ 134 Billy McMullen RC	10.00	3.00
❑ 135 Bobby Wade RC	12.00	3.60
❑ 136 Brandon Lloyd RC	15.00	4.50
❑ 137 Bryant Johnson RC	12.00	3.60
❑ 138 Charles Rogers RC	15.00	4.50
❑ 139 Doug Gabriel RC	12.00	3.60
❑ 140 Justin Gage RC	12.00	3.60
❑ 141 Kareem Kelly RC	10.00	3.00
❑ 142 Kelley Washington RC	12.00	3.60
❑ 143 Kevin Curtis RC	12.00	3.60
❑ 144 Nate Burleson RC	20.00	6.00
❑ 145 Sam Aiken RC	10.00	3.00
❑ 146 Shaun McDonald RC	12.00	3.60
❑ 147 Talman Gardner RC	12.00	3.60
❑ 148 Taylor Jacobs RC	12.00	3.60
❑ 149 Terrence Edwards RC	10.00	3.00
❑ 150 Tyrone Calico RC	15.00	4.50
❑ 151 Walter Young RC	6.00	1.80
❑ 152 Ryan Hoag/100 RC	30.00	9.00
❑ 153 Paul Arnold/100 RC	30.00	9.00
❑ 154 Bennie Joppru RC	12.00	3.60
❑ 155 Dallas Clark RC	12.00	3.60
❑ 156 George Wrighster RC	10.00	3.00
❑ 157 Jason Witten RC	20.00	6.00
❑ 158 Mike Pinkard RC	6.00	1.80
❑ 159 Robert Johnson/100 RC	30.00	9.00
❑ 160 Teyo Johnson RC	12.00	3.60
❑ 161 Andrew Williams RC	10.00	3.00
❑ 162 Chris Kelsay RC	12.00	3.60
❑ 163 Cory Redding RC	10.00	3.00
❑ 164 DeWayne Robertson RC	12.00	3.60
❑ 165 DeWayne White RC	10.00	3.00
❑ 166 Jerome McDougle RC	12.00	3.60
❑ 167 Kenny Peterson RC	10.00	3.00
❑ 168 Kindal Moorehead RC	10.00	3.00
❑ 169 Michael Haynes RC	12.00	3.60
❑ 170 Terrell Suggs RC	20.00	6.00
❑ 171 Tully Banta-Cain RC	10.00	3.00
❑ 172 Jimmy Kennedy RC	12.00	3.60
❑ 173 Johnathan Sullivan RC	6.00	1.80
❑ 174 Kevin Williams RC	12.00	3.60
❑ 175 Nick Eason/100 RC	30.00	9.00
❑ 176 Rien Long RC	6.00	1.80
❑ 177 Ty Warren RC	12.00	3.60
❑ 178 William Joseph RC	12.00	3.60
❑ 179 Boss Bailey RC	15.00	4.50
❑ 180 Bradie James RC	12.00	3.60
❑ 181 Victor Hobson RC	12.00	3.60
❑ 182 Clifton Smith/100 RC	30.00	9.00
❑ 183 E.J. Henderson/100 RC	30.00	9.00
❑ 184 Gerald Hayes/100 RC	30.00	9.00
❑ 185 LaMarcus McDonald/100 RC	30.00	9.00
❑ 186 Nick Barnett RC	20.00	6.00
❑ 187 Terry Pierce RC	10.00	3.00
❑ 188 Andre Woolfolk RC	12.00	3.60
❑ 189 Dennis Weathersby RC	6.00	1.80
❑ 190 Drayton Florence/100 RC	30.00	9.00
❑ 191 Eugene Wilson RC	10.00	3.00
❑ 192 Marcus Trufant RC	12.00	3.60
❑ 193 Rashean Mathis RC	10.00	3.00
❑ 194 Ricky Manning RC	12.00	3.60
❑ 195 Sammy Davis/100 RC	30.00	9.00
❑ 196 Terence Newman RC	25.00	7.50
❑ 197 Julian Battle RC	10.00	3.00
❑ 198 Ken Hamlin RC	12.00	3.60
❑ 199 Mike Doss RC	12.00	3.60
❑ 200 Troy Polamalu/100 RC	40.00	12.00

2003 Donruss Elite Aspirations

Nm-Mt Ex-Mt

*STARS/70-99: 8X TO 20X BASIC CARDS
*ROOKIES/70-99: .5X TO 1.2X
*STARS/45-69: 10X TO 25X
*ROOKIES/45-69: .6X TO 1.5X
*ROOKIES/30-44: .8X TO 2X
*STARS/20-29: 20X TO 50X
*ROOKIES/20-29: 1X TO 2.5X
UNPRICED GOLD ASPIRATIONS OF 1 EXIST

2003 Donruss Elite Status

	Nm-Mt	Ex-Mt
*STARS/70-99: 8X TO 20X BASIC CARDS		
*ROOKIES/70-99: .5X TO 1.2X		
*STARS/45-69: 10X TO 25X		
*ROOKIES/45-69: .6X TO 1.5X		
*STARS/30-44: 15X TO 40X		
*ROOKIES/30-44: .8X TO 2X		
*STARS/20-29: 20X TO 50X		
*ROOKIES/20-29: 1X TO 2.5X		

2004 Donruss Elite

	Nm-Mt	Ex-Mt
COMP.SET w/o SP's (100)	20.00	6.00
ROOKIE PRINT RUN 500 SER.#'d SETS		
1 Emmitt Smith	2.00	.60
2 Anquan Boldin	1.00	.30
3 Michael Vick	2.00	.60
4 Peerless Price	.60	.18
5 T.J. Duckett	.60	.18
6 Warrick Dunn	.60	.18
7 Jamal Lewis	1.00	.30
8 Kyle Boller	1.00	.30
9 Todd Heap	.60	.18
10 Ray Lewis	1.00	.30
11 Drew Bledsoe	1.00	.30
12 Eric Moulds	.60	.18
13 Travis Henry	.60	.18
14 Jake Delhomme	1.00	.30
15 Stephen Davis	.60	.18
16 Steve Smith	.60	.18
17 Anthony Thomas	.60	.18
18 Brian Urlacher	1.25	.35
19 Rex Grossman	1.00	.30
20 Chad Johnson	.60	.18
21 Carson Palmer	1.25	.35
22 Rudi Johnson	.60	.18
23 Peter Warrick	.60	.18
24 Andre Davis	.40	.12
25 Tim Couch	.40	.12
26 Quincy Carter	.60	.18
27 Roy Williams S	.60	.18
28 Terence Newman	.60	.18
29 Clinton Portis	1.00	.30
30 Jake Plummer	.60	.18
31 Rod Smith	.60	.18
32 Charles Rogers	.60	.18
33 Joey Harrington	1.00	.30
34 Ahman Green	1.00	.30
35 Brett Favre	2.50	.75
36 Javon Walker	.60	.18
37 Andre Johnson	1.00	.30
38 David Carr	1.00	.30
39 Domanick Davis	1.00	.30
40 Edgerrin James	1.00	.30
41 Marvin Harrison	1.00	.30
42 Peyton Manning	1.50	.45
43 Reggie Wayne	.60	.18
44 Byron Leftwich	2.00	.60
45 Fred Taylor	.60	.18
46 Jimmy Smith	.60	.18
47 Priest Holmes	1.25	.35
48 Tony Gonzalez	.60	.18
49 Trent Green	.60	.18
50 Chris Chambers	.60	.18
51 Ricky Williams	1.00	.30
52 Zach Thomas	1.00	.30
53 Daunte Culpepper	1.00	.30
54 Michael Bennett	.60	.18
55 Moe Williams	.40	.12
56 Randy Moss	1.25	.35
57 Deion Branch	1.00	.30
58 Tom Brady	1.50	.45
59 Tedy Bruschi	.60	.18
60 Aaron Brooks	.60	.18
61 Deuce McAllister	1.00	.30
62 Joe Horn	.60	.18
63 Jeremy Shockey	1.00	.30
64 Kerry Collins	.60	.18
65 Michael Strahan	.60	.18
66 Tiki Barber	.60	.18
67 Chad Pennington	1.25	.35
68 Curtis Martin	1.00	.30
69 Santana Moss	.60	.18
70 Jerry Porter	.60	.18
71 Jerry Rice	2.00	.60
72 Tim Brown	1.00	.30
73 Brian Westbrook	.60	.18
74 Correll Buckhalter	.60	.18
75 Donovan McNabb	1.25	.35
76 Hines Ward	1.00	.30
77 Kendrell Bell	.60	.18
78 Plaxico Burress	.60	.18
79 David Boston	.60	.18
80 Drew Brees	1.00	.30
81 LaDainian Tomlinson	1.00	.30
82 Jeff Garcia	1.00	.30
83 Kevan Barlow	.60	.18
84 Terrell Owens	1.00	.30
85 Koren Robinson	.60	.18
86 Matt Hasselbeck	.60	.18
87 Shaun Alexander	1.00	.30
88 Isaac Bruce	.60	.18
89 Marc Bulger	1.00	.30
90 Marshall Faulk	1.00	.30
91 Torry Holt	1.00	.30
92 Brad Johnson	.60	.18
93 Derrick Brooks	.60	.18
94 Keenan McCardell	.40	.12
95 Derrick Mason	.60	.18
96 Eddie George	.60	.18
97 Steve McNair	1.00	.30
98 Jevon Kearse	.60	.18
99 Laveranues Coles	.60	.18
100 Patrick Ramsey	.60	.18
101 Adimchinobe Echemandu RC	6.00	1.80
102 Ahmad Carroll RC	10.00	3.00
103 Antwan Odom RC	8.00	2.40
104 B.J. Johnson RC	6.00	1.80
105 Ben Roethlisberger RC	80.00	24.00
106 Ben Troupe RC	8.00	2.40
107 Ben Watson RC	8.00	2.40
108 Bernard Berrian RC	8.00	2.40
109 Bob Sanders RC	8.00	2.40
110 Brandon Everage RC	6.00	1.80
111 Brandon Miree RC	6.00	1.80
112 Carlos Francis RC	6.00	1.80
113 Cedric Cobbs RC	8.00	2.40
114 Chad Lavalais RC	6.00	1.80
115 Chris Collins RC	6.00	1.80
116 Chris Gamble RC	10.00	3.00
117 Chris Perry RC	15.00	4.50
118 Cody Pickett RC	8.00	2.40
119 Craig Krenzel RC	8.00	2.40
120 D.J. Hackett RC	6.00	1.80
121 D.J. Williams RC	10.00	3.00
122 Darius Watts RC	10.00	3.00
123 Darnell Dockett RC	6.00	1.80
124 DeAngelo Hall RC	10.00	3.00
125 Derek Abney RC	8.00	2.40
126 Derrick Hamilton RC	6.00	1.80
127 Derrick Strait RC	8.00	2.40
128 Devard Darling RC	8.00	2.40
129 Devery Henderson RC	6.00	1.80
130 Dontarrious Thomas RC	8.00	2.40
131 Drew Henson RC	25.00	7.50
132 Dunta Robinson RC	8.00	2.40
133 Dwan Edwards RC	4.00	1.20
134 Eli Manning RC	50.00	15.00
135 Ernest Wilford RC	8.00	2.40
136 Fred Russell RC	8.00	2.40
137 Greg Jones RC	8.00	2.40
138 Igor Olshansky RC	8.00	2.40
139 J.P. Losman RC	20.00	6.00
140 Jared Lorenzen RC	6.00	1.80
141 Jarrett Payton RC	8.00	2.40
142 Jason Babin RC	8.00	2.40
143 Jason Fife RC	6.00	1.80
144 Jeff Smoker RC	12.00	3.60
145 Jeremy LeSueur RC	6.00	1.80
146 Jerricho Cotchery RC	8.00	2.40
147 John Navarre RC	8.00	2.40
148 John Standeford RC	6.00	1.80
149 Johnnie Morant RC	8.00	2.40
150 Jonathan Vilma RC	8.00	2.40
151 Josh Davis RC	6.00	1.80
152 Josh Harris RC	8.00	2.40
153 Julius Jones RC	30.00	9.00
154 Justin Jenkins RC	6.00	1.80
155 Karlos Dansby RC	8.00	2.40
156 Keary Colbert RC	10.00	3.00
157 Keith Smith RC	6.00	1.80
158 Keiwan Ratliff RC	6.00	1.80
159 Kellen Winslow RC	20.00	6.00
160 Kendrick Starling RC	4.00	1.20
161 Kenechi Udeze RC	8.00	2.40
162 Kevin Jones RC	25.00	7.50
163 Larry Fitzgerald RC	30.00	9.00
164 Lee Evans RC	12.00	3.60
165 Luke McCown RC	8.00	2.40
166 Marquise Hill RC	6.00	1.80
167 Matt Schaub RC	12.00	3.60
168 Matt Ware RC	8.00	2.40
169 Matt Mauck RC	8.00	2.40
170 Maurice Mann RC	6.00	1.80
171 Mewelde Moore RC	10.00	3.00
172 Michael Boulware RC	8.00	2.40
173 Michael Clayton RC	20.00	6.00
174 Michael Jenkins RC	8.00	2.40
175 Michael Turner RC	6.00	1.80
176 B.J. Symons RC	8.00	2.40
177 Nathan Vasher RC	8.00	2.40
178 P.K. Sam RC	6.00	1.80
179 Philip Rivers RC	25.00	7.50
180 Quincy Wilson RC	6.00	1.80
181 Ran Carthon RC	6.00	1.80
182 Randy Starks RC	6.00	1.80
183 Rashaun Woods RC	10.00	3.00
184 Reggie Williams RC	10.00	3.00
185 Ricardo Colclough RC	8.00	2.40
186 Robert Kent RC	4.00	1.20
187 Roy Williams RC	30.00	9.00
188 Samie Parker RC	8.00	2.40
189 Scott Rislov RC	8.00	2.40
190 Sean Jones RC	6.00	1.80
191 Sean Taylor RC	10.00	3.00
192 Steven Jackson RC	25.00	7.50
193 Stuart Schweigert RC	8.00	2.40
194 Tatum Bell RC	12.00	3.60
195 Teddy Lehman RC	8.00	2.40
196 Tommie Harris RC	10.00	3.00
197 Troy Fleming RC	6.00	1.80
198 Vince Wilfork RC	10.00	3.00
199 Will Poole RC	8.00	2.40
200 Will Smith RC	8.00	2.40

2004 Donruss Elite Aspirations

	Nm-Mt	Ex-Mt
*STARS/70-99: 4X TO 10X BASIC CARDS		
*ROOKIES/70-99: .8X TO 2X		
*STARS/45-69: 5X TO 12X		
*ROOKIES/45-69: 1X TO 2.5X		
*ROOKIES/30-44: 1.2X TO 3X		
*STARS/20-29: 8X TO 20X		
*ROOKIES/20-29: 1.5X TO 4X		
CARDS #'d/19 or LESS NOT PRICED DUE TO SCARCITY		

2004 Donruss Elite Status

	Nm-Mt	Ex-Mt
*STARS/70-99: 4X TO 10X BASIC CARDS		
*ROOKIES/70-99: .8X TO 2X		
*STARS/45-69: 5X TO 12X		

*ROOKIES/45-69: 1X TO 2.5X
*STARS/30-44: 6X TO 15X
*ROOKIES/30-44: 1.2X TO 3X
*STARS/20-29: 8X TO 20X
*ROOKIES/20-29: 1.5X TO 4X
CARDS #'d/19 or LESS NOT PRICED DUE TO SCARCITY

1997 E-X2000

	Nm-Mt	Ex-Mt
COMPLETE SET (60)	30.00	13.50
❑ 1 Jake Plummer RC	10.00	4.50
❑ 2 Jamal Anderson	1.50	.70
❑ 3 Rae Carruth RC	.60	.25
❑ 4 Kerry Collins	1.50	.70
❑ 5 Darnell Autry RC	1.50	.70
❑ 6 Rashaan Salaam	.60	.25
❑ 7 Troy Aikman	3.00	1.35
❑ 8 Deion Sanders	1.50	.70
❑ 9 Emmitt Smith	5.00	2.20
❑ 10 Herman Moore	1.00	.45
❑ 11 Barry Sanders	5.00	2.20
❑ 12 Mark Chmura	1.00	.45
❑ 13 Brett Favre	6.00	2.70
❑ 14 Antonio Freeman	1.50	.70
❑ 15 Reggie White	1.50	.70
❑ 16 Cris Carter	1.50	.70
❑ 17 Brad Johnson	1.50	.70
❑ 18 Troy Davis RC	1.00	.45
❑ 19 Danny Wuerffel RC	1.50	.70
❑ 20 Dave Brown	.60	.25
❑ 21 Ike Hilliard RC	3.00	1.35
❑ 22 Ty Detmer	1.00	.45
❑ 23 Ricky Watters	1.00	.45
❑ 24 Tony Banks	1.00	.45
❑ 25 Eddie Kennison	1.00	.45
❑ 26 Jim Druckenmiller RC	1.00	.45
❑ 27 Jerry Rice	3.00	1.35
❑ 28 Steve Young	2.00	.90
❑ 29 Trent Dilfer	1.50	.70
❑ 30 Warrick Dunn RC	6.00	2.70
❑ 31 Terry Allen	1.50	.70
❑ 32 Gus Frerotte	.60	.25
❑ 33 Vinny Testaverde	1.00	.45
❑ 34 Antowain Smith RC	6.00	2.70
❑ 35 Thurman Thomas	1.50	.70
❑ 36 Jeff Blake	1.00	.45
❑ 37 Carl Pickens	1.00	.45
❑ 38 Terrell Davis	2.00	.90
❑ 39 John Elway	6.00	2.70
❑ 40 Eddie George	1.50	.70
❑ 41 Steve McNair	2.00	.90
❑ 42 Marshall Faulk	2.00	.90
❑ 43 Marvin Harrison	1.50	.70
❑ 44 Mark Brunell	2.00	.90
❑ 45 Marcus Allen	1.50	.70
❑ 46 Elvis Grbac	1.00	.45
❑ 47 Karim Abdul-Jabbar	1.00	.45
❑ 48 Dan Marino	6.00	2.70
❑ 49 Drew Bledsoe	2.00	.90
❑ 50 Terry Glenn	1.50	.70
❑ 51 Curtis Martin	2.00	.90
❑ 52 Keyshawn Johnson	1.50	.70
❑ 53 Tim Brown	1.50	.70
❑ 54 Jeff George	1.00	.45
❑ 55 Jerome Bettis	1.50	.70
❑ 56 Kordell Stewart	1.50	.70
❑ 57 Stan Humphries	1.00	.45
❑ 58 Junior Seau	1.50	.70
❑ 59 Joey Galloway	1.00	.45
❑ 60 Chris Warren	1.00	.45

1997 E-X2000 Essential Credentials

Nm-Mt Ex-Mt

*STARS: 8X TO 20X BASIC CARDS
*RCs: 2.5X TO 6X BASIC CARDS

1998 E-X2001

	Nm-Mt	Ex-Mt
COMPLETE SET (60)	50.00	22.00
❑ 1 Kordell Stewart	.75	.35
❑ 2 Steve Young	1.50	.70
❑ 3 Mark Brunell	.75	.35
❑ 4 Brett Favre	5.00	2.20
❑ 5 Barry Sanders	4.00	1.80
❑ 6 Warrick Dunn	.75	.35
❑ 7 Jerry Rice	2.50	1.10
❑ 8 Dan Marino	5.00	2.20
❑ 9 Emmitt Smith	4.00	1.80
❑ 10 John Elway	5.00	2.20
❑ 11 Eddie George	.75	.35
❑ 12 Jake Plummer	.75	.35
❑ 13 Terrell Davis	.75	.35
❑ 14 Curtis Martin	.75	.35
❑ 15 Troy Aikman	2.50	1.10
❑ 16 Terry Glenn	.75	.35
❑ 17 Mike Alstott	.75	.35
❑ 18 Drew Bledsoe	2.00	.90
❑ 19 Keyshawn Johnson	.75	.35
❑ 20 Dorsey Levens	.75	.35
❑ 21 Elvis Grbac	.50	.23
❑ 22 Ricky Watters	.50	.23
❑ 23 Robert Smith	.75	.35
❑ 24 Trent Dilfer	.75	.35
❑ 25 Joey Galloway	.50	.23
❑ 26 Rob Moore	.50	.23
❑ 27 Steve McNair	.75	.35
❑ 28 Jim Harbaugh	.50	.23
❑ 29 Troy Davis	.30	.14
❑ 30 Rob Johnson	.50	.23
❑ 31 Shannon Sharpe	.50	.23
❑ 32 Jerome Bettis	.75	.35
❑ 33 Tim Brown	.75	.35
❑ 34 Kerry Collins	.50	.23
❑ 35 Garrison Hearst	.75	.35
❑ 36 Antonio Freeman	.75	.35
❑ 37 Charlie Garner	.50	.23
❑ 38 Glenn Foley	.50	.23
❑ 39 Yatil Green	.30	.14
❑ 40 Tiki Barber	.75	.35
❑ 41 Bobby Hoying	.50	.23
❑ 42 Corey Dillon	.75	.35
❑ 43 Antowain Smith	.75	.35
❑ 44 Robert Edwards RC	2.50	1.10
❑ 45 Jammi German RC	1.50	.70
❑ 46 Ahman Green RC	15.00	6.75
❑ 47 Hines Ward RC	8.00	3.60
❑ 48 Skip Hicks RC	2.50	1.10
❑ 49 Brian Griese RC	6.00	2.70
❑ 50 Charlie Batch RC	3.00	1.35
❑ 51 Jacquez Green RC	2.50	1.10
❑ 52 John Avery RC	2.50	1.10
❑ 53 Kevin Dyson RC	3.00	1.35
❑ 54 Peyton Manning RC	30.00	13.50
❑ 55 Randy Moss RC	15.00	6.75
❑ 56 Ryan Leaf RC	3.00	1.35
❑ 57 Curtis Enis RC	1.50	.70
❑ 58 Charles Woodson RC	4.00	1.80
❑ 59 Robert Holcombe RC	2.50	1.10
❑ 60 Fred Taylor RC	5.00	2.20
❑ NNO Jake Plummer PROMO	1.00	.30
❑ NNO Checklist Card 1	.30	.14
❑ NNO Checklist Card 2	.30	.14

1998 E-X2001 Essential Credentials Future

	Nm-Mt	Ex-Mt
❑ 1 Kordell Stewart/60	50.00	22.00
❑ 2 Steve Young/59	80.00	36.00
❑ 3 Mark Brunell/58	80.00	36.00
❑ 4 Brett Favre/57	150.00	70.00
❑ 5 Barry Sanders/56	120.00	55.00
❑ 6 Warrick Dunn/55	50.00	22.00
❑ 7 Jerry Rice/54	120.00	55.00
❑ 8 Dan Marino/53	150.00	70.00
❑ 9 Emmitt Smith/52	150.00	70.00
❑ 10 John Elway/51	150.00	70.00
❑ 11 Eddie George/50	80.00	36.00
❑ 12 Jake Plummer/49	80.00	36.00
❑ 13 Terrell Davis/48	80.00	36.00
❑ 14 Curtis Martin/47	50.00	22.00
❑ 15 Troy Aikman/46	80.00	36.00
❑ 16 Terry Glenn/45	50.00	22.00
❑ 17 Mike Alstott/44	50.00	22.00
❑ 18 Drew Bledsoe/43	80.00	36.00
❑ 19 Keyshawn Johnson/42	50.00	22.00
❑ 20 Dorsey Levens/41	50.00	22.00
❑ 21 Elvis Grbac/40	40.00	18.00
❑ 22 Ricky Watters/39	40.00	18.00
❑ 23 Robert Smith/38	40.00	18.00
❑ 24 Trent Dilfer/37	50.00	22.00
❑ 25 Joey Galloway/36	50.00	22.00
❑ 26 Rob Moore/35	50.00	22.00
❑ 27 Steve McNair/34	80.00	36.00
❑ 28 Jim Harbaugh/33	50.00	22.00
❑ 29 Troy Davis/32	40.00	18.00
❑ 30 Rob Johnson/31	50.00	22.00
❑ 31 Shannon Sharpe/30	50.00	22.00
❑ 32 Jerome Bettis/29	120.00	55.00
❑ 33 Tim Brown/28	120.00	55.00
❑ 34 Kerry Collins/27	50.00	22.00
❑ 35 Garrison Hearst/26	80.00	36.00
❑ 36 Antonio Freeman/25	80.00	36.00
❑ 37 Charlie Garner/24	50.00	22.00
❑ 38 Glenn Foley/23	50.00	22.00
❑ 39 Yatil Green/22	50.00	22.00
❑ 40 Tiki Barber/21	80.00	36.00
❑ 41 Bobby Hoying/20	50.00	22.00

1999 E-X Century

	Nm-Mt	Ex-Mt
COMPLETE SET (90)	120.00	55.00
COMP.SET w/o SP's (60)	40.00	18.00
❑ 1 Keyshawn Johnson	1.25	.55
❑ 2 Natrone Means	.75	.35
❑ 3 Antonio Freeman	1.25	.55
❑ 4 Muhsin Muhammad	.75	.35
❑ 5 Curtis Martin	1.25	.55
❑ 6 Chris Chandler	.75	.35
❑ 7 Priest Holmes	2.00	.90
❑ 8 Vinny Testaverde	.75	.35

	Nm-Mt	Ex-Mt
❑ 9 Tim Brown	1.25	.55
❑ 10 Eddie George	1.25	.55
❑ 11 Brad Johnson	1.25	.55
❑ 12 Mike Alstott	1.25	.55
❑ 13 Dorsey Levens	1.25	.55
❑ 14 Jamal Anderson	1.25	.55
❑ 15 Herman Moore	.75	.35
❑ 16 Brett Favre	4.00	1.80
❑ 17 John Elway	4.00	1.80
❑ 18 Steve Young	1.50	.70
❑ 19 Warrick Dunn	1.25	.55
❑ 20 Fred Taylor	1.25	.55
❑ 21 Charlie Batch	1.25	.55
❑ 22 Jimmy Smith	.75	.35
❑ 23 Steve McNair	1.25	.55
❑ 24 Jerry Rice	2.50	1.10
❑ 25 Dan Marino	4.00	1.80
❑ 26 Jake Plummer	.75	.35
❑ 27 Marshall Faulk	1.50	.70
❑ 28 Garrison Hearst	.75	.35
❑ 29 Terrell Davis	1.25	.55
❑ 30 Barry Sanders	4.00	1.80
❑ 31 Carl Pickens	.75	.35
❑ 32 Jerome Bettis	1.25	.55
❑ 33 Scott Mitchell	.50	.23
❑ 34 Duce Staley	1.25	.55
❑ 35 Robert Smith	1.25	.55
❑ 36 Wayne Chrebet	.75	.35
❑ 37 Steve Beuerlein	.50	.23
❑ 38 Elvis Grbac	.75	.35
❑ 39 Troy Aikman	2.50	1.10
❑ 40 Emmitt Smith	2.50	1.10
❑ 41 Joey Galloway	.75	.35
❑ 42 Ryan Leaf	1.25	.55
❑ 43 Skip Hicks	.50	.23
❑ 44 Cris Carter	1.25	.55
❑ 45 Shannon Sharpe	.75	.35
❑ 46 Mark Brunell	1.25	.55
❑ 47 Kerry Collins	.75	.35
❑ 48 Corey Dillon	1.25	.55
❑ 49 Kordell Stewart	.75	.35
❑ 50 Randy Moss	3.00	1.35
❑ 51 Jon Kitna	1.25	.55
❑ 52 Deion Sanders	1.25	.55
❑ 53 Rod Smith	.75	.35
❑ 54 Drew Bledsoe	1.50	.70
❑ 55 Terrell Owens	1.25	.55
❑ 56 Napoleon Kaufman	1.25	.55
❑ 57 Trent Green	1.25	.55
❑ 58 Ricky Watters	.75	.35
❑ 59 Randall Cunningham	1.25	.55
❑ 60 Peyton Manning	4.00	1.80
❑ 61 Tim Couch RC	4.00	1.80
❑ 62 Amos Zereoue RC	4.00	1.80
❑ 63 Cade McNown RC	3.00	1.35
❑ 64 Donovan McNabb RC	15.00	6.75
❑ 65 Ricky Williams RC	6.00	2.70
❑ 66 Daunte Culpepper RC	12.00	5.50
❑ 67 Troy Edwards RC	3.00	1.35
❑ 68 Peerless Price RC	6.00	2.70
❑ 69 Edgerrin James RC	12.00	5.50
❑ 70 Champ Bailey RC	5.00	2.20
❑ 71 Akili Smith RC	3.00	1.35
❑ 72 Kevin Johnson RC	4.00	1.80
❑ 73 Cecil Collins RC	2.00	.90
❑ 74 David Boston RC	4.00	1.80
❑ 75 Torry Holt RC	10.00	4.50
❑ 76 James Johnson RC	3.00	1.35
❑ 77 Na Brown RC	3.00	1.35
❑ 78 Rob Konrad RC	3.00	1.35
❑ 79 Mike Cloud RC	3.00	1.35
❑ 80 Craig Yeast RC	3.00	1.35
❑ 81 Brock Huard RC	4.00	1.80
❑ 82 Chris McAlister RC	3.00	1.35
❑ 83 Shaun King RC	3.00	1.35
❑ 84 Wane McGarity RC	2.00	.90
❑ 85 Joe Germaine RC	3.00	1.35
❑ 86 D'Wayne Bates RC	3.00	1.35
❑ 87 Kevin Faulk RC	4.00	1.80
❑ 88 Antoine Winfield RC	3.00	1.35
❑ 89 Reginald Kelly RC	2.00	.90
❑ 90 Antuan Edwards RC	2.00	.90
❑ P1 Jake Plummer Promo	1.00	.45

1999 E-X Century Essential Credentials Future

Nm-Mt Ex-Mt

*STARS/70-90: 8X TO 20X BASIC CARDS
*STARS/45-69: 12X TO 30X
*STARS/31-44: 20X TO 50X
*ROOKIES/20-30: 5X TO 10X
*ROOKIES/10-19: 6X TO 12X

1999 E-X Century Essential Credentials Now

Nm-Mt Ex-Mt

*ROOKIES/70-90: 2X TO 5X BASIC CARDS
*STARS/45-69: 12X TO 30X
*ROOKIES/45-69: 2.5X TO 6X
*STARS/30-44: 20X TO 50X
*STARS/20-29: 25X TO 60X
*STARS/10-19: 30X TO 80X
CARDS #'d UNDER 10 NOT PRICED

1999 E-X Century Authen-Kicks

	Nm-Mt	Ex-Mt
❑ 1AK Travis McGriff/235	15.00	6.75
❑ 2AK Trent Green/190	30.00	13.50
❑ 3AK Brock Huard/280	15.00	6.75
❑ 4AK Randall Cunningham/290	25.00	11.00
❑ 5AK Donovan McNabb/210	60.00	27.00
❑ 6AK Torry Holt/285	40.00	18.00
❑ 7AK Joe Germaine/280	15.00	6.75
❑ 8AK Cade McNown/260	15.00	6.75
❑ 9AK Doug Flutie/215	30.00	13.50
❑ 10AK O.J. McDuffie/285	15.00	6.75
❑ 11AK Ricky Williams/215	30.00	13.50
❑ 12AK Dan Marino/285	80.00	36.00

2000 E-X

	Nm-Mt	Ex-Mt
COMPLETE SET (150)	400.00	180.00
COMP.SET w/o SP's (100)	15.00	6.75
❑ 1 Tim Couch	.50	.23
❑ 2 Daunte Culpepper	1.00	.45
❑ 3 Jake Reed	.50	.23
❑ 4 Donovan McNabb	1.25	.55
❑ 5 Terry Glenn	.50	.23
❑ 6 Vinny Testaverde	.50	.23
❑ 7 Michael Westbrook	.50	.23
❑ 8 Errict Rhett	.50	.23
❑ 9 Joey Galloway	.50	.23
❑ 10 O.J. McDuffie	.50	.23
❑ 11 Rob Johnson	.50	.23
❑ 12 Warren Sapp	.50	.23
❑ 13 Brian Griese	.75	.35
❑ 14 Derrick Mayes	.50	.23
❑ 15 Ike Hilliard	.50	.23
❑ 16 Kevin Dyson	.50	.23
❑ 17 Shannon Sharpe	.50	.23
❑ 18 Cade McNown	.30	.14
❑ 19 Damon Huard	.75	.35
❑ 20 James Stewart	.50	.23
❑ 21 Kevin Johnson	.75	.35
❑ 22 Muhsin Muhammad	.50	.23
❑ 23 Shaun King	.30	.14
❑ 24 Corey Dillon	.75	.35
❑ 25 Fred Taylor	.75	.35
❑ 26 Peyton Manning	2.00	.90
❑ 27 Steve McNair	.75	.35
❑ 28 Tim Brown	.75	.35
❑ 29 Brad Johnson	.75	.35
❑ 30 Edgerrin James	1.25	.55
❑ 31 Germane Crowell	.30	.14
❑ 32 Kordell Stewart	.50	.23
❑ 33 Randy Moss	1.50	.70
❑ 34 Tony Banks	.50	.23
❑ 35 Akili Smith	.30	.14
❑ 36 Charlie Batch	.75	.35
❑ 37 Duce Staley	.75	.35
❑ 38 Jerome Bettis	.75	.35
❑ 39 Rich Gannon	.75	.35
❑ 40 Steve Young	1.00	.45
❑ 41 Tony Gonzalez	.50	.23
❑ 42 Curtis Martin	.75	.35
❑ 43 Eddie George	.75	.35
❑ 44 Marshall Faulk	1.00	.45
❑ 45 Troy Edwards	.30	.14
❑ 46 Curtis Enis	.30	.14
❑ 47 Jake Plummer	.50	.23
❑ 48 Jon Kitna	.75	.35
❑ 49 Qadry Ismail	.50	.23
❑ 50 Terrell Davis	.75	.35
❑ 51 Troy Aikman	1.50	.70
❑ 52 Elvis Grbac	.50	.23
❑ 53 Jeff Blake	.50	.23
❑ 54 Kurt Warner	1.50	.70
❑ 55 Ricky Watters	.50	.23
❑ 56 Torry Holt	.75	.35
❑ 57 Brett Favre	2.50	1.10
❑ 58 Chris Chandler	.50	.23
❑ 59 Eric Moulds	.75	.35
❑ 60 Jimmy Smith	.50	.23
❑ 61 Ricky Williams	.75	.35
❑ 62 Antonio Freeman	.75	.35
❑ 63 Curtis Conway	.50	.23
❑ 64 Emmitt Smith	1.50	.70
❑ 65 Kerry Collins	.50	.23
❑ 66 Marvin Harrison	.75	.35
❑ 67 Tyrone Wheatley	.50	.23
❑ 68 Charlie Garner	.50	.23
❑ 69 Derrick Alexander	.50	.23
❑ 70 Jamal Anderson	.75	.35
❑ 71 Mike Alstott	.75	.35
❑ 72 Ryan Leaf	.50	.23
❑ 73 Tim Biakabutuka	.50	.23
❑ 74 Amani Toomer	.50	.23
❑ 75 Dorsey Levens	.50	.23
❑ 76 Frank Sanders	.50	.23
❑ 77 Junior Seau	.75	.35
❑ 78 Steve Beuerlein	.30	.14
❑ 79 Wayne Chrebet	.50	.23
❑ 80 Carl Pickens	.50	.23
❑ 81 Drew Bledsoe	1.00	.45
❑ 82 Isaac Bruce	.75	.35
❑ 83 Marcus Robinson	.75	.35
❑ 84 Stephen Davis	.75	.35
❑ 85 Cris Carter	.75	.35
❑ 86 Ed McCaffrey	.75	.35
❑ 87 Jerry Rice	1.50	.70
❑ 88 Mark Brunell	.75	.35
❑ 89 Peerless Price	.75	.35
❑ 90 Terance Mathis	.50	.23
❑ 91 Tony Martin	.50	.23
❑ 92 Jevon Kearse	.75	.35
❑ 93 Robert Smith	.75	.35
❑ 94 Rob Moore	.50	.23
❑ 95 Charles Johnson	.50	.23
❑ 96 Doug Flutie	.75	.35
❑ 97 Sean Dawkins	.30	.14
❑ 98 Keenan McCardell	.50	.23
❑ 99 Bill Schroeder	.50	.23
❑ 100 Rod Smith	.50	.23
❑ 101 Peter Warrick RC	8.00	3.60
❑ 102 Corey Simon RC	8.00	3.60
❑ 103 Danny Farmer RC	6.00	2.70
❑ 104 Jamal Lewis RC	20.00	9.00
❑ 105 Jerry Porter RC	10.00	4.50
❑ 106 Joe Hamilton RC	6.00	2.70
❑ 107 Marc Bulger RC	15.00	6.75
❑ 108 R.Jay Soward RC	6.00	2.70
❑ 109 Ron Dugans RC	4.00	1.80

Card	Nm-Mt	Ex-Mt
❑ 110 Shaun Alexander RC	20.00	9.00
❑ 111 Travis Prentice RC	6.00	2.70
❑ 112 Anthony Becht RC	8.00	3.60
❑ 113 Bubba Franks RC	8.00	3.60
❑ 114 Chris Redman RC	6.00	2.70
❑ 115 Dennis Northcutt RC	8.00	3.60
❑ 116 Dez White RC	8.00	3.60
❑ 117 Gari Scott RC	4.00	1.80
❑ 118 Mareno Philyaw RC	4.00	1.80
❑ 119 Ron Dayne RC	8.00	3.60
❑ 120 Shyrone Stith RC	6.00	2.70
❑ 121 Tee Martin RC	8.00	3.60
❑ 122 Tom Brady RC	80.00	36.00
❑ 123 Trung Canidate RC	6.00	2.70
❑ 124 Chad Pennington RC	30.00	13.50
❑ 125 Chris Cole RC	6.00	2.70
❑ 126 Courtney Brown RC	8.00	3.60
❑ 127 Doug Chapman RC	6.00	2.70
❑ 128 Giovanni Carmazzi RC	6.00	2.70
❑ 129 J.R. Redmond RC	6.00	2.70
❑ 130 Michael Wiley RC	6.00	2.70
❑ 131 Reuben Droughns RC	10.00	4.50
❑ 132 Terrelle Smith RC	6.00	2.70
❑ 133 Thomas Jones RC	12.00	5.50
❑ 134 Travis Taylor RC	8.00	3.60
❑ 135 Anthony Lucas RC	4.00	1.80
❑ 136 Curtis Keaton RC	6.00	2.70
❑ 137 Frank Moreau RC	6.00	2.70
❑ 138 Darrell Jackson RC	15.00	6.75
❑ 139 Laveranues Coles RC	10.00	4.50
❑ 140 Brian Urlacher RC	30.00	13.50
❑ 141 Plaxico Burress RC	15.00	6.75
❑ 142 Sammy Morris RC	6.00	2.70
❑ 143 Sylvester Morris RC	6.00	2.70
❑ 144 Tim Rattay RC	15.00	6.75
❑ 145 Todd Pinkston RC	8.00	3.60
❑ 146 Troy Walters RC	8.00	3.60
❑ 147 Sebastian Janikowski RC	8.00	3.60
❑ 148 JaJuan Dawson RC	4.00	1.80
❑ 149 Trevor Gaylor RC	6.00	2.70
❑ 150 Rondell Mealey RC	4.00	1.80

2000 E-X Essential Credentials

	Nm-Mt	Ex-Mt
*ESS.CRED.STARS: 12X TO 30X HI COL.		

2001 E-X

	Nm-Mt	Ex-Mt
COMP.SET w/o SP's (90)	25.00	7.50
❑ 1 Jamal Anderson	.75	.23
❑ 2 Tim Couch	.50	.15
❑ 3 Jeff Garcia	.75	.23
❑ 4 Brett Favre	2.50	.75
❑ 5 Donovan McNabb	1.00	.30
❑ 6 Kerry Collins	.50	.15
❑ 7 Doug Flutie	.75	.23
❑ 8 Steve McNair	.75	.23
❑ 9 Kordell Stewart	.50	.15
❑ 10 Daunte Culpepper	.75	.23
❑ 11 Rich Gannon	.75	.23
❑ 12 Kurt Warner	1.50	.45
❑ 13 Brian Griese	.75	.23
❑ 14 Brad Johnson	.75	.23
❑ 15 Jake Plummer	.50	.15
❑ 16 Mark Brunell	.75	.23
❑ 17 Peyton Manning	2.00	.60
❑ 18 Keyshawn Johnson	.75	.23
❑ 19 Derrick Alexander	.50	.15
❑ 20 Emmitt Smith	1.50	.45
❑ 21 Rob Johnson	.50	.15
❑ 22 Aaron Brooks	.75	.23
❑ 23 Charlie Garner	.50	.15
❑ 24 Lamar Smith	.50	.15
❑ 25 Eddie George	.75	.23
❑ 26 Marshall Faulk	1.00	.30
❑ 27 Tiki Barber	.50	.15
❑ 28 Terrell Davis	.75	.23
❑ 29 Jamal Lewis	1.25	.35
❑ 30 Edgerrin James	1.00	.30
❑ 31 Duce Staley	.75	.23
❑ 32 Ricky Williams	.75	.23
❑ 33 Dorsey Levens	.50	.15
❑ 34 Jerome Bettis	.75	.23
❑ 35 Ron Dayne	.75	.23
❑ 36 Mike Anderson	.75	.23
❑ 37 Peter Warrick	.75	.23
❑ 38 Mike Alstott	.75	.23
❑ 39 Fred Taylor	.75	.23
❑ 40 Curtis Martin	.75	.23
❑ 41 Warrick Dunn	.75	.23
❑ 42 Vinny Testaverde	.50	.15
❑ 43 Stephen Davis	.75	.23
❑ 44 Ahman Green	.75	.23
❑ 45 James Stewart	.50	.15
❑ 46 Ricky Watters	.50	.15
❑ 47 Ray Lewis	.75	.23
❑ 48 Thomas Jones	.50	.15
❑ 49 Zach Thomas	.75	.23
❑ 50 Junior Seau	.75	.23
❑ 51 Brian Urlacher	1.25	.35
❑ 52 Isaac Bruce	.75	.23
❑ 53 Corey Dillon	.75	.23
❑ 54 Cris Carter	.75	.23
❑ 55 Terrell Owens	.75	.23
❑ 56 Drew Bledsoe	1.00	.30
❑ 57 Torry Holt	.75	.23
❑ 58 Charlie Batch	.75	.23
❑ 59 Germane Crowell	.30	.09
❑ 60 Jimmy Smith	.50	.15
❑ 61 Tim Biakabutuka	.50	.15
❑ 62 Jay Fiedler	.75	.23
❑ 63 Joey Galloway	.50	.15
❑ 64 Michael Westbrook	.50	.15
❑ 65 Shaun Alexander	1.00	.30
❑ 66 Matt Hasselbeck	.50	.15
❑ 67 Elvis Grbac	.50	.15
❑ 68 Derrick Mason	.50	.15
❑ 69 Trent Green	.75	.23
❑ 70 Wayne Chrebet	.50	.15
❑ 71 Rod Smith	.50	.15
❑ 72 Jerry Rice	1.50	.45
❑ 73 Tim Brown	.75	.23
❑ 74 Shannon Sharpe	.50	.15
❑ 75 Joe Horn	.50	.15
❑ 76 Randy Moss	1.50	.45
❑ 77 Amani Toomer	.50	.15
❑ 78 Antonio Freeman	.75	.23
❑ 79 Ed McCaffrey	.75	.23
❑ 80 Marvin Harrison	.75	.23
❑ 81 Muhsin Muhammad	.50	.15
❑ 82 Chad Pennington	1.25	.35
❑ 83 Kevin Johnson	.50	.15
❑ 84 Tony Gonzalez	.50	.15
❑ 85 Terry Glenn	.50	.15
❑ 86 David Boston	.75	.23
❑ 87 Jevon Kearse	.50	.15
❑ 88 Marcus Robinson	.75	.23
❑ 89 Warren Sapp	.50	.15
❑ 90 Eric Moulds	.50	.15
❑ 91 Andre Carter/1250 RC	10.00	3.00
❑ 92 Kevan Barlow/1250 RC	10.00	3.00
❑ 93 Michael Bennett/1000 RC	20.00	6.00
❑ 94 Josh Booty/1500 RC	10.00	3.00
❑ 95 Drew Brees/1000 RC	20.00	6.00
❑ 96 C.Buckhalter RC/1500	12.00	3.60
❑ 97 Quincy Carter/1250 RC	10.00	3.00
❑ 98 Chris Chambers/1000 RC	12.00	3.60
❑ 99 Nick Goings/1500 RC	10.00	3.00
❑ 100 Kevin Kasper/1500 RC	10.00	3.00
❑ 101 Dave Dickenson/1500 RC	6.00	1.80
❑ 102 R.Ferguson RC/1250	10.00	3.00
❑ 103 Jamar Fletcher/1500 RC	6.00	1.80
❑ 104 Rod Gardner/1250 RC	10.00	3.00
❑ 105 J.McCareins RC/1250	10.00	3.00
❑ 106 Jason Brookins/1500 RC	10.00	3.00
❑ 107 Todd Heap/1500 RC	10.00	3.00
❑ 108 Travis Henry/1000 RC	15.00	4.50
❑ 109 Gerard Warren/1500 RC	10.00	3.00
❑ 110 James Jackson/1250 RC	10.00	3.00
❑ 111 Chad Johnson/1250 RC	20.00	6.00
❑ 112 Rudi Johnson/1500 RC	15.00	4.50
❑ 113 LaMont Jordan/1250 RC	12.00	3.60
❑ 114 D.McAllister RC/1250	25.00	7.50
❑ 115 Mike McMahon/1250 RC	10.00	3.00
❑ 116 Snoop Minnis/1000 RC	6.00	1.80
❑ 117 Travis Minor/1500 RC	6.00	1.80
❑ 118 Freddie Mitchell/1000 RC	10.00	3.00
❑ 119 Quincy Morgan/1250 RC	10.00	3.00
❑ 120 Santana Moss/1250 RC	15.00	4.50
❑ 121 Cedrick Wilson/1500 RC	10.00	3.00
❑ 122 Jesse Palmer/1500 RC	10.00	3.00
❑ 123 K.Rambo RC/1500	6.00	1.80
❑ 124 Jamal Reynolds/1500 RC	10.00	3.00
❑ 125 Koren Robinson/1250 RC	12.00	3.60
❑ 126 Sage Rosenfels/1500 RC	10.00	3.00
❑ 127 Dan Morgan/1250 RC	10.00	3.00
❑ 128 Justin Smith/1500 RC	10.00	3.00
❑ 129 Fred Smoot/1500 RC	10.00	3.00
❑ 130 V.Sutherland RC/1500	6.00	1.80
❑ 131 David Terrell/1000 RC	10.00	3.00
❑ 132 A.Thomas RC/1250	15.00	4.50
❑ 133 L.Tomlinson RC/1000	40.00	12.00
❑ 134 Dan Alexander/1500 RC	10.00	3.00
❑ 135 M.Tuiasosopo RC/1250	10.00	3.00
❑ 136 Michael Vick/1000 RC	80.00	24.00
❑ 137 Steve Smith/1250 RC	12.00	3.60
❑ 138 Reggie Wayne/1250 RC	15.00	4.50
❑ 139 Chris Weinke/1000 RC	10.00	3.00
❑ 140 Alex Bannister/1250 RC	6.00	1.80

2001 E-X Essential Credentials

	Nm-Mt	Ex-Mt
*STARS: 4X TO 10X BASIC CARDS		
*ROOKIES: 1.5X TO 4X		

1995 Finest

	Nm-Mt	Ex-Mt
COMPLETE SET (275)	80.00	36.00
COMP.SERIES 1 (165)	20.00	9.00
COMP.SERIES 2 (110)	60.00	27.00
❑ 1 Natrone Means	.60	.25
❑ 2 Dave Meggett	.25	.11
❑ 3 Tim Bowens	.25	.11
❑ 4 Jay Novacek	.60	.25
❑ 5 Michael Jackson	.60	.25
❑ 6 Calvin Williams	.60	.25
❑ 7 Neil Smith	.60	.25
❑ 8 Chris Gardocki	.25	.11
❑ 9 Jeff Burris	.25	.11
❑ 10 Warren Moon	.60	.25
❑ 11 Gary Anderson K	.25	.11
❑ 12 Bert Emanuel	1.25	.55
❑ 13 Rick Tuten	.25	.11
❑ 14 Steve Wallace	.25	.11
❑ 15 Marion Butts	.25	.11
❑ 16 Johnnie Morton	.60	.25

❑ 17 Rob Moore .60 .25
❑ 18 Wayne Gandy .25 .11
❑ 19 Quentin Coryatt .60 .25
❑ 20 Richmond Webb .25 .11
❑ 21 Errict Rhett .60 .25
❑ 22 Joe Johnson .25 .11
❑ 23 Gary Brown .25 .11
❑ 24 Jeff Hostetler .60 .25
❑ 25 Larry Centers .60 .25
❑ 26 Tom Carter .25 .11
❑ 27 Steve Atwater .25 .11
❑ 28 Doug Pelfrey .25 .11
❑ 29 Bryce Paup .60 .25
❑ 30 Erik Williams .25 .11
❑ 31 Henry Jones .25 .11
❑ 32 Stanley Richard .25 .11
❑ 33 Marcus Allen 1.25 .55
❑ 34 Antonio Langham .25 .11
❑ 35 Lewis Tillman .25 .11
❑ 36 Thomas Randolph .25 .11
❑ 37 Byron Bam Morris .25 .11
❑ 38 David Palmer .60 .25
❑ 39 Ricky Watters .60 .25
❑ 40 Brett Perriman .60 .25
❑ 41 Will Wolford .25 .11
❑ 42 Burt Grossman .25 .11
❑ 43 Vincent Brisby .25 .11
❑ 44 Ronnie Lott .60 .25
❑ 45 Brian Blades .60 .25
❑ 46 Brent Jones .25 .11
❑ 47 Anthony Newman .25 .11
❑ 48 Willie Roaf .25 .11
❑ 49 Paul Gruber .25 .11
❑ 50 Jeff George .60 .25
❑ 51 Jamir Miller .25 .11
❑ 52 Anthony Miller .60 .25
❑ 53 Darrell Green .25 .11
❑ 54 Steve Wisniewski .25 .11
❑ 55 Dan Wilkinson .60 .25
❑ 56 Brett Favre 5.00 2.20
❑ 57 Leslie O'Neal .60 .25
❑ 58 Keith Byars .25 .11
❑ 59 James Washington .25 .11
❑ 60 Andre Reed .60 .25
❑ 61 Ken Norton Jr. .60 .25
❑ 62 John Randle .60 .25
❑ 63 Lake Dawson .60 .25
❑ 64 Greg Montgomery .25 .11
❑ 65 Erric Pegram .60 .25
❑ 66 Steve Everitt .25 .11
❑ 67 Chris Brantley .25 .11
❑ 68 Rod Woodson .60 .25
❑ 69 Eugene Robinson .25 .11
❑ 70 Dave Brown .60 .25
❑ 71 Ricky Reynolds .25 .11
❑ 72 Rohn Stark .25 .11
❑ 73 Randal Hill .25 .11
❑ 74 Brian Washington .25 .11
❑ 75 Heath Shuler .60 .25
❑ 76 Darion Conner .25 .11
❑ 77 Terry McDaniel .25 .11
❑ 78 Al Del Greco .25 .11
❑ 79 Allen Aldridge .25 .11
❑ 80 Trace Armstrong .25 .11
❑ 81 Darnay Scott .60 .25
❑ 82 Charlie Garner 1.25 .55
❑ 83 Harold Bishop .25 .11
❑ 84 Reggie White 1.25 .55
❑ 85 Shawn Jefferson .25 .11
❑ 86 Irving Spikes .60 .25
❑ 87 Mel Gray .25 .11
❑ 88 D.J. Johnson .25 .11
❑ 89 Daryl Johnston .60 .25
❑ 90 Joe Montana 5.00 2.20
❑ 91 Michael Strahan 1.25 .55
❑ 92 Robert Blackmon .25 .11
❑ 93 Ryan Yarborough .60 .25
❑ 94 Terry Allen .60 .25
❑ 95 Michael Haynes .60 .25
❑ 96 Jim Harbaugh .60 .25
❑ 97 Micheal Barrow .25 .11
❑ 98 John Thierry .25 .11
❑ 99 Seth Joyner .25 .11
❑ 100 Deion Sanders 2.00 .90
❑ 101 Eric Turner .25 .11
❑ 102 LeShon Johnson .60 .25
❑ 103 John Copeland .25 .11
❑ 104 Cornelius Bennett .60 .25
❑ 105 Sean Gilbert .60 .25
❑ 106 Herschel Walker .60 .25
❑ 107 Henry Ellard .60 .25
❑ 108 Neil O'Donnell .60 .25
❑ 109 Charles Wilson .25 .11
❑ 110 Willie McGinest .60 .25
❑ 111 Tim Brown 1.25 .55
❑ 112 Simon Fletcher .25 .11
❑ 113 Broderick Thomas .25 .11
❑ 114 Tom Waddle .25 .11
❑ 115 Jessie Tuggle .25 .11
❑ 116 Maurice Hurst .25 .11
❑ 117 Aubrey Beavers .25 .11
❑ 118 Donnell Bennett .60 .25
❑ 119 Shante Carver .25 .11
❑ 120 Eric Metcalf .60 .25
❑ 121 John Carney .25 .11
❑ 122 Thomas Lewis .60 .25
❑ 123 Johnny Mitchell .25 .11
❑ 124 Trent Dilfer 1.25 .55
❑ 125 Marshall Faulk 3.00 1.35
❑ 126 Ernest Givins .25 .11
❑ 127 Aeneas Williams .25 .11
❑ 128 Bucky Brooks .25 .11
❑ 129 Todd Steussie .25 .11
❑ 130 Randall Cunningham 1.25 .55
❑ 131 Reggie Brooks .60 .25
❑ 132 Morten Andersen .25 .11
❑ 133 James Jett .60 .25
❑ 134 George Teague .25 .11
❑ 135 John Taylor .25 .11
❑ 136 Charles Johnson .60 .25
❑ 137 Isaac Bruce 2.50 1.10
❑ 138 Jason Elam .60 .25
❑ 139 Carl Pickens .60 .25
❑ 140 Chris Warren .60 .25
❑ 141 Bruce Armstrong .25 .11
❑ 142 Mark Carrier DB .25 .11
❑ 143 Irving Fryar .60 .25
❑ 144 Van Malone .25 .11
❑ 145 Charles Haley .60 .25
❑ 146 Chris Calloway .25 .11
❑ 147 J.J. Birden .25 .11
❑ 148 Tony Bennett .25 .11
❑ 149 Lincoln Kennedy .25 .11
❑ 150 Stan Humphries .60 .25
❑ 151 Hardy Nickerson .25 .11
❑ 152 Randall McDaniel .25 .11
❑ 153 Marcus Robertson .25 .11
❑ 154 Ronald Moore .25 .11
❑ 155 Thurman Thomas 1.25 .55
❑ 156 Tommy Vardell .25 .11
❑ 157 Ken Ruettgers .25 .11
❑ 158 Rob Fredrickson .25 .11
❑ 159 Johnny Bailey .25 .11
❑ 160 Greg Lloyd .60 .25
❑ 161 David Alexander .25 .11
❑ 162 Kevin Mawae .25 .11
❑ 163 Derek Brown RBK .25 .11
❑ 164 William Floyd .60 .25
❑ 165 Aaron Glenn .25 .11
❑ 166 Joey Galloway RC 8.00 3.60
❑ 167 Troy Drayton .25 .11
❑ 168 Dermontti Dawson .60 .25
❑ 169 Ronald Moore .25 .11
❑ 170 Dan Marino 5.00 2.20
❑ 171 Dennis Gibson .25 .11
❑ 172 Raymont Harris .25 .11
❑ 173 Shannon Sharpe .60 .25
❑ 174 Kevin Williams .60 .25
❑ 175 Jim Everett .25 .11
❑ 176 Rocket Ismail .60 .25
❑ 177 Mark Fields RC 1.25 .55
❑ 178 George Koonce .25 .11
❑ 179 Chris Hudson .25 .11
❑ 180 Jerry Rice 2.50 1.10
❑ 181 Dewayne Washington .60 .25
❑ 182 Dale Carter .60 .25
❑ 183 Pete Stoyanovich .25 .11
❑ 184 Blake Brockermeyer .25 .11
❑ 185 Troy Aikman 2.50 1.10
❑ 186 Jeff Blake RC 2.50 1.10
❑ 187 Troy Vincent .25 .11
❑ 188 Lamar Lathon .25 .11
❑ 189 Tony Boselli 1.25 .55
❑ 190 Emmitt Smith 4.00 1.80
❑ 191 Bobby Houston .25 .11
❑ 192 Edgar Bennett .60 .25
❑ 193 Derrick Brooks RC 8.00 3.60
❑ 194 Ricky Proehl .25 .11
❑ 195 Rodney Hampton .60 .25
❑ 196 Dave Krieg .25 .11
❑ 197 Vinny Testaverde .60 .25
❑ 198 Erik Kramer .25 .11
❑ 199 Ben Coates .60 .25
❑ 200 Steve Young 2.00 .90
❑ 201 Glyn Milburn .25 .11
❑ 202 Bryan Cox .25 .11
❑ 203 Luther Elliss .25 .11
❑ 204 Mark McMillian .25 .11
❑ 205 Jerome Bettis 1.25 .55
❑ 206 Craig Heyward .60 .25
❑ 207 Ray Buchanan .25 .11
❑ 208 Kimble Anders .60 .25
❑ 209 Kevin Greene .60 .25
❑ 210 Eric Allen .25 .11
❑ 211 Ricardo McDonald .25 .11
❑ 212 Ruben Brown RC 1.50 .70
❑ 213 Harvey Williams .25 .11
❑ 214 Broderick Thomas .25 .11
❑ 215 Frank Reich .25 .11
❑ 216 Frank Sanders RC UER 1.50 .70
Plays Wide Receiver
Defensive Record on Back
❑ 217 Craig Newsome .25 .11
❑ 218 Merton Hanks .25 .11
❑ 219 Chris Miller .25 .11
❑ 220 John Elway 5.00 2.20
❑ 221 Ernest Givins .25 .11
❑ 222 Boomer Esiason .60 25
❑ 223 Reggie Roby .25 .11
❑ 224 Qadry Ismail .60 .25
❑ 225 Ki-Jana Carter RC 1.50 .70
❑ 226 Leon Lett .25 .11
❑ 227 Eric Hill .25 .11
❑ 228 Scott Mitchell .60 .25
❑ 229 Craig Erickson .25 .11
❑ 230 Drew Bledsoe 2.00 .90
❑ 231 Sean Landeta .25 .11
❑ 232 Barrett Brooks .25 .11
❑ 233 Brian Mitchell .25 .11
❑ 234 Tyrone Poole 1.25 .55
❑ 235 Desmond Howard .60 .25
❑ 236 Wayne Simmons .25 .11
❑ 237 Michael Westbrook RC 1.50 .70
❑ 238 Quinn Early .60 .25
❑ 239 Willie Davis .60 .25
❑ 240 Rashaan Salaam RC .75 .35
❑ 241 Devin Bush .25 .11
❑ 242 Dana Stubblefield .60 .25
❑ 243 Dexter Carter .25 .11
❑ 244 Shane Conlan .25 .11
❑ 245 Keith Elias RC .25 .11
❑ 246 Robert Brooks 1.25 .55
❑ 247 Garrison Hearst 1.25 .55
❑ 248 Eric Zeier RC 1.50 .70
❑ 249 Nate Newton .60 .25
❑ 250 Barry Sanders 4.00 1.80
❑ 251 Dave Meggett .25 .11
❑ 252 Courtney Hawkins .25 .11
❑ 253 Cortez Kennedy .60 .25
❑ 254 Mario Bates .60 .25
❑ 255 Junior Seau 1.25 .55
❑ 256 Brian Washington .25 .11
❑ 257 Darius Holland .25 .11
❑ 258 Jeff Graham .25 .11
❑ 259 Rob Moore .60 .25
❑ 260 Andre Rison .60 .25
❑ 261 Kerry Collins RC 8.00 3.60
❑ 262 Roosevelt Potts .25 .11
❑ 263 Cris Carter 1.25 .55
❑ 264 Curtis Martin RC 15.00 6.75
❑ 265 Rick Mirer .60 .25
❑ 266 Mo Lewis .25 .11

❑ 267 Mike Sherrard .25 .11
❑ 268 Herman Moore 1.25 .55
❑ 269 Eric Metcalf .60 .25
❑ 270 Ray Childress .25 .11
❑ 271 Chris Slade .25 .11
❑ 272 Michael Irvin 1.25 .55
❑ 273 Jim Kelly 1.25 .55
❑ 274 Terance Mathis .60 .25
❑ 275 LeRoy Butler .25 .11

1995 Finest Refractors

	Nm-Mt	Ex-Mt
COMPLETE SET (275)	600.00	275.00
COMP.SERIES 1 (165)	200.00	90.00
COMP.SERIES 2 (110)	400.00	180.00

*REFRACT.STARS: 2.5X to 6 BASIC CARDS
*REFRACTOR RCs: 1.5X to 4X BASIC CARDS

1996 Finest

	Nm-Mt	Ex-Mt
COMPLETE SET (359)	400.00	180.00
COMP.SERIES 1 (191)	250.00	110.00
COMP.SERIES 2 (168)	150.00	70.00
COMP.BRONZE SER.1 (110)	40.00	18.00
COMP.BRONZE SER.2 (110)	40.00	18.00

❑ B2 Jay Novacek B .60 .25
❑ B3 Ray Buchanan B .30 .14
❑ B5 Phil Hansen B .30 .14
❑ B6 Mike Mamula B .30 .14
❑ B9 Bernie Parmalee B .30 .14
❑ B10 Herman Moore B .60 .25
❑ B11 Shawn Jefferson B .30 .14
❑ B12 Chris Doleman B .30 .14
❑ B13 Erik Kramer B .60 .25
❑ B15 Orlando Thomas B .30 .14
❑ B16 Terrell Davis B 4.00 1.80
❑ B18 Roman Phifer B .30 .14
❑ B19 Trent Dilfer B .60 .25
❑ B21 Darnay Scott B .60 .25
❑ B22 Steve McNair B 4.00 1.80
❑ B23 Lamar Lathon B .30 .14
❑ B26 Thomas Randolph B .30 .14
❑ B27 Michael Jackson B .60 .25
❑ B28 Seth Joyner B .30 .14
❑ B29 Jeff Lageman B .30 .14
❑ B30 Darryl Williams B .30 .14
❑ B32 Erric Pegram B .60 .25
❑ B34 Sean Dawkins B .60 .25
❑ B38 Dan Saleaumua B UER .30 .14
card misnumbered 28
❑ B39 Henry Thomas B .30 .14
❑ B43 Pat Swilling B .30 .14
❑ B44 Marty Carter B .30 .14
❑ B45 Anthony Miller B .60 .25
❑ B48 Chris Warren B .60 .25
❑ B49 Derek Brown RBK B .30 .14
❑ B51 Blaine Bishop B .30 .14
❑ B52 Jake Reed B .60 .25
❑ B55 Vencie Glenn B .30 .14
❑ B58 Derrick Alexander WR B .60 .25
❑ B64 Jessie Tuggle B .30 .14
❑ B65 Terrance Shaw B .30 .14
❑ B66 David Sloan B .60 .25
❑ B68 Brent Jones B .30 .14
❑ B70 William Thomas B .30 .14
❑ B71 Robert Smith B .60 .25
❑ B72 Wayne Simmons B .30 .14
❑ B73 Jim Harbaugh B .60 .25
❑ B76 Wayne Chrebet B 2.00 .90
❑ B77 Chris Hudson B .30 .14
❑ B79 Stevon Moore B .30 .14
❑ B80 Chris Calloway B .30 .14
❑ B81 Tom Carter B .30 .14
❑ B82 Dave Meggett B .30 .14
❑ B83 Sam Mills B .60 .25
❑ B86 Renaldo Turnbull B .30 .14
❑ B87 Derrick Brooks B 1.00 .45
❑ B89 Eugene Robinson B .30 .14
❑ B91 Rodney Thomas B .30 .14
❑ B92 Dan Wilkinson B .30 .14
❑ B93 Mark Fields B .30 .14
❑ B94 Warren Sapp B .30 .14
❑ B95 Curtis Martin B 4.00 1.80
❑ B97 Ray Crockett B .30 .14
❑ B98 Ed McDaniel B .30 .14
❑ B101 Craig Heyward B .30 .14
❑ B102 Ellis Johnson B .30 .14
❑ B104 O.J. McDuffie B .60 .25
❑ B105 J.J. Stokes B 1.00 .45
❑ B106 Mo Lewis B .30 .14
❑ B108 Rob Moore B .60 .25
❑ B110 Tyrone Wheatley B .60 .25
❑ B111 Ken Harvey B .30 .14
❑ B113 Willie Green B .30 .14
❑ B114 Willie Davis B .60 .25
❑ B115 Andy Harmon B .30 .14
❑ B117 Bryan Cox B .30 .14
❑ B119 Bert Emanuel B .60 .25
❑ B120 Greg Lloyd B .60 .25
❑ B122 Willie Jackson B .60 .25
❑ B123 Lorenzo Lynch B .30 .14
❑ B124 Pepper Johnson B .30 .14
❑ B128 Tyrone Poole B .30 .14
❑ B129 Neil Smith B .60 .25
❑ B130 Eddie Robinson B .30 .14
❑ B131 Bryce Paup B .60 .25
❑ B134 Troy Aikman B 5.00 2.20
❑ B136 Chris Sanders B .60 .25
❑ B138 Jim Everett B .30 .14
❑ B139 Frank Sanders B .60 .25
❑ B141 Cortez Kennedy B .60 .25
❑ B143 Derrick Alexander DE B .30 .14
❑ B144 Rob Fredrickson B .30 .14
❑ B145 Chris Zorich B .30 .14
❑ B146 Devin Bush B .30 .14
❑ B149 Troy Vincent B .30 .14
❑ B151 Deion Sanders B 2.50 1.10
❑ B152 James O. Stewart B .60 .25
❑ B156 Lawrence Dawsey B .30 .14
❑ B157 Robert Brooks B 1.00 .45
❑ B158 Rashaan Salaam B .60 .25
❑ B161 Tim Brown B .60 .25
❑ B162 Brendan Stai B .30 .14
❑ B163 Sean Gilbert B .30 .14
❑ B169 Calvin Williams B .60 .25
❑ B171 Ruben Brown B .30 .14
❑ B172 Eric Green B .30 .14
❑ B175 Jerry Rice B 5.00 2.20
❑ B176 Bruce Smith B 1.00 .45
❑ B177 Mark Bruener B .30 .14
❑ B179 Lamont Warren B .30 .14
❑ B180 Tamarick Vanover B 1.00 .45
❑ B182 Scott Mitchell B .60 .25
❑ B186 Terry Wooden B .30 .14
❑ B187 Ken Norton B .60 .25
❑ B188 Jeff Herrod B .30 .14
❑ B192 Gus Frerotte B .60 .25
❑ B194 Brett Maxie B .30 .14
❑ B198 Eddie Kennison B RC 1.25 .55
❑ B201 Marcus Jones B RC .30 .14
❑ B202 Terry Allen B .60 .25
❑ B203 Leroy Hoard B .30 .14
❑ B205 Reggie White B 1.00 .45
❑ B206 Larry Centers B .60 .25
❑ B208 Vincent Brisby B .30 .14
❑ B209 Michael Timpson B .30 .14
❑ B211 John Mobley B RC .30 .14
❑ B212 Clay Matthews B .60 .25
❑ B213 Shannon Sharpe B .60 .25
❑ B214 Tony Bennett B .30 .14
❑ B216 Mickey Washington B .30 .14
❑ B217 Fred Barnett B .60 .25
❑ B218 Michael Haynes B .60 .25
❑ B219 Stan Humphries B .60 .25
❑ B221 Winston Moss B .30 .14
❑ B222 Tim Biakabutuka B RC 1.25 .55
❑ B223 Leeland McElroy B RC .60 .25
❑ B224 Vinnie Clark B .30 .14
❑ B225 Keyshawn Johnson 5.00 2.20
B RC
❑ B228 Tony Woods B .30 .14
❑ B231 Anthony Pleasant B .30 .14
❑ B232 Jeff George B .60 .25
❑ B233 Curtis Conway B 1.00 .45
❑ B235 Jeff Lewis B RC .60 .25
❑ B236 Edgar Bennett B .60 .25
❑ B237 Regan Upshaw B RC .30 .14
❑ B238 William Fuller B .30 .14
❑ B241 Willie Anderson B RC .30 .14
❑ B242 Derrick Thomas B .60 .25
❑ B243 Marvin Harrison B RC 10.00 4.50
❑ B244 Darion Conner B .30 .14
❑ B245 Antonio Langham B .30 .14
❑ B246 Rodney Peete B .30 .14
❑ B247 Tim McDonald B .30 .14
❑ B248 Robert Jones B .30 .14
❑ B251 Mark Carrier DB B .30 .14
❑ B252 Stephen Grant B .30 .14
❑ B254 Jeff Hostetler B .60 .25
❑ B255 Darrell Green B .30 .14
❑ B261 Eric Swann B .60 .25
❑ B263 Irv Smith B .30 .14
❑ B264 Tim McKyer B .30 .14
❑ B266 Sean Jones B .30 .14
❑ B271 Yancey Thigpen B .60 .25
❑ B273 Quentin Coryatt B .30 .14
❑ B274 Hardy Nickerson B .30 .14
❑ B275 Ricardo McDonald B .30 .14
❑ B277 Robert Blackmon B .30 .14
❑ B279 Alonzo Spellman B .30 .14
❑ B281 Rickey Dudley B RC 1.25 .55
❑ B282 Joe Cain B .30 .14
❑ B284 John Randle B .60 .25
❑ B286 Vinny Testaverde B .60 .25
❑ B289 Henry Jones B .30 .14
❑ B290 Simeon Rice B RC 3.00 1.35
❑ B295 Leslie O'Neal B .30 .14
❑ B297 Greg Hill B .60 .25
❑ B301 Eric Metcalf B .60 .25
❑ B303 Jerome Woods B RC .30 .14
❑ B306 Anthony Smith B .30 .14
❑ B307 Darren Perry B .30 .14
❑ B311 James Hasty B .30 .14
❑ B312 Cris Carter B 1.00 .45
❑ B314 Lawrence Phillips B RC .60 .25
❑ B317 Aeneas Williams B .30 .14
❑ B318 Eric Hill B .30 .14
❑ B319 Kevin Hardy B RC 1.25 .55
❑ B321 Chris Chandler B .60 .25
❑ B322 Rocket Ismail B .60 .25
❑ B323 Anthony Parker B .30 .14
❑ B324 John Thierry B .30 .14
❑ B325 Micheal Barrow B .30 .14
❑ B326 Henry Ford B .30 .14
❑ B327 Aaron Hayden B RC .30 .14
❑ B328 Terance Mathis B .30 .14
❑ B329 Kirk Pointer B RC .30 .14
❑ B330 Ray Mickens B RC .30 .14
❑ B331 J.Mayberry B RC .30 .14
❑ B332 Mario Bates B .60 .25
❑ B333 Carlton Gray B .30 .14
❑ B334 Derek Loville B .30 .14
❑ B335 Mike Alstott B RC 5.00 2.20
❑ B336 Eric Guliford B .30 .14
❑ B337 Marvcus Patton B .30 .14
❑ B338 Terrell Owens B RC 12.00 5.50
❑ B339 Lance Johnstone B RC .60 .25
❑ B340 Lake Dawson B .60 .25
❑ B341 Winslow Oliver B RC .30 .14
❑ B342 Adrian Murrell B .60 .25
❑ B343 Jason Belser B .30 .14
❑ B344 Brian Dawkins B RC 5.00 2.20
❑ B345 Reggie Brown B RC .30 .14
❑ B346 Shaun Gayle B .30 .14
❑ B347 Tony Brackens B RC 1.25 .55

Card	Nm-Mt	Ex-Mt
❑ B348 Thomas Lewis B	.30	.14
❑ B349 Kelvin Pritchett B	.30	.14
❑ B350 Bobby Engram B RC	1.25	.55
❑ B351 Moe Williams B RC	3.00	1.35
❑ B352 Thomas Smith B	.30	.14
❑ B353 Dexter Carter B	.30	.14
❑ B354 Qadry Ismail B	.60	.25
❑ B355 Marco Battaglia B RC	.30	.14
❑ B356 Levon Kirkland B	.30	.14
❑ B357 Eric Allen B	.30	.14
❑ B358 Bobby Hoying B RC	1.25	.55
❑ B359 Checklist B	.30	.14
❑ G1 Kordell Stewart G	5.00	2.20
❑ G7 Kimble Anders G	1.50	.70
❑ G8 Merton Hanks G	1.50	.70
❑ G17 Rick Mirer G	3.00	1.35
❑ G33 Craig Newsome G	1.50	.70
❑ G36 Bryce Paup G	3.00	1.35
❑ G40 Dan Marino G	20.00	9.00
❑ G42 Andre Coleman G	1.50	.70
❑ G47 Kevin Carter G	1.50	.70
❑ G60 Mark Brunell G	8.00	3.60
❑ G61 David Palmer G	3.00	1.35
❑ G75 Carnell Lake G	1.50	.70
❑ G96 Joey Galloway G	5.00	2.20
❑ G112 Melvin Tuten G	1.50	.70
❑ G121 Aaron Glenn G	1.50	.70
❑ G132 Brett Favre G	20.00	9.00
❑ G133 Ken Dilger G	3.00	1.35
❑ G140 Barry Sanders G	20.00	9.00
❑ G142 Glyn Milburn G	1.50	.70
❑ G148 Brett Perriman G	3.00	1.35
❑ G160 Kerry Collins G	5.00	2.20
❑ G164 Lee Woodall G	1.50	.70
❑ G173 Marshall Faulk G	6.00	2.70
❑ G178 Troy Aikman G	12.00	5.50
❑ G190 Drew Bledsoe G	8.00	3.60
❑ G191 Checklist G	1.50	.70
❑ G193 Michael Irvin G	5.00	2.20
❑ G196 Warren Moon G	3.00	1.35
❑ G200 Steve Young G	10.00	4.50
❑ G207 Alex Van Dyke G RC	3.00	1.35
❑ G220 Cris Carter G	5.00	2.20
❑ G230 John Elway G	20.00	9.00
❑ G234 Charles Haley G	3.00	1.35
❑ G240 Jim Kelly G	5.00	2.20
❑ G250 Rodney Hampton G	3.00	1.35
❑ G256 Errict Rhett G	3.00	1.35
❑ G257 Alex Molden G	1.50	.70
❑ G260 Kevin Hardy G	3.00	1.35
❑ G267 Bryant Young G	3.00	1.35
❑ G268 Jeff Blake G	5.00	2.20
❑ G270 Keyshawn Johnson G	5.00	2.20
❑ G278 Junior Seau G	5.00	2.20
❑ G285 Terry Kirby G	3.00	1.35
❑ G293 Hugh Douglas G	3.00	1.35
❑ G296 Reggie White G	5.00	2.20
❑ G298 Elvis Grbac G	5.00	2.20
❑ G300 Emmitt Smith G	15.00	6.75
❑ G309 Ricky Watters G	3.00	1.35
❑ S4 Brett Favre S	15.00	6.75
❑ S14 Chester McGlockton S	.75	.35
❑ S20 Tyrone Hughes S	.75	.35
❑ S24 Ty Law S	3.00	1.35
❑ S25 Brian Mitchell S	.75	.35
❑ S31 Darren Woodson S	1.50	.70
❑ S35 Brian Mitchell S	.75	.35
❑ S37 Dana Stubblefield S	1.50	.70
❑ S41 Kerry Collins S	3.00	1.35
❑ S46 Orlando Thomas S	.75	.35
❑ S50 Jerry Rice S	8.00	3.60
❑ S53 Willie McGinest S	.75	.35
❑ S54 Blake Brockermeyer S	.75	.35
❑ S56 Michael Westbrook S	3.00	1.35
❑ S57 Garrison Hearst S	3.00	1.35
❑ S59 Kyle Brady S	1.50	.70
❑ S62 Tim Brown S	1.50	.70
❑ S63 Jeff Graham S	.75	.35
❑ S67 Dan Marino S	15.00	6.75
❑ S69 Tamarick Vanover S	3.00	1.35
❑ S74 Daryl Johnston S	1.50	.70
❑ S78 Frank Sanders S	1.50	.70
❑ S84 Darryll Lewis S	.75	.35
❑ S85 Carl Pickens S	1.50	.70
❑ S88 Jerome Bettis S	3.00	1.35
❑ S90 Terrell Davis S	6.00	2.70
❑ S99 Napoleon Kaufman S	3.00	1.35
❑ S100 Rashaan Salaam S	1.50	.70
❑ S103 Barry Sanders S	15.00	6.75
❑ S107 Tony Boselli S	1.50	.70
❑ S109 Eric Zeier S	1.50	.70
❑ S116 Bruce Smith S	3.00	1.35
❑ S118 Zack Crockett S	.75	.35
❑ S125 Joey Galloway S	3.00	1.35
❑ S126 Heath Shuler S	1.50	.70
❑ S127 Curtis Martin S	6.00	2.70
❑ S135 Greg Lloyd S	1.50	.70
❑ S137 Marshall Faulk S	4.00	1.80
❑ S147 Tyrone Poole S	.75	.35
❑ S150 J.J. Stokes S	3.00	1.35
❑ S153 Drew Bledsoe S	5.00	2.20
❑ S154 Terry McDaniel S	.75	.35
❑ S155 Terrell Fletcher S	.75	.35
❑ S159 Dave Brown S	.75	.35
❑ S165 Jim Harbaugh S	1.50	.70
❑ S166 Larry Brown S	.75	.35
❑ S167 Neil Smith S	1.50	.70
❑ S168 Herman Moore S	1.50	.70
❑ S170 Deion Sanders S	5.00	2.20
❑ S174 Mark Chmura S	1.50	.70
❑ S181 Chris Warren S	1.50	.70
❑ S183 Robert Brooks S	3.00	1.35
❑ S184 Steve McNair S	6.00	2.70
❑ S185 Kordell Stewart S	3.00	1.35
❑ S189 Charlie Garner S	1.50	.70
❑ S195 Harvey Williams S	.75	.35
❑ S197 Jeff George S	1.50	.70
❑ S199 Ricky Watters S	1.50	.70
❑ S204 Steve Bono S	1.50	.70
❑ S210 Jeff Blake S	3.00	1.35
❑ S215 Phillippi Sparks S	.75	.35
❑ S226 William Floyd S	1.50	.70
❑ S227 Troy Drayton S	.75	.35
❑ S229 Rodney Hampton S	1.50	.70
❑ S239 Duane Clemons S RC	.75	.35
❑ S249 Curtis Conway S	3.00	1.35
❑ S253 John Mobley S	.75	.35
❑ S258 Chris Slade S	.75	.35
❑ S259 Derrick Thomas S	1.50	.70
❑ S262 Eric Metcalf S	1.50	.70
❑ S265 Emmitt Smith S	12.00	5.50
❑ S269 Jeff Hostetler S	1.50	.70
❑ S272 Thurman Thomas S	3.00	1.35
❑ S276 Steve Atwater S	.75	.35
❑ S280 Isaac Bruce S	3.00	1.35
❑ S283 Neil O'Donnell S	1.50	.70
❑ S287 Jim Kelly S	3.00	1.35
❑ S288 Lawrence Phillips S	3.00	1.35
❑ S291 Terance Mathis S	.75	.35
❑ S292 Errict Rhett S	1.50	.70
❑ S294 Santo Stephens S	.75	.35
❑ S299 Walt Harris S RC	.75	.35
❑ S302 Jamir Miller S	.75	.35
❑ S304 Ben Coates S	1.50	.70
❑ S305 Marcus Allen S	3.00	1.35
❑ S308 Jonathan Ogden S RC	3.00	1.35
❑ S310 John Elway S	15.00	6.75
❑ S313 Irving Fryar S	1.50	.70
❑ S315 Junior Seau S	3.00	1.35
❑ S316 Alex Molden S RC	.75	.35
❑ S320 Steve Young S	6.00	2.70

1996 Finest Refractors

	Nm-Mt	Ex-Mt
COMP.BRONZE SET (220)	1000.00	450.00
COMP.BRONZE SER.1 (110)	500.00	220.00
COMP.BRONZE SER.2 (110)	500.00	220.00

*BRONZE REF.STARS: 4X TO 10X
*BRONZE REF.RCs: 1.5X TO 4X
*GOLD REFRACTORS: 1X TO 2.5X
*SILVER REF.STARS: 2.5X TO 6X

1997 Finest

	Nm-Mt	Ex-Mt
COMPLETE SET (350)	500.00	220.00
COMP.SERIES 1 SET (175)	250.00	110.00
COMP.SERIES 2 SET (175)	250.00	110.00
COMP.BRONZE SER.1 (100)	25.00	11.00
COMP.BRONZE SER.2 (100)	40.00	18.00

Card	Nm-Mt	Ex-Mt
❑ 1 Mark Brunell B	2.00	.90
❑ 2 Chris Slade B	.60	.25
❑ 3 Chris Doleman B	.60	.25
❑ 4 Chris Hudson B	.60	.25
❑ 5 Karim Abdul-Jabbar B	1.00	.45
❑ 6 Darren Perry B	.60	.25
❑ 7 Daryl Johnston B	1.00	.45
❑ 8 Rob Moore B UER listed as uncommon	1.00	.45
❑ 9 Robert Smith B	1.00	.45
❑ 10 Terry Allen B	1.50	.70
❑ 11 Jason Dunn B	.60	.25
❑ 12 Henry Thomas B	.60	.25
❑ 13 Rod Stephens B	.60	.25
❑ 14 Ray Mickens B	.60	.25
❑ 15 Ty Detmer B	1.00	.45
❑ 16 Fred Barnett B	.60	.25
❑ 17 Derrick Alexander WR B	1.00	.45
❑ 18 Marcus Robertson B	.60	.25
❑ 19 Robert Blackmon B	.60	.25
❑ 20 Isaac Bruce B	1.50	.70
❑ 21 Chester McGlockton B	.60	.25
❑ 22 Stan Humphries B	1.00	.45
❑ 23 Lonnie Marts B	.60	.25
❑ 24 Jason Sehorn B	1.00	.45
❑ 25 Bobby Engram B UER listed as uncommon	1.00	.45
❑ 26 Brett Perriman B UER listed as uncommon	.60	.25
❑ 27 Stevon Moore B	.60	.25
❑ 28 Jamal Anderson B	1.50	.70
❑ 29 Wayne Martin B	.60	.25
❑ 30 Michael Irvin B UER listed as uncommon	1.50	.70
❑ 31 Thomas Smith B	.60	.25
❑ 32 Tony Brackens B	.60	.25
❑ 33 Eric Davis B	.60	.25
❑ 34 James O.Stewart B	1.00	.45
❑ 35 Ki-Jana Carter B	.60	.25
❑ 36 Ken Norton B	.60	.25
❑ 37 William Thomas B	.60	.25
❑ 38 Tim Brown B	1.50	.70
❑ 39 Lawrence Phillips B	.60	.25
❑ 40 Ricky Watters B	1.00	.45
❑ 41 Tony Bennett B	.60	.25
❑ 42 Jessie Armstead B	.60	.25
❑ 43 Trent Dilfer B	1.50	.70
❑ 44 Rodney Hampton B	1.00	.45
❑ 45 Sam Mills B	.60	.25
❑ 46 Rodney Harrison B RC	3.00	1.35
❑ 47 Rob Fredrickson B	.60	.25
❑ 48 Eric Hill B	.60	.25
❑ 49 Bennie Blades B	.60	.25
❑ 50 Eddie George B	1.50	.70
❑ 51 Dave Brown B	.60	.25
❑ 52 Raymont Harris B	.60	.25
❑ 53 Steve Tovar B	.60	.25
❑ 54 Thurman Thomas B	1.50	.70
❑ 55 Leeland McElroy B	.60	.25
❑ 56 Brian Mitchell B UER listed as uncommon	.60	.25
❑ 57 Eric Allen B	.60	.25
❑ 58 Vinny Testaverde B	1.00	.45
❑ 59 Marvin Washington B	.60	.25
❑ 60 Junior Seau B	1.50	.70
❑ 61 Bert Emanuel B	1.00	.45
❑ 62 Kevin Carter B	.60	.25

❑ 63 Mark Carrier DB B .60 .25
❑ 64 Andre Coleman B .60 .25
❑ 65 Chris Warren B 1.00 .45
❑ 66 Aeneas Williams B .60 .25
❑ 67 Eugene Robinson B .60 .25
❑ 68 Darren Woodson B .60 .25
❑ 69 Anthony Johnson B .60 .25
❑ 70 Terry Glenn B 1.50 .70
❑ 71 Troy Vincent B .60 .25
❑ 72 John Copeland B .60 .25
❑ 73 Warren Sapp B 1.00 .45
❑ 74 Bobby Hebert B .60 .25
❑ 75 Jeff Hostetler B .60 .25
❑ 76 Willie Davis B .60 .25
❑ 77 Mickey Washington B .60 .25
❑ 78 Cortez Kennedy B .60 .25
❑ 79 Michael Strahan B 1.00 .45
❑ 80 Jerome Bettis B 1.50 .70
❑ 81 Andre Hastings B UER .60 .25
listed as uncommon
❑ 82 Simeon Rice B 1.00 .45
❑ 83 Cornelius Bennett B .60 .25
❑ 84 Napoleon Kaufman B 1.50 .70
❑ 85 Jim Harbaugh B 1.00 .45
❑ 86 Aaron Hayden B .60 .25
❑ 87 Gus Frerotte B .60 .25
❑ 88 Jeff Blake B 1.00 .45
❑ 89 Anthony Miller B UER .60 .25
listed as uncommon
❑ 90 Deion Sanders B 1.50 .70
❑ 91 Curtis Conway B 1.00 .45
❑ 92 William Floyd B 1.00 .45
❑ 93 Eric Moulds B UER 1.50 .70
listed as uncommon
❑ 94 Mel Gray B .60 .25
❑ 95 Andre Rison B UER 1.00 .45
listed as uncommon
❑ 96 Eugene Daniel B .60 .25
❑ 97 Jason Belser B .60 .25
❑ 98 Mike Mamula B .60 .25
❑ 99 Jim Everett B .60 .25
❑ 100 Checklist B .60 .25
❑ 101 Drew Bledsoe S 4.00 1.80
❑ 102 Shannon Sharpe S 2.00 .90
❑ 103 Ken Harvey S 1.25 .55
❑ 104 Isaac Bruce S 3.00 1.35
❑ 105 Terry Allen S 3.00 1.35
❑ 106 Lawyer Milloy S 2.00 .90
❑ 107 Ashley Ambrose S 1.25 .55
❑ 108 Alfred Williams S 1.25 .55
❑ 109 Hugh Douglas S 1.25 .55
❑ 110 Junior Seau S 3.00 1.35
❑ 111 Kordell Stewart S 3.00 1.35
❑ 112 Adrian Murrell S 2.00 .90
❑ 113 Byron Bam Morris S 1.25 .55
❑ 114 Terrell Buckley S 1.25 .55
❑ 115 Dan Marino S 12.00 5.50
❑ 116 Willie Clay S 1.25 .55
❑ 117 Neil Smith S 2.00 .90
❑ 118 Blaine Bishop S 1.25 .55
❑ 119 John Mobley S 1.25 .55
❑ 120 Herman Moore S 2.00 .90
❑ 121 Keyshawn Johnson S 3.00 1.35
❑ 122 Boomer Esiason S 2.00 .90
❑ 123 Marshall Faulk S 4.00 1.80
❑ 124 Keith Jackson S 1.25 .55
❑ 125 Ricky Watters S 2.00 .90
❑ 126 Carl Pickens S 2.00 .90
❑ 127 Cris Carter S 3.00 1.35
❑ 128 Mike Alstott S 3.00 1.35
❑ 129 Simeon Rice S 2.00 .90
❑ 130 Troy Aikman S 6.00 2.70
❑ 131 Tamarick Vanover S 2.00 .90
❑ 132 Marquez Pope S 1.25 .55
❑ 133 Winslow Oliver S 1.25 .55
❑ 134 Edgar Bennett S 2.00 .90
❑ 135 Dave Meggett S 1.25 .55
❑ 136 Marcus Allen S 3.00 1.35
❑ 137 Jerry Rice S 6.00 2.70
❑ 138 Steve Atwater S 1.25 .55
❑ 139 Tim McDonald S 1.25 .55
❑ 140 Barry Sanders S 10.00 4.50
❑ 141 Eddie George S 3.00 1.35
❑ 142 Wesley Walls S 1.25 .55
❑ 143 Jerome Bettis S 3.00 1.35
❑ 144 Kevin Greene S 2.00 .90
❑ 145 Terrell Davis S 4.00 1.80
❑ 146 Gus Frerotte S 2.00 .90
❑ 147 Joey Galloway S 2.00 .90
❑ 148 Vinny Testaverde S 2.00 .90
❑ 149 Hardy Nickerson S 1.25 .55
❑ 150 Brett Favre S 12.00 5.50
❑ 151 Desmond Howard G 1.50 .70
❑ 152 Keyshawn Johnson G 5.00 2.20
❑ 153 Tony Banks G 5.00 2.20
❑ 154 Chris Spielman G 1.50 .70
❑ 155 Reggie White G 5.00 2.20
❑ 156 Zach Thomas G 5.00 2.20
❑ 157 Carl Pickens G 3.00 1.35
❑ 158 Karim Abdul-Jabbar G 5.00 2.20
❑ 159 Chad Brown G 1.50 .70
❑ 160 Kerry Collins G 5.00 2.20
❑ 161 Marvin Harrison G 5.00 2.20
❑ 162 Steve Young G 6.00 2.70
❑ 163 Deion Sanders G 5.00 2.20
❑ 164 Trent Dilfer G 5.00 2.20
❑ 165 Barry Sanders G 15.00 6.75
❑ 166 Cris Carter G 5.00 2.20
❑ 167 Keenan McCardell G 3.00 1.35
❑ 168 Terry Glenn G 5.00 2.20
❑ 169 Emmitt Smith G 15.00 6.75
❑ 170 John Elway G 20.00 9.00
❑ 171 Jerry Rice G 10.00 4.50
❑ 172 Troy Aikman G 10.00 4.50
❑ 173 Curtis Martin G 6.00 2.70
❑ 174 Darrell Green G 1.50 .70
❑ 175 Mark Brunell G 6.00 2.70
❑ 176 Corey Dillon B RC 12.00 5.50
❑ 177 Tyrone Poole B .60 .25
❑ 178 Anthony Pleasant B .60 .25
❑ 179 Frank Sanders B 1.00 .45
❑ 180 Troy Aikman B 3.00 1.35
❑ 181 Bill Romanowski B .60 .25
❑ 182 Ty Law B 1.00 .45
❑ 183 Orlando Thomas B .60 .25
❑ 184 Quentin Coryatt B .60 .25
❑ 185 Kenny Holmes B RC 1.25 .55
❑ 186 Bryant Young B .60 .25
❑ 187 Michael Sinclair B .60 .25
❑ 188 Mike Tomczak B .60 .25
❑ 189 Bobby Taylor B .60 .25
❑ 190 Brett Favre B 6.00 2.70
❑ 191 Kent Graham B .60 .25
❑ 192 Jessie Tuggle B .60 .25
❑ 193 Jimmy Smith B 1.00 .45
❑ 194 Greg Hill B .60 .25
❑ 195 Yatil Green B RC .75 .35
❑ 196 Mark Fields B .60 .25
❑ 197 Phillippi Sparks B .60 .25
❑ 198 Aaron Glenn B .60 .25
❑ 199 Pat Swilling B .60 .25
❑ 200 Barry Sanders B 5.00 2.20
❑ 201 Mark Chmura B 1.00 .45
❑ 202 Marco Coleman B .60 .25
❑ 203 Merton Hanks B .60 .25
❑ 204 Brian Blades B .60 .25
❑ 205 Errict Rhett B .60 .25
❑ 206 Henry Ellard B .60 .25
❑ 207 Andre Reed B 1.00 .45
❑ 208 Bryan Cox B .60 .25
❑ 209 Darnay Scott B 1.00 .45
❑ 210 John Elway B 6.00 2.70
❑ 211 Glyn Milburn B .60 .25
❑ 212 Don Beebe B .60 .25
❑ 213 Kevin Lockett B RC .75 .35
❑ 214 Dorsey Levens B 1.50 .70
❑ 215 Kordell Stewart B 1.50 .70
❑ 216 Larry Centers B 1.00 .45
❑ 217 Cris Carter B 1.50 .70
❑ 218 Willie McGinest B .60 .25
❑ 219 Renaldo Wynn B RC .30 .14
❑ 220 Jerry Rice B 3.00 1.35
❑ 221 Reidel Anthony B RC .75 .35
❑ 222 Mark Carrier WR B .60 .25
❑ 223 Quinn Early B .60 .25
❑ 224 Chris Sanders B .60 .25
❑ 225 Shawn Springs B RC .75 .35
❑ 226 Kevin Smith B .60 .25
❑ 227 Ben Coates B 1.00 .45
❑ 228 Tyrone Wheatley B 1.00 .45
❑ 229 Antonio Freeman B 1.50 .70
❑ 230 Dan Marino B 6.00 2.70
❑ 231 Dwayne Rudd B RC 1.25 .55
❑ 232 Leslie O'Neal B .60 .25
❑ 233 Brent Jones B .60 .25
❑ 234 Jake Plummer B RC 10.00 4.50
❑ 235 Kerry Collins B 1.50 .70
❑ 236 Rashaan Salaam B .60 .25
❑ 237 Tyrone Braxton B .60 .25
❑ 238 Herman Moore B 1.00 .45
❑ 239 Keyshawn Johnson B 1.50 .70
❑ 240 Drew Bledsoe B 2.00 .90
❑ 241 Rickey Dudley B 1.00 .45
❑ 242 Antowain Smith B RC 5.00 2.20
❑ 243 Jeff Lageman B .60 .25
❑ 244 Chris T. Jones B .60 .25
❑ 245 Steve Young B 2.00 .90
❑ 246 Eddie Robinson B .60 .25
❑ 247 Chad Cota B .60 .25
❑ 248 Michael Jackson B 1.00 .45
❑ 249 Robert Porcher B .60 .25
❑ 250 Reggie White B 1.50 .70
❑ 251 Carnell Lake B .60 .25
❑ 252 Chris Calloway B .60 .25
❑ 253 Terance Mathis B 1.00 .45
❑ 254 Carl Pickens B 1.00 .45
❑ 255 Curtis Martin B 2.00 .90
❑ 256 Jeff Graham B .60 .25
❑ 257 Regan Upshaw B RC .30 .14
❑ 258 Sean Gilbert B .60 .25
❑ 259 Will Blackwell B RC .75 .35
❑ 260 Emmitt Smith B 5.00 2.20
❑ 261 Reinard Wilson B RC .75 .35
❑ 262 Darrell Russell B RC .30 .14
❑ 263 Wayne Chrebet B 1.00 .45
❑ 264 Kevin Hardy B .60 .25
❑ 265 Shannon Sharpe B 1.00 .45
❑ 266 Harvey Williams B .60 .25
❑ 267 John Randle B 1.00 .45
❑ 268 Tim Bowens B .60 .25
❑ 269 Tony Gonzalez B RC 6.00 2.70
❑ 270 Warrick Dunn B RC 5.00 2.20
❑ 271 Sean Dawkins B .60 .25
❑ 272 Darryll Lewis B .60 .25
❑ 273 Alonzo Spellman B .60 .25
❑ 274 Mark Collins B .60 .25
❑ 275 Checklist Card B .60 .25
❑ 276 Pat Barnes S RC 2.00 .90
❑ 277 Dana Stubblefield S 2.00 .90
❑ 278 Dan Wilkinson S 1.25 .55
❑ 279 Bryce Paup S 1.25 .55
❑ 280 Kerry Collins S 3.00 1.35
❑ 281 Derrick Brooks S 3.00 1.35
❑ 282 Walter Jones S RC 3.00 1.35
❑ 283 Terry McDaniel S 1.25 .55
❑ 284 James Farrior S RC 3.00 1.35
❑ 285 Curtis Martin S 4.00 1.80
❑ 286 O.J. McDuffie S 2.00 .90
❑ 287 Natrone Means S 2.00 .90
❑ 288 Bryant Westbrook S RC 2.00 .90
❑ 289 Peter Boulware S RC 3.00 1.35
❑ 290 Emmitt Smith S 10.00 4.50
❑ 291 Joey Kent S RC 3.00 1.35
❑ 292 Eddie Kennison S 2.00 .90
❑ 293 LeRoy Butler S 1.25 .55
❑ 294 Dale Carter S 1.25 .55
❑ 295 Jim Druckenmiller S RC 2.00 .90
❑ 296 Byron Hanspard S RC 2.00 .90
❑ 297 Jeff Blake S 2.00 .90
❑ 298 Levon Kirkland S 1.25 .55
❑ 299 Michael Westbrook S 2.00 .90
❑ 300 John Elway S 12.00 5.50
❑ 301 Lamar Lathon S 1.25 .55
❑ 302 Ray Lewis S 5.00 2.20
❑ 303 Steve McNair S 4.00 1.80
❑ 304 Shawn Springs S 2.00 .90
❑ 305 Karim Abdul-Jabbar S 2.00 .90
❑ 306 Orlando Pace S RC 3.00 1.35
❑ 307 Scott Mitchell S 1.25 .55
❑ 308 Walt Harris S 1.25 .55
❑ 309 Bruce Smith S 2.00 .90
❑ 310 Reggie White S 3.00 1.35

❑ 311 Eric Swann S	1.25	.55
❑ 312 Derrick Thomas S	2.00	.90
❑ 313 Tony Martin S	2.00	.90
❑ 314 Darrell Russell S RC	2.00	.90
❑ 315 Mark Brunell S	4.00	1.80
❑ 316 Trent Dilfer S	3.00	1.35
❑ 317 Irving Fryar S	1.25	.55
❑ 318 Amani Toomer S	2.00	.90
❑ 319 Jake Reed S	2.00	.90
❑ 320 Steve Young S	4.00	1.80
❑ 321 Troy Davis S RC	2.00	.90
❑ 322 Jim Harbaugh S	2.00	.90
❑ 323 Neil O'Donnell S	1.25	.55
❑ 324 Terry Glenn S	3.00	1.35
❑ 325 Deion Sanders S	3.00	1.35
❑ 326 Gus Frerotte G	3.00	1.35
❑ 327 Tom Knight G RC	3.00	1.35
❑ 328 Peter Boulware G	3.00	1.35
❑ 329 Jerome Bettis G	5.00	2.20
❑ 330 Orlando Pace G	5.00	2.20
❑ 331 Darnell Autry G RC	3.00	1.35
❑ 332 Ike Hilliard G RC	12.00	5.50
❑ 333 David LaFleur G RC	1.50	.70
❑ 334 Jim Harbaugh G	3.00	1.35
❑ 335 Eddie George G	5.00	2.20
❑ 336 Vinny Testaverde G	3.00	1.35
❑ 337 Terry Allen G	3.00	1.35
❑ 338 Jim Druckenmiller G	3.00	1.35
❑ 339 Ricky Watters G	3.00	1.35
❑ 340 Brett Favre G	20.00	9.00
❑ 341 Simeon Rice G	3.00	1.35
❑ 342 Shannon Sharpe G	3.00	1.35
❑ 343 Kordell Stewart G	5.00	2.20
❑ 344 Isaac Bruce G	5.00	2.20
❑ 345 Drew Bledsoe G	6.00	2.70
❑ 346 Jeff Blake G	3.00	1.35
❑ 347 Herman Moore G	3.00	1.35
❑ 348 Junior Seau G	5.00	2.20
❑ 349 Rae Carruth G RC	1.50	.70
❑ 350 Dan Marino G	20.00	9.00
❑ P5 K.Abdul-Jabbar Promo	1.50	.70
❑ P32 Tony Brackens Promo	1.50	.70
❑ P45 Sam Mills Promo	1.50	.70
❑ P70 Terry Glenn Promo	1.50	.70
❑ P87 Gus Frerotte Promo	1.50	.70

1997 Finest Embossed

	Nm-Mt	Ex-Mt
COMPLETE SET (150)	800.00	350.00
COMP.SERIES 1 (75)	300.00	135.00
COMP.SERIES 2 (75)	500.00	220.00

*SILVER STARS: .8X TO 2X BASIC CARDS
*SILVER RCs: .6X TO X BASIC CARDS
*GOLD STARS: .5X TO 1.25X BASIC CARDS
*GOLD RCs: SAME PRICE

1997 Finest Embossed Refractors

Nm-Mt Ex-Mt

*SILVER STARS: 2X TO 5X BASIC CARDS
*SILVER RCs: 1X TO 2.5X BASIC CARDS
*GOLD DC STARS: 2.5X TO 6X
*GOLD DC RCs: 1.2X TO 3X

1997 Finest Refractors

	Nm-Mt	Ex-Mt
COMP.BRONZE SER.1 (100)	250.00	110.00
COMP.BRONZE SER.2 (100)	400.00	180.00

*BRONZE STARS: 1.5X TO 4X
*BRONZE RCs: .8X TO 2X
*SILVER STARS: .8X TO 2X
*SILVER RCs: .6X TO 1.5X
*GOLD STARS: 1X TO 2.5X
*GOLD RCs: .6X TO 1.5X

1998 Finest

	Nm-Mt	Ex-Mt
COMPLETE SET (270)	80.00	36.00
COMP.SERIES 1 (150)	50.00	22.00
COMP.SERIES 2 (120)	30.00	13.50

❑ 1 John Elway	4.00	1.80
❑ 2 Terance Mathis	.60	.25
❑ 3 Jermaine Lewis	.60	.25
❑ 4 Fred Lane	.40	.18
❑ 5 Simeon Rice	.60	.25
❑ 6 David Dunn	.40	.18
❑ 7 Dexter Coakley	.40	.18
❑ 8 Carl Pickens	.60	.25
❑ 9 Antonio Freeman	1.00	.45
❑ 10 Herman Moore	.60	.25
❑ 11 Kevin Hardy	.40	.18
❑ 12 Tony Gonzalez	1.00	.45
❑ 13 O.J. McDuffie	.60	.25
❑ 14 David Palmer	.40	.18
❑ 15 Lawyer Milloy	.60	.25
❑ 16 Danny Kanell	.60	.25
❑ 17 Randal Hill	.40	.18
❑ 18 Chris Slade	.40	.18
❑ 19 Charlie Garner	.60	.25
❑ 20 Mark Brunell	1.00	.45
❑ 21 Donnell Woolford	.40	.18
❑ 22 Freddie Jones	.40	.18
❑ 23 Ken Norton	.40	.18
❑ 24 Tony Banks	.60	.25
❑ 25 Isaac Bruce	1.00	.45
❑ 26 Willie Davis	.40	.18
❑ 27 Cris Dishman	.40	.18
❑ 28 Aeneas Williams	.40	.18
❑ 29 Michael Booker	.40	.18
❑ 30 Cris Carter	1.00	.45
❑ 31 Michael McCrary	.40	.18
❑ 32 Eric Moulds	1.00	.45
❑ 33 Rae Carruth	.40	.18
❑ 34 Bobby Engram	.60	.25
❑ 35 Jeff Blake	.60	.25
❑ 36 Deion Sanders	1.00	.45
❑ 37 Rod Smith	.60	.25
❑ 38 Bryant Westbrook	.40	.18
❑ 39 Mark Chmura	.60	.25
❑ 40 Tim Brown	1.00	.45
❑ 41 Bobby Taylor	.40	.18
❑ 42 James Stewart	.60	.25
❑ 43 Kimble Anders	.60	.25
❑ 44 Karim Abdul-Jabbar	1.00	.45
❑ 45 Willie McGinest	.40	.18
❑ 46 Jessie Armstead	.40	.18
❑ 47 Brad Johnson	1.00	.45
❑ 48 Greg Lloyd	.40	.18
❑ 49 Stephen Davis	.40	.18
❑ 50 Jerome Bettis	1.00	.45
❑ 51 Warren Sapp	.60	.25
❑ 52 Horace Copeland	.40	.18
❑ 53 Chad Brown	.40	.18
❑ 54 Chris Canty	.40	.18
❑ 55 Robert Smith	1.00	.45
❑ 56 Pete Mitchell	.40	.18
❑ 57 Aaron Bailey	.40	.18
❑ 58 Robert Porcher	.40	.18
❑ 59 John Mobley	.40	.18
❑ 60 Tony Martin	.60	.25
❑ 61 Michael Irvin	1.00	.45
❑ 62 Charles Way	.40	.18
❑ 63 Raymont Harris	.40	.18
❑ 64 Chuck Smith	.40	.18
❑ 65 Larry Centers	.40	.18
❑ 66 Greg Hill	.40	.18
❑ 67 Kenny Holmes	.40	.18
❑ 68 John Lynch	.60	.25
❑ 69 Michael Sinclair	.40	.18
❑ 70 Steve Young	1.25	.55
❑ 71 Michael Strahan	.60	.25
❑ 72 Levon Kirkland	.40	.18
❑ 73 Rickey Dudley	.40	.18
❑ 74 Marcus Allen	1.00	.45
❑ 75 John Randle	.60	.25
❑ 76 Erik Kramer	.40	.18
❑ 77 Neil Smith	.60	.25
❑ 78 Byron Hanspard	.40	.18
❑ 79 Quinn Early	.40	.18
❑ 80 Warren Moon	1.00	.45
❑ 81 William Thomas	.40	.18
❑ 82 Ben Coates	.60	.25
❑ 83 Lake Dawson	.40	.18
❑ 84 Steve McNair	1.00	.45
❑ 85 Gus Frerotte	.40	.18
❑ 86 Rodney Harrison	.60	.25
❑ 87 Reggie White	1.00	.45
❑ 88 Derrick Thomas	.60	.25
❑ 89 Dale Carter	.40	.18
❑ 90 Warrick Dunn	1.00	.45
❑ 91 Will Blackwell	.40	.18
❑ 92 Troy Vincent	.40	.18
❑ 93 Johnnie Morton	.60	.25
❑ 94 David LaFleur	.40	.18
❑ 95 Tony McGee	.40	.18
❑ 96 Lonnie Johnson	.40	.18
❑ 97 Thurman Thomas	1.00	.45
❑ 98 Chris Chandler	.60	.25
❑ 99 Jamal Anderson	1.00	.45
❑ 100 Checklist	.40	.18
❑ 101 Marshall Faulk	1.50	.70
❑ 102 Chris Calloway	.40	.18
❑ 103 Chris Spielman	.40	.18
❑ 104 Zach Thomas	1.00	.45
❑ 105 Jeff George	.60	.25
❑ 106 Darrell Russell	.40	.18
❑ 107 Darryll Lewis	.40	.18
❑ 108 Reidel Anthony	.60	.25
❑ 109 Terrell Owens	1.00	.45
❑ 110 Rob Moore	.60	.25
❑ 111 Darrell Green	.60	.25
❑ 112 Merton Hanks	.40	.18
❑ 113 Shawn Jefferson	.40	.18
❑ 114 Chris Sanders	.40	.18
❑ 115 Scott Mitchell	.60	.25
❑ 116 Vaughn Hebron	.40	.18
❑ 117 Ed McCaffrey	.60	.25
❑ 118 Bruce Smith	.60	.25
❑ 119 Peter Boulware	.40	.18
❑ 120 Brett Favre	4.00	1.80
❑ 121 Peyton Manning RC	25.00	11.00
❑ 122 Brian Griese RC	5.00	2.20
❑ 123 Tavian Banks RC	1.50	.70
❑ 124 Duane Starks RC	1.00	.45
❑ 125 Robert Holcombe RC	1.50	.70
❑ 126 Brian Simmons RC	1.50	.70
❑ 127 Skip Hicks RC	1.50	.70
❑ 128 Keith Brooking RC	2.50	1.10
❑ 129 Ahman Green RC	12.00	5.50
❑ 130 Jerome Pathon RC	2.50	1.10
❑ 131 Curtis Enis RC	1.00	.45
❑ 132 Grant Wistrom RC	1.50	.70
❑ 133 Germane Crowell RC	1.50	.70
❑ 134 Jacquez Green RC	1.50	.70
❑ 135 Randy Moss RC	12.00	5.50
❑ 136 Jason Peter RC	1.00	.45
❑ 137 John Avery RC	1.50	.70
❑ 138 Takeo Spikes RC	2.50	1.10
❑ 139 Pat Johnson RC	1.50	.70
❑ 140 Andre Wadsworth RC	1.50	.70
❑ 141 Fred Taylor RC	4.00	1.80
❑ 142 Charles Woodson RC	3.00	1.35
❑ 143 Marcus Nash RC	1.00	.45
❑ 144 Robert Edwards RC	1.50	.70
❑ 145 Kevin Dyson RC	2.50	1.10
❑ 146 Joe Jurevicius RC	2.50	1.10
❑ 147 Anthony Simmons RC	1.50	.70
❑ 148 Hines Ward RC	6.00	2.70
❑ 149 Greg Ellis RC	1.00	.45
❑ 150 Ryan Leaf RC	2.50	1.10
❑ 151 Jerry Rice	2.00	.90
❑ 152 Tony Martin	.60	.25
❑ 153 Checklist	.40	.18
❑ 154 Rob Johnson	.60	.25
❑ 155 Shannon Sharpe	.60	.25

❑ 156 Bert Emanuel	.60	.25
❑ 157 Eric Metcalf	.40	.18
❑ 158 Natrone Means	.60	.25
❑ 159 Derrick Alexander	.60	.25
❑ 160 Emmitt Smith	3.00	1.35
❑ 161 Jeff Burris	.40	.18
❑ 162 Chris Warren	.60	.25
❑ 163 Corey Fuller	.40	.18
❑ 164 Courtney Hawkins	.40	.18
❑ 165 James McKnight	1.00	.45
❑ 166 Shawn Springs	.40	.18
❑ 167 Wayne Martin	.40	.18
❑ 168 Michael Westbrook	.60	.25
❑ 169 Michael Jackson	.40	.18
❑ 170 Dan Marino	4.00	1.80
❑ 171 Amp Lee	.40	.18
❑ 172 James Jett	.60	.25
❑ 173 Ty Law	.60	.25
❑ 174 Kerry Collins	.60	.25
❑ 175 Robert Brooks	.60	.25
❑ 176 Blaine Bishop	.40	.18
❑ 177 Stephen Boyd	.40	.18
❑ 178 Keyshawn Johnson	1.00	.45
❑ 179 Deon Figures	.40	.18
❑ 180 Allen Aldridge	.40	.18
❑ 181 Corey Miller	.40	.18
❑ 182 Chad Lewis	.60	.25
❑ 183 Derrick Rodgers	.40	.18
❑ 184 Troy Drayton	.40	.18
❑ 185 Darren Woodson	.40	.18
❑ 186 Ken Dilger	.40	.18
❑ 187 Elvis Grbac	.60	.25
❑ 188 Terrell Fletcher	.40	.18
❑ 189 Frank Sanders	.60	.25
❑ 190 Curtis Martin	1.00	.45
❑ 191 Derrick Brooks	1.00	.45
❑ 192 Darrien Gordon	.40	.18
❑ 193 Andre Reed	.60	.25
❑ 194 Darnay Scott	.60	.25
❑ 195 Curtis Conway	.60	.25
❑ 196 Tim McDonald	.40	.18
❑ 197 Sean Dawkins	.40	.18
❑ 198 Napoleon Kaufman	1.00	.45
❑ 199 Willie Clay	.40	.18
❑ 200 Terrell Davis	1.00	.45
❑ 201 Wesley Walls	.60	.25
❑ 202 Santana Dotson	.40	.18
❑ 203 Frank Wycheck	.40	.18
❑ 204 Wayne Chrebet	1.00	.45
❑ 205 Andre Rison	.60	.25
❑ 206 Jason Sehorn	.60	.25
❑ 207 Jessie Tuggle	.40	.18
❑ 208 Kevin Turner	.40	.18
❑ 209 Jason Taylor	.60	.25
❑ 210 Yancey Thigpen	.40	.18
❑ 211 Jake Reed	.60	.25
❑ 212 Carnell Lake	.40	.18
❑ 213 Joey Galloway	.60	.25
❑ 214 Andre Hastings	.40	.18
❑ 215 Terry Allen	1.00	.45
❑ 216 Jim Harbaugh	.60	.25
❑ 217 Tony Banks	.60	.25
❑ 218 Greg Clark	.40	.18
❑ 219 Corey Dillon	1.00	.45
❑ 220 Troy Aikman	2.00	.90
❑ 221 Antowain Smith	1.00	.45
❑ 222 Steve Atwater	.40	.18
❑ 223 Trent Dilfer	1.00	.45
❑ 224 Junior Seau	1.00	.45
❑ 225 Garrison Hearst	1.00	.45
❑ 226 Eric Allen	.40	.18
❑ 227 Chad Cota	.40	.18
❑ 228 Vinny Testaverde	.60	.25
❑ 229 Duce Staley	1.25	.55
❑ 230 Drew Bledsoe	1.50	.70
❑ 231 Charles Johnson	.40	.18
❑ 232 Jake Plummer	1.00	.45
❑ 233 Errict Rhett	.60	.25
❑ 234 Doug Evans	.40	.18
❑ 235 Phillippi Sparks	.40	.18
❑ 236 Ashley Ambrose	.40	.18
❑ 237 Bryan Cox	.40	.18
❑ 238 Kevin Smith	.40	.18
❑ 239 Hardy Nickerson	.40	.18
❑ 240 Terry Glenn	1.00	.45
❑ 241 Lee Woodall	.40	.18
❑ 242 Andre Coleman	.40	.18
❑ 243 Michael Bates	.40	.18
❑ 244 Mark Fields	.40	.18
❑ 245 Eddie Kennison	.60	.25
❑ 246 Dana Stubblefield	.40	.18
❑ 247 Bobby Hoying	.60	.25
❑ 248 Mo Lewis	.40	.18
❑ 249 Derrick Mayes	.60	.25
❑ 250 Eddie George	1.00	.45
❑ 251 Mike Alstott	1.00	.45
❑ 252 J.J. Stokes	.60	.25
❑ 253 Adrian Murrell	.60	.25
❑ 254 Kevin Greene	.60	.25
❑ 255 LeRoy Butler	.40	.18
❑ 256 Glenn Foley	.60	.25
❑ 257 Jimmy Smith	.60	.25
❑ 258 Tiki Barber	1.00	.45
❑ 259 Irving Fryar	.60	.25
❑ 260 Ricky Watters	.60	.25
❑ 261 Jeff Graham	.40	.18
❑ 262 Kordell Stewart	1.00	.45
❑ 263 Rod Woodson	.60	.25
❑ 264 Leslie Shepherd	.40	.18
❑ 265 Ryan McNeil	.40	.18
❑ 266 Ike Hilliard	.60	.25
❑ 267 Keenan McCardell	.60	.25
❑ 268 Marvin Harrison	1.00	.45
❑ 269 Dorsey Levens	1.00	.45
❑ 270 Barry Sanders	3.00	1.35

1998 Finest No-Protectors

	Nm-Mt	Ex-Mt
COMPLETE SET (270)	300.00	135.00

*NO-PROTECTOR STARS: 1.25X TO 3X BASIC CARDS
*NO-PROTECTOR RCs: .5X TO 1.2X BASIC CARDS

1998 Finest No-Protectors Refractors

	Nm-Mt	Ex-Mt
COMPLETE SET (270)	1800.00	800.00

*NP REF STARS: 6X TO 15X BASIC CARDS
*NP REF RC'S: 1.5X TO 4X BASIC CARDS

1998 Finest Refractors

	Nm-Mt	Ex-Mt
COMP.REFRACT.SET (270)	1000.00	450.00

*REFRACT.STARS: 3X TO 8X
*REFRACTOR RCs: 1X TO 2.5X

1999 Finest

	Nm-Mt	Ex-Mt
COMPLETE SET (175)	80.00	36.00
COMP.SET w/o SPs (124)	30.00	13.50
❑ 1 Peyton Manning	3.00	1.35
❑ 2 Priest Holmes	1.50	.70
❑ 3 Kordell Stewart	.60	.25
❑ 4 Shannon Sharpe	.60	.25
❑ 5 Andre Rison	.60	.25
❑ 6 Rickey Dudley	.40	.18
❑ 7 Duce Staley	1.00	.45
❑ 8 Randall Cunningham	1.00	.45
❑ 9 Warrick Dunn	1.00	.45
❑ 10 Dan Marino	3.00	1.35
❑ 11 Kevin Greene	.40	.18
❑ 12 Garrison Hearst	.60	.25
❑ 13 Eric Moulds	1.00	.45
❑ 14 Marvin Harrison	1.00	.45
❑ 15 Eddie George	1.00	.45
❑ 16 Vinny Testaverde	.60	.25
❑ 17 Brad Johnson	1.00	.45
❑ 18 Derrick Thomas	.60	.25
❑ 19 Chris Chandler	.60	.25
❑ 20 Troy Aikman	2.00	.90
❑ 21 Terance Mathis	.60	.25
❑ 22 Terrell Owens	1.00	.45
❑ 23 Junior Seau	1.00	.45
❑ 24 Cris Carter	1.00	.45
❑ 25 Fred Taylor	1.00	.45
❑ 26 Adrian Murrell	.60	.25
❑ 27 Terry Glenn	1.00	.45
❑ 28 Rod Smith	.60	.25
❑ 29 Darnay Scott	.60	.25
❑ 30 Brett Favre	3.00	1.35
❑ 31 Cam Cleeland	.40	.18
❑ 32 Ricky Watters	.60	.25
❑ 33 Derrick Alexander	.60	.25
❑ 34 Bruce Smith	.60	.25
❑ 35 Steve McNair	1.00	.45
❑ 36 Wayne Chrebet	.60	.25
❑ 37 Herman Moore	.60	.25
❑ 38 Bert Emanuel	.60	.25
❑ 39 Michael Irvin	.60	.25
❑ 40 Steve Young	1.25	.55
❑ 41 Napoleon Kaufman	1.00	.45
❑ 42 Tim Biakabutuka	.60	.25
❑ 43 Isaac Bruce	1.00	.45
❑ 44 J.J. Stokes	.60	.25
❑ 45 Antonio Freeman	1.00	.45
❑ 46 John Randle	.60	.25
❑ 47 Frank Sanders	.60	.25
❑ 48 O.J. McDuffie	.60	.25
❑ 49 Keenan McCardell	.60	.25
❑ 50 Randy Moss	2.50	1.10
❑ 51 Ed McCaffrey	.60	.25
❑ 52 Yancey Thigpen	.40	.18
❑ 53 Curtis Conway	.60	.25
❑ 54 Mike Alstott	1.00	.45
❑ 55 Deion Sanders	1.00	.45
❑ 56 Dorsey Levens	1.00	.45
❑ 57 Joey Galloway	.60	.25
❑ 58 Natrone Means	.60	.25
❑ 59 Tim Brown	1.00	.45
❑ 60 Jerry Rice	2.00	.90
❑ 61 Robert Smith	1.00	.45
❑ 62 Carl Pickens	.60	.25
❑ 63 Ben Coates	.60	.25
❑ 64 Jerome Bettis	1.00	.45
❑ 65 Corey Dillon	1.00	.45
❑ 66 Curtis Martin	1.00	.45
❑ 67 Jimmy Smith	.60	.25
❑ 68 Keyshawn Johnson	1.00	.45
❑ 69 Charlie Batch	1.00	.45
❑ 70 Jamal Anderson	1.00	.45
❑ 71 Mark Brunell	1.00	.45
❑ 72 Antowain Smith	1.00	.45
❑ 73 Aeneas Williams	.40	.18
❑ 74 Wesley Walls	.60	.25
❑ 75 Jake Plummer	.60	.25
❑ 76 Oronde Gadsden	.60	.25
❑ 77 Gary Brown	.40	.18
❑ 78 Peter Boulware	.40	.18
❑ 79 Stephen Alexander	.40	.18
❑ 80 Barry Sanders	3.00	1.35
❑ 81 Warren Sapp	.60	.25
❑ 82 Michael Sinclair	.40	.18
❑ 83 Freddie Jones	.40	.18
❑ 84 Ike Hilliard	.40	.18
❑ 85 Jake Reed	.60	.25
❑ 86 Tim Dwight	1.00	.45
❑ 87 Johnnie Morton	.60	.25
❑ 88 Robert Brooks	.60	.25
❑ 89 Rocket Ismail	.60	.25
❑ 90 Emmitt Smith	2.00	.90
❑ 91 Ricky Proehl	.40	.18
❑ 92 James Jett	.60	.25
❑ 93 Karim Abdul-Jabbar	.60	.25
❑ 94 Mark Chmura	.40	.18

Card	Nm-Mt	Ex-Mt
❑ 95 Andre Reed	.60	.25
❑ 96 Michael Westbrook	.60	.25
❑ 97 Michael Strahan	.60	.25
❑ 98 Chad Brown	.40	.18
❑ 99 Trent Dilfer	.60	.25
❑ 100 Terrell Davis	1.00	.45
❑ 101 Aaron Glenn	.40	.18
❑ 102 Skip Hicks	.40	.18
❑ 103 Tony Gonzalez	1.00	.45
❑ 104 Ty Law	.60	.25
❑ 105 Jermaine Lewis	.60	.25
❑ 106 Ray Lewis	1.00	.45
❑ 107 Zach Thomas	1.00	.45
❑ 108 Reidel Anthony	.60	.25
❑ 109 Levon Kirkland	.40	.18
❑ 110 Drew Bledsoe	1.25	.55
❑ 111 Bobby Engram	.60	.25
❑ 112 Jerome Pathon	.40	.18
❑ 113 Muhsin Muhammad	.60	.25
❑ 114 Vonnie Holliday	.40	.18
❑ 115 Bill Romanowski	.40	.18
❑ 116 Marshall Faulk	1.25	.55
❑ 117 Ty Detmer	.60	.25
❑ 118 Mo Lewis	.40	.18
❑ 119 Charles Woodson	1.00	.45
❑ 120 Doug Flutie	1.00	.45
❑ 121 Jon Kitna	1.00	.45
❑ 122 Courtney Hawkins	.40	.18
❑ 123 Trent Green	1.00	.45
❑ 124 John Elway	3.00	1.35
❑ 125 Barry Sanders GM	5.00	2.20
❑ 126 Brett Favre GM	5.00	2.20
❑ 127 Curtis Martin GM	1.50	.70
❑ 128 Dan Marino GM	5.00	2.20
❑ 129 Eddie George GM	1.00	.45
❑ 130 Emmitt Smith GM	5.00	2.20
❑ 131 Jamal Anderson GM	1.50	.70
❑ 132 Jerry Rice GM	3.00	1.35
❑ 133 John Elway GM	5.00	2.20
❑ 134 Terrell Davis GM	2.50	1.10
❑ 135 Troy Aikman GM	3.00	1.35
❑ 136 Skip Hicks SN	.40	.18
❑ 137 Charles Woodson SN	1.00	.45
❑ 138 Charlie Batch SN	2.50	1.10
❑ 139 Curtis Enis SN	1.50	.70
❑ 140 Fred Taylor SN	2.50	1.10
❑ 141 Jake Plummer SN	1.50	.70
❑ 142 Peyton Manning SN	5.00	2.20
❑ 143 Randy Moss SN	4.00	1.80
❑ 144 Corey Dillon SN	1.50	.70
❑ 145 Priest Holmes SN	1.50	.70
❑ 146 Warrick Dunn SN	1.50	.70
❑ 147 Jevon Kearse RC	4.00	1.80
❑ 148 Chris Claiborne RC	1.50	.70
❑ 149 Akili Smith RC	1.50	.70
❑ 150 Brock Huard RC	3.00	1.35
❑ 151 Daunte Culpepper RC	10.00	4.50
❑ 152 Edgerrin James RC	10.00	4.50
❑ 153 Cecil Collins RC	1.50	.70
❑ 154 Kevin Faulk RC	3.00	1.35
❑ 155 Amos Zereoue RC	3.00	1.35
❑ 156 James Johnson RC	2.50	1.10
❑ 157 Sedrick Irvin RC	1.50	.70
❑ 158 Ricky Williams RC	5.00	2.20
❑ 159 Mike Cloud RC	2.50	1.10
❑ 160 Chris McAlister	1.50	.70
❑ 161 Rob Konrad RC	2.50	1.10
❑ 162 Champ Bailey RC	3.00	1.35
❑ 163 Ebenezer Ekuban RC	2.50	1.10
❑ 164 Tim Couch RC	3.00	1.35
❑ 165 Cade McNown RC	2.50	1.10
❑ 166 Donovan McNabb RC	12.00	5.50
❑ 167 Joe Germaine RC	2.50	1.10
❑ 168 Shaun King RC	2.50	1.10
❑ 169 Peerless Price RC	4.00	1.80
❑ 170 Kevin Johnson RC	2.50	1.10
❑ 171 Troy Edwards RC	2.50	1.10
❑ 172 Karsten Bailey RC	2.50	1.10
❑ 173 David Boston RC	3.00	1.35
❑ 174 D'Wayne Bates RC	2.50	1.10
❑ 175 Torry Holt RC	6.00	2.70

1999 Finest Gold Refractors

Nm-Mt Ex-Mt

*STARS: 12.5X TO 30X BASIC CARDS
*GEMS: 8X TO 20X BASIC CARDS
*SENSATIONS: 6X TO 15X BASIC CARDS
*RCs: 3X TO 8X BASIC CARDS

1999 Finest Refractors

Nm-Mt Ex-Mt

*STARS: 3X TO 8X BASIC CARDS
*GEMS: 2.5X TO 6X BASIC CARDS
*SENSATIONS: 2X TO 5X BASIC CARDS
*RCs: 1.5X TO 3X BASIC CARDS

2000 Finest

Card	Nm-Mt	Ex-Mt
COMPLETE SET (205)	400.00	180.00
❑ 1 Tim Dwight	.75	.35
❑ 2 Cade McNown	.30	.14
❑ 3 Drew Bledsoe	1.00	.45
❑ 4 Torry Holt	.75	.35
❑ 5 Derrick Mayes	.50	.23
❑ 6 Vinny Testaverde	.50	.23
❑ 7 Patrick Jeffers	.75	.35
❑ 8 Dorsey Levens	.50	.23
❑ 9 James Johnson	.30	.14
❑ 10 Champ Bailey	.50	.23
❑ 11 Jeff George	.50	.23
❑ 12 Shawn Jefferson	.30	.14
❑ 13 Terrence Wilkins	.30	.14
❑ 14 J.J. Stokes	.50	.23
❑ 15 Doug Flutie	.75	.35
❑ 16 Corey Dillon	.75	.35
❑ 17 Rod Smith	.50	.23
❑ 18 Jimmy Smith	.50	.23
❑ 19 Amani Toomer	.50	.23
❑ 20 Curtis Conway	.50	.23
❑ 21 Brad Johnson	.75	.35
❑ 22 Edgerrin James	1.25	.55
❑ 23 Derrick Alexander	.50	.23
❑ 24 Terrell Owens	.75	.35
❑ 25 Kurt Warner	1.50	.70
❑ 26 Frank Sanders	.50	.23
❑ 27 Tony Banks	.50	.23
❑ 28 Troy Aikman	1.50	.70
❑ 29 Curtis Enis	.30	.14
❑ 30 Eddie George	.75	.35
❑ 31 Bill Schroeder	.50	.23
❑ 32 Kent Graham	.30	.14
❑ 33 Mike Alstott	.75	.35
❑ 34 Steve Young	1.00	.45
❑ 35 Jacquez Green	.30	.14
❑ 36 Frank Wycheck	.30	.14
❑ 37 Kerry Collins	.50	.23
❑ 38 Stephen Davis	.75	.35
❑ 39 Tony Gonzalez	.50	.23
❑ 40 Tyrone Wheatley	.50	.23
❑ 41 Brett Favre	2.50	1.10
❑ 42 Joey Galloway	.50	.23
❑ 43 Terrell Davis	.75	.35
❑ 44 Marvin Harrison	.75	.35
❑ 45 Zach Thomas	.75	.35
❑ 46 Jerry Rice	1.50	.70
❑ 47 Keyshawn Johnson	.75	.35
❑ 48 Rob Johnson	.50	.23
❑ 49 Rocket Ismail	.50	.23
❑ 50 Elvis Grbac	.50	.23
❑ 51 Warrick Dunn	.75	.35
❑ 52 Jevon Kearse	.75	.35
❑ 53 Albert Connell	.30	.14
❑ 54 Muhsin Muhammad	.50	.23
❑ 55 Carl Pickens	.50	.23
❑ 56 Peyton Manning	2.00	.90
❑ 57 Daunte Culpepper	1.00	.45
❑ 58 Ike Hilliard	.50	.23
❑ 59 Steve McNair	.75	.35
❑ 60 Sean Dawkins	.30	.14
❑ 61 Steve Beuerlein	.50	.23
❑ 62 Priest Holmes	1.00	.45
❑ 63 Jim Harbaugh	.50	.23
❑ 64 Germane Crowell	.30	.14
❑ 65 Cris Carter	.75	.35
❑ 66 Jamal Anderson	.75	.35
❑ 67 Kevin Johnson	.75	.35
❑ 68 Herman Moore	.50	.23
❑ 69 Ricky Williams	.75	.35
❑ 70 Rich Gannon	.75	.35
❑ 71 Isaac Bruce	.75	.35
❑ 72 Peerless Price	.75	.35
❑ 73 Az-Zahir Hakim	.50	.23
❑ 74 Mark Brunell	.75	.35
❑ 75 Rob Moore	.50	.23
❑ 76 Antowain Smith	.50	.23
❑ 77 Tim Biakabutuka	.50	.23
❑ 78 Ed McCaffrey	.75	.35
❑ 79 Tony Martin	.50	.23
❑ 80 Marcus Robinson	.75	.35
❑ 81 Kevin Dyson	.50	.23
❑ 82 Wesley Walls	.30	.14
❑ 83 Chris Chandler	.50	.23
❑ 84 Keenan McCardell	.50	.23
❑ 85 Napoleon Kaufman	.50	.23
❑ 86 Emmitt Smith	1.50	.70
❑ 87 James Stewart	.50	.23
❑ 88 Tim Brown	.75	.35
❑ 89 Ricky Watters	.50	.23
❑ 90 Johnnie Morton	.50	.23
❑ 91 Jake Plummer	.50	.23
❑ 92 Olandis Gary	.75	.35
❑ 93 Jerome Bettis	.75	.35
❑ 94 Terry Glenn	.50	.23
❑ 95 Kordell Stewart	.50	.23
❑ 96 Charlie Garner	.50	.23
❑ 97 Yancey Thigpen	.30	.14
❑ 98 Michael Westbrook	.50	.23
❑ 99 Bobby Engram	.50	.23
❑ 100 Eric Moulds	.75	.35
❑ 101 Darnay Scott	.50	.23
❑ 102 Antonio Freeman	.75	.35
❑ 103 Wayne Chrebet	.50	.23
❑ 104 Akili Smith	.30	.14
❑ 105 Jeff Blake	.50	.23
❑ 106 Curtis Martin	.75	.35
❑ 107 Errict Rhett	.50	.23
❑ 108 Damon Huard	.75	.35
❑ 109 Jeff Graham	.30	.14
❑ 110 Terance Mathis	.50	.23
❑ 111 Jon Kitna	.75	.35
❑ 112 Tim Couch	.50	.23
❑ 113 Fred Taylor	.75	.35
❑ 114 Qadry Ismail	.50	.23
❑ 115 Donovan McNabb	1.25	.55
❑ 116 Charles Johnson	.50	.23
❑ 117 Troy Edwards	.30	.14
❑ 118 Shaun King	.30	.14
❑ 119 Charlie Batch	.75	.35
❑ 120 Robert Smith	.75	.35
❑ 121 Marshall Faulk	1.00	.45
❑ 122 Brian Griese	.75	.35
❑ 123 O.J. McDuffie	.50	.23
❑ 124 Randy Moss	1.50	.70
❑ 125 Duce Staley	.75	.35
❑ 126 Peter Warrick RC	8.00	3.60
❑ 127 Dez White RC	8.00	3.60
❑ 128 Ron Dayne RC	8.00	3.60
❑ 129 J.R. Redmond RC	6.00	2.70
❑ 130 Thomas Jones RC	12.00	5.50
❑ 131 Plaxico Burress RC	15.00	6.75
❑ 132 Reuben Droughns RC	10.00	4.50
❑ 133 Shaun Alexander RC	20.00	9.00

Card	Nm-Mt	Ex-Mt
❑ 134 Ron Dugans RC	6.00	2.70
❑ 135 Travis Prentice RC	6.00	2.70
❑ 136 Joe Hamilton RC	6.00	2.70
❑ 137 Curtis Keaton RC	6.00	2.70
❑ 138 Chris Redman RC	6.00	2.70
❑ 139 Chad Pennington RC	30.00	13.50
❑ 140 Travis Taylor RC	8.00	3.60
❑ 141 Bubba Franks RC	8.00	3.60
❑ 142 Dennis Northcutt RC	8.00	3.60
❑ 143 Jerry Porter RC	10.00	4.50
❑ 144 Sylvester Morris RC	6.00	2.70
❑ 145 Anthony Becht RC	8.00	3.60
❑ 146 Trung Canidate RC	6.00	2.70
❑ 147 Jamal Lewis RC	20.00	9.00
❑ 148 R.Jay Soward RC	6.00	2.70
❑ 149 Tee Martin RC	8.00	3.60
❑ 150 Courtney Brown RC	8.00	3.60
❑ 151 Brian Urlacher RC	30.00	13.50
❑ 152 Danny Farmer RC	6.00	2.70
❑ 153 Laveranues Coles RC	10.00	4.50
❑ 154 Todd Pinkston RC	8.00	3.60
❑ 155 Corey Simon RC	8.00	3.60
❑ 156 Spergon Wynn RC	6.00	2.70
❑ 157 Tim Rattay RC	15.00	6.75
❑ 158 Todd Husak RC	8.00	3.60
❑ 159 Aaron Shea RC	6.00	2.70
❑ 160 Giovanni Carmazzi RC	6.00	2.70
❑ 161 Trevor Gaylor RC	6.00	2.70
❑ 162 JaJuan Dawson RC	6.00	2.70
❑ 163 Jarious Jackson RC	6.00	2.70
❑ 164 Chris Samuels RC	6.00	2.70
❑ 165 Rob Morris RC	6.00	2.70
❑ 166 Peter Warrick Randy Moss	2.00	.90
❑ 167 Randy Moss Peter Warrick	2.00	.90
❑ 168 Travis Prentice Stephen Davis	1.50	.70
❑ 169 Stephen Davis Travis Prentice	1.50	.70
❑ 170 Chris Redman Kurt Warner	1.50	.70
❑ 171 Kurt Warner Chris Redman	1.50	.70
❑ 172 Sylvester Morris Jimmy Smith	1.50	.70
❑ 173 Jimmy Smith Sylvester Morris	1.50	.70
❑ 174 Chad Pennington Peyton Manning	4.00	1.80
❑ 175 Peyton Manning Chad Pennington	4.00	1.80
❑ 176 R.Jay Soward Marvin Harrison	1.50	.70
❑ 177 Marvin Harrison R.Jay Soward	1.50	.70
❑ 178 Ron Dayne Jamal Anderson	1.50	.70
❑ 179 Jamal Anderson Ron Dayne	1.50	.70
❑ 180 Shaun Alexander Eddie George	2.00	.90
❑ 181 Eddie George Shaun Alexander	2.00	.90
❑ 182 Courtney Brown Bruce Smith	1.50	.70
❑ 183 Bruce Smith Courtney Brown	1.50	.70
❑ 184 Jamal Lewis Edgerrin James	3.00	1.35
❑ 185 Edgerrin James Jamal Lewis	3.00	1.35
❑ 186 Trung Canidate Emmitt Smith	3.00	1.35
❑ 187 Emmitt Smith Trung Canidate	3.00	1.35
❑ 188 Travis Taylor Cris Carter	2.00	.90
❑ 189 Cris Carter Travis Taylorr	2.00	.90
❑ 190 Curtis Keaton Marshall Faulk	2.00	.90
❑ 191 Marshall Faulk Curtis Keaton	2.00	.90
❑ 192 Plaxico Burress Jerry Rice	3.00	1.35
❑ 193 Jerry Rice Plaxico Burress	3.00	1.35
❑ 194 Thomas Jones Terrell Davis	2.00	.90
❑ 195 Terrell Davis Thomas Jones	2.00	.90
❑ 196 Peyton Manning GM	5.00	2.20
❑ 197 Randy Moss GM	4.00	1.80
❑ 198 Terrell Davis GM	1.50	.70
❑ 199 Marshall Faulk GM	2.50	1.10
❑ 200 Edgerrin James GM	4.00	1.80
❑ 201 Emmitt Smith GM	4.00	1.80
❑ 202 Ricky Williams GM	1.50	.70
❑ 203 Kurt Warner GM	3.00	1.35
❑ 204 Eddie George GM	1.50	.70
❑ 205 Brett Favre GM	6.00	2.70

2000 Finest Gold/Refractors

	Nm-Mt	Ex-Mt
*GOLD REF.STARS: 8X TO 20X BASIC CARDS		
*GOLD REF.RCs: 1X TO 2.5X		
*GOLD REF.IFs: 5X TO 12X		
*GOLD REF.GM's: 6X TO 15X BASIC CARDS		

2001 Finest

	Nm-Mt	Ex-Mt
COMP.SET w/o SP's (100)	40.00	12.00
❑ 1 Eddie George	1.25	.35
❑ 2 Jay Fiedler	1.25	.35
❑ 3 Peter Warrick	1.25	.35
❑ 4 Vinny Testaverde	.75	.23
❑ 5 Charles Johnson	.50	.15
❑ 6 Ahman Green	1.25	.35
❑ 7 Isaac Bruce	1.25	.35
❑ 8 Junior Seau	1.25	.35
❑ 9 Daunte Culpepper	1.25	.35
❑ 10 Ike Hilliard	.75	.23
❑ 11 Tony Banks	.75	.23
❑ 12 Steve Beuerlein	.75	.23
❑ 13 Jamal Anderson	1.25	.35
❑ 14 Tyrone Wheatley	.75	.23
❑ 15 Sylvester Morris	.50	.15
❑ 16 Edgerrin James	1.50	.45
❑ 17 Shaun King	.50	.15
❑ 18 Terrell Owens	1.25	.35
❑ 19 Donovan Mcnabb	1.50	.45
❑ 20 Cade Mcnown	.50	.15
❑ 21 Elvis Grbac	.75	.23
❑ 22 James Stewart	.75	.23
❑ 23 Joe Horn	.75	.23
❑ 24 Randy Moss	2.50	.75
❑ 25 Matt Hasselbeck	.75	.23
❑ 26 Jerome Bettis	1.25	.35
❑ 27 Bill Schroeder	.75	.23
❑ 28 Jake Plummer	.75	.23
❑ 29 Rod Smith	.75	.23
❑ 30 Akili Smith	.50	.15
❑ 31 Jimmy Smith	.75	.23
❑ 32 Oronde Gadsden	.75	.23
❑ 33 Kerry Collins	.75	.23
❑ 34 Warrick Dunn	1.25	.35
❑ 35 Jeff Graham	.50	.15
❑ 36 Ray Lewis	1.25	.35
❑ 37 Joey Galloway	.75	.23
❑ 38 Tim Brown	1.25	.35
❑ 39 Derrick Alexander	.75	.23
❑ 40 Jerry Rice	2.50	.75
❑ 41 Muhsin Muhammad	.75	.23
❑ 42 Shawn Jefferson	.50	.15
❑ 43 Curtis Martin	1.25	.35
❑ 44 Terry Glenn	.75	.23
❑ 45 Marvin Harrison	1.25	.35
❑ 46 Mike Anderson	1.25	.35
❑ 47 Stephen Davis	1.25	.35
❑ 48 Chad Lewis	.50	.15
❑ 49 Fred Taylor	1.25	.35
❑ 50 Corey Dillon	1.25	.35
❑ 51 Charlie Batch	1.25	.35
❑ 52 Kevin Johnson	.75	.23
❑ 53 Brett Favre	4.00	1.20
❑ 54 Marshall Faulk	1.50	.45
❑ 55 Kordell Stewart	.75	.23
❑ 56 Steve McNair	1.25	.35
❑ 57 Jeff Blake	.75	.23
❑ 58 Eric Moulds	.75	.23
❑ 59 Emmitt Smith	2.50	.75
❑ 60 David Boston	1.25	.35
❑ 61 Cris Carter	1.25	.35
❑ 62 Peyton Manning	3.00	.90
❑ 63 Keyshawn Johnson	1.25	.35
❑ 64 Doug Flutie	1.25	.35
❑ 65 Drew Bledsoe	1.50	.45
❑ 66 Ricky Williams	1.25	.35
❑ 67 Keenan Mccardell	.50	.15
❑ 68 Brian Urlacher	2.00	.60
❑ 69 Jamal Lewis	2.00	.60
❑ 70 Ed McCaffrey	1.25	.35
❑ 71 Antonio Freeman	1.25	.35
❑ 72 Darrell Jackson	1.25	.35
❑ 73 Jeff George	.75	.23
❑ 74 Chris Chandler	.75	.23
❑ 75 Germane Crowell	.50	.15
❑ 76 Tim Biakabutuka	.75	.23
❑ 77 Jon Kitna	.75	.23
❑ 78 Troy Brown	.75	.23
❑ 79 Lamar Smith	.75	.23
❑ 80 Derrick Mason	.75	.23
❑ 81 Hines Ward	1.25	.35
❑ 82 Mark Brunell	1.25	.35
❑ 83 Trent Dilfer	.75	.23
❑ 84 Tim Couch	.75	.23
❑ 85 Donald Hayes	.50	.15
❑ 86 Amani Toomer	.75	.23
❑ 87 Tony Gonzalez	.75	.23
❑ 88 Rich Gannon	1.25	.35
❑ 89 Rob Johnson	.75	.23
❑ 90 Torry Holt	1.25	.35
❑ 91 Jeff Garcia	1.25	.35
❑ 92 Kurt Warner	2.50	.75
❑ 93 Aaron Brooks	1.25	.35
❑ 94 Brian Griese	1.25	.35
❑ 95 James Allen	.75	.23
❑ 96 Wayne Chrebet	.75	.23
❑ 97 Tiki Barber	.75	.23
❑ 98 Brad Johnson	1.25	.35
❑ 99 Ricky Watters	.75	.23
❑ 100 Charlie Garner	.75	.23
❑ 101 Andre Carter RC	10.00	3.00
❑ 102 Dan Morgan RC	10.00	3.00
❑ 103 Gerard Warren RC	10.00	3.00
❑ 104 Jesse Palmer RC	10.00	3.00
❑ 105 Josh Heupel RC	10.00	3.00
❑ 106 Justin Smith RC	10.00	3.00
❑ 107 LaMont Jordan RC	12.00	3.60
❑ 108 Leonard Davis RC	6.00	1.80
❑ 109 Marques Tuiasosopo RC	10.00	3.00
❑ 110 Snoop Minnis RC	6.00	1.80
❑ 111 Quincy Carter RC	10.00	3.00
❑ 112 Quincy Morgan RC	10.00	3.00
❑ 113 Richard Seymour RC	10.00	3.00
❑ 114 Rudi Johnson RC	20.00	6.00
❑ 115 Sage Rosenfels RC	10.00	3.00
❑ 116 Todd Heap RC	10.00	3.00
❑ 117 Travis Minor RC	6.00	1.80
❑ 118 Will Allen RC	6.00	1.80
❑ 119 Jamal Reynolds RC	10.00	3.00
❑ 120 Scotty Anderson RC	6.00	1.80
❑ 121 Anthony Thomas RC	15.00	4.50
❑ 122 Chad Johnson RC	20.00	6.00

❑ 123 Chris Chambers RC	12.00	3.60
❑ 124 Chris Weinke RC	10.00	3.00
❑ 125 David Terrell RC	10.00	3.00
❑ 126 Deuce McAllister RC	25.00	7.50
❑ 127 Drew Brees RC	20.00	6.00
❑ 128 Freddie Mitchell RC	10.00	3.00
❑ 129 James Jackson RC	10.00	3.00
❑ 130 Kevan Barlow RC	10.00	3.00
❑ 131 Koren Robinson RC	12.00	3.60
❑ 132 LaDainian Tomlinson RC	30.00	9.00
❑ 133 Michael Bennett RC	20.00	6.00
❑ 134 Michael Vick RC	60.00	18.00
❑ 135 Mike McMahon RC	10.00	3.00
❑ 136 Reggie Wayne RC	15.00	4.50
❑ 137 Robert Ferguson RC	10.00	3.00
❑ 138 Rod Gardner RC	10.00	3.00
❑ 139 Santana Moss RC	15.00	4.50
❑ 140 Travis Henry RC	12.00	3.60

2002 Finest

	Nm-Mt	Ex-Mt
COMP.SET w/o SP's (62)	40.00	12.00
❑ 1 Peyton Manning	2.50	.75
❑ 2 Troy Brown	.75	.23
❑ 3 Curtis Martin	1.25	.35
❑ 4 Kordell Stewart	.75	.23
❑ 5 Michael Pittman	.50	.15
❑ 6 Rod Gardner	.75	.23
❑ 7 Germane Crowell	.50	.15
❑ 8 Terrell Davis	1.25	.35
❑ 9 Eric Moulds	.75	.23
❑ 10 Jake Plummer	.75	.23
❑ 11 Tony Gonzalez	.75	.23
❑ 12 Ricky Williams	1.25	.35
❑ 13 Deuce McAllister	1.50	.45
❑ 14 Jerry Rice	2.50	.75
❑ 15 Torry Holt	1.25	.35
❑ 16 Michael Vick	4.00	1.20
❑ 17 David Terrell	1.25	.35
❑ 18 Terry Glenn	.75	.23
❑ 19 Mark Brunell	1.25	.35
❑ 20 Vinny Testaverde	.75	.23
❑ 21 Jerome Bettis	1.25	.35
❑ 22 Randy Moss	2.50	.75
❑ 23 Marvin Harrison	1.25	.35
❑ 24 Chris Weinke	.75	.23
❑ 25 Tiki Barber	.75	.23
❑ 26 Corey Bradford	.50	.15
❑ 27 David Boston	1.25	.35
❑ 28 Emmitt Smith	3.00	.90
❑ 29 Santana Moss	1.25	.35
❑ 30 Brian Griese	1.25	.35
❑ 31 Priest Holmes	1.50	.45
❑ 32 Rich Gannon	1.25	.35
❑ 33 Antowain Smith	.75	.23
❑ 34 Marcus Robinson	.75	.23
❑ 35 Warrick Dunn	1.25	.35
❑ 36 Daunte Culpepper	1.25	.35
❑ 37 Shaun Alexander	1.25	.35
❑ 38 Kurt Warner	1.25	.35
❑ 39 Quincy Carter	.75	.23
❑ 40 Ray Lewis	1.25	.35
❑ 41 Aaron Brooks	1.25	.35
❑ 42 Plaxico Burress	.75	.23
❑ 43 Jamal Lewis	1.25	.35
❑ 44 Ahman Green	1.25	.35
❑ 45 Rod Smith	.75	.23
❑ 46 Tim Couch	.75	.23
❑ 47 Muhsin Muhammad	.75	.23
❑ 48 Drew Bledsoe	1.50	.45
❑ 49 Anthony Thomas	1.25	.35
❑ 50 Tom Brady	3.00	.90
❑ 51 Trent Green	.75	.23
❑ 52 Charlie Garner	.75	.23
❑ 53 Darrell Jackson	.75	.23
❑ 54 Mike McMahon	1.25	.35
❑ 55 Donovan McNabb	1.50	.45
❑ 56 Fred Taylor	1.25	.35
❑ 57 Corey Dillon	.75	.23
❑ 58 Keyshawn Johnson	1.25	.35
❑ 59 Drew Brees	1.25	.35
❑ 60 Steve McNair	1.25	.35
❑ 61 Jimmy Smith	.75	.23
❑ 62 Terrell Owens	1.25	.35
❑ 63 Eddie George JSY/499	20.00	6.00
❑ 64 Jeff Garcia JSY/999	15.00	4.50
❑ 65 LaDain Tomlinson JSY/999	20.00	6.00
❑ 66 Cris Carter JSY/499	20.00	6.00
❑ 67 Chris Chambers JSY/499	20.00	6.00
❑ 68 Brian Urlacher JSY/999	25.00	7.50
❑ 69 Tim Brown JSY/999	15.00	4.50
❑ 70 Marshall Faulk JSY/999	20.00	6.00
❑ 71 Stephen Davis JSY/999	12.00	3.60
❑ 72 Jevon Kearse JSY/999	12.00	3.60
❑ 73 Edgerrin James JSY/999	15.00	4.50
❑ 74 Mike Anderson JSY/999	15.00	4.50
❑ 75 Warren Sapp JSY/499	20.00	6.00
❑ 76 Brett Favre JSY/499	30.00	9.00
❑ 77 Julius Peppers RC	6.00	1.80
❑ 78 Tim Carter RC	3.00	.90
❑ 79 Travis Stephens RC	3.00	.90
❑ 80 Jabar Gaffney RC	4.00	1.20
❑ 81 Cliff Russell RC	3.00	.90
❑ 82 Reche Caldwell RC	4.00	1.20
❑ 83 Maurice Morris RC	4.00	1.20
❑ 84 Antwaan Randle El RC	5.00	1.50
❑ 85 Ladell Betts RC	4.00	1.20
❑ 86 Daniel Graham RC	4.00	1.20
❑ 87 Jeremy Shockey RC	12.00	3.60
❑ 88 Mike Williams RC	3.00	.90
❑ 89 Josh McCown RC	5.00	1.50
❑ 90 Rohan Davey RC	4.00	1.20
❑ 91 David Garrard RC	4.00	1.20
❑ 92 Dwight Freeney RC	5.00	1.50
❑ 93 Leonard Henry RC	3.00	.90
❑ 94 Albert Haynesworth RC	3.00	.90
❑ 95 Herb Haygood RC	2.00	.60
❑ 96 Kurt Kittner RC	3.00	.90
❑ 97 Jason McAddley RC	3.00	.90
❑ 98 Bryan Thomas RC	3.00	.90
❑ 99 Wendell Bryant RC	4.00	1.20
❑ 100 Mike Rumph RC	4.00	1.20
❑ 101 Chad Hutchinson RC	4.00	1.20
❑ 102 Brian Westbrook RC	6.00	1.80
❑ 103 Deion Branch RC	8.00	2.40
❑ 104 John Henderson RC	4.00	1.20
❑ 105 Jerramy Stevens RC	4.00	1.20
❑ 106 Tracey Wistrom RC	3.00	.90
❑ 107 Phillip Buchanon RC	4.00	1.20
❑ 108 Matt Schobel RC	3.00	.90
❑ 109 Ed Reed RC	6.00	1.80
❑ 110 Randy Fasani RC	3.00	.90
❑ 111 Josh Scobey RC	4.00	1.20
❑ 112 Luke Staley RC	3.00	.90
❑ 113 Anthony Weaver RC	3.00	.90
❑ 114 Kyle Johnson RC	2.00	.60
❑ 115 David Carr AU RC	60.00	18.00
❑ 116 Joey Harrington AU RC	60.00	18.00
❑ 117 Donte Stallworth AU RC	30.00	9.00
❑ 118 Ashley Lelie AU RC	40.00	12.00
❑ 119 Patrick Ramsey AU RC	40.00	12.00
❑ 120 William Green AU RC	40.00	12.00
❑ 121 Josh Reed AU RC	20.00	6.00
❑ 122 Clinton Portis AU RC	60.00	18.00
❑ 123 Antonio Bryant AU RC	20.00	6.00
❑ 124 Javon Walker AU RC	50.00	15.00
❑ 125 Roy Williams AU RC	40.00	12.00
❑ 126 Marquise Walker AU RC	20.00	6.00
❑ 127 Quentin Jammer AU RC	20.00	6.00
❑ 128 DeShaun Foster AU RC	25.00	7.50
❑ 129 Andre Davis AU RC	20.00	6.00
❑ 130 Ron Johnson AU RC	20.00	6.00
❑ 131 Lamar Gordon AU RC	20.00	6.00
❑ 132 T.J. Duckett AU/300 RC	60.00	18.00
❑ 133 Freddie Milons AU RC	20.00	6.00
❑ 134 Eric Crouch AU RC	30.00	9.00
❑ 135 Adrian Peterson AU RC	25.00	7.50
❑ 136 Damien Anderson AU RC	20.00	6.00

2002 Finest Refractors

	Nm-Mt	Ex-Mt
*STARS 1-62: 3X TO 8X BASIC CARDS		
*63-76 JSY/499: .5X TO 1.2X		
*63-76 JSY/999: .6X TO 1.5X		
*ROOKIES 77-114: 1.2X TO 3X		
*ROOKIE AU 115-136: .6X TO 1.5X		
❑ 115 David Carr AU	150.00	45.00
❑ 116 Joey Harrington AU	150.00	45.00
❑ 117 Donte Stallworth AU	50.00	15.00
❑ 118 Ashley Lelie AU	60.00	18.00
❑ 119 Patrick Ramsey AU	60.00	18.00
❑ 120 William Green AU	60.00	18.00
❑ 121 Josh Reed AU	30.00	9.00
❑ 122 Clinton Portis AU	150.00	45.00
❑ 123 Antonio Bryant AU	30.00	9.00
❑ 124 Javon Walker AU	80.00	24.00
❑ 125 Roy Williams AU	60.00	18.00
❑ 126 Marquise Walker AU	30.00	9.00
❑ 127 Quentin Jammer AU	30.00	9.00
❑ 128 DeShaun Foster AU	40.00	12.00
❑ 129 Andre Davis AU	30.00	9.00
❑ 130 Ron Johnson AU	30.00	9.00
❑ 131 Lamar Gordon AU	30.00	9.00
❑ 132 T.J. Duckett AU	100.00	30.00
❑ 133 Freddie Milons AU	30.00	9.00
❑ 134 Eric Crouch AU	50.00	15.00
❑ 135 Adrian Peterson AU	40.00	12.00
❑ 136 Damien Anderson AU	30.00	9.00

2002 Finest Refractors Gold

	Nm-Mt	Ex-Mt
*STARS 1-62: 12X TO 30X BASIC CARDS		
*JSY/999: 2X TO 5X BASIC CARDS		
*JSY/499: 1.5X TO 4X BASIC CARDS		
*ROOKIES: 4X TO 10X BASIC CARDS		
*ROOKIE AUTO: 2X TO 4X HI COL.		
❑ 115 David Carr AU	300.00	90.00
❑ 116 Joey Harrington AU	300.00	90.00
❑ 122 Clinton Portis AU	300.00	90.00

2003 Finest

	MINT	NRMT
COMP.SET w/o SP's (100)	50.00	22.00
101-118 GROUP A ODDS 1:171 MINI-BOXES		
101-118 GROUP B ODDS 1:38 MINI-BOXES		
101-118 GROUP C ODDS 1:4 MINI-BOXES		
ROOKIE AU/399 ODDS 1:30 MINI-BOXES		
ROOKIE AU/999 ODDS 1:3 MINI-BOXES		
❑ 1 Chad Pennington	1.50	.70
❑ 2 Tommy Maddox	1.25	.55
❑ 3 Brett Favre	3.00	1.35
❑ 4 Eric Moulds	.75	.35
❑ 5 Randy Moss	2.00	.90
❑ 6 Duce Staley	.75	.35
❑ 7 Derrick Mason	.75	.35
❑ 8 Shaun Alexander	1.25	.55
❑ 9 Peyton Manning	2.00	.90
❑ 10 Kerry Collins	.75	.35
❑ 11 Joe Horn	.75	.35

❑ 12 Laveranues Coles	.75	.35
❑ 13 Marty Booker	.75	.35
❑ 14 Emmitt Smith	3.00	1.35
❑ 15 Edgerrin James	1.25	.55
❑ 16 Aaron Brooks	1.25	.55
❑ 17 Curtis Martin	1.25	.55
❑ 18 Hines Ward	1.25	.55
❑ 19 Rod Smith	.75	.35
❑ 20 Priest Holmes	1.50	.70
❑ 21 Jerry Rice	2.50	1.10
❑ 22 Peerless Price	.75	.35
❑ 23 Mark Brunell	.75	.35
❑ 24 Trent Green	.75	.35
❑ 25 David Boston	.75	.35
❑ 26 Chris Chambers	1.25	.55
❑ 27 Marshall Faulk	1.25	.55
❑ 28 Fred Taylor	1.25	.55
❑ 29 Tim Couch	.50	.23
❑ 30 Amani Toomer	.75	.35
❑ 31 Travis Henry	.75	.35
❑ 32 Jeff Blake	.50	.23
❑ 33 Troy Brown	.75	.35
❑ 34 Charlie Garner	.75	.35
❑ 35 Tom Brady	2.00	.90
❑ 36 Warrick Dunn	.75	.35
❑ 37 Plaxico Burress	.75	.35
❑ 38 Marvin Harrison	1.25	.55
❑ 39 Clinton Portis	2.00	.90
❑ 40 Deuce McAllister	1.25	.55
❑ 41 Matt Hasselbeck	.75	.35
❑ 42 Jeff Garcia	1.25	.55
❑ 43 David Carr	2.00	.90
❑ 44 Ahman Green	1.25	.55
❑ 45 Eddie George	.75	.35
❑ 46 Drew Brees	1.25	.55
❑ 47 Tiki Barber	.75	.35
❑ 48 Jay Fiedler	.75	.35
❑ 49 Curtis Conway	.75	.35
❑ 50 Steve McNair	1.25	.55
❑ 51 Donald Driver	.75	.35
❑ 52 Jake Plummer	.75	.35
❑ 53 Jamal Lewis	1.25	.55
❑ 54 Corey Dillon	.75	.35
❑ 55 Stephen Davis	.75	.35
❑ 56 Terrell Owens	1.25	.55
❑ 57 Torry Holt	1.25	.55
❑ 58 Chad Johnson	.75	.35
❑ 59 Chad Hutchinson	.75	.35
❑ 60 Kurt Warner	1.25	.55
❑ 61 Troy Polamalu RC	3.00	1.35
❑ 62 Eugene Wilson RC	2.50	1.10
❑ 63 Juston Wood RC	1.50	.70
❑ 64 Anquan Boldin RC	8.00	3.60
❑ 65 Doug Gabriel RC	3.00	1.35
❑ 66 Domanick Davis RC	6.00	2.70
❑ 67 J.R. Tolver RC	2.50	1.10
❑ 68 Jerome McDougle RC	3.00	1.35
❑ 69 Keenan Howry RC	3.00	1.35
❑ 70 Teyo Johnson RC	3.00	1.35
❑ 71 Bethel Johnson RC	5.00	2.20
❑ 72 Ken Hamlin RC	2.50	1.10
❑ 73 L.J. Smith RC	3.00	1.35
❑ 74 Rashean Mathis RC	1.50	.70
❑ 75 Amaz Battle RC	3.00	1.35
❑ 76 B.J. Askew RC	3.00	1.35
❑ 77 Mike Doss RC	3.00	1.35
❑ 78 Kevin Curtis RC	3.00	1.35
❑ 79 Terence Newman RC	6.00	2.70
❑ 80 Shaun McDonald RC	3.00	1.35
❑ 81 Kevin Williams RC	3.00	1.35
❑ 82 Nate Burleson RC	5.00	2.20
❑ 83 Tyrone Calico RC	4.00	1.80
❑ 84 DeWayne White RC	2.50	1.10
❑ 85 Marcus Trufant RC	3.00	1.35
❑ 86 Nick Barnett RC	5.00	2.20
❑ 87 Bennie Joppru RC	3.00	1.35
❑ 88 Andre Woolfolk RC	3.00	1.35
❑ 89 Billy McMullen RC	2.50	1.10
❑ 90 Boss Bailey RC	4.00	1.80
❑ 91 William Joseph RC	3.00	1.35
❑ 92 Michael Haynes RC	3.00	1.35
❑ 93 DeWayne Robertson RC	3.00	1.35
❑ 94 LaTarence Dunbar RC	2.50	1.10
❑ 95 David Tyree RC	2.50	1.10
❑ 96 Walter Young RC	1.50	.70
❑ 97 E.J. Henderson RC	3.00	1.35
❑ 98 Ty Warren RC	3.00	1.35
❑ 99 Zuriel Smith RC	1.50	.70
❑ 100 Brock Forsey RC	3.00	1.35
❑ 101 Ricky Williams JSY C	12.00	5.50
❑ 102 Drew Bledsoe JSY C	12.00	5.50
❑ 103 Joey Harrington JSY C	15.00	6.75
❑ 104 Tim Brown JSY C	15.00	6.75
❑ 105 Brian Urlacher JSY C	20.00	9.00
❑ 106 Zach Thomas JSY C	12.00	5.50
❑ 107 Jeremy Shockey JSY C	15.00	6.75
❑ 108 Michael Strahan JSY A	12.00	5.50
❑ 109 Jason Taylor JSY C	12.00	5.50
❑ 110 Donovan McNabb JSY C	20.00	9.00
❑ 111 LaDainian Tomlinson JSY B	15.00	6.75
❑ 112 Rich Gannon JSY C	12.00	5.50
❑ 113 Brad Johnson JSY C	12.00	5.50
❑ 114 Daunte Culpepper JSY C	12.00	5.50
❑ 115 Michael Vick JSY C	25.00	11.00
❑ 116 Jimmy Smith JSY B	10.00	4.50
❑ 117 Keyshawn Johnson JSY C	12.00	5.50
❑ 118 Keith Brooking JSY C	10.00	4.50
❑ 119 Carson Palmer AU/399 RC	100.00	45.00
❑ 120 Byron Leftwich AU/399 RC	120.00	55.00
❑ 121 Chris Simms AU/399 RC	60.00	27.00
❑ 122 Kyle Boller AU/399 RC	60.00	27.00
❑ 123 Justin Fargas AU RC	15.00	6.75
❑ 124 Seneca Wallace AU RC	15.00	6.75
❑ 125 Larry Johnson AU RC	40.00	18.00
❑ 126 Kareem Kelly AU RC	15.00	6.75
❑ 127 Willis McGahee AU/399 RC	75.00	34.00
❑ 128 Kelley Washington AU RC	20.00	9.00
❑ 129 Brian St.Pierre AU RC	15.00	6.75
❑ 130 Kliff Kingsbury AU RC	15.00	6.75
❑ 131 Ken Dorsey AU RC	30.00	13.50
❑ 132 Bryant Johnson AU RC	15.00	6.75
❑ 133 Dallas Clark AU RC	15.00	6.75
❑ 134 Chris Brown AU RC	40.00	18.00
❑ 135 Taylor Jacobs AU RC	20.00	9.00
❑ 136 Artose Pinner AU RC	15.00	6.75
❑ 137 Lee Suggs AU RC	30.00	13.50
❑ 138 LaBrandon Toefield AU RC	15.00	6.75
❑ 139 Jason Witten AU RC	30.00	13.50
❑ 140 Brad Banks AU RC	15.00	6.75
❑ 141 Earnest Graham AU RC	15.00	6.75
❑ 142 Bobby Wade AU RC	15.00	6.75
❑ 143 Talman Gardner AU RC	15.00	6.75
❑ 144 Justin Gage AU RC	15.00	6.75
❑ 145 Sam Aiken AU RC	15.00	6.75
❑ 146 Musa Smith AU RC	15.00	6.75
❑ 147 Terrell Suggs AU RC	25.00	11.00
❑ 148 Brandon Lloyd AU RC	30.00	13.50
❑ 150 Rex Grossman AU RC	40.00	18.00

2003 Finest Refractors

	MINT	NRMT
*STARS: 2.5X TO 6X BASIC CARDS		
*ROOKIES 61-100: 1.5X TO 4X		
*JSY 101-118: .5X TO 1.2X		
*ROOKIE AU/399: .5X TO 1.2X		
*ROOKIE AU/999: .8X TO 2X		
❑ 150 Rex Grossman AU	80.00	36.00

2003 Finest Refractors Gold

	MINT	NRMT
*STARS: 6X TO 15X BASIC CARDS		
*ROOKIES 61-100: 3X TO 8X		
*JSY 101-118: .6X TO 1.5X		
*ROOKIE AU/399: .6X TO 1.5X		
*ROOKIE AU/999: 1.2X TO 3X		
❑ 150 Rex Grossman AU	150.00	70.00

2003 Finest Xfractors

	MINT	NRMT
*STARS: 3X TO 8X BASIC CARDS		
*ROOKIES 61-100: 2X TO 5X		
*JSY 101-118: .6X TO 1.5X		
*ROOKIE AU/399: .6X TO 1.5X		
*ROOKIE AU/999: 1.2X TO 3X		
❑ 150 Rex Grossman AU	150.00	70.00

2004 Finest

	Nm-Mt	Ex-Mt
COMP.SET w/o SP's (100)	40.00	12.00
COMP.SET w/o RC's (60)	12.00	3.60
COMMON CARD (1-60)	.30	.09
SEMISTARS	.50	.15
UNLISTED STARS	.75	.23
VETERAN JERSEY STATED ODDS 1:36		
108-134 AU/399 RC STATED ODDS 1:120		
108-134 AU/999 RC STATED ODDS 1:12		
UNPRICED PRINT PLATES #'d TO 1		
❑ 1 Steve McNair	.75	.23
❑ 2 Corey Dillon	.50	.15
❑ 3 Joey Harrington	.75	.23
❑ 4 Travis Henry	.50	.15
❑ 5 Donovan McNabb	1.00	.30
❑ 6 Jamal Lewis	.75	.23
❑ 7 Jeff Garcia	.75	.23
❑ 8 Fred Taylor	.50	.15
❑ 9 Aaron Brooks	.50	.15
❑ 10 Marc Bulger	.75	.23
❑ 11 Keenan McCardell	.30	.09
❑ 12 David Carr	.75	.23
❑ 13 Charles Rogers	.50	.15
❑ 14 Ray Lewis	.75	.23
❑ 15 Priest Holmes	1.00	.30
❑ 16 Curtis Martin	.75	.23
❑ 17 Plaxico Burress	.50	.15
❑ 18 Shaun Alexander	.75	.23
❑ 19 Brad Johnson	.50	.15
❑ 20 Marvin Harrison	.75	.23
❑ 21 Rod Smith	.50	.15
❑ 22 Jake Delhomme	.75	.23
❑ 23 Santana Moss	.50	.15
❑ 24 Trent Green	.50	.15
❑ 25 Michael Vick	1.50	.45
❑ 26 Tim Rattay	.50	.15
❑ 27 Chris Chambers	.50	.15
❑ 28 Robert Ferguson	.30	.09
❑ 29 Tiki Barber	.50	.15
❑ 30 Terrell Owens	.75	.23
❑ 31 Marshall Faulk	.75	.23
❑ 32 Quincy Carter	.50	.15
❑ 33 Stephen Davis	.50	.15
❑ 34 Josh McCown	.50	.15
❑ 35 Jeremy Shockey	.75	.23
❑ 36 Tommy Maddox	.50	.15
❑ 37 Derrick Mason	.50	.15
❑ 38 Kerry Collins	.50	.15
❑ 39 Jimmy Smith	.50	.15
❑ 40 Chad Pennington	1.00	.30
❑ 41 Domanick Davis	.75	.23
❑ 42 Darrell Jackson	.50	.15
❑ 43 Steve Smith	.50	.15
❑ 44 Drew Bledsoe	.75	.23
❑ 45 Deuce McAllister	.75	.23
❑ 46 Jerry Porter	.50	.15
❑ 47 Peerless Price	.50	.15
❑ 48 Eric Moulds	.50	.15
❑ 49 Garrison Hearst	.50	.15
❑ 50 Brett Favre	2.00	.60
❑ 51 Amani Toomer	.50	.15
❑ 52 Andre Johnson	.75	.23
❑ 53 Edgerrin James	.75	.23
❑ 54 Rex Grossman	.75	.23
❑ 55 Daunte Culpepper	.75	.23
❑ 56 Tony Gonzalez	.50	.15

❑ 57 Byron Leftwich	1.25	.35
❑ 58 Mark Brunell	.50	.15
❑ 59 Laveranues Coles	.50	.15
❑ 60 Matt Hasselbeck	.50	.15
❑ 61 Chris Gamble RC	2.50	.75
❑ 62 Michael Turner RC	1.50	.45
❑ 63 Julius Jones RC	12.00	3.60
❑ 64 Dunta Robinson RC	2.00	.60
❑ 65 Sean Taylor RC	2.50	.75
❑ 66 Ahmad Carroll RC	2.50	.75
❑ 67 Derrick Strait RC	2.00	.60
❑ 68 Dontarrious Thomas RC	2.00	.60
❑ 69 Jason Babin RC	2.00	.60
❑ 70 Reggie Williams RC	2.50	.75
❑ 71 Dwan Edwards RC	1.00	.30
❑ 72 Rashaun Woods RC	2.50	.75
❑ 73 Ricardo Colclough RC	2.00	.60
❑ 74 Will Smith RC	2.00	.60
❑ 75 Kellen Winslow RC	5.00	1.50
❑ 76 Roy Williams RC	6.00	1.80
❑ 77 B.J. Symons RC	2.00	.60
❑ 78 Carlos Francis RC	1.50	.45
❑ 79 Triandos Luke RC	2.00	.60
❑ 80 Drew Henson RC	5.00	1.50
❑ 81 Keiwan Ratliff RC	1.50	.45
❑ 82 Will Poole RC	2.00	.60
❑ 83 Tommie Harris RC	2.50	.75
❑ 84 Steven Jackson RC	6.00	1.80
❑ 85 Greg Jones RC	2.00	.60
❑ 86 Vince Wilfork RC	2.50	.75
❑ 87 DeAngelo Hall RC	2.50	.75
❑ 88 Daryl Smith RC	2.00	.60
❑ 89 Teddy Lehman RC	2.00	.60
❑ 90 Casey Bramlet RC	1.50	.45
❑ 91 Marcus Tubbs RC	2.00	.60
❑ 92 Andy Hall RC	1.50	.45
❑ 93 Jim Sorgi RC	2.00	.60
❑ 94 Kenechi Udeze RC	2.00	.60
❑ 95 Darius Watts RC	2.50	.75
❑ 96 Tank Johnson RC	1.50	.45
❑ 97 Matt Mauck RC	2.00	.60
❑ 98 Bradlee Van Pelt RC	2.00	.60
❑ 99 D.J. Williams RC	2.50	.75
❑ 100 Larry Fitzgerald RC	6.00	1.80
❑ 101 Peyton Manning JSY	15.00	4.50
❑ 102 Clinton Portis JSY	8.00	2.40
❑ 103 Chad Johnson JSY	6.00	1.80
❑ 104 Randy Moss JSY	10.00	3.00
❑ 105 Tom Brady JSY	20.00	6.00
❑ 106 LaDainian Tomlinson JSY	8.00	2.40
❑ 107 Ahman Green JSY	8.00	2.40
❑ 108 Ben Roethlisberger AU/399 RC	300.00	90.00
❑ 109 Philip Rivers AU/399 RC	60.00	18.00
❑ 110 Eli Manning AU/399 RC	150.00	45.00
❑ 111 Kevin Jones AU/399 RC	80.00	24.00
❑ 112 Bernard Berrian AU RC	15.00	4.50
❑ 113 Jeff Smoker AU RC	20.00	6.00
❑ 114 Mewelde Moore AU RC	20.00	6.00
❑ 115 Michael Clayton AU RC	40.00	12.00
❑ 116 Jonathan Vilma AU RC	15.00	4.50
❑ 117 Johnnie Morant AU RC EXCH	15.00	4.50
❑ 118 Devard Darling AU RC	15.00	4.50
❑ 119 Cedric Cobbs AU RC	15.00	4.50
❑ 120 Chris Perry AU/399 RC	30.00	9.00
❑ 121 Ernest Wilford AU RC	15.00	4.50
❑ 122 Michael Jenkins AU RC	20.00	6.00
❑ 123 Jerricho Cotchery AU RC	15.00	4.50
❑ 124 P.K. Sam AU RC	15.00	4.50
❑ 125 Tatum Bell AU RC	30.00	9.00
❑ 126 Derrick Hamilton AU RC	15.00	4.50
❑ 127 Luke McCown AU RC	15.00	4.50
❑ 128 Devery Henderson AU RC	15.00	4.50
❑ 129 Craig Krenzel AU RC	20.00	6.00
❑ 130 J.P. Losman AU RC	40.00	12.00
❑ 131 Lee Evans AU RC	25.00	7.50
❑ 132 Matt Schaub AU RC	20.00	6.00
❑ 133 Robert Gallery AU RC	20.00	6.00
❑ 134 Keary Colbert AU RC	20.00	6.00

2004 Finest Refractors

Nm-Mt Ex-Mt

*STARS: 2.5X TO 6X BASE CARD HI
*ROOKIES 61-100: 1.5X TO 4X
1-100 SER.#'d TO 199, STATED ODDS 1:12
*VETERAN JSY: .5X TO 1.2X BASE JSYs
VETERAN JERSEY STATED ODDS 1:168
*ROOKIE AUs: .6X TO 1.5X BASE AU/999
ROOKIE AUTO SER.#'d TO 199, ODDS 1:48

2004 Finest Refractors Gold

Nm-Mt Ex-Mt

*STARS: 6X TO 15X BASE CARD HI
*ROOKIES 61-100: 3X TO 8X BASE CARD HI
1-100 SER.#'d TO 50, STATED ODDS 1:48
*VETERAN JSY: 1.2X TO 3X BASE CARD HI
VETERAN JERSEY STATED ODDS 1:684
*ROOKIE AUs: 1.5X TO 3X BASE AU/999
ROOKIE AUTO SER.#'d TO 50, ODDS 1:180

2004 Finest Uncirculated Gold Xfractors

Nm-Mt Ex-Mt

*STARS: 5X TO 12X BASE CARD HI
*ROOKIES: 3X TO 8X BASE CARD HI
STATED PRINT RUN 150 SER.#'d SETS

2002 Flair

	Nm-Mt	Ex-Mt
COMP.SET w/o SP's (100)	25.00	7.50
❑ 1 Jeff Garcia	1.25	.35
❑ 2 Jevon Kearse	.75	.23
❑ 3 Chris Weinke	.75	.23
❑ 4 Ray Lewis	1.25	.35
❑ 5 Donovan McNabb	1.50	.45
❑ 6 Tiki Barber	.75	.23
❑ 7 Rich Gannon	1.25	.35
❑ 8 Jamal Anderson	.75	.23
❑ 9 Curtis Martin	1.25	.35
❑ 10 Darrell Jackson	.75	.23
❑ 11 Ricky Williams	1.25	.35
❑ 12 Drew Brees	1.25	.35
❑ 13 Mark Brunell	1.25	.35
❑ 14 Johnnie Morton	.75	.23
❑ 15 Quincy Carter	.75	.23
❑ 16 Brian Urlacher	2.00	.60
❑ 17 Peerless Price	.75	.23
❑ 18 Drew Bledsoe	1.50	.45
❑ 19 Aaron Brooks	1.25	.35
❑ 20 Derrick Mason	.75	.23
❑ 21 Charlie Garner	.75	.23
❑ 22 Mike Alstott	1.25	.35
❑ 23 Freddie Mitchell	.75	.23
❑ 24 Isaac Bruce	1.25	.35
❑ 25 Hines Ward	1.25	.35
❑ 26 Doug Flutie	1.25	.35
❑ 27 Terrell Owens	1.25	.35
❑ 28 Peyton Manning	2.50	.75
❑ 29 Ron Dayne	.75	.23
❑ 30 Peter Warrick	.75	.23
❑ 31 Randy Moss	2.50	.75
❑ 32 Priest Holmes	1.50	.45
❑ 33 Joey Galloway	.75	.23
❑ 34 Jimmy Smith	.75	.23
❑ 35 Marvin Harrison	1.25	.35
❑ 36 Junior Seau	1.25	.35
❑ 37 Zach Thomas	1.25	.35
❑ 38 Antowain Smith	.75	.23
❑ 39 Marty Booker	.75	.23
❑ 40 Deuce McAllister	1.50	.45
❑ 41 Rod Smith	.75	.23
❑ 42 Michael Westbrook	.50	.15
❑ 43 Antonio Freeman	1.25	.35
❑ 44 Kerry Collins	.75	.23
❑ 45 Koren Robinson	.75	.23
❑ 46 Jamal Lewis	1.25	.35
❑ 47 Duce Staley	1.25	.35
❑ 48 Jerome Bettis	1.25	.35
❑ 49 David Terrell	1.25	.35
❑ 50 Daunte Culpepper	1.25	.35
❑ 51 Tim Couch	.75	.23
❑ 52 Brian Griese	1.25	.35
❑ 53 Marshall Faulk	1.25	.35
❑ 54 Brad Johnson	.75	.23
❑ 55 Eddie George	1.25	.35
❑ 56 Kurt Warner	1.25	.35
❑ 57 Steve McNair	1.25	.35
❑ 58 Stephen Davis	.75	.23
❑ 59 Corey Dillon	.75	.23
❑ 60 Troy Brown	.75	.23
❑ 61 Warrick Dunn	1.25	.35
❑ 62 Ed McCaffrey	1.25	.35
❑ 63 Amani Toomer	.75	.23
❑ 64 Rod Gardner	.75	.23
❑ 65 Mike McMahon	1.25	.35
❑ 66 Wayne Chrebet	.75	.23
❑ 67 Jake Plummer	.75	.23
❑ 68 Edgerrin James	1.50	.45
❑ 69 Eric Moulds	.75	.23
❑ 70 Tony Gonzalez	.75	.23
❑ 71 Marcus Robinson	.75	.23
❑ 72 Muhsin Muhammad	.75	.23
❑ 73 Trent Dilfer	.75	.23
❑ 74 Kevin Johnson	.75	.23
❑ 75 Fred Taylor	1.25	.35
❑ 76 Terrell Davis	1.25	.35
❑ 77 Emmitt Smith	3.00	.90
❑ 78 Az-Zahir Hakim	.50	.15
❑ 79 Tim Brown	1.25	.35
❑ 80 Jerry Rice	2.50	.75
❑ 81 Warren Sapp	.75	.23
❑ 82 Michael Strahan	.75	.23
❑ 83 Garrison Hearst	.75	.23
❑ 84 David Boston	1.25	.35
❑ 85 Michael Vick	4.00	1.20
❑ 86 Anthony Thomas	1.25	.35
❑ 87 Ahman Green	1.25	.35
❑ 88 Chris Chambers	1.25	.35
❑ 89 Tom Brady	3.00	.90
❑ 90 Plaxico Burress	.75	.23
❑ 91 LaDainian Tomlinson	2.00	.60
❑ 92 Shaun Alexander	1.25	.35
❑ 93 Torry Holt	1.25	.35
❑ 94 Kordell Stewart	.75	.23
❑ 95 Chad Pennington	1.50	.45
❑ 96 Chris Redman	.50	.15
❑ 97 Kendrell Bell	1.25	.35
❑ 98 Michael Bennett	.75	.23
❑ 99 Joe Horn	.75	.23
❑ 100 Brett Favre	3.00	.90
❑ 101 David Carr RC	20.00	6.00
❑ 102 Joey Harrington RC	20.00	6.00
❑ 103 Ashley Lelie RC	12.00	3.60
❑ 104 Javon Walker RC	12.00	3.60
❑ 105 Reche Caldwell RC	6.00	1.80
❑ 106 Andre Davis RC	6.00	1.80
❑ 107 William Green RC	10.00	3.00
❑ 108 Antonio Bryant RC	6.00	1.80
❑ 109 Clinton Portis RC	20.00	6.00
❑ 110 Luke Staley RC	5.00	1.50
❑ 111 Josh Reed RC	6.00	1.80
❑ 112 Ron Johnson RC	5.00	1.50
❑ 113 Lamar Gordon RC	6.00	1.80
❑ 114 Cliff Russell RC	5.00	1.50
❑ 115 Eric Crouch RC	10.00	3.00
❑ 116 Ladell Betts RC	6.00	1.80
❑ 117 Patrick Ramsey RC	12.00	3.60
❑ 118 Adrian Peterson RC	6.00	1.80
❑ 119 DeShaun Foster RC	6.00	1.80
❑ 120 Tim Carter RC	5.00	1.50
❑ 121 Jabar Gaffney RC	6.00	1.80
❑ 122 T.J. Duckett RC	10.00	3.00
❑ 123 Julius Peppers RC	12.00	3.60
❑ 124 Rohan Davey RC	6.00	1.80
❑ 125 Antwaan Randle El RC	8.00	2.40

❑ 126 Jeremy Shockey RC	20.00	6.00
❑ 127 Donte Stallworth RC	12.00	3.60
❑ 128 Marquise Walker RC	5.00	1.50
❑ 129 Brian Westbrook RC	10.00	3.00
❑ 130 Randy Fasani RC	5.00	1.50
❑ 131 Jonathan Wells RC	6.00	1.80
❑ 132 Travis Stephens RC	5.00	1.50
❑ 133 Daniel Graham RC	6.00	1.80
❑ 134 Maurice Morris RC	6.00	1.80
❑ 135 David Garrard RC	6.00	1.80

2003 Flair

	Nm-Mt	Ex-Mt
COMP.SET w/o SP's (90)	25.00	7.50
❑ 1 Jamal Lewis	1.25	.35
❑ 2 Aaron Brooks	1.25	.35
❑ 3 Joey Harrington	2.00	.60
❑ 4 Brett Favre	3.00	.90
❑ 5 Donovan McNabb	1.50	.45
❑ 6 Marcel Shipp	.75	.23
❑ 7 Michael Vick	3.00	.90
❑ 8 David Carr	2.00	.60
❑ 9 Tommy Maddox	1.25	.35
❑ 10 Drew Brees	1.25	.35
❑ 11 Chad Pennington	1.50	.45
❑ 12 Drew Bledsoe	1.25	.35
❑ 13 Rich Gannon	.75	.23
❑ 14 Kurt Warner	1.25	.35
❑ 15 Brian Griese	1.25	.35
❑ 16 William Green	.75	.23
❑ 17 Jake Plummer	.75	.23
❑ 18 Eric Moulds	.75	.23
❑ 19 Peyton Manning	2.00	.60
❑ 20 Keyshawn Johnson	1.25	.35
❑ 21 Travis Henry	.75	.23
❑ 22 Tiki Barber	.75	.23
❑ 23 Emmitt Smith	3.00	.90
❑ 24 Michael Bennett	.75	.23
❑ 25 Curtis Martin	1.25	.35
❑ 26 Donald Driver	.75	.23
❑ 27 Clinton Portis	2.00	.60
❑ 28 Eddie George	.75	.23
❑ 29 Marshall Faulk	1.25	.35
❑ 30 Jeremy Shockey	2.00	.60
❑ 31 Ahman Green	1.25	.35
❑ 32 Priest Holmes	1.50	.45
❑ 33 Edgerrin James	1.25	.35
❑ 34 Plaxico Burress	.75	.23
❑ 35 Ricky Williams	1.25	.35
❑ 36 Anthony Thomas	1.25	.35
❑ 37 Jerome Bettis	1.25	.35
❑ 38 Shaun Alexander	1.25	.35
❑ 39 Fred Taylor	1.25	.35
❑ 40 Isaac Bruce	1.25	.35
❑ 41 Mike Alstott	1.25	.35
❑ 42 Peerless Price	.75	.23
❑ 43 Corey Dillon	.75	.23
❑ 44 Amani Toomer	.75	.23
❑ 45 Warrick Dunn	.75	.23
❑ 46 Tim Brown	1.25	.35
❑ 47 Deuce McAllister	1.25	.35
❑ 48 Terrell Owens	1.25	.35
❑ 49 Stephen Davis	.75	.23
❑ 50 Torry Holt	1.25	.35
❑ 51 Duce Staley	.75	.23
❑ 52 Jimmy Smith	.75	.23
❑ 53 Ray Lewis	1.25	.35
❑ 54 Brian Urlacher	2.00	.60
❑ 55 Zach Thomas	1.25	.35
❑ 56 Joey Galloway	.75	.23
❑ 57 LaDainian Tomlinson	1.25	.35
❑ 58 Chris Chambers	1.25	.35
❑ 59 Ronde Barber	.50	.15
❑ 60 Randy Moss	2.00	.60
❑ 61 Tom Brady	2.00	.60
❑ 62 Jerry Porter	.75	.23
❑ 63 Patrick Ramsey	1.25	.35
❑ 64 Derrick Mason	.75	.23
❑ 65 Daunte Culpepper	1.25	.35
❑ 66 Marty Booker	.75	.23
❑ 67 Steve McNair	1.25	.35
❑ 68 Hines Ward	1.25	.35
❑ 69 Matt Hasselbeck	.75	.23
❑ 70 Joe Horn	.75	.23
❑ 71 Mark Brunell	.75	.23
❑ 72 Laveranues Coles	.75	.23
❑ 73 Chad Hutchinson	.75	.23
❑ 74 Tony Gonzalez	.75	.23
❑ 75 Jeff Garcia	1.25	.35
❑ 76 Kendrell Bell	.75	.23
❑ 77 Kerry Collins	.75	.23
❑ 78 Warren Sapp	.75	.23
❑ 79 Tim Couch	.50	.15
❑ 80 Jerry Rice	2.50	.75
❑ 81 Koren Robinson	.75	.23
❑ 82 Antwaan Randle El	1.25	.35
❑ 83 Donte Stallworth	1.25	.35
❑ 84 Shannon Sharpe	.75	.23
❑ 85 Chad Johnson	.75	.23
❑ 86 Todd Heap	.75	.23
❑ 87 Rod Gardner	.75	.23
❑ 88 Marvin Harrison	1.25	.35
❑ 89 David Boston	.75	.23
❑ 90 Julius Peppers	1.25	.35
❑ 91 Byron Leftwich RC	50.00	15.00
❑ 92 Terrell Suggs RC	20.00	6.00
❑ 93 Kelley Washington RC	12.00	3.60
❑ 94 Brandon Lloyd RC	15.00	4.50
❑ 95 Kliff Kingsbury RC	10.00	3.00
❑ 96 Willis McGahee RC	30.00	9.00
❑ 97 Terence Newman RC	25.00	7.50
❑ 98 Bryant Johnson RC	12.00	3.60
❑ 99 Musa Smith RC	12.00	3.60
❑ 100 Ken Dorsey RC	20.00	6.00
❑ 101 Larry Johnson RC	25.00	7.50
❑ 102 DeWayne Robertson RC	12.00	3.60
❑ 103 Onterrio Smith RC	15.00	4.50
❑ 104 Tyrone Calico RC	15.00	4.50
❑ 105 Kareem Kelly RC	10.00	3.00
❑ 106 Chris Brown RC	25.00	7.50
❑ 107 Andrew Pinnock RC	10.00	3.00
❑ 108 Taylor Jacobs RC	12.00	3.60
❑ 109 Dallas Clark RC	12.00	3.60
❑ 110 Marcus Trufant RC	12.00	3.60
❑ 111 Charles Rogers RC	15.00	4.50
❑ 112 Lee Suggs RC	25.00	7.50
❑ 113 Rex Grossman RC	30.00	9.00
❑ 114 Doug Gabriel RC	12.00	3.60
❑ 115 Arnaz Battle RC	12.00	3.60
❑ 116 William Joseph RC	12.00	3.60
❑ 117 Justin Fargas RC	12.00	3.60
❑ 118 Anquan Boldin RC	30.00	9.00
❑ 119 Teyo Johnson RC	12.00	3.60
❑ 120 Bobby Wade RC	12.00	3.60
❑ 121 Brian St.Pierre RC	12.00	3.60
❑ 122 Carson Palmer RC	40.00	12.00
❑ 123 Kyle Boller RC	30.00	9.00
❑ 124 Andre Johnson RC	30.00	9.00
❑ 125 Dave Ragone RC	12.00	3.60
❑ 126 Chris Simms RC	25.00	7.50
❑ 127 Seneca Wallace RC	12.00	3.60
❑ 128 Justin Gage RC	12.00	3.60
❑ 129 LaBrandon Toefield RC	12.00	3.60
❑ 130 Talman Gardner RC	12.00	3.60

2004 Flair

	Nm-Mt	Ex-Mt
COMP.SET w/o SP's (60)	40.00	12.00
ROOKIE STATED ODDS 1:100 RETAIL		
ROOKIE PRINT RUN 799 SER.#'d SETS		
❑ 1 Clinton Portis	2.00	.60
❑ 2 Deuce McAllister	2.00	.60

❑ 3 Marshall Faulk	2.00	.60
❑ 4 Tom Brady	3.00	.90
❑ 5 Ahman Green	2.00	.60
❑ 6 LaDainian Tomlinson	2.00	.60
❑ 7 Lee Suggs	2.00	.60
❑ 8 Amani Toomer	1.25	.35
❑ 9 Priest Holmes	2.50	.75
❑ 10 Peerless Price	1.25	.35
❑ 11 Warren Sapp	1.25	.35
❑ 12 Andre Davis	.75	.23
❑ 13 Chad Pennington	2.50	.75
❑ 14 Quincy Carter	1.25	.35
❑ 15 Santana Moss	1.25	.35
❑ 16 Antonio Bryant	1.25	.35
❑ 17 Jerry Porter	1.25	.35
❑ 18 Laveranues Coles	1.25	.35
❑ 19 Daunte Culpepper	2.00	.60
❑ 20 Stephen Davis	1.25	.35
❑ 21 Rich Gannon	1.25	.35
❑ 22 Chad Johnson	1.25	.35
❑ 23 Ashley Lelie	1.25	.35
❑ 24 Ray Lewis	2.00	.60
❑ 25 Joey Harrington	2.00	.60
❑ 26 Brian Westbrook	1.25	.35
❑ 27 Marvin Harrison	2.00	.60
❑ 28 Torry Holt	2.00	.60
❑ 29 Kevan Barlow	1.25	.35
❑ 30 Peyton Manning	3.00	.90
❑ 31 Andre Johnson	2.00	.60
❑ 32 Steve Smith	1.25	.35
❑ 33 Troy Brown	1.25	.35
❑ 34 Brian Urlacher	2.50	.75
❑ 35 Anquan Boldin	2.00	.60
❑ 36 Matt Hasselbeck	1.25	.35
❑ 37 Edgerrin James	2.00	.60
❑ 38 Dante Hall	2.00	.60
❑ 39 Brad Johnson	1.25	.35
❑ 40 Jamal Lewis	2.00	.60
❑ 41 Rudi Johnson	1.25	.35
❑ 42 Michael Strahan	1.25	.35
❑ 43 Donovan McNabb	2.50	.75
❑ 44 Steve McNair	2.00	.60
❑ 45 Ricky Williams	2.00	.60
❑ 46 Jake Delhomme	2.00	.60
❑ 47 Patrick Ramsey	1.25	.35
❑ 48 Randy Moss	2.50	.75
❑ 49 David Carr	2.00	.60
❑ 50 Jeff Garcia	2.00	.60
❑ 51 Shaun Alexander	2.00	.60
❑ 52 Byron Leftwich	3.00	.90
❑ 53 Michael Vick	4.00	1.20
❑ 54 Brett Favre	5.00	1.50
❑ 55 Hines Ward	2.00	.60
❑ 56 Chris Chambers	1.25	.35
❑ 57 Eddie George	1.25	.35
❑ 58 Eric Moulds	1.25	.35
❑ 59 Plaxico Burress	1.25	.35
❑ 60 Charles Rogers	1.25	.35
❑ 61 Eli Manning RC	25.00	7.50
❑ 62 Larry Fitzgerald RC	15.00	4.50
❑ 63 Chris Perry RC	10.00	3.00
❑ 64 Ben Roethlisberger RC	50.00	15.00
❑ 65 Roy Williams RC	15.00	4.50
❑ 66 Kellen Winslow RC	12.00	3.60
❑ 67 Steven Jackson RC	15.00	4.50
❑ 68 Kevin Jones RC	15.00	4.50
❑ 69 Reggie Williams RC	6.00	1.80
❑ 70 Michael Clayton RC	12.00	3.60

❑ 71 Rashaun Woods RC	6.00	1.80
❑ 72 Ben Troupe RC	5.00	1.50
❑ 73 Greg Jones RC	5.00	1.50
❑ 74 J.P. Losman RC	12.00	3.60
❑ 75 Philip Rivers RC	15.00	4.50
❑ 76 Michael Jenkins RC	5.00	1.50
❑ 77 Darius Watts RC	6.00	1.80
❑ 78 Michael Turner RC	4.00	1.20
❑ 79 Lee Evans RC	8.00	2.40
❑ 80 Drew Henson RC	12.00	3.60
❑ 81 Luke McCown RC	5.00	1.50
❑ 82 Julius Jones RC	20.00	6.00
❑ 83 Bernard Berrian RC	5.00	1.50
❑ 84 Keary Colbert RC	6.00	1.80
❑ 85 Tatum Bell RC	8.00	2.40

2004 Flair Collection Row 1

	Nm-Mt	Ex-Mt

*STARS: 2X TO 5X BASIC CARDS
*ROOKIES: 1X TO 2.5X BASIC CARDS
ROW 1/2 OVERALL ODDS 1:7H, 1:55R
ROW 1 PRINT RUN 100 SER.#'d SETS
UNPRICED ROW 2 PRINT RUN 1 SET

1999 Flair Showcase

	Nm-Mt	Ex-Mt
COMPLETE SET (192)	600.00	275.00
COMP.SET w/o SPs (160)	50.00	22.00
❑ 1 Troy Aikman PW	2.00	.90
❑ 2 Jamal Anderson PW	.40	.18
❑ 3 Charlie Batch PW	1.00	.45
❑ 4 Jerome Bettis PW	.40	.18
❑ 5 Drew Bledsoe PW	1.25	.55
❑ 6 Mark Brunell PW	1.00	.45
❑ 7 Randall Cunningham PW	1.00	.45
❑ 8 Terrell Davis PW	1.00	.45
❑ 9 Corey Dillon PW	1.00	.45
❑ 10 Warrick Dunn PW	1.00	.45
❑ 11 Curtis Enis PW	.40	.18
❑ 12 Marshall Faulk PW	1.25	.55
❑ 13 Brett Favre PW	3.00	1.35
❑ 14 Doug Flutie PW	1.00	.45
❑ 15 Eddie George PW	1.00	.45
❑ 16 Brian Griese PW	1.00	.45
❑ 17 Keyshawn Johnson PW	1.00	.45
❑ 18 Peyton Manning PW	3.00	1.35
❑ 19 Dan Marino PW	3.00	1.35
❑ 20 Curtis Martin PW	1.00	.45
❑ 21 Steve McNair PW	1.00	.45
❑ 22 Randy Moss PW	2.50	1.10
❑ 23 Terrell Owens PW	1.00	.45
❑ 24 Jake Plummer PW	.60	.25
❑ 25 Jerry Rice PW	2.00	.90
❑ 26 Barry Sanders PW	3.00	1.35
❑ 27 Antowain Smith PW	1.00	.45
❑ 28 Emmitt Smith PW	2.00	.90
❑ 29 Kordell Stewart PW	.60	.25
❑ 30 J.J. Stokes PW	.60	.25
❑ 31 Fred Taylor PW	1.00	.45
❑ 32 Steve Young PW	1.25	.55
❑ 33 Troy Aikman PN	2.00	.90
❑ 34 Mike Alstott PN	1.00	.45
❑ 35 Jamal Anderson PN	1.00	.45
❑ 36 Charlie Batch PN	1.00	.45
❑ 37 Jerome Bettis PN	1.00	.45
❑ 38 Drew Bledsoe PN	1.25	.55
❑ 39 Mark Brunell PN	1.00	.45
❑ 40 Cris Carter PN	1.00	.45
❑ 41 Mark Chmura PN	.40	.18
❑ 42 Wayne Chrebet PN	.60	.25
❑ 43 Kerry Collins PN	.40	.18
❑ 44 Randall Cunningham PN	1.00	.45
❑ 45 Terrell Davis PN	1.00	.45
❑ 46 Trent Dilfer PN	.60	.25
❑ 47 Corey Dillon PN	1.00	.45
❑ 48 Warrick Dunn PN	1.00	.45
❑ 49 Kevin Dyson PN	.60	.25
❑ 50 Curtis Enis PN	.40	.18
❑ 51 Marshall Faulk PN	1.25	.55
❑ 52 Brett Favre PN	3.00	1.35
❑ 53 Doug Flutie PN	1.00	.45
❑ 54 Antonio Freeman PN	1.00	.45
❑ 55 Eddie George PN	1.00	.45
❑ 56 Terry Glenn PN	1.00	.45
❑ 57 Tony Gonzalez PN	1.00	.45
❑ 58 Elvis Grbac PN	.60	.25
❑ 59 Jacquez Green PN	.40	.18
❑ 60 Brian Griese PN	1.00	.45
❑ 61 Marvin Harrison PN	1.00	.45
❑ 62 Garrison Hearst PN	.60	.25
❑ 63 Skip Hicks PN	.40	.18
❑ 64 Priest Holmes PN	1.50	.70
❑ 65 Michael Irvin PN	.60	.25
❑ 66 Brad Johnson PN	.60	.25
❑ 67 Keyshawn Johnson PN	1.00	.45
❑ 68 Napoleon Kaufman PN	1.00	.45
❑ 69 Dorsey Levens PN	1.00	.45
❑ 70 Peyton Manning PN	3.00	1.35
❑ 71 Dan Marino PN	3.00	1.35
❑ 72 Curtis Martin PN	1.00	.45
❑ 73 Ed McCaffrey PN	.60	.25
❑ 74 Keenan McCardell PN	.60	.25
❑ 75 O.J. McDuffie PN	.60	.25
❑ 76 Steve McNair PN	1.00	.45
❑ 77 Scott Mitchell PN	.40	.18
❑ 78 Randy Moss PN	2.50	1.10
❑ 79 Eric Moulds PN	1.00	.45
❑ 80 Terrell Owens PN	1.00	.45
❑ 81 Lawrence Phillips PN	.60	.25
❑ 82 Jake Plummer PN	.60	.25
❑ 83 Jerry Rice PN	2.00	.90
❑ 84 Andre Rison PN	.60	.25
❑ 85 Barry Sanders PN	3.00	1.35
❑ 86 Shannon Sharpe PN	.60	.25
❑ 87 Antowain Smith PN	1.00	.45
❑ 88 Emmitt Smith PN	2.00	.90
❑ 89 Rod Smith PN	.60	.25
❑ 90 Duce Staley PN	1.00	.45
❑ 91 Kordell Stewart PN	.60	.25
❑ 92 J.J. Stokes PN	.60	.25
❑ 93 Fred Taylor PN	1.00	.45
❑ 94 Vinny Testaverde PN	.60	.25
❑ 95 Ricky Watters PN	.60	.25
❑ 96 Steve Young PN	1.25	.55
❑ 97 Mike Alstott	1.00	.45
❑ 98 Jamal Anderson	1.00	.45
❑ 99 Charlie Batch	1.00	.45
❑ 100 Jerome Bettis	1.00	.45
❑ 101 Tim Biakabutuka	.60	.25
❑ 102 Drew Bledsoe	1.25	.55
❑ 103 Tim Brown	1.00	.45
❑ 104 Mark Brunell	1.00	.45
❑ 105 Cris Carter	1.00	.45
❑ 106 Chris Chandler	.60	.25
❑ 107 Mark Chmura	.40	.18
❑ 108 Wayne Chrebet	.60	.25
❑ 109 Ben Coates	.60	.25
❑ 110 Kerry Collins	.60	.25
❑ 111 Randall Cunningham	1.00	.45
❑ 112 Trent Dilfer	.60	.25
❑ 113 Corey Dillon	1.00	.45
❑ 114 Warrick Dunn	1.00	.45
❑ 115 Kevin Dyson	.60	.25
❑ 116 Curtis Enis	.40	.18
❑ 117 Marshall Faulk	1.25	.55
❑ 118 Doug Flutie	1.00	.45
❑ 119 Antonio Freeman	1.00	.45
❑ 120 Joey Galloway	.60	.25
❑ 121 Rich Gannon	1.00	.45
❑ 122 Eddie George	1.00	.45
❑ 123 Terry Glenn	1.00	.45
❑ 124 Tony Gonzalez	1.00	.45
❑ 125 Elvis Grbac	.60	.25
❑ 126 Jacquez Green	.40	.18
❑ 127 Brian Griese	1.00	.45
❑ 128 Marvin Harrison	1.00	.45
❑ 129 Garrison Hearst	.60	.25
❑ 130 Skip Hicks	.40	.18
❑ 131 Priest Holmes	1.50	.70
❑ 132 Michael Irvin	.60	.25
❑ 133 Brad Johnson	.60	.25
❑ 134 Napoleon Kaufman	1.00	.45
❑ 135 Terry Kirby	.40	.18
❑ 136 Dorsey Levens	1.00	.45
❑ 137 Curtis Martin	1.00	.45
❑ 138 Ed McCaffrey	.60	.25
❑ 139 Keenan McCardell	.60	.25
❑ 140 O.J. McDuffie	.60	.25
❑ 141 Steve McNair	1.00	.45
❑ 142 Natrone Means	.60	.25
❑ 143 Scott Mitchell	.40	.18
❑ 144 Herman Moore	.60	.25
❑ 145 Eric Moulds	1.00	.45
❑ 146 Terrell Owens	1.00	.45
❑ 147 Lawrence Phillips	.60	.25
❑ 148 Jerry Rice	2.00	.90
❑ 149 Andre Rison	.60	.25
❑ 150 Deion Sanders	1.00	.45
❑ 151 Shannon Sharpe	.60	.25
❑ 152 Antowain Smith	1.00	.45
❑ 153 Rod Smith	.60	.25
❑ 154 Duce Staley	1.00	.45
❑ 155 Kordell Stewart	.60	.25
❑ 156 J.J. Stokes	.60	.25
❑ 157 Vinny Testaverde	.60	.25
❑ 158 Yancey Thigpen	.40	.18
❑ 159 Ricky Watters	.60	.25
❑ 160 Steve Young	1.25	.55
❑ 161 Troy Aikman SP	12.00	5.50
❑ 162 Champ Bailey RC	12.00	5.50
❑ 163 Karsten Bailey RC	8.00	3.60
❑ 164 D'Wayne Bates RC	8.00	3.60
❑ 165 David Boston RC	10.00	4.50
❑ 166 Mike Cloud RC	8.00	3.60
❑ 167 Cecil Collins RC	5.00	2.20
❑ 168 Tim Couch RC	10.00	4.50
❑ 169 Daunte Culpepper RC	40.00	18.00
❑ 170 Terrell Davis SP	6.00	2.70
❑ 171 Troy Edwards RC	8.00	3.60
❑ 172 Kevin Faulk RC	10.00	4.50
❑ 173 Brett Favre SP	20.00	9.00
❑ 174 Torry Holt RC	25.00	11.00
❑ 175 Sedrick Irvin RC	5.00	2.20
❑ 176 Edgerrin James RC	40.00	18.00
❑ 177 James Johnson RC	8.00	3.60
❑ 178 Kevin Johnson RC	10.00	4.50
❑ 179 Keyshawn Johnson SP	5.00	2.20
❑ 180 Peyton Manning SP	20.00	9.00
❑ 181 Dan Marino SP	20.00	9.00
❑ 182 Donovan McNabb RC	50.00	22.00
❑ 183 Cade McNown RC	8.00	3.60
❑ 184 Joe Montgomery RC	8.00	3.60
❑ 185 Randy Moss SP	15.00	6.75
❑ 186 Jake Plummer SP	6.00	2.70
❑ 187 Peerless Price RC	15.00	6.75
❑ 188 Barry Sanders SP	20.00	9.00
❑ 189 Akili Smith RC	8.00	3.60
❑ 190 Emmitt Smith SP	12.00	5.50
❑ 191 Fred Taylor SP	8.00	3.60
❑ 192 Ricky Williams RC	20.00	9.00
❑ P24 Jake Plummer PW Promo	1.00	.30
❑ P82 Jake Plummer PN Promo	1.00	.30
❑ P147 Jake Plummer Promo	1.00	.30

1999 Flair Showcase Legacy Collection

	Nm-Mt	Ex-Mt

*STARS: 6X TO 15X BASIC CARDS
*SP STARS: 2X TO 5X BASIC CARDS
*RCs: .6X TO 1.5X

1960 Fleer

	NM	Ex
COMPLETE SET (132)	750.00	350.00
WRAPPER (5-CENT)	25.00	11.00
❑ 1 Harvey White RC	20.00	5.00

❑ 2 Tom Corky Tharp	3.50	1.55
❑ 3 Dan McGrew	3.50	1.55
❑ 4 Bob White	3.50	1.55
❑ 5 Dick Jamieson	3.50	1.55
❑ 6 Sam Salerno	3.50	1.55
❑ 7 Sid Gillman CO RC	20.00	9.00
❑ 8 Ben Preston	3.50	1.55
❑ 9 George Blanch	3.50	1.55
❑ 10 Bob Stransky	3.50	1.55
❑ 11 Fran Curci	3.50	1.55
❑ 12 George Shirkey	3.50	1.55
❑ 13 Paul Larson	3.50	1.55
❑ 14 John Stolte	3.50	1.55
❑ 15 Serafino(Foge) Fazio RC	5.00	2.20
❑ 16 Tom Dimitroff	3.50	1.55
❑ 17 Elbert Dubenion RC	12.00	5.50
❑ 18 Hogan Wharton	3.50	1.55
❑ 19 Tom O'Connell	3.50	1.55
❑ 20 Sammy Baugh CO	50.00	22.00
❑ 21 Tony Sardisco	3.50	1.55
❑ 22 Alan Cann	3.50	1.55
❑ 23 Mike Hudock	3.50	1.55
❑ 24 Bill Atkins	3.50	1.55
❑ 25 Charlie Jackson	3.50	1.55
❑ 26 Frank Tripucka	6.00	2.70
❑ 27 Tony Teresa	3.50	1.55
❑ 28 Joe Amstutz	3.50	1.55
❑ 29 Bob Fee RC	3.50	1.55
❑ 30 Jim Baldwin	3.50	1.55
❑ 31 Jim Yates	3.50	1.55
❑ 32 Don Flynn	3.50	1.55
❑ 33 Ken Adamson	3.50	1.55
❑ 34 Ron Drzewiecki	3.50	1.55
❑ 35 J.W. Slack	3.50	1.55
❑ 36 Bob Yates	3.50	1.55
❑ 37 Gary Cobb	3.50	1.55
❑ 38 Jacky Lee RC	5.00	2.20
❑ 39 Jack Spikes RC	5.00	2.20
❑ 40 Jim Padgett	3.50	1.55
❑ 41 Jack Larscheid UER RC (name misspelled Larsheid)	3.50	1.55
❑ 42 Bob Reifsnyder RC	3.50	1.55
❑ 43 Fran Rogel	3.50	1.55
❑ 44 Ray Moss	3.50	1.55
❑ 45 Tony Banfield RC	5.00	2.20
❑ 46 George Herring	3.50	1.55
❑ 47 Willie Smith RC	3.50	1.55
❑ 48 Buddy Allen	3.50	1.55
❑ 49 Bill Brown	3.50	1.55
❑ 50 Ken Ford RC	3.50	1.55
❑ 51 Billy Kinard	3.50	1.55
❑ 52 Buddy Mayfield	3.50	1.55
❑ 53 Bill Krisher	3.50	1.55
❑ 54 Frank Bernardi	3.50	1.55
❑ 55 Lou Saban CO RC	5.00	2.20
❑ 56 Gene Cockrell	3.50	1.55
❑ 57 Sam Sanders	3.50	1.55
❑ 58 George Blanda	50.00	22.00
❑ 59 Sherrill Headrick RC	5.00	2.20
❑ 60 Carl Larpenter	3.50	1.55
❑ 61 Gene Prebola	3.50	1.55
❑ 62 Dick Chorovich	3.50	1.55
❑ 63 Bob McNamara	3.50	1.55
❑ 64 Tom Saidock	3.50	1.55
❑ 65 Willie Evans	3.50	1.55
❑ 66 Billy Cannon RC UER (Hometown: Istruma, should be Istrouma)	18.00	8.00
❑ 67 Sam McCord	3.50	1.55
❑ 68 Mike Simmons	3.50	1.55
❑ 69 Jim Swink RC	5.00	2.20
❑ 70 Don Hitt	3.50	1.55
❑ 71 Gerhard Schwedes	3.50	1.55
❑ 72 Thurlow Cooper	3.50	1.55
❑ 73 Abner Haynes RC	18.00	8.00
❑ 74 Billy Shoemake	3.50	1.55
❑ 75 Marv Lasater	3.50	1.55
❑ 76 Paul Lowe RC	15.00	6.75
❑ 77 Bruce Hartman	3.50	1.55
❑ 78 Blanche Martin	3.50	1.55
❑ 79 Gene Grabosky	3.50	1.55
❑ 80 Lou Rymkus CO	5.00	2.20
❑ 81 Chris Burford RC	8.00	3.60
❑ 82 Don Allen	3.50	1.55
❑ 83 Bob Nelson	3.50	1.55
❑ 84 Jim Woodard	3.50	1.55
❑ 85 Tom Rychlec	3.50	1.55
❑ 86 Bob Cox	3.50	1.55
❑ 87 Jerry Cornelison	3.50	1.55
❑ 88 Jack Work	3.50	1.55
❑ 89 Sam DeLuca	3.50	1.55
❑ 90 Rommie Loudd	3.50	1.55
❑ 91 Teddy Edmondson	3.50	1.55
❑ 92 Buster Ramsey CO	3.50	1.55
❑ 93 Doug Asad	3.50	1.55
❑ 94 Jimmy Harris	3.50	1.55
❑ 95 Larry Cundiff	3.50	1.55
❑ 96 Richie Lucas RC	6.00	2.70
❑ 97 Don Norwood	3.50	1.55
❑ 98 Larry Grantham RC	5.00	2.20
❑ 99 Bill Mathis RC	6.00	2.70
❑ 100 Mel Branch RC	5.00	2.20
❑ 101 Marvin Terrell	3.50	1.55
❑ 102 Charlie Flowers	3.50	1.55
❑ 103 John McMullan	3.50	1.55
❑ 104 Charlie Kaaihue	3.50	1.55
❑ 105 Joe Schaffer	3.50	1.55
❑ 106 Al Day	3.50	1.55
❑ 107 Johnny Carson	3.50	1.55
❑ 108 Alan Goldstein	3.50	1.55
❑ 109 Doug Cline	3.50	1.55
❑ 110 Al Carmichael	3.50	1.55
❑ 111 Bob Dee	3.50	1.55
❑ 112 John Bredice	3.50	1.55
❑ 113 Don Floyd	3.50	1.55
❑ 114 Ronnie Cain	3.50	1.55
❑ 115 Stan Flowers	3.50	1.55
❑ 116 Hank Stram CO RC	40.00	18.00
❑ 117 Bob Dougherty	3.50	1.55
❑ 118 Ron Mix RC	40.00	18.00
❑ 119 Roger Ellis	3.50	1.55
❑ 120 Elvin Caldwell	3.50	1.55
❑ 121 Bill Kimber	3.50	1.55
❑ 122 Jim Matheny	3.50	1.55
❑ 123 Curley Johnson RC	3.50	1.55
❑ 124 Jack Kemp RC	175.00	80.00
❑ 125 Ed Denk	3.50	1.55
❑ 126 Jerry McFarland	3.50	1.55
❑ 127 Dan Lanphear	3.50	1.55
❑ 128 Paul Maguire RC	18.00	8.00
❑ 129 Ray Collins	3.50	1.55
❑ 130 Ron Burton RC	6.00	2.70
❑ 131 Eddie Erdelatz CO	3.50	1.55
❑ 132 Ron Beagle RC	15.00	3.70

1961 Fleer

	NM	Ex
COMPLETE SET (220)	1600.00	700.00
COMMON CARD (1-132)	4.00	1.80
COMMON CARD (133-220)	6.00	2.70
WRAPPER (5-CENT, SER.1)	25.00	11.00
WRAPPER (5-CENT, SER.2)	30.00	13.50
❑ 1 Ed Brown	15.00	3.70
❑ 2 Rick Casares	6.00	2.70
❑ 3 Willie Galimore	6.00	2.70
❑ 4 Jim Dooley	4.00	1.80
❑ 5 Harlon Hill	4.00	1.80
❑ 6 Stan Jones	7.00	3.10
❑ 7 J.C. Caroline	4.00	1.80
❑ 8 Joe Fortunato	4.00	1.80
❑ 9 Doug Atkins	8.00	3.60
❑ 10 Milt Plum	6.00	2.70
❑ 11 Jim Brown	150.00	70.00
❑ 12 Bobby Mitchell	10.00	4.50
❑ 13 Ray Renfro	6.00	2.70
❑ 14 Gern Nagler	4.00	1.80
❑ 15 Jim Shofner	4.00	1.80
❑ 16 Vince Costello	4.00	1.80
❑ 17 Galen Fiss	4.00	1.80
❑ 18 Walt Michaels	6.00	2.70
❑ 19 Bob Gain	4.00	1.80
❑ 20 Mal Hammack	4.00	1.80
❑ 21 Frank Mestnik RC	4.00	1.80
❑ 22 Bobby Joe Conrad	6.00	2.70
❑ 23 John David Crow	6.00	2.70
❑ 24 Sonny Randle RC	6.00	2.70
❑ 25 Don Gillis	4.00	1.80
❑ 26 Jerry Norton	4.00	1.80
❑ 27 Bill Stacy	4.00	1.80
❑ 28 Leo Sugar	4.00	1.80
❑ 29 Frank Fuller	4.00	1.80
❑ 30 John Unitas	60.00	27.00
❑ 31 Alan Ameche	7.00	3.10
❑ 32 Lenny Moore	15.00	6.75
❑ 33 Raymond Berry	15.00	6.75
❑ 34 Jim Mutscheller	4.00	1.80
❑ 35 Jim Parker	7.00	3.10
❑ 36 Bill Pellington	4.00	1.80
❑ 37 Gino Marchetti	10.00	4.50
❑ 38 Gene Lipscomb	7.00	3.10
❑ 39 Art Donovan	15.00	6.75
❑ 40 Eddie LeBaron	6.00	2.70
❑ 41 Don Meredith RC	150.00	70.00
❑ 42 Don McIlhenny	4.00	1.80
❑ 43 L.G. Dupre	4.00	1.80
❑ 44 Fred Dugan	4.00	1.80
❑ 45 Billy Howton	6.00	2.70
❑ 46 Duane Putnam	4.00	1.80
❑ 47 Gene Cronin	4.00	1.80
❑ 48 Jerry Tubbs	4.00	1.80
❑ 49 Clarence Peaks	4.00	1.80
❑ 50 Ted Dean RC	4.00	1.80
❑ 51 Tommy McDonald	8.00	3.60
❑ 52 Bill Barnes	4.00	1.80
❑ 53 Pete Retzlaff	6.00	2.70
❑ 54 Bobby Walston	4.00	1.80
❑ 55 Chuck Bednarik	12.00	5.50
❑ 56 Maxie Baughan RC	6.00	2.70
❑ 57 Bob Pellegrini	4.00	1.80
❑ 58 Jesse Richardson	4.00	1.80
❑ 59 John Brodie RC	50.00	22.00
❑ 60 J.D. Smith RB	6.00	2.70
❑ 61 Ray Norton RC	4.00	1.80
❑ 62 Monty Stickles RC	4.00	1.80
❑ 63 Bob St. Clair	7.00	3.10
❑ 64 Dave Baker	4.00	1.80
❑ 65 Abe Woodson	4.00	1.80
❑ 66 Matt Hazeltine	4.00	1.80
❑ 67 Leo Nomellini	10.00	4.50
❑ 68 Charley Conerly	10.00	4.50
❑ 69 Kyle Rote	7.00	3.10
❑ 70 Jack Stroud	4.00	1.80
❑ 71 Roosevelt Brown	7.00	3.10
❑ 72 Jim Patton	4.00	1.80
❑ 73 Erich Barnes	4.00	1.80
❑ 74 Sam Huff	15.00	6.75
❑ 75 Andy Robustelli	10.00	4.50
❑ 76 Dick Modzelewski	4.00	1.80
❑ 77 Roosevelt Grier	7.00	3.10
❑ 78 Earl Morrall	7.00	3.10
❑ 79 Jim Ninowski	4.00	1.80
❑ 80 Nick Pietrosante RC	6.00	2.70
❑ 81 Howard Cassady	6.00	2.70
❑ 82 Jim Gibbons	4.00	1.80
❑ 83 Gail Cogdill RC	6.00	2.70
❑ 84 Dick Lane	7.00	3.10

❑ 85 Yale Lary 7.00 3.10
❑ 86 Joe Schmidt 8.00 3.60
❑ 87 Darris McCord 4.00 1.80
❑ 88 Bart Starr 60.00 27.00
❑ 89 Jim Taylor 50.00 22.00
❑ 90 Paul Hornung 55.00 25.00
❑ 91 Tom Moore RC 8.00 3.60
❑ 92 Boyd Dowler RC 15.00 6.75
❑ 93 Max McGee 7.00 3.10
❑ 94 Forrest Gregg 8.00 3.60
❑ 95 Jerry Kramer 10.00 4.50
❑ 96 Jim Ringo 8.00 3.60
❑ 97 Bill Forester 6.00 2.70
❑ 98 Frank Ryan 6.00 2.70
❑ 99 Ollie Matson 12.00 5.50
❑ 100 Jon Arnett 6.00 2.70
❑ 101 Dick Bass RC 6.00 2.70
❑ 102 Jim Phillips 4.00 1.80
❑ 103 Del Shofner 6.00 2.70
❑ 104 Art Hunter 4.00 1.80
❑ 105 Lindon Crow 4.00 1.80
❑ 106 Les Richter 6.00 2.70
❑ 107 Lou Michaels 4.00 1.80
❑ 108 Ralph Guglielmi 4.00 1.80
❑ 109 Don Bosseler 4.00 1.80
❑ 110 John Olszewski 4.00 1.80
❑ 111 Bill Anderson 4.00 1.80
❑ 112 Joe Walton 4.00 1.80
❑ 113 Jim Schrader 4.00 1.80
❑ 114 Gary Glick 4.00 1.80
❑ 115 Ralph Felton 4.00 1.80
❑ 116 Bob Toneff 4.00 1.80
❑ 117 Bobby Layne 40.00 18.00
❑ 118 John Henry Johnson 7.00 3.10
❑ 119 Tom Tracy 6.00 2.70
❑ 120 Jimmy Orr RC 7.00 3.10
❑ 121 John Nisby 4.00 1.80
❑ 122 Dean Derby 4.00 1.80
❑ 123 John Reger 4.00 1.80
❑ 124 George Tarasovic 4.00 1.80
❑ 125 Ernie Stautner 10.00 4.50
❑ 126 George Shaw 4.00 1.80
❑ 127 Hugh McElhenny 12.00 5.50
❑ 128 Dick Haley 4.00 1.80
❑ 129 Dave Middleton 4.00 1.80
❑ 130 Perry Richards 4.00 1.80
❑ 131 Gene Johnson 4.00 1.80
❑ 132 Don Joyce 4.00 1.80
❑ 133 Johnny Green 8.00 3.60
❑ 134 Wray Carlton RC 8.00 3.60
❑ 135 Richie Lucas 8.00 3.60
❑ 136 Elbert Dubenion 8.00 3.60
❑ 137 Tom Rychlec 6.00 2.70
❑ 138 Mack Yoho 6.00 2.70
❑ 139 Phil Blazer 6.00 2.70
❑ 140 Dan McGrew 6.00 2.70
❑ 141 Bill Atkins 6.00 2.70
❑ 142 Archie Matsos RC 6.00 2.70
❑ 143 Gene Grabosky 6.00 2.70
❑ 144 Frank Tripucka 10.00 4.50
❑ 145 Al Carmichael 6.00 2.70
❑ 146 Bob McNamara 6.00 2.70
❑ 147 Lionel Taylor RC 15.00 6.75
❑ 148 Eldon Danenhauer 6.00 2.70
❑ 149 Willie Smith 6.00 2.70
❑ 150 Carl Larpenter 6.00 2.70
❑ 151 Ken Adamson 6.00 2.70
❑ 152 Goose Gonsoulin RC UER 10.00 4.50
(Photo actually Darryl Rodgers)
❑ 153 Joe Young 6.00 2.70
❑ 154 Gordy Holz RC 6.00 2.70
❑ 155 Jack Kemp 120.00 55.00
❑ 156 Charlie Flowers 6.00 2.70
❑ 157 Paul Lowe 10.00 4.50
❑ 158 Don Norton 6.00 2.70
❑ 159 Howard Clark 6.00 2.70
❑ 160 Paul Maguire 15.00 6.75
❑ 161 Ernie Wright RC 8.00 3.60
❑ 162 Ron Mix 15.00 6.75
❑ 163 Fred Cole 6.00 2.70
❑ 164 Jim Sears 6.00 2.70
❑ 165 Volney Peters 6.00 2.70
❑ 166 George Blanda 45.00 20.00
❑ 167 Jacky Lee 8.00 3.60
❑ 168 Bob White 6.00 2.70
❑ 169 Doug Cline 6.00 2.70
❑ 170 Dave Smith 6.00 2.70
❑ 171 Billy Cannon 15.00 6.75
❑ 172 Bill Groman 6.00 2.70
❑ 173 Al Jamison 6.00 2.70
❑ 174 Jim Norton 6.00 2.70
❑ 175 Dennit Morris 6.00 2.70
❑ 176 Don Floyd 6.00 2.70
❑ 177 Butch Songin 6.00 2.70
❑ 178 Billy Lott 6.00 2.70
❑ 179 Ron Burton 10.00 4.50
❑ 180 Jim Colclough 6.00 2.70
❑ 181 Charley Leo 6.00 2.70
❑ 182 Walt Cudzik 6.00 2.70
❑ 183 Fred Bruney 6.00 2.70
❑ 184 Ross O'Hanley 6.00 2.70
❑ 185 Tony Sardisco 6.00 2.70
❑ 186 Harry Jacobs 6.00 2.70
❑ 187 Bob Dee 6.00 2.70
❑ 188 Tom Flores RC 30.00 13.50
❑ 189 Jack Larscheid 6.00 2.70
❑ 190 Dick Christy 6.00 2.70
❑ 191 Alan Miller RC 6.00 2.70
❑ 192 James Smith 6.00 2.70
❑ 193 Gerald Burch 6.00 2.70
❑ 194 Gene Prebola 6.00 2.70
❑ 195 Alan Goldstein 6.00 2.70
❑ 196 Don Manoukian 6.00 2.70
❑ 197 Jim Otto RC 75.00 34.00
❑ 198 Wayne Crow 6.00 2.70
❑ 199 Cotton Davidson RC 8.00 3.60
❑ 200 Randy Duncan RC 8.00 3.60
❑ 201 Jack Spikes 8.00 3.60
❑ 202 Johnny Robinson RC 15.00 6.75
❑ 203 Abner Haynes 15.00 6.75
❑ 204 Chris Burford 8.00 3.60
❑ 205 Bill Krisher 6.00 2.70
❑ 206 Marvin Terrell 6.00 2.70
❑ 207 Jimmy Harris 6.00 2.70
❑ 208 Mel Branch 8.00 3.60
❑ 209 Paul Miller 6.00 2.70
❑ 210 Al Dorow 6.00 2.70
❑ 211 Dick Jamieson 6.00 2.70
❑ 212 Pete Hart 6.00 2.70
❑ 213 Bill Shockley 6.00 2.70
❑ 214 Dewey Bohling 6.00 2.70
❑ 215 Don Maynard RC 80.00 36.00
❑ 216 Bob Mischak 6.00 2.70
❑ 217 Mike Hudock 6.00 2.70
❑ 218 Bob Reifsnyder 6.00 2.70
❑ 219 Tom Saidock 6.00 2.70
❑ 220 Sid Youngelman 20.00 5.00

1962 Fleer

	NM	Ex
COMPLETE SET (88)	900.00	400.00
WRAPPER (5-CENT)	200.00	90.00

❑ 1 Billy Lott 16.00 4.00
❑ 2 Ron Burton 10.00 4.50
❑ 3 Gino Cappelletti RC 15.00 6.75
❑ 4 Babe Parilli 10.00 4.50
❑ 5 Jim Colclough 7.00 3.10
❑ 6 Tony Sardisco 7.00 3.10
❑ 7 Walt Cudzik 7.00 3.10
❑ 8 Bob Dee 7.00 3.10
❑ 9 Tommy Addison RC 8.00 3.60
❑ 10 Harry Jacobs 7.00 3.10
❑ 11 Ross O'Hanley 7.00 3.10
❑ 12 Art Baker 7.00 3.10
❑ 13 Johnny Green 7.00 3.10
❑ 14 Elbert Dubenion 10.00 4.50
❑ 15 Tom Rychlec 7.00 3.10
❑ 16 Billy Shaw RC 30.00 13.50
❑ 17 Ken Rice 7.00 3.10
❑ 18 Bill Atkins 7.00 3.10
❑ 19 Richie Lucas 8.00 3.60
❑ 20 Archie Matsos 7.00 3.10
❑ 21 Laverne Torczon 7.00 3.10
❑ 22 Warren Rabb 7.00 3.10
❑ 23 Jack Spikes 8.00 3.60
❑ 24 Cotton Davidson 8.00 3.60
❑ 25 Abner Haynes 15.00 6.75
❑ 26 Jimmy Saxton 7.00 3.10
❑ 27 Chris Burford 8.00 3.60
❑ 28 Bill Miller 7.00 3.10
❑ 29 Sherrill Headrick 8.00 3.60
❑ 30 E.J. Holub RC 8.00 3.60
❑ 31 Jerry Mays RC 10.00 4.50
❑ 32 Mel Branch 8.00 3.60
❑ 33 Paul Rochester RC 7.00 3.10
❑ 34 Frank Tripucka 10.00 4.50
❑ 35 Gene Mingo 7.00 3.10
❑ 36 Lionel Taylor 12.00 5.50
❑ 37 Ken Adamson 7.00 3.10
❑ 38 Eldon Danenhauer 7.00 3.10
❑ 39 Goose Gonsoulin 10.00 4.50
❑ 40 Gordy Holz 7.00 3.10
❑ 41 Bud McFadin 8.00 3.60
❑ 42 Jim Stinnette 7.00 3.10
❑ 43 Bob Hudson RC 7.00 3.10
❑ 44 George Herring 7.00 3.10
❑ 45 Charley Tolar RC 7.00 3.10
❑ 46 George Blanda 50.00 22.00
❑ 47 Billy Cannon 15.00 6.75
❑ 48 Charlie Hennigan RC 15.00 6.75
❑ 49 Bill Groman 7.00 3.10
❑ 50 Al Jamison 7.00 3.10
❑ 51 Tony Banfield 7.00 3.10
❑ 52 Jim Norton 7.00 3.10
❑ 53 Dennit Morris 7.00 3.10
❑ 54 Don Floyd 7.00 3.10
❑ 55 Ed Husmann UER 7.00 3.10
(Misspelled Hussman
on both sides)
❑ 56 Robert Brooks 7.00 3.10
❑ 57 Al Dorow 7.00 3.10
❑ 58 Dick Christy 7.00 3.10
❑ 59 Don Maynard 50.00 22.00
❑ 60 Art Powell 10.00 4.50
❑ 61 Mike Hudock 7.00 3.10
❑ 62 Bill Mathis 8.00 3.60
❑ 63 Butch Songin 7.00 3.10
❑ 64 Larry Grantham 7.00 3.10
❑ 65 Nick Mumley 7.00 3.10
❑ 66 Tom Saidock 7.00 3.10
❑ 67 Alan Miller 7.00 3.10
❑ 68 Tom Flores 15.00 6.75
❑ 69 Bob Coolbaugh 7.00 3.10
❑ 70 George Fleming 7.00 3.10
❑ 71 Wayne Hawkins RC 8.00 3.60
❑ 72 Jim Otto 40.00 18.00
❑ 73 Wayne Crow 7.00 3.10
❑ 74 Fred Williamson RC 30.00 13.50
❑ 75 Tom Louderback 7.00 3.10
❑ 76 Volney Peters 7.00 3.10
❑ 77 Charley Powell 7.00 3.10
❑ 78 Don Norton 7.00 3.10
❑ 79 Jack Kemp 200.00 90.00
❑ 80 Paul Lowe 10.00 4.50
❑ 81 Dave Kocourek 7.00 3.10
❑ 82 Ron Mix 15.00 6.75
❑ 83 Ernie Wright 10.00 4.50
❑ 84 Dick Harris 7.00 3.10
❑ 85 Bill Hudson 7.00 3.10
❑ 86 Ernie Ladd RC 25.00 11.00
❑ 87 Earl Faison RC 8.00 3.60
❑ 88 Ron Nery 18.00 4.50

1963 Fleer

	NM	Ex
COMPLETE SET (88)	1800.00	800.00
WRAPPER (5-CENT)	120.00	55.00

❑ 1 Larry Garron RC 20.00 5.00
❑ 2 Babe Parilli 10.00 4.50
❑ 3 Ron Burton 12.00 5.50
❑ 4 Jim Colclough 8.00 3.60
❑ 5 Gino Cappelletti 12.00 5.50
❑ 6 Charles Long RC SP 150.00 70.00
❑ 7 Bill Neighbors RC 8.00 3.60
❑ 8 Dick Felt 8.00 3.60

9 Tommy Addison	8.00	3.60
10 Nick Buoniconti RC	80.00	36.00
11 Larry Eisenhauer RC	8.00	3.60
12 Bill Mathis	8.00	3.60
13 Lee Grosscup RC	10.00	4.50
14 Dick Christy	8.00	3.60
15 Don Maynard	50.00	22.00
16 Alex Kroll RC	8.00	3.60
17 Bob Mischak	8.00	3.60
18 Dainard Paulson	8.00	3.60
19 Lee Riley	8.00	3.60
20 Larry Grantham	10.00	4.50
21 Hubert Bobo	8.00	3.60
22 Nick Mumley	8.00	3.60
23 Cookie Gilchrist RC	50.00	22.00
24 Jack Kemp	150.00	70.00
25 Wray Carlton	8.00	3.60
26 Elbert Dubenion	10.00	4.50
27 Ernie Warlick RC	10.00	4.50
28 Billy Shaw	15.00	6.75
29 Ken Rice	8.00	3.60
30 Booker Edgerson	8.00	3.60
31 Ray Abruzzese	8.00	3.60
32 Mike Stratton RC	15.00	6.75
33 Tom Sestak RC	10.00	4.50
34 Charley Tolar	8.00	3.60
35 Dave Smith	8.00	3.60
36 George Blanda	55.00	25.00
37 Billy Cannon	15.00	6.75
38 Charlie Hennigan	10.00	4.50
39 Bob Talamini RC	8.00	3.60
40 Jim Norton	8.00	3.60
41 Tony Banfield	8.00	3.60
42 Doug Cline	8.00	3.60
43 Don Floyd	8.00	3.60
44 Ed Husmann	8.00	3.60
45 Curtis McClinton RC	15.00	6.75
46 Jack Spikes	10.00	4.50
47 Len Dawson RC	200.00	90.00
48 Abner Haynes	15.00	6.75
49 Chris Burford	10.00	4.50
50 Fred Arbanas RC	12.00	5.50
51 Johnny Robinson	10.00	4.50
52 E.J. Holub	10.00	4.50
53 Sherrill Headrick	10.00	4.50
54 Mel Branch	10.00	4.50
55 Jerry Mays	10.00	4.50
56 Cotton Davidson	10.00	4.50
57 Clem Daniels RC	15.00	6.75
58 Bo Roberson RC	10.00	4.50
59 Art Powell	12.00	5.50
60 Bob Coolbaugh	8.00	3.60
61 Wayne Hawkins	8.00	3.60
62 Jim Otto	30.00	13.50
63 Fred Williamson	20.00	9.00
64 Bob Dougherty SP	120.00	55.00
65 Dalva Allen	8.00	3.60
66 Chuck McMurtry	8.00	3.60
67 Gerry McDougall RC	8.00	3.60
68 Tobin Rote	10.00	4.50
69 Paul Lowe	12.00	5.50
70 Keith Lincoln RC	40.00	18.00
71 Dave Kocourek	8.00	3.60
72 Lance Alworth RC	250.00	110.00
73 Ron Mix	25.00	11.00
74 Charley McNeil RC	8.00	3.60
75 Emil Karas	8.00	3.60
76 Ernie Ladd	20.00	9.00
77 Earl Faison	8.00	3.60
78 Jim Stinnette	8.00	3.60
79 Frank Tripucka	12.00	5.50
80 Don Stone	8.00	3.60
81 Bob Scarpitto	8.00	3.60
82 Lionel Taylor	12.00	5.50
83 Jerry Tarr	8.00	3.60
84 Eldon Danenhauer	8.00	3.60
85 Goose Gonsoulin	10.00	4.50
86 Jim Fraser	8.00	3.60
87 Chuck Gavin	8.00	3.60
88 Bud McFadin	20.00	5.00
NNO Checklist Card SP	350.00	90.00

1990 Fleer Update

	Nm-Mt	Ex-Mt
COMP.FACT.SET (120)	25.00	11.00
U1 Albert Bentley	.08	.04
U2 Dean Biasucci	.08	.04
U3 Ray Donaldson	.08	.04
U4 Jeff George	1.25	.55
U5 Ray Agnew RC	.08	.04
U6 Greg McMurtry RC	.08	.04
U7 Chris Singleton RC	.08	.04
U8 James Francis RC	.08	.04
U9 Harold Green RC	.30	.14
U10 John Elliott	.08	.04
U11 Rodney Hampton RC	.30	.14
U12 Gary Reasons	.08	.04
U13 Lewis Tillman	.08	.04
U14 Everson Walls	.08	.04
U15 David Alexander RC	.08	.04
U16 Jim McMahon	.15	.07
U17 Ben Smith RC	.08	.04
U18 Andre Waters	.08	.04
U19 Calvin Williams RC	.15	.07
U20 Earnest Byner	.08	.04
U21 Andre Collins RC	.08	.04
U22 Russ Grimm	.08	.04
U23 Stan Humphries RC	.30	.14
U24 Martin Mayhew RC	.08	.04
U25 Barry Foster RC	.30	.14
U26 Eric Green RC	.15	.07
U27 Tunch Ilkin	.08	.04
U28 Hardy Nickerson	.15	.07
U29 Jerrol Williams	.08	.04
U30 Mike Baab	.08	.04
U31 Leroy Hoard RC	.50	.23
U32 Eddie Johnson RC	.08	.04
U33 William Fuller	.15	.07
U34 Haywood Jeffires RC	.30	.14
U35 Don Maggs RC	.08	.04
U36 Allen Pinkett	.08	.04
U37 Robert Awalt	.08	.04
U38 Dennis McKinnon	.08	.04
U39 Ken Norton RC	.30	.14
U40 Emmitt Smith RC	20.00	9.00
U41 Alexander Wright RC	.08	.04
U42 Eric Hill	.08	.04
U43 Johnny Johnson RC	.15	.07
U44 Timm Rosenbach	.08	.04
U45 Anthony Thompson RC	.08	.04
U46 Dexter Carter RC	.08	.04
U47 Eric Davis RC UER (Listed as WR on front, DB on back)	.15	.07
U48 Keith DeLong	.08	.04
U49 Brent Jones RC	.30	.14
U50 Darryl Pollard RC	.08	.04
U51 Steve Wallace RC	.30	.14
U52 Bern Brostek RC	.08	.04
U53 Aaron Cox	.08	.04
U54 Cleveland Gary	.08	.04
U55 Fred Strickland RC	.08	.04
U56 Pat Terrell RC	.08	.04
U57 Steve Broussard RC	.08	.04
U58 Scott Case	.08	.04
U59 Brian Jordan RC	.15	.07
U60 Andre Rison	.30	.14
U61 Kevin Haverdink	.08	.04
U62 Rueben Mayes	.08	.04
U63 Steve Walsh	.15	.07
U64 Greg Bell	.08	.04
U65 Tim Brown	.30	.14
U66 Willie Gault	.15	.07
U67 Vance Mueller RC	.08	.04
U68 Bill Pickel	.08	.04
U69 Aaron Wallace RC	.08	.04
U70 Glenn Parker RC	.08	.04
U71 Frank Reich	.30	.14
U72 Leon Seals RC	.08	.04
U73 Darryl Talley	.08	.04
U74 Brad Baxter RC	.08	.04
U75 Jeff Criswell	.08	.04
U76 Jeff Lageman	.08	.04
U77 Rob Moore RC	1.50	.70
U78 Blair Thomas	.15	.07
U79 Louis Oliver	.08	.04
U80 Tony Paige	.08	.04
U81 Richmond Webb RC	.08	.04
U82 Robert Blackmon RC	.08	.04
U83 Derrick Fenner RC	.08	.04
U84 Andy Heck	.08	.04
U85 Cortez Kennedy RC	.30	.14
U86 Terry Wooden RC	.08	.04
U87 Jeff Donaldson	.08	.04
U88 Tim Grunhard RC	.08	.04
U89 Emile Harry RC	.08	.04
U90 Dan Saleaumua	.08	.04
U91 Percy Snow	.08	.04
U92 Andre Ware	.30	.14
U93 Darrell Fullington RC	.08	.04
U94 Mike Merriweather	.08	.04
U95 Henry Thomas	.08	.04
U96 Robert Brown	.08	.04
U97 LeRoy Butler RC	.30	.14
U98 Anthony Dilweg	.08	.04
U99 Darrell Thompson RC	.08	.04
U100 Keith Woodside	.08	.04
U101 Gary Plummer	.08	.04
U102 Junior Seau RC	5.00	2.20
U103 Billy Joe Tolliver	.08	.04
U104 Mark Vlasic	.08	.04
U105 Gary Anderson RB	.08	.04
U106 Ian Beckles RC	.08	.04
U107 Reggie Cobb RC	.08	.04
U108 Keith McCants RC	.08	.04
U109 Mark Bortz RC	.08	.04
U110 Maury Buford	.08	.04
U111 Mark Carrier DB RC	.30	.14
U112 Dan Hampton	.15	.07
U113 William Perry	.15	.07
U114 Ron Rivera	.08	.04
U115 Lemuel Stinson	.08	.04
U116 Melvin Bratton RC	.08	.04
U117 Gary Kubiak RC	.08	.04
U118 Alton Montgomery RC	.08	.04
U119 Ricky Nattiel	.08	.04
U120 Checklist 1-132	.08	.04

2000 Fleer Focus

	Nm-Mt	Ex-Mt
COMPLETE SET (260)	400.00	180.00

Card	Player	Price	Price
	COMP.SET w/o SPs (200)	25.00	11.00
❑ 1	Tim Couch	.40	.18
❑ 2	Germane Crowell	.25	.11
❑ 3	Curtis Martin	.60	.25
❑ 4	Samari Rolle	.25	.11
❑ 5	Brian Griese	.60	.25
❑ 6	Kerry Collins	.40	.18
❑ 7	Jevon Kearse	.60	.25
❑ 8	Rocket Ismail	.40	.18
❑ 9	Cam Cleeland	.25	.11
❑ 10	Warrick Dunn	.60	.25
❑ 11	Carl Pickens	.40	.18
❑ 12	Cris Carter	.60	.25
❑ 13	Mike Pritchard	.25	.11
❑ 14	Corey Dillon	.60	.25
❑ 15	Randy Moss	1.25	.55
❑ 16	Derrick Mayes	.40	.18
❑ 17	Marcus Robinson	.60	.25
❑ 18	Thurman Thomas	.40	.18
❑ 19	J.J. Stokes	.40	.18
❑ 20	Muhsin Muhammad	.40	.18
❑ 21	Derrick Alexander	.40	.18
❑ 22	Curtis Conway	.40	.18
❑ 23	Qadry Ismail	.40	.18
❑ 24	Ken Dilger	.25	.11
❑ 25	Troy Edwards	.25	.11
❑ 26	Shawn Jefferson	.25	.11
❑ 27	Terrence Wilkins	.25	.11
❑ 28	Duce Staley	.60	.25
❑ 29	Aeneas Williams	.25	.11
❑ 30	Antonio Freeman	.60	.25
❑ 31	Tim Brown	.60	.25
❑ 32	Darrell Green	.25	.11
❑ 33	Herman Moore	.40	.18
❑ 34	Vinny Testaverde	.40	.18
❑ 35	Yancey Thigpen	.25	.11
❑ 36	Emmitt Smith	1.25	.55
❑ 37	Ricky Williams	.60	.25
❑ 38	Keyshawn Johnson	.60	.25
❑ 39	Eddie Kennison	.25	.11
❑ 40	Zach Thomas	.60	.25
❑ 41	Shawn Springs	.25	.11
❑ 42	Wesley Walls	.25	.11
❑ 43	Andre Rison	.40	.18
❑ 44	Jerry Rice	1.25	.55
❑ 45	Rob Johnson	.40	.18
❑ 46	Keenan McCardell	.40	.18
❑ 47	Ryan Leaf	.40	.18
❑ 48	Michael McCrary	.25	.11
❑ 49	Marvin Harrison	.60	.25
❑ 50	Donovan McNabb	1.00	.45
❑ 51	Curtis Enis	.25	.11
❑ 52	Tony Martin	.40	.18
❑ 53	Jeff Garcia	.60	.25
❑ 54	Tim Biakabutuka	.40	.18
❑ 55	Tony Gonzalez	.40	.18
❑ 56	Jim Harbaugh	.40	.18
❑ 57	Peerless Price	.60	.25
❑ 58	Fred Taylor	.60	.25
❑ 59	Kordell Stewart	.40	.18
❑ 60	Chris Chandler	.40	.18
❑ 61	Bill Schroeder	.40	.18
❑ 62	Charles Woodson	.40	.18
❑ 63	Terance Mathis	.40	.18
❑ 64	Brett Favre	2.00	.90
❑ 65	Rickey Dudley	.25	.11
❑ 66	Rob Moore	.40	.18
❑ 67	Charlie Batch	.60	.25
❑ 68	Wayne Chrebet	.40	.18
❑ 69	Jeff George	.40	.18
❑ 70	Olandis Gary	.60	.25
❑ 71	Amani Toomer	.40	.18
❑ 72	Kevin Dyson	.40	.18
❑ 73	Darrin Chiaverini	.25	.11
❑ 74	Willie McGinest	.25	.11
❑ 75	Ricky Proehl	.25	.11
❑ 76	Craig Yeast	.25	.11
❑ 77	Dwayne Rudd	.25	.11
❑ 78	Marshall Faulk	.75	.35
❑ 79	Bobby Engram	.40	.18
❑ 80	Jay Fiedler	.60	.25
❑ 81	Jon Kitna	.60	.25
❑ 82	Patrick Jeffers	.60	.25
❑ 83	James Johnson	.25	.11
❑ 84	Charlie Garner	.40	.18
❑ 85	Eric Moulds	.60	.25
❑ 86	Mark Brunell	.60	.25
❑ 87	Richard Huntley	.25	.11
❑ 88	Frank Sanders	.40	.18
❑ 89	Robert Porcher	.25	.11
❑ 90	Aaron Glenn	.25	.11
❑ 91	Stephen Davis	.60	.25
❑ 92	Ed McCaffrey	.60	.25
❑ 93	Pete Mitchell	.25	.11
❑ 94	Frank Wycheck	.25	.11
❑ 95	David LaFleur	.25	.11
❑ 96	Jake Delhomme RC	2.50	1.10
❑ 97	John Lynch	.40	.18
❑ 98	Michael Pittman	.25	.11
❑ 99	Andy Katzenmoyer	.25	.11
❑ 100	Isaac Bruce	.60	.25
❑ 101	Terry Kirby	.25	.11
❑ 102	Kevin Faulk	.40	.18
❑ 103	Kevin Carter	.40	.18
❑ 104	Darnay Scott	.40	.18
❑ 105	Robert Smith	.60	.25
❑ 106	Brian Mitchell	.25	.11
❑ 107	Shane Matthews	.25	.11
❑ 108	O.J. McDuffie	.40	.18
❑ 109	Bryant Young	.25	.11
❑ 110	Jay Riemersma	.25	.11
❑ 111	Elvis Grbac	.40	.18
❑ 112	Jermaine Fazande	.25	.11
❑ 113	Jonathan Linton	.25	.11
❑ 114	Kyle Brady	.25	.11
❑ 115	Junior Seau	.60	.25
❑ 116	Shannon Sharpe	.40	.18
❑ 117	Jerome Pathon	.40	.18
❑ 118	Jerome Bettis	.60	.25
❑ 119	O.J. Santiago	.25	.11
❑ 120	Ahman Green	.60	.25
❑ 121	Troy Vincent	.25	.11
❑ 122	David Boston	.60	.25
❑ 123	James Stewart	.40	.18
❑ 124	Ray Lucas	.40	.18
❑ 125	Brad Johnson	.60	.25
❑ 126	Rod Smith	.40	.18
❑ 127	Joe Jurevicius	.25	.11
❑ 128	Eddie George	.60	.25
❑ 129	Darren Woodson	.25	.11
❑ 130	Jake Reed	.40	.18
❑ 131	Mike Alstott	.60	.25
❑ 132	Leslie Shepherd	.25	.11
❑ 133	Terry Glenn	.40	.18
❑ 134	Az-Zahir Hakim	.40	.18
❑ 135	Alonzo Mayes	.25	.11
❑ 136	Sam Madison	.25	.11
❑ 137	Ricky Watters	.40	.18
❑ 138	Antowain Smith	.40	.18
❑ 139	Jimmy Smith	.40	.18
❑ 140	Hines Ward	.60	.25
❑ 141	Priest Holmes	.75	.35
❑ 142	Edgerrin James	1.00	.45
❑ 143	Charles Johnson	.40	.18
❑ 144	Jamal Anderson	.60	.25
❑ 145	Dorsey Levens	.40	.18
❑ 146	Rich Gannon	.60	.25
❑ 147	Champ Bailey	.40	.18
❑ 148	Bill Romanowski	.25	.11
❑ 149	Jason Sehorn	.25	.11
❑ 150	Steve McNair	.60	.25
❑ 151	Jermaine Lewis	.40	.18
❑ 152	Cornelius Bennett	.25	.11
❑ 153	Torrance Small	.25	.11
❑ 154	Tim Dwight	.60	.25
❑ 155	Corey Bradford	.40	.18
❑ 156	Napoleon Kaufman	.40	.18
❑ 157	Jake Plummer	.40	.18
❑ 158	David Sloan	.25	.11
❑ 159	Dedric Ward	.25	.11
❑ 160	Michael Westbrook	.40	.18
❑ 161	Terrell Davis	.60	.25
❑ 162	Ike Hilliard	.40	.18
❑ 163	Derrick Brooks	.60	.25
❑ 164	Greg Ellis	.25	.11
❑ 165	Keith Poole	.25	.11
❑ 166	Jacquez Green	.25	.11
❑ 167	Joey Galloway	.40	.18
❑ 168	Lawyer Milloy	.40	.18
❑ 169	Warren Sapp	.40	.18
❑ 170	Takeo Spikes	.25	.11
❑ 171	John Randle	.40	.18
❑ 172	Torry Holt	.60	.25
❑ 173	Cade McNown	.25	.11
❑ 174	Damon Huard	.60	.25
❑ 175	Terrell Owens	.60	.25
❑ 176	Steve Beuerlein	.40	.18
❑ 177	Tony Richardson RC	.40	.18
❑ 178	Jeff Graham	.40	.18
❑ 179	Doug Flutie	.60	.25
❑ 180	Kevin Hardy	.25	.11
❑ 181	Mark Bruener	.25	.11
❑ 182	Tony Banks	.40	.18
❑ 183	Peyton Manning	1.50	.70
❑ 184	Hugh Douglas	.25	.11
❑ 185	Simeon Rice	.40	.18
❑ 186	Terry Fair	.25	.11
❑ 187	James Jett	.25	.11
❑ 188	Albert Connell	.25	.11
❑ 189	Troy Aikman	1.50	.70
❑ 190	Jeff Blake	.40	.18
❑ 191	Shaun King	.25	.11
❑ 192	Kevin Johnson	.60	.25
❑ 193	Drew Bledsoe	.75	.35
❑ 194	Kurt Warner	1.25	.55
❑ 195	Akili Smith	.25	.11
❑ 196	Daunte Culpepper	.75	.35
❑ 197	Sean Dawkins	.25	.11
❑ 198	Natrone Means	.25	.11
❑ 199	Kimble Anders	.25	.11
❑ 200	Steve Young	.75	.35
❑ 201	Courtney Brown RC	4.00	1.80
❑ 202	Chris Samuels RC	3.00	1.35
❑ 203	Corey Simon RC	4.00	1.80
❑ 204	Deon Grant RC	4.00	1.80
❑ 205	Darren Howard RC	3.00	1.35
❑ 206	Rob Morris RC	4.00	1.80
❑ 207	Ahmed Plummer RC	4.00	1.80
❑ 208	Anthony Becht RC	4.00	1.80
❑ 209	Brian Urlacher RC	15.00	6.75
❑ 210	Shaun Ellis RC	4.00	1.80
❑ 211	Bubba Franks RC	4.00	1.80
❑ 212	Plaxico Burress RC	15.00	6.75
❑ 213	R.Jay Soward RC	8.00	3.60
❑ 214	Dez White RC	8.00	3.60
❑ 215	Peter Warrick RC	8.00	3.60
❑ 216	Jerry Porter RC	10.00	4.50
❑ 217	Ron Dugans RC	6.00	2.70
❑ 218	Laveranues Coles RC	10.00	4.50
❑ 219	Travis Taylor RC	8.00	3.60
❑ 220	Anthony Lucas RC	6.00	2.70
❑ 221	Sylvester Morris RC	8.00	3.60
❑ 222	Dennis Northcutt RC	8.00	3.60
❑ 223	Chafie Fields RC	6.00	2.70
❑ 224	Danny Farmer RC	8.00	3.60
❑ 225	Chris Cole RC	6.00	2.70
❑ 226	Sherrod Gideon RC	6.00	2.70
❑ 227	Todd Pinkston RC	8.00	3.60
❑ 228	Gari Scott RC	6.00	2.70
❑ 229	Darrell Jackson RC	15.00	6.75
❑ 230	JaJuan Dawson RC	6.00	2.70
❑ 231	Trevor Gaylor RC	6.00	2.70
❑ 232	Bashir Yamini RC	6.00	2.70
❑ 233	Quinton Spotwood RC	6.00	2.70
❑ 234	Michael Wiley RC	5.00	2.20
❑ 235	Ron Dayne RC	6.00	2.70
❑ 236	Thomas Jones RC	10.00	4.50
❑ 237	Jamal Lewis RC	20.00	9.00
❑ 238	Travis Prentice RC	5.00	2.20
❑ 239	J.R. Redmond RC	5.00	2.20
❑ 240	Trung Canidate RC	5.00	2.20
❑ 241	Shaun Alexander RC	20.00	9.00
❑ 242	Frank Murphy RC	4.00	1.80
❑ 243	Shyrone Stith RC	6.00	2.70
❑ 244	Rondell Mealey RC	4.00	1.80
❑ 245	Terrelle Smith RC	5.00	2.20
❑ 246	Reuben Droughns RC	8.00	3.60
❑ 247	Chad Morton RC	6.00	2.70
❑ 248	Mike Anderson RC	6.00	2.70
❑ 249	Paul Smith RC	5.00	2.20
❑ 250	Curtis Keaton RC	5.00	2.20
❑ 251	Jarious Jackson RC	6.00	2.70
❑ 252	Marc Bulger RC	10.00	4.50
❑ 253	Tee Martin RC	6.00	2.70
❑ 254	Todd Husak RC	6.00	2.70
❑ 255	Joe Hamilton RC	6.00	2.70
❑ 256	Doug Johnson RC	6.00	2.70
❑ 257	Giovanni Carmazzi RC	6.00	2.70
❑ 258	Chris Redman RC	6.00	2.70
❑ 259	Tim Rattay RC	15.00	6.75
❑ 260	Chad Pennington RC	25.00	11.00
❑ P16	Tim Couch Promo	1.00	.45

2001 Fleer Focus

	Nm-Mt	Ex-Mt
COMP.SET w/o SP's (180)	25.00	7.50
❑ 1 Marshall Faulk	.75	.23
❑ 2 Randy Moss	1.25	.35
❑ 3 Cade McNown	.25	.07
❑ 4 Jeff Graham	.25	.07
❑ 5 Donovan McNabb	.75	.23
❑ 6 Shannon Sharpe	.40	.12
❑ 7 Todd Pinkston	.40	.12
❑ 8 Terrence Wilkins	.25	.07
❑ 9 Michael Strahan	.40	.12
❑ 10 Rich Gannon	.60	.18
❑ 11 Germane Crowell	.25	.07
❑ 12 Warren Sapp	.40	.12
❑ 13 La'Roi Glover	.25	.07
❑ 14 Peter Warrick	.60	.18
❑ 15 Shaun Alexander	.75	.23
❑ 16 Ray Lucas	.25	.07
❑ 17 Muhsin Muhammad	.40	.12
❑ 18 Curtis Conway	.40	.12
❑ 19 R.Jay Soward	.25	.07
❑ 20 Jamal Lewis	1.00	.30
❑ 21 Tony Gonzalez	.40	.12
❑ 22 Bill Schroeder	.40	.12
❑ 23 Frank Sanders	.25	.07
❑ 24 Charles Woodson	.40	.12
❑ 25 Johnnie Morton	.40	.12
❑ 26 Frank Wycheck	.25	.07
❑ 27 Ron Dayne	.60	.18
❑ 28 Travis Prentice	.25	.07
❑ 29 Isaac Bruce	.60	.18
❑ 30 Drew Bledsoe	.75	.23
❑ 31 James Allen	.40	.12
❑ 32 Matt Hasselbeck	.40	.12
❑ 33 Zach Thomas	.60	.18
❑ 34 Shawn Bryson	.25	.07
❑ 35 Jerry Rice	1.25	.35
❑ 36 Mike Cloud	.25	.07
❑ 37 Sammy Morris	.25	.07
❑ 38 Corey Simon	.40	.12
❑ 39 Peyton Manning	1.50	.45
❑ 40 Thomas Jones	.40	.12
❑ 41 Tyrone Wheatley	.40	.12
❑ 42 Herman Moore	.40	.12
❑ 43 Jeff George	.40	.12
❑ 44 Kerry Collins	.40	.12
❑ 45 Rocket Ismail	.40	.12
❑ 46 Andre Rison	.40	.12
❑ 47 David Sloan	.25	.07
❑ 48 Michael Westbrook	.40	.12
❑ 49 Ron Dixon	.25	.07
❑ 50 Randall Cunningham	.60	.18
❑ 51 Keyshawn Johnson	.60	.18
❑ 52 Aaron Brooks	.60	.18
❑ 53 Corey Dillon	.60	.18
❑ 54 John Randle	.40	.12
❑ 55 Cris Carter	.60	.18
❑ 56 Donald Hayes	.25	.07
❑ 57 Hines Ward	.60	.18
❑ 58 Edgerrin James	.75	.23
❑ 59 Terance Mathis	.25	.07
❑ 60 Doug Johnson	.25	.07
❑ 61 Rod Smith	.40	.12
❑ 62 Kevin Dyson	.40	.12
❑ 63 Amani Toomer	.40	.12
❑ 64 Courtney Brown	.40	.12
❑ 65 Mike Alstott	.60	.18
❑ 66 Kevin Faulk	.40	.12
❑ 67 Shane Matthews	.25	.07
❑ 68 Ricky Watters	.40	.12
❑ 69 Peter Boulware	.25	.07
❑ 70 Tim Biakabutuka	.40	.12
❑ 71 Troy Aikman	1.00	.30
❑ 72 Keenan McCardell	.25	.07
❑ 73 Priest Holmes	.75	.23
❑ 74 Duce Staley	.60	.18
❑ 75 Antonio Freeman	.60	.18
❑ 76 David Boston	.60	.18
❑ 77 Chad Pennington	1.00	.30
❑ 78 Brian Griese	.60	.18
❑ 79 Stephen Davis	.60	.18
❑ 80 Curtis Martin	.60	.18
❑ 81 Tony Banks	.40	.12
❑ 82 Warrick Dunn	.60	.18
❑ 83 Willie McGinest	.25	.07
❑ 84 Marty Booker	.25	.07
❑ 85 James Williams	.25	.07
❑ 86 Oronde Gadsden	.40	.12
❑ 87 Patrick Jeffers	.40	.12
❑ 88 Junior Seau	.60	.18
❑ 89 Frank Moreau	.25	.07
❑ 90 Ray Lewis	.60	.18
❑ 91 Doug Flutie	.60	.18
❑ 92 Jimmy Smith	.40	.12
❑ 93 Qadry Ismail	.40	.12
❑ 94 Jeremiah Trotter	.40	.12
❑ 95 Dorsey Levens	.40	.12
❑ 96 Michael Pittman	.25	.07
❑ 97 Wayne Chrebet	.40	.12
❑ 98 Mike Anderson	.60	.18
❑ 99 Derrick Mason	.40	.12
❑ 100 Jason Sehorn	.25	.07
❑ 101 Kevin Johnson	.40	.12
❑ 102 Terrell Owens	.60	.18
❑ 103 Lamar Smith	.40	.12
❑ 104 Eric Moulds	.40	.12
❑ 105 Jerome Bettis	.60	.18
❑ 106 Marvin Harrison	.60	.18
❑ 107 Shawn Jefferson	.25	.07
❑ 108 Rickey Dudley	.25	.07
❑ 109 James Stewart	.40	.12
❑ 110 Bruce Smith	.25	.07
❑ 111 Matthew Hatchette	.25	.07
❑ 112 Emmitt Smith	1.25	.35
❑ 113 Steve McNair	.60	.18
❑ 114 Ricky Williams	.60	.18
❑ 115 Tim Couch	.40	.12
❑ 116 Darrell Jackson	.60	.18
❑ 117 Doug Chapman	.25	.07
❑ 118 Jeff Lewis	.25	.07
❑ 119 Freddie Jones	.25	.07
❑ 120 Sylvester Morris	.25	.07
❑ 121 Elvis Grbac	.40	.12
❑ 122 Plaxico Burress	.60	.18
❑ 123 Marcus Pollard	.25	.07
❑ 124 Chris Chandler	.40	.12
❑ 125 James Thrash	.40	.12
❑ 126 Brett Favre	2.00	.60
❑ 127 Jake Plummer	.40	.12
❑ 128 Vinny Testaverde	.40	.12
❑ 129 Terrell Davis	.60	.18
❑ 130 Jevon Kearse	.40	.12
❑ 131 Albert Connell	.25	.07
❑ 132 Dennis Northcutt	.40	.12
❑ 133 Az-Zahir Hakim	.40	.12
❑ 134 J.R. Redmond	.25	.07
❑ 135 Marcus Robinson	.60	.18
❑ 136 Eddie George	.60	.18
❑ 137 Ike Hilliard	.40	.12
❑ 138 Hugh Douglas	.25	.07
❑ 139 Kurt Warner	1.25	.35
❑ 140 Terry Glenn	.40	.12
❑ 141 Brian Urlacher	1.00	.30
❑ 142 Charlie Garner	.40	.12
❑ 143 Jay Fiedler	.60	.18
❑ 144 Rob Johnson	.40	.12
❑ 145 Kordell Stewart	.40	.12
❑ 146 Mark Brunell	.60	.18
❑ 147 Travis Taylor	.40	.12
❑ 148 Laveranues Coles	.60	.18
❑ 149 Ed McCaffrey	.60	.18
❑ 150 Jacquez Green	.25	.07
❑ 151 Joe Horn	.40	.12
❑ 152 Darnay Scott	.40	.12
❑ 153 Torry Holt	.60	.18
❑ 154 Daunte Culpepper	.60	.18
❑ 155 Wesley Walls	.25	.07
❑ 156 Jeff Garcia	.60	.18
❑ 157 Derrick Alexander	.40	.12
❑ 158 Peerless Price	.40	.12
❑ 159 Bobby Shaw	.25	.07
❑ 160 Fred Taylor	.60	.18
❑ 161 Chris Redman	.25	.07
❑ 162 Tim Brown	.60	.18
❑ 163 Charlie Batch	.60	.18
❑ 164 Champ Bailey	.40	.12
❑ 165 Tiki Barber	.40	.12
❑ 166 Joey Galloway	.40	.12
❑ 167 Brad Johnson	.60	.18
❑ 168 Jeff Blake	.40	.12
❑ 169 Jon Kitna	.40	.12
❑ 170 Trent Green	.60	.18
❑ 171 Troy Brown	.40	.12
❑ 172 Eddie Kennison	.40	.12
❑ 173 J.J. Stokes	.40	.12
❑ 174 James McKnight	.40	.12
❑ 175 Jeremy McDaniel	.25	.07
❑ 176 Richard Huntley	.25	.07
❑ 177 Kyle Brady	.25	.07
❑ 178 Jamal Anderson	.60	.18
❑ 179 Chad Lewis	.25	.07
❑ 180 Ahman Green	.60	.18
❑ 181 Michael Vick RC	25.00	7.50
❑ 182 Deuce McAllister RC	12.00	3.60
❑ 183 David Terrell RC	5.00	1.50
❑ 184 Koren Robinson RC	6.00	1.80
❑ 185 LaDainian Tomlinson RC	15.00	4.50
❑ 186 Michael Bennett RC	10.00	3.00
❑ 187 Chris Chambers RC	6.00	1.80
❑ 188 Chad Johnson RC	10.00	3.00
❑ 189 Santana Moss RC	8.00	2.40
❑ 190 Todd Heap RC	5.00	1.50
❑ 191 Freddie Mitchell RC	5.00	1.50
❑ 192 Quincy Morgan RC	5.00	1.50
❑ 193 Rod Gardner RC	5.00	1.50
❑ 194 Kevan Barlow RC	5.00	1.50
❑ 195 Drew Brees RC	10.00	3.00
❑ 196 Robert Ferguson RC	5.00	1.50
❑ 197 Ken-Yon Rambo RC	3.00	.90
❑ 198 Travis Henry RC	6.00	1.80
❑ 199 LaMont Jordan RC	6.00	1.80
❑ 200 Chris Weinke RC	5.00	1.50
❑ 201 Sage Rosenfels RC	5.00	1.50
❑ 202 Josh Heupel RC	5.00	1.50
❑ 203 Quincy Carter RC	5.00	1.50
❑ 204 Jesse Palmer RC	5.00	1.50
❑ 205 Mike McMahon RC	5.00	1.50
❑ 206 Rudi Johnson RC	10.00	3.00
❑ 207 Anthony Thomas RC	8.00	2.40
❑ 208 James Jackson RC	5.00	1.50
❑ 209 Snoop Minnis RC	3.00	.90
❑ 210 Derek Combs RC	3.00	.90
❑ 211 Ronney Daniels RC	3.00	.90
❑ 212 Alex Bannister RC	3.00	.90
❑ 213 Cedrick Wilson RC	5.00	1.50
❑ 214 Travis Minor RC	3.00	.90
❑ 215 Marques Tuiasosopo RC	5.00	1.50
❑ 216 Reggie Wayne RC	8.00	2.40
❑ 217 Josh Booty RC	5.00	1.50
❑ 218 Jamal Reynolds RC	5.00	1.50
❑ 219 Gerard Warren RC	5.00	1.50
❑ 220 Justin Smith RC	5.00	1.50
❑ 221 Andre Carter RC	5.00	1.50
❑ 222 Milton Wynn RC	3.00	.90
❑ 223 Fred Smoot RC	5.00	1.50
❑ 224 Jamar Fletcher RC	3.00	.90
❑ 225 Dan Morgan RC	5.00	1.50
❑ 226 Jonathan Carter RC	3.00	.90
❑ 227 Correll Buckhalter RC	6.00	1.80
❑ 228 Kevin Kasper RC	5.00	1.50
❑ 229 Derrick Blaylock RC	5.00	1.50
❑ 230 Justin McCareins RC	5.00	1.50

2002 Fleer Focus JE

	Nm-Mt	Ex-Mt
COMP.SET w/o SP's (100)	20.00	6.00
❑ 1 Tom Brady	2.50	.75
❑ 2 Curtis Martin	1.00	.30
❑ 3 Brett Favre	2.50	.75
❑ 4 Michael Pittman	.40	.12
❑ 5 Donovan McNabb	1.25	.35
❑ 6 Quincy Carter	.60	.18
❑ 7 Trent Dilfer	.60	.18
❑ 8 Troy Brown	.60	.18

❑ 9 Ed McCaffrey	1.00	.30
❑ 10 Shaun Alexander	1.00	.30
❑ 11 Daunte Culpepper	1.00	.30
❑ 12 Marty Booker	.60	.18
❑ 13 Junior Seau	1.00	.30
❑ 14 Zach Thomas	1.00	.30
❑ 15 Muhsin Muhammad	.60	.18
❑ 16 Kordell Stewart	.60	.18
❑ 17 Jimmy Smith	.60	.18
❑ 18 David Boston	1.00	.30
❑ 19 Laveranues Coles	.60	.18
❑ 20 Emmitt Smith	2.50	.75
❑ 21 Darrell Jackson	.60	.18
❑ 22 Charlie Garner	.60	.18
❑ 23 Marcus Robinson	.60	.18
❑ 24 Drew Brees	1.00	.30
❑ 25 Tony Gonzalez	.60	.18
❑ 26 James Allen	.60	.18
❑ 27 Steve McNair	1.00	.30
❑ 28 Kerry Collins	.60	.18
❑ 29 Az-Zahir Hakim	.40	.12
❑ 30 Marshall Faulk	1.00	.30
❑ 31 Derrick Mason	.60	.18
❑ 32 Rod Smith	.60	.18
❑ 33 Torry Holt	1.00	.30
❑ 34 Jake Plummer	.60	.18
❑ 35 Kevin Johnson	.60	.18
❑ 36 Kevan Barlow	.60	.18
❑ 37 Priest Holmes	1.25	.35
❑ 38 Anthony Thomas	1.00	.30
❑ 39 Jerome Bettis	1.00	.30
❑ 40 Johnnie Morton	.60	.18
❑ 41 Eric Moulds	.60	.18
❑ 42 James Thrash	.40	.12
❑ 43 Jamie Sharper	.40	.12
❑ 44 Eddie George	1.00	.30
❑ 45 Randy Moss	2.00	.60
❑ 46 Tim Couch	.60	.18
❑ 47 Terrell Owens	1.00	.30
❑ 48 Jay Fiedler	.60	.18
❑ 49 Travis Henry	1.00	.30
❑ 50 Hines Ward	1.00	.30
❑ 51 Ricky Williams	1.00	.30
❑ 52 Brian Urlacher	1.50	.45
❑ 53 LaDainian Tomlinson	1.50	.45
❑ 54 Trent Green	.60	.18
❑ 55 Chris Redman	.40	.12
❑ 56 Deuce McAllister	1.25	.35
❑ 57 Mark Brunell	.60	.18
❑ 58 Jamal Lewis	1.00	.30
❑ 59 Freddie Mitchell	.60	.18
❑ 60 Peyton Manning	2.00	.60
❑ 61 Stephen Davis	.60	.18
❑ 62 Tiki Barber	.60	.18
❑ 63 Terry Glenn	.60	.18
❑ 64 Keyshawn Johnson	1.00	.30
❑ 65 Aaron Brooks	1.00	.30
❑ 66 Brian Griese	1.00	.30
❑ 67 Koren Robinson	.60	.18
❑ 68 Michael Bennett	.60	.18
❑ 69 Ray Lewis	1.00	.30
❑ 70 Rich Gannon	1.00	.30
❑ 71 Marvin Harrison	1.00	.30
❑ 72 Rod Gardner	.60	.18
❑ 73 Chad Pennington	1.25	.35
❑ 74 Terrell Davis	1.00	.30
❑ 75 Isaac Bruce	1.00	.30
❑ 76 Peter Warrick	.60	.18
❑ 77 Jeff Garcia	1.00	.30
❑ 78 Chris Chambers	1.00	.30
❑ 79 Chris Weinke	.60	.18
❑ 80 Plaxico Burress	1.00	.30
❑ 81 Edgerrin James	1.25	.35
❑ 82 Drew Bledsoe	1.25	.35
❑ 83 Duce Staley	1.00	.30
❑ 84 Fred Taylor	1.00	.30
❑ 85 Warrick Dunn	1.00	.30
❑ 86 Jerry Rice	2.00	.60
❑ 87 Ahman Green	1.00	.30
❑ 88 Warren Sapp	.60	.18
❑ 89 Michael Strahan	.60	.18
❑ 90 Bill Schroeder	.60	.18
❑ 91 Kurt Warner	1.00	.30
❑ 92 Antowain Smith	.60	.18
❑ 93 Corey Dillon	.60	.18
❑ 94 Garrison Hearst	.60	.18
❑ 95 Joey Galloway	.60	.18
❑ 96 Michael Vick	3.00	.90
❑ 97 Tim Brown	1.00	.30
❑ 98 Corey Bradford	.40	.12
❑ 99 Brad Johnson	.60	.18
❑ 100 Joe Horn	.60	.18
❑ 101 Quentin Jammer RC	4.00	1.20
❑ 102 Rohan Davey RC	4.00	1.20
❑ 103 David Garrard RC	4.00	1.20
❑ 104 Ron Johnson RC	3.00	.90
❑ 105 Jeremy Shockey RC	12.00	3.60
❑ 106 Marquise Walker RC	3.00	.90
❑ 107 Luke Staley RC	3.00	.90
❑ 108 Josh Scobey RC	4.00	1.20
❑ 109 Adrian Peterson RC	5.00	1.50
❑ 110 Lito Sheppard RC	4.00	1.20
❑ 111 Daniel Graham RC	3.00	.90
❑ 112 Ryan Sims RC	4.00	1.20
❑ 113 William Green RC	6.00	1.80
❑ 114 Ashley Lelie RC	8.00	2.40
❑ 115 Deion Branch RC	8.00	2.40
❑ 116 Omar Easy RC	4.00	1.20
❑ 117 Jake Schifino RC	3.00	.90
❑ 118 Donte Stallworth RC	8.00	2.40
❑ 119 Craig Nall RC	4.00	1.20
❑ 120 Clinton Portis RC	12.00	3.60
❑ 121 Brandon Doman RC	4.00	1.20
❑ 122 Eric Crouch RC	6.00	1.80
❑ 123 Josh McCown RC	5.00	1.50
❑ 124 Cliff Russell RC	3.00	.90
❑ 125 T.J. Duckett RC	6.00	1.80
❑ 126 Jason McAddley RC	3.00	.90
❑ 127 Chad Hutchinson RC	4.00	1.20
❑ 128 Jonathan Wells RC	4.00	1.20
❑ 129 Antwaan Randle El RC	5.00	1.50
❑ 130 Terry Charles RC	3.00	.90
❑ 131 Lamar Gordon RC	4.00	1.20
❑ 132 Antonio Bryant RC	4.00	1.20
❑ 133 Brian Westbrook RC	6.00	1.80
❑ 134 Javon Walker RC	8.00	2.40
❑ 135 J.T. O'Sullivan RC	3.00	.90
❑ 136 Maurice Morris RC	4.00	1.20
❑ 137 Tim Carter RC	3.00	.90
❑ 138 Antwoine Womack RC	3.00	.90
❑ 139 Ladell Betts RC	4.00	1.20
❑ 140 Joey Harrington RC	12.00	3.60
❑ 141 Chester Taylor RC	4.00	1.20
❑ 142 David Carr RC	12.00	3.60
❑ 143 Roy Williams RC	10.00	3.00
❑ 144 Reche Caldwell RC	4.00	1.20
❑ 145 Lamont Brightful RC	2.00	.60
❑ 146 Patrick Ramsey RC	8.00	2.40
❑ 147 Travis Stephens RC	3.00	.90
❑ 148 Andre Davis RC	4.00	1.20
❑ 149 Herb Haygood RC	2.00	.60
❑ 150 Randy Fasani RC	3.00	.90
❑ 151 Jabar Gaffney RC	4.00	1.20
❑ 152 Kahlil Hill RC	3.00	.90
❑ 153 Julius Peppers RC	8.00	2.40
❑ 154 Kurt Kittner RC	3.00	.90
❑ 155 DeShaun Foster RC	4.00	1.20
❑ 156 Verron Haynes RC	4.00	1.20
❑ 157 Josh Reed RC	4.00	1.20
❑ 158 Freddie Milons RC	3.00	.90
❑ 159 Robert Thomas RC	4.00	1.20
❑ 160 Sam Simmons RC	2.00	.60

2003 Fleer Focus

	MINT	NRMT
COMP.SET w/o SP's (120)	25.00	11.00
❑ 1 Tony Gonzalez	.60	.25
❑ 2 Aaron Brooks	1.00	.45
❑ 3 Joey Harrington	1.50	.70
❑ 4 Brett Favre	2.50	1.10
❑ 5 Donovan McNabb	1.25	.55
❑ 6 Jerome Bettis	1.00	.45
❑ 7 Michael Vick	2.50	1.10
❑ 8 Travis Taylor	.60	.25
❑ 9 Jay Fiedler	.60	.25
❑ 10 David Boston	.60	.25
❑ 11 Peerless Price	.60	.25
❑ 12 Kevan Barlow	.60	.25
❑ 13 LaDainian Tomlinson	1.00	.45
❑ 14 Jevon Kearse	.60	.25
❑ 15 Peyton Manning	1.50	.70
❑ 16 T.J. Duckett	.60	.25
❑ 17 Drew Brees	1.00	.45
❑ 18 Brian Dawkins	.40	.18
❑ 19 Charles Woodson	.60	.25
❑ 20 Emmitt Smith	2.50	1.10
❑ 21 Joe Jurevicius	.40	.18
❑ 22 Duce Staley	.60	.25
❑ 23 Rod Gardner	.60	.25
❑ 24 Jamal Lewis	1.00	.45
❑ 25 Jeff Garcia	1.00	.45
❑ 26 Clinton Portis	1.50	.70
❑ 27 Priest Holmes	1.25	.55
❑ 28 Mike Alstott	1.00	.45
❑ 29 Shaun Alexander	1.00	.45
❑ 30 Randy Moss	1.50	.70
❑ 31 Eric Moulds	.60	.25
❑ 32 Troy Brown	.60	.25
❑ 33 Michael Bennett	.60	.25
❑ 34 Ricky Williams	1.00	.45
❑ 35 Champ Bailey	.60	.25
❑ 36 Hugh Douglas	.40	.18
❑ 37 Travis Henry	.60	.25
❑ 38 Daunte Culpepper	1.00	.45
❑ 39 Koren Robinson	.60	.25
❑ 40 Todd Heap	.60	.25
❑ 41 John Abraham	.40	.18
❑ 42 Drew Bledsoe	1.00	.45
❑ 43 Tom Brady	1.50	.70
❑ 44 Torry Holt	1.00	.45
❑ 45 Jake Delhomme	1.00	.45
❑ 46 Joe Horn	.60	.25
❑ 47 Julius Peppers	1.00	.45
❑ 48 Ray Lewis	1.00	.45
❑ 49 Deuce McAllister	1.00	.45
❑ 50 Marshall Faulk	1.00	.45
❑ 51 Takeo Spikes	.40	.18
❑ 52 Kordell Stewart	.60	.25
❑ 53 Brian Urlacher	1.50	.70
❑ 54 Zach Thomas	1.00	.45
❑ 55 Kurt Warner	1.00	.45
❑ 56 Peter Warrick	.60	.25
❑ 57 Marty Booker	.60	.25
❑ 58 Warren Sapp	.60	.25
❑ 59 Jon Kitna	.60	.25
❑ 60 Chad Johnson	.60	.25
❑ 61 Jeremy Shockey	1.50	.70
❑ 62 Keyshawn Johnson	1.00	.45
❑ 63 Kelly Holcomb	.60	.25
❑ 64 Corey Dillon	.60	.25
❑ 65 Tiki Barber	.60	.25
❑ 66 Eddie George	.60	.25
❑ 67 Joey Galloway	.60	.25
❑ 68 Tim Couch	.40	.18
❑ 69 Amani Toomer	.60	.25
❑ 70 Steve McNair	1.00	.45
❑ 71 Troy Hambrick	.40	.18
❑ 72 William Green	.60	.25
❑ 73 Chad Pennington	1.25	.55

❑ 74 Laveranues Coles	.60	.25
❑ 75 Quincy Carter	.60	.25
❑ 76 Antonio Bryant	.60	.25
❑ 77 Curtis Martin	1.00	.45
❑ 78 Terrell Owens	1.00	.45
❑ 79 Patrick Ramsey	1.00	.45
❑ 80 Ashley Lelie	1.00	.45
❑ 81 Donte Stallworth	1.00	.45
❑ 82 Roy Williams	1.00	.45
❑ 83 Charlie Garner	.60	.25
❑ 84 Chris Chambers	1.00	.45
❑ 85 Warrick Dunn	.60	.25
❑ 86 Shannon Sharpe	.60	.25
❑ 87 Rod Smith	.60	.25
❑ 88 Marvin Harrison	1.00	.45
❑ 89 Rich Gannon	.60	.25
❑ 90 Stephen Davis	.60	.25
❑ 91 James Stewart	.60	.25
❑ 92 Tim Brown	1.00	.45
❑ 93 Anthony Thomas	1.00	.45
❑ 94 Stacey Mack	.40	.18
❑ 95 Jake Plummer	.60	.25
❑ 96 Jerry Rice	2.00	.90
❑ 97 Quincy Morgan	.60	.25
❑ 98 Dwight Freeney	.40	.18
❑ 99 Jason Taylor	.40	.18
❑ 100 Ahman Green	1.00	.45
❑ 101 Hines Ward	1.00	.45
❑ 102 Kerry Collins	.60	.25
❑ 103 Plaxico Burress	.60	.25
❑ 104 Santana Moss	.60	.25
❑ 105 Michael Strahan	.60	.25
❑ 106 Donald Driver	.60	.25
❑ 107 Tommy Maddox	1.00	.45
❑ 108 Jerry Porter	.60	.25
❑ 109 David Carr	1.50	.70
❑ 110 Garrison Hearst	.60	.25
❑ 111 Edgerrin James	1.00	.45
❑ 112 Isaac Bruce	1.00	.45
❑ 113 Marc Bulger	1.00	.45
❑ 114 Brad Johnson	.60	.25
❑ 115 Fred Taylor	1.00	.45
❑ 116 Derrick Brooks	.60	.25
❑ 117 Jimmy Smith	.60	.25
❑ 118 Derrick Mason	.60	.25
❑ 119 Mark Brunell	.60	.25
❑ 120 Trent Green	.60	.25
❑ 121 Mike Doss RC	5.00	2.20
❑ 122 Carson Palmer RC	20.00	9.00
❑ 123 Charles Rogers RC	6.00	2.70
❑ 124 Andre Johnson RC	15.00	6.75
❑ 125 Tony Hollings RC	5.00	2.20
❑ 126 Terence Newman RC	10.00	4.50
❑ 127 Byron Leftwich RC	20.00	9.00
❑ 128 Terrell Suggs RC	8.00	3.60
❑ 129 Bryant Johnson RC	5.00	2.20
❑ 130 Kyle Boller RC	12.00	5.50
❑ 131 Rex Grossman RC	15.00	6.75
❑ 132 Willis McGahee RC	12.00	5.50
❑ 133 Dallas Clark RC	5.00	2.20
❑ 134 Bobby Wade RC	5.00	2.20
❑ 135 Tony Romo RC	5.00	2.20
❑ 136 Michael Haynes RC	5.00	2.20
❑ 137 Bethel Johnson RC	8.00	3.60
❑ 138 Anquan Boldin RC	12.00	5.50
❑ 139 Seneca Wallace RC	5.00	2.20
❑ 140 Nick Barnett RC	8.00	3.60
❑ 141 Teyo Johnson RC	5.00	2.20
❑ 142 Kelley Washington RC	5.00	2.20
❑ 143 Nate Burleson RC	8.00	3.60
❑ 144 Ken Dorsey RC	8.00	3.60
❑ 145 Dewayne White RC	4.00	1.80
❑ 146 Chris Kelsay RC	5.00	2.20
❑ 147 Dave Ragone RC	5.00	2.20
❑ 148 David Tyree RC	4.00	1.80
❑ 149 Billy McMullen RC	4.00	1.80
❑ 150 Chris Simms RC	10.00	4.50
❑ 151 Onterrio Smith RC	6.00	2.70
❑ 152 Marcus Trufant RC	5.00	2.20
❑ 153 Jason Witten RC	8.00	3.60
❑ 154 Johnathan Sullivan RC	4.00	1.80
❑ 155 Kevin Williams RC	5.00	2.20
❑ 156 Justin Fargas RC	5.00	2.20
❑ 157 Domanick Davis RC	10.00	4.50
❑ 158 LaBrandon Toefield RC	5.00	2.20
❑ 159 Shaun McDonald RC	5.00	2.20
❑ 160 Brandon Lloyd RC	6.00	2.70

2003 Fleer Focus Anniversary Gold

	MINT	NRMT
*STARS: 5X TO 12X BASIC CARDS		
*ROOKIES: .8X TO 2X		

2003 Fleer Focus Numbers Century

	MINT	NRMT
*STARS: 3X TO 8X BASIC CARDS		
*ROOKIES: .5X TO 1.2X		

2001 Fleer Genuine

	Nm-Mt	Ex-Mt
COMP.SET w/o SP's (125)	25.00	7.50
❑ 1 Donovan McNabb	1.25	.35
❑ 2 Daunte Culpepper	1.00	.30
❑ 3 Derrick Alexander	.60	.18
❑ 4 Jessie Armstead	.40	.12
❑ 5 Hines Ward	1.00	.30
❑ 6 Peter Warrick	1.00	.30
❑ 7 Jay Fiedler	1.00	.30
❑ 8 Cris Carter	1.00	.30
❑ 9 Az-Zahir Hakim	.40	.12
❑ 10 Michael Westbrook	.60	.18
❑ 11 Akili Smith	.40	.12
❑ 12 Lamar Smith	.60	.18
❑ 13 Eric Moulds	.60	.18
❑ 14 Shaun Alexander	1.25	.35
❑ 15 Jeff George	.60	.18
❑ 16 Brad Hoover	.40	.12
❑ 17 Brian Griese	1.00	.30
❑ 18 Keenan McCardell	.40	.12
❑ 19 Freddie Jones	.40	.12
❑ 20 Brian Urlacher	1.50	.45
❑ 21 Thomas Jones	.60	.18
❑ 22 Charlie Batch	1.00	.30
❑ 23 Aaron Brooks	1.00	.30
❑ 24 Hugh Douglas	.40	.12
❑ 25 Mike Alstott	1.00	.30
❑ 26 Darrell Russell	.40	.12
❑ 27 Muhsin Muhammad	.60	.18
❑ 28 Rocket Ismail	.60	.18
❑ 29 Fred Taylor	1.00	.30
❑ 30 Tyrone Wheatley	.60	.18
❑ 31 Rodney Harrison	.40	.12
❑ 32 Curtis Martin	1.00	.30
❑ 33 Jason Sehorn	.40	.12
❑ 34 James McKnight	.60	.18
❑ 35 Jimmy Smith	.60	.18
❑ 36 Laveranues Coles	1.00	.30
❑ 37 Jeff Garcia	1.00	.30
❑ 38 Sam Cowart	.40	.12
❑ 39 Joey Galloway	.60	.18
❑ 40 Mark Brunell	1.00	.30
❑ 41 Vinny Testaverde	.60	.18
❑ 42 Terrell Owens	1.00	.30
❑ 43 Ray Lewis	1.00	.30
❑ 44 Ahman Green	1.00	.30
❑ 45 Ron Dayne	1.00	.30
❑ 46 Samari Rolle	.40	.12
❑ 47 Shawn Bryson	.40	.12
❑ 48 Emmitt Smith	2.00	.60
❑ 49 Terrence Wilkins	.40	.12
❑ 50 Charlie Garner	.60	.18
❑ 51 Rob Johnson	.60	.18
❑ 52 Courtney Brown	.60	.18
❑ 53 Edgerrin James	1.25	.35
❑ 54 Kurt Warner	2.00	.60
❑ 55 Michael McCrary	.40	.12
❑ 56 Dennis Northcutt	.60	.18
❑ 57 Marvin Harrison	1.00	.30
❑ 58 Rich Gannon	1.00	.30
❑ 59 Marshall Faulk	1.25	.35
❑ 60 Travis Prentice	.40	.12
❑ 61 Terrell Davis	1.00	.30
❑ 62 Charles Woodson	.60	.18
❑ 63 Isaac Bruce	1.00	.30
❑ 64 Tim Couch	.60	.18
❑ 65 Oronde Gadsden	.60	.18
❑ 66 Randy Moss	2.00	.60
❑ 67 Torry Holt	1.00	.30
❑ 68 Shannon Sharpe	.60	.18
❑ 69 Antonio Freeman	1.00	.30
❑ 70 Michael Strahan	.60	.18
❑ 71 Jevon Kearse	.60	.18
❑ 72 Jamal Lewis	1.50	.45
❑ 73 Peyton Manning	2.50	.75
❑ 74 Amani Toomer	.40	.12
❑ 75 Derrick Mason	.60	.18
❑ 76 Jake Plummer	.60	.18
❑ 77 Rod Smith	.60	.18
❑ 78 Terry Glenn	.60	.18
❑ 79 Plaxico Burress	1.00	.30
❑ 80 Warren Sapp	.60	.18
❑ 81 Jamal Anderson	1.00	.30
❑ 82 James Stewart	.60	.18
❑ 83 Ricky Williams	1.00	.30
❑ 84 Chad Lewis	.40	.12
❑ 85 Shaun King	.40	.12
❑ 86 Wesley Walls	.40	.12
❑ 87 Mike Anderson	1.00	.30
❑ 88 Corey Simon	.60	.18
❑ 89 Wayne Chrebet	.60	.18
❑ 90 Junior Seau	1.00	.30
❑ 91 Terance Mathis	.60	.18
❑ 92 Germane Crowell	.40	.12
❑ 93 Joe Horn	.60	.18
❑ 94 Duce Staley	1.00	.30
❑ 95 Keyshawn Johnson	1.00	.30
❑ 96 Qadry Ismail	.60	.18
❑ 97 Dorsey Levens	1.00	.30
❑ 98 Kerry Collins	.60	.18
❑ 99 Corey Dillon	1.00	.30
❑ 100 Zach Thomas	1.00	.30
❑ 101 Chad Pennington	1.50	.45
❑ 102 Ricky Watters	.60	.18
❑ 103 Bruce Smith	.40	.12
❑ 104 David Boston	1.00	.30
❑ 105 Ed McCaffrey	1.00	.30
❑ 106 Kevin Faulk	1.00	.30
❑ 107 Jerome Bettis	1.00	.30
❑ 108 Warrick Dunn	1.00	.30
❑ 109 Tim Brown	1.00	.30
❑ 110 Marcus Robinson	1.00	.30
❑ 111 Tony Gonzalez	.60	.18
❑ 112 Drew Bledsoe	1.25	.35
❑ 113 Darrell Jackson	1.00	.30
❑ 114 Stephen Davis	1.00	.30
❑ 115 Doug Johnson	.40	.12
❑ 116 Brett Favre	3.00	.90
❑ 117 Darren Howard	.40	.12
❑ 118 Cade McNown	.40	.12
❑ 119 Steve McNair	1.00	.30
❑ 120 James Allen	.60	.18
❑ 121 Sylvester Morris	.40	.12
❑ 122 J.R. Redmond	.40	.12
❑ 123 Jacquez Green	.40	.12
❑ 124 Champ Bailey	.60	.18
❑ 125 Eddie George	1.00	.30
❑ 126 Michael Vick JSY RC	60.00	18.00
❑ 127 David Terrell JSY RC	12.00	3.60
❑ 128 Deuce McAllister JSY RC	25.00	7.50
❑ 129 Koren Robinson JSY RC	15.00	4.50
❑ 130 Rod Gardner JSY RC	12.00	3.60
❑ 131 Chris Chambers JSY RC	15.00	4.50
❑ 132 Santana Moss JSY RC	20.00	6.00
❑ 133 Reggie Wayne JSY RC	20.00	6.00
❑ 134 Quincy Morgan JSY RC	12.00	3.60
❑ 135 Rudi Johnson JSY RC	25.00	7.50
❑ 136 Robert Ferguson JSY RC	12.00	3.60
❑ 137 Todd Heap JSY RC	12.00	3.60
❑ 138 Michael Bennett JSY RC	25.00	7.50
❑ 139 Jesse Palmer JSY RC	12.00	3.60
❑ 140 Drew Brees JSY RC	25.00	7.50
❑ 141 James Jackson JSY RC	12.00	3.60

☐ 142 Chris Weinke JSY RC	12.00	3.60
☐ 143 L.Tomlinson JSY RC	40.00	12.00
☐ 144 Chad Johnson JSY RC	25.00	7.50
☐ 145 Quincy Carter JSY RC	12.00	3.60
☐ 146 Freddie Mitchell JSY RC	12.00	3.60
☐ 147 Anthony Thomas JSY RC	20.00	6.00
☐ 148 Travis Henry JSY RC	15.00	4.50
☐ 149 Snoop Minnis JSY RC	12.00	3.60
☐ 150 M.Tuiasosopo JSY RC	12.00	3.60
☐ 151 Travis Minor JSY RC	12.00	3.60
☐ 152 Mike McMahon JSY RC	12.00	3.60
☐ 153 Josh Heupel JSY RC	12.00	3.60
☐ 154 Sage Rosenfels JSY RC	12.00	3.60
☐ 155 Kevan Barlow JSY RC	12.00	3.60

2002 Fleer Genuine

	Nm-Mt	Ex-Mt
COMP.SET w/o SP's (125)	20.00	6.00
☐ 1 Brian Urlacher	1.50	.45
☐ 2 Keyshawn Johnson	1.00	.30
☐ 3 Donovan McNabb	1.25	.35
☐ 4 Tim Couch	.60	.18
☐ 5 Junior Seau	1.00	.30
☐ 6 Eric Moulds	.60	.18
☐ 7 Randy Moss	2.00	.60
☐ 8 Rod Smith	.60	.18
☐ 9 Torry Holt	1.00	.30
☐ 10 Plaxico Burress	1.00	.30
☐ 11 Kordell Stewart	.60	.18
☐ 12 Brett Favre	2.50	.75
☐ 13 Stephen Davis	.60	.18
☐ 14 Santana Moss	1.00	.30
☐ 15 Kurt Warner	1.00	.30
☐ 16 Jake Plummer	.60	.18
☐ 17 Jimmy Smith	.60	.18
☐ 18 Quincy Carter	.60	.18
☐ 19 Marvin Harrison	1.00	.30
☐ 20 Fred Taylor	1.00	.30
☐ 21 Warren Sapp	.60	.18
☐ 22 Curtis Martin	1.00	.30
☐ 23 Isaac Bruce	1.00	.30
☐ 24 Drew Brees	1.00	.30
☐ 25 Ray Lewis	1.00	.30
☐ 26 Hines Ward	1.00	.30
☐ 27 Koren Robinson	.60	.18
☐ 28 Jevon Kearse	.60	.18
☐ 29 Jerry Rice	2.00	.60
☐ 30 Jeff Garcia	1.00	.30
☐ 31 Edgerrin James	1.25	.35
☐ 32 Warrick Dunn	1.00	.30
☐ 33 Ricky Williams	1.00	.30
☐ 34 Doug Flutie	1.00	.30
☐ 35 Brian Griese	1.00	.30
☐ 36 Chad Pennington	1.25	.35
☐ 37 Duce Staley	1.00	.30
☐ 38 Eddie George	1.00	.30
☐ 39 Daunte Culpepper	1.00	.30
☐ 40 Jerome Bettis	1.00	.30
☐ 41 Michael Vick	3.00	.90
☐ 42 Tim Brown	1.00	.30
☐ 43 Tom Brady	2.50	.75
☐ 44 Steve McNair	1.00	.30
☐ 45 Terrell Owens	1.00	.30
☐ 46 Corey Dillon	.60	.18
☐ 47 Peyton Manning	2.00	.60
☐ 48 Rich Gannon	1.00	.30
☐ 49 Emmitt Smith	2.50	.75
☐ 50 David Boston	1.00	.30
☐ 51 Mark Brunell	1.00	.30
☐ 52 Ron Dayne	.60	.18
☐ 53 Wayne Chrebet	.60	.18
☐ 54 Terrell Davis	1.00	.30
☐ 55 Zach Thomas	1.00	.30
☐ 56 Kevin Johnson	.60	.18
☐ 57 Marshall Faulk	1.00	.30
☐ 58 Anthony Thomas	1.00	.30
☐ 59 Deuce McAllister	1.25	.35
☐ 60 LaDainian Tomlinson	1.50	.45
☐ 61 Thomas Jones	.60	.18
☐ 62 Ahman Green	1.00	.30
☐ 63 Aaron Brooks	1.00	.30
☐ 64 Courtney Brown	.60	.18
☐ 65 Chris Chambers	1.00	.30
☐ 66 Jamal Lewis	1.00	.30
☐ 67 David Terrell	1.00	.30
☐ 68 Tony Gonzalez	.60	.18
☐ 69 Laveranues Coles	.60	.18
☐ 70 Shaun Alexander	1.00	.30
☐ 71 Chris Weinke	.60	.18
☐ 72 Antowain Smith	.60	.18
☐ 73 Rod Gardner	.60	.18
☐ 74 Mike Anderson	1.00	.30
☐ 75 Antonio Freeman	1.00	.30
☐ 76 Kevan Barlow	.60	.18
☐ 77 Jim Miller	.60	.18
☐ 78 Bill Schroeder	.60	.18
☐ 79 Joe Horn	.60	.18
☐ 80 Travis Henry	1.00	.30
☐ 81 Michael Bennett	.60	.18
☐ 82 Michael Pittman	.40	.12
☐ 83 Keenan McCardell	.40	.12
☐ 84 Amani Toomer	.60	.18
☐ 85 Peerless Price	.60	.18
☐ 86 Az-Zahir Hakim	.40	.12
☐ 87 James Thrash	.60	.18
☐ 88 Drew Bledsoe	1.25	.35
☐ 89 Mike McMahon	1.00	.30
☐ 90 Derrick Mason	.60	.18
☐ 91 Joey Galloway	.60	.18
☐ 92 Snoop Minnis	.40	.12
☐ 93 Ed McCaffrey	1.00	.30
☐ 94 Johnnie Morton	.60	.18
☐ 95 Richard Huntley	.40	.12
☐ 96 Troy Brown	.60	.18
☐ 97 Shane Matthews	.40	.12
☐ 98 Muhsin Muhammad	.60	.18
☐ 99 David Patten	.40	.12
☐ 100 Jon Kitna	.60	.18
☐ 101 Terrence Wilkins	.40	.12
☐ 102 Kerry Collins	.60	.18
☐ 103 Tiki Barber	.60	.18
☐ 104 Fred Beasley	.40	.12
☐ 105 Trent Dilfer	.60	.18
☐ 106 Chris Redman	.40	.12
☐ 107 Jay Fiedler	.60	.18
☐ 108 Charlie Garner	.60	.18
☐ 109 Mike Alstott	1.00	.30
☐ 110 Darnay Scott	.40	.12
☐ 111 Garrison Hearst	.60	.18
☐ 112 James Jackson	.40	.12
☐ 113 Darrell Jackson	.60	.18
☐ 114 Freddie Mitchell	.60	.18
☐ 115 Brad Johnson	.60	.18
☐ 116 Olandis Gary	.60	.18
☐ 117 Priest Holmes	1.25	.35
☐ 118 Vinny Testaverde	.60	.18
☐ 119 Takeo Spikes	.40	.12
☐ 120 Marty Booker	.60	.18
☐ 121 Curtis Conway	.40	.12
☐ 122 Jacquez Green	.40	.12
☐ 123 Champ Bailey	.60	.18
☐ 124 Trent Green	.60	.18
☐ 125 Terry Glenn	.60	.18
☐ 126 Ladell Betts RC	6.00	1.80
☐ 127 DeShaun Foster RC	6.00	1.80
☐ 128 Maurice Morris RC	6.00	1.80
☐ 129 Chester Taylor RC	6.00	1.80
☐ 130 Randy McMichael RC	10.00	3.00
☐ 131 Verron Haynes RC	6.00	1.80
☐ 132 Cliff Russell RC	5.00	1.50
☐ 133 Brandon Doman RC	6.00	1.80
☐ 134 Ashley Lelie RC	12.00	3.60
☐ 135 Roy Williams RC	15.00	4.50
☐ 136 Antonio Bryant RC	6.00	1.80
☐ 137 William Green RC	10.00	3.00
☐ 138 Clinton Portis RC	20.00	6.00
☐ 139 J.T. O'Sullivan RC	5.00	1.50
☐ 140 Javon Walker RC	12.00	3.60
☐ 141 Randy Fasani RC	5.00	1.50
☐ 142 Chad Hutchinson RC	6.00	1.80
☐ 143 Ben Leber RC	6.00	1.80
☐ 144 Tim Carter RC	5.00	1.50
☐ 145 Jason McAddley RC	5.00	1.50
☐ 146 Donte Stallworth RC	12.00	3.60
☐ 147 Andre Davis RC	6.00	1.80
☐ 148 Julius Peppers RC	12.00	3.60
☐ 149 Patrick Ramsey RC	12.00	3.60
☐ 150 Deion Branch RC	12.00	3.60
☐ 151 Jonathan Wells RC	6.00	1.80
☐ 152 Jabar Gaffney RC	6.00	1.80
☐ 153 Josh McCown RC	8.00	2.40
☐ 154 Jeremy Shockey RC	20.00	6.00
☐ 155 Eric Crouch RC	10.00	3.00
☐ 156 Joey Harrington RC	20.00	6.00
☐ 157 Jerramy Stevens RC	6.00	1.80
☐ 158 T.J. Duckett RC	10.00	3.00
☐ 159 Ron Johnson RC	5.00	1.50
☐ 160 Josh Reed RC	6.00	1.80
☐ 161 Reche Caldwell RC	6.00	1.80
☐ 162 Lamar Gordon RC	6.00	1.80
☐ 163 David Garrard RC	6.00	1.80
☐ 164 Freddie Milons RC	5.00	1.50
☐ 165 Marquise Walker RC	5.00	1.50
☐ 166 Rohan Davey RC	6.00	1.80
☐ 167 Coy Wire RC	6.00	1.80
☐ 168 Quentin Jammer RC	6.00	1.80
☐ 169 Omar Easy RC	6.00	1.80
☐ 170 Kurt Kittner RC	5.00	1.50
☐ 171 Travis Stephens RC	5.00	1.50
☐ 172 David Carr RC	20.00	6.00
☐ 173 Daniel Graham RC	6.00	1.80
☐ 174 Antwaan Randle El RC	8.00	2.40
☐ 175 Brian Westbrook RC	10.00	3.00

2004 Fleer Genuine

	Nm-Mt	Ex-Mt
76-100 ROOKIE PRINT RUN 500 SER.#'d SETS		
☐ 1 Anquan Boldin	1.00	.30
☐ 2 Rod Smith	.60	.18
☐ 3 Randy Moss	1.25	.35
☐ 4 Drew Brees	1.00	.30
☐ 5 Jamal Lewis	1.00	.30
☐ 6 Ahman Green	1.00	.30
☐ 7 Aaron Brooks	.60	.18
☐ 8 Torry Holt	1.00	.30
☐ 9 Steve Smith	.60	.18
☐ 10 Marvin Harrison	1.00	.30
☐ 11 Santana Moss	.60	.18
☐ 12 Eddie George	.60	.18
☐ 13 Lee Suggs	1.00	.30
☐ 14 Randy McMichael	.40	.12
☐ 15 Hines Ward	1.00	.30
☐ 16 Drew Bledsoe	1.00	.30
☐ 17 Andre Johnson	1.00	.30
☐ 18 Jeremy Shockey	1.00	.30
☐ 19 Mike Alstott	.60	.18
☐ 20 Chad Johnson	.60	.18
☐ 21 Priest Holmes	1.25	.35
☐ 22 Brian Westbrook	.60	.18
☐ 23 Rudi Johnson	.60	.18
☐ 24 Keyshawn Johnson	.60	.18
☐ 25 Chris Chambers	.60	.18
☐ 26 LaDainian Tomlinson	1.00	.30
☐ 27 Ray Lewis	1.00	.30
☐ 28 Brett Favre	2.50	.75
☐ 29 Deuce McAllister	1.00	.30
☐ 30 Marshall Faulk	1.00	.30

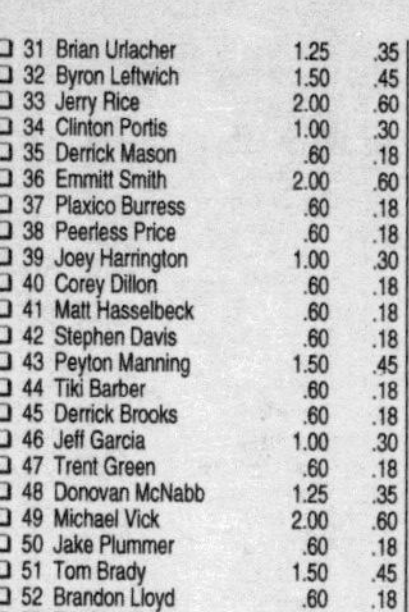

❑ 31 Brian Urlacher	1.25	.35
❑ 32 Byron Leftwich	1.50	.45
❑ 33 Jerry Rice	2.00	.60
❑ 34 Clinton Portis	1.00	.30
❑ 35 Derrick Mason	.60	.18
❑ 36 Emmitt Smith	2.00	.60
❑ 37 Plaxico Burress	.60	.18
❑ 38 Peerless Price	.60	.18
❑ 39 Joey Harrington	1.00	.30
❑ 40 Corey Dillon	.60	.18
❑ 41 Matt Hasselbeck	.60	.18
❑ 42 Stephen Davis	.60	.18
❑ 43 Peyton Manning	1.50	.45
❑ 44 Tiki Barber	.60	.18
❑ 45 Derrick Brooks	.60	.18
❑ 46 Jeff Garcia	1.00	.30
❑ 47 Trent Green	.60	.18
❑ 48 Donovan McNabb	1.25	.35
❑ 49 Michael Vick	2.00	.60
❑ 50 Jake Plummer	.60	.18
❑ 51 Tom Brady	1.50	.45
❑ 52 Brandon Lloyd	.60	.18
❑ 53 Eric Moulds	.60	.18
❑ 54 David Carr	1.00	.30
❑ 55 Joe Horn	.60	.18
❑ 56 Isaac Bruce	.60	.18
❑ 57 Rex Grossman	1.00	.30
❑ 58 Fred Taylor	.60	.18
❑ 59 Rich Gannon	.60	.18
❑ 60 Laveranues Coles	.60	.18
❑ 61 T.J. Duckett	.60	.18
❑ 62 Charles Rogers	.60	.18
❑ 63 Deion Branch	1.00	.30
❑ 64 Shaun Alexander	1.00	.30
❑ 65 Jake Delhomme	1.00	.30
❑ 66 Edgerrin James	1.00	.30
❑ 67 Chad Pennington	1.25	.35
❑ 68 Steve McNair	1.00	.30
❑ 69 Carson Palmer	1.25	.35
❑ 70 Tony Gonzalez	.60	.18
❑ 71 Terrell Owens	1.00	.30
❑ 72 Josh McCown	.60	.18
❑ 73 Ashley Lelie	.60	.18
❑ 74 Daunte Culpepper	1.00	.30
❑ 75 Kevan Barlow	.60	.18
❑ 76 Eli Manning RC	20.00	6.00
❑ 77 Larry Fitzgerald RC	12.00	3.60
❑ 78 Philip Rivers RC	12.00	3.60
❑ 79 Kellen Winslow RC	10.00	3.00
❑ 80 Roy Williams RC	12.00	3.60
❑ 81 Reggie Williams RC	5.00	1.50
❑ 82 Ben Roethlisberger RC	40.00	12.00
❑ 83 Lee Evans RC	6.00	1.80
❑ 84 Michael Clayton RC	10.00	3.00
❑ 85 J.P. Losman RC	10.00	3.00
❑ 86 Steven Jackson RC	12.00	3.60
❑ 87 Chris Perry RC	8.00	2.40
❑ 88 Michael Jenkins RC	4.00	1.20
❑ 89 Kevin Jones RC	12.00	3.60
❑ 90 Rashaun Woods RC	5.00	1.50
❑ 91 Ben Watson RC	4.00	1.20
❑ 92 Ben Troupe RC	4.00	1.20
❑ 93 Tatum Bell RC	6.00	1.80
❑ 94 Julius Jones RC	15.00	4.50
❑ 95 Devery Henderson RC	3.00	.90
❑ 96 Darius Watts RC	5.00	1.50
❑ 97 Greg Jones RC	4.00	1.20
❑ 98 Keary Colbert RC	5.00	1.50
❑ 99 Derrick Hamilton RC	3.00	.90
❑ 100 Drew Henson RC	10.00	3.00

2001 Fleer Hot Prospects

	Nm-Mt	Ex-Mt
COMP.SET w/o SP's (100)	25.00	7.50
❑ 1 Aaron Brooks	1.00	.30
❑ 2 Tim Couch	.60	.18
❑ 3 Jeff George	.60	.18
❑ 4 Brett Favre	3.00	.90
❑ 5 Donovan McNabb	1.25	.35
❑ 6 Ray Lucas	.40	.12
❑ 7 Doug Flutie	1.00	.30
❑ 8 Mark Brunell	1.00	.30
❑ 9 Steve McNair	1.00	.30
❑ 10 Trent Green	1.00	.30
❑ 11 Daunte Culpepper	1.00	.30
❑ 12 Rich Gannon	1.00	.30
❑ 13 Kurt Warner	2.00	.60

❑ 14 Brian Griese	1.00	.30
❑ 15 Kerry Collins	.60	.18
❑ 16 Vinny Testaverde	.60	.18
❑ 17 David Boston	1.00	.30
❑ 18 Peyton Manning	2.50	.75
❑ 19 Keyshawn Johnson	1.00	.30
❑ 20 Tim Biakabutuka	.60	.18
❑ 22 Emmitt Smith	2.00	.60
❑ 23 Terry Glenn	.60	.18
❑ 24 Tony Gonzalez	.60	.18
❑ 25 Charlie Garner	.60	.18
❑ 26 Lamar Smith	.60	.18
❑ 27 Eddie George	1.00	.30
❑ 28 Fred Taylor	1.00	.30
❑ 29 Marvin Harrison	1.00	.30
❑ 30 Terrell Davis	1.00	.30
❑ 31 Marcus Robinson	1.00	.30
❑ 32 Edgerrin James	1.25	.35
❑ 33 Ed McCaffrey	1.00	.30
❑ 34 Ricky Williams	1.00	.30
❑ 36 Jerome Bettis	1.00	.30
❑ 37 Shaun Alexander	1.25	.35
❑ 38 Mike Anderson	1.00	.30
❑ 39 Keenan McCardell	.40	.12
❑ 40 Mike Alstott	1.00	.30
❑ 41 Terrell Fletcher	.40	.12
❑ 42 Kevin Johnson	.60	.18
❑ 43 Wesley Walls	.40	.12
❑ 44 Derrick Mason	.60	.18
❑ 45 Sammy Morris	.40	.12
❑ 46 Joey Galloway	.60	.18
❑ 47 Sylvester Morris	.40	.12
❑ 48 Stephen Davis	1.00	.30
❑ 49 Terrell Owens	1.00	.30
❑ 50 Troy Edwards	.40	.12
❑ 51 Amani Toomer	.60	.18
❑ 52 Ray Lewis	1.00	.30
❑ 53 Terance Mathis	.60	.18
❑ 54 Brian Urlacher	1.50	.45
❑ 55 Junior Seau	1.00	.30
❑ 56 Rocket Ismail	.60	.18
❑ 57 Wayne Chrebet	.60	.18
❑ 58 Peter Warrick	1.00	.30
❑ 59 Andre Rison	.60	.18
❑ 60 Desmond Howard	.40	.12
❑ 61 Eric Moulds	.60	.18
❑ 62 Jerry Rice	2.00	.60
❑ 63 Stephen Alexander	.40	.12
❑ 64 Isaac Bruce	1.00	.30
❑ 65 Travis Prentice	.40	.12
❑ 66 James Stewart	.60	.18
❑ 67 Jamal Anderson	1.00	.30
❑ 68 Ricky Watters	.40	.12
❑ 69 Jamal Lewis	1.50	.45
❑ 70 Priest Holmes	1.25	.35
❑ 71 Ahman Green	1.00	.30
❑ 72 Marshall Faulk	1.25	.35
❑ 73 Warrick Dunn	1.00	.30
❑ 74 Curtis Martin	1.00	.30
❑ 75 Corey Dillon	1.00	.30
❑ 76 Ron Dayne	1.00	.30
❑ 77 Thomas Jones	.60	.18
❑ 78 Duce Staley	1.00	.30
❑ 79 Tiki Barber	.60	.18
❑ 80 Cris Carter	1.00	.30
❑ 81 Tim Brown	1.00	.30
❑ 82 Jimmy Smith	.60	.18
❑ 83 Elvis Grbac	.60	.18
❑ 84 Randy Moss	2.00	.60
❑ 85 Tim Dwight	1.00	.30
❑ 86 Antonio Freeman	1.00	.30
❑ 87 Muhsin Muhammad	.60	.18
❑ 88 Torry Holt	1.00	.30
❑ 89 Frank Wycheck	.40	.12
❑ 90 Jake Plummer	.60	.18
❑ 91 Brad Johnson	1.00	.30
❑ 92 Chris Chandler	.60	.18
❑ 93 Drew Bledsoe	1.25	.35
❑ 94 Rob Johnson	.60	.18
❑ 95 Matt Hasselbeck	.60	.18
❑ 96 Jon Kitna	.60	.18
❑ 97 Kordell Stewart	.60	.18
❑ 98 Charlie Batch	1.00	.30
❑ 99 Cade McNown	.40	.12
❑ 100 Jeff Garcia	1.00	.30
❑ 101 Quincy Morgan RC	3.00	.90
❑ 102 Jesse Palmer RC	3.00	.90
❑ 103 Reggie Wayne RC	5.00	1.50
❑ 104 Deuce McAllister RC	8.00	2.40
❑ 105 Chad Johnson RC	6.00	1.80
❑ 106 Chris Weinke RC	3.00	.90
❑ 107 Michael Bennett RC	6.00	1.80
❑ 108 Rod Gardner RC	3.00	.90
❑ 109 Michael Vick RC	20.00	6.00
❑ 110 Anthony Thomas RC	5.00	1.50
❑ 111 Santana Moss RC	5.00	1.50
❑ 112 Kevan Barlow RC	3.00	.90
❑ 113 Koren Robinson RC	4.00	1.20
❑ 114 Rudi Johnson RC	6.00	1.80
❑ 115 Josh Heupel RC	3.00	.90
❑ 116 James Jackson RC	3.00	.90
❑ 117 Freddie Mitchell RC	3.00	.90
❑ 118 LaDainian Tomlinson RC	10.00	3.00
❑ 119 Marques Tuiasosopo RC	3.00	.90
❑ 120 Drew Brees RC	6.00	1.80
❑ 121 David Terrell RC	3.00	.90
❑ 122 Chris Chambers RC	4.00	1.20
❑ 123 Mike McMahon RC	3.00	.90
❑ 124 Robert Ferguson RC	3.00	.90
❑ 125 Justin Smith RC	3.00	.90
❑ 126 Leonard Davis RC	2.00	.60
❑ 127 Todd Heap RC	3.00	.90
❑ 128 Dan Morgan RC	3.00	.90
❑ 129 Gerard Warren RC	3.00	.90
❑ 130 Travis Henry RC	4.00	1.20
❑ 131 Travis Minor RC	2.00	.60
❑ 132 Richard Seymour RC	3.00	.90
❑ 133 Quincy Carter RC	3.00	.90
❑ 134 Snoop Minnis RC	2.00	.60
❑ 135 Sage Rosenfels RC	3.00	.90
❑ CL1 Checklist	.10	.03

2002 Fleer Hot Prospects

	Nm-Mt	Ex-Mt
COMP.SET w/o SP's (80)	25.00	7.50
❑ 1 Donovan McNabb	1.50	.45
❑ 2 Drew Brees	1.25	.35
❑ 3 Curtis Martin	1.25	.35
❑ 4 Priest Holmes	1.50	.45
❑ 5 Quincy Carter	.75	.23
❑ 6 Chris Weinke	.75	.23
❑ 7 Marshall Faulk	1.25	.35
❑ 8 Jake Plummer	.75	.23
❑ 9 Tom Brady	3.00	.90
❑ 10 Ahman Green	1.25	.35
❑ 11 Brian Urlacher	2.00	.60
❑ 12 Keyshawn Johnson	1.25	.35
❑ 13 Jerome Bettis	1.25	.35
❑ 14 Tiki Barber	.75	.23
❑ 15 Edgerrin James	1.50	.45
❑ 16 Jamal Lewis	1.25	.35

❑ 17 Terrell Owens	1.25	.35
❑ 18 Joe Horn	.75	.23
❑ 19 Daunte Culpepper	1.25	.35
❑ 20 Terrell Davis	1.25	.35
❑ 21 Fred Taylor	1.25	.35
❑ 22 Emmitt Smith	3.00	.90
❑ 23 Jamal Anderson	.75	.23
❑ 24 Garrison Hearst	.75	.23
❑ 25 Chad Pennington	1.50	.45
❑ 26 Michael Bennett	.75	.23
❑ 27 James Allen	.75	.23
❑ 28 Marty Booker	.50	.15
❑ 29 Warren Sapp	.75	.23
❑ 30 Jerry Rice	2.50	.75
❑ 31 Antowain Smith	.75	.23
❑ 32 Marvin Harrison	1.25	.35
❑ 33 Tim Couch	.75	.23
❑ 34 Stephen Davis	.75	.23
❑ 35 Kordell Stewart	.75	.23
❑ 36 Tony Gonzalez	.75	.23
❑ 37 Mike McMahon	1.25	.35
❑ 38 Eric Moulds	.75	.23
❑ 39 Kurt Warner	1.25	.35
❑ 40 Ricky Williams	1.25	.35
❑ 41 Michael Strahan	.75	.23
❑ 42 Trent Green	.75	.23
❑ 43 Brian Griese	1.25	.35
❑ 44 David Boston	1.25	.35
❑ 45 LaDainian Tomlinson	2.00	.60
❑ 46 Tim Brown	1.25	.35
❑ 47 Deuce McAllister	1.50	.45
❑ 48 Jamie Sharper	.50	.15
❑ 49 Rod Gardner	.75	.23
❑ 50 Isaac Bruce	1.25	.35
❑ 51 Freddie Mitchell	.75	.23
❑ 52 Kerry Collins	.75	.23
❑ 53 Mark Brunell	1.25	.35
❑ 54 Corey Dillon	.75	.23
❑ 55 Steve McNair	1.25	.35
❑ 56 Aaron Brooks	1.25	.35
❑ 57 Chris Chambers	1.25	.35
❑ 58 Bill Schroeder	.75	.23
❑ 59 Ray Lewis	1.25	.35
❑ 60 Shaun Alexander	1.25	.35
❑ 61 Kevin Johnson	.75	.23
❑ 62 Michael Vick	4.00	1.20
❑ 63 Jeff Garcia	1.25	.35
❑ 64 Laveranues Coles	.75	.23
❑ 65 Jimmy Smith	.75	.23
❑ 66 Brett Favre	3.00	.90
❑ 67 Anthony Thomas	1.25	.35
❑ 68 Torry Holt	1.25	.35
❑ 69 Duce Staley	1.25	.35
❑ 70 Randy Moss	2.50	.75
❑ 71 Peyton Manning	2.50	.75
❑ 72 Peter Warrick	.75	.23
❑ 73 Eddie George	1.25	.35
❑ 74 Plaxico Burress	.75	.23
❑ 75 Troy Brown	.75	.23
❑ 76 Rod Smith	.75	.23
❑ 77 Drew Bledsoe	1.50	.45
❑ 78 Darrell Jackson	.75	.23
❑ 79 Rich Gannon	1.25	.35
❑ 80 Jay Fiedler	.75	.23
❑ 81 David Carr/250 RC	60.00	18.00
❑ 82 Andre Davis JSY RC	10.00	3.00
❑ 83 Daniel Graham JSY RC	10.00	3.00
❑ 84 Ron Johnson JSY RC	8.00	2.40
❑ 85 Julius Peppers JSY RC	20.00	6.00
❑ 86 Josh Reed JSY RC	10.00	3.00
❑ 87 Travis Stephens JSY RC	8.00	2.40
❑ 88 Mike Williams JSY RC	8.00	2.40
❑ 89 Antonio Bryant JSY RC	10.00	3.00
❑ 90 Eric Crouch JSY RC	15.00	4.50
❑ 91 DeShaun Foster JSY RC	10.00	3.00
❑ 92 Joey Harrington JSY RC	25.00	7.50
❑ 93 Josh McCown JSY RC	15.00	4.50
❑ 94 Patrick Ramsey JSY RC	20.00	6.00
❑ 95 Jeremy Shockey JSY RC	25.00	7.50
❑ 96 Marquise Walker JSY RC	8.00	2.40
❑ 97 Reche Caldwell JSY RC	10.00	3.00
❑ 98 Rohan Davey JSY RC	10.00	3.00
❑ 99 Jabar Gaffney JSY RC	10.00	3.00
❑ 100 David Garrard JSY RC	10.00	3.00
❑ 101 Maurice Morris JSY RC	10.00	3.00
❑ 102 Antwaan Randle El JSY RC	12.00	3.60
❑ 103 Donte Stallworth JSY RC	20.00	6.00
❑ 104 Roy Williams JSY RC	25.00	7.50
❑ 105 Ladell Betts JSY RC	10.00	3.00
❑ 106 Tim Carter JSY RC	8.00	2.40
❑ 107 T.J. Duckett JSY RC	20.00	6.00
❑ 108 William Green JSY RC	20.00	6.00
❑ 109 Ashley Lelie JSY RC	20.00	6.00
❑ 110 Clinton Portis JSY RC	25.00	7.50
❑ 111 Cliff Russell JSY RC	8.00	2.40
❑ 112 Javon Walker JSY RC	20.00	6.00

2003 Fleer Hot Prospects

	MINT	NRMT
COMP.SET w/o SP's (80)	20.00	9.00
❑ 1 Emmitt Smith	2.50	1.10
❑ 2 Terrell Owens	1.00	.45
❑ 3 Tiki Barber	.60	.25
❑ 4 Trent Green	.60	.25
❑ 5 Quincy Morgan	.60	.25
❑ 6 Eric Moulds	.60	.25
❑ 7 Simeon Rice	.60	.25
❑ 8 Hines Ward	1.00	.45
❑ 9 Michael Bennett	.60	.25
❑ 10 Donald Driver	.60	.25
❑ 11 Stephen Davis	.60	.25
❑ 12 Steve McNair	1.00	.45
❑ 13 David Boston	.60	.25
❑ 14 Deuce McAllister	1.00	.45
❑ 15 Marvin Harrison	1.00	.45
❑ 16 Peerless Price	.60	.25
❑ 17 Matt Hasselbeck	.60	.25
❑ 18 Jerry Rice	2.00	.90
❑ 19 Junior Seau	1.00	.45
❑ 20 Clinton Portis	1.50	.70
❑ 21 Fred Taylor	1.00	.45
❑ 22 William Green	.60	.25
❑ 23 Warrick Dunn	.60	.25
❑ 24 Koren Robinson	.60	.25
❑ 25 Jeremy Shockey	1.50	.70
❑ 26 Chris Chambers	1.00	.45
❑ 27 Brett Favre	2.50	1.10
❑ 28 Julius Peppers	1.00	.45
❑ 29 Eddie George	.60	.25
❑ 30 Todd Pinkston	.60	.25
❑ 31 Tom Brady	1.50	.70
❑ 32 Edgerrin James	1.00	.45
❑ 33 Chad Johnson	.60	.25
❑ 34 Laveranues Coles	.60	.25
❑ 35 LaDainian Tomlinson	1.00	.45
❑ 36 Priest Holmes	1.25	.55
❑ 37 Shannon Sharpe	.60	.25
❑ 38 Jamal Lewis	1.00	.45
❑ 39 Warren Sapp	.60	.25
❑ 40 Tim Brown	1.00	.45
❑ 41 Kerry Collins	.60	.25
❑ 42 Jimmy Smith	.60	.25
❑ 43 Chad Hutchinson	.60	.25
❑ 44 Marcel Shipp	.60	.25
❑ 45 Jeff Garcia	1.00	.45
❑ 46 Donovan McNabb	1.25	.55
❑ 47 Randy Moss	1.50	.70
❑ 48 Ahman Green	1.00	.45
❑ 49 Travis Henry	.60	.25
❑ 50 Brad Johnson	.60	.25
❑ 51 Tommy Maddox	1.00	.45
❑ 52 Aaron Brooks	1.00	.45
❑ 53 Peyton Manning	1.50	.70
❑ 54 Brian Urlacher	1.50	.70
❑ 55 Rod Gardner	.60	.25
❑ 56 Chad Pennington	1.25	.55
❑ 57 Ricky Williams	1.00	.45
❑ 58 James Stewart	.60	.25
❑ 59 Todd Heap	.60	.25
❑ 60 Marshall Faulk	1.00	.45
❑ 61 Corey Dillon	.60	.25
❑ 62 Michael Vick	2.50	1.10
❑ 63 Shaun Alexander	1.00	.45
❑ 64 Curtis Martin	1.00	.45
❑ 65 Mark Brunell	.60	.25
❑ 66 Joey Harrington	1.50	.70
❑ 67 Drew Bledsoe	1.00	.45
❑ 68 Keyshawn Johnson	1.00	.45
❑ 69 Jerome Bettis	1.00	.45
❑ 70 Daunte Culpepper	1.00	.45
❑ 71 David Carr	1.50	.70
❑ 72 Marty Booker	.60	.25
❑ 73 Patrick Ramsey	1.00	.45
❑ 74 Drew Brees	1.00	.45
❑ 75 Donte Stallworth	1.00	.45
❑ 76 Jake Plummer	.60	.25
❑ 77 Ray Lewis	1.00	.45
❑ 78 Kurt Warner	1.00	.45
❑ 79 Rich Gannon	.60	.25
❑ 80 Tony Gonzalez	.60	.25
❑ 92 Dallas Clark JSY RC	8.00	3.60
❑ 93 Terence Newman JSY RC	15.00	6.75
❑ 94 Rex Grossman JSY RC	20.00	9.00
❑ 95 Kelley Washington JSY RC	10.00	4.50
❑ 96 Kyle Boller JSY RC	15.00	6.75
❑ 97 Carson Palmer JSY RC	25.00	11.00
❑ 98 Charles Rogers JSY RC	10.00	4.50
❑ 99 Chris Simms JSY RC	15.00	6.75
❑ 100 Larry Johnson JSY RC	15.00	6.75
❑ 101 Andre Johnson JSY RC	20.00	9.00
❑ 102 Taylor Jacobs JSY RC	8.00	3.60
❑ 103 Byron Leftwich JSY RC	25.00	11.00
❑ 110 Tyrone Calico RC	6.00	2.70
❑ 111 Billy McMullen RC	4.00	1.80
❑ 112 Jerome McDougle RC	5.00	2.20
❑ 113 Willis McGahee RC	12.00	5.50
❑ 114 Anquan Boldin RC	12.00	5.50
❑ 115 Artose Pinner RC	5.00	2.20
❑ 116 Kevin Williams RC	5.00	2.20
❑ 117 Bethel Johnson RC	8.00	3.60
❑ 118 Quentin Griffin RC	12.00	5.50
❑ 119 Nate Burleson RC	8.00	3.60
❑ 120 DeWayne Robertson RC	5.00	2.20

2004 Fleer Hot Prospects

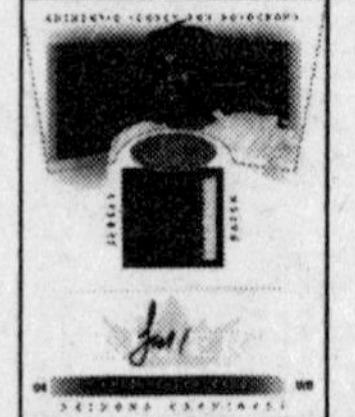

	Nm-Mt	Ex-Mt
COMP.SET w/o SP's (70)	20.00	6.00

71-94 AU JSY RC ODDS 1:20H, 1:840R
95-102 JSY RC ODDS 1:42H, 1:420R
95-102 JSY RC PRINT RUN 350 #'d SETS
103-112 ROOKIE ODDS 1:18H, 1:1440R
103-112 RC PRINT RUN 1000 SER. #'d SETS
UNPRICED WHITE HOTS #'d OF 1

❑ 1 Donovan McNabb	1.00	.30
❑ 2 Charlie Garner	.50	.15
❑ 3 Tim Rattay	.50	.15
❑ 4 Drew Brees	.75	.23
❑ 5 Jerry Rice	1.50	.45
❑ 6 Aaron Brooks	.50	.15
❑ 7 Chris Chambers	.50	.15
❑ 8 Byron Leftwich	1.25	.35
❑ 9 Andre Johnson	.75	.23
❑ 10 Edgerrin James	.75	.23
❑ 11 Charles Rogers	.50	.15
❑ 12 Quentin Griffin	.75	.23
❑ 13 Carson Palmer	1.00	.30
❑ 14 Ray Lewis	.75	.23
❑ 15 Clinton Portis	.75	.23

Card	Nm-Mt	Ex-Mt
❑ 16 Marc Bulger	.75	.23
❑ 17 Matt Hasselbeck	.50	.15
❑ 18 Plaxico Burress	.50	.15
❑ 19 Priest Holmes	1.00	.30
❑ 20 David Carr	.75	.23
❑ 21 Ahman Green	.75	.23
❑ 22 Roy Williams S	.50	.15
❑ 23 Travis Henry	.50	.15
❑ 24 Michael Vick	1.50	.45
❑ 25 Eddie George	.50	.15
❑ 26 Marshall Faulk	.75	.23
❑ 27 Kevan Barlow	.50	.15
❑ 28 Shaun Alexander	.75	.23
❑ 29 Hines Ward	.75	.23
❑ 30 Anquan Boldin	.75	.23
❑ 31 Chad Pennington	1.00	.30
❑ 32 Randy Moss	1.00	.30
❑ 33 Fred Taylor	.50	.15
❑ 34 Marvin Harrison	.75	.23
❑ 35 Joey Harrington	.75	.23
❑ 36 Rich Gannon	.50	.15
❑ 37 Deuce McAllister	.75	.23
❑ 38 Deion Branch	.75	.23
❑ 39 Tony Gonzalez	.50	.15
❑ 40 Brett Favre	2.00	.60
❑ 41 Keyshawn Johnson	.50	.15
❑ 42 Lee Suggs	.75	.23
❑ 43 Jake Delhomme	.75	.23
❑ 44 Rex Grossman	.75	.23
❑ 45 Drew Bledsoe	.75	.23
❑ 46 Warrick Dunn	.50	.15
❑ 47 Steve McNair	.75	.23
❑ 48 Torry Holt	.75	.23
❑ 49 Brian Westbrook	.50	.15
❑ 50 Santana Moss	.50	.15
❑ 51 Jeremy Shockey	.75	.23
❑ 52 Daunte Culpepper	.75	.23
❑ 53 Jeff Garcia	.75	.23
❑ 54 Stephen Davis	.50	.15
❑ 55 Eric Moulds	.50	.15
❑ 56 Emmitt Smith	1.50	.45
❑ 57 Keenan McCardell	.30	.09
❑ 58 LaDainian Tomlinson	.75	.23
❑ 59 Terrell Owens	.75	.23
❑ 60 Curtis Martin	.75	.23
❑ 61 Joe Horn	.50	.15
❑ 62 Tiki Barber	.50	.15
❑ 63 Tom Brady	1.25	.35
❑ 64 Ricky Williams	.75	.23
❑ 65 Peyton Manning	1.25	.35
❑ 66 Jake Plummer	.50	.15
❑ 67 Chad Johnson	.50	.15
❑ 68 Brian Urlacher	1.00	.30
❑ 69 Jamal Lewis	.75	.23
❑ 70 Laveranues Coles	.50	.15
❑ 71 Tatum Bell JSY AU/350 RC	100.00	30.00
❑ 72 Bernard Berrian JSY AU RC/344	40.00	12.00
❑ 73 Michael Clayton JSY AU RC/350	100.00	30.00
❑ 74 Lee Evans JSY AU/350 RC	80.00	24.00
❑ 75 Larry Fitzgerald JSY AU RC/140	175.00	52.50
❑ 76 Devery Henderson JSY AU RC/350	30.00	9.00
❑ 77 Drew Henson JSY AU RC/331	60.00	18.00
❑ 78 Steven Jackson JSY AU RC/300	150.00	45.00
❑ 79 Michael Jenkins JSY AU RC/349	50.00	15.00
❑ 80 Greg Jones JSY AU/289 RC	50.00	15.00
❑ 81 Kevin Jones JSY AU RC/278	150.00	45.00
❑ 82 J.P. Losman JSY AU RC/350	120.00	36.00
❑ 83 Eli Manning JSY AU/350 RC	200.00	60.00
❑ 84 Chris Perry JSY AU/350 RC	60.00	18.00
❑ 85 Philip Rivers JSY AU RC/350	150.00	45.00
❑ 86 Ben Roethlisberger JSY AU RC/150	600.00	180.00
❑ 87 Reggie Williams JSY AU RC/350	60.00	18.00
❑ 88 Roy Williams JSY AU RC/350	150.00	45.00
❑ 89 Kellen Winslow JSY AU RC/50	225.00	70.00
❑ 90 Rashaun Woods JSY AU RC/350	60.00	18.00
❑ 91 Julius Jones JSY AU RC/350	200.00	60.00
❑ 92 Luke McCown JSY AU RC EXCH	40.00	12.00
❑ 93 Keary Colbert JSY AU RC/349	50.00	15.00
❑ 94 Matt Schaub JSY AU RC/120	80.00	24.00
❑ 95 Cedric Cobbs JSY RC	15.00	4.50
❑ 96 Darius Watts JSY RC	20.00	6.00
❑ 97 DeAngelo Hall JSY RC	25.00	7.50
❑ 98 Derrick Hamilton JSY RC	12.00	3.60
❑ 99 Devard Darling JSY RC	15.00	4.50
❑ 100 Ben Troupe JSY RC	15.00	4.50
❑ 101 Mewelde Moore JSY RC	25.00	7.50
❑ 102 Ben Watson JSY RC	15.00	4.50
❑ 103 Sean Taylor RC	6.00	1.80
❑ 104 Ricky Ray RC	4.00	1.20
❑ 105 Carlos Francis RC	4.00	1.20
❑ 106 Samie Parker RC	5.00	1.50
❑ 107 Jerricho Cotchery RC	5.00	1.50
❑ 108 Ernest Wilford RC	5.00	1.50
❑ 109 Craig Krenzel RC	5.00	1.50
❑ 110 Robert Gallery RC	8.00	2.40
❑ 111 Dunta Robinson RC	5.00	1.50
❑ 112 Jonathan Vilma RC	5.00	1.50

2004 Fleer Inscribed

	Nm-Mt	Ex-Mt
COMP.SET w/o SP's (75)	25.00	7.50

76-100 RC ODDS: 1:12 HOB, 1:100 RET
76-100 RC PRINT RUN 750 SER.#'d SETS
UNPRICED RED PRINT RUN 5 SETS

Card	Nm-Mt	Ex-Mt
❑ 1 Terrell Owens	1.00	.30
❑ 2 David Carr	1.00	.30
❑ 3 Jerry Porter	.60	.18
❑ 4 Charles Rogers	.60	.18
❑ 5 Torry Holt	1.00	.30
❑ 6 Byron Leftwich	1.50	.45
❑ 7 Laveranues Coles	.60	.18
❑ 8 Edgerrin James	1.00	.30
❑ 9 Brian Urlacher	1.25	.35
❑ 10 Hines Ward	1.00	.30
❑ 11 LaDainian Tomlinson	1.00	.30
❑ 12 Ahman Green	1.00	.30
❑ 13 Kevan Barlow	.60	.18
❑ 14 Trent Green	.60	.18
❑ 15 Deuce McAllister	1.00	.30
❑ 16 Lee Suggs	1.00	.30
❑ 17 Drew Brees	1.00	.30
❑ 18 Randy Moss	1.25	.35
❑ 19 Brandon Lloyd	.60	.18
❑ 20 Jeff Garcia	1.00	.30
❑ 21 Roy Williams S	.60	.18
❑ 22 Daunte Culpepper	1.00	.30
❑ 23 Matt Hasselbeck	.60	.18
❑ 24 Keyshawn Johnson	.60	.18
❑ 25 Michael Vick	2.00	.60
❑ 26 Shaun Alexander	1.00	.30
❑ 27 Chad Pennington	1.25	.35
❑ 28 Ashley Lelie	.60	.18
❑ 29 Anquan Boldin	1.00	.30
❑ 30 Carson Palmer	1.25	.35
❑ 31 Jeremy Shockey	1.00	.30
❑ 32 Peerless Price	.60	.18
❑ 33 Chad Johnson	.60	.18
❑ 34 Tiki Barber	.60	.18
❑ 35 Warrick Dunn	.60	.18
❑ 36 Jamal Lewis	1.00	.30
❑ 37 Brian Westbrook	.60	.18
❑ 38 Stephen Davis	.60	.18
❑ 39 Steve McNair	1.00	.30
❑ 40 Donovan McNabb	1.25	.35
❑ 41 Fred Taylor	.60	.18
❑ 42 Clinton Portis	1.00	.30
❑ 43 Santana Moss	.60	.18
❑ 44 Rod Smith	.60	.18
❑ 45 Josh McCown	.60	.18
❑ 46 Ray Lewis	1.00	.30
❑ 47 Marshall Faulk	1.00	.30
❑ 48 Eric Moulds	.60	.18
❑ 49 Jerry Rice	2.00	.60
❑ 50 Jake Delhomme	1.00	.30
❑ 51 Tony Gonzalez	.60	.18
❑ 52 Aaron Brooks	.60	.18
❑ 53 Randy McMichael	.40	.12
❑ 54 David Boston	.60	.18
❑ 55 Plaxico Burress	.60	.18
❑ 56 Rich Gannon	.60	.18
❑ 57 Brett Favre	2.50	.75
❑ 58 Isaac Bruce	.60	.18
❑ 59 Tom Brady	1.50	.45
❑ 60 Priest Holmes	1.25	.35
❑ 61 Joe Horn	.60	.18
❑ 62 Troy Brown	.60	.18
❑ 63 Jake Plummer	.60	.18
❑ 64 Derrick Brooks	.60	.18
❑ 65 Marvin Harrison	1.00	.30
❑ 66 LaVar Arrington	2.00	.60
❑ 67 Drew Bledsoe	1.00	.30
❑ 68 Steve Smith	.60	.18
❑ 69 Peyton Manning	1.50	.45
❑ 70 Rex Grossman	1.00	.30
❑ 71 Corey Dillon	.60	.18
❑ 72 Mike Alstott	.60	.18
❑ 73 Andre Johnson	1.00	.30
❑ 74 Joey Harrington	1.00	.30
❑ 75 Tyrone Calico	.60	.18
❑ 76 Eli Manning RC	25.00	7.50
❑ 77 Larry Fitzgerald RC	15.00	4.50
❑ 78 Philip Rivers RC	15.00	4.50
❑ 79 Kellen Winslow RC	12.00	3.60
❑ 80 Roy Williams RC	15.00	4.50
❑ 81 Reggie Williams RC	6.00	1.80
❑ 82 Ben Roethlisberger RC	50.00	15.00
❑ 83 Lee Evans RC	8.00	2.40
❑ 84 Michael Clayton RC	12.00	3.60
❑ 85 J.P. Losman RC	12.00	3.60
❑ 86 Steven Jackson RC	15.00	4.50
❑ 87 Chris Perry RC	10.00	3.00
❑ 88 Michael Jenkins RC	5.00	1.50
❑ 89 Kevin Jones RC	15.00	4.50
❑ 90 Rashaun Woods RC	6.00	1.80
❑ 91 Ben Watson RC	5.00	1.50
❑ 92 Ben Troupe RC	5.00	1.50
❑ 93 Tatum Bell RC	8.00	2.40
❑ 94 Julius Jones RC	20.00	6.00
❑ 95 Devery Henderson RC	4.00	1.20
❑ 96 Darius Watts RC	6.00	1.80
❑ 97 Greg Jones RC	5.00	1.50
❑ 98 Keary Colbert RC	6.00	1.80
❑ 99 Derrick Hamilton RC	4.00	1.20
❑ 100 Bernard Berrian RC	5.00	1.50

2004 Fleer Inscribed Black Border Gold

Nm-Mt Ex-Mt

*STARS: 2X TO 5X BASE CARD HI
*ROOKIES: .6X TO 1.5X BASE CARD HI
STATED PRINT RUN 199 SER.#'d SETS

2004 Fleer Inscribed Autographs Purple

CARDS SER.#'d TO JERSEY NUMBER
CARDS #'d UNDER 25 NOT PRICED

Card	Nm-Mt	Ex-Mt
❑ AB Antonio Bryant/88	20.00	6.00
❑ AL Ashley Lelie/85 EXCH	20.00	6.00
❑ AV Adam Vinatieri/4		
❑ BW Brian Westbrook/36 EXCH	30.00	9.00
❑ CB Champ Bailey/21 EXCH		
❑ CC Chris Chambers/84 EXCH	20.00	6.00
❑ CJ Chad Johnson/85 EXCH	25.00	7.50
❑ DF DeShaun Foster/26		
❑ DH Dante Hall/82	25.00	7.50
❑ DS Donte Stallworth/83	25.00	7.50

	Nm-Mt	Ex-Mt
❑ JP Jerry Porter/84 EXCH	20.00	6.00
❑ JW1 Javon Walker/84 EXCH	30.00	9.00
❑ JW2 Jason Witten/82 EXCH	30.00	9.00
❑ KW Kelley Washington/87	20.00	6.00
❑ LM Luke McCown/12		
❑ SM Santana Moss/83 EXCH	20.00	6.00
❑ TC Tyrone Calico/87 EXCH	20.00	6.00
❑ WM Willis McGahee/21		

2001 Fleer Legacy

	Nm-Mt	Ex-Mt
COMP.SET w/o SP's (90)	25.00	7.50
❑ 1 Donovan McNabb	1.25	.35
❑ 2 Doug Flutie	1.00	.30
❑ 3 Amani Toomer	.60	.18
❑ 4 Jay Fiedler	1.00	.30
❑ 5 Antonio Freeman	1.00	.30
❑ 6 Jon Kitna	.60	.18
❑ 7 Jake Plummer	.60	.18
❑ 8 Ricky Watters	.60	.18
❑ 9 Jerry Rice	2.00	.60
❑ 10 Troy Brown	.60	.18
❑ 11 Jimmy Smith	.60	.18
❑ 12 Edgerrin James	1.25	.35
❑ 13 Todd Pinkston	.60	.18
❑ 14 Eric Moulds	.60	.18
❑ 15 Stephen Davis	1.00	.30
❑ 16 Matt Hasselbeck	.60	.18
❑ 17 Vinny Testaverde	.60	.18
❑ 18 Priest Holmes	1.25	.35
❑ 19 Mike Anderson	1.00	.30
❑ 20 Shane Matthews	.40	.12
❑ 21 Qadry Ismail	.60	.18
❑ 22 Torry Holt	1.00	.30
❑ 23 Duce Staley	1.00	.30
❑ 24 Ahman Green	1.00	.30
❑ 25 Corey Dillon	1.00	.30
❑ 26 Peerless Price	.60	.18
❑ 27 Steve McNair	1.00	.30
❑ 28 Junior Seau	1.00	.30
❑ 29 Doug Chapman	.40	.12
❑ 30 Mark Brunell	1.00	.30
❑ 31 Joey Galloway	.60	.18
❑ 32 James Allen	.60	.18
❑ 33 David Boston	1.00	.30
❑ 34 Marshall Faulk	1.25	.35
❑ 35 Shaun Alexander	1.25	.35
❑ 36 Wayne Chrebet	.60	.18
❑ 37 Randy Moss	2.00	.60
❑ 38 Marvin Harrison	1.00	.30
❑ 39 Tim Couch	.60	.18
❑ 40 Jamal Anderson	1.00	.30
❑ 41 Warren Sapp	.60	.18
❑ 42 Brad Johnson	1.00	.30
❑ 43 Kerry Collins	.60	.18
❑ 44 Derrick Alexander	.60	.18
❑ 45 Terrell Davis	1.00	.30
❑ 46 Tiki Barber	.60	.18
❑ 47 Trent Green	1.00	.30
❑ 48 James Stewart	.60	.18
❑ 49 Kevin Johnson	.60	.18
❑ 50 Ray Lewis	1.00	.30
❑ 51 Warrick Dunn	1.00	.30
❑ 52 Tim Brown	1.00	.30
❑ 53 Daunte Culpepper	1.00	.30
❑ 54 Fred Taylor	1.00	.30
❑ 55 Brian Griese	1.00	.30
❑ 56 Wesley Walls	.40	.12
❑ 57 Rob Johnson	.60	.18
❑ 58 Travis Taylor	.60	.18
❑ 59 Jeff Garcia	1.00	.30
❑ 60 Rich Gannon	1.00	.30
❑ 61 Cris Carter	1.00	.30
❑ 62 Peyton Manning	2.50	.75
❑ 63 Peter Warrick	1.00	.30
❑ 64 Terance Mathis	.40	.12
❑ 65 Kurt Warner	2.00	.60
❑ 66 Kordell Stewart	.60	.18
❑ 67 Aaron Brooks	1.00	.30
❑ 68 JaJuan Dawson	.40	.12
❑ 69 Elvis Grbac	.60	.18
❑ 70 Keyshawn Johnson	1.00	.30
❑ 71 Terrell Owens	1.00	.30
❑ 72 Curtis Martin	1.00	.30
❑ 73 Lamar Smith	.60	.18
❑ 74 Rod Smith	.60	.18
❑ 75 Tim Biakabutuka	.60	.18
❑ 76 Thomas Jones	.60	.18
❑ 77 Isaac Bruce	1.00	.30
❑ 78 Joe Horn	.60	.18
❑ 79 Drew Bledsoe	1.25	.35
❑ 80 Oronde Gadsden	.60	.18
❑ 81 Brett Favre	3.00	.90
❑ 82 Emmitt Smith	2.00	.60
❑ 83 Muhsin Muhammad	.60	.18
❑ 84 Eddie George	1.00	.30
❑ 85 Jerome Bettis	1.00	.30
❑ 86 Ricky Williams	1.00	.30
❑ 87 Tony Gonzalez	.60	.18
❑ 88 Germane Crowell	.40	.12
❑ 89 Brian Urlacher	1.50	.45
❑ 90 Shawn Jefferson	.40	.12
❑ 91 Michael Vick RC	50.00	15.00
❑ 92 David Terrell RC	8.00	2.40
❑ 93 Chris Chambers RC	10.00	3.00
❑ 94 Freddie Mitchell RC	8.00	2.40
❑ 95 Drew Brees RC	15.00	4.50
❑ 96 LaMont Jordan RC	10.00	3.00
❑ 97 Quincy Carter RC	8.00	2.40
❑ 98 Anthony Thomas RC	12.00	3.60
❑ 99 LaDainian Tomlinson RC	25.00	7.50
❑ 100 Santana Moss RC	12.00	3.60
❑ 101 Rod Gardner RC	8.00	2.40
❑ 102 Nick Goings RC	8.00	2.40
❑ 103 Sage Rosenfels RC	8.00	2.40
❑ 104 Mike McMahon RC	8.00	2.40
❑ 105 Snoop Minnis RC	5.00	1.50
❑ 106 Michael Bennett RC	15.00	4.50
❑ 107 Todd Heap RC	8.00	2.40
❑ 108 Kevan Barlow RC	8.00	2.40
❑ 109 Travis Henry RC	10.00	3.00
❑ 110 Jason Brookins RC	8.00	2.40
❑ 111 Rudi Johnson RC	15.00	4.50
❑ 112 Reggie Wayne RC	12.00	3.60
❑ 113 Koren Robinson RC	10.00	3.00
❑ 114 Chad Johnson RC	15.00	4.50
❑ 115 Quincy Morgan RC	8.00	2.40
❑ 116 Robert Ferguson RC	8.00	2.40
❑ 117 Chris Weinke RC	8.00	2.40
❑ 118 Jesse Palmer RC	8.00	2.40
❑ 119 James Jackson RC	8.00	2.40
❑ 120 Deuce McAllister RC	20.00	6.00

2001 Fleer Legacy Ultimate Legacy

	Nm-Mt	Ex-Mt
*STARS: 3X TO 8X BASIC CARDS		
*ROOKIES: .5X TO 1.2X		

1999 Fleer Mystique

	Nm-Mt	Ex-Mt
COMPLETE SET (160)	400.00	180.00
COMP.SHORT SET (100)	50.00	22.00
❑ 1 Terrell Davis SP	2.00	.90
❑ 2 Jerome Bettis SP	2.00	.90
❑ 3 J.J. Stokes	.75	.35
❑ 4 Frank Wycheck	.50	.23
❑ 5 O.J. McDuffie	.75	.35
❑ 6 Johnnie Morton	.75	.35
❑ 7 Marshall Faulk SP	2.50	1.10
❑ 8 Ryan Leaf	1.25	.55
❑ 9 Sean Dawkins	.50	.23
❑ 10 Brett Favre SP	6.00	2.70
❑ 11 Steve Young SP	2.50	1.10
❑ 12 Jimmy Smith	.75	.35
❑ 13 Isaac Bruce	1.25	.55
❑ 14 Trent Dilfer	.75	.35
❑ 15 Brian Mitchell	.50	.23
❑ 16 Kordell Stewart SP	1.50	.70
❑ 17 Herman Moore	.75	.35
❑ 18 Troy Aikman SP	4.00	1.80
❑ 19 Cris Carter	1.25	.55
❑ 20 Barry Sanders SP	6.00	2.70
❑ 21 Tony Gonzalez	1.25	.55
❑ 22 Skip Hicks	.50	.23
❑ 23 Steve McNair SP	2.00	.90
❑ 24 Brad Johnson	.75	.35
❑ 25 Mark Chmura	.50	.23
❑ 26 Randall Cunningham SP	2.00	.90
❑ 27 Jerry Rice SP	4.00	1.80
❑ 28 Jamie Asher	.50	.23
❑ 29 Brian Griese SP	2.00	.90
❑ 30 Peyton Manning SP	6.00	2.70
❑ 31 Keith Poole	.50	.23
❑ 32 Wayne Chrebet	.75	.35
❑ 33 Rich Gannon	1.25	.55
❑ 34 Michael Irvin	.75	.35
❑ 35 Yancey Thigpen	.50	.23
❑ 36 Corey Dillon	1.25	.55
❑ 37 Steve Beuerlein	.50	.23
❑ 38 Terry Kirby	.50	.23
❑ 39 Jacquez Green	.50	.23
❑ 40 Mark Brunell SP	1.50	.70
❑ 41 Rickey Dudley	.50	.23
❑ 42 Shannon Sharpe	.75	.35
❑ 43 Andre Rison	.75	.35
❑ 44 Chris Chandler	.75	.35
❑ 45 Fred Taylor SP	2.00	.90
❑ 46 Kerry Collins	.75	.35
❑ 47 Antowain Smith SP	1.50	.70
❑ 48 Wesley Walls	.50	.23
❑ 49 Rob Moore	.75	.35
❑ 50 Dan Marino SP	6.00	2.70
❑ 51 Robert Smith	1.25	.55
❑ 52 Keenan McCardell	.75	.35
❑ 53 Joey Galloway	.75	.35
❑ 54 Fred Lane	.50	.23
❑ 55 Napoleon Kaufman	1.25	.55
❑ 56 Curtis Martin	1.25	.55
❑ 57 Rod Smith	.75	.35
❑ 58 Curtis Conway	.75	.35
❑ 59 Kevin Dyson	.75	.35
❑ 60 Warrick Dunn SP	2.00	.90
❑ 61 Ahman Green	1.25	.55
❑ 62 Duce Staley	1.25	.55
❑ 63 Emmitt Smith SP	4.00	1.80
❑ 64 Adrian Murrell	.75	.35
❑ 65 Dorsey Levens	1.25	.55
❑ 66 Drew Bledsoe SP	2.50	1.10
❑ 67 Ed McCaffrey	.75	.35
❑ 68 Natrone Means	.75	.35
❑ 69 Deion Sanders	1.25	.55
❑ 70 Keyshawn Johnson SP	2.00	.90
❑ 71 Antonio Freeman	1.25	.55
❑ 72 James Stewart	.75	.35
❑ 73 Ben Coates	.75	.35
❑ 74 Priest Holmes	2.00	.90
❑ 75 Jake Reed	.75	.35
❑ 76 Mike Alstott	1.25	.55
❑ 77 Vinny Testaverde	.75	.35
❑ 78 Ricky Watters	.75	.35
❑ 79 Garrison Hearst	.75	.35
❑ 80 Junior Seau	1.25	.55
❑ 81 Tim Brown	1.25	.55
❑ 82 Jamal Anderson	1.25	.55
❑ 83 Robert Brooks	.75	.35
❑ 84 Marc Edwards	.50	.23

Card	Nm-Mt	Ex-Mt
85 Curtis Enis	.50	.23
86 Doug Flutie	1.25	.55
87 Terry Glenn	.50	.23
88 Charlie Batch SP	1.50	.70
89 Marvin Harrison	1.25	.55
90 Jake Plummer SP	1.50	.70
91 Terrell Owens	1.25	.55
92 Scott Mitchell	.50	.23
93 Tim Dwight	.75	.35
94 Eddie George SP	2.00	.90
95 Ike Hilliard	.50	.23
96 Robert Holcombe	.50	.23
97 Charles Johnson	.50	.23
98 Eric Moulds	1.25	.55
99 Michael Westbrook	.75	.35
100 Randy Moss SP	5.00	2.20
101 Tim Couch RC	8.00	3.60
102 Donovan McNabb RC	30.00	13.50
103 Akili Smith RC	4.00	1.80
104 Cade McNown RC	6.00	2.70
105 Daunte Culpepper RC	25.00	11.00
106 Ricky Williams RC	12.00	5.50
107 Edgerrin James RC	25.00	11.00
108 Kevin Faulk RC	8.00	3.60
109 Torry Holt RC	20.00	9.00
110 David Boston RC	8.00	3.60
111 Chris Claiborne RC	4.00	1.80
112 Mike Cloud RC	6.00	2.70
113 Joe Germaine RC	6.00	2.70
114 Cecil Collins RC	4.00	1.80
115 Tim Alexander RC	4.00	1.80
116 Brandon Stokley RC	10.00	4.50
117 Lamarr Glenn RC	4.00	1.80
118 Shawn Bryson RC	8.00	3.60
119 Jeff Paulk RC	4.00	1.80
120 Kevin Johnson RC	8.00	3.60
121 Charlie Rogers RC	6.00	2.70
122 Joe Montgomery RC	6.00	2.70
123 Travis McGriff RC	4.00	1.80
124 Dee Miller RC	4.00	1.80
125 Rob Konrad RC	8.00	3.60
126 Peerless Price RC	12.00	5.50
127 D'Wayne Bates RC	6.00	2.70
128 Craig Yeast RC	6.00	2.70
129 Malcolm Johnson RC	4.00	1.80
130 Brock Huard RC	8.00	3.60
131 Sedrick Irvin RC	1.50	.70
132 Troy Smith RC	4.00	1.80
133 Troy Edwards RC	6.00	2.70
134 Al Wilson RC	6.00	2.70
135 Terry Jackson RC	6.00	2.70
136 Dameane Douglas RC	6.00	2.70
137 Amos Zereoue RC	8.00	3.60
138 Shaun King RC	6.00	2.70
139 James Johnson RC	6.00	2.70
140 Jermaine Fazande RC	6.00	2.70
141 Autry Denson RC	6.00	2.70
142 Darran Hall RC	4.00	1.80
143 Na Brown RC	6.00	2.70
144 Mike Lucky RC	4.00	1.80
145 Karsten Bailey RC	6.00	2.70
146 Kevin Daft RC	6.00	2.70
147 Sean Bennett RC	4.00	1.80
148 Madre Hill RC	4.00	1.80
149 Michael Bishop RC	8.00	3.60
150 Scott Covington RC	8.00	3.60
151 Randy Moss STAR	12.00	5.50
152 Fred Taylor STAR	4.00	1.80
153 Brett Favre STAR	15.00	6.75
154 Dan Marino STAR	15.00	6.75
155 Terrell Davis STAR	4.00	1.80
156 Barry Sanders STAR	15.00	6.75
157 Emmitt Smith STAR	10.00	4.50
158 Jake Plummer STAR	3.00	1.35
159 Warrick Dunn STAR	4.00	1.80
160 Troy Aikman STAR	10.00	4.50
P86 Doug Flutie Promo	1.25	.55

2000 Fleer Mystique

	Nm-Mt	Ex-Mt
COMPLETE SET (145)	250.00	110.00
COMP.SET w/o SP's (100)	15.00	6.75
1 Tim Couch	.60	.25
2 Edgerrin James	1.50	.70
3 Terrell Davis	1.25	.55
4 Eddie George	1.00	.45
5 Jevon Kearse	1.00	.45

Card	Nm-Mt	Ex-Mt
6 Mike Alstott	1.00	.45
7 Tony Martin	.60	.25
8 Jermaine Fazande	.40	.18
9 Akili Smith	.40	.18
10 Damon Huard	1.00	.45
11 Kordell Stewart	.60	.25
12 Peyton Manning	2.50	1.10
13 Michael Westbrook	.60	.25
14 Tim Biakabutuka	.60	.25
15 Curtis Martin	1.00	.45
16 Shaun King	.40	.18
17 Jamal Anderson	1.00	.45
18 Terry Allen	.60	.25
19 Sean Dawkins	.40	.18
20 Muhsin Muhammad	.60	.25
21 Vinny Testaverde	.60	.25
22 Warren Sapp	.60	.25
23 Wesley Walls	.60	.25
24 Mark Brunell	1.00	.45
25 Tim Brown	1.00	.45
26 Kevin Dyson	.60	.25
27 Curtis Enis	.40	.18
28 Keenan McCardell	.60	.25
29 Rich Gannon	1.00	.45
30 Jermaine Lewis	.60	.25
31 Johnnie Morton	.60	.25
32 Kerry Collins	.60	.25
33 Az-Zahir Hakim	.40	.18
34 Cade McNown	.40	.18
35 Jimmy Smith	.60	.25
36 Tyrone Wheatley	.60	.25
37 Marcus Robinson	1.00	.45
38 Fred Taylor	1.00	.45
39 Donovan McNabb	1.50	.70
40 Steve McNair	1.00	.45
41 Corey Dillon	1.00	.45
42 Tony Gonzalez	.60	.25
43 Duce Staley	1.00	.45
44 Albert Connell	.40	.18
45 Isaac Bruce	1.00	.45
46 Troy Aikman	2.00	.90
47 Charlie Garner	.60	.25
48 Kevin Johnson	1.00	.45
49 Cris Carter	1.00	.45
50 Ryan Leaf	.60	.25
51 Doug Flutie	1.00	.45
52 Brett Favre	3.00	1.35
53 Joe Montgomery	.40	.18
54 Torry Holt	1.00	.45
55 Jonathan Linton	.40	.18
56 Antonio Freeman	1.00	.45
57 Amani Toomer	.60	.25
58 Kurt Warner	2.00	.90
59 Jake Plummer	.60	.25
60 Rob Johnson	.60	.25
61 Randy Moss	2.00	.90
62 Jerry Rice	2.00	.90
63 Chris Chandler	.60	.25
64 Joey Galloway	.60	.25
65 Olandis Gary	.60	.25
66 Drew Bledsoe	1.25	.55
67 Steve Beuerlein	.40	.18
68 Marvin Harrison	1.00	.45
69 Keyshawn Johnson	1.00	.45
70 Warrick Dunn	1.00	.45
71 Tim Dwight	1.00	.45
72 Brian Griese	1.00	.45
73 Terry Glenn	.60	.25
74 Jon Kitna	1.00	.45
75 Qadry Ismail	.60	.25
76 Germane Crowell	.40	.18
77 Ricky Williams	1.00	.45
78 Marshall Faulk	1.25	.55
79 Karim Abdul-Jabbar	.60	.25
80 James Johnson	.40	.18
81 Hines Ward	1.00	.45
82 Frank Sanders	.60	.25
83 Emmitt Smith	2.00	.90
84 Robert Smith	1.00	.45
85 Steve Young	1.25	.55
86 Darnay Scott	.60	.25
87 Tamarick Vanover	.40	.18
88 Troy Edwards	.40	.18
89 Brad Johnson	1.00	.45
90 Tony Banks	.60	.25
91 Charlie Batch	1.00	.45
92 Jeff Blake	.60	.25
93 Ricky Watters	.60	.25
94 Carl Pickens	.60	.25
95 Elvis Grbac	.60	.25
96 Jerome Bettis	1.00	.45
97 Eric Moulds	1.00	.45
98 Dorsey Levens	.60	.25
99 Wayne Chrebet	.60	.25
100 Stephen Davis	1.00	.45
101 Shaun Alexander RC	10.00	4.50
102 Sebastian Janikowski RC	4.00	1.80
103 Tom Brady RC	40.00	18.00
104 Courtney Brown RC	4.00	1.80
105 Marc Bulger RC	8.00	3.60
106 Plaxico Burress RC	8.00	3.60
107 Trung Canidate RC	3.00	1.35
108 Giovanni Carmazzi RC	3.00	1.35
109 Trevor Gaylor RC	3.00	1.35
110 Laveranues Coles RC	5.00	2.20
111 Ron Dayne RC	4.00	1.80
112 Reuben Droughns RC	5.00	2.20
113 Danny Farmer RC	3.00	1.35
114 Chafie Fields RC	2.00	.90
115 Bubba Franks RC	4.00	1.80
116 Sherrod Gideon RC	2.00	.90
117 Joe Hamilton RC	3.00	1.35
118 Chris Cole RC	3.00	1.35
119 Darrell Jackson RC	8.00	3.60
120 Thomas Jones RC	6.00	2.70
121 Jamal Lewis RC	10.00	4.50
122 Anthony Lucas RC	2.00	.90
123 Tee Martin RC	4.00	1.80
124 Frank Murphy RC	2.00	.90
125 Rondell Mealey RC	2.00	.90
126 Sylvester Morris RC	3.00	1.35
127 Dennis Northcutt RC	4.00	1.80
128 Chad Pennington RC	15.00	6.75
129 Travis Prentice RC	3.00	1.35
130 Tim Rattay RC	8.00	3.60
131 Chris Redman RC	3.00	1.35
132 J.R. Redmond RC	3.00	1.35
133 R.Jay Soward RC	3.00	1.35
134 Quinton Spotwood RC	2.00	.90
135 Shyrone Stith RC	3.00	1.35
136 Travis Taylor RC	4.00	1.80
137 Troy Walters RC	4.00	1.80
138 Peter Warrick RC	4.00	1.80
139 Dez White RC	4.00	1.80
140 Michael Wiley RC	3.00	1.35
141 Jerry Porter RC	5.00	2.20
142 Mareno Philyaw RC	2.00	.90
143 Anthony Becht RC	4.00	1.80
144 JaJuan Dawson RC	2.00	.90
145 Ron Dugans RC	5.00	2.20

2000 Fleer Mystique Gold

Nm-Mt Ex-Mt

*GOLD STARS: 1.5X TO 4X BASIC CARDS
*GOLD RC STARS: .4X TO 1X

2002 Fleer Platinum

	Nm-Mt	Ex-Mt
COMP.SET w/o SP's (230)	30.00	9.00
1 Donovan McNabb	1.25	.35
2 Tom Brady	2.50	.75
3 Kurt Warner	1.00	.30
4 Jerry Porter	.40	.12
5 LaDainian Tomlinson	1.50	.45
6 Rod Gardner	.60	.18
7 Dorsey Levens	.60	.18
8 Drew Bledsoe	1.25	.35
9 David Terrell	1.00	.30

❑ 10 Ahman Green 1.00 .30
❑ 11 D'Wayne Bates .40 .12
❑ 12 Wayne Chrebet .60 .18
❑ 13 Doug Flutie 1.00 .30
❑ 14 Steve McNair 1.00 .30
❑ 15 Nate Clements .40 .12
❑ 16 Gerard Warren .40 .12
❑ 17 James Allen .60 .18
❑ 18 David Patten .40 .12
❑ 19 Jerry Rice 2.00 .60
❑ 20 Garrison Hearst .60 .18
❑ 21 Samari Rolle .40 .12
❑ 22 Jay Riemersma .40 .12
❑ 23 Quincy Carter .60 .18
❑ 24 Lamar Smith .60 .18
❑ 25 Jacquez Green .40 .12
❑ 26 John Abraham .60 .18
❑ 27 Kevin Dyson .60 .18
❑ 28 James Thrash .60 .18
❑ 29 Todd Heap .60 .18
❑ 30 Gus Frerotte .40 .12
❑ 31 Terry Glenn .60 .18
❑ 32 Mark Brunell 1.00 .30
❑ 33 Randy Moss 2.00 .60
❑ 34 John Lynch .60 .18
❑ 35 Curtis Conway .40 .12
❑ 36 Bill Romanowski .40 .12
❑ 37 Thomas Jones .60 .18
❑ 38 Dez White .40 .12
❑ 39 Greg Ellis .40 .12
❑ 40 Trent Green .60 .18
❑ 41 Deuce McAllister 1.25 .35
❑ 42 Hines Ward 1.00 .30
❑ 43 Isaac Bruce 1.00 .30
❑ 44 Edgerrin James 1.25 .35
❑ 45 Chad Lewis .40 .12
❑ 46 Ray Lewis 1.00 .30
❑ 47 Corey Dillon .60 .18
❑ 48 Brett Favre 2.50 .75
❑ 49 Daunte Culpepper 1.00 .30
❑ 50 Vinny Testaverde .60 .18
❑ 51 Warren Sapp .60 .18
❑ 52 Corey Simon .40 .12
❑ 53 Chris McAlister .40 .12
❑ 54 Peter Warrick .60 .18
❑ 55 Luther Elliss .40 .12
❑ 56 Sam Madison .40 .12
❑ 57 Will Allen .40 .12
❑ 58 Michael Pittman .40 .12
❑ 59 Jamal Lewis 1.00 .30
❑ 60 Takeo Spikes .40 .12
❑ 61 Robert Porcher .40 .12
❑ 62 Peyton Manning 2.00 .60
❑ 63 Robert Edwards .40 .12
❑ 64 Rob Johnson .40 .12
❑ 65 Willie Jackson .40 .12
❑ 66 Dan Morgan .40 .12
❑ 67 Ian Gold .40 .12
❑ 68 Donald Driver .60 .18
❑ 69 Fred Taylor 1.00 .30
❑ 70 Dante Hall 1.00 .30
❑ 71 Jerome Pathon .60 .18
❑ 72 Amos Zereoue 1.00 .30
❑ 73 Darrell Jackson .60 .18
❑ 74 Chris Redman .40 .12
❑ 75 Chad Johnson 1.00 .30
❑ 76 Az-Zahir Hakim .40 .12
❑ 77 Jermaine Lewis .40 .12
❑ 78 Zach Thomas 1.00 .30
❑ 79 Michael Strahan .60 .18
❑ 80 Junior Seau 1.00 .30
❑ 81 Brad Johnson .60 .18
❑ 82 Keith Brooking .40 .12
❑ 83 Shawn Springs .40 .12
❑ 84 Tim Couch 1.25 .35
❑ 85 Bill Schroeder .60 .18
❑ 86 Jamie Sharper .40 .12
❑ 87 Ricky Williams 1.00 .30
❑ 88 Ron Dayne .60 .18
❑ 89 Brian Finneran .40 .12
❑ 90 Kevin Johnson .60 .18
❑ 91 Scotty Anderson .40 .12
❑ 92 Chris Chambers 1.00 .30
❑ 93 Amani Toomer .60 .18
❑ 94 Jeff Garcia 1.00 .30
❑ 95 Chad Brown .40 .12
❑ 96 Rodney Peete .60 .18
❑ 97 Dennis Northcutt .60 .18
❑ 98 Jamel White .40 .12
❑ 99 Patrick Johnson .40 .12
❑ 100 Ty Law .60 .18
❑ 101 Charles Woodson .60 .18
❑ 102 Stephen Davis .60 .18
❑ 103 Charlie Garner .60 .18
❑ 104 Courtney Brown .60 .18
❑ 105 Aaron Glenn .40 .12
❑ 106 Antowain Smith .60 .18
❑ 107 Tim Brown 1.00 .30
❑ 108 Shane Matthews .40 .12
❑ 109 Warrick Dunn 1.00 .30
❑ 110 Wesley Walls .40 .12
❑ 111 Jason Elam .40 .12
❑ 112 Jay Fiedler .60 .18
❑ 113 Kerry Collins .60 .18
❑ 114 Jerome Bettis 1.00 .30
❑ 115 Koren Robinson .60 .18
❑ 116 Patrick Kerney .40 .12
❑ 117 Muhsin Muhammad .60 .18
❑ 118 Mike McMahon 1.00 .30
❑ 119 Qadry Ismail .60 .18
❑ 120 Oronde Gadsden .60 .18
❑ 121 Tiki Barber .60 .18
❑ 122 Kordell Stewart .60 .18
❑ 123 Shaun Alexander 1.00 .30
❑ 124 Jake Plummer .60 .18
❑ 125 Marty Booker .60 .18
❑ 126 La'Roi Glover .40 .12
❑ 127 Marvin Harrison 1.00 .30
❑ 128 Bobby Shaw .40 .12
❑ 129 Kevin Faulk .60 .18
❑ 130 Drew Brees 1.00 .30
❑ 131 Marshall Faulk 1.00 .30
❑ 132 MarTay Jenkins .40 .12
❑ 133 Anthony Thomas 1.00 .30
❑ 134 Brian Griese 1.00 .30
❑ 135 Johnnie Morton .60 .18
❑ 136 Aaron Brooks 1.00 .30
❑ 137 Ernie Conwell .40 .12
❑ 138 Rod Smith .60 .18
❑ 139 Antonio Freeman 1.00 .30
❑ 140 Travis Taylor .60 .18
❑ 141 Jon Kitna .60 .18
❑ 142 Robert Ferguson .40 .12
❑ 143 Derrick Alexander .60 .18
❑ 144 Laveranues Coles .60 .18
❑ 145 Keyshawn Johnson 1.00 .30
❑ 146 Freddie Jones .40 .12
❑ 147 Jim Miller .40 .12
❑ 148 Mike Anderson 1.00 .30
❑ 149 Marcus Pollard .40 .12
❑ 150 Priest Holmes 1.25 .35
❑ 151 Joe Horn .60 .18
❑ 152 Plaxico Burress .60 .18
❑ 153 Shannon Sharpe .60 .18
❑ 154 Michael Vick 3.00 .90
❑ 155 Steve Smith .40 .12
❑ 156 Ed McCaffrey 1.00 .30
❑ 157 Eddie Kennison .40 .12
❑ 158 Darren Howard .40 .12
❑ 159 Trent Dilfer .60 .18
❑ 160 Peerless Price .60 .18
❑ 161 Quincy Morgan .60 .18
❑ 162 Corey Bradford .40 .12
❑ 163 Jimmy Smith .60 .18
❑ 164 Troy Brown .60 .18
❑ 165 Rich Gannon .60 .18
❑ 166 Kevan Barlow .60 .18
❑ 167 Jevon Kearse 1.00 .30
❑ 168 David Boston 1.00 .30
❑ 169 Marcel Shipp 1.00 .30
❑ 170 Joey Galloway .60 .18
❑ 171 Kyle Brady .40 .12
❑ 172 Donald Hayes .40 .12
❑ 173 Chad Scott .40 .12
❑ 174 Torry Holt 1.00 .30
❑ 175 Champ Bailey .60 .18
❑ 176 Travis Henry 1.00 .30
❑ 177 Troy Hambrick .40 .12
❑ 178 Hardy Nickerson .40 .12
❑ 179 Michael Bennett .60 .18
❑ 180 Chad Pennington 1.25 .35
❑ 181 Eric Johnson .40 .12
❑ 182 Derrick Mason .40 .12
❑ 183 Kwamie Lassiter .40 .12
❑ 184 Brian Urlacher 1.50 .45
❑ 185 Olandis Gary .60 .18
❑ 186 Tony Gonzalez .60 .18
❑ 187 David Sloan .40 .12
❑ 188 Kendrell Bell 1.00 .30
❑ 189 Jamie Martin .40 .12
❑ 190 Eric Moulds .60 .18
❑ 191 Emmitt Smith 2.50 .75
❑ 192 Bubba Franks .60 .18
❑ 193 Byron Chamberlain .40 .12
❑ 194 Santana Moss 1.00 .30
❑ 195 Dana Stubblefield .40 .12
❑ 196 Eddie George 1.00 .30
❑ 197 Brian Dawkins .40 .12
❑ 198 Stephen Alexander .40 .12
❑ 199 Terrell Owens 1.00 .30
❑ 200 Curtis Martin 1.00 .30
❑ 201 Larry Izzo UH .40 .12
❑ 202 Brian Simmons UH .40 .12
❑ 203 Jason Fisk UH RC .60 .18
❑ 204 Carlos Emmons UH .40 .12
❑ 205 Justin McCareins UH .60 .18
❑ 206 Adam Vinatieri UH 1.00 .30
❑ 207 Cornelius Griffin UH .40 .12
❑ 208 Trevor Pryce UH .40 .12
❑ 209 Sam Shade UH .40 .12
❑ 210 Rod Smart UH RC 1.00 .30
❑ 211 Tony Richardson UH .40 .12
❑ 212 Kevin Kasper UH .40 .12
❑ 213 Rodney Harrison UH .40 .12
❑ 214 Patrick Surtain UH .40 .12
❑ 215 Fred Beasley UH .40 .12
❑ 216 James Farrior UH .40 .12
❑ 217 Rosevelt Colvin UH RC 1.00 .30
❑ 218 Anthony McFarland UH .40 .12
❑ 219 Dat Nguyen UH .40 .12
❑ 220 Greg Comella UH .40 .12
❑ 221 Rob Konrad UH .40 .12
❑ 222 London Fletcher UH .40 .12
❑ 223 Omar Stoutmire UH .40 .12
❑ 224 Warrick Holdman UH .40 .12
❑ 225 Bob Christian UH .40 .12
❑ 226 David Akers UH .40 .12
❑ 227 Tony Brackens UH .40 .12
❑ 228 Deon Grant UH .40 .12
❑ 229 Olin Kreutz UH RC 1.00 .30
❑ 230 Gary Walker UH .40 .12
❑ 231 Lito Sheppard RC 3.00 .90
❑ 232 Kalimba Edwards RC 3.00 .90
❑ 233 Hayden Epstein RC 2.50 .75
❑ 234 Napoleon Harris RC 3.00 .90
❑ 235 Josh McCown RC 4.00 1.20
❑ 236 J.T. O'Sullivan RC 2.50 .75
❑ 237 Omar Easy RC 3.00 .90
❑ 238 Adrian Peterson RC 3.00 .90
❑ 239 Jarrod Baxter RC 2.50 .75
❑ 240 John Henderson RC 3.00 .90
❑ 241 Jon McGraw RC 1.50 .45
❑ 242 Terry Jones RC 2.50 .75
❑ 243 Ron Johnson RC 2.50 .75
❑ 244 Josh Reed RC 3.00 .90
❑ 245 Jason McAddley RC 2.50 .75
❑ 246 Sheldon Brown RC 3.00 .90
❑ 247 Rocky Bernard RC 3.00 .90
❑ 248 Nick Davis RC 1.50 .45
❑ 249 Robert Thomas RC 3.00 .90
❑ 250 Rohan Davey RC 3.00 .90
❑ 251 Seth Burford RC 2.50 .75
❑ 252 Najeh Davenport RC 3.00 .90
❑ 253 Verron Haynes RC 3.00 .90
❑ 254 Tellis Redmon RC 2.50 .75
❑ 255 Vernon Fox RC 1.50 .45
❑ 256 Willie Offord RC 3.00 .90

❑ 257 Marquise Walker RC	2.50	.75
❑ 258 Antonio Bryant RC	3.00	.90
❑ 259 Andre Davis RC	3.00	.90
❑ 260 Eddie Drummond RC	2.50	.75
❑ 261 Marques Anderson RC	3.00	.90
❑ 262 Charles Stackhouse RC	2.50	.75
❑ 263 Rocky Calmus RC	3.00	.90
❑ 264 Mike Williams RC	2.50	.75
❑ 265 Brandon Doman RC	3.00	.90
❑ 266 Maurice Morris RC	3.00	.90
❑ 267 Ladell Betts RC	3.00	.90
❑ 268 Ricky Williams RC	2.50	.75
❑ 269 Tony Fisher RC	3.00	.90
❑ 270 Michael Lewis RC	3.00	.90
❑ 271 Jerramy Stevens RC	3.00	.90
❑ 272 Reche Caldwell RC	3.00	.90
❑ 273 Antwaan Randle El RC	4.00	1.20
❑ 274 Charles Grant RC	3.00	.90
❑ 275 Lee Mays RC	2.50	.75
❑ 276 Phillip Buchanon RC	3.00	.90
❑ 277 Carlos Hall RC	3.00	.90
❑ 278 Billy Cundiff RC	10.00	3.00
❑ 279 Saleem Rasheed RC	3.00	.90
❑ 280 David Garrard RC	3.00	.90
❑ 281 Preston Parsons RC	1.50	.45
❑ 282 Travis Stephens RC	2.50	.75
❑ 283 Clinton Portis RC	10.00	3.00
❑ 284 James Mungro RC	3.00	.90
❑ 285 Tank Williams RC	2.50	.75
❑ 286 Ed Reed RC	5.00	1.50
❑ 287 Javon Walker RC	6.00	1.80
❑ 288 Cliff Russell RC	2.50	.75
❑ 289 Daryl Jones RC	2.50	.75
❑ 290 Freddie Milons RC	2.50	.75
❑ 291 Dwight Freeney RC	6.00	1.80
❑ 292 Lamar Gordon RC	5.00	1.50
❑ 293 Donte Stallworth RC	10.00	3.00
❑ 294 Craig Nall RC	5.00	1.50
❑ 295 Coy Wire RC	5.00	1.50
❑ 296 T.J. Duckett RC	8.00	2.40
❑ 297 Jeremy Shockey RC	15.00	4.50
❑ 298 Patrick Ramsey RC	10.00	3.00
❑ 299 Chester Taylor RC	5.00	1.50
❑ 300 Tim Carter RC	4.00	1.20
❑ 301 Joey Harrington RC	20.00	6.00
❑ 302 Roy Williams RC	15.00	4.50
❑ 303 Julius Peppers RC	12.00	3.60
❑ 304 William Green RC	10.00	3.00
❑ 305 Ashley Lelie RC	12.00	3.60
❑ 306 Rock Cartwright RC	8.00	2.40
❑ 307 DeShaun Foster RC	3.00	.90
❑ 308 Marc Boerigter RC	20.00	6.00
❑ 309 Chad Hutchinson RC	8.00	2.40
❑ 310 Daniel Graham RC	8.00	2.40
❑ 311 Ryan Sims RC	10.00	3.00
❑ 312 Kurt Kittner RC	10.00	3.00
❑ 313 Jabar Gaffney RC	10.00	3.00
❑ 314 David Carr RC	30.00	9.00
❑ 315 Brian Westbrook RC	15.00	4.50
❑ 316 Randy Fasani RC	10.00	3.00
❑ 317 Randy McMichael RC	15.00	4.50
❑ 318 Ben Leber RC	8.00	2.40
❑ 319 Jonathan Wells RC	10.00	3.00
❑ 320 Deion Branch RC	20.00	6.00

2002 Fleer Platinum Finish

	Nm-Mt	Ex-Mt

*STARS: 3X TO 8X BASIC CARDS
*ROOKIES 231-290: 1.5X TO 4X
*ROOKIES 291-300: 1X TO 2.5X
*ROOKIES 301-310: .8X TO 2X
*ROOKIES 311-320: .5X TO 1.2X

2003 Fleer Platinum

	MINT	NRMT
COMP.SET w/o SP's (210)	30.00	13.50
❑ 1 Donovan McNabb	1.25	.55
❑ 2 Jonathan Wells	.40	.18
❑ 3 Amos Zereoue	.60	.25
❑ 4 Ray Lewis	1.00	.45
❑ 5 Trent Green	.60	.25
❑ 6 Jeff Garcia	1.00	.45
❑ 7 Marty Booker	.60	.25
❑ 8 Antowain Smith	.60	.25
❑ 9 Brad Johnson	.60	.25
❑ 10 Joey Galloway	.60	.25
❑ 11 Chad Pennington	1.25	.55
❑ 12 Patrick Ramsey	1.00	.45
❑ 13 James Stewart	.60	.25
❑ 14 Charles Woodson	.60	.25
❑ 15 Warrick Dunn	.60	.25
❑ 16 Marvin Harrison	1.00	.45
❑ 17 Jerome Bettis	1.00	.45
❑ 18 Muhsin Muhammad	.60	.25
❑ 19 Zach Thomas	1.00	.45
❑ 20 Darrell Jackson	.60	.25
❑ 21 Kelly Holcomb	.60	.25
❑ 22 Deuce McAllister	1.00	.45
❑ 23 Mike Alstott	1.00	.45
❑ 24 Kabeer Gbaja-Biamila	.60	.25
❑ 25 Todd Pinkston	.60	.25
❑ 26 Chris Redman	.40	.18
❑ 27 Jimmy Smith	.60	.25
❑ 28 Tim Dwight	.60	.25
❑ 29 Kordell Stewart	.60	.25
❑ 30 Daunte Culpepper	1.00	.45
❑ 31 Isaac Bruce	1.00	.45
❑ 32 William Green	.60	.25
❑ 33 Tiki Barber	.60	.25
❑ 34 Jevon Kearse	.60	.25
❑ 35 Ashley Lelie	1.00	.45
❑ 36 Charlie Garner	.60	.25
❑ 37 Marcel Shipp	.60	.25
❑ 38 Corey Bradford	.40	.18
❑ 39 Hines Ward	1.00	.45
❑ 40 Josh Reed	.60	.25
❑ 41 Jay Fiedler	.60	.25
❑ 42 Matt Hasselbeck	.60	.25
❑ 43 Corey Dillon	.60	.25
❑ 44 David Patten	.40	.18
❑ 45 Warren Sapp	.60	.25
❑ 46 Chad Johnson	.60	.25
❑ 47 Troy Brown	.60	.25
❑ 48 Keyshawn Johnson	1.00	.45
❑ 49 Roy Williams	1.00	.45
❑ 50 Curtis Martin	1.00	.45
❑ 51 Rod Gardner	.60	.25
❑ 52 David Carr	1.50	.70
❑ 53 Tommy Maddox	1.00	.45
❑ 54 Todd Heap	.60	.25
❑ 55 Hugh Douglas	.40	.18
❑ 56 Julian Peterson	.40	.18
❑ 57 Julius Peppers	1.00	.45
❑ 58 Sam Madison	.40	.18
❑ 59 Jerramy Stevens	.40	.18
❑ 60 Andre Davis	.40	.18
❑ 61 Joe Horn	.60	.25
❑ 62 Ronde Barber	.40	.18
❑ 63 Joey Harrington	1.50	.70
❑ 64 Jerry Porter	.60	.25
❑ 65 T.J. Duckett	.60	.25
❑ 66 Edgerrin James	1.00	.45
❑ 67 Joey Porter	.40	.18
❑ 68 Brian Urlacher	1.50	.70
❑ 69 Randy Moss	1.50	.70
❑ 70 Torry Holt	1.00	.45
❑ 71 Quincy Morgan	.60	.25
❑ 72 Amani Toomer	.60	.25
❑ 73 Derrick Mason	.60	.25
❑ 74 Donald Driver	.60	.25
❑ 75 Duce Staley	.60	.25
❑ 76 Peerless Price	.60	.25
❑ 77 Mark Brunell	.60	.25
❑ 78 David Boston	.60	.25
❑ 79 Takeo Spikes	.40	.18
❑ 80 Ricky Williams	1.00	.45
❑ 81 Shaun Alexander	1.00	.45
❑ 82 Jon Kitna	.60	.25
❑ 83 Deion Branch	1.00	.45
❑ 84 Derrick Brooks	.60	.25
❑ 85 Rod Smith	.60	.25
❑ 86 Rich Gannon	.60	.25
❑ 87 Jason McAddley	.40	.18
❑ 88 Jabar Gaffney	.40	.18
❑ 89 Plaxico Burress	.60	.25
❑ 90 Troy Hambrick	.40	.18
❑ 91 Santana Moss	.60	.25
❑ 92 Champ Bailey	.60	.25
❑ 93 Bubba Franks	.60	.25
❑ 94 Brian Westbrook	.60	.25
❑ 95 Ed Reed	.60	.25
❑ 96 Priest Holmes	1.25	.55
❑ 97 Terrell Owens	1.00	.45
❑ 98 Anthony Thomas	1.00	.45
❑ 99 Michael Bennett	.60	.25
❑ 100 Marshall Faulk	1.00	.45
❑ 101 Kevin Johnson	.60	.25
❑ 102 Kerry Collins	.60	.25
❑ 103 Eddie George	.60	.25
❑ 104 Shannon Sharpe	.60	.25
❑ 105 Tim Brown	1.00	.45
❑ 106 Brian Finneran	.40	.18
❑ 107 Reggie Wayne	.60	.25
❑ 108 Drew Brees	1.00	.45
❑ 109 Jake Delhomme	1.00	.45
❑ 110 Chris Chambers	1.00	.45
❑ 111 Maurice Morris	.40	.18
❑ 112 Antonio Bryant	.60	.25
❑ 113 Michael Strahan	.60	.25
❑ 114 Laveranues Coles	.60	.25
❑ 115 Ahman Green	1.00	.45
❑ 116 Jeff Blake	.40	.18
❑ 117 Jamal Lewis	1.00	.45
❑ 118 Fred Taylor	1.00	.45
❑ 119 Marcellus Wiley	.40	.18
❑ 120 Stephen Davis	.60	.25
❑ 121 Randy McMichael	1.00	.45
❑ 122 Kurt Warner	1.00	.45
❑ 123 Tim Couch	.40	.18
❑ 124 Aaron Brooks	1.00	.45
❑ 125 John Lynch	.60	.25
❑ 126 Clinton Portis	1.50	.70
❑ 127 Wayne Chrebet	.60	.25
❑ 128 Emmitt Smith	2.50	1.10
❑ 129 Aaron Glenn	.40	.18
❑ 130 Antwaan Randle El	1.00	.45
❑ 131 Travis Henry	.60	.25
❑ 132 Tony Gonzalez	.60	.25
❑ 133 Garrison Hearst	.60	.25
❑ 134 Drew Bledsoe	1.00	.45
❑ 135 Eddie Kennison	.40	.18
❑ 136 Kevan Barlow	.60	.25
❑ 137 David Terrell	.60	.25
❑ 138 Tom Brady	1.50	.70
❑ 139 Joe Jurevicius	.40	.18
❑ 140 Terry Glenn	.40	.18
❑ 141 Curtis Conway	.40	.18
❑ 142 Trung Canidate	.60	.25
❑ 143 Javon Walker	.60	.25
❑ 144 Brian Dawkins	.40	.18
❑ 145 Keith Brooking	.40	.18
❑ 146 Dwight Freeney	.40	.18
❑ 147 LaDainian Tomlinson	1.00	.45
❑ 148 Kevin Dyson	.40	.18
❑ 149 Jason Taylor	.40	.18
❑ 150 Koren Robinson	.60	.25
❑ 151 Dennis Northcutt	.60	.25
❑ 152 Donte Stallworth	1.00	.45
❑ 153 Steve McNair	1.00	.45
❑ 154 Ed McCaffrey	1.00	.45
❑ 155 Jerry Rice	2.00	.90
❑ 156 Travis Taylor	.60	.25
❑ 157 Kyle Brady	.40	.18
❑ 158 Quentin Jammer	.40	.18
❑ 159 DeShaun Foster	.40	.18
❑ 160 Derrius Thompson	.40	.18
❑ 161 Marc Bulger	1.00	.45
❑ 162 Chad Hutchinson	.60	.25
❑ 163 Jeremy Shockey	1.50	.70
❑ 164 Frank Wycheck	.40	.18
❑ 165 Brett Favre	2.50	1.10
❑ 166 Phillip Buchanon	.40	.18
❑ 167 Michael Vick	2.50	1.10
❑ 168 Peyton Manning	1.50	.70
❑ 169 Kendrell Bell	.60	.25
❑ 170 Eric Moulds	.60	.25

171	Johnnie Morton	.60	.25
172	Tai Streets	.40	.18
173	Ron Dugans	.40	.18
174	Ty Law	.60	.25
175	Simeon Rice	.60	.25
176	Jake Plummer	.60	.25
177	John Abraham	.40	.18
178	Fred Smoot	.40	.18
179	Arizona TC/Shipp	.40	.18
180	Atlanta TC/Vick	1.25	.55
181	Baltimore TC/Lewis	.40	.18
182	Buffalo TC/Bledsoe	.60	.25
183	Carolina TC/Weinke	.40	.18
184	Chicago TC/Thomas	.40	.18
185	Cincinnati TC/Dillon	.40	.18
186	Cleveland TC/J.White	.40	.18
187	Dallas TC/Hambrick	.40	.18
188	Denver TC/Wilson	.40	.18
189	Detroit TC/Schlesinger	.40	.18
190	Green Bay TC/Fisher	.40	.18
191	Houston TC/Carr	1.00	.45
192	Indianapolis TC/Manning	.60	.25
193	Jacksonville TC/Taylor	.40	.18
194	Kansas City TC/Green	.40	.18
195	Miami TC/Fiedler	.40	.18
196	Minnesota TC/Williams	.40	.18
197	New England TC/Johnson	.40	.18
198	New Orleans TC/McAllister	.40	.18
199	NY Giants TC/Barrow	.40	.18
200	NY Jets TC/Jordan	.60	.25
201	Oakland TC/Wheatley	.40	.18
202	Philadelphia TC/Staley	.40	.18
203	Pittsburgh TC/Maddox	.40	.18
204	San Diego TC/Tomlinson	.40	.18
205	San Francisco TC/Hearst	.40	.18
206	Seattle TC/Hasselbeck	.40	.18
207	St. Louis TC/Warner	.40	.18
208	Tampa Bay TC/Stecker	.40	.18
209	Tennessee TC/Smith	.40	.18
210	Washington TC/Ramsey	.40	.18
211	L.J. Smith RC	3.00	1.35
212	Taylor Jacobs RC	3.00	1.35
213	J.R. Tolver RC	4.00	1.80
214	Musa Smith RC	3.00	1.35
215	Bennie Joppru RC	3.00	1.35
216	Ken Dorsey RC	5.00	2.20
217	Kareem Kelly RC	2.50	1.10
218	Andre Woolfolk RC	3.00	1.35
219	Brian St.Pierre RC	3.00	1.35
220	Jerome McDougle RC	3.00	1.35
221	Avon Cobourne RC	2.50	1.10
222	William Joseph RC	3.00	1.35
223	Dallas Clark RC	5.00	2.20
224	Anquan Boldin RC	8.00	3.60
225	Mike Doss RC	3.00	1.35
226	Cecil Sapp RC	2.50	1.10
227	Domanick Davis RC	6.00	2.70
228	Brad Banks RC	2.50	1.10
229	Justin Gage RC	3.00	1.35
230	Nate Burleson RC	5.00	2.20
231	Earnest Graham RC	2.50	1.10
232	DeWayne White RC	2.50	1.10
233	Kevin Williams RC	3.00	1.35
234	Billy McMullen RC	2.50	1.10
235	Talman Gardner RC	3.00	1.35
236	Marcus Trufant RC	3.00	1.35
237	Quentin Griffin RC	8.00	3.60
238	LaBrandon Toefield RC	3.00	1.35
239	Kliff Kingsbury RC	2.50	1.10
240	Doug Gabriel RC	3.00	1.35
241	Kyle Boller RC	12.00	5.50
242	Dave Ragone RC	5.00	2.20
243	Larry Johnson RC	10.00	4.50
244	Lee Suggs RC	10.00	4.50
245	Charles Rogers RC	6.00	2.70
246	Jimmy Kennedy RC	5.00	2.20
247	Onterrio Smith RC	6.00	2.70
248	Artose Pinner RC	5.00	2.20
249	Tyrone Calico RC	6.00	2.70
250	Terence Newman RC	10.00	4.50
251	Byron Leftwich RC	25.00	11.00
252	Kelley Washington RC	6.00	2.70
253	Justin Fargas RC	5.00	2.20
254	DeWayne Robertson RC	6.00	2.70
255	Boss Bailey RC	8.00	3.60
256	Sam Aiken RC	6.00	2.70
257	Bryant Johnson RC	6.00	2.70
258	Rex Grossman RC	15.00	6.75
259	Teyo Johnson RC	6.00	2.70
260	Willis McGahee RC	15.00	6.75
261	Carson Palmer RC	25.00	11.00
262	Chris Simms RC	15.00	6.75
263	Andre Johnson RC	20.00	9.00
264	Seneca Wallace RC	8.00	3.60
265	Terrell Suggs RC	12.00	5.50
266	Chris Brown RC	15.00	6.75
267	Kevin Curtis RC	8.00	3.60
268	Brandon Lloyd RC	10.00	4.50
269	Jason Witten RC	12.00	5.50
270	Bobby Wade RC	8.00	3.60

2003 Fleer Platinum Finish

MINT NRMT

*STARS: 5X TO 12X BASIC CARDS
*ROOKIES 211-240: 1.5X TO 4X
*ROOKIES 241-250: 1X TO 2.5X
*ROOKIES 251-260: .8X TO 2X
*ROOKIES 261-270: .6X TO 1.5X

2004 Fleer Platinum

		Nm-Mt	Ex-Mt
COMP.SET w/o SP's (135)		20.00	6.00

136-145 RC PRINT RUN 299 SER.#'d SETS
146-155 RC PRINT RUN 499 SER.#'d SETS
156-165 RC PRINT RUN 799 SER.#'d SETS
166-185 RC PRINT RUN 999 SER.#'d SETS

1	Joey Harrington	.75	.23
2	Kyle Boller	.75	.23
3	Randy McMichael	.30	.09
4	David Tyree	.30	.09
5	Darrell Jackson	.50	.15
6	Brian Urlacher	1.00	.30
7	Ahman Green	.75	.23
8	Onterrio Smith	.50	.15
9	Jevon Kearse	.50	.15
10	Eddie George	.50	.15
11	Julius Peppers	.75	.23
12	Donald Driver	.50	.15
13	Randy Moss	1.00	.30
14	Brian Westbrook	.50	.15
15	Derrick Brooks	.50	.15
16	Jamal Lewis	.75	.23
17	Artose Pinner	.30	.09
18	Ricky Williams	.75	.23
19	Chad Pennington	1.00	.30
20	Matt Hasselbeck	.50	.15
21	Josh McCown	.50	.15
22	Carson Palmer	1.00	.30
23	Byron Leftwich	1.25	.35
24	Tedy Bruschi	.50	.15
25	Duce Staley	.50	.15
26	Laveranues Coles	.50	.15
27	Drew Bledsoe	.75	.23
28	Shannon Sharpe	.50	.15
29	A.J. Feeley	.75	.23
30	Santana Moss	.50	.15
31	Adam Archuleta	.30	.09
32	Travis Henry	.50	.15
33	Ashley Lelie	.50	.15
34	Dante Hall	.75	.23
35	Curtis Martin	.75	.23
36	Isaac Bruce	.50	.15
37	Eric Moulds	.50	.15
38	Jake Plummer	.50	.15
39	Trent Green	.50	.15
40	Shaun Ellis	.30	.09
41	Torry Holt	.75	.23
42	T.J. Duckett	.50	.15
43	Quincy Morgan	.50	.15
44	Jabar Gaffney	.50	.15
45	Tiki Barber	.50	.15
46	Tim Rattay	.50	.15
47	Champ Bailey	.50	.15
48	Tony Gonzalez	.50	.15
49	Rich Gannon	.50	.15
50	Marshall Faulk	.75	.23
51	Jake Delhomme	.75	.23
52	Antonio Bryant	.50	.15
53	Priest Holmes	1.00	.30
54	Jerry Rice	1.50	.45
55	Marc Bulger	.75	.23
56	Stephen Davis	.50	.15
57	Roy Williams S	.50	.15
58	Willis McGahee	.75	.23
59	Julian Peterson	.30	.09
60	Thomas Jones	.50	.15
61	Dre Bly	.30	.09
62	Corey Dillon	.50	.15
63	Tommy Maddox	.50	.15
64	Derrick Mason	.50	.15
65	Marty Booker	.50	.15
66	Brett Favre	2.00	.60
67	Tom Brady	1.25	.35
68	Correll Buckhalter	.50	.15
69	Steve McNair	.75	.23
70	Alge Crumpler	.50	.15
71	Quincy Carter	.50	.15
72	Andre Johnson	.75	.23
73	Jeremy Shockey	.75	.23
74	Kevan Barlow	.50	.15
75	Jerry Porter	.50	.15
76	Ray Lewis	.75	.23
77	Keyshawn Johnson	.50	.15
78	Domanick Davis	.75	.23
79	Michael Strahan	.50	.15
80	Brandon Lloyd	.50	.15
81	Anquan Boldin	.75	.23
82	Chad Johnson	.50	.15
83	Jimmy Smith	.50	.15
84	Troy Brown	.50	.15
85	Hines Ward	.75	.23
86	Tyrone Calico	.50	.15
87	Marcel Shipp	.50	.15
88	Peter Warrick	.50	.15
89	Reggie Wayne	.50	.15
90	Aaron Brooks	.50	.15
91	Antwaan Randle El	.50	.15
92	Mark Brunell	.50	.15
93	Todd Heap	.50	.15
94	Charles Rogers	.50	.15
95	Chris Chambers	.50	.15
96	Amani Toomer	.50	.15
97	Shaun Alexander	.75	.23
98	Michael Vick	1.50	.45
99	Jeff Garcia	.75	.23
100	Edgerrin James	.75	.23
101	Deuce McAllister	.75	.23
102	LaDainian Tomlinson	.75	.23
103	Warrick Dunn	.50	.15
104	Andre Davis	.30	.09
105	Peyton Manning	1.25	.35
106	Boo Williams	.30	.09
107	Drew Brees	.75	.23
108	Rex Grossman	.75	.23
109	Javon Walker	.50	.15
110	Michael Bennett	.50	.15
111	Terrell Owens	.75	.23
112	Michael Pittman	.30	.09
113	Emmitt Smith	1.50	.45
114	Rudi Johnson	.50	.15
115	Fred Taylor	.50	.15
116	Deion Branch	.75	.23
117	Plaxico Burress	.50	.15
118	Clinton Portis	.75	.23
119	DeShaun Foster	.50	.15
120	Najeh Davenport	.30	.09
121	Daunte Culpepper	.75	.23
122	Donovan McNabb	1.00	.30
123	Charles Lee	.30	.09
124	Peerless Price	.50	.15
125	Lee Suggs	.75	.23
126	Marvin Harrison	.75	.23
127	Joe Horn	.50	.15
128	Antonio Gates	.75	.23
129	Steve Smith	.50	.15
130	David Carr	.75	.23

- ❑ 131 Jason Taylor .30 .09
- ❑ 132 Phillip Buchanon .30 .09
- ❑ 133 Brad Johnson .50 .15
- ❑ 134 Takeo Spikes .30 .09
- ❑ 135 Koren Robinson .50 .15
- ❑ 136 Eli Manning RC 40.00 12.00
- ❑ 137 Ben Roethlisberger RC 75.00 22.00
- ❑ 138 Drew Henson RC 20.00 6.00
- ❑ 139 Kellen Winslow RC 20.00 6.00
- ❑ 140 Kevin Jones RC 25.00 7.50
- ❑ 141 Larry Fitzgerald RC 25.00 7.50
- ❑ 142 Roy Williams RC 25.00 7.50
- ❑ 143 Philip Rivers RC 25.00 7.50
- ❑ 144 Lee Evans RC 12.00 3.60
- ❑ 145 Julius Jones RC 30.00 9.00
- ❑ 146 Chris Perry RC 10.00 3.00
- ❑ 147 Michael Clayton RC 12.00 3.60
- ❑ 148 Sean Taylor RC 6.00 1.80
- ❑ 149 Reggie Williams RC 6.00 1.80
- ❑ 150 Steven Jackson RC 15.00 4.50
- ❑ 151 Tatum Bell RC 8.00 2.40
- ❑ 152 Keary Colbert RC 6.00 1.80
- ❑ 153 J.P. Losman RC 12.00 3.60
- ❑ 154 Devery Henderson RC 4.00 1.20
- ❑ 155 Ben Troupe RC 5.00 1.50
- ❑ 156 Luke McCown RC 4.00 1.20
- ❑ 157 Greg Jones RC 4.00 1.20
- ❑ 158 Ben Watson RC 4.00 1.20
- ❑ 159 Bernard Berrian RC 4.00 1.20
- ❑ 160 Devard Darling RC 4.00 1.20
- ❑ 161 Cedric Cobbs RC 4.00 1.20
- ❑ 162 Darius Watts RC 5.00 1.50
- ❑ 163 Derrick Hamilton RC 3.00 .90
- ❑ 164 Matt Schaub RC 6.00 1.80
- ❑ 165 Mewelde Moore RC 5.00 1.50
- ❑ 166 Michael Jenkins RC 3.00 .90
- ❑ 167 Rashaun Woods RC 5.00 1.50
- ❑ 168 Quincy Wilson RC 2.50 .75
- ❑ 169 Jonathan Vilma RC 3.00 .90
- ❑ 170 Jerricho Cotchery RC 3.00 .90
- ❑ 171 John Navarre RC 3.00 .90
- ❑ 172 Josh Harris RC 3.00 .90
- ❑ 173 Teddy Lehman RC 3.00 .90
- ❑ 174 Ernest Wilford RC 3.00 .90
- ❑ 175 P.K. Sam RC 2.50 .75
- ❑ 176 Jeff Smoker RC 5.00 1.50
- ❑ 177 Chris Gamble RC 4.00 1.20
- ❑ 178 Johnnie Morant RC 3.00 .90
- ❑ 179 DeAngelo Hall RC 5.00 1.50
- ❑ 180 Vince Wilfork RC 4.00 1.20
- ❑ 181 Michael Turner RC 2.50 .75
- ❑ 182 Robert Gallery RC 5.00 1.50
- ❑ 183 Ricardo Colclough RC 3.00 .90
- ❑ 184 Kenechi Udeze RC 3.00 .90
- ❑ 185 Dunta Robinson RC 3.00 .90

2004 Fleer Platinum Finish

Nm-Mt Ex-Mt

*STARS: 4X TO 10X BASE CARD HI
*ROOKIES 136-145: .5X TO 1.2X BASE RCs
*ROOKIES 146-155: .8X TO 2X BASE RCs
*ROOKIES 156-165: 1X TO 2.5X BASE RCs
*ROOKIES 166-185: 1.2X TO 3X BASE RCs
STATED PRINT RUN 100 SER.#'d SETS

2001 Fleer Premium

Nm-Mt Ex-Mt

COMP.SET w/o SP's (200) 25.00 7.50

- ❑ 1 Ricky Williams .60 .18
- ❑ 2 Dez White .25 .07
- ❑ 3 Jay Riemersma .25 .07
- ❑ 4 Derrick Mason .40 .12
- ❑ 5 Chad Lewis .25 .07
- ❑ 6 Shaun King .25 .07
- ❑ 7 Jevon Kearse .40 .12
- ❑ 8 Bobby Engram .25 .07
- ❑ 9 Warrick Dunn .60 .18
- ❑ 10 Randall Cunningham .60 .18
- ❑ 11 Stephen Alexander .25 .07
- ❑ 12 Jimmy Smith .40 .12
- ❑ 13 Az-Zahir Hakim .40 .12
- ❑ 14 Antonio Freeman .60 .18
- ❑ 15 Curtis Conway .40 .12
- ❑ 16 Tim Biakabutuka .40 .12
- ❑ 17 Peter Warrick .60 .18
- ❑ 18 Kurt Warner 1.25 .35
- ❑ 19 Brian Urlacher 1.00 .30
- ❑ 20 Rod Smith .40 .12
- ❑ 21 Frank Sanders .25 .07
- ❑ 22 Trevor Pryce .25 .07
- ❑ 23 Sammy Morris .25 .07
- ❑ 24 Cade McNown .25 .07
- ❑ 25 Keyshawn Johnson .60 .18
- ❑ 26 Tim Couch .40 .12
- ❑ 27 Dedric Ward .25 .07
- ❑ 28 Bill Schroeder .40 .12
- ❑ 29 John Randle .40 .12
- ❑ 30 Donovan McNabb .75 .23
- ❑ 31 Marvin Harrison .60 .18
- ❑ 32 Trent Dilfer .40 .12
- ❑ 33 David Boston .60 .18
- ❑ 34 Donnell Bennett .25 .07
- ❑ 35 Trace Armstrong .25 .07
- ❑ 36 Sam Adams .25 .07
- ❑ 37 Jeremiah Trotter .40 .12
- ❑ 38 Zach Thomas .60 .18
- ❑ 39 Shawn Jefferson .25 .07
- ❑ 40 J.J. Stokes .40 .12
- ❑ 41 Akili Smith .25 .07
- ❑ 42 Tony Siragusa .25 .07
- ❑ 43 William Roaf .25 .07
- ❑ 44 Muhsin Muhammad .40 .12
- ❑ 45 Terance Mathis .40 .12
- ❑ 46 Tee Martin .40 .12
- ❑ 47 Ray Lewis .60 .18
- ❑ 48 Matt Hasselbeck .40 .12
- ❑ 49 Todd Pinkston .25 .07
- ❑ 50 Rob Johnson .40 .12
- ❑ 51 Edgerrin James .75 .23
- ❑ 52 Rocket Ismail .40 .12
- ❑ 53 Trent Green .60 .18
- ❑ 54 Tim Dwight .60 .18
- ❑ 55 Anthony Becht .25 .07
- ❑ 56 Jessie Armstead .25 .07
- ❑ 57 Mike Anderson .60 .18
- ❑ 58 Jamal Anderson .60 .18
- ❑ 59 Anthony Wright .25 .07
- ❑ 60 Regan Upshaw .25 .07
- ❑ 61 John Holecek .25 .07
- ❑ 62 Shaun Alexander .75 .23
- ❑ 63 Troy Aikman 1.00 .30
- ❑ 64 Peter Boulware .25 .07
- ❑ 65 Hines Ward .60 .18
- ❑ 66 Michael Strahan .40 .12
- ❑ 67 Herman Moore .40 .12
- ❑ 68 Rich Gannon .60 .18
- ❑ 69 Ken Dilger .25 .07
- ❑ 70 Terrell Davis .60 .18
- ❑ 71 Terrence Wilkins .25 .07
- ❑ 72 Fred Taylor .60 .18
- ❑ 73 Napoleon Kaufman .25 .07
- ❑ 74 Tony Horne .25 .07
- ❑ 75 Ahman Green .60 .18
- ❑ 76 Jay Fiedler .60 .18
- ❑ 77 Albert Connell .25 .07
- ❑ 78 Charlie Batch .60 .18
- ❑ 79 James Allen .40 .12
- ❑ 80 Sylvester Morris .25 .07
- ❑ 81 Isaac Bruce .60 .18
- ❑ 82 Charles Woodson .40 .12
- ❑ 83 Lamar Smith .40 .12
- ❑ 84 Peyton Manning 1.50 .45
- ❑ 85 Sam Madison .25 .07
- ❑ 86 Olandis Gary .40 .12
- ❑ 87 Kevin Faulk .40 .12
- ❑ 88 Jeff Garcia .60 .18
- ❑ 89 JaJuan Dawson .25 .07
- ❑ 90 Sam Cowart .25 .07
- ❑ 91 David Sloan .25 .07
- ❑ 92 Bobby Shaw .25 .07
- ❑ 93 Travis Prentice .25 .07
- ❑ 94 Terrell Owens .60 .18
- ❑ 95 John Lynch .40 .12
- ❑ 96 Jim Harbaugh .40 .12
- ❑ 97 Brian Griese .60 .18
- ❑ 98 Jeff Graham .25 .07
- ❑ 99 La'Roi Glover .25 .07
- ❑ 100 Joey Galloway .40 .12
- ❑ 101 Wesley Walls .25 .07
- ❑ 102 Vinny Testaverde .40 .12
- ❑ 103 Jason Taylor .25 .07
- ❑ 104 Darnay Scott .25 .07
- ❑ 105 Samari Rolle .25 .07
- ❑ 106 Adrian Murrell .25 .07
- ❑ 107 Eric Moulds .40 .12
- ❑ 108 Keenan McCardell .25 .07
- ❑ 109 Donald Hayes .25 .07
- ❑ 110 Brett Favre 2.00 .60
- ❑ 111 Troy Edwards .25 .07
- ❑ 112 Ron Dayne .60 .18
- ❑ 113 Daunte Culpepper .60 .18
- ❑ 114 Chris Chandler .40 .12
- ❑ 115 Mark Brunell .60 .18
- ❑ 116 Courtney Brown .40 .12
- ❑ 117 Aaron Brooks .60 .18
- ❑ 118 Fred Beasley .25 .07
- ❑ 119 Mike Alstott .60 .18
- ❑ 120 Tyrone Wheatley .40 .12
- ❑ 121 R.Jay Soward .25 .07
- ❑ 122 Deion Sanders .60 .18
- ❑ 123 Jake Reed .40 .12
- ❑ 124 Jamal Lewis 1.00 .30
- ❑ 125 Tony Gonzalez .40 .12
- ❑ 126 Terrell Fletcher .25 .07
- ❑ 127 Wayne Chrebet .40 .12
- ❑ 128 Cris Carter .60 .18
- ❑ 129 Drew Bledsoe .75 .23
- ❑ 130 Tiki Barber .40 .12
- ❑ 131 Derrick Alexander .40 .12
- ❑ 132 Frank Wycheck .25 .07
- ❑ 133 Jerome Pathon .40 .12
- ❑ 134 Warren Sapp .40 .12
- ❑ 135 Joe Horn .40 .12
- ❑ 136 Ricky Watters .40 .12
- ❑ 137 Amani Toomer .40 .12
- ❑ 138 Bruce Smith .40 .12
- ❑ 139 Andre Rison .40 .12
- ❑ 140 J.R. Redmond .25 .07
- ❑ 141 Steve McNair .60 .18
- ❑ 142 Michael McCrary .25 .07
- ❑ 143 Ike Hilliard .40 .12
- ❑ 144 Charlie Garner .40 .12
- ❑ 145 Mark Bruener .25 .07
- ❑ 146 Emmitt Smith 1.25 .35
- ❑ 147 Darren Sharper .25 .07
- ❑ 148 Peerless Price .60 .18
- ❑ 149 Johnnie Morton .40 .12
- ❑ 150 Curtis Martin .60 .18
- ❑ 151 Joe Johnson .25 .07
- ❑ 152 MarTay Jenkins .25 .07
- ❑ 153 Priest Holmes .75 .23
- ❑ 154 Terry Glenn .40 .12
- ❑ 155 Oronde Gadsden .40 .12
- ❑ 156 Germane Crowell .25 .07
- ❑ 157 Steve Beuerlein .25 .07
- ❑ 158 Champ Bailey .40 .12
- ❑ 159 Troy Vincent .25 .07
- ❑ 160 James Stewart .40 .12
- ❑ 161 Jerry Rice 1.25 .35
- ❑ 162 Randy Moss 1.25 .35
- ❑ 163 Dave Moore .25 .07
- ❑ 164 Ed McCaffrey .60 .18
- ❑ 165 Thomas Jones .40 .12
- ❑ 166 Rickey Dudley .25 .07
- ❑ 167 Hugh Douglas .25 .07
- ❑ 168 Stephen Davis .60 .18
- ❑ 169 Kerry Collins .40 .12
- ❑ 170 Cam Cleeland .25 .07
- ❑ 171 Stephen Boyd .25 .07
- ❑ 172 Jerome Bettis .60 .18
- ❑ 173 Aeneas Williams .25 .07
- ❑ 174 Chad Pennington 1.00 .30
- ❑ 175 Dorsey Levens .40 .12
- ❑ 176 Desmond Howard .25 .07
- ❑ 177 Torry Holt .60 .18
- ❑ 178 Plaxico Burress .60 .18

Card	Nm-Mt	Ex-Mt
179 Kevin Johnson	.40	.12
180 Kyle Brady	.25	.07
181 Jake Plummer	.40	.12
182 Brad Johnson	.60	.18
183 Eddie George	.60	.18
184 Corey Dillon	.60	.18
185 Curtis Enis	.25	.07
186 Tim Brown	.60	.18
187 Tony Boselli	.25	.07
188 Duce Staley	.60	.18
189 Junior Seau	.60	.18
190 Marshall Faulk	.75	.23
191 Kordell Stewart	.40	.12
192 Corey Simon	.40	.12
193 Shannon Sharpe	.40	.12
194 Marcus Robinson	.60	.18
195 Carl Pickens	.25	.07
196 Doug Flutie	.60	.18
197 Freddie Jones	.25	.07
198 Patrick Jeffers	.40	.12
199 Shawn Bryson	.25	.07
200 Kevin Dyson	.40	.12
201 David Terrell RC	5.00	1.50
202 Dan Morgan RC	5.00	1.50
203 Chris Weinke RC	5.00	1.50
204 Correll Buckhalter RC	6.00	1.80
205 Chad Johnson RC	10.00	3.00
206 LaDainian Tomlinson RC	15.00	4.50
207 Reggie Wayne RC	8.00	2.40
208 Tim Hasselbeck RC	5.00	1.50
209 Michael Vick RC	30.00	9.00
210 Heath Evans RC	3.00	.90
211 Damione Lewis RC	3.00	.90
212 Richard Seymour RC	5.00	1.50
213 Quincy Morgan RC	5.00	1.50
214 Drew Brees RC	10.00	3.00
215 Freddie Mitchell RC	5.00	1.50
216 Justin McCareins RC	5.00	1.50
217 Mike McMahon RC	5.00	1.50
218 Derrick Gibson RC	3.00	.90
219 Rudi Johnson RC	10.00	3.00
220 Todd Heap RC	5.00	1.50
221 Josh Booty RC	5.00	1.50
222 Justin Smith RC	5.00	1.50
223 Marcus Stroud RC	5.00	1.50
224 Rod Gardner RC	5.00	1.50
225 Vinny Sutherland RC	3.00	.90
226 Marques Tuiasosopo RC	5.00	1.50
227 Anthony Thomas RC	8.00	2.40
228 Bobby Newcombe RC	3.00	.90
229 Michael Bennett RC	10.00	3.00
230 Snoop Minnis RC	3.00	.90
231 Travis Minor RC	3.00	.90
232 Travis Henry RC	6.00	1.80
233 Kevan Barlow RC	5.00	1.50
234 Gerard Warren RC	5.00	1.50
235 Sage Rosenfels RC	5.00	1.50
236 Chris Chambers RC	6.00	1.80
237 James Jackson RC	5.00	1.50
238 Deuce McAllister RC	12.00	3.60
239 Koren Robinson RC	6.00	1.80
240 Andre Carter RC	5.00	1.50
241 Santana Moss RC	8.00	2.40
242 LaMont Jordan RC	6.00	1.80
243 Ken-Yon Rambo RC	3.00	.90
244 Jamal Reynolds RC	5.00	1.50
245 Fred Smoot RC	5.00	1.50
246 Robert Ferguson RC	5.00	1.50
247 Alex Bannister RC	3.00	.90
248 Dan Alexander RC	5.00	1.50
249 Nate Clements RC	5.00	1.50
250 Quincy Carter RC	5.00	1.50

2001 Fleer Premium Star Ruby

	Nm-Mt	Ex-Mt

*STARS: 6X TO 15X BASIC CARDS
*ROOKIES: 1.2X TO 3X

2002 Fleer Premium

Card	Nm-Mt	Ex-Mt
COMP.SET w/o SP's (160)	40.00	12.00
1 Kevin Dyson	.60	.18
2 Kerry Collins	.60	.18
3 Marty Booker	.60	.18
4 Curtis Conway	.40	.12
5 Drew Bledsoe	1.25	.35

Card	Nm-Mt	Ex-Mt
6 Kurt Warner	1.00	.30
7 Hines Ward	1.00	.30
8 Terrell Owens	1.00	.30
9 Todd Pinkston	.60	.18
10 Eric Moulds	.60	.18
11 Quincy Morgan	.40	.12
12 Fred Taylor	1.00	.30
13 Santana Moss	1.00	.30
14 Peyton Manning	2.00	.60
15 Qadry Ismail	.60	.18
16 Mike McMahon	1.00	.30
17 David Patten	.40	.12
18 Wayne Chrebet	.60	.18
19 David Terrell	1.00	.30
20 Corey Bradford	.40	.12
21 Derrick Mason	.60	.18
22 Anthony Thomas	1.00	.30
23 James Allen	.60	.18
24 Vinny Testaverde	.60	.18
25 Trent Green	.60	.18
26 Thomas Jones	.60	.18
27 Rocket Ismail	.60	.18
28 Duce Staley	1.00	.30
29 Drew Brees	1.00	.30
30 Chris Chandler	.60	.18
31 Kordell Stewart	.60	.18
32 Koren Robinson	.60	.18
33 Jon Kitna	.60	.18
34 Jamie Sharper	.40	.12
35 Germane Crowell	.40	.12
36 Lamar Smith	.60	.18
37 LaDainian Tomlinson	1.50	.45
38 Freddie Mitchell	.60	.18
39 Corey Dillon	.60	.18
40 Isaac Bruce	1.00	.30
41 James Thrash	.60	.18
42 Brian Griese	1.00	.30
43 Marvin Harrison	1.00	.30
44 Aaron Brooks	1.00	.30
45 Rich Gannon	1.00	.30
46 Mike Alstott	1.00	.30
47 Shannon Sharpe	.60	.18
48 Travis Henry	1.00	.30
49 Keyshawn Johnson	1.00	.30
50 Daunte Culpepper	1.00	.30
51 James Jackson	.40	.12
52 Justin McCareins	.60	.18
53 Quincy Carter	.60	.18
54 Stephen Davis	.60	.18
55 Joey Galloway	.60	.18
56 Joe Horn	.60	.18
57 Plaxico Burress	.60	.18
58 Brett Favre	2.50	.75
59 Brian Urlacher	1.50	.45
60 David Boston	1.00	.30
61 Darrell Jackson	.60	.18
62 Trung Canidate	.60	.18
63 Shaun Alexander	1.00	.30
64 Steve McNair	1.00	.30
65 Doug Flutie	1.00	.30
66 LaMont Jordan	1.00	.30
67 Rod Smith	.60	.18
68 Marshall Faulk	1.00	.30
69 Tiki Barber	.60	.18
70 James Stewart	.60	.18
71 Frank Wycheck	.40	.12
72 Peerless Price	.60	.18
73 Derrick Alexander	.60	.18
74 Charlie Garner	.60	.18
75 Peter Warrick	.60	.18
76 Warren Sapp	.60	.18
77 Kevan Barlow	.60	.18
78 Edgerrin James	1.25	.35
79 Willie Jackson	.40	.12
80 Keenan McCardell	.40	.12
81 Bill Schroeder	.40	.12
82 Curtis Martin	1.00	.30
83 Torry Holt	1.00	.30
84 Tony Gonzalez	.60	.18
85 Jeff Garcia	1.00	.30
86 Travis Taylor	.60	.18
87 Johnnie Morton	.60	.18
88 Tim Couch	.60	.18
89 Troy Brown	.60	.18
90 Emmitt Smith	2.50	.75
91 Aeneas Williams	.40	.12
92 Rod Gardner	.60	.18
93 Brandon Stokley	.60	.18
94 Warrick Dunn	1.00	.30
95 Jay Riemersma	.40	.12
96 Kevin Johnson	.60	.18
97 Antowain Smith	.60	.18
98 James McKnight	.40	.12
99 Amani Toomer	.60	.18
100 Ricky Williams	1.00	.30
101 Priest Holmes	1.25	.35
102 Muhsin Muhammad	.60	.18
103 Jake Plummer	.60	.18
104 Marcus Robinson	.60	.18
105 Donovan McNabb	1.25	.35
106 Tom Brady	2.50	.75
107 Jimmy Smith	.60	.18
108 Jamal Lewis	1.00	.30
109 Antonio Freeman	1.00	.30
110 Ron Dayne	.60	.18
111 Tim Brown	1.00	.30
112 Chris Chambers	1.00	.30
113 Garrison Hearst	.60	.18
114 Michael Vick	3.00	.90
115 Snoop Minnis	.40	.12
116 Terrell Davis	1.00	.30
117 Ahman Green	1.00	.30
118 Donald Hayes	.40	.12
119 Jermaine Lewis	.40	.12
120 Chad Johnson	1.00	.30
121 Jay Fiedler	.60	.18
122 Randy Moss	2.00	.60
123 Wesley Walls	.40	.12
124 Eddie George	1.00	.30
125 Jerry Rice	2.00	.60
126 Michael Bennett	.60	.18
127 Jerome Bettis	1.00	.30
128 Mark Brunell	1.00	.30
129 Adam Vinatieri	1.00	.30
130 Ed McCaffrey	1.00	.30
131 Maurice Morris RC	5.00	1.50
132 Ron Johnson RC	4.00	1.20
133 Antwaan Randle El RC	6.00	1.80
134 Brian Westbrook RC	8.00	2.40
135 Julius Peppers RC	10.00	3.00
136 Travis Stephens RC	4.00	1.20
137 David Carr RC	15.00	4.50
138 Clinton Portis RC	15.00	4.50
139 Reche Caldwell RC	5.00	1.50
140 Tim Carter RC	4.00	1.20
141 Daniel Graham RC	5.00	1.50
142 Rohan Davey RC	5.00	1.50
143 T.J. Duckett RC	8.00	2.40
144 Luke Staley RC	4.00	1.20
145 Ashley Lelie RC	10.00	3.00
146 Josh Reed RC	5.00	1.50
147 Randy Fasani RC	4.00	1.20
148 Andre Davis RC	5.00	1.50
149 Joey Harrington RC	15.00	4.50
150 David Garrard RC	5.00	1.50
151 Ladell Betts RC	5.00	1.50
152 Donte Stallworth RC	10.00	3.00
153 Adrian Peterson RC	5.00	1.50
154 Lamar Gordon RC	5.00	1.50
155 Jonathan Wells RC	5.00	1.50
156 Jabar Gaffney RC	5.00	1.50
157 Patrick Ramsey RC	10.00	3.00
158 Roy Williams RC	12.00	3.60
159 Jeremy Shockey RC	15.00	4.50
160 Javon Walker RC	10.00	3.00
161 Marquise Walker RC	4.00	1.20
162 Antonio Bryant RC	5.00	1.50
163 Josh McCown RC	6.00	1.80
164 Najeh Davenport RC	5.00	1.50

❑ 165 William Green RC	8.00	2.40
❑ 166 Jerramy Stevens RC	5.00	1.50
❑ 167 DeShaun Foster RC	5.00	1.50
❑ 168 Cliff Russell RC	4.00	1.20
❑ 169 Kurt Kittner RC	4.00	1.20
❑ 170 Eric Crouch RC	8.00	2.40
❑ 171 Michael Pittman PP	.40	.12
❑ 172 Darnay Scott PP	.40	.12
❑ 173 Charles Woodson PP	.60	.18
❑ 174 Ty Law PP	.40	.12
❑ 175 Tony Boselli PP	.40	.12
❑ 176 Zach Thomas PP	1.00	.30
❑ 177 Trent Dilfer PP	.60	.18
❑ 178 Bubba Franks PP	.60	.18
❑ 179 Laveranues Coles PP	.60	.18
❑ 180 John Lynch PP	.60	.18
❑ 181 Kendrell Bell PP	1.00	.30
❑ 182 Mike Anderson PP	1.00	.30
❑ 183 Amos Zereoue PP	1.00	.30
❑ 184 Michael Strahan PP	.60	.18
❑ 185 Chad Lewis PP	.40	.12
❑ 186 Travis Minor PP	.40	.12
❑ 187 Jevon Kearse PP	.60	.18
❑ 188 Darren Sharper PP	.40	.12
❑ 189 Az-Zahir Hakim PP	.40	.12
❑ 190 Ray Lewis PP	1.00	.30
❑ 191 Deuce McAllister PP	1.25	.35
❑ 192 Chris Weinke PP	.60	.18
❑ 193 Desmond Howard PP	.40	.12
❑ 194 Dominic Rhodes PP	.60	.18
❑ 195 Joe Jurevicius PP	.40	.12
❑ 196 Tim Dwight PP	1.00	.30
❑ 197 Jeff Zgonina PP	.40	.12
❑ 198 Junior Seau PP	1.00	.30
❑ 199 Rosevelt Colvin PP RC	1.00	.30
❑ 200 Chad Pennington PP	1.25	.35

2000 Fleer Showcase

	Nm-Mt	Ex-Mt
COMP.SET w/o SP's (100)	25.00	11.00
❑ 1 Tim Couch	.50	.23
❑ 2 Deion Sanders	.75	.35
❑ 3 Darnay Scott	.50	.23
❑ 4 Brett Favre	2.50	1.10
❑ 5 Mark Brunell	.75	.35
❑ 6 Randy Moss	1.50	.70
❑ 7 Tyrone Wheatley	.50	.23
❑ 8 Isaac Bruce	.75	.35
❑ 9 Eddie George	.75	.35
❑ 10 Troy Aikman	1.50	.70
❑ 11 Charlie Batch	.75	.35
❑ 12 Marvin Harrison	.75	.35
❑ 13 Terry Glenn	.50	.23
❑ 14 Charles Johnson	.50	.23
❑ 15 Jerry Rice	1.50	.70
❑ 16 Kurt Warner	1.50	.70
❑ 17 Kevin Johnson	.75	.35
❑ 18 Jay Fiedler	.75	.35
❑ 19 Vinny Testaverde	.50	.23
❑ 20 Curtis Enis	.30	.14
❑ 21 Elvis Grbac	.50	.23
❑ 22 Kordell Stewart	.50	.23
❑ 23 Jamal Anderson	.75	.35
❑ 24 Dorsey Levens	.50	.23
❑ 25 Derrick Mayes	.50	.23
❑ 26 Marcus Robinson	.75	.35
❑ 27 Cam Cleeland	.30	.14
❑ 28 Charlie Garner	.50	.23
❑ 29 Germane Crowell	.30	.14
❑ 30 Cade McNown	.30	.14
❑ 31 Tony Gonzalez	.50	.23
❑ 32 Shaun King	.30	.14
❑ 33 Wayne Chrebet	.50	.23
❑ 34 Muhsin Muhammad	.50	.23
❑ 35 Olandis Gary	.75	.35
❑ 36 Ray Lewis	.75	.35
❑ 37 Terrell Davis	.75	.35
❑ 38 Steve Beuerlein	.50	.23
❑ 39 James Stewart	.50	.23
❑ 40 Jon Kitna	.75	.35
❑ 41 Tim Biakabutuka	.50	.23
❑ 42 Ryan Leaf	.50	.23
❑ 43 Mike Alstott	.75	.35
❑ 44 Yancey Thigpen	.30	.14
❑ 45 Champ Bailey	.50	.23
❑ 46 Peerless Price	.75	.35
❑ 47 Ken Dilger	.30	.14
❑ 48 Derrick Alexander	.50	.23
❑ 49 Drew Bledsoe	1.00	.45
❑ 50 Jerome Bettis	.75	.35
❑ 51 Jermaine Fazande	.30	.14
❑ 52 Joey Galloway	.50	.23
❑ 53 Jeff Blake	.50	.23
❑ 54 Emmitt Smith	1.50	.70
❑ 55 Ricky Williams	.75	.35
❑ 56 Marshall Faulk	1.25	.55
❑ 57 Stephen Davis	.75	.35
❑ 58 Rob Johnson	.50	.23
❑ 59 Brian Griese	.75	.35
❑ 60 Damon Huard	.75	.35
❑ 61 Jevon Kearse	.75	.35
❑ 62 Doug Flutie	.75	.35
❑ 63 Curtis Martin	.75	.35
❑ 64 Torry Holt	.75	.35
❑ 65 David Boston	.75	.35
❑ 66 Cris Carter	.75	.35
❑ 67 Jason Sehorn	.30	.14
❑ 68 Keyshawn Johnson	.75	.35
❑ 69 Chris Chandler	.50	.23
❑ 70 Antonio Freeman	.75	.35
❑ 71 Kerry Collins	.50	.23
❑ 72 Akili Smith	.30	.14
❑ 73 Troy Edwards	.30	.14
❑ 74 Tim Dwight	.75	.35
❑ 75 Donovan McNabb	1.25	.55
❑ 76 Tony Banks	.50	.23
❑ 77 Ed McCaffrey	.75	.35
❑ 78 Errict Rhett	.30	.14
❑ 79 Fred Taylor	.75	.35
❑ 80 Terrell Owens	.75	.35
❑ 81 Steve McNair	.75	.35
❑ 82 Rob Moore	.50	.23
❑ 83 Jimmy Smith	.50	.23
❑ 84 Daunte Culpepper	1.00	.45
❑ 85 Carl Pickens	.50	.23
❑ 86 Moses Moreno	.30	.14
❑ 87 Brad Johnson	.75	.35
❑ 88 Jake Plummer	.50	.23
❑ 89 Edgerrin James	1.25	.55
❑ 90 Zach Thomas	.75	.35
❑ 91 Rich Gannon	.75	.35
❑ 92 Warrick Dunn	.75	.35
❑ 93 Shannon Sharpe	.50	.23
❑ 94 Peyton Manning	2.00	.90
❑ 95 Keenan McCardell	.50	.23
❑ 96 Tony Simmons	.30	.14
❑ 97 Duce Staley	.75	.35
❑ 98 Corey Dillon	.75	.35
❑ 99 Tim Brown	.75	.35
❑ 100 Ricky Watters	.50	.23
❑ 101 Peter Warrick RC	10.00	4.50
❑ 102 Shaun Alexander RC	25.00	11.00
❑ 103 Anthony Becht RC	10.00	4.50
❑ 104 Courtney Brown RC	10.00	4.50
❑ 105 Plaxico Burress RC	20.00	9.00
❑ 106 Trung Canidate RC	8.00	3.60
❑ 107 Giovanni Carmazzi RC	8.00	3.60
❑ 108 Laveranues Coles RC	12.00	5.50
❑ 109 Ron Dayne RC	10.00	4.50
❑ 110 Reuben Droughns RC	12.00	5.50
❑ 111 Danny Farmer RC	8.00	3.60
❑ 112 Bubba Franks RC	10.00	4.50
❑ 113 Thomas Jones RC	15.00	6.75
❑ 114 Jamal Lewis RC	25.00	11.00
❑ 115 Sylvester Morris RC	8.00	3.60
❑ 116 Chad Pennington RC	40.00	18.00
❑ 117 Travis Prentice RC	8.00	3.60
❑ 118 J.R. Redmond RC	8.00	3.60
❑ 119 R.Jay Soward RC	8.00	3.60
❑ 120 Dez White RC	10.00	4.50
❑ 121 Sebastian Janikowski RC	5.00	2.20
❑ 122 Todd Pinkston RC	5.00	2.20
❑ 123 Marc Bulger RC	10.00	4.50
❑ 124 Ron Dugans RC	2.50	1.10
❑ 125 Joe Hamilton RC	4.00	1.80
❑ 126 Curtis Keaton RC	4.00	1.80
❑ 127 Tee Martin RC	5.00	2.20
❑ 128 Dennis Northcutt RC	5.00	2.20
❑ 129 Corey Simon RC	5.00	2.20
❑ 130 Chris Redman RC	4.00	1.80
❑ 131 Brian Urlacher RC	20.00	9.00
❑ 132 Travis Taylor RC	5.00	2.20
❑ 133 Michael Wiley RC	4.00	1.80
❑ 134 Tim Rattay RC	10.00	4.50
❑ 135 Jerry Porter RC	6.00	2.70
❑ 136 Tom Brady RC	60.00	27.00
❑ 137 Deon Dyer RC	4.00	1.80
❑ 138 Mareno Philyaw RC	2.50	1.10
❑ 139 Spergon Wynn RC	4.00	1.80
❑ 140 John Abraham RC	5.00	2.20
❑ 141 Ahmed Plummer RC	5.00	2.20
❑ 142 Chris Hovan RC	4.00	1.80
❑ 143 Rob Morris RC	4.00	1.80
❑ 144 Keith Bulluck RC	5.00	2.20
❑ 145 JaJuan Dawson RC	2.50	1.10
❑ 146 Chris Cole RC	4.00	1.80
❑ 147 Chafie Fields RC	2.50	1.10
❑ 148 Darrell Jackson RC	10.00	4.50
❑ 149 Marcus Knight RC	4.00	1.80
❑ 150 Gari Scott RC	2.50	1.10
❑ 151 Kwame Cavil RC	2.50	1.10
❑ 152 Frank Moreau RC	4.00	1.80
❑ 153 Doug Chapman RC	4.00	1.80
❑ 154 Erron Kinney RC	5.00	2.20
❑ 155 Ron Dixon RC	4.00	1.80
❑ 156 Ben Kelly RC	2.50	1.10
❑ 157 Bashir Yamini RC	2.50	1.10
❑ 158 Anthony Lucas RC	2.50	1.10
❑ 159 Avion Black RC	4.00	1.80
❑ 160 Ian Gold RC	4.00	1.80

2001 Fleer Showcase

	Nm-Mt	Ex-Mt
COMP.SET w/o SP's (100)	25.00	7.50
❑ 1 Cris Carter	1.00	.30
❑ 2 Sylvester Morris	.40	.12
❑ 3 Vinny Testaverde	.60	.18
❑ 4 Jevon Kearse	.60	.18
❑ 5 Terance Mathis	.40	.12
❑ 6 Mike Anderson	1.00	.30
❑ 7 Aaron Brooks	1.00	.30
❑ 8 Jerry Rice	2.00	.60
❑ 9 Mike Alstott	1.00	.30
❑ 10 Jon Kitna	.60	.18
❑ 11 Derrick Alexander	.60	.18
❑ 12 Shaun Alexander	1.25	.35
❑ 13 Thomas Jones	.60	.18
❑ 14 James Stewart	.60	.18
❑ 15 Ron Dayne	1.00	.30
❑ 16 Az-Zahir Hakim	.60	.18
❑ 17 Terrell Owens	1.00	.30
❑ 18 Travis Prentice	.40	.12
❑ 19 Lamar Smith	.60	.18
❑ 20 James Thrash	.60	.18
❑ 21 Doug Flutie	1.00	.30
❑ 22 Derrick Mason	.60	.18
❑ 23 Ray Lewis	1.00	.30
❑ 24 Ed McCaffrey	1.00	.30

Card	Nm-Mt	Ex-Mt
❑ 25 Ricky Williams	1.00	.30
❑ 26 Tyrone Wheatley	.60	.18
❑ 27 Chris Chandler	.60	.18
❑ 28 Rod Smith	.60	.18
❑ 29 Joe Horn	.60	.18
❑ 30 Jerome Bettis	1.00	.30
❑ 31 Brian Urlacher	1.50	.45
❑ 32 Dorsey Levens	.60	.18
❑ 33 Kordell Stewart	.60	.18
❑ 34 Michael Westbrook	.60	.18
❑ 35 Jamal Anderson	1.00	.30
❑ 36 Charlie Batch	1.00	.30
❑ 37 Kerry Collins	.60	.18
❑ 38 Jake Plummer	.60	.18
❑ 39 Robert Porcher	.40	.12
❑ 40 Jason Sehorn	.40	.12
❑ 41 Junior Seau	1.00	.30
❑ 42 Warren Sapp	.60	.18
❑ 43 Champ Bailey	.60	.18
❑ 44 Jamal Lewis	1.50	.45
❑ 45 Tony Banks	.60	.18
❑ 46 Doug Chapman	.40	.12
❑ 47 Stephen Davis	1.00	.30
❑ 48 Elvis Grbac	.60	.18
❑ 49 Joey Galloway	.60	.18
❑ 50 Terry Glenn	.60	.18
❑ 51 Todd Pinkston	.60	.18
❑ 52 JaJuan Dawson	.40	.12
❑ 53 Zach Thomas	1.00	.30
❑ 54 Tim Couch	.60	.18
❑ 55 Cade McNown	.40	.12
❑ 56 Charlie Garner	.60	.18
❑ 57 Jeff George	.60	.18
❑ 58 Peerless Price	.60	.18
❑ 59 Tony Gonzalez	.60	.18
❑ 60 Rob Johnson	.40	.12
❑ 61 Keenan McCardell	.40	.12
❑ 62 Eric Moulds	.60	.18
❑ 63 Jimmy Smith	.60	.18
❑ 64 Jeff Garcia	1.00	.30
❑ 65 Rod Woodson	.60	.18
❑ 66 Brian Griese	1.00	.30
❑ 67 Kevin Faulk	.60	.18
❑ 68 Plaxico Burress	1.00	.30
❑ 69 Isaac Bruce	1.00	.30
❑ 70 Keyshawn Johnson	1.00	.30
❑ 71 Tim Biakabutuka	.60	.18
❑ 72 Mark Brunell	1.00	.30
❑ 73 Wesley Walls	.40	.12
❑ 74 Jerome Pathon	.60	.18
❑ 75 Wayne Chrebet	.60	.18
❑ 76 Muhsin Muhammad	.60	.18
❑ 77 Marvin Harrison	1.00	.30
❑ 78 David Boston	1.00	.30
❑ 79 Germane Crowell	.40	.12
❑ 80 Tiki Barber	.60	.18
❑ 81 Laveranues Coles	1.00	.30
❑ 82 Tim Brown	1.00	.30
❑ 83 Matt Hasselbeck	.60	.18
❑ 84 Brad Johnson	1.00	.30
❑ 85 Marcus Robinson	1.00	.30
❑ 86 Ahman Green	1.00	.30
❑ 87 Curtis Martin	1.00	.30
❑ 88 Peter Warrick	1.00	.30
❑ 89 Ray Lucas	.40	.12
❑ 90 Duce Staley	1.00	.30
❑ 91 Darrell Jackson	.40	.12
❑ 92 Steve McNair	1.00	.30
❑ 93 Rickey Dudley	.40	.12
❑ 94 Jason Taylor	.40	.12
❑ 95 Rich Gannon	1.00	.30
❑ 96 Torry Holt	1.00	.30
❑ 97 James Allen	.60	.18
❑ 98 Antonio Freeman	1.00	.30
❑ 99 Trent Green	.60	.18
❑ 100 Ricky Watters	.60	.18
❑ 101 Corey Dillon AC	4.00	1.20
❑ 102 Emmitt Smith AC	8.00	2.40
❑ 103 Terrell DACis AV	4.00	1.20
❑ 104 Brett FACre AV	12.00	3.60
❑ 105 Peyton Manning AC	10.00	3.00
❑ 106 Edgerrin James AC	5.00	1.50
❑ 107 Fred Taylor AC	4.00	1.20
❑ 108 Daunte Culpepper AC	4.00	1.20
❑ 109 Randy Moss AC	8.00	2.40
❑ 110 Drew Bledsoe AC	5.00	1.50
❑ 111 Donovan McNabb AC	5.00	1.50
❑ 112 Kurt Warner AC	8.00	2.40
❑ 113 Marshall Faulk AC	5.00	1.50
❑ 114 Warrick Dunn AC	4.00	1.20
❑ 115 Eddie George AC	4.00	1.20
❑ 116 Michael Vick AC RC	100.00	30.00
❑ 117 DACid Terrell AV RC	15.00	4.50
❑ 118 Deuce McAllister AC RC	30.00	9.00
❑ 119 Koren Robinson AC RC	20.00	6.00
❑ 120 Rod Gardner AC RC	15.00	4.50
❑ 121 Santana Moss AC RC	25.00	7.50
❑ 122 Drew Brees AC RC	25.00	7.50
❑ 123 Chris Weinke AC RC	15.00	4.50
❑ 124 LaDainian Tomlinson AC RC	50.00	15.00
❑ 125 Freddie Mitchell AC RC	15.00	4.50
❑ 126 Chris Chambers RC	10.00	3.00
❑ 127 Reggie Wayne RC	12.00	3.60
❑ 128 Quincy Morgan RC	6.00	1.80
❑ 129 Rudi Johnson RC	15.00	4.50
❑ 130 Robert Ferguson RC	6.00	1.80
❑ 131 Todd Heap RC	6.00	1.80
❑ 132 Michael Bennett RC	15.00	4.50
❑ 133 Jesse Palmer RC	6.00	1.80
❑ 134 James Jackson RC	6.00	1.80
❑ 135 Chad Johnson RC	15.00	4.50
❑ 136 LaMont Jordan RC	8.00	2.40
❑ 137 Anthony Thomas RC	12.00	3.60
❑ 138 Travis Henry RC	10.00	3.00
❑ 139 Snoop Minnis RC	6.00	1.80
❑ 140 Marques Tuiasosopo RC	6.00	1.80
❑ 141 Travis Minor RC	6.00	1.80
❑ 142 Mike McMahon RC	6.00	1.80
❑ 143 Josh Heupel RC	6.00	1.80
❑ 144 Sage Rosenfels RC	6.00	1.80
❑ 145 Quincy Carter RC	6.00	1.80
❑ 146 Alge Crumpler RC	8.00	2.40
❑ 147 Kevan Barlow RC	6.00	1.80
❑ 148 Heath Evans RC	4.00	1.20
❑ 149 Correll Buckhalter RC	8.00	2.40
❑ 150 Justin McCareins RC	6.00	1.80
❑ 151 Reggie Germany RC	4.00	1.20
❑ 152 Vinny Sutherland RC	4.00	1.20
❑ 153 Scotty Anderson RC	4.00	1.20
❑ 154 Tim Hasselbeck RC	6.00	1.80
❑ 155 Alex Bannister RC	4.00	1.20
❑ 156 Andre Carter RC	6.00	1.80
❑ 157 Adam Archuleta RC	6.00	1.80
❑ 158 Ken-Yon Rambo RC	4.00	1.20
❑ 159 Gerard Warren RC	6.00	1.80
❑ 160 Justin Smith RC	6.00	1.80
❑ NNO Donovan McNabb AU/300	60.00	18.00

2001 Fleer Showcase Legacy

Nm-Mt Ex-Mt

*STARS: 6X TO 15X BASIC CARDS
*STARS AC 101-115: 1.5X TO 4X
*ROOKIES 116-125: .8X TO 2X
*ROOKIES 126-145: 1.5X TO 4X
*ROOKIES 146-160: 2X TO 5X

2002 Fleer Showcase

Card	Nm-Mt	Ex-Mt
COMP.SET w/o SP's (125)	25.00	7.50
❑ 1 Kevin Johnson	.60	.18
❑ 2 Chris Walsh	.40	.12
❑ 3 Vinny Testaverde	.60	.18
❑ 4 Kordell Stewart	.60	.18
❑ 5 Chris Redman	.40	.12
❑ 6 Johnnie Morton	.60	.18
❑ 7 Tony Gonzalez	.60	.18
❑ 8 Torry Holt	1.00	.30
❑ 9 Champ Bailey	.60	.18
❑ 10 Eric Moulds	.60	.18
❑ 11 Az-Zahir Hakim	.40	.12
❑ 12 Mark Brunell	1.00	.30
❑ 13 Laveranues Coles	.60	.18
❑ 14 Kevan Barlow	.60	.18
❑ 15 Stephen Davis	.60	.18
❑ 16 Benjamin Gay	.60	.18
❑ 17 Randy Moss	2.00	.60
❑ 18 Hines Ward	1.00	.30
❑ 19 Brian Urlacher	1.50	.45
❑ 20 Dominic Rhodes	.60	.18
❑ 21 David Patten	.40	.12
❑ 22 Tim Brown	1.00	.30
❑ 23 Trent Dilfer	.60	.18
❑ 24 David Boston	1.00	.30
❑ 25 Quincy Carter	.60	.18
❑ 26 Daunte Culpepper	1.00	.30
❑ 27 Plaxico Burress	.60	.18
❑ 28 Michael Pittman	.40	.12
❑ 29 Joey Galloway	.60	.18
❑ 30 Jason Taylor	.40	.12
❑ 31 Drew Brees	1.00	.30
❑ 32 Jamal Anderson	.60	.18
❑ 33 Dat Nguyen	.40	.12
❑ 34 Chris Chambers	1.00	.30
❑ 35 Tiki Barber	.60	.18
❑ 36 LaDainian Tomlinson	1.50	.45
❑ 37 Peter Warrick	.60	.18
❑ 38 Bubba Franks	.60	.18
❑ 39 Joe Horn	.60	.18
❑ 40 Correll Buckhalter	.60	.18
❑ 41 Mike Alstott	1.00	.30
❑ 42 Brian Finneran	.40	.12
❑ 43 Troy Hambrick	.40	.12
❑ 44 Zach Thomas	1.00	.30
❑ 45 Kerry Collins	.60	.18
❑ 46 Junior Seau	1.00	.30
❑ 47 Alvis Whitted	.40	.12
❑ 48 Terrell Davis	1.00	.30
❑ 49 Ricky Williams	1.00	.30
❑ 50 Curtis Conway	.40	.12
❑ 51 Travis Taylor	.60	.18
❑ 52 Brian Griese	1.00	.30
❑ 53 Sylvester Morris	.40	.12
❑ 54 Amani Toomer	.60	.18
❑ 55 Jeff Garcia	1.00	.30
❑ 56 Michael McCrary	.40	.12
❑ 57 Ahman Green	1.00	.30
❑ 58 Trent Green	.60	.18
❑ 59 Trung Canidate	.60	.18
❑ 60 Jamal Lewis	1.00	.30
❑ 61 Larry Foster	.40	.12
❑ 62 Priest Holmes	1.25	.35
❑ 63 Isaac Bruce	1.00	.30
❑ 64 Bruce Smith	.40	.12
❑ 65 Darnay Scott	.40	.12
❑ 66 Terry Glenn	.60	.18
❑ 67 Darren Howard	.40	.12
❑ 68 Hugh Douglas	.40	.12
❑ 69 Milton Wynn	.40	.12
❑ 70 Tim Couch	.60	.18
❑ 71 Bill Schroeder	.60	.18
❑ 72 Michael Strahan	.60	.18
❑ 73 James Thrash	.60	.18
❑ 74 Steve McNair	1.00	.30
❑ 75 Patrick Jeffers	.40	.12
❑ 76 Marcus Pollard	.40	.12
❑ 77 Willie McGinest	.40	.12
❑ 78 Santana Moss	1.00	.30
❑ 79 Grant Wistrom	.40	.12
❑ 80 Jim Miller	.40	.12
❑ 81 Marvin Harrison	1.00	.30
❑ 82 Troy Brown	.60	.18
❑ 83 Rich Gannon	1.00	.30
❑ 84 Shaun Alexander	1.00	.30
❑ 85 Jake Plummer	.60	.18
❑ 86 Quincy Morgan	.40	.12
❑ 87 Michael Bennett	.60	.18
❑ 88 Jerome Bettis	1.00	.30
❑ 89 Marty Booker	.40	.12
❑ 90 Trevor Insley	.40	.12
❑ 91 Adam Vinatieri	1.00	.30
❑ 92 Charles Woodson	.60	.18
❑ 93 Darrell Jackson	.60	.18
❑ 94 Corey Dillon	.60	.18
❑ 95 Corey Bradford	.40	.12
❑ 96 Deuce McAllister	1.25	.35
❑ 97 Todd Pinkston	.60	.18

❑ 98 Warren Sapp	.60	.18
❑ 99 Alex Van Pelt	.60	.18
❑ 100 Mike McMahon	1.00	.30
❑ 101 Fred Taylor	1.00	.30
❑ 102 Ron Dayne	.60	.18
❑ 103 Ernie Conwell	.40	.12
❑ 104 Rod Gardner	.60	.18
❑ 105 Muhsin Muhammad	.60	.18
❑ 106 Reggie Wayne	.60	.18
❑ 107 Antowain Smith	.60	.18
❑ 108 Chad Pennington	1.25	.35
❑ 109 Koren Robinson	.60	.18
❑ 110 Travis Henry	1.00	.30
❑ 111 Ed McCaffrey	1.00	.30
❑ 112 Keenan McCardell	.40	.12
❑ 113 Curtis Martin	1.00	.30
❑ 114 Bryant Young	.40	.12
❑ 115 Derrick Mason	.60	.18
❑ 116 Anthony Thomas	1.00	.30
❑ 117 Jermaine Lewis	.40	.12
❑ 118 Aaron Brooks	1.00	.30
❑ 119 Charlie Garner	.60	.18
❑ 120 Keyshawn Johnson	1.00	.30
❑ 121 Chris Weinke	.60	.18
❑ 122 Rod Smith	.60	.18
❑ 123 Jimmy Smith	.60	.18
❑ 124 Terrell Owens	1.00	.30
❑ 125 Eddie George	1.00	.30
❑ 126 Tom Brady AC	10.00	3.00
❑ 127 Donovan McNabb AC	5.00	1.50
❑ 128 Kurt Warner AC	4.00	1.20
❑ 129 Peyton Manning AC	8.00	2.40
❑ 130 Marshall Faulk AC	4.00	1.20
❑ 131 Michael Vick AC	12.00	3.60
❑ 132 Emmitt Smith AC	10.00	3.00
❑ 133 Jerry Rice AC	8.00	2.40
❑ 134 Edgerrin James AC	5.00	1.50
❑ 135 Brett Favre AC	10.00	3.00
❑ 136 David Carr AC RC	30.00	9.00
❑ 137 Joey Harrington AC RC	30.00	9.00
❑ 138 Ashley Lelie AC RC	20.00	6.00
❑ 139 William Green AC RC	20.00	6.00
❑ 140 T.J. Duckett AC RC	20.00	6.00
❑ 141 Donte Stallworth AC RC	20.00	6.00
❑ 142 Ron Johnson RC	6.00	1.80
❑ 143 Jeremy Shockey RC	25.00	7.50
❑ 144 Daniel Graham RC	8.00	2.40
❑ 145 Reche Caldwell RC	8.00	2.40
❑ 146 Antonio Bryant RC	8.00	2.40
❑ 147 DeShaun Foster RC	8.00	2.40
❑ 148 Clinton Portis RC	25.00	7.50
❑ 149 Patrick Ramsey RC	15.00	4.50
❑ 150 Lamar Gordon RC	8.00	2.40
❑ 151 Josh Reed RC	8.00	2.40
❑ 152 Ladell Betts RC	8.00	2.40
❑ 153 Kurt Kittner RC	6.00	1.80
❑ 154 Jabar Gaffney RC	8.00	2.40
❑ 155 Josh McCown RC	10.00	3.00
❑ 156 Marquise Walker RC	6.00	1.80
❑ 157 Brian Westbrook RC	12.00	3.60
❑ 158 Andre Davis RC	8.00	2.40
❑ 159 David Garrard RC	8.00	2.40
❑ 160 Cliff Russell RC	6.00	1.80
❑ 161 Julius Peppers RC	15.00	4.50
❑ 162 Adrian Peterson RC	8.00	2.40
❑ 163 Antwaan Randle El RC	10.00	3.00
❑ 164 Javon Walker RC	15.00	4.50
❑ 165 Rohan Davey RC	8.00	2.40
❑ 166 Luke Staley RC	6.00	1.80

2002 Fleer Showcase Legacy

Nm-Mt Ex-Mt

*STARS: 5X TO 12X BASIC CARDS
*STARS AC: 1.5X TO 4X
*ROOKIES 136-141: .6X TO 1.5X
*ROOKIES 142-166: 1.2X TO 3X
UNPRICED MASTERPIECES #d of 1

2003 Fleer Showcase

	Nm-Mt	Ex-Mt
COMP.SET w/o SP's (90)	25.00	7.50
❑ 1 Edgerrin James	1.00	.30
❑ 2 Donald Driver	.60	.18
❑ 3 Drew Brees	1.00	.30
❑ 4 Corey Dillon	.60	.18
❑ 5 Jerome Bettis	1.00	.30
❑ 6 Charlie Garner	.60	.18

❑ 7 Eddie George	.60	.18
❑ 8 Mark Brunell	.60	.18
❑ 9 David Boston	.60	.18
❑ 10 Todd Heap	.60	.18
❑ 11 Terrell Owens	1.00	.30
❑ 12 Tommy Maddox	1.00	.30
❑ 13 Keyshawn Johnson	1.00	.30
❑ 14 Jamal Lewis	1.00	.30
❑ 15 Zach Thomas	.60	.18
❑ 16 Isaac Bruce	1.00	.30
❑ 17 Michael Bennett	.60	.18
❑ 18 Rod Smith	.60	.18
❑ 19 Eric Moulds	.60	.18
❑ 20 T.J Duckett	.60	.18
❑ 21 Hines Ward	1.00	.30
❑ 22 Tiki Barber	.60	.18
❑ 23 Julius Peppers	1.00	.30
❑ 24 Rich Gannon	.60	.18
❑ 25 Rod Gardner	.60	.18
❑ 26 Curtis Martin	1.00	.30
❑ 27 Donte Stallworth	1.00	.30
❑ 28 Anthony Thomas	1.00	.30
❑ 29 Warren Sapp	.60	.18
❑ 30 Jake Plummer	.60	.18
❑ 31 Patrick Ramsey	1.00	.30
❑ 32 Tai Streets	.40	.12
❑ 33 Matt Hasselbeck	.60	.18
❑ 34 James Stewart	.60	.18
❑ 35 Chad Hutchinson	.60	.18
❑ 36 Hugh Douglas	.40	.12
❑ 37 Jimmy Smith	.60	.18
❑ 38 Kerry Collins	.60	.18
❑ 39 Junior Seau	1.00	.30
❑ 40 Ed McCaffrey	.60	.18
❑ 41 Marshall Faulk	1.00	.30
❑ 42 Deuce McAllister	1.00	.30
❑ 43 Drew Bledsoe	1.00	.30
❑ 44 Brian Urlacher	1.50	.45
❑ 45 William Green	.60	.18
❑ 46 Chris Chambers	1.00	.30
❑ 47 Daunte Culpepper	1.00	.30
❑ 48 Warrick Dunn	.60	.18
❑ 49 Antwaan Randle El	1.00	.30
❑ 50 Joey Harrington	1.50	.45
❑ 51 Tim Brown	1.00	.30
❑ 52 Duce Staley	.60	.18
❑ 53 Laveranues Coles	.60	.18
❑ 54 Ray Lewis	1.00	.30
❑ 55 Marvin Harrison	1.00	.30
❑ 56 Tony Gonzalez	.60	.18
❑ 57 Torry Holt	1.00	.30
❑ 58 Jeff Garcia	1.00	.30
❑ 59 Peerless Price	.60	.18
❑ 60 Marcel Shipp	.60	.18
❑ 61 Brian Finneran	.40	.12
❑ 62 Fred Taylor	1.00	.30
❑ 63 Koren Robinson	.40	.12
❑ 64 Shaun Alexander	1.00	.30
❑ 65 Plaxico Burress	.60	.18
❑ 66 Ahman Green	1.00	.30
❑ 67 Simeon Rice	.60	.18
❑ 68 Joe Horn	.60	.18
❑ 69 Steve McNair	1.00	.30
❑ 70 Amani Toomer	.60	.18
❑ 71 Kendrell Bell	.60	.18
❑ 72 Marty Booker	.60	.18
❑ 73 Stephen Davis	.60	.18
❑ 74 David Carr	1.50	.45
❑ 75 Garrison Hearst	.60	.18
❑ 76 Joey Galloway	.60	.18
❑ 77 Aaron Brooks	1.00	.30
❑ 78 Mike Alstott	1.00	.30
❑ 79 Shannon Sharpe	.60	.18
❑ 80 Derrick Mason	.60	.18
❑ 81 Tim Couch	.40	.12
❑ 82 Chad Johnson	.60	.18
❑ 83 Jason Taylor	.40	.12
❑ 84 Travis Henry	.60	.18
❑ 85 Curtis Conway	.40	.12
❑ 86 Peyton Manning	1.50	.45
❑ 87 Kurt Warner	1.00	.30
❑ 88 LaDainian Tomlinson	1.00	.30
❑ 89 Emmitt Smith	2.50	.75
❑ 90 Priest Holmes	1.25	.35
❑ 91 Ricky Williams AC	5.00	1.50
❑ 92 Brett Favre AC	12.00	3.60
❑ 93 Clinton Portis AC	8.00	2.40
❑ 94 Randy Moss AC	8.00	2.40
❑ 95 Tom Brady AC	8.00	2.40
❑ 96 Chad Pennington AC	8.00	2.40
❑ 97 Michael Vick AC	15.00	4.50
❑ 98 Jeremy Shockey AC	10.00	3.00
❑ 99 Donovan McNabb AC	8.00	2.40
❑ 100 Jerry Rice AC	12.00	3.60
❑ 101 Carson Palmer AC/350 RC	40.00	12.00
❑ 102 Lee Suggs AC/350 RC	25.00	7.50
❑ 103 Larry Johnson AC/350 RC	25.00	7.50
❑ 104 Taylor Jacobs AC/650 RC	5.00	1.50
❑ 105 Andre Johnson AC/350 RC	30.00	9.00
❑ 106 Justin Fargas AC/650 RC	10.00	3.00
❑ 107 Charles Rogers AC/350 RC	25.00	7.50
❑ 108 Willis McGahee AC/650 RC	25.00	7.50
❑ 109 Byron Leftwich AC/350 RC	50.00	15.00
❑ 110 Kyle Boller AC/650 RC	25.00	7.50
❑ 111 Bobby Wade RC	8.00	2.40
❑ 112 Brian St.Pierre RC	8.00	2.40
❑ 113 Doug Gabriel RC	8.00	2.40
❑ 114 Chris Brown RC	15.00	4.50
❑ 115 DeWayne Robertson RC	8.00	2.40
❑ 116 Anquan Boldin RC	20.00	6.00
❑ 117 Brandon Lloyd RC	10.00	3.00
❑ 118 Brad Banks RC	6.00	1.80
❑ 119 Dallas Clark RC	8.00	2.40
❑ 120 Artose Pinner RC	8.00	2.40
❑ 121 Dave Ragone RC	8.00	2.40
❑ 122 Arnaz Battle RC	8.00	2.40
❑ 123 Andrew Pinnock RC	6.00	1.80
❑ 124 Billy McMullen RC	6.00	1.80
❑ 125 Avon Cobourne RC	6.00	1.80
❑ 126 Terence Newman RC	15.00	4.50
❑ 127 Jimmy Kennedy RC	8.00	2.40
❑ 128 Terrell Suggs RC	12.00	3.60
❑ 129 Rex Grossman RC	20.00	6.00
❑ 130 Musa Smith RC	8.00	2.40
❑ 131 William Joseph RC	8.00	2.40
❑ 132 Tyrone Calico RC	10.00	3.00
❑ 133 Teyo Johnson RC	8.00	2.40
❑ 134 Onterrio Smith RC	10.00	3.00
❑ 135 Mike Doss RC	8.00	2.40
❑ 136 Kliff Kingsbury RC	6.00	1.80
❑ 137 Kelley Washington RC	8.00	2.40
❑ 138 Kareem Kelly RC	6.00	1.80
❑ 139 Jason Gesser RC	8.00	2.40
❑ 140 Chris Simms RC	15.00	4.50

2003 Fleer Showcase Legacy

Nm-Mt Ex-Mt

*STARS: 3X TO 8X BASIC CARDS
*AC STARS 91-95: .8X TO 2X
*AC STARS 96-100: ..6X TO 1.5X
*AC/350 ROOKIES: .4X TO 1X
*AC/650 ROOKIES: .6X TO 1.5X
*ROOKIES 111-140: .8X TO 2X
UNPRICED MASTERPIECES of 1 EXIST

2004 Fleer Showcase

	Nm-Mt	Ex-Mt
COMP.SET w/o SP's (100)	25.00	7.50

101-148 ROOKIE STATED ODDS 1:10H, 1:75R
101-148 ROOKIE PRINT RUN 599 SER.#'d SETS

❑ 1 Jamal Lewis	1.00	.30
❑ 2 Kevan Barlow	.60	.18
❑ 3 Travis Henry	.60	.18
❑ 4 Jon Kitna	.60	.18
❑ 5 David Boston	.60	.18
❑ 6 Andre Davis	.40	.12
❑ 7 Steve McNair	1.00	.30

❑ 8 Freddie Mitchell .60 .18
❑ 9 Plaxico Burress .60 .18
❑ 10 Jake Delhomme 1.00 .30
❑ 11 Andre Johnson 1.00 .30
❑ 12 T.J. Duckett .60 .18
❑ 13 Ray Lewis 1.00 .30
❑ 14 Shaun Alexander 1.00 .30
❑ 15 Stephen Davis .60 .18
❑ 16 Priest Holmes 1.25 .35
❑ 17 Edgerrin James 1.00 .30
❑ 18 Josh McCown .60 .18
❑ 19 Jerry Rice 2.00 .60
❑ 20 Fred Taylor .60 .18
❑ 21 Marty Booker .60 .18
❑ 22 Eddie George .60 .18
❑ 23 Jake Plummer .60 .18
❑ 24 LaDainian Tomlinson 1.00 .30
❑ 25 David Carr 1.00 .30
❑ 26 Keenan McCardell .40 .12
❑ 27 Jerry Porter .60 .18
❑ 28 Drew Bledsoe 1.00 .30
❑ 29 Brian Dawkins .40 .12
❑ 30 Curtis Martin 1.00 .30
❑ 31 Troy Brown .60 .18
❑ 32 Peyton Manning 1.50 .45
❑ 33 Clinton Portis 1.00 .30
❑ 34 Brett Favre 2.50 .75
❑ 35 Joey Harrington 1.00 .30
❑ 36 Tiki Barber .60 .18
❑ 37 Hines Ward 1.00 .30
❑ 38 Laveranues Coles .60 .18
❑ 39 Deuce McAllister 1.00 .30
❑ 40 Kyle Boller 1.00 .30
❑ 41 Jeff Garcia 1.00 .30
❑ 42 Julius Peppers 1.00 .30
❑ 43 Chris Chambers .60 .18
❑ 44 Willis McGahee 1.00 .30
❑ 45 Michael Vick 2.00 .60
❑ 46 Carson Palmer 1.25 .35
❑ 47 Ricky Williams 1.00 .30
❑ 48 Matt Hasselbeck .60 .18
❑ 49 Anquan Boldin 1.00 .30
❑ 50 Tony Gonzalez .60 .18
❑ 51 Marvin Harrison 1.00 .30
❑ 52 Santana Moss .60 .18
❑ 53 Ahman Green 1.00 .30
❑ 54 Eric Moulds .60 .18
❑ 55 Byron Leftwich 1.50 .45
❑ 56 Daunte Culpepper 1.00 .30
❑ 57 Terrell Owens 1.00 .30
❑ 58 Kerry Collins .60 .18
❑ 59 Tommy Maddox .60 .18
❑ 60 Chad Johnson .60 .18
❑ 61 Rich Gannon .60 .18
❑ 62 Patrick Ramsey .60 .18
❑ 63 Quincy Morgan .60 .18
❑ 64 Koren Robinson .60 .18
❑ 65 Deion Branch 1.00 .30
❑ 66 Rex Grossman 1.00 .30
❑ 67 Damerien McCants .40 .12
❑ 68 Ashley Lelie .60 .18
❑ 69 Roy Williams S .60 .18
❑ 70 Michael Bennett .60 .18
❑ 71 Domanick Davis 1.00 .30
❑ 72 Warren Sapp .60 .18
❑ 73 Randy Moss 1.25 .35
❑ 74 Drew Brees 1.00 .30
❑ 75 Brian Westbrook .60 .18
❑ 76 Kelly Holcomb .60 .18
❑ 77 Jason Taylor .40 .12
❑ 78 Charles Rogers .60 .18
❑ 79 Marc Bulger 1.00 .30
❑ 80 Donald Driver .60 .18
❑ 81 Trent Green .60 .18
❑ 82 Peerless Price .60 .18
❑ 83 Quincy Carter .60 .18
❑ 84 Torry Holt 1.00 .30
❑ 85 Derrick Mason .60 .18
❑ 86 Donte Stallworth .60 .18
❑ 87 Derrick Brooks .60 .18
❑ 88 Dre Bly .40 .12
❑ 89 Antonio Bryant .60 .18
❑ 90 DeShaun Foster .60 .18
❑ 91 Emmitt Smith 2.00 .60
❑ 92 Chad Pennington 1.25 .35
❑ 93 Jeremy Shockey 1.00 .30
❑ 94 Aaron Brooks .60 .18
❑ 95 Marshall Faulk 1.00 .30
❑ 96 Dante Hall 1.00 .30
❑ 97 Brian Urlacher 1.25 .35
❑ 98 Corey Dillon .60 .18
❑ 99 Donovan McNabb 1.25 .35
❑ 100 Tom Brady 1.50 .45
❑ 101 Derrick Strait RC 6.00 1.80
❑ 102 Michael Clayton RC 15.00 4.50
❑ 103 Larry Fitzgerald RC 20.00 6.00
❑ 104 Chris Gamble RC 8.00 2.40
❑ 105 Devery Henderson RC 5.00 1.50
❑ 106 Steven Jackson RC 20.00 6.00
❑ 107 Michael Jenkins RC 6.00 1.80
❑ 108 Greg Jones RC 6.00 1.80
❑ 109 Kevin Jones RC 20.00 6.00
❑ 110 Eli Manning RC 30.00 9.00
❑ 111 Chris Perry RC 12.00 3.60
❑ 112 Philip Rivers RC 20.00 6.00
❑ 113 Ben Roethlisberger RC 50.00 15.00
❑ 114 Bernard Berrian RC 6.00 1.80
❑ 115 Sean Taylor RC 8.00 2.40
❑ 116 Reggie Williams RC 8.00 2.40
❑ 117 Roy Williams RC 20.00 6.00
❑ 118 Kellen Winslow RC 15.00 4.50
❑ 119 Rashaun Woods RC 8.00 2.40
❑ 120 J.P. Losman RC 15.00 4.50
❑ 121 Will Poole RC 6.00 1.80
❑ 122 Will Smith RC 6.00 1.80
❑ 123 Devard Darling RC 6.00 1.80
❑ 124 Jonathan Vilma RC 6.00 1.80
❑ 125 Drew Henson RC 15.00 4.50
❑ 126 Michael Turner RC 5.00 1.50
❑ 127 Lee Evans RC 10.00 3.00
❑ 128 Ernest Wilford RC 6.00 1.80
❑ 129 Cedric Cobbs RC 6.00 1.80
❑ 130 Ricardo Colclough RC 6.00 1.80
❑ 131 Ryan Dinwiddie RC 5.00 1.50
❑ 132 DeAngelo Hall RC 8.00 2.40
❑ 133 Cody Pickett RC 6.00 1.80
❑ 134 Quincy Wilson RC 5.00 1.50
❑ 135 Ahmad Carroll RC 8.00 2.40
❑ 136 Robert Gallery RC 10.00 3.00
❑ 137 John Navarre RC 6.00 1.80
❑ 138 P.K. Sam RC 5.00 1.50
❑ 139 Jeff Smoker RC 10.00 3.00
❑ 140 Ben Troupe RC 6.00 1.80
❑ 141 Marquise Hill RC 5.00 1.50
❑ 142 D.J. Williams RC 8.00 2.40
❑ 143 Tommie Harris RC 8.00 2.40
❑ 144 Ben Watson RC 6.00 1.80
❑ 145 Tatum Bell RC 10.00 3.00
❑ 146 B.J. Symons RC 6.00 1.80
❑ 147 Matt Schaub RC 10.00 3.00
❑ 148 Casey Clausen RC 8.00 2.40

2004 Fleer Showcase Legacy

Nm-Mt Ex-Mt
*LEGACY STARS: 3X TO 8X BASIC CARDS
*LEGACY RCs: .6X TO 1.5X BASE CARD HI
STATED PRINT RUN 125 SER.#'d SETS
UNPRICED MASTERPIECES #'d OF 1

2004 Fleer Sweet Sigs

Nm-Mt Ex-Mt
COMP.SET w/o RC's (75) 15.00 4.50
76-100 RC ODDS 1:7 HOB, 1:50 RET
76-100 RC PRINT RUN 999 SER.#'d SETS

❑ 1 Brett Favre 2.00 .60
❑ 2 Daunte Culpepper .75 .23
❑ 3 Marshall Faulk .75 .23
❑ 4 Ashley Lelie .50 .15
❑ 5 Rex Grossman .75 .23
❑ 6 Jeff Garcia .75 .23
❑ 7 Jake Plummer .50 .15
❑ 8 Tony Gonzalez .50 .15
❑ 9 Terrell Owens .75 .23
❑ 10 Plaxico Burress .50 .15
❑ 11 Michael Vick 1.50 .45
❑ 12 Carson Palmer 1.00 .30
❑ 13 Charles Rogers .50 .15
❑ 14 Corey Dillon .50 .15
❑ 15 Aaron Brooks .50 .15
❑ 16 Torry Holt .75 .23
❑ 17 Joey Galloway .50 .15
❑ 18 Mark Brunell .50 .15
❑ 19 Anquan Boldin .75 .23
❑ 20 Domanick Davis .75 .23
❑ 21 Edgerrin James .75 .23
❑ 22 Hines Ward .75 .23
❑ 23 Kyle Boller .75 .23
❑ 24 Kurt Warner .75 .23
❑ 25 Matt Hasselbeck .50 .15
❑ 26 Chris Chambers .50 .15
❑ 27 Deuce McAllister .75 .23
❑ 28 Chad Pennington 1.00 .30
❑ 29 Eddie George .50 .15
❑ 30 Ray Lewis .75 .23
❑ 31 Ahman Green .75 .23
❑ 32 Marvin Harrison .75 .23
❑ 33 Tiki Barber .50 .15
❑ 34 Jerry Rice 1.50 .45
❑ 35 Emmitt Smith 1.50 .45
❑ 36 Chad Johnson .50 .15
❑ 37 Roy Williams S .50 .15
❑ 38 Peyton Manning 1.25 .35
❑ 39 Stephen Davis .50 .15
❑ 40 Jamal Lewis .75 .23
❑ 41 David Carr .75 .23
❑ 42 A.J. Feeley .75 .23
❑ 43 Jerry Porter .50 .15
❑ 44 Willis McGahee .75 .23
❑ 45 Quincy Morgan .50 .15
❑ 46 Fred Taylor .50 .15
❑ 47 Trent Green .50 .15
❑ 48 Donovan McNabb 1.00 .30
❑ 49 Marc Bulger .75 .23
❑ 50 LaVar Arrington 1.50 .45
❑ 51 Joey Harrington .75 .23
❑ 52 Jake Delhomme .75 .23
❑ 53 Jeremy Shockey .75 .23
❑ 54 LaDainian Tomlinson .75 .23
❑ 55 Brian Urlacher 1.00 .30
❑ 56 Rudi Johnson .50 .15
❑ 57 Shaun Alexander .75 .23
❑ 58 Charlie Garner .50 .15
❑ 59 Eric Moulds .50 .15

❑ 60 Tom Brady	1.25	.35
❑ 61 Curtis Martin	.75	.23
❑ 62 Koren Robinson	.50	.15
❑ 63 Steve McNair	.75	.23
❑ 64 Travis Henry	.50	.15
❑ 65 Julius Peppers	.75	.23
❑ 66 Keyshawn Johnson	.50	.15
❑ 67 Andre Johnson	.75	.23
❑ 68 Priest Holmes	1.00	.30
❑ 69 Drew Brees	.75	.23
❑ 70 Rich Gannon	.50	.15
❑ 71 Randy Moss	1.00	.30
❑ 72 Peerless Price	.50	.15
❑ 73 Drew Bledsoe	.75	.23
❑ 74 Byron Leftwich	1.25	.35
❑ 75 Clinton Portis	.75	.23
❑ 76 Roy Williams RC	12.00	3.60
❑ 77 Eli Manning RC	20.00	6.00
❑ 78 Kevin Jones RC	12.00	3.60
❑ 79 Tatum Bell RC	8.00	2.40
❑ 80 DeAngelo Hall RC	5.00	1.50
❑ 81 Michael Clayton RC	10.00	3.00
❑ 82 Rashaun Woods RC	5.00	1.50
❑ 83 Darius Watts RC	5.00	1.50
❑ 84 J.P. Losman RC	10.00	3.00
❑ 85 Drew Henson RC	10.00	3.00
❑ 86 Philip Rivers RC	12.00	3.60
❑ 87 Ben Roethlisberger RC	40.00	12.00
❑ 88 Larry Fitzgerald RC	12.00	3.60
❑ 89 Chris Perry RC	8.00	2.40
❑ 90 Devery Henderson RC	3.00	.90
❑ 91 Sean Taylor RC	5.00	1.50
❑ 92 Reggie Williams RC	5.00	1.50
❑ 93 Lee Evans RC	6.00	1.80
❑ 94 Julius Jones RC	15.00	4.50
❑ 95 Dunta Robinson RC	4.00	1.20
❑ 96 Michael Jenkins RC	4.00	1.20
❑ 97 Greg Jones RC	4.00	1.20
❑ 98 Kellen Winslow RC	10.00	3.00
❑ 99 Steven Jackson RC	12.00	3.60
❑ 100 Matt Schaub RC	6.00	1.80

2004 Fleer Sweet Sigs Black

Nm-Mt Ex-Mt

*STARS/80-90: 4X TO 10X BASIC CARDS
*ROOKIES/80-83: .8X TO 2X
*STARS/48-56: 5X TO 12X
*STARS/26-37: 6X TO 15X
*ROOKIES/26-39: 1.2X TO 3X
CARDS SER.#'d TO JERSEY NUMBER
CARDS #'d UNDER 25 NOT PRICED

2004 Fleer Sweet Sigs Gold

Nm-Mt Ex-Mt

*STARS: 4X TO 10X BASE CARD HI
*ROOKIES: .6X TO 1.5X BASE CARD HI
STATED PRINT RUN 99 SER.#'d SETS

2002 Fleer Throwbacks

	Nm-Mt	Ex-Mt
COMP.SET w/o SP's (100)	30.00	9.00
❑ 1 Terry Bradshaw	2.50	.75
❑ 2 Franco Harris	2.00	.60
❑ 3 Y.A. Tittle	1.50	.45
❑ 4 Tony Dorsett	1.50	.45
❑ 5 Paul Hornung	1.50	.45
❑ 6 Rocky Bleier	1.50	.45
❑ 7 Archie Griffin	.75	.23
❑ 8 Dwight Clark	1.25	.35
❑ 9 Bo Jackson	2.50	.75
❑ 10 Fran Tarkenton	2.00	.60
❑ 11 Howie Long	2.00	.60
❑ 12 Bob Griese	1.50	.45
❑ 13 George Rogers	.75	.23
❑ 14 Roger Craig	1.25	.35
❑ 15 Jim Plunkett	1.25	.35
❑ 16 Eric Dickerson	1.25	.35
❑ 17 Marcus Allen	2.00	.60
❑ 18 Roger Staubach	2.50	.75
❑ 19 Lawrence Taylor	1.50	.45
❑ 20 Joe Greene	1.50	.45
❑ 21 Earl Campbell	1.50	.45
❑ 22 Dave Casper	.75	.23
❑ 23 Charles White	.75	.23
❑ 24 Fred Biletnikoff	1.50	.45
❑ 25 Dan Pastorini	.75	.23
❑ 26 John Cappelletti	.75	.23
❑ 27 Paul Warfield	1.50	.45
❑ 28 Ozzie Newsome	1.25	.35
❑ 29 Johnny Rodgers	1.50	.45
❑ 30 William Perry	1.25	.35
❑ 31 Charley Taylor	1.25	.35
❑ 32 Deacon Jones	1.25	.35
❑ 33 Bubba Smith	1.25	.35
❑ 34 James Lofton	.75	.23
❑ 35 Mike Rozier	.75	.23
❑ 36 Ray Nitschke	1.50	.45
❑ 37 Dan Fouts	1.50	.45
❑ 38 Bob Lilly	1.25	.35
❑ 39 Ronnie Lott	1.25	.35
❑ 40 Barry Sanders	2.50	.75
❑ 41 Troy Aikman	2.50	.75
❑ 42 John Elway	5.00	1.50
❑ 43 Irving Fryar	.75	.23
❑ 44 Jim Kelly	2.00	.60
❑ 45 Jim McMahon	2.00	.60
❑ 46 Joe Montana	6.00	1.80
❑ 47 Warren Moon	1.50	.45
❑ 48 Jay Novacek	.75	.23
❑ 49 Mel Renfro	.75	.23
❑ 50 Mike Singletary	1.25	.35
❑ 51 Johnny Unitas	2.50	.75
❑ 52 Steve Young	2.00	.60
❑ 53 Walter Payton	6.00	1.80
❑ 54 Dan Marino	5.00	1.50
❑ 55 Torry Holt	1.00	.30
❑ 56 Rod Smith	.60	.18
❑ 57 Priest Holmes	1.25	.35
❑ 58 Anthony Thomas	1.00	.30
❑ 59 Curtis Martin	1.00	.30
❑ 60 LaDainian Tomlinson	1.50	.45
❑ 61 Antowain Smith	.60	.18
❑ 62 Terrell Owens	1.00	.30
❑ 63 Tony Gonzalez	.60	.18
❑ 64 Steve McNair	1.00	.30
❑ 65 Jerome Bettis	1.00	.30
❑ 66 Rich Gannon	1.00	.30
❑ 67 Jake Plummer	.60	.18
❑ 68 Jamal Lewis	1.00	.30
❑ 69 Drew Brees	1.50	.45
❑ 70 Jevon Kearse	.60	.18
❑ 71 Keyshawn Johnson	1.00	.30
❑ 72 Kordell Stewart	.60	.18
❑ 73 Tim Brown	1.00	.30
❑ 74 Vinny Testaverde	.60	.18
❑ 75 Tom Brady	2.50	.75
❑ 76 Drew Bledsoe	1.25	.35
❑ 77 Stephen Davis	1.00	.30
❑ 78 Marvin Harrison	1.00	.30
❑ 79 Brian Griese	1.00	.30
❑ 80 Michael Vick	3.00	.90
❑ 81 Emmitt Smith	2.50	.75
❑ 82 Edgerrin James	1.25	.35
❑ 83 Mark Brunell	1.00	.30
❑ 84 Tim Couch	.60	.18
❑ 85 Randy Moss	2.00	.60
❑ 86 Brian Urlacher	1.50	.45
❑ 87 Marshall Faulk	1.00	.30
❑ 88 Corey Dillon	.60	.18
❑ 89 Eddie George	1.00	.30
❑ 90 Terrell Davis	1.00	.30
❑ 91 Brett Favre	2.50	.75
❑ 92 Peyton Manning	2.00	.60
❑ 93 Fred Taylor	1.00	.30
❑ 94 Daunte Culpepper	1.00	.30
❑ 95 Ricky Williams	1.50	.45
❑ 96 Jerry Rice	2.00	.60
❑ 97 Donovan McNabb	1.25	.35
❑ 98 Doug Flutie	1.00	.30
❑ 99 Jeff Garcia	1.00	.30
❑ 100 Kurt Warner	1.50	.45
❑ 101 Antonio Bryant RC	2.50	.75
❑ 102 Reche Caldwell RC	2.50	.75
❑ 103 David Carr RC	8.00	2.40
❑ 104 Tim Carter RC	1.25	.35
❑ 105 Rohan Davey RC	2.50	.75
❑ 106 Andre Davis RC	2.50	.75
❑ 107 T.J. Duckett RC	4.00	1.20
❑ 108 DeShaun Foster RC	2.50	.75
❑ 109 Jabar Gaffney RC	2.50	.75
❑ 110 William Green RC	4.00	1.20
❑ 111 Joey Harrington RC	8.00	2.40
❑ 112 Ron Johnson RC	1.25	.35
❑ 113 Ashley Lelie RC	5.00	1.50
❑ 114 Josh McCown RC	3.00	.90
❑ 115 Julius Peppers RC	5.00	1.50
❑ 116 Clinton Portis RC	8.00	2.40
❑ 117 Patrick Ramsey RC	5.00	1.50
❑ 118 Antwaan Randle El RC	2.50	.75
❑ 119 Josh Reed RC	2.50	.75
❑ 120 Cliff Russell RC	1.25	.35
❑ 121 Jeremy Shockey RC	8.00	2.40
❑ 122 Donte Stallworth RC	5.00	1.50
❑ 123 Travis Stephens RC	1.25	.35
❑ 124 Javon Walker RC	5.00	1.50
❑ 125 Marquise Walker RC	1.25	.35

1999 Fleer Tradition

	Nm-Mt	Ex-Mt
COMPLETE SET (300)	40.00	18.00
❑ 1 Randy Moss	1.25	.55
❑ 2 Peyton Manning	1.50	.70
❑ 3 Barry Sanders	1.50	.70
❑ 4 Terrell Davis	.50	.23
❑ 5 Brett Favre	1.50	.70
❑ 6 Fred Taylor	.50	.23
❑ 7 Jake Plummer	.30	.14
❑ 8 John Elway	1.50	.70
❑ 9 Emmitt Smith	1.00	.45
❑ 10 Kerry Collins	.30	.14
❑ 11 Peter Boulware	.20	.09
❑ 12 Jamal Anderson	.50	.23
❑ 13 Doug Flutie	.50	.23
❑ 14 Michael Bates	.20	.09
❑ 15 Corey Dillon	.50	.23
❑ 16 Curtis Conway	.30	.14
❑ 17 Ty Detmer	.30	.14
❑ 18 Robert Brooks	.30	.14
❑ 19 Dale Carter	.20	.09
❑ 20 Charlie Batch	.50	.23
❑ 21 Ken Dilger	.20	.09
❑ 22 Troy Aikman	1.00	.45
❑ 23 Tavian Banks	.20	.09
❑ 24 Cris Carter	.50	.23
❑ 25 Derrick Alexander WR	.30	.14
❑ 26 Chris Bordano RC	.20	.09
❑ 27 Karim Abdul-Jabbar	.30	.14
❑ 28 Jessie Armstead	.20	.09
❑ 29 Drew Bledsoe	.60	.25
❑ 30 Brian Dawkins	.30	.14
❑ 31 Wayne Chrebet	.30	.14
❑ 32 Garrison Hearst	.30	.14
❑ 33 Eric Allen	.20	.09
❑ 34 Tony Banks	.30	.14
❑ 35 Jerome Bettis	.50	.23
❑ 36 Stephen Alexander	.20	.09
❑ 37 Rodney Harrison	.20	.09
❑ 38 Mike Alstott	.50	.23

❑ 39 Chad Brown .20 .09
❑ 40 Johnny McWilliams .20 .09
❑ 41 Kevin Dyson .30 .14
❑ 42 Keith Brooking .20 .09
❑ 43 Jim Harbaugh .30 .14
❑ 44 Bobby Engram .30 .14
❑ 45 John Holecek .20 .09
❑ 46 Steve Beuerlein .20 .09
❑ 47 Tony McGee .20 .09
❑ 48 Greg Ellis .20 .09
❑ 49 Corey Fuller .20 .09
❑ 50 Stephen Boyd .20 .09
❑ 51 Marshall Faulk .60 .25
❑ 52 LeRoy Butler .20 .09
❑ 53 Reggie Barlow .20 .09
❑ 54 Randall Cunningham .50 .23
❑ 55 Aeneas Williams .20 .09
❑ 56 Kimble Anders .30 .14
❑ 57 Cam Cleeland .20 .09
❑ 58 John Avery .20 .09
❑ 59 Gary Brown .20 .09
❑ 60 Ben Coates .30 .14
❑ 61 Koy Detmer .20 .09
❑ 62 Bryan Cox .20 .09
❑ 63 Edgar Bennett .20 .09
❑ 64 Tim Brown .50 .23
❑ 65 Isaac Bruce .50 .23
❑ 66 Eddie George .50 .23
❑ 67 Reidel Anthony .30 .14
❑ 68 Charlie Jones .20 .09
❑ 69 Terry Allen .30 .14
❑ 70 Joey Galloway .30 .14
❑ 71 Jamir Miller .20 .09
❑ 72 Will Blackwell .20 .09
❑ 73 Ray Buchanan .20 .09
❑ 74 Priest Holmes .75 .35
❑ 75 Michael Irvin .30 .14
❑ 76 Jonathan Linton .20 .09
❑ 77 Curtis Enis .20 .09
❑ 78 Neil O'Donnell .30 .14
❑ 79 Tim Biakabutuka .30 .14
❑ 80 Terry Kirby .20 .09
❑ 81 Germane Crowell .20 .09
❑ 82 Jason Elam .20 .09
❑ 83 Mark Chmura .20 .09
❑ 84 Marvin Harrison .50 .23
❑ 85 Jimmy Hitchcock .20 .09
❑ 86 Tony Brackens .20 .09
❑ 87 Sean Dawkins .20 .09
❑ 88 Tony Gonzalez .50 .23
❑ 89 Kent Graham .20 .09
❑ 90 Oronde Gadsden .30 .14
❑ 91 Hugh Douglas .20 .09
❑ 92 Robert Edwards .20 .09
❑ 93 R.W. McQuarters .20 .09
❑ 94 Aaron Glenn .20 .09
❑ 95 Kevin Carter .20 .09
❑ 96 Rickey Dudley .20 .09
❑ 97 Derrick Brooks .50 .23
❑ 98 Mark Bruener .20 .09
❑ 99 Darrell Green .20 .09
❑ 100 Jessie Tuggle .20 .09
❑ 101 Freddie Jones .20 .09
❑ 102 Rob Moore .30 .14
❑ 103 Ahman Green .50 .23
❑ 104 Chris Chandler .30 .14
❑ 105 Steve McNair .50 .23
❑ 106 Kevin Greene .20 .09
❑ 107 Jermaine Lewis .30 .14
❑ 108 Erik Kramer .20 .09
❑ 109 Eric Moulds .50 .23
❑ 110 Terry Fair .20 .09
❑ 111 Carl Pickens .30 .14
❑ 112 La'Roi Glover RC
❑ 113 Chris Spielman .20 .09
❑ 114 Leroy Hoard .20 .09
❑ 115 Mark Brunell .50 .23
❑ 116 Patrick Jeffers RC 3.00 1.35
❑ 117 Elvis Grbac .30 .14
❑ 118 Ike Hilliard .20 .09
❑ 119 Sam Madison .20 .09
❑ 120 Terrell Owens .50 .23
❑ 121 Rich Gannon .50 .23
❑ 122 Skip Hicks .20 .09
❑ 123 Eric Green .20 .09
❑ 124 Trent Dilfer .30 .14
❑ 125 Terry Glenn .50 .23
❑ 126 Trent Green .50 .23
❑ 127 Charles Johnson .20 .09
❑ 128 Adrian Murrell .30 .14
❑ 129 Jason Gildon .20 .09
❑ 130 Tim Dwight .50 .23
❑ 131 Ryan Leaf .50 .23
❑ 132 Rocket Ismail .30 .14
❑ 133 Jon Kitna .50 .23
❑ 134 Alonzo Mayes .20 .09
❑ 135 Yancey Thigpen .20 .09
❑ 136 David LaFleur .20 .09
❑ 137 Ray Lewis .50 .23
❑ 138 Herman Moore .30 .14
❑ 139 Brian Griese .50 .23
❑ 140 Antonio Freeman .50 .23
❑ 141 Darnay Scott .20 .09
❑ 142 Ed McDaniel .20 .09
❑ 143 Andre Reed .30 .14
❑ 144 Andre Hastings .20 .09
❑ 145 Chris Warren .20 .09
❑ 146 Kevin Hardy .20 .09
❑ 147 Joe Jurevicius .30 .14
❑ 148 Jerome Pathon .20 .09
❑ 149 Duce Staley .50 .23
❑ 150 Dan Marino 1.50 .70
❑ 151 Jerry Rice 1.00 .45
❑ 152 Byron Bam Morris .20 .09
❑ 153 Az-Zahir Hakim .20 .09
❑ 154 Ty Law .30 .14
❑ 155 Warrick Dunn .50 .23
❑ 156 Keyshawn Johnson .50 .23
❑ 157 Brian Mitchell .20 .09
❑ 158 James Jett .30 .14
❑ 159 Fred Lane .20 .09
❑ 160 Courtney Hawkins .20 .09
❑ 161 Andre Wadsworth .20 .09
❑ 162 Natrone Means .30 .14
❑ 163 Andrew Glover .20 .09
❑ 164 Anthony Simmons .20 .09
❑ 165 Leon Lett .20 .09
❑ 166 Frank Wycheck .20 .09
❑ 167 Barry Minter .20 .09
❑ 168 Michael McCrary .20 .09
❑ 169 Johnnie Morton .30 .14
❑ 170 Jay Riemersma .20 .09
❑ 171 Vonnie Holliday .20 .09
❑ 172 Brian Simmons .20 .09
❑ 173 Joe Johnson .20 .09
❑ 174 Ed McCaffrey .30 .14
❑ 175 Jason Sehorn .20 .09
❑ 176 Keenan McCardell .30 .14
❑ 177 Bobby Taylor .20 .09
❑ 178 Andre Rison .30 .14
❑ 179 Greg Hill .20 .09
❑ 180 O.J. McDuffie .30 .14
❑ 181 Darren Woodson .20 .09
❑ 182 Willie McGinest .20 .09
❑ 183 J.J. Stokes .30 .14
❑ 184 Leon Johnson .20 .09
❑ 185 Bert Emanuel .30 .14
❑ 186 Napoleon Kaufman .50 .23
❑ 187 Leslie Shepherd .20 .09
❑ 188 Levon Kirkland .20 .09
❑ 189 Simeon Rice .30 .14
❑ 190 Mikhael Ricks .20 .09
❑ 191 Robert Smith .50 .23
❑ 192 Michael Sinclair .20 .09
❑ 193 Muhsin Muhammad .30 .14
❑ 194 Duane Starks .20 .09
❑ 195 Terance Mathis .30 .14
❑ 196 Antowain Smith .50 .23
❑ 197 Tony Parrish .20 .09
❑ 198 Takeo Spikes .20 .09
❑ 199 Ernie Mills .20 .09
❑ 200 John Mobley .20 .09
❑ 202 Pete Mitchell .20 .09
❑ 203 Darick Holmes .20 .09
❑ 204 Derrick Thomas .30 .14
❑ 205 David Palmer .20 .09
❑ 206 Jason Taylor .20 .09
❑ 207 Sammy Knight .20 .09
❑ 208 Dwayne Rudd .20 .09
❑ 209 Lawyer Milloy .30 .14
❑ 210 Michael Strahan .30 .14
❑ 211 Mo Lewis .20 .09
❑ 212 William Thomas .20 .09
❑ 213 Darrell Russell .20 .09
❑ 214 Brad Johnson .50 .23
❑ 215 Kordell Stewart .30 .14
❑ 216 Robert Holcombe .20 .09
❑ 217 Junior Seau .50 .23
❑ 218 Jacquez Green .20 .09
❑ 219 Shawn Springs .20 .09
❑ 220 Michael Westbrook .30 .14
❑ 221 Rod Woodson .30 .14
❑ 222 Frank Sanders .30 .14
❑ 223 Bruce Smith .30 .14
❑ 224 Eugene Robinson .20 .09
❑ 225 Bill Romanowski .20 .09
❑ 226 Wesley Walls .30 .14
❑ 227 Jimmy Smith .30 .14
❑ 228 Deion Sanders .50 .23
❑ 229 Lamar Thomas .20 .09
❑ 230 Dorsey Levens .50 .23
❑ 231 Tony Simmons .20 .09
❑ 232 John Randle .30 .14
❑ 233 Curtis Martin .50 .23
❑ 234 Bryant Young .20 .09
❑ 235 Charles Woodson .50 .23
❑ 236 Charles Way .20 .09
❑ 237 Zach Thomas .50 .23
❑ 238 Ricky Proehl .20 .09
❑ 239 Ricky Watters .30 .14
❑ 240 Hardy Nickerson .20 .09
❑ 241 Shannon Sharpe .30 .14
❑ 242 O.J. Santiago .20 .09
❑ 243 Vinny Testaverde .30 .14
❑ 244 Roell Preston .20 .09
❑ 245 James Stewart .30 .14
❑ 246 Jake Reed .30 .14
❑ 247 Steve Young .60 .25
❑ 248 Shaun Williams .20 .09
❑ 249 Rod Smith .30 .14
❑ 250 Warren Sapp .30 .14
❑ 251 Champ Bailey RC 1.50 .70
❑ 252 Karsten Bailey RC .75 .35
❑ 253 D'Wayne Bates RC .75 .35
❑ 254 Michael Bishop RC 1.25 .55
❑ 255 David Boston RC 1.25 .55
❑ 256 Na Brown RC .75 .35
❑ 257 Fernando Bryant RC .75 .35
❑ 258 Shawn Bryson RC 1.25 .55
❑ 259 Darrin Chiaverini RC .75 .35
❑ 260 Chris Claiborne RC .40 .18
❑ 261 Mike Cloud RC .75 .35
❑ 262 Cecil Collins RC .40 .18
❑ 263 Tim Couch RC 1.25 .55
❑ 264 Scott Covington RC 1.25 .55
❑ 265 Daunte Culpepper RC 5.00 2.20
❑ 266 Antuan Edwards RC .40 .18
❑ 267 Troy Edwards RC .75 .35
❑ 268 Ebenezer Ekuban RC .75 .35
❑ 269 Kevin Faulk RC 1.25 .55
❑ 270 Jermaine Fazande RC .75 .35
❑ 271 Joe Germaine RC .75 .35
❑ 272 Martin Gramatica RC .40 .18
❑ 273 Torry Holt RC 3.00 1.35
❑ 274 Brock Huard RC 1.25 .55
❑ 275 Sedrick Irvin RC .40 .18
❑ 276 Sheldon Jackson RC .75 .35
❑ 277 Edgerrin James RC 5.00 2.20
❑ 278 James Johnson RC .75 .35
❑ 279 Kevin Johnson RC 1.25 .55
❑ 280 Malcolm Johnson RC .40 .18
❑ 281 Andy Katzenmoyer RC .75 .35
❑ 282 Jevon Kearse RC 2.00 .90
❑ 283 Patrick Kerney RC 1.25 .55
❑ 284 Shaun King RC .75 .35
❑ 285 Jim Kleinsasser RC 1.25 .55
❑ 286 Rob Konrad RC 1.25 .55
❑ 287 Chris McAlister RC .75 .35
❑ 288 Donovan McNabb RC 6.00 2.70
❑ 289 Cade McNown RC .75 .35
❑ 290 Dee Miller RC .40 .18
❑ 291 Joe Montgomery RC .75 .35
❑ 292 De'Mond Parker RC .40 .18
❑ 293 Peerless Price RC 2.00 .90
❑ 294 Akili Smith RC .75 .35
❑ 295 Justin Swift RC .40 .18
❑ 296 Jerame Tuman RC .75 .35
❑ 297 Ricky Williams RC 2.50 1.10
❑ 298 Antoine Winfield .75 .35
❑ 299 Craig Yeast RC .75 .35
❑ 300 Amos Zereoue RC 1.25 .55
❑ P6 Fred Taylor Promo 1.00 .45

2000 Fleer Tradition

	Nm-Mt	Ex-Mt
COMPLETE SET (400)	60.00	27.00
❑ 1 Kevin Johnson	.50	.23
❑ 2 Chris Chandler	.30	.14
❑ 3 Peerless Price	.50	.23
❑ 4 Andre Rison	.30	.14
❑ 5 Curtis Enis	.20	.09
❑ 6 Tim Couch	.30	.14
❑ 7 Brian Dawkins	.20	.09
❑ 8 Akili Smith	.20	.09
❑ 9 Kevin Faulk	.30	.14
❑ 10 Joey Galloway	.30	.14
❑ 11 Bill Romanowski	.20	.09
❑ 12 Charlie Batch	.50	.23
❑ 13 Terrence Wilkins	.20	.09
❑ 14 Kevin Hardy	.20	.09
❑ 15 Cade McNown	.20	.09
❑ 16 Elvis Grbac	.30	.14
❑ 17 Cris Carter	.50	.23
❑ 18 Willie McGinest	.20	.09
❑ 19 Michael Bishop	.20	.09
❑ 20 Lee Woodall	.20	.09
❑ 21 Jake Reed	.30	.14
❑ 22 Bryan Cox	.20	.09
❑ 23 Chris Sanders	.20	.09
❑ 24 Tavian Banks	.20	.09
❑ 25 Levon Kirkland	.20	.09
❑ 26 James Hundon	.20	.09
❑ 27 Junior Seau	.50	.23
❑ 28 Darren Woodson	.20	.09
❑ 29 Kevin Carter	.20	.09
❑ 30 Joe Jurevicius	.20	.09
❑ 31 John Lynch	.30	.14
❑ 32 Steve McNair	.50	.23
❑ 33 Jake Plummer	.30	.14
❑ 34 Antonio Freeman	.50	.23
❑ 35 Peter Boulware	.20	.09
❑ 36 Brad Johnson	.50	.23
❑ 37 Bobby Engram	.30	.14
❑ 38 David Boston	.50	.23
❑ 39 Jason Tucker	.20	.09
❑ 40 Troy Brown	.30	.14
❑ 41 Brian Griese	.50	.23
❑ 42 Dorsey Levens	.30	.14
❑ 43 Cornelius Bennett	.20	.09
❑ 44 Donovan McNabb	.75	.35
❑ 45 Rob Johnson	.30	.14
❑ 46 Robert Smith	.50	.23
❑ 47 Stanley Pritchett	.20	.09
❑ 48 Tedy Bruschi	.50	.23
❑ 49 Dan Marino	1.50	.70
❑ 50 Amani Toomer	.30	.14
❑ 51 Aaron Glenn	.20	.09
❑ 52 Rickey Dudley	.20	.09
❑ 53 Tim Brown	.50	.23
❑ 54 Jim Harbaugh	.30	.14
❑ 55 Terrell Owens	.50	.23
❑ 56 Jason Sehorn	.20	.09
❑ 57 Cortez Kennedy	.20	.09
❑ 58 London Fletcher RC	.30	.14
❑ 59 Simeon Rice	.30	.14
❑ 60 Shaun King	.20	.09
❑ 61 Stephen Davis	.50	.23
❑ 62 Andre Wadsworth	.20	.09
❑ 63 Kyle Brady	.20	.09
❑ 64 Priest Holmes	.60	.25
❑ 65 Patrick Jeffers	.50	.23
❑ 66 Barry Minter	.20	.09
❑ 67 Curtis Martin	.50	.23
❑ 68 Darrin Chiaverini	.20	.09
❑ 69 Robert Thomas	.20	.09
❑ 70 Samari Rolle	.20	.09
❑ 71 Robert Porcher	.20	.09
❑ 72 Jerry Rice	1.00	.45
❑ 73 Bill Schroeder	.30	.14
❑ 74 Chad Bratzke	.20	.09
❑ 75 Tony Brackens	.20	.09
❑ 76 O.J. McDuffie	.30	.14
❑ 77 John Randle	.30	.14
❑ 78 Michael Pittman	.20	.09
❑ 79 Drew Bledsoe	.60	.25
❑ 80 Ike Hilliard	.30	.14
❑ 81 Victor Green	.20	.09
❑ 82 Duce Staley	.50	.23
❑ 83 Bruce Smith	.30	.14
❑ 84 Amos Zereoue	.50	.23
❑ 85 Charlie Garner	.30	.14
❑ 86 Shawn Springs	.20	.09
❑ 87 Kurt Warner	1.00	.45
❑ 88 Eddie George	.50	.23
❑ 89 Michael Westbrook	.30	.14
❑ 90 Dexter Coakley	.20	.09
❑ 91 Rob Moore	.30	.14
❑ 92 Duane Starks	.20	.09
❑ 93 Steve Beuerlein	.30	.14
❑ 94 Marty Booker	.30	.14
❑ 95 Karim Abdul-Jabbar	.30	.14
❑ 96 Troy Aikman	1.00	.45
❑ 97 Germane Crowell	.20	.09
❑ 98 Matt Hasselbeck	.30	.14
❑ 99 E.G. Green	.20	.09
❑ 100 Mark Brunell	.50	.23
❑ 101 Tony Martin	.30	.14
❑ 102 Darrell Green	.20	.09
❑ 103 Ricky Williams	.50	.23
❑ 104 Michael Strahan	.30	.14
❑ 105 Vinny Testaverde	.30	.14
❑ 106 Charles Johnson	.30	.14
❑ 107 Hines Ward	.50	.23
❑ 108 Bryant Young	.20	.09
❑ 109 Mo Lewis	.20	.09
❑ 110 Greg Clark	.20	.09
❑ 111 Jon Kitna	.50	.23
❑ 112 Jacquez Green	.20	.09
❑ 113 Kevin Dyson	.30	.14
❑ 114 Stephen Alexander	.20	.09
❑ 115 Cam Cleeland	.20	.09
❑ 116 Keith Poole	.20	.09
❑ 117 Az-Zahir Hakim	.30	.14
❑ 118 Tim Dwight	.50	.23
❑ 119 Corey Bradford	.20	.09
❑ 120 Carlos Emmons	.20	.09
❑ 121 Trent Dilfer	.30	.14
❑ 122 Lance Schulters	.20	.09
❑ 123 Byron Hanspard	.20	.09
❑ 124 Tim Biakabutuka	.30	.14
❑ 125 Eddie Kennison	.30	.14
❑ 126 Terry Kirby	.20	.09
❑ 127 Mike McKenzie	.20	.09
❑ 128 Fred Beasley	.20	.09
❑ 129 Chad Brown	.20	.09
❑ 130 Terrell Davis	.50	.23
❑ 131 Herman Moore	.30	.14
❑ 132 Vonnie Holliday	.20	.09
❑ 133 Jim Miller	.20	.09
❑ 134 Peyton Manning	1.25	.55
❑ 135 Derrick Alexander	.30	.14
❑ 136 Oronde Gadsden	.30	.14
❑ 137 Robert Griffith	.20	.09
❑ 138 Troy Edwards	.20	.09
❑ 139 Damon Huard	.50	.23
❑ 140 Jessie Armstead	.20	.09
❑ 141 Charles Woodson	.30	.14
❑ 142 Troy Vincent	.20	.09
❑ 143 Natrone Means	.20	.09
❑ 144 Jeff Garcia	.50	.23
❑ 145 Terry Glenn	.30	.14
❑ 146 Marshall Faulk	.60	.25
❑ 147 Pat Johnson	.20	.09
❑ 148 Frank Wycheck	.20	.09
❑ 149 Champ Bailey	.30	.14
❑ 150 Jamal Anderson	.50	.23
❑ 151 Doug Flutie	.50	.23
❑ 152 Michael Bates	.20	.09
❑ 153 Corey Dillon	.50	.23
❑ 154 Keith McKenzie	.20	.09
❑ 155 Orpheus Roye	.20	.09
❑ 156 Olandis Gary	.50	.23
❑ 157 Johnnie Morton	.30	.14
❑ 158 Brett Favre	1.50	.70
❑ 159 Adrian Murrell	.20	.09
❑ 160 Fred Taylor	.50	.23
❑ 161 Tony Gonzalez	.30	.14
❑ 162 Zach Thomas	.50	.23
❑ 163 Randy Moss	1.00	.45
❑ 164 Marcus Robinson	.50	.23
❑ 165 Tiki Barber	.30	.14
❑ 166 Rich Gannon	.50	.23
❑ 167 Jeremiah Trotter RC	1.50	.70
❑ 168 Jermaine Fazande	.20	.09
❑ 169 Steve Young	.60	.25
❑ 170 Isaac Bruce	.50	.23
❑ 171 Warrick Dunn	.50	.23
❑ 172 Yancey Thigpen	.20	.09
❑ 173 Rod Smith	.30	.14
❑ 174 Albert Connell	.20	.09
❑ 175 Freddie Jones	.20	.09
❑ 176 Terance Mathis	.30	.14
❑ 177 Eric Moulds	.50	.23
❑ 178 Brian Mitchell	.20	.09
❑ 179 Wesley Walls	.20	.09
❑ 180 Carl Pickens	.30	.14
❑ 181 Errict Rhett	.30	.14
❑ 182 Madre Hill	.20	.09
❑ 183 Jason Elam	.20	.09
❑ 184 Greg Ellis	.20	.09
❑ 185 David Sloan	.20	.09
❑ 186 Edgerrin James	.75	.35
❑ 187 Jimmy Smith	.30	.14
❑ 188 Tony Richardson RC	.30	.14
❑ 189 James Hasty	.20	.09
❑ 190 Sam Madison	.20	.09
❑ 191 Tony Simmons	.20	.09
❑ 192 Andre Hastings	.20	.09
❑ 193 Keyshawn Johnson	.50	.23
❑ 194 Na Brown	.20	.09
❑ 195 Napoleon Kaufman	.30	.14
❑ 196 Torrance Small	.20	.09
❑ 197 Curtis Conway	.30	.14
❑ 198 Jeff Graham	.20	.09
❑ 199 Jason Hanson	.20	.09
❑ 200 Derrick Mayes	.30	.14
❑ 201 Torry Holt	.50	.23
❑ 202 Warren Sapp	.30	.14
❑ 203 Kimble Anders	.20	.09
❑ 204 Blaine Bishop	.20	.09
❑ 205 Leroy Hoard	.20	.09
❑ 206 Larry Centers	.20	.09
❑ 207 O.J. Santiago	.20	.09
❑ 208 Antowain Smith	.30	.14
❑ 209 Chuck Smith	.20	.09
❑ 210 Takeo Spikes	.20	.09
❑ 211 Rocket Ismail	.30	.14
❑ 212 Ed McCaffrey	.50	.23
❑ 213 Karsten Bailey	.20	.09
❑ 214 Terry Fair	.20	.09
❑ 215 Ken Dilger	.20	.09
❑ 216 Jamie Martin	.30	.14
❑ 217 Cris Dishman	.20	.09
❑ 218 Jay Fiedler	.30	.14
❑ 219 Lawyer Milloy	.30	.14
❑ 220 Jake Delhomme RC	2.50	1.10
❑ 221 Wayne Chrebet	.30	.14
❑ 222 Darrell Russell	.20	.09
❑ 223 Christian Fauria	.20	.09
❑ 224 Jerome Bettis	.50	.23
❑ 225 Ryan Leaf	.30	.14
❑ 226 Ricky Watters	.30	.14
❑ 227 Keenan McCardell	.30	.14
❑ 228 Grant Wistrom	.20	.09
❑ 229 Jevon Kearse	.50	.23
❑ 230 Frank Sanders	.30	.14
❑ 231 Shannon Sharpe	.30	.14
❑ 232 Jonathan Linton	.20	.09
❑ 233 Alonzo Mayes	.20	.09
❑ 234 Jason Garrett	.20	.09
❑ 235 Kordell Stewart	.30	.14
❑ 236 David LaFleur	.20	.09
❑ 237 Kenny Bynum	.20	.09
❑ 238 Byron Chamberlain	.20	.09
❑ 239 Tyrone Davis	.20	.09
❑ 240 Jerome Pathon	.30	.14
❑ 241 Alvis Whitted	.20	.09
❑ 242 Kevin Lockett	.20	.09
❑ 243 Matthew Hatchette	.20	.09

❑ 244 Rod Woodson .30 .14
❑ 245 Joe Horn .30 .14
❑ 246 Ronnie Powell .20 .09
❑ 247 Dedric Ward .20 .09
❑ 248 James Johnson .20 .09
❑ 249 James Jett .20 .09
❑ 250 Bobby Shaw RC .60 .25
❑ 251 J.J. Stokes .30 .14
❑ 252 Paul Shields RC .20 .09
❑ 253 Sean Dawkins .20 .09
❑ 254 Hardy Nickerson .20 .09
❑ 255 Stephen Boyd .20 .09
❑ 256 Chris Warren .20 .09
❑ 257 Kerry Collins .30 .14
❑ 258 Isaac Byrd .20 .09
❑ 259 Bobby Hoying .20 .09
❑ 260 Daunte Culpepper .60 .25
❑ 261 Moe Williams .30 .14
❑ 262 Kamil Loud .20 .09
❑ 263 Derrick Brooks .50 .23
❑ 264 Jay Riemersma .20 .09
❑ 265 Ray Lucas .30 .14
❑ 266 Jason Gildon .20 .09
❑ 267 James Stewart .30 .14
❑ 268 Marcellus Wiley .20 .09
❑ 269 Craig Yeast .20 .09
❑ 270 Michael Basnight .20 .09
❑ 271 Tyrone Wheatley .30 .14
❑ 272 Martin Gramatica .20 .09
❑ 273 Phillip Daniels RC .30 .14
❑ 274 Richard Huntley .20 .09
❑ 275 Muhsin Muhammad .30 .14
❑ 276 Todd Lyght .20 .09
❑ 277 Carlester Crumpler .20 .09
❑ 278 Jeff Lewis .20 .09
❑ 279 Jeff George .30 .14
❑ 280 Jeff Blake .30 .14
❑ 281 Michael McCrary .20 .09
❑ 282 Shawn Jefferson .20 .09
❑ 283 Mark Bruener .20 .09
❑ 284 Donnie Abraham .20 .09
❑ 285 Yatil Green .20 .09
❑ 286 Jermaine Lewis .20 .09
❑ 287 Rob Fredrickson .20 .09
❑ 288 Thurman Thomas .30 .14
❑ 289 Kent Graham .20 .09
❑ 290 Darnay Scott .30 .14
❑ 291 Tony Graziani .20 .09
❑ 292 Qadry Ismail .30 .14
❑ 293 Aeneas Williams .20 .09
❑ 294 Marvin Harrison .50 .23
❑ 295 Jimmy Hitchcock .20 .09
❑ 296 Bob Christian .20 .09
❑ 297 Pete Mitchell .20 .09
❑ 298 Mike Alstott .50 .23
❑ 299 Emmitt Smith 1.00 .45
❑ 300 Trevor Pryce .20 .09
❑ 301 Tony Banks .30 .14
❑ 302 Mikhael Ricks .20 .09
❑ 303 Randall Cunningham .50 .23
❑ 304 Thomas Jones RC 1.25 .55
❑ 305 Mark Simoneau RC .60 .25
❑ 306 Jamal Lewis RC 2.00 .90
❑ 307 Kwame Cavil RC .40 .18
❑ 308 Rashard Anderson RC .60 .25
❑ 309 Brian Urlacher RC 3.00 1.35
❑ 310 Peter Warrick RC .75 .35
❑ 311 Courtney Brown RC .75 .35
❑ 312 Michael Wiley RC .60 .25
❑ 313 Chris Cole RC .60 .25
❑ 314 Reuben Droughns RC 1.00 .45
❑ 315 Bubba Franks RC .75 .35
❑ 316 Rob Morris RC .60 .25
❑ 317 R.Jay Soward RC .60 .25
❑ 318 Sylvester Morris RC .60 .25
❑ 319 Ben Kelly RC .40 .18
❑ 320 Doug Chapman RC .60 .25
❑ 321 J.R. Redmond RC .60 .25
❑ 322 Darren Howard RC .60 .25
❑ 323 Ron Dayne RC .75 .35
❑ 324 Chad Pennington RC 3.00 1.35
❑ 325 Jerry Porter RC 1.00 .45
❑ 326 Corey Simon RC .75 .35
❑ 327 Plaxico Burress RC 1.50 .70
❑ 328 Trung Canidate RC .60 .25
❑ 329 Rogers Beckett RC .60 .25
❑ 330 Giovanni Carmazzi RC .60 .25
❑ 331 Shaun Alexander RC 2.00 .90
❑ 332 Joe Hamilton RC .60 .25
❑ 333 Keith Bulluck RC .75 .35
❑ 334 Todd Husak RC .75 .35
❑ 335 Darwin Walker RC .60 .25
Raynoch Thompson RC
❑ 336 Mareno Philyaw RC .40 .18
Anthony Midget RC
❑ 337 Chris Redman RC .75 .35
Travis Taylor RC
❑ 338 Sammy Morris RC .60 .25
Avion Black RC
❑ 339 Deon Grant RC .60 .25
Alvin McKinley RC
❑ 340 Dez White RC .75 .35
Frank Murphy RC
❑ 341 Curtis Keaton RC 1.00 .45
Ron Dugans RC
❑ 342 Travis Prentice RC .60 .25
Dennis Northcutt RC
❑ 343 Orantes Grant RC .40 .18
Dwayne Goodrich RC
❑ 344 Deltha O'Neal RC .75 .35
Ian Gold RC
❑ 345 Stockar McDougle RC .40 .18
Barrett Green RC
❑ 346 Anthony Lucas RC .60 .25
Na'il Diggs RC
❑ 347 Marcus Washington RC .40 .18
Don Kendra RC
❑ 348 T.J. Slaughter RC .60 .25
Shyrone Stith RC
❑ 349 William Bartee RC .60 .25
Frank Moreau RC
❑ 350 Deon Dyer RC .60 .25
Todd Wade RC
❑ 351 Chris Hovan RC .75 .35
Troy Walters RC
❑ 352 David Stachelski RC 20.00 9.00
Tom Brady RC
❑ 353 Marc Bulger RC 1.50 .70
Terrelle Smith RC
❑ 354 Cornelius Griffin RC .60 .25
Ron Dixon RC
❑ 355 Laveranues Coles RC .75 .35
Anthony Becht RC
❑ 356 Sebastian Janikowski RC .75 .35
Shane Lechler RC
❑ 357 Todd Pinkston RC .75 .35
Gari Scott RC
❑ 358 Danny Farmer RC .60 .25
Tee Martin RC
❑ 359 Brian Young RC .60 .25
Jacoby Shepherd RC
❑ 360 JaJuan Seider RC .60 .25
Trevor Gaylor RC
❑ 361 Tim Rattay RC 1.50 .70
Chafie Fields RC
❑ 362 Darrell Jackson RC 1.25 .55
James Williams RC
❑ 363 Nate Webster RC .40 .18
James Whalen RC
❑ 364 Erron Kinney RC .75 .35
Chris Coleman RC
❑ 365 Chris Samuels RC .60 .25
Leon Murray RC
❑ 366 Arizona Cardinals IA .30 .14
Jake Plummer
❑ 367 Atlanta Falcons IA .30 .14
Chris Chandler
Jamal Anderson
❑ 368 Baltimore Ravens IA .20 .09
Peter Boulware
❑ 369 Buffalo Bills IA .30 .14
Doug Flutie
❑ 370 Carolina Panthers IA .30 .14
Steve Beuerlein
❑ 371 Chicago Bears IA .20 .09
Cade McNown
❑ 372 Cincinnati Bengals IA .30 .14
Corey Dillon
❑ 373 Cleveland Browns IA .30 .14
Tim Couch
❑ 374 Dallas Cowboys IA .50 .23
Emmitt Smith
❑ 375 Denver Broncos IA .30 .14
Olandis Gary
❑ 376 Detroit Lions IA .30 .14
Charlie Batch
❑ 377 Green Bay Packers IA .30 .14
Dorsey Levens
❑ 378 Indianapolis Colts IA .60 .25
Edgerrin James
❑ 379 Jacksonville Jaguars IA .20 .09
Tony Brackens
❑ 380 Kansas City Chiefs IA .20 .09
Elvis Grbac
❑ 381 Miami Dolphins IA .75 .35
Dan Marino
❑ 382 Minnesota Vikings IA .30 .14
Robert Smith
❑ 383 New England Patriots IA .30 .14
Drew Bledsoe
❑ 384 New Orleans Saints IA .50 .23
Ricky Williams
❑ 385 New York Giants IA .20 .09
Jessie Armstead
❑ 386 New York Jets IA .30 .14
Curtis Martin
❑ 387 Oakland Raiders IA .30 .14
Napoleon Kaufman
❑ 388 Philadelphia Eagles IA .30 .14
Donovan McNabb
❑ 389 Pittsburgh Steelers IA .30 .14
Jerome Bettis
❑ 390 St. Louis Rams IA .50 .23
Marshall Faulk
❑ 391 San Diego Chargers IA .20 .09
Jermaine Fazande
❑ 392 San Francisco 49ers IA .30 .14
Charlie Garner
❑ 393 Seattle Seahawks IA .20 .09
Cortez Kennedy
❑ 394 Tampa Bay Bucs IA .30 .14
Mike Alstott
❑ 395 Tennessee Titans IA .30 .14
Steve McNair
❑ 396 Washington Redskins IA .30 .14
Stephen Davis
❑ 397 Tim Couch CL .30 .14
❑ 398 Peyton Manning CL .60 .25
❑ 399 Kurt Warner CL .50 .23
❑ 400 Randy Moss CL .50 .23

2001 Fleer Tradition

	Nm-Mt	Ex-Mt
COMPLETE SET (450)	40.00	12.00
❑ 1 Thomas Jones	.40	.12
❑ 2 Bruce Smith	.25	.07
❑ 3 Marvin Harrison	.60	.18
❑ 4 Darrell Jackson	.60	.18
❑ 5 Trent Green	.60	.18
❑ 6 Wesley Walls	.25	.07
❑ 7 Jimmy Smith	.40	.12
❑ 8 Isaac Bruce	.60	.18
❑ 9 Jamal Anderson	.60	.18
❑ 10 Marty Booker	.25	.07
❑ 11 Elvis Grbac	.40	.12
❑ 12 Joe Jurevicius	.25	.07
❑ 13 Reidel Anthony	.25	.07
❑ 14 Darnay Scott	.25	.07
❑ 15 Oronde Gadsden	.40	.12
❑ 16 Shawn Bryson	.25	.07
❑ 17 Jonathan Ogden	.25	.07
❑ 18 Aaron Shea	.25	.07
❑ 19 Randy Moss	1.25	.35
❑ 20 Eddie George	.60	.18
❑ 21 Stephen Davis	.60	.18
❑ 22 Emmitt Smith	1.25	.35

❑ 23 Willie McGinest .25 .07
❑ 24 Trent Dilfer .40 .12
❑ 25 Peter Boulware .25 .07
❑ 26 Rod Smith .40 .12
❑ 27 Ricky Williams .60 .18
❑ 28 Albert Connell .25 .07
❑ 29 Robert Porcher .25 .07
❑ 30 Jessie Armstead .25 .07
❑ 31 Shane Matthews .25 .07
❑ 32 Eric Moulds .40 .12
❑ 33 Kurt Schulz .25 .07
❑ 34 Richie Anderson .25 .07
❑ 35 Ron Dugans .25 .07
❑ 36 Steve Beuerlein .40 .12
❑ 37 Darren Sharper .25 .07
❑ 38 Andre Rison .40 .12
❑ 39 Courtney Brown .40 .12
❑ 40 Eddie Kennison .40 .12
❑ 41 Ken Dilger .25 .07
❑ 42 Charles Johnson .25 .07
❑ 43 Dexter Coakley .25 .07
❑ 44 Akili Smith .25 .07
❑ 45 R.Jay Soward .25 .07
❑ 46 Danny Farmer .25 .07
❑ 47 Dez White .25 .07
❑ 48 Olandis Gary .40 .12
❑ 49 Wali Rainer .25 .07
❑ 50 Derrick Alexander .40 .12
❑ 51 Donnie Abraham .25 .07
❑ 52 David Sloan .25 .07
❑ 53 Larry Allen .25 .07
❑ 54 Sam Madison .25 .07
❑ 55 Troy Edwards .25 .07
❑ 56 Ryan Longwell .25 .07
❑ 57 Brian Griese .60 .18
❑ 58 John Randle .40 .12
❑ 59 Reggie Jones .25 .07
❑ 60 Mike Peterson .25 .07
❑ 61 Bill Romanowski .25 .07
❑ 62 Kevin Faulk .40 .12
❑ 63 Tai Streets .25 .07
❑ 64 Tony Brackens .25 .07
❑ 65 James Stewart .40 .12
❑ 66 Joe Horn .40 .12
❑ 67 Kurt Warner 1.25 .35
❑ 68 Eric Hicks RC .25 .07
❑ 69 Bryan Westbrook .25 .07
❑ 70 Tiki Barber .40 .12
❑ 71 Frank Sanders .25 .07
❑ 72 Olindo Mare .25 .07
❑ 73 Bill Schroeder .40 .12
❑ 74 Anthony Becht .25 .07
❑ 75 Rob Johnson .40 .12
❑ 76 Troy Brown .40 .12
❑ 77 Chad Bratzke .25 .07
❑ 78 Rickey Dudley .25 .07
❑ 79 Doug Johnson .25 .07
❑ 80 Joe Johnson .25 .07
❑ 81 Keenan McCardell .25 .07
❑ 82 Tim Brown .60 .18
❑ 83 Blaine Bishop .25 .07
❑ 84 Ron Dixon .25 .07
❑ 85 Michael Cloud .25 .07
❑ 86 Todd Pinkston .25 .07
❑ 87 Shannon Sharpe .40 .12
❑ 88 Marvin Jones .25 .07
❑ 89 Zach Thomas .60 .18
❑ 90 Kordell Stewart .40 .12
❑ 91 Champ Bailey .40 .12
❑ 92 Jacquez Green .25 .07
❑ 93 Daunte Culpepper .60 .18
❑ 94 Freddie Jones .25 .07
❑ 95 Donald Hayes .25 .07
❑ 96 Rich Gannon .60 .18
❑ 97 Ty Law .40 .12
❑ 98 Grant Wistrom .25 .07
❑ 99 James Allen .40 .12
❑ 100 Corey Simon .40 .12
❑ 101 Jeff Blake .40 .12
❑ 102 Bryant Young .25 .07
❑ 103 Craig Yeast .25 .07
❑ 104 Bobby Shaw .25 .07
❑ 105 Kerry Collins .40 .12
❑ 106 Brock Huard .25 .07
❑ 107 JaJuan Dawson .25 .07
❑ 108 Jeff Graham .25 .07
❑ 109 Chad Pennington 1.00 .30
❑ 110 Jake Plummer .40 .12
❑ 111 James McKnight .40 .12
❑ 112 Terrell Owens .60 .18
❑ 113 Mo Lewis .25 .07
❑ 114 Jeremy McDaniel .25 .07
❑ 115 Ed McCaffrey .60 .18
❑ 116 Ricky Watters .25 .07
❑ 117 Jerry Porter .40 .12
❑ 118 Shawn Jefferson .25 .07
❑ 119 Charlie Batch .60 .18
❑ 120 Justin Watson .25 .07
❑ 121 Donovan McNabb .75 .23
❑ 122 Shaun King .25 .07
❑ 123 Brett Favre 2.00 .60
❑ 124 Ronald McKinnon .25 .07
❑ 125 Richard Huntley .25 .07
❑ 126 Ray Lewis .60 .18
❑ 127 Jerome Pathon .40 .12
❑ 128 Sam Cowart .25 .07
❑ 129 Ryan Leaf .40 .12
❑ 130 Greg Clark .25 .07
❑ 131 Tony Boselli .25 .07
❑ 132 Frank Wycheck .25 .07
❑ 133 Charlie Garner .40 .12
❑ 134 Tony Siragusa .25 .07
❑ 135 Sylvester Morris .25 .07
❑ 136 Qadry Ismail .40 .12
❑ 137 Jon Kitna .40 .12
❑ 138 James Thrash .40 .12
❑ 139 Lamar Smith .40 .12
❑ 140 Brad Johnson .60 .18
❑ 141 London Fletcher .25 .07
❑ 142 Tim Biakabutuka .40 .12
❑ 143 Ed McDaniel .25 .07
❑ 144 Tony Parrish .25 .07
❑ 145 David Boston .60 .18
❑ 146 Brian Urlacher 1.00 .30
❑ 147 Drew Bledsoe .75 .23
❑ 148 David Patten .25 .07
❑ 149 Marcellus Wiley .25 .07
❑ 150 Peter Warrick .60 .18
❑ 151 La'Roi Glover .25 .07
❑ 152 Troy Aikman 1.00 .30
❑ 153 Chris Chandler .40 .12
❑ 154 Travis Prentice .25 .07
❑ 155 Ike Hilliard .40 .12
❑ 156 John Mobley .25 .07
❑ 157 Warren Sapp .40 .12
❑ 158 Joey Galloway .40 .12
❑ 159 Laveranues Coles .60 .18
❑ 160 Germane Crowell .25 .07
❑ 161 Jamal Lewis 1.00 .30
❑ 162 Mike Anderson .60 .18
❑ 163 Charles Woodson .40 .12
❑ 164 Antonio Freeman .60 .18
❑ 165 Derrick Mason .40 .12
❑ 166 Chris Claiborne .25 .07
❑ 167 Brian Mitchell .25 .07
❑ 168 Mike Vanderjagt .25 .07
❑ 169 Rod Woodson .40 .12
❑ 170 Doug Chapman .25 .07
❑ 171 John Lynch .40 .12
❑ 172 Kevin Hardy .25 .07
❑ 173 Sam Shade .25 .07
❑ 174 Edgerrin James .75 .23
❑ 175 Brian Dawkins .25 .07
❑ 176 Donnie Edwards .25 .07
❑ 177 Patrick Jeffers .40 .12
❑ 178 Mark Brunell .60 .18
❑ 179 Junior Seau .60 .18
❑ 180 Trace Armstrong .25 .07
❑ 181 Marcus Robinson .60 .18
❑ 182 Tony Gonzalez .40 .12
❑ 183 J.J. Stokes .40 .12
❑ 184 Jake Reed .40 .12
❑ 185 Corey Dillon .60 .18
❑ 186 Jay Fiedler .60 .18
❑ 187 Christian Fauria .25 .07
❑ 188 Sammy Knight .25 .07
❑ 189 Kevin Johnson .40 .12
❑ 190 Matthew Hatchette .25 .07
❑ 191 Az-Zahir Hakim .40 .12
❑ 192 Keith Hamilton .25 .07
❑ 193 Darren Woodson .25 .07
❑ 194 Terry Glenn .40 .12
❑ 195 Simeon Rice .40 .12
❑ 196 Keyshawn Johnson .60 .18
❑ 197 Terrell Davis .60 .18
❑ 198 William Roaf .25 .07
❑ 199 Doug Flutie .60 .18
❑ 200 Kevin Carter .25 .07
❑ 201 Stephen Boyd .25 .07
❑ 202 Michael Strahan .40 .12
❑ 203 Ray Buchanan .25 .07
❑ 204 Tyrone Wheatley .40 .12
❑ 205 Jason Hanson .25 .07
❑ 206 Wayne Chrebet .40 .12
❑ 207 Samari Rolle .25 .07
❑ 208 Duce Staley .60 .18
❑ 209 Dorsey Levens .40 .12
❑ 210 Sebastian Janikowski .25 .07
❑ 211 Duane Starks .25 .07
❑ 212 Jason Gildon .25 .07
❑ 213 Terrence Wilkins .25 .07
❑ 214 Eric Allen .25 .07
❑ 215 Deion Sanders .60 .18
❑ 216 Curtis Conway .40 .12
❑ 217 Fred Taylor .60 .18
❑ 218 Troy Vincent .25 .07
❑ 219 Mike Minter RC .40 .12
❑ 220 Jeff Garcia .60 .18
❑ 221 Tony Richardson .25 .07
❑ 222 Jerome Bettis .60 .18
❑ 223 Chad Morton .25 .07
❑ 224 Tony Horne .25 .07
❑ 225 Dave Moore .25 .07
❑ 226 Victor Green .25 .07
❑ 227 Chris Sanders .25 .07
❑ 228 Marshall Faulk .75 .23
❑ 229 Cris Carter .60 .18
❑ 230 Rodney Harrison .25 .07
❑ 231 Tim Couch .40 .12
❑ 232 Antowain Smith .40 .12
❑ 233 Lawyer Milloy .40 .12
❑ 234 Lance Schulters .25 .07
❑ 235 Michael Wiley .25 .07
❑ 236 Steve McNair .60 .18
❑ 237 Aaron Brooks .60 .18
❑ 238 Anthony Simmons .25 .07
❑ 239 Dwayne Carswell .25 .07
❑ 240 Priest Holmes .75 .23
❑ 241 Amani Toomer .40 .12
❑ 242 Aeneas Williams .25 .07
❑ 243 MarTay Jenkins .25 .07
❑ 244 Jeff George .40 .12
❑ 245 Vinny Testaverde .40 .12
❑ 246 Peerless Price .40 .12
❑ 247 Bubba Franks .40 .12
❑ 248 Randall Cunningham .60 .18
❑ 249 Aaron Glenn .25 .07
❑ 250 Terance Mathis .40 .12
❑ 251 Peyton Manning 1.50 .45
❑ 252 Terrell Buckley .25 .07
❑ 253 Greg Biekert .25 .07
❑ 254 Martin Gramatica .25 .07
❑ 255 Kyle Brady .25 .07
❑ 256 Johnnie Morton .40 .12
❑ 257 Jeremiah Trotter .40 .12
❑ 258 Travis Taylor .40 .12
❑ 259 Frank Moreau .25 .07
❑ 260 LeRoy Butler .25 .07
❑ 261 Plaxico Burress .60 .18
❑ 262 Randall Godfrey .25 .07
❑ 263 Jason Taylor .25 .07
❑ 264 Jeff Burris .25 .07
❑ 265 Jim Harbaugh .40 .12
❑ 266 Marco Coleman .25 .07
❑ 267 Robert Smith .40 .12
❑ 268 Mike Hollis .25 .07
❑ 269 Jerry Rice 1.25 .35
❑ 270 Muhsin Muhammad .40 .12
❑ 271 J.R. Redmond .25 .07
❑ 272 Brian Walker .25 .07
❑ 273 Orlando Pace .25 .07
❑ 274 Cade McNown .25 .07
❑ 275 Darren Howard .25 .07
❑ 276 Ron Dayne .60 .18
❑ 277 Shaun Alexander .75 .23
❑ 278 Brandon Bennett .25 .07
❑ 279 Jason Sehorn .25 .07
❑ 280 Matt Hasselbeck .40 .12
❑ 281 Michael Pittman .25 .07
❑ 282 Dennis Northcutt .40 .12
❑ 283 Dedric Ward .25 .07
❑ 284 Curtis Martin .60 .18
❑ 285 Sammy Morris .25 .07
❑ 286 Rocket Ismail .40 .12

❑ 287 Jon Ritchie .25 .07
❑ 288 Shaun Ellis .25 .07
❑ 289 Tim Dwight .60 .18
❑ 290 Trevor Pryce .25 .07
❑ 291 Warrick Dunn .60 .18
❑ 292 Napoleon Kaufman .40 .12
❑ 293 Mike Alstott .60 .18
❑ 294 Herman Moore .40 .12
❑ 295 Chad Lewis .25 .07
❑ 296 Hugh Douglas .25 .07
❑ 297 Chris Redman .25 .07
❑ 298 Ahman Green .60 .18
❑ 299 Hines Ward .60 .18
❑ 300 Mark Bruener .25 .07
❑ 301 Jevon Kearse .40 .12
❑ 302 Jermaine Fazande .25 .07
❑ 303 Terrell Fletcher .25 .07
❑ 304 Torry Holt .60 .18
❑ 305 Chris McAlister .25 .07
❑ 306 Jason Elam .25 .07
❑ 307 Fred Beasley .25 .07
❑ 308 Frank Wycheck UH .25 .07
❑ 309 Michael McCrary UH .25 .07
❑ 310 Mark Brunell UH .60 .18
❑ 311 Tim Couch UH .40 .12
❑ 312 Takeo Spikes UH .25 .07
❑ 313 Jerome Bettis UH .40 .12
❑ 314 Zach Thomas UH .60 .18
❑ 315 Drew Bledsoe UH .60 .18
❑ 316 Wayne Chrebet UH .25 .07
❑ 317 Jay Riemersma UH .25 .07
❑ 318 Marvin Harrison UH .40 .12
❑ 319 Ed McCaffrey UH .40 .12
❑ 320 Tony Gonzalez UH .25 .07
❑ 321 Tim Brown UH .40 .12
❑ 322 Junior Seau UH .40 .12
❑ 323 Shawn Springs UH .25 .07
❑ 324 Troy Aikman UH .40 .12
❑ 325 Pat Tillman UH RC 20.00 6.00
❑ 326 David Akers UH RC .40 .12
❑ 327 Michael Strahan UH .40 .12
❑ 328 Darrell Green UH .25 .07
❑ 329 Kurt Warner UH .60 .18
❑ 330 Jeff Garcia UH .40 .12
❑ 331 Aaron Brooks UH .40 .12
❑ 332 Jamal Anderson UH .40 .12
❑ 333 Brad Hoover UH .25 .07
❑ 334 Cris Carter UH .40 .12
❑ 335 Derrick Brooks UH .60 .18
❑ 336 Antonio Freeman UH .40 .12
❑ 337 Luther Elliss UH .25 .07
❑ 338 James Allen UH .25 .07
❑ 339 Arizona Cardinals TC .40 .12
❑ 340 Atlanta Falcons TC .40 .12
❑ 341 Baltimore Ravens TC .25 .07
❑ 342 Buffalo Bills TC .25 .07
❑ 343 Carolina Panthers TC .25 .07
❑ 344 Chicago Bears TC .60 .18
❑ 345 Cincinnati Bengals TC .40 .12
❑ 346 Cleveland Browns TC .25 .07
❑ 347 Dallas Cowboys TC .60 .18
❑ 348 Denver Broncos TC .40 .12
❑ 349 Detroit Lions TC .25 .07
❑ 350 Green Bay Packers TC 1.00 .30
❑ 351 Indianapolis Colts TC .60 .18
❑ 352 Jacksonville Jaguars TC .60 .18
❑ 353 Kansas City Chiefs TC .25 .07
❑ 354 Miami Dolphins TC .40 .12
❑ 355 Minnesota Vikings TC .60 .18
❑ 356 New England Patriots TC .60 .18
❑ 357 New Orleans Saints TC .40 .12
❑ 358 New York Giants TC .40 .12
❑ 359 New York Jets TC .40 .12
❑ 360 Oakland Raiders TC .40 .12
❑ 361 Philadelphia Eagles TC .60 .18
❑ 362 Pittsburgh Steelers TC .40 .12
❑ 363 San Diego Chargers TC .25 .07
❑ 364 San Francisco 49ers TC .25 .07
❑ 365 Seattle Seahawks TC .25 .07
❑ 366 St. Louis Rams TC .60 .18
❑ 367 T.B. Buccaneers TC .40 .12
❑ 368 Tennessee Titans TC .40 .12
❑ 369 Washington Redskins TC .40 .12
❑ 370 Buffalo Bills TL .25 .07
❑ 371 Indianapolis Colts TL .60 .18
❑ 372 Miami Dolphins TL .25 .07
❑ 373 New England Patriots TL .40 .12
❑ 374 New York Jets TL .40 .12
❑ 375 Baltimore Ravens TL .40 .12
❑ 376 Cincinnati Bengals TL .25 .07
❑ 377 Cleveland Browns TL .25 .07
❑ 378 Jacksonville Jaguars TL .40 .12
❑ 379 Pittsburgh Steelers TL .40 .12
❑ 380 Tennessee Titans TL .40 .12
❑ 381 Denver Broncos TL .40 .12
❑ 382 Kansas City Chiefs TL .40 .12
❑ 383 Oakland Raiders TL .40 .12
❑ 384 San Diego Chargers TL .40 .12
❑ 385 Seattle Seahawks TL .25 .07
❑ 386 Arizona Cardinals TL .25 .07
❑ 387 Dallas Cowboys TL .60 .18
❑ 388 New York Giants TL .40 .12
❑ 389 Philadelphia Eagles TL .40 .12
❑ 390 Washington Redskins TL .40 .12
❑ 391 Chicago Bears TL .25 .07
❑ 392 Detroit Lions TL .25 .07
❑ 393 Green Bay Packers TL .60 .18
❑ 394 Minnesota Vikings TL .60 .18
❑ 395 T.B. Buccaneers TL .40 .12
❑ 396 Atlanta Falcons TL .25 .07
❑ 397 Carolina Panthers TL .25 .07
❑ 398 New Orleans Saints TL .40 .12
❑ 399 San Francisco 49ersTL .40 .12
❑ 400 St. Louis Rams TL .60 .18
❑ 401 Michael Vick RC 8.00 2.40
❑ 402 Drew Brees RC 2.50 .75
❑ 403 Michael Bennett RC 2.50 .75
❑ 404 David Terrell RC 1.25 .35
❑ 405 Deuce McAllister RC 2.50 .75
❑ 406 Santana Moss RC 2.00 .60
❑ 407 Koren Robinson RC 1.50 .45
❑ 408 Chris Weinke RC 1.25 .35
❑ 409 Reggie Wayne RC 2.00 .60
❑ 410 Rod Gardner RC 1.25 .35
❑ 411 James Jackson RC 1.25 .35
❑ 412 Travis Henry RC 1.50 .45
❑ 413 Josh Heupel RC 1.25 .35
❑ 414 LaDainian Tomlinson RC 4.00 1.20
❑ 415 Chad Johnson RC 2.50 .75
❑ 416 Sage Rosenfels RC 1.25 .35
❑ 417 Quincy Morgan RC 1.25 .35
❑ 418 Ken-Yon Rambo RC .75 .23
❑ 419 LaMont Jordan RC 1.50 .45
❑ 420 Anthony Thomas RC 2.00 .60
❑ 421 Dave Dickenson RC .75 .23
❑ 422 Travis Minor RC .75 .23
❑ 423 Kevan Barlow RC 1.25 .35
❑ 424 Chris Chambers RC 1.50 .45
❑ 425 Richard Seymour RC 1.25 .35
❑ 426 Gerard Warren RC 1.25 .35
❑ 427 Jamar Fletcher RC .75 .23
❑ 428 Freddie Mitchell RC 1.25 .35
❑ 429 Jamal Reynolds RC 1.25 .35
❑ 430 Marques Tuiasosopo RC 1.25 .35
❑ 431 Snoop Minnis RC .75 .23
❑ 432 Mike McMahon RC 1.25 .35
❑ 433 Robert Ferguson RC 1.25 .35
❑ 434 Ronney Daniels RC .50 .15
❑ 435 Rudi Johnson RC 2.50 .75
❑ 436 Vinny Sutherland RC .75 .23
❑ 437 Josh Booty RC 1.25 .35
❑ 438 Reggie White RC .75 .23
❑ 439 Todd Heap RC 1.25 .35
❑ 440 Justin Smith RC 1.25 .35
❑ 441 Andre Carter RC 1.25 .35
❑ 442 Bobby Newcombe RC .75 .23
❑ 443 Alex Bannister RC .75 .23
❑ 444 Correll Buckhalter RC 1.50 .45
❑ 445 Quincy Carter RC 1.25 .35
❑ 446 Jesse Palmer RC 1.25 .35
❑ 447 Heath Evans RC .75 .23
❑ 448 Dan Morgan RC 1.25 .35
❑ 449 Justin McCareins RC 1.25 .35
❑ 450 Alge Crumpler RC 1.50 .45

2001 Fleer Tradition Glossy

Nm-Mt Ex-Mt

COMP.SET w/o SP's (400) 40.00 12.00

❑ 1 Thomas Jones .50 .15
❑ 2 Bruce Smith .30 .09
❑ 3 Marvin Harrison .75 .23
❑ 4 Darrell Jackson .75 .23
❑ 5 Trent Green .75 .23
❑ 6 Wesley Walls .30 .09
❑ 7 Jimmy Smith .50 .15

❑ 8 Isaac Bruce .75 .23
❑ 9 Jamal Anderson .75 .23
❑ 10 Marty Booker .30 .09
❑ 11 Elvis Grbac .50 .15
❑ 12 Joe Jurevicius .30 .09
❑ 13 Reidel Anthony .30 .09
❑ 14 Darnay Scott .30 .09
❑ 15 Oronde Gadsden .50 .15
❑ 16 Shawn Bryson .30 .09
❑ 17 Jonathan Ogden .30 .09
❑ 18 Aaron Shea .30 .09
❑ 19 Randy Moss 1.50 .45
❑ 20 Eddie George .75 .23
❑ 21 Stephen Davis .75 .23
❑ 22 Emmitt Smith 1.50 .45
❑ 23 Willie McGinest .30 .09
❑ 24 Trent Dilfer .50 .15
❑ 25 Peter Boulware .30 .09
❑ 26 Rod Smith .50 .15
❑ 27 Ricky Williams .75 .23
❑ 28 Albert Connell .30 .09
❑ 29 Robert Porcher .30 .09
❑ 30 Jessie Armstead .30 .09
❑ 31 Shane Matthews .30 .09
❑ 32 Eric Moulds .50 .15
❑ 33 Kurt Schulz .30 .09
❑ 34 Richie Anderson .30 .09
❑ 35 Ron Dugans .30 .09
❑ 36 Steve Beuerlein .50 .15
❑ 37 Darren Sharper .30 .09
❑ 38 Andre Rison .50 .15
❑ 39 Courtney Brown .50 .15
❑ 40 Eddie Kennison .50 .15
❑ 41 Ken Dilger .30 .09
❑ 42 Charles Johnson .30 .09
❑ 43 Dexter Coakley .30 .09
❑ 44 Akili Smith .30 .09
❑ 45 R.Jay Soward .30 .09
❑ 46 Danny Farmer .30 .09
❑ 47 Dez White .30 .09
❑ 48 Olandis Gary .50 .15
❑ 49 Wali Rainer .30 .09
❑ 50 Derrick Alexander .50 .15
❑ 51 Donnie Abraham .30 .09
❑ 52 David Sloan .30 .09
❑ 53 Larry Allen .30 .09
❑ 54 Sam Madison .30 .09
❑ 55 Troy Edwards .30 .09
❑ 56 Ryan Longwell .30 .09
❑ 57 Brian Griese .75 .23
❑ 58 John Randle .50 .15
❑ 59 Reggie Jones .30 .09
❑ 60 Mike Peterson .30 .09
❑ 61 Bill Romanowski .30 .09
❑ 62 Kevin Faulk .50 .15
❑ 63 Tai Streets .30 .09
❑ 64 Tony Brackens .30 .09
❑ 65 James Stewart .50 .15
❑ 66 Joe Horn .50 .15
❑ 67 Kurt Warner 1.50 .45
❑ 68 Eric Hicks RC .30 .09
❑ 69 Bryan Westbrook .30 .09
❑ 70 Tiki Barber .50 .15
❑ 71 Frank Sanders .30 .09
❑ 72 Olindo Mare .30 .09
❑ 73 Bill Schroeder .50 .15
❑ 74 Anthony Becht .30 .09
❑ 75 Rob Johnson .50 .15
❑ 76 Troy Brown .50 .15
❑ 77 Chad Bratzke .30 .09
❑ 78 Rickey Dudley .30 .09

❏ 79 Doug Johnson .30 .09
❏ 80 Joe Johnson .30 .09
❏ 81 Keenan McCardell .30 .09
❏ 82 Tim Brown .75 .23
❏ 83 Blaine Bishop .30 .09
❏ 84 Ron Dixon .30 .09
❏ 85 Michael Cloud .30 .09
❏ 86 Todd Pinkston .30 .09
❏ 87 Shannon Sharpe .50 .15
❏ 88 Marvin Jones .30 .09
❏ 89 Zach Thomas .75 .23
❏ 90 Kordell Stewart .50 .15
❏ 91 Champ Bailey .50 .15
❏ 92 Jacquez Green .30 .09
❏ 93 Daunte Culpepper .75 .23
❏ 94 Freddie Jones .30 .09
❏ 95 Donald Hayes .30 .09
❏ 96 Rich Gannon .75 .23
❏ 97 Ty Law .50 .15
❏ 98 Grant Wistrom .30 .09
❏ 99 James Allen .50 .15
❏ 100 Corey Simon .50 .15
❏ 101 Jeff Blake .50 .15
❏ 102 Bryant Young .30 .09
❏ 103 Craig Yeast .30 .09
❏ 104 Bobby Shaw .30 .09
❏ 105 Kerry Collins .50 .15
❏ 106 Brock Huard .30 .09
❏ 107 JaJuan Dawson .30 .09
❏ 108 Jeff Graham .30 .09
❏ 109 Chad Pennington 1.25 .35
❏ 110 Jake Plummer .50 .15
❏ 111 James McKnight .50 .15
❏ 112 Terrell Owens .75 .23
❏ 113 Mo Lewis .30 .09
❏ 114 Jeremy McDaniel .30 .09
❏ 115 Ed McCaffrey .75 .23
❏ 116 Ricky Watters .30 .09
❏ 117 Jerry Porter .50 .15
❏ 118 Shawn Jefferson .30 .09
❏ 119 Charlie Batch .75 .23
❏ 120 Justin Watson .30 .09
❏ 121 Donovan McNabb 1.00 .30
❏ 122 Shaun King .30 .09
❏ 123 Brett Favre 2.50 .75
❏ 124 Ronald McKinnon .30 .09
❏ 125 Richard Huntley .30 .09
❏ 126 Ray Lewis .75 .23
❏ 127 Jerome Pathon .50 .15
❏ 128 Sam Cowart .30 .09
❏ 129 Ryan Leaf .50 .15
❏ 130 Greg Clark .30 .09
❏ 131 Tony Boselli .30 .09
❏ 132 Frank Wycheck .30 .09
❏ 133 Charlie Garner .50 .15
❏ 134 Tony Siragusa .30 .09
❏ 135 Sylvester Morris .30 .09
❏ 136 Qadry Ismail .50 .15
❏ 137 Jon Kitna .50 .15
❏ 138 James Thrash .50 .15
❏ 139 Lamar Smith .50 .15
❏ 140 Brad Johnson .75 .23
❏ 141 London Fletcher .30 .09
❏ 142 Tim Biakabutuka .50 .15
❏ 143 Ed McDaniel .30 .09
❏ 144 Tony Parrish .30 .09
❏ 145 David Boston .75 .23
❏ 146 Brian Urlacher 1.25 .35
❏ 147 Drew Bledsoe 1.00 .30
❏ 148 David Patten .30 .09
❏ 149 Marcellus Wiley .30 .09
❏ 150 Peter Warrick .75 .23
❏ 151 La'Roi Glover .30 .09
❏ 152 Troy Aikman 1.25 .35
❏ 153 Chris Chandler .50 .15
❏ 154 Travis Prentice .30 .09
❏ 155 Ike Hilliard .50 .15
❏ 156 John Mobley .30 .09
❏ 157 Warren Sapp .50 .15
❏ 158 Joey Galloway .50 .15
❏ 159 Laveranues Coles .75 .23
❏ 160 Germane Crowell .30 .09
❏ 161 Jamal Lewis 1.25 .35
❏ 162 Mike Anderson .75 .23
❏ 163 Charles Woodson .50 .15
❏ 164 Antonio Freeman .75 .23
❏ 165 Derrick Mason .50 .15
❏ 166 Chris Claiborne .30 .09
❏ 167 Brian Mitchell .30 .09
❏ 168 Mike Vanderjagt .30 .09
❏ 169 Rod Woodson .50 .15
❏ 170 Doug Chapman .30 .09
❏ 171 John Lynch .50 .15
❏ 172 Kevin Hardy .30 .09
❏ 173 Sam Shade .30 .09
❏ 174 Edgerrin James 1.00 .30
❏ 175 Brian Dawkins .30 .09
❏ 176 Donnie Edwards .30 .09
❏ 177 Patrick Jeffers .50 .15
❏ 178 Mark Brunell .75 .23
❏ 179 Junior Seau .75 .23
❏ 180 Trace Armstrong .30 .09
❏ 181 Marcus Robinson .75 .23
❏ 182 Tony Gonzalez .50 .15
❏ 183 J.J. Stokes .50 .15
❏ 184 Jake Reed .50 .15
❏ 185 Corey Dillon .75 .23
❏ 186 Jay Fiedler .75 .23
❏ 187 Christian Fauria .30 .09
❏ 188 Sammy Knight .30 .09
❏ 189 Kevin Johnson .50 .15
❏ 190 Matthew Hatchette .30 .09
❏ 191 Az-Zahir Hakim .50 .15
❏ 192 Keith Hamilton .30 .09
❏ 193 Darren Woodson .30 .09
❏ 194 Terry Glenn .50 .15
❏ 195 Simeon Rice .50 .15
❏ 196 Keyshawn Johnson .75 .23
❏ 197 Terrell Davis .75 .23
❏ 198 William Roaf .30 .09
❏ 199 Doug Flutie .75 .23
❏ 200 Kevin Carter .30 .09
❏ 201 Stephen Boyd .30 .09
❏ 202 Michael Strahan .50 .15
❏ 203 Ray Buchanan .30 .09
❏ 204 Tyrone Wheatley .50 .15
❏ 205 Jason Hanson .30 .09
❏ 206 Wayne Chrebet .50 .15
❏ 207 Samari Rolle .30 .09
❏ 208 Duce Staley .75 .23
❏ 209 Dorsey Levens .50 .15
❏ 210 Sebastian Janikowski .30 .09
❏ 211 Duane Starks .30 .09
❏ 212 Jason Gildon .30 .09
❏ 213 Terrence Wilkins .30 .09
❏ 214 Eric Allen .30 .09
❏ 215 Deion Sanders .75 .23
❏ 216 Curtis Conway .50 .15
❏ 217 Fred Taylor .75 .23
❏ 218 Troy Vincent .30 .09
❏ 219 Mike Minter .50 .15
❏ 220 Jeff Garcia .75 .23
❏ 221 Tony Richardson .30 .09
❏ 222 Jerome Bettis .75 .23
❏ 223 Chad Morton .30 .09
❏ 224 Tony Horne .30 .09
❏ 225 Dave Moore .30 .09
❏ 226 Victor Green .30 .09
❏ 227 Chris Sanders .30 .09
❏ 228 Marshall Faulk 1.00 .30
❏ 229 Cris Carter .75 .23
❏ 230 Rodney Harrison .30 .09
❏ 231 Tim Couch .50 .15
❏ 232 Antowain Smith .50 .15
❏ 233 Lawyer Milloy .50 .15
❏ 234 Lance Schulters .30 .09
❏ 235 Michael Wiley .30 .09
❏ 236 Steve McNair .75 .23
❏ 237 Aaron Brooks .75 .23
❏ 238 Anthony Simmons .30 .09
❏ 239 Dwayne Carswell .30 .09
❏ 240 Priest Holmes 1.00 .30
❏ 241 Amani Toomer .50 .15
❏ 242 Aeneas Williams .30 .09
❏ 243 MarTay Jenkins .30 .09
❏ 244 Jeff George .50 .15
❏ 245 Vinny Testaverde .50 .15
❏ 246 Peerless Price .50 .15
❏ 247 Bubba Franks .50 .15
❏ 248 Randall Cunningham .75 .23
❏ 249 Aaron Glenn .30 .09
❏ 250 Terance Mathis .50 .15
❏ 251 Peyton Manning 2.00 .60
❏ 252 Terrell Buckley .30 .09
❏ 253 Greg Biekert .30 .09
❏ 254 Martin Gramatica .30 .09
❏ 255 Kyle Brady .30 .09
❏ 256 Johnnie Morton .50 .15
❏ 257 Jeremiah Trotter .50 .15
❏ 258 Travis Taylor .50 .15
❏ 259 Frank Moreau .30 .09
❏ 260 LeRoy Butler .30 .09
❏ 261 Plaxico Burress .75 .23
❏ 262 Randall Godfrey .30 .09
❏ 263 Jason Taylor .30 .09
❏ 264 Jeff Burris .30 .09
❏ 265 Jim Harbaugh .50 .15
❏ 266 Marco Coleman .30 .09
❏ 267 Robert Smith .50 .15
❏ 268 Mike Hollis .30 .09
❏ 269 Jerry Rice 1.50 .45
❏ 270 Muhsin Muhammad .50 .15
❏ 271 J.R. Redmond .30 .09
❏ 272 Brian Walker .30 .09
❏ 273 Orlando Pace .30 .09
❏ 274 Cade McNown .30 .09
❏ 275 Darren Howard .30 .09
❏ 276 Ron Dayne .75 .23
❏ 277 Shaun Alexander 1.00 .30
❏ 278 Brandon Bennett .30 .09
❏ 279 Jason Sehorn .30 .09
❏ 280 Matt Hasselbeck .50 .15
❏ 281 Michael Pittman .30 .09
❏ 282 Dennis Northcutt .50 .15
❏ 283 Dedric Ward .30 .09
❏ 284 Curtis Martin .75 .23
❏ 285 Sammy Morris .30 .09
❏ 286 Rocket Ismail .50 .15
❏ 287 Jon Ritchie .30 .09
❏ 288 Shaun Ellis .30 .09
❏ 289 Tim Dwight .75 .23
❏ 290 Trevor Pryce .30 .09
❏ 291 Warrick Dunn .75 .23
❏ 292 Napoleon Kaufman .50 .15
❏ 293 Mike Alstott .75 .23
❏ 294 Herman Moore .50 .15
❏ 295 Chad Lewis .30 .09
❏ 296 Hugh Douglas .30 .09
❏ 297 Chris Redman .30 .09
❏ 298 Ahman Green .75 .23
❏ 299 Hines Ward .75 .23
❏ 300 Mark Bruener .30 .09
❏ 301 Jevon Kearse .50 .15
❏ 302 Jermaine Fazande .30 .09
❏ 303 Terrell Fletcher .30 .09
❏ 304 Torry Holt .75 .23
❏ 305 Chris McAlister .30 .09
❏ 306 Jason Elam .30 .09
❏ 307 Fred Beasley .30 .09
❏ 308 Frank Wycheck UH .30 .09
❏ 309 Michael McCrary UH .30 .09
❏ 310 Mark Brunell UH .75 .23
❏ 311 Tim Couch UH .50 .15
❏ 312 Takeo Spikes UH .30 .09
❏ 313 Jerome Bettis UH .50 .15
❏ 314 Zach Thomas UH .75 .23
❏ 315 Drew Bledsoe UH .75 .23
❏ 316 Wayne Chrebet UH .30 .09
❏ 317 Jay Riemersma UH .30 .09
❏ 318 Marvin Harrison UH .50 .15
❏ 319 Ed McCaffrey UH .50 .15
❏ 320 Tony Gonzalez UH .30 .09
❏ 321 Tim Brown UH .50 .15
❏ 322 Junior Seau UH .50 .15
❏ 323 Shawn Springs UH .30 .09
❏ 324 Troy Aikman UH .75 .23
❏ 325 Pat Tillman UH RC 20.00 6.00
❏ 326 David Akers UH .30 .09
❏ 327 Michael Strahan UH .50 .15
❏ 328 Darrell Green UH .30 .09
❏ 329 Kurt Warner UH 1.00 .30
❏ 330 Jeff Garcia UH .50 .15
❏ 331 Aaron Brooks UH .50 .15
❏ 332 Jamal Anderson UH .50 .15
❏ 333 Brad Hoover UH .30 .09
❏ 334 Cris Carter UH .50 .15
❏ 335 Derrick Brooks UH .75 .23
❏ 336 Antonio Freeman UH .50 .15
❏ 337 Luther Elliss UH .30 .09
❏ 338 James Allen UH .30 .09
❏ 339 Arizona Cardinals TC .50 .15
❏ 340 Atlanta Falcons TC .50 .15
❏ 341 Baltimore Ravens TC .30 .09
❏ 342 Buffalo Bills TC .30 .09

❑ 343 Carolina Panthers TC .30 .09
❑ 344 Chicago Bears TC .75 .23
❑ 345 Cincinnati Bengals TC .50 .15
❑ 346 Cleveland Browns TC .30 .09
❑ 347 Dallas Cowboys TC .75 .23
❑ 348 Denver Broncos TC .50 .15
❑ 349 Detroit Lions TC .30 .09
❑ 350 Green Bay Packers TC 1.25 .35
❑ 351 Indianapolis Colts TC .75 .23
❑ 352 Jacksonville Jaguars TC .75 .23
❑ 353 Kansas City Chiefs TC .30 .09
❑ 354 Miami Dolphins TC .50 .15
❑ 355 Minnesota Vikings TC .75 .23
❑ 356 New England Patriots TC .75 .23
❑ 357 New Orleans Saints TC .50 .15
❑ 358 New York Giants TC .50 .15
❑ 359 New York Jets TC .50 .15
❑ 360 Oakland Raiders TC .50 .15
❑ 361 Philadelphia Eagles TC .75 .23
❑ 362 Pittsburgh Steelers TC .50 .15
❑ 363 San Diego Chargers TC .30 .09
❑ 364 San Francisco 49ers TC .30 .09
❑ 365 Seattle Seahawks TC .30 .09
❑ 366 St. Louis Rams TC .75 .23
❑ 367 T.B. Buccaneers TC .50 .15
❑ 368 Tennessee Titans TC .50 .15
❑ 369 Washington Redskins TC .50 .15
❑ 370 Buffalo Bills TL .50 .15
❑ 371 Indianapolis Colts TL .75 .23
❑ 372 Miami Dolphins TL .30 .09
❑ 373 New England Patriots TL .50 .15
❑ 374 New York Jets TL .50 .15
❑ 375 Baltimore Ravens TL .50 .15
❑ 376 Cincinnati Bengals TL .30 .09
❑ 377 Cleveland Browns TL .30 .09
❑ 378 Jacksonville Jaguars TL .50 .15
❑ 379 Pittsburgh Steelers TL .50 .15
❑ 380 Tennessee Titans TL .50 .15
❑ 381 Denver Broncos TL .50 .15
❑ 382 Kansas City Chiefs TL .50 .15
❑ 383 Oakland Raiders TL .50 .15
❑ 384 San Diego Chargers TL .50 .15
❑ 385 Seattle Seahawks TL .30 .09
❑ 386 Arizona Cardinals TL .30 .09
❑ 387 Dallas Cowboys TL .75 .23
❑ 388 New York Giants TL .50 .15
❑ 389 Philadelphia Eagles TL .50 .15
❑ 390 Washington Redskins TL .50 .15
❑ 391 Chicago Bears TL .30 .09
❑ 392 Detroit Lions TL .30 .09
❑ 393 Green Bay Packers TL .75 .23
❑ 394 Minnesota Vikings TL .75 .23
❑ 395 T.B. Buccaneers TL .50 .15
❑ 396 Atlanta Falcons TL .30 .09
❑ 397 Carolina Panthers TL .30 .09
❑ 398 New Orleans Saints TL .50 .15
❑ 399 San Francisco 49ersTL .50 .15
❑ 400 St. Louis Rams TL .75 .23
❑ 401 Michael Vick RC 30.00 9.00
❑ 402 Drew Brees RC 10.00 3.00
❑ 403 Michael Bennett RC 10.00 3.00
❑ 404 David Terrell RC 4.00 1.20
❑ 405 Deuce McAllister RC 10.00 3.00
❑ 406 Santana Moss RC 8.00 2.40
❑ 407 Koren Robinson RC 6.00 1.80
❑ 408 Chris Weinke RC 4.00 1.20
❑ 409 Reggie Wayne RC 8.00 2.40
❑ 410 Rod Gardner RC 4.00 1.20
❑ 411 James Jackson RC 4.00 1.20
❑ 412 Travis Henry RC 6.00 1.80
❑ 413 Josh Heupel RC 4.00 1.20
❑ 414 LaDainian Tomlinson RC 15.00 4.50
❑ 415 Chad Johnson RC 10.00 3.00
❑ 416 Sage Rosenfels RC 4.00 1.20
❑ 417 Quincy Morgan RC 4.00 1.20
❑ 418 Ken-Yon Rambo RC 3.00 .90
❑ 419 LaMont Jordan RC 5.00 1.50
❑ 420 Anthony Thomas RC 8.00 2.40
❑ 421 Dave Dickenson RC 3.00 .90
❑ 422 Travis Minor RC 3.00 .90
❑ 423 Kevan Barlow RC 4.00 1.20
❑ 424 Chris Chambers RC 6.00 1.80
❑ 425 Richard Seymour RC 4.00 1.20
❑ 426 Gerard Warren RC 4.00 1.20
❑ 427 Jamar Fletcher RC 3.00 .90
❑ 428 Freddie Mitchell RC 4.00 1.20
❑ 429 Jamal Reynolds RC 4.00 1.20
❑ 430 Marques Tuiasosopo RC 4.00 1.20
❑ 431 Snoop Minnis RC 3.00 .90
❑ 432 Mike McMahon RC 4.00 1.20
❑ 433 Robert Ferguson RC 4.00 1.20
❑ 434 Ronney Daniels RC 3.00 .90
❑ 435 Rudi Johnson RC 10.00 3.00
❑ 436 Vinny Sutherland RC 3.00 .90
❑ 437 Josh Booty RC 4.00 1.20
❑ 438 Reggie White RC 3.00 .90
❑ 439 Todd Heap RC 4.00 1.20
❑ 440 Justin Smith RC 4.00 1.20
❑ 441 Andre Carter RC 4.00 1.20
❑ 442 Bobby Newcombe RC 3.00 .90
❑ 443 Alex Bannister RC 3.00 .90
❑ 444 Correll Buckhalter RC 6.00 1.80
❑ 445 Quincy Carter RC 4.00 1.20
❑ 446 Jesse Palmer RC 4.00 1.20
❑ 447 Heath Evans RC 3.00 .90
❑ 448 Dan Morgan RC 4.00 1.20
❑ 449 Justin McCareins RC 4.00 1.20
❑ 450 Alge Crumpler RC 5.00 1.50

2002 Fleer Tradition

	Nm-Mt	Ex-Mt
COMPLETE SET (300)	80.00	24.00

❑ 1 Jeff Garcia .60 .18
❑ 2 Brian Simmons .25 .07
❑ 3 Kordell Stewart .40 .12
❑ 4 Chris Weinke .40 .12
❑ 5 Donovan McNabb .75 .23
❑ 6 Antoine Winfield .25 .07
❑ 7 Ray Lewis .60 .18
❑ 8 Drew Brees .60 .18
❑ 9 Frank Sanders .25 .07
❑ 10 Rich Gannon .60 .18
❑ 11 Jamal Anderson .40 .12
❑ 12 Curtis Martin .60 .18
❑ 13 Darrell Jackson .40 .12
❑ 14 Micheal Barrow .25 .07
❑ 15 Jeff Wilkins .25 .07
❑ 16 Ricky Williams .60 .18
❑ 17 Brad Johnson .40 .12
❑ 18 Tedy Bruschi .60 .18
❑ 19 Frank Wycheck .25 .07
❑ 20 Byron Chamberlain .25 .07
❑ 21 Terry Glenn .25 .07
❑ 22 James McKnight .25 .07
❑ 23 Thomas Jones .40 .12
❑ 24 Jamie Sharper .25 .07
❑ 25 Trent Green .40 .12
❑ 26 Mike Rucker RC 1.00 .30
❑ 27 Mark Brunell .60 .18
❑ 28 Takeo Spikes .25 .07
❑ 29 Dominic Rhodes .40 .12
❑ 30 Jim Miller .25 .07
❑ 31 Corey Bradford .25 .07
❑ 32 Jamir Miller .25 .07
❑ 33 Johnnie Morton .40 .12
❑ 34 Rocket Ismail .40 .12
❑ 35 Mike Anderson .60 .18
❑ 36 James Allen .40 .12
❑ 37 Quincy Carter .40 .12
❑ 38 Germane Crowell .25 .07
❑ 39 Quincy Morgan .25 .07
❑ 40 Kabeer Gbaja-Biamila .25 .07
❑ 41 Reggie Wayne .40 .12
❑ 42 Brian Urlacher 1.00 .30
❑ 43 Stacey Mack .25 .07
❑ 44 Justin Smith .25 .07
❑ 45 Snoop Minnis .25 .07
❑ 46 Donald Hayes .25 .07
❑ 47 Jay Fiedler .40 .12
❑ 48 Nate Clements .25 .07
❑ 49 Drew Bledsoe .75 .23
❑ 50 Peter Boulware .25 .07
❑ 51 Lawyer Milloy .40 .12
❑ 52 Michael Pittman .25 .07
❑ 53 Aaron Brooks .60 .18
❑ 54 Maurice Smith .40 .12
❑ 55 Ike Hilliard .40 .12
❑ 56 Derrick Mason .40 .12
❑ 57 LaMont Jordan .60 .18
❑ 58 Charlie Garner .40 .12
❑ 59 Mike Alstott .60 .18
❑ 60 Freddie Mitchell .40 .12
❑ 61 Isaac Bruce .60 .18
❑ 62 Hines Ward .60 .18
❑ 63 John Randle .25 .07
❑ 64 Doug Flutie .60 .18
❑ 65 Terrell Owens .60 .18
❑ 66 Garrison Hearst .40 .12
❑ 67 Rodney Harrison .25 .07
❑ 68 Koren Robinson .40 .12
❑ 69 Amos Zereoue .60 .18
❑ 70 Aeneas Williams .25 .07
❑ 71 Hugh Douglas .25 .07
❑ 72 Jacquez Green .25 .07
❑ 73 Sebastian Janikowski .25 .07
❑ 74 Kevin Dyson .40 .12
❑ 75 Terance Mathis .25 .07
❑ 76 Vinny Testaverde .40 .12
❑ 77 Kwamie Lassiter .25 .07
❑ 78 Ron Dayne .40 .12
❑ 79 Jonathan Ogden .25 .07
❑ 80 Charlie Clemons RC .25 .07
❑ 81 Peter Warrick .40 .12
❑ 82 Adam Vinatieri .60 .18
❑ 83 Ted Washington .25 .07
❑ 84 Randy Moss 1.25 .35
❑ 85 Rosevelt Colvin RC 1.00 .30
❑ 86 Oronde Gadsden .40 .12
❑ 87 Anthony Henry .25 .07
❑ 88 Priest Holmes .75 .23
❑ 89 Joey Galloway .40 .12
❑ 90 Jimmy Smith .40 .12
❑ 91 Bill Romanowski .25 .07
❑ 92 Chris Claiborne .40 .12
❑ 93 Marvin Harrison .60 .18
❑ 94 Vonnie Holliday .25 .07
❑ 95 Darren Sharper .25 .07
❑ 96 Chad Bratzke .25 .07
❑ 97 James Stewart .40 .12
❑ 98 Fred Taylor .60 .18
❑ 99 Jason Elam .25 .07
❑ 100 Keyshawn Johnson .60 .18
❑ 101 Dexter Coakley .25 .07
❑ 102 Zach Thomas .60 .18
❑ 103 Jamel White .25 .07
❑ 104 Antowain Smith .40 .12
❑ 105 Marty Booker .25 .07
❑ 106 Deuce McAllister .75 .23
❑ 107 Adam Archuleta .25 .07
❑ 108 Rod Smith .40 .12
❑ 109 Tony Boselli .25 .07
❑ 110 Joe Johnson .25 .07
❑ 111 Simeon Rice .40 .12
❑ 112 Cory Schlesinger .25 .07
❑ 113 La'Roi Glover .25 .07
❑ 114 Tiki Barber .40 .12
❑ 115 Michael Westbrook .25 .07
❑ 116 Antonio Freeman .60 .18
❑ 117 Kerry Collins .40 .12
❑ 118 Laveranues Coles .40 .12
❑ 119 Jay Feeley .25 .07
❑ 120 Champ Bailey .40 .12
❑ 121 Peyton Manning 1.25 .35
❑ 122 Chad Pennington .75 .23
❑ 123 Anthony Dorsett .25 .07
❑ 124 Jamal Lewis .60 .18
❑ 125 Marcus Pollard .25 .07
❑ 126 Charles Woodson .40 .12
❑ 127 Duce Staley .60 .18
❑ 128 Travis Henry .60 .18
❑ 129 Tony Brackens .25 .07
❑ 130 Jeremiah Trotter .25 .07
❑ 131 Jerome Bettis .60 .18
❑ 132 Chad Johnson .60 .18
❑ 133 Lamar Smith .40 .12
❑ 134 Joey Porter .25 .07

❑ 135 Curtis Conway .25 .07
❑ 136 David Terrell .60 .18
❑ 137 Daunte Culpepper .60 .18
❑ 138 Chris Fuamatu-Ma'afala .25 .07
❑ 139 J.J. Stokes .25 .07
❑ 140 Tim Couch .40 .12
❑ 141 Ty Law .40 .12
❑ 142 Vinny Sutherland .25 .07
❑ 143 Trung Canidate .40 .12
❑ 144 Larry Allen .25 .07
❑ 145 Darren Howard .25 .07
❑ 146 Ricky Watters .40 .12
❑ 147 Grant Wistrom .25 .07
❑ 148 Brian Griese .60 .18
❑ 149 Jason Sehorn .25 .07
❑ 150 Marshall Faulk .60 .18
❑ 151 Martin Gramatica .25 .07
❑ 152 Robert Porcher .25 .07
❑ 153 Richie Anderson .25 .07
❑ 154 Derrick Brooks .60 .18
❑ 155 Jevon Kearse .40 .12
❑ 156 Bill Schroeder .40 .12
❑ 157 Marvin Jones .25 .07
❑ 158 Eddie George .60 .18
❑ 159 Keith Brooking .25 .07
❑ 160 Ryan Longwell .25 .07
❑ 161 Brian Dawkins .25 .07
❑ 162 Chris Redman .25 .07
❑ 163 Az-Zahir Hakim .25 .07
❑ 164 James Thrash .40 .12
❑ 165 Rob Johnson .40 .12
❑ 166 Hardy Nickerson .25 .07
❑ 167 Chad Scott .25 .07
❑ 168 Jon Kitna .40 .12
❑ 169 Donnie Edwards .25 .07
❑ 170 Andre Carter .25 .07
❑ 171 Warrick Holdman .25 .07
❑ 172 Jason Taylor .25 .07
❑ 173 Levon Kirkland .25 .07
❑ 174 Mike Brown .60 .18
❑ 175 David Patten .25 .07
❑ 176 Kurt Warner .60 .18
❑ 177 Fred Smoot .25 .07
❑ 178 Dat Nguyen .25 .07
❑ 179 Joe Horn .40 .12
❑ 180 John Lynch .40 .12
❑ 181 Troy Hambrick .25 .07
❑ 182 John Carney .25 .07
❑ 183 Wesley Walls .25 .07
❑ 184 Deltha O'Neal .25 .07
❑ 185 Joe Jurevicius .25 .07
❑ 186 Steve McNair .60 .18
❑ 187 Scotty Anderson .25 .07
❑ 188 John Abraham .40 .12
❑ 189 Stephen Davis .40 .12
❑ 190 Nate Wayne .25 .07
❑ 191 Corey Simon .25 .07
❑ 192 Joel Makovicka .25 .07
❑ 193 Rob Morris .25 .07
❑ 194 Correll Buckhalter .40 .12
❑ 195 Qadry Ismail .40 .12
❑ 196 Keenan McCardell .25 .07
❑ 197 Jason Gildon .25 .07
❑ 198 Peerless Price .40 .12
❑ 199 Tony Richardson .25 .07
❑ 200 Kevan Barlow .40 .12
❑ 201 Corey Dillon .40 .12
❑ 202 Sam Madison .25 .07
❑ 203 Chad Brown .25 .07
❑ 204 Dez White .25 .07
❑ 205 Troy Brown .40 .12
❑ 206 Orlando Pace .25 .07
❑ 207 Jermaine Lewis .25 .07
❑ 208 Willie Jackson .25 .07
❑ 209 Warrick Dunn .60 .18
❑ 210 James Jackson .25 .07
❑ 211 Sammy Knight .25 .07
❑ 212 Ronde Barber .25 .07
❑ 213 Ed McCaffrey .60 .18
❑ 214 Amani Toomer .40 .12
❑ 215 Rod Gardner .40 .12
❑ 216 Mike McMahon .60 .18
❑ 217 Wayne Chrebet .40 .12
❑ 218 Jake Plummer .40 .12
❑ 219 Bubba Franks .40 .12
❑ 220 Shane Lechler .40 .12
❑ 221 Travis Taylor .40 .12
❑ 222 Edgerrin James .75 .23
❑ 223 David Akers .25 .07
❑ 224 Eric Moulds .40 .12
❑ 225 Mike Vanderjagt .25 .07
❑ 226 Kendrell Bell .60 .18
❑ 227 Darnay Scott .25 .07
❑ 228 Tony Gonzalez .40 .12
❑ 229 Marcellus Wiley .25 .07
❑ 230 Marcus Robinson .40 .12
❑ 231 Muhsin Muhammad .40 .12
❑ 232 Trent Dilfer .40 .12
❑ 233 Kevin Johnson .40 .12
❑ 234 Travis Minor .25 .07
❑ 235 London Fletcher .25 .07
❑ 236 Reggie Swinton .25 .07
❑ 237 Michael Bennett .40 .12
❑ 238 Brett Favre DD 1.50 .45
❑ 239 Terrell Davis DD .60 .18
❑ 240 Emmitt Smith DD 1.50 .45
❑ 241 Shannon Sharpe DD .40 .12
❑ 242 Cris Carter DD .60 .18
❑ 243 Tim Brown DD .60 .18
❑ 244 Jerry Rice DD 1.25 .35
❑ 245 Bruce Smith DD .40 .12
❑ 246 Warren Sapp DD .40 .12
❑ 247 Michael Strahan DD .40 .12
❑ 248 Junior Seau DD .60 .18
❑ 249 Darrell Green DD .25 .07
❑ 250 Rod Woodson DD .40 .12
❑ 251 David Boston BB .60 .18
❑ 252 Michael Vick BB 2.00 .60
❑ 253 Anthony Thomas BB .60 .18
❑ 254 Ahman Green BB .60 .18
❑ 255 Chris Chambers BB .60 .18
❑ 256 Tom Brady BB 1.50 .45
❑ 257 Plaxico Burress BB .40 .12
❑ 258 LaDainian Tomlinson BB 1.00 .30
❑ 259 Shaun Alexander BB .60 .18
❑ 260 Torry Holt BB .60 .18
❑ 261 Julius Peppers RC 4.00 1.20
❑ 262 William Green RC 3.00 .90
❑ 263 Joey Harrington RC 6.00 1.80
❑ 264 Jabar Gaffney RC 2.00 .60
❑ 265 T.J. Duckett RC 3.00 .90
❑ 266 Antwaan Randle El RC 2.50 .75
❑ 267 Javon Walker RC 4.00 1.20
❑ 268 David Carr RC 6.00 1.80
❑ 269 DeShaun Foster RC 2.00 .60
❑ 270 Donte Stallworth RC 4.00 1.20
❑ 271 Antonio Bryant RC 2.00 .60
❑ 272 Clinton Portis RC 6.00 1.80
❑ 273 Josh Reed RC 2.00 .60
❑ 274 Ashley Lelie RC 4.00 1.20
❑ 275 Patrick Ramsey RC 4.00 1.20
❑ 276 Jonathan Wells RC 2.00 .60
Adrian Peterson RC
❑ 277 Quentin Jammer RC 5.00 1.50
Roy Williams RC
❑ 278 Jeremy Shockey RC 6.00 1.80
Daniel Graham RC
❑ 279 Eric Crouch RC 2.50 .75
Major Applewhite RC
❑ 280 Phillip Buchanon RC 2.00 .60
Lito Sheppard RC
❑ 281 Kahlil Hill RC 4.00 1.20
Deion Branch RC
❑ 282 Ryan Sims RC 2.00 .60
Wendell Bryant RC
❑ 283 Josh Scobey RC 3.00 .90
Brian Westbrook RC
❑ 284 Ladell Betts RC 2.00 .60
Omar Easy RC
❑ 285 Andre Davis RC 2.00 .60
Daryl Jones RC
❑ 286 Cliff Russell RC 2.00 .60
Chester Taylor RC
❑ 287 Jason McAddley RC 2.50 .75
Josh McCown RC
❑ 288 David Garrard RC 2.50 .75
Rohan Davey RC
❑ 289 Marquise Walker RC 1.50 .45
Ron Johnson RC
❑ 290 Luke Staley RC 2.00 .60
Lamar Gordon RC
❑ 291 Reche Caldwell RC 2.00 .60
Lee Mays RC
❑ 292 Robert Thomas RC 2.00 .60
Napoleon Harris RC
❑ 293 Maurice Morris RC 2.00 .60
Jerramy Stevens RC
❑ 294 Kurt Kittner RC 1.50 .45
Randy Fasani RC
❑ 295 Rocky Calmus RC 2.00 .60
Jake Schifino RC
❑ 296 Tim Carter RC 1.50 .45
Freddie Milons RC
❑ 297 Tracey Wistrom RC 2.00 .60
Travis Stephens RC
❑ 298 Mike Williams RC 2.50 .75
Dwight Freeney RC
❑ 299 John Henderson RC 2.00 .60
Albert Haynesworth RC
❑ 300 Najeh Davenport RC 2.00 .60
Craig Nall RC

2003 Fleer Tradition

	MINT	NRMT
COMPLETE SET (300)	40.00	18.00
❑ 1 Aaron Glenn	.25	.11
❑ 2 Jerry Rice	1.25	.55
❑ 3 Chad Hutchinson	.40	.18
❑ 4 Kris Jenkins	.25	.11
❑ 5 Ed Reed	.40	.18
❑ 6 Ed McCaffrey	.60	.25
❑ 7 Rod Gardner	.40	.18
❑ 8 Aaron Brooks	.60	.25
❑ 9 Chad Pennington	.75	.35
❑ 10 Jevon Kearse	.40	.18
❑ 11 Kurt Warner	.60	.25
❑ 12 Eddie George	.40	.18
❑ 13 Ron Dugans	.25	.11
❑ 14 Adam Vinatieri	.60	.25
❑ 15 Jimmy Smith	.40	.18
❑ 16 Chad Johnson	.40	.18
❑ 17 Kyle Brady	.25	.11
❑ 18 Eddie Kennison	.25	.11
❑ 19 Joe Jurevicius	.25	.11
❑ 20 Ronde Barber	.25	.11
❑ 21 Adam Archuleta	.25	.11
❑ 22 Champ Bailey	.40	.18
❑ 23 Joe Horn	.40	.18
❑ 24 Ladell Betts	.40	.18
❑ 25 Edgerrin James	.60	.25
❑ 26 Rosevelt Colvin	.25	.11
❑ 27 Ahman Green	.60	.25
❑ 28 Joey Porter	.25	.11
❑ 29 Charles Woodson	.40	.18
❑ 30 Lance Schulters	.25	.11
❑ 31 Edgerton Hartwell	.25	.11
❑ 32 Joey Galloway	.40	.18
❑ 33 Roy Williams	.60	.25
❑ 34 Al Wilson	.25	.11
❑ 35 Charlie Garner	.40	.18
❑ 36 John Lynch	.25	.11
❑ 37 La'Roi Glover	.25	.11
❑ 38 Emmitt Smith	1.50	.70
❑ 39 Ryan Longwell	.25	.11
❑ 40 Alge Crumpler	.40	.18
❑ 41 John Abraham	.25	.11
❑ 42 Chris Hovan	.25	.11
❑ 43 Laveranues Coles	.40	.18
❑ 44 Eric Hicks	.25	.11
❑ 45 Johnnie Morton	.40	.18
❑ 46 Sam Madison	.25	.11
❑ 47 Amani Toomer	.40	.18
❑ 48 Chris Redman	.25	.11
❑ 49 Jon Kitna	.40	.18
❑ 50 Leonard Little	.25	.11
❑ 51 Eric Moulds	.40	.18

❑	52	Santana Moss	.40	.18
❑	53	Amos Zereoue	.40	.18
❑	54	Jonathan Wells	.25	.11
❑	55	Chris Chambers	.60	.25
❑	56	London Fletcher	.25	.11
❑	57	Frank Wycheck	.25	.11
❑	58	Josh McCown	.40	.18
❑	59	Shannon Sharpe	.25	.11
❑	60	Andre Carter	.25	.11
❑	61	Corey Dillon	.40	.18
❑	62	Josh Reed	.40	.18
❑	63	Marc Boerigter	.40	.18
❑	64	Fred Smoot	.25	.11
❑	65	Shaun Alexander	.60	.25
❑	66	Andre Davis	.25	.11
❑	67	Julian Peterson	.25	.11
❑	68	Corey Bradford	.25	.11
❑	69	Marc Bulger	.60	.25
❑	70	Fred Taylor	.60	.25
❑	71	Junior Seau	.60	.25
❑	72	Simeon Rice	.40	.18
❑	73	Anthony Thomas	.60	.25
❑	74	Correll Buckhalter	.40	.18
❑	75	Justin Smith	.25	.11
❑	76	Marcel Shipp	.40	.18
❑	77	Garrison Hearst	.40	.18
❑	78	Stacey Mack	.25	.11
❑	79	Antowain Smith	.40	.18
❑	80	Kabeer Gbaja-Biamila	.40	.18
❑	81	Curtis Martin	.60	.25
❑	82	Marcellus Wiley	.25	.11
❑	83	Gary Walker	.25	.11
❑	84	Kalimba Edwards	.25	.11
❑	85	Stephen Davis	.40	.18
❑	86	Antwaan Randle El	.60	.25
❑	87	Curtis Conway	.25	.11
❑	88	Keith Brooking	.25	.11
❑	89	Mark Word RC	.25	.11
❑	90	Greg Ellis	.25	.11
❑	91	Steve McNair	.60	.25
❑	92	Ashley Lelie	.60	.25
❑	93	Kelly Holcomb	.40	.18
❑	94	Darrell Jackson	.40	.18
❑	95	Mark Brunell	.40	.18
❑	96	Hugh Douglas	.25	.11
❑	97	Kendrell Bell	.40	.18
❑	98	Steve Smith	.40	.18
❑	99	Bill Schroeder	.40	.18
❑	100	Darren Howard	.25	.11
❑	101	Kevan Barlow	.40	.18
❑	102	Marshall Faulk	.60	.25
❑	103	Ike Hilliard	.25	.11
❑	104	T.J. Duckett	.40	.18
❑	105	Bobby Taylor	.25	.11
❑	106	Kevin Carter	.25	.11
❑	107	Darren Sharper	.25	.11
❑	108	Marty Booker	.40	.18
❑	109	Isaac Bruce	.60	.25
❑	110	Kevin Hardy	.25	.11
❑	111	Tai Streets	.25	.11
❑	112	Brad Johnson	.40	.18
❑	113	Daunte Culpepper	.60	.25
❑	114	Kevin Johnson	.40	.18
❑	115	Matt Hasselbeck	.40	.18
❑	116	Jabar Gaffney	.40	.18
❑	117	Takeo Spikes	.25	.11
❑	118	Brett Favre	1.50	.70
❑	119	Keyshawn Johnson	.60	.25
❑	120	David Akers	.25	.11
❑	121	Maurice Morris	.25	.11
❑	122	Jake Delhomme	.60	.25
❑	123	Kordell Stewart	.40	.18
❑	124	Terrell Davis	.60	.25
❑	125	Brian Kelly	.25	.11
❑	126	David Terrell	.40	.18
❑	127	Koren Robinson	.40	.18
❑	128	Michael Strahan	.40	.18
❑	129	Jake Plummer	.40	.18
❑	130	Terrell Owens	.60	.25
❑	131	Brian Urlacher	1.00	.45
❑	132	David Patten	.25	.11
❑	133	Michael Vick	1.50	.70
❑	134	Jamal Lewis	.60	.25
❑	135	Terry Glenn	.25	.11
❑	136	Brian Simmons	.25	.11
❑	137	David Boston	.40	.18
❑	138	Michael Bennett	.40	.18
❑	139	James Stewart	.40	.18
❑	140	Tiki Barber	.40	.18
❑	141	Brian Griese	.60	.25
❑	142	Deion Branch	.60	.25
❑	143	Mike Peterson	.25	.11
❑	144	James Mungro	.25	.11
❑	145	Tim Couch	.25	.11
❑	146	Brian Dawkins	.25	.11
❑	147	Dennis Northcutt	.40	.18
❑	148	Mike Alstott	.60	.25
❑	149	James Thrash	.25	.11
❑	150	Tim Brown	.60	.25
❑	151	Brian Finneran	.25	.11
❑	152	Derrick Brooks	.40	.18
❑	153	Muhsin Muhammad	.40	.18
❑	154	Jason Elam	.25	.11
❑	155	Tim Dwight	.40	.18
❑	156	Bruce Smith	.40	.18
❑	157	Derrick Mason	.40	.18
❑	158	Napoleon Harris	.25	.11
❑	159	Jason Gildon	.25	.11
❑	160	Todd Heap	.40	.18
❑	161	Aaron Schobel	.40	.18
❑	162	Derrius Thompson	.25	.11
❑	163	Nate Clements	.25	.11
❑	164	Jason McAddley	.25	.11
❑	165	Todd Pinkston	.40	.18
❑	166	Bubba Franks	.40	.18
❑	167	Deuce McAllister	.60	.25
❑	168	Patrick Surtain	.25	.11
❑	169	Javon Walker	.40	.18
❑	170	Tom Brady	1.00	.45
❑	171	Dexter Coakley	.25	.11
❑	172	Patrick Kerney	.25	.11
❑	173	Jay Fiedler	.40	.18
❑	174	Tommy Maddox	.60	.25
❑	175	Donald Driver	.40	.18
❑	176	Patrick Ramsey	.60	.25
❑	177	Olandis Gary	.40	.18
❑	178	Tony Gonzalez	.40	.18
❑	179	Donnie Edwards	.25	.11
❑	180	Peter Boulware	.25	.11
❑	181	Jeff Blake	.25	.11
❑	182	Torry Holt	.60	.25
❑	183	Donovan McNabb	.75	.35
❑	184	Peter Warrick	.25	.11
❑	185	Jeff Garcia	.60	.25
❑	186	Travis Henry	.40	.18
❑	187	Doug Jolley	.25	.11
❑	188	Peyton Manning	1.00	.45
❑	189	Jerome Bettis	.60	.25
❑	190	Travis Taylor	.40	.18
❑	191	Drew Brees	.60	.25
❑	192	Phillip Buchanon	.25	.11
❑	193	Jerramy Stevens	.25	.11
❑	194	Trent Green	.40	.18
❑	195	Duce Staley	.40	.18
❑	196	Plaxico Burress	.40	.18
❑	197	Jerry Porter	.40	.18
❑	198	Trevor Pryce	.25	.11
❑	199	Dwight Freeney	.25	.11
❑	200	Quincy Morgan	.40	.18
❑	201	Troy Vincent	.25	.11
❑	202	Randy McMichael	.40	.18
❑	203	Troy Hambrick	.25	.11
❑	204	Randy Moss	1.00	.45
❑	205	Troy Brown	.40	.18
❑	206	Ray Lewis	.60	.25
❑	207	Trung Canidate	.40	.18
❑	208	Raynoch Thompson	.25	.11
❑	209	Ty Law	.40	.18
❑	210	Reggie Wayne	.40	.18
❑	211	Warren Sapp	.40	.18
❑	212	Richard Seymour	.25	.11
❑	213	Warrick Dunn	.40	.18
❑	214	Robert Ferguson	.25	.11
❑	215	Wayne Chrebet	.40	.18
❑	216	Rod Coleman RC	.60	.25
❑	217	Will Allen	.25	.11
❑	218	Rod Woodson	.40	.18
❑	219	Zach Thomas	.60	.25
❑	220	Rod Smith	.40	.18
❑	221	Ricky Williams	.60	.25
❑	222	LaDainian Tomlinson	.60	.25
❑	223	Priest Holmes	.75	.35
❑	224	Rich Gannon	.40	.18
❑	225	Drew Bledsoe	.60	.25
❑	226	Kerry Collins	.40	.18
❑	227	Marvin Harrison	.60	.25
❑	228	Hines Ward	.60	.25
❑	229	Peerless Price	.40	.18
❑	230	Jason Taylor	.25	.11
❑	231	Jeremy Shockey	1.00	.45
❑	232	Clinton Portis	1.00	.45
❑	233	Antonio Bryant	.40	.18
❑	234	Donte Stallworth	.60	.25
❑	235	David Carr	1.00	.45
❑	236	Joey Harrington	1.00	.45
❑	237	William Green	.40	.18
❑	238	Julius Peppers	.60	.25
❑	239	Marcel Shipp	.25	.11
		Raynoch Thompson		
		Adrian Wilson		
❑	240	Michael Vick	.75	.35
		Warrick Dunn		
		Brian Finneran		
		Keith Brooking		
❑	241	Jamal Lewis	.40	.18
		Edgerton Hartwell		
		Travis Taylor		
		Ed Reed		
❑	242	Drew Bledsoe	.40	.18
		Travis Henry		
		Eric Moulds		
		London Fletcher		
❑	243	Julius Peppers	.40	.18
		Steve Smith		
		Muhsin Muhammad		
❑	244	Marty Booker	.60	.25
		Brian Urlacher		
		Anthony Thomas		
❑	245	Corey Dillon	.40	.18
		Justin Smith		
		Chad Johnson		
		Jon Kitna		
❑	246	Tim Couch	.40	.18
		William Green		
		Quincy Morgan		
		Mark Word		
❑	247	Chad Hutchinson	.25	.11
		Joey Galloway		
		Roy Williams		
		Greg Ellis		
❑	248	Clinton Portis	.60	.25
		Rod Smith		
		Al Wilson		
❑	249	Joey Harrington	.60	.25
		James Stewart		
		Bill Schroeder		
		Kalimba Edwards		
❑	250	Brett Favre	.75	.35
		Ahman Green		
		Donald Driver		
		KGB		
❑	251	David Carr	.60	.25
		Jonathan Wells		
		Corey Bradford		
		Aaron Glenn		
❑	252	Peyton Manning	.60	.25
		Edgerrin James		
		Marvin Harrison		
		Dwight Freeney		
❑	253	Mark Brunell	.25	.11
		Fred Taylor		
		Jimmy Smith		
		Marlon McCree		
❑	254	Treent Green	.40	.18
		Priest Holmes		
		Eddie Kennison		
		Eric Hicks		
❑	255	Ricky Williams	.60	.25
		Chris Chambers		
		Zach Thomas		
		Jason Taylor		
❑	256	Daunte Culpepper	.60	.25
		Michael Bennett		
		Randy Moss		
		Moe Williams		
❑	257	Tom Brady	.60	.25
		Antowain Smith		
		Troy Brown		
		Adam Vinatieri		
❑	258	Aaron Brooks	.25	.11
		Deuce McAllister		
		Joe Horn		
		Darren Howard		
❑	259	Kerry Collins	.25	.11

Tiki Barber
Amani Toomer
Michael Strahan
❑ 260 Chad Pennington .40 .18
Curtis Martin
Wayne Chrebet
John Abraham
❑ 261 Rich Gannon .60 .25
Charlie Garner
Jerry Rice
Rod Woodson
❑ 262 Donovan McNabb .40 .18
Duce Staley
Todd Pinkston
Bobby Taylor
❑ 263 Tommy Maddox .40 .18
Amos Zereoue
Hines Ward
Jason Gildon
Jerry Porter
❑ 264 Drew Brees .60 .25
LaDainian Tomlinson
Donnie Edwards
❑ 265 Jeff Garcia .40 .18
Garrison Hearst
Terrell Owens
Andre Carter
❑ 266 Matt Hasselbeck .25 .11
Shaun Alexander
Koren Robinson
Reggie Tongue
❑ 267 Marc Bulger .60 .25
Marshall Faulk
Torry Holt
Leonard Little
❑ 268 Brad Johnson .40 .18
Keyshawn Johnson
Simeon Rice
Brian Kelly
❑ 269 Steve McNair .25 .11
Eddie George
Derrick Mason
Lance Schulters
❑ 270 Patrick Ramsey .25 .11
Rod Gardner
Fred Smoot
❑ 271 Carson Palmer RC 4.00 1.80
❑ 272 Kyle Boller RC 3.00 1.35
❑ 273 Byron Leftwich RC 5.00 2.20
❑ 274 Willis McGahee RC 3.00 1.35
❑ 275 Larry Johnson RC 2.50 1.10
❑ 276 Charles Rogers RC 1.50 .70
❑ 277 Andre Johnson RC 3.00 1.35
❑ 278 Bryant Johnson RC 1.25 .55
❑ 279 Rex Grossman RC 3.00 1.35
❑ 280 Taylor Jacobs RC 1.25 .55
❑ 281 Dewayne Robertson RC 1.25 .55
Johnathan Sullivan RC
Kevin Williams RC
❑ 282 Bennie Joppru RC 3.00 1.35
Domanick Davis RC
Dave Ragone RC
❑ 283 Jason Witten RC 1.25 .55
Dallas Clark RC
L.J.Smith RC
❑ 284 Terrence Edwards RC 1.25 .55
Musa Smith RC
Boss Bailey RC
❑ 285 Lee Suggs RC 3.00 1.35
Chris Brown RC
Onterrio Smith RC
❑ 286 Quentin Griffin RC 3.00 1.35
Artose Pinner RC
B.J. Askew RC
❑ 287 Justin Fargas RC 1.25 .55
Doug Gabriel RC
Teyo Johnson RC
❑ 288 Jimmy Kennedy RC 1.25 .55
William Joseph RC
Ty Warren RC
❑ 289 Terrell Suggs RC 2.00 .90
Michael Haynes RC
Jerome McDougle RC
❑ 290 Kelley Washington RC 2.00 .90
Kevin Curtis RC
Nate Burleson RC
❑ 291 Seneca Wallace RC 2.50 1.10
Ken Dorsey RC
Chris Simms RC
❑ 292 Bobby Wade RC 1.25 .55
Sam Aiken RC
Justin Gage RC
❑ 293 Sultan McCullough RC 1.00 .45
Cecil Sapp RC
Earnest Graham RC
❑ 294 Kareem Kelly RC 1.00 .45
Talman Gardner RC
J.R. Tolver RC
❑ 295 Bethel Johnson RC 3.00 1.35
Anquan Boldin RC
Tyrone Calico RC
❑ 296 Brandon Lloyd RC 2.00 .90
Billy McMullen RC
Shaun McDonald RC
❑ 297 Chris Kelsay RC 1.25 .55
Dewayne White RC
Mike Doss RC
❑ 298 Terence Newman RC 2.50 1.10
Marcus Trufant RC
Andre Woolfolk RC
❑ 299 Kliff Kingsbury RC 1.25 .55
Tony Romo RC
Brian St. Pierre RC
❑ 300 Andrew Pinnock RC 1.25 .55
LaBrandon Toefield RC
Avon Cobourne RC

2004 Fleer Tradition

	Nm-Mt	Ex-Mt
COMPLETE SET (360)	100.00	30.00
COMP.SET w/o SP's (330)	30.00	9.00

331-ROOKIE STATED ODDS 1:4
351-360 ROOKIE STATED ODDS 1:18H, 1:24R

❑ 1 Ricky Williams TL .40 .12
Chris Chambers
Adewale Ogunleye
Patrick Surtain
❑ 2 Drew Bledsoe TL .40 .12
Travis Henry
Bobby Shaw
Aaron Schobel
❑ 3 Tom Brady TL .60 .18
Mike Cloud
David Givens
Mike Vrabel
❑ 4 Chad Pennington TL .40 .12
Curtis Martin
Santana Moss
Shaun Ellis
❑ 5 Peyton Manning TL .60 .18
Edgerrin James
Marvin Harrison
Dwight Freeney
❑ 6 Byron Leftwich TL .40 .12
Fred Taylor
Jimmy Smith
Mike Peterson
❑ 7 Steve McNair TL .25 .07
Eddie George
Derrick Mason
Samari Rolle
❑ 8 David Carr TL .40 .12
Domanick Davis
Andre Johnson
Marcus Coleman
❑ 9 Rich Gannon TL .60 .18
Zack Crockett
Jerry Rice
Phillip Buchanon
❑ 10 Jake Plummer TL .40 .12
Clinton Portis
Shannon Sharpe
Bert Berry
❑ 11 Trent Green TL .40 .12
Priest Holmes
Tony Gonzalez
Vonnie Holliday
❑ 12 Drew Brees TL .40 .12
LaDainian Tomlinson
David Boston
Quentin Jammer
❑ 13 Tommy Maddox TL .40 .12
Jerome Bettis
Hines Ward
Kimo von Oelhoffen
❑ 14 Kelly Holcomb TL .25 .07
William Green
Dennis Northcutt
Earl Little
❑ 15 Jon Kitna TL .25 .07
Rudi Johnson
Chad Johnson
Tory James
❑ 16 Kyle Boller TL .40 .12
Jamal Lewis
Terrell Suggs
Ray Lewis
❑ 17 Donovan McNabb TL .40 .12
Correll Buckhalter
Brian Westbrook
Corey Simon
❑ 18 Kerry Collins TL .25 .07
Tiki Barber
Amani Toomer
Michael Strahan
❑ 19 Patrick Ramsey TL .40 .12
Trung Canidate
Laveranues Coles
Fred Smoot
❑ 20 Quincy Carter TL .40 .12
Troy Hambrick
Terry Glenn
Terence Newman
❑ 21 Daunte Culpepper TL .60 .18
Moe Williams
Randy Moss
Kevin Williams
❑ 22 Brett Favre TL .75 .23
Ahman Green
Javon Walker
Kabeer Gbaja-Biamila
❑ 23 Kordell Stewart TL .60 .18
Anthony Thomas
Marty Booker
Brian Urlacher
❑ 24 Joey Harrington TL .40 .12
Shawn Bryson
Az-Zahir Hakim
Dre' Bly
❑ 25 Jeff Garcia TL .40 .12
Kevan Barlow
Terrell Owens
Julian Peterson
❑ 26 Marc Bulger TL .40 .12
Marshall Faulk
Torry Holt
Leonard Little
❑ 27 Matt Hasselbeck TL .25 .07
Shaun Alexander
Darrell Jackson
Chike Okeafor
❑ 28 Jeff Blake TL .25 .07
Marcel Shipp
Anquan Boldin
Dexter Jackson
❑ 29 Jake Delhomme TL .25 .07
Stephen Davis
Steve Smith
Mike Rucker
❑ 30 Brad Johnson TL .25 .07
Michael Pittman
Keenan McCardell
Simeon Rice
❑ 31 Doug Johnson TL .25 .07
T.J. Duckett
Peerless Price

Card	Player	Price 1	Price 2
	Keith Brooking		
❑ 32	Aaron Brooks TL	.40	.12
	Deuce McAllister		
	Joe Horn		
	Charles Grant		
❑ 33	Anquan Boldin	.60	.18
❑ 34	Michael Vick	1.25	.35
❑ 35	Kyle Boller	.60	.18
❑ 36	Aeneas Williams	.25	.07
❑ 37	Jake Delhomme	.60	.18
❑ 38	Rex Grossman	.60	.18
❑ 39	Carson Palmer	.75	.23
❑ 40	Quincy Morgan	.40	.12
❑ 41	Terry Glenn	.25	.07
❑ 42	Jake Plummer	.40	.12
❑ 43	Joey Harrington	.60	.18
❑ 44	Brett Favre	1.50	.45
❑ 45	Jeff Garcia	.60	.18
❑ 46	Peyton Manning	1.00	.30
❑ 47	Byron Leftwich	1.00	.30
❑ 48	Trent Green	.40	.12
❑ 49	A.J. Feeley	.60	.18
❑ 50	Daunte Culpepper	.60	.18
❑ 51	Tom Brady	1.00	.30
❑ 52	Aaron Brooks	.40	.12
❑ 53	Kerry Collins	.40	.12
❑ 54	Chad Pennington	.75	.23
❑ 55	Rich Gannon	.40	.12
❑ 56	Donovan McNabb	.75	.23
❑ 57	Tommy Maddox	.40	.12
❑ 58	Drew Brees	.60	.18
❑ 59	Terrell Owens	.60	.18
❑ 60	Matt Hasselbeck	.40	.12
❑ 61	Kurt Warner	.60	.18
❑ 62	Brad Johnson	.40	.12
❑ 63	Jerome Bettis	.60	.18
❑ 64	Keith Bulluck	.25	.07
❑ 65	Rod Gardner	.40	.12
❑ 66	Eddie George	.40	.12
❑ 67	Warren Sapp	.40	.12
❑ 68	Marc Bulger	.60	.18
❑ 69	Shaun Alexander	.60	.18
❑ 70	Tai Streets	.25	.07
❑ 71	LaDainian Tomlinson	.60	.18
❑ 72	Steve McNair	.60	.18
❑ 73	Brian Westbrook	.40	.12
❑ 74	Jerry Rice	1.25	.35
❑ 75	Santana Moss	.40	.12
❑ 76	Moe Williams	.25	.07
❑ 77	Deuce McAllister	.60	.18
❑ 78	Adam Vinatieri	.60	.18
❑ 79	Randy Moss	.75	.23
❑ 80	Ricky Williams	.60	.18
❑ 81	Priest Holmes	.75	.23
❑ 82	Jimmy Smith	.40	.12
❑ 83	Edgerrin James	.60	.18
❑ 84	Andre Johnson	.60	.18
❑ 85	Ahman Green	.60	.18
❑ 86	Charles Rogers	.40	.12
❑ 87	Champ Bailey	.40	.12
❑ 88	Roy Williams S	.40	.12
❑ 89	Tim Couch	.25	.07
❑ 90	Corey Dillon	.40	.12
❑ 91	Thomas Jones	.40	.12
❑ 92	Stephen Davis	.40	.12
❑ 93	Travis Henry	.40	.12
❑ 94	Jamal Lewis	.60	.18
❑ 95	Warrick Dunn	.40	.12
❑ 96	Emmitt Smith	1.25	.35
❑ 97	Mark Brunell	.40	.12
❑ 98	Willis McGahee	.60	.18
❑ 99	Duce Staley	.40	.12
❑ 100	Lee Suggs	.60	.18
❑ 101	Rod Smith	.40	.12
❑ 102	Marvin Harrison	.60	.18
❑ 103	Larry Johnson	.40	.12
❑ 104	Michael Bennett	.40	.12
❑ 105	Donte Stallworth	.40	.12
❑ 106	DeShaun Foster	.40	.12
❑ 107	Hines Ward	.60	.18
❑ 108	T.J. Duckett	.40	.12
❑ 109	Brian Urlacher	.75	.23
❑ 110	Boss Bailey	.40	.12
❑ 111	Tim Brown	.60	.18
❑ 112	David Boston	.40	.12
❑ 113	Marshall Faulk	.60	.18
❑ 114	Jason Witten	.40	.12
❑ 115	Richard Seymour	.25	.07
❑ 116	Domanick Davis	.60	.18
❑ 117	Jon Kitna	.40	.12
❑ 118	Ray Lewis	.60	.18
❑ 119	Tedy Bruschi	.40	.12
❑ 120	Chris Chambers	.40	.12
❑ 121	Freddie Mitchell	.40	.12
❑ 122	Amani Toomer	.40	.12
❑ 123	Curtis Martin	.60	.18
❑ 124	Eric Moulds	.40	.12
❑ 125	Darrell Jackson	.40	.12
❑ 126	Clinton Portis	.60	.18
❑ 127	Jay Fiedler	.25	.07
❑ 128	Todd Heap	.40	.12
❑ 129	Dexter Jackson	.25	.07
❑ 130	James Jackson	.25	.07
❑ 131	Shannon Sharpe	.40	.12
❑ 132	Donald Driver	.40	.12
❑ 133	Billy Miller	.25	.07
❑ 134	Dante Hall	.60	.18
❑ 135	Onterrio Smith	.40	.12
❑ 136	Joe Horn	.40	.12
❑ 137	Shaun Ellis	.25	.07
❑ 138	L.J. Smith	.40	.12
❑ 139	Jerry Porter	.40	.12
❑ 140	Reggie Wayne	.40	.12
❑ 141	Derrick Brooks	.40	.12
❑ 142	Terrell Suggs	.40	.12
❑ 143	Randy McMichael	.25	.07
❑ 144	Mike Alstott	.40	.12
❑ 145	Nate Poole RC	.60	.18
❑ 146	Chris Brown	.60	.18
❑ 147	Torry Holt	.60	.18
❑ 148	Adewale Ogunleye	.40	.12
❑ 149	Peter Warrick	.40	.12
❑ 150	Alge Crumpler	.40	.12
❑ 151	Charlie Garner	.40	.12
❑ 152	Jeremy Shockey	.60	.18
❑ 153	Simeon Rice	.40	.12
❑ 154	Julian Peterson	.25	.07
❑ 155	Patrick Ramsey	.40	.12
❑ 156	Shawn Springs	.25	.07
❑ 157	Marcus Stroud	.25	.07
❑ 158	Keyshawn Johnson	.40	.12
❑ 159	Steve Smith	.40	.12
❑ 160	Ty Law	.40	.12
❑ 161	Derrick Mason	.40	.12
❑ 162	Josh Reed	.25	.07
❑ 163	Fred Smoot	.25	.07
❑ 164	Muhsin Muhammad	.40	.12
❑ 165	Justin Gage	.40	.12
❑ 166	Chad Johnson	.40	.12
❑ 167	Dennis Northcutt	.25	.07
❑ 168	Joey Galloway	.40	.12
❑ 169	Ashley Lelie	.40	.12
❑ 170	Casey Fitzsimmons	.25	.07
❑ 171	Dwight Freeney	.25	.07
❑ 172	Nick Barnett	.40	.12
❑ 173	LaBrandon Toefield	.25	.07
❑ 174	Jabar Gaffney	.40	.12
❑ 175	Tony Gonzalez	.40	.12
❑ 176	Zach Thomas	.60	.18
❑ 177	Nate Burleson	.60	.18
❑ 178	Deion Branch	.60	.18
❑ 179	Boo Williams	.25	.07
❑ 180	Michael Strahan	.40	.12
❑ 181	Anthony Becht	.25	.07
❑ 182	Charles Woodson	.40	.12
❑ 183	Sheldon Brown	.25	.07
❑ 184	Kendrell Bell	.40	.12
❑ 185	Kassim Osgood	.25	.07
❑ 186	Tony Parrish	.25	.07
❑ 187	Marcel Shipp	.40	.12
❑ 188	Bobby Engram	.25	.07
❑ 189	Keith Brooking	.25	.07
❑ 190	Isaac Bruce	.40	.12
❑ 191	Travis Taylor	.25	.07
❑ 192	Charles Lee	.25	.07
❑ 193	Takeo Spikes	.25	.07
❑ 194	Justin McCareins	.25	.07
❑ 195	Julius Peppers	.60	.18
❑ 196	LaVar Arrington	1.25	.35
❑ 197	Dez White	.40	.12
❑ 198	Rudi Johnson	.40	.12
❑ 199	Andre Davis	.25	.07
❑ 200	Quincy Carter	.40	.12
❑ 201	Quentin Griffin	.60	.18
❑ 202	Dallas Clark	.40	.12
❑ 203	Artose Pinner	.25	.07
❑ 204	Kevin Johnson	.25	.07
❑ 205	Kabeer Gbaja-Biamila	.40	.12
❑ 206	Marcus Coleman	.25	.07
❑ 207	Johnnie Morton	.40	.12
❑ 208	Jason Taylor	.25	.07
❑ 209	Kevin Williams	.25	.07
❑ 210	David Givens	.40	.12
❑ 211	Charles Grant	.25	.07
❑ 212	Ike Hilliard	.25	.07
❑ 213	Wayne Chrebet	.40	.12
❑ 214	Teyo Johnson	.25	.07
❑ 215	Brian Dawkins	.25	.07
❑ 216	Antwaan Randle El	.40	.12
❑ 217	Eric Parker	.25	.07
❑ 218	Josh McCown	.40	.12
❑ 219	Tim Rattay	.40	.12
❑ 220	Brian Finneran	.25	.07
❑ 221	Chad Brown	.25	.07
❑ 222	Ed Reed	.40	.12
❑ 223	Dane Looker	.40	.12
❑ 224	Aaron Schobel	.40	.12
❑ 225	Joe Jurevicius	.25	.07
❑ 226	Ricky Manning	.25	.07
❑ 227	Jevon Kearse	.40	.12
❑ 228	Laveranues Coles	.40	.12
❑ 229	Kelley Washington	.25	.07
❑ 230	William Green	.40	.12
❑ 231	Terence Newman	.40	.12
❑ 232	Bryant Johnson	.25	.07
❑ 233	Peerless Price	.40	.12
❑ 234	Peter Boulware	.40	.12
❑ 235	Drew Bledsoe	.60	.18
❑ 236	Kris Jenkins	.25	.07
❑ 237	Marty Booker	.40	.12
❑ 238	Matt Schobel	.25	.07
❑ 239	Earl Little	.25	.07
❑ 240	Antonio Bryant	.40	.12
❑ 241	Al Wilson	.25	.07
❑ 242	Dre Bly	.25	.07
❑ 243	Javon Walker	.40	.12
❑ 244	David Carr	.60	.18
❑ 245	Mike Vanderjagt	.25	.07
❑ 246	Fred Taylor	.40	.12
❑ 247	Eddie Kennison	.25	.07
❑ 248	Patrick Surtain	.25	.07
❑ 249	Jim Kleinsasser	.25	.07
❑ 250	Daniel Graham	.25	.07
❑ 251	Jerome Pathon	.25	.07
❑ 252	Tiki Barber	.40	.12
❑ 253	John Abraham	.25	.07
❑ 254	Justin Fargas	.40	.12
❑ 255	Correll Buckhalter	.40	.12
❑ 256	Plaxico Burress	.40	.12
❑ 257	Quentin Jammer	.25	.07
❑ 258	Kevan Barlow	.40	.12
❑ 259	Koren Robinson	.40	.12
❑ 260	Leonard Little	.25	.07
❑ 261	John Lynch	.40	.12
❑ 262	Tyrone Calico	.40	.12
❑ 263	Taylor Jacobs	.40	.12
❑ 264	Joey Porter	.25	.07
❑ 265	Freddie Jones	.25	.07
❑ 266	Marcus Pollard	.25	.07
❑ 267	Mike Peterson	.25	.07
❑ 268	Justin Griffith	.25	.07
❑ 269	Shawn Bryson	.25	.07
❑ 270	Will Allen	.25	.07
❑ 271	Antonio Gates	.60	.18
❑ 272	Chris McAlister	.25	.07
❑ 273	Tony Hollings	.25	.07
❑ 274	Cedrick Wilson	.25	.07
❑ 275	Adam Archuleta	.25	.07
❑ 276	London Fletcher	.25	.07
❑ 277	Drew Bennett	.40	.12
❑ 278	Rod Smart	.25	.07
❑ 279	LaMont Jordan	.40	.12
❑ 280	Jerry Azumah	.25	.07
❑ 281	Bubba Franks	.40	.12
❑ 282	Troy Edwards	.25	.07
❑ 283	Willie McGinest	.25	.07
❑ 284	Morten Andersen	.25	.07
❑ 285	Dat Nguyen	.25	.07
❑ 286	Samari Rolle	.25	.07
❑ 287	Brian Simmons	.25	.07
❑ 288	Chike Okeafor	.25	.07
❑ 289	Rodney Harrison	.25	.07
❑ 290	Jason Elam	.25	.07
❑ 291	Tim Dwight	.40	.12

❑ 292 Corey Bradford	.25	.07
❑ 293 Charles Tillman	.40	.12
❑ 294 Tim Carter	.25	.07
❑ 295 Ahmed Plummer	.25	.07
❑ 296 Troy Walters	.25	.07
❑ 297 Michael Lewis	.25	.07
❑ 298 Tory James	.25	.07
❑ 299 Doug Flutie	.60	.18
❑ 300 Az-Zahir Hakim	.25	.07
❑ 301 Itula Mili	.25	.07
❑ 302 Jamie Sharper	.25	.07
❑ 303 Vonnie Holliday	.25	.07
❑ 304 Brian Russell RC	.60	.18
❑ 305 Bryan Gilmore	.25	.07
❑ 306 Darren Sharper	.25	.07
❑ 307 Kyle Brady	.25	.07
❑ 308 David Tyree	.25	.07
❑ 309 Andre Carter	.25	.07
❑ 310 Lawyer Milloy	.40	.12
❑ 311 David Terrell	.40	.12
❑ 312 Richie Anderson	.25	.07
❑ 313 Darren Howard	.25	.07
❑ 314 Sebastian Janikowski	.25	.07
❑ 315 Kimo von Oelhoffen	.25	.07
❑ 316 Donnie Edwards	.25	.07
❑ 317 Brandon Lloyd	.40	.12
❑ 318 Robert Ferguson	.25	.07
❑ 319 Derek Smith	.25	.07
❑ 320 Anthony Thomas	.40	.12
❑ 321 Ken Hamlin	.25	.07
❑ 322 Ronde Barber	.25	.07
❑ 323 Erron Kinney	.25	.07
❑ 324 Tom Brady AW	.60	.18
❑ 325 Peyton Manning AW	.60	.18
❑ 326 Steve McNair AW	.40	.12
❑ 327 Jamal Lewis AW	.40	.12
❑ 328 Ray Lewis AW	.40	.12
❑ 329 Anquan Boldin AW	.25	.07
❑ 330 Terrell Suggs AW	.25	.07
❑ 331 Eli Manning RC	10.00	3.00
❑ 332 Larry Fitzgerald RC	6.00	1.80
❑ 333 Ben Roethlisberger RC	20.00	6.00
❑ 334 Tatum Bell RC	4.00	1.20
❑ 335 Roy Williams RC	6.00	1.80
❑ 336 Drew Henson RC	5.00	1.50
❑ 337 Philip Rivers RC	6.00	1.80
❑ 338 Rashaun Woods RC	2.50	.75
❑ 339 Kevin Jones RC	6.00	1.80
❑ 340 Sean Taylor RC	2.50	.75
❑ 341 Steven Jackson RC	6.00	1.80
❑ 342 Kellen Winslow RC	5.00	1.50
❑ 343 Chris Perry RC	4.00	1.20
❑ 344 J.P. Losman RC	5.00	1.50
❑ 345 Greg Jones RC	2.00	.60
❑ 346 Reggie Williams RC	2.50	.75
❑ 347 Michael Clayton RC	5.00	1.50
❑ 348 Jonathan Vilma RC	2.00	.60
❑ 349 Julius Jones RC	8.00	2.40
❑ 350 Michael Jenkins RC	2.00	.60
❑ 351 Eli Manning Philip Rivers Ben Roethlisberger	25.00	7.50
❑ 352 Larry Fitzgerald Reggie Williams Roy Williams WR	8.00	2.40
❑ 353 Lee Evans RC Bernard Berrian RC Derrick Hamilton RC	5.00	1.50
❑ 354 Kenechi Udeze RC Will Poole RC Keary Colbert RC	3.00	.90
❑ 355 Chris Gamble RC Dunta Robinson RC DeAngelo Hall RC	3.00	.90
❑ 356 Ben Troupe RC Ben Watson RC Ben Hartsock RC	3.00	.90
❑ 357 Devard Darling RC Johnnie Morant RC Ernest Wilford RC	3.00	.90
❑ 358 Luke McCown RC Cody Pickett RC Matt Schaub RC	4.00	1.20
❑ 359 Tatum Bell Michael Turner RC Cedric Cobbs RC	5.00	1.50
❑ 360 Mewelde Moore RC Quincy Wilson RC Derrick Knight RC	3.00	.90

2004 Fleer Tradition Blue

Nm-Mt Ex-Mt

*STARS: 1X TO 2.5X BASE CARD HI
*ROOKIES 331-350: .6X TO 1.5X BASE CARD HI
*ROOKIES 351-360: .6X TO 1.5X BASE CARD HI

2004 Fleer Tradition Crystal

Nm-Mt Ex-Mt

*STARS: 5X TO 12X BASE CARD HI
*ROOKIES 331-350: 2.5X TO 6X BASIC CARDS
*ROOKIES 351-360: 3X TO 8X BASIC CARDS
1-330 PRINT RUN 150 SER.#'d SETS
331-350 PRINT RUN 75 SER.#'d SETS
351-360 PRINT RUN 25 SER.#'d SETS

2004 Fleer Tradition Draft Day

Nm-Mt Ex-Mt

*ROOKIES 331-350: 1X TO 2.5X BASE CARD HI
*ROOKIES 351-360: 1X TO 2.5X BASE CARD HI
STATED ODDS ONE PER HOT PACK
STATED PRINT RUN 375 SER.#'d SETS

2004 Fleer Tradition Green

Nm-Mt Ex-Mt

*STARS: 1.5X TO 4X BASE CARD HI
*ROOKIES 331-350: 1X TO 2.5X BASE CARD HI
*ROOKIES 351-360: 1X TO 2.5X BASE CARD HI

2000 Greats of the Game

	Nm-Mt	Ex-Mt
COMP.SET w/o SP's (100)	40.00	18.00
❑ 1 Terry Bradshaw	1.50	.70
❑ 2 Paul Hornung	.60	.25
❑ 3 Tony Dorsett	.60	.25
❑ 4 L.C. Greenwood	.40	.18
❑ 5 Ozzie Newsome	.25	.11
❑ 6 Michael Irvin	.40	.18
❑ 7 Art Donovan	.40	.18
❑ 8 Don Maynard	.40	.18
❑ 9 Bobby Mitchell	.40	.18
❑ 10 Bob Lilly	.40	.18
❑ 11 Earl Morrall	.25	.11
❑ 12 Harvey Martin	.25	.11
❑ 13 Dan Fouts	.60	.25
❑ 14 Joe Theismann	.60	.25
❑ 15 Roger Staubach	1.50	.70
❑ 16 Otto Graham	.40	.18
❑ 17 Cliff Branch	.40	.18
❑ 18 Sonny Jurgensen	.60	.25
❑ 19 Eric Dickerson	.40	.18
❑ 20 Lee Roy Selmon	.25	.11
❑ 21 Roger Craig	.40	.18
❑ 22 Raymond Berry	.40	.18
❑ 23 Bob Hayes	.40	.18
❑ 24 Steve Largent	.60	.25
❑ 25 Lenny Moore	.40	.18
❑ 26 Chuck Bednarik	.40	.18
❑ 27 Ken Stabler	1.25	.55
❑ 28 William Perry	.40	.18
❑ 29 Joe Greene	.60	.25
❑ 30 Joe Namath	1.50	.70
❑ 31 Jim Kelly	.75	.35
❑ 32 Steve Young	1.25	.55
❑ 33 Randy White	.40	.18
❑ 34 Lawrence Taylor	.60	.25
❑ 35 Franco Harris	.75	.35
❑ 36 Marcus Allen	.60	.25
❑ 37 Mike Singletary	.60	.25
❑ 38 Fran Tarkenton	1.25	.55
❑ 39 Mel Renfro	.25	.11
❑ 40 Len Dawson	.60	.25
❑ 41 Carl Eller	.25	.11
❑ 42 Chuck Foreman	.25	.11
❑ 43 Gino Marchetti	.25	.11
❑ 44 Jim Marshall	.25	.11
❑ 45 Jack Ham	.40	.18
❑ 46 Mercury Morris	.25	.11
❑ 47 Anthony Munoz	.40	.18
❑ 48 Herschel Walker	.40	.18
❑ 49 Drew Pearson	.40	.18
❑ 50 John Elway	2.50	1.10
❑ 51 George Blanda	.60	.25
❑ 52 Earl Campbell	.60	.25
❑ 53 Bart Starr	2.00	.90
❑ 54 Dan Marino	2.50	1.10
❑ 55 Johnny Unitas	1.50	.70
❑ 56 Sammy Baugh	.60	.25
❑ 57 Steve Van Buren	.40	.18
❑ 58 Mel Blount	.40	.18
❑ 59 Fred Biletnikoff	.60	.25
❑ 60 John Brodie	.25	.11
❑ 61 Daryle Lamonica	.25	.11
❑ 62 James Lofton	.25	.11
❑ 63 Ronnie Lott	.40	.18
❑ 64 Gale Sayers	1.25	.55
❑ 65 Art Monk	.40	.18
❑ 66 Jim Plunkett	.40	.18
❑ 67 Charlie Joiner	.25	.11

Card	Nm-Mt	Ex-Mt
❑ 68 Deacon Jones	.40	.18
❑ 69 Paul Warfield	.60	.25
❑ 70 Jim Otto	.25	.11
❑ 71 Billy Kilmer	.40	.18
❑ 72 Archie Manning	.40	.18
❑ 73 Alex Karras	.40	.18
❑ 74 Tom Matte	.25	.11
❑ 75 Jay Novacek	.25	.11
❑ 76 Charley Taylor	.40	.18
❑ 77 Sam Huff	.40	.18
❑ 78 Jack Lambert	.60	.25
❑ 79 Mike Ditka	.60	.25
❑ 80 Frank Gifford	.60	.25
❑ 81 Jim Thorpe	.60	.25
❑ 82 Walter Payton	3.00	1.35
❑ 83 Doak Walker	.60	.25
❑ 84 Sid Luckman	.40	.18
❑ 85 Bronko Nagurski	.60	.25
❑ 86 Alan Ameche	.25	.11
❑ 87 Merlin Olsen	.40	.18
❑ 88 Dick Butkus	1.25	.55
❑ 89 Elroy Hirsch	.40	.18
❑ 90 Max McGee	.40	.18
❑ 91 Ray Nitschke	.60	.25
❑ 92 Phil Simms	.40	.18
❑ 93 Vince Lombardi CC	1.25	.55
❑ 94 Tom Landry CC	.75	.35
❑ 95 Bill Walsh CC	.40	.18
❑ 96 Mike Ditka CC	.60	.25
❑ 97 Jimmy Johnson CC	.40	.18
❑ 98 Chuck Noll CC	.40	.18
❑ 99 Dan Reeves CC	.40	.18
❑ 100 Don Shula CC	.60	.25
❑ 101 Peter Warrick RC	8.00	3.60
❑ 102 Thomas Jones RC	12.00	5.50
❑ 103 Jamal Lewis RC	20.00	9.00
❑ 104 Chad Pennington RC	30.00	13.50
❑ 105 Chris Redman RC	6.00	2.70
❑ 106 Ron Dayne RC	8.00	3.60
❑ 107 Trung Canidate RC	6.00	2.70
❑ 108 Shaun Alexander RC	20.00	9.00
❑ 109 Plaxico Burress RC	15.00	6.75
❑ 110 J.R. Redmond RC	6.00	2.70
❑ 111 Travis Taylor RC	8.00	3.60
❑ 112 Dez White RC	8.00	3.60
❑ 113 Todd Pinkston RC	8.00	3.60
❑ 114 Laveranues Coles RC	10.00	4.50
❑ 115 Dennis Northcutt RC	8.00	3.60
❑ 116 Jerry Porter RC	10.00	4.50
❑ 117 R.Jay Soward RC	6.00	2.70
❑ 118 Sylvester Morris RC	6.00	2.70
❑ 119 Ron Dugans RC	6.00	2.70
❑ 120 Travis Prentice RC	6.00	2.70
❑ 121 Tee Martin RC	8.00	3.60
❑ 122 James Williams RC	6.00	2.70
❑ 123 Trevor Gaylor RC	6.00	2.70
❑ 124 Shyrone Stith RC	6.00	2.70
❑ 125 Frank Moreau RC	6.00	2.70
❑ 126 Kwame Cavil RC	6.00	2.70
❑ 127 Ron Dixon RC	6.00	2.70
❑ 128 Darrell Jackson RC	15.00	6.75
❑ 129 Sammy Morris RC	6.00	2.70
❑ 130 JaJuan Dawson RC	6.00	2.70
❑ 131 Doug Johnson RC	40.00	18.00
❑ 132 Brian Urlacher RC	80.00	36.00
❑ 133 Brad Hoover RC	40.00	18.00
❑ 134 Mike Anderson AUTO RC	40.00	18.00

2004 Greats of the Game

	Nm-Mt	Ex-Mt
COMP.SET w/o RC's (66)	40.00	12.00

ROOKIE STATED ODDS: 1:15 HOB, 1:24 RET
ROOKIE PRINT RUN 999 SER.#'d SETS
CARDS #35/39/41 NOT PRICED

Card	Nm-Mt	Ex-Mt
❑ 1 Jim Brown	3.00	.90
❑ 2 Jim Thorpe	2.00	.60
❑ 3 Terry Bradshaw	3.00	.90
❑ 4 Fran Tarkenton	2.50	.75
❑ 5 Joe Namath	3.00	.90
❑ 6 Joe Montana	6.00	1.80
❑ 7 George Rogers	1.00	.30
❑ 8 Marcus Allen	2.00	.60
❑ 9 Walter Payton	6.00	1.80
❑ 10 Dick Butkus	3.00	.90
❑ 11 Dan Fouts	2.00	.60
❑ 12 Kellen Winslow Sr.	1.50	.45
❑ 13 Sammy Baugh	2.00	.60
❑ 14 Bart Starr	4.00	1.20
❑ 15 Steve Young	2.50	.75
❑ 16 Sid Luckman	2.00	.60
❑ 17 Y.A. Tittle	2.00	.60
❑ 18 Dan Marino	5.00	1.50
❑ 19 Paul Hornung	2.00	.60
❑ 20 John Elway	3.00	.90
❑ 21 Earl Campbell	2.00	.60
❑ 22 Max McGee	1.50	.45
❑ 23 Alan Ameche	1.00	.30
❑ 24 Bronko Nagurski	2.00	.60
❑ 25 Elroy Hirsch	1.50	.45
❑ 26 Jack Lambert	2.50	.75
❑ 27 Sam Huff	1.50	.45
❑ 28 Jay Novacek	1.50	.45
❑ 29 Roger Staubach	3.00	.90
❑ 30 Bob Hayes	1.50	.45
❑ 31 Ken Stabler	2.50	.75
❑ 32 Chuck Bednarik	1.50	.45
❑ 33 Ronnie Lott	2.00	.60
❑ 34 Steve Van Buren	1.50	.45
❑ 36 Gale Sayers	2.50	.75
❑ 37 Jim Otto	1.00	.30
❑ 38 Jim Plunkett	1.50	.45
❑ 40 Don Maynard	1.50	.45
❑ 42 Billy Sims	1.50	.45
❑ 43 Franco Harris	2.50	.75
❑ 44 Tony Dorsett	2.00	.60
❑ 45 Wilbert Montgomery	1.00	.30
❑ 46 Eric Dickerson SP	4.00	1.20
❑ 47 Jim Taylor	2.00	.60
❑ 48 George Blanda	2.00	.60
❑ 49 Cris Carter	2.00	.60
❑ 50 Mike Quick	1.00	.30
❑ 51 James Lofton	1.00	.30
❑ 52 Lawrence Taylor	2.00	.60
❑ 53 Roger Craig	2.00	.60
❑ 54 Paul Warfield	1.50	.45
❑ 55 Dan Pastorini	1.00	.30
❑ 56 Ozzie Newsome	1.50	.45
❑ 57 Charley Taylor	1.50	.45
❑ 58 Deacon Jones	1.50	.45
❑ 59 Bob Lilly	2.00	.60
❑ 60 Mike Singletary	2.00	.60
❑ 61 Warren Moon	1.50	.45
❑ 62 Charles White	1.00	.30
❑ 63 Bob Griese	2.00	.60
❑ 64 Dwight Clark	1.50	.45
❑ 65 Joe Greene	2.00	.60
❑ 66 Dave Casper	1.00	.30
❑ 67 Harold Carmichael	1.00	.30
❑ 68 Drew Pearson	1.50	.45
❑ 69 Tony Hill	1.00	.30
❑ 70 Ray Nitschke	2.00	.60
❑ 71 Eli Manning RC	20.00	6.00
❑ 72 Philip Rivers RC	12.00	3.60
❑ 73 Ben Roethlisberger RC	40.00	12.00
❑ 74 Julius Jones RC	15.00	4.50
❑ 75 Larry Fitzgerald RC	12.00	3.60
❑ 76 Steven Jackson RC	12.00	3.60
❑ 77 Kevin Jones RC	12.00	3.60
❑ 78 Tatum Bell RC	6.00	1.80
❑ 79 Rashaun Woods RC	5.00	1.50
❑ 80 Roy Williams RC	12.00	3.60
❑ 81 Lee Evans RC	6.00	1.80
❑ 82 Michael Clayton RC	10.00	3.00
❑ 83 J.P. Losman RC	10.00	3.00
❑ 84 Drew Henson RC	10.00	3.00
❑ 85 Kellen Winslow RC	10.00	3.00
❑ 86 Chris Perry RC	8.00	2.40
❑ 87 Reggie Williams RC	5.00	1.50
❑ 88 Michael Jenkins RC	4.00	1.20
❑ 89 Darius Watts RC	5.00	1.50
❑ 90 Keary Colbert RC	5.00	1.50

2004 Greats of the Game Green/Red

Nm-Mt Ex-Mt

*STARS: 1.2X TO 3X BASE CARD HI
VETERAN GREEN PRINT RUN 500 SETS
*ROOKIES: 1X TO 2.5X BASE CARD HI
ROOKIE RED PRINT RUN 99 SETS
STATED ODDS 1:7.5 HOB, 1:24 RET

2002 Gridiron Kings

Card	Nm-Mt	Ex-Mt
COMPLETE SET (175)	150.00	45.00
COMP.SET w/o SP's (100)	40.00	12.00
❑ 1 David Boston	1.25	.35
❑ 2 Jake Plummer	.75	.23
❑ 3 Michael Vick	4.00	1.20
❑ 4 Warrick Dunn	1.25	.35
❑ 5 Jamal Lewis	1.25	.35
❑ 6 Ray Lewis	1.25	.35
❑ 7 Drew Bledsoe	1.50	.45
❑ 8 Travis Henry	1.25	.35
❑ 9 Eric Moulds	.75	.23
❑ 10 Chris Weinke	.75	.23
❑ 11 Lamar Smith	.75	.23
❑ 12 Anthony Thomas	1.25	.35
❑ 13 Chris Chandler	.75	.23
❑ 14 Brian Urlacher	2.00	.60
❑ 15 Corey Dillon	.75	.23
❑ 16 Peter Warrick	.75	.23
❑ 17 Tim Couch	.75	.23
❑ 18 James Jackson	.50	.15
❑ 19 Kevin Johnson	.75	.23
❑ 20 Quincy Carter	.75	.23
❑ 21 Emmitt Smith	3.00	.90
❑ 22 Joey Galloway	.75	.23
❑ 23 Brian Griese	1.25	.35
❑ 24 Terrell Davis	1.25	.35
❑ 25 Ed McCaffrey	1.25	.35
❑ 26 Rod Smith	.75	.23
❑ 27 Mike McMahon	1.25	.35
❑ 28 Az-Zahir Hakim	.50	.15
❑ 29 Germane Crowell	.50	.15
❑ 30 Brett Favre	3.00	.90
❑ 31 Terry Glenn	.75	.23
❑ 32 Ahman Green	1.25	.35
❑ 33 James Allen	.75	.23

❑ 34 Tony Simmons	.50	.15
❑ 35 Peyton Manning	2.50	.75
❑ 36 Edgerrin James	1.50	.45
❑ 37 Marvin Harrison	1.25	.35
❑ 38 Dominic Rhodes	.75	.23
❑ 39 Mark Brunell	1.25	.35
❑ 40 Jimmy Smith	.75	.23
❑ 41 Keenan McCardell	.50	.15
❑ 42 Fred Taylor	1.25	.35
❑ 43 Priest Holmes	1.50	.45
❑ 44 Snoop Minnis	.50	.15
❑ 45 Trent Green	.75	.23
❑ 46 Tony Gonzalez	.75	.23
❑ 47 Chris Chambers	1.25	.35
❑ 48 Ricky Williams	1.25	.35
❑ 49 Jay Fiedler	.75	.23
❑ 50 Zach Thomas	1.25	.35
❑ 51 Randy Moss	2.50	.75
❑ 52 Cris Carter	1.25	.35
❑ 53 Daunte Culpepper	1.25	.35
❑ 54 Michael Bennett	1.25	.35
❑ 55 Tom Brady	3.00	.90
❑ 56 Antowain Smith	.75	.23
❑ 57 Troy Brown	.75	.23
❑ 58 Aaron Brooks	1.25	.35
❑ 59 Deuce McAllister	1.50	.45
❑ 60 Joe Horn	.75	.23
❑ 61 Kerry Collins	.75	.23
❑ 62 Ron Dayne	.75	.23
❑ 63 Michael Strahan	.75	.23
❑ 64 Vinny Testaverde	.75	.23
❑ 65 Curtis Martin	1.25	.35
❑ 66 Wayne Chrebet	.75	.23
❑ 67 Rich Gannon	1.25	.35
❑ 68 Tim Brown	1.25	.35
❑ 69 Jerry Rice	2.50	.75
❑ 70 Charlie Garner	.75	.23
❑ 71 Donovan McNabb	1.50	.45
❑ 72 Duce Staley	1.25	.35
❑ 73 Freddie Mitchell	.75	.23
❑ 74 Kordell Stewart	.75	.23
❑ 75 Jerome Bettis	1.25	.35
❑ 76 Plaxico Burress	1.25	.35
❑ 77 Kendrell Bell	1.25	.35
❑ 78 LaDainian Tomlinson	2.00	.60
❑ 79 Drew Brees	1.25	.35
❑ 80 Doug Flutie	1.25	.35
❑ 81 Junior Seau	1.25	.35
❑ 82 Jeff Garcia	1.25	.35
❑ 83 Terrell Owens	1.25	.35
❑ 84 Garrison Hearst	.75	.23
❑ 85 Trent Dilfer	.75	.23
❑ 86 Shaun Alexander	1.25	.35
❑ 87 Koren Robinson	.75	.23
❑ 88 Marshall Faulk	1.25	.35
❑ 89 Kurt Warner	1.25	.35
❑ 90 Torry Holt	1.25	.35
❑ 91 Isaac Bruce	1.25	.35
❑ 92 Brad Johnson	.75	.23
❑ 93 Keyshawn Johnson	1.25	.35
❑ 94 Mike Alstott	1.25	.35
❑ 95 Warren Sapp	.75	.23
❑ 96 Steve McNair	1.25	.35
❑ 97 Eddie George	1.25	.35
❑ 98 Jevon Kearse	1.25	.35
❑ 99 Stephen Davis	.75	.23
❑ 100 Rod Gardner	.75	.23
❑ 101 David Carr RC	12.00	3.60
❑ 102 Joey Harrington RC	12.00	3.60
❑ 103 Patrick Ramsey RC	8.00	2.40
❑ 104 Josh McCown RC	5.00	1.50
❑ 105 David Garrard RC	4.00	1.20
❑ 106 Rohan Davey RC	4.00	1.20
❑ 107 Randy Fasani RC	3.00	.90
❑ 108 Kurt Kittner RC	3.00	.90
❑ 109 William Green RC	6.00	1.80
❑ 110 T.J. Duckett RC	6.00	1.80
❑ 111 DeShaun Foster RC	1.25	.35
❑ 112 Clinton Portis RC	12.00	3.60
❑ 113 Maurice Morris RC	4.00	1.20
❑ 114 Ladell Betts RC	4.00	1.20
❑ 115 Lamar Gordon RC	4.00	1.20
❑ 116 Brian Westbrook RC	6.00	1.80
❑ 117 Jonathan Wells RC	4.00	1.20
❑ 118 Travis Stephens RC	3.00	.90
❑ 119 Josh Scobey RC	4.00	1.20
❑ 120 Donte Stallworth RC	8.00	2.40
❑ 121 Ashley Lelie RC	8.00	2.40
❑ 122 Javon Walker RC	8.00	2.40
❑ 123 Jabar Gaffney RC	4.00	1.20
❑ 124 Josh Reed RC	4.00	1.20
❑ 125 Tim Carter RC	3.00	.90
❑ 126 Andre Davis RC	4.00	1.20
❑ 127 Reche Caldwell RC	4.00	1.20
❑ 128 Antwaan Randle El RC	5.00	1.50
❑ 129 Antonio Bryant RC	4.00	1.20
❑ 130 Deion Branch RC	8.00	2.40
❑ 131 Marquise Walker RC	3.00	.90
❑ 132 Cliff Russell RC	3.00	.90
❑ 133 Eric Crouch RC	6.00	1.80
❑ 134 Ron Johnson RC	3.00	.90
❑ 135 Terry Charles RC	3.00	.90
❑ 136 Jeremy Shockey RC	12.00	3.60
❑ 137 Daniel Graham RC	4.00	1.20
❑ 138 Julius Peppers RC	8.00	2.40
❑ 139 Dwight Freeney RC	5.00	1.50
❑ 140 Ryan Sims RC	4.00	1.20
❑ 141 John Henderson RC	4.00	1.20
❑ 142 Wendell Bryant RC	4.00	1.20
❑ 143 Albert Haynesworth RC	3.00	.90
❑ 144 Quentin Jammer RC	4.00	1.20
❑ 145 Phillip Buchanon RC	4.00	1.20
❑ 146 Lito Sheppard RC	4.00	1.20
❑ 147 Roy Williams RC	10.00	3.00
❑ 148 Ed Reed RC	6.00	1.80
❑ 149 Napoleon Harris RC	4.00	1.20
❑ 150 Mike Williams RC	3.00	.90
❑ 151 Art Monk	4.00	1.20
❑ 152 Barry Sanders	8.00	2.40
❑ 153 Bob Griese	5.00	1.50
❑ 154 Dan Marino	10.00	3.00
❑ 155 Dick Butkus	10.00	3.00
❑ 156 Earl Campbell	5.00	1.50
❑ 157 Eric Dickerson	5.00	1.50
❑ 158 Fran Tarkenton	5.00	1.50
❑ 159 Franco Harris	5.00	1.50
❑ 160 Herschel Walker	4.00	1.20
❑ 161 Joe Montana	15.00	4.50
❑ 162 Ronnie Lott	4.00	1.20
❑ 163 Joe Theismann	4.00	1.20
❑ 164 John Elway	10.00	3.00
❑ 165 John Riggins	5.00	1.50
❑ 166 Ken Stabler	6.00	1.80
❑ 167 Len Dawson	5.00	1.50
❑ 168 Marcus Allen	4.00	1.20
❑ 169 Mike Singletary	4.00	1.20
❑ 170 Roger Staubach	6.00	1.80
❑ 171 Walter Payton	12.00	3.60
❑ 172 Steve Largent	5.00	1.50
❑ 173 Terry Bradshaw	6.00	1.80
❑ 174 Thurman Thomas	4.00	1.20
❑ 175 Tony Dorsett	5.00	1.50

2003 Gridiron Kings

	MINT	NRMT
COMPLETE SET (175)	250.00	110.00
COMP.SET w/o SP's (100)	30.00	13.50
❑ 1 David Boston	.75	.35
❑ 2 Marcel Shipp	.75	.35
❑ 3 Jake Plummer	.75	.35
❑ 4 Michael Vick	3.00	1.35
❑ 5 T.J. Duckett	.75	.35
❑ 6 Warrick Dunn	.75	.35
❑ 7 Ray Lewis	1.25	.55
❑ 8 Jamal Lewis	1.25	.55
❑ 9 Todd Heap	.75	.35
❑ 10 Drew Bledsoe	1.25	.55
❑ 11 Eric Moulds	.75	.35
❑ 12 Travis Henry	.75	.35
❑ 13 Julius Peppers	1.25	.55
❑ 14 Steve Smith	.50	.23
❑ 15 Muhsin Muhammad	.75	.35
❑ 16 Anthony Thomas	1.25	.55
❑ 17 David Terrell	.75	.35
❑ 18 Brian Urlacher	2.00	.90
❑ 19 Corey Dillon	.75	.35
❑ 20 Chad Johnson	.75	.35
❑ 21 William Green	.75	.35
❑ 22 Tim Couch	.50	.23
❑ 23 Quincy Morgan	.75	.35
❑ 24 Roy Williams	1.25	.55
❑ 25 Emmitt Smith	3.00	1.35
❑ 26 Antonio Bryant	.75	.35
❑ 27 Clinton Portis	2.00	.90
❑ 28 Ashley Lelie	1.25	.55
❑ 29 Rod Smith	.75	.35
❑ 30 Brian Griese	1.25	.55
❑ 31 Joey Harrington	2.00	.90
❑ 32 James Stewart	.75	.35
❑ 33 Az-Zahir Hakim	.50	.23
❑ 34 Brett Favre	3.00	1.35
❑ 35 Ahman Green	1.25	.55
❑ 36 Donald Driver	.75	.35
❑ 37 Javon Walker	.75	.35
❑ 38 David Carr	2.00	.90
❑ 39 Jabar Gaffney	.75	.35
❑ 40 Jonathan Wells	.50	.23
❑ 41 Edgerrin James	1.25	.55
❑ 42 Marvin Harrison	1.25	.55
❑ 43 Peyton Manning	2.00	.90
❑ 44 Mark Brunell	.75	.35
❑ 45 Jimmy Smith	.75	.35
❑ 46 Fred Taylor	1.25	.55
❑ 47 Priest Holmes	1.50	.70
❑ 48 Tony Gonzalez	.75	.35
❑ 49 Trent Green	.75	.35
❑ 50 Jay Fiedler	.75	.35
❑ 51 Chris Chambers	1.25	.55
❑ 52 Zach Thomas	1.25	.55
❑ 53 Ricky Williams	1.25	.55
❑ 54 Randy Moss	2.00	.90
❑ 55 Daunte Culpepper	1.25	.55
❑ 56 Michael Bennett	.75	.35
❑ 57 Tom Brady	2.00	.90
❑ 58 Deion Branch	1.25	.55
❑ 59 Antowain Smith	.50	.23
❑ 60 Donte Stallworth	1.25	.55
❑ 61 Deuce McAllister	1.25	.55
❑ 62 Aaron Brooks	1.25	.55
❑ 63 Kerry Collins	.75	.35
❑ 64 Jeremy Shockey	2.00	.90
❑ 65 Tiki Barber	.75	.35
❑ 66 Curtis Martin	1.25	.55
❑ 67 Chad Pennington	1.50	.70
❑ 68 Santana Moss	.75	.35
❑ 69 Jerry Rice	2.50	1.10
❑ 70 Rich Gannon	.75	.35
❑ 71 Tim Brown	1.25	.55
❑ 72 Charlie Garner	.75	.35
❑ 73 Donovan McNabb	1.50	.70
❑ 74 Duce Staley	.75	.35
❑ 75 Antonio Freeman	.75	.35
❑ 76 Tommy Maddox	1.25	.55
❑ 77 Jerome Bettis	1.25	.55
❑ 78 Antwaan Randle El	1.25	.55
❑ 79 Plaxico Burress	.75	.35
❑ 80 LaDainian Tomlinson	1.25	.55
❑ 81 Junior Seau	1.25	.55
❑ 82 Drew Brees	1.25	.55
❑ 83 Terrell Owens	1.25	.55
❑ 84 Jeff Garcia	1.25	.55
❑ 85 Garrison Hearst	.75	.35
❑ 86 Koren Robinson	.75	.35
❑ 87 Shaun Alexander	1.25	.55
❑ 88 Trent Dilfer	.75	.35
❑ 89 Marshall Faulk	1.25	.55
❑ 90 Kurt Warner	1.25	.55
❑ 91 Isaac Bruce	1.25	.55
❑ 92 Brad Johnson	.75	.35
❑ 93 Keyshawn Johnson	1.25	.55
❑ 94 Warren Sapp	.75	.35
❑ 95 Steve McNair	1.25	.55
❑ 96 Derrick Mason	.75	.35
❑ 97 Eddie George	.75	.35
❑ 98 Bruce Smith	.75	.35
❑ 99 Rod Gardner	.75	.35

❑ 100 Patrick Ramsey	1.25	.55
❑ 101 Carson Palmer RC	10.00	4.50
❑ 102 Byron Leftwich RC	12.00	5.50
❑ 103 Kyle Boller RC	8.00	3.60
❑ 104 Chris Simms RC	6.00	2.70
❑ 105 Dave Ragone RC	3.00	1.35
❑ 106 Rex Grossman RC	8.00	3.60
❑ 107 Brian St.Pierre RC	3.00	1.35
❑ 108 Kliff Kingsbury RC	2.50	1.10
❑ 109 Seneca Wallace RC	3.00	1.35
❑ 110 Larry Johnson RC	6.00	2.70
❑ 111 Lee Suggs RC	6.00	2.70
❑ 112 Justin Fargas RC	3.00	1.35
❑ 113 Onterrio Smith RC	4.00	1.80
❑ 114 Willis McGahee RC	8.00	3.60
❑ 115 Chris Brown RC	6.00	2.70
❑ 116 Musa Smith RC	3.00	1.35
❑ 117 Artose Pinner RC	3.00	1.35
❑ 118 Domanick Davis RC	6.00	2.70
❑ 119 Charles Rogers RC	4.00	1.80
❑ 120 Andre Johnson RC	8.00	3.60
❑ 121 Taylor Jacobs RC	3.00	1.35
❑ 122 Bryant Johnson RC	3.00	1.35
❑ 123 Kelley Washington RC	3.00	1.35
❑ 124 Brandon Lloyd RC	4.00	1.80
❑ 125 Tyrone Calico RC	4.00	1.80
❑ 126 Kevin Curtis RC	3.00	1.35
❑ 127 Bethel Johnson RC	5.00	2.20
❑ 128 Anquan Boldin RC	8.00	3.60
❑ 129 Nate Burleson RC	5.00	2.20
❑ 130 Jason Witten RC	5.00	2.20
❑ 131 Bennie Joppru RC	3.00	1.35
❑ 132 Teyo Johnson RC	3.00	1.35
❑ 133 Dallas Clark RC	3.00	1.35
❑ 134 Terrell Suggs RC	5.00	2.20
❑ 135 Chris Kelsay RC	3.00	1.35
❑ 136 Jerome McDougle RC	3.00	1.35
❑ 137 Michael Haynes RC	3.00	1.35
❑ 138 Calvin Pace RC	2.50	1.10
❑ 139 Jimmy Kennedy RC	3.00	1.35
❑ 140 Kevin Williams RC	3.00	1.35
❑ 141 DeWayne Robertson RC	3.00	1.35
❑ 142 William Joseph RC	3.00	1.35
❑ 143 Johnathan Sullivan RC	2.50	1.10
❑ 144 Boss Bailey RC	4.00	1.80
❑ 145 E.J. Henderson RC	3.00	1.35
❑ 146 Terence Newman RC	6.00	2.70
❑ 147 Marcus Trufant RC	3.00	1.35
❑ 148 Andre Woolfolk RC	3.00	1.35
❑ 149 Troy Polamalu RC	3.00	1.35
❑ 150 Mike Doss RC	3.00	1.35
❑ 151 Andre Reed	3.00	1.35
❑ 152 Bo Jackson	5.00	2.20
❑ 153 Dan Marino	10.00	4.50
❑ 154 Deacon Jones	3.00	1.35
❑ 155 Deion Sanders	4.00	1.80
❑ 156 Doak Walker	3.00	1.35
❑ 157 Don Maynard	3.00	1.35
❑ 158 Frank Gifford	3.00	1.35
❑ 159 Fred Biletnikoff	3.00	1.35
❑ 160 Gale Sayers	3.00	1.35
❑ 161 Jack Lambert	4.00	1.80
❑ 162 Jim Brown	4.00	1.80
❑ 163 Jim Kelly	5.00	2.20
❑ 164 Joe Greene	3.00	1.35
❑ 165 Joe Montana	12.00	5.50
❑ 166 John Elway	10.00	4.50
❑ 167 John Riggins	4.00	1.80
❑ 168 Johnny Unitas	3.00	1.35
❑ 169 Larry Csonka	3.00	1.35
❑ 170 Lawrence Taylor	3.00	1.35
❑ 171 Mike Ditka	3.00	1.35
❑ 172 Ozzie Newsome	3.00	1.35
❑ 173 Red Grange	3.00	1.35
❑ 174 Troy Aikman	5.00	2.20
❑ 175 Warren Moon	3.00	1.35

2003 Gridiron Kings Bronze

MINT NRMT

*STARS: 1.2X TO 3X BASIC CARDS
*ROOKIES: .5X TO 1.2X
*STARS 151-175: .8X TO 2X

2003 Gridiron Kings Gold

MINT NRMT

*STARS: 5X TO 12X BASIC CARDS
*ROOKIES: 1.5X TO 4X
*STARS 151-175: 4X TO 10X

2003 Gridiron Kings Silver

MINT NRMT

*STARS: 2X TO 5X BASIC CARDS
*ROOKIES: .6X TO 1.5X
*STARS 151-175: 1.2X TO 3X

2000 Impact

	Nm-Mt	Ex-Mt
COMPLETE SET (199)	30.00	13.50
❑ 1 Kurt Warner	1.00	.45
❑ 2 Dan Marino	1.50	.70
❑ 3 Sedrick Irvin	.20	.09
❑ 4 Chris Redman RC	.50	.23
❑ 5 Robert Smith	.50	.23
❑ 6 Amani Toomer	.20	.09
❑ 7 Richard Huntley	.20	.09
❑ 8 Ahman Green	.50	.23
❑ 9 Fred Lane	.20	.09
❑ 10 Eddie George	.50	.23
❑ 11 Rocket Ismail	.30	.14
❑ 12 Shannon Sharpe	.30	.14
❑ 13 Shawn Jefferson	.20	.09
❑ 14 Michael Wiley RC	.50	.23
❑ 15 Jeff Graham	.20	.09
❑ 16 Steve Beuerlein	.30	.14
❑ 17 Tim Biakabutuka	.30	.14
❑ 18 Chris Watson	.20	.09
❑ 19 Kevin Faulk	.30	.14
❑ 20 Emmitt Smith	1.00	.45
❑ 21 Plaxico Burress RC	1.25	.55
❑ 22 Hines Ward	.50	.23
❑ 23 Jacquez Green	.20	.09
❑ 24 Doug Flutie	.50	.23
❑ 25 Leslie Shepherd	.20	.09
❑ 26 Johnnie Morton	.30	.14
❑ 27 Tom Brady RC	15.00	6.75
❑ 28 Jeff George	.30	.14
❑ 29 Derrick Mason	.30	.14
❑ 30 Marshall Faulk	.75	.35
❑ 31 Derrick Mayes	.30	.14
❑ 32 Jerome Bettis	.50	.23
❑ 33 Adrian Murrell	.30	.14
❑ 34 Curtis Enis	.20	.09
❑ 35 Kimble Anders	.20	.09
❑ 36 Travis Prentice RC	.50	.23
❑ 37 Curtis Martin	.50	.23
❑ 38 Ronnie Powell	.20	.09
❑ 39 Steve Christie	.20	.09
❑ 40 Brett Favre	1.50	.70
❑ 41 Michael Bates	.20	.09
❑ 42 Rondell Mealey RC	.40	.18
❑ 43 Randall Cunningham	.50	.23
❑ 44 Kerry Collins	.30	.14
❑ 45 William Thomas	.20	.09
❑ 46 Ricky Watters	.30	.14
❑ 47 Marvin Harrison	.50	.23
❑ 48 Corey Bradford	.30	.14
❑ 49 Terry Kirby	.20	.09
❑ 50 Troy Aikman	1.00	.45
❑ 51 Cris Carter	.50	.23
❑ 52 Jamal Lewis RC	1.50	.70
❑ 53 Duce Staley	.50	.23
❑ 54 Isaac Bruce	.50	.23
❑ 55 Yancey Thigpen	.20	.09
❑ 56 R.Jay Soward RC	.50	.23
❑ 57 Jermaine Lewis	.20	.09
❑ 58 Zach Thomas	.50	.23
❑ 59 Sylvester Morris RC	.50	.23
❑ 60 Steve McNair	.50	.23
❑ 61 Tiki Barber	.30	.14
❑ 62 Torrance Small	.20	.09
❑ 63 Champ Bailey	.30	.14
❑ 64 Tim Dwight	.50	.23
❑ 65 Willie Jackson	.20	.09
❑ 66 Edgerrin James	.75	.35
❑ 67 Ron Dayne RC	.60	.25
❑ 68 Rich Gannon	.50	.23
❑ 69 Junior Seau	.50	.23
❑ 70 Warren Sapp	.30	.14
❑ 71 Rob Johnson	.30	.14
❑ 72 Antonio Freeman	.50	.23
❑ 73 O.J. McDuffie	.30	.14
❑ 74 Tamarick Vanover	.20	.09
❑ 75 Courtney Brown RC	.60	.25
❑ 76 Donovan McNabb	.75	.35
❑ 77 Az-Zahir Hakim	.30	.14
❑ 78 Albert Connell	.20	.09
❑ 79 Qadry Ismail	.30	.14
❑ 80 Terrell Davis	.50	.23
❑ 81 Dorsey Levens	.30	.14
❑ 82 Tony Martin	.30	.14
❑ 83 Laveranues Coles RC	.75	.35
❑ 84 Karim Abdul-Jabbar	.30	.14
❑ 85 Charles Johnson	.30	.14
❑ 86 Torry Holt	.50	.23
❑ 87 Stephen Davis	.50	.23
❑ 88 Tony Banks	.30	.14
❑ 89 Akili Smith	.20	.09
❑ 90 Tim Couch	.30	.14
❑ 91 Bill Schroeder	.30	.14
❑ 92 Andre Hastings	.20	.09
❑ 93 Eddie Kennison	.20	.09
❑ 94 Randy Moss	1.00	.45
❑ 95 Tony Horne	.20	.09
❑ 96 Sherrod Gideon RC	.40	.18
❑ 97 Wesley Walls	.20	.09
❑ 98 Brian Griese	.50	.23
❑ 99 Jake Delhomme RC	2.00	.90
❑ 100 Peyton Manning	1.25	.55
❑ 101 Brad Johnson	.50	.23
❑ 102 Trung Canidate RC	.50	.23
❑ 103 Freddie Jones	.20	.09
❑ 104 Muhsin Muhammad	.30	.14
❑ 105 Eric Moulds	.50	.23
❑ 106 Ed McCaffrey	.50	.23
❑ 107 Joe Montgomery	.20	.09
❑ 108 Olandis Gary	.50	.23
❑ 109 J.J. Stokes	.20	.09
❑ 110 Ricky Williams	.50	.23
❑ 111 Jim Harbaugh	.30	.14
❑ 112 Mike Alstott	.50	.23
❑ 113 Errict Rhett	.30	.14
❑ 114 Terance Mathis	.30	.14
❑ 115 Kevin Johnson	.50	.23
❑ 116 Tremain Mack	.20	.09
❑ 117 Peter Warrick RC	.60	.25
❑ 118 Lamont Warren	.20	.09
❑ 119 Damon Huard	.50	.23
❑ 120 Cade McNown	.20	.09
❑ 121 Natrone Means	.20	.09
❑ 122 Ken Oxendine	.20	.09
❑ 123 J.R. Redmond RC	.50	.23
❑ 124 Ken Dilger	.20	.09
❑ 125 James Johnson	.20	.09
❑ 126 Napoleon Kaufman	.30	.14
❑ 127 Ryan Leaf	.30	.14
❑ 128 Michael Westbrook	.30	.14
❑ 129 Mario Bates	.20	.09
❑ 130 Jake Plummer	.30	.14
❑ 131 James Jett	.20	.09
❑ 132 Darnay Scott	.30	.14
❑ 133 Curtis Conway	.30	.14
❑ 134 Fred Taylor	.50	.23
❑ 135 Wayne Chrebet	.30	.14
❑ 136 Sean Dawkins	.20	.09
❑ 138 Keenan McCardell	.30	.14
❑ 139 Donnell Bennett	.20	.09
❑ 140 Jerry Rice	1.00	.45
❑ 141 Vinny Testaverde	.30	.14
❑ 142 Chad Pennington RC	2.50	1.10
❑ 143 Jonathan Linton	.20	.09
❑ 144 Herman Moore	.30	.14
❑ 145 David Patten	.30	.14
❑ 146 Troy Edwards	.20	.09
❑ 147 Jon Kitna	.50	.23
❑ 148 Jimmy Smith	.30	.14
❑ 149 Tee Martin RC	.60	.25

❑ 150 Jevon Kearse	.50	.23
❑ 151 Frank Sanders	.20	.09
❑ 152 Marcus Robinson	.50	.23
❑ 153 Mike Hollis	.20	.09
❑ 154 Frank Wycheck	.20	.09
❑ 155 Tim Rattay RC	1.25	.55
❑ 156 Dedric Ward	.20	.09
❑ 157 Terrell Owens	.50	.23
❑ 158 Chris Chandler	.30	.14
❑ 159 Damon Griffin	.20	.09
❑ 160 Mike Vanderjagt	.20	.09
❑ 161 Elvis Grbac	.20	.09
❑ 162 Rickey Dudley	.20	.09
❑ 163 Jeff Garcia	.50	.23
❑ 164 Thomas Jones RC	1.00	.45
❑ 165 Tyrone Wheatley	.30	.14
❑ 166 Rod Smith	.30	.14
❑ 167 Bubba Franks RC	.60	.25
❑ 168 Chris Warren	.20	.09
❑ 169 Anthony Lucas RC	.20	.09
❑ 170 Terry Glenn	.30	.14
❑ 171 John Carney	.20	.09
❑ 172 Warrick Dunn	.50	.23
❑ 173 Shaun Alexander RC	1.50	.70
❑ 174 David Boston	.50	.23
❑ 175 Bobby Engram	.20	.09
❑ 176 Travis Taylor RC	.60	.25
❑ 177 Derrick Alexander	.30	.14
❑ 178 Keyshawn Johnson	.50	.23
❑ 179 Steve Young	.60	.25
❑ 180 Deion Sanders	.50	.23
❑ 181 Charlie Batch	.50	.23
❑ 182 Drew Bledsoe	.60	.25
❑ 183 Reuben Droughns RC	.75	.35
❑ 184 Ray Lucas	.30	.14
❑ 185 Shaun King	.20	.09
❑ 186 Jamal Anderson	.50	.23
❑ 187 Corey Dillon	.50	.23
❑ 188 Joe Hamilton RC	.50	.23
❑ 189 Terrence Wilkins	.20	.09
❑ 190 Mark Brunell	.50	.23
❑ 191 Tony Gonzalez	.30	.14
❑ 192 Tim Brown	.50	.23
❑ 193 Charlie Garner	.30	.14
❑ 194 Antowain Smith	.30	.14
❑ 195 David LaFleur	.20	.09
❑ 196 Germane Crowell	.20	.09
❑ 197 Terry Allen	.30	.14
❑ 198 Marc Bulger RC	1.25	.55
❑ 199 Kevin Dyson	.30	.14
❑ 200 Kordell Stewart	.30	.14

1948 Leaf

	ExMt	VgEx
COMPLETE SET (98)	6000.00	2700.00
COMMON CARD (1-49)	30.00	13.50
COMMON CARD (50-98)	175.00	80.00
VAR (8B/12B/14B)	50.00	25.00
WRAPPER (5-CENT)	160.00	70.00
❑ 1 Sid Luckman RC	400.00	100.00
❑ 2 Steve Suhey	30.00	13.50
❑ 3A Bulldog Turner RC (Red background)	125.00	55.00
❑ 3B Bulldog Turner RC (White background)	175.00	80.00
❑ 4 Doak Walker RC	200.00	90.00
❑ 5 Levi Jackson RC	40.00	18.00
❑ 6 Bobby Layne RC UER (Name spelled Bobbie on front)	400.00	180.00
❑ 7 Bill Fischer	30.00	13.50
❑ 8A Vince Banonis (Black name on front)	30.00	13.50
❑ 8B Vince Banonis (White name on front)	50.00	22.00
❑ 9 Tommy Thompson RC	40.00	18.00
❑ 10 Perry Moss	30.00	13.50
❑ 11 Terry Brennan RC	40.00	18.00
❑ 12A William Swiacki RC (Black name on front)	30.00	13.50
❑ 12B William Swiacki RC (White name on front)	50.00	22.00
❑ 13A Johnny Lujack RC	200.00	90.00
❑ 13B Johnny Lujack RC ERR (misspelled Jonny on front; thought to be a salesmen's sample)	300.00	150.00
❑ 14A Mal Kutner RC (Black name on front)	30.00	13.50
❑ 14B Mal Kutner RC (White name on front)	50.00	22.00
❑ 15 Charlie Justice RC	90.00	40.00
❑ 16 Pete Pihos RC	150.00	70.00
❑ 17A Kenny Washington RC (Black name on front)	55.00	25.00
❑ 17B Kenny Washington RC (White name on front)	80.00	36.00
❑ 18 Harry Gilmer RC	50.00	22.00
❑ 19A George McAfee COR RC	150.00	70.00
❑ 19B George McAfee RC ERR (Listed as Gorgeous George on front)	200.00	90.00
❑ 20 George Taliaferro RC	40.00	18.00
❑ 21 Paul Christman RC	50.00	22.00
❑ 22 Steve Van Buren RC	250.00	110.00
❑ 23 Ken Kavanaugh RC	40.00	18.00
❑ 24 Jim Martin RC	40.00	18.00
❑ 25 Elmer Bud Angsman RC	40.00	18.00
❑ 26A Bob Waterfield RC	250.00	110.00
❑ 26B Bob Waterfield RC (White name on front)	450.00	220.00
❑ 27A Fred Davis (Yellow background)	30.00	13.50
❑ 27B Fred Davis (White background)	50.00	22.00
❑ 28 Whitey Wistert RC	40.00	18.00
❑ 29 Charley Trippi RC	110.00	50.00
❑ 30 Paul Governali RC	40.00	18.00
❑ 31 Tom McWilliams	30.00	13.50
❑ 32 Leroy Zimmerman	30.00	13.50
❑ 33 Pat Harder RC UER (Misspelled Harber on front)	55.00	25.00
❑ 34 Sammy Baugh RC	600.00	275.00
❑ 35 Ted Fritsch Sr. RC	40.00	18.00
❑ 36 Bill Dudley RC	125.00	55.00
❑ 37 George Connor RC	100.00	45.00
❑ 38 Frank Dancewicz	30.00	13.50
❑ 39 Billy Dewell	30.00	13.50
❑ 40 John Nolan	30.00	13.50
❑ 41A Harry Szulborski Yellow jersey	30.00	13.50
❑ 41B Harry Szulborski Orange jersey	50.00	22.00
❑ 42 Tex Coulter RC	40.00	18.00
❑ 43A Robert Nussbaumer (Maroon Jersey)	30.00	13.50
❑ 43B Robert Nussbaumer (Red Jersey)	50.00	22.00
❑ 44 Bob Mann	30.00	13.50
❑ 45 Jim White	30.00	13.50
❑ 46 Jack Jacobs	30.00	13.50
❑ 47 John Clement	30.00	13.50
❑ 48 Frank Reagan	30.00	13.50
❑ 49 Frank Tripucka RC	45.00	20.00
❑ 50 John Rauch RC	175.00	80.00
❑ 51 Mike Dimitro	175.00	80.00
❑ 52 Leo Nomellini RC	450.00	200.00
❑ 53 Charley Conerly RC	450.00	200.00
❑ 54 Chuck Bednarik RC	500.00	220.00
❑ 55 Chick Jagade	175.00	80.00
❑ 56 Bob Folsom RC	200.00	90.00
❑ 57 Gene Rossides RC	200.00	90.00
❑ 58 Art Weiner	175.00	80.00
❑ 59 Alex Sarkistian	175.00	80.00
❑ 60 Dick Harris	175.00	80.00
❑ 61 Len Younce	175.00	80.00
❑ 62 Gene Derricotte	175.00	80.00
❑ 63 Roy Rebel Steiner	175.00	80.00
❑ 64 Frank Seno	175.00	80.00
❑ 65 Bob Hendren RC	175.00	80.00
❑ 66 Jack Cloud	175.00	80.00
❑ 67 Harrell Collins	175.00	80.00
❑ 68A Clyde LeForce ERR RC (Red Background) (name misspelled LaForce)	175.00	80.00
❑ 68B Clyde LeForce ERR RC (White Background) (name misspelled LaForce)	200.00	100.00
❑ 69 Larry Joe	175.00	80.00
❑ 70 Phil O'Reilly	175.00	80.00
❑ 71 Paul Campbell	175.00	80.00
❑ 72 Ray Evans	175.00	80.00
❑ 73 Jackie Jensen RC UER Spelled Jackey on card front	400.00	180.00
❑ 74 Russ Steger	175.00	80.00
❑ 75 Tony Minisi	175.00	80.00
❑ 76 Clayton Tonnemaker	175.00	80.00
❑ 77 George Savitsky	175.00	80.00
❑ 78 Clarence Self	175.00	80.00
❑ 79 Rod Franz	175.00	80.00
❑ 80 Jim Youle	175.00	80.00
❑ 81 Billy Bye	175.00	80.00
❑ 82 Fred Enke	175.00	80.00
❑ 83 Fred Folger	175.00	80.00
❑ 84 Jug Girard RC	200.00	90.00
❑ 85 Joe Scott	175.00	80.00
❑ 86 Bob Demoss	175.00	80.00
❑ 87 Dave Templeton	175.00	80.00
❑ 88 Herb Siegert	175.00	80.00
❑ 89 Bucky O'Conner	175.00	80.00
❑ 90 Joe Whisler	175.00	80.00
❑ 91 Leon Hart RC	250.00	110.00
❑ 92 Earl Banks	175.00	80.00
❑ 93 Frank Aschenbrenner	175.00	80.00
❑ 94 John Goldsberry	175.00	80.00
❑ 95 Porter Payne	175.00	80.00
❑ 96 Pete Perini	175.00	80.00
❑ 97 Jay Rhodemyre	175.00	80.00
❑ 98 Al DiMarco RC	250.00	60.00

1949 Leaf

	ExMt	VgEx
COMPLETE SET (49)	2200.00	1000.00
WRAPPER (5-CENT)	300.00	135.00
❑ 1 Bob Hendren	80.00	20.00
❑ 2 Joe Scott	25.00	11.00
❑ 3 Frank Reagan	25.00	11.00
❑ 4 John Rauch	25.00	11.00
❑ 7 Bill Fischer	25.00	11.00
❑ 9 Elmer Bud Angsman	35.00	16.00
❑ 10 Billy Dewell	25.00	11.00
❑ 13 Tommy Thompson	35.00	16.00
❑ 15 Sid Luckman	125.00	55.00
❑ 16 Charley Trippi	55.00	25.00
❑ 17 Bob Mann	25.00	11.00
❑ 19 Paul Christman	35.00	16.00
❑ 22 Bill Dudley	55.00	25.00
❑ 23 Clyde LeForce	25.00	11.00
❑ 26 Sammy Baugh	300.00	135.00
❑ 28 Pete Pihos	70.00	32.00
❑ 31 Tex Coulter	35.00	16.00
❑ 32 Mal Kutner	35.00	16.00
❑ 35 Whitey Wistert	35.00	16.00
❑ 37 Ted Fritsch Sr.	35.00	16.00
❑ 38 Vince Banonis	25.00	11.00
❑ 39 Jim White	25.00	11.00
❑ 40 George Connor	55.00	25.00
❑ 41 George McAfee	55.00	25.00
❑ 43 Frank Tripucka	45.00	20.00
❑ 47 Fred Enke	25.00	11.00
❑ 49 Charley Conerly	100.00	45.00
❑ 51 Ken Kavanaugh	35.00	16.00
❑ 52 Bob Demoss	25.00	11.00
❑ 56 John Lujack	100.00	45.00
❑ 57 Jim Youle	25.00	11.00

❑ 62 Harry Gilmer	35.00	16.00
❑ 65 Robert Nussbaumer	25.00	11.00
❑ 67 Bobby Layne	200.00	90.00
❑ 70 Herb Siegert	25.00	11.00
❑ 74 Tony Minisi	25.00	11.00
❑ 79 Steve Van Buren	150.00	70.00
❑ 81 Perry Moss	25.00	11.00
❑ 89 Bob Waterfield	125.00	55.00
❑ 90 Jack Jacobs	25.00	11.00
❑ 95 Kenny Washington	45.00	20.00
❑ 101 Pat Harder UER (Misspelled Harber on front)	35.00	16.00
❑ 110 Bill Swiacki	35.00	16.00
❑ 118 Fred Davis	25.00	11.00
❑ 126 Jay Rhodemyre	25.00	11.00
❑ 127 Frank Seno	25.00	11.00
❑ 134 Chuck Bednarik	175.00	80.00
❑ 144 George Savitsky	25.00	11.00
❑ 150 Bulldog Turner	150.00	38.00

1999 Leaf Certified

	Nm-Mt	Ex-Mt
COMPLETE SET (225)	200.00	90.00
COMP.SET w/o RCs 175)	40.00	18.00
❑ 1 Simeon Rice	.60	.25
❑ 2 Frank Sanders	.60	.25
❑ 3 Andre Wadsworth	.40	.18
❑ 4 Larry Centers	.40	.18
❑ 5 Byron Hanspard	.40	.18
❑ 6 Terance Mathis	.60	.25
❑ 7 O.J. Santiago	.40	.18
❑ 8 Chris Calloway	.40	.18
❑ 9 Michael Jackson	.40	.18
❑ 10 Rod Woodson	.60	.25
❑ 11 Pat Johnson	.40	.18
❑ 12 Rob Johnson	.60	.25
❑ 13 Andre Reed	.60	.25
❑ 14 Tim Biakabutuka	.60	.25
❑ 15 Rae Carruth	.40	.18
❑ 16 Fred Lane	.40	.18
❑ 17 Muhsin Muhammad	.60	.25
❑ 18 Wesley Walls	.60	.25
❑ 19 Edgar Bennett	.40	.18
❑ 20 Curtis Conway	.60	.25
❑ 21 Bobby Engram	.60	.25
❑ 22 Jeff Blake	.60	.25
❑ 23 Darnay Scott	.40	.18
❑ 24 Ty Detmer	.60	.25
❑ 25 Sedrick Shaw	.40	.18
❑ 26 Leslie Shepherd	.40	.18
❑ 27 Terry Kirby	.40	.18
❑ 28 Chris Warren	.40	.18
❑ 29 Rocket Ismail	.60	.25
❑ 30 Marcus Nash	.40	.18
❑ 31 Neil Smith	.60	.25
❑ 32 Bubby Brister	.40	.18
❑ 33 Brian Griese	1.00	.45
❑ 34 Germane Crowell	.40	.18
❑ 35 Johnnie Morton	.60	.25
❑ 36 Gus Frerotte	.40	.18
❑ 37 Robert Brooks	.60	.25
❑ 38 Mark Chmura	.40	.18
❑ 39 Derrick Mayes	.40	.18
❑ 40 Jerome Pathon	.40	.18
❑ 41 Jimmy Smith	.60	.25
❑ 42 James Stewart	.60	.25
❑ 43 Tavian Banks	.40	.18
❑ 44 Derrick Alexander WR	.60	.25
❑ 45 Kimble Anders	.60	.25
❑ 46 Elvis Grbac	.60	.25
❑ 47 Derrick Thomas	.60	.25
❑ 48 Byron Bam Morris	.40	.18
❑ 49 Tony Gonzalez	1.00	.45
❑ 50 John Avery	.40	.18
❑ 51 Tyrone Wheatley	.60	.25
❑ 52 Zach Thomas	1.00	.45
❑ 53 Lamar Thomas	.40	.18
❑ 54 Jeff George	.60	.25
❑ 55 John Randle	.60	.25
❑ 56 Jake Reed	.60	.25
❑ 57 Leroy Hoard	.40	.18
❑ 58 Robert Edwards	.40	.18
❑ 59 Ben Coates	.60	.25
❑ 60 Tony Simmons	.40	.18
❑ 61 Shawn Jefferson	.40	.18
❑ 62 Eddie Kennison	.60	.25
❑ 63 Lamar Smith	.60	.25
❑ 64 Tiki Barber	.60	.25
❑ 65 Kerry Collins	.60	.25
❑ 66 Ike Hilliard	.40	.18
❑ 67 Gary Brown	.40	.18
❑ 68 Joe Jurevicius	.60	.25
❑ 69 Kent Graham	.40	.18
❑ 70 Dedric Ward	.40	.18
❑ 71 Terry Allen	.60	.25
❑ 72 Neil O'Donnell	.60	.25
❑ 73 Desmond Howard	.60	.25
❑ 74 James Jett	.60	.25
❑ 75 Jon Ritchie	.40	.18
❑ 76 Rickey Dudley	.40	.18
❑ 77 Charles Johnson	.40	.18
❑ 78 Chris Fuamatu-Ma'afala	.40	.18
❑ 79 Hines Ward	1.00	.45
❑ 80 Ryan Leaf	1.00	.45
❑ 81 Jim Harbaugh	.60	.25
❑ 82 Junior Seau	1.00	.45
❑ 83 Mikhael Ricks	.40	.18
❑ 84 J.J. Stokes	.60	.25
❑ 85 Ahman Green	1.00	.45
❑ 86 Tony Banks	.60	.25
❑ 87 Robert Holcombe	.40	.18
❑ 88 Az-Zahir Hakim	.40	.18
❑ 89 Greg Hill	.40	.18
❑ 90 Trent Green	1.00	.45
❑ 91 Eric Zeier	.40	.18
❑ 92 Reidel Anthony	.60	.25
❑ 93 Bert Emanuel	.60	.25
❑ 94 Warren Sapp	.40	.18
❑ 95 Kevin Dyson	.60	.25
❑ 96 Yancey Thigpen	.40	.18
❑ 97 Frank Wycheck	.40	.18
❑ 98 Michael Westbrook	.60	.25
❑ 99 Albert Connell	.40	.18
❑ 100 Darrell Green	.40	.18
❑ 101 Rob Moore	.60	.25
❑ 102 Adrian Murrell	.60	.25
❑ 103 Jake Plummer	1.00	.45
❑ 104 Chris Chandler	.60	.25
❑ 105 Jamal Anderson	1.00	.45
❑ 106 Tim Dwight	1.00	.45
❑ 107 Jermaine Lewis	1.00	.45
❑ 108 Priest Holmes	2.50	1.10
❑ 109 Bruce Smith	1.00	.45
❑ 110 Eric Moulds	1.00	.45
❑ 111 Antowain Smith	1.50	.70
❑ 112 Curtis Enis	1.00	.45
❑ 113 Corey Dillon	1.50	.70
❑ 114 Michael Irvin	1.00	.45
❑ 115 Ed McCaffrey	1.00	.45
❑ 116 Shannon Sharpe	1.00	.45
❑ 117 Terrell Davis	1.50	.70
❑ 118 Charlie Batch	1.50	.70
❑ 119 Antonio Freeman	1.00	.45
❑ 120 Dorsey Levens	1.00	.45
❑ 121 Marvin Harrison	1.50	.70
❑ 122 Peyton Manning	5.00	2.20
❑ 123 Keenan McCardell	1.00	.45
❑ 124 Fred Taylor	1.50	.70
❑ 125 Andre Rison	1.00	.45
❑ 126 O.J. McDuffie	1.00	.45
❑ 127 Karim Abdul-Jabbar	1.00	.45
❑ 128 Randy Moss	4.00	1.80
❑ 129 Terry Glenn	1.00	.45
❑ 130 Vinny Testaverde	1.00	.45
❑ 131 Keyshawn Johnson	1.00	.45
❑ 132 Curtis Martin	1.00	.45
❑ 133 Wayne Chrebet	1.00	.45
❑ 134 Napoleon Kaufman	1.00	.45
❑ 135 Charles Woodson	1.00	.45
❑ 136 Duce Staley	1.50	.70
❑ 137 Kordell Stewart	1.00	.45
❑ 138 Terrell Owens	1.50	.70
❑ 139 Ricky Watters	1.00	.45
❑ 140 Joey Galloway	1.00	.45
❑ 141 Jon Kitna	1.00	.45
❑ 142 Isaac Bruce	1.50	.70
❑ 143 Jacquez Green	1.00	.45
❑ 144 Warrick Dunn	1.00	.45
❑ 145 Mike Alstott	1.00	.45
❑ 146 Trent Dilfer	1.00	.45
❑ 147 Steve McNair	1.00	.45
❑ 148 Eddie George	1.50	.70
❑ 149 Skip Hicks	1.00	.45
❑ 150 Brad Johnson	1.50	.70
❑ 151 Doug Flutie	1.50	.70
❑ 152 Thurman Thomas	1.00	.45
❑ 153 Carl Pickens	1.00	.45
❑ 154 Emmitt Smith	5.00	2.20
❑ 155 Troy Aikman	5.00	2.20
❑ 156 Deion Sanders	1.50	.70
❑ 157 John Elway	8.00	3.60
❑ 158 Rod Smith	1.00	.45
❑ 159 Barry Sanders	8.00	3.60
❑ 160 Herman Moore	1.50	.70
❑ 161 Brett Favre	8.00	3.60
❑ 162 Mark Brunell	1.50	.70
❑ 163 Warren Moon	1.50	.70
❑ 164 Dan Marino	8.00	3.60
❑ 165 Randall Cunningham	1.50	.70
❑ 166 Robert Smith	1.50	.70
❑ 167 Cris Carter	1.50	.70
❑ 168 Drew Bledsoe	3.00	1.35
❑ 169 Tim Brown	1.50	.70
❑ 170 Jerome Bettis	1.50	.70
❑ 171 Natrone Means	1.00	.45
❑ 172 Jerry Rice	5.00	2.20
❑ 173 Steve Young	3.00	1.35
❑ 174 Garrison Hearst	1.50	.70
❑ 175 Marshall Faulk	3.00	1.35
❑ 176 David Boston RC	5.00	2.20
❑ 177 Jeff Paulk RC	2.00	.90
❑ 178 Reginald Kelly RC	2.00	.90
❑ 179 Scott Covington RC	5.00	2.20
❑ 180 Chris McAlister RC	3.00	1.35
❑ 181 Shawn Bryson RC	5.00	2.20
❑ 182 Peerless Price RC	8.00	3.60
❑ 183 Cade McNown RC	3.00	1.35
❑ 184 Michael Bishop RC	5.00	2.20
❑ 185 D'Wayne Bates RC	3.00	1.35
❑ 186 Marty Booker RC	5.00	2.20
❑ 187 Akili Smith RC	2.00	.90
❑ 188 Craig Yeast RC	3.00	1.35
❑ 189 Tim Couch RC	5.00	2.20
❑ 190 Kevin Johnson RC	5.00	2.20
❑ 191 Wane McGarity RC	2.00	.90
❑ 192 Olandis Gary RC	5.00	2.20
❑ 193 Travis McGriff RC	2.00	.90
❑ 194 Sedrick Irvin RC	2.00	.90
❑ 195 Chris Claiborne RC	2.00	.90
❑ 196 De'Mond Parker RC	2.00	.90
❑ 197 Dee Miller RC	2.00	.90
❑ 198 Edgerrin James RC	15.00	6.75
❑ 199 Mike Cloud RC	3.00	1.35
❑ 200 Larry Parker RC	5.00	2.20
❑ 201 Cecil Collins RC	2.00	.90
❑ 202 James Johnson RC	3.00	1.35
❑ 203 Rob Konrad RC	5.00	2.20
❑ 204 Daunte Culpepper RC	15.00	6.75
❑ 205 Jim Kleinsasser RC	5.00	2.20
❑ 206 Kevin Faulk RC	5.00	2.20
❑ 207 Andy Katzenmoyer RC	3.00	1.35
❑ 208 Ricky Williams RC	8.00	3.60
❑ 209 Joe Montgomery RC	3.00	1.35
❑ 210 Sean Bennett RC	2.00	.90
❑ 211 Dameane Douglas RC	5.00	2.20
❑ 212 Donovan McNabb RC	20.00	9.00
❑ 213 Na Brown RC	3.00	1.35
❑ 214 Amos Zereoue RC	5.00	2.20
❑ 215 Troy Edwards RC	3.00	1.35
❑ 216 Jermaine Fazande RC	3.00	1.35
❑ 217 Tai Streets RC	5.00	2.20
❑ 218 Brock Huard RC	5.00	2.20
❑ 219 Charlie Rogers RC	3.00	1.35
❑ 220 Karsten Bailey RC	3.00	1.35
❑ 221 Joe Germaine RC	3.00	1.35
❑ 222 Torry Holt RC	10.00	4.50

223 Shaun King RC	3.00	1.35
224 Jevon Kearse RC	8.00	3.60
225 Champ Bailey RC	6.00	2.70

2000 Leaf Certified

	Nm-Mt	Ex-Mt
COMP.SET w/o RC's (150)	40.00	18.00
1 Frank Sanders	.40	.18
2 Rob Moore	.60	.25
3 Simeon Rice	.60	.25
4 David Boston	1.00	.45
5 Tim Dwight	1.00	.45
6 Jamal Anderson	1.00	.45
7 Chris Chandler	.40	.18
8 Terance Mathis	.60	.25
9 Priest Holmes	1.25	.55
10 Rod Woodson	.60	.25
11 Tony Banks	.40	.18
12 Jermaine Lewis	.40	.18
13 Shannon Sharpe	.40	.18
14 Qadry Ismail	.60	.25
15 Doug Flutie	1.00	.45
16 Antowain Smith	.60	.25
17 Peerless Price	1.00	.45
18 Rob Johnson	.40	.18
19 Muhsin Muhammad	.60	.25
20 Wesley Walls	.40	.18
21 Tim Biakabutuka	.40	.18
22 Steve Beuerlein	.40	.18
23 Patrick Jeffers	.40	.18
24 Natrone Means	.40	.18
25 Curtis Enis	.40	.18
26 Bobby Engram	.40	.18
27 Marcus Robinson	1.00	.45
28 Eddie Kennison	.40	.18
29 Marty Booker	.60	.25
30 Darnay Scott	.40	.18
31 Carl Pickens	.40	.18
32 Karim Abdul-Jabbar	.40	.18
33 Errict Rhett	.40	.18
34 Darrin Chiaverini	.40	.18
35 Randall Cunningham	.40	.18
36 Michael Irvin	.40	.18
37 Rocket Ismail	.40	.18
38 Ed McCaffrey	1.00	.45
39 Rod Smith	.40	.18
40 Herman Moore	.60	.25
41 Johnnie Morton	.40	.18
42 James Stewart	.40	.18
43 Bill Schroeder	.60	.25
44 Ahman Green	1.00	.45
45 Terrence Wilkins	.40	.18
46 Keenan McCardell	.40	.18
47 Derrick Alexander	.40	.18
48 Elvis Grbac	.40	.18
49 Tony Gonzalez	.40	.18
50 O.J. McDuffie	.40	.18
51 Tony Martin	.40	.18
52 James Johnson	.40	.18
53 Thurman Thomas	.40	.18
54 Jay Fiedler	1.00	.45
55 Damon Huard	.40	.18
56 Leroy Hoard	.40	.18
57 Terry Glenn	.60	.25
58 Kevin Faulk	.40	.18
59 Jeff Blake	.40	.18
60 Jake Reed	.40	.18
61 Amani Toomer	.40	.18
62 Kerry Collins	.40	.18
63 Ike Hilliard	.40	.18
64 Joe Montgomery	.40	.18
65 Vinny Testaverde	.40	.18
66 Wayne Chrebet	.40	.18
67 Ray Lucas	.60	.25
68 Napoleon Kaufman	.60	.25
69 Charles Woodson	.40	.18
70 Tyrone Wheatley	.40	.18
71 Rich Gannon	1.00	.45
72 Duce Staley	1.00	.45
73 Kordell Stewart	.60	.25
74 Jerome Bettis	1.00	.45
75 Troy Edwards	.40	.18
76 Junior Seau	1.00	.45
77 Jim Harbaugh	.40	.18
78 Curtis Conway	.60	.25
79 Jermaine Fazande	.40	.18
80 Terrell Owens	1.00	.45
81 Charlie Garner	.60	.25
82 Garrison Hearst	.40	.18
83 Jeff Garcia	1.00	.45
84 Derrick Mayes	.40	.18
85 Az-Zahir Hakim	.40	.18
86 Mike Alstott	1.00	.45
87 Warrick Dunn	1.00	.45
88 Jacquez Green	.40	.18
89 Warren Sapp	.40	.18
90 Yancey Thigpen	.40	.18
91 Kevin Dyson	.40	.18
92 Frank Wycheck	.40	.18
93 Jevon Kearse	1.00	.45
94 Adrian Murrell	.40	.18
95 Bruce Smith	.40	.18
96 Michael Westbrook	.40	.18
97 Albert Connell	.40	.18
98 Champ Bailey	.60	.25
99 Jeff George	.40	.18
100 Deion Sanders	1.00	.45
101 Jake Plummer	1.00	.45
102 Eric Moulds	1.50	.70
103 Cade McNown	.40	.18
104 Corey Dillon	1.50	.70
105 Akili Smith	.60	.25
106 Tim Couch	1.00	.45
107 Kevin Johnson	1.50	.70
108 Emmitt Smith	3.00	1.35
109 Troy Aikman	3.00	1.35
110 Joey Galloway	1.00	.45
111 John Elway	5.00	2.20
112 Terrell Davis	1.00	.45
113 Olandis Gary	1.50	.70
114 Brian Griese	1.00	.45
115 Charlie Batch	1.50	.70
116 Barry Sanders	4.00	1.80
117 Germane Crowell	.60	.25
118 Brett Favre	5.00	2.20
119 Dorsey Levens	.60	.25
120 Antonio Freeman	1.50	.70
121 Peyton Manning	4.00	1.80
122 Edgerrin James	2.50	1.10
123 Marvin Harrison	1.50	.70
124 Mark Brunell	1.00	.45
125 Fred Taylor	1.00	.45
126 Jimmy Smith	1.00	.45
127 Dan Marino	5.00	2.20
128 Randy Moss	3.00	1.35
129 Daunte Culpepper	2.00	.90
130 Cris Carter	1.50	.70
131 Robert Smith	1.50	.70
132 Drew Bledsoe	2.00	.90
133 Ricky Williams	1.00	.45
134 Curtis Martin	1.50	.70
135 Tim Brown	1.50	.70
136 Donovan McNabb	2.50	1.10
137 Jerry Rice	3.00	1.35
138 Steve Young	2.00	.90
139 Jon Kitna	1.50	.70
140 Ricky Watters	.60	.25
141 Kurt Warner	3.00	1.35
142 Marshall Faulk	2.00	.90
143 Torry Holt	1.50	.70
144 Isaac Bruce	1.50	.70
145 Shaun King	.40	.18
146 Keyshawn Johnson	1.50	.70
147 Eddie George	1.00	.45
148 Steve McNair	1.50	.70
149 Stephen Davis	1.50	.70
150 Brad Johnson	1.50	.70
151 Rogers Beckett RC	4.00	1.80
152 Erik Flowers RC	4.00	1.80
153 Demario Brown RC	2.50	1.10
154 Doug Johnson RC	5.00	2.20
155 Deon Grant RC	4.00	1.80
156 Ian Gold RC	4.00	1.80
157 Brian Urlacher RC	20.00	9.00
158 Frank Murphy RC	2.50	1.10
159 James Whalen RC	2.50	1.10
160 JaJuan Dawson RC	2.50	1.10
161 William Bartee RC	4.00	1.80
162 Aaron Shea RC	1.00	.45
163 Deltha O'Neal RC	5.00	2.20
164 Jarious Jackson RC	4.00	1.80
165 Muneer Moore RC	2.50	1.10
166 Hank Poteat RC	4.00	1.80
167 Jacoby Shepherd RC	2.50	1.10
168 Ben Kelly RC	2.50	1.10
169 Orantes Grant RC	2.50	1.10
170 Chris Hovan RC	4.00	1.80
171 Leon Murray RC	2.50	1.10
172 Marc Bulger RC	10.00	4.50
173 Chad Morton RC	5.00	2.20
174 Na'il Diggs RC	4.00	1.80
175 Shaun Ellis RC	5.00	2.20
176 John Abraham RC	5.00	2.20
177 Fred Robbins RC	2.50	1.10
178 Marcus Knight RC	4.00	1.80
179 Thomas Hamner RC	2.50	1.10
180 Cornelius Griffin RC	4.00	1.80
181 Raynoch Thompson RC	4.00	1.80
182 Paul Smith RC	4.00	1.80
183 Ahmed Plummer RC	5.00	2.20
184 John Engelberger RC	4.00	1.80
185 Darren Howard RC	4.00	1.80
186 Corey Moore RC	2.50	1.10
187 Joe Hamilton RC	4.00	1.80
188 Rob Morris RC	4.00	1.80
189 Keith Bulluck RC	5.00	2.20
190 Todd Husak RC	5.00	2.20
191 Mareno Philyaw RC	3.00	1.35
192 Kwame Cavil RC	3.00	1.35
193 Sammy Morris RC	5.00	2.20
194 Avion Black RC	5.00	2.20
195 Bashir Yamini RC	3.00	1.35
196 Curtis Keaton RC	5.00	2.20
197 Mike Anderson RC	6.00	2.70
198 Bubba Franks RC	6.00	2.70
199 Anthony Lucas RC	3.00	1.35
200 Rondell Mealey RC	3.00	1.35
201 Terrelle Smith RC	5.00	2.20
202 Frank Moreau RC	5.00	2.20
203 Deon Dyer RC	5.00	2.20
204 Quinton Spotwood RC	3.00	1.35
205 Troy Walters RC	10.00	4.50
206 Doug Chapman RC	5.00	2.20
207 Tom Brady RC	80.00	36.00
208 Sherrod Gideon RC	3.00	1.35
209 Ron Dixon RC	5.00	2.20
210 Anthony Becht RC	6.00	2.70
211 James Williams RC	5.00	2.20
212 Sebastian Janikowski RC	6.00	2.70
213 Corey Simon RC	6.00	2.70
214 Gari Scott RC	3.00	1.35
215 Dante Hall RC	12.00	5.50
216 Tim Rattay RC	12.00	5.50
217 Chafie Fields RC	3.00	1.35
218 Trung Canidate RC	5.00	2.20
219 Chris Coleman RC	6.00	2.70
220 Erron Kinney RC	6.00	2.70
221 Thomas Jones RC	15.00	6.75
222 Travis Taylor RC	10.00	4.50
223 Chris Redman RC	8.00	3.60
224 Jamal Lewis RC	25.00	11.00
225 Dez White RC	10.00	4.50
226 Peter Warrick RC	10.00	4.50
227 Ron Dugans RC	8.00	3.60
228 Courtney Brown RC	10.00	4.50
229 Travis Prentice RC	8.00	3.60
230 Dennis Northcutt RC	10.00	4.50
231 Michael Wiley RC	8.00	3.60
232 Chris Cole RC	8.00	3.60
233 Reuben Droughns RC	12.00	5.50
234 R.Jay Soward RC	8.00	3.60
235 Shyrone Stith RC	8.00	3.60
236 Sylvester Morris RC	8.00	3.60
237 J.R. Redmond RC	8.00	3.60
238 Ron Dayne RC	10.00	4.50
239 Chad Pennington RC	40.00	18.00

❑ 240 Laveranues Coles RC	12.00	5.50
❑ 241 Jerry Porter RC	12.00	5.50
❑ 242 Todd Pinkston RC	10.00	4.50
❑ 243 Plaxico Burress RC	20.00	9.00
❑ 244 Danny Farmer RC	8.00	3.60
❑ 245 Tee Martin RC	10.00	4.50
❑ 246 Trevor Gaylor RC	8.00	3.60
❑ 247 Giovanni Carmazzi RC	8.00	3.60
❑ 248 Darrell Jackson RC	20.00	9.00
❑ 249 Shaun Alexander RC	25.00	11.00
❑ 250 Chris Samuels RC	8.00	3.60

2000 Leaf Certified Mirror Gold

Nm-Mt Ex-Mt

*1-STAR 1-100: 20X TO 50X BASIC CARDS
*2-STAR 101-150: 12X TO 30X BASIC CARDS
*3-STAR 151-190: 2.5X TO 6X BASIC CARDS
*4-STAR 191-220: 2X TO 5X BASIC CARDS
*5-STAR 221-250: 1X TO 2.5X BASIC CARDS

2000 Leaf Certified Mirror Red

Nm-Mt Ex-Mt

*1-STAR 1-100: 2X TO 5X BASIC CARDS
*2-STAR 101-150: 1.5X TO 4X BASIC CARDS
*3-STAR 151-190: .5X TO 1.2X BASIC CARDS
*4-STAR 191-220: .5X TO 1.2X BASIC CARDS
*5-STAR 221-250: .3X TO .8X BASIC CARDS

2000 Leaf Certified Rookie Die Cuts

Nm-Mt Ex-Mt

*3-STAR 151-190: 1X TO 2.5X BASIC CARDS
*4-STAR 191-220: .75X TO 2X BASIC CARDS
*5-STAR 221-250: .4X TO 1X BASIC CARDS

2001 Leaf Certified Materials

	Nm-Mt	Ex-Mt
COMP.SET w/o SPs (100)	30.00	9.00
❑ 1 Aaron Brooks	1.00	.30
❑ 2 Ahman Green	1.00	.30
❑ 3 Akili Smith	.40	.12
❑ 4 Amani Toomer	.60	.18
❑ 5 Antonio Freeman	1.00	.30
❑ 6 Barry Sanders	2.00	.60
❑ 7 Brad Johnson	1.00	.30
❑ 8 Brett Favre	3.00	.90
❑ 9 Brian Griese	1.00	.30
❑ 10 Brian Urlacher	1.50	.45
❑ 11 Bruce Smith	.40	.12
❑ 12 Cade McNown	.40	.12
❑ 13 Chad Pennington	1.50	.45
❑ 14 Charlie Batch	1.00	.30
❑ 15 Charlie Garner	.60	.18
❑ 16 Corey Dillon	1.00	.30
❑ 17 Cris Carter	1.00	.30
❑ 18 Curtis Martin	1.00	.30
❑ 19 Dan Marino	3.00	.90
❑ 20 Darrell Jackson	.40	.12
❑ 21 Daunte Culpepper	1.00	.30
❑ 22 David Boston	1.00	.30
❑ 23 Derrick Alexander	.60	.18
❑ 24 Donovan McNabb	1.25	.35
❑ 25 Dorsey Levens	.60	.18
❑ 26 Doug Flutie	1.00	.30
❑ 27 Drew Bledsoe	1.25	.35
❑ 28 Ed McCaffrey	1.00	.30
❑ 29 Eddie George	1.00	.30
❑ 30 Edgerrin James	1.25	.35
❑ 31 Elvis Grbac	.60	.18
❑ 32 Emmitt Smith	2.00	.60
❑ 33 Eric Moulds	1.00	.30
❑ 34 Frank Wycheck	.40	.12
❑ 35 Fred Taylor	1.00	.30
❑ 36 Ike Hilliard	.60	.18
❑ 37 Isaac Bruce	1.00	.30
❑ 38 Jacquez Green	.40	.12
❑ 39 Jake Plummer	.60	.18
❑ 40 Jamal Anderson	1.00	.30
❑ 41 Jamal Lewis	1.50	.45
❑ 42 James Stewart	.60	.18
❑ 43 Jay Fiedler	1.00	.30
❑ 44 Jeff Garcia	1.00	.30
❑ 45 Jeff George	.60	.18
❑ 46 Jerome Bettis	1.00	.30
❑ 47 Jerry Rice	2.00	.60
❑ 48 Jevon Kearse	.60	.18
❑ 49 Jimmy Smith	.60	.18
❑ 50 Joe Horn	.60	.18
❑ 51 Joey Galloway	.60	.18
❑ 52 John Elway	3.00	.90
❑ 53 Junior Seau	1.00	.30
❑ 54 Keenan McCardell	.40	.12
❑ 55 Kerry Collins	1.00	.30
❑ 56 Keyshawn Johnson	1.00	.30
❑ 57 Kurt Warner	2.00	.60
❑ 58 Lamar Smith	.60	.18
❑ 59 Laveranues Coles	1.00	.30
❑ 60 Marcus Robinson	1.00	.30
❑ 61 Mark Brunell	1.00	.30
❑ 62 Marshall Faulk	1.25	.35
❑ 63 Marvin Harrison	1.00	.30
❑ 64 Matt Hasselbeck	.60	.18
❑ 65 Mike Alstott	1.00	.30
❑ 66 Mike Anderson	1.00	.30
❑ 67 Muhsin Muhammad	.60	.18
❑ 68 Peter Warrick	1.00	.30
❑ 69 Peyton Manning	2.50	.75
❑ 70 Plaxico Burress	1.00	.30
❑ 71 Randy Moss	2.00	.60
❑ 72 Ray Lewis	1.00	.30
❑ 73 Rich Gannon	1.00	.30
❑ 74 Ricky Watters	.60	.18
❑ 75 Ricky Williams	1.00	.30
❑ 76 Rob Johnson	1.00	.30
❑ 77 Rod Smith	.60	.18
❑ 78 Ron Dayne	1.00	.30
❑ 79 Shannon Sharpe	.60	.18
❑ 80 Shaun Alexander	1.25	.35
❑ 81 Stephen Davis	1.00	.30
❑ 82 Steve McNair	1.00	.30
❑ 83 Steve Young	1.00	.30
❑ 84 Sylvester Morris	.40	.12
❑ 85 Terrell Davis	1.00	.30
❑ 86 Terrell Owens	1.00	.30
❑ 87 Terry Glenn	.60	.18
❑ 88 Thomas Jones	.60	.18
❑ 89 Tiki Barber	.60	.18
❑ 90 Tim Brown	1.00	.30
❑ 91 Tim Couch	.60	.18
❑ 92 Tony Gonzalez	.60	.18
❑ 93 Torry Holt	1.00	.30
❑ 94 Travis Taylor	.60	.18
❑ 95 Troy Aikman	1.50	.45
❑ 96 Tyrone Wheatley	.60	.18
❑ 97 Vinny Testaverde	.60	.18
❑ 98 Warren Sapp	.60	.18
❑ 99 Warrick Dunn	1.00	.30
❑ 100 Wayne Chrebet	.60	.18
❑ 101 Chris Taylor RC	6.00	1.80
❑ 102 Ken-Yon Rambo RC	6.00	1.80
❑ 103 Correll Buckhalter RC	12.00	3.60
❑ 104 A.J. Feeley RC	10.00	3.00
❑ 105 Josh Booty RC	10.00	3.00
❑ 106 LaMont Jordan RC	15.00	4.50
❑ 107 Alge Crumpler RC	12.00	3.60
❑ 108 Jamal Reynolds RC	10.00	3.00
❑ 109 Nate Clements RC	10.00	3.00
❑ 110 Will Allen RC	6.00	1.80
❑ 111 Santana Moss FF RC	25.00	7.50
❑ 112 Chad Johnson FF RC	30.00	9.00
❑ 113 Chris Chambers FF RC	20.00	6.00
❑ 114 David Terrell FF RC	15.00	4.50
❑ 115 Freddie Mitchell FF RC	15.00	4.50
❑ 116 Koren Robinson FF RC	20.00	6.00
❑ 117 Quincy Morgan FF RC	15.00	4.50
❑ 118 Reggie Wayne FF RC	25.00	7.50
❑ 119 Robert Ferguson FF RC	15.00	4.50
❑ 120 Rod Gardner FF RC	15.00	4.50
❑ 121 Snoop Minnis FF RC	10.00	3.00
❑ 122 Josh Heupel FF RC	15.00	4.50
❑ 123 Anthony Thomas FF RC	25.00	7.50
❑ 124 Deuce McAllister FF RC	30.00	9.00
❑ 125 James Jackson FF RC	15.00	4.50
❑ 126 Travis Minor FF RC	10.00	3.00
❑ 127 Kevan Barlow FF RC	15.00	4.50
❑ 128 L.Tomlinson FF RC	50.00	15.00
❑ 129 Todd Heap FF RC	15.00	4.50
❑ 130 Michael Bennett FF RC	30.00	9.00
❑ 131 Rudi Johnson FF RC	30.00	9.00
❑ 132 Travis Henry FF RC	20.00	6.00
❑ 133 Michael Vick FF RC	80.00	24.00
❑ 134 Drew Brees FF RC	30.00	9.00
❑ 135 Chris Weinke FF RC	15.00	4.50
❑ 136 Quincy Carter FF RC	15.00	4.50
❑ 137 Mike McMahon FF RC	15.00	4.50
❑ 138 Jesse Palmer FF RC	15.00	4.50
❑ 139 M.Tuiasosopo FF RC	15.00	4.50
❑ 140 Dan Morgan FF RC	15.00	4.50
❑ 141 Gerard Warren FF RC	15.00	4.50
❑ 142 Leonard Davis FF RC	10.00	3.00
❑ 143 Andre Carter FF RC	15.00	4.50
❑ 144 Justin Smith FF RC	15.00	4.50
❑ 145 Sage Rosenfels FF RC	15.00	4.50

2001 Leaf Certified Materials Mirror Gold

Nm-Mt Ex-Mt

*STARS: 12.5X TO 30X BASIC CARDS
*ROOKIES 101-110: 1.2X TO 3X

❑ 111 Santana Moss FF	150.00	45.00
❑ 112 Chad Johnson FF	150.00	45.00
❑ 113 Chris Chambers FF	120.00	36.00
❑ 114 David Terrell FF	80.00	24.00
❑ 115 Freddie Mitchell FF	80.00	24.00
❑ 116 Koren Robinson FF	80.00	24.00
❑ 117 Quincy Morgan FF	80.00	24.00
❑ 118 Reggie Wayne FF	150.00	45.00
❑ 119 Robert Ferguson FF	80.00	24.00
❑ 120 Rod Gardner FF	80.00	24.00
❑ 121 Snoop Minnis FF	50.00	15.00
❑ 122 Josh Heupel FF	80.00	24.00
❑ 123 Anthony Thomas FF	150.00	45.00
❑ 124 Deuce McAllister FF	200.00	60.00
❑ 125 James Jackson FF	80.00	24.00
❑ 126 Travis Minor FF	50.00	15.00
❑ 127 Kevan Barlow FF	80.00	24.00
❑ 128 LaDainian Tomlinson FF RC	250.00	75.00
❑ 129 Todd Heap FF	80.00	24.00
❑ 130 Michael Bennett FF	150.00	45.00
❑ 131 Rudi Johnson FF	150.00	45.00
❑ 132 Travis Henry FF	120.00	36.00
❑ 133 Michael Vick FF	300.00	90.00
❑ 134 Drew Brees FF	150.00	45.00
❑ 135 Chris Weinke FF	80.00	24.00
❑ 136 Quincy Carter FF	80.00	24.00
❑ 137 Mike McMahon FF	80.00	24.00
❑ 138 Jesse Palmer FF	80.00	24.00
❑ 139 Marques Tuiasosopo FF RC	80.00	24.00
❑ 140 Dan Morgan FF	80.00	24.00
❑ 141 Gerard Warren FF	80.00	24.00
❑ 142 Leonard Davis FF	50.00	15.00
❑ 143 Andre Carter FF	80.00	24.00
❑ 144 Justin Smith FF	80.00	24.00
❑ 145 Sage Rosenfels FF	80.00	24.00

2001 Leaf Certified Materials Mirror Red

Nm-Mt Ex-Mt

*STARS 1-100: 5X TO 12X BASIC CARDS
*ROOKIES 101-110: .6X TO 1.5X BASIC CARDS
1-110 PRINT RUN 75 SERIAL #'d SETS

❑ 111 Santana Moss FF AU	40.00	12.00
❑ 112 Chad Johnson FF AU	50.00	15.00
❑ 113 Chris Chambers FF AU	30.00	9.00
❑ 114 David Terrell FF AU	25.00	7.50
❑ 115 Freddie Mitchell FF AU	25.00	7.50

- ❑ 116 Koren Robinson FF AU 25.00 7.50
- ❑ 117 Quincy Morgan FF AU 25.00 7.50
- ❑ 118 Reggie Wayne FF AU 40.00 12.00
- ❑ 119 Robert Ferguson FF AU 25.00 7.50
- ❑ 120 Rod Gardner FF AU 25.00 7.50
- ❑ 121 Snoop Minnis FF AU 20.00 6.00
- ❑ 122 Josh Heupel FF AU 25.00 7.50
- ❑ 123 Anthony Thomas FF AU 40.00 12.00
- ❑ 124 Deuce McAllister FF AU 80.00 24.00
- ❑ 125 James Jackson FF AU 25.00 7.50
- ❑ 126 Travis Minor FF AU 20.00 6.00
- ❑ 127 Kevan Barlow FF AU 25.00 7.50
- ❑ 128 L.Tomlinson FF AU 120.00 36.00
- ❑ 129 Todd Heap FF AU 25.00 7.50
- ❑ 130 Michael Bennett FF AU 50.00 15.00
- ❑ 131 Rudi Johnson FF AU 50.00 15.00
- ❑ 132 Travis Henry FF AU 30.00 9.00
- ❑ 133 Michael Vick FF AU 250.00 75.00
- ❑ 134 Drew Brees FF AU 60.00 18.00
- ❑ 135 Chris Weinke FF AU 25.00 7.50
- ❑ 136 Quincy Carter FF AU 25.00 7.50
- ❑ 137 Mike McMahon FF AU 25.00 7.50
- ❑ 138 Jesse Palmer FF AU 25.00 7.50
- ❑ 139 M.Tuiasosopo FF AU 40.00 12.00
- ❑ 140 Dan Morgan FF AU 25.00 7.50
- ❑ 141 Gerard Warren FF AU 25.00 7.50
- ❑ 142 Leonard Davis FF AU EXCH 20.00 6.00
- ❑ 143 Andre Carter FF AU EXCH
- ❑ 144 Justin Smith FF AU 25.00 7.50
- ❑ 145 Sage Rosenfels FF AU 25.00 7.50

2002 Leaf Certified

	Nm-Mt	Ex-Mt
COMP.SET w/o SP's (100)	25.00	7.50
❑ 1 David Boston	1.00	.30
❑ 2 Jake Plummer	.60	.18
❑ 3 Michael Vick	3.00	.90
❑ 4 Jamal Anderson	.60	.18
❑ 5 Chris Redman	.40	.12
❑ 6 Ray Lewis	1.00	.30
❑ 7 Eric Moulds	.60	.18
❑ 8 Travis Henry	1.00	.30
❑ 9 Nate Clements	.40	.12
❑ 10 Chris Weinke	.60	.18
❑ 11 Muhsin Muhammad	.60	.18
❑ 12 Wesley Walls	.40	.12
❑ 13 Anthony Thomas	1.00	.30
❑ 14 Brian Urlacher	1.50	.45
❑ 15 Dez White	.40	.12
❑ 16 Corey Dillon	.60	.18
❑ 17 Peter Warrick	.60	.18
❑ 18 Tim Couch	.60	.18
❑ 19 Kevin Johnson	.60	.18
❑ 20 James Jackson	.40	.12
❑ 21 Emmitt Smith	2.50	.75
❑ 22 Quincy Carter	.60	.18
❑ 23 Brian Griese	1.00	.30
❑ 24 Ed McCaffrey	1.00	.30
❑ 25 Rod Smith	.60	.18
❑ 26 Terrell Davis	1.00	.30
❑ 27 Mike Anderson	1.00	.30
❑ 28 Germane Crowell	.40	.12
❑ 29 James Stewart	.60	.18
❑ 30 Charlie Batch	.60	.18
❑ 31 Antonio Freeman	1.00	.30
❑ 32 Brett Favre	2.50	.75
❑ 33 Ahman Green	1.00	.30
❑ 34 LeRoy Butler	.40	.12
❑ 35 Edgerrin James	1.25	.35
❑ 36 Marvin Harrison	1.00	.30
❑ 37 Peyton Manning	2.00	.60
❑ 38 Fred Taylor	1.00	.30
❑ 39 Jimmy Smith	.60	.18
❑ 40 Mark Brunell	1.00	.30
❑ 41 Keenan McCardell	.40	.12
❑ 42 Tony Gonzalez	.60	.18
❑ 43 Priest Holmes	1.25	.35
❑ 44 Jay Fiedler	.60	.18
❑ 45 Chris Chambers	1.00	.30
❑ 46 Zach Thomas	1.00	.30
❑ 47 Travis Minor	.40	.12
❑ 48 Cris Carter	1.00	.30
❑ 49 Daunte Culpepper	1.00	.30
❑ 50 Randy Moss	2.00	.60
❑ 51 Drew Bledsoe	1.25	.35
❑ 52 Tom Brady	2.50	.75
❑ 53 Antowain Smith	.60	.18
❑ 54 Troy Brown	.40	.12
❑ 55 Aaron Brooks	1.00	.30
❑ 56 Ricky Williams	1.00	.30
❑ 57 Ron Dayne	.60	.18
❑ 58 Kerry Collins	.60	.18
❑ 59 Michael Strahan	.60	.18
❑ 60 Amani Toomer	.60	.18
❑ 61 Chad Pennington	1.25	.35
❑ 62 Curtis Martin	1.00	.30
❑ 63 Vinny Testaverde	.60	.18
❑ 64 Wayne Chrebet	.60	.18
❑ 65 Charles Woodson	.60	.18
❑ 66 Rich Gannon	1.00	.30
❑ 67 Tim Brown	1.00	.30
❑ 68 Jerry Rice	2.00	.60
❑ 69 Tyrone Wheatley	.60	.18
❑ 70 Donovan McNabb	1.25	.35
❑ 71 Duce Staley	1.00	.30
❑ 72 Todd Pinkston	.60	.18
❑ 73 Correll Buckhalter	.60	.18
❑ 74 Jerome Bettis	1.00	.30
❑ 75 Kordell Stewart	.60	.18
❑ 76 Plaxico Burress	.60	.18
❑ 77 Hines Ward	1.00	.30
❑ 78 Junior Seau	1.00	.30
❑ 79 LaDainian Tomlinson	1.50	.45
❑ 80 Doug Flutie	1.00	.30
❑ 81 Terrell Owens	1.00	.30
❑ 82 Jeff Garcia	1.00	.30
❑ 83 Ricky Watters	.60	.18
❑ 84 Shaun Alexander	1.00	.30
❑ 85 Koren Robinson	.60	.18
❑ 86 Isaac Bruce	1.00	.30
❑ 87 Kurt Warner	1.00	.30
❑ 88 Marshall Faulk	1.00	.30
❑ 89 Torry Holt	1.00	.30
❑ 90 Keyshawn Johnson	1.00	.30
❑ 91 Mike Alstott	1.00	.30
❑ 92 Warren Sapp	.60	.18
❑ 93 Brad Johnson	.60	.18
❑ 94 Eddie George	1.00	.30
❑ 95 Jevon Kearse	.60	.18
❑ 96 Steve McNair	1.00	.30
❑ 97 Derrick Mason	.60	.18
❑ 98 Frank Wycheck	.40	.12
❑ 99 Champ Bailey	.60	.18
❑ 100 Stephen Davis	.60	.18
❑ 101 Ladell Betts JSY RC	8.00	2.40
❑ 102 Antonio Bryant JSY RC	8.00	2.40
❑ 103 Reche Caldwell JSY RC	8.00	2.40
❑ 104 David Carr JSY RC	25.00	7.50
❑ 105 Tim Carter JSY RC	5.00	1.50
❑ 106 Eric Crouch JSY RC	12.00	3.60
❑ 107 Rohan Davey JSY RC	8.00	2.40
❑ 108 Andre Davis JSY RC	8.00	2.40
❑ 109 T.J. Duckett JSY RC	12.00	3.60
❑ 110 DeShaun Foster JSY RC	8.00	2.40
❑ 111 Jabar Gaffney JSY RC	8.00	2.40
❑ 112 Daniel Graham JSY RC	8.00	2.40
❑ 113 William Green FB RC	12.00	3.60
❑ 114 Joey Harrington JSY RC	25.00	7.50
❑ 115 David Garrard JSY RC	8.00	2.40
❑ 116 Ron Johnson JSY RC	5.00	1.50
❑ 117 Ashley Lelie JSY RC	15.00	4.50
❑ 118 Josh McCown JSY RC	10.00	3.00
❑ 119 Maurice Morris JSY RC	8.00	2.40
❑ 120 Julius Peppers JSY RC	15.00	4.50
❑ 121 Clinton Portis JSY RC	25.00	7.50
❑ 122 Patrick Ramsey JSY RC	15.00	4.50
❑ 123 Antwaan Randle El JSY RC	10.00	3.00
❑ 124 Josh Reed JSY RC	8.00	2.40
❑ 125 Cliff Russell JSY RC	5.00	1.50
❑ 126 Jeremy Shockey JSY RC	25.00	7.50
❑ 127 Donte Stallworth JSY RC	15.00	4.50
❑ 128 Travis Stephens JSY RC	5.00	1.50
❑ 129 Javon Walker JSY RC	15.00	4.50
❑ 130 Marquise Walker JSY RC	5.00	1.50
❑ 131 Roy Williams JSY RC	20.00	6.00
❑ 132 Mike Williams JSY RC	5.00	1.50

2002 Leaf Certified Mirror Red

Nm-Mt Ex-Mt

*RED STARS: 6X TO 15X BASIC CARDS
*RED ROOKIES: .8X TO 2X BASE CARD HI
*MIRR.BLUE STARS: .8X TO 2X MIRR.RED
MIRROR BLUE 1-100 PRINT RUN 50 SETS
*MIRROR BLUE ROOKIES: .8X TO 2X
MIRROR BLUE 101-132 PRINT RUN 100 SETS
*MIRR.GOLD STARS: 1.5X TO 4X MIRR.RED
*MIRR.GOLD ROOKIES: 1.5X TO 3X MIRR.RED
MIRROR GOLD PRINT RUN 25 SER.#'d SETS

	Nm-Mt	Ex-Mt
❑ 101 Ladell Betts	15.00	4.50
❑ 102 Antonio Bryant	15.00	4.50
❑ 103 Reche Caldwell	15.00	4.50
❑ 104 David Carr	50.00	15.00
❑ 105 Tim Carter	10.00	3.00
❑ 106 Eric Crouch	25.00	7.50
❑ 107 Rohan Davey	15.00	4.50
❑ 108 Andre Davis	15.00	4.50
❑ 109 T.J. Duckett	25.00	7.50
❑ 110 DeShaun Foster	15.00	4.50
❑ 111 Jabar Gaffney	15.00	4.50
❑ 112 Daniel Graham	15.00	4.50
❑ 113 William Green	25.00	7.50
❑ 114 Joey Harrington	50.00	15.00
❑ 115 David Garrard	15.00	4.50
❑ 116 Ron Johnson	10.00	3.00
❑ 117 Ashley Lelie	30.00	9.00
❑ 118 Josh McCown	20.00	6.00
❑ 119 Maurice Morris	15.00	4.50
❑ 120 Julius Peppers	30.00	9.00
❑ 121 Clinton Portis	50.00	15.00
❑ 122 Patrick Ramsey	30.00	9.00
❑ 123 Antwaan Randle El	20.00	6.00
❑ 124 Josh Reed	15.00	4.50
❑ 125 Cliff Russell	10.00	3.00
❑ 126 Jeremy Shockey	50.00	15.00
❑ 127 Donte Stallworth	30.00	9.00
❑ 128 Travis Stephens	10.00	3.00
❑ 129 Javon Walker	30.00	9.00
❑ 130 Marquise Walker	10.00	3.00
❑ 131 Roy Williams	40.00	12.00
❑ 132 Mike Williams	10.00	3.00

2003 Leaf Certified Materials

	MINT	NRMT
COMP.SET w/o SP's (150)	30.00	13.50
❑ 1 Jake Plummer	.60	.25
❑ 2 David Boston	.60	.25
❑ 3 MarTay Jenkins	.40	.18
❑ 4 Marcel Shipp	.60	.25
❑ 5 Michael Vick	2.50	1.10
❑ 6 T.J. Duckett	.60	.25
❑ 7 Chris Redman	.40	.18
❑ 8 Ray Lewis	1.00	.45
❑ 9 Jamal Lewis	1.00	.45
❑ 10 Eric Moulds	.60	.25

❑	11	Nate Clements	.40	.18
❑	12	Travis Henry	.60	.25
❑	13	Drew Bledsoe	1.00	.45
❑	14	Peerless Price	.60	.25
❑	15	Josh Reed	.60	.25
❑	16	Wesley Walls	.40	.18
❑	17	Muhsin Muhammad	.60	.25
❑	18	Julius Peppers	1.00	.45
❑	19	Dez White	.40	.18
❑	20	Mike Brown	.60	.25
❑	21	Brian Urlacher	1.50	.70
❑	22	Anthony Thomas	1.00	.45
❑	23	David Terrell	.60	.25
❑	24	Corey Dillon	.60	.25
❑	25	Peter Warrick	.60	.25
❑	26	Josh McCown	.60	.25
❑	27	Dennis Northcutt	.60	.25
❑	28	Kevin Johnson	.60	.25
❑	29	Tim Couch	.40	.18
❑	30	Gerard Warren	.40	.18
❑	31	William Green	.60	.25
❑	32	Antonio Bryant	.60	.25
❑	33	Darren Woodson	.40	.18
❑	34	Emmitt Smith	2.50	1.10
❑	35	Quincy Carter	.60	.25
❑	36	Roy Williams	1.00	.45
❑	37	Brian Griese	1.00	.45
❑	38	Ed McCaffrey	1.00	.45
❑	39	Mike Anderson	.60	.25
❑	40	Rod Smith	.60	.25
❑	41	Clinton Portis	1.50	.70
❑	42	Ashley Lelie	1.00	.45
❑	43	Cory Schlesinger	.40	.18
❑	44	Germane Crowell	.40	.18
❑	45	James Stewart	.60	.25
❑	46	Scotty Anderson	.40	.18
❑	47	Joey Harrington	1.50	.70
❑	48	Brett Favre	2.50	1.10
❑	49	Terry Glenn	.40	.18
❑	50	Ahman Green	1.00	.45
❑	51	Donald Driver	.60	.25
❑	52	Javon Walker	.60	.25
❑	53	David Carr	1.50	.70
❑	54	Ron Dayne	.40	.18
❑	55	Terrell Davis	1.00	.45
❑	56	Edgerrin James	1.00	.45
❑	57	Marvin Harrison	1.00	.45
❑	58	Peyton Manning	1.50	.70
❑	59	Fred Taylor	1.00	.45
❑	60	Jimmy Smith	.60	.25
❑	61	Kyle Brady	.40	.18
❑	62	Mark Brunell	.60	.25
❑	63	Tony Gonzalez	.60	.25
❑	64	Priest Holmes	1.25	.55
❑	65	Trent Green	.60	.25
❑	66	Jason Taylor	.40	.18
❑	67	Jay Fiedler	.60	.25
❑	68	Zach Thomas	1.00	.45
❑	69	Chris Chambers	1.00	.45
❑	70	Ricky Williams	1.00	.45
❑	71	Randy McMichael	.60	.25
❑	72	Daunte Culpepper	1.00	.45
❑	73	Randy Moss	1.50	.70
❑	74	Michael Bennett	.60	.25
❑	75	Ty Law	.60	.25
❑	76	Tom Brady	1.50	.70
❑	77	Troy Brown	.60	.25
❑	78	Antowain Smith	.60	.25
❑	79	Aaron Brooks	1.00	.45
❑	80	Donte Stallworth	1.00	.45
❑	81	Joe Horn	.60	.25
❑	82	Deuce McAllister	1.00	.45
❑	83	Amani Toomer	.60	.25
❑	84	Kerry Collins	.60	.25
❑	85	Michael Strahan	.60	.25
❑	86	Tiki Barber	.60	.25
❑	87	Jeremy Shockey	1.50	.70
❑	88	Chad Pennington	1.25	.55
❑	89	Curtis Martin	1.00	.45
❑	90	Laveranues Coles	.60	.25
❑	91	Vinny Testaverde	.60	.25
❑	92	Santana Moss	.60	.25
❑	93	Charles Woodson	.60	.25
❑	94	Sebastian Janikowski	.40	.18
❑	95	Tim Brown	1.00	.45
❑	96	Rich Gannon	.60	.25
❑	97	Jerry Rice	2.00	.90
❑	98	Donovan McNabb	1.25	.55
❑	99	Duce Staley	.60	.25
❑	100	Todd Pinkston	.40	.18
❑	101	Chad Lewis	.40	.18
❑	102	A.J. Feeley	.40	.18
❑	103	Jerome Bettis	1.00	.45
❑	104	Plaxico Burress	.60	.25
❑	105	Hines Ward	1.00	.45
❑	106	Antwaan Randle El	1.00	.45
❑	107	Kendrell Bell	.60	.25
❑	108	Junior Seau	1.00	.45
❑	109	LaDainian Tomlinson	1.00	.45
❑	110	Doug Flutie	1.00	.45
❑	111	Drew Brees	1.00	.45
❑	112	Terrell Owens	1.00	.45
❑	113	Jeff Garcia	1.00	.45
❑	114	Garrison Hearst	.60	.25
❑	115	Koren Robinson	.60	.25
❑	116	Shaun Alexander	1.00	.45
❑	117	Isaac Bruce	1.00	.45
❑	118	Kurt Warner	1.00	.45
❑	119	Marshall Faulk	1.00	.45
❑	120	Torry Holt	1.00	.45
❑	121	Keyshawn Johnson	1.00	.45
❑	122	Warren Sapp	.60	.25
❑	123	Mike Alstott	1.00	.45
❑	124	Brad Johnson	.60	.25
❑	125	Eddie George	.60	.25
❑	126	Jevon Kearse	.60	.25
❑	127	Steve McNair	1.00	.45
❑	128	Derrick Mason	.60	.25
❑	129	Keith Bulluck	.40	.18
❑	130	Champ Bailey	.60	.25
❑	131	Darrell Green	.40	.18
❑	132	Stephen Davis	.60	.25
❑	133	Rod Gardner	.60	.25
❑	134	Barry Sanders	2.50	1.10
❑	135	Cris Carter	1.00	.45
❑	136	Dan Marino	5.00	2.20
❑	137	Deion Sanders	1.25	.55
❑	138	Jim Kelly	2.00	.90
❑	139	Joe Montana	6.00	2.70
❑	140	John Elway	5.00	2.20
❑	141	Marcus Allen	1.25	.55
❑	142	Reggie White	1.00	.45
❑	143	Sterling Sharpe	1.00	.45
❑	144	Steve Young	1.50	.70
❑	145	Thurman Thomas	1.00	.45
❑	146	Troy Aikman	2.00	.90
❑	147	Warren Moon	1.00	.45
❑	148	Drew Bledsoe	1.00	.45
❑	149	Jerry Rice	2.00	.90
❑	150	Ricky Williams	1.00	.45
❑	151	Carson Palmer JSY RC	25.00	11.00
❑	152	Byron Leftwich JSY RC	30.00	13.50
❑	153	Kyle Boller JSY RC	15.00	6.75
❑	154	Rex Grossman JSY RC	20.00	9.00
❑	155	Dave Ragone JSY RC	8.00	3.60
❑	156	Kliff Kingsbury JSY RC	8.00	3.60
❑	157	Seneca Wallace JSY RC	8.00	3.60
❑	158	Larry Johnson JSY RC	15.00	6.75
❑	159	Willis McGahee JSY RC	20.00	9.00
❑	160	Justin Fargas JSY RC	8.00	3.60
❑	161	Onterrio Smith JSY RC	10.00	4.50
❑	162	Chris Brown JSY RC	15.00	6.75
❑	163	Musa Smith JSY RC	8.00	3.60
❑	164	Artose Pinner JSY RC	8.00	3.60
❑	165	Andre Johnson JSY RC	20.00	9.00
❑	166	Kelley Washington JSY RC	8.00	3.60
❑	167	Taylor Jacobs JSY RC	8.00	3.60
❑	168	Bryant Johnson JSY RC	8.00	3.60
❑	169	Tyrone Calico JSY RC	10.00	4.50
❑	170	Anquan Boldin JSY RC	20.00	9.00
❑	171	Bethel Johnson JSY RC	12.00	5.50
❑	172	Nate Burleson JSY RC	12.00	5.50
❑	173	Kevin Curtis JSY RC	8.00	3.60
❑	174	Dallas Clark JSY RC	8.00	3.60
❑	175	Teyo Johnson JSY RC	8.00	3.60
❑	176	Terrell Suggs JSY RC	12.00	5.50
❑	177	DeWayne Robertson JSY RC	8.00	3.60
❑	178	Brian St.Pierre JSY RC	8.00	3.60
❑	179	Terence Newman JSY RC	15.00	6.75
❑	180	Marcus Trufant JSY RC	8.00	3.60

2003 Leaf Certified Materials Mirror Red

MINT NRMT

*RED ACTIVE STARS: 6X TO 15X BASIC CARD
*RED RETIRED: 5X TO 12X BASIC CARD
*RED ROOKIES: .6X TO 1.5X BASIC CARDS
*MIR.BLUE STARS: .8X TO 2X MIR.REDS
*MIR.BLUE ROOKIES: 1X TO 2.5X
BLUE PRINT RUN 50 SER.#'d SETS
*MIR.GOLD STARS: 1.5X TO 4X MIR.REDS
*MIR.GOLD ROOKIES: 2.5X TO 6X
GOLD PRINT RUN 25 SER.#'d SETS
UNPRICED MIRROR BLACK #'d TO 1
UNPRICED MIRROR EMERALD #'d TO 5

2004 Leaf Certified Materials

	Nm-Mt	Ex-Mt
COMP.SET w/o SP's (150)	30.00	9.00

151-200 PRINT RUN 1000 SER.#'d SETS
201-233 PRINT RUN 1250 SER.#'d SETS
UNPRICED MIRROR BLACK #'d OF 1
UNPRICED MIRROR EMERALD #'d OF 5

	No.	Player	Nm-Mt	Ex-Mt
❑	1	Anquan Boldin	1.00	.30
❑	2	Emmitt Smith	2.00	.60
❑	3	Josh McCown	.60	.18
❑	4	Marcel Shipp	.60	.18
❑	5	Michael Vick	2.00	.60
❑	6	Peerless Price	.60	.18
❑	7	T.J. Duckett	.60	.18
❑	8	Warrick Dunn	.60	.18
❑	9	Jamal Lewis	1.00	.30
❑	10	Kyle Boller	1.00	.30
❑	11	Ray Lewis	1.00	.30
❑	12	Terrell Suggs	.60	.18
❑	13	Todd Heap	.60	.18
❑	14	Drew Bledsoe	1.00	.30
❑	15	Eric Moulds	.60	.18
❑	16	Travis Henry	.60	.18
❑	17	Julius Peppers	1.00	.30
❑	18	Muhsin Muhammad	.60	.18
❑	19	Stephen Davis	.60	.18
❑	20	Anthony Thomas	.60	.18
❑	21	Brian Urlacher	1.25	.35
❑	22	Rex Grossman	1.00	.30
❑	23	Chad Johnson	.60	.18
❑	24	Corey Dillon	.60	.18
❑	25	Peter Warrick	.60	.18
❑	26	Jeff Garcia	1.00	.30
❑	27	Tim Couch	.40	.12
❑	28	William Green	.60	.18
❑	29	Antonio Bryant	.60	.18
❑	30	Keyshawn Johnson	.60	.18
❑	31	Quincy Carter	.60	.18
❑	32	Roy Williams S	.60	.18
❑	33	Terence Newman	.60	.18
❑	34	Ashley Lelie	.60	.18
❑	35	Ed McCaffrey	.60	.18
❑	36	Jake Plummer	.60	.18
❑	37	Mike Anderson	.60	.18
❑	38	Rod Smith	.60	.18
❑	39	Charles Rogers	.60	.18
❑	40	Joey Harrington	1.00	.30
❑	41	Ahman Green	1.00	.30
❑	42	Brett Favre	2.50	.75
❑	43	Donald Driver	.60	.18
❑	44	Javon Walker	.60	.18
❑	45	Robert Ferguson	.40	.12
❑	46	Andre Johnson	1.00	.30
❑	47	David Carr	1.00	.30
❑	48	Edgerrin James	1.00	.30
❑	49	Marvin Harrison	1.00	.30
❑	50	Peyton Manning	1.50	.45

❑ 51 Reggie Wayne .60 .18
❑ 52 Byron Leftwich 1.50 .45
❑ 53 Fred Taylor .60 .18
❑ 54 Jimmy Smith .60 .18
❑ 55 Dante Hall 1.00 .30
❑ 56 Priest Holmes 1.25 .35
❑ 57 Tony Gonzalez .60 .18
❑ 58 Trent Green .60 .18
❑ 59 A.J. Feeley 1.00 .30
❑ 60 Chris Chambers .60 .18
❑ 61 David Boston .60 .18
❑ 62 Jason Taylor .40 .12
❑ 63 Jay Fiedler .40 .12
❑ 64 Junior Seau 1.00 .30
❑ 65 Randy McMichael .40 .12
❑ 66 Ricky Williams 1.00 .30
❑ 67 Zach Thomas 1.00 .30
❑ 68 Daunte Culpepper 1.00 .30
❑ 69 Michael Bennett .60 .18
❑ 70 Randy Moss 1.25 .35
❑ 71 Tom Brady 1.50 .45
❑ 72 Troy Brown .60 .18
❑ 73 Ty Law .60 .18
❑ 74 Aaron Brooks .60 .18
❑ 75 Deuce McAllister 1.00 .30
❑ 76 Donte Stallworth .60 .18
❑ 77 Amani Toomer .60 .18
❑ 78 Jeremy Shockey 1.00 .30
❑ 79 Kerry Collins .60 .18
❑ 80 Michael Strahan .60 .18
❑ 81 Tiki Barber .60 .18
❑ 82 Chad Pennington 1.25 .35
❑ 83 Curtis Martin 1.00 .30
❑ 84 Justin McCareins .40 .12
❑ 85 Santana Moss .60 .18
❑ 86 Charles Woodson .60 .18
❑ 87 Jerry Rice 2.00 .60
❑ 88 Rich Gannon .60 .18
❑ 89 Tim Brown 1.00 .30
❑ 90 Warren Sapp .60 .18
❑ 91 Correll Buckhalter .60 .18
❑ 92 Donovan McNabb 1.25 .35
❑ 93 Freddie Mitchell .60 .18
❑ 94 Jevon Kearse .60 .18
❑ 95 Terrell Owens 1.00 .30
❑ 96 Antwaan Randle El .60 .18
❑ 97 Duce Staley .60 .18
❑ 98 Hines Ward 1.00 .30
❑ 99 Jerome Bettis 1.00 .30
❑ 100 Plaxico Burress .60 .18
❑ 101 Doug Flutie 1.00 .30
❑ 102 LaDainian Tomlinson 1.00 .30
❑ 103 Koren Robinson .60 .18
❑ 104 Matt Hasselbeck .60 .18
❑ 105 Shaun Alexander 1.00 .30
❑ 106 Isaac Bruce .60 .18
❑ 107 Kurt Warner 1.00 .30
❑ 108 Marc Bulger 1.00 .30
❑ 109 Marshall Faulk 1.00 .30
❑ 110 Torry Holt 1.00 .30
❑ 111 Brad Johnson .60 .18
❑ 112 Mike Alstott .60 .18
❑ 113 Derrick Mason .60 .18
❑ 114 Drew Bennett .60 .18
❑ 115 Eddie George .60 .18
❑ 116 Frank Wycheck .40 .12
❑ 117 Keith Bulluck .40 .12
❑ 118 Steve McNair 1.00 .30
❑ 119 Tyrone Calico .60 .18
❑ 120 Clinton Portis 1.00 .30
❑ 121 LaVar Arrington 2.00 .60
❑ 122 Laveranues Coles .60 .18
❑ 123 Mark Brunell .60 .18
❑ 124 Patrick Ramsey .60 .18
❑ 125 Rod Gardner .60 .18
❑ 126 Jake Plummer FLB .60 .18
❑ 127 Thomas Jones FLB .60 .18
❑ 128 Priest Holmes FLB 1.25 .35
❑ 129 Jim Kelly FLB 2.00 .60
❑ 130 Doug Flutie FLB 1.00 .30
❑ 131 Walter Payton FLB 6.00 1.80
❑ 132 Troy Aikman FLB 2.50 .75
❑ 133 John Elway FLB 4.00 1.20
❑ 134 Barry Sanders FLB 3.00 .90
❑ 135 Mark Brunell FLB .60 .18
❑ 136 Earl Campbell FLB 1.50 .45
❑ 137 Joe Montana FLB 6.00 1.80
❑ 138 Dan Marino FLB 5.00 1.50
❑ 139 Curtis Martin FLB 1.00 .30
❑ 140 Drew Bledsoe FLB 1.00 .30
❑ 141 Ricky Williams FLB 1.00 .30
❑ 142 Junior Seau FLB 1.00 .30
❑ 143 Charlie Garner FLB .60 .18
❑ 144 Jerry Rice FLB 2.00 .60
❑ 145 Ahman Green FLB 1.00 .30
❑ 146 Jerome Bettis FLB 1.00 .30
❑ 147 Trent Green FLB .60 .18
❑ 148 Warrick Dunn FLB .60 .18
❑ 149 Deion Sanders FLB 1.50 .45
❑ 150 Stephen Davis FLB .60 .18
❑ 151 A. Echemandu AU RC 10.00 3.00
❑ 152 Ahmad Carroll RC 8.00 2.40
❑ 153 Andy Hall AU RC 10.00 3.00
❑ 154 B.J. Johnson AU RC 10.00 3.00
❑ 155 B.J. Symons AU RC 12.00 3.60
❑ 156 Bradlee Van Pelt AU RC 12.00 3.60
❑ 157 Brandon Miree AU RC 10.00 3.00
❑ 158 Bruce Perry AU RC 10.00 3.00
❑ 159 Carlos Francis AU RC 10.00 3.00
❑ 160 Casey Bramlet AU RC 10.00 3.00
❑ 161 Chris Gamble RC 8.00 2.40
❑ 162 Clarence Moore AU RC 12.00 3.60
❑ 163 Cody Pickett AU RC 12.00 3.60
❑ 164 Craig Krenzel AU RC 12.00 3.60
❑ 165 D.J. Hackett RC 5.00 1.50
❑ 166 D.J. Williams RC 8.00 2.40
❑ 167 Derrick Ward AU RC 8.00 2.40
❑ 168 Drew Carter AU RC 12.00 3.60
❑ 169 Ernest Wilford RC 6.00 1.80
❑ 170 Drew Henson RC 15.00 4.50
❑ 171 Jamaar Taylor AU RC 12.00 3.60
❑ 172 Jared Lorenzen AU RC 10.00 3.00
❑ 173 Jarrett Payton AU RC 12.00 3.60
❑ 174 Jason Babin AU RC EXCH 12.00 3.60
❑ 175 Jeff Smoker AU RC 25.00 7.50
❑ 176 Jeris McIntyre AU RC 10.00 3.00
❑ 177 Jerricho Cotchery RC 6.00 1.80
❑ 178 Jim Sorgi AU RC 12.00 3.60
❑ 179 John Navarre AU RC 12.00 3.60
❑ 180 Patrick Crayton AU RC 12.00 3.60
❑ 181 Johnnie Morant RC 6.00 1.80
❑ 182 Sean Taylor RC 8.00 2.40
❑ 183 Jonathan Vilma RC 6.00 1.80
❑ 184 Josh Harris RC 6.00 1.80
❑ 185 Kenechi Udeze RC 8.00 2.40
❑ 186 Mark Jones AU RC 10.00 3.00
❑ 187 Matt Mauck AU RC 12.00 3.60
❑ 188 Maurice Mann AU RC 10.00 3.00
❑ 189 Michael Turner RC 5.00 1.50
❑ 190 P.K. Sam RC 5.00 1.50
❑ 191 Quincy Wilson RC 5.00 1.50
❑ 192 Ran Carthon AU RC 10.00 3.00
❑ 193 Ryan Krause AU RC 10.00 3.00
❑ 194 Samie Parker RC 6.00 1.80
❑ 195 Sloan Thomas AU RC 10.00 3.00
❑ 196 Tommie Harris RC 8.00 2.40
❑ 197 Triandos Luke AU RC 12.00 3.60
❑ 198 Troy Fleming AU RC 10.00 3.00
❑ 199 Vince Wilfork RC 8.00 2.40
❑ 200 Will Smith RC 6.00 1.80
❑ 201 Larry Fitzgerald JSY RC 20.00 6.00
❑ 202 DeAngelo Hall JSY RC 10.00 3.00
❑ 203 Matt Schaub JSY RC 10.00 3.00
❑ 204 Michael Jenkins JSY RC 8.00 2.40
❑ 205 Devard Darling JSY RC 8.00 2.40
❑ 206 J.P. Losman JSY RC 15.00 4.50
❑ 207 Lee Evans JSY RC 10.00 3.00
❑ 208 Keary Colbert JSY RC 10.00 3.00
❑ 209 Bernard Berrian JSY RC 8.00 2.40
❑ 210 Chris Perry JSY RC 12.00 3.60
❑ 211 Kellen Winslow JSY RC 15.00 4.50
❑ 212 Luke McCown JSY RC 8.00 2.40
❑ 213 Julius Jones JSY RC 25.00 7.50
❑ 214 Darius Watts JSY RC 10.00 3.00
❑ 215 Tatum Bell JSY RC 10.00 3.00
❑ 216 Kevin Jones JSY RC 20.00 6.00
❑ 217 Roy Williams JSY RC 20.00 6.00
❑ 218 Dunta Robinson JSY RC 8.00 2.40
❑ 219 Greg Jones JSY RC 8.00 2.40
❑ 220 Reggie Williams JSY RC 10.00 3.00
❑ 221 Mewelde Moore JSY RC 10.00 3.00
❑ 222 Ben Watson JSY RC 8.00 2.40
❑ 223 Cedric Cobbs JSY RC 8.00 2.40
❑ 224 Devery Henderson JSY RC 8.00 2.40
❑ 225 Eli Manning JSY RC 30.00 9.00
❑ 226 Robert Gallery JSY RC 10.00 3.00
❑ 227 Ben Roethlisberger JSY RC 50.00 15.00
❑ 228 Philip Rivers JSY RC 20.00 6.00
❑ 229 Derrick Hamilton JSY RC 8.00 2.40
❑ 230 Rashaun Woods JSY RC 10.00 3.00
❑ 231 Steven Jackson JSY RC 20.00 6.00
❑ 232 Michael Clayton JSY RC 15.00 4.50
❑ 233 Ben Troupe JSY RC 8.00 2.40

2004 Leaf Certified Materials Mirror Blue

Nm-Mt Ex-Mt
*STARS 1-150: 1X TO 2.5X MIRROR WHITE
*ROOKIES 151-200: .6X TO 1.5X MIRROR WHITE
STATED PRINT RUN 50 SER.#'d SETS

2004 Leaf Certified Materials Mirror Gold

Nm-Mt Ex-Mt
*STARS 1-150: 1.5X TO 4X MIRROR WHITE
*ROOKIES 151-200: 1X TO 2.5X MIRROR WHITE
STATED PRINT RUN 25 SER.#'d SETS

2004 Leaf Certified Materials Mirror Red

Nm-Mt Ex-Mt
*STARS 1-150: .5X TO 1.2X MIRROR WHITE
*ROOKIES 151-200: .5X TO 1.2X MIRROR WHITE
STATED PRINT RUN 100 SER.#'d SETS

2004 Leaf Certified Materials Mirror White

Nm-Mt Ex-Mt
*STARS 1-150: 2X TO 5X BASE CARD HI
COMMON ROOKIE (151-200) 5.00 1.50
ROOKIE SEMISTARS 151-200 8.00 2.40
ROOKIE UNL.STARS 151-200 10.00 3.00
STATED PRINT RUN 150 SER.#'d SETS

2000 Leaf Limited

Nm-Mt Ex-Mt
COMP.SET w/o SPs (200) 120.00 55.00
❑ 1 Ben Coates .50 .23
❑ 2 Joe Horn .75 .35
❑ 3 Jonathan Linton .50 .23
❑ 4 Derrick Mason .75 .35
❑ 5 Ray Lucas .75 .35
❑ 6 Brock Huard .75 .35
❑ 7 Frank Wycheck .50 .23
❑ 8 Michael Strahan .75 .35
❑ 9 Jessie Armstead .50 .23
❑ 10 Stephen Alexander .50 .23
❑ 11 Larry Centers .50 .23
❑ 12 Michael Pittman .50 .23
❑ 13 Priest Holmes 1.50 .70
❑ 14 Jermaine Lewis .75 .35
❑ 15 Jay Riemersma .50 .23
❑ 16 Wesley Walls .50 .23
❑ 17 Curtis Enis .50 .23
❑ 18 Bobby Engram .75 .35
❑ 19 Jim Miller .50 .23
❑ 20 Eddie Kennison .75 .35
❑ 21 Errict Rhett .50 .23
❑ 22 Chris Warren .50 .23
❑ 23 Byron Chamberlain .50 .23
❑ 24 Desmond Howard .50 .23

❑ 25 Lamar Smith .75 .35
❑ 26 Robert Porcher .50 .23
❑ 27 Corey Bradford .75 .35
❑ 28 Donald Driver 1.25 .55
❑ 29 Ahman Green 1.25 .55
❑ 30 Ken Dilger .50 .23
❑ 31 James McKnight .75 .35
❑ 32 Kimble Anders .50 .23
❑ 33 Zach Thomas 1.25 .55
❑ 34 James Johnson .50 .23
❑ 35 Lawyer Milloy .75 .35
❑ 36 Ty Law .75 .35
❑ 37 Willie McGinest .50 .23
❑ 38 Jason Sehorn .75 .35
❑ 39 Andre Rison .75 .35
❑ 40 Rickey Dudley .50 .23
❑ 41 Patrick Jeffers 1.25 .55
❑ 42 Darrell Russell .50 .23
❑ 43 Charles Johnson .75 .35
❑ 44 Michael Westbrook .75 .35
❑ 45 Levon Kirkland .50 .23
❑ 46 Ryan Leaf .75 .35
❑ 47 Sean Dawkins .50 .23
❑ 48 Todd Lyght .50 .23
❑ 49 Kevin Carter .50 .23
❑ 50 Neil O'Donnell .50 .23
❑ 51 Randall Cunningham 1.50 .70
❑ 52 Oronde Gadsden 1.00 .45
❑ 53 O.J. McDuffie 1.00 .45
❑ 54 Jake Reed 1.00 .45
❑ 55 Brian Mitchell .60 .25
❑ 56 Kordell Stewart 1.00 .45
❑ 57 Derrick Mayes 1.00 .45
❑ 58 Az-Zahir Hakim .60 .25
❑ 59 Jacquez Green .60 .25
❑ 60 Andre Reed 1.00 .45
❑ 61 Deion Sanders 1.50 .70
❑ 62 Frank Sanders 1.00 .45
❑ 63 Rob Moore 1.00 .45
❑ 64 Shawn Jefferson .60 .25
❑ 65 Pat Johnson .60 .25
❑ 66 Peter Boulware .60 .25
❑ 67 Donald Hayes .60 .25
❑ 68 Marty Booker 1.00 .45
❑ 69 Leslie Shepherd .60 .25
❑ 70 Jason Tucker .60 .25
❑ 71 Johnnie Morton 1.00 .45
❑ 72 Germane Crowell .60 .25
❑ 73 Herman Moore 1.00 .45
❑ 74 Bill Schroeder 1.00 .45
❑ 75 E.G. Green .60 .25
❑ 76 Jerome Pathon 1.00 .45
❑ 77 Tony Brackens .60 .25
❑ 78 Tony Richardson RC .60 .25
❑ 79 Sam Madison .60 .25
❑ 80 Jeff George 1.00 .45
❑ 81 Matthew Hatchette .60 .25
❑ 82 Kevin Faulk 1.00 .45
❑ 83 Jeff Blake 1.00 .45
❑ 84 Ike Hilliard 1.00 .45
❑ 85 Napoleon Kaufman 1.00 .45
❑ 86 Charles Woodson 1.00 .45
❑ 87 Na Brown .60 .25
❑ 88 Hines Ward 1.50 .70
❑ 89 Troy Edwards .60 .25
❑ 90 Curtis Conway 1.00 .45
❑ 91 Junior Seau 1.50 .70
❑ 92 Jim Harbaugh 1.00 .45
❑ 93 J.J. Stokes 1.00 .45
❑ 94 Jon Kitna 1.50 .70
❑ 95 Reidel Anthony .60 .25
❑ 96 Warrick Dunn 1.50 .70
❑ 97 Carl Pickens 1.00 .45
❑ 98 Yancey Thigpen .60 .25
❑ 99 Albert Connell .60 .25
❑ 100 Irving Fryar 1.00 .45
❑ 101 Qadry Ismail 1.25 .55
❑ 102 Shannon Sharpe 1.25 .55
❑ 103 Joey Galloway 1.25 .55
❑ 104 Ed McCaffrey 2.00 .90
❑ 105 Rod Smith 1.25 .55
❑ 106 Terrell Owens 2.00 .90
❑ 107 Warren Sapp 1.25 .55
❑ 108 Jevon Kearse 2.00 .90
❑ 109 Bruce Smith 1.25 .55
❑ 110 Champ Bailey 1.25 .55
❑ 111 David Boston 2.00 .90
❑ 112 Tim Dwight 2.00 .90
❑ 113 Terance Mathis 1.25 .55
❑ 114 Tony Banks 1.25 .55
❑ 115 Shawn Bryson .75 .35
❑ 116 Peerless Price 2.00 .90
❑ 117 Muhsin Muhammad 1.25 .55
❑ 118 Tim Biakabutuka 1.25 .55
❑ 119 Steve Beuerlein 1.25 .55
❑ 120 Corey Dillon 2.00 .90
❑ 121 Kevin Johnson 2.00 .90
❑ 122 Rocket Ismail 1.25 .55
❑ 123 Charlie Batch 2.00 .90
❑ 124 James Stewart 1.25 .55
❑ 125 Terrence Wilkins .75 .35
❑ 126 Keenan McCardell 1.25 .55
❑ 127 Mark Brunell 2.00 .90
❑ 128 Fred Taylor 2.00 .90
❑ 129 Derrick Alexander 1.25 .55
❑ 130 Tony Gonzalez 1.25 .55
❑ 131 Warren Moon 2.00 .90
❑ 132 Thurman Thomas 1.25 .55
❑ 133 Tony Martin 1.25 .55
❑ 134 Jay Fiedler 2.00 .90
❑ 135 John Randle 1.25 .55
❑ 136 Troy Brown 1.25 .55
❑ 137 Amani Toomer 1.25 .55
❑ 138 Kerry Collins 1.25 .55
❑ 139 Tiki Barber 1.25 .55
❑ 140 Wayne Chrebet 1.25 .55
❑ 141 Tyrone Wheatley 1.25 .55
❑ 142 Duce Staley 2.00 .90
❑ 143 Jermaine Fazande .75 .35
❑ 144 Charlie Garner 1.25 .55
❑ 145 Torry Holt 2.00 .90
❑ 146 Mike Alstott 2.00 .90
❑ 147 Shaun King .50 .23
❑ 148 Darrell Green .75 .35
❑ 149 Brad Johnson 2.00 .90
❑ 150 Olandis Gary 2.00 .90
❑ 151 Jake Plummer 1.50 .70
❑ 152 Chris Chandler 1.50 .70
❑ 153 Jamal Anderson 2.50 1.10
❑ 154 Eric Moulds 2.50 1.10
❑ 155 Doug Flutie 2.50 1.10
❑ 156 Rob Johnson 1.50 .70
❑ 157 Marcus Robinson 2.50 1.10
❑ 158 Cade McNown 1.00 .45
❑ 159 Akili Smith 1.00 .45
❑ 160 Tim Couch 1.50 .70
❑ 161 Emmitt Smith 5.00 2.20
❑ 162 Troy Aikman 5.00 2.20
❑ 163 Brian Griese 2.50 1.10
❑ 164 John Elway 8.00 3.60
❑ 165 Terrell Davis 2.50 1.10
❑ 166 Dorsey Levens 1.50 .70
❑ 167 Antonio Freeman 2.50 1.10
❑ 168 Brett Favre 8.00 3.60
❑ 169 Marvin Harrison 2.50 1.10
❑ 170 Peyton Manning 6.00 2.70
❑ 171 Edgerrin James 4.00 1.80
❑ 172 Jimmy Smith 1.50 .70
❑ 173 Elvis Grbac 1.50 .70
❑ 174 Dan Marino 8.00 3.60
❑ 175 Randy Moss 5.00 2.20
❑ 176 Cris Carter 2.50 1.10
❑ 177 Robert Smith 2.50 1.10
❑ 178 Daunte Culpepper 3.00 1.35
❑ 179 Terry Glenn 1.50 .70
❑ 180 Drew Bledsoe 3.00 1.35
❑ 181 Ricky Williams 1.25 .55
❑ 182 Jake Delhomme RC 8.00 3.60
❑ 183 Curtis Martin 2.50 1.10
❑ 184 Vinny Testaverde 1.50 .70
❑ 185 Tim Brown 2.50 1.10
❑ 186 Rich Gannon 2.50 1.10
❑ 187 Donovan McNabb 3.00 1.35
❑ 188 Jerome Bettis 2.50 1.10
❑ 189 Bobby Shaw RC 3.00 1.35
❑ 190 Jerry Rice 5.00 2.20
❑ 191 Steve Young 3.00 1.35
❑ 192 Jeff Garcia 2.50 1.10
❑ 193 Ricky Watters 1.00 .45
❑ 194 Isaac Bruce 2.50 1.10
❑ 195 Marshall Faulk 3.00 1.35
❑ 196 Kurt Warner 5.00 2.20
❑ 197 Keyshawn Johnson 2.50 1.10
❑ 198 Eddie George 2.50 1.10
❑ 199 Steve McNair 2.50 1.10
❑ 200 Stephen Davis 2.50 1.10
❑ 201 Bobby Brooks RC 3.00 1.35
❑ 202 Cornelius Griffin RC 4.00 1.80
❑ 203 Danny Clark RC 3.00 1.35
❑ 204 Pat Dennis RC 3.00 1.35
❑ 205 Tommy Hendricks RC 5.00 2.20
❑ 206 Fred Jones RC 3.00 1.35
❑ 207 Isaiah Kacyvenski RC 3.00 1.35
❑ 208 Keith Miller RC 3.00 1.35
❑ 209 Andre O' Neal RC 3.00 1.35
❑ 210 Justin Snow RC 3.00 1.35
❑ 211 Armegis Spearman RC 4.00 1.80
❑ 212 Lester Towns RC 3.00 1.35
❑ 213 Antonio Wilson RC 3.00 1.35
❑ 214 Greg Wesley RC 4.00 1.80
❑ 215 Jabari Issa RC 3.00 1.35
❑ 216 Darwin Walker RC 3.00 1.35
❑ 217 Reggie Grimes RC 3.00 1.35
❑ 218 Rian Lindell RC 3.00 1.35
❑ 219 Chris Combs RC 3.00 1.35
❑ 220 Rashard Anderson RC 4.00 1.80
❑ 221 Erik Flowers RC 4.00 1.80
❑ 222 Corey Moore RC 3.00 1.35
❑ 223 Rob Meier RC 3.00 1.35
❑ 224 John Milem RC 3.00 1.35
❑ 225 Jeremiah Parker RC 3.00 1.35
❑ 226 Neil Rackers RC 3.00 1.35
❑ 227 Josh Taves RC 4.00 1.80
❑ 228 Mao Tosi RC 3.00 1.35
❑ 229 Gary Berry RC 3.00 1.35
❑ 230 Matt Bowen RC 3.00 1.35
❑ 231 Ralph Brown RC 3.00 1.35
❑ 232 Tony Darden RC 3.00 1.35
❑ 233 Arturo Freeman RC 3.00 1.35
❑ 234 David Gibson RC 3.00 1.35
❑ 235 Demario Brown RC 3.00 1.35
❑ 236 Deveron Harper RC 3.00 1.35
❑ 237 Johnnie Harris RC 3.00 1.35
❑ 238 Marcus Knight RC 4.00 1.80
❑ 239 Ronnie Heard RC 4.00 1.80
❑ 240 Eric Johnson RC 4.00 1.80
❑ 241 John Keith RC 3.00 1.35
❑ 242 Anthony Malbrough RC 3.00 1.35
❑ 243 Anthony Mitchell RC 3.00 1.35
❑ 244 Aric Morris RC 3.00 1.35
❑ 245 Bobby Myers RC 3.00 1.35
❑ 246 Erik Olson RC 3.00 1.35
❑ 247 Lewis Sanders RC 3.00 1.35
❑ 248 Tony Scott RC 3.00 1.35
❑ 249 David Terrell RC 3.00 1.35
❑ 250 Travares Tillman RC 3.00 1.35
❑ 251 David Stachelski RC 4.00 1.80
❑ 252 Darren Howard RC 5.00 2.20
❑ 253 Frank Chamberlin RC 4.00 1.80
❑ 254 Na'il Diggs RC 5.00 2.20
❑ 255 Orantes Grant RC 4.00 1.80
❑ 256 Barrett Green RC 4.00 1.80
❑ 257 Kory Minor RC 4.00 1.80
❑ 258 Deon Grant RC 5.00 2.20
❑ 259 Mark Simoneau RC 5.00 2.20
❑ 260 Raynoch Thompson RC 5.00 2.20
❑ 261 Kenyatta Wright RC 4.00 1.80
❑ 262 Marcus Bell LB RC 4.00 1.80
❑ 263 Jack Golden RC 4.00 1.80
❑ 264 Thomas Hamner RC 4.00 1.80
❑ 265 Sekou Sanyika RC 4.00 1.80
❑ 266 Marcus Washington RC 5.00 2.20
❑ 267 Tim Seder RC 5.00 2.20
❑ 268 Paul Edinger RC 6.00 2.70
❑ 269 Michael Boireau RC 4.00 1.80
❑ 270 Byron Frisch RC 4.00 1.80
❑ 271 Ketric Sanford RC 4.00 1.80
❑ 272 Frank Murphy RC 4.00 1.80
❑ 273 Robaire Smith RC 4.00 1.80
❑ 274 Adalius Thomas RC 4.00 1.80
❑ 275 William Bartee RC 5.00 2.20
❑ 276 Robert Bean RC 5.00 2.20
❑ 277 Tyrone Carter RC 5.00 2.20
❑ 278 Ike Charlton RC 4.00 1.80
❑ 279 Mario Edwards RC 5.00 2.20
❑ 280 Dwayne Goodrich RC 4.00 1.80
❑ 281 Michael Hawthorne RC 4.00 1.80
❑ 282 Kareem Larrimore RC 4.00 1.80
❑ 283 Mark Roman RC 4.00 1.80
❑ 284 Jacoby Shepherd RC 4.00 1.80
❑ 285 Jason Webster RC 4.00 1.80
❑ 286 Jimmy Wyrick RC 4.00 1.80
❑ 287 Rashidi Barnes RC 4.00 1.80
❑ 288 David Barrett RC 4.00 1.80

❑ 289 Ainsley Battles RC	4.00	1.80
❑ 290 Lamar Chapman RC	4.00	1.80
❑ 291 Todd Franz RC	4.00	1.80
❑ 292 Michael Green RC	4.00	1.80
❑ 293 Antwan Harris RC	4.00	1.80
❑ 294 Brandon Jennings RC	4.00	1.80
❑ 295 Darrick Vaughn RC	4.00	1.80
❑ 296 David Macklin RC	4.00	1.80
❑ 297 Bobby Brown RC	4.00	1.80
❑ 298 Reggie Stephens RC	4.00	1.80
❑ 299 Kenoy Kennedy RC	4.00	1.80
❑ 300 Raion Hill RC	4.00	1.80
❑ 301 Windrell Hayes RC	8.00	3.60
❑ 302 DaShon Polk RC	6.00	2.70
❑ 303 Tywan Mitchell RC	8.00	3.60
❑ 304 Casey Crawford RC	6.00	2.70
❑ 305 Hank Poteat RC	8.00	3.60
❑ 306 Mondriel Fulcher RC	6.00	2.70
❑ 307 Cory Geason RC	6.00	2.70
❑ 308 James Hill RC	6.00	2.70
❑ 309 Brian Jennings RC	6.00	2.70
❑ 310 John Jones RC	8.00	3.60
❑ 311 Anthony Lucas RC	6.00	2.70
❑ 312 Mike Leach RC	6.00	2.70
❑ 313 Dustin Lyman RC	6.00	2.70
❑ 314 Derek Rackley RC	6.00	2.70
❑ 315 Sebastian Janikowski RC	10.00	4.50
❑ 316 Brad St.Louis RC	6.00	2.70
❑ 317 Jay Tant RC	6.00	2.70
❑ 318 Austin Wheatley RC	6.00	2.70
❑ 319 Jermaine Wiggins RC	10.00	4.50
❑ 320 Todd Yoder RC	8.00	3.60
❑ 321 Deon Dyer RC	8.00	3.60
❑ 322 Jim Finn	6.00	2.70
❑ 323 Herbert Goodman RC	8.00	3.60
❑ 324 Mike Green RC	8.00	3.60
❑ 325 Dante Hall RC	20.00	9.00
❑ 326 Thabiti Davis RC	6.00	2.70
❑ 327 Kevin Houser RC	8.00	3.60
❑ 328 Jonas Lewis RC	6.00	2.70
❑ 329 Chad Morton RC	10.00	4.50
❑ 330 Patrick Pass RC	8.00	3.60
❑ 331 Maurice Smith RC	10.00	4.50
❑ 332 Paul Smith RC	8.00	3.60
❑ 333 Terrelle Smith RC	8.00	3.60
❑ 334 Craig Walendy RC	6.00	2.70
❑ 335 Jamel White RC	8.00	3.60
❑ 336 Jarious Jackson RC	8.00	3.60
❑ 337 Matt Lytle RC	8.00	3.60
❑ 338 Ron Powlus RC	10.00	4.50
❑ 339 Ian Gold RC	8.00	3.60
❑ 340 Brandon Short RC	8.00	3.60
❑ 341 T.J. Slaughter RC	6.00	2.70
❑ 342 Nate Webster RC	6.00	2.70
❑ 343 John Engelberger RC	8.00	3.60
❑ 344 Rogers Beckett RC	8.00	3.60
❑ 345 Mike Brown RC	15.00	6.75
❑ 346 Anthony Wright RC	12.00	5.50
❑ 347 Danny Farmer RC	8.00	3.60
❑ 348 Clint Stoerner RC	8.00	3.60
❑ 349 Julian Peterson RC	10.00	4.50
❑ 350 Ahmed Plummer RC	10.00	4.50
❑ 351 Avion Black RC	10.00	4.50
❑ 352 Kwame Cavil RC	8.00	3.60
❑ 353 Chris Cole RC	10.00	4.50
❑ 354 Chris Coleman RC	8.00	3.60
❑ 355 Trevor Gaylor RC	10.00	4.50
❑ 356 Damon Hodge RC	10.00	4.50
❑ 357 Darrell Jackson RC	25.00	11.00
❑ 358 Reggie Jones RC	8.00	3.60
❑ 359 Charles Lee RC	8.00	3.60
❑ 360 Jerry Porter RC	15.00	6.75
❑ 361 Bobby Shaw	10.00	4.50
❑ 362 Ron Dugans RC	8.00	3.60
❑ 363 James Williams RC	10.00	4.50
❑ 364 Bashir Yamini RC	8.00	3.60
❑ 365 Anthony Becht RC	12.00	5.50
❑ 366 Erron Kinney RC	12.00	5.50
❑ 367 Aaron Shea RC	10.00	4.50
❑ 368 Chris Samuels RC	10.00	4.50
❑ 369 Trung Canidate RC	10.00	4.50
❑ 370 Obafemi Ayanbadejo RC	10.00	4.50
❑ 371 Doug Chapman RC	10.00	4.50
❑ 372 Ronney Jenkins RC	10.00	4.50
❑ 373 Curtis Keaton RC	10.00	4.50
❑ 374 Kevin McDougal RC	10.00	4.50
❑ 375 Frank Moreau RC	10.00	4.50
❑ 376 Aaron Stecker RC	12.00	5.50
❑ 377 Shyrone Stith RC	10.00	4.50
❑ 378 Tom Brady RC	175.00	80.00
❑ 379 Giovanni Carmazzi RC	10.00	4.50
❑ 380 Joe Hamilton RC	10.00	4.50
❑ 381 Todd Husak RC	12.00	5.50
❑ 382 Doug Johnson RC	12.00	5.50
❑ 383 Tee Martin RC	12.00	5.50
❑ 384 Chad Pennington RC	80.00	36.00
❑ 385 Tim Rattay RC	25.00	11.00
❑ 386 Chris Redman RC	10.00	4.50
❑ 387 Billy Volek RC	20.00	9.00
❑ 388 Spergon Wynn RC	10.00	4.50
❑ 389 John Abraham RC	12.00	5.50
❑ 390 Keith Bulluck RC	12.00	5.50
❑ 391 Rob Morris RC	10.00	4.50
❑ 392 JaJuan Dawson RC	8.00	3.60
❑ 393 Chris Hovan RC	10.00	4.50
❑ 394 Shaun Ellis RC	12.00	5.50
❑ 395 Deltha O'Neal RC	12.00	5.50
❑ 396 Gari Scott RC	8.00	3.60
❑ 397 Dialleo Burks RC	8.00	3.60
❑ 398 Shockmain Davis RC	8.00	3.60
❑ 399 Brad Hoover RC	10.00	4.50
❑ 400 Brian Finneran RC	12.00	5.50
❑ 401 Sylvester Morris J/FB/750 RC	8.00	3.60
❑ 402 Denn Northcutt J/FB/500 RC	25.00	11.00
❑ 403 Todd Pinkston J/FB/100 RC	20.00	9.00
❑ 404 Larry Foster J/FB/500 RC	20.00	9.00
❑ 405 R.Jay Soward J/FB/1000 RC	12.00	5.50
❑ 406 Travis Taylor J/FB/250 RC	40.00	18.00
❑ 407 Peter Warrick J/FB/1000 RC	20.00	9.00
❑ 408 Dez White J/FB/1000 RC	20.00	9.00
❑ 409 Ron Dayne J/FB/1000 RC	20.00	9.00
❑ 410 Thomas Jones J/FB/500 RC	25.00	11.00
❑ 411 Jamal Lewis J/FB/1000 RC	30.00	13.50
❑ 412 Sammy Morris J/FB/500 RC	20.00	9.00
❑ 413 Travis Prentice J/FB/500 RC	20.00	9.00
❑ 414 J.R. Redmond J/FB/250 RC	25.00	11.00
❑ 415 Michael Wiley FB/1000 RC	12.00	5.50
❑ 416 Laver Coles J/FB/250 RC	40.00	18.00
❑ 417 Bubba Franks J/FB/500 RC	20.00	9.00
❑ 418 Mike Anderson J/FB/250 RC	40.00	18.00
❑ 419 Plaxico Burress J/FB/250 RC	60.00	27.00
❑ 420 Ron Dixon J/FB/1000 RC	12.00	5.50
❑ 421 Troy Walters J/FB/1000 RC	12.00	5.50
❑ 422 Sha Alexander J/FB/1000 RC	30.00	13.50
❑ 423 Brian Urlacher J/FB/1000 RC	40.00	18.00
❑ 424 Corey Simon J/FB/1000 RC	12.00	5.50
❑ 425 Courtney Brown J/FB/500 RC	25.00	11.00

2000 Leaf Limited Limited Series

	Nm-Mt	Ex-Mt

*1-50 LIM.SER.STARS: 8X TO 20X BASIC CARDS
*51-100 LIM.SER.STARS: 6X TO 15X BASIC CARDS
*101-150 LIM.SER.STARS: 5X TO 12X HI COL.
*151-200 LIM.SER.STARS: 4X TO 10X BASIC CARDS
*151-200 LIM.SER.RCs: 1X TO 2.5X BASIC CARDS
*201-250 LIM.SER.RCs: 2X TO 5X BASIC CARDS
*251-300 LIM.SER.RCs: 1.5X TO 4X BASIC CARDS
*301-350 LIM.SER.RCs: 1X TO 2.5X BASIC CARDS
*351-400 LIM.SER.RCs: .8X TO 2X BASIC CARDS

❑ 401 Sylvester Morris	60.00	27.00
❑ 402 Dennis Northcutt	60.00	27.00
❑ 403 Todd Pinkston	60.00	27.00
❑ 404 Larry Foster	40.00	18.00
❑ 405 R.Jay Soward	50.00	22.00
❑ 406 Travis Taylor	60.00	27.00
❑ 407 Peter Warrick	60.00	27.00
❑ 408 Dez White	60.00	27.00
❑ 409 Ron Dayne	80.00	36.00
❑ 410 Thomas Jones	100.00	45.00
❑ 411 Jamal Lewis	200.00	90.00
❑ 412 Sammy Morris	50.00	22.00
❑ 413 Travis Prentice	60.00	27.00
❑ 414 J.R. Redmond	50.00	22.00
❑ 415 Michael Wiley	50.00	22.00
❑ 416 Laveranues Coles	80.00	36.00
❑ 417 Bubba Franks	60.00	27.00
❑ 418 Mike Anderson	100.00	45.00
❑ 419 Plaxico Burress	150.00	70.00
❑ 420 Ron Dixon	50.00	22.00
❑ 421 Troy Walters	60.00	27.00
❑ 422 Shaun Alexander	150.00	70.00
❑ 423 Brian Urlacher	225.00	100.00
❑ 424 Corey Simon	60.00	27.00
❑ 425 Courtney Brown	60.00	27.00

2003 Leaf Limited

	MINT	NRMT
COMP.SET w/o SP's (100)	250.00	110.00
❑ 1 Emmitt Smith	10.00	4.50
❑ 2 Michael Vick	10.00	4.50
❑ 3 Peerless Price	2.50	1.10
❑ 4 T.J. Duckett	2.50	1.10
❑ 5 Jamal Lewis	4.00	1.80
❑ 6 Drew Bledsoe	4.00	1.80
❑ 7 Eric Moulds	2.50	1.10
❑ 8 Travis Henry	2.50	1.10
❑ 9 Jim Kelly	8.00	3.60
❑ 10 Julius Peppers	4.00	1.80
❑ 11 Dick Butkus	6.00	2.70
❑ 12 Mike Singletary	4.00	1.80
❑ 13 Walter Payton	15.00	6.75
❑ 14 Anthony Thomas	4.00	1.80
❑ 15 Brian Urlacher	6.00	2.70
❑ 16 Marty Booker	2.50	1.10

❑ 17 Corey Dillon	2.50	1.10
❑ 18 Jim Thorpe	5.00	2.20
❑ 19 Jim Brown	10.00	4.50
❑ 20 Tim Couch	2.50	1.10
❑ 21 William Green	2.50	1.10
❑ 22 Deion Sanders	4.00	1.80
❑ 23 Michael Irvin	4.00	1.80
❑ 24 Roger Staubach	8.00	3.60
❑ 25 Troy Aikman	6.00	2.70
❑ 26 Tony Dorsett	6.00	2.70
❑ 27 Antonio Bryant	2.50	1.10
❑ 28 Clinton Portis	6.00	2.70
❑ 29 Jake Plummer	2.50	1.10
❑ 30 Rod Smith	2.50	1.10
❑ 31 Barry Sanders	8.00	3.60
❑ 32 Doak Walker	4.00	1.80
❑ 33 Joey Harrington	6.00	2.70
❑ 34 Bart Starr	8.00	3.60
❑ 35 Ahman Green	4.00	1.80
❑ 36 Brett Favre	10.00	4.50
❑ 37 Donald Driver	2.50	1.10
❑ 38 David Carr	6.00	2.70
❑ 39 Don Shula	5.00	2.20
❑ 40 Johnny Unitas	8.00	3.60
❑ 41 Edgerrin James	4.00	1.80
❑ 42 Marvin Harrison	4.00	1.80
❑ 43 Peyton Manning	6.00	2.70
❑ 44 Fred Taylor	4.00	1.80
❑ 45 Jimmy Smith	2.50	1.10
❑ 46 Mark Brunell	2.50	1.10
❑ 47 Marcus Allen	4.00	1.80
❑ 48 Priest Holmes	5.00	2.20
❑ 49 Tony Gonzalez	2.50	1.10
❑ 50 Trent Green	2.50	1.10
❑ 51 Dan Marino	12.00	5.50
❑ 52 Bob Griese	5.00	2.20
❑ 53 Chris Chambers	4.00	1.80
❑ 54 Ricky Williams	4.00	1.80
❑ 55 Fran Tarkenton	5.00	2.20
❑ 56 Daunte Culpepper	4.00	1.80
❑ 57 Michael Bennett	2.50	1.10
❑ 58 Randy Moss	6.00	2.70
❑ 59 Tom Brady	6.00	2.70
❑ 60 Aaron Brooks	4.00	1.80
❑ 61 Deuce McAllister	4.00	1.80
❑ 62 Donte Stallworth	4.00	1.80
❑ 63 Mark Bavaro	2.50	1.10
❑ 64 Jeremy Shockey	6.00	2.70
❑ 65 Kerry Collins	2.50	1.10
❑ 66 Tiki Barber	2.50	1.10
❑ 67 Joe Namath	8.00	3.60
❑ 68 Chad Pennington	5.00	2.20
❑ 69 Curtis Martin	4.00	1.80
❑ 70 Jerry Porter	2.50	1.10
❑ 71 Jerry Rice	8.00	3.60
❑ 72 Rich Gannon	2.50	1.10
❑ 73 Tim Brown	4.00	1.80
❑ 74 Donovan McNabb	5.00	2.20
❑ 75 Terry Bradshaw	8.00	3.60
❑ 76 Antwaan Randle El	4.00	1.80
❑ 77 Plaxico Burress	2.50	1.10
❑ 78 Tommy Maddox	4.00	1.80
❑ 79 David Boston	2.50	1.10
❑ 80 Drew Brees	4.00	1.80
❑ 81 LaDainian Tomlinson	4.00	1.80
❑ 82 Joe Montana	20.00	9.00
❑ 83 Steve Young	5.00	2.20
❑ 84 Jeff Garcia	4.00	1.80
❑ 85 Terrell Owens	4.00	1.80
❑ 86 Koren Robinson	2.50	1.10
❑ 87 Matt Hasselbeck	2.50	1.10
❑ 88 Shaun Alexander	4.00	1.80
❑ 89 Isaac Bruce	4.00	1.80
❑ 90 Kurt Warner	4.00	1.80
❑ 91 Marshall Faulk	4.00	1.80
❑ 92 Torry Holt	4.00	1.80
❑ 93 Brad Johnson	2.50	1.10
❑ 94 Keyshawn Johnson	4.00	1.80
❑ 95 Earl Campbell	4.00	1.80
❑ 96 Eddie George	2.50	1.10
❑ 97 Steve McNair	4.00	1.80
❑ 98 John Riggins	6.00	2.70
❑ 99 Laveranues Coles	2.50	1.10
❑ 100 Patrick Ramsey	4.00	1.80
❑ 101 LaTarence Dunbar RC	5.00	2.20
❑ 102 Sam Aiken RC	5.00	2.20
❑ 103 Bobby Wade RC	6.00	2.70
❑ 104 Justin Gage RC	6.00	2.70
❑ 105 Lee Suggs RC	12.00	5.50
❑ 106 Jason Witten RC	10.00	4.50
❑ 107 Quentin Griffin RC	15.00	6.75
❑ 108 Domanick Davis RC	12.00	5.50
❑ 109 LaBrandon Toefield RC	6.00	2.70
❑ 110 J.R. Tolver RC	5.00	2.20
❑ 111 Kliff Kingsbury RC	5.00	2.20
❑ 112 Talman Gardner RC	6.00	2.70
❑ 113 Teyo Johnson RC	6.00	2.70
❑ 114 Billy McMullen RC	5.00	2.20
❑ 115 L.J. Smith RC	6.00	2.70
❑ 116 Brian St.Pierre RC	6.00	2.70
❑ 117 Brandon Lloyd RC	8.00	3.60
❑ 118 Seneca Wallace RC	6.00	2.70
❑ 119 Kevin Curtis RC	6.00	2.70
❑ 120 Shaun McDonald RC	6.00	2.70
❑ 121 Terrell Suggs RC	10.00	4.50
❑ 122 Terence Newman RC	12.00	5.50
❑ 123 Tony Romo RC	6.00	2.70
❑ 124 DeWayne Robertson RC	6.00	2.70
❑ 125 Marcus Trufant RC	6.00	2.70
❑ 126 Artose Pinner AU RC	25.00	11.00
❑ 127 Bryant Johnson AU RC	25.00	11.00
❑ 128 Kelley Washington AU RC	25.00	11.00
❑ 129 Dallas Clark AU RC	25.00	11.00
❑ 130 Onterrio Smith AU RC	40.00	18.00
❑ 131 Tony Hollings AU RC	30.00	13.50
❑ 132 Tyrone Calico AU RC	40.00	18.00
❑ 133 Carson Palmer AU RC	100.00	45.00
❑ 134 Byron Leftwich AU RC	120.00	55.00
❑ 135 Rex Grossman AU RC	100.00	45.00
❑ 136 Kyle Boller AU RC	60.00	27.00
❑ 137 Chris Simms AU RC	50.00	22.00
❑ 138 Dave Ragone AU RC	25.00	11.00
❑ 139 Ken Dorsey AU RC	35.00	16.00
❑ 140 Willis McGahee AU RC	80.00	36.00
❑ 141 Larry Johnson AU RC	60.00	27.00
❑ 142 Musa Smith AU RC	25.00	11.00
❑ 143 Chris Brown AU RC	50.00	22.00
❑ 144 Charles Rogers AU RC	50.00	22.00
❑ 145 Andre Johnson AU RC	60.00	27.00
❑ 146 Taylor Jacobs AU RC	25.00	11.00
❑ 147 Anquan Boldin AU RC	80.00	36.00
❑ 148 Bethel Johnson AU RC	40.00	18.00
❑ 149 Justin Fargas AU RC	25.00	11.00
❑ 150 Nate Burleson AU RC	50.00	22.00

2003 Leaf Limited Bronze Spotlight

MINT NRMT

*STARS: .8X TO 2X BASIC CARDS
*ROOKIES: .6X TO 1.5X

2003 Leaf Limited Gold Spotlight

MINT NRMT

*STARS: 3X TO 8X BASIC CARDS
*ROOKIES 101-125: 2.5X TO 6X BASIC CARDS

2003 Leaf Limited Silver Spotlight

MINT NRMT

*STARS: 1.2X TO 3X BASIC CARDS
*ROOKIES: 1X TO 2.5X

2004 Leaf Limited

1-150 PRINT RUN 799 SER.#'d SETS
151-200 PRINT RUN 350 SER.#'d SETS
201-233 JSY AU PRINT RUN 150 SETS
EXCH EXPIRATION: 7/1/2006

	Nm-Mt	Ex-Mt
❑ 1 A.J. Feeley	4.00	1.20
❑ 2 Aaron Brooks	3.00	.90
❑ 3 Ahman Green	4.00	1.20
❑ 4 Andre Johnson	4.00	1.20
❑ 5 Anquan Boldin	4.00	1.20
❑ 6 Antwaan Randle El	3.00	.90
❑ 7 Ashley Lelie	3.00	.90
❑ 8 Brad Johnson	3.00	.90
❑ 9 Brett Favre	10.00	3.00
❑ 10 Brian Urlacher	5.00	1.50
❑ 11 Brian Westbrook	3.00	.90
❑ 12 Byron Leftwich	6.00	1.80
❑ 13 Carson Palmer	5.00	1.50
❑ 14 Chad Johnson	3.00	.90
❑ 15 Chad Pennington	5.00	1.50
❑ 16 Charlie Garner	3.00	.90
❑ 17 Charles Rogers	3.00	.90
❑ 18 Chris Brown	4.00	1.20
❑ 19 Chris Chambers	3.00	.90
❑ 20 Clinton Portis	4.00	1.20
❑ 21 Corey Dillon	3.00	.90
❑ 22 Deion Sanders	4.00	1.20
❑ 23 Curtis Martin	4.00	1.20
❑ 24 Daunte Culpepper	4.00	1.20
❑ 25 David Terrell	3.00	.90
❑ 26 David Carr	4.00	1.20
❑ 27 Deion Branch	4.00	1.20
❑ 28 Derrick Mason	3.00	.90
❑ 29 DeShaun Foster	3.00	.90
❑ 30 Deuce McAllister	4.00	1.20
❑ 31 Domanick Davis	4.00	1.20
❑ 32 Donovan McNabb	5.00	1.50
❑ 33 Donte Stallworth	3.00	.90
❑ 34 Drew Bledsoe	4.00	1.20
❑ 35 Duce Staley	3.00	.90
❑ 36 Eddie George	3.00	.90
❑ 37 Edgerrin James	4.00	1.20
❑ 38 Emmitt Smith	8.00	2.40
❑ 39 Eric Moulds	3.00	.90
❑ 40 Fred Taylor	3.00	.90
❑ 41 Hines Ward	4.00	1.20
❑ 42 Isaac Bruce	4.00	1.20
❑ 43 Jake Delhomme	4.00	1.20
❑ 44 Jake Plummer	3.00	.90
❑ 45 Javon Walker	3.00	.90
❑ 46 Jeff Garcia	4.00	1.20
❑ 47 Jeremy Shockey	4.00	1.20
❑ 48 Jerome Bettis	4.00	1.20
❑ 49 Jerry Porter	3.00	.90
❑ 50 Jerry Rice	8.00	2.40
❑ 51 Jevon Kearse	3.00	.90
❑ 52 Jimmy Smith	3.00	.90
❑ 53 Joe Horn	3.00	.90
❑ 54 Joey Harrington	4.00	1.20
❑ 55 Josh McCown	3.00	.90
❑ 56 Kevan Barlow	3.00	.90
❑ 57 Koren Robinson	3.00	.90
❑ 58 Kyle Boller	4.00	1.20
❑ 59 LaDainian Tomlinson	4.00	1.20
❑ 60 LaVar Arrington	8.00	2.40
❑ 61 Laveranues Coles	3.00	.90
❑ 62 Lee Suggs	4.00	1.20
❑ 63 Marc Bulger	4.00	1.20
❑ 64 Mark Brunell	3.00	.90
❑ 65 Marshall Faulk	4.00	1.20
❑ 66 Marvin Harrison	4.00	1.20
❑ 67 Matt Hasselbeck	3.00	.90
❑ 68 Michael Bennett	3.00	.90
❑ 69 Michael Strahan	3.00	.90
❑ 70 Michael Vick	8.00	2.40
❑ 71 Peerless Price	3.00	.90
❑ 72 Peter Warrick	3.00	.90
❑ 73 Peyton Manning	6.00	1.80
❑ 74 Priest Holmes	5.00	1.50
❑ 75 Quentin Griffin	4.00	1.20
❑ 76 Randy Moss	5.00	1.50
❑ 77 Ray Lewis	4.00	1.20
❑ 78 Rex Grossman	4.00	1.20
❑ 79 Lamar Gordon	2.50	.75
❑ 80 Rod Smith	3.00	.90
❑ 81 Roy Williams S	3.00	.90
❑ 82 Rudi Johnson	3.00	.90

❑ 83 Santana Moss 3.00 .90
❑ 84 Shaun Alexander 4.00 1.20
❑ 85 Stephen Davis 3.00 .90
❑ 86 Steve McNair 4.00 1.20
❑ 87 Steve Smith 3.00 .90
❑ 88 T.J. Duckett 3.00 .90
❑ 89 Terrell Owens 4.00 1.20
❑ 90 Thomas Jones 3.00 .90
❑ 91 Tiki Barber 3.00 .90
❑ 92 Tim Brown 4.00 1.20
❑ 93 Tom Brady 6.00 1.80
❑ 94 Tony Gonzalez 3.00 .90
❑ 95 Torry Holt 4.00 1.20
❑ 96 Travis Henry 3.00 .90
❑ 97 Trent Green 3.00 .90
❑ 98 Warren Sapp 3.00 .90
❑ 99 William Green 3.00 .90
❑ 100 Willis McGahee 4.00 1.20
❑ 101 Barry Sanders 8.00 2.40
❑ 102 Bart Starr 10.00 3.00
❑ 103 Bo Jackson 8.00 2.40
❑ 104 Bob Griese 5.00 1.50
❑ 105 Bronko Nagurski 5.00 1.50
❑ 106 Dan Marino 12.00 3.60
❑ 107 Deion Sanders 8.00 2.40
❑ 108 Dick Butkus 8.00 2.40
❑ 109 Doak Walker 5.00 1.50
❑ 110 Don Maynard 4.00 1.20
❑ 111 Don Shula 5.00 1.50
❑ 112 Earl Campbell 5.00 1.50
❑ 113 Fran Tarkenton 6.00 1.80
❑ 114 Franco Harris 6.00 1.80
❑ 115 Fred Biletnikoff 5.00 1.50
❑ 116 Gale Sayers 6.00 1.80
❑ 117 Herman Edwards 4.00 1.20
❑ 118 Jim Brown 8.00 2.40
❑ 119 Jim Kelly 6.00 1.80
❑ 120 Jim Thorpe 5.00 1.50
❑ 121 Jimmy Johnson 4.00 1.20
❑ 122 Joe Greene 5.00 1.50
❑ 123 Joe Montana 15.00 4.50
❑ 124 Joe Namath 8.00 2.40
❑ 125 John Elway 8.00 2.40
❑ 126 John Riggins 6.00 1.80
❑ 127 Johnny Unitas 8.00 2.40
❑ 128 Larry Csonka 5.00 1.50
❑ 129 Lawrence Taylor 5.00 1.50
❑ 130 Marcus Allen 5.00 1.50
❑ 131 Mark Bavaro 3.00 .90
❑ 132 Michael Irvin 5.00 1.50
❑ 133 Mike Ditka 5.00 1.50
❑ 134 Mike Singletary 5.00 1.50
❑ 135 Ozzie Newsome 4.00 1.20
❑ 136 Paul Warfield 4.00 1.20
❑ 137 Randall Cunningham 4.00 1.20
❑ 138 Ray Nitschke 5.00 1.50
❑ 139 Red Grange 6.00 1.80
❑ 140 Reggie White 5.00 1.50
❑ 141 Roger Staubach 8.00 2.40
❑ 142 Sterling Sharpe 4.00 1.20
❑ 143 Steve Largent 5.00 1.50
❑ 144 Terrell Davis 5.00 1.50
❑ 145 Terry Bradshaw 8.00 2.40
❑ 146 Thurman Thomas 4.00 1.20
❑ 147 Tony Dorsett 5.00 1.50
❑ 148 Troy Aikman 6.00 1.80
❑ 149 Walter Payton 15.00 4.50
❑ 150 Warren Moon 4.00 1.20
❑ 151 Ahmad Carroll RC 12.00 3.60
❑ 152 Andy Hall RC 8.00 2.40
❑ 153 Antwan Odom RC 10.00 3.00
❑ 154 B.J. Symons RC 10.00 3.00
❑ 155 Carlos Francis RC 8.00 2.40
❑ 156 Casey Bramlet RC 8.00 2.40
❑ 157 Chris Cooley RC 10.00 3.00
❑ 158 Chris Gamble RC 12.00 3.60
❑ 159 Clarence Moore RC 10.00 3.00
❑ 160 Cody Pickett RC 10.00 3.00
❑ 161 Courtney Watson RC 10.00 3.00
❑ 162 Craig Krenzel RC 10.00 3.00
❑ 163 D.J. Hackett RC 8.00 2.40
❑ 164 D.J. Williams RC 12.00 3.60
❑ 165 Derrick Strait RC 10.00 3.00
❑ 166 Dontarrious Thomas RC 10.00 3.00
❑ 167 Drew Henson RC 25.00 7.50
❑ 168 Ernest Wilford RC 10.00 3.00
❑ 169 Jamaar Taylor RC 10.00 3.00
❑ 170 Jason Babin RC 10.00 3.00
❑ 171 Jeff Smoker RC 15.00 4.50
❑ 172 Jerricho Cotchery RC 10.00 3.00
❑ 173 Jim Sorgi RC 10.00 3.00
❑ 174 Joey Thomas RC 10.00 3.00
❑ 175 John Navarre RC 10.00 3.00
❑ 176 Johnnie Morant RC 10.00 3.00
❑ 177 Jonathan Vilma RC 10.00 3.00
❑ 178 Josh Harris RC 10.00 3.00
❑ 179 Keiwan Ratliff RC 8.00 2.40
❑ 180 Kenechi Udeze RC 10.00 3.00
❑ 181 Kris Wilson RC 10.00 3.00
❑ 182 Marcus Tubbs RC 10.00 3.00
❑ 183 Marquise Hill RC 8.00 2.40
❑ 184 Matt Mauck RC 10.00 3.00
❑ 185 Maurice Mann RC 8.00 2.40
❑ 186 Michael Boulware RC 10.00 3.00
❑ 187 Michael Turner RC 8.00 2.40
❑ 188 P.K. Sam RC 8.00 2.40
❑ 189 Patrick Crayton RC 10.00 3.00
❑ 190 Ricardo Colclough RC 10.00 3.00
❑ 191 Richard Smith RC 8.00 2.40
❑ 192 Samie Parker RC 10.00 3.00
❑ 193 Sean Taylor RC 12.00 3.60
❑ 194 Teddy Lehman RC 10.00 3.00
❑ 195 Thomas Tapeh RC 8.00 2.40
❑ 196 Tommie Harris RC 12.00 3.60
❑ 197 Triandos Luke RC 10.00 3.00
❑ 198 Troy Fleming RC 8.00 2.40
❑ 199 Vince Wilfork RC 12.00 3.60
❑ 200 Will Smith RC 10.00 3.00
❑ 201 Larry Fitzgerald JSY AU RC 100.00 30.00
❑ 202 DeAngelo Hall JSY AU RC 40.00 12.00
❑ 203 Matt Schaub JSY AU RC 50.00 15.00
❑ 204 Michael Jenkins JSY AU RC 40.00 12.00
❑ 205 Devard Darling JSY AU RC 30.00 9.00
❑ 206 J.P. Losman JSY AU RC 100.00 30.00
❑ 207 Lee Evans JSY AU RC 50.00 15.00
❑ 208 Keary Colbert JSY AU RC 40.00 12.00
❑ 209 Bernard Berrian JSY AU RC 30.00 9.00
❑ 210 Chris Perry JSY AU RC 50.00 15.00
❑ 211 Kellen Winslow JSY AU RC EXCH 60.00 18.00
❑ 212 Luke McCown JSY AU RC 30.00 9.00
❑ 213 Julius Jones JSY AU RC 175.00 52.50
❑ 214 Darius Watts JSY AU RC EXCH 40.00 12.00
❑ 215 Tatum Bell JSY AU RC EXCH 60.00 18.00
❑ 216 Kevin Jones JSY AU RC 135.00 40.00
❑ 217 Roy Williams WR JSY AU RC 120.00 36.00
❑ 218 Dunta Robinson JSY AU RC EXCH 30.00 9.00
❑ 219 Greg Jones JSY AU RC 30.00 9.00
❑ 220 Reggie Williams JSY AU RC 40.00 12.00
❑ 221 Mewelde Moore JSY AU RC 40.00 12.00
❑ 222 Ben Watson JSY AU RC 30.00 9.00
❑ 223 Cedric Cobbs JSY AU RC 30.00 9.00
❑ 224 Devery Henderson JSY AU RC 25.00 7.50
❑ 225 Eli Manning JSY AU RC 200.00 60.00
❑ 226 Robert Gallery JSY AU RC 40.00 12.00
❑ 227 Ben Roethlisberger JSY AU RC 400.00 120.00
❑ 228 Philip Rivers JSY AU RC 125.00 38.00
❑ 229 Derrick Hamilton JSY AU RC 25.00 7.50
❑ 230 Rashaun Woods JSY AU RC 40.00 12.00
❑ 231 Steven Jackson JSY AU RC 120.00 36.00
❑ 232 Michael Clayton JSY AU RC 80.00 24.00
❑ 233 Ben Troupe JSY AU RC 30.00 9.00

2004 Leaf Limited Bronze Spotlight

Nm-Mt Ex-Mt
*STARS 1-100: .8X TO 2X BASE CARD HI
*RETIRED STARS 101-150: .8X TO 2X
*ROOKIES 151-200: .5X TO 1.2X BASE CARD HI
1-200 PRINT RUN 100 SER.#'d SETS
*ROOKIE JSY AU: .5X TO 1.2X
201-233 JSY AU PRINT RUN 25 SETS
EXCH EXPIRATION: 7/1/2006

❑ 213 Julius Jones JSY AU 200.00 60.00
❑ 216 Kevin Jones JSY AU 150.00 45.00
❑ 217 Roy Williams WR JSY AU 150.00 45.00
❑ 225 Eli Manning JSY AU 300.00 90.00
❑ 227 Ben Roethlisberger JSY AU 600.00 180.00
❑ 228 Philip Rivers JSY AU 150.00 45.00

2004 Leaf Limited Gold Spotlight

Nm-Mt Ex-Mt
*STARS 1-100: 2X TO 5X BASE CARD HI
*RETIRED STARS 101-150: 2X TO 5X
*ROOKIES 151-200: 1X TO 2.5X BASE CARD HI
1-200 PRINT RUN 25 SER.#'d SETS
UNPRICED JSY AU PRINT RUN 10 SETS
EXCH EXPIRATION: 7/1/2006

2004 Leaf Limited Silver Spotlight

Nm-Mt Ex-Mt
*STARS 1-100: 1.2X TO 3X BASE CARD HI
*RETIRED STARS 101-150: 1.2X TO 3X
*ROOKIES 151-200: .6X TO 1.5X BASE CARD HI
1-150 PRINT RUN 50 SER.#'d SETS
UNPRICED JSY AU PRINT RUN 15 SETS
EXCH EXPIRATION: 7/1/2006

1998 Leaf Rookies and Stars

Nm-Mt Ex-Mt
COMPLETE SET (300) 250.00 110.00
❑ 1 Keyshawn Johnson .60 .25
❑ 2 Marvin Harrison .60 .25
❑ 3 Eddie Kennison .40 .18
❑ 4 Bryant Young .25 .11
❑ 5 Darren Woodson .25 .11
❑ 6 Tyrone Wheatley .40 .18
❑ 7 Michael Westbrook .40 .18
❑ 8 Charles Way .25 .11
❑ 9 Ricky Watters .40 .18
❑ 10 Chris Warren .40 .18
❑ 11 Wesley Walls .40 .18
❑ 12 Tamarick Vanover .25 .11
❑ 13 Zach Thomas .60 .25
❑ 14 Derrick Thomas .40 .18
❑ 15 Yancey Thigpen .25 .11
❑ 16 Vinny Testaverde .40 .18
❑ 17 Dana Stubblefield .25 .11
❑ 18 J.J. Stokes .40 .18
❑ 19 James Stewart .40 .18
❑ 20 Jeff George .40 .18
❑ 21 John Randle .40 .18
❑ 22 Gary Brown .25 .11
❑ 23 Ed McCaffrey .40 .18
❑ 24 James Jett .40 .18
❑ 25 Rob Johnson .40 .18
❑ 26 Daryl Johnston .40 .18
❑ 27 Jermaine Lewis .40 .18

❑	28 Tony Martin	.40	.18
❑	29 Derrick Mayes	.40	.18
❑	30 Keenan McCardell	.40	.18
❑	31 O.J. McDuffie	.40	.18
❑	32 Chris Chandler	.40	.18
❑	33 Doug Flutie	.60	.25
❑	34 Scott Mitchell	.40	.18
❑	35 Warren Moon	.60	.25
❑	36 Rob Moore	.40	.18
❑	37 Johnnie Morton	.40	.18
❑	38 Neil O'Donnell	.40	.18
❑	39 Rich Gannon	.60	.25
❑	40 Andre Reed	.40	.18
❑	41 Jake Reed	.40	.18
❑	42 Errict Rhett	.40	.18
❑	43 Simeon Rice	.40	.18
❑	44 Andre Rison	.40	.18
❑	45 Eric Moulds	.60	.25
❑	46 Frank Sanders	.40	.18
❑	47 Darnay Scott	.40	.18
❑	48 Junior Seau	.60	.25
❑	49 Shannon Sharpe	.40	.18
❑	50 Bruce Smith	.40	.18
❑	51 Jimmy Smith	.40	.18
❑	52 Robert Smith	.60	.25
❑	53 Derrick Alexander	.40	.18
❑	54 Kimble Anders	.40	.18
❑	55 Jamal Anderson	.60	.25
❑	56 Mario Bates	.40	.18
❑	57 Edgar Bennett	.25	.11
❑	58 Tim Biakabutuka	.40	.18
❑	59 Ki-Jana Carter	.25	.11
❑	60 Larry Centers	.25	.11
❑	61 Mark Chmura	.40	.18
❑	62 Wayne Chrebet	.60	.25
❑	63 Ben Coates	.40	.18
❑	64 Curtis Conway	.40	.18
❑	65 Randall Cunningham	.60	.25
❑	66 Rickey Dudley	.25	.11
❑	67 Bert Emanuel	.40	.18
❑	68 Bobby Engram	.40	.18
❑	69 William Floyd	.25	.11
❑	70 Irving Fryar	.40	.18
❑	71 Elvis Grbac	.40	.18
❑	72 Kevin Greene	.40	.18
❑	73 Jim Harbaugh	.40	.18
❑	74 Raymont Harris	.25	.11
❑	75 Garrison Hearst	.60	.25
❑	76 Greg Hill	.25	.11
❑	77 Desmond Howard	.40	.18
❑	78 Bobby Hoying	.40	.18
❑	79 Michael Jackson	.25	.11
❑	80 Terry Allen	.60	.25
❑	81 Jerome Bettis	.60	.25
❑	82 Jeff Blake	.40	.18
❑	83 Robert Brooks	.40	.18
❑	84 Tim Brown	.60	.25
❑	85 Isaac Bruce	.60	.25
❑	86 Cris Carter	.60	.25
❑	87 Ty Detmer	.40	.18
❑	88 Trent Dilfer	.60	.25
❑	89 Marshall Faulk	.75	.35
❑	90 Antonio Freeman	.60	.25
❑	91 Gus Frerotte	.25	.11
❑	92 Joey Galloway	.40	.18
❑	93 Michael Irvin	.60	.25
❑	94 Brad Johnson	.60	.25
❑	95 Danny Kanell	.40	.18
❑	96 Napoleon Kaufman	.60	.25
❑	97 Dorsey Levens	.60	.25
❑	98 Natrone Means	.40	.18
❑	99 Herman Moore	.40	.18
❑	100 Adrian Murrell	.40	.18
❑	101 Carl Pickens	.40	.18
❑	102 Rod Smith	.40	.18
❑	103 Thurman Thomas	.60	.25
❑	104 Reggie White	.60	.25
❑	105 Jim Druckenmiller	.25	.11
❑	106 Antowain Smith	.60	.25
❑	107 Reidel Anthony	.40	.18
❑	108 Ike Hilliard	.40	.18
❑	109 Rae Carruth	.25	.11
❑	110 Troy Davis	.25	.11
❑	111 Terance Mathis	.40	.18
❑	112 Brett Favre	2.50	1.10
❑	113 Dan Marino	2.50	1.10
❑	114 Emmitt Smith	2.00	.90
❑	115 Barry Sanders	2.00	.90
❑	116 Eddie George	.60	.25
❑	117 Drew Bledsoe	1.00	.45
❑	118 Troy Aikman	1.25	.55
❑	119 Terrell Davis	.60	.25
❑	120 John Elway	2.50	1.10
❑	121 Mark Brunell	.60	.25
❑	122 Jerry Rice	1.25	.55
❑	123 Kordell Stewart	.60	.25
❑	124 Steve McNair	.60	.25
❑	125 Curtis Martin	.60	.25
❑	126 Steve Young	.75	.35
❑	127 Kerry Collins	.40	.18
❑	128 Terry Glenn	.60	.25
❑	129 Deion Sanders	.60	.25
❑	130 Mike Alstott	.60	.25
❑	131 Tony Banks	.40	.18
❑	132 Karim Abdul-Jabbar	.60	.25
❑	133 Terrell Owens	.60	.25
❑	134 Yatil Green	.25	.11
❑	135 Tony Gonzalez	.60	.25
❑	136 Byron Hanspard	.25	.11
❑	137 David LaFleur	.25	.11
❑	138 Danny Wuerffel	.40	.18
❑	139 Tiki Barber	.60	.25
❑	140 Peter Boulware	.25	.11
❑	141 Will Blackwell	.25	.11
❑	142 Warrick Dunn	.60	.25
❑	143 Corey Dillon	.60	.25
❑	144 Jake Plummer	.60	.25
❑	145 Neil Smith	.40	.18
❑	146 Charles Johnson	.25	.11
❑	147 Fred Lane	.25	.11
❑	148 Dan Wilkinson	.25	.11
❑	149 Ken Norton	.25	.11
❑	150 Stephen Davis	.25	.11
❑	151 Gilbert Brown	.25	.11
❑	152 Kenny Bynum RC	.25	.11
❑	153 Derrick Cullors	.25	.11
❑	154 Charlie Garner	.40	.18
❑	155 Jeff Graham	.25	.11
❑	156 Warren Sapp	.40	.18
❑	157 Jerald Moore	.25	.11
❑	158 Sean Dawkins	.25	.11
❑	159 Charlie Jones	.25	.11
❑	160 Kevin Lockett	.25	.11
❑	161 James McKnight	.60	.25
❑	162 Chris Penn	.25	.11
❑	163 Leslie Shepherd	.25	.11
❑	164 Karl Williams	.25	.11
❑	165 Mark Bruener	.25	.11
❑	166 Ernie Conwell	.25	.11
❑	167 Ken Dilger	.25	.11
❑	168 Troy Drayton	.25	.11
❑	169 Freddie Jones	.25	.11
❑	170 Dale Carter	.25	.11
❑	171 Charles Woodson RC	8.00	3.60
❑	172 Alonzo Mayes RC	2.50	1.10
❑	173 Andre Wadsworth RC	4.00	1.80
❑	174 Grant Wistrom RC	4.00	1.80
❑	175 Greg Ellis RC	2.50	1.10
❑	176 Chris Howard RC	2.50	1.10
❑	177 Keith Brooking RC	6.00	2.70
❑	178 Takeo Spikes RC	6.00	2.70
❑	179 Anthony Simmons RC	4.00	1.80
❑	180 Brian Simmons RC	4.00	1.80
❑	181 Sam Cowart RC	4.00	1.80
❑	182 Ken Oxendine RC	2.50	1.10
❑	183 Vonnie Holliday RC	4.00	1.80
❑	184 Terry Fair RC	4.00	1.80
❑	185 Shaun Williams RC	4.00	1.80
❑	186 Tremayne Stephens RC	2.50	1.10
❑	187 Duane Starks RC	2.50	1.10
❑	188 Jason Peter RC	2.50	1.10
❑	189 Tebucky Jones RC	2.50	1.10
❑	190 Donovin Darius RC	4.00	1.80
❑	191 R.W. McQuarters RC	4.00	1.80
❑	192 Corey Chavous RC	6.00	2.70
❑	193 Cameron Cleeland RC	2.50	1.10
❑	194 Stephen Alexander RC	4.00	1.80
❑	195 Rod Rutledge RC	2.50	1.10
❑	196 Scott Frost RC	2.50	1.10
❑	197 Fred Beasley RC	2.50	1.10
❑	198 Dorian Boose RC	2.50	1.10
❑	199 Randy Moss RC	30.00	13.50
❑	200 Jacquez Green RC	4.00	1.80
❑	201 Marcus Nash RC	2.50	1.10
❑	202 Hines Ward RC	15.00	6.75
❑	203 Kevin Dyson RC	6.00	2.70
❑	204 E.G. Green RC	4.00	1.80
❑	205 Germane Crowell RC	4.00	1.80
❑	206 Joe Jurevicius RC	6.00	2.70
❑	207 Tony Simmons RC	4.00	1.80
❑	208 Tim Dwight RC	6.00	2.70
❑	209 Az-Zahir Hakim RC	6.00	2.70
❑	210 Jerome Pathon RC	6.00	2.70
❑	211 Pat Johnson RC	4.00	1.80
❑	212 Mikhael Ricks RC	4.00	1.80
❑	213 Donald Hayes RC	4.00	1.80
❑	214 Jammi German RC	2.50	1.10
❑	215 Larry Shannon RC	2.50	1.10
❑	216 Brian Alford RC	2.50	1.10
❑	217 Curtis Enis RC	2.50	1.10
❑	218 Fred Taylor RC	10.00	4.50
❑	219 Robert Edwards RC	4.00	1.80
❑	220 Ahman Green RC	30.00	13.50
❑	221 Tavian Banks RC	4.00	1.80
❑	222 Skip Hicks RC	4.00	1.80
❑	223 Robert Holcombe RC	4.00	1.80
❑	224 John Avery RC	4.00	1.80
❑	225 C.Fuamatu-Ma'afala RC	4.00	1.80
❑	226 Michael Pittman RC	8.00	3.60
❑	227 Rashaan Shehee RC	4.00	1.80
❑	228 Jonathan Linton RC	4.00	1.80
❑	229 Jon Ritchie RC	4.00	1.80
❑	230 Chris Floyd RC	2.50	1.10
❑	231 Wilmont Perry RC	2.50	1.10
❑	232 Raymond Priester RC	2.50	1.10
❑	233 Peyton Manning RC	60.00	27.00
❑	234 Ryan Leaf RC	6.00	2.70
❑	235 Brian Griese RC	12.00	5.50
❑	236 Jeff Ogden RC	6.00	2.70
❑	237 Charlie Batch RC	6.00	2.70
❑	238 Moses Moreno RC	2.50	1.10
❑	239 Jonathan Quinn RC UER back Jonathon	6.00	2.70
❑	240 Flozell Adams RC	2.50	1.10
❑	241 Brett Favre PT	12.00	5.50
❑	242 Dan Marino PT	12.00	5.50
❑	243 Emmitt Smith PT	10.00	4.50
❑	244 Barry Sanders PT	10.00	4.50
❑	245 Eddie George PT	2.50	1.10
❑	246 Drew Bledsoe PT	5.00	2.20
❑	247 Troy Aikman PT	6.00	2.70
❑	248 Terrell Davis PT	2.50	1.10
❑	249 John Elway PT	12.00	5.50
❑	250 Carl Pickens PT	2.50	1.10
❑	251 Jerry Rice PT	6.00	2.70
❑	252 Kordell Stewart PT	2.50	1.10
❑	253 Steve McNair PT	2.50	1.10
❑	254 Curtis Martin PT	2.50	1.10
❑	255 Steve Young PT	4.00	1.80
❑	256 Herman Moore PT	2.50	1.10
❑	257 Dorsey Levens PT	2.50	1.10
❑	258 Deion Sanders PT	2.50	1.10
❑	259 Napoleon Kaufman PT	2.50	1.10
❑	260 Warrick Dunn PT	2.50	1.10
❑	261 Corey Dillon PT	2.50	1.10
❑	262 Jerome Bettis PT	2.50	1.10
❑	263 Tim Brown PT	2.50	1.10
❑	264 Cris Carter PT	2.50	1.10
❑	265 Antonio Freeman PT	2.50	1.10
❑	266 Randy Moss PT	12.00	5.50
❑	267 Curtis Enis PT	2.50	1.10
❑	268 Fred Taylor PT	4.00	1.80
❑	269 Robert Edwards PT	2.50	1.10
❑	270 Peyton Manning PT	25.00	11.00
❑	271 Barry Sanders TL	1.00	.45
❑	272 Eddie George TL	.40	.18
❑	273 Troy Aikman TL	.60	.25
❑	274 Mark Brunell TL	.60	.25
❑	275 Kordell Stewart TL	.60	.25
❑	276 Tim Biakabutuka TL	.25	.11
❑	277 Terry Glenn TL	.25	.11
❑	278 Mike Alstott TL	.25	.11
❑	279 Tony Banks TL	.25	.11
❑	280 Karim Abdul-Jabbar TL	.25	.11
❑	281 Terrell Owens TL	.40	.18
❑	282 Byron Hanspard TL	.25	.11
❑	283 Jake Plummer TL	.40	.18
❑	284 Terry Allen TL	.25	.11
❑	285 Jeff Blake TL	.25	.11
❑	286 Brad Johnson TL	.25	.11
❑	287 Danny Kanell TL	.25	.11
❑	288 Natrone Means TL	.25	.11
❑	289 Rod Smith TL	.25	.11
❑	290 Thurman Thomas TL	.25	.11

❑ 291 Reggie White TL	.25	.11
❑ 292 Troy Davis TL	.25	.11
❑ 293 Curtis Conway TL	.25	.11
❑ 294 Irving Fryar TL	.25	.11
❑ 295 Jim Harbaugh TL	.25	.11
❑ 296 Andre Rison TL	.25	.11
❑ 297 Ricky Watters TL	.25	.11
❑ 298 Keyshawn Johnson TL	.25	.11
❑ 299 Jeff George TL	.25	.11
❑ 300 Marshall Faulk TL	.60	.25

1998 Leaf Rookies and Stars Longevity

	Nm-Mt	Ex-Mt

*LONGEVITY STARS: 40X TO 100X BASIC
*LONGEVITY RCs: 1.5X TO 4X BASIC
*LONGEV.PT STARS: 8X TO 20X BASIC PT'S
*LONGEV.PT ROOKIES: 2X TO 5X BASIC CARDS

1998 Leaf Rookies and Stars True Blue

	Nm-Mt	Ex-Mt
COMPLETE SET (300)	800.00	350.00

*TRUE BLUE STARS: 4X TO 10X BASIC CARDS
*TRUE BLUE RCs: .3X TO .8X BASIC CARDS
*TRUE BLUE POWER TOOLS: .8X TO 2X BASIC CARDS

1999 Leaf Rookies and Stars

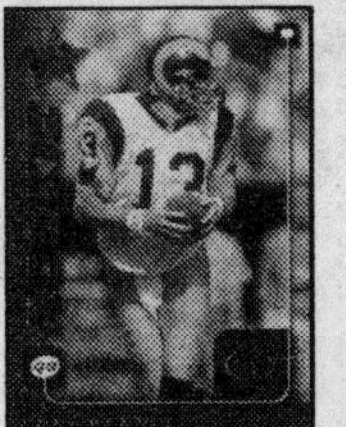

	Nm-Mt	Ex-Mt
COMPLETE SET (300)	200.00	90.00
COMP.SET w/o SP's (200)	30.00	13.50
❑ 1 Frank Sanders	.40	.18
❑ 2 Adrian Murrell	.40	.18
❑ 3 Rob Moore	.40	.18
❑ 4 Simeon Rice	.40	.18
❑ 5 Michael Pittman	.25	.11
❑ 6 Jake Plummer	.40	.18
❑ 7 Chris Chandler	.40	.18
❑ 8 Tim Dwight	.40	.18
❑ 9 Chris Calloway	.25	.11
❑ 10 Terance Mathis	.40	.18
❑ 11 Jamal Anderson	.60	.25
❑ 12 Byron Hanspard	.25	.11
❑ 13 O.J. Santiago	.25	.11
❑ 14 Ken Oxendine	.25	.11
❑ 15 Priest Holmes	1.00	.45
❑ 16 Scott Mitchell	.25	.11
❑ 17 Tony Banks	.40	.18
❑ 18 Patrick Johnson	.25	.11
❑ 19 Rod Woodson	.40	.18
❑ 20 Jermaine Lewis	.40	.18
❑ 21 Errict Rhett	.40	.18
❑ 22 Stoney Case	.25	.11
❑ 23 Andre Reed	.40	.18
❑ 24 Eric Moulds	.40	.18
❑ 25 Rob Johnson	.40	.18
❑ 26 Doug Flutie	.60	.25
❑ 27 Bruce Smith	.40	.18
❑ 28 Jay Riemersma	.25	.11
❑ 29 Antowain Smith	.25	.11
❑ 30 Thurman Thomas	.40	.18
❑ 31 Jonathan Linton	.25	.11
❑ 32 Muhsin Muhammad	.40	.18
❑ 33 Rae Carruth	.25	.11
❑ 34 Wesley Walls	.40	.18
❑ 35 Fred Lane	.25	.11
❑ 36 Kevin Greene	.25	.11
❑ 37 Tim Biakabutuka	.40	.18
❑ 38 Curtis Enis	.25	.11
❑ 39 Shane Matthews	.40	.18
❑ 40 Bobby Engram	.40	.18
❑ 41 Curtis Conway	.40	.18
❑ 42 Marcus Robinson	1.25	.55
❑ 43 Darnay Scott	.25	.11
❑ 44 Carl Pickens	.40	.18
❑ 45 Corey Dillon	.60	.25
❑ 46 Jeff Blake	.40	.18
❑ 47 Terry Kirby	.25	.11
❑ 48 Ty Detmer	.40	.18
❑ 49 Leslie Shepherd	.25	.11
❑ 50 Karim Abdul-Jabbar	.40	.18
❑ 51 Emmitt Smith	1.25	.55
❑ 52 Deion Sanders	.60	.25
❑ 53 Michael Irvin	.40	.18
❑ 54 Rocket Ismail	.40	.18
❑ 55 David LaFleur	.25	.11
❑ 56 Troy Aikman	1.25	.55
❑ 57 Ed McCaffrey	.40	.18
❑ 58 Rod Smith	.40	.18
❑ 59 Shannon Sharpe	.40	.18
❑ 60 Brian Griese	.60	.25
❑ 61 John Elway	2.00	.90
❑ 62 Bubby Brister	.25	.11
❑ 63 Neil Smith	.40	.18
❑ 64 Terrell Davis	.60	.25
❑ 65 John Avery	.25	.11
❑ 66 Derek Loville	.25	.11
❑ 67 Ron Rivers	.25	.11
❑ 68 Herman Moore	.40	.18
❑ 69 Johnnie Morton	.40	.18
❑ 70 Charlie Batch	.60	.25
❑ 71 Barry Sanders	2.00	.90
❑ 72 Germane Crowell	.25	.11
❑ 73 Greg Hill	.25	.11
❑ 74 Gus Frerotte	.40	.18
❑ 75 Corey Bradford	.25	.11
❑ 76 Dorsey Levens	.60	.25
❑ 77 Antonio Freeman	.60	.25
❑ 78 Mark Chmura	.25	.11
❑ 79 Brett Favre	2.00	.90
❑ 80 Bill Schroeder	.40	.18
❑ 81 Matt Hasselbeck	.60	.25
❑ 82 E.G. Green	.25	.11
❑ 83 Ken Dilger	.25	.11
❑ 84 Jerome Pathon	.25	.11
❑ 85 Marvin Harrison	.60	.25
❑ 86 Peyton Manning	2.00	.90
❑ 87 Tavian Banks	.25	.11
❑ 88 Keenan McCardell	.40	.18
❑ 89 Mark Brunell	.60	.25
❑ 90 Fred Taylor	.60	.25
❑ 91 Jimmy Smith	.40	.18
❑ 92 James Stewart	.40	.18
❑ 93 Kyle Brady	.25	.11
❑ 94 Derrick Thomas	.40	.18
❑ 95 Rashaan Shehee	.25	.11
❑ 96 Derrick Alexander WR	.40	.18
❑ 97 Byron Bam Morris	.25	.11
❑ 98 Andre Rison	.40	.18
❑ 99 Elvis Grbac	.40	.18
❑ 100 Tony Gonzalez	.60	.25
❑ 101 Donnell Bennett	.25	.11
❑ 102 Warren Moon	.60	.25
❑ 103 Zach Thomas	.60	.25
❑ 104 Oronde Gadsden	.40	.18
❑ 105 Dan Marino	2.00	.90
❑ 106 O.J. McDuffie	.40	.18
❑ 107 Tony Martin	.40	.18
❑ 108 Randy Moss	1.50	.70
❑ 109 Cris Carter	.60	.25
❑ 110 Robert Smith	.60	.25
❑ 111 Randall Cunningham	.60	.25
❑ 112 Jake Reed	.40	.18
❑ 113 John Randle	.40	.18
❑ 114 Leroy Hoard	.25	.11
❑ 115 Jeff George	.40	.18
❑ 116 Ty Law	.40	.18
❑ 117 Shawn Jefferson	.25	.11
❑ 118 Troy Brown	.40	.18
❑ 119 Robert Edwards	.25	.11
❑ 120 Tony Simmons	.25	.11
❑ 121 Terry Glenn	.60	.25
❑ 122 Ben Coates	.40	.18
❑ 123 Drew Bledsoe	.75	.35
❑ 124 Terry Allen	.40	.18
❑ 125 Cameron Cleeland	.25	.11
❑ 126 Eddie Kennison	.40	.18
❑ 127 Amani Toomer	.25	.11
❑ 128 Kerry Collins	.40	.18
❑ 129 Joe Jurevicius	.40	.18
❑ 130 Tiki Barber	.40	.18
❑ 131 Ike Hilliard	.25	.11
❑ 132 Michael Strahan	.40	.18
❑ 133 Gary Brown	.25	.11
❑ 134 Jason Sehorn	.25	.11
❑ 135 Curtis Martin	.60	.25
❑ 136 Vinny Testaverde	.40	.18
❑ 137 Dedric Ward	.25	.11
❑ 138 Keyshawn Johnson	.60	.25
❑ 139 Wayne Chrebet	.40	.18
❑ 140 Tyrone Wheatley	.40	.18
❑ 141 Napoleon Kaufman	.60	.25
❑ 142 Tim Brown	.60	.25
❑ 143 Rickey Dudley	.25	.11
❑ 144 Jon Ritchie	.25	.11
❑ 145 James Jett	.25	.11
❑ 146 Rich Gannon	.60	.25
❑ 147 Charles Woodson	.60	.25
❑ 148 Charles Johnson	.25	.11
❑ 149 Duce Staley	.60	.25
❑ 150 Will Blackwell	.25	.11
❑ 151 Kordell Stewart	.40	.18
❑ 152 Jerome Bettis	.60	.25
❑ 153 Hines Ward	.60	.25
❑ 154 Richard Huntley	.40	.18
❑ 155 Natrone Means	.40	.18
❑ 156 Mikhael Ricks	.25	.11
❑ 157 Junior Seau	.60	.25
❑ 158 Jim Harbaugh	.40	.18
❑ 159 Ryan Leaf	.60	.25
❑ 160 Erik Kramer	.25	.11
❑ 161 Terrell Owens	.60	.25
❑ 162 J.J. Stokes	.40	.18
❑ 163 Lawrence Phillips	.40	.18
❑ 164 Charlie Garner	.40	.18
❑ 165 Jerry Rice	1.25	.55
❑ 166 Garrison Hearst	.40	.18
❑ 167 Steve Young	.75	.35
❑ 168 Derrick Mayes	.40	.18
❑ 169 Ahman Green	.60	.25
❑ 170 Joey Galloway	.40	.18
❑ 171 Ricky Watters	.40	.18
❑ 172 Jon Kitna	.60	.25
❑ 173 Sean Dawkins	.25	.11
❑ 174 Az-Zahir Hakim	.25	.11
❑ 175 Robert Holcombe	.25	.11
❑ 176 Isaac Bruce	.60	.25
❑ 177 Amp Lee	.25	.11
❑ 178 Marshall Faulk	.75	.35
❑ 179 Trent Green	.60	.25
❑ 180 Eric Zeier	.40	.18
❑ 181 Bert Emanuel	.40	.18
❑ 182 Jacquez Green	.25	.11
❑ 183 Reidel Anthony	.40	.18
❑ 184 Warren Sapp	.25	.11
❑ 185 Mike Alstott	.60	.25
❑ 186 Warrick Dunn	.60	.25
❑ 187 Trent Dilfer	.60	.25
❑ 188 Neil O'Donnell	.40	.18
❑ 189 Eddie George	.60	.25
❑ 190 Yancey Thigpen	.25	.11
❑ 191 Steve McNair	.60	.25
❑ 192 Kevin Dyson	.40	.18
❑ 193 Frank Wycheck	.25	.11
❑ 194 Stephen Davis	.60	.25
❑ 195 Stephen Alexander	.25	.11
❑ 196 Darrell Green	.25	.11
❑ 197 Skip Hicks	.25	.11
❑ 198 Brad Johnson	.60	.25
❑ 199 Michael Westbrook	.40	.18
❑ 200 Albert Connell	.25	.11
❑ 201 David Boston RC	3.00	1.35
❑ 202 Joel Makovicka RC	3.00	1.35
❑ 203 Chris Greisen RC	2.50	1.10
❑ 204 Jeff Paulk RC	1.50	.70
❑ 205 Reginald Kelly RC	2.50	1.10
❑ 206 Chris McAlister RC	2.50	1.10
❑ 207 Brandon Stokley RC	4.00	1.80
❑ 208 Antoine Winfield RC	2.50	1.10
❑ 209 Bobby Collins RC	1.50	.70
❑ 210 Peerless Price RC	8.00	3.60
❑ 211 Shawn Bryson RC	3.00	1.35

❑ 212 Sheldon Jackson RC	2.50	1.10
❑ 213 Kamil Loud RC	1.50	.70
❑ 214 D'Wayne Bates RC	2.50	1.10
❑ 215 Jerry Azumah RC	2.50	1.10
❑ 216 Marty Booker RC	3.00	1.35
❑ 217 Cade McNown RC	2.50	1.10
❑ 218 James Allen RC	3.00	1.35
❑ 219 Nick Williams RC	2.50	1.10
❑ 220 Akili Smith RC	2.50	1.10
❑ 221 Craig Yeast RC	2.50	1.10
❑ 222 Damon Griffen RC	2.50	1.10
❑ 223 Scott Covington RC	3.00	1.35
❑ 224 Michael Basnight RC	1.50	.70
❑ 225 Ronnie Powell RC	1.50	.70
❑ 226 Rahim Abdullah RC	2.50	1.10
❑ 227 Tim Couch RC	3.00	1.35
❑ 228 Kevin Johnson RC	3.00	1.35
❑ 229 Darrin Chiaverini RC	2.50	1.10
❑ 230 Mark Campbell RC	2.50	1.10
❑ 231 Mike Lucky RC	2.50	1.10
❑ 232 Robert Thomas RC	2.50	1.10
❑ 233 Ebenezer Ekuban RC	2.50	1.10
❑ 234 Dat Nguyen RC	3.00	1.35
❑ 235 Wane McGarity RC	1.50	.70
❑ 236 Jason Tucker RC	2.50	1.10
❑ 237 Olandis Gary RC	3.00	1.35
❑ 238 Al Wilson RC	3.00	1.35
❑ 239 Travis McGriff RC	1.50	.70
❑ 240 Desmond Clark RC	3.00	1.35
❑ 241 Andre Cooper RC	1.50	.70
❑ 242 Chris Watson RC	1.50	.70
❑ 243 Sedrick Irvin RC	1.50	.70
❑ 244 Chris Claiborne RC	1.50	.70
❑ 245 Cory Sauter RC	1.50	.70
❑ 246 Brock Olivo RC	1.50	.70
❑ 247 De'Mond Parker RC	1.50	.70
❑ 248 Aaron Brooks RC	15.00	6.75
❑ 249 Antuan Edwards RC	2.50	1.10
❑ 250 Basil Mitchell RC	1.50	.70
❑ 251 Terrence Wilkins RC	2.50	1.10
❑ 252 Edgerrin James RC	15.00	6.75
❑ 253 Fernando Bryant RC	2.50	1.10
❑ 254 Mike Cloud RC	2.50	1.10
❑ 255 Larry Parker RC	3.00	1.35
❑ 256 Rob Konrad RC	3.00	1.35
❑ 257 Cecil Collins RC	1.50	.70
❑ 258 James Johnson RC	2.50	1.10
❑ 259 Jim Kleinsasser RC	3.00	1.35
❑ 260 Daunte Culpepper RC	15.00	6.75
❑ 261 Michael Bishop RC	3.00	1.35
❑ 262 Andy Katzenmoyer RC	2.50	1.10
❑ 263 Kevin Faulk RC	3.00	1.35
❑ 264 Brett Bech RC	1.50	.70
❑ 265 Ricky Williams RC	8.00	3.60
❑ 266 Sean Bennett RC	1.50	.70
❑ 267 Joe Montgomery RC	2.50	1.10
❑ 268 Dan Campbell RC	1.50	.70
❑ 269 Ray Lucas RC	3.00	1.35
❑ 270 Scott Dreisbach RC	2.50	1.10
❑ 271 Jed Weaver RC	1.50	.70
❑ 272 Dameane Douglas RC	2.50	1.10
❑ 273 Cecil Martin RC	2.50	1.10
❑ 274 Donovan McNabb RC	20.00	9.00
❑ 275 Na Brown RC	2.50	1.10
❑ 276 Jerame Tuman RC	2.50	1.10
❑ 277 Amos Zereoue RC	3.00	1.35
❑ 278 Troy Edwards RC	2.50	1.10
❑ 279 Jermaine Fazande RC	2.50	1.10
❑ 280 Steve Heiden RC	1.50	.70
❑ 281 Jeff Garcia RC	20.00	9.00
❑ 282 Terry Jackson RC	2.50	1.10
❑ 283 Charlie Rogers RC	2.50	1.10
❑ 284 Brock Huard RC	3.00	1.35
❑ 285 Karsten Bailey RC	2.50	1.10
❑ 286 Lamar King RC	1.50	.70
❑ 287 Justin Watson RC	1.50	.70
❑ 288 Kurt Warner RC	20.00	9.00
❑ 289 Torry Holt RC	12.00	5.50
❑ 290 Joe Germaine RC	2.50	1.10
❑ 291 Dre' Bly RC	3.00	1.35
❑ 292 Martin Gramatica RC	1.50	.70
❑ 293 Rabih Abdullah RC	2.50	1.10
❑ 294 Shaun King RC	2.50	1.10
❑ 295 Anthony McFarland RC	2.50	1.10
❑ 296 Darnell McDonald RC	2.50	1.10
❑ 297 Kevin Daft RC	2.50	1.10
❑ 298 Jevon Kearse RC	8.00	3.60
❑ 299 Mike Sellers	.25	.11
❑ 300 Champ Bailey RC	6.00	2.70

1999 Leaf Rookies and Stars Longevity

	Nm-Mt	Ex-Mt

*STARS: 20X TO 50X BASIC CARDS
*RCs: 2X TO 5X

2000 Leaf Rookies and Stars

	Nm-Mt	Ex-Mt
COMP.SET w/o SP's (100)	15.00	6.75
❑ 1 Jake Plummer	.40	.18
❑ 2 David Boston	.60	.25
❑ 3 Tim Dwight	.60	.25
❑ 4 Jamal Anderson	.60	.25
❑ 5 Chris Chandler	.40	.18
❑ 6 Tony Banks	.40	.18
❑ 7 Qadry Ismail	.40	.18
❑ 8 Eric Moulds	.60	.25
❑ 9 Doug Flutie	.60	.25
❑ 10 Lamar Smith	.40	.18
❑ 11 Peerless Price	.60	.25
❑ 12 Rob Johnson	.40	.18
❑ 13 Reggie White	.60	.25
❑ 14 Muhsin Muhammad	.40	.18
❑ 15 Steve Beuerlein	.40	.18
❑ 16 Cade McNown	.25	.11
❑ 17 Derrick Alexander	.40	.18
❑ 18 Marcus Robinson	.60	.25
❑ 19 Corey Dillon	.60	.25
❑ 20 Akili Smith	.25	.11
❑ 21 Tim Couch	.40	.18
❑ 22 Kevin Johnson	.60	.25
❑ 23 Emmitt Smith	1.25	.55
❑ 24 Troy Aikman	1.25	.55
❑ 25 Joey Galloway	.40	.18
❑ 26 Rocket Ismail	.40	.18
❑ 27 John Elway	2.00	.90
❑ 28 Terrell Davis	.60	.25
❑ 29 Brian Griese	.60	.25
❑ 30 Olandis Gary	.60	.25
❑ 31 Ed McCaffrey	.60	.25
❑ 32 Rod Smith	.40	.18
❑ 33 Barry Sanders	1.50	.70
❑ 34 Charlie Batch	.60	.25
❑ 35 Germane Crowell	.25	.11
❑ 36 James Stewart	.40	.18
❑ 37 Brett Favre	2.00	.90
❑ 38 Dorsey Levens	.40	.18
❑ 39 Antonio Freeman	.60	.25
❑ 40 Peyton Manning	1.50	.70
❑ 41 Edgerrin James	1.00	.45
❑ 42 Marvin Harrison	.60	.25
❑ 43 Fred Taylor	.60	.25
❑ 44 Mark Brunell	.60	.25
❑ 45 Jimmy Smith	.40	.18
❑ 46 Elvis Grbac	.40	.18
❑ 47 Tony Gonzalez	.40	.18
❑ 48 Dan Marino	2.00	.90
❑ 49 Joe Horn	.40	.18
❑ 50 Jay Fiedler	.60	.25
❑ 51 James Allen	.40	.18
❑ 52 Randy Moss	1.25	.55
❑ 53 Daunte Culpepper	.75	.35
❑ 54 Cris Carter	.60	.25
❑ 55 Robert Smith	.60	.25
❑ 56 Drew Bledsoe	.75	.35
❑ 57 Terry Glenn	.60	.25
❑ 58 Ricky Williams	.60	.25
❑ 59 Amani Toomer	.40	.18
❑ 60 Kerry Collins	.40	.18
❑ 61 Curtis Martin	.60	.25
❑ 62 Vinny Testaverde	.40	.18
❑ 63 Wayne Chrebet	.40	.18
❑ 64 Tim Brown	.60	.25
❑ 65 Tyrone Wheatley	.40	.18
❑ 66 Rich Gannon	.60	.25
❑ 67 Donovan McNabb	1.00	.45
❑ 68 Duce Staley	.60	.25
❑ 69 Jerome Bettis	.60	.25
❑ 70 Donald Hayes	.25	.11
❑ 71 Junior Seau	.60	.25
❑ 72 Jermaine Fazande	.25	.11
❑ 73 Jerry Rice	1.25	.55
❑ 74 Steve Young	.75	.35
❑ 75 Terrell Owens	.60	.25
❑ 76 Charlie Garner	.40	.18
❑ 77 Jeff Garcia	.60	.25
❑ 78 Tim Biakabutuka	.40	.18
❑ 79 Tiki Barber	.40	.18
❑ 80 Ricky Watters	.40	.18
❑ 81 Kurt Warner	1.25	.55
❑ 82 Marshall Faulk	.75	.35
❑ 83 Isaac Bruce	.60	.25
❑ 84 Torry Holt	.60	.25
❑ 85 Mike Alstott	.60	.25
❑ 86 Warrick Dunn	.60	.25
❑ 87 Shaun King	.25	.11
❑ 88 Keyshawn Johnson	.60	.25
❑ 89 Warren Sapp	.40	.18
❑ 90 Eddie George	.60	.25
❑ 91 Jevon Kearse	.60	.25
❑ 92 Steve McNair	.60	.25
❑ 93 Carl Pickens	.40	.18
❑ 94 Deion Sanders	.60	.25
❑ 95 Stephen Davis	.60	.25
❑ 96 Brad Johnson	.60	.25
❑ 97 Bruce Smith	.40	.18
❑ 98 Michael Westbrook	.40	.18
❑ 99 Albert Connell	.25	.11
❑ 100 Jeff George	.40	.18
❑ 101 Thomas Jones RC	15.00	6.75
❑ 102 Bashir Yamini RC	5.00	2.20
❑ 103 Jamal Lewis RC	25.00	11.00
❑ 104 Travis Taylor RC	10.00	4.50
❑ 105 Chris Redman RC	8.00	3.60
❑ 106 Avion Black RC	8.00	3.60
❑ 107 Sammy Morris RC	8.00	3.60
❑ 108 Dez White RC	10.00	4.50
❑ 109 Peter Warrick RC	10.00	4.50
❑ 110 Ron Dugans RC	5.00	2.20
❑ 111 Curtis Keaton RC	8.00	3.60
❑ 112 Danny Farmer RC	8.00	3.60
❑ 113 Courtney Brown RC	10.00	4.50
❑ 114 Dennis Northcutt RC	10.00	4.50
❑ 115 Travis Prentice RC	8.00	3.60
❑ 116 JaJuan Dawson RC	5.00	2.20
❑ 117 Spergon Wynn RC	8.00	3.60
❑ 118 Michael Wiley RC	8.00	3.60
❑ 119 Chris Cole RC	8.00	3.60
❑ 120 Mike Anderson RC	10.00	4.50
❑ 121 Muneer Moore RC	5.00	2.20
❑ 122 Reuben Droughns RC	12.00	5.50
❑ 123 Bubba Franks RC	10.00	4.50
❑ 124 Anthony Lucas RC	5.00	2.20
❑ 125 Charles Lee RC	5.00	2.20
❑ 126 R.Jay Soward RC	8.00	3.60
❑ 127 Shyrone Stith RC	8.00	3.60
❑ 128 Sylvester Morris RC	8.00	3.60
❑ 129 Frank Moreau RC	8.00	3.60
❑ 130 Dante Hall RC	20.00	9.00
❑ 131 Doug Chapman RC	8.00	3.60
❑ 132 Troy Walters RC	10.00	4.50
❑ 133 J.R. Redmond RC	8.00	3.60
❑ 134 Tom Brady RC	100.00	45.00
❑ 135 Terrelle Smith RC	8.00	3.60
❑ 136 Chad Morton RC	10.00	4.50
❑ 137 Ron Dayne RC	10.00	4.50
❑ 138 Ron Dixon RC	8.00	3.60
❑ 139 Chad Pennington RC	40.00	18.00
❑ 140 Anthony Becht RC	10.00	4.50
❑ 141 Laveranues Coles RC	12.00	5.50
❑ 142 Windrell Hayes RC	8.00	3.60
❑ 143 Sebastian Janikowski RC	10.00	4.50
❑ 144 Jerry Porter RC	12.00	5.50
❑ 145 Corey Simon RC	10.00	4.50
❑ 146 Todd Pinkston RC	10.00	4.50

❑	147 Gari Scott RC	5.00	2.20
❑	148 Plaxico Burress RC	20.00	9.00
❑	149 Tee Martin RC	10.00	4.50
❑	150 Trevor Gaylor RC	8.00	3.60
❑	151 Ronney Jenkins RC	8.00	3.60
❑	152 Giovanni Carmazzi RC	8.00	3.60
❑	153 Tim Rattay RC	20.00	9.00
❑	154 Shaun Alexander RC	25.00	11.00
❑	155 Darrell Jackson RC	15.00	6.75
❑	156 James Williams RC	8.00	3.60
❑	157 Trung Canidate RC	8.00	3.60
❑	158 Joe Hamilton RC	8.00	3.60
❑	159 Erron Kinney RC	10.00	4.50
❑	160 Todd Husak RC	10.00	4.50
❑	161 Raynoch Thompson RC	8.00	3.60
❑	162 Darwin Walker RC	5.00	2.20
❑	163 Jay Tant RC	5.00	2.20
❑	164 Doug Johnson RC	10.00	4.50
❑	165 Robert Bean RC	8.00	3.60
❑	166 Mark Simoneau RC	8.00	3.60
❑	167 John Jones RC	8.00	3.60
❑	168 Obafemi Ayanbadejo RC	8.00	3.60
❑	169 Mike Brown RC	15.00	6.75
❑	170 Shockmain Davis RC	5.00	2.20
❑	171 Erik Flowers RC	8.00	3.60
❑	172 Corey Moore RC	5.00	2.20
❑	173 Drew Haddad RC	5.00	2.20
❑	174 Kwame Cavil RC	5.00	2.20
❑	175 Pat Dennis RC	5.00	2.20
❑	176 Rashard Anderson RC	8.00	3.60
❑	177 Brian Finneran RC	10.00	4.50
❑	178 Na'il Diggs RC	8.00	3.60
❑	179 Marc Bulger RC	20.00	9.00
❑	180 Mondriel Fulcher RC	5.00	2.20
❑	181 Dwayne Carswell	5.00	2.20
❑	182 Brian Urlacher RC	25.00	11.00
❑	183 Paul Edinger RC	10.00	4.50
❑	184 Karon Coleman RC	8.00	3.60
❑	185 Aaron Shea RC	8.00	3.60
❑	186 Fabien Bownes RC	5.00	2.20
❑	187 Damon Hodge RC	8.00	3.60
❑	188 Dwayne Goodrich RC	5.00	2.20
❑	189 Clint Stoerner RC	8.00	3.60
❑	190 James Whalen RC	5.00	2.20
❑	191 Deltha O'Neal RC	10.00	4.50
❑	192 Ian Gold RC	8.00	3.60
❑	193 Kenoy Kennedy RC	5.00	2.20
❑	194 Jarious Jackson RC	8.00	3.60
❑	195 Leroy Fields RC	5.00	2.20
❑	196 Barrett Green RC	5.00	2.20
❑	197 Joey Jamison RC	5.00	2.20
❑	198 Rondell Mealey RC	5.00	2.20
❑	199 Rob Morris RC	8.00	3.60
❑	200 Marcus Washington RC	8.00	3.60
❑	201 Trevor Insley RC	5.00	2.20
❑	202 Jamel White RC	8.00	3.60
❑	203 Kevin McDougal RC	8.00	3.60
❑	204 Ibn Green RC	5.00	2.20
❑	205 T.J. Slaughter RC	5.00	2.20
❑	206 Emanuel Smith RC	5.00	2.20
❑	207 Herbert Goodman RC	8.00	3.60
❑	208 William Bartee RC	8.00	3.60
❑	209 Orantes Grant RC	5.00	2.20
❑	210 Brad Hoover RC	8.00	3.60
❑	211 Deon Dyer RC	8.00	3.60
❑	212 Jonas Lewis RC	5.00	2.20
❑	213 Chris Hovan RC	8.00	3.60
❑	214 Fred Robbins RC	5.00	2.20
❑	215 Michael Boireau RC	5.00	2.20
❑	216 Giles Cole RC	5.00	2.20
❑	217 Dave Stachelski RC	5.00	2.20
❑	218 Patrick Pass RC	8.00	3.60
❑	219 Darren Howard RC	8.00	3.60
❑	220 Austin Wheatley RC	5.00	2.20
❑	221 Kevin Houser RC	8.00	3.60
❑	222 Rian Lindell RC	5.00	2.20
❑	223 Jake Delhomme RC	50.00	22.00
❑	224 Cornelius Griffin RC	8.00	3.60
❑	225 Shaun Ellis RC	10.00	4.50
❑	226 John Abraham RC	10.00	4.50
❑	227 Travares Tillman RC	5.00	2.20
❑	228 Julian Peterson RC	10.00	4.50
❑	229 Marcus Knight RC	8.00	3.60
❑	230 Thomas Hamner RC	5.00	2.20
❑	231 Hank Poteat RC	8.00	3.60
❑	232 Neil Rackers RC	5.00	2.20
❑	233 Bobby Shaw RC	8.00	3.60
❑	234 Rogers Beckett RC	8.00	3.60
❑	235 Reggie Jones RC	5.00	2.20
❑	236 Tim Seder RC	8.00	3.60
❑	237 Durell Price RC	5.00	2.20
❑	238 Ahmed Plummer RC	10.00	4.50
❑	239 John Engelberger RC	8.00	3.60
❑	240 Paul Smith RC	8.00	3.60
❑	241 Chafie Fields RC	5.00	2.20
❑	242 Kevin Feterik RC	5.00	2.20
❑	243 Jacoby Shepherd RC	5.00	2.20
❑	244 Nate Webster RC	5.00	2.20
❑	245 Ketric Sanford RC	5.00	2.20
❑	246 Tavarus Hogans RC	5.00	2.20
❑	247 Keith Bulluck RC	10.00	4.50
❑	248 Mike Green RC	8.00	3.60
❑	249 Chris Coleman RC	10.00	4.50
❑	250 Demario Brown RC	5.00	2.20
❑	251 Billy Volek RC	15.00	6.75
❑	252 Mareno Philyaw RC	5.00	2.20
❑	253 Ethan Howell RC	5.00	2.20
❑	254 Chris Samuels RC	8.00	3.60
❑	255 Brandon Short RC	8.00	3.60
❑	256 Maurice Smith RC	8.00	3.60
❑	257 Frank Murphy RC	5.00	2.20
❑	258 Darrick Vaughn RC	5.00	2.20
❑	259 Payton Williams RC	5.00	2.20
❑	260 JaJuan Seider RC	5.00	2.20
❑	261 Antonio Banks EP RC	2.00	.90
❑	262 Jonathan Brown EP RC	2.00	.90
❑	263 Ontiwaun Carter EP RC	2.00	.90
❑	264 Jeremaine Copeland EP	2.00	.90
❑	265 Ralph Dawkins EP RC	3.00	1.35
❑	266 Marques Douglas EP RC	2.00	.90
❑	267 Kevin Drake EP RC	2.00	.90
❑	268 Damon Dunn EP RC	3.00	1.35
❑	269 Todd Floyd EP RC	2.00	.90
❑	270 Tony Graziani EP	3.00	1.35
❑	271 Derrick Ham EP RC	3.00	1.35
❑	272 Duane Hawthorne EP RC	3.00	1.35
❑	273 Alonzo Johnson EP RC	2.00	.90
❑	274 Mark Kacmarynski EP RC	2.00	.90
❑	275 Eric Kresser EP	2.00	.90
❑	276 Jim Kubiak EP RC	3.00	1.35
❑	277 Blaine McElmurry EP RC	2.00	.90
❑	278 Scott Milanovich EP	3.00	1.35
❑	279 Norman Miller EP RC	2.00	.90
❑	280 Sean Morey EP RC	3.00	1.35
❑	281 Jeff Ogden EP	3.00	1.35
❑	282 Pepe Pearson EP RC	3.00	1.35
❑	283 Ron Powlus EP RC	4.00	1.80
❑	284 Jason Shelley EP RC	2.00	.90
❑	285 Ben Snell EP RC	2.00	.90
❑	286 Aaron Stecker EP RC	4.00	1.80
❑	287 L.C. Stevens EP	2.00	.90
❑	288 Mike Sutton EP RC	2.00	.90
❑	289 Damian Vaughn EP RC	2.00	.90
❑	290 Ted White EP	2.00	.90
❑	291 Marcus Crandell EP RC	3.00	1.35
❑	292 Darryl Daniel EP RC	3.00	1.35
❑	293 Jesse Haynes EP	2.00	.90
❑	294 Matt Lytle EP RC	3.00	1.35
❑	295 Deon Mitchell EP RC	3.00	1.35
❑	296 Kendrick Nord EP RC	2.00	.90
❑	297 Ronnie Powell EP	2.00	.90
❑	298 Selucio Sanford EP RC	3.00	1.35
❑	299 Corey Thomas EP	2.00	.90
❑	300 Vershan Jackson EP RC	2.00	.90
❑	301 Michael Vick XRC	60.00	27.00
❑	302 Drew Brees XRC	25.00	11.00
❑	303 Quincy Carter XRC	12.00	5.50
❑	304 Marques Tuiasosopa XRC	15.00	6.75
❑	305 Chris Weinke XRC	10.00	4.50
❑	306 LaDainian Tomlinson	50.00	22.00
❑	307 Deuce McAllister XRC	30.00	13.50
❑	308 Michael Bennett XRC	25.00	11.00
❑	309 Anthony Thomas XRC	20.00	9.00
❑	310 LaMont Jordan XRC	20.00	9.00
❑	311 David Terrell XRC	12.00	5.50
❑	312 Koren Robinson XRC	15.00	6.75
❑	313 Rod Gardner XRC	15.00	6.75
❑	314 Santana Moss XRC	20.00	9.00
❑	315 Freddie Mitchell XRC	10.00	4.50
❑	316 Gerard Warren XRC	10.00	4.50
❑	317 Justin Smith XRC	10.00	4.50
❑	318 Richard Seymour XRC	20.00	9.00
❑	319 Andre Carter XRC	10.00	4.50
❑	320 Jamal Reynolds XRC	10.00	4.50

2000 Leaf Rookies and Stars Longevity

Nm-Mt Ex-Mt

*LONGEVITY STARS: 12X TO 30X BASIC CARDS

*LONGEVITY RC's: 1X TO 2.5X BASIC CARDS

*LONGEVITY EP's: 1.5X TO 4X BASIC CARDS

2000 Leaf Rookies and Stars Autographs

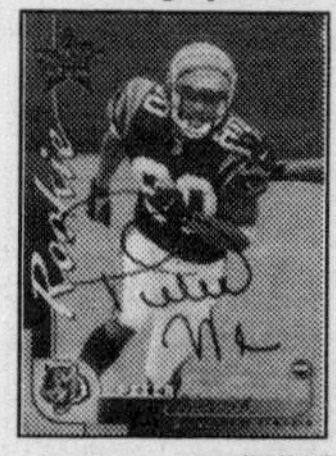

		Nm-Mt	Ex-Mt
❑	101 Thomas Jones EXCH	5.00	2.20
❑	103 Jamal Lewis	60.00	27.00
❑	104 Travis Taylor	30.00	13.50
❑	105 Chris Redman	25.00	11.00
❑	108 Dez White EXCH		
❑	109 Peter Warrick	40.00	18.00
❑	110 Ron Dugans EXCH		
❑	112 Danny Farmer EXCH		
❑	113 Courtney Brown	30.00	13.50
❑	115 Travis Prentice EXCH		
❑	116 JaJuan Dawson EXCH		
❑	120 Mike Anderson	30.00	13.50
❑	123 Bubba Franks	30.00	13.50
❑	126 R.Jay Soward	20.00	9.00
❑	127 Shyrone Stith EXCH		
❑	128 Sylvester Morris EXCH		
❑	133 J.R. Redmond EXCH		
❑	137 Ron Dayne	30.00	13.50
❑	138 Ron Dixon EXCH		
❑	139 Chad Pennington	100.00	45.00
❑	141 Laveranues Coles	40.00	18.00
❑	144 Jerry Porter	40.00	18.00
❑	145 Corey Simon	30.00	13.50
❑	146 Todd Pinkston	30.00	9.00
❑	148 Plaxico Burress	50.00	22.00
❑	152 Giovanni Carmazzi EXCH		
❑	154 Shaun Alexander	80.00	36.00
❑	155 Darrell Jackson EXCH		
❑	157 Trung Canidate	25.00	11.00
❑	261 Antonio Banks	12.00	5.50
❑	262 Jonathan Brown	12.00	5.50
❑	263 Ontiwaun Carter	12.00	5.50
❑	264 Jeremaine Copeland	12.00	5.50
❑	265 Ralph Dawkins EXCH		
❑	266 Marques Douglas	12.00	5.50
❑	267 Kevin Drake	12.00	5.50
❑	268 Damon Dunn	12.00	5.50
❑	269 Todd Floyd	12.00	5.50
❑	270 Tony Graziani	12.00	5.50
❑	271 Derrick Ham EXCH		
❑	272 Duane Hawthorne	12.00	5.50
❑	273 Alonzo Johnson EXCH		
❑	274 Mark Kacmarynski	12.00	5.50
❑	275 Eric Kresser	12.00	5.50
❑	276 Jim Kubiak	12.00	5.50
❑	277 Blaine McElmurry EXCH		
❑	278 Scott Milanovich EXCH		
❑	279 Norman Miller	12.00	5.50
❑	280 Sean Morey	12.00	5.50
❑	281 Jeff Ogden	12.00	5.50
❑	282 Pepe Pearson	12.00	5.50
❑	283 Ron Powlus	20.00	9.00
❑	284 Jason Shelley	12.00	5.50
❑	285 Ben Snell	12.00	5.50
❑	286 Aaron Stecker	15.00	6.75
❑	287 L.C. Stevens	12.00	5.50
❑	288 Mike Sutton	12.00	5.50

❑ 289 Damian Vaughn EXCH		
❑ 290 Ted White	12.00	5.50
❑ 291 Marcus Crandell EXCH		
❑ 292 Darryl Daniel	12.00	5.50
❑ 293 Jesse Haynes EXCH		
❑ 294 Matt Lytle	12.00	5.50
❑ 295 Deon Mitchell	12.00	5.50
❑ 296 Kendrick Nord	12.00	5.50
❑ 297 Ronnie Powell EXCH		
❑ 298 Selucio Sanford	12.00	5.50
❑ 299 Corey Thomas	12.00	5.50
❑ 300 Vershan Jackson	12.00	5.50

2001 Leaf Rookies and Stars

	Nm-Mt	Ex-Mt
COMP.SET w/o SP's (100)	20.00	6.00
❑ 1 Aaron Brooks	.60	.18
❑ 2 Ahman Green	.60	.18
❑ 3 Antonio Freeman	.60	.18
❑ 4 Brad Johnson	.60	.18
❑ 5 Brett Favre	2.00	.60
❑ 6 Brian Griese	.60	.18
❑ 7 Brian Urlacher	1.00	.30
❑ 8 Bruce Smith	.25	.07
❑ 9 Cade McNown	.25	.07
❑ 10 Chad Pennington	1.00	.30
❑ 11 Champ Bailey	.40	.12
❑ 12 Charles Woodson	.40	.12
❑ 13 Charlie Batch	.60	.18
❑ 14 Charlie Garner	.40	.12
❑ 15 Corey Dillon	.60	.18
❑ 16 Cris Carter	.60	.18
❑ 17 Curtis Martin	.60	.18
❑ 18 Dan Marino	2.50	.75
❑ 19 Daunte Culpepper	.60	.18
❑ 20 David Boston	.60	.18
❑ 21 Deion Sanders	.60	.18
❑ 22 Donovan McNabb	.75	.23
❑ 23 Doug Flutie	.60	.18
❑ 24 Drew Bledsoe	.75	.23
❑ 25 Duce Staley	.60	.18
❑ 26 Ed McCaffrey	.60	.18
❑ 27 Eddie George	.60	.18
❑ 28 Edgerrin James	.75	.23
❑ 29 Elvis Grbac	.40	.12
❑ 30 Emmitt Smith	1.25	.35
❑ 31 Eric Moulds	.40	.12
❑ 32 Fred Taylor	.60	.18
❑ 33 Germane Crowell	.25	.07
❑ 34 Ike Hilliard	.40	.12
❑ 35 Isaac Bruce	.60	.18
❑ 36 Jake Plummer	.40	.12
❑ 37 Jamal Anderson	.60	.18
❑ 38 Jamal Lewis	1.00	.30
❑ 39 James Allen	.40	.12
❑ 40 James Stewart	.40	.12
❑ 41 Jay Fiedler	.60	.18
❑ 42 Jeff Garcia	.60	.18
❑ 43 Jeff George	.40	.12
❑ 44 Jeff Lewis	.25	.07
❑ 45 Jerome Bettis	.60	.18
❑ 46 Jerry Rice	1.25	.35
❑ 47 Jevon Kearse	.40	.12
❑ 48 Jimmy Smith	.40	.12
❑ 49 Joey Galloway	.40	.12
❑ 50 John Elway	2.50	.75
❑ 51 Junior Seau	.60	.18
❑ 52 Keenan McCardell	.25	.07
❑ 53 Kerry Collins	.40	.12
❑ 54 Kevin Johnson	.40	.12
❑ 55 Keyshawn Johnson	.60	.18
❑ 56 Kordell Stewart	.40	.12
❑ 57 Kurt Warner	1.25	.35
❑ 58 Lamar Smith	.40	.12
❑ 59 Marcus Robinson	.60	.18
❑ 60 Mark Brunell	.60	.18
❑ 61 Marshall Faulk	.75	.23
❑ 62 Marvin Harrison	.60	.18
❑ 63 Matt Hasselbeck	.40	.12
❑ 64 Mike Alstott	.60	.18
❑ 65 Mike Anderson	.60	.18
❑ 66 Muhsin Muhammad	.40	.12
❑ 67 Peter Warrick	.60	.18
❑ 68 Peyton Manning	1.50	.45
❑ 69 Priest Holmes	.75	.23
❑ 70 Randy Moss	1.25	.35
❑ 71 Ray Lewis	.60	.18
❑ 72 Rich Gannon	.60	.18
❑ 73 Ricky Watters	.40	.12
❑ 74 Ricky Williams	.60	.18
❑ 75 Rob Johnson	.40	.12
❑ 76 Rod Smith	.40	.12
❑ 77 Ron Dayne	.60	.18
❑ 78 Shannon Sharpe	.40	.12
❑ 79 Shaun Alexander	.75	.23
❑ 80 Stephen Davis	.60	.18
❑ 81 Steve McNair	.60	.18
❑ 82 Steve Young	.75	.23
❑ 83 Sylvester Morris	.25	.07
❑ 84 Terrell Davis	.60	.18
❑ 85 Terrell Owens	.60	.18
❑ 86 Thomas Jones	.40	.12
❑ 87 Tim Brown	.60	.18
❑ 88 Tim Couch	.40	.12
❑ 89 Tony Banks	.40	.12
❑ 90 Tony Gonzalez	.40	.12
❑ 91 Torry Holt	.60	.18
❑ 92 Travis Taylor	.40	.12
❑ 93 Trent Green	.60	.18
❑ 94 Troy Aikman	1.00	.30
❑ 95 Tyrone Wheatley	.40	.12
❑ 96 Vinny Testaverde	.40	.12
❑ 97 Warren Sapp	.40	.12
❑ 98 Warrick Dunn	.60	.18
❑ 99 Wayne Chrebet	.40	.12
❑ 100 Zach Thomas	.60	.18
❑ 101 A.J. Feeley RC	6.00	1.80
❑ 102 Josh Booty RC	6.00	1.80
❑ 103 Roderick Robinson RC	4.00	1.20
❑ 104 Renaldo Hill RC	2.50	.75
❑ 105 Harold Blackmon RC	2.50	.75
❑ 106 Rudi Johnson RC	10.00	3.00
❑ 107 Curtis Fuller RC	2.50	.75
❑ 108 Dan Alexander RC	6.00	1.80
❑ 109 Anthony Thomas RPS	6.00	1.80
❑ 110 Travis Minor RPS	3.00	.90
❑ 111 Heath Evans RC	4.00	1.20
❑ 112 Joe Walker RC	2.50	.75
❑ 113 Moran Norris RC	2.50	.75
❑ 114 Quincy Carter RPS	4.00	1.20
❑ 115 Michael Vick RPS	25.00	7.50
❑ 116 Vinny Sutherland RC	4.00	1.20
❑ 117 Scotty Anderson RC	4.00	1.20
❑ 118 Eddie Berlin RC	4.00	1.20
❑ 119 Jonathan Carter RC	4.00	1.20
❑ 120 Monty Beisel RC	6.00	1.80
❑ 121 T.J. Houshmandzadeh RC	6.00	1.80
❑ 122 Rodney Bailey RC	2.50	.75
❑ 123 Reggie Germany RC	4.00	1.20
❑ 124 Ellis Wyms RC	2.50	.75
❑ 125 Koren Robinson RPS	5.00	1.50
❑ 126 Antonio Pierce RC	8.00	2.40
❑ 127 Arnold Jackson RC	4.00	1.20
❑ 128 Andre Rone RC	2.50	.75
❑ 129 Richard Newsome RC	2.50	.75
❑ 130 Ifeanyi Ohalete RC	2.50	.75
❑ 131 Dan O'Leary RC	4.00	1.20
❑ 132 Shad Meier RC	4.00	1.20
❑ 133 Jay Feeley RC	2.50	.75
❑ 134 B.Manumaleuna RC	4.00	1.20
❑ 135 Riall Johnson RC	2.50	.75
❑ 136 Snoop Minnis RPS	4.00	1.20
❑ 137 Jermaine Hampton RC	2.50	.75
❑ 138 Johnny Huggins RC	2.50	.75
❑ 139 Marcellus Rivers RC	4.00	1.20
❑ 140 Andre Carter RPS	6.00	1.80
❑ 141 Michael Stone RC	2.50	.75
❑ 142 Tony Dixon RC	4.00	1.20
❑ 143 Bhawoh Jue RC	6.00	1.80
❑ 144 Will Peterson RC	4.00	1.20
❑ 145 Anthony Henry RC	6.00	1.80
❑ 146 M.Tuiasosopo RPS	4.00	1.20
❑ 147 Reggie Swinton RC	4.00	1.20
❑ 148 Robert Carswell RC	2.50	.75
❑ 149 Freddie Mitchell RPS	3.00	.90
❑ 150 Idrees Bashir RC	2.50	.75
❑ 151 James Boyd RC	2.50	.75
❑ 152 Chris Chambers RPS	5.00	1.50
❑ 153 Aaron Schobel RC	6.00	1.80
❑ 154 Dominic Raiola RC	2.50	.75
❑ 155 Derrick Burgess RC	6.00	1.80
❑ 156 DeLawrence Grant RC	2.50	.75
❑ 157 Karon Riley RC	2.50	.75
❑ 158 Cedric Scott RC	4.00	1.20
❑ 159 Patrick Washington RC	4.00	1.20
❑ 160 Eric Johnson RC	12.00	3.60
❑ 161 Tevita Ofahengaue RC	2.50	.75
❑ 162 Chris Cooper RC	4.00	1.20
❑ 163 Fred Wakefield RC	4.00	1.20
❑ 164 Kenny Smith RC	4.00	1.20
❑ 165 Marcus Bell RC	4.00	1.20
❑ 166 Mario Fatafehi RC	4.00	1.20
❑ 167 Anthony Herron RC	2.50	.75
❑ 168 Joe Tafoya RC	2.50	.75
❑ 169 Morlon Greenwood RC	4.00	1.20
❑ 170 Orlando Huff RC	2.50	.75
❑ 171 Carlos Polk RC	2.50	.75
❑ 172 Edgerton Hartwell RC	2.50	.75
❑ 173 Zeke Moreno RC	6.00	1.80
❑ 174 Alex Lincoln RC	4.00	1.20
❑ 175 Quinton Caver RC	4.00	1.20
❑ 176 Matt Stewart RC	2.50	.75
❑ 177 Markus Steele RC	4.00	1.20
❑ 178 Dwight Smith RC	2.50	.75
❑ 179 Reggie Wayne RPS	6.00	1.80
❑ 180 Jerametrius Butler RC	4.00	1.20
❑ 181 Jason Doering RC	2.50	.75
❑ 182 John Howell RC	2.50	.75
❑ 183 Alvin Porter RC	2.50	.75
❑ 184 Eric Downing RC	2.50	.75
❑ 185 John Nix RC	2.50	.75
❑ 186 Tim Baker RC	2.50	.75
❑ 187 Robert Garza RC	2.50	.75
❑ 188 Randy Chevrier RC	2.50	.75
❑ 189 Drew Brees RPS	8.00	2.40
❑ 190 Shawn Worthen RC	2.50	.75
❑ 191 Drew Bennett RC	20.00	6.00
❑ 192 Marlon McCree RC	2.50	.75
❑ 193 David Terrell RPS	4.00	1.20
❑ 194 Jeff Backus RC	4.00	1.20
❑ 195 Otis Leverette RC	2.50	.75
❑ 196 Jason Glenn RC	6.00	1.80
❑ 197 Rashad Holman RC	2.50	.75
❑ 198 T.J. Turner RC	2.50	.75
❑ 199 Lynn Scott RC	6.00	1.80
❑ 200 Bill Gramatica RC	2.50	.75
❑ 201 Michael Vick RC	50.00	15.00
❑ 202 Drew Brees RC	15.00	4.50
❑ 203 Quincy Carter RC	8.00	2.40
❑ 204 Jesse Palmer RC	8.00	2.40
❑ 205 Mike McMahon RC	8.00	2.40
❑ 206 Dave Dickenson RC	4.00	1.20
❑ 207 Jameel Cook RC	5.00	1.50
❑ 208 Marques Tuiasosopo RC	8.00	2.40
❑ 209 Chris Weinke RC	6.00	1.80
❑ 210 Sage Rosenfels RC	6.00	1.80
❑ 211 Josh Heupel RC	8.00	2.40
❑ 212 LaDainian Tomlinson RC	25.00	7.50
❑ 213 Michael Bennett RC	15.00	4.50
❑ 214 Anthony Thomas RC	12.00	3.60
❑ 215 Travis Henry RC	10.00	3.00
❑ 216 James Jackson RC	6.00	1.80
❑ 217 Correll Buckhalter RC	10.00	3.00
❑ 218 Derrick Blaylock RC	8.00	2.40
❑ 219 Dee Brown RC	8.00	2.40
❑ 220 LeVar Woods RC	5.00	1.50
❑ 221 Deuce McAllister RC	20.00	6.00
❑ 222 LaMont Jordan RC	10.00	3.00
❑ 223 Kevan Barlow RC	8.00	2.40
❑ 224 Travis Minor RC	5.00	1.50
❑ 225 David Terrell RC	8.00	2.40
❑ 226 Koren Robinson RC	10.00	3.00
❑ 227 Rod Gardner RC	8.00	2.40
❑ 228 Santana Moss RC	12.00	3.60
❑ 229 Freddie Mitchell RC	8.00	2.40
❑ 230 Reggie Wayne RC	12.00	3.60

❑ 231 Quincy Morgan RC	8.00	2.40
❑ 232 Chris Chambers RC	10.00	3.00
❑ 233 Steve Smith RC	10.00	3.00
❑ 234 Snoop Minnis RC	5.00	1.50
❑ 235 Justin McCareins RC	8.00	2.40
❑ 236 Onome Ojo RC	5.00	1.50
❑ 237 Damerien McCants RC	5.00	1.50
❑ 238 Mike McMahon RPS	3.00	.90
❑ 239 Cedrick Wilson RC	8.00	2.40
❑ 240 Kevin Kasper RC	6.00	1.80
❑ 241 Chris Taylor RC	5.00	1.50
❑ 242 Ken-Yon Rambo RC	5.00	1.50
❑ 243 Richmond Flowers RC	5.00	1.50
❑ 244 Andre King RC	5.00	1.50
❑ 245 Boo Williams RC	5.00	1.50
❑ 246 Adrian Wilson RC	3.00	.90
❑ 247 Cory Bird RC	8.00	2.40
❑ 248 Alex Bannister RC	5.00	1.50
❑ 249 Elvis Joseph RC	5.00	1.50
❑ 250 Chad Johnson RC	15.00	4.50
❑ 251 Robert Ferguson RC	8.00	2.40
❑ 252 David Martin RC	5.00	1.50
❑ 253 Quentin McCord RC	5.00	1.50
❑ 254 Todd Heap RC	8.00	2.40
❑ 255 Alge Crumpler RC	10.00	3.00
❑ 256 Nate Clements RC	8.00	2.40
❑ 257 Will Allen RC	5.00	1.50
❑ 258 Willie Middlebrooks RC	5.00	1.50
❑ 259 Fred Smoot RC	8.00	2.40
❑ 260 Andre Dyson RC	3.00	.90
❑ 261 Gary Baxter RC	5.00	1.50
❑ 262 Jamar Fletcher RC	5.00	1.50
❑ 263 Ken Lucas RC	5.00	1.50
❑ 264 Tay Cody RC	3.00	.90
❑ 265 Eric Kelly RC	3.00	.90
❑ 266 Adam Archuleta RC	8.00	2.40
❑ 267 Derrick Gibson RC	5.00	1.50
❑ 268 Jarrod Cooper RC	8.00	2.40
❑ 269 Hakim Akbar RC	3.00	.90
❑ 270 Tony Driver RC	5.00	1.50
❑ 271 Justin Smith RC	8.00	2.40
❑ 272 Andre Carter RC	8.00	2.40
❑ 273 Jamal Reynolds RC	8.00	2.40
❑ 274 Gerard Warren RC	8.00	2.40
❑ 275 Richard Seymour RC	8.00	2.40
❑ 276 Damione Lewis RC	5.00	1.50
❑ 277 Casey Hampton RC	5.00	1.50
❑ 278 Marcus Stroud RC	8.00	2.40
❑ 279 Benjamin Gay RC	6.00	1.80
❑ 280 Shaun Rogers RC	8.00	2.40
❑ 281 Dan Morgan RC	8.00	2.40
❑ 282 Kendrell Bell RC	20.00	6.00
❑ 283 Tommy Polley RC	8.00	2.40
❑ 284 Jamie Winborn RC	5.00	1.50
❑ 285 Sedrick Hodge RC	3.00	.90
❑ 286 Torrance Marshall RC	8.00	2.40
❑ 287 Eric Westmoreland RC	5.00	1.50
❑ 288 Brian Allen RC	3.00	.90
❑ 289 Brandon Spoon RC	8.00	2.40
❑ 290 Henry Burris RC	5.00	1.50
❑ 291 Leonard Davis RC	5.00	1.50
❑ 292 Kenyatta Walker RC	3.00	.90
❑ 293 Cedric James RC	5.00	1.50
❑ 294 Sean Brewer RC	3.00	.90
❑ 295 Jason Brookins RC	6.00	1.80
❑ 296 Kyle Vanden Bosch RC	8.00	2.40
❑ 297 Nick Goings RC	8.00	2.40
❑ 298 Kris Jenkins RC	8.00	2.40
❑ 299 Dominic Rhodes RC	8.00	2.40
❑ 300 Leonard Myers RC	3.00	.90

2001 Leaf Rookies and Stars Longevity

	Nm-Mt	Ex-Mt
*STARS: 10X TO 25X BASIC CARDS		
*201-300 ROOKIES: 2X TO 5X		

2002 Leaf Rookies and Stars

	Nm-Mt	Ex-Mt
COMPLETE SET (300)	250.00	75.00
COMP.SET w/o SP's (100)	25.00	7.50
❑ 1 Jake Plummer	.50	.15
❑ 2 David Boston	.75	.23
❑ 3 Thomas Jones	.50	.15
❑ 4 Michael Vick	2.50	.75
❑ 5 Warrick Dunn	.75	.23
❑ 6 Jamal Lewis	.75	.23

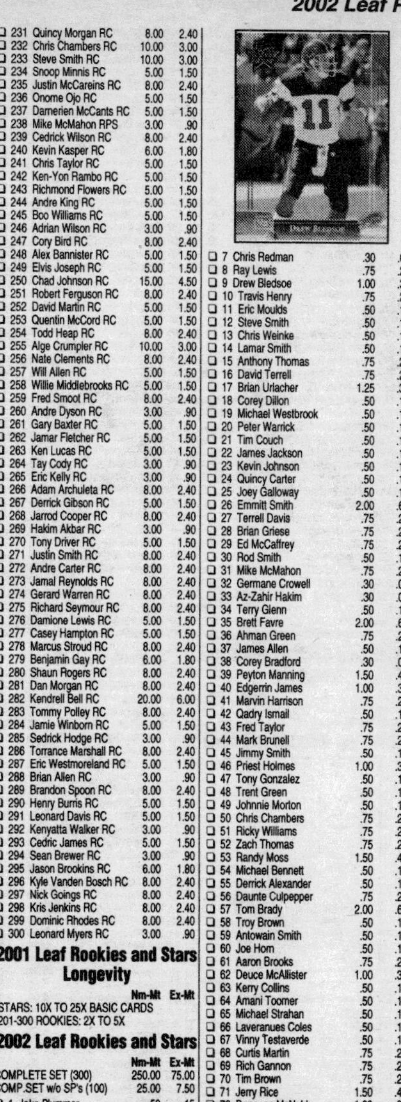

❑ 7 Chris Redman	.30	.09
❑ 8 Ray Lewis	.75	.23
❑ 9 Drew Bledsoe	1.00	.30
❑ 10 Travis Henry	.75	.23
❑ 11 Eric Moulds	.50	.15
❑ 12 Steve Smith	.50	.15
❑ 13 Chris Weinke	.50	.15
❑ 14 Lamar Smith	.50	.15
❑ 15 Anthony Thomas	.75	.23
❑ 16 David Terrell	.75	.23
❑ 17 Brian Urlacher	1.25	.35
❑ 18 Corey Dillon	.50	.15
❑ 19 Michael Westbrook	.50	.15
❑ 20 Peter Warrick	.50	.15
❑ 21 Tim Couch	.50	.15
❑ 22 James Jackson	.50	.15
❑ 23 Kevin Johnson	.50	.15
❑ 24 Quincy Carter	.50	.15
❑ 25 Joey Galloway	.50	.15
❑ 26 Emmitt Smith	2.00	.60
❑ 27 Terrell Davis	.75	.23
❑ 28 Brian Griese	.75	.23
❑ 29 Ed McCaffrey	.75	.23
❑ 30 Rod Smith	.50	.15
❑ 31 Mike McMahon	.75	.23
❑ 32 Germane Crowell	.30	.09
❑ 33 Az-Zahir Hakim	.30	.09
❑ 34 Terry Glenn	.50	.15
❑ 35 Brett Favre	2.00	.60
❑ 36 Ahman Green	.75	.23
❑ 37 James Allen	.50	.15
❑ 38 Corey Bradford	.30	.09
❑ 39 Peyton Manning	1.50	.45
❑ 40 Edgerrin James	1.00	.30
❑ 41 Marvin Harrison	.75	.23
❑ 42 Qadry Ismail	.50	.15
❑ 43 Fred Taylor	.75	.23
❑ 44 Mark Brunell	.75	.23
❑ 45 Jimmy Smith	.50	.15
❑ 46 Priest Holmes	1.00	.30
❑ 47 Tony Gonzalez	.50	.15
❑ 48 Trent Green	.50	.15
❑ 49 Johnnie Morton	.50	.15
❑ 50 Chris Chambers	.75	.23
❑ 51 Ricky Williams	.75	.23
❑ 52 Zach Thomas	.75	.23
❑ 53 Randy Moss	1.50	.45
❑ 54 Michael Bennett	.50	.15
❑ 55 Derrick Alexander	.50	.15
❑ 56 Daunte Culpepper	.75	.23
❑ 57 Tom Brady	2.00	.60
❑ 58 Troy Brown	.50	.15
❑ 59 Antowain Smith	.50	.15
❑ 60 Joe Horn	.50	.15
❑ 61 Aaron Brooks	.75	.23
❑ 62 Deuce McAllister	1.00	.30
❑ 63 Kerry Collins	.50	.15
❑ 64 Amani Toomer	.50	.15
❑ 65 Michael Strahan	.50	.15
❑ 66 Laveranues Coles	.50	.15
❑ 67 Vinny Testaverde	.50	.15
❑ 68 Curtis Martin	.75	.23
❑ 69 Rich Gannon	.75	.23
❑ 70 Tim Brown	.75	.23
❑ 71 Jerry Rice	1.50	.45
❑ 72 Donovan McNabb	1.00	.30
❑ 73 Freddie Mitchell	.50	.15
❑ 74 Duce Staley	.75	.23
❑ 75 Kordell Stewart	.50	.15
❑ 76 Jerome Bettis	.75	.23
❑ 77 Plaxico Burress	.50	.15
❑ 78 Drew Brees	.75	.23
❑ 79 LaDainian Tomlinson	1.25	.35
❑ 80 Junior Seau	.75	.23
❑ 81 Jeff Garcia	.75	.23
❑ 82 Garrison Hearst	.50	.15
❑ 83 Terrell Owens	.75	.23
❑ 84 Shaun Alexander	.75	.23
❑ 85 Koren Robinson	.50	.15
❑ 86 Kurt Warner	.75	.23
❑ 87 Marshall Faulk	.75	.23
❑ 88 Isaac Bruce	.75	.23
❑ 89 Torry Holt	.75	.23
❑ 90 Rob Johnson	.50	.15
❑ 91 Brad Johnson	.50	.15
❑ 92 Keyshawn Johnson	.75	.23
❑ 93 Mike Alstott	.75	.23
❑ 94 Eddie George	.75	.23
❑ 95 Steve McNair	.75	.23
❑ 96 Derrick Mason	.50	.15
❑ 97 Jevon Kearse	.50	.15
❑ 98 Stephen Davis	.50	.15
❑ 99 Sage Rosenfels	.30	.09
❑ 100 Rod Gardner	.50	.15
❑ 101 Adrian Peterson RC	5.00	1.50
❑ 102 Nick Rolovich RC	4.00	1.20
❑ 103 Lew Thomas RC	2.50	.75
❑ 104 David Carr RC	15.00	4.50
❑ 105 Daryl Jones RC	4.00	1.20
❑ 106 Brandon Doman RC	5.00	1.50
❑ 107 Ed Reed RC	8.00	2.40
❑ 108 Tellis Redmon RC	4.00	1.20
❑ 109 Andra Davis RC	4.00	1.20
❑ 110 Kendall Newson RC	2.50	.75
❑ 111 Joe Burns RC	5.00	1.50
❑ 112 Maurice Morris RC	5.00	1.50
❑ 113 Craig Nall RC	5.00	1.50
❑ 114 Phillip Buchanon RC	5.00	1.50
❑ 115 Mike Echols RC	2.50	.75
❑ 116 Terry Jones Jr. RC	4.00	1.20
❑ 117 Anthony Weaver RC	4.00	1.20
❑ 118 Jeb Putzier RC	5.00	1.50
❑ 119 Tony Fisher RC	5.00	1.50
❑ 120 Joey Harrington RC	15.00	4.50
❑ 121 Lamar Gordon RC	5.00	1.50
❑ 122 Tracey Wistrom RC	4.00	1.20
❑ 123 Ashley Lelie RC	10.00	3.00
❑ 124 Will Witherspoon RC	5.00	1.50
❑ 125 Travis Stephens RC	4.00	1.20
❑ 126 J.T. O'Sullivan RC	4.00	1.20
❑ 127 Brian Westbrook RC	8.00	2.40
❑ 128 James Mungro RC	5.00	1.50
❑ 129 Lamont Thompson RC	4.00	1.20
❑ 130 Jarrod Baxter RC	4.00	1.20
❑ 131 Andre Lott RC	5.00	1.50
❑ 132 Steve Bellisari RC	5.00	1.50
❑ 133 David Garrard RC	5.00	1.50
❑ 134 Michael Lewis RC	5.00	1.50
❑ 135 James Allen RC	2.50	.75
❑ 136 Bryant McKinnie RC	4.00	1.20
❑ 137 Marques Anderson RC	5.00	1.50
❑ 138 Rohan Davey RC	5.00	1.50
❑ 139 Kyle Johnson RC	2.50	.75
❑ 140 Dusty Bonner RC	2.50	.75
❑ 141 DeShaun Foster RC	5.00	1.50
❑ 142 Chad Hutchinson RC	5.00	1.50
❑ 143 Jack Brewer RC	4.00	1.20
❑ 144 Eddie Freeman RC	2.50	.75
❑ 145 Seth Burford RC	4.00	1.20
❑ 146 Roosevelt Williams RC	2.50	.75
❑ 147 Jamin Elliott RC	2.50	.75
❑ 148 Charles Grant RC	5.00	1.50
❑ 149 Jeff Kelly RC	4.00	1.20
❑ 150 Cliff Russell RC	4.00	1.20
❑ 151 Josh Scobey RC	5.00	1.50
❑ 152 Tank Williams RC	4.00	1.20
❑ 153 Larry Tripplett RC	2.50	.75
❑ 154 Clinton Portis RC	15.00	4.50
❑ 155 Javin Hunter RC	2.50	.75
❑ 156 Deveren Johnson RC	4.00	1.20
❑ 157 Reche Caldwell RC	5.00	1.50
❑ 158 Ronald Curry RC	5.00	1.50
❑ 159 Chris Hope RC	4.00	1.20
❑ 160 Damien Anderson RC	4.00	1.20
❑ 161 Saleem Rasheed RC	5.00	1.50
❑ 162 Albert Haynesworth RC	4.00	1.20
❑ 163 Bryan Gilmore RC	4.00	1.20
❑ 164 Wes Pate RC	2.50	.75
❑ 165 Deion Branch RC	10.00	3.00

❑ 166 Ben Leber RC 5.00 1.50
❑ 167 Andre Davis RC 5.00 1.50
❑ 168 Darrell Hill RC 4.00 1.20
❑ 169 Rodney Wright RC 2.50 .75
❑ 170 Demontray Carter RC 2.50 .75
❑ 171 Zak Kustok RC 5.00 1.50
❑ 172 James Wofford RC 4.00 1.20
❑ 173 David Priestley RC 4.00 1.20
❑ 174 Donte Stallworth RC 10.00 3.00
❑ 175 Marc Boerigter RC 15.00 4.50
❑ 176 Freddie Milons RC 4.00 1.20
❑ 177 John Simon RC 4.00 1.20
❑ 178 Josh Norman RC 5.00 1.50
❑ 179 Jabar Gaffney RC 5.00 1.50
❑ 180 Doug Jolley RC 5.00 1.50
❑ 181 Preston Parsons RC 2.50 .75
❑ 182 Chris Baker RC 4.00 1.20
❑ 183 Javon Walker RC 10.00 3.00
❑ 184 Justin Peelle RC 2.50 .75
❑ 185 Josh Reed RC 5.00 1.50
❑ 186 Omar Easy RC 5.00 1.50
❑ 187 Jerramy Stevens RC 5.00 1.50
❑ 188 Shaun Hill RC 5.00 1.50
❑ 189 David Thornton RC 2.50 .75
❑ 190 John Henderson RC 5.00 1.50
❑ 191 Verron Haynes RC 5.00 1.50
❑ 192 Dennis Johnson RC 2.50 .75
❑ 193 Napoleon Harris RC 5.00 1.50
❑ 194 Jonathan Wells RC 5.00 1.50
❑ 195 Howard Green RC 2.50 .75
❑ 196 Travis Fisher RC 5.00 1.50
❑ 197 Anton Palepoi RC 2.50 .75
❑ 198 Ed Stansbury RC 2.50 .75
❑ 199 Josh McCown RC 6.00 1.80
❑ 200 Alex Brown RC 5.00 1.50
❑ 201 Joseph Jefferson RC 4.00 1.20
❑ 202 Julius Peppers RC 10.00 3.00
❑ 203 Larry Ned RC 4.00 1.20
❑ 204 Rock Cartwright RC 6.00 1.80
❑ 205 Kalimba Edwards RC 5.00 1.50
❑ 206 Matt Schobel RC 4.00 1.20
❑ 207 Maurice Jackson RC 2.50 .75
❑ 208 Kelly Campbell RC 4.00 1.20
❑ 209 Mel Mitchell RC 4.00 1.20
❑ 210 Ken Simonton RC 2.50 .75
❑ 211 Brian Allen RC 4.00 1.20
❑ 212 Darnell Sanders RC 4.00 1.20
❑ 213 Jesse Chatman RC 5.00 1.50
❑ 214 Keyuo Craver RC 4.00 1.20
❑ 215 Chester Taylor RC 5.00 1.50
❑ 216 Kurt Kittner RC 4.00 1.20
❑ 217 Derek Ross RC 4.00 1.20
❑ 218 Charles Hill RC 2.50 .75
❑ 219 Jarvis Green RC 4.00 1.20
❑ 220 Mike Jenkins RC 2.50 .75
❑ 221 Robert Royal RC 5.00 1.50
❑ 222 Ladell Betts RC 5.00 1.50
❑ 223 Antwoine Womack RC 4.00 1.20
❑ 224 Raonall Smith RC 4.00 1.20
❑ 225 Charles Stackhouse RC 4.00 1.20
❑ 226 Quinn Gray RC 2.50 .75
❑ 227 Lito Sheppard RC 5.00 1.50
❑ 228 Ryan Van Dyke RC 5.00 1.50
❑ 229 Will Overstreet RC 2.50 .75
❑ 230 Leonard Henry RC 4.00 1.20
❑ 231 Dorsett Davis RC 2.50 .75
❑ 232 Marquand Manuel RC 2.50 .75
❑ 233 Luke Staley RC 4.00 1.20
❑ 234 Carlos Hall RC 5.00 1.50
❑ 235 Marcus Brady RC 4.00 1.20
❑ 236 Ryan Denney RC 2.50 .75
❑ 237 Eric McCoo RC 2.50 .75
❑ 238 Major Applewhite RC 5.00 1.50
❑ 239 Adam Tate RC 2.50 .75
❑ 240 Marquise Walker RC 4.00 1.20
❑ 241 John Flowers RC 2.50 .75
❑ 242 Levar Fisher RC 2.50 .75
❑ 243 Ricky Williams RC 4.00 1.20
❑ 244 Mike Rumph RC 5.00 1.50
❑ 245 Delvin Joyce RC 4.00 1.20
❑ 246 Bryan Thomas RC 4.00 1.20
❑ 247 Mike Williams RC 4.00 1.20
❑ 248 Sam Brandon RC 4.00 1.20
❑ 249 Eddie Drummond RC 4.00 1.20
❑ 250 Najeh Davenport RC 5.00 1.50
❑ 251 Brian Williams RC 2.50 .75
❑ 252 Scott Fujita RC 12.00 3.60
❑ 253 Dwight Freeney RC 6.00 1.80
❑ 254 Herb Haygood RC 2.50 .75
❑ 255 Patrick Ramsey RC 10.00 3.00
❑ 256 Atnaf Harris RC 2.50 .75
❑ 257 Jason McAddley RC 4.00 1.20
❑ 258 Pete Rebstock RC 2.50 .75
❑ 259 Quentin Jammer RC 5.00 1.50
❑ 260 Luke Butkus RC 2.50 .75
❑ 261 Jeremy Allen RC 5.00 1.50
❑ 262 Jake Schifino RC 4.00 1.20
❑ 263 Randy Fasani RC 4.00 1.20
❑ 264 Bryan Fletcher RC 2.50 .75
❑ 265 Jeremy Shockey RC 15.00 4.50
❑ 266 Kevin Bentley RC 2.50 .75
❑ 267 Jon McGraw RC 2.50 .75
❑ 268 Robert Thomas RC 5.00 1.50
❑ 269 Coy Wire RC 5.00 1.50
❑ 270 Brian Poli-Dixon RC 4.00 1.20
❑ 271 Willie Offord RC 5.00 1.50
❑ 272 Rocky Calmus RC 5.00 1.50
❑ 273 Sheldon Brown RC 5.00 1.50
❑ 274 Terry Charles RC 4.00 1.20
❑ 275 Ron Johnson RC 4.00 1.20
❑ 276 Roy Williams RC 12.00 3.60
❑ 277 Sam Simmons RC 2.50 .75
❑ 278 Andre Goodman RC 5.00 1.50
❑ 279 Ryan Sims RC 5.00 1.50
❑ 280 Antwaan Randle El RC 6.00 1.80
❑ 281 Alan Harper RC 2.50 .75
❑ 282 Tavon Mason RC 2.50 .75
❑ 283 Kahlil Hill RC 4.00 1.20
❑ 284 Antonio Bryant RC 5.00 1.50
❑ 285 Akin Ayodele RC 2.50 .75
❑ 286 T.J. Duckett RC 8.00 2.40
❑ 287 Kenyon Coleman RC 2.50 .75
❑ 288 Tim Carter RC 4.00 1.20
❑ 289 Lamont Brightful RC 2.50 .75
❑ 290 Trev Faulk RC 2.50 .75
❑ 291 Randy McMichael RC 8.00 2.40
❑ 292 Daniel Graham RC 5.00 1.50
❑ 293 Wendell Bryant RC 5.00 1.50
❑ 294 Jamar Martin RC 4.00 1.20
❑ 295 Chris Luzar RC 4.00 1.20
❑ 296 William Green RC 8.00 2.40
❑ 297 Lee Mays RC 4.00 1.20
❑ 298 Eric Crouch RC 8.00 2.40
❑ 299 Steve Smith RC 2.50 .75
❑ 300 Woody Dantzler RC 5.00 1.50

2002 Leaf Rookies and Stars Longevity

Nm-Mt Ex-Mt

*STARS: 10X TO 25X BASIC CARDS
*ROOKIES: 2X TO 5X

2003 Leaf Rookies and Stars

MINT NRMT

COMP.SET w/o SP's (100) 20.00 9.00
❑ 1 Emmitt Smith 2.00 .90
❑ 2 Michael Vick 2.00 .90
❑ 3 Peerless Price .50 .23
❑ 4 T.J. Duckett .50 .23
❑ 5 Warrick Dunn .50 .23
❑ 6 Jamal Lewis .75 .35
❑ 7 Ray Lewis .75 .35
❑ 8 Drew Bledsoe .75 .35
❑ 9 Eric Moulds .50 .23
❑ 10 Josh Reed .50 .23
❑ 11 Travis Henry .50 .23
❑ 12 Julius Peppers .75 .35
❑ 13 Anthony Thomas .75 .35
❑ 14 Brian Urlacher 1.25 .55
❑ 15 Marty Booker .50 .23
❑ 16 Kordell Stewart .50 .23
❑ 17 Corey Dillon .50 .23
❑ 18 Chad Johnson .50 .23
❑ 19 Tim Couch .30 .14
❑ 20 William Green .50 .23
❑ 21 Antonio Bryant .50 .23
❑ 22 Roy Williams .75 .35
❑ 23 Ashley Lelie .75 .35
❑ 24 Clinton Portis 1.25 .55
❑ 25 Ed McCaffrey .75 .35
❑ 26 Jake Plummer .50 .23
❑ 27 Rod Smith .50 .23
❑ 28 Joey Harrington 1.25 .55
❑ 29 Ahman Green .75 .35
❑ 30 Brett Favre 2.00 .90
❑ 31 Donald Driver .50 .23
❑ 32 Javon Walker .50 .23
❑ 33 David Carr 1.25 .55
❑ 34 Edgerrin James .75 .35
❑ 35 Marvin Harrison .75 .35
❑ 36 Peyton Manning 1.25 .55
❑ 37 Fred Taylor .75 .35
❑ 38 Jimmy Smith .50 .23
❑ 39 Mark Brunell .50 .23
❑ 40 Priest Holmes 1.25 .55
❑ 41 Tony Gonzalez .50 .23
❑ 42 Trent Green .50 .23
❑ 43 Chris Chambers .75 .35
❑ 44 Jay Fiedler .50 .23
❑ 45 Junior Seau .75 .35
❑ 46 Ricky Williams .75 .35
❑ 47 Zach Thomas .75 .35
❑ 48 Daunte Culpepper .75 .35
❑ 49 Michael Bennett .50 .23
❑ 50 Randy Moss 1.25 .55
❑ 51 Tom Brady 1.25 .55
❑ 52 Troy Brown .50 .23
❑ 53 Aaron Brooks .75 .35
❑ 54 Deuce McAllister .75 .35
❑ 55 Donte Stallworth .75 .35
❑ 56 Joe Horn .50 .23
❑ 57 Jeremy Shockey 1.25 .55
❑ 58 Kerry Collins .50 .23
❑ 59 Michael Strahan .50 .23
❑ 60 Tiki Barber .50 .23
❑ 61 Chad Pennington 1.00 .45
❑ 62 Curtis Martin .75 .35
❑ 63 Santana Moss .50 .23
❑ 64 Charles Woodson .50 .23
❑ 65 Jerry Rice 1.50 .70
❑ 66 Rich Gannon .50 .23
❑ 67 Tim Brown .75 .35
❑ 68 Donovan McNabb 1.00 .45
❑ 69 Antwaan Randle El .75 .35
❑ 70 Tommy Maddox .75 .35
❑ 71 Jerome Bettis .75 .35
❑ 72 Kendrell Bell .50 .23
❑ 73 Plaxico Burress .50 .23
❑ 74 David Boston .50 .23
❑ 75 Drew Brees .75 .35
❑ 76 LaDainian Tomlinson .75 .35
❑ 77 Kevan Barlow .50 .23
❑ 78 Jeff Garcia .75 .35
❑ 79 Terrell Owens .75 .35
❑ 80 Matt Hasselbeck .50 .23
❑ 81 Koren Robinson .50 .23
❑ 82 Shaun Alexander .75 .35
❑ 83 Isaac Bruce .75 .35
❑ 84 Kurt Warner .75 .35
❑ 85 Marshall Faulk .75 .35
❑ 86 Torry Holt .75 .35
❑ 87 Brad Johnson .50 .23
❑ 88 Keyshawn Johnson .75 .35
❑ 89 Mike Alstott .75 .35
❑ 90 Warren Sapp .50 .23
❑ 91 Eddie George .50 .23
❑ 92 Jevon Kearse .50 .23
❑ 93 Steve McNair .75 .35
❑ 94 Laveranues Coles .50 .23
❑ 95 Rod Gardner .50 .23
❑ 96 Patrick Ramsey .75 .35
❑ 97 Kyle Boller .75 .35
Terrell Suggs
Musa Smith CL
❑ 98 Rex Grossman .75 .35
Taylor Jacobs CL

❑ 99 Anquan Boldin .75 .35
Bryant Johnson CL
❑ 100 Tyrone Calico .75 .35
Chris Brown CL
❑ 101 Charles Tillman RC 6.00 2.70
❑ 102 Justin Griffith RC 3.00 1.35
❑ 103 Ovie Mughelli RC 2.00 .90
❑ 104 Chris Edmonds RC 2.00 .90
❑ 105 Jeremi Johnson RC 3.00 1.35
❑ 106 Malaefou MacKenzie RC 2.00 .90
❑ 107 James Lynch RC 3.00 1.35
❑ 108 B.J. Askew RC 4.00 1.80
❑ 109 Andrew Pinnock RC 3.00 1.35
❑ 110 Chris Davis RC 3.00 1.35
❑ 111 Dan Curley RC 2.00 .90
❑ 112 Lenny Walls RC 3.00 1.35
❑ 113 Travis Fisher RC 2.00 .90
❑ 114 Ahmaad Galloway RC 3.00 1.35
❑ 115 Joe Smith RC 2.00 .90
❑ 116 Reno Mahe RC 4.00 1.80
❑ 117 Torrie Cox RC 3.00 1.35
❑ 118 Kerry Carter RC 3.00 1.35
❑ 119 Dwone Hicks RC 2.00 .90
❑ 120 Cato June RC 3.00 1.35
❑ 121 Terry Pierce RC 3.00 1.35
❑ 122 Eddie Moore RC 3.00 1.35
❑ 123 Mike Seidman RC 2.00 .90
❑ 124 Michael Nattiel RC 4.00 1.80
❑ 125 Casey Fitzsimmons RC 4.00 1.80
❑ 126 George Wrighster RC 3.00 1.35
❑ 127 Mike Pinkard RC 2.00 .90
❑ 128 Donald Lee RC 3.00 1.35
❑ 129 Sean Berton RC 2.00 .90
❑ 130 Soloman Bates RC 2.00 .90
❑ 131 Zach Hilton RC 3.00 1.35
❑ 132 Antonio Gates RC 20.00 9.00
❑ 133 Aaron Walker RC 3.00 1.35
❑ 134 Richard Angulo RC 3.00 1.35
❑ 135 Will Heller RC 3.00 1.35
❑ 136 Theo Sanders RC 2.00 .90
❑ 137 Jimmy Farris RC 3.00 1.35
❑ 138 Ryan Nece RC 4.00 1.80
❑ 139 Antonio Brown RC 2.00 .90
❑ 140 Clarence Coleman RC 2.00 .90
❑ 141 Lawrence Hamilton RC 2.00 .90
❑ 142 C.J. Jones RC 2.00 .90
❑ 143 Frisman Jackson RC 4.00 1.80
❑ 144 Antonio Chatman RC 4.00 1.80
❑ 145 Rocky Boiman RC 3.00 1.35
❑ 146 Tron LaFavor RC 2.00 .90
❑ 147 Derick Armstrong RC 4.00 1.80
❑ 148 J.J. Moses RC 3.00 1.35
❑ 149 Aaron Moorehead RC 4.00 1.80
❑ 150 Brad Pyatt RC 3.00 1.35
❑ 151 Arland Bruce RC 2.00 .90
❑ 152 Chris Horn RC 2.00 .90
❑ 153 Kareem Kelly RC 3.00 1.35
❑ 154 Talman Gardner RC 4.00 1.80
❑ 155 David Tyree RC 3.00 1.35
❑ 156 Willie Ponder RC 2.00 .90
❑ 157 Greg Lewis RC 6.00 2.70
❑ 158 Eric Parker RC 4.00 1.80
❑ 159 Kassim Osgood RC 4.00 1.80
❑ 160 Jason Willis RC 2.00 .90
❑ 161 Akbar Gbaja-Biamila RC 4.00 1.80
❑ 162 Mike Furrey RC 6.00 2.70
❑ 163 Chris Kelsay RC 4.00 1.80
❑ 164 Cory Redding RC 3.00 1.35
❑ 165 Kenny Peterson RC 3.00 1.35
❑ 166 Osi Umenyiora RC 4.00 1.80
❑ 167 Tyler Brayton RC 4.00 1.80
❑ 168 DeWayne White RC 3.00 1.35
❑ 169 Kevin Williams RC 4.00 1.80
❑ 170 Dan Klecko RC 6.00 2.70
❑ 171 Johnathan Sullivan RC 3.00 1.35
❑ 172 William Joseph RC 4.00 1.80
❑ 173 Rien Long RC 2.00 .90
❑ 174 Angelo Crowell RC 3.00 1.35
❑ 175 Chaun Thompson RC 2.00 .90
❑ 176 Bradie James RC 4.00 1.80
❑ 177 Antwan Peek RC 3.00 1.35
❑ 178 Kawicka Mitchell RC 3.00 1.35
❑ 179 Cie Grant RC 4.00 1.80
❑ 180 E.J. Henderson RC 4.00 1.80
❑ 181 Victor Hobson RC 4.00 1.80
❑ 182 Alonzo Jackson RC 3.00 1.35
❑ 183 Matt Wilhelm RC 4.00 1.80
❑ 184 Pisa Tinoisamoa RC 6.00 2.70
❑ 185 Ricky Manning RC 4.00 1.80
❑ 186 Dennis Weathersby RC 2.00 .90
❑ 187 Donald Strickland RC 2.00 .90
❑ 188 Asante Samuel RC 4.00 1.80
❑ 189 Eugene Wilson RC 3.00 1.35
❑ 190 Nnamdi Asomugha RC 3.00 1.35
❑ 191 Ike Taylor RC 3.00 1.35
❑ 192 Drayton Florence RC 2.00 .90
❑ 193 DeJuan Groce RC 4.00 1.80
❑ 194 Shane Walton RC 2.00 .90
❑ 195 Terrence Holt RC 3.00 1.35
❑ 196 Rashean Mathis RC 3.00 1.35
❑ 197 Julian Battle RC 3.00 1.35
❑ 198 Hanik Milligan RC 3.00 1.35
❑ 199 Terrence Kiel RC 4.00 1.80
❑ 200 David Kircus RC 3.00 1.35
❑ 201 Lee Suggs RC 12.00 5.50
❑ 202 Charles Rogers RC 8.00 3.60
❑ 203 Brandon Lloyd RC 8.00 3.60
❑ 204 Terrence Edwards RC 5.00 2.20
❑ 205 Tony Romo RC 6.00 2.70
❑ 206 Brooks Bollinger RC 6.00 2.70
❑ 207 Jerome McDougle RC 6.00 2.70
❑ 208 Jimmy Kennedy RC 6.00 2.70
❑ 209 Ken Dorsey RC 10.00 4.50
❑ 210 Kirk Farmer RC 3.00 1.35
❑ 211 Mike Doss RC 6.00 2.70
❑ 212 Chris Simms RC 12.00 5.50
❑ 213 Cecil Sapp RC 5.00 2.20
❑ 214 Justin Gage RC 6.00 2.70
❑ 215 Sam Aiken RC 5.00 2.20
❑ 216 Doug Gabriel RC 6.00 2.70
❑ 217 Jason Witten RC 10.00 4.50
❑ 218 Bennie Joppru RC 6.00 2.70
❑ 219 Jason Gesser RC 6.00 2.70
❑ 220 Brock Forsey RC 6.00 2.70
❑ 221 Quentin Griffin RC 15.00 6.75
❑ 222 Avon Cobourne RC 3.00 1.35
❑ 223 Domanick Davis RC 12.00 5.50
❑ 224 Boss Bailey RC 8.00 3.60
❑ 225 Tony Hollings RC 6.00 2.70
❑ 226 LaBrandon Toefield RC 6.00 2.70
❑ 227 Arlen Harris RC 6.00 2.70
❑ 228 Sultan McCullough RC 5.00 2.20
❑ 229 Visanthe Shiancoe RC 5.00 2.20
❑ 230 L.J. Smith RC 6.00 2.70
❑ 231 LaTarence Dunbar RC 5.00 2.20
❑ 232 Walter Young RC 3.00 1.35
❑ 233 Bobby Wade RC 6.00 2.70
❑ 234 Zuriel Smith RC 3.00 1.35
❑ 235 Adrian Madise RC 5.00 2.20
❑ 236 Ken Hamlin RC 6.00 2.70
❑ 237 Carl Ford RC 3.00 1.35
❑ 238 Cortez Hankton RC 5.00 2.20
❑ 239 J.R. Tolver RC 5.00 2.20
❑ 240 Keenan Howry RC 6.00 2.70
❑ 241 Billy McMullen RC 5.00 2.20
❑ 242 Arnaz Battle RC 6.00 2.70
❑ 243 Shaun McDonald RC 6.00 2.70
❑ 244 Andre Woolfolk RC 6.00 2.70
❑ 245 Sammy Davis RC 6.00 2.70
❑ 246 Calvin Pace RC 5.00 2.20
❑ 247 Michael Haynes RC 6.00 2.70
❑ 248 Ty Warren RC 6.00 2.70
❑ 249 Nick Barnett RC 10.00 4.50
❑ 250 Troy Polamalu RC 6.00 2.70
❑ 251 Carson Palmer JSY RC 25.00 11.00
❑ 252 Byron Leftwich JSY RC 25.00 11.00
❑ 253 Kyle Boller JSY RC 15.00 6.75
❑ 254 Rex Grossman JSY RC 20.00 9.00
❑ 255 Dave Ragone JSY RC 6.00 2.70
❑ 256 Brian St.Pierre JSY RC 6.00 2.70
❑ 257 Kliff Kingsbury JSY RC 6.00 2.70
❑ 258 Seneca Wallace JSY RC 6.00 2.70
❑ 259 Larry Johnson JSY RC 12.00 5.50
❑ 260 Willis McGahee JSY RC 15.00 6.75
❑ 261 Justin Fargas JSY RC 6.00 2.70
❑ 262 Onterrio Smith JSY RC 8.00 3.60
❑ 263 Chris Brown JSY RC 15.00 6.75
❑ 264 Musa Smith JSY RC 6.00 2.70
❑ 265 Artose Pinner JSY RC 6.00 2.70
❑ 266 Andre Johnson JSY RC 20.00 9.00
❑ 267 Kelley Washington JSY RC 8.00 3.60
❑ 268 Taylor Jacobs JSY RC 6.00 2.70
❑ 269 Bryant Johnson JSY RC 8.00 3.60
❑ 270 Tyrone Calico JSY RC 10.00 4.50
❑ 271 Anquan Boldin JSY RC 20.00 9.00
❑ 272 Bethel Johnson JSY RC 12.00 5.50
❑ 273 Nate Burleson JSY RC 12.00 5.50
❑ 274 Kevin Curtis JSY RC 6.00 2.70
❑ 275 Dallas Clark JSY RC 6.00 2.70
❑ 276 Teyo Johnson JSY RC 6.00 2.70
❑ 277 Terrell Suggs JSY RC 10.00 4.50
❑ 278 DeWayne Robertson JSY RC 6.00 2.70
❑ 279 Terence Newman JSY RC 12.00 5.50
❑ 280 Marcus Trufant JSY RC 6.00 2.70
❑ 281 Carson Palmer 30.00 13.50
Byron Leftwich JSY
❑ 282 Kyle Boller 10.00 4.50
Dave Ragone JSY
❑ 283 Rex Grossman 10.00 4.50
Brian St.Pierre JSY
❑ 284 Kliff Kingsbury 10.00 4.50
Seneca Wallace JSY
❑ 285 Larry Johnson 15.00 6.75
Willis McGahee JSY
❑ 286 Justin Fargas 10.00 4.50
Onterrio Smith JSY
❑ 287 Chris Brown 12.00 5.50
Musa Smith JSY
❑ 288 Artose Pinner 15.00 6.75
Andre Johnson JSY
❑ 289 Kelley Washington 10.00 4.50
Taylor Jacobs JSY
❑ 290 Bryant Johnson 12.00 5.50
Tyrone Calico JSY
❑ 291 Anquan Boldin 25.00 11.00
Bryant Johnson JSY
❑ 292 Nate Burleson 12.00 5.50
Kevin Curtis JSY
❑ 293 Dallas Clark 10.00 4.50
Teyo Johnson JSY
❑ 294 Terrell Suggs 10.00 4.50
DeWayne Robertson JSY
❑ 295 Terence Newman 12.00 5.50
Marcus Trufant JSY

2003 Leaf Rookies and Stars Longevity

MINT NRMT

*STARS 1-100: 5X TO 12X BASIC CARDS
*ROOKIES 101-200: 2.5X TO 6X
SERIAL #'d UNDER 26 NOT PRICED

2004 Leaf Rookies and Stars

Nm-Mt Ex-Mt

COMP.SET w/o SP's (200) 60.00 18.00
COMP.SET w/o RC's (100) 20.00 6.00
201-250 RC PRINT RUN 750 SER.#'d SETS
251-283 JSY PRINT RUN 750 SER.#'d SETS
284-299 PRINT RUN 500 SER.#'d SETS

❑ 1 Anquan Boldin .75 .23
❑ 2 Emmitt Smith 1.50 .45
❑ 3 Josh McCown .50 .15
❑ 4 Michael Vick 1.50 .45
❑ 5 Peerless Price .50 .15
❑ 6 T.J. Duckett .50 .15
❑ 7 Warrick Dunn .50 .15
❑ 8 Jamal Lewis .75 .23
❑ 9 Kyle Boller .75 .23
❑ 10 Ray Lewis .75 .23
❑ 11 Drew Bledsoe .75 .23
❑ 12 Eric Moulds .50 .15
❑ 13 Travis Henry .50 .15
❑ 14 Jake Delhomme .75 .23
❑ 15 Stephen Davis .50 .15
❑ 16 Steve Smith .50 .15
❑ 17 Brian Urlacher 1.00 .30

❑	18	Rex Grossman	.75	.23
❑	19	Thomas Jones	.50	.15
❑	20	Carson Palmer	1.00	.30
❑	21	Chad Johnson	.50	.15
❑	22	Rudi Johnson	.50	.15
❑	23	Jeff Garcia	.75	.23
❑	24	William Green	.50	.15
❑	25	Keyshawn Johnson	.50	.15
❑	26	Terence Newman	.50	.15
❑	27	Roy Williams S	.50	.15
❑	28	Jake Plummer	.50	.15
❑	29	Quentin Griffin	.75	.23
❑	30	Rod Smith	.50	.15
❑	31	Charles Rogers	.50	.15
❑	32	Joey Harrington	.75	.23
❑	33	Ahman Green	.75	.23
❑	34	Brett Favre	2.00	.60
❑	35	Javon Walker	.50	.15
❑	36	Andre Johnson	.75	.23
❑	37	David Carr	.75	.23
❑	38	Domanick Davis	.75	.23
❑	39	Edgerrin James	.75	.23
❑	40	Marvin Harrison	.75	.23
❑	41	Peyton Manning	1.25	.35
❑	42	Byron Leftwich	1.25	.35
❑	43	Fred Taylor	.50	.15
❑	44	Jimmy Smith	.50	.15
❑	45	Priest Holmes	1.00	.30
❑	46	Tony Gonzalez	.50	.15
❑	47	Trent Green	.50	.15
❑	48	A.J. Feeley	.75	.23
❑	49	Chris Chambers	.50	.15
❑	50	Deion Sanders	1.00	.30
❑	51	Daunte Culpepper	.75	.23
❑	52	Michael Bennett	.50	.15
❑	53	Randy Moss	1.00	.30
❑	54	Corey Dillon	.50	.15
❑	55	Deion Branch	.75	.23
❑	56	Tom Brady	1.25	.35
❑	57	Aaron Brooks	.50	.15
❑	58	Deuce McAllister	.75	.23
❑	59	Joe Horn	.50	.15
❑	60	Jeremy Shockey	.75	.23
❑	61	Michael Strahan	.50	.15
❑	62	Tiki Barber	.50	.15
❑	63	Chad Pennington	1.00	.30
❑	64	Curtis Martin	.75	.23
❑	65	Santana Moss	.50	.15
❑	66	Jerry Porter	.50	.15
❑	67	Jerry Rice	1.50	.45
❑	68	Warren Sapp	.50	.15
❑	69	Donovan McNabb	1.00	.30
❑	70	Jevon Kearse	.50	.15
❑	71	Terrell Owens	.75	.23
❑	72	Duce Staley	.50	.15
❑	73	Hines Ward	.75	.23
❑	74	Jerome Bettis	.75	.23
❑	75	LaDainian Tomlinson	.75	.23
❑	76	Kevan Barlow	.50	.15
❑	77	Tim Rattay	.50	.15
❑	78	Koren Robinson	.50	.15
❑	79	Matt Hasselbeck	.50	.15
❑	80	Shaun Alexander	.75	.23
❑	81	Isaac Bruce	.50	.15
❑	82	Marc Bulger	.75	.23
❑	83	Marshall Faulk	.75	.23
❑	84	Torry Holt	.75	.23
❑	85	Brad Johnson	.50	.15
❑	86	Derrick Brooks	.50	.15
❑	87	Chris Brown	.75	.23
❑	88	Derrick Mason	.50	.15
❑	89	Eddie George	.50	.15
❑	90	Steve McNair	.75	.23
❑	91	Clinton Portis	.75	.23
❑	92	LaVar Arrington	1.50	.45
❑	93	Laveranues Coles	.50	.15
❑	94	Mark Brunell	.50	.15
❑	95	DeAngelo Hall CL	.75	.23
		Matt Schaub		
		Michael Jenkins		
❑	96	J.P. Losman CL	1.25	.35
		Lee Evans		
❑	97	Kellen Winslow Jr. CL	1.50	.45
		Luke McCown		
❑	98	Darius Watts CL	.75	.23
		Tatum Bell		
❑	99	Kevin Jones CL	2.00	.60
		Roy Williams WR		
❑	100	Greg Jones CL	.75	.23
		Reggie Williams		
❑	101	Darnell Dockett RC	3.00	.90
❑	102	Karlos Dansby RC	4.00	1.20
❑	103	Larry Croom RC	3.00	.90
❑	104	Chad Lavalais RC	3.00	.90
❑	105	Demorrio Williams RC	4.00	1.20
❑	106	B.J. Sams RC	4.00	1.20
❑	107	Dwan Edwards RC	2.00	.60
❑	108	Jason Peters RC	4.00	1.20
❑	109	Shaud Williams RC	3.00	.90
❑	110	Tim Anderson RC	4.00	1.20
❑	111	Tim Euhus RC	4.00	1.20
❑	112	Michael Gaines RC	3.00	.90
❑	113	Rod Rutherford RC	3.00	.90
❑	114	Leon Joe RC	2.00	.60
❑	115	Nathan Vasher RC	4.00	1.20
❑	116	Caleb Miller RC	3.00	.90
❑	117	Jamall Broussard RC	2.00	.60
❑	118	Keiwan Ratliff RC	3.00	.90
❑	119	Landon Johnson RC	3.00	.90
❑	120	Madieu Williams RC	3.00	.90
❑	121	Matthias Askew RC	3.00	.90
❑	122	Robert Geathers RC	3.00	.90
❑	123	Richard Alston RC	3.00	.90
❑	124	Bruce Thornton RC	2.00	.60
❑	125	Patrick Crayton RC	4.00	1.20
❑	126	Bradlee Van Pelt RC	4.00	1.20
❑	127	Charlie Adams RC	2.00	.60
❑	128	Nate Jackson RC	2.00	.60
❑	129	Roc Alexander RC	2.00	.60
❑	130	Romar Crenshaw RC	2.00	.60
❑	131	Keith Smith RC	3.00	.90
❑	132	Joey Thomas RC	4.00	1.20
❑	133	Kelvin Kight RC	2.00	.60
❑	134	Scott McBrien RC	2.00	.60
❑	135	Andrae Thurman RC	2.00	.60
❑	136	Derick Armstrong	3.00	.90
❑	137	Glenn Earl RC	3.00	.90
❑	138	Kendrick Starling RC	2.00	.60
❑	139	Ben Hartsock RC	4.00	1.20
❑	140	Gilbert Gardner RC	3.00	.90
❑	141	Jason David RC	4.00	1.20
❑	142	Daryl Smith RC	4.00	1.20
❑	143	Jared Allen RC	4.00	1.20
❑	144	Jeris McIntyre RC	3.00	.90
❑	145	John Booth RC	3.00	.90
❑	146	Jonathan Smith RC	3.00	.90
❑	147	Junior Siavii RC	4.00	1.20
❑	148	Keyaron Fox RC	3.00	.90
❑	149	Kris Wilson RC	4.00	1.20
❑	150	Doug Easlick RC	3.00	.90
❑	151	Fred Russell RC	4.00	1.20
❑	152	Tony Bua RC	3.00	.90
❑	153	Will Poole RC	4.00	1.20
❑	154	Ben Nelson RC	2.00	.60
❑	155	Brock Lesnar RC	5.00	1.50
❑	156	Butchie Wallace RC	3.00	.90
❑	157	Darrion Scott RC	4.00	1.20
❑	158	Dontarrious Thomas RC	4.00	1.20
❑	159	Richard Owens RC	2.00	.60
❑	160	Rod Davis RC	2.00	.60
❑	161	Dexter Reid RC	2.00	.60
❑	162	Kory Chapman RC	3.00	.90
❑	163	Marquise Hill RC	3.00	.90
❑	164	Courtney Watson RC	4.00	1.20
❑	165	Mike Karney RC	3.00	.90
❑	166	Gibril Wilson RC	4.00	1.20
❑	167	Reggie Torbor RC	3.00	.90
❑	168	Darrell McClover RC	3.00	.90
❑	169	Derrick Strait RC	4.00	1.20
❑	170	Erik Coleman RC	4.00	1.20
❑	171	Johnathan Reese RC	2.00	.60
❑	172	Rashad Washington RC	3.00	.90
❑	173	Courtney Anderson RC	3.00	.90
❑	174	Stuart Schweigert RC	4.00	1.20
❑	175	J.R. Reed RC	3.00	.90
❑	176	Justin Jenkins RC	3.00	.90
❑	177	Matt Ware RC	4.00	1.20
❑	178	Nate Lawrie RC	3.00	.90
❑	179	Thomas Tapeh RC	3.00	.90
❑	180	Matt Kranchick RC	4.00	1.20
❑	181	Willie Parker RC	4.00	1.20
❑	182	Igor Olshansky RC	4.00	1.20
❑	183	Ryan Krause RC	3.00	.90
❑	184	Shaun Phillips RC	3.00	.90
❑	185	Wes Welker RC	4.00	1.20
❑	186	Richard Seigler RC	3.00	.90
❑	187	Shawntae Spencer RC	4.00	1.20
❑	188	Marcus Tubbs RC	4.00	1.20
❑	189	Niko Koutouvides RC	3.00	.90
❑	190	Brandon Chillar RC	3.00	.90
❑	191	Tony Hargrove RC	3.00	.90
❑	192	Mark Jones RC	3.00	.90
❑	193	Marquis Cooper RC	3.00	.90
❑	194	Antwan Odom RC	4.00	1.20
❑	195	Michael Waddell RC	2.00	.60
❑	196	Randy Starks RC	3.00	.90
❑	197	Rich Gardner RC	3.00	.90
❑	198	Travis Laboy RC	4.00	1.20
❑	199	Vick King RC	3.00	.90
❑	200	Chris Cooley RC	4.00	1.20
❑	201	Adimchinobe Echemandu RC	5.00	1.50
❑	202	Ahmad Carroll RC	8.00	2.40
❑	203	Andy Hall RC	5.00	1.50
❑	204	B.J. Johnson RC	5.00	1.50
❑	205	B.J. Symons RC	6.00	1.80
❑	206	Brandon Miree RC	5.00	1.50
❑	207	Bruce Perry RC	5.00	1.50
❑	208	Carlos Francis RC	5.00	1.50
❑	209	Casey Bramlet RC	5.00	1.50
❑	210	Chris Gamble RC	8.00	2.40
❑	211	Clarence Moore RC	6.00	1.80
❑	212	Cody Pickett RC	6.00	1.80
❑	213	Craig Krenzel RC	6.00	1.80
❑	214	D.J. Hackett RC	5.00	1.50
❑	215	D.J. Williams RC	8.00	2.40
❑	216	Derrick Ward RC	3.00	.90
❑	217	Drew Carter RC	6.00	1.80
❑	218	Drew Henson RC	15.00	4.50
❑	219	Ernest Wilford RC	6.00	1.80
❑	220	Jamaar Taylor RC	6.00	1.80
❑	221	Jared Lorenzen RC	5.00	1.50
❑	222	Jarrett Payton RC	6.00	1.80
❑	223	Jason Babin RC	6.00	1.80
❑	224	Jeff Smoker RC	10.00	3.00
❑	225	Jerricho Cotchery RC	6.00	1.80
❑	226	Jim Sorgi RC	6.00	1.80
❑	227	John Navarre RC	6.00	1.80
❑	228	Johnnie Morant RC	6.00	1.80
❑	229	Jonathan Vilma RC	6.00	1.80
❑	230	Josh Harris RC	6.00	1.80
❑	231	Kenechi Udeze RC	6.00	1.80
❑	232	Matt Mauck RC	6.00	1.80
❑	233	Maurice Mann RC	5.00	1.50
❑	234	Michael Turner RC	5.00	1.50
❑	235	P.K. Sam RC	5.00	1.50
❑	236	Quincy Wilson RC	5.00	1.50
❑	237	Ran Carthon RC	5.00	1.50
❑	238	Ricardo Colclough RC	6.00	1.80
❑	239	Samie Parker RC	6.00	1.80
❑	240	Sean Jones RC	5.00	1.50
❑	241	Sean Taylor RC	8.00	2.40
❑	242	Sloan Thomas RC	5.00	1.50
❑	243	Tommie Harris RC	8.00	2.40
❑	244	Triandos Luke RC	6.00	1.80
❑	245	Troy Fleming RC	5.00	1.50
❑	246	Vince Wilfork RC	8.00	2.40
❑	247	Will Smith RC	6.00	1.80
❑	248	Michael Boulware RC	6.00	1.80
❑	249	Richard Smith RC	5.00	1.50
❑	250	Teddy Lehman RC	6.00	1.80
❑	251	Larry Fitzgerald JSY RC	20.00	6.00
❑	252	DeAngelo Hall JSY RC	10.00	3.00
❑	253	Matt Schaub JSY RC	10.00	3.00
❑	254	Michael Jenkins JSY RC	8.00	2.40
❑	255	Devard Darling JSY RC	8.00	2.40
❑	256	J.P. Losman JSY RC	15.00	4.50
❑	257	Lee Evans JSY RC	12.00	3.60
❑	258	Keary Colbert JSY RC	10.00	3.00
❑	259	Bernard Berrian JSY RC	8.00	2.40
❑	260	Chris Perry JSY RC	12.00	3.60
❑	261	Kellen Winslow Jr. JSY RC	15.00	4.50
❑	262	Luke McCown JSY RC	8.00	2.40
❑	263	Julius Jones JSY RC	25.00	7.50
❑	264	Darius Watts JSY RC	10.00	3.00
❑	265	Tatum Bell JSY RC	12.00	3.60
❑	266	Kevin Jones JSY RC	20.00	6.00
❑	267	Roy Williams JSY RC	20.00	6.00
❑	268	Dunta Robinson JSY RC	8.00	2.40
❑	269	Greg Jones JSY RC	8.00	2.40
❑	270	Reggie Williams JSY RC	10.00	3.00
❑	271	Mewelde Moore JSY RC	10.00	3.00
❑	272	Ben Watson JSY RC	8.00	2.40
❑	273	Cedric Cobbs JSY RC	8.00	2.40
❑	274	Devery Henderson JSY RC	6.00	1.80

❑ 275 Eli Manning JSY RC 30.00 9.00
❑ 276 Robert Gallery JSY RC 10.00 3.00
❑ 277 Ben Roethlisberger JSY RC 50.00 15.00
❑ 278 Philip Rivers JSY RC 20.00 6.00
❑ 279 Derrick Hamilton JSY RC 6.00 1.80
❑ 280 Rashaun Woods JSY RC 10.00 3.00
❑ 281 Steven Jackson JSY RC 20.00 6.00
❑ 282 Michael Clayton JSY RC 15.00 4.50
❑ 283 Ben Troupe JSY RC 8.00 2.40
❑ 284 Eli Manning JSY 30.00 9.00
Philip Rivers JSY
❑ 285 Larry Fitzgerald JSY 25.00 7.50
Roy Williams JSY
❑ 286 Kellen Winslow Jr. JSY 20.00 6.00
Greg Jones JSY
❑ 287 DeAngelo Hall JSY 10.00 3.00
Dunta Robinson JSY
❑ 288 Reggie Williams JSY 10.00 3.00
Devard Darling JSY
❑ 289 Ben Roethlisberger JSY 50.00 15.00
J.P. Losman JSY
❑ 290 Michael Clayton JSY 15.00 4.50
Devery Henderson JSY
❑ 291 Steven Jackson JSY 20.00 6.00
Chris Perry JSY
❑ 292 Lee Evans JSY 12.00 3.60
Michael Jenkins JSY
❑ 293 Rashaun Woods JSY 12.00 3.60
Tatum Bell JSY
❑ 294 Kevin Jones JSY 25.00 7.50
Bernard Berrian JSY
❑ 295 Ben Watson JSY 8.00 2.40
Ben Troupe JSY
❑ 296 Julius Jones JSY 25.00 7.50
Mewelde Moore JSY
❑ 297 Matt Schaub JSY 12.00 3.60
Derrick Hamilton JSY
❑ 298 Luke McCown JSY 8.00 2.40
Darius Watts JSY
❑ 299 Keary Colbert JSY 8.00 2.40
Cedric Cobbs JSY

2004 Leaf Rookies and Stars Longevity Parallel

Nm-Mt Ex-Mt

*STARS 1-100: 3X TO 8X BASE CARD HI
1-100 PRINT RUN 125 SER.#'d SETS
*ROOKIES 101-200: 2X TO 5X BASE CARD HI
101-200 PRINT RUN 75 SER.#'d SETS
201-250 AU PRINT RUN 50 SER.#'d SETS
UNPRICED 251-283 AU PRINT RUN 10 SETS
*ROOKIES JSY 284-299: 1.2X TO 3X
284-299 JSY PRINT RUN 25 SER.#'d SETS
EXCH EXPIRATION: 6/1/2006

2004 Leaf Rookies and Stars Longevity Holofoil Parallel

Nm-Mt Ex-Mt

*STARS 1-100: 4X TO 10X BASE CARD HI
1-100 PRINT RUN 75 SER.#'d SETS
*ROOKIES 101-200: 2.5X TO 6X
101-200 PRINT RUN 25 SER.#'d SETS
UNPRICED 201-250 AU PRINT RUN 10 SETS
UNPRICED 251-283 JSY AU PRINT RUN 5 SETS
UNPRICED 284-299 JSY PRINT RUN 10 SETS
EXCH EXPIRATION: 6/1/2006

2004 Leaf Rookies and Stars Longevity True Blue Parallel

Nm-Mt Ex-Mt

*STARS 1-100: 2X TO 5X BASE CARD HI
1-100 PRINT RUN 249 SER.#'d SETS
*ROOKIES 101-200: 2X TO 5X
101-200 PRINT RUN 75 SER.#'d SETS
*ROOKIES 201-250: 2.5X TO 6X
201-250 PRINT RUN 25 SER.#'d SETS

Nm-Mt Ex-Mt

COMP.SET w/o RCs (100) 30.00 9.00
*STARS 1-100: .8X TO 2X BASIC CARDS
*ROOKIES 101-200: .5X TO 1.2X BASIC CARDS
101-200 RC PRINT RUN 999 SER.#'d SETS
*ROOKIES 201-250: .5X TO 1.2X BASIC CARDS
201-250 RC PRINT RUN 499 SER.#'d SETS
*ROOKIES 251-283: .5X TO 1.2X BASIC CARDS
251-283 JSY RC PRINT RUN 299 SER.#'d SETS

2004 Leaf Rookies and Stars Longevity Black

Nm-Mt Ex-Mt

*STARS 1-100: 3X TO 8X BASIC CARDS
1-100 PRINT RUN 75 SER.#'d SETS
*ROOKIES 101-200: 1.5X TO 4X BASIC CARDS
101-200 PRINT RUN 50 SER.#'d SETS
*ROOKIES 201-250: 1.5X TO 4X BASIC CARDS
201-250 PRINT RUN 25 SER.#'d SETS
251-283 UNPRICED JSY PRINT RUN 10 SETS

2004 Leaf Rookies and Stars Longevity Emerald

Nm-Mt Ex-Mt

*STARS 1-100: 2.5X TO 6X BASIC CARDS
1-100 PRINT RUN 99 SER.#'d SETS
*ROOKIES 101-200: 1.2X TO 3X BASIC CARDS
101-200 PRINT RUN 75 SER.#'d SETS
*ROOKIES 201-250: 1X TO 2.5X BASIC CARDS
201-250 PRINT RUN 50 SER.#'d SETS
*ROOKIES 251-283: 1.2X TO 3X BASIC CARDS
251-283 JSY PRINT RUN 25 SER.#'d SETS

2004 Leaf Rookies and Stars Longevity Gold

Nm-Mt Ex-Mt

*STARS 1-100: 1.5X TO 4X BASIC CARDS
1-100 PRINT RUN 150 SER.#'d SETS
*ROOKIES 101-200: 1X TO 2.5X BASIC CARDS
101-200 PRINT RUN 99 SER.#'d SETS
*ROOKIES 201-250: .8X TO 2X BASIC CARDS
201-250 PRINT RUN 75 SER.#'d SETS
*ROOKIES 251-283: .8X TO 2X BASIC CARDS
251-283 JSY PRINT RUN 50 SER.#'d SETS

2004 Leaf Rookies and Stars Longevity Ruby

Nm-Mt Ex-Mt

*STARS 1-100: 1X TO 2.5X BASIC CARDS
1-100 PRINT RUN 250 SER.#'d SETS
*ROOKIES 101-200: .6X TO 1.5X BASIC CARDS
101-200 PRINT RUN 199 SER.#'d SETS
*ROOKIES 201-250: .5X TO 1.2X BASIC CARDS
201-250 PRINT RUN 150 SER.#'d SETS
*ROOKIES 251-283: .5X TO 1.2X BASIC CARDS
251-283 JSY PRINT RUN 99 SER.#'d SETS

2004 Leaf Rookies and Stars Longevity Sapphire

Nm-Mt Ex-Mt

*STARS 1-100: 1.2X TO 3X BASIC CARDS
1-100 PRINT RUN 199 SER.#'d SETS
*ROOKIES 101-200: .8X TO 2X BASIC CARDS
101-200 PRINT RUN 150 SER.#'d SETS
*ROOKIES 201-250: .6X TO 1.5X BASIC CARDS
201-250 PRINT RUN 99 SER.#'d SETS
*ROOKIES 251-283: .6X TO 1.5X BASIC CARDS
251-283 JSY PRINT RUN 75 SER.#'d SETS

1999 Metal Universe

	Nm-Mt	Ex-Mt
COMPLETE SET (250)	40.00	18.00
❑ 1 Eric Moulds	.50	.23
❑ 2 David Palmer	.20	.09
❑ 3 Ricky Watters	.30	.14
❑ 4 Antonio Freeman	.50	.23
❑ 5 Hugh Douglas	.20	.09
❑ 6 Johnnie Morton	.30	.14
❑ 7 Corey Fuller	.20	.09
❑ 8 J.J. Stokes	.30	.14
❑ 9 Keith Poole	.20	.09
❑ 10 Steve Beuerlein	.20	.09
❑ 11 Keenan McCardell	.30	.14
❑ 12 Carl Pickens	.30	.14
❑ 13 Mark Bruener	.20	.09
❑ 14 Warren Sapp	.30	.14
❑ 15 Rich Gannon	.50	.23
❑ 16 Bruce Smith	.30	.14
❑ 17 Mark Chmura	.20	.09
❑ 18 Drew Bledsoe	.60	.25
❑ 19 Charles Woodson	.50	.23
❑ 20 Ahman Green	.50	.23
❑ 21 Ricky Proehl	.20	.09
❑ 22 Corey Dillon	.50	.23
❑ 23 Terry Fair	.20	.09
❑ 24 Mark Brunell	.50	.23
❑ 25 Leroy Hoard	.20	.09
❑ 26 La'Roi Glover RC	.50	.23
❑ 27 Tim Brown	.50	.23
❑ 28 Kevin Turner	.20	.09
❑ 29 Terrell Owens	.50	.23
❑ 30 Mike Alstott	.50	.23
❑ 31 Rob Moore	.30	.14
❑ 32 Troy Aikman	1.00	.45
❑ 33 Derrick Alexander	.20	.09
❑ 34 Chris Calloway	.20	.09
❑ 35 Kordell Stewart	.30	.14
❑ 36 Reidel Anthony	.30	.14
❑ 37 Michael Westbrook	.30	.14
❑ 38 Ray Lewis	.50	.23
❑ 39 Alonzo Mayes	.20	.09
❑ 40 Rod Smith	.30	.14
❑ 41 Reggie Barlow	.20	.09
❑ 42 Sean Dawkins	.20	.09
❑ 43 Duce Staley	.50	.23
❑ 44 R.W. McQuarters	.20	.09
❑ 45 Robert Holcombe	.20	.09
❑ 46 Priest Holmes	.75	.35
❑ 47 Erik Kramer	.20	.09
❑ 48 Shannon Sharpe	.30	.14
❑ 49 Mike Vanderjagt	.20	.09
❑ 50 Cris Carter	.50	.23
❑ 51 Billy Joe Tolliver	.20	.09
❑ 52 Vinny Testaverde	.30	.14

❑ 53 Antonio Langham .20 .09
❑ 54 Damon Gibson .20 .09
❑ 55 Garrison Hearst .30 .14
❑ 56 Brad Johnson .50 .23
❑ 57 Randall Cunningham .50 .23
❑ 58 Jim Harbaugh .30 .14
❑ 59 Curtis Enis .20 .09
❑ 60 Bill Romanowski .20 .09
❑ 61 Marcus Pollard .20 .09
❑ 62 Zach Thomas .50 .23
❑ 63 Cameron Cleeland .20 .09
❑ 64 Curtis Martin .50 .23
❑ 65 Charlie Garner .30 .14
❑ 66 Jerris McPhail .20 .09
❑ 67 Jon Kitna .50 .23
❑ 68 Chris Chandler .30 .14
❑ 69 Emmitt Smith 1.00 .45
❑ 70 Andre Rison .30 .14
❑ 71 Wayne Chrebet .30 .14
❑ 72 Mikhael Ricks .20 .09
❑ 73 Yancey Thigpen .20 .09
❑ 74 Peter Boulware .20 .09
❑ 75 Bobby Engram .30 .14
❑ 76 John Mobley .20 .09
❑ 77 Peyton Manning 1.50 .70
❑ 78 O.J. McDuffie .30 .14
❑ 79 Tony Simmons .20 .09
❑ 80 Mo Lewis .20 .09
❑ 81 Bryan Still .20 .09
❑ 82 Eugene Robinson .20 .09
❑ 83 Curtis Conway .30 .14
❑ 84 Ed McCaffrey .30 .14
❑ 85 Marvin Harrison .50 .23
❑ 86 Dan Marino 1.50 .70
❑ 87 Ty Law .30 .14
❑ 88 Leon Johnson .20 .09
❑ 89 Junior Seau .50 .23
❑ 90 Terance Mathis .30 .14
❑ 91 Wesley Walls .30 .14
❑ 92 John Elway 1.50 .70
❑ 93 Marshall Faulk .60 .25
❑ 94 Oronde Gadsden .30 .14
❑ 95 Keyshawn Johnson .50 .23
❑ 96 Muhsin Muhammad .30 .14
❑ 97 Dorsey Levens .50 .23
❑ 98 Shawn Jefferson .20 .09
❑ 99 Rocket Ismail .30 .14
❑ 100 Vonnie Holliday .20 .09
❑ 101 Terry Glenn .50 .23
❑ 102 Shawn Springs .20 .09
❑ 103 Tim Dwight .50 .23
❑ 104 Terrell Davis .50 .23
❑ 105 Karim Abdul-Jabbar .30 .14
❑ 106 Bryan Cox .20 .09
❑ 107 Steve McNair .50 .23
❑ 108 Tony Martin .30 .14
❑ 109 Jason Elam .20 .09
❑ 110 John Avery .20 .09
❑ 111 Aaron Glenn .20 .09
❑ 112 Eddie George .50 .23
❑ 113 Larry Centers .20 .09
❑ 114 Darnay Scott .20 .09
❑ 115 Jimmy Smith .30 .14
❑ 116 Tiki Barber .30 .14
❑ 117 Charles Johnson .20 .09
❑ 118 Mike Archie RC .30 .14
❑ 119 Adrian Murrell .30 .14
❑ 120 Dexter Coakley .20 .09
❑ 121 Dale Carter .20 .09
❑ 122 Kent Graham .20 .09
❑ 123 Hines Ward .50 .23
❑ 124 Greg Hill .20 .09
❑ 125 Skip Hicks .20 .09
❑ 126 Doug Flutie .50 .23
❑ 127 Leslie Shepherd .20 .09
❑ 128 Neil O'Donnell .30 .14
❑ 129 Herman Moore .30 .14
❑ 130 Kevin Hardy .20 .09
❑ 131 Randy Moss 1.25 .55
❑ 132 Andre Hastings .20 .09
❑ 133 Rickey Dudley .20 .09
❑ 134 Jerome Bettis .50 .23
❑ 135 Jerry Rice 1.00 .45
❑ 136 Jake Plummer .30 .14
❑ 137 Billy Davis .20 .09
❑ 138 Tony Gonzalez .50 .23
❑ 139 Ike Hilliard .20 .09
❑ 140 Freddie Jones .20 .09
❑ 141 Isaac Bruce .50 .23
❑ 142 Darrell Green .20 .09
❑ 143 Trent Green .50 .23
❑ 144 Jamal Anderson .50 .23
❑ 145 Deion Sanders .50 .23
❑ 146 Byron Bam Morris .20 .09
❑ 147 Charles Way .20 .09
❑ 148 Natrone Means .30 .14
❑ 149 Frank Wycheck .20 .09
❑ 150 Brett Favre 1.50 .70
❑ 151 Michael Bates .20 .09
❑ 152 Ben Coates .30 .14
❑ 153 Koy Detmer .20 .09
❑ 154 Eddie Kennison .30 .14
❑ 155 Eric Metcalf .20 .09
❑ 156 Takeo Spikes .20 .09
❑ 157 Fred Taylor .50 .23
❑ 158 Gary Brown .20 .09
❑ 159 Levon Kirkland .20 .09
❑ 160 Trent Dilfer .30 .14
❑ 161 Antowain Smith .50 .23
❑ 162 Robert Brooks .30 .14
❑ 163 Robert Smith .50 .23
❑ 164 Napoleon Kaufman .50 .23
❑ 165 Chad Brown .20 .09
❑ 166 Warrick Dunn .50 .23
❑ 167 Joey Galloway .30 .14
❑ 168 Frank Sanders .30 .14
❑ 169 Michael Irvin .30 .14
❑ 170 Elvis Grbac .30 .14
❑ 171 Michael Strahan .30 .14
❑ 172 Ryan Leaf .50 .23
❑ 173 Stephen Alexander .20 .09
❑ 174 Andre Reed .30 .14
❑ 175 Barry Sanders 1.50 .70
❑ 176 Jake Reed .30 .14
❑ 177 James Jett .30 .14
❑ 178 Steve Young .60 .25
❑ 179 Jermaine Lewis .30 .14
❑ 180 Charlie Batch .50 .23
❑ 181 Jacquez Green .20 .09
❑ 182 Kevin Dyson .30 .14
❑ 183 Roell Preston PD .20 .09
❑ 184 Randall Cunningham PD .50 .23
❑ 185 Charlie Batch PD .50 .23
❑ 186 Kordell Stewart PD .30 .14
❑ 187 Bennie Thompson PD .20 .09
❑ 188 Deion Sanders PD .50 .23
❑ 189 Jake Plummer PD .30 .14
❑ 190 Eric Moulds PD .50 .23
❑ 191 Derrick Brooks PD .50 .23
❑ 192 Steve McNair PD .50 .23
❑ 193 Ryan Leaf PD .30 .14
❑ 194 Keyshawn Johnson PD .50 .23
❑ 195 Eddie George PD .30 .14
❑ 196 Warrick Dunn PD .50 .23
❑ 197 Jessie Tuggle PD .20 .09
❑ 198 Rodney Harrison PD .20 .09
❑ 199 Vinny Testaverde PD .30 .14
❑ 200 Marshall Faulk PD .60 .25
❑ 201 Ray Buchanan PD .20 .09
❑ 202 Garrison Hearst PD .30 .14
❑ 203 John Randle PD .30 .14
❑ 204 Drew Bledsoe PD .50 .23
❑ 205 Sam Gash PD .20 .09
❑ 206 Troy Aikman PD .50 .23
❑ 207 Michael McCrary .20 .09
❑ 208 Chris Claiborne RC .40 .18
❑ 209 Ricky Williams RC 2.50 1.10
❑ 210 Tim Couch RC 1.25 .55
❑ 211 Champ Bailey RC 1.50 .70
❑ 212 Torry Holt RC 3.00 1.35
❑ 213 Donovan McNabb RC 6.00 2.70
❑ 214 David Boston RC 1.25 .55
❑ 215 Chris McAlister RC .75 .35
❑ 216 Aaron Gibson RC .20 .09
❑ 217 Daunte Culpepper RC 5.00 2.20
❑ 218 Matt Stinchcomb RC .40 .18
❑ 219 Edgerrin James RC 5.00 2.20
❑ 220 Jevon Kearse RC 2.00 .90
❑ 221 Ebenezer Ekuban RC .75 .35
❑ 222 Kris Farris RC .40 .18
❑ 223 Chris Terry RC .40 .18
❑ 224 Cecil Collins RC .40 .18
❑ 225 Akili Smith RC .75 .35
❑ 226 Shaun King RC .75 .35
❑ 227 Rahim Abdullah RC .75 .35
❑ 228 Peerless Price RC 2.00 .90
❑ 229 Antoine Winfield RC .75 .35
❑ 230 Antuan Edwards RC .40 .18
❑ 231 Rob Konrad RC .75 .35
❑ 232 Troy Edwards RC .75 .35
❑ 233 John Thornton RC .40 .18
❑ 234 Fred Vinson RC .40 .18
❑ 235 Gary Stills RC .40 .18
❑ 236 Desmond Clark RC 1.25 .55
❑ 237 Lamar King RC .40 .18
❑ 238 Jared DeVries RC .75 .35
❑ 239 Martin Gramatica RC .40 .18
❑ 240 Montae Reagor RC .40 .18
❑ 241 Andy Katzenmoyer RC .75 .35
❑ 242 Rufus French RC .40 .18
❑ 243 D'Wayne Bates RC .75 .35
❑ 244 Amos Zereoue RC 1.25 .55
❑ 245 Dre' Bly RC 1.25 .55
❑ 246 Kevin Johnson RC 1.25 .55
❑ 247 Cade McNown RC .75 .35
❑ 248 Kordell Stewart CL .30 .14
❑ 249 Deion Sanders CL .50 .23
❑ 250 Vinny Testaverde CL .30 .14
❑ P1 Doug Flutie Promo 1.00 .45

2000 Metal

	Nm-Mt	Ex-Mt
COMPLETE SET (300)	80.00	36.00
COMP.SET w/o SP's (250)	15.00	6.75
❑ 1 Tim Couch	.30	.14
❑ 2 Olandis Gary	.50	.23
❑ 3 Andre Hastings	.20	.09
❑ 4 Donovan McNabb	.75	.35
❑ 5 Bobby Engram	.30	.14
❑ 6 Bert Emanuel	.20	.09
❑ 7 Levon Kirkland	.20	.09
❑ 8 Chris Chandler	.30	.14
❑ 9 Herman Moore	.30	.14
❑ 10 Jeff Blake	.30	.14
❑ 11 Cortez Kennedy	.20	.09
❑ 12 Antowain Smith	.30	.14
❑ 13 Marvin Harrison	.50	.23
❑ 14 Bryant Young	.20	.09
❑ 15 Peerless Price	.50	.23
❑ 16 Peyton Manning	1.25	.55
❑ 17 Darrell Russell	.20	.09
❑ 18 Darrell Green	.20	.09
❑ 19 James Allen	.30	.14
❑ 20 Tedy Bruschi	.50	.23
❑ 21 Jon Kitna	.50	.23
❑ 22 Doug Flutie	.50	.23
❑ 23 Bill Schroeder	.30	.14
❑ 24 Curtis Martin	.50	.23
❑ 25 Kevin Lockett	.20	.09
❑ 26 Errict Rhett	.30	.14
❑ 27 Kevin Faulk	.30	.14
❑ 28 J.J. Stokes	.30	.14
❑ 29 Jonathan Linton	.20	.09
❑ 30 Jimmy Smith	.30	.14
❑ 31 Brian Dawkins	.20	.09
❑ 32 Michael Westbrook	.30	.14
❑ 33 Randall Cunningham	.50	.23
❑ 34 Oronde Gadsden	.30	.14
❑ 35 Shawn Springs	.20	.09
❑ 36 Shannon Sharpe	.30	.14
❑ 37 Terrence Wilkins	.20	.09
❑ 38 Aaron Glenn	.20	.09
❑ 39 Torrance Small	.20	.09
❑ 40 Sean Dawkins	.20	.09
❑ 41 Terrell Davis	.50	.23
❑ 42 Ike Hilliard	.30	.14

Card	Player	Price 1	Price 2
❑ 43	Warrick Dunn	.50	.23
❑ 44	Jeremiah Trotter RC	1.50	.70
❑ 45	O.J. McDuffie	.30	.14
❑ 46	Richard Huntley	.20	.09
❑ 47	Aeneas Williams	.20	.09
❑ 48	Rocket Ismail	.30	.14
❑ 49	Terry Glenn	.50	.23
❑ 50	Derrick Mayes	.30	.14
❑ 51	Wayne Chrebet	.30	.14
❑ 52	Kevin Dyson	.30	.14
❑ 53	Takeo Spikes	.20	.09
❑ 54	Matthew Hatchette	.20	.09
❑ 55	Shawn Bryson	.20	.09
❑ 56	Qadry Ismail	.30	.14
❑ 57	Jerome Pathon	.30	.14
❑ 58	Rich Gannon	.50	.23
❑ 59	Stephen Davis	.50	.23
❑ 60	Marcus Robinson	.50	.23
❑ 61	Damon Huard	.50	.23
❑ 62	Junior Seau	.50	.23
❑ 63	Curtis Enis	.20	.09
❑ 64	Tony Richardson RC	.20	.09
❑ 65	Troy Edwards	.20	.09
❑ 66	Robert Brooks	.30	.14
❑ 67	Antonio Freeman	.50	.23
❑ 68	Kerry Collins	.30	.14
❑ 69	Jacquez Green	.20	.09
❑ 70	Akili Smith	.20	.09
❑ 71	Zach Thomas	.50	.23
❑ 72	Kordell Stewart	.30	.14
❑ 73	Deion Sanders	.50	.23
❑ 74	David Patten	.30	.14
❑ 75	Drew Bledsoe	.60	.25
❑ 76	Shaun King	.20	.09
❑ 77	Eddie Kennison	.30	.14
❑ 78	Stacey Mack	.30	.14
❑ 79	Jim Harbaugh	.30	.14
❑ 80	Shawn Jefferson	.20	.09
❑ 81	James Stewart	.30	.14
❑ 82	Pete Mitchell	.20	.09
❑ 83	Mike Alstott	.50	.23
❑ 84	Marty Booker	.30	.14
❑ 85	Hardy Nickerson	.20	.09
❑ 86	Charles Johnson	.30	.14
❑ 87	Jeff George	.30	.14
❑ 88	Jermaine Lewis	.30	.14
❑ 89	Edgerrin James	.75	.35
❑ 90	Rickey Dudley	.20	.09
❑ 91	Eddie George	.50	.23
❑ 92	Darren Woodson	.20	.09
❑ 93	Willie McGinest	.20	.09
❑ 94	Jeff Garcia	.50	.23
❑ 95	Eric Moulds	.50	.23
❑ 96	Tony Brackens	.20	.09
❑ 97	Charles Woodson	.30	.14
❑ 98	Warren Sapp	.30	.14
❑ 99	Corey Dillon	.50	.23
❑ 100	Tony Martin	.30	.14
❑ 101	Bruce Smith	.30	.14
❑ 102	Troy Aikman	1.00	.45
❑ 103	Daunte Culpepper	.60	.25
❑ 104	Christian Fauria	.20	.09
❑ 105	Steve Beuerlein	.30	.14
❑ 106	Fred Taylor	.50	.23
❑ 107	Ricky Watters	.30	.14
❑ 108	Brian Mitchell	.20	.09
❑ 109	Emmitt Smith	1.00	.45
❑ 110	Robert Smith	.50	.23
❑ 111	Jerry Rice	1.00	.45
❑ 112	Priest Holmes	.60	.25
❑ 113	Jay Fiedler	.50	.23
❑ 114	Curtis Conway	.30	.14
❑ 115	Jamal Anderson	.50	.23
❑ 116	E.G. Green	.20	.09
❑ 117	Kent Graham	.20	.09
❑ 118	Frank Wycheck	.20	.09
❑ 119	Jake Plummer	.30	.14
❑ 120	Randy Moss	1.00	.45
❑ 121	Charlie Garner	.30	.14
❑ 122	Frank Sanders	.30	.14
❑ 123	Germane Crowell	.20	.09
❑ 124	Jason Sehorn	.20	.09
❑ 125	Marshall Faulk	.60	.25
❑ 126	David Sloan	.20	.09
❑ 127	Cris Carter	.50	.23
❑ 128	Robert Chancey	.20	.09
❑ 129	Tony Banks	.30	.14
❑ 130	Ken Dilger	.20	.09
❑ 131	Dedric Ward	.20	.09
❑ 132	Yancey Thigpen	.20	.09
❑ 133	Jeremy McDaniel	.30	.14
❑ 134	John Randle	.20	.09
❑ 135	Jerome Bettis	.50	.23
❑ 136	Tim Dwight	.50	.23
❑ 137	Charlie Batch	.50	.23
❑ 138	Mark Brunell	.50	.23
❑ 139	Tyrone Wheatley	.30	.14
❑ 140	Champ Bailey	.30	.14
❑ 141	Brian Griese	.50	.23
❑ 142	Keith Poole	.20	.09
❑ 143	Kurt Warner	1.00	.45
❑ 144	Tim Biakabutuka	.30	.14
❑ 145	Elvis Grbac	.30	.14
❑ 146	Cade McNown	.20	.09
❑ 147	Albert Connell	.20	.09
❑ 148	Donald Driver	.50	.23
❑ 149	Donald Hayes	.20	.09
❑ 150	Terrell Owens	.50	.23
❑ 151	Johnnie Morton	.30	.14
❑ 152	Tiki Barber	.30	.14
❑ 153	Keyshawn Johnson	.50	.23
❑ 154	Carl Pickens	.30	.14
❑ 155	Thurman Thomas	.30	.14
❑ 156	Jeff Graham	.20	.09
❑ 157	Peter Boulware	.20	.09
❑ 158	Brett Favre	1.50	.70
❑ 159	Vinny Testaverde	.30	.14
❑ 160	Derrick Brooks	.50	.23
❑ 161	Wesley Walls	.20	.09
❑ 162	Derrick Alexander	.30	.14
❑ 163	Duce Staley	.50	.23
❑ 164	Troy Brown	.30	.14
❑ 165	Keenan McCardell	.30	.14
❑ 166	James Jett	.20	.09
❑ 167	Simeon Rice	.30	.14
❑ 168	Rod Smith	.30	.14
❑ 169	Ricky Williams	.50	.23
❑ 170	Az-Zahir Hakim	.20	.09
❑ 171	Muhsin Muhammad	.30	.14
❑ 172	Andre Rison	.30	.14
❑ 173	Tim Brown	.50	.23
❑ 174	Brad Johnson	.50	.23
❑ 175	Darrin Chiaverini	.20	.09
❑ 176	Jake Reed	.30	.14
❑ 177	Kevin Carter	.20	.09
❑ 178	Jay Riemersma	.20	.09
❑ 179	Tony Gonzalez	.30	.14
❑ 180	Hines Ward	.50	.23
❑ 181	David Boston	.50	.23
❑ 182	Ed McCaffrey	.50	.23
❑ 183	Amani Toomer	.20	.09
❑ 184	Torry Holt	.50	.23
❑ 185	Rob Johnson	.30	.14
❑ 186	Kevin Hardy	.20	.09
❑ 187	Napoleon Kaufman	.30	.14
❑ 188	Jevon Kearse	.50	.23
❑ 189	Terance Mathis	.30	.14
❑ 190	Dorsey Levens	.30	.14
❑ 191	Kyle Brady	.20	.09
❑ 192	Steve McNair	.50	.23
❑ 193	Kevin Johnson	.50	.23
❑ 194	Lamar Smith	.30	.14
❑ 195	Ryan Leaf	.30	.14
❑ 196	Rod Woodson	.30	.14
❑ 197	Corey Bradford	.20	.09
❑ 198	Joe Horn	.30	.14
❑ 199	Isaac Bruce	.50	.23
❑ 200	Steve Young Dan Marino	1.50	.70
❑ 201	DeMario Brown RC	.60	.25
❑ 202	Chad Morton RC	1.25	.55
❑ 203	Quinton Spotwood RC	.60	.25
❑ 204	Mike Anderson RC	1.25	.55
❑ 205	Jarious Jackson RC	1.00	.45
❑ 206	Hank Poteat RC	1.00	.45
❑ 207	Rogers Beckett RC	1.00	.45
❑ 208	Deon Dyer RC	1.00	.45
❑ 209	Charles Lee RC	.60	.25
❑ 210	Barrett Green RC	.60	.25
❑ 211	T.J. Slaughter RC	.60	.25
❑ 212	Chris Hovan RC	1.00	.45
❑ 213	Mark Simoneau	1.00	.45
❑ 214	Rashard Anderson RC	1.00	.45
❑ 215	Trevor Insley RC	.60	.25
❑ 216	Paul Smith RC	1.00	.45
❑ 217	Doug Johnson RC	1.25	.55
❑ 218	Dwayne Goodrich RC	.60	.25
❑ 219	Julian Peterson RC	1.25	.55
❑ 220	Keith Bulluck RC	1.25	.55
❑ 221	Chris Samuels RC	1.00	.45
❑ 222	Shaun Ellis RC	1.25	.55
❑ 223	Na'il Diggs RC	1.00	.45
❑ 224	William Bartee RC	1.00	.45
❑ 225	John Abraham RC	1.25	.55
❑ 226	Trevor Gaylor RC	1.00	.45
❑ 227	Dante Hall RC	2.50	1.10
❑ 228	Marcus Knight RC	1.00	.45
❑ 229	Patrick Pass RC	1.00	.45
❑ 230	Bashir Yamini RC	.60	.25
❑ 231	Deltha O'Neal RC	1.25	.55
❑ 232	Vaughn Sanders RC	.60	.25
❑ 233	Todd Husak RC	1.25	.55
❑ 234	Thomas Hamner RC	.60	.25
❑ 235	Chafie Fields RC	.60	.25
❑ 236	Orantes Grant RC	.60	.25
❑ 237	Muneer Moore RC	.60	.25
❑ 238	Kwame Cavil RC	.60	.25
❑ 239	Spergon Wynn RC	1.00	.45
❑ 240	Leon Murray RC	.60	.25
❑ 241	Rob Morris RC	1.00	.45
❑ 242	Ben Kelly RC	.60	.25
❑ 243	Darren Howard RC	1.00	.45
❑ 244	Raynoch Thompson RC	1.00	.45
❑ 245	Mike Green RC	1.00	.45
❑ 246	Sammy Morris RC	1.00	.45
❑ 247	Ahmed Plummer RC	1.25	.55
❑ 248	Ian Gold RC	1.00	.45
❑ 249	Chris Coleman RC	1.25	.55
❑ 250	Ron Dixon RC	1.00	.45
❑ 251	Peter Warrick RC	2.00	.90
❑ 252	Joe Hamilton RC	1.50	.70
❑ 253	Dennis Northcutt RC	2.00	.90
❑ 254	Laveranues Coles RC	2.50	1.10
❑ 255	Michael Wiley RC	1.00	.45
❑ 256	Plaxico Burress RC	4.00	1.80
❑ 257	Danny Farmer RC	1.50	.70
❑ 258	Aaron Shea RC	1.00	.45
❑ 259	Sebastian Janikowski RC	2.00	.90
❑ 260	Corey Simon RC	1.25	.55
❑ 261	Frank Murphy RC	1.00	.45
❑ 262	JaJuan Dawson RC	1.00	.45
❑ 263	Ron Dayne RC	2.00	.90
❑ 264	Tim Rattay RC	2.50	1.10
❑ 265	Troy Walters RC	2.00	.90
❑ 266	J.R. Redmond RC	1.50	.70
❑ 267	Tom Brady RC	25.00	11.00
❑ 268	Jamal Lewis RC	5.00	2.20
❑ 269	Anthony Lucas RC	1.00	.45
❑ 270	Reuben Droughns RC	2.50	1.10
❑ 271	James Williams RC	1.50	.70
❑ 272	Shyrone Stith RC	1.50	.70
❑ 273	Jerry Porter RC	2.50	1.10
❑ 274	Brian Urlacher RC	8.00	3.60
❑ 275	Avion Black RC	1.50	.70
❑ 276	Thomas Jones RC	3.00	1.35
❑ 277	Chad Pennington RC	8.00	3.60
❑ 278	Travis Prentice RC	1.50	.70
❑ 279	Chris Redman RC	1.00	.45
❑ 280	Travis Taylor RC	1.25	.55
❑ 281	Giovanni Carmazzi RC	1.50	.70
❑ 282	Sherrod Gideon RC	1.00	.45
❑ 283	Bubba Franks RC	2.00	.90
❑ 284	Sylvester Morris RC	1.00	.45
❑ 285	Curtis Keaton RC	1.50	.70
❑ 286	Frank Moreau RC	1.50	.70
❑ 287	Terrelle Smith RC	1.50	.70
❑ 288	Shaun Alexander RC	5.00	2.20
❑ 289	Tee Martin RC	1.25	.55
❑ 290	R.Jay Soward RC	1.50	.70
❑ 291	Dez White RC	2.00	.90
❑ 292	Trung Canidate RC	1.50	.70
❑ 293	Darrell Jackson RC	4.00	1.80
❑ 294	Marc Bulger RC	4.00	1.80
❑ 295	Courtney Brown RC	1.25	.55
❑ 296	Todd Pinkston RC	2.00	.90
❑ 297	Anthony Becht RC	2.00	.90
❑ 298	Doug Chapman RC	1.50	.70
❑ 299	Gari Scott RC	1.00	.45
❑ 300	Chris Cole RC	1.50	.70

1991 Pacific

	Nm-Mt	Ex-Mt
COMPLETE SET (660)	15.00	6.75
COMP.SERIES 1 (550)	8.00	3.60
COMP.FACT.SER.1 (550)	10.00	4.50
COMP.SERIES 2 (110)	8.00	3.60
COMP.FACT.SER.2 (110)	12.00	5.50
COMP.CHECKLIST SET (5)	15.00	6.75

❑ 1 Deion Sanders .40 .18
❑ 2 Steve Broussard .05 .02
❑ 3 Aundray Bruce .05 .02
❑ 4 Rick Bryan .05 .02
❑ 5 John Rade .05 .02
❑ 6 Scott Case .05 .02
❑ 7 Tony Casillas .05 .02
❑ 8 Shawn Collins .05 .02
❑ 9 Darion Conner .05 .02
❑ 10 Tory Epps .05 .02
❑ 11 Bill Fralic .05 .02
❑ 12 Mike Gann .05 .02
❑ 13 Tim Green UER .05 .02
(Listed as DT
should say DE)
❑ 14 Chris Hinton .05 .02
❑ 15 Houston Hoover UER .05 .02
(Deion misspelled as
Deon on card back)
❑ 16 Chris Miller .10 .05
❑ 17 Andre Rison .10 .05
❑ 18 Mike Rozier .05 .02
❑ 19 Jessie Tuggle .05 .02
❑ 20 Don Beebe .05 .02
❑ 21 Ray Bentley .05 .02
❑ 22 Shane Conlan .05 .02
❑ 23 Kent Hull .05 .02
❑ 24 Mark Kelso .05 .02
❑ 25 James Lofton UER .10 .05
(Photo on front
actually Flip Johnson)
❑ 26 Scott Norwood .05 .02
❑ 27 Andre Reed .10 .05
❑ 28 Leonard Smith .05 .02
❑ 29 Bruce Smith .25 .11
❑ 30 Leon Seals .05 .02
❑ 31 Darryl Talley .05 .02
❑ 32 Steve Tasker .10 .05
❑ 33 Thurman Thomas .25 .11
❑ 34 James Williams .05 .02
❑ 35 Will Wolford .05 .02
❑ 36 Frank Reich .10 .05
❑ 37 Jeff Wright RC .05 .02
❑ 38 Neal Anderson .10 .05
❑ 39 Trace Armstrong .05 .02
❑ 40 Johnny Bailey UER .05 .02
(Gained 5320 yards in
college, should be 6320)
❑ 41 Mark Bortz UER .05 .02
(Johnny Bailey misspelled
as Johhny on cardback)
❑ 42 Cap Boso RC .05 .02
❑ 43 Kevin Butler .05 .02
❑ 44 Mark Carrier DB .10 .05
❑ 45 Jim Covert .05 .02
❑ 46 Wendell Davis .05 .02
❑ 47 Richard Dent .10 .05
❑ 48 Shaun Gayle .05 .02
❑ 49 Jim Harbaugh .25 .11
❑ 50 Jay Hilgenberg .05 .02
❑ 51 Brad Muster .05 .02
❑ 52 William Perry .10 .05
❑ 53 Mike Singletary UER .10 .05
(No College listed
should say Baylor)
❑ 54 Peter Tom Willis .05 .02
❑ 55 Donnell Woolford .05 .02
❑ 56 Steve McMichael .10 .05
❑ 57 Eric Ball .05 .02
❑ 58 Lewis Billups .05 .02
❑ 59 Jim Breech .05 .02
❑ 60 James Brooks .10 .05
❑ 61 Eddie Brown .05 .02
❑ 62 Rickey Dixon .05 .02
❑ 63 Boomer Esiason .10 .05
❑ 64 James Francis .05 .02
❑ 65 David Fulcher .05 .02
❑ 66 David Grant .05 .02
❑ 67 Harold Green UER .05 .02
(Misplaced apostrophe
in Gamecocks)
❑ 68 Rodney Holman .05 .02
❑ 69 Stanford Jennings .05 .02
❑ 70A Tim Krumrie ERR .50 .23
(Misspelled Krumprie
on card front)
❑ 70B Tim Krumrie COR .30 .14
❑ 71 Tim McGee .05 .02
❑ 72 Anthony Munoz .10 .05
❑ 73 Mitchell Price RC .05 .02
❑ 74 Eric Thomas .05 .02
❑ 75 Ickey Woods .05 .02
❑ 76 Mike Baab .05 .02
❑ 77 Thane Gash .05 .02
❑ 78 David Grayson .05 .02
❑ 79 Mike Johnson .05 .02
❑ 80 Reggie Langhorne .05 .02
❑ 81 Kevin Mack .05 .02
❑ 82 Clay Matthews .10 .05
❑ 83A Eric Metcalf ERR .50 .23
("Terry is the son of Terry")
❑ 83B Eric Metcalf COR .30 .14
("Eric is the son of Terry")
❑ 84 Frank Minnifield .05 .02
❑ 85 Mike Oliphant .05 .02
❑ 86 Mike Pagel .05 .02
❑ 87 John Talley .05 .02
❑ 88 Lawyer Tillman .05 .02
❑ 89 Gregg Rakoczy UER .05 .02
(Misspelled Greg on
both sides of card)
❑ 90 Bryan Wagner .05 .02
❑ 91 Rob Burnett RC .10 .05
❑ 92 Tommie Agee .05 .02
❑ 93 Troy Aikman UER .75 .35
(4328 yards is career
total not season; text
has him breaking passing
record which is not true)
❑ 94A Bill Bates ERR .50 .23
(Black line on cardfront)
❑ 94B Bill Bates COR .30 .14
(No black line
on cardfront)
❑ 95 Jack Del Rio .10 .05
❑ 96 Issiac Holt UER .05 .02
(Photo on back
actually Timmy Newsome)
❑ 97 Michael Irvin .25 .11
❑ 98 Jim Jeffcoat UER .05 .02
(On back, red line
has Jeff not Jim)
❑ 99 Jimmie Jones .05 .02
❑ 100 Kelvin Martin .05 .02
❑ 101 Nate Newton .10 .05
❑ 102 Danny Noonan .05 .02
❑ 103 Ken Norton Jr. .10 .05
❑ 104 Jay Novacek .25 .11
❑ 105 Mike Saxon .05 .02
❑ 106 Derrick Shepard .05 .02
❑ 107 Emmitt Smith 2.00 .90
❑ 108 Daniel Stubbs .05 .02
❑ 109 Tony Tolbert .05 .02
❑ 110 Alexander Wright .05 .02
❑ 111 Steve Atwater .05 .02
❑ 112 Melvin Bratton .05 .02
❑ 113 Tyrone Braxton UER .05 .02
(Went to North Dakota
State, not South Dakota)
❑ 114 Alphonso Carreker .05 .02
❑ 115 John Elway 1.25 .55
❑ 116 Simon Fletcher .05 .02
❑ 117 Bobby Humphrey .05 .02
❑ 118 Mark Jackson .05 .02
❑ 119 Vance Johnson .05 .02
❑ 120 Greg Kragen UER .05 .02
(Recovered 20 fumbles
in '89, yet 11 in career)
❑ 121 Karl Mecklenburg UER .05 .02
(Misspelled Mecklenberg
on card front)
❑ 122A Orson Mobley ERR .50 .23
(Misspelled Orsen)
❑ 122B Orson Mobley COR .10 .05
❑ 123 Alton Montgomery .05 .02
❑ 124 Ricky Nattiel .05 .02
❑ 125 Steve Sewell .05 .02
❑ 126 Shannon Sharpe .50 .23
❑ 127 Dennis Smith .05 .02
❑ 128A A.Townsend RC ERR .50 .23
Misspelled Andie
on card front
❑ 128B A.Townsend COR RC .10 .05
❑ 129 Mike Horan .05 .02
❑ 130 Jerry Ball .05 .02
❑ 131 Bennie Blades .05 .02
❑ 132 Lomas Brown .05 .02
❑ 133 Jeff Campbell UER .05 .02
(No NFL totals line)
❑ 134 Robert Clark .05 .02
❑ 135 Michael Cofer .05 .02
❑ 136 Dennis Gibson .05 .02
❑ 137 Mel Gray .10 .05
❑ 138 LeRoy Irvin UER .05 .02
(Misspelled LEROY;
spent 10 years with
Rams, not 11)
❑ 139 George Jamison RC .05 .02
❑ 140 Richard Johnson .05 .02
❑ 141 Eddie Murray .05 .02
❑ 142 Dan Owens .05 .02
❑ 143 Rodney Peete .10 .05
❑ 144 Barry Sanders 1.25 .55
❑ 145 Chris Spielman .10 .05
❑ 146 Marc Spindler .05 .02
❑ 147 Andre Ware .10 .05
❑ 148 William White .05 .02
❑ 149 Tony Bennett .10 .05
❑ 150 Robert Brown .05 .02
❑ 151 LeRoy Butler .10 .05
❑ 152 Anthony Dilweg .05 .02
❑ 153 Michael Haddix .05 .02
❑ 154 Ron Hallstrom .05 .02
❑ 155 Tim Harris .05 .02
❑ 156 Johnny Holland .05 .02
❑ 157 Chris Jacke .05 .02
❑ 158 Perry Kemp .05 .02
❑ 159 Mark Lee .05 .02
❑ 160 Don Majkowski .05 .02
❑ 161 Tony Mandarich UER .05 .02
(United Stated on back)
❑ 162 Mark Murphy .05 .02
❑ 163 Brian Noble .05 .02
❑ 164 Shawn Patterson .05 .02
❑ 165 Jeff Query .05 .02
❑ 166 Sterling Sharpe .25 .11
❑ 167 Darrell Thompson .05 .02
❑ 168 Ed West .05 .02
❑ 169 Ray Childress UER .05 .02
(Front DE, back DT)
❑ 170A Cris Dishman RC ERR .10 .05
(Misspelled Chris
on both sides)
❑ 170B C.Dishman RC COR/ERR .10 .05
Misspelled Chris
on back only
❑ 170C Cris Dishman RC COR .10 .05
❑ 171 Curtis Duncan .05 .02
❑ 172 William Fuller .10 .05
❑ 173 Ernest Givins UER .10 .05
(Missing a highlight
line on back)
❑ 174 Drew Hill .05 .02
❑ 175A Haywood Jeffires ERR .25 .11
(Misspelled Jeffries
on both sides of card)
❑ 175B Haywood Jeffires COR .25 .11
❑ 176 Sean Jones .10 .05

❑ 177 Lamar Lathon .05 .02
❑ 178 Bruce Matthews .10 .05
❑ 179 Bubba McDowell .05 .02
❑ 180 Johnny Meads .05 .02
❑ 181 Warren Moon UER .25 .11
(Birth listed as '65, should be '56)
❑ 182 Mike Munchak .10 .05
❑ 183 Allen Pinkett .05 .02
❑ 184 Dean Steinkuhler UER .05 .02
(Oakland, should be Outland)
❑ 185 Lorenzo White UER .05 .02
(Rout misspelled as route on card back)
❑ 186A John Grimsley ERR .50 .23
(Misspelled Grimsby)
❑ 186B John Grimsley COR .10 .05
❑ 187 Pat Beach .05 .02
❑ 188 Albert Bentley .05 .02
❑ 189 Dean Biasucci .05 .02
❑ 190 Duane Bickett .05 .02
❑ 191 Bill Brooks .05 .02
❑ 192 Eugene Daniel .05 .02
❑ 193 Jeff George .25 .11
❑ 194 Jon Hand .05 .02
❑ 195 Jeff Herrod .05 .02
❑ 196A Jessie Hester ERR .30 .14
(Misspelled Jesse)
❑ 196B Jessie Hester ERR .10 .05
(Name corrected; 6-year player, not 7; no NFL total line)
❑ 197 Mike Prior .05 .02
❑ 198 Stacey Simmons .05 .02
❑ 199 Rohn Stark .05 .02
❑ 200 Pat Tomberlin .05 .02
❑ 201 Clarence Verdin .05 .02
❑ 202 Keith Taylor .05 .02
❑ 203 Jack Trudeau .05 .02
❑ 204 Chip Banks .05 .02
❑ 205 John Alt .05 .02
❑ 206 Deron Cherry .05 .02
❑ 207 Steve DeBerg .05 .02
❑ 208 Tim Grunhard .05 .02
❑ 209 Albert Lewis .05 .02
❑ 210 Nick Lowery UER .05 .02
(12 years NFL exp., should be 13)
❑ 211 Bill Maas .05 .02
❑ 212 Chris Martin .05 .02
❑ 213 Todd McNair .05 .02
❑ 214 Christian Okoye .05 .02
❑ 215 Stephone Paige .05 .02
❑ 216 Steve Pelluer .05 .02
❑ 217 Kevin Porter .05 .02
❑ 218 Kevin Ross .05 .02
❑ 219 Dan Saleaumua .05 .02
❑ 220 Neil Smith .25 .11
❑ 221 David Szott UER .05 .02
(Listed as Off. Guard)
❑ 222 Derrick Thomas .25 .11
❑ 223 Barry Word .05 .02
❑ 224 Percy Snow .05 .02
❑ 225 Marcus Allen .25 .11
❑ 226 Eddie Anderson UER .05 .02
(Began career with Seahawks, not Raiders)
❑ 227 Steve Beuerlein UER .10 .05
(Not injured during '90 season, but was inactive)
❑ 228A Tim Brown ERR .25 .11
(No position on card)
❑ 228B Tim Brown COR .25 .11
❑ 229 Scott Davis .05 .02
❑ 230 Mike Dyal .05 .02
❑ 231 Mervyn Fernandez UER .05 .02
(Card says free agent in '87, but was drafted in '83)
❑ 232 Willie Gault UER .05 .02
(Text says 60 catches in '90, stats say 50)
❑ 233 Ethan Horton UER .05 .02
(No height and weight listings)
❑ 234 Bo Jackson UER .30 .14
(Drafted in '87, not '86)
❑ 235 Howie Long .25 .11
❑ 236 Terry McDaniel .05 .02
❑ 237 Max Montoya .05 .02
❑ 238 Don Mosebar .05 .02
❑ 239 Jay Schroeder .05 .02
❑ 240 Steve Smith .05 .02
❑ 241 Greg Townsend .05 .02
❑ 242 Aaron Wallace .05 .02
❑ 243 Lionel Washington .05 .02
❑ 244A Steve Wisniewski ERR .10 .05
(Misspelled Winsniewski on both sides; Drafted, should say traded to)
❑ 244B Steve Wisniewski ERR .75 .35
(Misspelled Winsniewski on card back)
❑ 244C Steve Wisniewski COR .10 .05
❑ 245 Flipper Anderson .05 .02
❑ 246 Latin Berry RC .05 .02
❑ 247 Robert Delpino .05 .02
❑ 248 Marcus Dupree .05 .02
❑ 249 Henry Ellard .10 .05
❑ 250 Jim Everett .10 .05
❑ 251 Cleveland Gary .05 .02
❑ 252 Jerry Gray .05 .02
❑ 253 Kevin Greene .10 .05
❑ 254 Pete Holohan UER .05 .02
(Photo on back actually Kevin Greene)
❑ 255 Buford McGee .05 .02
❑ 256 Tom Newberry .05 .02
❑ 257A Irv Pankey ERR .50 .23
(Misspelled as Panky on both sides of card)
❑ 257B Irv Pankey COR .10 .05
❑ 258 Jackie Slater .05 .02
❑ 259 Doug Smith .05 .02
❑ 260 Frank Stams .05 .02
❑ 261 Michael Stewart .05 .02
❑ 262 Fred Strickland .05 .02
❑ 263 J.B. Brown UER .05 .02
(No periods after initials on card front)
❑ 264 Mark Clayton .10 .05
❑ 265 Jeff Cross .05 .02
❑ 266 Mark Dennis RC .05 .02
❑ 267 Mark Duper .10 .05
❑ 268 Ferrell Edmunds .05 .02
❑ 269 Dan Marino 1.25 .55
❑ 270 John Offerdahl .05 .02
❑ 271 Louis Oliver .05 .02
❑ 272 Tony Paige .05 .02
❑ 273 Reggie Roby .05 .02
❑ 274 Sammie Smith .05 .02
(Picture is sideways on the card)
❑ 275 Keith Sims .05 .02
❑ 276 Brian Sochia .05 .02
❑ 277 Pete Stoyanovich .05 .02
❑ 278 Richmond Webb .05 .02
❑ 279 Jarvis Williams .05 .02
❑ 280 Tim McKyer .05 .02
❑ 281A Jim C. Jensen ERR .50 .23
(Misspelled Jenson on card back)
❑ 281B Jim C. Jensen COR .10 .05
(Plays a skill position, not skilled)
❑ 282 Scott Secules RC .05 .02
❑ 283 Ray Berry .05 .02
❑ 284 Joey Browner UER .05 .02
(Safetys, sic)
❑ 285 Anthony Carter .10 .05
❑ 286A Cris Carter ERR .50 .23
(Misspelled Chris on both sides)
❑ 286B Cris Carter ERR/COR 1.50 .70
(Misspelled Chris on card back)
❑ 286C Cris Carter COR .50 .23
❑ 287 Chris Doleman .05 .02
❑ 288 Mark Dusbabek UER .05 .02
(Front DT, back LB)
❑ 289 Hassan Jones .05 .02
❑ 290 Steve Jordan .05 .02
❑ 291 Carl Lee .05 .02
❑ 292 Kirk Lowdermilk .05 .02
❑ 293 Randall McDaniel .05 .02
❑ 294 Mike Merriweather .05 .02
❑ 295A Keith Millard UER .20 .09
(No position on card)
❑ 295B Keith Millard COR 2.50 1.10
❑ 296 Al Noga UER .05 .02
(Card says DT, should say DE)
❑ 297 Scott Studwell UER .05 .02
(83 career tackles, but bio says 156 tackles in '81 season)
❑ 298 Henry Thomas .05 .02
❑ 299 Herschel Walker .10 .05
❑ 300 Gary Zimmerman .05 .02
❑ 301 Rick Gannon .25 .11
❑ 302 Wade Wilson UER .10 .05
(Led AFC, should say led NFC)
❑ 303 Vincent Brown .05 .02
❑ 304 Marv Cook .05 .02
❑ 305 Hart Lee Dykes .05 .02
❑ 306 Irving Fryar .10 .05
❑ 307 Tommy Hodson UER .05 .02
(No NFL totals line)
❑ 308 Maurice Hurst .05 .02
❑ 309 Ronnie Lippett UER .05 .02
(On back,reserves should be reserve)
❑ 310 Fred Marion .05 .02
❑ 311 Greg McMurtry .05 .02
❑ 312 Johnny Rembert .05 .02
❑ 313 Chris Singleton .05 .02
❑ 314 Ed Reynolds .05 .02
❑ 315 Andre Tippett .05 .02
❑ 316 Garin Veris .05 .02
❑ 317 Brent Williams .05 .02
❑ 318A John Stephens ERR .10 .05
(Misspelled Stevens on both sides of card)
❑ 318B J.Stephens COR/ERR .75 .35
Misspelled Stevens on card back
❑ 318C John Stephens COR .10 .05
❑ 319 Sammy Martin .05 .02
❑ 320 Bruce Armstrong .05 .02
❑ 321A Morten Andersen ERR .30 .14
(Misspelled Anderson on both sides of card)
❑ 321B M.Andersen ERR/COR .75 .35
Misspelled Anderson on card back
❑ 321C Morten Andersen COR .10 .05
❑ 322 Gene Atkins UER .05 .02
(No NFL Exp. line)
❑ 323 Vince Buck .05 .02
❑ 324 John Fourcade .05 .02
❑ 325 Kevin Haverdink .05 .02
❑ 326 Bobby Hebert .05 .02
❑ 327 Craig Heyward .10 .05
❑ 328 Dalton Hilliard .05 .02
❑ 329 Rickey Jackson .05 .02
❑ 330A Vaughan Johnson ERR .20 .09
(Misspelled Vaughn)
❑ 330B Vaughan Johnson COR 2.50 1.10
❑ 331 Eric Martin .05 .02
❑ 332 Wayne Martin .05 .02
❑ 333 Rueben Mayes UER .05 .02
(Misspelled Reuben on card back)
❑ 334 Sam Mills .05 .02
❑ 335 Brett Perriman .25 .11
❑ 336 Pat Swilling .10 .05
❑ 337 Renaldo Turnbull .05 .02
❑ 338 Lonzell Hill .05 .02
❑ 339 Steve Walsh UER .05 .02
(19 of 20 for 70.3, should be 95 percent)
❑ 340 Carl Banks UER .05 .02
(Led defensive in tackles should say defense)
❑ 341 Mark Bavaro UER .05 .02
(Weight on back 145, should say 245)
❑ 342 Maurice Carthon .05 .02
❑ 343 Pat Harlow RC .05 .02
❑ 344 Eric Dorsey .05 .02
❑ 345 John Elliott .05 .02

❑ 346 Rodney Hampton .25 .11
❑ 347 Jeff Hostetler .10 .05
❑ 348 Erik Howard UER .05 .02
(Listed as DT, should be NT)
❑ 349 Pepper Johnson .05 .02
❑ 350A Sean Landeta ERR .10 .05
(Misspelled Landetta on both sides of card)
❑ 350B Sean Landeta COR .50 .23
❑ 351 Leonard Marshall .05 .02
❑ 352 Dave Meggett .10 .05
❑ 353A Bart Oates ERR .10 .05
(Misspelled Oats on both sides; misspelled Megget in Did You Know)
❑ 353B Bart Oates COR/ERR .75 .35
(Misspelled Oats on card back; misspelled Megget in Did You Know)
❑ 353C Bart Oates COR .10 .05
(Dave Meggett still misspelled as Megget)
❑ 354 Gary Reasons .05 .02
❑ 355 Phil Simms .10 .05
❑ 356 Lawrence Taylor .25 .11
❑ 357 Reyna Thompson .05 .02
❑ 358 Brian Williams OL UER .05 .02
(Front C-G, back G)
❑ 359 Matt Bahr .05 .02
❑ 360 Mark Ingram .10 .05
❑ 361 Brad Baxter .05 .02
❑ 362 Mark Boyer .05 .02
❑ 363 Dennis Byrd .05 .02
❑ 364 Dave Cadigan UER .05 .02
(Terance misspelled as Terrance on back)
❑ 365 Kyle Clifton .05 .02
❑ 366 James Hasty .05 .02
❑ 367 Joe Kelly UER .05 .02
(Front 50, back 58)
❑ 368 Jeff Lageman .05 .02
❑ 369 Pat Leahy UER .05 .02
(Career-best FG in '65, should say '85)
❑ 370 Terance Mathis .10 .05
❑ 371 Erik McMillan .05 .02
❑ 372 Rob Moore .25 .11
❑ 373 Ken O'Brien .05 .02
❑ 374 Tony Stargell .05 .02
❑ 375 Jim Sweeney UER .05 .02
(Landetta, sic)
❑ 376 Al Toon .10 .05
❑ 377 Johnny Hector .05 .02
❑ 378 Jeff Criswell .05 .02
❑ 379 Mike Haight RC .05 .02
❑ 380 Troy Benson .05 .02
❑ 381 Eric Allen .05 .02
❑ 382 Fred Barnett .25 .11
❑ 383 Jerome Brown .05 .02
❑ 384 Keith Byars .05 .02
❑ 385 Randall Cunningham .25 .11
❑ 386 Byron Evans .05 .02
❑ 387 Wes Hopkins .05 .02
❑ 388 Keith Jackson .10 .05
❑ 389 Seth Joyner UER .10 .05
(Fumble recovery line not aligned)
❑ 390 Bobby Wilson RC .05 .02
❑ 391 Heath Sherman .05 .02
❑ 392 Clyde Simmons UER .05 .02
(Listed as DT, should say DE)
❑ 393 Ben Smith .05 .02
❑ 394 Andre Waters .05 .02
❑ 395 Reggie White UER .25 .11
(Derrick Thomas holds NFL record with 7 sacks)
❑ 396 Calvin Williams .10 .05
❑ 397 Al Harris .05 .02
❑ 398 Anthony Toney .05 .02
❑ 399 Mike Quick .05 .02
❑ 400 Anthony Bell .05 .02
❑ 401 Rich Camarillo .05 .02
❑ 402 Roy Green .05 .02
❑ 403 Ken Harvey .10 .05
❑ 404 Eric Hill .05 .02
❑ 405 Garth Jax RC UER .05 .02
(Should have comma before "the" and after "Cowboys" on cardback)
❑ 406 Ernie Jones .05 .02
❑ 407A Cedric Mack ERR .20 .09
(Misspelled Cedrick on card front)
❑ 407B Cedric Mack COR 2.50 1.10
(NFL Exp. line is red instead of black)
❑ 408 Dexter Manley .05 .02
❑ 409 Tim McDonald .05 .02
❑ 410 Freddie Joe Nunn .05 .02
❑ 411 Ricky Proehl .05 .02
❑ 412 Moe Gardner RC .05 .02
❑ 413 Timm Rosenbach .05 .02
❑ 414 Luis Sharpe UER .05 .02
(Lomiller, sic)
❑ 415 Vai Sikahema UER .05 .02
(Front RB, back PR)
❑ 416 Anthony Thompson .05 .02
❑ 417 Ron Wolfley UER .05 .02
(Missing NFL fact line under vital stats)
❑ 418 Lonnie Young .05 .02
❑ 419 Gary Anderson K .05 .02
❑ 420 Bubby Brister .05 .02
❑ 421 Thomas Everett .05 .02
❑ 422 Eric Green .05 .02
❑ 423 Delton Hall .05 .02
❑ 424 Bryan Hinkle .05 .02
❑ 425 Merril Hoge .05 .02
❑ 426 Carnell Lake .05 .02
❑ 427 Louis Lipps .05 .02
❑ 428 David Little .05 .02
❑ 429 Greg Lloyd .25 .11
❑ 430 Mike Mularkey .05 .02
❑ 431 Keith Willis UER .05 .02
(No period after C in L.C. Greenwood on back)
❑ 432 Dwayne Woodruff .05 .02
❑ 433 Rod Woodson UER .25 .11
(No NFL experience listed on card)
❑ 434 Tim Worley .05 .02
❑ 435 Warren Williams .05 .02
❑ 436 Terry Long UER .05 .02
(Not 5th NFL team, tied for 7th)
❑ 437 Martin Bayless .05 .02
❑ 438 Jarrod Bunch RC .05 .02
❑ 439 Marion Butts .10 .05
❑ 440 Gill Byrd UER .05 .02
(Pickoffs misspelled as two words)
❑ 441 Arthur Cox .05 .02
❑ 442 John Friesz .25 .11
❑ 443 Leo Goeas .05 .02
❑ 444 Burt Grossman .05 .02
❑ 445 Courtney Hall UER .05 .02
(In DYK section, is should be in)
❑ 446 Ronnie Harmon .05 .02
❑ 447 Nate Lewis RC .05 .02
❑ 448 Anthony Miller .10 .05
❑ 449 Leslie O'Neal .10 .05
❑ 450 Gary Plummer .05 .02
❑ 451 Junior Seau .25 .11
❑ 452 Billy Ray Smith .05 .02
❑ 453 Billy Joe Tolliver .05 .02
❑ 454 Broderick Thompson .05 .02
❑ 455 Lee Williams .05 .02
❑ 456 Michael Carter .05 .02
❑ 457 Mike Cofer .05 .02
❑ 458 Kevin Fagan .05 .02
❑ 459 Charles Haley .10 .05
❑ 460 Pierce Holt .05 .02
❑ 461 Johnnie Jackson RC UER .05 .02
Johnny on front
❑ 462 Brent Jones .25 .11
❑ 463 Guy McIntyre .05 .02
❑ 464 Joe Montana 1.25 .55
❑ 465A Bubba Paris ERR .10 .05
(Misspelled Parris; reversed negative)
❑ 465B Bubba Paris ERR/COR .50 .23
(Misspelled Parris; photo corrected
❑ 465C Bubba Paris COR .10 .05
❑ 466 Tom Rathman UER .05 .02
(Born 10/7/62, not 11/7/62)
❑ 467 Jerry Rice UER .75 .35
(4th to catch 100, should say 2nd)
❑ 468 Mike Sherrard .05 .02
❑ 469 John Taylor UER .10 .05
(AL1-Time, sic)
❑ 470 Steve Young .75 .35
❑ 471 Dennis Brown .05 .02
❑ 472 Dexter Carter .05 .02
❑ 473 Bill Romanowski .05 .02
❑ 474 Dave Waymer .05 .02
❑ 475 Robert Blackmon .05 .02
❑ 476 Derrick Fenner .05 .02
❑ 477 Nesby Glasgow UER .05 .02
(Missing total line for fumbles)
❑ 478 Jacob Green .05 .02
❑ 479 Andy Heck .05 .02
❑ 480 Norm Johnson UER .05 .02
(They own and operate card store, not run)
❑ 481 Tommy Kane .05 .02
❑ 482 Cortez Kennedy .25 .11
❑ 483A Dave Krieg ERR .20 .09
(Misspelled Kreig on both sides)
❑ 483B Dave Krieg COR 2.50 1.10
❑ 484 Bryan Millard .05 .02
❑ 485 Joe Nash .05 .02
❑ 486 Rufus Porter .05 .02
❑ 487 Eugene Robinson .05 .02
❑ 488 Mike Tice RC .05 .02
❑ 489 Chris Warren .25 .11
❑ 490 John L. Williams UER .05 .02
(No period after L on card front)
❑ 491 Terry Wooden .05 .02
❑ 492 Tony Woods .05 .02
❑ 493 Brian Blades .10 .05
❑ 494 Paul Skansi .05 .02
❑ 495 Gary Anderson RB .05 .02
❑ 496 Mark Carrier WR .25 .11
❑ 497 Chris Chandler .25 .11
❑ 498 Steve Christie .05 .02
❑ 499 Reggie Cobb .05 .02
❑ 500 Reuben Davis .05 .02
❑ 501 Willie Drewrey UER .05 .02
(Misspelled Drewery on both sides of card)
❑ 502 Randy Grimes .05 .02
❑ 503 Paul Gruber .05 .02
❑ 504 Wayne Haddix .05 .02
❑ 505 Ron Hall .05 .02
❑ 506 Harry Hamilton .05 .02
❑ 507 Bruce Hill .05 .02
❑ 508 Eugene Marve .05 .02
❑ 509 Keith McCants .05 .02
❑ 510 Winston Moss .05 .02
❑ 511 Kevin Murphy .05 .02
❑ 512 Mark Robinson .05 .02
❑ 513 Vinny Testaverde .10 .05
❑ 514 Broderick Thomas .05 .02
❑ 515A Jeff Bostic UER .10 .05
(Lomiller, sic; on back, word "goal" touches lower border)
❑ 515B Jeff Bostic UER .10 .05
(Lomiller, sic; on back, word "goal" is away from border)
❑ 516 Todd Bowles .05 .02
❑ 517 Earnest Byner .05 .02
❑ 518 Gary Clark .25 .11
❑ 519 Craig Erickson RC .25 .11
❑ 520 Darryl Grant .05 .02
❑ 521 Darrell Green .05 .02
❑ 522 Russ Grimm .05 .02
❑ 523 Stan Humphries .25 .11
❑ 524 Joe Jacoby UER .05 .02
(Lomiller, sic)
❑ 525 Jim Lachey .05 .02
❑ 526 Chip Lohmiller .05 .02

❑ 527 Charles Mann .05 .02
❑ 528 Wilber Marshall .05 .02
❑ 529A Art Monk .10 .05
(On back, "y" in history
touches copyright symbol)
❑ 529B Art Monk .10 .05
(On back, "y" in history
is away from symbol)
❑ 530 Tracy Rocker .05 .02
❑ 531 Mark Rypien .10 .05
❑ 532 Ricky Sanders UER .05 .02
(Stats say caught 56,
text says 57)
❑ 533 Alvin Walton UER .05 .02
(Listed as WR,
should be S)
❑ 534 Todd Marinovich RC UER .05 .02
17 percent, should
be 71 percent
❑ 535 Mike Dumas RC .05 .02
❑ 536A R.Maryland RC ERR .25 .11
No highlight line
❑ 536B R.Maryland RC COR .25 .11
Highlight line added
❑ 537 Eric Turner RC UER .10 .05
(Don Rogers misspelled
as Rodgers)
❑ 538 Ernie Mills RC .10 .05
❑ 539 Ed King RC .05 .02
❑ 540 Mike Stonebreaker .05 .02
❑ 541 Chris Zorich RC .25 .11
❑ 542A Mike Croel RC UER .05 .02
(Missing highlight line
under bio notes; front
photo reversed negative;
on back, "y" in weekly
inside copyright)
❑ 542B Mike Croel RC UER .05 .02
(Missing highlight line
under bio notes; front
photo reversed negative;
on back, "y" in weekly
barely touches copyright)
❑ 543 Eric Moten RC .05 .02
❑ 544 Dan McGwire RC .05 .02
❑ 545 Keith Cash RC .05 .02
❑ 546 Kenny Walker RC UER .05 .02
(Drafted 8th round,
not 7th)
❑ 547 Leroy Hoard UER .10 .05
(LeROY on card;
not a draft pick)
❑ 548 Luis Cristobal UER .05 .02
(front LB, back G)
❑ 549 Stacy Danley .05 .02
❑ 550 Todd Lyght RC .05 .02
❑ 551 Brett Favre RC 8.00 3.60
❑ 552 Mike Pritchard RC .25 .11
❑ 553 Moe Gardner .05 .02
❑ 554 Tim McKyer .05 .02
❑ 555 Erric Pegram RC .25 .11
❑ 556 Norm Johnson .05 .02
❑ 557 Bruce Pickens RC .05 .02
❑ 558 Henry Jones RC .10 .05
❑ 559 Phil Hansen RC .05 .02
❑ 560 Cornelius Bennett .10 .05
❑ 561 Stan Thomas .05 .02
❑ 562 Chris Zorich .10 .05
❑ 563 Anthony Morgan RC .05 .02
❑ 564 Darren Lewis RC .05 .02
❑ 565 Mike Stonebreaker .05 .02
❑ 566 Alfred Williams RC .05 .02
❑ 567 Lamar Rogers RC .05 .02
❑ 568 Erik Wilhelm RC UER .05 .02
(No NFL Experience
line on card back)
❑ 569 Ed King .05 .02
❑ 570 Michael Jackson RC .25 .11
❑ 571 James Jones RC .05 .02
❑ 572 Russell Maryland .25 .11
❑ 573 Dixon Edwards RC .05 .02
❑ 574 Darrick Brownlow RC .05 .02
❑ 575 Larry Brown DB RC .10 .05
❑ 576 Mike Croel .05 .02
❑ 577 Keith Traylor RC .05 .02
❑ 578 Kenny Walker .05 .02
❑ 579 Reggie Johnson RC .05 .02
❑ 580 Herman Moore RC .25 .11
❑ 581 Kelvin Pritchett RC .10 .05
❑ 582 Kevin Scott RC .05 .02
❑ 583 Vinnie Clark RC .05 .02
❑ 584 Esera Tuaolo RC .05 .02
❑ 585 Don Davey .05 .02
❑ 586 Blair Kiel RC .05 .02
❑ 587 Mike Dumas .05 .02
❑ 588 Darryll Lewis RC .10 .05
❑ 589 John Flannery RC .05 .02
❑ 590 Kevin Donnalley RC .05 .02
❑ 591 Shane Curry .05 .02
❑ 592 Mark Vander Poel RC .05 .02
❑ 593 Dave McCloughan .05 .02
❑ 594 Mel Agee RC .05 .02
❑ 595 Kerry Cash RC .05 .02
❑ 596 Harvey Williams RC .25 .11
❑ 597 Joe Valerio .05 .02
❑ 598 Tim Barnett RC UER .05 .02
(Harvey Williams
pictured on front)
❑ 599 Todd Marinovich .10 .05
❑ 600 Nick Bell RC .05 .02
❑ 601 Roger Craig .10 .05
❑ 602 Ronnie Lott .10 .05
❑ 603 Mike Jones RC .05 .02
❑ 604 Todd Lyght .05 .02
❑ 605 Roman Phifer RC .05 .02
❑ 606 David Lang RC .05 .02
❑ 607 Aaron Craver RC .05 .02
❑ 608 Mark Higgs RC .05 .02
❑ 609 Chris Green .05 .02
❑ 610 Randy Baldwin RC .05 .02
❑ 611 Pat Harlow .05 .02
❑ 612 Leonard Russell RC .25 .11
❑ 613 Jerome Henderson RC .05 .02
❑ 614 Scott Zolak RC UER .05 .02
(Bio says drafted in
1984, should be 1991)
❑ 615 Jon Vaughn RC .05 .02
❑ 616 Harry Colon RC .05 .02
❑ 617 Wesley Carroll RC .05 .02
❑ 618 Quinn Early .10 .05
❑ 619 Reginald Jones RC .05 .02
❑ 620 Jarrod Bunch .05 .02
❑ 621 Kanavis McGhee RC .05 .02
❑ 622 Ed McCaffrey RC 2.00 .90
❑ 623 Browning Nagle RC .05 .02
❑ 624 Mo Lewis RC .10 .05
❑ 625 Blair Thomas .05 .02
❑ 626 Antone Davis RC .05 .02
❑ 627 Jim McMahon .10 .05
❑ 628 Scott Kowalkowski RC .05 .02
❑ 629 Brad Goebel RC .05 .02
❑ 630 William Thomas RC .05 .02
❑ 631 Eric Swann RC .25 .11
❑ 632 Mike Jones DE RC .05 .02
❑ 633 Aeneas Williams RC .25 .11
❑ 634 Dexter Davis RC .05 .02
❑ 635 Tom Tupa UER .05 .02
(Did play in 1990,
but not as QB)
❑ 636 Johnny Johnson .05 .02
❑ 637 Randal Hill RC .10 .05
❑ 638 Jeff Graham RC .25 .11
❑ 639 Ernie Mills .05 .02
❑ 640 Adrian Cooper RC .05 .02
❑ 641 Stanley Richard RC .05 .02
❑ 642 Eric Bieniemy RC .05 .02
❑ 643 Eric Moten .05 .02
❑ 644 Shawn Jefferson RC .10 .05
❑ 645 Ted Washington RC .05 .02
❑ 646 John Johnson RC .05 .02
❑ 647 Dan McGwire .05 .02
❑ 648 Doug Thomas RC .05 .02
❑ 649 David Daniels RC .05 .02
❑ 650 John Kasay RC .10 .05
❑ 651 Jeff Kemp .05 .02
❑ 652 Charles McRae RC .05 .02
❑ 653 Lawrence Dawsey RC .10 .05
❑ 654 Robert Wilson RC .05 .02
❑ 655 Dexter Manley .05 .02
❑ 656 Chuck Weatherspoon .05 .02
❑ 657 Tim Ryan RC .05 .02
❑ 658 Bobby Wilson .05 .02
❑ 659 Ricky Ervins RC .10 .05
❑ 660 Matt Millen .10 .05

1999 Pacific

	Nm-Mt	Ex-Mt
COMPLETE SET (450)	80.00	36.00
❑ 1 Mario Bates	.25	.11
❑ 2 Larry Centers	.25	.11
❑ 3 Chris Gedney	.25	.11
❑ 4 Kwamie Lassiter RC	.60	.25
❑ 5 Johnny McWilliams	.25	.11
❑ 6 Eric Metcalf	.25	.11
❑ 7 Rob Moore	.40	.18
❑ 8 Adrian Murrell	.40	.18
❑ 9 Jake Plummer	.40	.18
❑ 10 Simeon Rice	.40	.18
❑ 11 Frank Sanders	.40	.18
❑ 12 Andre Wadsworth	.25	.11
❑ 13 Aeneas Williams	.25	.11
❑ 14 Michael Pittman Ronnie Anderson RC	1.25	.55
❑ 15 Morten Andersen	.25	.11
❑ 16 Jamal Anderson	.60	.25
❑ 17 Lester Archambeau	.25	.11
❑ 18 Chris Chandler	.40	.18
❑ 19 Bob Christian	.25	.11
❑ 20 Steve DeBerg	.25	.11
❑ 21 Tim Dwight	.60	.25
❑ 22 Tony Martin	.40	.18
❑ 23 Terance Mathis	.40	.18
❑ 24 Eugene Robinson	.25	.11
❑ 25 O.J. Santiago	.25	.11
❑ 26 Chuck Smith	.25	.11
❑ 27 Jessie Tuggle	.25	.11
❑ 28 Jammi German Ken Oxendine	.25	.11
❑ 29 Peter Boulware	.25	.11
❑ 30 Jay Graham	.25	.11
❑ 31 Jim Harbaugh	.40	.18
❑ 32 Priest Holmes	1.00	.45
❑ 33 Michael Jackson	.25	.11
❑ 34 Jermaine Lewis	.40	.18
❑ 35 Ray Lewis	.60	.25
❑ 36 Michael McCrary	.25	.11
❑ 37 Jonathan Ogden	.25	.11
❑ 38 Errict Rhett	.25	.11
❑ 39 James Roe RC	1.00	.45
❑ 40 Floyd Turner	.25	.11
❑ 41 Rod Woodson	.40	.18
❑ 42 Eric Zeier	.25	.11
❑ 43 Wally Richardson Patrick Johnson	.25	.11
❑ 44 Ruben Brown	.25	.11
❑ 45 Quinn Early	.25	.11
❑ 46 Doug Flutie	.60	.25
❑ 47 Sam Gash	.25	.11
❑ 48 Phil Hansen	.25	.11
❑ 49 Lonnie Johnson	.25	.11
❑ 50 Rob Johnson	.40	.18
❑ 51 Eric Moulds	.60	.25
❑ 52 Andre Reed	.40	.18
❑ 53 Jay Riemersma	.25	.11
❑ 54 Antowain Smith	.60	.25
❑ 55 Bruce Smith	.40	.18
❑ 56 Thurman Thomas	.40	.18
❑ 57 Ted Washington	.25	.11
❑ 58 Jonathan Linton Kamil Loud RC	1.00	.45
❑ 59 Michael Bates	.25	.11
❑ 60 Steve Beuerlein	.25	.11
❑ 61 Tim Biakabutuka	.40	.18
❑ 62 Mark Carrier WR	.25	.11
❑ 63 Eric Davis	.25	.11

❑ 64 William Floyd	.25	.11
❑ 65 Sean Gilbert	.25	.11
❑ 66 Kevin Greene	.25	.11
❑ 67 Rocket Ismail	.40	.18
❑ 68 Anthony Johnson	.25	.11
❑ 69 Fred Lane	.25	.11
❑ 70 Muhsin Muhammad	.40	.18
❑ 71 Winslow Oliver	.25	.11
❑ 72 Wesley Walls	.40	.18
❑ 73 Dameyune Craig RC	1.50	.70
Shane Matthews		
❑ 74 Edgar Bennett	.25	.11
❑ 75 Curtis Conway	.40	.18
❑ 76 Bobby Engram	.40	.18
❑ 77 Curtis Enis	.25	.11
❑ 78 Ty Hallock RC	1.00	.45
❑ 79 Walt Harris	.25	.11
❑ 80 Jeff Jaeger	.25	.11
❑ 81 Erik Kramer	.25	.11
❑ 82 Glyn Milburn	.25	.11
❑ 83 Chris Penn	.25	.11
❑ 84 Steve Stenstrom	.25	.11
❑ 85 Ryan Wetnight	.25	.11
❑ 86 James Allen RC	1.50	.70
Moses Moreno		
❑ 87 Ashley Ambrose	.25	.11
❑ 88 Brandon Bennett RC	1.00	.45
❑ 89 Eric Bieniemy	.25	.11
❑ 90 Jeff Blake	.40	.18
❑ 91 Corey Dillon	.60	.25
❑ 92 Paul Justin	.25	.11
❑ 93 Eric Kresser RC	1.00	.45
❑ 94 Tremain Mack	.25	.11
❑ 95 Tony McGee	.25	.11
❑ 96 Neil O'Donnell	.40	.18
❑ 97 Carl Pickens	.40	.18
❑ 98 Darnay Scott	.25	.11
❑ 99 Takeo Spikes	.25	.11
❑ 100 Ty Detmer	.25	.11
❑ 101 Chris Gardocki	.25	.11
❑ 102 Damon Gibson	.25	.11
❑ 103 Antonio Langham	.25	.11
❑ 104 Jerris McPhail	.25	.11
❑ 105 Irv Smith	.25	.11
❑ 106 Freddie Solomon	.25	.11
❑ 107 Scott Milanovich	1.00	.45
Fred Brock RC		
❑ 108 Troy Aikman	1.25	.55
❑ 109 Larry Allen	.25	.11
❑ 110 111	.25	.11
❑ 111 Billy Davis	.25	.11
❑ 112 Michael Irvin	.40	.18
❑ 113 David LaFleur	.25	.11
❑ 114 Ernie Mills	.25	.11
❑ 115 Nate Newton	.25	.11
❑ 116 Deion Sanders	.60	.25
❑ 117 Emmitt Smith	1.25	.55
❑ 118 Chris Warren	.25	.11
❑ 119 Bubby Brister	.40	.18
❑ 120 Terrell Davis	.60	.25
❑ 121 Jason Elam	.25	.11
❑ 122 John Elway	2.00	.90
❑ 123 Willie Green	.25	.11
❑ 124 Howard Griffith	.25	.11
❑ 125 Vaughn Hebron	.25	.11
❑ 126 Ed McCaffrey	.40	.18
❑ 127 John Mobley	.25	.11
❑ 128 Bill Romanowski	.25	.11
❑ 129 Shannon Sharpe	.40	.18
❑ 130 Neil Smith	.40	.18
❑ 131 Rod Smith	.40	.18
❑ 132 Brian Griese	.60	.25
Marcus Nash		
❑ 133 Charlie Batch	.60	.25
❑ 134 Stephen Boyd	.25	.11
❑ 135 Mark Carrier DB	.25	.11
❑ 136 Germane Crowell	.25	.11
❑ 137 Terry Fair	.25	.11
❑ 138 Jason Hanson	.25	.11
❑ 139 Greg Jeffries RC	1.00	.45
❑ 140 Herman Moore	.40	.18
❑ 141 Johnnie Morton	.40	.18
❑ 142 Robert Porcher	.25	.11
❑ 143 Ron Rivers	.25	.11
❑ 144 Barry Sanders	2.00	.90
❑ 145 Tommy Vardell	.25	.11
❑ 146 Bryant Westbrook	.25	.11
❑ 147 Robert Brooks	.40	.18
❑ 148 LeRoy Butler	.25	.11
❑ 149 Mark Chmura	.25	.11
❑ 150 Tyrone Davis	.25	.11
❑ 151 Brett Favre	2.00	.90
❑ 152 Antonio Freeman	.60	.25
❑ 153 Raymont Harris	.25	.11
❑ 154 Vonnie Holliday	.25	.11
❑ 155 Darick Holmes	.25	.11
❑ 156 Dorsey Levens	.60	.25
❑ 157 Brian Manning	.25	.11
❑ 158 Derrick Mayes	.25	.11
❑ 159 Roell Preston	.25	.11
❑ 160 Jeff Thomason	.25	.11
❑ 161 Tyrone Williams	.25	.11
❑ 162 Corey Bradford	1.50	.70
Michael Blair RC		
❑ 163 Aaron Bailey	.25	.11
❑ 164 Ken Dilger	.25	.11
❑ 165 Marshall Faulk	.75	.35
❑ 166 E.G. Green	.25	.11
❑ 167 Marvin Harrison	.60	.25
❑ 168 Craig Heyward	.25	.11
❑ 169 Peyton Manning	2.00	.90
❑ 170 Jerome Pathon	.40	.18
❑ 171 Marcus Pollard	.25	.11
❑ 172 Torrance Small	.25	.11
❑ 173 Mike Vanderjagt	.25	.11
❑ 174 Lamont Warren	.25	.11
❑ 175 Tavian Banks	.25	.11
❑ 176 Reggie Barlow	.25	.11
❑ 177 Tony Boselli	.25	.11
❑ 178 Tony Brackens	.25	.11
❑ 179 Mark Brunell	.60	.25
❑ 180 Kevin Hardy	.25	.11
❑ 181 Damon Jones	.25	.11
❑ 182 Jamie Martin	.60	.25
❑ 183 Keenan McCardell	.40	.18
❑ 184 Pete Mitchell	.25	.11
❑ 185 Bryce Paup	.25	.11
❑ 186 Jimmy Smith	.40	.18
❑ 187 Fred Taylor	.60	.25
❑ 188 Alvis Whitted	.25	.11
Chris Howard		
❑ 189 Derrick Alexander WR	.40	.18
❑ 190 Kimble Anders	.40	.18
❑ 191 Donnell Bennett	.25	.11
❑ 192 Dale Carter	.25	.11
❑ 193 Rich Gannon	.60	.25
❑ 194 Tony Gonzalez	.60	.25
❑ 195 Elvis Grbac	.40	.18
❑ 196 Joe Horn	.40	.18
❑ 197 Kevin Lockett	.25	.11
❑ 198 Byron Bam Morris	.25	.11
❑ 199 Andre Rison	.40	.18
❑ 200 Derrick Thomas	.40	.18
❑ 201 Tamarick Vanover	.25	.11
❑ 202 Gregory Favors	.25	.11
Rashaan Shehee		
❑ 203 Karim Abdul-Jabbar	.40	.18
❑ 204 Trace Armstrong	.25	.11
❑ 205 John Avery	.25	.11
❑ 206 Lorenzo Bromell RC	.60	.25
❑ 207 Terrell Buckley	.25	.11
❑ 208 Oronde Gadsden	.40	.18
❑ 209 Sam Madison	.25	.11
❑ 210 Dan Marino	2.00	.90
❑ 211 O.J. McDuffie	.40	.18
❑ 212 Ed Perry	.25	.11
❑ 213 Jason Taylor	.25	.11
❑ 214 Lamar Thomas	.25	.11
❑ 215 Zach Thomas	.60	.25
❑ 216 Henry Lusk	1.00	.45
Nate Jacquet RC		
❑ 217 Damon Huard	1.50	.70
Todd Doxzon RC		
❑ 218 Gary Anderson	.25	.11
❑ 219 Cris Carter	.60	.25
❑ 220 Randall Cunningham	.60	.25
❑ 221 Andrew Glover	.25	.11
❑ 222 Matthew Hatchette	.25	.11
❑ 223 Brad Johnson	.60	.25
❑ 224 Ed McDaniel	.25	.11
❑ 225 Randall McDaniel	.25	.11
❑ 226 Randy Moss	1.50	.70
❑ 227 David Palmer	.25	.11
❑ 228 John Randle	.40	.18
❑ 229 Jake Reed	.40	.18
❑ 230 Robert Smith	.60	.25
❑ 231 Todd Steussie	.25	.11
❑ 232 Stalin Colinet RC	.25	.11
Kivuusama Mays		
❑ 233 Jay Fiedler RC	6.00	2.70
Todd Bouman RC		
❑ 234 Drew Bledsoe	.75	.35
❑ 235 Troy Brown	.40	.18
❑ 236 Ben Coates	.40	.18
❑ 237 Derrick Cullors	.25	.11
❑ 238 Robert Edwards	.25	.11
❑ 239 Terry Glenn	.60	.25
❑ 240 Shawn Jefferson	.25	.11
❑ 241 Ty Law	.40	.18
❑ 242 Lawyer Milloy	.40	.18
❑ 243 Lovett Purnell RC	1.00	.45
❑ 244 Sedrick Shaw	.25	.11
❑ 245 Tony Simmons	.25	.11
❑ 246 Chris Slade	.25	.11
❑ 247 Rod Rutledge	1.00	.45
Anthony Ladd RC		
❑ 248 Chris Floyd	.25	.11
Harold Shaw		
❑ 249 Ink Aleaga RC	1.00	.45
❑ 250 Cameron Cleeland	.25	.11
❑ 251 Kerry Collins	.40	.18
❑ 252 Troy Davis	.25	.11
❑ 253 Sean Dawkins	.25	.11
❑ 254 Mark Fields	.25	.11
❑ 255 Andre Hastings	.25	.11
❑ 256 Sammy Knight	.25	.11
❑ 257 Keith Poole	.25	.11
❑ 258 William Roaf	.25	.11
❑ 259 Lamar Smith	.40	.18
❑ 260 Danny Wuerffel	.25	.11
❑ 261 Josh Wilcox RC	1.00	.45
Brett Bech RC		
❑ 262 Chris Bordano RC	1.00	.45
Wilmont Perry		
❑ 263 Jessie Armstead	.25	.11
❑ 264 Tiki Barber	.40	.18
❑ 265 Chad Bratzke	.25	.11
❑ 266 Gary Brown	.25	.11
❑ 267 Chris Calloway	.25	.11
❑ 268 Howard Cross	.25	.11
❑ 269 Kent Graham	.25	.11
❑ 270 Ike Hilliard	.25	.11
❑ 271 Danny Kanell	.40	.18
❑ 272 Michael Strahan	.40	.18
❑ 273 Amani Toomer	.25	.11
❑ 274 Charles Way	.25	.11
❑ 275 Mike Cherry	1.50	.70
Greg Comella RC		
❑ 276 Kyle Brady	.25	.11
❑ 277 Keith Byars	.25	.11
❑ 278 Chad Cascadden	.25	.11
❑ 279 Wayne Chrebet	.40	.18
❑ 280 Bryan Cox	.25	.11
❑ 281 Glenn Foley	.40	.18
❑ 282 Aaron Glenn	.25	.11
❑ 283 Keyshawn Johnson	.60	.25
❑ 284 Leon Johnson	.25	.11
❑ 285 Mo Lewis	.25	.11
❑ 286 Curtis Martin	.60	.25
❑ 287 Otis Smith	.25	.11
❑ 288 Vinny Testaverde	.40	.18
❑ 289 Dedric Ward	.25	.11
❑ 290 Tim Brown	.60	.25
❑ 291 Rickey Dudley	.25	.11
❑ 292 Jeff George	.40	.18
❑ 293 Desmond Howard	.40	.18
❑ 294 James Jett	.40	.18
❑ 295 Lance Johnstone	.25	.11
❑ 296 Randy Jordan	.25	.11
❑ 297 Napoleon Kaufman	.60	.25
❑ 298 Lincoln Kennedy	.25	.11
❑ 299 Terry Mickens	.25	.11
❑ 300 Darrell Russell	.25	.11
❑ 301 Harvey Williams	.25	.11
❑ 302 Jon Ritchie	.60	.25
Charles Woodson		
❑ 303 Rodney Williams	.25	.11
Jermaine Williams		
❑ 304 Koy Detmer	.25	.11
❑ 305 Hugh Douglas	.25	.11
❑ 306 Jason Dunn	.25	.11
❑ 307 Irving Fryar	.40	.18
❑ 308 Charlie Garner	.40	.18
❑ 309 Jeff Graham	.25	.11

❑ 310 Bobby Hoying .40 .18
❑ 311 Rodney Peete .25 .11
❑ 312 Allen Rossum .25 .11
❑ 313 Duce Staley .60 .25
❑ 314 William Thomas .25 .11
❑ 315 Kevin Turner .25 .11
❑ 316 Kaseem Sinceno RC 1.00 .45
Corey Walker RC
❑ 317 Jahine Arnold .25 .11
❑ 318 Jerome Bettis .60 .25
❑ 319 Will Blackwell .25 .11
❑ 320 Mark Bruener .25 .11
❑ 321 Dermontti Dawson .25 .11
❑ 322 Chris Fuamatu-Ma'afala .25 .11
❑ 323 Courtney Hawkins .25 .11
❑ 324 Richard Huntley .40 .18
❑ 325 Charles Johnson .25 .11
❑ 326 Levon Kirkland .25 .11
❑ 327 Kordell Stewart .40 .18
❑ 328 Hines Ward .60 .25
❑ 329 Dewayne Washington .25 .11
❑ 330 Tony Banks .40 .18
❑ 331 Steve Bono .25 .11
❑ 332 Isaac Bruce .60 .25
❑ 333 June Henley RC 1.25 .55
❑ 334 Robert Holcombe .25 .11
❑ 335 Mike Jones LB .25 .11
❑ 336 Eddie Kennison .40 .18
❑ 337 Amp Lee .25 .11
❑ 338 Jerald Moore .25 .11
❑ 339 Ricky Proehl .25 .11
❑ 340 J.T. Thomas .25 .11
❑ 341 Derrick Harris .40 .18
Az-Zahir Hakim
❑ 342 Roland Williams .25 .11
Grant Wistrom
❑ 343 Kurt Warner RC 12.00 5.50
Tony Horne
❑ 344 Terrell Fletcher .25 .11
❑ 345 Greg Jackson .25 .11
❑ 346 Charlie Jones .25 .11
❑ 347 Freddie Jones .25 .11
❑ 348 Ryan Leaf .60 .25
❑ 349 Natrone Means .40 .18
❑ 350 Mikhael Ricks .25 .11
❑ 351 Junior Seau .60 .25
❑ 352 Bryan Still .25 .11
❑ 353 Tremayne Stephens 1.25 .55
Ryan Thelwell RC
❑ 354 Greg Clark .25 .11
❑ 355 Marc Edwards .25 .11
❑ 356 Merton Hanks .25 .11
❑ 357 Garrison Hearst .40 .18
❑ 358 R.W. McQuarters .25 .11
❑ 359 Ken Norton Jr. .25 .11
❑ 360 Terrell Owens .60 .25
❑ 361 Jerry Rice 1.25 .55
❑ 362 J.J. Stokes .40 .18
❑ 363 Bryant Young .25 .11
❑ 364 Steve Young .75 .35
❑ 365 Chad Brown .25 .11
❑ 366 Christian Fauria .25 .11
❑ 367 Joey Galloway .40 .18
❑ 368 Ahman Green .60 .25
❑ 369 Cortez Kennedy .25 .11
❑ 370 Jon Kitna .60 .25
❑ 371 James McKnight .40 .18
❑ 372 Mike Pritchard .25 .11
❑ 373 Michael Sinclair .25 .11
❑ 374 Shawn Springs .25 .11
❑ 375 Ricky Watters .40 .18
❑ 376 Darryl Williams .25 .11
❑ 377 Robert Wilson 1.50 .70
Kerry Joseph RC
❑ 378 Mike Alstott .60 .25
❑ 379 Reidel Anthony .40 .18
❑ 380 Derrick Brooks .60 .25
❑ 381 Trent Dilfer .60 .25
❑ 382 Warrick Dunn .60 .25
❑ 383 Bert Emanuel .40 .18
❑ 384 Jacquez Green .25 .11
❑ 385 Patrick Hape .25 .11
❑ 386 John Lynch .40 .18
❑ 387 Dave Moore .25 .11
❑ 388 Hardy Nickerson .25 .11
❑ 389 Warren Sapp .40 .18
❑ 390 Karl Williams .25 .11
❑ 391 Blaine Bishop .25 .11
❑ 392 Joe Bowden .25 .11
❑ 393 Isaac Byrd 1.00 .45
❑ 394 Willie Davis .25 .11
❑ 395 Al Del Greco .25 .11
❑ 396 Kevin Dyson .40 .18
❑ 397 Eddie George .60 .25
❑ 398 Jackie Harris .25 .11
❑ 399 Dave Krieg .25 .11
❑ 400 Steve McNair .60 .25
❑ 401 Michael Roan .25 .11
❑ 402 Yancey Thigpen .25 .11
❑ 403 Frank Wycheck .25 .11
❑ 404 Derrick Mason .40 .18
Steve Matthews
❑ 405 Stephen Alexander .25 .11
❑ 406 Terry Allen .40 .18
❑ 407 Jamie Asher .25 .11
❑ 408 Stephen Davis .60 .25
❑ 409 Darrell Green .25 .11
❑ 410 Trent Green .60 .25
❑ 411 Skip Hicks .25 .11
❑ 412 Brian Mitchell .25 .11
❑ 413 Leslie Shepherd .25 .11
❑ 414 Michael Westbrook .40 .18
❑ 415 Terry Hardy 1.00 .45
Rabih Abdullah RC
❑ 416 Corey Thomas RC 1.00 .45
Mike Quinn RC
❑ 417 Jonathan Quinn 8.00 3.60
Kelly Holcomb RC
❑ 418 Brian Alford 1.00 .45
Blake Spence
❑ 419 Andy Haase RC 1.00 .45
Carlos King
❑ 420 James Thrash RC 1.50 .70
Karl Hankton
❑ 421 Fred Beasley 1.25 .55
Itula Mili RC
❑ 422 Champ Bailey RC 2.00 .90
❑ 423 D'Wayne Bates RC 1.25 .55
❑ 424 Michael Bishop RC 1.50 .70
❑ 425 David Boston RC 1.50 .70
❑ 426 Shawn Bryson RC 1.50 .70
❑ 427 Tim Couch RC 1.50 .70
❑ 428 Scott Covington RC 1.50 .70
❑ 429 Daunte Culpepper RC 6.00 2.70
❑ 430 Autry Denson RC 1.25 .55
❑ 431 Troy Edwards RC 1.25 .55
❑ 432 Kevin Faulk RC 1.50 .70
❑ 433 Joe Germaine RC 1.25 .55
❑ 434 Torry Holt RC 4.00 1.80
❑ 435 Brock Huard RC 1.50 .70
❑ 436 Sedrick Irvin RC 1.00 .45
❑ 437 Edgerrin James RC 6.00 2.70
❑ 438 Andy Katzenmoyer RC 1.25 .55
❑ 439 Shaun King RC 1.25 .55
❑ 440 Rob Konrad RC 1.25 .55
❑ 441 Donovan McNabb RC 8.00 3.60
❑ 442 Cade McNown RC 1.25 .55
❑ 443 Billy Miller RC 1.00 .45
❑ 444 Dee Miller RC 1.00 .45
❑ 445 Sirr Parker RC 1.00 .45
❑ 446 Peerless Price RC 2.50 1.10
❑ 447 Akili Smith RC 1.25 .55
❑ 448 Tai Streets RC 1.50 .70
❑ 449 Ricky Williams RC 3.00 1.35
❑ 450 Amos Zereoue RC 1.50 .70
❑ S1 Warrick Dunn Sample .60 .25

1999 Pacific Copper

Nm-Mt Ex-Mt
*COPPER STARS: 12.5X TO 30X
*COPPER RCs: 2.5X TO 6X
❑ 343 Kurt Warner/Tony Horne 80.00 36.00

1999 Pacific Gold

Nm-Mt Ex-Mt
*GOLD STARS: 10X TO 25X BASIC CARDS
*GOLD RCs: 2X TO 5X
❑ 343 Kurt Warner 60.00 27.00
Tony Horne

1999 Pacific Opening Day

Nm-Mt Ex-Mt
*OPEN.DAY STARS: 20X TO 50X
*OPEN.DAY RCs: 5X TO 12X
❑ 343 Kurt Warner 150.00 70.00
Tony Horne

1999 Pacific Platinum Blue

Nm-Mt Ex-Mt
*PLAT.BLUE STARS: 12X TO 30X HI COL.
*PLAT.BLUE RCs: 2.5X TO 6X
❑ 343 Kurt Warner 100.00 45.00
Tony Horne

1999 Pacific Red

Nm-Mt Ex-Mt
*RED STARS: 10X TO 25X BASIC CARDS
*RED RCs: 2X TO 5X
❑ 343 Kurt Warner 60.00 27.00
Tony Horne

2000 Pacific

Nm-Mt Ex-Mt
COMPLETE SET (450) 60.00 27.00
❑ 1 Mario Bates .25 .11
❑ 2 David Boston .60 .25
❑ 3 Rob Fredrickson .25 .11
❑ 4 Terry Hardy .25 .11
❑ 5 Rob Moore .40 .18
❑ 6 Adrian Murrell .40 .18
❑ 7 Michael Pittman .25 .11
❑ 8 Jake Plummer .40 .18
❑ 9 Simeon Rice .40 .18
❑ 10 Frank Sanders .40 .18
❑ 11 Aeneas Williams .25 .11
❑ 12 Mac Cody .25 .11
Andy McCullough
❑ 13 Dennis McKinley RC .60 .25
Joel Makovicka
❑ 14 Jamal Anderson .60 .25
❑ 15 Chris Calloway .25 .11
❑ 16 Chris Chandler .40 .18
❑ 17 Bob Christian .25 .11
❑ 18 Tim Dwight .60 .25
❑ 19 Jammi German .25 .11
❑ 20 Ronnie Harris .25 .11
❑ 21 Terance Mathis .40 .18
❑ 22 Ken Oxendine .25 .11
❑ 23 O.J. Santiago .25 .11
❑ 24 Bob Whitfield .25 .11
❑ 25 Eugene Baker .25 .11
Reggie Kelly
❑ 26 Justin Armour .25 .11
❑ 27 Tony Banks .40 .18
❑ 28 Peter Boulware .25 .11
❑ 29 Stoney Case .25 .11
❑ 30 Priest Holmes .75 .35
❑ 31 Qadry Ismail .40 .18
❑ 32 Patrick Johnson .25 .11
❑ 33 Michael McCrary .25 .11
❑ 34 Jonathan Ogden .25 .11
❑ 35 Errict Rhett .40 .18
❑ 36 Duane Starks .25 .11
❑ 37 Doug Flutie .60 .25
❑ 38 Rob Johnson .40 .18
❑ 39 Jonathan Linton .25 .11
❑ 40 Eric Moulds .60 .25
❑ 41 Peerless Price .60 .25
❑ 42 Andre Reed .40 .18
❑ 43 Jay Riemersma .25 .11
❑ 44 Antowain Smith .40 .18
❑ 45 Bruce Smith .40 .18
❑ 46 Thurman Thomas .40 .18

47	Kevin Williams	.25	.11
48	Bobby Collins	.25	.11
	Sheldon Jackson		
49	Michael Bates	.25	.11
50	Steve Beuerlein	.40	.18
51	Tim Biakabutuka	.40	.18
52	Antonio Edwards	.25	.11
53	Donald Hayes	.25	.11
54	Patrick Jeffers	.60	.25
55	Anthony Johnson	.25	.11
56	Jeff Lewis	.25	.11
57	Eric Metcalf	.25	.11
58	Muhsin Muhammad	.40	.18
59	Jason Peter	.25	.11
60	Wesley Walls	.25	.11
61	John Allred	.25	.11
62	Marty Booker	.40	.18
63	Curtis Conway	.40	.18
64	Bobby Engram	.25	.11
65	Curtis Enis	.25	.11
66	Shane Matthews	.40	.18
67	Cade McNown	.25	.11
68	Glyn Milburn	.25	.11
69	Jim Miller	.25	.11
70	Marcus Robinson	.60	.25
71	Ryan Wetnight	.25	.11
72	James Allen	.40	.18
	Macey Brooks		
73	Jeff Blake	.40	.18
74	Corey Dillon	.60	.25
75	Rodney Heath RC	.40	.18
76	Willie Jackson	.25	.11
77	Tremain Mack	.25	.11
78	Tony McGee	.25	.11
79	Carl Pickens	.40	.18
80	Darnay Scott	.40	.18
81	Akili Smith	.25	.11
82	Takeo Spikes	.25	.11
83	Craig Yeast	.25	.11
84	Michael Basnight	.25	.11
	Nick Williams		
85	Karim Abdul-Jabbar	.40	.18
86	Darrin Chiaverini	.25	.11
87	Tim Couch	.40	.18
88	Marc Edwards	.25	.11
89	Kevin Johnson	.60	.25
90	Terry Kirby	.25	.11
91	Daylon McCutcheon	.25	.11
92	Jamir Miller	.25	.11
93	Leslie Shepherd	.25	.11
94	Irv Smith	.25	.11
95	Mark Campbell	.25	.11
	James Dearth		
96	Zola Davis RC	.40	.18
	Damon Dunn RC		
97	Madre Hill	.25	.11
	Tarek Saleh RC		
98	Troy Aikman	1.25	.55
99	Eric Bjornson	.25	.11
100	Dexter Coakley	.25	.11
101	Greg Ellis	.25	.11
102	Rocket Ismail	.40	.18
103	David LaFleur	.25	.11
104	Ernie Mills	.25	.11
105	Jeff Ogden	.40	.18
106	Ryan Neufeld RC	.40	.18
	Robert Thomas		
107	Deion Sanders	.60	.25
108	Emmitt Smith	1.25	.55
109	Chris Warren	.25	.11
110	Mike Lucky	.25	.11
	Jason Tucker		
111	Byron Chamberlain	.25	.11
112	Terrell Davis	.60	.25
113	Jason Elam	.25	.11
114	Olandis Gary	.60	.25
115	Brian Griese	.60	.25
116	Ed McCaffrey	.60	.25
117	Trevor Pryce	.25	.11
118	Bill Romanowski	.25	.11
119	Shannon Sharpe	.40	.18
120	Rod Smith	.40	.18
121	Al Wilson	.25	.11
122	Andre Cooper	.25	.11
	Chris Watson		
123	Charlie Batch	.60	.25
124	Stephen Boyd	.25	.11
125	Chris Claiborne	.25	.11
126	Germane Crowell	.25	.11
127	Terry Fair	.25	.11
128	Gus Frerotte	.25	.11
129	Jason Hanson	.25	.11
130	Greg Hill	.25	.11
131	Herman Moore	.40	.18
132	Johnnie Morton	.40	.18
133	Barry Sanders	1.50	.70
134	David Sloan	.25	.11
135	Brock Olivo	.25	.11
	Cory Sauter		
136	Corey Bradford	.40	.18
137	Tyrone Davis	.25	.11
138	Brett Favre	2.00	.90
139	Antonio Freeman	.60	.25
140	Vonnie Holliday	.25	.11
141	Dorsey Levens	.40	.18
142	Keith McKenzie	.25	.11
143	Mike McKenzie	.25	.11
144	Bill Schroeder	.40	.18
145	Jeff Thomason	.25	.11
146	Frank Winters	.25	.11
147	Cornelius Bennett	.25	.11
148	Tony Blevins RC	.40	.18
149	Chad Bratzke	.25	.11
150	Ken Dilger	.25	.11
151	Tarik Glenn	.25	.11
152	E.G. Green	.25	.11
153	Marvin Harrison	.60	.25
154	Edgerrin James	1.00	.45
155	Peyton Manning	1.50	.70
156	Jerome Pathon	.40	.18
157	Marcus Pollard	.25	.11
158	Terrence Wilkins	.25	.11
159	Isaac Jones RC	.60	.25
	Paul Shields RC		
160	Reggie Barlow	.25	.11
161	Aaron Beasley	.25	.11
162	Tony Boselli	.25	.11
163	Tony Brackens	.25	.11
164	Kyle Brady	.25	.11
165	Mark Brunell	.60	.25
166	Jay Fiedler	.60	.25
167	Kevin Hardy	.25	.11
168	Carnell Lake	.25	.11
169	Keenan McCardell	.40	.18
170	Jonathan Quinn	.25	.11
171	Jimmy Smith	.40	.18
172	James Stewart	.40	.18
173	Fred Taylor	.60	.25
174	Lenzie Jackson RC	.60	.25
	Stacey Mack		
175	Derrick Alexander	.40	.18
176	Donnell Bennett	.25	.11
177	Donnie Edwards	.25	.11
178	Tony Gonzalez	.40	.18
179	Elvis Grbac	.40	.18
180	James Hasty	.25	.11
181	Joe Horn	.40	.18
182	Lonnie Johnson	.25	.11
183	Kevin Lockett	.25	.11
184	Larry Parker	.25	.11
185	Tony Richardson RC	.40	.18
186	Rashaan Shehee	.25	.11
187	Tamarick Vanover	.25	.11
188	Trace Armstrong	.25	.11
189	Oronde Gadsden	.40	.18
190	Damon Huard	.60	.25
191	Nate Jacquet	.25	.11
192	James Johnson	.25	.11
193	Rob Konrad	.25	.11
194	Sam Madison	.25	.11
195	Dan Marino	2.00	.90
196	Tony Martin	.40	.18
197	O.J. McDuffie	.40	.18
198	Stanley Pritchett	.25	.11
199	Tim Ruddy	.25	.11
200	Patrick Surtain	.25	.11
201	Zach Thomas	.60	.25
202	Cris Carter	.60	.25
203	Duane Clemons	.25	.11
204	Carlester Crumpler	.25	.11
205	Daunte Culpepper	.75	.35
206	Jeff George	.40	.18
207	Matthew Hatchette	.25	.11
208	Leroy Hoard	.25	.11
209	Randy Moss	1.25	.55
210	John Randle	.40	.18
211	Jake Reed	.40	.18
212	Robert Smith	.60	.25
213	Robert Tate	.25	.11
214	Terry Allen	.40	.18
215	Bruce Armstrong	.25	.11
216	Drew Bledsoe	.75	.35
217	Ben Coates	.25	.11
218	Kevin Faulk	.40	.18
219	Terry Glenn	.40	.18
220	Shawn Jefferson	.25	.11
221	Andy Katzenmoyer	.25	.11
222	Ty Law	.40	.18
223	Willie McGinest	.25	.11
224	Lawyer Milloy	.40	.18
225	Tony Simmons	.25	.11
226	Michael Bishop	.40	.18
	Sean Morey RC		
227	Cameron Cleeland	.25	.11
228	Troy Davis	.25	.11
229	Jake Delhomme RC	2.50	1.10
230	Andre Hastings	.25	.11
231	Eddie Kennison	.40	.18
232	Wilmont Perry	.25	.11
233	Dino Philyaw	.25	.11
234	Keith Poole	.25	.11
235	William Roaf	.25	.11
236	Billy Joe Tolliver	.25	.11
237	Fred Weary	.25	.11
238	Ricky Williams	.60	.25
239	P.J. Franklin RC	.60	.25
	Marvin Powell RC		
240	Jessie Armstead	.25	.11
241	Tiki Barber	.40	.18
242	Daniel Campbell	.25	.11
243	Kerry Collins	.40	.18
244	Percy Ellsworth	.25	.11
245	Kent Graham	.25	.11
246	Ike Hilliard	.40	.18
247	Cedric Jones	.25	.11
248	Bashir Levingston RC	.60	.25
249	Pete Mitchell	.25	.11
250	Michael Strahan	.40	.18
251	Amani Toomer	.25	.11
252	Charles Way	.25	.11
253	Andre Weathers RC	.40	.18
254	Richie Anderson	.40	.18
255	Wayne Chrebet	.40	.18
256	Marcus Coleman	.25	.11
257	Bryan Cox	.25	.11
258	Jason Fabini RC	.40	.18
259	Robert Farmer RC	.60	.25
260	Keyshawn Johnson	.60	.25
261	Ray Lucas	.40	.18
262	Curtis Martin	.60	.25
263	Kevin Mawae	.25	.11
264	Eric Ogbogu	.25	.11
265	Bernie Parmalee	.25	.11
266	Vinny Testaverde	.40	.18
267	Dedric Ward	.25	.11
268	Eric Barton RC	.40	.18
269	Tim Brown	.60	.25
270	Tony Bryant	.25	.11
271	Rickey Dudley	.25	.11
272	Rich Gannon	.60	.25
273	Bobby Hoying	.40	.18
274	James Jett	.25	.11
275	Napoleon Kaufman	.40	.18
276	Jon Ritchie	.25	.11
277	Darrell Russell	.25	.11
278	Kenny Shedd	.25	.11
279	Marquis Walker RC	.40	.18
280	Tyrone Wheatley	.40	.18
281	Charles Woodson	.40	.18
282	Luther Broughton RC	.40	.18
283	Al Harris RC	.25	.11
284	Greg Jefferson	.25	.11
285	Dietrich Jells	.25	.11
286	Charles Johnson	.40	.18
287	Chad Lewis	.25	.11
288	Mike Mamula	.25	.11
289	Donovan McNabb	1.00	.45
290	Doug Pederson	.25	.11
291	Allen Rossum	.25	.11
292	Torrance Small	.25	.11
293	Duce Staley	.60	.25
294	Jerome Bettis	.60	.25
295	Kris Brown	.25	.11
296	Mark Bruener	.25	.11

❑ 297 Troy Edwards .25 .11
❑ 298 Jason Gildon .25 .11
❑ 299 Richard Huntley .25 .11
❑ 300 Bobby Shaw RC .60 .25
❑ 301 Scott Shields RC .40 .18
❑ 302 Kordell Stewart .40 .18
❑ 303 Hines Ward .60 .25
❑ 304 Amos Zereoue .60 .25
❑ 305 Matt Cushing RC .40 .18
Jerame Tuman
❑ 306 Pete Gonzalez 2.00 .90
Anthony Wright RC
❑ 307 Isaac Bruce .60 .25
❑ 308 Kevin Carter .25 .11
❑ 309 Marshall Faulk .75 .35
❑ 310 London Fletcher RC .40 .18
❑ 311 Joe Germaine .25 .11
❑ 312 Az-Zahir Hakim .40 .18
❑ 313 Torry Holt .60 .25
❑ 314 Tony Horne .25 .11
❑ 315 Mike Jones LB .25 .11
❑ 316 Dexter McCleon RC .60 .25
❑ 317 Orlando Pace .25 .11
❑ 318 Ricky Proehl .25 .11
❑ 319 Kurt Warner 1.25 .55
❑ 320 Roland Williams .25 .11
❑ 321 Grant Wistrom .25 .11
❑ 322 James Hodgins RC .25 .11
Justin Watson
❑ 323 Jermaine Fazande .25 .11
❑ 324 Jeff Graham .25 .11
❑ 325 Jim Harbaugh .40 .18
❑ 326 Raylee Johnson .25 .11
❑ 327 Charlie Jones .25 .11
❑ 328 Freddie Jones .25 .11
❑ 329 Natrone Means .25 .11
❑ 330 Chris Penn .25 .11
❑ 331 Mikhael Ricks .25 .11
❑ 332 Junior Seau .60 .25
❑ 333 Reggie Davis RC .40 .18
Robert Reed RC
❑ 334 Fred Beasley .25 .11
❑ 335 Brentson Buckner .25 .11
❑ 336 Greg Clark .25 .11
❑ 337 Dave Fiore RC .25 .11
❑ 338 Charlie Garner .40 .18
❑ 339 Mark Harris RC .60 .25
❑ 340 Ramos McDonald RC .40 .18
❑ 341 Terrell Owens .60 .25
❑ 342 Jerry Rice 1.25 .55
❑ 343 Lance Schulters .25 .11
❑ 344 J.J. Stokes .40 .18
❑ 345 Bryant Young .25 .11
❑ 346 Steve Young .75 .35
❑ 347 Jeff Garcia .60 .25
❑ 348 Fabien Bownes RC .25 .11
❑ 349 Chad Brown .25 .11
❑ 350 Reggie Brown .25 .11
❑ 351 Sean Dawkins .25 .11
❑ 352 Christian Fauria .25 .11
❑ 353 Ahman Green .60 .25
❑ 354 Walter Jones .25 .11
❑ 355 Cortez Kennedy .25 .11
❑ 356 Jon Kitna .60 .25
❑ 357 Derrick Mayes .40 .18
❑ 358 Charlie Rogers .25 .11
❑ 359 Shawn Springs .25 .11
❑ 360 Ricky Watters .40 .18
❑ 361 Donne Abraham .25 .11
❑ 362 Mike Alstott .60 .25
❑ 363 Reidel Anthony .25 .11
❑ 364 Ronde Barber .25 .11
❑ 365 Derrick Brooks .60 .25
❑ 366 Warrick Dunn .60 .25
❑ 367 Jacquez Green .25 .11
❑ 368 Marcus Jones .25 .11
❑ 369 Shaun King .25 .11
❑ 370 John Lynch .40 .18
❑ 371 Warren Sapp .40 .18
❑ 372 Steve White RC .25 .11
❑ 373 Martin Gramatica .40 .18
Kevin McLeod RC
❑ 374 Blaine Bishop .25 .11
❑ 375 Al Del Greco .25 .11
❑ 376 Kevin Dyson .40 .18
❑ 377 Eddie George .60 .25
❑ 378 Jevon Kearse .60 .25
❑ 379 Derrick Mason .40 .18

❑ 380 Bruce Matthews .25 .11
❑ 381 Steve McNair .60 .25
❑ 382 Neil O'Donnell .25 .11
❑ 383 Yancey Thigpen .25 .11
❑ 384 Frank Wycheck .25 .11
❑ 385 Devin Daft .25 .11
Larry Brown
❑ 386 Stephen Alexander .25 .11
❑ 387 Champ Bailey .40 .18
❑ 388 Larry Centers .25 .11
❑ 389 Marco Coleman .25 .11
❑ 390 Albert Connell .25 .11
❑ 391 Stephen Davis .60 .25
❑ 392 Irving Fryar .40 .18
❑ 393 Skip Hicks .25 .11
❑ 394 Brad Johnson .60 .25
❑ 395 Michael Westbrook .40 .18
❑ 396 Obafemi Ayanbadejo RC .40 .18
Lennox Gordon RC
❑ 397 Donald Driver .60 .25
Ronnie Powell
❑ 398 Todd Bouman .60 .25
Jeremy Brigham RC
❑ 399 Brock Huard .25 .11
Sherdrick Bonner
❑ 400 Mike Sellers .40 .18
Spencer George RC
❑ 401 Shaun Alexander RC 3.00 1.35
❑ 402 LaVar Arrington RC 8.00 3.60
❑ 403 Tom Brady RC 20.00 9.00
❑ 404 Demario Brown RC .60 .25
❑ 405 Plaxico Burress RC 2.50 1.10
❑ 406 Trung Canidate RC 1.00 .45
❑ 407 Giovanni Carmazzi RC 1.00 .45
❑ 408 Kwame Cavil RC .60 .25
❑ 409 Chrys Chukwuma RC 1.25 .55
❑ 410 Ron Dayne RC 1.25 .55
❑ 411 Reuben Droughns RC 1.50 .70
❑ 412 Ron Dugans RC .60 .25
❑ 413 Deon Dyer RC 1.00 .45
❑ 414 Danny Farmer RC 1.00 .45
❑ 415 Chafie Fields RC .60 .25
❑ 416 Trevor Gaylor RC 1.00 .45
❑ 417 Sherrod Gideon RC .60 .25
❑ 418 Joey Goodspeed RC .60 .25
❑ 419 Joe Hamilton RC 1.00 .45
❑ 420 Tony Hartley RC .60 .25
❑ 421 Todd Husak RC 1.25 .55
❑ 422 Trevor Insley RC .60 .25
❑ 423 Thomas Jones RC 2.00 .90
❑ 424 Marcus Knight RC 1.00 .45
❑ 425 Jamal Lewis RC 3.00 1.35
❑ 426 Anthony Lucas RC 1.50 .70
❑ 427 Tee Martin RC 1.25 .55
❑ 428 Rondell Mealey RC .60 .25
❑ 429 Sylvester Morris RC 1.00 .45
❑ 430 Chad Morton RC 1.25 .55
❑ 431 Dennis Northcutt RC 1.25 .55
❑ 432 Chad Pennington RC 5.00 2.20
❑ 433 Rodnick Phillips RC .60 .25
❑ 434 Mareno Philyaw RC .60 .25
❑ 435 Jerry Porter RC 1.50 .70
❑ 436 Travis Prentice RC 1.00 .45
❑ 437 Tim Rattay RC 2.50 1.10
❑ 438 Chris Redman RC 1.00 .45
❑ 439 J.R. Redmond RC 1.00 .45
❑ 440 Gari Scott RC .60 .25
❑ 441 Keith Smith RC .60 .25
❑ 442 Terrelle Smith RC 1.00 .45
❑ 443 R.Jay Soward RC 1.00 .45
❑ 444 Q.Spotwood RC UER .60 .25
yardage totals reads 3080
❑ 445 Shyrone Stith RC 1.00 .45
❑ 446 Travis Taylor RC 1.25 .55
❑ 447 Troy Walters RC 1.25 .55
❑ 448 Peter Warrick RC 1.25 .55
❑ 449 Dez White RC 1.25 .55
❑ 450 Michael Wiley RC 1.00 .45

2001 Pacific

	Nm-Mt	Ex-Mt
COMP.SET w/o SP's (450)	50.00	15.00

❑ 1 David Boston .60 .25
❑ 2 Mac Cody .25 .11
❑ 3 Chris Gedney .25 .11
❑ 4 Chris Greisen .25 .11
❑ 5 Terry Hardy .25 .11

❑ 6 MarTay Jenkins .25 .11
❑ 7 Thomas Jones .60 .25
❑ 8 Joel Makovicka .25 .11
❑ 9 Tywan Mitchell .25 .11
❑ 10 Rob Moore .40 .18
❑ 11 Michael Pittman .25 .11
❑ 12 Jake Plummer .40 .18
❑ 13 Frank Sanders .25 .11
❑ 14 Aeneas Williams .25 .11
❑ 15 Jamal Anderson .60 .25
❑ 16 Eugene Baker .25 .11
❑ 17 Chris Chandler .40 .18
❑ 18 Tim Dwight .60 .25
❑ 19 Brian Finneran .25 .11
❑ 20 Jammi German .25 .11
❑ 21 Shawn Jefferson .25 .11
❑ 22 Doug Johnson .25 .11
❑ 23 Danny Kanell .25 .11
❑ 24 Reggie Kelly .25 .11
❑ 25 Terance Mathis .40 .18
❑ 26 Derek Rackley .25 .11
❑ 27 Ron Rivers .25 .11
❑ 28 Maurice Smith .40 .18
❑ 29 Sam Adams .25 .11
❑ 30 Obafemi Ayanbadejo .25 .11
❑ 31 Tony Banks .40 .18
❑ 32 Trent Dilfer .40 .18
❑ 33 Sam Gash .25 .11
❑ 34 Priest Holmes .75 .35
❑ 35 Qadry Ismail .40 .18
❑ 36 Pat Johnson .25 .11
❑ 37 Jamal Lewis 1.00 .45
❑ 38 Jermaine Lewis .25 .11
❑ 39 Ray Lewis .60 .25
❑ 40 Chris Redman .25 .11
❑ 41 Shannon Sharpe .40 .18
❑ 42 Brandon Stokley .40 .18
❑ 43 Travis Taylor .40 .18
❑ 44 Shawn Bryson .25 .11
❑ 45 Kwame Cavil .25 .11
❑ 46 Sam Cowart .25 .11
❑ 47 Doug Flutie .60 .25
❑ 48 Rob Johnson .40 .18
❑ 49 Jonathan Linton .25 .11
❑ 50 Jeremy McDaniel .25 .11
❑ 51 Sammy Morris .25 .11
❑ 52 Eric Moulds .60 .25
❑ 53 Peerless Price .60 .25
❑ 54 Jay Riemersma .25 .11
❑ 55 Antowain Smith .40 .18
❑ 56 Chris Watson .25 .11
❑ 57 Marcellus Wiley .25 .11
❑ 58 Michael Bates .25 .11
❑ 59 Steve Beuerlein .40 .18
❑ 60 Tim Biakabutuka .40 .18
❑ 61 Isaac Byrd .25 .11
❑ 62 Dameyune Craig .25 .11
❑ 63 William Floyd .25 .11
❑ 64 Karl Hankton .25 .11
❑ 65 Donald Hayes .25 .11
❑ 66 Chris Hetherington RC .40 .18
❑ 67 Brad Hoover .25 .11
❑ 68 Patrick Jeffers .60 .25
❑ 69 Muhsin Muhammad .40 .18
❑ 70 Iheanyi Uwaezuoke .25 .11
❑ 71 Wesley Walls .25 .11
❑ 72 James Allen .40 .18
❑ 73 Marlon Barnes .25 .11
❑ 74 D'Wayne Bates .25 .11
❑ 75 Marty Booker .25 .11
❑ 76 Macey Brooks .25 .11

	Card	Player	Hi	Lo
❑	77	Bobby Engram	.40	.18
❑	78	Curtis Enis	.25	.11
❑	79	Mark Hartsell RC	.40	.18
❑	80	Eddie Kennison	.25	.11
❑	81	Shane Matthews	.25	.11
❑	82	Cade McNown	.25	.11
❑	83	Jim Miller	.25	.11
❑	84	Marcus Robinson	.60	.25
❑	85	Brian Urlacher	1.00	.45
❑	86	Dez White	.25	.11
❑	87	Brandon Bennett	.25	.11
❑	88	Steve Bush RC	.40	.18
❑	89	Corey Dillon	.60	.25
❑	90	Ron Dugans	.25	.11
❑	91	Danny Farmer	.25	.11
❑	92	Damon Griffin	.25	.11
❑	93	Clif Groce	.40	.18
❑	94	Curtis Keaton	.25	.11
❑	95	Scott Mitchell	.25	.11
❑	96	Darnay Scott	.40	.18
❑	97	Akili Smith	.25	.11
❑	98	Peter Warrick	.60	.25
❑	99	Nick Williams	.25	.11
❑	100	Craig Yeast	.25	.11
❑	101	Bobby Brown	.25	.11
❑	102	Darrin Chiaverini	.25	.11
❑	103	Tim Couch	.40	.18
❑	104	JaJuan Dawson	.25	.11
❑	105	Marc Edwards	.25	.11
❑	106	Kevin Johnson	.40	.18
❑	107	Dennis Northcutt	.40	.18
❑	108	David Patten	.25	.11
❑	109	Doug Pederson	.25	.11
❑	110	Travis Prentice	.25	.11
❑	111	Errict Rhett	.25	.11
❑	112	Aaron Shea	.25	.11
❑	113	Kevin Thompson	.25	.11
❑	114	Jamel White	.25	.11
❑	115	Spergon Wynn	.25	.11
❑	116	Troy Aikman	1.00	.45
❑	117	Chris Brazzell	.25	.11
❑	118	Randall Cunningham	.60	.25
❑	119	Jackie Harris	.25	.11
❑	120	Damon Hodge	.25	.11
❑	121	Rocket Ismail	.40	.18
❑	122	David LaFleur	.25	.11
❑	123	Wane McGarity	.25	.11
❑	124	James McKnight	.40	.18
❑	125	Emmitt Smith	1.25	.55
❑	126	Clint Stoerner	.25	.11
❑	127	Jason Tucker	.25	.11
❑	128	Michael Wiley	.25	.11
❑	129	Anthony Wright	.25	.11
❑	130	Mike Anderson	.60	.25
❑	131	Dwayne Carswell	.25	.11
❑	132	Byron Chamberlain	.25	.11
❑	133	Desmond Clark	.25	.11
❑	134	Chris Cole	.25	.11
❑	135	KaRon Coleman	.25	.11
❑	136	Terrell Davis	.60	.25
❑	137	Gus Frerotte	.40	.18
❑	138	Olandis Gary	.60	.25
❑	139	Brian Griese	.60	.25
❑	140	Howard Griffith	.25	.11
❑	141	Jarious Jackson	.40	.18
❑	142	Ed McCaffrey	.60	.25
❑	143	Scottie Montgomery RC	.40	.18
❑	144	Rod Smith	.40	.18
❑	145	Charlie Batch	.60	.25
❑	146	Stoney Case	.25	.11
❑	147	Germane Crowell	.25	.11
❑	148	Larry Foster	.25	.11
❑	149	Desmond Howard	.25	.11
❑	150	Sedrick Irvin	.25	.11
❑	151	Herman Moore	.40	.18
❑	152	Johnnie Morton	.40	.18
❑	153	Robert Porcher	.25	.11
❑	154	Cory Sauter	.25	.11
❑	155	Cory Schlesinger	.25	.11
❑	156	David Sloan	.25	.11
❑	157	Brian Stablein	.25	.11
❑	158	James Stewart	.40	.18
❑	159	Corey Bradford	.25	.11
❑	160	Tyrone Davis	.25	.11
❑	161	Donald Driver	.40	.18
❑	162	Brett Favre	2.00	.90
❑	163	Bubba Franks	.40	.18
❑	164	Antonio Freeman	.60	.25
❑	165	Herbert Goodman	.25	.11
❑	166	Ahman Green	.60	.25
❑	167	Matt Hasselbeck	.40	.18
❑	168	William Henderson	.25	.11
❑	169	Charles Lee	.25	.11
❑	170	Dorsey Levens	.40	.18
❑	171	Bill Schroeder	.40	.18
❑	172	Darren Sharper	.25	.11
❑	173	Matt Snider	.25	.11
❑	174	Danny Wuerffel	.25	.11
❑	175	Ken Dilger	.25	.11
❑	176	Jim Finn	.25	.11
❑	177	Lennox Gordon	.25	.11
❑	178	E.G. Green	.25	.11
❑	179	Marvin Harrison	.60	.25
❑	180	Kelly Holcomb	.60	.25
❑	181	Trevor Insley	.25	.11
❑	182	Edgerrin James	.75	.35
❑	183	Peyton Manning	1.50	.70
❑	184	Kevin McDougal	.25	.11
❑	185	Jerome Pathon	.40	.18
❑	186	Marcus Pollard	.25	.11
❑	187	Justin Snow	.25	.11
❑	188	Terrence Wilkins	.25	.11
❑	189	Reggie Barlow	.25	.11
❑	190	Kyle Brady	.25	.11
❑	191	Mark Brunell	.60	.25
❑	192	Kevin Hardy	.25	.11
❑	193	Anthony Johnson	.25	.11
❑	194	Stacey Mack	.25	.11
❑	195	Jamie Martin	.40	.18
❑	196	Keenan McCardell	.25	.11
❑	197	Daimon Shelton	.25	.11
❑	198	Jimmy Smith	.40	.18
❑	199	R.Jay Soward	.25	.11
❑	200	Shyrone Stith	.25	.11
❑	201	Fred Taylor	.60	.25
❑	202	Alvis Whitted	.25	.11
❑	203	Jermaine Williams	.25	.11
❑	204	Derrick Alexander	.40	.18
❑	205	Kimble Anders	.25	.11
❑	206	Donnell Bennett	.25	.11
❑	207	Mike Cloud	.25	.11
❑	208	Todd Collins	.25	.11
❑	209	Tony Gonzalez	.40	.18
❑	210	Elvis Grbac	.40	.18
❑	211	Dante Hall	.60	.25
❑	212	Kevin Lockett	.25	.11
❑	213	Warren Moon	.40	.18
❑	214	Frank Moreau	.25	.11
❑	215	Sylvester Morris	.25	.11
❑	216	Larry Parker	.25	.11
❑	217	Tony Richardson	.25	.11
❑	218	Trace Armstrong	.25	.11
❑	219	Autry Denson	.25	.11
❑	220	Bert Emanuel	.25	.11
❑	221	Jay Fiedler	.60	.25
❑	222	Oronde Gadsden	.40	.18
❑	223	Damon Huard	.60	.25
❑	224	James Johnson	.25	.11
❑	225	Rob Konrad	.25	.11
❑	226	Tony Martin	.25	.11
❑	227	O.J. McDuffie	.25	.11
❑	228	Mike Quinn	.25	.11
❑	229	Lamar Smith	.25	.11
❑	230	Jason Taylor	.25	.11
❑	231	Thurman Thomas	.40	.18
❑	232	Zach Thomas	.60	.25
❑	233	Todd Bouman	.40	.18
❑	234	Bubby Brister	.25	.11
❑	235	Cris Carter	.60	.25
❑	236	Daunte Culpepper	.60	.25
❑	237	John Davis RC	.40	.18
❑	238	Robert Griffith	.25	.11
❑	239	Matthew Hatchette	.25	.11
❑	240	Jim Kleinsasser	.25	.11
❑	241	Randy Moss	1.25	.55
❑	242	John Randle	.25	.11
❑	243	Robert Smith	.60	.25
❑	244	Chris Walsh RC	.25	.11
❑	245	Troy Walters	.25	.11
❑	246	Moe Williams	.40	.18
❑	247	Michael Bishop	.25	.11
❑	248	Drew Bledsoe	.75	.35
❑	249	Troy Brown	.40	.18
❑	250	Tedy Bruschi	.50	.23
❑	251	Tony Carter	.25	.11
❑	252	Shockmain Davis	.25	.11
❑	253	Kevin Faulk	.40	.18
❑	254	Terry Glenn	.40	.18
❑	255	Ty Law	.40	.18
❑	256	Lawyer Milloy	.40	.18
❑	257	J.R. Redmond	.25	.11
❑	258	Harold Shaw	.25	.11
❑	259	Tony Simmons	.25	.11
❑	260	Jermaine Wiggins	.40	.18
❑	261	Jeff Blake	.25	.11
❑	262	Aaron Brooks	.60	.25
❑	263	Cam Cleeland	.25	.11
❑	264	Andrew Glover	.25	.11
❑	265	La'Roi Glover	.25	.11
❑	266	Joe Horn	.40	.18
❑	267	Kevin Houser	.25	.11
❑	268	Willie Jackson	.25	.11
❑	269	Jerald Moore	.25	.11
❑	270	Chad Morton	.25	.11
❑	271	Keith Poole	.25	.11
❑	272	Terrelle Smith	.25	.11
❑	273	Ricky Williams	.60	.25
❑	274	Robert Wilson	.25	.11
❑	275	Jessie Armstead	.25	.11
❑	276	Tiki Barber	.40	.18
❑	277	Mike Cherry	.25	.11
❑	278	Kerry Collins	.40	.18
❑	279	Greg Comella	.25	.11
❑	280	Thabiti Davis	.25	.11
❑	281	Ron Dayne	.60	.25
❑	282	Ron Dixon	.25	.11
❑	283	Ike Hilliard	.25	.11
❑	284	Joe Jurevicius	.25	.11
❑	285	Jason Sehorn	.25	.11
❑	286	Michael Strahan	.40	.18
❑	287	Amani Toomer	.25	.11
❑	288	Craig Walendy	.25	.11
❑	289	Damon Washington RC	.40	.18
❑	290	Richie Anderson	.25	.11
❑	291	Anthony Becht	.25	.11
❑	292	Wayne Chrebet	.40	.18
❑	293	Laveranues Coles	.60	.25
❑	294	Bryan Cox	.25	.11
❑	295	Marvin Jones	.25	.11
❑	296	Mo Lewis	.25	.11
❑	297	Ray Lucas	.25	.11
❑	298	Curtis Martin	.60	.25
❑	299	Bernie Parmalee	.25	.11
❑	300	Chad Pennington	1.00	.45
❑	301	Jerald Sowell	.25	.11
❑	302	Dwight Stone	.25	.11
❑	303	Vinny Testaverde	.40	.18
❑	304	Dedric Ward	.25	.11
❑	305	Tim Brown	.60	.25
❑	306	Zack Crockett	.25	.11
❑	307	Scott Dreisbach	.25	.11
❑	308	Rickey Dudley	.25	.11
❑	309	David Dunn	.25	.11
❑	310	Mondriel Fulcher	.25	.11
❑	311	Rich Gannon	.60	.25
❑	312	James Jett	.25	.11
❑	313	Randy Jordan	.25	.11
❑	314	Napoleon Kaufman	.40	.18
❑	315	Rodney Peete	.25	.11
❑	316	Jerry Porter	.40	.18
❑	317	Andre Rison	.40	.18
❑	318	Tyrone Wheatley	.25	.11
❑	319	Charles Woodson	.25	.11
❑	320	Darnell Autry	.25	.11
❑	321	Na Brown	.25	.11
❑	322	Hugh Douglas	.25	.11
❑	323	Charles Johnson	.25	.11
❑	324	Chad Lewis	.25	.11
❑	325	Cecil Martin	.25	.11
❑	326	Donovan McNabb	.75	.35
❑	327	Brian Mitchell	.25	.11
❑	328	Todd Pinkston	.25	.11
❑	329	Ron Powlus	.25	.11
❑	330	Stanley Pritchett	.25	.11
❑	331	Torrance Small	.25	.11
❑	332	Duce Staley	.60	.25
❑	333	Troy Vincent	.25	.11
❑	334	Chris Warren	.25	.11
❑	335	Jerome Bettis	.60	.25
❑	336	Plaxico Burress	.60	.25
❑	337	Troy Edwards	.25	.11
❑	338	Chris Fuamatu-Ma'afala	.25	.11
❑	339	Cory Geason	.25	.11
❑	340	Kent Graham	.25	.11

❑ 341 Courtney Hawkins .25 .11
❑ 342 Richard Huntley .25 .11
❑ 343 Tee Martin .40 .18
❑ 344 Bobby Shaw .25 .11
❑ 345 Kordell Stewart .40 .18
❑ 346 Hines Ward .60 .25
❑ 347 Destry Wright RC .40 .18
❑ 348 Amos Zereoue .60 .25
❑ 349 Isaac Bruce .60 .25
❑ 350 Trung Canidate .40 .18
❑ 351 Marshall Faulk .75 .35
❑ 352 London Fletcher .25 .11
❑ 353 Joe Germaine .25 .11
❑ 354 Trent Green .60 .25
❑ 355 Az-Zahir Hakim .25 .11
❑ 356 James Hodgins .25 .11
❑ 357 Robert Holcombe .25 .11
❑ 358 Torry Holt .60 .25
❑ 359 Tony Horne .25 .11
❑ 360 Ricky Proehl .25 .11
❑ 361 Chris Thomas RC .40 .18
❑ 362 Kurt Warner 1.25 .55
❑ 363 Justin Watson .25 .11
❑ 364 Kenny Bynum .25 .11
❑ 365 Robert Chancey .25 .11
❑ 366 Curtis Conway .40 .18
❑ 367 Jermaine Fazande .25 .11
❑ 368 Terrell Fletcher .25 .11
❑ 369 Trevor Gaylor .25 .11
❑ 370 Jeff Graham .25 .11
❑ 371 Jim Harbaugh .40 .18
❑ 372 Rodney Harrison .25 .11
❑ 373 Ronney Jenkins .25 .11
❑ 374 Freddie Jones .25 .11
❑ 375 Reggie Jones .25 .11
❑ 376 Ryan Leaf .40 .18
❑ 377 Junior Seau .60 .25
❑ 378 Fred Beasley .25 .11
❑ 379 Greg Clark .25 .11
❑ 380 Jeff Garcia .60 .25
❑ 381 Charlie Garner .40 .18
❑ 382 Terry Jackson .25 .11
❑ 383 Brian Jennings .25 .11
❑ 384 Travis Jervey .25 .11
❑ 385 Jonas Lewis .25 .11
❑ 386 Terrell Owens .60 .25
❑ 387 Jerry Rice 1.25 .55
❑ 388 Paul Smith .25 .11
❑ 389 J.J. Stokes .40 .18
❑ 390 Tai Streets .25 .11
❑ 391 Justin Swift .25 .11
❑ 392 Shaun Alexander .75 .35
❑ 393 Karsten Bailey .25 .11
❑ 394 Chad Brown .25 .11
❑ 395 Sean Dawkins .25 .11
❑ 396 Christian Fauria .25 .11
❑ 397 Brock Huard .25 .11
❑ 398 Darrell Jackson .25 .11
❑ 399 Jon Kitna .60 .25
❑ 400 Derrick Mayes .25 .11
❑ 401 Itula Mili .25 .11
❑ 402 Charlie Rogers .25 .11
❑ 403 Mack Strong .25 .11
❑ 404 Ricky Watters .25 .11
❑ 405 James Williams WR .25 .11
❑ 406 Rabih Abdullah .25 .11
❑ 407 Mike Alstott .60 .25
❑ 408 Reidel Anthony .25 .11
❑ 409 Derrick Brooks .60 .25
❑ 410 Warrick Dunn .60 .25
❑ 411 Jacquez Green .25 .11
❑ 412 Joe Hamilton .25 .11
❑ 413 Keyshawn Johnson .60 .25
❑ 414 Shaun King .25 .11
❑ 415 Charles Kirby RC .60 .25
❑ 416 Warren Sapp .40 .18
❑ 417 Aaron Stecker .25 .11
❑ 418 Todd Yoder .25 .11
❑ 419 Eric Zeier .25 .11
❑ 420 Chris Coleman .25 .11
❑ 421 Kevin Dyson .40 .18
❑ 422 Eddie George .60 .25
❑ 423 Jevon Kearse .40 .18
❑ 424 Erron Kinney .25 .11
❑ 425 Mike Leach .25 .11
❑ 426 Derrick Mason .40 .18
❑ 427 Steve McNair .60 .25
❑ 428 Lorenzo Neal .25 .11
❑ 429 Carl Pickens .40 .18
❑ 430 Chris Sanders .25 .11
❑ 431 Yancey Thigpen .25 .11
❑ 432 Rodney Thomas .25 .11
❑ 433 Frank Wycheck .25 .11
❑ 434 Stephen Alexander .25 .11
❑ 435 Champ Bailey .40 .18
❑ 436 Larry Centers .25 .11
❑ 437 Albert Connell .25 .11
❑ 438 Stephen Davis .60 .25
❑ 439 Zeron Flemister RC .40 .18
❑ 440 Irving Fryar .40 .18
❑ 441 Jeff George .40 .18
❑ 442 Skip Hicks .25 .11
❑ 443 Todd Husak .25 .11
❑ 444 Brad Johnson .40 .18
❑ 445 Adrian Murrell .25 .11
❑ 446 Deion Sanders .60 .25
❑ 447 Mike Sellers .25 .11
❑ 448 Derrius Thompson .25 .11
❑ 449 James Thrash .40 .18
❑ 450 Michael Westbrook .25 .11
❑ 451 Alex Bannister 10.00 4.50
AUTO RC/1750
❑ 452 Kevan Barlow 12.00 5.50
AUTO RC/1500
❑ 453 Drew Brees 30.00 13.50
AU RC/1000
❑ 454 Travis Henry 20.00 9.00
AUTO RC/1500
❑ 455 Chad Johnson 25.00 11.00
AUTO RC/1750
❑ 456 Mike McMahon 10.00 4.50
AUTO RC/1000
❑ 457 Bobby Newcombe 12.00 5.50
AUTO RC/1750
❑ 458 Sage Rosenfels 20.00 9.00
AUTO RC/1000
❑ 459 LaDainian Tomlinson 50.00 22.00
AU RC/1500
❑ 460 Chris Weinke 12.00 5.50
AUTO RC/1000
❑ 461 Tay Cody RC 2.00 .90
❑ 462 Adam Archuleta RC 5.00 2.20
❑ 463 Will Allen RC 2.50 1.10
❑ 464 Moran Norris RC 2.00 .90
❑ 465 Tommy Polley RC 5.00 2.20
❑ 466 Ennis Davis RC 2.00 .90
❑ 467 Jamar Fletcher RC 2.50 1.10
❑ 468 Derrick Gibson RC 2.50 1.10
❑ 469 Sedrick Hodge RC 2.00 .90
❑ 470 Willie Howard RC 2.50 1.10
❑ 471 Steve Hutchinson RC 2.50 1.10
❑ 472 Michael Stone RC 2.00 .90
❑ 473 Vinny Sutherland RC/1750 3.00 1.35
❑ 474 Joe Tafoya RC 2.00 .90
❑ 475 Maurice Williams RC 2.00 .90
❑ 476 Pork Chop Womack RC 2.00 .90
❑ 477 Chad Ward RC 2.00 .90
❑ 478 Scotty Anderson RC/1750 3.00 1.35
❑ 479 Gary Baxter RC 2.50 1.10
❑ 480 Marques Tuiasosopo 6.00 2.70
RC/1000
❑ 481 Tim Hasselbeck RC/1000 6.00 2.70
❑ 482 Clevan Thomas RC 2.00 .90
❑ 483 Marcus Stroud RC 5.00 2.20
❑ 484 John Schlecht RC 2.00 .90
❑ 485 Brandon Spoon RC 5.00 2.20
❑ 486 Alex Lincoln RC 2.50 1.10
❑ 487 Anthony Thomas RC/1750 10.00 4.50
❑ 488 Freddie Mitchell RC/1750 4.00 1.80
❑ 489 Brian Allen RC 2.50 1.10
❑ 490 Zeke Moreno RC 5.00 2.20
❑ 491 Tony Driver RC 5.00 2.20
❑ 492 Kynan Forney RC 2.00 .90
❑ 493 Reggie Wayne/1750 RC 8.00 3.60
❑ 494 Larry Casher RC 2.50 1.10
❑ 495 Fred Wakefield RC 2.50 1.10
❑ 496 Jeff Backus RC 2.50 1.10
❑ 497 Jarrod Cooper RC 5.00 2.20
❑ 498 Heath Evans RC 5.00 2.20
❑ 499 James Jackson RC/1500 3.00 1.35
❑ 500 Jabari Holloway RC 5.00 2.20
❑ 501 Quincy Morgan/1750 RC 4.00 1.80
❑ 502 Josh Booty/1000 RC 6.00 2.70
❑ 503 Ja'Mar Toombs RC 2.50 1.10
❑ 504 Jason McKinley/1000 RC 4.00 1.80
❑ 505 Reggie White/1500 RC 3.00 1.35
❑ 506 Todd Heap/1750 RC 4.00 1.80
❑ 507 Rudi Johnson/1500 RC 10.00 4.50
❑ 508 Snoop Minnis/1750 RC 3.00 1.35
❑ 509 David Terrell/1750 RC 4.00 1.80
❑ 510 Torrance Marshall RC 5.00 2.20
❑ 511 Michael Bennett RC/1500 10.00 4.50
❑ 512 Chris Chambers/1750 RC 8.00 3.60
❑ 513 Ben Leard/1000 RC 4.00 1.80
❑ 514 Rod Gardner/1750 RC 4.00 1.80
❑ 515 Michael Vick/1000 RC 50.00 22.00
❑ 516 Josh Heupel/1000 RC 6.00 2.70
❑ 517 Jesse Palmer/1000 RC 6.00 2.70
❑ 518 Quincy Carter/1000 RC 6.00 2.70
❑ 519 A.J. Feeley/1000 RC 6.00 2.70
❑ 520 David Rivers/1000 RC 6.00 2.70
❑ 521 D.McAllister RC/1500 15.00 6.75
❑ 522 LaMont Jordan/1500 RC 5.00 2.20
❑ 523 David Allen/1500 RC 8.00 3.60
❑ 524 Correll Buckhalter/1500 RC 12.00 5.50
❑ 525 Travis Minor/1500 6.00 2.70
❑ 526 Koren Robinson/1750 RC 8.00 3.60
❑ 527 Santana Moss/1750 RC 8.00 3.60
❑ 528 Robert Ferguson/1750 RC 4.00 1.80
❑ 529 T.J. Houshmandzadeh 4.00 1.80
RC/1750
❑ 530 Cedrick Wilson/1750 RC 4.00 1.80

2002 Pacific

	Nm-Mt	Ex-Mt
COMPLETE SET (500)	100.00	30.00

❑ 1 David Boston .60 .18
❑ 2 Arnold Jackson .25 .07
❑ 3 MarTay Jenkins .25 .07
❑ 4 Thomas Jones .40 .12
❑ 5 Kwamie Lassiter .25 .07
❑ 6 Joel Makovicka .25 .07
❑ 7 Ronald McKinnon .25 .07
❑ 8 Tywan Mitchell .25 .07
❑ 9 Michael Pittman .25 .07
❑ 10 Jake Plummer .40 .12
❑ 11 Frank Sanders .25 .07
❑ 12 Kyle Vanden Bosch .25 .07
❑ 13 Jamal Anderson .40 .12
❑ 14 Keith Brooking .25 .07
❑ 15 Chris Chandler .40 .12
❑ 16 Bob Christian .25 .07
❑ 17 Alge Crumpler .40 .12
❑ 18 Brian Finneran .25 .07
❑ 19 Shawn Jefferson .25 .07
❑ 20 Patrick Kerney .25 .07
❑ 21 Terance Mathis .25 .07
❑ 22 Maurice Smith .40 .12
❑ 23 Rodney Thomas .25 .07
❑ 24 Darrick Vaughn .25 .07
❑ 25 Michael Vick 2.00 .60
❑ 26 Sam Adams .25 .07
❑ 27 Terry Allen .25 .07
❑ 28 Obafemi Ayanbadejo .25 .07
❑ 29 Peter Boulware .25 .07
❑ 30 Jason Brookins .25 .07
❑ 31 Randall Cunningham .60 .18
❑ 32 Elvis Grbac .40 .12
❑ 33 Todd Heap .25 .07
❑ 34 Qadry Ismail .40 .12
❑ 35 Jamal Lewis .60 .18
❑ 36 Ray Lewis .60 .18
❑ 37 Chris Redman .25 .07
❑ 38 Shannon Sharpe .40 .12
❑ 39 Brandon Stokley .40 .12
❑ 40 Travis Taylor .40 .12

❑ 41 Moe Williams .25 .07
❑ 42 Rod Woodson .40 .12
❑ 43 Shawn Bryson .25 .07
❑ 44 Larry Centers .25 .07
❑ 45 Nate Clements .25 .07
❑ 46 London Fletcher .25 .07
❑ 47 Reggie Germany .25 .07
❑ 48 Travis Henry .60 .18
❑ 49 Jeremy McDaniel .25 .07
❑ 50 Sammy Morris .25 .07
❑ 51 Eric Moulds .40 .12
❑ 52 Peerless Price .40 .12
❑ 53 Jay Riemersma .25 .07
❑ 54 Alex Van Pelt .25 .07
❑ 55 Tim Biakabutuka .25 .07
❑ 56 Isaac Byrd .25 .07
❑ 57 Doug Evans .25 .07
❑ 58 Donald Hayes .25 .07
❑ 59 Chris Hetherington .25 .07
❑ 60 Brad Hoover .25 .07
❑ 61 Richard Huntley .25 .07
❑ 62 Patrick Jeffers .25 .07
❑ 63 Matt Lytle .25 .07
❑ 64 Dan Morgan .25 .07
❑ 65 Muhsin Muhammad .40 .12
❑ 66 Mike Rucker RC 1.00 .30
❑ 67 Steve Smith .40 .12
❑ 68 Wesley Walls .25 .07
❑ 69 Chris Weinke .40 .12
❑ 70 James Allen .40 .12
❑ 71 Fred Baxter .25 .07
❑ 72 Marty Booker .25 .07
❑ 73 Mike Brown .60 .18
❑ 74 Rosevelt Colvin RC 1.00 .30
❑ 75 Phillip Daniels .25 .07
❑ 76 Leon Johnson .25 .07
❑ 77 Shane Matthews .25 .07
❑ 78 Jim Miller .25 .07
❑ 79 Tony Parrish .25 .07
❑ 80 Marcus Robinson .40 .12
❑ 81 David Terrell .60 .18
❑ 82 Anthony Thomas .60 .18
❑ 83 Brian Urlacher 1.00 .30
❑ 84 Ted Washington .25 .07
❑ 85 Dez White .25 .07
❑ 86 Brandon Bennett .25 .07
❑ 87 Corey Dillon .40 .12
❑ 88 Ron Dugans .25 .07
❑ 89 Danny Farmer .25 .07
❑ 90 T.J. Houshmandzadeh .40 .12
❑ 91 Chad Johnson .60 .18
❑ 92 Curtis Keaton .25 .07
❑ 93 Jon Kitna .40 .12
❑ 94 Tony McGee .25 .07
❑ 95 Lorenzo Neal .25 .07
❑ 96 Darnay Scott .25 .07
❑ 97 Akili Smith .25 .07
❑ 98 Justin Smith .25 .07
❑ 99 Takeo Spikes .25 .07
❑ 100 Peter Warrick .40 .12
❑ 101 Tim Couch .40 .12
❑ 102 JaJuan Dawson .25 .07
❑ 103 Benjamin Gay .40 .12
❑ 104 Anthony Henry .25 .07
❑ 105 James Jackson .25 .07
❑ 106 Kevin Johnson .40 .12
❑ 107 Andre King .25 .07
❑ 108 Jamir Miller .25 .07
❑ 109 Quincy Morgan .25 .07
❑ 110 Dennis Northcutt .25 .07
❑ 111 O.J. Santiago .25 .07
❑ 112 Jamel White .25 .07
❑ 113 Quincy Carter .40 .12
❑ 114 Darrin Chiaverini .60 .18
❑ 115 Dexter Coakley .25 .07
❑ 116 Joey Galloway .40 .12
❑ 117 Troy Hambrick .25 .07
❑ 118 Rocket Ismail .40 .12
❑ 119 Dat Nguyen .25 .07
❑ 120 Ken-Yon Rambo .25 .07
❑ 121 Emmitt Smith 1.50 .45
❑ 122 Reggie Swinton .25 .07
❑ 123 Robert Thomas .25 .07
❑ 124 Michael Wiley .25 .07
❑ 125 Anthony Wright .25 .07
❑ 126 Mike Anderson .60 .18
❑ 127 Dwayne Carswell .25 .07
❑ 128 Desmond Clark .25 .07
❑ 129 Chris Cole .25 .07
❑ 130 Terrell Davis .60 .18
❑ 131 Gus Frerotte .25 .07
❑ 132 Olandis Gary .40 .12
❑ 133 Brian Griese .60 .18
❑ 134 Kevin Kasper .25 .07
❑ 135 Ed McCaffrey .60 .18
❑ 136 Phil McGeoghan RC .40 .12
❑ 137 John Mobley .25 .07
❑ 138 Scottie Montgomery .25 .07
❑ 139 Deltha O'Neal .25 .07
❑ 140 Trevor Pryce .25 .07
❑ 141 Rod Smith .40 .12
❑ 142 Al Wilson .25 .07
❑ 143 Scotty Anderson .25 .07
❑ 144 Charlie Batch .40 .12
❑ 145 Aveion Cason .60 .18
❑ 146 Germane Crowell .25 .07
❑ 147 Reuben Droughns .60 .18
❑ 148 Bert Emanuel .25 .07
❑ 149 Larry Foster .25 .07
❑ 150 Az-Zahir Hakim .25 .07
❑ 151 Desmond Howard .25 .07
❑ 152 Mike McMahon .60 .18
❑ 153 Herman Moore .40 .12
❑ 154 Johnnie Morton .40 .12
❑ 155 Robert Porcher .25 .07
❑ 156 Cory Schlesinger .25 .07
❑ 157 David Sloan .25 .07
❑ 158 James Stewart .40 .12
❑ 159 Lamont Warren .25 .07
❑ 160 Donald Driver .40 .12
❑ 161 Brett Favre 1.50 .45
❑ 162 Bubba Franks .40 .12
❑ 163 Antonio Freeman .60 .18
❑ 164 Kabeer Gbaja-Biamila .25 .07
❑ 165 Terry Glenn .40 .12
❑ 166 Ahman Green .60 .18
❑ 167 William Henderson .25 .07
❑ 168 Dorsey Levens .40 .12
❑ 169 David Martin .25 .07
❑ 170 Rondell Mealey .25 .07
❑ 171 Bill Schroeder .40 .12
❑ 172 Darren Sharper .25 .07
❑ 173 Avion Black .25 .07
❑ 174 Tony Boselli .25 .07
❑ 175 Corey Bradford .25 .07
❑ 176 Marcus Coleman .25 .07
❑ 177 Leomont Evans .25 .07
❑ 178 Aaron Glenn .25 .07
❑ 179 Trevor Insley .25 .07
❑ 180 Jermaine Lewis .25 .07
❑ 181 Anthony Malbrough .25 .07
❑ 182 Frank Moreau .25 .07
❑ 183 Mike Quinn .25 .07
❑ 184 Charlie Rogers .25 .07
❑ 185 Jamie Sharper .25 .07
❑ 186 Matt Snider .25 .07
❑ 187 Gary Walker .25 .07
❑ 188 Kevin Williams RC .40 .12
❑ 189 Kailee Wong .25 .07
❑ 190 Chad Bratzke .25 .07
❑ 191 Ken Dilger .25 .07
❑ 192 Marvin Harrison .60 .18
❑ 193 Edgerrin James .75 .23
❑ 194 Kevin McDougal .25 .07
❑ 195 Rob Morris .25 .07
❑ 196 Jerome Pathon .25 .07
❑ 197 Marcus Pollard .25 .07
❑ 198 Dominic Rhodes .40 .12
❑ 199 Marcus Washington .25 .07
❑ 200 Reggie Wayne .40 .12
❑ 201 Terrence Wilkins .25 .07
❑ 202 Tony Brackens .25 .07
❑ 203 Kyle Brady .25 .07
❑ 204 Mark Brunell .60 .18
❑ 205 Donovin Darius .25 .07
❑ 206 Sean Dawkins .25 .07
❑ 207 Damon Gibson .25 .07
❑ 208 Elvis Joseph .25 .07
❑ 209 Stacey Mack .25 .07
❑ 210 Keenan McCardell .25 .07
❑ 211 Hardy Nickerson .25 .07
❑ 212 Jonathan Quinn .25 .07
❑ 213 Micah Ross RC .40 .12
❑ 214 Jimmy Smith .40 .12
❑ 215 Fred Taylor .60 .18
❑ 216 Patrick Washington .25 .07
❑ 217 Derrick Alexander .40 .12
❑ 218 Mike Cloud .25 .07
❑ 219 Donnie Edwards .25 .07
❑ 220 Tony Gonzalez .40 .12
❑ 221 Trent Green .40 .12
❑ 222 Dante Hall .60 .18
❑ 223 Priest Holmes .75 .23
❑ 224 Eddie Kennison .25 .07
❑ 225 Snoop Minnis .25 .07
❑ 226 Larry Parker .25 .07
❑ 227 Marvcus Patton .25 .07
❑ 228 Tony Richardson .25 .07
❑ 229 Mikhael Ricks .25 .07
❑ 230 Chris Chambers .60 .18
❑ 231 Jay Fiedler .40 .12
❑ 232 Oronde Gadsden .40 .12
❑ 233 Rob Konrad .25 .07
❑ 234 Sam Madison .25 .07
❑ 235 Brock Marion .25 .07
❑ 236 James McKnight .25 .07
❑ 237 Travis Minor .25 .07
❑ 238 Jeff Ogden .25 .07
❑ 239 Lamar Smith .40 .12
❑ 240 Jason Taylor .25 .07
❑ 241 Zach Thomas .60 .18
❑ 242 Dedric Ward .25 .07
❑ 243 Ricky Williams .60 .18
❑ 244 Michael Bennett .40 .12
❑ 245 Todd Bouman .25 .07
❑ 246 Cris Carter .60 .18
❑ 247 Byron Chamberlain .25 .07
❑ 248 Doug Chapman .25 .07
❑ 249 Kenny Clark RC .40 .12
❑ 250 Daunte Culpepper .60 .18
❑ 251 Nate Jacquet .25 .07
❑ 252 Jim Kleinsasser .25 .07
❑ 253 Harold Morrow .25 .07
❑ 254 Randy Moss 1.25 .35
❑ 255 Jake Reed .25 .07
❑ 256 Spergon Wynn .25 .07
❑ 257 Drew Bledsoe .75 .23
❑ 258 Tom Brady 1.50 .45
❑ 259 Troy Brown .40 .12
❑ 260 Fred Coleman .25 .07
❑ 261 Marc Edwards .25 .07
❑ 262 Kevin Faulk .40 .12
❑ 263 Bobby Hamilton .25 .07
❑ 264 Ty Law .40 .12
❑ 265 Lawyer Milloy .40 .12
❑ 266 David Patten .25 .07
❑ 267 J.R. Redmond .25 .07
❑ 268 Antowain Smith .40 .12
❑ 269 Adam Vinatieri .60 .18
❑ 270 Jermaine Wiggins .25 .07
❑ 271 Aaron Brooks .60 .18
❑ 272 Cam Cleeland .25 .07
❑ 273 Charlie Clemons RC .25 .07
❑ 274 James Fenderson RC .40 .12
❑ 275 La'Roi Glover .25 .07
❑ 276 Joe Horn .40 .12
❑ 277 Willie Jackson .25 .07
❑ 278 Sammy Knight .25 .07
❑ 279 Michael Lewis .25 .07
❑ 280 Deuce McAllister .75 .23
❑ 281 Terrelle Smith .25 .07
❑ 282 Boo Williams .25 .07
❑ 283 Robert Wilson .25 .07
❑ 284 Tiki Barber .40 .12
❑ 285 Micheal Barrow .25 .07
❑ 286 Kerry Collins .40 .12
❑ 287 Greg Comella .25 .07
❑ 288 Thabiti Davis .25 .07
❑ 289 Ron Dayne .40 .12
❑ 290 Ron Dixon .25 .07
❑ 291 Ike Hilliard .40 .12
❑ 292 Joe Jurevicius .25 .07
❑ 293 Michael Strahan .40 .12
❑ 294 Amani Toomer .40 .12
❑ 295 Damon Washington .25 .07
❑ 296 John Abraham .40 .12
❑ 297 Richie Anderson .25 .07
❑ 298 Anthony Becht .25 .07
❑ 299 Wayne Chrebet .40 .12
❑ 300 Laveranues Coles .40 .12
❑ 301 James Farrior .25 .07
❑ 302 Marvin Jones .25 .07
❑ 303 LaMont Jordan .60 .18
❑ 304 Curtis Martin .60 .18

❑ 305 Santana Moss .60 .18
❑ 306 Chad Pennington .75 .23
❑ 307 Kevin Swayne .25 .07
❑ 308 Vinny Testaverde .40 .12
❑ 309 Craig Yeast .25 .07
❑ 310 Greg Biekert .25 .07
❑ 311 Tim Brown .60 .18
❑ 312 Zack Crockett .25 .07
❑ 313 Rich Gannon .60 .18
❑ 314 Charlie Garner .40 .12
❑ 315 Sebastian Janikowski .25 .07
❑ 316 Randy Jordan .25 .07
❑ 317 Terry Kirby .25 .07
❑ 318 Jerry Porter .25 .07
❑ 319 Jerry Rice 1.25 .35
❑ 320 Jon Ritchie .25 .07
❑ 321 Tyrone Wheatley .40 .12
❑ 322 Roland Williams .25 .07
❑ 323 Charles Woodson .40 .12
❑ 324 Correll Buckhalter .40 .12
❑ 325 Brian Dawkins .25 .07
❑ 326 Hugh Douglas .25 .07
❑ 327 A.J. Feeley .60 .18
❑ 328 Chad Lewis .25 .07
❑ 329 Cecil Martin .25 .07
❑ 330 Brian Mitchell .25 .07
❑ 331 Freddie Mitchell .40 .12
❑ 332 Todd Pinkston .40 .12
❑ 333 Rod Smart RC .25 .07
❑ 334 Duce Staley .60 .18
❑ 335 James Thrash .40 .12
❑ 336 Jeremiah Trotter .25 .07
❑ 337 Troy Vincent .25 .07
❑ 338 Kendrell Bell .60 .18
❑ 339 Jerome Bettis .60 .18
❑ 340 Demetrius Brown RC .40 .12
❑ 341 Plaxico Burress .40 .12
❑ 342 Troy Edwards .25 .07
❑ 343 Chris Fuamatu-Ma'afala .25 .07
❑ 344 Jason Gildon .25 .07
❑ 345 Earl Holmes .25 .07
❑ 346 Joey Porter .25 .07
❑ 347 Chad Scott .25 .07
❑ 348 Bobby Shaw .25 .07
❑ 349 Kordell Stewart .40 .12
❑ 350 Hines Ward .60 .18
❑ 351 Amos Zereoue .60 .18
❑ 352 Adam Archuleta .25 .07
❑ 353 Dre' Bly .25 .07
❑ 354 Isaac Bruce .60 .18
❑ 355 Trung Canidate .40 .12
❑ 356 Ernie Conwell .25 .07
❑ 357 Marshall Faulk .60 .18
❑ 358 Torry Holt .60 .18
❑ 359 Leonard Little .25 .07
❑ 360 Yo Murphy .25 .07
❑ 361 Ricky Proehl .25 .07
❑ 362 Kurt Warner .60 .18
❑ 363 Aeneas Williams .25 .07
❑ 364 Drew Brees .60 .18
❑ 365 Curtis Conway .25 .07
❑ 366 Tim Dwight .40 .12
❑ 367 Terrell Fletcher .25 .07
❑ 368 Doug Flutie .60 .18
❑ 369 Jeff Graham .25 .07
❑ 370 Rodney Harrison .25 .07
❑ 371 Ronney Jenkins .25 .07
❑ 372 Raylee Johnson .25 .07
❑ 373 Freddie Jones .25 .07
❑ 374 Ryan McNeil .25 .07
❑ 375 Junior Seau .60 .18
❑ 376 LaDainian Tomlinson 1.00 .30
❑ 377 Marcellus Wiley .25 .07
❑ 378 Kevan Barlow .40 .12
❑ 379 Fred Beasley .25 .07
❑ 380 Zack Bronson RC .40 .12
❑ 381 Andre Carter .25 .07
❑ 382 Jeff Garcia .60 .18
❑ 383 Garrison Hearst .40 .12
❑ 384 Terry Jackson .25 .07
❑ 385 Eric Johnson .40 .12
❑ 386 Saladin McCullough RC .25 .07
❑ 387 Terrell Owens .60 .18
❑ 388 Ahmed Plummer .25 .07
❑ 389 J.J. Stokes .25 .07
❑ 390 Tai Streets .25 .07
❑ 391 Vinny Sutherland .25 .07
❑ 392 Bryant Young .25 .07
❑ 393 Shaun Alexander .60 .18
❑ 394 Chad Brown .25 .07
❑ 395 Kerwin Cook RC .40 .12
❑ 396 Trent Dilfer .40 .12
❑ 397 Bobby Engram .25 .07
❑ 398 Christian Fauria .25 .07
❑ 399 Matt Hasselbeck .40 .12
❑ 400 Darrell Jackson .40 .12
❑ 401 John Randle .25 .07
❑ 402 Koren Robinson .40 .12
❑ 403 Anthony Simmons .25 .07
❑ 404 Mack Strong .25 .07
❑ 405 Ricky Watters .25 .07
❑ 406 James Williams WR .25 .07
❑ 407 Mike Alstott .60 .18
❑ 408 Ronde Barber .25 .07
❑ 409 Derrick Brooks .60 .18
❑ 410 Jameel Cook .25 .07
❑ 411 Warrick Dunn .60 .18
❑ 412 Jacquez Green .25 .07
❑ 413 Brad Johnson .40 .12
❑ 414 Keyshawn Johnson .60 .18
❑ 415 Rob Johnson .40 .12
❑ 416 John Lynch .40 .12
❑ 417 Dave Moore .25 .07
❑ 418 Warren Sapp .40 .12
❑ 419 Aaron Stecker .25 .07
❑ 420 Karl Williams .25 .07
❑ 421 Drew Bennett .60 .18
❑ 422 Eddie Berlin .25 .07
❑ 423 Rafael Cooper RC .40 .12
❑ 424 Kevin Dyson .40 .12
❑ 425 Eddie George .60 .18
❑ 426 Mike Green .25 .07
❑ 427 Skip Hicks .25 .07
❑ 428 Jevon Kearse .40 .12
❑ 429 Erron Kinney .25 .07
❑ 430 Derrick Mason .40 .12
❑ 431 Justin McCareins .40 .12
❑ 432 Steve McNair .60 .18
❑ 433 Neil O'Donnell .25 .07
❑ 434 Frank Wycheck .25 .07
❑ 435 Reidel Anthony .25 .07
❑ 436 Jessie Armstead .25 .07
❑ 437 Champ Bailey .40 .12
❑ 438 Tony Banks .25 .07
❑ 439 Michael Bates .25 .07
❑ 440 Donnell Bennett .25 .07
❑ 441 Ki-Jana Carter .25 .07
❑ 442 Stephen Davis .40 .12
❑ 443 Zeron Flemister .25 .07
❑ 444 Rod Gardner .40 .12
❑ 445 Kevin Lockett .25 .07
❑ 446 Eric Metcalf .25 .07
❑ 447 Sage Rosenfels .25 .07
❑ 448 Fred Smoot .25 .07
❑ 449 Michael Westbrook .25 .07
❑ 450 Danny Wuerffel .25 .07
❑ 451 Jason McAddley RC 1.50 .45
❑ 452 Freddie Milons RC 1.50 .45
❑ 453 Bryan Thomas RC 1.50 .45
❑ 454 Levi Jones RC 1.50 .45
❑ 455 William Green RC 3.00 .90
❑ 456 Luke Staley RC 1.50 .45
❑ 457 Daniel Graham RC 2.00 .60
❑ 458 David Garrard RC 2.00 .60
❑ 459 Reche Caldwell RC 2.00 .60
❑ 460 Andra Davis RC 1.50 .45
❑ 461 Lito Sheppard RC 2.00 .60
❑ 462 Chris Hope RC 1.50 .45
❑ 463 Javon Walker RC 4.00 1.20
❑ 464 David Carr RC 6.00 1.80
❑ 465 Alan Harper RC 1.00 .30
❑ 466 Adrian Peterson RC 2.00 .60
❑ 467 Kelly Campbell RC 1.50 .45
❑ 468 Ashley Lelie RC 4.00 1.20
❑ 469 Kurt Kittner RC 1.50 .45
❑ 470 Antwaan Randle El RC 2.50 .75
❑ 471 Ladell Betts RC 2.00 .60
❑ 472 Josh Reed RC 2.00 .60
❑ 473 Clinton Portis RC 6.00 1.80
❑ 474 Ron Johnson RC 1.50 .45
❑ 475 Eric Crouch RC 3.00 .90
❑ 476 Tracey Wistrom RC 1.50 .45
❑ 477 David Neill RC 1.50 .45
❑ 478 Ronald Curry RC 2.00 .60
❑ 479 Lamar Gordon RC 2.00 .60
❑ 480 Damien Anderson RC 1.50 .45
❑ 481 Napoleon Harris RC 2.00 .60
❑ 482 Zak Kustok RC 2.00 .60
❑ 483 Rocky Calmus RC 2.00 .60
❑ 484 Roy Williams RC 5.00 1.50
❑ 485 Joey Harrington RC 6.00 1.80
❑ 486 Maurice Morris RC 2.00 .60
❑ 487 Antonio Bryant RC 2.00 .60
❑ 488 Josh McCown RC 2.50 .75
❑ 489 John Henderson RC 2.00 .60
❑ 490 Quentin Jammer RC 2.00 .60
❑ 491 Mike Williams RC 1.50 .45
❑ 492 Patrick Ramsey RC 4.00 1.20
❑ 493 Kenyon Coleman RC 1.00 .30
❑ 494 DeShaun Foster RC 2.00 .60
❑ 495 Brian Poli-Dixon RC 1.50 .45
❑ 496 Cliff Russell RC 1.50 .45
❑ 497 Brian Westbrook RC 3.00 .90
❑ 498 Andre Davis RC 2.00 .60
❑ 499 Larry Tripplett RC 1.00 .30
❑ 500 Lamont Thompson RC 1.50 .45
❑ 501 T.J. Duckett RC 3.00 .90
❑ 502 Dameon Hunter RC 1.00 .30
❑ 503 Javin Hunter RC 1.00 .30
❑ 504 Tellis Redmon RC 1.50 .45
❑ 505 Chester Taylor RC 2.00 .60
❑ 506 Randy Fasani RC 1.50 .45
❑ 507 Julius Peppers RC 4.00 1.20
❑ 508 Jamin Elliott RC 1.00 .30
❑ 509 Chad Hutchinson RC 2.00 .60
❑ 510 Eddie Drummond RC 1.50 .45
❑ 511 Craig Nall RC 2.00 .60
❑ 512 Jabar Gaffney RC 2.00 .60
❑ 513 Jonathan Wells RC 2.00 .60
❑ 514 Shaun Hill RC 2.00 .60
❑ 515 Deion Branch RC 4.00 1.20
❑ 516 Rohan Davey RC 2.00 .60
❑ 517 J.T. O'Sullivan RC 1.50 .45
❑ 518 Tim Carter RC 1.50 .45
❑ 519 Daryl Jones RC 1.50 .45
❑ 520 Jeremy Shockey RC 6.00 1.80
❑ 521 Seth Burford RC 1.50 .45
❑ 522 Brandon Doman RC 2.00 .60
❑ 523 Jerramy Stevens RC 2.00 .60
❑ 524 Travis Stephens RC 1.50 .45
❑ 525 Marquise Walker RC 1.50 .45

2002 Pacific Adrenaline

	Nm-Mt	Ex-Mt
COMPLETE SET (288)	50.00	15.00
❑ 1 Damien Anderson RC	1.50	.45
❑ 2 David Boston	.75	.23
❑ 3 Wendell Bryant RC	2.00	.60
❑ 4 Thomas Jones	.50	.15
❑ 5 Jason McAddley RC	1.50	.45
❑ 6 Josh McCown RC	2.50	.75
❑ 7 Jake Plummer	.50	.15
❑ 8 Frank Sanders	.30	.09
❑ 9 Josh Scobey RC	2.00	.60
❑ 10 Keith Brooking	.30	.09
❑ 11 T.J. Duckett RC	3.00	.90
❑ 12 Warrick Dunn	.75	.23
❑ 13 Brian Finneran	.30	.09
❑ 14 Kahlil Hill RC	1.50	.45
❑ 15 Shawn Jefferson	.30	.09
❑ 16 Kurt Kittner RC	1.50	.45
❑ 17 Will Overstreet RC	1.00	.30
❑ 18 Michael Vick	2.50	.75
❑ 19 Ron Johnson RC	1.50	.45
❑ 20 Jamal Lewis	.75	.23
❑ 21 Ray Lewis	.75	.23

❑ 22 Chris Redman .30 .09
❑ 23 Tellis Redmon RC 1.50 .45
❑ 24 Brandon Stokley .50 .15
❑ 25 Chester Taylor RC 2.00 .60
❑ 26 Travis Taylor .50 .15
❑ 27 Anthony Weaver RC 1.50 .45
❑ 28 Drew Bledsoe 1.00 .30
❑ 29 Shawn Bryson .30 .09
❑ 30 Larry Centers .30 .09
❑ 31 Ryan Denney RC 1.00 .30
❑ 32 Travis Henry .75 .23
❑ 33 Richard Huntley .30 .09
❑ 34 Eric Moulds .50 .15
❑ 35 Peerless Price .50 .15
❑ 36 Josh Reed RC 2.00 .60
❑ 37 Isaac Byrd .30 .09
❑ 38 Randy Fasani RC 1.50 .45
❑ 39 DeShaun Foster RC 2.00 .60
❑ 40 Kyle Johnson RC 1.00 .30
❑ 41 Muhsin Muhammad .50 .15
❑ 42 Julius Peppers RC 4.00 1.20
❑ 43 Lamar Smith .50 .15
❑ 44 Steve Smith .50 .15
❑ 45 Chris Weinke .50 .15
❑ 46 Marty Booker .50 .15
❑ 47 Chris Chandler .50 .15
❑ 48 Eric McCoo RC 1.00 .30
❑ 49 Jim Miller .30 .09
❑ 50 Adrian Peterson RC 2.00 .60
❑ 51 Marcus Robinson .50 .15
❑ 52 David Terrell .75 .23
❑ 53 Anthony Thomas .75 .23
❑ 54 Brian Urlacher 1.25 .35
❑ 55 Corey Dillon .50 .15
❑ 56 Gus Frerotte .30 .09
❑ 57 Chad Johnson .75 .23
❑ 58 Jon Kitna .50 .15
❑ 59 Justin Smith .30 .09
❑ 60 Takeo Spikes .30 .09
❑ 61 Lamont Thompson RC 1.50 .45
❑ 62 Peter Warrick .50 .15
❑ 63 Michael Westbrook .30 .09
❑ 64 Tim Couch .50 .15
❑ 65 Andre Davis RC 2.00 .60
❑ 66 JaJuan Dawson .30 .09
❑ 67 William Green RC 3.00 .90
❑ 68 James Jackson .30 .09
❑ 69 Kevin Johnson .50 .15
❑ 70 Jamir Miller .30 .09
❑ 71 Quincy Morgan .30 .09
❑ 72 Jamel White .30 .09
❑ 73 Antonio Bryant RC 2.00 .60
❑ 74 Quincy Carter .50 .15
❑ 75 Woody Dantzler RC 2.00 .60
❑ 76 Joey Galloway .50 .15
❑ 77 Ennis Haywood RC 1.50 .45
❑ 78 Chad Hutchinson RC 2.00 .60
❑ 79 Rocket Ismail .50 .15
❑ 80 Emmitt Smith 2.00 .60
❑ 81 Roy Williams RC 5.00 1.50
❑ 82 Mike Anderson .75 .23
❑ 83 Terrell Davis .75 .23
❑ 84 Brian Griese .75 .23
❑ 85 Herb Haygood RC 1.00 .30
❑ 86 Ashley Lelie RC 4.00 1.20
❑ 87 Ed McCaffrey .75 .23
❑ 88 Deltha O'Neal .30 .09
❑ 89 Clinton Portis RC 6.00 1.80
❑ 90 Rod Smith .50 .15
❑ 91 Scotty Anderson .30 .09
❑ 92 Eddie Drummond RC 1.50 .45
❑ 93 Az-Zahir Hakim .30 .09
❑ 94 Joey Harrington RC 6.00 1.80
❑ 95 Mike McMahon .75 .23
❑ 96 James Mungro RC 2.00 .60
❑ 97 Bill Schroeder .30 .09
❑ 98 Luke Staley RC 1.50 .45
❑ 99 James Stewart .50 .15
❑ 100 Marques Anderson RC 2.00 .60
❑ 101 Najeh Davenport RC 2.00 .60
❑ 102 Brett Favre 2.00 .60
❑ 103 Robert Ferguson .30 .09
❑ 104 Bubba Franks .50 .15
❑ 105 Terry Glenn .50 .15
❑ 106 Ahman Green .75 .23
❑ 107 Craig Nall RC 2.00 .60
❑ 108 Javon Walker RC 4.00 1.20
❑ 109 James Allen .50 .15
❑ 110 Jarrod Baxter RC 1.50 .45
❑ 111 Corey Bradford .30 .09
❑ 112 David Carr RC 6.00 1.80
❑ 113 Delvon Flowers RC 1.50 .45
❑ 114 Jabar Gaffney RC 2.00 .60
❑ 115 Jermaine Lewis .30 .09
❑ 116 Travis Prentice .30 .09
❑ 117 Jonathan Wells RC 2.00 .60
❑ 118 Brian Allen RC 1.50 .45
❑ 119 Chad Bratzke .30 .09
❑ 120 Marvin Harrison .75 .23
❑ 121 Qadry Ismail .50 .15
❑ 122 Edgerrin James 1.00 .30
❑ 123 Peyton Manning 1.50 .45
❑ 124 Rob Morris .30 .09
❑ 125 Dominic Rhodes .50 .15
❑ 126 Reggie Wayne .50 .15
❑ 127 Tony Brackens .30 .09
❑ 128 Mark Brunell .75 .23
❑ 129 Donovin Darius .30 .09
❑ 130 David Garrard RC 2.00 .60
❑ 131 John Henderson RC 2.00 .60
❑ 132 Stacey Mack .30 .09
❑ 133 Bobby Shaw .30 .09
❑ 134 Jimmy Smith .50 .15
❑ 135 Fred Taylor .75 .23
❑ 136 Omar Easy RC 2.00 .60
❑ 137 Eddie Freeman RC 1.00 .30
❑ 138 Tony Gonzalez .50 .15
❑ 139 Trent Green .50 .15
❑ 140 Priest Holmes 1.00 .30
❑ 141 Eddie Kennison .30 .09
❑ 142 Snoop Minnis .30 .09
❑ 143 Johnnie Morton .50 .15
❑ 144 Ryan Sims RC 2.00 .60
❑ 145 Chris Chambers .75 .23
❑ 146 Jay Fiedler .50 .15
❑ 147 Oronde Gadsden .30 .09
❑ 148 Leonard Henry RC 1.50 .45
❑ 149 James McKnight .30 .09
❑ 150 Travis Minor .30 .09
❑ 151 Sam Simmons RC 1.00 .30
❑ 152 Zach Thomas .75 .23
❑ 153 Ricky Williams .75 .23
❑ 154 Derrick Alexander .50 .15
❑ 155 Jeremy Allen RC 2.00 .60
❑ 156 Atrews Bell RC 1.00 .30
❑ 157 Michael Bennett .50 .15
❑ 158 Kelly Campbell RC 1.50 .45
❑ 159 Byron Chamberlain .30 .09
❑ 160 Doug Chapman .30 .09
❑ 161 Daunte Culpepper .75 .23
❑ 162 Randy Moss 1.50 .45
❑ 163 Tom Brady 2.00 .60
❑ 164 Deion Branch RC 4.00 1.20
❑ 165 Troy Brown .50 .15
❑ 166 Rohan Davey RC 2.00 .60
❑ 167 Kevin Faulk .50 .15
❑ 168 Daniel Graham RC 2.00 .60
❑ 169 David Patten .30 .09
❑ 170 Antowain Smith .50 .15
❑ 171 Antwoine Womack RC 1.50 .45
❑ 172 Aaron Brooks .75 .23
❑ 173 Charlie Clemons .30 .09
❑ 174 Joe Horn .50 .15
❑ 175 Sammy Knight .30 .09
❑ 176 Deuce McAllister 1.00 .30
❑ 177 J.T. O'Sullivan RC 1.50 .45
❑ 178 Jerome Pathon .50 .15
❑ 179 Donte Stallworth RC 4.00 1.20
❑ 180 Ricky Williams RC 1.50 .45
❑ 181 Tiki Barber .50 .15
❑ 182 Tim Carter RC 1.50 .45
❑ 183 Kerry Collins .50 .15
❑ 184 Ron Dayne .50 .15
❑ 185 Ike Hilliard .50 .15
❑ 186 Daryl Jones RC 1.50 .45
❑ 187 Jeremy Shockey RC 6.00 1.80
❑ 188 Michael Strahan .50 .15
❑ 189 Amani Toomer .50 .15
❑ 190 Wayne Chrebet .50 .15
❑ 191 Laveranues Coles .50 .15
❑ 192 Alan Harper RC 1.00 .30
❑ 193 LaMont Jordan .75 .23
❑ 194 Curtis Martin .75 .23
❑ 195 Chad Morton .30 .09
❑ 196 Santana Moss .75 .23
❑ 197 Vinny Testaverde .50 .15
❑ 198 Bryan Thomas RC 1.50 .45
❑ 199 Tim Brown .75 .23
❑ 200 Ronald Curry RC 2.00 .60
❑ 201 Rich Gannon .75 .23
❑ 202 Charlie Garner .50 .15
❑ 203 Napoleon Harris RC 2.00 .60
❑ 204 Larry Ned RC 1.50 .45
❑ 205 Jerry Rice 1.50 .45
❑ 206 Tyrone Wheatley .50 .15
❑ 207 Charles Woodson .50 .15
❑ 208 Michael Lewis RC 2.00 .60
❑ 209 Donovan McNabb 1.00 .30
❑ 210 Freddie Milons RC 1.50 .45
❑ 211 Freddie Mitchell .50 .15
❑ 212 Todd Pinkston .50 .15
❑ 213 Lito Sheppard RC 2.00 .60
❑ 214 Duce Staley .75 .23
❑ 215 James Thrash .50 .15
❑ 216 Brian Westbrook RC 3.00 .90
❑ 217 Kendrell Bell .75 .23
❑ 218 Jerome Bettis .75 .23
❑ 219 Plaxico Burress .50 .15
❑ 220 Verron Haynes RC 2.00 .60
❑ 221 Chris Hope RC 1.50 .45
❑ 222 Lee Mays RC 1.50 .45
❑ 223 Antwaan Randle El RC 2.50 .75
❑ 224 Kordell Stewart .50 .15
❑ 225 Hines Ward .75 .23
❑ 226 Isaac Bruce .75 .23
❑ 227 Eric Crouch RC 3.00 .90
❑ 228 Marshall Faulk .75 .23
❑ 229 Lamar Gordon RC 2.00 .60
❑ 230 Torry Holt .75 .23
❑ 231 Leonard Little .30 .09
❑ 232 Robert Thomas RC 2.00 .60
❑ 233 Kurt Warner .75 .23
❑ 234 Terrence Wilkins .30 .09
❑ 235 Drew Brees .75 .23
❑ 236 Seth Burford RC 1.50 .45
❑ 237 Reche Caldwell RC 2.00 .60
❑ 238 Curtis Conway .30 .09
❑ 239 Doug Flutie .75 .23
❑ 240 Quentin Jammer RC 2.00 .60
❑ 241 Brian Poli-Dixon RC 1.50 .45
❑ 242 Junior Seau .75 .23
❑ 243 LaDainian Tomlinson 1.25 .35
❑ 244 Kevan Barlow .50 .15
❑ 245 Andre Carter .30 .09
❑ 246 Brandon Doman RC 2.00 .60
❑ 247 Jeff Garcia .75 .23
❑ 248 Garrison Hearst .50 .15
❑ 249 Terrell Owens .75 .23
❑ 250 Derek Smith RC 1.00 .30
❑ 251 J.J. Stokes .50 .15
❑ 252 Vinny Sutherland .30 .09
❑ 253 Shaun Alexander .75 .23
❑ 254 Chad Brown .30 .09
❑ 255 Trent Dilfer .50 .15
❑ 256 Bobby Engram .30 .09
❑ 257 Darrell Jackson .50 .15
❑ 258 Nakoa McElrath RC 1.50 .45
❑ 259 Maurice Morris RC 2.00 .60
❑ 260 Koren Robinson .50 .15
❑ 261 Jerramy Stevens RC 2.00 .60
❑ 262 Mike Alstott .75 .23
❑ 263 Derrick Brooks .75 .23
❑ 264 Brad Johnson .50 .15
❑ 265 Keyshawn Johnson .75 .23
❑ 266 Keenan McCardell .30 .09
❑ 267 Michael Pittman .30 .09
❑ 268 Warren Sapp .50 .15
❑ 269 Travis Stephens RC 1.50 .45
❑ 270 Marquise Walker RC 1.50 .45
❑ 271 Rocky Calmus RC 2.00 .60
❑ 272 Kevin Dyson .50 .15
❑ 273 Eddie George .75 .23
❑ 274 Albert Haynesworth RC 1.50 .45
❑ 275 Derrick Mason .50 .15
❑ 276 Steve McNair .75 .23
❑ 277 Dicenzo Miller RC 1.00 .30
❑ 278 Jake Schifino RC 1.50 .45
❑ 279 Tank Williams RC 1.50 .45
❑ 280 Champ Bailey .50 .15
❑ 281 Ladell Betts RC 2.00 .60
❑ 282 Stephen Davis .50 .15
❑ 283 Rod Gardner .50 .15
❑ 284 Jacquez Green .30 .09
❑ 285 Shane Matthews .30 .09

Card	Nm-Mt	Ex-Mt
❑ 286 Patrick Ramsey RC	4.00	1.20
❑ 287 Cliff Russell RC	1.50	.45
❑ 288 Jeremiah Trotter	.30	.09

2001 Pacific Dynagon

	Nm-Mt	Ex-Mt
COMP.SET w/o SP's (100)	40.00	12.00
❑ 1 David Boston	1.25	.35
❑ 2 Thomas Jones	.75	.23
❑ 3 Jake Plummer	.75	.23
❑ 4 Jamal Anderson	1.25	.35
❑ 5 Tim Dwight	1.25	.35
❑ 6 Elvis Grbac	.75	.23
❑ 7 Jamal Lewis	2.00	.60
❑ 8 Ray Lewis	1.25	.35
❑ 9 Shannon Sharpe	.75	.23
❑ 10 Rob Johnson	.75	.23
❑ 11 Eric Moulds	.75	.23
❑ 12 Peerless Price	.75	.23
❑ 13 Tim Biakabutuka	.75	.23
❑ 14 Patrick Jeffers	.75	.23
❑ 15 Muhsin Muhammad	.75	.23
❑ 16 James Allen	.75	.23
❑ 17 Cade McNown	.50	.15
❑ 18 Marcus Robinson	1.25	.35
❑ 19 Brian Urlacher	2.00	.60
❑ 20 Corey Dillon	1.25	.35
❑ 21 Akili Smith	.50	.15
❑ 22 Peter Warrick	1.25	.35
❑ 23 Tim Couch	.75	.23
❑ 24 Kevin Johnson	.75	.23
❑ 25 Randall Cunningham	1.25	.35
❑ 26 Emmitt Smith	2.50	.75
❑ 27 Mike Anderson	1.25	.35
❑ 28 Terrell Davis	1.25	.35
❑ 29 Brian Griese	1.25	.35
❑ 30 Ed McCaffrey	1.25	.35
❑ 31 Rod Smith	.75	.23
❑ 32 Charlie Batch	1.25	.35
❑ 33 Johnnie Morton	.75	.23
❑ 34 James Stewart	.75	.23
❑ 35 Brett Favre	4.00	1.20
❑ 36 Antonio Freeman	1.25	.35
❑ 37 Ahman Green	1.25	.35
❑ 38 Marvin Harrison	1.25	.35
❑ 39 Edgerrin James	1.50	.45
❑ 40 Peyton Manning	3.00	.90
❑ 41 Mark Brunell	1.25	.35
❑ 42 Keenan McCardell	.50	.15
❑ 43 Jimmy Smith	.75	.23
❑ 44 Fred Taylor	1.25	.35
❑ 45 Derrick Alexander	.75	.23
❑ 46 Tony Gonzalez	.75	.23
❑ 47 Sylvester Morris	.50	.15
❑ 48 Jay Fiedler	1.25	.35
❑ 49 Oronde Gadsden	.75	.23
❑ 50 Lamar Smith	.75	.23
❑ 51 Cris Carter	1.25	.35
❑ 52 Daunte Culpepper	1.25	.35
❑ 53 Randy Moss	2.50	.75
❑ 54 Drew Bledsoe	1.50	.45
❑ 55 Terry Glenn	.50	.15
❑ 56 J.R. Redmond	.50	.15
❑ 57 Aaron Brooks	1.25	.35
❑ 58 Joe Horn	.75	.23
❑ 59 Ricky Williams	1.25	.35
❑ 60 Tiki Barber	.75	.23
❑ 61 Kerry Collins	.75	.23
❑ 62 Ron Dayne	1.25	.35
❑ 63 Amani Toomer	.50	.15
❑ 64 Wayne Chrebet	.75	.23
❑ 65 Curtis Martin	1.25	.35
❑ 66 Vinny Testaverde	.75	.23
❑ 67 Tim Brown	1.25	.35
❑ 68 Rich Gannon	1.25	.35
❑ 69 Tyrone Wheatley	.75	.23
❑ 70 Charles Johnson	.50	.15
❑ 71 Donovan McNabb	1.50	.45
❑ 72 Duce Staley	1.25	.35
❑ 73 Jerome Bettis	1.25	.35
❑ 74 Plaxico Burress	1.25	.35
❑ 75 Kordell Stewart	.75	.23
❑ 76 Isaac Bruce	1.25	.35
❑ 77 Marshall Faulk	1.50	.45
❑ 78 Torry Holt	1.25	.35
❑ 79 Kurt Warner	2.50	.75
❑ 80 Curtis Conway	.75	.23
❑ 81 Doug Flutie	1.25	.35
❑ 82 Jeff Garcia	1.25	.35
❑ 83 Charlie Garner	.75	.23
❑ 84 Terrell Owens	1.25	.35
❑ 85 Jerry Rice	2.50	.75
❑ 86 Shaun Alexander	1.50	.45
❑ 87 Matt Hasselbeck	.75	.23
❑ 88 Darrell Jackson	1.25	.35
❑ 89 Mike Alstott	1.25	.35
❑ 90 Warrick Dunn	1.25	.35
❑ 91 Brad Johnson	1.25	.35
❑ 92 Keyshawn Johnson	1.25	.35
❑ 93 Shaun King	.50	.15
❑ 94 Eddie George	1.25	.35
❑ 95 Jevon Kearse	.75	.23
❑ 96 Derrick Mason	.75	.23
❑ 97 Steve McNair	1.25	.35
❑ 98 Stephen Davis	1.25	.35
❑ 99 Jeff George	.75	.23
❑ 100 Deion Sanders	1.25	.35
❑ 101 Michael Bennett AU RC	40.00	12.00
❑ 102 Drew Brees AU RC	60.00	18.00
❑ 103 Chris Chambers AU RC	30.00	9.00
❑ 104 LaMont Jordan AU RC	40.00	12.00
❑ 105 Deuce McAllister AU RC	60.00	18.00
❑ 106 Koren Robinson AU RC	25.00	7.50
❑ 107 David Terrell AU RC	25.00	7.50
❑ 108 L.Tomlinson AU RC	120.00	36.00
❑ 109 M.Tuiasosopo AU RC	30.00	9.00
❑ 110 Michael Vick AU RC	200.00	60.00
❑ 111 Chris Weinke AU RC	25.00	7.50
❑ 112 Kevan Barlow AU RC	25.00	7.50
❑ 113 Josh Booty AU RC	20.00	6.00
❑ 114 Rod Gardner AU RC	25.00	7.50
❑ 115 Todd Heap AU RC	20.00	6.00
❑ 116 Travis Henry AU RC	30.00	9.00
❑ 117 James Jackson AU RC	20.00	6.00
❑ 118 Chad Johnson AU RC	40.00	12.00
❑ 119 Rudi Johnson AU RC	40.00	12.00
❑ 120 Ben Leard AU RC	12.00	3.60
❑ 121 Quincy Morgan AU RC	20.00	6.00
❑ 122 Snoop Minnis AU RC	12.00	3.60
❑ 123 Freddie Mitchell AU RC	20.00	6.00
❑ 124 Sage Rosenfels AU RC	20.00	6.00
❑ 125 Anthony Thomas AU RC	40.00	12.00
❑ 126 Reggie Wayne AU RC	30.00	9.00
❑ 127 Dan Alexander AU RC	12.00	3.60
❑ 128 Will Allen AU RC	10.00	3.00
❑ 129 Scotty Anderson AU RC	10.00	3.00
❑ 130 Adam AAU RChuleta RC	12.00	3.60
❑ 131 Alex Bannister AU RC	10.00	3.00
❑ 133 Tay Cody AU RC	8.00	2.40
❑ 134 Tony Dixon AU RC	10.00	3.00
❑ 135 Heath Evans AU RC	10.00	3.00
❑ 137 Derrick Gibson AU RC	10.00	3.00
❑ 138 Edgerton Hartwell AU RC	8.00	2.40
❑ 139 Tim Hasselbeck AU RC	12.00	3.60
❑ 140 Jabari Holloway AU RC	10.00	3.00
❑ 141 Torrance Marshall AU RC	12.00	3.60
❑ 142 Jason McKinley AU RC	10.00	3.00
❑ 143 Mike McMahon AU RC	20.00	6.00
❑ 144 Bobby Newcombe AU RC	10.00	3.00
❑ 145 Moran Norris AU RC	8.00	2.40
❑ 146 Tommy Polley AU RC	12.00	3.60
❑ 147 Vinny Sutherland AU RC	10.00	3.00
❑ 149 Reggie White AU RC	10.00	3.00
❑ 150 Cedrick Wilson AU RC	12.00	3.60

2001 Pacific Dynagon Retail

	Nm-Mt	Ex-Mt
COMP.SET w/o SPs (100)	25.00	7.50
*RETAIL STARS 1-100: .3X TO .8X HOBBY		
❑ 101 Michael Bennett RC	5.00	1.50
❑ 102 Drew Brees RC	5.00	1.50
❑ 103 Chris Chambers RC	3.00	.90
❑ 104 LaMont Jordan RC	3.00	.90
❑ 105 Deuce McAllister RC	5.00	1.50
❑ 106 Koren Robinson RC	3.00	.90
❑ 107 David Terrell RC	2.50	.75
❑ 108 LaDainian Tomlinson RC	8.00	2.40
❑ 109 Marques Tuiasosopo RC	2.50	.75
❑ 110 Michael Vick RC	15.00	4.50
❑ 111 Chris Weinke RC	2.50	.75
❑ 112 Kevan Barlow RC	2.50	.75
❑ 113 Josh Booty RC	2.50	.75
❑ 114 Rod Gardner RC	2.50	.75
❑ 115 Todd Heap RC	2.50	.75
❑ 116 Travis Henry RC	3.00	.90
❑ 117 James Jackson RC	2.50	.75
❑ 118 Chad Johnson RC	5.00	1.50
❑ 119 Rudi Johnson RC	5.00	1.50
❑ 120 Ben Leard RC	1.50	.45
❑ 121 Quincy Morgan RC	2.50	.75
❑ 122 Snoop Minnis RC	1.50	.45
❑ 123 Freddie Mitchell RC	2.50	.75
❑ 124 Sage Rosenfels RC	2.50	.75
❑ 125 Anthony Thomas RC	4.00	1.20
❑ 126 Reggie Wayne RC	4.00	1.20
❑ 127 Dan Alexander RC	2.50	.75
❑ 128 Will Allen RC	1.50	.45
❑ 129 Scotty Anderson RC	1.50	.45
❑ 130 Adam Archuleta RC	2.50	.75
❑ 131 Alex Bannister RC	1.50	.45
❑ 132 Gary Baxter RC	1.50	.45
❑ 133 Tay Cody RC	1.00	.30
❑ 134 Tony Dixon RC	1.50	.45
❑ 135 Heath Evans RC	1.50	.45
❑ 136 Jamar Fletcher RC	1.50	.45
❑ 137 Derrick Gibson RC	1.50	.45
❑ 138 Edgerton Hartwell RC	1.00	.30
❑ 139 Tim Hasselbeck RC	2.50	.75
❑ 140 Jabari Holloway RC	1.50	.45
❑ 141 Torrance Marshall RC	2.50	.75
❑ 142 Jason McKinley RC	1.50	.45
❑ 143 Mike McMahon RC	2.50	.75
❑ 144 Bobby Newcombe RC	1.50	.45
❑ 145 Moran Norris RC	1.00	.30
❑ 146 Tommy Polley RC	2.50	.75
❑ 147 Vinny Sutherland RC	1.50	.45
❑ 148 Ja'Mar Toombs RC	1.50	.45
❑ 149 Reggie White RC	1.50	.45
❑ 150 Cedrick Wilson RC	2.50	.75

2002 Pacific Exclusive

	Nm-Mt	Ex-Mt
❑ 1 David Boston	1.50	.45
❑ 2 Thomas Jones	1.00	.30
❑ 3 Jake Plummer	1.00	.30
❑ 4 Frank Sanders	1.00	.30
❑ 5 Josh Scobey RC	2.50	.75
❑ 6 Warrick Dunn	1.50	.45
❑ 7 Brian Finneran	.60	.18
❑ 8 Kahlil Hill RC	2.00	.60
❑ 9 Shawn Jefferson	.60	.18
❑ 10 Kurt Kittner RC	2.00	.60
❑ 11 Michael Vick	5.00	1.50
❑ 12 Ron Johnson RC	2.00	.60

❑ 13 Jamal Lewis 1.50 .45
❑ 14 Ray Lewis 1.50 .45
❑ 15 Chris Redman .60 .18
❑ 16 Brandon Stokley 1.00 .30
❑ 17 Chester Taylor RC 2.50 .75
❑ 18 Travis Taylor .60 .18
❑ 19 Drew Bledsoe 2.00 .60
❑ 20 Travis Henry 1.50 .45
❑ 21 Eric Moulds 1.00 .30
❑ 22 Peerless Price 1.00 .30
❑ 23 Randy Fasani RC 2.00 .60
❑ 24 Muhsin Muhammad 1.00 .30
❑ 25 Lamar Smith 1.00 .30
❑ 26 Steve Smith 1.00 .30
❑ 27 Chris Weinke 1.00 .30
❑ 28 Marty Booker 1.00 .30
❑ 29 Jim Miller 1.00 .30
❑ 30 Adrian Peterson RC 2.50 .75
❑ 31 Marcus Robinson 1.00 .30
❑ 32 David Terrell 1.50 .45
❑ 33 Anthony Thomas 1.50 .45
❑ 34 Brian Urlacher 2.50 .75
❑ 35 Corey Dillon 1.00 .30
❑ 36 Chad Johnson 1.50 .45
❑ 37 Jon Kitna 1.00 .30
❑ 38 Michael Westbrook .60 .18
❑ 39 Peter Warrick 1.00 .30
❑ 40 Tim Couch 1.00 .30
❑ 41 JaJuan Dawson .60 .18
❑ 42 James Jackson .60 .18
❑ 43 Kevin Johnson 1.00 .30
❑ 44 Quincy Morgan 1.00 .30
❑ 45 Quincy Carter 1.00 .30
❑ 46 Joey Galloway 1.00 .30
❑ 47 Troy Hambrick .60 .18
❑ 48 Chad Hutchinson RC 2.50 .75
❑ 49 Rocket Ismail 1.00 .30
❑ 50 Emmitt Smith 4.00 1.20
❑ 51 Mike Anderson 1.50 .45
❑ 52 Terrell Davis 1.50 .45
❑ 53 Brian Griese 1.50 .45
❑ 54 Herb Haygood RC 1.25 .35
❑ 55 Ed McCaffrey 1.50 .45
❑ 56 Rod Smith 1.00 .30
❑ 57 Germane Crowell .60 .18
❑ 58 Az-Zahir Hakim .60 .18
❑ 59 Mike McMahon 1.50 .45
❑ 60 Bill Schroeder 1.00 .30
❑ 61 Luke Staley RC 2.00 .60
❑ 62 James Stewart 1.00 .30
❑ 63 Brett Favre 4.00 1.20
❑ 64 Robert Ferguson .60 .18
❑ 65 Bubba Franks 1.00 .30
❑ 66 Terry Glenn 1.00 .30
❑ 67 Ahman Green 1.50 .45
❑ 68 Craig Nall RC 2.50 .75
❑ 69 James Allen 1.00 .30
❑ 70 Corey Bradford .60 .18
❑ 71 Jermaine Lewis .60 .18
❑ 72 Travis Prentice .60 .18
❑ 73 Brian Allen RC 2.00 .60
❑ 74 Marvin Harrison 1.50 .45
❑ 75 Edgerrin James 2.00 .60
❑ 76 Peyton Manning 3.00 .90
❑ 77 Reggie Wayne 1.00 .30
❑ 78 Mark Brunell 1.50 .45
❑ 79 Patrick Johnson .60 .18
❑ 80 Jimmy Smith 1.00 .30
❑ 81 Fred Taylor 1.50 .45
❑ 82 Tony Gonzalez 1.00 .30
❑ 83 Trent Green 1.00 .30
❑ 84 Priest Holmes 2.00 .60
❑ 85 Johnnie Morton 1.00 .30
❑ 86 Chris Chambers 1.50 .45
❑ 87 Jay Fiedler 1.00 .30
❑ 88 Oronde Gadsden 1.00 .30
❑ 89 Leonard Henry RC 2.00 .60
❑ 90 Travis Minor .60 .18
❑ 91 Sam Simmons RC 1.25 .35
❑ 92 Ricky Williams 1.50 .45
❑ 93 Derrick Alexander 1.00 .30
❑ 94 Michael Bennett 1.50 .45
❑ 95 Daunte Culpepper 1.50 .45
❑ 96 Randy Moss 3.00 .90
❑ 97 Tom Brady 4.00 1.20
❑ 98 Deion Branch RC 5.00 1.50
❑ 99 Troy Brown 1.00 .30
❑ 100 Rohan Davey RC 2.50 .75
❑ 101 Donald Hayes .60 .18
❑ 102 David Patten .60 .18
❑ 103 Antowain Smith 1.00 .30
❑ 104 Antwoine Womack RC 2.00 .60
❑ 105 Aaron Brooks 1.50 .45
❑ 106 Joe Horn 1.00 .30
❑ 107 Deuce McAllister 1.50 .45
❑ 108 J.T. O'Sullivan RC 2.00 .60
❑ 109 Jerome Pathon 1.00 .30
❑ 110 Tiki Barber 1.00 .30
❑ 111 Tim Carter RC 2.00 .60
❑ 112 Kerry Collins 1.00 .30
❑ 113 Ron Dayne 1.00 .30
❑ 114 Ike Hilliard 1.00 .30
❑ 115 Amani Toomer 1.00 .30
❑ 116 Wayne Chrebet 1.00 .30
❑ 117 Laveranues Coles 1.00 .30
❑ 118 Curtis Martin 1.50 .45
❑ 119 Santana Moss 1.50 .45
❑ 120 Vinny Testaverde 1.00 .30
❑ 121 Tim Brown 1.50 .45
❑ 122 Ronald Curry RC 2.50 .75
❑ 123 Rich Gannon 1.50 .45
❑ 124 Charlie Garner 1.00 .30
❑ 125 Larry Ned RC 2.00 .60
❑ 126 Jerry Rice 3.00 .90
❑ 127 Tyrone Wheatley 1.00 .30
❑ 128 Donovan McNabb 2.00 .60
❑ 129 Freddie Mitchell 1.00 .30
❑ 130 Todd Pinkston 1.00 .30
❑ 131 Duce Staley 1.50 .45
❑ 132 James Thrash 1.00 .30
❑ 133 Jerome Bettis 1.50 .45
❑ 134 Plaxico Burress 1.50 .45
❑ 135 Kordell Stewart 1.00 .30
❑ 136 Hines Ward 1.50 .45
❑ 137 Amos Zereoue 1.50 .45
❑ 138 Isaac Bruce 1.50 .45
❑ 139 Trung Canidate 1.00 .30
❑ 140 Eric Crouch RC 4.00 1.20
❑ 141 Marshall Faulk 1.50 .45
❑ 142 Lamar Gordon RC 2.50 .75
❑ 143 Torry Holt 1.50 .45
❑ 144 Kurt Warner 1.50 .45
❑ 145 Terrence Wilkins .60 .18
❑ 146 Drew Brees 1.50 .45
❑ 147 Seth Burford RC 2.00 .60
❑ 148 Reche Caldwell RC 2.50 .75
❑ 149 Curtis Conway 1.00 .30
❑ 150 Tim Dwight 1.00 .30
❑ 151 Doug Flutie 1.50 .45
❑ 152 LaDainian Tomlinson 2.50 .75
❑ 153 Kevan Barlow 1.00 .30
❑ 154 Brandon Doman RC 2.50 .75
❑ 155 Jeff Garcia 1.50 .45
❑ 156 Garrison Hearst 1.00 .30
❑ 157 Terrell Owens 1.50 .45
❑ 158 J.J. Stokes 1.00 .30
❑ 159 Shaun Alexander 1.50 .45
❑ 160 Trent Dilfer 1.00 .30
❑ 161 Darrell Jackson 1.00 .30
❑ 162 Koren Robinson 1.00 .30
❑ 163 Mike Alstott 1.50 .45
❑ 164 Brad Johnson 1.00 .30
❑ 165 Keyshawn Johnson 1.50 .45
❑ 166 Keenan McCardell .60 .18
❑ 167 Michael Pittman .60 .18
❑ 168 Travis Stephens RC 2.00 .60
❑ 169 Marquise Walker RC 2.00 .60
❑ 170 Kevin Dyson 1.00 .30
❑ 171 Eddie George 1.50 .45
❑ 172 Derrick Mason 1.00 .30
❑ 173 Steve McNair 1.50 .45
❑ 174 Reidel Anthony .60 .18
❑ 175 Ladell Betts RC 2.50 .75
❑ 176 Stephen Davis 1.00 .30
❑ 177 Rod Gardner 1.00 .30
❑ 178 Jacquez Green .60 .18
❑ 179 Shane Matthews .60 .18
❑ 180 Cliff Russell RC 2.00 .60
❑ 181 Josh McCown AU/779 RC 25.00 7.50
❑ 182 T.J. Duckett RC 4.00 1.20
❑ 183 Josh Reed RC 2.50 .75
❑ 184 DeShaun Foster AU/105 RC 40.00 12.00
❑ 185 Andre Davis AU/778 RC 20.00 6.00
❑ 186 William Green RC 4.00 1.20
❑ 187 Antonio Bryant AU/575 RC 25.00 7.50
❑ 188 Ashley Lelie AU/100 RC 100.00 30.00
❑ 189 Clinton Portis AU/524 RC 80.00 24.00
❑ 190 Joey Harrington RC 8.00 2.40
❑ 191 Javon Walker AU/519 RC 50.00 15.00
❑ 192 David Carr AU/100 RC 200.00 60.00
❑ 193 Jabar Gaffney AU/103 RC 25.00 7.50
❑ 194 Jonathan Wells AU/615 RC 20.00 6.00
❑ 195 David Garrard AU/787 RC 20.00 6.00
❑ 196 Donte Stallworth RC 5.00 1.50
❑ 197 Brian Westbrook AU/930 RC 40.00 12.00
❑ 198 Ant Randle El AU/788 RC 30.00 9.00
❑ 199 Maurice Morris AU/1045 RC 15.00 4.50
❑ 200 Patrick Ramsey RC 5.00 1.50

2002 Pacific Heads Up

	Nm-Mt	Ex-Mt
COMP.SET w/o SP's (100)	25.00	7.50

❑ 1 David Boston 1.00 .30
❑ 2 Thomas Jones .60 .18
❑ 3 Jake Plummer .60 .18
❑ 4 Jamal Anderson .60 .18
❑ 5 Warrick Dunn 1.00 .30
❑ 6 Shawn Jefferson .40 .12
❑ 7 Michael Vick 3.00 .90
❑ 8 Jamal Lewis 1.00 .30
❑ 9 Chris Redman .40 .12
❑ 10 Brandon Stokley .60 .18
❑ 11 Travis Taylor .60 .18
❑ 12 Drew Bledsoe 1.25 .35
❑ 13 Travis Henry 1.00 .30
❑ 14 Eric Moulds .60 .18
❑ 15 Peerless Price .60 .18
❑ 16 Alex Van Pelt .40 .12
❑ 17 Muhsin Muhammad .60 .18
❑ 18 Lamar Smith .60 .18
❑ 19 Steve Smith .60 .18
❑ 20 Chris Weinke .60 .18
❑ 21 Marty Booker .40 .12
❑ 22 Jim Miller .40 .12
❑ 23 David Terrell 1.00 .30
❑ 24 Anthony Thomas 1.00 .30
❑ 25 Corey Dillon .60 .18
❑ 26 Chad Johnson 1.00 .30
❑ 27 Jon Kitna .60 .18
❑ 28 Peter Warrick .60 .18
❑ 29 Tim Couch .60 .18
❑ 30 James Jackson .40 .12
❑ 31 Kevin Johnson .60 .18
❑ 32 Quincy Morgan .40 .12
❑ 33 Quincy Carter .60 .18
❑ 34 Joey Galloway .60 .18
❑ 35 Rocket Ismail .60 .18
❑ 36 Emmitt Smith 2.50 .75
❑ 37 Terrell Davis 1.00 .30
❑ 38 Brian Griese 1.00 .30
❑ 39 Ed McCaffrey 1.00 .30
❑ 40 Rod Smith .60 .18
❑ 41 Scotty Anderson .40 .12
❑ 42 Az-Zahir Hakim .40 .12
❑ 43 Mike McMahon 1.00 .30
❑ 44 Bill Schroeder .60 .18
❑ 45 Brett Favre 2.50 .75
❑ 46 Robert Ferguson .40 .12
❑ 47 Terry Glenn .60 .18
❑ 48 Ahman Green 1.00 .30
❑ 49 James Allen .60 .18
❑ 50 Corey Bradford .40 .12
❑ 51 Jermaine Lewis .40 .12
❑ 52 Marvin Harrison 1.00 .30
❑ 53 Edgerrin James 1.25 .35
❑ 54 Peyton Manning 2.00 .60

❑ 55 Reggie Wayne .60 .18
❑ 56 Mark Brunell 1.00 .30
❑ 57 Keenan McCardell .40 .12
❑ 58 Jimmy Smith .60 .18
❑ 59 Fred Taylor 1.00 .30
❑ 60 Derrick Alexander .60 .18
❑ 61 Tony Gonzalez .60 .18
❑ 62 Trent Green .60 .18
❑ 63 Priest Holmes 1.25 .35
❑ 64 Chris Chambers 1.00 .30
❑ 65 Jay Fiedler .60 .18
❑ 66 James McKnight .40 .12
❑ 67 Ricky Williams 1.00 .30
❑ 68 Michael Bennett .60 .18
❑ 69 Daunte Culpepper 1.00 .30
❑ 70 Randy Moss 2.00 .60
❑ 71 Tom Brady 2.50 .75
❑ 72 Troy Brown .60 .18
❑ 73 Antowain Smith .60 .18
❑ 74 Aaron Brooks 1.00 .30
❑ 75 Joe Horn .60 .18
❑ 76 Willie Jackson .40 .12
❑ 77 Deuce McAllister 1.25 .35
❑ 78 Tiki Barber .60 .18
❑ 79 Kerry Collins .60 .18
❑ 80 Ron Dayne .60 .18
❑ 81 Ike Hilliard .60 .18
❑ 82 Wayne Chrebet .60 .18
❑ 83 Laveranues Coles .60 .18
❑ 84 Curtis Martin 1.00 .30
❑ 85 Vinny Testaverde .60 .18
❑ 86 Tim Brown 1.00 .30
❑ 87 Rich Gannon 1.00 .30
❑ 88 Charlie Garner .60 .18
❑ 89 Jerry Rice 2.00 .60
❑ 90 Correll Buckhalter .60 .18
❑ 91 Donovan McNabb 1.25 .35
❑ 92 Duce Staley 1.00 .30
❑ 93 James Thrash .60 .18
❑ 94 Jerome Bettis 1.00 .30
❑ 95 Plaxico Burress .60 .18
❑ 96 Kordell Stewart .60 .18
❑ 97 Hines Ward 1.00 .30
❑ 98 Isaac Bruce 1.00 .30
❑ 99 Marshall Faulk 1.00 .30
❑ 100 Torry Holt 1.00 .30
❑ 101 Kurt Warner 1.00 .30
❑ 102 Drew Brees 1.00 .30
❑ 103 Tim Dwight .60 .18
❑ 104 Doug Flutie 1.00 .30
❑ 105 LaDainian Tomlinson 1.50 .45
❑ 106 Jeff Garcia 1.00 .30
❑ 107 Garrison Hearst .60 .18
❑ 108 Terrell Owens 1.00 .30
❑ 109 J.J. Stokes .60 .18
❑ 110 Shaun Alexander 1.00 .30
❑ 111 Trent Dilfer .60 .18
❑ 112 Darrell Jackson .60 .18
❑ 113 Koren Robinson .60 .18
❑ 114 Mike Alstott 1.00 .30
❑ 115 Brad Johnson .60 .18
❑ 116 Keyshawn Johnson 1.00 .30
❑ 117 Michael Pittman .40 .12
❑ 118 Kevin Dyson .60 .18
❑ 119 Eddie George 1.00 .30
❑ 120 Derrick Mason .60 .18
❑ 121 Steve McNair 1.00 .30
❑ 122 Reidel Anthony .40 .12
❑ 123 Stephen Davis .60 .18
❑ 124 Rod Gardner .60 .18
❑ 125 Jacquez Green .40 .12
❑ 126 Jason McAddley RC 4.00 1.20
❑ 127 Josh McCown RC 6.00 1.80
❑ 128 T.J. Duckett RC 8.00 2.40
❑ 129 Kahlil Hill RC 4.00 1.20
❑ 130 Kurt Kittner RC 4.00 1.20
❑ 131 Ron Johnson RC 4.00 1.20
❑ 132 Chester Taylor RC 5.00 1.50
❑ 133 Josh Reed RC 5.00 1.50
❑ 134 Randy Fasani RC 4.00 1.20
❑ 135 DeShaun Foster RC 5.00 1.50
❑ 136 Julius Peppers RC 10.00 3.00
❑ 137 Eric McCoo RC 2.50 .75
❑ 138 Adrian Peterson RC 5.00 1.50
❑ 139 Andre Davis RC 5.00 1.50
❑ 140 William Green RC 8.00 2.40
❑ 141 Antonio Bryant RC 5.00 1.50
❑ 142 Roy Williams RC 12.00 3.60
❑ 143 Ashley Lelie RC 10.00 3.00
❑ 144 Clinton Portis RC 15.00 4.50
❑ 145 Joey Harrington RC 15.00 4.50
❑ 146 Luke Staley RC 4.00 1.20
❑ 147 Javon Walker RC 10.00 3.00
❑ 148 David Carr RC 15.00 4.50
❑ 149 Jabar Gaffney RC 5.00 1.50
❑ 150 Jonathan Wells RC 5.00 1.50
❑ 151 David Garrard RC 5.00 1.50
❑ 152 Leonard Henry RC 4.00 1.20
❑ 153 Major Applewhite RC 5.00 1.50
❑ 154 Deion Branch RC 10.00 3.00
❑ 155 Rohan Davey RC 5.00 1.50
❑ 156 Daniel Graham RC 5.00 1.50
❑ 157 Antwoine Womack RC 4.00 1.20
❑ 158 J.T. O'Sullivan RC 4.00 1.20
❑ 159 Donte Stallworth RC 10.00 3.00
❑ 160 Jeremy Shockey RC 15.00 4.50
❑ 161 Ronald Curry RC 5.00 1.50
❑ 162 Larry Ned RC 4.00 1.20
❑ 163 Freddie Milons RC 4.00 1.20
❑ 164 Brian Westbrook RC 8.00 2.40
❑ 165 Lee Mays RC 4.00 1.20
❑ 166 Antwaan Randle El RC 6.00 1.80
❑ 167 Eric Crouch RC 8.00 2.40
❑ 168 Lamar Gordon RC 5.00 1.50
❑ 169 Reche Caldwell RC 5.00 1.50
❑ 170 Maurice Morris RC 5.00 1.50
❑ 171 Travis Stephens RC 4.00 1.20
❑ 172 Marquise Walker RC 4.00 1.20
❑ 173 Ladell Betts RC 5.00 1.50
❑ 174 Patrick Ramsey RC 10.00 3.00
❑ 175 Cliff Russell RC 4.00 1.20
❑ 176 Dameon Hunter RC 2.50 .75
❑ 177 Javin Hunter RC 2.50 .75
❑ 178 Tellis Redmon RC 4.00 1.20
❑ 179 Ed Reed RC 8.00 2.40
❑ 180 Jamin Elliott RC 2.50 .75
❑ 181 Chad Hutchinson RC 5.00 1.50
❑ 182 Eddie Drummond RC 4.00 1.20
❑ 183 Najeh Davenport RC 5.00 1.50
❑ 184 Craig Nall RC 5.00 1.50
❑ 185 Jarrod Baxter RC 4.00 1.20
❑ 186 Marc Boerigter RC 15.00 4.50
❑ 187 Kelly Campbell RC 4.00 1.20
❑ 188 Shaun Hill RC 5.00 1.50
❑ 189 Tim Carter RC 4.00 1.20
❑ 190 Daryl Jones RC 4.00 1.20
❑ 191 Phillip Buchanon RC 5.00 1.50
❑ 192 Napoleon Harris RC 5.00 1.50
❑ 193 Seth Burford RC 4.00 1.20
❑ 194 Brandon Doman RC 5.00 1.50
❑ 195 Jerramy Stevens RC 5.00 1.50

2001 Pacific Impressions

	Nm-Mt	Ex-Mt
COMP.SET w/o SP's (144)	80.00	24.00

❑ 1 David Boston 1.50 .45
❑ 2 Thomas Jones 1.00 .30
❑ 3 Rob Moore 1.00 .30
❑ 4 Michael Pittman .60 .18
❑ 5 Jake Plummer 1.00 .30
❑ 6 Jamal Anderson 1.50 .45
❑ 7 Chris Chandler 1.00 .30
❑ 8 Shawn Jefferson .60 .18
❑ 9 Terance Mathis .60 .18
❑ 10 Elvis Grbac 1.00 .30
❑ 11 Qadry Ismail 1.00 .30
❑ 12 Jamal Lewis 2.50 .75
❑ 13 Ray Lewis 1.50 .45
❑ 14 Shannon Sharpe 1.00 .30
❑ 15 Shawn Bryson .60 .18
❑ 16 Rob Johnson 1.00 .30
❑ 17 Sammy Morris .60 .18
❑ 18 Eric Moulds 1.00 .30
❑ 19 Peerless Price 1.00 .30
❑ 20 Tim Biakabutuka 1.00 .30
❑ 21 Richard Huntley .60 .18
❑ 22 Patrick Jeffers 1.00 .30
❑ 23 Dameyune Craig .60 .18
❑ 24 Muhsin Muhammad 1.00 .30
❑ 25 James Allen 1.00 .30
❑ 26 Marcus Robinson 1.50 .45
❑ 27 Brian Urlacher 2.50 .75
❑ 28 Corey Dillon 1.50 .45
❑ 29 Jon Kitna 1.00 .30
❑ 30 Akili Smith .60 .18
❑ 31 Peter Warrick 1.50 .45
❑ 32 Tim Couch 1.00 .30
❑ 33 Kevin Johnson 1.00 .30
❑ 34 Dennis Northcutt 1.00 .30
❑ 35 JaJuan Dawson .60 .18
❑ 36 Joey Galloway 1.00 .30
❑ 37 Rocket Ismail 1.00 .30
❑ 38 Emmitt Smith 3.00 .90
❑ 39 Mike Anderson 1.50 .45
❑ 40 Terrell Davis 1.50 .45
❑ 41 Brian Griese 1.50 .45
❑ 42 Ed McCaffrey 1.50 .45
❑ 43 Rod Smith 1.00 .30
❑ 44 Charlie Batch 1.50 .45
❑ 45 Germane Crowell .60 .18
❑ 46 Herman Moore 1.00 .30
❑ 47 Johnnie Morton 1.00 .30
❑ 48 James Stewart 1.00 .30
❑ 49 Brett Favre 5.00 1.50
❑ 50 Antonio Freeman 1.50 .45
❑ 51 Ahman Green 1.50 .45
❑ 52 Dorsey Levens 1.00 .30
❑ 53 Bill Schroeder 1.00 .30
❑ 54 Marvin Harrison 1.50 .45
❑ 55 Edgerrin James 2.00 .60
❑ 56 Peyton Manning 4.00 1.20
❑ 57 Jerome Pathon 1.00 .30
❑ 58 Terrence Wilkins .60 .18
❑ 59 Mark Brunell 1.50 .45
❑ 60 Keenan McCardell .60 .18
❑ 61 Jimmy Smith 1.00 .30
❑ 62 Fred Taylor 1.50 .45
❑ 63 Derrick Alexander 1.00 .30
❑ 64 Tony Gonzalez 1.00 .30
❑ 65 Trent Green 1.50 .45
❑ 66 Priest Holmes 2.00 .60
❑ 67 Jay Fiedler 1.50 .45
❑ 68 Oronde Gadsden 1.00 .30
❑ 69 O.J. McDuffie .60 .18
❑ 70 Cade McNown .60 .18
❑ 71 Lamar Smith 1.00 .30
❑ 72 Zach Thomas 1.50 .45
❑ 73 Cris Carter 1.50 .45
❑ 74 Daunte Culpepper 1.50 .45
❑ 75 Randy Moss 3.00 .90
❑ 76 Travis Prentice .60 .18
❑ 77 Drew Bledsoe 2.00 .60
❑ 78 Kevin Faulk 1.00 .30
❑ 79 Charles Johnson .60 .18
❑ 80 J.R. Redmond .60 .18
❑ 81 Jeff Blake 1.00 .30
❑ 82 Aaron Brooks 1.50 .45
❑ 83 Albert Connell .60 .18
❑ 84 Joe Horn 1.00 .30
❑ 85 Ricky Williams 1.50 .45
❑ 86 Tiki Barber 1.00 .30
❑ 87 Kerry Collins 1.00 .30
❑ 88 Ron Dayne 1.50 .45
❑ 89 Ike Hilliard 1.00 .30
❑ 90 Amani Toomer 1.00 .30
❑ 91 Richie Anderson .60 .18
❑ 92 Wayne Chrebet 1.00 .30
❑ 93 Laveranues Coles 1.50 .45
❑ 94 Curtis Martin 1.50 .45
❑ 95 Chad Pennington 2.50 .75
❑ 96 Vinny Testaverde 1.00 .30
❑ 97 Tim Brown 1.50 .45
❑ 98 Rich Gannon 1.50 .45
❑ 99 Charlie Garner 1.00 .30
❑ 100 Jerry Rice 3.00 .90
❑ 101 Tyrone Wheatley 1.00 .30

❑ 102 Charles Woodson 1.00 .30
❑ 103 Todd Pinkston 1.00 .30
❑ 104 Donovan McNabb 2.00 .60
❑ 105 Duce Staley 1.50 .45
❑ 106 James Thrash 1.00 .30
❑ 107 Jerome Bettis 1.50 .45
❑ 108 Plaxico Burress 1.50 .45
❑ 109 Bobby Shaw .60 .18
❑ 110 Kordell Stewart 1.00 .30
❑ 111 Hines Ward 1.50 .45
❑ 112 Isaac Bruce 1.50 .45
❑ 113 Marshall Faulk 2.00 .60
❑ 114 Az-Zahir Hakim .60 .18
❑ 115 Torry Holt 1.50 .45
❑ 116 Kurt Warner 3.00 .90
❑ 117 Curtis Conway 1.00 .30
❑ 118 Tim Dwight 1.50 .45
❑ 119 Doug Flutie 1.50 .45
❑ 120 Jeff Graham 1.00 .30
❑ 121 Jeff Garcia 1.50 .45
❑ 122 Garrison Hearst 1.00 .30
❑ 123 Terrell Owens 1.50 .45
❑ 124 J.J. Stokes 1.00 .30
❑ 125 Tai Streets .60 .18
❑ 126 Shaun Alexander 2.00 .60
❑ 127 Matt Hasselbeck 1.00 .30
❑ 128 Darrell Jackson 1.50 .45
❑ 129 Ricky Watters 1.00 .30
❑ 130 Mike Alstott 1.50 .45
❑ 131 Warrick Dunn 1.50 .45
❑ 132 Jacquez Green .60 .18
❑ 133 Brad Johnson 1.50 .45
❑ 134 Keyshawn Johnson 1.50 .45
❑ 135 Warren Sapp 1.00 .30
❑ 136 Kevin Dyson 1.00 .30
❑ 137 Eddie George 1.50 .45
❑ 138 Jevon Kearse 1.00 .30
❑ 139 Derrick Mason 1.00 .30
❑ 140 Steve McNair 1.50 .45
❑ 141 Champ Bailey 1.50 .45
❑ 142 Stephen Davis 1.50 .45
❑ 143 Jeff George 1.00 .30
❑ 144 Michael Westbrook 1.00 .30
❑ 145 Bobby Newcombe RC 10.00 3.00
❑ 146 Corey Brown RC 10.00 3.00
❑ 147 Quentin McCord RC 10.00 3.00
❑ 148 Vinny Sutherland RC 10.00 3.00
❑ 149 Michael Vick RC 100.00 30.00
❑ 150 Chris Barnes RC 10.00 3.00
❑ 151 Tim Hasselbeck RC 15.00 4.50
❑ 152 Todd Heap RC 15.00 4.50
❑ 153 Nate Clements RC 15.00 4.50
❑ 154 Reggie Germany RC 10.00 3.00
❑ 155 Travis Henry RC 20.00 6.00
❑ 156 Dee Brown RC 15.00 4.50
❑ 157 Dan Morgan RC 15.00 4.50
❑ 158 Steve Smith RC 20.00 6.00
❑ 159 Chris Weinke RC 15.00 4.50
❑ 160 David Terrell RC 15.00 4.50
❑ 161 Anthony Thomas RC 25.00 7.50
❑ 162 T.J. Houshmandzadeh RC 15.00 4.50
❑ 163 Chad Johnson RC 30.00 9.00
❑ 164 Rudi Johnson RC 30.00 9.00
❑ 165 James Jackson RC 15.00 4.50
❑ 166 Andre King RC 10.00 3.00
❑ 167 Quincy Morgan RC 15.00 4.50
❑ 168 Quincy Carter RC 15.00 4.50
❑ 169 Kevin Kasper RC 15.00 4.50
❑ 170 Scotty Anderson RC 10.00 3.00
❑ 171 Mike McMahon RC 15.00 4.50
❑ 172 Robert Ferguson RC 15.00 4.50
❑ 173 Jamal Reynolds RC 15.00 4.50
❑ 174 Reggie Wayne RC 25.00 7.50
❑ 175 Marcus Stroud RC 15.00 4.50
❑ 176 Derrick Blaylock RC 15.00 4.50
❑ 177 Ryan Helming RC 10.00 3.00
❑ 178 Snoop Minnis RC 10.00 3.00
❑ 179 Chris Chambers RC 20.00 6.00
❑ 180 Josh Heupel RC 15.00 4.50
❑ 181 Travis Minor RC 10.00 3.00
❑ 182 Michael Bennett RC 30.00 9.00
❑ 183 Deuce McAllister RC 30.00 9.00
❑ 184 Onome Ojo RC 10.00 3.00
❑ 185 Will Allen RC 10.00 3.00
❑ 186 Jonathan Carter RC 10.00 3.00
❑ 187 Jesse Palmer RC 15.00 4.50
❑ 188 Corey Alston RC 6.00 1.80
❑ 189 LaMont Jordan RC 20.00 6.00
❑ 190 Santana Moss RC 25.00 7.50
❑ 191 Derek Combs RC 10.00 3.00
❑ 192 Derrick Gibson RC 10.00 3.00
❑ 193 Ken-Yon Rambo RC 10.00 3.00
❑ 194 Marques Tuiasosopo RC 15.00 4.50
❑ 195 Correll Buckhalter RC 20.00 6.00
❑ 196 Freddie Mitchell RC 15.00 4.50
❑ 197 Chris Taylor RC 10.00 3.00
❑ 198 Adam Archuleta RC 15.00 4.50
❑ 199 Damione Lewis RC 10.00 3.00
❑ 200 Francis St.Paul RC 10.00 3.00
❑ 201 Milton Wynn RC 10.00 3.00
❑ 202 Drew Brees RC 30.00 9.00
❑ 203 LaDainian Tomlinson RC 50.00 15.00
❑ 204 Kevan Barlow RC 15.00 4.50
❑ 205 Andre Carter RC 15.00 4.50
❑ 206 Cedrick Wilson RC 15.00 4.50
❑ 207 Alex Bannister RC 10.00 3.00
❑ 208 Josh Booty RC 15.00 4.50
❑ 209 Heath Evans RC 10.00 3.00
❑ 210 Ken Lucas RC 10.00 3.00
❑ 211 Koren Robinson RC 20.00 6.00
❑ 212 Dan Alexander RC 15.00 4.50
❑ 213 Eddie Berlin RC 10.00 3.00
❑ 214 Rod Gardner RC 15.00 4.50
❑ 215 Damerien McCants RC 10.00 3.00
❑ 216 Sage Rosenfels RC 15.00 4.50

2001 Pacific Invincible

	Nm-Mt	Ex-Mt
COMP.SET w/o SP's (250)	150.00	45.00

❑ 1 David Boston 3.00 .90
❑ 2 MarTay Jenkins 1.25 .35
❑ 3 Thomas Jones 2.00 .60
❑ 4 Rob Moore 2.00 .60
❑ 5 Michael Pittman 1.25 .35
❑ 6 Jake Plummer 2.00 .60
❑ 7 Frank Sanders 1.25 .35
❑ 8 Jamal Anderson 3.00 .90
❑ 9 Chris Chandler 2.00 .60
❑ 10 Jammi German 1.25 .35
❑ 11 Shawn Jefferson 1.25 .35
❑ 12 Doug Johnson 1.25 .35
❑ 13 Terance Mathis 2.00 .60
❑ 14 Rodney Thomas 1.25 .35
❑ 15 Elvis Grbac 2.00 .60
❑ 16 Qadry Ismail 2.00 .60
❑ 17 Jamal Lewis 5.00 1.50
❑ 18 Jermaine Lewis 1.25 .35
❑ 19 Ray Lewis 3.00 .90
❑ 20 Chris Redman 1.25 .35
❑ 21 Shannon Sharpe 2.00 .60
❑ 22 Travis Taylor 2.00 .60
❑ 23 Shawn Bryson 1.25 .35
❑ 24 Larry Centers 1.25 .35
❑ 25 Rob Johnson 2.00 .60
❑ 26 Jeremy McDaniel 1.25 .35
❑ 27 Sammy Morris 1.25 .35
❑ 28 Eric Moulds 2.00 .60
❑ 29 Peerless Price 2.00 .60
❑ 30 Antowain Smith 2.00 .60
❑ 31 Michael Bates 1.25 .35
❑ 32 Tim Biakabutuka 2.00 .60
❑ 33 Isaac Byrd 1.25 .35
❑ 34 Brad Hoover 1.25 .35
❑ 35 Patrick Jeffers 2.00 .60
❑ 36 Jeff Lewis 1.25 .35
❑ 37 Muhsin Muhammad 2.00 .60
❑ 38 Wesley Walls 1.25 .35
❑ 39 James Allen 2.00 .60
❑ 40 Marty Booker 1.25 .35
❑ 41 Macey Brooks 1.25 .35
❑ 42 Bobby Engram 1.25 .35
❑ 43 Cade McNown 1.25 .35
❑ 44 Marcus Robinson 3.00 .90
❑ 45 Brian Urlacher 5.00 1.50
❑ 46 Dez White 1.25 .35
❑ 47 Brandon Bennett 1.25 .35
❑ 48 Corey Dillon 3.00 .90
❑ 49 Danny Farmer 1.25 .35
❑ 50 Jon Kitna 3.00 .90
❑ 51 Darnay Scott 2.00 .60
❑ 52 Akili Smith 1.25 .35
❑ 53 Peter Warrick 3.00 .90
❑ 54 Craig Yeast 1.25 .35
❑ 55 Tim Couch 2.00 .60
❑ 56 JaJuan Dawson 1.25 .35
❑ 57 Curtis Enis 1.25 .35
❑ 58 Kevin Johnson 2.00 .60
❑ 59 Dennis Northcutt 2.00 .60
❑ 60 Travis Prentice 1.25 .35
❑ 61 Errict Rhett 1.25 .35
❑ 62 Tony Banks 2.00 .60
❑ 63 Randall Cunningham 3.00 .90
❑ 64 Rocket Ismail 2.00 .60
❑ 65 Wane McGarity 1.25 .35
❑ 66 Carl Pickens 1.25 .35
❑ 67 Emmitt Smith 6.00 1.80
❑ 68 Jason Tucker 1.25 .35
❑ 69 Michael Wiley 1.25 .35
❑ 70 Mike Anderson 3.00 .90
❑ 71 Terrell Davis 3.00 .90
❑ 72 Gus Frerotte 1.25 .35
❑ 73 Olandis Gary 2.00 .60
❑ 74 Brian Griese 3.00 .90
❑ 75 Eddie Kennison 1.25 .35
❑ 76 Ed McCaffrey 3.00 .90
❑ 77 Rod Smith 2.00 .60
❑ 78 Charlie Batch 3.00 .90
❑ 79 Germane Crowell 1.25 .35
❑ 80 Larry Foster 1.25 .35
❑ 81 Desmond Howard 1.25 .35
❑ 82 Herman Moore 2.00 .60
❑ 83 Johnnie Morton 2.00 .60
❑ 84 Robert Porcher 1.25 .35
❑ 85 James Stewart 2.00 .60
❑ 86 Donald Driver 2.00 .60
❑ 87 Brett Favre 10.00 3.00
❑ 88 Bubba Franks 2.00 .60
❑ 89 Antonio Freeman 3.00 .90
❑ 90 Ahman Green 3.00 .90
❑ 91 William Henderson 1.25 .35
❑ 92 Dorsey Levens 2.00 .60
❑ 93 Bill Schroeder 2.00 .60
❑ 94 Ken Dilger 1.25 .35
❑ 95 E.G. Green 1.25 .35
❑ 96 Marvin Harrison 3.00 .90
❑ 97 Edgerrin James 4.00 1.20
❑ 98 Peyton Manning 8.00 2.40
❑ 99 Jerome Pathon 2.00 .60
❑ 100 Marcus Pollard 1.25 .35
❑ 101 Terrence Wilkins 1.25 .35
❑ 102 Kyle Brady 1.25 .35
❑ 103 Mark Brunell 3.00 .90
❑ 104 Stacey Mack 1.25 .35
❑ 105 Keenan McCardell 1.25 .35
❑ 106 Jimmy Smith 2.00 .60
❑ 107 R. Jay Soward 1.25 .35
❑ 108 Shyrone Stith 1.25 .35
❑ 109 Fred Taylor 3.00 .90
❑ 110 Derrick Alexander WR 1.25 .35
❑ 111 Kimble Anders 1.25 .35
❑ 112 Todd Collins 1.25 .35
❑ 113 Tony Gonzalez 2.00 .60
❑ 114 Trent Green 3.00 .90
❑ 115 Priest Holmes 4.00 1.20
❑ 116 Tony Horne 1.25 .35
❑ 117 Frank Moreau 1.25 .35
❑ 118 Sylvester Morris 1.25 .35
❑ 119 Tony Richardson 1.25 .35
❑ 120 Jay Fiedler 3.00 .90
❑ 121 Oronde Gadsden 2.00 .60
❑ 122 James Johnson 1.25 .35
❑ 123 Ray Lucas 1.25 .35
❑ 124 Tony Martin 2.00 .60
❑ 125 O.J. McDuffie 1.25 .35
❑ 126 James McKnight 2.00 .60
❑ 127 Lamar Smith 2.00 .60

❑ 128 Jason Taylor	1.25	.35
❑ 129 Zach Thomas	3.00	.90
❑ 130 Dedric Ward	1.25	.35
❑ 131 Cris Carter	3.00	.90
❑ 132 Daunte Culpepper	3.00	.90
❑ 133 Randy Moss	6.00	1.80
❑ 134 Chris Walsh RC	1.25	.35
❑ 135 Troy Walters	1.25	.35
❑ 136 Moe Williams	2.00	.60
❑ 137 Drew Bledsoe	4.00	1.20
❑ 138 Troy Brown	2.00	.60
❑ 139 Kevin Faulk	2.00	.60
❑ 140 Terry Glenn	2.00	.60
❑ 141 Ty Law	2.00	.60
❑ 142 Lawyer Milloy	2.00	.60
❑ 143 David Patten	1.25	.35
❑ 144 J.R. Redmond	1.25	.35
❑ 145 Tony Simmons	1.25	.35
❑ 146 Jeff Blake	2.00	.60
❑ 147 Aaron Brooks	3.00	.90
❑ 148 Albert Connell	1.25	.35
❑ 149 Joe Horn	2.00	.60
❑ 150 Willie Jackson	1.25	.35
❑ 151 Chad Morton	1.25	.35
❑ 152 Keith Poole	1.25	.35
❑ 153 Ricky Williams	3.00	.90
❑ 154 Robert Wilson	1.25	.35
❑ 155 Jessie Armstead	1.25	.35
❑ 156 Tiki Barber	2.00	.60
❑ 157 Kerry Collins	2.00	.60
❑ 158 Ron Dayne	3.00	.90
❑ 159 Ron Dixon	1.25	.35
❑ 160 Ike Hilliard	2.00	.60
❑ 161 Jason Sehorn	1.25	.35
❑ 162 Michael Strahan	2.00	.60
❑ 163 Amani Toomer	1.25	.35
❑ 164 Richie Anderson	1.25	.35
❑ 165 Wayne Chrebet	2.00	.60
❑ 166 Laveranues Coles	3.00	.90
❑ 167 Matthew Hatchette	1.25	.35
❑ 168 Marvin Jones	1.25	.35
❑ 169 Curtis Martin	3.00	.90
❑ 170 Chad Pennington	5.00	1.50
❑ 171 Vinny Testaverde	2.00	.60
❑ 172 Tim Brown	3.00	.90
❑ 173 Zack Crockett	1.25	.35
❑ 174 Rich Gannon	3.00	.90
❑ 175 Charlie Garner	2.00	.60
❑ 176 James Jett	1.25	.35
❑ 177 Randy Jordan	1.25	.35
❑ 178 Andre Rison	2.00	.60
❑ 179 Tyrone Wheatley	2.00	.60
❑ 180 Charles Woodson	2.00	.60
❑ 181 Darnell Autry	1.25	.35
❑ 182 Charles Johnson	1.25	.35
❑ 183 Chad Lewis	1.25	.35
❑ 184 Donovan McNabb	4.00	1.20
❑ 185 Todd Pinkston	1.25	.35
❑ 186 Stanley Pritchett	1.25	.35
❑ 187 Torrance Small	1.25	.35
❑ 188 Duce Staley	3.00	.90
❑ 189 James Thrash	2.00	.60
❑ 190 Jerome Bettis	3.00	.90
❑ 191 Plaxico Burress	3.00	.90
❑ 192 Troy Edwards	1.25	.35
❑ 193 Courtney Hawkins	1.25	.35
❑ 194 Richard Huntley	1.25	.35
❑ 195 Bobby Shaw	1.25	.35
❑ 196 Kordell Stewart	2.00	.60
❑ 197 Hines Ward	3.00	.90
❑ 198 Isaac Bruce	3.00	.90
❑ 199 Trung Canidate	2.00	.60
❑ 200 Marshall Faulk	4.00	1.20
❑ 201 Az-Zahir Hakim	1.25	.35
❑ 202 Torry Holt	3.00	.90
❑ 203 Ricky Proehl	1.25	.35
❑ 204 Kurt Warner	6.00	1.80
❑ 205 Aeneas Williams	1.25	.35
❑ 206 Curtis Conway	2.00	.60
❑ 207 Tim Dwight	3.00	.90
❑ 208 Jermaine Fazande	1.25	.35
❑ 209 Terrell Fletcher	1.25	.35
❑ 210 Doug Flutie	3.00	.90
❑ 211 Jeff Graham	1.25	.35
❑ 212 Freddie Jones	1.25	.35
❑ 213 Reggie Jones	1.25	.35
❑ 214 Junior Seau	3.00	.90
❑ 215 Fred Beasley	1.25	.35
❑ 216 Jeff Garcia	3.00	.90
❑ 217 Terrell Owens	3.00	.90
❑ 218 Jerry Rice	6.00	1.80
❑ 219 Paul Smith	1.25	.35
❑ 220 J.J. Stokes	2.00	.60
❑ 221 Tai Streets	1.25	.35
❑ 222 Shaun Alexander	4.00	1.20
❑ 223 Karsten Bailey	1.25	.35
❑ 224 Matt Hasselbeck	2.00	.60
❑ 225 Brock Huard	1.25	.35
❑ 226 Darrell Jackson	3.00	.90
❑ 227 Shawn Springs	1.25	.35
❑ 228 Ricky Watters	2.00	.60
❑ 229 James Williams WR	1.25	.35
❑ 230 Mike Alstott	3.00	.90
❑ 231 Reidel Anthony	1.25	.35
❑ 232 Warrick Dunn	3.00	.90
❑ 233 Jacquez Green	1.25	.35
❑ 234 Brad Johnson	3.00	.90
❑ 235 Keyshawn Johnson	3.00	.90
❑ 236 Shaun King	1.25	.35
❑ 237 Warren Sapp	2.00	.60
❑ 238 Kevin Dyson	2.00	.60
❑ 239 Eddie George	3.00	.90
❑ 240 Jevon Kearse	2.00	.60
❑ 241 Derrick Mason	2.00	.60
❑ 242 Steve McNair	3.00	.90
❑ 243 Chris Sanders	1.25	.35
❑ 244 Frank Wycheck	1.25	.35
❑ 245 Stephen Alexander	1.25	.35
❑ 246 Stephen Davis	3.00	.90
❑ 247 Irving Fryar	2.00	.60
❑ 248 Jeff George	2.00	.60
❑ 249 Kevin Lockett	1.25	.35
❑ 250 Michael Westbrook	2.00	.60
❑ 251 Bobby Newcombe RC	6.00	1.80
❑ 252 Alge Crumpler RC	12.00	3.60
❑ 253 Vinny Sutherland RC	6.00	1.80
❑ 254 Michael Vick RC	100.00	30.00
❑ 255 Travis Henry RC	12.00	3.60
❑ 256 Dan Morgan RC	10.00	3.00
❑ 257 Chris Weinke JSY RC	15.00	4.50
❑ 258 David Terrell RC	10.00	3.00
❑ 259 Anthony Thomas JSY RC	40.00	12.00
❑ 260 T.J. Houshmandzadeh RC	10.00	3.00
❑ 261 Chad Johnson RC	20.00	6.00
❑ 262 Rudi Johnson RC	20.00	6.00
❑ 263 James Jackson RC	10.00	3.00
❑ 264 Quincy Morgan RC	10.00	3.00
❑ 265 Scotty Anderson RC	6.00	1.80
❑ 266 Mike McMahon RC	10.00	3.00
❑ 267 Robert Ferguson RC	10.00	3.00
❑ 268 Reggie Wayne RC	15.00	4.50
❑ 269 Snoop Minnis RC	6.00	1.80
❑ 270 Chris Chambers RC	12.00	3.60
❑ 271 Josh Heupel RC	10.00	3.00
❑ 272 Travis Minor RC	6.00	1.80
❑ 273 Michael Bennett RC	20.00	6.00
❑ 274 Ben Leard RC	6.00	1.80
❑ 275 Deuce McAllister RC	25.00	7.50
❑ 276 Moran Norris RC	4.00	1.20
❑ 277 Jesse Palmer RC	10.00	3.00
❑ 278 LaMont Jordan RC	12.00	3.60
❑ 279 Santana Moss RC	15.00	4.50
❑ 280 Ken-Yon Rambo RC	6.00	1.80
❑ 281 M.Tuiasosopo JSY RC	25.00	7.50
❑ 282 Correll Buckhalter RC	12.00	3.60
❑ 283 A.J. Feeley RC	10.00	3.00
❑ 284 Freddie Mitchell JSY RC	15.00	4.50
❑ 285 Joey Getherall RC	6.00	1.80
❑ 286 Chris Taylor RC	6.00	1.80
❑ 287 Adam Archuleta RC	10.00	3.00
❑ 288 David Rivers RC	6.00	1.80
❑ 289 Drew Brees JSY RC	40.00	12.00
❑ 290 L.Tomlinson JSY RC	60.00	18.00
❑ 291 David Allen RC	6.00	1.80
❑ 292 Kevan Barlow RC	10.00	3.00
❑ 293 Cedrick Wilson RC	10.00	3.00
❑ 294 Alex Bannister RC	6.00	1.80
❑ 295 Josh Booty RC	10.00	3.00
❑ 296 Heath Evans RC	6.00	1.80
❑ 297 Koren Robinson RC	12.00	3.60
❑ 298 Dan Alexander RC	10.00	3.00
❑ 299 Rod Gardner RC	10.00	3.00
❑ 300 Sage Rosenfels RC	10.00	3.00

2001 Pacific Invincible Blue

	Nm-Mt	Ex-Mt
*STARS: .8X TO 2X BASIC INSERTS		
*ROOKIES: .8X TO 2X		
❑ 1 David Boston JSY	10.00	3.00
❑ 4 Rob Moore JSY	10.00	3.00
❑ 8 Jamal Anderson JSY	12.00	3.60
❑ 9 Chris Chandler JSY	10.00	3.00
❑ 25 Rob Johnson JSY	10.00	3.00
❑ 28 Eric Moulds JSY	12.00	3.60
❑ 32 Tim Biakabutuka JSY	12.00	3.60
❑ 39 James Allen JSY	10.00	3.00
❑ 42 Bobby Engram JSY	10.00	3.00
❑ 55 Tim Couch JSY	15.00	4.50
❑ 58 Kevin Johnson JSY	10.00	3.00
❑ 67 Emmitt Smith JSY	40.00	12.00
❑ 70 Mike Anderson JSY	12.00	3.60
❑ 71 Terrell Davis JSY	20.00	6.00
❑ 74 Brian Griese JSY	20.00	6.00
❑ 78 Charlie Batch JSY	12.00	3.60
❑ 85 James Stewart JSY	10.00	3.00
❑ 87 Brett Favre JSY	60.00	18.00
❑ 103 Mark Brunell JSY	12.00	3.60
❑ 105 Keenan McCardell JSY	10.00	3.00
❑ 106 Jimmy Smith JSY	10.00	3.00
❑ 110 Derrick Alexander JSY	12.00	3.60
❑ 118 Sylvester Morris JSY	10.00	3.00
❑ 120 Jay Fiedler JSY	12.00	3.60
❑ 131 Cris Carter JSY	25.00	7.50
❑ 132 Daunte Culpepper JSY	15.00	4.50
❑ 133 Randy Moss JSY	50.00	15.00
❑ 146 Jeff Blake JSY	10.00	3.00
❑ 149 Joe Horn JSY	10.00	3.00
❑ 153 Ricky Williams JSY	12.00	3.60
❑ 156 Tiki Barber JSY	10.00	3.00
❑ 157 Kerry Collins JSY	12.00	3.60
❑ 163 Amani Toomer JSY	12.00	3.60
❑ 169 Curtis Martin JSY	12.00	3.60
❑ 170 Chad Pennington JSY	30.00	9.00
❑ 171 Vinny Testaverde JSY	12.00	3.60
❑ 172 Tim Brown JSY	12.00	3.60
❑ 174 Rich Gannon JSY	12.00	3.60
❑ 179 Tyrone Wheatley JSY	10.00	3.00
❑ 201 Az-Zahir Hakim JSY	10.00	3.00
❑ 204 Kurt Warner JSY	25.00	7.50
❑ 210 Doug Flutie JSY	15.00	4.50
❑ 214 Junior Seau JSY	12.00	3.60
❑ 218 Jerry Rice JSY	40.00	12.00
❑ 222 Shaun Alexander JSY	20.00	6.00
❑ 226 Darrell Jackson JSY	12.00	3.60
❑ 228 Ricky Watters JSY	10.00	3.00
❑ 238 Kevin Dyson JSY	10.00	3.00
❑ 239 Eddie George JSY	20.00	6.00
❑ 242 Steve McNair JSY	12.00	3.60
❑ 257 Chris Weinke	20.00	6.00
❑ 259 Anthony Thomas	30.00	9.00
❑ 281 Marques Tuiasosopo	30.00	9.00
❑ 284 Freddie Mitchell	25.00	7.50
❑ 289 Drew Brees	50.00	15.00
❑ 290 LaDainian Tomlinson	80.00	24.00

2001 Pacific Invincible Premiere Date

	Nm-Mt	Ex-Mt
*STARS: 2X TO 5X BASIC CARDS		
*ROOKIES: 1X TO 2.5X		
❑ 257 Chris Weinke	25.00	7.50
❑ 259 Anthony Thomas	50.00	15.00
❑ 281 Marques Tuiasosopo	40.00	12.00
❑ 284 Freddie Mitchell	30.00	9.00
❑ 289 Drew Brees	60.00	18.00
❑ 290 LaDainian Tomlinson	100.00	30.00

2001 Pacific Invincible Red

	Nm-Mt	Ex-Mt
*STARS: .4X TO 1X BASIC INSERTS		
*ROOKIES: .4X TO 1X		
❑ 2 MarTay Jenkins JSY	8.00	2.40
❑ 5 Michael Pittman JSY	8.00	2.40
❑ 10 Jammi German JSY	8.00	2.40
❑ 11 Shawn Jefferson JSY	8.00	2.40
❑ 15 Elvis Grbac JSY	12.00	3.60
❑ 23 Shawn Bryson JSY	10.00	3.00
❑ 29 Peerless Price JSY	12.00	3.60
❑ 33 Isaac Byrd JSY	8.00	2.40

❑ 35 Patrick Jeffers JSY	10.00	3.00
❑ 37 Muhsin Muhammad JSY	10.00	3.00
❑ 41 Macey Brooks JSY	8.00	2.40
❑ 44 Marcus Robinson JSY	12.00	3.60
❑ 51 Darnay Scott JSY	10.00	3.00
❑ 52 Akili Smith JSY	8.00	2.40
❑ 54 Craig Yeast JSY	8.00	2.40
❑ 57 Curtis Enis JSY	8.00	2.40
❑ 59 Dennis Northcutt JSY	10.00	3.00
❑ 64 Rocket Ismail JSY	10.00	3.00
❑ 69 Michael Wiley JSY	8.00	2.40
❑ 75 Eddie Kennison JSY	8.00	2.40
❑ 76 Ed McCaffrey JSY	12.00	3.60
❑ 77 Rod Smith JSY	10.00	3.00
❑ 79 Germane Crowell JSY	8.00	2.40
❑ 82 Herman Moore JSY	10.00	3.00
❑ 89 Antonio Freeman JSY	12.00	3.60
❑ 93 Bill Schroeder JSY	12.00	3.60
❑ 102 Kyle Brady JSY	10.00	3.00
❑ 107 R. Jay Soward JSY	8.00	2.40
❑ 108 Shyrone Stith JSY	8.00	2.40
❑ 111 Kimble Anders JSY	10.00	3.00
❑ 121 Oronde Gadsden JSY	10.00	3.00
❑ 125 O.J. McDuffie JSY	8.00	2.40
❑ 126 James McKnight JSY	10.00	3.00
❑ 151 Chad Morton JSY	8.00	2.40
❑ 159 Ron Dixon JSY	8.00	2.40
❑ 164 Richie Anderson JSY	8.00	2.40
❑ 165 Wayne Chrebet JSY	12.00	3.60
❑ 167 Matthew Hatchette JSY	8.00	2.40
❑ 178 Andre Rison JSY	12.00	3.60
❑ 180 Charles Woodson JSY	15.00	4.50
❑ 199 Trung Canidate JSY	10.00	3.00
❑ 203 Ricky Proehl JSY	10.00	3.00
❑ 206 Curtis Conway JSY	8.00	2.40
❑ 207 Tim Dwight JSY	12.00	3.60
❑ 208 Jermaine Fazande JSY	8.00	2.40
❑ 220 J.J. Stokes JSY	10.00	3.00
❑ 221 Tai Streets JSY	10.00	3.00
❑ 223 Karsten Bailey JSY	8.00	2.40
❑ 241 Derrick Mason JSY	15.00	4.50
❑ 249 Kevin Lockett JSY	12.00	3.60
❑ 257 Chris Weinke	12.00	3.60
❑ 259 Anthony Thomas	20.00	6.00
❑ 268 Reggie Wayne	15.00	4.50
❑ 281 Marques Tuiasosopo	15.00	4.50
❑ 284 Freddie Mitchell	12.00	3.60
❑ 289 Drew Brees	25.00	7.50
❑ 290 LaDainian Tomlinson	40.00	12.00

1999 Pacific Omega

	Nm-Mt	Ex-Mt
COMPLETE SET (250)	40.00	18.00
❑ 1 Mario Bates	.25	.11
❑ 2 David Boston RC	1.25	.55
❑ 3 Rob Moore	.40	.18
❑ 4 Adrian Murrell	.40	.18
❑ 5 Jake Plummer	.40	.18
❑ 6 Frank Sanders	.40	.18
❑ 7 Aeneas Williams	.25	.11
❑ 8 Joel Makovicka RC Lonnie Shelton RC	1.25	.55
❑ 9 Jamal Anderson	.60	.25
❑ 10 Ray Buchanan	.25	.11
❑ 11 Chris Chandler	.40	.18
❑ 12 Tim Dwight	.60	.25
❑ 13 Byron Hanspard	.25	.11
❑ 14 Terance Mathis	.40	.18
❑ 15 O.J. Santiago	.25	.11
❑ 16 Danny Kanell Chris Calloway	.25	.11
❑ 17 Peter Boulware	.25	.11
❑ 18 Priest Holmes	1.00	.45
❑ 19 Patrick Johnson	.25	.11
❑ 20 Jermaine Lewis	.40	.18
❑ 21 Ray Lewis	.60	.25
❑ 22 Michael McCrary	.25	.11
❑ 23 Jonathan Ogden	.25	.11
❑ 24 Tony Banks Scott Mitchell	.25	.11
❑ 25 Doug Flutie	.60	.25
❑ 26 Rob Johnson	.40	.18
❑ 27 Eric Moulds	.60	.25
❑ 28 Andre Reed	.40	.18
❑ 29 Antowain Smith	.60	.25
❑ 30 Bruce Smith	.40	.18
❑ 31 Kevin Williams	.25	.11
❑ 32 Shawn Bryson RC Peerless Price RC	2.00	.90
❑ 33 Steve Beuerlein	.25	.11
❑ 34 Tim Biakabutuka	.40	.18
❑ 35 Rae Carruth	.25	.11
❑ 36 Dameyune Craig RC	2.00	.90
❑ 37 William Floyd	.25	.11
❑ 38 Kevin Greene	.25	.11
❑ 39 Muhsin Muhammad	.40	.18
❑ 40 Wesley Walls	.40	.18
❑ 41 Edgar Bennett	.25	.11
❑ 42 Robert Chancey RC	1.50	.70
❑ 43 Curtis Conway	.40	.18
❑ 44 Bobby Engram	.40	.18
❑ 45 Curtis Enis	.25	.11
❑ 46 Cade McNown RC	1.00	.45
❑ 47 Ryan Wetnight	.25	.11
❑ 48 D'Wayne Bates RC Marty Booker RC	1.25	.55
❑ 49 Jeff Blake	.40	.18
❑ 50 Scott Covington RC	1.25	.55
❑ 51 Corey Dillon	.60	.25
❑ 52 James Hundon	.40	.18
❑ 53 Carl Pickens	.40	.18
❑ 54 Darnay Scott	.25	.11
❑ 55 Akili Smith RC	1.00	.45
❑ 56 Craig Yeast RC	1.00	.45
❑ 57 Tim Couch RC	1.25	.55
❑ 58 Ty Detmer	.40	.18
❑ 59 Marc Edwards	.25	.11
❑ 60 Kevin Johnson RC	1.25	.55
❑ 61 Terry Kirby	.25	.11
❑ 62 Sedrick Shaw	.25	.11
❑ 63 Leslie Shepherd	.25	.11
❑ 64 Darrin Chiaverini RC Daylon McCutcheon RC	1.00	.45
❑ 65 Troy Aikman	1.25	.55
❑ 66 Michael Irvin	.40	.18
❑ 67 David LaFleur	.25	.11
❑ 68 Wane McGarity RC	.50	.23
❑ 69 Ernie Mills	.25	.11
❑ 70 Deion Sanders	.60	.25
❑ 71 Emmitt Smith	1.25	.55
❑ 72 Rocket Ismail James McKnight	.40	.18
❑ 73 Bubby Brister	.25	.11
❑ 74 Byron Chamberlain RC	1.00	.45
❑ 75 Terrell Davis	.60	.25
❑ 76 Olandis Gary RC	1.25	.55
❑ 77 Brian Griese	.60	.25
❑ 78 Ed McCaffrey	.40	.18
❑ 79 Shannon Sharpe	.40	.18
❑ 80 Rod Smith	.40	.18
❑ 81 Travis McGriff RC Al Wilson RC	.50	.23
❑ 82 Charlie Batch	.60	.25
❑ 83 Chris Claiborne RC	.50	.23
❑ 84 Germane Crowell	.25	.11
❑ 85 Terry Fair	.25	.11
❑ 86 Sedrick Irvin RC	.50	.23
❑ 87 Herman Moore	.40	.18
❑ 88 Johnnie Morton	.40	.18
❑ 89 Barry Sanders	2.00	.90
❑ 90 Mark Chmura	.25	.11
❑ 91 Brett Favre	2.00	.90
❑ 92 Antonio Freeman	.60	.25
❑ 93 Desmond Howard	.40	.18
❑ 94 Dorsey Levens	.60	.25
❑ 95 Derrick Mayes	.25	.11
❑ 96 Bill Schroeder	.60	.25
❑ 97 Aaron Brooks RC Dee Miller RC	4.00	1.80
❑ 98 E.G. Green	.25	.11
❑ 99 Marvin Harrison	.60	.25
❑ 100 Edgerrin James RC	5.00	2.20
❑ 101 Peyton Manning	2.00	.90
❑ 102 Jerome Pathon	.25	.11
❑ 103 Marcus Pollard	.25	.11
❑ 104 Ken Dilger	.25	.11
❑ 105 Derrick Alexander WR	.40	.18
❑ 106 Reggie Barlow	.25	.11
❑ 107 Tony Boselli	.25	.11
❑ 108 Mark Brunell	.60	.25
❑ 109 George Jones	.25	.11
❑ 110 Keenan McCardell	.40	.18
❑ 111 Jimmy Smith	.40	.18
❑ 112 James Stewart	.40	.18
❑ 113 Fred Taylor	.60	.25
❑ 114 Kimble Anders	.40	.18
❑ 115 Mike Cloud RC	1.00	.45
❑ 116 Tony Gonzalez	.60	.25
❑ 117 Elvis Grbac	.40	.18
❑ 118 Byron Bam Morris	.25	.11
❑ 119 Andre Rison	.40	.18
❑ 120 Derrick Thomas	.40	.18
❑ 121 Karim Abdul-Jabbar	.40	.18
❑ 122 Oronde Gadsden	.40	.18
❑ 123 James Johnson RC	1.00	.45
❑ 124 Rob Konrad RC	1.25	.55
❑ 125 Dan Marino	2.00	.90
❑ 126 O.J. McDuffie	.40	.18
❑ 127 Lamar Thomas	.25	.11
❑ 128 Zach Thomas	.60	.25
❑ 129 Cris Carter	.60	.25
❑ 130 Daunte Culpepper RC	5.00	2.20
❑ 131 Randall Cunningham	.60	.25
❑ 132 Matthew Hatchette	.25	.11
❑ 133 Leroy Hoard	.25	.11
❑ 134 David Palmer	.25	.11
❑ 135 John Randle	.40	.18
❑ 136 Randy Moss	1.50	.70
❑ 137 Robert Smith	.60	.25
❑ 138 Drew Bledsoe	.75	.35
❑ 139 Ben Coates	.40	.18
❑ 140 Kevin Faulk RC	1.25	.55
❑ 141 Terry Glenn	.60	.25
❑ 142 Shawn Jefferson	.25	.11
❑ 143 Ty Law	.40	.18
❑ 144 Tony Simmons	.25	.11
❑ 145 Michael Bishop RC Andy Katzenmoyer RC	1.25	.55
❑ 146 Cameron Cleeland	.25	.11
❑ 147 Andre Hastings	.25	.11
❑ 148 Billy Joe Hobert	.25	.11
❑ 149 Joe Johnson	.25	.11
❑ 150 Keith Poole	.25	.11
❑ 151 William Roaf	.25	.11
❑ 152 Billy Joe Tolliver	.25	.11
❑ 153 Ricky Williams RC	2.50	1.10
❑ 154 Tiki Barber	.40	.18
❑ 155 Gary Brown	.25	.11
❑ 156 Kent Graham	.25	.11
❑ 157 Ike Hilliard	.25	.11
❑ 158 David Patten	.40	.18
❑ 159 Jason Sehorn	.25	.11
❑ 160 Amani Toomer	.25	.11
❑ 161 Joe Montgomery RC Luke Petitgout RC	1.00	.45
❑ 162 Wayne Chrebet	.40	.18
❑ 163 Bryan Cox	.25	.11
❑ 164 Aaron Glenn	.25	.11
❑ 165 Keyshawn Johnson	.60	.25
❑ 166 Leon Johnson	.25	.11
❑ 167 Curtis Martin	.60	.25
❑ 168 Vinny Testaverde	.40	.18
❑ 169 Dedric Ward	.25	.11
❑ 170 Tim Brown	.60	.25
❑ 171 Rickey Dudley	.25	.11
❑ 172 James Jett	.40	.18
❑ 173 Napoleon Kaufman	.60	.25
❑ 174 Jon Ritchie	.25	.11
❑ 175 Darrell Russell	.25	.11
❑ 176 Charles Woodson	.60	.25
❑ 177 Rich Gannon Heath Shuler	.60	.25
❑ 178 Hugh Douglas	.25	.11
❑ 179 Donovan McNabb RC	6.00	2.70
❑ 180 Allen Rossum	.25	.11
❑ 181 Duce Staley	.40	.18

❑ 182 Kevin Turner .25 .11
❑ 183 Charles Johnson .25 .11
Doug Pederson
❑ 184 Barry Gardner RC 1.25 .55
Cecil Martin RC
❑ 185 Jerome Bettis .60 .25
❑ 186 Mark Bruener .25 .11
❑ 187 Troy Edwards RC 1.00 .45
❑ 188 Courtney Hawkins .25 .11
❑ 189 Levon Kirkland .25 .11
❑ 190 Kordell Stewart .40 .18
❑ 191 Hines Ward .60 .25
❑ 192 Malcolm Johnson RC 1.25 .55
Amos Zereoue RC
❑ 193 Greg Clark .25 .11
❑ 194 Terrell Fletcher .25 .11
❑ 195 Charlie Jones .25 .11
❑ 196 Cecil Collins RC .50 .23
❑ 197 Natrone Means .40 .18
❑ 198 Mikhael Ricks .25 .11
❑ 199 Junior Seau .60 .25
❑ 200 Bryan Still .25 .11
❑ 201 Ryan Thelwell RC 1.00 .45
❑ 202 Garrison Hearst .40 .18
❑ 203 Terry Jackson RC 1.00 .45
❑ 204 R.W. McQuarters .25 .11
❑ 205 Terrell Owens .60 .25
❑ 206 Jerry Rice 1.25 .55
❑ 207 J.J. Stokes .40 .18
❑ 208 Lawrence Phillips .25 .11
Tommy Vardell
❑ 209 Steve Young .75 .35
❑ 210 Karsten Bailey RC 1.00 .45
❑ 211 Chad Brown .25 .11
❑ 212 Christian Fauria .25 .11
❑ 213 Joey Galloway .40 .18
❑ 214 Ahman Green .60 .25
❑ 215 Brock Huard RC 1.25 .55
❑ 216 Cortez Kennedy .25 .11
❑ 217 Jon Kitna .60 .25
❑ 218 Ricky Watters .40 .18
❑ 219 Isaac Bruce .60 .25
❑ 220 Az-Zahir Hakim .25 .11
❑ 221 June Henley RC .25 .11
❑ 222 Greg Hill .25 .11
❑ 223 Torry Holt RC 3.00 1.35
❑ 224 Amp Lee .25 .11
❑ 225 Ricky Proehl .25 .11
❑ 226 Marshall Faulk .75 .35
Trent Green
❑ 227 Mike Alstott .60 .25
❑ 228 Reidel Anthony .40 .18
❑ 229 Trent Dilfer .40 .18
❑ 230 Warrick Dunn .60 .25
❑ 231 Bert Emanuel .40 .18
❑ 232 Jacquez Green .25 .11
❑ 233 Warren Sapp .25 .11
❑ 234 Shaun King RC 1.25 .55
Anthony McFarland RC
❑ 235 Mike Archie RC .50 .23
❑ 236 Kevin Dyson .40 .18
❑ 237 Eddie George .60 .25
❑ 238 Derrick Mason .40 .18
❑ 239 Steve McNair .60 .25
❑ 240 Yancey Thigpen .25 .11
❑ 241 Frank Wycheck .25 .11
❑ 242 Darran Hall 2.00 .90
Jevon Kearse RC
❑ 243 Stephen Alexander .25 .11
❑ 244 Champ Bailey RC 1.50 .70
❑ 245 Stephen Davis .60 .25
❑ 246 Skip Hicks .25 .11
❑ 247 James Thrash RC 1.25 .55
❑ 248 Michael Westbrook .40 .18
❑ 249 Dan Wilkinson .25 .11
❑ 250 Brad Johnson .60 .25
Larry Centers

2000 Pacific Omega

	Nm-Mt	Ex-Mt
COMP.SET w/o SP's (150)	20.00	9.00

❑ 1 David Boston .60 .25
❑ 2 Dave Brown .25 .11
❑ 3 Rob Moore .40 .18
❑ 4 Jake Plummer .40 .18
❑ 5 Simeon Rice .40 .18
❑ 6 Frank Sanders .40 .18
❑ 7 Jamal Anderson .60 .25
❑ 8 Chris Chandler .40 .18
❑ 9 Tim Dwight .60 .25
❑ 10 Terance Mathis .40 .18
❑ 11 Tony Banks .40 .18
❑ 12 Peter Boulware .25 .11
❑ 13 Priest Holmes .75 .35
❑ 14 Qadry Ismail .40 .18
❑ 15 Doug Flutie .60 .25
❑ 16 Rob Johnson .40 .18
❑ 17 Jonathan Linton .25 .11
❑ 18 Eric Moulds .60 .25
❑ 19 Peerless Price .60 .25
❑ 20 Antowain Smith .60 .25
❑ 21 Steve Beuerlein .25 .11
❑ 22 Tim Biakabutuka .40 .18
❑ 23 Patrick Jeffers .60 .25
❑ 24 Muhsin Muhammad .40 .18
❑ 25 Wesley Walls .40 .18
❑ 26 Bobby Engram .40 .18
❑ 27 Curtis Enis .25 .11
❑ 28 Cade McNown .25 .11
❑ 29 Marcus Robinson .60 .25
❑ 30 Willie Anderson .25 .11
❑ 31 Michael Basnight .25 .11
❑ 32 Corey Dillon .60 .25
❑ 33 Akili Smith .25 .11
❑ 34 Tim Couch .40 .18
❑ 35 Kevin Johnson .60 .25
❑ 36 Wali Rainer .25 .11
❑ 37 Troy Aikman 1.25 .55
❑ 38 Dexter Coakley .25 .11
❑ 39 Rocket Ismail .40 .18
❑ 40 Emmitt Smith 1.25 .55
❑ 41 Chris Warren .25 .11
❑ 42 Terrell Davis .60 .25
❑ 43 Olandis Gary .60 .25
❑ 44 Brian Griese .60 .25
❑ 45 Ed McCaffrey .60 .25
❑ 46 Rod Smith .40 .18
❑ 47 Charlie Batch .60 .25
❑ 48 Germane Crowell .25 .11
❑ 49 Herman Moore .40 .18
❑ 50 Johnnie Morton .40 .18
❑ 51 Barry Sanders 1.50 .70
❑ 52 Corey Bradford .40 .18
❑ 53 Brett Favre 2.00 .90
❑ 54 Antonio Freeman .60 .25
❑ 55 Dorsey Levens .40 .18
❑ 56 Bill Schroeder .40 .18
❑ 57 Ken Dilger .25 .11
❑ 58 Marvin Harrison .60 .25
❑ 59 Edgerrin James 1.00 .45
❑ 60 Peyton Manning 1.50 .70
❑ 61 Jerome Pathon .40 .18
❑ 62 Terrence Wilkins .25 .11
❑ 63 Mark Brunell .60 .25
❑ 64 Keenan McCardell .40 .18
❑ 65 Jimmy Smith .40 .18
❑ 66 Fred Taylor .60 .25
❑ 67 Derrick Alexander .40 .18
❑ 68 Donnell Bennett .25 .11
❑ 69 Tony Gonzalez .40 .18
❑ 70 Elvis Grbac .40 .18
❑ 71 Tony Richardson RC .25 .11
❑ 72 Oronde Gadsden .40 .18
❑ 73 Damon Huard .60 .25
❑ 74 James Johnson .25 .11
❑ 75 Dan Marino 2.00 .90
❑ 76 Tony Martin .40 .18
❑ 77 O.J. McDuffie .40 .18
❑ 78 Cris Carter .60 .25
❑ 79 Daunte Culpepper .75 .35
❑ 80 Randy Moss 1.25 .55
❑ 81 Robert Smith .60 .25
❑ 82 Drew Bledsoe .75 .35
❑ 83 Kevin Faulk .40 .18
❑ 84 Terry Glenn .40 .18
❑ 85 P.J. Franklin RC .40 .18
❑ 86 Keith Poole .40 .18
❑ 87 Ricky Williams .60 .25
❑ 88 Tiki Barber .40 .18
❑ 89 Kerry Collins .40 .18
❑ 90 Ike Hilliard .40 .18
❑ 91 Amani Toomer .40 .18
❑ 92 Wayne Chrebet .40 .18
❑ 93 Ray Lucas .40 .18
❑ 94 Curtis Martin .60 .25
❑ 95 Vinny Testaverde .40 .18
❑ 96 Tim Brown .60 .25
❑ 97 Rich Gannon .60 .25
❑ 98 James Jett .25 .11
❑ 99 Napoleon Kaufman .40 .18
❑ 100 Tyrone Wheatley .40 .18
❑ 101 Charles Woodson .40 .18
❑ 102 Brian Dawkins .25 .11
❑ 103 Charles Johnson .40 .18
❑ 104 Donovan McNabb 1.00 .45
❑ 105 Torrance Small .25 .11
❑ 106 Duce Staley .60 .25
❑ 107 Jerome Bettis .60 .25
❑ 108 Troy Edwards .25 .11
❑ 109 Richard Huntley .25 .11
❑ 110 Kordell Stewart .40 .18
❑ 111 Hines Ward .60 .25
❑ 112 Isaac Bruce .60 .25
❑ 113 Marshall Faulk .75 .35
❑ 114 Az-Zahir Hakim .40 .18
❑ 115 Torry Holt .60 .25
❑ 116 Tony Horne .25 .11
❑ 117 Kurt Warner 1.25 .55
❑ 118 Jermaine Fazande .25 .11
❑ 119 Jeff Graham .25 .11
❑ 120 Jim Harbaugh .40 .18
❑ 121 Mikhael Ricks .25 .11
❑ 122 Junior Seau .60 .25
❑ 123 Jeff Garcia .60 .25
❑ 124 Charlie Garner .40 .18
❑ 125 Terrell Owens .60 .25
❑ 126 Jerry Rice 1.25 .55
❑ 127 J.J. Stokes .40 .18
❑ 128 Jon Kitna .60 .25
❑ 129 Derrick Mayes .40 .18
❑ 130 Charlie Rogers .25 .11
❑ 131 Shawn Springs .25 .11
❑ 132 Ricky Watters .40 .18
❑ 133 Mike Alstott .60 .25
❑ 134 Reidel Anthony .25 .11
❑ 135 Warrick Dunn .60 .25
❑ 136 Jacquez Green .25 .11
❑ 137 Shaun King .25 .11
❑ 138 Warren Sapp .40 .18
❑ 139 Kevin Dyson .40 .18
❑ 140 Eddie George .60 .25
❑ 141 Jevon Kearse .60 .25
❑ 142 Steve McNair .60 .25
❑ 143 Yancey Thigpen .25 .11
❑ 144 Frank Wycheck .25 .11
❑ 145 Champ Bailey .40 .18
❑ 146 Larry Centers .25 .11
❑ 147 Albert Connell .25 .11
❑ 148 Stephen Davis .60 .25
❑ 149 Brad Johnson .60 .25
❑ 150 Michael Westbrook .40 .18
❑ 151 Thomas Jones RC 12.00 5.50
❑ 152 Jay Tant RC 4.00 1.80
❑ 153 Doug Johnson RC 8.00 3.60
❑ 154 Mareno Philyaw RC 4.00 1.80
❑ 155 Jamal Lewis RC 20.00 9.00
❑ 156 Chris Redman RC 6.00 2.70
❑ 157 Travis Taylor RC 8.00 3.60
❑ 158 Kwame Cavil RC 4.00 1.80
❑ 159 Corey Moore RC 4.00 1.80
❑ 160 Deon Grant RC 6.00 2.70
❑ 161 Frank Murphy RC 4.00 1.80
❑ 162 Dez White RC 8.00 3.60
❑ 163 Ron Dugans RC 4.00 1.80
❑ 164 Tony Hartley RC 4.00 1.80
❑ 165 Curtis Keaton RC 6.00 2.70

❑ 166 Peter Warrick RC 8.00 3.60
❑ 167 Courtney Brown RC 8.00 3.60
❑ 168 JaJuan Dawson RC 4.00 1.80
❑ 169 Dennis Northcutt RC 8.00 3.60
❑ 170 Travis Prentice RC 6.00 2.70
❑ 171 Aaron Shea RC 6.00 2.70
❑ 172 Michael Wiley RC 6.00 2.70
❑ 173 Chris Cole RC 6.00 2.70
❑ 174 Jarious Jackson RC 6.00 2.70
❑ 175 Deltha O'Neal RC 8.00 3.60
❑ 176 Reuben Droughns RC 8.00 3.60
❑ 177 Bubba Franks RC 8.00 3.60
❑ 178 Anthony Lucas RC 4.00 1.80
❑ 179 Rondell Mealey RC 4.00 1.80
❑ 180 Ibn Green RC 4.00 1.80
❑ 181 Kevin McDougal RC 6.00 2.70
❑ 182 R.Jay Soward RC 6.00 2.70
❑ 183 Shyrone Stith RC 6.00 2.70
❑ 184 Dante Hall RC 15.00 6.75
❑ 185 Frank Moreau RC 6.00 2.70
❑ 186 Sylvester Morris RC 6.00 2.70
❑ 187 Deon Dyer RC 6.00 2.70
❑ 188 Ben Kelly RC 4.00 1.80
❑ 189 Quinton Spotwood RC 4.00 1.80
❑ 190 Troy Walters RC 8.00 3.60
❑ 191 Tom Brady RC 80.00 36.00
❑ 192 J.R. Redmond RC 6.00 2.70
❑ 193 David Stachelski RC 4.00 1.80
❑ 194 Marc Bulger RC 15.00 6.75
❑ 195 Sherrod Gideon RC 4.00 1.80
❑ 196 Chad Morton RC 8.00 3.60
❑ 197 Ron Dayne RC 8.00 3.60
❑ 198 Anthony Becht RC 8.00 3.60
❑ 199 Laveranues Coles RC 10.00 4.50
❑ 200 Chad Pennington RC 30.00 13.50
❑ 201 Sebastian Janikowski RC 8.00 3.60
❑ 202 Marcus Knight RC 6.00 2.70
❑ 203 Jerry Porter RC 10.00 4.50
❑ 204 Todd Pinkston RC 8.00 3.60
❑ 205 Gari Scott RC 4.00 1.80
❑ 206 Plaxico Burress RC 15.00 6.75
❑ 207 Danny Farmer RC 6.00 2.70
❑ 208 Tee Martin RC 8.00 3.60
❑ 209 Hank Poteat RC 6.00 2.70
❑ 210 Trung Canidate RC 6.00 2.70
❑ 211 Patrick Batteaux RC 4.00 1.80
❑ 212 Trevor Gaylor RC 6.00 2.70
❑ 213 Ronney Jenkins RC 6.00 2.70
❑ 214 Terrence McCaskey RC 4.00 1.80
❑ 215 JaJuan Seider RC 4.00 1.80
❑ 216 Giovanni Carmazzi RC 6.00 2.70
❑ 217 Chafie Fields RC 4.00 1.80
❑ 218 Jonas Lewis RC 4.00 1.80
❑ 219 Tim Rattay RC 15.00 6.75
❑ 220 Shaun Alexander RC 25.00 11.00
❑ 221 Darrell Jackson RC 15.00 6.75
❑ 222 James Williams RC 6.00 2.70
❑ 223 Joe Hamilton RC 6.00 2.70
❑ 224 Erron Kinney RC 8.00 3.60
❑ 225 Todd Husak RC 8.00 3.60
❑ 226 Plaxico Burress 8.00 3.60
Danny Farmer
❑ 227 Ron Dayne 3.00 1.35
Joe Hamilton
❑ 228 Peter Warrick 4.00 1.80
Ron Dugans
❑ 229 Thomas Jones 6.00 2.70
Curtis Keaton
❑ 230 Shaun Alexander 12.00 5.50
Reuben Droughns
❑ 231 Travis Taylor 8.00 3.60
Darrell Jackson
❑ 232 Giovanni Carmazzi 8.00 3.60
Tim Rattay
❑ 233 Trung Canidate 3.00 1.35
J.R. Redmond
❑ 234 Sylvester Morris 3.00 1.35
R.Jay Soward
❑ 235 Travis Prentice 3.00 1.35
Trevor Gaylor
❑ 236 Todd Pinkston 4.00 1.80
Sherrod Gideon
❑ 237 Frank Murphy 4.00 1.80
Dez White
❑ 238 Chris Redman 40.00 18.00
Tom Brady
❑ 239 Jamal Lewis 12.00 5.50
Tee Martin
❑ 240 Rondell Mealey 3.00 1.35
Shyrone Stith
❑ 241 Michael Wiley 3.00 1.35
Chad Morton
❑ 242 Laveranues Coles 4.00 1.80
Sebastian Janikowski
❑ 243 Troy Walters 4.00 1.80
Todd Husak
❑ 244 Marc Bulger 10.00 4.50
Jerry Porter
❑ 245 Mareno Philyaw 4.00 1.80
Doug Johnson
❑ 246 Dennis Northcutt 4.00 1.80
Courtney Brown
❑ 247 Jarious Jackson 3.00 1.35
Chris Cole
❑ 248 JaJuan Dawson 2.00 .90
Gari Scott
❑ 249 Quinton Spotwood 2.00 .90
Chafie Fields
❑ 250 Chad Pennington 15.00 6.75
James Williams

1997 Pacific Philadelphia

	Nm-Mt	Ex-Mt
COMPLETE SET (330)	50.00	22.00
❑ 1 Kevin Butler	.20	.09
❑ 2 Larry Centers	.30	.14
❑ 3 Kent Graham	.20	.09
❑ 4 Leeland McElroy	.20	.09
❑ 5 Ronald McKinnon RC	.30	.14
❑ 6 Johnny McWilliams	.20	.09
❑ 7 Brad Otis	.20	.09
❑ 8 Frank Sanders	.30	.14
❑ 9 Rob Selby	.20	.09
❑ 10 Cedric Smith	.20	.09
❑ 11 Joe Staysniak	.20	.09
❑ 12 Cornelius Bennett	.20	.09
❑ 13 David Brandon	.20	.09
❑ 14 Tyrone Brown	.20	.09
❑ 15 John Burrough	.20	.09
❑ 16 Browning Nagle	.20	.09
❑ 17 Dan Owens	.20	.09
❑ 18 Anthony Phillips	.20	.09
❑ 19 Roell Preston	.20	.09
❑ 20 Darnell Walker	.20	.09
❑ 21 Bob Whitfield	.20	.09
❑ 22 Mike Zandofsky	.20	.09
❑ 23 Vashone Adams	.20	.09
❑ 24 Derrick Alexander WR	.30	.14
❑ 25 Harold Bishop	.20	.09
❑ 26 Jeff Blackshear	.20	.09
❑ 27 Donald Brady RC	.20	.09
❑ 28 Mike Frederick	.20	.09
❑ 29 Tim Goad	.20	.09
❑ 30 DeRon Jenkins	.20	.09
❑ 31 Ray Lewis	.75	.35
❑ 32 Rick Lyle	.20	.09
❑ 33 Byron Bam Morris	.20	.09
❑ 34 Chris Brantley	.20	.09
❑ 35 Jeff Burris	.20	.09
❑ 36 Todd Collins	.20	.09
❑ 37 Rob Coons	.20	.09
❑ 38 Corbin Lacina RC	.20	.09
❑ 39 Emanuel Martin	.20	.09
❑ 40 Marlo Perry	.20	.09
❑ 41 Shawn Price	.20	.09
❑ 42 Thomas Smith	.20	.09
❑ 43 Matt Stevens RC	.20	.09
❑ 44 Thurman Thomas	.50	.23
❑ 45 Jay Barker	.20	.09
❑ 46 Tim Biakabutuka	.30	.14
❑ 47 Kerry Collins	.50	.23
❑ 48 Matt Elliott	.20	.09
❑ 49 Howard Griffith	.20	.09
❑ 50 Anthony Johnson	.20	.09
❑ 51 John Kasay	.20	.09
❑ 52 Muhsin Muhammad	.30	.14
❑ 53 Winslow Oliver	.20	.09
❑ 54 Walter Rasby	.20	.09
❑ 55 Gerald Williams	.20	.09
❑ 56 Mark Butterfield	.20	.09
❑ 57 Bryan Cox	.20	.09
❑ 58 Mike Faulkerson	.20	.09
❑ 59 Paul Grasmanis	.20	.09
❑ 60 Robert Green	.20	.09
❑ 61 Jack Jackson	.20	.09
❑ 62 Bobby Neely	.20	.09
❑ 63 Todd Perry	.20	.09
❑ 64 Evan Pilgrim	.20	.09
❑ 65 Octus Polk	.20	.09
❑ 66 Rashaan Salaam	.20	.09
❑ 67 Willie Anderson	.20	.09
❑ 68 Jeff Blake	.30	.14
❑ 69 Scott Brumfield	.20	.09
❑ 70 Jeff Cothran	.20	.09
❑ 71 Gerald Dixon	.20	.09
❑ 72 Garrison Hearst	.30	.14
❑ 73 James Hundon RC	.50	.23
❑ 74 Brian Milne	.20	.09
❑ 75 Troy Sadowski	.20	.09
❑ 76 Tom Tumulty	.20	.09
❑ 77 Kimo von Oelhoffen RC	.50	.23
❑ 78 Troy Aikman	1.00	.45
❑ 79 Dale Hellestrae	.20	.09
❑ 80 Roger Harper	.20	.09
❑ 81 Michael Irvin	.50	.23
❑ 82 John Jett	.20	.09
❑ 83 Kelvin Martin	.20	.09
❑ 84 Deion Sanders	.50	.23
❑ 85 Darrin Smith	.20	.09
❑ 86 Emmitt Smith	1.50	.70
❑ 87 Herschel Walker	.30	.14
❑ 88 Charlie Williams	.20	.09
❑ 89 Glenn Cadrez	.20	.09
❑ 90 Dwayne Carswell RC	.50	.23
❑ 91 Terrell Davis	.60	.25
❑ 92 David Diaz-infante	.20	.09
❑ 93 John Elway	2.00	.90
❑ 94 Harald Hasselback	.20	.09
❑ 95 Tory James	.20	.09
❑ 96 Bill Musgrave	.20	.09
❑ 97 Ralph Tamm	.20	.09
❑ 98 Maa Tanuvasa RC	.20	.09
❑ 99 Gary Zimmerman	.20	.09
❑ 100 Shane Bonham	.20	.09
❑ 101 Stephen Boyd RC	.20	.09
❑ 102 Jeff Hartings RC	.50	.23
❑ 103 Hessley Hempstead	.20	.09
❑ 104 Scott Kowalkowski	.20	.09
❑ 105 Herman Moore	.30	.14
❑ 106 Barry Sanders	1.50	.70
❑ 107 Tony Semple	.20	.09
❑ 108 Ryan Stewart	.20	.09
❑ 109 Mike Wells	.20	.09
❑ 110 Richard Woodley	.20	.09
❑ 111 Brett Favre	2.00	.90
❑ 112 Bernardo Harris RC	.30	.14
❑ 113 Keith McKenzie RC	.20	.09
❑ 114 Terry Mickens	.20	.09
❑ 115 Doug Pederson RC	.50	.23
❑ 116 Jeff Thomason RC	.20	.09
❑ 117 Adam Timmerman RC	.20	.09
❑ 118 Reggie White	.50	.23
❑ 119 Bruce Wilkerson	.20	.09
❑ 120 Gabe Wilkins RC	.20	.09
❑ 121 Tyrone Williams RC	.20	.09
❑ 122 Al Del Greco	.20	.09
❑ 123 Anthony Dorsett	.20	.09
❑ 124 Josh Evans	.20	.09
❑ 125 Eddie George	.50	.23
❑ 126 Lemanski Hall RC	.20	.09
❑ 127 Ronnie Harmon	.20	.09
❑ 128 Steve McNair	.60	.25
❑ 129 Michael Roan	.20	.09
❑ 130 Marcus Robertson	.20	.09
❑ 131 Jon Runyan	.20	.09
❑ 132 Chris Sanders	.20	.09

❑ 133 Kerwin Bell .20 .09
❑ 134 Marshall Faulk .60 .25
❑ 135 Clif Groce RC .20 .09
❑ 136 Jim Harbaugh .30 .14
❑ 137 Marvin Harrison .50 .23
❑ 138 Eric Mahlum .20 .09
❑ 139 Tony Mandarich .20 .09
❑ 140 Dedric Mathis .20 .09
❑ 141 Marcus Pollard RC .20 .09
❑ 142 Scott Slutzker .20 .09
❑ 143 Mark Stock .20 .09
❑ 144 Bucky Brooks .20 .09
❑ 145 Mark Brunell .60 .25
❑ 146 Kendricke Bullard .20 .09
❑ 147 Randy Jordan .20 .09
❑ 148 Jeff Kopp .20 .09
❑ 149 Le'Shai Maston .20 .09
❑ 150 Keenan McCardell .30 .14
❑ 151 Clyde Simmons .20 .09
❑ 152 Jimmy Smith .30 .14
❑ 153 Rich Tylski RC .20 .09
❑ 154 Dave Widell .20 .09
❑ 155 Marcus Allen .50 .23
❑ 156 Keith Cash .20 .09
❑ 157 Donnie Edwards .30 .14
❑ 158 Trezelle Jenkins .20 .09
❑ 159 Sean LaChapelle .20 .09
❑ 160 Greg Manusky .20 .09
❑ 161 Steve Matthews .20 .09
❑ 162 Pellom McDaniels .20 .09
❑ 163 Chris Penn .20 .09
❑ 164 Danny Villa .20 .09
❑ 165 Jerome Woods .20 .09
❑ 166 Karim Abdul-Jabbar .50 .23
❑ 167 John Bock .20 .09
❑ 168 O.J. Brigance RC .20 .09
❑ 169 Norman Hand RC .20 .09
❑ 170 Anthony Harris .20 .09
❑ 171 Larry Izzo RC .20 .09
❑ 172 Charles Jordan .20 .09
❑ 173 Dan Marino 2.00 .90
❑ 174 Everett McIver .20 .09
❑ 175 Joe Nedney RC .20 .09
❑ 176 Robert Wilson RC .20 .09
❑ 177 David Dixon .20 .09
❑ 178 Charles Evans .20 .09
❑ 179 Hunter Goodwin RC .20 .09
❑ 180 Ben Hanks .20 .09
❑ 181 Warren Moon .50 .23
❑ 182 Harold Morrow RC .50 .23
❑ 183 Fernando Smith .20 .09
❑ 184 Robert Smith .30 .14
❑ 185 Sean Vanhorse .20 .09
❑ 186 Jay Walker .20 .09
❑ 187 Dewayne Washington .20 .09
❑ 188 Moe Williams .50 .23
❑ 189 Mike Bartrum .20 .09
❑ 190 Drew Bledsoe .60 .25
❑ 191 Troy Brown .30 .14
❑ 192 Chad Eaton RC .20 .09
❑ 193 Sam Gash .20 .09
❑ 194 Mike Gisler .20 .09
❑ 195 Curtis Martin .60 .25
❑ 196 David Richards .20 .09
❑ 197 Todd Rucci .20 .09
❑ 198 Chris Sullivan .20 .09
❑ 199 Adam Vinatieri RC 40.00 18.00
❑ 200 Doug Brien .20 .09
❑ 201 Derek Brown RBK .20 .09
❑ 202 Lee DeRamus .20 .09
❑ 203 Jim Everett .20 .09
❑ 204 Mercury Hayes .20 .09
❑ 205 Joe Johnson .20 .09
❑ 206 Henry Lusk RC .20 .09
❑ 207 Andy McCollum .20 .09
❑ 208 Alex Molden .20 .09
❑ 209 Ray Zellars .20 .09
❑ 210 Marcus Buckley .20 .09
❑ 211 Doug Coleman RC .20 .09
❑ 212 Percy Ellsworth RC .20 .09
❑ 213 Rodney Hampton .30 .14
❑ 214 Brian Saxton .20 .09
❑ 215 Jason Sehorn .30 .14
❑ 216 Stan White .20 .09
❑ 217 Corey Widmer .20 .09
❑ 218 Rodney Young .20 .09
❑ 219 Rob Zatechka .20 .09
❑ 220 Henry Bailey .20 .09
❑ 221 Chad Cascadden RC .20 .09
❑ 222 Wayne Chrebet .50 .23
❑ 223 Tyrone Davis .20 .09
❑ 224 Kwame Ellis .20 .09
❑ 225 Glenn Foley .30 .14
❑ 226 Erik Howard .20 .09
❑ 227 Gary Jones .20 .09
❑ 228 Adrian Murrell .30 .14
❑ 229 Marc Spindler .20 .09
❑ 230 Lonnie Young .20 .09
❑ 231 Eric Zomalt .20 .09
❑ 232 Tim Brown .50 .23
❑ 233 Aundray Bruce .20 .09
❑ 234 Darren Carrington .20 .09
❑ 235 Rick Cunningham .20 .09
❑ 236 Rob Holmberg .20 .09
❑ 237 Jeff Hostetler .20 .09
❑ 238 Lorenzo Lynch .20 .09
❑ 239 Barrett Robbins .20 .09
❑ 240 Dan Turk .20 .09
❑ 241 Harvey Williams .20 .09
❑ 242 Brian Dawkins .50 .23
❑ 243 Ty Detmer .30 .14
❑ 244 Troy Drake .20 .09
❑ 245 Rhett Hall .20 .09
❑ 246 Joe Panos .20 .09
❑ 247 Johnny Thomas .20 .09
❑ 248 Kevin Turner .20 .09
❑ 249 Ricky Watters .30 .14
❑ 250 Derrick Witherspoon RC .20 .09
❑ 251 Sylvester Wright .20 .09
❑ 252 Jerome Bettis .50 .23
❑ 253 Carlos Emmons RC .20 .09
❑ 254 Jason Gildon .20 .09
❑ 255 Jonathan Hayes .20 .09
❑ 256 Kevin Henry .20 .09
❑ 257 Jerry Olsavsky .20 .09
❑ 258 Erric Pegram .20 .09
❑ 259 Brendan Stai .20 .09
❑ 260 Justin Strzelczyk .20 .09
❑ 261 Mike Tomczak .20 .09
❑ 262 Tony Banks .30 .14
❑ 263 Hayward Clay .20 .09
❑ 264 Percell Gaskins .20 .09
❑ 265 Eddie Kennison .30 .14
❑ 266 Aaron Laing .20 .09
❑ 267 Keith Lyle .20 .09
❑ 268 Jamie Martin RC 2.50 1.10
❑ 269 Lawrence Phillips .20 .09
❑ 270 Zach Wiegert .20 .09
❑ 271 Toby Wright .20 .09
❑ 272 Darren Bennett .20 .09
❑ 273 Tony Berti .20 .09
❑ 274 Freddie Bradley .20 .09
❑ 275 Joe Cocozzo .20 .09
❑ 276 Andre Coleman .20 .09
❑ 277 Marco Coleman .20 .09
❑ 278 Rodney Harrison RC 1.00 .45
❑ 279 David Hendrix .20 .09
❑ 280 Leonard Russell .20 .09
❑ 281 Sean Salisbury .20 .09
❑ 282 Dennis Brown .20 .09
❑ 283 Chris Dalman .20 .09
❑ 284 Brent Jones .30 .14
❑ 285 Sean Manuel .20 .09
❑ 286 Marquez Pope .20 .09
❑ 287 Jerry Rice 1.00 .45
❑ 288 Kirk Scrafford .20 .09
❑ 289 Iheanyi Uwaezuoke .30 .14
❑ 290 Tommy Vardell .20 .09
❑ 291 Steve Young .60 .25
❑ 292 James Atkins .20 .09
❑ 293 T.J. Cunningham .20 .09
❑ 294 Stan Gelbaugh .20 .09
❑ 295 James Logan .20 .09
❑ 296 James McKnight RC 1.50 .70
❑ 297 Rick Mirer .20 .09
❑ 298 Todd Peterson .20 .09
❑ 299 Fred Thomas .20 .09
❑ 300 Rick Tuten .20 .09
❑ 301 Chris Warren .30 .14
❑ 302 Donnie Abraham RC .50 .23
❑ 303 Trent Dilfer .50 .23
❑ 304 Kenneth Gant .20 .09
❑ 305 Jeff Gooch .30 .14
❑ 306 Courtney Hawkins .20 .09
❑ 307 Tyoka Jackson .20 .09
❑ 308 Melvin Johnson RC .20 .09
❑ 309 Lonnie Marts .20 .09
❑ 310 Hardy Nickerson .20 .09
❑ 311 Errict Rhett .20 .09
❑ 312 Terry Allen .50 .23
❑ 313 Flipper Anderson .20 .09
❑ 314 William Bell .20 .09
❑ 315 Scott Blanton .20 .09
❑ 316 Leomont Evans RC .20 .09
❑ 317 Gus Frerotte .20 .09
❑ 318 Darryl Morrison .20 .09
❑ 319 Matt Turk .20 .09
❑ 320 Jeff Uhlenhake .20 .09
❑ 321 Brian Walker RC .20 .09
❑ 322 Mark Brunell LL .50 .23
❑ 323 Barry Sanders LL .75 .35
❑ 324 Isaac Bruce LL .50 .23
❑ 325 Terry Allen LL .30 .14
❑ 326 Steve Young LL .50 .23
❑ 327 Jerry Rice LL .50 .23
❑ 328 Ricky Watters LL .30 .14
❑ 329 Kevin Greene LL .20 .09
❑ 330 Brett Favre LL 1.00 .45
❑ S1 Mark Brunell Sample 2.00 .90

1995 Pacific Prisms

	Nm-Mt	Ex-Mt
COMPLETE SET (216)	80.00	36.00
COMP.SERIES 1 (108)	40.00	18.00
COMP.SERIES 2 (108)	40.00	18.00

❑ 1 Chuck Levy .25 .11
❑ 2 Ronald Moore .25 .11
❑ 3 Jay Schroeder .25 .11
❑ 4 Bert Emanuel 1.00 .45
❑ 5 Terance Mathis .50 .23
❑ 6 Andre Rison .50 .23
❑ 7 Bucky Brooks .25 .11
❑ 8 Jeff Burris .25 .11
❑ 9 Jim Kelly 1.00 .45
❑ 10 Lewis Tillman .25 .11
❑ 11 Steve Walsh .25 .11
❑ 12 Chris Zorich .25 .11
❑ 13 Jeff Blake RC 2.50 1.10
❑ 14 Steve Broussard .25 .11
❑ 15 Jeff Cothran .25 .11
❑ 16 Earnest Byner .25 .11
❑ 17 Leroy Hoard .25 .11
❑ 18 Vinny Testaverde .50 .23
❑ 19 Troy Aikman 2.50 1.10
❑ 20 Alvin Harper .25 .11
❑ 21 Leon Lett .25 .11
❑ 22 Jay Novacek .50 .23
❑ 23 John Elway 5.00 2.20
❑ 24 Karl Mecklenburg .25 .11
❑ 25 Leonard Russell .25 .11
❑ 26 Mel Gray .25 .11
❑ 27 Dave Krieg .25 .11
❑ 28 Barry Sanders 4.00 1.80
❑ 29 Chris Spielman .50 .23
❑ 30 Robert Brooks 1.00 .45
❑ 31 LeShon Johnson .50 .23
❑ 32 Sterling Sharpe .50 .23
❑ 33 Ernest Givins .25 .11
❑ 34 Billy Joe Tolliver .25 .11
❑ 35 Lorenzo White .25 .11
❑ 36 Charles Arbuckle .25 .11
❑ 37 Sean Dawkins .50 .23
❑ 38 Marshall Faulk 3.00 1.35
❑ 39 Marcus Allen 1.00 .45
❑ 40 Donnell Bennett .50 .23
❑ 41 Matt Blundin RC .25 .11

❑ 42 Greg Hill .50 .23
❑ 43 Tim Brown 1.00 .45
❑ 44 Billy Joe Hobert .50 .23
❑ 45 Rocket Ismail .50 .23
❑ 46 James Jett .50 .23
❑ 47 Tim Bowens .25 .11
❑ 48 Irving Fryar .50 .23
❑ 49 O.J. McDuffie 1.00 .45
❑ 50 Irving Spikes .50 .23
❑ 51 Terry Allen .50 .23
❑ 52 Cris Carter 1.00 .45
❑ 53 Amp Lee .25 .11
❑ 54 Drew Bledsoe 1.50 .70
❑ 55 Willie McGinest .50 .23
❑ 56 Leroy Thompson .25 .11
❑ 57 Michael Timpson .25 .11
❑ 58 Michael Haynes .50 .23
❑ 59 Derrell Mitchell RC .25 .11
❑ 60 Dave Brown .50 .23
❑ 61 Thomas Lewis .50 .23
❑ 62 Dave Meggett .25 .11
❑ 63 Boomer Esiason .50 .23
❑ 64 Aaron Glenn .25 .11
❑ 65 Ronnie Lott .50 .23
❑ 66 Randall Cunningham 1.00 .45
❑ 67 Charlie Garner 1.00 .45
❑ 68 Herschel Walker .50 .23
❑ 69 Barry Foster .50 .23
❑ 70 Charles Johnson .50 .23
❑ 71 Jim Miller RC 3.00 1.35
❑ 72 Rod Woodson .50 .23
❑ 73 Andre Coleman .25 .11
❑ 74 Natrone Means .50 .23
❑ 75 Shannon Mitchell RC .25 .11
❑ 76 Junior Seau 1.00 .45
❑ 77 Elvis Grbac 1.00 .45
❑ 78 Deion Sanders 1.50 .70
❑ 79 Adam Walker RC .25 .11
❑ 80 Ricky Watters .50 .23
❑ 81 Michael Bates .25 .11
❑ 82 Brian Blades .50 .23
❑ 83 Eugene Robinson .25 .11
❑ 84 Chris Warren .50 .23
❑ 85 Jerome Bettis 1.00 .45
❑ 86 Troy Drayton .25 .11
❑ 87 Chris Miller .25 .11
❑ 88 Trent Dilfer 1.00 .45
❑ 89 Hardy Nickerson .25 .11
❑ 90 Errict Rhett .50 .23
❑ 91 Henry Ellard .50 .23
❑ 92 Gus Frerotte .50 .23
❑ 93 Ricky Ervins .25 .11
❑ 94 Dave Barr RC .25 .11
❑ 95 Kyle Brady RC 1.00 .45
❑ 96 Mark Bruener RC .50 .23
❑ 97 Ki-Jana Carter RC 1.00 .45
❑ 98 Kerry Collins RC 5.00 2.20
❑ 99 Joey Galloway RC 5.00 2.20
❑ 100 Napoleon Kaufman RC 4.00 1.80
❑ 101 Steve McNair RC 10.00 4.50
❑ 102 Craig Newsome RC .25 .11
❑ 103 Rashaan Salaam RC .50 .23
❑ 104 Kordell Stewart RC 5.00 2.20
❑ 105 J.J. Stokes RC 1.00 .45
❑ 106 Rodney Thomas RC .50 .23
❑ 107 Michael Westbrook RC 1.00 .45
❑ 108 Tyrone Wheatley RC 4.00 1.80
❑ 109 Larry Centers .50 .23
❑ 110 Garrison Hearst 1.00 .45
❑ 111 Jamir Miller .25 .11
❑ 112 Jeff George .50 .23
❑ 113 Craig Heyward .50 .23
❑ 114 Cornelius Bennett .50 .23
❑ 115 Andre Reed .50 .23
❑ 116 Randy Baldwin .25 .11
❑ 117 Tommy Barnhardt .25 .11
❑ 118 Sam Mills .50 .23
❑ 119 Brian O'Neal .25 .11
❑ 120 Frank Reich .25 .11
❑ 121 Tony Smith .25 .11
❑ 122 Lawyer Tillman .25 .11
❑ 123 Jack Trudeau .25 .11
❑ 124 Vernon Turner .25 .11
❑ 125 Curtis Conway 1.00 .45
❑ 126 Erik Kramer .25 .11
❑ 127 Nate Lewis .25 .11
❑ 128 Carl Pickens .50 .23
❑ 129 Darnay Scott .50 .23
❑ 130 Dan Wilkinson .50 .23
❑ 131 Derrick Alexander WR 1.00 .45
❑ 132 Carl Banks .25 .11
❑ 133 Michael Irvin 1.00 .45
❑ 134 Emmitt Smith 4.00 1.80
❑ 135 Kevin Williams WR .50 .23
❑ 136 Glyn Milburn .25 .11
❑ 137 Anthony Miller .50 .23
❑ 138 Shannon Sharpe .50 .23
❑ 139 Scott Mitchell .50 .23
❑ 140 Herman Moore 1.00 .45
❑ 141 Edgar Bennett .50 .23
❑ 142 Brett Favre 5.00 2.20
❑ 143 Reggie White 1.00 .45
❑ 144 Gary Brown .25 .11
❑ 145 Haywood Jeffires .25 .11
❑ 146 Webster Slaughter .25 .11
❑ 147 Craig Erickson .25 .11
❑ 148 Paul Justin .25 .11
❑ 149 Lamont Warren .25 .11
❑ 150 Steve Beuerlein .50 .23
❑ 151 Derek Brown TE .25 .11
❑ 152 Mark Brunell 1.50 .70
❑ 153 Reggie Cobb .25 .11
❑ 154 Desmond Howard .50 .23
❑ 155 Kelvin Pritchett .25 .11
❑ 156 James O. Stewart RC 4.00 1.80
❑ 157 Cedric Tillman .25 .11
❑ 158 Kimble Anders .50 .23
❑ 159 Lake Dawson .50 .23
❑ 160 Keith Byars .25 .11
❑ 161 Dan Marino 5.00 2.20
❑ 162 Bernie Parmalee .50 .23
❑ 163 Qadry Ismail .50 .23
❑ 164 Warren Moon .50 .23
❑ 165 Jake Reed .50 .23
❑ 166 Marion Butts .25 .11
❑ 167 Ben Coates .50 .23
❑ 168 Mario Bates .50 .23
❑ 169 Quinn Early .50 .23
❑ 170 Jim Everett .25 .11
❑ 171 Rodney Hampton .50 .23
❑ 172 Mike Horan .25 .11
❑ 173 Mike Sherrard .25 .11
❑ 174 Johnny Johnson .25 .11
❑ 175 Adrian Murrell .50 .23
❑ 176 Andrew Glover RC .25 .11
❑ 177 Jeff Hostetler .50 .23
❑ 178 Harvey Williams .25 .11
❑ 179 Fred Barnett .50 .23
❑ 180 Vaughn Hebron .25 .11
❑ 181 Jeff Sydner .25 .11
❑ 182 Kevin Greene .50 .23
❑ 183 Byron Bam Morris .25 .11
❑ 184 Neil O'Donnell .50 .23
❑ 185 Stan Humphries .50 .23
❑ 186 Tony Martin .50 .23
❑ 187 Mark Seay .50 .23
❑ 188 William Floyd .50 .23
❑ 189 Rickey Jackson .25 .11
❑ 190 Jerry Rice 2.50 1.10
❑ 191 Steve Young 2.00 .90
❑ 192 Cortez Kennedy .50 .23
❑ 193 Rick Mirer .50 .23
❑ 194 Jessie Hester .25 .11
❑ 195 Curtis Martin RC 10.00 4.50
❑ 196 Horace Copeland .25 .11
❑ 197 Charles Wilson .25 .11
❑ 198 Reggie Brooks .50 .23
❑ 199 Brian Mitchell .25 .11
❑ 200 Heath Shuler .50 .23
❑ 201 Justin Armour RC .25 .11
❑ 202 Jay Barker RC .25 .11
❑ 203 Zack Crockett RC .50 .23
❑ 204 Christian Fauria RC .50 .23
❑ 205 Antonio Freeman RC 4.00 1.80
❑ 206 Chad May RC .25 .11
❑ 207 Frank Sanders RC 1.00 .45
❑ 208 Steve Stenstrom RC .25 .11
❑ 209 Lorenzo Styles RC .25 .11
❑ 210 Sherman Williams RC .25 .11
❑ 211 Ray Zellars RC .50 .23
❑ 212 Eric Zeier RC 1.00 .45
❑ 213 Joey Galloway 2.00 .90
❑ 214 Napoleon Kaufman 1.50 .70
❑ 215 Rashaan Salaam .50 .23
❑ 216 J.J. Stokes 1.00 .45
❑ NNO Steve Beuerlein EE 1.00 .45
❑ NNO Barry Foster EE 1.00 .45
❑ P1 Natrone Means Promo 1.00 .45
Silver foil
❑ P2 Natrone Means Promo 1.00 .45
Gold foil

1999 Pacific Prisms

	Nm-Mt	Ex-Mt
COMPLETE SET (150)	80.00	36.00
❑ 1 David Boston RC	2.00	.90
❑ 2 Rob Moore	.60	.25
❑ 3 Adrian Murrell	.60	.25
❑ 4 Jake Plummer	.60	.25
❑ 5 Frank Sanders	.60	.25
❑ 6 Jamal Anderson	1.00	.45
❑ 7 Chris Chandler	.60	.25
❑ 8 Tim Dwight	.60	.25
❑ 9 Terance Mathis	.60	.25
❑ 10 Peter Boulware	.40	.18
❑ 11 Priest Holmes	1.50	.70
❑ 12 Pat Johnson	.40	.18
❑ 13 Jermaine Lewis	.60	.25
❑ 14 Doug Flutie	1.00	.45
❑ 15 Eric Moulds	1.00	.45
❑ 16 Peerless Price RC	3.00	1.35
❑ 17 Antowain Smith	1.00	.45
❑ 18 Bruce Smith	.60	.25
❑ 19 Steve Beuerlein	.40	.18
❑ 20 Tim Biakabutuka	.60	.25
❑ 21 Muhsin Muhammad	.60	.25
❑ 22 Wesley Walls	.60	.25
❑ 23 Edgar Bennett	.40	.18
❑ 24 Curtis Conway	.60	.25
❑ 25 Bobby Engram	.60	.25
❑ 26 Curtis Enis	.40	.18
❑ 27 Cade McNown RC	1.00	.45
❑ 28 Jeff Blake	.60	.25
❑ 29 Scott Covington RC	2.00	.90
❑ 30 Corey Dillon	1.00	.45
❑ 31 Carl Pickens	.60	.25
❑ 32 Akili Smith RC	1.00	.45
❑ 33 Craig Yeast RC	1.00	.45
❑ 34 Tim Couch RC	2.00	.90
❑ 35 Ty Detmer	.60	.25
❑ 36 Kevin Johnson RC	2.00	.90
❑ 37 Terry Kirby	.40	.18
❑ 38 Leslie Shepherd	.40	.18
❑ 39 Troy Aikman	2.00	.90
❑ 40 Michael Irvin	.60	.25
❑ 41 Deion Sanders	1.00	.45
❑ 42 Emmitt Smith	2.00	.90
❑ 43 Bubby Brister	.40	.18
❑ 44 Terrell Davis	1.00	.45
❑ 45 Brian Griese	1.00	.45
❑ 46 Ed McCaffrey	.60	.25
❑ 47 Shannon Sharpe	.60	.25
❑ 48 Rod Smith	.60	.25
❑ 49 Charlie Batch	1.00	.45
❑ 50 Germane Crowell	.40	.18
❑ 51 Sedrick Irvin RC	1.50	.70
❑ 52 Herman Moore	.60	.25
❑ 53 Johnnie Morton	.60	.25
❑ 54 Barry Sanders	3.00	1.35
❑ 55 Mark Chmura	.40	.18
❑ 56 Brett Favre	3.00	1.35
❑ 57 Antonio Freeman	1.00	.45
❑ 58 Dorsey Levens	1.00	.45
❑ 59 Ken Dilger	.40	.18
❑ 60 Marvin Harrison	1.00	.45
❑ 61 Edgerrin James RC	6.00	2.70

❑ 62 Peyton Manning	3.00	1.35
❑ 63 Jerome Pathon	.40	.18
❑ 64 Mark Brunell	1.00	.45
❑ 65 Keenan McCardell	.60	.25
❑ 66 Jimmy Smith	.60	.25
❑ 67 Fred Taylor	1.00	.45
❑ 68 Derrick Alexander	.60	.25
❑ 69 Mike Cloud RC	1.00	.45
❑ 70 Tony Gonzalez	1.00	.45
❑ 71 Elvis Grbac	.60	.25
❑ 72 Andre Rison	.60	.25
❑ 73 Cecil Collins RC	1.50	.70
❑ 74 Oronde Gadsden	.60	.25
❑ 75 James Johnson RC	1.00	.45
❑ 76 Dan Marino	3.00	1.35
❑ 77 O.J. McDuffie	.60	.25
❑ 78 Lamar Thomas	.40	.18
❑ 79 Cris Carter	1.00	.45
❑ 80 Daunte Culpepper RC	6.00	2.70
❑ 81 Randall Cunningham	1.00	.45
❑ 82 Matthew Hatchette	.40	.18
❑ 83 Randy Moss	2.50	1.10
❑ 84 John Randle	.60	.25
❑ 85 Robert Smith	1.00	.45
❑ 86 Drew Bledsoe	1.25	.55
❑ 87 Ben Coates	.60	.25
❑ 88 Kevin Faulk RC	2.00	.90
❑ 89 Terry Glenn	1.00	.45
❑ 90 Shawn Jefferson	.40	.18
❑ 91 Cam Cleeland	.40	.18
❑ 92 Billy Joe Hobert	.40	.18
❑ 93 Keith Poole	.40	.18
❑ 94 Ricky Williams RC	3.00	1.35
❑ 95 Gary Brown	.40	.18
❑ 96 Kent Graham	.40	.18
❑ 97 Ike Hilliard	.40	.18
❑ 98 Amani Toomer	.40	.18
❑ 99 Wayne Chrebet	.60	.25
❑ 100 Keyshawn Johnson	1.00	.45
❑ 101 Curtis Martin	1.00	.45
❑ 102 Vinny Testaverde	.60	.25
❑ 103 Tim Brown	1.00	.45
❑ 104 James Jett	.60	.25
❑ 105 Napoleon Kaufman	1.00	.45
❑ 106 Charles Woodson	1.00	.45
❑ 107 Koy Detmer	.40	.18
❑ 108 Donovan McNabb RC	8.00	3.60
❑ 109 Duce Staley	1.00	.45
❑ 110 Kevin Turner	.40	.18
❑ 111 Jerome Bettis	1.00	.45
❑ 112 Mark Bruener	.40	.18
❑ 113 Troy Edwards RC	1.00	.45
❑ 114 Levon Kirkland	.40	.18
❑ 115 Kordell Stewart	.60	.25
❑ 116 Amos Zereoue RC	2.00	.90
❑ 117 Isaac Bruce	1.00	.45
❑ 118 Marshall Faulk	1.25	.55
❑ 119 Joe Germaine RC	1.00	.45
❑ 120 Trent Green	1.00	.45
❑ 121 Torry Holt RC	5.00	2.20
❑ 122 Ryan Leaf	1.00	.45
❑ 123 Natrone Means	.60	.25
❑ 124 Mikhael Ricks	.40	.18
❑ 125 Junior Seau	1.00	.45
❑ 126 Garrison Hearst	.60	.25
❑ 127 Terrell Owens	1.00	.45
❑ 128 Jerry Rice	2.00	.90
❑ 129 J.J. Stokes	.60	.25
❑ 130 Steve Young	1.25	.55
❑ 131 Chad Brown	.40	.18
❑ 132 Joey Galloway	.60	.25
❑ 133 Brock Huard RC	2.00	.90
❑ 134 Jon Kitna	1.00	.45
❑ 135 Ricky Watters	.60	.25
❑ 136 Mike Alstott	1.00	.45
❑ 137 Reidel Anthony	.60	.25
❑ 138 Trent Dilfer	.60	.25
❑ 139 Warrick Dunn	1.00	.45
❑ 140 Jacquez Green	.40	.18
❑ 141 Shaun King RC	1.00	.45
❑ 142 Darnell McDonald RC	1.00	.45
❑ 143 Eddie George	1.00	.45
❑ 144 Steve McNair	1.00	.45
❑ 145 Yancey Thigpen	.40	.18
❑ 146 Frank Wycheck	.40	.18
❑ 147 Champ Bailey RC	2.50	1.10
❑ 148 Albert Connell	.40	.18
❑ 149 Skip Hicks	.40	.18
❑ 150 Michael Westbrook	.40	.18

2001 Pacific Prism Atomic

	Nm-Mt	Ex-Mt
COMP.SET w/o SP's (148)	60.00	18.00
❑ 1 David Boston	1.50	.45
❑ 2 Thomas Jones	1.00	.30
❑ 3 Rob Moore	1.00	.30
❑ 4 Michael Pittman	.60	.18
❑ 5 Jake Plummer	1.00	.30
❑ 6 Jamal Anderson	1.50	.45
❑ 7 Chris Chandler	1.00	.30
❑ 8 Shawn Jefferson	.60	.18
❑ 9 Terance Mathis	.60	.18
❑ 10 Elvis Grbac	1.00	.30
❑ 11 Qadry Ismail	1.00	.30
❑ 12 Jamal Lewis	2.50	.75
❑ 13 Ray Lewis	1.50	.45
❑ 14 Shannon Sharpe	1.00	.30
❑ 15 Shawn Bryson	.60	.18
❑ 16 Rob Johnson	1.00	.30
❑ 17 Sammy Morris	.60	.18
❑ 18 Eric Moulds	1.00	.30
❑ 19 Peerless Price	1.00	.30
❑ 20 Tim Biakabutuka	1.00	.30
❑ 21 Richard Huntley	.60	.18
❑ 22 Patrick Jeffers	1.00	.30
❑ 23 Jeff Lewis	.60	.18
❑ 24 Muhsin Muhammad	1.00	.30
❑ 25 James Allen	1.00	.30
❑ 26 Cade McNown	.60	.18
❑ 27 Marcus Robinson	1.50	.45
❑ 28 Brian Urlacher	2.50	.75
❑ 29 Corey Dillon	1.50	.45
❑ 30 Jon Kitna	1.00	.30
❑ 31 Akili Smith	.60	.18
❑ 32 Peter Warrick	1.50	.45
❑ 33 Tim Couch	1.00	.30
❑ 34 Kevin Johnson	1.00	.30
❑ 35 Dennis Northcutt	1.00	.30
❑ 36 Travis Prentice	.60	.18
❑ 37 Tony Banks	1.00	.30
❑ 38 Joey Galloway	1.00	.30
❑ 39 Rocket Ismail	1.00	.30
❑ 40 Emmitt Smith	3.00	.90
❑ 41 Anthony Wright	.60	.18
❑ 42 Mike Anderson	1.50	.45
❑ 43 Terrell Davis	1.50	.45
❑ 44 Olandis Gary	1.00	.30
❑ 45 Brian Griese	1.50	.45
❑ 46 Ed McCaffrey	1.50	.45
❑ 47 Rod Smith	1.00	.30
❑ 48 Charlie Batch	1.50	.45
❑ 49 Germane Crowell	.60	.18
❑ 50 Herman Moore	1.00	.30
❑ 51 Johnnie Morton	1.00	.30
❑ 52 James Stewart	1.00	.30
❑ 53 Brett Favre	5.00	1.50
❑ 54 Antonio Freeman	1.50	.45
❑ 55 Ahman Green	1.50	.45
❑ 56 Dorsey Levens	1.00	.30
❑ 57 Bill Schroeder	1.00	.30
❑ 58 Marvin Harrison	1.50	.45
❑ 59 Edgerrin James	2.00	.60
❑ 60 Peyton Manning	4.00	1.20
❑ 61 Jerome Pathon	1.00	.30
❑ 62 Terrence Wilkins	.60	.18
❑ 63 Mark Brunell	1.50	.45
❑ 64 Keenan McCardell	.60	.18
❑ 65 Jimmy Smith	1.00	.30
❑ 66 Fred Taylor	1.50	.45
❑ 67 Derrick Alexander	.60	.18
❑ 68 Tony Gonzalez	1.00	.30
❑ 69 Trent Green	1.50	.45
❑ 70 Priest Holmes	2.00	.60
❑ 71 Sylvester Morris	.60	.18
❑ 72 Jay Fiedler	1.50	.45
❑ 73 Oronde Gadsden	1.00	.30
❑ 74 O.J. McDuffie	.60	.18
❑ 75 Lamar Smith	1.00	.30
❑ 76 Zach Thomas	1.50	.45
❑ 77 Cris Carter	1.50	.45
❑ 78 Daunte Culpepper	1.50	.45
❑ 79 Randy Moss	3.00	.90
❑ 80 Chris Walsh RC	.60	.18
❑ 81 Moe Williams	1.00	.30
❑ 82 Drew Bledsoe	2.00	.60
❑ 83 Kevin Faulk	1.00	.30
❑ 84 Terry Glenn	1.00	.30
❑ 85 Charles Johnson	.60	.18
❑ 86 J.R. Redmond	.60	.18
❑ 87 Jeff Blake	1.00	.30
❑ 88 Aaron Brooks	1.50	.45
❑ 89 Albert Connell	.60	.18
❑ 90 Joe Horn	1.00	.30
❑ 91 Ricky Williams	1.50	.45
❑ 92 Tiki Barber	1.00	.30
❑ 93 Kerry Collins	1.00	.30
❑ 94 Ron Dayne	1.50	.45
❑ 95 Ike Hilliard	1.00	.30
❑ 96 Amani Toomer	1.00	.30
❑ 97 Richie Anderson	.60	.18
❑ 98 Wayne Chrebet	1.00	.30
❑ 99 Curtis Martin	1.50	.45
❑ 100 Chad Pennington	2.50	.75
❑ 101 Vinny Testaverde	1.00	.30
❑ 102 Tim Brown	1.50	.45
❑ 103 Rich Gannon	1.50	.45
❑ 104 Charlie Garner	1.00	.30
❑ 105 Jerry Rice	3.00	.90
❑ 106 Tyrone Wheatley	1.00	.30
❑ 107 Charles Woodson	1.00	.30
❑ 108 Darnell Autry	.60	.18
❑ 109 Donovan McNabb	2.00	.60
❑ 110 Duce Staley	1.50	.45
❑ 111 James Thrash	1.00	.30
❑ 112 Jerome Bettis	1.50	.45
❑ 113 Plaxico Burress	1.50	.45
❑ 114 Bobby Shaw	.60	.18
❑ 115 Kordell Stewart	1.00	.30
❑ 116 Hines Ward	1.50	.45
❑ 117 Isaac Bruce	1.50	.45
❑ 118 Marshall Faulk	2.00	.60
❑ 119 Az-Zahir Hakim	1.00	.30
❑ 120 Torry Holt	1.50	.45
❑ 121 Kurt Warner	3.00	.90
❑ 122 Curtis Conway	1.00	.30
❑ 123 Tim Dwight	1.50	.45
❑ 124 Doug Flutie	1.50	.45
❑ 125 Dave Dickenson RC	6.00	1.80
❑ 126 Jeff Garcia	1.50	.45
❑ 127 Terrell Owens	1.50	.45
❑ 128 J.J. Stokes	1.00	.30
❑ 129 Tai Streets	.60	.18
❑ 130 Shaun Alexander	2.00	.60
❑ 131 Trent Dilfer	1.00	.30
❑ 132 Matt Hasselbeck	1.00	.30
❑ 133 Darrell Jackson	1.50	.45
❑ 134 Ricky Watters	1.00	.30
❑ 135 Mike Alstott	1.50	.45
❑ 136 Warrick Dunn	1.50	.45
❑ 137 Brad Johnson	1.50	.45
❑ 138 Keyshawn Johnson	1.50	.45
❑ 139 Warren Sapp	1.00	.30
❑ 140 Kevin Dyson	1.00	.30
❑ 141 Eddie George	1.50	.45
❑ 142 Jevon Kearse	1.00	.30
❑ 143 Derrick Mason	1.00	.30
❑ 144 Steve McNair	1.50	.45
❑ 145 Champ Bailey	1.00	.30
❑ 146 Stephen Davis	1.50	.45
❑ 147 Jeff George	1.00	.30
❑ 148 Michael Westbrook	1.00	.30
❑ 149 Quentin McCord RC	6.00	1.80
❑ 150 Vinny Sutherland RC	6.00	1.80
❑ 151 Michael Vick RC	60.00	18.00
❑ 152 Chris Barnes RC	6.00	1.80

❑ 153 Reggie Germany RC 6.00 1.80
❑ 154 Travis Henry RC 12.00 3.60
❑ 155 Dee Brown RC 10.00 3.00
❑ 156 Dan Morgan RC 10.00 3.00
❑ 157 Steve Smith RC 12.00 3.60
❑ 158 Chris Weinke RC 10.00 3.00
❑ 159 David Terrell RC 10.00 3.00
❑ 160 Anthony Thomas RC 15.00 4.50
❑ 161 Chad Johnson RC 20.00 6.00
❑ 162 Rudi Johnson RC 20.00 6.00
❑ 163 James Jackson RC 10.00 3.00
❑ 164 Andre King RC 6.00 1.80
❑ 165 Quincy Morgan RC 10.00 3.00
❑ 166 Quincy Carter RC 10.00 3.00
❑ 167 Kevin Kasper RC 10.00 3.00
❑ 168 Scotty Anderson RC 6.00 1.80
❑ 169 Mike McMahon RC 10.00 3.00
❑ 170 Robert Ferguson RC 10.00 3.00
❑ 171 Reggie Wayne RC 15.00 4.50
❑ 172 Derrick Blaylock RC 10.00 3.00
❑ 173 Snoop Minnis RC 6.00 1.80
❑ 174 Chris Chambers RC 12.00 3.60
❑ 175 Josh Heupel RC 10.00 3.00
❑ 176 Travis Minor RC 6.00 1.80
❑ 177 Michael Bennett RC 20.00 6.00
❑ 178 Deuce McAllister RC 25.00 7.50
❑ 179 Jonathan Carter RC 6.00 1.80
❑ 180 Jesse Palmer RC 10.00 3.00
❑ 181 LaMont Jordan RC 12.00 3.60
❑ 182 Santana Moss RC 15.00 4.50
❑ 183 Ken-Yon Rambo RC 6.00 1.80
❑ 184 Marques Tuiasosopo RC 10.00 3.00
❑ 185 Correll Buckhalter RC 12.00 3.60
❑ 186 Freddie Mitchell RC 10.00 3.00
❑ 187 Milton Wynn RC 6.00 1.80
❑ 188 Drew Brees RC 20.00 6.00
❑ 189 LaDainian Tomlinson RC 30.00 9.00
❑ 190 Kevan Barlow RC 10.00 3.00
❑ 191 Cedrick Wilson RC 10.00 3.00
❑ 192 Alex Bannister RC 6.00 1.80
❑ 193 Josh Booty RC 10.00 3.00
❑ 194 Koren Robinson RC 12.00 3.60
❑ 195 Eddie Berlin RC 6.00 1.80
❑ 196 Rod Gardner RC 10.00 3.00
❑ 197 Damerien McCants RC 6.00 1.80
❑ 198 Sage Rosenfels RC 10.00 3.00
❑ NNO Eddie George SAMPLE 1.25 .35
❑ NNO Jamal Lewis SAMPLE 2.00 .60
❑ NNO Randy Moss SAMPLE 2.50 .75
❑ NNO Emmitt Smith SAMPLE 2.50 .75

2001 Pacific Prism Atomic Blue

Nm-Mt Ex-Mt
*STARS: 12X TO 30X BASIC CARDS
*1-148 ROOKIES: 1.2X TO 3X
149-198 NOT PRICED DUE TO SCARCITY

2001 Pacific Prism Atomic Gold

Nm-Mt Ex-Mt
*STARS: 3X TO 8X BASIC CARDS
*1-148 ROOKIES: .6X TO 1.5X
*149-196 ROOKIES: .4X TO 1X

2001 Pacific Prism Atomic Red

Nm-Mt Ex-Mt
*STARS: 2.5X TO 6X BASIC CARDS
*ROOKIES: .5X TO 1.2X

2000 Pacific Prism Prospects

Nm-Mt Ex-Mt
COMP.SET w/o SP's (100) 25.00 11.00
❑ 1 David Boston .75 .35
❑ 2 Jake Plummer .50 .23
❑ 3 Jamal Anderson .75 .35
❑ 4 Chris Chandler .50 .23
❑ 5 Tim Dwight .75 .35
❑ 6 Terance Mathis .50 .23
❑ 7 Tony Banks .50 .23
❑ 8 Priest Holmes 1.00 .45
❑ 9 Doug Flutie .75 .35
❑ 10 Rob Johnson .50 .23

❑ 11 Eric Moulds .75 .35
❑ 12 Antowain Smith .50 .23
❑ 13 Steve Beuerlein .50 .23
❑ 14 Tim Biakabutuka .50 .23
❑ 15 Muhsin Muhammad .50 .23
❑ 16 Bobby Engram .50 .23
❑ 17 Curtis Enis .30 .14
❑ 18 Cade McNown .30 .14
❑ 19 Marcus Robinson .75 .35
❑ 20 Corey Dillon .75 .35
❑ 21 Akili Smith .30 .14
❑ 22 Tim Couch .50 .23
❑ 23 Kevin Johnson .75 .35
❑ 24 Troy Aikman 1.50 .70
❑ 25 Joey Galloway .50 .23
❑ 26 Rocket Ismail .50 .23
❑ 27 Emmitt Smith 1.50 .70
❑ 28 Terrell Davis .75 .35
❑ 29 Olandis Gary .75 .35
❑ 30 Brian Griese .75 .35
❑ 31 Charlie Batch .75 .35
❑ 32 Herman Moore .50 .23
❑ 33 Johnnie Morton .50 .23
❑ 34 Brett Favre 2.50 1.10
❑ 35 Antonio Freeman .75 .35
❑ 36 Dorsey Levens .50 .23
❑ 37 Marvin Harrison .75 .35
❑ 38 Edgerrin James 1.25 .55
❑ 39 Peyton Manning 2.00 .90
❑ 40 Mark Brunell .75 .35
❑ 41 Keenan McCardell .50 .23
❑ 42 Jimmy Smith .50 .23
❑ 43 Fred Taylor .75 .35
❑ 44 Donnell Bennett .30 .14
❑ 45 Tony Gonzalez .50 .23
❑ 46 Elvis Grbac .50 .23
❑ 47 Damon Huard .75 .35
❑ 48 James Johnson .30 .14
❑ 49 Cris Carter .75 .35
❑ 50 Daunte Culpepper 1.00 .45
❑ 51 Randy Moss 1.50 .70
❑ 52 Robert Smith .75 .35
❑ 53 Drew Bledsoe 1.00 .45
❑ 54 Kevin Faulk .50 .23
❑ 55 Terry Glenn .50 .23
❑ 56 Jeff Blake .50 .23
❑ 57 Ricky Williams .75 .35
❑ 58 Kerry Collins .50 .23
❑ 59 Ike Hilliard .50 .23
❑ 60 Amani Toomer .50 .23
❑ 61 Wayne Chrebet .50 .23
❑ 62 Curtis Martin .75 .35
❑ 63 Vinny Testaverde .50 .23
❑ 64 Tim Brown .75 .35
❑ 65 Rich Gannon .75 .35
❑ 66 Napoleon Kaufman .50 .23
❑ 67 Tyrone Wheatley .50 .23
❑ 68 Donovan McNabb 1.25 .55
❑ 69 Duce Staley .75 .35
❑ 70 Jerome Bettis .75 .35
❑ 71 Troy Edwards .30 .14
❑ 72 Kordell Stewart .50 .23
❑ 73 Isaac Bruce .75 .35
❑ 74 Torry Holt .75 .35
❑ 75 Marshall Faulk 1.00 .45
❑ 76 Kurt Warner 1.50 .70
❑ 77 Jermaine Fazande .30 .14
❑ 78 Jim Harbaugh .50 .23
❑ 79 Ryan Leaf .50 .23
❑ 80 Junior Seau .75 .35
❑ 81 Jeff Garcia .75 .35
❑ 82 J.J. Stokes .50 .23
❑ 83 Terrell Owens .75 .35
❑ 84 Jerry Rice 1.50 .70
❑ 85 Jon Kitna .75 .35
❑ 86 Derrick Mayes .50 .23
❑ 87 Ricky Watters .50 .23
❑ 88 Mike Alstott .75 .35
❑ 89 Warrick Dunn .75 .35
❑ 90 Jacquez Green .30 .14
❑ 91 Shaun King .30 .14
❑ 92 Eddie George .75 .35
❑ 93 Jevon Kearse .75 .35
❑ 94 Steve McNair .75 .35
❑ 95 Carl Pickens .50 .23
❑ 96 Stephen Davis .75 .35
❑ 97 Jeff George .50 .23
❑ 98 Brad Johnson .75 .35
❑ 99 Deion Sanders .75 .35
❑ 100 Michael Westbrook .50 .23
❑ 101 Jabari Issa RC 3.00 1.35
❑ 102 Thomas Jones RC 10.00 4.50
❑ 103 Sekou Sanyika RC 3.00 1.35
❑ 104 Jay Tant RC 3.00 1.35
❑ 105 Raynoch Thompson RC 5.00 2.20
❑ 106 Doug Johnson RC 6.00 2.70
❑ 107 Mark Simoneau RC 5.00 2.20
❑ 108 Jamal Lewis RC 15.00 6.75
❑ 109 Chris Redman RC 5.00 2.20
❑ 110 Travis Taylor RC 6.00 2.70
❑ 111 Kwame Cavil RC 3.00 1.35
❑ 112 Corey Moore RC 3.00 1.35
❑ 113 Rashard Anderson RC 5.00 2.20
❑ 114 Lester Towns RC 3.00 1.35
❑ 115 Paul Edinger RC 6.00 2.70
❑ 116 Brian Urlacher RC 25.00 11.00
❑ 117 Dez White RC 6.00 2.70
❑ 118 Ron Dugans RC 3.00 1.35
❑ 119 Danny Farmer RC 5.00 2.20
❑ 120 Curtis Keaton RC 5.00 2.20
❑ 121 Peter Warrick RC 6.00 2.70
❑ 122 Courtney Brown RC 6.00 2.70
❑ 123 Lamar Chapman RC 3.00 1.35
❑ 124 JaJuan Dawson RC 3.00 1.35
❑ 125 Dennis Northcutt RC 6.00 2.70
❑ 126 Travis Prentice RC 5.00 2.20
❑ 127 Aaron Shea RC 5.00 2.20
❑ 128 Spergon Wynn RC 5.00 2.20
❑ 129 Dwayne Goodrich RC 3.00 1.35
❑ 130 Orantes Grant RC 3.00 1.35
❑ 131 Kareem Larrimore RC 3.00 1.35
❑ 132 Michael Wiley RC 5.00 2.20
❑ 133 Mike Anderson RC 6.00 2.70
❑ 134 Chris Cole RC 5.00 2.20
❑ 135 Jarious Jackson RC 5.00 2.20
❑ 136 Jerry Johnson RC 3.00 1.35
❑ 137 Kenoy Kennedy RC 3.00 1.35
❑ 138 Deltha O'Neal RC 6.00 2.70
❑ 139 Reuben Droughns RC 8.00 3.60
❑ 140 Barrett Green RC 3.00 1.35
❑ 141 Bubba Franks RC 6.00 2.70
❑ 142 Kevin McDougal RC 5.00 2.20
❑ 143 Marcus Washington RC 5.00 2.20
❑ 144 T.J. Slaughter RC 3.00 1.35
❑ 145 R.Jay Soward RC 5.00 2.20
❑ 146 Shyrone Stith RC 5.00 2.20
❑ 147 William Bartee RC 5.00 2.20
❑ 148 Dante Hall RC 12.00 5.50
❑ 149 Frank Moreau RC 5.00 2.20
❑ 150 Sylvester Morris RC 5.00 2.20
❑ 151 Deon Dyer RC 5.00 2.20
❑ 152 Ben Kelly RC 3.00 1.35
❑ 153 Tyrone Carter RC 5.00 2.20
❑ 154 Doug Chapman RC 5.00 2.20
❑ 155 Troy Walters RC 6.00 2.70
❑ 156 Tom Brady RC 60.00 27.00
❑ 157 Patrick Pass RC 5.00 2.20
❑ 158 J.R. Redmond RC 5.00 2.20
❑ 159 Marc Bulger RC 12.00 5.50
❑ 160 Darren Howard RC 5.00 2.20
❑ 161 Chad Morton RC 6.00 2.70
❑ 162 Mareno Philyaw RC 3.00 1.35
❑ 163 Terrelle Smith RC 5.00 2.20
❑ 164 Ralph Brown RC 3.00 1.35
❑ 165 Ron Dayne RC 6.00 2.70
❑ 166 Brandon Short RC 5.00 2.20
❑ 167 John Abraham RC 6.00 2.70
❑ 168 Anthony Becht RC 6.00 2.70
❑ 169 Laveranues Coles RC 8.00 3.60

❑ 170 Shaun Ellis RC 6.00 2.70
❑ 171 Chad Pennington RC 25.00 11.00
❑ 172 Sebastian Janikowski RC 6.00 2.70
❑ 173 Jerry Porter RC 8.00 3.60
❑ 174 Todd Pinkston RC 6.00 2.70
❑ 175 Gari Scott RC 3.00 1.35
❑ 176 Corey Simon RC 6.00 2.70
❑ 177 Plaxico Burress RC 12.00 5.50
❑ 178 Tee Martin RC 6.00 2.70
❑ 179 Hank Poteat RC 5.00 2.20
❑ 180 Rogers Beckett RC 5.00 2.20
❑ 181 Trevor Gaylor RC 5.00 2.20
❑ 182 Ronney Jenkins RC 5.00 2.20
❑ 183 Giovanni Carmazzi RC 5.00 2.20
❑ 184 Chafie Fields RC 3.00 1.35
❑ 185 Ahmed Plummer RC 6.00 2.70
❑ 186 Tim Rattay RC 12.00 5.50
❑ 187 Jeff Ulbrich RC 3.00 1.35
❑ 188 Shaun Alexander RC 15.00 6.75
❑ 189 Darrell Jackson RC 12.00 5.50
❑ 190 Rodnick Phillips RC 3.00 1.35
❑ 191 James Williams RC 5.00 2.20
❑ 192 Trung Canidate RC 5.00 2.20
❑ 193 Joe Hamilton RC 5.00 2.20
❑ 194 DeMario Brown RC 3.00 1.35
❑ 195 Keith Bulluck RC 6.00 2.70
❑ 196 Chris Coleman RC 6.00 2.70
❑ 197 Erron Kinney RC 6.00 2.70
❑ 198 Billy Volek RC 10.00 4.50
❑ 199 Todd Husak RC 6.00 2.70
❑ 200 Chris Samuels RC 5.00 2.20

1998 Paramount

	Nm-Mt	Ex-Mt
COMPLETE SET (250)	60.00	27.00
❑ 1 Larry Centers	.20	.09
❑ 2 Chris Gedney	.20	.09
❑ 3 Rob Moore	.30	.14
❑ 4 Jake Plummer	.50	.23
❑ 5 Simeon Rice	.30	.14
❑ 6 Frank Sanders	.30	.14
❑ 7 Mark Smith DE	.20	.09
❑ 8 Eric Swann	.20	.09
❑ 9 Jamal Anderson	.50	.23
❑ 10 Chris Chandler	.30	.14
❑ 11 Bert Emanuel	.30	.14
❑ 12 Tony Graziani	.20	.09
❑ 13 Byron Hanspard	.20	.09
❑ 14 Terance Mathis	.30	.14
❑ 15 O.J. Santiago	.20	.09
❑ 16 Chuck Smith	.20	.09
❑ 17 Derrick Alexander WR	.30	.14
❑ 18 Peter Boulware	.20	.09
❑ 19 Jay Graham	.20	.09
❑ 20 Priest Holmes RC	25.00	11.00
❑ 21 Michael Jackson	.20	.09
❑ 22 Byron Bam Morris	.20	.09
❑ 23 Vinny Testaverde	.30	.14
❑ 24 Eric Zeier	.30	.14
❑ 25 Todd Collins	.20	.09
❑ 26 Quinn Early	.20	.09
❑ 27 Bryce Paup	.20	.09
❑ 28 Andre Reed	.30	.14
❑ 29 Jay Riemersma	.20	.09
❑ 30 Antowain Smith	.50	.23
❑ 31 Bruce Smith	.30	.14
❑ 32 Thurman Thomas	.50	.23
❑ 33 Michael Bates	.20	.09
❑ 34 Mark Carrier WR	.20	.09
❑ 35 Rae Carruth	.20	.09
❑ 36 Kerry Collins	.30	.14
❑ 37 Fred Lane	.20	.09
❑ 38 Lamar Lathon	.20	.09
❑ 39 Muhsin Muhammad	.30	.14
❑ 40 Wesley Walls	.30	.14
❑ 41 Darnell Autry	.20	.09
❑ 42 Curtis Conway	.30	.14
❑ 43 Raymont Harris	.20	.09
❑ 44 Tyrone Hughes	.20	.09
❑ 45 Chris Penn	.20	.09
❑ 46 Ricky Proehl	.20	.09
❑ 47 Steve Stenstrom	.20	.09
❑ 48 Ryan Wetnight RC	.20	.09
❑ 49 Jeff Blake	.30	.14
❑ 50 Ki-Jana Carter	.20	.09
❑ 51 Corey Dillon	.50	.23
❑ 52 David Dunn	.20	.09
❑ 53 Boomer Esiason	.20	.09
❑ 54 Brian Milne	.20	.09
❑ 55 Carl Pickens	.30	.14
❑ 56 Darnay Scott	.30	.14
❑ 57 Troy Aikman	1.00	.45
❑ 58 Eric Bjornson	.20	.09
❑ 59 Michael Irvin	.50	.23
❑ 60 Daryl Johnston	.30	.14
❑ 61 Anthony Miller	.20	.09
❑ 62 Deion Sanders	.50	.23
❑ 63 Emmitt Smith	1.50	.70
❑ 64 Omar Stoutmire RC	.20	.09
❑ 65 Sherman Williams	.20	.09
❑ 66 Terrell Davis	.50	.23
❑ 67 John Elway	2.00	.90
❑ 68 Darrien Gordon	.20	.09
❑ 69 Ed McCaffrey	.30	.14
❑ 70 Bill Romanowski	.20	.09
❑ 71 Shannon Sharpe	.30	.14
❑ 72 Neil Smith	.30	.14
❑ 73 Rod Smith WR	.30	.14
❑ 74 Maa Tanuvasa	.20	.09
❑ 75 Tommie Boyd	.20	.09
❑ 76 Glyn Milburn	.20	.09
❑ 77 Scott Mitchell	.30	.14
❑ 78 Herman Moore	.30	.14
❑ 79 Johnnie Morton	.30	.14
❑ 80 Robert Porcher	.20	.09
❑ 81 Barry Sanders	1.50	.70
❑ 82 Bryant Westbrook	.20	.09
❑ 83 Robert Brooks	.30	.14
❑ 84 LeRoy Butler	.20	.09
❑ 85 Mark Chmura	.30	.14
❑ 86 Brett Favre	2.00	.90
❑ 87 Antonio Freeman	.50	.23
❑ 88 Dorsey Levens	.50	.23
❑ 89 Eugene Robinson	.20	.09
❑ 90 Bill Schroeder RC	1.50	.70
❑ 91 Reggie White	.50	.23
❑ 92 Aaron Bailey	.20	.09
❑ 93 Quentin Coryatt	.20	.09
❑ 94 Zack Crockett	.20	.09
❑ 95 Sean Dawkins	.20	.09
❑ 96 Ken Dilger	.20	.09
❑ 97 Marshall Faulk	.60	.25
❑ 98 Jim Harbaugh	.30	.14
❑ 99 Marvin Harrison	.50	.23
❑ 100 Bryan Barker	.20	.09
❑ 101 Tony Boselli	.20	.09
❑ 102 Tony Brackens	.20	.09
❑ 103 Mark Brunell	.50	.23
❑ 104 Mike Hollis	.20	.09
❑ 105 Keenan McCardell	.30	.14
❑ 106 Natrone Means	.30	.14
❑ 107 Jimmy Smith	.30	.14
❑ 108 James Stewart	.30	.14
❑ 109 Marcus Allen	.50	.23
❑ 110 Kimble Anders	.30	.14
❑ 111 Dale Carter	.20	.09
❑ 112 Tony Gonzalez	.50	.23
❑ 113 Elvis Grbac	.30	.14
❑ 114 Greg Hill	.20	.09
❑ 115 Andre Rison	.30	.14
❑ 116 Will Shields	.20	.09
❑ 117 Derrick Thomas	.30	.14
❑ 118 Karim Abdul-Jabbar	.50	.23
❑ 119 Trace Armstrong	.20	.09
❑ 120 Damon Huard RC	2.00	.90
❑ 121 Charles Jordan	.20	.09
❑ 122 Dan Marino	2.00	.90
❑ 123 O.J. McDuffie	.30	.14
❑ 124 Irving Spikes	.20	.09
❑ 125 Zach Thomas	.50	.23
❑ 126 Cris Carter	.50	.23
❑ 127 Charles Woodson RC	2.00	.90
❑ 128 Brad Johnson	.50	.23
❑ 129 Randall McDaniel	.20	.09
❑ 130 John Randle	.30	.14
❑ 131 Jake Reed	.30	.14
❑ 132 Robert Smith	.50	.23
❑ 133 Todd Steussie	.20	.09
❑ 134 Bruce Armstrong	.20	.09
❑ 135 Drew Bledsoe	.75	.35
❑ 136 Ben Coates	.30	.14
❑ 137 Derrick Cullors RC	.20	.09
❑ 138 Terry Glenn	.50	.23
❑ 139 Shawn Jefferson	.20	.09
❑ 140 Curtis Martin	.50	.23
❑ 141 Chris Slade	.20	.09
❑ 142 Larry Whigham	.20	.09
❑ 143 Troy Davis	.20	.09
❑ 144 Andre Hastings	.20	.09
❑ 145 Randal Hill	.20	.09
❑ 146 Sammy Knight RC	.50	.23
❑ 147 William Roaf	.20	.09
❑ 148 Heath Shuler	.20	.09
❑ 149 Danny Wuerffel	.30	.14
❑ 150 Ray Zellars	.20	.09
❑ 151 Jessie Armstead	.20	.09
❑ 152 Tiki Barber	.50	.23
❑ 153 Chris Calloway	.20	.09
❑ 154 Danny Kanell	.30	.14
❑ 155 David Patten RC	1.50	.70
❑ 156 Michael Strahan	.30	.14
❑ 157 Charles Way	.20	.09
❑ 158 Tyrone Wheatley	.30	.14
❑ 159 Kyle Brady	.20	.09
❑ 160 Wayne Chrebet	.50	.23
❑ 161 Glenn Foley	.30	.14
❑ 162 Aaron Glenn	.20	.09
❑ 163 Leon Johnson	.20	.09
❑ 164 Adrian Murrell	.30	.14
❑ 165 Neil O'Donnell	.30	.14
❑ 166 Dedric Ward	.20	.09
❑ 167 Tim Brown	.50	.23
❑ 168 Rickey Dudley	.20	.09
❑ 169 Jeff George	.30	.14
❑ 170 Desmond Howard	.30	.14
❑ 171 James Jett	.30	.14
❑ 172 Napoleon Kaufman	.50	.23
❑ 173 Chester McGlockton	.20	.09
❑ 174 Darrell Russell	.20	.09
❑ 175 Ty Detmer	.30	.14
❑ 176 Irving Fryar	.30	.14
❑ 177 Charlie Garner	.30	.14
❑ 178 Bobby Hoying	.30	.14
❑ 179 Chad Lewis	.30	.14
❑ 180 Duce Staley	.60	.25
❑ 181 Kevin Turner	.20	.09
❑ 182 Ricky Watters	.30	.14
❑ 183 Jerome Bettis	.50	.23
❑ 184 Will Blackwell	.20	.09
❑ 185 Charles Johnson	.20	.09
❑ 186 George Jones	.20	.09
❑ 187 Levon Kirkland	.20	.09
❑ 188 Carnell Lake	.20	.09
❑ 189 Kordell Stewart	.50	.23
❑ 190 Yancey Thigpen	.20	.09
❑ 191 Tony Banks	.30	.14
❑ 192 Isaac Bruce	.50	.23
❑ 193 Ernie Conwell	.20	.09
❑ 194 Craig Heyward	.20	.09
❑ 195 Eddie Kennison	.30	.14
❑ 196 Amp Lee	.20	.09
❑ 197 Orlando Pace	.20	.09
❑ 198 Torrance Small	.20	.09
❑ 199 Gary Brown	.20	.09
❑ 200 Kenny Bynum RC	.20	.09
❑ 201 Freddie Jones	.20	.09
❑ 202 Tony Martin	.30	.14
❑ 203 Eric Metcalf	.20	.09
❑ 204 Junior Seau	.50	.23
❑ 205 Craig Whelihan RC	.20	.09
❑ 206 William Floyd	.20	.09
❑ 207 Merton Hanks	.20	.09
❑ 208 Garrison Hearst	.50	.23
❑ 209 Brent Jones	.20	.09
❑ 210 Terrell Owens	.50	.23
❑ 211 Jerry Rice	1.00	.45

❑ 212 J.J. Stokes	.30	.14
❑ 213 Rod Woodson	.30	.14
❑ 214 Steve Young	.50	.23
❑ 215 Steve Broussard	.20	.09
❑ 216 Joey Galloway	.30	.14
❑ 217 Cortez Kennedy	.20	.09
❑ 218 Jon Kitna	.50	.23
❑ 219 James McKnight	.50	.23
❑ 220 Warren Moon	.50	.23
❑ 221 Michael Sinclair	.20	.09
❑ 222 Ryan Leaf RC	1.25	.55
❑ 223 Darryl Williams	.20	.09
❑ 224 Mike Alstott	.50	.23
❑ 225 Reidel Anthony	.30	.14
❑ 226 Derrick Brooks	.50	.23
❑ 227 Horace Copeland	.20	.09
❑ 228 Trent Dilfer	.50	.23
❑ 229 Warrick Dunn	.50	.23
❑ 230 Hardy Nickerson	.20	.09
❑ 231 Warren Sapp	.30	.14
❑ 232 Karl Williams	.20	.09
❑ 233 Blaine Bishop	.20	.09
❑ 234 Willie Davis	.20	.09
❑ 235 Eddie George	.50	.23
❑ 236 Derrick Mason	.30	.14
❑ 237 Bruce Matthews	.20	.09
❑ 238 Steve McNair	.50	.23
❑ 239 Chris Sanders	.20	.09
❑ 240 Rodney Thomas	.20	.09
❑ 241 Frank Wycheck	.20	.09
❑ 242 Terry Allen	.50	.23
❑ 243 Jamie Asher	.20	.09
❑ 244 Larry Bowie	.20	.09
❑ 245 Albert Connell	.20	.09
❑ 246 Stephen Davis	.20	.09
❑ 247 Gus Frerotte	.20	.09
❑ 248 Ken Harvey	.20	.09
❑ 249 Leslie Shepherd	.20	.09
❑ 250 Michael Westbrook	.30	.14
❑ S1 Mark Brunell Sample	1.00	.45

1999 Paramount

	Nm-Mt	Ex-Mt
COMPLETE SET (250)	50.00	22.00
❑ 1 David Boston RC	1.25	.55
❑ 2 Larry Centers	.20	.09
❑ 3 Joel Makovicka RC	1.25	.55
❑ 4 Eric Metcalf	.20	.09
❑ 5 Rob Moore	.30	.14
❑ 6 Adrian Murrell	.30	.14
❑ 7 Jake Plummer	.30	.14
❑ 8 Frank Sanders	.30	.14
❑ 9 Aeneas Williams	.20	.09
❑ 10 Morten Andersen	.20	.09
❑ 11 Jamal Anderson	.50	.23
❑ 12 Chris Chandler	.30	.14
❑ 13 Tim Dwight	.50	.23
❑ 14 Terance Mathis	.30	.14
❑ 15 Jeff Paulk RC	.40	.18
❑ 16 O.J. Santiago	.20	.09
❑ 17 Chuck Smith	.20	.09
❑ 18 Peter Boulware	.20	.09
❑ 19 Priest Holmes	.75	.35
❑ 20 Michael Jackson	.20	.09
❑ 21 Jermaine Lewis	.30	.14
❑ 22 Ray Lewis	.50	.23
❑ 23 Michael McCrary	.20	.09
❑ 24 Bennie Thompson	.20	.09
❑ 25 Rod Woodson	.30	.14
❑ 26 Shawn Bryson RC	1.25	.55
❑ 27 Doug Flutie	.50	.23
❑ 28 Eric Moulds	.50	.23
❑ 29 Peerless Price RC	2.00	.90
❑ 30 Andre Reed	.30	.14
❑ 31 Jay Riemersma	.20	.09
❑ 32 Antowain Smith	.50	.23
❑ 33 Bruce Smith	.30	.14
❑ 34 Michael Bates	.20	.09
❑ 35 Steve Beuerlein	.20	.09
❑ 36 Tim Biakabutuka	.30	.14
❑ 37 Kevin Greene	.20	.09
❑ 38 Anthony Johnson	.20	.09
❑ 39 Fred Lane	.20	.09
❑ 40 Muhsin Muhammad	.30	.14
❑ 41 Wesley Walls	.30	.14
❑ 42 D'Wayne Bates RC	.75	.35
❑ 43 Edgar Bennett	.20	.09
❑ 44 Marty Booker RC	1.25	.55
❑ 45 Curtis Conway	.30	.14
❑ 46 Bobby Engram	.30	.14
❑ 47 Curtis Enis	.20	.09
❑ 48 Erik Kramer	.20	.09
❑ 49 Cade McNown RC	.75	.35
❑ 50 Jeff Blake	.30	.14
❑ 51 Scott Covington RC	1.25	.55
❑ 52 Corey Dillon	.50	.23
❑ 53 Quincy Jackson RC	.40	.18
❑ 54 Carl Pickens	.30	.14
❑ 55 Darnay Scott	.20	.09
❑ 56 Akili Smith RC	.75	.35
❑ 57 Craig Yeast RC	.75	.35
❑ 58 Jerry Ball	.20	.09
❑ 59 Darrin Chiaverini RC	.75	.35
❑ 60 Tim Couch RC	1.25	.55
❑ 61 Ty Detmer	.30	.14
❑ 62 Kevin Johnson RC	1.25	.55
❑ 63 Terry Kirby	.20	.09
❑ 64 Daylon McCutcheon RC	.40	.18
❑ 65 Irv Smith	.20	.09
❑ 66 Troy Aikman	1.00	.45
❑ 67 Ebenezer Ekuban RC	.75	.35
❑ 68 Michael Irvin	.30	.14
❑ 69 Daryl Johnston	.20	.09
❑ 70 Wane McGarity RC	.40	.18
❑ 71 Dat Nguyen RC	1.25	.55
❑ 72 Deion Sanders	.50	.23
❑ 73 Emmitt Smith	1.00	.45
❑ 74 Bubby Brister	.20	.09
❑ 75 Terrell Davis	.50	.23
❑ 76 Jason Elam	.20	.09
❑ 77 Olandis Gary RC	1.25	.55
❑ 78 Brian Griese	.50	.23
❑ 79 Ed McCaffrey	.30	.14
❑ 80 Travis McGriff RC	.40	.18
❑ 81 Shannon Sharpe	.30	.14
❑ 82 Rod Smith	.30	.14
❑ 83 Charlie Batch	.50	.23
❑ 84 Chris Claiborne RC	.40	.18
❑ 85 Germane Crowell	.20	.09
❑ 86 Sedrick Irvin RC	.40	.18
❑ 87 Herman Moore	.30	.14
❑ 88 Johnnie Morton	.30	.14
❑ 89 Barry Sanders	1.50	.70
❑ 90 Robert Brooks	.30	.14
❑ 91 Aaron Brooks RC	4.00	1.80
❑ 92 Mark Chmura	.20	.09
❑ 93 Brett Favre	1.50	.70
❑ 94 Antonio Freeman	.50	.23
❑ 95 Vonnie Holliday	.20	.09
❑ 96 Dorsey Levens	.50	.23
❑ 97 De'Mond Parker RC	.40	.18
❑ 98 Ken Dilger	.20	.09
❑ 99 Marvin Harrison	.50	.23
❑ 100 Edgerrin James RC	5.00	2.20
❑ 101 Peyton Manning	1.50	.70
❑ 102 Jerome Pathon	.20	.09
❑ 103 Mike Peterson RC	.75	.35
❑ 104 Marcus Pollard	.20	.09
❑ 105 Tavian Banks	.20	.09
❑ 106 Reggie Barlow	.20	.09
❑ 107 Tony Boselli	.20	.09
❑ 108 Mark Brunell	.50	.23
❑ 109 Keenan McCardell	.30	.14
❑ 110 Bryce Paup	.20	.09
❑ 111 Jimmy Smith	.30	.14
❑ 112 Fred Taylor	.50	.23
❑ 113 Dave Thomas RC	.20	.09
❑ 114 Kimble Anders	.30	.14
❑ 115 Donnell Bennett	.20	.09
❑ 116 Mike Cloud RC	.75	.35
❑ 117 Tony Gonzalez	.50	.23
❑ 118 Elvis Grbac	.30	.14
❑ 119 Larry Parker RC	1.25	.55
❑ 120 Andre Rison	.30	.14
❑ 121 Brian Shay RC	.40	.18
❑ 122 Karim Abdul-Jabbar	.30	.14
❑ 123 Oronde Gadsden	.30	.14
❑ 124 James Johnson RC	.75	.35
❑ 125 Rob Konrad RC	.75	.35
❑ 126 Dan Marino	1.50	.70
❑ 127 O.J. McDuffie	.30	.14
❑ 128 Zach Thomas	.50	.23
❑ 129 Cris Carter	.50	.23
❑ 130 Daunte Culpepper RC	5.00	2.20
❑ 131 Randall Cunningham	.50	.23
❑ 132 Matthew Hatchette	.20	.09
❑ 133 Leroy Hoard	.20	.09
❑ 134 Randy Moss	1.25	.55
❑ 135 John Randle	.30	.14
❑ 136 Jake Reed	.30	.14
❑ 137 Robert Smith	.50	.23
❑ 138 Michael Bishop RC	1.25	.55
❑ 139 Drew Bledsoe	.60	.25
❑ 140 Ben Coates	.30	.14
❑ 141 Kevin Faulk RC	1.25	.55
❑ 142 Terry Glenn	.50	.23
❑ 143 Shawn Jefferson	.20	.09
❑ 144 Andy Katzenmoyer RC	.75	.35
❑ 145 Tony Simmons	.20	.09
❑ 146 Cuncho Brown RC	.40	.18
❑ 147 Cam Cleeland	.20	.09
❑ 148 Mark Fields	.20	.09
❑ 149 La'Roi Glover RC	.50	.23
❑ 150 Andre Hastings	.20	.09
❑ 151 Billy Joe Hobert	.20	.09
❑ 152 William Roaf	.20	.09
❑ 153 Billy Joe Tolliver	.20	.09
❑ 154 Ricky Williams RC	2.50	1.10
❑ 155 Jessie Armstead	.20	.09
❑ 156 Tiki Barber	.30	.14
❑ 157 Gary Brown	.20	.09
❑ 158 Kent Graham	.20	.09
❑ 159 Ike Hilliard	.20	.09
❑ 160 Joe Montgomery RC	.75	.35
❑ 161 Amani Toomer	.20	.09
❑ 162 Charles Way	.20	.09
❑ 163 Wayne Chrebet	.30	.14
❑ 164 Bryan Cox	.20	.09
❑ 165 Aaron Glenn	.20	.09
❑ 166 Keyshawn Johnson	.50	.23
❑ 167 Leon Johnson	.20	.09
❑ 168 Curtis Martin	.50	.23
❑ 169 Vinny Testaverde	.30	.14
❑ 170 Dedric Ward	.20	.09
❑ 171 Tim Brown	.50	.23
❑ 172 Dameane Douglas RC	1.25	.55
❑ 173 Rickey Dudley	.20	.09
❑ 174 James Jett	.30	.14
❑ 175 Napoleon Kaufman	.50	.23
❑ 176 Darrell Russell	.20	.09
❑ 177 Harvey Williams	.20	.09
❑ 178 Charles Woodson	.50	.23
❑ 179 Na Brown RC	.75	.35
❑ 180 Hugh Douglas	.20	.09
❑ 181 Cecil Martin RC	.75	.35
❑ 182 Donovan McNabb RC	6.00	2.70
❑ 183 Duce Staley	.50	.23
❑ 184 Kevin Turner	.20	.09
❑ 185 Jerome Bettis	.50	.23
❑ 186 Troy Edwards RC	.75	.35
❑ 187 Jason Gildon	.20	.09
❑ 188 Courtney Hawkins	.20	.09
❑ 189 Malcolm Johnson RC	.40	.18
❑ 190 Kordell Stewart	.30	.14
❑ 191 Jerame Tuman RC	.75	.35
❑ 192 Amos Zereoue RC	1.25	.55
❑ 193 Isaac Bruce	.50	.23
❑ 194 Kevin Carter	.20	.09
❑ 195 Jeremaine Copeland RC	.40	.18
❑ 196 Joe Germaine RC	.75	.35
❑ 197 Az-Zahir Hakim	.20	.09
❑ 198 Torry Holt RC	3.00	1.35
❑ 199 Amp Lee	.20	.09
❑ 200 Ricky Proehl	.20	.09
❑ 201 Charlie Jones	.20	.09
❑ 202 Freddie Jones	.20	.09

❑ 203 Ryan Leaf .50 .23
❑ 204 Natrone Means .30 .14
❑ 205 Mikhael Ricks .20 .09
❑ 206 Junior Seau .50 .23
❑ 207 Bryan Still .20 .09
❑ 208 Garrison Hearst .30 .14
❑ 209 Terry Jackson RC .75 .35
❑ 210 R.W. McQuarters .20 .09
❑ 211 Ken Norton Jr. .20 .09
❑ 212 Terrell Owens .50 .23
❑ 213 Jerry Rice 1.00 .45
❑ 214 J.J. Stokes .30 .14
❑ 215 Tai Streets RC 1.25 .55
❑ 216 Steve Young .60 .25
❑ 217 Karsten Bailey RC .75 .35
❑ 218 Chad Brown .20 .09
❑ 219 Joey Galloway .30 .14
❑ 220 Ahman Green .50 .23
❑ 221 Brock Huard RC 1.25 .55
❑ 222 Cortez Kennedy .20 .09
❑ 223 Jon Kitna .50 .23
❑ 224 Shawn Springs .20 .09
❑ 225 Ricky Watters .30 .14
❑ 226 Mike Alstott .50 .23
❑ 227 Reidel Anthony .30 .14
❑ 228 Trent Dilfer .30 .14
❑ 229 Warrick Dunn .50 .23
❑ 230 Bert Emanuel .30 .14
❑ 231 Martin Gramatica RC .40 .18
❑ 232 Jacquez Green .20 .09
❑ 233 Shaun King RC .75 .35
❑ 234 Anthony McFarland RC 1.25 .55
❑ 235 Warren Sapp .30 .14
❑ 236 Willie Davis .20 .09
❑ 237 Kevin Dyson .30 .14
❑ 238 Eddie George .50 .23
❑ 239 Darran Hall RC .40 .18
❑ 240 Jackie Harris .20 .09
❑ 241 Steve McNair .50 .23
❑ 242 Yancey Thigpen .20 .09
❑ 243 Frank Wycheck .20 .09
❑ 244 Stephen Alexander .20 .09
❑ 245 Champ Bailey RC 1.50 .70
❑ 246 Stephen Davis .50 .23
❑ 247 Darrell Green .20 .09
❑ 248 Skip Hicks .20 .09
❑ 249 Brian Mitchell .20 .09
❑ 250 Michael Westbrook .30 .14

2000 Paramount

	Nm-Mt	Ex-Mt
COMPLETE SET (249)	40.00	18.00

❑ 1 David Boston .50 .23
❑ 2 Thomas Jones RC 1.25 .55
❑ 3 Rob Moore .30 .14
❑ 4 Jake Plummer .30 .14
❑ 5 Simeon Rice .30 .14
❑ 6 Frank Sanders .30 .14
❑ 7 Raynoch Thompson RC .30 .14
❑ 8 Jamal Anderson .50 .23
❑ 9 Chris Chandler .30 .14
❑ 10 Bob Christian .20 .09
❑ 11 Tim Dwight .50 .23
❑ 12 Byron Hanspard .20 .09
❑ 13 Terance Mathis .30 .14
❑ 14 Mareno Philyaw RC .60 .25
❑ 15 Tony Banks .30 .14
❑ 16 Priest Holmes .60 .25
❑ 17 Qadry Ismail .30 .14
❑ 18 Pat Johnson .20 .09
❑ 19 Jamal Lewis RC 2.00 .90
❑ 20 Chris Redman RC .60 .25
❑ 21 Shannon Sharpe .30 .14
❑ 22 Travis Taylor RC .75 .35
❑ 23 Erik Flowers RC 1.00 .45
❑ 24 Doug Flutie .50 .23
❑ 25 Rob Johnson .30 .14
❑ 26 Jonathan Linton .20 .09
❑ 27 Corey Moore RC .60 .25
❑ 28 Eric Moulds .50 .23
❑ 29 Peerless Price .50 .23
❑ 30 Jay Riemersma .20 .09
❑ 31 Antowain Smith .30 .14
❑ 32 Rashard Anderson RC .60 .25
❑ 33 Steve Beuerlein .30 .14
❑ 34 Tim Biakabutuka .30 .14
❑ 35 Donald Hayes .20 .09
❑ 36 Patrick Jeffers .50 .23
❑ 37 Jeff Lewis .20 .09
❑ 38 Muhsin Muhammad .30 .14
❑ 39 Wesley Walls .20 .09
❑ 40 Bobby Engram .30 .14
❑ 41 Curtis Enis .20 .09
❑ 42 Cade McNown .20 .09
❑ 43 Jim Miller .20 .09
❑ 44 Marcus Robinson .50 .23
❑ 45 Brian Urlacher RC 3.00 1.35
❑ 46 Dez White RC .75 .35
❑ 47 Michael Basnight .20 .09
❑ 48 Corey Dillon .50 .23
❑ 49 Ron Dugans RC .60 .25
❑ 50 Willie Jackson .20 .09
❑ 51 Darnay Scott .30 .14
❑ 52 Akili Smith .20 .09
❑ 53 Peter Warrick RC .75 .35
❑ 54 Courtney Brown RC .75 .35
❑ 55 Darrin Chiaverini .20 .09
❑ 56 Tim Couch .30 .14
❑ 57 Kevin Johnson .50 .23
❑ 58 Terry Kirby .20 .09
❑ 59 Dennis Northcutt RC .75 .35
❑ 60 Travis Prentice RC .60 .25
❑ 61 Leslie Shepherd .20 .09
❑ 62 Troy Aikman 1.00 .45
❑ 63 Joey Galloway .30 .14
❑ 64 Rocket Ismail .30 .14
❑ 65 David LaFleur .20 .09
❑ 66 Emmitt Smith 1.00 .45
❑ 67 Jason Tucker .20 .09
❑ 68 Chris Warren .20 .09
❑ 69 Michael Wiley RC .60 .25
❑ 70 Desmond Clark .30 .14
❑ 71 Chris Cole RC .60 .25
❑ 72 Terrell Davis .50 .23
❑ 73 Olandis Gary .50 .23
❑ 74 Brian Griese .50 .23
❑ 75 Jarious Jackson RC .60 .25
❑ 76 Ed McCaffrey .50 .23
❑ 77 Deltha O'Neal RC .75 .35
❑ 78 Rod Smith .30 .14
❑ 79 Charlie Batch .50 .23
❑ 80 Germane Crowell .20 .09
❑ 81 Reuben Droughns RC 1.00 .45
❑ 82 Terry Fair .20 .09
❑ 83 Herman Moore .30 .14
❑ 84 Johnnie Morton .30 .14
❑ 85 Barry Sanders 1.25 .55
❑ 86 James Stewart .30 .14
❑ 87 Corey Bradford .30 .14
❑ 88 Tyrone Davis .20 .09
❑ 89 Brett Favre 1.50 .70
❑ 90 Bubba Franks RC .75 .35
❑ 91 Antonio Freeman .50 .23
❑ 92 Matt Hasselbeck .30 .14
❑ 93 Dorsey Levens .30 .14
❑ 94 Anthony Lucas RC .60 .25
❑ 95 Bill Schroeder .30 .14
❑ 96 Ken Dilger .20 .09
❑ 97 E.G. Green .20 .09
❑ 98 Marvin Harrison .50 .23
❑ 99 Edgerrin James .75 .35
❑ 100 Peyton Manning 1.25 .55
❑ 101 Jerome Pathon .30 .14
❑ 102 Marcus Washington RC .75 .35
❑ 103 Terrence Wilkins .20 .09
❑ 104 Kyle Brady .20 .09
❑ 105 Mark Brunell .50 .23
❑ 106 Kevin Hardy .20 .09
❑ 107 Keenan McCardell .30 .14
❑ 108 Jimmy Smith .30 .14
❑ 109 R.Jay Soward RC .60 .25
❑ 110 Shyrone Stith RC .60 .25
❑ 111 Fred Taylor .50 .23
❑ 112 Alvis Whitted .20 .09
❑ 113 Derrick Alexander .30 .14
❑ 114 Kimble Anders .20 .09
❑ 115 Donnell Bennett .20 .09
❑ 116 Tony Gonzalez .30 .14
❑ 117 Elvis Grbac .30 .14
❑ 118 Kevin Lockett .20 .09
❑ 119 Sylvester Morris RC .60 .25
❑ 120 Tony Richardson RC .30 .14
❑ 121 Deon Dyer RC .60 .25
❑ 122 Oronde Gadsden .30 .14
❑ 123 Damon Huard .50 .23
❑ 124 James Johnson .20 .09
❑ 125 Dan Marino 1.50 .70
❑ 126 Tony Martin .30 .14
❑ 127 O.J. McDuffie .30 .14
❑ 128 Zach Thomas .50 .23
❑ 129 Cris Carter .50 .23
❑ 130 Daunte Culpepper .60 .25
❑ 131 Leroy Hoard .20 .09
❑ 132 Chris Hovan RC .60 .25
❑ 133 Randy Moss 1.00 .45
❑ 134 John Randle .30 .14
❑ 135 Robert Smith .50 .23
❑ 136 Troy Walters RC .75 .35
❑ 137 Drew Bledsoe .60 .25
❑ 138 Tom Brady RC 20.00 9.00
❑ 139 Troy Brown .30 .14
❑ 140 Kevin Faulk .20 .09
❑ 141 Terry Glenn .30 .14
❑ 142 J.R. Redmond RC .60 .25
❑ 143 Tony Simmons .20 .09
❑ 144 David Stachelski RC .60 .25
❑ 145 Jeff Blake .30 .14
❑ 146 Marc Bulger RC 1.50 .70
❑ 147 Cam Cleeland .20 .09
❑ 148 Sherrod Gideon RC .60 .25
❑ 149 Darren Howard RC .60 .25
❑ 150 Chad Morton RC .75 .35
❑ 151 Keith Poole .20 .09
❑ 152 Ricky Williams .50 .23
❑ 153 Tiki Barber .30 .14
❑ 154 Kerry Collins .30 .14
❑ 155 Ron Dayne RC .75 .35
❑ 156 Ike Hilliard .30 .14
❑ 157 Joe Jurevicius .20 .09
❑ 158 Pete Mitchell .20 .09
❑ 159 Joe Montgomery .20 .09
❑ 160 Amani Toomer .30 .14
❑ 161 John Abraham RC .75 .35
❑ 162 Anthony Becht RC .75 .35
❑ 163 Wayne Chrebet .30 .14
❑ 164 Laveranues Coles RC 1.00 .45
❑ 165 Ray Lucas .30 .14
❑ 166 Curtis Martin .50 .23
❑ 167 Chad Pennington RC 3.00 1.35
❑ 168 Vinny Testaverde .30 .14
❑ 169 Dedric Ward .20 .09
❑ 170 Tim Brown .50 .23
❑ 171 Rich Gannon .50 .23
❑ 172 Bobby Hoying .30 .14
❑ 173 James Jett .20 .09
❑ 174 Napoleon Kaufman .30 .14
❑ 175 Jerry Porter RC 1.00 .45
❑ 176 Tyrone Wheatley .30 .14
❑ 177 Charles Woodson .50 .23
❑ 178 Dameane Douglas .20 .09
❑ 179 Charles Johnson .30 .14
❑ 180 Donovan McNabb .75 .35
❑ 181 Todd Pinkston RC .75 .35
❑ 182 Gari Scott RC .60 .25
❑ 183 Torrance Small .20 .09
❑ 184 Duce Staley .50 .23
❑ 185 Jerome Bettis .50 .23
❑ 186 Plaxico Burress RC 1.50 .70
❑ 187 Troy Edwards .20 .09
❑ 188 Danny Farmer RC .60 .25
❑ 189 Richard Huntley .20 .09
❑ 190 Tee Martin RC .75 .35
❑ 191 Kordell Stewart .30 .14
❑ 192 Hines Ward .50 .23
❑ 193 Isaac Bruce .50 .23
❑ 194 Trung Canidate RC .60 .25

Card	NM	Ex
❑ 195 Marshall Faulk	.60	.25
❑ 196 Az-Zahir Hakim	.30	.14
❑ 197 Torry Holt	.50	.23
❑ 198 Tony Horne	.20	.09
❑ 199 Ricky Proehl	.20	.09
❑ 200 Kurt Warner	1.00	.45
❑ 201 Jermaine Fazande	.20	.09
❑ 202 Trevor Gaylor RC	.60	.25
❑ 203 Jeff Graham	.20	.09
❑ 204 Jim Harbaugh	.30	.14
❑ 205 Freddie Jones	.20	.09
❑ 206 Mikhael Ricks	.20	.09
❑ 207 Junior Seau	.50	.23
❑ 208 Fred Beasley	.20	.09
❑ 209 Giovanni Carmazzi RC	.60	.25
❑ 210 Jeff Garcia	.50	.23
❑ 211 Charlie Garner	.30	.14
❑ 212 Terrell Owens	.50	.23
❑ 213 Tim Rattay RC	1.50	.70
❑ 214 Jerry Rice	1.00	.45
❑ 215 J.J. Stokes	.30	.14
❑ 216 Steve Young	.60	.25
❑ 217 Shaun Alexander RC	2.00	.90
❑ 218 Sean Dawkins	.20	.09
❑ 219 Darrell Jackson RC	1.50	.70
❑ 220 Jon Kitna	.50	.23
❑ 221 Derrick Mayes	.30	.14
❑ 222 Charlie Rogers	.20	.09
❑ 223 Shawn Springs	.20	.09
❑ 224 Ricky Watters	.30	.14
❑ 225 Mike Alstott	.50	.23
❑ 226 Reidel Anthony	.20	.09
❑ 227 Warrick Dunn	.50	.23
❑ 228 Jacquez Green	.20	.09
❑ 229 Joe Hamilton RC	.60	.25
❑ 230 Keyshawn Johnson	.50	.23
❑ 231 Shaun King	.20	.09
❑ 232 Warren Sapp	.30	.14
❑ 233 Keith Bulluck RC	.75	.35
❑ 234 Kevin Dyson	.30	.14
❑ 235 Eddie George	.50	.23
❑ 236 Jevon Kearse	.50	.23
❑ 237 Erron Kinney RC	.75	.35
❑ 238 Steve McNair	.50	.23
❑ 239 Neil O'Donnell	.20	.09
❑ 240 Yancy Thigpen	.20	.09
❑ 241 Frank Wycheck	.20	.09
❑ 243 Champ Bailey	.30	.14
❑ 244 Larry Centers	.20	.09
❑ 245 Albert Connell	.20	.09
❑ 246 Stephen Davis	.50	.23
❑ 247 Todd Husak RC	.75	.35
❑ 248 Brad Johnson	.50	.23
❑ 249 Chris Samuels RC	.60	.25
❑ 250 Michael Westbrook	.30	.14

1964 Philadelphia

	NM	Ex
COMPLETE SET (198)	900.00	400.00
WRAPPER (1-CENT)	40.00	18.00
WRAPPER (5-CENT)	20.00	9.00
❑ 1 Raymond Berry	20.00	9.00
❑ 2 Tom Gilburg	2.50	1.10
❑ 3 John Mackey RC	30.00	13.50
❑ 4 Gino Marchetti	5.00	2.20
❑ 5 Jim Martin	2.50	1.10
❑ 6 Tom Matte RC	6.00	2.70
❑ 7 Jimmy Orr	3.00	1.35
❑ 8 Jim Parker	4.00	1.80
❑ 9 Bill Pellington	2.50	1.10
❑ 10 Alex Sandusky	2.50	1.10
❑ 11 Dick Szymanski	2.50	1.10
❑ 12 John Unitas	45.00	20.00
❑ 13 Baltimore Colts Team Card	3.00	1.35
❑ 14 Baltimore Colts Play Card (Don Shula)	35.00	16.00
❑ 15 Doug Atkins	5.00	2.20
❑ 16 Ronnie Bull	2.50	1.10
❑ 17 Mike Ditka	40.00	18.00
❑ 18 Joe Fortunato	2.50	1.10
❑ 19 Willie Galimore	3.00	1.35
❑ 20 Joe Marconi	2.50	1.10
❑ 21 Bennie McRae RC	2.50	1.10
❑ 22 Johnny Morris	2.50	1.10
❑ 23 Richie Petitbon	2.50	1.10
❑ 24 Mike Pyle	2.50	1.10
❑ 25 Roosevelt Taylor RC	4.00	1.80
❑ 26 Bill Wade	3.00	1.35
❑ 27 Chicago Bears Team Card	3.00	1.35
❑ 28 Chicago Bears Play Card (George Halas)	12.00	5.50
❑ 29 Johnny Brewer	2.50	1.10
❑ 30 Jim Brown	90.00	40.00
❑ 31 Gary Collins RC	8.00	3.60
❑ 32 Vince Costello	2.50	1.10
❑ 33 Galen Fiss	2.50	1.10
❑ 34 Bill Glass	2.50	1.10
❑ 35 Ernie Green RC	3.00	1.35
❑ 36 Rich Kreitling	2.50	1.10
❑ 37 John Morrow	2.50	1.10
❑ 38 Frank Ryan	3.00	1.35
❑ 39 Charlie Scales RC	2.50	1.10
❑ 40 Dick Schafrath RC	2.50	1.10
❑ 41 Cleveland Browns Team Card	3.00	1.35
❑ 42 Cleveland Browns Play Card (Blanton Collier)	2.50	1.10
❑ 43 Don Bishop	2.50	1.10
❑ 44 Frank Clarke RC	3.00	1.35
❑ 45 Mike Connelly	2.50	1.10
❑ 46 Lee Folkins	2.50	1.10
❑ 47 Cornell Green RC	8.00	3.60
❑ 48 Bob Lilly	40.00	18.00
❑ 49 Amos Marsh	2.50	1.10
❑ 50 Tommy McDonald	5.00	2.20
❑ 51 Don Meredith	35.00	16.00
❑ 52 Pettis Norman RC	3.00	1.35
❑ 53 Don Perkins	4.00	1.80
❑ 54 Guy Reese	2.50	1.10
❑ 55 Dallas Cowboys Team Card	3.00	1.35
❑ 56 Dallas Cowboys Play Card (Tom Landry)	20.00	9.00
❑ 57 Terry Barr	2.50	1.10
❑ 58 Roger Brown	3.00	1.35
❑ 59 Gail Cogdill	2.50	1.10
❑ 60 John Gordy	2.50	1.10
❑ 61 Dick Lane	4.00	1.80
❑ 62 Yale Lary	4.00	1.80
❑ 63 Dan Lewis	2.50	1.10
❑ 64 Darris McCord	2.50	1.10
❑ 65 Earl Morrall	3.00	1.35
❑ 66 Joe Schmidt	5.00	2.20
❑ 67 Pat Studstill RC	3.00	1.35
❑ 68 Wayne Walker RC	3.00	1.35
❑ 69 Detroit Lions Team Card	3.00	1.35
❑ 70 Detroit Lions Play Card (George Wilson CO)	2.50	1.10
❑ 71 Herb Adderley RC	35.00	16.00
❑ 72 Willie Davis RC	30.00	13.50
❑ 73 Forrest Gregg	5.00	2.20
❑ 74 Paul Hornung	35.00	16.00
❑ 75 Hank Jordan	5.00	2.20
❑ 76 Jerry Kramer	6.00	2.70
❑ 77 Tom Moore	3.00	1.35
❑ 78 Jim Ringo UER (Green Bay on front& Philadelphia on back)	5.00	2.20
❑ 79 Bart Starr	60.00	27.00
❑ 80 Jim Taylor	25.00	11.00
❑ 81 Jesse Whittenton RC	3.00	1.35
❑ 82 Willie Wood	8.00	3.60
❑ 83 Green Bay Packers Team Card	6.00	2.70
❑ 84 Green Bay Packers Play Card (Vince Lombardi)	35.00	16.00
❑ 85 Jon Arnett	2.50	1.10
❑ 86 Pervis Atkins RC	2.50	1.10
❑ 87 Dick Bass	3.00	1.35
❑ 88 Carroll Dale	4.00	1.80
❑ 89 Roman Gabriel	6.00	2.70
❑ 90 Ed Meador	2.50	1.10
❑ 91 Merlin Olsen RC	50.00	22.00
❑ 92 Jack Pardee RC	4.00	1.80
❑ 93 Jim Phillips	2.50	1.10
❑ 94 Carver Shannon	2.50	1.10
❑ 95 Frank Varrichione	2.50	1.10
❑ 96 Danny Villanueva	2.50	1.10
❑ 97 Los Angeles Rams Team Card	3.00	1.35
❑ 98 Los Angeles Rams Play Card (Harland Svare)	2.50	1.10
❑ 99 Grady Alderman RC	3.00	1.35
❑ 100 Larry Bowie	2.50	1.10
❑ 101 Bill Brown RC	6.00	2.70
❑ 102 Paul Flatley RC	2.50	1.10
❑ 103 Rip Hawkins	2.50	1.10
❑ 104 Jim Marshall	8.00	3.60
❑ 105 Tommy Mason	3.00	1.35
❑ 106 Jim Prestel	2.50	1.10
❑ 107 Jerry Reichow	2.50	1.10
❑ 108 Ed Sharockman	2.50	1.10
❑ 109 Fran Tarkenton	35.00	16.00
❑ 110 Mick Tingelhoff RC	6.00	2.70
❑ 111 Minnesota Vikings Team Card	3.00	1.35
❑ 112 Minnesota Vikings Play Card (Norm Van Brocklin)	4.00	1.80
❑ 113 Erich Barnes	2.50	1.10
❑ 114 Roosevelt Brown	4.00	1.80
❑ 115 Don Chandler	2.50	1.10
❑ 116 Darrell Dess	2.50	1.10
❑ 117 Frank Gifford	35.00	16.00
❑ 118 Dick James	2.50	1.10
❑ 119 Jim Katcavage	2.50	1.10
❑ 120 John Lovetere	2.50	1.10
❑ 121 Dick Lynch RC	3.00	1.35
❑ 122 Jim Patton	2.50	1.10
❑ 123 Del Shofner	2.50	1.10
❑ 124 Y.A. Tittle	20.00	9.00
❑ 125 New York Giants Team Card	3.00	1.35
❑ 126 New York Giants Play Card (Allie Sherman)	2.50	1.10
❑ 127 Sam Baker	2.50	1.10
❑ 128 Maxie Baughan	2.50	1.10
❑ 129 Timmy Brown	3.00	1.35
❑ 130 Mike Clark	2.50	1.10
❑ 131 Irv Cross RC	3.00	1.35
❑ 132 Ted Dean	2.50	1.10
❑ 133 Ron Goodwin	2.50	1.10
❑ 134 King Hill	2.50	1.10
❑ 135 Clarence Peaks	2.50	1.10
❑ 136 Pete Retzlaff	3.00	1.35
❑ 137 Jim Schrader	2.50	1.10
❑ 138 Norm Snead	3.00	1.35
❑ 139 Philadelphia Eagles Team Card	3.00	1.35
❑ 140 Philadelphia Eagles Play Card (Nick Skorich)	2.50	1.10
❑ 141 Gary Ballman RC	2.50	1.10
❑ 142 Charley Bradshaw RC	2.50	1.10
❑ 143 Ed Brown	3.00	1.35
❑ 144 John Henry Johnson	4.00	1.80
❑ 145 Joe Krupa	2.50	1.10
❑ 146 Bill Mack	2.50	1.10
❑ 147 Lou Michaels	2.50	1.10
❑ 148 Buzz Nutter	2.50	1.10
❑ 149 Myron Pottios	2.50	1.10
❑ 150 John Reger	2.50	1.10
❑ 151 Mike Sandusky	2.50	1.10
❑ 152 Clendon Thomas	2.50	1.10
❑ 153 Pittsburgh Steelers	3.00	1.35

Team Card
- ❑ 154 Pittsburgh Steelers Play Card (Buddy Parker) 2.50 1.10
- ❑ 155 Kermit Alexander RC 3.00 1.35
- ❑ 156 Bernie Casey 3.00 1.35
- ❑ 157 Dan Colchico 2.50 1.10
- ❑ 158 Clyde Conner 2.50 1.10
- ❑ 159 Tommy Davis 2.50 1.10
- ❑ 160 Matt Hazeltine 2.50 1.10
- ❑ 161 Jim Johnson RC 20.00 6.75
- ❑ 162 Don Lisbon RC 2.50 1.10
- ❑ 163 Lamar McHan 2.50 1.10
- ❑ 164 Bob St. Clair 4.00 1.80
- ❑ 165 J.D. Smith 2.50 1.10
- ❑ 166 Abe Woodson 2.50 1.10
- ❑ 167 San Francisco 49ers Team Card 3.00 1.35
- ❑ 168 San Francisco 49ers Play Card (Red Hickey) 2.50 1.10
- ❑ 169 Garland Boyette UER (Photo on front is not Boyette) 2.50 1.10
- ❑ 170 Bobby Joe Conrad 3.00 1.35
- ❑ 171 Bob DeMarco RC 2.50 1.10
- ❑ 172 Ken Gray RC 2.50 1.10
- ❑ 173 Jimmy Hill 2.50 1.10
- ❑ 174 Charlie Johnson UER (Misspelled Charley on both sides) 3.00 1.35
- ❑ 175 Ernie McMillan 2.50 1.10
- ❑ 176 Dale Meinert 2.50 1.10
- ❑ 177 Luke Owens 2.50 1.10
- ❑ 178 Sonny Randle 2.50 1.10
- ❑ 179 Joe Robb 2.50 1.10
- ❑ 180 Bill Stacy 2.50 1.10
- ❑ 181 St. Louis Cardinals Team Card 3.00 1.35
- ❑ 182 St. Louis Cardinals Play Card (Wally Lemm) 2.50 1.10
- ❑ 183 Bill Barnes 2.50 1.10
- ❑ 184 Don Bosseler 2.50 1.10
- ❑ 185 Sam Huff 6.00 2.70
- ❑ 186 Sonny Jurgensen 20.00 9.00
- ❑ 187 Bob Khayat 2.50 1.10
- ❑ 188 Riley Mattson 2.50 1.10
- ❑ 189 Bobby Mitchell 6.00 2.70
- ❑ 190 John Nisby 2.50 1.10
- ❑ 191 Vince Promuto 2.50 1.10
- ❑ 192 Joe Rutgens 2.50 1.10
- ❑ 193 Lonnie Sanders 2.50 1.10
- ❑ 194 Jim Steffen 2.50 1.10
- ❑ 195 Washington Redskins Team Card 3.00 1.35
- ❑ 196 Washington Redskins Play Card (Bill McPeak) 2.50 1.10
- ❑ 197 Checklist 1 UER (Dated 1963) 30.00 13.50
- ❑ 198 Checklist 2 UER (Dated 1963& 174 Charley Johnson should be Charlie) 55.00 25.00

1965 Philadelphia

	NM	Ex
COMPLETE SET (198)	800.00	350.00
WRAPPER (5-CENT)	20.00	9.00

- ❑ 1 Baltimore Colts Team Card 15.00 6.75
- ❑ 2 Raymond Berry 10.00 4.50
- ❑ 3 Bob Boyd 2.00 .90
- ❑ 4 Wendell Harris 2.00 .90
- ❑ 5 Jerry Logan 2.00 .90
- ❑ 6 Tony Lorick 2.00 .90
- ❑ 7 Lou Michaels 2.00 .90
- ❑ 8 Lenny Moore 8.00 3.60
- ❑ 9 Jimmy Orr 3.00 1.35
- ❑ 10 Jim Parker 4.00 1.80
- ❑ 11 Dick Szymanski 2.00 .90
- ❑ 12 John Unitas 40.00 18.00
- ❑ 13 Bob Vogel RC 2.00 .90
- ❑ 14 Baltimore Colts Play Card (Don Shula) 20.00 9.00
- ❑ 15 Chicago Bears Team Card 3.00 1.35
- ❑ 16 Jon Arnett 2.00 .90
- ❑ 17 Doug Atkins 5.00 2.20
- ❑ 18 Rudy Bukich RC 3.00 1.35
- ❑ 19 Mike Ditka 40.00 18.00
- ❑ 20 Dick Evey 2.00 .90
- ❑ 21 Joe Fortunato 2.00 .90
- ❑ 22 Bobby Joe Green RC 2.00 .90
- ❑ 23 Johnny Morris 2.00 .90
- ❑ 24 Mike Pyle 2.00 .90
- ❑ 25 Roosevelt Taylor 3.00 1.35
- ❑ 26 Bill Wade 3.00 1.35
- ❑ 27 Bob Wetoska 2.00 .90
- ❑ 28 Chicago Bears Play Card (George Halas) 8.00 3.60
- ❑ 29 Cleveland Browns Team Card 3.00 1.35
- ❑ 30 Walter Beach 2.00 .90
- ❑ 31 Jim Brown 80.00 34.00
- ❑ 32 Gary Collins 3.00 1.35
- ❑ 33 Bill Glass 2.00 .90
- ❑ 34 Ernie Green 2.00 .90
- ❑ 35 Jim Houston RC 2.00 .90
- ❑ 36 Dick Modzelewski 2.00 .90
- ❑ 37 Bernie Parrish 2.00 .90
- ❑ 38 Walter Roberts 2.00 .90
- ❑ 39 Frank Ryan 3.00 1.35
- ❑ 40 Dick Schafrath 2.00 .90
- ❑ 41 Paul Warfield RC 90.00 40.00
- ❑ 42 Cleveland Browns Play Card (Blanton Collier) 2.00 .90
- ❑ 43 Dallas Cowboys Team Card UER (Cowboys Dallas on back) 3.00 1.35
- ❑ 44 Frank Clarke 3.00 1.35
- ❑ 45 Mike Connelly 2.00 .90
- ❑ 46 Buddy Dial 2.00 .90
- ❑ 47 Bob Lilly 35.00 16.00
- ❑ 48 Tony Liscio RC 2.00 .90
- ❑ 49 Tommy McDonald 5.00 2.20
- ❑ 50 Don Meredith 25.00 11.00
- ❑ 51 Pettis Norman 2.00 .90
- ❑ 52 Don Perkins 4.00 1.80
- ❑ 53 Mel Renfro RC 40.00 18.00
- ❑ 54 Jim Ridlon 2.00 .90
- ❑ 55 Jerry Tubbs 2.00 .90
- ❑ 56 Dallas Cowboys Play Card (Tom Landry) 15.00 6.75
- ❑ 57 Detroit Lions Team Card 3.00 1.35
- ❑ 58 Terry Barr 2.00 .90
- ❑ 59 Roger Brown 2.00 .90
- ❑ 60 Gail Cogdill 2.00 .90
- ❑ 61 Jim Gibbons 2.00 .90
- ❑ 62 John Gordy 2.00 .90
- ❑ 63 Yale Lary 4.00 1.80
- ❑ 64 Dick LeBeau RC 3.00 1.35
- ❑ 65 Earl Morrall 3.00 1.35
- ❑ 66 Nick Pietrosante 2.00 .90
- ❑ 67 Pat Studstill 2.00 .90
- ❑ 68 Wayne Walker 3.00 1.35
- ❑ 69 Tom Watkins 2.00 .90
- ❑ 70 Detroit Lions Play Card (Harry Gilmer CO) 3.00 1.35
- ❑ 71 Green Bay Packers Team Card 6.00 2.70
- ❑ 72 Herb Adderley 8.00 3.60
- ❑ 73 Willie Davis 8.00 3.60
- ❑ 74 Boyd Dowler 4.00 1.80
- ❑ 75 Forrest Gregg 5.00 2.20
- ❑ 76 Paul Hornung 35.00 16.00
- ❑ 77 Hank Jordan 5.00 2.20
- ❑ 78 Tom Moore 3.00 1.35
- ❑ 79 Ray Nitschke 20.00 9.00
- ❑ 80 Elijah Pitts RC 8.00 3.60
- ❑ 81 Bart Starr 50.00 22.00
- ❑ 82 Jim Taylor 20.00 9.00
- ❑ 83 Willie Wood 6.00 2.70
- ❑ 84 Green Bay Packers Play Card (Vince Lombardi) 20.00 9.00
- ❑ 85 Los Angeles Rams Team Card 3.00 1.35
- ❑ 86 Dick Bass 3.00 1.35
- ❑ 87 Roman Gabriel 5.00 2.20
- ❑ 88 Roosevelt Grier 4.00 1.80
- ❑ 89 Deacon Jones 10.00 4.50
- ❑ 90 Lamar Lundy RC 4.00 1.80
- ❑ 91 Marlin McKeever 2.00 .90
- ❑ 92 Ed Meador 2.00 .90
- ❑ 93 Bill Munson RC 4.00 1.80
- ❑ 94 Merlin Olsen 15.00 6.75
- ❑ 95 Bobby Smith 2.00 .90
- ❑ 96 Frank Varrichione 2.00 .90
- ❑ 97 Ben Wilson 2.00 .90
- ❑ 98 Los Angeles Rams Play Card (Harland Svare) 2.00 .90
- ❑ 99 Minnesota Vikings Team Card 3.00 1.35
- ❑ 100 Grady Alderman 2.00 .90
- ❑ 101 Hal Bedsole RC 2.00 .90
- ❑ 102 Bill Brown 3.00 1.35
- ❑ 103 Bill Butler 2.00 .90
- ❑ 104 Fred Cox RC 3.00 1.35
- ❑ 105 Carl Eller RC 30.00 13.50
- ❑ 106 Paul Flatley 2.00 .90
- ❑ 107 Jim Marshall 6.00 2.70
- ❑ 108 Tommy Mason 2.00 .90
- ❑ 109 George Rose 2.00 .90
- ❑ 110 Fran Tarkenton 25.00 11.00
- ❑ 111 Mick Tingelhoff 3.00 1.35
- ❑ 112 Minnesota Vikings Play Card (Norm Van Brocklin) 4.00 1.80
- ❑ 113 New York Giants Team Card 3.00 1.35
- ❑ 114 Erich Barnes 2.00 .90
- ❑ 115 Roosevelt Brown 4.00 1.80
- ❑ 116 Clarence Childs 2.00 .90
- ❑ 117 Jerry Hillebrand 2.00 .90
- ❑ 118 Greg Larson RC 2.00 .90
- ❑ 119 Dick Lynch 2.00 .90
- ❑ 120 Joe Morrison RC 4.00 1.80
- ❑ 121 Lou Slaby 2.00 .90
- ❑ 122 Aaron Thomas RC 2.00 .90
- ❑ 123 Steve Thurlow 2.00 .90
- ❑ 124 Ernie Wheelwright RC 2.00 .90
- ❑ 125 Gary Wood RC 3.00 1.35
- ❑ 126 New York Giants Play Card (Allie Sherman) 2.00 .90
- ❑ 127 Philadelphia Eagles Team Card 3.00 1.35
- ❑ 128 Sam Baker 2.00 .90
- ❑ 129 Maxie Baughan 2.00 .90
- ❑ 130 Timmy Brown 3.00 1.35
- ❑ 131 Jack Concannon RC 2.00 .90
- ❑ 132 Irv Cross 3.00 1.35
- ❑ 133 Earl Gros 2.00 .90
- ❑ 134 Dave Lloyd 2.00 .90
- ❑ 135 Floyd Peters RC 2.00 .90
- ❑ 136 Nate Ramsey 2.00 .90
- ❑ 137 Pete Retzlaff 3.00 1.35
- ❑ 138 Jim Ringo 4.00 1.80
- ❑ 139 Norm Snead 4.00 1.80
- ❑ 140 Philadelphia Eagles Play Card (Joe Kuharich) 2.00 .90
- ❑ 141 Pittsburgh Steelers Team Card 3.00 1.35
- ❑ 142 John Baker 2.00 .90
- ❑ 143 Gary Ballman 2.00 .90
- ❑ 144 Charley Bradshaw 2.00 .90

Card	NM	Ex
❑ 145 Ed Brown	2.00	.90
❑ 146 Dick Haley	2.00	.90
❑ 147 John Henry Johnson	4.00	1.80
❑ 148 Brady Keys	2.00	.90
❑ 149 Ray Lemek	2.00	.90
❑ 150 Ben McGee	2.00	.90
❑ 151 Clarence Peaks	2.00	.90
❑ 152 Myron Pottios	2.00	.90
❑ 153 Clendon Thomas	2.00	.90
❑ 154 Pittsburgh Steelers Play Card (Buddy Parker)	2.00	.90
❑ 155 St. Louis Cardinals Team Card	3.00	1.35
❑ 156 Jim Bakken RC	3.00	1.35
❑ 157 Joe Childress	2.00	.90
❑ 158 Bobby Joe Conrad	3.00	1.35
❑ 159 Bob DeMarco	2.00	.90
❑ 160 Pat Fischer RC	4.00	1.80
❑ 161 Irv Goode	2.00	.90
❑ 162 Ken Gray	2.00	.90
❑ 163 Charlie Johnson UER (Misspelled Charley on both sides)	3.00	1.35
❑ 164 Bill Koman	2.00	.90
❑ 165 Dale Meinert	2.00	.90
❑ 166 Jerry Stovall RC	3.00	1.35
❑ 167 Abe Woodson	2.00	.90
❑ 168 St. Louis Cardinals Play Card (Wally Lemm)	2.00	.90
❑ 169 San Francisco 49ers Team Card	3.00	1.35
❑ 170 Kermit Alexander	2.00	.90
❑ 171 John Brodie	10.00	4.50
❑ 172 Bernie Casey	3.00	1.35
❑ 173 John David Crow	3.00	1.35
❑ 174 Tommy Davis	2.00	.90
❑ 175 Matt Hazeltine	2.00	.90
❑ 176 Jim Johnson	4.00	1.80
❑ 177 Charlie Krueger RC	2.00	.90
❑ 178 Roland Lakes	2.00	.90
❑ 179 George Mira RC	3.00	1.35
❑ 180 Dave Parks RC	3.00	1.35
❑ 181 John Thomas RC	2.00	.90
❑ 182 San Francisco 49ers Play Card (Jack Christiansen)	2.00	.90
❑ 183 Washington Redskins Team Card	3.00	1.35
❑ 184 Pervis Atkins	2.00	.90
❑ 185 Preston Carpenter	2.00	.90
❑ 186 Angelo Coia	2.00	.90
❑ 187 Sam Huff	6.00	2.70
❑ 188 Sonny Jurgensen	15.00	6.75
❑ 189 Paul Krause RC	20.00	9.00
❑ 190 Jim Martin	2.00	.90
❑ 191 Bobby Mitchell	5.00	2.20
❑ 192 John Nisby	2.00	.90
❑ 193 John Paluck	2.00	.90
❑ 194 Vince Promuto	2.00	.90
❑ 195 Charley Taylor RC	50.00	22.00
❑ 196 Washington Redskins Play Card (Bill McPeak)	2.00	.90
❑ 197 Checklist 1	30.00	13.50
❑ 198 Checklist 2 UER (163 Charley Johnson should be Charlie)	50.00	22.00

1966 Philadelphia

	NM	Ex
COMPLETE SET (198)	900.00	400.00
WRAPPER (5-CENT)	20.00	9.00
❑ 1 Atlanta Falcons Insignia	12.00	5.50
❑ 2 Larry Benz	2.00	.90
❑ 3 Dennis Claridge	2.00	.90
❑ 4 Perry Lee Dunn	2.00	.90
❑ 5 Dan Grimm	2.00	.90
❑ 6 Alex Hawkins	2.00	.90
❑ 7 Ralph Heck	2.00	.90
❑ 8 Frank Lasky	2.00	.90
❑ 9 Guy Reese	2.00	.90
❑ 10 Bob Richards	2.00	.90
❑ 11 Ron Smith RC	2.00	.90
❑ 12 Ernie Wheelwright	2.00	.90
❑ 13 Atlanta Falcons Roster	3.00	1.35
❑ 14 Baltimore Colts Team Card	3.00	1.35
❑ 15 Raymond Berry	8.00	3.60
❑ 16 Bob Boyd	2.00	.90
❑ 17 Jerry Logan	2.00	.90
❑ 18 John Mackey	6.00	2.70
❑ 19 Tom Matte	4.00	1.80
❑ 20 Lou Michaels	2.00	.90
❑ 21 Lenny Moore	8.00	3.60
❑ 22 Jimmy Orr	3.00	1.35
❑ 23 Jim Parker	4.00	1.80
❑ 24 John Unitas	40.00	18.00
❑ 25 Bob Vogel	2.00	.90
❑ 26 Baltimore Colts Play Card (Lenny Moore Jim Parker)	4.00	1.80
❑ 27 Chicago Bears Team Card	3.00	1.35
❑ 28 Doug Atkins	4.00	1.80
❑ 29 Rudy Bukich	2.00	.90
❑ 30 Ronnie Bull	2.00	.90
❑ 31 Dick Butkus RC	250.00	110.00
❑ 32 Mike Ditka	35.00	16.00
❑ 33 Joe Fortunato	2.00	.90
❑ 34 Bobby Joe Green	2.00	.90
❑ 35 Roger LeClerc	2.00	.90
❑ 36 Johnny Morris	2.00	.90
❑ 37 Mike Pyle	2.00	.90
❑ 38 Gale Sayers RC	225.00	100.00
❑ 39 Chicago Bears Play Card (Gale Sayers)	35.00	16.00
❑ 40 Cleveland Browns Team Card	3.00	1.35
❑ 41 Jim Brown	80.00	36.00
❑ 42 Gary Collins	3.00	1.35
❑ 43 Ross Fichtner	2.00	.90
❑ 44 Ernie Green	2.00	.90
❑ 45 Gene Hickerson RC	3.00	1.35
❑ 46 Jim Houston	2.00	.90
❑ 47 John Morrow	2.00	.90
❑ 48 Walter Roberts	2.00	.90
❑ 49 Frank Ryan	3.00	1.35
❑ 50 Dick Schafrath	2.00	.90
❑ 51 Paul Wiggin RC	2.00	.90
❑ 52 Cleveland Browns Play Card (Ernie Green sweep)	2.00	.90
❑ 53 Dallas Cowboys Team Card	3.00	1.35
❑ 54 George Andrie RC UER (Text says startling& should be starting)	3.00	1.35
❑ 55 Frank Clarke	3.00	1.35
❑ 56 Mike Connelly	2.00	.90
❑ 57 Cornell Green	4.00	1.80
❑ 58 Bob Hayes RC	50.00	22.00
❑ 59 Chuck Howley RC	18.00	8.00
❑ 60 Bob Lilly	20.00	9.00
❑ 61 Don Meredith	25.00	11.00
❑ 62 Don Perkins	3.00	1.35
❑ 63 Mel Renfro	15.00	6.75
❑ 64 Danny Villanueva	2.00	.90
❑ 65 Dallas Cowboys Play Card (Danny Villanueva)	2.00	.90
❑ 66 Detroit Lions Team Card	3.00	1.35
❑ 67 Roger Brown	2.00	.90
❑ 68 John Gordy	2.00	.90
❑ 69 Alex Karras	10.00	4.50
❑ 70 Dick LeBeau	2.00	.90
❑ 71 Amos Marsh	2.00	.90
❑ 72 Milt Plum	3.00	1.35
❑ 73 Bobby Smith	2.00	.90
❑ 74 Wayne Rasmussen	2.00	.90
❑ 75 Pat Studstill	2.00	.90
❑ 76 Wayne Walker	2.00	.90
❑ 77 Tom Watkins	2.00	.90
❑ 78 Detroit Lions Play Card (George Izo pass)	2.00	.90
❑ 79 Green Bay Packers Team Card	6.00	2.70
❑ 80 Herb Adderley UER (Adderly on back)	6.00	2.70
❑ 81 Lee Roy Caffey RC	4.00	1.80
❑ 82 Don Chandler	3.00	1.35
❑ 83 Willie Davis	6.00	2.70
❑ 84 Boyd Dowler	4.00	1.80
❑ 85 Forrest Gregg	4.00	1.80
❑ 86 Tom Moore	3.00	1.35
❑ 87 Ray Nitschke	15.00	6.75
❑ 88 Bart Starr	50.00	22.00
❑ 89 Jim Taylor	20.00	9.00
❑ 90 Willie Wood	6.00	2.70
❑ 91 Green Bay Packers Play Card (Don Chandler FG)	2.00	.90
❑ 92 Los Angeles Rams Team Card	3.00	1.35
❑ 93 Willie Brown WR	2.00	.90
❑ 94 Dick Bass and Roman Gabriel	4.00	1.80
❑ 95 Bruce Gossett RC (Tom Landry small photo on back)	3.00	1.35
❑ 96 Deacon Jones	6.00	2.70
❑ 97 Tommy McDonald	5.00	2.20
❑ 98 Marlin McKeever	2.00	.90
❑ 99 Aaron Martin	2.00	.90
❑ 100 Ed Meador	2.00	.90
❑ 101 Bill Munson	3.00	1.35
❑ 102 Merlin Olsen	8.00	3.60
❑ 103 Jim Stiger	2.00	.90
❑ 104 Los Angeles Rams Play Card (Willie Brown run)	3.00	1.35
❑ 105 Minnesota Vikings Team Card	3.00	1.35
❑ 106 Grady Alderman	2.00	.90
❑ 107 Bill Brown	3.00	1.35
❑ 108 Fred Cox	2.00	.90
❑ 109 Paul Flatley	2.00	.90
❑ 110 Rip Hawkins	2.00	.90
❑ 111 Tommy Mason	2.00	.90
❑ 112 Ed Sharockman	2.00	.90
❑ 113 Gordon Smith	2.00	.90
❑ 114 Fran Tarkenton	30.00	13.50
❑ 115 Mick Tingelhoff	3.00	1.35
❑ 116 Bobby Walden RC**/C	2.00	.90
❑ 117 Minnesota Vikings Play Card (Bill Brown run)	2.00	.90
❑ 118 New York Giants Team Card	3.00	1.35
❑ 119 Roosevelt Brown	4.00	1.80
❑ 120 Henry Carr RC	3.00	1.35
❑ 121 Clarence Childs	2.00	.90
❑ 122 Tucker Frederickson RC	3.00	1.35
❑ 123 Jerry Hillebrand	2.00	.90
❑ 124 Greg Larson	2.00	.90
❑ 125 Spider Lockhart RC	3.00	1.35
❑ 126 Dick Lynch	2.00	.90
❑ 127 Earl Morrall and Bob Scholtz	3.00	1.35
❑ 128 Joe Morrison	2.00	.90
❑ 129 Steve Thurlow	2.00	.90
❑ 130 New York Giants Play Card (Chuck Mercein over)	2.00	.90
❑ 131 Philadelphia Eagles Team Card	3.00	1.35
❑ 132 Sam Baker	2.00	.90
❑ 133 Maxie Baughan	2.00	.90
❑ 134 Bob Brown OT RC	12.00	5.50

❑ 135 Timmy Brown 3.00 1.35
(Lou Groza small photo on back)
❑ 136 Irv Cross 3.00 1.35
❑ 137 Earl Gros 2.00 .90
❑ 138 Ray Poage 2.00 .90
❑ 139 Nate Ramsey 2.00 .90
❑ 140 Pete Retzlaff 3.00 1.35
❑ 141 Jim Ringo 4.00 1.80
(Joe Schmidt small photo on back)
❑ 142 Norm Snead 4.00 1.80
(Norm Van Brocklin small photo on back)
❑ 143 Philadelphia Eagles Play Card 2.00 .90
(Earl Gros tackled)
❑ 144 Pittsburgh Steelers Team Card 3.00 1.35
(Lee Roy Jordan small photo on back)
❑ 145 Gary Ballman 2.00 .90
❑ 146 Charley Bradshaw 2.00 .90
❑ 147 Jim Butler 2.00 .90
❑ 148 Mike Clark 2.00 .90
❑ 149 Dick Hoak RC 2.00 .90
❑ 150 Roy Jefferson RC 3.00 1.35
❑ 151 Frank Lambert 2.00 .90
❑ 152 Mike Lind 2.00 .90
❑ 153 Bill Nelsen RC 4.00 1.80
❑ 154 Clarence Peaks 2.00 .90
❑ 155 Clendon Thomas 2.00 .90
❑ 156 Pittsburgh Steelers Play Card 2.00 .90
(Gary Ballman scores)
❑ 157 St. Louis Cardinals Team Card 3.00 1.35
❑ 158 Jim Bakken 2.00 .90
❑ 159 Bobby Joe Conrad 3.00 1.35
❑ 160 Willis Crenshaw RC 2.00 .90
❑ 161 Bob DeMarco 2.00 .90
❑ 162 Pat Fischer 3.00 1.35
❑ 163 Charlie Johnson UER 3.00 1.35
(Misspelled Charley on both sides)
❑ 164 Dale Meinert 2.00 .90
❑ 165 Sonny Randle 2.00 .90
❑ 166 Sam Silas RC 2.00 .90
❑ 167 Bill Triplett 2.00 .90
❑ 168 Larry Wilson 4.00 1.80
❑ 169 St. Louis Cardinals Play Card 2.00 .90
(Bill Triplett tackled by Roosevelt Davis and Roger LaLonde)
❑ 170 San Francisco 49ers Team Card 3.00 1.35
(Vince Lombardi small photo on back)
❑ 171 Kermit Alexander 2.00 .90
❑ 172 Bruce Bosley 2.00 .90
❑ 173 John Brodie 6.00 2.70
❑ 174 Bernie Casey 3.00 1.35
❑ 175 John David Crow 4.00 1.80
(Don Shula small photo on back)
❑ 176 Tommy Davis 2.00 .90
❑ 177 Jim Johnson 4.00 1.80
❑ 178 Gary Lewis RC 2.00 .90
❑ 179 Dave Parks 2.00 .90
❑ 180 Walter Rock 3.00 1.35
(Paul Hornung small photo on back)
❑ 181 Ken Willard RC 4.00 1.80
(George Halas small photo on back)
❑ 182 San Francisco 49ers Play Card 2.00 .90
(Tommy Davis FG)
❑ 183 Washington Redskins Team Card 3.00 1.35
❑ 184 Rickie Harris 2.00 .90
❑ 185 Sonny Jurgensen 8.00 3.60
❑ 186 Paul Krause 6.00 2.70
❑ 187 Bobby Mitchell 6.00 2.70
❑ 188 Vince Promuto 2.00 .90
❑ 189 Pat Richter RC 2.00 .90
(Craig Morton small photo on back)
❑ 190 Joe Rutgens 2.00 .90
❑ 191 Johnny Sample 2.00 .90
❑ 192 Lonnie Sanders 2.00 .90
❑ 193 Jim Steffen 2.00 .90
❑ 194 Charley Taylor UER 15.00 6.75
(Called Charley and Charlie on card back
❑ 195 Washington Redskins Play Card 2.00 .90
(Dan Lewis tackled by Roger LaLonde)
❑ 196 Referee Signals 3.00 1.35
❑ 197 Checklist 1 25.00 11.00
❑ 198 Checklist 2 UER 50.00 22.00
(163 Charley Johnson should be Charlie)

1967 Philadelphia

	NM	Ex
COMPLETE SET (198)	650.00	300.00
WRAPPER (5-CENT)	20.00	9.00

❑ 1 Atlanta Falcons Team Card 10.00 4.50
❑ 2 Junior Coffey RC 3.00 1.35
❑ 3 Alex Hawkins 2.00 .90
❑ 4 Randy Johnson RC 3.00 1.35
❑ 5 Lou Kirouac 2.00 .90
❑ 6 Billy Martin RC 2.00 .90
❑ 7 Tommy Nobis RC 20.00 9.00
❑ 8 Jerry Richardson RC 4.00 1.80
❑ 9 Marion Rushing 2.00 .90
❑ 10 Ron Smith 2.00 .90
❑ 11 Ernie Wheelwright UER 2.00 .90
(Misspelled Wheelright on both sides)
❑ 12 Atlanta Falcons Insignia 2.00 .90
❑ 13 Baltimore Colts Team Card 3.00 1.35
❑ 14 Raymond Berry UER 7.00 3.10
(Photo actually Bob Boyd
❑ 15 Bob Boyd 2.00 .90
❑ 16 Ordell Braase 2.00 .90
❑ 17 Alvin Haymond 2.00 .90
❑ 18 Tony Lorick 2.00 .90
❑ 19 Lenny Lyles 2.00 .90
❑ 20 John Mackey 5.00 2.20
❑ 21 Tom Matte 3.00 1.35
❑ 22 Lou Michaels 2.00 .90
❑ 23 John Unitas 40.00 18.00
❑ 24 Baltimore Colts Insignia 2.00 .90
❑ 25 Chicago Bears Team Card 3.00 1.35
❑ 26 Rudy Bukich UER 2.00 .90
(Misspelled Buckich on card back)
❑ 27 Ronnie Bull 2.00 .90
❑ 28 Dick Butkus 75.00 34.00
❑ 29 Mike Ditka 30.00 13.50
❑ 30 Dick Gordon RC 3.00 1.35
❑ 31 Roger LeClerc 2.00 .90
❑ 32 Bennie McRae 2.00 .90
❑ 33 Richie Petitbon 2.00 .90
❑ 34 Mike Pyle 2.00 .90
❑ 35 Gale Sayers 75.00 34.00
❑ 36 Chicago Bears Insignia 2.00 .90
❑ 37 Cleveland Browns Team Card 3.00 1.35
❑ 38 Johnny Brewer 2.00 .90
❑ 39 Gary Collins 3.00 1.35
❑ 40 Ross Fichtner 2.00 .90
❑ 41 Ernie Green 2.00 .90
❑ 42 Gene Hickerson 2.00 .90
❑ 43 Leroy Kelly RC 40.00 18.00
❑ 44 Frank Ryan 3.00 1.35
❑ 45 Dick Schafrath 2.00 .90
❑ 46 Paul Warfield 18.00 8.00
❑ 47 John Wooten 2.00 .90
❑ 48 Cleveland Browns Insignia 2.00 .90
❑ 49 Dallas Cowboys Team Card 3.00 1.35
❑ 50 George Andrie 2.00 .90
❑ 51 Cornell Green 3.00 1.35
❑ 52 Bob Hayes 20.00 9.00
❑ 53 Chuck Howley 4.00 1.80
❑ 54 Lee Roy Jordan RC 20.00 9.00
❑ 55 Bob Lilly 15.00 6.75
❑ 56 Dave Manders RC 2.00 .90
❑ 57 Don Meredith 25.00 11.00
❑ 58 Dan Reeves RC 30.00 13.50
❑ 59 Mel Renfro 6.00 2.70
❑ 60 Dallas Cowboys Insignia 3.00 1.35
❑ 61 Detroit Lions Team Card 3.00 1.35
❑ 62 Roger Brown 3.00 1.35
❑ 63 Gail Cogdill 2.00 .90
❑ 64 John Gordy 2.00 .90
❑ 65 Ron Kramer 2.00 .90
❑ 66 Dick LeBeau 2.00 .90
❑ 67 Mike Lucci RC 4.00 1.80
❑ 68 Amos Marsh 2.00 .90
❑ 69 Tom Nowatzke 2.00 .90
❑ 70 Pat Studstill 2.00 .90
❑ 71 Karl Sweetan 2.00 .90
❑ 72 Detroit Lions Insignia 2.00 .90
❑ 73 Green Bay Packers Team Card 5.00 2.20
❑ 74 Herb Adderley UER 6.00 2.70
(Adderly on back)
❑ 75 Lee Roy Caffey 3.00 1.35
❑ 76 Willie Davis 5.00 2.20
❑ 77 Forrest Gregg 4.00 1.80
❑ 78 Hank Jordan 4.00 1.80
❑ 79 Ray Nitschke 12.00 5.50
❑ 80 Dave Robinson RC 6.00 2.70
❑ 81 Bob Skoronski 3.00 1.35
❑ 82 Bart Starr 50.00 22.00
❑ 83 Willie Wood 5.00 2.20
❑ 84 Green Bay Packers Insignia 3.00 1.35
❑ 85 Los Angeles Rams Team Card 3.00 1.35
❑ 86 Dick Bass 3.00 1.35
❑ 87 Maxie Baughan 2.00 .90
❑ 88 Roman Gabriel 4.00 1.80
❑ 89 Bruce Gossett 2.00 .90
❑ 90 Deacon Jones 5.00 2.20
❑ 91 Tommy McDonald 5.00 2.20
❑ 92 Marlin McKeever 2.00 .90
❑ 93 Tom Moore 2.00 .90
❑ 94 Merlin Olsen 6.00 2.70
❑ 95 Clancy Williams 2.00 .90
❑ 96 Los Angeles Rams Insignia 2.00 .90
❑ 97 Minnesota Vikings Team Card 3.00 1.35
❑ 98 Grady Alderman 2.00 .90
❑ 99 Bill Brown 3.00 1.35
❑ 100 Fred Cox 2.00 .90
❑ 101 Paul Flatley 2.00 .90
❑ 102 Dale Hackbart RC 2.00 .90
❑ 103 Jim Marshall 4.00 1.80
❑ 104 Tommy Mason 2.00 .90
❑ 105 Milt Sunde RC 2.00 .90
❑ 106 Fran Tarkenton 20.00 9.00
❑ 107 Mick Tingelhoff 3.00 1.35
❑ 108 Minnesota Vikings Insignia 2.00 .90
❑ 109 New York Giants Team Card 3.00 1.35
❑ 110 Henry Carr 2.00 .90
❑ 111 Clarence Childs 2.00 .90

❑ 112 Allen Jacobs	2.00	.90
❑ 113 Homer Jones RC	3.00	1.35
❑ 114 Tom Kennedy	2.00	.90
❑ 115 Spider Lockhart	2.00	.90
❑ 116 Joe Morrison	2.00	.90
❑ 117 Francis Peay	2.00	.90
❑ 118 Jeff Smith	2.00	.90
❑ 119 Aaron Thomas	2.00	.90
❑ 120 New York Giants Insignia	2.00	.90
❑ 121 New Orleans Saints Insignia (See also card 132)	3.00	1.35
❑ 122 Charley Bradshaw	2.00	.90
❑ 123 Paul Hornung	25.00	11.00
❑ 124 Elbert Kimbrough	2.00	.90
❑ 125 Earl Leggett RC	2.00	.90
❑ 126 Obert Logan	2.00	.90
❑ 127 Riley Mattson	2.00	.90
❑ 128 John Morrow	2.00	.90
❑ 129 Bob Scholtz	2.00	.90
❑ 130 Dave Whitsell RC	2.00	.90
❑ 131 Gary Wood	2.00	.90
❑ 132 New Orleans Saints Roster UER (121 on back)	3.00	1.35
❑ 133 Philadelphia Eagles Team Card	3.00	1.35
❑ 134 Sam Baker	2.00	.90
❑ 135 Bob Brown OT	5.00	2.20
❑ 136 Timmy Brown	3.00	1.35
❑ 137 Earl Gros	2.00	.90
❑ 138 Dave Lloyd	2.00	.90
❑ 139 Floyd Peters	2.00	.90
❑ 140 Pete Retzlaff	3.00	1.35
❑ 141 Joe Scarpati	2.00	.90
❑ 142 Norm Snead	3.00	1.35
❑ 143 Jim Skaggs	2.00	.90
❑ 144 Philadelphia Eagles Insignia	2.00	.90
❑ 145 Pittsburgh Steelers Team Card	3.00	1.35
❑ 146 Bill Asbury	2.00	.90
❑ 147 John Baker	2.00	.90
❑ 148 Gary Ballman	2.00	.90
❑ 149 Mike Clark	2.00	.90
❑ 150 Riley Gunnels	2.00	.90
❑ 151 John Hilton	2.00	.90
❑ 152 Roy Jefferson	3.00	1.35
❑ 153 Brady Keys	2.00	.90
❑ 154 Ben McGee	2.00	.90
❑ 155 Bill Nelsen	3.00	1.35
❑ 156 Pittsburgh Steelers Insignia	2.00	.90
❑ 157 St. Louis Cardinals Team Card	3.00	1.35
❑ 158 Jim Bakken	2.00	.90
❑ 159 Bobby Joe Conrad	3.00	1.35
❑ 160 Ken Gray	2.00	.90
❑ 161 Charlie Johnson UER (Misspelled Charley on both sides)	3.00	1.35
❑ 162 Joe Robb	2.00	.90
❑ 163 Johnny Roland RC	3.00	1.35
❑ 164 Roy Shivers	2.00	.90
❑ 165 Jackie Smith RC	15.00	6.75
❑ 166 Jerry Stovall	2.00	.90
❑ 167 Larry Wilson	4.00	1.80
❑ 168 St. Louis Cardinals Insignia	2.00	.90
❑ 169 San Francisco 49ers Team Card	3.00	1.35
❑ 170 Kermit Alexander	2.00	.90
❑ 171 Bruce Bosley	2.00	.90
❑ 172 John Brodie	6.00	2.70
❑ 173 Bernie Casey	3.00	1.35
❑ 174 Tommy Davis	2.00	.90
❑ 175 Howard Mudd	2.00	.90
❑ 176 Dave Parks	2.00	.90
❑ 177 John Thomas	2.00	.90
❑ 178 Dave Wilcox RC	10.00	4.50
❑ 179 Ken Willard	3.00	1.35
❑ 180 San Francisco 49ers Insignia	2.00	.90
❑ 181 Washington Redskins Team Card	3.00	1.35
❑ 182 Charlie Gogolak RC	2.00	.90
❑ 183 Chris Hanburger RC	5.00	2.20
❑ 184 Len Hauss RC	3.00	1.35
❑ 185 Sonny Jurgensen	7.00	3.10
❑ 186 Bobby Mitchell	5.00	2.20
❑ 187 Brig Owens	2.00	.90
❑ 188 Jim Shorter	2.00	.90
❑ 189 Jerry Smith RC	3.00	1.35
❑ 190 Charley Taylor	8.00	3.60
❑ 191 A.D. Whitfield	2.00	.90
❑ 192 Washington Redskins Insignia	2.00	.90
❑ 193 Cleveland Browns Play Card (Leroy Kelly)	6.00	2.70
❑ 194 New York Giants Play Card (Joe Morrison)	2.00	.90
❑ 195 Atlanta Falcons Play Card (Ernie Wheelright)	2.00	.90
❑ 196 Referee Signals	3.00	1.35
❑ 197 Checklist 1	20.00	9.00
❑ 198 Checklist 2 UER (161 Charley Johnson should be Charlie)	40.00	18.00

1993 Pinnacle Rookies

	Nm-Mt	Ex-Mt
COMPLETE SET (25)	200.00	90.00
❑ 1 Drew Bledsoe UER Card has drafted in 92 He was 1st pick of 93 draft	60.00	27.00
❑ 2 Garrison Hearst	25.00	11.00
❑ 3 John Copeland	6.00	2.70
❑ 4 Eric Curry	8.00	3.60
❑ 5 Curtis Conway	10.00	4.50
❑ 6 Lincoln Kennedy	6.00	2.70
❑ 7 Jerome Bettis	50.00	22.00
❑ 8 Dan Williams	6.00	2.70
❑ 9 Patrick Bates	6.00	2.70
❑ 10 Brad Hopkins	6.00	2.70
❑ 11 Wayne Simmons	6.00	2.70
❑ 12 Rick Mirer	10.00	4.50
❑ 13 Tom Carter	6.00	2.70
❑ 14 Irv Smith	8.00	3.60
❑ 15 Marvin Jones	6.00	2.70
❑ 16 Deon Figures	6.00	2.70
❑ 17 Leonard Renfro	6.00	2.70
❑ 18 O.J.McDuffie	10.00	4.50
❑ 19 Dana Stubblefield	10.00	4.50
❑ 20 Carlton Gray	6.00	2.70
❑ 21 Demetrius DuBose	6.00	2.70
❑ 22 Troy Drayton	6.00	2.70
❑ 23 Natrone Means	10.00	4.50
❑ 24 Reggie Brooks	8.00	3.60
❑ 25 Glyn Milburn	10.00	4.50

1997 Pinnacle Totally Certified Platinum Red

	Nm-Mt	Ex-Mt
COMPLETE SET (150)	150.00	70.00
❑ 1 Emmitt Smith	12.00	5.50
❑ 2 Dan Marino	15.00	6.75
❑ 3 Brett Favre	15.00	6.75
❑ 4 Steve Young	5.00	2.20
❑ 5 Kerry Collins	4.00	1.80
❑ 6 Troy Aikman	8.00	3.60
❑ 7 Drew Bledsoe	5.00	2.20
❑ 8 Eddie George	4.00	1.80
❑ 9 Jerry Rice	8.00	3.60

❑ 10 John Elway	15.00	6.75
❑ 11 Barry Sanders	12.00	5.50
❑ 12 Mark Brunell	5.00	2.20
❑ 13 Elvis Grbac	2.50	1.10
❑ 14 Tony Banks	2.50	1.10
❑ 15 Vinny Testaverde	2.50	1.10
❑ 16 Rick Mirer	1.50	.70
❑ 17 Carl Pickens	2.50	1.10
❑ 18 Deion Sanders	4.00	1.80
❑ 19 Terry Glenn	4.00	1.80
❑ 20 Heath Shuler	1.50	.70
❑ 21 Dave Brown	1.50	.70
❑ 22 Keyshawn Johnson	4.00	1.80
❑ 23 Jeff George	2.50	1.10
❑ 24 Ricky Watters	2.50	1.10
❑ 25 Kordell Stewart	4.00	1.80
❑ 26 Junior Seau	4.00	1.80
❑ 27 Terrell Owens	5.00	2.20
❑ 28 Warren Moon	4.00	1.80
❑ 29 Isaac Bruce	4.00	1.80
❑ 30 Steve McNair	5.00	2.20
❑ 31 Gus Frerotte	1.50	.70
❑ 32 Trent Dilfer	4.00	1.80
❑ 33 Shannon Sharpe	2.50	1.10
❑ 34 Scott Mitchell	2.50	1.10
❑ 35 Antonio Freeman	4.00	1.80
❑ 36 Jim Harbaugh	2.50	1.10
❑ 37 Natrone Means	2.50	1.10
❑ 38 Marcus Allen	4.00	1.80
❑ 39 Karim Abdul-Jabbar	4.00	1.80
❑ 40 Tim Biakabutuka	2.50	1.10
❑ 41 Jeff Blake	2.50	1.10
❑ 42 Michael Irvin	4.00	1.80
❑ 43 Herschel Walker	2.50	1.10
❑ 44 Curtis Martin	5.00	2.20
❑ 45 Eddie Kennison	2.50	1.10
❑ 46 Napoleon Kaufman	4.00	1.80
❑ 47 Larry Centers	2.50	1.10
❑ 48 Jamal Anderson	4.00	1.80
❑ 49 Derrick Alexander WR	2.50	1.10
❑ 50 Bruce Smith	2.50	1.10
❑ 51 Wesley Walls	2.50	1.10
❑ 52 Rod Smith WR	4.00	1.80
❑ 53 Keenan McCardell	2.50	1.10
❑ 54 Robert Brooks	2.50	1.10
❑ 55 Willie Green	1.50	.70
❑ 56 Jake Reed	2.50	1.10
❑ 57 Joey Galloway	2.50	1.10
❑ 58 Eric Metcalf	2.50	1.10
❑ 59 Chris Sanders	1.50	.70
❑ 60 Jeff Hostetler	1.50	.70
❑ 61 Kevin Greene	2.50	1.10
❑ 62 Frank Sanders	2.50	1.10
❑ 63 Dorsey Levens	4.00	1.80
❑ 64 Sean Dawkins	1.50	.70
❑ 65 Cris Carter	4.00	1.80
❑ 66 Andre Hastings	1.50	.70
❑ 67 Amani Toomer	2.50	1.10
❑ 68 Adrian Murrell	2.50	1.10
❑ 69 Ty Detmer	2.50	1.10
❑ 70 Yancey Thigpen	1.50	.70
❑ 71 Jim Everett	1.50	.70
❑ 72 Todd Collins	1.50	.70
❑ 73 Curtis Conway	2.50	1.10
❑ 74 Herman Moore	2.50	1.10
❑ 75 Neil O'Donnell	2.50	1.10
❑ 76 Rod Woodson	2.50	1.10
❑ 77 Tony Martin	2.50	1.10
❑ 78 Kent Graham	1.50	.70
❑ 79 Andre Reed	2.50	1.10
❑ 80 Reggie White	4.00	1.80

❑ 81 Thurman Thomas	4.00	1.80
❑ 82 Garrison Hearst	2.50	1.10
❑ 83 Chris Warren	2.50	1.10
❑ 84 Wayne Chrebet	4.00	1.80
❑ 85 Chris T. Jones	1.50	.70
❑ 86 Anthony Miller	1.50	.70
❑ 87 Chris Chandler	2.50	1.10
❑ 88 Terrell Davis	5.00	2.20
❑ 89 Mike Alstott	4.00	1.80
❑ 90 Terry Allen	4.00	1.80
❑ 91 Jerome Bettis	4.00	1.80
❑ 92 Stan Humphries	2.50	1.10
❑ 93 Andre Rison	2.50	1.10
❑ 94 Marshall Faulk	5.00	2.20
❑ 95 Erik Kramer	1.50	.70
❑ 96 O.J. McDuffie	2.50	1.10
❑ 97 Robert Smith	2.50	1.10
❑ 98 Keith Byars	1.50	.70
❑ 99 Rodney Hampton	2.50	1.10
❑ 100 Desmond Howard	2.50	1.10
❑ 101 Lawrence Phillips	1.50	.70
❑ 102 Michael Westbrook	2.50	1.10
❑ 103 Johnnie Morton	2.50	1.10
❑ 104 Ben Coates	2.50	1.10
❑ 105 J.J. Stokes	2.50	1.10
❑ 106 Terance Mathis	2.50	1.10
❑ 107 Errict Rhett	1.50	.70
❑ 108 Tim Brown	4.00	1.80
❑ 109 Marvin Harrison	4.00	1.80
❑ 110 Muhsin Muhammad	2.50	1.10
❑ 111 Byron Bam Morris	1.50	.70
❑ 112 Mario Bates	1.50	.70
❑ 113 Jimmy Smith	2.50	1.10
❑ 114 Irving Fryar	2.50	1.10
❑ 115 Tamarick Vanover	2.50	1.10
❑ 116 Brad Johnson	4.00	1.80
❑ 117 Rashaan Salaam	1.50	.70
❑ 118 Ki-Jana Carter	1.50	.70
❑ 119 Tyrone Wheatley	2.50	1.10
❑ 120 John Friesz	1.50	.70
❑ 121 Orlando Pace RC	4.00	1.80
❑ 122 Jim Druckenmiller RC	2.00	.90
❑ 123 Byron Hanspard RC	2.50	1.10
❑ 124 David LaFleur RC	1.00	.45
❑ 125 Reidel Anthony RC	4.00	1.80
❑ 126 Antowain Smith RC	10.00	4.50
❑ 127 Bryant Westbrook RC	1.00	.45
❑ 128 Fred Lane RC	2.00	.90
❑ 129 Tiki Barber RC	15.00	6.75
❑ 130 Shawn Springs RC	2.00	.90
❑ 131 Ike Hilliard RC	6.00	2.70
❑ 132 James Farrior RC	4.00	1.80
❑ 133 Darrell Russell RC	1.00	.45
❑ 134 Walter Jones RC	4.00	1.80
❑ 135 Tom Knight RC	1.00	.45
❑ 136 Yatil Green RC	2.00	.90
❑ 137 Joey Kent RC	2.00	.90
❑ 138 Kevin Lockett RC	2.00	.90
❑ 139 Troy Davis RC	2.00	.90
❑ 140 Darnell Autry RC	2.00	.90
❑ 141 Pat Barnes RC	4.00	1.80
❑ 142 Rae Carruth RC	1.00	.45
❑ 143 Will Blackwell RC	2.00	.90
❑ 144 Warrick Dunn RC	10.00	4.50
❑ 145 Corey Dillon RC	25.00	11.00
❑ 146 Dwayne Rudd RC	4.00	1.80
❑ 147 Reinard Wilson RC	2.00	.90
❑ 148 Peter Boulware RC	4.00	1.80
❑ 149 Tony Gonzalez RC	12.00	5.50
❑ 150 Danny Wuerffel RC	4.00	1.80

1997 Pinnacle Totally Certified Platinum Blue

	Nm-Mt	Ex-Mt
COMPLETE SET (150)	400.00	180.00

*PLATINUM BLUE CARDS: .75X TO 2X
*CERTIFIED BLUE RCs: .6X TO 1.5X

1997 Pinnacle Totally Certified Platinum Gold

Nm-Mt Ex-Mt

*PLAT.GOLD STARS: 8X TO 20X BASIC CARDS
*PLAT.GOLD RCs: 4X TO 10X BASIC CARDS

1993 Playoff

	Nm-Mt	Ex-Mt
COMPLETE SET (315)	25.00	11.00
❑ 1 Troy Aikman	1.50	.70
❑ 2 Jerry Rice	2.00	.90
❑ 3 Keith Jackson	.20	.09
❑ 4 Sean Gilbert	.20	.09
❑ 5 Jim Kelly	.40	.18
❑ 6 Junior Seau	.40	.18
❑ 7 Deion Sanders	1.00	.45
❑ 8 Joe Montana	3.00	1.35
❑ 9 Terrell Buckley	.10	.05
❑ 10 Emmitt Smith	3.00	1.35
❑ 11 Pete Stoyanovich	.10	.05
❑ 12 Randall Cunningham	.40	.18
❑ 13 Boomer Esiason	.20	.09
❑ 14 Mike Saxon	.10	.05
❑ 15 Chuck Cecil	.10	.05
❑ 16 Vinny Testaverde	.20	.09
❑ 17 Jeff Hostetler	.20	.09
❑ 18 Mark Clayton	.10	.05
❑ 19 Nick Bell	.10	.05
❑ 20 Frank Reich	.20	.09
❑ 21 Henry Ellard	.20	.09
❑ 22 Andre Reed	.20	.09
❑ 23 Mark Ingram	.10	.05
❑ 24 Mike Brim	.10	.05
❑ 25A Bernie Kosar UER (Name spelled Kozar on both sides)	.20	.09
❑ 25B Bernie Kosar COR	.20	.09
❑ 26 Jeff George	.40	.18
❑ 27 Tommy Maddox	.40	.18
❑ 28 Kent Graham RC	.40	.18
❑ 29 David Klingler	.10	.05
❑ 30 Robert Delpino	.10	.05
❑ 31 Kevin Fagan	.10	.05
❑ 32 Mark Bavaro	.10	.05
❑ 33 Harold Green	.10	.05
❑ 34 Shawn McCarthy	.10	.05
❑ 35 Ricky Proehl	.10	.05
❑ 36 Eugene Robinson	.10	.05
❑ 37 Phil Simms	.20	.09
❑ 38 David Lang	.10	.05
❑ 39 Santana Dotson	.20	.09
❑ 40 Brett Perriman	.40	.18
❑ 41 Jim Harbaugh	.40	.18
❑ 42 Keith Byars	.10	.05
❑ 43 Quentin Coryatt	.20	.09
❑ 44 Louis Oliver	.10	.05
❑ 45 Howie Long	.40	.18
❑ 46 Mike Sherrard	.10	.05
❑ 47 Earnest Byner	.10	.05
❑ 48 Neil Smith	.40	.18
❑ 49 Audray McMillian	.10	.05
❑ 50 Vaughn Dunbar	.10	.05
❑ 51 Ronnie Lott	.20	.09
❑ 52 Clyde Simmons	.10	.05
❑ 53 Kevin Scott	.10	.05
❑ 54 Bubby Brister	.10	.05
❑ 55 Randal Hill	.10	.05
❑ 56 Pat Swilling	.10	.05
❑ 57 Steve Beuerlein	.20	.09
❑ 58 Gary Clark	.20	.09
❑ 59 Brian Noble	.10	.05
❑ 60 Leslie O'Neal	.20	.09
❑ 61 Vincent Brown	.10	.05
❑ 62 Edgar Bennett	.40	.18
❑ 63 Anthony Carter	.20	.09
❑ 64 Glenn Cadrez RC UER (Name misspelled Cadez on front)	.10	.05
❑ 65 Dalton Hilliard	.10	.05
❑ 66 James Lofton	.20	.09
❑ 67 Walter Stanley	.10	.05
❑ 68 Tim Harris	.10	.05
❑ 69 Carl Banks	.10	.05
❑ 70 Andre Ware	.10	.05
❑ 71 Karl Mecklenburg	.10	.05
❑ 72 Russell Maryland	.10	.05
❑ 73 Leroy Thompson	.10	.05
❑ 74 Tommy Kane	.10	.05
❑ 75 Dan Marino	3.00	1.35
❑ 76 Darrell Fullington	.10	.05
❑ 77 Jessie Tuggle	.10	.05
❑ 78 Bruce Smith	.40	.18
❑ 79 Neal Anderson	.10	.05
❑ 80 Kevin Mack	.10	.05
❑ 81 Shane Dronett	.10	.05
❑ 82 Nick Lowery	.10	.05
❑ 83 Sheldon White	.10	.05
❑ 84 Flipper Anderson	.10	.05
❑ 85 Jeff Herrod	.10	.05
❑ 86 Dwight Stone	.10	.05
❑ 87 Dave Krieg	.20	.09
❑ 88 Bryan Cox	.10	.05
❑ 89 Greg McMurtry	.10	.05
❑ 90 Rickey Jackson	.10	.05
❑ 91 Ernie Mills	.10	.05
❑ 92 Browning Nagle	.10	.05
❑ 93 John Taylor	.20	.09
❑ 94 Eric Dickerson	.20	.09
❑ 95 Johnny Holland	.10	.05
❑ 96 Anthony Miller	.20	.09
❑ 97 Fred Barnett	.20	.09
❑ 98 Ricky Ervins UER (Name misspelled Rickey on back)	.10	.05
❑ 99 Leonard Russell	.20	.09
❑ 100 Lawrence Taylor	.40	.18
❑ 101 Tony Casillas	.10	.05
❑ 102 John Elway	3.00	1.35
❑ 103 Bennie Blades	.10	.05
❑ 104 Harry Sydney	.10	.05
❑ 105 Bubba McDowell	.10	.05
❑ 106 Todd McNair	.10	.05
❑ 107 Steve Smith	.10	.05
❑ 108 Jim Everett	.20	.09
❑ 109 Bobby Humphrey	.10	.05
❑ 110 Rich Gannon	.40	.18
❑ 111 Marv Cook	.10	.05
❑ 112 Wayne Martin	.10	.05
❑ 113 Sean Landeta	.10	.05
❑ 114 Brad Baxter UER (Reversed negative on front)	.10	.05
❑ 115 Reggie White	.40	.18
❑ 116 Johnny Johnson	.10	.05
❑ 117 Jeff Graham	.20	.09
❑ 118 Darren Carrington RC	.10	.05
❑ 119 Ricky Watters	.40	.18
❑ 120 Art Monk UER (Reversed negative on back)	.20	.09
❑ 121 Cornelius Bennett	.20	.09
❑ 122 Wade Wilson	.10	.05
❑ 123 Daniel Stubbs	.10	.05
❑ 124 Brad Muster	.10	.05
❑ 125 Mike Tomczak	.10	.05
❑ 126 Jay Novacek	.20	.09
❑ 127 Shannon Sharpe	.40	.18
❑ 128 Rodney Peete	.10	.05
❑ 129 Daryl Johnston	.40	.18
❑ 130 Warren Moon	.40	.18
❑ 131 Willie Gault	.10	.05
❑ 132 Tony Martin	.40	.18
❑ 133 Terry Allen	.40	.18
❑ 134 Hugh Millen	.10	.05
❑ 135 Rob Moore	.20	.09
❑ 136 Andy Harmon RC	.20	.09
❑ 137 Kelvin Martin	.10	.05
❑ 138 Rod Woodson	.40	.18
❑ 139 Nate Lewis	.10	.05
❑ 140 Darryl Talley	.10	.05
❑ 141 Guy McIntyre	.10	.05

❑ 142 John L. Williams .10 .05
❑ 143 Brad Edwards .10 .05
❑ 144 Trace Armstrong .10 .05
❑ 145 Kenneth Davis .10 .05
❑ 146 Clay Matthews .20 .09
❑ 147 Gaston Green .10 .05
❑ 148 Chris Spielman .20 .09
❑ 149 Cody Carlson .10 .05
❑ 150 Derrick Thomas .40 .18
❑ 151 Terry McDaniel .10 .05
❑ 152 Kevin Greene .20 .09
❑ 153 Roger Craig .20 .09
❑ 154 Craig Heyward .20 .09
❑ 155 Rodney Hampton .20 .09
❑ 156 Heath Sherman .10 .05
❑ 157 Mark Stepnoski .10 .05
❑ 158 Chris Chandler .20 .09
❑ 159 Rod Bernstine .10 .05
❑ 160 Pierce Holt .10 .05
❑ 161 Wilber Marshall .10 .05
❑ 162 Reggie Cobb .10 .05
❑ 163 Tom Rathman .10 .05
❑ 164 Michael Haynes .20 .09
❑ 165 Nate Odomes .10 .05
❑ 166 Tom Waddle .10 .05
❑ 167 Eric Ball .10 .05
❑ 168 Brett Favre UER 4.00 1.80
(Photo of Don Majkowski on back)
❑ 169 Michael Jackson .20 .09
❑ 170 Lorenzo White .10 .05
❑ 171 Cleveland Gary .10 .05
❑ 172 Jay Schroeder .10 .05
❑ 173 Tony Paige .10 .05
❑ 174 Jack Del Rio .10 .05
❑ 175 Jon Vaughn .10 .05
❑ 176 Morten Andersen UER .10 .05
(Misspelled Morton)
❑ 177 Chris Burkett .10 .05
❑ 178 Vai Sikahema .10 .05
❑ 179 Ronnie Harmon .10 .05
❑ 180 Amp Lee .10 .05
❑ 181 Chip Lohmiller .10 .05
❑ 182 Steve Broussard .10 .05
❑ 183 Don Beebe .10 .05
❑ 184 Tommy Vardell .10 .05
❑ 185 Keith Jennings .10 .05
❑ 186 Simon Fletcher .10 .05
❑ 187 Mel Gray .20 .09
❑ 188 Vince Workman .10 .05
❑ 189 Haywood Jeffires .20 .09
❑ 190 Barry Word .10 .05
❑ 191 Ethan Horton .10 .05
❑ 192 Mark Higgs .10 .05
❑ 193 Irving Fryar .20 .09
❑ 194 Charles Haley .20 .09
❑ 195 Steve Bono .20 .09
❑ 196 Mike Golic .10 .05
❑ 197 Gary Anderson K .10 .05
❑ 198 Sterling Sharpe .40 .18
❑ 199 Andre Tippett .10 .05
❑ 200 Thurman Thomas .40 .18
❑ 201 Chris Miller .20 .09
❑ 202 Henry Jones .10 .05
❑ 203 Mo Lewis .10 .05
❑ 204 Marion Butts .10 .05
❑ 205 Mike Johnson .10 .05
❑ 206 Alvin Harper .20 .09
❑ 207 Ray Childress .10 .05
❑ 208 Anthony Johnson .20 .09
❑ 209 Tony Bennett .10 .05
❑ 210 Anthony Newman RC .10 .05
❑ 211 Christian Okoye .10 .05
❑ 212 Marcus Allen .40 .18
❑ 213 Jackie Harris .10 .05
❑ 214 Mark Duper .10 .05
❑ 215 Cris Carter .40 .18
❑ 216 John Stephens .10 .05
❑ 217 Barry Sanders 2.50 1.10
❑ 218A Herman Moore ERR 1.25 .55
(First name misspelled Sherman)
❑ 218B Herman Moore COR 2.50 1.10
name spelled correctly
❑ 219 Marvin Washington .10 .05
❑ 220 Calvin Williams .20 .09
❑ 221 John Randle .20 .09
❑ 222 Marco Coleman .10 .05
❑ 223 Eric Martin .10 .05
❑ 224 Dave Meggett .10 .05
❑ 225 Brian Washington .10 .05
❑ 226 Barry Foster .20 .09
❑ 227 Michael Zordich .10 .05
❑ 228 Stan Humphries .20 .09
❑ 229 Mike Cofer .10 .05
❑ 230 Chris Warren .20 .09
❑ 231 Keith McCants .10 .05
❑ 232 Mark Rypien .10 .05
❑ 233 James Francis .10 .05
❑ 234 Andre Rison .20 .09
❑ 235 William Perry .20 .09
❑ 236 Chip Banks .10 .05
❑ 237 Willie Davis .40 .18
❑ 238 Chris Doleman .10 .05
❑ 239 Tim Brown .40 .18
❑ 240 Darren Perry .10 .05
❑ 241 Johnny Bailey .10 .05
❑ 242 Ernest Givins UER .20 .09
(Spelled Givens on back)
❑ 243 John Carney .10 .05
❑ 244 Cortez Kennedy .20 .09
❑ 245 Lawrence Dawsey .10 .05
❑ 246 Martin Mayhew .10 .05
❑ 247 Shane Conlan .10 .05
❑ 248 J.J. Birden .10 .05
❑ 249 Quinn Early .20 .09
❑ 250 Michael Irvin .40 .18
❑ 251 Neil O'Donnell .40 .18
❑ 252 Stan Gelbaugh .10 .05
❑ 253 Drew Hill .10 .05
❑ 254 Wendell Davis .10 .05
❑ 255 Tim Johnson .10 .05
❑ 256 Seth Joyner .10 .05
❑ 257 Derrick Fenner .10 .05
❑ 258 Steve Young 1.50 .70
❑ 259 Jackie Slater .10 .05
❑ 260 Eric Metcalf .20 .09
❑ 261 Rufus Porter .10 .05
❑ 262 Ken Norton Jr. .20 .09
❑ 263 Tim McDonald .10 .05
❑ 264 Mark Jackson .10 .05
❑ 265 Hardy Nickerson .20 .09
❑ 266 Anthony Munoz .20 .09
❑ 267 Mark Carrier WR .20 .09
❑ 268 Mike Pritchard .20 .09
❑ 269 Steve Emtman .10 .05
❑ 270 Ricky Sanders .10 .05
❑ 271 Robert Massey .10 .05
❑ 272 Pete Metzelaars .10 .05
❑ 273 Reggie Langhorne .10 .05
❑ 274 Tim McGee .10 .05
❑ 275 Reggie Rivers RC .10 .05
❑ 276 Jimmie Jones .10 .05
❑ 277 Lorenzo White TB .10 .05
❑ 278 Emmitt Smith TB 2.00 .90
❑ 279 Thurman Thomas TB .40 .18
❑ 280 Barry Sanders TB UER 1.50 .70
Ten TD's in '92; should be nine)
❑ 281 Rodney Hampton TB .20 .09
❑ 282 Barry Foster TB .20 .09
❑ 283 Troy Aikman PC 1.00 .45
❑ 284 Michael Irvin PC .20 .09
❑ 285 Brett Favre PC 2.50 1.10
❑ 286 Sterling Sharpe PC .20 .09
❑ 287 Steve Young PC 1.00 .45
❑ 288 Jerry Rice PC 1.25 .55
❑ 289 Stan Humphries PC .20 .09
❑ 290 Anthony Miller PC .20 .09
❑ 291 Dan Marino PC 2.00 .90
❑ 292 Keith Jackson PC .10 .05
❑ 293 Patrick Bates RC .10 .05
❑ 294 Jerome Bettis RC 6.00 2.70
❑ 295 Drew Bledsoe RC 6.00 2.70
❑ 296 Tom Carter RC .20 .09
❑ 297 Curtis Conway RC 1.00 .45
❑ 298 John Copeland RC .20 .09
❑ 299 Eric Curry RC .10 .05
❑ 300 Reggie Brooks RC .20 .09
❑ 301 Steve Everitt RC .10 .05
❑ 302 Deon Figures RC .10 .05
❑ 303 Garrison Hearst RC 2.00 .90
❑ 304 Qadry Ismail RC UER .40 .18
(Misspelled Quadry on both sides)
❑ 305 Marvin Jones RC .10 .05
❑ 306 Lincoln Kennedy RC .10 .05
❑ 307 O.J. McDuffie RC .40 .18
❑ 308 Rick Mirer RC .40 .18
❑ 309 Wayne Simmons RC .10 .05
❑ 310 Irv Smith RC .10 .05
❑ 311 Robert Smith RC 3.00 1.35
❑ 312 Dana Stubblefield RC .40 .18
❑ 313 George Teague RC .20 .09
❑ 314 Dan Williams RC .10 .05
❑ 315 Kevin Williams RC .40 .18
❑ NNO Santa Claus 2.00 .90

1998 Playoff Contenders Ticket

	Nm-Mt	Ex-Mt
COMP.SET w/o SPs (80)	60.00	27.00
❑ 1 Rob Moore	1.25	.55
❑ 2 Jake Plummer	2.00	.90
❑ 3 Jamal Anderson	2.00	.90
❑ 4 Terance Mathis	1.25	.55
❑ 5 Priest Holmes RC	80.00	36.00
❑ 6 Michael Jackson	.75	.35
❑ 7 Eric Zeier	1.25	.55
❑ 8 Andre Reed	1.25	.55
❑ 9 Antowain Smith	2.00	.90
❑ 10 Bruce Smith	1.25	.55
❑ 11 Thurman Thomas	2.00	.90
❑ 12 Rocket Ismail	.75	.35
❑ 13 Wesley Walls	1.25	.55
❑ 14 Curtis Conway	1.25	.55
❑ 15 Jeff Blake	1.25	.55
❑ 16 Corey Dillon	2.00	.90
❑ 17 Carl Pickens	1.25	.55
❑ 18 Troy Aikman	4.00	1.80
❑ 19 Michael Irvin	2.00	.90
❑ 20 Ernie Mills	.75	.35
❑ 21 Deion Sanders	2.00	.90
❑ 22 Emmitt Smith	6.00	2.70
❑ 23 Terrell Davis	2.00	.90
❑ 24 John Elway	8.00	3.60
❑ 25 Neil Smith	1.25	.55
❑ 26 Rod Smith WR	1.25	.55
❑ 27 Herman Moore	1.25	.55
❑ 28 Johnnie Morton	1.25	.55
❑ 29 Barry Sanders	6.00	2.70
❑ 30 Robert Brooks	1.25	.55
❑ 31 Brett Favre	8.00	3.60
❑ 32 Antonio Freeman	2.00	.90
❑ 33 Dorsey Levens	2.00	.90
❑ 34 Reggie White	2.00	.90
❑ 35 Marshall Faulk	2.50	1.10
❑ 36 Mark Brunell	2.00	.90
❑ 37 Jimmy Smith	1.25	.55
❑ 38 James Stewart	1.25	.55
❑ 39 Donnell Bennett	.75	.35
❑ 40 Andre Rison	1.25	.55
❑ 41 Derrick Thomas	1.25	.55
❑ 42 Karim Abdul-Jabbar	2.00	.90
❑ 43 Dan Marino	8.00	3.60
❑ 44 Cris Carter	2.00	.90
❑ 45 Brad Johnson	2.00	.90
❑ 46 Robert Smith	2.00	.90
❑ 47 Drew Bledsoe	3.00	1.35
❑ 48 Terry Glenn	2.00	.90

❑ 49 Lamar Smith 1.25 .55
❑ 50 Ike Hilliard 1.25 .55
❑ 51 Danny Kanell 1.25 .55
❑ 52 Wayne Chrebet 2.00 .90
❑ 53 Keyshawn Johnson 2.00 .90
❑ 54 Curtis Martin 2.00 .90
❑ 55 Tim Brown 2.00 .90
❑ 56 Rickey Dudley .75 .35
❑ 57 Jeff George 1.25 .55
❑ 58 Napoleon Kaufman 2.00 .90
❑ 59 Irving Fryar 1.25 .55
❑ 60 Jerome Bettis 2.00 .90
❑ 61 Charles Johnson .75 .35
❑ 62 Kordell Stewart 2.00 .90
❑ 63 Natrone Means 1.25 .55
❑ 64 Bryan Still .75 .35
❑ 65 Garrison Hearst 2.00 .90
❑ 66 Jerry Rice 4.00 1.80
❑ 67 Steve Young 2.50 1.10
❑ 68 Joey Galloway 1.25 .55
❑ 69 Warren Moon 2.00 .90
❑ 70 Ricky Watters 1.25 .55
❑ 71 Isaac Bruce 2.00 .90
❑ 72 Mike Alstott 2.00 .90
❑ 73 Reidel Anthony 1.25 .55
❑ 74 Trent Dilfer 2.00 .90
❑ 75 Warrick Dunn 2.00 .90
❑ 76 Warren Sapp 1.25 .55
❑ 77 Eddie George 2.00 .90
❑ 78 Steve McNair 2.00 .90
❑ 79 Terry Allen 2.00 .90
❑ 80 Gus Frerotte .75 .35
❑ 81 Andre Wadsworth AUTO 25.00 11.00
❑ 82 Tim Dwight AUTO 40.00 18.00
❑ 83 Curtis Enis AUTO/400 40.00 18.00
❑ 85 Charlie Batch AUTO 40.00 18.00
❑ 86 Germane Crowell AUTO 25.00 11.00
❑ 87 Peyton Manning AUTO/200 1200.00 550.00
❑ 88 Jerome Pathon AUTO 40.00 18.00
❑ 89 Fred Taylor AUTO 100.00 45.00
❑ 90 Tavian Banks AUTO 25.00 11.00
❑ 92 Randy Moss AUTO/300 600.00 275.00
❑ 93 Robert Edwards AUTO 25.00 11.00
❑ 94 Hines Ward AUTO 175.00 80.00
❑ 95 Ryan Leaf AUTO/200 60.00 27.00
❑ 96 Mikhael Ricks AUTO 25.00 11.00
❑ 97 Ahman Green AUTO 150.00 70.00
❑ 98 Jacquez Green AUTO 25.00 11.00
❑ 99 Kevin Dyson AUTO 40.00 18.00
❑ 100 Skip Hicks AUTO 25.00 11.00
❑ 103 Chris Fuamatu-Ma'afala AUTO 25.00 11.00

1998 Playoff Contenders Ticket Red

Nm-Mt Ex-Mt
COMP.RED SET (99) 400.00 180.00
*RED STARS: 1X TO 2.5X BASIC CARDS
❑ 5 Priest Holmes 80.00 36.00
❑ 81 Andre Wadsworth 6.00 2.70
❑ 82 Tim Dwight 8.00 3.60
❑ 83 Curtis Enis 5.00 2.20
❑ 85 Charlie Batch 8.00 3.60
❑ 86 Germane Crowell 6.00 2.70
❑ 87 Peyton Manning 80.00 36.00
❑ 88 Jerome Pathon 8.00 3.60
❑ 89 Fred Taylor 12.00 5.50
❑ 90 Tavian Banks 6.00 2.70
❑ 92 Randy Moss 50.00 22.00
❑ 93 Robert Edwards 6.00 2.70
❑ 94 Hines Ward 25.00 11.00
❑ 95 Ryan Leaf 8.00 3.60
❑ 96 Mikhael Ricks 6.00 2.70
❑ 97 Ahman Green 50.00 22.00
❑ 98 Jacquez Green 6.00 2.70
❑ 99 Kevin Dyson 8.00 3.60
❑ 100 Skip Hicks 6.00 2.70
❑ 103 Chris Fuamatu-Ma'afala 6.00 2.70

1999 Playoff Contenders SSD

Nm-Mt Ex-Mt
COMPLETE SET (200) 2000.00 900.00

COMP.SET w/o RC/PT's (141) 60.00 27.00
❑ 1 Randy Moss 5.00 2.20
❑ 2 Randall Cunningham 2.00 .90
❑ 3 Cris Carter 2.00 .90
❑ 4 Robert Smith 2.00 .90
❑ 5 Jake Reed 1.25 .55
❑ 6 Albert Connell .75 .35
❑ 7 Jeff George 1.25 .55
❑ 8 Brett Favre 6.00 2.70
❑ 9 Antonio Freeman 2.00 .90
❑ 10 Dorsey Levens 2.00 .90
❑ 11 Mark Chmura 1.25 .55
❑ 12 Mike Alstott 2.00 .90
❑ 13 Warrick Dunn 2.00 .90
❑ 14 Trent Dilfer 1.25 .55
❑ 15 Jacquez Green .75 .35
❑ 16 Reidel Anthony .75 .35
❑ 17 Warren Sapp 1.25 .55
❑ 18 Amani Toomer .75 .35
❑ 19 Curtis Enis .75 .35
❑ 20 Curtis Conway 1.25 .55
❑ 21 Bobby Engram 1.25 .55
❑ 22 Barry Sanders 6.00 2.70
❑ 23 Charlie Batch 2.00 .90
❑ 24 Herman Moore 1.25 .55
❑ 25 Johnnie Morton 1.25 .55
❑ 26 Greg Hill .75 .35
❑ 27 Germane Crowell .75 .35
❑ 28 Kerry Collins 1.25 .55
❑ 29 Ike Hilliard .75 .35
❑ 30 Joe Jurevicius 1.25 .55
❑ 31 Stephen Davis 2.00 .90
❑ 32 Brad Johnson 2.00 .90
❑ 33 Skip Hicks .75 .35
❑ 34 Michael Westbrook 1.25 .55
❑ 35 Jake Plummer 1.25 .55
❑ 36 Adrian Murrell .75 .35
❑ 37 Frank Sanders 1.25 .55
❑ 38 Rob Moore 1.25 .55
❑ 39 Gary Brown .75 .35
❑ 40 Duce Staley 2.00 .90
❑ 41 Charles Johnson 1.25 .55
❑ 42 Emmitt Smith 4.00 1.80
❑ 43 Troy Aikman 4.00 1.80
❑ 44 Michael Irvin 1.25 .55
❑ 45 Deion Sanders 2.00 .90
❑ 46 Rocket Ismail 1.25 .55
❑ 47 Jerry Rice 4.00 1.80
❑ 48 Terrell Owens 2.00 .90
❑ 49 Steve Young 2.50 1.10
❑ 50 Garrison Hearst 1.25 .55
❑ 51 J.J. Stokes 1.25 .55
❑ 52 Lawrence Phillips 1.25 .55
❑ 53 Jamal Anderson 2.00 .90
❑ 54 Chris Chandler 1.25 .55
❑ 55 Terance Mathis 1.25 .55
❑ 56 Tim Dwight 2.00 .90
❑ 57 Charlie Garner 1.25 .55
❑ 58 Chris Calloway 1.25 .55
❑ 59 Eddie Kennison 1.25 .55
❑ 60 Billy Joe Hobert .75 .35
❑ 61 Tim Biakabutuka 1.25 .55
❑ 62 Muhsin Muhammad 1.25 .55
❑ 63 Olandis Gary/1825 RC 25.00 11.00
❑ 64 Wesley Walls 1.25 .55
❑ 65 Isaac Bruce 2.00 .90
❑ 66 Marshall Faulk 2.50 1.10
❑ 67 Kordell Stewart 1.25 .55
❑ 68 Jerome Bettis 2.00 .90
❑ 69 Hines Ward 2.00 .90
❑ 70 Corey Dillon 2.00 .90
❑ 71 Carl Pickens 1.25 .55
❑ 72 Darnay Scott 1.25 .55
❑ 73 Steve McNair 2.00 .90
❑ 74 Eddie George 2.00 .90
❑ 75 Yancey Thigpen .75 .35
❑ 76 Kevin Dyson 1.25 .55
❑ 77 Fred Taylor 2.00 .90
❑ 78 Mark Brunell 2.00 .90
❑ 79 Jimmy Smith 1.25 .55
❑ 80 Keenan McCardell 1.25 .55
❑ 81 James Stewart 1.25 .55
❑ 82 Jermaine Lewis 1.25 .55
❑ 83 Priest Holmes 3.00 1.35
❑ 84 Stoney Case .75 .35
❑ 85 Errict Rhett 1.25 .55
❑ 86 Bill Schroeder 2.00 .90
❑ 87 Terry Kirby .75 .35
❑ 88 Leslie Shepherd .75 .35
❑ 89 Terrence Wilkins/825 RC 20.00 9.00
❑ 90 Dan Marino 6.00 2.70
❑ 91 O.J. McDuffie 1.25 .55
❑ 92 Karim Abdul-Jabbar 1.25 .55
❑ 93 Zach Thomas 2.00 .90
❑ 94 Terry Allen 1.25 .55
❑ 95 Tony Martin 1.25 .55
❑ 96 Drew Bledsoe 2.50 1.10
❑ 97 Terry Glenn 2.00 .90
❑ 98 Ben Coates 1.25 .55
❑ 99 Tony Simmons .75 .35
❑ 100 Curtis Martin 2.00 .90
❑ 101 Keyshawn Johnson 2.00 .90
❑ 102 Vinny Testaverde 1.25 .55
❑ 103 Wayne Chrebet 2.00 .90
❑ 104 Peyton Manning 6.00 2.70
❑ 105 Marvin Harrison 2.00 .90
❑ 106 E.G. Green .75 .35
❑ 107 Doug Flutie 2.00 .90
❑ 108 Thurman Thomas 1.25 .55
❑ 109 Andre Reed 1.25 .55
❑ 110 Eric Moulds 2.00 .90
❑ 111 Antowain Smith 2.00 .90
❑ 112 Bruce Smith 1.25 .55
❑ 113 Terrell Davis 2.00 .90
❑ 114 John Elway 6.00 2.70
❑ 115 Ed McCaffrey 1.25 .55
❑ 116 Rod Smith 1.25 .55
❑ 117 Shannon Sharpe 1.25 .55
❑ 118 Jeff Garcia AU/325 RC 120.00 55.00
❑ 119 Brian Griese 2.00 .90
❑ 120 Justin Watson/325 RC 25.00 11.00
❑ 121 Bubby Brister 1.25 .55
❑ 122 Ryan Leaf 2.00 .90
❑ 123 Natrone Means 1.25 .55
❑ 124 Mikhael Ricks .75 .35
❑ 125 Junior Seau 2.00 .90
❑ 126 Jim Harbaugh 1.25 .55
❑ 127 Andre Rison 1.25 .55
❑ 128 Elvis Grbac 1.25 .55
❑ 129 Bam Morris .75 .35
❑ 130 Rashaan Shehee .75 .35
❑ 131 Warren Moon 2.00 .90
❑ 132 Tony Gonzalez 2.00 .90
❑ 133 Derrick Alexander 1.25 .55
❑ 134 Jon Kitna 2.00 .90
❑ 135 Ricky Watters 1.25 .55
❑ 136 Joey Galloway 1.25 .55
❑ 137 Ahman Green 2.00 .90
❑ 138 Derrick Mayes 1.25 .55
❑ 139 Tyrone Wheatley 1.25 .55
❑ 140 Napoleon Kaufman 2.00 .90
❑ 141 Tim Brown 2.00 .90
❑ 142 Charles Woodson 2.00 .90
❑ 143 Rich Gannon 2.00 .90
❑ 144 Rickey Dudley .75 .35
❑ 145 Az-Zahir Hakim .75 .35
❑ 146 Kurt Warner AU/1825 RC 80.00 36.00
❑ 147 S.Bennett AU/1325 RC 15.00 6.75
❑ 148 Brandon Stokley AU/1325 RC 30.00 13.50
❑ 149 A.Zereoue AU/1325 RC 25.00 11.00
❑ 150 Brock Huard AU/1325 RC 25.00 11.00

❑ 151 Tim Couch AU/1025 RC 40.00 18.00
❑ 152 Ricky Williams AU/725 RC 60.00 27.00
❑ 153 Donovan McNabb AU/525 RC 225.00 100.00
❑ 154 Edgerrin James AU/525 RC 150.00 70.00
❑ 155 Torry Holt AU/1025 RC 80.00 36.00
❑ 156 Daunte Culpepper AU/1025 RC 135.00 60.00
❑ 157 Akili Smith AU/1025 RC 20.00 9.00
❑ 158 Champ Bailey AU/1725 RC 30.00 13.50
❑ 159 Chris Claiborne AU/1825 RC 20.00 9.00
❑ 160A Chris McAlister No AU/1825 RC 15.00 6.75
❑ 160B Jason Tucker AU/1825 15.00 6.75
❑ 161 Troy Edwards AU/1225 RC 20.00 9.00
❑ 162 Jevon Kearse AU/325 RC 80.00 36.00
❑ 163 Darnell McDonald AU/1825 RC 20.00 9.00
❑ 164 David Boston AU/1025 RC 25.00 11.00
❑ 165 Peerless Price AU/1325 RC 40.00 18.00
❑ 166 Cecil Collins AU/1025 RC 15.00 6.75
❑ 167 Rob Konrad AU/1325 RC 20.00 9.00
❑ 168 Cade McNown AU/1025 RC 20.00 9.00
❑ 169 Shawn Bryson AU/1825 RC 20.00 9.00
❑ 170 Kevin Faulk AU/1325 RC 25.00 11.00
❑ 171 Corby Jones AU/1825 RC 15.00 6.75
❑ 172A James Johnson No AU/1325 RC 15.00 6.75
❑ 172B Patrick Jeffers AU/1325 25.00 11.00
❑ 173 Autry Denson AU/1825 RC 20.00 9.00
❑ 174 Sedrick Irvin AU/1825 RC 15.00 6.75
❑ 175 Michael Bishop AU/1825 RC 25.00 11.00
❑ 176 Joe Germaine AU/825 RC 25.00 11.00
❑ 177 De'Mond Parker AU/1325 RC 15.00 6.75
❑ 178A Shaun King No AU/1825 RC 15.00 6.75
❑ 178B Ray Lucas AU/1825 25.00 11.00
❑ 179 D'Wayne Bates AU/1825 RC 20.00 9.00
❑ 180 Tai Streets AU/1825 RC 25.00 11.00
❑ 181 Na Brown AU/1825 RC 20.00 9.00
❑ 182 Desmond Clark AU/1825 RC 20.00 9.00
❑ 183 Jim Kleinsasser AU/1825 RC 20.00 9.00
❑ 184 Kevin Johnson AU/1325 RC 25.00 11.00
❑ 185 Joe Montgomery AU/1325 RC 20.00 9.00
❑ 186 John Elway PT 10.00 4.50
❑ 187 Dan Marino PT 10.00 4.50
❑ 188 Jerry Rice PT 6.00 2.70
❑ 189 Barry Sanders PT 10.00 4.50
❑ 190 Steve Young PT 4.00 1.80
❑ 191 Doug Flutie PT 2.50 1.10
❑ 192 Troy Aikman PT 6.00 2.70
❑ 193 Drew Bledsoe PT 4.00 1.80
❑ 194 Brett Favre PT 10.00 4.50
❑ 195 Randall Cunningham PT 2.50 1.10
❑ 196 Terrell Davis PT 2.50 1.10
❑ 197 Kordell Stewart PT 2.50 1.10
❑ 198 Keyshawn Johnson PT 2.50 1.10
❑ 199 Jake Plummer PT 2.50 1.10
❑ 200 Peyton Manning PT 10.00 4.50
❑ 201 Jay Fiedler/1825 AU 25.00 11.00
❑ 202 Kevin Daft/325 AU 40.00 18.00

1999 Playoff Contenders SSD Finesse Gold

Nm-Mt Ex-Mt
*STARS: 10X TO 25X BASIC CARDS
*PT STARS: 5X TO 12X
❑ 63 Olandis Gary 75.00 34.00
❑ 89 Terrence Wilkins 50.00 22.00
❑ 118 Jeff Garcia 250.00 110.00
❑ 120 Justin Watson 120.00 55.00
❑ 146 Kurt Warner 250.00 110.00
❑ 147 Sean Bennett 40.00 18.00
❑ 148 Brandon Stokley 100.00 45.00
❑ 150 Brock Huard 75.00 34.00
❑ 151 Tim Couch 75.00 34.00
❑ 152 Ricky Williams 200.00 90.00
❑ 153 Donovan McNabb 600.00 275.00
❑ 154 Edgerrin James 400.00 180.00
❑ 155 Torry Holt 150.00 70.00
❑ 156 Daunte Culpepper 400.00 180.00
❑ 157 Akili Smith 50.00 22.00
❑ 160A Chris McAlister No AU 40.00 18.00
❑ 160B Jason Tucker
❑ 162 Jevon Kearse 120.00 55.00
❑ 164 David Boston 75.00 34.00
❑ 165 Peerless Price 120.00 55.00
❑ 166 Cecil Collins No AU 25.00 11.00
❑ 168 Cade McNown 50.00 22.00
❑ 171 Corby Jones 40.00 18.00
❑ 172A James Johnson No AU 60.00 27.00
❑ 172B Patrick Jeffers 80.00 36.00
❑ 175 Michael Bishop 75.00 34.00
❑ 177 De'Mond Parker 40.00 18.00
❑ 178B Ray Lucas 60.00 27.00
❑ 179 D'Wayne Bates 50.00 22.00
❑ 180 Tai Streets 100.00 45.00
❑ 181 Na Brown 40.00 18.00
❑ 184 Kevin Johnson 75.00 34.00
❑ 185 Joe Montgomery 50.00 22.00
❑ 201 Jay Fiedler 75.00 34.00
❑ 202 Kevin Daft 80.00 36.00

1999 Playoff Contenders SSD Power Blue

Nm-Mt Ex-Mt
*STARS: 5X TO 12X BASIC CARDS
*PT STARS: 4X TO 10X
❑ 63 Olandis Gary 50.00 22.00
❑ 89 Terrence Wilkins 30.00 13.50
❑ 118 Jeff Garcia 150.00 70.00
❑ 120 Justin Watson 80.00 36.00
❑ 146 Kurt Warner 150.00 70.00
❑ 147 Sean Bennett 25.00 11.00
❑ 148 Brandon Stokley 60.00 27.00
❑ 150 Brock Huard 50.00 22.00
❑ 151 Tim Couch 80.00 36.00
❑ 152 Ricky Williams 120.00 55.00
❑ 153 Donovan McNabb 300.00 135.00
❑ 154 Edgerrin James 250.00 110.00
❑ 155 Torry Holt 150.00 70.00
❑ 156 Daunte Culpepper 250.00 110.00
❑ 157 Akili Smith 30.00 13.50
❑ 160A Chris McAlister No AU 25.00 11.00
❑ 160B Jason Tucker 30.00 13.50
❑ 162 Jevon Kearse 100.00 45.00
❑ 164 David Boston 50.00 22.00
❑ 165 Peerless Price 100.00 45.00
❑ 166 Cecil Collins No AU 8.00 3.60
❑ 168 Cade McNown 30.00 13.50
❑ 171 Corby Jones 25.00 11.00
❑ 172A James Johnson No AU 30.00 13.50
❑ 172B Patrick Jeffers 50.00 22.00
❑ 175 Michael Bishop 50.00 22.00
❑ 177 De'Mond Parker 25.00 11.00
❑ 178B Ray Lucas 50.00 22.00
❑ 179 D'Wayne Bates 30.00 13.50
❑ 180 Tai Streets 50.00 22.00
❑ 181 Na Brown 25.00 11.00
❑ 184 Kevin Johnson 30.00 13.50
❑ 185 Joe Montgomery 30.00 13.50
❑ 201 Jay Fiedler 50.00 22.00
❑ 202 Kevin Daft 50.00 22.00

1999 Playoff Contenders SSD Speed Red

Nm-Mt Ex-Mt
*STARS: 3X TO 8X BASIC CARDS
COMMON ROOKIE AUTO 20.00 9.00
ROOKIE SEMISTARS AUTO 25.00 11.00
ROOKIE UNL.STARS AUTO 30.00 13.50

*PT STARS: 2X TO 5X
❑ 63 Olandis Gary 30.00 13.50
❑ 89 Terrence Wilkins 25.00 11.00
❑ 118 Jeff Garcia 100.00 45.00
❑ 120 Justin Watson 60.00 27.00
❑ 146 Kurt Warner 100.00 45.00
❑ 147 Sean Bennett 20.00 9.00
❑ 148 Brandon Stokley 40.00 18.00
❑ 150 Brock Huard 30.00 13.50
❑ 151 Tim Couch 50.00 22.00
❑ 152 Ricky Williams 80.00 36.00
❑ 153 Donovan McNabb 250.00 110.00
❑ 154 Edgerrin James 150.00 70.00
❑ 155 Torry Holt 100.00 45.00
❑ 156 Daunte Culpepper 200.00 90.00
❑ 157 Akili Smith 25.00 11.00
❑ 160A Chris McAlister No AU 15.00 6.75
❑ 160B Jason Tucker 25.00 11.00
❑ 162 Jevon Kearse 75.00 34.00
❑ 164 David Boston 30.00 13.50
❑ 165 Peerless Price 75.00 34.00
❑ 166 Cecil Collins No AU 5.00 2.20
❑ 168 Cade McNown 25.00 11.00
❑ 171 Corby Jones 20.00 9.00
❑ 172A James Johnson No AU 30.00 13.50
❑ 172B Patrick Jeffers 40.00 18.00
❑ 175 Michael Bishop 30.00 13.50
❑ 177 De'Mond Parker 20.00 9.00
❑ 178B Ray Lucas 30.00 13.50
❑ 179 D'Wayne Bates 25.00 11.00
❑ 180 Tai Streets 30.00 13.50
❑ 181 Na Brown 20.00 9.00
❑ 184 Kevin Johnson 30.00 13.50
❑ 185 Joe Montgomery 25.00 11.00
❑ 201 Jay Fiedler 30.00 13.50
❑ 202 Kevin Daft 40.00 18.00

2000 Playoff Contenders

Nm-Mt Ex-Mt
COMP.SET w/o SP's (100) 20.00 9.00
❑ 1 David Boston .75 .35
❑ 2 Jake Plummer .50 .23
❑ 3 Chris Chandler .50 .23
❑ 4 Jamal Anderson .75 .35
❑ 5 Tim Dwight .75 .35
❑ 6 Qadry Ismail .50 .23
❑ 7 Tony Banks .50 .23
❑ 8 Lamar Smith .50 .23
❑ 9 Doug Flutie .75 .35
❑ 10 Eric Moulds .75 .35

❑ 11 Peerless Price	.75	.35
❑ 12 Rob Johnson	.50	.23
❑ 13 Muhsin Muhammad	.50	.23
❑ 14 Reggie White	.75	.35
❑ 15 Steve Beuerlein	.50	.23
❑ 16 Cade McNown	.30	.14
❑ 17 Derrick Alexander	.50	.23
❑ 18 Marcus Robinson	.50	.23
❑ 19 Akili Smith	.30	.14
❑ 20 Corey Dillon	.75	.35
❑ 21 Kevin Johnson	.75	.35
❑ 22 Tim Couch	.50	.23
❑ 23 Emmitt Smith	1.50	.70
❑ 24 Joey Galloway	.50	.23
❑ 25 Rocket Ismail	.50	.23
❑ 26 Troy Aikman	1.50	.70
❑ 27 Brian Griese	.75	.35
❑ 28 Ed McCaffrey	.75	.35
❑ 29 John Elway	2.50	1.10
❑ 30 Olandis Gary	.75	.35
❑ 31 Rod Smith	.50	.23
❑ 32 Terrell Davis	.75	.35
❑ 33 Charlie Batch	.75	.35
❑ 34 Germane Crowell	.30	.14
❑ 35 James Stewart	.50	.23
❑ 36 Barry Sanders	2.00	.90
❑ 37 Antonio Freeman	.75	.35
❑ 38 Brett Favre	2.50	1.10
❑ 39 Dorsey Levens	.50	.23
❑ 40 Edgerrin James	1.25	.55
❑ 41 Marvin Harrison	.75	.35
❑ 42 Peyton Manning	2.00	.90
❑ 43 Fred Taylor	.75	.35
❑ 44 Jimmy Smith	.50	.23
❑ 45 Mark Brunell	.75	.35
❑ 46 Elvis Grbac	.50	.23
❑ 47 Tony Gonzalez	.50	.23
❑ 48 Dan Marino	2.50	1.10
❑ 49 Joe Horn	.50	.23
❑ 50 Jay Fiedler	.75	.35
❑ 51 Thurman Thomas	.50	.23
❑ 52 Cris Carter	.75	.35
❑ 53 Daunte Culpepper	1.00	.45
❑ 54 Randy Moss	1.50	.70
❑ 55 Robert Smith	.75	.35
❑ 56 Drew Bledsoe	1.00	.45
❑ 57 Terry Glenn	.50	.23
❑ 58 Ricky Williams	.75	.35
❑ 59 Amani Toomer	.30	.14
❑ 60 Kerry Collins	.50	.23
❑ 61 Curtis Martin	.75	.35
❑ 62 Vinny Testaverde	.50	.23
❑ 63 Wayne Chrebet	.50	.23
❑ 64 Rich Gannon	.75	.35
❑ 65 Tim Brown	.75	.35
❑ 66 Tyrone Wheatley	.50	.23
❑ 67 Donovan McNabb	1.25	.55
❑ 68 Duce Staley	.75	.35
❑ 69 Jerome Bettis	.75	.35
❑ 70 Jermaine Fazande	.30	.14
❑ 71 Junior Seau	.75	.35
❑ 72 Donald Hayes	.30	.14
❑ 73 Charlie Garner	.50	.23
❑ 74 Jeff Garcia	.75	.35
❑ 75 Jerry Rice	1.50	.70
❑ 76 Steve Young	1.00	.45
❑ 77 Terrell Owens	.75	.35
❑ 78 Tiki Barber	.50	.23
❑ 79 Tim Biakabutuka	.50	.23
❑ 80 Ricky Watters	.50	.23
❑ 81 Isaac Bruce	.75	.35
❑ 82 Kurt Warner	1.50	.70
❑ 83 Marshall Faulk	1.00	.45
❑ 84 Torry Holt	.75	.35
❑ 85 Keyshawn Johnson	.75	.35
❑ 86 Mike Alstott	.75	.35
❑ 87 Shaun King	.30	.14
❑ 88 Warren Sapp	.50	.23
❑ 89 Warrick Dunn	.75	.35
❑ 90 Eddie George	.75	.35
❑ 91 Jevon Kearse	.75	.35
❑ 92 Steve McNair	.75	.35
❑ 93 Carl Pickens	.50	.23
❑ 94 Albert Connell	.30	.14
❑ 95 Brad Johnson	.75	.35
❑ 96 Bruce Smith	.50	.23
❑ 97 Deion Sanders	.75	.35
❑ 98 Jeff George	.50	.23
❑ 99 Michael Westbrook	.50	.23
❑ 100 Stephen Davis	.75	.35
❑ 101 Courtney Brown AU RC	80.00	36.00
❑ 102 Corey Simon AU RC	20.00	9.00
❑ 103 Brian Urlacher AU RC	80.00	36.00
❑ 104 Deon Grant AU RC	15.00	6.75
❑ 105 Peter Warrick AU RC	40.00	18.00
❑ 106 Jamal Lewis AU RC	60.00	27.00
❑ 107 Thomas Jones EXCH		
❑ 108 Plaxico Burress AU RC	50.00	22.00
❑ 109 Travis Taylor AU RC	25.00	11.00
❑ 110 Ron Dayne AU RC	40.00	18.00
❑ 111 Bubba Franks AU RC	40.00	18.00
❑ 112 Chad Pennington AU RC	100.00	45.00
❑ 113 Shaun Alexander AU RC	75.00	34.00
❑ 114 Sylvester Morris AU RC	15.00	6.75
❑ 115 Mike Anderson AU RC	30.00	13.50
❑ 116 R.Jay Soward AU RC	15.00	6.75
❑ 117 Trung Canidate AU RC	15.00	6.75
❑ 118 Dennis Northcutt AU RC	20.00	9.00
❑ 119 Todd Pinkston AU RC	20.00	9.00
❑ 120 Jerry Porter AU RC	50.00	22.00
❑ 121 Travis Prentice AU RC	15.00	6.75
❑ 122 Giovanni Carmazzi AU RC	15.00	6.75
❑ 123 Ron Dugans AU RC	10.00	4.50
❑ 124 Dez White AU RC	20.00	9.00
❑ 125 Chris Cole AU RC	15.00	6.75
❑ 126 Ron Dixon AU RC	15.00	6.75
❑ 127 Chris Redman AU RC	15.00	6.75
❑ 128 J.R. Redmond AU RC	20.00	9.00
❑ 129 Laveranues Coles AU RC	30.00	13.50
❑ 130 JaJuan Dawson AU RC	10.00	4.50
❑ 131 Darrell Jackson AU RC	30.00	13.50
❑ 132 Reuben Droughns AU RC	30.00	13.50
❑ 133 Doug Chapman AU RC	15.00	6.75
❑ 134 Curtis Keaton AU RC	15.00	6.75
❑ 135 Gari Scott AU RC	10.00	4.50
❑ 136 Danny Farmer AU RC	15.00	6.75
❑ 137 Trevor Gaylor AU RC	15.00	6.75
❑ 138 Avion Black AU RC	15.00	6.75
❑ 139 Michael Wiley AU RC	15.00	6.75
❑ 140 Sammy Morris AU RC	15.00	6.75
❑ 141 Tee Martin AU RC	20.00	9.00
❑ 142 Troy Walters AU RC	20.00	9.00
❑ 143 Marc Bulger AU RC	60.00	27.00
❑ 144 Tom Brady AU RC	350.00	160.00
❑ 145 Todd Husak AU RC	20.00	9.00
❑ 146 Tim Rattay AU RC	40.00	18.00
❑ 147 Jarious Jackson AU RC	15.00	6.75
❑ 148 Joe Hamilton AU RC	15.00	6.75
❑ 149 Shyrone Stith AU RC	15.00	6.75
❑ 150 Kwame Cavil AU RC	10.00	4.50
❑ 151 Antonio Banks ET AU RC	6.00	2.70
❑ 152 Jonathan Brown ET AU RC	6.00	2.70
❑ 153 Ontiwaun Carter ET AU RC	6.00	2.70
❑ 154 Jeremaine Copeland ET	6.00	2.70
❑ 155 Ralph Dawkins ET AU RC	8.00	3.60
❑ 156 Marques Douglas ET AU RC	6.00	2.70
❑ 157 Kevin Drake ET AU RC	6.00	2.70
❑ 158 Damon Dunn ET AU RC	8.00	3.60
❑ 159 Todd Floyd ET AU RC	6.00	2.70
❑ 160 Tony Graziani ET AU	8.00	3.60
❑ 161 Derrick Ham ET EXCH		
❑ 162 Duane Hawthorne ET AU RC	8.00	3.60
❑ 163 Alonzo Johnson ET AU RC	6.00	2.70
❑ 164 Mark Kacmarynski ET AU RC	6.00	2.70
❑ 165 Eric Kresser ET AU	6.00	2.70
❑ 166 Jim Kubiak ET AU RC	8.00	3.60
❑ 167 Blaine McElmurry ET AU RC	6.00	2.70
❑ 168 Scott Milanovich ET AU	10.00	4.50
❑ 169 Norman Miller ET AU RC	6.00	2.70
❑ 170 Sean Morey ET AU RC	8.00	3.60
❑ 171 Jeff Ogden ET AU	8.00	3.60
❑ 172 Pepe Pearson ET AU RC	8.00	3.60
❑ 173 Ron Powlus ET AU RC	10.00	4.50
❑ 174 Jason Shelley ET AU RC	8.00	3.60
❑ 175 Ben Snell ET AU RC	8.00	3.60
❑ 176 Aaron Stecker ET AU RC	8.00	3.60
❑ 177 L.C. Stevens ET AU	6.00	2.70
❑ 178 Mike Sutton ET AU RC	6.00	2.70
❑ 179 Damian Vaughn ET AU RC	6.00	2.70
❑ 180 Ted White ET AU	6.00	2.70
❑ 181 Marcus Crandell ET AU RC	8.00	3.60
❑ 182 Darryl Daniel ET AU RC	8.00	3.60
❑ 183 Jesse Haynes ET AU	6.00	2.70
❑ 184 Matt Lytle ET AU RC	8.00	3.60
❑ 185 Deon Mitchell ET AU RC	8.00	3.60
❑ 186 Kendrick Nord ET AU RC	6.00	2.70
❑ 187 Ronnie Powell EXCH		
❑ 188 Selucio Sanford ET AU RC	8.00	3.60
❑ 189 Corey Thomas ET AU	6.00	2.70
❑ 190 V.Jackson ET AU RC	6.00	2.70
❑ 191 Jake Plummer PT	20.00	9.00
❑ 192 Jim Kelly PT AU	40.00	18.00
❑ 193 Bernie Kosar PT AU	40.00	18.00
❑ 194 Marvin Harrison PT AU	40.00	18.00
❑ 195 Fred Taylor PT EXCH		
❑ 196 Kerry Collins PT AU	30.00	13.50
❑ 197 Kurt Warner PT AU	60.00	27.00
❑ 198 Jevon Kearse PT AUTO	30.00	13.50
❑ 199 Brad Johnson PT AU	30.00	13.50
❑ 200 Jeff George PT AU	30.00	13.50

2000 Playoff Contenders Championship Ticket

*CHAMP.TIC.STARS: 5X TO 12X HI COL.
*CHAMP.TICKET ET AUTOS: .6X TO 1.5X

Card	Nm-Mt	Ex-Mt
❑ 101 Courtney Brown AU	50.00	22.00
❑ 102 Corey Simon AU	30.00	13.50
❑ 103 Brian Urlacher AU	120.00	55.00
❑ 104 Deon Grant AU	20.00	9.00
❑ 105 Peter Warrick AU	30.00	13.50
❑ 106 Jamal Lewis AU	100.00	45.00
❑ 107 Thomas Jones AU EXCH		
❑ 108 Plaxico Burress AU	80.00	36.00
❑ 109 Travis Taylor AU	30.00	13.50
❑ 110 Ron Dayne AU	30.00	13.50
❑ 111 Bubba Franks AU	30.00	13.50
❑ 112 Chad Pennington AU	120.00	55.00
❑ 113 Shaun Alexander AU	100.00	45.00
❑ 114 Sylvester Morris AU	20.00	9.00
❑ 115 Mike Anderson AU	30.00	13.50
❑ 116 R.Jay Soward AU	20.00	9.00
❑ 117 Trung Canidate AU	20.00	9.00
❑ 118 Dennis Northcutt AU	30.00	13.50
❑ 119 Todd Pinkston AU	30.00	13.50
❑ 120 Jerry Porter AU	50.00	22.00
❑ 121 Travis Prentice AU	20.00	9.00
❑ 122 Giovanni Carmazzi AU	30.00	13.50
❑ 123 Ron Dugans AU	12.00	5.50
❑ 124 Dez White AU	30.00	13.50
❑ 125 Chris Cole AU	20.00	9.00

❑ 126 Ron Dixon AU 20.00 9.00
❑ 127 Chris Redman AU 20.00 9.00
❑ 128 J.R. Redmond EXCH
❑ 129 Laveranues Coles AU 40.00 18.00
❑ 130 JaJuan Dawson AU 12.00 5.50
❑ 131 Darrell Jackson AU 50.00 22.00
❑ 132 Reuben Droughns AU 50.00 22.00
❑ 133 Doug Chapman AU 20.00 9.00
❑ 134 Curtis Keaton AU 20.00 9.00
❑ 135 Gari Scott AU 12.00 5.50
❑ 136 Danny Farmer AU 20.00 9.00
❑ 137 Trevor Gaylor AU 20.00 9.00
❑ 138 Avion Black AU 20.00 9.00
❑ 139 Michael Wiley AU 20.00 9.00
❑ 140 Sammy Morris AU 20.00 9.00
❑ 141 Tee Martin AU 30.00 13.50
❑ 142 Troy Walters AU 30.00 13.50
❑ 143 Marc Bulger AU 100.00 45.00
❑ 144 Tom Brady AU 600.00 275.00
❑ 145 Todd Husak AU 30.00 13.50
❑ 146 Tim Rattay AU 80.00 36.00
❑ 147 Jarious Jackson AU 20.00 9.00
❑ 148 Joe Hamilton AU 20.00 9.00
❑ 149 Shyrone Stith AU 20.00 9.00
❑ 150 Kwame Cavil AU 12.00 5.50
❑ 191 Jake Plummer PT 20.00 9.00
❑ 192 Jim Kelly AU PT 50.00 22.00
❑ 193 Bernie Kosar AU PT 40.00 18.00
❑ 194 Marvin Harrison AU PT 40.00 18.00
❑ 195 Fred Taylor PT EXCH
❑ 196 Kerry Collins AU PT 25.00 11.00
❑ 197 Kurt Warner AU PT 80.00 36.00
❑ 198 Jevon Kearse PT AU 25.00 11.00
❑ 199 Brad Johnson AU PT 25.00 11.00
❑ 200 Jeff George PT AU 25.00 11.00

2001 Playoff Contenders

Nm-Mt Ex-Mt
COMP.SET w/o SP's (100) 25.00 7.50
❑ 1 David Boston 1.00 .30
❑ 2 Jake Plummer .60 .18
❑ 3 Jamal Anderson 1.00 .30
❑ 4 Chris Chandler .60 .18
❑ 5 Elvis Grbac .60 .18
❑ 6 Brandon Stokley .60 .18
❑ 7 Travis Taylor .60 .18
❑ 8 Ray Lewis 1.00 .30
❑ 9 Rob Johnson .60 .18
❑ 10 Eric Moulds .60 .18
❑ 11 Tim Biakabutuka .60 .18
❑ 12 Muhsin Muhammad .60 .18
❑ 13 James Allen .60 .18
❑ 14 Brian Urlacher 1.50 .45
❑ 15 Peter Warrick 1.00 .30
❑ 16 Corey Dillon 1.00 .30
❑ 17 Tim Couch .60 .18
❑ 18 Kevin Johnson .60 .18
❑ 19 Rickey Dudley .40 .12
❑ 20 Emmitt Smith 2.00 .60
❑ 21 Joey Galloway .60 .18
❑ 22 Brian Griese 1.00 .30
❑ 23 Terrell Davis 1.00 .30
❑ 24 Mike Anderson 1.00 .30
❑ 25 Ed McCaffrey 1.00 .30
❑ 26 Rod Smith .60 .18
❑ 27 Charlie Batch 1.00 .30
❑ 28 James Stewart .60 .18
❑ 29 Germane Crowell .40 .12
❑ 30 Johnnie Morton .60 .18
❑ 31 Brett Favre 3.00 .90
❑ 32 Ahman Green 1.00 .30
❑ 33 Antonio Freeman 1.00 .30
❑ 34 Peyton Manning 2.50 .75
❑ 35 Edgerrin James 1.25 .35
❑ 36 Marvin Harrison 1.00 .30
❑ 37 Jerome Pathon .60 .18
❑ 38 Mark Brunell 1.00 .30
❑ 39 Fred Taylor 1.00 .30
❑ 40 Keenan McCardell .40 .12
❑ 41 Jimmy Smith .60 .18
❑ 42 Trent Green 1.00 .30
❑ 43 Priest Holmes 1.25 .35
❑ 44 Tony Gonzalez .60 .18
❑ 45 Derrick Alexander .60 .18
❑ 46 Jay Fiedler 1.00 .30
❑ 47 Lamar Smith .60 .18
❑ 48 Zach Thomas 1.00 .30
❑ 49 Oronde Gadsden .60 .18
❑ 50 Daunte Culpepper 1.00 .30
❑ 51 Randy Moss 2.00 .60
❑ 52 Cris Carter 1.00 .30
❑ 53 Drew Bledsoe 1.25 .35
❑ 54 J.R. Redmond .40 .12
❑ 55 Troy Brown .60 .18
❑ 56 Aaron Brooks 1.00 .30
❑ 57 Ricky Williams 1.00 .30
❑ 58 Joe Horn .60 .18
❑ 59 Kerry Collins .60 .18
❑ 60 Tiki Barber .60 .18
❑ 61 Ron Dayne 1.00 .30
❑ 62 Ike Hilliard .60 .18
❑ 63 Vinny Testaverde .60 .18
❑ 64 Curtis Martin 1.00 .30
❑ 65 Wayne Chrebet .60 .18
❑ 66 Laveranues Coles 1.00 .30
❑ 67 Rich Gannon 1.00 .30
❑ 68 Tyrone Wheatley .60 .18
❑ 69 Tim Brown 1.00 .30
❑ 70 Jerry Rice 2.00 .60
❑ 71 Donovan McNabb 1.25 .35
❑ 72 Duce Staley 1.00 .30
❑ 73 Todd Pinkston .60 .18
❑ 74 Kordell Stewart .60 .18
❑ 75 Jerome Bettis 1.00 .30
❑ 76 Plaxico Burress 1.00 .30
❑ 77 Doug Flutie 1.00 .30
❑ 78 Junior Seau 1.00 .30
❑ 79 Jeff Garcia 1.00 .30
❑ 80 Garrison Hearst .60 .18
❑ 81 Terrell Owens 1.00 .30
❑ 82 Matt Hasselbeck .60 .18
❑ 83 Ricky Watters .60 .18
❑ 84 Shaun Alexander 1.25 .35
❑ 85 Darrell Jackson 1.00 .30
❑ 86 Kurt Warner 2.00 .60
❑ 87 Marshall Faulk 1.25 .35
❑ 88 Isaac Bruce 1.00 .30
❑ 89 Torry Holt 1.00 .30
❑ 90 Brad Johnson 1.00 .30
❑ 91 Keyshawn Johnson 1.00 .30
❑ 92 Warrick Dunn 1.00 .30
❑ 93 Warren Sapp .60 .18
❑ 94 Steve McNair 1.00 .30
❑ 95 Eddie George 1.00 .30
❑ 96 Derrick Mason .60 .18
❑ 97 Jevon Kearse .60 .18
❑ 98 Stephen Davis 1.00 .30
❑ 99 Bruce Smith .60 .18
❑ 100 Michael Westbrook .60 .18
❑ 101 Adam Archuleta/50 RC 100.00 30.00
❑ 102 Alex Bannister AU RC 15.00 4.50
❑ 103 Alge Crumpler AU RC 30.00 9.00
❑ 104 Andre Carter AU/100 RC 50.00 15.00
❑ 105 Anthony Thomas AU/600 RC 50.00 15.00
❑ 106 Ben Leard AU RC 10.00 3.00
❑ 107 Bobby Newcombe AU RC 15.00 4.50
❑ 108 Brian Allen AU RC 10.00 3.00
❑ 109 Carlos Polk AU RC 10.00 3.00
❑ 110 Casey Hampton No Auto RC 15.004.50
❑ 111 Cedric Scott AU RC 10.00 3.00
❑ 112 Cedrick Wilson AU RC 25.00 7.50
❑ 113 Chad Johnson AU RC 60.00 18.00
❑ 114 Chris Chambers AU/170 RC 150.00 45.00
❑ 115 Chris Weinke AU/350 RC 30.00 9.00
❑ 116 Correll Buckhalter AU/590 RC 30.00 9.00
❑ 117 Damione Lewis AU RC 25.00 7.50
❑ 118 Dan Morgan AU RC 50.00 15.00
❑ 119 Daniel Guy AU RC 10.00 3.00
❑ 120 David Allen AU RC 10.00 3.00
❑ 121 David Terrell AU/500 RC 30.00 9.00
❑ 122 Ken Lucas AU/276 RC 10.00 3.00
❑ 123 Deuce McAllister AU/500 RC 120.00 36.00
❑ 124 Drew Brees AU/500 RC 80.00 24.00
❑ 125 Eddie Berlin AU RC 10.00 3.00
❑ 126 Boo Williams AU/50 RC 60.00 18.00
❑ 127 Ennis Davis AU RC 10.00 3.00
❑ 128 Freddie Mitchell AU RC 25.00 7.50
❑ 129 Gary Baxter AU RC 15.00 4.50
❑ 130 Gerard Warren AU/200 RC 40.0012.00
❑ 131 Hakim Akbar AU RC 10.00 3.00
❑ 132 Heath Evans AU RC 10.00 3.00
❑ 133 Jabari Holloway AU RC 15.00 4.50
❑ 134 Jamal Reynolds AU/500 RC 15.004.50
❑ 135 James Jackson AU RC 15.00 4.50
❑ 136 Jamie Winborn AU RC 10.00 3.00
❑ 137 Javon Green AU RC 10.00 3.00
❑ 138 Jesse Palmer AU RC 25.00 7.50
❑ 139 Dominic Rhodes AU/300 RC 40.00 12.00
❑ 140 Josh Heupel AU/150 RC 50.00 15.00
❑ 141 Justin Smith AU RC 15.00 4.50
❑ 142 Karon Riley AU RC 10.00 3.00
❑ 143 Keith Adams/50 RC 80.00 24.00
❑ 144 Kendrell Bell AU RC 40.00 12.00
❑ 145 Kenny Smith AU RC 15.00 4.50
❑ 146 Kenyatta Walker AU/50 RC 80.0024.00
❑ 147 Ken-Yon Rambo AU RC 10.00 3.00
❑ 148 Kevan Barlow AU RC 40.00 12.00
❑ 149 Koren Robinson AU/400 RC 40.00 12.00
❑ 150 LaDainian Tomlinson AU RC/600 200.00 60.00
❑ 151 LaMont Jordan AU/50 RC 350.00 105.00
❑ 152 Leonard Davis/50 RC 100.00 30.00
❑ 153 Marcus Stroud AU RC 25.00 7.50
❑ 154 Marques Tuiasosopo AU RC 30.009.00
❑ 155 Snoop Minnis AU/295 RC 15.00 4.50
❑ 156 Michael Bennett AU/600 RC 60.00 18.00
❑ 157 Michael Vick AU/327 RC 400.00120.00
❑ 158 Mike McMahon AU/529 RC 30.00 9.00
❑ 159 Moran Norris AU RC 10.00 3.00
❑ 160 Morlon Greenwood AU RC 10.00 3.00
❑ 161 Nate Clements/50 RC 100.00 30.00
❑ 162 Quincy Carter AU SP RC 250.00 75.00
❑ 163 Quincy Morgan AU RC 25.00 7.50
❑ 164 Jamar Fletcher/50 RC 80.00 24.00
❑ 165 Reggie Germany AU RC 10.00 3.00
❑ 166 Reggie Wayne AU/400 RC 60.0018.00
❑ 167 Reggie White AU RC 10.00 3.00
❑ 168 Richard Seymour/50 RC 100.00 30.00
❑ 169 Robert Carswell/50 RC 80.00 24.00
❑ 170 Robert Ferguson AU RC 25.00 7.50
❑ 171 Rod Gardner AU/75 RC 200.00 60.00
❑ 172 Ronney Daniels AU RC 10.00 3.00
❑ 173 Rudi Johnson AU RC 50.00 15.00
❑ 174 Sage Rosenfels AU/400 RC 15.004.50
❑ 175 Santana Moss AU/500 RC 50.00 15.00
❑ 176 Shaun Rogers AU RC 25.00 7.50
❑ 177 T.J. Houshmandzadeh AU RC 30.00 9.00
❑ 178 Tim Hasselbeck AU RC 25.00 7.50
❑ 179 Todd Heap AU/169 RC 120.00 36.00
❑ 180 Tony Stewart AU RC 15.00 4.50
❑ 181 Torrance Marshall AU RC 15.00 4.50
❑ 182 Travis Henry AU/369 RC 60.00 18.00
❑ 183 Travis Minor AU RC 25.00 7.50
❑ 184 Vinny Sutherland AU RC 15.00 4.50
❑ 185 Will Allen AU RC 15.00 4.50
❑ 186 Willie Howard AU RC 10.00 3.00
❑ 187 Middlebrooks RC/50 60.00 18.00
❑ 188 Derrick Blaylock AU/200 RC 50.00 15.00
❑ 189 A.J. Feeley AU/200 RC 120.00 36.00
❑ 190 Steve Smith AU/300 RC 60.00 18.00
❑ 191 Onome Ojo AU/200 RC 15.00 4.50
❑ 192 Dee Brown AU 300 RC 25.00 7.50

❑ 193 Kevin Kasper AU/200 RC	25.00	7.50
❑ 194 Dave Dickenson AU/300 RC	30.00	9.00
❑ 195 Chris Barnes AU/200 RC	25.00	7.50
❑ 196 Scotty Anderson AU/300 RC	25.00	7.50
❑ 197 Chris Taylor AU/300 RC	15.00	4.50
❑ 198 Cedric James AU/300 SP RC	25.00	7.50
❑ 199 Justin McCareins AU/200 RC	50.00	15.00
❑ 200 Tommy Polley AU/200 RC	25.00	7.50

2001 Playoff Contenders Championship Ticket

	Nm-Mt	Ex-Mt
*STARS: 3X TO 8X BASIC CARDS		
❑ 101 Adam Archuleta	12.00	3.60
❑ 102 Alex Bannister	10.00	3.00
❑ 103 Alge Crumpler	15.00	4.50
❑ 104 Andre Carter	12.00	3.60
❑ 105 Anthony Thomas	25.00	7.50
❑ 106 Ben Leard	10.00	3.00
❑ 107 Bobby Newcombe	10.00	3.00
❑ 108 Brian Allen	6.00	1.80
❑ 109 Carlos Polk	6.00	1.80
❑ 110 Casey Hampton	10.00	3.00
❑ 111 Cedric Scott	10.00	3.00
❑ 112 Cedrick Wilson	12.00	3.60
❑ 113 Chad Johnson	30.00	9.00
❑ 114 Chris Chambers	20.00	6.00
❑ 115 Chris Weinke	12.00	3.60
❑ 116 Correll Buckhalter	20.00	6.00
❑ 117 Damione Lewis	10.00	3.00
❑ 118 Dan Morgan	12.00	3.60
❑ 119 Daniel Guy	6.00	1.80
❑ 120 David Allen	10.00	3.00
❑ 121 David Terrell	12.00	3.60
❑ 122 Ken Lucas	10.00	3.00
❑ 123 Deuce McAllister	40.00	12.00
❑ 124 Drew Brees	30.00	9.00
❑ 125 Eddie Berlin	10.00	3.00
❑ 126 Boo Williams	10.00	3.00
❑ 127 Ennis Davis	6.00	1.80
❑ 128 Freddie Mitchell	12.00	3.60
❑ 129 Gary Baxter	10.00	3.00
❑ 130 Gerard Warren	12.00	3.60
❑ 131 Hakim Akbar	6.00	1.80
❑ 132 Heath Evans	10.00	3.00
❑ 133 Jabari Holloway	10.00	3.00
❑ 134 Jamal Reynolds	12.00	3.60
❑ 135 James Jackson	12.00	3.60
❑ 136 Jamie Winborn	10.00	3.00
❑ 137 Javon Green	10.00	3.00
❑ 138 Jesse Palmer	12.00	3.60
❑ 139 Dominic Rhodes	20.00	6.00
❑ 140 Josh Heupel	12.00	3.60
❑ 141 Justin Smith	12.00	3.60
❑ 142 Karon Riley	6.00	1.80
❑ 143 Keith Adams	6.00	1.80
❑ 144 Kendrell Bell	40.00	12.00
❑ 145 Kenny Smith	10.00	3.00
❑ 146 Kenyatta Walker	6.00	1.80
❑ 147 Ken-Yon Rambo	10.00	3.00
❑ 148 Kevan Barlow	12.00	3.60
❑ 149 Koren Robinson		
❑ 150 LaDainian Tomlinson	50.00	15.00
❑ 151 LaMont Jordan	15.00	4.50
❑ 152 Leonard Davis	10.00	3.00
❑ 153 Marcus Stroud	12.00	3.60
❑ 154 Marques Tuiasosopo	12.00	3.60
❑ 155 Snoop Minnis	10.00	3.00
❑ 156 Michael Bennett	30.00	9.00
❑ 157 Michael Vick	150.00	45.00
❑ 158 Mike McMahon	12.00	3.60
❑ 159 Moran Norris	6.00	1.80
❑ 160 Morlon Greenwood	10.00	3.00
❑ 161 Nate Clements	12.00	3.60
❑ 162 Quincy Carter	12.00	3.60
❑ 163 Quincy Morgan	12.00	3.60
❑ 164 Jamar Fletcher	10.00	3.00
❑ 165 Reggie Germany	10.00	3.00
❑ 166 Reggie Wayne	25.00	7.50
❑ 167 Reggie White	10.00	3.00
❑ 168 Richard Seymour	12.00	3.60
❑ 169 Robert Carswell	6.00	1.80
❑ 170 Robert Ferguson	12.00	3.60
❑ 171 Rod Gardner	12.00	3.60
❑ 172 Ronney Daniels	6.00	1.80
❑ 173 Rudi Johnson	30.00	9.00
❑ 174 Sage Rosenfels	12.00	3.60
❑ 175 Santana Moss	25.00	7.50
❑ 176 Shaun Rogers	12.00	3.60
❑ 177 T.J. Houshmandzadeh	12.00	3.60
❑ 178 Tim Hasselbeck	12.00	3.60
❑ 179 Todd Heap	12.00	3.60
❑ 180 Tony Stewart	12.00	3.60
❑ 181 Torrance Marshall	12.00	3.60
❑ 182 Travis Henry	20.00	6.00
❑ 183 Travis Minor	10.00	3.00
❑ 184 Vinny Sutherland	10.00	3.00
❑ 185 Will Allen	10.00	3.00
❑ 186 Willie Howard	10.00	3.00
❑ 187 Willie Middlebrooks	10.00	3.00
❑ 188 Derrick Blaylock	12.00	3.60
❑ 189 A.J. Feeley	40.00	12.00
❑ 190 Steve Smith	20.00	6.00
❑ 191 Onome Ojo	10.00	3.00
❑ 192 Dee Brown	12.00	3.60
❑ 193 Kevin Kasper	12.00	3.60
❑ 194 Dave Dickenson	10.00	3.00
❑ 195 Chris Barnes	10.00	3.00
❑ 196 Scotty Anderson	10.00	3.00
❑ 197 Chris Taylor	10.00	3.00
❑ 198 Cedric James	10.00	3.00
❑ 199 Justin McCareins	12.00	3.60
❑ 200 Tommy Polley	12.00	3.60

2001 Playoff Contenders Legendary Contenders Autographs

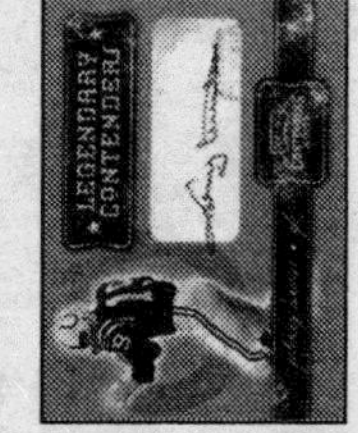

	Nm-Mt	Ex-Mt
❑ 1 Archie Griffin	40.00	12.00
❑ 2 Archie Manning/50	40.00	12.00
❑ 3 Art Monk/25	80.00	24.00
❑ 4 Bart Starr/25	250.00	75.00
❑ 5 Billy Sims	25.00	7.50
❑ 6 Bob Griese/25	60.00	18.00
❑ 7 Charlie Joiner/50		
❑ 8 Charley Taylor/50	40.00	12.00
❑ 9 Cris Collinsworth/50	40.00	12.00
❑ 10 Craig Morton	25.00	7.50
❑ 11 Dan Fouts/25	60.00	18.00
❑ 12 Deacon Jones/25	80.00	24.00
❑ 13 Dick Butkus/225	50.00	15.00
❑ 14 Don Maynard/25	50.00	15.00
❑ 15 Drew Pearson/25	40.00	12.00
❑ 16 Dwight Clark/50	40.00	12.00
❑ 17 Earl Campbell/225	40.00	12.00
❑ 18 Eric Dickerson/25	60.00	18.00
❑ 19 Fran Tarkenton/25		
❑ 20 Franco Harris/50	80.00	24.00
❑ 21 Frank Gifford/25	80.00	24.00
❑ 22 Fred Biletnikoff/125	40.00	12.00
❑ 23 John Fuqua	40.00	12.00
❑ 24 Gale Sayers/125	40.00	12.00
❑ 25 George Blanda/125	40.00	12.00
❑ 26 Harvey Martin No Auto	8.00	2.40
❑ 27 Henry Ellard	20.00	6.00
❑ 28 Irving Fryar	25.00	7.50
❑ 29 James Lofton/25	60.00	18.00
❑ 30 Jim Brown/150	100.00	30.00
❑ 31 Jim Plunkett/125	40.00	12.00
❑ 32 Joe Greene/125	80.00	24.00
❑ 33 Joe Montana/50	175.00	52.50
❑ 34 Joe Namath/100	120.00	36.00
❑ 35 Joe Theismann/125	40.00	12.00
❑ 36 John Hadl	20.00	6.00
❑ 37 John Stallworth/50	80.00	24.00
❑ 38 Johnny Unitas SP/25	200.00	60.00
❑ 39 Kellen Winslow	40.00	12.00
❑ 40 Ken Anderson/50	40.00	12.00
❑ 41 Ken Stabler/100	60.00	18.00
❑ 42 Lance Alworth/125	40.00	12.00
❑ 43 Warren Moon/72	60.00	18.00
❑ 44 Mike Singletary/125	40.00	12.00
❑ 45 Otto Graham/125	50.00	15.00
❑ 46 Ozzie Newsome/25	50.00	15.00
❑ 47 Paul Hornung/125	60.00	18.00
❑ 48 Paul Warfield/125	40.00	12.00
❑ 49 Raymond Berry/125	40.00	12.00
❑ 50 Rocky Bleier	50.00	15.00
❑ 51 Roger Craig/25	100.00	30.00
❑ 52 Roger Staubach/25	150.00	45.00
❑ 53 Ronnie Lott/50	50.00	15.00
❑ 54 Sammy Baugh/125	75.00	22.00
❑ 55 Sonny Jurgensen/25	100.00	30.00
❑ 56 Steve Largent/25	80.00	24.00
❑ 57 Terry Bradshaw/25	150.00	45.00
❑ 58 Todd Christensen	20.00	6.00
❑ 59 Tony Dorsett/25	120.00	36.00
❑ 60 Y.A. Tittle/125	40.00	12.00
❑ 61 Larry Csonka/225	50.00	15.00
❑ 62 Lawrence Taylor/52	80.00	24.00
❑ 63 Marcus Allen/50	60.00	18.00
❑ 64 Barry Sanders/50	125.00	38.00
❑ 65 Boomer Esiason/159	25.00	7.50
❑ 66 Dan Marino/59	150.00	45.00
❑ 67 Jim Kelly/58	60.00	18.00
❑ 68 John Elway/53	120.00	36.00
❑ 69 Michael Irvin	40.00	12.00
❑ 70 Phil Simms/57	40.00	12.00
❑ 71 Steve Young/54	80.00	24.00

2002 Playoff Contenders

	Nm-Mt	Ex-Mt
COMP.SET w/o SP's (100)	25.00	7.50
❑ 1 Drew Bledsoe	1.25	.35
❑ 2 Travis Henry	1.00	.30
❑ 3 Eric Moulds	.60	.18
❑ 4 Chris Chambers	1.00	.30
❑ 5 Ricky Williams	1.00	.30
❑ 6 Zach Thomas	1.00	.30
❑ 7 Tom Brady	2.50	.75
❑ 8 Antowain Smith	.60	.18
❑ 9 Troy Brown	.60	.18
❑ 10 Curtis Martin	1.00	.30
❑ 11 Vinny Testaverde	.60	.18
❑ 12 Chad Pennington	1.25	.35
❑ 13 Jeff Blake	.40	.12
❑ 14 Jamal Lewis	1.00	.30
❑ 15 Ray Lewis	1.00	.30
❑ 16 Michael Westbrook	.40	.12
❑ 17 Corey Dillon	.60	.18
❑ 18 Peter Warrick	.60	.18
❑ 19 Tim Couch	.60	.18
❑ 20 Quincy Morgan	.60	.18
❑ 21 Kevin Johnson	.60	.18
❑ 22 Kordell Stewart	.60	.18

- ❑ 23 Plaxico Burress .60 .18
- ❑ 24 Jerome Bettis 1.00 .30
- ❑ 25 James Allen .60 .18
- ❑ 26 Corey Bradford .40 .12
- ❑ 27 Mark Brunell 1.00 .30
- ❑ 28 Fred Taylor 1.00 .30
- ❑ 29 Jimmy Smith .60 .18
- ❑ 30 Peyton Manning 2.00 .60
- ❑ 31 Reggie Wayne .60 .18
- ❑ 32 Marvin Harrison 1.00 .30
- ❑ 33 Edgerrin James 1.25 .35
- ❑ 34 Steve McNair 1.00 .30
- ❑ 35 Eddie George 1.00 .30
- ❑ 36 Jevon Kearse .60 .18
- ❑ 37 Derrick Mason .60 .18
- ❑ 38 Brian Griese 1.00 .30
- ❑ 39 Terrell Davis 1.00 .30
- ❑ 40 Ed McCaffrey 1.00 .30
- ❑ 41 Rod Smith .60 .18
- ❑ 42 Trent Green .60 .18
- ❑ 43 Priest Holmes 1.25 .35
- ❑ 44 Johnnie Morton .60 .18
- ❑ 45 Tony Gonzalez .60 .18
- ❑ 46 Rich Gannon 1.00 .30
- ❑ 47 Tim Brown 1.00 .30
- ❑ 48 Jerry Rice 2.00 .60
- ❑ 49 Charlie Garner .60 .18
- ❑ 50 Drew Brees 1.00 .30
- ❑ 51 LaDainian Tomlinson 1.50 .45
- ❑ 52 Junior Seau 1.00 .30
- ❑ 53 Quincy Carter .60 .18
- ❑ 54 Emmitt Smith 2.50 .75
- ❑ 55 Joey Galloway .60 .18
- ❑ 56 Kerry Collins .60 .18
- ❑ 57 Tiki Barber .60 .18
- ❑ 58 Michael Strahan .60 .18
- ❑ 59 Donovan McNabb 1.25 .35
- ❑ 60 Duce Staley 1.00 .30
- ❑ 61 Antonio Freeman 1.00 .30
- ❑ 62 Derrius Thompson .40 .12
- ❑ 63 Stephen Davis .60 .18
- ❑ 64 Rod Gardner .60 .18
- ❑ 65 Anthony Thomas 1.00 .30
- ❑ 66 Marty Booker .60 .18
- ❑ 67 Brian Urlacher 1.50 .45
- ❑ 68 James Stewart .60 .18
- ❑ 69 Az-Zahir Hakim .40 .12
- ❑ 70 Brett Favre 2.50 .75
- ❑ 71 Ahman Green 1.00 .30
- ❑ 72 Donald Driver .60 .18
- ❑ 73 Daunte Culpepper 1.00 .30
- ❑ 74 Michael Bennett .60 .18
- ❑ 75 Randy Moss 2.00 .60
- ❑ 76 Michael Vick 3.00 .90
- ❑ 77 Warrick Dunn 1.00 .30
- ❑ 78 Chris Weinke .60 .18
- ❑ 79 Lamar Smith .60 .18
- ❑ 80 Steve Smith .60 .18
- ❑ 81 Aaron Brooks 1.00 .30
- ❑ 82 Deuce McAllister 1.25 .35
- ❑ 83 Joe Horn .60 .18
- ❑ 84 Brad Johnson .60 .18
- ❑ 85 Keyshawn Johnson 1.00 .30
- ❑ 86 Mike Alstott 1.00 .30
- ❑ 87 Warren Sapp .60 .18
- ❑ 88 Jake Plummer .60 .18
- ❑ 89 Thomas Jones .60 .18
- ❑ 90 David Boston 1.00 .30
- ❑ 91 Kurt Warner 1.00 .30
- ❑ 92 Marshall Faulk 1.00 .30
- ❑ 93 Isaac Bruce 1.00 .30
- ❑ 94 Torry Holt 1.00 .30
- ❑ 95 Jeff Garcia 1.00 .30
- ❑ 96 Garrison Hearst .60 .18
- ❑ 97 Kevan Barlow .60 .18
- ❑ 98 Terrell Owens 1.00 .30
- ❑ 99 Trent Dilfer .60 .18
- ❑ 100 Shaun Alexander 1.00 .30
- ❑ 101 Adrian Peterson AU/360 RC 30.009.00
- ❑ 102 Albert Haynesworth No Auto RC 30.00 9.00
- ❑ 103 Alex Brown AU/410 RC 30.00 9.00
- ❑ 104 Andra Davis AU/510 RC 15.00 4.50
- ❑ 105 Andre Davis AU/360 RC 30.00 9.00
- ❑ 106 Andre Lott AU/750 RC 15.00 4.50
- ❑ 107 Anthony Weaver AU/450 RC 15.00 4.50
- ❑ 108 Antonio Bryant AU/165 RC 80.0024.00
- ❑ 109 Antwaan Randle El/135 AU RC 100.00 30.00
- ❑ 110 Ashley Lelie AU/360 RC 100.00 30.00
- ❑ 111 Brian Poli-Dixon AU/460 RC 25.00 7.50
- ❑ 112 Brian Westbrook AU/600 RC 80.00 24.00
- ❑ 113 Bryant McKinnie AU/600 RC 30.009.00
- ❑ 114 Chad Hutchinson AU/450 RC 25.00 7.50
- ❑ 115 Charles Grant AU/450 RC 30.00 9.00
- ❑ 116 Chester Taylor AU/315 RC 40.0012.00
- ❑ 117 Cliff Russell AU/545 RC 25.00 7.50
- ❑ 118 Clinton Portis AU/360 RC 200.0060.00
- ❑ 119 Randy McMichael AU/400 RC 50.00 15.00
- ❑ 120 Damien Anderson AU/460 RC 15.00 4.50
- ❑ 121 Daniel Graham AU/185 RC 60.0018.00
- ❑ 122 David Carr AU/250 RC 200.00 60.00
- ❑ 123 David Garrard AU/310 RC 60.00 18.00
- ❑ 124 Deion Branch AU/650 RC 60.00 18.00
- ❑ 125 John Simon AU/400 RC 25.00 7.50
- ❑ 126 DeShaun Foster AU/310 RC 100.00 30.00
- ❑ 127 Donte Stallworth AU/302 RC 60.00 18.00
- ❑ 128 Dwight Freeney AU/410 RC 50.00 15.00
- ❑ 129 Ed Reed AU/550 RC 50.00 15.00
- ❑ 130 Eric Crouch AU/280 RC 60.00 18.00
- ❑ 131 Freddie Milons AU/380 RC 25.00 7.50
- ❑ 132 Jabar Gaffney AU/315 RC 30.00 9.00
- ❑ 133 Javon Walker AU/435 RC 100.0030.00
- ❑ 134 Jeremy Shockey AU/160 200.00 60.00
- ❑ 135 Jerramy Stevens AU/250 RC 30.00 9.00
- ❑ 136 Joey Harrington AU/250 RC 200.00 60.00
- ❑ 137 John Henderson AU/560 RC 30.00 9.00
- ❑ 138 Jonathan Wells AU/485 RC 50.0015.00
- ❑ 139 Josh McCown AU/595 RC 40.00 12.00
- ❑ 140 Josh Reed AU/290 RC 40.00 12.00
- ❑ 141 Josh Scobey AU/615 RC 15.00 4.50
- ❑ 142 Julius Peppers AU/40 RC 350.00105.00
- ❑ 143 Kalimba Edwards AU/510 RC 25.00 7.50
- ❑ 144 Kelly Campbell AU/360 RC 30.00 9.00
- ❑ 145 Ken Simonton AU/650 RC 15.00 4.50
- ❑ 146 Keyuo Craver AU/850 RC 15.00 4.50
- ❑ 147 Kahlil Hill AU/850 RC 25.00 7.50
- ❑ 148 Kurt Kittner AU/235 RC 25.00 7.50
- ❑ 149 Ladell Betts AU/600 RC 40.00 12.00
- ❑ 150 Lamar Gordon AU/600 RC 30.00 9.00
- ❑ 151 Levar Fisher AU/760 RC 15.00 4.50
- ❑ 152 Lito Sheppard AU/410 RC 30.00 9.00
- ❑ 153 Luke Staley AU/360 RC 25.00 7.50
- ❑ 154 Marquise Walker AU/330 RC 50.00 15.00
- ❑ 155 Maurice Morris AU/153 RC 80.0024.00
- ❑ 156 Mike Rumph AU/510 RC 30.00 9.00
- ❑ 157 Mike Williams AU/500 RC 25.00 7.50
- ❑ 158 Najeh Davenport AU/460 RC 30.00 9.00
- ❑ 159 Napoleon Harris AU/900 RC 25.007.50
- ❑ 160 Patrick Ramsey AU/575 RC 80.0024.00
- ❑ 161 Phillip Buchanon No Auto/310 RC 50.00 15.00
- ❑ 162 Quentin Jammer AU/300 RC 30.009.00
- ❑ 163 Randy Fasani AU/500 RC 25.00 7.50
- ❑ 164 Reche Caldwell AU/340 RC 30.00 9.00
- ❑ 165 Robert Thomas AU/460 RC 30.00 9.00
- ❑ 166 Rocky Calmus AU/385 RC 30.00 9.00
- ❑ 167 Rohan Davey AU/295 RC 50.00 15.00
- ❑ 168 Ron Johnson AU/385 RC 25.00 7.50
- ❑ 169 Roy Williams AU/250 RC 125.00 38.00
- ❑ 170 Ryan Sims No Auto/360 RC 30.009.00
- ❑ 171 Tavon Mason AU/690 RC 15.00 4.50
- ❑ 172 Terry Charles AU/750 RC 15.00 4.50
- ❑ 173 T.J. Duckett AU/335 RC 60.00 18.00
- ❑ 174 Tim Carter AU/600 RC 25.00 7.50
- ❑ 175 Travis Stephens AU/170 RC 60.00 18.00
- ❑ 176 Trev Faulk AU/600 RC 15.00 4.50
- ❑ 177 Wendell Bryant AU/560 RC 15.00 4.50
- ❑ 178 William Green AU/317 RC 50.00 15.00
- ❑ 179 Woody Dantzler AU/185 RC 60.00 18.00
- ❑ 180 Tony Fisher AU/340 RC 30.00 9.00
- ❑ 181 Javin Hunter AU/400 RC 15.00 4.50
- ❑ 182 Daryl Jones AU/400 RC 25.00 7.50
- ❑ 183 Jesse Chatman AU/400 RC 30.00 9.00
- ❑ 184 J.T. O'Sullivan AU/340 RC 25.00 7.50
- ❑ 185 Josh Norman AU/340 RC 30.00 9.00
- ❑ 186 James Mungro AU/100 RC 100.00 30.00

2002 Playoff Contenders Championship Ticket

Nm-Mt Ex-Mt

*STARS: 2.5X TO 6X BASIC CARDS

- ❑ 101 Adrian Peterson 20.00 6.00
- ❑ 102 Albert Haynesworth 15.00 4.50
- ❑ 103 Alex Brown 20.00 6.00
- ❑ 104 Andra Davis 15.00 4.50
- ❑ 105 Andre Davis 20.00 6.00
- ❑ 106 Andre Lott 20.00 6.00
- ❑ 107 Anthony Weaver 10.00 3.00
- ❑ 108 Antonio Bryant 20.00 6.00
- ❑ 109 Antwaan Randle El 25.00 7.50
- ❑ 110 Ashley Lelie 40.00 12.00
- ❑ 111 Brian Poli-Dixon 15.00 4.50
- ❑ 112 Brian Westbrook 30.00 9.00
- ❑ 113 Bryant McKinnie 15.00 4.50
- ❑ 114 Chad Hutchinson 20.00 6.00
- ❑ 115 Charles Grant 20.00 6.00
- ❑ 116 Chester Taylor 20.00 6.00
- ❑ 117 Cliff Russell 15.00 4.50
- ❑ 118 Clinton Portis 80.00 24.00
- ❑ 119 Randy McMichael 30.00 9.00
- ❑ 120 Damien Anderson 15.00 4.50
- ❑ 121 Daniel Graham 20.00 6.00
- ❑ 122 David Carr 80.00 24.00
- ❑ 123 David Garrard 20.00 6.00
- ❑ 124 Deion Branch 40.00 12.00
- ❑ 125 John Simon 15.00 4.50
- ❑ 126 DeShaun Foster 20.00 6.00
- ❑ 127 Donte Stallworth 50.00 15.00
- ❑ 128 Dwight Freeney 25.00 7.50
- ❑ 129 Ed Reed 50.00 15.00
- ❑ 130 Eric Crouch 30.00 9.00
- ❑ 131 Freddie Milons 15.00 4.50
- ❑ 132 Jabar Gaffney 20.00 6.00
- ❑ 133 Javon Walker 40.00 12.00
- ❑ 134 Jeremy Shockey 60.00 18.00
- ❑ 135 Jerramy Stevens 20.00 6.00
- ❑ 136 Joey Harrington 80.00 24.00
- ❑ 137 John Henderson 20.00 6.00
- ❑ 138 Jonathan Wells 20.00 6.00
- ❑ 139 Josh McCown 25.00 7.50
- ❑ 140 Josh Reed 20.00 6.00
- ❑ 141 Josh Scobey 20.00 6.00
- ❑ 142 Julius Peppers 40.00 12.00
- ❑ 143 Kalimba Edwards 20.00 6.00
- ❑ 144 Kelly Campbell 15.00 4.50
- ❑ 145 Ken Simonton 10.00 3.00
- ❑ 146 Keyuo Craver 15.00 4.50
- ❑ 147 Kahlil Hill 15.00 4.50
- ❑ 148 Kurt Kittner 15.00 4.50

❑ 149 Ladell Betts	20.00	6.00
❑ 150 Lamar Gordon	20.00	6.00
❑ 151 Levar Fisher	10.00	3.00
❑ 152 Lito Sheppard	20.00	6.00
❑ 153 Luke Staley	15.00	4.50
❑ 154 Marquise Walker	15.00	4.50
❑ 155 Maurice Morris	20.00	6.00
❑ 156 Mike Rumph	20.00	6.00
❑ 157 Mike Williams	15.00	4.50
❑ 158 Najeh Davenport	20.00	6.00
❑ 159 Napoleon Harris	20.00	6.00
❑ 160 Patrick Ramsey	40.00	12.00
❑ 161 Phillip Buchanon	20.00	6.00
❑ 162 Quentin Jammer	20.00	6.00
❑ 163 Randy Fasani	15.00	4.50
❑ 164 Reche Caldwell	20.00	6.00
❑ 165 Robert Thomas	20.00	6.00
❑ 166 Rocky Calmus	20.00	6.00
❑ 167 Rohan Davey	20.00	6.00
❑ 168 Ron Johnson	15.00	4.50
❑ 169 Roy Williams	50.00	15.00
❑ 170 Ryan Sims	20.00	6.00
❑ 171 Tavon Mason	10.00	3.00
❑ 172 Terry Charles	15.00	4.50
❑ 173 T.J. Duckett	30.00	9.00
❑ 174 Tim Carter	15.00	4.50
❑ 175 Travis Stephens	15.00	4.50
❑ 176 Trev Faulk	10.00	3.00
❑ 177 Wendell Bryant	20.00	6.00
❑ 178 William Green	30.00	9.00
❑ 179 Woody Dantzler	20.00	6.00
❑ 180 Tony Fisher	20.00	6.00
❑ 181 Javin Hunter	10.00	3.00
❑ 182 Daryl Jones	15.00	4.50
❑ 183 Jesse Chatman	20.00	6.00
❑ 184 J.T. O'Sullivan	15.00	4.50
❑ 185 Josh Norman	20.00	6.00
❑ 186 James Mungro	20.00	6.00

2003 Playoff Contenders

	MINT	NRMT
COMP.SET w/o SP's (100)	20.00	9.00
❑ 1 Roy Williams	.75	.35
❑ 2 Antonio Bryant	.50	.23
❑ 3 Jeremy Shockey	1.25	.55
❑ 4 Kerry Collins	.50	.23
❑ 5 Tiki Barber	.50	.23
❑ 6 Michael Strahan	.50	.23
❑ 7 Donovan McNabb	1.00	.45
❑ 8 Duce Staley	.50	.23
❑ 9 Todd Pinkston	.50	.23
❑ 10 Patrick Ramsey	.75	.35
❑ 11 Laveranues Coles	.50	.23
❑ 12 Rod Gardner	.50	.23
❑ 13 Drew Bledsoe	.75	.35
❑ 14 Travis Henry	.50	.23
❑ 15 Eric Moulds	.50	.23
❑ 16 Josh Reed	.50	.23
❑ 17 Ricky Williams	.75	.35
❑ 18 Jay Fiedler	.50	.23
❑ 19 Chris Chambers	.75	.35
❑ 20 Zach Thomas	.75	.35
❑ 21 Junior Seau	.75	.35
❑ 22 Tom Brady	1.25	.55
❑ 23 Troy Brown	.50	.23
❑ 24 Chad Pennington	1.00	.45
❑ 25 Curtis Martin	.75	.35
❑ 26 Santana Moss	.50	.23
❑ 27 Emmitt Smith	2.00	.90
❑ 28 Jeff Garcia	.75	.35
❑ 29 Terrell Owens	.75	.35
❑ 30 Kevan Barlow	.50	.23
❑ 31 Shaun Alexander	.75	.35
❑ 32 Matt Hasselbeck	.50	.23
❑ 33 Koren Robinson	.50	.23
❑ 34 Kurt Warner	.75	.35
❑ 35 Marshall Faulk	.75	.35
❑ 36 Torry Holt	.75	.35
❑ 37 Isaac Bruce	.75	.35
❑ 38 Clinton Portis	1.25	.55
❑ 39 Jake Plummer	.50	.23
❑ 40 Rod Smith	.50	.23
❑ 41 Ed McCaffrey	.75	.35
❑ 42 Ashley Lelie	.75	.35
❑ 43 Priest Holmes	1.00	.45
❑ 44 Trent Green	.50	.23
❑ 45 Tony Gonzalez	.50	.23
❑ 46 Jerry Rice	1.50	.70
❑ 47 Rich Gannon	.50	.23
❑ 48 Tim Brown	.75	.35
❑ 49 Jerry Porter	.50	.23
❑ 50 Charles Woodson	.50	.23
❑ 51 LaDainian Tomlinson	.75	.35
❑ 52 Drew Brees	.75	.35
❑ 53 David Boston	.50	.23
❑ 54 Brian Urlacher	1.25	.55
❑ 55 Kordell Stewart	.50	.23
❑ 56 Marty Booker	.50	.23
❑ 57 Joey Harrington	1.25	.55
❑ 58 Brett Favre	2.00	.90
❑ 59 Ahman Green	.75	.35
❑ 60 Donald Driver	.50	.23
❑ 61 Javon Walker	.50	.23
❑ 62 Randy Moss	1.25	.55
❑ 63 Daunte Culpepper	.75	.35
❑ 64 Michael Bennett	.50	.23
❑ 65 Jamal Lewis	.75	.35
❑ 66 Ray Lewis	.75	.35
❑ 67 Corey Dillon	.50	.23
❑ 68 Chad Johnson	.50	.23
❑ 69 William Green	.50	.23
❑ 70 Tim Couch	.30	.14
❑ 71 Quincy Morgan	.50	.23
❑ 72 Plaxico Burress	.50	.23
❑ 73 Tommy Maddox	.75	.35
❑ 74 Hines Ward	.75	.35
❑ 75 Antwaan Randle El	.75	.35
❑ 76 Michael Vick	2.00	.90
❑ 77 Peerless Price	.50	.23
❑ 78 Warrick Dunn	.50	.23
❑ 79 T.J. Duckett	.50	.23
❑ 80 Julius Peppers	.75	.35
❑ 81 Stephen Davis	.50	.23
❑ 82 Deuce McAllister	.75	.35
❑ 83 Aaron Brooks	.75	.35
❑ 84 Joe Horn	.50	.23
❑ 85 Donte Stallworth	.75	.35
❑ 86 Mike Alstott	.75	.35
❑ 87 Brad Johnson	.50	.23
❑ 88 Keyshawn Johnson	.75	.35
❑ 89 Warren Sapp	.50	.23
❑ 90 David Carr	1.25	.55
❑ 91 Jabar Gaffney	.50	.23
❑ 92 Peyton Manning	1.25	.55
❑ 93 Edgerrin James	.75	.35
❑ 94 Marvin Harrison	.75	.35
❑ 95 Mark Brunell	.50	.23
❑ 96 Fred Taylor	.75	.35
❑ 97 Jimmy Smith	.50	.23
❑ 98 Steve McNair	.75	.35
❑ 99 Eddie George	.50	.23
❑ 100 Jevon Kearse	.50	.23
❑ 101 Lee Suggs AU/499 RC	100.00	45.00
❑ 102 Charles Rogers AU/204 RC	150.00	70.00
❑ 103 Brandon Lloyd AU/589 RC	50.00	22.00
❑ 104 Terrence Edwards AU/399 RC	15.00	6.75
❑ 105 Mike Pinkard AU/849 RC	12.00	5.50
❑ 106 DeWayne White AU/524 RC	12.00	5.50
❑ 107 Jerome McDougle AU/339 RC	20.00	9.00
❑ 108 Jimmy Kennedy AU/514 RC	20.00	9.00
❑ 109 William Joseph AU/764 RC	15.00	6.75
❑ 110 E.J. Henderson AU/774 RC	20.00	9.00
❑ 111 Mike Doss AU/574 RC	20.00	9.00
❑ 112 Chris Simms AU/389 RC	100.00	45.00
❑ 113 Cecil Sapp AU/474 RC	15.00	6.75
❑ 114 Justin Gage AU/579 RC	20.00	9.00
❑ 115 Sam Aiken AU/664 RC	15.00	6.75
❑ 116 Doug Gabriel AU/389 RC	50.00	22.00
❑ 117 Jason Witten AU/599 RC	50.00	22.00
❑ 118 Bennie Joppru AU/449 RC	20.00	9.00
❑ 119 Chris Kelsay AU/864 RC	15.00	6.75
❑ 120 Johnathan Sullivan EXCH	20.00	9.00
❑ 121 Kevin Williams AU/764 RC	20.00	9.00
❑ 122 Rien Long AU/849 RC	12.00	5.50
❑ 123 Kenny Peterson EXCH	15.00	6.75
❑ 124 Boss Bailey AU/564 RC	20.00	9.00
❑ 125 Dennis Weathersby AU/774 RC	12.00	5.50
❑ 126 Carson Palmer AU/194 RC	250.00	110.00
❑ 127 Byron Leftwich AU/169 RC	350.00	160.00
❑ 128 Kyle Boller AU/439 RC	80.00	36.00
❑ 129 Rex Grossman AU/494 RC	100.00	45.00
❑ 130 Dave Ragone AU/344 RC	20.00	9.00
❑ 131 Brian St.Pierre AU/554 RC	15.00	6.75
❑ 132 Kliff Kingsbury AU/879 RC	20.00	9.00
❑ 133 Seneca Wallace AU/864 RC	15.00	6.75
❑ 134 Larry Johnson AU/344 RC	80.00	36.00
❑ 135 Willis McGahee AU/369 RC	120.00	55.00
❑ 136 Justin Fargas AU/354 RC	20.00	9.00
❑ 137 Onterrio Smith AU/414 RC	50.00	22.00
❑ 138 Chris Brown AU/279 RC	120.00	55.00
❑ 139 Musa Smith AU/379 RC	20.00	9.00
❑ 140 Artose Pinner AU/364 RC	40.00	18.00
❑ 141 Andre Johnson AU/199 RC	175.00	80.00
❑ 142 Kelley Washington AU/472 RC	30.00	13.50
❑ 143 Taylor Jacobs AU/349 RC	20.00	9.00
❑ 144 Bryant Johnson AU/389 RC	20.00	9.00
❑ 145 Tyrone Calico AU/499 RC	40.00	18.00
❑ 146 Anquan Boldin AU/524 RC	80.00	36.00
❑ 147 Bethel Johnson AU/484 RC	40.00	18.00
❑ 148 Nate Burleson AU/549 RC	60.00	27.00
❑ 149 Kevin Curtis AU/455 RC	20.00	9.00
❑ 150 Dallas Clark AU/539 RC	20.00	9.00
❑ 151 Teyo Johnson AU/389 RC	20.00	9.00
❑ 152 Terrell Suggs AU/564 RC	30.00	13.50
❑ 153 DeWayne Robertson EXCH	30.00	13.50
❑ 154 Terence Newman AU/364 RC	50.00	22.00
❑ 155 Marcus Trufant AU/739 RC	20.00	9.00
❑ 156 Tony Romo AU/999 RC	20.00	9.00
❑ 157 Brooks Bollinger AU/974 RC	15.00	6.75
❑ 158 Ken Dorsey AU/774 RC	40.00	18.00
❑ 159 Kirk Farmer AU/999 RC	15.00	6.75
❑ 160 Jason Gesser AU/999 RC	15.00	6.75
❑ 161 Brock Forsey AU/999 RC	15.00	6.75
❑ 162 Quentin Griffin AU/999 RC	50.00	22.00
❑ 163 Avon Cobourne AU/974 RC	12.00	5.50
❑ 164 Domanick Davis AU/999 RC	50.00	22.00
❑ 165 Tony Hollings AU/974 RC	20.00	9.00
❑ 166 LaBrandon Toefield AU/799 RC	20.00	9.00
❑ 167 Arlen Harris AU/974 RC	20.00	9.00
❑ 168 Sultan McCullough AU/989 RC	15.00	6.75
❑ 169 Visant Shiancoe AU/999 RC	12.00	5.50
❑ 170 L.J. Smith AU/974 RC	20.00	9.00
❑ 171 LaTarence Dunbar AU/999 RC	12.00	5.50
❑ 172 Walter Young AU/889 RC	12.00	5.50
❑ 173 Bobby Wade AU/989 RC	15.00	6.75
❑ 174 Zuriel Smith AU/989 RC	12.00	5.50
❑ 175 Adrian Madise AU/999 RC	15.00	6.75

❑ 176 Ken Hamlin AU/989 RC 15.00 6.75
❑ 177 Carl Ford AU/999 RC 12.00 5.50
❑ 178 Cortez Hankton AU/989 RC 15.00 6.75
❑ 179 J.R. Tolver AU/889 RC 15.00 6.75
❑ 180 Keenan Howry AU/999 RC 15.00 6.75
❑ 181 Billy McMullen AU/899 RC 15.00 6.75
❑ 182 Arnaz Battle AU/989 RC 20.00 9.00
❑ 183 Shaun McDonald AU/899 RC 15.00 6.75
❑ 184 Andre Woolfolk AU/989 RC 15.00 6.75
❑ 185 Sammy Davis AU/999 RC 12.00 5.50
❑ 186 Calvin Pace AU/999 RC 12.00 5.50
❑ 187 Michael Haynes AU/999 RC 15.00 6.75
❑ 188 Ty Warren AU/999 RC 15.00 6.75
❑ 189 Nick Barnett EXCH 40.00 18.00
❑ 190 Troy Polamalu AU/989 RC 50.00 22.00
❑ 191 Eric Parker AU/589 RC 20.00 9.00
❑ 192 Justin Griffith AU/589 RC 15.00 6.75
❑ 193 David Tyree AU/599 RC 15.00 6.75
❑ 194 Pisa Tinoisamoa EXCH 20.00 9.00
❑ 195 Rashean Mathis AU/589 RC 12.00 5.50
❑ 196 Mike Sherman AU/574 RC 30.00 13.50
❑ 197 Dave Wannstedt AU/574 RC 20.00 9.00
❑ 198 Dick Vermeil AU/574 RC 30.00 13.50
❑ 199 Tony Dungy AU/574 RC 30.00 13.50
❑ 200 Mike Martz AU/574 RC 20.00 9.00

2003 Playoff Contenders Playoff Ticket

MINT NRMT

*STARS: 4X TO 10X BASIC CARDS
UNPRICED CHAMPION.TICKET #'d TO 1

❑ 101 Lee Suggs 60.00 27.00
❑ 102 Charles Rogers 40.00 18.00
❑ 103 Brandon Lloyd 40.00 18.00
❑ 104 Terrence Edwards 25.00 11.00
❑ 105 Mike Pinkard 15.00 6.75
❑ 106 DeWayne White 25.00 11.00
❑ 107 Jerome McDougle 30.00 13.50
❑ 108 Jimmy Kennedy 30.00 13.50
❑ 109 William Joseph 30.00 13.50
❑ 110 E.J. Henderson 30.00 13.50
❑ 111 Mike Doss 30.00 13.50
❑ 112 Chris Simms 60.00 27.00
❑ 113 Cecil Sapp 25.00 11.00
❑ 114 Justin Gage 30.00 13.50
❑ 115 Sam Aiken 25.00 11.00
❑ 116 Doug Gabriel 30.00 13.50
❑ 117 Jason Witten 50.00 22.00
❑ 118 Bennie Joppru 30.00 13.50
❑ 119 Chris Kelsay 30.00 13.50
❑ 120 Johnathan Sullivan 25.00 11.00
❑ 121 Kevin Williams 30.00 13.50
❑ 122 Rien Long 15.00 6.75
❑ 123 Kenny Peterson 25.00 11.00
❑ 124 Boss Bailey 40.00 18.00
❑ 125 Dennis Weathersby 15.00 6.75
❑ 126 Carson Palmer 120.00 55.00
❑ 127 Byron Leftwich 120.00 55.00
❑ 128 Kyle Boller 80.00 36.00
❑ 129 Rex Grossman 100.00 45.00
❑ 130 Dave Ragone 30.00 13.50
❑ 131 Brian St.Pierre 30.00 13.50
❑ 132 Kliff Kingsbury 25.00 11.00
❑ 133 Seneca Wallace 30.00 13.50
❑ 134 Larry Johnson 50.00 22.00
❑ 135 Willis McGahee 80.00 36.00
❑ 136 Justin Fargas 30.00 13.50
❑ 137 Onterrio Smith 40.00 18.00
❑ 138 Chris Brown 60.00 27.00
❑ 139 Musa Smith 30.00 13.50
❑ 140 Artose Pinner 30.00 13.50
❑ 141 Andre Johnson 100.00 45.00
❑ 142 Kelley Washington 30.00 13.50
❑ 143 Taylor Jacobs 30.00 13.50
❑ 144 Bryant Johnson 30.00 13.50
❑ 145 Tyrone Calico 40.00 18.00
❑ 146 Anquan Boldin 80.00 36.00
❑ 147 Bethel Johnson 50.00 22.00
❑ 148 Nate Burleson 60.00 27.00
❑ 149 Kevin Curtis 30.00 13.50
❑ 150 Dallas Clark 30.00 13.50
❑ 151 Teyo Johnson 30.00 13.50
❑ 152 Terrell Suggs 50.00 22.00
❑ 153 DeWayne Robertson 30.00 13.50
❑ 154 Terence Newman 60.00 27.00
❑ 155 Marcus Trufant 30.00 13.50
❑ 156 Tony Romo 30.00 13.50
❑ 157 Brooks Bollinger 30.00 13.50
❑ 158 Ken Dorsey 50.00 22.00
❑ 159 Kirk Farmer 15.00 6.75
❑ 160 Jason Gesser 30.00 13.50
❑ 161 Brock Forsey 30.00 13.50
❑ 162 Quentin Griffin 80.00 36.00
❑ 163 Avon Cobourne 15.00 6.75
❑ 164 Domanick Davis 60.00 27.00
❑ 165 Tony Hollings 30.00 13.50
❑ 166 LaBrandon Toefield 30.00 13.50
❑ 167 Arlen Harris 30.00 13.50
❑ 168 Sultan McCullough 25.00 11.00
❑ 169 Visanthe Shiancoe 25.00 11.00
❑ 170 L.J. Smith 30.00 13.50
❑ 171 LaTarence Dunbar 25.00 11.00
❑ 172 Walter Young 15.00 6.75
❑ 173 Bobby Wade 30.00 13.50
❑ 174 Zuriel Smith 15.00 6.75
❑ 175 Adrian Madise 25.00 11.00
❑ 176 Ken Hamlin 30.00 13.50
❑ 177 Carl Ford 15.00 6.75
❑ 178 Cortez Hankton 25.00 11.00
❑ 179 J.R. Tolver 25.00 11.00
❑ 180 Keenan Howry 30.00 13.50
❑ 181 Billy McMullen 25.00 11.00
❑ 182 Arnaz Battle 30.00 13.50
❑ 183 Shaun McDonald 30.00 13.50
❑ 184 Andre Woolfolk 30.00 13.50
❑ 185 Sammy Davis 30.00 13.50
❑ 186 Calvin Pace 25.00 11.00
❑ 187 Michael Haynes 30.00 13.50
❑ 188 Ty Warren 30.00 13.50
❑ 189 Nick Barnett 50.00 22.00
❑ 190 Troy Polamalu 30.00 13.50
❑ 191 Eric Parker 30.00 13.50
❑ 192 Justin Griffith 25.00 11.00
❑ 193 David Tyree 25.00 11.00
❑ 194 Pisa Tinoisamoa 50.00 22.00
❑ 195 Rashean Mathis 25.00 11.00
❑ 196 Mike Sherman 30.00 13.50
❑ 197 Dave Wannstedt 25.00 11.00
❑ 198 Dick Vermeil 30.00 13.50
❑ 199 Tony Dungy 30.00 13.50
❑ 200 Mike Martz 25.00 11.00

2004 Playoff Contenders

Nm-Mt Ex-Mt

COMP.SET w/o SP's (100) 20.00 6.00
EXCH EXPIRATION: 7/01/2006
UNPRICED CHAMP.TICKET PRINT RUN 1
AU PRINT RUNS ANNOUNCED BY PLAYOFF

❑ 1 Anquan Boldin .75 .23
❑ 2 Emmitt Smith 1.50 .45
❑ 3 Josh McCown .50 .15
❑ 4 Michael Vick 1.50 .45
❑ 5 Peerless Price .50 .15
❑ 6 T.J. Duckett .50 .15
❑ 7 Warrick Dunn .50 .15
❑ 8 Jamal Lewis .75 .23
❑ 9 Kyle Boller .75 .23
❑ 10 Ray Lewis .75 .23
❑ 11 Drew Bledsoe .75 .23
❑ 12 Eric Moulds .50 .15
❑ 13 Travis Henry .50 .15
❑ 14 Willis McGahee .75 .23
❑ 15 DeShaun Foster .50 .15
❑ 16 Jake Delhomme .75 .23
❑ 17 Stephen Davis .50 .15
❑ 18 Steve Smith .50 .15
❑ 19 Brian Urlacher 1.00 .30
❑ 20 Rex Grossman .75 .23
❑ 21 Thomas Jones .50 .15
❑ 22 Carson Palmer 1.00 .30
❑ 23 Chad Johnson .50 .15
❑ 24 Rudi Johnson .50 .15
❑ 25 Jeff Garcia .75 .23
❑ 26 Lee Suggs .75 .23
❑ 27 William Green .50 .15
❑ 28 Keyshawn Johnson .50 .15
❑ 29 Roy Williams S .50 .15
❑ 30 Eddie George .50 .15
❑ 31 Ashley Lelie .50 .15
❑ 32 Jake Plummer .50 .15
❑ 33 Quentin Griffin .75 .23
❑ 34 Rod Smith .50 .15
❑ 35 Charles Rogers .50 .15
❑ 36 Joey Harrington .75 .23
❑ 37 Ahman Green .75 .23
❑ 38 Brett Favre 2.00 .60
❑ 39 Javon Walker .50 .15
❑ 40 Andre Johnson .75 .23
❑ 41 David Carr .75 .23
❑ 42 Domanick Davis .75 .23
❑ 43 Edgerrin James .75 .23
❑ 44 Marvin Harrison .75 .23
❑ 45 Peyton Manning 1.25 .35
❑ 46 Byron Leftwich 1.25 .35
❑ 47 Fred Taylor .50 .15
❑ 48 Jimmy Smith .50 .15
❑ 49 Priest Holmes 1.00 .30
❑ 50 Tony Gonzalez .50 .15
❑ 51 Trent Green .50 .15
❑ 52 A.J. Feeley .75 .23
❑ 53 Chris Chambers .50 .15
❑ 54 Deion Sanders .75 .23
❑ 55 Daunte Culpepper .75 .23
❑ 56 Michael Bennett .50 .15
❑ 57 Randy Moss 1.00 .30
❑ 58 Corey Dillon .50 .15
❑ 59 Deion Branch .75 .23
❑ 60 Tom Brady 1.25 .35
❑ 61 Aaron Brooks .50 .15
❑ 62 Deuce McAllister .75 .23
❑ 63 Donte Stallworth .50 .15
❑ 64 Joe Horn .50 .15
❑ 65 Amani Toomer .50 .15
❑ 66 Jeremy Shockey .75 .23
❑ 67 Michael Strahan .50 .15
❑ 68 Tiki Barber .50 .15
❑ 69 Chad Pennington 1.00 .30
❑ 70 Curtis Martin .75 .23
❑ 71 Santana Moss .50 .15
❑ 72 Jerry Porter .50 .15
❑ 73 Jerry Rice 1.50 .45

Card	Nm-Mt	Ex-Mt
❑ 74 Warren Sapp	.50	.15
❑ 75 Brian Westbrook	.50	.15
❑ 76 Donovan McNabb	1.00	.30
❑ 77 Jevon Kearse	.50	.15
❑ 78 Terrell Owens	.75	.23
❑ 79 Antwaan Randle El	.50	.15
❑ 80 Hines Ward	.75	.23
❑ 81 Jerome Bettis	.75	.23
❑ 82 LaDainian Tomlinson	.75	.23
❑ 83 Kevan Barlow	.50	.15
❑ 84 Tim Rattay	.50	.15
❑ 85 Koren Robinson	.50	.15
❑ 86 Matt Hasselbeck	.50	.15
❑ 87 Shaun Alexander	.75	.23
❑ 88 Isaac Bruce	.50	.15
❑ 89 Marc Bulger	.75	.23
❑ 90 Marshall Faulk	.75	.23
❑ 91 Torry Holt	.75	.23
❑ 92 Brad Johnson	.50	.15
❑ 93 Mike Alstott	.50	.15
❑ 94 Chris Brown	.75	.23
❑ 95 Derrick Mason	.50	.15
❑ 96 Steve McNair	.75	.23
❑ 97 Clinton Portis	.75	.23
❑ 98 LaVar Arrington	1.50	.45
❑ 99 Laveranues Coles	.50	.15
❑ 100 Mark Brunell	.50	.15
❑ 101 Adimchinobe Echemandu AU RC	15.00	4.50
❑ 102 Ahmad Carroll AU/574 RC	25.00	7.50
❑ 103 Andy Hall AU RC	20.00	6.00
❑ 104 B.J. Johnson AU RC	15.00	4.50
❑ 105 B.J. Symons AU RC	20.00	6.00
❑ 106 Ben Roethlisberger AU/541 RC	400.00	120.00
❑ 107 Ben Troupe AU/540 RC	25.00	7.50
❑ 108 Ben Watson AU/660 RC	25.00	7.50
❑ 109 Bernard Berrian AU/653 RC	20.00	6.00
❑ 110 Brandon Miree AU RC	15.00	4.50
❑ 111 Bruce Perry AU RC	15.00	4.50
❑ 112 Carlos Francis AU RC	20.00	6.00
❑ 113 Casey Bramlet AU RC	15.00	4.50
❑ 114 Cedric Cobbs AU/630 RC	25.00	7.50
❑ 115 Chris Gamble AU/490 RC	25.00	7.50
❑ 116 Chris Perry AU/478 RC	40.00	12.00
❑ 117 Clarence Moore AU RC	20.00	6.00
❑ 118 Cody Pickett AU RC	20.00	6.00
❑ 119 Craig Krenzel AU RC	20.00	6.00
❑ 120 D.J. Hackett AU/325 RC	20.00	6.00
❑ 121 D.J. Williams AU/490 RC	25.00	7.50
❑ 122 Darius Watts AU RC	25.00	7.50
❑ 123 DeAngelo Hall AU RC	30.00	9.00
❑ 124 Derrick Hamilton AU/373 RC	20.00	6.00
❑ 125 Derrick Ward AU RC	12.00	3.60
❑ 126 Devard Darling AU/325 RC	25.00	7.50
❑ 127 Devery Henderson AU/475 RC	30.00	9.00
❑ 128 Drew Carter AU RC	15.00	4.50
❑ 129 Drew Henson AU/415 RC	60.00	18.00
❑ 130 Dunta Robinson AU/660 RC EXCH	25.00	7.50
❑ 131 Eli Manning AU/372 RC	300.00	90.00
❑ 132 Ernest Wilford AU/365 RC	30.00	9.00
❑ 133 Greg Jones AU/553 RC	30.00	9.00
❑ 134 J.P. Losman AU/358 RC	135.00	40.00
❑ 135 Jamaar Taylor AU RC	20.00	6.00
❑ 136 Jared Lorenzen AU RC	15.00	4.50
❑ 137 Jarrett Payton AU RC	20.00	6.00
❑ 138 Jason Babin AU RC	25.00	7.50
❑ 139 Jeff Smoker AU RC	25.00	7.50
❑ 140 Jerricho Cotchery AU/325 RC	30.00	9.00
❑ 141 Jim Sorgi AU RC	20.00	6.00
❑ 142 John Navarre AU RC	20.00	6.00
❑ 143 Johnnie Morant AU/325 RC	30.00	9.00
❑ 144 Jonathan Vilma AU SP RC	30.00	9.00
❑ 145 Josh Harris AU/555 RC	20.00	6.00
❑ 146 Julius Jones AU/252 RC	300.00	90.00
❑ 147 Keary Colbert AU/495 RC	50.00	15.00
❑ 148 Kellen Winslow AU/135 RC	225.00	70.00
❑ 149 Kenechi Udeze AU/475 RC	25.00	7.50
❑ 150 Kevin Jones AU/327 RC	150.00	45.00
❑ 151 Larry Fitzgerald AU/50 RC	500.00	150.00
❑ 152 Lee Evans AU/375 RC	60.00	18.00
❑ 153 Luke McCown AU/543 RC	25.00	7.50
❑ 154 Matt Mauck AU RC	20.00	6.00
❑ 155 Matt Schaub AU/367 RC	50.00	15.00
❑ 156 Maurice Mann AU RC	15.00	4.50
❑ 157 Mewelde Moore AU/435 RC	40.00	12.00
❑ 158 Michael Clayton AU/325 RC	100.00	30.00
❑ 159 Michael Jenkins AU/412 RC	40.00	12.00
❑ 160 Michael Turner AU/535 RC	25.00	7.50
❑ 161 P.K. Sam AU/300 RC	25.00	7.50
❑ 162 Philip Rivers AU/556 RC	120.00	36.00
❑ 163 Quincy Wilson AU/350 RC	25.00	7.50
❑ 164 Ran Carthon AU RC	15.00	4.50
❑ 165 Rashaun Woods AU RC	25.00	7.50
❑ 166 Reggie Williams AU/336 RC	60.00	18.00
❑ 167 Ricardo Colclough AU/640 RC	20.00	6.00
❑ 168 Robert Gallery AU/310 RC	40.00	12.00
❑ 169 Roy Williams AU/564 RC	120.00	36.00
❑ 170 Samie Parker AU/356 RC	30.00	9.00
❑ 171 Sean Jones AU RC	20.00	6.00
❑ 172 Sean Taylor AU/575 RC EXCH	50.00	15.00
❑ 173 Sloan Thomas AU RC	15.00	4.50
❑ 174 Steven Jackson AU/333 RC	150.00	45.00
❑ 175 Tatum Bell AU/539 RC	100.00	30.00
❑ 176 Tommie Harris AU/365 RC	25.00	7.50
❑ 177 Triandos Luke AU RC	20.00	6.00
❑ 178 Troy Fleming AU RC	15.00	4.50
❑ 179 Vince Wilfork AU/315 RC	30.00	9.00
❑ 180 Will Smith AU/565 RC	20.00	6.00
❑ 181 Marcus Tubbs AU RC	25.00	7.50
❑ 182 Michael Boulware AU RC	20.00	6.00
❑ 183 Kris Wilson AU RC	20.00	6.00
❑ 184 Richard Smith AU RC	15.00	4.50
❑ 185 Teddy Lehman AU RC	20.00	6.00
❑ 186 Chris Cooley AU RC	20.00	6.00
❑ 187 Thomas Tapeh AU RC	15.00	4.50
❑ 188 Willie Parker AU RC	25.00	7.50
❑ 189 Patrick Crayton AU RC	20.00	6.00
❑ 190 Kendrick Starling AU RC	15.00	4.50
❑ 191 B.J. Sams AU RC	20.00	6.00
❑ 192 Derick Armstrong AU EXCH	15.00	4.50
❑ 193 Wes Welker AU RC	20.00	6.00
❑ 194 Erik Coleman AU RC	20.00	6.00
❑ 195 Gibril Wilson AU RC	20.00	6.00
❑ 196 Andy Reid AU/335 RC	30.00	9.00
❑ 197 Brian Billick AU/585 RC	30.00	9.00
❑ 198 Jeff Fisher AU/585 RC	25.00	7.50
❑ 199 Jon Gruden AU/585 RC	25.00	7.50
❑ 200 Marvin Lewis AU/585 RC	25.00	7.50

2004 Playoff Contenders Playoff Ticket

*STARS: 3X TO 8X BASE CARD HI
1-100 PRINT RUN 150 SER.#'d SETS
101-200 PRINT RUN 50 SER.#'d SETS

Card	Nm-Mt	Ex-Mt
❑ 101 Adimchinobe Echemandu	10.00	3.00
❑ 102 Ahmad Carroll	15.00	4.50
❑ 103 Andy Hall	10.00	3.00
❑ 104 B.J. Johnson	10.00	3.00
❑ 105 B.J. Symons	12.00	3.60
❑ 106 Ben Roethlisberger	120.00	36.00
❑ 107 Ben Troupe	12.00	3.60
❑ 108 Ben Watson	12.00	3.60
❑ 109 Bernard Berrian	12.00	3.60
❑ 110 Brandon Miree	10.00	3.00
❑ 111 Bruce Perry	10.00	3.00
❑ 112 Carlos Francis	10.00	3.00
❑ 113 Casey Bramlet	10.00	3.00
❑ 114 Cedric Cobbs	12.00	3.60
❑ 115 Chris Gamble	15.00	4.50
❑ 116 Chris Perry	25.00	7.50
❑ 117 Clarence Moore	12.00	3.60
❑ 118 Cody Pickett	12.00	3.60
❑ 119 Craig Krenzel	12.00	3.60
❑ 120 D.J. Hackett	10.00	3.00
❑ 121 D.J. Williams	15.00	4.50
❑ 122 Darius Watts	15.00	4.50
❑ 123 DeAngelo Hall	15.00	4.50
❑ 124 Derrick Hamilton	10.00	3.00
❑ 125 Derrick Ward	6.00	1.80
❑ 126 Devard Darling	12.00	3.60
❑ 127 Devery Henderson	10.00	3.00
❑ 128 Drew Carter	12.00	3.60
❑ 129 Drew Henson	30.00	9.00
❑ 130 Dunta Robinson	12.00	3.60
❑ 131 Eli Manning	60.00	18.00
❑ 132 Ernest Wilford	12.00	3.60
❑ 133 Greg Jones	12.00	3.60
❑ 134 J.P. Losman	30.00	9.00
❑ 135 Jamaar Taylor	12.00	3.60
❑ 136 Jared Lorenzen	10.00	3.00
❑ 137 Jarrett Payton	12.00	3.60
❑ 138 Jason Babin	12.00	3.60
❑ 139 Jeff Smoker	20.00	6.00
❑ 140 Jerricho Cotchery	12.00	3.60
❑ 141 Jim Sorgi	12.00	3.60
❑ 142 John Navarre	12.00	3.60
❑ 143 Johnnie Morant	12.00	3.60
❑ 144 Jonathan Vilma	12.00	3.60
❑ 145 Josh Harris	12.00	3.60
❑ 146 Julius Jones	50.00	15.00
❑ 147 Keary Colbert	15.00	4.50
❑ 148 Kellen Winslow Jr.	30.00	9.00
❑ 149 Kenechi Udeze	12.00	3.60
❑ 150 Kevin Jones	40.00	12.00
❑ 151 Larry Fitzgerald	40.00	12.00
❑ 152 Lee Evans	20.00	6.00
❑ 153 Luke McCown	12.00	3.60
❑ 154 Matt Mauck	12.00	3.60
❑ 155 Matt Schaub	20.00	6.00
❑ 156 Maurice Mann	10.00	3.00
❑ 157 Mewelde Moore	15.00	4.50
❑ 158 Michael Clayton	30.00	9.00
❑ 159 Michael Jenkins	12.00	3.60
❑ 160 Michael Turner	10.00	3.00
❑ 161 P.K. Sam	10.00	3.00
❑ 162 Philip Rivers	40.00	12.00
❑ 163 Quincy Wilson	10.00	3.00
❑ 164 Ran Carthon	10.00	3.00
❑ 165 Rashaun Woods	15.00	4.50
❑ 166 Reggie Williams	15.00	4.50
❑ 167 Ricardo Colclough	12.00	3.60
❑ 168 Robert Gallery	20.00	6.00
❑ 169 Roy Williams WR	40.00	12.00
❑ 170 Samie Parker	12.00	3.60
❑ 171 Sean Jones	10.00	3.00
❑ 172 Sean Taylor	15.00	4.50
❑ 173 Sloan Thomas	10.00	3.00
❑ 174 Steven Jackson	40.00	12.00
❑ 175 Tatum Bell	20.00	6.00
❑ 176 Tommie Harris	15.00	4.50
❑ 177 Triandos Luke	12.00	3.60
❑ 178 Troy Fleming	10.00	3.00
❑ 179 Vince Wilfork	15.00	4.50
❑ 180 Will Smith	12.00	3.60
❑ 181 Marcus Tubbs	12.00	3.60
❑ 182 Michael Boulware	12.00	3.60
❑ 183 Kris Wilson	12.00	3.60
❑ 184 Richard Smith	10.00	3.00
❑ 185 Teddy Lehman	12.00	3.60
❑ 186 Chris Cooley	12.00	3.60
❑ 187 Thomas Tapeh	10.00	3.00
❑ 188 Willie Parker	12.00	3.60
❑ 189 Patrick Crayton	12.00	3.60
❑ 190 Kendrick Starling	6.00	1.80
❑ 191 B.J. Sams	12.00	3.60
❑ 192 Derick Armstrong	6.00	1.80
❑ 193 Wes Welker	12.00	3.60
❑ 194 Erik Coleman	12.00	3.60
❑ 195 Gibril Wilson	12.00	3.60
❑ 196 Andy Reid	15.00	4.50
❑ 197 Brian Billick	12.00	3.60
❑ 198 Jeff Fisher	12.00	3.60
❑ 199 Jon Gruden	12.00	3.60
❑ 200 Marvin Lewis	12.00	3.60

2004 Playoff Contenders Legendary Contenders Orange

Nm-Mt Ex-Mt

ORANGE PRINT RUN 2000 SER.#'d SETS
*BLUE: .6X TO 1.5X ORANGE
BLUE PRINT RUN 250 SER.#'d SETS
*GREEN: 1X TO 2.5X ORANGE
GREEN PRINT RUN 100 SER.#'d SETS
*RED: .5X TO 1.2X ORANGE
RED PRINT RUN 750 SER.#'d SETS

❑ LC1 Barry Sanders	8.00	2.40
❑ LC2 Don Shula	3.00	.90
❑ LC3 Gale Sayers	4.00	1.20
❑ LC4 Herman Edwards	2.50	.75
❑ LC5 Joe Montana	10.00	3.00
❑ LC6 Joe Namath	5.00	1.50
❑ LC7 Larry Csonka	3.00	.90
❑ LC8 Mark Bavaro	2.50	.75
❑ LC9 Michael Irvin	3.00	.90
❑ LC10 Roger Staubach	6.00	1.80

2003 Playoff Hogg Heaven

	MINT	NRMT
COMP.SET w/o SP's (150)	30.00	13.50
❑ 1 Emmitt Smith	2.50	1.10
❑ 2 Marcel Shipp	.60	.25
❑ 3 Michael Vick	2.50	1.10
❑ 4 Warrick Dunn	.60	.25
❑ 5 T.J. Duckett	.60	.25
❑ 6 Peerless Price	.60	.25
❑ 7 Brian Finneran	.40	.18
❑ 8 Chris Redman	.40	.18
❑ 9 Jamal Lewis	1.00	.45
❑ 10 Todd Heap	.60	.25
❑ 11 Travis Taylor	.60	.25
❑ 12 Ray Lewis	1.00	.45
❑ 13 Peter Boulware	.40	.18
❑ 14 Ed Reed	.60	.25
❑ 15 Drew Bledsoe	1.00	.45
❑ 16 Travis Henry	.60	.25
❑ 17 Eric Moulds	.60	.25
❑ 18 Josh Reed	.60	.25
❑ 19 Takeo Spikes	.40	.18
❑ 20 Julius Peppers	1.00	.45
❑ 21 Stephen Davis	.60	.25
❑ 22 Muhsin Muhammad	.60	.25
❑ 23 Wesley Walls	.40	.18
❑ 24 Anthony Thomas	1.00	.45
❑ 25 Brian Urlacher	1.50	.70
❑ 26 Marty Booker	.60	.25
❑ 27 Mike Brown	.60	.25
❑ 28 Kordell Stewart	.60	.25
❑ 29 Dez White	.40	.18
❑ 30 Corey Dillon	.60	.25
❑ 31 Chad Johnson	.60	.25
❑ 32 Peter Warrick	.60	.25
❑ 33 Tim Couch	.40	.18
❑ 34 William Green	.60	.25
❑ 35 Andre Davis	.40	.18
❑ 36 Quincy Morgan	.60	.25
❑ 37 Kevin Johnson	.60	.25
❑ 38 Dennis Northcutt	.40	.18
❑ 39 Antonio Bryant	.60	.25
❑ 40 Terry Glenn	.40	.18
❑ 41 Joey Galloway	.60	.25
❑ 42 Roy Williams	1.00	.45
❑ 43 Darren Woodson	.40	.18
❑ 44 Jake Plummer	.60	.25
❑ 45 Clinton Portis	1.50	.70
❑ 46 Mike Anderson	.60	.25
❑ 47 Rod Smith	.60	.25
❑ 48 Ed McCaffrey	.60	.25
❑ 49 Ashley Lelie	1.00	.45
❑ 50 Shannon Sharpe	.60	.25
❑ 51 Al Wilson	.40	.18
❑ 52 Joey Harrington	1.50	.70
❑ 53 James Stewart	.60	.25
❑ 54 Brett Favre	2.50	1.10
❑ 55 Ahman Green	1.00	.45
❑ 56 Darren Sharper	.40	.18
❑ 57 Donald Driver	.60	.25
❑ 58 Javon Walker	.60	.25
❑ 59 Robert Ferguson	.40	.18
❑ 60 David Carr	1.50	.70
❑ 61 Jabar Gaffney	.60	.25
❑ 62 Stacey Mack	.40	.18
❑ 63 Marvin Harrison	1.00	.45
❑ 64 Peyton Manning	1.50	.70
❑ 65 Edgerrin James	1.00	.45
❑ 66 Reggie Wayne	.60	.25
❑ 67 Fred Taylor	1.00	.45
❑ 68 Mark Brunell	.60	.25
❑ 69 Jimmy Smith	.60	.25
❑ 70 Hugh Douglas	.40	.18
❑ 71 Priest Holmes	1.25	.55
❑ 72 Trent Green	.60	.25
❑ 73 Tony Gonzalez	.60	.25
❑ 74 Marc Boerigter	.60	.25
❑ 75 Ricky Williams	1.00	.45
❑ 76 Jay Fiedler	.60	.25
❑ 77 Chris Chambers	1.00	.45
❑ 78 Zach Thomas	1.00	.45
❑ 79 Jason Taylor	.40	.18
❑ 80 Junior Seau	1.00	.45
❑ 81 Randy McMichael	.60	.25
❑ 82 Patrick Surtain	.40	.18
❑ 83 Randy Moss	1.50	.70
❑ 84 Michael Bennett	.60	.25
❑ 85 Daunte Culpepper	1.00	.45
❑ 86 Tom Brady	1.50	.70
❑ 87 Troy Brown	.60	.25
❑ 88 Ty Law	.60	.25
❑ 89 Aaron Brooks	1.00	.45
❑ 90 Deuce McAllister	1.00	.45
❑ 91 Donte Stallworth	1.00	.45
❑ 92 Joe Horn	.60	.25
❑ 93 Michael Strahan	.60	.25
❑ 94 Kerry Collins	.60	.25
❑ 95 Tiki Barber	.60	.25
❑ 96 Amani Toomer	.60	.25
❑ 97 Jeremy Shockey	1.50	.70
❑ 98 Chad Pennington	1.25	.55
❑ 99 Curtis Martin	1.00	.45
❑ 100 Santana Moss	.60	.25
❑ 101 Rich Gannon	.60	.25
❑ 102 Jerry Rice	2.00	.90
❑ 103 Tim Brown	1.00	.45
❑ 104 Jerry Porter	.60	.25
❑ 105 Charlie Garner	.60	.25
❑ 106 Charles Woodson	.60	.25
❑ 107 Donovan McNabb	1.25	.55
❑ 108 Duce Staley	.60	.25
❑ 109 James Thrash	.40	.18
❑ 110 Chad Lewis	.40	.18
❑ 111 Troy Vincent	.40	.18
❑ 112 Tommy Maddox	1.00	.45
❑ 113 Plaxico Burress	.60	.25
❑ 114 Hines Ward	1.00	.45
❑ 115 Antwaan Randle El	1.00	.45
❑ 116 Jerome Bettis	1.00	.45
❑ 117 Kendrell Bell	.60	.25
❑ 118 LaDainian Tomlinson	1.00	.45
❑ 119 Drew Brees	1.00	.45
❑ 120 David Boston	.60	.25
❑ 121 Jeff Garcia	1.00	.45
❑ 122 Terrell Owens	1.00	.45
❑ 123 Tai Streets	.60	.25
❑ 124 Kevan Barlow	.60	.25
❑ 125 Matt Hasselbeck	.60	.25
❑ 126 Koren Robinson	.60	.25
❑ 127 Shaun Alexander	1.00	.45
❑ 128 Kurt Warner	1.00	.45
❑ 129 Marc Bulger	1.00	.45
❑ 130 Marshall Faulk	1.00	.45
❑ 131 Torry Holt	1.00	.45
❑ 132 Isaac Bruce	1.00	.45
❑ 133 Brad Johnson	.60	.25
❑ 134 Keyshawn Johnson	1.00	.45
❑ 135 Warren Sapp	.60	.25
❑ 136 Derrick Brooks	.60	.25
❑ 137 John Lynch	.60	.25
❑ 138 Michael Pittman	.40	.18
❑ 139 Mike Alstott	1.00	.45
❑ 140 Steve McNair	1.00	.45
❑ 141 Eddie George	.60	.25
❑ 142 Jevon Kearse	.60	.25
❑ 143 Keith Bulluck	.40	.18
❑ 144 Derrick Mason	.60	.25
❑ 145 Patrick Ramsey	1.00	.45
❑ 146 Ladell Betts	.60	.25
❑ 147 Laveranues Coles	.60	.25
❑ 148 Rod Gardner	.60	.25
❑ 149 Champ Bailey	.60	.25
❑ 150 Bruce Smith	.40	.18
❑ 151 Ken Dorsey RC	10.00	4.50
❑ 152 Lee Suggs RC	12.00	5.50
❑ 153 Domanick Davis RC	12.00	5.50
❑ 154 Quentin Griffin RC	15.00	6.75
❑ 155 LaBrandon Toefield RC	6.00	2.70
❑ 156 B.J. Askew RC	6.00	2.70
❑ 157 Jason Witten RC	10.00	4.50
❑ 158 Bennie Joppru RC	6.00	2.70
❑ 159 L.J. Smith RC	6.00	2.70
❑ 160 Billy McMullen RC	5.00	2.20
❑ 161 Shaun McDonald RC	6.00	2.70
❑ 162 Brandon Lloyd RC	8.00	3.60
❑ 163 Sam Aiken RC	5.00	2.20
❑ 164 Bobby Wade RC	6.00	2.70
❑ 165 Justin Gage RC	6.00	2.70
❑ 166 Doug Gabriel RC	6.00	2.70
❑ 167 David Kircus RC	5.00	2.20
❑ 168 Arnaz Battle RC	6.00	2.70
❑ 169 Kareem Kelly RC	5.00	2.20
❑ 170 Talman Gardner RC	6.00	2.70
❑ 171 Ryan Hoag RC	3.00	1.35
❑ 172 LaTarence Dunbar RC	5.00	2.20
❑ 173 Johnathan Sullivan RC	5.00	2.20
❑ 174 Kevin Williams RC	6.00	2.70
❑ 175 Jimmy Kennedy RC	8.00	3.60
❑ 176 Ty Warren RC	6.00	2.70
❑ 177 William Joseph RC	6.00	2.70
❑ 178 Michael Haynes RC	6.00	2.70
❑ 179 Jerome McDougle RC	6.00	2.70
❑ 180 Calvin Pace RC	3.00	1.35
❑ 181 Tyler Brayton RC	6.00	2.70
❑ 182 Chris Kelsay RC	6.00	2.70
❑ 183 DeWayne White RC	5.00	2.20
❑ 184 E.J. Henderson RC	6.00	2.70
❑ 185 Charles Rogers RC	8.00	3.60
❑ 186 Terry Pierce RC	5.00	2.20
❑ 187 Nick Barnett RC	10.00	4.50
❑ 188 Boss Bailey RC	8.00	3.60
❑ 189 Pisa Tinoisamoa RC	10.00	4.50
❑ 190 Chaun Thompson RC	3.00	1.35
❑ 191 Andre Woolfolk RC	6.00	2.70
❑ 192 Sammy Davis RC	6.00	2.70
❑ 193 Eugene Wilson RC	5.00	2.20
❑ 194 Drayton Florence RC	3.00	1.35
❑ 195 Ricky Manning RC	6.00	2.70
❑ 196 Donald Strickland RC	3.00	1.35
❑ 197 Dennis Weathersby RC	3.00	1.35
❑ 198 Troy Polamalu RC	6.00	2.70
❑ 199 Ken Hamlin RC	6.00	2.70
❑ 200 Mike Doss RC	6.00	2.70
❑ 201 Carson Palmer JSY RC	25.00	11.00
❑ 202 Byron Leftwich JSY RC	30.00	13.50
❑ 203 Kyle Boller JSY RC	20.00	9.00
❑ 204 Rex Grossman JSY RC	20.00	9.00

❑ 205 Andre Johnson JSY RC	20.00	9.00
❑ 206 Bryant Johnson JSY RC	8.00	3.60
❑ 207 Larry Johnson JSY RC	15.00	6.75
❑ 208 Taylor Jacobs JSY RC	8.00	3.60
❑ 209 Bethel Johnson JSY RC	12.00	5.50
❑ 210 Anquan Boldin JSY RC	20.00	9.00
❑ 211 Tyrone Calico JSY RC	10.00	4.50
❑ 212 Teyo Johnson JSY RC	8.00	3.60
❑ 213 Kelley Washington JSY RC	8.00	3.60
❑ 214 Musa Smith JSY RC	8.00	3.60
❑ 215 Chris Brown JSY RC	15.00	6.75
❑ 216 Justin Fargas JSY RC	8.00	3.60
❑ 217 Artose Pinner JSY RC	8.00	3.60
❑ 218 Onterrio Smith JSY RC	10.00	4.50
❑ 219 Brian St.Pierre JSY RC	8.00	3.60
❑ 220 Dave Ragone JSY RC	8.00	3.60
❑ 221 Dallas Clark JSY RC	8.00	3.60
❑ 222 Seneca Wallace JSY RC	8.00	3.60
❑ 223 Terrell Suggs JSY RC	12.00	5.50
❑ 224 Terence Newman JSY RC	15.00	6.75
❑ 225 DeWayne Robertson JSY RC	8.00	3.60
❑ 226 Marcus Trufant JSY RC	8.00	3.60
❑ 227 Kliff Kingsbury JSY RC	6.00	2.70
❑ 228 Kevin Curtis JSY RC	8.00	3.60
❑ 229 Willis McGahee JSY RC	20.00	9.00
❑ 230 Nate Burleson JSY RC	12.00	5.50

2003 Playoff Hogg Heaven Hogg Wild

MINT NRMT

*STARS: 3X TO 8X BASIC CARDS
*ROOKIES: 151-200: .8X TO 2X
*ROOKIES 201-230: 1.2X TO 3X

2004 Playoff Hogg Heaven

	Nm-Mt	Ex-Mt
COMP.SET w/o SP's (100)	30.00	9.00

101-150 RC PRINT RUN 750 SER.#'d SETS
151-180 RPH RC PRINT RUN 750 SER.#'d SETS

❑ 1 Anquan Boldin	1.00	.30
❑ 2 Emmitt Smith	2.00	.60
❑ 3 Josh McCown	.60	.18
❑ 4 Michael Vick	2.00	.60
❑ 5 Peerless Price	.60	.18
❑ 6 T.J. Duckett	.60	.18
❑ 7 Jamal Lewis	1.00	.30
❑ 8 Kyle Boller	1.00	.30
❑ 9 Ray Lewis	1.00	.30
❑ 10 Terrell Owens	1.00	.30
❑ 11 Drew Bledsoe	1.00	.30
❑ 12 Eric Moulds	.60	.18
❑ 13 Travis Henry	.60	.18
❑ 14 Jake Delhomme	1.00	.30
❑ 15 Stephen Davis	.60	.18
❑ 16 Steve Smith	.60	.18
❑ 17 Anthony Thomas	.60	.18
❑ 18 Brian Urlacher	1.25	.35
❑ 19 Rex Grossman	1.00	.30
❑ 20 Carson Palmer	1.25	.35
❑ 21 Chad Johnson	.60	.18
❑ 22 Peter Warrick	.60	.18
❑ 23 Rudi Johnson	.60	.18
❑ 24 Andre Davis	.40	.12
❑ 25 Lee Suggs	1.00	.30
❑ 26 Keyshawn Johnson	.60	.18
❑ 27 Quincy Carter	.60	.18
❑ 28 Roy Williams S	.60	.18
❑ 29 Ashley Lelie	.60	.18
❑ 30 Jake Plummer	.60	.18
❑ 31 Rod Smith	.60	.18
❑ 32 Charles Rogers	.60	.18
❑ 33 Joey Harrington	1.00	.30
❑ 34 Ahman Green	1.00	.30
❑ 35 Brett Favre	2.50	.75
❑ 36 Javon Walker	.60	.18
❑ 37 Andre Johnson	1.00	.30
❑ 38 David Carr	1.00	.30
❑ 39 Domanick Davis	1.00	.30
❑ 40 Edgerrin James	1.00	.30
❑ 41 Marvin Harrison	1.00	.30
❑ 42 Peyton Manning	1.50	.45
❑ 43 Reggie Wayne	.60	.18
❑ 44 Byron Leftwich	1.50	.45
❑ 45 Fred Taylor	.60	.18
❑ 46 Jimmy Smith	.60	.18
❑ 47 Priest Holmes	1.25	.35
❑ 48 Tony Gonzalez	.60	.18
❑ 49 Trent Green	.60	.18
❑ 50 A.J. Feeley	1.00	.30
❑ 51 Chris Chambers	.60	.18
❑ 52 Ricky Williams	1.00	.30
❑ 53 Zach Thomas	1.00	.30
❑ 54 Daunte Culpepper	1.00	.30
❑ 55 Michael Bennett	.60	.18
❑ 56 Randy Moss	1.25	.35
❑ 57 Deion Branch	1.00	.30
❑ 58 Tom Brady	1.50	.45
❑ 59 Ty Law	.60	.18
❑ 60 Aaron Brooks	.60	.18
❑ 61 Deuce McAllister	1.00	.30
❑ 62 Joe Horn	.60	.18
❑ 63 Jeremy Shockey	1.00	.30
❑ 64 Kerry Collins	.60	.18
❑ 65 Michael Strahan	.60	.18
❑ 66 Tiki Barber	.60	.18
❑ 67 Chad Pennington	1.25	.35
❑ 68 Curtis Martin	1.00	.30
❑ 69 Santana Moss	.60	.18
❑ 70 Jerry Rice	2.00	.60
❑ 71 Rich Gannon	.60	.18
❑ 72 Tim Brown	1.00	.30
❑ 73 Brian Westbrook	.60	.18
❑ 74 Donovan McNabb	1.25	.35
❑ 75 Jevon Kearse	.60	.18
❑ 76 Hines Ward	1.00	.30
❑ 77 Jerome Bettis	1.00	.30
❑ 78 Kendrell Bell	.60	.18
❑ 79 David Boston	.60	.18
❑ 80 Drew Brees	1.00	.30
❑ 81 LaDainian Tomlinson	1.00	.30
❑ 82 Jeff Garcia	1.00	.30
❑ 83 Kevan Barlow	.60	.18
❑ 84 Tim Rattay	.60	.18
❑ 85 Koren Robinson	.60	.18
❑ 86 Matt Hasselbeck	.60	.18
❑ 87 Shaun Alexander	1.00	.30
❑ 88 Isaac Bruce	.60	.18
❑ 89 Marc Bulger	1.00	.30
❑ 90 Marshall Faulk	1.00	.30
❑ 91 Torry Holt	1.00	.30
❑ 92 Brad Johnson	.60	.18
❑ 93 Keenan McCardell	.40	.12
❑ 94 Warren Sapp	.60	.18
❑ 95 Derrick Mason	.60	.18
❑ 96 Steve McNair	1.00	.30
❑ 97 Eddie George	.60	.18
❑ 98 Clinton Portis	1.00	.30
❑ 99 Laveranues Coles	.60	.18
❑ 100 Mark Brunell	.60	.18
❑ 101 Adimchinobe Echemandu RC	5.00	1.50
❑ 102 Ahmad Carroll RC	8.00	2.40
❑ 103 Andy Hall RC	5.00	1.50
❑ 104 B.J. Symons RC	6.00	1.80
❑ 105 Bradlee Van Pelt RC	8.00	2.40
❑ 106 Brandon Miree RC	5.00	1.50
❑ 107 Bruce Perry RC	5.00	1.50
❑ 108 Carlos Francis RC	5.00	1.50
❑ 109 Casey Bramlet RC	5.00	1.50
❑ 110 Chris Gamble RC	8.00	2.40
❑ 111 Clarence Moore RC	6.00	1.80
❑ 112 Cody Pickett RC	6.00	1.80
❑ 113 Craig Krenzel RC	6.00	1.80
❑ 114 D.J. Hackett RC	5.00	1.50
❑ 115 D.J. Williams RC	8.00	2.40
❑ 116 Derrick Ward RC	3.00	.90
❑ 117 Drew Carter RC	6.00	1.80
❑ 118 Ernest Wilford RC	6.00	1.80
❑ 119 Drew Henson RC	15.00	4.50
❑ 120 Jamaar Taylor RC	6.00	1.80
❑ 121 Jared Lorenzen RC	5.00	1.50
❑ 122 Jarrett Payton RC	6.00	1.80
❑ 123 Jason Babin RC	6.00	1.80
❑ 124 Jeff Smoker RC	10.00	3.00
❑ 125 Jeris McIntyre RC	5.00	1.50
❑ 126 Jerricho Cotchery RC	6.00	1.80
❑ 127 Jim Sorgi RC	6.00	1.80
❑ 128 John Navarre RC	6.00	1.80
❑ 129 Johnnie Morant RC	6.00	1.80
❑ 130 Sean Taylor RC	8.00	2.40
❑ 131 Jonathan Vilma RC	6.00	1.80
❑ 132 Josh Harris RC	6.00	1.80
❑ 133 Kenechi Udeze RC	6.00	1.80
❑ 134 Marcus Tubbs RC	6.00	1.80
❑ 135 Mark Jones RC	5.00	1.50
❑ 136 Matt Mauck RC	6.00	1.80
❑ 137 Maurice Mann RC	5.00	1.50
❑ 138 Michael Turner RC	5.00	1.50
❑ 139 P.K. Sam RC	5.00	1.50
❑ 140 Patrick Crayton RC	6.00	1.80
❑ 141 Quincy Wilson RC	5.00	1.50
❑ 142 Ran Carthon RC	5.00	1.50
❑ 143 Ryan Krause RC	5.00	1.50
❑ 144 Samie Parker RC	6.00	1.80
❑ 145 Sloan Thomas RC	5.00	1.50
❑ 146 Tommie Harris RC	8.00	2.40
❑ 147 Triandos Luke RC	6.00	1.80
❑ 148 Troy Fleming RC	5.00	1.50
❑ 149 Vince Wilfork RC	8.00	2.40
❑ 150 Will Smith RC	6.00	1.80
❑ 151 Larry Fitzgerald RPH RC	20.00	6.00
❑ 152 DeAngelo Hall RPH RC	8.00	2.40
❑ 153 Matt Schaub RPH RC	10.00	3.00
❑ 154 Michael Jenkins RPH RC	6.00	1.80
❑ 155 Devard Darling RPH RC	6.00	1.80
❑ 156 J.P. Losman RPH RC	15.00	4.50
❑ 157 Lee Evans RPH RC	10.00	3.00
❑ 158 Keary Colbert RPH RC	8.00	2.40
❑ 159 Bernard Berrian RPH RC	6.00	1.80
❑ 160 Chris Perry RPH RC	12.00	3.60
❑ 161 Kellen Winslow RPH RC	15.00	4.50
❑ 162 Luke McCown RPH RC	6.00	1.80
❑ 163 Julius Jones RPH RC	25.00	7.50
❑ 164 Darius Watts RPH RC	8.00	2.40
❑ 165 Tatum Bell RPH RC	10.00	3.00
❑ 166 Kevin Jones RPH RC	20.00	6.00
❑ 167 Roy Williams RPH RC	20.00	6.00
❑ 168 Greg Jones RPH RC	6.00	1.80
❑ 169 Reggie Williams RPH RC	8.00	2.40
❑ 170 Ben Watson RPH RC	6.00	1.80
❑ 171 Cedric Cobbs RPH RC	6.00	1.80
❑ 172 Devery Henderson RPH RC	5.00	1.50
❑ 173 Eli Manning RPH RC	30.00	9.00
❑ 174 Ben Roethlisberger RPH RC	50.00	15.00
❑ 175 Philip Rivers RPH RC	20.00	6.00
❑ 176 Derrick Hamilton RPH RC	5.00	1.50
❑ 177 Rashaun Woods RPH RC	8.00	2.40
❑ 178 Steven Jackson RPH RC	20.00	6.00
❑ 179 Michael Clayton RPH RC	15.00	4.50
❑ 180 Ben Troupe RPH RC	6.00	1.80

2004 Playoff Hogg Heaven Hogg Wild

Nm-Mt Ex-Mt

*STARS 1-100: 3X TO 8X BASE CARD HI
*ROOKIES 101-150: .8X TO 2X BASE CARD HI
101-150 PRINT RUN 125 SER.#'d SETS
*ROOKIES 151-180: 1.2X TO 3X BASE RCs
151-180 PRINT RUN 25 SER.#'d SETS

2001 Playoff Honors

	Nm-Mt	Ex-Mt
COMP.SET w/o SP's (100)	25.00	7.50
❑ 1 Rob Johnson	.60	.18
❑ 2 Eric Moulds	.60	.18
❑ 3 Marvin Harrison	1.00	.30
❑ 4 Edgerrin James	1.25	.35
❑ 5 Peyton Manning	2.50	.75
❑ 6 Jay Fiedler	1.00	.30
❑ 7 Lamar Smith	.60	.18
❑ 8 Zach Thomas	1.00	.30
❑ 9 Dan Marino	3.00	.90
❑ 10 Drew Bledsoe	1.25	.35
❑ 11 Terry Glenn	.60	.18
❑ 12 Wayne Chrebet	.60	.18
❑ 13 Curtis Martin	1.00	.30
❑ 14 Chad Pennington	1.50	.45
❑ 15 Vinny Testaverde	.60	.18
❑ 16 Corey Dillon	1.00	.30
❑ 17 Jon Kitna	1.00	.30
❑ 18 Akili Smith	.40	.12
❑ 19 Peter Warrick	1.00	.30
❑ 20 Kevin Johnson	.60	.18
❑ 21 Tim Couch	.60	.18
❑ 22 Eddie George	1.00	.30
❑ 23 Steve McNair	1.00	.30
❑ 24 Jevon Kearse	.60	.18
❑ 25 Jerome Bettis	1.00	.30
❑ 26 Kordell Stewart	.60	.18
❑ 27 Plaxico Burress	1.00	.30
❑ 28 Mark Brunell	1.00	.30
❑ 29 Keenan McCardell	.40	.12
❑ 30 Jimmy Smith	.60	.18
❑ 31 Fred Taylor	1.00	.30
❑ 32 Elvis Grbac	.60	.18
❑ 33 Jamal Lewis	1.50	.45
❑ 34 Ray Lewis	1.00	.30
❑ 35 Mike Anderson	1.00	.30
❑ 36 Terrell Davis	1.00	.30
❑ 37 John Elway	3.00	.90
❑ 38 Brian Griese	1.00	.30
❑ 39 Ed McCaffrey	1.00	.30
❑ 40 Tony Gonzalez	.60	.18
❑ 41 Trent Green	1.00	.30
❑ 42 Sylvester Morris	.40	.12
❑ 43 Tim Brown	1.00	.30
❑ 44 Rich Gannon	1.00	.30
❑ 45 Charlie Garner	.60	.18
❑ 46 Tyrone Wheatley	.60	.18
❑ 47 Charles Woodson	.60	.18
❑ 48 Tim Dwight	1.00	.30
❑ 49 Doug Flutie	1.00	.30
❑ 50 Junior Seau	1.00	.30
❑ 51 Shaun Alexander	1.25	.35
❑ 52 Matt Hasselbeck	.60	.18
❑ 53 Ricky Watters	.60	.18
❑ 54 Tony Banks	.60	.18
❑ 55 Joey Galloway	.60	.18
❑ 56 Emmitt Smith	2.00	.60
❑ 57 Troy Aikman	1.50	.45
❑ 58 Kerry Collins	.60	.18
❑ 59 Ron Dayne	1.00	.30
❑ 60 Donovan McNabb	1.25	.35
❑ 61 Duce Staley	1.00	.30
❑ 62 David Boston	1.00	.30
❑ 63 Thomas Jones	.60	.18
❑ 64 Jake Plummer	.60	.18
❑ 65 Stephen Davis	1.00	.30
❑ 66 Jeff George	.60	.18
❑ 67 Michael Westbrook	.60	.18
❑ 68 Deion Sanders	1.00	.30
❑ 69 James Allen	.60	.18
❑ 70 Cade McNown	.40	.12
❑ 71 Marcus Robinson	1.00	.30
❑ 72 Brian Urlacher	1.50	.45
❑ 73 Germane Crowell	.40	.12
❑ 74 Charlie Batch	1.00	.30
❑ 75 James Stewart	.60	.18
❑ 76 Brett Favre	3.00	.90
❑ 77 Antonio Freeman	1.00	.30
❑ 78 Ahman Green	1.00	.30
❑ 79 Cris Carter	1.00	.30
❑ 80 Daunte Culpepper	1.00	.30
❑ 81 Randy Moss	2.00	.60
❑ 82 Mike Alstott	1.00	.30
❑ 83 Warrick Dunn	1.00	.30
❑ 84 Brad Johnson	1.00	.30
❑ 85 Keyshawn Johnson	1.00	.30
❑ 86 Warren Sapp	.60	.18
❑ 87 Jamal Anderson	1.00	.30
❑ 88 Chris Chandler	.60	.18
❑ 89 Isaac Bruce	1.00	.30
❑ 90 Marshall Faulk	1.25	.35
❑ 91 Torry Holt	1.00	.30
❑ 92 Kurt Warner	2.00	.60
❑ 93 Aaron Brooks	1.00	.30
❑ 94 Albert Connell	.40	.12
❑ 95 Ricky Williams	1.00	.30
❑ 96 Jeff Garcia	1.00	.30
❑ 97 Terrell Owens	1.00	.30
❑ 98 Steve Young	1.00	.30
❑ 99 Jerry Rice	2.00	.60
❑ 100 Jeff Lewis	.40	.12
❑ 101 Rashard Casey RC	6.00	1.80
❑ 102 A.J. Feeley RC	10.00	3.00
❑ 103 Josh Booty RC	10.00	3.00
❑ 104 LaMont Jordan RC	12.00	3.60
❑ 105 Ben Leard RC	6.00	1.80
❑ 106 David Rivers RC	6.00	1.80
❑ 107 Tim Hasselbeck RC	10.00	3.00
❑ 108 Jason McKinley RC	6.00	1.80
❑ 109 Correll Buckhalter RC	12.00	3.60
❑ 110 Dan Alexander RC	10.00	3.00
❑ 111 Derrick Blaylock RC	10.00	3.00
❑ 112 Chris Barnes RC	6.00	1.80
❑ 113 Dee Brown RC	10.00	3.00
❑ 114 Derek Combs RC	6.00	1.80
❑ 115 David Allen RC	6.00	1.80
❑ 116 DeAngelo Evans RC	6.00	1.80
❑ 117 Reggie White RC	6.00	1.80
❑ 118 Heath Evans RC	6.00	1.80
❑ 119 George Layne RC	6.00	1.80
❑ 120 Moran Norris RC	4.00	1.20
❑ 121 Bhawoh Jue RC	10.00	3.00
❑ 122 Dustin McClintock RC	6.00	1.80
❑ 123 Ja'Mar Toombs RC	6.00	1.80
❑ 124 Steve Smith RC	12.00	3.60
❑ 125 Milton Wynn RC	6.00	1.80
❑ 126 Justin McCareins RC	10.00	3.00
❑ 127 Jarrod Cooper RC	10.00	3.00
❑ 128 Vinny Sutherland RC	6.00	1.80
❑ 129 Alex Bannister RC	6.00	1.80
❑ 130 Scotty Anderson RC	6.00	1.80
❑ 131 Onome Ojo RC	6.00	1.80
❑ 132 Damerien McCants RC	6.00	1.80
❑ 133 Eddie Berlin RC	6.00	1.80
❑ 134 Jonathan Carter RC	6.00	1.80
❑ 135 Bobby Newcombe RC	10.00	3.00
❑ 136 Cedrick Wilson RC	10.00	3.00
❑ 137 Kevin Kasper RC	10.00	3.00
❑ 138 Francis St. Paul RC	6.00	1.80
❑ 139 David Martin RC	6.00	1.80
❑ 140 T.J. Houshmandzadeh RC	10.00	3.00
❑ 141 John Capel RC	6.00	1.80
❑ 142 Reggie Germany RC	6.00	1.80
❑ 143 Chris Taylor RC	6.00	1.80
❑ 144 Ken-Yon Rambo RC	6.00	1.80
❑ 145 Richmond Flowers RC	6.00	1.80
❑ 146 Quentin McCord RC	6.00	1.80
❑ 147 Andre King RC	6.00	1.80
❑ 148 Boo Williams RC	6.00	1.80
❑ 149 Daniel Guy RC	4.00	1.20
❑ 150 Javon Green RC	6.00	1.80
❑ 151 Ronney Daniels RC	4.00	1.20
❑ 152 Alge Crumpler RC	12.00	3.60
❑ 153 Tony Driver RC	6.00	1.80
❑ 154 Shad Meier RC	6.00	1.80
❑ 155 Jabari Holloway RC	6.00	1.80
❑ 156 Ryan Pickett RC	4.00	1.20
❑ 157 Cedric James RC	6.00	1.80
❑ 158 Tony Stewart RC	10.00	3.00
❑ 159 Sean Brewer RC	4.00	1.20
❑ 160 Orlando Huff RC	4.00	1.20
❑ 161 Nate Clements RC	10.00	3.00
❑ 162 Will Allen RC	6.00	1.80
❑ 163 Willie Middlebrooks RC	6.00	1.80
❑ 164 Jamar Fletcher RC	6.00	1.80
❑ 165 Ken Lucas RC	6.00	1.80
❑ 166 Fred Smoot RC	10.00	3.00
❑ 167 Michael Stone RC	4.00	1.20
❑ 168 Tony Dixon RC	6.00	1.80
❑ 169 Andre Dyson RC	4.00	1.20
❑ 170 Gary Baxter RC	6.00	1.80
❑ 171 Adam Archuleta RC	10.00	3.00
❑ 172 Derrick Gibson RC	6.00	1.80
❑ 173 Edgerton Hartwell RC	4.00	1.20
❑ 174 Jamal Reynolds RC	10.00	3.00
❑ 175 Richard Seymour RC	10.00	3.00
❑ 176 B.Manumaleuna RC	6.00	1.80
❑ 177 Idrees Bashir RC	4.00	1.20
❑ 178 DeLawrence Grant RC	4.00	1.20
❑ 179 Karon Riley RC	4.00	1.20
❑ 180 Cedric Scott RC	6.00	1.80
❑ 181 Damione Lewis RC	6.00	1.80
❑ 182 Marcus Stroud RC	10.00	3.00
❑ 183 Casey Hampton RC	6.00	1.80
❑ 184 Willie Howard RC	6.00	1.80
❑ 185 Shaun Rogers RC	10.00	3.00
❑ 186 Kenny Smith RC	6.00	1.80
❑ 187 Marcus Bell DT RC	6.00	1.80
❑ 188 Mario Fatafehi RC	6.00	1.80
❑ 189 Kendrell Bell RC	20.00	6.00
❑ 190 Tommy Polley RC	10.00	3.00
❑ 191 Jamie Winborn RC	6.00	1.80
❑ 192 Sedrick Hodge RC	4.00	1.20
❑ 193 Torrance Marshall RC	10.00	3.00
❑ 194 Eric Westmoreland RC	6.00	1.80
❑ 195 Brian Allen RC	4.00	1.20
❑ 196 Morlon Greenwood RC	6.00	1.80
❑ 197 Brandon Spoon RC	10.00	3.00
❑ 198 Carlos Polk RC	4.00	1.20
❑ 199 Alex Lincoln RC	6.00	1.80
❑ 200 Keith Adams RC	4.00	1.20
❑ 201 Kevan Barlow JSY RC	10.00	3.00
❑ 202 Michael Bennett JSY RC	20.00	6.00
❑ 203 Drew Brees JSY RC	20.00	6.00
❑ 204 Quincy Carter JSY RC	10.00	3.00
❑ 205 Andre Carter JSY RC	10.00	3.00
❑ 206 Chris Chambers JSY RC	12.00	3.60
❑ 207 Robert Ferguson JSY RC	10.00	3.00
❑ 208 Rod Gardner JSY RC	10.00	3.00
❑ 210 Travis Henry JSY RC	12.00	3.60
❑ 212 Chad Johnson JSY RC	20.00	6.00
❑ 213 Rudi Johnson JSY RC	20.00	6.00
❑ 214 Sage Rosenfels JSY RC	10.00	3.00
❑ 215 Deuce McAllister JSY RC	20.00	6.00
❑ 216 Mike McMahon JSY RC	10.00	3.00
❑ 217 Snoop Minnis JSY RC	6.00	1.80
❑ 218 Travis Minor JSY RC	6.00	1.80
❑ 219 Freddie Mitchell JSY RC	10.00	3.00
❑ 220 Quincy Morgan JSY RC	10.00	3.00
❑ 222 Santana Moss JSY RC	15.00	4.50
❑ 223 Jesse Palmer JSY RC	10.00	3.00
❑ 224 Koren Robinson JSY RC	12.00	3.60
❑ 225 Josh Heupel JSY RC	10.00	3.00
❑ 226 Justin Smith JSY RC	10.00	3.00
❑ 227 David Terrell JSY RC	10.00	3.00
❑ 228 Anthony Thomas JSY RC	15.00	4.50
❑ 229 L.Tomlinson JSY RC	30.00	9.00
❑ 230 M.Tuiasosopo JSY RC	10.00	3.00
❑ 231 Michael Vick JSY RC	50.00	15.00
❑ 232 Gerard Warren JSY RC	10.00	3.00
❑ 233 Reggie Wayne JSY RC	15.00	4.50
❑ 234 Chris Weinke JSY RC	10.00	3.00
❑ 235 Leonard Davis JSY RC	6.00	1.80

2002 Playoff Honors

	Nm-Mt	Ex-Mt
COMP.SET w/o SP's (100)	25.00	7.50
❑ 1 David Boston	1.00	.30
❑ 2 Jake Plummer	.60	.18
❑ 3 Warrick Dunn	1.00	.30
❑ 4 Michael Vick	3.00	.90
❑ 5 Jamal Lewis	1.00	.30
❑ 6 Chris Redman	.40	.12
❑ 7 Ray Lewis	1.00	.30
❑ 8 Drew Bledsoe	1.25	.35
❑ 9 Travis Henry	1.00	.30
❑ 10 Eric Moulds	.60	.18
❑ 11 Lamar Smith	.60	.18
❑ 12 Steve Smith	.60	.18
❑ 13 Chris Weinke	.60	.18
❑ 14 Chris Chandler	.60	.18
❑ 15 David Terrell	1.00	.30
❑ 16 Anthony Thomas	1.00	.30
❑ 17 Brian Urlacher	1.50	.45
❑ 18 Corey Dillon	.60	.18
❑ 19 Peter Warrick	.60	.18
❑ 20 Tim Couch	.60	.18
❑ 21 James Jackson	.40	.12
❑ 22 Kevin Johnson	.60	.18
❑ 23 Quincy Carter	.60	.18
❑ 24 Joey Galloway	.60	.18
❑ 25 Emmitt Smith	2.50	.75
❑ 26 Terrell Davis	1.00	.30
❑ 27 Brian Griese	1.00	.30
❑ 28 Rod Smith	.60	.18
❑ 29 Germane Crowell	.40	.12
❑ 30 Az-Zahir Hakim	.40	.12
❑ 31 Mike McMahon	1.00	.30
❑ 32 Brett Favre	2.50	.75
❑ 33 Terry Glenn	.60	.18
❑ 34 Ahman Green	1.00	.30
❑ 35 James Allen	.60	.18
❑ 36 Corey Bradford	.40	.12
❑ 37 Marvin Harrison	1.00	.30
❑ 38 Peyton Manning	2.00	.60
❑ 39 Edgerrin James	1.25	.35
❑ 40 Reggie Wayne	.60	.18
❑ 41 Mark Brunell	1.00	.30
❑ 42 Fred Taylor	1.00	.30
❑ 43 Jimmy Smith	.60	.18
❑ 44 Tony Gonzalez	.60	.18
❑ 45 Trent Green	.60	.18
❑ 46 Priest Holmes	1.25	.35
❑ 47 Snoop Minnis	.40	.12
❑ 48 Chris Chambers	1.00	.30
❑ 49 Jay Fiedler	.60	.18
❑ 50 Ricky Williams	1.00	.30
❑ 51 Zach Thomas	1.00	.30
❑ 52 Randy Moss	2.00	.60
❑ 53 Daunte Culpepper	1.00	.30
❑ 54 Michael Bennett	.60	.18
❑ 55 Tom Brady	2.50	.75
❑ 56 Troy Brown	.60	.18
❑ 57 Antowain Smith	.60	.18
❑ 58 Aaron Brooks	1.00	.30
❑ 59 Deuce McAllister	1.00	.30
❑ 60 Tiki Barber	.60	.18
❑ 61 Kerry Collins	.60	.18
❑ 62 Amani Toomer	.60	.18
❑ 63 Michael Strahan	.60	.18
❑ 64 Curtis Martin	1.00	.30
❑ 65 Vinny Testaverde	.60	.18
❑ 66 Chad Pennington	1.25	.35
❑ 67 Laveranues Coles	.60	.18
❑ 68 Tim Brown	1.00	.30
❑ 69 Rich Gannon	1.00	.30
❑ 70 Jerry Rice	2.00	.60
❑ 71 Donovan McNabb	1.25	.35
❑ 72 Freddie Mitchell	.60	.18
❑ 73 Duce Staley	1.00	.30
❑ 74 Jerome Bettis	1.00	.30
❑ 75 Plaxico Burress	.60	.18
❑ 76 Kordell Stewart	.60	.18
❑ 77 Drew Brees	1.00	.30
❑ 78 Doug Flutie	1.00	.30
❑ 79 LaDainian Tomlinson	1.50	.45
❑ 80 Jeff Garcia	1.00	.30
❑ 81 Garrison Hearst	.60	.18
❑ 82 Terrell Owens	1.00	.30
❑ 83 Shaun Alexander	1.00	.30
❑ 84 Trent Dilfer	.60	.18
❑ 85 Koren Robinson	.60	.18
❑ 86 Isaac Bruce	1.00	.30
❑ 87 Marshall Faulk	1.00	.30
❑ 88 Torry Holt	1.00	.30
❑ 89 Kurt Warner	1.00	.30
❑ 90 Mike Alstott	1.00	.30
❑ 91 Brad Johnson	.60	.18
❑ 92 Keyshawn Johnson	1.00	.30
❑ 93 Keenan McCardell	.40	.12
❑ 94 Steve McNair	1.00	.30
❑ 95 Eddie George	1.00	.30
❑ 96 Jevon Kearse	.60	.18
❑ 97 Derrick Mason	.60	.18
❑ 98 Stephen Davis	.60	.18
❑ 99 Sage Rosenfels	.40	.12
❑ 100 Rod Gardner	.60	.18
❑ 101 Randy Fasani RC	5.00	1.50
❑ 102 Kurt Kittner RC	5.00	1.50
❑ 103 Brandon Doman RC	6.00	1.80
❑ 104 Craig Nall RC	6.00	1.80
❑ 105 J.T. O'Sullivan RC	5.00	1.50
❑ 106 Seth Burford RC	5.00	1.50
❑ 107 Jeff Kelly RC	5.00	1.50
❑ 108 Ronald Curry RC	6.00	1.80
❑ 109 Wes Pate RC	3.00	.90
❑ 110 Chad Hutchinson RC	6.00	1.80
❑ 111 Major Applewhite RC	6.00	1.80
❑ 112 Preston Parsons RC	3.00	.90
❑ 113 David Priestley RC	5.00	1.50
❑ 114 Lamar Gordon RC	6.00	1.80
❑ 115 Brian Westbrook RC	10.00	3.00
❑ 116 Jonathan Wells RC	6.00	1.80
❑ 117 Omar Easy RC	6.00	1.80
❑ 118 Verron Haynes RC	6.00	1.80
❑ 119 Josh Scobey RC	6.00	1.80
❑ 120 Larry Ned RC	5.00	1.50
❑ 121 Adrian Peterson RC	6.00	1.80
❑ 122 Brian Allen RC	5.00	1.50
❑ 123 Chester Taylor RC	6.00	1.80
❑ 124 Luke Staley RC	5.00	1.50
❑ 125 Antwoine Womack RC	5.00	1.50
❑ 126 Leonard Henry RC	5.00	1.50
❑ 127 Jesse Chatman RC	6.00	1.80
❑ 128 Damien Anderson RC	5.00	1.50
❑ 129 Eric McCoo RC	3.00	.90
❑ 130 Tellis Redmon RC	5.00	1.50
❑ 131 Joe Burns RC	6.00	1.80
❑ 132 Delvon Flowers RC	5.00	1.50
❑ 133 Ken Simonton RC	3.00	.90
❑ 134 Ricky Williams RC	5.00	1.50
❑ 135 Dicenzo Miller RC	3.00	.90
❑ 136 James Mungro RC	6.00	1.80
❑ 137 Randy McMichael RC	10.00	3.00
❑ 138 Deion Branch RC	12.00	3.60
❑ 139 Terry Charles RC	5.00	1.50
❑ 140 Herb Haygood RC	3.00	.90
❑ 141 Jason McAddley RC	5.00	1.50
❑ 142 Jake Schifino RC	5.00	1.50
❑ 143 Freddie Milons RC	5.00	1.50
❑ 144 Kahlil Hill RC	5.00	1.50
❑ 145 Lamont Brightful RC	3.00	.90
❑ 146 Chris Luzar RC	5.00	1.50
❑ 147 Daryl Jones RC	5.00	1.50
❑ 148 Woody Dantzler RC	6.00	1.80
❑ 149 Kelly Campbell RC	5.00	1.50
❑ 150 Brian Poli-Dixon RC	5.00	1.50
❑ 151 Atrews Bell RC	3.00	.90
❑ 152 Jarrod Baxter RC	5.00	1.50
❑ 153 Eddie Drummond RC	5.00	1.50
❑ 154 Jerramy Stevens RC	6.00	1.80
❑ 155 Doug Jolley RC	6.00	1.80
❑ 156 Jamar Martin RC	5.00	1.50
❑ 157 Najeh Davenport RC	6.00	1.80
❑ 158 Dwight Freeney RC	8.00	2.40
❑ 159 Bryan Thomas RC	5.00	1.50
❑ 160 Charles Grant RC	6.00	1.80
❑ 161 Kalimba Edwards RC	6.00	1.80
❑ 162 Ryan Denney RC	3.00	.90
❑ 163 Will Overstreet RC	3.00	.90
❑ 164 Dennis Johnson RC	3.00	.90
❑ 165 Alex Brown RC	6.00	1.80
❑ 166 Kenyon Coleman RC	3.00	.90
❑ 167 Ryan Sims RC	6.00	1.80
❑ 168 John Henderson RC	6.00	1.80
❑ 169 Wendell Bryant RC	6.00	1.80
❑ 170 Albert Haynesworth RC	5.00	1.50
❑ 171 Larry Tripplett RC	3.00	.90
❑ 172 Eddie Freeman RC	3.00	.90
❑ 173 Anthony Weaver RC	5.00	1.50
❑ 174 Quentin Jammer RC	6.00	1.80
❑ 175 Phillip Buchanon RC	6.00	1.80
❑ 176 Lito Sheppard RC	6.00	1.80
❑ 177 Mike Rumph RC	5.00	1.50
❑ 178 Roosevelt Williams RC	3.00	.90
❑ 179 Derek Ross RC	5.00	1.50
❑ 180 Mike Echols RC	3.00	.90
❑ 181 Keyou Craver RC	5.00	1.50
❑ 182 Ed Reed RC	10.00	3.00
❑ 183 Lamont Thompson RC	5.00	1.50
❑ 184 Tank Williams RC	5.00	1.50
❑ 185 Michael Lewis RC	6.00	1.80
❑ 186 Napoleon Harris RC	6.00	1.80
❑ 187 Robert Thomas RC	6.00	1.80
❑ 188 Raonall Smith RC	5.00	1.50
❑ 189 Levar Fisher RC	3.00	.90
❑ 190 Rocky Calmus RC	6.00	1.80
❑ 191 Andra Davis RC	5.00	1.50
❑ 192 Nick Rolovich RC	5.00	1.50
❑ 193 Zak Kustok RC	6.00	1.80
❑ 194 Dusty Bonner RC	3.00	.90
❑ 195 Tony Fisher RC	6.00	1.80
❑ 196 Sam Simmons RC	3.00	.90
❑ 197 Lee Mays RC	5.00	1.50
❑ 198 Jamin Elliott RC	3.00	.90
❑ 199 Javin Hunter RC	3.00	.90
❑ 200 Kendall Newson RC	3.00	.90
❑ 201 Ladell Betts JSY RC	10.00	3.00
❑ 202 Antonio Bryant JSY RC	10.00	3.00
❑ 203 Reche Caldwell JSY RC	10.00	3.00
❑ 204 David Carr JSY RC	30.00	9.00
❑ 205 Tim Carter JSY RC	8.00	2.40
❑ 206 Eric Crouch JSY RC	15.00	4.50
❑ 207 Rohan Davey JSY RC	10.00	3.00
❑ 208 Andre Davis JSY RC	10.00	3.00
❑ 209 T.J. Duckett JSY RC	15.00	4.50
❑ 210 DeShaun Foster JSY RC	10.00	3.00
❑ 211 Jabar Gaffney JSY RC	10.00	3.00
❑ 212 David Garrard JSY RC	10.00	3.00
❑ 213 Daniel Graham JSY RC	10.00	3.00
❑ 214 William Green JSY RC	15.00	4.50
❑ 215 Joey Harrington JSY RC	30.00	9.00
❑ 216 Ron Johnson JSY RC	8.00	2.40
❑ 217 Ashley Lelie JSY RC	20.00	6.00
❑ 218 Josh McCown JSY RC	12.00	3.60
❑ 219 Maurice Morris JSY RC	10.00	3.00
❑ 220 Julius Peppers JSY RC	20.00	6.00
❑ 221 Clinton Portis JSY RC	30.00	9.00
❑ 222 Patrick Ramsey JSY RC	20.00	6.00
❑ 223 Antwaan Randle El JSY RC	12.00	3.60
❑ 224 Josh Reed JSY RC	10.00	3.00
❑ 225 Cliff Russell JSY RC	8.00	2.40
❑ 226 Jeremy Shockey JSY RC	30.00	9.00
❑ 227 Donte Stallworth JSY RC	20.00	6.00
❑ 228 Travis Stephens JSY RC	8.00	2.40
❑ 229 Javon Walker JSY RC	20.00	6.00
❑ 230 Marquise Walker JSY RC	8.00	2.40
❑ 231 Roy Williams JSY RC	25.00	7.50

❑ 232 Mike Williams JSY RC	8.00	2.40
❑ RWH1 Walter Payton/250 Emmitt Smith Run With History dual jersey	120.00	36.00
❑ RWH1A Walter Payton Emmitt Smith AUTO/22 Run With History dual jersey (22 signed by Emmitt Smith only)	400.00	120.00

2002 Playoff Honors O's

Nm-Mt Ex-Mt

*STARS: 4X TO 10X HI COL.
*ROOKIES 101-200: 1.2X TO 3X

2002 Playoff Honors X's

Nm-Mt Ex-Mt

*STARS: 4X TO 10X BASIC CARDS
*ROOKIES 101-200: 1.2X TO 3X

2003 Playoff Honors

	MINT	NRMT
COMP.SET w/o SP's (100)	20.00	9.00
❑ 1 Aaron Brooks	1.00	.45
❑ 2 Ahman Green	1.00	.45
❑ 3 Amani Toomer	.60	.25
❑ 4 Anthony Thomas	1.00	.45
❑ 5 Antonio Bryant	.60	.25
❑ 6 Antwaan Randle El	1.00	.45
❑ 7 Ashley Lelie	1.00	.45
❑ 8 Brad Johnson	.60	.25
❑ 9 Brett Favre	2.50	1.10
❑ 10 Brian Urlacher	1.50	.70
❑ 11 Bruce Smith	.60	.25
❑ 12 Chad Johnson	.60	.25
❑ 13 Chad Pennington	1.25	.55
❑ 14 Charlie Garner	.60	.25
❑ 15 Chris Chambers	1.00	.45
❑ 16 Clinton Portis	1.50	.70
❑ 17 Corey Dillon	.60	.25
❑ 18 Curtis Martin	1.00	.45
❑ 19 Daunte Culpepper	1.00	.45
❑ 20 David Boston	.60	.25
❑ 21 David Carr	1.50	.70
❑ 22 Deuce McAllister	1.00	.45
❑ 23 Donald Driver	.60	.25
❑ 24 Donovan McNabb	1.25	.55
❑ 25 Donte Stallworth	1.00	.45
❑ 26 Drew Bledsoe	1.00	.45
❑ 27 Drew Brees	1.00	.45
❑ 28 Duce Staley	.60	.25
❑ 29 Ed McCaffrey	1.00	.45
❑ 30 Eddie George	.60	.25
❑ 31 Edgerrin James	1.00	.45
❑ 32 Emmitt Smith	2.50	1.10
❑ 33 Eric Moulds	.60	.25
❑ 34 Fred Taylor	1.00	.45
❑ 35 Garrison Hearst	.60	.25
❑ 36 Hines Ward	1.00	.45
❑ 37 Isaac Bruce	1.00	.45
❑ 38 Jabar Gaffney	.60	.25
❑ 39 Jake Plummer	.60	.25
❑ 40 Jamal Lewis	1.00	.45
❑ 41 Jay Fiedler	.60	.25
❑ 42 Jeff Garcia	1.00	.45
❑ 43 Jeremy Shockey	1.50	.70
❑ 44 Jerome Bettis	1.00	.45
❑ 45 Jerry Porter	.60	.25
❑ 46 Jerry Rice	2.00	.90
❑ 47 Jevon Kearse	.60	.25
❑ 48 Jimmy Smith	.60	.25
❑ 49 Joe Horn	.60	.25
❑ 50 Joey Harrington	1.50	.70
❑ 51 Josh Reed	.60	.25
❑ 52 Julius Peppers	1.00	.45
❑ 53 Kendrell Bell	.60	.25
❑ 54 Kerry Collins	.60	.25
❑ 55 Keyshawn Johnson	1.00	.45
❑ 56 Kordell Stewart	.60	.25
❑ 57 Koren Robinson	.60	.25
❑ 58 Kurt Warner	1.00	.45
❑ 59 LaDainian Tomlinson	1.00	.45
❑ 60 Laveranues Coles	.60	.25
❑ 61 Mark Brunell	.60	.25
❑ 62 Marshall Faulk	1.00	.45
❑ 63 Marvin Harrison	1.00	.45
❑ 64 Matt Hasselbeck	.60	.25
❑ 65 Michael Bennett	.60	.25
❑ 66 Michael Strahan	.60	.25
❑ 67 Michael Vick	2.50	1.10
❑ 68 Mike Alstott	1.00	.45
❑ 69 Patrick Ramsey	1.00	.45
❑ 70 Peerless Price	.60	.25
❑ 71 Peyton Manning	1.50	.70
❑ 72 Plaxico Burress	.60	.25
❑ 73 Priest Holmes	1.25	.55
❑ 74 Randy Moss	1.50	.70
❑ 75 Ray Lewis	1.00	.45
❑ 76 Rich Gannon	.60	.25
❑ 77 Ricky Williams	1.00	.45
❑ 78 Rod Gardner	.60	.25
❑ 79 Rod Smith	.60	.25
❑ 80 Roy Williams	1.00	.45
❑ 81 Shaun Alexander	1.00	.45
❑ 82 Stephen Davis	.60	.25
❑ 83 Steve McNair	1.00	.45
❑ 84 T.J. Duckett	.60	.25
❑ 85 Terrell Owens	1.00	.45
❑ 86 Tiki Barber	.60	.25
❑ 87 Tim Brown	1.00	.45
❑ 88 Tim Couch	.40	.18
❑ 89 Todd Heap	.60	.25
❑ 90 Tom Brady	1.50	.70
❑ 91 Tommy Maddox	1.00	.45
❑ 92 Tony Gonzalez	.60	.25
❑ 93 Torry Holt	1.00	.45
❑ 94 Travis Henry	.60	.25
❑ 95 Trent Green	.60	.25
❑ 96 Troy Brown	.60	.25
❑ 97 Warren Sapp	.60	.25
❑ 98 Warrick Dunn	.60	.25
❑ 99 William Green	.60	.25
❑ 100 Zach Thomas	1.00	.45
❑ 101 Chris Simms RC	10.00	4.50
❑ 102 Brooks Bollinger RC	5.00	2.20
❑ 103 Gibran Hamdan RC	2.50	1.10
❑ 104 Ken Dorsey RC	8.00	3.60
❑ 105 Jason Gesser RC	5.00	2.20
❑ 106 Brad Banks RC	4.00	1.80
❑ 107 Tony Romo RC	5.00	2.20
❑ 108 B.J. Askew RC	5.00	2.20
❑ 109 Domanick Davis RC	10.00	4.50
❑ 110 Lee Suggs RC	10.00	4.50
❑ 111 LaBrandon Toefield RC	5.00	2.20
❑ 112 Brock Forsey RC	5.00	2.20
❑ 113 Malaefou MacKenzie RC	2.50	1.10
❑ 114 Andrew Pinnock RC	4.00	1.80
❑ 115 Ahmaad Galloway RC	4.00	1.80
❑ 116 Tony Hollings RC	5.00	2.20
❑ 117 Charles Rogers RC	6.00	2.70
❑ 118 Billy McMullen RC	4.00	1.80
❑ 119 Shaun McDonald RC	5.00	2.20
❑ 120 Brandon Lloyd RC	6.00	2.70
❑ 121 Sam Aiken RC	4.00	1.80
❑ 122 Bobby Wade RC	5.00	2.20
❑ 123 Justin Gage RC	5.00	2.20
❑ 124 Adrian Madise RC	4.00	1.80
❑ 125 Jon Olinger RC	2.50	1.10
❑ 126 Doug Gabriel RC	5.00	2.20
❑ 127 J.R. Tolver RC	4.00	1.80
❑ 128 David Kircus RC	4.00	1.80
❑ 129 Zuriel Smith RC	2.50	1.10
❑ 130 LaTarence Dunbar RC	4.00	1.80
❑ 131 Arnaz Battle RC	5.00	2.20
❑ 132 Willie Ponder RC	2.50	1.10
❑ 133 Kareem Kelly RC	4.00	1.80
❑ 134 David Tyree RC	4.00	1.80
❑ 135 Keenan Howry RC	5.00	2.20
❑ 136 Taco Wallace RC	4.00	1.80
❑ 137 Walter Young RC	2.50	1.10
❑ 138 Talman Gardner RC	5.00	2.20
❑ 139 DeAndrew Rubin RC	2.50	1.10
❑ 140 Kevin Walter RC	4.00	1.80
❑ 141 Carl Ford RC	2.50	1.10
❑ 142 Travis Anglin RC	2.50	1.10
❑ 143 Ryan Hoag RC	2.50	1.10
❑ 144 Terrence Edwards RC	4.00	1.80
❑ 145 Bennie Joppru RC	5.00	2.20
❑ 146 L.J. Smith RC	5.00	2.20
❑ 147 Jason Witten RC	8.00	3.60
❑ 148 Andre Woolfolk RC	5.00	2.20
❑ 149 Nnamdi Asomugha RC	4.00	1.80
❑ 150 Troy Polamalu RC	5.00	2.20
❑ 151 Nate Hybl RC	10.00	4.50
❑ 152 Curt Anes RC	5.00	2.20
❑ 153 Avon Cobourne RC	5.00	2.20
❑ 154 Cecil Sapp RC	8.00	3.60
❑ 155 Casey Urlacher RC	10.00	4.50
❑ 156 Dwone Hicks RC	5.00	2.20
❑ 157 Jeremi Johnson RC	8.00	3.60
❑ 158 Kirk Farmer RC	8.00	3.60
❑ 159 James MacPherson RC	10.00	4.50
❑ 160 Chris Davis RC	8.00	3.60
❑ 161 Brandon Drumm RC	5.00	2.20
❑ 162 J.T. Wall RC	5.00	2.20
❑ 163 Casey Moore RC	8.00	3.60
❑ 164 Mike Seidman RC	5.00	2.20
❑ 165 Visanthe Shiancoe RC	8.00	3.60
❑ 166 George Wrighster RC	8.00	3.60
❑ 167 Dan Curley RC	5.00	2.20
❑ 168 Donald Lee RC	8.00	3.60
❑ 169 Aaron Walker RC	8.00	3.60
❑ 170 Trent Smith RC	5.00	2.20
❑ 171 Spencer Nead RC	8.00	3.60
❑ 172 Richard Angulo RC	8.00	3.60
❑ 173 Mike Pinkard RC	5.00	2.20
❑ 174 Johnathan Sullivan RC	8.00	3.60
❑ 175 Kevin Williams RC	10.00	4.50
❑ 176 Jimmy Kennedy RC	10.00	4.50
❑ 177 Ty Warren RC	10.00	4.50
❑ 178 William Joseph RC	10.00	4.50
❑ 179 Michael Haynes RC	10.00	4.50
❑ 180 Jerome McDougle RC	10.00	4.50
❑ 181 Calvin Pace RC	8.00	3.60
❑ 182 Tyler Brayton RC	10.00	4.50
❑ 183 Chris Kelsay RC	10.00	4.50
❑ 184 Osi Umenyiora RC	10.00	4.50
❑ 185 Alonzo Jackson RC	8.00	3.60
❑ 186 DeWayne White RC	8.00	3.60
❑ 187 Kenny Peterson RC	8.00	3.60
❑ 188 Nick Barnett RC	15.00	6.75
❑ 189 Boss Bailey RC	12.00	5.50
❑ 190 E.J. Henderson RC	10.00	4.50
❑ 191 Pisa Tinoisamoa RC	15.00	6.75
❑ 192 Sammy Davis RC	10.00	4.50
❑ 193 Charles Tillman RC	15.00	6.75
❑ 194 Eugene Wilson RC	8.00	3.60
❑ 195 Drayton Florence RC	5.00	2.20
❑ 196 Ricky Manning RC	10.00	4.50
❑ 197 Rashean Mathis RC	8.00	3.60
❑ 198 Ken Hamlin RC	10.00	4.50
❑ 199 Mike Doss RC	10.00	4.50
❑ 200 Julian Battle RC	8.00	3.60
❑ 201 Andre Johnson JSY RC	20.00	9.00
❑ 202 Anquan Boldin JSY RC	20.00	9.00
❑ 203 Artose Pinner JSY RC	8.00	3.60
❑ 204 Bethel Johnson JSY RC	12.00	5.50
❑ 205 Brian St.Pierre JSY RC	8.00	3.60
❑ 206 Bryant Johnson JSY RC	8.00	3.60
❑ 207 Byron Leftwich JSY RC	30.00	13.50
❑ 208 Carson Palmer JSY RC	25.00	11.00
❑ 209 Chris Brown JSY RC	15.00	6.75
❑ 210 Dallas Clark JSY RC	8.00	3.60
❑ 211 Dave Ragone JSY RC	8.00	3.60
❑ 212 DeWayne Robertson JSY RC	8.00	3.60

❑ 213 Justin Fargas JSY RC	8.00	3.60
❑ 214 Kelley Washington JSY RC	8.00	3.60
❑ 215 Kevin Curtis JSY RC	8.00	3.60
❑ 216 Kliff Kingsbury JSY RC	6.00	2.70
❑ 217 Kyle Boller JSY RC	20.00	9.00
❑ 218 Larry Johnson JSY RC	15.00	6.75
❑ 219 Marcus Trufant JSY RC	8.00	3.60
❑ 220 Musa Smith JSY RC	8.00	3.60
❑ 221 Nate Burleson JSY RC	12.00	5.50
❑ 222 Onterrio Smith JSY RC	10.00	4.50
❑ 223 Rex Grossman JSY RC	20.00	9.00
❑ 224 Seneca Wallace JSY RC	8.00	3.60
❑ 225 Taylor Jacobs JSY RC	8.00	3.60
❑ 226 Terrell Suggs JSY RC	12.00	5.50
❑ 227 Terence Newman JSY RC	15.00	6.75
❑ 228 Teyo Johnson JSY RC	8.00	3.60
❑ 229 Tyrone Calico JSY RC	10.00	4.50
❑ 230 Willis McGahee JSY RC	20.00	9.00

2003 Playoff Honors X's

	MINT	NRMT

*STARS: 2X TO 5X BASIC CARDS
*ROOKIES 101-150: 1.2X TO 3X
*ROOKIES 201-230: 1.2X TO 3X

2004 Playoff Honors

	Nm-Mt	Ex-Mt
COMP.SET w/o SP's (100)	20.00	6.00

101-150 INSERTS IN HOBBY PACKS ONLY
101-150 RC PRINT RUN 750 #'d SETS
151-200 INSERTS IN RETAIL PACKS ONLY
151-200 RC PRINT RUN 425 #'d SETS
201-233 JSY RC PRINT RUN 750 #'d SETS

❑ 1 Anquan Boldin	1.00	.30
❑ 2 Emmitt Smith	2.00	.60
❑ 3 Josh McCown	.60	.18
❑ 4 Michael Vick	2.00	.60
❑ 5 Peerless Price	.60	.18
❑ 6 T.J. Duckett	.60	.18
❑ 7 Warrick Dunn	.60	.18
❑ 8 Jamal Lewis	1.00	.30
❑ 9 Kyle Boller	1.00	.30
❑ 10 Ray Lewis	1.00	.30
❑ 11 Drew Bledsoe	1.00	.30
❑ 12 Eric Moulds	.60	.18
❑ 13 Travis Henry	.60	.18
❑ 14 DeShaun Foster	.60	.18
❑ 15 Jake Delhomme	1.00	.30
❑ 16 Steve Smith	.60	.18
❑ 17 Stephen Davis	.60	.18
❑ 18 Brian Urlacher	1.25	.35
❑ 19 Rex Grossman	1.00	.30
❑ 20 Thomas Jones	.60	.18
❑ 21 Carson Palmer	1.25	.35
❑ 22 Chad Johnson	.60	.18
❑ 23 Rudi Johnson	.60	.18
❑ 24 Jeff Garcia	1.00	.30
❑ 25 Lee Suggs	1.00	.30
❑ 26 Keyshawn Johnson	.60	.18
❑ 27 Quincy Carter	.60	.18
❑ 28 Roy Williams S	.60	.18
❑ 29 Jake Plummer	.60	.18
❑ 30 Quentin Griffin	1.00	.30
❑ 31 Rod Smith	.60	.18
❑ 32 Charles Rogers	.60	.18
❑ 33 Joey Harrington	1.00	.30
❑ 34 Ahman Green	1.00	.30
❑ 35 Brett Favre	2.50	.75
❑ 36 Javon Walker	.60	.18
❑ 37 Andre Johnson	1.00	.30
❑ 38 David Carr	1.00	.30
❑ 39 Domanick Davis	1.00	.30
❑ 40 Edgerrin James	1.00	.30
❑ 41 Marvin Harrison	1.00	.30
❑ 42 Peyton Manning	1.50	.45
❑ 43 Byron Leftwich	1.50	.45
❑ 44 Fred Taylor	.60	.18
❑ 45 Jimmy Smith	.60	.18
❑ 46 Priest Holmes	1.25	.35
❑ 47 Tony Gonzalez	.60	.18
❑ 48 Trent Green	.60	.18
❑ 49 A.J. Feeley	1.00	.30
❑ 50 Chris Chambers	.60	.18
❑ 51 Ricky Williams	1.00	.30
❑ 52 Daunte Culpepper	1.00	.30
❑ 53 Michael Bennett	.60	.18
❑ 54 Randy Moss	1.25	.35
❑ 55 Corey Dillon	.60	.18
❑ 56 Deion Branch	1.00	.30
❑ 57 Tom Brady	1.50	.45
❑ 58 Aaron Brooks	.60	.18
❑ 59 Deuce McAllister	1.00	.30
❑ 60 Joe Horn	.60	.18
❑ 61 Jeremy Shockey	1.00	.30
❑ 62 Michael Strahan	.60	.18
❑ 63 Tiki Barber	.60	.18
❑ 64 Chad Pennington	1.25	.35
❑ 65 Curtis Martin	1.00	.30
❑ 66 Santana Moss	.60	.18
❑ 67 Jerry Rice	2.00	.60
❑ 68 Justin Fargas	.60	.18
❑ 69 Kerry Collins	.60	.18
❑ 70 Tim Brown	1.00	.30
❑ 71 Brian Westbrook	.60	.18
❑ 72 Donovan McNabb	1.25	.35
❑ 73 Jevon Kearse	.60	.18
❑ 74 Terrell Owens	1.00	.30
❑ 75 Duce Staley	.60	.18
❑ 76 Hines Ward	1.00	.30
❑ 77 Jerome Bettis	1.00	.30
❑ 78 Tommy Maddox	.60	.18
❑ 79 Drew Brees	1.00	.30
❑ 80 LaDainian Tomlinson	1.00	.30
❑ 81 Kevan Barlow	.60	.18
❑ 82 Tim Rattay	.60	.18
❑ 83 Koren Robinson	.60	.18
❑ 84 Matt Hasselbeck	.60	.18
❑ 85 Shaun Alexander	1.00	.30
❑ 86 Isaac Bruce	.60	.18
❑ 87 Marc Bulger	1.00	.30
❑ 88 Marshall Faulk	1.00	.30
❑ 89 Torry Holt	1.00	.30
❑ 90 Brad Johnson	.60	.18
❑ 91 Charlie Garner	.60	.18
❑ 92 Keenan McCardell	.40	.12
❑ 93 Chris Brown	1.00	.30
❑ 94 Derrick Mason	.60	.18
❑ 95 Eddie George	.60	.18
❑ 96 Steve McNair	1.00	.30
❑ 97 Clinton Portis	1.00	.30
❑ 98 LaVar Arrington	2.00	.60
❑ 99 Laveranues Coles	.60	.18
❑ 100 Mark Brunell	.60	.18
❑ 101 Drew Henson RC	15.00	4.50
❑ 102 Craig Krenzel RC	6.00	1.80
❑ 103 Andy Hall RC	5.00	1.50
❑ 104 Josh Harris RC	6.00	1.80
❑ 105 Jim Sorgi RC	6.00	1.80
❑ 106 Jeff Smoker RC	10.00	3.00
❑ 107 John Navarre RC	6.00	1.80
❑ 108 Cody Pickett RC	6.00	1.80
❑ 109 Casey Bramlet RC	5.00	1.50
❑ 110 Matt Mauck RC	6.00	1.80
❑ 111 B.J. Symons RC	6.00	1.80
❑ 112 Bradlee Van Pelt RC	6.00	1.80
❑ 113 Michael Turner RC	5.00	1.50
❑ 114 Troy Fleming RC	5.00	1.50
❑ 115 Adimchinobe Echemandu RC	5.00	1.50
❑ 116 Quincy Wilson RC	5.00	1.50
❑ 117 Derrick Ward RC	3.00	.90
❑ 118 Bruce Perry RC	5.00	1.50
❑ 119 Brandon Miree RC	5.00	1.50
❑ 120 Carlos Francis RC	5.00	1.50
❑ 121 Samie Parker RC	6.00	1.80
❑ 122 Jerricho Cotchery RC	6.00	1.80
❑ 123 Ernest Wilford RC	6.00	1.80
❑ 124 Johnnie Morant RC	6.00	1.80
❑ 125 Maurice Mann RC	5.00	1.50
❑ 126 D.J. Hackett RC	5.00	1.50
❑ 127 Drew Carter RC	6.00	1.80
❑ 128 P.K. Sam RC	5.00	1.50
❑ 129 Jamaar Taylor RC	6.00	1.80
❑ 130 Ryan Krause RC	5.00	1.50
❑ 131 Triandos Luke RC	6.00	1.80
❑ 132 Jeris McIntyre RC	5.00	1.50
❑ 133 Clarence Moore RC	6.00	1.80
❑ 134 Mark Jones RC	5.00	1.50
❑ 135 Sloan Thomas RC	5.00	1.50
❑ 136 Jonathan Smith RC	5.00	1.50
❑ 137 Patrick Crayton RC	6.00	1.80
❑ 138 Derek Abney RC	6.00	1.80
❑ 139 Kris Wilson RC	6.00	1.80
❑ 140 Sean Taylor RC	8.00	2.40
❑ 141 Jonathan Vilma RC	6.00	1.80
❑ 142 Tommie Harris RC	8.00	2.40
❑ 143 D.J. Williams RC	8.00	2.40
❑ 144 Will Smith RC	6.00	1.80
❑ 145 Kenechi Udeze RC	6.00	1.80
❑ 146 Vince Wilfork RC	8.00	2.40
❑ 147 Marcus Tubbs RC	6.00	1.80
❑ 148 Ahmad Carroll RC	8.00	2.40
❑ 149 Jason Babin RC	6.00	1.80
❑ 150 Chris Gamble RC	8.00	2.40
❑ 151 Willie Parker RC	10.00	3.00
❑ 152 Darnell Dockett RC	8.00	2.40
❑ 153 Nate Poole RC	5.00	1.50
❑ 154 Matt Kegel RC	10.00	3.00
❑ 155 Kendrick Starling RC	5.00	1.50
❑ 156 Tramon Douglas RC	5.00	1.50
❑ 157 Ryan Dinwiddie RC	8.00	2.40
❑ 158 Brian Gaither RC	5.00	1.50
❑ 159 Ran Carthon RC	8.00	2.40
❑ 160 Derick Armstrong	5.00	1.50
❑ 161 Chris Cooley RC	10.00	3.00
❑ 162 Casey Clausen RC	12.00	3.60
❑ 163 Omar Jenkins RC	5.00	1.50
❑ 164 Justin Jenkins RC	8.00	2.40
❑ 165 Wes Welker RC	10.00	3.00
❑ 166 Terrance Copper RC	8.00	2.40
❑ 167 Jarrett Payton RC	10.00	3.00
❑ 168 Zamir Cobb RC	10.00	3.00
❑ 169 Derrick Knight RC	8.00	2.40
❑ 170 Romby Bryant RC	5.00	1.50
❑ 171 Larry Croom RC	8.00	2.40
❑ 172 Thomas Tapeh RC	8.00	2.40
❑ 173 Brock Lesnar RC	10.00	3.00
❑ 174 Richard Smith RC	8.00	2.40
❑ 175 Ricky Ray RC	8.00	2.40
❑ 176 John Booth RC	5.00	1.50
❑ 177 Huey Whittaker RC	10.00	3.00
❑ 178 Fred Russell RC	10.00	3.00
❑ 179 Ben Hartsock RC	10.00	3.00
❑ 180 Tim Euhus RC	10.00	3.00
❑ 181 Ricardo Colclough RC	10.00	3.00
❑ 182 Keiwan Ratliff RC	8.00	2.40
❑ 183 Shawntae Spencer RC	10.00	3.00
❑ 184 Joey Thomas RC	10.00	3.00
❑ 185 Keith Smith RC	8.00	2.40
❑ 186 Derrick Strait RC	10.00	3.00
❑ 187 Jeremy LeSueur RC	8.00	2.40
❑ 188 Matt Ware RC	10.00	3.00
❑ 189 Rich Gardner RC	8.00	2.40
❑ 190 Daryl Smith RC	10.00	3.00
❑ 191 Dontarrious Thomas RC	10.00	3.00
❑ 192 Courtney Watson RC	10.00	3.00
❑ 193 Karlos Dansby RC	10.00	3.00
❑ 194 Teddy Lehman RC	10.00	3.00
❑ 195 Michael Boulware RC	10.00	3.00
❑ 196 Bob Sanders RC	8.00	2.40
❑ 197 Travis LaBoy RC	10.00	3.00
❑ 198 Antwan Odom RC	10.00	3.00
❑ 199 Marquise Hill RC	8.00	2.40
❑ 200 Terry Johnson RC	8.00	2.40
❑ 201 Larry Fitzgerald JSY RC	20.00	6.00

❑ 202 DeAngelo Hall JSY RC 10.00 3.00
❑ 203 Matt Schaub JSY RC 10.00 3.00
❑ 204 Michael Jenkins JSY RC 8.00 2.40
❑ 205 Devard Darling JSY RC 8.00 2.40
❑ 206 J.P. Losman JSY RC 15.00 4.50
❑ 207 Lee Evans JSY RC 10.00 3.00
❑ 208 Keary Colbert JSY RC 10.00 3.00
❑ 209 Bernard Berrian JSY RC 8.00 2.40
❑ 210 Chris Perry JSY RC 12.00 3.60
❑ 211 Kellen Winslow JSY RC 15.00 4.50
❑ 212 Luke McCown JSY RC 8.00 2.40
❑ 213 Julius Jones JSY RC 25.00 7.50
❑ 214 Darius Watts JSY RC 10.00 3.00
❑ 215 Tatum Bell JSY RC 10.00 3.00
❑ 216 Kevin Jones JSY RC 20.00 6.00
❑ 217 Roy Williams JSY RC 20.00 6.00
❑ 218 Dunta Robinson JSY RC 8.00 2.40
❑ 219 Greg Jones JSY RC 8.00 2.40
❑ 220 Reggie Williams JSY RC 10.00 3.00
❑ 221 Mewelde Moore JSY RC 10.00 3.00
❑ 222 Ben Watson JSY RC 8.00 2.40
❑ 223 Cedric Cobbs JSY RC 8.00 2.40
❑ 224 Devery Henderson JSY RC 6.00 1.80
❑ 225 Eli Manning JSY RC 30.00 9.00
❑ 226 Robert Gallery JSY RC 10.00 3.00
❑ 227 Ben Roethlisberger JSY RC 60.00 18.00
❑ 228 Philip Rivers JSY RC 20.00 6.00
❑ 229 Derrick Hamilton JSY RC 6.00 1.80
❑ 230 Rashaun Woods JSY RC 10.00 3.00
❑ 231 Steven Jackson JSY RC 20.00 6.00
❑ 232 Michael Clayton JSY RC 15.00 4.50
❑ 233 Ben Troupe JSY RC 8.00 2.40

2004 Playoff Honors X's

Nm-Mt Ex-Mt

*STARS 1-100: 2X TO 5X BASE CARD HI
1-100 PRINT RUN 199 SER.#'d SETS
*ROOKIES 101-150: .6X TO 1.5X BASE CARD HI
101-150 PRINT RUN 99 SER.#'d SETS
*ROOKIE JSY 201-233: 1.5X TO 4X
201-233 JSY PRINT RUN 25 #'d SETS
INSERTS IN HOBBY PACKS ONLY

1998 Playoff Momentum Hobby

Nm-Mt Ex-Mt

COMPLETE SET (250) 250.00 110.00
❑ 1 Jake Plummer 2.50 1.10
❑ 2 Eric Metcalf 1.00 .45
❑ 3 Adrian Murrell 1.50 .70
❑ 4 Larry Centers 1.00 .45
❑ 5 Frank Sanders 1.50 .70
❑ 6 Rob Moore 1.50 .70
❑ 7 Andre Wadsworth RC 4.00 1.80
❑ 8 Chris Chandler 1.50 .70
❑ 9 Jamal Anderson 2.50 1.10
❑ 10 Tony Martin 1.50 .70
❑ 11 Terance Mathis 1.50 .70
❑ 12 Tim Dwight RC 5.00 2.20
❑ 13 Jammi German RC 2.50 1.10
❑ 14 O.J. Santiago 1.00 .45
❑ 15 Jim Harbaugh 1.50 .70
❑ 16 Eric Zeier 1.50 .70
❑ 17 Duane Starks RC 2.50 1.10
❑ 18 Rod Woodson 1.50 .70
❑ 19 Errict Rhett 1.50 .70
❑ 20 Jay Graham 1.00 .45
❑ 21 Ray Lewis 2.50 1.10
❑ 22 Michael Jackson 1.00 .45
❑ 23 Jermaine Lewis 1.50 .70
❑ 24 Pat Johnson RC 4.00 1.80
❑ 25 Eric Green 1.00 .45
❑ 26 Doug Flutie 2.50 1.10
❑ 27 Rob Johnson 1.50 .70
❑ 28 Antowain Smith 2.50 1.10
❑ 29 Thurman Thomas 2.50 1.10
❑ 30 Jonathan Linton RC 4.00 1.80
❑ 31 Bruce Smith 1.50 .70
❑ 32 Eric Moulds 2.50 1.10
❑ 33 Kevin Williams 1.00 .45
❑ 34 Andre Reed 1.50 .70
❑ 35 Steve Beuerlein 1.50 .70
❑ 36 Kerry Collins 1.50 .70
❑ 37 Anthony Johnson 1.00 .45
❑ 38 Fred Lane 1.00 .45
❑ 39 William Floyd 1.00 .45
❑ 40 Rocket Ismail 1.00 .45
❑ 41 Wesley Walls 1.50 .70
❑ 42 Muhsin Muhammad 1.50 .70
❑ 43 Rae Carruth 1.00 .45
❑ 44 Kevin Greene 1.50 .70
❑ 45 Greg Lloyd 1.00 .45
❑ 46 Moses Moreno RC 2.50 1.10
❑ 47 Erik Kramer 1.00 .45
❑ 48 Edgar Bennett 1.00 .45
❑ 49 Curtis Enis RC 2.50 1.10
❑ 50 Curtis Conway 1.50 .70
❑ 51 Bobby Engram 1.50 .70
❑ 52 Alonzo Mayes RC 2.50 1.10
❑ 53 Jeff Blake 1.50 .70
❑ 54 Neil O'Donnell 1.50 .70
❑ 55 Corey Dillon 2.50 1.10
❑ 56 Takeo Spikes RC 5.00 2.20
❑ 57 Carl Pickens 1.50 .70
❑ 58 Tony McGee 1.00 .45
❑ 59 Darnay Scott 1.50 .70
❑ 60 Troy Aikman 5.00 2.20
❑ 61 Deion Sanders 2.50 1.10
❑ 62 Emmitt Smith 8.00 3.60
❑ 63 Darren Woodson 1.00 .45
❑ 64 Chris Warren 1.50 .70
❑ 65 Daryl Johnston 1.50 .70
❑ 66 Ernie Mills 1.00 .45
❑ 67 Billy Davis 1.00 .45
❑ 68 Michael Irvin 2.50 1.10
❑ 69 David LaFleur 1.00 .45
❑ 70 John Elway 10.00 4.50
❑ 71 Brian Griese RC 10.00 4.50
❑ 72 Steve Atwater 1.00 .45
❑ 73 Terrell Davis 2.50 1.10
❑ 74 Rod Smith 1.50 .70
❑ 75 Marcus Nash RC 2.50 1.10
❑ 76 Shannon Sharpe 1.50 .70
❑ 77 Ed McCaffrey 1.50 .70
❑ 78 Neil Smith 1.50 .70
❑ 79 Charlie Batch RC 5.00 2.20
❑ 80 Germane Crowell RC 4.00 1.80
❑ 81 Scott Mitchell 1.50 .70
❑ 82 Barry Sanders 8.00 3.60
❑ 83 Terry Fair RC 4.00 1.80
❑ 84 Herman Moore 1.50 .70
❑ 85 Johnnie Morton 1.50 .70
❑ 86 Brett Favre 10.00 4.50
❑ 87 Rick Mirer 1.00 .45
❑ 88 Dorsey Levens 2.50 1.10
❑ 89 William Henderson 1.50 .70
❑ 90 Derrick Mayes 1.50 .70
❑ 91 Antonio Freeman 2.50 1.10
❑ 92 Robert Brooks 1.50 .70
❑ 93 Mark Chmura 1.50 .70
❑ 94 Vonnie Holliday RC 4.00 1.80
❑ 95 Reggie White 2.50 1.10
❑ 96 E.G. Green RC 4.00 1.80
❑ 97 Jerome Pathon RC 5.00 2.20
❑ 98 Peyton Manning RC 50.00 22.00
❑ 99 Marshall Faulk 3.00 1.35
❑ 100 Zack Crockett 1.00 .45
❑ 101 Ken Dilger 1.00 .45
❑ 102 Marvin Harrison 2.50 1.10
❑ 103 Mark Brunell 2.50 1.10
❑ 104 Jonathan Quinn RC 5.00 2.20
❑ 105 Tavian Banks RC 4.00 1.80
❑ 106 Fred Taylor RC 8.00 3.60
❑ 107 James Stewart 1.50 .70
❑ 108 Jimmy Smith 1.50 .70
❑ 109 Keenan McCardell 1.50 .70
❑ 110 Elvis Grbac 1.50 .70
❑ 111 Rich Gannon 2.50 1.10
❑ 112 Rashaan Shehee RC 4.00 1.80
❑ 113 Donnell Bennett 1.00 .45
❑ 114 Kimble Anders 1.50 .70
❑ 115 Derrick Thomas 1.50 .70
❑ 116 Kevin Lockett 1.00 .45
❑ 117 Derrick Alexander WR 1.50 .70
❑ 118 Tony Gonzalez 2.50 1.10
❑ 119 Andre Rison 1.50 .70
❑ 120 Craig Erickson 1.00 .45
❑ 121 Dan Marino 10.00 4.50
❑ 122 John Avery RC 4.00 1.80
❑ 123 Karim Abdul-Jabbar 2.50 1.10
❑ 124 Zach Thomas 2.50 1.10
❑ 125 O.J. McDuffie 1.50 .70
❑ 126 Troy Drayton 1.00 .45
❑ 127 Randall Cunningham 2.50 1.10
❑ 128 Brad Johnson 2.50 1.10
❑ 129 Robert Smith 2.50 1.10
❑ 130 Cris Carter 2.50 1.10
❑ 131 Randy Moss RC 25.00 11.00
❑ 132 Jake Reed 1.50 .70
❑ 133 John Randle 1.50 .70
❑ 134 Drew Bledsoe 4.00 1.80
❑ 135 Tony Simmons RC 4.00 1.80
❑ 136 Sedrick Shaw 1.00 .45
❑ 137 Chris Floyd RC 2.50 1.10
❑ 138 Robert Edwards RC 4.00 1.80
❑ 139 Rod Rutledge RC 2.50 1.10
❑ 140 Shawn Jefferson 1.00 .45
❑ 141 Ben Coates 1.50 .70
❑ 142 Terry Glenn 2.50 1.10
❑ 143 Heath Shuler 1.00 .45
❑ 144 Danny Wuerffel 1.50 .70
❑ 145 Troy Davis 1.00 .45
❑ 146 Qadry Ismail 1.50 .70
❑ 147 Ray Zellars 1.00 .45
❑ 148 Lamar Smith 1.50 .70
❑ 149 Cameron Cleeland RC 2.50 1.10
❑ 150 Sean Dawkins 1.00 .45
❑ 151 Andre Hastings 1.00 .45
❑ 152 Danny Kanell 1.50 .70
❑ 153 Tiki Barber 2.50 1.10
❑ 154 Tyrone Wheatley 1.50 .70
❑ 155 Charles Way 1.00 .45
❑ 156 Gary Brown 1.00 .45
❑ 157 Shaun Williams RC 4.00 1.80
❑ 158 Chris Calloway 1.00 .45
❑ 159 Amani Toomer 1.50 .70
❑ 160 Brian Alford RC 2.50 1.10
❑ 161 Joe Jurevicius RC 5.00 2.20
❑ 162 Ike Hilliard 1.50 .70
❑ 163 Michael Strahan 1.50 .70
❑ 164 Glenn Foley 1.50 .70
❑ 165 Vinny Testaverde 1.50 .70
❑ 166 Keyshawn Johnson 2.50 1.10
❑ 167 Curtis Martin 2.50 1.10
❑ 168 Leon Johnson 1.00 .45
❑ 169 Keith Byars 1.00 .45
❑ 170 Wayne Chrebet 2.50 1.10
❑ 171 Kyle Brady 1.00 .45
❑ 172 Dedric Ward 1.00 .45
❑ 173 Jeff George 1.50 .70
❑ 174 Charles Woodson RC 10.00 4.50
❑ 175 Napoleon Kaufman 2.50 1.10
❑ 176 Jon Ritchie RC 4.00 1.80
❑ 177 Tim Brown 2.50 1.10
❑ 178 James Jett 1.50 .70
❑ 179 Rickey Dudley 1.00 .45
❑ 180 Bobby Hoying 1.50 .70
❑ 181 Duce Staley 3.00 1.35
❑ 182 Charlie Garner 1.50 .70
❑ 183 Irving Fryar 1.50 .70
❑ 184 Jeff Graham 1.00 .45
❑ 185 Jason Dunn 1.00 .45
❑ 186 Kordell Stewart 2.50 1.10

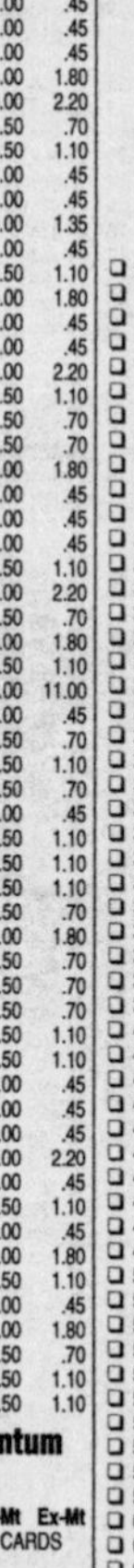

Card	Nm-Mt	Ex-Mt
❑ 187 Jerome Bettis	2.50	1.10
❑ 188 Andre Coleman	1.00	.45
❑ 189 C.Fuamatu-Ma'afala RC	4.00	1.80
❑ 190 Charles Johnson	1.00	.45
❑ 191 Hines Ward RC	12.00	5.50
❑ 192 Mark Bruener	1.00	.45
❑ 193 Courtney Hawkins	1.00	.45
❑ 194 Will Blackwell	1.00	.45
❑ 195 Levon Kirkland	1.00	.45
❑ 196 Mikhael Ricks RC	4.00	1.80
❑ 197 Ryan Leaf RC	5.00	2.20
❑ 198 Natrone Means	1.50	.70
❑ 199 Junior Seau	2.50	1.10
❑ 200 Bryan Still	1.00	.45
❑ 201 Freddie Jones	1.00	.45
❑ 202 Steve Young	3.00	1.35
❑ 203 Jim Druckenmiller	1.00	.45
❑ 204 Garrison Hearst	2.50	1.10
❑ 205 R.W. McQuarters RC	4.00	1.80
❑ 206 Merton Hanks	1.00	.45
❑ 207 Marc Edwards	1.00	.45
❑ 208 Jerry Rice	5.00	2.20
❑ 209 Terrell Owens	2.50	1.10
❑ 210 J.J. Stokes	1.50	.70
❑ 211 Tony Banks	1.50	.70
❑ 212 Robert Holcombe RC	4.00	1.80
❑ 213 Greg Hill	1.00	.45
❑ 214 Amp Lee	1.00	.45
❑ 215 Jerald Moore	1.00	.45
❑ 216 Isaac Bruce	2.50	1.10
❑ 217 Az-Zahir Hakim RC	5.00	2.20
❑ 218 Eddie Kennison	1.50	.70
❑ 219 Grant Wistrom RC	4.00	1.80
❑ 220 Warren Moon	2.50	1.10
❑ 221 Ahman Green RC	25.00	11.00
❑ 222 Steve Broussard	1.00	.45
❑ 223 Ricky Watters	1.50	.70
❑ 224 James McKnight	2.50	1.10
❑ 225 Joey Galloway	1.50	.70
❑ 226 Mike Pritchard	1.00	.45
❑ 227 Trent Dilfer	2.50	1.10
❑ 228 Warrick Dunn	2.50	1.10
❑ 229 Mike Alstott	2.50	1.10
❑ 230 John Lynch	1.50	.70
❑ 231 Jacquez Green RC	4.00	1.80
❑ 232 Reidel Anthony	1.50	.70
❑ 233 Bert Emanuel	1.50	.70
❑ 234 Warren Sapp	1.50	.70
❑ 235 Steve McNair	2.50	1.10
❑ 236 Eddie George	2.50	1.10
❑ 237 Chris Sanders	1.00	.45
❑ 238 Yancey Thigpen	1.00	.45
❑ 239 Willie Davis	1.00	.45
❑ 240 Kevin Dyson RC	5.00	2.20
❑ 241 Frank Wycheck	1.00	.45
❑ 242 Trent Green	2.50	1.10
❑ 243 Gus Frerotte	1.00	.45
❑ 244 Skip Hicks RC	4.00	1.80
❑ 245 Terry Allen	2.50	1.10
❑ 246 Stephen Davis	1.00	.45
❑ 247 Stephen Alexander RC	4.00	1.80
❑ 248 Michael Westbrook	1.50	.70
❑ 249 Dana Stubblefield SP	2.50	1.10
❑ 250 Dan Wilkinson SP	2.50	1.10

1998 Playoff Momentum Hobby Gold

Nm-Mt Ex-Mt

*GOLD STARS: 12X TO 30X BASIC CARDS
*GOLD RCs: 2.5X TO 6X

1999 Playoff Momentum SSD

	Nm-Mt	Ex-Mt
COMPLETE SET (200)	300.00	135.00
COMP.SHORT SET (150)	100.00	45.00
❑ 1 Rob Moore	.50	.23
❑ 2 Adrian Murrell	.50	.23
❑ 3 Frank Sanders	.50	.23
❑ 4 Andre Wadsworth	.30	.14
❑ 5 Tim Dwight	.75	.35
❑ 6 Terance Mathis	.50	.23
❑ 7 Priest Holmes	1.25	.55
❑ 8 Jermaine Lewis	.50	.23

Card	Nm-Mt	Ex-Mt
❑ 9 Scott Mitchell	.30	.14
❑ 10 Patrick Johnson	.30	.14
❑ 11 Tony Banks	.50	.23
❑ 12 Thurman Thomas	.50	.23
❑ 13 Andre Reed	.50	.23
❑ 14 Bruce Smith	.50	.23
❑ 15 Tim Biakabutuka	.50	.23
❑ 16 Muhsin Muhammad	.50	.23
❑ 17 Wesley Walls	.50	.23
❑ 18 Rae Carruth	.30	.14
❑ 19 Curtis Conway	.50	.23
❑ 20 Bobby Engram	.50	.23
❑ 21 Jeff Blake	.50	.23
❑ 22 Darnay Scott	.30	.14
❑ 23 Ty Detmer	.50	.23
❑ 24 Leslie Shepherd	.30	.14
❑ 25 Sedrick Shaw	.30	.14
❑ 26 Michael Irvin	.50	.23
❑ 27 Rocket Ismail	.50	.23
❑ 28 Ed McCaffrey	.50	.23
❑ 29 Marcus Nash	.30	.14
❑ 30 Shannon Sharpe	.50	.23
❑ 31 Neil Smith	.50	.23
❑ 32 Rod Smith	.50	.23
❑ 33 Bubby Brister	.30	.14
❑ 34 Germane Crowell	.30	.14
❑ 35 Johnnie Morton	.50	.23
❑ 36 Bill Schroeder	.75	.35
❑ 37 Mark Chmura	.30	.14
❑ 38 Marvin Harrison	.75	.35
❑ 39 E.G. Green	.30	.14
❑ 40 Jerome Pathon	.30	.14
❑ 41 Keenan McCardell	.50	.23
❑ 42 Jimmy Smith	.50	.23
❑ 43 Kyle Brady	.30	.14
❑ 44 Tavian Banks	.30	.14
❑ 45 Warren Moon	.75	.35
❑ 46 Derrick Alexander WR	.50	.23
❑ 47 Elvis Grbac	.50	.23
❑ 48 Andre Rison	.50	.23
❑ 49 Byron Bam Morris	.30	.14
❑ 50 Rashaan Shehee	.30	.14
❑ 51 Karim Abdul-Jabbar	.50	.23
❑ 52 John Avery	.30	.14
❑ 53 Tony Martin	.50	.23
❑ 54 O.J. McDuffie	.50	.23
❑ 55 Oronde Gadsden	.50	.23
❑ 56 Robert Smith	.75	.35
❑ 57 Jeff George	.50	.23
❑ 58 Jake Reed	.50	.23
❑ 59 Leroy Hoard	.30	.14
❑ 60 Terry Allen	.50	.23
❑ 61 Terry Glenn	.75	.35
❑ 62 Ben Coates	.50	.23
❑ 63 Tony Simmons	.30	.14
❑ 64 Cameron Cleeland	.30	.14
❑ 65 Eddie Kennison	.50	.23
❑ 66 Billy Joe Hobert	.30	.14
❑ 67 Amani Toomer	.30	.14
❑ 68 Kerry Collins	.50	.23
❑ 69 Ike Hilliard	.30	.14
❑ 70 Gary Brown	.30	.14
❑ 71 Joe Jurevicius	.50	.23
❑ 72 Wayne Chrebet	.50	.23
❑ 73 Vinny Testaverde	.50	.23
❑ 74 Charles Woodson	.75	.35
❑ 75 James Jett	.50	.23
❑ 76 Charles Johnson	.30	.14
❑ 77 Duce Staley	.75	.35
❑ 78 Hines Ward	.75	.35
❑ 79 Jim Harbaugh	.50	.23
❑ 80 Ryan Leaf	.75	.35
❑ 81 Junior Seau	.75	.35
❑ 82 Mikhael Ricks	.30	.14
❑ 83 Garrison Hearst	.50	.23
❑ 84 J.J. Stokes	.50	.23
❑ 85 Lawrence Phillips	.50	.23
❑ 86 Derrick Mayes	.30	.14
❑ 87 Mike Pritchard	.30	.14
❑ 88 Ahman Green	.75	.35
❑ 89 Ricky Watters	.50	.23
❑ 90 Robert Holcombe	.30	.14
❑ 91 Isaac Bruce	.75	.35
❑ 92 Trent Dilfer	.50	.23
❑ 93 Reidel Anthony	.30	.14
❑ 94 Jacquez Green	.30	.14
❑ 95 Warren Sapp	.30	.14
❑ 96 Kevin Dyson	.50	.23
❑ 97 Yancey Thigpen	.30	.14
❑ 98 Stephen Davis	.75	.35
❑ 99 Irving Fryar	.50	.23
❑ 100 Michael Westbrook	.50	.23
❑ 101 Jake Plummer	.75	.35
❑ 102 Jamal Anderson	1.25	.55
❑ 103 Chris Chandler	.75	.35
❑ 104 Doug Flutie	.75	.35
❑ 105 Eric Moulds	1.25	.55
❑ 106 Antowain Smith	1.25	.55
❑ 107 Jonathan Linton	.50	.23
❑ 108 Curtis Enis	.50	.23
❑ 109 Corey Dillon	1.25	.55
❑ 110 Carl Pickens	.75	.35
❑ 111 Emmitt Smith	2.50	1.10
❑ 112 Troy Aikman	2.50	1.10
❑ 113 Deion Sanders	1.25	.55
❑ 114 John Elway	4.00	1.80
❑ 115 Terrell Davis	1.25	.55
❑ 116 Brian Griese	1.25	.55
❑ 117 Barry Sanders	4.00	1.80
❑ 118 Charlie Batch	.75	.35
❑ 119 Herman Moore	.75	.35
❑ 120 Brett Favre	4.00	1.80
❑ 121 Antonio Freeman	1.25	.55
❑ 122 Dorsey Levens	1.25	.55
❑ 123 Peyton Manning	4.00	1.80
❑ 124 Fred Taylor	1.25	.55
❑ 125 Mark Brunell	.75	.35
❑ 126 Dan Marino	4.00	1.80
❑ 127 Randy Moss	3.00	1.35
❑ 128 Cris Carter	1.25	.55
❑ 129 Randall Cunningham	1.25	.55
❑ 130 Drew Bledsoe	1.50	.70
❑ 131 Keyshawn Johnson	1.25	.55
❑ 132 Curtis Martin	1.25	.55
❑ 133 Tim Brown	1.25	.55
❑ 134 Napoleon Kaufman	1.25	.55
❑ 135 Kordell Stewart	.75	.35
❑ 136 Jerome Bettis	1.25	.55
❑ 137 Natrone Means	.75	.35
❑ 138 Jerry Rice	2.50	1.10
❑ 139 Steve Young	1.50	.70
❑ 140 Terrell Owens	1.25	.55
❑ 141 Joey Galloway	.75	.35
❑ 142 Jon Kitna	.75	.35
❑ 143 Marshall Faulk	1.50	.70
❑ 144 Kurt Warner RC	12.00	5.50
❑ 145 Warrick Dunn	1.25	.55
❑ 146 Mike Alstott	1.25	.55
❑ 147 Eddie George	.75	.35
❑ 148 Steve McNair	1.25	.55
❑ 149 Brad Johnson	1.25	.55
❑ 150 Skip Hicks	.50	.23
❑ 151 Tim Couch RC	5.00	2.20
❑ 152 Donovan McNabb RC	20.00	9.00
❑ 153 Akili Smith RC	.75	.35
❑ 154 Edgerrin James RC	15.00	6.75
❑ 155 Ricky Williams RC	8.00	3.60
❑ 156 Torry Holt RC	10.00	4.50
❑ 157 Champ Bailey RC	6.00	2.70
❑ 158 David Boston RC	5.00	2.20
❑ 159 Chris Claiborne RC	2.50	1.10

❑ 160 Chris McAlister RC 4.00 1.80
❑ 161 Daunte Culpepper RC 15.00 6.75
❑ 162 Cade McNown RC 4.00 1.80
❑ 163 Troy Edwards RC 4.00 1.80
❑ 164 Jevon Kearse RC 8.00 3.60
❑ 165 Kevin Johnson RC 5.00 2.20
❑ 166 James Johnson RC 4.00 1.80
❑ 167 Reginald Kelly RC 2.50 1.10
❑ 168 Rob Konrad RC 5.00 2.20
❑ 169 Jim Kleinsasser RC 5.00 2.20
❑ 170 Kevin Faulk RC 5.00 2.20
❑ 171 Joe Montgomery RC 4.00 1.80
❑ 172 Shaun King RC 4.00 1.80
❑ 173 Peerless Price RC 8.00 3.60
❑ 174 Mike Cloud RC 4.00 1.80
❑ 175 Jermaine Fazande RC 4.00 1.80
❑ 176 D'Wayne Bates RC 4.00 1.80
❑ 177 Brock Huard RC 5.00 2.20
❑ 178 Marty Booker RC 5.00 2.20
❑ 179 Karsten Bailey RC 4.00 1.80
❑ 180 Shawn Bryson RC 5.00 2.20
❑ 181 Jeff Paulk RC 2.50 1.10
❑ 182 Travis McGriff RC 2.50 1.10
❑ 183 Amos Zereoue RC 5.00 2.20
❑ 184 Craig Yeast RC 4.00 1.80
❑ 185 Joe Germaine RC 4.00 1.80
❑ 186 Dameane Douglas RC 4.00 1.80
❑ 187 Sedrick Irvin RC 2.50 1.10
❑ 188 Brandon Stokley RC 6.00 2.70
❑ 189 Larry Parker RC 5.00 2.20
❑ 190 Sean Bennett RC 2.50 1.10
❑ 191 Wane McGarity RC 2.50 1.10
❑ 192 Olandis Gary RC 5.00 2.20
❑ 193 Na Brown RC 4.00 1.80
❑ 194 Aaron Brooks RC 12.00 5.50
❑ 195 Cecil Collins RC 2.50 1.10
❑ 196 Darrin Chiaverini RC 4.00 1.80
❑ 197 Kevin Daft RC 4.00 1.80
❑ 198 Darnell McDonald RC 4.00 1.80
❑ 199 Joel Makovicka RC 5.00 2.20
❑ 200 Michael Bishop RC 5.00 2.20

2000 Playoff Momentum

	Nm-Mt	Ex-Mt
COMP.SET w/o SP's	15.00	6.75

❑ 1 David Boston .60 .25
❑ 2 Jake Plummer .40 .18
❑ 3 Chris Chandler .40 .18
❑ 4 Jamal Anderson .60 .25
❑ 5 Tim Dwight .60 .25
❑ 6 Qadry Ismail .40 .18
❑ 7 Peerless Price .60 .25
❑ 8 Antowain Smith .40 .18
❑ 9 Eric Moulds .60 .25
❑ 10 Rob Johnson .40 .18
❑ 11 Natrone Means .25 .11
❑ 12 Muhsin Muhammad .40 .18
❑ 13 Steve Beuerlein .40 .18
❑ 14 Patrick Jeffers .60 .25
❑ 15 Curtis Enis .25 .11
❑ 16 Cade McNown .25 .11
❑ 17 Marcus Robinson .60 .25
❑ 18 Corey Dillon .60 .25
❑ 19 Akili Smith .25 .11
❑ 20 Carl Pickens .40 .18
❑ 21 Tim Couch .40 .18
❑ 22 Kevin Johnson .60 .25
❑ 23 Troy Aikman 1.25 .55
❑ 24 Emmitt Smith 1.25 .55
❑ 25 Joey Galloway .40 .18
❑ 26 Rocket Ismail .40 .18
❑ 27 Olandis Gary .60 .25
❑ 28 John Elway 2.00 .90
❑ 29 Brian Griese .60 .25
❑ 30 Ed McCaffrey .60 .25
❑ 31 Terrell Davis .60 .25
❑ 32 Charlie Batch .60 .25
❑ 33 James Stewart .40 .18
❑ 34 Germane Crowell .25 .11
❑ 35 Barry Sanders 1.50 .70
❑ 36 Herman Moore .40 .18
❑ 37 Antonio Freeman .60 .25
❑ 38 Dorsey Levens .40 .18
❑ 39 Brett Favre 2.00 .90
❑ 40 Edgerrin James 1.00 .45
❑ 41 Marvin Harrison .60 .25
❑ 42 Peyton Manning 1.50 .70
❑ 43 Fred Taylor .60 .25
❑ 44 Keenan McCardell .40 .18
❑ 45 Mark Brunell .60 .25
❑ 46 Jimmy Smith .40 .18
❑ 47 Elvis Grbac .40 .18
❑ 48 Tony Gonzalez .40 .18
❑ 49 James Johnson .25 .11
❑ 50 Dan Marino 2.00 .90
❑ 51 Thurman Thomas .40 .18
❑ 52 Cris Carter .60 .25
❑ 53 Robert Smith .60 .25
❑ 54 Randy Moss 1.25 .55
❑ 55 Daunte Culpepper .75 .35
❑ 56 Terry Glenn .40 .18
❑ 57 Kevin Faulk .40 .18
❑ 58 Drew Bledsoe .75 .35
❑ 59 Ricky Williams .60 .25
❑ 60 Amani Toomer .40 .18
❑ 61 Kerry Collins .40 .18
❑ 62 Vinny Testaverde .40 .18
❑ 63 Curtis Martin .60 .25
❑ 64 Rich Gannon .60 .25
❑ 65 Tyrone Wheatley .40 .18
❑ 66 Napoleon Kaufman .40 .18
❑ 67 Tim Brown .60 .25
❑ 68 Duce Staley .60 .25
❑ 69 Donovan McNabb 1.00 .45
❑ 70 Kordell Stewart .40 .18
❑ 71 Troy Edwards .25 .11
❑ 72 Jerome Bettis .60 .25
❑ 73 Jim Harbaugh .40 .18
❑ 74 Jermaine Fazande .25 .11
❑ 75 Steve Young .75 .35
❑ 76 Charlie Garner .40 .18
❑ 77 Terrell Owens .60 .25
❑ 78 Jerry Rice 1.25 .55
❑ 79 Jeff Garcia .60 .25
❑ 80 Ricky Watters .40 .18
❑ 81 Jon Kitna .60 .25
❑ 82 Marshall Faulk .75 .35
❑ 83 Isaac Bruce .60 .25
❑ 84 Torry Holt .60 .25
❑ 85 Kurt Warner 1.25 .55
❑ 86 Keyshawn Johnson .60 .25
❑ 87 Warrick Dunn .60 .25
❑ 88 Mike Alstott .60 .25
❑ 89 Warren Sapp .40 .18
❑ 90 Shaun King .25 .11
❑ 91 Eddie George .60 .25
❑ 92 Steve McNair .60 .25
❑ 93 Jevon Kearse .60 .25
❑ 94 Bruce Smith .40 .18
❑ 95 Deion Sanders .60 .25
❑ 96 Albert Connell .25 .11
❑ 97 Michael Westbrook .40 .18
❑ 98 Brad Johnson .60 .25
❑ 99 Jeff George .40 .18
❑ 100 Stephen Davis .60 .25
❑ 101 Peter Warrick RC 8.00 3.60
❑ 102 Jamal Lewis RC 20.00 9.00
❑ 103 Thomas Jones RC 12.00 5.50
❑ 104 Plaxico Burress RC 15.00 6.75
❑ 105 Travis Taylor RC 8.00 3.60
❑ 106 Ron Dayne RC 8.00 3.60
❑ 107 Bubba Franks RC 8.00 3.60
❑ 108 Sebastian Janikowski RC 8.00 3.60
❑ 109 Chad Pennington RC 30.00 13.50
❑ 110 Shaun Alexander RC 20.00 9.00
❑ 111 Sylvester Morris RC 6.00 2.70
❑ 112 Anthony Becht RC 8.00 3.60
❑ 113 R.Jay Soward RC 6.00 2.70
❑ 114 Trung Canidate RC 6.00 2.70
❑ 115 Dennis Northcutt RC 8.00 3.60
❑ 116 Todd Pinkston RC 8.00 3.60
❑ 117 Jerry Porter RC 10.00 4.50
❑ 118 Travis Prentice RC 6.00 2.70
❑ 119 Giovanni Carmazzi RC 6.00 2.70
❑ 120 Ron Dugans RC 4.00 1.80
❑ 121 Erron Kinney RC 8.00 3.60
❑ 122 Dez White RC 8.00 3.60
❑ 123 Chris Cole RC 6.00 2.70
❑ 124 Ron Dixon RC 6.00 2.70
❑ 125 Chris Redman RC 6.00 2.70
❑ 126 J.R. Redmond RC 6.00 2.70
❑ 127 Laveranues Coles RC 10.00 4.50
❑ 128 JaJuan Dawson RC 4.00 1.80
❑ 129 Darrell Jackson RC 15.00 6.75
❑ 130 Reuben Droughns RC 10.00 4.50
❑ 131 Doug Chapman RC 6.00 2.70
❑ 132 Terrelle Smith RC 6.00 2.70
❑ 133 Curtis Keaton RC 6.00 2.70
❑ 134 Gari Scott RC 4.00 1.80
❑ 135 Courtney Brown RC 8.00 3.60
❑ 136 Corey Simon RC 8.00 3.60
❑ 137 Brian Urlacher RC 30.00 13.50
❑ 138 Shaun Ellis RC 8.00 3.60
❑ 139 John Abraham RC 8.00 3.60
❑ 140 Deltha O'Neal RC 8.00 3.60
❑ 141 Rashard Anderson RC 6.00 2.70
❑ 142 Ahmed Plummer RC 8.00 3.60
❑ 143 Chris Hovan RC 6.00 2.70
❑ 144 Erik Flowers RC 6.00 2.70
❑ 145 Rob Morris RC 6.00 2.70
❑ 146 Keith Bulluck RC 8.00 3.60
❑ 147 Darren Howard RC 6.00 2.70
❑ 148 John Engelberger RC 6.00 2.70
❑ 149 Ian Gold RC 6.00 2.70
❑ 150 Raynoch Thompson RC 6.00 2.70
❑ 151 Cornelius Griffin RC 6.00 2.70
❑ 152 Rogers Beckett RC 6.00 2.70
❑ 153 Dwayne Goodrich RC 4.00 1.80
❑ 154 Barrett Green RC 4.00 1.80
❑ 155 Kevin Thompson RC 4.00 1.80
❑ 156 Ben Kelly RC 4.00 1.80
❑ 157 Danny Farmer RC 6.00 2.70
❑ 158 Aaron Shea RC 6.00 2.70
❑ 159 Trevor Gaylor RC 6.00 2.70
❑ 160 Mike Brown RC 12.00 5.50
❑ 161 Frank Moreau RC 6.00 2.70
❑ 162 Deon Dyer RC 6.00 2.70
❑ 163 Avion Black RC 6.00 2.70
❑ 164 Spergon Wynn RC 6.00 2.70
❑ 165 Billy Volek RC 12.00 5.50
❑ 166 Michael Wiley RC 6.00 2.70
❑ 167 Dante Hall RC 15.00 6.75
❑ 168 Ronney Jenkins RC 6.00 2.70
❑ 169 Sammy Morris RC 6.00 2.70
❑ 170 Kevin McDougal RC 6.00 2.70
❑ 171 Tee Martin RC 8.00 3.60
❑ 172 Troy Walters RC 8.00 3.60
❑ 173 Chad Morton RC 8.00 3.60
❑ 174 Jamel White RC 6.00 2.70
❑ 175 Shockmain Davis RC 4.00 1.80
❑ 176 Mario Edwards RC 6.00 2.70
❑ 177 Brandon Short RC 6.00 2.70
❑ 178 James Williams RC 6.00 2.70
❑ 179 Mike Anderson RC 8.00 3.60
❑ 180 Tom Brady RC 80.00 36.00
❑ 181 Na'il Diggs RC 6.00 2.70
❑ 182 Todd Husak RC 8.00 3.60
❑ 183 JaJuan Seider RC 4.00 1.80
❑ 184 Tim Rattay RC 15.00 6.75
❑ 185 Jarious Jackson RC 6.00 2.70
❑ 186 Joe Hamilton RC 6.00 2.70
❑ 187 Shyrone Stith RC 6.00 2.70
❑ 188 Mondriel Fulcher RC 4.00 1.80
❑ 189 Bashir Yamini RC 4.00 1.80
❑ 190 Herbert Goodman RC 6.00 2.70

❑ 191 Mike Green RC	6.00	2.70
❑ 192 Demario Brown RC	4.00	1.80
❑ 193 Charles Lee RC	4.00	1.80
❑ 194 Doug Johnson RC	8.00	3.60
❑ 195 Windrell Hayes RC	6.00	2.70
❑ 196 Julian Peterson RC	8.00	3.60
❑ 197 Kwame Cavil RC	4.00	1.80
❑ 198 Hank Poteat RC	6.00	2.70
❑ 199 Clint Stoerner RC	6.00	2.70
❑ 200 Mark Simoneau RC	6.00	2.70

2000 Playoff Momentum O's

Nm-Mt Ex-Mt

*STARS/80-120: 10X TO 25X BASIC CARDS
*ROOKIES/80-120: .6X TO 1.5X BASIC CARDS
*STARS/70: 12X TO 30X BASIC CARDS
*ROOKIES/70: .6X TO 1.5X BASIC CARDS
*STARS/60: 15X TO 40X BASIC CARDS
*ROOKIES/60: .8X TO 2X BASIC CARDS
*STARS/50: 15X TO 40X BASIC CARDS
*ROOKIES/50: .8X TO 2X BASIC CARDS
*STARS/40: 20X TO 50X BASIC CARDS
*ROOKIES/40: 1X TO 2.5X BASIC CARDS
*STARS/30: 25X TO 60X BASIC CARDS
*ROOKIES/30: 1X TO 2.5X BASIC CARDS
*STARS/20: 40X TO 80X BASIC CARDS
*ROOKIES/20: 1.2X TO 3X BASIC CARDS
CARDS SER.#'d UNDER 20 NOT PRICED

2000 Playoff Momentum X's

CARDS SER.#'d UNDER 20 NOT PRICED

	Nm-Mt	Ex-Mt
❑ 2 Jake Plummer/42	20.00	9.00
❑ 3 Chris Chandler/76	8.00	3.60
❑ 4 Jamal Anderson/201	5.00	2.20
❑ 5 Tim Dwight/114	10.00	4.50
❑ 6 Qadry Ismail/53	12.00	5.50
❑ 7 Peerless Price/53	12.00	5.50
❑ 8 Antowain Smith/23	25.00	11.00
❑ 9 Eric Moulds/24	40.00	18.00
❑ 10 Rob Johnson/99	8.00	3.60
❑ 11 Natrone Means/42	12.00	5.50
❑ 12 Muhsin Muhammad/43	20.00	9.00
❑ 13 Steve Beuerlein/110	6.00	2.70
❑ 14 Patrick Jeffers/159	5.00	2.20
❑ 17 Marcus Robinson/108	10.00	4.50
❑ 18 Corey Dillon/43	30.00	13.50
❑ 20 Carl Pickens/31	20.00	9.00
❑ 22 Kevin Johnson/32	30.00	13.50
❑ 26 Rocket Ismail/100	6.00	2.70
❑ 27 Olandis Gary/127	10.00	4.50
❑ 29 Brian Griese/91	12.00	5.50
❑ 30 Ed McCaffrey/83	12.00	5.50
❑ 31 Terrell Davis/196	8.00	3.60
❑ 32 Charlie Batch/60	20.00	9.00
❑ 34 Germane Crowell/50	8.00	3.60
❑ 37 Antonio Freeman/90	12.00	5.50
❑ 38 Dorsey Levens/149	8.00	3.60
❑ 39 Brett Favre/33	100.00	45.00
❑ 44 Keenan McCardell/326	3.00	1.35
❑ 45 Mark Brunell/119	10.00	4.50
❑ 46 Jimmy Smith/36	20.00	9.00
❑ 47 Elvis Grbac/220	3.00	1.35
❑ 49 James Johnson/39	12.00	5.50
❑ 50 Dan Marino/27	120.00	55.00
❑ 51 Thurman Thomas/40	20.00	9.00
❑ 53 Robert Smith/22	25.00	11.00
❑ 54 Randy Moss/21	100.00	45.00
❑ 57 Kevin Faulk/46	12.00	5.50
❑ 60 Amani Toomer/34	20.00	9.00
❑ 63 Curtis Martin/74	12.00	5.50
❑ 64 Rich Gannon/98	12.00	5.50
❑ 68 Duce Staley/71	12.00	5.50
❑ 70 Kordell Stewart/60	12.00	5.50
❑ 73 Jim Harbaugh/26	25.00	11.00
❑ 74 Jermaine Fazande/60	8.00	3.60
❑ 76 Charlie Garner/42	20.00	9.00
❑ 77 Terrell Owens/89	12.00	5.50
❑ 79 Jeff Garcia/254	5.00	2.20
❑ 80 Ricky Watters/45	12.00	5.50
❑ 81 Jon Kitna/241	3.00	1.35
❑ 83 Isaac Bruce/33	30.00	13.50
❑ 88 Mike Alstott/35	30.00	13.50
❑ 90 Shaun King/50	8.00	3.60
❑ 96 Albert Connell/115	6.00	2.70
❑ 98 Brad Johnson/227	5.00	2.20
❑ 100 Stephen Davis/102	10.00	4.50
❑ 111 Sylvester Morris/21	25.00	11.00
❑ 112 Anthony Becht/27	40.00	18.00
❑ 113 R.Jay Soward/29	25.00	11.00
❑ 114 Trung Canidate/31	20.00	9.00
❑ 115 Dennis Northcutt/32	30.00	13.50
❑ 116 Todd Pinkston/36	30.00	13.50
❑ 117 Jerry Porter/47	25.00	11.00
❑ 118 Travis Prentice/63	12.00	5.50
❑ 119 Giovanni Carmazzi/65	12.00	5.50
❑ 120 Ron Dugans/66	8.00	3.60
❑ 121 Erron Kinney/68	12.00	5.50
❑ 122 Dez White/69	20.00	9.00
❑ 123 Chris Cole/70	8.00	3.60
❑ 124 Ron Dixon/73	8.00	3.60
❑ 125 Chris Redman/75	8.00	3.60
❑ 126 J.R. Redmond/76	8.00	3.60
❑ 127 Laveranues Coles/78	15.00	6.75
❑ 128 JaJuan Dawson/79	5.00	2.20
❑ 129 Darrell Jackson/80	20.00	9.00
❑ 130 Reuben Droughns/81	12.00	5.50
❑ 131 Doug Chapman/88	8.00	3.60
❑ 132 Terrelle Smith/96	8.00	3.60
❑ 133 Curtis Keaton/97	8.00	3.60
❑ 134 Gari Scott/99	5.00	2.20
❑ 141 Rashard Anderson/23	25.00	11.00
❑ 142 Ahmed Plummer/24	40.00	18.00
❑ 143 Chris Hovan/25	25.00	11.00
❑ 144 Erik Flowers/26	25.00	11.00
❑ 145 Rob Morris/28	25.00	11.00
❑ 146 Keith Bulluck/30	30.00	13.50
❑ 147 Darren Howard/33	20.00	9.00
❑ 148 John Engelberger/35	20.00	9.00
❑ 149 Ian Gold/40	20.00	9.00
❑ 150 Raynoch Thompson/41	20.00	9.00
❑ 151 Cornelius Griffin/42	20.00	9.00
❑ 152 Rogers Beckett/43	20.00	9.00
❑ 153 Dwayne Goodrich/49	8.00	3.60
❑ 154 Barrett Green/50	8.00	3.60
❑ 155 Kevin Thompson/255	2.00	.90
❑ 156 Ben Kelly/84	5.00	2.20
❑ 157 Danny Farmer/103	6.00	2.70
❑ 158 Aaron Shea/110	6.00	2.70
❑ 159 Trevor Gaylor/111	6.00	2.70
❑ 160 Mike Brown/39	30.00	13.50
❑ 161 Frank Moreau/115	6.00	2.70
❑ 162 Deon Dyer/117	6.00	2.70
❑ 163 Avion Black/121	6.00	2.70
❑ 164 Spergon Wynn/183	5.00	2.20
❑ 165 Billy Volek/255	8.00	3.60
❑ 166 Michael Wiley/144	5.00	2.20
❑ 167 Dante Hall/153	12.00	5.50
❑ 168 Ronney Jenkins/255	3.00	1.35
❑ 169 Sammy Morris/156	5.00	2.20
❑ 170 Kevin McDougal/255	3.00	1.35
❑ 171 Tee Martin/163	8.00	3.60
❑ 172 Troy Walters/165	8.00	3.60
❑ 173 Chad Morton/166	8.00	3.60
❑ 174 Jamel White/255	3.00	1.35
❑ 175 Shockmain Davis/255	2.00	.90
❑ 176 Mario Edwards/180	5.00	2.20
❑ 177 Brandon Short/105	6.00	2.70
❑ 178 James Williams/175	5.00	2.20
❑ 179 Mike Anderson/189	20.00	9.00
❑ 180 Tom Brady/199	100.00	45.00
❑ 181 Na'il Diggs/98	8.00	3.60
❑ 182 Todd Husak/202	5.00	2.20
❑ 183 JaJuan Seider/205	2.00	.90
❑ 184 Tim Rattay/212	10.00	4.50
❑ 185 Jarious Jackson/214	3.00	1.35
❑ 186 Joe Hamilton/234	3.00	1.35
❑ 187 Shyrone Stith/243	3.00	1.35
❑ 188 Mondriel Fulcher/227	2.00	.90
❑ 189 Bashir Yamini/255	2.00	.90
❑ 190 Herbert Goodman/255	2.00	.90
❑ 191 Mike Green/213	3.00	1.35
❑ 192 Demario Brown/255	2.00	.90
❑ 193 Charles Lee/242	2.00	.90
❑ 194 Doug Johnson/255	5.00	2.20
❑ 195 Windrell Hayes/143	5.00	2.20
❑ 196 Julian Peterson/16	50.00	22.00
❑ 197 Kwame Cavil/255	2.00	.90
❑ 198 Hank Poteat/77	8.00	3.60
❑ 199 Clint Stoerner/255	3.00	1.35
❑ 200 Mark Simoneau/67	12.00	5.50

2001 Playoff Preferred

	Nm-Mt	Ex-Mt
COMP.SET w/o SP's (100)	60.00	18.00
❑ 1 Elvis Grbac	.75	.23
❑ 2 Ray Lewis	1.25	.35
❑ 3 Travis Taylor	.75	.23
❑ 4 Rob Johnson	.75	.23
❑ 5 Eric Moulds	.75	.23
❑ 6 Corey Dillon	1.25	.35
❑ 7 Peter Warrick	1.25	.35
❑ 8 Tim Couch	.75	.23
❑ 9 Kevin Johnson	.75	.23
❑ 10 Brian Griese	1.25	.35
❑ 11 Mike Anderson	1.25	.35
❑ 12 Rod Smith	.75	.23
❑ 13 Terrell Davis	1.25	.35
❑ 14 Olandis Gary	.75	.23
❑ 15 Peyton Manning	3.00	.90
❑ 16 Edgerrin James	1.50	.45
❑ 17 Marvin Harrison	1.25	.35
❑ 18 Terrence Wilkins	.50	.15
❑ 19 Mark Brunell	1.25	.35
❑ 20 Fred Taylor	1.25	.35
❑ 21 Keenan McCardell	.50	.15
❑ 22 Jimmy Smith	.75	.23
❑ 23 Stacey Mack	.50	.15
❑ 24 Trent Green	1.25	.35
❑ 25 Priest Holmes	1.50	.45
❑ 26 Tony Gonzalez	.75	.23
❑ 27 Jay Fiedler	1.25	.35
❑ 28 Lamar Smith	.75	.23
❑ 29 Zach Thomas	1.25	.35
❑ 30 Drew Bledsoe	1.50	.45
❑ 31 Antowain Smith	.75	.23
❑ 32 Troy Brown	.75	.23
❑ 33 Tom Brady	12.00	3.60
❑ 34 Vinny Testaverde	.75	.23
❑ 35 Wayne Chrebet	.75	.23
❑ 36 Curtis Martin	1.25	.35
❑ 37 Rich Gannon	1.25	.35
❑ 38 Tyrone Wheatley	.75	.23
❑ 39 Jerry Rice	2.50	.75
❑ 40 Tim Brown	1.25	.35
❑ 41 Charles Woodson	.75	.23
❑ 42 Charlie Garner	.75	.23
❑ 43 Kordell Stewart	.75	.23
❑ 44 Jerome Bettis	1.25	.35
❑ 45 Doug Flutie	1.25	.35
❑ 46 Junior Seau	1.25	.35
❑ 47 Matt Hasselbeck	.75	.23
❑ 48 Trent Dilfer	.75	.23
❑ 49 Shaun Alexander	1.50	.45
❑ 50 Ricky Watters	.75	.23
❑ 51 Eddie George	1.25	.35
❑ 52 Steve McNair	1.25	.35
❑ 53 Jevon Kearse	.75	.23
❑ 54 David Boston	1.25	.35
❑ 55 Jake Plummer	.75	.23
❑ 56 Chris Chandler	.75	.23
❑ 57 Maurice Smith	.50	.15
❑ 58 Muhsin Muhammad	.75	.23
❑ 59 Wesley Walls	.50	.15

❑ 60 James Allen .75 .23
❑ 61 Marcus Robinson 1.25 .35
❑ 62 Brian Urlacher 2.00 .60
❑ 63 Clint Stoerner .50 .15
❑ 64 Ryan Leaf .75 .23
❑ 65 Emmitt Smith 2.50 .75
❑ 66 Joey Galloway .75 .23
❑ 67 Charlie Batch 1.25 .35
❑ 68 James Stewart .75 .23
❑ 69 Brett Favre 4.00 1.20
❑ 70 Ahman Green 1.25 .35
❑ 71 Bill Schroeder .75 .23
❑ 72 Bubba Franks .75 .23
❑ 73 Daunte Culpepper 1.25 .35
❑ 74 Randy Moss 2.50 .75
❑ 75 Cris Carter 1.25 .35
❑ 76 Aaron Brooks 1.25 .35
❑ 77 Ricky Williams 1.25 .35
❑ 78 Albert Connell .50 .15
❑ 79 Kerry Collins .75 .23
❑ 80 Ron Dayne 1.25 .35
❑ 81 Jason Sehorn .50 .15
❑ 82 Amani Toomer .75 .23
❑ 83 Donovan McNabb 1.50 .45
❑ 84 James Thrash .75 .23
❑ 85 Duce Staley 1.25 .35
❑ 86 Jeff Garcia 1.25 .35
❑ 87 Garrison Hearst .75 .23
❑ 88 Terrell Owens 1.25 .35
❑ 89 Kurt Warner 2.50 .75
❑ 90 Marshall Faulk 1.50 .45
❑ 91 Torry Holt 1.25 .35
❑ 92 Isaac Bruce 1.25 .35
❑ 93 Brad Johnson 1.25 .35
❑ 94 Warrick Dunn 1.25 .35
❑ 95 Mike Alstott 1.25 .35
❑ 96 Keyshawn Johnson 1.25 .35
❑ 97 Warren Sapp .75 .23
❑ 98 Tony Banks .75 .23
❑ 99 Stephen Davis 1.25 .35
❑ 100 Champ Bailey .75 .23
❑ 101 Michael Vick RC 40.00 12.00
❑ 102 Drew Brees RC 12.00 3.60
❑ 103 Marques Tuiasosopo RC 6.00 1.80
❑ 104 Sage Rosenfels RC 6.00 1.80
❑ 105 Jesse Palmer RC 6.00 1.80
❑ 106 Mike McMahon RC 6.00 1.80
❑ 107 A.J. Feeley RC 6.00 1.80
❑ 108 Josh Booty RC 6.00 1.80
❑ 109 Josh Heupel RC 6.00 1.80
❑ 110 Henry Burris RC 4.00 1.20
❑ 111 Roderick Robinson RC 4.00 1.20
❑ 112 Tory Woodbury RC 4.00 1.20
❑ 113 Dave Dickenson RC 4.00 1.20
❑ 114 Deuce McAllister RC 12.00 3.60
❑ 115 Michael Bennett RC 12.00 3.60
❑ 116 Rudi Johnson RC 12.00 3.60
❑ 117 Derrick Blaylock RC 6.00 1.80
❑ 118 Dee Brown RC 6.00 1.80
❑ 119 Eric Kelly RC 2.50 .75
❑ 120 Dominic Rhodes RC 8.00 2.40
❑ 121 Jason Brookins RC 6.00 1.80
❑ 122 Nick Goings RC 6.00 1.80
❑ 123 Markus Steele RC 4.00 1.20
❑ 124 Benjamin Gay RC 6.00 1.80
❑ 125 Tony Taylor RC 4.00 1.20
❑ 126 Elvis Joseph RC 4.00 1.20
❑ 127 Tay Cody RC 2.50 .75
❑ 128 Heath Evans RC 4.00 1.20
❑ 129 George Layne RC 4.00 1.20
❑ 130 Moran Norris RC 2.50 .75
❑ 131 Jameel Cook RC 4.00 1.20
❑ 132 Patrick Washington RC 4.00 1.20
❑ 133 Chad Johnson RC 12.00 3.60
❑ 134 Santana Moss RC 10.00 3.00
❑ 135 Reggie Wayne RC 10.00 3.00
❑ 136 Robert Ferguson RC 6.00 1.80
❑ 137 Steve Smith RC 8.00 2.40
❑ 138 Justin McCareins RC 6.00 1.80
❑ 139 Vinny Sutherland RC 4.00 1.20
❑ 140 Alex Bannister RC 4.00 1.20
❑ 141 Scotty Anderson RC 4.00 1.20
❑ 142 Onome Ojo RC 4.00 1.20
❑ 143 Darnerien McCants RC 4.00 1.20
❑ 144 Eddie Berlin RC 4.00 1.20
❑ 145 Cedrick Wilson RC 6.00 1.80
❑ 146 Kevin Kasper RC 6.00 1.80
❑ 147 T.J. Houshmandzadeh RC 6.00 1.80
❑ 148 Reggie Germany RC 4.00 1.20
❑ 149 Chris Taylor RC 4.00 1.20
❑ 150 Ken-Yon Rambo RC 4.00 1.20
❑ 151 Quentin McCord RC 4.00 1.20
❑ 152 Andre King RC 4.00 1.20
❑ 153 Arnold Jackson RC 4.00 1.20
❑ 154 Tim Baker RC 2.50 .75
❑ 155 Drew Bennett RC 20.00 6.00
❑ 156 Cedric James RC 4.00 1.20
❑ 157 Todd Heap RC 6.00 1.80
❑ 158 Alge Crumpler RC 8.00 2.40
❑ 159 Sean Brewer RC 2.50 .75
❑ 160 Shad Meier RC 4.00 1.20
❑ 161 B.Manumaleuna RC 4.00 1.20
❑ 162 Tony Stewart RC 6.00 1.80
❑ 163 David Martin RC 4.00 1.20
❑ 164 Matt Dominguez RC 4.00 1.20
❑ 165 Boo Williams RC 4.00 1.20
❑ 166 Justin Smith RC 6.00 1.80
❑ 167 Andre Carter RC 6.00 1.80
❑ 168 Jamal Reynolds RC 6.00 1.80
❑ 169 Ryan Pickett RC 2.50 .75
❑ 170 Aaron Schobel RC 6.00 1.80
❑ 171 Derrick Burgess RC 6.00 1.80
❑ 172 DeLawrence Grant RC 2.50 .75
❑ 173 Karon Riley RC 2.50 .75
❑ 174 Richard Seymour RC 6.00 1.80
❑ 175 Marcus Stroud RC 6.00 1.80
❑ 176 Casey Hampton RC 4.00 1.20
❑ 177 Shaun Rogers RC 6.00 1.80
❑ 178 Kris Jenkins RC 6.00 1.80
❑ 179 Eric Downing RC 2.50 .75
❑ 180 Kenny Smith RC 4.00 1.20
❑ 181 Marcus Bell RC 4.00 1.20
❑ 182 Dan Morgan RC 6.00 1.80
❑ 183 Kendrell Bell RC 15.00 4.50
❑ 184 Tommy Polley RC 6.00 1.80
❑ 185 Jamie Winborn RC 4.00 1.20
❑ 186 Quinton Caver RC 4.00 1.20
❑ 187 Sedrick Hodge RC 2.50 .75
❑ 188 Brian Allen RC 2.50 .75
❑ 189 Torrance Marshall RC 6.00 1.80
❑ 190 Willie Middlebrooks RC 4.00 1.20
❑ 191 Jamar Fletcher RC 4.00 1.20
❑ 192 Ken Lucas RC 4.00 1.20
❑ 193 Fred Smoot RC 6.00 1.80
❑ 194 Andre Dyson RC 2.50 .75
❑ 195 Anthony Henry RC 6.00 1.80
❑ 196 Adam Archuleta RC 6.00 1.80
❑ 197 Idrees Bashir RC 2.50 .75
❑ 198 Adrian Wilson RC 2.50 .75
❑ 199 Cory Bird RC 6.00 1.80
❑ 200 Jarrod Cooper RC 6.00 1.80
❑ 201 LaDainian Tomlinson JSY/400 RC 40.00 12.00
❑ 202 Chris Weinke JSY/400 RC 10.00 3.00
❑ 203 Anthony Thomas FB/400 RC 20.00 6.00
❑ 204 Koren Robinson JSY/400 RC 15.00 4.50
❑ 205 James Jackson JSY/400 RC 10.00 3.00
❑ 206 Kevan Barlow FB/400 RC 10.00 3.00
❑ 207 Quincy Morgan JSY/400 RC 12.00 3.60
❑ 208 Nate Clements JSY/400 RC 8.00 2.40
❑ 209 Travis Henry JSY/400 RC 15.00 4.50
❑ 210 Damione Lewis FB/400 RC 8.00 2.40
❑ 211 Snoop Minnis FB/400 RC 10.00 3.00
❑ 212 David Terrell FB/600 RC 10.00 3.00
❑ 213 Gerard Warren JSY/600 RC 8.00 2.40
❑ 214 Chris Chambers JSY/600 RC 12.00 3.60
❑ 215 Will Allen FB/750 RC 6.00 1.80
❑ 216 Leonard Davis JSY/750 RC 6.00 1.80
❑ 217 Travis Minor JSY/750 RC 8.00 2.40
❑ 218 Will Peterson FB/750 RC 6.00 1.80
❑ 219 Rod Gardner FB/750 RC 8.00 2.40
❑ 220 Freddie Mitchell FB/750 RC 8.00 2.40
❑ 221 Derrick Gibson FB/750 RC 6.00 1.80
❑ 222 Kyle Vanden Bosch JSY/750 RC 10.00 3.00
❑ 223 LaMont Jordan FB/750 RC 10.00 3.00
❑ 224 Quincy Carter FB/750 RC 8.00 2.40
❑ 225 Correll Buckhalter FB/750 RC 12.00 3.60

2001 Playoff Preferred Signatures Bronze

Nm-Mt Ex-Mt
❑ 1 A.J. Feeley 30.00 9.00
❑ 2 Alan Page 30.00 9.00
❑ 3 Andre Carter SP 20.00 6.00
❑ 7 Bart Starr SP
❑ 8 Bob Griese SP
❑ 9 Brian Griese SP
❑ 10 Cedric James 10.00 3.00
❑ 11 Charlie Batch 10.00 3.00
❑ 12 Chris Barnes 10.00 3.00
❑ 13 Chris Chambers 25.00 7.50
❑ 14 Chris Taylor SP
❑ 15 Chris Weinke SP
❑ 16 Corey Dillon SP 25.00 7.50
❑ 17 Damione Lewis 10.00 3.00
❑ 18 Dan Alexander 20.00 6.00
❑ 19 Dan Fouts SP 40.00 12.00
❑ 21 Dave Dickenson 12.00 3.60
❑ 22 Deacon Jones SP
❑ 23 Dee Brown 12.00 3.60
❑ 24 Derrick Blaylock SP
❑ 25 Don Maynard SP
❑ 27 Earl Campbell SP 40.00 12.00
❑ 32 Frank Gifford SP 40.00 12.00
❑ 34 Freddie Mitchell SP
❑ 35 George Blanda SP 50.00 15.00
❑ 37 Jim Brown SP 60.00 18.00
❑ 39 Joe Montana SP 150.00 45.00
❑ 40 Joe Namath SP 80.00 24.00
❑ 42 Johnny Unitas SP 200.00 60.00
❑ 43 Jonathan Carter 10.00 3.00
❑ 44 Josh Booty 10.00 3.00
❑ 45 Justin McCareins SP
❑ 46 Kellen Winslow SP
❑ 47 Kevin Kasper SP
❑ 48 LaMont Jordan SP 30.00 9.00
❑ 50 Larry Csonka SP 60.00 18.00
❑ 51 Lawrence Taylor SP 50.00 15.00
❑ 52 Marcus Allen SP 50.00 15.00
❑ 53 Marshall Faulk SP
❑ 54 Marvin Harrison SP 50.00 15.00
❑ 56 Onome Ojo SP
❑ 58 Ozzie Newsome SP
❑ 59 Paul Hornung SP
❑ 61 Ray Lewis SP 50.00 15.00
❑ 63 Rod Gardner SP
❑ 64 Roger Craig SP 80.00 24.00
❑ 65 Roger Staubach SP 80.00 24.00
❑ 66 Ronnie Lott SP 40.00 12.00

Card	Nm-Mt	Ex-Mt
❑ 68 Scotty Anderson		
❑ 71 Steve Smith	25.00	7.50
❑ 72 Terry Bradshaw SP	80.00	24.00
❑ 73 Tim Brown SP		
❑ 74 Tommy Polley	10.00	3.00
❑ 75 Tony Dorsett SP	50.00	15.00
❑ 76 Tony Gonzalez SP	40.00	12.00
❑ 77 Torry Holt	20.00	6.00
❑ 79 Chad Pennington	40.00	12.00
❑ 80 Cris Carter SP	40.00	12.00
❑ 81 Laveranues Coles	20.00	6.00
❑ 82 Correll Buckhalter	20.00	6.00
❑ 83 Jamal Anderson SP		
❑ 84 Jamal Lewis SP		
❑ 85 Marcus Robinson	20.00	6.00
❑ 87 Wesley Walls	10.00	3.00
❑ 88 Terrell Owens SP	40.00	12.00
❑ 89 Thurman Thomas SP		
❑ 90 Doug Johnson	10.00	3.00
❑ 91 Ron Dugans	10.00	3.00
❑ 93 Kenyatta Walker	20.00	6.00
❑ 94 Reggie Germany	10.00	3.00
❑ 96 Justin Smith	12.00	3.60
❑ 97 Heath Evans	10.00	3.00
❑ 98 Eddie Berlin		
❑ 100 Alge Crumpler	25.00	7.50
❑ 101 Shaun Rogers	10.00	3.00
❑ 102 Will Allen	10.00	3.00
❑ 103 Moran Norris	10.00	3.00
❑ 104 Travis Minor	12.00	3.60
❑ 105 Brian Allen SP	10.00	3.00
❑ 109 Anthony Thomas SP	30.00	9.00
❑ 110 James Jackson	12.00	3.60

2001 Playoff Preferred Signatures Silver

Card	Nm-Mt	Ex-Mt
❑ 1 A.J. Feeley	50.00	15.00
❑ 2 Alan Page	30.00	9.00
❑ 3 Andre Carter	15.00	4.50
❑ 5 Archie Manning	40.00	12.00
❑ 6 Art Monk	30.00	9.00
❑ 10 Cedric James		
❑ 11 Charlie Batch	15.00	4.50
❑ 12 Chris Barnes		
❑ 13 Chris Chambers	40.00	12.00
❑ 14 Chris Taylor	15.00	4.50
❑ 16 Corey Dillon	30.00	9.00
❑ 17 Damione Lewis	15.00	4.50
❑ 18 Dan Alexander	15.00	4.50
❑ 19 Dan Fouts	40.00	12.00
❑ 21 Dave Dickenson	20.00	6.00
❑ 23 Dee Brown	20.00	6.00
❑ 28 Boo Williams	15.00	4.50
❑ 30 Eric Dickerson	40.00	12.00
❑ 31 Fran Tarkenton	40.00	12.00
❑ 35 George Blanda	50.00	15.00
❑ 43 Jonathan Carter	15.00	4.50
❑ 44 Josh Booty	30.00	9.00
❑ 50 Larry Csonka	60.00	18.00
❑ 52 Marcus Allen	50.00	15.00
❑ 58 Ozzie Newsome	30.00	9.00
❑ 65 Roger Staubach	100.00	30.00
❑ 68 Scotty Anderson	15.00	4.50
❑ 69 Sonny Jurgensen	40.00	12.00
❑ 70 Steve Largent	40.00	12.00
❑ 71 Steve Smith	40.00	12.00
❑ 74 Tommy Polley	15.00	4.50
❑ 76 Tony Gonzalez	30.00	9.00
❑ 77 Torry Holt	30.00	9.00
❑ 79 Chad Pennington	40.00	12.00
❑ 80 Cris Carter	40.00	12.00
❑ 81 Laveranues Coles		
❑ 82 Correll Buckhalter	30.00	9.00
❑ 85 Marcus Robinson	30.00	9.00
❑ 87 Wesley Walls	15.00	4.50
❑ 88 Terrell Owens	30.00	9.00
❑ 90 Doug Johnson	15.00	4.50
❑ 91 Ron Dugans	15.00	4.50
❑ 93 Kenyatta Walker		
❑ 94 Reggie Germany	15.00	4.50
❑ 95 Mike McMahon	30.00	9.00
❑ 96 Justin Smith	20.00	6.00
❑ 97 Heath Evans	15.00	4.50
❑ 98 Eddie Berlin	15.00	4.50
❑ 100 Alge Crumpler	40.00	12.00
❑ 101 Shaun Rogers	15.00	4.50
❑ 102 Will Allen	15.00	4.50
❑ 103 Moran Norris	15.00	4.50
❑ 104 Travis Minor	20.00	6.00
❑ 105 Brian Allen	15.00	4.50
❑ 108 Alex Bannister		
❑ 109 Anthony Thomas	40.00	12.00
❑ 110 James Jackson	20.00	6.00

1999 Playoff Prestige EXP

	Nm-Mt	Ex-Mt
COMPLETE SET (200)	50.00	22.00
❑ 1 Anthony McFarland RC	1.50	.70
❑ 2 Al Wilson RC	1.00	.45
❑ 3 Jevon Kearse RC	2.50	1.10
❑ 4 Aaron Brooks RC	5.00	2.20
❑ 5 Travis McGriff RC	.75	.35
❑ 6 Jeff Paulk RC	.75	.35
❑ 7 Shawn Bryson RC	1.50	.70
❑ 8 Karsten Bailey RC	1.00	.45
❑ 9 Mike Cloud RC	1.00	.45
❑ 10 James Johnson RC	1.00	.45
❑ 11 Tai Streets RC	1.50	.70
❑ 12 Jermaine Fazande RC	1.00	.45
❑ 13 Ebenezer Ekuban RC	1.00	.45
❑ 14 Joe Montgomery RC	1.00	.45
❑ 15 Craig Yeast RC	1.00	.45
❑ 16 Joe Germaine RC	1.00	.45
❑ 17 Andy Katzenmoyer RC	1.00	.45
❑ 18 Kevin Faulk RC	1.50	.70
❑ 19 Chris McAlister RC	1.00	.45
❑ 20 Sedrick Irvin RC	.75	.35
❑ 21 Brock Huard RC	1.50	.70
❑ 22 Cade McNown RC	1.00	.45
❑ 23 Shaun King RC	1.00	.45
❑ 24 Amos Zereoue RC	1.50	.70
❑ 25 Dameane Douglas RC	1.00	.45
❑ 26 D'Wayne Bates RC	1.00	.45
❑ 27 Kevin Johnson RC	1.50	.70
❑ 28 Rob Konrad RC	1.50	.70
❑ 29 Troy Edwards RC	1.00	.45
❑ 30 Peerless Price RC	2.50	1.10
❑ 31 Daunte Culpepper RC	6.00	2.70
❑ 32 Akili Smith RC	1.00	.45
❑ 33 David Boston RC	1.50	.70
❑ 34 Chris Claiborne RC	.75	.35
❑ 35 Torry Holt RC	4.00	1.80
❑ 36 Champ Bailey RC	2.00	.90
❑ 37 Edgerrin James RC	6.00	2.70
❑ 38 Donovan McNabb RC	8.00	3.60
❑ 39 Ricky Williams RC	3.00	1.35
❑ 40 Tim Couch RC	1.50	.70
❑ 41 Charles Woodson RP	1.00	.45
❑ 42 Skip Hicks RP	.40	.18
❑ 43 Brian Griese RP	1.00	.45
❑ 44 Tim Dwight RP	1.00	.45
❑ 45 Ryan Leaf RP	.60	.25
❑ 46 Curtis Enis RP	.40	.18
❑ 47 Charlie Batch RP	1.00	.45
❑ 48 Fred Taylor RP	1.00	.45
❑ 49 Peyton Manning RP	1.50	.70
❑ 50 Randy Moss RP	1.25	.55
❑ 51 Jim Harbaugh	.60	.25
❑ 52 Warren Moon	1.00	.45
❑ 53 Jeff George	.60	.25
❑ 54 Rich Gannon	1.00	.45
❑ 55 Scott Mitchell	.40	.18
❑ 56 Kerry Collins	.60	.25
❑ 57 Brad Johnson	1.00	.45
❑ 58 Charles Johnson	.40	.18
❑ 59 Chris Calloway	.40	.18
❑ 60 Tyrone Wheatley	.60	.25
❑ 61 Michael Westbrook	.60	.25
❑ 62 Skip Hicks	.40	.18
❑ 63 Terry Allen	.60	.25
❑ 64 Albert Connell	.40	.18
❑ 65 Kevin Dyson	.60	.25
❑ 66 Frank Wycheck	.40	.18
❑ 67 Yancey Thigpen	.40	.18
❑ 68 Steve McNair	1.00	.45
❑ 69 Eddie George	1.00	.45
❑ 70 Eric Zeier	.40	.18
❑ 71 Jacquez Green	.40	.18
❑ 72 Reidel Anthony	.60	.25
❑ 73 Warren Sapp	.60	.25
❑ 74 Mike Alstott	1.00	.45
❑ 75 Warrick Dunn	1.00	.45
❑ 76 Trent Dilfer	.60	.25
❑ 77 Ahman Green	1.00	.45
❑ 78 Joey Galloway	.60	.25
❑ 79 Ricky Watters	.60	.25
❑ 80 Jon Kitna	1.00	.45
❑ 81 Amp Lee	.40	.18
❑ 82 Isaac Bruce	1.00	.45
❑ 83 Robert Holcombe	.40	.18
❑ 84 Greg Hill	.40	.18
❑ 85 Marshall Faulk	1.25	.55
❑ 86 Trent Green	1.00	.45
❑ 87 J.J. Stokes	.60	.25
❑ 88 Terrell Owens	1.00	.45
❑ 89 Jerry Rice	2.00	.90
❑ 90 Garrison Hearst	.60	.25
❑ 91 Steve Young	1.25	.55
❑ 92 Junior Seau	1.00	.45
❑ 93 Mikhael Ricks	.40	.18
❑ 94 Natrone Means	.60	.25
❑ 95 Ryan Leaf	1.00	.45
❑ 96 Courtney Hawkins	.40	.18
❑ 97 C.Fuamatu-Ma'afala UER	.40	.18
❑ 98 Jerome Bettis	1.00	.45
❑ 99 Kordell Stewart	.60	.25
❑ 100 Bobby Hoying	.60	.25
❑ 101 Charlie Garner	.60	.25
❑ 102 Duce Staley	1.00	.45
❑ 103 Charles Woodson	1.00	.45
❑ 104 James Jett	.60	.25
❑ 105 Rickey Dudley	.40	.18
❑ 106 Tim Brown	1.00	.45
❑ 107 Napoleon Kaufman	1.00	.45
❑ 108 Wayne Chrebet	.60	.25
❑ 109 Keyshawn Johnson	1.00	.45
❑ 110 Vinny Testaverde	.60	.25
❑ 111 Curtis Martin	1.00	.45
❑ 112 Joe Jurevicius	.60	.25
❑ 113 Tiki Barber	.60	.25
❑ 114 Ike Hilliard	.40	.18
❑ 115 Kent Graham	.40	.18
❑ 116 Gary Brown	.40	.18
❑ 117 Lamar Smith	.60	.25
❑ 118 Eddie Kennison	.60	.25
❑ 119 Cam Cleeland	.40	.18

❑ 120 Tony Simmons	.40	.18
❑ 121 Ben Coates	.60	.25
❑ 122 Darick Holmes	.40	.18
❑ 123 Terry Glenn	1.00	.45
❑ 124 Drew Bledsoe	1.25	.55
❑ 125 Leroy Hoard	.40	.18
❑ 126 Jake Reed	.60	.25
❑ 127 Randy Moss	2.50	1.10
❑ 128 Cris Carter	1.00	.45
❑ 129 Robert Smith	1.00	.45
❑ 130 Randall Cunningham	1.00	.45
❑ 131 Lamar Thomas	.40	.18
❑ 132 John Avery	.40	.18
❑ 133 O.J. McDuffie	.60	.25
❑ 134 Dan Marino	3.00	1.35
❑ 135 Karim Abdul-Jabbar	.60	.25
❑ 136 Rashaan Shehee	.40	.18
❑ 137 Derrick Alexander WR	.60	.25
❑ 138 Byron Bam Morris	.40	.18
❑ 139 Andre Rison	.60	.25
❑ 140 Elvis Grbac	.60	.25
❑ 141 Tavian Banks	.40	.18
❑ 142 Keenan McCardell	.60	.25
❑ 143 Jimmy Smith	.60	.25
❑ 144 Fred Taylor	1.00	.45
❑ 145 Mark Brunell	1.00	.45
❑ 146 Jerome Pathon	.40	.18
❑ 147 Marvin Harrison	1.00	.45
❑ 148 Peyton Manning	3.00	1.35
❑ 149 Robert Brooks	.60	.25
❑ 150 Mark Chmura	.40	.18
❑ 151 Antonio Freeman	1.00	.45
❑ 152 Dorsey Levens	1.00	.45
❑ 153 Brett Favre	3.00	1.35
❑ 154 Johnnie Morton	.60	.25
❑ 155 Germane Crowell	.40	.18
❑ 156 Barry Sanders	3.00	1.35
❑ 157 Herman Moore	.60	.25
❑ 158 Charlie Batch	1.00	.45
❑ 159 Marcus Nash	.40	.18
❑ 160 Shannon Sharpe	.60	.25
❑ 161 Rod Smith	.60	.25
❑ 162 Ed McCaffrey	.60	.25
❑ 163 Terrell Davis	1.00	.45
❑ 164 John Elway	3.00	1.35
❑ 165 Ernie Mills	.40	.18
❑ 166 Michael Irvin	.60	.25
❑ 167 Deion Sanders	1.00	.45
❑ 168 Emmitt Smith	2.00	.90
❑ 169 Troy Aikman	2.00	.90
❑ 170 Chris Spielman	.40	.18
❑ 171 Terry Kirby	.40	.18
❑ 172 Ty Detmer	.60	.25
❑ 173 Leslie Shepherd	.40	.18
❑ 174 Damay Scott	.40	.18
❑ 175 Jeff Blake	.60	.25
❑ 176 Carl Pickens	.60	.25
❑ 177 Corey Dillon	1.00	.45
❑ 178 Bobby Engram	.60	.25
❑ 179 Curtis Conway	.60	.25
❑ 180 Curtis Enis	.40	.18
❑ 181 Muhsin Muhammad	.60	.25
❑ 182 Steve Beuerlein	.40	.18
❑ 183 Tim Biakabutuka	.60	.25
❑ 184 Bruce Smith	.60	.25
❑ 185 Andre Reed	.60	.25
❑ 186 Thurman Thomas	.60	.25
❑ 187 Eric Moulds	1.00	.45
❑ 188 Antowain Smith	1.00	.45
❑ 189 Doug Flutie	1.00	.45
❑ 190 Jermaine Lewis	.60	.25
❑ 191 Priest Holmes	1.50	.70
❑ 192 O.J. Santiago	.40	.18
❑ 193 Tim Dwight	1.00	.45
❑ 194 Terance Mathis	.60	.25
❑ 195 Chris Chandler	.60	.25
❑ 196 Jamal Anderson	1.00	.45
❑ 197 Rob Moore	.60	.25
❑ 198 Frank Sanders	.60	.25
❑ 199 Adrian Murrell	.60	.25
❑ 200 Jake Plummer	.60	.25
❑ RR1 Barry Sanders (Run For the Record Insert)	20.00	9.00

1999 Playoff Prestige SSD

	Nm-Mt	Ex-Mt
COMPLETE SET (200)	150.00	70.00
COMP.SET w/o SP's (150)	50.00	22.00
❑ 1 Jake Plummer	.75	.35
❑ 2 Adrian Murrell	.75	.35
❑ 3 Frank Sanders	.75	.35
❑ 4 Rob Moore	.75	.35
❑ 5 Jamal Anderson	1.25	.55
❑ 6 Chris Chandler	.75	.35
❑ 7 Terance Mathis	.75	.35
❑ 8 Tim Dwight	1.25	.55
❑ 9 O.J. Santiago	.50	.23
❑ 10 Priest Holmes	2.00	.90
❑ 11 Jermaine Lewis	.75	.35
❑ 12 Doug Flutie	1.25	.55
❑ 13 Antowain Smith	1.25	.55
❑ 14 Eric Moulds	1.25	.55
❑ 15 Thurman Thomas	.75	.35
❑ 16 Andre Reed	.75	.35
❑ 17 Bruce Smith	.75	.35
❑ 18 Tim Biakabutuka	.75	.35
❑ 19 Steve Beuerlein	.50	.23
❑ 20 Muhsin Muhammad	.75	.35
❑ 21 Curtis Enis	.50	.23
❑ 22 Curtis Conway	.75	.35
❑ 23 Bobby Engram	.75	.35
❑ 24 Corey Dillon	1.25	.55
❑ 25 Carl Pickens	.75	.35
❑ 26 Jeff Blake	.75	.35
❑ 27 Damay Scott	.50	.23
❑ 28 Leslie Shepherd	.50	.23
❑ 29 Ty Detmer	.75	.35
❑ 30 Terry Kirby	.50	.23
❑ 31 Chris Spielman	.50	.23
❑ 32 Troy Aikman	3.00	1.35
❑ 33 Emmitt Smith	3.00	1.35
❑ 34 Deion Sanders	1.25	.55
❑ 35 Michael Irvin	.75	.35
❑ 36 Ernie Mills	.50	.23
❑ 37 John Elway	5.00	2.20
❑ 38 Terrell Davis	1.25	.55
❑ 39 Ed McCaffrey	.75	.35
❑ 40 Rod Smith	.75	.35
❑ 41 Shannon Sharpe	.75	.35
❑ 42 Marcus Nash	.50	.23
❑ 43 Charlie Batch	1.25	.55
❑ 44 Herman Moore	.75	.35
❑ 45 Barry Sanders	5.00	2.20
❑ 46 Germane Crowell	.50	.23
❑ 47 Johnnie Morton	.75	.35
❑ 48 Brett Favre	5.00	2.20
❑ 49 Dorsey Levens	1.25	.55
❑ 50 Antonio Freeman	1.25	.55
❑ 51 Mark Chmura	.50	.23
❑ 52 Robert Brooks	.75	.35
❑ 53 Peyton Manning	5.00	2.20
❑ 54 Marvin Harrison	1.25	.55
❑ 55 Jerome Pathon	.50	.23
❑ 56 Mark Brunell	1.25	.55
❑ 57 Fred Taylor	1.25	.55
❑ 58 Jimmy Smith	.75	.35
❑ 59 Keenan McCardell	.75	.35
❑ 60 Tavian Banks	.50	.23
❑ 61 Elvis Grbac	.75	.35
❑ 62 Andre Rison	.75	.35
❑ 63 Byron Bam Morris	.50	.23
❑ 64 Derrick Alexander WR	.75	.35
❑ 65 Rashaan Shehee	.50	.23
❑ 66 Karim Abdul-Jabbar	.75	.35
❑ 67 Dan Marino	5.00	2.20
❑ 68 O.J. McDuffie	.75	.35
❑ 69 John Avery	.50	.23
❑ 70 Lamar Thomas	.50	.23
❑ 71 Randall Cunningham	1.25	.55
❑ 72 Robert Smith	1.25	.55
❑ 73 Cris Carter	1.25	.55
❑ 74 Randy Moss	4.00	1.80
❑ 75 Jake Reed	.75	.35
❑ 76 Leroy Hoard	.50	.23
❑ 77 Drew Bledsoe	2.00	.90
❑ 78 Terry Glenn	1.25	.55
❑ 79 Darick Holmes	.50	.23
❑ 80 Ben Coates	.75	.35
❑ 81 Tony Simmons	.50	.23
❑ 82 Cam Cleeland	.50	.23
❑ 83 Eddie Kennison	.75	.35
❑ 84 Lamar Smith	.75	.35
❑ 85 Gary Brown	.50	.23
❑ 86 Kent Graham	.50	.23
❑ 87 Ike Hilliard	.50	.23
❑ 88 Tiki Barber	.75	.35
❑ 89 Joe Jurevicius	.75	.35
❑ 90 Curtis Martin	1.25	.55
❑ 91 Vinny Testaverde	.75	.35
❑ 92 Keyshawn Johnson	1.25	.55
❑ 93 Wayne Chrebet	.75	.35
❑ 94 Napoleon Kaufman	1.25	.55
❑ 95 Tim Brown	1.25	.55
❑ 96 Rickey Dudley	.50	.23
❑ 97 James Jett	.75	.35
❑ 98 Charles Woodson	1.25	.55
❑ 99 Duce Staley	1.25	.55
❑ 100 Charlie Garner	.75	.35
❑ 101 Bobby Hoying	.75	.35
❑ 102 Kordell Stewart	.75	.35
❑ 103 Jerome Bettis	1.25	.55
❑ 104 Chris Fuamatu-Ma'afala	.50	.23
❑ 105 Courtney Hawkins	.50	.23
❑ 106 Ryan Leaf	1.25	.55
❑ 107 Natrone Means	.75	.35
❑ 108 Mikhael Ricks	.50	.23
❑ 109 Junior Seau	1.25	.55
❑ 110 Steve Young	2.00	.90
❑ 111 Garrison Hearst	.75	.35
❑ 112 Jerry Rice	3.00	1.35
❑ 113 Terrell Owens	1.25	.55
❑ 114 J.J. Stokes	.75	.35
❑ 115 Trent Green	1.25	.55
❑ 116 Marshall Faulk	1.50	.70
❑ 117 Greg Hill	.50	.23
❑ 118 Robert Holcombe	.50	.23
❑ 119 Isaac Bruce	1.25	.55
❑ 120 Amp Lee	.50	.23
❑ 121 Jon Kitna	1.25	.55
❑ 122 Ricky Watters	.75	.35
❑ 123 Joey Galloway	.75	.35
❑ 124 Ahman Green	1.25	.55
❑ 125 Trent Dilfer	.75	.35
❑ 126 Warrick Dunn	1.25	.55
❑ 127 Mike Alstott	1.25	.55
❑ 128 Warren Sapp	.75	.35
❑ 129 Reidel Anthony	.75	.35
❑ 130 Jacquez Green	.50	.23
❑ 131 Eric Zeier	.50	.23
❑ 132 Eddie George	1.25	.55
❑ 133 Steve McNair	1.25	.55
❑ 134 Yancey Thigpen	.50	.23
❑ 135 Frank Wycheck	.50	.23
❑ 136 Kevin Dyson	.75	.35
❑ 137 Albert Connell	.50	.23
❑ 138 Terry Allen	.75	.35
❑ 139 Skip Hicks	.50	.23
❑ 140 Michael Westbrook	.75	.35
❑ 141 Tyrone Wheatley	.75	.35
❑ 142 Chris Calloway	.50	.23
❑ 143 Charles Johnson	.50	.23
❑ 144 Brad Johnson	1.25	.55
❑ 145 Kerry Collins	.75	.35
❑ 146 Scott Mitchell	.50	.23

❑ 147 Rich Gannon 1.25 .55
❑ 148 Jeff George .75 .35
❑ 149 Warren Moon 1.25 .55
❑ 150 Jim Harbaugh .75 .35
❑ 151 Randy Moss RP 6.00 2.70
❑ 152 Peyton Manning RP 8.00 3.60
❑ 153 Fred Taylor RP 2.50 1.10
❑ 154 Charlie Batch RP 2.50 1.10
❑ 155 Curtis Enis RP 1.50 .70
❑ 156 Ryan Leaf RP 1.50 .70
❑ 157 Tim Dwight RP 1.50 .70
❑ 158 Brian Griese RP 2.50 1.10
❑ 159 Skip Hicks RP 1.50 .70
❑ 160 Charles Woodson RP 2.50 1.10
❑ 161 Tim Couch RC 4.00 1.80
❑ 162 Ricky Williams RC 6.00 2.70
❑ 163 Donovan McNabb RC 15.00 6.75
❑ 164 Edgerrin James RC 12.00 5.50
❑ 165 Champ Bailey RC 5.00 2.20
❑ 166 Torry Holt RC 8.00 3.60
❑ 167 Chris Claiborne RC 2.00 .90
❑ 168 David Boston RC 4.00 1.80
❑ 169 Akili Smith RC 1.50 .70
❑ 170 Daunte Culpepper RC 12.00 5.50
❑ 171 Peerless Price RC 6.00 2.70
❑ 172 Troy Edwards RC 3.00 1.35
❑ 173 Rob Konrad RC 4.00 1.80
❑ 174 Kevin Johnson RC 4.00 1.80
❑ 175 D'Wayne Bates RC 3.00 1.35
❑ 176 Dameane Douglas RC 3.00 1.35
❑ 177 Amos Zereoue RC 4.00 1.80
❑ 178 Shaun King RC 3.00 1.35
❑ 179 Cade McNown RC 3.00 1.35
❑ 180 Brock Huard RC 4.00 1.80
❑ 181 Sedrick Irvin RC 2.00 .90
❑ 182 Chris McAlister RC 3.00 1.35
❑ 183 Kevin Faulk RC 4.00 1.80
❑ 184 Andy Katzenmoyer RC 3.00 1.35
❑ 185 Joe Germaine RC 3.00 1.35
❑ 186 Craig Yeast RC 3.00 1.35
❑ 187 Joe Montgomery RC 3.00 1.35
❑ 188 Ebenezer Ekuban RC 3.00 1.35
❑ 189 Jermaine Fazande RC 3.00 1.35
❑ 190 Tai Streets RC 4.00 1.80
❑ 191 James Johnson RC 3.00 1.35
❑ 192 Mike Cloud RC 3.00 1.35
❑ 193 Karsten Bailey RC 3.00 1.35
❑ 194 Shawn Bryson RC 4.00 1.80
❑ 195 Jeff Paulk RC 2.00 .90
❑ 196 Travis McGriff RC 2.00 .90
❑ 197 Aaron Brooks RC 10.00 4.50
❑ 198 Jevon Kearse RC 6.00 2.70
❑ 199 Al Wilson RC 3.00 1.35
❑ 200 Anthony McFarland RC 4.00 1.80

2000 Playoff Prestige

	Nm-Mt	Ex-Mt
COMPLETE SET (300)	350.00	160.00
COMP.SET w/o SP's (200)	25.00	11.00

❑ 1 Frank Sanders .40 .18
❑ 2 Rob Moore .40 .18
❑ 3 Michael Pittman .25 .11
❑ 4 Jake Plummer .40 .18
❑ 5 David Boston .60 .25
❑ 6 Chris Chandler .40 .18
❑ 7 Tim Dwight .60 .25
❑ 8 Shawn Jefferson .25 .11
❑ 9 Terance Mathis .40 .18
❑ 10 Jamal Anderson .60 .25
❑ 11 Byron Hanspard .25 .11
❑ 12 Ken Oxendine .25 .11
❑ 13 Priest Holmes .75 .35
❑ 14 Tony Banks .40 .18
❑ 15 Shannon Sharpe .40 .18
❑ 16 Rod Woodson .40 .18
❑ 17 Jermaine Lewis .40 .18
❑ 18 Qadry Ismail .40 .18
❑ 19 Eric Moulds .60 .25
❑ 20 Doug Flutie .60 .25
❑ 21 Jay Riemersma .25 .11
❑ 22 Antowain Smith .40 .18
❑ 23 Jonathan Linton .25 .11
❑ 24 Peerless Price .60 .25
❑ 25 Rob Johnson .40 .18
❑ 26 Muhsin Muhammad .40 .18
❑ 27 Wesley Walls .25 .11
❑ 28 Tim Biakabutuka .40 .18
❑ 29 Steve Beuerlein .40 .18
❑ 30 Patrick Jeffers .60 .25
❑ 31 Natrone Means .25 .11
❑ 32 Curtis Enis .25 .11
❑ 33 Bobby Engram .40 .18
❑ 34 Marcus Robinson .60 .25
❑ 35 Marty Booker .40 .18
❑ 36 Cade McNown .25 .11
❑ 37 Darnay Scott .40 .18
❑ 38 Carl Pickens .40 .18
❑ 39 Corey Dillon .60 .25
❑ 40 Akili Smith .25 .11
❑ 41 Michael Basnight .25 .11
❑ 42 Karim Abdul-Jabbar .40 .18
❑ 43 Tim Couch .40 .18
❑ 44 Kevin Johnson .60 .25
❑ 45 Darrin Chiaverini .25 .11
❑ 46 Errict Rhett .40 .18
❑ 47 Emmitt Smith 1.25 .55
❑ 48 Deion Sanders .60 .25
❑ 49 Michael Irvin .40 .18
❑ 50 Rocket Ismail .40 .18
❑ 51 Troy Aikman 1.25 .55
❑ 52 Jason Tucker .25 .11
❑ 53 Joey Galloway .40 .18
❑ 54 David LaFleur .25 .11
❑ 55 Wane McGarity .25 .11
❑ 56 Ed McCaffrey .60 .25
❑ 57 Rod Smith .40 .18
❑ 58 Brian Griese .60 .25
❑ 59 John Elway 2.00 .90
❑ 60 Gus Frerotte .25 .11
❑ 61 Neil Smith .25 .11
❑ 62 Terrell Davis .60 .25
❑ 63 Olandis Gary .60 .25
❑ 64 Johnnie Morton .40 .18
❑ 65 Charlie Batch .60 .25
❑ 66 Barry Sanders 1.50 .70
❑ 67 James Stewart .40 .18
❑ 68 Germane Crowell .25 .11
❑ 69 Sedrick Irvin .25 .11
❑ 70 Herman Moore .40 .18
❑ 71 Corey Bradford .40 .18
❑ 72 Dorsey Levens .40 .18
❑ 73 Antonio Freeman .60 .25
❑ 74 Brett Favre 2.00 .90
❑ 75 De'Mond Parker .25 .11
❑ 76 Bill Schroeder .40 .18
❑ 77 Donald Driver .60 .25
❑ 78 E.G. Green .25 .11
❑ 79 Marvin Harrison .60 .25
❑ 80 Peyton Manning 1.50 .70
❑ 81 Terrence Wilkins .25 .11
❑ 82 Edgerrin James 1.00 .45
❑ 83 Keenan McCardell .40 .18
❑ 84 Mark Brunell .60 .25
❑ 85 Fred Taylor .60 .25
❑ 86 Jimmy Smith .40 .18
❑ 87 Derrick Alexander .40 .18
❑ 88 Andre Rison .40 .18
❑ 89 Elvis Grbac .40 .18
❑ 90 Tony Gonzalez .40 .18
❑ 91 Donnell Bennett .25 .11
❑ 92 Warren Moon .60 .25
❑ 93 Kimble Anders .25 .11
❑ 94 Tony Richardson RC .40 .18
❑ 95 Jay Fiedler .60 .25
❑ 96 Zach Thomas .60 .25
❑ 97 Oronde Gadsden .40 .18
❑ 98 Dan Marino 2.00 .90
❑ 99 O.J. McDuffie .40 .18
❑ 100 Tony Martin .40 .18
❑ 101 James Johnson .25 .11
❑ 102 Rob Konrad .25 .11
❑ 103 Damon Huard .60 .25
❑ 104 Thurman Thomas .40 .18
❑ 105 Randy Moss 1.25 .55
❑ 106 Cris Carter .60 .25
❑ 107 Robert Smith .60 .25
❑ 108 Randall Cunningham .60 .25
❑ 109 John Randle .40 .18
❑ 110 Leroy Hoard .25 .11
❑ 111 Daunte Culpepper .75 .35
❑ 112 Matthew Hatchette .25 .11
❑ 113 Troy Brown .40 .18
❑ 114 Tony Simmons .25 .11
❑ 115 Terry Glenn .40 .18
❑ 116 Ben Coates .25 .11
❑ 117 Drew Bledsoe .75 .35
❑ 118 Terry Allen .40 .18
❑ 119 Kevin Faulk .25 .11
❑ 120 Ricky Williams .60 .25
❑ 121 Jake Delhomme RC 2.50 1.10
❑ 122 Jake Reed .40 .18
❑ 123 Jeff Blake .40 .18
❑ 124 Amani Toomer .40 .18
❑ 125 Kerry Collins .40 .18
❑ 126 Tiki Barber .40 .18
❑ 127 Ike Hilliard .40 .18
❑ 128 Joe Montgomery .25 .11
❑ 129 Sean Bennett .25 .11
❑ 130 Curtis Martin .60 .25
❑ 131 Vinny Testaverde .40 .18
❑ 132 Wayne Chrebet .40 .18
❑ 133 Ray Lucas .40 .18
❑ 134 Tyrone Wheatley .40 .18
❑ 135 Napoleon Kaufman .40 .18
❑ 136 Tim Brown .60 .25
❑ 137 Rickey Dudley .25 .11
❑ 138 James Jett .25 .11
❑ 139 Rich Gannon .60 .25
❑ 140 Charles Woodson .40 .18
❑ 141 Duce Staley .60 .25
❑ 142 Donovan McNabb 1.00 .45
❑ 143 Na Brown .25 .11
❑ 144 Kordell Stewart .40 .18
❑ 145 Jerome Bettis .60 .25
❑ 146 Hines Ward .60 .25
❑ 147 Troy Edwards .25 .11
❑ 148 Curtis Conway .40 .18
❑ 149 Junior Seau .60 .25
❑ 150 Jim Harbaugh .40 .18
❑ 151 Jermaine Fazande .25 .11
❑ 152 Terrell Owens .60 .25
❑ 153 J.J. Stokes .40 .18
❑ 154 Charlie Garner .40 .18
❑ 155 Jerry Rice 1.25 .55
❑ 156 Garrison Hearst .40 .18
❑ 157 Steve Young .75 .35
❑ 158 Jeff Garcia .60 .25
❑ 159 Derrick Mayes .40 .18
❑ 160 Ahman Green .60 .25
❑ 161 Ricky Watters .40 .18
❑ 162 Jon Kitna .60 .25
❑ 163 Karsten Bailey .25 .11
❑ 164 Sean Dawkins .25 .11
❑ 165 Az-Zahir Hakim .40 .18
❑ 166 Isaac Bruce .60 .25
❑ 167 Marshall Faulk .75 .35
❑ 168 Trent Green .60 .25
❑ 169 Kurt Warner 1.25 .55
❑ 170 Torry Holt .60 .25
❑ 171 Robert Holcombe .25 .11
❑ 172 Kevin Carter .25 .11
❑ 173 Keyshawn Johnson .60 .25
❑ 174 Jacquez Green .25 .11
❑ 175 Reidel Anthony .25 .11
❑ 176 Warren Sapp .40 .18

❑ 177 Mike Alstott .60 .25
❑ 178 Warrick Dunn .60 .25
❑ 179 Trent Dilfer .40 .18
❑ 180 Shaun King .25 .11
❑ 181 Neil O'Donnell .25 .11
❑ 182 Eddie George .60 .25
❑ 183 Yancey Thigpen .25 .11
❑ 184 Steve McNair .60 .25
❑ 185 Kevin Dyson .40 .18
❑ 186 Frank Wycheck .25 .11
❑ 187 Jevon Kearse .60 .25
❑ 188 Adrian Murrell .25 .11
❑ 189 Jeff George .40 .18
❑ 190 Stephen Davis .60 .25
❑ 191 Stephen Alexander .25 .11
❑ 192 Darrell Green .25 .11
❑ 193 Skip Hicks .25 .11
❑ 194 Brad Johnson .60 .25
❑ 195 Michael Westbrook .40 .18
❑ 196 Albert Connell .25 .11
❑ 197 Irving Fryar .40 .18
❑ 198 Bruce Smith .40 .18
❑ 199 Champ Bailey .40 .18
❑ 200 Larry Centers .25 .11
❑ 201 Jake Plummer PP 1.25 .55
❑ 202 Doug Flutie PP 1.25 .55
❑ 203 Eric Moulds PP 1.25 .55
❑ 204 Muhsin Muhammad PP 1.25 .55
❑ 205 Marcus Robinson PP 1.25 .55
❑ 206 Cade McNown PP 1.25 .55
❑ 207 Corey Dillon PP 1.25 .55
❑ 208 Tim Couch PP 1.25 .55
❑ 209 Kevin Johnson PP 1.25 .55
❑ 210 Emmitt Smith PP 3.00 1.35
❑ 211 Troy Aikman PP 3.00 1.35
❑ 212 Brian Griese PP 1.25 .55
❑ 213 Olandis Gary PP 1.25 .55
❑ 214 Germane Crowell PP 1.25 .55
❑ 215 Brett Favre PP 5.00 2.20
❑ 216 Charlie Batch PP 1.25 .55
❑ 217 Antonio Freeman PP 1.25 .55
❑ 218 Dorsey Levens PP 1.25 .55
❑ 219 Peyton Manning PP 4.00 1.80
❑ 220 Edgerrin James PP 2.50 1.10
❑ 221 Marvin Harrison PP 1.25 .55
❑ 222 Fred Taylor PP 1.25 .55
❑ 223 Mark Brunell PP 1.25 .55
❑ 224 Jimmy Smith PP 1.25 .55
❑ 225 Dan Marino PP 5.00 2.20
❑ 226 Randy Moss PP 3.00 1.35
❑ 227 Cris Carter PP 1.25 .55
❑ 228 Robert Smith PP 1.25 .55
❑ 229 Drew Bledsoe PP 2.00 .90
❑ 230 Terry Glenn PP 1.25 .55
❑ 231 Ricky Williams PP 1.25 .55
❑ 232 Amani Toomer PP 1.25 .55
❑ 233 Keyshawn Johnson PP 1.25 .55
❑ 234 Curtis Martin PP 1.25 .55
❑ 235 Ray Lucas PP 1.25 .55
❑ 236 Tim Brown PP 1.25 .55
❑ 237 Duce Staley PP 1.25 .55
❑ 238 Donovan McNabb PP 2.50 1.10
❑ 239 Jerry Rice PP 3.00 1.35
❑ 240 Jon Kitna PP 1.25 .55
❑ 241 Isaac Bruce PP 1.25 .55
❑ 242 Kurt Warner PP 3.00 1.35
❑ 243 Torry Holt PP 1.25 .55
❑ 244 Mike Alstott PP 1.25 .55
❑ 245 Marshall Faulk PP 2.00 .90
❑ 246 Shaun King PP .25 .11
❑ 247 Eddie George PP 1.25 .55
❑ 248 Steve McNair PP 1.25 .55
❑ 249 Stephen Davis PP 1.25 .55
❑ 250 Brad Johnson PP 1.25 .55
❑ 251 Rondell Mealey RC 2.50 1.10
❑ 252 Peter Warrick RC 4.00 1.80
❑ 253 Courtney Brown RC 1.25 .55
❑ 254 Plaxico Burress RC 8.00 3.60
❑ 255 Corey Simon RC 1.25 .55
❑ 256 Thomas Jones RC 6.00 2.70
❑ 257 Travis Taylor RC 1.25 .55
❑ 258 Shaun Alexander RC 10.00 4.50
❑ 259 Chris Redman RC 1.25 .55
❑ 260 Chad Pennington RC 15.00 6.75
❑ 261 Jamal Lewis RC 10.00 4.50
❑ 262 Bubba Franks RC 4.00 1.80
❑ 263 Dez White RC 4.00 1.80
❑ 264 Ron Dayne RC 4.00 1.80
❑ 265 Sylvester Morris RC 3.00 1.35
❑ 266 R.Jay Soward RC 3.00 1.35
❑ 267 Sherrod Gideon RC 2.50 1.10
❑ 268 Travis Prentice RC 3.00 1.35
❑ 269 Darrell Jackson RC 8.00 3.60
❑ 270 Giovanni Carmazzi RC 3.00 1.35
❑ 271 Anthony Lucas RC 2.50 1.10
❑ 272 Danny Farmer RC 3.00 1.35
❑ 273 Dennis Northcutt RC 4.00 1.80
❑ 274 Troy Walters RC 4.00 1.80
❑ 275 Laveranues Coles RC 5.00 2.20
❑ 276 Tee Martin RC 4.00 1.80
❑ 277 J.R. Redmond RC 3.00 1.35
❑ 278 Jerry Porter RC 5.00 2.20
❑ 279 Sebastian Janikowski RC 4.00 1.80
❑ 280 Michael Wiley RC 3.00 1.35
❑ 281 Reuben Droughns RC 5.00 2.20
❑ 282 Trung Canidate RC 3.00 1.35
❑ 283 Shyrone Stith RC 3.00 1.35
❑ 284 Trevor Gaylor RC 3.00 1.35
❑ 285 Marc Bulger RC 8.00 3.60
❑ 286 Tom Brady RC 40.00 18.00
❑ 287 Todd Husak RC 4.00 1.80
❑ 288 Jarious Jackson RC 3.00 1.35
❑ 289 Terrelle Smith RC 3.00 1.35
❑ 290 Chad Morton RC 4.00 1.80
❑ 291 Chris Cole RC 4.00 1.80
❑ 292 Kwame Cavil RC 2.50 1.10
❑ 293 JaJuan Dawson RC 2.50 1.10
❑ 294 Curtis Keaton RC 3.00 1.35
❑ 295 Tim Rattay RC 8.00 3.60
❑ 296 Joe Hamilton RC 3.00 1.35
❑ 297 Gari Scott RC 2.50 1.10
❑ 298 Mike Anderson RC 4.00 1.80
❑ 299 Ron Dugans RC 2.50 1.10
❑ 300 Todd Pinkston RC 4.00 1.80

2002 Playoff Prestige

	Nm-Mt	Ex-Mt
COMP.SET w/o SP's (150)	40.00	12.00
❑ 1 David Boston	1.25	.35
❑ 2 MarTay Jenkins	.50	.15
❑ 3 Jake Plummer	.75	.23
❑ 4 Chris Chandler	.75	.23
❑ 5 Jamal Anderson	.75	.23
❑ 6 Michael Vick	4.00	1.20
❑ 7 Maurice Smith	.75	.23
❑ 8 Elvis Grbac	.75	.23
❑ 9 Jamal Lewis	1.25	.35
❑ 10 Todd Heap	.50	.15
❑ 11 Qadry Ismail	.75	.23
❑ 12 Shannon Sharpe	.75	.23
❑ 13 Ray Lewis	1.25	.35
❑ 14 Rod Woodson	.75	.23
❑ 15 Travis Henry	1.25	.35
❑ 16 Rob Johnson	.75	.23
❑ 17 Eric Moulds	.75	.23
❑ 18 Nate Clements	.50	.15
❑ 19 Donald Hayes	.50	.15
❑ 20 Muhsin Muhammad	.75	.23
❑ 21 Steve Smith	.75	.23
❑ 22 Wesley Walls	.50	.15
❑ 23 Chris Weinke	.75	.23
❑ 24 James Allen	.75	.23
❑ 25 David Terrell	1.25	.35
❑ 26 Anthony Thomas	1.25	.35
❑ 27 Dez White	.50	.15
❑ 28 Brian Urlacher	2.00	.60
❑ 29 Mike Brown	1.25	.35
❑ 30 Corey Dillon	.75	.23
❑ 31 Chad Johnson	1.25	.35
❑ 32 Peter Warrick	.75	.23
❑ 33 Justin Smith	.50	.15
❑ 34 Tim Couch	.75	.23
❑ 35 James Jackson	.50	.15
❑ 36 Quincy Morgan	.50	.15
❑ 37 Kevin Johnson	.75	.23
❑ 38 Gerard Warren	.50	.15
❑ 39 Anthony Henry	.50	.15
❑ 40 Quincy Carter	.75	.23
❑ 41 Joey Galloway	.75	.23
❑ 42 Rocket Ismail	.75	.23
❑ 43 Ryan Leaf	.75	.23
❑ 44 Emmitt Smith	3.00	.90
❑ 45 Troy Hambrick	.50	.15
❑ 46 Mike Anderson	1.25	.35
❑ 47 Terrell Davis	1.25	.35
❑ 48 Brian Griese	1.25	.35
❑ 49 Rod Smith	.75	.23
❑ 50 Ed McCaffrey	1.25	.35
❑ 51 Charlie Batch	.75	.23
❑ 52 Johnnie Morton	.75	.23
❑ 53 Germane Crowell	.50	.15
❑ 54 James Stewart	.75	.23
❑ 55 Shaun Rogers	.50	.15
❑ 56 Brett Favre	3.00	.90
❑ 57 Antonio Freeman	1.25	.35
❑ 58 Ahman Green	1.25	.35
❑ 59 Bill Schroeder	.75	.23
❑ 60 Kabeer Gbaja-Biamila	.75	.23
❑ 61 Marvin Harrison	1.25	.35
❑ 62 Terrence Wilkins	.50	.15
❑ 63 Dominic Rhodes	.75	.23
❑ 64 Reggie Wayne	.75	.23
❑ 65 Edgerrin James	1.50	.45
❑ 66 Mark Brunell	1.25	.35
❑ 67 Keenan McCardell	.50	.15
❑ 68 Jimmy Smith	.75	.23
❑ 69 Fred Taylor	1.25	.35
❑ 70 Derrick Alexander	.75	.23
❑ 71 Tony Gonzalez	.75	.23
❑ 72 Trent Green	.75	.23
❑ 73 Priest Holmes	1.50	.45
❑ 74 Snoop Minnis	.50	.15
❑ 75 Chris Chambers	1.25	.35
❑ 76 Jay Fiedler	.75	.23
❑ 77 Travis Minor	.50	.15
❑ 78 Lamar Smith	.75	.23
❑ 79 Zach Thomas	1.25	.35
❑ 80 Michael Bennett	.75	.23
❑ 81 Cris Carter	1.25	.35
❑ 82 Daunte Culpepper	1.25	.35
❑ 83 Randy Moss	2.50	.75
❑ 84 Drew Bledsoe	1.50	.45
❑ 85 Tom Brady	3.00	.90
❑ 86 Troy Brown	.75	.23
❑ 87 Antowain Smith	.75	.23
❑ 88 Aaron Brooks	1.25	.35
❑ 89 Joe Horn	.75	.23
❑ 90 Deuce McAllister	1.50	.45
❑ 91 Ricky Williams	1.25	.35
❑ 92 Kerry Collins	.75	.23
❑ 93 Ron Dayne	.75	.23
❑ 94 Michael Strahan	.75	.23
❑ 95 Jason Sehorn	.50	.15
❑ 96 Wayne Chrebet	.75	.23
❑ 97 Laveranues Coles	.75	.23
❑ 98 LaMont Jordan	1.25	.35
❑ 99 Curtis Martin	1.25	.35
❑ 100 Santana Moss	1.25	.35
❑ 101 Vinny Testaverde	.75	.23
❑ 102 Tim Brown	1.25	.35
❑ 103 Jerry Porter	.50	.15
❑ 104 Jerry Rice	2.50	.75
❑ 105 Charlie Garner	.75	.23
❑ 106 Tyrone Wheatley	.75	.23
❑ 107 Charles Woodson	.75	.23

❑ 108 Correll Buckhalter	.75	.23
❑ 109 Todd Pinkston	.75	.23
❑ 110 Freddie Mitchell	.75	.23
❑ 111 James Thrash	.75	.23
❑ 112 Duce Staley	1.25	.35
❑ 113 Jerome Bettis	1.25	.35
❑ 114 Plaxico Burress	.75	.23
❑ 115 Kordell Stewart	.75	.23
❑ 116 Hines Ward	1.25	.35
❑ 117 Kendrell Bell	1.25	.35
❑ 118 Drew Brees	1.25	.35
❑ 119 Curtis Conway	.50	.15
❑ 120 Doug Flutie	1.25	.35
❑ 121 LaDainian Tomlinson	2.00	.60
❑ 122 Junior Seau	1.25	.35
❑ 123 Kevan Barlow	.75	.23
❑ 124 Jeff Garcia	1.25	.35
❑ 125 Garrison Hearst	.75	.23
❑ 126 Terrell Owens	1.25	.35
❑ 127 Andre Carter	.50	.15
❑ 128 Shaun Alexander	1.25	.35
❑ 129 Matt Hasselbeck	.75	.23
❑ 130 Koren Robinson	.75	.23
❑ 131 Ricky Watters	.75	.23
❑ 132 Isaac Bruce	1.25	.35
❑ 133 Trung Canidate	.75	.23
❑ 134 Marshall Faulk	1.25	.35
❑ 135 Torry Holt	1.25	.35
❑ 136 Kurt Warner	1.25	.35
❑ 137 Mike Alstott	1.25	.35
❑ 138 Warrick Dunn	1.25	.35
❑ 139 Brad Johnson	.75	.23
❑ 140 Keyshawn Johnson	1.25	.35
❑ 141 Warren Sapp	.75	.23
❑ 142 Eddie George	1.25	.35
❑ 143 Derrick Mason	.75	.23
❑ 144 Steve McNair	1.25	.35
❑ 145 Jevon Kearse	.75	.23
❑ 146 Stephen Davis	.75	.23
❑ 147 Rod Gardner	.75	.23
❑ 148 Champ Bailey	.75	.23
❑ 149 Bruce Smith	.50	.15
❑ 150 Houston Texans	1.50	.45
❑ 151 David Carr RC	12.00	3.60
❑ 152 Julius Peppers RC	8.00	2.40
❑ 153 Joey Harrington RC	12.00	3.60
❑ 154 Quentin Jammer RC	4.00	1.20
❑ 155 Ryan Sims RC	4.00	1.20
❑ 156 Bryant McKinnie RC	3.00	.90
❑ 157 Roy Williams RC	10.00	3.00
❑ 158 John Henderson RC	4.00	1.20
❑ 159 Dwight Freeney RC	5.00	1.50
❑ 160 Wendell Bryant RC	4.00	1.20
❑ 161 Donte Stallworth RC	8.00	2.40
❑ 162 Jeremy Shockey RC	12.00	3.60
❑ 163 Albert Haynesworth RC	3.00	.90
❑ 164 William Green RC	6.00	1.80
❑ 165 Phillip Buchanon RC	4.00	1.20
❑ 166 T.J. Duckett RC	6.00	1.80
❑ 167 Ashley Lelie RC	8.00	2.40
❑ 168 Javon Walker RC	8.00	2.40
❑ 169 Daniel Graham RC	4.00	1.20
❑ 170 Napoleon Harris RC	4.00	1.20
❑ 171 Lito Sheppard RC	4.00	1.20
❑ 172 Robert Thomas RC	4.00	1.20
❑ 173 Patrick Ramsey RC	8.00	2.40
❑ 174 Jabar Gaffney RC	4.00	1.20
❑ 175 DeShaun Foster RC	4.00	1.20
❑ 176 Kalimba Edwards RC	4.00	1.20
❑ 177 Josh Reed RC	4.00	1.20
❑ 178 Larry Tripplett RC	2.00	.60
❑ 179 Andre Davis RC	4.00	1.20
❑ 180 Reche Caldwell RC	4.00	1.20
❑ 181 Levar Fisher RC	2.00	.60
❑ 182 Clinton Portis RC	12.00	3.60
❑ 183 Anthony Weaver RC	3.00	.90
❑ 184 Maurice Morris RC	4.00	1.20
❑ 185 Ladell Betts RC	4.00	1.20
❑ 186 Antwaan Randle El RC	5.00	1.50
❑ 187 Antonio Bryant RC	4.00	1.20
❑ 188 Rocky Calmus RC	4.00	1.20
❑ 189 Josh McCown RC	5.00	1.50
❑ 190 Lamar Gordon RC	4.00	1.20
❑ 191 Marquise Walker RC	3.00	.90
❑ 192 Cliff Russell RC	3.00	.90
❑ 193 Eric Crouch RC	6.00	1.80
❑ 194 Dennis Johnson RC	2.00	.60
❑ 195 Alex Brown RC	4.00	1.20
❑ 196 David Garrard RC	4.00	1.20
❑ 197 Rohan Davey RC	4.00	1.20
❑ 198 Alan Harper RC	2.00	.60
❑ 199 Ron Johnson RC	3.00	.90
❑ 200 Andra Davis RC	3.00	.90
❑ 201 Kurt Kittner RC	3.00	.90
❑ 202 Freddie Milons RC	3.00	.90
❑ 203 Adrian Peterson RC	4.00	1.20
❑ 204 Luke Staley RC	3.00	.90
❑ 205 Tracey Wistrom RC	3.00	.90
❑ 206 Woody Dantzler RC	4.00	1.20
❑ 207 Chad Hutchinson RC	4.00	1.20
❑ 208 Zak Kustok RC	4.00	1.20
❑ 209 Damien Anderson RC	3.00	.90
❑ 210 James Mungro RC	4.00	1.20
❑ 211 Cortlen Johnson RC	2.00	.60
❑ 212 Demontray Carter RC	2.00	.60
❑ 213 Kelly Campbell RC	3.00	.90
❑ 214 Brian Poli-Dixon RC	3.00	.90
❑ 215 Mike Rumph RC	4.00	1.20
❑ 216 Najeh Davenport RC	4.00	1.20

2002 Playoff Prestige Stars of the NFL Autographs

	Nm-Mt	Ex-Mt
#'d/13 OR LESS NOT PRICED DUE TO SCARCITY		
❑ SN4 Brett Favre/4		
❑ SN7 John Elway/7		
❑ SN8 Troy Aikman/8		
❑ SN11 Stephen Davis/48	60.00	18.00
❑ SN13 Dan Marino/13		
❑ SN14 Brian Urlacher/54	150.00	45.00
❑ SN15 Mike Anderson/38	80.00	24.00
❑ SN16 Jevon Kearse/90	60.00	18.00
❑ SN17 Terrell Owens/81	60.00	18.00
❑ SN19 Ricky Williams/34	80.00	24.00

2003 Playoff Prestige

	Nm-Mt	Ex-Mt
COMP.SET w/o SP's (150)	30.00	9.00
❑ 1 David Boston	.75	.23
❑ 2 Thomas Jones	.75	.23
❑ 3 Jake Plummer	.75	.23
❑ 4 Marcel Shipp	.75	.23
❑ 5 T.J. Duckett	.75	.23
❑ 6 Warrick Dunn	.75	.23
❑ 7 Michael Vick	3.00	.90
❑ 8 Jeff Blake	.50	.15
❑ 9 Todd Heap	.75	.23
❑ 10 Jamal Lewis	1.25	.35
❑ 11 Ray Lewis	1.25	.35
❑ 12 Drew Bledsoe	1.25	.35
❑ 13 Travis Henry	.75	.23
❑ 14 Eric Moulds	.75	.23
❑ 15 Peerless Price	.75	.23
❑ 16 Josh Reed	.75	.23
❑ 17 DeShaun Foster	.50	.15
❑ 18 Muhsin Muhammad	.75	.23
❑ 19 Steve Smith	.50	.15
❑ 20 Julius Peppers	1.25	.35
❑ 21 Marty Booker	.75	.23
❑ 22 David Terrell	.75	.23
❑ 23 Anthony Thomas	1.25	.35
❑ 24 Brian Urlacher	2.00	.60
❑ 25 Corey Dillon	.75	.23
❑ 26 Chad Johnson	.75	.23
❑ 27 Jon Kitna	.75	.23
❑ 28 Peter Warrick	.75	.23
❑ 29 Tim Couch	.50	.15
❑ 30 Andre Davis	.50	.15
❑ 31 William Green	.75	.23
❑ 32 Quincy Morgan	.75	.23
❑ 33 Dennis Northcutt	.75	.23
❑ 34 Antonio Bryant	.75	.23
❑ 35 Quincy Carter	.75	.23
❑ 36 Troy Hambrick	.50	.15
❑ 37 Chad Hutchinson	.75	.23
❑ 38 Emmitt Smith	3.00	.90
❑ 39 Roy Williams	1.25	.35
❑ 40 Brian Griese	1.25	.35
❑ 41 Ashley Lelie	1.25	.35
❑ 42 Ed McCaffrey	.75	.23
❑ 43 Clinton Portis	2.00	.60
❑ 44 Rod Smith	.75	.23
❑ 45 Germane Crowell	.50	.15
❑ 46 Az-Zahir Hakim	.50	.15
❑ 47 Joey Harrington	2.00	.60
❑ 48 James Stewart	.75	.23
❑ 49 Donald Driver	.75	.23
❑ 50 Brett Favre	3.00	.90
❑ 51 Terry Glenn	.50	.15
❑ 52 Ahman Green	1.25	.35
❑ 53 Javon Walker	.75	.23
❑ 54 Corey Bradford	.50	.15
❑ 55 David Carr	2.00	.60
❑ 56 Jabar Gaffney	.75	.23
❑ 57 Jonathan Wells	.50	.15
❑ 58 Marvin Harrison	1.25	.35
❑ 59 Edgerrin James	1.25	.35
❑ 60 Peyton Manning	2.00	.60
❑ 61 James Mungro	.50	.15
❑ 62 Reggie Wayne	.75	.23
❑ 63 Mark Brunell	.75	.23
❑ 64 David Garrard	.50	.15
❑ 65 Stacey Mack	.50	.15
❑ 66 Jimmy Smith	.75	.23
❑ 67 Fred Taylor	1.25	.35
❑ 68 Marc Boerigter	.75	.23
❑ 69 Tony Gonzalez	.75	.23
❑ 70 Trent Green	.75	.23
❑ 71 Priest Holmes	1.50	.45
❑ 72 Eddie Kennison	.50	.15
❑ 73 Cris Carter	1.25	.35
❑ 74 Chris Chambers	1.25	.35
❑ 75 Jay Fiedler	.75	.23
❑ 76 Randy McMichael	.75	.23
❑ 77 Zach Thomas	.75	.23
❑ 78 Ricky Williams	1.25	.35
❑ 79 Michael Bennett	.75	.23
❑ 80 Todd Bouman	.50	.15
❑ 81 Daunte Culpepper	1.25	.35
❑ 82 Randy Moss	2.00	.60
❑ 83 Tom Brady	2.00	.60
❑ 84 Deion Branch	1.25	.35
❑ 85 Troy Brown	.75	.23
❑ 86 Kevin Faulk	.50	.15
❑ 87 Antowain Smith	.75	.23
❑ 88 Aaron Brooks	1.25	.35

❑ 89 Joe Horn	.75	.23
❑ 90 Deuce McAllister	1.25	.35
❑ 91 Donte Stallworth	1.25	.35
❑ 92 Tiki Barber	.75	.23
❑ 93 Kerry Collins	.75	.23
❑ 94 Jeremy Shockey	2.00	.60
❑ 95 Michael Strahan	.75	.23
❑ 96 Amani Toomer	.75	.23
❑ 97 Laveranues Coles	.75	.23
❑ 98 LaMont Jordan	.75	.23
❑ 99 Curtis Martin	1.25	.35
❑ 100 Santana Moss	.75	.23
❑ 101 Chad Pennington	1.50	.45
❑ 102 Tim Brown	1.25	.35
❑ 103 Rich Gannon	.75	.23
❑ 104 Charlie Garner	.75	.23
❑ 105 Jerry Rice	2.50	.75
❑ 106 Charles Woodson	.75	.23
❑ 107 Antonio Freeman	.75	.23
❑ 108 Dorsey Levens	.50	.15
❑ 109 Donovan McNabb	1.50	.45
❑ 110 Duce Staley	.75	.23
❑ 111 James Thrash	.50	.15
❑ 112 Jerome Bettis	1.25	.35
❑ 113 Plaxico Burress	.75	.23
❑ 114 Tommy Maddox	1.25	.35
❑ 115 Antwaan Randle El	1.25	.35
❑ 116 Kordell Stewart	.75	.23
❑ 117 Hines Ward	1.25	.35
❑ 118 Drew Brees	1.25	.35
❑ 119 Curtis Conway	.50	.15
❑ 120 Junior Seau	1.25	.35
❑ 121 LaDainian Tomlinson	1.25	.35
❑ 122 Kevan Barlow	.75	.23
❑ 123 Jeff Garcia	1.25	.35
❑ 124 Garrison Hearst	.75	.23
❑ 125 Terrell Owens	1.25	.35
❑ 126 Shaun Alexander	1.25	.35
❑ 127 Trent Dilfer	.75	.23
❑ 128 Darrell Jackson	.75	.23
❑ 129 Maurice Morris	.50	.15
❑ 130 Koren Robinson	.50	.15
❑ 131 Isaac Bruce	1.25	.35
❑ 132 Marc Bulger	1.25	.35
❑ 133 Marshall Faulk	1.25	.35
❑ 134 Torry Holt	1.25	.35
❑ 135 Kurt Warner	1.25	.35
❑ 136 Mike Alstott	1.25	.35
❑ 137 Brad Johnson	.75	.23
❑ 138 Keyshawn Johnson	1.25	.35
❑ 139 Dexter Jackson RC	1.25	.35
❑ 140 Warren Sapp	.75	.23
❑ 141 Kevin Dyson	.75	.23
❑ 142 Eddie George	.75	.23
❑ 143 Jevon Kearse	.75	.23
❑ 144 Derrick Mason	.75	.23
❑ 145 Steve McNair	1.25	.35
❑ 146 Stephen Davis	.75	.23
❑ 147 Rod Gardner	.75	.23
❑ 148 Shane Matthews	.50	.15
❑ 149 Patrick Ramsey	1.25	.35
❑ 150 Derrius Thompson	.50	.15
❑ 151 Byron Leftwich RC	12.00	3.60
❑ 152 Carson Palmer RC	10.00	3.00
❑ 153 Chris Simms RC	6.00	1.80
❑ 154 Kliff Kingsbury RC	2.50	.75
❑ 155 Dave Ragone RC	3.00	.90
❑ 156 Jason Gesser RC	3.00	.90
❑ 157 Ken Dorsey RC	5.00	1.50
❑ 158 Kyle Boller RC	8.00	2.40
❑ 159 Brad Banks RC	2.50	.75
❑ 160 Rex Grossman RC	8.00	2.40
❑ 161 Seneca Wallace RC	3.00	.90
❑ 162 Brian St.Pierre RC	3.00	.90
❑ 163 Larry Johnson RC	6.00	1.80
❑ 164 Earnest Graham RC	2.50	.75
❑ 165 Musa Smith RC	3.00	.90
❑ 166 Lee Suggs RC	6.00	1.80
❑ 167 Willis McGahee RC	8.00	2.40
❑ 168 Onterrio Smith RC	4.00	1.20
❑ 170 Sultan McCullough RC	2.50	.75
❑ 171 Chris Brown RC	6.00	1.80
❑ 172 Justin Fargas RC	3.00	.90
❑ 173 Avon Cobourne RC	1.50	.45
❑ 174 Dahrran Diedrick RC	3.00	.90
❑ 175 LaBrandon Toefield RC	3.00	.90
❑ 176 Artose Pinner RC	3.00	.90
❑ 177 Quentin Griffin RC	8.00	2.40
❑ 178 ReShard Lee RC	3.00	.90
❑ 179 Andrew Pinnock RC	2.50	.75
❑ 180 B.J. Askew RC	3.00	.90
❑ 181 Andre Johnson RC	8.00	2.40
❑ 182 Brandon Lloyd RC	4.00	1.20
❑ 183 Bryant Johnson RC	3.00	.90
❑ 184 Charles Rogers RC	4.00	1.20
❑ 185 Doug Gabriel RC	3.00	.90
❑ 186 Justin Gage RC	3.00	.90
❑ 187 Kareem Kelly RC	2.50	.75
❑ 188 Kelley Washington RC	3.00	.90
❑ 189 Taylor Jacobs RC	3.00	.90
❑ 190 Terrence Edwards RC	2.50	.75
❑ 191 Anquan Boldin RC	8.00	2.40
❑ 192 Billy McMullen RC	2.50	.75
❑ 193 Talman Gardner RC	3.00	.90
❑ 194 Amaz Battle RC	3.00	.90
❑ 195 Sam Aiken RC	2.50	.75
❑ 196 Bobby Wade RC	3.00	.90
❑ 197 Mike Bush RC	1.50	.45
❑ 198 Keenan Howry RC	3.00	.90
❑ 199 Jerel Myers RC	1.50	.45
❑ 200 Dallas Clark RC	3.00	.90
❑ 201 Mike Pinkard RC	1.50	.45
❑ 202 Teyo Johnson RC	3.00	.90
❑ 203 Trent Smith RC	2.50	.75
❑ 204 George Wrighster RC	2.50	.75
❑ 205 Jason Witten RC	5.00	1.50
❑ 206 Cory Redding RC	2.50	.75
❑ 207 DeWayne White RC	2.50	.75
❑ 208 Jerome McDougle RC	3.00	.90
❑ 209 Michael Haynes RC	3.00	.90
❑ 210 Chris Kelsay RC	3.00	.90
❑ 211 Calvin Pace RC	2.50	.75
❑ 212 Kenny King RC	2.50	.75
❑ 213 Jimmy Kennedy RC	3.00	.90
❑ 214 William Joseph RC	3.00	.90
❑ 215 DeWayne Robertson RC	3.00	.90
❑ 216 Jarret Johnson RC	2.50	.75
❑ 217 Rien Long RC	1.50	.45
❑ 218 Boss Bailey RC	4.00	1.20
❑ 219 Terrell Suggs RC	5.00	1.50
❑ 220 Terry Pierce RC	2.50	.75
❑ 221 Bradie James RC	3.00	.90
❑ 222 Angelo Crowell RC	2.50	.75
❑ 223 Andre Woolfolk RC	3.00	.90
❑ 224 Dennis Weathersby RC	1.50	.45
❑ 225 Marcus Trufant RC	3.00	.90
❑ 226 Terence Newman RC	6.00	1.80
❑ 227 Ricky Manning RC	3.00	.90
❑ 228 Mike Doss RC	3.00	.90
❑ 229 Julian Battle RC	2.50	.75
❑ 230 Rashean Mathis RC	2.50	.75

2003 Playoff Prestige Xtra Points Green

	Nm-Mt	Ex-Mt
*STARS: 3X TO 8X BASIC CARDS		
*ROOKIES: 2.5X TO 6X		

2003 Playoff Prestige Xtra Points Purple

	Nm-Mt	Ex-Mt
*STARS: 3X TO 8X BASIC CARDS		
*ROOKIES: 2.5X TO 6X		

2004 Playoff Prestige

	Nm-Mt	Ex-Mt
COMP.SET w/o RC's (150)	25.00	7.50
❑ 1 Anquan Boldin	1.00	.30
❑ 2 Emmitt Smith	2.00	.60
❑ 3 Jeff Blake	.40	.12
❑ 4 Marcel Shipp	.60	.18
❑ 5 Michael Vick	2.00	.60
❑ 6 Peerless Price	.60	.18
❑ 7 T.J. Duckett	.60	.18
❑ 8 Warrick Dunn	.60	.18
❑ 9 Ed Reed	.60	.18
❑ 10 Jamal Lewis	1.00	.30
❑ 11 Kyle Boller	1.00	.30
❑ 12 Ray Lewis	1.00	.30
❑ 13 Todd Heap	.60	.18
❑ 14 Drew Bledsoe	1.00	.30
❑ 15 Eric Moulds	.60	.18
❑ 16 Josh Reed	.40	.12
❑ 17 Travis Henry	.60	.18
❑ 18 DeShaun Foster	.60	.18
❑ 19 Stephen Davis	.60	.18
❑ 20 Jake Delhomme	1.00	.30
❑ 21 Julius Peppers	1.00	.30
❑ 22 Steve Smith	.60	.18
❑ 23 Anthony Thomas	.60	.18
❑ 24 Brian Urlacher	1.25	.35
❑ 25 Marty Booker	.60	.18
❑ 26 Rex Grossman	1.00	.30
❑ 27 Chad Johnson	.60	.18
❑ 28 Corey Dillon	.60	.18
❑ 29 Carson Palmer	1.25	.35
❑ 30 Peter Warrick	.60	.18
❑ 31 Rudi Johnson	.60	.18
❑ 32 Andre Davis	.40	.12
❑ 33 Quincy Morgan	.60	.18
❑ 34 William Green	.60	.18
❑ 35 Kelly Holcomb	.60	.18
❑ 36 Antonio Bryant	.60	.18
❑ 37 Quincy Carter	.60	.18
❑ 38 Roy Williams S	.60	.18
❑ 39 Terence Newman	.60	.18
❑ 40 Terry Glenn	.40	.12
❑ 41 Troy Hambrick	.40	.12
❑ 42 Ashley Lelie	.60	.18
❑ 43 Clinton Portis	1.00	.30
❑ 44 Rod Smith	.60	.18
❑ 45 Shannon Sharpe	.60	.18
❑ 46 Mike Anderson	.60	.18
❑ 47 Jake Plummer	.60	.18
❑ 48 Charles Rogers	.60	.18
❑ 49 Joey Harrington	1.00	.30
❑ 50 Ahman Green	1.00	.30
❑ 51 Brett Favre	2.50	.75
❑ 52 Donald Driver	.60	.18
❑ 53 Javon Walker	.60	.18
❑ 54 Robert Ferguson	.40	.12
❑ 55 Andre Johnson	1.00	.30
❑ 56 David Carr	1.00	.30
❑ 57 Domanick Davis	1.00	.30
❑ 58 Jabar Gaffney	.60	.18
❑ 59 Dwight Freeney	.40	.12
❑ 60 Dallas Clark	.60	.18
❑ 61 Edgerrin James	1.00	.30
❑ 62 Marvin Harrison	1.00	.30
❑ 63 Peyton Manning	1.50	.45
❑ 64 Reggie Wayne	.60	.18
❑ 65 Byron Leftwich	1.50	.45
❑ 66 Fred Taylor	.60	.18
❑ 67 Jimmy Smith	.60	.18
❑ 68 Johnnie Morton	.60	.18
❑ 69 Priest Holmes	1.25	.35
❑ 70 Tony Gonzalez	.60	.18
❑ 71 Trent Green	.60	.18
❑ 72 Chris Chambers	.60	.18
❑ 73 Jay Fiedler	.40	.12
❑ 74 Randy McMichael	.40	.12
❑ 75 Ricky Williams	1.00	.30
❑ 76 Zach Thomas	1.00	.30

❑ 77 Daunte Culpepper 1.00 .30
❑ 78 Kelly Campbell .40 .12
❑ 79 Michael Bennett .60 .18
❑ 80 Moe Williams .40 .12
❑ 81 Nate Burleson 1.00 .30
❑ 82 Randy Moss 1.25 .35
❑ 83 Deion Branch 1.00 .30
❑ 84 Kevin Faulk .40 .12
❑ 85 Tom Brady 1.50 .45
❑ 86 Troy Brown .60 .18
❑ 87 Tedy Bruschi .60 .18
❑ 88 Aaron Brooks .60 .18
❑ 89 Deuce McAllister 1.00 .30
❑ 90 Donte Stallworth .60 .18
❑ 91 Joe Horn .60 .18
❑ 92 Amani Toomer .60 .18
❑ 93 Ike Hilliard .40 .12
❑ 94 Jeremy Shockey 1.00 .30
❑ 95 Kerry Collins .60 .18
❑ 96 Michael Strahan .60 .18
❑ 97 Tiki Barber .60 .18
❑ 98 Chad Pennington 1.25 .35
❑ 99 Curtis Martin 1.00 .30
❑ 100 LaMont Jordan .60 .18
❑ 101 Santana Moss .60 .18
❑ 102 Charlie Garner .60 .18
❑ 103 Jerry Porter .60 .18
❑ 104 Jerry Rice 2.00 .60
❑ 105 Justin Fargas .60 .18
❑ 106 Rich Gannon .60 .18
❑ 107 Rod Woodson .60 .18
❑ 108 Tim Brown 1.00 .30
❑ 109 Brian Westbrook .60 .18
❑ 110 Correll Buckhalter .60 .18
❑ 111 Donovan McNabb 1.25 .35
❑ 112 Freddie Mitchell .60 .18
❑ 113 James Thrash .40 .12
❑ 114 Amos Zereoue .40 .12
❑ 115 Antwaan Randle El .60 .18
❑ 116 Hines Ward 1.00 .30
❑ 117 Joey Porter .40 .12
❑ 118 Kendrell Bell .60 .18
❑ 119 Plaxico Burress .60 .18
❑ 120 David Boston .60 .18
❑ 121 Drew Brees 1.00 .30
❑ 122 LaDainian Tomlinson 1.00 .30
❑ 123 Jeff Garcia 1.00 .30
❑ 124 Kevan Barlow .60 .18
❑ 125 Tai Streets .40 .12
❑ 126 Terrell Owens 1.00 .30
❑ 127 Tim Rattay .60 .18
❑ 128 Darrell Jackson .60 .18
❑ 129 Koren Robinson .60 .18
❑ 130 Matt Hasselbeck .60 .18
❑ 131 Shaun Alexander 1.00 .30
❑ 132 Isaac Bruce .60 .18
❑ 133 Marc Bulger 1.00 .30
❑ 134 Marshall Faulk 1.00 .30
❑ 135 Torry Holt 1.00 .30
❑ 136 Brad Johnson .60 .18
❑ 137 Derrick Brooks .60 .18
❑ 138 Keenan McCardell .40 .12
❑ 139 Keyshawn Johnson .60 .18
❑ 140 Mike Alstott .60 .18
❑ 141 Derrick Mason .60 .18
❑ 142 Drew Bennett .60 .18
❑ 143 Jevon Kearse .60 .18
❑ 144 Justin McCareins .40 .12
❑ 145 Steve McNair 1.00 .30
❑ 146 Tyrone Calico .60 .18
❑ 147 Bruce Smith .60 .18
❑ 148 Laveranues Coles .60 .18
❑ 149 Patrick Ramsey .60 .18
❑ 150 LaVar Arrington 2.00 .60
❑ 151 Eli Manning RC 12.00 3.60
❑ 152 Larry Fitzgerald RC 8.00 2.40
❑ 153 Philip Rivers RC 8.00 2.40
❑ 154 Sean Taylor RC 3.00 .90
❑ 155 Kellen Winslow RC 6.00 1.80
❑ 156 Roy Williams RC 8.00 2.40
❑ 157 DeAngelo Hall RC 3.00 .90
❑ 158 Reggie Williams RC 3.00 .90
❑ 159 Ben Roethlisberger RC 20.00 6.00
❑ 160 Jonathan Vilma RC 2.50 .75
❑ 161 Lee Evans RC 4.00 1.20
❑ 162 Tommie Harris RC 3.00 .90
❑ 163 Michael Clayton RC 6.00 1.80
❑ 164 D.J. Williams SP RC 30.00 9.00
❑ 165 Will Smith RC 2.50 .75
❑ 166 Kenechi Udeze RC 2.50 .75
❑ 167 Vince Wilfork SP RC 30.00 9.00
❑ 168 J.P. Losman RC 6.00 1.80
❑ 169 Steven Jackson SP RC 50.00 15.00
❑ 170 Ahmad Carroll RC 3.00 .90
❑ 171 Chris Perry RC 5.00 1.50
❑ 172 Jason Babin SP RC 30.00 9.00
❑ 173 Chris Gamble RC 3.00 .90
❑ 174 Michael Jenkins RC 2.50 .75
❑ 175 Kevin Jones RC 8.00 2.40
❑ 176 Rashaun Woods RC 3.00 .90
❑ 177 Ben Watson RC 2.50 .75
❑ 178 Karlos Dansby RC 2.50 .75
❑ 179 Teddy Lehman RC 2.50 .75
❑ 180 Ricardo Colclough SP RC 30.00 9.00
❑ 181 Daryl Smith RC 2.50 .75
❑ 182 Ben Troupe RC 2.50 .75
❑ 183 Tatum Bell RC 4.00 1.20
❑ 184 Julius Jones RC 10.00 3.00
❑ 185 Bob Sanders RC 2.50 .75
❑ 186 Devery Henderson RC 2.00 .60
❑ 187 Dwan Edwards RC 1.25 .35
❑ 188 Michael Boulware RC 2.50 .75
❑ 189 Darius Watts RC 3.00 .90
❑ 190 Greg Jones RC 2.50 .75
❑ 191 Antwan Odom RC 2.50 .75
❑ 192 Sean Jones SP RC 25.00 7.50
❑ 193 Courtney Watson RC 2.50 .75
❑ 194 Keary Colbert RC 3.00 .90
❑ 195 Keith Smith RC 2.00 .60
❑ 196 Derrick Strait RC 2.50 .75
❑ 197 Bernard Berrian RC 2.50 .75
❑ 198 Devard Darling RC 2.50 .75
❑ 199 Matt Schaub RC 4.00 1.20
❑ 200 Will Poole RC 2.50 .75
❑ 201 Samie Parker RC 2.50 .75
❑ 202 Luke McCown SP RC 30.00 9.00
❑ 203 Jerricho Cotchery RC 2.50 .75
❑ 204 Mewelde Moore RC 3.00 .90
❑ 205 Ernest Wilford RC 2.50 .75
❑ 206 Cedric Cobbs SP RC 30.00 9.00
❑ 207 Johnnie Morant RC 2.50 .75
❑ 208 Craig Krenzel RC 2.50 .75
❑ 209 Michael Turner RC 2.00 .60
❑ 210 D.J. Hackett RC 2.00 .60
❑ 211 P.K. Sam RC 2.00 .60
❑ 212 Josh Harris RC 2.50 .75
❑ 213 Drew Henson RC 6.00 1.80
❑ 214 Jeff Smoker RC 4.00 1.20
❑ 215 John Navarre RC 2.50 .75
❑ 216 Cody Pickett RC 2.50 .75
❑ 217 Quincy Wilson RC 2.00 .60
❑ 218 Derek Abney RC 2.50 .75
❑ 219 Maurice Clarett SP RC 60.00 18.00
❑ 220 Mike Williams SP RC 135.00 40.00
❑ 221 B.J. Johnson RC 2.00 .60
❑ 222 Brandon Everage RC 2.00 .60
❑ 223 Derek McCoy RC 2.00 .60
❑ 224 Jared Lorenzen RC 2.00 .60
❑ 225 Jarrett Payton RC 2.50 .75
❑ 226 Jason Fife RC 2.00 .60
❑ 227 Robert Kent RC 1.25 .35

2004 Playoff Prestige Xtra Points Black

Nm-Mt Ex-Mt
*VETERANS: 10X TO 25X BASE CARD HI
*ROOKIES: 6X TO 15X BASE CARD HI
*ROOKIE SPs: .5X TO 1.2X BASE CARD HI
PRINT RUN 25 SER.#'d SETS HOB ONLY

❑ 19 Stephen Davis AU 50.00 15.00
❑ 38 Roy Williams S AU 80.00 24.00
❑ 57 Domanick Davis AU 60.00 18.00
❑ 67 Jimmy Smith AU 40.00 12.00
❑ 72 Chris Chambers AU 50.00 15.00
❑ 88 Aaron Brooks AU 40.00 12.00
❑ 97 Tiki Barber AU 60.00 18.00
❑ 116 Hines Ward AU 100.00 30.00
❑ 141 Derrick Mason AU 40.00 12.00
❑ 213 Drew Henson AU 150.00 45.00

2004 Playoff Prestige Xtra Points Green

Nm-Mt Ex-Mt
*VETERANS: 10X TO 25X BASE CARD HI
*ROOKIES: 6X TO 15X BASE CARD HI
*ROOKIE SPs: .5X TO 1.2X BASE CARD HI
PRINT RUN 25 SER.#'d SETS RETAIL ONLY

2004 Playoff Prestige Xtra Points Purple

Nm-Mt Ex-Mt
*VETERANS: 4X TO 10X BASE CARD HI
*ROOKIES: 2.5X TO 6X BASE CARD HI
*ROOKIE SPs: .4X TO 1X BASE CARD HI
PRINT RUN 75 SER.#'d SETS HOBBY ONLY

2004 Playoff Prestige Xtra Points Red

Nm-Mt Ex-Mt
*VETERANS: 3X TO 8X BASE CARD HI
*ROOKIES: 2X TO 5X BASE CARD HI
*ROOKIE SPs: .4X TO 1X BASE CARD HI
PRINT RUN 100 SER.#'d SETS RETAIL ONLY

2005 Playoff Prestige

Nm-Mt Ex-Mt
COMP.SET w/o SP's (234) 100.00 30.00
COMP.SET w/o RC's (150) 25.00 7.50
ONE 151-244 DRAFT PICK PER PACK

❑ 1 Anquan Boldin .60 .18
❑ 2 Emmitt Smith 2.00 .60
❑ 3 Josh McCown .60 .18
❑ 4 Larry Fitzgerald 1.00 .30
❑ 5 Michael Vick 1.50 .45
❑ 6 Peerless Price .60 .18
❑ 7 Alge Crumpler .60 .18
❑ 8 T.J. Duckett .60 .18
❑ 9 Warrick Dunn .60 .18
❑ 10 Ed Reed .60 .18
❑ 11 Jamal Lewis 1.00 .30
❑ 12 Kyle Boller .60 .18
❑ 13 Ray Lewis 1.00 .30
❑ 14 Todd Heap .60 .18
❑ 15 Drew Bledsoe 1.00 .30
❑ 16 Eric Moulds .60 .18
❑ 17 Lee Evans .60 .18
❑ 18 Travis Henry .60 .18
❑ 19 Willis McGahee 1.00 .30
❑ 20 Anthony Thomas .60 .18
❑ 21 Brian Urlacher 1.00 .30
❑ 22 Rex Grossman .60 .18
❑ 23 David Terrell .60 .18
❑ 24 Thomas Jones .60 .18
❑ 25 Carson Palmer 1.00 .30
❑ 26 Chad Johnson .60 .18
❑ 27 Peter Warrick .60 .18
❑ 28 Rudi Johnson .60 .18
❑ 29 Antonio Bryant .50 .15
❑ 30 William Green .50 .15
❑ 31 Jeff Garcia .60 .18
❑ 32 Kellen Winslow 1.00 .30
❑ 33 Lee Suggs .60 .18

❑ 34 Drew Henson .60 .18
❑ 35 Julius Jones 1.50 .45
❑ 36 Jason Witten .60 .18
❑ 37 Keyshawn Johnson .60 .18
❑ 38 Roy Williams S .60 .18
❑ 39 Ashley Lelie .60 .18
❑ 40 Champ Bailey .60 .18
❑ 41 Jake Plummer .60 .18
❑ 42 Reuben Droughns .60 .18
❑ 43 Rod Smith .60 .18
❑ 44 Charles Rogers .60 .18
❑ 45 Joey Harrington 1.00 .30
❑ 46 Kevin Jones 1.25 .35
❑ 47 Roy Williams WR 1.25 .35
❑ 48 Ahman Green 1.00 .30
❑ 49 Donald Driver .60 .18
❑ 50 Javon Walker .60 .18
❑ 51 Brett Favre 2.50 .75
❑ 52 Andre Johnson .60 .18
❑ 53 David Carr 1.00 .30
❑ 54 Domanick Davis .60 .18
❑ 55 Jabar Gaffney .60 .18
❑ 56 Edgerrin James 1.00 .30
❑ 57 Marvin Harrison 1.00 .30
❑ 58 Brandon Stokley .60 .18
❑ 59 Peyton Manning 1.50 .45
❑ 60 Reggie Wayne .60 .18
❑ 61 Byron Leftwich 1.00 .30
❑ 62 Fred Taylor .60 .18
❑ 63 Jimmy Smith .60 .18
❑ 64 Priest Holmes 1.00 .30
❑ 65 Tony Gonzalez .60 .18
❑ 66 Johnnie Morton .60 .18
❑ 67 Trent Green .60 .18
❑ 68 Chris Chambers .60 .18
❑ 69 Randy McMichael .50 .15
❑ 70 A.J. Feeley .60 .18
❑ 71 Zach Thomas 1.00 .30
❑ 72 Daunte Culpepper 1.00 .30
❑ 73 Marcus Robinson .60 .18
❑ 74 Mewelde Moore .60 .18
❑ 75 Nate Burleson .60 .18
❑ 76 Onterrio Smith .60 .18
❑ 77 Randy Moss 1.25 .35
❑ 78 Corey Dillon .60 .18
❑ 79 Tom Brady 2.00 .60
❑ 80 Deion Branch .60 .18
❑ 81 Tedy Bruschi .60 .18
❑ 82 David Givens .60 .18
❑ 83 David Patten .50 .15
❑ 84 Aaron Brooks .60 .18
❑ 85 Deuce McAllister 1.00 .30
❑ 86 Donte Stallworth .60 .18
❑ 87 Joe Horn .60 .18
❑ 88 Eli Manning 2.00 .60
❑ 89 Jeremy Shockey 1.00 .30
❑ 90 Kurt Warner .60 .18
❑ 91 Michael Strahan .60 .18
❑ 92 Tiki Barber .60 .18
❑ 93 Amani Toomer .60 .18
❑ 94 Chad Pennington 1.25 .35
❑ 95 Curtis Martin 1.00 .30
❑ 96 Santana Moss .60 .18
❑ 97 Justin McCareins .50 .15
❑ 98 Charles Woodson .60 .18
❑ 99 Kerry Collins .60 .18
❑ 100 Warren Sapp .60 .18
❑ 101 Jerry Porter .60 .18
❑ 102 Donovan McNabb 1.25 .35
❑ 103 Jevon Kearse .60 .18
❑ 104 Terrell Owens 1.00 .30
❑ 105 Brian Westbrook .60 .18
❑ 106 Todd Pinkston .50 .15
❑ 107 Duce Staley .60 .18
❑ 108 Hines Ward 1.00 .30
❑ 109 Jerome Bettis 1.00 .30
❑ 110 Joey Porter .50 .15
❑ 111 Plaxico Burress .60 .18
❑ 112 Ben Roethlisberger 3.00 .90
❑ 113 Drew Brees 1.00 .30
❑ 114 LaDainian Tomlinson 1.00 .30
❑ 115 Keenan McCardell .50 .15
❑ 116 Philip Rivers 1.00 .30
❑ 117 Antonio Gates 1.00 .30
❑ 118 Eric Johnson .60 .18
❑ 119 Kevan Barlow .60 .18
❑ 120 Brandon Lloyd .50 .15
❑ 121 Tim Rattay .60 .18
❑ 122 Darrell Jackson .60 .18
❑ 123 Koren Robinson .60 .18
❑ 124 Jerry Rice 2.00 .60
❑ 125 Matt Hasselbeck .60 .18
❑ 126 Shaun Alexander 1.00 .30
❑ 127 Isaac Bruce .60 .18
❑ 128 Marc Bulger 1.00 .30
❑ 129 Marshall Faulk 1.00 .30
❑ 130 Steven Jackson 1.25 .35
❑ 131 Torry Holt 1.00 .30
❑ 132 Derrick Brooks .60 .18
❑ 133 Michael Clayton 1.00 .30
❑ 134 Michael Pittman .50 .15
❑ 135 Chris Simms .60 .18
❑ 136 Chris Brown .60 .18
❑ 137 Derrick Mason .60 .18
❑ 138 Drew Bennett .60 .18
❑ 139 Steve McNair 1.00 .30
❑ 140 Clinton Portis 1.00 .30
❑ 141 LaVar Arrington 1.00 .30
❑ 142 Laveranues Coles .60 .18
❑ 143 Patrick Ramsey .60 .18
❑ 144 Rod Gardner .60 .18
❑ 145 DeShaun Foster .60 .18
❑ 146 Stephen Davis .60 .18
❑ 147 Jake Delhomme 1.00 .30
❑ 148 Muhsin Muhammad .60 .18
❑ 149 Steve Smith .60 .18
❑ 150 Keary Colbert .60 .18
❑ 151 Aaron Rodgers SP RC 60.00 18.00
❑ 152 Adrian McPherson SP RC 40.00 12.00
❑ 153 Alex Smith QB RC 12.00 3.60
❑ 154 Andrew Walter RC 4.00 1.20
❑ 155 Brock Berlin RC 2.50 .75
❑ 156 Charlie Frye SP RC 40.00 12.00
❑ 157 Chris Rix RC 2.50 .75
❑ 158 Dan Orlovsky RC 3.00 .90
❑ 159 Darian Durant RC 2.50 .75
❑ 160 David Greene RC 3.00 .90
❑ 161 Derek Anderson RC 2.50 .75
❑ 162 Gino Guidugli RC 2.00 .60
❑ 163 Jason Campbell RC 5.00 1.50
❑ 164 Jason White RC 4.00 1.20
❑ 165 Kyle Orton RC 4.00 1.20
❑ 166 Matt Jones SP RC 50.00 15.00
❑ 167 Ryan Fitzpatrick RC 2.50 .75
❑ 168 Stefan LeFors RC 3.00 .90
❑ 169 Timmy Chang RC 3.00 .90
❑ 170 Alvin Pearman RC 2.00 .60
❑ 171 Anthony Davis RC 2.50 .75
❑ 172 Brandon Jacobs RC 2.50 .75
❑ 173 Carnell Williams RC 8.00 2.40
❑ 174 Cedric Benson RC 8.00 2.40
❑ 175 Cedric Houston RC 2.50 .75
❑ 176 Ciatrick Fason RC 3.00 .90
❑ 177 Damien Nash RC 2.00 .60
❑ 178 Darren Sproles RC 3.00 .90
❑ 179 Eric Shelton SP RC 25.00 7.50
❑ 180 Frank Gore SP RC 30.00 9.00
❑ 181 J.J. Arrington SP RC 40.00 12.00
❑ 182 Kay-Jay Harris RC 2.00 .60
❑ 183 Marion Barber RC 2.50 .75
❑ 184 Ronnie Brown RC 8.00 2.40
❑ 185 Ryan Moats RC 2.50 .75
❑ 186 T.A. McLendon RC 2.00 .60
❑ 187 Vernand Morency RC 2.50 .75
❑ 188 Walter Reyes RC 2.50 .75
❑ 189 Braylon Edwards RC 8.00 2.40
❑ 190 Charles Frederick RC 2.00 .60
❑ 191 Chris Henry RC 2.50 .75
❑ 192 Courtney Roby RC 2.50 .75
❑ 193 Craig Bragg RC 2.50 .75
❑ 194 Craphonso Thorpe SP RC 25.00 7.50
❑ 195 Dante Ridgeway RC 2.00 .60
❑ 196 Fred Amey RC 2.00 .60
❑ 197 Fred Gibson RC 3.00 .90
❑ 198 J.R. Russell RC 2.00 .60
❑ 199 Jerome Mathis SP RC 25.00 7.50
❑ 200 Josh Davis RC 2.00 .60
❑ 201 Larry Brackins RC 1.25 .35
❑ 202 Mark Bradley RC 3.00 .90
❑ 203 Mark Clayton SP RC 50.00 15.00
❑ 204 Mike Williams 8.00 2.40
❑ 205 Reggie Brown RC 3.00 .90
❑ 206 Roddy White RC 2.50 .75
❑ 207 Roscoe Parrish RC 3.00 .90
❑ 208 Roydell Williams RC 2.00 .60
❑ 209 Steve Savoy RC 2.00 .60
❑ 210 Tab Perry RC 2.00 .60
❑ 211 Taylor Stubblefield RC 2.00 .60
❑ 212 Terrence Murphy RC 2.50 .75
❑ 213 Troy Williamson RC 5.00 1.50
❑ 214 Vincent Jackson RC 2.50 .75
❑ 215 Alex Smith TE RC 2.50 .75
❑ 216 Heath Miller RC 4.00 1.20
❑ 217 Dan Cody RC 3.00 .90
❑ 218 David Pollack RC 4.00 1.20
❑ 219 Erasmus James RC 3.00 .90
❑ 220 Justin Tuck RC 2.00 .60
❑ 221 Marcus Spears RC 3.00 .90
❑ 222 Matt Roth RC 2.50 .75
❑ 223 Anttaj Hawthorne RC 2.00 .60
❑ 224 Mike Patterson RC 2.50 .75
❑ 225 Shaun Cody RC 2.50 .75
❑ 226 Travis Johnson RC 2.50 .75
❑ 227 Channing Crowder RC 2.50 .75
❑ 228 Darryl Blackstock RC 2.00 .60
❑ 229 Demarcus Ware RC 3.00 .90
❑ 230 Derrick Johnson RC 4.00 1.20
❑ 231 Kevin Burnett RC 2.50 .75
❑ 232 Shawne Merriman RC 3.00 .90
❑ 233 Adam Jones RC 3.00 .90
❑ 234 Antrel Rolle RC 3.00 .90
❑ 235 Brandon Browner RC 1.25 .35
❑ 236 Bryant McFadden RC 2.50 .75
❑ 237 Carlos Rogers RC 3.00 .90
❑ 238 Corey Webster RC 2.50 .75
❑ 239 Fabian Washington RC 2.50 .75
❑ 240 Justin Miller RC 2.50 .75
❑ 241 Marlin Jackson RC 2.50 .75
❑ 242 Ernest Shazor RC 2.50 .75
❑ 243 Josh Bullocks RC 2.50 .75
❑ 244 Thomas Davis RC 2.50 .75

2005 Playoff Prestige Xtra Points Black

Nm-Mt Ex-Mt

*VETERANS: 8X TO 20X BASIC CARDS
*ROOKIES: 4X TO 10X BASIC CARDS
*ROOKIE SPs: .5X TO 1.2X BASIC CARDS
STATED PRINT RUN 25 SER.#'d SETS

2005 Playoff Prestige Xtra Points Green

Nm-Mt Ex-Mt

*VETERANS: 5X TO 12X BASIC CARDS
*ROOKIES: 2.5X TO 6X BASIC CARDS
*ROOKIE SPs: .4X TO 1X BASIC CARDS
STATED PRINT RUN 50 SER.#'d SETS

2005 Playoff Prestige Xtra Points Purple

Nm-Mt Ex-Mt

*VETERANS: 3X TO 8X BASIC CARDS
*ROOKIES: 1.5X TO 4X BASIC CARDS
*ROOKIE SPs: .3X TO .8X BASIC CARDS
STATED PRINT RUN 100 SER.#'d SETS

2005 Playoff Prestige Xtra Points Red

Nm-Mt Ex-Mt

*VETERANS: 3X TO 8X BASIC CARDS
*ROOKIES: 1.5X TO 4X BASIC CARDS
*ROOKIE SPs: .3X TO .8X BASIC CARDS
STATED PRINT RUN 125 SER.#'d SETS

2005 Playoff Prestige Changing Stripes

Nm-Mt Ex-Mt

STATED PRINT RUN 250 SER.#'d SETS
*PRIME: 1X TO 2.5X BASIC INSERTS

PRIME PRINT RUN 25 SER.#'d SETS

❑ CS1 Ahman Green	20.00	6.00
❑ CS2 Clinton Portis	20.00	6.00
❑ CS3 Duce Staley	20.00	6.00
❑ CS4 Jevon Kearse	15.00	4.50
❑ CS5 Terrell Owens	20.00	6.00
❑ CS6 Jeff Garcia	15.00	4.50
❑ CS7 Keyshawn Johnson	15.00	4.50
❑ CS8 Drew Bledsoe	20.00	6.00
❑ CS9 Jake Plummer	15.00	4.50
❑ CS10 Marshall Faulk	20.00	6.00

2005 Playoff Prestige Draft Picks

	Nm-Mt	Ex-Mt
COMPLETE SET (10)	40.00	12.00

STATED ODDS 1:24
*FOIL: 1X TO 2.5X BASIC INSERTS
FOIL PRINT RUN 100 SER.#'d SETS
*HOLOFOIL: 2.5X TO 6X BASIC INSERTS
HOLOFOIL PRINT RUN 25 SER.#'d SETS

❑ DP1 Alex Smith QB	12.00	3.60
❑ DP2 Aaron Rodgers	10.00	3.00
❑ DP3 Charlie Frye	4.00	1.20
❑ DP4 Cedric Benson	8.00	2.40
❑ DP5 Ronnie Brown	8.00	2.40
❑ DP6 Carnell Williams	8.00	2.40
❑ DP7 Vernand Morency	2.50	.75
❑ DP8 Braylon Edwards	8.00	2.40
❑ DP9 Troy Williamson	5.00	1.50
❑ DP10 Roddy White	2.50	.75

2005 Playoff Prestige Draft Picks Rights Autographs

STATED PRINT RUN 50 SER.#'d SETS

	Nm-Mt	Ex-Mt
❑ DP1 Alex Smith QB EXCH	250.00	75.00
❑ DP2 Aaron Rodgers EXCH	200.00	60.00
❑ DP3 Charlie Frye EXCH	60.00	18.00
❑ DP4 Cedric Benson EXCH	200.00	60.00
❑ DP5 Ronnie Brown	150.00	45.00
❑ DP6 Carnell Williams EXCH	150.00	45.00
❑ DP7 Vernand Morency EXCH	50.00	15.00
❑ DP8 Braylon Edwards EXCH	200.00	60.00
❑ DP9 Troy Williamson EXCH	80.00	24.00
❑ DP10 Roddy White EXCH	50.00	15.00

2005 Playoff Prestige Fans of the Game

	Nm-Mt	Ex-Mt
COMPLETE SET (4)	10.00	3.00

STATED ODDS 1:24

❑ FG1 Rick Reilly	2.50	.75
❑ FG2 Heather Mitts	3.00	.90
❑ FG3 Rulon Gardner	2.00	.60
❑ FG4 Sue Bird	3.00	.90

2005 Playoff Prestige Fans of the Game Autographs

STATED ODDS 1:625

	Nm-Mt	Ex-Mt
❑ FG1 Rick Reilly	50.00	15.00
❑ FG2 Heather Mitts	60.00	18.00
❑ FG3 Rulon Gardner	40.00	12.00
❑ FG4 Sue Bird	60.00	18.00

2005 Playoff Prestige Game Day Jerseys

STATED ODDS 1:49

	Nm-Mt	Ex-Mt
❑ GJ1 David Carr	12.00	3.60
❑ GJ2 Peyton Manning	20.00	6.00
❑ GJ3 Randy Moss	15.00	4.50
❑ GJ4 Donovan McNabb	15.00	4.50
❑ GJ5 Tom Brady	25.00	7.50
❑ GJ6 Larry Fitzgerald	12.00	3.60
❑ GJ7 Shaun Alexander	12.00	3.60
❑ GJ8 Anquan Boldin	10.00	3.00
❑ GJ9 Daunte Culpepper	12.00	3.60
❑ GJ10 Chris Brown	10.00	3.00
❑ GJ11 Isaac Bruce	12.00	3.60
❑ GJ12 Rod Smith	10.00	3.00
❑ GJ13 Roy Williams S	12.00	3.60
❑ GJ14 Tony Gonzalez	10.00	3.00
❑ GJ15 Torry Holt	12.00	3.60
❑ GJ16 John Abraham	10.00	3.00
❑ GJ17 Ike Hilliard	8.00	2.40
❑ GJ18 Jimmy Smith	10.00	3.00
❑ GJ19 Byron Leftwich	12.00	3.60
❑ GJ20 Stephen Davis	10.00	3.00
❑ GJ21 T.J. Duckett	8.00	2.40
❑ GJ22 Travis Henry	10.00	3.00
❑ GJ23 Julius Peppers	12.00	3.60
❑ GJ24 Charles Rogers	10.00	3.00
❑ GJ25 Eric Moulds	10.00	3.00
❑ GJ26 Freddie Mitchell	8.00	2.40
❑ GJ27 Anthony Thomas	8.00	2.40
❑ GJ28 Steve McNair	12.00	3.60
❑ GJ29 Brian Urlacher	12.00	3.60
❑ GJ30 Donte Stallworth	10.00	3.00

2005 Playoff Prestige Gridiron Heritage

STATED ODDS 1:24
*FOIL: .6X TO 1.5X BASIC INSERTS
FOIL PRINT RUN 100 SER.#'d SETS
*HOLOFOIL: 2X TO 5X BASIC INSERTS
HOLOFOIL PRINT RUN 25 SER.#'d SETS

	Nm-Mt	Ex-Mt
❑ GH1 Brett Favre	8.00	2.40
❑ GH2 Edgerrin James	3.00	.90
❑ GH3 Byron Leftwich	3.00	.90
❑ GH4 Peyton Manning	5.00	1.50
❑ GH5 Larry Fitzgerald	3.00	.90
❑ GH6 Shaun Alexander	3.00	.90
❑ GH7 Daunte Culpepper	3.00	.90
❑ GH8 Marshall Faulk	3.00	.90
❑ GH9 Steve McNair	3.00	.90
❑ GH10 Zach Thomas	3.00	.90
❑ GH11 Mike Alstott	2.00	.60
❑ GH12 Jeremiah Trotter	1.50	.45
❑ GH13 Drew Brees	3.00	.90
❑ GH14 Isaac Bruce	2.00	.60
❑ GH15 Chris Chambers	2.00	.60
❑ GH16 Santana Moss	2.00	.60
❑ GH17 Peerless Price	2.00	.60
❑ GH18 Donald Driver	2.00	.60
❑ GH19 Amani Toomer	2.00	.60
❑ GH20 Todd Pinkston	1.50	.45
❑ GH21 Derrick Mason	2.00	.60
❑ GH22 Jimmy Smith	2.00	.60
❑ GH23 Michael Vick	5.00	1.50
❑ GH24 Andre Johnson	2.00	.60
❑ GH25 Josh McCown	2.00	.60

2005 Playoff Prestige Gridiron Heritage Jerseys

STATED ODDS 1:60

	Nm-Mt	Ex-Mt
❑ GH1 Brett Favre	25.00	7.50
❑ GH2 Edgerrin James	10.00	3.00
❑ GH3 Byron Leftwich	10.00	3.00
❑ GH4 Peyton Manning	15.00	4.50
❑ GH5 Larry Fitzgerald	10.00	3.00
❑ GH6 Shaun Alexander	10.00	3.00
❑ GH7 Daunte Culpepper	10.00	3.00
❑ GH8 Marshall Faulk	10.00	3.00
❑ GH9 Steve McNair	10.00	3.00
❑ GH10 Zach Thomas	10.00	3.00
❑ GH11 Mike Alstott	8.00	2.40
❑ GH12 Jeremiah Trotter	8.00	2.40
❑ GH13 Drew Brees	10.00	3.00
❑ GH14 Isaac Bruce	10.00	3.00
❑ GH15 Chris Chambers	8.00	2.40
❑ GH16 Santana Moss	8.00	2.40
❑ GH17 Peerless Price	8.00	2.40
❑ GH18 Donald Driver	8.00	2.40
❑ GH19 Amani Toomer	8.00	2.40
❑ GH20 Todd Pinkston	8.00	2.40
❑ GH21 Derrick Mason	8.00	2.40
❑ GH22 Jimmy Smith	8.00	2.40
❑ GH23 Michael Vick	15.00	4.50
❑ GH24 Andre Johnson	8.00	2.40
❑ GH25 Josh McCown	8.00	2.40

2005 Playoff Prestige League Leaders

STATED ODDS 1:24
*FOIL: .6X TO 1.5X BASIC INSERTS
FOIL PRINT RUN 100 SER.#'d SETS
*HOLOFOIL: 2X TO 5X BASIC INSERTS
HOLOFOIL PRINT RUN 25 SER.#'d SETS

	Nm-Mt	Ex-Mt
❑ LL1 Peyton Manning Trent Green	5.00	1.50
❑ LL2 Daunte Culpepper Brett Favre	8.00	2.40
❑ LL3 Donovan McNabb	4.00	1.20

Aaron Brooks		
❑ LL4 Jake Plummer Drew Bledsoe	3.00	.90
❑ LL5 Tom Brady David Carr	6.00	1.80
❑ LL6 Marc Bulger Matt Hasselbeck	3.00	.90
❑ LL7 Carson Palmer Byron Leftwich	3.00	.90
❑ LL8 Shaun Alexander Clinton Portis	3.00	.90
❑ LL9 Edgerrin James Corey Dillon	3.00	.90
❑ LL10 Curtis Martin LaDainian Tomlinson	3.00	.90
❑ LL11 Tiki Barber Ahman Green	3.00	.90
❑ LL12 Rudi Johnson Fred Taylor	2.00	.60
❑ LL13 Willis McGahee Domanick Davis	3.00	.90
❑ LL14 Kevin Jones Deuce McAllister	4.00	1.20
❑ LL15 Keyshawn Johnson Laveranues Coles	2.00	.60
❑ LL16 Javon Walker Torry Holt	3.00	.90
❑ LL17 Chad Johnson Drew Bennett	2.00	.60
❑ LL18 Isaac Bruce Terrell Owens	3.00	.90
❑ LL19 Rod Smith Plaxico Burress	2.00	.60
❑ LL20 Michael Clayton Darrell Jackson	3.00	.90
❑ LL21 Curtis Martin Corey Dillon Shaun Alexander#Tiki Barber	4.00	1.20
❑ LL22 Edgerrin James LaDainian Tomlinson Clinton Portis#Ahman Green	4.00	1.20
❑ LL23 Rudi Johnson Fred Taylor Kevin Jones#Deuce McAllister	5.00	1.50
❑ LL24 Trent Green Peyton Manning Brett Favre#Daunte Culpepper	10.00	3.00
❑ LL25 Jake Plummer Tom Brady Jake Delhomme#Donovan McNabb	8.00	2.40
❑ LL26 David Carr Carson Palmer Marc Bulger#Aaron Brooks	4.00	1.20
❑ LL27 Chad Johnson Drew Bennett Keyshawn Johnson#Laveranues Coles	2.50	.75
❑ LL28 Tony Gonzalez Plaxico Burress Javon Walker#Torry Holt	2.50	.75
❑ LL29 Jimmy Smith Rod Smith Isaac Bruce#Donald Driver	2.50	.75
❑ LL30 Derrick Mason Andre Johnson Terrell Owens#Michael Clayton	4.00	1.20

2005 Playoff Prestige League Leaders Jerseys

STATED PRINT RUN 250 SER.#'d SETS
*PRIME: 1X TO 2.5X BASIC JERSEYS
PRIME PRINT RUN 25 SER.#'d SETS

	Nm-Mt	Ex-Mt
❑ LL1 Peyton Manning Trent Green	20.00	6.00
❑ LL2 Daunte Culpepper Brett Favre	30.00	9.00
❑ LL3 Donovan McNabb Aaron Brooks	15.00	4.50
❑ LL4 Jake Plummer Drew Bledsoe	12.00	3.60
❑ LL5 Tom Brady David Carr	25.00	7.50
❑ LL6 Marc Bulger Matt Hasselbeck	12.00	3.60
❑ LL7 Carson Palmer Byron Leftwich	12.00	3.60
❑ LL8 Shaun Alexander Clinton Portis	12.00	3.60
❑ LL9 Edgerrin James Corey Dillon	12.00	3.60
❑ LL10 Curtis Martin LaDainian Tomlinson	12.00	3.60
❑ LL11 Tiki Barber Ahman Green	12.00	3.60
❑ LL12 Rudi Johnson Fred Taylor	10.00	3.00
❑ LL13 Willis McGahee Domanick Davis	10.00	3.00
❑ LL14 Kevin Jones Deuce McAllister	15.00	4.50
❑ LL15 Keyshawn Johnson Laveranues Coles	10.00	3.00
❑ LL16 Javon Walker Torry Holt	12.00	3.60
❑ LL17 Chad Johnson Drew Bennett	10.00	3.00
❑ LL18 Isaac Bruce Terrell Owens	12.00	3.60
❑ LL19 Rod Smith Plaxico Burress	12.00	3.60
❑ LL20 Michael Clayton Darrell Jackson	12.00	3.60
❑ LL21 Curtis Martin Corey Dillon Shaun Alexander#Tiki Barber	20.00	6.00
❑ LL22 Edgerrin James LaDainian Tomlinson Clinton Portis#Ahman Green	20.00	6.00
❑ LL23 Rudi Johnson Fred Taylor Kevin Jones#Deuce McAllister	20.00	6.00
❑ LL24 Trent Green Peyton Manning Brett Favre#Daunte Culpepper	50.00	15.00
❑ LL25 Jake Plummer Tom Brady Jake Delhomme#Donovan McNabb	40.00	12.00
❑ LL26 David Carr Carson Palmer Marc Bulger#Aaron Brooks	20.00	6.00
❑ LL27 Chad Johnson Drew Bennett Keyshawn Johnson#Laveranues Coles	15.00	4.50
❑ LL28 Tony Gonzalez Plaxico Burress Javon Walker#Torry Holt	20.00	6.00
❑ LL29 Jimmy Smith Rod Smith Isaac Bruce#Donald Driver	20.00	6.00
❑ LL30 Derrick Mason Andre Johnson Terrell Owens#Michael Clayton	20.00	6.00

2005 Playoff Prestige Prestigious Pros Orange

Nm-Mt Ex-Mt

ORANGE PRINT RUN 500 SER.#'d SETS
*BLUE: .6X TO 1.5X ORANGE

BLUE PRINT RUN 250 SER.#'d SETS
*GOLD: 2X TO 5X BASIC INSERTS
GOLD PRINT RUN 25 SER.#'d SETS
*GREEN: 1X TO 2.5X BASIC INSERTS
GREEN PRINT RUN 75 SER.#'d SETS
UNPRICED PLATINUM PRINT RUN 10 SETS
*PURPLE: 1X TO 2.5X BASIC INSERTS
PURPLE PRINT RUN 100 SER.#'d SETS
*RED: .8X TO 2X BASIC INSERTS
RED PRINT RUN 150 SER.#'d SETS
*SILVER: 1.2X TO 3X BASIC INSERTS
SILVER PRINT RUN 50 SER.#'d SETS

	Nm-Mt	Ex-Mt
❑ PP1 Aaron Brooks	1.50	.45
❑ PP2 Andre Johnson	1.50	.45
❑ PP3 Ben Roethlisberger	8.00	2.40
❑ PP4 Brett Favre	6.00	1.80
❑ PP5 Brian Urlacher	2.50	.75
❑ PP6 Byron Leftwich	2.50	.75
❑ PP7 Carson Palmer	2.50	.75
❑ PP8 Chad Pennington	3.00	.90
❑ PP9 Corey Dillon	1.50	.45
❑ PP10 Daunte Culpepper	2.50	.75
❑ PP11 David Carr	2.50	.75
❑ PP12 Deuce McAllister	2.50	.75
❑ PP13 Donovan McNabb	3.00	.90
❑ PP14 Drew Bledsoe	2.50	.75
❑ PP15 Drew Brees	2.50	.75
❑ PP16 Duce Staley	1.50	.45
❑ PP17 Edgerrin James	2.50	.75
❑ PP18 Hines Ward	2.50	.75
❑ PP19 Isaac Bruce	1.50	.45
❑ PP20 Jake Plummer	1.50	.45
❑ PP21 Jamal Lewis	2.50	.75
❑ PP22 Javon Walker	1.50	.45
❑ PP23 Jeff Garcia	1.50	.45
❑ PP24 Jeremy Shockey	2.50	.75
❑ PP25 Jevon Kearse	1.50	.45
❑ PP26 Joey Harrington	2.50	.75
❑ PP27 Keyshawn Johnson	1.50	.45
❑ PP28 LaDainian Tomlinson	2.50	.75
❑ PP29 LaVar Arrington	2.50	.75
❑ PP30 Lee Suggs	1.50	.45
❑ PP31 Marc Bulger	2.50	.75
❑ PP32 Marshall Faulk	2.50	.75
❑ PP33 Marvin Harrison	2.50	.75
❑ PP34 Matt Hasselbeck	1.50	.45
❑ PP35 Michael Vick	4.00	1.20
❑ PP36 Peyton Manning	4.00	1.20
❑ PP37 Plaxico Burress	1.50	.45
❑ PP38 Priest Holmes	2.50	.75
❑ PP39 Randy Moss	3.00	.90
❑ PP40 Ray Lewis	2.50	.75
❑ PP41 Rex Grossman	1.50	.45
❑ PP42 Rudi Johnson	1.50	.45
❑ PP43 Shaun Alexander	2.50	.75
❑ PP44 Steve McNair	2.50	.75
❑ PP45 Terrell Owens	2.50	.75
❑ PP46 Tiki Barber	1.50	.45
❑ PP47 Tom Brady	5.00	1.50
❑ PP48 Tony Gonzalez	1.50	.45
❑ PP49 Torry Holt	2.50	.75
❑ PP50 Trent Green	1.50	.45

2005 Playoff Prestige Prestigious Pros Gold Jerseys

GOLD PRINT RUN 100 SER.#'d SETS
UNPRICED PLATINUM PRINT RUN 10 SETS

	Nm-Mt	Ex-Mt
❑ PP1 Aaron Brooks	10.00	3.00
❑ PP2 Andre Johnson	10.00	3.00
❑ PP3 Ben Roethlisberger	40.00	12.00
❑ PP4 Brett Favre	30.00	9.00
❑ PP5 Brian Urlacher	12.00	3.60
❑ PP6 Byron Leftwich	12.00	3.60
❑ PP7 Carson Palmer	12.00	3.60
❑ PP8 Chad Pennington	15.00	4.50
❑ PP9 Corey Dillon	12.00	3.60
❑ PP10 Daunte Culpepper	12.00	3.60
❑ PP11 David Carr	12.00	3.60
❑ PP12 Deuce McAllister	12.00	3.60
❑ PP13 Donovan McNabb	15.00	4.50
❑ PP14 Drew Bledsoe	12.00	3.60
❑ PP15 Drew Brees	10.00	3.00
❑ PP16 Duce Staley	12.00	3.60
❑ PP17 Edgerrin James	12.00	3.60
❑ PP18 Hines Ward	12.00	3.60
❑ PP19 Isaac Bruce	12.00	3.60
❑ PP20 Jake Plummer	12.00	3.60
❑ PP21 Jamal Lewis	12.00	3.60
❑ PP22 Javon Walker	10.00	3.00
❑ PP23 Jeff Garcia	10.00	3.00
❑ PP24 Jeremy Shockey	12.00	3.60
❑ PP25 Jevon Kearse	10.00	3.00
❑ PP26 Joey Harrington	12.00	3.60
❑ PP27 Keyshawn Johnson	10.00	3.00
❑ PP28 LaDainian Tomlinson	12.00	3.60
❑ PP29 LaVar Arrington	12.00	3.60
❑ PP30 Lee Suggs	10.00	3.00
❑ PP31 Marc Bulger	12.00	3.60
❑ PP32 Marshall Faulk	12.00	3.60
❑ PP33 Marvin Harrison	12.00	3.60
❑ PP34 Matt Hasselbeck	10.00	3.00
❑ PP35 Michael Vick	20.00	6.00
❑ PP36 Peyton Manning	20.00	6.00
❑ PP37 Plaxico Burress	12.00	3.60
❑ PP38 Priest Holmes	12.00	3.60
❑ PP39 Randy Moss	15.00	4.50
❑ PP40 Ray Lewis	12.00	3.60
❑ PP41 Rex Grossman	10.00	3.00
❑ PP42 Rudi Johnson	10.00	3.00
❑ PP43 Shaun Alexander	12.00	3.60
❑ PP44 Steve McNair	12.00	3.60
❑ PP45 Terrell Owens	12.00	3.60
❑ PP46 Tiki Barber	10.00	3.00
❑ PP47 Tom Brady	25.00	7.50
❑ PP48 Tony Gonzalez	10.00	3.00
❑ PP49 Torry Holt	12.00	3.60
❑ PP50 Trent Green	10.00	3.00

2005 Playoff Prestige Stars of the NFL

Nm-Mt Ex-Mt

STATED ODDS 1:24
*FOIL: .8X TO 2X BASIC INSERTS
FOIL PRINT RUN 100 SER.#'d SETS
*HOLOFOIL: 2X TO 5X BASIC INSERTS

HOLOFOIL PRINT RUN 25 SER.#'d SETS

	Nm-Mt	Ex-Mt
❑ 1 Aaron Brooks	2.00	.60
❑ 2 Andre Johnson	2.00	.60
❑ 3 Brett Favre	8.00	2.40
❑ 4 Brian Urlacher	3.00	.90
❑ 5 Byron Leftwich	3.00	.90
❑ 6 Chad Johnson	2.00	.60
❑ 7 Chad Pennington	4.00	1.20
❑ 8 Chris Brown	2.00	.60
❑ 9 Daunte Culpepper	3.00	.90
❑ 10 David Carr	3.00	.90
❑ 11 Donovan McNabb	4.00	1.20
❑ 12 Drew Bledsoe	3.00	.90
❑ 13 Edgerrin James	3.00	.90
❑ 14 Isaac Bruce	2.00	.60
❑ 15 Jake Delhomme	3.00	.90
❑ 16 Javon Walker	2.00	.60
❑ 17 Jeremy Shockey	3.00	.90
❑ 18 LaDainian Tomlinson	3.00	.90
❑ 19 Marvin Harrison	3.00	.90
❑ 20 Matt Hasselbeck	2.00	.60
❑ 21 Michael Vick	5.00	1.50
❑ 22 Peyton Manning	5.00	1.50
❑ 23 Randy Moss	4.00	1.20
❑ 24 Priest Holmes	3.00	.90
❑ 25 Tom Brady	6.00	1.80

2005 Playoff Prestige Stars of the NFL Jersey

STATED ODDS 1:104
*PRIME: 1X TO 2.5X BASIC INSERTS
PRIME PRINT RUN 25 SER.#'d SETS

	Nm-Mt	Ex-Mt
❑ 1 Aaron Brooks	10.00	3.00
❑ 2 Andre Johnson	10.00	3.00
❑ 3 Brett Favre	30.00	9.00
❑ 4 Brian Urlacher	12.00	3.60
❑ 5 Byron Leftwich	12.00	3.60
❑ 6 Chad Johnson	10.00	3.00
❑ 7 Chad Pennington	15.00	4.50
❑ 8 Chris Brown	10.00	3.00
❑ 9 Daunte Culpepper	12.00	3.60
❑ 10 David Carr	12.00	3.60
❑ 11 Donovan McNabb	15.00	4.50
❑ 12 Drew Bledsoe	12.00	3.60
❑ 13 Edgerrin James	12.00	3.60
❑ 14 Isaac Bruce	12.00	3.60
❑ 15 Jake Delhomme	12.00	3.60
❑ 16 Javon Walker	10.00	3.00
❑ 17 Jeremy Shockey	12.00	3.60
❑ 18 LaDainian Tomlinson	12.00	3.60
❑ 19 Marvin Harrison	12.00	3.60
❑ 20 Matt Hasselbeck	10.00	3.00
❑ 21 Michael Vick	20.00	6.00
❑ 22 Peyton Manning	20.00	6.00
❑ 23 Randy Moss	15.00	4.50
❑ 24 Priest Holmes	12.00	3.60
❑ 25 Tom Brady	25.00	7.50

2005 Playoff Prestige Super Bowl Heroes

	Nm-Mt	Ex-Mt
COMPLETE SET (10)	20.00	6.00

STATED ODDS 1:24
*FOIL: .8X TO 2X BASIC INSERTS

FOIL PRINT RUN 100 SER.#'d SETS

	Nm-Mt	Ex-Mt
❑ SB1 Tom Brady	6.00	1.80
❑ SB2 Deion Branch	2.00	.60
❑ SB3 Corey Dillon	2.00	.60
❑ SB4 David Givens	2.00	.60
❑ SB5 Mike Vrabel	3.00	.90
❑ SB6 Tedy Bruschi	2.00	.60
❑ SB7 Rodney Harrison	2.00	.60
❑ SB8 Adam Vinatieri	3.00	.90
❑ SB9 Donovan McNabb	4.00	1.20
❑ SB10 Terrell Owens	3.00	.90

2005 Playoff Prestige Super Bowl Heroes Holofoil

HOLOFOIL PRINT RUN 25 SER.#'d SETS

	Nm-Mt	Ex-Mt
❑ SB1 Tom Brady SP	80.00	24.00
❑ SB1AU Tom Brady AU	200.00	60.00
❑ SB2 Deion Branch	10.00	3.00
❑ SB3 Corey Dillon AU	60.00	18.00
❑ SB4 David Givens	10.00	3.00
❑ SB5 Mike Vrabel	15.00	4.50
❑ SB6 Tedy Bruschi SP	25.00	7.50
❑ SB6AU Tedy Bruschi AU SP	150.00	45.00
❑ SB7 Rodney Harrison	10.00	3.00
❑ SB8 Adam Vinatieri SP	40.00	12.00
❑ SB8AU Adam Vinatieri AU SP	100.00	30.00
❑ SB9 Donovan McNabb AU	80.00	24.00
❑ SB10 Terrell Owens	15.00	4.50

2005 Playoff Prestige Turning Pro Jerseys

STATED PRINT RUN 250 SER.#'d SETS
*PRIME: 1X TO 2.5X BASIC INSERTS
PRIME PRINT RUN 25 SER.#'d SETS

	Nm-Mt	Ex-Mt
❑ TP1 Lee Suggs	15.00	4.50
❑ TP2 Barry Sanders	40.00	12.00
❑ TP3 Andre Johnson	20.00	6.00
❑ TP4 Kyle Boller	15.00	4.50
❑ TP5 Carson Palmer	20.00	6.00
❑ TP6 Michael Vick	30.00	9.00
❑ TP7 Laveranues Coles	15.00	4.50
❑ TP8 Clinton Portis	20.00	6.00
❑ TP9 Edgerrin James	20.00	6.00
❑ TP10 Marshall Faulk	20.00	6.00

2002 Playoff Prime Signatures

	Nm-Mt	Ex-Mt
❑ 1 Aaron Brooks	5.00	1.50
❑ 2 Brett Favre	12.00	3.60
❑ 3 Drew Bledsoe	6.00	1.80
❑ 4 Jake Plummer	3.00	.90
❑ 5 Jeff Blake	2.00	.60
❑ 6 Jevon Kearse	3.00	.90
❑ 7 Ricky Williams	5.00	1.50
❑ 8 Terrell Davis	6.00	1.80
❑ 9 Chris Chambers	5.00	1.50
❑ 10 Cris Carter	5.00	1.50
❑ 11 Emmitt Smith	12.00	3.60
❑ 12 Randall Cunningham	3.00	.90
❑ 13 Corey Dillon	3.00	.90
❑ 14 Brian Griese	5.00	1.50
❑ 15 Isaac Bruce	5.00	1.50
❑ 16 Koren Robinson	3.00	.90
❑ 17 David Terrell	5.00	1.50
❑ 18 Mark Brunell	5.00	1.50
❑ 19 Eric Moulds	3.00	.90
❑ 20 Kevan Barlow	3.00	.90
❑ 21 David Boston	5.00	1.50
❑ 22 LaMont Jordan	5.00	1.50
❑ 23 Jimmy Smith	3.00	.90
❑ 24 Marvin Harrison	5.00	1.50
❑ 25 Marcus Robinson	3.00	.90
❑ 26 Ray Lewis	5.00	1.50
❑ 27 Mike Anderson	5.00	1.50
❑ 28 Randy Moss	10.00	3.00
❑ 29 Michael Bennett	3.00	.90
❑ 30 Quincy Carter	3.00	.90
❑ 31 Tim Brown	5.00	1.50
❑ 32 Michael Strahan	3.00	.90
❑ 33 Tony Gonzalez	3.00	.90
❑ 34 Santana Moss	5.00	1.50
❑ 35 Torry Holt	5.00	1.50
❑ 36 Anthony Thomas	5.00	1.50
❑ 37 Chris Weinke	3.00	.90
❑ 38 Deuce McAllister	6.00	1.80
❑ 39 Drew Brees	5.00	1.50
❑ 40 Edgerrin James	6.00	1.80
❑ 41 Freddie Mitchell	3.00	.90
❑ 42 James Jackson	2.00	.60
❑ 43 Kendrell Bell	5.00	1.50
❑ 44 LaDainian Tomlinson	8.00	2.40
❑ 45 Mike McMahon	5.00	1.50
❑ 46 Quincy Morgan	3.00	.90
❑ 47 Robert Ferguson	2.00	.60
❑ 48 Steve Smith	3.00	.90
❑ 49 Terrell Owens	5.00	1.50
❑ 50 Eddie George	5.00	1.50
❑ 51 Kurt Warner	5.00	1.50
❑ 52 Chad Johnson	5.00	1.50
❑ 53 Dan Marino	15.00	4.50
❑ 54 Jim Kelly	8.00	2.40
❑ 55 John Elway	15.00	4.50
❑ 56 Michael Irvin	5.00	1.50
❑ 57 Phil Simms	3.00	.90
❑ 58 Steve Young	8.00	2.40
❑ 59 Troy Aikman	8.00	2.40
❑ 60 Warren Moon	5.00	1.50
❑ 61 Barry Sanders	8.00	2.40
❑ 62 Joe Montana	20.00	6.00
❑ 63 Joe Namath	6.00	1.80
❑ 64 Thurman Thomas	3.00	.90
❑ 65 T.J. Duckett RC	30.00	9.00
❑ 66 William Green RC	30.00	9.00
❑ 67 Travis Stephens RC	12.00	3.60
❑ 68 Tim Carter RC	12.00	3.60
❑ 69 Terry Charles RC	12.00	3.60
❑ 70 Roy Williams RC	40.00	12.00
❑ 71 Marquise Walker RC	12.00	3.60
❑ 72 Rohan Davey RC	15.00	4.50
❑ 73 Quentin Jammer RC	15.00	4.50
❑ 74 Reche Caldwell RC	15.00	4.50
❑ 75 Maurice Morris RC	15.00	4.50
❑ 76 Woody Dantzler RC	15.00	4.50
❑ 77 Patrick Ramsey RC	30.00	9.00
❑ 78 Tavon Mason RC	8.00	2.40
❑ 79 Ladell Betts RC	15.00	4.50
❑ 80 Kahlil Hill RC	12.00	3.60
❑ 81 Josh Scobey RC	15.00	4.50
❑ 82 Brian Westbrook RC	25.00	7.50
❑ 83 Javon Walker RC	30.00	9.00
❑ 84 DeShaun Foster RC	15.00	4.50
❑ 85 Kelly Campbell RC	12.00	3.60
❑ 86 Ashley Lelie RC	30.00	9.00
❑ 87 Donte Stallworth RC	30.00	9.00
❑ 88 David Carr RC	60.00	18.00
❑ 89 Kurt Kittner RC	12.00	3.60
❑ 90 Clinton Portis RC	60.00	18.00
❑ 91 Josh Reed RC	15.00	4.50
❑ 92 Joey Harrington RC	60.00	18.00
❑ 93 Antwaan Randle El RC	20.00	6.00
❑ 94 Randy Fasani RC	12.00	3.60
❑ 95 Cliff Russell RC	12.00	3.60
❑ 96 John Henderson RC	15.00	4.50
❑ 97 Luke Staley RC	12.00	3.60
❑ 98 Antonio Bryant RC	15.00	4.50
❑ 99 Jonathan Wells RC	15.00	4.50
❑ 100 Chester Taylor RC	15.00	4.50
❑ 101 Lamar Gordon RC	15.00	4.50
❑ 102 Deion Branch RC	30.00	9.00
❑ 103 Josh McCown RC	20.00	6.00
❑ 104 Andre Davis RC	15.00	4.50
❑ 105 Freddie Milons RC	12.00	3.60
❑ 106 David Garrard RC	15.00	4.50
❑ 107 Chad Hutchinson RC	15.00	4.50
❑ 108 Jabar Gaffney RC	15.00	4.50
❑ 109 Eric Crouch RC	25.00	7.50
❑ 110 Albert Haynesworth RC	12.00	3.60
❑ NNO Jeff Garcia TIN	5.00	1.50

2004 Playoff Prime Signatures

1-100 PRINT RUN 999 SER.#'d SETS
101-125 AU PRINT RUN 199 SER.#'d SETS
126-158 AU PRINT RUN 99 SER.#'d SETS

	Nm-Mt	Ex-Mt
❑ 1 Anquan Boldin	4.00	1.20
❑ 2 Josh McCown	3.00	.90
❑ 3 Alge Crumpler	3.00	.90
❑ 4 Michael Vick	8.00	2.40
❑ 5 Jamal Lewis	4.00	1.20
❑ 6 Todd Heap	3.00	.90
❑ 7 Jim Kelly	6.00	1.80
❑ 8 Thurman Thomas	4.00	1.20
❑ 9 Travis Henry	3.00	.90
❑ 10 Jake Delhomme	4.00	1.20
❑ 11 Stephen Davis	3.00	.90
❑ 12 Steve Smith	3.00	.90
❑ 13 Brian Urlacher	5.00	1.50
❑ 14 Dick Butkus	6.00	1.80
❑ 15 Gale Sayers	6.00	1.80
❑ 16 Mike Ditka	5.00	1.50
❑ 17 Mike Singletary	5.00	1.50
❑ 18 Rex Grossman	4.00	1.20
❑ 19 Richard Dent	3.00	.90
❑ 20 Chad Johnson	3.00	.90
❑ 21 Rudi Johnson	3.00	.90
❑ 22 Jim Brown	8.00	2.40
❑ 23 Lee Suggs	4.00	1.20
❑ 24 Ozzie Newsome	4.00	1.20
❑ 25 Paul Warfield	4.00	1.20
❑ 26 Quincy Morgan	3.00	.90
❑ 27 William Green	3.00	.90
❑ 28 Antonio Bryant	3.00	.90
❑ 29 Herschel Walker	4.00	1.20
❑ 30 Jimmy Johnson	4.00	1.20
❑ 31 Keyshawn Johnson	3.00	.90
❑ 32 Roger Staubach	8.00	2.40
❑ 33 Terence Newman	3.00	.90
❑ 34 Tony Dorsett	5.00	1.50
❑ 35 Terrell Davis	4.00	1.20
❑ 36 Joey Harrington	4.00	1.20
❑ 37 Ahman Green	4.00	1.20
❑ 38 Javon Walker	3.00	.90
❑ 39 Paul Hornung	5.00	1.50
❑ 40 Reggie White	5.00	1.50
❑ 41 Robert Ferguson	2.50	.75
❑ 42 Sterling Sharpe	4.00	1.20
❑ 43 David Carr	4.00	1.20
❑ 44 Domanick Davis	4.00	1.20
❑ 45 Earl Campbell	5.00	1.50
❑ 46 Peyton Manning	6.00	1.80
❑ 47 Reggie Wayne	3.00	.90
❑ 48 Dante Hall	4.00	1.20
❑ 49 Priest Holmes	5.00	1.50
❑ 50 Trent Green	3.00	.90
❑ 51 A.J. Feeley	4.00	1.20
❑ 52 Don Shula	5.00	1.50
❑ 53 Chris Chambers	3.00	.90
❑ 54 Travis Minor	2.50	.75
❑ 55 Fran Tarkenton	6.00	1.80
❑ 56 Bill Belichick	5.00	1.50
❑ 57 Tom Brady	6.00	1.80
❑ 58 Aaron Brooks	3.00	.90
❑ 59 Deuce McAllister	4.00	1.20
❑ 60 Boo Williams	2.50	.75
❑ 61 Joe Horn	3.00	.90
❑ 62 Lawrence Taylor	5.00	1.50
❑ 63 Mark Bavaro	2.50	.75
❑ 64 Michael Strahan	3.00	.90
❑ 65 Tiki Barber	3.00	.90
❑ 66 Herman Edwards	4.00	1.20
❑ 67 Joe Namath	8.00	2.40
❑ 68 Justin McCareins	2.50	.75
❑ 69 LaMont Jordan	3.00	.90
❑ 70 Santana Moss	3.00	.90
❑ 71 Bo Jackson	8.00	2.40
❑ 72 Fred Biletnikoff	5.00	1.50
❑ 73 George Blanda	5.00	1.50
❑ 74 Jim Plunkett	4.00	1.20
❑ 75 Marcus Allen	5.00	1.50
❑ 76 Barry Switzer	10.00	3.00
❑ 77 Correll Buckhalter	3.00	.90
❑ 78 Donovan McNabb	5.00	1.50
❑ 79 Antwaan Randle El	3.00	.90
❑ 80 Bill Cowher	4.00	1.20
❑ 81 Franco Harris	6.00	1.80
❑ 82 Jack Lambert	6.00	1.80
❑ 83 Joe Greene	5.00	1.50
❑ 84 Kendrell Bell	3.00	.90
❑ 85 L.C. Greenwood	4.00	1.20
❑ 86 Mel Blount	4.00	1.20
❑ 87 Terry Bradshaw	8.00	2.40
❑ 88 LaDainian Tomlinson	4.00	1.20
❑ 89 Andre Carter	2.50	.75
❑ 90 Bill Walsh	5.00	1.50
❑ 91 Shaun Alexander	4.00	1.20
❑ 92 Steve Largent	5.00	1.50
❑ 93 Matt Hasselbeck	3.00	.90
❑ 94 Torry Holt	4.00	1.20
❑ 95 Clinton Portis	4.00	1.20
❑ 96 Laveranues Coles	3.00	.90
❑ 97 Mark Brunell	3.00	.90
❑ 98 Patrick Ramsey	3.00	.90
❑ 99 Reuben Droughns	3.00	.90
❑ 100 Sonny Jurgensen	4.00	1.20
❑ 101 Matt Mauck AU RC	25.00	7.50
Triandos Luke AU RC		
❑ 102 D.J. Williams AU RC	20.00	6.00
Brandon Miree AU RC		
❑ 103 Carlos Francis AU RC	25.00	7.50
Johnnie Morant AU RC		
❑ 104 Jonathan Vilma AU RC	25.00	7.50
Derrick Ward AU RC		
❑ 105 Vince Wilfork AU RC	20.00	6.00
P.K. Sam AU RC		
❑ 106 Jim Sorgi AU RC	25.00	7.50
Ran Carthon AU RC		
❑ 107 Troy Fleming AU RC	25.00	7.50
Jarrett Payton AU RC		
❑ 108 Jason Babin AU RC	25.00	7.50

B.J. Symons AU RC
❑ 109 Josh Harris AU RC 25.00 7.50
Clarence Moore AU RC
❑ 110 Maurice Mann AU RC 20.00 6.00
Casey Bramlet AU RC
❑ 111 Sean Jones AU RC 20.00 6.00
Adimchinobe Echemandu AU RC
❑ 112 Andy Hall AU RC 20.00 6.00
Bruce Perry AU RC
❑ 113 Jamaar Taylor AU RC 25.00 7.50
Jared Lorenzen AU RC
❑ 114 Chris Gamble AU RC 25.00 7.50
Drew Carter AU RC
❑ 115 Drew Henson AU RC 40.00 12.00
Craig Krenzel AU RC
❑ 116 Tommie Harris AU RC 25.00 7.50
Ahmad Carroll AU RC
❑ 117 Jeff Smoker AU RC 25.00 7.50
D.J. Hackett AU RC
❑ 118 Ernest Wilford AU RC 25.00 7.50
Jerricho Cotchery AU RC
❑ 119 Will Smith AU RC 25.00 7.50
Kenechi Udeze AU RC
❑ 120 Samie Parker AU RC 25.00 7.50
Michael Turner AU RC
❑ 121 Sloan Thomas AU RC 20.00 6.00
B.J. Johnson AU RC
❑ 122 John Navarre AU RC 25.00 7.50
Cody Pickett AU RC
❑ 123 Ricardo Colclough AU RC 25.00 7.50
Quincy Wilson AU RC
❑ 124 Sean Taylor RC 25.00 7.50
Chris Cooley AU RC
❑ 125 Michael Boulware AU RC 20.00 6.00
Teddy Lehman RC
❑ 126 J.P. Losman AU RC 135.00 40.00
❑ 127 Lee Evans AU RC 80.00 24.00
❑ 128 Ben Watson AU RC 40.00 12.00
❑ 129 Cedric Cobbs AU RC 40.00 12.00
❑ 130 Devard Darling AU RC 40.00 12.00
❑ 131 Chris Perry AU RC 60.00 18.00
❑ 132 Kellen Winslow AU RC 100.00 30.00
❑ 133 Luke McCown AU RC 40.00 12.00
❑ 134 Ben Roethlisberger AU RC 600.00 180.00
❑ 135 Dunta Robinson AU RC 50.00 15.00
❑ 136 Greg Jones AU RC 50.00 15.00
❑ 137 Reggie Williams AU RC 50.00 15.00
❑ 138 Ben Troupe AU RC 40.00 12.00
❑ 139 Tatum Bell AU RC 100.00 30.00
❑ 140 Darius Watts AU RC 50.00 15.00
❑ 141 Robert Gallery AU RC 50.00 15.00
❑ 142 Philip Rivers AU RC 150.00 45.00
❑ 143 Julius Jones AU RC 200.00 60.00
❑ 144 Eli Manning AU RC 300.00 90.00
❑ 145 Bernard Berrian AU RC 40.00 12.00
❑ 146 Roy Williams AU RC 150.00 45.00
❑ 147 Kevin Jones AU RC 150.00 45.00
❑ 148 Mewelde Moore AU RC 60.00 18.00
❑ 149 DeAngelo Hall AU RC 50.00 15.00
❑ 150 Michael Jenkins AU RC 50.00 15.00
❑ 151 Matt Schaub AU RC 60.00 18.00
❑ 152 Keary Colbert AU RC 60.00 18.00
❑ 153 Devery Henderson AU RC 30.00 9.00
❑ 154 Michael Clayton AU RC 100.00 30.00
❑ 155 Larry Fitzgerald AU RC 150.00 45.00
❑ 156 Rashaun Woods AU RC 50.00 15.00
❑ 157 Derrick Hamilton AU RC 40.00 12.00
❑ 158 Steven Jackson AU RC 150.00 45.00

2004 Playoff Prime Signatures Bronze Proofs

Nm-Mt Ex-Mt
*STARS: 1.2X TO 3X BASE CARD HI
*RETIRED STARS: 1.2X TO 3X
STATED PRINT RUN 50 SER.#'d SETS

2004 Playoff Prime Signatures Gold Proofs

Nm-Mt Ex-Mt
1-100 PRINT RUN 5 SER.#'d SETS
*GOLD DUAL AUTOS: .6X TO 1.5X
101-125 AU PRINT RUN 50 SER.#'d SETS
126-158 AU PRINT RUN 5 SER.#'d SETS

2004 Playoff Prime Signatures Silver Proofs

Nm-Mt Ex-Mt
*STARS: 2X TO 5X BASE CARD HI
*RETIRED STARS: 1.5X TO 4X
SILVER PRINT RUN 25 SER.#'d SETS

1993 Power Update Prospects

Nm-Mt Ex-Mt
COMPLETE SET (60) 15.00 6.75
❑ 1 Drew Bledsoe RC 2.50 1.10
❑ 2 Rick Mirer RC .25 .11
❑ 3 Trent Green RC 10.00 4.50
❑ 4 Mark Brunell RC 1.50 .70
❑ 5 Billy Joe Hobert RC UER .25 .11
Name spelled Hebert on back
❑ 6 Ronald Moore RC .10 .05
❑ 7 Elvis Grbac RC UER 1.50 .70
(Spelled Grback on both sides)
❑ 8 Garrison Hearst RC .75 .35
❑ 9 Jerome Bettis RC 2.50 1.10
❑ 10 Reggie Brooks RC .10 .05
❑ 11 Robert Smith RC 1.25 .55
❑ 12 Vaughn Hebron RC .05 .02
❑ 13 Derek Brown RBK RC .10 .05
❑ 14 Roosevelt Potts RC .10 .05
❑ 15 Terry Kirby RC UER .10 .05
(Card says wide receiver; he is a running back)
❑ 16 Glyn Milburn RC .10 .05
❑ 17 Greg Robinson RC .05 .02
❑ 18 Natrone Means RC .25 .11
❑ 19 Curtis Conway RC .40 .18
❑ 20 James Jett RC .25 .11
❑ 21 O.J. McDuffie RC .25 .11
❑ 22 Rocket Ismail .25 .11
❑ 23 Qadry Ismail RC .25 .11
❑ 24 Kevin Williams RC .10 .05
❑ 25 Victor Bailey RC UER .05 .02
(Name spelled Baily on front)
❑ 26 Vincent Brisby RC .25 .11
❑ 27 Irv Smith RC .05 .02
❑ 28 Troy Drayton RC .05 .02
❑ 29 Wayne Simmons RC .05 .02
❑ 30 Marvin Jones RC .05 .02
❑ 31 Demetrius DuBose RC .05 .02
❑ 32 Chad Brown RC .10 .05
❑ 33 Micheal Barrow RC .25 .11
❑ 34 Darrin Smith RC .05 .02

2000 Private Stock

Nm-Mt Ex-Mt
COMP.SET w/o SP's (100) 25.00 11.00
❑ 1 Rob Moore .60 .25
❑ 2 Jake Plummer .60 .25
❑ 3 Frank Sanders .60 .25
❑ 4 Jamal Anderson 1.00 .45
❑ 5 Chris Chandler .60 .25
❑ 6 Tim Dwight 1.00 .45
❑ 7 Tony Banks .60 .25
❑ 8 Priest Holmes 1.25 .55
❑ 9 Doug Flutie 1.00 .45
❑ 10 Rob Johnson .60 .25

❑ 11 Eric Moulds 1.00 .45
❑ 12 Antowain Smith .60 .25
❑ 13 Steve Beuerlein .40 .18
❑ 14 Tim Biakabutuka .60 .25
❑ 15 Patrick Jeffers 1.00 .45
❑ 16 Muhsin Muhammad .60 .25
❑ 17 Curtis Enis .40 .18
❑ 18 Cade McNown .40 .18
❑ 19 Marcus Robinson 1.00 .45
❑ 20 Corey Dillon 1.00 .45
❑ 21 Akili Smith .40 .18
❑ 22 Tim Couch .60 .25
❑ 23 Kevin Johnson 1.00 .45
❑ 24 Troy Aikman 2.00 .90
❑ 25 Rocket Ismail .60 .25
❑ 26 Emmitt Smith 2.00 .90
❑ 27 Terrell Davis 1.00 .45
❑ 28 Olandis Gary 1.00 .45
❑ 29 Brian Griese 1.00 .45
❑ 30 Ed McCaffrey .60 .25
❑ 31 Charlie Batch 1.00 .45
❑ 32 Germane Crowell .40 .18
❑ 33 Herman Moore .60 .25
❑ 34 Barry Sanders 2.50 1.10
❑ 35 Brett Favre 3.00 1.35
❑ 36 Antonio Freeman 1.00 .45
❑ 37 Dorsey Levens .60 .25
❑ 38 Marvin Harrison 1.00 .45
❑ 39 Edgerrin James 1.50 .70
❑ 40 Peyton Manning 2.50 1.10
❑ 41 Terrence Wilkins .40 .18
❑ 42 Mark Brunell 1.00 .45
❑ 43 Keenan McCardell .60 .25
❑ 44 Jimmy Smith .60 .25
❑ 45 Fred Taylor 1.00 .45
❑ 46 Derrick Alexander .60 .25
❑ 47 Donnell Bennett .40 .18
❑ 48 Tony Gonzalez .60 .25
❑ 49 Elvis Grbac .60 .25
❑ 50 Damon Huard 1.00 .45
❑ 51 James Johnson .40 .18
❑ 52 Dan Marino 3.00 1.35
❑ 53 O.J. McDuffie .60 .25
❑ 54 Cris Carter 1.00 .45
❑ 55 Daunte Culpepper 1.25 .55
❑ 56 Randy Moss 2.00 .90
❑ 57 Robert Smith 1.00 .45
❑ 58 Drew Bledsoe 1.25 .55
❑ 59 Kevin Faulk .60 .25
❑ 60 Terry Glenn .60 .25
❑ 61 Keith Poole .60 .25
❑ 62 Ricky Williams 1.00 .45
❑ 63 Kerry Collins .60 .25
❑ 64 Ike Hilliard .60 .25
❑ 65 Amani Toomer .60 .25
❑ 66 Wayne Chrebet .60 .25
❑ 67 Ray Lucas .60 .25
❑ 68 Curtis Martin 1.00 .45
❑ 69 Tim Brown 1.00 .45
❑ 70 Rich Gannon 1.00 .45
❑ 71 Napoleon Kaufman .60 .25
❑ 72 Donovan McNabb 1.50 .70
❑ 73 Duce Staley 1.00 .45
❑ 74 Jerome Bettis 1.00 .45
❑ 75 Troy Edwards .40 .18
❑ 76 Kordell Stewart .60 .25
❑ 77 Isaac Bruce 1.00 .45

❑ 78 Marshall Faulk	1.25	.55
❑ 79 Torry Holt	1.00	.45
❑ 80 Kurt Warner	2.00	.90
❑ 81 Jermaine Fazande	.40	.18
❑ 82 Jim Harbaugh	.60	.25
❑ 83 Junior Seau	1.00	.45
❑ 84 Charlie Garner	.60	.25
❑ 85 Terrell Owens	1.00	.45
❑ 86 Jerry Rice	2.00	.90
❑ 87 Jon Kitna	1.00	.45
❑ 88 Derrick Mayes	.60	.25
❑ 89 Ricky Watters	.60	.25
❑ 90 Mike Alstott	1.00	.45
❑ 91 Warrick Dunn	1.00	.45
❑ 92 Jacquez Green	.40	.18
❑ 93 Shaun King	.40	.18
❑ 94 Eddie George	1.00	.45
❑ 95 Jevon Kearse	1.00	.45
❑ 96 Steve McNair	1.00	.45
❑ 97 Yancey Thigpen	.40	.18
❑ 98 Stephen Davis	1.00	.45
❑ 99 Brad Johnson	1.00	.45
❑ 100 Michael Westbrook	.60	.25
❑ 101 Thomas Jones RC	25.00	11.00
❑ 102 Doug Johnson RC	15.00	6.75
❑ 103 Mareno Philyaw RC	10.00	4.50
❑ 104 Jamal Lewis RC	40.00	18.00
❑ 105 Chris Redman RC	12.00	5.50
❑ 106 Travis Taylor RC	15.00	6.75
❑ 107 Frank Murphy RC	10.00	4.50
❑ 108 Dez White RC	15.00	6.75
❑ 109 Ron Dugans RC	10.00	4.50
❑ 110 Curtis Keaton RC	12.00	5.50
❑ 111 Peter Warrick RC	15.00	6.75
❑ 112 Courtney Brown RC	15.00	6.75
❑ 113 JaJuan Dawson RC	10.00	4.50
❑ 114 Dennis Northcutt RC	15.00	6.75
❑ 115 Travis Prentice RC	12.00	5.50
❑ 116 Michael Wiley RC	12.00	5.50
❑ 117 Chris Cole RC	12.00	5.50
❑ 118 Jarious Jackson RC	12.00	5.50
❑ 119 Reuben Droughns RC	20.00	9.00
❑ 120 Bubba Franks RC	15.00	6.75
❑ 121 Anthony Lucas RC	10.00	4.50
❑ 122 Rondell Mealey RC	10.00	4.50
❑ 123 R.Jay Soward RC	12.00	5.50
❑ 124 Shyrone Stith RC	12.00	5.50
❑ 125 Sylvester Morris RC	12.00	5.50
❑ 126 Quinton Spotwood RC	10.00	4.50
❑ 127 Troy Walters RC	15.00	6.75
❑ 128 Tom Brady RC	120.00	55.00
❑ 129 J.R. Redmond RC	12.00	5.50
❑ 130 Marc Bulger RC	30.00	13.50
❑ 131 Sherrod Gideon RC	10.00	4.50
❑ 132 Ron Dayne RC	15.00	6.75
❑ 133 Anthony Becht RC	15.00	6.75
❑ 134 Laveranues Coles RC	20.00	9.00
❑ 135 Chad Pennington RC	60.00	27.00
❑ 136 Sebastian Janikowski RC	15.00	6.75
❑ 137 Jerry Porter RC	20.00	9.00
❑ 138 Todd Pinkston RC	15.00	6.75
❑ 139 Gari Scott RC	10.00	4.50
❑ 140 Plaxico Burress RC	30.00	13.50
❑ 141 Danny Farmer RC	12.00	5.50
❑ 142 Tee Martin RC	15.00	6.75
❑ 143 Trung Canidate RC	12.00	5.50
❑ 144 Trevor Gaylor RC	12.00	5.50
❑ 145 Giovanni Carmazzi RC	12.00	5.50
❑ 146 Tim Rattay RC	30.00	13.50
❑ 147 Shaun Alexander RC	40.00	18.00
❑ 148 Darrell Jackson RC	25.00	11.00
❑ 149 Joe Hamilton RC	12.00	5.50
❑ 150 Todd Husak RC	15.00	6.75
❑ S1 Jon Kitna Sample	1.00	.45

2001 Private Stock

	Nm-Mt	Ex-Mt
COMP.SET w/o SP's (100)	60.00	18.00
❑ 1 David Boston	1.25	.35
❑ 2 Thomas Jones	.75	.23
❑ 3 Jake Plummer	.75	.23
❑ 4 Jamal Anderson	1.25	.35
❑ 5 Chris Chandler	.75	.23

❑ 6 Eric Zeier	.50	.15
❑ 7 Elvis Grbac	.75	.23
❑ 8 Jamal Lewis	2.00	.60
❑ 9 Shannon Sharpe	.75	.23
❑ 10 Rob Johnson	.75	.23
❑ 11 Eric Moulds	1.25	.35
❑ 12 Peerless Price	.75	.23
❑ 13 Tim Biakabutuka	.75	.23
❑ 14 Jeff Lewis	.50	.15
❑ 15 Muhsin Muhammad	.75	.23
❑ 16 James Allen	.75	.23
❑ 17 Cade McNown	.50	.15
❑ 18 Marcus Robinson	1.25	.35
❑ 19 Brian Urlacher	2.00	.60
❑ 20 Corey Dillon	1.25	.35
❑ 21 Jon Kitna	1.25	.35
❑ 22 Akili Smith	.50	.15
❑ 23 Peter Warrick	1.25	.35
❑ 24 Tim Couch	.75	.23
❑ 25 Kevin Johnson	.75	.23
❑ 26 Travis Prentice	.50	.15
❑ 27 Rocket Ismail	.75	.23
❑ 28 Emmitt Smith	2.50	.75
❑ 29 Mike Anderson	1.25	.35
❑ 30 Terrell Davis	1.25	.35
❑ 31 Brian Griese	1.25	.35
❑ 32 Ed McCaffrey	1.25	.35
❑ 33 Charlie Batch	1.25	.35
❑ 34 Germane Crowell	.50	.15
❑ 35 James Stewart	.75	.23
❑ 36 Brett Favre	4.00	1.20
❑ 37 Antonio Freeman	1.25	.35
❑ 38 Ahman Green	1.25	.35
❑ 39 Marvin Harrison	1.25	.35
❑ 40 Edgerrin James	1.50	.45
❑ 41 Peyton Manning	3.00	.90
❑ 42 Mark Brunell	1.25	.35
❑ 43 Jimmy Smith	.75	.23
❑ 44 Fred Taylor	1.25	.35
❑ 45 Derrick Alexander	.75	.23
❑ 46 Tony Gonzalez	.75	.23
❑ 47 Trent Green	1.25	.35
❑ 48 Priest Holmes	1.50	.45
❑ 49 Jay Fiedler	1.25	.35
❑ 50 Oronde Gadsden	.75	.23
❑ 51 Lamar Smith	.75	.23
❑ 52 Cris Carter	1.25	.35
❑ 53 Daunte Culpepper	1.25	.35
❑ 54 Randy Moss	2.50	.75
❑ 55 Drew Bledsoe	1.50	.45
❑ 56 Kevin Faulk	.75	.23
❑ 57 Terry Glenn	.75	.23
❑ 58 Jeff Blake	.75	.23
❑ 59 Aaron Brooks	1.25	.35
❑ 60 Joe Horn	.75	.23
❑ 61 Ricky Williams	1.25	.35
❑ 62 Tiki Barber	.75	.23
❑ 63 Kerry Collins	.75	.23
❑ 64 Ron Dayne	1.25	.35
❑ 65 Amani Toomer	.75	.23
❑ 66 Wayne Chrebet	.75	.23
❑ 67 Curtis Martin	1.25	.35
❑ 68 Vinny Testaverde	.75	.23
❑ 69 Tim Brown	1.25	.35
❑ 70 Rich Gannon	1.25	.35
❑ 71 Charlie Garner	.75	.23
❑ 72 Jerry Rice	2.50	.75
❑ 73 Tyrone Wheatley	.75	.23
❑ 74 Donovan McNabb	1.50	.45
❑ 75 Duce Staley	1.25	.35
❑ 76 Jerome Bettis	1.25	.35
❑ 77 Kordell Stewart	.75	.23
❑ 78 Hines Ward	1.25	.35
❑ 79 Isaac Bruce	1.25	.35
❑ 80 Marshall Faulk	1.50	.45
❑ 81 Torry Holt	1.25	.35
❑ 82 Kurt Warner	2.50	.75
❑ 83 Curtis Conway	.75	.23
❑ 84 Doug Flutie	1.25	.35
❑ 85 Jeff Garcia	1.25	.35
❑ 86 Terrell Owens	1.25	.35
❑ 87 Shaun Alexander	1.50	.45
❑ 88 Matt Hasselbeck	.75	.23
❑ 89 Darrell Jackson	1.25	.35
❑ 90 Ricky Watters	.75	.23
❑ 91 Mike Alstott	1.25	.35
❑ 92 Warrick Dunn	1.25	.35
❑ 93 Keyshawn Johnson	1.25	.35
❑ 94 Brad Johnson	1.25	.35
❑ 95 Eddie George	1.25	.35
❑ 96 Derrick Mason	.75	.23
❑ 97 Steve McNair	1.25	.35
❑ 98 Stephen Davis	1.25	.35
❑ 99 Jeff George	.75	.23
❑ 100 Michael Westbrook	.75	.23
❑ 101 Bobby Newcombe RC	12.00	3.60
❑ 102 Corey Brown RC	12.00	3.60
❑ 103 Alge Crumpler RC	25.00	7.50
❑ 104 Vinny Sutherland RC	12.00	3.60
❑ 105 Michael Vick RC	100.00	30.00
❑ 106 Chris Barnes RC	12.00	3.60
❑ 107 Todd Heap RC	20.00	6.00
❑ 108 Nate Clements RC	20.00	6.00
❑ 109 Tim Hasselbeck RC	20.00	6.00
❑ 110 Travis Henry RC	25.00	7.50
❑ 111 Dee Brown RC	20.00	6.00
❑ 112 Dan Morgan RC	20.00	6.00
❑ 113 Steve Smith RC	25.00	7.50
❑ 114 Chris Weinke RC	20.00	6.00
❑ 115 John Capel RC	12.00	3.60
❑ 116 David Terrell RC	20.00	6.00
❑ 117 Anthony Thomas RC	30.00	9.00
❑ 118 T.J. Houshmandzadeh RC	20.00	6.00
❑ 119 Chad Johnson RC	40.00	12.00
❑ 120 Rudi Johnson RC	40.00	12.00
❑ 121 James Jackson RC	20.00	6.00
❑ 122 Quincy Morgan RC	20.00	6.00
❑ 123 Quincy Carter RC	20.00	6.00
❑ 124 Kevin Kasper RC	20.00	6.00
❑ 125 Scotty Anderson RC	12.00	3.60
❑ 126 Mike McMahon RC	20.00	6.00
❑ 127 Robert Ferguson RC	20.00	6.00
❑ 128 David Martin RC	12.00	3.60
❑ 129 Jamal Reynolds RC	20.00	6.00
❑ 130 Reggie Wayne RC	30.00	9.00
❑ 131 Richmond Flowers RC	12.00	3.60
❑ 132 Marcus Stroud RC	20.00	6.00
❑ 133 Derrick Blaylock RC	20.00	6.00
❑ 134 Snoop Minnis RC	12.00	3.60
❑ 135 Chris Chambers RC	25.00	7.50
❑ 136 Jamar Fletcher RC	12.00	3.60
❑ 137 Josh Heupel RC	20.00	6.00
❑ 138 Travis Minor RC	12.00	3.60
❑ 139 Michael Bennett RC	40.00	12.00
❑ 140 Deuce McAllister RC	50.00	15.00
❑ 141 Moran Norris RC	8.00	2.40
❑ 142 Onomo Ojo RC	12.00	3.60
❑ 143 Will Allen RC	12.00	3.60
❑ 144 Jonathan Carter RC	12.00	3.60
❑ 145 Jesse Palmer RC	20.00	6.00
❑ 146 LaMont Jordan RC	25.00	7.50
❑ 147 Santana Moss RC	30.00	9.00
❑ 148 Derek Combs RC	12.00	3.60
❑ 149 Derrick Gibson RC	12.00	3.60
❑ 150 Javon Green RC	12.00	3.60
❑ 151 Ken-Yon Rambo RC	12.00	3.60
❑ 152 Marques Tuiasosopo RC	20.00	6.00
❑ 153 Correll Buckhalter RC	25.00	7.50
❑ 154 Freddie Mitchell RC	20.00	6.00
❑ 155 Joey Getherall RC	12.00	3.60
❑ 156 Chris Taylor RC	12.00	3.60

Card	Nm-Mt	Ex-Mt
❑ 157 Adam Archuleta RC	20.00	6.00
❑ 158 David Rivers RC	12.00	3.60
❑ 159 Francis St. Paul RC	12.00	3.60
❑ 160 Drew Brees RC	40.00	12.00
❑ 161 LaDainian Tomlinson RC	60.00	18.00
❑ 162 David Allen RC	12.00	3.60
❑ 163 Kevan Barlow RC	20.00	6.00
❑ 164 Andre Carter RC	20.00	6.00
❑ 165 Cedrick Wilson RC	20.00	6.00
❑ 166 Alex Bannister RC	12.00	3.60
❑ 167 Josh Booty RC	20.00	6.00
❑ 168 Heath Evans RC	12.00	3.60
❑ 169 Koren Robinson RC	25.00	7.50
❑ 170 Margin Hooks RC	8.00	2.40
❑ 171 Dan Alexander RC	20.00	6.00
❑ 172 Eddie Berlin RC	12.00	3.60
❑ 173 Rod Gardner RC	20.00	6.00
❑ 174 Damerien McCants RC	12.00	3.60
❑ 175 Sage Rosenfels RC	20.00	6.00

2001 Private Stock Blue Framed

Nm-Mt Ex-Mt

*STARS: 5X TO 12X BASIC CARDS
*ROOKIES: .4X TO 1X

2001 Private Stock Gold Framed

Nm-Mt Ex-Mt

*STARS: 6X TO 15X BASIC CARDS
*ROOKIES: .5X TO 1.2X

2001 Private Stock Premiere Date

Nm-Mt Ex-Mt

*STARS: 3X TO 8X BASIC CARDS
*ROOKIES: .3X TO .8X

2001 Private Stock Retail

Card	Nm-Mt	Ex-Mt
COMP.SET w/o SPs (100)	60.00	18.00
*RETAIL STARS: .4X TO 1X HOBBY		
❑ 101 Bobby Newcombe RC	8.00	2.40
❑ 102 Corey Brown RC	8.00	2.40
❑ 103 Alge Crumpler RC	15.00	4.50
❑ 104 Vinny Sutherland RC	8.00	2.40
❑ 105 Michael Vick RC	50.00	15.00
❑ 106 Chris Barnes RC	8.00	2.40
❑ 107 Todd Heap RC	12.00	3.60
❑ 108 Nate Clements RC	12.00	3.60
❑ 109 Tim Hasselbeck RC	12.00	3.60
❑ 110 Travis Henry RC	15.00	4.50
❑ 111 Dee Brown RC	12.00	3.60
❑ 112 Dan Morgan RC	12.00	3.60
❑ 113 Steve Smith RC	15.00	4.50
❑ 114 Chris Weinke RC	12.00	3.60
❑ 115 John Capel RC	8.00	2.40
❑ 116 David Terrell RC	12.00	3.60
❑ 117 Anthony Thomas RC	20.00	6.00
❑ 118 T.J. Houshmandzadeh RC	12.00	3.60
❑ 119 Chad Johnson RC	25.00	7.50
❑ 120 Rudi Johnson RC	25.00	7.50
❑ 121 James Jackson RC	12.00	3.60
❑ 122 Quincy Morgan RC	12.00	3.60
❑ 123 Quincy Carter RC	12.00	3.60
❑ 124 Kevin Kasper RC	12.00	3.60
❑ 125 Scotty Anderson RC	8.00	2.40
❑ 126 Mike McMahon RC	12.00	3.60
❑ 127 Robert Ferguson RC	12.00	3.60
❑ 128 David Martin RC	8.00	2.40
❑ 129 Jamal Reynolds RC	12.00	3.60
❑ 130 Reggie Wayne RC	20.00	6.00
❑ 131 Richmond Flowers RC	8.00	2.40
❑ 132 Marcus Stroud RC	12.00	3.60
❑ 133 Derrick Blaylock RC	12.00	3.60
❑ 134 Snoop Minnis RC	8.00	2.40
❑ 135 Chris Chambers RC	15.00	4.50
❑ 136 Jamar Fletcher RC	8.00	2.40
❑ 137 Josh Heupel RC	12.00	3.60
❑ 138 Travis Minor RC	8.00	2.40
❑ 139 Michael Bennett RC	25.00	7.50
❑ 140 Deuce McAllister RC	25.00	7.50
❑ 141 Moran Norris RC	5.00	1.50
❑ 142 Onomo Ojo RC	8.00	2.40
❑ 143 Will Allen RC	8.00	2.40
❑ 144 Jonathan Carter RC	8.00	2.40
❑ 145 Jesse Palmer RC	12.00	3.60
❑ 146 LaMont Jordan RC	15.00	4.50
❑ 147 Santana Moss RC	20.00	6.00
❑ 148 Derek Combs RC	8.00	2.40
❑ 149 Derrick Gibson RC	8.00	2.40
❑ 150 Javon Green RC	8.00	2.40
❑ 151 Ken-Yon Rambo RC	8.00	2.40
❑ 152 Marques Tuiasosopo RC	12.00	3.60
❑ 153 Correll Buckhalter RC	15.00	4.50
❑ 154 Freddie Mitchell RC	12.00	3.60
❑ 155 Joey Getherall RC	8.00	2.40
❑ 156 Chris Taylor RC	8.00	2.40
❑ 157 Adam Archuleta RC	12.00	3.60
❑ 158 David Rivers RC	8.00	2.40
❑ 159 Francis St. Paul RC	8.00	2.40
❑ 160 Drew Brees RC	25.00	7.50
❑ 161 LaDainian Tomlinson RC	40.00	12.00
❑ 162 David Allen RC	8.00	2.40
❑ 163 Kevan Barlow RC	12.00	3.60
❑ 164 Andre Carter RC	12.00	3.60
❑ 165 Cedrick Wilson RC	12.00	3.60
❑ 166 Alex Bannister RC	8.00	2.40
❑ 167 Josh Booty RC	12.00	3.60
❑ 168 Heath Evans RC	8.00	2.40
❑ 169 Koren Robinson RC	15.00	4.50
❑ 170 Margin Hooks RC	5.00	1.50
❑ 171 Dan Alexander RC	12.00	3.60
❑ 172 Eddie Berlin RC	8.00	2.40
❑ 173 Rod Gardner RC	12.00	3.60
❑ 174 Damerien McCants RC	8.00	2.40
❑ 175 Sage Rosenfels RC	12.00	3.60

2001 Private Stock Silver Framed

Nm-Mt Ex-Mt

*STARS: 3X TO 8X BASE RETAIL
*ROOKIES: .5X TO 1.2X BASE RETAIL

2002 Private Stock

Card	Nm-Mt	Ex-Mt
COMP.SET w/o SP's (100)	40.00	12.00
❑ 1 David Boston	1.50	.45
❑ 2 Thomas Jones	1.00	.30
❑ 3 Jake Plummer	1.00	.30
❑ 4 Jamal Anderson	1.00	.30
❑ 5 Warrick Dunn	1.50	.45
❑ 6 Shawn Jefferson	.60	.18
❑ 7 Michael Vick	5.00	1.50
❑ 8 Jamal Lewis	1.50	.45
❑ 9 Chris Redman	.60	.18
❑ 10 Travis Taylor	1.00	.30
❑ 11 Travis Henry	1.50	.45
❑ 12 Eric Moulds	1.00	.30
❑ 13 Peerless Price	1.00	.30
❑ 14 Muhsin Muhammad	1.00	.30
❑ 15 Lamar Smith	1.00	.30
❑ 16 Chris Weinke	1.00	.30
❑ 17 Marty Booker	.60	.18
❑ 18 Jim Miller	.60	.18
❑ 19 Anthony Thomas	1.50	.45
❑ 20 Corey Dillon	1.00	.30
❑ 21 Darnay Scott	.60	.18
❑ 22 Peter Warrick	1.00	.30
❑ 23 Tim Couch	1.00	.30
❑ 24 James Jackson	.60	.18
❑ 25 Kevin Johnson	1.00	.30
❑ 26 Quincy Carter	1.00	.30
❑ 27 Rocket Ismail	1.00	.30
❑ 28 Emmitt Smith	4.00	1.20
❑ 29 Mike Anderson	1.50	.45
❑ 30 Terrell Davis	1.50	.45
❑ 31 Brian Griese	1.50	.45
❑ 32 Rod Smith	1.00	.30
❑ 33 Mike McMahon	1.50	.45
❑ 34 Johnnie Morton	1.00	.30
❑ 35 Brett Favre	4.00	1.20
❑ 36 Antonio Freeman	1.50	.45
❑ 37 Ahman Green	1.50	.45
❑ 38 Corey Bradford	.60	.18
❑ 39 Jermaine Lewis	.60	.18
❑ 40 Jamie Sharper	.60	.18
❑ 41 Marvin Harrison	1.50	.45
❑ 42 Edgerrin James	2.00	.60
❑ 43 Mark Brunell	1.50	.45
❑ 44 Jimmy Smith	1.00	.30
❑ 45 Fred Taylor	1.50	.45
❑ 46 Tony Gonzalez	1.00	.30
❑ 47 Trent Green	1.00	.30
❑ 48 Priest Holmes	2.00	.60
❑ 49 Chris Chambers	1.50	.45
❑ 50 Jay Fiedler	1.00	.30
❑ 51 James McKnight	.60	.18
❑ 52 Ricky Williams	1.50	.45
❑ 53 Michael Bennett	1.00	.30
❑ 54 Cris Carter	1.50	.45
❑ 55 Daunte Culpepper	1.50	.45
❑ 56 Randy Moss	3.00	.90
❑ 57 Drew Bledsoe	1.50	.45
❑ 58 Tom Brady	4.00	1.20
❑ 59 Troy Brown	1.00	.30
❑ 60 Antowain Smith	1.00	.30
❑ 61 Aaron Brooks	1.50	.45
❑ 62 Joe Horn	1.00	.30
❑ 63 Deuce McAllister	2.00	.60
❑ 64 Tiki Barber	1.00	.30
❑ 65 Kerry Collins	1.00	.30
❑ 66 Ron Dayne	1.00	.30
❑ 67 Laveranues Coles	1.00	.30
❑ 68 Curtis Martin	1.50	.45
❑ 69 Vinny Testaverde	1.00	.30
❑ 70 Tim Brown	1.50	.45
❑ 71 Rich Gannon	1.50	.45
❑ 72 Jerry Rice	3.00	.90
❑ 73 Correll Buckhalter	1.00	.30
❑ 74 Duce Staley	1.50	.45
❑ 75 James Thrash	1.00	.30
❑ 76 Jerome Bettis	1.50	.45
❑ 77 Plaxico Burress	1.00	.30
❑ 78 Kordell Stewart	1.00	.30
❑ 79 Hines Ward	1.50	.45
❑ 80 Isaac Bruce	1.50	.45
❑ 81 Marshall Faulk	1.50	.45
❑ 82 Torry Holt	1.50	.45
❑ 83 Kurt Warner	1.50	.45
❑ 84 Drew Brees	1.50	.45
❑ 85 Doug Flutie	1.50	.45
❑ 86 LaDainian Tomlinson	2.50	.75
❑ 87 Jeff Garcia	1.50	.45
❑ 88 Garrison Hearst	1.00	.30
❑ 89 Terrell Owens	1.50	.45
❑ 90 Shaun Alexander	1.50	.45
❑ 91 Trent Dilfer	1.00	.30
❑ 92 Darrell Jackson	1.00	.30
❑ 93 Ricky Watters	1.00	.30
❑ 94 Brad Johnson	1.00	.30
❑ 95 Keyshawn Johnson	1.50	.45
❑ 96 Eddie George	1.50	.45
❑ 97 Derrick Mason	1.00	.30
❑ 98 Steve McNair	1.50	.45
❑ 99 Stephen Davis	1.00	.30
❑ 100 Rod Gardner	1.00	.30
❑ 101 Damien Anderson FB/20		
❑ 102 Ladell Betts FB/46	50.00	15.00
❑ 103 Antonio Bryant FB/80	40.00	12.00
❑ 104 Wendell Bryant FB/77	40.00	12.00
❑ 105 Reche Caldwell FB/17		

❑ 106 Kelly Campbell FB/6		
❑ 107 David Carr FB/8		
❑ 108 Eric Crouch FB/7		
❑ 109 Ronald Curry FB/1		
❑ 110 Rohan Davey FB/6		
❑ 111 Andre Davis FB/88	50.00	15.00
❑ 112 T.J. Duckett FB/8		
❑ 113 DeShaun Foster FB/26	80.00	24.00
❑ 114 Jabar Gaffney FB/10		
❑ 115 David Garrard FB/9		
❑ 116 Lamar Gordon FB/28	60.00	18.00
❑ 117 Daniel Graham FB/89	50.00	15.00
❑ 118 William Green FB/1		
❑ 119 Joey Harrington FB/3		
❑ 120 Napoleon Harris FB/8		
❑ 121 Verron Haynes FB/35	50.00	15.00
❑ 122 John Henderson FB/98	40.00	12.00
❑ 123 Kahlil Hill FB/3		
❑ 124 Quentin Jammer FB/6		
❑ 125 Ron Johnson FB/3		
❑ 126 Kurt Kittner FB/15		
❑ 127 Zak Kustok FB/10		
❑ 128 Ashley Lelie FB/8		
❑ 129 Josh McCown FB/12		
❑ 130 Freddie Milons FB/15		
❑ 131 Maurice Morris FB/9		
❑ 132 James Mungro FB/23	50.00	15.00
❑ 133 David Neill FB/11		
❑ 134 Adrian Peterson FB/3		
❑ 135 Brian Poli-Dixon FB/82	40.00	12.00
❑ 136 Clinton Portis FB/28	150.00	45.00
❑ 137 Patrick Ramsey FB/7		
❑ 138 Antwaan Randle El FB/11		
❑ 139 Josh Reed FB/25	50.00	15.00
❑ 140 Cliff Russell FB/1		
❑ 141 Josh Scobey FB/1		
❑ 142 Lito Sheppard FB/3		
❑ 143 Jeremy Shockey FB/88	60.00	18.00
❑ 144 Luke Staley FB/6		
❑ 145 Donte Stallworth FB/4		
❑ 146 Lamont Thompson FB/19		
❑ 147 Javon Walker FB/80	60.00	18.00
❑ 148 Marquise Walker FB/4		
❑ 149 Brian Westbrook FB/20		
❑ 150 Roy Williams FB/38	80.00	24.00

1991 Pro Line Portraits Autographs

	Nm-Mt	Ex-Mt
COMPLETE SET (300)	5500.00	2500.00
❑ 1 Ray Agnew	10.00	4.50
❑ 2 Troy Aikman	80.00	36.00
❑ 3 Eric Allen	12.00	5.50
❑ 4 Morten Andersen	12.00	5.50
❑ 5 Flipper Anderson	12.00	5.50
❑ 6 Gary Anderson K	12.00	5.50
❑ 7 Gary Anderson RB	12.00	5.50
❑ 8 Neal Anderson	15.00	6.75
❑ 9 Ottis Anderson	12.00	5.50
❑ 10 Bruce Armstrong	10.00	4.50
❑ 11 Steve Atwater	12.00	5.50
❑ 12 Robert Awalt	10.00	4.50
❑ 13 Carl Banks	12.00	5.50
❑ 14 Reggie Barrett	10.00	4.50
❑ 15 Harris Barton	10.00	4.50
❑ 16 Martin Bayless	10.00	4.50
❑ 17 Bill Belichick CO	75.00	34.00
❑ 18 Nick Bell	10.00	4.50
❑ 19 Cornelius Bennett	15.00	6.75
❑ 20 Albert Bentley	10.00	4.50
❑ 21 Rod Bernstine	10.00	4.50
❑ 22 Dean Biasucci	10.00	4.50
❑ 23 Duane Bickett	10.00	4.50
❑ 24 Bennie Blades	10.00	4.50
❑ 25 Brian Blades	12.00	5.50
❑ 26 Mel Blount RET	25.00	11.00
❑ 27 Mark Bortz	10.00	4.50
❑ 28 Bubby Brister	12.00	5.50
(Signed Bubby 6)		
❑ 29 James Brooks	12.00	5.50
❑ 30 Steve Broussard	10.00	4.50
❑ 31 Lomas Brown	10.00	4.50
❑ 32 Maury Buford	10.00	4.50
❑ 33 Joe Bugel CO	10.00	4.50
❑ 34 Jarrod Bunch	10.00	4.50
❑ 35 Jerry Burns CO	10.00	4.50
❑ 36 Kevin Butler	15.00	6.75
❑ 37 Marion Butts	12.00	5.50
❑ 38 Keith Byars	12.00	5.50
❑ 39 Earnest Byner	12.00	5.50
❑ 40 Mark Carrier DB	100.00	45.00
(released in 1992 Pro Line)		
❑ 41 Mark Carrier WR	12.00	5.50
❑ 42 Anthony Carter	15.00	6.75
(Signatures usually miscut)		
❑ 43 Dexter Carter	10.00	4.50
❑ 44 Deron Cherry	10.00	4.50
❑ 45 Ray Childress	12.00	5.50
❑ 46 Vinnie Clark	10.00	4.50
❑ 47 Mark Clayton	15.00	6.75
❑ 48 Michael Cofer	10.00	4.50
❑ 49 Monte Coleman	10.00	4.50
❑ 50 Andre Collins	10.00	4.50
❑ 51 Shane Conlan	10.00	4.50
❑ 52 Darion Conner	10.00	4.50
❑ 53 Bruce Coslet CO	10.00	4.50
❑ 54 Jim Covert	10.00	4.50
❑ 55 Roger Craig	15.00	6.75
❑ 56 Randall Cunningham	25.00	11.00
❑ 57 Steve DeBerg	12.00	5.50
❑ 58 Eric Dickerson	40.00	18.00
❑ 59 Mike Ditka CO	30.00	13.50
❑ 60 Ray Donaldson	10.00	4.50
❑ 61 Eric Dorsey	10.00	4.50
❑ 62 Mike Dumas	10.00	4.50
❑ 63 Marcus Dupree	12.00	5.50
❑ 64 Hart Lee Dykes	10.00	4.50
❑ 65 Ferrell Edmunds	10.00	4.50
❑ 66 Henry Ellard	12.00	5.50
❑ 67 Jumbo Elliott	10.00	4.50
❑ 68 John Elway	120.00	55.00
❑ 69 Boomer Esiason	15.00	6.75
❑ 70 Jim Everett	12.00	5.50
❑ 71 Thomas Everett	10.00	4.50
❑ 72 Kevin Fagan	10.00	4.50
❑ 73 Paul Farren	10.00	4.50
❑ 74 Wayne Fontes CO	10.00	4.50
❑ 75 John Fourcade	10.00	4.50
❑ 76 Bill Fralic	10.00	4.50
❑ 77 James Francis	300.00	135.00
(released in 1992 Pro Line)		
❑ 78 Irving Fryar	15.00	6.75
❑ 79 David Fulcher	10.00	4.50
❑ 80 Cleveland Gary	10.00	4.50
❑ 81 Shaun Gayle	10.00	4.50
❑ 82 Jeff George	15.00	6.75
❑ 83 Joe Gibbs CO	30.00	13.50
❑ 84 Ernest Givins	12.00	5.50
❑ 85 Jerry Glanville CO	12.00	5.50
❑ 86 Bob Golic	12.00	5.50
❑ 87 Mel Gray	12.00	5.50
❑ 88 Jacob Green	10.00	4.50
❑ 89 Kevin Greene	15.00	6.75
❑ 90 Burt Grossman	10.00	4.50
❑ 91 Tim Grunhard	10.00	4.50
(Two different signatures known for this card)		
❑ 92 Myron Guyton	10.00	4.50
❑ 93 Ray Handley CO	10.00	4.50
❑ 94 Jim Harbaugh	15.00	6.75
❑ 95 Franco Harris RET	50.00	22.00
Most signatures are cut off		
❑ 96 Andy Heck	10.00	4.50
❑ 97 Dan Henning CO	10.00	4.50
❑ 98 Alonzo Highsmith	120.00	55.00
(released in 1992 Pro Line)		
❑ 99 Jay Hilgenberg	10.00	4.50
(released via mail promotion)		
❑ 100 Bruce Hill	10.00	4.50
❑ 101 Derek Hill	10.00	4.50
❑ 102 Randal Hill	12.00	5.50
❑ 103 Dalton Hilliard	12.00	5.50
(Signatures usually miscut)		
❑ 104 Bryan Hinkle	10.00	4.50
❑ 105 Chris Hinton	10.00	4.50
❑ 106 Leroy Hoard	15.00	6.75
❑ 107 Merril Hoge	15.00	6.75
❑ 108 Rodney Holman	300.00	135.00
(released in 1992 Pro Line)		
❑ 109 Issiac Holt	10.00	4.50
❑ 110 Pierce Holt	10.00	4.50
❑ 111 Jeff Hostetler	12.00	5.50
❑ 112 Erik Howard	10.00	4.50
❑ 113 Bobby Humphrey	10.00	4.50
(released via mail promotion)		
❑ 114 Lindy Infante CO	10.00	4.50
❑ 115 Michael Irvin	25.00	11.00
❑ 116 Mark Jackson	12.00	5.50
❑ 117 Rickey Jackson	12.00	5.50
❑ 118 Haywood Jeffires	12.00	5.50
❑ 119 D.J. Johnson	10.00	4.50
❑ 120 Jimmy Johnson CO	40.00	18.00
❑ 121 Pepper Johnson	12.00	5.50
(released via mail promotion)		
❑ 122 Tracy Johnson	10.00	4.50
❑ 123 Vaughan Johnson	10.00	4.50
❑ 124 Brent Jones	12.00	5.50
❑ 125 Henry Jones	10.00	4.50
❑ 126 Keith Jones	10.00	4.50
❑ 127A Jim Kelly	15.00	6.75
(Autopenned)		
❑ 127B Jim Kelly	250.00	110.00
(Real signature)		
❑ 128 Jack Kemp RET	30.00	13.50
(Autopenned)		
❑ 129 Cortez Kennedy	12.00	5.50
❑ 130 Chuck Knox CO	12.00	5.50
❑ 131 Bernie Kosar	20.00	9.00
❑ 132 Rich Kotite CO	10.00	4.50
❑ 133 Greg Kragen	12.00	5.50
❑ 134 Dave Krieg	12.00	5.50
❑ 135 Jim Lachey	12.00	5.50
❑ 136 Carnell Lake	12.00	5.50
❑ 137 Sean Landeta	10.00	4.50
❑ 138 Reggie Langhorne	50.00	22.00
(released in 1992 Pro Line)		
❑ 139 Steve Largent RET	30.00	13.50
❑ 140 Albert Lewis	50.00	22.00
Most signatures are cut off		
❑ 141 Louis Lipps	12.00	5.50
❑ 142 David Little	15.00	6.75
❑ 143 Eugene Lockhart	10.00	4.50
❑ 144 James Lofton	15.00	6.75
❑ 145 Chip Lohmiller	10.00	4.50
❑ 146 Howie Long	40.00	18.00
❑ 147 Ronnie Lott	20.00	9.00
❑ 148 Nick Lowery	10.00	4.50
(May be autopenned)		
❑ 149 Dick MacPherson CO	10.00	4.50
❑ 150 Ed McCaffrey	15.00	6.75
❑ 151 Keith McCants	10.00	4.50
❑ 152 Vann McElroy	10.00	4.50
❑ 153 Tim McGee	10.00	4.50
❑ 154 Kanavis McGhee	10.00	4.50
❑ 155 Dan McGwire	10.00	4.50
❑ 156 Guy McIntyre	80.00	36.00
(released at Super Bowl Show)		
❑ 157 Jim McMahon	300.00	135.00
❑ 158 Steve McMichael	12.00	5.50
❑ 159 Erik McMillan	10.00	4.50
❑ 160 Bill Maas	10.00	4.50
❑ 161 Tony Mandarich	12.00	5.50
❑ 162 Charles Mann	10.00	4.50
❑ 163 Dan Marino	150.00	70.00

❑ 164 Leonard Marshall 12.00 5.50
(Frequently miscut)
❑ 165 Eric Martin 10.00 4.50
❑ 166 Russell Maryland 12.00 5.50
❑ 167 Tim McDonald SP
❑ 168 Ron Meyer CO 10.00 4.50
❑ 169 Matt Millen 12.00 5.50
❑ 170 Anthony Miller 12.00 5.50
❑ 171 Chris Miller 12.00 5.50
❑ 172 Sam Mills 30.00 13.50
❑ 173 Warren Moon 30.00 13.50
❑ 174 Herman Moore 25.00 11.00
❑ 175 Rob Moore 15.00 6.75
❑ 176 Jim Mora CO 10.00 4.50
❑ 177 Jim Morrissey 10.00 4.50
❑ 178 Anthony Munoz 15.00 6.75
❑ 179 Mark Murphy 10.00 4.50
❑ 180 Browning Nagle 10.00 4.50
❑ 181 Tom Newberry 10.00 4.50
❑ 182 Brian Noble 10.00 4.50
❑ 183 Chuck Noll CO 40.00 18.00
❑ 184 Danny Noonan 10.00 4.50
❑ 185 Ken O'Brien 12.00 5.50
❑ 186 Leslie O'Neal 12.00 5.50
❑ 187 Bart Oates 10.00 4.50
❑ 188 Christian Okoye 12.00 5.50
❑ 189 Louis Oliver 10.00 4.50
❑ 190 Stephone Paige 10.00 4.50
❑ 191 Irv Pankey 10.00 4.50
❑ 192 Jack Pardee CO 10.00 4.50
❑ 193 Walter Payton RET 175.00 80.00
❑ 194 Drew Pearson RET 15.00 6.75
❑ 195 Danny Peebles 10.00 4.50
❑ 196 Rodney Peete 12.00 5.50
❑ 197 Michael Dean Perry 12.00 5.50
(released via mail promotion)
❑ 198 William Perry 30.00 13.50
❑ 199 Roman Phifer 10.00 4.50
❑ 200 Bill Pickel 10.00 4.50
❑ 201 Gary Plummer 10.00 4.50
❑ 202 Kevin Porter 10.00 4.50
❑ 203 Rufus Porter 10.00 4.50
❑ 204 Mike Pritchard 10.00 4.50
❑ 205 Ricky Proehl 12.00 5.50
❑ 206 Ahmad Rashad RET 175.00 80.00
(released in 1992 Pro Line)
❑ 207 Tom Rathman 15.00 6.75
❑ 208 Andre Reed 15.00 6.75
❑ 209 Dan Reeves CO 15.00 6.75
❑ 210 Johnny Rembert 10.00 4.50
❑ 211 Jerry Rice 100.00 45.00
(released at Super Bowl Show)
❑ 212 Doug Riesenberg 10.00 4.50
❑ 213 John Riggins RET 60.00 27.00
❑ 214 Andre Rison 12.00 5.50
(Ball-point pen)
❑ 215 Andre Rison 30.00 13.50
(Signed in Sharpie)
❑ 216 William Roberts 10.00 4.50
(released via mail promotion)
❑ 217 Eugene Robinson 12.00 5.50
❑ 218 John Robinson CO 12.00 5.50
❑ 219 Reggie Roby 15.00 6.75
❑ 220 John Roper 10.00 4.50
❑ 221 Timm Rosenbach 10.00 4.50
❑ 222 Kevin Ross 10.00 4.50
❑ 223 Ricky Sanders 10.00 4.50
❑ 224 Dan Saleaumua 10.00 4.50
❑ 225 Gale Sayers RET 30.00 13.50
❑ 226 Mike Schad 10.00 4.50
❑ 227 Marty Schottenheimer CO 12.00 5.50
❑ 228 Jay Schroeder 10.00 4.50
❑ 229 Junior Seau 25.00 11.00
❑ 230 George Seifert CO 15.00 6.75
❑ 231 Art Shell CO 15.00 6.75
❑ 232 Mike Sherrard 10.00 4.50
❑ 233 Don Shula CO 40.00 18.00
❑ 234 O.J. Simpson RET 200.00 90.00
(released in 1992 Pro Line)
❑ 235 Phil Simms 30.00 13.50
(released via mail promotion)
❑ 236 Keith Sims 10.00 4.50
❑ 237 Mike Singletary 60.00 27.00
(released at Super Bowl Show)
❑ 238 Jackie Slater 15.00 6.75
❑ 239 Webster Slaughter 12.00 5.50
❑ 240 Al Smith 10.00 4.50
❑ 241 Billy Ray Smith 10.00 4.50
❑ 242 Bruce Smith 25.00 11.00
(released via mail promotion)
❑ 243 Dennis Smith 12.00 5.50
❑ 244 J.T. Smith 10.00 4.50
❑ 245 Emmitt Smith SP 200.00 60.00
❑ 246 Neil Smith 60.00 27.00
(Most signatures are cut off)
❑ 247 Steve Smith 10.00 4.50
❑ 248 Ernest Spears 10.00 4.50
❑ 249 Chris Spielman 15.00 6.75
❑ 250 Rohn Stark 10.00 4.50
❑ 251 Roger Staubach RET 100.00 45.00
(released at Super Bowl Show)
❑ 252 Eric Swann 12.00 5.50
❑ 253 Pat Swilling 12.00 5.50
❑ 254 Darryl Talley 12.00 5.50
❑ 255 Steve Tasker 15.00 6.75
❑ 256 John Taylor 15.00 6.75
❑ 257 Lawrence Taylor 30.00 13.50
❑ 258 Vinny Testaverde 12.00 5.50
❑ 259 Tom Thayer 10.00 4.50
❑ 260 Joe Theismann RET 30.00 13.50
❑ 261 Blair Thomas 10.00 4.50
❑ 262 Broderick Thomas 10.00 4.50
❑ 263 Derrick Thomas 50.00 22.00
❑ 264 Eric Thomas 10.00 4.50
❑ 265 Thurman Thomas 30.00 13.50
❑ 266 Anthony Thompson 10.00 4.50
❑ 267 Andre Tippett 10.00 4.50
❑ 268 Billy Joe Tolliver 10.00 4.50
❑ 269 Al Toon 12.00 5.50
❑ 270 Greg Townsend 175.00 80.00
(released in 1992 Pro Line)
❑ 271 David Treadwell 10.00 4.50
❑ 272 Jack Trudeau 10.00 4.50
❑ 273 Renaldo Turnbull 12.00 5.50
❑ 274 Eric Turner 12.00 5.50
❑ 275 Clarence Verdin 10.00 4.50
❑ 276 Everson Walls 12.00 5.50
❑ 277 Steve Walsh 10.00 4.50
❑ 278 Alvin Walton 10.00 4.50
❑ 279 Andre Ware 15.00 6.75
❑ 280 Paul Warfield RET 15.00 6.75
❑ 281 Don Warren 10.00 4.50
❑ 282 Lionel Washington 150.00 70.00
Most signatures are cut off
❑ 283 Ted Washington 12.00 5.50
❑ 284 Andre Waters 10.00 4.50
❑ 285 Lorenzo White 10.00 4.50
❑ 286 David Whitmore 10.00 4.50
❑ 287 Alfred Williams 10.00 4.50
❑ 288 Lee Williams 10.00 4.50
❑ 289 Richard Williamson CO 10.00 4.50
❑ 290 Wade Wilson 10.00 4.50
❑ 291 Ickey Woods 12.00 5.50
❑ 292 Tony Woods 10.00 4.50
❑ 293 Rod Woodson 35.00 16.00
❑ 294 Donnell Woolford 10.00 4.50
❑ 295 Barry Word 10.00 4.50
❑ 296 Tim Worley 12.00 5.50
❑ 297 Sam Wyche CO 12.00 5.50
❑ 298 David Wyman 10.00 4.50
❑ 299 Lonnie Young 10.00 4.50
❑ 300 Steve Young 60.00 27.00
❑ 301 Gary Zimmerman 10.00 4.50
❑ 302 Chris Zorich 12.00 5.50
❑ PLC2 Payne Stewart 200.00 90.00
Golfer
❑ NNO Santa Claus Sendaway 30.00 13.50
(Signed, not numbered)
❑ NNO Santa Claus/2000 50.00 22.00

1992 Pro Line Portraits Autographs

Nm-Mt Ex-Mt
COMPLETE SET (161) 1200.00 550.00
❑ 1 Kurt Barber 8.00 3.60
❑ 2 Fred Barnett 12.00 5.50
❑ 3 Lem Barney RET 12.00 5.50
❑ 4 Brad Baxter 8.00 3.60
❑ 5 Edgar Bennett 15.00 6.75
❑ 6 Fred Biletnikoff RET 150.00 70.00
❑ 7 Lewis Billups 8.00 3.60
❑ 8 Brian Brennan 8.00 3.60
❑ 9 Bill Brooks 12.00 5.50
❑ 10 Derek Brown TE 8.00 3.60
❑ 11 Terrell Buckley 12.00 5.50
❑ 12 Rob Burnett 8.00 3.60
❑ 13 Dick Butkus RET 25.00 11.00
❑ 14 LeRoy Butler 15.00 6.75
❑ 15 Jeff Carlson 8.00 3.60
❑ 16 Cris Carter 25.00 11.00
❑ 17 Dale Carter 12.00 5.50
❑ 18 Toby Caston 8.00 3.60
❑ 19 Eugene Chung 8.00 3.60
❑ 20 Gary Clark 12.00 5.50
❑ 21 Greg Clark 8.00 3.60
❑ 22 Marco Coleman 12.00 5.50
❑ 23 Cary Conklin 8.00 3.60
❑ 24 Marv Cook 8.00 3.60
❑ 25 Quentin Coryatt 12.00 5.50
❑ 26 Bill Cowher CO 40.00 18.00
❑ 27 Aaron Cox 8.00 3.60
❑ 28 Ray Crockett 8.00 3.60
❑ 29 Jeff Cross 8.00 3.60
❑ 30 Joe DeLamielleure RET 12.00 5.50
❑ 31 Keith DeLong 8.00 3.60
❑ 32 Steve DeOssie 8.00 3.60
❑ 33 Al Davis OWN 350.00 160.00
❑ 34 Antone Davis 8.00 3.60
❑ 35 Wendell Davis 8.00 3.60
❑ 36 Robert Delpino 8.00 3.60
❑ 37 Chris Doleman 12.00 5.50
❑ 38 Tony Dorsett RET 25.00 11.00
❑ 39 Vaughn Dunbar 8.00 3.60
❑ 40 Al Edwards 8.00 3.60
❑ 41 Steve Emtman 8.00 3.60
❑ 42 Ricky Ervins 8.00 3.60
❑ 43 Gill Fenerty 8.00 3.60
❑ 44 Derrick Fenner 8.00 3.60
❑ 45 John Fina 8.00 3.60
❑ 46 Tom Flores CO 12.00 5.50
❑ 47 Dan Fouts RET 20.00 9.00
❑ 48 Mike Fox 8.00 3.60
❑ 49 Mitch Frerotte 8.00 3.60
❑ 50 John Friesz 8.00 3.60
❑ 51 William Fuller 12.00 5.50
❑ 52 Willie Gault 15.00 6.75
❑ 53 John Gesek 8.00 3.60
❑ 54 Sean Gilbert 8.00 3.60
❑ 55 Otto Graham RET 30.00 13.50
❑ 56 Eric Green 8.00 3.60
❑ 57 Harold Green 8.00 3.60
❑ 58 Paul Gruber 8.00 3.60
❑ 59 Dino Hackett 8.00 3.60
❑ 60 Charles Haley 15.00 6.75
❑ 61 Jason Hanson 15.00 6.75
❑ 62 Alvin Harper 12.00 5.50
❑ 63 Michael Haynes 12.00 5.50
❑ 64 Keith Henderson 8.00 3.60
❑ 65 Jeff Herrod 8.00 3.60
❑ 66 Jessie Hester 8.00 3.60
(Signed in ball-point pen)
❑ 67 Craig Heyward 12.00 5.50
❑ 68 Mark Higgs 8.00 3.60

❑ 69 Tommy Hodson 8.00 3.60
❑ 70 Mike Holmgren CO 25.00 11.00
❑ 71 Ethan Horton 8.00 3.60
❑ 72 Patrick Hunter 8.00 3.60
❑ 73 Steve Israel 8.00 3.60
❑ 74 Keith Jackson 12.00 5.50
❑ 75 Joe Jacoby 15.00 6.75
❑ 76 Jim C. Jensen 8.00 3.60
❑ 77 Vance Johnson 8.00 3.60
❑ 78 Ernie Jones 8.00 3.60
❑ 79 Robert Jones 8.00 3.60
❑ 80 Sean Jones 12.00 5.50
❑ 81 Brian Jordan 15.00 6.75
❑ 82 Sonny Jurgensen RET 25.00 11.00
❑ 83 David Klingler 8.00 3.60
❑ 84 Chuck Knox CO 8.00 3.60
❑ 85 Tim Krumrie 8.00 3.60
❑ 86 Eddie LeBaron RET 15.00 6.75
❑ 87 Darren Lewis 8.00 3.60
❑ 88 Nate Lewis 8.00 3.60
❑ 89 Greg Lloyd 30.00 13.50
❑ 90 Bubba McDowell 8.00 3.60
❑ 91 Chester McGlockton 12.00 5.50
❑ 92 Tommy Maddox 25.00 11.00
❑ 93 Ted Marchibroda CO 15.00 6.75
❑ 94 Chris Martin 8.00 3.60
❑ 95 Mike Merriweather 8.00 3.60
❑ 96 Eric Metcalf 12.00 5.50
❑ 97 Chris Mims 8.00 3.60
❑ 98 Hugh Millen 8.00 3.60
❑ 99 Brian Mitchell 12.00 5.50
❑ 100 Johnny Mitchell 8.00 3.60
❑ 101 Joe Montana 120.00 55.00
❑ 102 Eric Moore 8.00 3.60
❑ 103 Brad Muster 8.00 3.60
❑ 104 Ken Norton Jr. 12.00 5.50
❑ 105 Jay Novacek 12.00 5.50
❑ 106 Neil O'Donnell 15.00 6.75
❑ 107 Marquez Pope 8.00 3.60
❑ 108 Robert Porcher 12.00 5.50
❑ 109 Mike Prior 8.00 3.60
❑ 110 Ervin Randle 8.00 3.60
❑ 111 Walter Reeves 8.00 3.60
❑ 112 Ricky Reynolds 8.00 3.60
❑ 113 Bobby Ross CO 12.00 5.50
❑ 114 Deion Sanders 40.00 18.00
(Deion also signed and numbered 200 cards from his personal stock; these are worth double)
❑ 115 Tracy Scroggins 8.00 3.60
❑ 116 Leon Searcy 8.00 3.60
❑ 117 Sterling Sharpe 15.00 6.75
❑ 118 David Shula CO 8.00 3.60
❑ 119 Chris Singleton 8.00 3.60
❑ 120 Greg Skrepenak 8.00 3.60
❑ 121 Chuck Smith 8.00 3.60
❑ 122 Doug Smith 8.00 3.60
❑ 123 Emmitt Smith 100.00 45.00
❑ 124 Kevin Smith 8.00 3.60
❑ 125 Lance Smith 8.00 3.60
❑ 126 Sammie Smith 8.00 3.60
❑ 127 Phillippi Sparks 8.00 3.60
❑ 128 Alonzo Spellman 8.00 3.60
❑ 129 Ken Stabler RET 30.00 13.50
❑ 130 Kelly Stouffer 8.00 3.60
❑ 131 Lynn Swann RET 75.00 34.00
❑ 132 Jim Sweeney 8.00 3.60
❑ 133 Harry Sydney 8.00 3.60
❑ 134 Charley Taylor RET 15.00 6.75
❑ 135 Pat Terrell 8.00 3.60
❑ 136 Henry Thomas 8.00 3.60
❑ 137 Stan Thomas 8.00 3.60
❑ 138 Y.A. Tittle RET 25.00 11.00
❑ 139 Mike Tomczak 8.00 3.60
❑ 140 Jessie Tuggle 8.00 3.60
❑ 141 Floyd Turner 8.00 3.60
❑ 142 Tommy Vardell 12.00 5.50
❑ 143 Jon Vaughn 8.00 3.60
❑ 144 Troy Vincent 15.00 6.75
❑ 145 Tom Waddle 8.00 3.60
❑ 146 Van Waiters 8.00 3.60
❑ 147 Aaron Wallace 8.00 3.60
❑ 148 Brian Washington 8.00 3.60
❑ 149 William White 8.00 3.60
❑ 150 Dave Widell 8.00 3.60
Doug Widell
❑ 151 Calvin Williams 12.00 5.50
❑ 152 Darryl Williams 8.00 3.60
❑ 153 Harvey Williams 8.00 3.60
❑ 154 John L. Williams 12.00 5.50
❑ 155 Warren Williams 8.00 3.60
❑ 156 Ken Willis 8.00 3.60
❑ 157 Kellen Winslow RET 20.00 9.00
❑ 158 Darren Woodson 15.00 6.75
❑ 159 Sam Wyche CO 12.00 5.50
❑ 160 Michael Young 8.00 3.60
❑ 161 Tony Zendejas 8.00 3.60
❑ NNO Santa Claus 15.00 6.75
❑ NNO Mrs. Santa Claus 15.00 6.75

1992 Pro Line Profiles Autographs

	Nm-Mt	Ex-Mt
TROY AIKMAN (181-189)	50.00	22.00
CARL BANKS (19-27)	5.00	2.20
BUBBY BRISTER (91-99)	8.00	3.60
KEITH BYARS (190-198)	5.00	2.20
EARNEST BYNER (478-486)	8.00	3.60
ANTHONY CARTER (64-72)	5.00	2.20
GARY CLARK (208-216)	8.00	3.60
RAND.CUNNINGHAM (469-477)	25.00	11.00
ERIC DICKERSON (379-387)	25.00	11.00
MIKE DITKA (487-495)	25.00	11.00
CHRIS DOLEMAN (217-225)	5.00	2.20
JOHN ELWAY (226-234)	80.00	36.00
BOOMER ESIASON (235-243)	15.00	6.75
JIM EVERETT (244-252)	12.00	5.50
JOE GIBBS (127-135)	40.00	18.00
JERRY GLANVILLE (262-270)	5.00	2.20
ERIC GREEN (253-261)	5.00	2.20
JIM HARBAUGH (163-171)	8.00	3.60
JEFF HOSTETLER (271-279)	5.00	2.20
MICHAEL IRVIN (289-297)	25.00	11.00
HAYWOOD JEFFIRES (280-288)	8.00	3.60
JACK KEMP (154-162)	30.00	13.50
BERNIE KOSAR (100-108)	25.00	11.00
STEVE LARGENT (298-306)	30.00	13.50
HOWIE LONG (388-396)	40.00	18.00
RONNIE LOTT (1-9)	15.00	6.75
DAN MCGWIRE (172-180)	5.00	2.20
ART MONK (496-504)	30.00	13.50
WARREN MOON (442-450)	20.00	9.00
ANTHONY MUNOZ (82-90)	8.00	3.60
KEN O'BRIEN (307-315)	5.00	2.20
CHRISTIAN OKOYE (316-324)	12.00	5.50
RODNEY PEETE (10-18)	5.00	2.20
MICHAEL D. PERRY (325-333)	5.00	2.20
JERRY RICE (46-54)	80.00	36.00
TIMM ROSENBACH (199-207)	8.00	3.60
DEION SANDERS (451-459)	40.00	18.00
JUNIOR SEAU (136-144)	25.00	11.00
STERLING SHARPE (73-81)	15.00	6.75
ART SHELL (109-117)	15.00	6.75
DON SHULA (118-126)	25.00	11.00
PHIL SIMMS (343-351)	15.00	6.75
MIKE SINGLETARY (397-405)	15.00	6.75
BRUCE SMITH (352-360)	30.00	13.50
ROGER STAUBACH (37-45)	40.00	18.00
PAT SWILLING (370-378)	5.00	2.20
JOHN TAYLOR (406-414)	5.00	2.20
LAWRENCE TAYLOR (460-468)	30.00	13.50
VINNY TESTAVERDE (55-63)	12.00	5.50
DERRICK THOMAS (361-369)	50.00	22.00
THURMAN THOMAS (28-36)	15.00	6.75
ANDRE TIPPETT (415-423)	5.00	2.20
AL TOON (145-153)	5.00	2.20

1993 Pro Line Live Autographs

	Nm-Mt	Ex-Mt
COMPLETE SET (38)	800.00	350.00
❑ 1 Troy Aikman/700	50.00	22.00
❑ 2 Neal Anderson/1050	20.00	9.00
❑ 3 Rod Bernstine/1000	12.00	5.50
❑ 4 Terrell Buckley/1050	12.00	5.50
❑ 5 Earnest Byner/750	15.00	6.75
❑ 6 Anthony Carter/950	20.00	9.00
❑ 7 Ray Childress/950	12.00	5.50
❑ 8 Gary Clark/1050	20.00	9.00
❑ 9 Marco Coleman/1000	12.00	5.50
❑ 10 Quentin Coryatt/900	20.00	9.00
❑ 11 Eric Dickerson/900	30.00	13.50
❑ 12 Chris Doleman/1000	12.00	5.50
❑ 13 Steve Emtman/800	15.00	6.75
❑ 14 Brett Favre/650	120.00	55.00
❑ 15 Barry Foster/750	25.00	11.00
❑ 16 Jeff George/1050	20.00	9.00
❑ 17 Rodney Hampton/650	20.00	9.00
❑ 18 Keith Jackson/650	15.00	6.75
❑ 19 Haywood Jeffires/950	20.00	9.00
❑ 20 David Klingler/1200	12.00	5.50
❑ 21 Howie Long/950	40.00	18.00
❑ 22 Ronnie Lott/1050	20.00	9.00
❑ 23 Tommy Maddox/1050	25.00	11.00
❑ 24 Art Monk/750	25.00	11.00
❑ 25 Joe Montana/600	100.00	45.00
❑ 26 Rob Moore/900	20.00	9.00
❑ 27 Neil O'Donnell/1050	20.00	9.00
❑ 28 Christian Okoye/900	12.00	5.50
❑ 29 Rodney Peete/1000	20.00	9.00
❑ 30 Andre Reed/1050	25.00	11.00
❑ 31 Deion Sanders/900	40.00	18.00
❑ 32 Junior Seau/900	25.00	11.00
❑ 33 Sterling Sharpe/1050	25.00	11.00
❑ 34 Neil Smith/1050	25.00	11.00
❑ 35 Pat Swilling/950	20.00	9.00
❑ 36 Vinny Testaverde/900	20.00	9.00
❑ 37 Derrick Thomas/550	60.00	27.00
❑ 38 Herschel Walker/400	25.00	11.00

1993 Pro Line Portraits Autographs

	Nm-Mt	Ex-Mt
COMPLETE SET (26)	700.00	325.00
❑ 1 Patrick Bates	20.00	9.00
❑ 2 Jerome Bettis	50.00	22.00
❑ 3 Steve Beuerlein	25.00	11.00
❑ 4 Tony Casillas	20.00	9.00
❑ 5 Chuck Cecil	20.00	9.00
❑ 6 Reggie Cobb	20.00	9.00
❑ 7 John Copeland	20.00	9.00
❑ 8 Eric Curry	20.00	9.00
❑ 9 Brett Favre	200.00	90.00
❑ 10 Gaston Green	20.00	9.00

	Nm-Mt	Ex-Mt
❑ 11 Rodney Hampton	25.00	11.00
❑ 12 Pat Harlow	20.00	9.00
❑ 13 Bert Jones TB	25.00	11.00
❑ 14 Marvin Jones	20.00	9.00
❑ 15 Lincoln Kennedy	20.00	9.00
❑ 16 Billy Kilmer TB	25.00	11.00
❑ 17 Jeff Lageman	20.00	9.00
❑ 18 Archie Manning TB	30.00	13.50
❑ 19 Harvey Martin TB	40.00	18.00
❑ 20 Terry McDaniel	20.00	9.00
❑ 21 Mike Munchak	35.00	16.00
❑ 22 Frank Reich	20.00	9.00
❑ 23 Willie Roaf	20.00	9.00
❑ 24 Shannon Sharpe	40.00	18.00
❑ 25 Tony Smith	20.00	9.00
❑ 26 Gino Torretta	30.00	13.50

1993 Pro Line Profiles Autographs

	Nm-Mt	Ex-Mt
RAY CHILDRESS (496-504)	10.00	3.00
JEFF GEORGE (505-513)	15.00	4.50
FRANCO HARRIS (514-521)	25.00	7.50
KEITH JACKSON (523-531)	10.00	3.00
J.JOHNSON (533/535/538-540)	12.00	5.50
J.JOHNSON (532/534/536/537)	50.00	22.00
JAY NOVACEK (568-576)	20.00	6.00
GALE SAYERS (577-585)	40.00	18.00

1994 Pro Line Live Autographs

	Nm-Mt	Ex-Mt
COMPLETE SET (134)	2500.00	1100.00
❑ 1 Troy Aikman/340	80.00	36.00
❑ 2 Derrick Alexander WR/950	15.00	6.75
❑ 3 Eric Allen/1980	15.00	6.75
❑ 4 Steve Atwater/1040	25.00	11.00
❑ 5 Victor Bailey/450	10.00	4.50
❑ 6 Harris Barton/2120	10.00	4.50
❑ 7 Mario Bates/1145	10.00	4.50
❑ 8 Brad Baxter/1070	10.00	4.50
❑ 9 Aubrey Beavers/1150	10.00	4.50
❑ 10 Donnell Bennett/1130	10.00	4.50
❑ 11 Rod Bernstine/1010	10.00	4.50
❑ 12 Steve Beuerlein/970	15.00	6.75
❑ 13 Drew Bledsoe/1150	40.00	18.00
❑ 14 Bill Brooks/1030	10.00	4.50
❑ 15 Bucky Brooks/1090	10.00	4.50
❑ 16 Reggie Brooks/460	15.00	6.75
❑ 17 Derek Brown RBK/449	10.00	4.50
❑ 18 Gary Brown/950	10.00	4.50
❑ 19 Tim Brown/1920	30.00	13.50
❑ 20 Jeff Burris/1140	10.00	4.50
❑ 21 Marion Butts/2040	10.00	4.50
❑ 22 Keith Byars/1020	15.00	6.75
❑ 23 Anthony Carter/1020	15.00	6.75
❑ 24 Dale Carter/1031	15.00	6.75
❑ 25 Tom Carter/460	10.00	4.50
❑ 26 Shante Carver/1160	10.00	4.50
❑ 27 Ray Childress/2240	15.00	6.75
❑ 28 Andre Coleman/1000	10.00	4.50
❑ 29 Andre Collins/1100	10.00	4.50
❑ 30 Shane Conlan/1110	10.00	4.50
❑ 31 Horace Copeland/450	10.00	4.50
❑ 32 Quentin Coryatt/970	15.00	6.75
❑ 33 Isaac Davis/1150	10.00	4.50
❑ 34 Kenneth Davis/1170	15.00	6.75
❑ 35 Lake Dawson/1100	15.00	6.75
❑ 36 Robert Delpino/1030	10.00	4.50
❑ 37 Trent Dilfer/2680	25.00	11.00
❑ 38 Troy Drayton/450	10.00	4.50
❑ 39 John Elliott/2150	10.00	4.50
❑ 40 John Elway/1000	100.00	45.00
❑ 41 Steve Emtman/1900	10.00	4.50
❑ 42 Boomer Esiason/920	25.00	11.00
❑ 43 Jim Everett/1265	15.00	6.75
❑ 44 Marshall Faulk/2230	50.00	22.00
❑ 45 Brett Favre/1130	100.00	45.00
❑ 46 William Floyd/950	15.00	6.75
❑ 47 Glenn Foley/890	10.00	4.50
❑ 48 Henry Ford/1110	10.00	4.50
❑ 49 Barry Foster/1080	15.00	6.75
❑ 50 Rob Fredrickson/1160	10.00	4.50
❑ 51 John Friesz/2150	10.00	4.50
❑ 52 Irving Fryar/1040	25.00	11.00
❑ 53 Wayne Gandy/1040	10.00	4.50
❑ 54 Charlie Garner/1130	25.00	11.00
❑ 55 Jeff George/2140	15.00	6.75
❑ 56 Aaron Glenn/1140	25.00	11.00
❑ 58 Rodney Hampton/1090	15.00	6.75
❑ 59 Garrison Hearst/1435	25.00	11.00
❑ 60 Mark Higgs/980	10.00	4.50
❑ 61 Greg Hill/1145	15.00	6.75
❑ 62 Pierce Holt/2020	10.00	4.50
❑ 63 Jeff Hostetler/955	15.00	6.75
❑ 64 Tyrone Hughes/470	10.00	4.50
❑ 65 Michael Irvin/450	30.00	13.50
❑ 66 Qadry Ismail/450	25.00	11.00
❑ 67 Steve Israel/2020	10.00	4.50
❑ 68 Keith Jackson/1020	15.00	6.75
❑ 69 Michael Jackson/1490	15.00	6.75
❑ 70 Willie Jackson/1140	15.00	6.75
❑ 71 Charles Johnson/950	15.00	6.75
❑ 72 Brent Jones/1880	15.00	6.75
❑ 73 Calvin Jones/960	15.00	6.75
❑ 74 Perry Klein/1000	10.00	4.50
❑ 75 David Klingler/2140	10.00	4.50
❑ 76 Erik Kramer/1020	15.00	6.75
❑ 77 Jim Lachey/1850	10.00	4.50
❑ 78 Carnell Lake/1985	10.00	4.50
❑ 79 Antonio Langham/1240	15.00	6.75
❑ 80 Kevin Lee/1190	10.00	4.50
❑ 81 Chuck Levy/950	15.00	6.75
❑ 82 Thomas Lewis/1140	10.00	4.50
❑ 83 Ronnie Lott/910	25.00	11.00
❑ 84 Ed McCaffrey/2030	15.00	6.75
❑ 85 Terry McDaniel/1980	10.00	4.50
❑ 86 Tim McDonald/2040	10.00	4.50
❑ 87 Willie McGinest/3520	25.00	11.00
❑ 88 Russell Maryland/1945	10.00	4.50
❑ 89 Clay Matthews/2000	15.00	6.75
❑ 90 Natrone Means/445	25.00	11.00
❑ 91 Glyn Milburn/440	10.00	4.50
❑ 92 Anthony Miller/2070	15.00	6.75
❑ 93 Sam Mills/1115	30.00	13.50
❑ 94 Joe Montana/920	100.00	45.00
❑ 95 Rob Moore/1025	15.00	6.75
❑ 96 Byron Bam Morris/1130	10.00	4.50
❑ 97 Johnnie Morton/2945	15.00	6.75
❑ 98 Hardy Nickerson/1175	10.00	4.50
❑ 99 Doug Nussmeier/1150	10.00	4.50
❑ 100 Leslie O'Neal/2050	10.00	4.50
❑ 101 David Palmer/950	10.00	4.50
❑ 102 Erric Pegram/1020	10.00	4.50
❑ 103 Roman Phifer/2140	10.00	4.50
❑ 104 Ricky Proehl/1020	15.00	6.75
❑ 105 Thomas Randolph/1100	10.00	4.50
❑ 106 Tom Rathman/2230	25.00	11.00
❑ 107 Errict Rhett/1120	15.00	6.75
❑ 108 Darnay Scott/1400	25.00	11.00
❑ 109 Jason Sehorn/950	25.00	11.00
❑ 110 Shannon Sharpe/1020	25.00	11.00
❑ 111 Sterling Sharpe/450	30.00	13.50
❑ 112 Heath Shuler/2020	15.00	6.75
❑ 113 Jackie Slater/1110	15.00	6.75
❑ 114 Emmitt Smith/925	100.00	45.00
❑ 115 Irv Smith/470	10.00	4.50
❑ 116 Lamar Smith/1130	15.00	6.75
❑ 117 Neil Smith/1000	25.00	11.00
❑ 118 Todd Steussie/2100	15.00	6.75
❑ 119 Aaron Taylor/950	10.00	4.50
❑ 120 John Taylor/1030	25.00	11.00
❑ 121 John Thierry/1150	10.00	4.50
❑ 122 Derrick Thomas/1087	50.00	22.00
❑ 123 Andre Tippett/1090	10.00	4.50
❑ 124 Renaldo Turnbull/945	10.00	4.50
❑ 125 Eric Turner/1030	15.00	6.75
❑ 126 Tommy Vardell/1000	10.00	4.50
❑ 127 D.Washington/1040	15.00	6.75
❑ 128 Richmond Webb/1020	15.00	6.75
❑ 129 Dan Wilkinson/1960	15.00	6.75
❑ 130 Steve Wisniewski/2150	10.00	4.50
❑ 131 Donnell Woolford/1000	10.00	4.50
❑ 132 Steve Young/925	50.00	22.00
❑ 132 Ronnie Woolfork/360	10.00	4.50
❑ 133 Troy Aikman Combo/345 Michael Irvin	120.00	55.00
❑ 134 Steve Young Combo/450 Jerry Rice	150.00	70.00

1995 Pro Line Autographs

	Nm-Mt	Ex-Mt
COMPLETE SET (128)	2400.00	1100.00
❑ 1 Troy Aikman/500	60.00	27.00
❑ 2A Eric Allen/1225	12.00	5.50
❑ 2B Eric Allen/2398AP	12.00	5.50
❑ 2C Eric Allen/745AP	12.00	5.50
❑ 3 Flipper Anderson/1140	8.00	3.60
❑ 4A Randy Baldwin/1435	8.00	3.60
❑ 4B Randy Baldwin/2405AP	8.00	3.60
❑ 4C Randy Baldwin/760AP	8.00	3.60
❑ 5 Mario Bates/1480	12.00	5.50
❑ 6A Don Beebe/1200	12.00	5.50
❑ 6B Don Beebe/275AP	12.00	5.50
❑ 7A Cornelius Bennett/1200	12.00	5.50
❑ 7B Cornelius Bennett/255AP	12.00	5.50
❑ 8 Edgar Bennett/1475	15.00	6.75
❑ 9 Tony Bennett/1475	8.00	3.60
❑ 10 Steve Beuerlein/1465	12.00	5.50
❑ 11 J.J. Birden/775	8.00	3.60
❑ 12 Brian Blades/1465	12.00	5.50
❑ 13 Jeff Blake/1200	15.00	6.75
❑ 14 Drew Bledsoe/515	40.00	18.00
❑ 15A Blake Brockermeyer 1445	8.00	3.60
❑ 15B Blake Brockermeyer 2315AP	8.00	3.60
❑ 16 Derrick Brooks/1470	20.00	9.00
❑ 17 Tim Brown/2410	20.00	9.00
❑ 18 Dale Carter/1400	12.00	5.50

- ❑ 19A Ray Childress/1200 8.00 3.60
- ❑ 19B Ray Childress/235AP 8.00 3.60
- ❑ 20 Ben Coates/1175 12.00 5.50
- ❑ 21 Mark Collins/1430 8.00 3.60
- ❑ 22 Kerry Collins/3300 15.00 6.75
- ❑ 23 Curtis Conway/1200 12.00 5.50
- ❑ 24 Quentin Coryatt/1400 12.00 5.50
- ❑ 25 R. Cunningham/470 30.00 13.50
- ❑ 26A Jack Del Rio/1480 8.00 3.60
- ❑ 26B Jack Del Rio/930AP 8.00 3.60
- ❑ 27 Willie Davis/1500 12.00 5.50
- ❑ 28A Derrick Deese/1200 8.00 3.60
- ❑ 28B Derrick Deese/2375AP 8.00 3.60
- ❑ 28C Derrick Deese/735AP 8.00 3.60
- ❑ 29A Trent Dilfer/2010 15.00 6.75
- ❑ 29B Trent Dilfer/306AP 15.00 6.75
- ❑ 30 Troy Drayton/1375 8.00 3.60
- ❑ 31 Quinn Early/1200 12.00 5.50
- ❑ 32 Henry Ellard/1440 12.00 5.50
- ❑ 33 John Elliott/2380 8.00 3.60
- ❑ 34 Luther Elliss/1470 8.00 3.60
- ❑ 35 John Elway/50 250.00 110.00
- ❑ 36 Bert Emanuel/1445 12.00 5.50
- ❑ 37 Steve Emtman/2365 8.00 3.60
- ❑ 38A Craig Erickson/630 12.00 5.50
- ❑ 38B Craig Erickson/890AP 8.00 3.60
- ❑ 39 Boomer Esiason/1700 15.00 6.75
- ❑ 40 Marshall Faulk/1030 50.00 22.00
- ❑ 41 Barry Foster/1455 12.00 5.50
- ❑ 42 Mike Fox/1445 8.00 3.60
- ❑ 43 Irving Fryar/1500 12.00 5.50
- ❑ 44 Joey Galloway/1445 15.00 6.75
- ❑ 45A Shaun Gayle/1200 8.00 3.60
- ❑ 45B Shaun Gayle/265AP 8.00 3.60
- ❑ 46 Jeff George/1295 12.00 5.50
- ❑ 47 Darrien Gordon/2400 8.00 3.60
- ❑ 48 Jeff Graham/1465 12.00 5.50
- ❑ 49 Eric Green/1460 8.00 3.60
- ❑ 50 Charles Haley/1420 12.00 5.50
- ❑ 51 Rodney Hampton/1120 12.00 5.50
- ❑ 52 Andy Harmon/1200 8.00 3.60
- ❑ 53 Courtney Hawkins/1445 8.00 3.60
- ❑ 54 Michael Haynes/1180 12.00 5.50
- ❑ 55 Garrison Hearst/1460 15.00 6.75
- ❑ 56A Craig Heyward/1200 8.00 3.60
- ❑ 56B Craig Heyward/265AP 12.00 5.50
- ❑ 57 Greg Hill/1455 12.00 5.50
- ❑ 58 Pierce Holt/1440 8.00 3.60
- ❑ 59 Patrick Hunter/2375 8.00 3.60
- ❑ 60 Michael Irvin/1490 15.00 6.75
- ❑ 61 Sean Jones/2385 8.00 3.60
- ❑ 62 Qadry Ismail/1170 12.00 5.50
- ❑ 63A Steve Israel/1200 8.00 3.60
- ❑ 63B Steve Israel/2413AP 8.00 3.60
- ❑ 63C Steve Israel/750AP 8.00 3.60
- ❑ 64 Jack Jackson/1475 8.00 3.60
- ❑ 65 Michael Jackson/1200 12.00 5.50
- ❑ 66A Shawn Jefferson/1200 8.00 3.60
- ❑ 66B Shawn Jefferson/240AP 12.00 5.50
- ❑ 67 Haywood Jeffires/1470 12.00 5.50
- ❑ 68 Trezelle Jenkins/1470 8.00 3.60
- ❑ 69A Rob Johnson/2815 12.00 5.50
- ❑ 69B Rob Johnson/500 12.00 5.50
- ❑ 70 Seth Joyner/1480 15.00 6.75
- ❑ 71 Jim Kelly/470 40.00 18.00
- ❑ 72 Cortez Kennedy/1380 12.00 5.50
- ❑ 73 Terry Kirby/1450 12.00 5.50
- ❑ 74 Dave Krieg/1470 12.00 5.50
- ❑ 75A Antonio Langham/1200 8.00 3.60
- ❑ 75B Antonio Langham/260AP 8.00 3.60
- ❑ 76 Ty Law/1460 30.00 13.50
- ❑ 77 Leon Lett/1550 8.00 3.60
- ❑ 78 Ronnie Lott/1900 15.00 6.75
- ❑ 79A K.McCardell/1235 12.00 5.50
- ❑ 79B Keenan McCardell/2403AP 12.00 5.50
- ❑ 80 Terry McDaniel/2340 8.00 3.60
- ❑ 81 Tony McGee/1385 12.00 5.50
- ❑ 82A Willie McGinest/1160 15.00 6.75
- ❑ 82B Willie McGinest/2407AP 15.00 6.75
- ❑ 82C Willie McGinest/754AP 15.00 6.75
- ❑ 83 Chester McGlockton/1280 12.00 5.50
- ❑ 84A Mark McMillian/1175 8.00 3.60
- ❑ 84B Mark McMillian/2400AP 8.00 3.60
- ❑ 84C Mark McMillian/825AP 8.00 3.60
- ❑ 85 Steve McNair/3490 25.00 11.00
- ❑ 86 Mike Mamula/1250 8.00 3.60
- ❑ 87A Arthur Marshall/1165 8.00 3.60
- ❑ 87B Arthur Marshall/2400AP 8.00 3.60
- ❑ 87C Arthur Marshall/870AP 8.00 3.60
- ❑ 88 Russell Maryland/1250 12.00 5.50
- ❑ 89 Clay Matthews/2385 12.00 5.50
- ❑ 90A Chad May/1180 8.00 3.60
- ❑ 90B Chad May/2410AP 8.00 3.60
- ❑ 91 Natrone Means/1058 12.00 5.50
- ❑ 92 Anthony Miller/2385 12.00 5.50
- ❑ 93 Sam Mills/1470 30.00 13.50
- ❑ 94 Herman Moore/2070 12.00 5.50
- ❑ 95 Byron Bam Morris/1430 8.00 3.60
- ❑ 96 Jay Novacek/1195 30.00 13.50
- ❑ 97A Brett Perriman/1380 8.00 3.60
- ❑ 97B Brett Perriman/935 8.00 3.60
- ❑ 98A Michael D. Perry/1200 15.00 6.75
- ❑ 98B Michael D.Perry/295AP 15.00 6.75
- ❑ 99 Roman Phifer/2395 8.00 3.60
- ❑ 100 Ricky Proehl/1475 12.00 5.50
- ❑ 101A John Randle/1170 12.00 5.50
- ❑ 101B John Randle/2400AP 12.00 5.50
- ❑ 101C John Randle/757AP 12.00 5.50
- ❑ 102 Andre Reed/1440 15.00 6.75
- ❑ 103 Jake Reed/1470 12.00 5.50
- ❑ 104 Errict Rhett/1400 12.00 5.50
- ❑ 105A Willie Roaf/1200 12.00 5.50
- ❑ 105B Willie Roaf/245AP 12.00 5.50
- ❑ 106 Bill Romanowski/1450 30.00 13.50
- ❑ 107 Rashaan Salaam/1320 12.00 5.50
- ❑ 108 Mike Sherrard/1450 8.00 3.60
- ❑ 109A Heath Shuler/2000 12.00 5.50
- ❑ 109B Heath Shuler/366AP 12.00 5.50
- ❑ 110 Clyde Simmons/735 12.00 5.50
- ❑ 111A Chris Slade/1100 8.00 3.60
- ❑ 111B Chris Slade/2417AP 8.00 3.60
- ❑ 111C Chris Slade/750AP 8.00 2.40
- ❑ 112 Al Smith/1360 8.00 3.60
- ❑ 113 Emmitt Smith/500 120.00 55.00
- ❑ 114 Neil Smith/1465 15.00 6.75
- ❑ 115 Mark Stepnoski/1500 8.00 3.60
- ❑ 116 J.J. Stokes/1435 15.00 6.75
- ❑ 117 Vinny Testaverde/1020 12.00 5.50
- ❑ 118 Henry Thomas/1420 8.00 3.60
- ❑ 119 Lewis Tillman/1170 8.00 3.60
- ❑ 120A Jessie Tuggle/1200 8.00 3.60
- ❑ 120B Jessie Tuggle/195AP 12.00 5.50
- ❑ 121 Tamarick Vanover/1155 12.00 5.50
- ❑ 122 Troy Vincent/1490 8.00 3.60
- ❑ 123 John Walsh/3340 8.00 3.60
- ❑ 124A Steve Walsh/1185 12.00 5.50
- ❑ 124B Steve Walsh/1015AP 12.00 5.50
- ❑ 125A Brian Williams LB/1175 8.00 3.60
- ❑ 125B Brian Williams LB/2670AP 8.00 3.60
- ❑ 125C Brian Williams LB/865AP 8.00 3.60
- ❑ 126 Calvin Williams/1200 12.00 5.50
- ❑ 127 Sherman Williams/1460 8.00 3.60
- ❑ 128 Steve Young/500 40.00 18.00
- ❑ 129 Eric Zeier/500 12.00 5.50

1995 Pro Line Autograph Printer's Proofs

	Nm-Mt	Ex-Mt
❑ 99 Steve McNair	100.00	45.00
❑ 175 Drew Bledsoe	100.00	45.00
❑ 197 Steve Young	120.00	55.00
❑ 210 Kerry Collins	60.00	27.00
❑ 230 Boomer Esiason	40.00	18.00
❑ 254 Troy Aikman	150.00	70.00
❑ 304 Emmitt Smith	250.00	110.00
❑ 311 Trent Dilfer	40.00	18.00

1996 Pro Line Autographs Gold

	Nm-Mt	Ex-Mt
❑ 1 Troy Aikman Emmitt Smith Gold Only	300.00	135.00
❑ 2 Eric Allen	12.00	5.50
❑ 3 Mike Alstott	30.00	13.50
❑ 4 Tony Banks	30.00	13.50
❑ 5 Blaine Bishop	12.00	5.50
❑ 6 Drew Bledsoe	80.00	36.00
❑ 7 Tim Brown	40.00	18.00
❑ 8 Marion Butts	12.00	5.50
❑ 9 Sedric Clark	12.00	5.50
❑ 10 Duane Clemons	12.00	5.50
❑ 11 Marco Coleman	12.00	5.50
❑ 12 Kerry Collins	30.00	9.00
❑ 13 Eric Davis	12.00	5.50
❑ 14 Derrick Deese	12.00	5.50
❑ 15 Jack Del Rio	12.00	5.50
❑ 16 Ty Detmer	20.00	9.00
❑ 17 Chris Doering	12.00	5.50
❑ 18 Jumbo Elliott	12.00	5.50
❑ 19 Marshall Faulk	50.00	22.00
❑ 20 Glenn Foley	12.00	5.50
❑ 21 John Friesz	12.00	5.50
❑ 22 Daryl Gardener	20.00	9.00
❑ 23 Randall Godfrey	12.00	5.50
❑ 24 Scott Greene	12.00	5.50
❑ 25 Rhett Hall	12.00	5.50
❑ 26 Merton Hanks	12.00	5.50
❑ 27 Kevin Hardy	12.00	5.50
❑ 28 Richard Huntley	20.00	9.00
❑ 29 Michael Jackson	12.00	5.50
❑ 30 Ron Jaworski	20.00	9.00
❑ 31 Andre Johnson	12.00	5.50
❑ 32 Keyshawn Johnson	30.00	13.50
❑ 33 Keyshawn Johnson Neil O'Donnell Gold Only	50.00	22.00
❑ 34 Mike Jones	12.00	5.50
❑ 35 Jim Kiick	30.00	13.50
❑ 36 Carnell Lake	20.00	6.00
❑ 37 Jeff Lewis	20.00	9.00
❑ 38 Tommy Maddox	30.00	13.50
❑ 39 Arthur Marshall	12.00	5.50
❑ 40 Russell Maryland	12.00	5.50
❑ 41 Derrick Mayes	20.00	9.00
❑ 42 Ed McCaffrey	20.00	9.00
❑ 43 Keenan McCardell	20.00	9.00
❑ 44 Terry McDaniel	12.00	5.50
❑ 45 Tim McDonald	12.00	5.50
❑ 46 Willie McGinest	30.00	13.50
❑ 47 Mark McMillian	12.00	5.50
❑ 48 Johnny McWilliams	12.00	5.50
❑ 49 Ray Mickens	12.00	5.50
❑ 50 Anthony Miller	12.00	5.50
❑ 51 Rick Mirer	20.00	9.00
❑ 52 Alex Molden	12.00	5.50
❑ 53 Johnnie Morton	20.00	9.00
❑ 54 Eric Moulds	20.00	9.00
❑ 55 Roman Oben	12.00	5.50
❑ 56 Neil O'Donnell Gold Only	30.00	13.50
❑ 57 Leslie O'Neal	12.00	5.50
❑ 58 Roman Phifer	12.00	5.50
❑ 59 Gary Plummer	12.00	5.50
❑ 60 Jim Plunkett	30.00	13.50
❑ 61 Stanley Pritchett	20.00	9.00
❑ 62 John Randle	20.00	9.00
❑ 63 Brian Roche	12.00	5.50
❑ 64 Orpheus Roye	12.00	5.50
❑ 65 Mark Seay	12.00	5.50

Card	Nm-Mt	Ex-Mt
❑ 66 Mike Sherrard	12.00	5.50
❑ 67 Chris Slade	12.00	5.50
❑ 68 Scott Slutzker	12.00	5.50
❑ 69 Emmitt Smith	250.00	110.00
Gold Only		
❑ 70 Steve Taneyhill	12.00	5.50
❑ 71 Robb Thomas	12.00	5.50
❑ 72 William Thomas	12.00	5.50
❑ 73 Alex Van Dyke	30.00	13.50
❑ 74 Randy White	30.00	13.50
❑ 75 Steve Young	100.00	45.00
Gold Only		

1996 Pro Line Autographs Blue

	Nm-Mt	Ex-Mt
COMP.BLUE SET (68)	600.00	275.00

*BLUE CARDS: .25X TO .6X GOLDS

1997 Pro Line Autographs

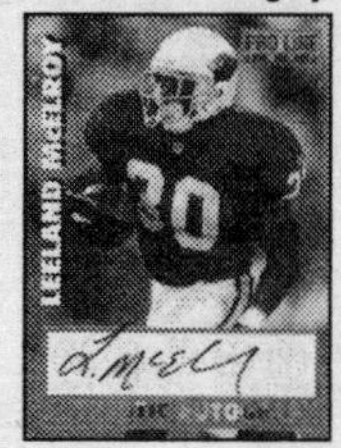

Card	Nm-Mt	Ex-Mt
❑ 1 Karim Abdul-Jabbar	20.00	9.00
❑ 2 Troy Aikman	120.00	55.00
❑ 3 Eric Allen	15.00	6.75
❑ 4 Mike Alstott	20.00	9.00
❑ 5 Marco Battaglia	10.00	4.50
❑ 6 Eric Bjornson	10.00	4.50
❑ 7 Peter Boulware	15.00	6.75
❑ 8 Ray Buchanon	20.00	9.00
❑ 9 Rae Carruth	10.00	4.50
❑ 10 Kerry Collins	20.00	9.00
❑ 11 Stephen Davis	30.00	13.50
❑ 12 Terrell Davis	40.00	18.00
❑ 13 Derrick Deese	10.00	4.50
❑ 14 Koy Detmer	15.00	6.75
❑ 15 Ken Dilger	10.00	4.50
❑ 16 Corey Dillon	40.00	18.00
❑ 17 Hugh Douglas	10.00	4.50
❑ 18 Jason Dunn	10.00	4.50
❑ 19 Warrick Dunn	20.00	9.00
❑ 20 Ray Farmer	10.00	4.50
❑ 21 Brett Favre	120.00	55.00
❑ 22 Joey Galloway	15.00	6.75
❑ 23 Norberto Garrido	10.00	4.50
❑ 24 Terry Glenn	20.00	9.00
❑ 25 Tony Gonzalez	20.00	9.00
❑ 26 Byron Hanspard	10.00	4.50
❑ 27 Kevin Hardy	10.00	4.50
❑ 28 Steve Israel	10.00	4.50
❑ 29 Brad Johnson	20.00	9.00
❑ 30 Keyshawn Johnson	20.00	9.00
❑ 31 Lance Johnstone	10.00	4.50
❑ 32 Greg Jones	10.00	4.50
❑ 33 Mike Jones	10.00	4.50
❑ 34 Danny Kanell	15.00	6.75
❑ 35 David LaFleur	10.00	4.50
❑ 36 Keenan McCardell	15.00	6.75
❑ 37 Leeland McElroy	10.00	4.50
❑ 38 Willie McGinest	20.00	9.00
❑ 39 Mark McMillian	10.00	4.50
❑ 40 Nate Newton	10.00	4.50
❑ 41 Jake Plummer	30.00	13.50
❑ 42 Trevor Pryce	20.00	9.00
❑ 43 John Randle	15.00	6.75
❑ 44 Simeon Rice	15.00	6.75
❑ 45 Jon Runyan	10.00	4.50
❑ 46 Chris Slade	10.00	4.50
❑ 47 Antowain Smith	20.00	9.00
❑ 48 Emmitt Smith	120.00	55.00
❑ 49 Jimmy Smith	15.00	6.75
❑ 50 Matt Stevens	10.00	4.50
❑ 51 Kordell Stewart	20.00	9.00
❑ 52 Mark Tuinei	20.00	9.00
❑ 53 Bryant Westbrook	10.00	4.50
❑ 54 Brian Williams LB	10.00	4.50
❑ 55 Dusty Zeigler	10.00	4.50
❑ 56 Troy Davis/5000	10.00	3.00

1997 Pro Line Autographs Emerald

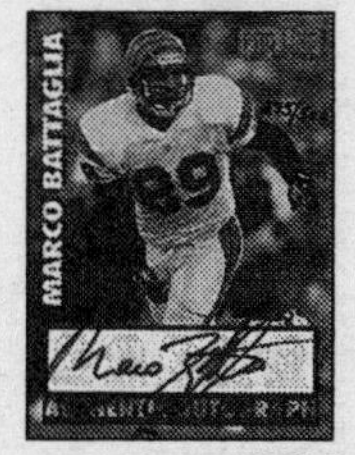

Card	Nm-Mt	Ex-Mt
❑ 1 Karim Abdul-Jabbar/190	30.00	13.50
❑ 2 Troy Aikman/40	300.00	135.00
❑ 3 Eric Allen/250	20.00	9.00
❑ 4 Marco Battaglia/500	20.00	9.00
❑ 5 Eric Bjornson/390	20.00	9.00
❑ 6 Peter Boulware/430	25.00	11.00
❑ 7 Ray Buchanon/390	30.00	13.50
❑ 8 Rae Carruth/525	20.00	9.00
❑ 9 Kerry Collins/170	40.00	18.00
❑ 10 Stephen Davis/530	50.00	22.00
❑ 11 Terrell Davis/100	100.00	45.00
❑ 14 Ken Dilger/525	20.00	9.00
❑ 15 Corey Dillon/470	40.00	18.00
❑ 16 Hugh Douglas/400	20.00	9.00
❑ 17 Jason Dunn/525	20.00	9.00
❑ 18 Warrick Dunn/430	40.00	18.00
❑ 19 Ray Farmer/340	20.00	9.00
❑ 20 Brett Favre/100	250.00	110.00
❑ 21 Joey Galloway/300	25.00	11.00
❑ 23 Terry Glenn/380	30.00	13.50
❑ 24 Byron Hanspard/500	25.00	11.00
❑ 25 Kevin Hardy/500	20.00	9.00
❑ 27 Brad Johnson/410	50.00	22.00
❑ 28 Keyshawn Johnson/100	80.00	36.00
❑ 29 Greg Jones/470	20.00	9.00
❑ 31 Danny Kanell/450	25.00	11.00
❑ 32 David LaFleur/500	20.00	9.00
❑ 33 Keenan McCardell/220	25.00	11.00
❑ 34 Leeland McElroy/440	20.00	9.00
❑ 35 Willie McGinest/210	30.00	13.50
❑ 37 Nate Newton/340	20.00	9.00
❑ 38 Jake Plummer/440	30.00	13.50
❑ 39 John Randle/400	25.00	11.00
❑ 40 Simeon Rice/375	25.00	11.00
❑ 41 Jon Runyan/500	20.00	9.00
❑ 42 Chris Slade/260	20.00	9.00
❑ 44 Emmitt Smith/200	150.00	70.00
❑ 45 Jimmy Smith/280	25.00	11.00
❑ 46 Matt Stevens/450	20.00	9.00
❑ 47 Kordell Stewart/130	50.00	22.00
❑ 48 Mark Tuinei/400	30.00	13.50
❑ 49 Bryant Westbrook/525	25.00	11.00
❑ 51 Dusty Zeigler/480	20.00	9.00

1996 Pro Line Memorabilia Rookie Autographs

Card	Nm-Mt	Ex-Mt
COMPLETE SET (16)	400.00	180.00
❑ 1 Tim Biakabutuka/210	30.00	13.50
❑ 2 Tim Biakabutuka/600	50.00	22.00
Eddie George		
❑ 3 Duane Clemons/1255	15.00	6.75
❑ 4 Daryl Gardener/1390	15.00	6.75
❑ 5 Eddie George/395	50.00	22.00
❑ 6 Terry Glenn/600	50.00	22.00
Keyshawn Johnson		
❑ 7 Kevin Hardy/940	20.00	9.00
❑ 8 Jeff Hartings/1370		
❑ 9 Andre Johnson/1370	15.00	6.75
❑ 10 Keyshawn Johnson/195	50.00	22.00
❑ 11 Pete Kendall/1495	15.00	6.75
❑ 12 Alex Molden/1320	15.00	6.75
❑ 13 Eric Moulds/1010	30.00	13.50
❑ 14 Jamain Stephens/795	15.00	6.75
❑ 15 Regan Upshaw	15.00	4.50
(not serial numbered)		
❑ 16 Jerome Woods/1375	15.00	6.75

1989 Pro Set

Card	Nm-Mt	Ex-Mt
COMPLETE SET (561)	25.00	11.00
COMP.SERIES 1 (440)	6.00	2.70
COMP.SERIES 2 (100)	20.00	9.00
COMP.FINAL FACT.SET (21)	2.00	.90
❑ 1 Stacey Bailey	.04	.02
❑ 2 Aundray Bruce RC	.04	.02
❑ 3 Rick Bryan	.04	.02
❑ 4 Bobby Butler	.04	.02
❑ 5 Scott Case RC	.04	.02
❑ 6 Tony Casillas	.04	.02
❑ 7 Floyd Dixon	.04	.02
❑ 8 Rick Donnelly	.04	.02
❑ 9 Bill Fralic	.04	.02

❑	10	Mike Gann	.04	.02
❑	11	Mike Kenn	.04	.02
❑	12	Chris Miller RC	.25	.11
❑	13	John Rade	.04	.02
❑	14	Gerald Riggs UER (Uniform number is 42 but 43 on back)	.10	.05
❑	15	John Settle RC	.04	.02
❑	16	Marion Campbell CO	.04	.02
❑	17	Cornelius Bennett	.10	.05
❑	18	Derrick Burroughs	.04	.02
❑	19	Shane Conlan	.04	.02
❑	20	Ronnie Harmon	.10	.05
❑	21	Kent Hull RC	.04	.02
❑	22	Jim Kelly	.50	.23
❑	23	Mark Kelso	.04	.02
❑	24	Pete Metzelaars	.04	.02
❑	25	Scott Norwood RC**	.04	.02
❑	26	Andre Reed	.25	.11
❑	27	Fred Smerlas	.04	.02
❑	28	Bruce Smith	.25	.11
❑	29	Leonard Smith	.04	.02
❑	30	Art Still	.04	.02
❑	31	Darryl Talley	.10	.05
❑	32	Thurman Thomas RC	1.00	.45
❑	33	Will Wolford RC	.04	.02
❑	34	Marv Levy CO	.04	.02
❑	35	Neal Anderson	.10	.05
❑	36	Kevin Butler	.04	.02
❑	37	Jim Covert	.04	.02
❑	38	Richard Dent	.10	.05
❑	39	Dave Duerson	.04	.02
❑	40	Dennis Gentry	.04	.02
❑	41	Dan Hampton	.10	.05
❑	42	Jay Hilgenberg	.04	.02
❑	43	Dennis McKinnon UER (Caught 20 or 21 passes as a rookie)	.04	.02
❑	44	Jim McMahon	.10	.05
❑	45	Steve McMichael	.10	.05
❑	46	Brad Muster RC	.04	.02
❑	47A	William Perry SP	6.00	2.70
❑	47B	Ron Morris RC	.04	.02
❑	48	Ron Rivera	.04	.02
❑	49	Vestee Jackson RC	.04	.02
❑	50	Mike Singletary	.10	.05
❑	51	Mike Tomczak	.10	.05
❑	52	Keith Van Horne RC	.04	.02
❑	53A	Mike Ditka CO (No HOF mention on card front)	.25	.11
❑	53B	Mike Ditka CO (HOF banner on front)	.25	.11
❑	54	Lewis Billups	.04	.02
❑	55	James Brooks	.10	.05
❑	56	Eddie Brown	.04	.02
❑	57	Jason Buck RC	.04	.02
❑	58	Boomer Esiason	.10	.05
❑	59	David Fulcher	.10	.05
❑	60A	Rodney Holman RC (BENGALS on front)	.10	.05
❑	60B	Rodney Holman RC (Bengals on front)	.25	.11
❑	61	Reggie Williams	.04	.02
❑	62	Joe Kelly RC	.04	.02
❑	63	Tim Krumrie	.04	.02
❑	64	Tim McGee	.04	.02
❑	65	Max Montoya	.04	.02
❑	66	Anthony Munoz	.10	.05
❑	67	Jim Skow	.04	.02
❑	68	Eric Thomas RC	.04	.02
❑	69	Leon White	.04	.02
❑	70	Ickey Woods RC	.10	.05
❑	71	Carl Zander	.04	.02
❑	72	Sam Wyche CO	.04	.02
❑	73	Brian Brennan	.04	.02
❑	74	Earnest Byner	.04	.02
❑	75	Hanford Dixon	.04	.02
❑	76	Mike Pagel	.04	.02
❑	77	Bernie Kosar	.10	.05
❑	78	Reggie Langhorne RC	.04	.02
❑	79	Kevin Mack	.04	.02
❑	80	Clay Matthews	.10	.05
❑	81	Gerald McNeil	.04	.02
❑	82	Frank Minnifield	.04	.02
❑	83	Cody Risien	.04	.02
❑	84	Webster Slaughter	.10	.05
❑	85	Felix Wright	.04	.02
❑	86	Bud Carson CO UER (NFLPA logo on back)	.04	.02
❑	87	Bill Bates	.10	.05
❑	88	Kevin Brooks	.04	.02
❑	89	Michael Irvin RC	1.25	.55
❑	90	Jim Jeffcoat	.04	.02
❑	91	Ed Too Tall Jones	.10	.05
❑	92	Eugene Lockhart RC	.04	.02
❑	93	Nate Newton RC	.10	.05
❑	94	Danny Noonan	.04	.02
❑	95	Steve Pelluer	.04	.02
❑	96	Herschel Walker	.10	.05
❑	97	Everson Walls	.04	.02
❑	98	Jimmy Johnson CO RC	.10	.05
❑	99	Keith Bishop	.04	.02
❑	100A	John Elway ERR (Drafted 1st Round)	6.00	2.70
❑	100B	John Elway COR (Acquired Trade)	2.00	.90
❑	101	Simon Fletcher RC	.04	.02
❑	102	Mike Harden	.04	.02
❑	103	Mike Horan	.04	.02
❑	104	Mark Jackson	.04	.02
❑	105	Vance Johnson	.10	.05
❑	106	Rulon Jones	.04	.02
❑	107	Clarence Kay	.04	.02
❑	108	Karl Mecklenburg	.04	.02
❑	109	Ricky Nattiel	.04	.02
❑	110	Steve Sewell RC	.04	.02
❑	111	Dennis Smith	.10	.05
❑	112	Gerald Willhite	.04	.02
❑	113	Sammy Winder	.04	.02
❑	114	Dan Reeves CO	.04	.02
❑	115	Jim Arnold	.04	.02
❑	116	Jerry Ball RC	.04	.02
❑	117	Bennie Blades RC	.04	.02
❑	118	Lomas Brown	.04	.02
❑	119	Mike Cofer	.04	.02
❑	120	Garry James	.04	.02
❑	121	James Jones	.04	.02
❑	122	Chuck Long	.04	.02
❑	123	Pete Mandley	.04	.02
❑	124	Eddie Murray	.04	.02
❑	125	Chris Spielman RC	.25	.11
❑	126	Dennis Gibson	.04	.02
❑	127	Wayne Fontes CO	.04	.02
❑	128	John Anderson	.04	.02
❑	129	Brent Fullwood RC	.04	.02
❑	130	Mark Cannon	.04	.02
❑	131	Tim Harris	.04	.02
❑	132	Mark Lee	.04	.02
❑	133	Don Majkowski RC	.10	.05
❑	134	Mark Murphy	.04	.02
❑	135	Brian Noble	.04	.02
❑	136	Ken Ruettgers RC	.04	.02
❑	137	Johnny Holland	.04	.02
❑	138	Randy Wright	.04	.02
❑	139	Lindy Infante CO	.04	.02
❑	140	Steve Brown	.04	.02
❑	141	Ray Childress (Sacking Joe Montana)	.04	.02
❑	142	Jeff Donaldson	.04	.02
❑	143	Ernest Givins	.10	.05
❑	144	John Grimsley	.04	.02
❑	145	Alonzo Highsmith	.04	.02
❑	146	Drew Hill	.04	.02
❑	147	Robert Lyles	.04	.02
❑	148	Bruce Matthews RC	.60	.25
❑	149	Warren Moon	.25	.11
❑	150	Mike Munchak	.10	.05
❑	151	Allen Pinkett RC	.04	.02
❑	152	Mike Rozier	.04	.02
❑	153	Tony Zendejas	.04	.02
❑	154	Jerry Glanville CO	.04	.02
❑	155	Albert Bentley	.04	.02
❑	156	Dean Biasucci	.04	.02
❑	157	Duane Bickett	.04	.02
❑	158	Bill Brooks	.10	.05
❑	159	Chris Chandler RC	1.00	.45
❑	160	Pat Beach	.04	.02
❑	161	Ray Donaldson	.04	.02
❑	162	Jon Hand	.04	.02
❑	163	Chris Hinton	.04	.02
❑	164	Rohn Stark	.04	.02
❑	165	Fredd Young	.04	.02
❑	166	Ron Meyer CO	.04	.02
❑	167	Lloyd Burruss	.04	.02
❑	168	Carlos Carson	.04	.02
❑	169	Deron Cherry	.10	.05
❑	170	Irv Eatman	.04	.02
❑	171	Dino Hackett	.04	.02
❑	172	Steve DeBerg	.04	.02
❑	173	Albert Lewis	.04	.02
❑	174	Nick Lowery	.04	.02
❑	175	Bill Maas	.04	.02
❑	176	Christian Okoye	.04	.02
❑	177	Stephone Paige	.04	.02
❑	178	Mark Adickes (Out of alphabetical sequence for his team)	.04	.02
❑	179	Kevin Ross RC	.10	.05
❑	180	Neil Smith RC	.50	.23
❑	181	M. Schottenheimer CO	.04	.02
❑	182	Marcus Allen	.25	.11
❑	183	Tim Brown RC	1.50	.70
❑	184	Willie Gault	.10	.05
❑	185	Bo Jackson	.30	.14
❑	186	Howie Long	.25	.11
❑	187	Vann McElroy	.04	.02
❑	188	Matt Millen	.10	.05
❑	189	Don Mosebar RC	.04	.02
❑	190	Bill Pickel	.04	.02
❑	191	Jerry Robinson UER (Stats show 1 TD, but text says 2 TD's)	.04	.02
❑	192	Jay Schroeder	.04	.02
❑	193A	Stacey Toran (No mention of death on card front)	.04	.02
❑	193B	Stacey Toran (1961-1989 banner on card front)	.50	.23
❑	194	Mike Shanahan CO RC	.10	.05
❑	195	Greg Bell	.04	.02
❑	196	Ron Brown	.04	.02
❑	197	Aaron Cox RC	.04	.02
❑	198	Henry Ellard	.25	.11
❑	199	Jim Everett	.10	.05
❑	200	Jerry Gray	.04	.02
❑	201	Kevin Greene	.25	.11
❑	202	Pete Holohan	.04	.02
❑	203	LeRoy Irvin	.04	.02
❑	204	Mike Lansford	.04	.02
❑	205	Tom Newberry RC	.04	.02
❑	206	Mel Owens	.04	.02
❑	207	Jackie Slater	.04	.02
❑	208	Doug Smith	.04	.02
❑	209	Mike Wilcher	.04	.02
❑	210	John Robinson CO	.04	.02
❑	211	John Bosa	.04	.02
❑	212	Mark Brown	.04	.02
❑	213	Mark Clayton	.10	.05
❑	214A	Ferrell Edmonds RC ERR, Misspelled Edmonds on front and back)	.50	.23
❑	214B	Ferrell Edmonds RC COR, spelled correctly	.04	.02
❑	215	Roy Foster	.04	.02
❑	216	Lorenzo Hampton	.04	.02
❑	217	Jim C. Jensen RC UER (Born Albington, should be Abington)	.04	.02
❑	218	William Judson	.04	.02
❑	219	Eric Kumerow RC	.04	.02
❑	220	Dan Marino	2.00	.90
❑	221	John Offerdahl	.04	.02
❑	222	Fuad Reveiz	.04	.02
❑	223	Reggie Roby	.04	.02
❑	224	Brian Sochia	.04	.02
❑	225	Don Shula CO RC	.25	.11
❑	226	Alfred Anderson	.04	.02
❑	227	Joey Browner	.04	.02
❑	228	Anthony Carter	.10	.05
❑	229	Chris Doleman	.10	.05

❑ 230 Hassan Jones RC .04 .02
❑ 231 Steve Jordan .04 .02
❑ 232 Tommy Kramer .04 .02
❑ 233 Carl Lee RC .04 .02
❑ 234 Kirk Lowdermilk RC .04 .02
❑ 235 Randall McDaniel RC .25 .11
❑ 236 Doug Martin .04 .02
❑ 237 Keith Millard .04 .02
❑ 238 Darrin Nelson .04 .02
❑ 239 Jesse Solomon .04 .02
❑ 240 Scott Studwell .04 .02
❑ 241 Wade Wilson .10 .05
❑ 242 Gary Zimmerman .04 .02
❑ 243 Jerry Burns CO .04 .02
❑ 244 Bruce Armstrong RC .04 .02
❑ 245 Raymond Clayborn .04 .02
❑ 246 Reggie Dupard .04 .02
❑ 247 Tony Eason .04 .02
❑ 248 Sean Farrell .04 .02
❑ 249 Doug Flutie .75 .35
❑ 250 Brent Williams RC .04 .02
❑ 251 Roland James .04 .02
❑ 252 Ronnie Lippett .04 .02
❑ 253 Fred Marion .04 .02
❑ 254 Larry McGrew .04 .02
❑ 255 Stanley Morgan .04 .02
❑ 256 Johnny Rembert RC .04 .02
❑ 257 John Stephens RC .04 .02
❑ 258 Andre Tippett .04 .02
❑ 259 Garin Veris .04 .02
❑ 260A Raymond Berry CO .04 .02
(No HOF mention
on card front)
❑ 260B Raymond Berry CO .04 .02
(HOF banner
on card front)
❑ 261 Morten Andersen .04 .02
❑ 262 Hoby Brenner .04 .02
❑ 263 Stan Brock .04 .02
❑ 264 Brad Edelman .04 .02
❑ 265 Jumpy Geathers .04 .02
❑ 266A Bobby Hebert ERR .50 .23
("passers" in 42-0)
❑ 266B Bobby Hebert COR .04 .02
("passes" in 42-0)
❑ 267 Craig Heyward RC .25 .11
❑ 268 Lonzell Hill .04 .02
❑ 269 Dalton Hilliard .04 .02
❑ 270 Rickey Jackson .10 .05
❑ 271 Steve Korte .04 .02
❑ 272 Eric Martin .04 .02
❑ 273 Rueben Mayes .04 .02
❑ 274 Sam Mills .10 .05
❑ 275 Brett Perriman RC .25 .11
❑ 276 Pat Swilling .10 .05
❑ 277 John Tice .04 .02
❑ 278 Jim Mora CO .04 .02
❑ 279 Eric Moore .04 .02
❑ 280 Carl Banks .04 .02
❑ 281 Mark Bavaro .10 .05
❑ 282 Maurice Carthon .04 .02
❑ 283 Mark Collins RC .04 .02
❑ 284 Erik Howard .04 .02
❑ 285 Terry Kinard .04 .02
❑ 286 Sean Landeta .04 .02
❑ 287 Lionel Manuel .04 .02
❑ 288 Leonard Marshall .04 .02
❑ 289 Joe Morris .04 .02
❑ 290 Bart Oates .04 .02
❑ 291 Phil Simms .10 .05
❑ 292 Lawrence Taylor .25 .11
❑ 293 Bill Parcells CO RC .10 .05
❑ 294 Dave Cadigan .04 .02
❑ 295 Kyle Clifton RC .04 .02
❑ 296 Alex Gordon .04 .02
❑ 297 James Hasty RC .04 .02
❑ 298 Johnny Hector .04 .02
❑ 299 Bobby Humphery .04 .02
❑ 300 Pat Leahy .04 .02
❑ 301 Marty Lyons .04 .02
❑ 302 Reggie McElroy RC .04 .02
❑ 303 Erik McMillan RC .04 .02
❑ 304 Freeman McNeil .04 .02
❑ 305 Ken O'Brien .04 .02
❑ 306 Pat Ryan .04 .02
❑ 307 Mickey Shuler .04 .02
❑ 308 Al Toon .10 .05
❑ 309 Jo Jo Townsell .04 .02
❑ 310 Roger Vick .04 .02
❑ 311 Joe Walton CO .04 .02
❑ 312 Jerome Brown .10 .05
❑ 313 Keith Byars .10 .05
❑ 314 Cris Carter RC 1.50 .70
❑ 315 Randall Cunningham .40 .18
❑ 316 Terry Hoage .04 .02
❑ 317 Wes Hopkins .04 .02
❑ 318 Keith Jackson RC .25 .11
❑ 319 Mike Quick .04 .02
❑ 320 Mike Reichenbach .04 .02
❑ 321 Dave Rimington .04 .02
❑ 322 John Teltschik .04 .02
❑ 323 Anthony Toney .04 .02
❑ 324 Andre Waters .04 .02
❑ 325 Reggie White .25 .11
❑ 326 Luis Zendejas .04 .02
❑ 327 Buddy Ryan CO .04 .02
❑ 328 Robert Awalt .04 .02
❑ 329 Tim McDonald RC .10 .05
❑ 330 Roy Green .10 .05
❑ 331 Neil Lomax .04 .02
❑ 332 Cedric Mack .04 .02
❑ 333 Stump Mitchell .04 .02
❑ 334 Niko Noga RC .04 .02
❑ 335 Jay Novacek RC .25 .11
❑ 336 Freddie Joe Nunn .04 .02
❑ 337 Luis Sharpe .04 .02
❑ 338 Vai Sikahema .04 .02
❑ 339 J.T. Smith .04 .02
❑ 340 Ron Wolfley .04 .02
❑ 341 Gene Stallings CO RC .10 .05
❑ 342 Gary Anderson K .04 .02
❑ 343 Bubby Brister RC .25 .11
❑ 344 Dermontti Dawson RC .10 .05
❑ 345 Thomas Everett RC .04 .02
❑ 346 Delton Hall RC .04 .02
❑ 347 Bryan Hinkle RC .04 .02
❑ 348 Merril Hoge RC .04 .02
❑ 349 Tunch Ilkin RC .04 .02
❑ 350 Aaron Jones RC .04 .02
❑ 351 Louis Lipps .10 .05
❑ 352 David Little .04 .02
❑ 353 Hardy Nickerson RC .25 .11
❑ 354 Rod Woodson RC .50 .23
❑ 355A Chuck Noll RC CO ERR .10 .05
("one of only three")
❑ 355B Chuck Noll RC CO COR .10 .05
("one of only two")
❑ 356 Gary Anderson RB .04 .02
❑ 357 Rod Bernstine RC .04 .02
❑ 358 Gill Byrd .04 .02
❑ 359 Vencie Glenn .04 .02
❑ 360 Dennis McKnight .04 .02
❑ 361 Lionel James .04 .02
❑ 362 Mark Malone .04 .02
❑ 363A Anthony Miller RC ERR .25 .11
(TD total 14.8)
❑ 363B Anthony Miller RC COR .25 .11
(TD total 3)
❑ 364 Ralf Mojsiejenko .04 .02
❑ 365 Leslie O'Neal .10 .05
❑ 366 Jamie Holland RC .04 .02
❑ 367 Lee Williams .04 .02
❑ 368 Dan Henning CO .04 .02
❑ 369 Harris Barton RC .04 .02
❑ 370 Michael Carter .04 .02
❑ 371 Mike Cofer RC .04 .02
(Joe Montana holding)
❑ 372 Roger Craig .25 .11
❑ 373 Riki Ellison RC .04 .02
❑ 374 Jim Fahnhorst .04 .02
❑ 375 John Frank .04 .02
❑ 376 Jeff Fuller .04 .02
❑ 377 Don Griffin .04 .02
❑ 378 Charles Haley .25 .11
❑ 379 Ronnie Lott .10 .05
❑ 380 Tim McKyer .04 .02
❑ 381 Joe Montana 2.00 .90
❑ 382 Tom Rathman .04 .02
❑ 383 Jerry Rice 1.50 .70
❑ 384 John Taylor RC .25 .11
❑ 385 Keena Turner .04 .02
❑ 386 Michael Walter .04 .02
❑ 387 Bubba Paris .04 .02
❑ 388 Steve Young 1.00 .45
❑ 389 George Seifert .10 .05
CO RC UER
(NFLPA logo on back)
❑ 390 Brian Blades RC .25 .11
❑ 391A Brian Bosworth ERR .30 .14
(Seattle on front)
❑ 391B Brian Bosworth COR .10 .05
(Listed by team nick-
name on front)
❑ 392 Jeff Bryant .04 .02
❑ 393 Jacob Green .04 .02
❑ 394 Norm Johnson .04 .02
❑ 395 Dave Krieg .10 .05
❑ 396 Steve Largent .25 .11
❑ 397 Bryan Millard RC .04 .02
❑ 398 Paul Moyer .04 .02
❑ 399 Joe Nash .04 .02
❑ 400 Rufus Porter RC .04 .02
❑ 401 Eugene Robinson RC .04 .02
❑ 402 Bruce Scholtz .04 .02
❑ 403 Kelly Stouffer RC .04 .02
❑ 404A Curt Warner ERR 1.25 .55
("yards 1455")
❑ 404B Curt Warner COR .10 .05
("yards 6074")
❑ 405 John L. Williams .04 .02
❑ 406 Tony Woods RC .04 .02
❑ 407 David Wyman .04 .02
❑ 408 Chuck Knox CO .04 .02
❑ 409 Mark Carrier WR RC .25 .11
❑ 410 Randy Grimes .04 .02
❑ 411 Paul Gruber RC .04 .02
❑ 412 Harry Hamilton .04 .02
❑ 413 Ron Holmes .04 .02
❑ 414 Donald Igwebuike .04 .02
❑ 415 Dan Turk .04 .02
❑ 416 Ricky Reynolds .04 .02
❑ 417 Bruce Hill RC .04 .02
❑ 418 Lars Tate .04 .02
❑ 419 Vinny Testaverde .30 .14
❑ 420 James Wilder .04 .02
❑ 421 Ray Perkins CO .04 .02
❑ 422 Jeff Bostic .04 .02
❑ 423 Kelvin Bryant .04 .02
❑ 424 Gary Clark .25 .11
❑ 425 Monte Coleman .04 .02
❑ 426 Darrell Green .10 .05
❑ 427 Joe Jacoby .04 .02
❑ 428 Jim Lachey .04 .02
❑ 429 Charles Mann .04 .02
❑ 430 Dexter Manley .04 .02
❑ 431 Darryl Grant .04 .02
❑ 432 Mark May RC .04 .02
❑ 433 Art Monk .10 .05
❑ 434 Mark Rypien RC .25 .11
❑ 435 Ricky Sanders .04 .02
❑ 436 Alvin Walton RC .04 .02
❑ 437 Don Warren .04 .02
❑ 438 Jamie Morris .04 .02
❑ 439 Doug Williams .10 .05
❑ 440 Joe Gibbs CO RC .10 .05
❑ 441 Marcus Cotton .04 .02
❑ 442 Joel Williams .04 .02
❑ 443 Joe Devlin .04 .02
❑ 444 Robb Riddick .04 .02
❑ 445 William Perry .10 .05
❑ 446 Thomas Sanders RC .04 .02
❑ 447 Brian Blados .04 .02
❑ 448 Cris Collinsworth .10 .05
❑ 449 Stanford Jennings .04 .02
❑ 450 Barry Krauss UER .04 .02
(Listed as playing for
Indianapolis 1979-88)
❑ 451 Ozzie Newsome .10 .05
❑ 452 Mike Oliphant RC .04 .02
❑ 453 Tony Dorsett .25 .11
❑ 454 Bruce McNorton .04 .02
❑ 455 Eric Dickerson .10 .05

Card	Nm-Mt	Ex-Mt
❑ 456 Keith Bostic	.04	.02
❑ 457 Sam Clancy RC	.04	.02
❑ 458 Jack Del Rio RC	.25	.11
❑ 459 Mike Webster	.10	.05
❑ 460 Bob Golic	.04	.02
❑ 461 Otis Wilson	.04	.02
❑ 462 Mike Haynes	.10	.05
❑ 463 Greg Townsend	.04	.02
❑ 464 Mark Duper	.10	.05
❑ 465 E.J. Junior	.04	.02
❑ 466 Troy Stradford	.04	.02
❑ 467 Mike Merriweather	.04	.02
❑ 468 Irving Fryar	.25	.11
❑ 469 Vaughan Johnson RC**	.04	.02
❑ 470 Pepper Johnson	.04	.02
❑ 471 Gary Reasons RC	.04	.02
❑ 472 Perry Williams RC	.04	.02
❑ 473 Wesley Walker	.04	.02
❑ 474 Anthony Bell RC	.04	.02
❑ 475 Earl Ferrell	.04	.02
❑ 476 Craig Wolfley	.04	.02
❑ 477 Billy Ray Smith	.04	.02
❑ 478A Jim McMahon (No mention of trade on card front)	.10	.05
❑ 478B Jim McMahon (Traded banner on card front)	.10	.05
❑ 478C Jim McMahon (Traded banner on card front but no line on back saying also see card 44)	40.00	18.00
❑ 479 Eric Wright	.04	.02
❑ 480A Earnest Byner (No mention of trade on card front)	.04	.02
❑ 480B Earnest Byner (Traded banner on card front)	.30	.14
❑ 480C Earnest Byner (Traded banner on card front but no line on back saying also see card 74)	40.00	18.00
❑ 481 Russ Grimm	.04	.02
❑ 482 Wilber Marshall	.04	.02
❑ 483A Gerald Riggs (No mention of trade on card front)	.10	.05
❑ 483B Gerald Riggs (Traded banner on card front)	.30	.14
❑ 483C Gerald Riggs (Traded banner on card front but no line on back saying also see card 14)	40.00	18.00
❑ 484 Brian Davis RC	.04	.02
❑ 485 Shawn Collins RC	.04	.02
❑ 486 Deion Sanders RC	2.00	.90
❑ 487 Trace Armstrong RC	.04	.02
❑ 488 Donnell Woolford RC	.10	.05
❑ 489 Eric Metcalf RC	.25	.11
❑ 490 Troy Aikman RC	6.00	2.70
❑ 491 Steve Walsh RC	.10	.05
❑ 492 Steve Atwater RC	.25	.11
❑ 493 B.Humphrey RC UER Jersey 41 on back should be 26	.04	.02
❑ 494 Barry Sanders RC	8.00	3.60
❑ 495 Tony Mandarich RC	.04	.02
❑ 496 David Williams RC	.04	.02
❑ 497 Andre Rison RC UER (Jersey number not listed on back)	1.00	.45
❑ 498 Derrick Thomas RC	1.50	.70
❑ 499 Cleveland Gary RC	.04	.02
❑ 500 Bill Hawkins RC	.04	.02
❑ 501 Louis Oliver RC	.10	.05
❑ 502 Sammie Smith RC	.04	.02
❑ 503 Hart Lee Dykes RC	.04	.02
❑ 504 Wayne Martin RC	.04	.02
❑ 505 Brian Williams OL RC	.04	.02
❑ 506 Jeff Lageman RC	.10	.05
❑ 507 Eric Hill RC	.04	.02
❑ 508 Joe Wolf RC	.04	.02
❑ 509 Timm Rosenbach RC	.04	.02
❑ 510 Tom Ricketts	.04	.02
❑ 511 Tim Worley RC	.04	.02
❑ 512 Burt Grossman RC	.04	.02
❑ 513 Keith DeLong RC	.04	.02
❑ 514 Andy Heck RC	.04	.02
❑ 515 Broderick Thomas RC	.25	.11
❑ 516 Don Beebe RC	.25	.11
❑ 517 James Thornton RC	.04	.02
❑ 518 Eric Kattus	.04	.02
❑ 519 Bruce Kozerski RC	.04	.02
❑ 520 Brian Washington RC	.04	.02
❑ 521 Rodney Peete RC UER (Jersey 19 on back, should be 9)	.50	.23
❑ 522 Erik Affholter RC	.04	.02
❑ 523 Anthony Dilweg RC	.04	.02
❑ 524 O'Brien Alston	.04	.02
❑ 525 Mike Elkins	.04	.02
❑ 526 Jonathan Hayes RC	.04	.02
❑ 527 Terry McDaniel RC	.04	.02
❑ 528 Frank Stams RC	.04	.02
❑ 529 Darryl Ingram RC	.04	.02
❑ 530 Henry Thomas	.04	.02
❑ 531 Eric Coleman DB	.04	.02
❑ 532 Sheldon White RC	.04	.02
❑ 533 Eric Allen RC	.25	.11
❑ 534 Robert Drummond	.04	.02
❑ 535A Gizmo Williams RC (Without Scouting Photo on front and "Footbal" misspelled on back)	10.00	4.50
❑ 535B Gizmo Williams RC (Without Scouting Photo on front but "Canadian Football" on back)	.25	.11
❑ 535C Gizmo Williams RC (With Scouting Photo on card front)	.04	.02
❑ 536 Billy Joe Tolliver RC	.04	.02
❑ 537 Daniel Stubbs RC	.04	.02
❑ 538 Wesley Walls RC	.40	.18
❑ 539A James Jefferson RC* ERR No Prospect banner on card front	.30	.14
❑ 539B James Jefferson RC* COR Prospect banner on card front	.04	.02
❑ 540 Tracy Rocker	.04	.02
❑ 541 Art Shell CO	.10	.05
❑ 542 Lemuel Stinson RC	.04	.02
❑ 543 Tyrone Braxton RC UER (back photo actually Ken Bell)	.04	.02
❑ 544 David Treadwell RC	.04	.02
❑ 545 Flipper Anderson RC	.25	.11
❑ 546 Dave Meggett RC	.25	.11
❑ 547 Lewis Tillman RC	.04	.02
❑ 548 Carnell Lake RC	.25	.11
❑ 549 Marion Butts RC	.10	.05
❑ 550 Sterling Sharpe RC	1.00	.45
❑ 551 Ezra Johnson	.04	.02
❑ 552 Clarence Verdin RC**	.04	.02
❑ 553 M.Fernandez RC**/C	.04	.02
❑ 554 Ottis Anderson	.10	.05
❑ 555 Gary Hogeboom	.04	.02
❑ 556 Paul Palmer TR	.04	.02
❑ 557 Jesse Solomon TR	.04	.02
❑ 558 Chip Banks TR	.04	.02
❑ 559 Steve Pelluer TR	.04	.02
❑ 560 Darrin Nelson TR	.04	.02
❑ 561 Herschel Walker TR	.10	.05
❑ CC1 Pete Rozelle SP (Commissioner)	.50	.23

1990 Pro Set

	Nm-Mt	Ex-Mt
COMPLETE SET (801)	25.00	11.00
COMP.SERIES 1 (377)	10.00	4.50
COMP.SERIES 2 (392)	10.00	4.50
COMP.FINAL SERIES (32)	4.00	1.80
COMP.FINAL FACT. (32)	5.00	2.20
❑ 1A Barry Sanders ROY (Issued at Hawaii Trade Show in February 1990; no ROY trophy on back)	80.00	36.00
❑ 1B Barry Sanders UER Rookie of the Year (TD total says 14, but adds up to 11)	.60	.25
❑ 2A Joe Montana ERR Player of the Year (Jim Kelly's stats in text)	.50	.23
❑ 2B Joe Montana COR Player of the Year (Corrected from 3521 yards to 3130)	.50	.23
❑ 3 Lindy Infante UER Coach of the Year (missing Coach next to Packers)	.04	.02
❑ 4 Warren Moon UER Man of the Year (missing R symbol)	.25	.11
❑ 5 Keith Millard Defensive Player of the Year	.04	.02
❑ 6 Derrick Thomas UER Defensive Rookie of the Year (no 1989 on front banner of card)	.25	.11
❑ 7 Ottis Anderson Comeback Player of the Year	.10	.05
❑ 8 Joe Montana Passing Leader	.50	.23
❑ 9 Christian Okoye Rushing Leader	.04	.02
❑ 10 Thurman Thomas Total Yardage Leader	.25	.11
❑ 11 Mike Cofer Kick Scoring Leader	.04	.02
❑ 12 Dalton Hilliard UER TD Scoring Leader (O.J. Simpson not listed in stats, but is mentioned in text)	.04	.02
❑ 13 Sterling Sharpe Receiving Leader	.25	.11
❑ 14 Rich Camarillo Punting Leader	.04	.02
❑ 15A Walter Stanley ERR Punt Return Leader (jersey on front reads 87, back says 8 or 86)	.50	.23
❑ 15B Walter Stanley COR Punt Return Leader	.04	.02
❑ 16 Rod Woodson Kickoff Return Leader	.25	.11
❑ 17 Felix Wright Interception Leader	.04	.02
❑ 18A Chris Doleman ERR Sack Leader (Townsent, Jeffcoact)	.50	.23
❑ 18B Chris Doleman COR Sack Leader	.50	.23

(Townsend, Jeffcoat)
❑ 19A Andre Ware RC .10 .05
Heisman Trophy
(No drafted stripe
on card front)
❑ 19B Andre Ware RC .10 .05
Heisman Trophy
(Drafted stripe
on card front)
❑ 20A Mo Elewonibi RC .04 .02
Outland Trophy
(No drafted stripe
on card front)
❑ 20B Mo Elewonibi RC .04 .02
Outland Trophy
(Drafted stripe
on card front)
❑ 21A Percy Snow .50 .23
Lombardi Award
(No drafted stripe
on card front)
❑ 21B Percy Snow .04 .02
Lombardi Award
(Drafted stripe
on card front)
❑ 22A Anthony Thompson RC .04 .02
Maxwell Award
(No drafted stripe
on card front)
❑ 22B Anthony Thompson RC .04 .02
Maxwell Award
(Drafted stripe
on card front)
❑ 23 Buck Buchanan .04 .02
(Sacking Bart Starr)
1990 HOF Selection
❑ 24 Bob Griese .10 .05
1990 HOF Selection
❑ 25A Franco Harris ERR .50 .23
1990 HOF Selection
(Born 2/7/50)
❑ 25B Franco Harris COR .10 .05
1990 HOF Selection
(Born 3/7/50)
❑ 26 Ted Hendricks .04 .02
1990 HOF Selection
❑ 27A Jack Lambert ERR .50 .23
1990 HOF Selection
(Born 7/2/52)
❑ 27B Jack Lambert COR .50 .23
1990 HOF Selection
(Born 7/8/52)
❑ 28 Tom Landry .10 .05
1990 HOF Selection
❑ 29 Bob St.Clair .04 .02
1990 HOF Selection
❑ 30 Aundray Bruce UER .04 .02
(Stats say Falcons)
❑ 31 Tony Casillas UER .04 .02
(Stats say Falcons)
❑ 32 Shawn Collins .04 .02
❑ 33 Marcus Cotton .04 .02
❑ 34 Bill Fralic .04 .02
❑ 35 Chris Miller .10 .05
❑ 36 Deion Sanders UER .50 .23
(Stats say Falcons)
❑ 37 John Settle .04 .02
❑ 38 Jerry Glanville CO .04 .02
❑ 39 Cornelius Bennett .10 .05
❑ 40 Jim Kelly .25 .11
❑ 41 Mark Kelso UER .04 .02
(No fumble rec. in '88;
mentioned in '89)
❑ 42 Scott Norwood .04 .02
❑ 43 Nate Odomes RC .10 .05
❑ 44 Scott Radecic .04 .02
❑ 45 Jim Ritcher RC .04 .02
❑ 46 Leonard Smith .04 .02
❑ 47 Darryl Talley .04 .02
❑ 48 Marv Levy CO .04 .02
❑ 49 Neal Anderson .10 .05
❑ 50 Kevin Butler .04 .02
❑ 51 Jim Covert .04 .02
❑ 52 Richard Dent .10 .05
❑ 53 Jay Hilgenberg .04 .02
❑ 54 Steve McMichael .10 .05
❑ 55 Ron Morris .04 .02
❑ 56 John Roper .04 .02
❑ 57 Mike Singletary .10 .05
❑ 58 Keith Van Horne .04 .02
❑ 59 Mike Ditka CO .25 .11
❑ 60 Lewis Billups .04 .02
❑ 61 Eddie Brown .04 .02
❑ 62 Jason Buck .04 .02
❑ 63A Rickey Dixon RC ERR .50 .23
(Info missing under
bio notes)
❑ 63B Rickey Dixon RC COR .50 .23
❑ 64 Tim McGee .04 .02
❑ 65 Eric Thomas .04 .02
❑ 66 Ickey Woods .04 .02
❑ 67 Carl Zander .04 .02
❑ 68A Sam Wyche CO ERR .50 .23
(Info missing under
bio notes)
❑ 68B Sam Wyche CO COR .50 .23
❑ 69 Paul Farren .04 .02
❑ 70 Thane Gash RC .04 .02
❑ 71 David Grayson .04 .02
❑ 72 Bernie Kosar .10 .05
❑ 73 Reggie Langhorne .04 .02
❑ 74 Eric Metcalf .25 .11
❑ 75A Ozzie Newsome ERR .50 .23
(Born Muscle Shoals)
❑ 75B Ozzie Newsome COR .50 .23
(Born Little Rock)
❑ 75C Cody Risien SP .50 .23
(withdrawn)
❑ 76 Felix Wright .04 .02
❑ 77 Bud Carson CO .04 .02
❑ 78 Troy Aikman .75 .35
❑ 79 Michael Irvin .25 .11
❑ 80 Jim Jeffcoat .04 .02
❑ 81 Crawford Ker .04 .02
❑ 82 Eugene Lockhart .04 .02
❑ 83 Kelvin Martin RC .04 .02
❑ 84 Ken Norton RC .25 .11
❑ 85 Jimmy Johnson CO .10 .05
❑ 86 Steve Atwater .04 .02
❑ 87 Tyrone Braxton .04 .02
❑ 88 John Elway 1.25 .55
❑ 89 Simon Fletcher .04 .02
❑ 90 Ron Holmes .04 .02
❑ 91 Bobby Humphrey .04 .02
❑ 92 Vance Johnson .04 .02
❑ 93 Ricky Nattiel .04 .02
❑ 94 Dan Reeves CO .04 .02
❑ 95 Jim Arnold .04 .02
❑ 96 Jerry Ball .04 .02
❑ 97 Bennie Blades .04 .02
❑ 98 Lomas Brown .04 .02
❑ 99 Michael Cofer .04 .02
❑ 100 Richard Johnson .04 .02
❑ 101 Eddie Murray .04 .02
❑ 102 Barry Sanders 1.25 .55
❑ 103 Chris Spielman .25 .11
❑ 104 William White RC .04 .02
❑ 105 Eric Williams RC .04 .02
❑ 106 Wayne Fontes CO UER .04 .02
(Says born in MO,
actually born in MA)
❑ 107 Brent Fullwood .04 .02
❑ 108 Ron Hallstrom RC .04 .02
❑ 109 Tim Harris .04 .02
❑ 110A Johnny Holland ERR .50 .23
(No name or position
at top of reverse)
❑ 110B Johnny Holland COR .50 .23
❑ 111A Perry Kemp ERR .50 .23
(Photo on back is
actually Ken Stiles,
wearing gray shirt)
❑ 111B Perry Kemp COR .50 .23
(Wearing green shirt)
❑ 112 Don Majkowski .04 .02
❑ 113 Mark Murphy .04 .02
❑ 114A Sterling Sharpe ERR .25 .11
(Born Glenville, Ga.)
❑ 114B Sterling Sharpe COR .50 .23
(Born Chicago)
❑ 115 Ed West RC .04 .02
❑ 116 Lindy Infante CO .04 .02
❑ 117 Steve Brown .04 .02
❑ 118 Ray Childress .04 .02
❑ 119 Ernest Givins .10 .05
❑ 120 John Grimsley .04 .02
❑ 121 Alonzo Highsmith .04 .02
❑ 122 Drew Hill .04 .02
❑ 123 Bubba McDowell .04 .02
❑ 124 Dean Steinkuhler .04 .02
❑ 125 Lorenzo White .10 .05
❑ 126 Tony Zendejas .04 .02
❑ 127 Jack Pardee CO .04 .02
❑ 128 Albert Bentley .04 .02
❑ 129 Dean Biasucci .04 .02
❑ 130 Duane Bickett .04 .02
❑ 131 Bill Brooks .04 .02
❑ 132 Jon Hand .04 .02
❑ 133 Mike Prior .04 .02
❑ 134A Andre Rison .25 .11
(No mention of trade
on card front)
❑ 134B Andre Rison .25 .11
(Traded banner on card
front; also reissued
with Final Update)
❑ 134C Andre Rison .25 .11
(Traded banner on card
front; message from
Lud Denny on back)
❑ 135 Rohn Stark .04 .02
❑ 136 Donnell Thompson .04 .02
❑ 137 Clarence Verdin .04 .02
❑ 138 Fredd Young .04 .02
❑ 139 Ron Meyer CO .04 .02
❑ 140 John Alt RC .04 .02
❑ 141 Steve DeBerg .04 .02
❑ 142 Irv Eatman .04 .02
❑ 143 Dino Hackett .04 .02
❑ 144 Nick Lowery .04 .02
❑ 145 Bill Maas .04 .02
❑ 146 Stephone Paige .04 .02
❑ 147 Neil Smith .25 .11
❑ 148 Marty Schottenheimer CO .04 .02
❑ 149 Steve Beuerlein .10 .05
❑ 150 Tim Brown .25 .11
❑ 151 Mike Dyal .04 .02
❑ 152A Mervyn Fernandez ERR .75 .35
(Acquired: Free
Agent '87)
❑ 152B Mervyn Fernandez COR .75 .35
(Acquired: Drafted
10th Round, 1983)
❑ 153 Willie Gault .10 .05
❑ 154 Bob Golic .04 .02
❑ 155 Bo Jackson .30 .14
❑ 156 Don Mosebar .04 .02
❑ 157 Steve Smith .04 .02
❑ 158 Greg Townsend .04 .02
❑ 159 Bruce Wilkerson RC .04 .02
❑ 160 Steve Wisniewski .10 .05
(Blocking for Bo Jackson)
❑ 161A Art Shell CO ERR .50 .23
(Born 11/25/46)
❑ 161B Art Shell CO COR .50 .23
(Born 11/26/46;
large HOF print on front)
❑ 161C Art Shell CO COR .50 .23
(Born 11/26/46;
small HOF print on front)
❑ 162 Flipper Anderson .04 .02
❑ 163 Greg Bell UER .04 .02
(Stats have 5 catches,
should be 9)
❑ 164 Henry Ellard .10 .05
❑ 165 Jim Everett .10 .05
❑ 166 Jerry Gray .04 .02
❑ 167 Kevin Greene .10 .05
❑ 168 Pete Holohan .04 .02
❑ 169 Larry Kelm RC .04 .02
❑ 170 Tom Newberry .04 .02
❑ 171 Vince Newsome RC .04 .02

❑ 172 Irv Pankey .04 .02
❑ 173 Jackie Slater .04 .02
❑ 174 Fred Strickland RC .04 .02
❑ 175 Mike Wilcher UER .04 .02 (Fumble rec. number different from 1989 Pro Set card)
❑ 176 John Robinson CO UER .04 .02 (Stats say Rams, should say L.A. Rams)
❑ 177 Mark Clayton .10 .05
❑ 178 Roy Foster .04 .02
❑ 179 Harry Galbreath RC .04 .02
❑ 180 Jim C. Jensen .04 .02
❑ 181 Dan Marino 1.25 .55
❑ 182 Louis Oliver .04 .02
❑ 183 Sammie Smith .04 .02
❑ 184 Brian Sochia .04 .02
❑ 185 Don Shula CO .10 .05
❑ 186 Joey Browner .04 .02
❑ 187 Anthony Carter .10 .05
❑ 188 Chris Doleman .04 .02
❑ 189 Steve Jordan .04 .02
❑ 190 Carl Lee .04 .02
❑ 191 Randall McDaniel .10 .05
❑ 192 Mike Merriweather .04 .02
❑ 193 Keith Millard .04 .02
❑ 194 Al Noga .04 .02
❑ 195 Scott Studwell .04 .02
❑ 196 Henry Thomas .04 .02
❑ 197 Herschel Walker .10 .05
❑ 198 Wade Wilson .10 .05
❑ 199 Gary Zimmerman .04 .02
❑ 200 Jerry Burns CO .04 .02
❑ 201 Vincent Brown RC .04 .02
❑ 202 Hart Lee Dykes .04 .02
❑ 203 Sean Farrell .04 .02
❑ 204A Fred Marion .04 .02 (Belt visible on John Taylor)
❑ 204B Fred Marion .04 .02 (Belt not visible)
❑ 205 Stanley Morgan UER .04 .02 (Text says he reached 10,000 yards fastest; 3 players did it in 10 seasons)
❑ 206 Eric Sievers RC .04 .02
❑ 207 John Stephens .04 .02
❑ 208 Andre Tippett .04 .02
❑ 209 Rod Rust CO .04 .02
❑ 210A Morten Andersen ERR .50 .23 (Card number and name on back in white)
❑ 210B Morten Andersen COR .50 .23 (Card number and name on back in black)
❑ 211 Brad Edelman .04 .02
❑ 212 John Fourcade .04 .02
❑ 213 Dalton Hilliard .04 .02
❑ 214 Rickey Jackson .10 .05 (Forcing Jim Kelly fumble)
❑ 215 Vaughan Johnson .04 .02
❑ 216A Eric Martin ERR .50 .23 (Card number and name on back in white)
❑ 216B Eric Martin COR .50 .23 (Card number and name on back in black)
❑ 217 Sam Mills .10 .05
❑ 218 Pat Swilling UER .10 .05 (Total fumble recoveries listed as 4, should be 5)
❑ 219 Frank Warren RC .04 .02
❑ 220 Jim Wilks .04 .02
❑ 221A Jim Mora CO ERR .50 .23 (Card number and name on back in white)
❑ 221B Jim Mora CO COR .50 .23 (Card number and name on back in black)
❑ 222 Raul Allegre .04 .02
❑ 223 Carl Banks .04 .02
❑ 224 John Elliott .04 .02
❑ 225 Erik Howard .04 .02
❑ 226 Pepper Johnson .04 .02
❑ 227 Leonard Marshall UER .04 .02 (In Super Bowl XXI, George Martin had the safety)
❑ 228 Dave Meggett .10 .05
❑ 229 Bart Oates .04 .02
❑ 230 Phil Simms .10 .05
❑ 231 Lawrence Taylor .25 .11
❑ 232 Bill Parcells CO .10 .05
❑ 233 Troy Benson .04 .02
❑ 234 Kyle Clifton UER .04 .02 (Born: Onley, should be Olney)
❑ 235 Johnny Hector .04 .02
❑ 236 Jeff Lageman .04 .02
❑ 237 Pat Leahy .04 .02
❑ 238 Freeman McNeil .04 .02
❑ 239 Ken O'Brien .04 .02
❑ 240 Al Toon .10 .05
❑ 241 Jo Jo Townsell .04 .02
❑ 242 Bruce Coslet CO .04 .02
❑ 243 Eric Allen .04 .02
❑ 244 Jerome Brown .04 .02
❑ 245 Keith Byars .04 .02
❑ 246 Cris Carter .50 .23
❑ 247 Randall Cunningham .25 .11
❑ 248 Keith Jackson .10 .05
❑ 249 Mike Quick .04 .02 (Darrell Green also in photo)
❑ 250 Clyde Simmons .04 .02
❑ 251 Andre Waters .04 .02
❑ 252 Reggie White .25 .11
❑ 253 Buddy Ryan CO .04 .02
❑ 254 Rich Camarillo .04 .02
❑ 255 Earl Ferrell .04 .02 (No mention of retirement on card front)
❑ 256 Roy Green .10 .05
❑ 257 Ken Harvey RC .25 .11
❑ 258 Ernie Jones RC .04 .02
❑ 259 Tim McDonald .04 .02
❑ 260 Timm Rosenbach UER .04 .02 (Born 1967; should be 1966)
❑ 261 Luis Sharpe .04 .02
❑ 262 Vai Sikahema .04 .02
❑ 263 J.T. Smith .04 .02
❑ 264 Ron Wolfley UER .04 .02 (Born Blaisdel, should be Blasdel)
❑ 265 Joe Bugel CO .04 .02
❑ 266 Gary Anderson K .04 .02
❑ 267 Bubby Brister .04 .02
❑ 268 Merril Hoge .04 .02
❑ 269 Carnell Lake .04 .02
❑ 270 Louis Lipps .10 .05
❑ 271 David Little .04 .02
❑ 272 Greg Lloyd .25 .11
❑ 273 Keith Willis .04 .02
❑ 274 Tim Worley .04 .02
❑ 275 Chuck Noll CO .10 .05
❑ 276 Marion Butts .10 .05
❑ 277 Gill Byrd .04 .02
❑ 278 Vencie Glenn UER .04 .02 (Sack total should be 2, not 2.5)
❑ 279 Burt Grossman .04 .02
❑ 280 Gary Plummer .04 .02
❑ 281 Billy Ray Smith .04 .02
❑ 282 Billy Joe Tolliver .04 .02
❑ 283 Dan Henning CO .04 .02
❑ 284 Harris Barton .04 .02
❑ 285 Michael Carter .04 .02
❑ 286 Mike Cofer .04 .02
❑ 287 Roger Craig .10 .05
❑ 288 Don Griffin .04 .02
❑ 289A Charles Haley ERR 10.00 4.50 (Fumble recoveries 1 in '86 and 4 total)
❑ 289B Charles Haley COR .75 .35 (Fumble recoveries 2 in '86 and 5 total)
❑ 290 Pierce Holt RC .04 .02
❑ 291 Ronnie Lott .10 .05
❑ 292 Guy McIntyre .04 .02
❑ 293 Joe Montana 1.25 .55
❑ 294 Tom Rathman .04 .02
❑ 295 Jerry Rice .75 .35
❑ 296 Jesse Sapolu RC .04 .02
❑ 297 John Taylor .10 .05
❑ 298 Michael Walter .04 .02
❑ 299 George Seifert CO .10 .05
❑ 300 Jeff Bryant .04 .02
❑ 301 Jacob Green .04 .02
❑ 302 Norm Johnson UER .04 .02 (Card shop not in Garden Grove, should say Fullerton)
❑ 303 Bryan Millard .04 .02
❑ 304 Joe Nash .04 .02
❑ 305 Eugene Robinson .04 .02
❑ 306 John L. Williams .04 .02
❑ 307 David Wyman .04 .02 (NFL EXP is in caps, inconsistent with rest of the set)
❑ 308 Chuck Knox CO .04 .02
❑ 309 Mark Carrier WR .25 .11
❑ 310 Paul Gruber .04 .02
❑ 311 Harry Hamilton .04 .02
❑ 312 Bruce Hill .04 .02
❑ 313 Donald Igwebuike .04 .02
❑ 314 Kevin Murphy .04 .02
❑ 315 Ervin Randle .04 .02
❑ 316 Mark Robinson .04 .02
❑ 317 Lars Tate .04 .02
❑ 318 Vinny Testaverde .10 .05
❑ 319A Ray Perkins CO ERR .75 .35 (No name or title at top of reverse)
❑ 319B Ray Perkins CO COR .04 .02
❑ 320 Earnest Byner .04 .02
❑ 321 Gary Clark .25 .11
❑ 322 Darryl Grant .04 .02
❑ 323 Darrell Green .10 .05
❑ 324 Jim Lachey .04 .02
❑ 325 Charles Mann .04 .02
❑ 326 Wilber Marshall .04 .02
❑ 327 Ralf Mojsiejenko .04 .02
❑ 328 Art Monk .10 .05
❑ 329 Gerald Riggs .10 .05
❑ 330 Mark Rypien .10 .05
❑ 331 Ricky Sanders .04 .02
❑ 332 Alvin Walton .04 .02
❑ 333 Joe Gibbs CO .10 .05
❑ 334 Aloha Stadium .04 .02 Site of Pro Bowl
❑ 335 Brian Blades PB .04 .02
❑ 336 James Brooks PB .04 .02
❑ 337 Shane Conlan PB .04 .02
❑ 338A Eric Dickerson PB SP 3.00 1.35 (Card withdrawn)
❑ 338B Lud Denny Promo 200.00 60.00
❑ 339 Ray Donaldson PB .04 .02
❑ 340 Ferrell Edmunds PB .04 .02
❑ 341 Boomer Esiason PB .04 .02
❑ 342 David Fulcher PB .04 .02
❑ 343A Chris Hinton PB .50 .23 (No mention of trade on card front)
❑ 343B Chris Hinton PB .04 .02 (Traded banner on card front)
❑ 344 Rodney Holman PB .04 .02
❑ 345 Kent Hull PB .04 .02
❑ 346 Tunch Ilkin PB .04 .02
❑ 347 Mike Johnson PB .04 .02
❑ 348 Greg Kragen PB .04 .02
❑ 349 Dave Krieg PB .10 .05
❑ 350 Albert Lewis PB .04 .02
❑ 351 Howie Long PB .10 .05
❑ 352 Bruce Matthews PB .04 .02
❑ 353 Clay Matthews PB .04 .02
❑ 354 Erik McMillan PB .04 .02
❑ 355 Karl Mecklenburg PB .04 .02
❑ 356 Anthony Miller PB .04 .02

❑ 357 Frank Minnifield PB .04 .02
❑ 358 Max Montoya PB .04 .02
❑ 359 Warren Moon PB .25 .11
❑ 360 Mike Munchak PB .04 .02
❑ 361 Anthony Munoz PB .04 .02
❑ 362 John Offerdahl PB .04 .02
❑ 363 Christian Okoye PB .04 .02
❑ 364 Leslie O'Neal PB .04 .02
❑ 365 Rufus Porter PB UER .04 .02
(TM logo missing)
❑ 366 Andre Reed PB .10 .05
❑ 367 Johnny Rembert PB .04 .02
❑ 368 Reggie Roby PB .04 .02
❑ 369 Kevin Ross PB .04 .02
❑ 370 Webster Slaughter PB .04 .02
❑ 371 Bruce Smith PB .10 .05
❑ 372 Dennis Smith PB .04 .02
❑ 373 Derrick Thomas PB .10 .05
❑ 374 Thurman Thomas PB .25 .11
❑ 375 David Treadwell PB .04 .02
❑ 376 Lee Williams PB .04 .02
❑ 377 Rod Woodson PB .10 .05
❑ 378 Bud Carson CO PB .04 .02
❑ 379 Eric Allen PB .04 .02
❑ 380 Neal Anderson PB .10 .05
❑ 381 Jerry Ball PB .04 .02
❑ 382 Joey Browner PB .04 .02
❑ 383 Rich Camarillo PB .04 .02
❑ 384 Mark Carrier WR PB .04 .02
❑ 385 Roger Craig PB .10 .05
❑ 386A R.Cunningham PB .50 .23
Small print on front
❑ 386B R.Cunningham PB .50 .23
Large print on front
❑ 387 Chris Doleman PB .04 .02
❑ 388 Henry Ellard PB .04 .02
❑ 389 Bill Fralic PB .04 .02
❑ 390 Brent Fullwood PB .04 .02
❑ 391 Jerry Gray PB .04 .02
❑ 392 Kevin Greene PB .10 .05
❑ 393 Tim Harris PB .04 .02
❑ 394 Jay Hilgenberg PB .04 .02
❑ 395 Dalton Hilliard PB .04 .02
❑ 396 Keith Jackson PB .10 .05
❑ 397 Vaughan Johnson PB .04 .02
❑ 398 Steve Jordan PB .04 .02
❑ 399 Carl Lee PB .04 .02
❑ 400 Ronnie Lott PB .10 .05
❑ 401 Don Majkowski PB .04 .02
❑ 402 Charles Mann PB .04 .02
❑ 403 Randall McDaniel PB .04 .02
❑ 404 Tim McDonald PB .04 .02
❑ 405 Guy McIntyre PB .04 .02
❑ 406 Dave Meggett PB .04 .02
❑ 407 Keith Millard PB .04 .02
❑ 408 Joe Montana PB .50 .23
(not pictured in Pro
Bowl uniform)
❑ 409 Eddie Murray PB .04 .02
❑ 410 Tom Newberry PB .04 .02
❑ 411 Jerry Rice PB .50 .23
❑ 412 Mark Rypien PB .04 .02
❑ 413 Barry Sanders PB .60 .25
❑ 414 Luis Sharpe PB .04 .02
❑ 415 Sterling Sharpe PB .04 .02
❑ 416 Mike Singletary PB .10 .05
❑ 417 Jackie Slater PB .04 .02
❑ 418 Doug Smith PB .04 .02
❑ 419 Chris Spielman PB .04 .02
❑ 420 Pat Swilling PB .04 .02
❑ 421 John Taylor PB .04 .02
❑ 422 Lawrence Taylor PB .10 .05
❑ 423 Reggie White PB .10 .05
❑ 424 Ron Wolfley PB .04 .02
❑ 425 Gary Zimmerman PB .04 .02
❑ 426 John Robinson CO PB .04 .02
❑ 427 Scott Case UER .04 .02
(front CB, back S)
❑ 428 Mike Kenn .04 .02
❑ 429 Mike Gann .04 .02
❑ 430 Tim Green RC .04 .02
❑ 431 Michael Haynes RC .25 .11
❑ 432 Jessie Tuggle RC UER .04 .02
(Front Jesse,
back Jessie)
❑ 433 John Rade .04 .02
❑ 434 Andre Rison .25 .11
❑ 435 Don Beebe .10 .05
❑ 436 Ray Bentley .04 .02
❑ 437 Shane Conlan .04 .02
❑ 438 Kent Hull .04 .02
❑ 439 Pete Metzelaars .04 .02
❑ 440 Andre Reed UER .25 .11
(Vance Johnson also had
more catches in '85)
❑ 441 Frank Reich .25 .11
❑ 442 Leon Seals RC .04 .02
❑ 443 Bruce Smith .25 .11
❑ 444 Thurman Thomas .25 .11
❑ 445 Will Wolford .04 .02
❑ 446 Trace Armstrong .04 .02
❑ 447 Mark Bortz RC .04 .02
❑ 448 Tom Thayer RC .04 .02
❑ 449A Dan Hampton ERR .50 .23
(Card back says DE)
❑ 449B Dan Hampton COR 10.00 4.50
(Card back says DT)
❑ 450 Shaun Gayle RC .04 .02
❑ 451 Dennis Gentry .04 .02
❑ 452 Jim Harbaugh .25 .11
❑ 453 Vestee Jackson .04 .02
❑ 454 Brad Muster .04 .02
❑ 455 William Perry .10 .05
❑ 456 Ron Rivera .04 .02
❑ 457 James Thornton .04 .02
❑ 458 Mike Tomczak .10 .05
❑ 459 Donnell Woolford .04 .02
❑ 460 Eric Ball .04 .02
❑ 461 James Brooks .10 .05
❑ 462 David Fulcher .04 .02
❑ 463 Boomer Esiason .10 .05
❑ 464 Rodney Holman .04 .02
❑ 465 Bruce Kozerski .04 .02
❑ 466 Tim Krumrie .04 .02
❑ 467 Anthony Munoz .10 .05
(Type on front smaller
compared to other cards)
❑ 468 Brian Blados .04 .02
❑ 469 Mike Baab .04 .02
❑ 470 Brian Brennan .04 .02
❑ 471 Raymond Clayborn .04 .02
❑ 472 Mike Johnson .04 .02
❑ 473 Kevin Mack .04 .02
❑ 474 Clay Matthews .10 .05
❑ 475 Frank Minnifield .04 .02
❑ 476 Gregg Rakoczy RC .04 .02
❑ 477 Webster Slaughter .10 .05
❑ 478 James Dixon .04 .02
❑ 479 Robert Awalt UER .04 .02
(front 89, back 46)
❑ 480 Dennis McKinnon UER .04 .02
(front 81, back 85)
❑ 481 Danny Noonan .04 .02
❑ 482 Jesse Solomon .04 .02
❑ 483 Daniel Stubbs UER .04 .02
(front 66, back 96)
❑ 484 Steve Walsh .10 .05
❑ 485 Michael Brooks RC .04 .02
❑ 486 Mark Jackson .04 .02
❑ 487 Greg Kragen .04 .02
❑ 488 Ken Lanier RC .04 .02
❑ 489 Karl Mecklenburg .04 .02
❑ 490 Steve Sewell .04 .02
❑ 491 Dennis Smith .04 .02
❑ 492 David Treadwell .04 .02
❑ 493 Michael Young RC .04 .02
❑ 494 Robert Clark RC .04 .02
❑ 495 Dennis Gibson .04 .02
❑ 496A Kevin Glover RC ERR .50 .23
(Card back says C/G)
❑ 496B Kevin Glover RC COR .04 .02
(Card back says C)
❑ 497 Mel Gray .10 .05
❑ 498 Rodney Peete .10 .05
❑ 499 Dave Brown DB .04 .02
❑ 500 Jerry Holmes .04 .02
❑ 501 Chris Jacke .04 .02
❑ 502 Alan Veingrad .04 .02
❑ 503 Mark Lee .04 .02
❑ 504 Tony Mandarich .04 .02
❑ 505 Brian Noble .04 .02
❑ 506 Jeff Query .04 .02
❑ 507 Ken Ruettgers .04 .02
❑ 508 Patrick Allen .04 .02
❑ 509 Curtis Duncan .04 .02
❑ 510 William Fuller .10 .05
❑ 511 Haywood Jeffires RC .25 .11
❑ 512 Sean Jones .10 .05
❑ 513 Terry Kinard .04 .02
❑ 514 Bruce Matthews .10 .05
❑ 515 Gerald McNeil .04 .02
❑ 516 Greg Montgomery RC .04 .02
❑ 517 Warren Moon .25 .11
❑ 518 Mike Munchak .10 .05
❑ 519 Allen Pinkett .04 .02
❑ 520 Pat Beach .04 .02
❑ 521 Eugene Daniel .04 .02
❑ 522 Kevin Call .04 .02
❑ 523 Ray Donaldson .04 .02
❑ 524 Jeff Herrod RC .04 .02
❑ 525 Keith Taylor .04 .02
❑ 526 Jack Trudeau .04 .02
❑ 527 Deron Cherry .04 .02
❑ 528 Jeff Donaldson .04 .02
❑ 529 Albert Lewis .04 .02
❑ 530 Pete Mandley .04 .02
❑ 531 Chris Martin RC .04 .02
❑ 532 Christian Okoye .04 .02
❑ 533 Steve Pelluer .04 .02
❑ 534 Kevin Ross .04 .02
❑ 535 Dan Saleaumua .04 .02
❑ 536 Derrick Thomas .25 .11
❑ 537 Mike Webster .10 .05
❑ 538 Marcus Allen .25 .11
❑ 539 Greg Bell .04 .02
❑ 540 Thomas Benson .04 .02
❑ 541 Ron Brown .04 .02
❑ 542 Scott Davis .04 .02
❑ 543 Riki Ellison .04 .02
❑ 544 Jamie Holland .04 .02
❑ 545 Howie Long .25 .11
❑ 546 Terry McDaniel .04 .02
❑ 547 Max Montoya .04 .02
❑ 548 Jay Schroeder .04 .02
❑ 549 Lionel Washington .04 .02
❑ 550 Robert Delpino .04 .02
❑ 551 Bobby Humphery .04 .02
❑ 552 Mike Lansford .04 .02
❑ 553 Michael Stewart RC .04 .02
❑ 554 Doug Smith .04 .02
❑ 555 Curt Warner .04 .02
❑ 556 Alvin Wright RC .04 .02
❑ 557 Jeff Cross .04 .02
❑ 558 Jeff Dellenbach RC .04 .02
❑ 559 Mark Duper .10 .05
❑ 560 Ferrell Edmunds .04 .02
❑ 561 Tim McKyer .04 .02
❑ 562 John Offerdahl .04 .02
❑ 563 Reggie Roby .04 .02
❑ 564 Pete Stoyanovich .04 .02
❑ 565 Alfred Anderson .04 .02
❑ 566 Ray Berry .04 .02
❑ 567 Rick Fenney .04 .02
❑ 568 Rich Gannon RC 1.50 .70
❑ 569 Tim Irwin .04 .02
❑ 570 Hassan Jones .04 .02
❑ 571 Cris Carter .50 .23
❑ 572 Kirk Lowdermilk .04 .02
❑ 573 Reggie Rutland RC .04 .02
❑ 574 Ken Stills .04 .02
❑ 575 Bruce Armstrong .04 .02
❑ 576 Irving Fryar .10 .05
❑ 577 Roland James .04 .02
❑ 578 Robert Perryman .04 .02
❑ 579 Cedric Jones .04 .02
❑ 580 Steve Grogan .10 .05
❑ 581 Johnny Rembert .04 .02
❑ 582 Ed Reynolds .04 .02
❑ 583 Brent Williams .04 .02
❑ 584 Marc Wilson .04 .02
❑ 585 Hoby Brenner .04 .02
❑ 586 Stan Brock .04 .02

❑ 587 Jim Dombrowski RC .04 .02
❑ 588 Joel Hilgenberg RC .04 .02
❑ 589 Robert Massey .04 .02
❑ 590 Floyd Turner .04 .02
❑ 591 Ottis Anderson .10 .05
❑ 592 Mark Bavaro .04 .02
❑ 593 Maurice Carthon .04 .02
❑ 594 Eric Dorsey RC .04 .02
❑ 595 Myron Guyton .04 .02
❑ 596 Jeff Hostetler RC .25 .11
❑ 597 Sean Landeta .04 .02
❑ 598 Lionel Manuel .04 .02
❑ 599 Odessa Turner RC .04 .02
❑ 600 Perry Williams .04 .02
❑ 601 James Hasty .04 .02
❑ 602 Erik McMillan .04 .02
❑ 603 Alex Gordon UER .04 .02
(reversed photo on back)
❑ 604 Ron Stallworth .04 .02
❑ 605 Byron Evans RC .04 .02
❑ 606 Ron Heller RC .04 .02
❑ 607 Wes Hopkins .04 .02
(Hitting Ottis Anderson)
❑ 608 Mickey Shuler UER .04 .02
(Reversed photo on back)
❑ 609 Seth Joyner .10 .05
❑ 610 Jim McMahon .10 .05
❑ 611 Mike Pitts .04 .02
❑ 612 Izel Jenkins RC .04 .02
❑ 613 Anthony Bell .04 .02
❑ 614 David Galloway .04 .02
❑ 615 Eric Hill .04 .02
❑ 616 Cedric Mack .04 .02
❑ 617 Freddie Joe Nunn .04 .02
❑ 618 Tootie Robbins .04 .02
❑ 619 Tom Tupa RC .04 .02
❑ 620 Joe Wolf .04 .02
❑ 621 Dermontti Dawson .10 .05
❑ 622 Thomas Everett .04 .02
❑ 623 Tunch Ilkin .04 .02
❑ 624 Hardy Nickerson .10 .05
❑ 625 Gerald Williams RC .04 .02
❑ 626 Rod Woodson .25 .11
❑ 627A Rod Bernstine TE ERR .50 .23
❑ 627B Rod Bernstine RB COR .04 .02
❑ 628 Courtney Hall .04 .02
❑ 629 Ronnie Harmon .10 .05
❑ 630A Anthony Miller ERR .25 .11
(Back says WR)
❑ 630B Anthony Miller COR .10 .05
(Back says WR-KR)
❑ 631 Joe Phillips .04 .02
❑ 632A Leslie O'Neal ERR .50 .23
(Listed as LB-DE on
front and back)
❑ 632B Leslie O'Neal ERR .15 .07
(Listed as LB-DE on
front and LB on back)
❑ 632C Leslie O'Neal COR .10 .05
(Listed as LB on
front and back)
❑ 633A David Richards RC ERR .15 .07
(Back says G-T)
❑ 633B D.Richards RC COR .15 .07
Back says G
❑ 634 Mark Vlasic .04 .02
❑ 635 Lee Williams .04 .02
❑ 636 Chet Brooks .04 .02
❑ 637 Keena Turner .04 .02
❑ 638 Kevin Fagan RC .04 .02
❑ 639 Brent Jones RC .25 .11
❑ 640 Matt Millen .10 .05
❑ 641 Bubba Paris .04 .02
❑ 642 Bill Romanowski RC 1.00 .45
❑ 643 Fred Smerlas UER .04 .02
(Front 67, back 76)
❑ 644 Dave Waymer .04 .02
❑ 645 Steve Young .50 .23
❑ 646 Brian Blades .10 .05
❑ 647 Andy Heck .04 .02
❑ 648 Dave Krieg .10 .05
❑ 649 Rufus Porter .04 .02
❑ 650 Kelly Stouffer .04 .02
❑ 651 Tony Woods .04 .02
❑ 652 Gary Anderson RB .04 .02
❑ 653 Reuben Davis .04 .02
❑ 654 Randy Grimes .04 .02
❑ 655 Ron Hall .04 .02
❑ 656 Eugene Marve .04 .02
❑ 657A Curt Jarvis ERR .50 .23
(No "Official NFL
Card" on front)
❑ 657B Curt Jarvis COR 10.00 4.50
❑ 658 Ricky Reynolds .04 .02
❑ 659 Broderick Thomas .04 .02
❑ 660 Jeff Bostic .04 .02
❑ 661 Todd Bowles RC .04 .02
❑ 662 Ravin Caldwell .04 .02
❑ 663 Russ Grimm UER .04 .02
(Back photo is act-
ually Jeff Bostic)
❑ 664 Joe Jacoby .04 .02
❑ 665 Mark May .04 .02
(Front G, back G/T)
❑ 666 Walter Stanley .04 .02
❑ 667 Don Warren .04 .02
❑ 668 Stan Humphries RC .25 .11
❑ 669A Jeff George SP 1.00 .45
(Illinois uniform;
issued in first series)
❑ 669B Jeff George RC .50 .23
(Colts uniform;
issued in second series)
❑ 670 Blair Thomas RC .10 .05
(No color stripe along
line with AFC symbol
and Jets logo)
❑ 671 Cortez Kennedy RC UER .25 .11
(No scouting photo
line on back)
❑ 672 Keith McCants RC .04 .02
❑ 673 Junior Seau RC 1.25 .55
❑ 674 Mark Carrier DB RC .25 .11
❑ 675 Andre Ware .10 .05
❑ 676 Chris Singleton RC UER .04 .02
(Parsippany High,
should be Parsippany
Hills High)
❑ 677 Richmond Webb RC .04 .02
❑ 678 Ray Agnew RC .04 .02
❑ 679 Anthony Smith RC .04 .02
❑ 680 James Francis RC .04 .02
❑ 681 Percy Snow .04 .02
❑ 682 Renaldo Turnbull RC .04 .02
❑ 683 Lamar Lathon RC .10 .05
❑ 684 James Williams DB RC .04 .02
❑ 685 Emmitt Smith RC 5.00 2.20
❑ 686 Tony Bennett RC .25 .11
❑ 687 Darrell Thompson RC .04 .02
❑ 688 Steve Broussard RC .04 .02
❑ 689 Eric Green RC .10 .05
❑ 690 Ben Smith RC .04 .02
❑ 691 Bern Brostek RC UER .04 .02
(Listed as Center but
is playing Guard)
❑ 692 Rodney Hampton RC .25 .11
❑ 693 Dexter Carter RC .04 .02
❑ 694 Rob Moore RC .50 .23
❑ 695 Alexander Wright RC .04 .02
❑ 696 Darion Conner RC .10 .05
❑ 697 Reggie Rembert RC UER .04 .02
(Missing Scouting Line
credit on the front)
❑ 698A Terry Wooden RC ERR .50 .23
(Number on back is 51)
❑ 698B Terry Wooden RC COR .04 .02
(Number on back is 90)
❑ 699 Reggie Cobb RC .04 .02
❑ 700 Anthony Thompson .04 .02
❑ 701 Fred Washington RC .04 .02
(Final Update version
mentions his death;
this card does not)
❑ 702 Ron Cox RC .04 .02
❑ 703 Robert Blackmon RC .04 .02
❑ 704 Dan Owens RC .04 .02
❑ 705 Anthony Johnson RC .25 .11
❑ 706 Aaron Wallace RC .04 .02
❑ 707 Harold Green RC .25 .11
❑ 708 Keith Sims RC .04 .02
❑ 709 Tim Grunhard RC .04 .02
❑ 710 Jeff Alm RC .04 .02
❑ 711 Carwell Gardner RC .04 .02
❑ 712 Kenny Davidson RC .04 .02
❑ 713 Vince Buck RC .04 .02
❑ 714 Leroy Hoard RC .25 .11
❑ 715 Andre Collins RC .04 .02
❑ 716 Dennis Brown RC .04 .02
❑ 717 LeRoy Butler RC .25 .11
❑ 718A Pat Terrell 41 ERR RC .50 .23
❑ 718B Pat Terrell 37 COR RC .04 .02
❑ 719 Mike Bellamy RC .04 .02
❑ 720 Mike Fox RC .04 .02
❑ 721 Alton Montgomery RC .04 .02
❑ 722 Eric Davis RC .10 .05
❑ 723A Oliver Barnett RC ERR .50 .23
(Front says DT)
❑ 723B Oliver Barnett RC COR .04 .02
(Front says NT)
❑ 724 Houston Hoover RC .04 .02
❑ 725 Howard Ballard RC .04 .02
❑ 726 Keith McKeller RC .04 .02
❑ 727 Wendell Davis RC .04 .02
(Pro Set Prospect in
white, not black)
❑ 728 Peter Tom Willis RC .04 .02
❑ 729 Bernard Clark .04 .02
❑ 730 Doug Widell RC .04 .02
❑ 731 Eric Andolsek .04 .02
❑ 732 Jeff Campbell RC .04 .02
❑ 733 Marc Spindler RC .04 .02
❑ 734 Keith Woodside .04 .02
❑ 735 Willis Peguese RC .04 .02
❑ 736 Frank Stams .04 .02
❑ 737 Jeff Uhlenhake .04 .02
❑ 738 Todd Kalis .04 .02
❑ 739 Tommy Hodson RC UER .04 .02
(Born Matthews,
should be Mathews)
❑ 740 Greg McMurtry RC .04 .02
❑ 741 Mike Buck RC .04 .02
❑ 742 Kevin Haverdink UER .04 .02
(Jersey says 70,
back says 74)
❑ 743A Johnny Bailey RC .10 .05
(Back says 46)
❑ 743B Johnny Bailey RC .10 .05
(Back says 22)
❑ 744A Eric Moore .15 .07
(No Pro Set Prospect
on front of card)
❑ 744B Eric Moore 10.00 4.50
(Pro Set Prospect
on front of card)
❑ 745 Tony Stargell RC .04 .02
❑ 746 Fred Barnett RC .25 .11
❑ 747 Walter Reeves .04 .02
❑ 748 Derek Hill .04 .02
❑ 749 Quinn Early .25 .11
❑ 750 Ronald Lewis .04 .02
❑ 751 Ken Clark RC .04 .02
❑ 752 Garry Lewis RC .04 .02
❑ 753 James Lofton .10 .05
❑ 754 Steve Tasker UER .25 .11
(Back says photo is
against Raiders, but
front shows a Steeler)
❑ 755 Jim Shofner CO .04 .02
❑ 756 Jimmie Jones RC .04 .02
❑ 757 Jay Novacek .25 .11
❑ 758 Jessie Hester RC .04 .02
❑ 759 Barry Word RC .04 .02
❑ 760 Eddie Anderson RC .04 .02
❑ 761 Cleveland Gary .04 .02
❑ 762 Marcus Dupree RC** .04 .02
❑ 763 David Griggs RC .04 .02
❑ 764 Rueben Mayes .04 .02
❑ 765 Stephen Baker .04 .02
❑ 766 Reyna Thompson RC UER .04 .02
(Front CB, back ST-CB)
❑ 767 Everson Walls .04 .02
❑ 768 Brad Baxter RC .04 .02

❑ 769 Steve Walsh .10 .05
❑ 770 Heath Sherman RC .04 .02
❑ 771 Johnny Johnson RC .10 .05
❑ 772A Dexter Manley 30.00 13.50
(Back mentions substance abuse violation)
❑ 772B Dexter Manley .04 .02
(Bio on back changed; doesn't mention substance abuse violation)
❑ 773 Ricky Proehl RC .25 .11
❑ 774 Frank Cornish .04 .02
❑ 775 Tommy Kane RC .04 .02
❑ 776 Derrick Fenner RC .04 .02
❑ 777 Steve Christie RC .04 .02
❑ 778 Wayne Haddix RC .04 .02
❑ 779 Richard Williamson UER .04 .02
(Experience is misspelled as esperience)
❑ 780 Brian Mitchell RC .25 .11
❑ 781 American Bowl/London .04 .02
Raiders vs. Saints
❑ 782 American Bowl/Berlin .04 .02
Rams vs. Chiefs
❑ 783 American Bowl/Tokyo .04 .02
Broncos vs. Seahawks
❑ 784 American Bowl/Montreal .04 .02
Steelers vs. Patriots
❑ 785A Berlin Wall .75 .35
Paul Tagliabue
("Peered through the Berlin Wall")
❑ 785B Berlin Wall .75 .35
Paul Tagliabue
("Posed at the Berlin Wall")
❑ 786 Raiders Stay in LA .04 .02
(Al Davis RC)
❑ 787 Falcons Back in Black .04 .02
(Jerry Glanville)
❑ 788 NFL Goes International .04 .02
World League Spring Debut
(Number on back is black, Newsreel cards are otherwise white; only Newsreel card with silver borders)
❑ 789 Overseas Appeal .04 .02
(Cheerleaders)
❑ 790 Photo Contest .04 .02
(Mike Mularkey awash)
❑ 791 Photo Contest .04 .02
(Gary Reasons hitting Bobby Humphrey)
❑ 792 Photo Contest .04 .02
(Maurice Hurst covering Drew Hill)
❑ 793 Photo Contest .04 .02
(Ronnie Lott celebrating)
❑ 794 Photo Contest .50 .23
(Felix Wright grabbing Barry Sanders' jersey)
❑ 795 Photo Contest .04 .02
(George Seifert in Gatorade Shower)
❑ 796 Photo Contest .04 .02
(Doug Smith praying)
❑ 797 Photo Contest .04 .02
(Doug Widell keeping cool)
❑ 798 Photo Contest .04 .02
(Todd Bowles covering Cris Carter)
❑ 799 Ronnie Lott .10 .05
(Stay in School)
❑ 800D Mark Carrier DB .10 .05
Defensive ROY
❑ 800O Emmitt Smith 1.50 .70
(Offensive ROY)
❑ 1990 Santa Claus SP .50 .23
(Second series only; No quote mark after Andre Ware)
❑ CC2 Paul Tagliabue SP .40 .18
NFL Commissioner
(First series only)
❑ CC3 Joe Robbie Mem SP .50 .23
(Second series only)
❑ SC Super Pro SP .50 .23
(Second series only)
❑ SC4 Fred Washington UER .04 .02
(Memorial to his death; word patches repeated in fourth line of text)
❑ SP1 Payne Stewart SP 1.00 .45
(First series only)
❑ NNO Lombardi Trophy SP 50.00 22.00
(Hologram: numbered out of 10,000)
❑ NNO Super Bowl XXIV Logo .04 .02

1991 Pro Set

	Nm-Mt	Ex-Mt
COMPLETE SET (850)	12.00	5.50
COMP.SERIES 1 (405)	6.00	2.70
COMP.SERIES 2 (407)	6.00	2.70
COMP.FINAL FACT. (38)	2.00	.90

❑ 1D Mark Carrier DB .10 .05
Defensive ROY
❑ 1O Emmitt Smith 1.00 .45
Offensive ROY
❑ 3 Joe Montana .50 .23
NFL Player of the Year
❑ 4 Art Shell .10 .05
NFL Coach of the Year
❑ 5 Mike Singletary .10 .05
NFL Man of the Year
❑ 6 Bruce Smith .10 .05
NFL Defensive Player of the Year
❑ 7 Barry Word .05 .02
NFL Comeback Player of the Year
❑ 8A Jim Kelly .25 .11
NFL Passing Leader
(NFLPA logo on back)
❑ 8B Jim Kelly .25 .11
NFL Passing Leader
(No NFLPA logo on back)
❑ 8C Jim Kelly 6.00 2.70
NFL Passing Leader
(No NFLPA logo on back but the registered symbol remains)
❑ 9 Warren Moon .10 .05
NFL Passing Yardage and TD Leader
❑ 10 Barry Sanders .50 .23
NFL Rushing and TD Leader
❑ 11 Jerry Rice .40 .18
NFL Receiving and Receiving Yardage Leader
❑ 12 Jay Novacek .10 .05
Tight End Leader
❑ 13 Thurman Thomas .10 .05
NFL Total Yardage Leader
❑ 14 Nick Lowery .05 .02
NFL Scoring Leader, Kickers
❑ 15 Mike Horan .05 .02
NFL Punting Leader
❑ 16 Clarence Verdin .05 .02
NFL Punt Return Leader
❑ 17 Kevin Clark RC .05 .02
NFL Kickoff Return Leader
❑ 18 Mark Carrier DB .10 .05
NFL Interception Leader
❑ 19A Derrick Thomas ERR 20.00 9.00
NFL Sack Leader
(Bills helmet on front)
❑ 19B Derrick Thomas COR .10 .05
NFL Sack Leader
(Chiefs helmet on front)
❑ 20 Ottis Anderson ML .10 .05
10000 Career Rushing Yards
❑ 21 Roger Craig ML .10 .05
Most Career Receptions by RB
❑ 22 Art Monk ML .10 .05
700 Career Receptions
❑ 23 Chuck Noll ML .10 .05
200 Victories
❑ 24 Randall Cunningham ML .10 .05
Leads team in rushing, fourth straight year
UER (586 rushes, should be 486; average 5.9, should be 7.1)
❑ 25 Dan Marino ML .50 .23
7th Straight 3000 yard season
❑ 26 49ers Road Record ML .05 .02
18 victories in row, still alive
❑ 27 Earl Campbell HOF .05 .02
❑ 28 John Hannah HOF .05 .02
❑ 29 Stan Jones HOF .05 .02
❑ 30 Tex Schramm HOF .05 .02
❑ 31 Jan Stenerud HOF .05 .02
❑ 32 Russell Maryland RC .10 .05
Outland Winner
❑ 33 Chris Zorich RC .10 .05
Lombardi Winner
❑ 34 Darryll Lewis RC UER .10 .05
Thorpe Winner
(Name misspelled Darryl on card)
❑ 35 Alfred Williams RC .05 .02
Butkus Winner
❑ 36 Raghib(Rocket) Ismail RC 1.00 .45
Walter Camp POY
❑ 37 Ty Detmer HH RC .40 .18
❑ 38 Andre Ware HH .10 .05
❑ 39 Barry Sanders HH .50 .23
❑ 40 Tim Brown HH UER .10 .05
(No "Official Photo and Stat Card of the NFL" on card back)
❑ 41 Vinny Testaverde HH .10 .05
❑ 42 Bo Jackson HH .30 .14
❑ 43 Mike Rozier HH .05 .02
❑ 44 Herschel Walker HH .10 .05
❑ 45 Marcus Allen HH .10 .05
❑ 46A James Lofton SB .10 .05
(NFLPA logo on back)
❑ 46B James Lofton SB .10 .05
(No NFLPA logo on back)
❑ 47A Bruce Smith SB .10 .05
(Official NFL Card in black letters)
❑ 47B Bruce Smith SB .10 .05
(Official NFL Card in white letters)
❑ 48 Myron Guyton SB .05 .02
❑ 49 Stephen Baker SB .05 .02
❑ 50 Mark Ingram SB UER .05 .02
(First repeated twice on back title)
❑ 51 Ottis Anderson SB .10 .05
❑ 52 Thurman Thomas SB .25 .11
❑ 53 Matt Bahr SB .05 .02
❑ 54 Scott Norwood SB .05 .02
❑ 55 Stephen Baker .05 .02

❑ 56 Carl Banks .05 .02
❑ 57 Mark Collins .05 .02
❑ 58 Steve DeOssie .05 .02
❑ 59 Eric Dorsey .05 .02
❑ 60 John Elliott .05 .02
❑ 61 Myron Guyton .05 .02
❑ 62 Rodney Hampton .25 .11
❑ 63 Jeff Hostetler .10 .05
❑ 64 Erik Howard .05 .02
❑ 65 Mark Ingram .10 .05
❑ 66 Greg Jackson RC .05 .02
❑ 67 Leonard Marshall .05 .02
❑ 68 David Meggett .10 .05
❑ 69 Eric Moore .05 .02
❑ 70 Bart Oates .05 .02
❑ 71 Gary Reasons .05 .02
❑ 72 Bill Parcells CO .10 .05
❑ 73 Howard Ballard .05 .02
❑ 74A Cornelius Bennett (NFLPA logo on back) .25 .11
❑ 74B Cornelius Bennett (No NFLPA logo on back) .05 .02
❑ 75 Shane Conlan .05 .02
❑ 76 Kent Hull .05 .02
❑ 77 Kirby Jackson RC .05 .02
❑ 78A Jim Kelly (NFLPA logo on back) .60 .25
❑ 78B Jim Kelly (No NFLPA logo on back) .25 .11
❑ 79 Mark Kelso .05 .02
❑ 80 Nate Odomes .05 .02
❑ 81 Andre Reed .10 .05
❑ 82 Jim Ritcher .05 .02
❑ 83 Bruce Smith .25 .11
❑ 84 Darryl Talley .05 .02
❑ 85 Steve Tasker .10 .05
❑ 86 Thurman Thomas .25 .11
❑ 87 James Williams .05 .02
❑ 88 Will Wolford .05 .02
❑ 89 Jeff Wright RC UER (Went to Central Missouri State, not Central Missouri) .05 .02
❑ 90 Marv Levy CO .05 .02
❑ 91 Steve Broussard .05 .02
❑ 92A Darion Conner ERR (Drafted 1st round, 19'99) 10.00 4.50
❑ 92B Darion Conner COR (Drafted 2nd round, 1990) .25 .11
❑ 93 Bill Fralic .05 .02
❑ 94 Tim Green .05 .02
❑ 95 Michael Haynes .25 .11
❑ 96 Chris Hinton .05 .02
❑ 97 Chris Miller UER (Two commas after city in his birth info) .10 .05
❑ 98 Deion Sanders UER (Career TD's 3, but only 2 in yearly stats) .40 .18
❑ 99 Jerry Glanville CO .05 .02
❑ 100 Kevin Butler .05 .02
❑ 101 Mark Carrier DB .10 .05
❑ 102 Jim Covert .05 .02
❑ 103 Richard Dent .10 .05
❑ 104 Jim Harbaugh .25 .11
❑ 105 Brad Muster .05 .02
❑ 106 Lemuel Stinson .05 .02
❑ 107 Keith Van Horne .05 .02
❑ 108 Mike Ditka CO UER (Winning percent in '87 was .733, not .753) .25 .11
❑ 109 Lewis Billups .05 .02
❑ 110 James Brooks .10 .05
❑ 111 Boomer Esiason .10 .05
❑ 112 James Francis .05 .02
❑ 113 David Fulcher .05 .02
❑ 114 Rodney Holman .05 .02
❑ 115 Tim McGee .05 .02
❑ 116 Anthony Munoz .10 .05
❑ 117 Sam Wyche CO .05 .02
❑ 118 Paul Farren .05 .02
❑ 119 Thane Gash .05 .02
❑ 120 Mike Johnson .05 .02
❑ 121A Bernie Kosar (NFLPA logo on back) .10 .05
❑ 121B Bernie Kosar (No NFLPA logo on back) .10 .05
❑ 122 Clay Matthews .10 .05
❑ 123 Eric Metcalf .10 .05
❑ 124 Frank Minnifield .05 .02
❑ 125A Webster Slaughter (NFLPA logo on back) .10 .05
❑ 125B Webster Slaughter (No NFLPA logo on back) .10 .05
❑ 126 Bill Belichick CO RC 1.50 .70
❑ 127 Tommie Agee .05 .02
❑ 128 Troy Aikman .75 .35
❑ 129 Jack Del Rio .10 .05
❑ 130 John Gesek RC .05 .02
❑ 131 Issiac Holt .05 .02
❑ 132 Michael Irvin .25 .11
❑ 133 Ken Norton .10 .05
❑ 134 Daniel Stubbs .05 .02
❑ 135 Jimmy Johnson CO .10 .05
❑ 136 Steve Atwater .05 .02
❑ 137 Michael Brooks .05 .02
❑ 138 John Elway 1.25 .55
❑ 139 Wymon Henderson .05 .02
❑ 140 Bobby Humphrey .05 .02
❑ 141 Mark Jackson .05 .02
❑ 142 Karl Mecklenburg .05 .02
❑ 143 Doug Widell .05 .02
❑ 144 Dan Reeves CO .05 .02
❑ 145 Eric Andolsek .05 .02
❑ 146 Jerry Ball .05 .02
❑ 147 Bennie Blades .05 .02
❑ 148 Lomas Brown .05 .02
❑ 149 Robert Clark .05 .02
❑ 150 Michael Cofer .05 .02
❑ 151 Dan Owens .05 .02
❑ 152 Rodney Peete .10 .05
❑ 153 Wayne Fontes CO .05 .02
❑ 154 Tim Harris .05 .02
❑ 155 Johnny Holland .05 .02
❑ 156 Don Majkowski .05 .02
❑ 157 Tony Mandarich .05 .02
❑ 158 Mark Murphy .05 .02
❑ 159 Brian Noble .05 .02
❑ 160 Jeff Query .05 .02
❑ 161 Sterling Sharpe .25 .11
❑ 162 Lindy Infante CO .05 .02
❑ 163 Ray Childress .05 .02
❑ 164 Ernest Givins .10 .05
❑ 165 Richard Johnson .05 .02
❑ 166 Bruce Matthews .10 .05
❑ 167 Warren Moon .25 .11
❑ 168 Mike Munchak .10 .05
❑ 169 Al Smith .05 .02
❑ 170 Lorenzo White .05 .02
❑ 171 Jack Pardee CO .05 .02
❑ 172 Albert Bentley .05 .02
❑ 173 Duane Bickett .05 .02
❑ 174 Bill Brooks .05 .02
❑ 175A Eric Dickerson (NFLPA logo on back) .40 .18
❑ 175B Eric Dickerson (No NFLPA logo on back and 667 yards rushing for 1990 in text) 1.25 .55
❑ 175C Eric Dickerson (No NFLPA logo on back and 677 yards rushing for 1990 in text) .25 .11
❑ 176 Ray Donaldson .05 .02
❑ 177 Jeff George .25 .11
❑ 178 Jeff Herrod .05 .02
❑ 179 Clarence Verdin .05 .02
❑ 180 Ron Meyer CO .05 .02
❑ 181 John Alt .05 .02
❑ 182 Steve DeBerg .05 .02
❑ 183 Albert Lewis .05 .02
❑ 184 Nick Lowery UER (In his 13th year, not 12th) .05 .02
❑ 185 Christian Okoye .05 .02
❑ 186 Stephone Paige .05 .02
❑ 187 Kevin Porter .05 .02
❑ 188 Derrick Thomas .25 .11
❑ 189 Marty Schottenheimer CO .05 .02
❑ 190 Willie Gault .10 .05
❑ 191 Howie Long .25 .11
❑ 192 Terry McDaniel .05 .02
❑ 193 Jay Schroeder UER (Passing total yards 13,863, should be 13,683) .05 .02
❑ 194 Steve Smith .05 .02
❑ 195 Greg Townsend .05 .02
❑ 196 Lionel Washington .05 .02
❑ 197 Steve Wisniewski UER (Back says drafted, should say traded to) .05 .02
❑ 198 Art Shell CO .10 .05
❑ 199 Henry Ellard .10 .05
❑ 200 Jim Everett .10 .05
❑ 201 Jerry Gray .05 .02
❑ 202 Kevin Greene .10 .05
❑ 203 Buford McGee .05 .02
❑ 204 Tom Newberry .05 .02
❑ 205 Frank Stams .05 .02
❑ 206 Alvin Wright .05 .02
❑ 207 John Robinson CO .05 .02
❑ 208 Jeff Cross .05 .02
❑ 209 Mark Duper .10 .05
❑ 210 Dan Marino 1.25 .55
❑ 211A Tim McKyer (No Traded box on front) .10 .05
❑ 211B Tim McKyer (Traded box on front) .25 .11
❑ 212 John Offerdahl .05 .02
❑ 213 Sammie Smith .05 .02
❑ 214 Richmond Webb .05 .02
❑ 215 Jarvis Williams .05 .02
❑ 216 Don Shula CO .10 .05
❑ 217A Darrell Fullington ERR (No registered symbol on card back) .10 .05
❑ 217B Darrell Fullington COR (Registered symbol on card back) .10 .05
❑ 218 Tim Irwin .05 .02
❑ 219 Mike Merriweather .05 .02
❑ 220 Keith Millard .05 .02
❑ 221 Al Noga .05 .02
❑ 222 Henry Thomas .05 .02
❑ 223 Wade Wilson .10 .05
❑ 224 Gary Zimmerman .05 .02
❑ 225 Jerry Burns CO .05 .02
❑ 226 Bruce Armstrong .05 .02
❑ 227 Marv Cook .05 .02
❑ 228 Hart Lee Dykes .05 .02
❑ 229 Tommy Hodson .05 .02
❑ 230 Ronnie Lippett .05 .02
❑ 231 Ed Reynolds .05 .02
❑ 232 Chris Singleton .05 .02
❑ 233 John Stephens .05 .02
❑ 234 Dick MacPherson CO .05 .02
❑ 235 Stan Brock .05 .02
❑ 236 Craig Heyward .10 .05
❑ 237 Vaughan Johnson .05 .02
❑ 238 Robert Massey .05 .02
❑ 239 Brett Maxie .05 .02
❑ 240 Rueben Mayes .05 .02
❑ 241 Pat Swilling .10 .05
❑ 242 Renaldo Turnbull .05 .02
❑ 243 Jim Mora CO .05 .02
❑ 244 Kyle Clifton .05 .02
❑ 245 Jeff Criswell .05 .02
❑ 246 James Hasty .05 .02
❑ 247 Erik McMillan .05 .02
❑ 248 Scott Mersereau RC .05 .02
❑ 249 Ken O'Brien .05 .02
❑ 250A Blair Thomas (NFLPA logo on back) .25 .11
❑ 250B Blair Thomas (No NFLPA logo on back) .10 .05
❑ 251 Al Toon .10 .05
❑ 252 Bruce Coslet CO .05 .02
❑ 253 Eric Allen .05 .02
❑ 254 Fred Barnett .25 .11
❑ 255 Keith Byars .05 .02
❑ 256 Randall Cunningham .25 .11
❑ 257 Seth Joyner .10 .05

❑ 258 Clyde Simmons .05 .02
❑ 259 Jessie Small .05 .02
❑ 260 Andre Waters .05 .02
❑ 261 Rich Kotite CO .05 .02
❑ 262 Roy Green .05 .02
❑ 263 Ernie Jones .05 .02
❑ 264 Tim McDonald .05 .02
❑ 265 Timm Rosenbach .05 .02
❑ 266 Rod Saddler .05 .02
❑ 267 Luis Sharpe .05 .02
❑ 268 Anthony Thompson UER .05 .02
(Terra Haute should
be Terre Haute)
❑ 269 Marcus Turner RC .05 .02
❑ 270 Joe Bugel CO .05 .02
❑ 271 Gary Anderson K .05 .02
❑ 272 Dermontti Dawson .05 .02
❑ 273 Eric Green .05 .02
❑ 274 Merril Hoge .05 .02
❑ 275 Tunch Ilkin .05 .02
❑ 276 D.J. Johnson .05 .02
❑ 277 Louis Lipps .05 .02
❑ 278 Rod Woodson .25 .11
❑ 279 Chuck Noll CO .10 .05
❑ 280 Martin Bayless .05 .02
❑ 281 Marion Butts UER .10 .05
(2 years exp.,
should be 3)
❑ 282 Gill Byrd .05 .02
❑ 283 Burt Grossman .05 .02
❑ 284 Courtney Hall .05 .02
❑ 285 Anthony Miller .10 .05
❑ 286 Leslie O'Neal .10 .05
❑ 287 Billy Joe Tolliver .05 .02
❑ 288 Dan Henning CO .05 .02
❑ 289 Dexter Carter .05 .02
❑ 290 Michael Carter .05 .02
❑ 291 Kevin Fagan .05 .02
❑ 292 Pierce Holt .05 .02
❑ 293 Guy McIntyre .05 .02
(Joe Montana also in photo)
❑ 294 Tom Rathman .05 .02
❑ 295 John Taylor .10 .05
❑ 296 Steve Young .75 .35
❑ 297 George Seifert CO .10 .05
❑ 298 Brian Blades .10 .05
❑ 299 Jeff Bryant .05 .02
❑ 300 Norm Johnson .05 .02
❑ 301 Tommy Kane .05 .02
❑ 302 Cortez Kennedy UER .25 .11
(Played for Seattle
in '90, not Miami)
❑ 303 Bryan Millard .05 .02
❑ 304 John L. Williams .05 .02
❑ 305 David Wyman .05 .02
❑ 306A Chuck Knox CO ERR .05 .02
(Has NFLPA logo,
but should not)
❑ 306B Chuck Knox CO COR .50 .23
(No NFLPA logo on back)
❑ 307 Gary Anderson RB .05 .02
❑ 308 Reggie Cobb .05 .02
❑ 309 Randy Grimes .05 .02
❑ 310 Harry Hamilton .05 .02
❑ 311 Bruce Hill .05 .02
❑ 312 Eugene Marve .05 .02
❑ 313 Ervin Randle .05 .02
❑ 314 Vinny Testaverde .10 .05
❑ 315 Richard Williamson CO .05 .02
UER (Coach: 1st year,
should be 2nd year)
❑ 316 Earnest Byner .05 .02
❑ 317 Gary Clark .25 .11
❑ 318A Andre Collins .10 .05
(NFLPA logo on back)
❑ 318B Andre Collins .10 .05
(No NFLPA logo on back)
❑ 319 Darryl Grant .05 .02
❑ 320 Chip Lohmiller .05 .02
❑ 321 Martin Mayhew .05 .02
❑ 322 Mark Rypien .10 .05
❑ 323 Alvin Walton .05 .02
❑ 324 Joe Gibbs CO UER .10 .05
(Has registered
symbol but should not)
❑ 325 Jerry Glanville REP .05 .02
❑ 326A John Elway REP 4.00 1.80
(NFLPA logo on back)
❑ 326B John Elway REP 2.00 .90
(No NFLPA logo on back)
❑ 327 Boomer Esiason REP .05 .02
❑ 328A Steve Tasker REP 4.00 1.80
(NFLPA logo on back)
❑ 328B Steve Tasker REP 2.00 .90
(No NFLPA logo on back)
❑ 329 Jerry Rice REP .40 .18
❑ 330 Jeff Rutledge REP .05 .02
❑ 331 K.C. Defense REP .05 .02
❑ 332 49ers Streak REP .05 .02
(Cleveland Gary)
❑ 333 Monday Meeting REP .05 .02
(John Taylor)
❑ 334A Randall Cunningham .05 .02
REP
(NFLPA logo on back)
❑ 334B Randall Cunningham .05 .02
REP
(No NFLPA logo on back)
❑ 335A Bo Jackson and .50 .23
Barry Sanders REP
(NFLPA logo on back)
❑ 335B Bo Jackson and .50 .23
Barry Sanders REP
(No NFLPA logo on back)
❑ 336 Lawrence Taylor REP .25 .11
❑ 337 Warren Moon REP .25 .11
❑ 338 Alan Grant REP .05 .02
❑ 339 Todd McNair REP .05 .02
❑ 340A Miami Dolphins REP .05 .02
(Mark Clayton;
TM symbol on Chiefs
player's shoulder)
❑ 340B Miami Dolphins REP .05 .02
(Mark Clayton;
TM symbol off Chiefs
player's shoulder)
❑ 341A Highest Scoring REP 4.00 1.80
Jim Kelly Passing
(NFLPA logo on back)
❑ 341B Highest Scoring REP 2.00 .90
Jim Kelly Passing
(No NFLPA logo on back)
❑ 342 Matt Bahr REP .05 .02
❑ 343 Robert Tisch NEW .05 .02
(With Wellington Mara)
❑ 344 Sam Jankovich NEW .05 .02
❑ 345 In-the-Grasp NEW .05 .02
(John Elway)
❑ 346 Bo Jackson NEW .10 .05
(Career in Jeopardy)
❑ 347 NFL Teacher of the .05 .02
Year Jack Williams
with Paul Tagliabue
❑ 348 Ronnie Lott NEW .10 .05
(Plan B Free Agent)
❑ 349 Super Bowl XXV .05 .02
Teleclinic NEW (Greg
Gumbel with Warren
Moon, Derrick Thomas,
and Wade Wilson)
❑ 350 W.Houston NEW RC .05 .02
❑ 351 U.S. Troops in .05 .02
Saudia Arabia NEW
(Troops watching TV
with gas masks)
❑ 352 Art McNally OFF .05 .02
❑ 353 Dick Jorgensen OFF .05 .02
❑ 354 Jerry Seeman OFF .05 .02
❑ 355 Jim Tunney OFF .05 .02
❑ 356 Gerry Austin OFF .05 .02
❑ 357 Gene Barth OFF .05 .02
❑ 358 Red Cashion OFF .05 .02
❑ 359 Tom Dooley OFF .05 .02
❑ 360 Johnny Grier OFF .05 .02
❑ 361 Pat Haggerty OFF .05 .02
❑ 362 Dale Hamer OFF .05 .02
❑ 363 Dick Hantak OFF .05 .02
❑ 364 Jerry Markbreit OFF .05 .02
❑ 365 Gordon McCarter OFF .05 .02
❑ 366 Bob McElwee OFF .05 .02
❑ 367 Howard Roe OFF .05 .02
(Illustrations on back
smaller than other
officials' cards)
❑ 368 Tom White OFF .05 .02
❑ 369 Norm Schachter OFF .05 .02
❑ 370A Warren Moon .25 .11
Crack Kills
(Small type on back)
❑ 370B Warren Moon .25 .11
Crack Kills
(Large type on back)
❑ 371A Boomer Esiason .50 .23
Don't Drink
(Small type on back)
❑ 371B Boomer Esiason .10 .05
Don't Drink
(Large type on back)
❑ 372A Troy Aikman .40 .18
Play It Straight
(Small type on back)
❑ 372B Troy Aikman .40 .18
Play It Straight
(Large type on back)
❑ 373A Carl Banks .50 .23
Read
(Small type on back)
❑ 373B Carl Banks .05 .02
Read
(Large type on back)
❑ 374A Jim Everett .50 .23
Study
(Small type on back)
❑ 374B Jim Everett .10 .05
Study
(Large type on back)
❑ 375A Anthony Munoz .10 .05
Quadante en la Escuela
(Dificul; small type)
❑ 375B Anthony Munoz .10 .05
Quadante en la Escuela
(Dificil; small type)
❑ 375C Anthony Munoz .10 .05
Quadante en la Escuela
(Dificil; large type)
❑ 375D Anthony Munoz .10 .05
Quedate en la Escuela
(Large type)
❑ 376A Ray Childress 1.25 .55
Don't Pollute
(Small type on back)
❑ 376B Ray Childress .05 .02
Don't Pollute
(Large type on back)
❑ 377A Charles Mann 1.25 .55
Steroids Destroy
(Small type on back)
❑ 377B Charles Mann .05 .02
Steroids Destroy
(Large type on back)
❑ 378A Jackie Slater 1.25 .55
Keep the Peace
(Small type on back)
❑ 378B Jackie Slater .05 .02
Keep the Peace
(Large type on back)
❑ 379 Jerry Rice NFC .40 .18
❑ 380 Andre Rison NFC .10 .05
❑ 381 Jim Lachey NFC .05 .02
❑ 382 Jackie Slater NFC .05 .02
❑ 383 Randall McDaniel NFC .05 .02
❑ 384 Mark Bortz NFC .05 .02
❑ 385 Jay Hilgenberg NFC .05 .02
❑ 386 Keith Jackson NFC .05 .02
❑ 387 Joe Montana NFC .50 .23
❑ 388 Barry Sanders NFC .50 .23
❑ 389 Neal Anderson NFC .05 .02
❑ 390 Reggie White NFC .25 .11
❑ 391 Chris Doleman NFC .05 .02
❑ 392 Jerome Brown NFC .05 .02
❑ 393 Charles Haley NFC .05 .02
❑ 394 Lawrence Taylor NFC .25 .11

❑ 395 Pepper Johnson NFC .05 .02
❑ 396 Mike Singletary NFC .10 .05
❑ 397 Darrell Green NFC .05 .02
❑ 398 Carl Lee NFC .05 .02
❑ 399 Joey Browner NFC .05 .02
❑ 400 Ronnie Lott NFC .10 .05
❑ 401 Sean Landeta NFC .05 .02
❑ 402 Morten Andersen NFC .05 .02
❑ 403 Mel Gray NFC .05 .02
❑ 404 Reyna Thompson NFC .05 .02
❑ 405 Jimmy Johnson CO NFC .10 .05
❑ 406 Andre Reed AFC .10 .05
❑ 407 Anthony Miller AFC .10 .05
❑ 408 Anthony Munoz AFC .10 .05
❑ 409 Bruce Armstrong AFC .05 .02
❑ 410 Bruce Matthews AFC .05 .02
❑ 411 Mike Munchak AFC .05 .02
❑ 412 Kent Hull AFC .05 .02
❑ 413 Rodney Holman AFC .05 .02
❑ 414 Warren Moon AFC .25 .11
❑ 415 Thurman Thomas AFC .25 .11
❑ 416 Marion Butts AFC .10 .05
❑ 417 Bruce Smith AFC .10 .05
❑ 418 Greg Townsend AFC .05 .02
❑ 419 Ray Childress AFC .05 .02
❑ 420 Derrick Thomas AFC .25 .11
❑ 421 Leslie O'Neal AFC .10 .05
❑ 422 John Offerdahl AFC .05 .02
❑ 423 Shane Conlan AFC .05 .02
❑ 424 Rod Woodson AFC .25 .11
❑ 425 Albert Lewis AFC .05 .02
❑ 426 Steve Atwater AFC .05 .02
❑ 427 David Fulcher AFC .05 .02
❑ 428 Rohn Stark AFC .05 .02
❑ 429 Nick Lowery AFC .05 .02
❑ 430 Clarence Verdin AFC .05 .02
❑ 431 Steve Tasker AFC .05 .02
❑ 432 Art Shell CO AFC .10 .05
❑ 433 Scott Case .05 .02
❑ 434 Tory Epps UER .05 .02
(No TM next to Pro Set on card back)
❑ 435 Mike Gann UER .05 .02
(Text has 2 fumble recoveries, stats say 3)
❑ 436 Brian Jordan UER .10 .05
(No TM next to Pro Set on card back)
❑ 437 Mike Kenn .05 .02
❑ 438 John Rade .05 .02
❑ 439 Andre Rison .10 .05
❑ 440 Mike Rozier .05 .02
❑ 441 Jessie Tuggle .05 .02
❑ 442 Don Beebe .05 .02
❑ 443 John Davis RC .05 .02
❑ 444 James Lofton .10 .05
❑ 445 Keith McKeller .05 .02
❑ 446 Jamie Mueller .05 .02
❑ 447 Scott Norwood .05 .02
❑ 448 Frank Reich .10 .05
❑ 449 Leon Seals .05 .02
❑ 450 Leonard Smith .05 .02
❑ 451 Neal Anderson .10 .05
❑ 452 Trace Armstrong .05 .02
❑ 453 Mark Bortz .05 .02
❑ 454 Wendell Davis .05 .02
❑ 455 Shaun Gayle .05 .02
❑ 456 Jay Hilgenberg .05 .02
❑ 457 Steve McMichael .10 .05
❑ 458 Mike Singletary .10 .05
❑ 459 Donnell Woolford .05 .02
❑ 460 Jim Breech .05 .02
❑ 461 Eddie Brown .05 .02
❑ 462 Barney Bussey RC .05 .02
❑ 463 Bruce Kozerski .05 .02
❑ 464 Tim Krumrie .05 .02
❑ 465 Bruce Reimers .05 .02
❑ 466 Kevin Walker RC .05 .02
❑ 467 Ickey Woods .05 .02
❑ 468 Carl Zander UER .05 .02
(DOB: 4/12/63, should be 3/23/63)
❑ 469 Mike Baab .05 .02
❑ 470 Brian Brennan .05 .02
❑ 471 Rob Burnett RC .10 .05
❑ 472 Raymond Clayborn .05 .02
❑ 473 Reggie Langhorne .05 .02
❑ 474 Kevin Mack .05 .02
❑ 475 Anthony Pleasant .05 .02
❑ 476 Joe Morris .05 .02
❑ 477 Dan Fike .05 .02
❑ 478 Ray Horton .05 .02
❑ 479 Jim Jeffcoat .05 .02
❑ 480 Jimmie Jones .05 .02
❑ 481 Kelvin Martin .05 .02
❑ 482 Nate Newton .10 .05
❑ 483 Danny Noonan .05 .02
❑ 484 Jay Novacek .25 .11
❑ 485 Emmitt Smith 2.00 .90
❑ 486 James Washington RC .05 .02
❑ 487 Simon Fletcher .05 .02
❑ 488 Ron Holmes .05 .02
❑ 489 Mike Horan .05 .02
❑ 490 Vance Johnson .05 .02
❑ 491 Keith Kartz .05 .02
❑ 492 Greg Kragen .05 .02
❑ 493 Ken Lanier .05 .02
❑ 494 Warren Powers .05 .02
❑ 495 Dennis Smith .05 .02
❑ 496 Jeff Campbell .05 .02
❑ 497 Ken Dallafior .05 .02
❑ 498 Dennis Gibson .05 .02
❑ 499 Kevin Glover .05 .02
❑ 500 Mel Gray .10 .05
❑ 501 Eddie Murray .05 .02
❑ 502 Barry Sanders 1.25 .55
❑ 503 Chris Spielman .10 .05
❑ 504 William White .05 .02
❑ 505 Matt Brock RC .05 .02
❑ 506 Robert Brown .05 .02
❑ 507 LeRoy Butler .10 .05
❑ 508 James Campen RC .05 .02
❑ 509 Jerry Holmes .05 .02
❑ 510 Perry Kemp .05 .02
❑ 511 Ken Ruettgers .05 .02
❑ 512 Scott Stephen RC .05 .02
❑ 513 Ed West .05 .02
❑ 514 Cris Dishman RC .05 .02
❑ 515 Curtis Duncan .05 .02
❑ 516 Drew Hill UER .05 .02
(Text says 390 catches and 6368 yards, stats say 450 and 7715)
❑ 517 Haywood Jeffires .10 .05
❑ 518 Sean Jones .10 .05
❑ 519 Lamar Lathon .05 .02
❑ 520 Don Maggs .05 .02
❑ 521 Bubba McDowell .05 .02
❑ 522 Johnny Meads .05 .02
❑ 523A Chip Banks ERR .50 .23
(No text)
❑ 523B Chip Banks COR .05 .02
❑ 524 Pat Beach .05 .02
❑ 525 Sam Clancy .05 .02
❑ 526 Eugene Daniel .05 .02
❑ 527 Jon Hand .05 .02
❑ 528 Jessie Hester .05 .02
❑ 529A Mike Prior ERR .50 .23
(No textual information)
❑ 529B Mike Prior COR .05 .02
❑ 530 Keith Taylor .05 .02
❑ 531 Donnell Thompson .05 .02
❑ 532 Dino Hackett .05 .02
❑ 533 David Lutz RC .05 .02
❑ 534 Chris Martin .05 .02
❑ 535 Kevin Ross .05 .02
❑ 536 Dan Saleaumua .05 .02
❑ 537 Neil Smith .25 .11
❑ 538 Percy Snow .05 .02
❑ 539 Robb Thomas .05 .02
❑ 540 Barry Word .05 .02
❑ 541 Marcus Allen .25 .11
❑ 542 Eddie Anderson .05 .02
❑ 543 Scott Davis .05 .02
❑ 544 Mervyn Fernandez .05 .02
❑ 545 Ethan Horton .05 .02
❑ 546 Ronnie Lott .10 .05
❑ 547 Don Mosebar .05 .02
❑ 548 Jerry Robinson .05 .02
❑ 549 Aaron Wallace .05 .02
❑ 550 Flipper Anderson .05 .02
❑ 551 Cleveland Gary .05 .02
❑ 552 Damone Johnson RC .05 .02
❑ 553 Duval Love RC .05 .02
❑ 554 Irv Pankey .05 .02
❑ 555 Mike Piel .05 .02
❑ 556 Jackie Slater .05 .02
❑ 557 Michael Stewart .05 .02
❑ 558 Pat Terrell .05 .02
❑ 559 J.B. Brown .05 .02
❑ 560 Mark Clayton .10 .05
❑ 561 Ferrell Edmunds .05 .02
❑ 562 Harry Galbreath .05 .02
❑ 563 David Griggs .05 .02
❑ 564 Jim C. Jensen .05 .02
❑ 565 Louis Oliver .05 .02
❑ 566 Tony Paige .05 .02
❑ 567 Keith Sims .05 .02
❑ 568 Joey Browner .05 .02
❑ 569 Anthony Carter .10 .05
❑ 570 Chris Doleman .05 .02
❑ 571 Rich Gannon UER .25 .11
(Acquired in '87, not '88 as in text)
❑ 572 Hassan Jones .05 .02
❑ 573 Steve Jordan .05 .02
❑ 574 Carl Lee .05 .02
❑ 575 Randall McDaniel .05 .02
❑ 576 Herschel Walker .10 .05
❑ 577 Ray Agnew .05 .02
❑ 578 Vincent Brown .05 .02
❑ 579 Irving Fryar .10 .05
❑ 580 Tim Goad .05 .02
❑ 581 Maurice Hurst .05 .02
❑ 582 Fred Marion .05 .02
❑ 583 Johnny Rembert .05 .02
❑ 584 Andre Tippett .05 .02
❑ 585 Brent Williams .05 .02
❑ 586 Morten Andersen .05 .02
❑ 587 Toi Cook RC .05 .02
❑ 588 Jim Dombrowski .05 .02
❑ 589 Dalton Hilliard .05 .02
❑ 590 Rickey Jackson .05 .02
❑ 591 Eric Martin .05 .02
❑ 592 Sam Mills .05 .02
❑ 593 Bobby Hebert .05 .02
❑ 594 Steve Walsh .05 .02
❑ 595 Ottis Anderson .10 .05
❑ 596 Pepper Johnson .05 .02
❑ 597 Bob Kratch RC .05 .02
❑ 598 Sean Landeta .05 .02
❑ 599 Doug Riesenberg .05 .02
❑ 600 William Roberts .05 .02
❑ 601 Phil Simms .10 .05
❑ 602 Lawrence Taylor .25 .11
❑ 603 Everson Walls .05 .02
❑ 604 Brad Baxter .05 .02
❑ 605 Dennis Byrd .05 .02
❑ 606 Jeff Lageman .05 .02
❑ 607 Pat Leahy .05 .02
❑ 608 Rob Moore .25 .11
❑ 609 Joe Mott .05 .02
❑ 610 Tony Stargell .05 .02
❑ 611 Brian Washington .05 .02
❑ 612 Marvin Washington RC .05 .02
❑ 613 David Alexander .05 .02
❑ 614 Jerome Brown .05 .02
❑ 615 Byron Evans .05 .02
❑ 616 Ron Heller .05 .02
❑ 617 Wes Hopkins .05 .02
❑ 618 Keith Jackson .10 .05
❑ 619 Heath Sherman .05 .02
❑ 620 Reggie White .25 .11
❑ 621 Calvin Williams .10 .05
❑ 622 Ken Harvey .10 .05
❑ 623 Eric Hill .05 .02
❑ 624 Johnny Johnson .05 .02
❑ 625 Freddie Joe Nunn .05 .02
❑ 626 Ricky Proehl .05 .02
❑ 627 Tootie Robbins .05 .02
❑ 628 Jay Taylor .05 .02
❑ 629 Tom Tupa .05 .02

❑ 630 Jim Wahler RC .05 .02
❑ 631 Bubby Brister .05 .02
❑ 632 Thomas Everett .05 .02
❑ 633 Bryan Hinkle .05 .02
❑ 634 Carnell Lake .05 .02
❑ 635 David Little .05 .02
❑ 636 Hardy Nickerson .10 .05
❑ 637 Gerald Williams .05 .02
❑ 638 Keith Willis .05 .02
❑ 639 Tim Worley .05 .02
❑ 640 Rod Bernstine .05 .02
❑ 641 Frank Cornish .05 .02
❑ 642 Gary Plummer .05 .02
❑ 643 Henry Rolling RC .05 .02
❑ 644 Sam Seale .05 .02
❑ 645 Junior Seau .25 .11
❑ 646 Billy Ray Smith .05 .02
❑ 647 Broderick Thompson .05 .02
❑ 648 Derrick Walker RC .05 .02
❑ 649 Todd Bowles .05 .02
❑ 650 Don Griffin .05 .02
❑ 651 Charles Haley .10 .05
❑ 652 Brent Jones UER .10 .05
(Born in Santa Clara,
not San Jose)
❑ 653 Joe Montana 1.25 .55
❑ 654 Jerry Rice .75 .35
❑ 655 Bill Romanowski .05 .02
❑ 656 Michael Walter .05 .02
❑ 657 Dave Waymer .05 .02
❑ 658 Jeff Chadwick .05 .02
❑ 659 Derrick Fenner .05 .02
❑ 660 Nesby Glasgow .05 .02
❑ 661 Jacob Green .05 .02
❑ 662 Dwayne Harper RC .05 .02
❑ 663 Andy Heck .05 .02
❑ 664 Dave Krieg .10 .05
❑ 665 Rufus Porter .05 .02
❑ 666 Eugene Robinson .05 .02
❑ 667 Mark Carrier WR .25 .11
❑ 668 Steve Christie .05 .02
❑ 669 Reuben Davis .05 .02
❑ 670 Paul Gruber .05 .02
❑ 671 Wayne Haddix .05 .02
❑ 672 Ron Hall .05 .02
❑ 673 Keith McCants UER .05 .02
(Senior All-American,
sic, left school
after junior year)
❑ 674 Ricky Reynolds .05 .02
❑ 675 Mark Robinson .05 .02
❑ 676 Jeff Bostic .05 .02
❑ 677 Darrell Green .05 .02
❑ 678 Markus Koch .05 .02
❑ 679 Jim Lachey .05 .02
❑ 680 Charles Mann .05 .02
❑ 681 Wilber Marshall .05 .02
❑ 682 Art Monk .10 .05
❑ 683 Gerald Riggs .05 .02
❑ 684 Ricky Sanders .05 .02
❑ 685 Ray Handley NEW .05 .02
(Replaces Bill Parcells as
Giants head coach)
❑ 686 NFL announces NEW .05 .02
expansion
❑ 687 Miami gets NEW .05 .02
Super Bowl XXIX
❑ 688 George Young NEW .05 .02
is named NFL Executive
of the Year by
The Sporting News
❑ 689 Five-millionth fan NEW .05 .02
visits Pro Football
Hall of Fame
❑ 690 Sports Illustrated NEW .05 .02
poll finds pro football
is America's Number 1
spectator sport
❑ 691 American Bowl NEW .05 .02
London Theme Art
❑ 692 American Bowl NEW .05 .02
Berlin Theme Art
❑ 693 American Bowl NEW .05 .02
Tokyo Theme Art

❑ 694A Russell Maryland .25 .11
(Says he runs a 4.91
40, card 32 has 4.8)
❑ 694B Joe Ferguson LEG .05 .02
❑ 695 Carl Hairston LEG .10 .05
❑ 696 Dan Hampton LEG .10 .05
❑ 697 Mike Haynes LEG .05 .02
❑ 698 Marty Lyons LEG .05 .02
❑ 699 Ozzie Newsome LEG .10 .05
❑ 700 Scott Studwell LEG .05 .02
❑ 701 Mike Webster LEG .05 .02
❑ 702 Dwayne Woodruff LEG .05 .02
❑ 703 Larry Kennan CO .05 .02
London Monarchs
❑ 704 Stan Gelbaugh RC LL .10 .05
London Monarchs
❑ 705 John Brantley LL .05 .02
Birmingham Fire
❑ 706 Danny Lockett LL .05 .02
London Monarchs
❑ 707 Anthony Parker RC LL .10 .05
NY/NJ Knights
❑ 708 Dan Crossman LL .05 .02
London Monarchs
❑ 709 Eric Wilkerson LL .05 .02
NY/NJ Knights
❑ 710 Judd Garrett RC LL .05 .02
London Monarchs
❑ 711 Tony Baker LL .05 .02
Frankfurt Galaxy
❑ 712 1st Place BW PHOTO .05 .02
Randall Cunningham
❑ 713 2nd Place BW PHOTO .05 .02
Mark Ingram
❑ 714 3rd Place BW PHOTO .05 .02
Pete Holohan
Barney Bussey
Carl Carter
❑ 715 1st Place Color PHOTO .05 .02
Action
Sterling Sharpe
❑ 716 2nd Place Color PHOTO .05 .02
Action
Jim Harbaugh
❑ 717 3rd Place Color PHOTO .05 .02
Action
Anthony Miller
David Fulcher
❑ 718 1st Place Color PHOTO .05 .02
Feature
Bill Parcells CO
Lawrence Taylor
❑ 719 2nd Place Color PHOTO .05 .02
Feature
Patriotic Crowd
❑ 720 3rd Place Color PHOTO .05 .02
Feature
Alfredo Roberts
❑ 721 Ray Bentley .05 .02
Read And Study
❑ 722 Earnest Byner .05 .02
Never Give Up
❑ 723 Bill Fralic .05 .02
Steroids Destroy
❑ 724 Joe Jacoby .05 .02
Don't Pollute
❑ 725 Howie Long .25 .11
Aids Kills
❑ 726 Dan Marino .50 .23
School's The Ticket
❑ 727 Ron Rivera .05 .02
Leer Y Estudiar
❑ 728 Mike Singletary .10 .05
Be The Best
❑ 729 Cornelius Bennett .10 .05
Chill
❑ 730 Russell Maryland .25 .11
❑ 731 Eric Turner RC .10 .05
❑ 732 Bruce Pickens RC UER .05 .02
(Wearing 38, but card
back lists 39)
❑ 733 Mike Croel RC .05 .02
❑ 734 Todd Lyght RC .05 .02
❑ 735 Eric Swann RC .25 .11

❑ 736 Charles McRae RC .05 .02
❑ 737 Antone Davis RC .05 .02
❑ 738 Stanley Richard RC .05 .02
❑ 739 Herman Moore RC .25 .11
❑ 740 Pat Harlow RC .05 .02
❑ 741 Alvin Harper RC .25 .11
❑ 742 Mike Pritchard RC .25 .11
❑ 743 Leonard Russell RC .25 .11
❑ 744 Huey Richardson RC .05 .02
❑ 745 Dan McGwire RC .05 .02
❑ 746 Bobby Wilson RC .05 .02
❑ 747 Alfred Williams .05 .02
❑ 748 Vinnie Clark RC .05 .02
❑ 749 Kelvin Pritchett RC .10 .05
❑ 750 Harvey Williams RC .25 .11
❑ 751 Stan Thomas .05 .02
❑ 752 Randal Hill RC .10 .05
❑ 753 Todd Marinovich RC .05 .02
❑ 754 Ted Washington RC .05 .02
❑ 755 Henry Jones RC .10 .05
❑ 756 Jarrod Bunch RC .05 .02
❑ 757 Mike Dumas RC .05 .02
❑ 758 Ed King RC .05 .02
❑ 759 Reggie Johnson RC .05 .02
❑ 760 Roman Phifer RC .05 .02
❑ 761 Mike Jones DE RC .05 .02
❑ 762 Brett Favre RC 8.00 3.60
❑ 763 Browning Nagle RC .05 .02
❑ 764 Esera Tuaolo RC .05 .02
❑ 765 George Thornton RC .05 .02
❑ 766 Dixon Edwards RC .05 .02
❑ 767 Darryll Lewis .10 .05
❑ 768 Eric Bieniemy RC .05 .02
❑ 769 Shane Curry .05 .02
❑ 770 Jerome Henderson RC .05 .02
❑ 771 Wesley Carroll RC .05 .02
❑ 772 Nick Bell RC .05 .02
❑ 773 John Flannery RC .05 .02
❑ 774 Ricky Watters RC 1.50 .70
❑ 775 Jeff Graham RC .25 .11
❑ 776 Eric Moten RC .05 .02
❑ 777 Jesse Campbell RC .05 .02
❑ 778 Chris Zorich .10 .05
❑ 779 Joe Valerio .05 .02
❑ 780 Doug Thomas RC .05 .02
❑ 781 Lamar Rogers RC UER .05 .02
(No "Official Card of
NFL" and TM on
card front)
❑ 782 John Johnson RC .05 .02
❑ 783 Phil Hansen RC .05 .02
❑ 784 Kanavis McGhee RC .05 .02
❑ 785 Calvin Stephens RC UER .05 .02
(Card says New England,
others say New England
Patriots)
❑ 786 James Jones RC .05 .02
❑ 787 Reggie Barrett .05 .02
❑ 788 Aeneas Williams RC .25 .11
❑ 789 Aaron Craver RC .05 .02
❑ 790 Keith Traylor RC .05 .02
❑ 791 Godfrey Myles RC .05 .02
❑ 792 Mo Lewis RC .10 .05
❑ 793 James Richards RC .05 .02
❑ 794 Carlos Jenkins RC .05 .02
❑ 795 Lawrence Dawsey RC .10 .05
❑ 796 Don Davey .05 .02
❑ 797 Jake Reed RC .50 .23
❑ 798 Dave McCloughan .05 .02
❑ 799 Erik Williams RC .10 .05
❑ 800 Steve Jackson RC .05 .02
❑ 801 Bob Dahl .05 .02
❑ 802 Ernie Mills RC .10 .05
❑ 803 David Daniels RC .05 .02
❑ 804 Rob Selby RC .05 .02
❑ 805 Ricky Ervins RC .10 .05
❑ 806 Tim Barnett RC .05 .02
❑ 807 Chris Gardocki .05 .02
❑ 808 Kevin Donnalley RC .05 .02
❑ 809 Robert Wilson RC .05 .02
❑ 810 Chuck Webb RC .05 .02
❑ 811 Darryl Wren RC .05 .02
❑ 812 Ed McCaffrey RC 2.00 .90
❑ 813 Shula's 300th Victory .05 .02

NEWS

❑ 814 Raiders-49ers sell out Coliseum NEWS .05 .02
❑ 815 NFL International NEWS .05 .02
❑ 816 Moe Gardner RC .05 .02
❑ 817 Tim McKyer .05 .02
❑ 818 Tom Waddle RC .05 .02
❑ 819 Michael Jackson RC .25 .11
❑ 820 Tony Casillas .05 .02
❑ 821 Gaston Green .05 .02
❑ 822 Kenny Walker RC .05 .02
❑ 823 Willie Green RC .05 .02
❑ 824 Erik Kramer RC .25 .11
❑ 825 William Fuller .10 .05
❑ 826 Allen Pinkett .05 .02
❑ 827 Rick Venturi CO .05 .02
❑ 828 Bill Maas .05 .02
❑ 829 Jeff Jaeger .05 .02
❑ 830 Robert Delpino .05 .02
❑ 831 Mark Higgs RC .05 .02
❑ 832 Reggie Roby .05 .02
❑ 833 Terry Allen RC 1.50 .70
❑ 834 Cris Carter .50 .23
(No indication when acquired on waivers)
❑ 835 John Randle RC .60 .25
❑ 836 Hugh Millen RC .05 .02
❑ 837 Jon Vaughn RC .05 .02
❑ 838 Gill Fenerty .05 .02
❑ 839 Floyd Turner .05 .02
❑ 840 Irv Eatman .05 .02
❑ 841 Lonnie Young .05 .02
❑ 842 Jim McMahon .10 .05
❑ 843 Randal Hill UER .05 .02
(Traded to Phoenix, not drafted)
❑ 844 Barry Foster .10 .05
❑ 845 Neil O'Donnell RC .25 .11
❑ 846 John Friesz UER .25 .11
(Wears 17, not 7)
❑ 847 Broderick Thomas .05 .02
❑ 848 Brian Mitchell .10 .05
❑ 849 Mike Utley RC .10 .05
❑ 850 Mike Croel ROY .05 .02
❑ SC1 Super Bowl XXVI Theme Art UER .25 .11
(Card says SB 26, should be 25)
❑ SC3 Jim Thorpe Pioneers of the Game .75 .35
❑ SC4 Otto Graham Pioneers of the Game .75 .35
❑ SC5 Paul Brown Pioneers of the Game .75 .35
❑ PSS1 Walter Payton and Team 34 .50 .23
❑ PSS2 Red Grange .50 .23
❑ MVPC25 Ottis Anderson MVP Super Bowl XXV .25 .11
❑ AU336 Lawrence Taylor REP (autographed/500) 175.00 80.00
❑ AU394 Lawrence Taylor PB (autographed/500) 175.00 80.00
❑ AU699 Ozzie Newsome (Certified autograph) 50.00 22.00
❑ AU824 Erik Kramer (Certified autograph) 50.00 22.00
❑ NNO Mini Pro Set Gazette .25 .11
❑ NNO Pro Set Gazette .25 .11
❑ NNO Santa Claus .50 .23
❑ NNO Super Bowl XXV Art .25 .11
❑ NNO Super Bowl XXV Logo .25 .11

2000 Quantum Leaf

	Nm-Mt	Ex-Mt
COMPLETE SET (350)	150.00	70.00
COMP.SET w/o SP's (300)	25.00	11.00
COMP.ROOKIE UPDATE (31)	20.00	9.00

❑ 1 Frank Sanders .75 .35
❑ 2 Adrian Murrell .75 .35
❑ 3 Rob Moore .75 .35
❑ 4 Simeon Rice .75 .35
❑ 5 Michael Pittman .50 .23
❑ 6 Jake Plummer .75 .35
❑ 7 David Boston 1.25 .55
❑ 8 Mario Bates .50 .23
❑ 9 Chris Chandler .75 .35
❑ 10 Tim Dwight 1.25 .55
❑ 11 Chris Calloway .50 .23
❑ 12 Terance Mathis .75 .35
❑ 13 Jamal Anderson 1.25 .55
❑ 14 Byron Hanspard .50 .23
❑ 15 Ken Oxendine .50 .23
❑ 16 Tony Graziani .50 .23
❑ 17 Bob Christian .50 .23
❑ 18 Priest Holmes 1.50 .70
❑ 19 Tony Banks .75 .35
❑ 20 Patrick Johnson .50 .23
❑ 21 Rod Woodson .75 .35
❑ 22 Jermaine Lewis .50 .23
❑ 23 Errict Rhett .75 .35
❑ 24 Stoney Case .50 .23
❑ 25 Peter Boulware .50 .23
❑ 26 Qadry Ismail .75 .35
❑ 27 Brandon Stokley .75 .35
❑ 28 Andre Reed .75 .35
❑ 29 Eric Moulds 1.25 .55
❑ 30 Doug Flutie 1.25 .55
❑ 31 Bruce Smith .75 .35
❑ 32 Jay Riemersma .50 .23
❑ 33 Antowain Smith .75 .35
❑ 34 Thurman Thomas .75 .35
❑ 35 Jonathan Linton .50 .23
❑ 36 Peerless Price 1.25 .55
❑ 37 Rob Johnson .75 .35
❑ 38 Sam Gash .50 .23
❑ 39 Muhsin Muhammad .75 .35
❑ 40 Wesley Walls .50 .23
❑ 41 Fred Lane .50 .23
❑ 42 Kevin Greene .50 .23
❑ 43 Tim Biakabutuka .75 .35
❑ 44 Steve Beuerlein .75 .35
❑ 45 Donald Hayes .50 .23
❑ 46 Patrick Jeffers 1.25 .55
❑ 47 Curtis Enis .50 .23
❑ 48 Bobby Engram .50 .23
❑ 49 Curtis Conway .75 .35
❑ 50 Marcus Robinson 1.25 .55
❑ 51 Marty Booker .75 .35
❑ 52 Cade McNown .50 .23
❑ 53 Shane Matthews .75 .35
❑ 54 Jim Miller .50 .23
❑ 55 Darnay Scott .75 .35
❑ 56 Carl Pickens .75 .35
❑ 57 Corey Dillon 1.25 .55
❑ 58 Jeff Blake .75 .35
❑ 59 Akili Smith .50 .23
❑ 60 Michael Basnight .50 .23
❑ 61 Karim Abdul-Jabbar .75 .35
❑ 62 Tim Couch .75 .35
❑ 63 Kevin Johnson 1.25 .55
❑ 64 Terry Kirby .50 .23
❑ 65 Ty Detmer .75 .35
❑ 66 Leslie Shepherd .50 .23
❑ 67 Darrin Chiaverini .50 .23
❑ 68 Emmitt Smith 2.50 1.10
❑ 69 Deion Sanders 1.25 .55
❑ 70 Michael Irvin .75 .35
❑ 71 Rocket Ismail .75 .35
❑ 72 Troy Aikman 2.50 1.10
❑ 73 Daryl Johnston .75 .35
❑ 74 Chris Warren .50 .23
❑ 75 Jason Garrett .75 .35
❑ 76 Jason Tucker .50 .23
❑ 77 Lawyer Milloy .75 .35
❑ 78 Dexter Coakley .50 .23
❑ 79 Greg Ellis .50 .23
❑ 80 David LaFleur .50 .23
❑ 81 Todd Lyght .50 .23
❑ 82 Ernie Mills .50 .23
❑ 83 Wane McGarity .50 .23
❑ 84 Chris Brazzell RC .75 .35
❑ 85 Ed McCaffrey 1.25 .55
❑ 86 Rod Smith .75 .35
❑ 87 Shannon Sharpe .75 .35
❑ 88 Brian Griese 1.25 .55
❑ 89 John Elway 4.00 1.80
❑ 90 Neil Smith .75 .35
❑ 91 Terrell Davis 1.25 .55
❑ 92 Olandis Gary 1.25 .55
❑ 93 Derek Loville .50 .23
❑ 94 John Avery .50 .23
❑ 95 Bubby Brister .50 .23
❑ 96 Byron Chamberlain .50 .23
❑ 97 Dale Carter .50 .23
❑ 98 Johnnie Morton .75 .35
❑ 99 Charlie Batch 1.25 .55
❑ 100 Barry Sanders 3.00 1.35
❑ 101 Germane Crowell .50 .23
❑ 102 Gus Frerotte .50 .23
❑ 103 Desmond Howard .50 .23
❑ 104 Terry Fair .50 .23
❑ 105 Ron Rivers .50 .23
❑ 106 Greg Hill .50 .23
❑ 107 Sedrick Irvin .50 .23
❑ 108 David Sloan .50 .23
❑ 109 Herman Moore .75 .35
❑ 110 Robert Porcher .50 .23
❑ 111 Corey Bradford .75 .35
❑ 112 Dorsey Levens .75 .35
❑ 113 Antonio Freeman 1.25 .55
❑ 114 Brett Favre 4.00 1.80
❑ 115 De'Mond Parker .50 .23
❑ 116 Bill Schroeder .75 .35
❑ 117 Matt Hasselbeck .75 .35
❑ 118 Donald Driver 1.25 .55
❑ 119 Basil Mitchell .50 .23
❑ 120 E.G. Green .50 .23
❑ 121 Ken Dilger .50 .23
❑ 122 Marvin Harrison 1.25 .55
❑ 123 Peyton Manning 3.00 1.35
❑ 124 Terrence Wilkins .50 .23
❑ 125 Edgerrin James 2.00 .90
❑ 126 Jerome Pathon .75 .35
❑ 127 Marcus Pollard .50 .23
❑ 128 Keenan McCardell .75 .35
❑ 129 Mark Brunell 1.25 .55
❑ 130 Fred Taylor 1.25 .55
❑ 131 Jimmy Smith .75 .35
❑ 132 James Stewart .75 .35
❑ 133 Kyle Brady .50 .23
❑ 134 Tony Brackens .50 .23
❑ 135 Derrick Thomas .75 .35
❑ 136 Rashaan Shehee .50 .23
❑ 137 Derrick Alexander .75 .35
❑ 138 Bam Morris .50 .23
❑ 139 Andre Rison .75 .35
❑ 140 Elvis Grbac .75 .35
❑ 141 Tony Gonzalez .75 .35
❑ 142 Donnell Bennett .50 .23
❑ 143 Warren Moon 1.25 .55
❑ 144 Tamarick Vanover .50 .23
❑ 145 Kimble Anders .50 .23
❑ 146 Tony Richardson RC .75 .35
❑ 147 Zach Thomas 1.25 .55
❑ 148 Oronde Gadsden .75 .35
❑ 149 Dan Marino 4.00 1.80
❑ 150 O.J. McDuffie .75 .35
❑ 151 Tony Martin .75 .35
❑ 152 Cecil Collins .50 .23
❑ 153 James Johnson .50 .23
❑ 154 Rob Konrad .50 .23
❑ 155 Yatil Green .50 .23
❑ 156 Damon Huard 1.25 .55
❑ 157 Nate Jacquet .50 .23

❑ 158 Stanley Pritchett .50 .23
❑ 159 Sam Madison .50 .23
❑ 160 Randy Moss 2.50 1.10
❑ 161 Cris Carter 1.25 .55
❑ 162 Robert Smith 1.25 .55
❑ 163 Randall Cunningham 1.25 .55
❑ 164 Jake Reed .75 .35
❑ 165 John Randle .75 .35
❑ 166 Leroy Hoard .50 .23
❑ 167 Jeff George .75 .35
❑ 168 Daunte Culpepper 1.50 .70
❑ 169 Matthew Hatchette .50 .23
❑ 170 Robert Tate .50 .23
❑ 171 Ty Law .75 .35
❑ 172 Troy Brown .75 .35
❑ 173 Tony Simmons .50 .23
❑ 174 Terry Glenn .75 .35
❑ 175 Ben Coates .50 .23
❑ 176 Drew Bledsoe 1.50 .70
❑ 177 Terry Allen .75 .35
❑ 178 Kevin Faulk .75 .35
❑ 179 Shawn Jefferson .50 .23
❑ 180 Andy Katzenmoyer .50 .23
❑ 181 Willie McGinest .50 .23
❑ 182 Cameron Cleeland .50 .23
❑ 183 Eddie Kennison .75 .35
❑ 184 Ricky Williams 1.25 .55
❑ 185 Danny Wuerffel .50 .23
❑ 186 Brett Bech .50 .23
❑ 187 Billy Joe Hobert .50 .23
❑ 188 Jake Delhomme RC 5.00 2.20
❑ 189 Wilmont Perry .50 .23
❑ 190 Keith Poole .50 .23
❑ 191 Ashley Ambrose .50 .23
❑ 192 Amani Toomer .50 .23
❑ 193 Kerry Collins .75 .35
❑ 194 Tiki Barber .75 .35
❑ 195 Ike Hilliard .75 .35
❑ 196 Jason Sehorn .50 .23
❑ 197 Joe Montgomery .50 .23
❑ 198 Joe Jurevicius .50 .23
❑ 199 Michael Strahan .75 .35
❑ 200 Sean Bennett .50 .23
❑ 201 Jessie Armstead .50 .23
❑ 202 Pete Mitchell .50 .23
❑ 203 Curtis Martin 1.25 .55
❑ 204 Vinny Testaverde .75 .35
❑ 205 Keyshawn Johnson 1.25 .55
❑ 206 Wayne Chrebet .75 .35
❑ 207 Ray Lucas .75 .35
❑ 208 Tyrone Wheatley .75 .35
❑ 209 Napoleon Kaufman .75 .35
❑ 210 Tim Brown 1.25 .55
❑ 211 Rickey Dudley .50 .23
❑ 212 James Jett .50 .23
❑ 213 Rich Gannon 1.25 .55
❑ 214 Charles Woodson .75 .35
❑ 215 Zack Crockett .50 .23
❑ 216 Darrell Russell .50 .23
❑ 217 Duce Staley 1.25 .55
❑ 218 Donovan McNabb 2.00 .90
❑ 219 Charles Johnson .75 .35
❑ 220 Dameane Douglas .50 .23
❑ 221 Doug Pederson .50 .23
❑ 222 Torrance Small .50 .23
❑ 223 Troy Vincent .50 .23
❑ 224 Na Brown .50 .23
❑ 225 Kordell Stewart .75 .35
❑ 226 Jerome Bettis 1.25 .55
❑ 227 Hines Ward 1.25 .55
❑ 228 Troy Edwards .50 .23
❑ 229 Richard Huntley .50 .23
❑ 230 Mark Bruener .50 .23
❑ 231 Pete Gonzalez .50 .23
❑ 232 Levon Kirkland .50 .23
❑ 233 Bobby Shaw RC 1.25 .55
❑ 234 Amos Zereoue 1.25 .55
❑ 235 Natrone Means .50 .23
❑ 236 Junior Seau 1.25 .55
❑ 237 Jim Harbaugh .75 .35
❑ 238 Ryan Leaf .75 .35
❑ 239 Mikhael Ricks .50 .23
❑ 240 Jermaine Fazande .50 .23
❑ 241 Jeff Graham .50 .23
❑ 242 Tremayne Stephens .50 .23
❑ 243 Terrell Owens 1.25 .55
❑ 244 J.J. Stokes .75 .35
❑ 245 Charlie Garner .75 .35
❑ 246 Jerry Rice 2.50 1.10
❑ 247 Garrison Hearst .75 .35
❑ 248 Steve Young 1.50 .70
❑ 249 Jeff Garcia 1.25 .55
❑ 250 Fred Beasley .50 .23
❑ 251 Bryant Young .50 .23
❑ 252 Derrick Mayes .75 .35
❑ 253 Ahman Green 1.25 .55
❑ 254 Joey Galloway .75 .35
❑ 255 Ricky Watters .75 .35
❑ 256 Jon Kitna 1.25 .55
❑ 257 Sean Dawkins .50 .23
❑ 258 Sam Adams .50 .23
❑ 259 Christian Fauria .50 .23
❑ 260 Shawn Springs .50 .23
❑ 261 Az-Zahir Hakim .75 .35
❑ 262 Isaac Bruce 1.25 .55
❑ 263 Marshall Faulk 1.50 .70
❑ 264 Trent Green 1.25 .55
❑ 265 Kurt Warner 2.50 1.10
❑ 266 Torry Holt 1.25 .55
❑ 267 Robert Holcombe .50 .23
❑ 268 Kevin Carter .50 .23
❑ 269 Amp Lee .50 .23
❑ 270 Roland Williams .50 .23
❑ 271 Jacquez Green .50 .23
❑ 272 Reidel Anthony .50 .23
❑ 273 Warren Sapp .75 .35
❑ 274 Mike Alstott 1.25 .55
❑ 275 Warrick Dunn 1.25 .55
❑ 276 Trent Dilfer .75 .35
❑ 277 Shaun King .50 .23
❑ 278 Bert Emanuel .50 .23
❑ 279 Eric Zeier .50 .23
❑ 280 Neil O'Donnell .50 .23
❑ 281 Eddie George 1.25 .55
❑ 282 Yancey Thigpen .50 .23
❑ 283 Steve McNair 1.25 .55
❑ 284 Kevin Dyson .75 .35
❑ 285 Frank Wycheck .50 .23
❑ 286 Jevon Kearse 1.25 .55
❑ 287 Bruce Matthews .50 .23
❑ 288 Lorenzo Neal .50 .23
❑ 289 Stephen Davis 1.25 .55
❑ 290 Stephen Alexander .50 .23
❑ 291 Darrell Green .50 .23
❑ 292 Skip Hicks .50 .23
❑ 293 Brad Johnson 1.25 .55
❑ 294 Michael Westbrook .75 .35
❑ 295 Albert Connell .50 .23
❑ 296 Irving Fryar .75 .35
❑ 297 Champ Bailey .75 .35
❑ 298 Larry Centers .50 .23
❑ 299 Brian Mitchell .50 .23
❑ 300 James Thrash 1.25 .55
❑ 301 LaVar Arrington RC 10.00 4.50
❑ 302 Peter Warrick RC 2.50 1.10
❑ 303 Courtney Brown RC 2.50 1.10
❑ 304 Plaxico Burress RC 5.00 2.20
❑ 305 Corey Simon RC 2.50 1.10
❑ 306 Thomas Jones RC 4.00 1.80
❑ 307 Travis Taylor RC 2.50 1.10
❑ 308 Shaun Alexander RC 6.00 2.70
❑ 309 Chris Redman RC 2.00 .90
❑ 310 Chad Pennington RC 10.00 4.50
❑ 311 Jamal Lewis RC 6.00 2.70
❑ 312 Brian Urlacher RC 10.00 4.50
❑ 313 Keith Bulluck RC 2.50 1.10
❑ 314 Bubba Franks RC 2.50 1.10
❑ 315 Dez White RC 2.50 1.10
❑ 316 Ahmed Plummer RC 2.50 1.10
❑ 317 Ron Dayne RC 2.50 1.10
❑ 318 Shaun Ellis RC 2.50 1.10
❑ 319 Sylvester Morris RC 2.00 .90
❑ 320 Deltha O'Neal RC 2.50 1.10
❑ 321 R.Jay Soward RC 2.00 .90
❑ 322 Sherrod Gideon RC 1.50 .70
❑ 323 John Abraham RC 2.50 1.10
❑ 324 Travis Prentice RC 2.00 .90
❑ 325 Darrell Jackson RC 5.00 2.20
❑ 326 Giovanni Carmazzi RC 2.00 .90
❑ 327 Anthony Lucas RC 1.50 .70
❑ 328 Danny Farmer RC 2.00 .90
❑ 329 Dennis Northcutt RC 2.50 1.10
❑ 330 Troy Walters RC 2.50 1.10
❑ 331 Laveranues Coles RC 3.00 1.35
❑ 332 Tee Martin RC 2.50 1.10
❑ 333 J.R. Redmond RC 2.00 .90
❑ 334 Jerry Porter RC 3.00 1.35
❑ 335 Sebastian Janikowski RC 2.00 .90
❑ 336 Michael Wiley RC 2.00 .90
❑ 337 Reuben Droughns RC 2.00 .90
❑ 338 Trung Canidate RC 2.00 .90
❑ 339 Shyrone Stith RC 1.50 .70
❑ 340 Trevor Gaylor RC 1.50 .70
❑ 341 Rob Morris RC 2.50 1.10
❑ 342 Marc Bulger RC 5.00 2.20
❑ 343 Tom Brady RC 25.00 11.00
❑ 344 Todd Husak RC 2.50 1.10
❑ 345 Gari Scott RC 1.50 .70
❑ 346 Erron Kinney RC 2.50 1.10
❑ 347 Julian Peterson RC 2.50 1.10
❑ 348 Doug Chapman RC 2.00 .90
❑ 349 Ron Dugans RC 1.50 .70
❑ 350 Todd Pinkston RC 2.50 1.10
❑ 351 Deon Grant RC 1.25 .55
❑ 352 Na'il Diggs RC 1.25 .55
❑ 353 Raynoch Thompson RC 1.25 .55
❑ 354 Mario Edwards RC 1.25 .55
❑ 355 John Engelberger RC 1.25 .55
❑ 356 Dwayne Goodrich RC .75 .35
❑ 357 Ben Kelly RC .75 .35
❑ 358 Sekou Sanyika RC .75 .35
❑ 359 Brandon Short RC 1.25 .55
❑ 360 Jabari Issa RC .75 .35
❑ 361 Darwin Walker RC .75 .35
❑ 362 Jerry Johnson RC .75 .35
❑ 363 Robaire Smith RC .75 .35
❑ 364 Mark Roman RC .75 .35
❑ 365 Leonardo Carson RC .75 .35
❑ 366 Mark Simoneau RC 1.25 .55
❑ 367 Hank Poteat RC 1.25 .55
❑ 368 Darren Howard RC 1.25 .55
❑ 369 David Macklin RC .75 .35
❑ 370 Adalius Thomas RC .75 .35
❑ 371 Ralph Brown RC .75 .35
❑ 372 Mondriel Fulcher RC .75 .35
❑ 373 Sammy Morris RC 1.25 .55
❑ 374 Rondell Mealey RC .75 .35
❑ 375 Deon Dyer RC 1.25 .55
❑ 376 Mareno Philyaw RC .75 .35
❑ 377 Thomas Hamner RC .75 .35
❑ 378 Jarious Jackson RC 1.25 .55
❑ 379 Joe Hamilton RC 1.25 .55
❑ 380 Tim Rattay RC 5.00 2.20
❑ 381 Chris Hovan RC 1.25 .55
❑ SB1 Kurt Warner MVP/1000 8.00 3.60
❑ SB1A Kurt Warner MVP AUTO/100 100.00 45.00
❑ NFL1 Kurt Warner MVP/1000 8.00 3.60
❑ NFL1A Kurt Warner MVP AUTO/100 100.00 45.00
❑ QLP10 Dan Marino Promo 3.00 1.35

2001 Quantum Leaf

	Nm-Mt	Ex-Mt
COMP.SET w/o SP's (200)	25.00	7.50

COMP.ROOKIE UPDATE (36)	20.00	6.00
❑ 1 David Boston	1.00	.45
❑ 2 Frank Sanders	.40	.18
❑ 3 Jake Plummer	.60	.25
❑ 4 Michael Pittman	.40	.18
❑ 5 Rob Moore	.60	.25
❑ 6 Thomas Jones	.60	.25
❑ 7 Chris Chandler	.60	.25
❑ 8 Doug Johnson	.40	.18
❑ 9 Jamal Anderson	1.00	.45
❑ 10 Tim Dwight	1.00	.45
❑ 11 Chris Redman	.40	.18
❑ 12 Jamal Lewis	1.50	.70
❑ 13 Qadry Ismail	.60	.25
❑ 14 Ray Lewis	1.00	.45
❑ 15 Rod Woodson	.60	.25
❑ 16 Shannon Sharpe	.60	.25
❑ 17 Travis Taylor	.60	.25
❑ 18 Trent Dilfer	.60	.25
❑ 19 Doug Flutie	1.00	.45
❑ 20 Eric Moulds	.60	.25
❑ 21 Jay Riemersma	.40	.18
❑ 22 Peerless Price	.60	.25
❑ 23 Rob Johnson	.60	.25
❑ 24 Sammy Morris	.40	.18
❑ 25 Shawn Bryson	.40	.18
❑ 26 Donald Hayes	.40	.18
❑ 27 Muhsin Muhammad	.60	.25
❑ 28 Patrick Jeffers	.60	.25
❑ 29 Reggie White DE	.60	.25
❑ 30 Steve Beuerlein	.60	.25
❑ 31 Tim Biakabutuka	.60	.25
❑ 32 Wesley Walls	.40	.18
❑ 33 Brian Urlacher	1.50	.70
❑ 34 Cade McNown	.40	.18
❑ 35 Dez White	.40	.18
❑ 36 James Allen	.60	.25
❑ 37 Marcus Robinson	1.00	.45
❑ 38 Marty Booker	.40	.18
❑ 39 Akili Smith	.40	.18
❑ 40 Corey Dillon	1.00	.45
❑ 41 Danny Farmer	.40	.18
❑ 42 Peter Warrick	1.00	.45
❑ 43 Ron Dugans	.40	.18
❑ 44 Courtney Brown	.60	.25
❑ 45 Dennis Northcutt	.60	.25
❑ 46 JaJuan Dawson	.40	.18
❑ 47 Kevin Johnson	.60	.25
❑ 48 Tim Couch	.60	.25
❑ 49 Travis Prentice	.40	.18
❑ 50 Anthony Wright	.40	.18
❑ 51 Emmitt Smith	2.00	.90
❑ 52 James McKnight	.60	.25
❑ 53 Joey Galloway	.60	.25
❑ 54 Rocket Ismail	.60	.25
❑ 55 Randall Cunningham	1.00	.45
❑ 56 Troy Aikman	1.50	.70
❑ 57 Brian Griese	1.00	.45
❑ 58 Ed McCaffrey	1.00	.45
❑ 59 Gus Frerotte	.40	.18
❑ 60 John Elway	3.00	1.35
❑ 61 Mike Anderson	1.00	.45
❑ 62 Olandis Gary	.60	.25
❑ 63 Rod Smith	.60	.25
❑ 64 Terrell Davis	1.00	.45
❑ 65 Barry Sanders	2.00	.90
❑ 66 Charlie Batch	1.00	.45
❑ 67 Germane Crowell	.40	.18
❑ 68 Herman Moore	.60	.25
❑ 69 James Stewart	.60	.25
❑ 70 Johnnie Morton	.60	.25
❑ 71 Ahman Green	1.00	.45
❑ 72 Antonio Freeman	1.00	.45
❑ 73 Bill Schroeder	.60	.25
❑ 74 Brett Favre	3.00	1.35
❑ 75 Dorsey Levens	.60	.25
❑ 76 Matt Hasselbeck	.60	.25
❑ 77 Edgerrin James	1.25	.55
❑ 78 Jerome Pathon	.60	.25
❑ 79 Ken Dilger	.40	.18
❑ 80 Marvin Harrison	1.00	.45
❑ 81 Peyton Manning	2.50	1.10
❑ 82 Fred Taylor	1.00	.45
❑ 83 Hardy Nickerson	.40	.18
❑ 84 Jimmy Smith	.60	.25
❑ 85 Keenan McCardell	.40	.18
❑ 86 Mark Brunell	1.00	.45
❑ 87 Tony Brackens	.40	.18
❑ 88 Derrick Alexander	.60	.25
❑ 89 Elvis Grbac	.60	.25
❑ 90 Sylvester Morris	.40	.18
❑ 91 Tony Gonzalez	.60	.25
❑ 92 Tony Richardson	.40	.18
❑ 93 Warren Moon	.60	.25
❑ 94 Dan Marino	3.00	1.35
❑ 95 Jay Fiedler	1.00	.45
❑ 96 Lamar Smith	.60	.25
❑ 97 Oronde Gadsden	.60	.25
❑ 98 Sam Madison	.40	.18
❑ 99 Thurman Thomas	.40	.18
❑ 100 Tony Martin	.60	.25
❑ 101 Zach Thomas	1.00	.45
❑ 102 Cris Carter	1.00	.45
❑ 103 Daunte Culpepper	1.00	.45
❑ 104 John Randle	.60	.25
❑ 105 Randy Moss	2.00	.90
❑ 106 Robert Smith	.60	.25
❑ 107 Drew Bledsoe	1.25	.55
❑ 108 J.R. Redmond	.40	.18
❑ 109 Kevin Faulk	.60	.25
❑ 110 Michael Bishop	.40	.18
❑ 111 Terry Glenn	.60	.25
❑ 112 Troy Brown	.60	.25
❑ 113 Aaron Brooks	1.00	.45
❑ 114 Jake Reed	.60	.25
❑ 115 Jeff Blake	.60	.25
❑ 116 Joe Horn	.60	.25
❑ 117 La'Roi Glover	.40	.18
❑ 118 Ricky Williams	1.00	.45
❑ 119 Willie Jackson	.40	.18
❑ 120 Amani Toomer	.40	.18
❑ 121 Ike Hilliard	.60	.25
❑ 122 Jason Sehorn	.40	.18
❑ 123 Kerry Collins	.60	.25
❑ 124 Michael Strahan	.60	.25
❑ 125 Ron Dayne	1.00	.45
❑ 126 Ron Dixon	.40	.18
❑ 127 Tiki Barber	.60	.25
❑ 128 Chad Pennington	1.50	.70
❑ 129 Curtis Martin	1.00	.45
❑ 130 Dedric Ward	.40	.18
❑ 131 Laveranues Coles	1.00	.45
❑ 132 Vinny Testaverde	.60	.25
❑ 133 Wayne Chrebet	.60	.25
❑ 134 Charles Woodson	.60	.25
❑ 135 Napoleon Kaufman	.60	.25
❑ 136 Rich Gannon	1.00	.45
❑ 137 Tim Brown	1.00	.45
❑ 138 Tyrone Wheatley	.60	.25
❑ 139 Charles Johnson	.40	.18
❑ 140 Donovan McNabb	1.25	.55
❑ 141 Duce Staley	1.00	.45
❑ 142 Hugh Douglas	.40	.18
❑ 143 Na Brown	.40	.18
❑ 144 Todd Pinkston	.40	.18
❑ 145 Bobby Shaw	.40	.18
❑ 146 Hines Ward	1.00	.45
❑ 147 Jerome Bettis	1.00	.45
❑ 148 Kordell Stewart	.60	.25
❑ 149 Levon Kirkland	.40	.18
❑ 150 Plaxico Burress	1.00	.45
❑ 151 Richard Huntley	.40	.18
❑ 152 Troy Edwards	.40	.18
❑ 153 Jim Harbaugh	.60	.25
❑ 154 Junior Seau	1.00	.45
❑ 155 Ryan Leaf	.60	.25
❑ 156 Charlie Garner	.60	.25
❑ 157 Jeff Garcia	1.00	.45
❑ 158 Jerry Rice	2.00	.90
❑ 159 Steve Young	1.25	.55
❑ 160 Terrell Owens	1.00	.45
❑ 161 Brock Huard	.40	.18
❑ 162 Darrell Jackson	1.00	.45
❑ 163 Derrick Mayes	.40	.18
❑ 164 Ricky Watters	.60	.25
❑ 165 Shaun Alexander	1.25	.55
❑ 166 Az-Zahir Hakim	.40	.18
❑ 167 Isaac Bruce	1.00	.45
❑ 168 Kurt Warner	2.00	.90
❑ 169 Marshall Faulk	1.25	.55
❑ 170 Torry Holt	1.00	.45
❑ 171 Trent Green	1.00	.45
❑ 172 Derrick Brooks	1.00	.45
❑ 173 Jacquez Green	.40	.18
❑ 174 John Lynch	.60	.25
❑ 175 Keyshawn Johnson	1.00	.45
❑ 176 Mike Alstott	1.00	.45
❑ 177 Reidel Anthony	.40	.18
❑ 178 Shaun King	.40	.18
❑ 179 Warren Sapp	.60	.25
❑ 180 Warrick Dunn	1.00	.45
❑ 181 Carl Pickens	.40	.18
❑ 182 Derrick Mason	.60	.25
❑ 183 Eddie George	1.00	.45
❑ 184 Frank Wycheck	.40	.18
❑ 185 Jevon Kearse	.60	.25
❑ 186 Neil O'Donnell	.40	.18
❑ 187 Steve McNair	1.00	.45
❑ 188 Yancey Thigpen	.40	.18
❑ 189 Albert Connell	.40	.18
❑ 190 Andre Reed	.40	.18
❑ 191 Brad Johnson	1.00	.45
❑ 192 Bruce Smith	.40	.18
❑ 193 Champ Bailey	.60	.25
❑ 194 Darrell Green	.40	.18
❑ 195 Deion Sanders	1.00	.45
❑ 196 Irving Fryar	.60	.25
❑ 197 James Thrash	.60	.25
❑ 198 Jeff George	.60	.25
❑ 199 Michael Westbrook	.60	.25
❑ 200 Stephen Davis	1.00	.45
❑ 201 Michael Vick RC	15.00	6.75
❑ 202 Drew Brees RC	4.00	1.80
❑ 203 Chris Weinke RC	2.00	.90
❑ 204 Sage Rosenfels RC	2.00	.90
❑ 205 Josh Heupel RC	2.00	.90
❑ 206 Marques Tuiasosopo RC	2.00	.90
❑ 207 Mike McMahon SP RC	40.00	18.00
❑ 208 Deuce McAllister SP RC	80.00	36.00
❑ 209 LaMont Jordan RC	2.50	1.10
❑ 210 LaDainian Tomlinson RC	6.00	2.70
❑ 211 James Jackson RC	2.00	.90
❑ 212 Anthony Thomas RC	3.00	1.35
❑ 213 Travis Henry RC	2.50	1.10
❑ 214 Travis Minor RC	1.25	.55
❑ 215 Rudi Johnson RC	4.00	1.80
❑ 216 Michael Bennett RC	4.00	1.80
❑ 217 Kevan Barlow RC	2.00	.90
❑ 218 Dan Alexander RC	1.25	.55
❑ 219 Correll Buckhalter SP RC	50.00	22.00
❑ 220 Moran Norris RC	.75	.35
❑ 221 Jesse Palmer RC	2.00	.90
❑ 222 Heath Evans RC	1.25	.55
❑ 223 David Terrell SP RC	50.00	22.00
❑ 224 Santana Moss RC	3.00	1.35
❑ 225 Rod Gardner RC	2.00	.90
❑ 226 Quincy Morgan SP RC	50.00	22.00
❑ 227 Freddie Mitchell RC	2.00	.90
❑ 228 Reggie Wayne RC	3.00	1.35
❑ 229 Bobby Newcombe RC	1.25	.55
❑ 230 Casey Hampton RC	1.25	.55
❑ 231 Robert Ferguson RC	2.00	.90
❑ 232 Ken-Yon Rambo RC	1.25	.55
❑ 233 Alex Bannister RC	1.25	.55
❑ 234 Koren Robinson RC	2.50	1.10
❑ 235 Chad Johnson RC	4.00	1.80
❑ 236 Chris Chambers RC	2.50	1.10
❑ 237 Snoop Minnis RC	1.25	.55
❑ 238 Vinny Sutherland RC	1.25	.55
❑ 239 Cedrick Wilson RC	2.00	.90
❑ 240 T.J. Houshmandzadeh RC	2.00	.90
❑ 241 Todd Heap RC	2.00	.90
❑ 242 Alge Crumpler RC	2.50	1.10
❑ 243 Jabari Holloway RC	1.25	.55
❑ 244 Tony Stewart RC	2.00	.90
❑ 245 Jamal Reynolds RC	2.00	.90
❑ 246 Andre Carter SP RC	50.00	22.00
❑ 247 Justin Smith SP RC	40.00	18.00
❑ 248 Richard Seymour RC	2.00	.90
❑ 249 Marcus Stroud RC	2.00	.90
❑ 250 Damione Lewis RC	1.25	.55
❑ 251 Gerard Warren SP RC	50.00	22.00

Card	Nm-Mt	Ex-Mt
❑ 252 Tommy Polley SP RC	40.00	18.00
❑ 253 Dan Morgan RC	2.00	.90
❑ 254 Jamar Fletcher RC	1.25	.55
❑ 255 Ken Lucas RC	2.00	.90
❑ 256 Fred Smoot SP RC	40.00	18.00
❑ 257 Nate Clements RC	2.00	.90
❑ 258 Will Allen RC	1.25	.55
❑ 259 Derrick Gibson RC	1.25	.55
❑ 260 Adam Archuleta RC	2.00	.90
❑ 261 Karon Riley RC	.75	.35
❑ 262 Cedric Scott RC	1.25	.55
❑ 263 Kenny Smith RC	1.25	.55
❑ 264 Willie Howard RC	1.25	.55
❑ 265 Shaun Rogers RC	2.00	.90
❑ 266 Ennis Davis RC	.75	.35
❑ 267 Morlon Greenwood RC	1.25	.55
❑ 268 Gary Baxter RC	1.25	.55
❑ 269 Keith Adams RC	.75	.35
❑ 270 Brian Allen RC	.75	.35
❑ 271 Carlos Polk RC	.75	.35
❑ 272 Torrance Marshall RC	2.00	.90
❑ 273 Jamie Winborn RC	1.25	.55
❑ 274 Hakim Akbar RC	.75	.35
❑ 275 David Rivers RC	1.25	.55
❑ 276 Ben Leard RC	1.25	.55
❑ 277 Tim Hasselbeck RC	2.00	.90
❑ 278 DeAngelo Evans RC	1.25	.55
❑ 279 David Allen RC	1.25	.55
❑ 280 Reggie White RC	1.25	.55
❑ 281 Ja'Mar Toombs RC	1.25	.55
❑ 282 Dustin McClintock RC	1.25	.55
❑ 283 Boo Williams RC	1.25	.55
❑ 284 Ronney Daniels RC	.75	.35
❑ 285 Daniel Guy RC	.75	.35
❑ 286 Javon Green RC	1.25	.55
❑ 287 Marcellus Rivers RC	1.25	.55
❑ 288 Rashon Burns RC	.75	.35
❑ 289 Jevaris Johnson RC	.75	.35
❑ 290 David Warren RC	.75	.35
❑ 291 John Capel RC	1.25	.35
❑ 292 Kendrell Bell RC	6.00	1.80
❑ 294 Willie Middlebrooks RC	1.25	.35
❑ 295 Reggie Germany RC	1.25	.35
❑ 296 Quincy Carter RC	2.00	.60

2001 Quantum Leaf Infinity Green

*1-100 STARS: 5X TO 12X
*101-200 STARS: 12X TO 30X
*201-296 ROOKIES: 3X TO 8X

Card	Nm-Mt	Ex-Mt
❑ 207 Mike McMahon	12.00	5.50
❑ 208 Deuce McAllister	60.00	27.00
❑ 219 Correll Buckhalter	40.00	18.00
❑ 223 David Terrell	25.00	11.00
❑ 226 Quincy Morgan	30.00	13.50
❑ 246 Andre Carter	20.00	9.00
❑ 247 Justin Smith	25.00	11.00
❑ 251 Gerard Warren	25.00	11.00
❑ 252 Tommy Polley	15.00	6.75
❑ 256 Fred Smoot	20.00	9.00

2001 Quantum Leaf Infinity Purple

*1-100 STARS: 12X TO 30X
*101-200 STARS: 8X TO 20X
*201-296 ROOKIES: 10X TO 25X

Card	Nm-Mt	Ex-Mt
❑ 207 Mike McMahon	40.00	18.00
❑ 208 Deuce McAllister	150.00	70.00
❑ 219 Correll Buckhalter	100.00	45.00
❑ 223 David Terrell	60.00	27.00
❑ 226 Quincy Morgan	80.00	36.00
❑ 246 Andre Carter	80.00	36.00
❑ 247 Justin Smith	80.00	36.00
❑ 251 Gerard Warren	60.00	27.00
❑ 252 Tommy Polley	50.00	22.00
❑ 256 Fred Smoot	100.00	45.00

2001 Quantum Leaf Infinity Red

*1-100 STARS: 8X TO 20X
*101-200 STARS: 5X TO 12X
*201-296 ROOKIES: 6X TO 15X

Card	Nm-Mt	Ex-Mt
❑ 207 Mike McMahon	25.00	11.00
❑ 208 Deuce McAllister	100.00	45.00
❑ 219 Correll Buckhalter	60.00	27.00
❑ 223 David Terrell	40.00	18.00
❑ 226 Quincy Morgan	50.00	22.00
❑ 246 Andre Carter	40.00	18.00
❑ 247 Justin Smith	50.00	22.00
❑ 251 Gerard Warren	50.00	22.00
❑ 252 Tommy Polley	30.00	13.50
❑ 256 Fred Smoot	40.00	18.00

2004 Reflections

Card	Nm-Mt	Ex-Mt
COMP.SET w/o SP's (100)	40.00	12.00

201-294 RC PRINT RUN 1150 SER.#'d SETS
OVERALL RC STATED ODDS 1:1

Card	Nm-Mt	Ex-Mt
❑ 1 Emmitt Smith	3.00	.90
❑ 2 Anquan Boldin	1.50	.45
❑ 3 Josh McCown	1.00	.30
❑ 4 Michael Vick	3.00	.90
❑ 5 Peerless Price	1.00	.30
❑ 6 T.J. Duckett	1.00	.30
❑ 7 Todd Heap	1.00	.30
❑ 8 Jamal Lewis	1.50	.45
❑ 9 Kyle Boller	1.50	.45
❑ 10 Drew Bledsoe	1.50	.45
❑ 11 Travis Henry	1.00	.30
❑ 12 Eric Moulds	1.00	.30
❑ 13 Jake Delhomme	1.50	.45
❑ 14 Steve Smith	1.00	.30
❑ 15 Stephen Davis	1.00	.30
❑ 16 Rex Grossman	1.50	.45
❑ 17 Brian Urlacher	2.00	.60
❑ 18 Anthony Thomas	1.00	.30
❑ 19 Rudi Johnson	1.00	.30
❑ 20 Carson Palmer	2.00	.60
❑ 21 Chad Johnson	1.00	.30
❑ 22 Jeff Garcia	1.50	.45
❑ 23 Andre Davis	.60	.18
❑ 24 Quincy Morgan	1.00	.30
❑ 25 Keyshawn Johnson	1.00	.30
❑ 26 Roy Williams S	1.00	.30
❑ 27 Quincy Carter	1.00	.30
❑ 28 Ashley Lelie	1.00	.30
❑ 29 Champ Bailey	1.00	.30
❑ 30 Jake Plummer	1.00	.30
❑ 31 Az-Zahir Hakim	.60	.18
❑ 32 Joey Harrington	1.50	.45
❑ 33 Charles Rogers	1.00	.30
❑ 34 Javon Walker	1.00	.30
❑ 35 Ahman Green	1.50	.45
❑ 36 Brett Favre	4.00	1.20
❑ 37 Domanick Davis	1.50	.45
❑ 38 David Carr	1.50	.45
❑ 39 Andre Johnson	1.50	.45
❑ 40 Edgerrin James	1.50	.45
❑ 41 Marvin Harrison	1.50	.45
❑ 42 Dwight Freeney	.60	.18
❑ 43 Peyton Manning	2.50	.75
❑ 44 Fred Taylor	1.00	.30
❑ 45 Jimmy Smith	1.00	.30
❑ 46 Byron Leftwich	2.50	.75
❑ 47 Dante Hall	1.50	.45
❑ 48 Tony Gonzalez	1.00	.30
❑ 49 Trent Green	1.00	.30
❑ 50 Priest Holmes	2.00	.60
❑ 51 Zach Thomas	1.50	.45
❑ 52 A.J. Feeley	1.50	.45
❑ 53 Chris Chambers	1.00	.30
❑ 54 Ricky Williams	1.50	.45
❑ 55 Randy Moss	2.00	.60
❑ 56 Onterrio Smith	1.00	.30
❑ 57 Daunte Culpepper	1.50	.45
❑ 58 Tom Brady	2.50	.75
❑ 59 Troy Brown	1.00	.30
❑ 60 Corey Dillon	1.00	.30
❑ 61 Donte Stallworth	1.00	.30
❑ 62 Deuce McAllister	1.50	.45
❑ 63 Aaron Brooks	1.00	.30
❑ 64 Amani Toomer	1.00	.30
❑ 65 Jeremy Shockey	1.50	.45
❑ 66 Michael Strahan	1.00	.30
❑ 67 Curtis Martin	1.50	.45
❑ 68 Chad Pennington	2.00	.60
❑ 69 Santana Moss	1.00	.30
❑ 70 Jerry Porter	1.00	.30
❑ 71 Jerry Rice	3.00	.90
❑ 72 Rich Gannon	1.00	.30
❑ 73 Tim Brown	1.50	.45
❑ 74 Terrell Owens	1.50	.45
❑ 75 Brian Westbrook	1.00	.30
❑ 76 Donovan McNabb	2.00	.60
❑ 77 Tommy Maddox	1.00	.30
❑ 78 Hines Ward	1.50	.45
❑ 79 Duce Staley	1.00	.30
❑ 80 Donnie Edwards	.60	.18
❑ 81 LaDainian Tomlinson	1.50	.45
❑ 82 Drew Brees	1.50	.45
❑ 83 Brandon Lloyd	1.00	.30
❑ 84 Tim Rattay	1.00	.30
❑ 85 Kevan Barlow	1.00	.30
❑ 86 Koren Robinson	1.00	.30
❑ 87 Shaun Alexander	1.50	.45
❑ 88 Matt Hasselbeck	1.00	.30
❑ 89 Torry Holt	1.50	.45
❑ 90 Marc Bulger	1.50	.45
❑ 91 Marshall Faulk	1.50	.45
❑ 92 Brad Johnson	1.00	.30
❑ 93 Keenan McCardell	.60	.18
❑ 94 Charlie Garner	1.00	.30
❑ 95 Steve McNair	1.50	.45
❑ 96 Chris Brown	1.50	.45
❑ 97 Eddie George	1.00	.30
❑ 98 Mark Brunell	1.00	.30
❑ 99 Laveranues Coles	1.00	.30
❑ 100 Clinton Portis	1.50	.45
❑ 101 Kris Wilson/750 RC	6.00	1.80
❑ 102 Carlos Francis/750 RC	5.00	1.50
❑ 103 D.J. Williams/750 RC	8.00	2.40
❑ 104 Devery Henderson/450 RC	6.00	1.80
❑ 105 Craig Krenzel/750 RC	6.00	1.80
❑ 106 Jonathan Vilma/750 RC	6.00	1.80
❑ 107 Luke McCown/750 RC	6.00	1.80
❑ 108 Michael Turner/750 RC	5.00	1.50
❑ 109 Richard Seigler/750 RC	5.00	1.50
❑ 110 Stuart Schweigert/750 RC	6.00	1.80
❑ 111 Ben Watson/750 RC	6.00	1.80
❑ 112 Chris Perry/450 RC	15.00	4.50
❑ 113 Jason Fife/750 RC	5.00	1.50
❑ 114 Eli Manning/450 RC	40.00	12.00
❑ 115 Matt Kegel/750 RC	6.00	1.80
❑ 116 Kellen Winslow/450 RC	20.00	6.00
❑ 117 Chris Cooley/750 RC	6.00	1.80
❑ 118 Quincy Wilson/750 RC	5.00	1.50
❑ 119 Samie Parker/750 RC	6.00	1.80
❑ 120 Vince Wilfork/750 RC	8.00	2.40
❑ 121 Bernard Berrian/750 RC	6.00	1.80
❑ 122 Ahmad Carroll/750 RC	8.00	2.40
❑ 123 Derrick Hamilton/750 RC	5.00	1.50
❑ 124 Rich Gardner/750 RC	5.00	1.50
❑ 125 Jeff Smoker/750 RC	10.00	3.00
❑ 126 Kenechi Udeze/750 RC	6.00	1.80
❑ 127 Mewelde Moore/750 RC	8.00	2.40

❑ 128 Keyaron Fox/750 RC	5.00	1.50
❑ 129 Sean Jones/750 RC	5.00	1.50
❑ 130 Will Poole/750 RC	6.00	1.80
❑ 131 Travelle Wharton/750 RC	3.00	.90
❑ 132 Demorrio Williams/750 RC	6.00	1.80
❑ 133 Jason Babin/750 RC	6.00	1.80
❑ 134 Ernest Wilford/750 RC	6.00	1.80
❑ 135 Jerricho Cotchery/750 RC	6.00	1.80
❑ 136 Kevin Jones/450 RC	25.00	7.50
❑ 137 Michael Boulware/750 RC	6.00	1.80
❑ 138 D.J. Hackett/750 RC	5.00	1.50
❑ 139 Sean Taylor/450 RC	10.00	3.00
❑ 140 Will Smith/750 RC	6.00	1.80
❑ 141 John Standeford/750 RC	5.00	1.50
❑ 142 Max Starks/750 RC	5.00	1.50
❑ 143 Cody Pickett/750 RC	6.00	1.80
❑ 144 Derrick Strait/750 RC	6.00	1.80
❑ 145 Greg Jones/450 RC	8.00	2.40
❑ 146 John Navarre/750 RC	6.00	1.80
❑ 147 Larry Fitzgerald/450 RC	25.00	7.50
❑ 148 Michael Clayton/450 RC	20.00	6.00
❑ 149 Rashaun Woods/450 RC	10.00	3.00
❑ 150 Shawn Andrews/750 RC	6.00	1.80
❑ 151 B.J. Symons/750 RC	6.00	1.80
❑ 152 Cedric Cobbs/450 RC	8.00	2.40
❑ 153 Darius Watts/750 RC	8.00	2.40
❑ 154 B.J. Johnson/750 RC	5.00	1.50
❑ 155 Ricardo Colclough/750 RC	6.00	1.80
❑ 156 Josh Harris/750 RC	6.00	1.80
❑ 157 Derek Abney/750 RC	6.00	1.80
❑ 158 Kendrick Starling/750 RC	3.00	.90
❑ 159 Robert Gallery/450 RC	12.00	3.60
❑ 160 Tatum Bell/450 RC	12.00	3.60
❑ 161 Ben Hartsock/750 RC	6.00	1.80
❑ 162 Dwan Edwards/750 RC	3.00	.90
❑ 163 Darnell Dockett/750 RC	5.00	1.50
❑ 164 Igor Olshansky/750 RC	6.00	1.80
❑ 165 Justin Smiley/750 RC	6.00	1.80
❑ 166 Julius Jones/450 RC	30.00	9.00
❑ 167 Matt Mauck/750 RC	6.00	1.80
❑ 168 Derek McCoy/750 RC	5.00	1.50
❑ 169 Chris Pittman/750 RC	6.00	1.80
❑ 170 Teddy Lehman/750 RC	6.00	1.80
❑ 171 Ben Troupe/450 RC	8.00	2.40
❑ 172 Chris Gamble/750 RC	8.00	2.40
❑ 173 DeAngelo Hall/750 RC	8.00	2.40
❑ 174 Dunta Robinson/750 RC	6.00	1.80
❑ 175 Jason Shivers/750 RC	5.00	1.50
❑ 176 Keary Colbert/450 RC	10.00	3.00
❑ 177 Jared Lorenzen/750 RC	5.00	1.50
❑ 178 Philip Rivers/450 RC	25.00	7.50
❑ 179 Roy Williams/450 RC	25.00	7.50
❑ 180 Bob Sanders/750 RC	6.00	1.80
❑ 181 Antwan Odom/750 RC	6.00	1.80
❑ 182 Josh Davis/750 RC	5.00	1.50
❑ 183 Courtney Watson/750 RC	6.00	1.80
❑ 184 Devard Darling/750 RC	6.00	1.80
❑ 185 J.P. Losman/450 RC	20.00	6.00
❑ 186 Johnnie Morant/750 RC	6.00	1.80
❑ 187 Lee Evans/450 RC	12.00	3.60
❑ 188 Michael Jenkins/450 RC	8.00	2.40
❑ 189 Reggie Williams/450 RC	10.00	3.00
❑ 190 Steven Jackson/450 RC	25.00	7.50
❑ 191 Ben Roethlisberger/450 RC	60.00	18.00
❑ 192 P.K. Sam/750 RC	5.00	1.50
❑ 193 Derrick Knight/750 RC	5.00	1.50
❑ 194 Drew Henson/450 RC	20.00	6.00
❑ 195 Marquise Hill/750 RC	5.00	1.50
❑ 196 Karlos Dansby/750 RC	6.00	1.80
❑ 197 Matt Schaub/750 RC	10.00	3.00
❑ 198 Ben Utecht/750 RC	3.00	.90
❑ 199 Darrion Scott/750 RC	6.00	1.80
❑ 200 Tommie Harris/750 RC	8.00	2.40
❑ 201 Andrae Thurman RC	3.00	.90
❑ 202 Matt Kranchick RC	6.00	1.80
❑ 203 Shaun Phillips RC	5.00	1.50
❑ 204 Landon Johnson RC	5.00	1.50
❑ 205 Jeff Dugan RC	3.00	.90
❑ 206 Wes Welker RC	6.00	1.80
❑ 207 Michael Gaines RC	5.00	1.50
❑ 208 Jamaar Taylor RC	6.00	1.80
❑ 209 Brandon Chillar RC	5.00	1.50
❑ 210 Jermaine Green RC	5.00	1.50
❑ 211 Triandos Luke RC	6.00	1.80
❑ 212 Brandon Miree RC	5.00	1.50
❑ 213 Dexter Reid RC	3.00	.90
❑ 214 Isaac Hilton RC	5.00	1.50
❑ 215 Adrian Jones RC	5.00	1.50
❑ 216 Grant Wiley RC	5.00	1.50
❑ 217 Matt Cherry RC	3.00	.90
❑ 218 Courtney Anderson RC	5.00	1.50
❑ 219 Antonio Smith RC	5.00	1.50
❑ 220 Sean Tufts RC	5.00	1.50
❑ 221 Johnny Lamar RC	6.00	1.80
❑ 222 Shawn Johnson RC	5.00	1.50
❑ 223 Jason Peters RC	6.00	1.80
❑ 224 Rodney Leisle RC	3.00	.90
❑ 225 Lane Danielsen RC	6.00	1.80
❑ 226 Zack Abron RC	5.00	1.50
❑ 227 Romar Crenshaw RC	3.00	.90
❑ 228 Keiwan Ratliff RC	5.00	1.50
❑ 229 Chad Lavalais RC	5.00	1.50
❑ 230 Jason Wright RC	5.00	1.50
❑ 231 Rayshun Reed RC	3.00	.90
❑ 232 Patrick Crayton RC	6.00	1.80
❑ 233 Casey Bramlet RC	5.00	1.50
❑ 234 Nathaniel Adibi RC	6.00	1.80
❑ 235 Dontarrious Thomas RC	6.00	1.80
❑ 236 B.J. Sander RC	5.00	1.50
❑ 237 Ryan McGuffey RC	3.00	.90
❑ 238 Shawntae Spencer RC	6.00	1.80
❑ 239 Amon Gordon RC	3.00	.90
❑ 240 Vernon Carey RC	5.00	1.50
❑ 241 Stanford Samuels RC	5.00	1.50
❑ 242 Thomas Tapeh RC	5.00	1.50
❑ 243 Keith Smith RC	5.00	1.50
❑ 244 Casey Clausen RC	8.00	2.40
❑ 245 Jake Grove RC	3.00	.90
❑ 246 Omar Nazel RC	5.00	1.50
❑ 247 Jammal Lord RC	6.00	1.80
❑ 248 Jeremy LeSueur RC	5.00	1.50
❑ 249 Daryl Smith RC	6.00	1.80
❑ 250 Nat Dorsey RC	3.00	.90
❑ 251 Tim Anderson RC	6.00	1.80
❑ 252 Chris Snee RC	5.00	1.50
❑ 253 Sean Ryan RC	5.00	1.50
❑ 254 Tank Johnson RC	5.00	1.50
❑ 255 Marquis Cooper RC	5.00	1.50
❑ 256 Josh Scobee RC	3.00	.90
❑ 257 Justin Jenkins RC	5.00	1.50
❑ 258 Nate Lawrie RC	5.00	1.50
❑ 259 Randy Starks RC	5.00	1.50
❑ 260 Caleb Miller RC	5.00	1.50
❑ 261 A.J. Ricker RC	3.00	.90
❑ 262 Andy Hall RC	5.00	1.50
❑ 263 Troy Fleming RC	5.00	1.50
❑ 264 Matt Ware RC	6.00	1.80
❑ 265 Christian Ferrara RC	5.00	1.50
❑ 266 Stacy Andrews RC	5.00	1.50
❑ 267 Reggie Torbor RC	5.00	1.50
❑ 268 Jeris McIntyre RC	5.00	1.50
❑ 269 Jarrett Payton RC	6.00	1.80
❑ 270 Ronald Jones RC	3.00	.90
❑ 271 Kelly Butler RC	5.00	1.50
❑ 272 Bryan Hickman RC	6.00	1.80
❑ 273 Chris Collins RC	5.00	1.50
❑ 274 Ryan Dinwiddie RC	5.00	1.50
❑ 275 Robert Geathers RC	5.00	1.50
❑ 276 Niko Koutouvides RC	5.00	1.50
❑ 277 Clarence Farmer RC	5.00	1.50
❑ 278 Jim Sorgi RC	6.00	1.80
❑ 279 Ran Carthon RC	5.00	1.50
❑ 280 Michael Waddell RC	3.00	.90
❑ 281 Andrew Strojny RC	3.00	.90
❑ 282 Sloan Thomas RC	5.00	1.50
❑ 283 Tim Euhus RC	6.00	1.80
❑ 284 Lawrence Richardson RC	6.00	1.80
❑ 285 Nate Kaeding RC	6.00	1.80
❑ 286 Ryan Krause RC	5.00	1.50
❑ 287 Derrick Ward RC	3.00	.90
❑ 288 Nathan Vasher RC	6.00	1.80
❑ 289 Bobby McCray RC	5.00	1.50
❑ 290 Scott Rislov RC	6.00	1.80
❑ 291 Ryan Boschetti RC	3.00	.90
❑ 292 Fred Russell RC	6.00	1.80
❑ 293 Von Hutchins RC	5.00	1.50
❑ 294 Derrick Crawford RC	3.00	.90

2004 Reflections Green

	Nm-Mt	Ex-Mt

*VETERANS: 3X TO 8X BASE CARD HI
*ROOKIES/450: .8X TO 2X BASE CARD HI
*ROOKIES/750: 1X TO 2.5X BASE CARD HI
*ROOKIES/1150: 1X TO 2.5X BASE CARD HI
STATED PRINT RUN 50 SER.#'d SETS

2004 Reflections Red

	Nm-Mt	Ex-Mt

*VETERANS: 2X TO 5X BASE CARD HI
*ROOKIES/450: .5X TO 1.2X BASE CARD HI
*ROOKIES/750: .6X TO 1.5X BASE CARD HI
*ROOKIES/1150: .6X TO 1.5X BASE CARD HI
STATED PRINT RUN 100 SER.#'d SETS

1999 Revolution

	Nm-Mt	Ex-Mt
COMPLETE SET (175)	100.00	45.00
❑ 1 David Boston SP RC	2.50	1.10
❑ 2 Joel Makovicka RC SP	3.00	1.35
❑ 3 Rob Moore	.75	.35
❑ 4 Adrian Murrell	.75	.35
❑ 5 Jake Plummer	.75	.35
❑ 6 Frank Sanders	.75	.35
❑ 7 Jamal Anderson	1.25	.55
❑ 8 Chris Chandler	.75	.35
❑ 9 Tim Dwight	1.25	.55
❑ 10 Terance Mathis	.75	.35
❑ 11 Jeff Paulk RC SP	1.50	.70
❑ 12 O.J. Santiago	.50	.23
❑ 13 Peter Boulware	.50	.23
❑ 14 Priest Holmes	2.00	.90
❑ 15 Michael Jackson	.50	.23
❑ 16 Jermaine Lewis	.75	.35
❑ 17 Doug Flutie	1.25	.55
❑ 18 Eric Moulds	1.25	.55
❑ 19 Peerless Price RC SP	5.00	2.20
❑ 20 Andre Reed	.75	.35
❑ 21 Antowain Smith	1.25	.55
❑ 22 Bruce Smith	.75	.35
❑ 23 Steve Beuerlein	.50	.23
❑ 24 Kevin Greene	.75	.35
❑ 25 Fred Lane	.50	.23
❑ 26 Muhsin Muhammad	.75	.35
❑ 27 Wesley Walls	.75	.35
❑ 28 Marty Booker RC SP	3.00	1.35
❑ 29 Curtis Conway	.75	.35
❑ 30 Bobby Engram	.75	.35
❑ 31 Curtis Enis	.50	.23
❑ 32 Erik Kramer	.50	.23
❑ 33 Cade McNown SP RC	2.00	.90
❑ 34 Scott Covington RC	2.50	1.10
❑ 35 Corey Dillon	1.25	.55
❑ 36 Carl Pickens	.75	.35
❑ 37 Darnay Scott	.50	.23
❑ 38 Akili Smith RC	2.00	.90
❑ 39 Craig Yeast RC SP	2.50	1.10
❑ 40 Darrin Chiaverini RC SP	2.50	1.10
❑ 41 Tim Couch SP RC	2.50	1.10
❑ 42 Ty Detmer	.75	.35
❑ 43 Kevin Johnson SP RC	2.50	1.10
❑ 44 Terry Kirby	.50	.23
❑ 45 D.McCutcheon RC SP	1.50	.70
❑ 46 Irv Smith	.50	.23

❑ 47 Troy Aikman 2.50 1.10
❑ 48 Michael Irvin .75 .35
❑ 49 Wane McGarity RC SP 1.50 .70
❑ 50 Dat Nguyen RC SP 3.00 1.35
❑ 51 Deion Sanders 1.25 .55
❑ 52 Emmitt Smith 2.50 1.10
❑ 53 Terrell Davis 1.25 .55
❑ 54 John Elway 4.00 1.80
❑ 55 Brian Griese 1.25 .55
❑ 56 Ed McCaffrey .75 .35
❑ 57 Travis McGriff RC SP 1.50 .70
❑ 58 Shannon Sharpe .75 .35
❑ 59 Rod Smith WR .75 .35
❑ 60 Charlie Batch 1.25 .55
❑ 61 Chris Claiborne RC 1.25 .55
❑ 62 Sedrick Irvin RC 1.25 .55
❑ 63 Herman Moore .75 .35
❑ 64 Johnnie Morton .75 .35
❑ 65 Barry Sanders 4.00 1.80
❑ 66 Aaron Brooks RC SP 10.00 4.50
❑ 67 Mark Chmura .50 .23
❑ 68 Brett Favre 4.00 1.80
❑ 69 Antonio Freeman 1.25 .55
❑ 70 Dorsey Levens 1.25 .55
❑ 71 De'Mond Parker RC SP 1.50 .70
❑ 72 Marvin Harrison 1.25 .55
❑ 73 Edgerrin James SP RC 8.00 3.60
❑ 74 Peyton Manning 4.00 1.80
❑ 75 Jerome Pathon .50 .23
❑ 76 Mike Peterson RC SP 2.50 1.10
❑ 77 Reggie Barlow .50 .23
❑ 78 Mark Brunell 1.25 .55
❑ 79 Keenan McCardell .75 .35
❑ 80 Jimmy Smith .75 .35
❑ 81 Fred Taylor 1.25 .55
❑ 82 Mike Cloud RC 2.00 .90
❑ 83 Tony Gonzalez 1.25 .55
❑ 84 Elvis Grbac .75 .35
❑ 85 Larry Parker RC SP 3.00 1.35
❑ 86 Andre Rison .75 .35
❑ 87 Brian Shay RC SP 1.50 .70
❑ 88 Karim Abdul-Jabbar .75 .35
❑ 89 Oronde Gadsden .75 .35
❑ 90 James Johnson SP RC 2.00 .90
❑ 91 Rob Konrad RC 2.00 .90
❑ 92 Dan Marino 4.00 1.80
❑ 93 O.J. McDuffie .75 .35
❑ 94 Cris Carter 1.25 .55
❑ 95 Daunte Culpepper SP RC 8.00 3.60
❑ 96 Randall Cunningham 1.25 .55
❑ 97 Jim Kleinsasser RC SP 2.50 1.10
❑ 98 Randy Moss 3.00 1.35
❑ 99 Jake Reed .75 .35
❑ 100 Robert Smith 1.25 .55
❑ 101 Drew Bledsoe 1.50 .70
❑ 102 Ben Coates .75 .35
❑ 103 Kevin Faulk SP RC 2.50 1.10
❑ 104 Terry Glenn 1.25 .55
❑ 105 Shawn Jefferson .50 .23
❑ 106 A.Katzenmoyer RC SP 2.50 1.10
❑ 107 Cameron Cleeland .50 .23
❑ 108 Andre Hastings .50 .23
❑ 109 Billy Joe Tolliver .50 .23
❑ 110 Ricky Williams RC 4.00 1.80
❑ 111 Gary Brown .50 .23
❑ 112 Kent Graham .50 .23
❑ 113 Ike Hilliard .50 .23
❑ 114 Joe Montgomery RC SP 2.50 1.10
❑ 115 Amani Toomer .50 .23
❑ 116 Wayne Chrebet .75 .35
❑ 117 Keyshawn Johnson 1.25 .55
❑ 118 Leon Johnson .50 .23
❑ 119 Curtis Martin 1.25 .55
❑ 120 Vinny Testaverde .75 .35
❑ 121 Dedric Ward .50 .23
❑ 122 Tim Brown 1.25 .55
❑ 123 D.Douglas RC SP 3.00 1.35
❑ 124 Rickey Dudley .50 .23
❑ 125 James Jett .75 .35
❑ 126 Napoleon Kaufman 1.25 .55
❑ 127 Charles Woodson 1.25 .55
❑ 128 Na Brown RC SP 2.50 1.10
❑ 129 Cecil Martin RC SP 2.50 1.10
❑ 130 Donovan McNabb SP RC 10.00 4.50
❑ 131 Duce Staley 1.25 .55
❑ 132 Kevin Turner .50 .23
❑ 133 Jerome Bettis 1.25 .55
❑ 134 Troy Edwards SP RC 2.00 .90
❑ 135 Courtney Hawkins .50 .23
❑ 136 Malcolm Johnson RC SP 1.50 .70
❑ 137 Kordell Stewart .75 .35
❑ 138 Jerame Tuman RC SP 2.50 1.10
❑ 139 Amos Zereoue RC 2.50 1.10
❑ 140 Isaac Bruce 1.25 .55
❑ 141 Joe Germaine RC 2.00 .90
❑ 142 Torry Holt RC SP 6.00 2.70
❑ 143 Amp Lee .50 .23
❑ 144 Ricky Proehl .50 .23
❑ 145 Freddie Jones .50 .23
❑ 146 Ryan Leaf 1.25 .55
❑ 147 Natrone Means .75 .35
❑ 148 Mikhael Ricks .50 .23
❑ 149 Garrison Hearst .75 .35
❑ 150 Terry Jackson RC SP 2.50 1.10
❑ 151 Terrell Owens 1.25 .55
❑ 152 Jerry Rice 2.50 1.10
❑ 153 J.J. Stokes .75 .35
❑ 154 Steve Young 1.50 .70
❑ 155 Karsten Bailey RC 2.00 .90
❑ 156 Joey Galloway .75 .35
❑ 157 Ahman Green 1.25 .55
❑ 158 Brock Huard SP RC 2.50 1.10
❑ 159 Jon Kitna 1.25 .55
❑ 160 Ricky Watters .75 .35
❑ 161 Mike Alstott 1.25 .55
❑ 162 Reidel Anthony .75 .35
❑ 163 Trent Dilfer .75 .35
❑ 164 Warrick Dunn 1.25 .55
❑ 165 Shaun King SP RC 2.00 .90
❑ 166 Anthony McFarland RC 2.50 1.10
❑ 167 Kevin Dyson .75 .35
❑ 168 Eddie George 1.25 .55
❑ 169 Darran Hall RC 1.25 .55
❑ 170 Steve McNair 1.25 .55
❑ 171 Frank Wycheck .50 .23
❑ 172 Stephen Alexander .50 .23
❑ 173 Champ Bailey RC 3.00 1.35
❑ 174 Skip Hicks .50 .23
❑ 175 Michael Westbrook .75 .35

2000 Revolution

	Nm-Mt	Ex-Mt
COMP.SET w/o SP's (100)	40.00	18.00

❑ 1 David Boston 1.25 .55
❑ 2 Jake Plummer .75 .35
❑ 3 Frank Sanders .75 .35
❑ 4 Jamal Anderson 1.25 .55
❑ 5 Chris Chandler .75 .35
❑ 6 Tim Dwight 1.25 .55
❑ 7 Terance Mathis .75 .35
❑ 8 Tony Banks .75 .35
❑ 9 Qadry Ismail .75 .35
❑ 10 Shannon Sharpe .50 .23
❑ 11 Rob Johnson .75 .35
❑ 12 Eric Moulds 1.25 .55
❑ 13 Peerless Price 1.25 .55
❑ 14 Antowain Smith .75 .35
❑ 15 Steve Beuerlein .75 .35
❑ 16 Tim Biakabutuka .75 .35
❑ 17 Muhsin Muhammad .75 .35
❑ 18 Curtis Enis .50 .23
❑ 19 Cade McNown .50 .23
❑ 20 Marcus Robinson 1.25 .55
❑ 21 Corey Dillon 1.25 .55
❑ 22 Akili Smith .50 .23
❑ 23 Tim Couch .75 .35
❑ 24 Kevin Johnson 1.25 .55
❑ 25 Troy Aikman 2.50 1.10
❑ 26 Rocket Ismail .75 .35
❑ 27 Emmitt Smith 2.50 1.10
❑ 28 Terrell Davis 1.25 .55
❑ 29 Brian Griese 1.25 .55
❑ 30 Ed McCaffrey 1.25 .55
❑ 31 Charlie Batch 1.25 .55
❑ 32 Herman Moore .75 .35
❑ 33 James Stewart .75 .35
❑ 34 Brett Favre 4.00 1.80
❑ 35 Antonio Freeman 1.25 .55
❑ 36 Dorsey Levens .75 .35
❑ 37 Marvin Harrison 1.25 .55
❑ 38 Edgerrin James 2.00 .90
❑ 39 Peyton Manning 3.00 1.35
❑ 40 Terrence Wilkins .50 .23
❑ 41 Mark Brunell 1.25 .55
❑ 42 Keenan McCardell .75 .35
❑ 43 Jimmy Smith .75 .35
❑ 44 Fred Taylor 1.25 .55
❑ 45 Derrick Alexander .75 .35
❑ 46 Tony Gonzalez .75 .35
❑ 47 Elvis Grbac .75 .35
❑ 48 Damon Huard 1.25 .55
❑ 49 James Johnson .50 .23
❑ 50 O.J. McDuffie .75 .35
❑ 51 Cris Carter 1.25 .55
❑ 52 Daunte Culpepper 1.50 .70
❑ 53 Randy Moss 2.50 1.10
❑ 54 Robert Smith 1.25 .55
❑ 55 Drew Bledsoe 1.50 .70
❑ 56 Terry Glenn .75 .35
❑ 57 Jeff Blake .75 .35
❑ 58 Ricky Williams 1.25 .55
❑ 59 Tiki Barber .75 .35
❑ 60 Kerry Collins .75 .35
❑ 61 Ike Hilliard .75 .35
❑ 62 Amani Toomer .50 .23
❑ 63 Wayne Chrebet .75 .35
❑ 64 Curtis Martin 1.25 .55
❑ 65 Vinny Testaverde .75 .35
❑ 66 Dedric Ward .50 .23
❑ 67 Tim Brown 1.25 .55
❑ 68 Napoleon Kaufman .75 .35
❑ 69 Tyrone Wheatley .75 .35
❑ 70 Charles Johnson .75 .35
❑ 71 Donovan McNabb 2.00 .90
❑ 72 Duce Staley 1.25 .55
❑ 73 Jerome Bettis 1.25 .55
❑ 74 Troy Edwards .50 .23
❑ 75 Kordell Stewart .75 .35
❑ 76 Isaac Bruce 1.25 .55
❑ 77 Marshall Faulk 1.50 .70
❑ 78 Az-Zahir Hakim .50 .23
❑ 79 Torry Holt 1.25 .55
❑ 80 Kurt Warner 2.50 1.10
❑ 81 Curtis Conway .75 .35
❑ 82 Jermaine Fazande .50 .23
❑ 83 Ryan Leaf .75 .35
❑ 84 Junior Seau 1.25 .55
❑ 85 Jeff Garcia 1.25 .55
❑ 86 Charlie Garner .75 .35
❑ 87 Terrell Owens 1.25 .55
❑ 88 Jerry Rice 2.50 1.10
❑ 89 Jon Kitna 1.25 .55
❑ 90 Derrick Mayes .75 .35
❑ 91 Ricky Watters .75 .35
❑ 92 Mike Alstott 1.25 .55
❑ 93 Warrick Dunn 1.25 .55
❑ 94 Keyshawn Johnson 1.25 .55
❑ 95 Shaun King .50 .23
❑ 96 Eddie George 1.25 .55
❑ 97 Jevon Kearse 1.25 .55
❑ 98 Steve McNair 1.25 .55
❑ 99 Stephen Davis 1.25 .55
❑ 100 Brad Johnson 1.25 .55
❑ 101 Thomas Jones RC 25.00 11.00
❑ 102 Doug Johnson RC 15.00 6.75

Card	Nm-Mt	Ex-Mt
❑ 103 Jamal Lewis RC	40.00	18.00
❑ 104 Chris Redman RC	12.00	5.50
❑ 105 Travis Taylor RC	15.00	6.75
❑ 106 Troy Walters RC	15.00	6.75
❑ 107 Kwame Cavil RC	8.00	3.60
❑ 108 Sammy Morris RC	12.00	5.50
❑ 109 Dez White RC	15.00	6.75
❑ 110 Ron Dugans RC	8.00	3.60
❑ 111 Danny Farmer RC	12.00	5.50
❑ 112 Curtis Keaton RC	12.00	5.50
❑ 113 Peter Warrick RC	15.00	6.75
❑ 114 Dennis Northcutt RC	15.00	6.75
❑ 115 Travis Prentice RC	12.00	5.50
❑ 116 Kevin Thompson RC	8.00	3.60
❑ 117 Spergon Wynn RC	12.00	5.50
❑ 118 Michael Wiley RC	12.00	5.50
❑ 119 Mike Anderson RC	15.00	6.75
❑ 120 Chris Cole RC	12.00	5.50
❑ 121 Jarious Jackson RC	12.00	5.50
❑ 122 Charles Lee RC	8.00	3.60
❑ 123 Anthony Lucas RC	8.00	3.60
❑ 124 R.Jay Soward RC	12.00	5.50
❑ 125 Shyrone Stith RC	12.00	5.50
❑ 126 Sylvester Morris RC	12.00	5.50
❑ 127 Doug Chapman RC	12.00	5.50
❑ 128 Tom Brady RC	150.00	70.00
❑ 129 Gari Scott RC	8.00	3.60
❑ 130 J.R. Redmond RC	12.00	5.50
❑ 131 Ron Dayne RC	15.00	6.75
❑ 132 Ron Dixon RC	12.00	5.50
❑ 133 Laveranues Coles RC	20.00	9.00
❑ 134 Ronney Jenkins RC	12.00	5.50
❑ 135 Chad Pennington RC	60.00	27.00
❑ 136 Jerry Porter RC	20.00	9.00
❑ 137 Todd Pinkston RC	15.00	6.75
❑ 138 Plaxico Burress RC	30.00	13.50
❑ 139 Trung Canidate RC	12.00	5.50
❑ 140 Troy Walters RC	15.00	6.75
❑ 141 Giovanni Carmazzi RC	12.00	5.50
❑ 142 Tim Rattay RC	30.00	13.50
❑ 143 Shaun Alexander RC	40.00	18.00
❑ 144 Darrell Jackson RC	30.00	13.50
❑ 145 James Williams RC	12.00	5.50
❑ 146 Joe Hamilton RC	12.00	5.50
❑ 147 Aaron Stecker RC	15.00	6.75
❑ 148 Erron Kinney RC	15.00	6.75
❑ 149 Billy Volek RC	25.00	11.00
❑ 150 Todd Husak RC	15.00	6.75

1989 Score

	Nm-Mt	Ex-Mt
COMPLETE SET (330)	100.00	45.00
COMP.FACT.SET (330)	120.00	55.00
❑ 1 Joe Montana	4.00	1.80
❑ 2 Bo Jackson	.60	.25
❑ 3 Boomer Esiason	.20	.09
❑ 4 Roger Craig	.50	.23
❑ 5 Ed Too Tall Jones	.20	.09
❑ 6 Phil Simms	.20	.09
❑ 7 Dan Hampton	.20	.09
❑ 8 John Settle RC	.10	.05
❑ 9 Bernie Kosar	.20	.09
❑ 10 Al Toon	.20	.09
❑ 11 Bubby Brister RC	1.00	.45
❑ 12 Mark Clayton	.20	.09
❑ 13 Dan Marino	4.00	1.80
❑ 14 Joe Morris	.10	.05
❑ 15 Warren Moon	.50	.23
❑ 16 Chuck Long	.10	.05
❑ 17 Mark Jackson	.10	.05
❑ 18 Michael Irvin RC	6.00	2.70
❑ 19 Bruce Smith	.50	.23
❑ 20 Anthony Carter	.20	.09
❑ 21 Charles Haley	.50	.23
❑ 22 Dave Duerson	.10	.05
❑ 23 Troy Stradford	.10	.05
❑ 24 Freeman McNeil	.10	.05
❑ 25 Jerry Gray	.10	.05
❑ 26 Bill Maas	.10	.05
❑ 27 Chris Chandler RC	5.00	2.20
❑ 28 Tom Newberry RC	.10	.05
❑ 29 Albert Lewis	.10	.05
❑ 30 Jay Schroeder	.10	.05
❑ 31 Dalton Hilliard	.10	.05
❑ 32 Tony Eason	.10	.05
❑ 33 Rick Donnelly UER (229.11 yards per punt)	.10	.05
❑ 34 Herschel Walker	.20	.09
❑ 35 Wesley Walker	.10	.05
❑ 36 Chris Doleman	.20	.09
❑ 37 Pat Swilling	.20	.09
❑ 38 Joey Browner	.10	.05
❑ 39 Shane Conlan	.10	.05
❑ 40 Mike Tomczak	.20	.09
❑ 41 Webster Slaughter	.20	.09
❑ 42 Ray Donaldson	.10	.05
❑ 43 Christian Okoye	.10	.05
❑ 44 John Bosa	.10	.05
❑ 45 Aaron Cox RC	.10	.05
❑ 46 Bobby Hebert	.20	.09
❑ 47 Carl Banks	.10	.05
❑ 48 Jeff Fuller	.10	.05
❑ 49 Gerald Willhite	.10	.05
❑ 50 Mike Singletary	.20	.09
❑ 51 Stanley Morgan	.10	.05
❑ 52 Mark Bavaro	.20	.09
❑ 53 Mickey Shuler	.10	.05
❑ 54 Keith Millard	.10	.05
❑ 55 Andre Tippett	.10	.05
❑ 56 Vance Johnson	.20	.09
❑ 57 Bennie Blades RC	.20	.09
❑ 58 Tim Harris	.10	.05
❑ 59 Hanford Dixon	.10	.05
❑ 60 Chris Miller RC	1.00	.45
❑ 61 Cornelius Bennett	.50	.23
❑ 62 Neal Anderson	.20	.09
❑ 63 Ickey Woods RC UER (Jersey is 31 but listed as 30 on card back)	.50	.23
❑ 64 Gary Anderson RB	.10	.05
❑ 65 Vaughan Johnson RC	.10	.05
❑ 66 Ronnie Lippett	.10	.05
❑ 67 Mike Quick	.10	.05
❑ 68 Roy Green	.20	.09
❑ 69 Tim Krumrie	.10	.05
❑ 70 Mark Malone	.10	.05
❑ 71 James Jones	.10	.05
❑ 72 Cris Carter RC	12.00	5.50
❑ 73 Ricky Nattiel	.10	.05
❑ 74 Jim Arnold UER (238.83 yards per punt)	.10	.05
❑ 75 Randall Cunningham	1.00	.45
❑ 76 John L. Williams	.10	.05
❑ 77 Paul Gruber RC	.10	.05
❑ 78 Rod Woodson RC	3.00	1.35
❑ 79 Ray Childress	.10	.05
❑ 80 Doug Williams	.20	.09
❑ 81 Deron Cherry	.20	.09
❑ 82 John Offerdahl	.10	.05
❑ 83 Louis Lipps	.20	.09
❑ 84 Neil Lomax	.10	.05
❑ 85 Wade Wilson	.20	.09
❑ 86 Tim Brown RC	12.00	5.50
❑ 87 Chris Hinton	.10	.05
❑ 88 Stump Mitchell	.10	.05
❑ 89 Tunch Ilkin RC	.10	.05
❑ 90 Steve Pelluer	.10	.05
❑ 91 Brian Noble	.10	.05
❑ 92 Reggie White	.50	.23
❑ 93 Aundray Bruce RC	.10	.05
❑ 94 Garry James	.10	.05
❑ 95 Drew Hill	.10	.05
❑ 96 Anthony Munoz	.20	.09
❑ 97 James Wilder	.10	.05
❑ 98 Dexter Manley	.10	.05
❑ 99 Lee Williams	.10	.05
❑ 100 Dave Krieg	.20	.09
❑ 101A Keith Jackson RC ERR (Listed as 84 on card back)	.50	.23
❑ 101B Keith Jackson RC COR (Listed as 88 on card back)	.50	.23
❑ 102 Luis Sharpe	.10	.05
❑ 103 Kevin Greene	.50	.23
❑ 104 Duane Bickett	.10	.05
❑ 105 Mark Rypien RC	.50	.23
❑ 106 Curt Warner	.10	.05
❑ 107 Jacob Green	.10	.05
❑ 108 Gary Clark	.50	.23
❑ 109 Bruce Matthews RC	2.50	1.10
❑ 110 Bill Fralic	.10	.05
❑ 111 Bill Bates	.20	.09
❑ 112 Jeff Bryant	.10	.05
❑ 113 Charles Mann	.10	.05
❑ 114 Richard Dent	.20	.09
❑ 115 Bruce Hill RC	.10	.05
❑ 116 Mark May RC	.10	.05
❑ 117 Mark Collins RC	.10	.05
❑ 118 Ron Holmes	.10	.05
❑ 119 Scott Case RC	.10	.05
❑ 120 Tom Rathman	.10	.05
❑ 121 Dennis McKinnon	.10	.05
❑ 122A Ricky Sanders ERR (Listed as 46 on card back)	.25	.11
❑ 122B Ricky Sanders COR (Listed as 83 on card back)	.50	.23
❑ 123 Michael Carter	.10	.05
❑ 124 Ozzie Newsome	.20	.09
❑ 125 Irving Fryar UER ("wide reveiver")	.20	.09
❑ 126A Ron Hall RC ERR (wrong photos on card)	.25	.11
❑ 126B Ron Hall RC COR (correct photos used)	.50	.23
❑ 127 Clay Matthews	.20	.09
❑ 128 Leonard Marshall	.10	.05
❑ 129 Kevin Mack	.10	.05
❑ 130 Art Monk	.20	.09
❑ 131 Garin Veris	.10	.05
❑ 132 Steve Jordan	.10	.05
❑ 133 Frank Minnifield	.10	.05
❑ 134 Eddie Brown	.10	.05
❑ 135 Stacey Bailey	.10	.05
❑ 136 Rickey Jackson	.20	.09
❑ 137 Henry Ellard	.20	.09
❑ 138 Jim Burt	.10	.05
❑ 139 Jerome Brown	.20	.09
❑ 140 Rodney Holman RC	.10	.05
❑ 141 Sammy Winder	.10	.05
❑ 142 Marcus Cotton	.10	.05
❑ 143 Jim Jeffcoat	.10	.05
❑ 144 Rueben Mayes	.10	.05
❑ 145 Jim McMahon	.20	.09
❑ 146 Reggie Williams	.10	.05
❑ 147 John Anderson	.10	.05
❑ 148 Harris Barton RC	.10	.05
❑ 149 Phillip Epps	.10	.05
❑ 150 Jay Hilgenberg	.10	.05
❑ 151 Earl Ferrell	.10	.05
❑ 152 Andre Reed	.50	.23
❑ 153 Dennis Gentry	.10	.05
❑ 154 Max Montoya	.10	.05
❑ 155 Darrin Nelson	.10	.05
❑ 156 Jeff Chadwick	.10	.05
❑ 157 James Brooks	.20	.09
❑ 158 Keith Bishop	.10	.05
❑ 159 Robert Awalt	.10	.05
❑ 160 Marty Lyons	.10	.05
❑ 161 Johnny Hector	.10	.05
❑ 162 Tony Casillas	.10	.05
❑ 163 Kyle Clifton RC	.10	.05

❑ 164 Cody Risien .10 .05
❑ 165 Jamie Holland RC .10 .05
❑ 166 Merril Hoge RC .10 .05
❑ 167 Chris Spielman RC 1.00 .45
❑ 168 Carlos Carson .10 .05
❑ 169 Jerry Ball RC .10 .05
❑ 170 Don Majkowski RC .50 .23
❑ 171 Everson Walls .10 .05
❑ 172 Mike Rozier .10 .05
❑ 173 Matt Millen .20 .09
❑ 174 Karl Mecklenburg .10 .05
❑ 175 Paul Palmer .10 .05
❑ 176 Brian Blades RC UER .50 .23
(Photo on back is
reversed negative)
❑ 177 Brent Fullwood RC .10 .05
❑ 178 Anthony Miller RC .50 .23
❑ 179 Brian Sochia .10 .05
❑ 180 Stephen Baker RC .10 .05
❑ 181 Jesse Solomon .10 .05
❑ 182 John Grimsley .10 .05
❑ 183 Timmy Newsome .10 .05
❑ 184 Steve Sewell RC .10 .05
❑ 185 Dean Biasucci .10 .05
❑ 186 Alonzo Highsmith .10 .05
❑ 187 Randy Grimes .10 .05
❑ 188A M.Carrier RC WR ERR 1.00 .45
Photo on back is
actually Bruce Hill
❑ 188B M.Carrier RC WR COR 1.00 .45
(Wearing helmet in
photo on back
❑ 189 Vann McElroy .10 .05
❑ 190 Greg Bell .10 .05
❑ 191 Quinn Early RC 1.00 .45
❑ 192 Lawrence Taylor .50 .23
❑ 193 Albert Bentley .10 .05
❑ 194 Ernest Givins .20 .09
❑ 195 Jackie Slater .10 .05
❑ 196 Jim Sweeney .10 .05
❑ 197 Freddie Joe Nunn .10 .05
❑ 198 Keith Byars .20 .09
❑ 199 Hardy Nickerson RC .50 .23
❑ 200 Steve Beuerlein RC 4.00 1.80
❑ 201 Bruce Armstrong RC .50 .23
❑ 202 Lionel Manuel .10 .05
❑ 203 J.T. Smith .10 .05
❑ 204 Mark Ingram RC .50 .23
❑ 205 Fred Smerlas .10 .05
❑ 206 Bryan Hinkle RC .10 .05
❑ 207 Steve McMichael .20 .09
❑ 208 Nick Lowery .10 .05
❑ 209 Jack Trudeau .10 .05
❑ 210 Lorenzo Hampton .10 .05
❑ 211 Thurman Thomas RC 6.00 2.70
❑ 212 Steve Young 1.50 .70
❑ 213 James Lofton .50 .23
❑ 214 Jim Covert .10 .05
❑ 215 Ronnie Lott .20 .09
❑ 216 Stephone Paige .10 .05
❑ 217 Mark Duper .20 .09
❑ 218A Willie Gault ERR .25 .11
(Front photo actually
93 Greg Townsend)
❑ 218B Willie Gault COR .50 .23
(83 clearly visible)
❑ 219 Ken Ruettgers RC .10 .05
❑ 220 Kevin Ross RC .10 .05
❑ 221 Jerry Rice 3.00 1.35
❑ 222 Billy Ray Smith .10 .05
❑ 223 Jim Kelly 1.00 .45
❑ 224 Vinny Testaverde 1.00 .45
❑ 225 Steve Largent .50 .23
❑ 226 Warren Williams RC .10 .05
❑ 227 Morten Andersen .10 .05
❑ 228 Bill Brooks .20 .09
❑ 229 Reggie Langhorne RC .10 .05
❑ 230 Pepper Johnson .10 .05
❑ 231 Pat Leahy .10 .05
❑ 232 Fred Marion .10 .05
❑ 233 Gary Zimmerman .10 .05
❑ 234 Marcus Allen .50 .23
❑ 235 Gaston Green RC .10 .05
❑ 236 John Stephens RC .10 .05
❑ 237 Terry Kinard .10 .05
❑ 238 John Taylor RC .50 .23
❑ 239 Brian Bosworth .20 .09
❑ 240 Anthony Toney .10 .05
❑ 241 Ken O'Brien .10 .05
❑ 242 Howie Long .50 .23
❑ 243 Doug Flutie 2.50 1.10
❑ 244 Jim Everett .50 .23
❑ 245 Broderick Thomas RC .10 .05
❑ 246 Deion Sanders RC 12.00 5.50
❑ 247 Donnell Woolford RC .10 .05
❑ 248 Wayne Martin RC .10 .05
❑ 249 David Williams RC .10 .05
❑ 250 Bill Hawkins RC .10 .05
❑ 251 Eric Hill RC .10 .05
❑ 252 Burt Grossman RC .10 .05
❑ 253 Tracy Rocker .10 .05
❑ 254 Steve Wisniewski RC .50 .23
❑ 255 Jessie Small RC .10 .05
❑ 256 David Braxton .10 .05
❑ 257 Barry Sanders RC 40.00 18.00
❑ 258 Derrick Thomas RC 6.00 2.70
❑ 259 Eric Metcalf RC 1.00 .45
❑ 260 Keith DeLong RC .10 .05
❑ 261 Hart Lee Dykes RC .10 .05
❑ 262 Sammie Smith RC .10 .05
❑ 263 Steve Atwater RC .50 .23
❑ 264 Eric Ball RC .10 .05
❑ 265 Don Beebe RC .50 .23
❑ 266 Brian Williams OL RC .10 .05
❑ 267 Jeff Lageman RC .10 .05
❑ 268 Tim Worley RC .10 .05
❑ 269 Tony Mandarich RC .10 .05
❑ 270 Troy Aikman RC 30.00 13.50
❑ 271 Andy Heck RC .10 .05
❑ 272 Andre Rison RC 5.00 2.20
❑ 273 AFC Championship .10 .05
Bengals over Bills
(Ickey Woods and
Boomer Esiason)
❑ 274 NFC Championship 1.00 .45
49ers over Bears
(Joe Montana)
❑ 275 Super Bowl XXIII 2.00 .90
49ers over Bengals
(Joe Montana and
Jerry Rice)
❑ 276 Rodney Carter .10 .05
❑ 277 Mark Jackson .10 .05
Vance Johnson
Ricky Nattiel
❑ 278 John L. Williams .10 .05
and Curt Warner
❑ 279 Joe Montana and 2.00 .90
Jerry Rice
❑ 280 Roy Green .10 .05
Neil Lomax
❑ 281 Randall Cunningham .10 .05
and Keith Jackson
❑ 282 Chris Doleman and .10 .05
Keith Millard
❑ 283 Mark Duper and .10 .05
Mark Clayton
❑ 284 Marcus Allen and .60 .25
Bo Jackson
❑ 285 Frank Minnifield AP .10 .05
❑ 286 Bruce Matthews AP .20 .09
❑ 287 Joey Browner AP .10 .05
❑ 288 Jay Hilgenberg AP .10 .05
❑ 289 Carl Lee AP RC .10 .05
❑ 290 Scott Norwood AP RC .10 .05
❑ 291 John Taylor AP .50 .23
❑ 292 Jerry Rice AP 1.50 .70
❑ 293A Keith Jackson AP ERR .50 .23
(Listed as 84
on card back)
❑ 293B Keith Jackson AP COR .50 .23
(Listed as 88
on card back)
❑ 294 Gary Zimmerman AP .10 .05
❑ 295 Lawrence Taylor AP .50 .23
❑ 296 Reggie White AP .50 .23
❑ 297 Roger Craig AP .20 .09
❑ 298 Boomer Esiason AP .20 .09
❑ 299 Cornelius Bennett AP .20 .09
❑ 300 Mike Horan AP .10 .05
❑ 301 Deron Cherry AP .10 .05
❑ 302 Tom Newberry AP .10 .05
❑ 303 Mike Singletary AP .20 .09
❑ 304 Shane Conlan AP .10 .05
❑ 305A Tim Brown ERR AP 2.00 .90
Photo on front act-
ually 80 James Lofton
❑ 305B Tim Brown COR AP 2.00 .90
(Dark jersey 81)
❑ 306 Henry Ellard AP .20 .09
❑ 307 Bruce Smith AP .20 .09
❑ 308 Tim Krumrie AP .10 .05
❑ 309 Anthony Munoz AP .20 .09
❑ 310 Darrell Green SPEED .10 .05
❑ 311 Anthony Miller SPEED .50 .23
❑ 312 Wesley Walker SPEED .10 .05
❑ 313 Ron Brown SPEED .10 .05
❑ 314 Bo Jackson SPEED .60 .25
❑ 315 Phillip Epps SPEED .10 .05
❑ 316A E.Thomas RC ERR SPEED .25 .11
Listed as 31
on card back
❑ 316B E.Thomas RC COR SPEED .50 .23
Listed as 22
on card back
❑ 317 Herschel Walker SPEED .20 .09
❑ 318 Jacob Green PRED .10 .05
❑ 319 Andre Tippett PRED .10 .05
❑ 320 Freddie Joe Nunn PRED .10 .05
❑ 321 Reggie White PRED .50 .23
❑ 322 Lawrence Taylor PRED .50 .23
❑ 323 Greg Townsend PRED .10 .05
❑ 324 Tim Harris PRED .10 .05
❑ 325 Bruce Smith PRED .20 .09
❑ 326 Tony Dorsett RB .50 .23
❑ 327 Steve Largent RB .50 .23
❑ 328 Tim Brown RB 2.00 .90
❑ 329 Joe Montana RB 1.50 .70
❑ 330 Tom Landry Tribute 1.00 .45

1989 Score Supplemental

	Nm-Mt	Ex-Mt
COMP.FACT.SET (110)	8.00	3.60
❑ 331S Herschel Walker	.40	.18
❑ 332S Allen Pinkett RC	.10	.05
❑ 333S Sterling Sharpe RC	3.00	1.35
❑ 334S Alvin Walton RC	.10	.05
❑ 335S Frank Reich RC	.40	.18
❑ 336S Jim Thornton RC	.10	.05
❑ 337S David Fulcher	.20	.09
❑ 338S Raul Allegre	.10	.05
❑ 339S John Elway	4.00	1.80
❑ 340S Michael Cofer	.10	.05
❑ 341S Jim Skow	.10	.05
❑ 342S Steve DeBerg	.10	.05
❑ 343S Mervyn Fernandez RC	.10	.05
❑ 344S Mike Lansford	.10	.05
❑ 345S Reggie Roby	.10	.05
❑ 346S Raymond Clayborn	.10	.05
❑ 347S Lonzell Hill	.10	.05
❑ 348S Ottis Anderson	.20	.09
❑ 349S Erik McMillan RC	.10	.05
❑ 350S Al Harris RC	.10	.05
❑ 351S Jack Del Rio RC	.40	.18
❑ 352S Gary Anderson K	.10	.05

Card	Nm-Mt	Ex-Mt
❑ 353S Jim McMahon	.20	.09
❑ 354S Keena Turner	.10	.05
❑ 355S Tony Woods RC	.10	.05
❑ 356S Donald Igwebuike	.10	.05
❑ 357S Gerald Riggs	.20	.09
❑ 358S Eddie Murray	.10	.05
❑ 359S Dino Hackett	.10	.05
❑ 360S Brad Muster RC	.10	.05
❑ 361S Paul Palmer	.10	.05
❑ 362S Jerry Robinson	.10	.05
❑ 363S Simon Fletcher RC	.20	.09
❑ 364S Tommy Kramer	.10	.05
❑ 365S Jim C. Jensen RC	.10	.05
❑ 366S Lorenzo White RC	.40	.18
❑ 367S Fredd Young	.10	.05
❑ 368S Ron Jaworski	.10	.05
❑ 369S Mel Owens	.10	.05
❑ 370S Dave Waymer	.10	.05
❑ 371S Sean Landeta	.10	.05
❑ 372S Sam Mills	.20	.09
❑ 373S Todd Blackledge	.10	.05
❑ 374S Jo Jo Townsell	.10	.05
❑ 375S Ron Wolfley	.10	.05
❑ 376S Ralf Mojsiejenko	.10	.05
❑ 377S Eric Wright	.10	.05
❑ 378S Nesby Glasgow	.10	.05
❑ 379S Darryl Talley	.20	.09
❑ 380S Eric Allen RC	.40	.18
❑ 381S Dennis Smith	.20	.09
❑ 382S John Tice	.10	.05
❑ 383S Jesse Solomon	.10	.05
❑ 384S Bo Jackson (FB/BB Pose)	1.00	.45
❑ 385S Mike Merriweather	.10	.05
❑ 386S Maurice Carthon	.10	.05
❑ 387S David Grayson	.10	.05
❑ 388S Wilber Marshall	.10	.05
❑ 389S David Wyman	.10	.05
❑ 390S Thomas Everett RC	.10	.05
❑ 391S Alex Gordon	.10	.05
❑ 392S D.J. Dozier	.10	.05
❑ 393S Scott Radecic RC	.10	.05
❑ 394S Eric Thomas	.10	.05
❑ 395S Mike Gann	.10	.05
❑ 396S William Perry	.20	.09
❑ 397S Carl Hairston	.10	.05
❑ 398S Billy Ard	.10	.05
❑ 399S Donnell Thompson	.10	.05
❑ 400S Mike Webster	.20	.09
❑ 401S Scott Davis RC	.10	.05
❑ 402S Sean Farrell	.10	.05
❑ 403S Mike Golic RC	.10	.05
❑ 404S Mike Kenn	.10	.05
❑ 405S Keith Van Horne RC	.10	.05
❑ 406S Bob Golic	.10	.05
❑ 407S Neil Smith RC	2.00	.90
❑ 408S Dermontti Dawson RC	.20	.09
❑ 409S Leslie O'Neal	.20	.09
❑ 410S Matt Bahr	.10	.05
❑ 411S Guy McIntyre RC	.10	.05
❑ 412S Bryan Millard	.10	.05
❑ 413S Joe Jacoby	.10	.05
❑ 414S Rob Taylor RC	.10	.05
❑ 415S Tony Zendejas	.10	.05
❑ 416S Vai Sikahema	.10	.05
❑ 417S Gary Reasons RC	.10	.05
❑ 418S Shawn Collins RC	.10	.05
❑ 419S Mark Green RC	.10	.05
❑ 420S Courtney Hall RC	.10	.05
❑ 421S Bobby Humphrey RC	.10	.05
❑ 422S Myron Guyton RC	.10	.05
❑ 423S Darryl Ingram RC	.10	.05
❑ 424S Chris Jacke RC	.10	.05
❑ 425S Keith Jones RC	.10	.05
❑ 426S Robert Massey RC	.10	.05
❑ 427S Bubba McDowell RC	.40	.18
❑ 428S Dave Meggett RC	.40	.18
❑ 429S Louis Oliver RC	.20	.09
❑ 430S Danny Peebles	.10	.05
❑ 431S Rodney Peete RC	.75	.35
❑ 432S Jeff Query RC	.10	.05
❑ 433S T.Rosenbach RC UER Photo actually Gary Hogeboom	.10	.05
❑ 434S Frank Stams RC	.10	.05
❑ 435S Lawyer Tillman RC	.10	.05
❑ 436S Billy Joe Tolliver RC	.10	.05
❑ 437S Floyd Turner RC	.20	.09
❑ 438S Steve Walsh RC	.20	.09
❑ 439S Joe Wolf RC	.10	.05
❑ 440S Trace Armstrong RC	.10	.05

1990 Score Supplemental

	Nm-Mt	Ex-Mt
COMP.FACT.SET (110)	80.00	36.00
❑ 1T Marcus Dupree RC**	.15	.07
❑ 2T Jerry Kauric	.15	.07
❑ 3T Everson Walls	.15	.07
❑ 4T Elliott Smith	.15	.07
❑ 5T Donald Evans RC UER (Misspelled Pittsburg on card back)	.30	.14
❑ 6T Jerry Holmes	.15	.07
❑ 7T Dan Stryzinski RC	.15	.07
❑ 8T Gerald McNeil	.15	.07
❑ 9T Rick Tuten RC	.15	.07
❑ 10T Mickey Shuler	.15	.07
❑ 11T Jay Novacek	.60	.25
❑ 12T Eric Williams RC	.15	.07
❑ 13T Stanley Morgan	.15	.07
❑ 14T Wayne Haddix RC	.15	.07
❑ 15T Gary Anderson RB	.15	.07
❑ 16T Stan Humphries RC	.60	.25
❑ 17T Raymond Clayborn	.15	.07
❑ 18T Mark Boyer RC	.15	.07
❑ 19T Dave Waymer	.15	.07
❑ 20T Andre Rison	.60	.25
❑ 21T Daniel Stubbs	.15	.07
❑ 22T Mike Rozier	.15	.07
❑ 23T Damian Johnson	.15	.07
❑ 24T Don Smith RBK RC	.15	.07
❑ 25T Max Montoya	.15	.07
❑ 26T Terry Kinard	.15	.07
❑ 27T Herb Welch	.15	.07
❑ 28T Cliff Odom	.15	.07
❑ 29T John Kidd	.15	.07
❑ 30T Barry Word RC	.15	.07
❑ 31T Rich Karlis	.15	.07
❑ 32T Mike Baab	.15	.07
❑ 33T Ronnie Harmon	.30	.14
❑ 34T Jeff Donaldson	.15	.07
❑ 35T Riki Ellison	.15	.07
❑ 36T Steve Walsh	.30	.14
❑ 37T Bill Lewis RC	.15	.07
❑ 38T Tim McKyer	.15	.07
❑ 39T James Wilder	.15	.07
❑ 40T Tony Paige	.15	.07
❑ 41T Derrick Fenner RC	.15	.07
❑ 42T Thane Gash RC	.15	.07
❑ 43T Dave Duerson	.15	.07
❑ 44T Clarence Weathers	.15	.07
❑ 45T Matt Bahr	.15	.07
❑ 46T Alonzo Highsmith	.15	.07
❑ 47T Joe Kelly	.15	.07
❑ 48T Chris Hinton	.15	.07
❑ 49T Bobby Humphery	.15	.07
❑ 50T Greg Bell	.15	.07
❑ 51T Fred Smerlas	.15	.07
❑ 52T Walter Stanley	.15	.07
❑ 53T Jim Skow	.15	.07
❑ 54T Renaldo Turnbull	.15	.07
❑ 55T Bern Brostek	.15	.07
❑ 56T Charles Wilson RC	.15	.07
❑ 57T Keith McCants	.15	.07
❑ 58T Alexander Wright	.30	.14
❑ 59T Ian Beckles RC	.15	.07
❑ 60T Eric Davis RC	.30	.14
❑ 61T Chris Singleton	.15	.07
❑ 62T Rob Moore RC	2.50	1.10
❑ 63T Darion Conner	.30	.14
❑ 64T Tim Grunhard	.15	.07
❑ 65T Junior Seau	6.00	2.70
❑ 66T Tony Stargell RC	.15	.07
❑ 67T Anthony Thompson	.15	.07
❑ 68T Cortez Kennedy	.60	.25
❑ 69T Darrell Thompson	.15	.07
❑ 70T Calvin Williams RC	.60	.25
❑ 71T Rodney Hampton	.60	.25
❑ 72T Terry Wooden	.15	.07
❑ 73T Leo Goeas RC	.15	.07
❑ 74T Ken Willis	.15	.07
❑ 75T Ricky Proehl	.60	.25
❑ 76T Steve Christie RC	.15	.07
❑ 77T Andre Ware	.60	.25
❑ 78T Jeff George	2.50	1.10
❑ 79T Walter Wilson	.15	.07
❑ 80T Johnny Bailey RC	.15	.07
❑ 81T Harold Green	.30	.14
❑ 82T Mark Carrier	.60	.25
❑ 83T Frank Cornish	.15	.07
❑ 84T James Williams	.15	.07
❑ 85T James Francis RC	.15	.07
❑ 86T Percy Snow	.15	.07
❑ 87T Anthony Johnson	.60	.25
❑ 88T Tim Ryan	.15	.07
❑ 89T Dan Owens RC	.15	.07
❑ 90T Aaron Wallace RC	.15	.07
❑ 91T Steve Broussard	.15	.07
❑ 92T Eric Green	.15	.07
❑ 93T Blair Thomas	.30	.14
❑ 94T Robert Blackmon RC	.15	.07
❑ 95T Alan Grant RC	.15	.07
❑ 96T Andre Collins	.15	.07
❑ 97T Dexter Carter	.15	.07
❑ 98T Reggie Cobb RC	.15	.07
❑ 99T Dennis Brown	.15	.07
❑ 100T Kenny Davidson RC	.15	.07
❑ 101T Emmitt Smith RC	60.00	27.00
❑ 102T Jeff Alm	.15	.07
❑ 103T Alton Montgomery	.15	.07
❑ 104T Tony Bennett	.60	.25
❑ 105T Johnny Johnson RC	.30	.14
❑ 106T Leroy Hoard RC	.60	.25
❑ 107T Ray Agnew	.15	.07
❑ 108T Richmond Webb	.15	.07
❑ 109T Keith Sims	.15	.07
❑ 110T Barry Foster	.60	.25

1991 Score

	Nm-Mt	Ex-Mt
COMPLETE SET (686)	8.00	3.60
COMP.FACT.SET (690)	15.00	6.75
❑ 1 Joe Montana	1.25	.55
❑ 2 Eric Allen	.04	.02
❑ 3 Rohn Stark	.04	.02
❑ 4 Frank Reich	.10	.05
❑ 5 Derrick Thomas	.25	.11
❑ 6 Mike Singletary	.10	.05

❑ 7 Boomer Esiason	.10	.05
❑ 8 Matt Millen	.10	.05
❑ 9 Chris Spielman	.10	.05
❑ 10 Gerald McNeil	.04	.02
❑ 11 Nick Lowery	.04	.02
❑ 12 Randall Cunningham	.25	.11
❑ 13 Marion Butts	.10	.05
❑ 14 Tim Brown	.25	.11
❑ 15 Emmitt Smith	2.00	.90
❑ 16 Rich Camarillo	.04	.02
❑ 17 Mike Merriweather	.04	.02
❑ 18 Derrick Fenner	.04	.02
❑ 19 Clay Matthews	.10	.05
❑ 20 Barry Sanders	1.25	.55
❑ 21 James Brooks	.10	.05
❑ 22 Alton Montgomery	.04	.02
❑ 23 Steve Atwater	.04	.02
❑ 24 Ron Morris	.04	.02
❑ 25 Brad Muster	.04	.02
❑ 26 Andre Rison	.10	.05
❑ 27 Brian Brennan	.04	.02
❑ 28 Leonard Smith	.04	.02
❑ 29 Kevin Butler	.04	.02
❑ 30 Tim Harris	.04	.02
❑ 31 Jay Novacek	.25	.11
❑ 32 Eddie Murray	.04	.02
❑ 33 Keith Woodside	.04	.02
❑ 34 Ray Crockett RC	.04	.02
❑ 35 Eugene Lockhart	.04	.02
❑ 36 Bill Romanowski	.04	.02
❑ 37 Eddie Brown	.04	.02
❑ 38 Eugene Daniel	.04	.02
❑ 39 Scott Fulhage	.04	.02
❑ 40 Harold Green	.10	.05
❑ 41 Mark Jackson	.04	.02
❑ 42 Sterling Sharpe	.25	.11
❑ 43 Mel Gray	.10	.05
❑ 44 Jerry Holmes	.04	.02
❑ 45 Allen Pinkett	.04	.02
❑ 46 Warren Powers	.04	.02
❑ 47 Rodney Peete	.10	.05
❑ 48 Lorenzo White	.04	.02
❑ 49 Dan Owens	.04	.02
❑ 50 James Francis	.04	.02
❑ 51 Ken Norton	.10	.05
❑ 52 Ed West	.04	.02
❑ 53 Andre Reed	.10	.05
❑ 54 John Grimsley	.04	.02
❑ 55 Michael Cofer	.04	.02
❑ 56 Chris Doleman	.04	.02
❑ 57 Pat Swilling	.10	.05
❑ 58 Jessie Tuggle	.04	.02
❑ 59 Mike Johnson	.04	.02
❑ 60 Steve Walsh	.04	.02
❑ 61 Sam Mills	.04	.02
❑ 62 Don Mosebar	.04	.02
❑ 63 Jay Hilgenberg	.04	.02
❑ 64 Cleveland Gary	.04	.02
❑ 65 Andre Tippett	.04	.02
❑ 66 Tom Newberry	.04	.02
❑ 67 Maurice Hurst	.04	.02
❑ 68 Louis Oliver	.04	.02
❑ 69 Fred Marion	.04	.02
❑ 70 Christian Okoye	.04	.02
❑ 71 Marv Cook	.04	.02
❑ 72 Darryl Talley	.04	.02
❑ 73 Rick Fenney	.04	.02
❑ 74 Kelvin Martin	.04	.02
❑ 75 Howie Long	.25	.11
❑ 76 Steve Wisniewski	.04	.02
❑ 77 Karl Mecklenburg	.04	.02
❑ 78 Dan Saleaumua	.04	.02
❑ 79 Ray Childress	.04	.02
❑ 80 Henry Ellard	.10	.05
❑ 81 Ernest Givins UER (3rd on Oilers in receiving, not 4th)	.10	.05
❑ 82 Ferrell Edmunds	.04	.02
❑ 83 Steve Jordan	.04	.02
❑ 84 Tony Mandarich	.04	.02
❑ 85 Eric Martin	.04	.02
❑ 86 Rich Gannon	.25	.11
❑ 87 Irving Fryar	.10	.05
❑ 88 Tom Rathman	.04	.02
❑ 89 Dan Hampton	.10	.05
❑ 90 Barry Word	.04	.02
❑ 91 Kevin Greene	.10	.05
❑ 92 Sean Landeta	.04	.02
❑ 93 Trace Armstrong	.04	.02
❑ 94 Dennis Byrd	.04	.02
❑ 95 Timm Rosenbach	.04	.02
❑ 96 Anthony Toney	.04	.02
❑ 97 Tim Krumrie	.04	.02
❑ 98 Jerry Ball	.04	.02
❑ 99 Tim Green	.04	.02
❑ 100 Bo Jackson	.30	.14
❑ 101 Myron Guyton	.04	.02
❑ 102 Mike Mularkey	.04	.02
❑ 103 Jerry Gray	.04	.02
❑ 104 Scott Stephen RC	.04	.02
❑ 105 Anthony Bell	.04	.02
❑ 106 Lomas Brown	.04	.02
❑ 107 David Little	.04	.02
❑ 108 Brad Baxter	.04	.02
❑ 109 Freddie Joe Nunn	.04	.02
❑ 110 Dave Meggett	.10	.05
❑ 111 Mark Rypien	.10	.05
❑ 112 Warren Williams	.04	.02
❑ 113 Ron Rivera	.04	.02
❑ 114 Terance Mathis	.10	.05
❑ 115 Anthony Munoz	.10	.05
❑ 116 Jeff Bryant	.04	.02
❑ 117 Issiac Holt	.04	.02
❑ 118 Steve Sewell	.04	.02
❑ 119 Tim Newton	.04	.02
❑ 120 Emile Harry	.04	.02
❑ 121 Gary Anderson K	.04	.02
❑ 122 Mark Lee	.04	.02
❑ 123 Alfred Anderson	.04	.02
❑ 124 Anthony Blaylock	.04	.02
❑ 125 Earnest Byner	.04	.02
❑ 126 Bill Maas	.04	.02
❑ 127 Keith Taylor	.04	.02
❑ 128 Cliff Odom	.04	.02
❑ 129 Bob Golic	.04	.02
❑ 130 Bart Oates	.04	.02
❑ 131 Jim Arnold	.04	.02
❑ 132 Jeff Herrod	.04	.02
❑ 133 Bruce Armstrong	.04	.02
❑ 134 Craig Heyward	.10	.05
❑ 135 Joey Browner	.04	.02
❑ 136 Darren Comeaux	.04	.02
❑ 137 Pat Beach	.04	.02
❑ 138 Dalton Hilliard	.04	.02
❑ 139 David Treadwell	.04	.02
❑ 140 Gary Anderson RB	.04	.02
❑ 141 Eugene Robinson	.04	.02
❑ 142 Scott Case	.04	.02
❑ 143 Paul Farren	.04	.02
❑ 144 Gill Fenerty	.04	.02
❑ 145 Tim Irwin	.04	.02
❑ 146 Norm Johnson	.04	.02
❑ 147 Willie Gault	.10	.05
❑ 148 Clarence Verdin	.04	.02
❑ 149 Jeff Uhlenhake	.04	.02
❑ 150 Erik McMillan	.04	.02
❑ 151 Kevin Ross	.04	.02
❑ 152 Pepper Johnson	.04	.02
❑ 153 Bryan Hinkle	.04	.02
❑ 154 Gary Clark	.25	.11
❑ 155 Robert Delpino	.04	.02
❑ 156 Doug Smith	.04	.02
❑ 157 Chris Martin	.04	.02
❑ 158 Ray Berry	.04	.02
❑ 159 Steve Christie	.04	.02
❑ 160 Don Smith	.04	.02
❑ 161 Greg McMurtry	.04	.02
❑ 162 Jack Del Rio	.10	.05
❑ 163 Floyd Dixon	.04	.02
❑ 164 Buford McGee	.04	.02
❑ 165 Brett Maxie	.04	.02
❑ 166 Morten Andersen	.04	.02
❑ 167 Kent Hull	.04	.02
❑ 168 Skip McClendon	.04	.02
❑ 169 Keith Sims	.04	.02
❑ 170 Leonard Marshall	.04	.02
❑ 171 Tony Woods	.04	.02
❑ 172 Byron Evans	.04	.02
❑ 173 Rob Burnett RC	.10	.05
❑ 174 Tory Epps	.04	.02
❑ 175 Toi Cook RC	.04	.02
❑ 176 John Elliott	.04	.02
❑ 177 Tommie Agee	.04	.02
❑ 178 Keith Van Horne	.04	.02
❑ 179 Dennis Smith	.04	.02
❑ 180 James Lofton	.10	.05
❑ 181 Art Monk	.10	.05
❑ 182 Anthony Carter	.10	.05
❑ 183 Louis Lipps	.04	.02
❑ 184 Bruce Hill	.04	.02
❑ 185 Michael Young	.04	.02
❑ 186 Eric Green	.04	.02
❑ 187 Barney Bussey RC	.04	.02
❑ 188 Curtis Duncan	.04	.02
❑ 189 Robert Awalt	.04	.02
❑ 190 Johnny Johnson	.04	.02
❑ 191 Jeff Cross	.04	.02
❑ 192 Keith McKeller	.04	.02
❑ 193 Robert Brown	.04	.02
❑ 194 Vincent Brown	.04	.02
❑ 195 Calvin Williams	.10	.05
❑ 196 Sean Jones	.10	.05
❑ 197 Willie Drewrey	.04	.02
❑ 198 Bubba McDowell	.04	.02
❑ 199 Al Noga	.04	.02
❑ 200 Ronnie Lott	.10	.05
❑ 201 Warren Moon	.25	.11
❑ 202 Chris Hinton	.04	.02
❑ 203 Jim Sweeney	.04	.02
❑ 204 Wayne Haddix	.04	.02
❑ 205 Tim Jorden RC	.04	.02
❑ 206 Marvin Allen	.04	.02
❑ 207 Jim Morrissey RC	.04	.02
❑ 208 Ben Smith	.04	.02
❑ 209 William White	.04	.02
❑ 210 Jim C. Jensen	.04	.02
❑ 211 Doug Reed	.04	.02
❑ 212 Ethan Horton	.04	.02
❑ 213 Chris Jacke	.04	.02
❑ 214 Johnny Hector	.04	.02
❑ 215 Drew Hill UER (Tied for the NFC lead, should say AFC)	.04	.02
❑ 216 Roy Green	.04	.02
❑ 217 Dean Steinkuhler	.04	.02
❑ 218 Cedric Mack	.04	.02
❑ 219 Chris Miller	.10	.05
❑ 220 Keith Byars	.04	.02
❑ 221 Lewis Billups	.04	.02
❑ 222 Roger Craig	.10	.05
❑ 223 Shaun Gayle	.04	.02
❑ 224 Mike Rozier	.04	.02
❑ 225 Troy Aikman	.75	.35
❑ 226 Bobby Humphrey	.04	.02
❑ 227 Eugene Marve	.04	.02
❑ 228 Michael Carter	.04	.02
❑ 229 Richard Johnson RC	.04	.02
❑ 230 Billy Joe Tolliver	.04	.02
❑ 231 Mark Murphy	.04	.02
❑ 232 John L. Williams	.04	.02
❑ 233 Ronnie Harmon	.04	.02
❑ 234 Thurman Thomas	.25	.11
❑ 235 Martin Mayhew	.04	.02
❑ 236 Richmond Webb	.04	.02
❑ 237 Gerald Riggs UER (Earnest Byner misspelled as Ernest)	.10	.05
❑ 238 Mike Prior	.04	.02
❑ 239 Mike Gann	.04	.02
❑ 240 Alvin Walton	.04	.02
❑ 241 Tim McGee	.04	.02
❑ 242 Bruce Matthews	.10	.05
❑ 243 Johnny Holland	.04	.02
❑ 244 Martin Bayless	.04	.02
❑ 245 Eric Metcalf	.10	.05
❑ 246 John Alt	.04	.02
❑ 247 Max Montoya	.04	.02
❑ 248 Rod Bernstine	.04	.02
❑ 249 Paul Gruber	.04	.02
❑ 250 Charles Haley	.10	.05
❑ 251 Scott Norwood	.04	.02
❑ 252 Michael Haddix	.04	.02

❑	253	Ricky Sanders	.04	.02
❑	254	Ervin Randle	.04	.02
❑	255	Duane Bickett	.04	.02
❑	256	Mike Munchak	.10	.05
❑	257	Keith Jones	.04	.02
❑	258	Riki Ellison	.04	.02
❑	259	Vince Newsome	.04	.02
❑	260	Lee Williams	.04	.02
❑	261	Steve Smith	.04	.02
❑	262	Sam Clancy	.04	.02
❑	263	Pierce Holt	.04	.02
❑	264	Jim Harbaugh	.25	.11
❑	265	Dino Hackett	.04	.02
❑	266	Andy Heck	.04	.02
❑	267	Leo Goeas	.04	.02
❑	268	Russ Grimm	.04	.02
❑	269	Gill Byrd	.04	.02
❑	270	Neal Anderson	.10	.05
❑	271	Jackie Slater	.04	.02
❑	272	Joe Nash	.04	.02
❑	273	Todd Bowles	.04	.02
❑	274	D.J. Dozier	.04	.02
❑	275	Kevin Fagan	.04	.02
❑	276	Don Warren	.04	.02
❑	277	Jim Jeffcoat	.04	.02
❑	278	Bruce Smith	.25	.11
❑	279	Cortez Kennedy	.25	.11
❑	280	Thane Gash	.04	.02
❑	281	Perry Kemp	.04	.02
❑	282	John Taylor	.10	.05
❑	283	Stephone Paige	.04	.02
❑	284	Paul Skansi	.04	.02
❑	285	Shawn Collins	.04	.02
❑	286	Mervyn Fernandez	.04	.02
❑	287	Daniel Stubbs	.04	.02
❑	288	Chip Lohmiller	.04	.02
❑	289	Brian Blades	.10	.05
❑	290	Mark Carrier WR	.25	.11
❑	291	Carl Zander	.04	.02
❑	292	David Wyman	.04	.02
❑	293	Jeff Bostic	.04	.02
❑	294	Irv Pankey	.04	.02
❑	295	Keith Millard	.04	.02
❑	296	Jamie Mueller	.04	.02
❑	297	Bill Fralic	.04	.02
❑	298	Wendell Davis	.04	.02
❑	299	Ken Clarke	.04	.02
❑	300	Wymon Henderson	.04	.02
❑	301	Jeff Campbell	.04	.02
❑	302	Cody Carlson RC	.04	.02
❑	303	Matt Brock RC	.04	.02
❑	304	Maurice Carthon	.04	.02
❑	305	Scott Mersereau RC	.04	.02
❑	306	Steve Wright RC	.04	.02
❑	307	J.B. Brown	.04	.02
❑	308	Ricky Reynolds	.04	.02
❑	309	Darryl Pollard	.04	.02
❑	310	Donald Evans	.04	.02
❑	311	Nick Bell RC	.04	.02
❑	312	Pat Harlow RC	.04	.02
❑	313	Dan McGwire RC	.04	.02
❑	314	Mike Dumas RC	.04	.02
❑	315	Mike Croel RC	.04	.02
❑	316	Chris Smith RC	.04	.02
❑	317	Kenny Walker RC	.04	.02
❑	318	Todd Lyght RC	.04	.02
❑	319	Mike Stonebreaker	.04	.02
❑	320	Randall Cunningham 90	.10	.05
❑	321	Terance Mathis 90	.25	.11
❑	322	Gaston Green 90	.04	.02
❑	323	Johnny Bailey 90	.04	.02
❑	324	Donnie Elder 90	.04	.02
❑	325	Dwight Stone 90 UER (No '91 copyright on card back)	.04	.02
❑	326	J.J. Birden 90 RC	.10	.05
❑	327	Alexander Wright 90	.04	.02
❑	328	Eric Metcalf 90	.10	.05
❑	329	Andre Rison TL	.10	.05
❑	330	Warren Moon TL UER (Not Blanda's record, should be Van Brocklin)	.10	.05
❑	331	Steve Tasker DT	.04	.02
❑	332	Mel Gray DT	.10	.05
❑	333	Nick Lowery DT	.04	.02
❑	334	Sean Landeta DT	.04	.02
❑	335	David Fulcher DT	.04	.02
❑	336	Joey Browner DT	.04	.02
❑	337	Albert Lewis DT	.04	.02
❑	338	Rod Woodson DT	.10	.05
❑	339	Shane Conlan DT	.04	.02
❑	340	Pepper Johnson DT	.04	.02
❑	341	Chris Spielman DT	.04	.02
❑	342	Derrick Thomas DT	.10	.05
❑	343	Ray Childress DT	.04	.02
❑	344	Reggie White DT	.10	.05
❑	345	Bruce Smith DT	.10	.05
❑	346	Darrell Green	.04	.02
❑	347	Ray Bentley	.04	.02
❑	348	Herschel Walker	.10	.05
❑	349	Rodney Holman	.04	.02
❑	350	Al Toon	.10	.05
❑	351	Harry Hamilton	.04	.02
❑	352	Albert Lewis	.04	.02
❑	353	Renaldo Turnbull	.04	.02
❑	354	Junior Seau	.25	.11
❑	355	Merril Hoge	.04	.02
❑	356	Shane Conlan	.04	.02
❑	357	Jay Schroeder	.04	.02
❑	358	Steve Broussard	.04	.02
❑	359	Mark Bavaro	.04	.02
❑	360	Jim Lachey	.04	.02
❑	361	Greg Townsend	.04	.02
❑	362	Dave Krieg	.10	.05
❑	363	Jessie Hester	.04	.02
❑	364	Steve Tasker	.10	.05
❑	365	Ron Hall	.04	.02
❑	366	Pat Leahy	.04	.02
❑	367	Jim Everett	.10	.05
❑	368	Felix Wright	.04	.02
❑	369	Ricky Proehl	.04	.02
❑	370	Anthony Miller	.10	.05
❑	371	Keith Jackson	.10	.05
❑	372	Pete Stoyanovich	.04	.02
❑	373	Tommy Kane	.04	.02
❑	374	Richard Johnson	.04	.02
❑	375	Randall McDaniel	.04	.02
❑	376	John Stephens	.04	.02
❑	377	Haywood Jeffires	.10	.05
❑	378	Rodney Hampton	.25	.11
❑	379	Tim Grunhard	.04	.02
❑	380	Jerry Rice	.75	.35
❑	381	Ken Harvey	.10	.05
❑	382	Vaughan Johnson	.04	.02
❑	383	J.T. Smith	.04	.02
❑	384	Carnell Lake	.04	.02
❑	385	Dan Marino	1.25	.55
❑	386	Kyle Clifton	.04	.02
❑	387	Wilber Marshall	.04	.02
❑	388	Pete Holohan	.04	.02
❑	389	Gary Plummer	.04	.02
❑	390	William Perry	.10	.05
❑	391	Mark Robinson	.04	.02
❑	392	Nate Odomes	.04	.02
❑	393	Ickey Woods	.04	.02
❑	394	Reyna Thompson	.04	.02
❑	395	Deion Sanders	.40	.18
❑	396	Harris Barton	.04	.02
❑	397	Sammie Smith	.04	.02
❑	398	Vinny Testaverde	.10	.05
❑	399	Ray Donaldson	.04	.02
❑	400	Tim McKyer	.04	.02
❑	401	Nesby Glasgow	.04	.02
❑	402	Brent Williams	.04	.02
❑	403	Rob Moore	.25	.11
❑	404	Bubby Brister	.04	.02
❑	405	David Fulcher	.04	.02
❑	406	Reggie Cobb	.04	.02
❑	407	Jerome Brown	.04	.02
❑	408	Erik Howard	.04	.02
❑	409	Tony Paige	.04	.02
❑	410	John Elway	1.25	.55
❑	411	Charles Mann	.04	.02
❑	412	Luis Sharpe	.04	.02
❑	413	Hassan Jones	.04	.02
❑	414	Frank Minnifield	.04	.02
❑	415	Steve DeBerg	.04	.02
❑	416	Mark Carrier DB	.10	.05
❑	417	Brian Jordan	.10	.05
❑	418	Reggie Langhorne	.04	.02
❑	419	Don Majkowski	.04	.02
❑	420	Marcus Allen	.25	.11
❑	421	Michael Brooks	.04	.02
❑	422	Vai Sikahema	.04	.02
❑	423	Dermontti Dawson	.04	.02
❑	424	Jacob Green	.04	.02
❑	425	Flipper Anderson	.04	.02
❑	426	Bill Brooks	.04	.02
❑	427	Keith McCants	.04	.02
❑	428	Ken O'Brien	.04	.02
❑	429	Fred Barnett	.25	.11
❑	430	Mark Duper	.10	.05
❑	431	Mark Kelso	.04	.02
❑	432	Leslie O'Neal	.10	.05
❑	433	Ottis Anderson	.10	.05
❑	434	Jesse Sapolu	.04	.02
❑	435	Gary Zimmerman	.04	.02
❑	436	Kevin Porter	.04	.02
❑	437	Anthony Thompson	.04	.02
❑	438	Robert Clark	.04	.02
❑	439	Chris Warren	.25	.11
❑	440	Gerald Williams	.04	.02
❑	441	Jim Skow	.04	.02
❑	442	Rick Donnelly	.04	.02
❑	443	Guy McIntyre	.04	.02
❑	444	Jeff Lageman	.04	.02
❑	445	John Offerdahl	.04	.02
❑	446	Clyde Simmons	.04	.02
❑	447	John Kidd	.04	.02
❑	448	Chip Banks	.04	.02
❑	449	Johnny Meads	.04	.02
❑	450	Rickey Jackson	.04	.02
❑	451	Lee Johnson	.04	.02
❑	452	Michael Irvin	.25	.11
❑	453	Leon Seals	.04	.02
❑	454	Darrell Thompson	.04	.02
❑	455	Everson Walls	.04	.02
❑	456	LeRoy Butler	.10	.05
❑	457	Marcus Dupree	.04	.02
❑	458	Kirk Lowdermilk	.04	.02
❑	459	Chris Singleton	.04	.02
❑	460	Seth Joyner	.10	.05
❑	461	Rueben Mayes UER (Hayes in bio should be Heyward)	.04	.02
❑	462	Ernie Jones	.04	.02
❑	463	Greg Kragen	.04	.02
❑	464	Bennie Blades	.04	.02
❑	465	Mark Bortz	.04	.02
❑	466	Tony Stargell	.04	.02
❑	467	Mike Cofer	.04	.02
❑	468	Randy Grimes	.04	.02
❑	469	Tim Worley	.04	.02
❑	470	Kevin Mack	.04	.02
❑	471	Wes Hopkins	.04	.02
❑	472	Will Wolford	.04	.02
❑	473	Sam Seale	.04	.02
❑	474	Jim Ritcher	.04	.02
❑	475	Jeff Hostetler	.25	.11
❑	476	Mitchell Price RC	.04	.02
❑	477	Ken Lanier	.04	.02
❑	478	Naz Worthen	.04	.02
❑	479	Ed Reynolds	.04	.02
❑	480	Mark Clayton	.10	.05
❑	481	Matt Bahr	.04	.02
❑	482	Gary Reasons	.04	.02
❑	483	David Szott	.04	.02
❑	484	Barry Foster	.10	.05
❑	485	Bruce Reimers	.04	.02
❑	486	Dean Biasucci	.04	.02
❑	487	Cris Carter	.50	.23
❑	488	Albert Bentley	.04	.02
❑	489	Robert Massey	.04	.02
❑	490	Al Smith	.04	.02
❑	491	Greg Lloyd	.25	.11
❑	492	Steve McMichael UER (Photo on back actually Dan Hampton)	.10	.05
❑	493	Jeff Wright RC	.04	.02
❑	494	Scott Davis	.04	.02
❑	495	Freeman McNeil	.04	.02
❑	496	Simon Fletcher	.04	.02

❑ 497	Terry McDaniel	.04	.02
❑ 498	Heath Sherman	.04	.02
❑ 499	Jeff Jaeger	.04	.02
❑ 500	Mark Collins	.04	.02
❑ 501	Tim Goad	.04	.02
❑ 502	Jeff George	.25	.11
❑ 503	Jimmie Jones	.04	.02
❑ 504	Henry Thomas	.04	.02
❑ 505	Steve Young	.75	.35
❑ 506	William Roberts	.04	.02
❑ 507	Neil Smith	.25	.11
❑ 508	Mike Saxon	.04	.02
❑ 509	Johnny Bailey	.04	.02
❑ 510	Broderick Thomas	.04	.02
❑ 511	Wade Wilson	.10	.05
❑ 512	Hart Lee Dykes	.04	.02
❑ 513	Hardy Nickerson	.10	.05
❑ 514	Tim McDonald	.04	.02
❑ 515	Frank Cornish	.04	.02
❑ 516	Jarvis Williams	.04	.02
❑ 517	Carl Lee	.04	.02
❑ 518	Carl Banks	.04	.02
❑ 519	Mike Golic	.04	.02
❑ 520	Brian Noble	.04	.02
❑ 521	James Hasty	.04	.02
❑ 522	Bubba Paris	.04	.02
❑ 523	Kevin Walker RC	.04	.02
❑ 524	William Fuller	.10	.05
❑ 525	Eddie Anderson	.04	.02
❑ 526	Roger Ruzek	.04	.02
❑ 527	Robert Blackmon	.04	.02
❑ 528	Vince Buck	.04	.02
❑ 529	Lawrence Taylor	.25	.11
❑ 530	Reggie Roby	.04	.02
❑ 531	Doug Riesenberg	.04	.02
❑ 532	Joe Jacoby	.04	.02
❑ 533	Kirby Jackson RC	.04	.02
❑ 534	Robb Thomas	.04	.02
❑ 535	Don Griffin	.04	.02
❑ 536	Andre Waters	.04	.02
❑ 537	Marc Logan	.04	.02
❑ 538	James Thornton	.04	.02
❑ 539	Ray Agnew	.04	.02
❑ 540	Frank Stams	.04	.02
❑ 541	Brett Perriman	.25	.11
❑ 542	Andre Ware	.10	.05
❑ 543	Kevin Haverdink	.04	.02
❑ 544	Greg Jackson RC	.04	.02
❑ 545	Tunch Ilkin	.04	.02
❑ 546	Dexter Carter	.04	.02
❑ 547	Rod Woodson	.25	.11
❑ 548	Donnell Woolford	.04	.02
❑ 549	Mark Boyer	.04	.02
❑ 550	Jeff Query	.04	.02
❑ 551	Burt Grossman	.04	.02
❑ 552	Mike Kenn	.04	.02
❑ 553	Richard Dent	.10	.05
❑ 554	Gaston Green	.04	.02
❑ 555	Phil Simms	.10	.05
❑ 556	Brent Jones	.25	.11
❑ 557	Ronnie Lippett	.04	.02
❑ 558	Mike Horan	.04	.02
❑ 559	Danny Noonan	.04	.02
❑ 560	Reggie White	.25	.11
❑ 561	Rufus Porter	.04	.02
❑ 562	Aaron Wallace	.04	.02
❑ 563	Vance Johnson	.04	.02
❑ 564A	Aaron Craver RC ERR (No copyright line on back)	.04	.02
❑ 564B	Aaron Craver COR RC	.04	.02
❑ 565A	R.Maryland RC ERR No copyright line on back	.25	.11
❑ 565B	R.Maryland COR RC	.25	.11
❑ 566	Paul Justin RC	.04	.02
❑ 567	Walter Dean	.04	.02
❑ 568	Herman Moore RC	.25	.11
❑ 569	Bill Musgrave RC	.04	.02
❑ 570	Rob Carpenter RC	.04	.02
❑ 571	Greg Lewis RC	.04	.02
❑ 572	Ed King RC	.04	.02
❑ 573	Ernie Mills RC	.10	.05
❑ 574	Jake Reed RC	.50	.23
❑ 575	Ricky Watters RC	1.50	.70
❑ 576	Derek Russell RC	.04	.02
❑ 577	Shawn Moore RC	.04	.02
❑ 578	Eric Bieniemy RC	.04	.02
❑ 579	Chris Zorich RC	.25	.11
❑ 580	Scott Miller	.04	.02
❑ 581	Jarrod Bunch RC	.04	.02
❑ 582	Ricky Ervins RC	.10	.05
❑ 583	Browning Nagle RC	.04	.02
❑ 584	Eric Turner RC	.10	.05
❑ 585	William Thomas RC	.04	.02
❑ 586	Stanley Richard RC	.04	.02
❑ 587	Adrian Cooper RC	.04	.02
❑ 588	Harvey Williams RC	.25	.11
❑ 589	Alvin Harper RC	.25	.11
❑ 590	John Carney	.04	.02
❑ 591	Mark Vander Poel RC	.04	.02
❑ 592	Mike Pritchard RC	.25	.11
❑ 593	Eric Moten RC	.04	.02
❑ 594	Moe Gardner RC	.04	.02
❑ 595	Wesley Carroll RC	.04	.02
❑ 596	Eric Swann RC	.25	.11
❑ 597	Joe Kelly	.04	.02
❑ 598	Steve Jackson RC	.04	.02
❑ 599	Kelvin Pritchett RC	.10	.05
❑ 600	Jesse Campbell RC	.04	.02
❑ 601	Darryll Lewis RC UER (Name misspelled Darryl)	.10	.05
❑ 602	Howard Griffith	.04	.02
❑ 603	Blaise Bryant	.04	.02
❑ 604	Vinnie Clark RC	.04	.02
❑ 605	Mel Agee RC	.04	.02
❑ 606	Bobby Wilson RC	.04	.02
❑ 607	Kevin Donnalley RC	.04	.02
❑ 608	Randal Hill RC	.10	.05
❑ 609	Stan Thomas	.04	.02
❑ 610	Mike Heldt	.04	.02
❑ 611	Brett Favre RC	8.00	3.60
❑ 612	Lawrence Dawsey RC UER (Went to Florida State not Florida)	.10	.05
❑ 613	Dennis Gibson	.04	.02
❑ 614	Dean Dingman	.04	.02
❑ 615	Bruce Pickens RC	.04	.02
❑ 616	Todd Marinovich RC	.04	.02
❑ 617	Gene Atkins	.04	.02
❑ 618	Marcus Dupree (Comeback Player)	.04	.02
❑ 619	Warren Moon (Man of the Year)	.10	.05
❑ 620	Joe Montana MVP	.50	.23
❑ 621	Neal Anderson MVP	.04	.02
❑ 622	James Brooks MVP	.10	.05
❑ 623	Thurman Thomas MVP	.10	.05
❑ 624	Bobby Humphrey MVP	.04	.02
❑ 625	Kevin Mack MVP	.04	.02
❑ 626	Mark Carrier WR MVP	.04	.02
❑ 627	Johnny Johnson MVP	.04	.02
❑ 628	Marion Butts MVP	.10	.05
❑ 629	Steve DeBerg MVP	.04	.02
❑ 630	Jeff George MVP	.10	.05
❑ 631	Troy Aikman MVP	.40	.18
❑ 632	Dan Marino MVP	.50	.23
❑ 633	R.Cunningham MVP	.10	.05
❑ 634	Andre Rison MVP	.10	.05
❑ 635	Pepper Johnson MVP	.04	.02
❑ 636	Pat Leahy MVP	.04	.02
❑ 637	Barry Sanders MVP	.50	.23
❑ 638	Warren Moon MVP	.10	.05
❑ 639	Sterling Sharpe MVP	.04	.02
❑ 640	Bruce Armstrong MVP	.04	.02
❑ 641	Bo Jackson MVP	.10	.05
❑ 642	Henry Ellard MVP	.10	.05
❑ 643	Earnest Byner MVP	.04	.02
❑ 644	Pat Swilling MVP	.04	.02
❑ 645	John L. Williams MVP	.04	.02
❑ 646	Rod Woodson MVP	.10	.05
❑ 647	Chris Doleman MVP	.04	.02
❑ 648	Joey Browner CC	.04	.02
❑ 649	Erik McMillan CC	.04	.02
❑ 650	David Fulcher CC	.04	.02
❑ 651A	Ronnie Lott CC ERR (Front 47, back 42)	.10	.05
❑ 651B	Ronnie Lott CC COR (Front 47, back 42 is now blacked out)	.10	.05
❑ 652	Louis Oliver CC	.04	.02
❑ 653	Mark Robinson CC	.04	.02
❑ 654	Dennis Smith CC	.04	.02
❑ 655	Reggie White SA ERR (listed as a QB)	.10	.05
❑ 656	Charles Haley SA	.04	.02
❑ 657	Leslie O'Neal SA	.10	.05
❑ 658	Kevin Greene SA	.10	.05
❑ 659	Dennis Byrd SA	.04	.02
❑ 660	Bruce Smith SA	.10	.05
❑ 661	Derrick Thomas SA	.10	.05
❑ 662	Steve DeBerg TL	.04	.02
❑ 663	Barry Sanders TL	.50	.23
❑ 664	Thurman Thomas TL	.10	.05
❑ 665	Jerry Rice TL	.40	.18
❑ 666	Derrick Thomas TL	.10	.05
❑ 667	Bruce Smith TL	.10	.05
❑ 668	Mark Carrier DB TL	.04	.02
❑ 669	Richard Johnson TL	.04	.02
❑ 670	Jan Stenerud HOF	.04	.02
❑ 671	Stan Jones HOF	.04	.02
❑ 672	John Hannah HOF	.04	.02
❑ 673	Tex Schramm HOF	.04	.02
❑ 674	Earl Campbell HOF	.25	.11
❑ 675	Mark Carrier and Emmitt Smith (Rookies of the Year)	.50	.23
❑ 676	Warren Moon DT	.10	.05
❑ 677	Barry Sanders DT	.50	.23
❑ 678	Thurman Thomas DT	.25	.11
❑ 679	Andre Reed DT	.10	.05
❑ 680	Andre Rison DT	.10	.05
❑ 681	Keith Jackson DT	.04	.02
❑ 682	Bruce Armstrong DT	.04	.02
❑ 683	Jim Lachey DT	.04	.02
❑ 684	Bruce Matthews DT	.04	.02
❑ 685	Mike Munchak DT	.04	.02
❑ 686	Don Mosebar DT	.04	.02
❑ B1	Jeff Hostetler SB	.25	.11
❑ B2	Matt Bahr SB	.04	.02
❑ B3	Ottis Anderson SB	.10	.05
❑ B4	Ottis Anderson SB	.10	.05

1999 Score

	Nm-Mt	Ex-Mt
COMPLETE SET (275)	60.00	27.00
COMP.SET w/o SP's (220)	15.00	6.75
❑ 1 Randy Moss	1.50	.70
❑ 2 Randall Cunningham	.60	.25
❑ 3 Cris Carter	.60	.25
❑ 4 Robert Smith	.60	.25
❑ 5 Jake Reed	.40	.18
❑ 6 Leroy Hoard	.25	.11
❑ 7 John Randle	.40	.18
❑ 8 Brett Favre	2.00	.90
❑ 9 Antonio Freeman	.60	.25
❑ 10 Dorsey Levens	.60	.25
❑ 11 Robert Brooks	.40	.18
❑ 12 Derrick Mayes	.40	.18
❑ 13 Mark Chmura	.40	.18
❑ 14 Darick Holmes	.25	.11
❑ 15 Vonnie Holliday	.25	.11
❑ 16 Mike Alstott	.60	.25
❑ 17 Warrick Dunn	.60	.25
❑ 18 Trent Dilfer	.40	.18

❑ 19 Jacquez Green	.25	.11
❑ 20 Reidel Anthony	.40	.18
❑ 21 Warren Sapp	.40	.18
❑ 22 Bert Emanuel	.40	.18
❑ 23 Curtis Enis	.25	.11
❑ 24 Curtis Conway	.40	.18
❑ 25 Bobby Engram	.40	.18
❑ 26 Erik Kramer	.40	.18
❑ 27 Moses Moreno	.25	.11
❑ 28 Edgar Bennett	.25	.11
❑ 29 Barry Sanders	2.00	.90
❑ 30 Charlie Batch	.60	.25
❑ 31 Herman Moore	.40	.18
❑ 32 Johnnie Morton	.40	.18
❑ 33 Germane Crowell	.25	.11
❑ 34 Terry Fair	.25	.11
❑ 35 Gary Brown	.25	.11
❑ 36 Kent Graham	.25	.11
❑ 37 Kerry Collins	.40	.18
❑ 38 Charles Way	.25	.11
❑ 39 Tiki Barber	.40	.18
❑ 40 Ike Hilliard	.25	.11
❑ 41 Joe Jurevicius	.40	.18
❑ 42 Michael Strahan	.40	.18
❑ 43 Jason Sehorn	.25	.11
❑ 44 Brad Johnson	.60	.25
❑ 45 Terry Allen	.40	.18
❑ 46 Skip Hicks	.25	.11
❑ 47 Michael Westbrook	.40	.18
❑ 48 Leslie Shepherd	.25	.11
❑ 49 Stephen Alexander	.25	.11
❑ 50 Albert Connell	.25	.11
❑ 51 Darrell Green	.40	.18
❑ 52 Jake Plummer	.40	.18
❑ 53 Adrian Murrell	.40	.18
❑ 54 Frank Sanders	.40	.18
❑ 55 Rob Moore	.40	.18
❑ 56 Larry Centers	.25	.11
❑ 57 Simeon Rice	.40	.18
❑ 58 Andre Wadsworth	.25	.11
❑ 59 Duce Staley	.60	.25
❑ 60 Charles Johnson	.25	.11
❑ 61 Charlie Garner	.40	.18
❑ 62 Bobby Hoying	.40	.18
❑ 63 Daryl Johnston	.40	.18
❑ 64 Emmitt Smith	1.25	.55
❑ 65 Troy Aikman	1.25	.55
❑ 66 Michael Irvin	.40	.18
❑ 67 Deion Sanders	.60	.25
❑ 68 Chris Warren	.25	.11
❑ 69 Darren Woodson	.25	.11
❑ 70 Rod Woodson	.40	.18
❑ 71 Travis Jervey	.25	.11
❑ 72 Jerry Rice	1.25	.55
❑ 73 Terrell Owens	.60	.25
❑ 74 Steve Young	.75	.35
❑ 75 Garrison Hearst	.40	.18
❑ 76 J.J. Stokes	.40	.18
❑ 77 Ken Norton	.25	.11
❑ 78 R.W. McQuarters	.25	.11
❑ 79 Bryant Young	.25	.11
❑ 80 Jamal Anderson	.60	.25
❑ 81 Chris Chandler	.40	.18
❑ 82 Terance Mathis	.40	.18
❑ 83 Tim Dwight	.60	.25
❑ 84 O.J. Santiago	.25	.11
❑ 85 Chris Calloway	.25	.11
❑ 86 Keith Brooking	.25	.11
❑ 87 Eddie Kennison	.40	.18
❑ 88 Willie Roaf	.25	.11
❑ 89 Cam Cleeland	.25	.11
❑ 90 Lamar Smith	.40	.18
❑ 91 Sean Dawkins	.25	.11
❑ 92 Tim Biakabutuka	.40	.18
❑ 93 Muhsin Muhammad	.40	.18
❑ 94 Steve Beuerlein	.25	.11
❑ 95 Rae Carruth	.25	.11
❑ 96 Wesley Walls	.40	.18
❑ 97 Kevin Greene	.40	.18
❑ 98 Trent Green	.60	.25
❑ 99 Tony Banks	.40	.18
❑ 100 Greg Hill	.25	.11
❑ 101 Robert Holcombe	.25	.11
❑ 102 Isaac Bruce	.60	.25
❑ 103 Amp Lee	.25	.11
❑ 104 Az-Zahir Hakim	.25	.11
❑ 105 Warren Moon	.60	.25
❑ 106 Jeff George	.40	.18
❑ 107 Rocket Ismail	.40	.18
❑ 108 Kordell Stewart	.40	.18
❑ 109 Jerome Bettis	.60	.25
❑ 110 Courtney Hawkins	.25	.11
❑ 111 Chris Fuamatu-Ma'afala	.25	.11
❑ 112 Levon Kirkland	.25	.11
❑ 113 Hines Ward	.60	.25
❑ 114 Will Blackwell	.25	.11
❑ 115 Corey Dillon	.60	.25
❑ 116 Carl Pickens	.40	.18
❑ 117 Neil O'Donnell	.40	.18
❑ 118 Jeff Blake	.40	.18
❑ 119 Darnay Scott	.25	.11
❑ 120 Takeo Spikes	.25	.11
❑ 121 Steve McNair	.60	.25
❑ 122 Frank Wycheck	.25	.11
❑ 123 Eddie George	.60	.25
❑ 124 Chris Sanders	.25	.11
❑ 125 Yancey Thigpen	.25	.11
❑ 126 Kevin Dyson	.40	.18
❑ 127 Blaine Bishop	.25	.11
❑ 128 Fred Taylor	.60	.25
❑ 129 Mark Brunell	.60	.25
❑ 130 Jimmy Smith	.40	.18
❑ 131 Keenan McCardell	.40	.18
❑ 132 Kyle Brady	.25	.11
❑ 133 Tavian Banks	.25	.11
❑ 134 James Stewart	.40	.18
❑ 135 Kevin Hardy	.25	.11
❑ 136 Jonathan Quinn	.25	.11
❑ 137 Jermaine Lewis	.40	.18
❑ 138 Priest Holmes	1.00	.45
❑ 139 Scott Mitchell	.40	.18
❑ 140 Eric Zeier	.40	.18
❑ 141 Patrick Johnson	.25	.11
❑ 142 Ray Lewis	.60	.25
❑ 143 Terry Kirby	.25	.11
❑ 144 Ty Detmer	.25	.11
❑ 145 Irv Smith	.25	.11
❑ 146 Chris Spielman	.25	.11
❑ 147 Antonio Langham	.25	.11
❑ 148 Dan Marino	2.00	.90
❑ 149 O.J. McDuffie	.40	.18
❑ 150 Oronde Gadsden	.40	.18
❑ 151 Karim Abdul-Jabbar	.40	.18
❑ 152 Yatil Green	.25	.11
❑ 153 Zach Thomas	.60	.25
❑ 154 John Avery	.25	.11
❑ 155 Lamar Thomas	.25	.11
❑ 156 Drew Bledsoe	.75	.35
❑ 157 Terry Glenn	.60	.25
❑ 158 Ben Coates	.40	.18
❑ 159 Shawn Jefferson	.25	.11
❑ 160 Sedrick Shaw	.25	.11
❑ 161 Tony Simmons	.25	.11
❑ 162 Ty Law	.40	.18
❑ 163 Robert Edwards	.25	.11
❑ 164 Curtis Martin	.60	.25
❑ 165 Keyshawn Johnson	.60	.25
❑ 166 Vinny Testaverde	.40	.18
❑ 167 Aaron Glenn	.25	.11
❑ 168 Wayne Chrebet	.40	.18
❑ 169 Dedric Ward	.25	.11
❑ 170 Peyton Manning	2.00	.90
❑ 171 Marshall Faulk	.75	.35
❑ 172 Marvin Harrison	.60	.25
❑ 173 Jerome Pathon	.25	.11
❑ 174 Ken Dilger	.25	.11
❑ 175 E.G. Green	.25	.11
❑ 176 Doug Flutie	.60	.25
❑ 177 Thurman Thomas	.40	.18
❑ 178 Andre Reed	.40	.18
❑ 179 Eric Moulds	.60	.25
❑ 180 Antowain Smith	.60	.25
❑ 181 Bruce Smith	.40	.18
❑ 182 Rob Johnson	.40	.18
❑ 183 Terrell Davis	.60	.25
❑ 184 John Elway	2.00	.90
❑ 185 Ed McCaffrey	.40	.18
❑ 186 Rod Smith	.40	.18
❑ 187 Shannon Sharpe	.40	.18
❑ 188 Marcus Nash	.25	.11
❑ 189 Brian Griese	.60	.25
❑ 190 Neil Smith	.40	.18
❑ 191 Bubby Brister	.25	.11
❑ 192 Ryan Leaf	.60	.25
❑ 193 Natrone Means	.40	.18
❑ 194 Mikhael Ricks	.25	.11
❑ 195 Junior Seau	.60	.25
❑ 196 Jim Harbaugh	.40	.18
❑ 197 Bryan Still	.25	.11
❑ 198 Freddie Jones	.25	.11
❑ 199 Andre Rison	.40	.18
❑ 200 Elvis Grbac	.40	.18
❑ 201 Byron Bam Morris	.25	.11
❑ 202 Rashaan Shehee	.25	.11
❑ 203 Kimble Anders	.40	.18
❑ 204 Donnell Bennett	.25	.11
❑ 205 Tony Gonzalez	.60	.25
❑ 206 Derrick Alexander WR	.40	.18
❑ 207 Jon Kitna	.60	.25
❑ 208 Ricky Watters	.40	.18
❑ 209 Joey Galloway	.40	.18
❑ 210 Ahman Green	.60	.25
❑ 211 Shawn Springs	.25	.11
❑ 212 Michael Sinclair	.25	.11
❑ 213 Napoleon Kaufman	.60	.25
❑ 214 Tim Brown	.60	.25
❑ 215 Charles Woodson	.60	.25
❑ 216 Harvey Williams	.25	.11
❑ 217 Jon Ritchie	.25	.11
❑ 218 Rich Gannon	.60	.25
❑ 219 Rickey Dudley	.25	.11
❑ 220 James Jett	.40	.18
❑ 221 Tim Couch RC	3.00	1.35
❑ 222 Ricky Williams RC	4.00	1.80
❑ 223 Donovan McNabb RC	10.00	4.50
❑ 224 Edgerrin James RC	8.00	3.60
❑ 225 Torry Holt RC	6.00	2.70
❑ 226 Daunte Culpepper RC	8.00	3.60
❑ 227 Akili Smith RC	2.00	.90
❑ 228 Champ Bailey RC	4.00	1.80
❑ 229 Chris Claiborne RC	1.25	.55
❑ 230 Chris McAlister RC	2.00	.90
❑ 231 Troy Edwards RC	2.00	.90
❑ 232 Jevon Kearse RC	5.00	2.20
❑ 233 Shaun King RC	2.00	.90
❑ 234 David Boston RC	3.00	1.35
❑ 235 Peerless Price RC	5.00	2.20
❑ 236 Cecil Collins RC	1.25	.55
❑ 237 Rob Konrad RC	2.00	.90
❑ 238 Cade McNown RC UER (college listed as UNLV)	2.00	.90
❑ 239 Shawn Bryson RC	3.00	1.35
❑ 240 Kevin Faulk RC	3.00	1.35
❑ 241 Scott Covington RC	3.00	1.35
❑ 242 James Johnson RC	2.00	.90
❑ 243 Mike Cloud RC	2.00	.90
❑ 244 Aaron Brooks RC	8.00	3.60
❑ 245 Sedrick Irvin RC	1.25	.55
❑ 246 Amos Zereoue RC	3.00	1.35
❑ 247 Jermaine Fazande RC	2.00	.90
❑ 248 Joe Germaine RC	2.00	.90
❑ 249 Brock Huard RC	3.00	1.35
❑ 250 Craig Yeast RC	2.00	.90
❑ 251 Travis McGriff RC	1.25	.55
❑ 252 D'Wayne Bates RC	2.00	.90
❑ 253 Na Brown RC	2.00	.90
❑ 254 Tai Streets RC	3.00	1.35
❑ 255 Andy Katzenmoyer RC	2.00	.90
❑ 256 Kevin Johnson RC	3.00	1.35
❑ 257 Joe Montgomery RC	2.00	.90
❑ 258 Karsten Bailey RC	2.00	.90
❑ 259 De'Mond Parker RC	1.25	.55
❑ 260 Reginald Kelly RC	1.25	.55
❑ 261 Eddie George AP	1.50	.70
❑ 262 Jamal Anderson AP	1.50	.70
❑ 263 Barry Sanders AP	6.00	2.70
❑ 264 Fred Taylor AP	1.50	.70
❑ 265 Keyshawn Johnson AP	1.50	.70
❑ 266 Jerry Rice AP	4.00	1.80
❑ 267 Doug Flutie AP	1.50	.70
❑ 268 Deion Sanders AP	1.50	.70
❑ 269 Randall Cunningham AP	1.50	.70

Card	Nm-Mt	Ex-Mt
❑ 270 Steve Young AP	2.50	1.10
❑ 271 John Elway GC Terrell Davis GC	5.00	2.20
❑ 272 Peyton Manning GC Marshall Faulk GC	5.00	2.20
❑ 273 Brett Favre GC Antonio Freeman GC	6.00	2.70
❑ 274 Troy Aikman GC Emmitt Smith GC	4.00	1.80
❑ 275 Cris Carter GC Randy Moss GC	4.00	1.80

1999 Score Supplemental

	Nm-Mt	Ex-Mt
COMPLETE SET (110)	25.00	11.00
COMP.FACT.SET (110)	30.00	13.50
❑ S1 Chris Greisen RC	1.00	.45
❑ S2 Sherdrick Bonner RC	.60	.25
❑ S3 Joel Makovicka RC	1.50	.70
❑ S4 Andy McCullough RC	.60	.25
❑ S5 Jeff Paulk RC	.60	.25
❑ S6 Brandon Stokley RC	2.00	.90
❑ S7 Sheldon Jackson RC	1.00	.45
❑ S8 Bobby Collins RC	.60	.25
❑ S9 Kamil Loud RC	.60	.25
❑ S10 Antoine Winfield RC	1.00	.45
❑ S11 Jerry Azumah RC	1.00	.45
❑ S12 James Allen RC	1.50	.70
❑ S13 Nick Williams RC	1.00	.45
❑ S14 Michael Basnight RC	.60	.25
❑ S15 Damon Griffin RC	1.00	.45
❑ S16 Ronnie Powell RC	.60	.25
❑ S17 Darrin Chiaverini RC	1.00	.45
❑ S18 Mark Campbell RC	1.00	.45
❑ S19 Mike Lucky RC	1.00	.45
❑ S20 Wane McGarity RC	.60	.25
❑ S21 Jason Tucker RC	1.00	.45
❑ S22 Ebenezer Ekuban RC	1.00	.45
❑ S23 Robert Thomas RC	1.00	.45
❑ S24 Dat Nguyen RC	1.00	.45
❑ S25 Olandis Gary RC	1.50	.70
❑ S26 Desmond Clark RC	1.50	.70
❑ S27 Andre Cooper RC	.60	.25
❑ S28 Chris Watson RC	.60	.25
❑ S29 Al Wilson RC	1.50	.70
❑ S30 Cory Sauter RC	.60	.25
❑ S31 Brock Olivo RC	.60	.25
❑ S32 Basil Mitchell RC	.60	.25
❑ S33 Matt Snider RC	.60	.25
❑ S34 Antuan Edwards RC	1.00	.45
❑ S35 Mike McKenzie RC	1.00	.45
❑ S36 Terrence Wilkins RC	1.00	.45
❑ S37 Fernando Bryant RC	1.00	.45
❑ S38 Larry Parker RC	1.50	.70
❑ S39 Autry Denson RC	1.00	.45
❑ S40 Jim Kleinsasser RC	1.50	.70
❑ S41 Michael Bishop RC	1.50	.70
❑ S42 Andy Katzenmoyer	.25	.11
❑ S43 Brett Bech RC	.60	.25
❑ S44 Sean Bennett RC	.60	.25
❑ S45 Dan Campbell RC	.60	.25
❑ S46 Ray Lucas RC	1.50	.70
❑ S47 Scott Dreisbach RC	1.00	.45
❑ S48 Cecil Martin RC	1.00	.45
❑ S49 Dameane Douglas RC	1.00	.45
❑ S50 Jed Weaver RC	1.00	.45
❑ S51 Jerame Tuman RC	1.00	.45
❑ S52 Steve Heiden RC	.60	.25
❑ S53 Jeff Garcia RC	4.00	1.80
❑ S54 Terry Jackson RC	1.00	.45
❑ S55 Charlie Rogers RC	1.00	.45
❑ S56 Lamar King RC	1.00	.45
❑ S57 Kurt Warner RC	8.00	3.60
❑ S58 Dre' Bly RC	1.50	.70
❑ S59 Justin Watson RC	.60	.25
❑ S60 Rabih Abdullah RC	1.00	.45
❑ S61 Martin Gramatica RC	.60	.25
❑ S62 Darnell McDonald RC	1.00	.45
❑ S63 Anthony McFarland RC	1.00	.45
❑ S64 Larry Brown TE RC	.60	.25
❑ S65 Kevin Daft RC	1.00	.45
❑ S66 Mike Sellers	.15	.07
❑ S67 Ken Oxendine	.15	.07
❑ S68 Errict Rhett	.25	.11
❑ S69 Stoney Case	.15	.07
❑ S70 Jonathan Linton	.15	.07
❑ S71 Marcus Robinson	1.00	.45
❑ S72 Shane Matthews	.25	.11
❑ S73 Cade McNown	1.00	.45
❑ S74 Akili Smith	.15	.07
❑ S75 Karim Abdul-Jabbar	.25	.11
❑ S76 Tim Couch	1.50	.70
❑ S77 Kevin Johnson	.40	.18
❑ S78 Ron Rivers	.15	.07
❑ S79 Bill Schroeder	.40	.18
❑ S80 Edgerrin James	2.50	1.10
❑ S81 Cecil Collins	.75	.35
❑ S82 Matthew Hatchette	.15	.07
❑ S83 Daunte Culpepper	2.50	1.10
❑ S84 Ricky Williams	1.25	.55
❑ S85 Tyrone Wheatley	.40	.18
❑ S86 Donovan McNabb	3.00	1.35
❑ S87 Marshall Faulk	.50	.23
❑ S88 Torry Holt	2.00	.90
❑ S89 Stephen Davis	.40	.18
❑ S90 Brad Johnson	.40	.18
❑ S91 Jake Plummer SS	.25	.11
❑ S92 Emmitt Smith SS	.75	.35
❑ S93 Troy Aikman SS	.75	.35
❑ S94 John Elway SS	1.25	.55
❑ S95 Terrell Davis SS	.40	.18
❑ S96 Barry Sanders SS	1.25	.55
❑ S97 Brett Favre SS	1.25	.55
❑ S98 Antonio Freeman SS	.40	.18
❑ S99 Peyton Manning SS	1.25	.55
❑ S100 Fred Taylor SS	.40	.18
❑ S101 Mark Brunell SS	.40	.18
❑ S102 Dan Marino SS	1.25	.55
❑ S103 Randy Moss SS	1.00	.45
❑ S104 Cris Carter SS	.40	.18
❑ S105 Drew Bledsoe SS	.50	.23
❑ S106 Terry Glenn SS	.40	.18
❑ S107 Keyshawn Johnson SS	.40	.18
❑ S108 Jerry Rice SS	.75	.35
❑ S109 Steve Young SS	.50	.23
❑ S110 Eddie George SS	.40	.18

2000 Score

	Nm-Mt	Ex-Mt
COMP.SET w/o SP's (220)	20.00	9.00
❑ 1 Michael Pittman	.25	.11
❑ 2 Jake Plummer	.40	.18
❑ 3 Rob Moore	.40	.18
❑ 4 David Boston	.60	.25
❑ 5 Frank Sanders	.40	.18
❑ 6 Jamal Anderson	.60	.25
❑ 7 Chris Chandler	.40	.18
❑ 8 Tim Dwight	.60	.25
❑ 9 Terance Mathis	.40	.18
❑ 10 Shawn Jefferson	.25	.11
❑ 11 Ashley Ambrose	.25	.11
❑ 12 Peter Boulware	.25	.11
❑ 13 Priest Holmes	.75	.35
❑ 14 Tony Banks	.40	.18
❑ 15 Qadry Ismail	.40	.18
❑ 16 Shannon Sharpe	.40	.18
❑ 17 Rod Woodson	.40	.18
❑ 18 Matt Stover	.25	.11
❑ 19 Michael McCrary	.25	.11
❑ 20 Doug Flutie	.60	.25
❑ 21 Rob Johnson	.40	.18
❑ 22 Eric Moulds	.60	.25
❑ 23 Peerless Price	.60	.25
❑ 24 Jonathan Linton	.25	.11
❑ 25 Antowain Smith	.40	.18
❑ 26 Jay Riemersma	.25	.11
❑ 27 Muhsin Muhammad	.40	.18
❑ 28 Tim Biakabutuka	.40	.18
❑ 29 Patrick Jeffers	.60	.25
❑ 30 Wesley Walls	.25	.11
❑ 31 Steve Beuerlein	.40	.18
❑ 32 John Kasay	.25	.11
❑ 33 Curtis Enis	.25	.11
❑ 34 Cade McNown	.25	.11
❑ 35 Marcus Robinson	.60	.25
❑ 36 Bobby Engram	.25	.11
❑ 37 Eddie Kennison	.25	.11
❑ 38 Akili Smith	.25	.11
❑ 39 Carl Pickens	.40	.18
❑ 40 Corey Dillon	.60	.25
❑ 41 Darnay Scott	.40	.18
❑ 42 Errict Rhett	.40	.18
❑ 43 Karim Abdul-Jabbar	.40	.18
❑ 44 Tim Couch	.40	.18
❑ 45 Kevin Johnson	.60	.25
❑ 46 Darrin Chiaverini	.25	.11
❑ 47 Terry Kirby	.25	.11
❑ 48 Jason Tucker	.25	.11
❑ 49 Rocket Ismail	.40	.18
❑ 50 Joey Galloway	.40	.18
❑ 51 Michael Irvin	.40	.18
❑ 52 Troy Aikman	1.25	.55
❑ 53 Emmitt Smith	1.25	.55
❑ 54 David LaFleur	.25	.11
❑ 55 Trevor Pryce	.25	.11
❑ 56 Brian Griese	.60	.25
❑ 57 Olandis Gary	.60	.25
❑ 58 Terrell Davis	.60	.25
❑ 59 Rod Smith	.40	.18
❑ 60 Ed McCaffrey	.60	.25
❑ 61 Gus Frerotte	.25	.11
❑ 62 Jason Elam	.25	.11
❑ 63 Kavika Pittman	.25	.11
❑ 64 James Stewart	.40	.18
❑ 65 Charlie Batch	.60	.25
❑ 66 Johnnie Morton	.40	.18
❑ 67 Herman Moore	.40	.18
❑ 68 Germane Crowell	.25	.11
❑ 69 Barry Sanders	1.50	.70
❑ 70 Chris Claiborne	.25	.11
❑ 71 Brett Favre	2.00	.90
❑ 72 Antonio Freeman	.60	.25
❑ 73 Dorsey Levens	.40	.18
❑ 74 De'Mond Parker	.25	.11
❑ 75 Corey Bradford	.40	.18
❑ 76 Basil Mitchell	.25	.11
❑ 77 Bill Schroeder	.40	.18
❑ 78 Peyton Manning	1.50	.70
❑ 79 Marvin Harrison	.60	.25
❑ 80 Terrence Wilkins	.25	.11
❑ 81 Edgerrin James	1.00	.45
❑ 82 E.G. Green	.25	.11
❑ 83 Chad Bratzke	.25	.11
❑ 84 Mark Brunell	.60	.25
❑ 85 Fred Taylor	.60	.25
❑ 86 Jimmy Smith	.40	.18
❑ 87 Keenan McCardell	.40	.18
❑ 88 Kevin Hardy	.25	.11

❑ 89 Aaron Beasley .25 .11
❑ 90 Elvis Grbac .40 .18
❑ 91 Derrick Alexander .40 .18
❑ 92 Tony Gonzalez .40 .18
❑ 93 Donnell Bennett .25 .11
❑ 94 Warren Moon .60 .25
❑ 95 Andre Rison .40 .18
❑ 96 James Hasty .25 .11
❑ 97 Dan Marino 2.00 .90
❑ 98 Thurman Thomas .40 .18
❑ 99 James Johnson .25 .11
❑ 100 O.J. McDuffie .40 .18
❑ 101 Tony Martin .40 .18
❑ 102 Oronde Gadsden .40 .18
❑ 103 Zach Thomas .60 .25
❑ 104 Sam Madison .25 .11
❑ 105 Jay Fiedler .60 .25
❑ 106 Damon Huard .60 .25
❑ 107 Robert Smith .60 .25
❑ 108 Leroy Hoard .25 .11
❑ 109 Randy Moss 1.25 .55
❑ 110 Cris Carter .60 .25
❑ 111 Daunte Culpepper .75 .35
❑ 112 John Randle .40 .18
❑ 113 Randall Cunningham .60 .25
❑ 114 Gary Anderson .25 .11
❑ 115 Drew Bledsoe DP .75 .35
❑ 116 Terry Glenn .40 .18
❑ 117 Kevin Faulk .40 .18
❑ 118 Terry Allen SP 15.00 6.75
❑ 119 Adam Vinatieri .60 .25
❑ 120 Ty Law .40 .18
❑ 121 Lawyer Milloy .40 .18
❑ 122 Troy Brown .40 .18
❑ 123 Ben Coates .25 .11
❑ 124 Cam Cleeland .25 .11
❑ 125 Jeff Blake .40 .18
❑ 126 Ricky Williams .60 .25
❑ 127 Jake Reed .40 .18
❑ 128 Jake Delhomme RC 2.50 1.10
❑ 129 Andrew Glover .25 .11
❑ 130 Keith Poole .25 .11
❑ 131 Joe Horn .40 .18
❑ 132 Kerry Collins .40 .18
❑ 133 Joe Montgomery .25 .11
❑ 134 Sean Bennett .25 .11
❑ 135 Amani Toomer .25 .11
❑ 136 Ike Hilliard .40 .18
❑ 137 Joe Jurevicius .25 .11
❑ 138 Tiki Barber .40 .18
❑ 139 Victor Green .25 .11
❑ 140 Ray Lucas .40 .18
❑ 141 Vinny Testaverde .40 .18
❑ 142 Curtis Martin .60 .25
❑ 143 Wayne Chrebet .40 .18
❑ 144 Tyrone Wheatley .40 .18
❑ 145 Rich Gannon .60 .25
❑ 146 Napoleon Kaufman .40 .18
❑ 147 Tim Brown .25 .11
❑ 148 Rickey Dudley .25 .11
❑ 149 Charles Woodson .60 .25
❑ 150 James Jett .25 .11
❑ 151 Duce Staley .60 .25
❑ 152 Charles Johnson .40 .18
❑ 153 Donovan McNabb 1.00 .45
❑ 154 Troy Vincent .25 .11
❑ 155 Troy Edwards .25 .11
❑ 156 Jerome Bettis .60 .25
❑ 157 Kordell Stewart .40 .18
❑ 158 Richard Huntley .25 .11
❑ 159 Hines Ward .60 .25
❑ 160 Levon Kirkland .25 .11
❑ 161 Ryan Leaf .40 .18
❑ 162 Jim Harbaugh .40 .18
❑ 163 Jermaine Fazande .25 .11
❑ 164 Natrone Means .25 .11
❑ 165 Junior Seau .60 .25
❑ 166 Curtis Conway .40 .18
❑ 167 Freddie Jones .25 .11
❑ 168 Jeff Graham .25 .11
❑ 169 Terrell Owens .60 .25
❑ 170 Jeff Garcia .60 .25
❑ 171 Jerry Rice 1.25 .55
❑ 172 Steve Young .75 .35
❑ 173 Garrison Hearst .40 .18
❑ 174 Charlie Garner .40 .18
❑ 175 Fred Beasley .25 .11
❑ 176 Bryant Young .25 .11
❑ 177 Derrick Mayes .40 .18
❑ 178 Sean Dawkins .25 .11
❑ 179 Jon Kitna .60 .25
❑ 180 Ricky Watters .40 .18
❑ 181 Charlie Rogers .25 .11
❑ 182 Kurt Warner 1.25 .55
❑ 183 Marshall Faulk .75 .35
❑ 184 Isaac Bruce .60 .25
❑ 185 Az-Zahir Hakim .40 .18
❑ 186 Trent Green .60 .25
❑ 187 Jeff Wilkins .25 .11
❑ 188 Torry Holt .60 .25
❑ 189 London Fletcher RC .40 .18
❑ 190 Robert Holcombe .25 .11
❑ 191 Todd Lyght .25 .11
❑ 192 Keyshawn Johnson .60 .25
❑ 193 Derrick Brooks .60 .25
❑ 194 Warren Sapp .40 .18
❑ 195 Shaun King .25 .11
❑ 196 Warrick Dunn .60 .25
❑ 197 Mike Alstott .60 .25
❑ 198 Jacquez Green .25 .11
❑ 199 Reidel Anthony .25 .11
❑ 200 Martin Gramatica .25 .11
❑ 201 Donnie Abraham .25 .11
❑ 202 Steve McNair .60 .25
❑ 203 Eddie George .60 .25
❑ 204 Jevon Kearse .60 .25
❑ 205 Frank Wycheck .25 .11
❑ 206 Kevin Dyson .40 .18
❑ 207 Yancey Thigpen .25 .11
❑ 208 Al Del Greco .25 .11
❑ 209 Jeff George .40 .18
❑ 210 Adrian Murrell .40 .18
❑ 211 Brad Johnson .60 .25
❑ 212 Stephen Davis .60 .25
❑ 213 Stephen Alexander .25 .11
❑ 214 Michael Westbrook .40 .18
❑ 215 Darrell Green .25 .11
❑ 216 Champ Bailey .60 .25
❑ 217 Albert Connell .25 .11
❑ 218 Larry Centers .25 .11
❑ 219 Bruce Smith .40 .18
❑ 220 Deion Sanders .60 .25
❑ 221 Ricky Williams SS .60 .25
❑ 222 Edgerrin James SS 1.00 .45
❑ 223 Tim Couch SS .40 .18
❑ 224 Cade McNown SS .30 .14
❑ 225 Olandis Gary SS .75 .35
❑ 226 Torry Holt SS .75 .35
❑ 227 Donovan McNabb SS 1.00 .45
❑ 228 Shaun King SS .25 .11
❑ 229 Kevin Johnson SS .75 .35
❑ 230 Kurt Warner SS 1.50 .70
❑ 231 Tony Gonzalez AP .50 .23
❑ 232 Frank Wycheck AP .30 .14
❑ 233 Eddie George AP .75 .35
❑ 234 Mark Brunell AP .75 .35
❑ 235 Corey Dillon AP .75 .35
❑ 236 Peyton Manning AP 2.00 .90
❑ 237 Keyshawn Johnson AP .75 .35
❑ 238 Rich Gannon AP .75 .35
❑ 239 Terry Glenn AP .50 .23
❑ 240 Tony Brackens AP .30 .14
❑ 241 Edgerrin James AP 1.00 .45
❑ 242 Tim Brown AP .75 .35
❑ 243 Michael Strahan AP .50 .23
❑ 244 Kurt Warner AP 1.50 .70
❑ 245 Brad Johnson AP .75 .35
❑ 246 Aeneas Williams AP .30 .14
❑ 247 Marshall Faulk AP 1.00 .45
❑ 248 Dexter Coakley AP .30 .14
❑ 249 Warren Sapp AP .50 .23
❑ 250 Mike Alstott AP .75 .35
❑ 251 David Sloan AP .30 .14
❑ 252 Cris Carter AP .75 .35
❑ 253 Muhsin Muhammad AP .30 .14
❑ 254 Isaac Bruce AP .75 .35
❑ 255 Wesley Walls AP .30 .14
❑ 256 Steve Beuerlein LL .50 .23
❑ 257 Kurt Warner LL 1.50 .70
❑ 258 Peyton Manning LL 2.00 .90
❑ 259 Brad Johnson LL .75 .35
❑ 260 Edgerrin James LL 1.00 .45
❑ 261 Curtis Martin LL .75 .35
❑ 262 Stephen Davis LL .75 .35
❑ 263 Emmitt Smith LL 1.50 .70
❑ 264 Marvin Harrison LL .75 .35
❑ 265 Jimmy Smith LL .50 .23
❑ 266 Randy Moss LL 1.50 .70
❑ 267 Marcus Robinson LL .75 .35
❑ 268 Kevin Carter LL .30 .14
❑ 269 Simeon Rice LL .50 .23
❑ 270 Robert Porcher LL .30 .14
❑ 271 Jevon Kearse LL .75 .35
❑ 272 Mike Vanderjagt LL .30 .14
❑ 273 Olindo Mare LL .30 .14
❑ 274 Todd Peterson LL .30 .14
❑ 275 Mike Hollis LL .30 .14
❑ 276 Mike Anderson RC/500 40.00 18.00
❑ 277 Peter Warrick RC 2.00 .90
❑ 278 Courtney Brown RC .75 .35
❑ 279 Plaxico Burress RC 4.00 1.80
❑ 280 Corey Simon RC .75 .35
❑ 281 Thomas Jones RC 3.00 1.35
❑ 282 Travis Taylor RC .75 .35
❑ 283 Shaun Alexander RC 5.00 2.20
❑ 284 Patrick Pass RC/500 25.00 11.00
❑ 285 Chris Redman RC .50 .23
❑ 286 Chad Pennington RC 8.00 3.60
❑ 287 Jamal Lewis RC 5.00 2.20
❑ 288 Brian Urlacher RC 8.00 3.60
❑ 289 Bubba Franks RC 2.00 .90
❑ 290 Dez White RC 2.00 .90
❑ 291 Frank Moreau RC/500 25.00 11.00
❑ 292 Ron Dayne RC 2.00 .90
❑ 293 Sylvester Morris RC .50 .23
❑ 294 R.Jay Soward RC 1.50 .70
❑ 295 Curtis Keaton RC 1.50 .70
❑ 296 Spergon Wynn RC/500 25.00 11.00
❑ 297 Rondell Mealey RC 1.50 .70
❑ 298 Travis Prentice RC 1.50 .70
❑ 299 Darrell Jackson RC 4.00 1.80
❑ 300 Giovanni Carmazzi RC 1.50 .70
❑ 301 Anthony Lucas RC 1.50 .70
❑ 302 Danny Farmer RC 1.50 .70
❑ 303 Dennis Northcutt RC 2.00 .90
❑ 304 Troy Walters RC 2.00 .90
❑ 305 Laveranues Coles RC 2.50 1.10
❑ 306 Kwame Cavil RC 1.50 .70
❑ 307 Tee Martin RC 2.00 .90
❑ 308 J.R. Redmond RC 1.50 .70
❑ 309 Tim Rattay RC 4.00 1.80
❑ 310 Jerry Porter RC 2.50 1.10
❑ 311 Michael Wiley RC 1.50 .70
❑ 312 Reuben Droughns RC 2.50 1.10
❑ 313 Trung Canidate RC 1.50 .70
❑ 314 Shyrone Stith RC 1.50 .70
❑ 315 Marc Bulger RC 4.00 1.80
❑ 316 Tom Brady RC 25.00 11.00
❑ 317 Doug Johnson RC 2.00 .90
❑ 318 Todd Husak RC 2.00 .90
❑ 319 Gari Scott RC 1.50 .70
❑ 320 Windrell Hayes RC/500 25.00 11.00
❑ 321 Chris Cole RC 1.50 .70
❑ 322 Sammy Morris RC 1.50 .70
❑ 323 Trevor Gaylor RC 1.50 .70
❑ 324 Jarious Jackson RC 1.50 .70
❑ 325 Doug Chapman RC/500 25.00 11.00
❑ 326 Ron Dugans RC 1.50 .70
❑ 327 Ron Dixon RC/500 25.00 11.00
❑ 328 Joe Hamilton RC 1.50 .70
❑ 329 Todd Pinkston RC 2.00 .90
❑ 330 Chad Morton RC 2.00 .90

2001 Score

	Nm-Mt	Ex-Mt
COMP.SET w/o SP's (220)	25.00	7.50
❑ 1 David Boston	.50	.15
❑ 2 Frank Sanders	.20	.06
❑ 3 Jake Plummer	.30	.09
❑ 4 Michael Pittman	.20	.06
❑ 5 Rob Moore	.30	.09

No.	Player	Price	Price
❑ 6	Thomas Jones	.30	.09
❑ 7	Chris Chandler	.30	.09
❑ 8	Doug Johnson	.20	.06
❑ 9	Jamal Anderson	.50	.15
❑ 10	Tim Dwight	.50	.15
❑ 11	Brandon Stokley	.30	.09
❑ 12	Chris Redman	.20	.06
❑ 13	Jamal Lewis	.75	.23
❑ 14	Qadry Ismail	.30	.09
❑ 15	Ray Lewis	.50	.15
❑ 16	Rod Woodson	.30	.09
❑ 17	Shannon Sharpe	.30	.09
❑ 18	Travis Taylor	.30	.09
❑ 19	Trent Dilfer	.30	.09
❑ 20	Elvis Grbac	.30	.09
❑ 21	Eric Moulds	.30	.09
❑ 22	Jay Riemersma	.20	.06
❑ 23	Peerless Price	.30	.09
❑ 24	Rob Johnson	.30	.09
❑ 25	Sam Cowart	.20	.06
❑ 26	Sammy Morris	.20	.06
❑ 27	Shawn Bryson	.20	.06
❑ 28	Donald Hayes	.20	.06
❑ 29	Muhsin Muhammad	.30	.09
❑ 30	Patrick Jeffers	.30	.09
❑ 31	Reggie White DE	.50	.15
❑ 32	Steve Beuerlein	.30	.09
❑ 33	Tim Biakabutuka	.30	.09
❑ 34	Wesley Walls	.20	.06
❑ 35	Brian Urlacher	.75	.23
❑ 36	Cade McNown	.20	.06
❑ 37	Dez White	.20	.06
❑ 38	James Allen	.30	.09
❑ 39	Marcus Robinson	.50	.15
❑ 40	Marty Booker	.20	.06
❑ 41	Akili Smith	.20	.06
❑ 42	Corey Dillon	.50	.15
❑ 43	Danny Farmer	.20	.06
❑ 44	Peter Warrick	.50	.15
❑ 45	Ron Dugans	.20	.06
❑ 46	Takeo Spikes	.20	.06
❑ 47	Courtney Brown	.30	.09
❑ 48	Dennis Northcutt	.30	.09
❑ 49	JaJuan Dawson	.20	.06
❑ 50	Kevin Johnson	.30	.09
❑ 51	Tim Couch	.30	.09
❑ 52	Travis Prentice	.20	.06
❑ 53	Anthony Wright	.20	.06
❑ 54	Emmitt Smith	1.00	.30
❑ 55	James McKnight	.30	.09
❑ 56	Joey Galloway	.30	.09
❑ 57	Rocket Ismail	.30	.09
❑ 58	Randall Cunningham	.50	.15
❑ 59	Troy Aikman	.75	.23
❑ 60	Brian Griese	.50	.15
❑ 61	Ed McCaffrey	.50	.15
❑ 62	Gus Frerotte	.20	.06
❑ 63	John Elway	1.50	.45
❑ 64	Mike Anderson	.50	.15
❑ 65	Olandis Gary	.30	.09
❑ 66	Rod Smith	.30	.09
❑ 67	Terrell Davis	.50	.15
❑ 68	Barry Sanders	1.00	.30
❑ 69	Charlie Batch	.50	.15
❑ 70	Germane Crowell	.20	.06
❑ 71	Herman Moore	.30	.09
❑ 72	James Stewart	.30	.09
❑ 73	Johnnie Morton	.30	.09
❑ 74	Robert Porcher	.20	.06
❑ 75	Jim Harbaugh	.30	.09
❑ 76	Ahman Green	.50	.15
❑ 77	Antonio Freeman	.50	.15
❑ 78	Bill Schroeder	.30	.09
❑ 79	Brett Favre	1.50	.45
❑ 80	Bubba Franks	.30	.09
❑ 81	Dorsey Levens	.30	.09
❑ 82	E.G. Green	.20	.06
❑ 83	Edgerrin James	.60	.18
❑ 84	Jerome Pathon	.30	.09
❑ 85	Ken Dilger	.20	.06
❑ 86	Marcus Pollard	.20	.06
❑ 87	Marvin Harrison	.50	.15
❑ 88	Peyton Manning	1.25	.35
❑ 89	Terrence Wilkins	.20	.06
❑ 90	Fred Taylor	.50	.15
❑ 91	Hardy Nickerson	.20	.06
❑ 92	Jimmy Smith	.30	.09
❑ 93	Keenan McCardell	.20	.06
❑ 94	Kyle Brady	.20	.06
❑ 95	Mark Brunell	.50	.15
❑ 96	Tony Brackens	.20	.06
❑ 97	Derrick Alexander	.30	.09
❑ 98	Sylvester Morris	.20	.06
❑ 99	Tony Gonzalez	.30	.09
❑ 100	Tony Richardson	.20	.06
❑ 101	Kimble Anders	.20	.06
❑ 102	Warren Moon	.50	.15
❑ 103	Dan Marino	1.50	.45
❑ 104	Jay Fiedler	.50	.15
❑ 105	Lamar Smith	.30	.09
❑ 106	O.J. McDuffie	.20	.06
❑ 107	Oronde Gadsden	.30	.09
❑ 108	Sam Madison	.20	.06
❑ 109	Thurman Thomas	.20	.06
❑ 110	Tony Martin	.20	.06
❑ 111	Zach Thomas	.50	.15
❑ 112	Cris Carter	.50	.15
❑ 113	Daunte Culpepper	.50	.15
❑ 114	Matthew Hatchette	.20	.06
❑ 115	Randy Moss	1.00	.30
❑ 116	Robert Smith	.50	.15
❑ 117	Drew Bledsoe	.60	.18
❑ 118	J.R. Redmond	.20	.06
❑ 119	Kevin Faulk	.30	.09
❑ 120	Michael Bishop	.20	.06
❑ 121	Terry Glenn	.30	.09
❑ 122	Troy Brown	.30	.09
❑ 123	Ty Law	.30	.09
❑ 124	Aaron Brooks	.50	.15
❑ 125	Darren Howard	.20	.06
❑ 126	Jake Reed	.30	.09
❑ 127	Jeff Blake	.30	.09
❑ 128	Joe Horn	.30	.09
❑ 129	La'Roi Glover	.20	.06
❑ 130	Ricky Williams	.50	.15
❑ 131	Willie Jackson	.20	.06
❑ 132	Albert Connell	.20	.06
❑ 133	Amani Toomer	.20	.06
❑ 134	Ike Hilliard	.30	.09
❑ 135	Jason Sehorn	.20	.06
❑ 136	Jessie Armstead	.20	.06
❑ 137	Kerry Collins	.30	.09
❑ 138	Michael Strahan	.30	.09
❑ 139	Ron Dayne	.50	.15
❑ 140	Ron Dixon	.20	.06
❑ 141	Tiki Barber	.30	.09
❑ 142	Anthony Becht	.20	.06
❑ 143	Chad Pennington	.75	.23
❑ 144	Curtis Martin	.50	.15
❑ 145	Dedric Ward	.20	.06
❑ 146	Laveranues Coles	.50	.15
❑ 147	Vinny Testaverde	.30	.09
❑ 148	Wayne Chrebet	.30	.09
❑ 149	Andre Rison	.30	.09
❑ 150	Charles Woodson	.30	.09
❑ 151	Darrell Russell	.20	.06
❑ 152	Napoleon Kaufman	.30	.09
❑ 153	Rich Gannon	.50	.15
❑ 154	Tim Brown	.50	.15
❑ 155	Tyrone Wheatley	.30	.09
❑ 156	Chad Lewis	.20	.06
❑ 157	Charles Johnson	.20	.06
❑ 158	Donovan McNabb	.60	.18
❑ 159	Duce Staley	.50	.15
❑ 160	Hugh Douglas	.20	.06
❑ 161	Na Brown	.20	.06
❑ 162	Todd Pinkston	.20	.06
❑ 163	James Thrash	.30	.09
❑ 164	Bobby Shaw	.20	.06
❑ 165	Hines Ward	.50	.15
❑ 166	Jerome Bettis	.50	.15
❑ 167	Kordell Stewart	.30	.09
❑ 168	Levon Kirkland	.20	.06
❑ 169	Plaxico Burress	.50	.15
❑ 170	Richard Huntley	.20	.06
❑ 171	Troy Edwards	.20	.06
❑ 172	Jeff Graham	.20	.06
❑ 173	Junior Seau	.50	.15
❑ 174	Doug Flutie	.50	.15
❑ 175	Charlie Garner	.30	.09
❑ 176	Jeff Garcia	.50	.15
❑ 177	Jerry Rice	1.00	.30
❑ 178	Steve Young	.50	.15
❑ 179	Terrell Owens	.50	.15
❑ 180	Brock Huard	.20	.06
❑ 181	Darrell Jackson	.50	.15
❑ 182	Derrick Mayes	.30	.09
❑ 183	Ricky Watters	.30	.09
❑ 184	Shaun Alexander	.60	.18
❑ 185	Matt Hasselbeck	.30	.09
❑ 186	John Randle	.30	.09
❑ 187	Az-Zahir Hakim	.20	.06
❑ 188	Isaac Bruce	.50	.15
❑ 189	Kurt Warner	1.00	.30
❑ 190	Marshall Faulk	.60	.18
❑ 191	Torry Holt	.50	.15
❑ 192	Trent Green	.50	.15
❑ 193	Derrick Brooks	.50	.15
❑ 194	Jacquez Green	.20	.06
❑ 195	John Lynch	.30	.09
❑ 196	Keyshawn Johnson	.50	.15
❑ 197	Mike Alstott	.50	.15
❑ 198	Reidel Anthony	.20	.06
❑ 199	Shaun King	.20	.06
❑ 200	Warren Sapp	.30	.09
❑ 201	Warrick Dunn	.50	.15
❑ 202	Ryan Leaf	.30	.09
❑ 203	Carl Pickens	.20	.06
❑ 204	Derrick Mason	.30	.09
❑ 205	Eddie George	.50	.15
❑ 206	Frank Wycheck	.20	.06
❑ 207	Jevon Kearse	.30	.09
❑ 208	Neil O'Donnell	.20	.06
❑ 209	Steve McNair	.50	.15
❑ 210	Yancey Thigpen	.20	.06
❑ 211	Andre Reed	.30	.09
❑ 212	Brad Johnson	.50	.15
❑ 213	Bruce Smith	.30	.09
❑ 214	Champ Bailey	.50	.15
❑ 215	Darrell Green	.20	.06
❑ 216	Deion Sanders	.50	.15
❑ 217	Irving Fryar	.30	.09
❑ 218	Jeff George	.30	.09
❑ 219	Michael Westbrook	.30	.09
❑ 220	Stephen Davis	.50	.15
❑ 221	Terrell Owens AP	1.00	.30
❑ 222	Peyton Manning AP	2.50	.75
❑ 223	Stephen Davis AP	1.00	.30
❑ 224	Marvin Harrison AP	1.00	.30
❑ 225	Donovan McNabb AP	1.25	.35
❑ 226	Edgerrin James AP	1.25	.35
❑ 227	Eric Moulds AP	.60	.18
❑ 228	Daunte Culpepper AP	1.00	.30
❑ 229	Eddie George AP	1.00	.30
❑ 230	Cris Carter AP	1.00	.30
❑ 231	Rich Gannon AP	1.00	.30
❑ 232	Jeff Garcia AP	1.00	.30
❑ 233	Jimmy Smith AP	.60	.18
❑ 234	Tony Gonzalez AP	.60	.18
❑ 235	Torry Holt AP	1.00	.30
❑ 236	Jevon Kearse AP	.60	.18
❑ 237	Ray Lewis AP	1.00	.30
❑ 238	Warren Sapp AP	.60	.18
❑ 239	Brian Urlacher AP	1.50	.45
❑ 240	Champ Bailey AP	.60	.18

❑ 241 Peyton Manning LL	2.50	.75
❑ 242 Jeff Garcia LL	1.00	.30
❑ 243 Elvis Grbac LL	.60	.18
❑ 244 Daunte Culpepper LL	1.00	.30
❑ 245 Brett Favre LL	3.00	.90
❑ 246 Edgerrin James LL	1.25	.35
❑ 247 Robert Smith LL	.60	.18
❑ 248 Eddie George LL	1.00	.30
❑ 249 Mike Anderson LL	1.00	.30
❑ 250 Corey Dillon LL	1.00	.30
❑ 251 Torry Holt LL	1.00	.30
❑ 252 Rod Smith LL	.60	.18
❑ 253 Isaac Bruce LL	1.00	.30
❑ 254 Terrell Owens LL	1.00	.30
❑ 255 Randy Moss LL	2.00	.60
❑ 256 La'Roi Glover LL	.40	.12
❑ 257 Trace Armstrong LL	.40	.12
❑ 258 Warren Sapp LL	.60	.18
❑ 259 Hugh Douglas LL	.40	.12
❑ 260 Jason Taylor LL	.40	.12
❑ 261 Mike Anderson SS	1.00	.30
❑ 262 Jamal Lewis SS	1.25	.35
❑ 263 Sylvester Morris SS	.40	.12
❑ 264 Darrell Jackson SS	1.00	.30
❑ 265 Peter Warrick SS	1.00	.30
❑ 266 Ron Dayne SS	1.00	.30
❑ 267 Shaun Alexander SS	1.25	.35
❑ 268 Plaxico Burress SS	1.00	.30
❑ 269 Brian Urlacher SS	1.50	.45
❑ 270 Courtney Brown SS	.60	.18
❑ 271 Michael Vick RC	12.00	3.60
❑ 272 Drew Brees RC	4.00	1.20
❑ 273 Chris Weinke RC	1.00	.30
❑ 274 Quincy Carter RC	2.00	.60
❑ 275 Sage Rosenfels RC	1.00	.30
❑ 276 Josh Heupel RC	2.00	.60
❑ 277 David Rivers RC	1.25	.35
❑ 278 Ben Leard RC	1.25	.35
❑ 279 Marques Tuiasosopo RC	2.00	.60
❑ 280 Mike McMahon RC	2.00	.60
❑ 281 Deuce McAllister RC	4.00	1.20
❑ 282 LaMont Jordan RC	2.50	.75
❑ 283 LaDainian Tomlinson RC	6.00	1.80
❑ 284 James Jackson RC	2.00	.60
❑ 285 Anthony Thomas RC	3.00	.90
❑ 286 Travis Henry RC	2.50	.75
❑ 287 Travis Minor RC	1.25	.35
❑ 288 Rudi Johnson RC	4.00	1.20
❑ 289 Michael Bennett RC	4.00	1.20
❑ 290 Kevan Barlow RC	2.00	.60
❑ 291 Reggie White RC	1.25	.35
❑ 292 Moran Norris RC	.75	.23
❑ 293 Ja'Mar Toombs RC	1.25	.35
❑ 294 Heath Evans RC	1.25	.35
❑ 295 David Terrell RC	2.00	.60
❑ 296 Santana Moss RC	3.00	.90
❑ 297 Rod Gardner RC	2.00	.60
❑ 298 Quincy Morgan RC	2.00	.60
❑ 299 Freddie Mitchell RC	2.00	.60
❑ 300 Boo Williams RC	1.25	.35
❑ 301 Reggie Wayne RC	3.00	.90
❑ 302 Ronney Daniels RC	.75	.23
❑ 303 Bobby Newcombe RC	1.25	.35
❑ 304 Vinny Sutherland RC	1.25	.35
❑ 305 Cedrick Wilson RC	2.00	.60
❑ 306 Robert Ferguson RC	2.00	.60
❑ 307 Ken-Yon Rambo RC	1.25	.35
❑ 308 Alex Bannister RC	1.25	.35
❑ 309 Koren Robinson RC	2.50	.75
❑ 310 Chad Johnson RC	4.00	1.20
❑ 311 Chris Chambers RC	2.50	.75
❑ 312 Javon Green RC	1.25	.35
❑ 313 Snoop Minnis RC	1.25	.35
❑ 314 Scotty Anderson RC	1.25	.35
❑ 315 Todd Heap RC	2.00	.60
❑ 316 Alge Crumpler RC	2.50	.75
❑ 317 Marcellus Rivers RC	1.25	.35
❑ 318 Rashon Burns RC	.75	.23
❑ 319 Jamal Reynolds RC	2.00	.60
❑ 320 Andre Carter RC	2.00	.60
❑ 321 Justin Smith RC	2.00	.60
❑ 322 Gerard Warren RC	2.00	.60
❑ 323 Tommy Polley RC	2.00	.60
❑ 324 Dan Morgan RC	1.00	.30
❑ 325 Torrance Marshall RC	2.00	.60
❑ 326 Correll Buckhalter RC	2.50	.75
❑ 327 Derrick Gibson RC	1.25	.35
❑ 328 Adam Archuleta RC	2.00	.60
❑ 329 Jamar Fletcher RC	1.25	.35
❑ 330 Nate Clements RC	2.00	.60

2002 Score

	Nm-Mt	Ex-Mt
COMPLETE SET (330)	50.00	15.00
❑ 1 David Boston	.50	.15
❑ 2 Arnold Jackson	.20	.06
❑ 3 MarTay Jenkins	.20	.06
❑ 4 Thomas Jones	.30	.09
❑ 5 Kwamie Lassiter	.20	.06
❑ 6 Michael Pittman	.20	.06
❑ 7 Jake Plummer	.30	.09
❑ 8 Chris Chandler	.30	.09
❑ 9 Alge Crumpler	.30	.09
❑ 10 Terance Mathis	.20	.06
❑ 11 Maurice Smith	.30	.09
❑ 12 Ray Buchanan	.20	.06
❑ 13 Jamal Anderson	.30	.09
❑ 14 Keith Brooking	.20	.06
❑ 15 Michael Vick	1.50	.45
❑ 16 Obafemi Ayanbadejo	.20	.06
❑ 17 Jason Brookins	.20	.06
❑ 18 Randall Cunningham	.20	.06
❑ 19 Elvis Grbac	.30	.09
❑ 20 Todd Heap	.20	.06
❑ 21 Qadry Ismail	.30	.09
❑ 22 Shannon Sharpe	.30	.09
❑ 23 Travis Taylor	.30	.09
❑ 24 Ray Lewis	.50	.15
❑ 25 Jamal Lewis	.50	.15
❑ 26 Larry Centers	.20	.06
❑ 27 Rob Johnson	.30	.09
❑ 28 Shawn Bryson	.20	.06
❑ 29 Eric Moulds	.30	.09
❑ 30 Peerless Price	.30	.09
❑ 31 Nate Clements	.20	.06
❑ 32 Travis Henry	.50	.15
❑ 33 Isaac Byrd	.20	.06
❑ 34 Nick Goings	.20	.06
❑ 35 Donald Hayes	.20	.06
❑ 36 Richard Huntley	.20	.06
❑ 37 Muhsin Muhammad	.30	.09
❑ 38 Steve Smith	.30	.09
❑ 39 Wesley Walls	.20	.06
❑ 40 Chris Weinke	.30	.09
❑ 41 James Allen	.30	.09
❑ 42 Marty Booker	.20	.06
❑ 43 Jim Miller	.20	.06
❑ 44 David Terrell	.50	.15
❑ 45 Dez White	.20	.06
❑ 46 Brian Urlacher	.75	.23
❑ 47 Mike Brown	.50	.15
❑ 48 Anthony Thomas	.50	.15
❑ 49 T.J. Houshmandzadeh	.30	.09
❑ 50 Chad Johnson	.50	.15
❑ 51 Darnay Scott	.20	.06
❑ 52 Peter Warrick	.30	.09
❑ 53 Akili Smith	.20	.06
❑ 54 Jon Kitna	.30	.09
❑ 55 Justin Smith	.20	.06
❑ 56 Corey Dillon	.30	.09
❑ 57 Benjamin Gay	.30	.09
❑ 58 Kevin Johnson	.30	.09
❑ 59 Quincy Morgan	.20	.06
❑ 60 James Jackson	.20	.06
❑ 61 Anthony Henry	.20	.06
❑ 62 Gerard Warren	.20	.06
❑ 63 Jamir Miller	.20	.06
❑ 64 Tim Couch	.30	.09
❑ 65 Quincy Carter	.30	.09
❑ 66 Joey Galloway	.30	.09
❑ 67 Troy Hambrick	.20	.06
❑ 68 Rocket Ismail	.30	.09
❑ 69 Dexter Coakley	.20	.06
❑ 70 Darren Woodson	.20	.06
❑ 71 Emmitt Smith	1.25	.35
❑ 72 Mike Anderson	.50	.15
❑ 73 Terrell Davis	.50	.15
❑ 74 Kevin Kasper	.20	.06
❑ 75 Rod Smith	.30	.09
❑ 76 Ed McCaffrey	.50	.15
❑ 77 Olandis Gary	.30	.09
❑ 78 Dwayne Carswell	.20	.06
❑ 79 Deltha O'Neal	.20	.06
❑ 80 Brian Griese	.50	.15
❑ 81 Scotty Anderson	.20	.06
❑ 82 Johnnie Morton	.30	.09
❑ 83 Cory Schlesinger	.20	.06
❑ 84 James Stewart	.30	.09
❑ 85 Shaun Rogers	.20	.06
❑ 86 Mike McMahon	.50	.15
❑ 87 Charlie Batch	.30	.09
❑ 88 Robert Porcher	.20	.06
❑ 89 Bubba Franks	.30	.09
❑ 90 Robert Ferguson	.20	.06
❑ 91 Antonio Freeman	.50	.15
❑ 92 Ahman Green	.50	.15
❑ 93 Bill Schroeder	.30	.09
❑ 94 Kabeer Gbaja-Biamila	.30	.09
❑ 95 Jamal Reynolds	.20	.06
❑ 96 Darren Sharper	.20	.06
❑ 97 Brett Favre	1.25	.35
❑ 98 Marvin Harrison	.50	.15
❑ 99 Dominic Rhodes	.30	.09
❑ 100 Edgerrin James	.60	.18
❑ 101 Reggie Wayne	.30	.09
❑ 102 Terrence Wilkins	.20	.06
❑ 103 Ken Dilger	.20	.06
❑ 104 Peyton Manning	1.00	.30
❑ 105 Elvis Joseph	.20	.06
❑ 106 Stacey Mack	.20	.06
❑ 107 Fred Taylor	.50	.15
❑ 108 Keenan McCardell	.20	.06
❑ 109 Jimmy Smith	.30	.09
❑ 110 Mark Brunell	.50	.15
❑ 111 Derrick Alexander	.30	.09
❑ 112 Tony Gonzalez	.30	.09
❑ 113 Trent Green	.30	.09
❑ 114 Snoop Minnis	.20	.06
❑ 115 Priest Holmes	.60	.18
❑ 116 Chris Chambers	.50	.15
❑ 117 Jay Fiedler	.30	.09
❑ 118 Oronde Gadsden	.30	.09
❑ 119 Travis Minor	.20	.06
❑ 120 Lamar Smith	.30	.09
❑ 121 Zach Thomas	.50	.15
❑ 122 Michael Bennett	.30	.09
❑ 123 Todd Bouman	.20	.06
❑ 124 Cris Carter	.50	.15
❑ 125 Byron Chamberlain	.20	.06
❑ 126 Randy Moss	1.00	.30
❑ 127 Jake Reed	.30	.09
❑ 128 Daunte Culpepper	.50	.15
❑ 129 Drew Bledsoe	.50	.15
❑ 130 Troy Brown	.30	.09
❑ 131 David Patten	.20	.06
❑ 132 J.R. Redmond	.20	.06
❑ 133 Antowain Smith	.30	.09
❑ 134 Ty Law	.30	.09
❑ 135 Richard Seymour	.20	.06
❑ 136 Adam Vinatieri	.50	.15
❑ 137 Tom Brady	1.25	.35
❑ 138 Joe Horn	.30	.09
❑ 139 Willie Jackson	.20	.06
❑ 140 Deuce McAllister	.60	.18
❑ 141 Boo Williams	.20	.06

❑ 142 Ricky Williams .50 .15
❑ 143 La'Roi Glover .20 .06
❑ 144 Sammy Knight .20 .06
❑ 145 Aaron Brooks .50 .15
❑ 146 Tiki Barber .30 .09
❑ 147 Ron Dayne .30 .09
❑ 148 Ike Hilliard .30 .09
❑ 149 Amani Toomer .30 .09
❑ 150 Will Allen .20 .06
❑ 151 Michael Strahan .30 .09
❑ 152 Jason Sehorn .20 .06
❑ 153 Kerry Collins .30 .09
❑ 154 Anthony Becht .20 .06
❑ 155 Wayne Chrebet .30 .09
❑ 156 Laveranues Coles .30 .09
❑ 157 LaMont Jordan .50 .15
❑ 158 Santana Moss .50 .15
❑ 159 Chad Pennington .60 .18
❑ 160 John Abraham .30 .09
❑ 161 Vinny Testaverde .30 .09
❑ 162 Curtis Martin .50 .15
❑ 163 Tim Brown .50 .15
❑ 164 Rich Gannon .50 .15
❑ 165 Charlie Garner .30 .09
❑ 166 Jerry Porter .20 .06
❑ 167 Marques Tuiasosopo .30 .09
❑ 168 Tyrone Wheatley .30 .09
❑ 169 Charles Woodson .30 .09
❑ 170 Jerry Rice 1.00 .30
❑ 171 Correll Buckhalter .30 .09
❑ 172 Chad Lewis .20 .06
❑ 173 Brian Mitchell .20 .06
❑ 174 Freddie Mitchell .30 .09
❑ 175 Todd Pinkston .30 .09
❑ 176 Duce Staley .50 .15
❑ 177 Tony Stewart .20 .06
❑ 178 James Thrash .30 .09
❑ 179 Hugh Douglas .20 .06
❑ 180 Donovan McNabb .60 .18
❑ 181 Plaxico Burress .30 .09
❑ 182 Chris Fuamatu-Ma'afala .20 .06
❑ 183 Kordell Stewart .30 .09
❑ 184 Hines Ward .50 .15
❑ 185 Amos Zereoue .50 .15
❑ 186 Kendrell Bell .50 .15
❑ 187 Casey Hampton .20 .06
❑ 188 Jerome Bettis .50 .15
❑ 189 Drew Brees .50 .15
❑ 190 Curtis Conway .20 .06
❑ 191 Tim Dwight .30 .09
❑ 192 Doug Flutie .50 .15
❑ 193 Junior Seau .50 .15
❑ 194 Marcellus Wiley .20 .06
❑ 195 Ryan McNeil .20 .06
❑ 196 Jeff Graham .20 .06
❑ 197 LaDainian Tomlinson .75 .23
❑ 198 Kevan Barlow .30 .09
❑ 199 Garrison Hearst .30 .09
❑ 200 Eric Johnson .30 .09
❑ 201 Terrell Owens .50 .15
❑ 202 J.J. Stokes .30 .09
❑ 203 Andre Carter .20 .06
❑ 204 Jeff Garcia .50 .15
❑ 205 Trent Dilfer .30 .09
❑ 206 Matt Hasselbeck .30 .09
❑ 207 Darrell Jackson .30 .09
❑ 208 Koren Robinson .30 .09
❑ 209 Ricky Watters .30 .09
❑ 210 John Randle .20 .06
❑ 211 Shaun Alexander .50 .15
❑ 212 Isaac Bruce .50 .15
❑ 213 Trung Canidate .30 .09
❑ 214 Marshall Faulk .50 .15
❑ 215 Az-Zahir Hakim .20 .06
❑ 216 Torry Holt .50 .15
❑ 217 Yo Murphy .20 .06
❑ 218 Ricky Proehl .20 .06
❑ 219 Adam Archuleta .20 .06
❑ 220 Dre Bly .20 .06
❑ 221 London Fletcher .20 .06
❑ 222 Tommy Polley .20 .06
❑ 223 Aeneas Williams .20 .06
❑ 224 Kurt Warner .50 .15
❑ 225 Mike Alstott .50 .15
❑ 226 Warrick Dunn .50 .15
❑ 227 Jacquez Green .20 .06
❑ 228 Derrick Brooks .50 .15
❑ 229 John Lynch .30 .09
❑ 230 Warren Sapp .30 .09
❑ 231 Ronde Barber .20 .06
❑ 232 Brad Johnson .30 .09
❑ 233 Keyshawn Johnson .50 .15
❑ 234 Drew Bennett .50 .15
❑ 235 Kevin Dyson .30 .09
❑ 236 Eddie George .50 .15
❑ 237 Derrick Mason .30 .09
❑ 238 Justin McCareins .30 .09
❑ 239 Frank Wycheck .20 .06
❑ 240 Jevon Kearse .30 .09
❑ 241 Samari Rolle .20 .06
❑ 242 Steve McNair .50 .15
❑ 243 Tony Banks .20 .06
❑ 244 Stephen Davis .30 .09
❑ 245 Michael Westbrook .20 .06
❑ 246 Champ Bailey .30 .09
❑ 247 Darrell Green .20 .06
❑ 248 Bruce Smith .20 .06
❑ 249 Fred Smoot .20 .06
❑ 250 Rod Gardner .30 .09
❑ 251 David Carr RC 4.00 1.20
❑ 252 Joey Harrington RC 4.00 1.20
❑ 253 Patrick Ramsey RC 2.50 .75
❑ 254 Kurt Kittner RC .60 .18
❑ 255 Eric Crouch RC 2.00 .60
❑ 256 Josh McCown RC 1.50 .45
❑ 257 David Garrard RC 1.25 .35
❑ 258 Rohan Davey RC 1.25 .35
❑ 259 Ronald Curry RC 1.25 .35
❑ 260 Chad Hutchinson RC 1.25 .35
❑ 261 William Green RC 2.00 .60
❑ 262 T.J. Duckett RC 2.00 .60
❑ 263 Clinton Portis RC 4.00 1.20
❑ 264 DeShaun Foster RC 1.25 .35
❑ 265 Luke Staley RC .60 .18
❑ 266 Wes Pate RC .50 .15
❑ 267 Travis Stephens RC .60 .18
❑ 268 Adrian Peterson RC 1.25 .35
❑ 269 Zak Kustok RC 1.25 .35
❑ 270 Maurice Morris RC 1.25 .35
❑ 271 Lamar Gordon RC 1.25 .35
❑ 272 Chester Taylor RC 1.25 .35
❑ 273 Najeh Davenport RC 1.25 .35
❑ 274 Ladell Betts RC 1.25 .35
❑ 275 Ashley Lelie RC 2.50 .75
❑ 276 Josh Reed RC 1.25 .35
❑ 277 Cliff Russell RC .60 .18
❑ 278 Javon Walker RC 2.50 .75
❑ 279 Ron Johnson RC .60 .18
❑ 280 Antwaan Randle El RC 1.50 .45
❑ 281 Andre Davis RC 1.25 .35
❑ 282 Marquise Walker RC .60 .18
❑ 283 Kelly Campbell RC .60 .18
❑ 284 Tavon Mason RC .50 .15
❑ 285 Antonio Bryant RC 1.25 .35
❑ 286 Jabar Gaffney RC 1.25 .35
❑ 287 Donte Stallworth RC 2.50 .75
❑ 288 Tim Carter RC .60 .18
❑ 289 Reche Caldwell RC 1.25 .35
❑ 290 Freddie Milons RC .60 .18
❑ 291 Brian Poli-Dixon RC .60 .18
❑ 292 Brian Westbrook RC 2.00 .60
❑ 293 Josh Scobey RC 1.25 .35
❑ 294 Jeremy Shockey RC 4.00 1.20
❑ 295 Daniel Graham RC 1.25 .35
❑ 296 Deion Branch RC 2.50 .75
❑ 297 Julius Peppers RC 2.50 .75
❑ 298 Kalimba Edwards RC 1.25 .35
❑ 299 Dwight Freeney RC 1.50 .45
❑ 300 Terry Charles RC .60 .18
❑ 301 Alex Brown RC 1.25 .35
❑ 302 Jason McAddley RC .60 .18
❑ 303 Michael Lewis RC 1.25 .35
❑ 304 Dennis Johnson RC .50 .15
❑ 305 Albert Haynesworth RC .60 .18
❑ 306 Ryan Sims RC 1.25 .35
❑ 307 Larry Tripplett RC .50 .15
❑ 308 Anthony Weaver RC .60 .18
❑ 309 Wendell Bryant RC 1.25 .35
❑ 310 John Henderson RC 1.25 .35
❑ 311 Alan Harper RC .50 .15
❑ 312 Napoleon Harris RC 1.25 .35
❑ 313 Bryan Thomas RC .60 .18
❑ 314 Andra Davis RC .60 .18
❑ 315 Levar Fisher RC .50 .15
❑ 316 Woody Dantzler RC 1.25 .35
❑ 317 Robert Thomas RC 1.25 .35
❑ 318 Quentin Jammer RC 1.25 .35
❑ 319 Lito Sheppard RC 1.25 .35
❑ 320 Travis Fisher RC 1.25 .35
❑ 321 Roy Williams RC 3.00 .90
❑ 322 Phillip Buchanon RC 1.25 .35
❑ 323 Joseph Jefferson RC .60 .18
❑ 324 Ed Reed RC 2.00 .60
❑ 325 Lamont Thompson RC .60 .18
❑ 326 Raonall Smith RC .60 .18
❑ 327 Mike Rumph RC 1.25 .35
❑ 328 Rocky Calmus RC 1.25 .35
❑ 329 Bryant McKinnie RC .60 .18
❑ 330 Mike Williams RC .60 .18

2003 Score

	Nm-Mt	Ex-Mt
COMPLETE SET (327)	50.00	15.00
❑ 1 Jeff Blake	.20	.06
❑ 2 Todd Heap	.30	.09
❑ 3 Ron Johnson	.20	.06
❑ 4 Jamal Lewis	.50	.15
❑ 5 Ray Lewis	.50	.15
❑ 6 Chris Redman	.20	.06
❑ 7 Ed Reed	.30	.09
❑ 8 Travis Taylor	.20	.06
❑ 9 Anthony Weaver	.20	.06
❑ 10 Drew Bledsoe	.50	.15
❑ 11 Larry Centers	.20	.06
❑ 12 Nate Clements	.20	.06
❑ 13 Travis Henry	.30	.09
❑ 14 Eric Moulds	.30	.09
❑ 15 Peerless Price	.30	.09
❑ 16 Josh Reed	.30	.09
❑ 17 Coy Wire	.20	.06
❑ 18 Corey Dillon	.30	.09
❑ 19 T.J. Houshmandzadeh	.20	.06
❑ 20 Chad Johnson	.30	.09
❑ 21 Jon Kitna	.30	.09
❑ 22 Lorenzo Neal	.20	.06
❑ 23 Peter Warrick	.30	.09
❑ 24 Nicolas Luchey RC	.20	.06
❑ 25 Tim Couch	.20	.06
❑ 26 Andre Davis	.20	.06
❑ 27 William Green	.30	.09
❑ 28 Kevin Johnson	.30	.09
❑ 29 Quincy Morgan	.30	.09
❑ 30 Dennis Northcutt	.30	.09
❑ 31 Jamel White	.20	.06
❑ 32 Mike Anderson	.30	.09
❑ 33 Steve Beuerlein	.20	.06
❑ 34 Jason Elam	.20	.06
❑ 35 Olandis Gary	.30	.09
❑ 36 Brian Griese	.50	.15
❑ 37 Ashley Lelie	.50	.15
❑ 38 Ed McCaffrey	.30	.09
❑ 39 Clinton Portis	.75	.23
❑ 40 Shannon Sharpe	.30	.09
❑ 41 Rod Smith	.30	.09
❑ 42 James Allen	.30	.09

❑	43	Corey Bradford	.20	.06
❑	44	David Carr	.75	.23
❑	45	JaJuan Dawson	.20	.06
❑	46	Jabar Gaffney	.30	.09
❑	47	Aaron Glenn	.20	.06
❑	48	Billy Miller	.20	.06
❑	49	Jonathan Wells	.20	.06
❑	50	Dwight Freeney	.20	.06
❑	51	Marvin Harrison	.50	.15
❑	52	Qadry Ismail	.30	.09
❑	53	Edgerrin James	.50	.15
❑	54	Peyton Manning	.75	.23
❑	55	James Mungro	.20	.06
❑	56	Marcus Pollard	.20	.06
❑	57	Reggie Wayne	.30	.09
❑	58	Kyle Brady	.20	.06
❑	59	Mark Brunell	.30	.09
❑	60	David Garrard	.20	.06
❑	61	John Henderson	.20	.06
❑	62	Stacey Mack	.20	.06
❑	63	Jimmy Smith	.30	.09
❑	64	Fred Taylor	.50	.15
❑	65	Marc Boerigter	.30	.09
❑	66	Tony Gonzalez	.30	.09
❑	67	Trent Green	.30	.09
❑	68	Priest Holmes	.60	.18
❑	69	Eddie Kennison	.20	.06
❑	70	Snoop Minnis	.20	.06
❑	71	Johnnie Morton	.30	.09
❑	72	Cris Carter	.50	.15
❑	73	Chris Chambers	.50	.15
❑	74	Robert Edwards	.20	.06
❑	75	Jay Fiedler	.30	.09
❑	76	Ray Lucas	.20	.06
❑	77	Randy McMichael	.30	.09
❑	78	Travis Minor	.20	.06
❑	79	Zach Thomas	.30	.09
❑	80	Ricky Williams	.50	.15
❑	81	Tom Brady	.75	.23
❑	82	Deion Branch	.50	.15
❑	83	Troy Brown	.30	.09
❑	84	Tedy Bruschi	.50	.15
❑	85	Kevin Faulk	.20	.06
❑	86	Daniel Graham	.20	.06
❑	87	David Patten	.20	.06
❑	88	Antowain Smith	.30	.09
❑	89	Adam Vinatieri	.50	.15
❑	90	Donnie Abraham	.20	.06
❑	91	Anthony Becht	.20	.06
❑	92	Wayne Chrebet	.30	.09
❑	93	Laveranues Coles	.30	.09
❑	94	LaMont Jordan	.30	.09
❑	95	Curtis Martin	.50	.15
❑	96	Chad Morton	.20	.06
❑	97	Santana Moss	.30	.09
❑	98	Chad Pennington	.60	.18
❑	99	Vinny Testaverde	.30	.09
❑	100	Tim Brown	.50	.15
❑	101	Phillip Buchanon	.20	.06
❑	102	Rich Gannon	.30	.09
❑	103	Charlie Garner	.30	.09
❑	104	Doug Jolley	.20	.06
❑	105	Jerry Porter	.30	.09
❑	106	Jerry Rice	1.00	.30
❑	107	Marques Tuiasosopo	.30	.09
❑	108	Charles Woodson	.30	.09
❑	109	Rod Woodson	.30	.09
❑	110	Kendrell Bell	.30	.09
❑	111	Jerome Bettis	.50	.15
❑	112	Plaxico Burress	.30	.09
❑	113	Tommy Maddox	.50	.15
❑	114	Joey Porter	.20	.06
❑	115	Antwaan Randle El	.50	.15
❑	116	Kordell Stewart	.30	.09
❑	117	Hines Ward	.50	.15
❑	118	Amos Zereoue	.30	.09
❑	119	Drew Brees	.50	.15
❑	120	Reche Caldwell	.20	.06
❑	121	Curtis Conway	.20	.06
❑	122	Tim Dwight	.30	.09
❑	123	Doug Flutie	.50	.15
❑	124	Quentin Jammer	.20	.06
❑	125	Ben Leber	.20	.06
❑	126	Josh Norman	.20	.06
❑	127	Junior Seau	.50	.15
❑	128	LaDainian Tomlinson	.50	.15
❑	129	Keith Bulluck	.20	.06
❑	130	Rocky Calmus	.20	.06
❑	131	Kevin Carter	.20	.06
❑	132	Kevin Dyson	.30	.09
❑	133	Eddie George	.30	.09
❑	134	Albert Haynesworth	.20	.06
❑	135	Jevon Kearse	.30	.09
❑	136	Derrick Mason	.30	.09
❑	137	Justin McCareins	.20	.06
❑	138	Steve McNair	.50	.15
❑	139	Frank Wycheck	.20	.06
❑	140	David Boston	.30	.09
❑	141	MarTay Jenkins	.20	.06
❑	142	Freddie Jones	.20	.06
❑	143	Thomas Jones	.30	.09
❑	144	Jason McAddley	.20	.06
❑	145	Josh McCown	.30	.09
❑	146	Jake Plummer	.30	.09
❑	147	Marcel Shipp	.30	.09
❑	148	Alge Crumpler	.30	.09
❑	149	T.J. Duckett	.30	.09
❑	150	Warrick Dunn	.30	.09
❑	151	Brian Finneran	.20	.06
❑	152	Trevor Gaylor	.20	.06
❑	153	Shawn Jefferson	.20	.06
❑	154	Michael Vick	1.25	.35
❑	155	Randy Fasani	.20	.06
❑	156	DeShaun Foster	.20	.06
❑	157	Muhsin Muhammad	.30	.09
❑	158	Rodney Peete	.20	.06
❑	159	Julius Peppers	.50	.15
❑	160	Lamar Smith	.20	.06
❑	161	Steve Smith	.20	.06
❑	162	Chris Weinke	.30	.09
❑	163	Wesley Walls	.20	.06
❑	164	Marty Booker	.30	.09
❑	165	Mike Brown	.30	.09
❑	166	Chris Chandler	.20	.06
❑	167	Jim Miller	.20	.06
❑	168	Marcus Robinson	.30	.09
❑	169	David Terrell	.30	.09
❑	170	Anthony Thomas	.50	.15
❑	171	Brian Urlacher	.75	.23
❑	172	Dez White	.20	.06
❑	173	Antonio Bryant	.30	.09
❑	174	Quincy Carter	.30	.09
❑	175	Dexter Coakley	.20	.06
❑	176	Joey Galloway	.30	.09
❑	177	La'Roi Glover	.20	.06
❑	178	Troy Hambrick	.20	.06
❑	179	Chad Hutchinson	.30	.09
❑	180	Rocket Ismail	.30	.09
❑	181	Emmitt Smith	1.25	.35
❑	182	Roy Williams	.50	.15
❑	183	Scotty Anderson	.20	.06
❑	184	Germane Crowell	.20	.06
❑	185	Az-Zahir Hakim	.20	.06
❑	186	Joey Harrington	.75	.23
❑	187	Cory Schlesinger	.20	.06
❑	188	Bill Schroeder	.30	.09
❑	189	James Stewart	.30	.09
❑	190	Marques Anderson	.20	.06
❑	191	Najeh Davenport	.20	.06
❑	192	Donald Driver	.30	.09
❑	193	Brett Favre	1.25	.35
❑	194	Bubba Franks	.30	.09
❑	195	Terry Glenn	.20	.06
❑	196	Ahman Green	.50	.15
❑	197	Darren Sharper	.20	.06
❑	198	Javon Walker	.30	.09
❑	199	D'Wayne Bates	.20	.06
❑	200	Michael Bennett	.30	.09
❑	201	Todd Bouman	.20	.06
❑	202	Byron Chamberlain	.20	.06
❑	203	Daunte Culpepper	.50	.15
❑	204	Randy Moss	.75	.23
❑	205	Kelly Campbell	.30	.09
❑	206	Aaron Brooks	.50	.15
❑	207	Charles Grant	.20	.06
❑	208	Joe Horn	.30	.09
❑	209	Michael Lewis	.20	.06
❑	210	Deuce McAllister	.50	.15
❑	211	Jerome Pathon	.30	.09
❑	212	Donte Stallworth	.50	.15
❑	213	Boo Williams	.20	.06
❑	214	Tiki Barber	.30	.09
❑	215	Tim Carter	.30	.09
❑	216	Kerry Collins	.30	.09
❑	217	Ron Dayne	.20	.06
❑	218	Jesse Palmer	.20	.06
❑	219	Will Peterson	.20	.06
❑	220	Jason Sehorn	.20	.06
❑	221	Jeremy Shockey	.75	.23
❑	222	Michael Strahan	.30	.09
❑	223	Amani Toomer	.30	.09
❑	224	Koy Detmer	.20	.06
❑	225	Antonio Freeman	.30	.09
❑	226	Dorsey Levens	.20	.06
❑	227	Chad Lewis	.20	.06
❑	228	Donovan McNabb	.60	.18
❑	229	Freddie Mitchell	.30	.09
❑	230	Duce Staley	.30	.09
❑	231	James Thrash	.20	.06
❑	232	Brian Westbrook	.30	.09
❑	233	Kevan Barlow	.30	.09
❑	234	Andre Carter	.20	.06
❑	235	Jeff Garcia	.50	.15
❑	236	Garrison Hearst	.30	.09
❑	237	Eric Johnson	.30	.09
❑	238	Terrell Owens	.50	.15
❑	239	Jamal Robertson	.30	.09
❑	240	Tai Streets	.20	.06
❑	241	Shaun Alexander	.50	.15
❑	242	Trent Dilfer	.30	.09
❑	243	Bobby Engram	.20	.06
❑	244	Matt Hasselbeck	.30	.09
❑	245	Darrell Jackson	.30	.09
❑	246	Maurice Morris	.20	.06
❑	247	Koren Robinson	.20	.06
❑	248	Jerramy Stevens	.20	.06
❑	249	Isaac Bruce	.50	.15
❑	250	Marc Bulger	.50	.15
❑	251	Marshall Faulk	.50	.15
❑	252	Lamar Gordon	.20	.06
❑	253	Torry Holt	.50	.15
❑	254	Ricky Proehl	.20	.06
❑	255	Kurt Warner	.50	.15
❑	256	Aeneas Williams	.20	.06
❑	257	Mike Alstott	.50	.15
❑	258	Ken Dilger	.20	.06
❑	259	Brad Johnson	.30	.09
❑	260	Keyshawn Johnson	.50	.15
❑	261	Rob Johnson	.30	.09
❑	262	John Lynch	.30	.09
❑	263	Keenan McCardell	.20	.06
❑	264	Michael Pittman	.20	.06
❑	265	Warren Sapp	.30	.09
❑	266	Marquise Walker	.20	.06
❑	267	Champ Bailey	.30	.09
❑	268	Stephen Davis	.30	.09
❑	269	Rod Gardner	.30	.09
❑	270	Darrell Green	.20	.06
❑	271	Shane Matthews	.20	.06
❑	272	Damerien McCants	.20	.06
❑	273	Patrick Ramsey	.50	.15
❑	274	Bruce Smith	.30	.09
❑	275	Kenny Watson	.20	.06
❑	276	Carson Palmer RC	4.00	1.20
❑	277	Byron Leftwich RC	5.00	1.50
❑	278	Kyle Boller RC	3.00	.90
❑	279	Chris Simms RC	2.50	.75
❑	280	Dave Ragone RC	1.25	.35
❑	281	Rex Grossman RC	3.00	.90
❑	282	Brian St.Pierre RC	1.25	.35
❑	283	Larry Johnson RC	2.50	.75
❑	284	Lee Suggs RC	2.50	.75
❑	285	Justin Fargas RC	1.25	.35
❑	286	Onterrio Smith RC	1.50	.45
❑	287	Willis McGahee RC	3.00	.90
❑	288	Chris Brown RC	2.50	.75
❑	289	Musa Smith RC	1.25	.35
❑	290	Artose Pinner RC	1.25	.35
❑	291	Cecil Sapp RC	1.00	.30
❑	293	LaBrandon Toefield RC	1.25	.35
❑	294	Charles Rogers RC	1.50	.45
❑	295	Andre Johnson RC	3.00	.90

❑ 296 Taylor Jacobs RC	1.25	.35
❑ 297 Bryant Johnson RC	1.25	.35
❑ 298 Kelley Washington RC	1.25	.35
❑ 299 Brandon Lloyd RC	1.50	.45
❑ 300 Justin Gage RC	1.25	.35
❑ 301 Tyrone Calico RC	1.50	.45
❑ 302 Kevin Curtis RC	1.25	.35
❑ 303 Sam Aiken RC	1.00	.30
❑ 304 Doug Gabriel RC	1.25	.35
❑ 305 Talman Gardner RC	1.25	.35
❑ 306 Jason Witten RC	2.00	.60
❑ 307 Mike Pinkard RC	.60	.18
❑ 308 Teyo Johnson RC	1.25	.35
❑ 309 Bennie Joppru RC	1.25	.35
❑ 310 Dallas Clark RC	1.25	.35
❑ 311 Terrell Suggs RC	2.00	.60
❑ 312 Chris Kelsay RC	1.25	.35
❑ 313 Jerome McDougle RC	1.25	.35
❑ 314 Andrew Williams RC	1.00	.30
❑ 315 Michael Haynes RC	1.25	.35
❑ 316 Jimmy Kennedy RC	1.25	.35
❑ 317 Kevin Williams RC	1.25	.35
❑ 318 Ken Dorsey RC	2.00	.60
❑ 319 William Joseph RC	1.25	.35
❑ 320 Kenny Peterson RC	1.00	.30
❑ 321 Rien Long RC	.60	.18
❑ 322 Boss Bailey RC	1.50	.45
❑ 324 Terence Newman RC	2.50	.75
❑ 325 Marcus Trufant RC	1.25	.35
❑ 326 Andre Woolfolk RC	1.25	.35
❑ 327 Dennis Weathersby RC	.60	.18
❑ 329 Mike Doss RC	1.25	.35
❑ 330 Rashean Mathis RC	1.00	.30

2003 Score Scorecard

	Nm-Mt	Ex-Mt

*STARS: 2.5X TO 6X BASIC CARDS
*RC's: 1X TO 2.5X

2004 Score

	Nm-Mt	Ex-Mt
COMPLETE SET (440)	80.00	24.00
ONE ROOKIE PER PACK		
❑ 1 Emmitt Smith	1.00	.30
❑ 2 Anquan Boldin	.50	.15
❑ 3 Bryant Johnson	.20	.06
❑ 4 Marcel Shipp	.30	.09
❑ 5 Josh McCown	.30	.09
❑ 6 Dexter Jackson	.20	.06
❑ 7 Bert Berry	.20	.06
❑ 8 Freddie Jones	.20	.06
❑ 9 Duane Starks	.20	.06
❑ 10 Michael Vick	1.00	.30
❑ 11 T.J. Duckett	.30	.09
❑ 12 Warrick Dunn	.30	.09
❑ 13 Peerless Price	.30	.09
❑ 14 Alge Crumpler	.30	.09
❑ 15 Brian Finneran	.20	.06
❑ 16 Jason Webster	.20	.06
❑ 17 Dez White	.30	.09
❑ 18 Keith Brooking	.20	.06
❑ 19 Rod Coleman	.20	.06
❑ 20 Jamal Lewis	.50	.15
❑ 21 Kyle Boller	.50	.15
❑ 22 Todd Heap	.30	.09
❑ 23 Jonathan Ogden	.20	.06
❑ 24 Travis Taylor	.20	.06
❑ 25 Ray Lewis	.50	.15
❑ 26 Peter Boulware	.30	.09
❑ 27 Terrell Suggs	.30	.09
❑ 28 Chris McAlister	.20	.06
❑ 29 Ed Reed	.30	.09
❑ 30 Drew Bledsoe	.50	.15
❑ 31 Travis Henry	.30	.09
❑ 32 Eric Moulds	.30	.09
❑ 33 Josh Reed	.20	.06
❑ 34 Willis McGahee	.50	.15
❑ 35 Takeo Spikes	.20	.06
❑ 36 Lawyer Milloy	.30	.09
❑ 37 Troy Vincent	.20	.06
❑ 38 Sam Adams	.20	.06
❑ 39 Nate Clements	.20	.06
❑ 40 Jake Delhomme	.50	.15
❑ 41 Stephen Davis	.30	.09
❑ 42 DeShaun Foster	.30	.09
❑ 43 Muhsin Muhammad	.30	.09
❑ 44 Steve Smith	.30	.09
❑ 45 Ricky Proehl	.20	.06
❑ 46 Julius Peppers	.50	.15
❑ 47 Kris Jenkins	.20	.06
❑ 48 Dan Morgan	.20	.06
❑ 49 Ricky Manning	.20	.06
❑ 50 Brad Hoover	.20	.06
❑ 51 Carson Palmer	.60	.18
❑ 52 Rudi Johnson	.30	.09
❑ 53 Corey Dillon	.30	.09
❑ 54 Chad Johnson	.30	.09
❑ 55 Peter Warrick	.30	.09
❑ 56 Kelley Washington	.20	.06
❑ 57 Kevin Hardy	.20	.06
❑ 58 Tory James	.20	.06
❑ 59 Ickey Woods	.50	.15
❑ 60 Anthony Thomas	.30	.09
❑ 61 Thomas Jones	.30	.09
❑ 62 Rex Grossman	.50	.15
❑ 63 Marty Booker	.30	.09
❑ 64 Justin Gage	.30	.09
❑ 65 David Terrell	.30	.09
❑ 66 Brian Urlacher	.60	.18
❑ 67 Mike Brown	.20	.06
❑ 68 Charles Tillman	.30	.09
❑ 69 Jeff Garcia	.50	.15
❑ 70 Lee Suggs	.50	.15
❑ 71 William Green	.30	.09
❑ 72 Kelly Holcomb	.30	.09
❑ 73 Quincy Morgan	.30	.09
❑ 74 Andre Davis	.20	.06
❑ 75 Dennis Northcutt	.20	.06
❑ 76 Gerard Warren	.20	.06
❑ 77 Courtney Brown	.30	.09
❑ 78 Joey Harrington	.50	.15
❑ 79 Shawn Bryson	.20	.06
❑ 80 Charles Rogers	.30	.09
❑ 81 Mikhael Ricks	.20	.06
❑ 82 Artose Pinner	.20	.06
❑ 83 Az-Zahir Hakim	.20	.06
❑ 84 Dre Bly	.20	.06
❑ 85 Fernando Bryant	.20	.06
❑ 86 Boss Bailey	.30	.09
❑ 87 Tai Streets	.20	.06
❑ 88 Jake Plummer	.30	.09
❑ 89 Quentin Griffin	.50	.15
❑ 90 Mike Anderson	.30	.09
❑ 91 Garrison Hearst	.30	.09
❑ 92 Rod Smith	.30	.09
❑ 93 Ashley Lelie	.30	.09
❑ 94 Shannon Sharpe	.30	.09
❑ 95 Al Wilson	.20	.06
❑ 96 Champ Bailey	.30	.09
❑ 97 Jason Elam	.20	.06
❑ 98 John Lynch	.30	.09
❑ 99 Quincy Carter	.30	.09
❑ 100 Antonio Bryant	.30	.09
❑ 101 Terry Glenn	.20	.06
❑ 102 Keyshawn Johnson	.30	.09
❑ 103 Jason Witten	.30	.09
❑ 104 La'Roi Glover	.20	.06
❑ 105 Dat Nguyen	.20	.06
❑ 106 Dexter Coakley	.20	.06
❑ 107 Terence Newman	.30	.09
❑ 108 Darren Woodson	.20	.06
❑ 109 Roy Williams S	.30	.09
❑ 110 Brett Favre	1.25	.35
❑ 111 Ahman Green	.50	.15
❑ 112 Najeh Davenport	.20	.06
❑ 113 Donald Driver	.30	.09
❑ 114 Robert Ferguson	.20	.06
❑ 115 Javon Walker	.30	.09
❑ 116 Bubba Franks	.30	.09
❑ 117 Kabeer Gbaja-Biamila	.30	.09
❑ 118 Darren Sharper	.20	.06
❑ 119 Mike McKenzie	.20	.06
❑ 120 Nick Barnett	.30	.09
❑ 121 David Carr	.50	.15
❑ 122 Domanick Davis	.50	.15
❑ 123 Andre Johnson	.50	.15
❑ 124 Corey Bradford	.20	.06
❑ 125 Jabar Gaffney	.30	.09
❑ 126 Billy Miller	.20	.06
❑ 127 Gary Walker	.20	.06
❑ 128 Jamie Sharper	.20	.06
❑ 129 Aaron Glenn	.20	.06
❑ 130 Robaire Smith	.20	.06
❑ 131 Peyton Manning	.75	.23
❑ 132 Edgerrin James	.50	.15
❑ 133 Dominic Rhodes	.30	.09
❑ 134 Marvin Harrison	.50	.15
❑ 135 Reggie Wayne	.30	.09
❑ 136 Brandon Stokley	.30	.09
❑ 137 Marcus Pollard	.20	.06
❑ 138 Dallas Clark	.30	.09
❑ 139 Mike Vanderjagt	.20	.06
❑ 140 Dwight Freeney	.20	.06
❑ 141 Mike Doss	.20	.06
❑ 142 Byron Leftwich	.75	.23
❑ 143 Fred Taylor	.30	.09
❑ 144 LaBrandon Toefield	.20	.06
❑ 145 Jimmy Smith	.30	.09
❑ 146 Kevin Johnson	.20	.06
❑ 147 Marcus Stroud	.20	.06
❑ 148 John Henderson	.20	.06
❑ 149 Donovin Darius	.20	.06
❑ 150 Deon Grant	.20	.06
❑ 151 Rashean Mathis	.20	.06
❑ 152 Trent Green	.30	.09
❑ 153 Priest Holmes	.60	.18
❑ 154 Johnnie Morton	.30	.09
❑ 155 Eddie Kennison	.20	.06
❑ 156 Marc Boerigter	.30	.09
❑ 157 Tony Gonzalez	.30	.09
❑ 158 Dante Hall	.50	.15
❑ 159 Tony Richardson	.20	.06
❑ 160 Gary Stills	.20	.06
❑ 161 Daunte Culpepper	.50	.15
❑ 162 Michael Bennett	.30	.09
❑ 163 Moe Williams	.20	.06
❑ 164 Onterrio Smith	.30	.09
❑ 165 Jim Kleinsasser	.20	.06
❑ 166 Antoine Winfield	.20	.06
❑ 167 Nate Burleson	.50	.15
❑ 168 Randy Moss	.60	.18
❑ 169 Marcus Robinson	.30	.09
❑ 170 Chris Hovan	.20	.06
❑ 171 Brian Russell RC	.50	.15
❑ 172 A.J. Feeley	.50	.15
❑ 173 Jay Fiedler	.20	.06
❑ 174 Ricky Williams	.50	.15
❑ 175 Chris Chambers	.30	.09
❑ 176 David Boston	.30	.09
❑ 177 Randy McMichael	.20	.06
❑ 178 Jason Taylor	.20	.06
❑ 179 Adewale Ogunleye	.30	.09
❑ 180 Zach Thomas	.50	.15
❑ 181 Junior Seau	.50	.15
❑ 182 Patrick Surtain	.20	.06
❑ 183 Tom Brady	.75	.23
❑ 184 Kevin Faulk	.20	.06
❑ 185 Troy Brown	.30	.09
❑ 186 Deion Branch	.50	.15
❑ 187 David Givens	.30	.09
❑ 188 Bethel Johnson	.30	.09
❑ 189 Richard Seymour	.20	.06
❑ 190 Tedy Bruschi	.30	.09
❑ 191 Ty Law	.30	.09

❑	192	Rodney Harrison	.20	.06
❑	193	Willie McGinest	.20	.06
❑	194	Adam Vinatieri	.50	.15
❑	195	Aaron Brooks	.30	.09
❑	196	Deuce McAllister	.50	.15
❑	197	Joe Horn	.30	.09
❑	198	Donte Stallworth	.30	.09
❑	199	Jerome Pathon	.20	.06
❑	200	Boo Williams	.20	.06
❑	201	Charles Grant	.20	.06
❑	202	Darren Howard	.20	.06
❑	203	Michael Lewis	.20	.06
❑	204	Johnathan Sullivan	.20	.06
❑	205	LeCharles Bentley	.20	.06
❑	206	Kerry Collins	.30	.09
❑	207	Tiki Barber	.30	.09
❑	208	Amani Toomer	.30	.09
❑	209	Ike Hilliard	.20	.06
❑	210	Tim Carter	.20	.06
❑	211	Jeremy Shockey	.50	.15
❑	212	Michael Strahan	.30	.09
❑	213	Will Allen	.20	.06
❑	214	Will Peterson	.20	.06
❑	215	William Joseph	.20	.06
❑	216	Chad Pennington	.60	.18
❑	217	Curtis Martin	.50	.15
❑	218	LaMont Jordan	.30	.09
❑	219	Santana Moss	.30	.09
❑	220	Justin McCareins	.20	.06
❑	221	Wayne Chrebet	.30	.09
❑	222	Anthony Becht	.20	.06
❑	223	Shaun Ellis	.20	.06
❑	224	John Abraham	.20	.06
❑	225	DeWayne Robertson	.20	.06
❑	226	Rich Gannon	.30	.09
❑	227	Justin Fargas	.30	.09
❑	228	Tyrone Wheatley	.20	.06
❑	229	Jerry Rice	1.00	.30
❑	230	Tim Brown	.50	.15
❑	231	Jerry Porter	.30	.09
❑	232	Teyo Johnson	.20	.06
❑	233	Charles Woodson	.30	.09
❑	234	Phillip Buchanon	.20	.06
❑	235	Rod Woodson	.30	.09
❑	236	Warren Sapp	.30	.09
❑	237	Donovan McNabb	.60	.18
❑	238	Brian Westbrook	.30	.09
❑	239	Correll Buckhalter	.30	.09
❑	240	Chad Lewis	.20	.06
❑	241	L.J. Smith	.30	.09
❑	242	Terrell Owens	.50	.15
❑	243	Todd Pinkston	.20	.06
❑	244	Freddie Mitchell	.30	.09
❑	245	Jevon Kearse	.30	.09
❑	246	Brian Dawkins	.20	.06
❑	247	Corey Simon	.30	.09
❑	248	Tommy Maddox	.30	.09
❑	249	Duce Staley	.30	.09
❑	250	Jerome Bettis	.50	.15
❑	251	Hines Ward	.50	.15
❑	252	Plaxico Burress	.30	.09
❑	253	Antwaan Randle El	.30	.09
❑	254	Kendrell Bell	.30	.09
❑	255	Joey Porter	.20	.06
❑	256	Alan Faneca	.20	.06
❑	257	Casey Hampton	.20	.06
❑	258	Drew Brees	.50	.15
❑	259	Doug Flutie	.50	.15
❑	260	LaDainian Tomlinson	.50	.15
❑	261	Reche Caldwell	.20	.06
❑	262	Tim Dwight	.30	.09
❑	263	Eric Parker	.20	.06
❑	264	Kevin Dyson	.20	.06
❑	265	Antonio Gates	.50	.15
❑	266	Quentin Jammer	.20	.06
❑	267	Zeke Moreno	.20	.06
❑	268	Tim Rattay	.30	.09
❑	269	Kevan Barlow	.30	.09
❑	270	Cedrick Wilson	.20	.06
❑	271	Brandon Lloyd	.30	.09
❑	272	Fred Beasley	.20	.06
❑	273	Andre Carter	.20	.06
❑	274	Julian Peterson	.20	.06
❑	275	Ahmed Plummer	.20	.06
❑	276	Tony Parrish	.20	.06
❑	277	Bryant Young	.20	.06
❑	278	Matt Hasselbeck	.30	.09
❑	279	Shaun Alexander	.50	.15
❑	280	Maurice Morris	.20	.06
❑	281	Koren Robinson	.30	.09
❑	282	Darrell Jackson	.30	.09
❑	283	Bobby Engram	.20	.06
❑	284	Grant Wistrom	.20	.06
❑	285	Chad Brown	.20	.06
❑	286	Marcus Trufant	.20	.06
❑	287	Bobby Taylor	.20	.06
❑	288	Marc Bulger	.50	.15
❑	289	Kurt Warner	.50	.15
❑	290	Marshall Faulk	.50	.15
❑	291	Lamar Gordon	.20	.06
❑	292	Torry Holt	.50	.15
❑	293	Isaac Bruce	.30	.09
❑	294	Leonard Little	.20	.06
❑	295	Aeneas Williams	.20	.06
❑	296	Orlando Pace	.20	.06
❑	297	Tommy Polley	.20	.06
❑	298	Pisa Tinoisamoa	.20	.06
❑	299	Brad Johnson	.30	.09
❑	300	Michael Pittman	.20	.06
❑	301	Charlie Garner	.30	.09
❑	302	Mike Alstott	.30	.09
❑	303	Keenan McCardell	.20	.06
❑	304	Joey Galloway	.30	.09
❑	305	Joe Jurevicius	.20	.06
❑	306	Anthony McFarland	.20	.06
❑	307	Derrick Brooks	.30	.09
❑	308	Ronde Barber	.20	.06
❑	309	Shelton Quarles	.20	.06
❑	310	Steve McNair	.50	.15
❑	311	Eddie George	.30	.09
❑	312	Chris Brown	.50	.15
❑	313	Derrick Mason	.30	.09
❑	314	Tyrone Calico	.30	.09
❑	315	Drew Bennett	.30	.09
❑	316	Kevin Carter	.20	.06
❑	317	Keith Bulluck	.20	.06
❑	318	Samari Rolle	.20	.06
❑	319	Albert Haynesworth	.20	.06
❑	320	Erron Kinney	.20	.06
❑	321	Mark Brunell	.30	.09
❑	322	Patrick Ramsey	.30	.09
❑	323	Laveranues Coles	.30	.09
❑	324	Rod Gardner	.30	.09
❑	325	Darnerien McCants	.20	.06
❑	326	Clinton Portis	.50	.15
❑	327	LaVar Arrington	1.00	.30
❑	328	Shawn Springs	.20	.06
❑	329	Fred Smoot	.20	.06
❑	330	James Thrash	.20	.06
❑	331	Marvin Harrison PB	.30	.09
❑	332	Steve McNair PB	.30	.09
❑	333	Ray Lewis PB	.30	.09
❑	334	Trent Green PB	.20	.06
❑	335	Peyton Manning PB	.50	.15
❑	336	Priest Holmes PB	.50	.15
❑	337	Clinton Portis PB	.50	.15
❑	338	Torry Holt PB	.30	.09
❑	339	Anquan Boldin PB	.20	.06
❑	340	Daunte Culpepper PB	.30	.09
❑	341	Ahman Green PB	.30	.09
❑	342	Brian Urlacher PB	.50	.15
❑	343	Donovan McNabb PB	.50	.15
❑	344	Marc Bulger PB	.30	.09
❑	345	Shaun Alexander PB	.30	.09
❑	346	Peyton Manning LL	.50	.15
❑	347	Daunte Culpepper LL	.30	.09
❑	348	Brett Favre LL	.60	.18
❑	349	Steve McNair LL	.30	.09
❑	350	Tom Brady LL	.50	.15
❑	351	Jamal Lewis LL	.30	.09
❑	352	Deuce McAllister LL	.30	.09
❑	353	Clinton Portis LL	.50	.15
❑	354	Ahman Green LL	.30	.09
❑	355	LaDainian Tomlinson LL	.30	.09
❑	356	Torry Holt LL	.30	.09
❑	357	Anquan Boldin LL	.20	.06
❑	358	Randy Moss LL	.50	.15
❑	359	Chad Johnson LL	.20	.06
❑	360	Marvin Harrison LL	.30	.09
❑	361	Peyton Manning HL	.50	.15
❑	362	Jamal Lewis HL	.30	.09
❑	363	Ray Lewis HL	.30	.09
❑	364	Anquan Boldin HL	.20	.06
❑	365	Terrell Suggs HL	.20	.06
❑	366	Jamal Lewis HL	.30	.09
❑	367	Priest Holmes HL	.50	.15
❑	368	Tom Brady HL	.50	.15
❑	369	Marc Bulger HL	.30	.09
❑	370	Steve McNair HL	.30	.09
❑	371	Eli Manning RC	6.00	1.80
❑	372	Robert Gallery RC	2.00	.60
❑	373	Larry Fitzgerald RC	4.00	1.20
❑	374	Philip Rivers RC	4.00	1.20
❑	375	Sean Taylor RC	1.50	.45
❑	376	Kellen Winslow RC	3.00	.90
❑	377	Roy Williams RC	4.00	1.20
❑	378	DeAngelo Hall RC	1.50	.45
❑	379	Reggie Williams RC	1.50	.45
❑	380	Dunta Robinson RC	1.25	.35
❑	381	Ben Roethlisberger RC	12.00	3.60
❑	382	Jonathan Vilma RC	1.25	.35
❑	383	Lee Evans RC	2.00	.60
❑	384	Tommie Harris RC	1.50	.45
❑	385	Michael Clayton RC	3.00	.90
❑	386	D.J. Williams RC	1.50	.45
❑	387	Will Smith RC	1.25	.35
❑	388	Kenechi Udeze RC	1.25	.35
❑	389	Vince Wilfork RC	1.50	.45
❑	390	J.P. Losman RC	3.00	.90
❑	391	Marcus Tubbs RC	1.25	.35
❑	392	Steven Jackson RC	4.00	1.20
❑	393	Ahmad Carroll RC	1.50	.45
❑	394	Chris Perry RC	2.50	.75
❑	395	Jason Babin RC	1.25	.35
❑	396	Chris Gamble RC	1.50	.45
❑	397	Michael Jenkins RC	1.25	.35
❑	398	Kevin Jones RC	4.00	1.20
❑	399	Rashaun Woods RC	1.50	.45
❑	400	Ben Watson RC	1.25	.35
❑	401	Karlos Dansby RC	1.25	.35
❑	402	Igor Olshansky RC	1.25	.35
❑	403	Junior Siavii RC	1.25	.35
❑	404	Teddy Lehman RC	1.25	.35
❑	405	Ricardo Colclough RC	1.25	.35
❑	406	Daryl Smith RC	1.25	.35
❑	407	Ben Troupe RC	1.25	.35
❑	408	Tatum Bell RC	2.00	.60
❑	409	Travis LaBoy RC	1.25	.35
❑	410	Julius Jones RC	5.00	1.50
❑	411	Mewelde Moore RC	1.50	.45
❑	412	Drew Henson RC	3.00	.90
❑	413	Dontarrious Thomas RC	1.25	.35
❑	414	Keiwan Ratliff RC	1.00	.30
❑	415	Devery Henderson RC	1.00	.30
❑	416	Dwan Edwards RC	.60	.18
❑	417	Michael Boulware RC	1.25	.35
❑	418	Darius Watts RC	1.50	.45
❑	419	Greg Jones RC	1.25	.35
❑	420	Madieu Williams RC	1.00	.30
❑	421	Antwan Odom RC	1.25	.35
❑	422	Shawntae Spencer RC	1.25	.35
❑	423	Sean Jones RC	1.00	.30
❑	424	Courtney Watson RC	1.25	.35
❑	425	Kris Wilson RC	1.25	.35
❑	426	Keary Colbert RC	1.50	.45
❑	427	Marquise Hill RC	1.00	.30
❑	428	Darnell Dockett RC	1.00	.30
❑	429	Stuart Schweigert RC	1.25	.35
❑	430	Ben Hartsock RC	1.25	.35
❑	431	Joey Thomas RC	1.25	.35
❑	432	Randy Starks RC	1.00	.30
❑	433	Keith Smith RC	1.00	.30
❑	434	Derrick Hamilton RC	1.00	.30
❑	435	Bernard Berrian RC	1.25	.35
❑	436	Chris Cooley RC	1.25	.35
❑	437	Devard Darling RC	1.25	.35
❑	438	Matt Schaub RC	2.00	.60
❑	439	Luke McCown RC	1.25	.35
❑	440	Cedric Cobbs RC	1.25	.35

2004 Score Glossy

	Nm-Mt	Ex-Mt
*STARS: 1.5X TO 4X BASE CARD HI		
*ROOKIES: .6X TO 1.5X BASE CARD HI		
ONE GLOSSY PER PACK		

2004 Score Scorecard

	Nm-Mt	Ex-Mt
*STARS: 2.5X TO 6X BASE CARD HI		
*ROOKIES: 1.2X TO 3X BASE CARD HI		
STATED PRINT RUN 625 SER.#'d SETS		

2004 Score Inscriptions

	Nm-Mt	Ex-Mt
EXCH EXPIRATION: 4/1/2006		
❑ 6 Dexter Jackson EXCH	15.00	4.50
❑ 7 Bert Berry EXCH	15.00	4.50
❑ 38 Sam Adams EXCH	15.00	4.50
❑ 59 Ickey Woods SP	20.00	6.00
❑ 147 Marcus Stroud EXCH	15.00	4.50
❑ 170 Chris Hovan EXCH	15.00	4.50
❑ 205 LeCharles Bentley EXCH	15.00	4.50
❑ 265 Antonio Gates	60.00	18.00
❑ 267 Zeke Moreno EXCH	15.00	4.50
❑ 320 Erron Kinney EXCH	15.00	4.50

2001 Score Select

	Nm-Mt	Ex-Mt
COMP.SET w/o SPs (220)	30.00	9.00
❑ 1 David Boston	.75	.23
❑ 2 Frank Sanders	.30	.09
❑ 3 Jake Plummer	.50	.15
❑ 4 Michael Pittman	.30	.09
❑ 5 Rob Moore	.50	.15
❑ 6 Thomas Jones	.50	.15
❑ 7 Chris Chandler	.50	.15
❑ 8 Doug Johnson	.30	.09
❑ 9 Jamal Anderson	.75	.23
❑ 10 Tim Dwight	.75	.23
❑ 11 Brandon Stokley	.50	.15
❑ 12 Chris Redman	.30	.09
❑ 13 Jamal Lewis	1.25	.35
❑ 14 Qadry Ismail	.50	.15
❑ 15 Ray Lewis	.75	.23
❑ 16 Rod Woodson	.50	.15
❑ 17 Shannon Sharpe	.50	.15
❑ 18 Travis Taylor	.50	.15
❑ 19 Trent Dilfer	.50	.15
❑ 20 Elvis Grbac	.50	.15
❑ 21 Eric Moulds	.50	.15
❑ 22 Jay Riemersma	.30	.09
❑ 23 Peerless Price	.50	.15
❑ 24 Rob Johnson	.50	.15
❑ 25 Sam Cowart	.30	.09
❑ 26 Sammy Morris	.30	.09
❑ 27 Shawn Bryson	.30	.09
❑ 28 Donald Hayes	.30	.09
❑ 29 Muhsin Muhammad	.50	.15
❑ 30 Patrick Jeffers	.50	.15
❑ 31 Reggie White DE	.75	.23
❑ 32 Steve Beuerlein	.50	.15
❑ 33 Tim Biakabutuka	.50	.15
❑ 34 Wesley Walls	.30	.09
❑ 35 Brian Urlacher	1.25	.35
❑ 36 Cade McNown	.30	.09
❑ 37 Dez White	.30	.09
❑ 38 James Allen	.50	.15
❑ 39 Marcus Robinson	.75	.23
❑ 40 Marty Booker	.30	.09
❑ 41 Akili Smith	.30	.09
❑ 42 Corey Dillon	.75	.23
❑ 43 Danny Farmer	.30	.09
❑ 44 Peter Warrick	.75	.23
❑ 45 Ron Dugans	.30	.09
❑ 46 Takeo Spikes	.30	.09
❑ 47 Courtney Brown	.50	.15
❑ 48 Dennis Northcutt	.50	.15
❑ 49 JaJuan Dawson	.30	.09
❑ 50 Kevin Johnson	.50	.15
❑ 51 Tim Couch	.50	.15
❑ 52 Travis Prentice	.30	.09
❑ 53 Anthony Wright	.30	.09
❑ 54 Emmitt Smith	1.50	.45
❑ 55 James McKnight	.50	.15
❑ 56 Joey Galloway	.50	.15
❑ 57 Rocket Ismail	.50	.15
❑ 58 Randall Cunningham	.75	.23
❑ 59 Troy Aikman	1.25	.35
❑ 60 Brian Griese	.75	.23
❑ 61 Ed McCaffrey	.75	.23
❑ 62 Gus Frerotte	.30	.09
❑ 63 John Elway	2.50	.75
❑ 64 Mike Anderson	.75	.23
❑ 65 Olandis Gary	.50	.15
❑ 66 Rod Smith	.50	.15
❑ 67 Terrell Davis	.75	.23
❑ 68 Barry Sanders	1.50	.45
❑ 69 Charlie Batch	.75	.23
❑ 70 Germane Crowell	.30	.09
❑ 71 Herman Moore	.50	.15
❑ 72 James Stewart	.50	.15
❑ 73 Johnnie Morton	.50	.15
❑ 74 Robert Porcher	.30	.09
❑ 75 Jim Harbaugh	.50	.15
❑ 76 Ahman Green	.75	.23
❑ 77 Antonio Freeman	.75	.23
❑ 78 Bill Schroeder	.50	.15
❑ 79 Brett Favre	2.50	.75
❑ 80 Bubba Franks	.50	.15
❑ 81 Dorsey Levens	.50	.15
❑ 82 E.G. Green	.30	.09
❑ 83 Edgerrin James	1.00	.30
❑ 84 Jerome Pathon	.50	.15
❑ 85 Ken Dilger	.30	.09
❑ 86 Marcus Pollard	.30	.09
❑ 87 Marvin Harrison	.75	.23
❑ 88 Peyton Manning	2.00	.60
❑ 89 Terrence Wilkins	.30	.09
❑ 90 Fred Taylor	.75	.23
❑ 91 Hardy Nickerson	.30	.09
❑ 92 Jimmy Smith	.50	.15
❑ 93 Keenan McCardell	.30	.09
❑ 94 Kyle Brady	.30	.09
❑ 95 Mark Brunell	.75	.23
❑ 96 Tony Brackens	.30	.09
❑ 97 Derrick Alexander WR	.50	.15
❑ 98 Sylvester Morris	.30	.09
❑ 99 Tony Gonzalez	.50	.15
❑ 100 Tony Richardson	.30	.09
❑ 101 Kimble Anders	.30	.09
❑ 102 Warren Moon	.75	.23
❑ 103 Dan Marino	2.50	.75
❑ 104 Jay Fiedler	.75	.23
❑ 105 Lamar Smith	.50	.15
❑ 106 O.J. McDuffie	.30	.09
❑ 107 Oronde Gadsden	.50	.15
❑ 108 Sam Madison	.30	.09
❑ 109 Thurman Thomas	.50	.15
❑ 110 Tony Martin	.30	.09
❑ 111 Zach Thomas	.75	.23
❑ 112 Cris Carter	.75	.23
❑ 113 Daunte Culpepper	.75	.23
❑ 114 Matthew Hatchette	.30	.09
❑ 115 Randy Moss	1.50	.45
❑ 116 Robert Smith	.75	.23
❑ 117 Drew Bledsoe	1.00	.30
❑ 118 J.R. Redmond	.30	.09
❑ 119 Kevin Faulk	.50	.15
❑ 120 Michael Bishop	.30	.09
❑ 121 Terry Glenn	.50	.15
❑ 122 Troy Brown	.50	.15
❑ 123 Ty Law	.50	.15
❑ 124 Aaron Brooks	.75	.23
❑ 125 Darren Howard	.30	.09
❑ 126 Jake Reed	.50	.15
❑ 127 Jeff Blake	.50	.15
❑ 128 Joe Horn	.50	.15
❑ 129 La'Roi Glover	.30	.09
❑ 130 Ricky Williams	.75	.23
❑ 131 Willie Jackson	.30	.09
❑ 132 Albert Connell	.30	.09
❑ 133 Amani Toomer	.50	.15
❑ 134 Ike Hilliard	.50	.15
❑ 135 Jason Sehorn	.30	.09
❑ 136 Jessie Armstead	.30	.09
❑ 137 Kerry Collins	.50	.15
❑ 138 Michael Strahan	.50	.15
❑ 139 Ron Dayne	.75	.23
❑ 140 Ron Dixon	.30	.09
❑ 141 Tiki Barber	.50	.15
❑ 142 Anthony Becht	.30	.09
❑ 143 Chad Pennington	1.25	.35
❑ 144 Curtis Martin	.75	.23
❑ 145 Dedric Ward	.30	.09
❑ 146 Laveranues Coles	.75	.23
❑ 147 Vinny Testaverde	.50	.15
❑ 148 Wayne Chrebet	.50	.15
❑ 149 Andre Rison	.50	.15
❑ 150 Charles Woodson	.50	.15
❑ 151 Darrell Russell	.30	.09
❑ 152 Napoleon Kaufman	.50	.15
❑ 153 Rich Gannon	.75	.23
❑ 154 Tim Brown	.75	.23
❑ 155 Tyrone Wheatley	.50	.15
❑ 156 Chad Lewis	.30	.09
❑ 157 Charles Johnson	.30	.09
❑ 158 Donovan McNabb	1.00	.30
❑ 159 Duce Staley	.75	.23
❑ 160 Hugh Douglas	.30	.09
❑ 161 Na Brown	.30	.09
❑ 162 Todd Pinkston	.30	.09
❑ 163 James Thrash	.50	.15
❑ 164 Bobby Shaw	.30	.09
❑ 165 Hines Ward	.75	.23
❑ 166 Jerome Bettis	.75	.23
❑ 167 Kordell Stewart	.50	.15
❑ 168 Levon Kirkland	.30	.09
❑ 169 Plaxico Burress	.75	.23
❑ 170 Richard Huntley	.30	.09
❑ 171 Troy Edwards	.30	.09
❑ 172 Jeff Graham	.30	.09
❑ 173 Junior Seau	.75	.23
❑ 174 Doug Flutie	.75	.23
❑ 175 Charlie Garner	.50	.15
❑ 176 Jeff Garcia	.75	.23
❑ 177 Jerry Rice	1.50	.45
❑ 178 Steve Young	1.00	.30
❑ 179 Terrell Owens	.75	.23
❑ 180 Brock Huard	.30	.09
❑ 181 Darrell Jackson	.75	.23
❑ 182 Derrick Mayes	.30	.09
❑ 183 Ricky Watters	.50	.15
❑ 184 Shaun Alexander	1.00	.30
❑ 185 Matt Hasselbeck	.50	.15
❑ 186 John Randle	.50	.15
❑ 187 Az-Zahir Hakim	.30	.09
❑ 188 Isaac Bruce	.75	.23
❑ 189 Kurt Warner	1.50	.45
❑ 190 Marshall Faulk	1.00	.30
❑ 191 Torry Holt	.75	.23
❑ 192 Trent Green	.75	.23
❑ 193 Derrick Brooks	.75	.23
❑ 194 Jacquez Green	.30	.09
❑ 195 John Lynch	.50	.15
❑ 196 Keyshawn Johnson	.75	.23
❑ 197 Mike Alstott	.75	.23
❑ 198 Reidel Anthony	.30	.09
❑ 199 Shaun King	.30	.09
❑ 200 Warren Sapp	.50	.15
❑ 201 Warrick Dunn	.75	.23
❑ 202 Ryan Leaf	.50	.15
❑ 203 Carl Pickens	.30	.09
❑ 204 Derrick Mason	.50	.15

❑ 205 Eddie George .75 .23
❑ 206 Frank Wycheck .30 .09
❑ 207 Jevon Kearse .50 .15
❑ 208 Neil O'Donnell .30 .09
❑ 209 Steve McNair .75 .23
❑ 210 Yancey Thigpen .30 .09
❑ 211 Andre Reed .50 .15
❑ 212 Brad Johnson .75 .23
❑ 213 Bruce Smith .50 .15
❑ 214 Champ Bailey .75 .23
❑ 215 Darrell Green .30 .09
❑ 216 Deion Sanders .75 .23
❑ 217 Irving Fryar .50 .15
❑ 218 Jeff George .50 .15
❑ 219 Michael Westbrook .50 .15
❑ 220 Stephen Davis .75 .23
❑ 221 Terrell Owens AP 2.00 .60
❑ 222 Peyton Manning AP 6.00 1.80
❑ 223 Stephen Davis AP 2.00 .60
❑ 224 Marvin Harrison AP 2.00 .60
❑ 225 Donovan McNabb AP 3.00 .90
❑ 226 Edgerrin James AP 3.00 .90
❑ 227 Eric Moulds AP 1.25 .35
❑ 228 Daunte Culpepper AP 2.00 .60
❑ 229 Eddie George AP 2.00 .60
❑ 230 Cris Carter AP 2.00 .60
❑ 231 Rich Gannon AP 2.00 .60
❑ 232 Jeff Garcia AP 2.00 .60
❑ 233 Jimmy Smith AP 1.25 .35
❑ 234 Tony Gonzalez AP 1.25 .35
❑ 235 Torry Holt AP 2.00 .60
❑ 236 Jevon Kearse AP 1.25 .35
❑ 237 Ray Lewis AP 2.00 .60
❑ 238 Warren Sapp AP 1.25 .35
❑ 239 Brian Urlacher AP 4.00 1.20
❑ 240 Champ Bailey AP 1.25 .35
❑ 241 Peyton Manning LL 6.00 1.80
❑ 242 Jeff Garcia LL 2.00 .60
❑ 243 Elvis Grbac LL 1.25 .35
❑ 244 Daunte Culpepper LL 2.00 .60
❑ 245 Brett Favre LL 8.00 2.40
❑ 246 Edgerrin James LL 3.00 .90
❑ 247 Robert Smith LL 1.25 .35
❑ 248 Eddie George LL 2.00 .60
❑ 249 Mike Anderson LL 2.00 .60
❑ 250 Corey Dillon LL 2.00 .60
❑ 251 Torry Holt LL 2.00 .60
❑ 252 Rod Smith LL 1.25 .35
❑ 253 Isaac Bruce LL 2.00 .60
❑ 254 Terrell Owens LL 2.00 .60
❑ 255 Randy Moss LL 5.00 1.50
❑ 256 La'Roi Glover LL .75 .23
❑ 257 Trace Armstrong LL .75 .23
❑ 258 Warren Sapp LL 1.25 .35
❑ 259 Hugh Douglas LL .75 .23
❑ 260 Jason Taylor LL .75 .23
❑ 261 Mike Anderson SS 2.00 .60
❑ 262 Jamal Lewis SS 3.00 .90
❑ 263 Sylvester Morris SS .75 .23
❑ 264 Darrell Jackson SS 2.00 .60
❑ 265 Peter Warrick SS 2.00 .60
❑ 266 Ron Dayne SS 2.00 .60
❑ 267 Shaun Alexander SS 3.00 .90
❑ 268 Plaxico Burress SS 2.00 .60
❑ 269 Brian Urlacher SS 4.00 1.20
❑ 270 Courtney Brown SS 1.25 .35
❑ 271 Michael Vick RC 60.00 18.00
❑ 272 Drew Brees RC 25.00 7.50
❑ 273 Chris Weinke RC 12.00 3.60
❑ 274 Quincy Carter RC 12.00 3.60
❑ 275 Sage Rosenfels RC 12.00 3.60
❑ 276 Josh Heupel RC 12.00 3.60
❑ 277 David Rivers RC 8.00 2.40
❑ 278 Ben Leard RC 8.00 2.40
❑ 279 Marques Tuiasosopo RC 12.00 3.60
❑ 280 Mike McMahon RC 12.00 3.60
❑ 281 Deuce McAllister RC 25.00 7.50
❑ 282 LaMont Jordan RC 15.00 4.50
❑ 283 LaDainian Tomlinson RC 40.00 12.00
❑ 284 James Jackson RC 12.00 3.60
❑ 285 Anthony Thomas RC 20.00 6.00
❑ 286 Travis Henry RC 15.00 4.50
❑ 287 Travis Minor RC 8.00 2.40
❑ 288 Rudi Johnson RC 25.00 7.50
❑ 289 Michael Bennett RC 25.00 7.50
❑ 290 Kevan Barlow RC 12.00 3.60
❑ 291 Reggie White RC 8.00 2.40
❑ 292 Moran Norris RC 5.00 1.50
❑ 293 Ja'Mar Toombs RC 8.00 2.40
❑ 294 Heath Evans RC 8.00 2.40
❑ 295 David Terrell RC 12.00 3.60
❑ 296 Santana Moss RC 20.00 6.00
❑ 297 Rod Gardner RC 12.00 3.60
❑ 298 Quincy Morgan RC 12.00 3.60
❑ 299 Freddie Mitchell RC 12.00 3.60
❑ 300 Boo Williams RC 8.00 2.40
❑ 301 Reggie Wayne RC 20.00 6.00
❑ 302 Ronney Daniels RC 5.00 1.50
❑ 303 Bobby Newcombe RC 8.00 2.40
❑ 304 Vinny Sutherland RC 8.00 2.40
❑ 305 Cedrick Wilson RC 12.00 3.60
❑ 306 Robert Ferguson RC 12.00 3.60
❑ 307 Ken-Yon Rambo RC 8.00 2.40
❑ 308 Alex Bannister RC 8.00 2.40
❑ 309 Koren Robinson RC 15.00 4.50
❑ 310 Chad Johnson RC 25.00 7.50
❑ 311 Chris Chambers RC 15.00 4.50
❑ 312 Javon Green RC 8.00 2.40
❑ 313 Snoop Minnis RC 8.00 2.40
❑ 314 Scotty Anderson RC 8.00 2.40
❑ 315 Todd Heap RC 12.00 3.60
❑ 316 Alge Crumpler RC 15.00 4.50
❑ 317 Marcellus Rivers RC 8.00 2.40
❑ 318 Rashon Burns RC 5.00 1.50
❑ 319 Jamal Reynolds RC 12.00 3.60
❑ 320 Andre Carter RC 12.00 3.60
❑ 321 Justin Smith RC 12.00 3.60
❑ 322 Gerard Warren RC 12.00 3.60
❑ 323 Tommy Polley RC 12.00 3.60
❑ 324 Dan Morgan RC 12.00 3.60
❑ 325 Torrance Marshall RC 12.00 3.60
❑ 326 Correll Buckhalter RC 15.00 4.50
❑ 327 Derrick Gibson RC 8.00 2.40
❑ 328 Adam Archuleta RC 12.00 3.60
❑ 329 Jamar Fletcher RC 8.00 2.40
❑ 330 Nate Clements RC 12.00 3.60

1993 Select

	Nm-Mt	Ex-Mt
COMPLETE SET (200)	20.00	9.00

❑ 1 Steve Young 2.00 .90
❑ 2 Andre Reed .40 .18
❑ 3 Deion Sanders 1.25 .55
❑ 4 Harold Green .20 .09
❑ 5 Wendell Davis .20 .09
❑ 6 Mike Johnson .20 .09
❑ 7 Troy Aikman 2.00 .90
❑ 8 Johnny Mitchell .20 .09
❑ 9 Dale Carter .20 .09
❑ 10 Bruce Matthews .20 .09
❑ 11 Terrell Buckley .20 .09
❑ 12 Steve Emtman .20 .09
❑ 13 Neil Smith .75 .35
❑ 14 Tim Brown .75 .35
❑ 15 Chris Doleman .20 .09
❑ 16 Dan Marino 4.00 1.80
❑ 17 Terry McDaniel .20 .09
❑ 18 Neal Anderson .20 .09
❑ 19 Phil Simms .40 .18
❑ 20 Jeff Lageman .20 .09
❑ 21 Jerry Rice 2.50 1.10
❑ 22 Dermontti Dawson .20 .09
❑ 23 Reggie Cobb .20 .09
❑ 24 Junior Seau .75 .35
❑ 25 Darrell Green .20 .09
❑ 26 Chris Warren .40 .18
❑ 27 Randall Cunningham .75 .35
❑ 28 Bruce Smith .75 .35
❑ 29 Bryan Cox .20 .09
❑ 30 David Klingler .20 .09
❑ 31 Chip Lohmiller .20 .09
❑ 32 Eric Metcalf .40 .18
❑ 33 Ken Norton Jr. .40 .18
❑ 34 John Elway 4.00 1.80
❑ 35 Harris Barton .20 .09
❑ 36 Tim Barnett .20 .09
❑ 37 Rodney Hampton .40 .18
❑ 38 Desmond Howard .40 .18
❑ 39 Tom Rathman .20 .09
❑ 40 Derrick Thomas .75 .35
❑ 41 Randal Hill .20 .09
❑ 42 Steve Wisniewski .20 .09
❑ 43 Brett Favre 5.00 2.20
❑ 44 Darryl Talley .20 .09
❑ 45 Shane Conlan .20 .09
❑ 46 Anthony Miller .40 .18
❑ 47 Randall McDaniel .20 .09
❑ 48 Rod Woodson .75 .35
❑ 49 Eric Martin .20 .09
❑ 50 Ronnie Lott .40 .18
❑ 51 Chris Spielman .40 .18
❑ 52 Vincent Brown .20 .09
❑ 53 Donnell Woolford .20 .09
❑ 54 Richmond Webb .20 .09
❑ 55 Emmitt Smith 3.00 1.35
❑ 56 Haywood Jeffires .40 .18
❑ 57 Jim Kelly .75 .35
❑ 58 James Francis .20 .09
❑ 59 Steve Wallace .20 .09
❑ 60 Jarrod Bunch .20 .09
❑ 61 Lawrence Dawsey .20 .09
❑ 62 Steve Atwater .20 .09
❑ 63 Art Monk .40 .18
❑ 64 Eric Green .20 .09
❑ 65 Lawrence Taylor .75 .35
❑ 66 Ronnie Harmon .20 .09
❑ 67 Fred Barnett .40 .18
❑ 68 Cortez Kennedy .40 .18
❑ 69 Mark Collins .20 .09
❑ 70 Howie Long .75 .35
❑ 71 Jackie Harris .20 .09
❑ 72 Irving Fryar .40 .18
❑ 73 Jim Everett .40 .18
❑ 74 Troy Vincent .20 .09
❑ 75 Cris Carter .75 .35
❑ 76 Boomer Esiason .40 .18
❑ 77 Sam Mills .20 .09
❑ 78 Lorenzo White .20 .09
❑ 79 Andre Rison .40 .18
❑ 80 Quentin Coryatt .40 .18
❑ 81 Steve McMichael .40 .18
❑ 82 Nick Lowery .20 .09
❑ 83 Michael Irvin .75 .35
❑ 84 Thurman Thomas .75 .35
❑ 85 Bill Romanowski .20 .09
❑ 86 Carl Pickens .40 .18
❑ 87 Tim McDonald .20 .09
❑ 88 Bernie Kosar .40 .18
❑ 89 Greg Lloyd .40 .18
❑ 90 Barry Sanders 3.00 1.35
❑ 91 Shannon Sharpe .75 .35
❑ 92 Henry Thomas .20 .09
❑ 93 Barry Foster .40 .18
❑ 94 Antone Davis .20 .09
❑ 95 Stan Humphries .40 .18
❑ 96 Eric Swann .40 .18
❑ 97 Mike Pritchard .40 .18
❑ 98 Reggie White .75 .35
❑ 99 Jeff Hostetler .40 .18
❑ 100 Flipper Anderson .20 .09
❑ 101 Gary Clark .40 .18
❑ 102 Morten Andersen .20 .09
❑ 103 Leonard Russell .40 .18
❑ 104 Chris Hinton .20 .09
❑ 105 John Stephens .20 .09

❑ 106 Byron Evans	.20	.09
❑ 107 Warren Moon	.75	.35
❑ 108 Marv Cook	.20	.09
❑ 109 Carlton Gray RC	.20	.09
❑ 110 Jay Novacek	.40	.18
❑ 111 Gary Anderson K	.20	.09
❑ 112 Andre Tippett	.20	.09
❑ 113 Cornelius Bennett	.40	.18
❑ 114 Clyde Simmons	.20	.09
❑ 115 Jeff George	.75	.35
❑ 116 Audray McMillian	.20	.09
❑ 117 Mark Carrier WR	.40	.18
❑ 118 Vaughan Johnson	.20	.09
❑ 119 Kevin Greene	.40	.18
❑ 120 John Taylor	.40	.18
❑ 121 Jerry Ball	.20	.09
❑ 122 Pat Swilling	.20	.09
❑ 123 George Teague RC	.40	.18
❑ 124 Ricky Reynolds	.20	.09
❑ 125 Marcus Allen	.75	.35
❑ 126 Henry Jones	.20	.09
❑ 127 Ricky Watters	.75	.35
❑ 128 Leon Searcy	.20	.09
❑ 129 Chris Miller	.40	.18
❑ 130 Jim Harbaugh	.75	.35
❑ 131 Luis Sharpe	.20	.09
❑ 132 Simon Fletcher	.20	.09
❑ 133 Eric Allen	.20	.09
❑ 134 Carlton Haselrig	.20	.09
❑ 135 Harvey Williams	.40	.18
❑ 136 Leslie O'Neal	.40	.18
❑ 137 Sterling Sharpe	.75	.35
❑ 138 Tim Harris	.20	.09
❑ 139 Mark Rypien	.20	.09
❑ 140 Harry Galbreath	.20	.09
❑ 141 Sean Gilbert	.40	.18
❑ 142 Keith Jackson	.40	.18
❑ 143 Mark Clayton	.20	.09
❑ 144 Guy McIntyre	.20	.09
❑ 145 Jessie Tuggle	.20	.09
❑ 146 Leonard Marshall	.20	.09
❑ 147 Willie Davis	.75	.35
❑ 148 Herman Moore	.75	.35
❑ 149 Charles Haley	.40	.18
❑ 150 Amp Lee	.20	.09
❑ 151 Gary Zimmerman	.20	.09
❑ 152 Bennie Blades	.20	.09
❑ 153 Pierce Holt	.20	.09
❑ 154 Edgar Bennett	.75	.35
❑ 155 Joe Montana	4.00	1.80
❑ 156 Ted Washington	.20	.09
❑ 157 Hardy Nickerson	.40	.18
❑ 158 Rohn Stark	.20	.09
❑ 159 Brent Jones	.40	.18
❑ 160 Eugene Robinson	.20	.09
❑ 161 Pepper Johnson	.20	.09
❑ 162 Dan Saleaumua	.20	.09
❑ 163 Seth Joyner	.20	.09
❑ 164 Bruce Armstrong	.20	.09
❑ 165 Mike Munchak	.40	.18
❑ 166 Drew Bledsoe RC	5.00	2.20
❑ 167 Curtis Conway RC	1.25	.55
❑ 168 Lincoln Kennedy RC	.20	.09
❑ 169 Dana Stubblefield RC	.75	.35
❑ 170 Wayne Simmons RC	.20	.09
❑ 171 Garrison Hearst RC	2.00	.90
❑ 172 Jerome Bettis RC	5.00	2.20
❑ 173 Eric Curry RC	.20	.09
❑ 174 Natrone Means RC	.75	.35
❑ 175 Glyn Milburn RC	.75	.35
❑ 176 Marvin Jones RC	.20	.09
❑ 177 O.J. McDuffie RC	.75	.35
❑ 178 Dan Williams RC	.20	.09
❑ 179 Rick Mirer RC	.75	.35
❑ 180 John Copeland RC	.40	.18
❑ 181 Willie Roaf RC	.40	.18
❑ 182 Patrick Bates RC	.20	.09
❑ 183 Troy Drayton RC	.40	.18
❑ 184 Vincent Brisby RC	.75	.35
❑ 185 Irv Smith RC	.20	.09
❑ 186 Marion Butts	.20	.09
❑ 187 Wayne Martin	.20	.09
❑ 188 Brian Blades	.40	.18
❑ 189 Mel Gray	.40	.18
❑ 190 Mark Stepnoski	.20	.09
❑ 191 Ernest Givins	.40	.18
❑ 192 Steve Tasker	.40	.18
❑ 193 Tim Grunhard	.20	.09
❑ 194 Stanley Richard	.20	.09
❑ 195 Jeff Wright	.20	.09
❑ 196 Rodney Peete	.20	.09
❑ 197 Tunch Ilkin	.20	.09
❑ 198 Rich Camarillo	.20	.09
❑ 199 Erik Williams	.20	.09
❑ 200 Pete Stoyanovich	.20	.09
❑ S21 Jerry Rice SAMPLE	2.50	.75

1994 Select

	Nm-Mt	Ex-Mt
COMPLETE SET (225)	15.00	6.75
❑ 1 Emmitt Smith	2.50	1.10
❑ 2 Bruce Smith	.40	.18
❑ 3 Randall McDaniel	.10	.05
❑ 4 Drew Bledsoe	1.25	.55
❑ 5 Rod Woodson	.20	.09
❑ 6 Richard Dent	.20	.09
❑ 7 Norm Johnson	.10	.05
❑ 8 Jim Everett	.20	.09
❑ 9 Harold Green	.10	.05
❑ 10 John Elway	3.00	1.35
❑ 11 Barry Sanders	2.50	1.10
❑ 12 Sterling Sharpe	.20	.09
❑ 13 Marcus Robertson	.10	.05
❑ 14 Steve Wisniewski	.10	.05
❑ 15 Irving Fryar	.20	.09
❑ 16 Tyrone Hughes	.20	.09
❑ 17 Garrison Hearst	.40	.18
❑ 18 Randall Cunningham	.40	.18
❑ 19 Junior Seau	.40	.18
❑ 20 Rick Mirer	.40	.18
❑ 21 Jerry Rice	1.50	.70
❑ 22 Eric Metcalf	.20	.09
❑ 23 Roosevelt Potts	.10	.05
❑ 24 Neil Smith	.20	.09
❑ 25 Jerome Bettis	.75	.35
❑ 26 Keith Hamilton	.10	.05
❑ 27 Hardy Nickerson	.20	.09
❑ 28 Steve Tasker	.20	.09
❑ 29 Johnny Johnson	.10	.05
❑ 30 Tom Carter	.10	.05
❑ 31 Andre Rison	.20	.09
❑ 32 Cortez Kennedy	.20	.09
❑ 33 Mark Carrier DB	.10	.05
❑ 34 Shannon Sharpe	.20	.09
❑ 35 Eric Swann	.20	.09
❑ 36 Steve Young	1.25	.55
❑ 37 Johnny Mitchell	.10	.05
❑ 38 Dermontti Dawson	.10	.05
❑ 39 Mike Johnson	.10	.05
❑ 40 Troy Aikman	1.50	.70
❑ 41 Pierce Holt	.10	.05
❑ 42 Derrick Thomas	.40	.18
❑ 43 Reggie Cobb	.10	.05
❑ 44 Michael Jackson	.20	.09
❑ 45 Lomas Brown	.10	.05
❑ 46 Jeff Hostetler	.20	.09
❑ 47 Pete Stoyanovich	.10	.05
❑ 48 Reggie White	.40	.18
❑ 49 Quentin Coryatt	.10	.05
❑ 50 Cris Carter	.75	.35
❑ 51 Sean Gilbert	.10	.05
❑ 52 Chris Slade	.10	.05
❑ 53 Ronnie Harmon	.10	.05
❑ 54 Renaldo Turnbull	.10	.05
❑ 55 Fred Barnett	.20	.09
❑ 56 John Elliott	.10	.05
❑ 57 Deion Sanders	.75	.35
❑ 58 John Carney	.10	.05
❑ 59 Louis Oliver	.10	.05
❑ 60 Greg Lloyd	.20	.09
❑ 61 Chris Hinton	.10	.05
❑ 62 Ronald Moore	.10	.05
❑ 63 Vincent Brown	.10	.05
❑ 64 Tony McGee	.10	.05
❑ 65 Erik Williams	.10	.05
❑ 66 Thurman Thomas	.40	.18
❑ 67 Neil O'Donnell	.40	.18
❑ 68 Scott Mitchell	.20	.09
❑ 69 Keith Byars	.10	.05
❑ 70 Henry Ellard	.20	.09
❑ 71 Chris Spielman	.20	.09
❑ 72 LeRoy Butler	.10	.05
❑ 73 Tim Brown	.40	.18
❑ 74 Darrell Green	.10	.05
❑ 75 Bruce Matthews	.10	.05
❑ 76 Stan Humphries	.20	.09
❑ 77 Will Wolford	.10	.05
❑ 78 John Taylor	.20	.09
❑ 79 Joe Montana	3.00	1.35
❑ 80 Chris Warren	.20	.09
❑ 81 Michael Brooks	.10	.05
❑ 82 Vance Johnson	.10	.05
❑ 83 Rob Moore	.20	.09
❑ 84 Herschel Walker	.20	.09
❑ 85 Alvin Harper	.20	.09
❑ 86 Wayne Martin	.10	.05
❑ 87 Leslie O'Neal	.10	.05
❑ 88 Flipper Anderson	.10	.05
❑ 89 Tommy Vardell	.10	.05
❑ 90 Mike Sherrard	.10	.05
❑ 91 Chris Jacke	.10	.05
❑ 92 Jim Kelly	.40	.18
❑ 93 Jeff Graham	.10	.05
❑ 94 Bryan Cox	.10	.05
❑ 95 Michael Irvin	.40	.18
❑ 96 Jeff Lageman	.10	.05
❑ 97 Webster Slaughter	.10	.05
❑ 98 Eugene Robinson	.10	.05
❑ 99 Vencie Glenn	.10	.05
❑ 100 Sean Jones	.10	.05
❑ 101 Calvin Williams	.20	.09
❑ 102 Jim Harbaugh	.40	.18
❑ 103 Eric Curry	.10	.05
❑ 104 Terry Allen	.20	.09
❑ 105 Darryl Williams	.10	.05
❑ 106 Gary Clark	.20	.09
❑ 107 Marcus Allen	.40	.18
❑ 108 Chip Lohmiller	.10	.05
❑ 109 Vaughan Johnson	.10	.05
❑ 110 Herman Moore	.40	.18
❑ 111 Barry Foster	.10	.05
❑ 112 Rocket Ismail	.20	.09
❑ 113 Erric Pegram	.10	.05
❑ 114 Anthony Miller	.20	.09
❑ 115 Shane Conlan	.10	.05
❑ 116 David Klingler	.10	.05
❑ 117 Mark Collins	.10	.05
❑ 118 Tony Bennett	.10	.05
❑ 119 Donnell Woolford	.10	.05
❑ 120 Reggie Brooks	.20	.09
❑ 121 Sam Mills	.10	.05
❑ 122 Greg Montgomery	.10	.05
❑ 123 Kevin Greene	.20	.09
❑ 124 Terry McDaniel	.10	.05
❑ 125 Henry Jones	.10	.05
❑ 126 Ricky Watters	.20	.09
❑ 127 Dan Marino	3.00	1.35
❑ 128 Steve Atwater	.10	.05
❑ 129 Ricky Proehl	.10	.05
❑ 130 Ernest Givins	.20	.09
❑ 131 John L. Williams	.10	.05
❑ 132 John Randle	.20	.09
❑ 133 Jay Novacek	.20	.09
❑ 134 Boomer Esiason	.20	.09
❑ 135 Jessie Hester	.10	.05

❑ 136 Courtney Hawkins	.10	.05
❑ 137 Ben Coates	.20	.09
❑ 138 Stevon Moore	.10	.05
❑ 139 Eric Allen	.10	.05
❑ 140 Jessie Tuggle	.10	.05
❑ 141 Marion Butts	.10	.05
❑ 142 Brett Favre	3.00	1.35
❑ 143 Andre Reed	.20	.09
❑ 144 Rodney Hampton	.20	.09
❑ 145 Keith Sims	.10	.05
❑ 146 Derek Brown RBK	.10	.05
❑ 147 Eric Green	.10	.05
❑ 148 Greg Robinson	.10	.05
❑ 149 Nate Newton	.10	.05
❑ 150 Mark Higgs	.10	.05
❑ 151 Nick Lowery	.10	.05
❑ 152 Craig Erickson	.10	.05
❑ 153 Anthony Carter	.20	.09
❑ 154 Simon Fletcher	.10	.05
❑ 155 Ronnie Lott	.20	.09
❑ 156 Gary Brown	.10	.05
❑ 157 Brent Jones	.20	.09
❑ 158 Jim Sweeney	.10	.05
❑ 159 Robert Brooks	.40	.18
❑ 160 Keith Jackson	.10	.05
❑ 161 Daryl Johnston	.20	.09
❑ 162 Tom Waddle	.10	.05
❑ 163 Eric Martin	.10	.05
❑ 164 Cornelius Bennett	.20	.09
❑ 165 Tim McDonald	.10	.05
❑ 166 Chris Doleman	.10	.05
❑ 167 Gary Zimmerman	.10	.05
❑ 168 Al Smith	.10	.05
❑ 169 Mark Carrier WR	.20	.09
❑ 170 Harris Barton	.10	.05
❑ 171 Ray Childress	.10	.05
❑ 172 Darryl Talley	.10	.05
❑ 173 James Jett	.10	.05
❑ 174 Mark Stepnoski	.10	.05
❑ 175 Jeff Query	.10	.05
❑ 176 Charles Haley	.20	.09
❑ 177 Rod Bernstine	.10	.05
❑ 178 Richmond Webb	.10	.05
❑ 179 Rich Camarillo	.10	.05
❑ 180 Pat Swilling	.10	.05
❑ 181 Chris Miller	.10	.05
❑ 182 Mike Pritchard	.10	.05
❑ 183 Checklist NFC	.10	.05
❑ 184 Natrone Means	.40	.18
❑ 185 Erik Kramer	.20	.09
❑ 186 Clyde Simmons	.10	.05
❑ 187 Checklist AFC/NFC	.10	.05
❑ 188 Warren Moon	.40	.18
❑ 189 Michael Haynes	.20	.09
❑ 190 Terry Kirby	.40	.18
❑ 191 Brian Blades	.20	.09
❑ 192 Haywood Jeffires	.20	.09
❑ 193 Thomas Everett	.10	.05
❑ 194 Morten Andersen	.10	.05
❑ 195 Dana Stubblefield	.20	.09
❑ 196 Ken Norton	.20	.09
❑ 197 Art Monk	.20	.09
❑ 198 Seth Joyner	.10	.05
❑ 199 Heath Shuler RC	.40	.18
❑ 200 Marshall Faulk RC	6.00	2.70
❑ 201 Charles Johnson RC	.40	.18
❑ 202 Der.Alexander WR RC	.40	.18
❑ 203 Greg Hill RC	.40	.18
❑ 204 Darnay Scott RC	1.00	.45
❑ 205 Willie McGinest RC	.40	.18
❑ 206 Thomas Randolph RC	.10	.05
❑ 207 Errict Rhett RC	.40	.18
❑ 208 William Floyd RC	.40	.18
❑ 209 Johnnie Morton RC	2.00	.90
❑ 210 David Palmer RC	.40	.18
❑ 211 Dan Wilkinson RC	.20	.09
❑ 212 Trent Dilfer RC	1.25	.55
❑ 213 Antonio Langham RC	.20	.09
❑ 214 Chuck Levy RC	.10	.05
❑ 215 John Thierry RC	.10	.05
❑ 216 Kevin Lee RC	.10	.05
❑ 217 Aaron Glenn RC	.40	.18
❑ 218 Charlie Garner RC	1.50	.70
❑ 219 Jeff Burris RC	.20	.09
❑ 220 LeShon Johnson RC	.20	.09
❑ 221 Thomas Lewis RC	.20	.09
❑ 222 Ryan Yarborough RC	.10	.05
❑ 223 Mario Bates RC	.40	.18
❑ 224 Checklist NFC/AFC	.10	.05
❑ 225 Checklist AFC	.10	.05
❑ SR1 Marshall Faulk SR	40.00	18.00
❑ SR2 Dan Wilkinson SR	8.00	3.60

1995 Select Certified

	Nm-Mt	Ex-Mt
COMPLETE SET (135)	40.00	18.00
❑ 1 Marshall Faulk	4.00	1.80
❑ 2 Heath Shuler	.50	.23
❑ 3 Garrison Hearst	1.00	.45
❑ 4 Errict Rhett	.50	.23
❑ 5 Jeff George	.50	.23
❑ 6 Jerome Bettis	1.00	.45
❑ 7 Jim Kelly	1.00	.45
❑ 8 Rick Mirer	.50	.23
❑ 9 Willie Davis	.50	.23
❑ 10 Steve Young	2.50	1.10
❑ 11 Erik Kramer	.25	.11
❑ 12 Natrone Means	.50	.23
❑ 13 Jeff Blake RC	3.00	1.35
❑ 14 Neil O'Donnell	.50	.23
❑ 15 Andre Rison	.50	.23
❑ 16 Randall Cunningham	1.00	.45
❑ 17 Emmitt Smith	5.00	2.20
❑ 18 Tim Brown	1.00	.45
❑ 19 Shannon Sharpe	.50	.23
❑ 20 Boomer Esiason	.50	.23
❑ 21 Barry Sanders	5.00	2.20
❑ 22 Rodney Hampton	.50	.23
❑ 23 Robert Brooks	1.00	.45
❑ 24 Jim Everett	.25	.11
❑ 25 Gary Brown	.25	.11
❑ 26 Drew Bledsoe	1.25	.55
❑ 27 Desmond Howard	.50	.23
❑ 28 Cris Carter	1.00	.45
❑ 29 Marcus Allen	1.00	.45
❑ 30 Dan Marino	6.00	2.70
❑ 31 Warren Moon	.50	.23
❑ 32 Dave Krieg	.25	.11
❑ 33 Ben Coates	.50	.23
❑ 34 Terance Mathis	.50	.23
❑ 35 Mario Bates	.50	.23
❑ 36 Andre Reed	.50	.23
❑ 37 Dave Brown	.50	.23
❑ 38 Jeff Graham	.25	.11
❑ 39 Johnny Mitchell	.25	.11
❑ 40 Carl Pickens	.50	.23
❑ 41 Jeff Hostetler	.50	.23
❑ 42 Vinny Testaverde	.50	.23
❑ 43 Ricky Watters	.50	.23
❑ 44 Troy Aikman	3.00	1.35
❑ 45 Byron Bam Morris	.25	.11
❑ 46 John Elway	6.00	2.70
❑ 47 Junior Seau	1.00	.45
❑ 48 Scott Mitchell	.50	.23
❑ 49 Jerry Rice	3.00	1.35
❑ 50 Brett Favre	6.00	2.70
❑ 51 Chris Warren	.50	.23
❑ 52 Chris Chandler	.50	.23
❑ 53 Lorenzo White	.25	.11
❑ 54 Craig Erickson	.25	.11
❑ 55 Alvin Harper	.25	.11
❑ 56 Steve Beuerlein	.50	.23
❑ 57 Edgar Bennett	.50	.23
❑ 58 Steve Bono	.50	.23
❑ 59 Eric Green	.25	.11
❑ 60 Jake Reed	.50	.23
❑ 61 Terry Kirby	.50	.23
❑ 62 Vincent Brisby	.25	.11
❑ 63 Lake Dawson	.50	.23
❑ 64 Torrance Small	.25	.11
❑ 65 Mark Brunell	1.25	.55
❑ 66 Haywood Jeffires	.25	.11
❑ 67 Flipper Anderson	.25	.11
❑ 68 Ronald Moore	.25	.11
❑ 69 LeShon Johnson	.50	.23
❑ 70 Rocket Ismail	.50	.23
❑ 71 Herman Moore	1.00	.45
❑ 72 Charlie Garner	1.00	.45
❑ 73 Anthony Miller	.50	.23
❑ 74 Greg Lloyd	.50	.23
❑ 75 Michael Irvin	1.00	.45
❑ 76 Stan Humphries	.50	.23
❑ 77 Leroy Hoard	.25	.11
❑ 78 Deion Sanders Card mailed to dealers	3.00	1.35
❑ 79 Darnay Scott	.50	.23
❑ 80 Chris Miller	.25	.11
❑ 81 Curtis Conway	1.00	.45
❑ 82 Trent Dilfer	1.00	.45
❑ 83 Bruce Smith	1.00	.45
❑ 84 Reggie Brooks	.50	.23
❑ 85 Frank Reich	.25	.11
❑ 86 Henry Ellard	.50	.23
❑ 87 Eric Metcalf	.50	.23
❑ 88 Sean Gilbert	.50	.23
❑ 89 Larry Centers	.50	.23
❑ 90 Ricky Ervins	.25	.11
❑ 91 Craig Heyward	.50	.23
❑ 92 Rod Woodson	.50	.23
❑ 93 Steve Walsh	.25	.11
❑ 94 Fred Barnett	.50	.23
❑ 95 William Floyd	.50	.23
❑ 96 Harvey Williams	.25	.11
❑ 97 Greg Hill	.50	.23
❑ 98 Irving Fryar	.50	.23
❑ 99 Kevin Williams	.50	.23
❑ 100 Herschel Walker	.50	.23
❑ 101 Sean Dawkins	.50	.23
❑ 102 Michael Haynes	.50	.23
❑ 103 Reggie White	1.00	.45
❑ 104 Robert Smith	1.00	.45
❑ 105 Todd Collins RC	1.00	.45
❑ 106 Michael Westbrook RC	2.00	.90
❑ 107 Frank Sanders RC	2.00	.90
❑ 108 Christian Fauria RC	1.00	.45
❑ 109 Stoney Case RC	.50	.23
❑ 110 Jimmy Oliver RC	.50	.23
❑ 111 Mark Bruener RC	1.00	.45
❑ 112 Rodney Thomas RC	1.00	.45
❑ 113 Chris T.Jones RC	.50	.23
❑ 114 James A.Stewart RC	.50	.23
❑ 115 Kevin Carter RC	2.00	.90
❑ 116 Eric Zeier RC	2.00	.90
❑ 117 Curtis Martin RC	15.00	6.75
❑ 118 James O. Stewart RC	5.00	2.20
❑ 119 Joe Aska RC	.50	.23
❑ 120 Ken Dilger RC	2.00	.90
❑ 121 Tyrone Wheatley RC	5.00	2.20
❑ 122 Ray Zellars RC	1.00	.45
❑ 123 Kyle Brady RC	2.00	.90
❑ 124 Chad May RC	.50	.23
❑ 125 Napoleon Kaufman RC	5.00	2.20
❑ 126 Terrell Davis RC	12.00	5.50
❑ 127 Warren Sapp RC	6.00	2.70
❑ 128 Sherman Williams RC	.50	.23
❑ 129 Kordell Stewart RC	8.00	3.60
❑ 130 Ki-Jana Carter RC	2.00	.90
❑ 131 Terrell Fletcher RC	.50	.23
❑ 132 Rashaan Salaam RC	1.00	.45
❑ 133 J.J. Stokes RC	2.00	.90
❑ 134 Kerry Collins RC	8.00	3.60
❑ 135 Joey Galloway RC	8.00	3.60
❑ P7 Dan Marino Promo Gold Team Card	5.00	2.20
❑ P10 Steve Young Promo	2.00	.90
❑ P44 Troy Aikman Promo	2.50	1.10

1995 Select Certified Mirror Gold

	Nm-Mt	Ex-Mt
COMPLETE SET (135)	300.00	135.00

*MIRROR GOLD STARS: 2X TO 5X BASIC CARDS
*MIRROR GOLD RCs: 1X TO 2.5X BASIC CARDS

1996 Select Certified

	Nm-Mt	Ex-Mt
COMPLETE SET (125)	50.00	22.00
❑ 1 Isaac Bruce	.75	.35
❑ 2 Rick Mirer	.40	.18
❑ 3 Jake Reed	.40	.18
❑ 4 Reggie White	.75	.35
❑ 5 Harvey Williams	.20	.09
❑ 6 Jim Everett	.20	.09
❑ 7 Tony Martin	.40	.18
❑ 8 Craig Heyward	.20	.09
❑ 9 Tamarick Vanover	.40	.18
❑ 10 Hugh Douglas	.40	.18
❑ 11 Erik Kramer	.20	.09
❑ 12 Charlie Garner	.40	.18
❑ 13 Erric Pegram	.20	.09
❑ 14 Scott Mitchell	.40	.18
❑ 15 Michael Westbrook	.75	.35
❑ 16 Robert Smith	.40	.18
❑ 17 Kerry Collins	.75	.35
❑ 18 Derek Loville	.20	.09
❑ 19 Jeff Blake	.75	.35
❑ 20 Terry Kirby	.40	.18
❑ 21 Bruce Smith	.40	.18
❑ 22 Stan Humphries	.40	.18
❑ 23 Rodney Thomas	.20	.09
❑ 24 Wayne Chrebet	1.00	.45
❑ 25 Napoleon Kaufman	.75	.35
❑ 26 Marshall Faulk	1.00	.45
❑ 27 Emmitt Smith	3.00	1.35
❑ 28 Natrone Means	.40	.18
❑ 29 Neil O'Donnell	.40	.18
❑ 30 Warren Moon	.40	.18
❑ 31 Junior Seau	.75	.35
❑ 32 Chris Sanders	.40	.18
❑ 33 Barry Sanders	3.00	1.35
❑ 34 Jeff Graham	.20	.09
❑ 35 Kordell Stewart	.75	.35
❑ 36 Jim Harbaugh	.40	.18
❑ 37 Chris Warren	.40	.18
❑ 38 Cris Carter	.75	.35
❑ 39 J.J. Stokes	.75	.35
❑ 40 Tyrone Wheatley	.40	.18
❑ 41 Terrell Davis	1.50	.70
❑ 42 Mark Brunell	1.25	.55
❑ 43 Steve Young	1.50	.70
❑ 44 Rodney Hampton	.40	.18
❑ 45 Drew Bledsoe	1.25	.55
❑ 46 Larry Centers	.40	.18
❑ 47 Ken Norton Jr.	.20	.09
❑ 48 Deion Sanders	1.25	.55
❑ 49 Alvin Harper	.20	.09
❑ 50 Trent Dilfer	.75	.35
❑ 51 Steve McNair	1.50	.70
❑ 52 Robert Brooks	.75	.35
❑ 53 Edgar Bennett	.40	.18
❑ 54 Troy Aikman	2.00	.90
❑ 55 Dan Marino	4.00	1.80
❑ 56 Steve Bono	.20	.09
❑ 57 Marcus Allen	.75	.35
❑ 58 Rodney Peete	.20	.09
❑ 59 Ben Coates	.40	.18
❑ 60 Yancey Thigpen	.40	.18
❑ 61 Tim Brown	.75	.35
❑ 62 Jerry Rice	2.00	.90
❑ 63 Quinn Early	.20	.09
❑ 64 Ricky Watters	.40	.18
❑ 65 Thurman Thomas	.75	.35
❑ 66 Greg Lloyd	.40	.18
❑ 67 Eric Metcalf	.20	.09
❑ 68 Jeff George	.40	.18
❑ 69 John Elway	4.00	1.80
❑ 70 Frank Sanders	.40	.18
❑ 71 Curtis Conway	.75	.35
❑ 72 Greg Hill	.40	.18
❑ 73 Darick Holmes	.20	.09
❑ 74 Herman Moore	.40	.18
❑ 75 Carl Pickens	.40	.18
❑ 76 Eric Zeier	.20	.09
❑ 77 Curtis Martin	1.50	.70
❑ 78 Rashaan Salaam	.40	.18
❑ 79 Joey Galloway	.75	.35
❑ 80 Jeff Hostetler	.20	.09
❑ 81 Jim Kelly	.75	.35
❑ 82 Dave Brown	.20	.09
❑ 83 Sean Dawkins	.20	.09
❑ 84 Michael Irvin	.75	.35
❑ 85 Brett Favre	4.00	1.80
❑ 86 Cedric Jones RC	.25	.11
❑ 87 Jeff Lewis RC	.50	.23
❑ 88 Alex Van Dyke RC	.50	.23
❑ 89 Regan Upshaw RC	.25	.11
❑ 90 Karim Abdul-Jabbar RC	1.00	.45
❑ 91 Marvin Harrison RC	10.00	4.50
❑ 92 Stephen Davis RC	8.00	3.60
❑ 93 Terry Glenn RC	4.00	1.80
❑ 94 Kevin Hardy RC	1.00	.45
❑ 95 Stanley Pritchett RC	.25	.11
❑ 96 Willie Anderson RC	.25	.11
❑ 97 Lawrence Phillips RC	.50	.23
❑ 98 Bobby Hoying RC	1.00	.45
❑ 99 Amani Toomer RC	4.00	1.80
❑ 100 Eddie George RC	6.00	2.70
❑ 101 Stepfret Williams RC	.25	.11
❑ 102 Eric Moulds RC	5.00	2.20
❑ 103 Simeon Rice RC	2.50	1.10
❑ 104 John Mobley RC	.25	.11
❑ 105 Keyshawn Johnson RC	4.00	1.80
❑ 106 Daryl Gardener RC	.25	.11
❑ 107 Tony Banks RC	1.00	.45
❑ 108 Bobby Engram RC	1.00	.45
❑ 109 Jonathan Ogden RC	1.00	.45
❑ 110 Eddie Kennison RC	1.00	.45
❑ 111 Danny Kanell RC	1.00	.45
❑ 112 Tony Brackens RC	1.00	.45
❑ 113 Tim Biakabutuka RC	1.00	.45
❑ 114 Leeland McElroy RC	.50	.23
❑ 115 Rickey Dudley RC	1.00	.45
❑ 116 Troy Aikman SS	1.00	.45
❑ 117 Brett Favre SS	2.00	.90
❑ 118 Drew Bledsoe SS	.75	.35
❑ 119 Steve Young SS	.75	.35
❑ 120 Kerry Collins SS	.75	.35
❑ 121 John Elway SS	2.00	.90
❑ 122 Dan Marino SS	2.00	.90
❑ 123 Kordell Stewart SS	.75	.35
❑ 124 Jeff Blake SS	.40	.18
❑ 125 Jim Harbaugh SS	.40	.18

1996 Select Certified Artist's Proofs

	Nm-Mt	Ex-Mt
COMPLETE SET (125)	400.00	180.00

*STARS: 2.5X TO 6X BASIC CARDS
*RCs: 1.2X TO 3X BASIC CARDS

1996 Select Certified Blue

	Nm-Mt	Ex-Mt
COMPLETE SET (125)	1000.00	450.00

*STARS: 6X TO 15X BASIC CARDS
*RCs: 2.5X TO 6X

1996 Select Certified Mirror Blue

Nm-Mt Ex-Mt

*MIR.BLUE STARS: 15X TO 40X BASIC CARDS
*MIR.BLUE RC'S: 6X TO 15X

1996 Select Certified Mirror Gold

Nm-Mt Ex-Mt

*MIR.GOLD STARS: 20X TO 50X BASIC CARDS
*MIR.GOLD RCs: 6X TO 15X BASIC CARDS

1996 Select Certified Mirror Red

	Nm-Mt	Ex-Mt
COMPLETE SET (125)	1500.00	700.00

*MIR.RED STARS: 8X TO 20X BASIC CARDS
*MIR.RED RCs: 3X TO 8X

1996 Select Certified Mirror Red Premium Stock

Nm-Mt Ex-Mt

*MIRROR RED PS STARS: 60X TO 120X
*MIRROR RED PS RCs: 25X TO 50X

1996 Select Certified Premium Stock

	Nm-Mt	Ex-Mt
COMPLETE SET (125)	8.00	3.60

*PREM.STOCK: .8X TO 2X BASIC CARDS

1996 Select Certified Red

	Nm-Mt	Ex-Mt
COMPLETE SET (125)	300.00	135.00

*STARS: 2X TO 5X BASIC CARDS
*RCs: 1X TO 2.5X BASIC CARDS

2000 SkyBox

	Nm-Mt	Ex-Mt
COMPLETE SET (300)	400.00	180.00
COMP.SET w/o SPs (250)	30.00	13.50
❑ 1 Tim Couch	.40	.18
❑ 2 Edgerrin James	1.00	.45
❑ 3 Wesley Walls	.25	.11
❑ 4 Brian Griese	.60	.25
❑ 5 Herman Moore	.40	.18
❑ 6 Mark Brunell	.60	.25
❑ 7 John Randle	.40	.18
❑ 8 Victor Green	.25	.11
❑ 9 Michael Sinclair	.25	.11
❑ 10 Jevon Kearse	.60	.25
❑ 11 Peter Boulware	.25	.11
❑ 12 Kevin Johnson	.60	.25
❑ 13 Vonnie Holliday	.25	.11
❑ 14 Jason Taylor	.40	.18
❑ 15 Cam Cleeland	.25	.11
❑ 16 Jeff Graham	.25	.11
❑ 17 Jacquez Green	.25	.11

❑	18 Chris McAlister	.25	.11
❑	19 Takeo Spikes	.25	.11
❑	20 Marvin Harrison	.60	.25
❑	21 Jay Fiedler	.60	.25
❑	22 Jake Reed	.40	.18
❑	23 Jerry Rice	1.25	.55
❑	24 Shaun King	.25	.11
❑	25 Donovan McNabb	1.00	.45
❑	26 David Boston	.60	.25
❑	27 Curtis Enis	.25	.11
❑	28 Olandis Gary	.60	.25
❑	29 James Stewart	.40	.18
❑	30 Jimmy Smith	.40	.18
❑	31 Randy Moss	1.25	.55
❑	32 Keyshawn Johnson	.60	.25
❑	33 Kevin Carter	.25	.11
❑	34 Stephen Davis	.60	.25
❑	35 Jay Riemersma	.25	.11
❑	36 Emmitt Smith	1.25	.55
❑	37 E.G. Green	.25	.11
❑	38 Dwayne Rudd	.25	.11
❑	39 Michael Strahan	.40	.18
❑	40 Troy Edwards	.25	.11
❑	41 Derrick Mayes	.40	.18
❑	42 Eddie George	.60	.25
❑	43 Bruce Smith	.40	.18
❑	44 Andre Wadsworth	.25	.11
❑	45 Bobby Engram	.40	.18
❑	46 Byron Chamberlain	.25	.11
❑	47 Antonio Freeman	.60	.25
❑	48 Hardy Nickerson	.25	.11
❑	49 Terry Glenn	.40	.18
❑	50 Wayne Chrebet	.40	.18
❑	51 London Fletcher RC	.40	.18
❑	52 Michael Westbrook	.40	.18
❑	53 Rob Moore	.40	.18
❑	54 Eddie Kennison	.40	.18
❑	55 Ed McCaffrey	.60	.25
❑	56 Dorsey Levens	.40	.18
❑	57 Andre Rison	.40	.18
❑	58 Willie McGinest	.25	.11
❑	59 Tyrone Wheatley	.40	.18
❑	60 Kurt Warner	1.25	.55
❑	61 Stephen Alexander	.25	.11
❑	62 Jessie Tuggle	.25	.11
❑	63 Jim Miller	.25	.11
❑	64 Luther Elliss	.25	.11
❑	65 Bill Schroeder	.40	.18
❑	66 Elvis Grbac	.40	.18
❑	67 Ty Law	.40	.18
❑	68 Tim Brown	.60	.25
❑	69 Marshall Faulk	.75	.35
❑	70 Champ Bailey	.40	.18
❑	71 Charlie Batch	.60	.25
❑	72 Steve Beuerlein	.40	.18
❑	73 Rocket Ismail	.40	.18
❑	74 Kevin Hardy	.25	.11
❑	75 Zach Thomas	.60	.25
❑	76 Aaron Glenn	.25	.11
❑	77 Jerome Bettis	.60	.25
❑	78 Chris Chandler	.40	.18
❑	79 Marcus Robinson	.60	.25
❑	80 Derrick Alexander	.40	.18
❑	81 Drew Bledsoe	.75	.35
❑	82 Charles Woodson	.40	.18
❑	83 Isaac Bruce	.60	.25
❑	84 Darrell Green	.25	.11
❑	85 Tim Dwight	.60	.25
❑	86 Darnay Scott	.40	.18
❑	87 Chris Claiborne	.25	.11
❑	88 Tony Gonzalez	.40	.18
❑	89 Tony Simmons	.25	.11
❑	90 Rich Gannon	.60	.25
❑	91 Torry Holt	.60	.25
❑	92 Jamal Anderson	.60	.25
❑	93 Akili Smith	.25	.11
❑	94 Germane Crowell	.25	.11
❑	95 Lawyer Milloy	.40	.18
❑	96 Napoleon Kaufman	.40	.18
❑	97 Grant Wistrom	.25	.11
❑	98 Terance Mathis	.40	.18
❑	99 Karim Abdul-Jabbar	.40	.18
❑	100 Kerry Collins	.40	.18
❑	101 Troy Vincent	.25	.11
❑	102 Jermaine Fazande	.25	.11
❑	103 Warren Sapp	.40	.18
❑	104 Tony Banks	.40	.18
❑	105 Darrin Chiaverini	.25	.11
❑	106 Corey Bradford	.40	.18
❑	107 Tony Martin	.40	.18
❑	108 Jeff Blake	.40	.18
❑	109 Torrance Small	.25	.11
❑	110 Freddie Jones	.25	.11
❑	111 Warrick Dunn	.60	.25
❑	112 Tim Biakabutuka	.40	.18
❑	113 Rod Smith	.40	.18
❑	114 Kyle Brady	.25	.11
❑	115 Oronde Gadsden	.40	.18
❑	116 Dedric Ward	.25	.11
❑	117 Mikhael Ricks	.25	.11
❑	118 Bryant Young	.25	.11
❑	119 Michael Bates	.25	.11
❑	120 Junior Seau	.60	.25
❑	121 Bill Romanowski	.25	.11
❑	122 Reggie Barlow	.25	.11
❑	123 Jeff Garcia	.60	.25
❑	124 Peerless Price	.60	.25
❑	125 Jeff George	.40	.18
❑	126 Cornelius Bennett	.25	.11
❑	127 Amani Toomer	.40	.18
❑	128 Charles Johnson	.40	.18
❑	129 Cortez Kennedy	.25	.11
❑	130 Samari Rolle	.25	.11
❑	131 Eric Moulds	.60	.25
❑	132 Joey Galloway	.40	.18
❑	133 Peyton Manning	1.50	.70
❑	134 Robert Smith	.60	.25
❑	135 Jessie Armstead	.25	.11
❑	136 Will Blackwell	.25	.11
❑	137 Jon Kitna	.60	.25
❑	138 Kevin Dyson	.40	.18
❑	139 Jake Plummer	.40	.18
❑	140 Cade McNown	.25	.11
❑	141 Terrell Davis	.60	.25
❑	142 Johnnie Morton	.40	.18
❑	143 Fred Taylor	.60	.25
❑	144 Ed McDaniel	.25	.11
❑	145 Vinny Testaverde	.40	.18
❑	146 Az-Zahir Hakim	.40	.18
❑	147 Brad Johnson	.60	.25
❑	148 Antowain Smith	.40	.18
❑	149 Rob Konrad	.25	.11
❑	150 Sam Cowart	.25	.11
❑	151 Cris Carter	.60	.25
❑	152 Jason Sehorn	.25	.11
❑	153 Levon Kirkland	.25	.11
❑	154 Shawn Springs	.25	.11
❑	155 Frank Wycheck	.25	.11
❑	156 Troy Aikman	1.25	.55
❑	157 Keenan McCardell	.40	.18
❑	158 Sam Madison	.25	.11
❑	159 Curtis Martin	.60	.25
❑	160 Hines Ward	.60	.25
❑	161 Steve Young	.75	.35
❑	162 Blaine Bishop	.25	.11
❑	163 Shannon Sharpe	.40	.18
❑	164 Michael Pittman	.25	.11
❑	165 Brett Favre	2.00	.90
❑	166 Damon Huard	.60	.25
❑	167 Keith Poole	.25	.11
❑	168 Curtis Conway	.40	.18
❑	169 Derrick Brooks	.60	.25
❑	170 Duce Staley	.60	.25
❑	171 Rob Johnson	.40	.18
❑	172 Pete Gonzalez	.25	.11
❑	173 Ken Dilger	.25	.11
❑	174 Ike Hilliard	.40	.18
❑	175 Bobby Taylor	.25	.11
❑	176 Ricky Watters	.40	.18
❑	177 Steve McNair	.60	.25
❑	178 Pat Johnson	.25	.11
❑	179 Carl Pickens	.40	.18
❑	180 Terrence Wilkins	.25	.11
❑	181 Rashaan Shehee	.25	.11
❑	182 Ricky Williams	.60	.25
❑	183 James Jett	.25	.11
❑	184 Terrell Owens	.60	.25
❑	185 John Lynch	.40	.18
❑	186 Muhsin Muhammad	.40	.18
❑	187 Ryan McNeil	.25	.11
❑	188 Jerome Pathon	.40	.18
❑	189 Daunte Culpepper	.75	.35
❑	190 Joe Jurevicius	.25	.11
❑	191 Kordell Stewart	.40	.18
❑	192 Christian Fauria	.25	.11
❑	193 Yancey Thigpen	.25	.11
❑	194 Patrick Jeffers	.60	.25
❑	195 Corey Dillon	.60	.25
❑	196 Tamarick Vanover	.25	.11
❑	197 Doug Flutie	.60	.25
❑	198 Rickey Dudley	.25	.11
❑	199 Charlie Garner	.40	.18
❑	200 Mike Alstott	.60	.25
❑	201 Courtney Brown RC	.75	.35
❑	201H Courtney Brown SP	8.00	3.60
❑	202 Peter Warrick RC	.75	.35
❑	202H Peter Warrick SP	8.00	3.60
❑	203 Thomas Jones RC	1.25	.55
❑	203H Thomas Jones SP	12.00	5.50
❑	204 Sylvester Morris RC	.50	.23
❑	204H Sylvester Morris SP	5.00	2.20
❑	205 Chad Pennington RC	3.00	1.35
❑	205H Chad Pennington SP	30.00	13.50
❑	206 Ron Dayne RC	.75	.35
❑	206H Ron Dayne SP	8.00	3.60
❑	207 Todd Pinkston RC	.75	.35
❑	207H Todd Pinkston SP	8.00	3.60
❑	208 Todd Husak RC	.75	.35
❑	208H Todd Husak SP	8.00	3.60
❑	209 Chris Redman RC	.50	.23
❑	209H Chris Redman SP	5.00	2.20
❑	210 Jerry Porter RC	1.00	.45
❑	210H Jerry Porter SP	10.00	4.50
❑	211 Michael Wiley RC	.50	.23
❑	211H Michael Wiley SP	5.00	2.20
❑	212 J.R. Redmond RC	.50	.23
❑	212H J.R. Redmond SP	5.00	2.20
❑	213 Dennis Northcutt RC	.75	.35
❑	213H Dennis Northcutt SP	8.00	3.60
❑	214 Gari Scott RC	.30	.14
❑	214H Gari Scott SP	3.00	1.35
❑	215 Bashir Yamini RC	.30	.14
❑	215H Bashir Yamini SP	3.00	1.35
❑	216 Danny Farmer RC	.50	.23
❑	216H Danny Farmer SP	5.00	2.20
❑	217 Corey Simon RC	.75	.35
❑	217H Corey Simon SP	8.00	3.60
❑	218 Plaxico Burress RC	1.50	.70
❑	218H Plaxico Burress SP	15.00	6.75
❑	219 Chad Morton RC	.75	.35
❑	219H Chad Morton SP	8.00	3.60
❑	220 Bubba Franks RC	.75	.35
❑	220H Bubba Franks SP	8.00	3.60
❑	221 Shaun Alexander RC	2.00	.90
❑	221H Shaun Alexander SP	20.00	9.00
❑	222 Dez White RC	.75	.35
❑	222H Dez White SP	8.00	3.60
❑	223 Mareno Philyaw RC	.30	.14
❑	223H Mareno Philyaw SP	3.00	1.35
❑	224 Travis Taylor RC	.75	.35
❑	224H Travis Taylor SP	.75	.35
❑	225 Brian Urlacher RC	3.00	1.35
❑	225H Brian Urlacher SP	30.00	13.50
❑	226 Jamal Lewis RC	2.00	.90
❑	226H Jamal Lewis SP	20.00	9.00
❑	227 Sherrod Gideon RC	.30	.14
❑	227H Sherrod Gideon SP	3.00	1.35
❑	228 Shyrone Stith RC	.50	.23
❑	228H Shyrone Stith SP	5.00	2.20
❑	229 Chris Cole RC	.50	.23
❑	229H Chris Cole SP	5.00	2.20
❑	230 Darrell Jackson RC	1.50	.70
❑	230H Darrell Jackson SP	15.00	6.75
❑	231 Quinton Spotwood RC	.30	.14
❑	231H Quinton Spotwood SP	3.00	1.35
❑	232 Tee Martin RC	.75	.35
❑	232H Tee Martin SP	8.00	3.60
❑	233 Tim Rattay RC	1.50	.70
❑	233H Tim Rattay SP	15.00	6.75
❑	234 Marc Bulger RC	1.50	.70
❑	234H Marc Bulger SP	15.00	6.75
❑	235 Doug Johnson RC	.75	.35

❑ 235H Doug Johnson SP 8.00 3.60
❑ 236 Joe Hamilton RC .50 .23
❑ 236H Joe Hamilton SP 5.00 2.20
❑ 237 Trevor Gaylor RC .50 .23
❑ 237H Trevor Gaylor SP 5.00 2.20
❑ 238 Travis Prentice RC .50 .23
❑ 238H Travis Prentice SP 5.00 2.20
❑ 239 R.Jay Soward RC .50 .23
❑ 239H R.Jay Soward SP 5.00 2.20
❑ 240 Trung Canidate RC .50 .23
❑ 240H Trung Canidate SP 5.00 2.20
❑ 241 Giovanni Carmazzi RC .50 .23
❑ 241H Giovanni Carmazzi SP 5.00 2.20
❑ 242 Reuben Droughns RC 1.00 .45
❑ 242H Reuben Droughns SP 8.00 3.60
❑ 243 Curtis Keaton RC .50 .23
❑ 243H Curtis Keaton SP 5.00 2.20
❑ 244 Laveranues Coles RC 1.00 .45
❑ 244H Laveranues Coles SP 10.00 4.50
❑ 245 Ron Dugans RC .30 .14
❑ 245H Ron Dugans SP 3.00 1.35
❑ 246 Mike Anderson RC .75 .35
❑ 246H Mike Anderson SP 8.00 3.60
❑ 247 Anthony Becht RC .75 .35
❑ 247H Anthony Becht SP 8.00 3.60
❑ 248 Raynoch Thompson RC .50 .23
❑ 248H Raynoch Thompson SP 5.00 2.20
❑ 249 Rob Morris RC .75 .35
❑ 249H Rob Morris SP 8.00 3.60
❑ 250 Chafie Fields RC .30 .14
❑ 250H Chafie Fields SP 3.00 1.35
❑ P1 Tim Couch Promo 1.00 .30

1999 SkyBox Dominion

Nm-Mt Ex-Mt
COMPLETE SET (250) 40.00 18.00
❑ 1 Randy Moss 1.25 .55
❑ 2 James Jett .30 .14
❑ 3 Lawyer Milloy .30 .14
❑ 4 Mike Alstott .50 .23
❑ 5 Courtney Hawkins .20 .09
❑ 6 Carl Pickens .30 .14
❑ 7 Marvin Harrison .50 .23
❑ 8 Robert Smith .50 .23
❑ 9 Fred Taylor .50 .23
❑ 10 Barry Sanders 1.50 .70
❑ 11 Tony Gonzalez .50 .23
❑ 12 Leroy Hoard .20 .09
❑ 13 Drew Bledsoe .60 .25
❑ 14 Cam Cleeland .20 .09
❑ 15 Steve Atwater .20 .09
❑ 16 Eric Moulds .50 .23
❑ 17 Herman Moore .30 .14
❑ 18 Rickey Dudley .20 .09
❑ 19 Jeff Blake .30 .14
❑ 20 Eddie George .50 .23
❑ 21 Antonio Freeman .50 .23
❑ 22 Stephen Alexander .20 .09
❑ 23 Larry Centers .20 .09
❑ 24 Chris Chandler .30 .14
❑ 25 James Stewart .30 .14
❑ 26 Randall Cunningham .50 .23
❑ 27 Mark Brunell .50 .23
❑ 28 David Palmer .20 .09
❑ 29 Eric Green .20 .09
❑ 30 Terry Glenn .50 .23
❑ 31 Jerry Rice 1.00 .45
❑ 32 Ricky Proehl .20 .09
❑ 33 Tony Banks .30 .14
❑ 34 John Elway 1.50 .70
❑ 35 Johnnie Morton .30 .14
❑ 36 Tony Simmons .20 .09
❑ 37 Jon Kitna .50 .23
❑ 38 Trent Green .50 .23
❑ 39 Peyton Manning 1.50 .70
❑ 40 Emmitt Smith 1.00 .45
❑ 41 Warrick Dunn .50 .23
❑ 42 Jerome Bettis .50 .23
❑ 43 Ricky Watters .30 .14
❑ 44 Rocket Ismail .30 .14
❑ 45 Ryan Leaf .50 .23
❑ 46 Jackie Harris .20 .09
❑ 47 Robert Holcombe .20 .09
❑ 48 Dorsey Levens .50 .23
❑ 49 Duce Staley .50 .23
❑ 50 Brett Favre 1.50 .70
❑ 51 Andre Rison .30 .14
❑ 52 Curtis Conway .30 .14
❑ 53 Mark Chmura .20 .09
❑ 54 Doug Flutie .50 .23
❑ 55 Ernie Mills .20 .09
❑ 56 Jeff George .30 .14
❑ 57 Chris Warren .20 .09
❑ 58 Alonzo Mayes .20 .09
❑ 59 Freddie Jones .20 .09
❑ 60 Shannon Sharpe .30 .14
❑ 61 O.J. Santiago .20 .09
❑ 62 Shawn Springs .20 .09
❑ 63 Kent Graham .20 .09
❑ 64 Muhsin Muhammad .30 .14
❑ 65 Keith Poole .20 .09
❑ 66 Chris Spielman .20 .09
❑ 67 Curtis Enis .20 .09
❑ 68 Lamar Smith .30 .14
❑ 69 Charles Johnson .20 .09
❑ 70 Kerry Collins .30 .14
❑ 71 Charlie Batch .50 .23
❑ 72 Keenan McCardell .30 .14
❑ 73 Ty Detmer .30 .14
❑ 74 Mark Bruener .20 .09
❑ 75 Lamar Thomas .20 .09
❑ 76 Kwamie Lassiter RC .50 .23
❑ 77 Byron Bam Morris .20 .09
❑ 78 Michael Sinclair .20 .09
❑ 79 Darnay Scott .20 .09
❑ 80 Napoleon Kaufman .50 .23
❑ 81 Ed McCaffrey .30 .14
❑ 82 Reidel Anthony .30 .14
❑ 83 Kevin Greene .20 .09
❑ 84 Michael Irvin .30 .14
❑ 85 Charles Way .20 .09
❑ 86 Tim Brown .50 .23
❑ 87 Johnny McWilliams .20 .09
❑ 88 Brad Johnson .50 .23
❑ 89 Antonio Langham .20 .09
❑ 90 Bruce Smith .30 .14
❑ 91 Reggie Barlow .20 .09
❑ 92 Ty Law .30 .14
❑ 93 Bobby Engram .30 .14
❑ 94 Kimble Anders .30 .14
❑ 95 Dale Carter .20 .09
❑ 96 Jimmy Smith .30 .14
❑ 97 Marc Edwards .20 .09
❑ 98 Ken Dilger .20 .09
❑ 99 Adrian Murrell .30 .14
❑ 100 Terance Mathis .30 .14
❑ 101 Gary Anderson .20 .09
❑ 102 Garrison Hearst .30 .14
❑ 103 Ahman Green .50 .23
❑ 104 Daryl Johnston .20 .09
❑ 105 O.J. McDuffie .30 .14
❑ 106 Matthew Hatchette .20 .09
❑ 107 Chris Doleman .20 .09
❑ 108 Steve McNair .50 .23
❑ 109 Leon Johnson .20 .09
❑ 110 Terrell Davis .50 .23
❑ 111 Rob Moore .30 .14
❑ 112 Troy Aikman 1.00 .45
❑ 113 John Avery .20 .09
❑ 114 Frank Wycheck .20 .09
❑ 115 Curtis Martin .50 .23
❑ 116 Jim Harbaugh .30 .14
❑ 117 Sean Dawkins .20 .09
❑ 118 Glenn Foley .30 .14
❑ 119 Warren Sapp .20 .09
❑ 120 R.W. McQuarters .20 .09
❑ 121 Yancey Thigpen .20 .09
❑ 122 Frank Sanders .30 .14
❑ 123 Tim Dwight .50 .23
❑ 124 Pete Mitchell .20 .09
❑ 125 Steve Beuerlein .20 .09
❑ 126 Tyrone Davis .20 .09
❑ 127 Jamie Asher .20 .09
❑ 128 Corey Dillon .50 .23
❑ 129 Doug Pederson .20 .09
❑ 130 Deion Sanders .50 .23
❑ 131 J.J. Stokes .30 .14
❑ 132 Jermaine Lewis .30 .14
❑ 133 Gary Brown .20 .09
❑ 134 Derrick Alexander .20 .09
❑ 135 Tony McGee .20 .09
❑ 136 Kyle Brady .20 .09
❑ 137 Mikhael Ricks .20 .09
❑ 138 Germane Crowell .20 .09
❑ 139 Skip Hicks .20 .09
❑ 140 Ben Coates .30 .14
❑ 141 Will Blackwell .20 .09
❑ 142 Al Del Greco .20 .09
❑ 143 Jake Plummer .30 .14
❑ 144 Marshall Faulk .60 .25
❑ 145 Antowain Smith .50 .23
❑ 146 Corey Fuller .20 .09
❑ 147 Keyshawn Johnson .50 .23
❑ 148 John Randle .30 .14
❑ 149 Terrell Buckley .20 .09
❑ 150 Terry Kirby .20 .09
❑ 151 Robert Brooks .30 .14
❑ 152 Karim Abdul-Jabbar .30 .14
❑ 153 Jason Sehorn .20 .09
❑ 154 Elvis Grbac .30 .14
❑ 155 Andre Reed .30 .14
❑ 156 Ike Hilliard .20 .09
❑ 157 Jamal Anderson .50 .23
❑ 158 Jake Reed .30 .14
❑ 159 Rich Gannon .50 .23
❑ 160 Michael Jackson .20 .09
❑ 161 Bert Emanuel .30 .14
❑ 162 Charles Woodson .50 .23
❑ 163 Ray Lewis .50 .23
❑ 164 Trent Dilfer .30 .14
❑ 165 Oronde Gadsden .30 .14
❑ 166 Wesley Walls .30 .14
❑ 167 Joey Galloway .30 .14
❑ 168 Mo Lewis .20 .09
❑ 169 Darren Woodson .20 .09
❑ 170 Cris Carter .50 .23
❑ 171 Brian Mitchell .20 .09
❑ 172 Tim Biakabutuka .30 .14
❑ 173 Michael Westbrook .30 .14
❑ 174 Dan Marino 1.50 .70
❑ 175 Greg Hill .20 .09
❑ 176 Priest Holmes .75 .35
❑ 177 Fred Lane .20 .09
❑ 178 Isaac Bruce .50 .23
❑ 179 Erik Kramer .20 .09
❑ 180 Steve Young .60 .25
❑ 181 Terry Fair .20 .09
❑ 182 Brian Griese .50 .23
❑ 183 Leslie Shepherd .20 .09
❑ 184 Kordell Stewart .30 .14
❑ 185 Charlie Jones .20 .09
❑ 186 Chris Calloway .20 .09
❑ 187 Wayne Chrebet .30 .14
❑ 188 Natrone Means .30 .14
❑ 189 David LaFleur .20 .09
❑ 190 Rod Smith WR .30 .14
❑ 191 Kevin Dyson .30 .14
❑ 192 Scott Mitchell .20 .09
❑ 193 Andre Wadsworth .20 .09
❑ 194 Vinny Testaverde .30 .14
❑ 195 Az-Zahir Hakim .20 .09
❑ 196 Joe Jurevicius .30 .14
❑ 197 Junior Seau .50 .23
❑ 198 Jason Elam .20 .09
❑ 199 Terrell Owens .50 .23

❑ 200 Jacquez Green	.20	.09
❑ 201 Tim Couch RC	1.00	.45
❑ 202 Donovan McNabb RC	6.00	2.70
❑ 203 Cade McNown RC	.75	.35
❑ 204 Akili Smith RC	.75	.35
❑ 205 Kevin Faulk RC	1.00	.45
❑ 206 Sedrick Irvin RC	.50	.23
❑ 207 Edgerrin James RC	5.00	2.20
❑ 208 Ricky Williams RC	2.50	1.10
❑ 209 D'Wayne Bates RC	.75	.35
❑ 210 David Boston RC	1.00	.45
❑ 211 Torry Holt RC	2.50	1.10
❑ 212 Peerless Price RC	1.50	.70
❑ 213 Daunte Culpepper RC	5.00	2.20
❑ 214 Troy Edwards RC	.75	.35
❑ 215 Rob Konrad RC	1.00	.45
❑ 216 Joe Germaine RC	.75	.35
❑ 217 James Johnson RC	.75	.35
❑ 218 Brock Huard RC	1.00	.45
❑ 219 Cecil Collins RC	.50	.23
❑ 220 Jeff Paulk RC	.50	.23
Eugene Baker RC		
❑ 221 Marty Booker RC	1.00	.45
Jim Finn RC		
❑ 222 Scott Covington RC	1.00	.45
Nick Williams RC		
❑ 223 Kevin Johnson RC	1.00	.45
Darrin Chiaverini RC		
❑ 224 Ebenezer Ekuban RC	.75	.35
Dat Nguyen RC		
❑ 225 Al Wilson RC	.50	.23
Chad Plummer RC		
❑ 226 Chris Claiborn RC	.50	.23
Aaron Gibson RC		
❑ 227 Aaron Brooks RC	4.00	1.80
De'Mond Parker RC		
❑ 228 John Tait RC	.75	.35
Mike Cloud RC		
❑ 229 Andy Katzenmoyer RC	.75	.35
Michael Bishop RC		
❑ 230 Joe Montgomery RC	.75	.35
Dan Campbell RC		
❑ 231 Na Brown RC	.75	.35
Cecil Martin RC		
❑ 232 Amos Zereoue RC	1.00	.45
Jerame Tuman RC		
❑ 233 Jermaine Fazande RC	.75	.35
Steve Heiden RC		
❑ 234 Karsten Bailey RC	.75	.35
Charlie Rogers RC		
❑ 235 Shaun King RC	.75	.35
Martin Gramatica RC		
❑ 236 Jevon Kearse RC	1.25	.55
Kevin Daft RC		
❑ 237 Champ Bailey RC	1.25	.55
Tim Alexander RC		
❑ 238 Karsten Bailey RC	.75	.35
Darnell McDonald RC		
❑ 239 Lamarr Glenn RC	.50	.23
Terry Jackson RC		
❑ 240 Troy Smith RC	.50	.23
Malcolm Johnson RC		
❑ 241 Rondel Menendez RC	.75	.35
Craig Yeast RC		
❑ 242 Jed Weaver RC	.50	.23
James Dearth RC		
❑ 243 Joel Makovicka RC	1.00	.45
Shawn Bryson RC		
❑ 244 Desmond Clark RC	1.00	.45
Jim Kleinsasser RC		
❑ 245 Sean Bennett RC	.50	.23
Autry Denson RC		
❑ 246 Billy Miller RC	.50	.23
Wane McGarity RC		
❑ 247 Mike Lucky RC	.50	.23
Justin Swift RC		
❑ 248 Travis McGriff RC	1.00	.45
MarTay Jenkins RC		
❑ 249 Donald Driver RC	2.00	.90
Larry Parker RC		
❑ 250 Antoine Winfield RC	1.00	.45
Dre' Bly RC		

2003 SkyBox LE

	Nm-Mt	Ex-Mt
COMP.SET w/o SP's (60)	20.00	6.00
❑ 1 Emmitt Smith	2.00	.60
❑ 2 Eric Moulds	.50	.15
❑ 3 William Green	.50	.15
❑ 4 Clinton Portis	1.25	.35
❑ 5 Tony Gonzalez	.50	.15
❑ 6 Aaron Brooks	.75	.23
❑ 7 Chad Pennington	1.00	.30
❑ 8 Jerry Rice	1.50	.45
❑ 9 LaDainian Tomlinson	.75	.23
❑ 10 Torry Holt	.75	.23
❑ 11 Warren Sapp	.50	.15
❑ 12 Steve McNair	.75	.23
❑ 13 Marc Bulger	.75	.23
❑ 14 Patrick Ramsey	.75	.23
❑ 15 Peerless Price	.50	.15
❑ 16 Jamal Lewis	.75	.23
❑ 17 Rich Gannon	.50	.15
❑ 18 Plaxico Burress	.50	.15
❑ 19 Drew Brees	.75	.23
❑ 20 Eddie George	.50	.15
❑ 21 Ray Lewis	.75	.23
❑ 22 Drew Bledsoe	.75	.23
❑ 23 Antonio Bryant	.50	.15
❑ 24 David Carr	1.25	.35
❑ 25 Priest Holmes	1.00	.30
❑ 26 Ricky Williams	.75	.23
❑ 27 Peyton Manning	1.25	.35
❑ 28 Daunte Culpepper	.75	.23
❑ 29 Jeremy Shockey	1.25	.35
❑ 30 Tiki Barber	.50	.15
❑ 31 Koren Robinson	.50	.15
❑ 32 Keyshawn Johnson	.75	.23
❑ 33 Laveranues Coles	.50	.15
❑ 34 Brian Urlacher	1.25	.35
❑ 35 Jake Plummer	.50	.15
❑ 36 Edgerrin James	.75	.23
❑ 37 Marvin Harrison	.75	.23
❑ 38 Tom Brady	1.25	.35
❑ 39 Curtis Martin	.75	.23
❑ 40 Donovan McNabb	1.00	.30
❑ 41 Hines Ward	.75	.23
❑ 42 Charlie Garner	.50	.15
❑ 43 Tommy Maddox	.75	.23
❑ 44 Terrell Owens	.75	.23
❑ 45 Shaun Alexander	.75	.23
❑ 46 Ahman Green	.75	.23
❑ 47 Fred Taylor	.75	.23
❑ 48 Randy Moss	1.25	.35
❑ 49 Deuce McAllister	.75	.23
❑ 50 Quincy Carter	.50	.15
❑ 51 Jeff Garcia	.75	.23
❑ 52 Marshall Faulk	.75	.23
❑ 53 Dante Hall	.75	.23
❑ 54 Michael Vick	2.00	.60
❑ 55 Stephen Davis	.50	.15
❑ 56 Corey Dillon	.50	.15
❑ 57 Travis Henry	.50	.15
❑ 58 Chad Johnson	.50	.15
❑ 59 Joey Harrington	1.25	.35
❑ 60 Brett Favre	2.00	.60
❑ 61 Bryant Johnson RC	25.00	7.50
❑ 62 Terence Newman RC	50.00	15.00
❑ 63 Labrandon Toefield RC	25.00	7.50
❑ 64 Visanthe Shiancoe RC	20.00	6.00
❑ 65 Josh Brown RC	40.00	12.00
❑ 66 Andre Woolfolk RC	25.00	7.50
❑ 67 Jeremi Johnson RC	20.00	6.00
❑ 68 Michael Doss RC	25.00	7.50
❑ 69 Talman Gardner RC	25.00	7.50
❑ 70 Arnaz Battle RC	25.00	7.50
❑ 71 Troy Polamalu RC	25.00	7.50
❑ 72 Brock Forsey RC	25.00	7.50
❑ 73 Domanick Davis RC	60.00	18.00
❑ 74 Onterrio Smith RC	30.00	9.00
❑ 75 Kassim Osgood RC	25.00	7.50
❑ 76 Asante Samuel RC	25.00	7.50
❑ 77 Terrell Suggs RC	40.00	12.00
❑ 78 Boss Bailey RC	30.00	9.00
❑ 79 Larry Johnson RC	50.00	15.00
❑ 80 Teyo Johnson RC	25.00	7.50
❑ 81 Chris Simms RC	50.00	15.00
❑ 82 Walter Young RC	20.00	6.00
❑ 83 Dave Ragone RC	25.00	7.50
❑ 84 E.J. Henderson RC	25.00	7.50
❑ 85 Billy McMullen RC	20.00	6.00
❑ 86 Taylor Jacobs RC	25.00	7.50
❑ 87 Sam Aiken RC	20.00	6.00
❑ 88 Avon Cobourne RC	20.00	6.00
❑ 89 J.R. Tolver RC	20.00	6.00
❑ 90 Doug Gabriel RC	25.00	7.50
❑ 91 Chris Brown RC	50.00	15.00
❑ 92 Musa Smith RC	25.00	7.50
❑ 93 Charles Rogers RC	30.00	9.00
❑ 94 Seth Marler RC	20.00	6.00
❑ 95 Dewayne Robertson RC	25.00	7.50
❑ 96 Shaun McDonald RC	25.00	7.50
❑ 97 Reno Mahe RC	25.00	7.50
❑ 98 Carson Palmer RC	80.00	24.00
❑ 99 Dallas Clark RC	25.00	7.50
❑ 100 Johnathan Sullivan RC	20.00	6.00
❑ 101 Brandon Lloyd RC	30.00	9.00
❑ 102 Ken Dorsey RC	40.00	12.00
❑ 103 Kelley Washington RC	25.00	7.50
❑ 104 Tony Hollings RC	25.00	7.50
❑ 105 Bethel Johnson RC	40.00	12.00
❑ 106 Antonio Gates RC	150.00	45.00
❑ 107 Tyler Brayton RC	25.00	7.50
❑ 108 Michael Haynes RC	25.00	7.50
❑ 109 Andre Johnson RC	60.00	18.00
❑ 110 Nate Burleson RC	60.00	18.00
❑ 111 Sammy Davis RC	25.00	7.50
❑ 112 Nick Barnett RC	40.00	12.00
❑ 113 Willis McGahee RC	60.00	18.00
❑ 114 Casey Fitzsimmons RC	25.00	7.50
❑ 115 Donald Lee RC	20.00	6.00
❑ 116 L.J. Smith RC	25.00	7.50
❑ 117 Tyrone Calico RC	30.00	9.00
❑ 118 Anquan Boldin RC	60.00	18.00
❑ 119 Jason Witten RC	40.00	12.00
❑ 120 George Wrighster RC	20.00	6.00
❑ 121 William Joseph RC	25.00	7.50
❑ 122 Kevin Curtis RC	25.00	7.50
❑ 123 Anthony Adams RC	20.00	6.00
❑ 124 Kyle Boller RC	60.00	18.00
❑ 125 Artose Pinner RC	25.00	7.50
❑ 126 Rashean Mathis RC	20.00	6.00
❑ 127 Justin Fargas RC	25.00	7.50
❑ 128 Pisa Tinoisamoa RC	40.00	12.00
❑ 129 Justin Griffith RC	20.00	6.00
❑ 130 Quentin Griffin RC	60.00	18.00
❑ 131 Cortez Hankton RC	20.00	6.00
❑ 132 B.J. Askew RC	25.00	7.50
❑ 133 Arlen Harris RC	25.00	7.50
❑ 134 Dan Klecko RC	25.00	7.50
❑ 135 Lee Suggs RC	50.00	15.00
❑ 136 Byron Leftwich RC	100.00	30.00
❑ 137 David Tyree RC	20.00	6.00
❑ 138 Aaron Walker RC	20.00	6.00
❑ 139 Marcus Trufant RC	25.00	7.50
❑ 140 Rex Grossman RC	60.00	18.00
❑ 141 Bennie Joppru RC	25.00	7.50
❑ 142 Kevin Williams RC	25.00	7.50
❑ 143 Jerome McDougle RC	25.00	7.50
❑ 144 Ken Hamlin RC	25.00	7.50
❑ 145 Zuriel Smith RC	20.00	6.00
❑ 146 Brooks Bollinger RC	25.00	7.50
❑ 147 Ivan Taylor RC	20.00	6.00

		Nm-Mt	Ex-Mt
❑ 148	Brad Pyatt RC	20.00	6.00
❑ 149	DeJuan Groce RC	25.00	7.50
❑ 150	Keenan Howry RC	25.00	7.50
❑ 151	Seneca Wallace RC	25.00	7.50
❑ 152	Richard Angulo RC	20.00	6.00
❑ 153	Jimmy Kennedy RC	25.00	7.50
❑ 154	Ty Warren RC	25.00	7.50
❑ 155	Nnamdi Asomugha RC	20.00	6.00
❑ 156	Chris Kelsay RC	25.00	7.50
❑ 157	Terry Pierce RC	20.00	6.00
❑ 158	Victor Hobson RC	25.00	7.50
❑ 159	Brian St.Pierre RC	25.00	7.50
❑ 160	Dewayne White RC	20.00	6.00

2003 SkyBox LE Artist Proofs

Nm-Mt Ex-Mt

*STARS: 8X TO 20X BASIC CARDS

2003 SkyBox LE Gold Proofs

Nm-Mt Ex-Mt

*STARS: 4X TO 10X BASIC CARDS

2004 SkyBox LE

		Nm-Mt	Ex-Mt
COMP.SET w/o SP's (60)		20.00	6.00

ROOKIE STATED ODDS 1:29
ROOKIE PRINT RUN 99 SER.#'d SETS
UNPRICED EXEC.PURPLE #'d OF 1

		Nm-Mt	Ex-Mt
❑ 1	Anquan Boldin	.75	.23
❑ 2	Quincy Carter	.50	.15
❑ 3	Chad Pennington	1.00	.30
❑ 4	Brett Favre	2.00	.60
❑ 5	Marc Bulger	.75	.23
❑ 6	David Carr	.75	.23
❑ 7	Byron Leftwich	1.25	.35
❑ 8	Hines Ward	.75	.23
❑ 9	Drew Bledsoe	.75	.23
❑ 10	Domanick Davis	.75	.23
❑ 11	Plaxico Burress	.50	.15
❑ 12	Mark Brunell	.50	.15
❑ 13	Terrell Owens	.75	.23
❑ 14	Peyton Manning	1.25	.35
❑ 15	Matt Hasselbeck	.50	.15
❑ 16	Willis McGahee	.75	.23
❑ 17	Fred Taylor	.50	.15
❑ 18	Torry Holt	.75	.23
❑ 19	Priest Holmes	1.00	.30
❑ 20	Charlie Garner	.50	.15
❑ 21	Brian Urlacher	1.00	.30
❑ 22	Corey Dillon	.50	.15
❑ 23	Daunte Culpepper	.75	.23
❑ 24	Clinton Portis	.75	.23
❑ 25	Chad Johnson	.50	.15
❑ 26	Tom Brady	1.25	.35
❑ 27	Deuce McAllister	.75	.23
❑ 28	Randy Moss	1.00	.30
❑ 29	A.J. Feeley	.75	.23
❑ 30	Steve McNair	.75	.23
❑ 31	Aaron Brooks	.50	.15
❑ 32	Carson Palmer	1.00	.30
❑ 33	Jeremy Shockey	.75	.23
❑ 34	Emmitt Smith	1.50	.45
❑ 35	Jeff Garcia	.75	.23
❑ 36	Kurt Warner	.75	.23
❑ 37	Andre Johnson	.75	.23
❑ 38	LaDainian Tomlinson	.75	.23
❑ 39	Ray Lewis	.75	.23
❑ 40	Charles Rogers	.50	.15
❑ 41	Rich Gannon	.50	.15
❑ 42	Jake Delhomme	.75	.23
❑ 43	Marvin Harrison	.75	.23
❑ 44	Shaun Alexander	.75	.23
❑ 45	Ricky Williams	.75	.23
❑ 46	Eddie George	.50	.15
❑ 47	Edgerrin James	.75	.23
❑ 48	Chris Chambers	.50	.15
❑ 49	Jamal Lewis	.75	.23
❑ 50	Joey Harrington	.75	.23
❑ 51	Jerry Rice	1.50	.45
❑ 52	Kyle Boller	.75	.23
❑ 53	Ahman Green	.75	.23
❑ 54	Donovan McNabb	1.00	.30
❑ 55	Stephen Davis	.50	.15
❑ 56	Tony Gonzalez	.50	.15
❑ 57	Marshall Faulk	.75	.23
❑ 58	Michael Vick	1.50	.45
❑ 59	Jake Plummer	.50	.15
❑ 60	Curtis Martin	.75	.23
❑ 61	Eli Manning RC	80.00	24.00
❑ 62	Robert Gallery RC	25.00	7.50
❑ 63	Larry Fitzgerald RC	50.00	15.00
❑ 64	Philip Rivers RC	50.00	15.00
❑ 65	Sean Taylor RC	20.00	6.00
❑ 66	Kellen Winslow RC	40.00	12.00
❑ 67	Roy Williams RC	50.00	15.00
❑ 68	DeAngelo Hall RC	20.00	6.00
❑ 69	Reggie Williams RC	20.00	6.00
❑ 70	Dunta Robinson RC	15.00	4.50
❑ 71	Ben Roethlisberger RC	120.00	36.00
❑ 72	Jonathan Vilma RC	15.00	4.50
❑ 73	Lee Evans RC	25.00	7.50
❑ 74	Tommie Harris RC	20.00	6.00
❑ 75	Michael Clayton RC	40.00	12.00
❑ 76	D.J. Williams RC	20.00	6.00
❑ 77	Tim Euhus RC	15.00	4.50
❑ 78	Kenechi Udeze RC	15.00	4.50
❑ 79	Vince Wilfork RC	20.00	6.00
❑ 80	J.P. Losman RC	40.00	12.00
❑ 81	Jared Lorenzen RC	12.00	3.60
❑ 82	Steven Jackson RC	50.00	15.00
❑ 83	Ricky Ray RC	12.00	3.60
❑ 84	Chris Perry RC	30.00	9.00
❑ 85	Jason Babin RC	15.00	4.50
❑ 86	Chris Gamble RC	20.00	6.00
❑ 87	Michael Jenkins RC	15.00	4.50
❑ 88	Kevin Jones RC	50.00	15.00
❑ 89	Rashaun Woods RC	20.00	6.00
❑ 90	Ben Watson RC	15.00	4.50
❑ 91	Karlos Dansby RC	15.00	4.50
❑ 92	Teddy Lehman RC	15.00	4.50
❑ 93	Ben Troupe RC	15.00	4.50
❑ 94	Tatum Bell RC	25.00	7.50
❑ 95	Julius Jones RC	60.00	18.00
❑ 96	Devery Henderson RC	12.00	3.60
❑ 97	Drew Henson RC	30.00	9.00
❑ 98	Darius Watts RC	20.00	6.00
❑ 99	Greg Jones RC	15.00	4.50
❑ 100	Luke McCown RC	15.00	4.50
❑ 101	Keary Colbert RC	20.00	6.00
❑ 102	Mewelde Moore RC	20.00	6.00
❑ 103	Ben Hartsock RC	15.00	4.50
❑ 104	Derrick Hamilton RC	12.00	3.60
❑ 105	Bernard Berrian RC	15.00	4.50
❑ 106	Chris Cooley RC	15.00	4.50
❑ 107	Devard Darling RC	15.00	4.50
❑ 108	Matt Schaub RC	25.00	7.50
❑ 109	Carlos Francis RC	12.00	3.60
❑ 110	Will Poole RC	15.00	4.50
❑ 111	Samie Parker RC	15.00	4.50
❑ 112	Derrick Knight RC	12.00	3.60
❑ 113	Jerricho Cotchery RC	15.00	4.50
❑ 114	Rod Rutherford RC	12.00	3.60
❑ 115	Ernest Wilford RC	15.00	4.50
❑ 116	Cedric Cobbs RC	15.00	4.50
❑ 117	Johnnie Morant RC	15.00	4.50
❑ 118	Craig Krenzel RC	15.00	4.50
❑ 119	Maurice Mann RC	12.00	3.60
❑ 120	Michael Turner RC	12.00	3.60
❑ 121	Ryan Dinwiddie RC	12.00	3.60
❑ 122	Drew Carter RC	15.00	4.50
❑ 123	P.K. Sam RC	12.00	3.60
❑ 124	Jamaar Taylor RC	15.00	4.50
❑ 125	Ryan Krause RC	12.00	3.60
❑ 126	Triandos Luke RC	15.00	4.50
❑ 127	Andy Hall RC	12.00	3.60
❑ 128	Josh Harris RC	15.00	4.50
❑ 129	Jim Sorgi RC	15.00	4.50
❑ 130	Jason Fife RC	12.00	3.60
❑ 131	Clarence Moore RC	15.00	4.50
❑ 132	Jeff Smoker RC	25.00	7.50
❑ 133	John Navarre RC	15.00	4.50
❑ 134	Justin Jenkins RC	12.00	3.60
❑ 135	Adimchinobe Echemandu RC	12.00	3.60
❑ 136	Jammal Lord RC	15.00	4.50
❑ 137	Erik Jensen RC	12.00	3.60
❑ 138	Cody Pickett RC	15.00	4.50
❑ 139	Casey Bramlet RC	12.00	3.60
❑ 140	Quincy Wilson RC	12.00	3.60
❑ 141	Thomas Tapeh RC	12.00	3.60
❑ 142	Matt Brandt RC	10.00	3.00
❑ 143	Bruce Perry RC	12.00	3.60
❑ 144	Mark Jones RC	12.00	3.60
❑ 145	Keith Smith RC	12.00	3.60
❑ 146	B.J. Symons RC	15.00	4.50
❑ 147	Patrick Crayton RC	15.00	4.50
❑ 148	Daryl Smith RC	15.00	4.50
❑ 149	Demorrio Williams RC	15.00	4.50
❑ 150	Casey Clausen RC	20.00	6.00
❑ 151	Jarrett Payton RC	15.00	4.50
❑ 152	Kris Wilson RC	15.00	4.50
❑ 153	Renaldo Works RC	15.00	4.50
❑ 154	Shawn Andrews RC	15.00	4.50
❑ 155	Ricardo Colclough RC	15.00	4.50
❑ 156	Travis LaBoy RC	15.00	4.50
❑ 157	Bob Sanders RC	12.00	3.60
❑ 158	Chad Lavalais RC	12.00	3.60
❑ 159	Derrick Strait RC	15.00	4.50
❑ 160	Darnell Dockett RC	12.00	3.60

2004 SkyBox LE Black Border Red

Nm-Mt Ex-Mt

*STARS: 6X TO 15X BASE CARD HI
*ROOKIES: .4X TO 1X BASE CARD HI
STATED PRINT RUN 50 SER.#'d SETS

2004 SkyBox LE Gold

Nm-Mt Ex-Mt

*STARS: 3X TO 8X BASE CARD HI
*ROOKIES: .25X TO .6X BASE CARD HI
STATED PRINT RUN 150 SER.#'d SETS

2004 SkyBox LE Black Border Platinum

Nm-Mt Ex-Mt

*STARS: 8X TO 20X BASE CARD HI
*ROOKIES: .5X TO 1.2X BASE CARD HI
STATED PRINT RUN 35 SER.#'d SETS

1999 SkyBox Molten Metal

		Nm-Mt	Ex-Mt
COMPLETE SET (151)		100.00	45.00
COMP.SET w/o SP's (125)		30.00	13.50
❑ 1	Terrell Davis	1.50	.70
❑ 2	Chris Chandler	1.00	.45

❑ 3 Terry Glenn 1.50 .70
❑ 4 Jon Kitna 1.50 .70
❑ 5 Bubby Brister 1.00 .45
❑ 6 Jermaine Lewis 1.00 .45
❑ 7 Doug Flutie 1.50 .70
❑ 8 Napoleon Kaufman 1.50 .70
❑ 9 Yancey Thigpen .60 .25
❑ 10 Bobby Engram 1.00 .45
❑ 11 Barry Sanders 5.00 2.20
❑ 12 Ben Coates .60 .25
❑ 13 Joey Galloway 1.00 .45
❑ 14 Charlie Batch 1.50 .70
❑ 15 Jerome Bettis 1.50 .70
❑ 16 Brad Johnson 1.50 .70
❑ 17 Brian Griese 1.50 .70
❑ 18 Jeff Lewis .60 .25
❑ 19 Jake Plummer 1.00 .45
❑ 20 Mark Brunell 1.50 .70
❑ 21 Robert Smith 1.50 .70
❑ 22 Steve Young 2.00 .90
❑ 23 Derrick Mayes 1.00 .45
❑ 24 Wayne Chrebet 1.50 .70
❑ 25 Rich Gannon 1.50 .70
❑ 26 Steve McNair 1.50 .70
❑ 27 Charles Johnson 1.00 .45
❑ 28 Stephen Alexander .60 .25
❑ 29 Jeff Blake 1.00 .45
❑ 30 Tony Gonzalez 1.50 .70
❑ 31 Eddie Kennison 1.00 .45
❑ 32 Hines Ward 1.50 .70
❑ 33 Isaac Bruce 1.50 .70
❑ 34 Peyton Manning 5.00 2.20
❑ 35 Doug Pederson 1.00 .45
❑ 36 Stephen Davis 1.50 .70
❑ 37 Terance Mathis 1.00 .45
❑ 38 Herman Moore 1.00 .45
❑ 39 Fred Taylor 1.50 .70
❑ 40 Courtney Hawkins .60 .25
❑ 41 Michael Westbrook 1.00 .45
❑ 42 Vinny Testaverde 1.00 .45
❑ 43 Jacquez Green .60 .25
❑ 44 Rocket Ismail 1.00 .45
❑ 45 Curtis Martin 1.50 .70
❑ 46 Tim Brown 1.50 .70
❑ 47 Kevin Dyson 1.00 .45
❑ 48 Steve Beuerlein 1.00 .45
❑ 49 Adrian Murrell 1.00 .45
❑ 50 Randall Cunningham 1.50 .70
❑ 51 Jerry Rice 3.00 1.35
❑ 52 Tim Biakabutuka 1.00 .45
❑ 53 Muhsin Muhammad 1.00 .45
❑ 54 Antonio Freeman 1.50 .70
❑ 55 Cris Carter 1.50 .70
❑ 56 Lawrence Phillips 1.00 .45
❑ 57 Michael Irvin 1.00 .45
❑ 58 Terrell Owens 1.50 .70
❑ 59 Warrick Dunn 1.50 .70
❑ 60 Leslie Shepherd .60 .25
❑ 61 O.J. McDuffie 1.00 .45
❑ 62 Byron Hanspard .60 .25
❑ 63 Trent Dilfer 1.00 .45
❑ 64 Eric Moulds 1.50 .70
❑ 65 Scott Mitchell 1.00 .45
❑ 66 Marc Edwards .60 .25
❑ 67 Dorsey Levens 1.50 .70
❑ 68 Dan Marino 5.00 2.20
❑ 69 Jason Sehorn .60 .25
❑ 70 Junior Seau 1.50 .70
❑ 71 Reidel Anthony .60 .25
❑ 72 Rob Moore 1.00 .45
❑ 73 Deion Sanders 1.50 .70
❑ 74 Rickey Dudley .60 .25
❑ 75 Keyshawn Johnson 1.50 .70
❑ 76 Eddie George 1.50 .70
❑ 77 E.G. Green .60 .25
❑ 78 Terry Kirby 1.00 .45
❑ 79 John Avery .60 .25
❑ 80 Pete Mitchell .60 .25
❑ 81 Natrone Means 1.00 .45
❑ 82 Mike Alstott 1.50 .70
❑ 83 Carl Pickens 1.00 .45
❑ 84 Karim Abdul-Jabbar 1.00 .45
❑ 85 Kerry Collins 1.00 .45
❑ 86 Erik Kramer .60 .25
❑ 87 Robert Holcombe .60 .25
❑ 88 Willie Jackson .60 .25
❑ 89 Marcus Pollard .60 .25
❑ 90 Bam Morris .60 .25
❑ 91 Gary Brown .60 .25
❑ 92 Freddie Jones .60 .25
❑ 93 Kurt Warner RC 10.00 4.50
❑ 94 Priest Holmes 2.50 1.10
❑ 95 Duce Staley 1.50 .70
❑ 96 Skip Hicks .60 .25
❑ 97 Frank Sanders 1.00 .45
❑ 98 Corey Dillon 1.50 .70
❑ 99 Shannon Sharpe 1.00 .45
❑ 100 Randy Moss 4.00 1.80
❑ 101 Sean Dawkins .60 .25
❑ 102 Marshall Faulk 2.00 .90
❑ 103 Mark Chmura .60 .25
❑ 104 Keenan McCardell 1.00 .45
❑ 105 Jimmy Smith 1.00 .45
❑ 106 Jim Harbaugh 1.00 .45
❑ 107 Jamal Anderson 1.50 .70
❑ 108 Elvis Grbac 1.00 .45
❑ 109 Ed McCaffrey 1.00 .45
❑ 110 Drew Bledsoe 2.00 .90
❑ 111 Curtis Conway 1.00 .45
❑ 112 Billy Joe Tolliver .60 .25
❑ 113 J.J. Stokes 1.00 .45
❑ 114 Curtis Enis .60 .25
❑ 115 Antowain Smith 1.50 .70
❑ 116 Troy Aikman 3.00 1.35
❑ 117 Ricky Watters 1.00 .45
❑ 118 Kordell Stewart 1.00 .45
❑ 119 Derrick Alexander 1.00 .45
❑ 120 Emmitt Smith 3.00 1.35
❑ 121 Billy Joe Hobert .60 .25
❑ 122 Johnnie Morton 1.00 .45
❑ 123 Rod Smith 1.00 .45
❑ 124 Marvin Harrison 1.50 .70
❑ 125 Brett Favre 5.00 2.20
❑ 126 Craig Yeast RC 2.00 .90
❑ 127 Ricky Williams RC 4.00 1.80
❑ 128 Brandon Stokley RC 3.00 1.35
❑ 129 Akili Smith RC 2.00 .90
❑ 130 Peerless Price RC 4.00 1.80
❑ 131 Joe Montgomery RC 2.00 .90
❑ 132 Cade McNown RC 2.00 .90
❑ 133 Donovan McNabb RC 10.00 4.50
❑ 134 Shaun King RC 2.00 .90
❑ 135 James Johnson RC 2.00 .90
❑ 136 Kevin Johnson RC 2.50 1.10
❑ 137 Edgerrin James RC 8.00 3.60
❑ 138 Terry Jackson RC 1.25 .55
❑ 139 Sedrick Irvin RC 1.25 .55
❑ 140 Brock Huard RC 2.50 1.10
❑ 141 Torry Holt RC 5.00 2.20
❑ 142 Amos Zereoue RC 2.50 1.10
❑ 143 Kevin Faulk RC 2.50 1.10
❑ 144 Troy Edwards RC 2.00 .90
❑ 145 Donald Driver RC 4.00 1.80
❑ 146 Daunte Culpepper RC 8.00 3.60
❑ 147 Tim Couch RC 2.50 1.10
❑ 148 Cecil Collins RC 1.25 .55
❑ 149 David Boston RC 2.50 1.10
❑ 150 Champ Bailey RC 3.00 1.35
❑ 151 Olandis Gary RC 2.50 1.10
❑ P133 Donovan McNabb Promo 3.00 1.35

1998 SkyBox Premium

	Nm-Mt	Ex-Mt
COMPLETE SET (250)	80.00	36.00

❑ 1 John Elway 2.50 1.10
❑ 2 Drew Bledsoe 1.00 .45
❑ 3 Antonio Freeman .60 .25
❑ 4 Merton Hanks .25 .11
❑ 5 James Jett .40 .18
❑ 6 Ricky Proehl .25 .11
❑ 7 Deion Sanders .60 .25
❑ 8 Frank Sanders .40 .18
❑ 9 Bruce Smith .40 .18
❑ 10 Tiki Barber .60 .25
❑ 11 Isaac Bruce .60 .25
❑ 12 Mark Brunell .60 .25
❑ 13 Quinn Early .25 .11
❑ 14 Terry Glenn .60 .25
❑ 15 Darrien Gordon .25 .11
❑ 16 Keith Byars .25 .11
❑ 17 Terrell Davis .60 .25
❑ 18 Charlie Garner .40 .18
❑ 19 Eddie Kennison .40 .18
❑ 20 Keenan McCardell .40 .18
❑ 21 Eric Moulds .60 .25
❑ 22 Jimmy Smith .40 .18
❑ 23 Reidel Anthony .40 .18
❑ 24 Rae Carruth .25 .11
❑ 25 Michael Irvin .60 .25
❑ 26 Dorsey Levens .60 .25
❑ 27 Derrick Mayes .40 .18
❑ 28 Adrian Murrell .40 .18
❑ 29 Dwayne Rudd .25 .11
❑ 30 Leslie Shepherd .25 .11
❑ 31 Jamal Anderson .60 .25
❑ 32 Robert Brooks .40 .18
❑ 33 Sean Dawkins .25 .11
❑ 34 Cris Dishman .25 .11
❑ 35 Rickey Dudley .25 .11
❑ 36 Bobby Engram .40 .18
❑ 37 Chester McGlockton .25 .11
❑ 38 Terrell Owens .60 .25
❑ 39 Wayne Chrebet .60 .25
❑ 40 Dexter Coakley .25 .11
❑ 41 Kerry Collins .40 .18
❑ 42 Trent Dilfer .60 .25
❑ 43 Bobby Hoying .40 .18
❑ 44 Glyn Milburn .25 .11
❑ 45 Rob Moore .40 .18
❑ 46 Jake Reed .40 .18
❑ 47 Dana Stubblefield .25 .11
❑ 48 Reggie White .60 .25
❑ 49 Natrone Means .40 .18
❑ 50 Troy Aikman 1.25 .55
❑ 51 Aaron Bailey .25 .11
❑ 52 William Floyd .25 .11
❑ 53 Eric Metcalf .25 .11
❑ 54 Warrick Dunn .60 .25
❑ 55 Chad Lewis .40 .18
❑ 56 Curtis Martin .60 .25
❑ 57 Tony Martin .40 .18
❑ 58 John Randle .40 .18
❑ 59 Jeff Burris .25 .11
❑ 60 Larry Centers .25 .11
❑ 61 Bert Emanuel .40 .18
❑ 62 Sean Gilbert .25 .11
❑ 63 David Palmer .25 .11
❑ 64 Eric Bieniemy .25 .11
❑ 65 Peter Boulware .25 .11
❑ 66 Charles Johnson .25 .11
❑ 67 Jerris McPhail .25 .11
❑ 68 Scott Mitchell .40 .18
❑ 69 Chris Sanders .25 .11
❑ 70 Ken Dilger .25 .11
❑ 71 Brad Johnson .60 .25
❑ 72 Danny Kanell .40 .18
❑ 73 Fred Lane .25 .11
❑ 74 Warren Sapp .40 .18
❑ 75 Carl Pickens .40 .18
❑ 76 Cris Carter .60 .25
❑ 77 Marshall Faulk .75 .35
❑ 78 Keyshawn Johnson .60 .25
❑ 79 Tony McGee .25 .11
❑ 80 Muhsin Muhammad .40 .18

❑ 81 Kordell Stewart	.60	.25
❑ 82 Karl Williams	.25	.11
❑ 83 Willie Davis	.25	.11
❑ 84 David Dunn	.25	.11
❑ 85 Marvin Harrison	.60	.25
❑ 86 Michael Jackson	.25	.11
❑ 87 John Mobley	.25	.11
❑ 88 Shawn Springs	.25	.11
❑ 89 Wesley Walls	.40	.18
❑ 90 Jermaine Lewis	.40	.18
❑ 91 Ed McCaffrey	.40	.18
❑ 92 Chris Calloway	.25	.11
❑ 93 Lamont Warren	.25	.11
❑ 94 Ricky Watters	.40	.18
❑ 95 Tony Banks	.40	.18
❑ 96 Tony Brackens	.25	.11
❑ 97 Gary Brown	.25	.11
❑ 98 Howard Griffith	.25	.11
❑ 99 Ray Lewis	.60	.25
❑ 100 Jeff Blake	.40	.18
❑ 101 Charlie Jones	.25	.11
❑ 102 Glenn Foley	.40	.18
❑ 103 Jay Graham	.25	.11
❑ 104 James McKnight	.60	.25
❑ 105 Steve McNair	.60	.25
❑ 106 Chad Scott	.25	.11
❑ 107 Rod Smith WR	.40	.18
❑ 108 Jason Taylor	.40	.18
❑ 109 Corey Dillon	.60	.25
❑ 110 Eddie George	.60	.25
❑ 111 Jim Harbaugh	.40	.18
❑ 112 Warren Moon	.60	.25
❑ 113 Shannon Sharpe	.40	.18
❑ 114 Darnell Autry	.25	.11
❑ 115 Brett Favre	2.50	1.10
❑ 116 Jeff George	.40	.18
❑ 117 Tony Gonzalez	.60	.25
❑ 118 Garrison Hearst	.60	.25
❑ 119 Randal Hill	.25	.11
❑ 120 Eric Swann	.25	.11
❑ 121 Jamie Asher	.25	.11
❑ 122 Tim Brown	.60	.25
❑ 123 Stephen Davis	.25	.11
❑ 124 Chris Chandler	.40	.18
❑ 125 Jerry Rice	1.25	.55
❑ 126 Troy Davis	.25	.11
❑ 127 Ronnie Harmon	.25	.11
❑ 128 Andre Rison	.40	.18
❑ 129 Duce Staley	.75	.35
❑ 130 Charles Way	.25	.11
❑ 131 Bryant Westbrook	.25	.11
❑ 132 Mike Alstott	.60	.25
❑ 133 Gus Frerotte	.25	.11
❑ 134 Travis Jervey	.40	.18
❑ 135 Daryl Johnston	.40	.18
❑ 136 Jake Plummer	.60	.25
❑ 137 Junior Seau	.60	.25
❑ 138 Robert Smith	.60	.25
❑ 139 Thurman Thomas	.60	.25
❑ 140 Karim Abdul-Jabbar	.60	.25
❑ 141 Jerome Bettis	.60	.25
❑ 142 Byron Hanspard	.25	.11
❑ 143 Raymont Harris	.25	.11
❑ 144 Willie McGinest	.25	.11
❑ 145 Barry Sanders	2.00	.90
❑ 146 Irv Smith	.25	.11
❑ 147 Michael Strahan	.40	.18
❑ 148 Frank Wycheck	.25	.11
❑ 149 Steve Broussard	.25	.11
❑ 150 Joey Galloway	.40	.18
❑ 151 Courtney Hawkins	.25	.11
❑ 152 O.J. McDuffie	.40	.18
❑ 153 Herman Moore	.40	.18
❑ 154 Chris Penn	.25	.11
❑ 155 O.J. Santiago	.25	.11
❑ 156 Yancey Thigpen	.25	.11
❑ 157 Jason Sehorn	.40	.18
❑ 158 Ben Coates	.40	.18
❑ 159 Ernie Conwell	.25	.11
❑ 160 Dale Carter	.25	.11
❑ 161 Jeff Graham	.25	.11
❑ 162 Rob Johnson	.40	.18
❑ 163 Damon Jones	.25	.11
❑ 164 Mark Chmura	.40	.18
❑ 165 Curtis Conway	.40	.18
❑ 166 Elvis Grbac	.40	.18
❑ 167 Andre Hastings	.25	.11
❑ 168 Terry Kirby	.25	.11
❑ 169 Aeneas Williams	.25	.11
❑ 170 Derrick Alexander WR	.40	.18
❑ 171 Troy Brown	.40	.18
❑ 172 Irving Fryar	.40	.18
❑ 173 Jerald Moore	.25	.11
❑ 174 Andre Reed	.40	.18
❑ 175 James Stewart	.40	.18
❑ 176 Chris Warren	.40	.18
❑ 177 Will Blackwell	.25	.11
❑ 178 Erik Kramer	.25	.11
❑ 179 Dan Marino	2.50	1.10
❑ 180 Terance Mathis	.40	.18
❑ 181 Johnnie Morton	.40	.18
❑ 182 J.J. Stokes	.40	.18
❑ 183 Rodney Thomas	.25	.11
❑ 184 Steve Young	.75	.35
❑ 185 Kimble Anders	.40	.18
❑ 186 Napoleon Kaufman	.60	.25
❑ 187 Orlando Pace	.25	.11
❑ 188 Antowain Smith	.60	.25
❑ 189 Emmitt Smith	2.00	.90
❑ 190 Terry Allen	.60	.25
❑ 191 Mark Bruener	.25	.11
❑ 192 Rodney Harrison	.40	.18
❑ 193 Billy Joe Hobert	.25	.11
❑ 194 Leon Johnson	.25	.11
❑ 195 Freddie Jones	.25	.11
❑ 196 John Elway OFA	1.00	.45
❑ 197 Brett Favre OFA Steve Atwater OFA	.75	.35
❑ 198 Brett Favre OFA Steve Atwater OFA	.75	.35
❑ 199 Dorsey Levens OFA Keith Traylor OFA	.40	.18
❑ 200 Packers Offense OFA Broncos Defense OFA	.60	.25
❑ 201 Mark Chmura OFA Tyrone Braxton OFA	.25	.11
❑ 202 Dorsey Levens OFA Steve Atwater OFA Bill Romanowski OFA	.40	.18
❑ 203 Robert Brooks OFA Ray Crockett OFA	.40	.18
❑ 204 Tim McKyer OFA	.25	.11
❑ 205 Allen Aldridge OFA	.25	.11
❑ 206 Terrell Davis OFA Rod Smith WR OFA	.60	.25
❑ 207 Bill Romanowski OFA	.25	.11
❑ 208 John Elway OFA Rod Smith WR OFA Ed McCaffrey OFA	1.00	.45
❑ 209 Ray Crockett OFA	.25	.11
❑ 210 John Elway OFA	1.00	.45
❑ 211 Robert Edwards RC	2.50	1.10
❑ 212 Roland Williams RC	2.00	.90
❑ 213 Joe Jurevicius RC	4.00	1.80
❑ 214 Wilmont Perry RC	2.00	.90
❑ 215 Robert Holcombe RC	2.50	1.10
❑ 216 Larry Shannon RC	2.00	.90
❑ 217 Skip Hicks RC	2.50	1.10
❑ 218 Pat Johnson RC	2.50	1.10
❑ 219 Pat Palmer RC	2.00	.90
❑ 220 John Dutton RC	2.00	.90
❑ 221 Az-Zahir Hakim RC	4.00	1.80
❑ 222 Mikhael Ricks RC	2.50	1.10
❑ 223 Rashaan Shehee RC	2.50	1.10
❑ 224 Ryan Leaf RC	4.00	1.80
❑ 225 Alvis Whitted RC	2.50	1.10
❑ 226 Marcus Nash RC	2.00	.90
❑ 227 Fred Taylor RC	6.00	2.70
❑ 228 Hines Ward RC	10.00	4.50
❑ 229 C.Fuamatu-Ma'afala RC	2.50	1.10
❑ 230 Jerome Pathon RC	4.00	1.80
❑ 231 Peyton Manning RC	40.00	18.00
❑ 232 Charles Woodson RC	5.00	2.20
❑ 233 Jon Ritchie RC	2.50	1.10
❑ 234 Scott Frost R RC	2.00	.90
❑ 235 John Avery RC	2.50	1.10
❑ 236 Jonathan Linton RC	2.50	1.10
❑ 237 Jacquez Green RC	2.50	1.10
❑ 238 Andre Wadsworth RC	2.50	1.10
❑ 239 Cam Quayle RC	2.00	.90
❑ 240 Randy Moss RC	20.00	9.00
❑ 241 Raymond Priester RC	2.00	.90
❑ 242 Donald Hayes RC	2.50	1.10
❑ 243 Brian Griese RC	8.00	3.60
❑ 244 Brian Alford RC	2.00	.90
❑ 245 Kevin Dyson RC	4.00	1.80
❑ 246 Jammi German RC	2.00	.90
❑ 247 Cameron Cleeland RC	2.00	.90
❑ 248 Curtis Enis RC	2.00	.90
❑ 249 Terry Hardy RC	2.00	.90
❑ 250 Tony Simmons RC	2.50	1.10
❑ NNO Checklist Card	.25	.11
❑ P136 Jake Plummer Promo	1.50	.70

1998 SkyBox Premium Star Rubies

	Nm-Mt	Ex-Mt

*RUBY STARS: 40X TO 100X
*RUBY RCs: 4X TO 10X

1999 SkyBox Premium

	Nm-Mt	Ex-Mt
COMPLETE SET (290)	300.00	135.00
COMP.SET w/o SPs (250)	50.00	22.00
❑ 1 Randy Moss	1.50	.70
❑ 2 Jamie Asher	.25	.11
❑ 3 Joey Galloway	.40	.18
❑ 4 Kent Graham	.25	.11
❑ 5 Leslie Shepherd	.25	.11
❑ 6 Levon Kirkland	.25	.11
❑ 7 Marcus Pollard	.25	.11
❑ 8 O.J. McDuffie	.40	.18
❑ 9 Bill Romanowski	.25	.11
❑ 10 Priest Holmes	1.00	.45
❑ 11 Tim Biakabutuka	.40	.18
❑ 12 Duce Staley	.60	.25
❑ 13 Isaac Bruce	.60	.25
❑ 14 Jay Riemersma	.25	.11
❑ 15 Karim Abdul-Jabbar	.40	.18
❑ 16 Kevin Dyson	.40	.18
❑ 17 Rickey Dudley	.25	.11
❑ 18 Rocket Ismail	.40	.18
❑ 19 Billy Davis	.25	.11
❑ 20 James Jett	.40	.18
❑ 21 Jerome Bettis	.60	.25
❑ 22 Michael McCrary	.25	.11
❑ 23 Michael Westbrook	.40	.18
❑ 24 Oronde Gadsden	.40	.18
❑ 25 Brad Johnson	.60	.25
❑ 26 Shawn Springs	.25	.11
❑ 27 Cris Carter	.60	.25
❑ 28 Ed McCaffrey	.40	.18
❑ 29 Gary Brown	.25	.11
❑ 30 Hines Ward	.60	.25
❑ 31 Hugh Douglas	.25	.11
❑ 32 Jamir Miller	.25	.11
❑ 33 Michael Bates	.25	.11
❑ 34 Peyton Manning	2.00	.90
❑ 35 Tony Banks	.40	.18
❑ 36 Charles Way	.25	.11
❑ 37 Charlie Batch	.60	.25
❑ 38 Jake Reed	.40	.18
❑ 39 Mark Brunell	.60	.25
❑ 40 Skip Hicks	.25	.11

❑ 41 Steve Young .75 .35
❑ 42 Wesley Walls .40 .18
❑ 43 Antonio Langham .25 .11
❑ 44 Antowain Smith .60 .25
❑ 45 Brian Griese .60 .25
❑ 46 Jessie Armstead .25 .11
❑ 47 Thurman Thomas .40 .18
❑ 48 Jeff George .40 .18
❑ 49 Jessie Tuggle .25 .11
❑ 50 Jim Harbaugh .40 .18
❑ 51 Marvin Harrison .60 .25
❑ 52 Randall Cunningham .60 .25
❑ 53 Stephen Alexander .25 .11
❑ 54 Tiki Barber .40 .18
❑ 55 Billy Joe Tolliver .25 .11
❑ 56 Bruce Smith .40 .18
❑ 57 Eddie George .60 .25
❑ 58 Eugene Robinson .25 .11
❑ 59 John Elway 2.00 .90
❑ 60 Kent Dilger .25 .11
❑ 61 Rodney Harrison .25 .11
❑ 62 Ty Detmer .40 .18
❑ 63 Andre Reed .40 .18
❑ 64 Dorsey Levens .60 .25
❑ 65 Eddie Kennison .40 .18
❑ 66 Freddie Jones .25 .11
❑ 67 Jacquez Green .25 .11
❑ 68 Jason Elam .25 .11
❑ 69 Marc Edwards .25 .11
❑ 70 Terance Mathis .40 .18
❑ 71 Alonzo Mayes .25 .11
❑ 72 Andre Wadsworth .25 .11
❑ 73 Barry Sanders 2.00 .90
❑ 74 Derrick Alexander .25 .11
❑ 75 Garrison Hearst .40 .18
❑ 76 Leon Johnson .25 .11
❑ 77 Mike Alstott .60 .25
❑ 78 Shawn Jefferson .25 .11
❑ 79 Andre Hastings .25 .11
❑ 80 Eric Moulds .60 .25
❑ 81 Ryan Leaf .60 .25
❑ 82 Takeo Spikes .25 .11
❑ 83 Terrell Davis .60 .25
❑ 84 Tim Dwight .60 .25
❑ 85 Trent Dilfer .40 .18
❑ 86 Vonnie Holliday .25 .11
❑ 87 Antonio Freeman .60 .25
❑ 88 Carl Pickens .40 .18
❑ 89 Chris Chandler .40 .18
❑ 90 Dale Carter .25 .11
❑ 91 La'Roi Glover RC .60 .25
❑ 92 Natrone Means .40 .18
❑ 93 Reidel Anthony .40 .18
❑ 94 Brett Favre 2.00 .90
❑ 95 Bubby Brister .25 .11
❑ 96 Cameron Cleeland .25 .11
❑ 97 Chris Calloway .25 .11
❑ 98 Corey Dillon .60 .25
❑ 99 Greg Hill .25 .11
❑ 100 Vinny Testaverde .40 .18
❑ 101 Trent Green .60 .25
❑ 102 Sam Gash .25 .11
❑ 103 Mikhael Ricks .25 .11
❑ 104 Emmitt Smith 1.25 .55
❑ 105 Doug Flutie .60 .25
❑ 106 Deion Sanders .60 .25
❑ 107 Charles Johnson .25 .11
❑ 108 Byron Bam Morris .25 .11
❑ 109 Andre Rison .40 .18
❑ 110 Doug Pederson .25 .11
❑ 111 Marshall Faulk .75 .35
❑ 112 Tim Brown .60 .25
❑ 113 Warren Sapp .25 .11
❑ 114 Bryan Still .25 .11
❑ 115 Chris Penn .25 .11
❑ 116 Jamal Anderson .60 .25
❑ 117 Keyshawn Johnson .60 .25
❑ 118 Ricky Proehl .25 .11
❑ 119 Robert Brooks .40 .18
❑ 120 Tony Gonzalez .60 .25
❑ 121 Ty Law .40 .18
❑ 122 Elvis Grbac .40 .18
❑ 123 Jeff Blake .40 .18
❑ 124 Mark Chmura .25 .11
❑ 125 Junior Seau .60 .25
❑ 126 Mo Lewis .25 .11
❑ 127 Ray Buchanan .25 .11
❑ 128 Robert Holcombe .25 .11
❑ 129 Tony Simmons .25 .11
❑ 130 David Palmer .25 .11
❑ 131 Ike Hilliard .25 .11
❑ 132 Mike Vanderjagt .25 .11
❑ 133 Rae Carruth .25 .11
❑ 134 Sean Dawkins .25 .11
❑ 135 Shannon Sharpe .40 .18
❑ 136 Curtis Conway .40 .18
❑ 137 Darrell Green .25 .11
❑ 138 Germane Crowell .25 .11
❑ 139 J.J. Stokes .40 .18
❑ 140 Kevin Hardy .25 .11
❑ 141 Rob Moore .40 .18
❑ 142 Robert Smith .60 .25
❑ 143 Wayne Chrebet .40 .18
❑ 144 Yancey Thigpen .25 .11
❑ 145 Jerome Pathon .25 .11
❑ 146 John Mobley .25 .11
❑ 147 Kerry Collins .40 .18
❑ 148 Peter Boulware .25 .11
❑ 149 Matthew Hatchette .25 .11
❑ 150 Kordell Stewart .40 .18
❑ 151 Koy Detmer .25 .11
❑ 152 Sedrick Shaw .25 .11
❑ 153 Steve Beuerlein .25 .11
❑ 154 Zach Thomas .60 .25
❑ 155 Adrian Murrell .40 .18
❑ 156 Bobby Engram .40 .18
❑ 157 Bryan Cox .25 .11
❑ 158 Drew Bledsoe .75 .35
❑ 159 Jerry Rice 1.25 .55
❑ 160 Keenan McCardell .40 .18
❑ 161 Steve McNair .60 .25
❑ 162 Terry Fair .25 .11
❑ 163 Derrick Brooks .60 .25
❑ 164 Eric Green .25 .11
❑ 165 Erik Kramer .25 .11
❑ 166 Frank Sanders .40 .18
❑ 167 Fred Taylor .60 .25
❑ 168 Johnnie Morton .40 .18
❑ 169 R.W. McQuarters .25 .11
❑ 170 Terry Glenn .60 .25
❑ 171 Frank Wycheck .25 .11
❑ 172 John Avery .25 .11
❑ 173 Kevin Turner .25 .11
❑ 174 Larry Centers .25 .11
❑ 175 Michael Irvin .40 .18
❑ 176 Rich Gannon .60 .25
❑ 177 Ricky Watters .40 .18
❑ 178 Rodney Thomas .25 .11
❑ 179 Scott Mitchell .25 .11
❑ 180 Chad Brown .25 .11
❑ 181 John Randle .40 .18
❑ 182 Michael Strahan .40 .18
❑ 183 Muhsin Muhammad .40 .18
❑ 184 Reggie Barlow .25 .11
❑ 185 Rod Smith .40 .18
❑ 186 Dan Marino 2.00 .90
❑ 187 Dexter Coakley .25 .11
❑ 188 Jermaine Lewis .40 .18
❑ 189 Jon Kitna .60 .25
❑ 190 Napoleon Kaufman .60 .25
❑ 191 Will Blackwell .25 .11
❑ 192 Aaron Glenn .25 .11
❑ 193 Ben Coates .40 .18
❑ 194 Curtis Enis .25 .11
❑ 195 Herman Moore .40 .18
❑ 196 Jake Plummer .40 .18
❑ 197 Jimmy Smith .40 .18
❑ 198 Terrell Owens .60 .25
❑ 199 Warrick Dunn .60 .25
❑ 200 Charles Woodson .60 .25
❑ 201 Ahman Green .60 .25
❑ 202 Mark Bruener .25 .11
❑ 203 Ray Lewis .60 .25
❑ 204 Tony Martin .40 .18
❑ 205 Troy Aikman 1.25 .55
❑ 206 Curtis Martin .60 .25
❑ 207 Darnay Scott .25 .11
❑ 208 Derrick Mayes .25 .11
❑ 209 Keith Poole .25 .11
❑ 210 Warren Moon .60 .25
❑ 211 Chris Claiborne RC .50 .23
❑ 211S Chris Claiborne SP 1.50 .70
❑ 212 Ricky Williams RC 2.50 1.10
❑ 212S Ricky Williams SP 8.00 3.60
❑ 213 Tim Couch RC 1.25 .55
❑ 213S Tim Couch SP 4.00 1.80
❑ 214 Champ Bailey RC 1.50 .70
❑ 214S Champ Bailey SP 5.00 2.20
❑ 215 Torry Holt RC 3.00 1.35
❑ 215S Torry Holt SP 10.00 4.50
❑ 216 Donovan McNabb RC 6.00 2.70
❑ 216S Donovan McNabb SP 20.00 9.00
❑ 217 David Boston RC 1.25 .55
❑ 217S David Boston SP 4.00 1.80
❑ 218 Chris McAlister RC .75 .35
❑ 218S Chris McAlister SP 2.50 1.10
❑ 219 Michael Bishop RC 1.25 .55
❑ 219S Michael Bishop SP 4.00 1.80
❑ 220 Daunte Culpepper RC 5.00 2.20
❑ 220S Daunte Culpepper SP 15.00 6.75
❑ 221 Joe Germaine RC .75 .35
❑ 221S Joe Germaine SP 2.50 1.10
❑ 222 Edgerrin James RC 5.00 2.20
❑ 222S Edgerrin James SP 15.00 6.75
❑ 223 Jevon Kearse RC 2.00 .90
❑ 223S Jevon Kearse SP 6.00 2.70
❑ 224 Ebenezer Ekuban RC .75 .35
❑ 224S Ebenezer Ekuban SP 2.50 1.10
❑ 225 Scott Covington RC 1.25 .55
❑ 225S Scott Covington SP 4.00 1.80
❑ 226 Aaron Brooks RC 4.00 1.80
❑ 226S Aaron Brooks SP 12.00 5.50
❑ 227 Cecil Collins RC .50 .23
❑ 227S Cecil Collins SP 1.50 .70
❑ 228 Akili Smith RC .75 .35
❑ 228S Akili Smith SP 2.50 1.10
❑ 229 Shaun King RC .75 .35
❑ 229S Shaun King SP 2.50 1.10
❑ 230 Chad Plummer RC .50 .23
❑ 230S Chad Plummer SP 1.50 .70
❑ 231 Peerless Price RC 2.00 .90
❑ 231S Peerless Price SP 6.00 2.70
❑ 232 Antoine Winfield RC .75 .35
❑ 232S Antoine Winfield SP 2.50 1.10
❑ 233 Antuan Edwards RC .50 .23
❑ 233S Antuan Edwards SP 1.50 .70
❑ 234 Rob Konrad RC 1.25 .55
❑ 234S Rob Konrad SP 4.00 1.80
❑ 235 Troy Edwards RC .75 .35
❑ 235S Troy Edwards SP 2.50 1.10
❑ 236 Terry Jackson RC .75 .35
❑ 236S Terry Jackson SP 2.50 1.10
❑ 237 Jim Kleinsasser RC 1.25 .55
❑ 237S Jim Kleinsasser SP 4.00 1.80
❑ 238 Joe Montgomery RC .75 .35
❑ 238S Joe Montgomery SP 2.50 1.10
❑ 239 Desmond Clark RC 1.25 .55
❑ 239S Desmond Clark SP 4.00 1.80
❑ 240 Lamar King RC .50 .23
❑ 240S Lamar King SP 1.50 .70
❑ 241 Dameane Douglas RC .75 .35
❑ 241S Dameane Douglas SP 2.50 1.10
❑ 242 Martin Gramatica RC .50 .23
❑ 242S Martin Gramatica SP 1.50 .70
❑ 243 Jim Finn RC .50 .23
❑ 243S Jim Finn SP 1.50 .70
❑ 244 Andy Katzenmoyer RC .75 .35
❑ 244S Andy Katzenmoyer SP 2.50 1.10
❑ 245 Dee Miller RC .50 .23
❑ 245S Dee Miller SP 1.50 .70
❑ 246 D'Wayne Bates RC .75 .35
❑ 246S D'Wayne Bates SP 2.50 1.10
❑ 247 Amos Zereoue RC 1.25 .55
❑ 247S Amos Zereoue SP 4.00 1.80
❑ 248 Karsten Bailey RC .75 .35
❑ 248S Karsten Bailey SP 2.50 1.10
❑ 249 Kevin Johnson RC 1.25 .55
❑ 249S Kevin Johnson SP 4.00 1.80
❑ 250 Cade McNown RC .75 .35
❑ 250S Cade McNown SP 2.50 1.10

1993 SP

	Nm-Mt	Ex-Mt
COMPLETE SET (270)	60.00	27.00
❑ 1 Curtis Conway FOIL RC	4.00	1.80
❑ 2 John Copeland FOIL RC	.75	.35
❑ 3 Kevin Williams FOIL RC	1.50	.70
❑ 4 Dan Williams FOIL RC	.75	.35
❑ 5 Patrick Bates FOIL RC	.75	.35
❑ 6 Jerome Bettis FOIL RC	25.00	11.00
❑ 7 O.J. McDuffie FOIL RC	3.00	1.35
❑ 8 Robert Smith FOIL RC	12.00	5.50
❑ 9 Drew Bledsoe FOIL RC	30.00	13.50
❑ 10 Irv Smith FOIL RC	.75	.35
❑ 11 Marvin Jones FOIL RC	.75	.35
❑ 12 Victor Bailey FOIL RC	.75	.35
❑ 13 Garrison Hearst FOIL RC	10.00	4.50
❑ 14 Natrone Means FOIL RC	3.00	1.35
❑ 15 Todd Kelly FOIL RC	.75	.35
❑ 16 Rick Mirer FOIL RC	3.00	1.35
❑ 17 Eric Curry FOIL RC	.75	.35
❑ 18 Reggie Brooks FOIL RC	1.50	.70
❑ 19 Eric Dickerson	.50	.23
❑ 20 Roger Harper RC	.30	.14
❑ 21 Michael Haynes	.50	.23
❑ 22 Bobby Hebert	.30	.14
❑ 23 Lincoln Kennedy RC	.30	.14
❑ 24 Chris Miller	.50	.23
❑ 25 Mike Pritchard	.50	.23
❑ 26 Andre Rison	.50	.23
❑ 27 Deion Sanders	1.50	.70
❑ 28 Cornelius Bennett	.50	.23
❑ 29 Kenneth Davis	.30	.14
❑ 30 Henry Jones	.30	.14
❑ 31 Jim Kelly	1.00	.45
❑ 32 John Parrella RC	.30	.14
❑ 33 Andre Reed	.50	.23
❑ 34 Bruce Smith	1.00	.45
❑ 35 Thomas Smith RC	.50	.23
❑ 36 Thurman Thomas	1.00	.45
❑ 37 Neal Anderson	.30	.14
❑ 38 Myron Baker RC	.30	.14
❑ 39 Mark Carrier DB	.30	.14
❑ 40 Richard Dent	.50	.23
❑ 41 Chris Gedney RC	.30	.14
❑ 42 Jim Harbaugh	1.00	.45
❑ 43 Craig Heyward	.50	.23
❑ 44 Carl Simpson RC	.30	.14
❑ 45 Alonzo Spellman	.30	.14
❑ 46 Derrick Fenner	.30	.14
❑ 47 Harold Green	.30	.14
❑ 48 David Klingler	.30	.14
❑ 49 Ricardo McDonald	.30	.14
❑ 50 Tony McGee RC	.50	.23
❑ 51 Carl Pickens	.50	.23
❑ 52 Steve Tovar RC	.30	.14
❑ 53 Alfred Williams	.30	.14
❑ 54 Darryl Williams	.30	.14
❑ 55 Jerry Ball	.30	.14
❑ 56 Mike Caldwell RC	.30	.14
❑ 57 Mark Carrier WR	.50	.23
❑ 58 Steve Everitt RC	.30	.14
❑ 59 Dan Footman RC	.30	.14
❑ 60 Pepper Johnson	.30	.14
❑ 61 Bernie Kosar	.50	.23
❑ 62 Eric Metcalf	.50	.23
❑ 63 Michael Dean Perry	.50	.23
❑ 64 Troy Aikman	2.50	1.10
❑ 65 Charles Haley	.50	.23
❑ 66 Michael Irvin	1.00	.45
❑ 67 Robert Jones	.30	.14
❑ 68 Derrick Lassic RC	.30	.14
❑ 69 Russell Maryland	.30	.14
❑ 70 Ken Norton Jr.	.50	.23
❑ 71 Darrin Smith RC	.50	.23
❑ 72 Emmitt Smith	5.00	2.20
❑ 73 Steve Atwater	.30	.14
❑ 74 Rod Bernstine	.30	.14
❑ 75 Jason Elam RC	1.00	.45
❑ 76 John Elway	5.00	2.20
❑ 77 Simon Fletcher	.30	.14
❑ 78 Tommy Maddox	1.00	.45
❑ 79 Glyn Milburn RC	1.00	.45
❑ 80 Derek Russell	.30	.14
❑ 81 Shannon Sharpe	1.00	.45
❑ 82 Bennie Blades	.30	.14
❑ 83 Willie Green	.30	.14
❑ 84 Antonio London RC	.30	.14
❑ 85 Ryan McNeil RC	1.00	.45
❑ 86 Herman Moore	1.00	.45
❑ 87 Rodney Peete	.30	.14
❑ 88 Barry Sanders	4.00	1.80
❑ 89 Chris Spielman	.50	.23
❑ 90 Pat Swilling	.30	.14
❑ 91 Mark Brunell RC	15.00	6.75
❑ 92 Terrell Buckley	.30	.14
❑ 93 Brett Favre	6.00	2.70
❑ 94 Jackie Harris	.30	.14
❑ 95 Sterling Sharpe	1.00	.45
❑ 96 John Stephens	.30	.14
❑ 97 Wayne Simmons RC	.30	.14
❑ 98 George Teague RC	.50	.23
❑ 99 Reggie White	1.00	.45
❑ 100 Micheal Barrow RC	1.00	.45
❑ 101 Cody Carlson	.30	.14
❑ 102 Ray Childress	.30	.14
❑ 103 Brad Hopkins RC	.30	.14
❑ 104 Haywood Jeffires	.50	.23
❑ 105 Wilber Marshall	.30	.14
❑ 106 Warren Moon	1.00	.45
❑ 107 Webster Slaughter	.30	.14
❑ 108 Lorenzo White	.30	.14
❑ 109 John Baylor	.30	.14
❑ 110 Duane Bickett	.30	.14
❑ 111 Quentin Coryatt	.50	.23
❑ 112 Steve Emtman	.30	.14
❑ 113 Jeff George	1.00	.45
❑ 114 Jessie Hester	.30	.14
❑ 115 Anthony Johnson	.50	.23
❑ 116 Reggie Langhorne	.30	.14
❑ 117 Roosevelt Potts RC	.30	.14
❑ 118 Marcus Allen	1.00	.45
❑ 119 J.J. Birden	.30	.14
❑ 120 Willie Davis	1.00	.45
❑ 121 Jaime Fields RC	.30	.14
❑ 122 Joe Montana	5.00	2.20
❑ 123 Will Shields RC	1.00	.45
❑ 124 Neil Smith	1.00	.45
❑ 125 Derrick Thomas	1.00	.45
❑ 126 Harvey Williams	.50	.23
❑ 127 Tim Brown	1.00	.45
❑ 128 Billy Joe Hobert RC	1.00	.45
❑ 129 Jeff Hostetler	.50	.23
❑ 130 Ethan Horton	.30	.14
❑ 131 Raghib Ismail	.50	.23
❑ 132 Howie Long	1.00	.45
❑ 133 Terry McDaniel	.30	.14
❑ 134 Greg Robinson RC	.30	.14
❑ 135 Anthony Smith	.30	.14
❑ 136 Flipper Anderson	.30	.14
❑ 137 Marc Boutte	.30	.14
❑ 138 Shane Conlan	.30	.14
❑ 139 Troy Drayton RC	.50	.23
❑ 140 Henry Ellard	.50	.23
❑ 141 Jim Everett	.50	.23
❑ 142 Cleveland Gary	.30	.14
❑ 143 Sean Gilbert	.50	.23
❑ 144 Robert Young	.30	.14
❑ 145 Marco Coleman	.30	.14
❑ 146 Bryan Cox	.30	.14
❑ 147 Irving Fryar	.50	.23
❑ 148 Keith Jackson	.50	.23
❑ 149 Terry Kirby RC	1.00	.45
❑ 150 Dan Marino	5.00	2.20
❑ 151 Scott Mitchell	1.00	.45
❑ 152 Louis Oliver	.30	.14
❑ 153 Troy Vincent	.30	.14
❑ 154 Anthony Carter	.50	.23
❑ 155 Cris Carter	1.00	.45
❑ 156 Roger Craig	.50	.23
❑ 157 Chris Doleman	.30	.14
❑ 158 Qadry Ismail RC	2.00	.90
❑ 159 Steve Jordan	.30	.14
❑ 160 Randall McDaniel	.30	.14
❑ 161 Audray McMillian	.30	.14
❑ 162 Barry Word	.30	.14
❑ 163 Vincent Brown	.30	.14
❑ 164 Marv Cook	.30	.14
❑ 165 Sam Gash RC	1.00	.45
❑ 166 Pat Harlow	.30	.14
❑ 167 Greg McMurtry	.30	.14
❑ 168 Todd Rucci RC	.30	.14
❑ 169 Leonard Russell	.50	.23
❑ 170 Scott Sisson RC	.30	.14
❑ 171 Chris Slade RC	.50	.23
❑ 172 Morten Andersen	.30	.14
❑ 173 Derek Brown RBK RC	.50	.23
❑ 174 Reggie Freeman RC	.30	.14
❑ 175 Rickey Jackson	.30	.14
❑ 176 Eric Martin	.30	.14
❑ 177 Wayne Martin	.30	.14
❑ 178 Brad Muster	.30	.14
❑ 179 Willie Roaf RC	.50	.23
❑ 180 Renaldo Turnbull	.30	.14
❑ 181 Derek Brown TE	.30	.14
❑ 182 Marcus Buckley RC	.30	.14
❑ 183 Jarrod Bunch	.30	.14
❑ 184 Rodney Hampton	.50	.23
❑ 185 Ed McCaffrey	1.00	.45
❑ 186 Kanavis McGhee	.30	.14
❑ 187 Mike Sherrard	.30	.14
❑ 188 Phil Simms	.50	.23
❑ 189 Lawrence Taylor	1.00	.45
❑ 190 Kurt Barber	.30	.14
❑ 191 Boomer Esiason	.50	.23
❑ 192 Johnny Johnson	.30	.14
❑ 193 Ronnie Lott	.50	.23
❑ 194 Johnny Mitchell	.30	.14
❑ 195 Rob Moore	.50	.23
❑ 196 Adrian Murrell RC	1.00	.45
❑ 197 Browning Nagle	.30	.14
❑ 198 Marvin Washington	.30	.14
❑ 199 Eric Allen	.30	.14
❑ 200 Fred Barnett	.50	.23
❑ 201 Randall Cunningham	1.00	.45
❑ 202 Byron Evans	.30	.14
❑ 203 Tim Harris	.30	.14
❑ 204 Seth Joyner	.30	.14
❑ 205 Leonard Renfro RC	.30	.14
❑ 206 Heath Sherman	.30	.14
❑ 207 Clyde Simmons	.30	.14
❑ 208 Johnny Bailey	.30	.14
❑ 209 Steve Beuerlein	.50	.23
❑ 210 Chuck Cecil	.30	.14
❑ 211 Larry Centers RC	1.00	.45
❑ 212 Gary Clark	.50	.23
❑ 213 Ernest Dye RC	.30	.14
❑ 214 Ken Harvey	.30	.14
❑ 215 Randal Hill	.30	.14
❑ 216 Ricky Proehl	.30	.14
❑ 217 Deon Figures RC	.30	.14
❑ 218 Barry Foster	.50	.23
❑ 219 Eric Green	.30	.14
❑ 220 Kevin Greene	.50	.23
❑ 221 Carlton Haselrig	.30	.14
❑ 222 Andre Hastings RC	.50	.23
❑ 223 Greg Lloyd	.50	.23
❑ 224 Neil O'Donnell	1.00	.45
❑ 225 Rod Woodson	1.00	.45
❑ 226 Marion Butts	.30	.14
❑ 227 Darren Carrington RC	.30	.14
❑ 228 Darrien Gordon RC	.30	.14
❑ 229 Ronnie Harmon	.30	.14
❑ 230 Stan Humphries	.50	.23
❑ 231 Anthony Miller	.50	.23

❑ 232	Chris Mims	.30	.14
❑ 233	Leslie O'Neal	.50	.23
❑ 234	Junior Seau	1.00	.45
❑ 235	Dana Hall	.30	.14
❑ 236	Adrian Hardy	.30	.14
❑ 237	Brent Jones	.50	.23
❑ 238	Tim McDonald	.30	.14
❑ 239	Tom Rathman	.30	.14
❑ 240	Jerry Rice	3.00	1.35
❑ 241	Dana Stubblefield RC	1.00	.45
❑ 242	Ricky Watters	1.00	.45
❑ 243	Steve Young	2.50	1.10
❑ 244	Brian Blades	.50	.23
❑ 245	Ferrell Edmunds	.30	.14
❑ 246	Carlton Gray RC	.30	.14
❑ 247	Cortez Kennedy	.50	.23
❑ 248	Kelvin Martin	.30	.14
❑ 249	Dan McGwire	.30	.14
❑ 250	Jon Vaughn	.30	.14
❑ 251	Chris Warren	.50	.23
❑ 252	John L. Williams	.30	.14
❑ 253	Reggie Cobb	.30	.14
❑ 254	Horace Copeland RC	.50	.23
❑ 255	Lawrence Dawsey	.30	.14
❑ 256	Demetrius DuBose RC	.30	.14
❑ 257	Craig Erickson	.50	.23
❑ 258	Courtney Hawkins	.30	.14
❑ 259	John Lynch RC	8.00	3.60
❑ 260	Hardy Nickerson	.50	.23
❑ 261	Lamar Thomas RC	.30	.14
❑ 262	Carl Banks	.30	.14
❑ 263	Tom Carter RC	.50	.23
❑ 264	Brad Edwards	.30	.14
❑ 265	Kurt Gouveia	.30	.14
❑ 266	Desmond Howard	.50	.23
❑ 267	Charles Mann	.30	.14
❑ 268	Art Monk	.50	.23
❑ 269	Mark Rypien	.30	.14
❑ 270	Ricky Sanders	.30	.14
❑ P1	Joe Montana Promo numbered 19	5.00	2.20

1994 SP

		Nm-Mt	Ex-Mt
COMPLETE SET (200)		50.00	22.00
❑ 1	Dan Wilkinson RC	1.25	.55
❑ 2	Heath Shuler RC	.75	.35
❑ 3	Marshall Faulk RC	20.00	9.00
❑ 4	Willie McGinest RC	1.25	.55
❑ 5	Trent Dilfer RC	5.00	2.20
❑ 6	Bryant Young RC	1.25	.55
❑ 7	Antonio Langham RC	.40	.18
❑ 8	John Thierry RC	.40	.18
❑ 9	Aaron Glenn RC	1.25	.55
❑ 10	Charles Johnson RC	1.25	.55
❑ 11	Dewayne Washington RC	.40	.18
❑ 12	Johnnie Morton RC	3.00	1.35
❑ 13	Greg Hill RC	.75	.35
❑ 14	William Floyd RC	.75	.35
❑ 15	Derrick Alexander WR RC	1.25	.55
❑ 16	Darnay Scott RC	1.25	.55
❑ 17	Errict Rhett RC	1.25	.55
❑ 18	Charlie Garner RC	4.00	1.80
❑ 19	Thomas Lewis RC	.40	.18
❑ 20	David Palmer RC	1.25	.55
❑ 21	Andre Reed	.30	.14
❑ 22	Thurman Thomas	.50	.23
❑ 23	Bruce Smith	.50	.23
❑ 24	Jim Kelly	.50	.23
❑ 25	Cornelius Bennett	.30	.14
❑ 26	Bucky Brooks RC	.15	.07
❑ 27	Jeff Burris RC	.30	.14
❑ 28	Jim Harbaugh	.50	.23
❑ 29	Tony Bennett	.15	.07
❑ 30	Quentin Coryatt	.15	.07
❑ 31	Floyd Turner	.15	.07
❑ 32	Roosevelt Potts	.15	.07
❑ 33	Jeff Herrod	.15	.07
❑ 34	Irving Fryar	.30	.14
❑ 35	Bryan Cox	.15	.07
❑ 36	Dan Marino	4.00	1.80
❑ 37	Terry Kirby	.50	.23
❑ 38	Michael Stewart	.15	.07
❑ 39	Bernie Kosar	.30	.14
❑ 40	Aubrey Beavers RC	.15	.07
❑ 41	Vincent Brisby	.30	.14
❑ 42	Ben Coates	.30	.14
❑ 43	Drew Bledsoe	2.00	.90
❑ 44	Marion Butts	.15	.07
❑ 45	Chris Slade	.15	.07
❑ 46	Michael Timpson	.15	.07
❑ 47	Ray Crittenden RC	.15	.07
❑ 48	Rob Moore	.30	.14
❑ 49	Johnny Mitchell	.15	.07
❑ 50	Art Monk	.30	.14
❑ 51	Boomer Esiason	.30	.14
❑ 52	Ronnie Lott	.30	.14
❑ 53	Ryan Yarborough RC	.15	.07
❑ 54	Carl Pickens	.30	.14
❑ 55	David Klingler	.15	.07
❑ 56	Harold Green	.15	.07
❑ 57	John Copeland	.15	.07
❑ 58	Louis Oliver	.15	.07
❑ 59	Corey Sawyer	.15	.07
❑ 60	Michael Jackson	.30	.14
❑ 61	Mark Rypien	.15	.07
❑ 62	Vinny Testaverde	.30	.14
❑ 63	Eric Metcalf	.30	.14
❑ 64	Eric Turner	.15	.07
❑ 65	Haywood Jeffires	.30	.14
❑ 66	Micheal Barrow	.15	.07
❑ 67	Cody Carlson	.15	.07
❑ 68	Gary Brown	.15	.07
❑ 69	Bucky Richardson	.15	.07
❑ 70	Al Smith	.15	.07
❑ 71	Eric Green	.15	.07
❑ 72	Neil O'Donnell	.50	.23
❑ 73	Barry Foster	.15	.07
❑ 74	Greg Lloyd	.30	.14
❑ 75	Rod Woodson	.30	.14
❑ 76	Byron Bam Morris RC	.30	.14
❑ 77	John L. Williams	.15	.07
❑ 78	Anthony Miller	.30	.14
❑ 79	Mike Pritchard	.15	.07
❑ 80	John Elway	4.00	1.80
❑ 81	Shannon Sharpe	.30	.14
❑ 82	Steve Atwater	.15	.07
❑ 83	Simon Fletcher	.15	.07
❑ 84	Glyn Milburn	.30	.14
❑ 85	Mark Collins	.15	.07
❑ 86	Keith Cash	.15	.07
❑ 87	Willie Davis	.30	.14
❑ 88	Joe Montana	4.00	1.80
❑ 89	Marcus Allen	.50	.23
❑ 90	Neil Smith	.30	.14
❑ 91	Derrick Thomas	.50	.23
❑ 92	Tim Brown	.50	.23
❑ 93	Jeff Hostetler	.30	.14
❑ 94	Terry McDaniel	.15	.07
❑ 95	Rocket Ismail	.30	.14
❑ 96	Rob Fredrickson RC	.30	.14
❑ 97	Harvey Williams	.30	.14
❑ 98	Steve Wisniewski	.15	.07
❑ 99	Stan Humphries	.30	.14
❑ 100	Natrone Means	.50	.23
❑ 101	Leslie O'Neal	.15	.07
❑ 102	Junior Seau	.50	.23
❑ 103	Ronnie Harmon	.15	.07
❑ 104	Shawn Jefferson	.15	.07
❑ 105	Howard Ballard	.15	.07
❑ 106	Rick Mirer	.50	.23
❑ 107	Cortez Kennedy	.30	.14
❑ 108	Chris Warren	.30	.14
❑ 109	Brian Blades	.30	.14
❑ 110	Sam Adams RC	.30	.14
❑ 111	Gary Clark	.30	.14
❑ 112	Steve Beuerlein	.30	.14
❑ 113	Ronald Moore	.15	.07
❑ 114	Eric Swann	.30	.14
❑ 115	Clyde Simmons	.15	.07
❑ 116	Seth Joyner	.15	.07
❑ 117	Troy Aikman	2.00	.90
❑ 118	Charles Haley	.30	.14
❑ 119	Alvin Harper	.30	.14
❑ 120	Michael Irvin	.50	.23
❑ 121	Daryl Johnston	.30	.14
❑ 122	Emmitt Smith	3.00	1.35
❑ 123	Shante Carver RC	.15	.07
❑ 124	Dave Brown	.30	.14
❑ 125	Rodney Hampton	.30	.14
❑ 126	Dave Meggett	.15	.07
❑ 127	Chris Calloway	.15	.07
❑ 128	Mike Sherrard	.15	.07
❑ 129	Carlton Bailey	.15	.07
❑ 130	Randall Cunningham	.50	.23
❑ 131	William Fuller	.15	.07
❑ 132	Eric Allen	.15	.07
❑ 133	Calvin Williams	.30	.14
❑ 134	Herschel Walker	.30	.14
❑ 135	Bernard Williams RC	.15	.07
❑ 136	Henry Ellard	.30	.14
❑ 137	Ethan Horton	.15	.07
❑ 138	Desmond Howard	.30	.14
❑ 139	Reggie Brooks	.30	.14
❑ 140	John Friesz	.30	.14
❑ 141	Tom Carter	.15	.07
❑ 142	Terry Allen	.30	.14
❑ 143	Adrian Cooper	.15	.07
❑ 144	Qadry Ismail	.50	.23
❑ 145	Warren Moon	.50	.23
❑ 146	Henry Thomas	.15	.07
❑ 147	Todd Steussie RC	.30	.14
❑ 148	Cris Carter	.75	.35
❑ 149	Andy Heck	.15	.07
❑ 150	Curtis Conway	.50	.23
❑ 151	Erik Kramer	.30	.14
❑ 152	Lewis Tillman	.15	.07
❑ 153	Dante Jones	.15	.07
❑ 154	Alonzo Spellman	.15	.07
❑ 155	Herman Moore	.50	.23
❑ 156	Broderick Thomas	.15	.07
❑ 157	Scott Mitchell	.30	.14
❑ 158	Barry Sanders	3.00	1.35
❑ 159	Chris Spielman	.30	.14
❑ 160	Pat Swilling	.15	.07
❑ 161	Bennie Blades	.15	.07
❑ 162	Sterling Sharpe	.30	.14
❑ 163	Brett Favre	4.00	1.80
❑ 164	Reggie Cobb	.15	.07
❑ 165	Reggie White	.50	.23
❑ 166	Sean Jones	.15	.07
❑ 167	George Teague	.15	.07
❑ 168	LeShon Johnson RC	.30	.14
❑ 169	Courtney Hawkins	.15	.07
❑ 170	Jackie Harris	.15	.07
❑ 171	Craig Erickson	.15	.07
❑ 172	Santana Dotson	.30	.14
❑ 173	Eric Curry	.15	.07
❑ 174	Hardy Nickerson	.30	.14
❑ 175	Derek Brown RBK	.15	.07
❑ 176	Jim Everett	.30	.14
❑ 177	Michael Haynes	.30	.14
❑ 178	Tyrone Hughes	.30	.14
❑ 179	Wayne Martin	.15	.07
❑ 180	Willie Roaf	.15	.07
❑ 181	Irv Smith	.15	.07
❑ 182	Jeff George	.50	.23
❑ 183	Andre Rison	.30	.14
❑ 184	Erric Pegram	.15	.07
❑ 185	Bret Emanuel RC	1.00	.45
❑ 186	Chris Doleman	.15	.07
❑ 187	Ron George	.15	.07
❑ 188	Chris Miller	.15	.07
❑ 189	Troy Drayton	.15	.07
❑ 190	Chris Chandler	.30	.14

	Nm-Mt	Ex-Mt
❑ 191 Jerome Bettis	1.00	.45
❑ 192 Jimmie Jones	.15	.07
❑ 193 Sean Gilbert	.15	.07
❑ 194 Jerry Rice	2.00	.90
❑ 195 Brent Jones	.30	.14
❑ 196 Deion Sanders	1.00	.45
❑ 197 Steve Young	1.50	.70
❑ 198 Ricky Watters	.30	.14
❑ 199 Dana Stubblefield	.30	.14
❑ 200 Ken Norton Jr.	.30	.14
❑ RB1 Dan Marino RB	25.00	11.00
❑ RB2 Jerry Rice RB	25.00	11.00
❑ P16 Joe Montana Promo	4.00	1.80

1994 SP Die Cuts

	Nm-Mt	Ex-Mt
COMPLETE SET (200)	80.00	36.00

*STARS: .8X TO 2X BASIC CARDS
*RCs: .5X TO 1.2X BASIC CARDS

1995 SP

	Nm-Mt	Ex-Mt
COMPLETE SET (200)	50.00	22.00
❑ 1 Ki-Jana Carter PP RC	2.00	.90
❑ 2 Eric Zeier PP RC UER Height listed at 6'11"	2.00	.90
❑ 3 Steve McNair PP RC	12.00	5.50
❑ 4 Michael Westbrook PP RC	2.00	.90
❑ 5 Kerry Collins PP RC	6.00	2.70
❑ 6 Joey Galloway PP RC	5.00	2.20
❑ 7 Kevin Carter PP RC	2.00	.90
❑ 8 Mike Mamula PP RC	.50	.23
❑ 9 Kyle Brady PP RC	2.00	.90
❑ 10 J.J. Stokes PP RC	2.00	.90
❑ 11 Tyrone Poole PP RC	2.00	.90
❑ 12 Rashaan Salaam PP RC	1.00	.45
❑ 13 Sherman Williams PP RC	.50	.23
❑ 14 Luther Elliss PP RC	.50	.23
❑ 15 James O. Stewart PP RC	4.00	1.80
❑ 16 Tamarick Vanover PP RC	2.00	.90
❑ 17 Napoleon Kaufman PP RC	4.00	1.80
❑ 18 Curtis Martin PP RC	12.00	5.50
❑ 19 Tyrone Wheatley PP RC	4.00	1.80
❑ 20 Frank Sanders PP RC	2.00	.90
❑ 21 Devin Bush	.20	.09
❑ 22 Terance Mathis	.40	.18
❑ 23 Bert Emanuel	.75	.35
❑ 24 Eric Metcalf	.40	.18
❑ 25 Craig Heyward	.40	.18
❑ 26 Jeff George	.40	.18
❑ 27 Mark Carrier WR	.40	.18
❑ 28 Pete Metzelaars	.20	.09
❑ 29 Frank Reich	.20	.09
❑ 30 Sam Mills	.40	.18
❑ 31 John Kasay	.20	.09
❑ 32 Willie Green	.40	.18
❑ 33 Jeff Graham	.20	.09
❑ 34 Curtis Conway	.75	.35
❑ 35 Steve Walsh	.20	.09
❑ 36 Erik Kramer	.20	.09
❑ 37 Michael Timpson	.20	.09
❑ 38 Mark Carrier	.20	.09
❑ 39 Troy Aikman	2.00	.90
❑ 40 Michael Irvin	.75	.35
❑ 41 Charles Haley	.40	.18
❑ 42 Deion Sanders	1.25	.55
❑ 43 Jay Novacek	.40	.18
❑ 44 Emmitt Smith	3.00	1.35
❑ 45 Herman Moore	.75	.35
❑ 46 Scott Mitchell UER front reads Mitcehill	.40	.18
❑ 47 Bennie Blades	.20	.09
❑ 48 Johnnie Morton	.40	.18
❑ 49 Chris Spielman	.40	.18
❑ 50 Barry Sanders	3.00	1.35
❑ 51 Edgar Bennett	.40	.18
❑ 52 Reggie White	.75	.35
❑ 53 Sean Jones	.20	.09
❑ 54 Mark Ingram	.20	.09
❑ 55 Robert Brooks	.75	.35
❑ 56 Brett Favre	4.00	1.80
❑ 57 Lovell Pinkney RC	.50	.23
❑ 58 Chris Miller	.20	.09
❑ 59 Isaac Bruce	1.25	.55
❑ 60 Roman Phifer	.20	.09
❑ 61 Sean Gilbert	.40	.18
❑ 62 Jerome Bettis	.75	.35
❑ 63 Derrick Alexander DE RC	.50	.23
❑ 64 Cris Carter	.75	.35
❑ 65 Jake Reed	.40	.18
❑ 66 Robert Smith	.75	.35
❑ 67 David Palmer	.40	.18
❑ 68 Warren Moon	.40	.18
❑ 69 Ray Zellars RC	1.00	.45
❑ 70 Jim Everett	.20	.09
❑ 71 Michael Haynes	.40	.18
❑ 72 Quinn Early	.40	.18
❑ 73 Willie Roaf	.20	.09
❑ 74 Mario Bates	.40	.18
❑ 75 Mike Sherrard	.20	.09
❑ 76 Chris Calloway	.20	.09
❑ 77 Dave Brown	.40	.18
❑ 78 Thomas Lewis	.40	.18
❑ 79 Herschel Walker	.40	.18
❑ 80 Rodney Hampton	.40	.18
❑ 81 Fred Barnett	.40	.18
❑ 82 Calvin Williams	.40	.18
❑ 83 Randall Cunningham	.75	.35
❑ 84 Charlie Garner	.75	.35
❑ 85 Bobby Taylor RC	3.00	1.35
❑ 86 Ricky Watters	.40	.18
❑ 87 Dave Krieg	.20	.09
❑ 88 Rob Moore	.40	.18
❑ 89 Eric Swann	.40	.18
❑ 90 Clyde Simmons	.20	.09
❑ 91 Seth Joyner	.20	.09
❑ 92 Garrison Hearst	.75	.35
❑ 93 Jerry Rice	2.00	.90
❑ 94 Bryant Young	.40	.18
❑ 95 Brent Jones	.20	.09
❑ 96 Ken Norton	.40	.18
❑ 97 William Floyd	.40	.18
❑ 98 Steve Young	1.50	.70
❑ 99 Warren Sapp RC	5.00	2.20
❑ 100 Trent Dilfer	.75	.35
❑ 101 Alvin Harper	.20	.09
❑ 102 Hardy Nickerson	.20	.09
❑ 103 Derrick Brooks RC	5.00	2.20
❑ 104 Errict Rhett	.40	.18
❑ 105 Henry Ellard	.40	.18
❑ 106 Ken Harvey	.20	.09
❑ 107 Gus Frerotte	.40	.18
❑ 108 Brian Mitchell	.20	.09
❑ 109 Terry Allen	.40	.18
❑ 110 Heath Shuler	.40	.18
❑ 111 Jim Kelly	.75	.35
❑ 112 Andre Reed	.40	.18
❑ 113 Bruce Smith	.75	.35
❑ 114 Darick Holmes RC	1.00	.45
❑ 115 Bryce Paup	.40	.18
❑ 116 Cornelius Bennett	.40	.18
❑ 117 Carl Pickens	.40	.18
❑ 118 Darnay Scott	.40	.18
❑ 119 Jeff Blake RC	2.00	.90
❑ 120 Steve Tovar	.20	.09
❑ 121 Tony McGee	.20	.09
❑ 122 Dan Wilkinson	.40	.18
❑ 123 Craig Powell RC	.20	.09
❑ 124 Vinny Testaverde	.40	.18
❑ 125 Eric Turner	.20	.09
❑ 126 Leroy Hoard	.20	.09
❑ 127 Lorenzo White	.20	.09
❑ 128 Andre Rison	.40	.18
❑ 129 Shannon Sharpe	.40	.18
❑ 130 Terrell Davis RC	10.00	4.50
❑ 131 Anthony Miller	.40	.18
❑ 132 Mike Pritchard	.20	.09
❑ 133 Steve Atwater	.20	.09
❑ 134 John Elway	4.00	1.80
❑ 135 Haywood Jeffires	.20	.09
❑ 136 Gary Brown	.20	.09
❑ 137 Al Smith	.20	.09
❑ 138 Rodney Thomas RC	1.00	.45
❑ 139 Chris Chandler	.40	.18
❑ 140 Mel Gray	.20	.09
❑ 141 Craig Erickson	.20	.09
❑ 142 Sean Dawkins	.40	.18
❑ 143 Ken Dilger RC	2.00	.90
❑ 144 Ellis Johnson RC UER front reads Elliss	.50	.23
❑ 145 Quentin Coryatt	.40	.18
❑ 146 Marshall Faulk	2.50	1.10
❑ 147 Tony Boselli RC	2.00	.90
❑ 148 Rob Johnson RC	3.00	1.35
❑ 149 Desmond Howard	.40	.18
❑ 150 Steve Beuerlein	.40	.18
❑ 151 Reggie Cobb	.20	.09
❑ 152 Jeff Lageman	.20	.09
❑ 153 Willie Davis	.40	.18
❑ 154 Marcus Allen	.75	.35
❑ 155 Neil Smith	.40	.18
❑ 156 Greg Hill	.40	.18
❑ 157 Steve Bono	.40	.18
❑ 158 Derrick Thomas	.40	.18
❑ 159 Jeff Hostetler	.40	.18
❑ 160 Harvey Williams	.20	.09
❑ 161 Rocket Ismail	.40	.18
❑ 162 Chester McGlockton	.40	.18
❑ 163 Terry McDaniel	.20	.09
❑ 164 Tim Brown	.75	.35
❑ 165 Terry Kirby	.40	.18
❑ 166 Irving Fryar	.40	.18
❑ 167 O.J. McDuffie	.75	.35
❑ 168 Bryan Cox	.20	.09
❑ 169 Eric Green	.20	.09
❑ 170 Dan Marino	4.00	1.80
❑ 171 Ben Coates	.40	.18
❑ 172 Vincent Brisby	.20	.09
❑ 173 Chris Slade	.20	.09
❑ 174 Ty Law RC	4.00	1.80
❑ 175 Vincent Brown	.20	.09
❑ 176 Drew Bledsoe	1.25	.55
❑ 177 Johnny Mitchell	.20	.09
❑ 178 Boomer Esiason	.40	.18
❑ 179 Wayne Chrebet RC	6.00	2.70
❑ 180 Mo Lewis	.20	.09
❑ 181 Ronald Moore	.20	.09
❑ 182 Aaron Glenn	.20	.09
❑ 183 Mark Bruener RC	1.00	.45
❑ 184 Neil O'Donnell	.40	.18
❑ 185 Charles Johnson	.40	.18
❑ 186 Greg Lloyd	.40	.18
❑ 187 Rod Woodson	.40	.18
❑ 188 Byron Bam Morris	.20	.09
❑ 189 Terrell Fletcher RC	.50	.23
❑ 190 Terrance Shaw RC UER front reads Terrence	.50	.23
❑ 191 Stan Humphries	.40	.18
❑ 192 Junior Seau	.75	.35
❑ 193 Leslie O'Neal	.40	.18
❑ 194 Natrone Means	.40	.18
❑ 195 Christian Fauria RC	1.00	.45
❑ 196 Rick Mirer	.40	.18
❑ 197 Sam Adams	.20	.09
❑ 198 Cortez Kennedy	.40	.18
❑ 199 Eugene Robinson	.20	.09
❑ 200 Chris Warren	.40	.18
❑ DM1 Dan Marino Tribute	20.00	9.00
❑ JM1 Joe Montana Salute	20.00	9.00
❑ JMAP Joe Montana Promo All-Pro Silver card	4.00	1.80
❑ NNO Dan Marino TRI Jumbo Card measures 3 1/2" by 5" Issued by Upper Deck Authenticated	25.00	11.00

Numbered of 10,000		
❑ NNO J.Montana SAL Jumbo	25.00	11.00
Card meaures 3 1/2" by 5"		
Issued by Upper Deck Authenticated		
Numbered of 10,000		
❑ P113 Dan Marino Promo	3.00	1.35

1996 SP

	Nm-Mt	Ex-Mt
COMPLETE SET (188)	100.00	45.00
❑ 1 Keyshawn Johnson PP RC	8.00	3.60
❑ 2 Kevin Hardy PP RC	.75	.35
❑ 3 Simeon Rice PP RC	3.00	1.35
❑ 4 Jonathan Ogden PP RC	1.25	.55
❑ 5 Eddie George PP RC	10.00	4.50
❑ 6 Terry Glenn PP RC	6.00	2.70
❑ 7 Terrell Owens PP RC	25.00	11.00
❑ 8 Tim Biakabutuka PP RC	2.00	.90
❑ 9 Lawrence Phillips PP RC	.75	.35
❑ 10 Alex Molden PP RC	.40	.18
❑ 11 Regan Upshaw PP RC	.40	.18
❑ 12 Rickey Dudley PP RC	1.25	.55
❑ 13 Duane Clemons PP RC	.40	.18
❑ 14 John Mobley PP RC	.75	.35
❑ 15 Eddie Kennison RC	1.25	.55
❑ 16 K.Abdul-Jabbar PP RC	1.25	.55
❑ 17 Eric Moulds PP RC	8.00	3.60
❑ 18 Marvin Harrison PP RC	15.00	6.75
❑ 19 Stepfret Williams PP RC	.40	.18
❑ 20 Stephen Davis PP RC	12.00	5.50
❑ 21 Deion Sanders	1.25	.55
❑ 22 Emmitt Smith	3.00	1.35
❑ 23 Troy Aikman	2.00	.90
❑ 24 Michael Irvin	.75	.35
❑ 25 Herschel Walker	.40	.18
❑ 26 Kavika Pittman RC	.20	.09
❑ 27 Andre Hastings	.20	.09
❑ 28 Jerome Bettis	.75	.35
❑ 29 Mike Tomczak	.20	.09
❑ 30 Kordell Stewart	.75	.35
❑ 31 Charles Johnson	.20	.09
❑ 32 Greg Lloyd	.40	.18
❑ 33 Brett Favre	4.00	1.80
❑ 34 Mark Chmura	.40	.18
❑ 35 Edgar Bennett	.40	.18
❑ 36 Robert Brooks	.40	.18
❑ 37 Craig Newsome	.20	.09
❑ 38 Reggie White	.75	.35
❑ 39 Jim Harbaugh	.40	.18
❑ 40 Marshall Faulk	1.00	.45
❑ 41 Sean Dawkins	.20	.09
❑ 42 Quentin Coryatt	.20	.09
❑ 43 Ray Buchanan	.20	.09
❑ 44 Ken Dilger	.40	.18
❑ 45 Jerry Rice	2.00	.90
❑ 46 J.J. Stokes	.75	.35
❑ 47 Steve Young	1.50	.70
❑ 48 Derek Loville	.20	.09
❑ 49 Terry Kirby	.40	.18
❑ 50 Ken Norton	.20	.09
❑ 51 Tamarick Vanover	.40	.18
❑ 52 Marcus Allen	.75	.35
❑ 53 Steve Bono	.20	.09
❑ 54 Neil Smith	.40	.18
❑ 55 Derrick Thomas	.40	.18
❑ 56 Dale Carter	.20	.09
❑ 57 Terance Mathis	.20	.09
❑ 58 Eric Metcalf	.20	.09
❑ 59 Jamal Anderson RC	1.50	.70
❑ 60 Bert Emanuel	.40	.18
❑ 61 Craig Heyward	.20	.09
❑ 62 Cornelius Bennett	.20	.09
❑ 63 Tony Martin	.40	.18
❑ 64 Stan Humphries	.40	.18
❑ 65 Andre Coleman	.20	.09
❑ 66 Junior Seau	.75	.35
❑ 67 Terrell Fletcher	.20	.09
❑ 68 John Carney	.20	.09
❑ 69 Charlie Jones RC	.40	.18
❑ 70 Ricky Watters	.40	.18
❑ 71 Charlie Garner	.40	.18
❑ 72 Bobby Hoying RC	.75	.35
❑ 73 Jason Dunn RC	.40	.18
❑ 74 Bobby Taylor	.20	.09
❑ 75 Irving Fryar	.40	.18
❑ 76 Jim Kelly	.75	.35
❑ 77 Thurman Thomas	.75	.35
❑ 78 Bruce Smith	.40	.18
❑ 79 Bryce Paup	.20	.09
❑ 80 Darick Holmes	.20	.09
❑ 81 Andre Reed	.40	.18
❑ 82 Glyn Milburn	.20	.09
❑ 83 Brett Perriman	.20	.09
❑ 84 Herman Moore	.40	.18
❑ 85 Scott Mitchell	.40	.18
❑ 86 Barry Sanders	3.00	1.35
❑ 87 Johnnie Morton	.40	.18
❑ 88 Dan Marino	4.00	1.80
❑ 89 O.J. McDuffie	.40	.18
❑ 90 Stanley Pritchett RC	.20	.09
❑ 91 Zach Thomas RC	4.00	1.80
❑ 92 Daryl Gardener RC	.20	.09
❑ 93 Rashaan Salaam	.40	.18
❑ 94 Erik Kramer	.20	.09
❑ 95 Curtis Conway	.75	.35
❑ 96 Bobby Engram RC	.75	.35
❑ 97 Walt Harris RC	.20	.09
❑ 98 Bryan Cox	.20	.09
❑ 99 John Elway	4.00	1.80
❑ 100 Terrell Davis	1.50	.70
❑ 101 Anthony Miller	.40	.18
❑ 102 Shannon Sharpe	.40	.18
❑ 103 Tory James RC	.75	.35
❑ 104 Jeff Lewis RC	.40	.18
❑ 105 Joey Galloway	.75	.35
❑ 106 Chris Warren	.40	.18
❑ 107 Rick Mirer	.40	.18
❑ 108 Cortez Kennedy	.20	.09
❑ 109 Michael Sinclair	.20	.09
❑ 110 John Friesz	.20	.09
❑ 111 Warren Moon	.40	.18
❑ 112 Cris Carter	.75	.35
❑ 113 Jake Reed	.40	.18
❑ 114 Robert Smith	.40	.18
❑ 115 John Randle	.40	.18
❑ 116 Orlando Thomas	.20	.09
❑ 117 Jeff Hostetler	.20	.09
❑ 118 Tim Brown	.75	.35
❑ 119 Joe Aska	.20	.09
❑ 120 Napoleon Kaufman	.75	.35
❑ 121 Terry McDaniel	.20	.09
❑ 122 Harvey Williams	.20	.09
❑ 123 Trent Dilfer	.75	.35
❑ 124 Reggie Brooks	.20	.09
❑ 125 Alvin Harper	.20	.09
❑ 126 Mike Alstott RC	5.00	2.20
❑ 127 Hardy Nickerson	.20	.09
❑ 128 Mario Bates	.40	.18
❑ 129 Jim Everett	.20	.09
❑ 130 Tyrone Hughes	.20	.09
❑ 131 Michael Haynes	.20	.09
❑ 132 Eric Allen	.20	.09
❑ 133 Isaac Bruce	.75	.35
❑ 134 Kevin Carter	.20	.09
❑ 135 Leslie O'Neal	.20	.09
❑ 136 Tony Banks RC	.75	.35
❑ 137 Chris Chandler	.40	.18
❑ 138 Steve McNair	1.50	.70
❑ 139 Chris Sanders	.40	.18
❑ 140 Ronnie Harmon	.20	.09
❑ 141 Willie Davis	.20	.09
❑ 142 Michael Westbrook	.75	.35
❑ 143 Terry Allen	.40	.18
❑ 144 Brian Mitchell	.20	.09
❑ 145 Henry Ellard	.20	.09
❑ 146 Gus Frerotte	.40	.18
❑ 147 Kerry Collins	.75	.35
❑ 148 Sam Mills	.20	.09
❑ 149 Wesley Walls	.40	.18
❑ 150 Kevin Greene	.40	.18
❑ 151 Muhsin Muhammad RC	4.00	1.80
❑ 152 Winslow Oliver	.20	.09
❑ 153 Jeff Blake	.75	.35
❑ 154 Carl Pickens	.40	.18
❑ 155 Darnay Scott	.40	.18
❑ 156 Garrison Hearst	.40	.18
❑ 157 Marco Battaglia RC	.20	.09
❑ 158 Drew Bledsoe	1.25	.55
❑ 159 Curtis Martin	1.50	.70
❑ 160 Shawn Jefferson	.20	.09
❑ 161 Ben Coates	.40	.18
❑ 162 Lawyer Milloy RC	2.50	1.10
❑ 163 Tyrone Wheatley	.40	.18
❑ 164 Rodney Hampton	.40	.18
❑ 165 Chris Calloway	.20	.09
❑ 166 Dave Brown	.20	.09
❑ 167 Amani Toomer RC	5.00	2.20
❑ 168 Vinny Testaverde	.40	.18
❑ 169 Michael Jackson	.40	.18
❑ 170 Eric Turner	.20	.09
❑ 171 DeRon Jenkins	.20	.09
❑ 172 Jermaine Lewis RC	.75	.35
❑ 173 Frank Sanders	.40	.18
❑ 174 Rob Moore	.40	.18
❑ 175 Kent Graham	.20	.09
❑ 176 Leeland McElroy RC	.40	.18
❑ 177 Larry Centers	.40	.18
❑ 178 Eric Swann	.20	.09
❑ 179 Mark Brunell	1.25	.55
❑ 180 Willie Jackson	.40	.18
❑ 181 James O. Stewart	.40	.18
❑ 182 Natrone Means	.40	.18
❑ 183 Tony Brackens RC	.75	.35
❑ 184 Adrian Murrell	.40	.18
❑ 185 Neil O'Donnell	.40	.18
❑ 186 Hugh Douglas	.40	.18
❑ 187 Wayne Chrebet	1.00	.45
❑ 188 Alex Van Dyke RC	.40	.18
❑ SP13 Dan Marino Promo	3.00	1.35

1997 SP Authentic

	Nm-Mt	Ex-Mt
COMPLETE SET (198)	150.00	70.00
❑ 1 Orlando Pace RC	2.00	.90
❑ 2 Darrell Russell RC	.50	.23
❑ 3 Shawn Springs RC	1.00	.45
❑ 4 Peter Boulware RC	4.00	1.80
❑ 5 Bryant Westbrook RC	1.00	.45
❑ 6 Walter Jones RC	2.00	.90
❑ 7 Ike Hilliard RC	4.00	1.80
❑ 8 James Farrior RC	2.00	.90
❑ 9 Tom Knight RC	.50	.23
❑ 10 Warrick Dunn RC	15.00	6.75
❑ 11 Tony Gonzalez RC	20.00	9.00
❑ 12 Reinard Wilson RC	1.00	.45
❑ 13 Yatil Green RC	1.00	.45
❑ 14 Reidel Anthony RC	2.00	.90
❑ 15 Kenny Holmes RC	.50	.23

❑ 16 Dwayne Rudd RC	.50	.23
❑ 17 Renaldo Wynn RC	.50	.23
❑ 18 David LaFleur RC	.50	.23
❑ 19 Antowain Smith RC	12.00	5.50
❑ 20 Jim Druckenmiller RC	1.00	.45
❑ 21 Rae Carruth RC	.50	.23
❑ 22 Byron Hanspard RC	1.00	.45
❑ 23 Jake Plummer RC	25.00	11.00
❑ 24 Joey Kent RC	1.00	.45
❑ 25 Corey Dillon RC	30.00	13.50
❑ 26 Danny Wuerffel RC	5.00	2.20
❑ 27 Will Blackwell RC	.50	.23
❑ 28 Troy Davis RC	1.00	.45
❑ 29 Darnell Autry RC	1.00	.45
❑ 30 Pat Barnes RC	1.00	.45
❑ 31 Kent Graham	.50	.23
❑ 32 Simeon Rice	.75	.35
❑ 33 Frank Sanders	.75	.35
❑ 34 Rob Moore	.75	.35
❑ 35 Eric Swann	.50	.23
❑ 36 Chris Chandler	.75	.35
❑ 37 Jamal Anderson	1.25	.55
❑ 38 Terance Mathis	.75	.35
❑ 39 Bert Emanuel	.75	.35
❑ 40 Michael Booker	.50	.23
❑ 41 Vinny Testaverde	.75	.35
❑ 42 Byron Bam Morris	.50	.23
❑ 43 Michael Jackson	.75	.35
❑ 44 Derrick Alexander WR	.75	.35
❑ 45 Jamie Sharper RC	2.00	.90
❑ 46 Kim Herring RC	.50	.23
❑ 47 Todd Collins	.50	.23
❑ 48 Thurman Thomas	1.25	.55
❑ 49 Andre Reed	.75	.35
❑ 50 Quinn Early	.50	.23
❑ 51 Bryce Paup	.50	.23
❑ 52 Lonnie Johnson	.50	.23
❑ 53 Kerry Collins	1.25	.55
❑ 54 Anthony Johnson	.50	.23
❑ 55 Tim Biakabutuka	.75	.35
❑ 56 Muhsin Muhammad	.75	.35
❑ 57 Sam Mills	.50	.23
❑ 58 Wesley Walls	.75	.35
❑ 59 Rick Mirer	.50	.23
❑ 60 Raymont Harris	.50	.23
❑ 61 Curtis Conway	.75	.35
❑ 62 Bobby Engram	.75	.35
❑ 63 Bryan Cox	.50	.23
❑ 64 John Allred RC	.50	.23
❑ 65 Jeff Blake	.75	.35
❑ 66 Ki-Jana Carter	.50	.23
❑ 67 Darnay Scott	.75	.35
❑ 68 Carl Pickens	.75	.35
❑ 69 Dan Wilkinson	.50	.23
❑ 70 Troy Aikman	2.50	1.10
❑ 71 Emmitt Smith	4.00	1.80
❑ 72 Michael Irvin	1.25	.55
❑ 73 Deion Sanders	1.25	.55
❑ 74 Anthony Miller	.50	.23
❑ 75 Antonio Anderson RC	.50	.23
❑ 76 John Elway	5.00	2.20
❑ 77 Terrell Davis	1.50	.70
❑ 78 Rod Smith WR	1.25	.55
❑ 79 Shannon Sharpe	.75	.35
❑ 80 Neil Smith	.75	.35
❑ 81 Trevor Pryce RC	2.00	.90
❑ 82 Scott Mitchell	.75	.35
❑ 83 Barry Sanders	4.00	1.80
❑ 84 Herman Moore	.75	.35
❑ 85 Johnnie Morton	.75	.35
❑ 86 Matt Russell RC	.50	.23
❑ 87 Brett Favre	5.00	2.20
❑ 88 Edgar Bennett	.75	.35
❑ 89 Robert Brooks	.75	.35
❑ 90 Antonio Freeman	1.25	.55
❑ 91 Reggie White	1.25	.55
❑ 92 Craig Newsome	.50	.23
❑ 93 Jim Harbaugh	.75	.35
❑ 94 Marshall Faulk	1.50	.70
❑ 95 Sean Dawkins	.50	.23
❑ 96 Marvin Harrison	1.25	.55
❑ 97 Quentin Coryatt	.50	.23
❑ 98 Tarik Glenn RC	.50	.23
❑ 99 Mark Brunell	1.50	.70
❑ 100 Natrone Means	.75	.35
❑ 101 Keenan McCardell	.75	.35
❑ 102 Jimmy Smith	.75	.35
❑ 103 Tony Brackens	.50	.23
❑ 104 Kevin Hardy	.50	.23
❑ 105 Elvis Grbac	.75	.35
❑ 106 Marcus Allen	1.25	.55
❑ 107 Greg Hill	.50	.23
❑ 108 Derrick Thomas	.75	.35
❑ 109 Dale Carter	.50	.23
❑ 110 Dan Marino	5.00	2.20
❑ 111 Karim Abdul-Jabbar	.75	.35
❑ 112 Brian Manning RC	.50	.23
❑ 113 Daryl Gardener	.50	.23
❑ 114 Troy Drayton	.50	.23
❑ 115 Zach Thomas	1.25	.55
❑ 116 Jason Taylor RC	12.00	5.50
❑ 117 Brad Johnson	1.25	.55
❑ 118 Robert Smith	.75	.35
❑ 119 John Randle	.75	.35
❑ 120 Cris Carter	1.25	.55
❑ 121 Jake Reed	.75	.35
❑ 122 Randall Cunningham	1.25	.55
❑ 123 Drew Bledsoe	1.50	.70
❑ 124 Curtis Martin	1.50	.70
❑ 125 Terry Glenn	1.25	.55
❑ 126 Willie McGinest	.50	.23
❑ 127 Chris Canty RC	.50	.23
❑ 128 Sedrick Shaw RC	1.00	.45
❑ 129 Heath Shuler	.50	.23
❑ 130 Mario Bates	.50	.23
❑ 131 Ray Zellars	.50	.23
❑ 132 Andre Hastings	.50	.23
❑ 133 Dave Brown	.50	.23
❑ 134 Tyrone Wheatley	.75	.35
❑ 135 Rodney Hampton	.75	.35
❑ 136 Chris Calloway	.50	.23
❑ 137 Tiki Barber RC	25.00	11.00
❑ 138 Neil O'Donnell	.75	.35
❑ 139 Adrian Murrell	.75	.35
❑ 140 Wayne Chrebet	1.25	.55
❑ 141 Keyshawn Johnson	1.25	.55
❑ 142 Hugh Douglas	.50	.23
❑ 143 Jeff George	.75	.35
❑ 144 Napoleon Kaufman	1.25	.55
❑ 145 Tim Brown	1.25	.55
❑ 146 Desmond Howard	.75	.35
❑ 147 Rickey Dudley	.75	.35
❑ 148 Terry McDaniel	.50	.23
❑ 149 Ty Detmer	.75	.35
❑ 150 Ricky Watters	.75	.35
❑ 151 Chris T. Jones	.50	.23
❑ 152 Irving Fryar	.75	.35
❑ 153 Mike Mamula	.50	.23
❑ 154 Jon Harris RC	.50	.23
❑ 155 Kordell Stewart	1.25	.55
❑ 156 Jerome Bettis	1.25	.55
❑ 157 Charles Johnson	.75	.35
❑ 158 Greg Lloyd	.50	.23
❑ 159 George Jones RC	.50	.23
❑ 160 Terrell Fletcher	.50	.23
❑ 161 Stan Humphries	.75	.35
❑ 162 Tony Martin	.75	.35
❑ 163 Eric Metcalf	.75	.35
❑ 164 Junior Seau	1.25	.55
❑ 165 Rod Woodson	.75	.35
❑ 166 Steve Young	1.50	.70
❑ 167 Terry Kirby	.75	.35
❑ 168 Garrison Hearst	.75	.35
❑ 169 Jerry Rice	2.50	1.10
❑ 170 Ken Norton	.50	.23
❑ 171 Kevin Greene	.75	.35
❑ 172 Lamar Smith	1.25	.55
❑ 173 Warren Moon	1.25	.55
❑ 174 Chris Warren	.75	.35
❑ 175 Cortez Kennedy	.50	.23
❑ 176 Joey Galloway	.75	.35
❑ 177 Tony Banks	.75	.35
❑ 178 Isaac Bruce	1.25	.55
❑ 179 Eddie Kennison	.75	.35
❑ 180 Kevin Carter	.50	.23
❑ 181 Craig Heyward	.50	.23
❑ 182 Trent Dilfer	1.25	.55
❑ 183 Errict Rhett	.50	.23
❑ 184 Mike Alstott	1.25	.55
❑ 185 Hardy Nickerson	.50	.23
❑ 186 Ronde Barber RC	15.00	6.75
❑ 187 Steve McNair	1.50	.70
❑ 188 Eddie George	1.25	.55
❑ 189 Chris Sanders	.50	.23
❑ 190 Blaine Bishop	.50	.23
❑ 191 Derrick Mason RC	15.00	6.75
❑ 192 Gus Frerotte	.50	.23
❑ 193 Terry Allen	1.25	.55
❑ 194 Brian Mitchell	.50	.23
❑ 195 Alvin Harper	.50	.23
❑ 196 Jeff Hostetler	.50	.23
❑ 197 Leslie Shepherd	.50	.23
❑ 198 Stephen Davis	1.25	.55
❑ A1 Aikman Audio Blue	4.00	1.80
❑ A2 Aikman Audio Pro Bowl	10.00	4.50
❑ A3 Aikman Audio White (500 cards made)	30.00	13.50

1998 SP Authentic

	Nm-Mt	Ex-Mt
COMP.SET w/o SP's (84)	40.00	18.00
*HAND NUMBERED RCs: .5X TO .8X		
❑ 1 Andre Wadsworth RC	25.00	11.00
❑ 2 Corey Chavous RC	40.00	18.00
❑ 3 Keith Brooking RC	40.00	18.00
❑ 4 Duane Starks RC	15.00	6.75
❑ 5 Pat Johnson RC	25.00	11.00
❑ 6 Jason Peter RC	15.00	6.75
❑ 7 Curtis Enis RC	15.00	6.75
❑ 8 Takeo Spikes RC	40.00	18.00
❑ 9 Greg Ellis RC	15.00	6.75
❑ 10 Marcus Nash RC	15.00	6.75
❑ 11 Brian Griese RC	50.00	22.00
❑ 12 Germane Crowell RC	25.00	11.00
❑ 13 Vonnie Holliday RC	25.00	11.00
❑ 14 Peyton Manning RC	600.00	275.00
❑ 15 Jerome Pathon RC	25.00	11.00
❑ 16 Fred Taylor RC	60.00	27.00
❑ 17 John Avery RC	25.00	11.00
❑ 18 Randy Moss RC	250.00	110.00
❑ 19 Robert Edwards RC	15.00	6.75
❑ 20 Tony Simmons RC	25.00	11.00
❑ 21 Shaun Williams RC	25.00	11.00
❑ 22 Joe Jurevicius RC	40.00	18.00
❑ 23 Charles Woodson RC	50.00	22.00
❑ 24 Tra Thomas RC	15.00	6.75
❑ 25 Grant Wistrom RC	25.00	11.00
❑ 26 Ryan Leaf RC	40.00	18.00
❑ 27 Ahman Green RC	120.00	55.00
❑ 28 Jacquez Green RC	25.00	11.00
❑ 29 Kevin Dyson RC	40.00	18.00
❑ 30 Stephen Alexander RC	25.00	11.00
❑ 31 John Elway TW	20.00	9.00
❑ 32 Jerry Rice TW	12.00	5.50
❑ 33 Emmitt Smith TW	20.00	9.00
❑ 34 Steve Young TW	8.00	3.60
❑ 35 Jerome Bettis TW	6.00	2.70
❑ 36 Deion Sanders TW	6.00	2.70
❑ 37 Andre Rison TW	4.00	1.80
❑ 38 Warren Moon TW	6.00	2.70
❑ 39 Mark Brunell TW	6.00	2.70
❑ 40 Ricky Watters TW	4.00	1.80
❑ 41 Dan Marino TW	25.00	11.00
❑ 42 Brett Favre TW	25.00	11.00
❑ 43 Jake Plummer	1.00	.45

❑ 44 Adrian Murrell	.60	.25
❑ 45 Eric Swann	.40	.18
❑ 46 Jamal Anderson	1.00	.45
❑ 47 Chris Chandler	.60	.25
❑ 48 Jim Harbaugh	.60	.25
❑ 49 Michael Jackson	.40	.18
❑ 50 Jermaine Lewis	.60	.25
❑ 51 Rob Johnson	.60	.25
❑ 52 Antowain Smith	1.00	.45
❑ 53 Thurman Thomas	1.00	.45
❑ 54 Kerry Collins	.60	.25
❑ 55 Fred Lane	.40	.18
❑ 56 Rae Carruth	.40	.18
❑ 57 Erik Kramer	.40	.18
❑ 58 Curtis Conway	.60	.25
❑ 59 Corey Dillon	1.00	.45
❑ 60 Neil O'Donnell	.60	.25
❑ 61 Carl Pickens	.60	.25
❑ 62 Troy Aikman	2.00	.90
❑ 63 Emmitt Smith	3.00	1.35
❑ 64 Deion Sanders	1.00	.45
❑ 65 Terrell Davis	1.00	.45
❑ 66 John Elway	4.00	1.80
❑ 67 Rod Smith	.60	.25
❑ 68 Scott Mitchell	.60	.25
❑ 69 Barry Sanders	3.00	1.35
❑ 70 Herman Moore	.60	.25
❑ 71 Brett Favre	4.00	1.80
❑ 72 Dorsey Levens	1.00	.45
❑ 73 Antonio Freeman	1.00	.45
❑ 74 Marshall Faulk	1.25	.55
❑ 75 Marvin Harrison	1.00	.45
❑ 76 Mark Brunell	1.00	.45
❑ 77 Keenan McCardell	.60	.25
❑ 78 Jimmy Smith	.60	.25
❑ 79 Andre Rison	.60	.25
❑ 80 Elvis Grbac	.60	.25
❑ 81 Derrick Alexander	.60	.25
❑ 82 Dan Marino	4.00	1.80
❑ 83 Karim Abdul-Jabbar	1.00	.45
❑ 84 O.J. McDuffie	.60	.25
❑ 85 Brad Johnson	1.00	.45
❑ 86 Cris Carter	1.00	.45
❑ 87 Robert Smith	1.00	.45
❑ 88 Drew Bledsoe	1.50	.70
❑ 89 Terry Glenn	1.00	.45
❑ 90 Ben Coates	.60	.25
❑ 91 Lamar Smith	.60	.25
❑ 92 Danny Wuerffel	.60	.25
❑ 93 Tiki Barber	1.00	.45
❑ 94 Danny Kanell	.60	.25
❑ 95 Ike Hilliard	.60	.25
❑ 96 Curtis Martin	1.00	.45
❑ 97 Keyshawn Johnson	1.00	.45
❑ 98 Glenn Foley	.60	.25
❑ 99 Jeff George	.60	.25
❑ 100 Tim Brown	1.00	.45
❑ 101 Napoleon Kaufman	1.00	.45
❑ 102 Bobby Hoying	.60	.25
❑ 103 Charlie Garner	.60	.25
❑ 104 Irving Fryar	.60	.25
❑ 105 Kordell Stewart	1.00	.45
❑ 106 Jerome Bettis	1.00	.45
❑ 107 Charles Johnson	.40	.18
❑ 108 Tony Banks	.60	.25
❑ 109 Isaac Bruce	1.00	.45
❑ 110 Natrone Means	.60	.25
❑ 111 Junior Seau	1.00	.45
❑ 112 Steve Young	1.25	.55
❑ 113 Jerry Rice	2.00	.90
❑ 114 Garrison Hearst	1.00	.45
❑ 115 Ricky Watters	.60	.25
❑ 116 Warren Moon	1.00	.45
❑ 117 Joey Galloway	.60	.25
❑ 118 Trent Dilfer	1.00	.45
❑ 119 Warrick Dunn	1.25	.55
❑ 120 Mike Alstott	1.00	.45
❑ 121 Steve McNair	1.00	.45
❑ 122 Eddie George	1.00	.45
❑ 123 Yancey Thigpen	.40	.18
❑ 124 Gus Frerotte	.40	.18
❑ 125 Terry Allen	1.00	.45
❑ 126 Michael Westbrook	.60	.25
❑ AE13 Dan Marino SAMPLE	2.00	.90

1998 SP Authentic Die Cuts

	Nm-Mt	Ex-Mt
*DIE CUT STARS 43-126: 3X TO 8X		
*DIE CUT TIME WARP 31-42: .6X TO 1.5X		
*UNLISTED DC RCs 1-30: .4X TO 1X		
❑ 11 Brian Griese	50.00	22.00
❑ 14 Peyton Manning	600.00	275.00
❑ 16 Fred Taylor	60.00	27.00
❑ 18 Randy Moss	250.00	110.00
❑ 27 Ahman Green	120.00	55.00

1999 SP Authentic

	Nm-Mt	Ex-Mt
COMPLETE SET (145)	1500.00	700.00
COMP.SET w/o SPs (90)	35.00	16.00
*HAND NUMBERED RCs: .5X TO .8X		
❑ 1 Jake Plummer	.60	.25
❑ 2 Adrian Murrell	.60	.25
❑ 3 Frank Sanders	.60	.25
❑ 4 Jamal Anderson	1.00	.45
❑ 5 Chris Chandler	.60	.25
❑ 6 Terance Mathis	.60	.25
❑ 7 Priest Holmes	1.50	.70
❑ 8 Jermaine Lewis	.60	.25
❑ 9 Antowain Smith	1.00	.45
❑ 10 Doug Flutie	1.00	.45
❑ 11 Eric Moulds	1.00	.45
❑ 12 Muhsin Muhammad	.60	.25
❑ 13 Tim Biakabutuka	.60	.25
❑ 14 Wesley Walls	.60	.25
❑ 15 Curtis Enis	.40	.18
❑ 16 Bobby Engram	.60	.25
❑ 17 Corey Dillon	1.00	.45
❑ 18 Darnay Scott	.60	.25
❑ 19 Terry Kirby	.40	.18
❑ 20 Ty Detmer	.60	.25
❑ 21 Troy Aikman	2.00	.90
❑ 22 Michael Irvin	.60	.25
❑ 23 Emmitt Smith	2.00	.90
❑ 24 Terrell Davis	1.00	.45
❑ 25 Brian Griese	1.00	.45
❑ 26 Rod Smith	.60	.25
❑ 27 Shannon Sharpe	.60	.25
❑ 28 Barry Sanders	3.00	1.35
❑ 29 Charlie Batch	1.00	.45
❑ 30 Herman Moore	.60	.25
❑ 31 Johnnie Morton	.60	.25
❑ 32 Brett Favre	3.00	1.35
❑ 33 Antonio Freeman	1.00	.45
❑ 34 Dorsey Levens	1.00	.45
❑ 35 Mark Chmura	.60	.25
❑ 36 Peyton Manning	3.00	1.35
❑ 37 Marvin Harrison	1.00	.45
❑ 38 Mark Brunell	1.00	.45
❑ 39 Fred Taylor	1.00	.45
❑ 40 Jimmy Smith	.60	.25
❑ 41 Elvis Grbac	.60	.25
❑ 42 Andre Rison	.60	.25
❑ 43 Dan Marino	3.00	1.35
❑ 44 O.J. McDuffie	.60	.25
❑ 45 Yatil Green	.40	.18
❑ 46 Randall Cunningham	1.00	.45
❑ 47 Randy Moss	3.00	1.35
❑ 48 Robert Smith	1.00	.45
❑ 49 Cris Carter	1.00	.45
❑ 50 Drew Bledsoe	1.25	.55
❑ 51 Ben Coates	.40	.18
❑ 52 Terry Glenn	1.00	.45
❑ 53 Eddie Kennison	.60	.25
❑ 54 Cam Cleeland	.40	.18
❑ 55 Ike Hilliard	.60	.25
❑ 56 Gary Brown	.40	.18
❑ 57 Kerry Collins	.60	.25
❑ 58 Vinny Testaverde	.60	.25
❑ 59 Keyshawn Johnson	1.00	.45
❑ 60 Wayne Chrebet	1.00	.45
❑ 61 Curtis Martin	1.00	.45
❑ 62 Tim Brown	1.00	.45
❑ 63 Napoleon Kaufman	1.00	.45
❑ 64 Charles Woodson	1.00	.45
❑ 65 Duce Staley	1.00	.45
❑ 66 Charles Johnson	.60	.25
❑ 67 Kordell Stewart	.60	.25
❑ 68 Jerome Bettis	1.00	.45
❑ 69 Marshall Faulk	1.25	.55
❑ 70 Isaac Bruce	1.00	.45
❑ 71 Trent Green	1.00	.45
❑ 72 Jim Harbaugh	.60	.25
❑ 73 Junior Seau	1.00	.45
❑ 74 Natrone Means	.60	.25
❑ 75 Steve Young	1.25	.55
❑ 76 Jerry Rice	2.00	.90
❑ 77 Terrell Owens	1.00	.45
❑ 78 Lawrence Phillips	.60	.25
❑ 79 Joey Galloway	.60	.25
❑ 80 Ricky Watters	.60	.25
❑ 81 Jon Kitna	1.00	.45
❑ 82 Warrick Dunn	1.00	.45
❑ 83 Trent Dilfer	.60	.25
❑ 84 Mike Alstott	1.00	.45
❑ 85 Eddie George	1.00	.45
❑ 86 Steve McNair	1.00	.45
❑ 87 Yancey Thigpen	.40	.18
❑ 88 Brad Johnson	1.00	.45
❑ 89 Skip Hicks	.40	.18
❑ 90 Michael Westbrook	.60	.25
❑ 91 Ricky Williams RC	50.00	22.00
❑ 92 Tim Couch RC	30.00	13.50
❑ 93 Akili Smith RC	20.00	9.00
❑ 94 Edgerrin James RC	80.00	36.00
❑ 95 Donovan McNabb RC	120.00	55.00
❑ 96 Torry Holt RC	60.00	27.00
❑ 97 Cade McNown RC	20.00	9.00
❑ 98 Shaun King RC	20.00	9.00
❑ 99 Daunte Culpepper RC	120.00	55.00
❑ 100 Brock Huard RC	25.00	11.00
❑ 101 Chris Claiborne RC	12.00	5.50
❑ 102 James Johnson RC	20.00	9.00
❑ 103 Rob Konrad RC	25.00	11.00
❑ 104 Peerless Price RC	50.00	22.00
❑ 105 Kevin Faulk RC	25.00	11.00
❑ 106 Andy Katzenmoyer RC	20.00	9.00
❑ 107 Troy Edwards RC	20.00	9.00
❑ 108 Kevin Johnson RC	25.00	11.00
❑ 109 Mike Cloud RC	20.00	9.00
❑ 110 David Boston RC	25.00	11.00
❑ 111 Champ Bailey RC	40.00	18.00
❑ 112 D'Wayne Bates RC	20.00	9.00
❑ 113 Joe Germaine RC	20.00	9.00
❑ 114 Antoine Winfield RC	20.00	9.00
❑ 115 Fernando Bryant RC	20.00	9.00
❑ 116 Jevon Kearse RC	40.00	18.00
❑ 117 Chris McAlister RC	20.00	9.00
❑ 118 Brandon Stokley RC	30.00	13.50
❑ 119 Karsten Bailey RC	20.00	9.00
❑ 120 Daylon McCutcheon RC	20.00	9.00
❑ 121 Jermaine Fazande RC	20.00	9.00
❑ 122 Joel Makovicka RC	25.00	11.00
❑ 123 Ebenezer Ekuban RC	20.00	9.00
❑ 124 Joe Montgomery RC	20.00	9.00
❑ 125 Sean Bennett RC	12.00	5.50
❑ 126 Na Brown RC	20.00	9.00
❑ 127 De'Mond Parker RC	12.00	5.50
❑ 128 Sedrick Irvin RC	12.00	5.50
❑ 129 Terry Jackson RC	20.00	9.00
❑ 130 Jeff Paulk RC	12.00	5.50
❑ 131 Cecil Collins RC	12.00	5.50
❑ 132 Bobby Collins RC	12.00	5.50
❑ 133 Amos Zereoue RC	25.00	11.00

❑ 134 Travis McGriff RC 12.00 5.50
❑ 135 Larry Parker RC 25.00 11.00
❑ 136 Wane McGarity RC 12.00 5.50
❑ 137 Cecil Martin RC 20.00 9.00
❑ 138 Al Wilson RC 20.00 9.00
❑ 139 Jim Kleinsasser RC 20.00 9.00
❑ 140 Dat Nguyen RC 20.00 9.00
❑ 141 Marty Booker RC 25.00 11.00
❑ 142 Reginald Kelly RC 12.00 5.50
❑ 143 Scott Covington RC 25.00 11.00
❑ 144 Antuan Edwards RC 20.00 9.00
❑ 145 Craig Yeast RC 20.00 9.00
❑ WPA W.Payton AU/100 400.00 180.00
❑ WPSP Walter Payton 1000.00 450.00
(Game Jersey AUTO/34)

1999 SP Authentic Excitement

	Nm-Mt	Ex-Mt
*STARS: 5X TO 12X BASIC CARDS		
❑ 91 Ricky Williams	120.00	55.00
❑ 92 Tim Couch	40.00	18.00
❑ 93 Akili Smith	25.00	11.00
❑ 94 Edgerrin James	200.00	90.00
❑ 95 Donovan McNabb	250.00	110.00
❑ 96 Torry Holt	80.00	36.00
❑ 97 Cade McNown	25.00	11.00
❑ 98 Shaun King	25.00	11.00
❑ 99 Daunte Culpepper	200.00	90.00
❑ 100 Brock Huard	30.00	13.50
❑ 101 Chris Claiborne	15.00	6.75
❑ 102 James Johnson	25.00	11.00
❑ 103 Rob Konrad	30.00	13.50
❑ 104 Peerless Price	60.00	27.00
❑ 105 Kevin Faulk	30.00	13.50
❑ 106 Andy Katzenmoyer	25.00	11.00
❑ 107 Troy Edwards	25.00	11.00
❑ 108 Kevin Johnson	30.00	13.50
❑ 109 Mike Cloud	25.00	11.00
❑ 110 David Boston	30.00	13.50
❑ 111 Champ Bailey	50.00	22.00
❑ 112 D'Wayne Bates	25.00	11.00
❑ 113 Joe Germaine	25.00	11.00
❑ 114 Antoine Winfield	25.00	11.00
❑ 115 Fernando Bryant	25.00	11.00
❑ 116 Jevon Kearse	50.00	22.00
❑ 117 Chris McAlister	25.00	11.00
❑ 118 Brandon Stokley	40.00	18.00
❑ 119 Karsten Bailey	25.00	11.00
❑ 120 Daylon McCutcheon	25.00	11.00
❑ 121 Jermaine Fazande	25.00	11.00
❑ 122 Joel Makovicka	30.00	13.50
❑ 123 Ebenezer Ekuban	25.00	11.00
❑ 124 Joe Montgomery	25.00	11.00
❑ 125 Sean Bennett	15.00	6.75
❑ 126 Na Brown	25.00	11.00
❑ 127 De'Mond Parker	15.00	6.75
❑ 128 Sedrick Irvin	15.00	6.75
❑ 129 Terry Jackson	25.00	11.00
❑ 130 Jeff Paulk	15.00	6.75
❑ 131 Cecil Collins	15.00	6.75
❑ 132 Bobby Collins	15.00	6.75
❑ 133 Amos Zereoue	30.00	13.50
❑ 134 Travis McGriff	15.00	6.75
❑ 135 Larry Parker	30.00	13.50
❑ 136 Wane McGarity	15.00	6.75
❑ 137 Cecil Martin	25.00	11.00
❑ 138 Al Wilson	25.00	11.00
❑ 139 Jim Kleinsasser	25.00	11.00
❑ 140 Dat Nguyen	25.00	11.00
❑ 141 Marty Booker	30.00	13.50
❑ 142 Reginald Kelly	15.00	6.75
❑ 143 Scott Covington	30.00	13.50
❑ 144 Antuan Edwards	25.00	11.00
❑ 145 Craig Yeast	25.00	11.00

1999 SP Authentic Excitement Gold

	Nm-Mt	Ex-Mt
*STARS: 30X TO 80X BASIC CARDS		
❑ 91 Ricky Williams	300.00	135.00
❑ 92 Tim Couch	100.00	45.00
❑ 93 Akili Smith	50.00	22.00
❑ 94 Edgerrin James	500.00	220.00
❑ 95 Donovan McNabb	600.00	275.00
❑ 96 Torry Holt	250.00	110.00
❑ 97 Cade McNown	50.00	22.00
❑ 98 Shaun King	50.00	22.00
❑ 99 Daunte Culpepper	500.00	220.00
❑ 100 Brock Huard	60.00	27.00
❑ 101 Chris Claiborne	30.00	13.50
❑ 102 James Johnson	50.00	22.00
❑ 103 Rob Konrad	60.00	27.00
❑ 104 Peerless Price	120.00	55.00
❑ 105 Kevin Faulk	60.00	27.00
❑ 106 Andy Katzenmoyer	50.00	22.00
❑ 107 Troy Edwards	50.00	22.00
❑ 108 Kevin Johnson	60.00	27.00
❑ 109 Mike Cloud	50.00	22.00
❑ 110 David Boston	60.00	27.00
❑ 111 Champ Bailey	100.00	45.00
❑ 112 D'Wayne Bates	50.00	22.00
❑ 113 Joe Germaine	50.00	22.00
❑ 114 Antoine Winfield	50.00	22.00
❑ 115 Fernando Bryant	50.00	22.00
❑ 116 Jevon Kearse	100.00	45.00
❑ 117 Chris McAlister	50.00	22.00
❑ 118 Brandon Stokley	80.00	36.00
❑ 119 Karsten Bailey	50.00	22.00
❑ 120 Daylon McCutcheon	50.00	22.00
❑ 121 Jermaine Fazande	50.00	22.00
❑ 122 Joel Makovicka	60.00	27.00
❑ 123 Ebenezer Ekuban	50.00	22.00
❑ 124 Joe Montgomery	50.00	22.00
❑ 125 Sean Bennett	30.00	13.50
❑ 126 Na Brown	50.00	22.00
❑ 127 De'Mond Parker	30.00	13.50
❑ 128 Sedrick Irvin	30.00	13.50
❑ 129 Terry Jackson	50.00	22.00
❑ 130 Jeff Paulk	30.00	13.50
❑ 131 Cecil Collins	30.00	13.50
❑ 132 Bobby Collins	30.00	13.50
❑ 133 Amos Zereoue	60.00	27.00
❑ 134 Travis McGriff	30.00	13.50
❑ 135 Larry Parker	60.00	27.00
❑ 136 Wane McGarity	30.00	13.50
❑ 137 Cecil Martin	50.00	22.00
❑ 138 Al Wilson	50.00	22.00
❑ 139 Jim Kleinsasser	50.00	22.00
❑ 140 Dat Nguyen	50.00	22.00
❑ 141 Marty Booker	60.00	27.00
❑ 142 Reginald Kelly	30.00	13.50
❑ 143 Scott Covington	60.00	27.00
❑ 144 Antuan Edwards	50.00	22.00
❑ 145 Craig Yeast	50.00	22.00

1999 SP Authentic Player's Ink Purple

	Nm-Mt	Ex-Mt
*LEVEL 2 PURPLES: .8X TO 2X BASIC AUTOS		
❑ RWA Ricky Williams	150.00	70.00

2000 SP Authentic

	Nm-Mt	Ex-Mt
COMP.SET w/o SP's (90)	15.00	6.75
❑ 1 Jake Plummer	.60	.25
❑ 2 David Boston	1.00	.45
❑ 3 Frank Sanders	.60	.25
❑ 4 Chris Chandler	.60	.25
❑ 5 Jamal Anderson	1.00	.45
❑ 6 Shawn Jefferson	.40	.18
❑ 7 Tony Banks	.60	.25
❑ 8 Shannon Sharpe	.60	.25
❑ 9 Rob Johnson	.60	.25
❑ 10 Antowain Smith	.60	.25
❑ 11 Muhsin Muhammad	.60	.25
❑ 12 Steve Beuerlein	.60	.25
❑ 13 Cade McNown	.40	.18
❑ 14 Curtis Enis	.40	.18
❑ 15 Marcus Robinson	1.00	.45
❑ 16 Akili Smith	.40	.18
❑ 17 Corey Dillon	1.00	.45
❑ 18 Tim Couch	.60	.25
❑ 19 Kevin Johnson	1.00	.45
❑ 20 Errict Rhett	.40	.18
❑ 21 Troy Aikman	2.00	.90
❑ 22 Emmitt Smith	2.50	1.10
❑ 23 Rocket Ismail	.60	.25
❑ 24 Joey Galloway	.60	.25
❑ 25 Terrell Davis	1.00	.45
❑ 26 Olandis Gary	1.00	.45
❑ 27 Ed McCaffrey	1.00	.45
❑ 28 Brian Griese	1.00	.45
❑ 29 Charlie Batch	1.00	.45
❑ 30 Germane Crowell	.40	.18
❑ 31 James O. Stewart	.60	.25
❑ 32 Brett Favre	3.00	1.35
❑ 33 Antonio Freeman	1.00	.45
❑ 34 Dorsey Levens	.60	.25
❑ 35 Peyton Manning	2.50	1.10
❑ 36 Edgerrin James	1.50	.70
❑ 37 Marvin Harrison	1.00	.45
❑ 38 Mark Brunell	1.00	.45
❑ 39 Fred Taylor	1.00	.45
❑ 40 Jimmy Smith	.60	.25
❑ 41 Elvis Grbac	.60	.25
❑ 42 Tony Gonzalez	.60	.25
❑ 43 James Johnson	.40	.18
❑ 44 Oronde Gadsden	.60	.25
❑ 45 Damon Huard	1.00	.45
❑ 46 Randy Moss	2.00	.90
❑ 47 Cris Carter	1.00	.45
❑ 48 Daunte Culpepper	1.25	.55
❑ 49 Drew Bledsoe	1.25	.55
❑ 50 Terry Glenn	.60	.25
❑ 51 Ricky Williams	1.00	.45
❑ 52 Jeff Blake	.60	.25
❑ 53 Keith Poole	.40	.18
❑ 54 Kerry Collins	.60	.25
❑ 55 Amani Toomer	.60	.25
❑ 56 Ike Hilliard	.60	.25
❑ 57 Wayne Chrebet	.60	.25
❑ 58 Curtis Martin	1.00	.45
❑ 59 Vinny Testaverde	.60	.25
❑ 60 Tim Brown	1.00	.45
❑ 61 Rich Gannon	1.00	.45
❑ 62 Tyrone Wheatley	.60	.25
❑ 63 Duce Staley	1.00	.45
❑ 64 Donovan McNabb	1.50	.70
❑ 65 Troy Edwards	.40	.18
❑ 66 Jerome Bettis	1.00	.45
❑ 67 Kordell Stewart	.60	.25
❑ 68 Marshall Faulk	1.25	.55
❑ 69 Kurt Warner	1.50	.70
❑ 70 Isaac Bruce	1.00	.45
❑ 71 Torry Holt	1.00	.45
❑ 72 Ryan Leaf	.60	.25
❑ 73 Jim Harbaugh	.60	.25
❑ 74 Jermaine Fazande	.40	.18
❑ 75 Jerry Rice	2.00	.90
❑ 76 Terrell Owens	1.00	.45
❑ 77 Jeff Garcia	1.00	.45
❑ 78 Ricky Watters	.60	.25
❑ 79 Jon Kitna	1.00	.45
❑ 80 Derrick Mayes	.60	.25
❑ 81 Shaun King	.40	.18
❑ 82 Mike Alstott	1.00	.45
❑ 83 Keyshawn Johnson	1.00	.45
❑ 84 Warrick Dunn	1.00	.45
❑ 85 Eddie George	1.00	.45
❑ 86 Steve McNair	1.00	.45
❑ 87 Jevon Kearse	1.00	.45

❑ 88 Brad Johnson 1.00 .45
❑ 89 Stephen Davis 1.00 .45
❑ 90 Michael Westbrook .60 .25
❑ 91 Anthony Lucas RC 10.00 4.50
❑ 92 Avion Black RC 15.00 6.75
❑ 93 Dante Hall RC 40.00 18.00
❑ 94 Darrell Jackson RC 30.00 13.50
❑ 95 Deltha O'Neal RC 20.00 9.00
❑ 96 Erron Kinney RC 20.00 9.00
❑ 97 Doug Chapman RC 15.00 6.75
❑ 98 Frank Murphy RC 10.00 4.50
❑ 99 Gari Scott RC 10.00 4.50
❑ 100 Giovanni Carmazzi RC 15.00 6.75
❑ 101 JaJuan Dawson RC 10.00 4.50
❑ 102 Jarious Jackson RC 15.00 6.75
❑ 103 Rashard Anderson RC 15.00 6.75
❑ 104 Michael Wiley RC 15.00 6.75
❑ 105 Spergon Wynn RC 15.00 6.75
❑ 106 Muneer Moore RC 10.00 4.50
❑ 107 Ahmed Plummer RC 20.00 9.00
❑ 108 Chad Morton RC 20.00 9.00
❑ 109 Rob Morris RC 15.00 6.75
❑ 110 Ron Dixon RC 15.00 6.75
❑ 111 Rondell Mealey RC 10.00 4.50
❑ 112 Sebastian Janikowski RC 20.00 9.00
❑ 113 Shaun Ellis RC 20.00 9.00
❑ 114 Rogers Beckett RC 15.00 6.75
❑ 115 Shyrone Stith RC 15.00 6.75
❑ 116 Tim Rattay RC 50.00 22.00
❑ 117 Todd Husak RC 20.00 9.00
❑ 118 Tom Brady RC 800.00 350.00
❑ 119 Trevor Gaylor RC 15.00 6.75
❑ 120 Windrell Hayes RC 15.00 6.75
❑ 121 Anthony Becht RC 20.00 9.00
❑ 122 Brian Urlacher RC 100.00 45.00
❑ 123 Bubba Franks RC 20.00 9.00
❑ 124 Chad Pennington RC 200.00 90.00
❑ 125 Chris Redman RC 15.00 6.75
❑ 126 Corey Simon RC 20.00 9.00
❑ 127 Curtis Keaton RC 15.00 6.75
❑ 128 Danny Farmer RC 15.00 6.75
❑ 129 Dennis Northcutt RC 20.00 9.00
❑ 130 Dez White RC 20.00 9.00
❑ 131 J.R. Redmond RC 15.00 6.75
❑ 132 Jamal Lewis RC 80.00 36.00
❑ 133 Jerry Porter RC 50.00 22.00
❑ 134 Joe Hamilton RC 15.00 6.75
❑ 135 Laveranues Coles RC 40.00 18.00
❑ 136 R.Jay Soward RC 15.00 6.75
❑ 137 Reuben Droughns RC 40.00 18.00
❑ 138 Ron Dayne RC 30.00 13.50
❑ 139 Ron Dugans RC 10.00 4.50
❑ 140 Shaun Alexander RC 100.00 45.00
❑ 141 Sylvester Morris RC 15.00 6.75
❑ 142 Tee Martin RC 20.00 9.00
❑ 143 Thomas Jones RC 40.00 18.00
❑ 144 Todd Pinkston RC 20.00 9.00
❑ 145 Travis Prentice RC 15.00 6.75
❑ 146 Travis Taylor RC 20.00 9.00
❑ 147 Trung Canidate RC 15.00 6.75
❑ 148 Courtney Brown RC 20.00 9.00
❑ 149 Plaxico Burress RC 50.00 22.00
❑ 150 Peter Warrick RC 20.00 9.00
❑ 151 Billy Volek RC 50.00 22.00
❑ 152 Bobby Shaw RC 10.00 4.50
❑ 153 Brad Hoover RC 15.00 6.75
❑ 154 Brian Finneran RC 20.00 9.00
❑ 155 Charles Lee RC 10.00 4.50
❑ 156 Chris Cole RC 10.00 4.50
❑ 157 Clint Stoerner RC 15.00 6.75
❑ 158 Doug Johnson RC 20.00 9.00
❑ 159 Frank Moreau RC 15.00 6.75
❑ 160 Jake Delhomme RC 60.00 27.00
❑ 161 KaRon Coleman RC 10.00 4.50
❑ 162 Kevin McDougal RC 10.00 4.50
❑ 163 Larry Foster RC 10.00 4.50
❑ 164 Mike Anderson RC 25.00 11.00
❑ 165 Patrick Pass RC 10.00 4.50
❑ 166 Reggie Jones RC 10.00 4.50
❑ 167 Sammy Morris RC 15.00 6.75
❑ 168 Shockmain Davis RC 10.00 4.50
❑ 169 Terrelle Smith RC 10.00 4.50
❑ 170 Ronney Jenkins RC 10.00 4.50
❑ 171 Troy Walters RC 15.00 6.75

2001 SP Authentic

Nm-Mt Ex-Mt
COMP.SET w/o SP's (90) 20.00 6.00
*SINGLE COLOR SWATCH: .3X TO .8X

❑ 1 Jake Plummer .60 .18
❑ 2 Thomas Jones .60 .18
❑ 3 Frank Sanders .40 .12
❑ 4 Jamal Anderson 1.00 .30
❑ 5 Chris Chandler .60 .18
❑ 6 Tony Martin .60 .18
❑ 7 Jamal Lewis 1.25 .35
❑ 8 Elvis Grbac .60 .18
❑ 9 Travis Taylor .60 .18
❑ 10 Peerless Price .60 .18
❑ 11 Rob Johnson .60 .18
❑ 12 Eric Moulds .60 .18
❑ 13 Muhsin Muhammad .60 .18
❑ 14 Isaac Byrd .40 .12
❑ 15 Wesley Walls .40 .12
❑ 16 James Allen .60 .18
❑ 17 Marcus Robinson 1.00 .30
❑ 18 Brian Urlacher 1.25 .35
❑ 19 Jon Kitna .60 .18
❑ 20 Peter Warrick 1.00 .30
❑ 21 Corey Dillon 1.00 .30
❑ 22 Kevin Johnson .60 .18
❑ 23 JaJuan Dawson .40 .12
❑ 24 Tim Couch .60 .18
❑ 25 Rocket Ismail .60 .18
❑ 26 Emmitt Smith 2.00 .60
❑ 27 Joey Galloway .60 .18
❑ 28 Terrell Davis 1.00 .30
❑ 29 Mike Anderson 1.00 .30
❑ 30 Brian Griese 1.00 .30
❑ 31 Ed McCaffrey 1.00 .30
❑ 32 Charlie Batch 1.00 .30
❑ 33 James O. Stewart .60 .18
❑ 34 Johnnie Morton .60 .18
❑ 35 Brett Favre 3.00 .90
❑ 36 Antonio Freeman 1.00 .30
❑ 37 Bill Schroeder .40 .12
❑ 38 Ahman Green 1.00 .30
❑ 39 Peyton Manning 2.50 .75
❑ 40 Edgerrin James 1.25 .35
❑ 41 Marvin Harrison 1.00 .30
❑ 42 Mark Brunell 1.00 .30
❑ 43 Fred Taylor 1.00 .30
❑ 44 Jimmy Smith .60 .18
❑ 45 Tony Gonzalez .60 .18
❑ 46 Trent Green 1.00 .30
❑ 47 Oronde Gadsden .60 .18
❑ 48 Jay Fiedler 1.00 .30
❑ 49 Lamar Smith .60 .18
❑ 50 Randy Moss 2.00 .60
❑ 51 Cris Carter 1.00 .30
❑ 52 Daunte Culpepper 1.00 .30
❑ 53 Drew Bledsoe 1.25 .35
❑ 54 Terry Glenn .60 .18
❑ 55 Antowain Smith .60 .18
❑ 56 Ricky Williams 1.00 .30
❑ 57 Joe Horn .60 .18
❑ 58 Aaron Brooks 1.00 .30
❑ 59 Kerry Collins .60 .18
❑ 60 Tiki Barber .60 .18
❑ 61 Ron Dayne 1.00 .30
❑ 62 Vinny Testaverde .60 .18
❑ 63 Wayne Chrebet .60 .18
❑ 64 Curtis Martin 1.00 .30
❑ 65 Tim Brown 1.00 .30
❑ 66 Rich Gannon 1.00 .30
❑ 67 Jerry Rice 2.00 .60
❑ 68 Duce Staley 1.00 .30
❑ 69 Donovan McNabb 1.25 .35
❑ 70 Kordell Stewart .60 .18
❑ 71 Jerome Bettis 1.00 .30
❑ 72 Marshall Faulk 1.25 .35
❑ 73 Kurt Warner 1.50 .45
❑ 74 Isaac Bruce 1.00 .30
❑ 75 Doug Flutie 1.00 .30
❑ 76 Junior Seau 1.00 .30
❑ 77 Jeff Garcia 1.00 .30
❑ 78 Garrison Hearst .60 .18
❑ 79 Terrell Owens 1.00 .30
❑ 80 Ricky Watters .60 .18
❑ 81 Matt Hasselbeck .60 .18
❑ 82 Brad Johnson 1.00 .30
❑ 83 Warrick Dunn 1.00 .30
❑ 84 Mike Alstott 1.00 .30
❑ 85 Kevin Dyson .60 .18
❑ 86 Eddie George 1.00 .30
❑ 87 Steve McNair 1.00 .30
❑ 88 Champ Bailey .60 .18
❑ 89 Michael Westbrook .60 .18
❑ 90 Stephen Davis 1.00 .30
❑ 91 Michael Vick JSY AU RC 1600.00 475.00
❑ 92 Rod Gardner JSY AU RC 120.00 36.00
❑ 93 F.Mitchell JSY AU RC 100.00 30.00
❑ 94 K.Robinson JSY RC/500 60.00 18.00
❑ 95 David Terrell JSY/500 RC 50.00 15.00
❑ 96 Michael Bennett JSY RC 80.00 24.00
❑ 97 Robert Ferguson JSY RC 40.00 12.00
❑ 98 Deuce McAllister JSY RC 100.00 30.00
❑ 99 Travis Henry JSY RC 60.00 18.00
❑ 100 Andre Carter JSY RC 25.00 7.50
❑ 101 Drew Brees JSY RC 100.00 30.00
❑ 102 S.Moss JSY RC/500 80.00 24.00
❑ 103 Chris Weinke JSY/390 RC 40.00 12.00
❑ 104 Chad Johnson JSY/160 RC 350.00 105.00
❑ 105 Reggie Wayne JSY RC 80.00 24.00
❑ 106 K.Barlow JSY RC/500 80.00 24.00
❑ 107 ChrisChambers JSY RC/500 80.00 24.00
❑ 108 Todd Heap JSY/500 RC 80.00 24.00
❑ 109 A.Thomas JSY RC/500 60.00 18.00
❑ 110 J.Jackson JSY RC/500 25.00 7.50
❑ 111 R.Johnson JSY RC/500 100.00 30.00
❑ 112 Mike McMahon JSY RC 40.00 12.00
❑ 113 Josh Heupel JSY RC 40.00 12.00
❑ 114 Travis Minor JSY/500 RC 50.00 15.00
❑ 115 Q.Morgan JSY RC/500 40.00 12.00
❑ 116 Dan Morgan JSY/500 RC 40.00 12.00
❑ 117 J.Palmer JSY RC/500 50.00 15.00
❑ 118 Sage Rosenfels JSY/300 RC 60.00 18.00
❑ 119 Marq Tuiasosopo JSY RC 25.00 7.50
❑ 120 LaDainian Tomlinson 400.00 120.00
JSY RC/500
❑ 121 Adam Archuleta EXCH
❑ 122 Alex Bannister EXCH
❑ 123 Alge Crumpler AU RC 30.00 9.00
❑ 124 Arnold Jackson AU RC 20.00 6.00
❑ 125 Bobby Newcombe AU RC 20.00 6.00
❑ 126 B.Manumaleuna AU RC 20.00 6.00
❑ 127 Cedrick Wilson AU RC 30.00 9.00
❑ 128 Brian Allen AU RC 15.00 4.50
❑ 129 Dee Brown AU RC 25.00 7.50
❑ 130 D.McCants AU RC 20.00 6.00
❑ 131 Dave Dickenson AU RC 20.00 6.00
❑ 132 Derrick Blaylock AU RC 40.00 12.00
❑ 133 Eddie Berlin AU RC 20.00 6.00
❑ 134 Francis St.Paul AU RC 20.00 6.00
❑ 135 Jamar Fletcher AU RC 20.00 6.00
❑ 136 Josh Booty AU RC 25.00 7.50
❑ 137 Scotty Anderson AU RC 20.00 6.00
❑ 138 Ken-Yon Rambo AU RC 20.00 6.00
❑ 139 Kenyatta Walker AU RC 15.00 4.50
❑ 140 Kevin Kasper AU RC 30.00 9.00
❑ 141 Snoop Minnis AU RC 20.00 6.00
❑ 142 T.J. Houshmandzadeh AU RC 30.00 9.00
❑ 143 Quincy Carter AU RC 40.00 12.00
❑ 144 Ronney Daniels AU RC 15.00 4.50
❑ 145 Sedrick Hodge AU RC 15.00 4.50

Card	Nm-Mt	Ex-Mt
❑ 146 Steve Smith AU RC	60.00	18.00
❑ 147 Tim Hasselbeck AU RC	25.00	7.50
❑ 148 Vinny Sutherland AU RC	20.00	6.00
❑ 149 Richard Seymour AU RC	60.00	18.00
❑ 150 Jamie Winborn AU	20.00	6.00
❑ 151 Gerard Warren RC	12.00	3.60
❑ 152 Justin Smith RC	12.00	3.60
❑ 153 David Martin RC	10.00	3.00
❑ 154 Jamal Reynolds RC	12.00	3.60
❑ 155 Dominic Rhodes RC	20.00	6.00
❑ 156 Nate Clements RC	12.00	3.60
❑ 157 Michael Lewis RC	12.00	3.60
❑ 158 Andre King RC	10.00	3.00
❑ 159 Benjamin Gay RC	12.00	3.60
❑ 160 Correll Buckhalter RC	30.00	9.00
❑ 161 Roderick Robinson RC	10.00	3.00
❑ 162 Moran Norris RC	8.00	2.40
❑ 163 Onome Ojo RC	10.00	3.00
❑ 164 Will Allen RC	10.00	3.00
❑ 165 Jonathan Carter RC	10.00	3.00
❑ 166 LaMont Jordan RC	75.00	22.00
❑ 167 DeLawrence Grant RC	8.00	2.40
❑ 168 Derrick Gibson RC	10.00	3.00
❑ 169 A.J. Feeley RC	30.00	9.00
❑ 170 Tim Baker RC	8.00	2.40
❑ 171 Kendrell Bell RC	30.00	9.00
❑ 172 Zeke Moreno RC	12.00	3.60
❑ 173 Carlos Polk RC	8.00	2.40
❑ 174 Ken Lucas RC	10.00	3.00
❑ 175 Heath Evans RC	10.00	3.00
❑ 176 Elvis Joseph RC	10.00	3.00
❑ 177 Damione Lewis RC	10.00	3.00
❑ 178 Tommy Polley RC	12.00	3.60
❑ 179 Fred Smoot RC	12.00	3.60
❑ 180 Jason Brookins RC	12.00	3.60
❑ 181 Nick Goings RC	12.00	3.60
❑ 182 Drew Bennett RC	30.00	9.00
❑ 183 Justin McCareins RC	20.00	6.00
❑ 184 Kabeer Gbaja-Biamila RC	25.00	7.50
❑ 185 Edgerton Hartwell RC	8.00	2.40
❑ 186 Robert Carswell RC	8.00	2.40
❑ 187 Aaron Schobel RC	12.00	3.60
❑ 188 Dan Alexander RC	12.00	3.60
❑ 189 Jamie Winborn RC	10.00	3.00
❑ 190 Karon Riley RC	8.00	2.40
❑ EG Eddie George SAMPLE	3.00	.90

2001 SP Authentic Rookie Gold 100

	Nm-Mt	Ex-Mt
❑ 91 Michael Vick	300.00	90.00
❑ 92 Rod Gardner	50.00	15.00
❑ 93 Freddie Mitchell	50.00	15.00
❑ 94 Koren Robinson	60.00	18.00
❑ 95 David Terrell	50.00	15.00
❑ 96 Michael Bennett	120.00	36.00
❑ 97 Robert Ferguson	50.00	15.00
❑ 98 Deuce McAllister	150.00	45.00
❑ 99 Travis Henry	80.00	24.00
❑ 100 Andre Carter	50.00	15.00
❑ 101 Drew Brees	150.00	45.00
❑ 102 Santana Moss	80.00	24.00
❑ 103 Chris Weinke	50.00	15.00
❑ 104 Chad Johnson	100.00	30.00
❑ 105 Reggie Wayne	100.00	30.00
❑ 106 Kevan Barlow	50.00	15.00
❑ 107 Chris Chambers	80.00	24.00
❑ 108 Todd Heap	50.00	15.00
❑ 109 Anthony Thomas	80.00	24.00
❑ 110 James Jackson	50.00	15.00
❑ 111 Rudi Johnson	100.00	30.00
❑ 112 Mike McMahon	50.00	15.00
❑ 113 Josh Heupel	50.00	15.00
❑ 114 Travis Minor	40.00	12.00
❑ 115 Quincy Morgan	50.00	15.00
❑ 116 Dan Morgan	50.00	15.00
❑ 117 Jesse Palmer	50.00	15.00
❑ 118 Sage Rosenfels	50.00	15.00
❑ 119 Marques Tuiasosopo	60.00	18.00
❑ 120 LaDainian Tomlinson	225.00	70.00
❑ 121 Adam Archuleta	50.00	15.00
❑ 122 Alex Bannister	40.00	12.00
❑ 123 Alge Crumpler	60.00	18.00
❑ 124 Arnold Jackson	40.00	12.00
❑ 125 Bobby Newcombe	40.00	12.00
❑ 126 Brandon Manumaleuna	40.00	12.00
❑ 127 Cedrick Wilson	50.00	15.00
❑ 128 Brian Allen	25.00	7.50
❑ 129 Dee Brown	50.00	15.00
❑ 130 Damerien McCants	40.00	12.00
❑ 131 Dave Dickenson	40.00	12.00
❑ 132 Derrick Blaylock	60.00	18.00
❑ 133 Eddie Berlin	40.00	12.00
❑ 134 Francis St.Paul	40.00	12.00
❑ 135 Jamar Fletcher	40.00	12.00
❑ 136 Josh Booty	50.00	15.00
❑ 137 Scotty Anderson	40.00	12.00
❑ 138 Ken-Yon Rambo	40.00	12.00
❑ 139 Kenyatta Walker	25.00	7.50
❑ 140 Kevin Kasper	50.00	15.00
❑ 141 Snoop Minnis	40.00	12.00
❑ 142 T.J. Houshmandzadeh	50.00	15.00
❑ 143 Quincy Carter	50.00	15.00
❑ 144 Ronney Daniels	25.00	7.50
❑ 145 Sedrick Hodge	25.00	7.50
❑ 146 Steve Smith	80.00	24.00
❑ 147 Tim Hasselbeck	50.00	15.00
❑ 148 Vinny Sutherland	40.00	12.00
❑ 149 Richard Seymour	60.00	18.00
❑ 150 Jamie Winborn	40.00	12.00
❑ 151 Gerard Warren	50.00	15.00
❑ 152 Justin Smith	50.00	15.00
❑ 153 David Martin	40.00	12.00
❑ 154 Jamal Reynolds	50.00	15.00
❑ 155 Dominic Rhodes	60.00	18.00
❑ 156 Nate Clements	50.00	15.00
❑ 157 Michael Lewis	50.00	15.00
❑ 158 Andre King	50.00	15.00
❑ 159 Benjamin Gay	50.00	15.00
❑ 160 Correll Buckhalter	60.00	18.00
❑ 161 Roderick Robinson	40.00	12.00
❑ 162 Moran Norris	25.00	7.50
❑ 163 Onome Ojo	40.00	12.00
❑ 164 Will Allen	40.00	12.00
❑ 165 Jonathan Carter	40.00	12.00
❑ 166 LaMont Jordan	100.00	30.00
❑ 167 DeLawrence Grant	25.00	7.50
❑ 168 Derrick Gibson	40.00	12.00
❑ 169 A.J. Feeley	50.00	15.00
❑ 170 Tim Baker	25.00	7.50
❑ 171 Kendrell Bell	80.00	24.00
❑ 172 Zeke Moreno	50.00	15.00
❑ 173 Carlos Polk	25.00	7.50
❑ 174 Ken Lucas	40.00	12.00
❑ 175 Heath Evans	50.00	15.00
❑ 176 Elvis Joseph	40.00	12.00
❑ 177 Damione Lewis	40.00	12.00
❑ 178 Tommy Polley	50.00	15.00
❑ 179 Fred Smoot	50.00	15.00
❑ 180 Jason Brookins	50.00	15.00
❑ 181 Nick Goings	50.00	15.00
❑ 182 Drew Bennett	100.00	30.00
❑ 183 Justin McCareins	50.00	15.00
❑ 184 Kabeer Gbaja-Biamila	50.00	15.00
❑ 185 Edgerton Hartwell	25.00	7.50
❑ 186 Robert Carswell	25.00	7.50
❑ 187 Aaron Schobel	50.00	15.00
❑ 188 Dan Alexander	50.00	15.00
❑ 189 Jamie Winborn	40.00	12.00
❑ 190 Karon Riley	25.00	7.50

2002 SP Authentic

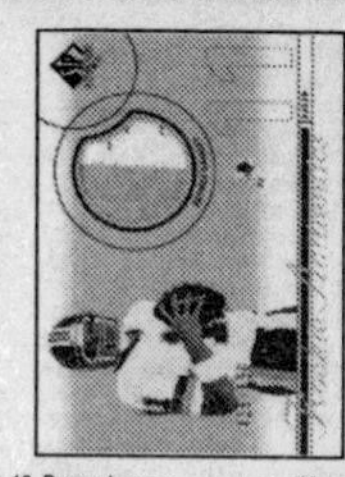

	Nm-Mt	Ex-Mt
COMP.SET w/o SP's (94)	25.00	7.50
❑ 1 Tom Brady	2.00	.60
❑ 2 Antowain Smith	.60	.18
❑ 3 Troy Brown	.60	.18
❑ 4 Kurt Warner	1.00	.30
❑ 5 Marshall Faulk	1.00	.30
❑ 6 Isaac Bruce	1.00	.30
❑ 7 Kordell Stewart	.60	.18
❑ 8 Jerome Bettis	1.00	.30
❑ 9 Plaxico Burress	.60	.18
❑ 10 Hines Ward	1.00	.30
❑ 11 Donovan McNabb	1.25	.35
❑ 12 Duce Staley	1.00	.30
❑ 13 Dorsey Levens	.60	.18
❑ 14 Antonio Freeman	1.00	.30
❑ 15 Jerry Rice	2.00	.60
❑ 16 Rich Gannon	1.00	.30
❑ 17 Tim Brown	1.00	.30
❑ 18 Jim Miller	.60	.18
❑ 19 Marty Booker	.60	.18
❑ 20 Brian Urlacher	1.25	.35
❑ 21 Jamal Lewis	1.00	.30
❑ 22 Chris Redman	.40	.12
❑ 23 Ray Lewis	1.00	.30
❑ 24 Brett Favre	2.50	.75
❑ 25 Ahman Green	1.00	.30
❑ 26 Terry Glenn	.60	.18
❑ 27 Keyshawn Johnson	1.00	.30
❑ 28 Keenan McCardell	.40	.12
❑ 29 Michael Pittman	.40	.12
❑ 30 Curtis Martin	1.00	.30
❑ 31 Vinny Testaverde	.60	.18
❑ 32 Chad Pennington	1.25	.35
❑ 33 Wayne Chrebet	.60	.18
❑ 34 Terrell Owens	1.00	.30
❑ 35 Garrison Hearst	.60	.18
❑ 36 Jay Fiedler	.60	.18
❑ 37 Ricky Williams	1.00	.30
❑ 38 Chris Chambers	1.00	.30
❑ 39 Shaun Alexander	1.00	.30
❑ 40 Darrell Jackson	.60	.18
❑ 41 Drew Bledsoe	1.25	.35
❑ 42 Travis Henry	1.00	.30
❑ 43 Eric Moulds	.60	.18
❑ 44 Stephen Davis	.60	.18
❑ 45 Rod Gardner	.60	.18
❑ 46 Brian Griese	1.00	.30
❑ 47 Olandis Gary	.60	.18
❑ 48 Shannon Sharpe	.60	.18
❑ 49 Tim Couch	.60	.18
❑ 50 Kevin Johnson	.60	.18
❑ 51 Steve McNair	1.00	.30
❑ 52 Eddie George	1.00	.30
❑ 53 Aaron Brooks	1.00	.30
❑ 54 Deuce McAllister	1.25	.35
❑ 55 Joe Horn	.60	.18
❑ 56 Michael Vick	2.50	.75
❑ 57 Warrick Dunn	1.00	.30
❑ 58 Kerry Collins	.60	.18
❑ 59 Tiki Barber	.60	.18
❑ 60 Amani Toomer	.60	.18
❑ 61 Jake Plummer	.60	.18
❑ 62 David Boston	1.00	.30
❑ 63 Thomas Jones	.60	.18
❑ 64 Edgerrin James	1.25	.35
❑ 65 Marvin Harrison	1.00	.30
❑ 66 Mark Brunell	1.00	.30
❑ 67 Jimmy Smith	.60	.18
❑ 68 Fred Taylor	1.00	.30
❑ 69 Corey Dillon	.60	.18
❑ 70 Jon Kitna	.60	.18
❑ 71 Michael Westbrook	.40	.12
❑ 72 Trent Green	.60	.18
❑ 73 Priest Holmes	1.25	.35
❑ 74 Tony Gonzalez	.60	.18
❑ 75 Daunte Culpepper	1.00	.30
❑ 76 Michael Bennett	.60	.18
❑ 77 Randy Moss	1.50	.45
❑ 78 Drew Brees	1.00	.30
❑ 79 Curtis Conway	.40	.12

		Nm-Mt	Ex-Mt
❑ 80	Junior Seau	1.00	.30
❑ 81	Quincy Carter	.60	.18
❑ 82	Emmitt Smith	2.50	.75
❑ 83	Joey Galloway	.60	.18
❑ 84	Cory Schlesinger	.40	.12
❑ 85	James Stewart	.60	.18
❑ 86	Az-Zahir Hakim	.40	.12
❑ 87	Rodney Peete	.60	.18
❑ 88	Lamar Smith	.60	.18
❑ 89	Corey Bradford	.40	.12
❑ 90	Jermaine Lewis	.40	.12
❑ 91	Peyton Manning AU	100.00	30.00
❑ 92	Anthony Thomas AU	25.00	7.50
❑ 93	LaDainian Tomlinson AU	40.00	12.00
❑ 94	Jeff Garcia AU	25.00	7.50
❑ 95	Kurt Warner SC	3.00	.90
❑ 96	Brett Favre SC	8.00	2.40
❑ 97	Michael Vick SC	10.00	3.00
❑ 98	Donovan McNabb SC	4.00	1.20
❑ 99	Daunte Culpepper SC	3.00	.90
❑ 100	Tom Brady SC	8.00	2.40
❑ 101	Drew Brees SC	3.00	.90
❑ 102	Kordell Stewart SC	2.00	.60
❑ 103	Steve McNair SC	3.00	.90
❑ 104	Peyton Manning SC	6.00	1.80
❑ 105	Mark Brunell SC	3.00	.90
❑ 106	Jeff Garcia SC	3.00	.90
❑ 107	Aaron Brooks SC	3.00	.90
❑ 108	Rich Gannon SC	3.00	.90
❑ 109	Tim Couch SC	2.00	.60
❑ 110	Jake Plummer SC	3.00	.90
❑ 111	Drew Bledsoe SC	4.00	1.20
❑ 112	Brian Griese SC	3.00	.90
❑ 113	Quincy Carter SC	2.00	.60
❑ 114	Vinny Testaverde SC	2.00	.60
❑ 115	Chad Pennington SC	4.00	1.20
❑ 116	Brad Johnson SC	2.00	.60
❑ 117	Trent Dilfer SC	2.00	.60
❑ 118	Jim Miller SC	2.00	.60
❑ 119	Tommy Maddox SC	8.00	2.40
❑ 120	Trent Green SC	2.00	.60
❑ 121	Rodney Peete SC	2.00	.60
❑ 122	Jay Fiedler SC	2.00	.60
❑ 123	Kerry Collins SC	2.00	.60
❑ 124	Chris Redman SC	2.00	.60
❑ 125	Marshall Faulk SS	4.00	1.20
❑ 126	Donovan McNabb SS	5.00	1.50
❑ 127	Michael Vick SS	12.00	3.60
❑ 128	Brett Favre SS	10.00	3.00
❑ 129	Peyton Manning SS	8.00	2.40
❑ 130	Kurt Warner SS	4.00	1.20
❑ 131	Curtis Martin SS	4.00	1.20
❑ 132	Randy Moss SS	8.00	2.40
❑ 133	Edgerrin James SS	5.00	1.50
❑ 134	Jerome Bettis SS	4.00	1.20
❑ 135	Emmitt Smith SS	10.00	3.00
❑ 136	LaDainian Tomlinson SS	6.00	1.80
❑ 137	Jeff Garcia SS	4.00	1.20
❑ 138	Kordell Stewart SS	2.50	.75
❑ 139	Anthony Thomas SS	4.00	1.20
❑ 140	Tom Brady SS	10.00	3.00
❑ 141	Daunte Culpepper SS	4.00	1.20
❑ 142	Drew Bledsoe SS	5.00	1.50
❑ 143	Ricky Williams SS	4.00	1.20
❑ 144	Warrick Dunn SS	4.00	1.20
❑ 145	Steve McNair SS	4.00	1.20
❑ 146	Rich Gannon SS	4.00	1.20
❑ 147	Jake Plummer SS	2.50	.75
❑ 148	Jerry Rice SS	8.00	2.40
❑ 149	Mark Brunell SS	4.00	1.20
❑ 150	Brian Griese SS	4.00	1.20
❑ 151	Eddie George SS	4.00	1.20
❑ 152	Tim Couch SS	2.50	.75
❑ 153	Keyshawn Johnson SS	4.00	1.20
❑ 154	Shannon Sharpe SS	2.50	.75
❑ 155	Phillip Buchanon RC	12.00	3.60
❑ 156	Brian Allen RC	10.00	3.00
❑ 157	Brian Westbrook RC	40.00	12.00
❑ 158	Lito Sheppard RC	12.00	3.60
❑ 159	Daryl Jones RC	10.00	3.00
❑ 160	Javin Hunter RC	6.00	1.80
❑ 161	Derrick Lewis RC	6.00	1.80
❑ 162	Javon Walker RC	30.00	9.00
❑ 163	Tank Williams RC	10.00	3.00
❑ 164	Shaun Hill RC	12.00	3.60
❑ 165	Napoleon Harris RC	12.00	3.60
❑ 166	Herb Haygood RC	6.00	1.80
❑ 167	Jake Schifino RC	10.00	3.00
❑ 168	Quentin Jammer RC	12.00	3.60
❑ 169	Jason McAddley RC	10.00	3.00
❑ 170	Jerramy Stevens RC	12.00	3.60
❑ 171	Jesse Chatman RC	12.00	3.60
❑ 172	Larry Ned RC	10.00	3.00
❑ 173	Najeh Davenport RC	12.00	3.60
❑ 174	Lamont Thompson RC	10.00	3.00
❑ 175	Darrell Hill RC	10.00	3.00
❑ 176	Ryan Sims RC	12.00	3.60
❑ 177	Ryan Denney RC	6.00	1.80
❑ 178	Jamin Elliott RC	6.00	1.80
❑ 179	Sam Simmons RC	6.00	1.80
❑ 180	Seth Burford RC	10.00	3.00
❑ 181	Tellis Redmon RC	10.00	3.00
❑ 182	Ben Leber RC	12.00	3.60
❑ 183	Kendall Newson RC	6.00	1.80
❑ 184	Marques Anderson RC	12.00	3.60
❑ 185	Adrian Peterson AU RC	25.00	7.50
❑ 186	Albert Haynesworth AU RC EXCH	20.00	6.00
❑ 187	Antwoine Womack AU RC	20.00	6.00
❑ 188	Brandon Doman AU RC	25.00	7.50
❑ 189	Craig Nall AU RC	30.00	9.00
❑ 190	Chad Hutchinson AU RC	25.00	7.50
❑ 191	Chester Taylor AU RC	25.00	7.50
❑ 192	Damien Anderson AU RC	20.00	6.00
❑ 193	Deion Branch AU RC	50.00	15.00
❑ 194	Dusty Bonner AU RC	15.00	4.50
❑ 195	Ed Reed AU RC	50.00	15.00
❑ 196	Eric McCoo AU RC	15.00	4.50
❑ 197	J.T. O'Sullivan AU RC	20.00	6.00
❑ 198	Kalimba Edwards AU RC	25.00	7.50
❑ 199	Jonathan Wells AU RC	25.00	7.50
❑ 200	Josh Scobey AU RC	20.00	6.00
❑ 201	Kelly Campbell AU RC	30.00	9.00
❑ 202	Kurt Kittner AU RC	20.00	6.00
❑ 203	Lamar Gordon AU RC	25.00	7.50
❑ 204	Lee Mays AU RC	20.00	6.00
❑ 205	Leonard Henry AU RC	20.00	6.00
❑ 206	Luke Staley AU RC	20.00	6.00
❑ 207	Justin Peelle AU RC	15.00	4.50
❑ 208	Randy Fasani AU RC	20.00	6.00
❑ 209	Ricky Williams AU RC	25.00	7.50
❑ 210	Ronald Curry AU RC	30.00	9.00
❑ 211	Travis Stephens AU RC	20.00	6.00
❑ 212	Wendell Bryant AU RC	25.00	7.50
❑ 213	Woody Dantzler AU RC	25.00	7.50
❑ 214	Kahlil Hill AU RC	20.00	6.00
❑ 215	Donte Stallworth JSY RC	50.00	15.00
❑ 216	Joey Harrington AU/280 RC	350.00	105.00
❑ 217	Cliff Russell JSY RC	30.00	9.00
❑ 218	Clinton Portis JSY RC	120.00	36.00
❑ 219	Daniel Graham JSY RC	40.00	12.00
❑ 220	David Garrard JSY RC	50.00	15.00
❑ 221	DeShaun Foster JSY RC	60.00	18.00
❑ 222	Julius Peppers JSY RC	50.00	15.00
❑ 223	Jeremy Shockey JSY RC	80.00	24.00
❑ 224	Patrick Ramsey JSY RC	60.00	18.00
❑ 225	Josh Reed JSY RC	30.00	9.00
❑ 226	LaDell Betts JSY RC	30.00	9.00
❑ 227	Mike Williams JSY/350 RC	30.00	9.00
❑ 228	Reche Caldwell JSY RC	30.00	9.00
❑ 229	Rohan Davey JSY RC	40.00	12.00
❑ 230	Ron Johnson JSY RC	30.00	9.00
❑ 231	Roy Williams JSY/350 RC	100.00	30.00
❑ 232	T.J. Duckett JSY RC	50.00	15.00
❑ 233	Tim Carter JSY RC	30.00	9.00
❑ 234	William Green JSY RC	40.00	12.00
❑ 235	Antwaan Randle El JSY AU RC	120.00	36.00
❑ 237	David Carr JSY AU RC	400.00	120.00
❑ 238	Andre Davis JSY AU RC	80.00	24.00
❑ 239	Eric Crouch JSY AU RC	80.00	24.00
❑ 240	Antonio Bryant JSY AU RC	100.00	30.00
❑ 241	Jabar Gaffney JSY AU RC	80.00	24.00
❑ 242	Marquise Walker JSY AU RC	80.00	24.00
❑ 243	Maurice Morris JSY AU RC	100.00	30.00
❑ 244	Josh McCown JSY AU RC	120.00	36.00
❑ AP1	Walter Payton AU/34	300.00	90.00
❑ SW1	Walter Payton JSY/150	120.00	36.00
❑ SW1	Walter Payton Gold JSY/34	200.00	60.00
❑ SCPS	Walter Payton JSY/250 Emmitt Smith	120.00	36.00
❑ SCPSG	Walter Payton Emmitt Smith Gold JSY/34	300.00	90.00

2002 SP Authentic Gold

*STARS 1-90: 12X TO 30X BASIC CARDS
*ROOKIE JSYs 215-234: .8X TO 2X

		Nm-Mt	Ex-Mt
❑ 91	Peyton Manning AU	150.00	45.00
❑ 92	Anthony Thomas AU	50.00	15.00
❑ 93	LaDainian Tomlinson AU	60.00	18.00
❑ 94	Jeff Garcia AU	50.00	15.00

2003 SP Authentic

		Nm-Mt	Ex-Mt
COMP.SET w/o SP's (150)		20.00	6.00
❑ 1	Donovan McNabb	1.25	.35
❑ 2	Tim Couch	.40	.12
❑ 3	Joey Harrington	1.25	.35
❑ 4	Brett Favre	2.50	.75
❑ 5	Jeff Garcia	1.00	.30
❑ 6	Kerry Collins	.60	.18
❑ 7	Michael Vick	2.00	.60
❑ 8	David Carr	1.25	.35
❑ 9	Steve McNair	1.00	.30
❑ 10	Chad Pennington	1.25	.35
❑ 11	Patrick Ramsey	1.00	.30
❑ 12	Rich Gannon	.60	.18
❑ 13	Kurt Warner	1.00	.30
❑ 14	Brad Johnson	.60	.18
❑ 15	Jay Fiedler	.60	.18
❑ 16	Jake Plummer	.60	.18
❑ 17	Mark Brunell	.60	.18
❑ 18	Peyton Manning	1.50	.45
❑ 19	Brian Griese	1.00	.30
❑ 20	Kordell Stewart	.60	.18
❑ 21	Kelly Holcomb	.60	.18
❑ 22	Josh McCown	.60	.18
❑ 23	Matt Hasselbeck	.60	.18
❑ 24	Marc Bulger	1.00	.30
❑ 25	Chris Redman	.40	.12
❑ 26	Rodney Peete	.60	.18
❑ 27	Jake Delhomme	1.00	.30
❑ 28	Jon Kitna	.60	.18
❑ 29	Trent Green	.60	.18
❑ 30	Quincy Carter	.60	.18
❑ 31	Chad Hutchinson	.60	.18
❑ 32	Edgerrin James	1.00	.30
❑ 33	Deuce McAllister	1.00	.30
❑ 34	Ricky Williams	1.00	.30
❑ 35	Priest Holmes	1.25	.35
❑ 36	Curtis Martin	1.00	.30
❑ 37	Shaun Alexander	1.00	.30
❑ 38	Eddie George	.60	.18
❑ 39	Marshall Faulk	1.00	.30
❑ 40	Garrison Hearst	.60	.18
❑ 41	Ahman Green	1.00	.30
❑ 42	Corey Dillon	.60	.18
❑ 43	Jamal Lewis	1.00	.30
❑ 44	William Green	.60	.18
❑ 45	Travis Henry	.60	.18

		Nm-Mt	Ex-Mt
❑ 46	Mike Alstott	1.00	.30
❑ 47	Amos Zereoue	.60	.18
❑ 48	Stephen Davis	.60	.18
❑ 49	Duce Staley	.60	.18
❑ 50	Fred Taylor	1.00	.30
❑ 51	Anthony Thomas	1.00	.30
❑ 52	Charlie Garner	.60	.18
❑ 53	Kevan Barlow	.60	.18
❑ 54	Brian Urlacher	1.25	.35
❑ 55	Junior Seau	1.00	.30
❑ 56	Zach Thomas	1.00	.30
❑ 57	Ray Lewis	1.00	.30
❑ 58	Jerry Porter	.60	.18
❑ 59	Marty Booker	.60	.18
❑ 60	Javon Walker	.60	.18
❑ 61	Donald Driver	.60	.18
❑ 62	Amani Toomer	.60	.18
❑ 63	Peerless Price	.60	.18
❑ 64	Santana Moss	.60	.18
❑ 65	Laveranues Coles	.60	.18
❑ 66	Troy Brown	.60	.18
❑ 67	Chris Chambers	1.00	.30
❑ 68	Rod Smith	.60	.18
❑ 69	Ashley Lelie	1.00	.30
❑ 70	Plaxico Burress	.60	.18
❑ 71	Keyshawn Johnson	1.00	.30
❑ 72	Isaac Bruce	1.00	.30
❑ 73	Torry Holt	1.00	.30
❑ 74	Koren Robinson	.60	.18
❑ 75	Derrick Mason	.60	.18
❑ 76	Kevin Johnson	.60	.18
❑ 77	Andre' Davis	.40	.12
❑ 78	Antonio Bryant	.60	.18
❑ 79	Eric Moulds	.60	.18
❑ 80	Jerry Rice	2.00	.60
❑ 81	Tim Brown	1.00	.30
❑ 82	Antwaan Randle El	1.00	.30
❑ 83	Donte Stallworth	1.00	.30
❑ 84	Randy Moss	1.50	.45
❑ 85	Chad Johnson	.60	.18
❑ 86	Hines Ward	1.00	.30
❑ 87	Rod Gardner	.60	.18
❑ 88	Marvin Harrison	1.00	.30
❑ 89	David Boston	.60	.18
❑ 90	Julius Peppers	1.00	.30
❑ 91	Dewayne White RC	5.00	1.50
❑ 92	Casey Fitzsimmons RC	6.00	1.80
❑ 93	Aaron Moorehead RC	6.00	1.80
❑ 94	Jimmy Farris RC	5.00	1.50
❑ 95	Eric Parker RC	6.00	1.80
❑ 96	Michael Haynes RC	6.00	1.80
❑ 97	J.J. Moses RC	5.00	1.50
❑ 98	Ken Hamlin RC	6.00	1.80
❑ 99	William Joseph RC	6.00	1.80
❑ 100	Alonzo Jackson RC	5.00	1.50
❑ 101	Tyler Brayton RC	6.00	1.80
❑ 102	Eddie Moore RC	5.00	1.50
❑ 103	Cleo Lemon RC	5.00	1.50
❑ 104	Arlen Harris RC	6.00	1.80
❑ 105	Cortez Hankton RC	5.00	1.50
❑ 106	Angelo Crowell RC	5.00	1.50
❑ 107	Johnathan Sullivan RC	5.00	1.50
❑ 108	Pisa Tinoisamoa RC	10.00	3.00
❑ 109	Boss Bailey RC	8.00	2.40
❑ 110	Tommy Jones RC	3.00	.90
❑ 111	E.J. Henderson RC	6.00	1.80
❑ 112	Jimmy Kennedy RC	6.00	1.80
❑ 113	Nnamdi Asomugha RC	5.00	1.50
❑ 114	Hanik Milligan RC	5.00	1.50
❑ 115	Sammy Davis RC	6.00	1.80
❑ 116	Drayton Florence RC	3.00	.90
❑ 117	Andre Woolfolk RC	6.00	1.80
❑ 118	Dennis Weathersby RC	3.00	.90
❑ 119	Mike Doss RC	6.00	1.80
❑ 120	Troy Polamalu RC	6.00	1.80
❑ 121	Clinton Portis SS	6.00	1.80
❑ 122	Daunte Culpepper SS	5.00	1.50
❑ 123	Jeremy Shockey SS	6.00	1.80
❑ 124	Drew Brees SS	5.00	1.50
❑ 125	Marshall Faulk SS	5.00	1.50
❑ 126	Emmitt Smith SS	10.00	3.00
❑ 127	Terrell Owens SS	5.00	1.50
❑ 128	Ricky Williams SS	5.00	1.50
❑ 129	Deuce McAllister SS	5.00	1.50
❑ 130	Ahman Green SS	5.00	1.50
❑ 131	Chad Pennington SS	5.00	1.50
❑ 132	Plaxico Burress SS	5.00	1.50
❑ 133	Steve McNair SS	5.00	1.50
❑ 134	Keyshawn Johnson SS	5.00	1.50
❑ 135	Jeff Garcia SS	5.00	1.50
❑ 136	Drew Bledsoe SS	5.00	1.50
❑ 137	Jerry Rice SS	8.00	2.40
❑ 138	Randy Moss SS	6.00	1.80
❑ 139	David Carr SS	6.00	1.80
❑ 140	Joey Harrington SS	6.00	1.80
❑ 141	Michael Vick SS	10.00	3.00
❑ 142	Tom Brady SS	6.00	1.80
❑ 143	Brian Urlacher SS	6.00	1.80
❑ 144	Brett Favre SS	10.00	3.00
❑ 145	Kurt Warner SS	5.00	1.50
❑ 146	LaDainian Tomlinson SS	5.00	1.50
❑ 147	Aaron Brooks SS	5.00	1.50
❑ 148	Edgerrin James SS	5.00	1.50
❑ 149	Peyton Manning SS	6.00	1.80
❑ 150	Donovan McNabb SS	5.00	1.50
❑ 151	Jason Gesser RC	12.00	3.60
❑ 152	Ken Dorsey RC	25.00	7.50
❑ 153	Jason Johnson RC	6.00	1.80
❑ 154	Avon Cobourne RC	6.00	1.80
❑ 155	Andrew Pinnock RC	10.00	3.00
❑ 156	Kirk Farmer RC	6.00	1.80
❑ 157	Reno Mahe RC	12.00	3.60
❑ 158	Lon Sheriff RC	6.00	1.80
❑ 159	Marquel Blackwell RC	6.00	1.80
❑ 160	Quentin Griffin RC	30.00	9.00
❑ 161	Rashean Mathis RC	10.00	3.00
❑ 162	Lee Suggs RC	30.00	9.00
❑ 163	Jeremi Johnson RC	10.00	3.00
❑ 164	Ovie Mughelli RC	6.00	1.80
❑ 165	Nick Barnett RC	20.00	6.00
❑ 166	Brock Forsey RC	12.00	3.60
❑ 167	Malaefou MacKenzie RC	6.00	1.80
❑ 168	Ahmad Galloway RC	10.00	3.00
❑ 169	Cecil Sapp RC	10.00	3.00
❑ 170	Kerry Carter RC	10.00	3.00
❑ 171	Dahrran Diedrick RC	12.00	3.60
❑ 171A	Terrence Edwards RC should be card 177	10.00	3.00
❑ 172	Joffrey Reynolds RC	6.00	1.80
❑ 173	Sultan McCullough RC	10.00	3.00
❑ 174	Brandon Drumm RC	6.00	1.80
❑ 175	Casey Moore RC	10.00	3.00
❑ 176	Gerald Hayes RC	6.00	1.80
❑ 178	Jamal Burke RC	6.00	1.80
❑ 179	Antonio Chatman RC	12.00	3.60
❑ 180	Reggie Newhouse RC	10.00	3.00
❑ 181	Chris Horn RC	6.00	1.80
❑ 182	Denero Marriott RC	6.00	1.80
❑ 183	DeAndrew Rubin RC	6.00	1.80
❑ 184	Taco Wallace RC	10.00	3.00
❑ 185	Doug Gabriel RC	12.00	3.60
❑ 186	Willie Ponder RC	6.00	1.80
❑ 187	David Tyree RC	10.00	3.00
❑ 188	Kevin Walter RC	10.00	3.00
❑ 189	Zuriel Smith RC	6.00	1.80
❑ 190	Keenan Howry RC	12.00	3.60
❑ 191	C.J. Jones RC	6.00	1.80
❑ 192	Arnaz Battle RC	12.00	3.60
❑ 193	Walter Young RC	6.00	1.80
❑ 194	Anthony Adams RC	10.00	3.00
❑ 195	Jerome McDougle RC	12.00	3.60
❑ 196	Will Heller RC	10.00	3.00
❑ 197	Cecil Moore RC	6.00	1.80
❑ 198	Mike Seidman RC	6.00	1.80
❑ 199	Jason Witten RC	20.00	6.00
❑ 200	L.J. Smith RC	12.00	3.60
❑ 201	Bennie Joppru RC	12.00	3.60
❑ 202	Donald Lee RC	10.00	3.00
❑ 203	Aaron Walker RC	10.00	3.00
❑ 204	Antonio Brown RC	6.00	1.80
❑ 205	George Wrighster RC	10.00	3.00
❑ 206	Danny Curley RC	6.00	1.80
❑ 207	Mike Banks RC	6.00	1.80
❑ 208	Mike Pinkard RC	6.00	1.80
❑ 209	Ryan Hoag RC	6.00	1.80
❑ 210	Brad Pyatt RC	10.00	3.00
❑ 211	Charles Rogers RC	20.00	6.00
❑ 212	Chris Simms AU/250 RC	150.00	45.00
❑ 213	Nate Hybl AU RC	20.00	6.00
❑ 214	Brandon Lloyd AU RC	40.00	12.00
❑ 215	ReShard Lee AU RC	25.00	7.50
❑ 216	Dwone Hicks AU RC	12.00	3.60
❑ 217	Tony Romo AU RC	20.00	6.00
❑ 218	Brett Engemann AU RC	12.00	3.60
❑ 219	Nick Maddox AU RC	12.00	3.60
❑ 220	James MacPherson AU RC	12.00	3.60
❑ 221	Juston Wood AU RC	12.00	3.60
❑ 222	Adrian Madise AU RC	15.00	4.50
❑ 223	Shaun McDonald AU RC	20.00	6.00
❑ 224	Carl Ford AU RC	12.00	3.60
❑ 225	Vishante Shiancoe AU RC	15.00	4.50
❑ 226	Gibran Hamdan AU RC	12.00	3.60
❑ 227	Brooks Bollinger AU RC	15.00	4.50
❑ 228	B.J. Askew AU RC	20.00	6.00
❑ 229	Domanick Davis AU RC	60.00	18.00
❑ 230	LaBrandon Toefield AU RC	20.00	6.00
❑ 231	Bobby Wade AU RC	20.00	6.00
❑ 232	Justin Gage AU RC	20.00	6.00
❑ 233	Billy McMullen AU RC	15.00	4.50
❑ 234	David Kircus AU RC	15.00	4.50
❑ 235	J.R. Tolver AU RC	15.00	4.50
❑ 236	Sam Aiken AU RC	15.00	4.50
❑ 237	LaTarence Dunbar AU RC	15.00	4.50
❑ 238	Kassim Osgood AU RC	20.00	6.00
❑ 239	Tony Hollings AU RC	25.00	7.50
❑ 240	Justin Griffith AU RC	15.00	4.50
❑ 241	Brian St.Pierre JSY RC	30.00	9.00
❑ 242	Kevin Curtis JSY RC	30.00	9.00
❑ 243	Dallas Clark JSY RC	30.00	9.00
❑ 244	Willis McGahee JSY RC	120.00	36.00
❑ 245	Terence Newman JSY RC	40.00	12.00
❑ 246	Justin Fargas JSY AU RC	80.00	24.00
❑ 247	Artose Pinner JSY RC	40.00	12.00
❑ 248	Kelley Washington JSY RC	40.00	12.00
❑ 249	DeWayne Robertson JSY RC	25.00	7.50
❑ 250	Nate Burleson JSY RC	60.00	18.00
❑ 251	Kliff Kingsbury JSY RC	25.00	7.50
❑ 252	Bethel Johnson JSY RC	50.00	15.00
❑ 253	Anquan Boldin JSY RC	60.00	18.00
❑ 254	Bryant Johnson JSY AU RC	80.00	24.00
❑ 255	Terrell Suggs EXCH	150.00	45.00
❑ 256	Musa Smith JSY RC	30.00	9.00
❑ 257	Chris Brown JSY RC	80.00	24.00
❑ 258	Marcus Trufant JSY RC	30.00	9.00
❑ 259	Teyo Johnson JSY RC	30.00	9.00
❑ 260	Tyrone Calico JSY RC	50.00	15.00
❑ 261	Dave Ragone JSY AU RC	80.00	24.00
❑ 262	Kyle Boller JSY AU RC	200.00	60.00
❑ 263	Onterrio Smith JSY AU RC	150.00	45.00
❑ 264	Rex Grossman JSY RC	120.00	36.00
❑ 265	Larry Johnson JSY RC	75.00	22.00
❑ 266	Seneca Wallace JSY AU RC	80.00	24.00
❑ 268	Taylor Jacobs JSY AU RC	80.00	24.00
❑ 269	Byron Leftwich JSY AU RC	550.00	160.00
❑ 270	Carson Palmer JSY AU RC	450.00	135.00

2003 SP Authentic Gold

Nm-Mt Ex-Mt

*STARS: 12X TO 30X BASE CARD HI
*SS STARS 121-150 : 2.5X TO 6X
*ROOKIES 91-120: 3X TO 8X BASE CARD HI
*ROOKIES 151-211: 1.5X TO 4X BASE CARD HI
*ROOKIE JSYs: 1X TO 2.5X BASE CARD HI
ROOKIE AUTOs TOO SCARCE TO PRICE

2004 SP Authentic

	Nm-Mt	Ex-Mt
COMP.SET w/o SP's (90)	25.00	7.50

91-150 RC PRINT RUN 1199 SER.#'d SETS
151-185 AU RC PRINT RUN 990 SER.#'d SETS
186-200 JSY AU RC PRINT RUN 799
201-206 JSY AU RC PRINT RUN 499
207-216 JSY AU RC PRINT RUN 299
EXCH EXPIRATION: 12/15/2007

Card	Nm-Mt	Ex-Mt
❑ 1 Josh McCown	.60	.18
❑ 2 Anquan Boldin	1.00	.30
❑ 3 Michael Vick	2.00	.60
❑ 4 Peerless Price	.60	.18
❑ 5 Todd Heap	.60	.18
❑ 6 Kyle Boller	1.00	.30
❑ 7 Jamal Lewis	1.00	.30
❑ 8 Drew Bledsoe	1.00	.30
❑ 9 Travis Henry	.60	.18
❑ 10 Eric Moulds	.60	.18
❑ 11 Steve Smith	.60	.18
❑ 12 Stephen Davis	.60	.18
❑ 13 Jake Delhomme	1.00	.30
❑ 14 Rex Grossman	1.00	.30
❑ 15 Brian Urlacher	1.25	.35
❑ 16 Thomas Jones	.60	.18
❑ 17 Chad Johnson	.60	.18
❑ 18 Rudi Johnson	.60	.18
❑ 19 Carson Palmer	1.25	.35
❑ 20 William Green	.60	.18
❑ 21 Andre Davis	.40	.12
❑ 22 Jeff Garcia	1.00	.30
❑ 23 Roy Williams S	.60	.18
❑ 24 Eddie George	.60	.18
❑ 25 Keyshawn Johnson	.60	.18
❑ 26 Ashley Lelie	.60	.18
❑ 27 Jake Plummer	.60	.18
❑ 28 Champ Bailey	.60	.18
❑ 29 Charles Rogers	.60	.18
❑ 30 Joey Harrington	1.00	.30
❑ 31 Ahman Green	1.00	.30
❑ 32 Brett Favre	2.50	.75
❑ 33 Javon Walker	.60	.18
❑ 34 David Carr	1.00	.30
❑ 35 Domanick Davis	1.00	.30
❑ 36 Andre Johnson	1.00	.30
❑ 37 Marvin Harrison	1.00	.30
❑ 38 Edgerrin James	1.00	.30
❑ 39 Peyton Manning	1.50	.45
❑ 40 Byron Leftwich	1.50	.45
❑ 41 Fred Taylor	.60	.18
❑ 42 Trent Green	.60	.18
❑ 43 Tony Gonzalez	.60	.18
❑ 44 Priest Holmes	1.25	.35
❑ 45 Ricky Williams	1.00	.30
❑ 46 Chris Chambers	.60	.18
❑ 47 Jay Fiedler	.40	.12
❑ 48 Daunte Culpepper	1.00	.30
❑ 49 Randy Moss	1.25	.35
❑ 50 Onterrio Smith	.60	.18
❑ 51 Tom Brady	1.50	.45
❑ 52 Troy Brown	.60	.18
❑ 53 Corey Dillon	.60	.18
❑ 54 Deuce McAllister	1.00	.30
❑ 55 Aaron Brooks	.60	.18
❑ 56 Joe Horn	.60	.18
❑ 57 Amani Toomer	.60	.18
❑ 58 Kurt Warner	1.00	.30
❑ 59 Jeremy Shockey	1.00	.30
❑ 60 Chad Pennington	1.25	.35
❑ 61 Santana Moss	.60	.18
❑ 62 Curtis Martin	1.00	.30
❑ 63 Rich Gannon	.60	.18
❑ 64 Jerry Rice	2.00	.60
❑ 65 Jerry Porter	.60	.18
❑ 66 Terrell Owens	1.00	.30
❑ 67 Jevon Kearse	.60	.18
❑ 68 Donovan McNabb	1.25	.35
❑ 69 Hines Ward	1.00	.30
❑ 70 Plaxico Burress	.60	.18
❑ 71 Tommy Maddox	.60	.18
❑ 72 Drew Brees	1.00	.30
❑ 73 LaDainian Tomlinson	1.00	.30
❑ 74 Tim Rattay	.60	.18
❑ 75 Brandon Lloyd	.60	.18
❑ 76 Kevan Barlow	.60	.18
❑ 77 Shaun Alexander	1.00	.30
❑ 78 Koren Robinson	.60	.18
❑ 79 Matt Hasselbeck	.60	.18
❑ 80 Marshall Faulk	1.00	.30
❑ 81 Torry Holt	1.00	.30
❑ 82 Marc Bulger	1.00	.30
❑ 83 Brad Johnson	.60	.18
❑ 84 Joey Galloway	.60	.18
❑ 85 Steve McNair	1.00	.30
❑ 86 Derrick Mason	.60	.18
❑ 87 Chris Brown	1.00	.30
❑ 88 Mark Brunell	.60	.18
❑ 89 Laveranues Coles	.60	.18
❑ 90 Clinton Portis	1.00	.30
❑ 91 Triandos Luke RC	8.00	2.40
❑ 92 Keith Smith RC	6.00	1.80
❑ 93 Shaun Phillips RC	6.00	1.80
❑ 94 D.J. Williams RC	10.00	3.00
❑ 95 Keiwan Ratliff RC	6.00	1.80
❑ 96 Madieu Williams RC	6.00	1.80
❑ 97 Chris Cooley RC	8.00	2.40
❑ 98 Stuart Schweigert RC	8.00	2.40
❑ 99 Sloan Thomas RC	6.00	1.80
❑ 100 Chad Lavalais RC	6.00	1.80
❑ 101 Jared Allen RC	8.00	2.40
❑ 102 Brian Jones RC	6.00	1.80
❑ 103 Matt Ware RC	8.00	2.40
❑ 104 Daryl Smith RC	8.00	2.40
❑ 105 J.R. Reed RC	6.00	1.80
❑ 106 D.J. Hackett RC	6.00	1.80
❑ 107 Jeris McIntyre RC	6.00	1.80
❑ 108 Dexter Reid RC	4.00	1.20
❑ 109 Courtney Anderson RC	6.00	1.80
❑ 110 Courtney Watson RC	8.00	2.40
❑ 111 Larry Croom RC	6.00	1.80
❑ 112 Jonathan Smith RC	6.00	1.80
❑ 113 Vernon Carey RC	6.00	1.80
❑ 114 Michael Gaines RC	6.00	1.80
❑ 115 Chris Snee RC	6.00	1.80
❑ 116 Nathan Vasher RC	8.00	2.40
❑ 117 Teddy Lehman RC	8.00	2.40
❑ 118 Marcus Tubbs RC	8.00	2.40
❑ 119 Ben Utecht RC	4.00	1.20
❑ 120 Maurice Mann RC	6.00	1.80
❑ 121 Thomas Tapeh RC	6.00	1.80
❑ 122 Will Allen RC	8.00	2.40
❑ 123 Demorrio Williams RC	8.00	2.40
❑ 124 Ran Carthon RC	6.00	1.80
❑ 125 Tim Euhus RC	8.00	2.40
❑ 126 Bradlee Van Pelt RC	8.00	2.40
❑ 127 Patrick Crayton RC	8.00	2.40
❑ 128 Ryan Krause RC	6.00	1.80
❑ 129 Joey Thomas RC	8.00	2.40
❑ 130 Antwan Odom RC	8.00	2.40
❑ 131 Karlos Dansby RC	8.00	2.40
❑ 132 Junior Siavii RC	8.00	2.40
❑ 133 Jamaar Taylor RC	8.00	2.40
❑ 134 Kendrick Starling RC	4.00	1.20
❑ 135 Wes Welker RC	8.00	2.40
❑ 136 Igor Olshansky RC	8.00	2.40
❑ 137 Mark Jones RC	6.00	1.80
❑ 138 Bruce Thornton RC	4.00	1.20
❑ 139 Michael Boulware RC	8.00	2.40
❑ 140 Matt Mauck RC	8.00	2.40
❑ 141 Clarence Moore RC	8.00	2.40
❑ 142 Derrick Strait RC	8.00	2.40
❑ 143 Jarrett Payton RC	8.00	2.40
❑ 144 Dontarrious Thomas RC	8.00	2.40
❑ 145 Shawntae Spencer RC	8.00	2.40
❑ 146 Bob Sanders RC	8.00	2.40
❑ 147 Darnell Dockett RC	6.00	1.80
❑ 148 Sean Taylor RC	10.00	3.00
❑ 149 Jason Babin RC	8.00	2.40
❑ 150 Ricardo Colclough RC	8.00	2.40
❑ 151 Brandon Chillar AU RC	15.00	4.50
❑ 152 Clarence Farmer AU RC	15.00	4.50
❑ 153 B.J. Symons AU RC	20.00	6.00
❑ 154 John Navarre AU RC	20.00	6.00
❑ 155 P.K. Sam AU RC EXCH	20.00	6.00
❑ 156 Casey Clausen AU RC	20.00	6.00
❑ 157 Drew Henson AU RC	40.00	12.00
❑ 158 Kris Wilson AU RC	20.00	6.00
❑ 159 Vince Wilfork AU RC	25.00	7.50
❑ 160 Michael Turner AU RC	20.00	6.00
❑ 161 Jonathan Vilma AU RC	30.00	9.00
❑ 162 Samie Parker AU RC	20.00	6.00
❑ 163 B.J. Sams AU RC	20.00	6.00
❑ 164 Adimchinobe Echemandu AU RC EXCH	15.00	4.50
❑ 165 Ernest Wilford AU RC	20.00	6.00
❑ 166 Troy Fleming AU RC	20.00	6.00
❑ 167 Tommie Harris AU RC	25.00	7.50
❑ 168 Jammal Lord AU RC	20.00	6.00
❑ 169 Kenechi Udeze AU RC	20.00	6.00
❑ 170 Chris Gamble AU RC	25.00	7.50
❑ 171 Carlos Francis AU RC	15.00	4.50
❑ 172 Mewelde Moore AU RC	30.00	9.00
❑ 173 Jared Lorenzen AU RC	15.00	4.50
❑ 174 Jeff Smoker AU RC	25.00	7.50
❑ 175 Ben Hartsock AU RC	20.00	6.00
❑ 176 Jerricho Cotchery AU RC	20.00	6.00
❑ 177 Josh Harris AU RC	20.00	6.00
❑ 178 Cody Pickett AU RC	20.00	6.00
❑ 179 Quincy Wilson AU RC	15.00	4.50
❑ 180 Will Smith AU RC EXCH	20.00	6.00
❑ 181 Ahmad Carroll AU RC	25.00	7.50
❑ 182 B.J. Johnson AU RC	15.00	4.50
❑ 183 Dunta Robinson AU RC	25.00	7.50
❑ 184 Craig Krenzel AU RC	20.00	6.00
❑ 185 Johnnie Morant AU RC	20.00	6.00
❑ 186 Cedric Cobbs JSY AU RC	60.00	18.00
❑ 187 Matt Schaub JSY AU RC	90.00	27.00
❑ 188 Bernard Berrian JSY AU RC	50.00	15.00
❑ 189 Devard Darling JSY AU RC	50.00	15.00
❑ 190 Ben Watson JSY AU RC	50.00	15.00
❑ 191 Darius Watts JSY AU RC	60.00	18.00
❑ 192 DeAngelo Hall JSY AU RC	60.00	18.00
❑ 193 Ben Troupe JSY AU RC	50.00	15.00
❑ 194 Michael Jenkins JSY AU RC	80.00	24.00
❑ 195 Keary Colbert JSY AU RC	60.00	18.00
❑ 196 Robert Gallery JSY AU RC	60.00	18.00
❑ 197 Greg Jones JSY AU RC	60.00	18.00
❑ 198 Michael Clayton JSY AU RC	120.00	36.00
❑ 199 Luke McCown JSY AU RC	60.00	18.00
❑ 200 Derrick Hamilton JSY AU RC	50.00	15.00
❑ 201 Rashaun Woods JSY AU RC	60.00	18.00
❑ 202 Chris Perry JSY AU RC	100.00	30.00
❑ 203 Devery Henderson JSY AU RC	60.00	18.00
❑ 204 Tatum Bell JSY AU RC	175.00	52.50
❑ 205 Lee Evans JSY AU RC	135.00	40.00
❑ 206 J.P. Losman JSY AU RC	250.00	75.00
❑ 207 Kellen Winslow JSY AU RC	150.00	45.00
❑ 208 Reggie Williams JSY AU RC	120.00	36.00
❑ 209 Julius Jones JSY AU RC	450.00	135.00
❑ 210 Steven Jackson JSY AU RC	400.00	120.00
❑ 211 Kevin Jones JSY AU RC	350.00	105.00
❑ 212 Roy Williams JSY AU RC	300.00	90.00
❑ 213 Ben Roethlisberger JSY AU RC	800.00	240.00
❑ 214 Philip Rivers JSY AU RC	350.00	105.00
❑ 215 Larry Fitzgerald JSY AU RC	300.00	90.00
❑ 216 Eli Manning JSY AU RC	600.00	180.00

2004 SP Authentic Gold

Nm-Mt Ex-Mt

*GOLD STARS: 6X TO 15X BASE CARD HI
*GOLD ROOKIES 91-150: 1.5X TO 4X

1-150 STATED PRINT RUN 50 SER.#'d SETS
*ROOKIE JSY AU 186-200: 1.2X TO 3X
*ROOKIE JSY AU 201-206: .8X TO 2X
*ROOKIE JSY AU 207-216: .6X TO 1.5X
186-216 JSY AU PRINT RUN 25 SER.#'d SETS
EXCH EXPIRATION: 12/15/2007

2001 SP Game Used Edition

	Nm-Mt	Ex-Mt
COMP.SET w/o SP's (90)	100.00	30.00
❑ 1 Jake Plummer	1.50	.45
❑ 2 David Boston	2.50	.75
❑ 3 Frank Sanders	1.00	.30
❑ 4 Jamal Anderson	2.50	.75
❑ 5 Doug Johnson	1.00	.30
❑ 6 Shawn Jefferson	1.00	.30
❑ 7 Jamal Lewis	4.00	1.20
❑ 8 Shannon Sharpe	1.50	.45
❑ 9 Qadry Ismail	1.50	.45
❑ 10 Shawn Bryson	1.00	.30
❑ 11 Rob Johnson	1.50	.45
❑ 12 Eric Moulds	1.50	.45
❑ 13 Muhsin Muhammad	1.50	.45
❑ 14 Brad Hoover	1.00	.30
❑ 15 Tim Biakabutuka	1.50	.45
❑ 16 Cade McNown	1.00	.30
❑ 17 Marcus Robinson	2.50	.75
❑ 18 Brian Urlacher	4.00	1.20
❑ 19 Akili Smith	1.00	.30
❑ 20 Peter Warrick	2.50	.75
❑ 21 Corey Dillon	2.50	.75
❑ 22 Kevin Johnson	1.50	.45
❑ 23 Rickey Dudley	1.00	.30
❑ 24 Tim Couch	1.50	.45
❑ 25 Tony Banks	1.00	.30
❑ 26 Emmitt Smith	5.00	1.50
❑ 27 Carl Pickens	1.00	.30
❑ 28 Terrell Davis	2.50	.75
❑ 29 Mike Anderson	2.50	.75
❑ 30 Brian Griese	2.50	.75
❑ 31 Ed McCaffrey	2.50	.75
❑ 32 Charlie Batch	2.50	.75
❑ 33 Germane Crowell	1.00	.30
❑ 34 James O. Stewart	1.50	.45
❑ 35 Brett Favre	8.00	2.40
❑ 36 Antonio Freeman	2.50	.75
❑ 37 Ahman Green	2.50	.75
❑ 38 Peyton Manning	6.00	1.80
❑ 39 Edgerrin James	3.00	.90
❑ 40 Marvin Harrison	2.50	.75
❑ 41 Mark Brunell	2.50	.75
❑ 42 Fred Taylor	2.50	.75
❑ 43 Jimmy Smith	1.50	.45
❑ 44 Tony Gonzalez	1.50	.45
❑ 45 Derrick Alexander	1.50	.45
❑ 46 Oronde Gadsden	1.50	.45
❑ 47 Ray Lucas	1.00	.30
❑ 48 Lamar Smith	1.50	.45
❑ 49 Randy Moss	5.00	1.50
❑ 50 Cris Carter	2.50	.75
❑ 51 Daunte Culpepper	2.50	.75
❑ 52 Drew Bledsoe	3.00	.90
❑ 53 Terry Glenn	1.50	.45
❑ 54 Ricky Williams	2.50	.75
❑ 55 Jeff Blake	1.50	.45
❑ 56 Joe Horn	1.50	.45
❑ 57 Aaron Brooks	2.50	.75
❑ 58 Kerry Collins	1.50	.45
❑ 59 Tiki Barber	1.50	.45
❑ 60 Ron Dayne	2.50	.75
❑ 61 Vinny Testaverde	1.50	.45
❑ 62 Wayne Chrebet	1.50	.45
❑ 63 Curtis Martin	2.50	.75
❑ 64 Tim Brown	2.50	.75
❑ 65 Rich Gannon	2.50	.75
❑ 66 Tyrone Wheatley	1.50	.45
❑ 67 Duce Staley	2.50	.75
❑ 68 Donovan McNabb	3.00	.90
❑ 69 Kordell Stewart	1.50	.45
❑ 70 Jerome Bettis	2.50	.75
❑ 71 Marshall Faulk	3.00	.90
❑ 72 Kurt Warner	5.00	1.50
❑ 73 Isaac Bruce	2.50	.75
❑ 74 Doug Flutie	2.50	.75
❑ 75 Curtis Conway	1.50	.45
❑ 76 Jeff Garcia	2.50	.75
❑ 77 Jerry Rice	5.00	1.50
❑ 78 Charlie Garner	1.50	.45
❑ 79 Terrell Owens	2.50	.75
❑ 80 Ricky Watters	1.00	.30
❑ 81 Matt Hasselbeck	1.50	.45
❑ 82 Levon Kirkland	1.00	.30
❑ 83 Keyshawn Johnson	2.50	.75
❑ 84 Brad Johnson	2.50	.75
❑ 85 Mike Alstott	2.50	.75
❑ 86 Eddie George	2.50	.75
❑ 87 Steve McNair	2.50	.75
❑ 88 Jeff George	1.50	.45
❑ 89 Michael Westbrook	2.50	.75
❑ 90 Stephen Davis	2.50	.75
❑ 91 Michael Vick JSY RC	100.00	30.00
❑ 92 Chris Weinke JSY RC	15.00	4.50
❑ 93 Drew Brees JSY RC	30.00	9.00
❑ 94 Deuce McAllister JSY RC	30.00	9.00
❑ 95 Michael Bennett JSY RC	30.00	9.00
❑ 96 LaDainian Tomlinson JSY RC	40.00	12.00
❑ 97 Kevan Barlow JSY RC	15.00	4.50
❑ 98 Travis Minor JSY RC	12.00	3.60
❑ 99 Rudi Johnson JSY RC	30.00	9.00
❑ 100 Todd Heap JSY RC	15.00	4.50
❑ 101 Freddie Mitchell JSY RC	15.00	4.50
❑ 102 Santana Moss JSY RC	25.00	7.50
❑ 103 Reggie Wayne JSY RC	25.00	7.50
❑ 104 Koren Robinson JSY RC	15.00	4.50
❑ 105 Josh Heupel JSY RC	15.00	4.50
❑ 106 Rod Gardner JSY RC	15.00	4.50
❑ 107 Quincy Morgan JSY RC	15.00	4.50
❑ 108 Chad Johnson JSY RC	30.00	9.00
❑ 109 Dan Morgan JSY RC	15.00	4.50
❑ 110 Gerard Warren JSY RC	15.00	4.50
❑ 111 Chris Chambers JSY RC	20.00	6.00
❑ 112 James Jackson JSY RC	15.00	4.50
❑ 113 Jesse Palmer JSY RC	15.00	4.50
❑ 114 Sage Rosenfels JSY RC	15.00	4.50
❑ 115 Mike McMahon JSY RC	15.00	4.50
❑ 116 M.Tuiasosopo JSY RC	15.00	4.50
❑ 117 Robert Ferguson JSY RC	15.00	4.50
❑ 118 Travis Henry JSY RC	20.00	6.00
❑ 119 Richard Seymour JSY RC	15.00	4.50
❑ 120 Andre Carter JSY RC	15.00	4.50
❑ 121 LaMont Jordan RC	10.00	3.00
❑ 122 Vinny Sutherland RC	5.00	1.50
❑ 123 Nate Clements RC	8.00	2.40
❑ 124 David Terrell RC	8.00	2.40
❑ 125 A.J. Feeley RC	8.00	2.40
❑ 126 David Rivers RC	5.00	1.50
❑ 127 Snoop Minnis RC	5.00	1.50
❑ 128 Josh Booty RC	8.00	2.40
❑ 129 Correll Buckhalter RC	10.00	3.00
❑ 130 Will Allen RC	5.00	1.50
❑ 131 Dan Alexander RC	8.00	2.40
❑ 132 Leonard Davis RC	5.00	1.50
❑ 133 Anthony Thomas RC	15.00	4.50
❑ 134 Alge Crumpler RC	10.00	3.00
❑ 135 Jamal Reynolds RC	8.00	2.40
❑ 136 Ken-Yon Rambo RC	5.00	1.50
❑ 137 Bobby Newcombe RC	5.00	1.50
❑ 138 Alex Bannister RC	5.00	1.50
❑ 139 Jabari Holloway RC	5.00	1.50
❑ 140 Jamar Fletcher RC	5.00	1.50
❑ 141 Adam Archuleta RC	8.00	2.40
❑ 142 Heath Evans RC	5.00	1.50
❑ 143 Scotty Anderson RC	5.00	1.50
❑ 144 Moran Norris RC	3.00	.90
❑ 145 Justin Smith RC	8.00	2.40
❑ 146 Quincy Carter RC	8.00	2.40
❑ 147 Ronney Daniels RC	3.00	.90
❑ 148 Ben Leard RC	5.00	1.50
❑ 149 Fred Smoot RC	8.00	2.40
❑ 150 Milton Wynn RC	5.00	1.50

2003 SP Game Used Edition

	Nm-Mt	Ex-Mt
COMP.SET w/o SP's (90)	60.00	18.00
❑ 1 Chad Hutchinson	2.00	.60
❑ 2 Quincy Carter	2.00	.60
❑ 3 Joey Galloway	2.00	.60
❑ 4 Kerry Collins	2.00	.60
❑ 5 Jeremy Shockey	5.00	1.50
❑ 6 Amani Toomer	2.00	.60
❑ 7 A.J. Feeley	2.00	.60
❑ 8 Duce Staley	2.00	.60
❑ 9 Dorsey Levens	1.25	.35
❑ 10 Ladell Betts	2.00	.60
❑ 11 Patrick Ramsey	3.00	.90
❑ 12 Anthony Thomas	3.00	.90
❑ 13 Marty Booker	2.00	.60
❑ 14 Brian Urlacher	5.00	1.50
❑ 15 Joey Harrington	5.00	1.50
❑ 16 James Stewart	2.00	.60
❑ 17 Az-Zahir Hakim	1.25	.35
❑ 18 Donald Driver	2.00	.60
❑ 19 Javon Walker	2.00	.60
❑ 20 Kordell Stewart	2.00	.60
❑ 21 Randy Moss	5.00	1.50
❑ 22 Shaun Hill	1.25	.35
❑ 23 Brian Finneran	1.25	.35
❑ 24 T.J. Duckett	2.00	.60
❑ 25 Warrick Dunn	2.00	.60
❑ 26 Rodney Peete	1.25	.35
❑ 27 Stephen Davis	2.00	.60
❑ 28 Muhsin Muhammad	2.00	.60
❑ 29 Aaron Brooks	3.00	.90
❑ 30 Deuce McAllister	3.00	.90
❑ 31 Joe Horn	2.00	.60
❑ 32 Keyshawn Johnson	3.00	.90
❑ 33 Brad Johnson	2.00	.60
❑ 34 Keenan McCardell	1.25	.35
❑ 35 Jake Plummer	2.00	.60
❑ 36 Josh McCown	2.00	.60
❑ 37 Thomas Jones	2.00	.60
❑ 38 Tai Streets	1.25	.35
❑ 39 Kevan Barlow	2.00	.60
❑ 40 Garrison Hearst	2.00	.60
❑ 41 Maurice Morris	1.25	.35
❑ 42 Matt Hasselbeck	2.00	.60
❑ 43 Koren Robinson	2.00	.60
❑ 44 Marc Bulger	3.00	.90
❑ 45 Trung Canidate	2.00	.60
❑ 46 Emmitt Smith	8.00	2.40
❑ 47 Alex Van Pelt	1.25	.35
❑ 48 Travis Henry	2.00	.60
❑ 49 Eric Moulds	2.00	.60
❑ 50 Jason Taylor	1.25	.35
❑ 51 Jay Fiedler	2.00	.60
❑ 52 Randy McMichael	2.00	.60
❑ 53 Tom Brady	5.00	1.50
❑ 54 Antowain Smith	2.00	.60

❑ 55 Troy Brown 2.00 .60
❑ 56 Curtis Martin 3.00 .90
❑ 57 Vinny Testaverde 2.00 .60
❑ 58 Santana Moss 2.00 .60
❑ 59 Jamal Lewis 3.00 .90
❑ 60 Chris Redman 1.25 .35
❑ 61 Ray Lewis 3.00 .90
❑ 62 Jon Kitna 2.00 .60
❑ 63 Peter Warrick 2.00 .60
❑ 64 Kelly Holcomb 2.00 .60
❑ 65 William Green 2.00 .60
❑ 66 Kevin Johnson 2.00 .60
❑ 67 Amos Zereoue 2.00 .60
❑ 68 Tommy Maddox 3.00 .90
❑ 69 Hines Ward 3.00 .90
❑ 70 Corey Bradford 1.25 .35
❑ 71 Jonathan Wells 1.25 .35
❑ 72 Jabar Gaffney 2.00 .60
❑ 73 Edgerrin James 3.00 .90
❑ 74 David Garrard 1.25 .35
❑ 75 Mark Brunell 2.00 .60
❑ 76 Jimmy Smith 2.00 .60
❑ 77 Steve McNair 3.00 .90
❑ 78 Kevin Dyson 2.00 .60
❑ 79 Terrell Davis 3.00 .90
❑ 80 Shannon Sharpe 2.00 .60
❑ 81 Rod Smith 2.00 .60
❑ 82 Trent Green 2.00 .60
❑ 83 Priest Holmes 4.00 1.20
❑ 84 Tony Gonzalez 2.00 .60
❑ 85 Jerry Rice 6.00 1.80
❑ 86 Charlie Garner 2.00 .60
❑ 87 Jerry Porter 2.00 .60
❑ 88 Reche Caldwell 1.25 .35
❑ 89 Tim Dwight 2.00 .60
❑ 90 Junior Seau 3.00 .90
❑ 91 Carson Palmer RC 40.00 12.00
❑ 92 Byron Leftwich RC 50.00 15.00
❑ 93 Dave Ragone RC 12.00 3.60
❑ 94 Kyle Boller RC 30.00 9.00
❑ 95 Rex Grossman RC 30.00 9.00
❑ 96 Chris Simms RC 25.00 7.50
❑ 97 Kliff Kingsbury RC 10.00 3.00
❑ 98 Jason Gesser RC 12.00 3.60
❑ 99 Brad Banks RC 10.00 3.00
❑ 100 Ken Dorsey RC 20.00 6.00
❑ 101 Juston Wood RC 6.00 1.80
❑ 102 Brian St.Pierre RC 12.00 3.60
❑ 103 Domanick Davis RC 25.00 7.50
❑ 104 Quentin Griffin RC 30.00 9.00
❑ 105 B.J. Askew RC 12.00 3.60
❑ 106 Onterrio Smith RC 15.00 4.50
❑ 107 Seneca Wallace RC 12.00 3.60
❑ 108 Artose Pinner RC 12.00 3.60
❑ 109 Justin Fargas RC 12.00 3.60
❑ 110 Chris Brown RC 25.00 7.50
❑ 111 Willis McGahee RC 30.00 9.00
❑ 112 Larry Johnson RC 25.00 7.50
❑ 113 Lee Suggs RC 25.00 7.50
❑ 114 Billy McMullen RC 10.00 3.00
❑ 115 Sultan McCullough RC 10.00 3.00
❑ 116 Musa Smith RC 12.00 3.60
❑ 117 Earnest Graham RC 10.00 3.00
❑ 118 Antwone Savage RC 6.00 1.80
❑ 119 Kirk Farmer RC 6.00 1.80
❑ 120 Kareem Kelly RC 10.00 3.00
❑ 121 J.R. Tolver RC 10.00 3.00
❑ 122 Tyrone Calico RC 15.00 4.50
❑ 123 Kevin Curtis RC 12.00 3.60
❑ 124 Bobby Wade RC 12.00 3.60
❑ 125 Justin Gage RC 12.00 3.60
❑ 126 Bryant Johnson RC 12.00 3.60
❑ 127 Doug Gabriel RC 12.00 3.60
❑ 128 Teyo Johnson RC 12.00 3.60
❑ 129 Brandon Lloyd RC 15.00 4.50
❑ 130 Kelley Washington RC 12.00 3.60
❑ 131 Talman Gardner RC 12.00 3.60
❑ 132 Anquan Boldin RC 30.00 9.00
❑ 133 Taylor Jacobs RC 12.00 3.60
❑ 134 Andre Johnson RC 30.00 9.00
❑ 135 Charles Rogers RC 15.00 4.50
❑ 136 Antonio Bryant JSY 12.00 3.60
❑ 137 Donovan McNabb JSY/99 30.00 9.00
❑ 138 Rod Gardner JSY 8.00 2.40
❑ 139 Ahman Green JSY 12.00 3.60
❑ 140 Brett Favre JSY/99 40.00 12.00
❑ 141 Daunte Culpepper JSY 12.00 3.60
❑ 142 Michael Bennett JSY 12.00 3.60
❑ 143 Michael Vick JSY/99 50.00 15.00
❑ 144 Jeff Garcia JSY 15.00 4.50
❑ 145 Terrell Owens JSY 12.00 3.60
❑ 146 Shaun Alexander JSY 12.00 3.60
❑ 147 Torry Holt JSY 12.00 3.60
❑ 148 Isaac Bruce JSY 10.00 3.00
❑ 149 Marshall Faulk JSY/99 20.00 6.00
❑ 150 Kurt Warner JSY/99 25.00 7.50
❑ 151 Drew Bledsoe JSY 12.00 3.60
❑ 152 Josh Reed JSY 10.00 3.00
❑ 153 Peerless Price JSY 10.00 3.00
❑ 154 David Boston JSY 10.00 3.00
❑ 155 Ricky Williams JSY/99 25.00 7.50
❑ 156 Chris Chambers JSY 12.00 3.60
❑ 157 Wayne Chrebet JSY 10.00 3.00
❑ 158 Chad Pennington JSY/99 25.00 7.50
❑ 159 Laveranues Coles JSY 10.00 3.00
❑ 160 Corey Dillon JSY 10.00 3.00
❑ 161 Tim Couch JSY 8.00 2.40
❑ 162 Jerome Bettis JSY 12.00 3.60
❑ 163 Plaxico Burress JSY 12.00 3.60
❑ 164 Antwaan Randle El JSY 12.00 3.60
❑ 165 David Carr JSY/99 30.00 9.00
❑ 166 Marvin Harrison JSY 10.00 3.00
❑ 167 Peyton Manning JSY 15.00 4.50
❑ 168 Fred Taylor JSY 10.00 3.00
❑ 169 Eddie George JSY 10.00 3.00
❑ 170 Clinton Portis JSY/99 30.00 9.00
❑ 171 Ashley Lelie JSY 10.00 3.00
❑ 172 Rich Gannon JSY 12.00 3.60
❑ 173 Phillip Buchanon JSY 10.00 3.00
❑ 174 Tim Brown JSY 12.00 3.60
❑ 175 LaDainian Tomlinson JSY 12.00 3.60
❑ 176 Drew Brees JSY/99 30.00 9.00
❑ 177 Jason Johnson RC 6.00 1.80
❑ 178 Sam Aiken RC 10.00 3.00
❑ 179 Nate Burleson RC 20.00 6.00
❑ 180 Tony Romo RC 12.00 3.60
❑ 181 Arnaz Battle RC 12.00 3.60

2003 SP Game Used Edition Gold Rookies

MINT NRMT

*GOLD: .8X TO 2X BASIC CARDS

2004 SP Game Used Edition

Nm-Mt Ex-Mt

ROOKIE STATED ODDS 1:4
ROOKIE PRINT RUN 425 SER.#'d SETS

❑ 1 Anquan Boldin 3.00 .90
❑ 2 Marcel Shipp 2.00 .60
❑ 3 Josh McCown 2.00 .60
❑ 4 Michael Vick 6.00 1.80
❑ 5 T.J. Duckett 2.00 .60
❑ 6 Peerless Price 2.00 .60
❑ 7 Jamal Lewis 3.00 .90
❑ 8 Todd Heap 2.00 .60
❑ 9 Kyle Boller 3.00 .90
❑ 10 Drew Bledsoe 3.00 .90
❑ 11 Travis Henry 2.00 .60
❑ 12 Eric Moulds 2.00 .60
❑ 13 Jake Delhomme 3.00 .90
❑ 14 Stephen Davis 2.00 .60
❑ 15 Julius Peppers 3.00 .90
❑ 16 Anthony Thomas 2.00 .60
❑ 17 Rex Grossman 3.00 .90
❑ 18 Brian Urlacher 4.00 1.20
❑ 19 Carson Palmer 4.00 1.20
❑ 20 Chad Johnson 2.00 .60
❑ 21 Rudi Johnson 2.00 .60
❑ 22 Jeff Garcia 3.00 .90
❑ 23 Dennis Northcutt 1.25 .35
❑ 24 Andre Davis 1.25 .35
❑ 25 Quincy Carter 2.00 .60
❑ 26 Roy Williams S 2.00 .60
❑ 27 Keyshawn Johnson 2.00 .60
❑ 28 Quentin Griffin 3.00 .90
❑ 29 Jake Plummer 2.00 .60
❑ 30 Ashley Lelie 2.00 .60
❑ 31 Shannon Sharpe 2.00 .60
❑ 32 Joey Harrington 3.00 .90
❑ 33 Charles Rogers 2.00 .60
❑ 34 Az-Zahir Hakim 1.25 .35
❑ 35 Brett Favre 8.00 2.40
❑ 36 Javon Walker 2.00 .60
❑ 37 Ahman Green 3.00 .90
❑ 38 Andre Johnson 3.00 .90
❑ 39 David Carr 3.00 .90
❑ 40 Domanick Davis 3.00 .90
❑ 41 Peyton Manning 5.00 1.50
❑ 42 Edgerrin James 3.00 .90
❑ 43 Marvin Harrison 3.00 .90
❑ 44 Byron Leftwich 5.00 1.50
❑ 45 Fred Taylor 2.00 .60
❑ 46 Jimmy Smith 2.00 .60
❑ 47 Priest Holmes 4.00 1.20
❑ 48 Trent Green 2.00 .60
❑ 49 Dante Hall 3.00 .90
❑ 50 Tony Gonzalez 2.00 .60
❑ 51 Ricky Williams 3.00 .90
❑ 52 Jay Fiedler 1.25 .35
❑ 53 Chris Chambers 2.00 .60
❑ 54 Randy Moss 4.00 1.20
❑ 55 Daunte Culpepper 3.00 .90
❑ 56 Moe Williams 1.25 .35
❑ 57 Tom Brady 5.00 1.50
❑ 58 Deion Branch 3.00 .90
❑ 59 Corey Dillon 2.00 .60
❑ 60 Deuce McAllister 3.00 .90
❑ 61 Aaron Brooks 2.00 .60
❑ 62 Joe Horn 2.00 .60
❑ 63 Jeremy Shockey 3.00 .90
❑ 64 Amani Toomer 2.00 .60
❑ 65 Michael Strahan 2.00 .60
❑ 66 Curtis Martin 3.00 .90
❑ 67 Chad Pennington 4.00 1.20
❑ 68 Santana Moss 2.00 .60
❑ 69 Jerry Rice 6.00 1.80
❑ 70 Tim Brown 3.00 .90
❑ 71 Warren Sapp 2.00 .60
❑ 72 Donovan McNabb 4.00 1.20
❑ 73 Brian Westbrook 2.00 .60
❑ 74 Terrell Owens 3.00 .90
❑ 75 Hines Ward 3.00 .90
❑ 76 Plaxico Burress 2.00 .60
❑ 77 Duce Staley 2.00 .60
❑ 78 LaDainian Tomlinson 3.00 .90
❑ 79 Quentin Jammer 1.25 .35

❑ 80 Drew Brees	3.00	.90
❑ 81 Brandon Lloyd	2.00	.60
❑ 82 Kevan Barlow	2.00	.60
❑ 83 Tim Rattay	2.00	.60
❑ 84 Matt Hasselbeck	2.00	.60
❑ 85 Shaun Alexander	3.00	.90
❑ 86 Darrell Jackson	2.00	.60
❑ 87 Marc Bulger	3.00	.90
❑ 88 Torry Holt	3.00	.90
❑ 89 Marshall Faulk	3.00	.90
❑ 90 Isaac Bruce	2.00	.60
❑ 91 Brad Johnson	2.00	.60
❑ 92 Derrick Brooks	2.00	.60
❑ 93 Joey Galloway	2.00	.60
❑ 94 Steve McNair	3.00	.90
❑ 95 Derrick Mason	2.00	.60
❑ 96 Eddie George	2.00	.60
❑ 97 Clinton Portis	3.00	.90
❑ 98 Mark Brunell	2.00	.60
❑ 99 Laveranues Coles	2.00	.60
❑ 100 LaVar Arrington	6.00	1.80
❑ 101 Ben Troupe RC	12.00	3.60
❑ 102 Chris Gamble RC	15.00	4.50
❑ 103 DeAngelo Hall RC	15.00	4.50
❑ 104 Dunta Robinson RC	12.00	3.60
❑ 105 Jason Shivers RC	6.00	1.80
❑ 106 Keary Colbert RC	15.00	4.50
❑ 107 Craig Krenzel RC	12.00	3.60
❑ 108 Philip Rivers RC	40.00	12.00
❑ 109 Roy Williams RC	40.00	12.00
❑ 110 Will Allen RC	12.00	3.60
❑ 111 Bob Sanders RC	12.00	3.60
❑ 112 Kris Wilson RC	12.00	3.60
❑ 113 D.J. Williams RC	15.00	4.50
❑ 114 Devery Henderson RC	10.00	3.00
❑ 115 Carlos Francis RC	10.00	3.00
❑ 116 Jonathan Vilma RC	12.00	3.60
❑ 117 Luke McCown RC	12.00	3.60
❑ 118 Michael Turner RC	10.00	3.00
❑ 119 Richard Seigler RC	10.00	3.00
❑ 120 Jared Lorenzen RC	10.00	3.00
❑ 121 P.K. Sam RC	10.00	3.00
❑ 122 Justin Smiley RC	12.00	3.60
❑ 123 Marquise Hill RC	10.00	3.00
❑ 124 Ernest Wilford RC	12.00	3.60
❑ 125 Jerricho Cotchery RC	12.00	3.60
❑ 126 Kevin Jones RC	40.00	12.00
❑ 127 Michael Boulware RC	12.00	3.60
❑ 128 Jarrett Payton RC	12.00	3.60
❑ 129 Sean Taylor RC	15.00	4.50
❑ 130 Will Smith RC	12.00	3.60
❑ 131 Bernard Berrian RC	12.00	3.60
❑ 132 Ahmad Carroll RC	15.00	4.50
❑ 133 Derrick Hamilton RC	10.00	3.00
❑ 134 Dwan Edwards RC	6.00	1.80
❑ 135 Jeff Smoker RC	20.00	6.00
❑ 136 Kenechi Udeze RC	15.00	4.50
❑ 137 Mewelde Moore RC	20.00	6.00
❑ 138 Joey Thomas RC	12.00	3.60
❑ 139 Sean Jones RC	10.00	3.00
❑ 140 Will Poole RC	12.00	3.60
❑ 141 Casey Clausen RC	15.00	4.50
❑ 142 Stuart Schweigert RC	12.00	3.60
❑ 143 Cody Pickett RC	12.00	3.60
❑ 144 Derrick Strait RC	12.00	3.60
❑ 145 Greg Jones RC	12.00	3.60
❑ 146 John Navarre RC	12.00	3.60
❑ 147 Larry Fitzgerald RC	40.00	12.00
❑ 148 Michael Clayton RC	30.00	9.00
❑ 149 Rashaun Woods RC	15.00	4.50
❑ 150 Shawn Andrews RC	12.00	3.60
❑ 151 B.J. Symons RC	12.00	3.60
❑ 152 Cedric Cobbs RC	12.00	3.60
❑ 153 Darius Watts RC	15.00	4.50
❑ 154 B.J. Johnson RC	10.00	3.00
❑ 155 Max Starks RC	10.00	3.00
❑ 156 Josh Harris RC	12.00	3.60
❑ 157 Kendrick Starling RC	6.00	1.80
❑ 158 Brandon Miree RC	10.00	3.00
❑ 159 Robert Gallery RC	20.00	6.00
❑ 160 Tatum Bell RC	20.00	6.00
❑ 161 Ben Hartsock RC	12.00	3.60
❑ 162 Derek Abney RC	12.00	3.60
❑ 163 Ricardo Colclough RC	12.00	3.60
❑ 164 Justin Jenkins RC	10.00	3.00
❑ 165 Chris Cooley RC	12.00	3.60
❑ 166 Julius Jones RC	50.00	15.00
❑ 167 Matt Mauck RC	12.00	3.60
❑ 168 Vernon Carey RC	10.00	3.00
❑ 169 John Standeford RC	10.00	3.00
❑ 170 Teddy Lehman RC	12.00	3.60
❑ 171 Ben Roethlisberger RC	120.00	36.00
❑ 172 Ben Utecht RC	6.00	1.80
❑ 173 D.J. Hackett RC	10.00	3.00
❑ 174 Drew Henson RC	30.00	9.00
❑ 175 Rich Gardner RC	10.00	3.00
❑ 176 Karlos Dansby RC	12.00	3.60
❑ 177 Matt Schaub RC	20.00	6.00
❑ 178 Darrion Scott RC	12.00	3.60
❑ 179 Keyaron Fox RC	10.00	3.00
❑ 180 Tommie Harris RC	15.00	4.50
❑ 181 Ben Watson RC	12.00	3.60
❑ 182 Chris Perry RC	25.00	7.50
❑ 183 Travelle Wharton RC	6.00	1.80
❑ 184 Eli Manning RC	80.00	24.00
❑ 185 Demorrio Williams RC	12.00	3.60
❑ 186 Kellen Winslow RC	30.00	9.00
❑ 187 Jason Babin RC	12.00	3.60
❑ 188 Quincy Wilson RC	10.00	3.00
❑ 189 Samie Parker RC	12.00	3.60
❑ 190 Vince Wilfork RC	12.00	3.60
❑ 191 Antwan Odom RC	12.00	3.60
❑ 192 Josh Davis RC	10.00	3.00
❑ 193 Courtney Watson RC	12.00	3.60
❑ 194 Devard Darling RC	12.00	3.60
❑ 195 J.P. Losman RC	30.00	9.00
❑ 196 Johnnie Morant RC	12.00	3.60
❑ 197 Lee Evans RC	20.00	6.00
❑ 198 Michael Jenkins RC	12.00	3.60
❑ 199 Reggie Williams RC	15.00	4.50
❑ 200 Steven Jackson RC	40.00	12.00

2004 SP Game Used Edition Gold

Nm-Mt Ex-Mt

*GOLD VETERANS: 1.2X TO 3X BASIC CARDS
VETERAN 1-100 STATED ODDS 1:7
VETERAN PRINT RUN 100 SER.#'d SETS
*GOLD ROOKIES: 1X TO 2.5X BASIC CARDS
ROOKIES PRINT RUN 50 SER.#'d SETS

2002 SP Legendary Cuts

	Nm-Mt	Ex-Mt
COMP.SET w/o SP's (90)	40.00	12.00
❑ 1 Tom Brady	3.00	.90
❑ 2 Antowain Smith	.75	.23
❑ 3 Troy Brown	.75	.23
❑ 4 Drew Bledsoe	1.50	.45
❑ 5 Travis Henry	1.25	.35
❑ 6 Eric Moulds	.75	.23
❑ 7 Ricky Williams	1.25	.35
❑ 8 Jay Fiedler	.75	.23
❑ 9 Chris Chambers	1.25	.35
❑ 10 Curtis Martin	1.25	.35
❑ 11 Chad Pennington	1.50	.45
❑ 12 Wayne Chrebet	.75	.23
❑ 13 Jerome Bettis	1.25	.35
❑ 14 Tommy Maddox	3.00	.90
❑ 15 Hines Ward	1.25	.35
❑ 16 Tim Couch	.75	.23
❑ 17 Kevin Johnson	.75	.23
❑ 18 Jamal Lewis	1.25	.35
❑ 19 Chris Redman	.50	.15
❑ 20 Corey Dillon	.75	.23
❑ 21 Michael Westbrook	.50	.15
❑ 22 Peyton Manning	2.50	.75
❑ 23 Edgerrin James	1.50	.45
❑ 24 Marvin Harrison	1.25	.35
❑ 25 Qadry Ismail	.75	.23
❑ 26 Mark Brunell	1.25	.35
❑ 27 Jimmy Smith	.75	.23
❑ 28 Stacey Mack	.50	.15
❑ 29 Fred Taylor	1.25	.35
❑ 30 Steve McNair	1.25	.35
❑ 31 Eddie George	1.25	.35
❑ 32 Kevin Dyson	.75	.23
❑ 33 James Allen	.75	.23
❑ 34 Corey Bradford	.50	.15
❑ 35 Shannon Sharpe	.75	.23
❑ 36 Brian Griese	1.25	.35
❑ 37 Ed McCaffrey	1.25	.35
❑ 38 Jerry Rice	2.50	.75
❑ 39 Rich Gannon	1.25	.35
❑ 40 Tim Brown	1.25	.35
❑ 41 Trent Green	.75	.23
❑ 42 Priest Holmes	1.50	.45
❑ 43 Tony Gonzalez	.75	.23
❑ 44 LaDainian Tomlinson	2.00	.60
❑ 45 Drew Brees	1.25	.35
❑ 46 Curtis Conway	.50	.15
❑ 47 Donovan McNabb	1.50	.45
❑ 48 Duce Staley	1.25	.35
❑ 49 Antonio Freeman	1.25	.35
❑ 50 James Thrash	.75	.23
❑ 51 Kerry Collins	.75	.23
❑ 52 Tiki Barber	.75	.23
❑ 53 Amani Toomer	.75	.23
❑ 54 Emmitt Smith	3.00	.90
❑ 55 Quincy Carter	.75	.23
❑ 56 Joey Galloway	.75	.23
❑ 57 Stephen Davis	.75	.23
❑ 58 Champ Bailey	.75	.23
❑ 59 Anthony Thomas	1.25	.35
❑ 60 Jim Miller	.75	.23
❑ 61 Brian Urlacher	2.00	.60
❑ 62 Brett Favre	3.00	.90
❑ 63 Ahman Green	1.25	.35
❑ 64 Robert Ferguson	.50	.15
❑ 65 Randy Moss	2.50	.75
❑ 66 Daunte Culpepper	1.25	.35
❑ 67 Moe Williams	.50	.15
❑ 68 James Stewart	.75	.23
❑ 69 Az-Zahir Hakim	.50	.15
❑ 70 Keyshawn Johnson	1.25	.35
❑ 71 Brad Johnson	.75	.23
❑ 72 Mike Alstott	1.25	.35
❑ 73 Michael Vick	4.00	1.20
❑ 74 Warrick Dunn	1.25	.35
❑ 75 Shawn Jefferson	.50	.15
❑ 76 Aaron Brooks	1.25	.35
❑ 77 Deuce McAllister	1.50	.45
❑ 78 Joe Horn	.75	.23
❑ 79 Rodney Peete	.75	.23
❑ 80 Steve Smith	.75	.23
❑ 81 Terrell Owens	1.25	.35
❑ 82 Jeff Garcia	1.25	.35
❑ 83 Garrison Hearst	.75	.23
❑ 84 Kurt Warner	1.25	.35
❑ 85 Marshall Faulk	1.25	.35
❑ 86 Torry Holt	1.25	.35
❑ 87 Jake Plummer	.75	.23
❑ 88 David Boston	1.25	.35
❑ 89 Shaun Alexander	1.25	.35
❑ 90 Trent Dilfer	.75	.23
❑ 91 Tom Brady VM	5.00	1.50
❑ 92 Michael Vick VM	6.00	1.80

Card	Nm-Mt	Ex-Mt
❑ 93 LaDainian Tomlinson VM	3.00	.90
❑ 94 Rich Gannon VM	2.00	.60
❑ 95 Randy Moss VM	4.00	1.20
❑ 96 Aaron Brooks VM	2.00	.60
❑ 97 Mark Brunell VM	2.00	.60
❑ 98 Jeff Garcia VM	2.00	.60
❑ 99 Ahman Green VM	2.00	.60
❑ 100 Shaun Alexander VM	2.00	.60
❑ 101 Ricky Williams TG	2.50	.75
❑ 102 Bruce Smith TG	1.50	.45
❑ 103 Curtis Martin TG	2.50	.75
❑ 104 Brian Urlacher TG	4.00	1.20
❑ 105 Jerome Bettis TG	2.50	.75
❑ 106 Ray Lewis TG	2.50	.75
❑ 107 Edgerrin James TG	3.00	.90
❑ 108 Junior Seau TG	2.50	.75
❑ 109 Priest Holmes TG	3.00	.90
❑ 110 Warren Sapp TG	1.50	.45
❑ 111 Emmitt Smith RI	10.00	3.00
❑ 112 Jerry Rice RI	8.00	2.40
❑ 113 Brett Favre RI	10.00	3.00
❑ 114 Marshall Faulk RI	4.00	1.20
❑ 115 Drew Bledsoe RI	5.00	1.50
❑ 116 Tim Brown RI	4.00	1.20
❑ 117 Donovan McNabb RI	5.00	1.50
❑ 118 Peyton Manning RI	8.00	2.40
❑ 119 Kurt Warner RI	4.00	1.20
❑ 120 Shannon Sharpe RI	2.50	.75
❑ 121 Andre Davis RC	8.00	2.40
❑ 122 Antonio Bryant RC	8.00	2.40
❑ 123 Antwaan Randle El RC	10.00	3.00
❑ 124 Ashley Lelie RC	15.00	4.50
❑ 125 Ben Leber RC	8.00	2.40
❑ 126 Chad Hutchinson RC	8.00	2.40
❑ 127 Clinton Portis RC	25.00	7.50
❑ 128 David Carr RC	25.00	7.50
❑ 129 Deion Branch RC	15.00	4.50
❑ 130 DeShaun Foster RC	8.00	2.40
❑ 131 Donte Stallworth RC	15.00	4.50
❑ 132 Jabar Gaffney RC	8.00	2.40
❑ 133 Javon Walker RC	15.00	4.50
❑ 134 Jeremy Shockey RC	25.00	7.50
❑ 135 Joey Harrington RC	25.00	7.50
❑ 136 Josh McCown RC	10.00	3.00
❑ 137 Josh Reed RC	8.00	2.40
❑ 138 Julius Peppers RC	15.00	4.50
❑ 139 Marquise Walker RC	8.00	2.40
❑ 140 Maurice Morris RC	8.00	2.40
❑ 141 Patrick Ramsey RC	15.00	4.50
❑ 142 Quentin Jammer RC	8.00	2.40
❑ 143 Randy Fasani RC	8.00	2.40
❑ 144 Reche Caldwell RC	8.00	2.40
❑ 145 Rohan Davey RC	8.00	2.40
❑ 146 Ron Johnson RC	8.00	2.40
❑ 147 Roy Williams RC	20.00	6.00
❑ 148 T.J. Duckett RC	12.00	3.60
❑ 149 Travis Stephens RC	8.00	2.40
❑ 150 William Green RC	12.00	3.60
❑ 151 Albert Haynesworth RC	4.00	1.20
❑ 152 Alex Brown RC	5.00	1.50
❑ 153 Andra Davis RC	4.00	1.20
❑ 154 Andre Gurode RC	4.00	1.20
❑ 155 Anthony Weaver RC	4.00	1.20
❑ 156 Brandon Doman RC	5.00	1.50
❑ 157 Brian Westbrook RC	8.00	2.40
❑ 158 Brian Williams RC	2.50	.75
❑ 159 Lamont Brightful RC	2.50	.75
❑ 160 Charles Grant RC	5.00	1.50
❑ 161 Chester Taylor RC	5.00	1.50
❑ 162 Cliff Russell RC	4.00	1.20
❑ 163 Daniel Graham RC	5.00	1.50
❑ 164 David Garrard RC	5.00	1.50
❑ 165 James Mungro RC	5.00	1.50
❑ 166 Dennis Johnson RC	2.50	.75
❑ 167 Derek Ross RC	4.00	1.20
❑ 168 Dwight Freeney RC	6.00	1.80
❑ 169 Ed Reed RC	8.00	2.40
❑ 170 Carlos Hall RC	5.00	1.50
❑ 171 Jarrod Baxter RC	4.00	1.20
❑ 172 Jason McAddley RC	4.00	1.20
❑ 173 Jerramy Stevens RC	5.00	1.50
❑ 174 Jesse Chatman RC	5.00	1.50
❑ 175 John Henderson RC	5.00	1.50
❑ 176 Jon McGraw RC	2.50	.75
❑ 177 Jonathan Wells RC	5.00	1.50
❑ 178 Justin Peelle RC	2.50	.75
❑ 179 Kalimba Edwards RC	5.00	1.50
❑ 180 Keyou Craver RC	4.00	1.20
❑ 181 Kurt Kittner RC	4.00	1.20
❑ 182 LaDell Betts RC	5.00	1.50
❑ 183 Lamar Gordon RC	5.00	1.50
❑ 184 Lamont Thompson RC	4.00	1.20
❑ 185 Larry Tripplett RC	2.50	.75
❑ 186 Randy McMichael RC	8.00	2.40
❑ 187 Lito Sheppard RC	5.00	1.50
❑ 188 Marques Anderson RC	5.00	1.50
❑ 189 Michael Lewis RC	5.00	1.50
❑ 190 Mike Pearson RC	2.50	.75
❑ 191 Mike Rumph RC	5.00	1.50
❑ 192 Najeh Davenport RC	5.00	1.50
❑ 193 Napoleon Harris RC	5.00	1.50
❑ 194 Phillip Buchanon RC	5.00	1.50
❑ 195 Quinn Gray RC	2.50	.75
❑ 196 Raonall Smith RC	4.00	1.20
❑ 197 Ricky Williams RC	4.00	1.20
❑ 198 Robert Thomas RC	5.00	1.50
❑ 199 Rocky Calmus RC	5.00	1.50
❑ 200 Ryan Denney RC	2.50	.75
❑ 201 Ryan Sims RC	5.00	1.50
❑ 202 Jamal Robertson RC	4.00	1.20
❑ 203 Shaun Hill RC	5.00	1.50
❑ 204 Tank Williams RC	4.00	1.20
❑ 205 Tellis Redmon RC	4.00	1.20
❑ 206 Tim Carter RC	4.00	1.20
❑ 207 Tony Fisher RC	5.00	1.50
❑ 208 Travis Fisher RC	5.00	1.50
❑ 209 Verron Haynes RC	5.00	1.50
❑ 210 Wendell Bryant RC	5.00	1.50

2002 SP Legendary Cuts Autographs

	Nm-Mt	Ex-Mt
❑ LCAH Arnie Herber/25	450.00	135.00
❑ LCAW Alex Wojciechowicz/28	250.00	75.00
❑ LCBG Bill George/8		
❑ LCBL Bobby Layne/4		
❑ LCBN Bronko Nagurski/75	300.00	90.00
❑ LCBU Buck Buchanan/8		
❑ LCBW Bob Waterfield/12		
❑ LCCN Jack Christiansen/3		
❑ LCDF Dan Fortmann/30	200.00	60.00
❑ LCJU Johnny Unitas/29	300.00	90.00
❑ LCKS Ken Strong/120	150.00	45.00
❑ LCLF Len Ford/4		
❑ LCLG Lou Groza/20		
❑ LCLL Link Lyman/11		
❑ LCMM Mike Michalske/7		
❑ LCMO Marion Motley/12		
❑ LCMU Johnny Unitas Peyton Manning/1		
❑ LCPS Emmitt Smith Walter Payton/1		
❑ LCPW Pop Warner/1		
❑ LCRB Red Badgro/57	150.00	45.00
❑ LCRF Ray Flaherty/25	200.00	60.00
❑ LCRG Red Grange/9		
❑ LCRN Ray Nitschke/115	200.00	60.00
❑ LCSL Sid Luckman/22		
❑ LCSO Steve Owen/5		
❑ LCTE Turk Edwards/12		
❑ LCTF Tom Fears/9		
❑ LCTL Tom Landry/20		
❑ LCVB Norm Van Brocklin/3		
❑ LCVL Vince Lombardi/240	350.00	105.00
❑ LCWP Walter Payton/65	500.00	150.00

1999 SP Signature

	Nm-Mt	Ex-Mt
COMPLETE SET (180)	400.00	180.00
COMP.SET w/o SP's (170)	100.00	45.00
❑ 1 Jake Plummer	1.00	.45
❑ 2 Mario Bates	.60	.25
❑ 3 Adrian Murrell	1.00	.45
❑ 4 Jamal Anderson	1.50	.70
❑ 5 Chris Chandler	1.00	.45
❑ 6 Bob Christian	.60	.25
❑ 7 O.J. Santiago	.60	.25
❑ 8 Jim Harbaugh	1.00	.45
❑ 9 Priest Holmes	2.50	1.10
❑ 10 Ray Lewis	1.50	.70
❑ 11 Michael Jackson	.60	.25
❑ 12 Tony Siragusa	.60	.25
❑ 13 Doug Flutie	1.50	.70
❑ 14 Antowain Smith	1.50	.70
❑ 15 Eric Moulds	1.50	.70
❑ 16 William Floyd	.60	.25
❑ 17 Fred Lane	.60	.25
❑ 18 Muhsin Muhammad	1.00	.45
❑ 19 Bobby Engram	1.00	.45
❑ 20 Curtis Enis	.60	.25
❑ 21 Curtis Conway	1.00	.45
❑ 22 Corey Dillon	1.50	.70
❑ 23 Carl Pickens	1.00	.45
❑ 24 Ashley Ambrose	.60	.25
❑ 25 Darnay Scott	.60	.25
❑ 26 Troy Aikman	3.00	1.35
❑ 27 Jason Garrett	.60	.25
❑ 28 Emmitt Smith	3.00	1.35
❑ 29 Deion Sanders	1.50	.70
❑ 30 John Elway	5.00	2.20
❑ 31 Terrell Davis	1.50	.70
❑ 32 Ed McCaffrey	1.00	.45
❑ 33 John Mobley	.60	.25
❑ 34 Maa Tanuvasa	.60	.25
❑ 35 Ray Crockett	.60	.25
❑ 36 Barry Sanders	5.00	2.20
❑ 37 Herman Moore	1.00	.45
❑ 38 Charlie Batch	1.50	.70
❑ 39 Robert Porcher	.60	.25
❑ 40 Tommy Vardell	.60	.25
❑ 41 Brett Favre	5.00	2.20
❑ 42 Antonio Freeman	1.50	.70
❑ 43 Darick Holmes	.60	.25
❑ 44 Robert Brooks	1.00	.45
❑ 45 Peyton Manning	6.00	2.70
❑ 46 Marshall Faulk	2.00	.90
❑ 47 Torrance Small	.60	.25
❑ 48 Lamont Warren	.60	.25
❑ 49 Zack Crockett	.60	.25

❑ 50 Mark Brunell	1.50	.70
❑ 51 Pete Mitchell	.60	.25
❑ 52 Fred Taylor	1.50	.70
❑ 53 Jimmy Smith	1.00	.45
❑ 54 Andre Rison	1.00	.45
❑ 55 Rich Gannon	1.50	.70
❑ 56 Donnell Bennett	.60	.25
❑ 57 Dan Marino	5.00	2.20
❑ 58 Karim Abdul-Jabbar	1.00	.45
❑ 59 Troy Drayton	.60	.25
❑ 60 Jason Taylor	.60	.25
❑ 61 Cris Carter	1.50	.70
❑ 62 Randy Moss	5.00	2.20
❑ 63 Robert Smith	1.50	.70
❑ 64 Leroy Hoard	.60	.25
❑ 65 Randall Cunningham	1.50	.70
❑ 66 Derrick Alexander DE	.60	.25
❑ 67 Drew Bledsoe	2.00	.90
❑ 68 Robert Edwards	.60	.25
❑ 69 Willie McGinest	.60	.25
❑ 70 Chris Slade	.60	.25
❑ 71 Terry Glenn	1.50	.70
❑ 72 Ty Law	1.00	.45
❑ 73 Kerry Collins	1.00	.45
❑ 74 Sean Dawkins	.60	.25
❑ 75 Cam Cleeland	.60	.25
❑ 76 Sammy Knight	.60	.25
❑ 77 Danny Kanell	.60	.25
❑ 78 Gary Brown	.60	.25
❑ 79 Chris Calloway	1.00	.45
❑ 80 Curtis Martin	1.50	.70
❑ 81 Keyshawn Johnson	1.50	.70
❑ 82 Vinny Testaverde	1.00	.45
❑ 83 Leon Johnson	.60	.25
❑ 84 Kyle Brady	.60	.25
❑ 85 Tim Brown	1.50	.70
❑ 86 Jeff George	1.00	.45
❑ 87 Rickey Dudley	.60	.25
❑ 88 Napoleon Kaufman	1.50	.70
❑ 89 James Jett	1.00	.45
❑ 90 Harvey Williams	.60	.25
❑ 91 Koy Detmer	.60	.25
❑ 92 Duce Staley	1.50	.70
❑ 93 Charlie Garner	1.00	.45
❑ 94 Jerome Bettis	1.50	.70
❑ 95 Kordell Stewart	1.00	.45
❑ 96 Courtney Hawkins	.60	.25
❑ 97 Hines Ward	1.50	.70
❑ 98 Isaac Bruce	1.50	.70
❑ 99 Tony Banks	1.00	.45
❑ 100 Greg Hill	.60	.25
❑ 101 Keith Lyle	.60	.25
❑ 102 Ryan Leaf	1.50	.70
❑ 103 Craig Whelihan	.60	.25
❑ 104 Charlie Jones	.60	.25
❑ 105 Junior Seau	1.50	.70
❑ 106 Natrone Means	1.00	.45
❑ 107 Rodney Harrison	.60	.25
❑ 108 Steve Young	2.00	.90
❑ 109 Garrison Hearst	1.00	.45
❑ 110 Jerry Rice	3.00	1.35
❑ 111 Chris Doleman	.60	.25
❑ 112 Roy Barker	.60	.25
❑ 113 Ricky Watters	1.00	.45
❑ 114 Jon Kitna	1.50	.70
❑ 115 Joey Galloway	1.00	.45
❑ 116 Chad Brown	.60	.25
❑ 117 Michael Sinclair	.60	.25
❑ 118 Warrick Dunn	1.50	.70
❑ 119 Mike Alstott	1.50	.70
❑ 120 Bert Emanuel	1.00	.45
❑ 121 Hardy Nickerson	.60	.25
❑ 122 Eddie George	1.50	.70
❑ 123 Steve McNair	1.50	.70
❑ 124 Yancey Thigpen	.60	.25
❑ 125 Frank Wycheck	.60	.25
❑ 126 Jackie Harris	.60	.25
❑ 127 Terry Allen	1.00	.45
❑ 128 Trent Green	1.50	.70
❑ 129 Jamie Asher	.60	.25
❑ 130 Brian Mitchell	.60	.25
❑ 131 Lance Alworth	1.50	.70
❑ 132 Fred Biletnikoff	1.50	.70
❑ 133 Mel Blount	.60	.25
❑ 134 Cliff Branch	.60	.25
❑ 135 Harold Carmichael	.60	.25
❑ 136 Larry Csonka	1.50	.70
❑ 137 Eric Dickerson	.60	.25
❑ 138 Randy Gradishar	.60	.25
❑ 139 Joe Greene	1.50	.70
❑ 140 Jack Ham	1.00	.45
❑ 141 Ted Hendricks	.60	.25
❑ 142 Charlie Joiner	.60	.25
❑ 143 Ed Jones	.60	.25
❑ 144 Billy Kilmer	.60	.25
❑ 145 Paul Krause	.60	.25
❑ 146 James Lofton	.60	.25
❑ 147 Archie Manning	1.00	.45
❑ 148 Don Maynard	.60	.25
❑ 149 Ozzie Newsome	.60	.25
❑ 150 Jim Otto	.60	.25
❑ 151 Lee Roy Selmon	.60	.25
❑ 152 Billy Sims	.60	.25
❑ 153 Mike Singletary	1.00	.45
❑ 154 Ken Stabler	1.50	.70
❑ 155 John Stallworth	1.00	.45
❑ 156 Roger Staubach	2.00	.90
❑ 157 Charley Taylor	.60	.25
❑ 158 Paul Warfield	1.50	.70
❑ 159 Kellen Winslow	.60	.25
❑ 160 Jack Youngblood	.60	.25
❑ 161 Bill Bergey	.60	.25
❑ 162 Raymond Berry	1.00	.45
❑ 163 Chuck Howley	.60	.25
❑ 164 Rocky Bleier	1.00	.45
❑ 165 Russ Francis	.60	.25
❑ 166 Drew Pearson	.60	.25
❑ 167 Mercury Morris	.60	.25
❑ 168 Dick Anderson	.60	.25
❑ 169 Earl Morrall	.60	.25
❑ 170 Jim Hart	.60	.25
❑ 171 Ricky Williams RC	12.00	5.50
❑ 172 Cade McNown RC	10.00	4.50
❑ 173 Tim Couch RC	12.00	5.50
❑ 174 Daunte Culpepper RC	25.00	11.00
❑ 175 Akili Smith RC	12.00	5.50
❑ 176 Brock Huard RC	12.00	5.50
❑ 177 Donovan McNabb RC	30.00	13.50
❑ 178 Michael Bishop RC	10.00	4.50
❑ 179 Shaun King RC	10.00	4.50
❑ 180 Torry Holt RC	20.00	9.00

1999 SP Signature Autographs

	Nm-Mt	Ex-Mt
❑ AA Ashley Ambrose	10.00	4.50
❑ AF Antonio Freeman	60.00	27.00
❑ AK Akili Smith	40.00	18.00
❑ AM Adrian Murrell	10.00	4.50
❑ AN Dick Anderson	10.00	4.50
❑ AS Antowain Smith	25.00	11.00
❑ BB Bill Bergey	15.00	6.75
❑ BC Bob Christian	10.00	4.50
❑ BE Bobby Engram	10.00	4.50
❑ BH Brock Huard	60.00	27.00
❑ BT Bert Emanuel	10.00	4.50
❑ CB Charlie Batch	10.00	4.50
❑ CC Chris Chandler	15.00	6.75
❑ CD Corey Dillon	25.00	11.00
❑ CE Curtis Enis	15.00	6.75
❑ CG Charlie Garner	15.00	6.75
❑ CJ Charlie Joiner	15.00	6.75
❑ CK Ray Crockett	10.00	4.50
❑ CL Cameron Cleeland	10.00	4.50
❑ CP Mike Singletary	25.00	11.00
❑ CS Chris Slade	10.00	4.50
❑ CT Charley Taylor	15.00	6.75
❑ CW Curtis Conway	15.00	6.75
❑ CY Chris Calloway	10.00	4.50
❑ DA Derrick Alexander DE	10.00	4.50
❑ DB Donnell Bennett	10.00	4.50
❑ DC Daunte Culpepper	250.00	110.00
❑ DE Roy Barker	10.00	4.50
❑ DH Darick Holmes	10.00	4.50
❑ DM Dan Marino	250.00	110.00
❑ DP Drew Pearson	25.00	11.00
❑ EG Eddie George	50.00	22.00
❑ EJ Ed Too Tall Jones	25.00	11.00
❑ EM Eric Moulds	25.00	11.00
❑ ES Emmitt Smith	300.00	135.00
❑ FL Fred Lane	25.00	11.00
❑ FW Frank Wycheck	15.00	6.75
❑ GA Joey Galloway	50.00	22.00
❑ GB Gary Brown	10.00	4.50
❑ GE Jeff George	40.00	18.00
❑ GH Garrison Hearst	25.00	11.00
❑ GN Trent Green	15.00	6.75
❑ GR Randy Gradishar	15.00	6.75
❑ HC Harold Carmichael	15.00	6.75
❑ HL Greg Hill	10.00	4.50
❑ HM Herman Moore	10.00	4.50
❑ HN Hardy Nickerson	10.00	4.50
❑ HT Jim Hart	15.00	6.75
❑ HV Harvey Williams	10.00	4.50
❑ HW Hines Ward	40.00	18.00
❑ HY Chuck Howley	15.00	6.75
❑ IB Isaac Bruce	25.00	11.00
❑ JG Jason Garrett	10.00	4.50
❑ JH Jack Ham	40.00	18.00
❑ JJ James Jett	10.00	4.50
❑ JK Jackie Harris	10.00	4.50
❑ JL James Lofton	25.00	11.00
❑ JM John Mobley	10.00	4.50
❑ JP Jake Plummer	100.00	45.00
❑ JR Junior Seau	150.00	70.00
❑ JS Jimmy Smith	15.00	6.75
❑ JT Jason Taylor	40.00	18.00
❑ JY Jack Youngblood	15.00	6.75
❑ KA Karim Abdul-Jabbar	10.00	4.50
❑ KB Kyle Brady	10.00	4.50
❑ KD Koy Detmer	15.00	6.75
❑ KI Jon Kitna	25.00	11.00
❑ KJ Keyshawn Johnson	50.00	22.00
❑ KL Keith Lyle	10.00	4.50
❑ KR Brian Mitchell	15.00	6.75
❑ KS Ken Stabler	30.00	13.50
❑ KW Kellen Winslow	25.00	11.00
❑ LB Chad Brown	10.00	4.50
❑ LH Leroy Hoard	10.00	4.50
❑ LJ Leon Johnson	10.00	4.50
❑ LS Lee Roy Selmon	15.00	6.75
❑ LW Lamont Warren	10.00	4.50
❑ MA Mike Alstott	60.00	27.00
❑ MB Mario Bates	10.00	4.50
❑ MF Marshall Faulk	60.00	27.00
❑ MG Archie Manning	25.00	11.00
❑ MI Michael Bishop	80.00	36.00
❑ MJ Michael Jackson	10.00	4.50
❑ MK Mark Brunell	50.00	22.00
❑ ML Mel Blount	30.00	13.50
❑ MM Muhsin Muhammad	25.00	11.00
❑ MN Donovan McNabb	300.00	135.00
❑ MO Earl Morrall	15.00	6.75
❑ MS Michael Sinclair	10.00	4.50
❑ MT Maa Tanuvasa	10.00	4.50
❑ MY Mercury Morris	15.00	6.75

❑ ND Ricky Watters	15.00	6.75
❑ NM Natrone Means	15.00	6.75
❑ NO Sean Dawkins	10.00	4.50
❑ NY Don Maynard	15.00	6.75
❑ OJ O.J. Santiago	10.00	4.50
❑ OZ Ozzie Newsome	25.00	11.00
❑ PH Priest Holmes	40.00	18.00
❑ PK Paul Krause	25.00	11.00
❑ PT Pete Mitchell	10.00	4.50
❑ PW Paul Warfield	25.00	11.00
❑ QB Cade McNown	30.00	13.50
❑ RB Robert Brooks	50.00	22.00
❑ RD Rickey Dudley	10.00	4.50
❑ RE Robert Edwards	15.00	6.75
❑ RF Russ Francis	15.00	6.75
❑ RH Rodney Harrison	25.00	11.00
❑ RL Ray Lewis	50.00	22.00
❑ RM Randy Moss	250.00	110.00
❑ RP Robert Porcher	10.00	4.50
❑ RW Ricky Williams	150.00	70.00
❑ RY Raymond Berry	25.00	11.00
❑ SD Charlie Jones	10.00	4.50
❑ SH Shaun King	50.00	22.00
❑ SK Sammy Knight	10.00	4.50
❑ ST Duce Staley	25.00	11.00
❑ SW John Stallworth	25.00	11.00
❑ TA Troy Aikman	150.00	70.00
❑ TB Tim Brown	100.00	45.00
❑ TC Tim Couch	120.00	55.00
❑ TD Terrell Davis UDA	40.00	18.00
❑ TE Jamie Asher	10.00	4.50
❑ TH Ted Hendricks	25.00	11.00
❑ TL Ty Law	30.00	13.50
❑ TO Torrance Small	10.00	4.50
❑ TR Troy Drayton	10.00	4.50
❑ TS Tony Siragusa	15.00	6.75
❑ TV Tommy Vardell	10.00	4.50
❑ WF William Floyd	10.00	4.50
❑ WH Craig Whelihan	10.00	4.50
❑ WM Willie McGinest	25.00	11.00
❑ WP Torry Holt	120.00	55.00
❑ ZC Zack Crockett	10.00	4.50

1999 SP Signature Autographs Gold

*UNLISTED GOLDS: .8X TO 2X BASIC INSERTS

	Nm-Mt	Ex-Mt
❑ AK Akili Smith	250.00	110.00
❑ BH Brock Huard	200.00	90.00
❑ DC Daunte Culpepper	500.00	220.00
❑ JR Junior Seau	400.00	180.00
❑ MI Michael Bishop	200.00	90.00
❑ MN Donovan McNabb	500.00	220.00
❑ QB Cade McNown	150.00	70.00
❑ RW Ricky Williams	300.00	135.00
❑ SH Shaun King	200.00	90.00
❑ TC Tim Couch	200.00	90.00
❑ WP Torry Holt	250.00	110.00

2003 SP Signature

	MINT	NRMT
❑ 1 Michael Vick	12.00	5.50
❑ 2 Aaron Brooks	5.00	2.20
❑ 3 Jim Brown	10.00	4.50
❑ 4 Steve Young	6.00	2.70
❑ 5 Jeff Garcia	5.00	2.20
❑ 6 Warren Moon	5.00	2.20
❑ 7 John Elway	15.00	6.75
❑ 8 Troy Aikman	8.00	3.60
❑ 9 Drew Brees	5.00	2.20
❑ 10 Chad Pennington	6.00	2.70
❑ 11 Fran Tarkenton	6.00	2.70
❑ 12 Joe Namath	10.00	4.50
❑ 13 Dan Marino	15.00	6.75
❑ 14 Terry Bradshaw	15.00	6.75
❑ 15 Edgerrin James	5.00	2.20
❑ 16 Joe Montana	20.00	9.00
❑ 17 Ken Stabler	10.00	4.50
❑ 18 Peyton Manning	8.00	3.60
❑ 19 Johnny Unitas	12.00	5.50
❑ 20 Barry Sanders	8.00	3.60
❑ 21 Jim Kelly	10.00	4.50
❑ 22 Michael Bennett	3.00	1.35
❑ 23 Phil Simms	8.00	3.60
❑ 24 David Carr	8.00	3.60
❑ 25 Deuce McAllister	5.00	2.20
❑ 26 Clinton Portis	8.00	3.60
❑ 27 Brad Johnson	3.00	1.35
❑ 28 Tim Couch	2.00	.90
❑ 29 Archie Manning	5.00	2.20
❑ 30 Ahman Green	5.00	2.20
❑ 31 Priest Holmes	6.00	2.70
❑ 32 Marcus Allen	6.00	2.70
❑ 33 Ricky Williams	5.00	2.20
❑ 34 Walter Payton	20.00	9.00
❑ 35 Anthony Thomas	5.00	2.20
❑ 36 Eddie George	3.00	1.35
❑ 37 Shaun Alexander	5.00	2.20
❑ 38 Rich Gannon	3.00	1.35
❑ 39 Jay Fiedler	3.00	1.35
❑ 40 Travis Henry	3.00	1.35
❑ 41 Chad Johnson	3.00	1.35
❑ 42 Eric Moulds	3.00	1.35
❑ 43 Julius Peppers	5.00	2.20
❑ 44 John Riggins	6.00	2.70
❑ 45 Antonio Bryant	3.00	1.35
❑ 46 Laveranues Coles	3.00	1.35
❑ 47 Josh McCown	3.00	1.35
❑ 48 Matt Hasselbeck	3.00	1.35
❑ 49 William Green	3.00	1.35
❑ 50 Peerless Price	3.00	1.35
❑ 51 Kerry Collins	3.00	1.35
❑ 52 Zach Thomas	3.00	1.35
❑ 53 Bruiser Kinard	5.00	2.20
❑ 54 Brian Urlacher	8.00	3.60
❑ 55 Junior Seau	5.00	2.20
❑ 56 Jamal Lewis	5.00	2.20
❑ 57 Duce Staley	3.00	1.35
❑ 58 Chris Redman	2.00	.90
❑ 59 Kordell Stewart	3.00	1.35
❑ 60 Chad Hutchinson	3.00	1.35
❑ 61 Kevan Barlow	3.00	1.35
❑ 62 Charlie Garner	3.00	1.35
❑ 63 Fred Taylor	5.00	2.20
❑ 64 Jerome Bettis	5.00	2.20
❑ 65 Donte Stallworth	5.00	2.20
❑ 66 Rod Smith	3.00	1.35
❑ 67 Antwaan Randle El	5.00	2.20
❑ 68 Brian Griese	5.00	2.20
❑ 69 Corey Dillon	3.00	1.35
❑ 70 Chris Chambers	5.00	2.20
❑ 71 Steve McNair	5.00	2.20
❑ 72 Jake Plummer	3.00	1.35
❑ 73 Keyshawn Johnson	5.00	2.20
❑ 74 Marvin Harrison	5.00	2.20
❑ 75 Plaxico Burress	3.00	1.35
❑ 76 Tim Brown	5.00	2.20
❑ 77 Mark Brunell	3.00	1.35
❑ 78 Curtis Martin	5.00	2.20
❑ 79 Cal Hubbard	5.00	2.20
❑ 80 Isaac Bruce	5.00	2.20
❑ 81 Terrell Owens	5.00	2.20
❑ 82 Santana Moss	3.00	1.35
❑ 83 Tommy Maddox	5.00	2.20
❑ 84 Randy Moss	8.00	3.60
❑ 85 Drew Bledsoe	5.00	2.20
❑ 86 Az-Zahir Hakim	2.00	.90
❑ 87 Rod Gardner	3.00	1.35
❑ 88 Tom Brady	8.00	3.60
❑ 89 David Boston	3.00	1.35
❑ 90 Trent Green	3.00	1.35
❑ 91 Jeremy Shockey	8.00	3.60
❑ 92 Daunte Culpepper	5.00	2.20
❑ 93 Emmitt Smith	12.00	5.50
❑ 94 Jerry Rice	10.00	4.50
❑ 95 LaDainian Tomlinson	5.00	2.20
❑ 96 Marshall Faulk	5.00	2.20
❑ 97 Kurt Warner	5.00	2.20
❑ 98 Brett Favre	12.00	5.50
❑ 99 Doak Walker	8.00	3.60
❑ 100 Donovan McNabb	6.00	2.70
❑ 101 Ken Dorsey RC	12.00	5.50
❑ 102 Kirk Farmer RC	4.00	1.80
❑ 103 Nate Hybl RC	8.00	3.60
❑ 104 Marquel Blackwell RC	4.00	1.80
❑ 105 Brett Engemann RC	4.00	1.80
❑ 106 Tony Romo RC	8.00	3.60
❑ 107 Derick Armstrong RC	8.00	3.60
❑ 108 Lon Sheriff RC	4.00	1.80
❑ 109 Casey Moore RC	6.00	2.70
❑ 110 Jason Gesser RC	8.00	3.60
❑ 111 Brock Forsey RC	10.00	4.50
❑ 112 Willis McGahee RC	20.00	9.00
❑ 113 Nick Maddox RC	4.00	1.80
❑ 114 LaBrandon Toefield RC	8.00	3.60
❑ 115 Kareem Kelly RC	6.00	2.70
❑ 116 Malaefou MacKenzie RC	4.00	1.80
❑ 117 Troy Polamalu RC	8.00	3.60
❑ 118 Terence Newman RC	15.00	6.75
❑ 119 Marcus Trufant RC	8.00	3.60
❑ 120 Terrell Suggs RC	12.00	5.50
❑ 121 DeWayne Robertson RC	8.00	3.60
❑ 122 Justin Griffith RC	6.00	2.70
❑ 123 Lee Suggs RC	15.00	6.75
❑ 124 Bryant Johnson RC	8.00	3.60
❑ 125 Andre Woolfolk RC	8.00	3.60
❑ 126 Cedric Henry RC	4.00	1.80
❑ 127 Billy McMullen RC	6.00	2.70
❑ 128 Charles Rogers RC	10.00	4.50
❑ 129 David Kircus RC	6.00	2.70
❑ 130 Jerome McDougle RC	8.00	3.60
❑ 131 Ryan Hoag RC	4.00	1.80
❑ 132 Mike Pinkard RC	4.00	1.80
❑ 133 Shaun McDonald RC	8.00	3.60
❑ 134 Bobby Wade RC	8.00	3.60
❑ 135 Kassim Osgood RC	8.00	3.60
❑ 136 Ovie Mughelli RC	4.00	1.80
❑ 137 Doug Gabriel RC	8.00	3.60
❑ 138 Aaron Walker RC	6.00	2.70
❑ 139 Brandon Lloyd RC	10.00	4.50
❑ 140 Donald Lee RC	6.00	2.70
❑ 141 George Wrighster RC	6.00	2.70
❑ 142 Antwone Savage RC	4.00	1.80
❑ 143 Keenan Howry RC	8.00	3.60
❑ 144 Kevin Walter RC	6.00	2.70
❑ 145 Gerald Hayes RC	4.00	1.80
❑ 146 Walter Young RC	4.00	1.80
❑ 147 Casey Fitzsimmons RC	8.00	3.60
❑ 148 Vishante Shiancoe RC	6.00	2.70
❑ 149 Lance Briggs RC	8.00	3.60
❑ 150 Zuriel Smith RC	4.00	1.80
❑ 151 Terrence Edwards RC	6.00	2.70
❑ 152 Arnaz Battle RC	8.00	3.60
❑ 153 DeAndrew Rubin RC	4.00	1.80
❑ 154 Pisa Tinoisamoa RC	12.00	5.50
❑ 155 David Tyree RC	6.00	2.70
❑ 156 Bradie James RC	8.00	3.60
❑ 157 Anquan Boldin RC	20.00	9.00
❑ 158 Kevin Curtis RC	8.00	3.60
❑ 159 Taylor Jacobs RC	8.00	3.60
❑ 160 Cato June RC	6.00	2.70
❑ 161 Jason Witten RC	12.00	5.50
❑ 162 Mike Seidman RC	4.00	1.80
❑ 163 Dallas Clark RC	10.00	4.50

		MINT	NRMT
❑ 164	Gibran Hamdan RC	4.00	1.80
❑ 165	Kliff Kingsbury RC	6.00	2.70
❑ 166	Brooks Bollinger RC	8.00	3.60
❑ 167	Nick Barnett RC	12.00	5.50
❑ 168	Rex Grossman RC	20.00	9.00
❑ 169	Byron Leftwich RC	25.00	11.00
❑ 170	Kyle Boller RC	20.00	9.00
❑ 171	Chris Brown RC	20.00	9.00
❑ 172	Carl Ford RC	5.00	2.20
❑ 173	Kelley Washington RC	10.00	4.50
❑ 174	Charles Tillman RC	20.00	9.00
❑ 175	Ken Hamlin RC	10.00	4.50
❑ 176	Bennie Joppru RC	10.00	4.50
❑ 177	Nate Burleson RC	15.00	6.75
❑ 178	Boss Bailey RC	12.00	5.50
❑ 179	LaTarence Dunbar RC	8.00	3.60
❑ 180	Adrian Madise RC	8.00	3.60
❑ 181	J.R. Tolver RC	8.00	3.60
❑ 182	Tyrone Calico RC	12.00	5.50
❑ 183	Justin Gage RC	10.00	4.50
❑ 184	Teyo Johnson RC	10.00	4.50
❑ 185	B.J. Askew RC	10.00	4.50
❑ 186	Sam Aiken RC	8.00	3.60
❑ 187	Andre Johnson RC	25.00	11.00
❑ 188	Bethel Johnson RC	15.00	6.75
❑ 189	Artose Pinner RC	10.00	4.50
❑ 190	Quentin Griffin RC	25.00	11.00
❑ 191	Musa Smith RC	10.00	4.50
❑ 192	Larry Johnson RC	20.00	9.00
❑ 193	Onterrio Smith RC	10.00	4.50
❑ 194	Justin Fargas RC	10.00	4.50
❑ 195	Dwone Hicks RC	5.00	2.20
❑ 196	Brian St.Pierre RC	10.00	4.50
❑ 197	Dave Ragone RC	10.00	4.50
❑ 198	Seneca Wallace RC	10.00	4.50
❑ 199	Chris Simms RC	20.00	9.00
❑ 200	Carson Palmer RC	30.00	13.50

2003 SP Signature Autographs Black Ink

*UNLISTED: .5X TO 1.2X BLUE INK

		MINT	NRMT
❑ AM	Archie Manning	40.00	18.00
❑ BJ	Brad Johnson SP	25.00	11.00
❑ CP	Chad Pennington	50.00	22.00
❑ CS	Chris Simms	40.00	18.00
❑ DA	David Boston SP/25*	50.00	22.00
❑ DB	Drew Brees SP/20*		
❑ DM	Dan Marino SP	200.00	90.00
❑ FT	Fran Tarkenton SP	50.00	22.00
❑ JM	Joe Montana	150.00	70.00
❑ JN	Joe Namath SP	150.00	70.00
❑ KS	Ken Stabler SP	50.00	22.00
❑ MC	Deuce McAllister	25.00	11.00
❑ PH	Priest Holmes SP/25*	125.00	55.00
❑ TM	Tommy Maddox SP/25*	50.00	22.00

2003 SP Signature Autographs Blue Ink

		MINT	NRMT
❑ AA	Aaron Brooks	15.00	6.75
❑ AB	Anquan Boldin	50.00	22.00
❑ AH	Az-Zahir Hakim	10.00	4.50
❑ AJ	Andre Johnson	50.00	22.00
❑ AM	Archie Manning SP/25*	60.00	27.00
❑ AP	Artose Pinner	15.00	6.75
❑ AR	Arnaz Battle	15.00	6.75
❑ AT	Anthony Thomas	20.00	9.00
❑ BB	Brad Banks	12.00	5.50
❑ BJ	Brad Johnson SP/25*	40.00	18.00
❑ BL	Brandon Lloyd	20.00	9.00
❑ BO	Brooks Bollinger	15.00	6.75
❑ BR	Bryant Johnson	15.00	6.75
❑ BY	Byron Leftwich	80.00	36.00
❑ CA	Tyrone Calico	20.00	9.00
❑ CB	Chris Brown	30.00	13.50
❑ CP	Chad Pennington SP	50.00	22.00
❑ CS	Chris Simms SP	60.00	27.00
❑ DB	Drew Brees SP	40.00	18.00
❑ DC	David Carr	40.00	18.00
❑ DO	Donovan McNabb SP/19*		
❑ DR	DeWayne Robertson	12.00	5.50
❑ EG	Earnest Graham	10.00	4.50
❑ FA	Justin Fargas	15.00	6.75
❑ IB	Isaac Bruce	15.00	6.75
❑ JB	Jim Brown SP	100.00	45.00
❑ JF	Jay Fiedler	15.00	6.75
❑ JG	Jeff Garcia SP/24*		
❑ JO	Teyo Johnson	15.00	6.75
❑ KA	Kareem Kelly	10.00	4.50
❑ KB	Kyle Boller	30.00	13.50
❑ KC	Kevin Curtis	10.00	4.50
❑ KD	Ken Dorsey	25.00	11.00
❑ KK	Kliff Kingsbury	12.00	5.50
❑ KW	Kelley Washington	15.00	6.75
❑ LJ	Larry Johnson	25.00	11.00
❑ LS	Lee Suggs	30.00	13.50
❑ MB	Michael Bennett	15.00	6.75
❑ MM	Malaefou MacKenzie	10.00	4.50
❑ MO	Warren Moon	40.00	18.00
❑ MS	Musa Smith	15.00	6.75
❑ MT	Marcus Trufant	15.00	6.75
❑ NB	Nate Burleson	25.00	11.00
❑ OS	Onterrio Smith	20.00	9.00
❑ PM	Peyton Manning	80.00	36.00
❑ PO	Clinton Portis SP/25*	100.00	45.00
❑ QG	Quentin Griffin	30.00	13.50
❑ RA	Dave Ragone	15.00	6.75
❑ RE	Rex Grossman	40.00	18.00
❑ RG	Rod Gardner	12.00	5.50
❑ RM	Randy Moss SP/10*		
❑ RW	Ricky Williams SP/25*		
❑ SA	Shaun Alexander	20.00	9.00
❑ SC	Carson Palmer	80.00	36.00
❑ SM	Santana Moss	20.00	9.00
❑ SP	Brian St.Pierre	15.00	6.75
❑ SW	Seneca Wallace	12.00	5.50
❑ TC	Tim Couch	10.00	4.50
❑ TJ	Taylor Jacobs	25.00	11.00
❑ TN	Terence Newman	30.00	13.50
❑ TS	Terrell Suggs	15.00	6.75
❑ WM	Willis McGahee SP	80.00	36.00

2003 SP Signature Autographs Blue Ink Numbered

*UNLISTED: .6X TO 1.5X BLUE INK

		MINT	NRMT
❑ AM	Archie Manning	50.00	22.00
❑ BF	Brett Favre/7		
❑ CP	Chad Pennington	50.00	22.00
❑ CS	Chris Simms	40.00	18.00
❑ JB	Jim Brown	100.00	45.00
❑ TG	Trent Green	25.00	11.00

2003 SP Signature Autographs Green Ink

*UNLISTED: 1X TO 2.5X BLUE INK

		MINT	NRMT
❑ AM	Archie Manning	80.00	36.00
❑ BA	Barry Sanders	150.00	70.00
❑ BJ	Brad Johnson	40.00	18.00
❑ BY	Byron Leftwich	200.00	90.00
❑ CP	Chad Pennington	70.00	32.00
❑ CS	Chris Simms	80.00	36.00
❑ DA	David Boston	25.00	11.00
❑ DB	Drew Brees	30.00	13.50
❑ DM	Dan Marino	200.00	90.00
❑ FT	Fran Tarkenton	80.00	36.00
❑ JB	Jim Brown	120.00	55.00
❑ JE	John Elway	200.00	90.00
❑ JK	Jim Kelly	80.00	36.00
❑ JM	Joe Montana	250.00	110.00
❑ JN	Joe Namath	150.00	70.00
❑ JR	John Riggins	60.00	27.00
❑ KS	Ken Stabler	60.00	27.00
❑ MA	Marcus Allen	50.00	22.00
❑ MC	Deuce McAllister	60.00	27.00
❑ PH	Priest Holmes	80.00	36.00
❑ PS	Phil Simms	40.00	18.00
❑ SC	Carson Palmer	150.00	70.00
❑ SW1	Seneca Wallace/50	40.00	18.00
❑ SW2	Seneca Wallace (without serial #)	20.00	9.00
❑ SY	Steve Young	80.00	36.00
❑ TB	Terry Bradshaw	100.00	45.00
❑ TG	Trent Green	40.00	18.00
❑ TM	Tommy Maddox	40.00	18.00
❑ TO	Terrell Owens	60.00	27.00
❑ WM	Willis McGahee	120.00	55.00

2003 SP Signature Autographs Red Ink

*UNLISTED: .6X TO 1.5X BLUE INK

		MINT	NRMT
❑ AM	Archie Manning	50.00	22.00
❑ BA	Barry Sanders	100.00	45.00
❑ BJ	Brad Johnson	30.00	13.50
❑ CP	Chad Pennington	50.00	22.00
❑ CS	Chris Simms	40.00	18.00
❑ DA	David Boston	20.00	9.00
❑ DB	Drew Brees	25.00	11.00
❑ FT	Fran Tarkenton	40.00	18.00
❑ JB	Jim Brown	100.00	45.00
❑ JE	John Elway	125.00	55.00
❑ JK	Jim Kelly		
❑ JM	Joe Montana	150.00	70.00
❑ JN	Joe Namath	120.00	55.00
❑ JR	John Riggins	40.00	18.00
❑ KS	Ken Stabler	50.00	22.00
❑ MA	Marcus Allen	50.00	22.00
❑ MC	Deuce McAllister	30.00	13.50
❑ MO	Warren Moon Purple Ink	60.00	27.00
❑ PH	Priest Holmes	60.00	27.00
❑ SY	Steve Young	60.00	27.00
❑ TB	Terry Bradshaw	80.00	36.00
❑ TG	Trent Green	25.00	11.00
❑ TM	Tommy Maddox	30.00	13.50
❑ TO	Terrell Owens	60.00	27.00
❑ WM	Willis McGahee	80.00	36.00

2003 SP Signature Dual Autographs

	MINT	NRMT
ABKK Aaron Brooks Kareem Kelly	25.00	11.00
BJAB Bryant Johnson Anquan Boldin	80.00	36.00
CPKW Carson Palmer Kelley Washington	100.00	45.00
CPSM Chad Pennington Santana Moss	80.00	36.00
CPVT Chad Pennington Vinny Testaverde	60.00	27.00
DBDB Drew Brees David Boston	30.00	13.50
DCAJ David Carr Andre Johnson	125.00	55.00
JMKD Joe Montana Ken Dorsey	200.00	90.00
JNCP Joe Namath Chad Pennington	200.00	90.00
KDTO Ken Dorsey Terrell Owens	60.00	27.00
MBOS Michael Bennett Onterrio Smith	40.00	18.00
PHLJ Priest Holmes Larry Johnson	80.00	36.00
PMAM Peyton Manning Archie Manning	150.00	70.00
PSCS Phil Simms Chris Simms	80.00	36.00
RGAT Rex Grossman Anthony Thomas	60.00	27.00
TMBS Tommy Maddox Brian St. Pierre	50.00	22.00

1999 Sports Illustrated

	Nm-Mt	Ex-Mt
COMPLETE SET (150)	75.00	34.00
1 Bart Starr MVP	.75	.35
2 Bart Starr MVP	.75	.35
3 Joe Namath MVP	.75	.35
4 Len Dawson MVP	.50	.23
5 Chuck Howley MVP	.30	.14
6 Roger Staubach MVP	.75	.35
7 Jake Scott MVP	.30	.14
8 Larry Csonka MVP	.50	.23
9 Franco Harris MVP	.50	.23
10 Fred Biletnikoff MVP	.50	.23
11 Harvey Martin MVP Randy White MVP	.30	.14
12 Terry Bradshaw MVP	.75	.35
13 Terry Bradshaw MVP	.75	.35
14 Jim Plunkett MVP	.30	.14
15 Joe Montana MVP	.75	.35
16 Marcus Allen MVP	.50	.23
17 Joe Montana MVP	.75	.35
18 Richard Dent MVP	.50	.23
19 Phil Simms MVP	.30	.14
20 Doug Williams MVP	.30	.14
21 Jerry Rice MVP	.75	.35
22 Joe Montana MVP	.75	.35
23 Ottis Anderson MVP	.30	.14
24 Mark Rypien MVP	.30	.14
25 Troy Aikman MVP	.75	.35
26 Emmitt Smith MVP	1.25	.55
27 Steve Young MVP	.75	.35
28 Larry Brown MVP	.30	.14
29 Desmond Howard MVP	.50	.23
30 Terrell Davis MVP	.75	.35
31 Y.A. Tittle	.75	.35
32 Paul Hornung	.50	.23
33 Gale Sayers	.50	.23
34 Garo Yepremian	.30	.14
35 Bert Jones	.30	.14
36 Joe Washington	.30	.14
37 Joe Theismann	.30	.14
38 Roger Craig	.30	.14
39 Mike Singletary	.30	.14
40 Bobby Bell	.30	.14
41 Ken Houston	.30	.14
42 Lenny Moore	.30	.14
43 Mark Moseley	.30	.14
44 Chuck Bednarik	.30	.14
45 Ted Hendricks	.30	.14
46 Steve Largent	.75	.35
47 Bob Lilly	.30	.14
48 Don Maynard	.30	.14
49 John Mackey	.30	.14
50 Anthony Munoz	.30	.14
51 Bobby Mitchell	.30	.14
52 Jim Brown	.75	.35
53 Otto Graham	.50	.23
54 Earl Morrall	.30	.14
55 Danny White	.30	.14
56 Karim Abdul-Jabbar	.50	.23
57 Charlie Garner	.50	.23
58 Jeff Blake	.50	.23
59 Reggie White	.75	.35
60 Derrick Thomas	.50	.23
61 Duce Staley	.75	.35
62 Tim Brown	.75	.35
63 Elvis Grbac	.50	.23
64 Tony Banks	.50	.23
65 Rob Johnson	.50	.23
66 Danny Kanell	.30	.14
67 Marshall Faulk	1.00	.45
68 Warrick Dunn	.75	.35
69 Dan Marino	3.00	1.35
70 Jimmy Smith	.50	.23
71 John Elway	3.00	1.35
72 Charles Way	.30	.14
73 Ricky Watters	.50	.23
74 Terry Glenn	.75	.35
75 Bobby Hoying	.50	.23
76 Curtis Martin	.75	.35
77 Trent Dilfer	.50	.23
78 Emmitt Smith	2.50	1.10
79 Irving Fryar	.50	.23
80 Troy Aikman	1.50	.70
81 Barry Sanders	2.50	1.10
82 Brett Favre	3.00	1.35
83 Robert Smith	.75	.35
84 Dorsey Levens	.75	.35
85 Cris Carter	.75	.35
86 Jeff George	.50	.23
87 Jerome Bettis	.75	.35
88 Warren Moon	.75	.35
89 Steve Young	1.00	.45
90 Fred Lane	.30	.14
91 Jerry Rice	1.50	.70
92 Natrone Means	.50	.23
93 Mike Alstott	.75	.35
94 Kordell Stewart	.50	.23
95 Jake Plummer	.50	.23
96 Jamal Anderson	.75	.35
97 Corey Dillon	1.00	.45
98 Deion Sanders	.75	.35
99 Mark Brunell	.75	.35
100 Garrison Hearst	.50	.23
101 Andre Rison	.50	.23
102 Antowain Smith	.75	.35
103 Drew Bledsoe	1.25	.55
104 Eddie George	.75	.35
105 Keyshawn Johnson	.75	.35
106 Isaac Bruce	.75	.35
107 Rob Moore	.50	.23
108 Steve McNair	.75	.35
109 Terrell Davis	.75	.35
110 Carl Pickens	.50	.23
111 Wayne Chrebet	.50	.23
112 Kerry Collins	.50	.23
113 Eric Metcalf	.30	.14
114 Joey Galloway	.50	.23
115 Shannon Sharpe	.50	.23
116 Robert Brooks	.50	.23
117 Glenn Foley	.50	.23
118 Yancey Thigpen	.30	.14
119 Frank Sanders	.50	.23
120 Herman Moore	.50	.23
121 Antonio Freeman	.75	.35
122 Michael Irvin	.50	.23
123 Brad Johnson	.75	.35
124 James Stewart	.50	.23
125 Jim Harbaugh	.50	.23
126 Peyton Manning FF	8.00	3.60
127 Ryan Leaf FF	1.00	.45
128 Curtis Enis FF	.60	.25
129 Fred Taylor FF	2.00	.90
130 Randy Moss FF	6.00	2.70
131 John Avery FF	.60	.25
132 Charles Woodson FF	2.00	.90
133 Robert Edwards FF	.60	.25
134 Charlie Batch FF	2.00	.90
135 Brian Griese FF	2.00	.90
136 Skip Hicks FF	.60	.25
137 Jacquez Green FF	.60	.25
138 Robert Holcombe FF	.60	.25
139 Kevin Dyson FF	2.00	.90
140 Rodney Williams FF	.60	.25
141 Ahman Green FF	2.00	.90
142 Tavian Banks FF	1.00	.45
143 Donald Hayes FF	1.00	.45
144 Tony Simmons FF	1.00	.45
145 Pat Johnson FF	1.00	.45
146 Marcus Nash FF	.60	.25
147 Germane Crowell FF	.60	.25
148 R.W. McQuarters FF	.60	.25
149 Jonathan Quinn FF	2.00	.90
150 Andre Wadsworth FF	.60	.25
P35 Gale Sayers Promo	3.00	1.35

1999 Sports Illustrated Autographs

	Nm-Mt	Ex-Mt
❑ 1 Ottis Anderson	15.00	6.75
❑ 2 Chuck Bednarik	20.00	9.00
❑ 3 Bobby Bell	15.00	6.75
❑ 4 Terry Bradshaw	300.00	135.00
❑ 5 Jim Brown	100.00	45.00
❑ 6 Roger Craig	20.00	9.00
❑ 7 Len Dawson	120.00	55.00
❑ 8 Otto Graham	50.00	22.00
❑ 9 Franco Harris	120.00	55.00
❑ 10 Ted Hendricks	20.00	9.00
❑ 11 Paul Hornung	120.00	55.00
❑ 12 Ken Houston	15.00	6.75
❑ 13 Bert Jones	15.00	6.75
❑ 14 Steve Largent	25.00	11.00
❑ 15 Bob Lilly	20.00	9.00
❑ 16 John Mackey	15.00	6.75
❑ 17 Don Maynard	20.00	9.00
❑ 18 Bobby Mitchell	20.00	9.00
❑ 19 Joe Montana	300.00	135.00
❑ 20 Lenny Moore	20.00	9.00
❑ 21 Earl Morrall	15.00	6.75
❑ 22 Mark Moseley	10.00	4.50
❑ 23 Anthony Munoz	15.00	6.75
❑ 24 Joe Namath	300.00	135.00
❑ 25 Jim Plunkett	20.00	9.00
❑ 26 Gale Sayers	40.00	18.00
❑ 27 Mike Singletary	80.00	36.00
❑ 28 Bart Starr	300.00	135.00
❑ 29 Roger Staubach	250.00	110.00
❑ 30 Joe Theismann	50.00	22.00
❑ 31 Y.A. Tittle	100.00	45.00
❑ 32 Joe Washington	10.00	4.50
❑ 33 Danny White	20.00	9.00
❑ 34 Doug Williams	50.00	22.00
❑ 35 Garo Yepremian	10.00	4.50

1996 SPx

	Nm-Mt	Ex-Mt
COMPLETE SET (50)	25.00	11.00
❑ 1 Frank Sanders	1.00	.45
❑ 2 Terance Mathis	.50	.23
❑ 3 Todd Collins	1.00	.45
❑ 4 Kerry Collins	2.00	.90
❑ 5 Carl Pickens	1.00	.45
❑ 6 Darnay Scott	1.00	.45
❑ 7 Ki-Jana Carter	1.00	.45
❑ 8 Eric Zeier	.50	.23
❑ 9 Andre Rison	1.00	.45
❑ 10 Sherman Williams	.50	.23
❑ 11 Troy Aikman	4.00	1.80
❑ 12 Michael Irvin	2.00	.90
❑ 13 Emmitt Smith	6.00	2.70
❑ 14 Shannon Sharpe	1.00	.45
❑ 15 John Elway	8.00	3.60
❑ 16 Barry Sanders	6.00	2.70
❑ 17 Brett Favre	8.00	3.60
❑ 18 Rodney Thomas	.50	.23
❑ 19 Marshall Faulk	2.50	1.10
❑ 20 James O.Stewart	1.00	.45
❑ 21 Greg Hill	1.00	.45
❑ 22 Tamarick Vanover	1.00	.45
❑ 23 Dan Marino	8.00	3.60
❑ 24 Cris Carter	2.00	.90
❑ 25 Warren Moon	1.00	.45
❑ 26 Drew Bledsoe	2.50	1.10
❑ 27 Ben Coates	1.00	.45
❑ 28 Curtis Martin	3.00	1.35
❑ 29 Mario Bates	1.00	.45
❑ 30 Tyrone Wheatley	1.00	.45
❑ 31 Rodney Hampton	1.00	.45
❑ 32 Kyle Brady	.50	.23
❑ 33 Jeff Hostetler	.50	.23
❑ 34 Napoleon Kaufman	2.00	.90
❑ 35 Tim Brown	2.00	.90
❑ 36 Charles Johnson	.50	.23
❑ 37 Rod Woodson UER Incorrect birth year	1.00	.45
❑ 38 Natrone Means	1.00	.45
❑ 39 J.J. Stokes	2.00	.90
❑ 40 Steve Young	4.00	1.80
❑ 41 Brent Jones	.50	.23
❑ 42 Jerry Rice	4.00	1.80
❑ 43 Joe Montana	8.00	3.60
❑ 44 Rick Mirer	1.00	.45
❑ 45 Chris Warren	1.00	.45
❑ 46 Joey Galloway	2.00	.90
❑ 47 Isaac Bruce	2.00	.90
❑ 48 Jerome Bettis	2.00	.90
❑ 49 Errict Rhett	1.00	.45
❑ 50 Michael Westbrook	2.00	.90
❑ UDT13 Dan Marino Record Breaker	15.00	6.75
❑ UDT13 Dan Marino AUTO Record Breaker signed	120.00	55.00
❑ UDT19 Joe Montana Tribute	15.00	6.75
❑ UDT19 Joe Montana AUTO Tribute card signed	100.00	45.00
❑ P1 Dan Marino Promo	5.00	2.20
❑ P2 Joe Montana Promo	5.00	2.20

1998 SPx Finite

	Nm-Mt	Ex-Mt
COMP.SERIES 1 (190)	750.00	350.00
COMP.SERIES 2 (180)	750.00	350.00
❑ 1 Jake Plummer	2.50	1.10
❑ 2 Eric Swann	1.00	.45
❑ 3 Rob Moore	1.50	.70
❑ 4 Jamal Anderson	2.50	1.10
❑ 5 Byron Hanspard	1.00	.45
❑ 6 Cornelius Bennett	1.00	.45
❑ 7 Michael Jackson	1.00	.45
❑ 8 Peter Boulware	1.00	.45
❑ 9 Jermaine Lewis	1.50	.70
❑ 10 Antowain Smith	2.50	1.10
❑ 11 Bruce Smith	1.50	.70
❑ 12 Bryce Paup	1.00	.45
❑ 13 Rae Carruth	1.00	.45
❑ 14 Michael Bates	1.00	.45
❑ 15 Fred Lane	1.00	.45
❑ 16 Darnell Autry	1.50	.70
❑ 17 Curtis Conway	1.50	.70
❑ 18 Erik Kramer	1.00	.45
❑ 19 Corey Dillon	2.50	1.10
❑ 20 Darnay Scott	1.50	.70
❑ 21 Reinard Wilson	1.00	.45
❑ 22 Troy Aikman	5.00	2.20
❑ 23 David LaFleur	1.00	.45
❑ 24 Emmitt Smith	8.00	3.60
❑ 25 John Elway	10.00	4.50
❑ 26 John Mobley	1.00	.45
❑ 27 Terrell Davis	2.50	1.10
❑ 28 Rod Smith	1.50	.70
❑ 29 Bryant Westbrook	1.00	.45
❑ 30 Scott Mitchell	1.50	.70
❑ 31 Barry Sanders	8.00	3.60
❑ 32 Dorsey Levens	2.50	1.10
❑ 33 Antonio Freeman	2.50	1.10
❑ 34 Reggie White	2.50	1.10
❑ 35 Marshall Faulk	3.00	1.35
❑ 36 Marvin Harrison	2.50	1.10
❑ 37 Ken Dilger	1.00	.45
❑ 38 Mark Brunell	2.50	1.10
❑ 39 Keenan McCardell	1.50	.70
❑ 40 Renaldo Wynn	1.00	.45
❑ 41 Marcus Allen	2.50	1.10
❑ 42 Elvis Grbac	1.50	.70
❑ 43 Andre Rison	1.50	.70
❑ 44 Yatil Green	1.00	.45
❑ 45 Zach Thomas	2.50	1.10
❑ 46 Karim Abdul-Jabbar UER Karim Abdul front and back	2.50	1.10
❑ 47 John Randle	1.50	.70
❑ 48 Brad Johnson	2.50	1.10
❑ 49 Jake Reed	1.50	.70
❑ 50 Danny Wuerffel	1.50	.70
❑ 51 Andre Hastings	1.00	.45
❑ 52 Drew Bledsoe	4.00	1.80
❑ 53 Terry Glenn	2.50	1.10
❑ 54 Ty Law	1.50	.70
❑ 55 Danny Kanell	1.50	.70
❑ 56 Tiki Barber	2.50	1.10
❑ 57 Jessie Armstead	1.00	.45
❑ 58 Glenn Foley	1.50	.70
❑ 59 James Farrior	1.00	.45
❑ 60 Wayne Chrebet	2.50	1.10
❑ 61 Tim Brown	2.50	1.10
❑ 62 Napoleon Kaufman	2.50	1.10
❑ 63 Darrell Russell	1.00	.45
❑ 64 Bobby Hoying	1.50	.70
❑ 65 Irving Fryar	1.50	.70
❑ 66 Charlie Garner	1.50	.70
❑ 67 Will Blackwell	1.00	.45
❑ 68 Kordell Stewart	2.50	1.10
❑ 69 Levon Kirkland	1.00	.45
❑ 70 Tony Banks	1.50	.70
❑ 71 Ryan McNeil	1.00	.45
❑ 72 Isaac Bruce	2.50	1.10
❑ 73 Tony Martin	1.50	.70
❑ 74 Junior Seau	2.50	1.10
❑ 75 Natrone Means	1.50	.70
❑ 76 Jerry Rice	5.00	2.20
❑ 77 Garrison Hearst	2.50	1.10
❑ 78 Terrell Owens	2.50	1.10
❑ 79 Warren Moon	2.50	1.10
❑ 80 Joey Galloway	1.50	.70
❑ 81 Chad Brown	1.00	.45
❑ 82 Warrick Dunn	2.50	1.10
❑ 83 Mike Alstott	2.50	1.10
❑ 84 Hardy Nickerson	1.00	.45
❑ 85 Steve McNair	2.50	1.10
❑ 86 Chris Sanders	1.00	.45
❑ 87 Darryll Lewis	1.00	.45
❑ 88 Gus Frerotte	1.00	.45
❑ 89 Terry Allen	2.50	1.10
❑ 90 Chris Dishman	1.00	.45
❑ 91 Kordell Stewart PM	3.00	1.35
❑ 92 Jerry Rice PM	6.00	2.70
❑ 93 Michael Irvin PM	3.00	1.35
❑ 94 Brett Favre PM	12.00	5.50
❑ 95 Jeff George PM	2.00	.90
❑ 96 Joey Galloway PM	2.00	.90
❑ 97 John Elway PM	12.00	5.50
❑ 98 Troy Aikman PM	6.00	2.70
❑ 99 Steve Young PM	4.00	1.80
❑ 100 Andre Rison PM	2.00	.90
❑ 101 Ben Coates PM	2.00	.90
❑ 102 Robert Brooks PM	2.00	.90
❑ 103 Dan Marino PM	12.00	5.50

❑	104	Isaac Bruce PM	3.00	1.35
❑	105	Junior Seau PM	3.00	1.35
❑	106	Jake Plummer PM	3.00	1.35
❑	107	Curtis Conway PM	2.00	.90
❑	108	Jeff Blake PM	2.00	.90
❑	109	Rod Smith PM	2.00	.90
❑	110	Barry Sanders PM	10.00	4.50
❑	111	Deion Sanders PM	3.00	1.35
❑	112	Drew Bledsoe PM	5.00	2.20
❑	113	Emmitt Smith PM	10.00	4.50
❑	114	Herman Moore PM	2.00	.90
❑	115	Dorsey Levens PM	3.00	1.35
❑	116	Jimmy Smith PM	2.00	.90
❑	117	Tony Martin PM	1.25	.55
❑	118	Carl Pickens PM	2.00	.90
❑	119	Keyshawn Johnson PM	3.00	1.35
❑	120	Cris Carter PM	3.00	1.35
❑	121	Warrick Dunn YM	5.00	2.20
❑	122	Marshall Faulk YM	6.00	2.70
❑	123	Trent Dilfer YM	5.00	2.20
❑	124	Napoleon Kaufman YM	5.00	2.20
❑	125	Corey Dillon YM	5.00	2.20
❑	126	Darrell Russell YM	2.00	.90
❑	127	Danny Kanell YM	3.00	1.35
❑	128	Reidel Anthony YM	3.00	1.35
❑	129	Steve McNair YM	5.00	2.20
❑	130	Ike Hilliard YM	3.00	1.35
❑	131	Tony Banks YM	3.00	1.35
❑	132	Yatil Green YM	2.00	.90
❑	133	J.J. Stokes YM	3.00	1.35
❑	134	Fred Lane YM	2.00	.90
❑	135	Bryant Westbrook YM	2.00	.90
❑	136	Jake Plummer YM	5.00	2.20
❑	137	Byron Hanspard YM	2.00	.90
❑	138	Rae Carruth YM	2.00	.90
❑	139	Keyshawn Johnson YM	5.00	2.20
❑	140	Jim Druckenmiller YM	2.00	.90
❑	141	Amani Toomer YM	3.00	1.35
❑	142	Troy Davis YM	2.00	.90
❑	143	Antowain Smith YM	5.00	2.20
❑	144	Shawn Springs YM	2.00	.90
❑	145	Rickey Dudley YM	2.00	.90
❑	146	Terry Glenn YM	5.00	2.20
❑	147	Johnnie Morton YM	3.00	1.35
❑	148	David LaFleur YM	2.00	.90
❑	149	Eddie Kennison YM	3.00	1.35
❑	150	Bobby Hoying YM	3.00	1.35
❑	151	Junior Seau PE	6.00	2.70
❑	152	Shannon Sharpe PE	4.00	1.80
❑	153	Bruce Smith PE	4.00	1.80
❑	154	Brett Favre PE	20.00	9.00
❑	155	Emmitt Smith PE	15.00	6.75
❑	156	Keenan McCardell PE	2.50	1.10
❑	157	Kordell Stewart PE	6.00	2.70
❑	158	Troy Aikman PE	10.00	4.50
❑	159	Steve Young PE	6.00	2.70
❑	160	Tim Brown PE	6.00	2.70
❑	161	Eddie George PE	6.00	2.70
❑	162	Herman Moore PE	4.00	1.80
❑	163	Dan Marino PE	20.00	9.00
❑	164	Dorsey Levens PE	6.00	2.70
❑	165	Jerry Rice PE	10.00	4.50
❑	166	Warren Sapp PE	4.00	1.80
❑	167	Robert Smith PE	6.00	2.70
❑	168	Mark Brunell PE	6.00	2.70
❑	169	Terrell Davis PE	6.00	2.70
❑	170	Jerome Bettis PE	6.00	2.70
❑	171	Dan Marino HG	30.00	13.50
❑	172	Barry Sanders HG	25.00	11.00
❑	173	Marcus Allen HG	8.00	3.60
❑	174	Brett Favre HG	30.00	13.50
❑	175	Warrick Dunn HG	8.00	3.60
❑	176	Eddie George HG	8.00	3.60
❑	177	John Elway HG	30.00	13.50
❑	178	Troy Aikman HG	15.00	6.75
❑	179	Cris Carter HG	8.00	3.60
❑	180	Terrell Davis HG	8.00	3.60
❑	181	Peyton Manning RC	200.00	90.00
❑	182	Ryan Leaf RC	25.00	11.00
❑	183	Andre Wadsworth RC	20.00	9.00
❑	184	Charles Woodson RC	30.00	13.50
❑	185	Curtis Enis RC	15.00	6.75
❑	186	Grant Wistrom RC	20.00	9.00
❑	187	Fred Taylor RC	40.00	18.00
❑	188	Takeo Spikes RC	25.00	11.00
❑	189	Kevin Dyson RC	25.00	11.00
❑	190	Robert Edwards RC	20.00	9.00
❑	191	Adrian Murrell	1.00	.45
❑	192	Simeon Rice	1.00	.45
❑	193	Frank Sanders	1.00	.45
❑	194	Chris Chandler	1.00	.45
❑	195	Terance Mathis	1.00	.45
❑	196	Keith Brooking RC	1.50	.70
❑	197	Jim Harbaugh	1.00	.45
❑	198	Errict Rhett	1.00	.45
❑	199	Pat Johnson RC	2.50	1.10
❑	200	Rob Johnson	1.00	.45
❑	201	Andre Reed	1.00	.45
❑	202	Thurman Thomas	1.50	.70
❑	203	Kerry Collins	1.00	.45
❑	204	William Floyd	.60	.25
❑	205	Sean Gilbert	.60	.25
❑	206	Bobby Engram	1.00	.45
❑	207	Edgar Bennett	1.00	.45
❑	208	Walt Harris	1.00	.45
❑	209	Carl Pickens	1.00	.45
❑	210	Neil O'Donnell	1.00	.45
❑	211	Tony McGee	.60	.25
❑	212	Deion Sanders	1.50	.70
❑	213	Michael Irvin	1.50	.70
❑	214	Greg Ellis RC	1.25	.55
❑	215	Shannon Sharpe	1.00	.45
❑	216	Neil Smith	1.00	.45
❑	217	Marcus Nash RC	1.25	.55
❑	218	Brian Griese RC	30.00	13.50
❑	219	Johnnie Morton	1.00	.45
❑	220	Herman Moore	1.50	.70
❑	221	Charlie Batch RC	20.00	9.00
❑	222	Robert Brooks	1.00	.45
❑	223	Mark Chmura	1.00	.45
❑	224	Brett Favre	6.00	2.70
❑	225	Jerome Pathon RC	5.00	2.20
❑	226	Zack Crockett	.60	.25
❑	227	Dan Footman	.60	.25
❑	228	Jimmy Smith	1.00	.45
❑	229	Bryce Paup	.60	.25
❑	230	James Stewart	1.00	.45
❑	231	Derrick Thomas	1.00	.45
❑	232	Derrick Alexander	1.00	.45
❑	233	Tony Gonzalez	1.50	.70
❑	234	Dan Marino	6.00	2.70
❑	235	O.J. McDuffie	1.00	.45
❑	236	Troy Drayton	.60	.25
❑	237	Cris Carter	1.50	.70
❑	238	Robert Smith	1.50	.70
❑	239	Randy Moss RC	80.00	36.00
❑	240	Lamar Smith	1.00	.45
❑	241	Sean Dawkins	.60	.25
❑	242	Alex Molden	.60	.25
❑	243	Ben Coates	1.00	.45
❑	244	Ted Johnson	.60	.25
❑	245	Sedrick Shaw	.60	.25
❑	246	Ike Hilliard	1.00	.45
❑	247	Jason Sehorn	1.00	.45
❑	248	Michael Strahan	1.00	.45
❑	249	Keyshawn Johnson	1.50	.70
❑	250	Curtis Martin	1.50	.70
❑	251	Jeff George	1.00	.45
❑	252	Rickey Dudley	.60	.25
❑	253	James Jett	1.00	.45
❑	254	Bobby Taylor	1.00	.45
❑	255	Rodney Peete	1.00	.45
❑	256	William Thomas	1.00	.45
❑	257	Jerome Bettis	1.50	.70
❑	258	Charles Johnson	.60	.25
❑	259	C.Fuamatu-Ma'afala RC	2.50	1.10
❑	260	Eddie Kennison	1.00	.45
❑	261	Az-Zahir Hakim RC	5.00	2.20
❑	262	Robert Holcombe RC	2.50	1.10
❑	263	Bryan Still	.60	.25
❑	264	Mikhael Ricks RC	2.50	1.10
❑	265	Charlie Jones	.60	.25
❑	266	J.J. Stokes	1.00	.45
❑	267	Marc Edwards	.60	.25
❑	268	Steve Young	2.00	.90
❑	269	Ricky Watters	1.00	.45
❑	270	Cortez Kennedy	.60	.25
❑	271	Shawn Springs	.60	.25
❑	272	Trent Dilfer	1.50	.70
❑	273	Warren Sapp	1.00	.45
❑	274	Reidel Anthony	1.00	.45
❑	275	Yancey Thigpen	.60	.25
❑	276	Chris Sanders	.60	.25
❑	277	Eddie George	1.50	.70
❑	278	Leslie Shepherd	.60	.25
❑	279	Skip Hicks RC	2.50	1.10
❑	280	Dana Stubblefield	.60	.25
❑	281	John Elway ET	8.00	3.60
❑	282	Brett Favre ET	8.00	3.60
❑	283	Junior Seau ET	2.00	.90
❑	284	Barry Sanders ET	6.00	2.70
❑	285	Jerry Rice ET	4.00	1.80
❑	286	Antonio Freeman ET	2.00	.90
❑	287	Peyton Manning ET	30.00	13.50
❑	288	Warrick Dunn ET	2.00	.90
❑	289	Steve Young ET	2.50	1.10
❑	290	Dan Marino ET	8.00	3.60
❑	291	Jerome Bettis ET	2.00	.90
❑	292	Ryan Leaf ET	2.00	.90
❑	293	Deion Sanders ET	2.00	.90
❑	294	Eddie George ET	2.00	.90
❑	295	Joey Galloway ET	1.25	.55
❑	296	Troy Aikman ET	4.00	1.80
❑	297	Andre Wadsworth ET	1.25	.55
❑	298	Terrell Davis ET	2.00	.90
❑	299	Steve McNair ET	2.00	.90
❑	300	Jake Plummer ET	2.00	.90
❑	301	Emmitt Smith ET	6.00	2.70
❑	302	Isaac Bruce ET	2.00	.90
❑	303	Kordell Stewart ET	2.00	.90
❑	304	Dorsey Levens ET	2.00	.90
❑	305	Antowain Smith ET	2.00	.90
❑	306	Drew Bledsoe ET	3.00	1.35
❑	307	Marshall Faulk ET	2.50	1.10
❑	308	Herman Moore ET	1.25	.55
❑	309	Mark Brunell ET	2.00	.90
❑	310	Charles Woodson ET	5.00	2.20
❑	311	Peyton Manning NS	30.00	13.50
❑	312	Curtis Enis NS	1.50	.70
❑	313	Terry Fair NS RC	2.50	1.10
❑	314	Andre Wadsworth NS	2.50	1.10
❑	315	A.Simmons NS RC	2.50	1.10
❑	316	Jacquez Green NS RC	8.00	3.60
❑	317	Takeo Spikes NS	5.00	2.20
❑	318	Vonnie Holliday NS RC	8.00	3.60
❑	319	Kyle Turley NS RC	5.00	2.20
❑	320	Keith Brooking NS	5.00	2.20
❑	321	Randy Moss NS	20.00	9.00
❑	322	Shaun Williams NS RC	2.50	1.10
❑	323	Greg Ellis NS	1.50	.70
❑	324	Mikhael Ricks NS	2.50	1.10
❑	325	Charles Woodson NS	8.00	3.60
❑	326	Corey Chavous NS RC	5.00	2.20
❑	327	S.Alexander NS RC	8.00	3.60
❑	328	Marcus Nash NS	1.50	.70
❑	329	Tra Thomas NS RC	2.50	1.10
❑	330	Duane Starks NS RC	5.00	2.20
❑	331	John Avery NS RC	2.50	1.10
❑	332	Kevin Dyson NS	5.00	2.20
❑	333	Fred Taylor NS	10.00	4.50
❑	334	Grant Wistrom NS	2.50	1.10
❑	335	Ryan Leaf NS	5.00	2.20
❑	336	Robert Edwards NS	2.50	1.10
❑	337	Jason Peter NS RC	2.50	1.10
❑	338	Brian Griese NS	12.00	5.50
❑	339	Charlie Batch NS	5.00	2.20
❑	340	Pat Johnson NS	2.50	1.10
❑	341	John Elway SS	15.00	6.75
❑	342	Curtis Enis SS	1.50	.70
❑	343	Antonio Freeman SS	4.00	1.80
❑	344	Mark Brunell SS	4.00	1.80
❑	345	Robert Edwards SS	2.50	1.10
❑	346	Ryan Leaf SS	4.00	1.80

	Nm-Mt	Ex-Mt
❑ 347 Steve Young SS	5.00	2.20
❑ 348 Jerome Bettis SS	4.00	1.80
❑ 349 Antowain Smith SS	4.00	1.80
❑ 350 Tim Brown SS	4.00	1.80
❑ 351 Peyton Manning SS	40.00	18.00
❑ 352 Troy Aikman SS	8.00	3.60
❑ 353 Natrone Means SS	2.50	1.10
❑ 354 Dan Marino SS	15.00	6.75
❑ 355 Junior Seau SS	1.50	.70
❑ 356 Brad Johnson SS	4.00	1.80
❑ 357 Jerry Rice SS	8.00	3.60
❑ 358 Drew Bledsoe SS	6.00	2.70
❑ 359 Fred Taylor SS	8.00	3.60
❑ 360 Emmitt Smith SS	12.00	5.50
❑ 361 Terrell Davis UV	8.00	3.60
❑ 362 Kordell Stewart UV	6.00	2.70
❑ 363 Barry Sanders UV	20.00	9.00
❑ 364 Jake Plummer UV	6.00	2.70
❑ 365 Brett Favre UV	25.00	11.00
❑ 366 Curtis Enis UV	6.00	2.70
❑ 367 Eddie George UV	6.00	2.70
❑ 368 Napoleon Kaufman UV	6.00	2.70
❑ 369 Randy Moss UV	40.00	18.00
❑ 370 Warrick Dunn UV	6.00	2.70
❑ S8 Troy Aikman Sample	1.00	.45
❑ S234 Dan Marino Sample	2.00	.90

1998 SPx Finite Radiance

Nm-Mt Ex-Mt

*1-90 RADIANCE STARS: .6X TO 1.5X HI
1-90 PRINT RUN 3800 SERIAL #'d SETS
*91-120 RADIANCE STARS: .6X TO 1.5X HI
91-120 PM PRINT RUN 2750 SERIAL #'d SETS
*121-150 RADIANCE STARS: .6X TO 1.5X HI
121-150 YM PRINT RUN 1500 SERIAL #'d SETS
*151-170 RADIANCE STARS: .8X TO 2X HI
151-170 PE PRINT RUN 1000 SERIAL #'d SETS
*171-180 RADIANCE STARS: 2X TO 5X
171-180 HG PRINT RUN 100 SERIAL #'d SETS
181-190 PRINT RUN 50 SERIAL #'d SETS
*191-280 RADIANCE STARS: .6X TO 1.5X
*191-280 RADIANCE RCs: .4X TO 1X
191-280 PRINT RUN 5050 SERIAL #'d SETS
218/221/239 PRINT RUN 1700 SER.#'d SETS
*281-310 RADIANCE STARS: .6X TO 1.5X
281-310 ET PRINT RUN 3600 SER.#'d SETS
*311-340 RADIANCE STARS: .6X TO 1.5X
311-340 NS PRINT RUN 2000 SER.#'d SETS
321/338/339 PRINT RUN 850 SER.#'d SETS
*341-360 RADIANCE STARS: .8X TO 2X
341-360 SS PRINT RUN 900 SER.#'d SETS
*361-370 RADIANCE STARS: .8X TO 2X
*361-370 RAD.ROOKIES: .6X TO 1.5X
361-370 UV PRINT RUN 540 SER.#'d SETS

	Nm-Mt	Ex-Mt
❑ 181 Peyton Manning	400.00	180.00
❑ 182 Ryan Leaf	60.00	27.00
❑ 183 Andre Wadsworth	50.00	22.00
❑ 184 Charles Woodson	80.00	36.00
❑ 185 Curtis Enis	40.00	18.00
❑ 186 Grant Wistrom	50.00	22.00
❑ 187 Fred Taylor	60.00	27.00
❑ 188 Takeo Spikes	60.00	27.00
❑ 189 Kevin Dyson	60.00	27.00
❑ 190 Robert Edwards	40.00	18.00
❑ 218 Brian Griese	80.00	36.00
❑ 221 Charlie Batch	30.00	13.50
❑ 239 Randy Moss	120.00	55.00

1999 SPx

	Nm-Mt	Ex-Mt
COMPLETE SET (135)	2000.00	900.00
COMP.SET w/o SP's (90)	25.00	11.00

*HAND NUMBERED RCs: .5X TO .8X

	Nm-Mt	Ex-Mt
❑ 1 Jake Plummer	1.00	.45
❑ 2 Adrian Murrell	1.00	.45
❑ 3 Frank Sanders	1.00	.45
❑ 4 Jamal Anderson	1.50	.70
❑ 5 Chris Chandler	1.00	.45
❑ 6 Terance Mathis	1.00	.45
❑ 7 Tony Banks	1.00	.45
❑ 8 Priest Holmes	2.50	1.10
❑ 9 Jermaine Lewis	1.00	.45
❑ 10 Antowain Smith	1.50	.70
❑ 11 Doug Flutie	1.50	.70
❑ 12 Eric Moulds	1.50	.70
❑ 13 Tim Biakabutuka	1.00	.45
❑ 14 Steve Beuerlein	1.00	.45
❑ 15 Muhsin Muhammad	1.00	.45
❑ 16 Bobby Engram	1.00	.45
❑ 17 Curtis Conway	1.00	.45
❑ 18 Curtis Enis	.60	.25
❑ 19 Corey Dillon	1.50	.70
❑ 20 Jeff Blake	1.00	.45
❑ 21 Carl Pickens	1.00	.45
❑ 22 Ty Detmer	1.00	.45
❑ 23 Terry Kirby	.60	.25
❑ 24 Leslie Shepherd	.60	.25
❑ 25 Troy Aikman	3.00	1.35
❑ 26 Emmitt Smith	3.00	1.35
❑ 27 Deion Sanders	1.50	.70
❑ 28 Terrell Davis	1.50	.70
❑ 29 Rod Smith	1.00	.45
❑ 30 Bubby Brister	1.00	.45
❑ 31 Barry Sanders	5.00	2.20
❑ 32 Herman Moore	1.00	.45
❑ 33 Charlie Batch	1.50	.70
❑ 34 Brett Favre	5.00	2.20
❑ 35 Antonio Freeman	1.50	.70
❑ 36 Dorsey Levens	1.50	.70
❑ 37 Peyton Manning	5.00	2.20
❑ 38 Marvin Harrison	1.50	.70
❑ 39 Jerome Pathon	.60	.25
❑ 40 Mark Brunell	1.50	.70
❑ 41 Jimmy Smith	1.00	.45
❑ 42 Fred Taylor	1.50	.70
❑ 43 Elvis Grbac	1.00	.45
❑ 44 Andre Rison	1.00	.45
❑ 45 Warren Moon	1.50	.70
❑ 46 Dan Marino	5.00	2.20
❑ 47 Karim Abdul-Jabbar	1.00	.45
❑ 48 O.J. McDuffie	1.00	.45
❑ 49 Randall Cunningham	1.50	.70
❑ 50 Robert Smith	1.50	.70
❑ 51 Randy Moss	4.00	1.80
❑ 52 Drew Bledsoe	2.00	.90
❑ 53 Terry Glenn	1.50	.70
❑ 54 Tony Simmons	.60	.25
❑ 55 Danny Wuerffel	.60	.25
❑ 56 Cam Cleeland	.60	.25
❑ 57 Kerry Collins	1.00	.45
❑ 58 Gary Brown	.60	.25
❑ 59 Ike Hilliard	.60	.25
❑ 60 Vinny Testaverde	1.00	.45
❑ 61 Curtis Martin	1.50	.70
❑ 62 Keyshawn Johnson	1.50	.70
❑ 63 Rich Gannon	1.50	.70
❑ 64 Napoleon Kaufman	1.50	.70
❑ 65 Tim Brown	1.50	.70
❑ 66 Duce Staley	1.50	.70
❑ 67 Doug Pederson	.60	.25
❑ 68 Charles Johnson	.60	.25
❑ 69 Kordell Stewart	1.00	.45
❑ 70 Jerome Bettis	1.50	.70
❑ 71 Trent Green	1.50	.70
❑ 72 Marshall Faulk	2.00	.90
❑ 73 Ryan Leaf	1.50	.70
❑ 74 Natrone Means	1.00	.45
❑ 75 Jim Harbaugh	1.00	.45
❑ 76 Steve Young	2.00	.90
❑ 77 Garrison Hearst	1.00	.45
❑ 78 Jerry Rice	3.00	1.35
❑ 79 Terrell Owens	1.50	.70
❑ 80 Ricky Watters	1.00	.45
❑ 81 Joey Galloway	1.00	.45
❑ 82 Jon Kitna	1.50	.70
❑ 83 Warrick Dunn	1.50	.70
❑ 84 Trent Dilfer	1.00	.45
❑ 85 Mike Alstott	1.50	.70
❑ 86 Steve McNair	1.50	.70
❑ 87 Eddie George	1.50	.70
❑ 88 Yancey Thigpen	.60	.25
❑ 89 Skip Hicks	.60	.25
❑ 90 Michael Westbrook	1.00	.45
❑ 91 Amos Zereoue RC	15.00	6.75
❑ 92 Chris Claiborne AU RC	25.00	11.00
❑ 93 Scott Covington RC	15.00	6.75
❑ 94 Jeff Paulk RC	10.00	4.50
❑ 95 Brandon Stokley AUTO RC	30.00	13.50
❑ 96 Antoine Winfield RC	10.00	4.50
❑ 97 Reginald Kelly RC	10.00	4.50
❑ 98 Jermaine Fazande AUTO RC	15.00	6.75
❑ 99 Andy Katzenmoyer RC	12.00	5.50
❑ 100 Craig Yeast RC	12.00	5.50
❑ 101 Joe Montgomery RC	12.00	5.50
❑ 102 Darrin Chiaverini RC	12.00	5.50
❑ 103 Travis McGriff RC	10.00	4.50
❑ 104 Jevon Kearse RC	30.00	13.50
❑ 105 Joel Makovicka AUTO RC	15.00	6.75
❑ 106 Aaron Brooks RC	40.00	18.00
❑ 107 Chris McAlister RC	12.00	5.50
❑ 108 Jim Kleinsasser RC	15.00	6.75
❑ 109 Ebenezer Ekuban RC	12.00	5.50
❑ 110 Karsten Bailey RC	12.00	5.50
❑ 111 Sedrick Irvin AU RC	12.00	5.50
❑ 112 D.Bates AUTO RC	12.00	5.50
❑ 113 Joe Germaine AU RC	15.00	6.75
❑ 114 Cecil Collins AU RC	15.00	6.75
❑ 115 Mike Cloud RC	12.00	5.50
❑ 116 James Johnson RC	12.00	5.50
❑ 117 Champ Bailey AU RC	40.00	18.00
❑ 118 Rob Konrad RC	15.00	6.75
❑ 119 Peerless Price AU RC	40.00	18.00
❑ 120 Kevin Faulk AU RC	25.00	11.00
❑ 121 Dameane Douglas RC	10.00	4.50
❑ 122 Kevin Johnson AU RC	15.00	6.75
❑ 123 Troy Edwards AU RC	25.00	11.00
❑ 124 Edgerrin James AUTO RC	120.00	55.00
❑ 125 David Boston AU RC	25.00	11.00
❑ 126 Michael Bishop AU RC	25.00	11.00
❑ 127 Shaun King AUTO RC SP	100.00	45.00
❑ 127X Shaun King EXCH	10.00	4.50
❑ 128 Brock Huard AU RC	15.00	6.75
❑ 129 Torry Holt AU RC	60.00	27.00
❑ 130 C.McNown AU/500 RC	50.00	22.00
❑ 131 Tim Couch AU/500 RC	80.00	36.00
❑ 132 Donovan McNabb AUTO RC	150.00	70.00
❑ 132X Donovan McNabb EXCH	5.00	1.50
❑ 133 Akili Smith AU/500 RC	50.00	22.00
❑ 134 Daunte Culpepper AUTO/500 RC	350.00	160.00
❑ 135 Ricky Williams AUTO/500 RC	120.00	55.00
❑ S8 Troy Aikman Sample	2.00	.90

1999 SPx Radiance

Nm-Mt Ex-Mt

*RADIANCE STARS: 6X TO 15X BASIC CARDS

Card	Nm-Mt	Ex-Mt
❑ 91 Amos Zereoue	30.00	13.50
❑ 92 Chris Claiborne	20.00	9.00
❑ 93 Scott Covington	30.00	13.50
❑ 94 Jeff Paulk	20.00	9.00
❑ 95 Brandon Stokley	30.00	13.50
❑ 96 Antoine Winfield	20.00	9.00
❑ 97 Reginald Kelly	20.00	9.00
❑ 98 Jermaine Fazande	25.00	11.00
❑ 99 Andy Katzenmoyer	25.00	11.00
❑ 100 Craig Yeast	25.00	11.00
❑ 101 Joe Montgomery	25.00	11.00
❑ 102 Darrin Chiaverini	25.00	11.00
❑ 103 Travis McGriff	20.00	9.00
❑ 104 Jevon Kearse	50.00	22.00
❑ 105 Joel Makovicka	30.00	13.50
❑ 106 Aaron Brooks	100.00	45.00
❑ 107 Chris McAlister	25.00	11.00
❑ 108 Jim Kleinsasser	30.00	13.50
❑ 109 Ebenezer Ekuban	25.00	11.00
❑ 110 Karsten Bailey	25.00	11.00
❑ 111 Sedrick Irvin	20.00	9.00
❑ 112 D'Wayne Bates	25.00	11.00
❑ 113 Joe Germaine	25.00	11.00
❑ 114 Cecil Collins	20.00	9.00
❑ 115 Mike Cloud	25.00	11.00
❑ 116 James Johnson	25.00	11.00
❑ 117 Champ Bailey	40.00	18.00
❑ 118 Rob Konrad	30.00	13.50
❑ 119 Peerless Price	50.00	22.00
❑ 120 Kevin Faulk	30.00	13.50
❑ 121 Dameane Douglas	20.00	9.00
❑ 122 Kevin Johnson	30.00	13.50
❑ 123 Troy Edwards	25.00	11.00
❑ 124 Edgerrin James	100.00	45.00
❑ 125 David Boston	30.00	13.50
❑ 126 Michael Bishop	30.00	13.50
❑ 127 Shaun King	25.00	11.00
❑ 128 Brock Huard	30.00	13.50
❑ 129 Torry Holt	80.00	36.00
❑ 130 Cade McNown	25.00	11.00
❑ 131 Tim Couch	30.00	13.50
❑ 132 Donovan McNabb	120.00	55.00
❑ 133 Akili Smith	25.00	11.00
❑ 134 Daunte Culpepper	100.00	45.00
❑ 135 Ricky Williams	60.00	27.00

2000 SPx

	Nm-Mt	Ex-Mt
COMP.SET w/o SP's (90)	20.00	9.00
❑ 1 Jake Plummer	.60	.25
❑ 2 David Boston	1.00	.45
❑ 3 Frank Sanders	.60	.25
❑ 4 Chris Chandler	.60	.25
❑ 5 Jamal Anderson	1.00	.45
❑ 6 Shawn Jefferson	.40	.18
❑ 7 Qadry Ismail	.60	.25
❑ 8 Tony Banks	.60	.25
❑ 9 Shannon Sharpe	.60	.25
❑ 10 Rob Johnson	.60	.25
❑ 11 Eric Moulds	1.00	.45
❑ 12 Muhsin Muhammad	.60	.25
❑ 13 Steve Beuerlein	.40	.18
❑ 14 Cade McNown	.40	.18
❑ 15 Marcus Robinson	1.00	.45
❑ 16 Akili Smith	.40	.18
❑ 17 Corey Dillon	1.00	.45
❑ 18 Darnay Scott	.60	.25
❑ 19 Tim Couch	.60	.25
❑ 20 Kevin Johnson	1.00	.45
❑ 21 Errict Rhett	.40	.18
❑ 22 Troy Aikman	2.00	.90
❑ 23 Emmitt Smith	2.00	.90
❑ 24 Joey Galloway	.60	.25
❑ 25 Terrell Davis	1.00	.45
❑ 26 Olandis Gary	1.00	.45
❑ 27 Brian Griese	1.00	.45
❑ 28 Charlie Batch	1.00	.45
❑ 29 Germane Crowell	.40	.18
❑ 30 James Stewart	.60	.25
❑ 31 Brett Favre	3.00	1.35
❑ 32 Antonio Freeman	1.00	.45
❑ 33 Dorsey Levens	.60	.25
❑ 34 Peyton Manning	2.50	1.10
❑ 35 Edgerrin James	1.50	.70
❑ 36 Marvin Harrison	1.00	.45
❑ 37 Mark Brunell	1.00	.45
❑ 38 Fred Taylor	1.00	.45
❑ 39 Jimmy Smith	.60	.25
❑ 40 Keenan McCardell	.60	.25
❑ 41 Elvis Grbac	.60	.25
❑ 42 Tony Gonzalez	.60	.25
❑ 43 Tony Martin	.60	.25
❑ 44 Jay Fiedler	1.00	.45
❑ 45 Damon Huard	1.00	.45
❑ 46 Randy Moss	2.00	.90
❑ 47 Robert Smith	1.00	.45
❑ 48 Cris Carter	1.00	.45
❑ 49 Daunte Culpepper	1.25	.55
❑ 50 Drew Bledsoe	1.25	.55
❑ 51 Terry Glenn	.60	.25
❑ 52 Ricky Williams	1.00	.45
❑ 53 Jeff Blake	.60	.25
❑ 54 Keith Poole	.40	.18
❑ 55 Kerry Collins	.60	.25
❑ 56 Amani Toomer	.60	.25
❑ 57 Ike Hilliard	.60	.25
❑ 58 Ray Lucas	.60	.25
❑ 59 Curtis Martin	1.00	.45
❑ 60 Vinny Testaverde	.60	.25
❑ 61 Tim Brown	1.00	.45
❑ 62 Rich Gannon	1.00	.45
❑ 63 Tyrone Wheatley	.60	.25
❑ 64 Napoleon Kaufman	.60	.25
❑ 65 Duce Staley	1.00	.45
❑ 66 Donovan McNabb	1.50	.70
❑ 67 Troy Edwards	.40	.18
❑ 68 Jerome Bettis	1.00	.45
❑ 69 Kordell Stewart	.60	.25
❑ 70 Marshall Faulk	1.25	.55
❑ 71 Kurt Warner	1.50	.70
❑ 72 Isaac Bruce	1.00	.45
❑ 73 Torry Holt	1.00	.45
❑ 74 Ryan Leaf	.60	.25
❑ 75 Jim Harbaugh	.60	.25
❑ 76 Jerry Rice	2.00	.90
❑ 77 Terrell Owens	1.00	.45
❑ 78 Jeff Garcia	1.00	.45
❑ 79 Ricky Watters	.60	.25
❑ 80 Jon Kitna	1.00	.45
❑ 81 Derrick Mayes	.60	.25
❑ 82 Shaun King	.40	.18
❑ 83 Mike Alstott	1.00	.45
❑ 84 Keyshawn Johnson	1.00	.45
❑ 85 Eddie George	1.00	.45
❑ 86 Steve McNair	1.00	.45
❑ 87 Jevon Kearse	1.00	.45
❑ 88 Brad Johnson	1.00	.45
❑ 89 Stephen Davis	1.00	.45
❑ 90 Michael Westbrook	.60	.25
❑ 91 Anthony Lucas RC	8.00	3.60
❑ 92 Avion Black RC	12.00	5.50
❑ 93 Corey Moore RC	8.00	3.60
❑ 94 Chris Cole RC	12.00	5.50
❑ 95 Chris Hovan RC	12.00	5.50
❑ 96 Dante Hall RC	30.00	13.50
❑ 97 Darrell Jackson RC	30.00	13.50
❑ 98 Deltha O'Neal RC	15.00	6.75
❑ 99 Doug Chapman RC	12.00	5.50
❑ 100 Doug Johnson RC	15.00	6.75
❑ 101 Erron Kinney RC	15.00	6.75
❑ 102 Frank Moreau RC	12.00	5.50
❑ 103 Patrick Pass RC	12.00	5.50
❑ 104 Gari Scott RC	8.00	3.60
❑ 105 Giovanni Carmazzi RC	12.00	5.50
❑ 106 JaJuan Dawson RC	8.00	3.60
❑ 107 James Williams RC	12.00	5.50
❑ 108 Jarious Jackson RC	12.00	5.50
❑ 109 John Abraham RC	20.00	9.00
❑ 110 Keith Bulluck RC	15.00	6.75
❑ 111 Jonas Lewis RC	8.00	3.60
❑ 112 Mike Green RC	12.00	5.50
❑ 113 Ronney Jenkins RC	12.00	5.50
❑ 114 Michael Wiley RC	12.00	5.50
❑ 115 Mike Anderson RC	15.00	6.75
❑ 116 Mareno Philyaw RC	8.00	3.60
❑ 117 Muneer Moore RC	8.00	3.60
❑ 118 Paul Smith RC	12.00	5.50
❑ 119 Raynoch Thompson RC	12.00	5.50
❑ 120 Rob Morris RC	12.00	5.50
❑ 121 Ron Dixon RC	12.00	5.50
❑ 122 Rondell Mealey RC	8.00	3.60
❑ 123 Sebastian Janikowski RC	15.00	6.75
❑ 124 Shaun Ellis RC	15.00	6.75
❑ 125 Charles Lee RC	12.00	5.50
❑ 126 Shyrone Stith RC	12.00	5.50
❑ 127 Thomas Hamner RC	8.00	3.60
❑ 128 Tim Rattay RC	30.00	13.50
❑ 129 Todd Husak RC	15.00	6.75
❑ 130 Tom Brady RC	250.00	110.00
❑ 131 Trevor Gaylor RC	12.00	5.50
❑ 132 Windrell Hayes RC	12.00	5.50
❑ 133 Anthony Becht JSY AU RC	25.00	11.00
❑ 134 Brian Urlacher JSY AU RC	100.00	45.00
❑ 135 Bubba Franks JSY AU RC	30.00	13.50
❑ 136 Chad Pennington JSY AU RC	120.00	55.00
❑ 137 Chris Redman JSY AU RC	25.00	11.00
❑ 138 Corey Simon JSY AU RC	30.00	13.50
❑ 139 Curtis Keaton JSY AU RC	25.00	11.00
❑ 140 Danny Farmer JSY AU RC	25.00	11.00
❑ 141 Dennis Northcutt JSY AU RC	30.00	13.50
❑ 142 Dez White JSY AU RC	30.00	13.50
❑ 143 J.R. Redmond JSY AU SP RC	25.00	11.00
❑ 144 Jamal Lewis JSY AU RC	60.00	27.00
❑ 145 Jerry Porter JSY AU RC	50.00	22.00
❑ 146 Joe Hamilton EXCH	3.00	1.35
❑ 147 Laveranues Coles JSY AU RC	50.00	22.00
❑ 148 R.Jay Soward JSY AU RC	25.00	11.00
❑ 149 Reuben Droughns JSY AU RC	40.00	18.00
❑ 150 Ron Dayne JSY AU RC	40.00	18.00
❑ 151 Ron Dugans JSY AU RC	20.00	9.00
❑ 152 Shaun Alexander JSY AU RC	80.00	36.00
❑ 153 Sylvester Morris JSY AU RC	25.00	11.00
❑ 154 Tee Martin JSY AU RC	30.00	13.50
❑ 155 Thomas Jones EXCH	6.00	2.70
❑ 156 Todd Pinkston JSY AU RC	30.00	13.50
❑ 157 Travis Prentice JSY AU RC	25.00	11.00
❑ 158 Travis Taylor JSY AU SP RC	50.00	22.00
❑ 159 Trung Canidate JSY AU RC	25.00	11.00
❑ 160 Courtney Brown JSY AU RC	40.00	18.00
❑ 161 Peter Warrick JSY AU RC/500	40.00	18.00
❑ 162 Plaxico Burress JSY AU RC	100.00	45.00
❑ S1 Peyton Manning Sample	4.00	1.20

2000 SPx Spectrum

	Nm-Mt	Ex-Mt
*SPECTRUM STARS: 20X TO 50X HI COL.		
❑ 91 Anthony Lucas	40.00	18.00
❑ 92 Avion Black	60.00	27.00
❑ 93 Corey Moore	40.00	18.00
❑ 94 Chris Cole	60.00	27.00

Card	Nm-Mt	Ex-Mt
❑ 95 Chris Hovan	60.00	27.00
❑ 96 Dante Hall	150.00	70.00
❑ 97 Darrell Jackson	120.00	55.00
❑ 98 Deltha O'Neal	80.00	36.00
❑ 99 Doug Chapman	60.00	27.00
❑ 100 Doug Johnson	80.00	36.00
❑ 101 Erron Kinney	80.00	36.00
❑ 102 Frank Moreau	60.00	27.00
❑ 103 Patrick Pass	60.00	27.00
❑ 104 Gari Scott	40.00	18.00
❑ 105 Giovanni Carmazzi	60.00	27.00
❑ 106 JaJuan Dawson	40.00	18.00
❑ 107 James Williams	60.00	27.00
❑ 108 Jarious Jackson	60.00	27.00
❑ 109 John Abraham	80.00	36.00
❑ 110 Keith Bulluck	80.00	36.00
❑ 111 Jonas Lewis	40.00	18.00
❑ 112 Mike Green	60.00	27.00
❑ 113 Ronney Jenkins	60.00	27.00
❑ 114 Michael Wiley	60.00	27.00
❑ 115 Mike Anderson	80.00	36.00
❑ 116 Mareno Philyaw	40.00	18.00
❑ 117 Muneer Moore	40.00	18.00
❑ 118 Paul Smith	60.00	27.00
❑ 119 Raynoch Thompson	60.00	27.00
❑ 120 Rob Morris	60.00	27.00
❑ 121 Ron Dixon	80.00	36.00
❑ 122 Rondell Mealey	40.00	18.00
❑ 123 Sebastian Janikowski	80.00	36.00
❑ 124 Shaun Ellis	80.00	36.00
❑ 125 Charles Lee	40.00	18.00
❑ 126 Shyrone Stith	60.00	27.00
❑ 127 Thomas Hamner	40.00	18.00
❑ 128 Tim Rattay	120.00	55.00
❑ 129 Todd Husak	80.00	36.00
❑ 130 Tom Brady	600.00	275.00
❑ 131 Trevor Gaylor	60.00	27.00
❑ 132 Windrell Hayes	60.00	27.00
❑ 133 Anthony Becht JSY AU	100.00	45.00
❑ 134 Brian Urlacher JSY AU	300.00	135.00
❑ 135 Bubba Franks JSY AU	80.00	36.00
❑ 136 Chad Pennington JSY AU	400.00	180.00
❑ 137 Chris Redman JSY AU	80.00	36.00
❑ 138 Corey Simon JSY AU	100.00	45.00
❑ 139 Curtis Keaton JSY AU	50.00	22.00
❑ 140 Danny Farmer JSY AU	80.00	36.00
❑ 141 Dennis Northcutt JSY AU	80.00	36.00
❑ 142 Dez White JSY AU	100.00	45.00
❑ 143 J.R. Redmond JSY AU	80.00	36.00
❑ 144 Jamal Lewis JSY AU	250.00	110.00
❑ 145 Jerry Porter JSY AU	150.00	70.00
❑ 146 Joe Hamilton JSY AU EXCH	2.00	.90
❑ 147 Laveranues Coles JSY AU	120.00	55.00
❑ 148 R.Jay Soward JSY AU	80.00	36.00
❑ 149 Reuben Droughns JSY AU	120.00	55.00
❑ 150 Ron Dayne JSY AU	120.00	55.00
❑ 151 Ron Dugans JSY AU	50.00	22.00
❑ 152 Shaun Alexander JSY AU	250.00	110.00
❑ 153 Sylvester Morris JSY AU	60.00	27.00
❑ 154 Tee Martin JSY AU	100.00	45.00
❑ 155 Thomas Jones JSY AU	150.00	70.00
❑ 156 Todd Pinkston JSY AU	100.00	45.00
❑ 157 Travis Prentice JSY AU	80.00	36.00
❑ 158 Travis Taylor JSY AU	100.00	45.00
❑ 159 Trung Canidate JSY AU	80.00	36.00
❑ 160 Courtney Brown JSY AU	150.00	70.00
❑ 161 Peter Warrick JSY AU	120.00	55.00
❑ 162 Plaxico Burress JSY AU	250.00	110.00

2000 SPx Winning Materials Autographs

	Nm-Mt	Ex-Mt
❑ AWMCP Chad Pennington	150.00	70.00
❑ AWMEG Eddie George	40.00	18.00
❑ AWMEJ Edgerrin James	60.00	27.00
❑ AWMJL Jamal Lewis	60.00	27.00
❑ AWMKJ Keyshawn Johnson	40.00	18.00
❑ AWMKW Kurt Warner	60.00	27.00
❑ AWMPM Peyton Manning	200.00	90.00
❑ AWMPW Peter Warrick	40.00	18.00

	Nm-Mt	Ex-Mt
❑ AWMRD Ron Dayne	40.00	18.00
❑ AWMRM Randy Moss	150.00	70.00
❑ AWMSA Shaun Alexander	100.00	45.00
❑ AWMTC Tim Couch	40.00	18.00
❑ AWMTD Terrell Davis	60.00	27.00
❑ AWMTM Tee Martin	40.00	18.00
❑ AWMTT Travis Taylor	40.00	18.00

2001 SPx

	Nm-Mt	Ex-Mt
COMP.SET w/o SP's (90)	20.00	6.00
❑ 1 Jake Plummer	.60	.18
❑ 2 David Boston	1.00	.30
❑ 3 Jamal Anderson	1.00	.30
❑ 4 Chris Chandler	.60	.18
❑ 5 Tony Martin	.60	.18
❑ 6 Elvis Grbac	.60	.18
❑ 7 Qadry Ismail	.60	.18
❑ 8 Ray Lewis	1.00	.30
❑ 9 Rob Johnson	.60	.18
❑ 10 Shawn Bryson	.40	.12
❑ 11 Eric Moulds	.60	.18
❑ 12 Tim Biakabutuka	.60	.18
❑ 13 Jeff Lewis	.40	.12
❑ 14 Muhsin Muhammad	.60	.18
❑ 15 Shane Matthews	.40	.12
❑ 16 Marcus Robinson	1.00	.30
❑ 17 Brian Urlacher	1.50	.45
❑ 18 Jon Kitna	.40	.12
❑ 19 Peter Warrick	1.00	.30
❑ 20 Corey Dillon	1.00	.30
❑ 21 Tim Couch	.60	.18
❑ 22 Travis Prentice	.40	.12
❑ 23 Kevin Johnson	.60	.18
❑ 24 Rocket Ismail	.60	.18
❑ 25 Emmitt Smith	2.00	.60
❑ 26 Joey Galloway	.60	.18
❑ 27 Terrell Davis	1.00	.30
❑ 28 Brian Griese	1.00	.30
❑ 29 Rod Smith	.60	.18
❑ 30 Ed McCaffrey	1.00	.30
❑ 31 Charlie Batch	1.00	.30
❑ 32 Germane Crowell	.40	.12
❑ 33 James O. Stewart	.60	.18
❑ 34 Brett Favre	3.00	.90
❑ 35 Antonio Freeman	1.00	.30
❑ 36 Ahman Green	1.00	.30
❑ 37 Peyton Manning	2.50	.75
❑ 38 Edgerrin James	1.25	.35
❑ 39 Marvin Harrison	1.00	.30
❑ 40 Mark Brunell	1.00	.30
❑ 41 Fred Taylor	1.00	.30
❑ 42 Jimmy Smith	.60	.18
❑ 43 Tony Gonzalez	.60	.18
❑ 44 Trent Green	1.00	.30
❑ 45 Priest Holmes	1.25	.35
❑ 46 Lamar Smith	.60	.18
❑ 47 Jay Fiedler	1.00	.30
❑ 48 Oronde Gadsden	.60	.18
❑ 49 Daunte Culpepper	1.00	.30
❑ 50 Randy Moss	2.00	.60
❑ 51 Cris Carter	1.00	.30
❑ 52 Drew Bledsoe	1.25	.35
❑ 53 Troy Brown	.60	.18
❑ 54 Ricky Williams	1.00	.30
❑ 55 Joe Horn	.60	.18
❑ 56 Aaron Brooks	1.00	.30
❑ 57 Albert Connell	.40	.12
❑ 58 Kerry Collins	.60	.18
❑ 59 Tiki Barber	.60	.18
❑ 60 Ron Dayne	1.00	.30
❑ 61 Vinny Testaverde	.60	.18
❑ 62 Wayne Chrebet	.60	.18
❑ 63 Curtis Martin	1.00	.30
❑ 64 Tim Brown	1.00	.30
❑ 65 Jerry Rice	2.00	.60
❑ 66 Rich Gannon	1.00	.30
❑ 67 Duce Staley	1.00	.30
❑ 68 Donovan McNabb	1.25	.35
❑ 69 Kordell Stewart	.60	.18
❑ 70 Jerome Bettis	1.00	.30
❑ 71 Marshall Faulk	1.25	.35
❑ 72 Kurt Warner	2.00	.60
❑ 73 Isaac Bruce	1.00	.30
❑ 74 Torry Holt	1.00	.30
❑ 75 Doug Flutie	1.00	.30
❑ 76 Junior Seau	1.00	.30
❑ 77 Jeff Garcia	1.00	.30
❑ 78 Garrison Hearst	.60	.18
❑ 79 Terrell Owens	1.00	.30
❑ 80 Ricky Watters	.60	.18
❑ 81 Matt Hasselbeck	.60	.18
❑ 82 Brad Johnson	1.00	.30
❑ 83 Keyshawn Johnson	1.00	.30
❑ 84 Warrick Dunn	1.00	.30
❑ 85 Mike Alstott	1.00	.30
❑ 86 Kevin Dyson	.60	.18
❑ 87 Eddie George	1.00	.30
❑ 88 Steve McNair	1.00	.30
❑ 89 Michael Westbrook	.60	.18
❑ 90 Stephen Davis	1.00	.30
❑ 91B Deuce McAllister JSY AU RC/250	120.00	36.00
❑ 91G Deuce McAllister JSY AU RC/250	120.00	36.00
❑ 92B Freddie Mitchell JSY AU RC/250	30.00	9.00
❑ 92G Freddie Mitchell JSY AU RC/250	30.00	9.00
❑ 93B Koren Robinson/999 RC	12.00	3.60
❑ 93G Koren Robinson/999 RC	12.00	3.60
❑ 94B David Terrell/999 RC	10.00	3.00
❑ 94G David Terrell/999 RC	10.00	3.00
❑ 95B Michael Vick JSY AU RC/250	400.00	120.00
❑ 95G Michael Vick JSY AU RC/250	400.00	120.00
❑ 96B Michael Bennett JSY AU RC/550	50.00	15.00
❑ 96G Michael Bennett JSY AU RC/550	50.00	15.00
❑ 97B Robert Ferguson/999 RC	10.00	3.00
❑ 97G Robert Ferguson/999 RC	10.00	3.00
❑ 98B Rod Gardner/999 RC	10.00	3.00
❑ 98G Rod Gardner/999 RC	10.00	3.00
❑ 99B Travis Henry JSY AU RC/550	40.00	12.00
❑ 99G Travis Henry JSY AU RC/550	40.00	12.00

❑ 100B Chad Johnson JSY AU RC/550 60.00 18.00
❑ 100G Chad Johnson JSY AU RC/550 60.00 18.00
❑ 101B Drew Brees JSY AU RC/250 120.00 36.00
❑ 101G Drew Brees JSY AU RC/250 120.00 36.00
❑ 102B Santana Moss JSY AU RC/550 40.00 12.00
❑ 102G Santana Moss JSY AU RC/550 40.00 12.00
❑ 103B Chris Weinke JSY AU RC/550 30.00 9.00
❑ 103G Chris Weinke JSY AU RC/550 30.00 9.00
❑ 104B Richard Seymour JSY AU RC/900 40.00 12.00
❑ 104G Richard Seymour JSY AU RC/900 40.00 12.00
❑ 105B Reggie Wayne/999 RC 15.00 4.50
❑ 105G Reggie Wayne/999 RC 15.00 4.50
❑ 106B Kevan Barlow JSY AU RC/550 30.00 9.00
❑ 106G Kevan Barlow JSY AU RC/550 30.00 9.00
❑ 107B Chris Chambers JSY AU RC/900 40.00 12.00
❑ 107G Chris Chambers JSY AU RC/900 40.00 12.00
❑ 108B Todd Heap JSY AU RC/900 40.00 12.00
❑ 108G Todd Heap JSY AU RC/900 40.00 12.00
❑ 109B Anthony Thomas JSY AU RC/550 40.00 12.00
❑ 109G Anthony Thomas JSY AU RC/550 40.00 12.00
❑ 110B James Jackson JSY AU RC/550 25.00 7.50
❑ 110G James Jackson JSY AU RC/550 25.00 7.50
❑ 111B Rudi Johnson JSY AU RC/900 50.00 15.00
❑ 111G Rudi Johnson JSY AU RC/900 50.00 15.00
❑ 112B Mike McMahon JSY AU RC/900 25.00 7.50
❑ 112G Mike McMahon JSY AU RC/900 25.00 7.50
❑ 113 Josh Heupel JSY AU/900 40.00 12.00
❑ 114B Travis Minor JSY AU RC/900 25.00 7.50
❑ 114G Travis Minor JSY AU RC/900 25.00 7.50
❑ 115B Quincy Morgan/999 RC 10.00 3.00
❑ 115G Quincy Morgan/999 RC 10.00 3.00
❑ 116B Dan Morgan JSY AU RC/900 20.00 6.00
❑ 116G Dan Morgan JSY AU RC/900 20.00 6.00
❑ 117B Jesse Palmer JSY AU RC/900 25.00 7.50
❑ 117G Jesse Palmer JSY AU RC/900 25.00 7.50
❑ 118B Sage Rosenfels JSY AU RC/900 20.00 6.00
❑ 118G Sage Rosenfels JSY AU RC/900 20.00 6.00
❑ 119B Marques Tuiasosopo JSY AU RC/900 30.00 9.00
❑ 119G Marques Tuiasosopo JSY AU RC/900 30.00 9.00
❑ 120B Damerien McCants RC/999 6.00 1.80
❑ 120G Damerien McCants RC/999 6.00 1.80
❑ 121B Snoop Minnis/999 RC 6.00 1.80
❑ 121G Snoop Minnis/999 RC 6.00 1.80
❑ 122B LaDainian Tomlinson JSY/250 RC 120.00 36.00
❑ 122G LaDainian Tomlinson JSY/250 RC 120.00 36.00
❑ 123B Quincy Carter/999 RC 10.00 3.00
❑ 123G Quincy Carter/999 RC 10.00 3.00
❑ 124B Arnold Jackson/999 RC 6.00 1.80
❑ 124G Arnold Jackson/999 RC 6.00 1.80
❑ 125B Justin McCareins RC/999 10.00 3.00
❑ 125G Justin McCareins RC/999 10.00 3.00
❑ 126B Eddie Berlin/999 RC 6.00 1.80
❑ 126G Eddie Berlin/999 RC 6.00 1.80
❑ 127B Quentin McCord RC/999 6.00 1.80
❑ 127G Quentin McCord RC/999 6.00 1.80
❑ 128B Vinny Sutherland RC/999 6.00 1.80
❑ 128G Vinny Sutherland RC/999 6.00 1.80
❑ 129B Willie Middlebrooks RC/999 6.00 1.80
❑ 129G Willie Middlebrooks RC/999 6.00 1.80
❑ 130B Dan Alexander/999 RC 10.00 3.00
❑ 130G Dan Alexander/999 RC 10.00 3.00
❑ 131B Dee Brown/999 RC 10.00 3.00
❑ 131G Dee Brown/999 RC 10.00 3.00
❑ 132B Andre Carter/999 RC 10.00 3.00
❑ 132G Andre Carter/999 RC 10.00 3.00
❑ 133B Justin Smith/999 RC 10.00 3.00
❑ 133G Justin Smith/999 RC 10.00 3.00
❑ 134B T.J. Houshmandzadeh RC/999 10.00 3.00
❑ 134G T.J. Houshmandzadeh RC/999 10.00 3.00
❑ 135B Andre King/999 RC 6.00 1.80
❑ 135G Andre King/999 RC 6.00 1.80
❑ 136B Nick Goings/999 RC 10.00 3.00
❑ 136G Nick Goings/999 RC 10.00 3.00
❑ 137B Scotty Anderson RC/999 6.00 1.80
❑ 137G Scotty Anderson RC/999 6.00 1.80
❑ 138B David Martin/999 RC 6.00 1.80
❑ 138G David Martin/999 RC 6.00 1.80
❑ 139B Derrick Blaylock/999 RC 12.00 3.60
❑ 139G Derrick Blaylock/999 RC 12.00 3.60
❑ 140B Onome Ojo/999 RC 6.00 1.80
❑ 140G Onome Ojo/999 RC 6.00 1.80
❑ 141B Jonathan Carter RC/999 6.00 1.80
❑ 141G Jonathan Carter RC/999 6.00 1.80
❑ 142B LaMont Jordan/999 RC 12.00 3.60
❑ 142G LaMont Jordan/999 RC 12.00 3.60
❑ 143B Dominic Rhodes RC/999 15.00 4.50
❑ 143G Dominic Rhodes RC/999 15.00 4.50
❑ 145B A.J. Feeley/999 RC 10.00 3.00
❑ 145G A.J. Feeley/999 RC 10.00 3.00
❑ 146B Correll Buckhalter RC/999 12.00 3.60
❑ 146G Correll Buckhalter RC/999 12.00 3.60
❑ 147B Steve Smith/999 RC 12.00 3.60
❑ 147G Steve Smith/999 RC 12.00 3.60
❑ 148B Dave Dickenson RC/999 6.00 1.80
❑ 148G Dave Dickenson RC/999 6.00 1.80
❑ 149B Cedrick Wilson/999 RC 10.00 3.00
❑ 149G Cedrick Wilson/999 RC 10.00 3.00
❑ 150B Jamie Winborn/999 RC 6.00 1.80
❑ 150G Jamie Winborn/999 RC 6.00 1.80
❑ 151B Alex Bannister/999 RC 6.00 1.80
❑ 151G Alex Bannister/999 RC 6.00 1.80
❑ 152B Heath Evans/999 RC 6.00 1.80
❑ 152G Heath Evans/999 RC 6.00 1.80
❑ 153B Josh Booty/999 RC 10.00 3.00
❑ 153G Josh Booty/999 RC 10.00 3.00
❑ 154B Adam Archuleta/999 RC 10.00 3.00
❑ 154G Adam Archuleta/999 RC 10.00 3.00
❑ 155B Francis St.Paul/999 RC 6.00 1.80
❑ 155G Francis St.Paul/999 RC 6.00 1.80
❑ 156B Andre Dyson/999 RC 4.00 1.20
❑ 156G Andre Dyson/999 RC 4.00 1.20
❑ RM Randy Moss SAMPLE 2.00 .60

2001 SPx Winning Materials

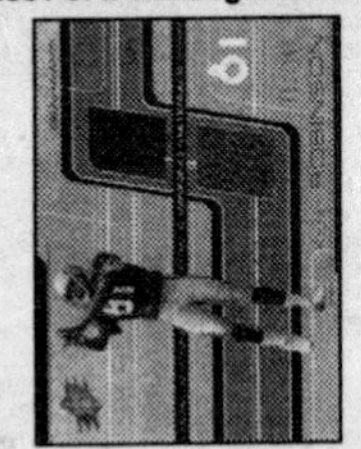

	Nm-Mt	Ex-Mt
❑ WMAC1 Andre Carter/750	12.00	3.60
❑ WMAC2 Andre Carter/250	20.00	6.00
❑ WMAS1 Akili Smith/300	12.00	3.60
❑ WMAS2 Akili Smith/20		
❑ WMAT1 Anthony Thomas/500	20.00	6.00
❑ WMAT2 Anthony Thomas/100	30.00	9.00
❑ WMBE1 Michael Bennett/500	20.00	6.00
❑ WMBE2 Michael Bennett/100	40.00	12.00
❑ WMBF1 Brett Favre/300	60.00	18.00
❑ WMBF2 Brett Favre/20		
❑ WMBO1 David Boston/300	20.00	6.00
❑ WMBO2 David Boston/20		
❑ WMCG1 Charlie Garner/500	10.00	3.00
❑ WMCG2 Charlie Garner/100	20.00	6.00
❑ WMCH1 Chris Chambers/500	30.00	9.00
❑ WMCH2 Chris Chambers/100	40.00	12.00
❑ WMCW1 Chris Weinke/750	12.00	3.60
❑ WMCW2 Chris Weinke/250	20.00	6.00
❑ WMDB1 Drew Brees/500	20.00	6.00
❑ WMDB2 Drew Brees/100	40.00	12.00
❑ WMDB3 Drew Brees/250	30.00	9.00
❑ WMDB4 Drew Brees/750	20.00	6.00
❑ WMDF1 Doug Flutie/750	20.00	6.00
❑ WMDF2 Doug Flutie/250	30.00	9.00
❑ WMDT1 David Terrell/750	10.00	3.00
❑ WMDT2 David Terrell/250	20.00	6.00
❑ WMDU1 Deuce McAllister/750	20.00	6.00
❑ WMDU2 Deuce McAllister/250	40.00	12.00
❑ WMEG1 Elvis Grbac/500	12.00	3.60
❑ WMEG2 Elvis Grbac/100	20.00	6.00
❑ WMEJ1 Edgerrin James/300	25.00	7.50
❑ WMEJ2 Edgerrin James/20		
❑ WMFM1 Freddie Mitchell/500	12.00	3.60
❑ WMFM2 Freddie Mitchell/100	20.00	6.00
❑ WMGA1 Rod Gardner/750	20.00	6.00
❑ WMGA2 Rod Gardner/250	25.00	7.50
❑ WMHE1 Travis Henry/300	20.00	6.00
❑ WMHE2 Travis Henry/20		
❑ WMJF1 Jay Fiedler/750	12.00	3.60
❑ WMJF2 Jay Fiedler/250	20.00	6.00
❑ WMJJ1 James Jackson/300	12.00	3.60
❑ WMJJ2 James Jackson/20		
❑ WMJP1 Jake Plummer/300	12.00	3.60
❑ WMJP2 Jake Plummer/20		
❑ WMJR1 Jerry Rice/750	30.00	9.00
❑ WMJR2 Jerry Rice/250	50.00	15.00
❑ WMJS1 Junior Seau/750	20.00	6.00
❑ WMJS2 Junior Seau/250	20.00	6.00
❑ WMKB1 Kevan Barlow/500	20.00	6.00
❑ WMKB2 Kevan Barlow/100	30.00	9.00
❑ WMKR1 Koren Robinson/750	12.00	3.60
❑ WMKR2 Koren Robinson/250	20.00	6.00
❑ WMKW1 Kurt Warner/300	30.00	9.00

❑ WMKW2 Kurt Warner/20
❑ WMLT1 LaDainian Tomlinson 30.00 9.00
300
❑ WMLT2 LaDainian Tomlinson
20
❑ WMMA1 Mike Alstott/750 20.00 6.00
❑ WMMA2 Mike Alstott/250 20.00 6.00
❑ WMMB1 Mark Brunell/300 20.00 6.00
❑ WMMB2 Mark Brunell/20
❑ WMMF1 Marshall Faulk/300 30.00 9.00
❑ WMMF2 Marshall Faulk/20
❑ WMMO1 Dan Morgan/500 10.00 3.00
❑ WMMO2 Dan Morgan/100 20.00 6.00
❑ WMMT1 Margues Tuiasosopo 20.00 6.00
750
❑ WMMT2 Margues Tuiasosopo 20.00 6.00
250
❑ WMMV1 Michael Vick/750 50.00 15.00
❑ WMMV2 Michael Vick/250 60.00 18.00
❑ WMPA1 Jesse Palmer/500 20.00 6.00
❑ WMPA2 Jesse Palmer/100 30.00 9.00
❑ WMPM1 Peyton Manning/750 30.00 9.00
❑ WMPM2 Peyton Manning/250 50.00 15.00
❑ WMPW1 Peter Warrick/300 20.00 6.00
❑ WMPW2 Peter Warrick/20
❑ WMQM1 Quincy Morgan/750 12.00 3.60
❑ WMQM2 Quincy Morgan/250 20.00 6.00
❑ WMRD1 Ron Dayne/500 20.00 6.00
❑ WMRD2 Ron Dayne/100 30.00 9.00
❑ WMRF1 Robert Ferguson/750 12.00 3.60
❑ WMRF2 Robert Ferguson/250 20.00 6.00
❑ WMRG1 Rich Gannon/300 20.00 6.00
❑ WMRG2 Rich Gannon/20
❑ WMSE1 Jason Sehorn/500 12.00 3.60
❑ WMSE2 Jason Sehorn/100 20.00 6.00
❑ WMSM1 Santana Moss/750 20.00 6.00
❑ WMSM2 Santana Moss/250 25.00 7.50
❑ WMTA1 Troy Aikman/300 30.00 9.00
❑ WMTA2 Troy Aikman/20
❑ WMTB1 Tiki Barber/750 12.00 3.60
❑ WMTB2 Tiki Barber/250 20.00 6.00
❑ WMTC1 Tim Couch/750 12.00 3.60
❑ WMTC2 Tim Couch/250 12.00 3.60
❑ WMTJ1 Thomas Jones/500 12.00 3.60
❑ WMTJ2 Thomas Jones/100 25.00 7.50
❑ WMTO1 Terrell Owens/300 20.00 6.00
❑ WMTO2 Terrell Owens/20
❑ WMWA1 Reggie Wayne/750 20.00 6.00
❑ WMWA2 Reggie Wayne/250 20.00 6.00

2002 SPx

	Nm-Mt	Ex-Mt
COMP.SET w/o SP's (90)	20.00	6.00
❑ 1 Drew Bledsoe	1.25	.35
❑ 2 Peerless Price	.60	.18
❑ 3 Travis Henry	1.00	.30
❑ 4 Ricky Williams	1.00	.30
❑ 5 Jay Fiedler	.60	.18
❑ 6 Tom Brady	2.50	.75
❑ 7 Troy Brown	.60	.18
❑ 8 Antowain Smith	.60	.18
❑ 9 Santana Moss	1.00	.30
❑ 10 Curtis Martin	1.00	.30
❑ 11 Vinny Testaverde	.60	.18
❑ 12 Jamal Lewis	1.00	.30
❑ 13 Chris Redman	.40	.12
❑ 14 Travis Taylor	.60	.18
❑ 15 Corey Dillon	.60	.18
❑ 16 T.J. Houshmandzadeh	.60	.18
❑ 17 Peter Warrick	.60	.18
❑ 18 Courtney Brown	.60	.18
❑ 19 Kevin Johnson	.60	.18
❑ 20 Tim Couch	.60	.18
❑ 21 Hines Ward	1.00	.30
❑ 22 Jerome Bettis	1.00	.30
❑ 23 Kordell Stewart	.60	.18
❑ 24 Corey Bradford	.40	.12
❑ 25 Jermaine Lewis	.40	.12
❑ 26 Edgerrin James	1.25	.35
❑ 27 Marvin Harrison	1.00	.30
❑ 28 Peyton Manning	2.00	.60
❑ 29 Jimmy Smith	.60	.18
❑ 30 Mark Brunell	1.00	.30
❑ 31 Fred Taylor	1.00	.30
❑ 32 Eddie George	1.00	.30
❑ 33 Steve McNair	1.00	.30
❑ 34 Brian Griese	1.00	.30
❑ 35 Shannon Sharpe	.60	.18
❑ 36 Rod Smith	.60	.18
❑ 37 Trent Green	.60	.18
❑ 38 Johnnie Morton	.60	.18
❑ 39 Priest Holmes	1.25	.35
❑ 40 Jerry Rice	2.00	.60
❑ 41 Rich Gannon	1.00	.30
❑ 42 Tim Brown	1.00	.30
❑ 43 Drew Brees	1.00	.30
❑ 44 Junior Seau	1.00	.30
❑ 45 LaDainian Tomlinson	1.50	.45
❑ 46 Emmitt Smith	2.50	.75
❑ 47 Quincy Carter	.60	.18
❑ 48 Rocket Ismail	.60	.18
❑ 49 Amani Toomer	.60	.18
❑ 50 Kerry Collins	.60	.18
❑ 51 Ron Dayne	.60	.18
❑ 52 Donovan McNabb	1.25	.35
❑ 53 Duce Staley	1.00	.30
❑ 54 Antonio Freeman	1.00	.30
❑ 55 Rod Gardner	.60	.18
❑ 56 Stephen Davis	.60	.18
❑ 57 Brian Urlacher	1.50	.45
❑ 58 Anthony Thomas	1.00	.30
❑ 59 Jim Miller	.60	.18
❑ 60 Marty Booker	.60	.18
❑ 61 Az-Zahir Hakim	.40	.12
❑ 62 James Stewart	.60	.18
❑ 63 Ahman Green	1.00	.30
❑ 64 Brett Favre	2.50	.75
❑ 65 Robert Ferguson	.40	.12
❑ 66 Terry Glenn	.60	.18
❑ 67 Randy Moss	2.00	.60
❑ 68 Daunte Culpepper	1.00	.30
❑ 69 Michael Bennett	.60	.18
❑ 70 Michael Vick	3.00	.90
❑ 71 Warrick Dunn	1.00	.30
❑ 72 Rodney Peete	.60	.18
❑ 73 Muhsin Muhammad	.60	.18
❑ 74 Aaron Brooks	1.00	.30
❑ 75 Deuce McAllister	1.25	.35
❑ 76 Keyshawn Johnson	1.00	.30
❑ 77 Michael Pittman	.40	.12
❑ 78 Brad Johnson	.60	.18
❑ 79 Thomas Jones	.60	.18
❑ 80 David Boston	1.00	.30
❑ 81 Jake Plummer	.60	.18
❑ 82 Terrell Owens	1.00	.30
❑ 83 Garrison Hearst	.60	.18
❑ 84 Jeff Garcia	1.00	.30
❑ 85 Darrell Jackson	.60	.18
❑ 86 Shaun Alexander	1.00	.30
❑ 87 Trent Dilfer	.60	.18
❑ 88 Isaac Bruce	1.00	.30
❑ 89 Kurt Warner	1.00	.30
❑ 90 Marshall Faulk	1.00	.30
❑ 91 Saleem Rasheed RC	10.00	3.00
❑ 92 Jason McAddley RC	8.00	2.40
❑ 93 Brandon Doman RC	10.00	3.00
❑ 94 Mike Rumph RC	10.00	3.00
❑ 95 Wendell Bryant RC	10.00	3.00
❑ 96 Bryan Thomas RC	8.00	2.40
❑ 97 Anthony Weaver RC	8.00	2.40
❑ 98 Chester Taylor RC	10.00	3.00
❑ 99 Ed Reed RC	15.00	4.50
❑ 100 Lamar Gordon RC	10.00	3.00
❑ 101 Tellis Redmon RC	8.00	2.40
❑ 102 Ben Leber RC	10.00	3.00
❑ 103 Javin Hunter RC	5.00	1.50
❑ 104 Javon Walker RC	20.00	6.00
❑ 105 Shaun Hill RC	10.00	3.00
❑ 106 Raonall Smith RC	8.00	2.40
❑ 107 Darrell Hill RC	8.00	2.40
❑ 108 Kalimba Edwards RC	10.00	3.00
❑ 109 Robert Thomas RC	10.00	3.00
❑ 110 Craig Nall RC	10.00	3.00
❑ 111 Marques Anderson RC	10.00	3.00
❑ 112 Najeh Davenport RC	10.00	3.00
❑ 113 Jonathan Wells RC	10.00	3.00
❑ 114 Dwight Freeney RC	12.00	3.60
❑ 115 Larry Tripplett RC	5.00	1.50
❑ 116 T.J. Duckett RC	15.00	4.50
❑ 117 John Henderson RC	10.00	3.00
❑ 118 Albert Haynesworth RC	8.00	2.40
❑ 119 Tank Williams RC	8.00	2.40
❑ 120 Ryan Sims RC	10.00	3.00
❑ 121 Leonard Henry RC	8.00	2.40
❑ 122 Clinton Portis RC	50.00	15.00
❑ 123 Josh Reed RC	10.00	3.00
❑ 124 Chad Hutchinson RC	10.00	3.00
❑ 125 Deion Branch RC	20.00	6.00
❑ 126 Rocky Calmus RC	10.00	3.00
❑ 127 Donte Stallworth RC	20.00	6.00
❑ 128 Daryl Jones RC	8.00	2.40
❑ 129 Joey Harrington RC	40.00	12.00
❑ 130 Napoleon Harris RC	10.00	3.00
❑ 131 Phillip Buchanon RC	10.00	3.00
❑ 132 Patrick Ramsey RC	20.00	6.00
❑ 133 Brian Westbrook RC	20.00	6.00
❑ 134 Freddie Milons RC	8.00	2.40
❑ 135 Lito Sheppard RC	10.00	3.00
❑ 136 Michael Lewis RC	10.00	3.00
❑ 137 Jamin Elliott RC	5.00	1.50
❑ 138 Lee Mays RC	10.00	3.00
❑ 139 Verron Haynes RC	10.00	3.00
❑ 140 Jesse Chatman RC	10.00	3.00
❑ 141 Quentin Jammer RC	10.00	3.00
❑ 142 Seth Burford RC	8.00	2.40
❑ 143 Julius Peppers RC	20.00	6.00
❑ 144 William Green RC	15.00	4.50
❑ 145 DeShaun Foster RC	10.00	3.00
❑ 146 Daniel Graham RC	10.00	3.00
❑ 147 David Garrard RC	10.00	3.00
❑ 148 Reche Caldwell RC	10.00	3.00
❑ 149 Randy Fasani RC	8.00	2.40
❑ 150 J.T. O'Sullivan RC	8.00	2.40
❑ 151 Josh McCown JSY AU RC	40.00	12.00
❑ 152 Kurt Kittner JSY AU RC	25.00	7.50
❑ 153 Kahlil Hill JSY AU RC	15.00	4.50
❑ 154 Ladell Betts JSY AU RC	30.00	9.00
❑ 155 Ron Johnson JSY AU RC	15.00	4.50
❑ 156 Maurice Morris JSY AU RC	25.00	7.50
❑ 157 Andre Davis JSY AU RC	30.00	9.00
❑ 158 Antonio Bryant JSY AU RC	30.00	9.00
❑ 159 Roy Williams JSY AU RC	60.00	18.00
❑ 160 Lamont Thompson JSY AU RC	15.00	4.50
❑ 161 Cliff Russell JSY AU RC	15.00	4.50
❑ 162 Woody Dantzler JSY AU RC	20.00	6.00
❑ 163 Travis Stephens JSY AU RC	15.00	4.50
❑ 164 Tony Fisher JSY AU RC	30.00	9.00
❑ 165 Eric McCoo JSY AU RC	15.00	4.50
❑ 166 Eric Crouch JSY AU RC	30.00	9.00
❑ 167 Rohan Davey JSY AU RC	25.00	7.50
❑ 168 Marquise Walker JSY AU RC	15.00	4.50
❑ 169 Jeremy Shockey JSY RC	50.00	15.00
❑ 170 Tim Carter JSY AU RC	20.00	6.00
❑ 171 Atrews Bell JSY AU RC	15.00	4.50
❑ 172 Ant Randle El JSY AU RC	60.00	18.00
❑ 173 Ricky Williams JSY AU RC	40.00	12.00

❑ 174 Mike Williams JSY AU	15.00	4.50
❑ 175 Adrian Peterson JSY AU RC	30.00	9.00
❑ 176 Jab Gaffney JSY AU/650 RC	30.00	9.00
❑ 177 Ashley Lelie JSY AU/250 RC	80.00	24.00
❑ 178 David Carr JSY AU/250 RC	250.00	75.00

2002 SPx Supreme Signatures

	Nm-Mt	Ex-Mt
❑ SSAG Ahman Green	50.00	15.00
❑ SSAM Archie Manning	30.00	9.00
❑ SSAT Anthony Thomas	25.00	7.50
❑ SSBE Michael Bennett	25.00	7.50
❑ SSBJ Brad Johnson	25.00	7.50
❑ SSBO0 David Boston	15.00	4.50
❑ SSCC Chris Chambers	25.00	7.50
❑ SSCW Chris Weinke	15.00	4.50
❑ SSDB0 Drew Brees	25.00	7.50
❑ SSFM0 Freddie Mitchell	12.00	3.60
❑ SSJB0 Jim Brown	80.00	24.00
❑ SSJE John Elway SP/52	200.00	60.00
❑ SSJG Jeff Garcia SP/62	100.00	30.00
❑ SSJL Jamal Lewis	25.00	7.50
❑ SSJR0 John Riggins	50.00	15.00
❑ SSKJ0 Kevin Johnson	15.00	4.50
❑ SSKS0 Kordell Stewart	25.00	7.50
❑ SSMM Mike McMahon	12.00	3.60
❑ SSMO Dan Morgan	12.00	3.60
❑ SSMT Marques Tuiasosopo	15.00	4.50
❑ SSMV Michael Vick	100.00	30.00
❑ SSPH Priest Holmes	40.00	12.00
❑ SSPM Peyton Manning	80.00	24.00
❑ SSQM Quincy Morgan	15.00	4.50
❑ SSSM Santana Moss	25.00	7.50
❑ SSSR Sage Rosenfels	12.00	3.60
❑ SSTC0 Tim Couch	15.00	4.50

2003 SPx

	MINT	NRMT
COMP.SET w/o SP's (110)	25.00	11.00
❑ 1 Peyton Manning	1.50	.70
❑ 2 Aaron Brooks	1.00	.45
❑ 3 Joey Harrington	1.50	.70
❑ 4 Tim Couch	.40	.18
❑ 5 Jeff Garcia	1.00	.45
❑ 6 Jay Fiedler	.60	.25
❑ 7 Chad Hutchinson	1.00	.45
❑ 8 Tommy Maddox	1.00	.45
❑ 9 Drew Brees	1.00	.45
❑ 10 Trent Green	.60	.25
❑ 11 Patrick Ramsey	1.00	.45
❑ 12 Daunte Culpepper	1.00	.45
❑ 13 Kurt Warner	1.00	.45
❑ 14 Brad Johnson	.60	.25
❑ 15 Rich Gannon	.60	.25
❑ 16 Jake Plummer	.60	.25
❑ 17 Steve McNair	1.00	.45
❑ 18 Mark Brunell	.60	.25
❑ 19 Drew Bledsoe	1.00	.45
❑ 20 Kordell Stewart	.60	.25
❑ 21 Kelly Holcomb	.60	.25
❑ 22 Josh McCown	.60	.25
❑ 23 Matt Hasselbeck	.60	.25
❑ 24 Marc Bulger	1.00	.45
❑ 25 Chris Redman	.40	.18
❑ 26 Rodney Peete	.60	.25
❑ 27 Jake Delhomme	1.00	.45
❑ 28 Jon Kitna	.60	.25
❑ 29 Kerry Collins	.60	.25
❑ 30 Quincy Carter	.60	.25
❑ 31 Ricky Williams	1.00	.45
❑ 32 Clinton Portis	1.50	.70
❑ 33 Deuce McAllister	1.00	.45
❑ 34 Ahman Green	1.00	.45
❑ 35 Priest Holmes	1.25	.55
❑ 36 Curtis Martin	1.00	.45
❑ 37 Michael Bennett	.60	.25
❑ 38 Eddie George	.60	.25
❑ 39 Marshall Faulk	1.00	.45
❑ 40 Garrison Hearst	.60	.25
❑ 41 Shaun Alexander	1.00	.45
❑ 42 Corey Dillon	.60	.25
❑ 43 Jamal Lewis	1.00	.45
❑ 44 William Green	.60	.25
❑ 45 Travis Henry	.60	.25
❑ 46 Randy Moss	1.50	.70
❑ 47 Terrell Owens	1.00	.45
❑ 48 Peerless Price	.60	.25
❑ 49 David Boston	.60	.25
❑ 50 Eric Moulds	.60	.25
❑ 51 Marvin Harrison	1.00	.45
❑ 52 Laveranues Coles	.60	.25
❑ 53 Santana Moss	.60	.25
❑ 54 Troy Brown	.60	.25
❑ 55 Chris Chambers	1.00	.45
❑ 56 Tim Brown	1.00	.45
❑ 57 Rod Smith	.60	.25
❑ 58 Hines Ward	1.00	.45
❑ 59 Keyshawn Johnson	1.00	.45
❑ 60 Isaac Bruce	1.00	.45
❑ 61 Torry Holt	1.00	.45
❑ 62 Koren Robinson	.60	.25
❑ 63 Chad Johnson	.60	.25
❑ 64 Derrick Mason	.60	.25
❑ 65 Antonio Bryant	.60	.25
❑ 66 Kevin Johnson	.60	.25
❑ 67 Todd Heap	.60	.25
❑ 68 Tony Gonzalez	.60	.25
❑ 69 Jeremy Shockey	1.50	.70
❑ 70 Brian Urlacher	1.50	.70
❑ 71 Emmitt Smith/500	20.00	9.00
❑ 72 Edgerrin James/500	10.00	4.50
❑ 73 LaDainian Tomlinson/500	8.00	3.60
❑ 74 Brett Favre/500	20.00	9.00
❑ 75 Donovan McNabb/500	10.00	4.50
❑ 76 Tom Brady/500	12.00	5.50
❑ 77 Michael Vick/500	20.00	9.00
❑ 78 David Carr/500	12.00	5.50
❑ 79 Jerry Rice/500	15.00	6.75
❑ 80 Chad Pennington/500	10.00	4.50
❑ 81 Joey Harrington XCT	1.50	.70
❑ 82 Clinton Portis XCT	1.50	.70
❑ 83 Jeremy Shockey XCT	1.50	.70
❑ 84 David Boston XCT	.60	.25
❑ 85 Marshall Faulk XCT	1.00	.45
❑ 86 Emmitt Smith XCT	2.50	1.10
❑ 87 Terrell Owens XCT	1.00	.45
❑ 88 Randy Moss XCT	1.50	.70
❑ 89 Deuce McAllister XCT	1.00	.45
❑ 90 Ahman Green XCT	1.00	.45
❑ 91 Peerless Price XCT	.60	.25
❑ 92 Plaxico Burress XCT	.60	.25
❑ 93 Marvin Harrison XCT	1.00	.45
❑ 94 Keyshawn Johnson XCT	1.00	.45
❑ 95 Laveranues Coles XCT	.60	.25
❑ 96 Drew Bledsoe XCT	1.00	.45
❑ 97 Eric Moulds XCT	.60	.25
❑ 98 Chad Pennington XCT	1.25	.55
❑ 99 Jerry Rice XCT	2.00	.90
❑ 100 David Carr XCT	1.50	.70
❑ 101 Michael Vick XCT	2.50	1.10
❑ 102 Tom Brady XCT	1.50	.70
❑ 103 Donovan McNabb XCT	1.25	.55
❑ 104 Brett Favre XCT	2.50	1.10
❑ 105 Kurt Warner XCT	1.00	.45
❑ 106 LaDainian Tomlinson XCT	1.00	.45
❑ 107 Drew Brees XCT	1.00	.45
❑ 108 Edgerrin James XCT	1.00	.45
❑ 109 Peyton Manning XCT	1.50	.70
❑ 110 Ricky Williams XCT	1.00	.45
❑ 111 Brooks Bollinger RC	10.00	4.50
❑ 112 Gibran Hamden RC	5.00	2.20
❑ 113 Jason Johnson RC	5.00	2.20
❑ 114 Tony Romo RC	10.00	4.50
❑ 115 Juston Wood RC	5.00	2.20
❑ 116 Kirk Farmer RC	5.00	2.20
❑ 117 Kliff Kingsbury RC	8.00	3.60
❑ 118 Jason Gesser RC	10.00	4.50
❑ 119 Brad Banks RC	8.00	3.60
❑ 120 Rob Adamson RC	5.00	2.20
❑ 121 Ken Dorsey RC	15.00	6.75
❑ 122 Curt Anes RC	5.00	2.20
❑ 123 George Wrighster RC	8.00	3.60
❑ 124 Brett Engemann RC	5.00	2.20
❑ 125 Aaron Walker RC	8.00	3.60
❑ 126 Nate Hybl RC	10.00	4.50
❑ 127 Chris Simms RC	20.00	9.00
❑ 128 Marquel Blackwell RC	5.00	2.20
❑ 129 Domanick Davis RC	20.00	9.00
❑ 130 Quentin Griffin RC	25.00	11.00
❑ 131 B.J. Askew RC	10.00	4.50
❑ 132 Earnest Graham RC	8.00	3.60
❑ 133 Sultan McCullough RC	8.00	3.60
❑ 134 Dahrran Diedrick RC	10.00	4.50
❑ 135 Cecil Sapp RC	8.00	3.60
❑ 136 LaBrandon Toefield RC	10.00	4.50
❑ 137 ReShard Lee RC	10.00	4.50
❑ 138 Dwone Hicks RC	5.00	2.20
❑ 139 Brock Forsey RC	10.00	4.50
❑ 140 Bethel Johnson RC	15.00	6.75
❑ 141 Andrew Pinnock RC	8.00	3.60
❑ 142 Ahmad Galloway RC	8.00	3.60
❑ 143 J.T. Wall RC	5.00	2.20
❑ 144 Tom Lopienski RC	8.00	3.60
❑ 145 Justin Griffith RC	8.00	3.60
❑ 146 Lee Suggs RC	20.00	9.00
❑ 147 Nick Maddox RC	5.00	2.20
❑ 148 Jeremi Johnson RC	8.00	3.60
❑ 149 Doug Gabriel RC	10.00	4.50
❑ 150 Bobby Wade RC	10.00	4.50
❑ 151 Justin Gage RC	10.00	4.50
❑ 152 Arnaz Battle RC	10.00	4.50
❑ 153 Brandon Lloyd RC	12.00	5.50
❑ 154 Talman Gardner RC	10.00	4.50
❑ 155 Kareem Kelly RC	8.00	3.60
❑ 156 Billy McMullen RC	8.00	3.60
❑ 157 Antwone Savage RC	5.00	2.20
❑ 158 J.R. Tolver RC	8.00	3.60
❑ 159 Kassim Osgood RC	10.00	4.50
❑ 160 Shaun McDonald RC	10.00	4.50
❑ 161 Sam Aiken RC	8.00	3.60
❑ 162 Adrian Madise RC	8.00	3.60
❑ 163 Charles Rogers RC	12.00	5.50
❑ 164 David Kircus RC	8.00	3.60
❑ 165 Zuriel Smith RC	5.00	2.20
❑ 166 LaTarence Dunbar RC	8.00	3.60
❑ 167 Willie Ponder RC	8.00	3.60
❑ 168 David Tyree RC	5.00	2.20
❑ 169 Kevin Walter RC	8.00	3.60

		MINT	NRMT
❑ 170	Keenan Howry RC	10.00	4.50
❑ 171	Walter Young RC	5.00	2.20
❑ 172	DeAndrew Rubin RC	5.00	2.20
❑ 173	Carl Ford RC	5.00	2.20
❑ 174	Taco Wallace RC	8.00	3.60
❑ 175	Travis Anglin RC	5.00	2.20
❑ 176	Ryan Hoag RC	5.00	2.20
❑ 177	Ronald Bellamy RC	8.00	3.60
❑ 178	Terrence Edwards RC	8.00	3.60
❑ 179	Jerel Myers RC	5.00	2.20
❑ 180	Mike Bush RC	8.00	3.60
❑ 181	Dan Curley RC	5.00	2.20
❑ 182	Carl Morris RC	5.00	2.20
❑ 183	Reggie Newhouse RC	8.00	3.60
❑ 184	Troy Polamalu RC	10.00	4.50
❑ 185	Cecil Moore RC	5.00	2.20
❑ 186	Bennie Joppru RC	10.00	4.50
❑ 187	Donald Lee RC	8.00	3.60
❑ 188	Jason Witten RC	15.00	6.75
❑ 189	Mike Seidman RC	5.00	2.20
❑ 190	Vishante Shiancoe RC	8.00	3.60
❑ 191	Anquan Boldin JSY AU RC	50.00	22.00
❑ 192	Kyle Boller JSY AU/450 RC	80.00	36.00
❑ 193	Chris Brown JSY AU RC	80.00	36.00
❑ 194	Nate Burleson JSY AU RC	50.00	22.00
❑ 195	Tyrone Calico JSY AU/450 RC	50.00	22.00
❑ 196	Dallas Clark JSY AU RC	30.00	13.50
❑ 197	Kevin Curtis JSY AU RC	30.00	13.50
❑ 198	Kliff Kingsbury JSY AU RC	25.00	11.00
❑ 199	Justin Fargas JSY AU RC	30.00	13.50
❑ 200	Rex Grossman JSY AU/450 RC	120.00	55.00
❑ 201	Taylor Jacobs JSY AU RC	30.00	13.50
❑ 202	Andre Johnson JSY AU/250 RC	150.00	70.00
❑ 203	Malaefou MacKenzie JSY AU RC	15.00	6.75
❑ 204	Bryant Johnson JSY AU RC	30.00	13.50
❑ 205	Larry Johnson JSY AU RC	60.00	27.00
❑ 206	Teyo Johnson JSY AU/450 RC	50.00	22.00
❑ 207	Byron Leftwich JSY AU/250 RC	250.00	110.00
❑ 208	Willis McGahee JSY AU/450 RC	125.00	55.00
❑ 210	Carson Palmer JSY AU/250 RC	200.00	90.00
❑ 211	Artose Pinner JSY AU RC	30.00	13.50
❑ 212	Dave Ragone JSY AU RC	30.00	13.50
❑ 213	Terrell Suggs JSY AU RC	40.00	18.00
❑ 215	Onterio Smith JSY AU RC	30.00	13.50
❑ 216	Musa Smith JSY AU RC	30.00	13.50
❑ 217	Brian St.Pierre JSY AU RC	30.00	13.50
❑ 218	Marcus Trufant JSY AU RC	30.00	13.50
❑ 219	Seneca Wallace JSY AU RC	30.00	13.50
❑ 220	Kelley Washington JSY AU RC	30.00	13.50

2003 SPx Spectrum

MINT NRMT

*STARS: 8X TO 20X BASIC CARDS
*STARS 71-80: 1.5X TO 4X
*ROOKIES 111-190: 1.2X TO 3X
ROOKIES/25 NOT PRICED DUE TO SCARCITY

2003 SPx Supreme Signatures

		MINT	NRMT
❑ SSAB	Aaron Brooks	20.00	9.00
❑ SSAH	Az-Zahir Hakim	15.00	6.75
❑ SSAM	Archie Manning	25.00	11.00
❑ SSBB	Brad Banks	15.00	6.75
❑ SSBJ	Bryant Johnson	20.00	9.00
❑ SSBL	Byron Leftwich	80.00	36.00
❑ SSBR	Brad Johnson	20.00	9.00
❑ SSBS	Brian St.Pierre	20.00	9.00
❑ SSCH	Chad Pennington	50.00	22.00
❑ SSCP	Carson Palmer	80.00	36.00
❑ SSCS	Chris Simms	40.00	18.00
❑ SSDC	David Carr SP	50.00	22.00
❑ SSDR	Dave Ragone	20.00	9.00
❑ SSEG	Earnest Graham	15.00	6.75
❑ SSIB	Isaac Bruce	20.00	9.00
❑ SSJG	Jeff Garcia	25.00	11.00
❑ SSJK	Jim Kelly SP		
❑ SSKB	Kyle Boller	40.00	18.00
❑ SSKB	Kevan Barlow	15.00	6.75
❑ SSKK	Kareem Kelly	15.00	6.75
❑ SSKL	Kliff Kingsbury	20.00	9.00
❑ SSKW	Kelley Washington	20.00	9.00
❑ SSLS	Lee Suggs	50.00	22.00
❑ SSMB	Mark Brunell	25.00	11.00
❑ SSMH	Matt Hasselbeck SP		
❑ SSMI	Michael Bennett SP	20.00	9.00
❑ SSMV	Michael Vick	80.00	36.00
❑ SSOS	Onterrio Smith	25.00	11.00
❑ SSPM	Peyton Manning	80.00	36.00
❑ SSPO	Clinton Portis	50.00	22.00
❑ SSQG	Quentin Griffin	30.00	13.50
❑ SSRG	Rod Gardner	15.00	6.75
❑ SSRS	Rod Smith SP	20.00	9.00
❑ SSTB	Tom Brady SP	175.00	80.00
❑ SSTC	Tim Couch	15.00	6.75
❑ SSTG	Trent Green	25.00	11.00
❑ SSTH	Travis Henry	15.00	6.75
❑ SSTJ	Taylor Jacobs	20.00	9.00
❑ SSTS	Terrell Suggs	20.00	9.00

2003 SPx Supreme Signatures Spectrum

MINT NRMT

*SPECTRUM: .6X TO 1.5X BASIC INSERTS

		MINT	NRMT
❑ SSJK	Jim Kelly	80.00	36.00
❑ SSMH	Matt Hasselbeck	60.00	27.00
❑ SSRS	Rod Smith	40.00	18.00
❑ SSTB	Tom Brady	125.00	55.00

2003 SPx Winning Materials Patches Autographs

		MINT	NRMT
❑ BL	Byron Leftwich/25	250.00	110.00
❑ CP	Chad Pennington/50	100.00	45.00
❑ DB	Drew Brees/50	80.00	36.00
❑ JG	Jeff Garcia/50	80.00	36.00
❑ JR	Jerry Rice/25	350.00	160.00
❑ LT	LaDainian Tomlinson/50	100.00	45.00
❑ MV0	Michael Vick/25	300.00	135.00
❑ PM	Peyton Manning/50	175.00	80.00
❑ RM	Randy Moss/50	150.00	70.00
❑ SA	Shaun Alexander/50	100.00	45.00
❑ SC	Carson Palmer/25	200.00	90.00
❑ TC	Tim Couch/50	60.00	27.00
❑ TO	Terrell Owens/50	80.00	36.00

2003 SPx Winning Materials Team Logos

MINT NRMT

*LOGOS/147-250: .5X TO 1.2X BASIC INSERTS

		MINT	NRMT
❑ CC	Chris Chambers/50	20.00	9.00
❑ CD	Corey Dillon/53	20.00	9.00
❑ DC	David Carr/99	25.00	11.00
❑ EJ	Edgerrin James/99	15.00	6.75
❑ KJ	Keyshawn Johnson/53	20.00	9.00
❑ MF	Marshall Faulk/99	15.00	6.75
❑ MV	Michael Vick/150	30.00	13.50
❑ RS	Rod Smith/94	15.00	6.75

2003 SPx Winning Materials Team Logos Spectrum

MINT NRMT

*SPECTRUM: .8X TO 2X BASIC WIN.MAT.

		MINT	NRMT
❑ MV	Michael Vick	60.00	27.00

2004 SPx

	Nm-Mt	Ex-Mt
COMP.SET w/o SP's (100)	30.00	9.00

101-165 RC PRINT RUN 1650 SER.#'d SETS
166-190 RC PRINT RUN 799 SER.#'d SETS
191-221 JSY AU RC #'d TO 1499 UNLESS NOTED

Card	Nm-Mt	Ex-Mt
❑ 1 Anquan Boldin	1.00	.30
❑ 2 Marcel Shipp	.60	.18
❑ 3 Josh McCown	.60	.18
❑ 4 Peerless Price	.60	.18
❑ 5 Michael Vick	2.00	.60
❑ 6 T.J. Duckett	.60	.18
❑ 7 Kyle Boller	1.00	.30
❑ 8 Todd Heap	.60	.18
❑ 9 Jamal Lewis	1.00	.30
❑ 10 Travis Henry	.60	.18
❑ 11 Drew Bledsoe	1.00	.30
❑ 12 Eric Moulds	.60	.18
❑ 13 Jake Delhomme	1.00	.30
❑ 14 Steve Smith	.60	.18
❑ 15 Stephen Davis	.60	.18
❑ 16 Brian Urlacher	1.25	.35
❑ 17 Rex Grossman	1.00	.30
❑ 18 Thomas Jones	.60	.18
❑ 19 Chad Johnson	.60	.18
❑ 20 Carson Palmer	1.25	.35
❑ 21 Rudi Johnson	.60	.18
❑ 22 William Green	.60	.18
❑ 23 Jeff Garcia	1.00	.30
❑ 24 Andre Davis	.40	.12
❑ 25 Roy Williams S	.60	.18
❑ 26 Eddie George	.60	.18
❑ 27 Keyshawn Johnson	.60	.18
❑ 28 Jake Plummer	.60	.18
❑ 29 Ashley Lelie	.60	.18
❑ 30 Quentin Griffin	1.00	.30
❑ 31 Charles Rogers	.60	.18
❑ 32 Olandis Gary	.40	.12
❑ 33 Joey Harrington	1.00	.30
❑ 34 Brett Favre	2.50	.75
❑ 35 Javon Walker	.60	.18
❑ 36 Ahman Green	1.00	.30
❑ 37 Andre Johnson	1.00	.30
❑ 38 Domanick Davis	1.00	.30
❑ 39 David Carr	1.00	.30
❑ 40 Peyton Manning	1.50	.45
❑ 41 Edgerrin James	1.00	.30
❑ 42 Marvin Harrison	1.00	.30
❑ 43 Byron Leftwich	1.50	.45
❑ 44 Jimmy Smith	.60	.18
❑ 45 Fred Taylor	.60	.18
❑ 46 Trent Green	.60	.18
❑ 47 Priest Holmes	1.25	.35
❑ 48 Dante Hall	1.00	.30
❑ 49 Tony Gonzalez	.60	.18
❑ 50 A.J. Feeley	1.00	.30
❑ 51 Marty Booker	.60	.18
❑ 52 Chris Chambers	.60	.18
❑ 53 Zach Thomas	1.00	.30
❑ 54 Randy Moss	1.25	.35
❑ 55 Daunte Culpepper	1.00	.30
❑ 56 Onterrio Smith	.60	.18
❑ 57 Troy Brown	.60	.18
❑ 58 Corey Dillon	.60	.18
❑ 59 Tom Brady	1.50	.45
❑ 60 Deuce McAllister	1.00	.30
❑ 61 Joe Horn	.60	.18
❑ 62 Aaron Brooks	.60	.18
❑ 63 Jeremy Shockey	1.00	.30
❑ 64 Kurt Warner	1.00	.30
❑ 65 Tiki Barber	.60	.18
❑ 66 Chad Pennington	1.25	.35
❑ 67 Curtis Martin	1.00	.30
❑ 68 Santana Moss	.60	.18
❑ 69 Rich Gannon	.60	.18
❑ 70 Jerry Rice	2.00	.60
❑ 71 Warren Sapp	.60	.18
❑ 72 Donovan McNabb	1.25	.35
❑ 73 Terrell Owens	1.00	.30
❑ 74 Jevon Kearse	.60	.18
❑ 75 Brian Westbrook	.60	.18
❑ 76 Hines Ward	1.00	.30
❑ 77 Duce Staley	.60	.18
❑ 78 Tommy Maddox	.60	.18
❑ 79 LaDainian Tomlinson	1.00	.30
❑ 80 Drew Brees	1.00	.30
❑ 81 Tim Rattay	.60	.18
❑ 82 Kevan Barlow	.60	.18
❑ 83 Brandon Lloyd	.60	.18
❑ 84 Shaun Alexander	1.00	.30
❑ 85 Matt Hasselbeck	.60	.18
❑ 86 Koren Robinson	.60	.18
❑ 87 Marc Bulger	1.00	.30
❑ 88 Marshall Faulk	1.00	.30
❑ 89 Torry Holt	1.00	.30
❑ 90 Isaac Bruce	.60	.18
❑ 91 Brad Johnson	.60	.18
❑ 92 Keenan McCardell	.40	.12
❑ 93 Derrick Brooks	.60	.18
❑ 94 Steve McNair	1.00	.30
❑ 95 Chris Brown	1.00	.30
❑ 96 Derrick Mason	.60	.18
❑ 97 Clinton Portis	1.00	.30
❑ 98 Mark Brunell	.60	.18
❑ 99 Laveranues Coles	.60	.18
❑ 100 LaVar Arrington	2.00	.60
❑ 101 B.J. Johnson RC	8.00	2.40
❑ 102 Craig Krenzel RC	10.00	3.00
❑ 103 Will Smith RC	10.00	3.00
❑ 104 Jamaar Taylor RC	10.00	3.00
❑ 105 Tommie Harris RC	12.00	3.60
❑ 106 Shawn Andrews RC	10.00	3.00
❑ 107 Kendrick Starling RC	5.00	1.50
❑ 108 Jeris McIntyre RC	8.00	2.40
❑ 109 Jason Babin RC	10.00	3.00
❑ 110 Marcus Tubbs RC	10.00	3.00
❑ 111 Triandos Luke RC	10.00	3.00
❑ 112 Karlos Dansby RC	10.00	3.00
❑ 113 Vernon Carey RC	8.00	2.40
❑ 114 Ryan Krause RC	8.00	2.40
❑ 115 Daryl Smith RC	10.00	3.00
❑ 116 Ricardo Colclough RC	10.00	3.00
❑ 117 Michael Boulware RC	10.00	3.00
❑ 118 Chris Cooley RC	10.00	3.00
❑ 119 Tank Johnson RC	8.00	2.40
❑ 120 Marquise Hill RC	8.00	2.40
❑ 121 Teddy Lehman RC	10.00	3.00
❑ 122 Antwan Odom RC	10.00	3.00
❑ 123 Sean Jones RC	8.00	2.40
❑ 124 Junior Siavii RC	10.00	3.00
❑ 125 Joey Thomas RC	10.00	3.00
❑ 126 Shawntae Spencer RC	10.00	3.00
❑ 127 Dontarrious Thomas RC	10.00	3.00
❑ 128 Travis LaBoy RC	10.00	3.00
❑ 129 Justin Jenkins RC	8.00	2.40
❑ 130 Dwan Edwards RC	5.00	1.50
❑ 131 Derrick Strait RC	10.00	3.00
❑ 132 Matt Ware RC	10.00	3.00
❑ 133 Jared Lorenzen RC	8.00	2.40
❑ 134 Demorrio Williams RC	10.00	3.00
❑ 135 Bob Sanders RC	10.00	3.00
❑ 136 Justin Smiley RC	10.00	3.00
❑ 137 Casey Bramlet RC	8.00	2.40
❑ 138 Jake Grove RC	5.00	1.50
❑ 139 Thomas Tapeh RC	8.00	2.40
❑ 140 Igor Olshansky RC	10.00	3.00
❑ 141 Stuart Schweigert RC	10.00	3.00
❑ 142 Cody Pickett RC	10.00	3.00
❑ 143 Derrick Ward RC	5.00	1.50
❑ 144 Gilbert Gardner RC	8.00	2.40
❑ 145 D.J. Hackett RC	8.00	2.40
❑ 146 Marquis Cooper RC	8.00	2.40
❑ 147 Courtney Watson RC	10.00	3.00
❑ 148 Jim Sorgi RC	10.00	3.00
❑ 149 Caleb Miller RC	8.00	2.40
❑ 150 Casey Clausen RC	12.00	3.60
❑ 151 Jammal Lord RC	10.00	3.00
❑ 152 Sloan Thomas RC	8.00	2.40
❑ 153 Keyaron Fox RC	8.00	2.40
❑ 154 Adimchinobe Echemandu RC	8.00	2.40
❑ 155 Ryan Dinwiddie RC	8.00	2.40
❑ 156 Kris Wilson RC	10.00	3.00
❑ 157 D.J. Williams RC	12.00	3.60
❑ 158 Tim Euhus RC	10.00	3.00
❑ 159 Bradlee Van Pelt RC	10.00	3.00
❑ 160 Keiwan Ratliff RC	8.00	2.40
❑ 161 Darnell Dockett RC	8.00	2.40
❑ 162 Troy Fleming RC	8.00	2.40
❑ 163 Tramon Douglas RC	5.00	1.50
❑ 164 Jeremy LeSueur RC	8.00	2.40
❑ 165 Matt Mauck RC	10.00	3.00
❑ 166 Sean Taylor RC	12.00	3.60
❑ 167 B.J. Symons RC	12.00	3.60
❑ 168 Quincy Wilson RC	10.00	3.00
❑ 169 Ernest Wilford RC	12.00	3.60
❑ 170 Jerricho Cotchery RC	12.00	3.60
❑ 171 Michael Turner RC	10.00	3.00
❑ 172 Samie Parker RC	12.00	3.60
❑ 173 Andy Hall RC	10.00	3.00
❑ 174 Keith Smith RC	10.00	3.00
❑ 175 Josh Harris RC	12.00	3.60
❑ 176 Maurice Mann RC	10.00	3.00
❑ 177 Jonathan Vilma RC	12.00	3.60
❑ 178 Jeff Smoker RC	20.00	6.00
❑ 179 Ben Hartsock RC	12.00	3.60
❑ 180 Chris Gamble RC	15.00	4.50
❑ 181 Derrick Hamilton RC	10.00	3.00
❑ 182 John Navarre RC	12.00	3.60
❑ 183 P.K. Sam RC	10.00	3.00
❑ 184 Kenechi Udeze RC	12.00	3.60
❑ 185 Mewelde Moore RC	15.00	4.50
❑ 186 Carlos Francis RC	10.00	3.00
❑ 187 Dunta Robinson RC	12.00	3.60
❑ 188 Johnnie Morant RC	12.00	3.60
❑ 189 Ahmad Carroll RC	15.00	4.50
❑ 190 Vince Wilfork RC	15.00	4.50
❑ 191 Tatum Bell JSY AU RC	50.00	15.00
❑ 192 Cedric Cobbs JSY AU RC	20.00	6.00
❑ 193 Darius Watts JSY AU RC	25.00	7.50
❑ 194 Julius Jones JSY AU/375 RC	225.00	70.00
❑ 195 Robert Gallery JSY AU RC	25.00	7.50
❑ 196 DeAngelo Hall JSY AU RC	30.00	9.00
❑ 197 Ben Watson JSY AU RC	20.00	6.00
❑ 198 Ben Troupe JSY AU RC	20.00	6.00
❑ 199 Matt Schaub JSY AU RC	25.00	7.50
❑ 200 Michael Jenkins JSY AU RC	25.00	7.50
❑ 201 Luke McCown JSY AU RC	20.00	6.00
❑ 202 Devery Henderson JSY AU RC	15.00	4.50

Card	Nm-Mt	Ex-Mt
❑ 203 Bernard Berrian JSY AU RC	20.00	6.00
❑ 204 Keary Colbert JSY AU RC	25.00	7.50
❑ 205 Devard Darling JSY AU RC	25.00	7.50
❑ 206 Lee Evans JSY AU RC	30.00	9.00
❑ 207 Greg Jones JSY AU RC	20.00	6.00
❑ 208 Michael Clayton JSY AU RC	50.00	15.00
❑ 209 Reggie Williams JSY AU RC	25.00	7.50
❑ 210 Chris Perry JSY AU/799 RC	40.00	12.00
❑ 211 Rashaun Woods JSY AU RC	25.00	7.50
❑ 212 J.P. Losman JSY AU RC	60.00	18.00
❑ 213 Kevin Jones JSY AU RC	60.00	18.00
❑ 214 Kellen Winslow JSY AU/375 RC	60.00	18.00
❑ 215 Steven Jackson JSY AU/375 RC	150.00	45.00
❑ 216 Derrick Hamilton JSY AU RC EXCH	15.00	4.50
❑ 217 Roy Williams JSY AU/375 RC	120.00	36.00
❑ 218 Philip Rivers JSY AU/375 RC	120.00	36.00
❑ 219 Larry Fitzgerald JSY AU/100 RC	300.00	90.00
❑ 220 Ben Roethlisberger JSY AU/375 RC	600.00	180.00
❑ 221 Eli Manning JSY AU/375 RC	300.00	90.00

2004 SPx Spectrum Gold

*STARS: 8X TO 20X BASE CARD HI
*ROOKIES 101-165: 1.2X TO 3X BASE CARD HI
*ROOKIES 166-190: 1X TO 2.5X BASE CARD HI
*ROOKIE AUs 191-221: 1.5X TO 4X AU/1499
STATED PRINT RUN 25 SER.#'d SETS

Card	Nm-Mt	Ex-Mt
❑ 194 Julius Jones JSY AU	500.00	150.00
❑ 210 Chris Perry JSY AU	120.00	36.00
❑ 213 Kevin Jones JSY AU	300.00	90.00
❑ 214 Kellen Winslow JSY AU	200.00	60.00
❑ 215 Steven Jackson JSY AU	300.00	90.00
❑ 217 Roy Williams WR JSY AU	300.00	90.00
❑ 218 Philip Rivers JSY AU	250.00	75.00
❑ 219 Larry Fitzgerald JSY AU	250.00	75.00
❑ 220 Ben Roethlisberger JSY AU	1000.00	300.00
❑ 221 Eli Manning JSY AU	600.00	180.00

2004 SPx Rookie Swatch Supremacy

STATED ODDS 1:18

Card	Nm-Mt	Ex-Mt
❑ SWRBB Bernard Berrian	6.00	1.80
❑ SWRBR Ben Roethlisberger	50.00	15.00
❑ SWRBT Ben Troupe	6.00	1.80
❑ SWRBW Ben Watson	6.00	1.80
❑ SWRCC Cedric Cobbs	6.00	1.80
❑ SWRCP Chris Perry	10.00	3.00
❑ SWRDD Devard Darling	6.00	1.80
❑ SWRDE Devery Henderson	6.00	1.80
❑ SWRDH DeAngelo Hall	8.00	2.40
❑ SWRDW Darius Watts	6.00	1.80
❑ SWREM Eli Manning	30.00	9.00
❑ SWRGJ Greg Jones	6.00	1.80
❑ SWRHA Derrick Hamilton	6.00	1.80
❑ SWRJJ Julius Jones	25.00	7.50
❑ SWRJP J.P. Losman	15.00	4.50
❑ SWRKC Keary Colbert	6.00	1.80
❑ SWRKJ Kevin Jones	20.00	6.00
❑ SWRKW Kellen Winslow Jr.	12.00	3.60
❑ SWRLE Lee Evans	8.00	2.40
❑ SWRLF Larry Fitzgerald	15.00	4.50
❑ SWRLM Luke McCown	6.00	1.80
❑ SWRMC Michael Clayton	15.00	4.50
❑ SWRMJ Michael Jenkins	6.00	1.80
❑ SWRPR Philip Rivers	20.00	6.00
❑ SWRRA Rashaun Woods	6.00	1.80
❑ SWRRG Robert Gallery	8.00	2.40
❑ SWRRO Roy Williams WR	20.00	6.00
❑ SWRRW Reggie Williams	8.00	2.40
❑ SWRSJ Steven Jackson	20.00	6.00
❑ SWRTB Tatum Bell	8.00	2.40

2004 SPx Rookie Winning Materials

STATED ODDS 1:126

Card	Nm-Mt	Ex-Mt
❑ WMRBB Bernard Berrian	8.00	2.40
❑ WMRBR Ben Roethlisberger	80.00	24.00
❑ WMRBT Ben Troupe	8.00	2.40
❑ WMRBW Ben Watson	8.00	2.40
❑ WMRCC Cedric Cobbs	8.00	2.40
❑ WMRCP Chris Perry	15.00	4.50
❑ WMRDD Devard Darling	8.00	2.40
❑ WMRDE Devery Henderson	8.00	2.40
❑ WMRDH DeAngelo Hall	10.00	3.00
❑ WMRDW Darius Watts	10.00	3.00
❑ WMREM Eli Manning	40.00	12.00
❑ WMRGJ Greg Jones	8.00	2.40
❑ WMRHA Derrick Hamilton	8.00	2.40
❑ WMRJJ Julius Jones	30.00	9.00
❑ WMRJP J.P. Losman	20.00	6.00
❑ WMRKC Keary Colbert	10.00	3.00
❑ WMRKJ Kevin Jones	25.00	7.50
❑ WMRKW Kellen Winslow Jr.	20.00	6.00
❑ WMRLE Lee Evans	12.00	3.60
❑ WMRLF Larry Fitzgerald	25.00	7.50
❑ WMRLM Luke McCown	8.00	2.40
❑ WMRMC Michael Clayton	20.00	6.00
❑ WMRMJ Michael Jenkins	8.00	2.40
❑ WMRPR Philip Rivers	25.00	7.50
❑ WMRRA Rashaun Woods	10.00	3.00
❑ WMRRG Robert Gallery	12.00	3.60
❑ WMRRO Roy Williams WR	25.00	7.50
❑ WMRRW Reggie Williams	10.00	3.00
❑ WMRSJ Steven Jackson	25.00	7.50
❑ WMRTB Tatum Bell	12.00	3.60

2004 SPx Super Scripts Autographs

STATED ODDS 1:54

Card	Nm-Mt	Ex-Mt
❑ SSAG Ahman Green	30.00	9.00
❑ SSAR Andy Reid CO	25.00	7.50
❑ SSBC Brandon Chillar	10.00	3.00
❑ SSBF Brett Favre SP	150.00	45.00
❑ SSBH Ben Hartsock	10.00	3.00
❑ SSBL Brandon Lloyd	10.00	3.00
❑ SSBW Brian Westbrook EXCH	25.00	7.50
❑ SSBY Byron Leftwich	30.00	9.00
❑ SSCC Chris Chambers	15.00	4.50
❑ SSCF Clarence Farmer	10.00	3.00
❑ SSCJ Chad Johnson	15.00	4.50
❑ SSCP Chad Pennington EXCH	40.00	12.00
❑ SSDB Drew Bledsoe	25.00	7.50
❑ SSDC David Carr	25.00	7.50
❑ SSDD Domanick Davis	15.00	4.50
❑ SSDE Deuce McAllister	25.00	7.50
❑ SSDH Dante Hall	15.00	4.50
❑ SSDM Derrick Mason	10.00	3.00
❑ SSDO Donovan McNabb SP	50.00	15.00
❑ SSEL Antwaan Randle El	25.00	7.50
❑ SSHE Todd Heap	15.00	4.50
❑ SSJF Justin Fargas EXCH	15.00	4.50
❑ SSJG Jon Gruden CO	15.00	4.50
❑ SSJH Joe Horn	10.00	3.00
❑ SSJJ Jimmy Johnson CO	25.00	7.50
❑ SSJO Joey Galloway	10.00	3.00
❑ SSJP Jesse Palmer	10.00	3.00
❑ SSJW Javon Walker EXCH	25.00	7.50
❑ SSKB Kyle Boller	15.00	4.50
❑ SSKD Ken Dorsey	10.00	3.00
❑ SSKW Kelley Washington	10.00	3.00
❑ SSLT LaDainian Tomlinson EXCH	25.00	7.50
❑ SSMB Mark Brunell	15.00	4.50
❑ SSMV Michael Vick SP	80.00	24.00
❑ SSPM Peyton Manning	80.00	24.00
❑ SSRG Rex Grossman	15.00	4.50
❑ SSRJ Rudi Johnson	15.00	4.50
❑ SSRW Roy Williams S	25.00	7.50
❑ SSSM Steve McNair	25.00	7.50
❑ SSTB Tom Brady SP	150.00	45.00
❑ SSTG Tony Gonzalez	15.00	4.50
❑ SSTH Travis Henry	10.00	3.00
❑ SSWM Willis McGahee	25.00	7.50
❑ SSZT Zach Thomas	25.00	7.50

2004 SPx Super Scripts Triple Autographs

STATED PRINT RUN 10-25 SER.#'d CARDS
SERIAL #'d TO 10 NOT PRICED

Card	Nm-Mt	Ex-Mt
❑ BFM Tom Brady/10 Brett Favre Peyton Manning		

Card	Nm-Mt	Ex-Mt
❑ EMN John Elway/10		
Joe Montana		
Joe Namath		
❑ GBL Rex Grossman/25	150.00	45.00
Kyle Boller		
Byron Leftwich		
❑ GSL Robert Gallery/25	250.00	75.00
Ken Stabler		
Howie Long		
❑ JGR Jimmy Johnson/25	150.00	45.00
Jon Gruden		
Andy Reid		
❑ JJJ Steven Jackson/25	300.00	90.00
Julius Jones		
Kevin Jones		
❑ MBM Steve McNair/25	150.00	45.00
Chris Brown		
Derrick Mason		
❑ MMM Archie Manning/10		
Peyton Manning		
Eli Manning		
❑ MVM Donovan McNabb/10		
Michael Vick		
Steve McNair		
❑ RRM Philip Rivers/25	800.00	240.00
Ben Roethlisberger		
Eli Manning		
❑ SAH Roger Staubach/10		
Troy Aikman		
Drew Henson		
❑ SEA Barry Sanders/25	600.00	180.00
John Elway		
Troy Aikman		
❑ TMG LaDainian Tomlinson/25		
Deuce McAllister		
Ahman Green		
❑ TST Joe Theismann/25	250.00	75.00
Ken Stabler		
Fran Tarkenton		
❑ WWE Roy Williams WR/25 EXCH	250.00	75.00
Reggie Williams		
Lee Evans		

2004 SPx Swatch Supremacy

STATED ODDS 1:18	Nm-Mt	Ex-Mt
❑ SWAG Ahman Green	8.00	2.40
❑ SWAR Antwaan Randle El	6.00	1.80
❑ SWBL Byron Leftwich	10.00	3.00
❑ SWBW Brian Westbrook	8.00	2.40
❑ SWCB Chris Brown	8.00	2.40
❑ SWCC Chris Chambers	6.00	1.80
❑ SWCJ Chad Johnson	6.00	1.80
❑ SWCP Chad Pennington	10.00	3.00
❑ SWDC Daunte Culpepper	8.00	2.40
❑ SWDD Domanick Davis	6.00	1.80
❑ SWDE Derrick Mason	6.00	1.80
❑ SWDH Dante Hall	8.00	2.40
❑ SWDM Deuce McAllister	8.00	2.40
❑ SWDO Donovan McNabb	10.00	3.00
❑ SWHE Todd Heap	6.00	1.80
❑ SWJG Joey Galloway	5.00	1.50
❑ SWJH Joe Horn	6.00	1.80
❑ SWJW Javon Walker	8.00	2.40
❑ SWKB Kyle Boller	6.00	1.80
❑ SWLT LaDainian Tomlinson	8.00	2.40
❑ SWMB Mark Brunell	6.00	1.80
❑ SWMV Michael Vick	15.00	4.50
❑ SWPM Peyton Manning	12.00	3.60
❑ SWRG Rex Grossman	8.00	2.40
❑ SWRJ Rudi Johnson	6.00	1.80
❑ SWRW Roy Williams S	8.00	2.40
❑ SWTB Tom Brady	20.00	6.00
❑ SWTG Tony Gonzalez	6.00	1.80
❑ SWTH Travis Henry	5.00	1.50
❑ SWZT Zach Thomas	8.00	2.40

2004 SPx Swatch Supremacy Autographs

STATED PRINT RUN 100 SER.#'d SETS	Nm-Mt	Ex-Mt
❑ SWAAG Ahman Green	50.00	15.00
❑ SWAAR Antwaan Randle El	40.00	12.00
❑ SWABL Byron Leftwich	50.00	15.00
❑ SWABW Brian Westbrook EXCH	30.00	9.00
❑ SWACB Chris Brown	40.00	12.00
❑ SWACC Chris Chambers	30.00	9.00
❑ SWACJ Chad Johnson	30.00	9.00
❑ SWACP Chad Pennington EXCH	50.00	15.00
❑ SWADC Daunte Culpepper	50.00	15.00
❑ SWADD Domanick Davis	30.00	9.00
❑ SWADE Derrick Mason	25.00	7.50
❑ SWADH Dante Hall	30.00	9.00
❑ SWADM Deuce McAllister	40.00	12.00
❑ SWADO Donovan McNabb	80.00	24.00
❑ SWAHE Todd Heap	30.00	9.00
❑ SWAJG Joey Galloway	25.00	7.50
❑ SWAJH Joe Horn	25.00	7.50
❑ SWAJW Javon Walker EXCH	40.00	12.00
❑ SWAKB Kyle Boller	30.00	9.00
❑ SWALT LaDainian Tomlinson	40.00	12.00
❑ SWAMB Mark Brunell	30.00	9.00
❑ SWAMV Michael Vick	100.00	30.00
❑ SWAPM Peyton Manning	120.00	36.00
❑ SWARG Rex Grossman	30.00	9.00
❑ SWARJ Rudi Johnson	30.00	9.00
❑ SWARW Roy Williams S	40.00	12.00
❑ SWATB Tom Brady	150.00	45.00
❑ SWATG Tony Gonzalez	30.00	9.00
❑ SWATH Travis Henry	25.00	7.50
❑ SWAZT Zach Thomas	40.00	12.00

2004 SPx Winning Materials

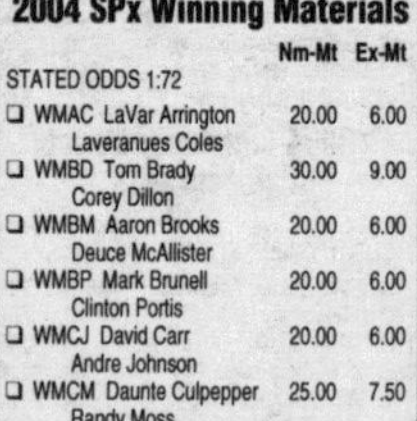

STATED ODDS 1:72	Nm-Mt	Ex-Mt
❑ WMAC LaVar Arrington	20.00	6.00
Laveranues Coles		
❑ WMBD Tom Brady	30.00	9.00
Corey Dillon		
❑ WMBM Aaron Brooks	20.00	6.00
Deuce McAllister		
❑ WMBP Mark Brunell	20.00	6.00
Clinton Portis		
❑ WMCJ David Carr	20.00	6.00
Andre Johnson		
❑ WMCM Daunte Culpepper	25.00	7.50
Randy Moss		

Card	Nm-Mt	Ex-Mt
❑ WMDF Stephen Davis	12.00	3.60
DeShaun Foster		
❑ WMDT Drew Bledsoe	20.00	6.00
Travis Henry		
❑ WMFG Brett Favre	30.00	9.00
Ahman Green		
❑ WMFH Marshall Faulk	20.00	6.00
Torry Holt		
❑ WMFM Brett Favre	30.00	9.00
Donovan McNabb		
❑ WMGG Trent Green	12.00	3.60
Tony Gonzalez		
❑ WMHA Matt Hasselbeck	12.00	3.60
Shaun Alexander		
❑ WMHR Joey Harrington	12.00	3.60
Charles Rogers		
❑ WMHW Priest Holmes	20.00	6.00
Ricky Williams		
❑ WMMJ Peyton Manning	25.00	7.50
Edgerrin James		
❑ WMMM Curtis Martin	20.00	6.00
Santana Moss		
❑ WMMO Donovan McNabb	25.00	7.50
Terrell Owens		
❑ WMMR Randy Moss	25.00	7.50
Jerry Rice		
❑ WMMV Steve McNair	25.00	7.50
Michael Vick		
❑ WMPG Jake Plummer	12.00	3.60
Quentin Griffin		
❑ WMPJ Carson Palmer	12.00	3.60
Rudi Johnson		
❑ WMPL Chad Pennington	25.00	7.50
Byron Leftwich		
❑ WMPS Peyton Manning	25.00	7.50
Steve McNair		
❑ WMRG Jerry Rice	25.00	7.50
Rich Gannon		
❑ WMSK Michael Strahan	12.00	3.60
Jevon Kearse		
❑ WMSU Junior Seau	25.00	7.50
Brian Urlacher		
❑ WMSW Jeremy Shockey	20.00	6.00
Kurt Warner		
❑ WMTH LaDainian Tomlinson	25.00	7.50
Priest Holmes		
❑ WMVB Michael Vick	40.00	12.00
Tom Brady		

2004 SPx Winning Materials Autographs

CARD NUMBERS HAVE WMA PREFIX
STATED PRINT RUN 25 SER.#'d SETS

Card	Nm-Mt	Ex-Mt
❑ BF Tom Brady	600.00	180.00
Brett Favre		
❑ BH Larry Fitzgerald	250.00	75.00
Reggie Williams		
❑ JJ Kevin Jones	250.00	75.00
Steven Jackson		
❑ MG Deuce McAllister	100.00	30.00
Ahman Green		
❑ MM Peyton Manning	250.00	75.00
Steve McNair		

❑ PE Peyton Manning Eli Manning	400.00	120.00
❑ PL Chad Pennington EXCH Byron Leftwich	125.00	38.00
❑ RR Philip Rivers Ben Roethlisberger	500.00	150.00
❑ SA Roger Staubach Troy Aikman	225.00	70.00
❑ TB Joe Theismann Mark Brunell	100.00	30.00
❑ TC Fran Tarkenton Daunte Culpepper	125.00	38.00
❑ TM LaDainian Tomlinson Deuce McAllister	100.00	30.00
❑ VM Michael Vick Donovan McNabb	300.00	90.00
❑ WJ Roy Williams WR Kevin Jones	250.00	75.00
❑ WW Kellen Winslow Jr. EXCH Kellen Winslow Sr.	125.00	38.00

1991 Stadium Club

	Nm-Mt	Ex-Mt
COMPLETE SET (500)	60.00	27.00
❑ 1 Pepper Johnson	.20	.09
❑ 2 Emmitt Smith	5.00	2.20
❑ 3 Deion Sanders	1.50	.70
❑ 4 Andre Collins	.20	.09
❑ 5 Eric Metcalf	.40	.18
❑ 6 Richard Dent	.40	.18
❑ 7 Eric Martin	.20	.09
❑ 8 Marcus Allen	.75	.35
❑ 9 Gary Anderson K	.20	.09
❑ 10 Joey Browner	.20	.09
❑ 11 Lorenzo White	.20	.09
❑ 12 Bruce Smith	.75	.35
❑ 13 Mark Boyer	.20	.09
❑ 14 Mike Piel	.20	.09
❑ 15 Albert Bentley	.20	.09
❑ 16 Bennie Blades	.20	.09
❑ 17 Jason Staurovsky	.20	.09
❑ 18 Anthony Toney	.20	.09
❑ 19 Dave Krieg	.40	.18
❑ 20 Harvey Williams RC	.75	.35
❑ 21 Bubba Paris	.20	.09
❑ 22 Tim McGee	.20	.09
❑ 23 Brian Noble	.20	.09
❑ 24 Vinny Testaverde	.40	.18
❑ 25 Doug Widell	.20	.09
❑ 26 John Jackson RC	.20	.09
❑ 27 Marion Butts	.40	.18
❑ 28 Deron Cherry	.20	.09
❑ 29 Don Warren	.20	.09
❑ 30 Rod Woodson	.75	.35
❑ 31 Mike Baab	.20	.09
❑ 32 Greg Jackson RC	.20	.09
❑ 33 Jerry Robinson	.20	.09
❑ 34 Dalton Hilliard	.20	.09
❑ 35 Brian Jordan	.40	.18
❑ 36 James Thornton UER (Misspelled Thorton on card back)	.20	.09
❑ 37 Michael Irvin	.75	.35
❑ 38 Billy Joe Tolliver	.20	.09
❑ 39 Jeff Herrod	.20	.09
❑ 40 Scott Norwood	.20	.09
❑ 41 Ferrell Edmunds	.20	.09
❑ 42 Andre Waters	.20	.09
❑ 43 Kevin Glover	.20	.09
❑ 44 Ray Berry	.20	.09
❑ 45 Timm Rosenbach	.20	.09
❑ 46 Reuben Davis	.20	.09
❑ 47 Charles Wilson	.20	.09
❑ 48 Todd Marinovich RC	.20	.09
❑ 49 Harris Barton	.20	.09
❑ 50 Jim Breech	.20	.09
❑ 51 Ron Holmes	.20	.09
❑ 52 Chris Singleton	.20	.09
❑ 53 Pat Leahy	.20	.09
❑ 54 Tom Newberry	.20	.09
❑ 55 Greg Montgomery	.20	.09
❑ 56 Robert Blackmon	.20	.09
❑ 57 Jay Hilgenberg	.20	.09
❑ 58 Rodney Hampton	.75	.35
❑ 59 Brett Perriman	.75	.35
❑ 60 Ricky Watters RC	6.00	2.70
❑ 61 Howie Long	.75	.35
❑ 62 Frank Cornish	.20	.09
❑ 63 Chris Miller	.40	.18
❑ 64 Keith Taylor	.20	.09
❑ 65 Tony Paige	.20	.09
❑ 66 Gary Zimmerman	.20	.09
❑ 67 Mark Royals RC	.20	.09
❑ 68 Ernie Jones	.20	.09
❑ 69 David Grant	.20	.09
❑ 70 Shane Conlan	.20	.09
❑ 71 Jerry Rice	2.50	1.10
❑ 72 Christian Okoye	.20	.09
❑ 73 Eddie Murray	.20	.09
❑ 74 Reggie White	.75	.35
❑ 75 Jeff Graham RC	1.00	.45
❑ 76 Mark Jackson	.20	.09
❑ 77 David Grayson	.20	.09
❑ 78 Dan Stryzinski	.20	.09
❑ 79 Sterling Sharpe	.75	.35
❑ 80 Cleveland Gary	.20	.09
❑ 81 Johnny Meads	.20	.09
❑ 82 Howard Cross	.20	.09
❑ 83 Ken O'Brien	.20	.09
❑ 84 Brian Blades	.40	.18
❑ 85 Ethan Horton	.20	.09
❑ 86 Bruce Armstrong	.20	.09
❑ 87 James Washington RC	.20	.09
❑ 88 Eugene Daniel	.20	.09
❑ 89 James Lofton	.40	.18
❑ 90 Louis Oliver	.20	.09
❑ 91 Boomer Esiason	.40	.18
❑ 92 Seth Joyner	.40	.18
❑ 93 Mark Carrier WR	.75	.35
❑ 94 Brett Favre RC UER (Favre misspelled as Farve)	50.00	22.00
❑ 95 Lee Williams	.20	.09
❑ 96 Neal Anderson	.40	.18
❑ 97 Brent Jones	.75	.35
❑ 98 John Alt	.20	.09
❑ 99 Rodney Peete	.40	.18
❑ 100 Steve Broussard	.20	.09
❑ 101 Cedric Mack	.20	.09
❑ 102 Pat Swilling	.40	.18
❑ 103 Stan Humphries	.75	.35
❑ 104 Darrell Thompson	.20	.09
❑ 105 Reggie Langhorne	.20	.09
❑ 106 Kenny Davidson	.20	.09
❑ 107 Jim Everett	.40	.18
❑ 108 Keith Millard	.20	.09
❑ 109 Garry Lewis	.20	.09
❑ 110 Jeff Hostetler	.40	.18
❑ 111 Lamar Lathon	.20	.09
❑ 112 Johnny Bailey	.20	.09
❑ 113 Cornelius Bennett	.40	.18
❑ 114 Travis McNeal	.20	.09
❑ 115 Jeff Lageman	.20	.09
❑ 116 Nick Bell RC	.20	.09
❑ 117 Calvin Williams	.40	.18
❑ 118 Shawn Lee RC	.20	.09
❑ 119 Anthony Munoz	.40	.18
❑ 120 Jay Novacek	.75	.35
❑ 121 Kevin Fagan	.20	.09
❑ 122 Leo Goeas	.20	.09
❑ 123 Vance Johnson	.20	.09
❑ 124 Brent Williams	.20	.09
❑ 125 Clarence Verdin	.20	.09
❑ 126 Luis Sharpe	.20	.09
❑ 127 Darrell Green	.20	.09
❑ 128 Barry Word	.20	.09
❑ 129 Steve Walsh	.20	.09
❑ 130 Bryan Hinkle	.20	.09
❑ 131 Ed West	.20	.09
❑ 132 Jeff Campbell	.20	.09
❑ 133 Dennis Byrd	.20	.09
❑ 134 Nate Odomes	.20	.09
❑ 135 Trace Armstrong	.20	.09
❑ 136 Jarvis Williams	.20	.09
❑ 137 Warren Moon	.75	.35
❑ 138 Eric Moten RC	.20	.09
❑ 139 Tony Woods	.20	.09
❑ 140 Phil Simms	.40	.18
❑ 141 Ricky Reynolds	.20	.09
❑ 142 Frank Stams	.20	.09
❑ 143 Kevin Mack	.20	.09
❑ 144 Wade Wilson	.40	.18
❑ 145 Shawn Collins	.20	.09
❑ 146 Roger Craig	.40	.18
❑ 147 Jeff Feagles RC	.20	.09
❑ 148 Norm Johnson	.20	.09
❑ 149 Terance Mathis	.40	.18
❑ 150 Reggie Cobb	.20	.09
❑ 151 Chip Banks	.20	.09
❑ 152 Darryl Pollard	.20	.09
❑ 153 Karl Mecklenburg	.20	.09
❑ 154 Ricky Proehl	.20	.09
❑ 155 Pete Stoyanovich	.20	.09
❑ 156 John Stephens	.20	.09
❑ 157 Ron Morris	.20	.09
❑ 158 Steve DeBerg	.20	.09
❑ 159 Mike Munchak	.40	.18
❑ 160 Brett Maxie	.20	.09
❑ 161 Don Beebe	.20	.09
❑ 162 Martin Mayhew	.20	.09
❑ 163 Merril Hoge	.20	.09
❑ 164 Kelvin Pritchett RC	.40	.18
❑ 165 Jim Jeffcoat	.20	.09
❑ 166 Myron Guyton	.20	.09
❑ 167 Ickey Woods	.20	.09
❑ 168 Andre Ware	.40	.18
❑ 169 Gary Plummer	.20	.09
❑ 170 Henry Ellard	.40	.18
❑ 171 Scott Davis	.20	.09
❑ 172 Randall McDaniel	.20	.09
❑ 173 Randal Hill RC	.40	.18
❑ 174 Anthony Bell	.20	.09
❑ 175 Gary Anderson RB	.20	.09
❑ 176 Byron Evans	.20	.09
❑ 177 Tony Mandarich	.20	.09
❑ 178 Jeff George	1.00	.45
❑ 179 Art Monk	.40	.18
❑ 180 Mike Kenn	.20	.09
❑ 181 Sean Landeta	.20	.09
❑ 182 Shaun Gayle	.20	.09

❑ 183 Michael Carter	.20	.09
❑ 184 Robb Thomas	.20	.09
❑ 185 Richmond Webb	.20	.09
❑ 186 Carnell Lake	.20	.09
❑ 187 Rueben Mayes	.20	.09
❑ 188 Issiac Holt	.20	.09
❑ 189 Leon Seals	.20	.09
❑ 190 Al Smith	.20	.09
❑ 191 Steve Atwater	.20	.09
❑ 192 Greg McMurtry	.20	.09
❑ 193 Al Toon	.40	.18
❑ 194 Cortez Kennedy	.75	.35
❑ 195 Gill Byrd	.20	.09
❑ 196 Carl Zander	.20	.09
❑ 197 Robert Brown	.20	.09
❑ 198 Buford McGee	.20	.09
❑ 199 Mervyn Fernandez	.20	.09
❑ 200 Mike Dumas RC	.20	.09
❑ 201 Rob Burnett RC	.40	.18
❑ 202 Brian Mitchell	.40	.18
❑ 203 Randall Cunningham	.75	.35
❑ 204 Sammie Smith	.20	.09
❑ 205 Ken Clarke	.20	.09
❑ 206 Floyd Dixon	.20	.09
❑ 207 Ken Norton	.40	.18
❑ 208 Tony Siragusa RC	.40	.18
❑ 209 Louis Lipps	.20	.09
❑ 210 Chris Martin	.20	.09
❑ 211 Jamie Mueller	.20	.09
❑ 212 Dave Waymer	.20	.09
❑ 213 Donnell Woolford	.20	.09
❑ 214 Paul Gruber	.20	.09
❑ 215 Ken Harvey	.40	.18
❑ 216 Henry Jones RC	.40	.18
❑ 217 Tommy Barnhardt RC	.20	.09
❑ 218 Arthur Cox	.20	.09
❑ 219 Pat Terrell	.20	.09
❑ 220 Curtis Duncan	.20	.09
❑ 221 Jeff Jaeger	.20	.09
❑ 222 Scott Stephen RC	.20	.09
❑ 223 Rob Moore	1.00	.45
❑ 224 Chris Hinton	.20	.09
❑ 225 Marv Cook	.20	.09
❑ 226 Patrick Hunter RC	.20	.09
❑ 227 Earnest Byner	.20	.09
❑ 228 Troy Aikman	3.00	1.35
❑ 229 Kevin Walker RC	.20	.09
❑ 230 Keith Jackson	.40	.18
❑ 231 Russell Maryland RC (UER, Card back says Dallas Cowboy)	.75	.35
❑ 232 Charles Haley	.40	.18
❑ 233 Nick Lowery	.20	.09
❑ 234 Erik Howard	.20	.09
❑ 235 Leonard Smith	.20	.09
❑ 236 Tim Irwin	.20	.09
❑ 237 Simon Fletcher	.20	.09
❑ 238 Thomas Everett	.20	.09
❑ 239 Reggie Roby	.20	.09
❑ 240 Leroy Hoard	.40	.18
❑ 241 Wayne Haddix	.20	.09
❑ 242 Gary Clark	.75	.35
❑ 243 Eric Andolsek	.20	.09
❑ 244 Jim Wahler RC	.20	.09
❑ 245 Vaughan Johnson	.20	.09
❑ 246 Kevin Butler	.20	.09
❑ 247 Steve Tasker	.40	.18
❑ 248 LeRoy Butler	.40	.18
❑ 249 Darion Conner	.20	.09
❑ 250 Eric Turner RC	.40	.18
❑ 251 Kevin Ross	.20	.09
❑ 252 Stephen Baker	.20	.09
❑ 253 Harold Green	.40	.18
❑ 254 Rohn Stark	.20	.09
❑ 255 Joe Nash	.20	.09
❑ 256 Jesse Sapolu	.20	.09
❑ 257 Willie Gault	.40	.18
❑ 258 Jerome Brown	.20	.09
❑ 259 Ken Willis	.20	.09
❑ 260 Courtney Hall	.20	.09
❑ 261 Hart Lee Dykes	.20	.09
❑ 262 William Fuller	.40	.18
❑ 263 Stan Thomas	.20	.09
❑ 264 Dan Marino	4.00	1.80
❑ 265 Ron Cox	.20	.09
❑ 266 Eric Green	.20	.09
❑ 267 Anthony Carter	.40	.18
❑ 268 Jerry Ball	.20	.09
❑ 269 Ron Hall	.20	.09
❑ 270 Dennis Smith	.20	.09
❑ 271 Eric Hill	.20	.09
❑ 272 Dan McGwire RC	.20	.09
❑ 273 Lewis Billups UER Louis on back	.20	.09
❑ 274 Rickey Jackson	.20	.09
❑ 275 Jim Sweeney	.20	.09
❑ 276 Pat Beach	.20	.09
❑ 277 Kevin Porter	.20	.09
❑ 278 Mike Sherrard	.20	.09
❑ 279 Andy Heck	.20	.09
❑ 280 Ron Brown	.20	.09
❑ 281 Lawrence Taylor	.75	.35
❑ 282 Anthony Pleasant	.20	.09
❑ 283 Wes Hopkins	.20	.09
❑ 284 Jim Lachey	.20	.09
❑ 285 Tim Harris	.20	.09
❑ 286 Tory Epps	.20	.09
❑ 287 Wendell Davis	.20	.09
❑ 288 Bubba McDowell	.20	.09
❑ 289 Bubby Brister	.20	.09
❑ 290 Chris Zorich RC	.75	.35
❑ 291 Mike Merriweather	.20	.09
❑ 292 Burt Grossman	.20	.09
❑ 293 Erik McMillan	.20	.09
❑ 294 John Elway	4.00	1.80
❑ 295 Toi Cook RC	.20	.09
❑ 296 Tom Rathman	.20	.09
❑ 297 Matt Bahr	.20	.09
❑ 298 Chris Spielman	.40	.18
❑ 299 Freddie Joe Nunn (Troy Aikman and Emmitt Smith shown in background)	.40	.18
❑ 300 Jim C. Jensen	.20	.09
❑ 301 David Fulcher UER (Rookie card should be '88, not '89)	.20	.09
❑ 302 Tommy Hodson	.20	.09
❑ 303 Stephone Paige	.20	.09
❑ 304 Greg Townsend	.20	.09
❑ 305 Dean Biasucci	.20	.09
❑ 306 Jimmie Jones	.20	.09
❑ 307 Eugene Marve	.20	.09
❑ 308 Flipper Anderson	.20	.09
❑ 309 Darryl Talley	.20	.09
❑ 310 Mike Croel RC	.20	.09
❑ 311 Thane Gash	.20	.09
❑ 312 Perry Kemp	.20	.09
❑ 313 Heath Sherman	.20	.09
❑ 314 Mike Singletary	.40	.18
❑ 315 Chip Lohmiller	.20	.09
❑ 316 Tunch Ilkin	.20	.09
❑ 317 Junior Seau	1.25	.55
❑ 318 Mike Gann	.20	.09
❑ 319 Tim McDonald	.20	.09
❑ 320 Kyle Clifton	.20	.09
❑ 321 Dan Owens	.20	.09
❑ 322 Tim Grunhard	.20	.09
❑ 323 Stan Brock	.20	.09
❑ 324 Rodney Holman	.20	.09
❑ 325 Mark Ingram	.40	.18
❑ 326 Browning Nagle RC	.20	.09
❑ 327 Joe Montana	5.00	2.20
❑ 328 Carl Lee	.20	.09
❑ 329 John L. Williams	.20	.09
❑ 330 David Griggs	.20	.09
❑ 331 Clarence Kay	.20	.09
❑ 332 Irving Fryar	.40	.18
❑ 333 Doug Smith DT RC**	.40	.18
❑ 334 Kent Hull	.20	.09
❑ 335 Mike Wilcher	.20	.09
❑ 336 Ray Donaldson	.20	.09
❑ 337 Mark Carrier DB UER (Rookie card should be '90, not '89)	.20	.09
❑ 338 Kelvin Martin	.20	.09
❑ 339 Keith Byars	.20	.09
❑ 340 Wilber Marshall	.20	.09
❑ 341 Ronnie Lott	.40	.18
❑ 342 Blair Thomas	.20	.09
❑ 343 Ronnie Harmon	.20	.09
❑ 344 Brian Brennan	.20	.09
❑ 345 Charles McRae RC	.20	.09
❑ 346 Michael Cofer	.20	.09
❑ 347 Keith Willis	.20	.09
❑ 348 Bruce Kozerski	.20	.09
❑ 349 Dave Meggett	.40	.18
❑ 350 John Taylor	.40	.18
❑ 351 Johnny Holland	.20	.09
❑ 352 Steve Christie	.20	.09
❑ 353 Ricky Ervins RC	.40	.18
❑ 354 Robert Massey	.20	.09
❑ 355 Derrick Thomas	.75	.35
❑ 356 Tommy Kane	.20	.09
❑ 357 Melvin Bratton	.20	.09
❑ 358 Bruce Matthews	.40	.18
❑ 359 Mark Duper	.40	.18
❑ 360 Jeff Wright RC	.20	.09
❑ 361 Barry Sanders	4.00	1.80
❑ 362 Chuck Webb RC	.20	.09
❑ 363 Darryl Grant	.20	.09
❑ 364 William Roberts	.20	.09
❑ 365 Reggie Rutland	.20	.09
❑ 366 Clay Matthews	.40	.18
❑ 367 Anthony Miller	.40	.18
❑ 368 Mike Prior	.20	.09
❑ 369 Jessie Tuggle	.20	.09
❑ 370 Brad Muster	.20	.09
❑ 371 Jay Schroeder	.20	.09
❑ 372 Greg Lloyd	.75	.35
❑ 373 Mike Cofer	.20	.09
❑ 374 James Brooks	.40	.18
❑ 375 Danny Noonan UER (Misspelled Noonen on card back)	.20	.09
❑ 376 Latin Berry RC	.20	.09
❑ 377 Brad Baxter	.20	.09
❑ 378 Godfrey Myles RC	.20	.09
❑ 379 Morten Andersen	.20	.09
❑ 380 Keith Woodside	.20	.09
❑ 381 Bobby Humphrey	.20	.09
❑ 382 Mike Golic	.20	.09
❑ 383 Keith McCants	.20	.09
❑ 384 Anthony Thompson	.20	.09
❑ 385 Mark Clayton	.40	.18
❑ 386 Neil Smith	.75	.35
❑ 387 Bryan Millard	.20	.09
❑ 388 Mel Gray UER (Wrong Mel Gray pictured on card back)	.40	.18
❑ 389 Ernest Givins	.40	.18
❑ 390 Reyna Thompson	.20	.09
❑ 391 Eric Bieniemy RC	.20	.09
❑ 392 Jon Hand	.20	.09
❑ 393 Mark Rypien	.40	.18
❑ 394 Bill Romanowski	.20	.09
❑ 395 Thurman Thomas	.75	.35
❑ 396 Jim Harbaugh	.75	.35
❑ 397 Don Mosebar	.20	.09
❑ 398 Andre Rison	.40	.18
❑ 399 Mike Johnson	.20	.09
❑ 400 Dermontti Dawson	.20	.09
❑ 401 Herschel Walker	.40	.18
❑ 402 Joe Prokop	.20	.09
❑ 403 Eddie Brown	.20	.09
❑ 404 Nate Newton	.40	.18
❑ 405 Damone Johnson RC	.20	.09
❑ 406 Jessie Hester	.20	.09
❑ 407 Jim Arnold	.20	.09
❑ 408 Ray Agnew	.20	.09
❑ 409 Michael Brooks	.20	.09
❑ 410 Keith Sims	.20	.09
❑ 411 Carl Banks	.20	.09

❑ 412 Jonathan Hayes .20 .09
❑ 413 Richard Johnson RC .20 .09
❑ 414 Darryll Lewis RC .40 .18
❑ 415 Jeff Bryant .20 .09
❑ 416 Leslie O'Neal .40 .18
❑ 417 Andre Reed .40 .18
❑ 418 Charles Mann .20 .09
❑ 419 Keith DeLong .20 .09
❑ 420 Bruce Hill .20 .09
❑ 421 Matt Brock RC .20 .09
❑ 422 Johnny Johnson .20 .09
❑ 423 Mark Bortz .20 .09
❑ 424 Ben Smith .20 .09
❑ 425 Jeff Cross .20 .09
❑ 426 Irv Pankey .20 .09
❑ 427 Hassan Jones .20 .09
❑ 428 Andre Tippett .20 .09
❑ 429 Tim Worley .20 .09
❑ 430 Daniel Stubbs .20 .09
❑ 431 Max Montoya .20 .09
❑ 432 Jumbo Elliott .20 .09
❑ 433 Duane Bickett .20 .09
❑ 434 Nate Lewis RC .20 .09
❑ 435 Leonard Russell RC .75 .35
❑ 436 Hoby Brenner .20 .09
❑ 437 Ricky Sanders .20 .09
❑ 438 Pierce Holt .20 .09
❑ 439 Derrick Fenner .20 .09
❑ 440 Drew Hill .20 .09
❑ 441 Will Wolford .20 .09
❑ 442 Albert Lewis .20 .09
❑ 443 James Francis .20 .09
❑ 444 Chris Jacke .20 .09
❑ 445 Mike Farr .20 .09
❑ 446 Stephen Braggs .20 .09
❑ 447 Michael Haynes .75 .35
❑ 448 Freeman McNeil UER .20 .09
(2,008 Pounds for weight)
❑ 449 Kevin Donnalley RC .20 .09
❑ 450 John Offerdahl .20 .09
❑ 451 Eric Allen .20 .09
❑ 452 Keith McKeller .20 .09
❑ 453 Kevin Greene .40 .18
❑ 454 Ronnie Lippett .20 .09
❑ 455 Ray Childress .20 .09
❑ 456 Mike Saxon .20 .09
❑ 457 Mark Robinson .20 .09
❑ 458 Greg Kragen .20 .09
❑ 459 Steve Jordan .20 .09
❑ 460 John Johnson RC .20 .09
❑ 461 Sam Mills .20 .09
❑ 462 Bo Jackson 1.00 .45
❑ 463 Mark Collins .20 .09
❑ 464 Percy Snow .20 .09
❑ 465 Jeff Bostic .20 .09
❑ 466 Jacob Green .20 .09
❑ 467 Dexter Carter .20 .09
❑ 468 Rich Camarillo .20 .09
❑ 469 Bill Brooks .20 .09
❑ 470 John Carney .20 .09
❑ 471 Don Majkowski .20 .09
❑ 472 Ralph Tamm RC .20 .09
❑ 473 Fred Barnett .75 .35
❑ 474 Jim Covert .20 .09
❑ 475 Kenneth Davis .20 .09
❑ 476 Jerry Gray .20 .09
❑ 477 Broderick Thomas .20 .09
❑ 478 Chris Doleman .20 .09
❑ 479 Haywood Jeffires .40 .18
❑ 480 Craig Heyward .40 .18
❑ 481 Markus Koch .20 .09
❑ 482 Tim Krumrie .20 .09
❑ 483 Robert Clark .20 .09
❑ 484 Mike Rozier .20 .09
❑ 485 Danny Villa .20 .09
❑ 486 Gerald Williams .20 .09
❑ 487 Steve Wisniewski .20 .09
❑ 488 J.B. Brown .20 .09
❑ 489 Eugene Robinson .20 .09
❑ 490 Ottis Anderson .40 .18
❑ 491 Tony Stargell .20 .09
❑ 492 Jack Del Rio .40 .18
❑ 493 Lamar Rogers RC .20 .09
❑ 494 Ricky Nattiel .20 .09
❑ 495 Dan Saleaumua .20 .09
❑ 496 Checklist 1-100 .20 .09
❑ 497 Checklist 101-200 .20 .09
❑ 498 Checklist 201-300 .20 .09
❑ 499 Checklist 301-400 .20 .09
❑ 500 Checklist 401-500 .20 .09

1992 Stadium Club

	Nm-Mt	Ex-Mt
COMPLETE SET (700)	120.00	55.00
COMP.SERIES 1 (300)	12.00	5.50
COMP.SERIES 2 (300)	12.00	5.50
COMP.HIGH SER.(100)	100.00	45.00

❑ 1 Mark Rypien .08 .04
❑ 2 Carlton Bailey RC .08 .04
❑ 3 Kevin Glover .08 .04
❑ 4 Vance Johnson .08 .04
❑ 5 Jim Jeffcoat .08 .04
❑ 6 Dan Saleaumua .08 .04
❑ 7 Darion Conner .08 .04
❑ 8 Don Maggs .08 .04
❑ 9 Richard Dent .15 .07
❑ 10 Mark Murphy .08 .04
❑ 11 Wesley Carroll .08 .04
❑ 12 Chris Burkett .08 .04
❑ 13 Steve Wallace .08 .04
❑ 14 Jacob Green .08 .04
❑ 15 Roger Ruzek .08 .04
❑ 16 J.B. Brown .08 .04
❑ 17 Dave Meggett .15 .07
❑ 18 D.J. Johnson .08 .04
❑ 19 Rich Gannon .30 .14
❑ 20 Kevin Mack .08 .04
❑ 21A Reggie Cobb ERR .08 .04
(Buccaneers upside down on card front)
❑ 21B Reggie Cobb COR .08 .04
❑ 22 Nate Lewis .08 .04
❑ 23 Doug Smith .08 .04
❑ 24 Irving Fryar .15 .07
❑ 25 Anthony Thompson .08 .04
❑ 26 Duane Bickett .08 .04
❑ 27 Don Majkowski .08 .04
❑ 28 Mark Schlereth RC .08 .04
❑ 29 Melvin Jenkins .08 .04
❑ 30 Michael Haynes .15 .07
❑ 31 Greg Lewis .08 .04
❑ 32 Kenneth Davis .08 .04
❑ 33 Derrick Thomas .30 .14
❑ 34 David Williams .08 .04
❑ 35 Neal Anderson .08 .04
❑ 36 Andre Collins .08 .04
❑ 37 Jesse Solomon .08 .04
❑ 38 Barry Sanders 2.50 1.10
❑ 39 Jeff Gossett .08 .04
❑ 40 Rickey Jackson .08 .04
❑ 41 Ray Berry .08 .04
❑ 42 Leroy Hoard .15 .07
❑ 43 Eric Thomas .08 .04
❑ 44 Brian Washington .08 .04
❑ 45 Pat Terrell .08 .04
❑ 46 Eugene Robinson .08 .04
❑ 47 Luis Sharpe .08 .04
❑ 48 Jerome Brown .08 .04
❑ 49 Mark Collins .08 .04
❑ 50 Johnny Holland .08 .04
❑ 51 Tony Paige .08 .04
❑ 52 Willie Green .08 .04
❑ 53 Steve Atwater .08 .04
❑ 54 Brad Muster .08 .04
❑ 55 Cris Dishman .08 .04
❑ 56 Eddie Anderson .08 .04
❑ 57 Sam Mills .08 .04
❑ 58 Donald Evans .08 .04
❑ 59 Jon Vaughn .08 .04
❑ 60 Marion Butts .08 .04
❑ 61 Rodney Holman .08 .04
❑ 62 Dwayne White RC .08 .04
❑ 63 Martin Mayhew .08 .04
❑ 64 Jonathan Hayes .08 .04
❑ 65 Andre Rison .15 .07
❑ 66 Calvin Williams .15 .07
❑ 67 James Washington .08 .04
❑ 68 Tim Harris .08 .04
❑ 69 Jim Ritcher .08 .04
❑ 70 Johnny Johnson .08 .04
❑ 71 John Offerdahl .08 .04
❑ 72 Herschel Walker .15 .07
❑ 73 Perry Kemp .08 .04
❑ 74 Erik Howard .08 .04
❑ 75 Lamar Lathon .08 .04
❑ 76 Greg Kragen .08 .04
❑ 77 Jay Schroeder .08 .04
❑ 78 Jim Arnold .08 .04
❑ 79 Chris Miller .15 .07
❑ 80 Deron Cherry .08 .04
❑ 81 Jim Harbaugh .30 .14
❑ 82 Gill Fenerty .08 .04
❑ 83 Fred Stokes .08 .04
❑ 84 Roman Phifer .08 .04
❑ 85 Clyde Simmons .08 .04
❑ 86 Vince Newsome .08 .04
❑ 87 Lawrence Dawsey .15 .07
❑ 88 Eddie Brown .08 .04
❑ 89 Greg Montgomery .08 .04
❑ 90 Jeff Lageman .08 .04
❑ 91 Terry Wooden .08 .04
❑ 92 Nate Newton .08 .04
❑ 93 David Richards .08 .04
❑ 94 Derek Russell .08 .04
❑ 95 Steve Jordan .08 .04
❑ 96 Hugh Millen .08 .04
❑ 97 Mark Duper .08 .04
❑ 98 Sean Landeta .08 .04
❑ 99 James Thornton .08 .04
❑ 100 Darrell Green .08 .04
❑ 101 Harris Barton .08 .04
❑ 102 John Alt .08 .04
❑ 103 Mike Farr .08 .04
❑ 104 Bob Golic .08 .04
❑ 105 Gene Atkins .08 .04
❑ 106 Gary Anderson K .08 .04
❑ 107 Norm Johnson .08 .04
❑ 108 Eugene Daniel .08 .04
❑ 109 Kent Hull .08 .04
❑ 110 John Elway 2.50 1.10
❑ 111 Rich Camarillo .08 .04
❑ 112 Charles Wilson .08 .04
❑ 113 Matt Bahr .08 .04
❑ 114 Mark Carrier WR .15 .07
❑ 115 Richmond Webb .08 .04
❑ 116 Charles Mann .08 .04
❑ 117 Tim McGee .08 .04
❑ 118 Wes Hopkins .08 .04
❑ 119 Mo Lewis .08 .04
❑ 120 Warren Moon .30 .14
❑ 121 Damone Johnson .08 .04
❑ 122 Kevin Gogan .08 .04
❑ 123 Joey Browner .08 .04
❑ 124 Tommy Kane .08 .04
❑ 125 Vincent Brown .08 .04
❑ 126 Barry Word .08 .04

❑	127	Michael Brooks	.08	.04
❑	128	Jumbo Elliott	.08	.04
❑	129	Marcus Allen	.30	.14
❑	130	Tom Waddle	.08	.04
❑	131	Jim Dombrowski	.08	.04
❑	132	Aeneas Williams	.15	.07
❑	133	Clay Matthews	.15	.07
❑	134	Thurman Thomas	.30	.14
❑	135	Dean Biasucci	.08	.04
❑	136	Moe Gardner	.08	.04
❑	137	James Campen	.08	.04
❑	138	Tim Johnson	.08	.04
❑	139	Erik Kramer	.15	.07
❑	140	Keith McCants	.08	.04
❑	141	John Carney	.08	.04
❑	142	Tunch Ilkin	.08	.04
❑	143	Louis Oliver	.08	.04
❑	144	Bill Maas	.08	.04
❑	145	Wendell Davis	.08	.04
❑	146	Pepper Johnson	.08	.04
❑	147	Howie Long	.30	.14
❑	148	Brett Maxie	.08	.04
❑	149	Tony Casillas	.08	.04
❑	150	Michael Carter	.08	.04
❑	151	Byron Evans	.08	.04
❑	152	Lorenzo White	.08	.04
❑	153	Larry Kelm	.08	.04
❑	154	Andy Heck	.08	.04
❑	155	Harry Newsome	.08	.04
❑	156	Chris Singleton	.08	.04
❑	157	Mike Kenn	.08	.04
❑	158	Jeff Faulkner	.08	.04
❑	159	Ken Lanier	.08	.04
❑	160	Darryl Talley	.08	.04
❑	161	Louie Aguiar RC	.08	.04
❑	162	Danny Copeland	.08	.04
❑	163	Kevin Porter	.08	.04
❑	164	Trace Armstrong	.08	.04
❑	165	Dermontti Dawson	.08	.04
❑	166	Fred McAfee RC	.08	.04
❑	167	Ronnie Lott	.15	.07
❑	168	Tony Mandarich	.08	.04
❑	169	Howard Cross	.08	.04
❑	170	Vestee Jackson	.08	.04
❑	171	Jeff Herrod	.08	.04
❑	172	Randy Hilliard RC	.08	.04
❑	173	Robert Wilson	.08	.04
❑	174	Joe Walter RC	.08	.04
❑	175	Chris Spielman	.15	.07
❑	176	Darryl Henley	.08	.04
❑	177	Jay Hilgenberg	.08	.04
❑	178	John Kidd	.08	.04
❑	179	Doug Widell	.08	.04
❑	180	Seth Joyner	.08	.04
❑	181	Nick Bell	.08	.04
❑	182	Don Griffin	.08	.04
❑	183	Johnny Meads	.08	.04
❑	184	Jeff Bostic	.08	.04
❑	185	Johnny Hector	.08	.04
❑	186	Jessie Tuggle	.08	.04
❑	187	Robb Thomas	.08	.04
❑	188	Shane Conlan	.08	.04
❑	189	Michael Zordich RC	.08	.04
❑	190	Emmitt Smith	3.00	1.35
❑	191	Robert Blackmon	.08	.04
❑	192	Carl Lee	.08	.04
❑	193	Harry Galbreath	.08	.04
❑	194	Ed King	.08	.04
❑	195	Stan Thomas	.08	.04
❑	196	Andre Waters	.08	.04
❑	197	Pat Harlow	.08	.04
❑	198	Zefross Moss	.08	.04
❑	199	Bobby Hebert	.08	.04
❑	200	Doug Riesenberg	.08	.04
❑	201	Mike Croel	.08	.04
❑	202	Jeff Jaeger	.08	.04
❑	203	Gary Plummer	.08	.04
❑	204	Chris Jacke	.08	.04
❑	205	Neil O'Donnell	.15	.07
❑	206	Mark Bortz	.08	.04
❑	207	Tim Barnett	.08	.04
❑	208	Jerry Ball	.08	.04
❑	209	Chip Lohmiller	.08	.04
❑	210	Jim Everett	.15	.07
❑	211	Tim McKyer	.08	.04
❑	212	Aaron Craver	.08	.04
❑	213	John L. Williams	.08	.04
❑	214	Simon Fletcher	.08	.04
❑	215	Walter Reeves	.08	.04
❑	216	Terance Mathis	.15	.07
❑	217	Mike Pitts	.08	.04
❑	218	Bruce Matthews	.08	.04
❑	219	Howard Ballard	.08	.04
❑	220	Leonard Russell	.15	.07
❑	221	Michael Stewart	.08	.04
❑	222	Mike Merriweather	.08	.04
❑	223	Ricky Sanders	.08	.04
❑	224	Ray Horton	.08	.04
❑	225	Michael Jackson	.15	.07
❑	226	Bill Romanowski	.08	.04
❑	227	Steve McMichael UER (His wife is former Mrs. Illinois, not Miss Illinois)	.15	.07
❑	228	Chris Martin	.08	.04
❑	229	Tim Green	.08	.04
❑	230	Karl Mecklenburg	.08	.04
❑	231	Felix Wright	.08	.04
❑	232	Charles McRae	.08	.04
❑	233	Pete Stoyanovich	.08	.04
❑	234	Stephen Baker	.08	.04
❑	235	Herman Moore	.30	.14
❑	236	Terry McDaniel	.08	.04
❑	237	Dalton Hilliard	.08	.04
❑	238	Gill Byrd	.08	.04
❑	239	Leon Seals	.08	.04
❑	240	Rod Woodson	.30	.14
❑	241	Curtis Duncan	.08	.04
❑	242	Keith Jackson	.15	.07
❑	243	Mark Stepnoski	.15	.07
❑	244	Art Monk	.15	.07
❑	245	Matt Stover	.08	.04
❑	246	John Roper	.08	.04
❑	247	Rodney Hampton	.15	.07
❑	248	Steve Wisniewski	.08	.04
❑	249	Bryan Millard	.08	.04
❑	250	Todd Lyght	.08	.04
❑	251	Marvin Washington	.08	.04
❑	252	Eric Swann	.15	.07
❑	253	Bruce Kozerski	.08	.04
❑	254	Jon Hand	.08	.04
❑	255	Scott Fulhage	.08	.04
❑	256	Chuck Cecil	.08	.04
❑	257	Eric Martin	.08	.04
❑	258	Eric Metcalf	.15	.07
❑	259	T.J. Turner	.08	.04
❑	260	Kirk Lowdermilk	.08	.04
❑	261	Keith McKeller	.08	.04
❑	262	Wymon Henderson	.08	.04
❑	263	David Alexander	.08	.04
❑	264	George Jamison	.08	.04
❑	265	Ken Norton Jr.	.15	.07
❑	266	Jim Lachey	.08	.04
❑	267	Bo Orlando RC	.08	.04
❑	268	Nick Lowery	.08	.04
❑	269	Keith Van Horne	.08	.04
❑	270	Dwight Stone	.08	.04
❑	271	Keith DeLong	.08	.04
❑	272	James Francis	.08	.04
❑	273	Greg McMurtry	.08	.04
❑	274	Ethan Horton	.08	.04
❑	275	Stan Brock	.08	.04
❑	276	Ken Harvey	.08	.04
❑	277	Ronnie Harmon	.08	.04
❑	278	Mike Pritchard	.15	.07
❑	279	Kyle Clifton	.08	.04
❑	280	Anthony Johnson	.15	.07
❑	281	Esera Tuaolo	.08	.04
❑	282	Vernon Turner	.08	.04
❑	283	David Griggs	.08	.04
❑	284	Dino Hackett	.08	.04
❑	285	Carwell Gardner	.08	.04
❑	286	Ron Hall	.08	.04
❑	287	Reggie White	.30	.14
❑	288	Checklist 1-100	.08	.04
❑	289	Checklist 101-200	.08	.04
❑	290	Checklist 201-300	.08	.04
❑	291	Mark Clayton MC	.08	.04
❑	292	Pat Swilling MC	.08	.04
❑	293	Ernest Givins MC	.08	.04
❑	294	Broderick Thomas MC	.08	.04
❑	295	John Friesz MC	.08	.04
❑	296	Cornelius Bennett MC	.08	.04
❑	297	Anthony Carter MC	.15	.07
❑	298	Earnest Byner MC	.08	.04
❑	299	Michael Irvin MC	.30	.14
❑	300	Cortez Kennedy MC	.08	.04
❑	301	Barry Sanders MC	1.50	.70
❑	302	Mike Croel MC	.08	.04
❑	303	Emmitt Smith MC	2.00	.90
❑	304	Leonard Russell MC	.08	.04
❑	305	Neal Anderson MC	.08	.04
❑	306	Derrick Thomas MC	.15	.07
❑	307	Mark Rypien MC	.08	.04
❑	308	Reggie White MC	.15	.07
❑	309	Rod Woodson MC	.15	.07
❑	310	Rodney Hampton MC	.15	.07
❑	311	Carnell Lake	.08	.04
❑	312	Robert Delpino	.08	.04
❑	313	Brian Blades	.15	.07
❑	314	Marc Spindler	.08	.04
❑	315	Scott Norwood	.08	.04
❑	316	Frank Warren	.08	.04
❑	317	David Treadwell	.08	.04
❑	318	Steve Broussard	.08	.04
❑	319	Lorenzo Lynch	.08	.04
❑	320	Ray Agnew	.08	.04
❑	321	Derrick Walker	.08	.04
❑	322	Vinson Smith RC	.08	.04
❑	323	Gary Clark	.30	.14
❑	324	Charles Haley	.15	.07
❑	325	Keith Byars	.08	.04
❑	326	Winston Moss	.08	.04
❑	327	Paul McJulien RC UER (Has Brett Perriman card back; see also 453)	.08	.04
❑	328	Tony Covington	.08	.04
❑	329	Mark Carrier DB	.08	.04
❑	330	Mark Tuinei	.08	.04
❑	331	Tracy Simien RC	.08	.04
❑	332	Jeff Wright	.08	.04
❑	333	Bryan Cox	.15	.07
❑	334	Lonnie Young	.08	.04
❑	335	Clarence Verdin	.08	.04
❑	336	Dan Fike	.08	.04
❑	337	Steve Sewell	.08	.04
❑	338	Gary Zimmerman	.08	.04
❑	339	Barney Bussey	.08	.04
❑	340	William Perry	.15	.07
❑	341	Jeff Hostetler	.15	.07
❑	342	Doug Smith	.08	.04
❑	343	Cleveland Gary	.08	.04
❑	344	Todd Marinovich	.08	.04
❑	345	Rich Moran	.08	.04
❑	346	Tony Woods	.08	.04
❑	347	Vaughan Johnson	.08	.04
❑	348	Marv Cook	.08	.04
❑	349	Pierce Holt	.08	.04
❑	350	Gerald Williams	.08	.04
❑	351	Kevin Butler	.08	.04
❑	352	William White	.08	.04
❑	353	Henry Rolling	.08	.04
❑	354	James Joseph	.08	.04
❑	355	Vinny Testaverde	.15	.07
❑	356	Scott Radecic	.08	.04
❑	357	Lee Johnson	.08	.04
❑	358	Steve Tasker	.15	.07
❑	359	David Lutz	.08	.04
❑	360	Audray McMillian UER (Name on back misspelled Audrey)	.08	.04
❑	361	Brad Baxter	.08	.04
❑	362	Mark Dennis	.08	.04

❑ 363 Erric Pegram	.15	.07
❑ 364 Sean Jones	.08	.04
❑ 365 William Roberts	.08	.04
❑ 366 Steve Young	1.00	.45
❑ 367 Joe Jacoby	.08	.04
❑ 368 Richard Brown RC	.08	.04
❑ 369 Keith Kartz	.08	.04
❑ 370 Freddie Joe Nunn	.08	.04
❑ 371 Darren Comeaux	.08	.04
❑ 372 Larry Brown DB	.08	.04
❑ 373 Haywood Jeffires	.15	.07
❑ 374 Tom Newberry	.08	.04
❑ 375 Steve Bono RC	.30	.14
❑ 376 Kevin Ross	.08	.04
❑ 377 Kelvin Pritchett	.08	.04
❑ 378 Jessie Hester	.08	.04
❑ 379 Mitchell Price	.08	.04
❑ 380 Barry Foster	.15	.07
❑ 381 Reyna Thompson	.08	.04
❑ 382 Cris Carter	.75	.35
❑ 383 Lemuel Stinson	.08	.04
❑ 384 Rod Bernstine	.08	.04
❑ 385 James Lofton	.15	.07
❑ 386 Kevin Murphy	.08	.04
❑ 387 Greg Townsend	.08	.04
❑ 388 Edgar Bennett RC	.30	.14
❑ 389 Rob Moore	.15	.07
❑ 390 Eugene Lockhart	.08	.04
❑ 391 Bern Brostek	.08	.04
❑ 392 Craig Heyward	.15	.07
❑ 393 Ferrell Edmunds	.08	.04
❑ 394 John Kasay	.08	.04
❑ 395 Jesse Sapolu	.08	.04
❑ 396 Jim Breech	.08	.04
❑ 397 Neil Smith	.30	.14
❑ 398 Bryce Paup	.30	.14
❑ 399 Tony Tolbert	.08	.04
❑ 400 Bubby Brister	.08	.04
❑ 401 Dennis Smith	.08	.04
❑ 402 Dan Owens	.08	.04
❑ 403 Steve Beuerlein	.15	.07
❑ 404 Rick Tuten	.08	.04
❑ 405 Eric Allen	.08	.04
❑ 406 Eric Hill	.08	.04
❑ 407 Don Warren	.08	.04
❑ 408 Greg Jackson	.08	.04
❑ 409 Chris Doleman	.08	.04
❑ 410 Anthony Munoz	.15	.07
❑ 411 Michael Young	.08	.04
❑ 412 Cornelius Bennett	.15	.07
❑ 413 Ray Childress	.08	.04
❑ 414 Kevin Call	.08	.04
❑ 415 Burt Grossman	.08	.04
❑ 416 Scott Miller	.08	.04
❑ 417 Tim Newton	.08	.04
❑ 418 Robert Young	.08	.04
❑ 419 Tommy Vardell RC	.08	.04
❑ 420 Michael Walter	.08	.04
❑ 421 Chris Port RC	.08	.04
❑ 422 Carlton Haselrig RC	.08	.04
❑ 423 Rodney Peete	.15	.07
❑ 424 Scott Stephen	.08	.04
❑ 425 Chris Warren	.30	.14
❑ 426 Scott Galbraith RC	.08	.04
❑ 427 Fuad Reveiz UER (Born in Colombia, not Columbia)	.08	.04
❑ 428 Irv Eatman	.08	.04
❑ 429 David Szott	.08	.04
❑ 430 Brent Williams	.08	.04
❑ 431 Mike Horan	.08	.04
❑ 432 Brent Jones	.15	.07
❑ 433 Paul Gruber	.08	.04
❑ 434 Carlos Huerta	.08	.04
❑ 435 Scott Case	.08	.04
❑ 436 Greg Davis	.08	.04
❑ 437 Ken Clarke	.08	.04
❑ 438 Alfred Williams	.08	.04
❑ 439 Jim C. Jensen	.08	.04
❑ 440 Louis Lipps	.08	.04
❑ 441 Larry Roberts	.08	.04
❑ 442 James Jones	.08	.04
❑ 443 Don Mosebar	.08	.04
❑ 444 Quinn Early	.15	.07
❑ 445 Robert Brown	.08	.04
❑ 446 Tom Thayer	.08	.04
❑ 447 Michael Irvin	.30	.14
❑ 448 Jarrod Bunch	.08	.04
❑ 449 Riki Ellison	.08	.04
❑ 450 Joe Phillips	.08	.04
❑ 451 Ernest Givins	.15	.07
❑ 452 Glenn Parker	.08	.04
❑ 453 Brett Perriman UER (Has Paul McJulien card back; see also 327)	.30	.14
❑ 454 Jayice Pearson RC	.08	.04
❑ 455 Mark Jackson	.08	.04
❑ 456 Siran Stacy RC	.08	.04
❑ 457 Rufus Porter	.08	.04
❑ 458 Michael Ball	.08	.04
❑ 459 Craig Taylor	.08	.04
❑ 460 George Thomas RC	.08	.04
❑ 461 Alvin Wright	.08	.04
❑ 462 Ron Hallstrom	.08	.04
❑ 463 Mike Mooney RC	.08	.04
❑ 464 Dexter Carter	.08	.04
❑ 465 Marty Carter RC	.08	.04
❑ 466 Pat Swilling	.08	.04
❑ 467 Mike Golic	.08	.04
❑ 468 Reggie Roby	.08	.04
❑ 469 Randall McDaniel	.08	.04
❑ 470 John Stephens	.08	.04
❑ 471 Ricardo McDonald RC	.08	.04
❑ 472 Wilber Marshall	.08	.04
❑ 473 Jim Sweeney	.08	.04
❑ 474 Ernie Jones	.08	.04
❑ 475 Bennie Blades	.08	.04
❑ 476 Don Beebe	.08	.04
❑ 477 Grant Feasel	.08	.04
❑ 478 Ernie Mills	.08	.04
❑ 479 Tony Jones	.08	.04
❑ 480 Jeff Uhlenhake	.08	.04
❑ 481 Gaston Green	.08	.04
❑ 482 John Taylor	.15	.07
❑ 483 Anthony Smith	.08	.04
❑ 484 Tony Bennett	.08	.04
❑ 485 David Brandon RC	.08	.04
❑ 486 Shawn Jefferson	.08	.04
❑ 487 Christian Okoye	.08	.04
❑ 488 Leonard Marshall	.08	.04
❑ 489 Jay Novacek	.15	.07
❑ 490 Harold Green	.08	.04
❑ 491 Bubba McDowell	.08	.04
❑ 492 Gary Anderson RB	.08	.04
❑ 493 Terrell Buckley RC	.08	.04
❑ 494 Jamie Dukes RC	.08	.04
❑ 495 Morten Andersen	.08	.04
❑ 496 Henry Thomas	.08	.04
❑ 497 Bill Lewis	.08	.04
❑ 498 Jeff Cross	.08	.04
❑ 499 Hardy Nickerson	.15	.07
❑ 500 Henry Ellard	.15	.07
❑ 501 Joe Bowden RC	.08	.04
❑ 502 Brian Noble	.08	.04
❑ 503 Mike Cofer	.08	.04
❑ 504 Jeff Bryant	.08	.04
❑ 505 Lomas Brown	.08	.04
❑ 506 Chip Banks	.08	.04
❑ 507 Keith Traylor	.08	.04
❑ 508 Mark Kelso	.08	.04
❑ 509 Dexter McNabb RC	.08	.04
❑ 510 Gene Chilton RC	.08	.04
❑ 511 George Thornton	.08	.04
❑ 512 Jeff Criswell	.08	.04
❑ 513 Brad Edwards	.08	.04
❑ 514 Ron Heller	.08	.04
❑ 515 Tim Brown	.30	.14
❑ 516 Keith Hamilton RC	.15	.07
❑ 517 Mark Higgs	.08	.04
❑ 518 Tommy Barnhardt	.08	.04
❑ 519 Brian Jordan	.15	.07
❑ 520 Ray Crockett	.08	.04
❑ 521 Karl Wilson	.08	.04
❑ 522 Ricky Reynolds	.08	.04
❑ 523 Max Montoya	.08	.04
❑ 524 David Little	.08	.04
❑ 525 Alonzo Mitz RC	.08	.04
❑ 526 Darryll Lewis	.08	.04
❑ 527 Keith Henderson	.08	.04
❑ 528 LeRoy Butler	.08	.04
❑ 529 Rob Burnett	.08	.04
❑ 530 Chris Chandler	.30	.14
❑ 531 Maury Buford	.08	.04
❑ 532 Mark Ingram	.08	.04
❑ 533 Mike Saxon	.08	.04
❑ 534 Bill Fralic	.08	.04
❑ 535 Craig Patterson RC	.08	.04
❑ 536 John Randle	.15	.07
❑ 537 Dwayne Harper	.08	.04
❑ 538 Chris Hakel RC	.08	.04
❑ 539 Maurice Hurst	.08	.04
❑ 540 Warren Powers UER (Front has photo of Ron Holmes)	.08	.04
❑ 541 Will Wolford	.08	.04
❑ 542 Dennis Gibson	.08	.04
❑ 543 Jackie Slater	.08	.04
❑ 544 Floyd Turner	.08	.04
❑ 545 Guy McIntyre	.08	.04
❑ 546 Eric Green	.08	.04
❑ 547 Rohn Stark	.08	.04
❑ 548 William Fuller	.08	.04
❑ 549 Alvin Harper	.15	.07
❑ 550 Mark Clayton	.15	.07
❑ 551 Natu Tuatagaloa RC	.08	.04
❑ 552 Fred Barnett	.30	.14
❑ 553 Bob Whitfield RC	.08	.04
❑ 554 Courtney Hall	.08	.04
❑ 555 Brian Mitchell	.15	.07
❑ 556 Patrick Hunter	.08	.04
❑ 557 Rick Bryan	.08	.04
❑ 558 Anthony Carter	.15	.07
❑ 559 Jim Wahler	.08	.04
❑ 560 Joe Morris	.08	.04
❑ 561 Tony Zendejas	.08	.04
❑ 562 Mervyn Fernandez	.08	.04
❑ 563 Jamie Williams	.08	.04
❑ 564 Darrell Thompson	.08	.04
❑ 565 Adrian Cooper	.08	.04
❑ 566 Chris Goode	.08	.04
❑ 567 Jeff Davidson RC	.08	.04
❑ 568 James Hasty	.08	.04
❑ 569 Chris Mims RC	.08	.04
❑ 570 Ray Seals RC	.08	.04
❑ 571 Myron Guyton	.08	.04
❑ 572 Todd McNair	.08	.04
❑ 573 Andre Tippett	.08	.04
❑ 574 Kirby Jackson	.08	.04
❑ 575 Mel Gray	.15	.07
❑ 576 Stephone Paige	.08	.04
❑ 577 Scott Davis	.08	.04
❑ 578 John Gesek	.08	.04
❑ 579 Earnest Byner	.08	.04
❑ 580 John Friesz	.15	.07
❑ 581 Al Smith	.08	.04
❑ 582 Flipper Anderson	.08	.04
❑ 583 Amp Lee RC	.08	.04
❑ 584 Greg Lloyd	.15	.07
❑ 585 Cortez Kennedy	.15	.07
❑ 586 Keith Sims	.08	.04
❑ 587 Terry Allen	.30	.14
❑ 588 David Fulcher	.08	.04
❑ 589 Chris Hinton	.08	.04
❑ 590 Tim McDonald	.08	.04
❑ 591 Bruce Armstrong	.08	.04
❑ 592 Sterling Sharpe	.30	.14
❑ 593 Tom Rathman	.08	.04
❑ 594 Bill Brooks	.08	.04
❑ 595 Broderick Thomas	.08	.04
❑ 596 Jim Wilks	.08	.04
❑ 597 Tyrone Braxton UER (Bio for Melvin Braxton)	.08	.04
❑ 598 Checklist 301-400 UER	.08	.04

Card	Nm-Mt	Ex-Mt
(Audray McMillian is misspelled Audrey)		
❑ 599 Checklist 401-500	.08	.04
❑ 600 Checklist 501-600	.08	.04
❑ 601 Andre Reed MC	.75	.35
❑ 602 Troy Aikman MC	4.00	1.80
❑ 603 Dan Marino MC	6.00	2.70
❑ 604 Randall Cunningham MC	.75	.35
❑ 605 Jim Kelly MC	1.50	.70
❑ 606 Deion Sanders MC	2.00	.90
❑ 607 Junior Seau MC	1.50	.70
❑ 608 Jerry Rice MC	4.00	1.80
❑ 609 Bruce Smith MC	.75	.35
❑ 610 Lawrence Taylor MC	1.50	.70
❑ 611 Todd Collins RC	.50	.23
❑ 612 Ty Detmer	1.50	.70
❑ 613 Browning Nagle	.50	.23
❑ 614 Tony Sacca RC UER (Reverse negative photo on back)	.50	.23
❑ 615 Boomer Esiason	.75	.35
❑ 616 Billy Joe Tolliver	.50	.23
❑ 617 Leslie O'Neal	.75	.35
❑ 618 Mark Wheeler RC	.50	.23
❑ 619 Eric Dickerson	.75	.35
❑ 620 Phil Simms	.75	.35
❑ 621 Troy Vincent RC	.50	.23
❑ 622 Jason Hanson RC	.75	.35
❑ 623 Andre Reed	.75	.35
❑ 624 Russell Maryland	.50	.23
❑ 625 Steve Emtman RC	.50	.23
❑ 626 Sean Gilbert RC	.75	.35
❑ 627 Dana Hall RC	.50	.23
❑ 628 Dan McGwire	.50	.23
❑ 629 Lewis Billups	.50	.23
❑ 630 Darryl Williams RC	.50	.23
❑ 631 Dwayne Sabb RC	.50	.23
❑ 632 Mark Royals	.50	.23
❑ 633 Cary Conklin	.50	.23
❑ 634 Al Toon	.75	.35
❑ 635 Junior Seau	1.50	.70
❑ 636 Greg Skrepenak RC UER (Card misnumbered 686)	.50	.23
❑ 637 Deion Sanders	3.00	1.35
❑ 638 Steve DeOssie	.50	.23
❑ 639 Randall Cunningham	1.50	.70
❑ 640 Jim Kelly	1.50	.70
❑ 641 Michael Brandon RC	.50	.23
❑ 642 Clayton Holmes RC	.50	.23
❑ 643 Webster Slaughter	.50	.23
❑ 644 Ricky Proehl	.50	.23
❑ 645 Jerry Rice	5.00	2.20
❑ 646 Carl Banks	.50	.23
❑ 647 J.J.Birden	.50	.23
❑ 648 Tracy Scroggins RC	.50	.23
❑ 649 Alonzo Spellman RC	.75	.35
❑ 650 Joe Montana	8.00	3.60
❑ 651 Courtney Hawkins RC	.75	.35
❑ 652 Corey Widmer RC	.50	.23
❑ 653 Robert Brooks RC	4.00	1.80
❑ 654 Darren Woodson RC	1.50	.70
❑ 655 Derrick Fenner	.50	.23
❑ 656 Steve Christie	.50	.23
❑ 657 Chester McGlockton RC	.75	.35
❑ 658 Steve Israel RC	.50	.23
❑ 659 Robert Harris RC	.50	.23
❑ 660 Dan Marino	8.00	3.60
❑ 661 Ed McCaffrey	5.00	2.20
❑ 662 Johnny Mitchell RC	.50	.23
❑ 663 Timm Rosenbach	.50	.23
❑ 664 Anthony Miller	.75	.35
❑ 665 Merril Hoge	.50	.23
❑ 666 Eugene Chung RC	.50	.23
❑ 667 Rueben Mayes	.50	.23
❑ 668 Martin Bayless	.50	.23
❑ 669 Ashley Ambrose RC	1.50	.70
❑ 670 Michael Cofer UER (Back shows card for Mike Cofer, the kicker)	.50	.23
❑ 671 Shane Dronett RC	.50	.23
❑ 672 Bernie Kosar	.75	.35
❑ 673 Mike Singletary	.75	.35
❑ 674 Mike Lodish RC	.50	.23
❑ 675 Phillippi Sparks RC	.50	.23
❑ 676 Joel Steed RC	.50	.23
❑ 677 Kevin Fagan	.50	.23
❑ 678 Randal Hill	.50	.23
❑ 679 Ken O'Brien	.50	.23
❑ 680 Lawrence Taylor	1.50	.70
❑ 681 Harvey Williams	1.50	.70
❑ 682 Quentin Coryatt RC	.50	.23
❑ 683 Brett Favre	80.00	36.00
❑ 684 Robert Jones RC	.50	.23
❑ 685 Michael Dean Perry	.75	.35
❑ 686 Bruce Smith	1.50	.70
❑ 687 Troy Auzenne RC	.50	.23
❑ 688 Thomas McLemore RC	.50	.23
❑ 689 Dale Carter RC	.75	.35
❑ 690 Marc Boutte RC	.50	.23
❑ 691 Jeff George	1.50	.70
❑ 692 Dion Lambert RC UER (Birthdate is 2/12/19; should be 2/12/69)	.50	.23
❑ 693 Vaughn Dunbar RC	.50	.23
❑ 694 Derek Brown TE RC	.50	.23
❑ 695 Troy Aikman	5.00	2.20
❑ 696 John Fina RC	.50	.23
❑ 697 Kevin Smith RC	.50	.23
❑ 698 Corey Miller RC	.50	.23
❑ 699 Lance Olberding RC	.50	.23
❑ 700 Checklist 601-700 UER (Numbering sequence off from 616 to 636)	.50	.23
❑ P1 Promo Sheet blue National July 10-12, 1992 Barry Sanders Gene Atkins Louis Oliver Paul Gruber Emmitt Smith Steve Jordan Warren Moon Seth Joyner Ronnie Lott	10.00	4.50
❑ P2 Promo Sheet red National July 9, 1992 Barry Sanders Gene Atkins Louis Oliver Paul Gruber Emmitt Smith Steve Jordan Warren Moon Seth Joyner Ronnie Lott	12.00	5.50

1993 Stadium Club

	Nm-Mt	Ex-Mt
COMPLETE SET (550)	40.00	18.00
COMP.SERIES 1 (250)	25.00	11.00
COMP.SERIES 2 (250)	15.00	6.75
COMP.HIGH SERIES (50)	8.00	3.60
COMP.HIGH FACT.SET (51)	12.00	5.50
❑ 1 Sterling Sharpe	.20	.09
❑ 2 Chris Burkett	.10	.05
❑ 3 Santana Dotson	.20	.09
❑ 4 Michael Jackson	.20	.09
❑ 5 Neal Anderson	.10	.05
❑ 6 Bryan Cox	.10	.05
❑ 7 Dennis Gibson	.10	.05
❑ 8 Jeff Graham	.20	.09
❑ 9 Roger Ruzek	.10	.05
❑ 10 Duane Bickett	.10	.05
❑ 11 Charles Mann	.10	.05
❑ 12 Tommy Maddox	.40	.18
❑ 13 Vaughn Dunbar	.10	.05
❑ 14 Gary Plummer	.10	.05
❑ 15 Chris Miller	.20	.09
❑ 16 Chris Warren	.20	.09
❑ 17 Alvin Harper	.20	.09
❑ 18 Eric Dickerson	.20	.09
❑ 19 Mike Jones	.10	.05
❑ 20 Ernest Givins	.20	.09
❑ 21 Natrone Means RC	.40	.18
❑ 22 Doug Riesenberg	.10	.05
❑ 23 Barry Word	.10	.05
❑ 24 Sean Salisbury	.10	.05
❑ 25 Derrick Fenner	.10	.05
❑ 26 David Howard	.10	.05
❑ 27 Mark Kelso	.10	.05
❑ 28 Todd Lyght	.10	.05
❑ 29 Dana Hall	.10	.05
❑ 30 Eric Metcalf	.20	.09
❑ 31 Jason Hanson	.10	.05
❑ 32 Dwight Stone	.10	.05
❑ 33 Johnny Mitchell	.10	.05
❑ 34 Reggie Roby	.10	.05
❑ 35 Terrell Buckley	.10	.05
❑ 36 Steve McMichael	.20	.09
❑ 37 Marty Carter	.10	.05
❑ 38 Seth Joyner	.10	.05
❑ 39 Rohn Stark	.10	.05
❑ 40 Eric Curry RC	.10	.05
❑ 41 Tommy Barnhardt	.10	.05
❑ 42 Karl Mecklenburg	.10	.05
❑ 43 Darion Conner	.10	.05
❑ 44 Ronnie Harmon	.10	.05
❑ 45 Cortez Kennedy	.20	.09
❑ 46 Tim Brown	.40	.18
❑ 47 Bill Lewis	.10	.05
❑ 48 Randall McDaniel	.10	.05
❑ 49 Curtis Duncan	.10	.05
❑ 50 Troy Aikman	1.50	.70
❑ 51 David Klingler	.10	.05
❑ 52 Brent Jones	.20	.09
❑ 53 Dave Krieg	.20	.09
❑ 54 Bruce Smith	.40	.18
❑ 55 Vincent Brown	.10	.05
❑ 56 O.J. McDuffie RC	.40	.18
❑ 57 Cleveland Gary	.10	.05
❑ 58 Larry Centers RC	.40	.18
❑ 59 Pepper Johnson	.10	.05
❑ 60 Dan Marino	3.00	1.35
❑ 61 Robert Porcher	.10	.05
❑ 62 Jim Harbaugh	.40	.18
❑ 63 Sam Mills	.10	.05
❑ 64 Gary Anderson RB	.10	.05
❑ 65 Neil O'Donnell	.20	.09
❑ 66 Keith Byars	.10	.05
❑ 67 Jeff Herrod	.10	.05
❑ 68 Marion Butts	.10	.05
❑ 69 Terry McDaniel	.10	.05
❑ 70 John Elway	3.00	1.35
❑ 71 Steve Broussard	.10	.05
❑ 72 Kelvin Martin	.10	.05
❑ 73 Tom Carter RC	.20	.09
❑ 74 Bryce Paup	.20	.09
❑ 75 Jim Kelly UER back shows 1992 Topps card as RC	.20	.09
❑ 76 Bill Romanowski	.10	.05
❑ 77 Andre Collins	.10	.05
❑ 78 Mike Farr	.10	.05
❑ 79 Henry Ellard	.20	.09
❑ 80 Dale Carter	.10	.05
❑ 81 Johnny Bailey	.10	.05

❑	82 Garrison Hearst RC	1.50	.70
❑	83 Brent Williams	.10	.05
❑	84 Ricardo McDonald	.10	.05
❑	85 Emmitt Smith	3.00	1.35
❑	86 Vai Sikahema	.10	.05
❑	87 Jackie Harris	.10	.05
❑	88 Alonzo Spellman	.10	.05
❑	89 Mark Wheeler	.10	.05
❑	90 Dalton Hilliard	.10	.05
❑	91 Mark Higgs	.10	.05
❑	92 Aaron Wallace	.10	.05
❑	93 Earnest Byner	.10	.05
❑	94 Stanley Richard	.10	.05
❑	95 Cris Carter	.40	.18
❑	96 Bobby Houston RC	.10	.05
❑	97 Craig Heyward	.20	.09
❑	98 Bernie Kosar	.20	.09
❑	99 Mike Croel	.10	.05
❑	100 Deion Sanders	1.00	.45
❑	101 Warren Moon	.20	.09
❑	102 Christian Okoye	.10	.05
❑	103 Ricky Watters	.40	.18
❑	104 Eric Swann	.20	.09
❑	105 Rodney Hampton	.20	.09
❑	106 Daryl Johnston	.20	.09
❑	107 Andre Reed	.20	.09
❑	108 Jerome Bettis RC	5.00	2.20
❑	109 Eugene Daniel	.10	.05
❑	110 Leonard Russell	.20	.09
❑	111 Darryl Williams	.10	.05
❑	112 Rod Woodson	.40	.18
❑	113 Boomer Esiason	.20	.09
❑	114 James Hasty	.10	.05
❑	115 Marc Boutte	.10	.05
❑	116 Tom Waddle	.10	.05
❑	117 Lawrence Dawsey	.10	.05
❑	118 Mark Collins	.10	.05
❑	119 Willie Gault	.10	.05
❑	120 Barry Sanders	2.50	1.10
❑	121 Leroy Hoard	.20	.09
❑	122 Anthony Munoz	.20	.09
❑	123 Jesse Sapolu	.10	.05
❑	124 Art Monk	.20	.09
❑	125 Randal Hill	.10	.05
❑	126 John Offerdahl	.10	.05
❑	127 Carlos Jenkins	.10	.05
❑	128 Al Smith	.10	.05
❑	129 Michael Irvin	.40	.18
❑	130 Kenneth Davis	.10	.05
❑	131 Curtis Conway RC	.75	.35
❑	132 Steve Atwater	.10	.05
❑	133 Neil Smith	.40	.18
❑	134 Steve Everitt RC	.10	.05
❑	135 Chris Mims	.10	.05
❑	136 Rickey Jackson	.10	.05
❑	137 Edgar Bennett	.40	.18
❑	138 Mike Pritchard	.20	.09
❑	139 Richard Dent	.20	.09
❑	140 Barry Foster	.20	.09
❑	141 Eugene Robinson	.10	.05
❑	142 Jackie Slater	.10	.05
❑	143 Paul Gruber	.10	.05
❑	144 Rob Moore	.20	.09
❑	145 Robert Smith RC	2.50	1.10
❑	146 Lorenzo White	.10	.05
❑	147 Tommy Vardell	.10	.05
❑	148 Dave Meggett	.10	.05
❑	149 Vince Workman	.10	.05
❑	150 Terry Allen	.40	.18
❑	151 Howie Long	.40	.18
❑	152 Charles Haley	.20	.09
❑	153 Pete Metzelaars	.10	.05
❑	154 John Copeland RC	.20	.09
❑	155 Aeneas Williams	.10	.05
❑	156 Ricky Sanders	.10	.05
❑	157 Andre Ware	.10	.05
❑	158 Tony Paige	.10	.05
❑	159 Jerome Henderson	.10	.05
❑	160 Harold Green	.10	.05
❑	161 Wymon Henderson	.10	.05
❑	162 Andre Rison	.20	.09
❑	163 Donald Evans	.10	.05
❑	164 Todd Scott	.10	.05
❑	165 Steve Emtman	.10	.05
❑	166 William Fuller	.10	.05
❑	167 Michael Dean Perry	.20	.09
❑	168 Randall Cunningham	.40	.18
❑	169 Toi Cook	.10	.05
❑	170 Browning Nagle	.10	.05
❑	171 Darryl Henley	.10	.05
❑	172 George Teague RC	.20	.09
❑	173 Derrick Thomas	.20	.09
❑	174 Jay Novacek	.20	.09
❑	175 Mark Carrier DB	.10	.05
❑	176 Kevin Fagan	.10	.05
❑	177 Nate Lewis	.10	.05
❑	178 Courtney Hawkins	.10	.05
❑	179 Robert Blackmon	.10	.05
❑	180 Rick Mirer RC	.40	.18
❑	181 Mike Lodish	.10	.05
❑	182 Jarrod Bunch	.10	.05
❑	183 Anthony Smith	.10	.05
❑	184 Brian Noble	.10	.05
❑	185 Eric Bieniemy	.10	.05
❑	186 Keith Jackson	.20	.09
❑	187 Eric Martin	.10	.05
❑	188 Vance Johnson	.10	.05
❑	189 Kevin Mack	.10	.05
❑	190 Rich Camarillo	.10	.05
❑	191 Ashley Ambrose	.10	.05
❑	192 Ray Childress	.10	.05
❑	193 Jim Arnold	.10	.05
❑	194 Ricky Ervins	.10	.05
❑	195 Gary Anderson K	.10	.05
❑	196 Eric Allen	.10	.05
❑	197 Roger Craig	.20	.09
❑	198 Jon Vaughn	.10	.05
❑	199 Tim McDonald	.10	.05
❑	200 Broderick Thomas	.10	.05
❑	201 Jessie Tuggle	.10	.05
❑	202 Alonzo Mitz	.10	.05
❑	203 Harvey Williams	.20	.09
❑	204 Russell Maryland	.10	.05
❑	205 Marvin Washington	.10	.05
❑	206 Jim Everett	.20	.09
❑	207 Trace Armstrong	.10	.05
❑	208 Steve Young	1.50	.70
❑	209 Tony Woods	.10	.05
❑	210 Brett Favre	4.00	1.80
❑	211 Nate Odomes	.10	.05
❑	212 Ricky Proehl	.10	.05
❑	213 Jim Dombrowski	.10	.05
❑	214 Anthony Carter	.20	.09
❑	215 Tracy Simien	.10	.05
❑	216 Clay Matthews	.20	.09
❑	217 Patrick Bates RC	.10	.05
❑	218 Jeff George	.40	.18
❑	219 David Fulcher	.10	.05
❑	220 Phil Simms	.20	.09
❑	221 Eugene Chung	.10	.05
❑	222 Reggie Cobb	.10	.05
❑	223 Jim Sweeney	.10	.05
❑	224 Greg Lloyd	.20	.09
❑	225 Sean Jones	.10	.05
❑	226 Marvin Jones RC	.10	.05
❑	227 Bill Brooks	.10	.05
❑	228 Moe Gardner	.10	.05
❑	229 Louis Oliver	.10	.05
❑	230 Flipper Anderson	.10	.05
❑	231 Marc Spindler	.10	.05
❑	232 Jerry Rice	2.00	.90
❑	233 Chip Lohmiller	.10	.05
❑	234 Nolan Harrison	.10	.05
❑	235 Heath Sherman	.10	.05
❑	236 Reyna Thompson	.10	.05
❑	237 Derrick Walker	.10	.05
❑	238 Rufus Porter	.10	.05
❑	239 Checklist 1-125	.10	.05
❑	240 Checklist 126-250	.10	.05
❑	241 John Elway MC	1.50	.70
❑	242 Troy Aikman MC	.75	.35
❑	243 Steve Emtman MC	.10	.05
❑	244 Ricky Watters MC	.20	.09
❑	245 Barry Foster MC	.10	.05
❑	246 Dan Marino MC	1.50	.70
❑	247 Reggie White MC	.20	.09
❑	248 Thurman Thomas MC	.20	.09
❑	249 Broderick Thomas MC	.10	.05
❑	250 Joe Montana MC	1.50	.70
❑	251 Tim Goad	.10	.05
❑	252 Joe Nash	.10	.05
❑	253 Anthony Johnson	.20	.09
❑	254 Carl Pickens	.20	.09
❑	255 Steve Beuerlein	.20	.09
❑	256 Anthony Newman	.10	.05
❑	257 Corey Miller	.10	.05
❑	258 Steve DeBerg	.10	.05
❑	259 Johnny Holland	.10	.05
❑	260 Jerry Ball	.10	.05
❑	261 Siupeli Malamala RC	.10	.05
❑	262 Steve Wisniewski	.10	.05
❑	263 Kelvin Pritchett	.10	.05
❑	264 Chris Gardocki	.10	.05
❑	265 Henry Thomas	.10	.05
❑	266 Arthur Marshall RC	.10	.05
❑	267 Quinn Early	.20	.09
❑	268 Jonathan Hayes	.10	.05
❑	269 Erric Pegram	.20	.09
❑	270 Clyde Simmons	.10	.05
❑	271 Eric Moten	.10	.05
❑	272 Brian Mitchell	.20	.09
❑	273 Adrian Cooper	.10	.05
❑	274 Gaston Green	.10	.05
❑	275 John Taylor	.20	.09
❑	276 Jeff Uhlenhake	.10	.05
❑	277 Phil Hansen	.10	.05
❑	278A K.Williams RC WR ERR	.40	.18
	missing draft pick logo on front		
❑	278B K.Williams RC WR COR	.40	.18
	with draft pick logo		
❑	279 Robert Massey	.10	.05
❑	280A Drew Bledsoe RC ERR	10.00	4.50
	missing draft pick logo on front		
❑	280B Drew Bledsoe RC COR	5.00	2.20
	(draft pick logo on front)		
❑	281 Walter Reeves	.10	.05
❑	282A Carlton Gray RC ERR	.25	.11
	(missing draft pick logo on front)		
❑	282B Carlton Gray RC COR	.15	.07
	(draft pick logo on front)		
❑	283 Derek Brown TE	.10	.05
❑	284 Martin Mayhew	.10	.05
❑	285 Sean Gilbert	.20	.09
❑	286 Jessie Hester	.10	.05
❑	287 Mark Clayton	.10	.05
❑	288 Blair Thomas	.10	.05
❑	289 J.J. Birden	.10	.05
❑	290 Shannon Sharpe	.40	.18
❑	291 Richard Fain RC	.10	.05
❑	292 Gene Atkins	.10	.05
❑	293 Burt Grossman	.10	.05
❑	294 Chris Doleman	.10	.05
❑	295 Pat Swilling	.10	.05
❑	296 Mike Kenn	.10	.05
❑	297 Merril Hoge	.10	.05
❑	298 Don Mosebar	.10	.05
❑	299 Kevin Smith	.20	.09
❑	300 Darrell Green	.10	.05
❑	301A Dan Footman RC ERR	.25	.11
	(missing draft pick logo on front)		
❑	301B Dan Footman RC COR	.15	.07
	draft pick logo on front)		
❑	302 Vestee Jackson	.10	.05
❑	303 Carwell Gardner	.10	.05
❑	304 Amp Lee	.10	.05
❑	305 Bruce Matthews	.10	.05
❑	306 Antone Davis	.10	.05
❑	307 Dean Biasucci	.10	.05
❑	308 Maurice Hurst	.10	.05
❑	309 John Kasay	.10	.05
❑	310 Lawrence Taylor	.20	.09
❑	311 Ken Harvey	.10	.05
❑	312 Willie Davis	.20	.09

❑ 313 Tony Bennett .10 .05
❑ 314 Jay Schroeder .10 .05
❑ 315 Darren Perry .10 .05
❑ 316A Troy Drayton RC ERR .25 .11
(missing draft pick logo on front)
❑ 316B Troy Drayton RC COR .15 .07
(draft pick logo on front)
❑ 317A Dan Williams RC ERR .25 .11
(missing draft pick logo on front)
❑ 317B Dan Williams RC COR .15 .07
(draft pick logo on front)
❑ 318 Michael Haynes .20 .09
❑ 319 Renaldo Turnbull .10 .05
❑ 320 Junior Seau .40 .18
❑ 321 Ray Crockett .10 .05
❑ 322 Will Furrer .10 .05
❑ 323 Byron Evans .10 .05
❑ 324 Jim McMahon .20 .09
❑ 325 Robert Jones .10 .05
❑ 326 Eric Davis .10 .05
❑ 327 Jeff Cross .10 .05
❑ 328 Kyle Clifton .10 .05
❑ 329 Haywood Jeffires .20 .09
❑ 330 Jeff Hostetler .20 .09
❑ 331 Darryl Talley .10 .05
❑ 332 Keith McCants .10 .05
❑ 333 Mo Lewis .10 .05
❑ 334 Matt Stover .10 .05
❑ 335 Ferrell Edmunds .10 .05
❑ 336 Matt Brock .10 .05
❑ 337 Ernie Mills .10 .05
❑ 338 Shane Dronett .10 .05
❑ 339 Brad Muster .10 .05
❑ 340 Jesse Solomon .10 .05
❑ 341 John Randle .20 .09
❑ 342 Chris Spielman .20 .09
❑ 343 David Whitmore .10 .05
❑ 344 Glenn Parker .10 .05
❑ 345 Marco Coleman .10 .05
❑ 346 Kenneth Gant .10 .05
❑ 347 Cris Dishman .10 .05
❑ 348 Kenny Walker .10 .05
❑ 349A R.Potts RC ERR .25 .11
missing draft pick logo on front
❑ 349B R.Potts RC COR .15 .07
draft pick logo on front
❑ 350 Reggie White .40 .18
❑ 351 Gerald Robinson .10 .05
❑ 352 Mark Rypien .10 .05
❑ 353 Stan Humphries .20 .09
❑ 354 Chris Singleton .10 .05
❑ 355 Herschel Walker .20 .09
❑ 356 Ron Hall .10 .05
❑ 357 Ethan Horton .10 .05
❑ 358 Anthony Pleasant .10 .05
❑ 359A Thomas Smith RC ERR .25 .11
(missing draft pick logo on front)
❑ 359B Thomas Smith RC COR .15 .07
(draft pick logo on front)
❑ 360 Audray McMillian .10 .05
❑ 361 D.J. Johnson .10 .05
❑ 362 Ron Heller .10 .05
❑ 363 Bern Brostek .10 .05
❑ 364 Ronnie Lott .20 .09
❑ 365 Reggie Johnson .10 .05
❑ 366 Lin Elliott .10 .05
❑ 367 Lemuel Stinson .10 .05
❑ 368 William White .10 .05
❑ 369 Ernie Jones .10 .05
❑ 370 Tom Rathman .10 .05
❑ 371 Tommy Kane .10 .05
❑ 372 David Brandon .10 .05
❑ 373 Lee Johnson .10 .05
❑ 374 Wade Wilson .10 .05
❑ 375 Nick Lowery .10 .05
❑ 376 Bubba McDowell .10 .05
❑ 377A W.Simmons RC ERR .25 .11
missing draft pick logo on front
❑ 377B W.Simmons RC COR .15 .07
draft pick logo on front
❑ 378 Calvin Williams .20 .09
❑ 379 Courtney Hall .10 .05
❑ 380 Troy Vincent .10 .05
❑ 381 Tim McGee .10 .05
❑ 382 Russell Freeman RC .10 .05
❑ 383 Steve Tasker .20 .09
❑ 384A M.Strahan RC ERR 2.00 .90
(missing draft pick logo on front)
❑ 384B Michael Strahan RC COR 2.00 .90
(draft pick logo on front)
❑ 385 Greg Skrepenak .10 .05
❑ 386 Jake Reed .20 .09
❑ 387 Pete Stoyanovich .10 .05
❑ 388 Levon Kirkland .10 .05
❑ 389 Mel Gray .20 .09
❑ 390 Brian Washington .10 .05
❑ 391 Don Griffin .10 .05
❑ 392 Desmond Howard .20 .09
❑ 393 Luis Sharpe .10 .05
❑ 394 Mike Johnson .10 .05
❑ 395 Andre Tippett .10 .05
❑ 396 Donnell Woolford .10 .05
❑ 397A D.DuBose RC ERR .25 .11
missing draft pick logo on front
❑ 397B D.DuBose RC COR .15 .07
(draft pick logo on front)
❑ 398 Pat Terrell .10 .05
❑ 399 Todd McNair .10 .05
❑ 400 Ken Norton .20 .09
❑ 401 Keith Hamilton .10 .05
❑ 402 Andy Heck .10 .05
❑ 403 Jeff Gossett .10 .05
❑ 404 Dexter McNabb .10 .05
❑ 405 Richmond Webb .10 .05
❑ 406 Irving Fryar .20 .09
❑ 407 Brian Hansen .10 .05
❑ 408 David Little .10 .05
❑ 409A Glyn Milburn RC ERR .40 .18
(missing draft pick logo on front)
❑ 409B Glyn Milburn RC COR .20 .09
(draft pick logo on front)
❑ 410 Doug Dawson .10 .05
❑ 411 Scott Mersereau .10 .05
❑ 412 Don Beebe .10 .05
❑ 413 Vaughan Johnson .10 .05
❑ 414 Jack Del Rio .10 .05
❑ 415A D.Gordon RC ERR .25 .11
missing draft pick logo on front
❑ 415B D.Gordon RC COR .15 .07
draft pick logo on front
❑ 416 Mark Schlereth .10 .05
❑ 417 Lomas Brown .10 .05
❑ 418 William Thomas .10 .05
❑ 419 James Francis .10 .05
❑ 420 Quentin Coryatt .20 .09
❑ 421 Tyji Armstrong .10 .05
❑ 422 Hugh Millen .10 .05
❑ 423 Adrian White RC .10 .05
❑ 424 Eddie Anderson .10 .05
❑ 425 Mark Ingram .10 .05
❑ 426 Ken O'Brien .10 .05
❑ 427 Simon Fletcher .10 .05
❑ 428 Tim McKyer .10 .05
❑ 429 Leonard Marshall .10 .05
❑ 430 Eric Green .10 .05
❑ 431 Leonard Harris .10 .05
❑ 432 Darin Jordan RC .10 .05
❑ 433 Erik Howard .10 .05
❑ 434 David Lang .10 .05
❑ 435 Eric Turner .10 .05
❑ 436 Michael Cofer .10 .05
❑ 437 Jeff Bryant .10 .05
❑ 438 Charles McRae .10 .05
❑ 439 Henry Jones .10 .05
❑ 440 Joe Montana 3.00 1.35
❑ 441 Morten Andersen .10 .05
❑ 442 Jeff Jaeger .10 .05
❑ 443 Leslie O'Neal .20 .09
❑ 444 LeRoy Butler .10 .05
❑ 445 Steve Jordan .10 .05
❑ 446 Brad Edwards .10 .05
❑ 447 J.B. Brown .10 .05
❑ 448 Kerry Cash .10 .05
❑ 449 Mark Tuinei .10 .05
❑ 450 Rodney Peete .10 .05
❑ 451 Sheldon White .10 .05
❑ 452 Wesley Carroll .10 .05
❑ 453 Brad Baxter .10 .05
❑ 454 Mike Pitts .10 .05
❑ 455 Greg Montgomery .10 .05
❑ 456 Kenny Davidson .10 .05
❑ 457 Scott Fulhage .10 .05
❑ 458 Greg Townsend .10 .05
❑ 459 Rod Bernstine .10 .05
❑ 460 Gary Clark .20 .09
❑ 461 Hardy Nickerson .20 .09
❑ 462 Sean Landeta .10 .05
❑ 463 Rob Burnett .10 .05
❑ 464 Fred Barnett .20 .09
❑ 465 John L. Williams .10 .05
❑ 466 Anthony Miller .20 .09
❑ 467 Roman Phifer .10 .05
❑ 468 Rich Moran .10 .05
❑ 469A Willie Roaf RC ERR .25 .11
(missing draft pick logo on front)
❑ 469B Willie Roaf RC COR .15 .07
(draft pick logo on front)
❑ 470 William Perry .20 .09
❑ 471 Marcus Allen .40 .18
❑ 472 Carl Lee .10 .05
❑ 473 Kurt Gouveia .10 .05
❑ 474 Jarvis Williams .10 .05
❑ 475 Alfred Williams .10 .05
❑ 476 Mark Stepnoski .10 .05
❑ 477 Steve Wallace .10 .05
❑ 478 Pat Harlow .10 .05
❑ 479 Chip Banks .10 .05
❑ 480 Cornelius Bennett .20 .09
❑ 481A Ryan McNeil RC ERR .15 .07
(missing draft pick logo on front)
❑ 481B Ryan McNeil RC COR .40 .18
(draft pick logo on front)
❑ 482 Norm Johnson .10 .05
❑ 483 Dermontti Dawson .10 .05
❑ 484 Dwayne White .10 .05
❑ 485 Derek Russell .10 .05
❑ 486 Lionel Washington .10 .05
❑ 487 Eric Hill .10 .05
❑ 488 Micheal Barrow RC .40 .18
❑ 489 Checklist 251-375 UER .10 .05
(No. 277 Hansen misspelled Hanson)
❑ 490 Checklist 376-500 UER .10 .05
(No. 488 Micheal Barrow misspelled Michael)
❑ 491 Emmitt Smith MC 1.50 .70
❑ 492 Derrick Thomas MC .20 .09
❑ 493 Deion Sanders MC .40 .18
❑ 494 Randall Cunningham MC .20 .09
❑ 495 Sterling Sharpe MC .20 .09
❑ 496 Barry Sanders MC 1.25 .55
❑ 497 Thurman Thomas MC .20 .09
❑ 498 Brett Favre MC 2.00 .90
❑ 499 Vaughan Johnson MC .10 .05
❑ 500 Steve Young MC .75 .35
❑ 501 Marvin Jones MC .10 .05
❑ 502 Reggie Brooks RC MC .20 .09
❑ 503 Eric Curry MC .10 .05
❑ 504 Drew Bledsoe MC 2.00 .90
❑ 505 Glyn Milburn MC .20 .09
❑ 506 Jerome Bettis MC 2.00 .90
❑ 507 Robert Smith MC 1.00 .45
❑ 508 Dana Stubblefield RC MC .40 .18
❑ 509 Tom Carter MC .20 .09
❑ 510 Rick Mirer MC .40 .18
❑ 511 Russell Copeland RC .20 .09
❑ 512 Deon Figures RC .10 .05
❑ 513 Tony McGee RC .20 .09
❑ 514 Derrick Lassic RC .10 .05
❑ 515 Everett Lindsay RC .10 .05
❑ 516 Derek Brown RC RBK .10 .05
❑ 517 Harold Alexander RC .10 .05
❑ 518 Tom Scott RC .10 .05
❑ 519 Elvis Grbac RC 3.00 1.35

❑ 520 Terry Kirby RC	.40	.18
❑ 521 Doug Pelfrey RC	.10	.05
❑ 522 Horace Copeland RC	.20	.09
❑ 523 Irv Smith RC	.10	.05
❑ 524 Lincoln Kennedy RC	.10	.05
❑ 525 Jason Elam RC	.40	.18
❑ 526 Qadry Ismail RC	.40	.18
❑ 527 Artie Smith RC	.10	.05
❑ 528 Tyrone Hughes RC	.20	.09
❑ 529 Lance Gunn RC	.10	.05
❑ 530 Vincent Brisby RC	.40	.18
❑ 531 Patrick Robinson RC	.10	.05
❑ 532 Raghib Ismail	.20	.09
❑ 533 Willie Beamon RC	.10	.05
❑ 534 Vaughn Hebron RC	.10	.05
❑ 535 Darren Drozdov RC	.40	.18
❑ 536 James Jett RC	.40	.18
❑ 537 Michael Bates RC	.10	.05
❑ 538 Tom Rouen RC	.10	.05
❑ 539 Michael Husted RC	.10	.05
❑ 540 Greg Robinson RC	.10	.05
❑ 541 Carl Banks	.10	.05
❑ 542 Kevin Greene	.20	.09
❑ 543 Scott Mitchell	.40	.18
❑ 544 Michael Brooks	.10	.05
❑ 545 Shane Conlan	.10	.05
❑ 546 Vinny Testaverde	.20	.09
❑ 547 Robert Delpino	.10	.05
❑ 548 Bill Fralic	.10	.05
❑ 549 Carlton Bailey	.10	.05
❑ 550 Johnny Johnson	.10	.05
❑ NNO Jerry Rice RB UER	10.00	4.50
(Wrong date for record touchdown)		
❑ P1 Promo Sheet	5.00	2.20
Johnny Bailey		
Vai Sikahema		
Richard Dent		
Sterling Sharpe		
Tommy Barnhardt		
Cris Carter		
Cortez Kennedy		
Christian Okoye		
Reggie Cobb		

1997 Stadium Club Co-Signers

	Nm-Mt	Ex-Mt
❑ CO1 Karim Abdul-Jabbar / Eddie George	250.00	110.00
❑ CO2 Trace Armstrong / Alonzo Spellman	30.00	13.50
❑ CO3 Steve Atwater / Kevin Hardy	30.00	13.50
❑ CO4 Fred Barnett / Lake Dawson	50.00	22.00
❑ CO5 Blaine Bishop / Darrell Green	30.00	13.50
❑ CO6 Jeff Blake / Gus Frerotte	100.00	45.00
❑ CO7 Steve Bono / Cris Carter	100.00	45.00
❑ CO8 Tim Brown / Isaac Bruce	120.00	55.00
❑ CO9 Wayne Chrebet / Mickey Washington	30.00	13.50
❑ CO10 Curtis Conway / Eddie Kennison	30.00	13.50
❑ CO11 Eric Davis / Jason Sehorn	50.00	22.00
❑ CO12 Terrell Davis / Thurman Thomas	100.00	45.00
❑ CO13 Ken Dilger / Kent Graham	50.00	22.00
❑ CO14 Stephen Grant / Marvcus Patton	30.00	13.50
❑ CO15 Keith Hamilton / Mike Tomczak	30.00	13.50
❑ CO16 Rodney Hampton / Dave Meggett	50.00	22.00
❑ CO17 Merton Hanks / Aeneas Williams	30.00	13.50
❑ CO19 Brent Jones / Wesley Walls	30.00	13.50
❑ CO20 Carnell Lake / Tim McDonald	30.00	13.50
❑ CO21 Thomas Lewis / Keith Lyle	30.00	13.50
❑ CO22 Leeland McElroy / Jeff Lageman	30.00	13.50
❑ CO23 Ray Mickens / Willie Davis	30.00	13.50
❑ CO24 Herman Moore / Desmond Howard	30.00	13.50
❑ CO25 Stevon Moore / William Thomas	30.00	13.50
❑ CO26 Adrian Murrell / Levon Kirkland	30.00	13.50
❑ CO27 Simeon Rice / Winslow Oliver	50.00	22.00
❑ CO28 Bill Romanowski / Gary Plummer	30.00	13.50
❑ CO29 Junior Seau / Chris Spielman	30.00	13.50
❑ CO30 Chris Slade / Kevin Greene	30.00	13.50
❑ CO31 Derrick Thomas / Chris T. Jones	80.00	36.00
❑ CO32 Orlando Thomas / Bobby Engram	50.00	22.00
❑ CO33 Amani Toomer / Thomas Randolph	50.00	22.00
❑ CO34 Steve Tovar / Ellis Johnson LB	30.00	13.50
❑ CO35 Herschel Walker / Anthony Johnson	50.00	22.00
❑ CO36 Darren Woodson / Aaron Glenn	50.00	22.00
❑ CO37 Karim Abdul-Jabbar / Thurman Thomas	80.00	36.00
❑ CO38 Blaine Bishop / Tim McDonald	30.00	13.50
❑ CO39 Jeff Blake / Derrick Thomas	80.00	36.00
❑ CO41 Cris Carter / Marvin Harrison	120.00	55.00
❑ CO42 Curtis Conway / Wesley Walls	40.00	18.00
❑ CO43 Willie Davis / Amani Toomer	40.00	18.00
❑ CO44 Lake Dawson / Ray Mickens	30.00	13.50
❑ CO45 Ken Dilger / Ellis Johnson LB	40.00	18.00
❑ CO46 Bobby Engram / Thomas Lewis	30.00	13.50
❑ CO47 Gus Frerotte / Chris T. Jones	80.00	36.00
❑ CO48 Eddie George / Terrell Davis	80.00	36.00
❑ CO49 Aaron Glenn / Eric Davis	30.00	13.50
❑ CO50 Kent Graham / Steve Tovar	40.00	18.00
❑ CO51 Darrell Green / Carnell Lake	30.00	13.50
❑ CO52 Kevin Greene / Steve Atwater	40.00	18.00
❑ CO53 Rodney Hampton / Anthony Johnson	40.00	18.00
❑ CO54 Kevin Hardy / Merton Hanks	30.00	13.50
❑ CO55 Desmond Howard / Tim Brown	80.00	36.00
❑ CO56 Eddie Kennison / Brent Jones	40.00	18.00
❑ CO57 Levon Kirkland / Simeon Rice	40.00	18.00
❑ CO58 Jeff Lageman / Adrian Murrell	30.00	13.50
❑ CO59 Keith Lyle / Wayne Chrebet	50.00	22.00
❑ CO60 Dave Meggett / Herschel Walker	50.00	22.00
❑ CO61 Herman Moore / Isaac Bruce	100.00	45.00
❑ CO62 Winslow Oliver / Leeland McElroy	30.00	13.50
❑ CO63 Marvcus Patton / Keith Hamilton	30.00	13.50
❑ CO64 Gary Plummer / Junior Seau	60.00	27.00
❑ CO65 Thomas Randolph / Fred Barnett	30.00	13.50
❑ CO66 Alonzo Spellman / Stephen Grant	30.00	13.50
❑ CO67 Chris Spielman / Stevon Moore	30.00	13.50
❑ CO68 William Thomas / Bill Romanowski	40.00	18.00
❑ CO69 Mike Tomczak / Trace Armstrong	30.00	13.50
❑ CO70 Mickey Washington / Orlando Thomas	30.00	13.50
❑ CO71 Aeneas Williams / Chris Slade	30.00	13.50
❑ CO72 Darren Woodson / Jason Sehorn	40.00	18.00
❑ CO73 Trace Armstrong / Keith Hamilton	15.00	6.75
❑ CO74 Steve Atwater / Chris Slade	15.00	6.75
❑ CO75 Fred Barnett / Amani Toomer	25.00	11.00
❑ CO76 Tim Brown / Herman Moore	80.00	36.00
❑ CO77 Isaac Bruce / Desmond Howard	60.00	27.00
❑ CO78 Wayne Chrebet / Thomas Lewis	25.00	11.00
❑ CO79 Eric Davis / Darren Woodson	15.00	6.75
❑ CO80 Terrell Davis / Karim Abdul-Jabbar	40.00	18.00
❑ CO81 Willie Davis / Lake Dawson	25.00	11.00
❑ CO82 Bobby Engram / Marvin Washington	15.00	6.75
❑ CO83 Stephen Grant / Mike Tomczak	15.00	6.75
❑ CO84 Merton Hanks / Kevin Greene	15.00	6.75
❑ CO85 Marvin Harrison / Steve Bono	50.00	22.00
❑ CO86 Anthony Johnson / Dave Meggett	15.00	6.75
❑ CO87 Ellis Johnson LB / Kent Graham	15.00	6.75
❑ CO88 Brent Jones / Curtis Conway	25.00	11.00
❑ CO89 Chris T. Jones / Jeff Blake	30.00	13.50
❑ CO90 Carnell Lake / Blaine Bishop	15.00	6.75
❑ CO91 Tim McDonald / Darrell Green	15.00	6.75
❑ CO92 Ray Mickens	15.00	6.75

Thomas Randolph		
❑ CO93 Stevon Moore	15.00	6.75
Gary Plummer		
❑ CO94 Adrian Murrell	15.00	6.75
Leeland McElroy		
❑ CO95 Winslow Oliver	15.00	6.75
Levon Kirkland		
❑ CO96 Marvcus Patton	15.00	6.75
Alonzo Spellman		
❑ CO98 Simeon Rice	25.00	11.00
Jeff Lageman		
❑ CO99 Junior Seau	30.00	13.50
Bill Romanowski		
❑ CO100 Jason Sehorn	15.00	6.75
Aaron Glenn		
❑ CO101 Derrick Thomas	40.00	18.00
Gus Frerotte		
❑ CO102 Orlando Thomas	15.00	6.75
Keith Lyle		
❑ CO103 Thurman Thomas	80.00	36.00
Eddie George		
❑ CO104 William Thomas	15.00	6.75
Chris Spielman		
❑ CO105 Steve Tovar	15.00	6.75
Ken Dilger		
❑ CO106 Herschel Walker	30.00	13.50
Rodney Hampton		
❑ CO107 Wesley Walls	30.00	13.50
Eddie Kennison		
❑ CO108 Aeneas Williams	15.00	6.75
Kevin Hardy		

1998 Stadium Club Co-Signers

	Nm-Mt	Ex-Mt
❑ CO1 Peyton Manning	400.00	180.00
Ryan Leaf		
❑ CO2 Dan Marino	400.00	180.00
Kordell Stewart		
❑ CO3 Eddie George	120.00	55.00
Corey Dillon		
❑ CO4 Dorsey Levens	150.00	70.00
Mike Alstott		
❑ CO5 Ryan Leaf	200.00	90.00
Dan Marino		
❑ CO6 Peyton Manning	250.00	110.00
Kordell Stewart		
❑ CO7 Eddie George	120.00	55.00
Mike Alstott		
❑ CO8 Dorsey Levens	80.00	36.00
Corey Dillon		
❑ CO9 Peyton Manning	500.00	220.00
Dan Marino		
❑ CO10 Ryan Leaf	50.00	22.00
Kordell Stewart		
❑ CO11 Eddie George	50.00	22.00
Dorsey Levens		
❑ CO12 Mike Alstott	50.00	22.00
Corey Dillon		

1999 Stadium Club

	Nm-Mt	Ex-Mt
COMPLETE SET (200)	60.00	27.00
COMP.SET w/o SP's (175)	20.00	9.00

UNPRICED 1/1 PRESS PLATES EXIST
FOUR DIFF.PP's PRODUCED PER CARD

❑ 1 Dan Marino	2.50	1.10
❑ 2 Andre Reed	.50	.23
❑ 3 Michael Westbrook	.50	.23
❑ 4 Isaac Bruce	.75	.35
❑ 5 Curtis Martin	.75	.35
❑ 6 Courtney Hawkins	.30	.14
❑ 7 Charles Way	.30	.14
❑ 8 Terrell Owens	.75	.35
❑ 9 Warrick Dunn	.75	.35
❑ 10 Jake Plummer	.50	.23
❑ 11 Chad Brown	.30	.14
❑ 12 Yancey Thigpen	.30	.14
❑ 13 Lamar Thomas	.30	.14
❑ 14 Keenan McCardell	.50	.23
❑ 15 Shannon Sharpe	.50	.23
❑ 16 Robert Brooks	.50	.23
❑ 17 Cameron Cleeland	.30	.14
❑ 18 Derrick Thomas	.50	.23
❑ 19 Mark Brunell	.75	.35
❑ 20 Jamal Anderson	.75	.35
❑ 21 Germane Crowell	.30	.14
❑ 22 Rod Smith	.50	.23
❑ 23 Ty Law	.50	.23
❑ 24 Cris Carter	.75	.35
❑ 25 Terrell Davis	.75	.35
❑ 26 Takeo Spikes	.30	.14
❑ 27 Tim Biakabutuka	.50	.23
❑ 28 Jermaine Lewis	.50	.23
❑ 29 Adrian Murrell	.50	.23
❑ 30 Doug Flutie	.75	.35
❑ 31 Curtis Enis	.30	.14
❑ 32 Skip Hicks	.30	.14
❑ 33 Steve McNair	.75	.35
❑ 34 Charles Woodson	.75	.35
❑ 35 Jessie Armstead	.30	.14
❑ 36 Shawn Springs	.30	.14
❑ 37 Levon Kirkland	.30	.14
❑ 38 Freddie Jones	.30	.14
❑ 39 Warren Sapp	.30	.14
❑ 40 Emmitt Smith	1.50	.70
❑ 41 Reidel Anthony	.50	.23
❑ 42 Tony Simmons	.30	.14
❑ 43 Andre Hastings	.30	.14
❑ 44 Byron Bam Morris	.30	.14
❑ 45 Jimmy Smith	.50	.23
❑ 46 Antonio Freeman	.75	.35
❑ 47 Herman Moore	.50	.23
❑ 48 Muhsin Muhammad	.50	.23
❑ 49 Chris Chandler	.50	.23
❑ 50 John Elway	2.50	1.10
❑ 51 Aeneas Williams	.30	.14
❑ 52 Bobby Engram	.50	.23
❑ 53 Keith Poole	.30	.14
❑ 54 Zach Thomas	.75	.35
❑ 55 Mike Alstott	.75	.35
❑ 56 Junior Seau	.75	.35
❑ 57 Aaron Glenn	.30	.14
❑ 58 Darrell Green	.30	.14
❑ 59 Thurman Thomas	.50	.23
❑ 60 Troy Aikman	1.50	.70
❑ 61 Bill Romanowski	.30	.14
❑ 62 Wesley Walls	.50	.23
❑ 63 Andre Wadsworth	.30	.14
❑ 64 Robert Smith	.75	.35
❑ 65 Elvis Grbac	.50	.23
❑ 66 Terry Fair	.30	.14
❑ 67 Ben Coates	.50	.23
❑ 68 Bert Emanuel	.50	.23
❑ 69 Jacquez Green	.30	.14
❑ 70 Barry Sanders	2.50	1.10
❑ 71 James Jett	.50	.23
❑ 72 Gary Brown	.30	.14
❑ 73 Stephen Alexander	.30	.14
❑ 74 Wayne Chrebet	.50	.23
❑ 75 Drew Bledsoe	1.00	.45
❑ 76 John Lynch	.50	.23
❑ 77 Jake Reed	.50	.23
❑ 78 Marvin Harrison	.75	.35
❑ 79 Johnnie Morton	.50	.23
❑ 80 Brett Favre	2.50	1.10
❑ 81 Charlie Batch	.75	.35
❑ 82 Antowain Smith	.75	.35
❑ 83 Mikhael Ricks	.30	.14
❑ 84 Derrick Mayes	.30	.14
❑ 85 John Mobley	.30	.14
❑ 86 Ernie Mills	.30	.14
❑ 87 Jeff Blake	.50	.23
❑ 88 Curtis Conway	.50	.23
❑ 89 Bruce Smith	.50	.23
❑ 90 Peyton Manning	2.50	1.10
❑ 91 Tyrone Davis	.30	.14
❑ 92 Ray Buchanan	.30	.14
❑ 93 Tim Dwight	.75	.35
❑ 94 O.J. McDuffie	.50	.23
❑ 95 Vonnie Holliday	.30	.14
❑ 96 Jon Kitna	.75	.35
❑ 97 Trent Dilfer	.50	.23
❑ 98 Jerome Bettis	.75	.35
❑ 99 Dedric Ward	.30	.14
❑ 100 Fred Taylor	.75	.35
❑ 101 Ike Hilliard	.30	.14
❑ 102 Frank Wycheck	.30	.14
❑ 103 Eric Moulds	.75	.35
❑ 104 Rob Moore	.50	.23
❑ 105 Ed McCaffrey	.50	.23
❑ 106 Carl Pickens	.50	.23
❑ 107 Priest Holmes	1.25	.55
❑ 108 Kevin Hardy	.30	.14
❑ 109 Terry Glenn	.75	.35
❑ 110 Keyshawn Johnson	.75	.35
❑ 111 Karim Abdul-Jabbar	.50	.23
❑ 112 Stephen Boyd	.30	.14
❑ 113 Ahman Green	.75	.35
❑ 114 Duce Staley	.75	.35
❑ 115 Vinny Testaverde	.50	.23
❑ 116 Napoleon Kaufman	.75	.35
❑ 117 Frank Sanders	.50	.23
❑ 118 Peter Boulware	.30	.14
❑ 119 Kevin Greene	.30	.14
❑ 120 Steve Young	1.00	.45
❑ 121 Darnay Scott	.30	.14
❑ 122 Deion Sanders	.75	.35
❑ 123 Corey Dillon	.75	.35
❑ 124 Randall Cunningham	.75	.35
❑ 125 Eddie George	.75	.35
❑ 126 Derrick Alexander	.30	.14
❑ 127 Mark Chmura	.30	.14
❑ 128 Michael Sinclair	.30	.14
❑ 129 Rickey Dudley	.30	.14
❑ 130 Joey Galloway	.50	.23
❑ 131 Michael Strahan	.50	.23
❑ 132 Ricky Proehl	.30	.14
❑ 133 Natrone Means	.50	.23
❑ 134 Dorsey Levens	.75	.35
❑ 135 Andre Rison	.50	.23
❑ 136 Alonzo Mayes	.30	.14
❑ 137 John Randle	.50	.23
❑ 138 Terance Mathis	.50	.23
❑ 139 Rae Carruth	.30	.14
❑ 140 Jerry Rice	1.50	.70
❑ 141 Michael Irvin	.50	.23
❑ 142 Oronde Gadsden	.50	.23
❑ 143 Jerome Pathon	.30	.14

❑ 144 Ricky Watters	.50	.23
❑ 145 J.J. Stokes	.50	.23
❑ 146 Kordell Stewart	.50	.23
❑ 147 Tim Brown	.75	.35
❑ 148 Garrison Hearst	.50	.23
❑ 149 Tony Gonzalez	.75	.35
❑ 150 Randy Moss	2.00	.90
❑ 151 Daunte Culpepper RC	6.00	2.70
❑ 152 Amos Zereoue RC	2.00	.90
❑ 153 Champ Bailey RC	2.50	1.10
❑ 154 Peerless Price RC	3.00	1.35
❑ 155 Edgerrin James RC	6.00	2.70
❑ 156 Joe Germaine RC	1.50	.70
❑ 157 David Boston RC	2.00	.90
❑ 158 Kevin Faulk RC	2.00	.90
❑ 159 Troy Edwards RC	1.50	.70
❑ 160 Akili Smith RC	1.50	.70
❑ 161 Kevin Johnson RC	2.00	.90
❑ 162 Rob Konrad RC	1.50	.70
❑ 163 Shaun King RC	1.50	.70
❑ 164 James Johnson RC	1.50	.70
❑ 165 Donovan McNabb RC	8.00	3.60
❑ 166 Torry Holt RC	4.00	1.80
❑ 167 Mike Cloud RC	1.50	.70
❑ 168 Sedrick Irvin RC	1.00	.45
❑ 169 Cade McNown RC	1.50	.70
❑ 170 Ricky Williams RC	3.00	1.35
❑ 171 Karsten Bailey RC	1.50	.70
❑ 172 Cecil Collins RC	1.00	.45
❑ 173 Brock Huard RC	2.00	.90
❑ 174 D'Wayne Bates RC	1.50	.70
❑ 175 Tim Couch RC	2.00	.90
❑ 176 Torrance Small	.30	.14
❑ 177 Warren Moon	.75	.35
❑ 178 Rocket Ismail	.50	.23
❑ 179 Marshall Faulk	1.00	.45
❑ 180 Trent Green	.75	.35
❑ 181 Sean Dawkins	.30	.14
❑ 182 Pete Mitchell	.30	.14
❑ 183 Jeff Graham	.30	.14
❑ 184 Eddie Kennison	.50	.23
❑ 185 Kerry Collins	.50	.23
❑ 186 Eric Green	.30	.14
❑ 187 Kyle Brady	.30	.14
❑ 188 Tony Martin	.50	.23
❑ 189 Jim Harbaugh	.50	.23
❑ 190 Erik Kramer	.30	.14
❑ 191 Steve Atwater	.30	.14
❑ 192 Chad Bratzke	.30	.14
❑ 193 Charles Johnson	.30	.14
❑ 194 Damon Gibson	.30	.14
❑ 195 Jeff George	.50	.23
❑ 196 Scott Mitchell	.30	.14
❑ 197 Terry Kirby	.30	.14
❑ 198 Rich Gannon	.75	.35
❑ 199 Chris Spielman	.30	.14
❑ 200 Brad Johnson	.75	.35
❑ PP4 Emmitt Smith PROMO	3.00	.90

1999 Stadium Club Co-Signers

	Nm-Mt	Ex-Mt
❑ CS1 Terrell Davis / Ricky Williams	100.00	45.00
❑ CS2 Terrell Davis / Edgerrin James	120.00	55.00
❑ CS3 Tim Couch / Dan Marino	200.00	90.00
❑ CS4 Tim Couch / Peyton Manning	150.00	70.00
❑ CS5 Randy Moss / Jerry Rice	250.00	110.00
❑ CS6 Dan Marino / Vinny Testaverde	150.00	70.00

1999 Stadium Club Lone Star Autographs

	Nm-Mt	Ex-Mt
❑ LS1 Randy Moss	80.00	36.00
❑ LS2 Jerry Rice	120.00	55.00
❑ LS3 Peyton Manning	120.00	55.00
❑ LS4 Vinny Testaverde	25.00	11.00
❑ LS5 Tim Couch	30.00	13.50
❑ LS6 Dan Marino	150.00	70.00
❑ LS7 Edgerrin James	60.00	27.00
❑ LS8 Fred Taylor	40.00	18.00
❑ LS9 Garrison Hearst	25.00	11.00
❑ LS10 Antonio Freeman	40.00	18.00
❑ LS11 Torry Holt	50.00	22.00

2000 Stadium Club

	Nm-Mt	Ex-Mt
COMPLETE SET (175)	50.00	22.00
COMP.SET w/o SP's (150)	20.00	9.00
❑ 1 Peyton Manning	1.50	.70
❑ 2 Pete Mitchell	.25	.11
❑ 3 Napoleon Kaufman	.40	.18
❑ 4 Mikhael Ricks	.25	.11
❑ 5 Mike Alstott	.60	.25
❑ 6 Brad Johnson	.60	.25
❑ 7 Tony Gonzalez	.40	.18
❑ 8 Germane Crowell	.25	.11
❑ 9 Marcus Robinson	.60	.25
❑ 10 Stephen Davis	.60	.25
❑ 11 Terance Mathis	.40	.18
❑ 12 Jake Plummer	.40	.18
❑ 13 Qadry Ismail	.40	.18
❑ 14 Cade McNown	.25	.11
❑ 15 Zach Thomas	.60	.25
❑ 16 Curtis Martin	.60	.25
❑ 17 Torrance Small	.25	.11
❑ 18 Steve McNair	.60	.25
❑ 19 Jim Harbaugh	.40	.18
❑ 20 Keyshawn Johnson	.60	.25
❑ 21 Antonio Freeman	.60	.25
❑ 22 Ed McCaffrey	.60	.25
❑ 23 Elvis Grbac	.40	.18
❑ 24 Peerless Price	.60	.25
❑ 25 Jerome Bettis	.60	.25
❑ 26 Yancey Thigpen	.25	.11
❑ 27 Jake Delhomme RC	2.50	1.10
❑ 28 Keith Poole	.25	.11
❑ 29 Carl Pickens	.40	.18
❑ 30 Jerry Rice	1.25	.55
❑ 31 Rob Moore	.40	.18
❑ 32 Reidel Anthony	.25	.11
❑ 33 Jimmy Smith	.40	.18
❑ 34 Ray Lucas	.40	.18
❑ 35 Troy Aikman	1.25	.55
❑ 36 Steve Beuerlein	.40	.18
❑ 37 Charlie Batch	.60	.25
❑ 38 Derrick Mayes	.40	.18
❑ 39 Tim Brown	.60	.25
❑ 40 Eddie George	.60	.25
❑ 41 O.J. McDuffie	.40	.18
❑ 42 Ike Hilliard	.40	.18
❑ 43 Bill Schroeder	.40	.18
❑ 44 Jim Miller	.25	.11
❑ 45 Chris Chandler	.40	.18
❑ 46 Fred Taylor	.60	.25
❑ 47 Ricky Watters	.40	.18
❑ 48 Tyrone Wheatley	.40	.18
❑ 49 Bruce Smith	.40	.18
❑ 50 Marshall Faulk	.75	.35
❑ 51 Kevin Carter	.25	.11
❑ 52 Champ Bailey	.40	.18
❑ 53 Troy Edwards	.25	.11
❑ 54 Doug Flutie	.60	.25
❑ 55 Charles Johnson	.40	.18
❑ 56 Michael Westbrook	.40	.18
❑ 57 Frank Wycheck	.25	.11
❑ 58 Drew Bledsoe	.75	.35
❑ 59 Terrence Wilkins	.25	.11
❑ 60 Ricky Williams	.60	.25
❑ 61 Rod Smith	.40	.18
❑ 62 Errict Rhett	.40	.18
❑ 63 Vinny Testaverde	.40	.18
❑ 64 Jacquez Green	.25	.11
❑ 65 Curtis Conway	.40	.18
❑ 66 Wayne Chrebet	.40	.18
❑ 67 Albert Connell	.25	.11
❑ 68 Kordell Stewart	.40	.18
❑ 69 Bert Emanuel	.25	.11
❑ 70 Randy Moss	1.25	.55
❑ 71 Akili Smith	.25	.11
❑ 72 Brian Griese	.60	.25
❑ 73 Frank Sanders	.40	.18
❑ 74 Wesley Walls	.25	.11
❑ 75 Michael Pittman	.25	.11
❑ 76 Steve Young	.75	.35
❑ 77 Jevon Kearse	.60	.25
❑ 78 Az-Zahir Hakim	.40	.18
❑ 79 James Stewart	.40	.18
❑ 80 Brett Favre	2.00	.90
❑ 81 Dan Marino	2.00	.90
❑ 82 Joe Horn	.40	.18
❑ 83 Mark Brunell	.60	.25
❑ 84 Eddie Kennison	.40	.18
❑ 85 Deion Sanders	.60	.25
❑ 86 Priest Holmes	.75	.35
❑ 87 Terry Glenn	.40	.18
❑ 88 Olandis Gary	.60	.25
❑ 89 Patrick Jeffers	.60	.25
❑ 90 Emmitt Smith	1.25	.55
❑ 91 J.J. Stokes	.40	.18
❑ 92 Warrick Dunn	.60	.25
❑ 93 Damon Huard	.60	.25
❑ 94 Herman Moore	.40	.18
❑ 95 Corey Dillon	.60	.25
❑ 96 Joey Galloway	.40	.18
❑ 97 Jamal Anderson	.60	.25
❑ 98 Junior Seau	.60	.25

❑ 99 Robert Smith	.60	.25
❑ 100 Edgerrin James	1.00	.45
❑ 101 Derrick Alexander	.40	.18
❑ 102 Johnnie Morton	.40	.18
❑ 103 Sean Dawkins	.25	.11
❑ 104 Derrick Brooks	.60	.25
❑ 105 Rickey Dudley	.25	.11
❑ 106 Keenan McCardell	.40	.18
❑ 107 Kerry Collins	.40	.18
❑ 108 Kevin Johnson	.60	.25
❑ 109 Eric Moulds	.60	.25
❑ 110 Terrell Davis	.60	.25
❑ 111 Shawn Jefferson	.25	.11
❑ 112 Donovan McNabb	1.00	.45
❑ 113 Torry Holt	.60	.25
❑ 114 Marvin Harrison	.60	.25
❑ 115 Amani Toomer	.40	.18
❑ 116 Tony Martin	.40	.18
❑ 117 Curtis Enis	.25	.11
❑ 118 Tiki Barber	.40	.18
❑ 119 Freddie Jones	.25	.11
❑ 120 Muhsin Muhammad	.40	.18
❑ 121 Shaun King	.25	.11
❑ 122 Isaac Bruce	.60	.25
❑ 123 Duce Staley	.60	.25
❑ 124 Hardy Nickerson	.25	.11
❑ 125 Corey Bradford	.40	.18
❑ 126 Kevin Hardy	.25	.11
❑ 127 Hines Ward	.60	.25
❑ 128 Charlie Garner	.40	.18
❑ 129 Warren Sapp	.40	.18
❑ 130 Tim Couch	.40	.18
❑ 131 Kevin Dyson	.40	.18
❑ 132 Rocket Ismail	.40	.18
❑ 133 Tim Dwight	.60	.25
❑ 134 Darnay Scott	.40	.18
❑ 135 Jeff George	.40	.18
❑ 136 Dorsey Levens	.40	.18
❑ 137 Jeff Blake	.40	.18
❑ 138 Jon Kitna	.60	.25
❑ 139 Rich Gannon	.60	.25
❑ 140 Cris Carter	.60	.25
❑ 141 Jeff Graham	.25	.11
❑ 142 James Johnson	.25	.11
❑ 143 Tim Biakabutuka	.40	.18
❑ 144 Bobby Engram	.40	.18
❑ 145 Tony Banks	.40	.18
❑ 146 Shannon Sharpe	.40	.18
❑ 147 Antowain Smith	.40	.18
❑ 148 Terrell Owens	.60	.25
❑ 149 Rob Johnson	.40	.18
❑ 150 Kurt Warner	1.25	.55
❑ 151 Thomas Jones RC	4.00	1.80
❑ 152 Chad Pennington RC	10.00	4.50
❑ 153 Ron Dayne RC	2.50	1.10
❑ 154 Tee Martin RC	2.50	1.10
❑ 155 Reuben Droughns RC	3.00	1.35
❑ 156 Jerry Porter RC	3.00	1.35
❑ 157 R.Jay Soward RC	2.00	.90
❑ 158 Sylvester Morris RC	2.00	.90
❑ 159 Todd Pinkston RC	2.50	1.10
❑ 160 Courtney Brown RC	2.50	1.10
❑ 161 Travis Taylor RC	2.50	1.10
❑ 162 Ron Dugans RC	2.00	.90
❑ 163 Laveranues Coles RC	3.00	1.35
❑ 164 Joe Hamilton RC	2.00	.90
❑ 165 Curtis Keaton RC	2.00	.90
❑ 166 Bubba Franks RC	2.50	1.10
❑ 167 Dennis Northcutt RC	2.50	1.10
❑ 168 Chris Redman RC	2.00	.90
❑ 169 Travis Prentice RC	2.00	.90
❑ 170 Shaun Alexander RC	6.00	2.70
❑ 171 Jamal Lewis RC	6.00	2.70
❑ 172 Peter Warrick RC	2.50	1.10
❑ 173 J.R. Redmond RC	2.00	.90
❑ 174 Trung Canidate RC	2.00	.90
❑ 175 Plaxico Burress RC	5.00	2.20

2000 Stadium Club Co-Signers

	Nm-Mt	Ex-Mt
❑ CS1 Peyton Manning Kurt Warner	250.00	110.00
❑ CS2 Edgerrin James Marshall Faulk	120.00	55.00
❑ CS3 Stephen Davis Eddie George	60.00	27.00
❑ CS4 Jimmy Smith Cris Carter	50.00	22.00
❑ CS5 Marvin Harrison Isaac Bruce	80.00	36.00
❑ CS6 Jon Kitna Cade McNown	50.00	22.00

2000 Stadium Club Lone Star Signatures

	Nm-Mt	Ex-Mt
❑ LS1 Edgerrin James	50.00	22.00
❑ LS2 Stephen Davis	20.00	9.00
❑ LS3 Marshall Faulk	40.00	18.00
❑ LS4 Eddie George	25.00	11.00
❑ LS5 Isaac Bruce	25.00	11.00
❑ LS6 Jimmy Smith	20.00	9.00
❑ LS7 Cris Carter	25.00	11.00
❑ LS8 Kurt Warner	50.00	22.00
❑ LS9 Marvin Harrison	25.00	11.00
❑ LS10 Kevin Carter	12.00	5.50
❑ LS11 Ron Dayne	20.00	9.00
❑ LS12 Chad Pennington	60.00	27.00
❑ LS13 Sylvester Morris	12.00	5.50
❑ LS14 Thomas Jones	25.00	11.00
❑ LS15 Shaun Alexander	40.00	18.00
❑ LS16 Chris Redman	12.00	5.50
❑ LS18 Peter Warrick	20.00	9.00
❑ LS19 Jon Kitna	20.00	9.00
❑ LS20 Cade McNown	12.00	5.50
❑ LS21 Az-Zahir Hakim	12.00	5.50
❑ LS22 Amani Toomer	20.00	9.00
❑ LS23 Wesley Walls	12.00	5.50
❑ LS24 Marcus Robinson	25.00	11.00
❑ LS25 Zach Thomas	25.00	11.00
❑ LS26 Tony Gonzalez	20.00	9.00
❑ LS27 Muhsin Muhammad	12.00	5.50
❑ LS28 Ed McCaffrey	25.00	11.00
❑ LS29 Eric Moulds	20.00	9.00
❑ LS30 Peyton Manning	120.00	55.00
❑ LS31 Joe Montana SP	150.00	70.00

2000 Stadium Club Pro Bowl Jerseys Autographs

	Nm-Mt	Ex-Mt
❑ APA1 Eddie George	120.00	55.00
❑ APA2 Edgerrin James	175.00	80.00
❑ APA3 Marshall Faulk	150.00	70.00
❑ APA4 Stephen Davis	100.00	45.00
❑ APA5 Isaac Bruce	100.00	45.00

2001 Stadium Club Common Threads Autographs

	Nm-Mt	Ex-Mt
❑ CTACR Daunte Culpepper David Rivers	100.00	30.00
❑ CTAHW Marvin Harrison Reggie Wayne	80.00	24.00
❑ CTAJB Edgerrin James Kevan Barlow	120.00	36.00
❑ CTMJ E.Moulds/C.Johnson	100.00	30.00

2001 Stadium Club Co-Signers

	Nm-Mt	Ex-Mt
❑ COAL Mike Anderson Jamal Lewis	40.00	12.00
❑ COCG Daunte Culpepper Jeff Garcia	60.00	18.00
❑ COFB Brett Favre Aaron Brooks	200.00	60.00
❑ COFJ Edgerrin James EXCH Marshall Faulk		
❑ COMO Randy Moss EXCH Terrell Owens		

2001 Stadium Club Lone Star Signatures

	Nm-Mt	Ex-Mt
❑ LSAT Anthony Thomas 8	25.00	7.50
❑ LSDA Dan Alexander 7	25.00	7.50
❑ LSDB Drew Brees 7	40.00	12.00
❑ LSDC Daunte Culpepper 2	40.00	12.00
❑ LSDM Deuce McAllister 1	50.00	15.00
❑ LSDT David Terrell 3	15.00	4.50

❑ LSEG Eddie George 3 20.00 6.00
❑ LSEJ Edgerrin James 1 40.00 12.00
❑ LSJB Josh Booty 10 12.00 3.60
❑ LSJH Joe Horn 7 12.00 3.60
❑ LSJP Jesse Palmer 10 15.00 4.50
❑ LSKB Kevan Barlow 9 20.00 6.00
❑ LSKW Kenyatta Walker 10 12.00 3.60
❑ LSLT LaDainian Tomlinson 7 60.00 18.00
❑ LSMA Mike Anderson 7 20.00 6.00
❑ LSMF Marshall Faulk 3 30.00 9.00
❑ LSMH Marvin Harrison 6 20.00 6.00
❑ LSMV Michael Vick 4 100.00 30.00
❑ LSQM Quincy Morgan 8 20.00 6.00
❑ LSRW Reggie Wayne 3 20.00 6.00
❑ LSSD Stephen Davis 4 20.00 6.00
❑ LSTH Travis Henry 7 25.00 7.50
❑ LSTO Terrell Owens 5 20.00 6.00

2001 Stadium Club Pro Bowl Jerseys Autographs

	Nm-Mt	Ex-Mt
❑ SPADC Daunte Culpepper	80.00	24.00
❑ SPAEJ Edgerrin James	80.00	24.00
❑ SPAMH Marvin Harrison	40.00	12.00

2002 Stadium Club Co-Signers

	Nm-Mt	Ex-Mt
❑ CSCH David Carr Joey Harrington	250.00	75.00
❑ CSFW Brett Favre Kurt Warner	250.00	75.00
❑ CSGF Willie Green DeShaun Foster	50.00	15.00
❑ CSOB Terrell Owens David Boston	80.00	24.00

❑ CSWB Kurt Warner#[Tom Brady 250.00 75.00

2002 Stadium Club Lone Star Signatures

	Nm-Mt	Ex-Mt
❑ LSAP Adrian Peterson	20.00	6.00
❑ LSAS Antowain Smith	20.00	6.00
❑ LSBF Brett Favre	175.00	52.50
❑ LSCC Chris Chambers	25.00	7.50
❑ LSDB David Boston	20.00	6.00

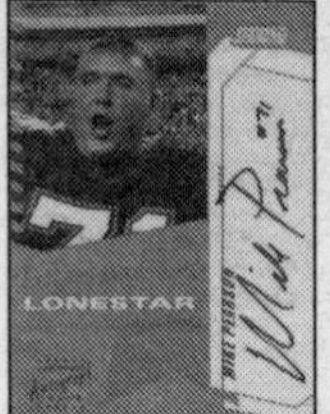

❑ LSDC David Carr 50.00 15.00
❑ LSDF DeShaun Foster 20.00 6.00
❑ LSJA John Abraham 20.00 6.00
❑ LSJH Joey Harrington 50.00 15.00
❑ LSJR Josh Reed 20.00 6.00
❑ LSJT James Thrash 30.00 9.00
❑ LSKK Kurt Kittner 15.00 4.50
❑ LSKW Kurt Warner 60.00 18.00
❑ LSMB Marty Booker 20.00 6.00
❑ LSMP Mike Pearson 12.00 3.60
❑ LSRW Roy Williams 50.00 15.00
❑ LSTB Tom Brady 125.00 38.00
❑ LSTO Terrell Owens 30.00 9.00
❑ LSWG William Green 20.00 6.00

1999 Stadium Club Chrome

	Nm-Mt	Ex-Mt
COMPLETE SET (150)	60.00	27.00
❑ 1 Dan Marino	4.00	1.80
❑ 2 Andre Reed	.75	.35
❑ 3 Michael Westbrook	.75	.35
❑ 4 Isaac Bruce	1.25	.55
❑ 5 Curtis Martin	1.25	.55
❑ 6 Terrell Owens	1.25	.55
❑ 7 Warrick Dunn	1.25	.55
❑ 8 Jake Plummer	.75	.35
❑ 9 Chad Brown	.50	.23
❑ 10 Yancey Thigpen	.75	.35
❑ 11 Keenan McCardell	.75	.35
❑ 12 Shannon Sharpe	.75	.35
❑ 13 Cameron Cleeland	.50	.23
❑ 14 Mark Brunell	1.25	.55
❑ 15 Jamal Anderson	1.25	.55
❑ 16 Germane Crowell	.50	.23
❑ 17 Rod Smith	.75	.35
❑ 18 Cris Carter	1.25	.55
❑ 19 Terrell Davis	1.25	.55
❑ 20 Tim Biakabutuka	.75	.35
❑ 21 Jermaine Lewis	.75	.35
❑ 22 Adrian Murrell	.75	.35
❑ 23 Doug Flutie	1.25	.55
❑ 24 Curtis Enis	.50	.23
❑ 25 Skip Hicks	.50	.23
❑ 26 Steve McNair	1.25	.55
❑ 27 Charles Woodson	1.25	.55
❑ 28 Freddie Jones	.50	.23
❑ 29 Warren Sapp	.75	.35
❑ 30 Emmitt Smith	2.50	1.10
❑ 31 Reidel Anthony	.50	.23
❑ 32 Tony Simmons	.50	.23
❑ 33 Andre Hastings	.50	.23
❑ 34 Byron Bam Morris	.50	.23
❑ 35 Jimmy Smith	.75	.35
❑ 36 Antonio Freeman	1.25	.55
❑ 37 Herman Moore	.75	.35
❑ 38 Muhsin Muhammad	.75	.35
❑ 39 Chris Chandler	.75	.35
❑ 40 John Elway	4.00	1.80
❑ 41 Bobby Engram	.75	.35
❑ 42 Keith Poole	.50	.23
❑ 43 Mike Alstott	1.25	.55
❑ 44 Junior Seau	1.25	.55
❑ 45 Thurman Thomas	.75	.35
❑ 46 Troy Aikman	2.50	1.10
❑ 47 Wesley Walls	.75	.35
❑ 48 Robert Smith	1.25	.55
❑ 49 Elvis Grbac	.75	.35
❑ 50 Ben Coates	.50	.23
❑ 51 Bert Emanuel	.75	.35
❑ 52 Jacquez Green	.50	.23
❑ 53 Barry Sanders	4.00	1.80
❑ 54 James Jett	.50	.23
❑ 55 Gary Brown	.50	.23
❑ 56 Stephen Alexander	.50	.23
❑ 57 Wayne Chrebet	1.25	.55
❑ 58 Drew Bledsoe	1.50	.70
❑ 59 Jake Reed	.75	.35
❑ 60 Marvin Harrison	1.25	.55
❑ 61 Johnnie Morton	.75	.35
❑ 62 Brett Favre	4.00	1.80
❑ 63 Charlie Batch	1.25	.55
❑ 64 Antowain Smith	1.25	.55
❑ 65 Ernie Mills	.50	.23
❑ 66 Jeff Blake	.75	.35
❑ 67 Curtis Conway	.75	.35
❑ 68 Bruce Smith	.75	.35
❑ 69 Peyton Manning	4.00	1.80
❑ 70 Tim Dwight	1.25	.55
❑ 71 O.J. McDuffie	.75	.35
❑ 72 Jon Kitna	1.25	.55
❑ 73 Trent Dilfer	.75	.35
❑ 74 Jerome Bettis	1.25	.55
❑ 75 Dedric Ward	.50	.23
❑ 76 Fred Taylor	1.25	.55
❑ 77 Ike Hilliard	.75	.35
❑ 78 Frank Wycheck	.50	.23
❑ 79 Eric Moulds	1.25	.55
❑ 80 Rob Moore	.75	.35
❑ 81 Ed McCaffrey	.75	.35
❑ 82 Carl Pickens	.75	.35
❑ 83 Priest Holmes	2.00	.90
❑ 84 Terry Glenn	1.25	.55
❑ 85 Keyshawn Johnson	1.25	.55
❑ 86 Karim Abdul-Jabbar	.75	.35
❑ 87 Ahman Green	1.25	.55
❑ 88 Duce Staley	1.25	.55
❑ 89 Vinny Testaverde	.75	.35
❑ 90 Napoleon Kaufman	1.25	.55
❑ 91 Frank Sanders	.75	.35
❑ 92 Steve Young	1.50	.70
❑ 93 Darnay Scott	.75	.35
❑ 94 Deion Sanders	1.25	.55
❑ 95 Corey Dillon	1.25	.55
❑ 96 Randall Cunningham	1.25	.55
❑ 97 Eddie George	1.25	.55
❑ 98 Derrick Alexander	.75	.35
❑ 99 Mark Chmura	.75	.35
❑ 100 Rickey Dudley	.50	.23
❑ 101 Joey Galloway	.75	.35
❑ 102 Ricky Proehl	.50	.23
❑ 103 Natrone Means	.75	.35
❑ 104 Dorsey Levens	1.25	.55
❑ 105 Andre Rison	.75	.35
❑ 106 John Randle	.75	.35
❑ 107 Terance Mathis	.75	.35
❑ 108 Rae Carruth	.50	.23
❑ 109 Jerry Rice	2.50	1.10
❑ 110 Michael Irvin	.75	.35
❑ 111 Oronde Gadsden	.75	.35

❑ 112 Jerome Pathon .50 .23
❑ 113 Ricky Watters .75 .35
❑ 114 J.J. Stokes .75 .35
❑ 115 Kordell Stewart .75 .35
❑ 116 Tim Brown 1.25 .55
❑ 117 Tony Gonzalez 1.25 .55
❑ 118 Randy Moss 3.00 1.35
❑ 119 Daunte Culpepper RC 8.00 3.60
❑ 120 Amos Zereoue RC 2.50 1.10
❑ 121 Champ Bailey RC 3.00 1.35
❑ 122 Peerless Price RC 4.00 1.80
❑ 123 Edgerrin James RC 8.00 3.60
❑ 124 Joe Germaine RC 2.00 .90
❑ 125 David Boston RC 2.50 1.10
❑ 126 Kevin Faulk RC 2.50 1.10
❑ 127 Troy Edwards RC 2.00 .90
❑ 128 Akili Smith RC 2.00 .90
❑ 129 Kevin Johnson RC 2.50 1.10
❑ 130 Rob Konrad RC 2.00 .90
❑ 131 Shaun King RC 2.00 .90
❑ 132 James Johnson RC 2.00 .90
❑ 133 Donovan McNabb RC 10.00 4.50
❑ 134 Torry Holt RC 5.00 2.20
❑ 135 Mike Cloud RC 2.00 .90
❑ 136 Sedrick Irvin RC 1.25 .55
❑ 137 Cade McNown RC 2.00 .90
❑ 138 Ricky Williams RC 4.00 1.80
❑ 139 Karsten Bailey RC 2.00 .90
❑ 140 Cecil Collins RC 1.25 .55
❑ 141 Brock Huard RC 2.50 1.10
❑ 142 D'Wayne Bates RC 2.00 .90
❑ 143 Tim Couch RC 2.50 1.10
❑ 144 Rocket Ismail .75 .35
❑ 145 Marshall Faulk 1.50 .70
❑ 146 Trent Green 1.25 .55
❑ 147 Tony Martin .75 .35
❑ 148 Jim Harbaugh .75 .35
❑ 149 Rich Gannon 1.25 .55
❑ 150 Brad Johnson 1.25 .55

2002 Sweet Spot

	Nm-Mt	Ex-Mt
COMP.SET w/o SP's (90)	30.00	9.00

❑ 1 Aaron Brooks 1.25 .35
❑ 2 Tim Couch .75 .23
❑ 3 Jon Kitna .75 .23
❑ 4 Brett Favre 3.00 .90
❑ 5 Donovan McNabb 1.50 .45
❑ 6 Jeff Garcia 1.25 .35
❑ 7 Michael Vick 4.00 1.20
❑ 8 Mark Brunell 1.25 .35
❑ 9 Steve McNair 1.25 .35
❑ 10 Kordell Stewart .75 .23
❑ 11 Drew Bledsoe 1.50 .45
❑ 12 Tom Brady 3.00 .90
❑ 13 Kurt Warner 1.25 .35
❑ 14 Brian Griese 1.25 .35
❑ 15 Jim Miller .75 .23
❑ 16 Jake Plummer .75 .23
❑ 17 Quincy Carter .75 .23
❑ 18 Peyton Manning 2.50 .75
❑ 19 Keyshawn Johnson 1.25 .35
❑ 20 Travis Henry 1.25 .35
❑ 21 LaDainian Tomlinson 2.00 .60
❑ 22 Emmitt Smith 3.00 .90
❑ 23 Michael Bennett .75 .23
❑ 24 Duce Staley 1.25 .35
❑ 25 Thomas Jones .75 .23
❑ 26 Deuce McAllister 1.50 .45
❑ 27 Eddie George 1.25 .35
❑ 28 Marshall Faulk 1.25 .35
❑ 29 Curtis Martin 1.25 .35
❑ 30 Ahman Green 1.25 .35
❑ 31 Priest Holmes 1.50 .45
❑ 32 Edgerrin James 1.50 .45
❑ 33 Antowain Smith .75 .23
❑ 34 Ricky Williams 1.25 .35
❑ 35 Anthony Thomas 1.25 .35
❑ 36 Jerome Bettis 1.25 .35
❑ 37 Shaun Alexander 1.25 .35
❑ 38 Kerry Collins .75 .23
❑ 39 Drew Brees 1.25 .35
❑ 40 Chris Redman .50 .15
❑ 41 Marc Bulger 1.25 .35
❑ 42 Jay Fiedler .75 .23
❑ 43 Trent Green .75 .23
❑ 44 Daunte Culpepper 1.25 .35
❑ 45 Rich Gannon 1.25 .35
❑ 46 Rodney Peete .75 .23
❑ 47 Vinny Testaverde .75 .23
❑ 48 Stephen Davis .75 .23
❑ 49 James Allen .75 .23
❑ 50 Tiki Barber .75 .23
❑ 51 Ron Dayne .75 .23
❑ 52 Ray Lewis 1.25 .35
❑ 53 Corey Dillon .75 .23
❑ 54 Brian Urlacher 2.00 .60
❑ 55 Junior Seau 1.25 .35
❑ 56 Warrick Dunn 1.25 .35
❑ 57 Fred Taylor 1.25 .35
❑ 58 Jamal Lewis 1.25 .35
❑ 59 Trent Dilfer .75 .23
❑ 60 James Stewart .75 .23
❑ 61 David Patten .50 .15
❑ 62 Eric Moulds .75 .23
❑ 63 Isaac Bruce 1.25 .35
❑ 64 Troy Brown .75 .23
❑ 65 Terrell Owens 1.25 .35
❑ 66 Moe Williams .50 .15
❑ 67 Joe Horn .75 .23
❑ 68 Az-Zahir Hakim .50 .15
❑ 69 Jimmy Smith .75 .23
❑ 70 Michael Westbrook .50 .15
❑ 71 Olandis Gary .75 .23
❑ 72 Chris Chambers 1.25 .35
❑ 73 Kevin Johnson .75 .23
❑ 74 Joey Galloway .75 .23
❑ 75 Hines Ward 1.25 .35
❑ 76 Garrison Hearst .75 .23
❑ 77 Wayne Chrebet .75 .23
❑ 78 Muhsin Muhammad .75 .23
❑ 79 Rod Gardner .75 .23
❑ 80 Jerry Rice 2.50 .75
❑ 81 Tim Brown 1.25 .35
❑ 82 Shannon Sharpe .75 .23
❑ 83 Terry Glenn .75 .23
❑ 84 Randy Moss 2.50 .75
❑ 85 Corey Bradford .50 .15
❑ 86 Marty Booker .75 .23
❑ 87 Keenan McCardell .50 .15
❑ 88 Marvin Harrison 1.25 .35
❑ 89 David Boston 1.25 .35
❑ 90 Eddie Kennison .50 .15
❑ 91 Tim Carter RC 5.00 1.50
❑ 92 Joey Harrington RC 20.00 6.00
❑ 93 Patrick Ramsey RC 12.00 3.60
❑ 94 David Garrard RC 6.00 1.80
❑ 95 Donte Stallworth RC 12.00 3.60
❑ 96 Reche Caldwell RC 6.00 1.80
❑ 97 William Green RC 10.00 3.00
❑ 98 Josh Reed RC 6.00 1.80
❑ 99 DeShaun Foster RC 6.00 1.80
❑ 100 Jeremy Shockey RC 20.00 6.00
❑ 101 Mike Williams RC 5.00 1.50
❑ 102 Daniel Graham RC 6.00 1.80
❑ 103 Josh McCown RC 8.00 2.40
❑ 104 Javon Walker RC 12.00 3.60
❑ 105 Travis Stephens RC 5.00 1.50
❑ 106 Marquise Walker RC 5.00 1.50
❑ 107 T.J. Duckett RC 10.00 3.00
❑ 108 Damien Anderson RC 5.00 1.50
❑ 109 Quentin Jammer RC 6.00 1.80
❑ 110 Bryan Thomas RC 5.00 1.50
❑ 111 Chad Hutchinson RC 6.00 1.80
❑ 112 Brian Westbrook RC 10.00 3.00
❑ 113 Lamar Gordon RC 6.00 1.80
❑ 114 Deion Branch RC 12.00 3.60
❑ 115 Ed Reed RC 10.00 3.00
❑ 116 Jonathan Wells RC 6.00 1.80
❑ 117 Phillip Buchanon RC 6.00 1.80
❑ 118 Wendell Bryant RC 6.00 1.80
❑ 119 Kurt Kittner RC 5.00 1.50
❑ 120 Randy McMichael RC 10.00 3.00
❑ 121 Brandon Doman RC 6.00 1.80
❑ 122 Adrian Peterson RC 6.00 1.80
❑ 123 Ricky Williams RC 5.00 1.50
❑ 124 Seth Burford RC 5.00 1.50
❑ 125 Shaun Hill RC 6.00 1.80
❑ 126 Anthony Weaver RC 5.00 1.50
❑ 127 Freddie Milons RC 5.00 1.50
❑ 128 Darrell Hill RC 5.00 1.50
❑ 129 Daryl Jones RC 5.00 1.50
❑ 130 Chester Taylor RC 6.00 1.80
❑ 131 Najeh Davenport RC 6.00 1.80
❑ 132 Jason McAddley RC 5.00 1.50
❑ 133 Preston Parsons RC 3.00 .90
❑ 134 Michael Lewis RC 6.00 1.80
❑ 135 Mike Rumph RC 6.00 1.80
❑ 136 Lamont Thompson RC 5.00 1.50
❑ 137 Dwight Freeney RC 8.00 2.40
❑ 138 Napoleon Harris RC 6.00 1.80
❑ 139 Tank Williams RC 5.00 1.50
❑ 140 Lee Mays RC 6.00 1.80
❑ 141 Robert Thomas RC 6.00 1.80
❑ 142 Tellis Redmon RC 5.00 1.50
❑ 143 Alex Brown RC 6.00 1.80
❑ 144 Ryan Sims RC 6.00 1.80
❑ 145 Larry Tripplett RC 3.00 .90
❑ 146 Quinn Gray RC 3.00 .90
❑ 147 Jesse Chatman RC 6.00 1.80
❑ 148 Jamin Elliott RC 3.00 .90
❑ 149 Ben Leber RC 6.00 1.80
❑ 150 Lito Sheppard RC 6.00 1.80
❑ 151 Antonio Bryant AU/550 RC 25.00 7.50
❑ 152 Rohan Davey AU/550 RC 20.00 6.00
❑ 153 Randy Fasani AU/550 RC 15.00 4.50
❑ 154 J.T. O'Sullivan AU/550 RC 20.00 6.00
❑ 155 Ron Johnson AU/550 RC 15.00 4.50
❑ 156 Maurice Morris AU/550 RC 25.00 7.50
❑ 157 Kahlil Hill AU/550 RC 15.00 4.50
❑ 158 Ant Randle El AU/550 RC 30.00 9.00
❑ 159 Cliff Russell AU/550 RC 15.00 4.50
❑ 160 Ladell Betts AU/550 RC 20.00 6.00
❑ 161 David Carr AU/125 RC 150.00 45.00
❑ 162 Andre Davis AU/125 RC 30.00 9.00
❑ 163 Julius Peppers AU/125 80.00 24.00
❑ 164 Ashley Lelie AU/125 RC 80.00 24.00
❑ 165 Jabar Gaffney AU/125 RC 30.00 9.00
❑ 166 Clinton Portis AU/125 RC 150.00 45.00

2003 Sweet Spot

	MINT	NRMT
COMP.SET w/o SP's (90)	30.00	13.50

❑ 1 Chad Pennington 1.50 .70
❑ 2 Aaron Brooks 1.25 .55
❑ 3 Joey Harrington 2.00 .90
❑ 4 Brett Favre 3.00 1.35
❑ 5 Donovan McNabb 1.50 .70
❑ 6 Jeff Garcia 1.25 .55
❑ 7 Michael Vick 3.00 1.35
❑ 8 David Carr 2.00 .90
❑ 9 Drew Brees 1.25 .55
❑ 10 Trent Green .75 .35
❑ 11 Patrick Ramsey 1.25 .55
❑ 12 Tom Brady 2.00 .90
❑ 13 Kurt Warner 1.25 .55

❑ 14 Brad Johnson .75 .35
❑ 15 Brian Griese 1.25 .55
❑ 16 Jake Plummer .75 .35
❑ 17 Drew Bledsoe 1.25 .55
❑ 18 Peyton Manning 2.00 .90
❑ 19 Tim Couch .50 .23
❑ 20 Kordell Stewart .75 .35
❑ 21 Jay Fiedler .75 .35
❑ 22 Rich Gannon .75 .35
❑ 23 Josh McCown .75 .35
❑ 24 Matt Hasselbeck .75 .35
❑ 25 Tommy Maddox 1.25 .55
❑ 26 Rodney Peete .50 .23
❑ 27 Jake Delhomme 1.25 .55
❑ 28 Chris Redman .50 .23
❑ 29 Mark Brunell .75 .35
❑ 30 Marc Bulger 1.25 .55
❑ 31 Kelly Holcomb .75 .35
❑ 32 Chad Hutchinson .75 .35
❑ 33 Quincy Carter .75 .35
❑ 34 Steve McNair 1.25 .55
❑ 35 Marshall Faulk 1.25 .55
❑ 36 Deuce McAllister 1.25 .55
❑ 37 Emmitt Smith 3.00 1.35
❑ 38 LaDainian Tomlinson 1.25 .55
❑ 39 Kevan Barlow .75 .35
❑ 40 Michael Bennett .75 .35
❑ 41 Shaun Alexander 1.25 .55
❑ 42 Edgerrin James 1.25 .55
❑ 43 Ricky Williams 1.25 .55
❑ 44 Priest Holmes 1.50 .70
❑ 45 Ahman Green 1.25 .55
❑ 46 Curtis Martin 1.25 .55
❑ 47 Anthony Thomas 1.25 .55
❑ 48 Travis Henry .75 .35
❑ 49 Jerome Bettis 1.25 .55
❑ 50 Fred Taylor 1.25 .55
❑ 51 Corey Dillon .75 .35
❑ 52 Jamal Lewis 1.25 .55
❑ 53 William Green .75 .35
❑ 54 Brian Urlacher 2.00 .90
❑ 55 Junior Seau 1.25 .55
❑ 56 Ray Lewis 1.25 .55
❑ 57 Julius Peppers 1.25 .55
❑ 58 Terrell Owens 1.25 .55
❑ 59 David Boston .75 .35
❑ 60 Isaac Bruce 1.25 .55
❑ 61 Marvin Harrison 1.25 .55
❑ 62 Chris Chambers 1.25 .55
❑ 63 Chad Johnson .75 .35
❑ 64 Peter Warrick .75 .35
❑ 65 Peerless Price .75 .35
❑ 66 Antonio Bryant .75 .35
❑ 67 Laveranues Coles .75 .35
❑ 68 Rod Gardner .75 .35
❑ 69 Hines Ward 1.25 .55
❑ 70 Plaxico Burress .75 .35
❑ 71 Keyshawn Johnson 1.25 .55
❑ 72 Jabar Gaffney .75 .35
❑ 73 Eric Moulds .75 .35
❑ 74 Santana Moss .75 .35
❑ 75 Koren Robinson .75 .35
❑ 76 Jimmy Smith .75 .35
❑ 77 Donte Stallworth 1.25 .55
❑ 78 Kevin Johnson .75 .35
❑ 79 Quincy Morgan .75 .35
❑ 80 Jerry Rice 2.50 1.10
❑ 81 Tim Brown 1.25 .55
❑ 82 Rod Smith .75 .35
❑ 83 Ashley Lelie 1.25 .55
❑ 84 Randy Moss 2.00 .90
❑ 85 Torry Holt 1.25 .55
❑ 86 Troy Brown .75 .35
❑ 87 Donald Driver .75 .35
❑ 88 Todd Heap .75 .35
❑ 89 Tony Gonzalez .75 .35
❑ 90 Jeremy Shockey 2.00 .90
❑ 91 Casey Moore RC 5.00 2.20
❑ 92 Chris Crocker RC 4.00 1.80
❑ 93 Pisa Tinoisamoa RC 10.00 4.50
❑ 94 Nnamdi Asomugha RC 5.00 2.20
❑ 95 Tyler Brayton RC 6.00 2.70
❑ 96 Eddie Moore RC 5.00 2.20
❑ 97 Terrence Kiel RC 6.00 2.70
❑ 98 Casey Fitzsimmons RC 6.00 2.70
❑ 99 George Foster RC 4.00 1.80
❑ 100 J.J. Moses RC 5.00 2.20
❑ 101 Dan Klecko RC 6.00 2.70
❑ 102 Terry Pierce RC 5.00 2.20
❑ 103 Brad Pyatt RC 5.00 2.20
❑ 104 Boss Bailey RC 8.00 3.60
❑ 105 Michael Haynes RC 6.00 2.70
❑ 106 Jimmy Kennedy RC 6.00 2.70
❑ 107 Jerome McDougle RC 6.00 2.70
❑ 108 William Joseph RC 6.00 2.70
❑ 109 Visanthe Shiancoe RC 5.00 2.20
❑ 110 L.J. Smith RC 6.00 2.70
❑ 111 Avon Cobourne RC 4.00 1.80
❑ 112 Bennie Joppru RC 6.00 2.70
❑ 113 Ken Hamlin RC 6.00 2.70
❑ 114 Jeremi Johnson RC 5.00 2.20
❑ 115 Justin Griffith RC 5.00 2.20
❑ 116 Joffrey Reynolds RC 4.00 1.80
❑ 117 Kassim Osgood RC 6.00 2.70
❑ 118 Donald Lee RC 5.00 2.20
❑ 119 Denero Marriott RC 4.00 1.80
❑ 120 Jamal Burke RC 4.00 1.80
❑ 121 Michael Vick SS 25.00 11.00
❑ 122 Donovan McNabb SS 12.00 5.50
❑ 123 Jerry Rice SS 20.00 9.00
❑ 124 Brett Favre SS 25.00 11.00
❑ 125 Kurt Warner SS 10.00 4.50
❑ 126 Marshall Faulk SS 10.00 4.50
❑ 127 Ricky Williams SS 10.00 4.50
❑ 128 Emmitt Smith SS 25.00 11.00
❑ 129 Tom Brady SS 15.00 6.75
❑ 130 Randy Moss SS 15.00 6.75
❑ 131 LaDainian Tomlinson SS 10.00 4.50
❑ 132 Jeff Garcia SS 10.00 4.50
❑ 133 Brian Urlacher SS 15.00 6.75
❑ 134 Drew Bledsoe SS 10.00 4.50
❑ 135 Peyton Manning SS 15.00 6.75
❑ 136 Dave Ragone RC 8.00 3.60
❑ 137 Brian St.Pierre RC 8.00 3.60
❑ 138 Kliff Kingsbury RC 6.00 2.70
❑ 139 Marquel Blackwell RC 4.00 1.80
❑ 140 Brett Engemann RC 4.00 1.80
❑ 141 Kirk Farmer RC 4.00 1.80
❑ 142 Andrew Pinnock RC 6.00 2.70
❑ 143 Tony Romo RC 8.00 3.60
❑ 144 Nate Hybl RC 8.00 3.60
❑ 145 Ken Dorsey RC 15.00 6.75
❑ 146 Brock Forsey RC 8.00 3.60
❑ 147 Musa Smith RC 8.00 3.60
❑ 148 Domanick Davis RC 15.00 6.75
❑ 149 LaBrandon Toefield RC 8.00 3.60
❑ 150 B.J. Askew RC 8.00 3.60
❑ 151 Quentin Griffin RC 20.00 9.00
❑ 152 Ahmaad Galloway RC 6.00 2.70
❑ 153 Cecil Sapp RC 6.00 2.70
❑ 154 Justin Fargas RC 8.00 3.60
❑ 155 Sultan McCullough RC 6.00 2.70
❑ 156 Malaefou MacKenzie RC 4.00 1.80
❑ 157 Tom Lopienski RC 6.00 2.70
❑ 158 Lee Suggs RC 15.00 6.75
❑ 159 Richard Angulo RC 6.00 2.70
❑ 160 Dwone Hicks RC 4.00 1.80
❑ 161 Nate Burleson RC 12.00 5.50
❑ 162 Billy McMullen RC 6.00 2.70
❑ 163 David Tyree RC 6.00 2.70
❑ 164 Gerald Hayes RC 4.00 1.80
❑ 165 Anthony Adams RC 6.00 2.70
❑ 166 George Wrighster RC 6.00 2.70
❑ 167 Tyrone Calico RC 10.00 4.50
❑ 168 Shaun McDonald RC 8.00 3.60
❑ 169 Bobby Wade RC 8.00 3.60
❑ 170 Larry Johnson RC 15.00 6.75
❑ 171 Ryan Hoag RC 4.00 1.80
❑ 172 Doug Gabriel RC 8.00 3.60
❑ 173 Antonio Gates RC 30.00 13.50
❑ 174 Brandon Lloyd RC 10.00 4.50
❑ 175 Arnaz Battle RC 8.00 3.60
❑ 176 Kelley Washington RC 8.00 3.60
❑ 177 Antwone Savage RC 4.00 1.80
❑ 178 Keenan Howry RC 8.00 3.60
❑ 179 Adrian Madise RC 6.00 2.70
❑ 180 LaTarence Dunbar RC 6.00 2.70
❑ 181 Walter Young RC 4.00 1.80
❑ 182 Travaris Robinson RC 4.00 1.80
❑ 183 DeAndrew Rubin RC 4.00 1.80
❑ 184 Carl Ford RC 4.00 1.80
❑ 185 Zuriel Smith RC 4.00 1.80
❑ 186 Willie Ponder RC 5.00 2.20
❑ 187 Gibran Hamdan RC 5.00 2.20
❑ 188 Aaron Moorehead RC 10.00 4.50
❑ 189 Nick Barnett RC 15.00 6.75
❑ 190 Chris Brown RC 20.00 9.00
❑ 191 ReShard Lee RC 10.00 4.50
❑ 192 Anquan Boldin RC 25.00 11.00
❑ 193 Kevin Curtis RC 10.00 4.50
❑ 194 Taylor Jacobs RC 10.00 4.50
❑ 195 Sam Aiken RC 8.00 3.60
❑ 196 Aaron Walker RC 8.00 3.60
❑ 197 Mike Seidman RC 5.00 2.20
❑ 198 Jason Witten RC 15.00 6.75
❑ 199 Dallas Clark RC 10.00 4.50
❑ 200 Rashean Mathis RC 8.00 3.60
❑ 201 Dewayne Robertson RC 10.00 4.50
❑ 202 Johnathan Sullivan RC 8.00 3.60
❑ 203 Drayton Florence RC 5.00 2.20
❑ 204 Sammy Davis RC 10.00 4.50
❑ 205 Andre Woolfolk RC 10.00 4.50
❑ 206 Terence Newman RC 20.00 9.00
❑ 207 Mike Doss RC 10.00 4.50
❑ 208 Troy Polamalu RC 10.00 4.50
❑ 209 Terrell Suggs RC 15.00 6.75
❑ 210 Marcus Trufant RC 10.00 4.50
❑ 211 Seneca Wallace RC 15.00 6.75
❑ 212 Brooks Bollinger RC 15.00 6.75
❑ 213 Jason Gesser RC 15.00 6.75
❑ 214 Onterrio Smith RC 20.00 9.00
❑ 215 Artose Pinner RC 15.00 6.75
❑ 216 J.R. Tolver RC 12.00 5.50
❑ 217 Kerry Carter RC 12.00 5.50
❑ 218 Tony Hollings RC 15.00 6.75
❑ 219 Teyo Johnson RC 15.00 6.75
❑ 220 Bethel Johnson RC 25.00 11.00
❑ 221 Rex Grossman RC 50.00 22.00
❑ 222 Andre Johnson RC 50.00 22.00
❑ 223 Terrence Edwards RC 12.00 5.50
❑ 224 Willis McGahee RC 40.00 18.00
❑ 225 Charles Rogers RC 20.00 9.00
❑ 226 Chris Simms AU RC 50.00 22.00
❑ 227 Bryant Johnson AU RC 25.00 11.00
❑ 228 Byron Leftwich AU RC 120.00 55.00
❑ 229 Carson Palmer AU RC 100.00 45.00
❑ 230 Justin Gage AU RC 40.00 18.00
❑ 231 Kyle Boller AU RC 60.00 27.00

2003 Sweet Spot Gold

MINT NRMT

*ROOKIES 136-185: 1.5X TO 4X BASE CARD HI

*ROOKIES 186-210: 1.2X TO 3X BASE CARD HI

*ROOKIES 211-225: .8X TO 2X BASE CARD HI
ROOKIE AUTOS 226-231 NOT PRICED

2003 Sweet Spot Jerseys

	MINT	NRMT
OVERALL JSY ODDS 1:12		
*GOLDS: 1X TO 2.5X BASIC INSERTS		
GOLD PRINT RUN 25 SER.#'d SETS		
❑ JCAB Aaron Brooks	10.00	4.50
❑ JCBF Brett Favre	30.00	13.50
❑ JCBG Brian Griese	10.00	4.50
❑ JCBO David Boston	10.00	4.50
❑ JCBU Brian Urlacher	15.00	6.75
❑ JCCP Chad Pennington	15.00	6.75
❑ JCDB Drew Brees	10.00	4.50
❑ JCDC David Carr	12.00	5.50
❑ JCDM Donovan McNabb	12.00	5.50
❑ JCEG Eddie George	8.00	3.60
❑ JCEJ Edgerrin James	10.00	4.50
❑ JCES Emmitt Smith	25.00	11.00
❑ JCJF Jay Fiedler	10.00	4.50
❑ JCJG Jeff Garcia	10.00	4.50
❑ JCJP Jake Plummer	10.00	4.50
❑ JCJR Jerry Rice	20.00	9.00
❑ JCJS Jeremy Shockey	12.00	5.50
❑ JCKC Kerry Collins	8.00	3.60
❑ JCKS Kordell Stewart	8.00	3.60
❑ JCKW Kurt Warner	10.00	4.50
❑ JCLC Laveranues Coles	8.00	3.60
❑ JCLT LaDainian Tomlinson	10.00	4.50
❑ JCMV Michael Vick	25.00	11.00
❑ JCPM Peyton Manning	20.00	9.00
❑ JCPO Clinton Portis	15.00	6.75
❑ JCRG Rich Gannon	10.00	4.50
❑ JCRL Ray Lewis	10.00	4.50
❑ JCRM Randy Moss	15.00	6.75
❑ JCSM Steve McNair	10.00	4.50
❑ JCTB Tom Brady	25.00	11.00
❑ JCTI Tim Brown	10.00	4.50
❑ JCTO Terrell Owens	10.00	4.50
❑ JCWD Warrick Dunn	10.00	4.50

2003 Sweet Spot Signatures

	MINT	NRMT
OVERALL SIGNATURES ODDS 1:24		
*GOLD: .8X TO 2X BASIC AUTOS		
*GOLD: .5X TO 1.2X AUTOS/60-100		
❑ SSAB Aaron Brooks	40.00	18.00

❑ SSAN Anquan Boldin/100	80.00	36.00
❑ SSBB Boss Bailey	25.00	11.00
❑ SSBL Drew Bledsoe	40.00	18.00
❑ SSBU Brian Urlacher	75.00	34.00
❑ SSCJ Chad Johnson	40.00	18.00
❑ SSCP Chad Pennington	60.00	27.00
❑ SSDB Drew Brees	40.00	18.00
❑ SSDC David Carr	60.00	27.00
❑ SSDE Deuce McAllister/75	60.00	27.00
❑ SSDH Dwone Hicks	20.00	9.00
❑ SSDM Donovan McNabb/99	100.00	45.00
❑ SSJB Jim Brown/75	120.00	55.00
❑ SSJG Jeff Garcia	40.00	18.00
❑ SSJM Joe Montana/60	250.00	110.00
❑ SSJR Jerry Rice/20		
❑ SSLD LaTarence Dunbar	20.00	9.00
❑ SSLS Lynn Swann	120.00	55.00
❑ SSMH Matt Hasselbeck	40.00	18.00
❑ SSMS Musa Smith	25.00	11.00
❑ SSOS Onterrio Smith	40.00	18.00
❑ SSPH0 Priest Holmes/450	80.00	36.00
❑ SSPM Peyton Manning	100.00	45.00
❑ SSPO Clinton Portis	40.00	18.00
❑ SSRI John Riggins/75	80.00	36.00
❑ SSRM Randy Moss/15 EXCH		
❑ SSRW Ricky Williams/75	100.00	45.00
❑ SSSW Seneca Wallace	25.00	11.00
❑ SSTA Troy Aikman	100.00	45.00
❑ SSTB0 Terry Bradshaw/65	100.00	45.00
❑ SSTB Tim Brown/75	60.00	27.00
❑ SSTC Tyrone Calico	40.00	18.00
❑ SSTG Trent Green	40.00	18.00
❑ SSTO Terrell Owens	40.00	18.00

2004 Sweet Spot

	Nm-Mt	Ex-Mt
COMP.SET w/o SP's (100)	30.00	9.00
101-112 LEGENDS/2499 STATED ODDS 1:12		
113-175 RC PRINT RUN 1299 SER.#'d SETS		
176-210 RC PRINT RUN 999 SER.#'d SETS		
211-230 RC PRINT RUN 499 SER.#'d SETS		
CARD #258 NOT RELEASED		
EXCH EXPIRATION: 1/7/2008		
❑ 1 Anquan Boldin	1.25	.35
❑ 2 Emmitt Smith	2.50	.75
❑ 3 Josh McCown	.75	.23
❑ 4 Michael Vick	2.50	.75
❑ 5 Warrick Dunn	.75	.23
❑ 6 Peerless Price	.75	.23
❑ 7 Jamal Lewis	1.25	.35
❑ 8 Deion Sanders	1.25	.35
❑ 9 Kyle Boller	1.25	.35
❑ 10 Drew Bledsoe	1.25	.35
❑ 11 Travis Henry	.75	.23
❑ 12 Eric Moulds	.75	.23
❑ 13 Jake Delhomme	1.25	.35
❑ 14 Stephen Davis	.75	.23
❑ 15 Julius Peppers	1.25	.35
❑ 16 Thomas Jones	.75	.23
❑ 17 Rex Grossman	1.25	.35
❑ 18 Brian Urlacher	1.50	.45
❑ 19 Carson Palmer	1.50	.45
❑ 20 Chad Johnson	.75	.23
❑ 21 Rudi Johnson	.75	.23
❑ 22 Jeff Garcia	1.25	.35
❑ 23 William Green	.75	.23
❑ 24 Andre Davis	.50	.15
❑ 25 Vinny Testaverde	.75	.23
❑ 26 Eddie George	.75	.23
❑ 27 Keyshawn Johnson	.75	.23
❑ 28 Reuben Droughns	.75	.23
❑ 29 Jake Plummer	.75	.23
❑ 30 Ashley Lelie	.75	.23
❑ 31 Rod Smith	.75	.23
❑ 32 Joey Harrington	1.25	.35
❑ 33 Artose Pinner	.50	.15
❑ 34 Az-Zahir Hakim	.50	.15
❑ 35 Brett Favre	3.00	.90
❑ 36 Javon Walker	.75	.23
❑ 37 Ahman Green	1.25	.35
❑ 38 Andre Johnson	1.25	.35
❑ 39 David Carr	1.25	.35
❑ 40 Domanick Davis	1.25	.35
❑ 41 Peyton Manning	2.00	.60
❑ 42 Edgerrin James	1.25	.35
❑ 43 Marvin Harrison	1.25	.35
❑ 44 Byron Leftwich	2.00	.60
❑ 45 Fred Taylor	.75	.23
❑ 46 Jimmy Smith	.75	.23
❑ 47 Priest Holmes	1.50	.45
❑ 48 Trent Green	.75	.23
❑ 49 Dante Hall	1.25	.35
❑ 50 Tony Gonzalez	.75	.23
❑ 51 Randy McMichael	.50	.15
❑ 52 Jay Fiedler	.50	.15
❑ 53 Chris Chambers	.75	.23
❑ 54 Randy Moss	1.50	.45
❑ 55 Daunte Culpepper	1.25	.35
❑ 56 Onterrio Smith	.75	.23
❑ 57 Tom Brady	2.00	.60
❑ 58 Deion Branch	1.25	.35
❑ 59 Corey Dillon	.75	.23
❑ 60 Deuce McAllister	1.25	.35
❑ 61 Aaron Brooks	.75	.23
❑ 62 Joe Horn	.75	.23
❑ 63 Jeremy Shockey	1.25	.35
❑ 64 Tiki Barber	.75	.23
❑ 65 Michael Strahan	.75	.23
❑ 66 Curtis Martin	1.25	.35
❑ 67 Chad Pennington	1.50	.45
❑ 68 Santana Moss	.75	.23
❑ 69 Charles Woodson	.75	.23
❑ 70 Kerry Collins	.75	.23
❑ 71 Warren Sapp	.75	.23
❑ 72 Donovan McNabb	1.50	.45
❑ 73 Brian Westbrook	.75	.23
❑ 74 Terrell Owens	1.25	.35
❑ 75 Hines Ward	1.25	.35
❑ 76 Plaxico Burress	.75	.23
❑ 77 Duce Staley	.75	.23
❑ 78 LaDainian Tomlinson	1.25	.35
❑ 79 Antonio Gates	1.25	.35
❑ 80 Drew Brees	1.25	.35
❑ 81 Eric Johnson	.75	.23
❑ 82 Kevan Barlow	.75	.23
❑ 83 Tim Rattay	.75	.23
❑ 84 Matt Hasselbeck	.75	.23
❑ 85 Shaun Alexander	1.25	.35
❑ 86 Jerry Rice	2.50	.75

Card	Player	Nm-Mt	Ex-Mt
❑ 87	Marc Bulger	1.25	.35
❑ 88	Torry Holt	1.25	.35
❑ 89	Marshall Faulk	1.25	.35
❑ 90	Isaac Bruce	.75	.23
❑ 91	Brad Johnson	.75	.23
❑ 92	Derrick Brooks	.75	.23
❑ 93	Joey Galloway	.75	.23
❑ 94	Steve McNair	1.25	.35
❑ 95	Derrick Mason	.75	.23
❑ 96	Chris Brown	1.25	.35
❑ 97	Clinton Portis	1.25	.35
❑ 98	Mark Brunell	.75	.23
❑ 99	Laveranues Coles	.75	.23
❑ 100	LaVar Arrington	2.50	.75
❑ 101	Roger Staubach	8.00	2.40
❑ 102	Troy Aikman	6.00	1.80
❑ 103	John Elway	10.00	3.00
❑ 104	Barry Sanders	10.00	3.00
❑ 105	Fran Tarkenton	6.00	1.80
❑ 106	Archie Manning	6.00	1.80
❑ 107	Joe Namath	8.00	2.40
❑ 108	Ken Stabler	6.00	1.80
❑ 109	Howie Long	6.00	1.80
❑ 110	Kellen Winslow Sr.	5.00	1.50
❑ 111	Joe Montana	15.00	4.50
❑ 112	Joe Theismann	5.00	1.50
❑ 113	Darnell Dockett RC	6.00	1.80
❑ 114	Randy Starks RC	6.00	1.80
❑ 115	Rashad Baker RC	8.00	2.40
❑ 116	Tim Anderson RC	8.00	2.40
❑ 117	Darrion Scott RC	8.00	2.40
❑ 118	Courtney Watson RC	8.00	2.40
❑ 119	Gilbert Gardner RC	6.00	1.80
❑ 120	Marquis Cooper RC	6.00	1.80
❑ 121	Caleb Miller RC	6.00	1.80
❑ 122	Jeff Shoate RC	4.00	1.20
❑ 123	Keyaron Fox RC	6.00	1.80
❑ 124	Landon Johnson RC	6.00	1.80
❑ 125	Reggie Torbor RC	6.00	1.80
❑ 126	Demorrio Williams RC	8.00	2.40
❑ 127	Niko Koutouvides RC	6.00	1.80
❑ 128	Richard Seigler RC	6.00	1.80
❑ 129	Brandon Chillar RC	6.00	1.80
❑ 130	Nate Kaeding RC	8.00	2.40
❑ 131	Dave Ball RC	4.00	1.20
❑ 132	Josh Thomas RC	8.00	2.40
❑ 133	Josh Scobee RC	4.00	1.20
❑ 134	Wes Welker RC	8.00	2.40
❑ 135	Darrell McClover RC	6.00	1.80
❑ 136	Ben Utecht RC	4.00	1.20
❑ 137	Chris Snee RC	6.00	1.80
❑ 138	Jake Grove RC	4.00	1.20
❑ 139	Justin Smiley RC	8.00	2.40
❑ 140	Max Starks RC	6.00	1.80
❑ 141	Randall Gay RC	12.00	3.60
❑ 142	Charlie Anderson RC	4.00	1.20
❑ 143	Alain Kashama RC	8.00	2.40
❑ 144	Eric Edwards RC	10.00	3.00
❑ 145	Jacques Reeves RC	6.00	1.80
❑ 146	Jarrett Payton RC	8.00	2.40
❑ 147	Curtis Deloatch RC	6.00	1.80
❑ 148	Michael Gaines RC	6.00	1.80
❑ 149	Erik Jensen RC	6.00	1.80
❑ 150	Courtney Anderson RC	6.00	1.80
❑ 151	Bruce Thornton RC	4.00	1.20
❑ 152	Glenn Earl RC	6.00	1.80
❑ 153	Michael Waddell RC	4.00	1.20
❑ 154	J.R. Reed RC	6.00	1.80
❑ 155	Dwight Anderson RC	8.00	2.40
❑ 156	Von Hutchins RC	6.00	1.80
❑ 157	Travis LaBoy RC	8.00	2.40
❑ 158	Terry Johnson RC	6.00	1.80
❑ 159	Dwan Edwards RC	4.00	1.20
❑ 160	Colby Bockwoldt RC	8.00	2.40
❑ 161	Madieu Williams RC	6.00	1.80
❑ 162	Will Poole RC	8.00	2.40
❑ 163	Igor Olshansky RC	8.00	2.40
❑ 164	Michael Boulware RC	8.00	2.40
❑ 165	Shaun Phillips RC	6.00	1.80
❑ 166	Keith Smith RC	6.00	1.80
❑ 167	Will Smith RC	8.00	2.40
❑ 168	D.J. Williams RC	10.00	3.00
❑ 169	Derrick Strait RC	8.00	2.40
❑ 170	Karlos Dansby RC	8.00	2.40
❑ 171	Ricardo Colclough RC	8.00	2.40
❑ 172	Chad Lavalais RC	6.00	1.80
❑ 173	Teddy Lehman RC	8.00	2.40
❑ 174	Jim Sorgi RC	8.00	2.40
❑ 175	Bob Sanders RC	8.00	2.40
❑ 176	Sean Taylor RC	12.00	3.60
❑ 177	Marcus Tubbs RC	10.00	3.00
❑ 178	Daryl Smith RC	10.00	3.00
❑ 179	Bradlee Van Pelt RC	10.00	3.00
❑ 180	Shawntae Spencer RC	10.00	3.00
❑ 181	Nathan Vasher RC	10.00	3.00
❑ 182	Jared Allen RC	10.00	3.00
❑ 183	Rod Davis RC	5.00	1.50
❑ 184	Brian Jones RC	8.00	2.40
❑ 185	Will Allen RC	10.00	3.00
❑ 186	Antwan Odom RC	10.00	3.00
❑ 187	Vernon Carey RC	8.00	2.40
❑ 188	Mike Karney RC	8.00	2.40
❑ 189	Joey Thomas RC	10.00	3.00
❑ 190	Casey Bramlet RC	8.00	2.40
❑ 191	Keiwan Ratliff RC	8.00	2.40
❑ 192	Rich Gardner RC	8.00	2.40
❑ 193	Jason Babin RC	10.00	3.00
❑ 194	Dontarrious Thomas RC	10.00	3.00
❑ 195	Dexter Reid RC	5.00	1.50
❑ 196	Marquise Hill RC	8.00	2.40
❑ 197	Jonathan Smith RC	8.00	2.40
❑ 198	Larry Croom RC	8.00	2.40
❑ 199	Gibril Wilson RC	10.00	3.00
❑ 200	Erik Coleman RC	10.00	3.00
❑ 201	B.J. Sams RC	10.00	3.00
❑ 202	Bruce Perry RC	8.00	2.40
❑ 203	Brock Lesnar RC	15.00	4.50
❑ 204	Brandon Miree RC	8.00	2.40
❑ 205	Clarence Moore RC	10.00	3.00
❑ 206	Mark Jones RC	8.00	2.40
❑ 207	Patrick Crayton RC	10.00	3.00
❑ 208	Jeff Dugan RC	5.00	1.50
❑ 209	Sean Ryan RC	8.00	2.40
❑ 210	Sloan Thomas RC	8.00	2.40
❑ 211	Triandos Luke RC	12.00	3.60
❑ 212	Dexter Wynn RC	10.00	3.00
❑ 213	Matt Kranchick RC	12.00	3.60
❑ 214	Tim Euhus RC	12.00	3.60
❑ 215	Ryan Krause RC	10.00	3.00
❑ 216	Junior Siavii RC	12.00	3.60
❑ 217	Ran Carthon RC	10.00	3.00
❑ 218	Derrick Pope RC	10.00	3.00
❑ 219	Alex Lewis RC	12.00	3.60
❑ 220	Chris Cooley RC	12.00	3.60
❑ 221	Jamaar Taylor RC	12.00	3.60
❑ 222	Stuart Schweigert RC	12.00	3.60
❑ 223	Jason David RC	12.00	3.60
❑ 224	Maurice Mann RC	10.00	3.00
❑ 225	Robert Geathers RC	10.00	3.00
❑ 226	Matt Mauck RC	12.00	3.60
❑ 227	Jammal Lord RC	12.00	3.60
❑ 228	Travelle Wharton RC	6.00	1.80
❑ 229	D.J. Hackett RC	10.00	3.00
❑ 230	Thomas Tapeh RC	10.00	3.00
❑ 231	Dunta Robinson AU/699 RC EXCH	25.00	7.50
❑ 232	Ahmad Carroll AU/699 RC	25.00	7.50
❑ 233	Kenechi Udeze AU/699 RC	20.00	6.00
❑ 234	Tommie Harris AU/699 RC	25.00	7.50
❑ 235	Jonathan Vilma AU/699 RC	30.00	9.00
❑ 236	Vince Wilfork AU/699 RC	25.00	7.50
❑ 237	B.J. Symons AU/699 RC	20.00	6.00
❑ 238	B.J. Johnson AU/699 RC	15.00	4.50
❑ 239	Kris Wilson AU/699 RC	20.00	6.00
❑ 240	Josh Harris AU/699 RC	20.00	6.00
❑ 241	Troy Fleming AU/699 RC	15.00	4.50
❑ 242	Johnnie Morant AU/699 RC EXCH	20.00	6.00
❑ 243	Craig Krenzel AU/699 RC	20.00	6.00
❑ 244	Quincy Wilson AU/699 RC EXCH	15.00	4.50
❑ 245	P.K. Sam AU/699 RC	15.00	4.50
❑ 246	Michael Turner AU/699 RC	15.00	4.50
❑ 247	Carlos Francis AU/699 RC	20.00	6.00
❑ 248	Jared Lorenzen AU/699 RC	15.00	4.50
❑ 249	John Navarre AU/675 RC	20.00	6.00
❑ 250	Jeff Smoker AU/699 RC	25.00	7.50
❑ 251	Ernest Wilford AU/559 RC	20.00	6.00
❑ 252	Mewelde Moore AU/699 RC	25.00	7.50
❑ 253	Chris Gamble AU/699 RC EXCH	25.00	7.50
❑ 254	Jerricho Cotchery AU/699 RC	20.00	6.00
❑ 255	Derrick Hamilton AU/699 RC	20.00	6.00
❑ 256	Samie Parker AU/699 RC	20.00	6.00
❑ 257	Cody Pickett AU/699 RC	25.00	7.50
❑ 259	Ben Hartsock AU/699 RC	20.00	6.00
❑ 260	Cedric Cobbs AU/699 RC	20.00	6.00
❑ 261	Matt Schaub AU/699 RC	30.00	9.00
❑ 262	Bernard Berrian AU/699 RC	20.00	6.00
❑ 263	Devard Darling AU/699 RC	20.00	6.00
❑ 264	Ben Watson AU/699 RC	20.00	6.00
❑ 265	Darius Watts AU/699 RC	25.00	7.50
❑ 266	DeAngelo Hall AU/399 RC	25.00	7.50
❑ 267	Ben Troupe AU/699 RC	20.00	6.00
❑ 268	Michael Jenkins AU/399 RC	25.00	7.50
❑ 269	Keary Colbert AU/699 RC	25.00	7.50
❑ 270	Robert Gallery AU/699 RC	25.00	7.50
❑ 271	Greg Jones AU/650 RC	25.00	7.50
❑ 272	Michael Clayton AU/699 RC	50.00	15.00
❑ 273	Luke McCown AU/699 RC EXCH	20.00	6.00
❑ 274	Rashaun Woods AU/699 RC	25.00	7.50
❑ 275	Reggie Williams AU/699 RC	25.00	7.50
❑ 276	Devery Henderson AU/699 RC	15.00	4.50
❑ 277	Tatum Bell AU/699 RC	40.00	12.00
❑ 278	Lee Evans AU/350 RC	50.00	15.00
❑ 279	J.P. Losman AU/199 RC EXCH	80.00	24.00
❑ 280	Drew Henson AU/199 RC	50.00	15.00
❑ 281	Kellen Winslow AU/125 RC	100.00	30.00
❑ 282	Chris Perry AU/199 RC	50.00	15.00
❑ 283	Julius Jones AU/199 RC	150.00	45.00
❑ 284	Steven Jackson AU/199 RC	120.00	36.00
❑ 285	Kevin Jones AU/199 RC EXCH	120.00	36.00
❑ 286	Roy Williams AU/149 RC	120.00	36.00
❑ 287	Ben Roethlisberger AU/199 RC	300.00	90.00
❑ 288	Philip Rivers AU/199 RC	100.00	30.00
❑ 289	Larry Fitzgerald AU/150 RC	100.00	30.00
❑ 290	Eli Manning AU/150 RC	200.00	60.00

2004 Sweet Spot Gold

Nm-Mt Ex-Mt

*STARS: 4X TO 10X BASE CARD HI
*LEGENDS: 1X TO 2.5X BASE CARD HI
*ROOKIES 113-175: 1X TO 2.5X BASE CARD HI
*ROOKIES 176-210: .8X TO 2X BASE CARD HI
*ROOKIES 211-230: .6X TO 1.5X BASE CARD HI
STATED PRINT RUN 50 SER.#'d SETS

2004 Sweet Spot Silver

Nm-Mt Ex-Mt

*STARS: 2.5X TO 6X BASE CARD HI
*LEGENDS: .6X TO 1.5X BASE CARD HI
*ROOKIES 113-175: .6X TO 1.5X BASE CARD HI
*ROOKIES 176-210: .5X TO 1.2X BASE CARD HI
*ROOKIES 211-230: .4X TO 1X BASE CARD HI
STATED PRINT RUN 100 SER.#'d SETS

2004 Sweet Spot Gold Rookie Autographs

STATED PRINT RUN 100 UNLESS NOTED
EXCH EXPIRATION: 1/7/2008

Card	Player	Nm-Mt	Ex-Mt
❑ 231	Dunta Robinson EXCH	40.00	12.00
❑ 232	Ahmad Carroll	40.00	12.00
❑ 233	Kenechi Udeze	30.00	9.00
❑ 234	Tommie Harris	40.00	12.00
❑ 235	Jonathan Vilma	50.00	15.00
❑ 236	Vince Wilfork	30.00	9.00
❑ 237	B.J. Symons	30.00	9.00
❑ 238	B.J. Johnson	25.00	7.50
❑ 239	Kris Wilson	30.00	9.00
❑ 240	Josh Harris	30.00	9.00

❑ 241 Troy Fleming	25.00	7.50
❑ 242 Johnnie Morant EXCH	30.00	9.00
❑ 243 Craig Krenzel	40.00	12.00
❑ 244 Quincy Wilson EXCH	25.00	7.50
❑ 245 P.K. Sam	25.00	7.50
❑ 246 Michael Turner	25.00	7.50
❑ 247 Carlos Francis	25.00	7.50
❑ 248 Jared Lorenzen	25.00	7.50
❑ 249 John Navarre	30.00	9.00
❑ 250 Jeff Smoker	40.00	12.00
❑ 251 Ernest Wilford	30.00	9.00
❑ 252 Mewelde Moore	40.00	12.00
❑ 253 Chris Gamble EXCH	40.00	12.00
❑ 254 Jerricho Cotchery	30.00	9.00
❑ 255 Derrick Hamilton	25.00	7.50
❑ 256 Samie Parker	30.00	9.00
❑ 257 Cody Pickett	30.00	9.00
❑ 259 Ben Hartsock	30.00	9.00
❑ 260 Cedric Cobbs	30.00	9.00
❑ 261 Matt Schaub	50.00	15.00
❑ 262 Bernard Berrian	30.00	9.00
❑ 263 Devard Darling	30.00	9.00
❑ 264 Ben Watson	30.00	9.00
❑ 265 Darius Watts	40.00	12.00
❑ 266 DeAngelo Hall	40.00	12.00
❑ 267 Ben Troupe	30.00	9.00
❑ 268 Michael Jenkins	30.00	9.00
❑ 269 Keary Colbert	40.00	12.00
❑ 270 Robert Gallery	40.00	12.00
❑ 271 Greg Jones	30.00	9.00
❑ 272 Michael Clayton	80.00	24.00
❑ 273 Luke McCown EXCH	30.00	9.00
❑ 274 Rashaun Woods	40.00	12.00
❑ 275 Reggie Williams	40.00	12.00
❑ 276 Devery Henderson	25.00	7.50
❑ 277 Tatum Bell	50.00	15.00
❑ 278 Lee Evans	50.00	15.00
❑ 279 J.P. Losman EXCH	100.00	30.00
❑ 280 Drew Henson	60.00	18.00
❑ 281 Kellen Winslow/50	120.00	36.00
❑ 282 Chris Perry	60.00	18.00
❑ 283 Julius Jones	135.00	40.00
❑ 284 Steven Jackson	120.00	36.00
❑ 285 Kevin Jones EXCH	120.00	36.00
❑ 286 Roy Williams WR	100.00	30.00
❑ 287 Ben Roethlisberger	250.00	75.00
❑ 288 Philip Rivers	100.00	30.00
❑ 289 Larry Fitzgerald/35	175.00	52.50
❑ 290 Eli Manning/50	300.00	90.00

2004 Sweet Spot Signatures

STATED ODDS 1:24
*GOLD: .5X TO 1.2X BASIC AUTOS
GOLD PRINT RUN 100 SER.#'d SETS
EXCH EXPIRATION: 1/7/2008

	Nm-Mt	Ex-Mt
❑ SSAG Ahman Green	50.00	15.00
❑ SSAP Alan Page	40.00	12.00
❑ SSBF Brett Favre	225.00	70.00
❑ SSBG Bob Griese	40.00	12.00
❑ SSBP Bill Parcells	50.00	15.00
❑ SSBS Barry Sanders SP	150.00	45.00
❑ SSBW Brian Westbrook EXCH	40.00	12.00
❑ SSCB Chris Brown EXCH	20.00	6.00
❑ SSCH Charlie Joiner	30.00	9.00
❑ SSCJ Chad Johnson	20.00	6.00
❑ SSCP Chad Pennington	50.00	15.00
❑ SSDA Dave Casper	30.00	9.00
❑ SSDD Domanick Davis	20.00	6.00
❑ SSDF Dan Fouts	50.00	15.00
❑ SSDM Donovan McNabb EXCH	80.00	24.00
❑ SSDP Drew Pearson	40.00	12.00
❑ SSFT Fran Tarkenton	60.00	18.00
❑ SSHL Howie Long	50.00	15.00
❑ SSJA Jack Ham	50.00	15.00
❑ SSJE John Elway SP	150.00	45.00
❑ SSJG Jon Gruden	30.00	9.00
❑ SSJJ Jimmy Johnson	50.00	15.00
❑ SSJN Joe Namath SP	100.00	30.00
❑ SSJO Joe Montana SP	225.00	70.00
❑ SSJT Joe Theismann SP	50.00	15.00
❑ SSKA Ken Anderson	30.00	9.00
❑ SSKE Kellen Winslow Sr.	40.00	12.00
❑ SSKS Ken Stabler	60.00	18.00
❑ SSLD Len Dawson	40.00	12.00
❑ SSLT LaDainian Tomlinson	60.00	18.00
❑ SSMA Dan Marino SP	200.00	60.00
❑ SSMC Mark Clayton	30.00	9.00
❑ SSMV Michael Vick SP	120.00	36.00
❑ SSPH0 Paul Hornung SP	60.00	18.00
❑ SSPM Peyton Manning SP	120.00	36.00
❑ SSRG Rex Grossman	30.00	9.00
❑ SSRJ Rudi Johnson	20.00	6.00
❑ SSRO Roy Williams S	40.00	12.00
❑ SSRS Roger Staubach SP	100.00	30.00
❑ SSRW Randy White	30.00	9.00
❑ SSTA Troy Aikman	80.00	24.00

2004 Sweet Spot Sweet Panel Signatures

STATED PRINT RUN 100 UNLESS NOTED
*GOLD: .6X TO 1.5X BASIC AUTOS
GOLD PRINT RUN 25 SER.#'d SETS
EXCH EXPIRATION: 1/7/2008

	Nm-Mt	Ex-Mt
❑ SPBL Byron Leftwich	40.00	12.00
❑ SPBR Ben Roethlisberger	250.00	75.00
❑ SPBS Bart Starr/80	150.00	45.00
❑ SPCH0 Chris Perry EXCH	30.00	9.00
❑ SPCP Chad Pennington	50.00	15.00
❑ SPDD Domanick Davis	40.00	12.00
❑ SPEM Eli Manning	150.00	45.00
❑ SPFT Fran Tarkenton	40.00	12.00
❑ SPHL Howie Long	60.00	18.00
❑ SPJP J.P. Losman	80.00	24.00
❑ SPJT Joe Theismann	60.00	18.00
❑ SPKJ Kevin Jones	80.00	24.00
❑ SPKW Kellen Winslow Jr.	50.00	15.00
❑ SPMV Michael Vick	100.00	30.00
❑ SPPH Paul Hornung	50.00	15.00
❑ SPPM Peyton Manning	120.00	36.00
❑ SPPR Philip Rivers	80.00	24.00
❑ SPRJ Rudi Johnson	30.00	9.00
❑ SPRO Roman Gabriel	40.00	12.00
❑ SPTA Tatum Bell	40.00	12.00
❑ SPZT Zach Thomas EXCH	40.00	12.00

2004 Sweet Spot Sweet Swatches

STATED ODDS 1:12

	Nm-Mt	Ex-Mt
❑ SWBR Ben Roethlisberger	80.00	24.00
❑ SWBT Ben Troupe	6.00	1.80
❑ SWBW Ben Watson	6.00	1.80
❑ SWCC Cedric Cobbs	6.00	1.80
❑ SWCP Chris Perry	10.00	3.00
❑ SWDD Devard Darling	6.00	1.80
❑ SWDE Devery Henderson	6.00	1.80
❑ SWDH DeAngelo Hall	8.00	2.40
❑ SWDW Darius Watts	6.00	1.80
❑ SWEM Eli Manning	30.00	9.00
❑ SWGJ Greg Jones	8.00	2.40
❑ SWHA Derrick Hamilton	6.00	1.80
❑ SWJJ Julius Jones	20.00	6.00
❑ SWJP J.P. Losman	12.00	3.60
❑ SWKC Keary Colbert	8.00	2.40
❑ SWKJ Kevin Jones SP	20.00	6.00
❑ SWKW Kellen Winslow Jr.	12.00	3.60
❑ SWLE Lee Evans	12.00	3.60
❑ SWLF Larry Fitzgerald	15.00	4.50
❑ SWLM Luke McCown	8.00	2.40
❑ SWMC Michael Clayton	12.00	3.60
❑ SWMJ Michael Jenkins	6.00	1.80
❑ SWMS Matt Schaub	10.00	3.00
❑ SWPR Philip Rivers	15.00	4.50
❑ SWRA Rashaun Woods	8.00	2.40
❑ SWRG Robert Gallery	10.00	3.00
❑ SWRO Roy Williams WR	15.00	4.50
❑ SWRW Reggie Williams SP	8.00	2.40
❑ SWSJ Steven Jackson	15.00	4.50
❑ SWTB Tatum Bell	10.00	3.00

2001 Titanium

	Nm-Mt	Ex-Mt
COMP.SET w/o SP's (144)	80.00	24.00
❑ 1 David Boston	1.50	.45
❑ 2 Thomas Jones	1.00	.30
❑ 3 Rob Moore	1.00	.30
❑ 4 Michael Pittman	.60	.18
❑ 5 Jake Plummer	1.00	.30
❑ 6 Jamal Anderson	1.50	.45
❑ 7 Chris Chandler	1.00	.30
❑ 8 Shawn Jefferson	.60	.18

❑ 9 Terance Mathis .60 .18
❑ 10 Terry Allen .60 .18
❑ 11 Jason Brookins UER RC 1.50 .45
(Chad Pennington wrongback, card number on back is #93)
❑ 12 Elvis Grbac 1.00 .30
❑ 13 Qadry Ismail 1.00 .30
❑ 14 Jamal Lewis 2.50 .75
❑ 15 Ray Lewis 1.50 .45
❑ 16 Shannon Sharpe 1.00 .30
❑ 17 Shawn Bryson .60 .18
❑ 18 Rob Johnson 1.00 .30
❑ 19 Sammy Morris .60 .18
❑ 20 Eric Moulds 1.00 .30
❑ 21 Peerless Price 1.00 .30
❑ 22 Tim Biakabutuka 1.00 .30
❑ 23 Patrick Jeffers 1.00 .30
❑ 24 Muhsin Muhammad 1.00 .30
❑ 25 James Allen 1.00 .30
❑ 26 Shane Matthews .60 .18
❑ 27 Marcus Robinson 1.50 .45
❑ 28 Brian Urlacher 2.50 .75
❑ 29 Corey Dillon 1.50 .45
❑ 30 Jon Kitna 1.00 .30
❑ 31 Akili Smith .60 .18
❑ 32 Peter Warrick 1.50 .45
❑ 33 Tim Couch 1.00 .30
❑ 34 Kevin Johnson 1.00 .30
❑ 35 Dennis Northcutt 1.00 .30
❑ 36 Joey Galloway 1.00 .30
❑ 37 Rocket Ismail 1.00 .30
❑ 38 Emmitt Smith 3.00 .90
❑ 39 Mike Anderson 1.50 .45
❑ 40 Terrell Davis 1.50 .45
❑ 41 Brian Griese 1.50 .45
❑ 42 Ed McCaffrey 1.50 .45
❑ 43 Rod Smith 1.00 .30
❑ 44 Charlie Batch 1.50 .45
❑ 45 Germane Crowell .60 .18
❑ 46 Herman Moore .60 .18
❑ 47 Johnnie Morton 1.00 .30
❑ 48 James Stewart 1.00 .30
❑ 49 Brett Favre 5.00 1.50
❑ 50 Antonio Freeman 1.50 .45
❑ 51 Ahman Green 1.50 .45
❑ 52 Bill Schroeder 1.00 .30
❑ 53 Marvin Harrison 1.50 .45
❑ 54 Edgerrin James 2.00 .60
❑ 55 Peyton Manning 4.00 1.20
❑ 56 Jerome Pathon 1.00 .30
❑ 57 Terrence Wilkins .60 .18
❑ 58 Mark Brunell 1.50 .45
❑ 59 Keenan McCardell .60 .18
❑ 60 Jimmy Smith 1.00 .30
❑ 61 Fred Taylor 1.50 .45
❑ 62 Derrick Alexander 1.00 .30
❑ 63 Tony Gonzalez 1.00 .30
❑ 64 Trent Green 1.50 .45
❑ 65 Priest Holmes 2.00 .60
❑ 66 Jay Fiedler 1.50 .45
❑ 67 Oronde Gadsden 1.00 .30
❑ 68 James McKnight .60 .18
❑ 69 Lamar Smith 1.00 .30
❑ 70 Zach Thomas 1.50 .45
❑ 71 Cris Carter 1.50 .45
❑ 72 Daunte Culpepper 1.50 .45
❑ 73 Randy Moss 3.00 .90
❑ 74 Drew Bledsoe 2.00 .60
❑ 75 Troy Brown 1.00 .30
❑ 76 Charles Johnson .60 .18
❑ 77 J.R. Redmond .60 .18
❑ 78 Antowain Smith 1.00 .30
❑ 79 Jeff Blake 1.00 .30
❑ 80 Aaron Brooks 1.50 .45
❑ 81 Albert Connell .60 .18
❑ 82 Joe Horn 1.00 .30
❑ 83 Ricky Williams 1.50 .45
❑ 84 Tiki Barber 1.00 .30
❑ 85 Kerry Collins 1.00 .30
❑ 86 Ron Dayne 1.50 .45
❑ 87 Ike Hilliard 1.00 .30
❑ 88 Amani Toomer 1.00 .30
❑ 89 Richie Anderson .60 .18
❑ 90 Wayne Chrebet 1.00 .30
❑ 91 Laveranues Coles 1.50 .45
❑ 92 Curtis Martin 1.50 .45
❑ 93 Chad Pennington UER 2.50 .75
(Jason Brookins wrongback, card number on back is #11)
❑ 94 Vinny Testaverde 1.00 .30
❑ 95 Tim Brown 1.50 .45
❑ 96 Rich Gannon 1.50 .45
❑ 97 Charlie Garner 1.00 .30
❑ 98 Jerry Rice 3.00 .90
❑ 99 Tyrone Wheatley 1.00 .30
❑ 100 Charles Woodson 1.00 .30
❑ 101 Donovan McNabb 2.00 .60
❑ 102 Todd Pinkston 1.00 .30
❑ 103 Duce Staley 1.50 .45
❑ 104 James Thrash 1.00 .30
❑ 105 Jerome Bettis 1.50 .45
❑ 106 Plaxico Burress 1.50 .45
❑ 107 Tommy Maddox 5.00 1.50
❑ 108 Bobby Shaw .60 .18
❑ 109 Kordell Stewart 1.00 .30
❑ 110 Hines Ward 1.50 .45
❑ 111 Isaac Bruce 1.50 .45
❑ 112 Marshall Faulk 2.00 .60
❑ 113 Az-Zahir Hakim .60 .18
❑ 114 Torry Holt 1.50 .45
❑ 115 Kurt Warner 3.00 .90
❑ 116 Curtis Conway 1.00 .30
❑ 117 Tim Dwight 1.50 .45
❑ 118 Doug Flutie 1.50 .45
❑ 119 Jeff Graham .60 .18
❑ 120 Jeff Garcia 1.50 .45
❑ 121 Garrison Hearst 1.00 .30
❑ 122 Terrell Owens 1.50 .45
❑ 123 J.J. Stokes 1.00 .30
❑ 124 Tai Streets .60 .18
❑ 125 Shaun Alexander 2.00 .60
❑ 126 Matt Hasselbeck 1.00 .30
❑ 127 Darrell Jackson 1.50 .45
❑ 128 Ricky Watters 1.00 .30
❑ 129 Mike Alstott 1.50 .45
❑ 130 Warrick Dunn 1.50 .45
❑ 131 Jacquez Green .60 .18
❑ 132 Brad Johnson 1.50 .45
❑ 133 Keyshawn Johnson 1.50 .45
❑ 134 Warren Sapp 1.00 .30
❑ 135 Kevin Dyson 1.00 .30
❑ 136 Eddie George 1.50 .45
❑ 137 Mike Green .60 .18
❑ 138 Jevon Kearse 1.00 .30
❑ 139 Derrick Mason 1.00 .30
❑ 140 Steve McNair 1.50 .45
❑ 141 Champ Bailey 1.00 .30
❑ 142 Tony Banks 1.00 .30
❑ 143 Stephen Davis 1.50 .45
❑ 144 Michael Westbrook 1.00 .30
❑ 145 Bill Gramatica JSY RC 20.00 6.00
❑ 146 Arnold Jackson JSY RC 20.00 6.00
❑ 147 Bobby Newcombe JSY RC 25.00 7.50
❑ 148 Marcel Shipp JSY RC 40.00 12.00
❑ 149 Quentin McCord JSY RC 20.00 6.00
❑ 150 Michael Vick JSY RC 250.00 75.00
❑ 151 Chris Barnes JSY RC 20.00 6.00
❑ 152 Todd Heap JSY RC 40.00 12.00
❑ 153 Reggie Germany JSY RC 20.00 6.00
❑ 154 Travis Henry JSY RC 50.00 15.00
❑ 155 Chris Taylor JSY RC 25.00 7.50
❑ 156 Dee Brown JSY RC 40.00 12.00
❑ 157 Dan Morgan JSY RC 40.00 12.00
❑ 158 Steve Smith JSY RC 60.00 18.00
❑ 159 Chris Weinke JSY RC 40.00 12.00
❑ 160 David Terrell JSY RC 40.00 12.00
❑ 161 Anthony Thomas JSY RC 60.00 18.00
❑ 162 T.J. Houshmandzadeh JSY RC 40.00 12.00
❑ 163 Chad Johnson JSY RC 80.00 24.00
❑ 164 Rudi Johnson JSY RC 80.00 24.00
❑ 165 James Jackson JSY RC 40.00 12.00
❑ 166 Andre King JSY RC 20.00 6.00
❑ 167 Quincy Morgan JSY RC 40.00 12.00
❑ 168 Quincy Carter JSY RC 40.00 12.00
❑ 169 Ken-Yon Rambo JSY RC 25.00 7.50
❑ 170 Kevin Kasper JSY RC 40.00 12.00
❑ 171 Scotty Anderson JSY RC 25.00 7.50
❑ 172 Mike McMahon JSY RC 40.00 12.00
❑ 173 Robert Ferguson JSY RC 40.00 12.00
❑ 174 David Martin JSY RC 20.00 6.00
❑ 175 Reggie Wayne JSY RC 60.00 18.00
❑ 176 Richmond Flowers JSY RC 20.00 6.00
❑ 177 Derrick Blaylock JSY RC 40.00 12.00
❑ 178 Snoop Minnis JSY RC 25.00 7.50
❑ 179 Chris Chambers JSY RC 50.00 15.00
❑ 180 Josh Heupel JSY RC 40.00 12.00
❑ 181 Travis Minor JSY RC 25.00 7.50
❑ 182 Michael Bennett JSY RC 100.00 30.00
❑ 183 Cedric James JSY RC 25.00 7.50
❑ 184 Deuce McAllister JSY RC 100.00 30.00
❑ 185 Onome Ojo JSY RC 25.00 7.50
❑ 186 Jonathan Carter JSY RC 20.00 6.00
❑ 187 Jesse Palmer JSY RC 40.00 12.00
❑ 188 LaMont Jordan JSY RC 60.00 18.00
❑ 189 Derek Combs JSY RC 20.00 6.00
❑ 190 Marques Tuiasosopo JSY RC 40.00 12.00
❑ 191 Correll Buckhalter JSY RC 60.00 18.00
❑ 192 Freddie Mitchell JSY RC 40.00 12.00
❑ 193 Adam Archuleta JSY RC 40.00 12.00
❑ 194 Francis St.Paul JSY RC 20.00 6.00
❑ 195 Drew Brees JSY RC 100.00 30.00
❑ 196 LaDainian Tomlinson JSY RC 150.00 45.00
❑ 197 Kevan Barlow JSY RC 40.00 12.00
❑ 198 Vinny Sutherland JSY RC 25.00 7.50
❑ 199 Cedrick Wilson JSY RC 40.00 12.00
❑ 200 Alex Bannister JSY RC 20.00 6.00
❑ 201 Koren Robinson JSY RC 40.00 12.00
❑ 202 Milton Wynn JSY RC 20.00 6.00
❑ 203 Dan Alexander JSY RC 40.00 12.00
❑ 204 Eddie Berlin JSY RC 40.00 12.00
❑ 205 Justin McCareins JSY RC 40.00 12.00
❑ 206 Rod Gardner JSY RC 40.00 12.00
❑ 207 Damerien McCants JSY RC 25.00 7.50
❑ 208 Sage Rosenfels JSY RC 40.00 12.00
❑ 209 Nick Goings JSY RC 40.00 12.00
❑ 210 Josh Booty JSY RC 40.00 12.00
❑ 211 Benjamin Gay JSY RC 40.00 12.00
❑ 212 Gerard Warren JSY RC 40.00 12.00
❑ 213 Jamal Reynolds JSY RC 40.00 12.00
❑ 214 Will Allen JSY RC 25.00 7.50
❑ 215 Santana Moss JSY RC 60.00 18.00
❑ 216 Andre Carter JSY RC 40.00 12.00

2001 Titanium Retail

Nm-Mt Ex-Mt

*RETAIL STARS: .3X TO .8X HOBBY

❑ 145 Bill Gramatica RC 2.00 .60
❑ 146 Arnold Jackson RC 3.00 .90
❑ 147 Bobby Newcombe RC 3.00 .90
❑ 148 Marcel Shipp RC 5.00 1.50
❑ 149 Quentin McCord RC 3.00 .90
❑ 150 Michael Vick RC 30.00 9.00
❑ 151 Chris Barnes RC 3.00 .90
❑ 152 Todd Heap RC 5.00 1.50
❑ 153 Reggie Germany RC 3.00 .90
❑ 154 Travis Henry RC 6.00 1.80
❑ 155 Chris Taylor RC 3.00 .90
❑ 156 Dee Brown RC 5.00 1.50
❑ 157 Dan Morgan RC 5.00 1.50
❑ 158 Steve Smith RC 6.00 1.80
❑ 159 Chris Weinke RC 5.00 1.50
❑ 160 David Terrell RC 5.00 1.50
❑ 161 Anthony Thomas RC 8.00 2.40
❑ 162 T.J. Houshmandzadeh RC 5.00 1.50
❑ 163 Chad Johnson RC 10.00 3.00
❑ 164 Rudi Johnson RC 10.00 3.00
❑ 165 James Jackson RC 5.00 1.50
❑ 166 Andre King RC 3.00 .90
❑ 167 Quincy Morgan RC 5.00 1.50
❑ 168 Quincy Carter RC 5.00 1.50
❑ 169 Ken-Yon Rambo RC 3.00 .90
❑ 170 Kevin Kasper RC 5.00 1.50

❑ 171 Scotty Anderson RC	3.00	.90
❑ 172 Mike McMahon RC	5.00	1.50
❑ 173 Robert Ferguson RC	5.00	1.50
❑ 174 David Martin RC	3.00	.90
❑ 175 Reggie Wayne RC	8.00	2.40
❑ 176 Richmond Flowers RC	3.00	.90
❑ 177 Derrick Blaylock RC	5.00	1.50
❑ 178 Snoop Minnis RC	3.00	.90
❑ 179 Chris Chambers RC	6.00	1.80
❑ 180 Josh Heupel RC	5.00	1.50
❑ 181 Travis Minor RC	3.00	.90
❑ 182 Michael Bennett RC	10.00	3.00
❑ 183 Cedric James RC	3.00	.90
❑ 184 Deuce McAllister RC	10.00	3.00
❑ 185 Onome Ojo RC	3.00	.90
❑ 186 Jonathan Carter RC	3.00	.90
❑ 187 Jesse Palmer RC	5.00	1.50
❑ 188 LaMont Jordan RC	6.00	1.80
❑ 189 Derek Combs RC	3.00	.90
❑ 190 Marques Tuiasosopo RC	5.00	1.50
❑ 191 Correll Buckhalter RC	6.00	1.80
❑ 192 Freddie Mitchell RC	5.00	1.50
❑ 193 Adam Archuleta RC	5.00	1.50
❑ 194 Francis St.Paul RC	3.00	.90
❑ 195 Drew Brees RC	10.00	3.00
❑ 196 LaDainian Tomlinson RC	15.00	4.50
❑ 197 Kevan Barlow RC	5.00	1.50
❑ 198 Vinny Sutherland RC	3.00	.90
❑ 199 Cedrick Wilson RC	5.00	1.50
❑ 200 Alex Bannister RC	3.00	.90
❑ 201 Koren Robinson RC	6.00	1.80
❑ 202 Milton Wynn RC	3.00	.90
❑ 203 Dan Alexander RC	5.00	1.50
❑ 204 Eddie Berlin RC	3.00	.90
❑ 205 Justin McCareins RC	5.00	1.50
❑ 206 Rod Gardner RC	5.00	1.50
❑ 207 Damerien McCants RC	3.00	.90
❑ 208 Sage Rosenfels RC	5.00	1.50
❑ 209 Nick Goings RC	5.00	1.50
❑ 210 Josh Booty RC	5.00	1.50
❑ 211 Benjamin Gay RC	5.00	1.50
❑ 212 Gerard Warren RC	5.00	1.50
❑ 213 Jamal Reynolds RC	5.00	1.50
❑ 214 Will Allen RC	3.00	.90
❑ 215 Santana Moss RC	8.00	2.40
❑ 216 Andre Carter RC	5.00	1.50

2002 Titanium

	Nm-Mt	Ex-Mt
COMP.SET w/o SP's (100)	60.00	18.00
❑ 1 David Boston	1.50	.45
❑ 2 Thomas Jones	1.00	.30
❑ 3 Jake Plummer	1.00	.30
❑ 4 Warrick Dunn	1.50	.45
❑ 5 Shawn Jefferson	.60	.18
❑ 6 Michael Vick	5.00	1.50
❑ 7 Jamal Lewis	1.50	.45
❑ 8 Chris Redman	.60	.18
❑ 9 Travis Taylor	1.00	.30
❑ 10 Drew Bledsoe	2.00	.60
❑ 11 Travis Henry	1.50	.45
❑ 12 Eric Moulds	1.00	.30
❑ 13 Peerless Price	1.00	.30
❑ 14 Muhsin Muhammad	1.00	.30
❑ 15 Rodney Peete	1.00	.30
❑ 16 Lamar Smith	1.00	.30
❑ 17 Chris Weinke	1.00	.30
❑ 18 Marty Booker	1.00	.30
❑ 19 Jim Miller	1.00	.30
❑ 20 Anthony Thomas	1.50	.45
❑ 21 Corey Dillon	1.00	.30
❑ 22 Gus Frerotte	.60	.18
❑ 23 Peter Warrick	1.00	.30
❑ 24 Tim Couch	1.00	.30
❑ 25 Kevin Johnson	1.00	.30
❑ 26 Jamel White	.60	.18
❑ 27 Quincy Carter	1.00	.30
❑ 28 Joey Galloway	1.00	.30
❑ 29 Emmitt Smith	4.00	1.20
❑ 30 Olandis Gary	1.00	.30
❑ 31 Brian Griese	1.50	.45
❑ 32 Ed McCaffrey	1.50	.45
❑ 33 Rod Smith	1.00	.30
❑ 34 Mike McMahon	1.50	.45
❑ 35 Bill Schroeder	1.00	.30
❑ 36 James Stewart	1.00	.30
❑ 37 Brett Favre	4.00	1.20
❑ 38 Terry Glenn	1.00	.30
❑ 39 Ahman Green	1.50	.45
❑ 40 James Allen	1.00	.30
❑ 41 Corey Bradford	.60	.18
❑ 42 Jermaine Lewis	.60	.18
❑ 43 Marvin Harrison	1.50	.45
❑ 44 Edgerrin James	2.00	.60
❑ 45 Peyton Manning	3.00	.90
❑ 46 Mark Brunell	1.50	.45
❑ 47 Jimmy Smith	1.00	.30
❑ 48 Fred Taylor	1.50	.45
❑ 49 Tony Gonzalez	1.00	.30
❑ 50 Trent Green	1.00	.30
❑ 51 Priest Holmes	2.00	.60
❑ 52 Chris Chambers	1.50	.45
❑ 53 Jay Fiedler	1.00	.30
❑ 54 Ricky Williams	1.50	.45
❑ 55 Michael Bennett	1.00	.30
❑ 56 Daunte Culpepper	1.50	.45
❑ 57 Randy Moss	3.00	.90
❑ 58 Tom Brady	4.00	1.20
❑ 59 Troy Brown	1.00	.30
❑ 60 Antowain Smith	1.00	.30
❑ 61 Aaron Brooks	1.50	.45
❑ 62 Joe Horn	1.00	.30
❑ 63 Deuce McAllister	2.00	.60
❑ 64 Tiki Barber	1.00	.30
❑ 65 Kerry Collins	1.00	.30
❑ 66 Amani Toomer	1.00	.30
❑ 67 Laveranues Coles	1.00	.30
❑ 68 Curtis Martin	1.50	.45
❑ 69 Vinny Testaverde	1.00	.30
❑ 70 Tim Brown	1.50	.45
❑ 71 Rich Gannon	1.50	.45
❑ 72 Jerry Rice	3.00	.90
❑ 73 Donovan McNabb	2.00	.60
❑ 74 Duce Staley	1.50	.45
❑ 75 James Thrash	1.00	.30
❑ 76 Jerome Bettis	1.50	.45
❑ 77 Kordell Stewart	1.00	.30
❑ 78 Hines Ward	1.50	.45
❑ 79 Isaac Bruce	1.50	.45
❑ 80 Marshall Faulk	1.50	.45
❑ 81 Torry Holt	1.50	.45
❑ 82 Kurt Warner	1.50	.45
❑ 83 Drew Brees	1.50	.45
❑ 84 LaDainian Tomlinson	2.50	.75
❑ 85 Jeff Garcia	1.50	.45
❑ 86 Garrison Hearst	1.00	.30
❑ 87 Terrell Owens	1.50	.45
❑ 88 Shaun Alexander	1.50	.45
❑ 89 Trent Dilfer	1.00	.30
❑ 90 Koren Robinson	1.00	.30
❑ 91 Brad Johnson	1.00	.30
❑ 92 Keyshawn Johnson	1.50	.45
❑ 93 Keenan McCardell	.60	.18
❑ 94 Eddie George	1.50	.45
❑ 95 Derrick Mason	1.00	.30
❑ 96 Steve McNair	1.50	.45
❑ 97 Stephen Davis	1.00	.30
❑ 98 Rod Gardner	1.00	.30
❑ 99 Shane Matthews	.60	.18
❑ 100 Derrius Thompson	.60	.18
❑ 101 Freddie Jones JSY Jason McAddley RC	8.00	2.40
❑ 102 Jake Plummer JSY Josh McCown RC	15.00	4.50
❑ 103 Kyle Vanden Bosch JSY Wendell Bryant RC	15.00	4.50
❑ 104 Thomas Jones JSY Chester Taylor RC	12.00	3.60
❑ 105 Bryan Gilmore JSY Tim Carter RC	10.00	3.00
❑ 106 Michael Vick JSY Kurt Kittner RC	25.00	7.50
❑ 107 Brandon Stokley JSY Ron Johnson RC	10.00	3.00
❑ 108 Chris Redman JSY Javin Hunter RC	8.00	2.40
❑ 109 Peerless Price JSY Josh Reed RC	12.00	3.60
❑ 110 Isaac Byrd JSY Julius Peppers RC	20.00	6.00
❑ 111 Dez White JSY Jamin Elliott RC	8.00	2.40
❑ 112 Rabih Abdullah JSY Adrian Peterson RC	8.00	2.40
❑ 113 Brian Urlacher JSY Napoleon Harris RC	15.00	4.50
❑ 114 Michael Westbrook JSY Lamont Thompson RC	10.00	3.00
❑ 115 Corey Dillon JSY T.J. Duckett RC	15.00	4.50
❑ 116 Takeo Spikes JSY Roy Williams RC	12.00	3.60
❑ 117 Akili Smith JSY Craig Nall RC	12.00	3.60
❑ 118 Tim Couch JSY André Davis RC	12.00	3.60
❑ 119 Jamel White JSY Tellis Redmon RC	8.00	2.40
❑ 120 Quincy Carter JSY Chad Hutchinson RC	15.00	4.50
❑ 121 Troy Hambrick JSY Antonio Bryant RC	15.00	4.50
❑ 122 Emmitt Smith JSY William Green RC	15.00	4.50
❑ 123 La'Roi Glover JSY John Henderson RC	12.00	3.60
❑ 124 Deltha O'Neal JSY Mike Rumph RC	8.00	2.40
❑ 125 Larry Foster JSY Eddie Drummond RC	10.00	3.00
❑ 126 Ahman Green JSY Najeh Davenport RC	20.00	6.00
❑ 127 Donald Driver JSY Javon Walker RC	20.00	6.00
❑ 128 Brett Favre JSY David Carr RC	30.00	9.00
❑ 129 James Allen JSY Jonathan Wells RC	8.00	2.40
❑ 130 Jermaine Lewis JSY Jabar Gaffney RC	10.00	3.00
❑ 131 Edgerrin James JSY Ricky Williams RC	12.00	3.60
❑ 132 Peyton Manning JSY Dwight Freeney RC	15.00	4.50
❑ 133 Mark Brunell JSY David Garrard RC	8.00	2.40
❑ 134 Jimmy Smith JSY Marquise Walker RC	8.00	2.40
❑ 135 Curtis Jackson JSY Marc Boerigter RC	25.00	7.50
❑ 136 Tony Richardson JSY Omar Easy RC	8.00	2.40
❑ 137 Desmond Clark JSY Randy McMichael RC	15.00	4.50
❑ 138 Zach Thomas JSY Robert Thomas RC	8.00	2.40

	ExMt	VG
❑ 139 Chris Walsh JSY	10.00	3.00
Shaun Hill RC		
❑ 140 Daunte Culpepper JSY	12.00	3.60
Randy Fasani RC		
❑ 141 Jim Kleinsasser JSY	12.00	3.60
Jarrod Baxter RC		
❑ 142 Randy Moss JSY	15.00	4.50
Donte Stallworth RC		
❑ 143 Corey Chavous JSY	8.00	2.40
Phillip Buchanon RC		
❑ 144 Christian Fauria JSY	8.00	2.40
Daniel Graham RC		
❑ 145 Damon Huard JSY	12.00	3.60
Rohan Davey RC		
❑ 146 Donald Hayes JSY	20.00	6.00
Deion Branch RC		
❑ 147 Terrelle Smith JSY	8.00	2.40
J.T. O'Sullivan RC		
❑ 148 Jonathan Carter JSY	8.00	2.40
Daryl Jones RC		
❑ 149 Ron Dayne JSY	20.00	6.00
Jeremy Shockey RC		
❑ 150 Anthony Becht JSY	8.00	2.40
Bryan Thomas RC		
❑ 151 Curtis Martin JSY	10.00	3.00
Dameon Hunter RC		
❑ 152 Jerry Rice JSY	20.00	6.00
Ashley Lelie RC		
❑ 153 Jon Ritchie JSY/1100	8.00	2.40
Ed Stansbury RC		
❑ 154 Cecil Martin JSY	10.00	3.00
Freddie Milons RC		
❑ 155 Donovan McNabb JSY	12.00	3.60
Lito Sheppard RC		
❑ 156 James Thrash JSY	15.00	4.50
Brian Westbrook RC		
❑ 157 Jerome Bettis JSY	8.00	2.40
Verron Haynes RC		
❑ 158 Kordell Stewart JSY	2.00	.60
Antwaan Randle El RC		
❑ 159 Marshall Faulk JSY	12.00	3.60
Lamar Gordon RC		
❑ 160 Kurt Warner JSY	20.00	6.00
Joey Harrington RC		
❑ 161 Drew Brees JSY	12.00	3.60
Quentin Jammer RC		
❑ 162 Fred McCrary JSY	8.00	2.40
Seth Burford RC		
❑ 163 Stephen Alexander JSY	8.00	2.40
Reche Caldwell RC		
❑ 164 LaDainian Tomlinson JSY	20.00	6.00
Clinton Portis RC		
❑ 165 Jeff Garcia JSY	12.00	3.60
Brandon Doman RC		
❑ 166 Paul Smith JSY	8.00	2.40
Lee Mays RC		
❑ 167 Shaun Alexander JSY	10.00	3.00
Maurice Morris RC		
❑ 168 Michael Pittman JSY	10.00	3.00
Travis Stephens RC		
❑ 169 Ken Dilger JSY	8.00	2.40
Jerramy Stevens RC		
❑ 170 Erron Kinney JSY	8.00	2.40
John Simon RC		
❑ 171 Steve McNair JSY	12.00	3.60
Albert Haynesworth RC		
❑ 172 Eddie George JSY	10.00	3.00
DeShaun Foster RC		
❑ 173 Jacquez Green JSY		
Ladell Betts RC		
❑ 174 Rod Gardner JSY	8.00	2.40
Cliff Russell RC		
❑ 175 Shane Matthews JSY	12.00	3.60
Patrick Ramsey RC		

1950 Topps Felt Backs

	ExMt	VG
COMPLETE SET (100)	7500.00	3400.00
WRAPPER (1-CENT)	500.00	220.00
❑ 1 Lou Allen	60.00	27.00

	ExMt	VG
❑ 2 Morris Bailey	60.00	27.00
❑ 3 George Bell	60.00	27.00
❑ 4 Lindy Berry HOR	60.00	27.00
❑ 5A Mike Boldin Brown	60.00	27.00
❑ 5B Mike Boldin Yellow	80.00	36.00
❑ 6A Bernie Botula Brown	60.00	27.00
❑ 6B Bernie Botula Yellow	80.00	36.00
❑ 7 Bob Bowlby	60.00	27.00
❑ 8 Bob Bucher	60.00	27.00
❑ 9A Al Burnett Brown	60.00	27.00
❑ 9B Al Burnett Yellow	80.00	36.00
❑ 10 Don Burson	60.00	27.00
❑ 11 Paul Campbell	60.00	27.00
❑ 12 Herb Carey	60.00	27.00
❑ 13A Bimbo Cecconi Brown	60.00	27.00
❑ 13B Bimbo Cecconi Yellow	80.00	36.00
❑ 14 Bill Chauncey	60.00	27.00
❑ 15 Dick Clark	60.00	27.00
❑ 16 Tom Coleman	60.00	27.00
❑ 17 Billy Conn	60.00	27.00
❑ 18 John Cox	60.00	27.00
❑ 19 Lou Creekmur RC	150.00	70.00
❑ 20 Richard Glen Davis RC	75.00	34.00
❑ 21 Warren Davis	60.00	27.00
❑ 22 Bob Deuber	60.00	27.00
❑ 23 Ray Dooney	60.00	27.00
❑ 24 Tom Dublinski	75.00	34.00
❑ 25 Jeff Fleischman	60.00	27.00
❑ 26 Jack Friedland	60.00	27.00
❑ 27 Bob Fuchs	60.00	27.00
❑ 28 Arnold Galiffa RC	75.00	34.00
❑ 29 Dick Gilman	60.00	27.00
❑ 30A Frank Gitschier Brown	60.00	27.00
❑ 30B Frank Gitschier Yellow	80.00	36.00
❑ 31 Gene Glick	60.00	27.00
❑ 32 Bill Gregus	60.00	27.00
❑ 33 Harold Hagan	60.00	27.00
❑ 34 Charles Hall	60.00	27.00
❑ 35A Leon Hart Brown	125.00	55.00
❑ 35B Leon Hart Yellow	175.00	80.00
❑ 36A Bob Hester Brown	60.00	27.00
❑ 36B Bob Hester Yellow	80.00	36.00
❑ 37 George Hughes	60.00	27.00
❑ 38 Levi Jackson	75.00	34.00
❑ 39A Jackie Jensen Brown	200.00	90.00
❑ 39B Jackie Jensen Yellow	300.00	135.00
❑ 40 Charlie Justice	150.00	70.00
❑ 41 Gary Kerkorian	60.00	27.00
❑ 42 Bernie Krueger	60.00	27.00
❑ 43 Bill Kuhn	60.00	27.00
❑ 44 Dean Laun	60.00	27.00
❑ 45 Chet Leach	60.00	27.00
❑ 46A Bobby Lee Brown	60.00	27.00
❑ 46B Bobby Lee Yellow	80.00	36.00
❑ 47 Roger Lehew	60.00	27.00
❑ 48 Glenn Lippman	60.00	27.00
❑ 49 Melvin Lyle	60.00	27.00
❑ 50 Len Makowski	60.00	27.00
❑ 51A Al Malekoff Brown	60.00	27.00
❑ 51B Al Malekoff Yellow	80.00	36.00
❑ 52A Jim Martin Brown	75.00	34.00
❑ 52B Jim Martin Yellow	100.00	45.00
❑ 53 Frank Mataya	60.00	27.00
❑ 54A Ray Mathews Brown RC	75.00	34.00
❑ 54B Ray Mathews Yellow RC	100.00	45.00
❑ 55A Dick McKissack Brown	60.00	27.00
❑ 55B Dick McKissack Yellow	80.00	36.00
❑ 56 Frank Miller	60.00	27.00
❑ 57A John Miller Brown	60.00	27.00
❑ 57B John Miller Yellow	80.00	36.00
❑ 58 Ed Modzelewski RC	75.00	34.00
❑ 59 Don Mouser	60.00	27.00
❑ 60 James Murphy	60.00	27.00
❑ 61A Ray Nagle Brown	60.00	27.00
❑ 61B Ray Nagle Yellow	80.00	36.00
❑ 62 Leo Nomellini	250.00	110.00
❑ 63 James O'Day	60.00	27.00
❑ 64 Joe Paterno RC	1800.00	800.00
❑ 65 Andy Pavich	60.00	27.00
❑ 66A Pete Perini Brown	60.00	27.00
❑ 66B Pete Perini Yellow	80.00	36.00
❑ 67 Jim Powers	60.00	27.00
❑ 68 Dave Rakestraw	60.00	27.00
❑ 69 Herb Rich	60.00	27.00
❑ 70 Fran Rogel RC	60.00	27.00
❑ 71A Darrell Royal Brown RC	300.00	110.00
❑ 71B Darrell Royal Yellow RC	400.00	180.00
❑ 72 Steve Sawle	60.00	27.00
❑ 73 Nick Sebek	60.00	27.00
❑ 74 Herb Seidell	60.00	27.00
❑ 75A Charles Shaw Brown	60.00	27.00
❑ 75B Charles Shaw Yellow	80.00	36.00
❑ 76A Emil Sitko Brown RC	75.00	34.00
❑ 76B Emil Sitko Yellow RC	100.00	45.00
❑ 77 Ed(Butch) Songin RC	75.00	34.00
❑ 78A Mariano Stalloni Brown	60.00	27.00
❑ 78B Mariano Stalloni Yellow	80.00	36.00
❑ 79 Ernie Stautner RC	250.00	110.00
❑ 80 Don Stehley	60.00	27.00
❑ 81 Gil Stevenson	60.00	27.00
❑ 82 Bishop Strickland	60.00	27.00
❑ 83 Harry Szulborski	60.00	27.00
❑ 84A Wally Teninga Brown	60.00	27.00
❑ 84B Wally Teninga Yellow	80.00	36.00
❑ 85 Clayton Tonnemaker	60.00	27.00
❑ 86A Deacon Dan Towler RC Brown	150.00	70.00
❑ 86B Deacon Dan Towler RC Yellow	250.00	110.00
❑ 87A Bert Turek Brown	60.00	27.00
❑ 87B Bert Turek Yellow	80.00	36.00
❑ 88 Harry Ulinski	60.00	27.00
❑ 89 Leon Van Billingham	60.00	27.00
❑ 90 Langdon Viracola	60.00	27.00
❑ 91 Leo Wagner	60.00	27.00
❑ 92A Doak Walker Brown	350.00	135.00
❑ 92B Doak Walker Yellow	500.00	200.00
❑ 93 Jim Ward	60.00	27.00
❑ 94 Art Weiner	60.00	27.00
❑ 95 Dick Weiss	60.00	27.00
❑ 96 Froggie Williams	60.00	27.00
❑ 97 Robert Red Wilson	60.00	27.00
❑ 98 Roger Red Wilson	60.00	27.00
❑ 99 Carl Wren	60.00	27.00
❑ 100A Pete Zinaich Brown	60.00	27.00
❑ 100B Pete Zinaich Yellow	80.00	36.00

1951 Topps Magic

	ExMt	VgEx
COMPLETE SET (75)	1100.00	500.00
*BACK UNSCRATCHED: 1.5X TO 2.5X		
WRAPPER (1-CENT)	200.00	90.00
WRAPPER (5-CENT)	300.00	135.00
❑ 1 Jimmy Monahan RC	30.00	13.50
❑ 2 Bill Wade RC	50.00	22.00
❑ 3 Bill Reichardt	18.00	8.00
❑ 4 Babe Parilli RC	50.00	22.00
❑ 5 Billie Burkhalter	18.00	8.00
❑ 6 Ed Weber	18.00	8.00
❑ 7 Tom Scott	25.00	11.00
❑ 8 Frank Guthridge	18.00	8.00
❑ 9 John Karras	18.00	8.00
❑ 10 Vic Janowicz RC	150.00	70.00
❑ 11 Lloyd Hill	18.00	8.00
❑ 12 Jim Weatherall RC	25.00	11.00
❑ 13 Howard Hansen	18.00	8.00
❑ 14 Lou D'Achille	18.00	8.00
❑ 15 Johnny Turco	18.00	8.00
❑ 16 Jerrell Price	18.00	8.00
❑ 17 John Coatta	18.00	8.00
❑ 18 Bruce Patton	18.00	8.00
❑ 19 Marion Campbell RC	35.00	16.00
❑ 20 Blaine Earon	18.00	8.00
❑ 21 Dewey McConnell	18.00	8.00
❑ 22 Ray Beck	18.00	8.00
❑ 23 Jim Prewett	18.00	8.00
❑ 24 Bob Steele	18.00	8.00
❑ 25 Art Betts	18.00	8.00
❑ 26 Walt Trillhaase	18.00	8.00
❑ 27 Gil Bartosh	18.00	8.00
❑ 28 Bob Bestwick	18.00	8.00
❑ 29 Tom Rushing	18.00	8.00
❑ 30 Bert Rechichar RC	35.00	16.00
❑ 31 Bill Owens	18.00	8.00
❑ 32 Mike Goggins	18.00	8.00
❑ 33 John Petitbon	18.00	8.00
❑ 34 Byron Townsend	18.00	8.00
❑ 35 Ed Rotticci	18.00	8.00
❑ 36 Steve Wadiak	18.00	8.00
❑ 37 Bobby Marlow RC	25.00	11.00
❑ 38 Bill Fuchs	18.00	8.00
❑ 39 Ralph Staub	18.00	8.00
❑ 40 Bill Vesprini	18.00	8.00
❑ 41 Zack Jordan	18.00	8.00
❑ 42 Bob Smith RC	25.00	11.00
❑ 43 Charles Hanson	18.00	8.00
❑ 44 Glenn Smith	18.00	8.00
❑ 45 Armand Kitto	18.00	8.00
❑ 46 Vinnie Drake	18.00	8.00
❑ 47 Bill Putich RC	18.00	8.00
❑ 48 George Young RC	40.00	18.00
❑ 49 Don McRae	18.00	8.00
❑ 50 Frank Smith RC	18.00	8.00
❑ 51 Dick Hightower	18.00	8.00
❑ 52 Clyde Pickard	18.00	8.00
❑ 53 Bob Reynolds	25.00	11.00
❑ 54 Dick Gregory	18.00	8.00
❑ 55 Dale Samuels	18.00	8.00
❑ 56 Gale Galloway	18.00	8.00
❑ 57 Vic Pujo	18.00	8.00
❑ 58 Dave Waters	18.00	8.00
❑ 59 Joe Ernest	18.00	8.00
❑ 60 Elmer Costa	18.00	8.00
❑ 61 Nick Liotta	18.00	8.00
❑ 62 John Dottley	18.00	8.00
❑ 63 Hi Faubion	18.00	8.00
❑ 64 David Harr	18.00	8.00
❑ 65 Bill Matthews	18.00	8.00
❑ 66 Carroll McDonald	18.00	8.00
❑ 67 Dick Dewing	18.00	8.00
❑ 68 Joe Johnson	18.00	8.00
❑ 69 Arnold Burwitz	18.00	8.00
❑ 70 Ed Dobrowolski	18.00	8.00
❑ 71 Joe Dudeck	18.00	8.00
❑ 72 Johnny Bright RC	25.00	11.00
❑ 73 Harold Loehlein	18.00	8.00
❑ 74 Lawrence Hairston	18.00	8.00
❑ 75 Bob Carey RC	25.00	11.00

1955 Topps All-American

	NM	Ex
COMPLETE SET (100)	3800.00	1700.00
WRAPPER (1-CENT)	300.00	135.00
WRAPPER (5-CENT)	250.00	110.00
❑ 1 Herman Hickman RC	125.00	31.00
❑ 2 John Kimbrough	18.00	8.00
❑ 3 Ed Weir	18.00	8.00
❑ 4 Erny Pinckert	18.00	8.00
❑ 5 Bobby Grayson	18.00	8.00
❑ 6 Nile Kinnick RC UER Spelled Niles	125.00	55.00
❑ 7 Andy Bershak	18.00	8.00
❑ 8 George Cafego RC	18.00	8.00
❑ 9 Tom Hamilton SP	30.00	13.50
❑ 10 Bill Dudley	40.00	18.00
❑ 11 Bobby Dodd SP	30.00	13.50
❑ 12 Otto Graham	175.00	80.00
❑ 13 Aaron Rosenberg	18.00	8.00
❑ 14A Gaynell Tinsley RC ERR (with Whizzer White bio)	100.00	45.00
❑ 14B Gaynell Tinsley RC COR (correct bio)	25.00	11.00
❑ 15 Ed Kaw SP	30.00	13.50
❑ 16 Knute Rockne	275.00	125.00
❑ 17 Bob Reynolds	18.00	8.00
❑ 18 Pudge Heffelfinger RC SP	40.00	18.00
❑ 19 Bruce Smith	35.00	16.00
❑ 20 Sammy Baugh	200.00	90.00
❑ 21A W.White RC SP ERR with Gaynell Tinsley bio	250.00	110.00
❑ 21B W.White RC SP COR correct bio	100.00	45.00
❑ 22 Brick Muller	18.00	8.00
❑ 23 Dick Kazmaier RC	18.00	8.00
❑ 24 Ken Strong	50.00	22.00
❑ 25 Casimir Myslinski SP	30.00	13.50
❑ 26 Larry Kelley RC SP	40.00	18.00
❑ 27 Red Grange UER Card says he was QB should say halfback	300.00	135.00
❑ 28 Mel Hein RC SP	75.00	34.00
❑ 29 Leo Nomellini SP	100.00	45.00
❑ 30 Wes Fesler	18.00	8.00
❑ 31 George Sauer Sr. RC	25.00	11.00
❑ 32 Hank Foldberg	18.00	8.00
❑ 33 Bob Higgins	18.00	8.00
❑ 34 Davey O'Brien RC	50.00	22.00
❑ 35 Tom Harmon RC SP	100.00	45.00
❑ 36 Turk Edwards SP	60.00	27.00
❑ 37 Jim Thorpe	400.00	180.00
❑ 38 Amos A. Stagg RC	75.00	34.00
❑ 39 Jerome Holland RC	25.00	11.00
❑ 40 Donn Moomaw	18.00	8.00
❑ 41 Joseph Alexander SP	30.00	13.50
❑ 42 Eddie Tryon RC SP	40.00	18.00
❑ 43 George Savitsky	18.00	8.00
❑ 44 Ed Garbisch	18.00	8.00
❑ 45 Elmer Oliphant	18.00	8.00
❑ 46 Arnold Lassman	18.00	8.00
❑ 47 Bo McMillin RC	25.00	11.00
❑ 48 Ed Widseth	18.00	8.00
❑ 49 Don Zimmerman	18.00	8.00
❑ 50 Ken Kavanaugh	25.00	11.00
❑ 51 Duane Purvis SP	30.00	13.50
❑ 52 John Lujack	90.00	40.00
❑ 53 John F. Green	18.00	8.00
❑ 54 Edwin Dooley SP	30.00	13.50
❑ 55 Frank Merritt SP	30.00	13.50
❑ 56 Ernie Nevers RC	125.00	55.00
❑ 57 Vic Hanson SP	30.00	13.50
❑ 58 Ed Franco	18.00	8.00
❑ 59 Doc Blanchard RC	50.00	22.00
❑ 60 Dan Hill	18.00	8.00
❑ 61 Charles Brickley SP	30.00	13.50
❑ 62 Harry Newman	18.00	8.00
❑ 63 Charlie Justice	35.00	16.00
❑ 64 Benny Friedman RC	30.00	11.00
❑ 65 Joe Donchess SP	30.00	13.50
❑ 66 Bruiser Kinard RC	35.00	16.00
❑ 67 Frankie Albert	25.00	11.00
❑ 68 Four Horsemen RC SP Jim Crowley Elmer Layden Don Miller Harry Stuhldreher	500.00	220.00
❑ 69 Frank Sinkwich RC	25.00	11.00
❑ 70 Bill Daddio	18.00	8.00
❑ 71 Bobby Wilson	18.00	8.00
❑ 72 Chub Peabody	18.00	8.00
❑ 73 Paul Governali	25.00	11.00
❑ 74 Gene McEver	18.00	8.00
❑ 75 Hugh Gallarneau	18.00	8.00
❑ 76 Angelo Bertelli RC	25.00	11.00
❑ 77 Bowden Wyatt SP	30.00	13.50
❑ 78 Jay Berwanger RC	35.00	16.00
❑ 79 Pug Lund	18.00	8.00
❑ 80 Bennie Oosterbaan	18.00	8.00
❑ 81 Cotton Warburton	18.00	8.00
❑ 82 Alex Wojciechowicz	35.00	16.00
❑ 83 Ted Coy SP	30.00	13.50
❑ 84 Ace Parker RC SP	50.00	22.00
❑ 85 Sid Luckman	150.00	70.00
❑ 86 Albie Booth SP	30.00	13.50
❑ 87 Adolph Schultz SP	30.00	13.50
❑ 88 Ralph Kercheval	18.00	8.00
❑ 89 Marshall Goldberg	25.00	11.00
❑ 90 Charlie O'Rourke	18.00	8.00
❑ 91 Bob Odell UER Photo actually Howard Odell	18.00	8.00
❑ 92 Biggie Munn	18.00	8.00
❑ 93 Willie Heston SP	40.00	18.00
❑ 94 Joe Bernard SP	40.00	18.00
❑ 95 Chris(Red) Cagle SP	40.00	18.00
❑ 96 Bill Hollenback SP	40.00	18.00
❑ 97 Don Hutson RC SP	225.00	100.00
❑ 98 Beattie Feathers SP	100.00	45.00
❑ 99 Don Whitmire SP	40.00	18.00
❑ 100 Fats Henry SP RC	200.00	50.00

1956 Topps

	NM	Ex
COMPLETE SET (120)	1800.00	800.00
WRAPPER (1-CENT)	250.00	110.00
WRAPPER (5-CENT)	50.00	22.00
❑ 1 Johnny Carson SP	80.00	20.00

❑ 2 Gordy Soltau	6.00	2.70
❑ 3 Frank Varrichione	6.00	2.70
❑ 4 Eddie Bell	6.00	2.70
❑ 5 Alex Webster RC	12.00	5.50
❑ 6 Norm Van Brocklin	30.00	13.50
❑ 7 Green Bay Packers Team Card	25.00	11.00
❑ 8 Lou Creekmur	15.00	6.75
❑ 9 Lou Groza	25.00	11.00
❑ 10 Tom Bienemann SP	25.00	11.00
❑ 11 George Blanda	50.00	22.00
❑ 12 Alan Ameche	12.00	5.50
❑ 13 Vic Janowicz SP	45.00	20.00
❑ 14 Dick Moegle	8.00	3.60
❑ 15 Fran Rogel	6.00	2.70
❑ 16 Harold Giancanelli	6.00	2.70
❑ 17 Emlen Tunnell	15.00	6.75
❑ 18 Tank Younger	12.00	5.50
❑ 19 Billy Howton	8.00	3.60
❑ 20 Jack Christiansen	15.00	6.75
❑ 21 Darrel Brewster	6.00	2.70
❑ 22 Chicago Cardinals SP Team Card	100.00	45.00
❑ 23 Ed Brown	8.00	3.60
❑ 24 Joe Campanella	6.00	2.70
❑ 25 Leon Heath SP	22.00	10.00
❑ 26 San Francisco 49ers Team Card	18.00	8.00
❑ 27 Dick Flanagan	6.00	2.70
❑ 28 Chuck Bednarik	25.00	11.00
❑ 29 Kyle Rote	12.00	5.50
❑ 30 Les Richter	8.00	3.60
❑ 31 Howard Ferguson	6.00	2.70
❑ 32 Dorne Dibble	6.00	2.70
❑ 33 Kenny Konz	6.00	2.70
❑ 34 Dave Mann SP	25.00	11.00
❑ 35 Rick Casares	12.00	5.50
❑ 36 Art Donovan	30.00	13.50
❑ 37 Chuck Drazenovich SP	22.00	10.00
❑ 38 Joe Arenas	6.00	2.70
❑ 39 Lynn Chandnois	6.00	2.70
❑ 40 Philadelphia Eagles Team Card	18.00	8.00
❑ 41 Roosevelt Brown RC	35.00	16.00
❑ 42 Tom Fears	25.00	11.00
❑ 43 Gary Knafelc	6.00	2.70
❑ 44 Joe Schmidt RC	50.00	20.00
❑ 45 Cleveland Browns Team Card UER (Card back does not credit the Browns with being Champs in 1955)	18.00	8.00
❑ 46 Len Teeuws RC SP	25.00	11.00
❑ 47 Bill George RC	30.00	13.50
❑ 48 Baltimore Colts Team Card	18.00	8.00
❑ 49 Eddie LeBaron SP	45.00	20.00
❑ 50 Hugh McElhenny	30.00	13.50
❑ 51 Ted Marchibroda	12.00	5.50
❑ 52 Adrian Burk	6.00	2.70
❑ 53 Frank Gifford	60.00	34.00
❑ 54 Charley Toogood	6.00	2.70
❑ 55 Tobin Rote	8.00	3.60
❑ 56 Bill Stits	6.00	2.70
❑ 57 Don Colo	6.00	2.70
❑ 58 Ollie Matson SP	75.00	34.00
❑ 59 Harlon Hill	8.00	3.60
❑ 60 Lenny Moore RC !	90.00	40.00
❑ 61 Washington Redskins SP Team Card	90.00	40.00
❑ 62 Billy Wilson	6.00	2.70
❑ 63 Pittsburgh Steelers Team Card	18.00	8.00
❑ 64 Bob Pellegrini	6.00	2.70
❑ 65 Ken MacAfee	6.00	2.70
❑ 66 Willard Sherman	6.00	2.70
❑ 67 Roger Zatkoff	6.00	2.70
❑ 68 Dave Middleton	6.00	2.70
❑ 69 Ray Renfro	8.00	3.60
❑ 70 Don Stonesifer SP	25.00	11.00
❑ 71 Stan Jones RC	30.00	13.50
❑ 72 Jim Mutscheller	6.00	2.70
❑ 73 Volney Peters SP	22.00	10.00
❑ 74 Leo Nomellini	20.00	9.00
❑ 75 Ray Mathews	6.00	2.70
❑ 76 Dick Bielski	6.00	2.70
❑ 77 Charley Conerly	25.00	11.00
❑ 78 Elroy Hirsch	30.00	13.50
❑ 79 Bill Forester RC	8.00	3.60
❑ 80 Jim Doran	6.00	2.70
❑ 81 Fred Morrison	6.00	2.70
❑ 82 Jack Simmons SP	25.00	11.00
❑ 83 Bill McColl	6.00	2.70
❑ 84 Bert Rechichar	6.00	2.70
❑ 85 Joe Scudero SP	22.00	10.00
❑ 86 Y.A. Tittle UER (misspelled Yelverton on back)	50.00	22.00
❑ 87 Ernie Stautner	20.00	9.00
❑ 88 Norm Willey	6.00	2.70
❑ 89 Bob Schnelker	6.00	2.70
❑ 90 Dan Towler	12.00	5.50
❑ 91 John Martinkovic	6.00	2.70
❑ 92 Detroit Lions Team Card	18.00	8.00
❑ 93 George Ratterman	8.00	3.60
❑ 94 Chuck Ulrich SP	25.00	11.00
❑ 95 Bobby Watkins	6.00	2.70
❑ 96 Buddy Young	12.00	5.50
❑ 97 Billy Wells SP	22.00	10.00
❑ 98 Bob Toneff	6.00	2.70
❑ 99 Bill McPeak	6.00	2.70
❑ 100 Bobby Thomason	6.00	2.70
❑ 101 Roosevelt Grier RC	40.00	18.00
❑ 102 Ron Waller	6.00	2.70
❑ 103 Bobby Dillon	6.00	2.70
❑ 104 Leon Hart	12.00	5.50
❑ 105 Mike McCormack	15.00	6.75
❑ 106 John Olszewski SP	25.00	11.00
❑ 107 Bill Wightkin	6.00	2.70
❑ 108 George Shaw RC	8.00	3.60
❑ 109 Dale Atkeson SP	22.00	10.00
❑ 110 Joe Perry	25.00	11.00
❑ 111 Dale Dodrill	6.00	2.70
❑ 112 Tom Scott	6.00	2.70
❑ 113 New York Giants Team Card	18.00	8.00
❑ 114 Los Angeles Rams Team Card UER (back incorrect, Rams were not 1955 champs)	18.00	8.00
❑ 115 Al Carmichael	6.00	2.70
❑ 116 Bobby Layne	50.00	22.00
❑ 117 Ed Modzelewski	6.00	2.70
❑ 118 Lamar McHan RC SP	25.00	11.00
❑ 119 Chicago Bears Team Card	18.00	8.00
❑ 120 Billy Vessels RC	40.00	10.00
❑ AD1 Advertising Panel Lou Groza Don Colo Darrel Brewster (no player on back)	250.00	110.00
❑ NNO Checklist Card SP (unnumbered)	400.00	100.00
❑ C1 Contest Card Sunday, October 14 Colts vs. Packers Cards vs. Redskins	80.00	36.00
❑ C2 Contest Card Sunday, October 14 Rams vs. Lions Giants vs. Browns	80.00	36.00
❑ C3 Contest Card Sunday, October 14 Eagles vs. Steelers 49ers vs. Bears	80.00	36.00
❑ CA Contest Card Sunday, November 25 Bears vs. Giants Rams vs. Colts	90.00	40.00
❑ CB Contest Card Sunday, November 25 Steelers vs. Cards 49ers vs. Eagles	110.00	50.00

1957 Topps

	NM	Ex
COMPLETE SET (154)	2200.00	1000.00
COMMON CARD (1-88)	4.00	1.80
COMMON CARD (89-154)	10.00	4.50
WRAPPER (1-CENT)	50.00	22.00
WRAPPER (5-CENT)	75.00	34.00
❑ 1 Eddie LeBaron	50.00	12.50
❑ 2 Pete Retzlaff RC	15.00	6.75
❑ 3 Mike McCormack	12.00	5.50
❑ 4 Lou Baldacci	4.00	1.80
❑ 5 Gino Marchetti	20.00	9.00
❑ 6 Leo Nomellini	20.00	9.00
❑ 7 Bobby Watkins	4.00	1.80
❑ 8 Dave Middleton	4.00	1.80
❑ 9 Bobby Dillon	4.00	1.80
❑ 10 Les Richter	6.00	2.70
❑ 11 Roosevelt Brown	20.00	9.00
❑ 12 Lavern Torgeson RC	4.00	1.80
❑ 13 Dick Bielski	4.00	1.80
❑ 14 Pat Summerall	20.00	9.00
❑ 15 Jack Butler RC	10.00	4.50
❑ 16 John Henry Johnson	15.00	6.75
❑ 17 Art Spinney	4.00	1.80
❑ 18 Bob St. Clair	12.00	5.50
❑ 19 Perry Jeter	4.00	1.80
❑ 20 Lou Creekmur	12.00	5.50
❑ 21 Dave Hanner	6.00	2.70
❑ 22 Norm Van Brocklin	30.00	13.50
❑ 23 Don Chandler RC	10.00	4.50
❑ 24 Al Dorow	4.00	1.80
❑ 25 Tom Scott	4.00	1.80
❑ 26 Ollie Matson	20.00	9.00
❑ 27 Fran Rogel	4.00	1.80
❑ 28 Lou Groza	25.00	11.00
❑ 29 Billy Vessels	6.00	2.70
❑ 30 Y.A. Tittle	40.00	18.00
❑ 31 George Blanda	40.00	18.00
❑ 32 Bobby Layne	40.00	18.00
❑ 33 Billy Howton	6.00	2.70
❑ 34 Bill Wade	10.00	4.50
❑ 35 Emlen Tunnell	15.00	6.75
❑ 36 Leo Elter	4.00	1.80
❑ 37 Clarence Peaks RC	6.00	2.70
❑ 38 Don Stonesifer	4.00	1.80
❑ 39 George Tarasovic	4.00	1.80
❑ 40 Darrel Brewster	4.00	1.80
❑ 41 Bert Rechichar	4.00	1.80
❑ 42 Billy Wilson	4.00	1.80
❑ 43 Ed Brown	6.00	2.70
❑ 44 Gene Gedman	4.00	1.80
❑ 45 Gary Knafelc	4.00	1.80
❑ 46 Elroy Hirsch	30.00	13.50
❑ 47 Don Heinrich	6.00	2.70
❑ 48 Gene Brito	4.00	1.80
❑ 49 Chuck Bednarik	25.00	11.00
❑ 50 Dave Mann	4.00	1.80
❑ 51 Bill McPeak	4.00	1.80
❑ 52 Kenny Konz	4.00	1.80
❑ 53 Alan Ameche	10.00	4.50
❑ 54 Gordy Soltau	4.00	1.80

❑ 55 Rick Casares	6.00	2.70
❑ 56 Charlie Ane	4.00	1.80
❑ 57 Al Carmichael	4.00	1.80
❑ 58A Willard Sherman ERR (no team on front)	300.00	135.00
❑ 58B Willard Sherman COR	4.00	1.80
❑ 59 Kyle Rote	10.00	4.50
❑ 60 Chuck Drazenovich	4.00	1.80
❑ 61 Bobby Walston	4.00	1.80
❑ 62 John Olszewski	4.00	1.80
❑ 63 Ray Mathews	4.00	1.80
❑ 64 Maurice Bassett	4.00	1.80
❑ 65 Art Donovan	25.00	11.00
❑ 66 Joe Arenas	4.00	1.80
❑ 67 Harlon Hill	6.00	2.70
❑ 68 Yale Lary	12.00	5.50
❑ 69 Bill Forester	6.00	2.70
❑ 70 Bob Boyd	4.00	1.80
❑ 71 Andy Robustelli	20.00	9.00
❑ 72 Sam Baker RC	6.00	2.70
❑ 73 Bob Pellegrini	4.00	1.80
❑ 74 Leo Sanford	4.00	1.80
❑ 75 Sid Watson	4.00	1.80
❑ 76 Ray Renfro	6.00	2.70
❑ 77 Carl Taseff	4.00	1.80
❑ 78 Clyde Conner	4.00	1.80
❑ 79 J.C. Caroline	4.00	1.80
❑ 80 Howard Cassady RC	15.00	6.75
❑ 81 Tobin Rote	6.00	2.70
❑ 82 Ron Waller	4.00	1.80
❑ 83 Jim Patton RC	6.00	2.70
❑ 84 Volney Peters	4.00	1.80
❑ 85 Dick Lane RC	50.00	22.00
❑ 86 Royce Womble	4.00	1.80
❑ 87 Duane Putnam RC	6.00	2.70
❑ 88 Frank Gifford	60.00	27.00
❑ 89 Steve Meilinger	10.00	4.50
❑ 90 Buck Lansford	10.00	4.50
❑ 91 Lindon Crow DP	8.00	3.60
❑ 92 Ernie Stautner DP	25.00	11.00
❑ 93 Preston Carpenter DP RC	8.00	3.60
❑ 94 Raymond Berry RC	135.00	60.00
❑ 95 Hugh McElhenny	30.00	13.50
❑ 96 Stan Jones	25.00	11.00
❑ 97 Dorne Dibble	10.00	4.50
❑ 98 Joe Scudero DP	8.00	3.60
❑ 99 Eddie Bell	10.00	4.50
❑ 100 Joe Childress DP	8.00	3.60
❑ 101 Elbert Nickel	12.00	5.50
❑ 102 Walt Michaels	12.00	5.50
❑ 103 Jim Mutscheller DP	8.00	3.60
❑ 104 Earl Morrall RC	50.00	22.00
❑ 105 Larry Strickland	10.00	4.50
❑ 106 Jack Christiansen	15.00	6.75
❑ 107 Fred Cone DP	8.00	3.60
❑ 108 Bud McFadin RC	12.00	5.50
❑ 109 Charley Conerly	30.00	13.50
❑ 110 Tom Runnels DP	8.00	3.60
❑ 111 Ken Keller DP	8.00	3.60
❑ 112 James Root	10.00	4.50
❑ 113 Ted Marchibroda DP	10.00	4.50
❑ 114 Don Paul	10.00	4.50
❑ 115 George Shaw	12.00	5.50
❑ 116 Dick Moegle	12.00	5.50
❑ 117 Don Bingham	10.00	4.50
❑ 118 Leon Hart	14.00	6.25
❑ 119 Bart Starr RC	450.00	200.00
❑ 120 Paul Miller DP	8.00	3.60
❑ 121 Alex Webster	12.00	5.50
❑ 122 Ray Wietecha DP	8.00	3.60
❑ 123 Johnny Carson	10.00	4.50
❑ 124 Tommy McDonald DP RC	30.00	11.00
❑ 125 Jerry Tubbs RC	12.00	5.50
❑ 126 Jack Scarbath	10.00	4.50
❑ 127 Ed Modzelewski DP	8.00	3.60
❑ 128 Lenny Moore	50.00	22.00
❑ 129 Joe Perry DP	25.00	11.00
❑ 130 Bill Wightkin	10.00	4.50
❑ 131 Jim Doran	10.00	4.50
❑ 132 Howard Ferguson UER (Name misspelled Furgeson on front)	10.00	4.50
❑ 133 Tom Wilson	10.00	4.50
❑ 134 Dick James	10.00	4.50
❑ 135 Jimmy Harris	10.00	4.50
❑ 136 Chuck Ulrich	10.00	4.50
❑ 137 Lynn Chandnois	10.00	4.50
❑ 138 John Unitas DP RC	450.00	200.00
❑ 139 Jim Ridlon DP	8.00	3.60
❑ 140 Zeke Bratkowski DP	10.00	4.50
❑ 141 Ray Krouse	10.00	4.50
❑ 142 John Martinkovic	10.00	4.50
❑ 143 Jim Cason DP	8.00	3.60
❑ 144 Ken MacAfee	10.00	4.50
❑ 145 Sid Youngelman RC	12.00	5.50
❑ 146 Paul Larson	10.00	4.50
❑ 147 Len Ford	30.00	13.50
❑ 148 Bob Toneff DP	8.00	3.60
❑ 149 Ronnie Knox DP	8.00	3.60
❑ 150 Jim David RC	12.00	5.50
❑ 151 Paul Hornung RC	400.00	180.00
❑ 152 Tank Younger	14.00	6.25
❑ 153 Bill Svoboda DP	8.00	3.60
❑ 154 Fred Morrison	70.00	17.50
❑ AD1 Advertising Panel Al Dorow Harlon Hill Bert Rechichar (Ollie Matson back)	175.00	80.00
❑ AD2 Advertising Panel Bobby Watkins Gino Marchetti Clarence Peaks (Ollie Matson back)	200.00	100.00
❑ NNO1 Checklist Card SP ! (Bazooka back)	750.00	190.00
❑ NNO2 Checklist Card SP ! (Twin Blony back)	750.00	375.00

1958 Topps

	NM	Ex
COMPLETE SET (132)	1250.00	550.00
WRAPPER (1-CENT)	60.00	27.00
WRAPPER (5-CENT)	125.00	55.00
❑ 1 Gene Filipski RC	15.00	3.70
❑ 2 Bobby Layne	35.00	16.00
❑ 3 Joe Schmidt	12.00	5.50
❑ 4 Bill Barnes	4.00	1.80
❑ 5 Milt Plum RC	8.00	3.60
❑ 6 Billy Howton UER (Misspelled Billie on card front)	5.00	2.20
❑ 7 Howard Cassady	5.00	2.20
❑ 8 Jim Dooley	4.00	1.80
❑ 9 Cleveland Browns Team Card	6.00	2.70
❑ 10 Lenny Moore	25.00	11.00
❑ 11 Darrel Brewster	4.00	1.80
❑ 12 Alan Ameche	8.00	3.60
❑ 13 Jim David	4.00	1.80
❑ 14 Jim Mutscheller	4.00	1.80
❑ 15 Andy Robustelli UER (Never played for San Francisco)	10.00	4.50
❑ 16 Gino Marchetti	12.00	5.50
❑ 17 Ray Renfro	5.00	2.20
❑ 18 Yale Lary	8.00	3.60
❑ 19 Gary Glick	4.00	1.80
❑ 20 Jon Arnett RC	8.00	3.60
❑ 21 Bob Boyd	4.00	1.80
❑ 22 John Unitas UER (College: Pittsburgh should be Louisville)	135.00	60.00
❑ 23 Zeke Bratkowski	5.00	2.20
❑ 24 Sid Youngelman UER (Misspelled Youngleman on card back)	4.00	1.80
❑ 25 Leo Elter	4.00	1.80
❑ 26 Kenny Konz	4.00	1.80
❑ 27 Washington Redskins Team Card	6.00	2.70
❑ 28 Carl Brettschneider UER (Misspelled on back as Brettschnieder)	4.00	1.80
❑ 29 Chicago Bears Team Card	6.00	2.70
❑ 30 Alex Webster	5.00	2.20
❑ 31 Al Carmichael	4.00	1.80
❑ 32 Bobby Dillon	4.00	1.80
❑ 33 Steve Meilinger	4.00	1.80
❑ 34 Sam Baker	4.00	1.80
❑ 35 Chuck Bednarik UER (Misspelled Bednarick on card back)	15.00	6.75
❑ 36 Bert Vic Zucco	4.00	1.80
❑ 37 George Tarasovic	4.00	1.80
❑ 38 Bill Wade	8.00	3.60
❑ 39 Dick Stanfel	5.00	2.20
❑ 40 Jerry Norton	4.00	1.80
❑ 41 San Francisco 49ers Team Card	6.00	2.70
❑ 42 Emlen Tunnell	10.00	4.50
❑ 43 Jim Doran	4.00	1.80
❑ 44 Ted Marchibroda	8.00	3.60
❑ 45 Chet Hanulak	4.00	1.80
❑ 46 Dale Dodrill	4.00	1.80
❑ 47 Johnny Carson	4.00	1.80
❑ 48 Dick Deschaine	4.00	1.80
❑ 49 Billy Wells UER (College should be Michigan State)	4.00	1.80
❑ 50 Larry Morris	4.00	1.80
❑ 51 Jack McClairen	4.00	1.80
❑ 52 Lou Groza	15.00	6.75
❑ 53 Rick Casares	5.00	2.20
❑ 54 Don Chandler	5.00	2.20
❑ 55 Duane Putnam	4.00	1.80
❑ 56 Gary Knafelc	4.00	1.80
❑ 57 Earl Morrall UER (Misspelled Morall on card back)	10.00	4.50
❑ 58 Ron Kramer RC	5.00	2.20
❑ 59 Mike McCormack	8.00	3.60
❑ 60 Gern Nagler	4.00	1.80
❑ 61 New York Giants Team Card	6.00	2.70
❑ 62 Jim Brown RC	450.00	200.00
❑ 63 Joe Marconi RC UER (Avg. gain should be 4.4)	4.00	1.80
❑ 64 R.C. Owens RC UER (Photo actually Don Owens)	5.00	2.20
❑ 65 Jimmy Carr RC	5.00	2.20
❑ 66 Bart Starr UER (Life and year stats reversed)	135.00	60.00
❑ 67 Tom Wilson	4.00	1.80
❑ 68 Lamar McHan	4.00	1.80
❑ 69 Chicago Cardinals Team Card	6.00	2.70
❑ 70 Jack Christiansen	8.00	3.60
❑ 71 Don McIlhenny RC	4.00	1.80
❑ 72 Ron Waller	4.00	1.80
❑ 73 Frank Gifford	50.00	22.00
❑ 74 Bert Rechichar	4.00	1.80
❑ 75 John Henry Johnson	10.00	4.50
❑ 76 Jack Butler	5.00	2.20

❑ 77 Frank Varrichione 4.00 1.80
❑ 78 Ray Mathews 4.00 1.80
❑ 79 Marv Matuszak UER 4.00 1.80
(Misspelled Matuzsak
on card front)
❑ 80 Harlon Hill UER 4.00 1.80
(Lifetime yards and
Avg. gain incorrect)
❑ 81 Lou Creekmur 8.00 3.60
❑ 82 Woodley Lewis UER 4.00 1.80
(misspelled Woodly on
front; end on front
and halfback on back)
❑ 83 Don Heinrich 4.00 1.80
❑ 84 Charley Conerly UER 15.00 6.75
(Misspelled Charlie
on card back)
❑ 85 Los Angeles Rams 6.00 2.70
Team Card
❑ 86 Y.A. Tittle 30.00 13.50
❑ 87 Bobby Walston 4.00 1.80
❑ 88 Earl Putman 4.00 1.80
❑ 89 Leo Nomellini 15.00 6.75
❑ 90 Sonny Jurgensen RC 100.00 45.00
❑ 91 Don Paul 4.00 1.80
❑ 92 Paige Cothren 4.00 1.80
❑ 93 Joe Perry 15.00 6.75
❑ 94 Tobin Rote 5.00 2.20
❑ 95 Billy Wilson 4.00 1.80
❑ 96 Green Bay Packers 6.00 2.70
Team Card
❑ 97 Lavern Torgeson 4.00 1.80
❑ 98 Milt Davis 4.00 1.80
❑ 99 Larry Strickland 4.00 1.80
❑ 100 Matt Hazeltine RC 5.00 2.20
❑ 101 Walt Yowarsky 4.00 1.80
❑ 102 Roosevelt Brown 8.00 3.60
❑ 103 Jim Ringo 10.00 4.50
❑ 104 Joe Krupa 4.00 1.80
❑ 105 Les Richter 5.00 2.20
❑ 106 Art Donovan 20.00 9.00
❑ 107 John Olszewski 4.00 1.80
❑ 108 Ken Keller 4.00 1.80
❑ 109 Philadelphia Eagles 6.00 2.70
Team Card
❑ 110 Baltimore Colts 6.00 2.70
Team Card
❑ 111 Dick Bielski 4.00 1.80
❑ 112 Eddie LeBaron 8.00 3.60
❑ 113 Gene Brito 4.00 1.80
❑ 114 Willie Galimore RC 8.00 3.60
❑ 115 Detroit Lions 6.00 2.70
Team Card
❑ 116 Pittsburgh Steelers 6.00 2.70
Team Card
❑ 117 L.G. Dupre 5.00 2.20
❑ 118 Babe Parilli 5.00 2.20
❑ 119 Bill George 10.00 4.50
❑ 120 Raymond Berry 40.00 18.00
❑ 121 Jim Podoley UER 4.00 1.80
(Photo actually
Volney Peters;
Podoly in cartoon)
❑ 122 Hugh McElhenny 15.00 6.75
❑ 123 Ed Brown 5.00 2.20
❑ 124 Dick Moegle 5.00 2.20
❑ 125 Tom Scott 4.00 1.80
❑ 126 Tommy McDonald 12.00 5.50
❑ 127 Ollie Matson 20.00 9.00
❑ 128 Preston Carpenter 4.00 1.80
❑ 129 George Blanda 30.00 13.50
❑ 130 Gordy Soltau 4.00 1.80
❑ 131 Dick Nolan RC 5.00 2.20
❑ 132 Don Bosseler RC 20.00 5.00
❑ NNO Free Felt Initial Card 25.00 11.00

1959 Topps

	NM	Ex
COMPLETE SET (176)	900.00	400.00
COMMON CARD (1-88)	3.00	1.35
COMMON CARD (89-176)	2.00	.90

WRAPPER (1-CENT) 90.00 40.00
WRAPPER (1-CENT, REP) 80.00 36.00
WRAPPER (5-CENT) 75.00 34.00

❑ 1 Johnny Unitas 150.00 38.00
❑ 2 Gene Brito 3.00 1.35
❑ 3 Detroit Lions 6.00 2.70
Team Card
(checklist back)
❑ 4 Max McGee RC 15.00 6.75
❑ 5 Hugh McElhenny 15.00 6.75
❑ 6 Joe Schmidt 8.00 3.60
❑ 7 Kyle Rote 6.00 2.70
❑ 8 Clarence Peaks 3.00 1.35
❑ 9 Pittsburgh Steelers 3.50 1.55
Pennant Card
❑ 10 Jim Brown 150.00 70.00
❑ 11 Ray Mathews 3.00 1.35
❑ 12 Bobby Dillon 3.00 1.35
❑ 13 Joe Childress 3.00 1.35
❑ 14 Terry Barr RC 3.00 1.35
❑ 15 Del Shofner RC 4.00 1.80
❑ 16 Bob Pellegrini UER 3.00 1.35
(Misspelled Pellagrini
on card back)
❑ 17 Baltimore Colts 6.00 2.70
Team Card
(checklist back)
❑ 18 Preston Carpenter 3.00 1.35
❑ 19 Leo Nomellini 10.00 4.50
❑ 20 Frank Gifford 40.00 18.00
❑ 21 Charlie Ane 3.00 1.35
❑ 22 Jack Butler 3.00 1.35
❑ 23 Bart Starr 60.00 27.00
❑ 24 Chicago Cardinals 3.50 1.55
Pennant Card
❑ 25 Bill Barnes 3.00 1.35
❑ 26 Walt Michaels 4.00 1.80
❑ 27 Clyde Conner UER 3.00 1.35
(Misspelled Connor
on card back)
❑ 28 Paige Cothren 3.00 1.35
❑ 29 Roosevelt Grier 6.00 2.70
❑ 30 Alan Ameche 6.00 2.70
❑ 31 Philadelphia Eagles 6.00 2.70
Team Card
(checklist back)
❑ 32 Dick Nolan 4.00 1.80
❑ 33 R.C. Owens 4.00 1.80
❑ 34 Dale Dodrill 3.00 1.35
❑ 35 Gene Gedman 3.00 1.35
❑ 36 Gene Lipscomb RC 10.00 4.50
❑ 37 Ray Renfro 4.00 1.80
❑ 38 Cleveland Browns 3.50 1.55
Pennant Card
❑ 39 Bill Forester 4.00 1.80
❑ 40 Bobby Layne 25.00 11.00
❑ 41 Pat Summerall 10.00 4.50
❑ 42 Jerry Mertens 3.00 1.35
❑ 43 Steve Myhra 3.00 1.35
❑ 44 John Henry Johnson 8.00 3.60
❑ 45 Woodley Lewis UER 3.00 1.35
(misspelled Woody)
❑ 46 Green Bay Packers 8.00 3.60
Team Card
(checklist back)
❑ 47 Don Owens UER 3.00 1.35
(Def.Tackle on front,
Linebacker on back)
❑ 48 Ed Beatty 3.00 1.35
❑ 49 Don Chandler 3.00 1.35
❑ 50 Ollie Matson 12.00 5.50
❑ 51 Sam Huff RC 50.00 22.00
❑ 52 Tom Miner 3.00 1.35
❑ 53 New York Giants 3.50 1.55
Pennant Card
❑ 54 Kenny Konz 3.00 1.35
❑ 55 Raymond Berry 20.00 9.00
❑ 56 Howard Ferguson UER 3.00 1.35
(Misspelled Fergeson
on card back)
❑ 57 Chuck Ulrich 3.00 1.35
❑ 58 Bob St. Clair 6.00 2.70
❑ 59 Don Burroughs RC 3.00 1.35
❑ 60 Lou Groza 15.00 6.75
❑ 61 San Francisco 49ers 6.00 2.70
Team Card
(checklist back)
❑ 62 Andy Nelson 3.00 1.35
❑ 63 Harold Bradley 3.00 1.35
❑ 64 Dave Hanner 4.00 1.80
❑ 65 Charley Conerly 10.00 4.50
❑ 66 Gene Cronin 3.00 1.35
❑ 67 Duane Putnam 3.00 1.35
❑ 68 Baltimore Colts 3.50 1.55
Pennant Card
❑ 69 Ernie Stautner 8.00 3.60
❑ 70 Jon Arnett 4.00 1.80
❑ 71 Ken Panfil 3.00 1.35
❑ 72 Matt Hazeltine 3.00 1.35
❑ 73 Harley Sewell 3.00 1.35
❑ 74 Mike McCormack 6.00 2.70
❑ 75 Jim Ringo 8.00 3.60
❑ 76 Los Angeles Rams 6.00 2.70
Team Card
(checklist back)
❑ 77 Bob Gain RC 3.00 1.35
❑ 78 Buzz Nutter 3.00 1.35
❑ 79 Jerry Norton 3.00 1.35
❑ 80 Joe Perry 12.00 5.50
❑ 81 Carl Brettschneider 3.00 1.35
❑ 82 Paul Hornung 60.00 27.00
❑ 83 Philadelphia Eagles 3.50 1.55
Pennant Card
❑ 84 Les Richter 4.00 1.80
❑ 85 Howard Cassady 4.00 1.80
❑ 86 Art Donovan 15.00 6.75
❑ 87 Jim Patton 4.00 1.80
❑ 88 Pete Retzlaff 4.00 1.80
❑ 89 Jim Mutscheller 2.00 .90
❑ 90 Zeke Bratkowski 3.00 1.35
❑ 91 Washington Redskins 4.00 1.80
Team Card
(Checklist back)
❑ 92 Art Hunter 2.00 .90
❑ 93 Gern Nagler 2.00 .90
❑ 94 Chuck Weber 2.00 .90
❑ 95 Lew Carpenter RC 3.00 1.35
❑ 96 Stan Jones 5.00 2.20
❑ 97 Ralph Guglielmi UER 3.00 1.35
(Misspelled Gugliemi
on card front)
❑ 98 Green Bay Packers 4.00 1.80
Pennant Card
❑ 99 Ray Wietecha 2.00 .90
❑ 100 Lenny Moore 12.00 5.50
❑ 101 Jim Ray Smith RC UER 3.00 1.35
(Lions logo on front)
❑ 102 Abe Woodson RC 3.00 1.35
❑ 103 Alex Karras RC 40.00 18.00
❑ 104 Chicago Bears 4.00 1.80
Team Card
(checklist back)
❑ 105 John David Crow RC 12.00 5.50
❑ 106 Joe Fortunato RC 2.00 .90
❑ 107 Babe Parilli 3.00 1.35

❑ 108 Proverb Jacobs	2.00	.90
❑ 109 Gino Marchetti	8.00	3.60
❑ 110 Bill Wade	3.00	1.35
❑ 111 San Francisco 49ers Pennant Card	3.00	1.35
❑ 112 Karl Rubke	2.00	.90
❑ 113 Dave Middleton UER (Browns logo in upper left corner)	2.00	.90
❑ 114 Roosevelt Brown	5.00	2.20
❑ 115 John Olszewski	2.00	.90
❑ 116 Jerry Kramer RC	30.00	13.50
❑ 117 King Hill RC	3.00	1.35
❑ 118 Chicago Cardinals Team Card (Checklist back)	4.00	1.80
❑ 119 Frank Varrichione	2.00	.90
❑ 120 Rick Casares	3.00	1.35
❑ 121 George Strugar	2.00	.90
❑ 122 Bill Glass RC UER (Center on front& tackle on back)	3.00	1.35
❑ 123 Don Bosseler	2.00	.90
❑ 124 John Reger	2.00	.90
❑ 125 Jim Ninowski RC	2.00	.90
❑ 126 Los Angeles Rams Pennant Card	3.00	1.35
❑ 127 Willard Sherman	2.00	.90
❑ 128 Bob Schnelker	2.00	.90
❑ 129 Ollie Spencer	2.00	.90
❑ 130 Y.A. Tittle	25.00	11.00
❑ 131 Yale Lary	5.00	2.20
❑ 132 Jim Parker RC	25.00	11.00
❑ 133 New York Giants Team Card (Checklist back)	4.00	1.80
❑ 134 Jim Schrader	2.00	.90
❑ 135 M.C. Reynolds	2.00	.90
❑ 136 Mike Sandusky	2.00	.90
❑ 137 Ed Brown	3.00	1.35
❑ 138 Al Barry	2.00	.90
❑ 139 Detroit Lions Pennant Card	3.00	1.35
❑ 140 Bobby Mitchell RC	35.00	16.00
❑ 141 Larry Morris	2.00	.90
❑ 142 Jim Phillips RC	3.00	1.35
❑ 143 Jim David	2.00	.90
❑ 144 Joe Krupa	2.00	.90
❑ 145 Willie Galimore	3.00	1.35
❑ 146 Pittsburgh Steelers Team Card (Checklist back)	4.00	1.80
❑ 147 Andy Robustelli	8.00	3.60
❑ 148 Billy Wilson	2.00	.90
❑ 149 Leo Sanford	2.00	.90
❑ 150 Eddie LeBaron	5.00	2.20
❑ 151 Bill McColl	2.00	.90
❑ 152 Buck Lansford UER (Tackle on front& guard on back)	2.00	.90
❑ 153 Chicago Bears Pennant Card	3.00	1.35
❑ 154 Leo Sugar	2.00	.90
❑ 155 Jim Taylor RC UER (Photo actually other Jim Taylor, Cardinal LB)	35.00	16.00
❑ 156 Lindon Crow	2.00	.90
❑ 157 Jack McClairen	2.00	.90
❑ 158 Vince Costello RC UER (Linebacker on front, Guard on back)	2.00	.90
❑ 159 Stan Wallace	2.00	.90
❑ 160 Mel Triplett RC	2.00	.90
❑ 161 Cleveland Browns Team Card (Checklist back)	4.00	1.80
❑ 162 Dan Currie RC	3.00	1.35
❑ 163 L.G. Dupre UER (Misspelled DuPre on back)	3.00	1.35
❑ 164 John Morrow UER (Center on front, Linebacker on back)	2.00	.90
❑ 165 Jim Podoley	2.00	.90
❑ 166 Bruce Bosley RC	2.00	.90
❑ 167 Harlon Hill	2.00	.90
❑ 168 Washington Redskins Pennant Card	3.00	1.35
❑ 169 Junior Wren	2.00	.90
❑ 170 Tobin Rote	3.00	1.35
❑ 171 Art Spinney	2.00	.90
❑ 172 Chuck Drazenovich UER (Linebacker on front, Defensive Back on back)	2.00	.90
❑ 173 Bobby Joe Conrad RC	3.00	1.35
❑ 174 Jesse Richardson	2.00	.90
❑ 175 Sam Baker	2.00	.90
❑ 176 Tom Tracy RC	8.00	2.00

1960 Topps

	NM	Ex
COMPLETE SET (132)	600.00	275.00
WRAPPER (1-CENT)	80.00	36.00
WRAPPER (1-CENT, REP)	300.00	135.00
WRAPPER (5-CENT)	75.00	34.00
❑ 1 John Unitas	80.00	20.00
❑ 2 Alan Ameche	4.00	1.80
❑ 3 Lenny Moore	10.00	4.50
❑ 4 Raymond Berry	12.00	5.50
❑ 5 Jim Parker	8.00	3.60
❑ 6 George Preas	2.50	1.10
❑ 7 Art Spinney	2.50	1.10
❑ 8 Bill Pellington RC	3.00	1.35
❑ 9 John Sample RC	3.00	1.35
❑ 10 Gene Lipscomb UER (Def. Tackle on front& Tackle on back)	3.00	1.35
❑ 11 Baltimore Colts Team Card (Checklist 67-132)	3.00	1.35
❑ 12 Ed Brown	3.00	1.35
❑ 13 Rick Casares	3.00	1.35
❑ 14 Willie Galimore	3.00	1.35
❑ 15 Jim Dooley	2.50	1.10
❑ 16 Harlon Hill UER (Lifetime yards and Avg. gain incorrect)	2.50	1.10
❑ 17 Stan Jones UER (Defensive ... All-Star Team& should be Offensive)	4.00	1.80
❑ 18 Bill George	4.00	1.80
❑ 19 Erich Barnes RC	3.00	1.35
❑ 20 Doug Atkins UER (reversed negative)	6.00	2.70
❑ 21 Chicago Bears Team Card (Checklist 1-66)	3.00	1.35
❑ 22 Milt Plum	3.00	1.35
❑ 23 Jim Brown	100.00	45.00
❑ 24 Sam Baker	2.50	1.10
❑ 25 Bobby Mitchell	10.00	4.50
❑ 26 Ray Renfro	3.00	1.35
❑ 27 Billy Howton	3.00	1.35
❑ 28 Jim Ray Smith	2.50	1.10
❑ 29 Jim Shofner RC	3.00	1.35
❑ 30 Bob Gain	2.50	1.10
❑ 31 Cleveland Browns Team Card (Checklist 1-66)	3.00	1.35
❑ 32 Don Heinrich	2.50	1.10
❑ 33 Ed Modzelewski UER (Lifetime yards and Avg. gain incorrect)	2.50	1.10
❑ 34 Fred Cone	2.50	1.10
❑ 35 L.G. Dupre	3.00	1.35
❑ 36 Dick Bielski	2.50	1.10
❑ 37 Charlie Ane UER (Misspelled Charley)	2.50	1.10
❑ 38 Jerry Tubbs	3.00	1.35
❑ 39 Doyle Nix	2.50	1.10
❑ 40 Ray Krouse	2.50	1.10
❑ 41 Earl Morrall	4.00	1.80
❑ 42 Howard Cassady	3.00	1.35
❑ 43 Dave Middleton	2.50	1.10
❑ 44 Jim Gibbons RC	3.00	1.35
❑ 45 Darris McCord	2.50	1.10
❑ 46 Joe Schmidt	6.00	2.70
❑ 47 Terry Barr	2.50	1.10
❑ 48 Yale Lary UER (Def.back on front, halfback on back)	4.00	1.80
❑ 49 Gil Mains	2.50	1.10
❑ 50 Detroit Lions Team Card (Checklist 1-66)	3.00	1.35
❑ 51 Bart Starr	45.00	20.00
❑ 52 Jim Taylor UER (photo actually Jim Taylor, Cardinal LB)	8.00	3.60
❑ 53 Lew Carpenter	3.00	1.35
❑ 54 Paul Hornung UER (Halfback on front, fullback on back)	45.00	20.00
❑ 55 Max McGee	4.00	1.80
❑ 56 Forrest Gregg RC	40.00	18.00
❑ 57 Jim Ringo	5.00	2.20
❑ 58 Bill Forester	3.00	1.35
❑ 59 Dave Hanner	3.00	1.35
❑ 60 Green Bay Packers Team Card (Checklist 67-132)	8.00	3.60
❑ 61 Bill Wade	3.00	1.35
❑ 62 Frank Ryan RC	4.00	1.80
❑ 63 Ollie Matson	10.00	4.50
❑ 64 Jon Arnett	3.00	1.35
❑ 65 Del Shofner	3.00	1.35
❑ 66 Jim Phillips	2.50	1.10
❑ 67 Art Hunter	2.50	1.10
❑ 68 Les Richter	3.00	1.35
❑ 69 Lou Michaels RC	3.00	1.35
❑ 70 John Baker	2.50	1.10
❑ 71 Los Angeles Rams Team Card (Checklist 1-66)	3.00	1.35
❑ 72 Charley Conerly	8.00	3.60
❑ 73 Mel Triplett	2.50	1.10
❑ 74 Frank Gifford	35.00	16.00
❑ 75 Alex Webster	3.00	1.35
❑ 76 Bob Schnelker	2.50	1.10
❑ 77 Pat Summerall	8.00	3.60
❑ 78 Roosevelt Brown	4.00	1.80
❑ 79 Jim Patton	2.50	1.10
❑ 80 Sam Huff UER (Def.tackle on front& linebacker on back)	20.00	9.00
❑ 81 Andy Robustelli	6.00	2.70
❑ 82 New York Giants Team Card (Checklist 1-66)	3.00	1.35
❑ 83 Clarence Peaks	2.50	1.10
❑ 84 Bill Barnes	2.50	1.10
❑ 85 Pete Retzlaff	3.00	1.35
❑ 86 Bobby Walston	2.50	1.10

❑ 87 Chuck Bednarik UER 8.00 3.60
(Misspelled Bednarick
on both sides of card)
❑ 88 Bob Pellegrini 2.50 1.10
(Misspelled Pellagrini
on both sides)
❑ 89 Tom Brookshier RC 3.00 1.35
❑ 90 Marion Campbell 3.00 1.35
❑ 91 Jesse Richardson 2.50 1.10
❑ 92 Philadelphia Eagles 3.00 1.35
Team Card
(Checklist 1-66)
❑ 93 Bobby Layne 30.00 13.50
❑ 94 John Henry Johnson 6.00 2.70
❑ 95 Tom Tracy UER 3.00 1.35
(Halfback on front&
fullback on back)
❑ 96 Preston Carpenter 2.50 1.10
❑ 97 Frank Varrichione UER 2.50 1.10
(Reversed negative)
❑ 98 John Nisby 2.50 1.10
❑ 99 Dean Derby 2.50 1.10
❑ 100 George Tarasovic 2.50 1.10
❑ 101 Ernie Stautner 5.00 2.20
❑ 102 Pittsburgh Steelers 3.00 1.35
Team Card
(Checklist 67-132)
❑ 103 King Hill 2.50 1.10
❑ 104 Mal Hammack 2.50 1.10
❑ 105 John David Crow 3.00 1.35
❑ 106 Bobby Joe Conrad 3.00 1.35
❑ 107 Woodley Lewis 2.50 1.10
❑ 108 Don Gillis 2.50 1.10
❑ 109 Carl Brettschneider 2.50 1.10
❑ 110 Leo Sugar 2.50 1.10
❑ 111 Frank Fuller 2.50 1.10
❑ 112 St. Louis Cardinals 3.00 1.35
Team Card
(Checklist 67-132)
❑ 113 Y.A. Tittle 30.00 13.50
❑ 114 Joe Perry 8.00 3.60
❑ 115 J.D. Smith RC 3.00 1.35
❑ 116 Hugh McElhenny 8.00 3.60
❑ 117 Billy Wilson 2.50 1.10
❑ 118 Bob St. Clair 4.00 1.80
❑ 119 Matt Hazeltine 2.50 1.10
❑ 120 Abe Woodson 2.50 1.10
❑ 121 Leo Nomellini 5.00 2.20
❑ 122 San Francisco 49ers 3.00 1.35
Team Card
(Checklist 67-132)
❑ 123 Ralph Guglielmi UER 2.50 1.10
(Misspelled Gugliemi
on card front)
❑ 124 Don Bosseler 2.50 1.10
❑ 125 John Olszewski 2.50 1.10
❑ 126 Bill Anderson UER 2.50 1.10
(Walt on back)
❑ 127 Joe Walton RC 3.00 1.35
❑ 128 Jim Schrader 2.50 1.10
❑ 129 Ralph Felton 2.50 1.10
❑ 130 Gary Glick 2.50 1.10
❑ 131 Bob Toneff 2.50 1.10
❑ 132 Washington Redskins 30.00 7.50
Team Card
(Checklist 67-132)
❑ AD1 Advertising Panel 125.00 55.00
Alan Ameche
Paul Hornung
Tom Tracy
(Gene Cronin back)
❑ AD2 Advertising Panel 90.00 40.00
Del Shofner
Milt Plum
Jim Patton
(Gene Cronin back)
❑ AD3 Advertising Panel 100.00 45.00
Bob St.Clair
Jim Shofner
Gil Mains
(Gene Cronin back)
❑ AD4 Advertising Panel 100.00 45.00
Tom Brookshier
Packers Team
George Preas
(Gene Cronin back)

1961 Topps

	NM	Ex
COMPLETE SET (198)	1000.00	450.00
COMMON CARD (1-132)	2.50	1.10
COMMON CARD (133-198)	3.00	1.35
WRAPPER (1-CENT)	275.00	125.00
WRAPPER (1-CENT, REP)	200.00	90.00
WRAPPER (5-CENT)	80.00	36.00

❑ 1 Johnny Unitas 100.00 25.00
❑ 2 Lenny Moore 12.00 5.50
❑ 3 Alan Ameche 4.00 1.80
❑ 4 Raymond Berry 12.00 5.50
❑ 5 Jim Mutscheller 2.50 1.10
❑ 6 Jim Parker 5.00 2.20
❑ 7 Gino Marchetti 6.00 2.70
❑ 8 Gene Lipscomb 4.00 1.80
❑ 9 Baltimore Colts 3.00 1.35
Team Card
❑ 10 Bill Wade 3.00 1.35
❑ 11 Johnny Morris RC UER 6.00 2.70
(Years pro and return
averages wrong)
❑ 12 Rick Casares 3.00 1.35
❑ 13 Harlon Hill 2.50 1.10
❑ 14 Stan Jones 4.00 1.80
❑ 15 Doug Atkins 5.00 2.20
❑ 16 Bill George 4.00 1.80
❑ 17 J.C. Caroline 2.50 1.10
❑ 18 Chicago Bears 3.00 1.35
Team Card
❑ 19 Big Time Football 3.00 1.35
Comes to Texas
(Eddie LeBaron)
❑ 20 Eddie LeBaron 3.00 1.35
❑ 21 Don McIlhenny 2.50 1.10
❑ 22 L.G. Dupre 3.00 1.35
❑ 23 Jim Doran 2.50 1.10
❑ 24 Billy Howton 3.00 1.35
❑ 25 Buzz Guy 2.50 1.10
❑ 26 Jack Patera RC 2.50 1.10
❑ 27 Tom Franckhauser UER 2.50 1.10
(misspelled Frankhauser)
❑ 28 Dallas Cowboys 15.00 6.75
Team Card
❑ 29 Jim Ninowski 2.50 1.10
❑ 30 Dan Lewis RC 2.50 1.10
❑ 31 Nick Pietrosante RC 3.00 1.35
❑ 32 Gail Cogdill RC 3.00 1.35
❑ 33 Jim Gibbons 2.50 1.10
❑ 34 Jim Martin 2.50 1.10
❑ 35 Alex Karras 15.00 6.75
❑ 36 Joe Schmidt 5.00 2.20
❑ 37 Detroit Lions 3.00 1.35
Team Card
❑ 38 Packers' Hornung 18.00 8.00
Sets NFL Scoring
Record
❑ 39 Bart Starr 40.00 18.00
❑ 40 Paul Hornung 40.00 18.00
❑ 41 Jim Taylor 35.00 13.50
❑ 42 Max McGee 4.00 1.80
❑ 43 Boyd Dowler RC 8.00 3.60
❑ 44 Jim Ringo 5.00 2.20
❑ 45 Hank Jordan RC 30.00 13.50
❑ 46 Bill Forester 3.00 1.35
❑ 47 Green Bay Packers 15.00 6.75
Team Card
❑ 48 Frank Ryan 3.00 1.35
❑ 49 Jon Arnett 3.00 1.35
❑ 50 Ollie Matson 8.00 3.60
❑ 51 Jim Phillips 2.50 1.10
❑ 52 Del Shofner 3.00 1.35
❑ 53 Art Hunter 2.50 1.10
❑ 54 Gene Brito 2.50 1.10
❑ 55 Lindon Crow 2.50 1.10
❑ 56 Los Angeles Rams 3.00 1.35
Team Card
❑ 57 Colts' Unitas 25.00 11.00
25 TD Passes
❑ 58 Y.A. Tittle 30.00 13.50
❑ 59 John Brodie RC 40.00 18.00
❑ 60 J.D. Smith 2.50 1.10
❑ 61 R.C. Owens 3.00 1.35
❑ 62 Clyde Conner 2.50 1.10
❑ 63 Bob St. Clair 4.00 1.80
❑ 64 Leo Nomellini 6.00 2.70
❑ 65 Abe Woodson 2.50 1.10
❑ 66 San Francisco 49ers 3.00 1.35
Team Card
❑ 67 Checklist Card 40.00 10.00
❑ 68 Milt Plum 3.00 1.35
❑ 69 Ray Renfro 3.00 1.35
❑ 70 Bobby Mitchell 8.00 3.60
❑ 71 Jim Brown 125.00 55.00
❑ 72 Mike McCormack 4.00 1.80
❑ 73 Jim Ray Smith 2.50 1.10
❑ 74 Sam Baker 2.50 1.10
❑ 75 Walt Michaels 3.00 1.35
❑ 76 Cleveland Browns 3.00 1.35
Team Card
❑ 77 Jimmy Brown Gains 35.00 16.00
1257 Yards
❑ 78 George Shaw 2.50 1.10
❑ 79 Hugh McElhenny 8.00 3.60
❑ 80 Clancy Osborne 2.50 1.10
❑ 81 Dave Middleton 2.50 1.10
❑ 82 Frank Youso 2.50 1.10
❑ 83 Don Joyce 2.50 1.10
❑ 84 Ed Culpepper 2.50 1.10
❑ 85 Charley Conerly 8.00 3.60
❑ 86 Mel Triplett 2.50 1.10
❑ 87 Kyle Rote 3.00 1.35
❑ 88 Roosevelt Brown 4.00 1.80
❑ 89 Ray Wietecha 2.50 1.10
❑ 90 Andy Robustelli 5.00 2.20
❑ 91 Sam Huff 8.00 3.60
❑ 92 Jim Patton 2.50 1.10
❑ 93 New York Giants 3.00 1.35
Team Card
❑ 94 Charley Conerly UER 6.00 2.70
Leads Giants for
13th Year
(Misspelled Charlie
on card)
❑ 95 Sonny Jurgensen 25.00 11.00
❑ 96 Tommy McDonald 5.00 2.20
❑ 97 Bill Barnes 2.50 1.10
❑ 98 Bobby Walston 2.50 1.10
❑ 99 Pete Retzlaff 3.00 1.35
❑ 100 Jim McCusker 2.50 1.10
❑ 101 Chuck Bednarik 8.00 3.60
❑ 102 Tom Brookshier 3.00 1.35
❑ 103 Philadelphia Eagles 3.00 1.35
Team Card
❑ 104 Bobby Layne 30.00 13.50
❑ 105 John Henry Johnson 4.00 1.80
❑ 106 Tom Tracy 3.00 1.35
❑ 107 Buddy Dial RC 2.50 1.10
❑ 108 Jimmy Orr RC 4.00 1.80

❑ 109 Mike Sandusky 2.50 1.10
❑ 110 John Reger 2.50 1.10
❑ 111 Junior Wren 2.50 1.10
❑ 112 Pittsburgh Steelers 3.00 1.35
Team Card
❑ 113 Bobby Layne Sets 10.00 4.50
New Passing Record
❑ 114 John Roach 2.50 1.10
❑ 115 Sam Etcheverry RC 3.00 1.35
❑ 116 John David Crow 3.00 1.35
❑ 117 Mal Hammack 2.50 1.10
❑ 118 Sonny Randle RC 3.00 1.35
❑ 119 Leo Sugar 2.50 1.10
❑ 120 Jerry Norton 2.50 1.10
❑ 121 St. Louis Cardinals 3.00 1.35
Team Card
❑ 122 Checklist Card 50.00 12.50
❑ 123 Ralph Guglielmi 2.50 1.10
❑ 124 Dick James 2.50 1.10
❑ 125 Don Bosseler 2.50 1.10
❑ 126 Joe Walton 2.50 1.10
❑ 127 Bill Anderson 2.50 1.10
❑ 128 Vince Promuto RC 2.50 1.10
❑ 129 Bob Toneff 2.50 1.10
❑ 130 John Paluck 2.50 1.10
❑ 131 Washington Redskins 3.00 1.35
Team Card
❑ 132 Browns' Plum Wins 2.50 1.10
NFL Passing Title
❑ 133 Abner Haynes 8.00 3.60
❑ 134 Mel Branch UER 4.00 1.80
(Def. Tackle on front&
Def. End on back)
❑ 135 Jerry Cornelison UER 3.00 1.35
(Misspelled Cornielson)
❑ 136 Bill Krisher 3.00 1.35
❑ 137 Paul Miller 3.00 1.35
❑ 138 Jack Spikes 4.00 1.80
❑ 139 Johnny Robinson RC 8.00 3.60
❑ 140 Cotton Davidson RC 4.00 1.80
❑ 141 Dave Smith 3.00 1.35
❑ 142 Bill Groman 3.00 1.35
❑ 143 Rich Michael 3.00 1.35
❑ 144 Mike Dukes 3.00 1.35
❑ 145 George Blanda 25.00 11.00
❑ 146 Billy Cannon 6.00 2.70
❑ 147 Dennit Morris 3.00 1.35
❑ 148 Jacky Lee UER 4.00 1.80
(Misspelled Jackie
on card back)
❑ 149 Al Dorow 3.00 1.35
❑ 150 Don Maynard RC 50.00 22.00
❑ 151 Art Powell RC 8.00 3.60
❑ 152 Sid Youngelman 3.00 1.35
❑ 153 Bob Mischak 3.00 1.35
❑ 154 Larry Grantham 3.00 1.35
❑ 155 Tom Saidock 3.00 1.35
❑ 156 Roger Donnahoo 3.00 1.35
❑ 157 Laverne Torczon 3.00 1.35
❑ 158 Archie Matsos RC 4.00 1.80
❑ 159 Elbert Dubenion 4.00 1.80
❑ 160 Wray Carlton RC 4.00 1.80
❑ 161 Rich McCabe 3.00 1.35
❑ 162 Ken Rice 3.00 1.35
❑ 163 Art Baker 3.00 1.35
❑ 164 Tom Rychlec 3.00 1.35
❑ 165 Mack Yoho 3.00 1.35
❑ 166 Jack Kemp 100.00 45.00
❑ 167 Paul Lowe 6.00 2.70
❑ 168 Ron Mix 10.00 4.50
❑ 169 Paul Maguire UER 6.00 2.70
(name misspelled McGuire)
❑ 170 Volney Peters 3.00 1.35
❑ 171 Ernie Wright RC 4.00 1.80
❑ 172 Ron Nery RC 3.00 1.35
❑ 173 Dave Kocourek RC 4.00 1.80
❑ 174 Jim Colclough 3.00 1.35
❑ 175 Babe Parilli 4.00 1.80
❑ 176 Billy Lott 3.00 1.35
❑ 177 Fred Bruney 3.00 1.35
❑ 178 Ross O'Hanley 3.00 1.35
❑ 179 Walt Cudzik 3.00 1.35
❑ 180 Charley Leo 3.00 1.35
❑ 181 Bob Dee 3.00 1.35
❑ 182 Jim Otto RC 40.00 18.00
❑ 183 Eddie Macon 3.00 1.35
❑ 184 Dick Christy 3.00 1.35
❑ 185 Alan Miller 3.00 1.35
❑ 186 Tom Flores RC 20.00 9.00
❑ 187 Joe Cannavino 3.00 1.35
❑ 188 Don Manoukian 3.00 1.35
❑ 189 Bob Coolbaugh 3.00 1.35
❑ 190 Lionel Taylor RC 8.00 3.60
❑ 191 Bud McFadin 3.00 1.35
❑ 192 Goose Gonsoulin RC 6.00 2.70
❑ 193 Frank Tripucka 4.00 1.80
❑ 194 Gene Mingo RC 4.00 1.80
❑ 195 Eldon Danenhauer 3.00 1.35
❑ 196 Bob McNamara 3.00 1.35
❑ 197 Dave Rolle UER 3.00 1.35
(End on front&
Fullback on back)
❑ 198 Checklist Card UER 100.00 25.00
(135 Cornielson)
❑ AD1 Advertising Panel 100.00 45.00
Jim Martin
George Shaw
Jim Ray Smith

1962 Topps

	NM	Ex
COMPLETE SET (176)	2000.00	900.00
WRAPPER (1-CENT)	250.00	110.00
WRAPPER (5-CENT,STARS)	50.00	22.00
WRAPPER (5-CENT, BUCKS)	40.00	18.00

❑ 1 John Unitas 200.00 50.00
❑ 2 Lenny Moore 12.00 5.50
❑ 3 Alex Hawkins RC SP 10.00 4.50
❑ 4 Joe Perry 8.00 3.60
❑ 5 Raymond Berry SP 40.00 18.00
❑ 6 Steve Myhra 4.00 1.80
❑ 7 Tom Gilburg SP 8.00 3.60
❑ 8 Gino Marchetti 8.00 3.60
❑ 9 Bill Pellington 4.00 1.80
❑ 10 Andy Nelson 4.00 1.80
❑ 11 Wendell Harris SP 8.00 3.60
❑ 12 Baltimore Colts 6.00 2.70
Team Card
❑ 13 Bill Wade SP 10.00 4.50
❑ 14 Willie Galimore 5.00 2.20
❑ 15 Johnny Morris SP 8.00 3.60
❑ 16 Rick Casares 5.00 2.20
❑ 17 Mike Ditka RC 225.00 100.00
❑ 18 Stan Jones 6.00 2.70
❑ 19 Roger LeClerc 4.00 1.80
❑ 20 Angelo Coia 4.00 1.80
❑ 21 Doug Atkins 7.00 3.10
❑ 22 Bill George 6.00 2.70
❑ 23 Richie Petitbon RC 5.00 2.20
❑ 24 Ronnie Bull RC SP 8.00 3.60
❑ 25 Chicago Bears 6.00 2.70
Team Card
❑ 26 Howard Cassady 5.00 2.20
❑ 27 Ray Renfro SP 10.00 4.50
❑ 28 Jim Brown 175.00 80.00
❑ 29 Rich Kreitling 4.00 1.80
❑ 30 Jim Ray Smith 4.00 1.80
❑ 31 John Morrow 4.00 1.80
❑ 32 Lou Groza 15.00 6.75
❑ 33 Bob Gain 4.00 1.80
❑ 34 Bernie Parrish 4.00 1.80
❑ 35 Jim Shofner 4.00 1.80
❑ 36 Ernie Davis RC SP 150.00 70.00
❑ 37 Cleveland Browns 6.00 2.70
Team Card
❑ 38 Eddie LeBaron 5.00 2.20
❑ 39 Don Meredith SP 100.00 45.00
❑ 40 J.W. Lockett SP 8.00 3.60
❑ 41 Don Perkins RC 10.00 4.50
❑ 42 Billy Howton 5.00 2.20
❑ 43 Dick Bielski 4.00 1.80
❑ 44 Mike Connelly RC 4.00 1.80
❑ 45 Jerry Tubbs SP 8.00 3.60
❑ 46 Don Bishop SP 8.00 3.60
❑ 47 Dick Moegle 4.00 1.80
❑ 48 Bobby Plummer SP 8.00 3.60
❑ 49 Dallas Cowboys 20.00 9.00
Team Card
❑ 50 Milt Plum 5.00 2.20
❑ 51 Dan Lewis 4.00 1.80
❑ 52 Nick Pietrosante SP 8.00 3.60
❑ 53 Gail Cogdill 4.00 1.80
❑ 54 Jim Gibbons 4.00 1.80
❑ 55 Jim Martin 4.00 1.80
❑ 56 Yale Lary 6.00 2.70
❑ 57 Darris McCord 4.00 1.80
❑ 58 Alex Karras 25.00 11.00
❑ 59 Joe Schmidt 7.00 3.10
❑ 60 Dick Lane 6.00 2.70
❑ 61 John Lomakoski SP 8.00 3.60
❑ 62 Detroit Lions SP 18.00 8.00
Team Card
❑ 63 Bart Starr SP 125.00 55.00
❑ 64 Paul Hornung SP 100.00 45.00
❑ 65 Tom Moore SP 12.00 5.50
❑ 66 Jim Taylor SP 50.00 22.00
❑ 67 Max McGee SP 12.00 5.50
❑ 68 Jim Ringo SP 15.00 6.75
❑ 69 Fuzzy Thurston RC SP 20.00 9.00
❑ 70 Forrest Gregg 7.00 3.10
❑ 71 Boyd Dowler 6.00 2.70
❑ 72 Hank Jordan SP 15.00 6.75
❑ 73 Bill Forester SP 10.00 4.50
❑ 74 Earl Gros SP 8.00 3.60
❑ 75 Green Bay Packers SP 35.00 16.00
Team Card
❑ 76 Checklist SP 80.00 20.00
❑ 77 Zeke Bratkowski SP 10.00 4.50
(Inset photo is
Johnny Unitas)
❑ 78 Jon Arnett SP 10.00 4.50
❑ 79 Ollie Matson SP 35.00 16.00
❑ 80 Dick Bass SP 10.00 4.50
❑ 81 Jim Phillips 4.00 1.80
❑ 82 Carroll Dale RC 5.00 2.20
❑ 83 Frank Varrichione 4.00 1.80
❑ 84 Art Hunter 4.00 1.80
❑ 85 Danny Villanueva RC 4.00 1.80
❑ 86 Les Richter SP 8.00 3.60
❑ 87 Lindon Crow 4.00 1.80
❑ 88 Roman Gabriel RC SP 60.00 27.00
(Inset photo is
Y.A. Tittle)
❑ 89 Los Angeles Rams SP 18.00 8.00
Team Card
❑ 90 F.Tarkenton SP RC UER 225.00 100.00
Small photo actually
Sonny Jurgensen
with airbrushed jersey
❑ 91 Jerry Reichow SP 8.00 3.60
❑ 92 Hugh McElhenny SP 30.00 13.50
❑ 93 Mel Triplett SP 8.00 3.60
❑ 94 Tommy Mason RC SP 12.00 5.50
❑ 95 Dave Middleton SP 8.00 3.60
❑ 96 Frank Youso SP 8.00 3.60
❑ 97 Mike Mercer SP 8.00 3.60
❑ 98 Rip Hawkins SP 8.00 3.60
❑ 99 Cliff Livingston SP 8.00 3.60
❑ 100 Roy Winston RC SP 8.00 3.60
❑ 101 Minnesota Vikings SP 25.00 11.00
Team Card
❑ 102 Y.A. Tittle 40.00 18.00
❑ 103 Joe Walton 4.00 1.80

Card	NM	Ex
❑ 104 Frank Gifford	50.00	22.00
❑ 105 Alex Webster	5.00	2.20
❑ 106 Del Shofner	5.00	2.20
❑ 107 Don Chandler	4.00	1.80
❑ 108 Andy Robustelli	7.00	3.10
❑ 109 Jim Katcavage RC	5.00	2.20
❑ 110 Sam Huff SP	40.00	18.00
❑ 111 Erich Barnes	4.00	1.80
❑ 112 Jim Patton	4.00	1.80
❑ 113 Jerry Hillebrand SP	8.00	3.60
❑ 114 New York Giants Team Card	6.00	2.70
❑ 115 Sonny Jurgensen	40.00	18.00
❑ 116 Tommy McDonald	8.00	3.60
❑ 117 Ted Dean SP	8.00	3.60
❑ 118 Clarence Peaks	4.00	1.80
❑ 119 Bobby Walston	4.00	1.80
❑ 120 Pete Retzlaff SP	10.00	4.50
❑ 121 Jim Schrader SP	8.00	3.60
❑ 122 J.D. Smith T	4.00	1.80
❑ 123 King Hill	4.00	1.80
❑ 124 Maxie Baughan	5.00	2.20
❑ 125 Pete Case SP	8.00	3.60
❑ 126 Philadelphia Eagles Team Card	6.00	2.70
❑ 127 Bobby Layne UER (Bears until 1958& should be Lions)	40.00	18.00
❑ 128 Tom Tracy	5.00	2.20
❑ 129 John Henry Johnson	6.00	2.70
❑ 130 Buddy Dial SP	10.00	4.50
❑ 131 Preston Carpenter	4.00	1.80
❑ 132 Lou Michaels SP	8.00	3.60
❑ 133 Gene Lipscomb SP	10.00	4.50
❑ 134 Ernie Stautner SP	20.00	9.00
❑ 135 John Reger SP	8.00	3.60
❑ 136 Myron Pottios RC	4.00	1.80
❑ 137 Bob Ferguson SP	8.00	3.60
❑ 138 Pittsburgh Steelers SP Team Card	18.00	8.00
❑ 139 Sam Etcheverry	5.00	2.20
❑ 140 John David Crow SP	10.00	4.50
❑ 141 Bobby Joe Conrad SP	10.00	4.50
❑ 142 Prentice Gautt RC SP	8.00	3.60
❑ 143 Frank Mestnik	4.00	1.80
❑ 144 Sonny Randle	5.00	2.20
❑ 145 Gerry Perry UER (T-K on both sides& but Def. End in bio)	4.00	1.80
❑ 146 Jerry Norton	4.00	1.80
❑ 147 Jimmy Hill	4.00	1.80
❑ 148 Bill Stacy	4.00	1.80
❑ 149 Fate Echols SP	8.00	3.60
❑ 150 St. Louis Cardinals Team Card	6.00	2.70
❑ 151 Bill Kilmer RC	35.00	16.00
❑ 152 John Brodie	18.00	8.00
❑ 153 J.D. Smith RB	5.00	2.20
❑ 154 C.R. Roberts SP	8.00	3.60
❑ 155 Monty Stickles	4.00	1.80
❑ 156 Clyde Conner UER (Misspelled Connor on card back)	4.00	1.80
❑ 157 Bob St. Clair	6.00	2.70
❑ 158 Tommy Davis RC	4.00	1.80
❑ 159 Leo Nomellini	8.00	3.60
❑ 160 Matt Hazeltine	4.00	1.80
❑ 161 Abe Woodson	4.00	1.80
❑ 162 Dave Baker	4.00	1.80
❑ 163 San Francisco 49ers Team Card	6.00	2.70
❑ 164 Norm Snead RC SP	30.00	13.50
❑ 165 Dick James (Inset photo is Don Bosseler)	5.00	2.20
❑ 166 Bobby Mitchell	8.00	3.60
❑ 167 Sam Horner	4.00	1.80
❑ 168 Bill Barnes	4.00	1.80
❑ 169 Bill Anderson	4.00	1.80
❑ 170 Fred Dugan	4.00	1.80
❑ 171 John Aveni SP	8.00	3.60
❑ 172 Bob Toneff	4.00	1.80
❑ 173 Jim Kerr	4.00	1.80
❑ 174 Leroy Jackson SP	8.00	3.60
❑ 175 Washington Redskins Team Card	6.00	2.70
❑ 176 Checklist	100.00	25.00

1963 Topps

	NM	Ex
COMPLETE SET (170)	1350.00	600.00
WRAPPER (1-CENT)	450.00	200.00
WRAPPER (5-CENT)	80.00	36.00
❑ 1 John Unitas	135.00	34.00
❑ 2 Lenny Moore	8.00	3.60
❑ 3 Jimmy Orr	3.00	1.35
❑ 4 Raymond Berry	8.00	3.60
❑ 5 Jim Parker	5.00	2.20
❑ 6 Alex Sandusky	2.50	1.10
❑ 7 Dick Szymanski RC	2.50	1.10
❑ 8 Gino Marchetti	6.00	2.70
❑ 9 Billy Ray Smith RC	3.00	1.35
❑ 10 Bill Pellington	2.50	1.10
❑ 11 Bob Boyd RC	2.50	1.10
❑ 12 Baltimore Colts SP Team Card	10.00	4.50
❑ 13 Frank Ryan SP	8.00	3.60
❑ 14 Jim Brown SP	200.00	90.00
❑ 15 Ray Renfro SP	8.00	3.60
❑ 16 Rich Kreitling SP	6.00	2.70
❑ 17 Mike McCormack SP	10.00	4.50
❑ 18 Jim Ray Smith SP	6.00	2.70
❑ 19 Lou Groza SP	25.00	11.00
❑ 20 Bill Glass SP	6.00	2.70
❑ 21 Galen Fiss SP	6.00	2.70
❑ 22 Don Fleming RC SP	8.00	3.60
❑ 23 Bob Gain SP	6.00	2.70
❑ 24 Cleveland Browns SP Team Card	10.00	4.50
❑ 25 Milt Plum	3.00	1.35
❑ 26 Dan Lewis	2.50	1.10
❑ 27 Nick Pietrosante	2.50	1.10
❑ 28 Gail Cogdill	2.50	1.10
❑ 29 Harley Sewell	2.50	1.10
❑ 30 Jim Gibbons	2.50	1.10
❑ 31 Carl Brettschneider	2.50	1.10
❑ 32 Dick Lane	5.00	2.20
❑ 33 Yale Lary	5.00	2.20
❑ 34 Roger Brown RC	3.00	1.35
❑ 35 Joe Schmidt	6.00	2.70
❑ 36 Detroit Lions SP Team Card	10.00	4.50
❑ 37 Roman Gabriel	8.00	3.60
❑ 38 Zeke Bratkowski	3.00	1.35
❑ 39 Dick Bass	3.00	1.35
❑ 40 Jon Arnett	3.00	1.35
❑ 41 Jim Phillips	2.50	1.10
❑ 42 Frank Varrichione	2.50	1.10
❑ 43 Danny Villanueva	2.50	1.10
❑ 44 Deacon Jones RC	50.00	22.00
❑ 45 Lindon Crow	2.50	1.10
❑ 46 Marlin McKeever	2.50	1.10
❑ 47 Ed Meador RC	2.50	1.10
❑ 48 Los Angeles Rams Team Card	4.00	1.80
❑ 49 Y.A. Tittle SP	50.00	22.00
❑ 50 Del Shofner SP	6.00	2.70
❑ 51 Alex Webster SP	8.00	3.60
❑ 52 Phil King SP	6.00	2.70
❑ 53 Jack Stroud SP	6.00	2.70
❑ 54 Darrell Dess SP	6.00	2.70
❑ 55 Jim Katcavage SP	6.00	2.70
❑ 56 Roosevelt Grier SP	10.00	4.50
❑ 57 Erich Barnes SP	6.00	2.70
❑ 58 Jim Patton SP	6.00	2.70
❑ 59 Sam Huff SP	20.00	9.00
❑ 60 New York Giants Team Card	4.00	1.80
❑ 61 Bill Wade	3.00	1.35
❑ 62 Mike Ditka	60.00	27.00
❑ 63 Johnny Morris	2.50	1.10
❑ 64 Roger LeClerc	2.50	1.10
❑ 65 Roger Davis RC	2.50	1.10
❑ 66 Joe Marconi	2.50	1.10
❑ 67 Herman Lee	2.50	1.10
❑ 68 Doug Atkins	6.00	2.70
❑ 69 Joe Fortunato	2.50	1.10
❑ 70 Bill George	5.00	2.20
❑ 71 Richie Petitbon	3.00	1.35
❑ 72 Chicago Bears SP Team Card	10.00	4.50
❑ 73 Eddie LeBaron SP	10.00	4.50
❑ 74 Don Meredith SP	60.00	27.00
❑ 75 Don Perkins SP	10.00	4.50
❑ 76 Amos Marsh SP	6.00	2.70
❑ 77 Billy Howton SP	8.00	3.60
❑ 78 Andy Cvercko SP	6.00	2.70
❑ 79 Sam Baker SP	6.00	2.70
❑ 80 Jerry Tubbs SP	6.00	2.70
❑ 81 Don Bishop SP	6.00	2.70
❑ 82 Bob Lilly RC SP	175.00	80.00
❑ 83 Jerry Norton SP	6.00	2.70
❑ 84 Dallas Cowboys SP Team Card	20.00	9.00
❑ 85 Checklist Card	25.00	6.25
❑ 86 Bart Starr	75.00	27.00
❑ 87 Jim Taylor	30.00	13.50
❑ 88 Boyd Dowler	5.00	2.20
❑ 89 Forrest Gregg	6.00	2.70
❑ 90 Fuzzy Thurston	6.00	2.70
❑ 91 Jim Ringo	6.00	2.70
❑ 92 Ron Kramer	3.00	1.35
❑ 93 Hank Jordan	6.00	2.70
❑ 94 Bill Forester	3.00	1.35
❑ 95 Willie Wood RC	40.00	18.00
❑ 96 Ray Nitschke RC	125.00	55.00
❑ 97 Green Bay Packers Team Card	15.00	6.75
❑ 98 Fran Tarkenton	60.00	27.00
❑ 99 Tommy Mason	3.00	1.35
❑ 100 Mel Triplett	2.50	1.10
❑ 101 Jerry Reichow	2.50	1.10
❑ 102 Frank Youso	2.50	1.10
❑ 103 Hugh McElhenny	8.00	3.60
❑ 104 Gerald Huth	2.50	1.10
❑ 105 Ed Sharockman	2.50	1.10
❑ 106 Rip Hawkins	2.50	1.10
❑ 107 Jim Marshall RC	35.00	16.00
❑ 108 Jim Prestel	2.50	1.10
❑ 109 Minnesota Vikings Team Card	4.00	1.80
❑ 110 Sonny Jurgensen SP	25.00	11.00
❑ 111 Tim Brown SP RC	10.00	4.50
❑ 112 Tommy McDonald SP	15.00	6.75
❑ 113 Clarence Peaks SP	6.00	2.70
❑ 114 Pete Retzlaff SP	8.00	3.60
❑ 115 Jim Schrader SP	6.00	2.70
❑ 116 Jim McCusker SP	6.00	2.70
❑ 117 Don Burroughs SP	6.00	2.70
❑ 118 Maxie Baughan SP	6.00	2.70
❑ 119 Riley Gunnels SP	6.00	2.70
❑ 120 Jimmy Carr SP	6.00	2.70
❑ 121 Philadelphia Eagles SP Team Card	10.00	4.50
❑ 122 Ed Brown SP	8.00	3.60
❑ 123 John Henry Johnson SP	15.00	6.75

Card	NM	Ex
❑ 124 Buddy Dial SP	6.00	2.70
❑ 125 Bill Red Mack SP	6.00	2.70
❑ 126 Preston Carpenter SP	6.00	2.70
❑ 127 Ray Lemek SP	6.00	2.70
❑ 128 Buzz Nutter SP	6.00	2.70
❑ 129 Ernie Stautner SP	15.00	6.75
❑ 130 Lou Michaels SP	6.00	2.70
❑ 131 Clendon Thomas RC SP	6.00	2.70
❑ 132 Tom Bettis SP	6.00	2.70
❑ 133 Pittsburgh Steelers SP Team Card	10.00	4.50
❑ 134 John Brodie	8.00	3.60
❑ 135 J.D. Smith	2.50	1.10
❑ 136 Bill Kilmer UER (College listed as San Francisco 49ers)	5.00	2.20
❑ 137 Bernie Casey RC	3.00	1.35
❑ 138 Tommy Davis	2.50	1.10
❑ 139 Ted Connolly	2.50	1.10
❑ 140 Bob St. Clair	5.00	2.20
❑ 141 Abe Woodson	2.50	1.10
❑ 142 Matt Hazeltine	2.50	1.10
❑ 143 Leo Nomellini	6.00	2.70
❑ 144 Dan Colchico	2.50	1.10
❑ 145 San Francisco 49ers SP Team Card	10.00	4.50
❑ 146 Charlie Johnson RC	8.00	3.60
❑ 147 John David Crow	3.00	1.35
❑ 148 Bobby Joe Conrad	3.00	1.35
❑ 149 Sonny Randle	2.50	1.10
❑ 150 Prentice Gautt	2.50	1.10
❑ 151 Taz Anderson	2.50	1.10
❑ 152 Ernie McMillan RC	3.00	1.35
❑ 153 Jimmy Hill	2.50	1.10
❑ 154 Bill Koman	2.50	1.10
❑ 155 Larry Wilson RC	20.00	9.00
❑ 156 Don Owens	2.50	1.10
❑ 157 St. Louis Cardinals SP Team Card	10.00	4.50
❑ 158 Norm Snead SP	10.00	4.50
❑ 159 Bobby Mitchell SP	15.00	6.75
❑ 160 Bill Barnes SP	6.00	2.70
❑ 161 Fred Dugan SP	6.00	2.70
❑ 162 Don Bosseler SP	6.00	2.70
❑ 163 John Nisby SP	6.00	2.70
❑ 164 Riley Mattson SP	6.00	2.70
❑ 165 Bob Toneff SP	6.00	2.70
❑ 166 Rod Breedlove SP	6.00	2.70
❑ 167 Dick James SP	6.00	2.70
❑ 168 Claude Crabb SP UER (Claud on front and back)	6.00	2.70
❑ 169 Washington Redskins SP Team Card	10.00	4.50
❑ 170 Checklist Card UER (108 Jim Prestal)	50.00	12.50
❑ AD1 Advertising Panel Charlie Johnson John David Crow Bobby Joe Conrad (Y.A. Tittle back)	100.00	45.00

1964 Topps

	NM	Ex
COMPLETE SET (176)	1500.00	700.00
WRAPPER (1-CENT)	40.00	18.00
WRAPPER (5-CENT, PENN)	90.00	40.00
WRAPPER (5-CENT, 8-CARD)	150.00	70.00
❑ 1 Tommy Addison SP	30.00	7.50
❑ 2 Houston Antwine RC	4.00	1.80
❑ 3 Nick Buoniconti	25.00	11.00
❑ 4 Ron Burton SP	10.00	4.50
❑ 5 Gino Cappelletti UER (Misspelled Cappalletti on card front)	5.00	2.20
❑ 6 Jim Colclough SP	6.00	2.70
❑ 7 Bob Dee SP	6.00	2.70
❑ 8 Larry Eisenhauer	4.00	1.80
❑ 9 Dick Felt SP	6.00	2.70
❑ 10 Larry Garron	4.00	1.80
❑ 11 Art Graham	4.00	1.80
❑ 12 Ron Hall	4.00	1.80
❑ 13 Charles Long	4.00	1.80
❑ 14 Don McKinnon	4.00	1.80
❑ 15 Don Oakes SP	6.00	2.70
❑ 16 Ross O'Hanley SP	6.00	2.70
❑ 17 Babe Parilli SP	10.00	4.50
❑ 18 Jesse Richardson SP	6.00	2.70
❑ 19 Jack Rudolph SP	6.00	2.70
❑ 20 Don Webb RC	4.00	1.80
❑ 21 Boston Patriots Team Card	6.00	2.70
❑ 22 Ray Abruzzese UER (photo is Ed Rutkowski)	4.00	1.80
❑ 23 Stew Barber RC	4.00	1.80
❑ 24 Dave Behrman	4.00	1.80
❑ 25 Al Bemiller	4.00	1.80
❑ 26 Elbert Dubenion SP	10.00	4.50
❑ 27 Jim Dunaway RC SP	6.00	2.70
❑ 28 Booker Edgerson SP	6.00	2.70
❑ 29 Cookie Gilchrist SP	25.00	11.00
❑ 30 Jack Kemp SP	120.00	80.00
❑ 31 Daryle Lamonica RC	75.00	34.00
❑ 32 Bill Miller	4.00	1.80
❑ 33 Herb Paterra RC	4.00	1.80
❑ 34 Ken Rice SP	6.00	2.70
❑ 35 Ed Rutkowski UER (photo is Ray Abruzzese)	4.00	1.80
❑ 36 George Saimes RC	4.00	1.80
❑ 37 Tom Sestak	4.00	1.80
❑ 38 Billy Shaw SP	15.00	6.75
❑ 39 Mike Stratton	5.00	2.20
❑ 40 Gene Sykes	4.00	1.80
❑ 41 John Tracey SP	6.00	2.70
❑ 42 Sid Youngelman SP	6.00	2.70
❑ 43 Buffalo Bills Team Card	6.00	2.70
❑ 44 Eldon Danenhauer SP	6.00	2.70
❑ 45 Jim Fraser SP	6.00	2.70
❑ 46 Chuck Gavin SP	6.00	2.70
❑ 47 Goose Gonsoulin SP	10.00	4.50
❑ 48 Ernie Barnes RC	4.00	1.80
❑ 49 Tom Janik	4.00	1.80
❑ 50 Billy Joe RC	5.00	2.20
❑ 51 Ike Lassiter RC	4.00	1.80
❑ 52 John McCormick SP	6.00	2.70
❑ 53 Bud McFadin SP	6.00	2.70
❑ 54 Gene Mingo SP	6.00	2.70
❑ 55 Charlie Mitchell	4.00	1.80
❑ 56 John Nocera SP	6.00	2.70
❑ 57 Tom Nomina	4.00	1.80
❑ 58 Harold Olson SP	6.00	2.70
❑ 59 Bob Scarpitto	4.00	1.80
❑ 60 John Sklopan	4.00	1.80
❑ 61 Mickey Slaughter	4.00	1.80
❑ 62 Don Stone	4.00	1.80
❑ 63 Jerry Sturm	4.00	1.80
❑ 64 Lionel Taylor SP	12.00	5.50
❑ 65 Denver Broncos SP Team Card	20.00	9.00
❑ 66 Scott Appleton RC	4.00	1.80
❑ 67 Tony Banfield SP	6.00	2.70
❑ 68 George Blanda SP	75.00	34.00
❑ 69 Billy Cannon	6.00	2.70
❑ 70 Doug Cline SP	6.00	2.70
❑ 71 Gary Cutsinger SP	6.00	2.70
❑ 72 Willard Dewveall SP	6.00	2.70
❑ 73 Don Floyd SP	6.00	2.70
❑ 74 Freddy Glick SP	6.00	2.70
❑ 75 Charlie Hennigan SP	10.00	4.50
❑ 76 Ed Husmann SP	6.00	2.70
❑ 77 Bobby Jancik SP	6.00	2.70
❑ 78 Jacky Lee SP	10.00	4.50
❑ 79 Bob McLeod SP	6.00	2.70
❑ 80 Rich Michael SP	6.00	2.70
❑ 81 Larry Onesti RC	4.00	1.80
❑ 82 Checklist Card UER (16 Ross O'Hanldy)	60.00	15.00
❑ 83 Bob Schmidt SP	6.00	2.70
❑ 84 Walt Suggs SP	6.00	2.70
❑ 85 Bob Talamini SP	6.00	2.70
❑ 86 Charley Tolar SP	6.00	2.70
❑ 87 Don Trull RC	4.00	1.80
❑ 88 Houston Oilers Team Card	6.00	2.70
❑ 89 Fred Arbanas	4.00	1.80
❑ 90 Bobby Bell RC	40.00	18.00
❑ 91 Mel Branch SP	10.00	4.50
❑ 92 Buck Buchanan RC	40.00	18.00
❑ 93 Ed Budde RC	4.00	1.80
❑ 94 Chris Burford SP	10.00	4.50
❑ 95 Walt Corey RC	5.00	2.20
❑ 96 Len Dawson SP	75.00	34.00
❑ 97 Dave Grayson RC	4.00	1.80
❑ 98 Abner Haynes	6.00	2.70
❑ 99 Sherrill Headrick SP	10.00	4.50
❑ 100 E.J. Holub	4.00	1.80
❑ 101 Bobby Hunt RC	4.00	1.80
❑ 102 Frank Jackson SP	6.00	2.70
❑ 103 Curtis McClinton	5.00	2.20
❑ 104 Jerry Mays SP	10.00	4.50
❑ 105 Johnny Robinson SP	12.00	5.50
❑ 106 Jack Spikes SP	6.00	2.70
❑ 107 Smokey Stover SP	6.00	2.70
❑ 108 Jim Tyrer RC	8.00	3.60
❑ 109 Duane Wood SP	6.00	2.70
❑ 110 Kansas City Chiefs Team Card	6.00	2.70
❑ 111 Dick Christy SP	6.00	2.70
❑ 112 Dan Ficca SP	6.00	2.70
❑ 113 Larry Grantham	4.00	1.80
❑ 114 Curley Johnson SP	6.00	2.70
❑ 115 Gene Heeter	4.00	1.80
❑ 116 Jack Klotz	4.00	1.80
❑ 117 Pete Liske RC	5.00	2.20
❑ 118 Bob McAdam	4.00	1.80
❑ 119 Dee Mackey SP	6.00	2.70
❑ 120 Bill Mathis SP	10.00	4.50
❑ 121 Don Maynard	35.00	16.00
❑ 122 Dainard Paulson SP	6.00	2.70
❑ 123 Gerry Philbin RC	5.00	2.20
❑ 124 Mark Smolinski SP	6.00	2.70
❑ 125 Matt Snell RC	20.00	9.00
❑ 126 Mike Taliaferro	4.00	1.80
❑ 127 Bake Turner RC SP	10.00	4.50
❑ 128 Jeff Ware	4.00	1.80
❑ 129 Clyde Washington	4.00	1.80
❑ 130 Dick Wood RC	4.00	1.80
❑ 131 New York Jets Team Card	6.00	2.70
❑ 132 Dalva Allen SP	6.00	2.70
❑ 133 Dan Birdwell	4.00	1.80
❑ 134 Dave Costa RC	4.00	1.80
❑ 135 Dobie Craig	4.00	1.80
❑ 136 Clem Daniels	5.00	2.20
❑ 137 Cotton Davidson SP	10.00	4.50
❑ 138 Claude Gibson	4.00	1.80
❑ 139 Tom Flores SP	15.00	6.75
❑ 140 Wayne Hawkins SP	6.00	2.70
❑ 141 Ken Herock	4.00	1.80
❑ 142 Jon Jelacic SP	6.00	2.70
❑ 143 Joe Krakoski	4.00	1.80
❑ 144 Archie Matsos SP	6.00	2.70
❑ 145 Mike Mercer	4.00	1.80
❑ 146 Alan Miller SP	6.00	2.70
❑ 147 Bob Mischak SP	6.00	2.70

Card	NM	Ex
❑ 148 Jim Otto SP	30.00	13.50
❑ 149 Clancy Osborne SP	6.00	2.70
❑ 150 Art Powell SP	12.00	5.50
❑ 151 Bo Roberson (Raider helmet placed over his foot)	4.00	1.80
❑ 152 Fred Williamson SP	30.00	11.00
❑ 153 Oakland Raiders Team Card	6.00	2.70
❑ 154 Chuck Allen RC SP	10.00	4.50
❑ 155 Lance Alworth	50.00	22.00
❑ 156 George Blair	4.00	1.80
❑ 157 Earl Faison	4.00	1.80
❑ 158 Sam Gruneisen	4.00	1.80
❑ 159 John Hadl RC	40.00	18.00
❑ 160 Dick Harris SP	6.00	2.70
❑ 161 Emil Karas SP	6.00	2.70
❑ 162 Dave Kocourek SP	6.00	2.70
❑ 163 Ernie Ladd	8.00	3.60
❑ 164 Keith Lincoln	6.00	2.70
❑ 165 Paul Lowe SP	12.00	5.50
❑ 166 Charley McNeil	4.00	1.80
❑ 167 Jacque MacKinnon SP RC	6.00	2.70
❑ 168 Ron Mix SP	20.00	9.00
❑ 169 Don Norton SP	6.00	2.70
❑ 170 Don Rogers SP	6.00	2.70
❑ 171 Tobin Rote SP	10.00	4.50
❑ 172 Henry Schmidt SP RC	6.00	2.70
❑ 173 Bud Whitehead	4.00	1.80
❑ 174 Ernie Wright SP	10.00	4.50
❑ 175 San Diego Chargers Team Card	6.00	2.70
❑ 176 Checklist SP UER (155 Lance Allworth)	160.00	40.00

1965 Topps

	NM	Ex
COMPLETE SET (176)	4000.00	1800.00
WRAPPER (5-CENT)	150.00	70.00
❑ 1 Tommy Addison SP	35.00	8.75
❑ 2 Houston Antwine SP	12.00	5.50
❑ 3 Nick Buoniconti SP	30.00	13.50
❑ 4 Ron Burton SP	20.00	9.00
❑ 5 Gino Cappelletti SP	20.00	9.00
❑ 6 Jim Colclough	7.00	3.10
❑ 7 Bob Dee SP	12.00	5.50
❑ 8 Larry Eisenhauer	7.00	3.10
❑ 9 J.D. Garrett	7.00	3.10
❑ 10 Larry Garron	7.00	3.10
❑ 11 Art Graham SP	12.00	5.50
❑ 12 Ron Hall	7.00	3.10
❑ 13 Charles Long	7.00	3.10
❑ 14 Jon Morris RC	10.00	4.50
❑ 15 Billy Neighbors SP	12.00	5.50
❑ 16 Ross O'Hanley	7.00	3.10
❑ 17 Babe Parilli SP	20.00	9.00
❑ 18 Tony Romeo SP	12.00	5.50
❑ 19 Jack Rudolph SP	12.00	5.50
❑ 20 Bob Schmidt	7.00	3.10
❑ 21 Don Webb SP	12.00	5.50
❑ 22 Jim Whalen SP	12.00	5.50
❑ 23 Stew Barber	7.00	3.10
❑ 24 Glenn Bass SP	12.00	5.50
❑ 25 Al Bemiller SP	12.00	5.50
❑ 26 Wray Carlton SP	12.00	5.50
❑ 27 Tom Day	7.00	3.10
❑ 28 Elbert Dubenion SP	15.00	6.75
❑ 29 Jim Dunaway	7.00	3.10
❑ 30 Pete Gogolak RC SP	20.00	9.00
❑ 31 Dick Hudson SP	12.00	5.50
❑ 32 Harry Jacobs SP	12.00	5.50
❑ 33 Billy Joe SP	15.00	6.75
❑ 34 Tom Keating RC SP	12.00	5.50
❑ 35 Jack Kemp SP	150.00	70.00
❑ 36 Daryle Lamonica SP	50.00	22.00
❑ 37 Paul Maguire SP	20.00	9.00
❑ 38 Ron McDole RC SP	12.00	5.50
❑ 39 George Saimes SP	12.00	5.50
❑ 40 Tom Sestak SP	12.00	5.50
❑ 41 Billy Shaw SP	20.00	9.00
❑ 42 Mike Stratton SP	12.00	5.50
❑ 43 John Tracey SP	12.00	5.50
❑ 44 Ernie Warlick	7.00	3.10
❑ 45 Odell Barry	7.00	3.10
❑ 46 Willie Brown RC SP	100.00	55.00
❑ 47 Gerry Bussell SP	12.00	5.50
❑ 48 Eldon Danenhauer SP	12.00	5.50
❑ 49 Al Denson SP	12.00	5.50
❑ 50 Hewritt Dixon RC SP	15.00	6.75
❑ 51 Cookie Gilchrist SP	30.00	13.50
❑ 52 Goose Gonsoulin SP	15.00	6.75
❑ 53 Abner Haynes SP	20.00	9.00
❑ 54 Jerry Hopkins	7.00	3.10
❑ 55 Ray Jacobs SP	12.00	5.50
❑ 56 Jacky Lee SP	15.00	6.75
❑ 57 John McCormick	7.00	3.10
❑ 58 Bob McCullough SP	12.00	5.50
❑ 59 John McGeever	7.00	3.10
❑ 60 Charlie Mitchell SP	12.00	5.50
❑ 61 Jim Perkins SP	12.00	5.50
❑ 62 Bob Scarpitto SP	12.00	5.50
❑ 63 Mickey Slaughter SP	12.00	5.50
❑ 64 Jerry Sturm SP	12.00	5.50
❑ 65 Lionel Taylor SP	20.00	9.00
❑ 66 Scott Appleton SP	12.00	5.50
❑ 67 Johnny Baker SP	12.00	5.50
❑ 68 Sonny Bishop SP	12.00	5.50
❑ 69 George Blanda SP	125.00	55.00
❑ 70 Sid Blanks SP	12.00	5.50
❑ 71 Ode Burrell SP	12.00	5.50
❑ 72 Doug Cline SP	12.00	5.50
❑ 73 Willard Dewveall	7.00	3.10
❑ 74 Larry Elkins RC	7.00	3.10
❑ 75 Don Floyd SP	12.00	5.50
❑ 76 Freddy Glick	7.00	3.10
❑ 77 Tom Goode SP	12.00	5.50
❑ 78 Charlie Hennigan SP	20.00	9.00
❑ 79 Ed Husmann	7.00	3.10
❑ 80 Bobby Jancik SP	12.00	5.50
❑ 81 Bud McFadin SP	12.00	5.50
❑ 82 Bob McLeod SP	12.00	5.50
❑ 83 Jim Norton SP	12.00	5.50
❑ 84 Walt Suggs	7.00	3.10
❑ 85 Bob Talamini	7.00	3.10
❑ 86 Charley Tolar SP	12.00	5.50
❑ 87 Checklist SP	175.00	45.00
❑ 88 Don Trull SP	12.00	5.50
❑ 89 Fred Arbanas SP	12.00	5.50
❑ 90 Pete Beathard RC SP	12.00	5.50
❑ 91 Bobby Bell SP	40.00	18.00
❑ 92 Mel Branch SP	12.00	5.50
❑ 93 Tommy Brooker SP	12.00	5.50
❑ 94 Buck Buchanan SP	35.00	16.00
❑ 95 Ed Budde SP	12.00	5.50
❑ 96 Chris Burford SP	12.00	5.50
❑ 97 Walt Corey	7.00	3.10
❑ 98 Jerry Cornelison	7.00	3.10
❑ 99 Len Dawson SP	100.00	45.00
❑ 100 Jon Gilliam SP	12.00	5.50
❑ 101 Sherrill Headrick SP UER (Name spelled Sherill on front)	12.00	5.50
❑ 102 Dave Hill SP	12.00	5.50
❑ 103 E.J. Holub SP	12.00	5.50
❑ 104 Bobby Hunt SP	12.00	5.50
❑ 105 Frank Jackson SP	12.00	5.50
❑ 106 Jerry Mays	10.00	4.50
❑ 107 Curtis McClinton SP	15.00	6.75
❑ 108 Bobby Ply SP	12.00	5.50
❑ 109 Johnny Robinson SP	15.00	6.75
❑ 110 Jim Tyrer SP	12.00	5.50
❑ 111 Bill Baird SP	12.00	5.50
❑ 112 Ralph Baker RC SP	12.00	5.50
❑ 113 Sam DeLuca SP	12.00	5.50
❑ 114 Larry Grantham SP	15.00	6.75
❑ 115 Gene Heeter SP	12.00	5.50
❑ 116 Winston Hill RC SP	20.00	9.00
❑ 117 John Huarte RC SP	30.00	13.50
❑ 118 Cosmo Iacavazzi SP	12.00	5.50
❑ 119 Curley Johnson SP	12.00	5.50
❑ 120 Dee Mackey UER (College WVU, should be East Texas State)	7.00	3.10
❑ 121 Don Maynard	50.00	22.00
❑ 122 Joe Namath SP RC	1600.00	700.00
❑ 123 Dainard Paulson	7.00	3.10
❑ 124 Gerry Philbin SP	12.00	5.50
❑ 125 Sherman Plunkett RC SP	15.00	6.75
❑ 126 Mark Smolinski	7.00	3.10
❑ 127 Matt Snell SP	30.00	13.50
❑ 128 Mike Taliaferro SP	12.00	5.50
❑ 129 Bake Turner SP	12.00	5.50
❑ 130 Clyde Washington SP	12.00	5.50
❑ 131 Verlon Biggs RC SP	12.00	5.50
❑ 132 Dalva Allen	7.00	3.10
❑ 133 Fred Biletnikoff RC SP	225.00	100.00
❑ 134 Billy Cannon SP	20.00	9.00
❑ 135 Dave Costa SP	12.00	5.50
❑ 136 Clem Daniels SP	15.00	6.75
❑ 137 Ben Davidson RC SP	60.00	27.00
❑ 138 Cotton Davidson SP	15.00	6.75
❑ 139 Tom Flores SP	20.00	9.00
❑ 140 Claude Gibson	7.00	3.10
❑ 141 Wayne Hawkins	7.00	3.10
❑ 142 Archie Matsos SP	12.00	5.50
❑ 143 Mike Mercer SP	12.00	5.50
❑ 144 Bob Mischak SP	12.00	5.50
❑ 145 Jim Otto	30.00	13.50
❑ 146 Art Powell UER (Photo actually Clem Daniels)	10.00	4.50
❑ 147 Warren Powers SP	12.00	5.50
❑ 148 Ken Rice SP	12.00	5.50
❑ 149 Bo Roberson SP	12.00	5.50
❑ 150 Harry Schuh RC	7.00	3.10
❑ 151 Larry Todd SP	12.00	5.50
❑ 152 Fred Williamson SP	30.00	9.00
❑ 153 J.R. Williamson	7.00	3.10
❑ 154 Chuck Allen	10.00	4.50
❑ 155 Lance Alworth	75.00	34.00
❑ 156 Frank Buncom	7.00	3.10
❑ 157 Steve DeLong RC SP	12.00	5.50
❑ 158 Earl Faison SP	15.00	6.75
❑ 159 Kenny Graham SP	12.00	5.50
❑ 160 George Gross SP	12.00	5.50
❑ 161 John Hadl SP	35.00	16.00
❑ 162 Emil Karas SP	12.00	5.50
❑ 163 Dave Kocourek SP	12.00	5.50
❑ 164 Ernie Ladd SP	20.00	9.00
❑ 165 Keith Lincoln SP	20.00	9.00
❑ 166 Paul Lowe SP	20.00	9.00
❑ 167 Jacque MacKinnon	7.00	3.10
❑ 168 Ron Mix	20.00	9.00
❑ 169 Don Norton SP	12.00	5.50
❑ 170 Bob Petrich	7.00	3.10
❑ 171 Rick Redman SP	12.00	5.50
❑ 172 Pat Shea	7.00	3.10
❑ 173 Walt Sweeney RC SP	15.00	6.75
❑ 174 Dick Westmoreland RC	7.00	3.10
❑ 175 Ernie Wright SP	20.00	9.00
❑ 176 Checklist SP	225.00	55.00

1966 Topps

	NM	Ex
COMPLETE SET (132)	1500.00	700.00
WRAPPER (5-CENT)	60.00	27.00
❑ 1 Tommy Addison	20.00	5.00

❑ 2 Houston Antwine 5.00 2.20
❑ 3 Nick Buoniconti 10.00 4.50
❑ 4 Gino Cappelletti 7.00 3.10
❑ 5 Bob Dee 5.00 2.20
❑ 6 Larry Garron 5.00 2.20
❑ 7 Art Graham 5.00 2.20
❑ 8 Ron Hall 5.00 2.20
❑ 9 Charles Long 5.00 2.20
❑ 10 Jon Morris 5.00 2.20
❑ 11 Don Oakes 5.00 2.20
❑ 12 Babe Parilli 7.00 3.10
❑ 13 Don Webb 5.00 2.20
❑ 14 Jim Whalen 5.00 2.20
❑ 15 Funny Ring Checklist 300.00 75.00
❑ 16 Stew Barber 5.00 2.20
❑ 17 Glenn Bass 5.00 2.20
❑ 18 Dave Behrman 5.00 2.20
❑ 19 Al Bemiller 5.00 2.20
❑ 20 George Butch Byrd RC 7.00 3.10
❑ 21 Wray Carlton 5.00 2.20
❑ 22 Tom Day 5.00 2.20
❑ 23 Elbert Dubenion 7.00 3.10
❑ 24 Jim Dunaway 5.00 2.20
❑ 25 Dick Hudson 5.00 2.20
❑ 26 Jack Kemp 150.00 70.00
❑ 27 Daryle Lamonica 20.00 9.00
❑ 28 Tom Sestak 5.00 2.20
❑ 29 Billy Shaw 10.00 4.50
❑ 30 Mike Stratton 5.00 2.20
❑ 31 Eldon Danenhauer 5.00 2.20
❑ 32 Cookie Gilchrist 10.00 4.50
❑ 33 Goose Gonsoulin 7.00 3.10
❑ 34 Wendell Hayes RC 10.00 4.50
❑ 35 Abner Haynes 10.00 4.50
❑ 36 Jerry Hopkins 5.00 2.20
❑ 37 Ray Jacobs 5.00 2.20
❑ 38 Charlie Janerette 5.00 2.20
❑ 39 Ray Kubala 5.00 2.20
❑ 40 John McCormick 5.00 2.20
❑ 41 Leroy Moore 5.00 2.20
❑ 42 Bob Scarpitto 5.00 2.20
❑ 43 Mickey Slaughter 5.00 2.20
❑ 44 Jerry Sturm 5.00 2.20
❑ 45 Lionel Taylor 10.00 4.50
❑ 46 Scott Appleton 5.00 2.20
❑ 47 Johnny Baker 5.00 2.20
❑ 48 George Blanda 35.00 16.00
❑ 49 Sid Blanks 5.00 2.20
❑ 50 Danny Brabham 5.00 2.20
❑ 51 Ode Burrell 5.00 2.20
❑ 52 Gary Cutsinger 5.00 2.20
❑ 53 Larry Elkins 5.00 2.20
❑ 54 Don Floyd 5.00 2.20
❑ 55 Willie Frazier RC 7.00 3.10
❑ 56 Freddy Glick 5.00 2.20
❑ 57 Charlie Hennigan 7.00 3.10
❑ 58 Bobby Jancik 5.00 2.20
❑ 59 Rich Michael 5.00 2.20
❑ 60 Don Trull 5.00 2.20
❑ 61 Checklist Card 55.00 14.00
❑ 62 Fred Arbanas 5.00 2.20
❑ 63 Pete Beathard 5.00 2.20
❑ 64 Bobby Bell 10.00 4.50
❑ 65 Ed Budde 5.00 2.20
❑ 66 Chris Burford 5.00 2.20
❑ 67 Len Dawson 40.00 18.00
❑ 68 Jon Gilliam 5.00 2.20
❑ 69 Sherrill Headrick 5.00 2.20
❑ 70 E.J. Holub UER 5.00 2.20
(College: TCU, should be Texas Tech)
❑ 71 Bobby Hunt 5.00 2.20
❑ 72 Curtis McClinton 7.00 3.10
❑ 73 Jerry Mays 5.00 2.20
❑ 74 Johnny Robinson 7.00 3.10
❑ 75 Otis Taylor RC 25.00 11.00
❑ 76 Tom Erlandson 7.00 3.10
❑ 77 Norm Evans RC UER 10.00 4.50
(Flanker on front, tackle on back)
❑ 78 Tom Goode 7.00 3.10
❑ 79 Mike Hudock 7.00 3.10
❑ 80 Frank Jackson 7.00 3.10
❑ 81 Billy Joe 7.00 3.10
❑ 82 Dave Kocourek 7.00 3.10
❑ 83 Bo Roberson 7.00 3.10
❑ 84 Jack Spikes 7.00 3.10
❑ 85 Jim Warren RC 7.00 3.10
❑ 86 Willie West RC 7.00 3.10
❑ 87 Dick Westmoreland 7.00 3.10
❑ 88 Eddie Wilson 7.00 3.10
❑ 89 Dick Wood 7.00 3.10
❑ 90 Verlon Biggs 7.00 3.10
❑ 91 Sam DeLuca 5.00 2.20
❑ 92 Winston Hill 5.00 2.20
❑ 93 Dee Mackey 5.00 2.20
❑ 94 Bill Mathis 5.00 2.20
❑ 95 Don Maynard 30.00 13.50
❑ 96 Joe Namath 250.00 110.00
❑ 97 Dainard Paulson 5.00 2.20
❑ 98 Gerry Philbin 7.00 3.10
❑ 99 Sherman Plunkett 5.00 2.20
❑ 100 Paul Rochester 5.00 2.20
❑ 101 George Sauer Jr. RC 15.00 6.75
❑ 102 Matt Snell 10.00 4.50
❑ 103 Jim Turner RC 7.00 3.10
❑ 104 Fred Biletnikoff UER 50.00 22.00
(Misspelled on back as Bilentnikoff)
❑ 105 Bill Budness 5.00 2.20
❑ 106 Billy Cannon 10.00 4.50
❑ 107 Clem Daniels 7.00 3.10
❑ 108 Ben Davidson 15.00 6.75
❑ 109 Cotton Davidson 7.00 3.10
❑ 110 Claude Gibson 5.00 2.20
❑ 111 Wayne Hawkins 5.00 2.20
❑ 112 Ken Herock 5.00 2.20
❑ 113 Bob Mischak 5.00 2.20
❑ 114 Gus Otto 5.00 2.20
❑ 115 Jim Otto 20.00 9.00
❑ 116 Art Powell 10.00 4.50
❑ 117 Harry Schuh 5.00 2.20
❑ 118 Chuck Allen 5.00 2.20
❑ 119 Lance Alworth 40.00 18.00
❑ 120 Frank Buncom 5.00 2.20
❑ 121 Steve DeLong 5.00 2.20
❑ 122 John Farris 5.00 2.20
❑ 123 Kenny Graham 5.00 2.20
❑ 124 Sam Gruneisen 5.00 2.20
❑ 125 John Hadl 10.00 4.50
❑ 126 Walt Sweeney 5.00 2.20
❑ 127 Keith Lincoln 10.00 4.50
❑ 128 Ron Mix 10.00 4.50
❑ 129 Don Norton 5.00 2.20
❑ 130 Pat Shea 5.00 2.20
❑ 131 Ernie Wright 10.00 4.50
❑ 132 Checklist Card 100.00 25.00

1967 Topps

	NM	Ex
COMPLETE SET (132)	700.00	325.00
WRAPPER (5-CENT)	60.00	27.00

❑ 1 John Huarte 18.00 4.50
❑ 2 Babe Parilli 4.00 1.80

❑ 3 Gino Cappelletti 4.00 1.80
❑ 4 Larry Garron 3.00 1.35
❑ 5 Tommy Addison 3.00 1.35
❑ 6 Jon Morris 3.00 1.35
❑ 7 Houston Antwine 3.00 1.35
❑ 8 Don Oakes 3.00 1.35
❑ 9 Larry Eisenhauer 3.00 1.35
❑ 10 Jim Hunt 3.00 1.35
❑ 11 Jim Whalen 3.00 1.35
❑ 12 Art Graham 3.00 1.35
❑ 13 Nick Buoniconti 6.00 2.70
❑ 14 Bob Dee 3.00 1.35
❑ 15 Keith Lincoln 6.00 2.70
❑ 16 Tom Flores 4.00 1.80
❑ 17 Art Powell 4.00 1.80
❑ 18 Stew Barber 3.00 1.35
❑ 19 Wray Carlton 3.00 1.35
❑ 20 Elbert Dubenion 4.00 1.80
❑ 21 Jim Dunaway 3.00 1.35
❑ 22 Dick Hudson 3.00 1.35
❑ 23 Harry Jacobs 3.00 1.35
❑ 24 Jack Kemp 80.00 36.00
❑ 25 Ron McDole 3.00 1.35
❑ 26 George Saimes 3.00 1.35
❑ 27 Tom Sestak 3.00 1.35
❑ 28 Billy Shaw 6.00 2.70
❑ 29 Mike Stratton 3.00 1.35
❑ 30 Nemiah Wilson RC 3.00 1.35
❑ 31 John McCormick 3.00 1.35
❑ 32 Rex Mirich 3.00 1.35
❑ 33 Dave Costa 3.00 1.35
❑ 34 Goose Gonsoulin 4.00 1.80
❑ 35 Abner Haynes 6.00 2.70
❑ 36 Wendell Hayes 4.00 1.80
❑ 37 Archie Matsos 3.00 1.35
❑ 38 John Bramlett 3.00 1.35
❑ 39 Jerry Sturm 3.00 1.35
❑ 40 Max Leetzow 3.00 1.35
❑ 41 Bob Scarpitto 3.00 1.35
❑ 42 Lionel Taylor 6.00 2.70
❑ 43 Al Denson 3.00 1.35
❑ 44 Miller Farr RC 3.00 1.35
❑ 45 Don Trull 3.00 1.35
❑ 46 Jacky Lee 4.00 1.80
❑ 47 Bobby Jancik 3.00 1.35
❑ 48 Ode Burrell 3.00 1.35
❑ 49 Larry Elkins 3.00 1.35
❑ 50 W.K. Hicks 3.00 1.35
❑ 51 Sid Blanks 3.00 1.35
❑ 52 Jim Norton 3.00 1.35
❑ 53 Bobby Maples RC 3.00 1.35
❑ 54 Bob Talamini 3.00 1.35
❑ 55 Walt Suggs 3.00 1.35
❑ 56 Gary Cutsinger 3.00 1.35
❑ 57 Danny Brabham 3.00 1.35
❑ 58 Ernie Ladd 6.00 2.70
❑ 59 Checklist Card 50.00 22.00
❑ 60 Pete Beathard 3.00 1.35
❑ 61 Len Dawson 30.00 13.50
❑ 62 Bobby Hunt 3.00 1.35
❑ 63 Bert Coan 3.00 1.35
❑ 64 Curtis McClinton 4.00 1.80
❑ 65 Johnny Robinson 4.00 1.80
❑ 66 E.J. Holub 3.00 1.35

❑ 67 Jerry Mays 3.00 1.35
❑ 68 Jim Tyrer 4.00 1.80
❑ 69 Bobby Bell 6.00 2.70
❑ 70 Fred Arbanas 3.00 1.35
❑ 71 Buck Buchanan 6.00 2.70
❑ 72 Chris Burford 3.00 1.35
❑ 73 Otis Taylor 6.00 2.70
❑ 74 Cookie Gilchrist 8.00 3.60
❑ 75 Earl Faison 3.00 1.35
❑ 76 George Wilson Jr. 4.00 1.80
❑ 77 Rick Norton 3.00 1.35
❑ 78 Frank Jackson 4.00 1.80
❑ 79 Joe Auer 3.00 1.35
❑ 80 Willie West 3.00 1.35
❑ 81 Jim Warren 3.00 1.35
❑ 82 Wahoo McDaniel RC 50.00 22.00
❑ 83 Ernie Park 3.00 1.35
❑ 84 Billy Neighbors 3.00 1.35
❑ 85 Norm Evans 4.00 1.80
❑ 86 Tom Nomina 3.00 1.35
❑ 87 Rich Zecher 3.00 1.35
❑ 88 Dave Kocourek 3.00 1.35
❑ 89 Bill Baird 3.00 1.35
❑ 90 Ralph Baker 3.00 1.35
❑ 91 Verlon Biggs 3.00 1.35
❑ 92 Sam DeLuca 3.00 1.35
❑ 93 Larry Grantham 4.00 1.80
❑ 94 Jim Harris 3.00 1.35
❑ 95 Winston Hill 3.00 1.35
❑ 96 Bill Mathis 3.00 1.35
❑ 97 Don Maynard 20.00 9.00
❑ 98 Joe Namath 150.00 70.00
❑ 99 Gerry Philbin 4.00 1.80
❑ 100 Paul Rochester 3.00 1.35
❑ 101 George Sauer Jr. 4.00 1.80
❑ 102 Matt Snell 6.00 2.70
❑ 103 Daryle Lamonica 10.00 4.50
❑ 104 Glenn Bass 3.00 1.35
❑ 105 Jim Otto 6.00 2.70
❑ 106 Fred Biletnikoff 30.00 13.50
❑ 107 Cotton Davidson 4.00 1.80
❑ 108 Larry Todd 3.00 1.35
❑ 109 Billy Cannon 6.00 2.70
❑ 110 Clem Daniels 4.00 1.80
❑ 111 Dave Grayson 3.00 1.35
❑ 112 Kent McCloughan RC 3.00 1.35
❑ 113 Bob Svihus 3.00 1.35
❑ 114 Ike Lassiter 3.00 1.35
❑ 115 Harry Schuh 3.00 1.35
❑ 116 Ben Davidson 8.00 3.60
❑ 117 Tom Day 3.00 1.35
❑ 118 Scott Appleton 3.00 1.35
❑ 119 Steve Tensi RC 3.00 1.35
❑ 120 John Hadl 6.00 2.70
❑ 121 Paul Lowe 4.00 1.80
❑ 122 Jim Allison 3.00 1.35
❑ 123 Lance Alworth 35.00 16.00
❑ 124 Jacque MacKinnon 3.00 1.35
❑ 125 Ron Mix 6.00 2.70
❑ 126 Bob Petrich 3.00 1.35
❑ 127 Howard Kindig 3.00 1.35
❑ 128 Steve DeLong 3.00 1.35
❑ 129 Chuck Allen 3.00 1.35
❑ 130 Frank Buncom 3.00 1.35
❑ 131 Speedy Duncan RC 4.00 1.80
❑ 132 Checklist Card 70.00 17.50

1968 Topps

	NM	Ex
COMPLETE SET (219)	550.00	250.00
COMMON CARD (1-131)	1.50	.70
COMMON CARD (132-219)	2.00	.90
WRAPPER (5-CENT, SER.1)	20.00	9.00
WRAPPER (5-CENT, SER.2)	30.00	13.50

❑ 1 Bart Starr 40.00 10.00
❑ 2 Dick Bass 2.00 .90
❑ 3 Grady Alderman 1.50 .70
❑ 4 Obert Logan 1.50 .70
❑ 5 Ernie Koy RC 2.00 .90
❑ 6 Don Hultz 1.50 .70
❑ 7 Earl Gros 1.50 .70
❑ 8 Jim Bakken 1.50 .70
❑ 9 George Mira 2.00 .90
❑ 10 Carl Kammerer 1.50 .70
❑ 11 Willie Frazier 1.50 .70
❑ 12 Kent McCloughan UER (McCloughlan on card back) 1.50 .70
❑ 13 George Sauer Jr. 2.00 .90
❑ 14 Jack Clancy 1.50 .70
❑ 15 Jim Tyrer 2.00 .90
❑ 16 Bobby Maples 1.50 .70
❑ 17 Bo Hickey 1.50 .70
❑ 18 Frank Buncom 1.50 .70
❑ 19 Keith Lincoln 2.00 .90
❑ 20 Jim Whalen 1.50 .70
❑ 21 Junior Coffey 1.50 .70
❑ 22 Billy Ray Smith 1.50 .70
❑ 23 Johnny Morris 1.50 .70
❑ 24 Ernie Green 1.50 .70
❑ 25 Don Meredith 25.00 11.00
❑ 26 Wayne Walker 1.50 .70
❑ 27 Carroll Dale 2.00 .90
❑ 28 Bernie Casey 2.00 .90
❑ 29 Dave Osborn RC 2.00 .90
❑ 30 Ray Poage 1.50 .70
❑ 31 Homer Jones 1.50 .70
❑ 32 Sam Baker 1.50 .70
❑ 33 Bill Saul 1.50 .70
❑ 34 Ken Willard 2.00 .90
❑ 35 Bobby Mitchell 4.00 1.80
❑ 36 Gary Garrison RC 2.00 .90
❑ 37 Billy Cannon 2.00 .90
❑ 38 Ralph Baker 1.50 .70
❑ 39 Howard Twilley RC 4.00 1.80
❑ 40 Wendell Hayes 2.00 .90
❑ 41 Jim Norton 1.50 .70
❑ 42 Tom Beer 1.50 .70
❑ 43 Chris Burford 1.50 .70
❑ 44 Stew Barber 1.50 .70
❑ 45 Leroy Mitchell UER (Lifetime Int. should be 3, not 2) 1.50 .70
❑ 46 Dan Grimm 1.50 .70
❑ 47 Jerry Logan 1.50 .70
❑ 48 Andy Livingston 1.50 .70
❑ 49 Paul Warfield 15.00 6.75
❑ 50 Don Perkins 3.00 1.35
❑ 51 Ron Kramer 1.50 .70
❑ 52 Bob Jeter RC 2.00 .90
❑ 53 Les Josephson RC 2.00 .90
❑ 54 Bobby Walden 1.50 .70
❑ 55 Checklist Card 15.00 3.70
❑ 56 Walter Roberts 1.50 .70
❑ 57 Henry Carr 1.50 .70
❑ 58 Gary Ballman 1.50 .70
❑ 59 J.R. Wilburn 1.50 .70
❑ 60 Jim Hart RC 10.00 4.50
❑ 61 Jim Johnson 3.00 1.35
❑ 62 Chris Hanburger 2.00 .90
❑ 63 John Hadl 3.00 1.35
❑ 64 Hewritt Dixon 2.00 .90
❑ 65 Joe Namath 80.00 36.00
❑ 66 Jim Warren 1.50 .70
❑ 67 Curtis McClinton 2.00 .90
❑ 68 Bob Talamini 1.50 .70
❑ 69 Steve Tensi 1.50 .70
❑ 70 Dick Van Raaphorst UER (Van Raap Horst on card back) 1.50 .70
❑ 71 Art Powell 2.00 .90
❑ 72 Jim Nance RC 4.00 1.80
❑ 73 Bob Riggle 1.50 .70
❑ 74 John Mackey 5.00 2.20
❑ 75 Gale Sayers 40.00 18.00
❑ 76 Gene Hickerson 1.50 .70
❑ 77 Dan Reeves 10.00 4.50
❑ 78 Tom Nowatzke 1.50 .70
❑ 79 Elijah Pitts 3.00 1.35
❑ 80 Lamar Lundy 2.00 .90
❑ 81 Paul Flatley 1.50 .70
❑ 82 Dave Whitsell 1.50 .70
❑ 83 Spider Lockhart 2.00 .90
❑ 84 Dave Lloyd 1.50 .70
❑ 85 Roy Jefferson 2.00 .90
❑ 86 Jackie Smith 6.00 2.70
❑ 87 John David Crow 2.00 .90
❑ 88 Sonny Jurgensen 6.00 2.70
❑ 89 Ron Mix 3.00 1.35
❑ 90 Clem Daniels 2.00 .90
❑ 91 Cornell Gordon 1.50 .70
❑ 92 Tom Goode 1.50 .70
❑ 93 Bobby Bell 3.00 1.35
❑ 94 Walt Suggs 1.50 .70
❑ 95 Eric Crabtree 1.50 .70
❑ 96 Sherrill Headrick 1.50 .70
❑ 97 Wray Carlton 1.50 .70
❑ 98 Gino Cappelletti 2.00 .90
❑ 99 Tommy McDonald 4.00 1.80
❑ 100 John Unitas 35.00 16.00
❑ 101 Richie Petitbon 1.50 .70
❑ 102 Erich Barnes 1.50 .70
❑ 103 Bob Hayes 8.00 3.60
❑ 104 Milt Plum 2.00 .90
❑ 105 Boyd Dowler 2.00 .90
❑ 106 Ed Meador 1.50 .70
❑ 107 Fred Cox 1.50 .70
❑ 108 Steve Stonebreaker RC 1.50 .70
❑ 109 Aaron Thomas 1.50 .70
❑ 110 Norm Snead 2.00 .90
❑ 111 Paul Martha RC 1.50 .70
❑ 112 Jerry Stovall 1.50 .70
❑ 113 Kay McFarland 1.50 .70
❑ 114 Pat Richter 1.50 .70
❑ 115 Rick Redman 1.50 .70
❑ 116 Tom Keating 1.50 .70
❑ 117 Matt Snell 2.00 .90
❑ 118 Dick Westmoreland 1.50 .70
❑ 119 Jerry Mays 1.50 .70
❑ 120 Sid Blanks 1.50 .70
❑ 121 Al Denson 1.50 .70
❑ 122 Bobby Hunt 1.50 .70
❑ 123 Mike Mercer 1.50 .70
❑ 124 Nick Buoniconti 3.00 1.35
❑ 125 Ron Vanderkelen RC 1.50 .70
❑ 126 Ordell Braase 1.50 .70
❑ 127 Dick Butkus 45.00 20.00
❑ 128 Gary Collins 2.00 .90
❑ 129 Mel Renfro 6.00 2.70
❑ 130 Alex Karras 5.00 2.20
❑ 131 Herb Adderley 5.00 2.20
❑ 132 Roman Gabriel 4.00 1.80
❑ 133 Bill Brown 2.50 1.10
❑ 134 Kent Kramer 2.00 .90
❑ 135 Tucker Frederickson 2.50 1.10
❑ 136 Nate Ramsey 2.00 .90
❑ 137 Marv Woodson 2.00 .90
❑ 138 Ken Gray 2.00 .90
❑ 139 John Brodie 5.00 2.20
❑ 140 Jerry Smith 2.00 .90
❑ 141 Brad Hubbert 2.00 .90
❑ 142 George Blanda 20.00 9.00
❑ 143 Pete Lammons RC 2.00 .90
❑ 144 Doug Moreau 2.00 .90
❑ 145 E.J. Holub 2.00 .90

Card	NM	Ex
146 Ode Burrell	2.00	.90
147 Bob Scarpitto	2.00	.90
148 Andre White	2.00	.90
149 Jack Kemp	50.00	22.00
150 Art Graham	2.00	.90
151 Tommy Nobis	6.00	2.70
152 Willie Richardson RC	2.50	1.10
153 Jack Concannon	2.00	.90
154 Bill Glass	2.00	.90
155 Craig Morton RC	10.00	4.50
156 Pat Studstill	2.00	.90
157 Ray Nitschke	10.00	4.50
158 Roger Brown	2.00	.90
159 Joe Kapp RC	5.00	2.20
160 Jim Taylor (Shown in uniform of Green Bay Packers)	15.00	6.75
161 Fran Tarkenton	20.00	9.00
162 Mike Ditka	30.00	13.50
163 Andy Russell RC	6.00	2.70
164 Larry Wilson	4.00	1.80
165 Tommy Davis	2.00	.90
166 Paul Krause	4.00	1.80
167 Speedy Duncan	2.00	.90
168 Fred Biletnikoff	15.00	6.75
169 Don Maynard	10.00	4.50
170 Frank Emanuel	2.00	.90
171 Len Dawson	15.00	6.75
172 Miller Farr	2.00	.90
173 Floyd Little RC	20.00	9.00
174 Lonnie Wright	2.00	.90
175 Paul Costa	2.00	.90
176 Don Trull	2.00	.90
177 Jerry Simmons	2.00	.90
178 Tom Matte	2.50	1.10
179 Bennie McRae	2.00	.90
180 Jim Kanicki	2.00	.90
181 Bob Lilly	15.00	6.75
182 Tom Watkins	2.00	.90
183 Jim Grabowski RC	4.00	1.80
184 Jack Snow RC	4.00	1.80
185 Gary Cuozzo RC	2.50	1.10
186 Bill Kilmer	4.00	1.80
187 Jim Katcavage	2.00	.90
188 Floyd Peters	2.00	.90
189 Bill Nelsen	2.50	1.10
190 Bobby Joe Conrad	2.50	1.10
191 Kermit Alexander	2.00	.90
192 Charley Taylor UER (Called Charley and Charlie on back)	6.00	2.70
193 Lance Alworth	20.00	9.00
194 Daryle Lamonica	5.00	2.20
195 Al Atkinson	2.00	.90
196 Bob Griese RC	90.00	40.00
197 Buck Buchanan	4.00	1.80
198 Pete Beathard	2.00	.90
199 Nemiah Wilson	2.00	.90
200 Ernie Wright	2.00	.90
201 George Saimes	2.00	.90
202 John Charles	2.00	.90
203 Randy Johnson	2.00	.90
204 Tony Lorick	2.00	.90
205 Dick Evey	2.00	.90
206 Leroy Kelly	10.00	4.50
207 Lee Roy Jordan	6.00	2.70
208 Jim Gibbons	2.00	.90
209 Donny Anderson RC	4.00	1.80
210 Maxie Baughan	2.00	.90
211 Joe Morrison	2.00	.90
212 Jim Snowden	2.00	.90
213 Lenny Lyles	2.00	.90
214 Bobby Joe Green	2.00	.90
215 Frank Ryan	2.50	1.10
216 Cornell Green	2.50	1.10
217 Karl Sweetan	2.00	.90
218 Dave Williams	2.00	.90
219A Checklist 132-218 (green print on back)	18.00	4.50
219B Checklist 132-218 (blue print on back)	20.00	5.00

1969 Topps

	NM	Ex
COMPLETE SET (263)	550.00	250.00
COMMON CARD (1-132)	1.50	.70
COMMON CARD (133-263)	2.00	.90
WRAPPER (5-CENT)	30.00	13.50
1 Leroy Kelly	20.00	5.00
2 Paul Flatley	1.50	.70
3 Jim Cadile	1.50	.70
4 Erich Barnes	1.50	.70
5 Willie Richardson	1.50	.70
6 Bob Hayes	5.00	2.20
7 Bob Jeter	1.50	.70
8 Jim Colclough	1.50	.70
9 Sherrill Headrick	1.50	.70
10 Jim Dunaway	1.50	.70
11 Bill Munson	2.00	.90
12 Jack Pardee	2.00	.90
13 Jim Lindsey	1.50	.70
14 Dave Whitsell	1.50	.70
15 Tucker Frederickson	1.50	.70
16 Alvin Haymond	2.00	.90
17 Andy Russell	2.00	.90
18 Tom Beer	1.50	.70
19 Bobby Maples	1.50	.70
20 Len Dawson	8.00	3.60
21 Willis Crenshaw	1.50	.70
22 Tommy Davis	1.50	.70
23 Rickie Harris	1.50	.70
24 Jerry Simmons	1.50	.70
25 John Unitas	40.00	18.00
26 Brian Piccolo RC UER (Misspelled Bryon on front and Bryan on back)	80.00	36.00
27 Bob Matheson	1.50	.70
28 Howard Twilley	2.00	.90
29 Jim Turner	2.00	.90
30 Pete Banaszak RC	2.00	.90
31 Lance Rentzel RC	2.00	.90
32 Bill Triplett	1.50	.70
33 Boyd Dowler	2.00	.90
34 Merlin Olsen	5.00	2.20
35 Joe Kapp	3.00	1.35
36 Dan Abramowicz RC	4.00	1.80
37 Spider Lockhart	2.00	.90
38 Tom Day	1.50	.70
39 Art Graham	1.50	.70
40 Bob Cappadona	1.50	.70
41 Gary Ballman	1.50	.70
42 Clendon Thomas	1.50	.70
43 Jackie Smith	4.00	1.80
44 Dave Wilcox	3.00	1.35
45 Jerry Smith	1.50	.70
46 Dan Grimm	1.50	.70
47 Tom Matte	2.00	.90
48 John Stofa	1.50	.70
49 Rex Mirich	1.50	.70
50 Miller Farr	1.50	.70
51 Gale Sayers	40.00	18.00
52 Bill Nelsen	2.00	.90
53 Bob Lilly	6.00	2.70
54 Wayne Walker	1.50	.70
55 Ray Nitschke	5.00	2.20
56 Ed Meador	1.50	.70
57 Lonnie Warwick	1.50	.70
58 Wendell Hayes	1.50	.70
59 Dick Anderson RC	5.00	2.20
60 Don Maynard	6.00	2.70
61 Tony Lorick	1.50	.70
62 Pete Gogolak	1.50	.70
63 Nate Ramsey	1.50	.70
64 Dick Shiner	1.50	.70
65 Larry Wilson	3.00	1.35
66 Ken Willard	2.00	.90
67 Charley Taylor UER (Led Redskins in pass interceptions)	5.00	2.20
68 Billy Cannon	2.00	.90
69 Lance Alworth	8.00	3.60
70 Jim Nance	2.00	.90
71 Nick Rassas	1.50	.70
72 Lenny Lyles	1.50	.70
73 Bennie McRae	1.50	.70
74 Bill Glass	1.50	.70
75 Don Meredith	25.00	11.00
76 Dick LeBeau	1.50	.70
77 Carroll Dale	2.00	.90
78 Ron McDole	1.50	.70
79 Charley King	1.50	.70
80 Checklist 1-132 UER (26 Bryon Piccolo)	15.00	3.70
81 Dick Bass	2.00	.90
82 Roy Winston	1.50	.70
83 Don McCall	1.50	.70
84 Jim Katcavage	2.00	.90
85 Norm Snead	2.00	.90
86 Earl Gros	1.50	.70
87 Don Brumm	1.50	.70
88 Sonny Bishop	1.50	.70
89 Fred Arbanas	1.50	.70
90 Karl Noonan	1.50	.70
91 Dick Witcher	1.50	.70
92 Vince Promuto	1.50	.70
93 Tommy Nobis	4.00	1.80
94 Jerry Hill	1.50	.70
95 Ed O'Bradovich RC	1.50	.70
96 Ernie Kellerman	1.50	.70
97 Chuck Howley	2.00	.90
98 Hewritt Dixon	1.50	.70
99 Ron Mix	3.00	1.35
100 Joe Namath	75.00	34.00
101 Billy Gambrell	1.50	.70
102 Elijah Pitts	2.00	.90
103 Billy Truax RC	2.00	.90
104 Ed Sharockman	1.50	.70
105 Doug Atkins	3.00	1.35
106 Greg Larson	1.50	.70
107 Israel Lang	1.50	.70
108 Houston Antwine	1.50	.70
109 Paul Guidry	1.50	.70
110 Al Denson	1.50	.70
111 Roy Jefferson	2.00	.90
112 Chuck Latourette	1.50	.70
113 Jim Johnson	3.00	1.35
114 Bobby Mitchell	4.00	1.80
115 Randy Johnson	1.50	.70
116 Lou Michaels	1.50	.70
117 Rudy Kuechenberg	1.50	.70
118 Walt Suggs	1.50	.70
119 Goldie Sellers	1.50	.70
120 Larry Csonka RC !	75.00	34.00
121 Jim Houston	1.50	.70
122 Craig Baynham	1.50	.70
123 Alex Karras	5.00	2.20
124 Jim Grabowski	2.00	.90
125 Roman Gabriel	3.00	1.35
126 Larry Bowie	1.50	.70
127 Dave Parks	2.00	.90
128 Ben Davidson	3.00	1.35
129 Steve DeLong	1.50	.70
130 Fred Hill	1.50	.70
131 Ernie Koy	2.00	.90
132A Checklist 133-263 (no border)	15.00	3.70

❑ 132B Checklist 133-263 (thin white border like second series)	20.00	5.00
❑ 133 Dick Hoak	2.00	.90
❑ 134 Larry Stallings RC	2.00	.90
❑ 135 Clifton McNeil RC	2.00	.90
❑ 136 Walter Rock	2.00	.90
❑ 137 Billy Lothridge	2.00	.90
❑ 138 Bob Vogel	2.00	.90
❑ 139 Dick Butkus	40.00	18.00
❑ 140 Frank Ryan	2.50	1.10
❑ 141 Larry Garron	2.00	.90
❑ 142 George Saimes	2.00	.90
❑ 143 Frank Buncom	2.00	.90
❑ 144 Don Perkins	2.50	1.10
❑ 145 Johnnie Robinson UER (Misspelled Johnny)	2.00	.90
❑ 146 Lee Roy Caffey	2.50	1.10
❑ 147 Bernie Casey	2.50	1.10
❑ 148 Billy Martin E	2.00	.90
❑ 149 Gene Howard	2.00	.90
❑ 150 Fran Tarkenton	20.00	9.00
❑ 151 Eric Crabtree	2.00	.90
❑ 152 W.K. Hicks	2.00	.90
❑ 153 Bobby Bell	4.00	1.80
❑ 154 Sam Baker	2.00	.90
❑ 155 Marv Woodson	2.00	.90
❑ 156 Dave Williams	2.00	.90
❑ 157 Bruce Bosley UER (Considered one of the three centers in all of pro football)	2.00	.90
❑ 158 Carl Kammerer	2.00	.90
❑ 159 Jim Burson	2.00	.90
❑ 160 Roy Hilton	2.00	.90
❑ 161 Bob Griese	25.00	11.00
❑ 162 Bob Talamini	2.00	.90
❑ 163 Jim Otto	4.00	1.80
❑ 164 Ronnie Bull	2.00	.90
❑ 165 Walter Johnson RC	2.00	.90
❑ 166 Lee Roy Jordan	4.00	1.80
❑ 167 Mike Lucci	2.50	1.10
❑ 168 Willie Wood	4.00	1.80
❑ 169 Maxie Baughan	2.00	.90
❑ 170 Bill Brown	2.50	1.10
❑ 171 John Hadl	4.00	1.80
❑ 172 Gino Cappelletti	2.50	1.10
❑ 173 George Butch Byrd	2.50	1.10
❑ 174 Steve Stonebreaker	2.00	.90
❑ 175 Joe Morrison	2.00	.90
❑ 176 Joe Scarpati	2.00	.90
❑ 177 Bobby Walden	2.00	.90
❑ 178 Roy Shivers	2.00	.90
❑ 179 Kermit Alexander	2.00	.90
❑ 180 Pat Richter	2.00	.90
❑ 181 Pete Perreault	2.00	.90
❑ 182 Pete Duranko	2.00	.90
❑ 183 Leroy Mitchell	2.00	.90
❑ 184 Jim Simon	2.00	.90
❑ 185 Billy Ray Smith	2.00	.90
❑ 186 Jack Concannon	2.00	.90
❑ 187 Ben Davis	2.00	.90
❑ 188 Mike Clark	2.00	.90
❑ 189 Jim Gibbons	2.00	.90
❑ 190 Dave Robinson	2.50	1.10
❑ 191 Otis Taylor	2.50	1.10
❑ 192 Nick Buoniconti	4.00	1.80
❑ 193 Matt Snell	2.50	1.10
❑ 194 Bruce Gossett	2.00	.90
❑ 195 Mick Tingelhoff	2.50	1.10
❑ 196 Earl Leggett	2.00	.90
❑ 197 Pete Case	2.00	.90
❑ 198 Tom Woodeshick RC	2.00	.90
❑ 199 Ken Kortas	2.00	.90
❑ 200 Jim Hart	4.00	1.80
❑ 201 Fred Biletnikoff	10.00	4.50
❑ 202 Jacque MacKinnon	2.00	.90
❑ 203 Jim Whalen	2.00	.90
❑ 204 Matt Hazeltine	2.00	.90
❑ 205 Charlie Gogolak	2.00	.90
❑ 206 Ray Ogden	2.00	.90
❑ 207 John Mackey	4.00	1.80
❑ 208 Roosevelt Taylor	2.00	.90
❑ 209 Gene Hickerson	2.00	.90
❑ 210 Dave Edwards RC	2.50	1.10
❑ 211 Tom Sestak	2.00	.90
❑ 212 Ernie Wright	2.00	.90
❑ 213 Dave Costa	2.00	.90
❑ 214 Tom Vaughn	2.00	.90
❑ 215 Bart Starr	35.00	16.00
❑ 216 Les Josephson	2.00	.90
❑ 217 Fred Cox	2.00	.90
❑ 218 Mike Tilleman	2.00	.90
❑ 219 Darrell Dess	2.00	.90
❑ 220 Dave Lloyd	2.00	.90
❑ 221 Pete Beathard	2.00	.90
❑ 222 Buck Buchanan	4.00	1.80
❑ 223 Frank Emanuel	2.00	.90
❑ 224 Paul Martha	2.00	.90
❑ 225 Johnny Roland	2.00	.90
❑ 226 Gary Lewis	2.00	.90
❑ 227 Sonny Jurgensen UER (Chiefs logo)	6.00	2.70
❑ 228 Jim Butler	2.00	.90
❑ 229 Mike Curtis RC	6.00	2.70
❑ 230 Richie Petitbon	2.00	.90
❑ 231 George Sauer Jr.	2.50	1.10
❑ 232 George Blanda	20.00	9.00
❑ 233 Gary Garrison	2.00	.90
❑ 234 Gary Collins	2.50	1.10
❑ 235 Craig Morton	4.00	1.80
❑ 236 Tom Nowatzke	2.00	.90
❑ 237 Donny Anderson	2.50	1.10
❑ 238 Deacon Jones	4.00	1.80
❑ 239 Grady Alderman	2.00	.90
❑ 240 Bill Kilmer	4.00	1.80
❑ 241 Mike Taliaferro	2.00	.90
❑ 242 Stew Barber	2.00	.90
❑ 243 Bobby Hunt	2.00	.90
❑ 244 Homer Jones	2.00	.90
❑ 245 Bob Brown OT	4.00	1.80
❑ 246 Bill Asbury	2.00	.90
❑ 247 Charlie Johnson UER (Misspelled Charley on both sides)	2.50	1.10
❑ 248 Chris Hanburger	2.50	1.10
❑ 249 John Brodie	6.00	2.70
❑ 250 Earl Morrall	2.50	1.10
❑ 251 Floyd Little	5.00	2.20
❑ 252 Jerrel Wilson RC	2.00	.90
❑ 253 Jim Keyes	2.00	.90
❑ 254 Mel Renfro	4.00	1.80
❑ 255 Herb Adderley	4.00	1.80
❑ 256 Jack Snow	2.50	1.10
❑ 257 Charlie Durkee	2.00	.90
❑ 258 Charlie Harper	2.00	.90
❑ 259 J.R. Wilburn	2.00	.90
❑ 260 Charlie Krueger	2.00	.90
❑ 261 Pete Jacques	2.00	.90
❑ 262 Gerry Philbin	2.00	.90
❑ 263 Daryle Lamonica	10.00	2.50

1970 Topps

	NM	Ex
COMPLETE SET (263)	475.00	210.00
COMMON CARD (1-132)	1.00	.45
COMMON CARD (133-263)	1.25	.55
WRAPPER (10-CENT)	12.00	5.50
❑ 1 Len Dawson UER (Cartoon caption says, "AFL AN NFL")	20.00	5.00
❑ 2 Doug Hart	1.00	.45
❑ 3 Verlon Biggs	1.00	.45
❑ 4 Ralph Neely RC	1.50	.70
❑ 5 Harmon Wages	1.00	.45
❑ 6 Dan Conners	1.00	.45
❑ 7 Gino Cappelletti	1.50	.70
❑ 8 Erich Barnes	1.00	.45
❑ 9 Checklist 1-132	10.00	2.50
❑ 10 Bob Griese	15.00	6.75
❑ 11 Ed Flanagan	1.00	.45
❑ 12 George Seals	1.00	.45
❑ 13 Harry Jacobs	1.00	.45
❑ 14 Mike Haffner	1.00	.45
❑ 15 Bob Vogel	1.00	.45
❑ 16 Bill Peterson	1.00	.45
❑ 17 Spider Lockhart	1.00	.45
❑ 18 Billy Truax	1.00	.45
❑ 19 Jim Beirne	1.00	.45
❑ 20 Leroy Kelly	6.00	2.70
❑ 21 Dave Lloyd	1.00	.45
❑ 22 Mike Tilleman	1.00	.45
❑ 23 Gary Garrison	1.00	.45
❑ 24 Larry Brown RC	8.00	3.60
❑ 25 Jan Stenerud RC	12.00	5.50
❑ 26 Rolf Krueger	1.00	.45
❑ 27 Roland Lakes	1.00	.45
❑ 28 Dick Hoak	1.00	.45
❑ 29 Gene Washington Vik RC	2.50	1.10
❑ 30 Bart Starr	20.00	9.00
❑ 31 Dave Grayson	1.00	.45
❑ 32 Jerry Rush	1.00	.45
❑ 33 Len St. Jean	1.00	.45
❑ 34 Randy Edmunds	1.00	.45
❑ 35 Matt Snell	1.50	.70
❑ 36 Paul Costa	1.00	.45
❑ 37 Mike Pyle	1.00	.45
❑ 38 Roy Hilton	1.00	.45
❑ 39 Steve Tensi	1.00	.45
❑ 40 Tommy Nobis	2.50	1.10
❑ 41 Pete Case	1.00	.45
❑ 42 Andy Rice	1.00	.45
❑ 43 Elvin Bethea RC	8.00	3.60
❑ 44 Jack Snow	1.50	.70
❑ 45 Mel Renfro	2.50	1.10
❑ 46 Andy Livingston	1.00	.45
❑ 47 Gary Ballman	1.00	.45
❑ 48 Bob DeMarco	1.00	.45
❑ 49 Steve DeLong	1.00	.45
❑ 50 Daryle Lamonica	4.00	1.80
❑ 51 Jim Lynch RC	1.00	.45
❑ 52 Mel Farr RC	1.00	.45
❑ 53 Bob Long RC	1.00	.45
❑ 54 John Elliott	1.00	.45
❑ 55 Ray Nitschke	5.00	2.20
❑ 56 Jim Shorter	1.00	.45
❑ 57 Dave Wilcox	2.50	1.10
❑ 58 Eric Crabtree	1.00	.45
❑ 59 Alan Page RC	30.00	13.50
❑ 60 Jim Nance	1.50	.70
❑ 61 Glen Ray Hines	1.00	.45
❑ 62 John Mackey	2.50	1.10
❑ 63 Ron McDole	1.00	.45
❑ 64 Tom Beier	1.00	.45
❑ 65 Bill Nelsen	1.50	.70
❑ 66 Paul Flatley	1.00	.45
❑ 67 Sam Brunelli	1.00	.45
❑ 68 Jack Pardee	1.50	.70
❑ 69 Brig Owens	1.00	.45
❑ 70 Gale Sayers	25.00	11.00
❑ 71 Lee Roy Jordan	2.50	1.10
❑ 72 Harold Jackson RC	5.00	2.20
❑ 73 John Hadl	2.50	1.10
❑ 74 Dave Parks	1.00	.45
❑ 75 Lem Barney RC	14.00	6.25

❑ 76 Johnny Roland 1.00 .45
❑ 77 Ed Budde 1.00 .45
❑ 78 Ben McGee 1.00 .45
❑ 79 Ken Bowman 1.00 .45
❑ 80 Fran Tarkenton 15.00 6.75
❑ 81 Gene Washington 49er RC 5.00 2.20
❑ 82 Larry Grantham 1.00 .45
❑ 83 Bill Brown 1.50 .70
❑ 84 John Charles 1.00 .45
❑ 85 Fred Biletnikoff 7.00 3.10
❑ 86 Royce Berry 1.00 .45
❑ 87 Bob Lilly 5.00 2.20
❑ 88 Earl Morrall 1.50 .70
❑ 89 Jerry LeVias RC 1.50 .70
❑ 90 O.J. Simpson RC 80.00 36.00
❑ 91 Mike Howell 1.00 .45
❑ 92 Ken Gray 1.00 .45
❑ 93 Chris Hanburger 1.00 .45
❑ 94 Larry Seiple RC 1.00 .45
❑ 95 Rich Jackson RC 1.00 .45
❑ 96 Rockne Freitas 1.00 .45
❑ 97 Dick Post RC 1.50 .70
❑ 98 Ben Hawkins RC 1.00 .45
❑ 99 Ken Reaves 1.00 .45
❑ 100 Roman Gabriel 2.50 1.10
❑ 101 Dave Rowe 1.00 .45
❑ 102 Dave Robinson 1.00 .45
❑ 103 Otis Taylor 1.50 .70
❑ 104 Jim Turner 1.00 .45
❑ 105 Joe Morrison 1.00 .45
❑ 106 Dick Evey 1.00 .45
❑ 107 Ray Mansfield 1.00 .45
❑ 108 Grady Alderman 1.00 .45
❑ 109 Bruce Gossett 1.00 .45
❑ 110 Bob Trumpy RC 4.00 1.80
❑ 111 Jim Hunt 1.00 .45
❑ 112 Larry Stallings 1.00 .45
❑ 113A Lance Rentzel (name in red) 1.50 .70
❑ 113B Lance Rentzel (name in black) 1.50 .70
❑ 114 Bubba Smith RC 25.00 11.00
❑ 115 Norm Snead 1.50 .70
❑ 116 Jim Otto 2.50 1.10
❑ 117 Bo Scott RC 1.00 .45
❑ 118 Rick Redman 1.00 .45
❑ 119 George Butch Byrd 1.00 .45
❑ 120 George Webster RC 1.50 .70
❑ 121 Chuck Walton RC 1.00 .45
❑ 122 Dave Costa 1.00 .45
❑ 123 Al Dodd 1.00 .45
❑ 124 Len Hauss 1.00 .45
❑ 125 Deacon Jones 2.50 1.10
❑ 126 Randy Johnson 1.00 .45
❑ 127 Ralph Heck 1.00 .45
❑ 128 Emerson Boozer RC 1.50 .70
❑ 129 Johnny Robinson 1.50 .70
❑ 130 John Brodie 5.00 2.20
❑ 131 Gale Gillingham RC 1.00 .45
❑ 132 Checklist 133-263 DP UER (145 Charley Taylor misspelled Charlie) 6.00 1.50
❑ 133 Chuck Walker 1.25 .55
❑ 134 Bennie McRae 1.25 .55
❑ 135 Paul Warfield 7.00 3.10
❑ 136 Dan Darragh 1.25 .55
❑ 137 Paul Robinson RC 1.25 .55
❑ 138 Ed Philpott 1.25 .55
❑ 139 Craig Morton 3.00 1.35
❑ 140 Tom Dempsey RC 2.00 .90
❑ 141 Al Nelson 1.25 .55
❑ 142 Tom Matte 2.00 .90
❑ 143 Dick Schafrath 1.25 .55
❑ 144 Willie Brown 4.00 1.80
❑ 145 Charley Taylor UER (Misspelled Charlie on both sides) 5.00 2.20
❑ 146 John Huard 1.25 .55
❑ 147 Dave Osborn 1.25 .55
❑ 148 Gene Mingo 1.25 .55
❑ 149 Larry Hand 1.25 .55
❑ 150 Joe Namath 50.00 22.00
❑ 151 Tom Mack RC 10.00 4.50
❑ 152 Kenny Graham 1.25 .55
❑ 153 Don Herrmann 1.25 .55
❑ 154 Bobby Bell 3.00 1.35
❑ 155 Hoyle Granger 1.25 .55
❑ 156 Claude Humphrey RC 2.00 .90
❑ 157 Clifton McNeil 1.25 .55
❑ 158 Mick Tingelhoff 2.00 .90
❑ 159 Don Horn RC 1.25 .55
❑ 160 Larry Wilson 3.00 1.35
❑ 161 Tom Neville 1.25 .55
❑ 162 Larry Csonka 20.00 9.00
❑ 163 Doug Buffone RC 1.25 .55
❑ 164 Cornell Green 2.00 .90
❑ 165 Haven Moses RC 2.00 .90
❑ 166 Bill Kilmer 3.00 1.35
❑ 167 Tim Rossovich RC 1.25 .55
❑ 168 Bill Bergey RC 4.00 1.80
❑ 169 Gary Collins 2.00 .90
❑ 170 Floyd Little 3.00 1.35
❑ 171 Tom Keating 1.25 .55
❑ 172 Pat Fischer 1.25 .55
❑ 173 Walt Sweeney 1.25 .55
❑ 174 Greg Larson 1.25 .55
❑ 175 Carl Eller 3.00 1.35
❑ 176 George Sauer Jr. 2.00 .90
❑ 177 Jim Hart 3.00 1.35
❑ 178 Bob Brown OT 3.00 1.35
❑ 179 Mike Garrett RC 2.00 .90
❑ 180 John Unitas 25.00 11.00
❑ 181 Tom Regner 1.25 .55
❑ 182 Bob Jeter 1.25 .55
❑ 183 Gail Cogdill 1.25 .55
❑ 184 Earl Gros 1.25 .55
❑ 185 Dennis Partee 1.25 .55
❑ 186 Charlie Krueger 1.25 .55
❑ 187 Martin Baccaglio 1.25 .55
❑ 188 Charles Long 1.25 .55
❑ 189 Bob Hayes 4.00 1.80
❑ 190 Dick Butkus 25.00 11.00
❑ 191 Al Bemiller 1.25 .55
❑ 192 Dick Westmoreland 1.25 .55
❑ 193 Joe Scarpati 1.25 .55
❑ 194 Ron Snidow 1.25 .55
❑ 195 Earl McCullouch RC 1.25 .55
❑ 196 Jake Kupp 1.25 .55
❑ 197 Bob Lurtsema 1.25 .55
❑ 198 Mike Current 1.25 .55
❑ 199 Charlie Smith 1.25 .55
❑ 200 Sonny Jurgensen 6.00 2.70
❑ 201 Mike Curtis 2.00 .90
❑ 202 Aaron Brown 1.25 .55
❑ 203 Richie Petitbon 1.25 .55
❑ 204 Walt Suggs 1.25 .55
❑ 205 Roy Jefferson 1.25 .55
❑ 206 Russ Washington RC 1.25 .55
❑ 207 Woody Peoples RC 1.25 .55
❑ 208 Dave Williams 1.25 .55
❑ 209 John Zook RC 1.25 .55
❑ 210 Tom Woodeshick 1.25 .55
❑ 211 Howard Fest 1.25 .55
❑ 212 Jack Concannon 1.25 .55
❑ 213 Jim Marshall 3.00 1.35
❑ 214 Jon Morris 1.25 .55
❑ 215 Dan Abramowicz 2.00 .90
❑ 216 Paul Martha 1.25 .55
❑ 217 Ken Willard 1.25 .55
❑ 218 Walter Rock 1.25 .55
❑ 219 Garland Boyette 1.25 .55
❑ 220 Buck Buchanan 3.00 1.35
❑ 221 Bill Munson 2.00 .90
❑ 222 David Lee RC 1.25 .55
❑ 223 Karl Noonan 1.25 .55
❑ 224 Harry Schuh 1.25 .55
❑ 225 Jackie Smith 3.00 1.35
❑ 226 Gerry Philbin 1.25 .55
❑ 227 Ernie Koy 1.25 .55
❑ 228 Chuck Howley 2.00 .90
❑ 229 Billy Shaw 3.00 1.35
❑ 230 Jerry Hillebrand 1.25 .55
❑ 231 Bill Thompson RC 2.00 .90
❑ 232 Carroll Dale 2.00 .90
❑ 233 Gene Hickerson 1.25 .55
❑ 234 Jim Butler 1.25 .55
❑ 235 Greg Cook RC 1.25 .55
❑ 236 Lee Roy Caffey 1.25 .55
❑ 237 Merlin Olsen 4.00 1.80
❑ 238 Fred Cox 1.25 .55
❑ 239 Nate Ramsey 1.25 .55
❑ 240 Lance Alworth 7.00 3.10
❑ 241 Chuck Hinton 1.25 .55
❑ 242 Jerry Smith 1.25 .55
❑ 243 Tony Baker 1.25 .55
❑ 244 Nick Buoniconti 3.00 1.35
❑ 245 Jim Johnson 3.00 1.35
❑ 246 Willie Richardson 1.25 .55
❑ 247 Fred Dryer RC 10.00 4.50
❑ 248 Bobby Maples 1.25 .55
❑ 249 Alex Karras 4.00 1.80
❑ 250 Joe Kapp 2.00 .90
❑ 251 Ben Davidson 3.00 1.35
❑ 252 Mike Stratton 1.25 .55
❑ 253 Les Josephson 1.25 .55
❑ 254 Don Maynard 6.00 2.70
❑ 255 Houston Antwine 1.25 .55
❑ 256 Mac Percival RC 1.25 .55
❑ 257 George Goeddeke 1.25 .55
❑ 258 Homer Jones 1.25 .55
❑ 259 Bob Berry 1.25 .55
❑ 260A Calvin Hill RC (Name in red) 15.00 6.75
❑ 260B Calvin Hill RC (Name in black) 20.00 9.00
❑ 261 Willie Wood 3.00 1.35
❑ 262 Ed Weisacosky 1.25 .55
❑ 263 Jim Tyrer 3.00 .75

1971 Topps

	NM	Ex
COMPLETE SET (263)	500.00	220.00
COMMON CARD (1-132)	.75	.35
COMMON CARD (133-263)	1.00	.45

❑ 1 John Unitas 30.00 7.50
❑ 2 Jim Butler .75 .35
❑ 3 Marty Schottenheimer RC 12.00 5.50
❑ 4 Joe O'Donnell .75 .35
❑ 5 Tom Dempsey 1.25 .55
❑ 6 Chuck Allen .75 .35
❑ 7 Ernie Kellerman .75 .35
❑ 8 Walt Garrison RC 2.00 .90
❑ 9 Bill Van Heusen .75 .35
❑ 10 Lance Alworth 8.00 3.60
❑ 11 Greg Landry RC 2.00 .90
❑ 12 Larry Krause .75 .35
❑ 13 Buck Buchanan 2.00 .90
❑ 14 Roy Gerela RC 1.25 .55
❑ 15 Clifton McNeil .75 .35
❑ 16 Bob Brown OT 2.00 .90
❑ 17 Lloyd Mumphord .75 .35
❑ 18 Gary Cuozzo .75 .35
❑ 19 Don Maynard 5.00 2.20
❑ 20 Larry Wilson 2.00 .90
❑ 21 Charlie Smith .75 .35
❑ 22 Ken Avery .75 .35

❑ 23 Billy Walik .75 .35
❑ 24 Jim Johnson 2.00 .90
❑ 25 Dick Butkus 25.00 11.00
❑ 26 Charley Taylor UER 4.00 1.80
(Misspelled Charlie
on both sides)
❑ 27 Checklist 1-132 UER 8.00 2.00
(26 Charlie Taylor
should be Charley)
❑ 28 Lionel Aldridge RC .75 .35
❑ 29 Billy Lothridge .75 .35
❑ 30 Terry Hanratty RC 1.25 .55
❑ 31 Lee Roy Jordan 2.00 .90
❑ 32 Rick Volk RC .75 .35
❑ 33 Howard Kindig .75 .35
❑ 34 Carl Garrett RC .75 .35
❑ 35 Bobby Bell 2.00 .90
❑ 36 Gene Hickerson .75 .35
❑ 37 Dave Parks .75 .35
❑ 38 Paul Martha .75 .35
❑ 39 George Blanda 15.00 6.75
❑ 40 Tom Woodeshick .75 .35
❑ 41 Alex Karras 3.00 1.35
❑ 42 Rick Redman .75 .35
❑ 43 Zeke Moore .75 .35
❑ 44 Jack Snow 1.25 .55
❑ 45 Larry Csonka 15.00 6.75
❑ 46 Karl Kassulke .75 .35
❑ 47 Jim Hart 2.00 .90
❑ 48 Al Atkinson .75 .35
❑ 49 Horst Muhlmann RC .75 .35
❑ 50 Sonny Jurgensen 5.00 2.20
❑ 51 Ron Johnson RC 1.25 .55
❑ 52 Cas Banaszek .75 .35
❑ 53 Bubba Smith 8.00 3.60
❑ 54 Bobby Douglass RC 1.25 .55
❑ 55 Willie Wood 2.00 .90
❑ 56 Bake Turner .75 .35
❑ 57 Mike Morgan .75 .35
❑ 58 George Butch Byrd 1.25 .55
❑ 59 Don Horn .75 .35
❑ 60 Tommy Nobis 2.00 .90
❑ 61 Jan Stenerud 4.00 1.80
❑ 62 Altie Taylor RC .75 .35
❑ 63 Gary Pettigrew .75 .35
❑ 64 Spike Jones RC .75 .35
❑ 65 Duane Thomas RC 2.00 .90
❑ 66 Marty Domres RC .75 .35
❑ 67 Dick Anderson 1.25 .55
❑ 68 Ken Iman .75 .35
❑ 69 Miller Farr .75 .35
❑ 70 Daryle Lamonica 3.00 1.35
❑ 71 Alan Page 12.00 5.50
❑ 72 Pat Matson .75 .35
❑ 73 Emerson Boozer .75 .35
❑ 74 Pat Fischer .75 .35
❑ 75 Gary Collins 1.25 .55
❑ 76 John Fuqua RC 1.25 .55
❑ 77 Bruce Gossett .75 .35
❑ 78 Ed O'Bradovich .75 .35
❑ 79 Bob Tucker RC 1.25 .55
❑ 80 Mike Curtis 1.25 .55
❑ 81 Rich Jackson .75 .35
❑ 82 Tom Janik .75 .35
❑ 83 Gale Gillingham .75 .35
❑ 84 Jim Mitchell .75 .35
❑ 85 Charlie Johnson 1.25 .55
❑ 86 Edgar Chandler .75 .35
❑ 87 Cyril Pinder .75 .35
❑ 88 Johnny Robinson 1.25 .55
❑ 89 Ralph Neely .75 .35
❑ 90 Dan Abramowicz .75 .35
❑ 91 Mercury Morris RC 5.00 2.20
❑ 92 Steve DeLong .75 .35
❑ 93 Larry Stallings .75 .35
❑ 94 Tom Mack 2.00 .90
❑ 95 Hewritt Dixon .75 .35
❑ 96 Fred Cox .75 .35
❑ 97 Chris Hanburger .75 .35
❑ 98 Gerry Philbin .75 .35
❑ 99 Ernie Wright .75 .35
❑ 100 John Brodie 4.00 1.80
❑ 101 Tucker Frederickson .75 .35
❑ 102 Bobby Walden .75 .35
❑ 103 Dick Gordon .75 .35
❑ 104 Walter Johnson .75 .35
❑ 105 Mike Lucci 1.25 .55
❑ 106 Checklist 133-263 DP 6.00 1.50
❑ 107 Ron Berger .75 .35
❑ 108 Dan Sullivan .75 .35
❑ 109 George Kunz RC .75 .35
❑ 110 Floyd Little 2.00 .90
❑ 111 Zeke Bratkowski 1.25 .55
❑ 112 Haven Moses 1.25 .55
❑ 113 Ken Houston RC 15.00 6.75
❑ 114 Willie Lanier RC 15.00 6.75
❑ 115 Larry Brown 2.00 .90
❑ 116 Tim Rossovich .75 .35
❑ 117 Errol Linden .75 .35
❑ 118 Mel Renfro 2.00 .90
❑ 119 Mike Garrett .75 .35
❑ 120 Fran Tarkenton 15.00 6.75
❑ 121 Garo Yepremian RC 2.00 .90
❑ 122 Glen Condren .75 .35
❑ 123 Johnny Roland .75 .35
❑ 124 Dave Herman .75 .35
❑ 125 Merlin Olsen 3.00 1.35
❑ 126 Doug Buffone .75 .35
❑ 127 Earl McCullouch .75 .35
❑ 128 Spider Lockhart .75 .35
❑ 129 Ken Willard .75 .35
❑ 130 Gene Washington Vik .75 .35
❑ 131 Mike Phipps RC 1.25 .55
❑ 132 Andy Russell 1.25 .55
❑ 133 Ray Nitschke 4.00 1.80
❑ 134 Jerry Logan 1.00 .45
❑ 135 MacArthur Lane RC 1.50 .70
❑ 136 Jim Turner 1.00 .45
❑ 137 Kent McCloughan 1.00 .45
❑ 138 Paul Guidry 1.00 .45
❑ 139 Otis Taylor 1.50 .70
❑ 140 Virgil Carter RC 1.00 .45
❑ 141 Joe Dawkins 1.00 .45
❑ 142 Steve Preece 1.00 .45
❑ 143 Mike Bragg RC 1.00 .45
❑ 144 Bob Lilly 5.00 2.20
❑ 145 Joe Kapp 1.50 .70
❑ 146 Al Dodd 1.00 .45
❑ 147 Nick Buoniconti 2.50 1.10
❑ 148 Speedy Duncan 1.00 .45
(Back mentions his
trade to Redskins)
❑ 149 Cedrick Hardman RC 1.00 .45
❑ 150 Gale Sayers 25.00 11.00
❑ 151 Jim Otto 2.50 1.10
❑ 152 Billy Truax 1.00 .45
❑ 153 John Elliott 1.00 .45
❑ 154 Dick LeBeau 1.00 .45
❑ 155 Bill Bergey 1.50 .70
❑ 156 Terry Bradshaw RC 200.00 90.00
❑ 157 Leroy Kelly 6.00 2.70
❑ 158 Paul Krause 2.50 1.10
❑ 159 Ted Vactor 1.00 .45
❑ 160 Bob Griese 15.00 6.75
❑ 161 Ernie McMillan 1.00 .45
❑ 162 Donny Anderson 1.50 .70
❑ 163 John Pitts 1.00 .45
❑ 164 Dave Costa 1.00 .45
❑ 165 Gene Washington 49er 1.50 .70
❑ 166 John Zook 1.00 .45
❑ 167 Pete Gogolak 1.00 .45
❑ 168 Erich Barnes 1.00 .45
❑ 169 Alvin Reed 1.00 .45
❑ 170 Jim Nance 1.50 .70
❑ 171 Craig Morton 2.50 1.10
❑ 172 Gary Garrison 1.00 .45
❑ 173 Joe Scarpati 1.00 .45
❑ 174 Adrian Young UER 1.00 .45
(Photo actually
Rick Duncan)
❑ 175 John Mackey 2.50 1.10
❑ 176 Mac Percival 1.00 .45
❑ 177 Preston Pearson RC 4.00 1.80
❑ 178 Fred Biletnikoff 8.00 3.60
❑ 179 Mike Battle RC 1.00 .45
❑ 180 Len Dawson 8.00 3.60
❑ 181 Les Josephson 1.00 .45
❑ 182 Royce Berry 1.00 .45
❑ 183 Herman Weaver 1.00 .45
❑ 184 Norm Snead 1.50 .70
❑ 185 Sam Brunelli 1.00 .45
❑ 186 Jim Kiick RC 5.00 2.20
❑ 187 Austin Denney 1.00 .45
❑ 188 Roger Wehrli RC 1.50 .70
❑ 189 Dave Wilcox 2.50 1.10
❑ 190 Bob Hayes 2.50 1.10
❑ 191 Joe Morrison 1.00 .45
❑ 192 Manny Sistrunk 1.00 .45
❑ 193 Don Cockroft RC 1.00 .45
❑ 194 Lee Bouggess 1.00 .45
❑ 195 Bob Berry 1.00 .45
❑ 196 Ron Sellers 1.00 .45
❑ 197 George Webster 1.00 .45
❑ 198 Hoyle Granger 1.00 .45
❑ 199 Bob Vogel 1.00 .45
❑ 200 Bart Starr 20.00 9.00
❑ 201 Mike Mercer 1.00 .45
❑ 202 Dave Smith 1.00 .45
❑ 203 Lee Roy Caffey 1.00 .45
❑ 204 Mick Tingelhoff 1.50 .70
❑ 205 Matt Snell 1.50 .70
❑ 206 Jim Tyrer 1.00 .45
❑ 207 Willie Brown 2.50 1.10
❑ 208 Bob Johnson RC 1.00 .45
❑ 209 Deacon Jones 2.50 1.10
❑ 210 Charlie Sanders RC 1.50 .70
❑ 211 Jake Scott RC 6.00 2.70
❑ 212 Bob Anderson RC 1.00 .45
❑ 213 Charlie Krueger 1.00 .45
❑ 214 Jim Bakken 1.00 .45
❑ 215 Harold Jackson 1.50 .70
❑ 216 Bill Brundige 1.00 .45
❑ 217 Calvin Hill 5.00 2.20
❑ 218 Claude Humphrey 1.00 .45
❑ 219 Glen Ray Hines 1.00 .45
❑ 220 Bill Nelsen 1.50 .70
❑ 221 Roy Hilton 1.00 .45
❑ 222 Don Herrmann 1.00 .45
❑ 223 John Bramlett 1.00 .45
❑ 224 Ken Ellis 1.00 .45
❑ 225 Dave Osborn 1.50 .70
❑ 226 Edd Hargett RC 1.00 .45
❑ 227 Gene Mingo 1.00 .45
❑ 228 Larry Grantham 1.00 .45
❑ 229 Dick Post 1.00 .45
❑ 230 Roman Gabriel 2.50 1.10
❑ 231 Mike Eischeid 1.00 .45
❑ 232 Jim Lynch 1.00 .45
❑ 233 Lemar Parrish RC 1.50 .70
❑ 234 Cecil Turner 1.00 .45
❑ 235 Dennis Shaw RC 1.00 .45
❑ 236 Mel Farr 1.00 .45
❑ 237 Curt Knight 1.00 .45
❑ 238 Chuck Howley 1.50 .70
❑ 239 Bruce Taylor RC 1.00 .45
❑ 240 Jerry LeVias 1.00 .45
❑ 241 Bob Lurtsema 1.00 .45
❑ 242 Earl Morrall 1.50 .70
❑ 243 Kermit Alexander 1.00 .45
❑ 244 Jackie Smith 2.50 1.10
❑ 245 Joe Greene RC 50.00 22.00
❑ 246 Harmon Wages 1.00 .45
❑ 247 Errol Mann 1.00 .45
❑ 248 Mike McCoy DT RC 1.00 .45
❑ 249 Milt Morin RC 1.00 .45
❑ 250 Joe Namath UER 60.00 27.00
In 9th line, Joe is
spelled in small letters
❑ 251 Jackie Burkett 1.00 .45
❑ 252 Steve Chomyszak 1.00 .45
❑ 253 Ed Sharockman 1.00 .45
❑ 254 Robert Holmes RC 1.00 .45
❑ 255 John Hadl 2.50 1.10

Card	NM	Ex
❑ 256 Cornell Gordon	1.00	.45
❑ 257 Mark Moseley RC	1.50	.70
❑ 258 Gus Otto	1.00	.45
❑ 259 Mike Taliaferro	1.00	.45
❑ 260 O.J. Simpson	25.00	11.00
❑ 261 Paul Warfield	8.00	3.60
❑ 262 Jack Concannon	1.00	.45
❑ 263 Tom Matte	2.50	.60

1972 Topps

	NM	Ex
COMPLETE SET (351)	2200.00	1000.00
COMMON CARD (1-132)	.50	.23
COMMON CARD (133-263)	.60	.25
COMMON CARD (264-351)	18.00	8.00
WRAPPER (10-CENT)	10.00	4.50
WRAPPER SER.3 (10-CENT)	20.00	9.00
❑ 1 AFC Rushing Leaders Floyd Little Larry Csonka Marv Hubbard	4.00	1.80
❑ 2 NFC Rushing Leaders John Brockington Steve Owens Willie Ellison	.50	.23
❑ 3 AFC Passing Leaders Bob Griese Len Dawson Virgil Carter	2.00	.90
❑ 4 NFC Passing Leaders Roger Staubach Greg Landry Bill Kilmer	5.00	2.20
❑ 5 AFC Receiving Leaders Fred Biletnikoff Otis Taylor Randy Vataha	1.00	.45
❑ 6 NFC Receiving Leaders Bob Tucker Ted Kwalick Harold Jackson Roy Jefferson	.50	.23
❑ 7 AFC Scoring Leaders Garo Yepremian Jan Stenerud Jim O'Brien	.50	.23
❑ 8 NFC Scoring Leaders Curt Knight Errol Mann Bruce Gossett	.50	.23
❑ 9 Jim Kiick	2.00	.90
❑ 10 Otis Taylor	1.00	.45
❑ 11 Bobby Joe Green	.50	.23
❑ 12 Ken Ellis	.50	.23
❑ 13 John Riggins RC	20.00	9.00
❑ 14 Dave Parks	.50	.23
❑ 15 John Hadl	2.00	.90
❑ 16 Ron Hornsby	.50	.23
❑ 17 Chip Myers RC	.50	.23
❑ 18 Bill Kilmer	2.00	.90
❑ 19 Fred Hoaglin	.50	.23
❑ 20 Carl Eller	2.00	.90
❑ 21 Steve Zabel	.50	.23
❑ 22 Vic Washington RC	.50	.23
❑ 23 Len St. Jean	.50	.23
❑ 24 Bill Thompson	.50	.23
❑ 25 Steve Owens RC	2.00	.90
❑ 26 Ken Burrough RC	1.00	.45
❑ 27 Mike Clark	.50	.23
❑ 28 Willie Brown	2.00	.90
❑ 29 Checklist 1-132	6.00	1.50
❑ 30 Marlin Briscoe RC	.50	.23
❑ 31 Jerry Logan	.50	.23
❑ 32 Donny Anderson	1.00	.45
❑ 33 Rich McGeorge	.50	.23
❑ 34 Charlie Durkee	.50	.23
❑ 35 Willie Lanier	4.00	1.80
❑ 36 Chris Farasopoulos	.50	.23
❑ 37 Ron Shanklin RC	.50	.23
❑ 38 Forrest Blue RC	.50	.23
❑ 39 Ken Reaves	.50	.23
❑ 40 Roman Gabriel	2.00	.90
❑ 41 Mac Percival	.50	.23
❑ 42 Lem Barney	3.00	1.35
❑ 43 Nick Buoniconti	2.00	.90
❑ 44 Charlie Gogolak	.50	.23
❑ 45 Bill Bradley RC	1.00	.45
❑ 46 Joe Jones	.50	.23
❑ 47 Dave Williams	.50	.23
❑ 48 Pete Athas	.50	.23
❑ 49 Virgil Carter	.50	.23
❑ 50 Floyd Little	2.00	.90
❑ 51 Curt Knight	.50	.23
❑ 52 Bobby Maples	.50	.23
❑ 53 Charlie West	.50	.23
❑ 54 Marv Hubbard RC	1.00	.45
❑ 55 Archie Manning RC	20.00	9.00
❑ 56 Jim O'Brien RC	1.00	.45
❑ 57 Wayne Patrick	.50	.23
❑ 58 Ken Bowman	.50	.23
❑ 59 Roger Wehrli	.50	.23
❑ 60 Charlie Sanders UER (Front WR, back TE)	.50	.23
❑ 61 Jan Stenerud	2.00	.90
❑ 62 Willie Ellison	.50	.23
❑ 63 Walt Sweeney	.50	.23
❑ 64 Ron Smith	.50	.23
❑ 65 Jim Plunkett RC	20.00	9.00
❑ 66 Herb Adderley UER (misspelled Adderly)	2.00	.90
❑ 67 Mike Reid RC	2.00	.90
❑ 68 Richard Caster RC	1.00	.45
❑ 69 Dave Wilcox	2.00	.90
❑ 70 Leroy Kelly	3.00	1.35
❑ 71 Bob Lee RC	.50	.23
❑ 72 Verlon Biggs	.50	.23
❑ 73 Henry Allison	.50	.23
❑ 74 Steve Ramsey	.50	.23
❑ 75 Claude Humphrey	1.00	.45
❑ 76 Bob Grim RC	.50	.23
❑ 77 John Fuqua	1.00	.45
❑ 78 Ken Houston	4.00	1.80
❑ 79 Checklist 133-263 DP	5.00	1.25
❑ 80 Bob Griese	8.00	3.60
❑ 81 Lance Rentzel	1.00	.45
❑ 82 Ed Podolak RC	1.00	.45
❑ 83 Ike Hill	.50	.23
❑ 84 George Farmer	.50	.23
❑ 85 John Brockington RC	2.00	.90
❑ 86 Jim Otto	2.00	.90
❑ 87 Richard Neal	.50	.23
❑ 88 Jim Hart	2.00	.90
❑ 89 Bob Babich	.50	.23
❑ 90 Gene Washington 49er	1.00	.45
❑ 91 John Zook	.50	.23
❑ 92 Bobby Duhon	.50	.23
❑ 93 Ted Hendricks RC	15.00	6.75
❑ 94 Rockne Freitas	.50	.23
❑ 95 Larry Brown	2.00	.90
❑ 96 Mike Phipps	1.00	.45
❑ 97 Julius Adams	.50	.23
❑ 98 Dick Anderson	1.00	.45
❑ 99 Fred Willis	.50	.23
❑ 100 Joe Namath	35.00	16.00
❑ 101 L.C. Greenwood RC	15.00	6.75
❑ 102 Mark Nordquist	.50	.23
❑ 103 Robert Holmes	.50	.23
❑ 104 Ron Yary RC	5.00	2.20
❑ 105 Bob Hayes	2.00	.90
❑ 106 Lyle Alzado RC	15.00	6.75
❑ 107 Bob Berry	.50	.23
❑ 108 Phil Villapiano RC	1.00	.45
❑ 109 Dave Elmendorf	.50	.23
❑ 110 Gale Sayers	20.00	9.00
❑ 111 Jim Tyrer	.50	.23
❑ 112 Mel Gray RC	2.00	.90
❑ 113 Gerry Philbin	.50	.23
❑ 114 Bob James	.50	.23
❑ 115 Garo Yepremian	1.00	.45
❑ 116 Dave Robinson	1.00	.45
❑ 117 Jeff Queen	.50	.23
❑ 118 Norm Snead	1.00	.45
❑ 119 Jim Nance IA	1.00	.45
❑ 120 Terry Bradshaw IA	15.00	6.75
❑ 121 Jim Kiick IA	1.00	.45
❑ 122 Roger Staubach IA	20.00	9.00
❑ 123 Bo Scott IA	.50	.23
❑ 124 John Brodie IA	2.00	.90
❑ 125 Rick Volk IA	.50	.23
❑ 126 John Riggins IA	6.00	2.70
❑ 127 Bubba Smith IA	2.00	.90
❑ 128 Roman Gabriel IA	1.00	.45
❑ 129 Calvin Hill IA	1.00	.45
❑ 130 Bill Nelsen IA	.50	.23
❑ 131 Tom Matte IA	1.00	.45
❑ 132 Bob Griese IA	4.00	1.80
❑ 133 AFC Semi-Final Dolphins 27, Chiefs 24	1.00	.45
❑ 134 NFC Semi-Final Cowboys 20, Vikings 12 (Duane Thomas getting tackled)	1.00	.45
❑ 135 AFC Semi-Final Colts 20, Browns 3 (Don Nottingham)	1.00	.45
❑ 136 NFC Semi-Final 49ers 24, Redskins 20	1.00	.45
❑ 137 AFC Title Game Dolphins 21, Colts 0 (Johnny Unitas getting tackled)	3.00	1.35
❑ 138 NFC Title Game Cowboys 14, 49ers 3 (Bob Lilly making tackle)	2.00	.90
❑ 139 Super Bowl Cowboys 24, Dolphins 3 (Roger Staubach rolling out)	5.00	2.20
❑ 140 Larry Csonka	8.00	3.60
❑ 141 Rick Volk	.60	.25
❑ 142 Roy Jefferson	1.00	.45
❑ 143 Raymond Chester RC	1.00	.45
❑ 144 Bobby Douglass	.60	.25
❑ 145 Bob Lilly	5.00	2.20
❑ 146 Harold Jackson	1.00	.45
❑ 147 Pete Gogolak	.60	.25
❑ 148 Art Malone	.60	.25
❑ 149 Ed Flanagan	.60	.25
❑ 150 Terry Bradshaw	40.00	18.00
❑ 151 MacArthur Lane	1.00	.45
❑ 152 Jack Snow	1.00	.45
❑ 153 Al Beauchamp	.60	.25
❑ 154 Bob Anderson	.60	.25
❑ 155 Ted Kwalick RC	.60	.25
❑ 156 Dan Pastorini RC	2.00	.90
❑ 157 Emmitt Thomas RC	2.00	.90
❑ 158 Randy Vataha RC	.60	.25
❑ 159 Al Atkinson	.60	.25

❑ 160 O.J. Simpson 15.00 6.75
❑ 161 Jackie Smith 2.00 .90
❑ 162 Ernie Kellerman .60 .25
❑ 163 Dennis Partee .60 .25
❑ 164 Jake Kupp .60 .25
❑ 165 John Unitas 20.00 9.00
❑ 166 Clint Jones RC .60 .25
❑ 167 Paul Warfield 6.00 2.70
❑ 168 Roland McDole .60 .25
❑ 169 Daryle Lamonica 2.00 .90
❑ 170 Dick Butkus 15.00 6.75
❑ 171 Jim Butler .60 .25
❑ 172 Mike McCoy .60 .25
❑ 173 Dave Smith .60 .25
❑ 174 Greg Landry 1.00 .45
❑ 175 Tom Dempsey 1.00 .45
❑ 176 John Charles .60 .25
❑ 177 Bobby Bell 2.00 .90
❑ 178 Don Horn .60 .25
❑ 179 Bob Trumpy 2.00 .90
❑ 180 Duane Thomas 1.00 .45
❑ 181 Merlin Olsen 3.00 1.35
❑ 182 Dave Herman .60 .25
❑ 183 Jim Nance 1.00 .45
❑ 184 Pete Beathard .60 .25
❑ 185 Bob Tucker .60 .25
❑ 186 Gene Upshaw RC 15.00 6.75
❑ 187 Bo Scott .60 .25
❑ 188 J.D. Hill RC .60 .25
❑ 189 Bruce Gossett .60 .25
❑ 190 Bubba Smith 4.00 1.80
❑ 191 Edd Hargett .60 .25
❑ 192 Gary Garrison .60 .25
❑ 193 Jake Scott 1.00 .45
❑ 194 Fred Cox .60 .25
❑ 195 Sonny Jurgensen 4.00 1.80
❑ 196 Greg Brezina RC .60 .25
❑ 197 Ed O'Bradovich .60 .25
❑ 198 John Rowser .60 .25
❑ 199 Altie Taylor UER .60 .25
(Taylor misspelled as Tayor on front)
❑ 200 Roger Staubach RC 175.00 80.00
❑ 201 Leroy Keyes RC .60 .25
❑ 202 Garland Boyette .60 .25
❑ 203 Tom Beer .60 .25
❑ 204 Buck Buchanan 2.00 .90
❑ 205 Larry Wilson 2.00 .90
❑ 206 Scott Hunter RC .60 .25
❑ 207 Ron Johnson .60 .25
❑ 208 Sam Brunelli .60 .25
❑ 209 Deacon Jones 2.00 .90
❑ 210 Fred Biletnikoff 6.00 2.70
❑ 211 Bill Nelsen 1.00 .45
❑ 212 George Nock .60 .25
❑ 213 Dan Abramowicz 1.00 .45
❑ 214 Irv Goode .60 .25
❑ 215 Isiah Robertson RC 1.00 .45
❑ 216 Tom Matte 1.00 .45
❑ 217 Pat Fischer .60 .25
❑ 218 Gene Washington Vik .60 .25
❑ 219 Paul Robinson .60 .25
❑ 220 John Brodie 4.00 1.80
❑ 221 Manny Fernandez RC 1.00 .45
❑ 222 Errol Mann .60 .25
❑ 223 Dick Gordon .60 .25
❑ 224 Calvin Hill 2.00 .90
❑ 225 Fran Tarkenton UER 12.00 5.50
(Plays in the Masters each spring)
❑ 226 Jim Turner .60 .25
❑ 227 Jim Mitchell .60 .25
❑ 228 Pete Liske .60 .25
❑ 229 Carl Garrett .60 .25
❑ 230 Joe Greene 20.00 9.00
❑ 231 Gale Gillingham .60 .25
❑ 232 Norm Bulaich RC 1.00 .45
❑ 233 Spider Lockhart .60 .25
❑ 234 Ken Willard .60 .25
❑ 235 George Blanda 12.00 5.50
❑ 236 Wayne Mulligan .60 .25
❑ 237 Dave Lewis .60 .25
❑ 238 Dennis Shaw .60 .25
❑ 239 Fair Hooker .60 .25
❑ 240 Larry Little RC 15.00 6.75
❑ 241 Mike Garrett .60 .25
❑ 242 Glen Ray Hines .60 .25
❑ 243 Myron Pottios .60 .25
❑ 244 Charlie Joiner RC 20.00 9.00
❑ 245 Len Dawson 6.00 2.70
❑ 246 W.K. Hicks .60 .25
❑ 247 Les Josephson .60 .25
❑ 248 Lance Alworth UER 6.00 2.70
(Front TE, back WR)
❑ 249 Frank Nunley .60 .25
❑ 250 Mel Farr IA .60 .25
❑ 251 Johnny Unitas IA 8.00 3.60
❑ 252 George Farmer IA .60 .25
❑ 253 Duane Thomas IA 1.00 .45
❑ 254 John Hadl IA 2.00 .90
❑ 255 Vic Washington IA .60 .25
❑ 256 Don Horn IA .60 .25
❑ 257 L.C. Greenwood IA 2.00 .90
❑ 258 Bob Lee IA .60 .25
❑ 259 Larry Csonka IA 4.00 1.80
❑ 260 Mike McCoy IA .60 .25
❑ 261 Greg Landry IA 1.00 .45
❑ 262 Ray May IA .60 .25
❑ 263 Bobby Douglass IA .60 .25
❑ 264 Charlie Sanders AP 30.00 13.50
❑ 265 Ron Yary AP 30.00 13.50
❑ 266 Rayfield Wright AP 30.00 13.50
❑ 267 Larry Little AP 35.00 16.00
❑ 268 John Niland AP 30.00 13.50
❑ 269 Forrest Blue AP 30.00 13.50
❑ 270 Otis Taylor AP 30.00 13.50
❑ 271 Paul Warfield AP 50.00 22.00
❑ 272 Bob Griese AP 70.00 32.00
❑ 273 John Brockington AP 30.00 13.50
❑ 274 Floyd Little AP 30.00 13.50
❑ 275 Garo Yepremian AP 30.00 13.50
❑ 276 Jerrel Wilson AP 18.00 8.00
❑ 277 Carl Eller AP 30.00 13.50
❑ 278 Bubba Smith AP 40.00 18.00
❑ 279 Alan Page AP 40.00 18.00
❑ 280 Bob Lilly AP 60.00 27.00
❑ 281 Ted Hendricks AP 50.00 22.00
❑ 282 Dave Wilcox AP 30.00 13.50
❑ 283 Willie Lanier AP 35.00 16.00
❑ 284 Jim Johnson AP 30.00 13.50
❑ 285 Willie Brown AP 35.00 16.00
❑ 286 Bill Bradley AP 30.00 13.50
❑ 287 Ken Houston AP 35.00 16.00
❑ 288 Mel Farr 18.00 8.00
❑ 289 Kermit Alexander 18.00 8.00
❑ 290 John Gilliam RC 25.00 11.00
❑ 291 Steve Spurrier RC 100.00 45.00
❑ 292 Walter Johnson 18.00 8.00
❑ 293 Jack Pardee 25.00 11.00
❑ 294 Checklist 264-351 UER 80.00 20.00
(334 Charlie Taylor should be Charley)
❑ 295 Winston Hill 18.00 8.00
❑ 296 Hugo Hollas 18.00 8.00
❑ 297 Ray May RC 18.00 8.00
❑ 298 Jim Bakken 18.00 8.00
❑ 299 Larry Carwell 18.00 8.00
❑ 300 Alan Page 50.00 22.00
❑ 301 Walt Garrison 25.00 11.00
❑ 302 Mike Lucci 25.00 11.00
❑ 303 Nemiah Wilson 18.00 8.00
❑ 304 Carroll Dale 25.00 11.00
❑ 305 Jim Kanicki 18.00 8.00
❑ 306 Preston Pearson 30.00 13.50
❑ 307 Lemar Parrish 25.00 11.00
❑ 308 Earl Morrall 25.00 11.00
❑ 309 Tommy Nobis 25.00 11.00
❑ 310 Rich Jackson 18.00 8.00
❑ 311 Doug Cunningham 18.00 8.00
❑ 312 Jim Marsalis 18.00 8.00
❑ 313 Jim Beirne 18.00 8.00
❑ 314 Tom McNeill 18.00 8.00
❑ 315 Milt Morin 18.00 8.00
❑ 316 Rayfield Wright RC 25.00 11.00
❑ 317 Jerry LeVias 25.00 11.00
❑ 318 Travis Williams RC 25.00 11.00
❑ 319 Edgar Chandler 18.00 8.00
❑ 320 Bob Wallace 18.00 8.00
❑ 321 Delles Howell 18.00 8.00
❑ 322 Emerson Boozer 25.00 11.00
❑ 323 George Atkinson RC 25.00 11.00
❑ 324 Mike Montler 18.00 8.00
❑ 325 Randy Johnson 18.00 8.00
❑ 326 Mike Curtis UER 25.00 11.00
(Text on back states he was named Super Bowl MVP in 1972. Chuck Howley won the award)
❑ 327 Miller Farr 18.00 8.00
❑ 328 Horst Muhlmann 18.00 8.00
❑ 329 John Niland RC 25.00 11.00
❑ 330 Andy Russell 30.00 13.50
❑ 331 Mercury Morris 40.00 18.00
❑ 332 Jim Johnson 30.00 13.50
❑ 333 Jerrel Wilson 18.00 8.00
❑ 334 Charley Taylor UER 40.00 18.00
(Misspelled Charlie on both sides)
❑ 335 Dick LeBeau 18.00 8.00
❑ 336 Jim Marshall 30.00 13.50
❑ 337 Tom Mack 30.00 13.50
❑ 338 Steve Spurrier IA 60.00 27.00
❑ 339 Floyd Little IA 25.00 11.00
❑ 340 Len Dawson IA 40.00 18.00
❑ 341 Dick Butkus IA 70.00 32.00
❑ 342 Larry Brown IA 25.00 11.00
❑ 343 Joe Namath IA 175.00 80.00
❑ 344 Jim Turner IA 18.00 8.00
❑ 345 Doug Cunningham IA 18.00 8.00
❑ 346 Edd Hargett IA 18.00 8.00
❑ 347 Steve Owens IA 18.00 8.00
❑ 348 George Blanda IA 50.00 22.00
❑ 349 Ed Podolak IA 18.00 8.00
❑ 350 Rich Jackson IA 18.00 8.00
❑ 351 Ken Willard IA 40.00 18.00

1973 Topps

	NM	Ex
COMPLETE SET (528)	400.00	180.00

❑ 1 Rushing Leaders 8.00 2.00
Larry Brown
O.J. Simpson
❑ 2 Passing Leaders 1.00 .45
Norm Snead
Earl Morrall
❑ 3 Receiving Leaders UER 1.50 .70
Harold Jackson
Fred Biletnikoff
(Charley Taylor misspelled as Charlie)
❑ 4 Scoring Leaders .50 .23
Chester Marcol
Bobby Howfield
❑ 5 Interception Leaders .50 .23
Bill Bradley
Mike Sensibaugh
❑ 6 Punting Leaders .50 .23

Dave Chapple
Jerrel Wilson
❑ 7 Bob Trumpy 1.50 .70
❑ 8 Mel Tom .50 .23
❑ 9 Clarence Ellis .50 .23
❑ 10 John Niland .50 .23
❑ 11 Randy Jackson .50 .23
❑ 12 Greg Landry 1.50 .70
❑ 13 Cid Edwards .50 .23
❑ 14 Phil Olsen .50 .23
❑ 15 Terry Bradshaw 25.00 11.00
❑ 16 Al Cowlings RC 1.50 .70
❑ 17 Walker Gillette .50 .23
❑ 18 Bob Atkins .50 .23
❑ 19 Diron Talbert RC .50 .23
❑ 20 Jim Johnson 1.50 .70
❑ 21 Howard Twilley 1.00 .45
❑ 22 Dick Enderle .50 .23
❑ 23 Wayne Colman .50 .23
❑ 24 John Schmitt .50 .23
❑ 25 George Blanda 10.00 4.50
❑ 26 Milt Morin .50 .23
❑ 27 Mike Current .50 .23
❑ 28 Rex Kern RC .50 .23
❑ 29 MacArthur Lane 1.00 .45
❑ 30 Alan Page 3.00 1.35
❑ 31 Randy Vataha .50 .23
❑ 32 Jim Kearney .50 .23
❑ 33 Steve Smith .50 .23
❑ 34 Ken Anderson RC 15.00 6.75
❑ 35 Calvin Hill 1.50 .70
❑ 36 Andy Maurer .50 .23
❑ 37 Joe Taylor .50 .23
❑ 38 Deacon Jones 1.50 .70
❑ 39 Mike Weger .50 .23
❑ 40 Roy Gerela 1.00 .45
❑ 41 Les Josephson .50 .23
❑ 42 Dave Washington .50 .23
❑ 43 Bill Curry RC 1.00 .45
❑ 44 Fred Heron .50 .23
❑ 45 John Brodie 3.00 1.35
❑ 46 Roy Winston .50 .23
❑ 47 Mike Bragg .50 .23
❑ 48 Mercury Morris 1.50 .70
❑ 49 Jim Files .50 .23
❑ 50 Gene Upshaw 3.00 1.35
❑ 51 Hugo Hollas .50 .23
❑ 52 Rod Sherman .50 .23
❑ 53 Ron Snidow .50 .23
❑ 54 Steve Tannen RC .50 .23
❑ 55 Jim Carter RC .50 .23
❑ 56 Lydell Mitchell RC 1.50 .70
❑ 57 Jack Rudnay RC .50 .23
❑ 58 Halvor Hagen .50 .23
❑ 59 Tom Dempsey 1.00 .45
❑ 60 Fran Tarkenton 10.00 4.50
❑ 61 Lance Alworth 5.00 2.20
❑ 62 Vern Holland .50 .23
❑ 63 Steve DeLong .50 .23
❑ 64 Art Malone .50 .23
❑ 65 Isiah Robertson 1.00 .45
❑ 66 Jerry Rush .50 .23
❑ 67 Bryant Salter .50 .23
❑ 68 Checklist 1-132 5.00 1.25
❑ 69 J.D. Hill .50 .23
❑ 70 Forrest Blue .50 .23
❑ 71 Myron Pottios .50 .23
❑ 72 Norm Thompson RC .50 .23
❑ 73 Paul Robinson .50 .23
❑ 74 Larry Grantham .50 .23
❑ 75 Manny Fernandez 1.00 .45
❑ 76 Kent Nix .50 .23
❑ 77 Art Shell RC 15.00 6.75
❑ 78 George Saimes .50 .23
❑ 79 Don Cockroft .50 .23
❑ 80 Bob Tucker 1.00 .45
❑ 81 Don McCauley RC .50 .23
❑ 82 Bob Brown DT .50 .23
❑ 83 Larry Carwell .50 .23
❑ 84 Mo Moorman .50 .23
❑ 85 John Gilliam 1.00 .45
❑ 86 Wade Key .50 .23
❑ 87 Ross Brupbacher .50 .23
❑ 88 Dave Lewis .50 .23
❑ 89 Franco Harris RC 50.00 22.00
❑ 90 Tom Mack 1.50 .70
❑ 91 Mike Tilleman .50 .23
❑ 92 Carl Mauck .50 .23
❑ 93 Larry Hand .50 .23
❑ 94 Dave Foley RC .50 .23
❑ 95 Frank Nunley .50 .23
❑ 96 John Charles .50 .23
❑ 97 Jim Bakken .50 .23
❑ 98 Pat Fischer 1.00 .45
❑ 99 Randy Rasmussen .50 .23
❑ 100 Larry Csonka 6.00 2.70
❑ 101 Mike Siani RC .50 .23
❑ 102 Tom Roussel .50 .23
❑ 103 Clarence Scott RC 1.00 .45
❑ 104 Charlie Johnson 1.00 .45
❑ 105 Rick Volk .50 .23
❑ 106 Willie Young .50 .23
❑ 107 Emmitt Thomas 1.00 .45
❑ 108 Jon Morris .50 .23
❑ 109 Clarence Williams .50 .23
❑ 110 Rayfield Wright 1.00 .45
❑ 111 Norm Bulaich .50 .23
❑ 112 Mike Eischeid .50 .23
❑ 113 Speedy Thomas .50 .23
❑ 114 Glen Holloway .50 .23
❑ 115 Jack Ham RC 30.00 13.50
❑ 116 Jim Nettles .50 .23
❑ 117 Errol Mann .50 .23
❑ 118 John Mackey 1.50 .70
❑ 119 George Kunz .50 .23
❑ 120 Bob James .50 .23
❑ 121 Garland Boyette .50 .23
❑ 122 Mel Phillips .50 .23
❑ 123 Johnny Roland .50 .23
❑ 124 Doug Swift .50 .23
❑ 125 Archie Manning 4.00 1.80
❑ 126 Dave Herman .50 .23
❑ 127 Carleton Oats .50 .23
❑ 128 Bill Van Heusen .50 .23
❑ 129 Rich Jackson .50 .23
❑ 130 Len Hauss 1.00 .45
❑ 131 Billy Parks RC .50 .23
❑ 132 Ray May .50 .23
❑ 133 NFC Semi-Final 5.00 2.20
(Cowboys 30, 49ers 28:
Roger Staubach dropping back)
❑ 134 AFC Semi-Final 2.50 1.10
(Steelers 13, Raiders 7:
Immaculate Reception Game)
❑ 135 NFC Semi-Final 1.00 .45
(Redskins 16, Packers 3:
Redskins defense)
❑ 136 AFC Semi-Final 2.00 .90
(Dolphins 20, Browns 14:
Bob Griese handing
off to Larry Csonka)
❑ 137 NFC Title Game 1.50 .70
(Redskins 26, Cowboys 3:
Billy Kilmer handing
off to Larry Brown)
❑ 138 AFC Title Game 1.00 .45
(Dolphins 21, Steelers 17:
Miami stops John Fuqua)
❑ 139 Super Bowl 1.50 .70
(Dolphins 14, Redskins 7:
Miami defense)
❑ 140 Dwight White RC UER 3.00 1.35
(College North Texas
State, should be
East Texas State)
❑ 141 Jim Marsalis .50 .23
❑ 142 Doug Van Horn .50 .23
❑ 143 Al Matthews .50 .23
❑ 144 Bob Windsor .50 .23
❑ 145 Dave Hampton RC .50 .23
❑ 146 Horst Muhlmann .50 .23
❑ 147 Wally Hilgenberg RC .50 .23
❑ 148 Ron Smith .50 .23
❑ 149 Coy Bacon RC 1.00 .45
❑ 150 Winston Hill .50 .23
❑ 151 Ron Jessie RC 1.00 .45
❑ 152 Ken Iman .50 .23
❑ 153 Ron Saul .50 .23
❑ 154 Jim Braxton RC 1.00 .45
❑ 155 Bubba Smith 2.50 1.10
❑ 156 Gary Cuozzo 1.00 .45
❑ 157 Charlie Krueger 1.00 .45
❑ 158 Tim Foley RC 1.00 .45
❑ 159 Lee Roy Jordan 1.50 .70
❑ 160 Bob Brown OT 1.50 .70
❑ 161 Margene Adkins .50 .23
❑ 162 Ron Widby .50 .23
❑ 163 Jim Houston .50 .23
❑ 164 Joe Dawkins .50 .23
❑ 165 L.C. Greenwood 4.00 1.80
❑ 166 Richmond Flowers RC .50 .23
❑ 167 Curley Culp RC 1.50 .70
❑ 168 Len St. Jean .50 .23
❑ 169 Walter Rock .50 .23
❑ 170 Bill Bradley 1.00 .45
❑ 171 Ken Riley RC 1.50 .70
❑ 172 Rich Coady .50 .23
❑ 173 Don Hansen .50 .23
❑ 174 Lionel Aldridge .50 .23
❑ 175 Don Maynard 4.00 1.80
❑ 176 Dave Osborn 1.00 .45
❑ 177 Jim Bailey .50 .23
❑ 178 John Pitts .50 .23
❑ 179 Dave Parks .50 .23
❑ 180 Chester Marcol RC .50 .23
❑ 181 Len Rohde .50 .23
❑ 182 Jeff Staggs .50 .23
❑ 183 Gene Hickerson .50 .23
❑ 184 Charlie Evans .50 .23
❑ 185 Mel Renfro 1.50 .70
❑ 186 Marvin Upshaw .50 .23
❑ 187 George Atkinson 1.00 .45
❑ 188 Norm Evans 1.00 .45
❑ 189 Steve Ramsey .50 .23
❑ 190 Dave Chapple .50 .23
❑ 191 Gerry Mullins .50 .23
❑ 192 John Didion .50 .23
❑ 193 Bob Gladieux .50 .23
❑ 194 Don Hultz .50 .23
❑ 195 Mike Lucci .50 .23
❑ 196 John Wilbur .50 .23
❑ 197 George Farmer .50 .23
❑ 198 Tommy Casanova RC 1.00 .45
❑ 199 Russ Washington .50 .23
❑ 200 Claude Humphrey 1.50 .70
Tackling Roger Staubach
❑ 201 Pat Hughes .50 .23
❑ 202 Zeke Moore .50 .23
❑ 203 Chip Glass .50 .23
❑ 204 Glenn Ressler .50 .23
❑ 205 Willie Ellison 1.00 .45
❑ 206 John Leypoldt .50 .23
❑ 207 Johnny Fuller .50 .23
❑ 208 Bill Hayhoe .50 .23
❑ 209 Ed Bell .50 .23
❑ 210 Willie Brown 1.50 .70
❑ 211 Carl Eller 1.50 .70
❑ 212 Mark Nordquist .50 .23
❑ 213 Larry Willingham .50 .23
❑ 214 Nick Buoniconti 1.50 .70
❑ 215 John Hadl 1.50 .70
❑ 216 Jethro Pugh RC 1.50 .70
❑ 217 Leroy Mitchell .50 .23
❑ 218 Billy Newsome .50 .23
❑ 219 John McMakin .50 .23
❑ 220 Larry Brown 1.50 .70
❑ 221 Clarence Scott RC .50 .23
❑ 222 Paul Naumoff .50 .23
❑ 223 Ted Fritsch Jr. .50 .23
❑ 224 Checklist 133-264 5.00 1.25
❑ 225 Dan Pastorini 1.50 .70
❑ 226 Joe Beauchamp UER .50 .23
(Safety on front,

Cornerback on back)
❑ 227 Pat Matson .50 .23
❑ 228 Tony McGee .50 .23
❑ 229 Mike Phipps 1.00 .45
❑ 230 Harold Jackson 1.50 .70
❑ 231 Willie Williams .50 .23
❑ 232 Spike Jones .50 .23
❑ 233 Jim Tyrer .50 .23
❑ 234 Roy Hilton .50 .23
❑ 235 Phil Villapiano 1.00 .45
❑ 236 Charley Taylor UER 3.00 1.35
(Misspelled Charlie
on both sides)
❑ 237 Malcolm Snider .50 .23
❑ 238 Vic Washington .50 .23
❑ 239 Grady Alderman .50 .23
❑ 240 Dick Anderson 1.00 .45
❑ 241 Ron Yankowski .50 .23
❑ 242 Billy Masters .50 .23
❑ 243 Herb Adderley 1.50 .70
❑ 244 David Ray .50 .23
❑ 245 John Riggins 8.00 3.60
❑ 246 Mike Wagner RC 1.50 .70
❑ 247 Don Morrison .50 .23
❑ 248 Earl McCullouch .50 .23
❑ 249 Dennis Wirgowski .50 .23
❑ 250 Chris Hanburger 1.00 .45
❑ 251 Pat Sullivan RC 1.50 .70
❑ 252 Walt Sweeney .50 .23
❑ 253 Willie Alexander .50 .23
❑ 254 Doug Dressler .50 .23
❑ 255 Walter Johnson .50 .23
❑ 256 Ron Hornsby .50 .23
❑ 257 Ben Hawkins .50 .23
❑ 258 Donnie Green RC .50 .23
❑ 259 Fred Hoaglin .50 .23
❑ 260 Jerrel Wilson .50 .23
❑ 261 Horace Jones .50 .23
❑ 262 Woody Peoples .50 .23
❑ 263 Jim Hill RC .50 .23
❑ 264 John Fuqua .50 .23
❑ 265 Donny Anderson KP 1.00 .45
❑ 266 Roman Gabriel KP 1.50 .70
❑ 267 Mike Garrett KP 1.00 .45
❑ 268 Rufus Mayes RC .50 .23
❑ 269 Chip Myrtle .50 .23
❑ 270 Bill Stanfill RC 1.00 .45
❑ 271 Clint Jones .50 .23
❑ 272 Miller Farr .50 .23
❑ 273 Harry Schuh .50 .23
❑ 274 Bob Hayes 1.50 .70
❑ 275 Bobby Douglass 1.00 .45
❑ 276 Gus Hollomon .50 .23
❑ 277 Del Williams .50 .23
❑ 278 Julius Adams .50 .23
❑ 279 Herman Weaver .50 .23
❑ 280 Joe Greene 8.00 3.60
❑ 281 Wes Chesson .50 .23
❑ 282 Charlie Harraway .50 .23
❑ 283 Paul Guidry .50 .23
❑ 284 Terry Owens .50 .23
❑ 285 Jan Stenerud 1.50 .70
❑ 286 Pete Athas .50 .23
❑ 287 Dale Lindsey .50 .23
❑ 288 Jack Tatum RC 15.00 6.75
❑ 289 Floyd Little 1.50 .70
❑ 290 Bob Johnson .50 .23
❑ 291 Tommy Hart RC .50 .23
❑ 292 Tom Mitchell .50 .23
❑ 293 Walt Patulski RC .50 .23
❑ 294 Jim Skaggs .50 .23
❑ 295 Bob Griese 6.00 2.70
❑ 296 Mike McCoy .50 .23
❑ 297 Mel Gray 1.00 .45
❑ 298 Bobby Bryant .50 .23
❑ 299 Blaine Nye RC .50 .23
❑ 300 Dick Butkus 12.00 5.50
❑ 301 Charlie Cowan RC .50 .23
❑ 302 Mark Lomas .50 .23
❑ 303 Josh Ashton .50 .23
❑ 304 Happy Feller .50 .23
❑ 305 Ron Shanklin .50 .23
❑ 306 Wayne Rasmussen .50 .23
❑ 307 Jerry Smith .50 .23
❑ 308 Ken Reaves .50 .23
❑ 309 Ron East .50 .23
❑ 310 Otis Taylor 1.50 .70
❑ 311 John Garlington .50 .23
❑ 312 Lyle Alzado 4.00 1.80
❑ 313 Remi Prudhomme .50 .23
❑ 314 Cornelius Johnson .50 .23
❑ 315 Lemar Parrish 1.00 .45
❑ 316 Jim Kiick 1.50 .70
❑ 317 Steve Zabel .50 .23
❑ 318 Alden Roche .50 .23
❑ 319 Tom Blanchard .50 .23
❑ 320 Fred Biletnikoff 4.00 1.80
❑ 321 Ralph Neely 1.00 .45
❑ 322 Dan Dierdorf RC 20.00 9.00
❑ 323 Richard Caster 1.00 .45
❑ 324 Gene Howard .50 .23
❑ 325 Elvin Bethea 1.50 .70
❑ 326 Carl Garrett 1.00 .45
❑ 327 Ron Billingsley .50 .23
❑ 328 Charlie West .50 .23
❑ 329 Tom Neville .50 .23
❑ 330 Ted Kwalick 1.00 .45
❑ 331 Rudy Redmond .50 .23
❑ 332 Henry Davis .50 .23
❑ 333 John Zook .50 .23
❑ 334 Jim Turner .50 .23
❑ 335 Len Dawson 5.00 2.20
❑ 336 Bob Chandler RC 1.00 .45
❑ 337 Al Beauchamp .50 .23
❑ 338 Tom Matte 1.00 .45
❑ 339 Paul Laaveg .50 .23
❑ 340 Ken Ellis .50 .23
❑ 341 Jim Langer RC 10.00 4.50
❑ 342 Ron Porter .50 .23
❑ 343 Jack Youngblood RC 15.00 6.75
❑ 344 Cornell Green 1.50 .70
❑ 345 Marv Hubbard 1.00 .45
❑ 346 Bruce Taylor .50 .23
❑ 347 Sam Havrilak .50 .23
❑ 348 Walt Sumner .50 .23
❑ 349 Steve O'Neal .50 .23
❑ 350 Ron Johnson 1.00 .45
❑ 351 Rockne Freitas .50 .23
❑ 352 Larry Stallings .50 .23
❑ 353 Jim Cadile .50 .23
❑ 354 Ken Burrough 1.00 .45
❑ 355 Jim Plunkett 4.00 1.80
❑ 356 Dave Long .50 .23
❑ 357 Ralph Anderson .50 .23
❑ 358 Checklist 265-396 5.00 1.25
❑ 359 Gene Washington Vik 1.00 .45
❑ 360 Dave Wilcox 1.50 .70
❑ 361 Paul Smith .50 .23
❑ 362 Alvin Wyatt .50 .23
❑ 363 Charlie Smith .50 .23
❑ 364 Royce Berry .50 .23
❑ 365 Dave Elmendorf .50 .23
❑ 366 Scott Hunter 1.00 .45
❑ 367 Bob Kuechenberg RC 3.00 1.35
❑ 368 Pete Gogolak .50 .23
❑ 369 Dave Edwards .50 .23
❑ 370 Lem Barney 2.50 1.10
❑ 371 Verlon Biggs .50 .23
❑ 372 John Reaves RC .50 .23
❑ 373 Ed Podolak 1.00 .45
❑ 374 Chris Farasopoulos .50 .23
❑ 375 Gary Garrison .50 .23
❑ 376 Tom Funchess .50 .23
❑ 377 Bobby Joe Green .50 .23
❑ 378 Don Brumm .50 .23
❑ 379 Jim O'Brien .50 .23
❑ 380 Paul Krause 1.50 .70
❑ 381 Leroy Kelly 2.50 1.10
❑ 382 Ray Mansfield .50 .23
❑ 383 Dan Abramowicz 1.00 .45
❑ 384 John Outlaw RC .50 .23
❑ 385 Tommy Nobis 1.50 .70
❑ 386 Tom Domres .50 .23
❑ 387 Ken Willard .50 .23
❑ 388 Mike Stratton .50 .23
❑ 389 Fred Dryer 2.50 1.10
❑ 390 Jake Scott 1.50 .70
❑ 391 Rich Houston .50 .23
❑ 392 Virgil Carter .50 .23
❑ 393 Tody Smith .50 .23
❑ 394 Ernie Calloway .50 .23
❑ 395 Charlie Sanders 1.00 .45
❑ 396 Fred Willis .50 .23
❑ 397 Curt Knight .50 .23
❑ 398 Nemiah Wilson .50 .23
❑ 399 Carroll Dale 1.00 .45
❑ 400 Joe Namath 30.00 13.50
❑ 401 Wayne Mulligan .50 .23
❑ 402 Jim Harrison .50 .23
❑ 403 Tim Rossovich .50 .23
❑ 404 David Lee .50 .23
❑ 405 Frank Pitts .50 .23
❑ 406 Jim Marshall 1.50 .70
❑ 407 Bob Brown TE .50 .23
❑ 408 John Rowser .50 .23
❑ 409 Mike Montler .50 .23
❑ 410 Willie Lanier 1.50 .70
❑ 411 Bill Bell .50 .23
❑ 412 Cedrick Hardman .50 .23
❑ 413 Bob Anderson .50 .23
❑ 414 Earl Morrall 1.50 .70
❑ 415 Ken Houston 1.50 .70
❑ 416 Jack Snow 1.00 .45
❑ 417 Dick Cunningham .50 .23
❑ 418 Greg Larson .50 .23
❑ 419 Mike Bass 1.00 .45
❑ 420 Mike Reid 1.50 .70
❑ 421 Walt Garrison 1.50 .70
❑ 422 Pete Liske .50 .23
❑ 423 Jim Yarbrough .50 .23
❑ 424 Rich McGeorge .50 .23
❑ 425 Bobby Howfield .50 .23
❑ 426 Pete Banaszak .50 .23
❑ 427 Willie Holman .50 .23
❑ 428 Dale Hackbart .50 .23
❑ 429 Fair Hooker .50 .23
❑ 430 Ted Hendricks 5.00 2.20
❑ 431 Mike Garrett 1.00 .45
❑ 432 Glen Ray Hines .50 .23
❑ 433 Fred Cox .50 .23
❑ 434 Bobby Walden .50 .23
❑ 435 Bobby Bell 1.50 .70
❑ 436 Dave Rowe .50 .23
❑ 437 Bob Berry .50 .23
❑ 438 Bill Thompson .50 .23
❑ 439 Jim Beirne .50 .23
❑ 440 Larry Little 3.00 1.35
❑ 441 Rocky Thompson .50 .23
❑ 442 Brig Owens .50 .23
❑ 443 Richard Neal .50 .23
❑ 444 Al Nelson .50 .23
❑ 445 Chip Myers .50 .23
❑ 446 Ken Bowman .50 .23
❑ 447 Jim Purnell .50 .23
❑ 448 Altie Taylor .50 .23
❑ 449 Linzy Cole .50 .23
❑ 450 Bob Lilly 5.00 2.20
❑ 451 Charlie Ford .50 .23
❑ 452 Milt Sunde .50 .23
❑ 453 Doug Wyatt .50 .23
❑ 454 Don Nottingham RC 1.00 .45
❑ 455 John Unitas 15.00 6.75
❑ 456 Frank Lewis RC 1.00 .45
❑ 457 Roger Wehrli 1.00 .45
❑ 458 Jim Cheyunski .50 .23
❑ 459 Jerry Sherk RC 1.00 .45
❑ 460 Gene Washington 49er 1.00 .45
❑ 461 Jim Otto 1.50 .70
❑ 462 Ed Budde .50 .23
❑ 463 Jim Mitchell 1.00 .45
❑ 464 Emerson Boozer 1.00 .45
❑ 465 Garo Yepremian 1.50 .70
❑ 466 Pete Duranko .50 .23

❑ 467 Charlie Joiner	8.00	3.60
❑ 468 Spider Lockhart	1.00	.45
❑ 469 Marty Domres	.50	.23
❑ 470 John Brockington	1.50	.70
❑ 471 Ed Flanagan	.50	.23
❑ 472 Roy Jefferson	1.00	.45
❑ 473 Julian Fagan	.50	.23
❑ 474 Bill Brown	1.00	.45
❑ 475 Roger Staubach	30.00	13.50
❑ 476 Jan White	.50	.23
❑ 477 Pat Holmes	.50	.23
❑ 478 Bob DeMarco	.50	.23
❑ 479 Merlin Olsen	2.50	1.10
❑ 480 Andy Russell	1.50	.70
❑ 481 Steve Spurrier	20.00	9.00
❑ 482 Nate Ramsey	.50	.23
❑ 483 Dennis Partee	.50	.23
❑ 484 Jerry Simmons	.50	.23
❑ 485 Donny Anderson	1.50	.70
❑ 486 Ralph Baker	.50	.23
❑ 487 Ken Stabler RC	60.00	27.00
❑ 488 Ernie McMillan	.50	.23
❑ 489 Ken Burrow	.50	.23
❑ 490 Jack Gregory RC	.50	.23
❑ 491 Larry Seiple	1.00	.45
❑ 492 Mick Tingelhoff	1.00	.45
❑ 493 Craig Morton	1.50	.70
❑ 494 Cecil Turner	.50	.23
❑ 495 Steve Owens	1.50	.70
❑ 496 Rickie Harris	.50	.23
❑ 497 Buck Buchanan	1.50	.70
❑ 498 Checklist 397-528	5.00	1.25
❑ 499 Billy Kilmer	1.50	.70
❑ 500 O.J. Simpson	15.00	6.75
❑ 501 Bruce Gossett	.50	.23
❑ 502 Art Thoms RC	.50	.23
❑ 503 Larry Kaminski	.50	.23
❑ 504 Larry Smith	.50	.23
❑ 505 Bruce Van Dyke	.50	.23
❑ 506 Alvin Reed	.50	.23
❑ 507 Delles Howell	.50	.23
❑ 508 Leroy Keyes	.50	.23
❑ 509 Bo Scott	1.00	.45
❑ 510 Ron Yary	1.50	.70
❑ 511 Paul Warfield	5.00	2.20
❑ 512 Mac Percival	.50	.23
❑ 513 Essex Johnson	.50	.23
❑ 514 Jackie Smith	1.50	.70
❑ 515 Norm Snead	1.50	.70
❑ 516 Charlie Stukes	.50	.23
❑ 517 Reggie Rucker RC	1.00	.45
❑ 518 Bill Sandeman UER (Should be a period between run and he instead of a comma)	.50	.23
❑ 519 Mel Farr	1.00	.45
❑ 520 Raymond Chester	1.00	.45
❑ 521 Fred Carr RC	1.00	.45
❑ 522 Jerry LeVias	1.00	.45
❑ 523 Jim Strong	.50	.23
❑ 524 Roland McDole	.50	.23
❑ 525 Dennis Shaw	.50	.23
❑ 526 Dave Manders	.50	.23
❑ 527 Skip Vanderbundt	.50	.23
❑ 528 Mike Sensibaugh RC	1.50	.35

1974 Topps

	NM	Ex
COMPLETE SET (528)	300.00	135.00
❑ 1 O.J. Simpson RB UER (Text on back says 100 years, should say 100 yards)	20.00	5.00
❑ 2 Blaine Nye	.40	.18
❑ 3 Don Hansen	.40	.18
❑ 4 Ken Bowman	.40	.18
❑ 5 Carl Eller	1.50	.70
❑ 6 Jerry Smith	.40	.18
❑ 7 Ed Podolak	.40	.18
❑ 8 Mel Gray	1.50	.70
❑ 9 Pat Matson	.40	.18
❑ 10 Floyd Little	1.50	.70
❑ 11 Frank Pitts	.40	.18
❑ 12 Vern Den Herder RC	.75	.35
❑ 13 John Fuqua	.75	.35
❑ 14 Jack Tatum	2.00	.90
❑ 15 Winston Hill	.40	.18
❑ 16 John Beasley	.40	.18
❑ 17 David Lee	.40	.18
❑ 18 Rich Coady	.40	.18
❑ 19 Ken Willard	.40	.18
❑ 20 Coy Bacon	.75	.35
❑ 21 Ben Hawkins	.40	.18
❑ 22 Paul Guidry	.40	.18
❑ 23 Norm Snead (Horizontal pose)	.75	.35
❑ 24 Jim Yarbrough	.40	.18
❑ 25 Jack Reynolds RC	3.00	1.35
❑ 26 Josh Ashton	.40	.18
❑ 27 Donnie Green	.40	.18
❑ 28 Bob Hayes	1.50	.70
❑ 29 John Zook	.40	.18
❑ 30 Bobby Bryant	.40	.18
❑ 31 Scott Hunter	.75	.35
❑ 32 Dan Dierdorf	6.00	2.70
❑ 33 Curt Knight	.40	.18
❑ 34 Elmo Wright RC	.40	.18
❑ 35 Essex Johnson	.40	.18
❑ 36 Walt Sumner	.40	.18
❑ 37 Marv Montgomery	.40	.18
❑ 38 Tim Foley	.75	.35
❑ 39 Mike Siani	.40	.18
❑ 40 Joe Greene	6.00	2.70
❑ 41 Bobby Howfield	.40	.18
❑ 42 Del Williams	.40	.18
❑ 43 Don McCauley	.40	.18
❑ 44 Randy Jackson	.40	.18
❑ 45 Ron Smith	.40	.18
❑ 46 Gene Washington 49er	.75	.35
❑ 47 Po James	.40	.18
❑ 48 Solomon Freelon	.40	.18
❑ 49 Bob Windsor (Horizontal pose)	.40	.18
❑ 50 John Hadl	1.50	.70
❑ 51 Greg Larson	.40	.18
❑ 52 Steve Owens	.75	.35
❑ 53 Jim Cheyunski	.40	.18
❑ 54 Rayfield Wright	.75	.35
❑ 55 Dave Hampton	.40	.18
❑ 56 Ron Widby	.40	.18
❑ 57 Milt Sunde	.40	.18
❑ 58 Billy Kilmer	1.50	.70
❑ 59 Bobby Bell	1.50	.70
❑ 60 Jim Bakken	.40	.18
❑ 61 Rufus Mayes	.40	.18
❑ 62 Vic Washington	.40	.18
❑ 63 Gene Washington Vik	.75	.35
❑ 64 Clarence Scott	.40	.18
❑ 65 Gene Upshaw	2.00	.90
❑ 66 Larry Seiple	.75	.35
❑ 67 John McMakin	.40	.18
❑ 68 Ralph Baker	.40	.18
❑ 69 Lydell Mitchell	.75	.35
❑ 70 Archie Manning	2.50	1.10
❑ 71 George Farmer	.40	.18
❑ 72 Ron East	.40	.18
❑ 73 Al Nelson	.40	.18
❑ 74 Pat Hughes	.40	.18
❑ 75 Fred Willis	.40	.18
❑ 76 Larry Walton	.40	.18
❑ 77 Tom Neville	.40	.18
❑ 78 Ted Kwalick	.40	.18
❑ 79 Walt Patulski	.40	.18
❑ 80 John Niland	.40	.18
❑ 81 Ted Fritsch Jr.	.40	.18
❑ 82 Paul Krause	1.50	.70
❑ 83 Jack Snow	.75	.35
❑ 84 Mike Bass	.40	.18
❑ 85 Jim Tyrer	.40	.18
❑ 86 Ron Yankowski	.40	.18
❑ 87 Mike Phipps	.75	.35
❑ 88 Al Beauchamp	.40	.18
❑ 89 Riley Odoms RC	1.50	.70
❑ 90 MacArthur Lane	.40	.18
❑ 91 Art Thoms	.40	.18
❑ 92 Marlin Briscoe	.40	.18
❑ 93 Bruce Van Dyke	.40	.18
❑ 94 Tom Myers RC	.40	.18
❑ 95 Calvin Hill	1.50	.70
❑ 96 Bruce Laird	.40	.18
❑ 97 Tony McGee	.40	.18
❑ 98 Len Rohde	.40	.18
❑ 99 Tom McNeill	.40	.18
❑ 100 Delles Howell	.40	.18
❑ 101 Gary Garrison	.40	.18
❑ 102 Dan Goich	.40	.18
❑ 103 Len St. Jean	.40	.18
❑ 104 Zeke Moore	.40	.18
❑ 105 Ahmad Rashad RC	20.00	9.00
❑ 106 Mel Renfro	1.50	.70
❑ 107 Jim Mitchell	.40	.18
❑ 108 Ed Budde	.40	.18
❑ 109 Harry Schuh	.40	.18
❑ 110 Greg Pruitt RC	4.00	1.80
❑ 111 Ed Flanagan	.40	.18
❑ 112 Larry Stallings	.40	.18
❑ 113 Chuck Foreman RC	4.00	1.80
❑ 114 Royce Berry	.40	.18
❑ 115 Gale Gillingham	.40	.18
❑ 116 Charlie Johnson (Horizontal pose)	1.50	.70
❑ 117 Checklist 1-132 UER (345 Hamburger)	4.00	1.00
❑ 118 Bill Butler	.40	.18
❑ 119 Roy Jefferson	.75	.35
❑ 120 Bobby Douglass	.75	.35
❑ 121 Harold Carmichael AP RC	12.00	5.50
❑ 122 George Kunz AP	.40	.18
❑ 123 Larry Little AP	2.00	.90
❑ 124 Forrest Blue AP	.40	.18
❑ 125 Ron Yary AP	1.50	.70
❑ 126 Tom Mack AP	1.50	.70
❑ 127 Bob Tucker AP	.75	.35
❑ 128 Paul Warfield AP	4.00	1.80
❑ 129 Fran Tarkenton AP	10.00	4.50
❑ 130 O.J. Simpson AP	12.00	5.50
❑ 131 Larry Csonka AP	6.00	2.70
❑ 132 Bruce Gossett AP	.40	.18
❑ 133 Bill Stanfill AP	.75	.35
❑ 134 Alan Page AP	2.50	1.10
❑ 135 Paul Smith AP	.40	.18
❑ 136 Claude Humphrey AP	.75	.35
❑ 137 Jack Ham AP	10.00	4.50
❑ 138 Lee Roy Jordan AP	1.50	.70
❑ 139 Phil Villapiano AP	.75	.35
❑ 140 Ken Ellis AP	.40	.18
❑ 141 Willie Brown AP	1.50	.70
❑ 142 Dick Anderson AP	.75	.35
❑ 143 Bill Bradley AP	.75	.35
❑ 144 Jerrel Wilson AP	.40	.18
❑ 145 Reggie Rucker	.75	.35
❑ 146 Marty Domres	.40	.18
❑ 147 Bob Kowalkowski	.40	.18
❑ 148 John Matuszak RC	6.00	2.70

❑ 149 Mike Adamle RC	.75	.35
❑ 150 John Unitas	15.00	6.75
❑ 151 Charlie Ford	.40	.18
❑ 152 Bob Klein RC	.40	.18
❑ 153 Jim Merlo	.40	.18
❑ 154 Willie Young	.40	.18
❑ 155 Donny Anderson	.75	.35
❑ 156 Brig Owens	.40	.18
❑ 157 Bruce Jarvis	.40	.18
❑ 158 Ron Carpenter RC	.40	.18
❑ 159 Don Cockroft	.40	.18
❑ 160 Tommy Nobis	1.50	.70
❑ 161 Craig Morton	1.50	.70
❑ 162 Jon Staggers	.40	.18
❑ 163 Mike Eischeid	.40	.18
❑ 164 Jerry Sisemore RC	.40	.18
❑ 165 Cedrick Hardman	.40	.18
❑ 166 Bill Thompson	.75	.35
❑ 167 Jim Lynch	.75	.35
❑ 168 Bob Moore	.40	.18
❑ 169 Glen Edwards	.40	.18
❑ 170 Mercury Morris	1.50	.70
❑ 171 Julius Adams	.40	.18
❑ 172 Cotton Speyrer	.40	.18
❑ 173 Bill Munson	.75	.35
❑ 174 Benny Johnson	.40	.18
❑ 175 Burgess Owens RC	.40	.18
❑ 176 Cid Edwards	.40	.18
❑ 177 Doug Buffone	.40	.18
❑ 178 Charlie Cowan	.40	.18
❑ 179 Bob Newland	.40	.18
❑ 180 Ron Johnson	.75	.35
❑ 181 Bob Rowe	.40	.18
❑ 182 Len Hauss	.40	.18
❑ 183 Joe DeLamielleure RC	8.00	3.60
❑ 184 Sherman White RC	.40	.18
❑ 185 Fair Hooker	.40	.18
❑ 186 Nick Mike-Mayer	.40	.18
❑ 187 Ralph Neely	.40	.18
❑ 188 Rich McGeorge	.40	.18
❑ 189 Ed Marinaro RC	4.00	1.80
❑ 190 Dave Wilcox	1.50	.70
❑ 191 Joe Owens RC	.40	.18
❑ 192 Bill Van Heusen	.40	.18
❑ 193 Jim Kearney	.40	.18
❑ 194 Otis Sistrunk RC	1.50	.70
❑ 195 Ron Shanklin	.40	.18
❑ 196 Bill Lenkaitis	.40	.18
❑ 197 Tom Drougas	.40	.18
❑ 198 Larry Hand	.40	.18
❑ 199 Mack Alston	.40	.18
❑ 200 Bob Griese	6.00	2.70
❑ 201 Earlie Thomas	.40	.18
❑ 202 Carl Gersbach	.40	.18
❑ 203 Jim Harrison	.40	.18
❑ 204 Jake Kupp	.40	.18
❑ 205 Merlin Olsen	2.00	.90
❑ 206 Spider Lockhart	.75	.35
❑ 207 Walker Gillette	.40	.18
❑ 208 Verlon Biggs	.40	.18
❑ 209 Bob James	.40	.18
❑ 210 Bob Trumpy	1.50	.70
❑ 211 Jerry Sherk	.40	.18
❑ 212 Andy Maurer	.40	.18
❑ 213 Fred Carr	.40	.18
❑ 214 Mick Tingelhoff	.75	.35
❑ 215 Steve Spurrier	15.00	6.75
❑ 216 Richard Harris	.40	.18
❑ 217 Charlie Greer	.40	.18
❑ 218 Buck Buchanan	1.50	.70
❑ 219 Ray Guy RC	10.00	4.50
❑ 220 Franco Harris	12.00	5.50
❑ 221 Darryl Stingley RC	1.50	.70
❑ 222 Rex Kern	.40	.18
❑ 223 Toni Fritsch	.75	.35
❑ 224 Levi Johnson	.40	.18
❑ 225 Bob Kuechenberg	.75	.35
❑ 226 Elvin Bethea	1.50	.70
❑ 227 Al Woodall RC	.75	.35
❑ 228 Terry Owens	.40	.18
❑ 229 Bivian Lee	.40	.18
❑ 230 Dick Butkus	10.00	4.50
❑ 231 Jim Bertelsen RC	.75	.35
❑ 232 John Mendenhall RC	.40	.18
❑ 233 Conrad Dobler RC	1.50	.70
❑ 234 J.D. Hill	.75	.35
❑ 235 Ken Houston	1.50	.70
❑ 236 Dave Lewis	.40	.18
❑ 237 John Garlington	.40	.18
❑ 238 Bill Sandeman	.40	.18
❑ 239 Alden Roche	.40	.18
❑ 240 John Gilliam	.75	.35
❑ 241 Bruce Taylor	.40	.18
❑ 242 Vern Winfield	.40	.18
❑ 243 Bobby Maples	.40	.18
❑ 244 Wendell Hayes	.40	.18
❑ 245 George Blanda	8.00	3.60
❑ 246 Dwight White	.75	.35
❑ 247 Sandy Durko	.40	.18
❑ 248 Tom Mitchell	.40	.18
❑ 249 Chuck Walton	.40	.18
❑ 250 Bob Lilly	4.00	1.80
❑ 251 Doug Swift	.40	.18
❑ 252 Lynn Dickey RC	1.50	.70
❑ 253 Jerome Barkum RC	.40	.18
❑ 254 Clint Jones	.40	.18
❑ 255 Billy Newsome	.40	.18
❑ 256 Bob Asher	.40	.18
❑ 257 Joe Scibelli	.40	.18
❑ 258 Tom Blanchard	.40	.18
❑ 259 Norm Thompson	.40	.18
❑ 260 Larry Brown	1.50	.70
❑ 261 Paul Seymour	.40	.18
❑ 262 Checklist 133-264	4.00	1.00
❑ 263 Doug Dieken RC	.40	.18
❑ 264 Lemar Parrish	.75	.35
❑ 265 Bob Lee UER (listed as Atlanta Hawks on card back)	.40	.18
❑ 266 Bob Brown DT	.40	.18
❑ 267 Roy Winston	.40	.18
❑ 268 Randy Beisler	.40	.18
❑ 269 Joe Dawkins	.40	.18
❑ 270 Tom Dempsey	.75	.35
❑ 271 Jack Rudnay	.40	.18
❑ 272 Art Shell	5.00	2.20
❑ 273 Mike Wagner	.75	.35
❑ 274 Rick Cash	.40	.18
❑ 275 Greg Landry	1.50	.70
❑ 276 Glenn Ressler	.40	.18
❑ 277 Billy Joe DuPree RC	3.00	1.35
❑ 278 Norm Evans	.40	.18
❑ 279 Billy Parks	.40	.18
❑ 280 John Riggins	6.00	2.70
❑ 281 Lionel Aldridge	.40	.18
❑ 282 Steve O'Neal	.40	.18
❑ 283 Craig Clemons	.40	.18
❑ 284 Willie Williams	.40	.18
❑ 285 Isiah Robertson	.75	.35
❑ 286 Dennis Shaw	.40	.18
❑ 287 Bill Brundige	.40	.18
❑ 288 John Leypoldt	.40	.18
❑ 289 John DeMarie	.40	.18
❑ 290 Mike Reid	1.50	.70
❑ 291 Greg Brezina	.40	.18
❑ 292 Willie Buchanon RC	.40	.18
❑ 293 Dave Osborn	.75	.35
❑ 294 Mel Phillips	.40	.18
❑ 295 Haven Moses	.75	.35
❑ 296 Wade Key	.40	.18
❑ 297 Marvin Upshaw	.40	.18
❑ 298 Ray Mansfield	.40	.18
❑ 299 Edgar Chandler	.40	.18
❑ 300 Marv Hubbard	.75	.35
❑ 301 Herman Weaver	.40	.18
❑ 302 Jim Bailey	.40	.18
❑ 303 D.D. Lewis RC	1.50	.70
❑ 304 Ken Burrough	.75	.35
❑ 305 Jake Scott	1.50	.70
❑ 306 Randy Rasmussen	.40	.18
❑ 307 Pettis Norman	.40	.18
❑ 308 Carl Johnson	.40	.18
❑ 309 Joe Taylor	.40	.18
❑ 310 Pete Gogolak	.40	.18
❑ 311 Tony Baker	.40	.18
❑ 312 John Richardson	.40	.18
❑ 313 Dave Robinson	.75	.35
❑ 314 Reggie McKenzie RC	1.50	.70
❑ 315 Isaac Curtis RC	1.50	.70
❑ 316 Thom Darden	.40	.18
❑ 317 Ken Reaves	.40	.18
❑ 318 Malcolm Snider	.40	.18
❑ 319 Jeff Siemon RC	.75	.35
❑ 320 Dan Abramowicz	.75	.35
❑ 321 Lyle Alzado	2.00	.90
❑ 322 John Reaves	.40	.18
❑ 323 Morris Stroud	.40	.18
❑ 324 Bobby Walden	.40	.18
❑ 325 Randy Vataha	.40	.18
❑ 326 Nemiah Wilson	.40	.18
❑ 327 Paul Naumoff	.40	.18
❑ 328 Rushing Leaders O.J. Simpson John Brockington	3.00	1.35
❑ 329 Passing Leaders Ken Stabler Roger Staubach	5.00	2.20
❑ 330 Receiving Leaders Fred Willis Harold Carmichael	1.50	.70
❑ 331 Scoring Leaders Roy Gerela David Ray	.75	.35
❑ 332 Interception Leaders Dick Anderson Mike Wagner Bobby Bryant	.75	.35
❑ 333 Punting Leaders Jerrel Wilson Tom Wittum	.75	.35
❑ 334 Dennis Nelson	.40	.18
❑ 335 Walt Garrison	.75	.35
❑ 336 Tody Smith	.40	.18
❑ 337 Ed Bell	.40	.18
❑ 338 Bryant Salter	.40	.18
❑ 339 Wayne Colman	.40	.18
❑ 340 Garo Yepremian	.75	.35
❑ 341 Bob Newton	.40	.18
❑ 342 Vince Clements RC	.40	.18
❑ 343 Ken Iman	.40	.18
❑ 344 Jim Tolbert	.40	.18
❑ 345 Chris Hanburger	.75	.35
❑ 346 Dave Foley	.40	.18
❑ 347 Tommy Casanova	.75	.35
❑ 348 John James	.40	.18
❑ 349 Clarence Williams	.40	.18
❑ 350 Leroy Kelly	1.50	.70
❑ 351 Stu Voigt RC	.75	.35
❑ 352 Skip Vanderbundt	.40	.18
❑ 353 Pete Duranko	.40	.18
❑ 354 John Outlaw	.40	.18
❑ 355 Jan Stenerud	1.50	.70
❑ 356 Barry Pearson	.40	.18
❑ 357 Brian Dowling RC	.40	.18
❑ 358 Dan Conners	.40	.18
❑ 359 Bob Bell	.40	.18
❑ 360 Rick Volk	.40	.18
❑ 361 Pat Toomay	.75	.35
❑ 362 Bob Gresham	.40	.18
❑ 363 John Schmitt	.40	.18
❑ 364 Mel Rogers	.40	.18
❑ 365 Manny Fernandez	.75	.35
❑ 366 Ernie Jackson	.40	.18
❑ 367 Gary Huff RC	.75	.35
❑ 368 Bob Grim	.40	.18
❑ 369 Ernie McMillan	.40	.18
❑ 370 Dave Elmendorf	.40	.18
❑ 371 Mike Bragg	.40	.18
❑ 372 John Skorupan	.40	.18
❑ 373 Howard Fest	.40	.18
❑ 374 Jerry Tagge RC	.75	.35
❑ 375 Art Malone	.40	.18
❑ 376 Bob Babich	.40	.18

❑ 377	Jim Marshall	1.50	.70
❑ 378	Bob Hoskins	.40	.18
❑ 379	Don Zimmerman	.40	.18
❑ 380	Ray May	.40	.18
❑ 381	Emmitt Thomas	.75	.35
❑ 382	Terry Hanratty	.75	.35
❑ 383	John Hannah RC	15.00	6.75
❑ 384	George Atkinson	.40	.18
❑ 385	Ted Hendricks	3.00	1.35
❑ 386	Jim O'Brien	.40	.18
❑ 387	Jethro Pugh	.75	.35
❑ 388	Elbert Drungo	.40	.18
❑ 389	Richard Caster	.75	.35
❑ 390	Deacon Jones	1.50	.70
❑ 391	Checklist 265-396	4.00	1.00
❑ 392	Jess Phillips	.40	.18
❑ 393	Garry Lyle UER (Misspelled Gary on card front)	.40	.18
❑ 394	Jim Files	.40	.18
❑ 395	Jim Hart	1.50	.70
❑ 396	Dave Chapple	.40	.18
❑ 397	Jim Langer	2.00	.90
❑ 398	John Wilbur	.40	.18
❑ 399	Dwight Harrison	.40	.18
❑ 400	John Brockington	.75	.35
❑ 401	Ken Anderson	6.00	2.70
❑ 402	Mike Tilleman	.40	.18
❑ 403	Charlie Hall	.40	.18
❑ 404	Tommy Hart	.40	.18
❑ 405	Norm Bulaich	.75	.35
❑ 406	Jim Turner	.40	.18
❑ 407	Mo Moorman	.40	.18
❑ 408	Ralph Anderson	.40	.18
❑ 409	Jim Otto	1.50	.70
❑ 410	Andy Russell	1.50	.70
❑ 411	Glenn Doughty	.40	.18
❑ 412	Altie Taylor	.40	.18
❑ 413	Marv Bateman	.40	.18
❑ 414	Willie Alexander	.40	.18
❑ 415	Bill Zapalac RC	.40	.18
❑ 416	Russ Washington	.40	.18
❑ 417	Joe Federspiel	.40	.18
❑ 418	Craig Cotton	.40	.18
❑ 419	Randy Johnson	.40	.18
❑ 420	Harold Jackson	1.50	.70
❑ 421	Roger Wehrli	.75	.35
❑ 422	Charlie Harraway	.40	.18
❑ 423	Spike Jones	.40	.18
❑ 424	Bob Johnson	.40	.18
❑ 425	Mike McCoy	.40	.18
❑ 426	Dennis Havig	.40	.18
❑ 427	Bob McKay	.40	.18
❑ 428	Steve Zabel	.40	.18
❑ 429	Horace Jones	.40	.18
❑ 430	Jim Johnson	1.50	.70
❑ 431	Roy Gerela	.75	.35
❑ 432	Tom Graham RC	.40	.18
❑ 433	Curley Culp	.75	.35
❑ 434	Ken Mendenhall	.40	.18
❑ 435	Jim Plunkett	2.50	1.10
❑ 436	Julian Fagan	.40	.18
❑ 437	Mike Garrett	.75	.35
❑ 438	Bobby Joe Green	.40	.18
❑ 439	Jack Gregory	.40	.18
❑ 440	Charlie Sanders	.75	.35
❑ 441	Bill Curry	.75	.35
❑ 442	Bob Pollard	.40	.18
❑ 443	David Ray	.40	.18
❑ 444	Terry Metcalf RC	3.00	1.35
❑ 445	Pat Fischer	.75	.35
❑ 446	Bob Chandler	.75	.35
❑ 447	Bill Bergey	.75	.35
❑ 448	Walter Johnson	.40	.18
❑ 449	Charle Young RC	1.50	.70
❑ 450	Chester Marcol	.40	.18
❑ 451	Ken Stabler	20.00	9.00
❑ 452	Preston Pearson	1.50	.70
❑ 453	Mike Current	.40	.18
❑ 454	Ron Bolton	.40	.18
❑ 455	Mark Lomas	.40	.18
❑ 456	Raymond Chester	.75	.35
❑ 457	Jerry LeVias	.75	.35
❑ 458	Skip Butler	.40	.18
❑ 459	Mike Livingston RC	.40	.18
❑ 460	AFC Semi-Finals Raiders 33; Steelers 14 Dolphins 34; Bengals 16	.75	.35
❑ 461	NFC Semi-Finals Vikings 27; Redskins 20 Cowboys 27; Rams 16 (Staubach)	4.00	1.80
❑ 462	Playoff Championship Dolphins 27; Raiders 10 Vikings 27; Cowboys 10 (Ken Stabler and Fran Tarkenton)	3.00	1.35
❑ 463	Super Bowl Dolphins 24; Vikings 7 (Tarkenton pictured)	2.00	.90
❑ 464	Wayne Mulligan	.40	.18
❑ 465	Horst Muhlmann	.40	.18
❑ 466	Milt Morin	.40	.18
❑ 467	Don Parish	.40	.18
❑ 468	Richard Neal	.40	.18
❑ 469	Ron Jessie	.75	.35
❑ 470	Terry Bradshaw	25.00	11.00
❑ 471	Fred Dryer	1.50	.70
❑ 472	Jim Carter	.40	.18
❑ 473	Ken Burrow	.40	.18
❑ 474	Wally Chambers RC	.75	.35
❑ 475	Dan Pastorini	1.50	.70
❑ 476	Don Morrison	.40	.18
❑ 477	Carl Mauck	.40	.18
❑ 478	Larry Cole RC	.75	.35
❑ 479	Jim Kiick	1.50	.70
❑ 480	Willie Lanier	1.50	.70
❑ 481	Don Herrmann	.75	.35
❑ 482	George Hunt	.40	.18
❑ 483	Bob Howard RC	.40	.18
❑ 484	Myron Pottios	.40	.18
❑ 485	Jackie Smith	1.50	.70
❑ 486	Vern Holland	.40	.18
❑ 487	Jim Braxton	.40	.18
❑ 488	Joe Reed	.40	.18
❑ 489	Wally Hilgenberg	.40	.18
❑ 490	Fred Biletnikoff	4.00	1.80
❑ 491	Bob DeMarco	.40	.18
❑ 492	Mark Nordquist	.40	.18
❑ 493	Larry Brooks	.40	.18
❑ 494	Pete Athas	.40	.18
❑ 495	Emerson Boozer	.75	.35
❑ 496	L.C. Greenwood	2.00	.90
❑ 497	Rockne Freitas	.40	.18
❑ 498	Checklist 397-528 UER (510 Charlie Taylor should be Charley)	4.00	1.00
❑ 499	Joe Schmiesing	.40	.18
❑ 500	Roger Staubach	25.00	11.00
❑ 501	Al Cowlings UER (Def. tackle on front, Def. End on back)	.75	.35
❑ 502	Sam Cunningham RC	1.50	.70
❑ 503	Dennis Partee	.40	.18
❑ 504	John Didion	.40	.18
❑ 505	Nick Buoniconti	1.50	.70
❑ 506	Carl Garrett	.75	.35
❑ 507	Doug Van Horn	.40	.18
❑ 508	Jamie Rivers	.40	.18
❑ 509	Jack Youngblood	4.00	1.80
❑ 510	Charley Taylor UER (Misspelled Charlie on both sides)	2.50	1.10
❑ 511	Ken Riley	1.50	.70
❑ 512	Joe Ferguson RC	3.00	1.35
❑ 513	Bill Lueck	.40	.18
❑ 514	Ray Brown	.40	.18
❑ 515	Fred Cox	.40	.18
❑ 516	Joe Jones	.40	.18
❑ 517	Larry Schreiber	.40	.18
❑ 518	Dennis Wirgowski	.40	.18
❑ 519	Leroy Mitchell	.40	.18
❑ 520	Otis Taylor	1.50	.70
❑ 521	Henry Davis	.40	.18
❑ 522	Bruce Barnes	.40	.18
❑ 523	Charlie Smith	.40	.18
❑ 524	Bert Jones RC	5.00	2.20
❑ 525	Lem Barney	2.00	.90
❑ 526	John Fitzgerald RC	.40	.18
❑ 527	Tom Funchess	.40	.18
❑ 528	Steve Tannen	1.50	.70

1975 Topps

		NM	Ex
COMPLETE SET (528)		300.00	135.00
❑ 1	Rushing Leaders Lawrence McCutcheon Otis Armstrong	1.50	.35
❑ 2	Passing Leaders Sonny Jurgensen Ken Anderson	1.50	.70
❑ 3	Receiving Leaders Charle Young Lydell Mitchell	1.50	.70
❑ 4	Scoring Leaders Chester Marcol Roy Gerela	.75	.35
❑ 5	Interception Leaders Ray Brown Emmitt Thomas	.75	.35
❑ 6	Punting Leaders Tom Blanchard Ray Guy	1.50	.70
❑ 7	George Blanda (Black jersey; highlights on back)	5.00	2.20
❑ 8	George Blanda (White jersey; career record on back)	5.00	2.20
❑ 9	Ralph Baker	.30	.14
❑ 10	Don Woods	.30	.14
❑ 11	Bob Asher	.30	.14
❑ 12	Mel Blount RC	20.00	9.00
❑ 13	Sam Cunningham	.75	.35
❑ 14	Jackie Smith	1.50	.70
❑ 15	Greg Landry	.75	.35
❑ 16	Buck Buchanan	1.50	.70
❑ 17	Haven Moses	.75	.35
❑ 18	Clarence Ellis	.30	.14
❑ 19	Jim Carter	.30	.14
❑ 20	Charley Taylor UER (Misspelled Charlie on card front)	2.00	.90
❑ 21	Jess Phillips	.30	.14
❑ 22	Larry Seiple	.30	.14
❑ 23	Doug Dieken	.30	.14
❑ 24	Ron Saul	.30	.14
❑ 25	Isaac Curtis UER (Misspelled Issac	1.50	.70

on card front)
❑ 26 Gary Larsen RC .30 .14
❑ 27 Bruce Jarvis .30 .14
❑ 28 Steve Zabel .30 .14
❑ 29 John Mendenhall .30 .14
❑ 30 Rick Volk .30 .14
❑ 31 Checklist 1-132 4.00 1.00
❑ 32 Dan Abramowicz .75 .35
❑ 33 Bubba Smith 1.50 .70
❑ 34 David Ray .30 .14
❑ 35 Dan Dierdorf 4.00 1.80
❑ 36 Randy Rasmussen .30 .14
❑ 37 Bob Howard .30 .14
❑ 38 Gary Huff .75 .35
❑ 39 Rocky Bleier RC 20.00 9.00
❑ 40 Mel Gray .75 .35
❑ 41 Tony McGee .30 .14
❑ 42 Larry Hand .30 .14
❑ 43 Wendell Hayes .30 .14
❑ 44 Doug Wilkerson RC .30 .14
❑ 45 Paul Smith .30 .14
❑ 46 Dave Robinson .75 .35
❑ 47 Bivian Lee .30 .14
❑ 48 Jim Mandich RC .75 .35
❑ 49 Greg Pruitt 1.50 .70
❑ 50 Dan Pastorini UER 1.50 .70
(5/26/39 birthdate
incorrect)
❑ 51 Ron Pritchard .30 .14
❑ 52 Dan Conners .30 .14
❑ 53 Fred Cox .30 .14
❑ 54 Tony Greene .30 .14
❑ 55 Craig Morton 1.50 .70
❑ 56 Jerry Sisemore .30 .14
❑ 57 Glenn Doughty .30 .14
❑ 58 Larry Schreiber .30 .14
❑ 59 Charlie Waters RC 4.00 1.80
❑ 60 Jack Youngblood 1.50 .70
❑ 61 Bill Lenkaitis .30 .14
❑ 62 Greg Brezina .30 .14
❑ 63 Bob Pollard .30 .14
❑ 64 Mack Alston .30 .14
❑ 65 Drew Pearson RC 20.00 9.00
❑ 66 Charlie Stukes .30 .14
❑ 67 Emerson Boozer .75 .35
❑ 68 Dennis Partee .30 .14
❑ 69 Bob Newton .30 .14
❑ 70 Jack Tatum 1.50 .70
❑ 71 Frank Lewis .30 .14
❑ 72 Bob Young .30 .14
❑ 73 Julius Adams .30 .14
❑ 74 Paul Naumoff .30 .14
❑ 75 Otis Taylor 1.50 .70
❑ 76 Dave Hampton .30 .14
❑ 77 Mike Current .30 .14
❑ 78 Brig Owens .30 .14
❑ 79 Bobby Scott .30 .14
❑ 80 Harold Carmichael 3.00 1.35
❑ 81 Bill Stanfill .30 .14
❑ 82 Bob Babich .30 .14
❑ 83 Vic Washington .30 .14
❑ 84 Mick Tingelhoff .75 .35
❑ 85 Bob Trumpy 1.50 .70
❑ 86 Earl Edwards .30 .14
❑ 87 Ron Hornsby .30 .14
❑ 88 Don McCauley .30 .14
❑ 89 Jim Johnson 1.50 .70
❑ 90 Andy Russell .75 .35
❑ 91 Cornell Green 1.50 .70
❑ 92 Charlie Cowan .30 .14
❑ 93 Jon Staggers .30 .14
❑ 94 Billy Newsome .30 .14
❑ 95 Willie Brown 1.50 .70
❑ 96 Carl Mauck .30 .14
❑ 97 Doug Buffone .30 .14
❑ 98 Preston Pearson .75 .35
❑ 99 Jim Bakken .30 .14
❑ 100 Bob Griese 5.00 2.20
❑ 101 Bob Windsor .30 .14
❑ 102 Rockne Freitas .30 .14
❑ 103 Jim Marsalis .30 .14
❑ 104 Bill Thompson .75 .35
❑ 105 Ken Burrow .30 .14
❑ 106 Diron Talbert .30 .14
❑ 107 Joe Federspiel .30 .14
❑ 108 Norm Bulaich .75 .35
❑ 109 Bob DeMarco .30 .14
❑ 110 Tom Wittum .30 .14
❑ 111 Larry Hefner .30 .14
❑ 112 Tody Smith .30 .14
❑ 113 Stu Voigt .30 .14
❑ 114 Horst Muhlmann .30 .14
❑ 115 Ahmad Rashad 6.00 2.70
❑ 116 Joe Dawkins .30 .14
❑ 117 George Kunz .30 .14
❑ 118 D.D. Lewis .75 .35
❑ 119 Levi Johnson .30 .14
❑ 120 Len Dawson 4.00 1.80
❑ 121 Jim Bertelsen .30 .14
❑ 122 Ed Bell .30 .14
❑ 123 Art Thoms .30 .14
❑ 124 Joe Beauchamp .30 .14
❑ 125 Jack Ham 6.00 2.70
❑ 126 Carl Garrett .30 .14
❑ 127 Roger Finnie .30 .14
❑ 128 Howard Twilley .75 .35
❑ 129 Bruce Barnes .30 .14
❑ 130 Nate Wright .30 .14
❑ 131 Jerry Tagge .30 .14
❑ 132 Floyd Little 1.50 .70
❑ 133 John Zook .30 .14
❑ 134 Len Hauss .30 .14
❑ 135 Archie Manning 1.50 .70
❑ 136 Po James .30 .14
❑ 137 Walt Sumner .30 .14
❑ 138 Randy Beisler .30 .14
❑ 139 Willie Alexander .30 .14
❑ 140 Garo Yepremian .75 .35
❑ 141 Chip Myers .30 .14
❑ 142 Jim Braxton .30 .14
❑ 143 Doug Van Horn .30 .14
❑ 144 Stan White .30 .14
❑ 145 Roger Staubach 20.00 9.00
❑ 146 Herman Weaver .30 .14
❑ 147 Marvin Upshaw .30 .14
❑ 148 Bob Klein .30 .14
❑ 149 Earlie Thomas .30 .14
❑ 150 John Brockington .75 .35
❑ 151 Mike Siani .30 .14
❑ 152 Sam Davis RC .30 .14
❑ 153 Mike Wagner .75 .35
❑ 154 Larry Stallings .30 .14
❑ 155 Wally Chambers .30 .14
❑ 156 Randy Vataha .30 .14
❑ 157 Jim Marshall 1.50 .70
❑ 158 Jim Turner .30 .14
❑ 159 Walt Sweeney .30 .14
❑ 160 Ken Anderson 4.00 1.80
❑ 161 Ray Brown .30 .14
❑ 162 John Didion .30 .14
❑ 163 Tom Dempsey .30 .14
❑ 164 Clarence Scott .30 .14
❑ 165 Gene Washington 49er .75 .35
❑ 166 Willie Rodgers RC .30 .14
❑ 167 Doug Swift .30 .14
❑ 168 Rufus Mayes .30 .14
❑ 169 Marv Bateman .30 .14
❑ 170 Lydell Mitchell .75 .35
❑ 171 Ron Smith .30 .14
❑ 172 Bill Munson .75 .35
❑ 173 Bob Grim .30 .14
❑ 174 Ed Budde .30 .14
❑ 175 Bob Lilly UER 4.00 1.80
(Was first draft,
not first player)
❑ 176 Jim Youngblood RC 1.50 .70
❑ 177 Steve Tannen .30 .14
❑ 178 Rich McGeorge .30 .14
❑ 179 Jim Tyrer .30 .14
❑ 180 Forrest Blue .30 .14
❑ 181 Jerry LeVias .75 .35
❑ 182 Joe Gilliam RC 1.50 .70
❑ 183 Jim Otis RC .75 .35
❑ 184 Mel Tom .30 .14
❑ 185 Paul Seymour .30 .14
❑ 186 George Webster .30 .14
❑ 187 Pete Duranko .30 .14
❑ 188 Essex Johnson .30 .14
❑ 189 Bob Lee .75 .35
❑ 190 Gene Upshaw 1.50 .70
❑ 191 Tom Myers .30 .14
❑ 192 Don Zimmerman .30 .14
❑ 193 John Garlington .30 .14
❑ 194 Skip Butler .30 .14
❑ 195 Tom Mitchell .30 .14
❑ 196 Jim Langer 1.50 .70
❑ 197 Ron Carpenter .30 .14
❑ 198 Dave Foley .30 .14
❑ 199 Bert Jones 1.50 .70
❑ 200 Larry Brown .75 .35
❑ 201 All Pro Receivers 2.00 .90
Charley Taylor
Fred Biletnikoff
❑ 202 All Pro Tackles .30 .14
Rayfield Wright
Russ Washington
❑ 203 All Pro Guards 1.50 .70
Tom Mack
Larry Little
❑ 204 All Pro Centers .30 .14
Jeff Van Note
Jack Rudnay
❑ 205 All Pro Guards 1.50 .70
Gale Gillingham
John Hannah
❑ 206 All Pro Tackles 1.50 .70
Dan Dierdorf
Winston Hill
❑ 207 All Pro Tight Ends .75 .35
Charle Young
Riley Odoms
❑ 208 All Pro Quarterbacks 4.00 1.80
Fran Tarkenton
Ken Stabler
❑ 209 All Pro Backs 3.00 1.35
Lawrence McCutcheon
O.J. Simpson
❑ 210 All Pro Backs .75 .35
Terry Metcalf
Otis Armstrong
❑ 211 All Pro Receivers .75 .35
Mel Gray
Isaac Curtis
❑ 212 All Pro Kickers .30 .14
Chester Marcol
Roy Gerela
❑ 213 All Pro Ends 1.50 .70
Jack Youngblood
Elvin Bethea
❑ 214 All Pro Tackles .75 .35
Alan Page
Otis Sistrunk
❑ 215 All Pro Tackles 1.50 .70
Merlin Olsen
Mike Reid
❑ 216 All Pro Ends 1.50 .70
Carl Eller
Lyle Alzado
❑ 217 All Pro Linebackers 1.50 .70
Ted Hendricks
Phil Villapiano
❑ 218 All Pro Linebackers 1.50 .70
Lee Roy Jordan
Willie Lanier
❑ 219 All Pro Linebackers .75 .35
Isiah Robertson
Andy Russell
❑ 220 All Pro Cornerbacks .30 .14
Nate Wright
Emmitt Thomas
❑ 221 All Pro Cornerbacks .30 .14
Willie Buchanon
Lemar Parrish

❑ 222 All Pro Safeties	.75	.35
Ken Houston		
Dick Anderson		
❑ 223 All Pro Safeties	1.50	.70
Cliff Harris		
Jack Tatum		
❑ 224 All Pro Punters	.75	.35
Tom Wittum		
Ray Guy		
❑ 225 All Pro Returners	.75	.35
Terry Metcalf		
Greg Pruitt		
❑ 226 Ted Kwalick	.30	.14
❑ 227 Spider Lockhart	.75	.35
❑ 228 Mike Livingston	.30	.14
❑ 229 Larry Cole	.30	.14
❑ 230 Gary Garrison	.30	.14
❑ 231 Larry Brooks	.30	.14
❑ 232 Bobby Howfield	.30	.14
❑ 233 Fred Carr	.30	.14
❑ 234 Norm Evans	.30	.14
❑ 235 Dwight White	.75	.35
❑ 236 Conrad Dobler	.75	.35
❑ 237 Garry Lyle	.30	.14
❑ 238 Darryl Stingley	1.50	.70
❑ 239 Tom Graham	.30	.14
❑ 240 Chuck Foreman	1.50	.70
❑ 241 Ken Riley	.75	.35
❑ 242 Don Morrison	.30	.14
❑ 243 Lynn Dickey	.75	.35
❑ 244 Don Cockroft	.30	.14
❑ 245 Claude Humphrey	.75	.35
❑ 246 John Skorupan	.30	.14
❑ 247 Raymond Chester	.75	.35
❑ 248 Cas Banaszek	.30	.14
❑ 249 Art Malone	.30	.14
❑ 250 Ed Flanagan	.30	.14
❑ 251 Checklist 133-264	4.00	1.00
❑ 252 Nemiah Wilson	.30	.14
❑ 253 Ron Jessie	.30	.14
❑ 254 Jim Lynch	.30	.14
❑ 255 Bob Tucker	.75	.35
❑ 256 Terry Owens	.30	.14
❑ 257 John Fitzgerald	.30	.14
❑ 258 Jack Snow	.75	.35
❑ 259 Garry Puetz	.30	.14
❑ 260 Mike Phipps	.75	.35
❑ 261 Al Matthews	.30	.14
❑ 262 Bob Kuechenberg	.30	.14
❑ 263 Ron Yankowski	.30	.14
❑ 264 Ron Shanklin	.30	.14
❑ 265 Bobby Douglass	.75	.35
❑ 266 Josh Ashton	.30	.14
❑ 267 Bill Van Heusen	.30	.14
❑ 268 Jeff Siemon	.30	.14
❑ 269 Bob Newland	.30	.14
❑ 270 Gale Gillingham	.30	.14
❑ 271 Zeke Moore	.30	.14
❑ 272 Mike Tilleman	.30	.14
❑ 273 John Leypoldt	.30	.14
❑ 274 Ken Mendenhall	.30	.14
❑ 275 Norm Snead	.75	.35
❑ 276 Bill Bradley	.75	.35
❑ 277 Jerry Smith	.30	.14
❑ 278 Clarence Davis	.30	.14
❑ 279 Jim Yarbrough	.30	.14
❑ 280 Lemar Parrish	.30	.14
❑ 281 Bobby Bell	1.50	.70
❑ 282 Lynn Swann RC UER	60.00	27.00
(Wide Reciever on front)		
❑ 283 John Hicks	.30	.14
❑ 284 Coy Bacon	.75	.35
❑ 285 Lee Roy Jordan	1.50	.70
❑ 286 Willie Buchanon	.30	.14
❑ 287 Al Woodall	.30	.14
❑ 288 Reggie Rucker	.75	.35
❑ 289 John Schmitt	.30	.14
❑ 290 Carl Eller	1.50	.70
❑ 291 Jake Scott	.75	.35
❑ 292 Donny Anderson	.75	.35
❑ 293 Charley Wade	.30	.14
❑ 294 John Tanner	.30	.14
❑ 295 Charlie Johnson	.75	.35
(Misspelled Charley		
on both sides)		
❑ 296 Tom Blanchard	.30	.14
❑ 297 Curley Culp	.75	.35
❑ 298 Jeff Van Note RC	.75	.35
❑ 299 Bob James	.30	.14
❑ 300 Franco Harris	8.00	3.60
❑ 301 Tim Berra	.75	.35
❑ 302 Bruce Gossett	.30	.14
❑ 303 Verlon Biggs	.30	.14
❑ 304 Bob Kowalkowski	.30	.14
❑ 305 Marv Hubbard	.30	.14
❑ 306 Ken Avery	.30	.14
❑ 307 Mike Adamle	.30	.14
❑ 308 Don Herrmann	.30	.14
❑ 309 Chris Fletcher	.30	.14
❑ 310 Roman Gabriel	1.50	.70
❑ 311 Billy Joe DuPree	1.50	.70
❑ 312 Fred Dryer	1.50	.70
❑ 313 John Riggins	5.00	2.20
❑ 314 Bob McKay	.30	.14
❑ 315 Ted Hendricks	1.50	.70
❑ 316 Bobby Bryant	.30	.14
❑ 317 Don Nottingham	.30	.14
❑ 318 John Hannah	4.00	1.80
❑ 319 Rich Coady	.30	.14
❑ 320 Phil Villapiano	.75	.35
❑ 321 Jim Plunkett	1.50	.70
❑ 322 Lyle Alzado	1.50	.70
❑ 323 Ernie Jackson	.30	.14
❑ 324 Billy Parks	.30	.14
❑ 325 Willie Lanier	1.50	.70
❑ 326 John James	.30	.14
❑ 327 Joe Ferguson	.75	.35
❑ 328 Ernie Holmes RC	1.50	.70
❑ 329 Bruce Laird	.30	.14
❑ 330 Chester Marcol	.30	.14
❑ 331 Dave Wilcox	1.50	.70
❑ 332 Pat Fischer	.75	.35
❑ 333 Steve Owens	.75	.35
❑ 334 Royce Berry	.30	.14
❑ 335 Russ Washington	.30	.14
❑ 336 Walker Gillette	.30	.14
❑ 337 Mark Nordquist	.30	.14
❑ 338 James Harris RC	1.50	.70
❑ 339 Warren Koegel	.30	.14
❑ 340 Emmitt Thomas	.75	.35
❑ 341 Walt Garrison	.75	.35
❑ 342 Thom Darden	.30	.14
❑ 343 Mike Eischeid	.30	.14
❑ 344 Ernie McMillan	.30	.14
❑ 345 Nick Buoniconti	1.50	.70
❑ 346 George Farmer	.30	.14
❑ 347 Sam Adams	.30	.14
❑ 348 Larry Cipa	.30	.14
❑ 349 Bob Moore	.30	.14
❑ 350 Otis Armstrong RC	1.50	.70
❑ 351 George Blanda RB	3.00	1.35
All Time Scoring		
Leader		
❑ 352 Fred Cox RB	.75	.35
151 Straight PAT's		
❑ 353 Tom Dempsey RB	.75	.35
63 Yard FG		
❑ 354 Ken Houston RB	1.50	.70
9th Int. for TD		
(Shown as Oiler,		
should be Redskin)		
❑ 355 O.J. Simpson RB	5.00	2.20
2003 Yard Season		
❑ 356 Ron Smith RB	.75	.35
All Time Return		
Yardage Mark		
❑ 357 Bob Atkins	.30	.14
❑ 358 Pat Sullivan	.75	.35
❑ 359 Joe DeLamielleure	2.50	1.10
❑ 360 L.McCutcheon RC	1.50	.70
❑ 361 David Lee	.30	.14
❑ 362 Mike McCoy	.30	.14
❑ 363 Skip Vanderbundt	.30	.14
❑ 364 Mark Moseley	.75	.35
❑ 365 Lem Barney	1.50	.70
❑ 366 Doug Dressler	.30	.14
❑ 367 Dan Fouts RC	40.00	18.00
❑ 368 Bob Hyland	.30	.14
❑ 369 John Outlaw	.30	.14
❑ 370 Roy Gerela	.30	.14
❑ 371 Isiah Robertson	.75	.35
❑ 372 Jerome Barkum	.30	.14
❑ 373 Ed Podolak	.30	.14
❑ 374 Milt Morin	.30	.14
❑ 375 John Niland	.30	.14
❑ 376 Checklist 265-396 UER	4.00	1.00
(295 Charlie Johnson		
misspelled as Charley)		
❑ 377 Ken Iman	.30	.14
❑ 378 Manny Fernandez	.75	.35
❑ 379 Dave Gallagher	.30	.14
❑ 380 Ken Stabler	15.00	6.75
❑ 381 Mack Herron	.30	.14
❑ 382 Bill McClard	.30	.14
❑ 383 Ray May	.30	.14
❑ 384 Don Hansen	.30	.14
❑ 385 Elvin Bethea	1.50	.70
❑ 386 Joe Scibelli	.30	.14
❑ 387 Neal Craig	.30	.14
❑ 388 Marty Domres	.30	.14
❑ 389 Ken Ellis	.30	.14
❑ 390 Charle Young	.75	.35
❑ 391 Tommy Hart	.30	.14
❑ 392 Moses Denson	.30	.14
❑ 393 Larry Walton	.30	.14
❑ 394 Dave Green	.30	.14
❑ 395 Ron Johnson	.75	.35
❑ 396 Ed Bradley	.30	.14
❑ 397 J.T. Thomas	.30	.14
❑ 398 Jim Bailey	.30	.14
❑ 399 Barry Pearson	.30	.14
❑ 400 Fran Tarkenton	8.00	3.60
❑ 401 Jack Rudnay	.30	.14
❑ 402 Rayfield Wright	.75	.35
❑ 403 Roger Wehrli	.75	.35
❑ 404 Vern Den Herder	.30	.14
❑ 405 Fred Biletnikoff	3.00	1.35
❑ 406 Ken Grandberry	.30	.14
❑ 407 Bob Adams	.30	.14
❑ 408 Jim Merlo	.30	.14
❑ 409 John Pitts	.30	.14
❑ 410 Dave Osborn	.75	.35
❑ 411 Dennis Havig	.30	.14
❑ 412 Bob Johnson	.30	.14
❑ 413 Ken Burrough UER	.75	.35
(Misspelled Burrow		
on card front)		
❑ 414 Jim Cheyunski	.30	.14
❑ 415 MacArthur Lane	.30	.14
❑ 416 Joe Theismann RC	25.00	11.00
❑ 417 Mike Boryla RC	.30	.14
❑ 418 Bruce Taylor	.30	.14
❑ 419 Chris Hanburger	.75	.35
❑ 420 Tom Mack	1.50	.70
❑ 421 Errol Mann	.30	.14
❑ 422 Jack Gregory	.30	.14
❑ 423 Harrison Davis	.30	.14
❑ 424 Burgess Owens	.30	.14
❑ 425 Joe Greene	5.00	2.20
❑ 426 Morris Stroud	.30	.14
❑ 427 John DeMarie	.30	.14
❑ 428 Mel Renfro	1.50	.70
❑ 429 Cid Edwards	.30	.14
❑ 430 Mike Reid	1.50	.70
❑ 431 Jack Mildren RC	.30	.14
❑ 432 Jerry Simmons	.30	.14
❑ 433 Ron Yary	1.50	.70
❑ 434 Howard Stevens	.30	.14
❑ 435 Ray Guy	2.00	.90
❑ 436 Tommy Nobis	1.50	.70
❑ 437 Solomon Freelon	.30	.14
❑ 438 J.D. Hill	.75	.35
❑ 439 Toni Linhart	.30	.14

	NM	Ex
❑ 440 Dick Anderson	.75	.35
❑ 441 Guy Morriss	.30	.14
❑ 442 Bob Hoskins	.30	.14
❑ 443 John Hadl	1.50	.70
❑ 444 Roy Jefferson	.30	.14
❑ 445 Charlie Sanders	.75	.35
❑ 446 Pat Curran	.30	.14
❑ 447 David Knight	.30	.14
❑ 448 Bob Brown DT	.30	.14
❑ 449 Pete Gogolak	.30	.14
❑ 450 Terry Metcalf	1.50	.70
❑ 451 Bill Bergey	1.50	.70
❑ 452 Dan Abramowicz HL 105 Straight Games	.75	.35
❑ 453 Otis Armstrong HL 183 Yard Game	.75	.35
❑ 454 Cliff Branch HL 13 TD Passes	1.50	.70
❑ 455 John James HL Record 96 Punts	.30	.14
❑ 456 Lydell Mitchell HL 13 Passes in Game	.75	.35
❑ 457 Lemar Parrish HL 3 TD Punt Returns	.75	.35
❑ 458 Ken Stabler HL 26 TD Passes in One Season	5.00	2.20
❑ 459 Lynn Swann HL 577 Yards in Punt Returns	8.00	3.60
❑ 460 Emmitt Thomas HL 73 Yd. Interception	.30	.14
❑ 461 Terry Bradshaw	20.00	9.00
❑ 462 Jerrel Wilson	.30	.14
❑ 463 Walter Johnson	.30	.14
❑ 464 Golden Richards	.75	.35
❑ 465 Tommy Casanova	.75	.35
❑ 466 Randy Jackson	.30	.14
❑ 467 Ron Bolton	.30	.14
❑ 468 Joe Owens	.30	.14
❑ 469 Wally Hilgenberg	.30	.14
❑ 470 Riley Odoms	.75	.35
❑ 471 Otis Sistrunk	.75	.35
❑ 472 Eddie Ray	.30	.14
❑ 473 Reggie McKenzie	.75	.35
❑ 474 Elbert Drungo	.30	.14
❑ 475 Mercury Morris	1.50	.70
❑ 476 Dan Dickel	.30	.14
❑ 477 Merritt Kersey	.30	.14
❑ 478 Mike Holmes	.30	.14
❑ 479 Clarence Williams	.30	.14
❑ 480 Billy Kilmer	1.50	.70
❑ 481 Altie Taylor	.30	.14
❑ 482 Dave Elmendorf	.30	.14
❑ 483 Bob Rowe	.30	.14
❑ 484 Pete Athas	.30	.14
❑ 485 Winston Hill	.30	.14
❑ 486 Bo Matthews	.30	.14
❑ 487 Earl Thomas	.30	.14
❑ 488 Jan Stenerud	1.50	.70
❑ 489 Steve Holden	.30	.14
❑ 490 Cliff Harris RC	4.00	1.80
❑ 491 Boobie Clark RC	.75	.35
❑ 492 Joe Taylor	.30	.14
❑ 493 Tom Neville	.30	.14
❑ 494 Wayne Colman	.30	.14
❑ 495 Jim Mitchell	.30	.14
❑ 496 Paul Krause	1.50	.70
❑ 497 Jim Otto	1.50	.70
❑ 498 John Rowser	.30	.14
❑ 499 Larry Little	1.50	.70
❑ 500 O.J. Simpson	10.00	4.50
❑ 501 John Dutton RC	1.50	.70
❑ 502 Pat Hughes	.30	.14
❑ 503 Malcolm Snider	.30	.14
❑ 504 Fred Willis	.30	.14
❑ 505 Harold Jackson	1.50	.70
❑ 506 Mike Bragg	.30	.14
❑ 507 Jerry Sherk	.75	.35
❑ 508 Mirro Roder	.30	.14
❑ 509 Tom Sullivan	.30	.14
❑ 510 Jim Hart	1.50	.70
❑ 511 Cedrick Hardman	.30	.14
❑ 512 Blaine Nye	.30	.14
❑ 513 Elmo Wright	.30	.14
❑ 514 Herb Orvis	.30	.14
❑ 515 Richard Caster	.75	.35
❑ 516 Doug Kotar RC	.30	.14
❑ 517 Checklist 397-528	4.00	1.00
❑ 518 Jesse Freitas	.30	.14
❑ 519 Ken Houston	1.50	.70
❑ 520 Alan Page	1.50	.70
❑ 521 Tim Foley	.75	.35
❑ 522 Bill Olds	.30	.14
❑ 523 Bobby Maples	.30	.14
❑ 524 Cliff Branch RC	15.00	6.75
❑ 525 Merlin Olsen	1.50	.70
❑ 526 AFC Champs Pittsburgh 24, Oakland 13 (Bradshaw and Franco Harris)	4.00	1.80
❑ 527 NFC Champs Minnesota 14; Los Angeles 10 (Chuck Foreman tackled)	1.50	.70
❑ 528 Super Bowl IX Steelers 16; Vikings 6 (Bradshaw watching pass)	5.00	1.25

1976 Topps

	NM	Ex
COMPLETE SET (528)	350.00	160.00
❑ 1 George Blanda RB First to Score 2000 Points	5.00	1.25
❑ 2 Neal Colzie RB Punt Returns	.75	.35
❑ 3 Chuck Foreman RB Catches 73 Passes	.75	.35
❑ 4 Jim Marshall RB 26th Fumble Recovery	.75	.35
❑ 5 Terry Metcalf RB Most all-purpose yards; season	.75	.35
❑ 6 O.J. Simpson RB 23 Touchdowns	3.00	1.35
❑ 7 Fran Tarkenton RB Most Attempts;Season	3.00	1.35
❑ 8 Charley Taylor RB Career Receptions	1.50	.70
❑ 9 Ernie Holmes	.75	.35
❑ 10 Ken Anderson AP	1.50	.70
❑ 11 Bobby Bryant	.30	.14
❑ 12 Jerry Smith	.75	.35
❑ 13 David Lee	.30	.14
❑ 14 Robert Newhouse RC	1.50	.70
❑ 15 Vern Den Herder	.30	.14
❑ 16 John Hannah	1.50	.70
❑ 17 J.D. Hill	.75	.35
❑ 18 James Harris	.75	.35
❑ 19 Willie Buchanon	.30	.14
❑ 20 Charle Young	.75	.35
❑ 21 Jim Yarbrough	.30	.14
❑ 22 Ronnie Coleman	.30	.14
❑ 23 Don Cockroft	.30	.14
❑ 24 Willie Lanier	1.50	.70
❑ 25 Fred Biletnikoff	3.00	1.35
❑ 26 Ron Yankowski	.30	.14
❑ 27 Spider Lockhart	.30	.14
❑ 28 Bob Johnson	.30	.14
❑ 29 J.T. Thomas	.30	.14
❑ 30 Ron Yary	1.50	.70
❑ 31 Brad Dusek RC	.30	.14
❑ 32 Raymond Chester	.75	.35
❑ 33 Larry Little	1.50	.70
❑ 34 Pat Leahy RC	1.50	.70
❑ 35 Steve Bartkowski RC	4.00	1.80
❑ 36 Tom Myers	.30	.14
❑ 37 Bill Van Heusen	.30	.14
❑ 38 Russ Washington	.30	.14
❑ 39 Tom Sullivan	.30	.14
❑ 40 Curley Culp	.75	.35
❑ 41 Johnnie Gray	.30	.14
❑ 42 Bob Klein	.30	.14
❑ 43 Lem Barney	1.50	.70
❑ 44 Harvey Martin RC	6.00	2.70
❑ 45 Reggie Rucker	.75	.35
❑ 46 Neil Clabo	.30	.14
❑ 47 Ray Hamilton	.30	.14
❑ 48 Joe Ferguson	.75	.35
❑ 49 Ed Podolak	.30	.14
❑ 50 Ray Guy AP	1.50	.70
❑ 51 Glen Edwards	.30	.14
❑ 52 Jim LeClair	.30	.14
❑ 53 Mike Barnes	.30	.14
❑ 54 Nat Moore RC	1.50	.70
❑ 55 Billy Kilmer	1.50	.70
❑ 56 Larry Stallings	.30	.14
❑ 57 Jack Gregory	.30	.14
❑ 58 Steve Mike-Mayer	.30	.14
❑ 59 Virgil Livers	.30	.14
❑ 60 Jerry Sherk	.75	.35
❑ 61 Guy Morriss	.30	.14
❑ 62 Barty Smith	.30	.14
❑ 63 Jerome Barkum	.30	.14
❑ 64 Ira Gordon	.30	.14
❑ 65 Paul Krause	1.50	.70
❑ 66 John McMakin	.30	.14
❑ 67 Checklist 1-132	3.00	.75
❑ 68 Charlie Johnson UER (Misspelled Charley on both sides)	.75	.35
❑ 69 Tommy Nobis	1.50	.70
❑ 70 Lydell Mitchell	.75	.35
❑ 71 Vern Holland	.30	.14
❑ 72 Tim Foley	.75	.35
❑ 73 Golden Richards	.75	.35
❑ 74 Bryant Salter	.30	.14
❑ 75 Terry Bradshaw	20.00	9.00
❑ 76 Ted Hendricks	1.50	.70
❑ 77 Rich Saul RC	.30	.14
❑ 78 John Smith RC	.30	.14
❑ 79 Altie Taylor	.30	.14
❑ 80 Cedrick Hardman	.30	.14
❑ 81 Ken Payne	.30	.14
❑ 82 Zeke Moore	.30	.14
❑ 83 Alvin Maxson	.30	.14
❑ 84 Wally Hilgenberg	.30	.14
❑ 85 John Niland	.30	.14
❑ 86 Mike Sensibaugh	.30	.14
❑ 87 Ron Johnson	.75	.35
❑ 88 Winston Hill	.30	.14
❑ 89 Charlie Joiner	4.00	1.80
❑ 90 Roger Wehrli	.75	.35
❑ 91 Mike Bragg	.30	.14
❑ 92 Dan Dickel	.30	.14
❑ 93 Earl Morrall	.75	.35
❑ 94 Pat Toomay	.30	.14
❑ 95 Gary Garrison	.30	.14
❑ 96 Ken Geddes	.30	.14
❑ 97 Mike Current	.30	.14
❑ 98 Bob Avellini RC	.75	.35
❑ 99 Dave Pureifory	.30	.14

❑ 100	Franco Harris AP	8.00	3.60
❑ 101	Randy Logan	.30	.14
❑ 102	John Fitzgerald	.30	.14
❑ 103	Gregg Bingham RC	.75	.35
❑ 104	Jim Plunkett	1.50	.70
❑ 105	Carl Eller	1.50	.70
❑ 106	Larry Walton	.30	.14
❑ 107	Clarence Scott	.30	.14
❑ 108	Skip Vanderbundt	.30	.14
❑ 109	Boobie Clark	.75	.35
❑ 110	Tom Mack	1.50	.70
❑ 111	Bruce Laird	.30	.14
❑ 112	Dave Dalby RC	.30	.14
❑ 113	John Leypoldt	.30	.14
❑ 114	Barry Pearson	.30	.14
❑ 115	Larry Brown	.75	.35
❑ 116	Jackie Smith	1.50	.70
❑ 117	Pat Hughes	.30	.14
❑ 118	Al Woodall	.30	.14
❑ 119	John Zook	.30	.14
❑ 120	Jake Scott	.75	.35
❑ 121	Rich Glover	.30	.14
❑ 122	Ernie Jackson	.30	.14
❑ 123	Otis Armstrong	1.50	.70
❑ 124	Bob Grim	.30	.14
❑ 125	Jeff Siemon	.75	.35
❑ 126	Harold Hart	.30	.14
❑ 127	John DeMarie	.30	.14
❑ 128	Dan Fouts	12.00	5.50
❑ 129	Jim Kearney	.30	.14
❑ 130	John Dutton AP	.75	.35
❑ 131	Calvin Hill	1.50	.70
❑ 132	Toni Fritsch	.30	.14
❑ 133	Ron Jessie	.30	.14
❑ 134	Don Nottingham	.30	.14
❑ 135	Lemar Parrish	.30	.14
❑ 136	Russ Francis RC	1.50	.70
❑ 137	Joe Reed	.30	.14
❑ 138	C.L. Whittington	.30	.14
❑ 139	Otis Sistrunk	.75	.35
❑ 140	Lynn Swann AP	20.00	9.00
❑ 141	Jim Carter	.30	.14
❑ 142	Mike Montler	.30	.14
❑ 143	Walter Johnson	.30	.14
❑ 144	Doug Kotar	.30	.14
❑ 145	Roman Gabriel	1.50	.70
❑ 146	Billy Newsome	.30	.14
❑ 147	Ed Bradley	.30	.14
❑ 148	Walter Payton RC	250.00	110.00
❑ 149	Johnny Fuller	.30	.14
❑ 150	Alan Page AP	1.50	.70
❑ 151	Frank Grant	.30	.14
❑ 152	Dave Green	.30	.14
❑ 153	Nelson Munsey	.30	.14
❑ 154	Jim Mandich	.30	.14
❑ 155	Lawrence McCutcheon	1.50	.70
❑ 156	Steve Ramsey	.30	.14
❑ 157	Ed Flanagan	.30	.14
❑ 158	Randy White RC	20.00	9.00
❑ 159	Gerry Mullins	.30	.14
❑ 160	Jan Stenerud AP	1.50	.70
❑ 161	Steve Odom	.30	.14
❑ 162	Roger Finnie	.30	.14
❑ 163	Norm Snead	.75	.35
❑ 164	Jeff Van Note	.75	.35
❑ 165	Bill Bergey	1.50	.70
❑ 166	Allen Carter	.30	.14
❑ 167	Steve Holden	.30	.14
❑ 168	Sherman White	.30	.14
❑ 169	Bob Berry	.30	.14
❑ 170	Ken Houston AP	1.50	.70
❑ 171	Bill Olds	.30	.14
❑ 172	Larry Seiple	.30	.14
❑ 173	Cliff Branch	4.00	1.80
❑ 174	Reggie McKenzie	.75	.35
❑ 175	Dan Pastorini	1.50	.70
❑ 176	Paul Naumoff	.30	.14
❑ 177	Checklist 133-264	3.00	.75
❑ 178	Durwood Keeton	.30	.14
❑ 179	Earl Thomas	.30	.14
❑ 180	L.C. Greenwood AP	1.50	.70
❑ 181	John Outlaw	.30	.14
❑ 182	Frank Nunley	.30	.14
❑ 183	Dave Jennings RC	.75	.35
❑ 184	MacArthur Lane	.30	.14
❑ 185	Chester Marcol	.30	.14
❑ 186	J.J. Jones	.30	.14
❑ 187	Tom DeLeone	.30	.14
❑ 188	Steve Zabel	.30	.14
❑ 189	Ken Johnson	.30	.14
❑ 190	Rayfield Wright	.75	.35
❑ 191	Brent McClanahan	.30	.14
❑ 192	Pat Fischer	.75	.35
❑ 193	Roger Carr RC	.75	.35
❑ 194	Manny Fernandez	.75	.35
❑ 195	Roy Gerela	.30	.14
❑ 196	Dave Elmendorf	.30	.14
❑ 197	Bob Kowalkowski	.30	.14
❑ 198	Phil Villapiano	.75	.35
❑ 199	Will Wynn	.30	.14
❑ 200	Terry Metcalf	1.50	.70
❑ 201	Passing Leaders Ken Anderson Fran Tarkenton	2.00	.90
❑ 202	Receiving Leaders Reggie Rucker Lydell Mitchell Chuck Foreman	.75	.35
❑ 203	Rushing Leaders O.J. Simpson Jim Otis	2.50	1.10
❑ 204	Scoring Leaders O.J. Simpson Chuck Foreman	2.50	1.10
❑ 205	Interception Leaders Mel Blount Paul Krause	1.50	.70
❑ 206	Punting Leaders Ray Guy Herman Weaver	.75	.35
❑ 207	Ken Ellis	.30	.14
❑ 208	Ron Saul	.30	.14
❑ 209	Toni Linhart	.30	.14
❑ 210	Jim Langer AP	1.50	.70
❑ 211	Jeff Wright	.30	.14
❑ 212	Moses Denson	.30	.14
❑ 213	Earl Edwards	.30	.14
❑ 214	Walker Gillette	.30	.14
❑ 215	Bob Trumpy	.75	.35
❑ 216	Emmitt Thomas	.75	.35
❑ 217	Lyle Alzado	1.50	.70
❑ 218	Carl Garrett	.75	.35
❑ 219	Van Green	.30	.14
❑ 220	Jack Lambert AP RC	35.00	16.00
❑ 221	Spike Jones	.30	.14
❑ 222	John Hadl	1.50	.70
❑ 223	Billy Johnson RC	1.50	.70
❑ 224	Tony McGee	.30	.14
❑ 225	Preston Pearson	.75	.35
❑ 226	Isiah Robertson	.75	.35
❑ 227	Errol Mann	.30	.14
❑ 228	Paul Seal	.30	.14
❑ 229	Roland Harper RC	.30	.14
❑ 230	Ed White AP RC	.75	.35
❑ 231	Joe Theismann	6.00	2.70
❑ 232	Jim Cheyunski	.30	.14
❑ 233	Bill Stanfill	.75	.35
❑ 234	Marv Hubbard	.30	.14
❑ 235	Tommy Casanova	.75	.35
❑ 236	Bob Hyland	.30	.14
❑ 237	Jesse Freitas	.30	.14
❑ 238	Norm Thompson	.30	.14
❑ 239	Charlie Smith	.30	.14
❑ 240	John James	.30	.14
❑ 241	Alden Roche	.30	.14
❑ 242	Gordon Jolley	.30	.14
❑ 243	Larry Ely	.30	.14
❑ 244	Richard Caster	.30	.14
❑ 245	Joe Greene	5.00	2.20
❑ 246	Larry Schreiber	.30	.14
❑ 247	Terry Schmidt	.30	.14
❑ 248	Jerrel Wilson	.30	.14
❑ 249	Marty Domres	.30	.14
❑ 250	Isaac Curtis	.75	.35
❑ 251	Harold McLinton	.30	.14
❑ 252	Fred Dryer	1.50	.70
❑ 253	Bill Lenkaitis	.30	.14
❑ 254	Don Hardeman	.30	.14
❑ 255	Bob Griese	4.00	1.80
❑ 256	Oscar Roan RC	.30	.14
❑ 257	Randy Gradishar RC	2.50	1.10
❑ 258	Bob Thomas RC	.30	.14
❑ 259	Joe Owens	.30	.14
❑ 260	Cliff Harris AP	1.50	.70
❑ 261	Frank Lewis	.30	.14
❑ 262	Mike McCoy	.30	.14
❑ 263	Rickey Young RC	.30	.14
❑ 264	Brian Kelley RC	.30	.14
❑ 265	Charlie Sanders	.75	.35
❑ 266	Jim Hart	1.50	.70
❑ 267	Greg Gantt	.30	.14
❑ 268	John Ward	.30	.14
❑ 269	Al Beauchamp	.30	.14
❑ 270	Jack Tatum	1.50	.70
❑ 271	Jim Lash	.30	.14
❑ 272	Diron Talbert	.30	.14
❑ 273	Checklist 265-396	3.00	.75
❑ 274	Steve Spurrier	8.00	3.60
❑ 275	Greg Pruitt	1.50	.70
❑ 276	Jim Mitchell	.30	.14
❑ 277	Jack Rudnay	.30	.14
❑ 278	Freddie Solomon RC	.75	.35
❑ 279	Frank LeMaster	.30	.14
❑ 280	Wally Chambers	.30	.14
❑ 281	Mike Collier	.30	.14
❑ 282	Clarence Williams	.30	.14
❑ 283	Mitch Hoopes	.30	.14
❑ 284	Ron Bolton	.30	.14
❑ 285	Harold Jackson	1.50	.70
❑ 286	Greg Landry	.75	.35
❑ 287	Tony Greene	.30	.14
❑ 288	Howard Stevens	.30	.14
❑ 289	Roy Jefferson	.30	.14
❑ 290	Jim Bakken	.30	.14
❑ 291	Doug Sutherland	.30	.14
❑ 292	Marvin Cobb RC	.30	.14
❑ 293	Mack Alston	.30	.14
❑ 294	Rod McNeill	.30	.14
❑ 295	Gene Upshaw	1.50	.70
❑ 296	Dave Gallagher	.30	.14
❑ 297	Larry Ball	.30	.14
❑ 298	Ron Howard	.30	.14
❑ 299	Don Strock RC	1.50	.70
❑ 300	O.J. Simpson AP	8.00	3.60
❑ 301	Ray Mansfield	.30	.14
❑ 302	Larry Marshall	.30	.14
❑ 303	Dick Himes	.30	.14
❑ 304	Ray Wersching RC	.30	.14
❑ 305	John Riggins	4.00	1.80
❑ 306	Bob Parsons	.30	.14
❑ 307	Ray Brown	.30	.14
❑ 308	Len Dawson	3.00	1.35
❑ 309	Andy Maurer	.30	.14
❑ 310	Jack Youngblood AP	1.50	.70
❑ 311	Essex Johnson	.30	.14
❑ 312	Stan White	.30	.14
❑ 313	Drew Pearson	5.00	2.20
❑ 314	Rockne Freitas	.30	.14
❑ 315	Mercury Morris	1.50	.70
❑ 316	Willie Alexander	.30	.14
❑ 317	Paul Warfield	3.00	1.35
❑ 318	Bob Chandler	.75	.35
❑ 319	Bobby Walden	.30	.14
❑ 320	Riley Odoms	.75	.35
❑ 321	Mike Boryla	.30	.14
❑ 322	Bruce Van Dyke	.30	.14
❑ 323	Pete Banaszak	.30	.14
❑ 324	Darryl Stingley	1.50	.70
❑ 325	John Mendenhall	.30	.14
❑ 326	Dan Dierdorf	2.00	.90
❑ 327	Bruce Taylor	.30	.14
❑ 328	Don McCauley	.30	.14
❑ 329	John Reaves UER	.30	.14

(24 attempts in '72; should be 224)
❑ 330 Chris Hanburger .75 .35
❑ 331 NFC Champions 3.00 1.35
Cowboys 37;
Rams 7
(Roger Staubach)
❑ 332 AFC Champions 2.00 .90
Steelers 16;
Raiders 10
(Franco Harris)
❑ 333 Super Bowl X 2.50 1.10
Steelers 21;
Cowboys 17
(Terry Bradshaw)
❑ 334 Godwin Turk .30 .14
❑ 335 Dick Anderson .75 .35
❑ 336 Woody Green .30 .14
❑ 337 Pat Curran .30 .14
❑ 338 Council Rudolph .30 .14
❑ 339 Joe Lavender .30 .14
❑ 340 John Gilliam .75 .35
❑ 341 Steve Furness RC .75 .35
❑ 342 D.D. Lewis .75 .35
❑ 343 Duane Carrell .30 .14
❑ 344 Jon Morris .30 .14
❑ 345 John Brockington .75 .35
❑ 346 Mike Phipps .75 .35
❑ 347 Lyle Blackwood RC .30 .14
❑ 348 Julius Adams .30 .14
❑ 349 Terry Hermeling .30 .14
❑ 350 R.Lawrence AP RC .30 .14
❑ 351 Glenn Doughty .30 .14
❑ 352 Doug Swift .30 .14
❑ 353 Mike Strachan .30 .14
❑ 354 Craig Morton 1.50 .70
❑ 355 George Blanda 5.00 2.20
❑ 356 Garry Puetz .30 .14
❑ 357 Carl Mauck .30 .14
❑ 358 Walt Patulski .30 .14
❑ 359 Stu Voigt .30 .14
❑ 360 Fred Carr .30 .14
❑ 361 Po James .30 .14
❑ 362 Otis Taylor 1.50 .70
❑ 363 Jeff West .30 .14
❑ 364 Gary Huff .75 .35
❑ 365 Dwight White .75 .35
❑ 366 Dan Ryczek .30 .14
❑ 367 Jon Keyworth RC .30 .14
❑ 368 Mel Renfro 1.50 .70
❑ 369 Bruce Coslet RC 1.50 .70
❑ 370 Len Hauss .30 .14
❑ 371 Rick Volk .30 .14
❑ 372 Howard Twilley .75 .35
❑ 373 Cullen Bryant RC .75 .35
❑ 374 Bob Babich .30 .14
❑ 375 Herman Weaver .30 .14
❑ 376 Steve Grogan RC 3.00 1.35
❑ 377 Bubba Smith 1.50 .70
❑ 378 Burgess Owens .30 .14
❑ 379 Al Matthews .30 .14
❑ 380 Art Shell 1.50 .70
❑ 381 Larry Brown .30 .14
❑ 382 Horst Muhlmann .30 .14
❑ 383 Ahmad Rashad 2.50 1.10
❑ 384 Bobby Maples .30 .14
❑ 385 Jim Marshall 1.50 .70
❑ 386 Joe Dawkins .30 .14
❑ 387 Dennis Partee .30 .14
❑ 388 Eddie McMillan RC .30 .14
❑ 389 Randy Johnson .30 .14
❑ 390 Bob Kuechenberg .30 .14
❑ 391 Rufus Mayes .30 .14
❑ 392 Lloyd Mumphord .30 .14
❑ 393 Ike Harris .30 .14
❑ 394 Dave Hampton .30 .14
❑ 395 Roger Staubach 20.00 9.00
❑ 396 Doug Buffone .30 .14
❑ 397 Howard Fest .30 .14
❑ 398 Wayne Mulligan .30 .14
❑ 399 Bill Bradley .75 .35
❑ 400 Chuck Foreman AP 1.50 .70
❑ 401 Jack Snow .75 .35
❑ 402 Bob Howard .30 .14
❑ 403 John Matuszak 1.50 .70
❑ 404 Bill Munson .75 .35
❑ 405 Andy Russell .75 .35
❑ 406 Skip Butler .30 .14
❑ 407 Hugh McKinnis .30 .14
❑ 408 Bob Penchion .30 .14
❑ 409 Mike Bass .30 .14
❑ 410 George Kunz .30 .14
❑ 411 Ron Pritchard .30 .14
❑ 412 Barry Smith .30 .14
❑ 413 Norm Bulaich .30 .14
❑ 414 Marv Bateman .30 .14
❑ 415 Ken Stabler 12.00 5.50
❑ 416 Conrad Dobler .75 .35
❑ 417 Bob Tucker .75 .35
❑ 418 Gene Washington 49er .75 .35
❑ 419 Ed Marinaro 1.50 .70
❑ 420 Jack Ham AP 4.00 1.80
❑ 421 Jim Turner .30 .14
❑ 422 Chris Fletcher .30 .14
❑ 423 Carl Barzilauskas .30 .14
❑ 424 Robert Brazile RC 1.50 .70
❑ 425 Harold Carmichael 2.00 .90
❑ 426 Ron Jaworski RC 5.00 2.20
❑ 427 Ed Too Tall Jones RC 20.00 9.00
❑ 428 Larry McCarren .30 .14
❑ 429 Mike Thomas RC .30 .14
❑ 430 Joe DeLamielleure 1.50 .70
❑ 431 Tom Blanchard .30 .14
❑ 432 Ron Carpenter .30 .14
❑ 433 Levi Johnson .30 .14
❑ 434 Sam Cunningham .75 .35
❑ 435 Garo Yepremian .75 .35
❑ 436 Mike Livingston .30 .14
❑ 437 Larry Csonka 4.00 1.80
❑ 438 Doug Dieken .75 .35
❑ 439 Bill Lueck .30 .14
❑ 440 Tom MacLeod .30 .14
❑ 441 Mick Tingelhoff .75 .35
❑ 442 Terry Hanratty .75 .35
❑ 443 Mike Siani .30 .14
❑ 444 Dwight Harrison .30 .14
❑ 445 Jim Otis .75 .35
❑ 446 Jack Reynolds .75 .35
❑ 447 Jean Fugett RC .75 .35
❑ 448 Dave Beverly .30 .14
❑ 449 Bernard Jackson RC .30 .14
❑ 450 Charley Taylor 2.00 .90
❑ 451 Atlanta Falcons 2.00 .50
Team Checklist
❑ 452 Baltimore Colts 2.00 .50
Team Checklist
❑ 453 Buffalo Bills 2.00 .50
Team Checklist
❑ 454 Chicago Bears 2.00 .50
Team Checklist
❑ 455 Cincinnati Bengals 2.00 .50
Team Checklist
❑ 456 Cleveland Browns 2.00 .50
Team Checklist
❑ 457 Dallas Cowboys 2.00 .50
Team Checklist
❑ 458 Denver Broncos UER 2.00 .50
Team Checklist
(Charlie Johnson
spelled Charley)
❑ 459 Detroit Lions 2.00 .50
Team Checklist
❑ 460 Green Bay Packers 2.00 .50
Team Checklist
❑ 461 Houston Oilers 2.00 .50
Team Checklist
❑ 462 Kansas City Chiefs 2.00 .50
Team Checklist
❑ 463 Los Angeles Rams 2.00 .50
Team Checklist
❑ 464 Miami Dolphins 2.00 .50
Team Checklist
❑ 465 Minnesota Vikings 2.00 .50
Team Checklist
❑ 466 New England Patriots 2.00 .50
Team Checklist
❑ 467 New Orleans Saints 2.00 .50
Team Checklist
❑ 468 New York Giants 2.00 .50
Team Checklist
❑ 469 New York Jets 2.00 .50
Team Checklist
❑ 470 Oakland Raiders 2.00 .50
Team Checklist
❑ 471 Philadelphia Eagles 2.00 .50
Team Checklist
❑ 472 Pittsburgh Steelers 2.00 .50
Team Checklist
❑ 473 St. Louis Cardinals 2.00 .50
Team Checklist
❑ 474 San Diego Chargers 2.00 .50
Team Checklist
❑ 475 San Francisco 49ers 2.00 .50
Team Checklist
❑ 476 Seattle Seahawks 2.00 .50
Team Checklist
❑ 477 Tampa Bay Buccaneers 2.00 .50
Team Checklist
❑ 478 Washington Redskins 2.00 .50
Team Checklist
❑ 479 Fred Cox .30 .14
❑ 480 Mel Blount AP 6.00 2.70
❑ 481 John Bunting RC .75 .35
❑ 482 Ken Mendenhall .30 .14
❑ 483 Will Harrell .30 .14
❑ 484 Marlin Briscoe .30 .14
❑ 485 Archie Manning 1.50 .70
❑ 486 Tody Smith .30 .14
❑ 487 George Hunt .30 .14
❑ 488 Roscoe Word .30 .14
❑ 489 Paul Seymour .30 .14
❑ 490 Lee Roy Jordan AP 1.50 .70
❑ 491 Chip Myers .30 .14
❑ 492 Norm Evans .30 .14
❑ 493 Jim Bertelsen .30 .14
❑ 494 Mark Moseley .75 .35
❑ 495 George Buehler .30 .14
❑ 496 Charlie Hall .30 .14
❑ 497 Marvin Upshaw .30 .14
❑ 498 Tom Banks RC .30 .14
❑ 499 Randy Vataha .30 .14
❑ 500 Fran Tarkenton AP 6.00 2.70
❑ 501 Mike Wagner .75 .35
❑ 502 Art Malone .30 .14
❑ 503 Fred Cook .30 .14
❑ 504 Rich McGeorge .30 .14
❑ 505 Ken Burrough .75 .35
❑ 506 Nick Mike-Mayer .30 .14
❑ 507 Checklist 397-528 3.00 .75
❑ 508 Steve Owens .75 .35
❑ 509 Brad Van Pelt RC .30 .14
❑ 510 Ken Riley .75 .35
❑ 511 Art Thoms .30 .14
❑ 512 Ed Bell .30 .14
❑ 513 Tom Wittum .30 .14
❑ 514 Jim Braxton .30 .14
❑ 515 Nick Buoniconti 1.50 .70
❑ 516 Brian Sipe RC 6.00 2.70
❑ 517 Jim Lynch .30 .14
❑ 518 Prentice McCray .30 .14
❑ 519 Tom Dempsey .30 .14
❑ 520 Mel Gray .75 .35
❑ 521 Nate Wright .30 .14
❑ 522 Rocky Bleier 6.00 2.70
❑ 523 Dennis Johnson RC .30 .14
❑ 524 Jerry Sisemore .30 .14
❑ 525 Bert Jones .30 .14
❑ 526 Perry Smith .30 .14
❑ 527 Blaine Nye .30 .14
❑ 528 Bob Moore 1.50 .35

1977 Topps

	Nm-Mt	Ex-Mt
COMPLETE SET (528)	250.00	110.00

❑ 1 Passing Leaders 2.50 .60
James Harris
Ken Stabler
❑ 2 Receiving Leaders 1.00 .45
Drew Pearson
MacArthur Lane
❑ 3 Rushing Leaders 10.00 4.50
Walter Payton
O.J. Simpson
❑ 4 Scoring Leaders .50 .23
Mark Moseley
Toni Linhart
❑ 5 Interception Leaders .50 .23
Monte Jackson
Ken Riley
❑ 6 Punting Leaders .25 .11
John James
Marv Bateman
❑ 7 Mike Phipps .50 .23
❑ 8 Rick Volk .25 .11
❑ 9 Steve Furness .50 .23
❑ 10 Isaac Curtis .50 .23
❑ 11 Nate Wright .50 .23
❑ 12 Jean Fugett .25 .11
❑ 13 Ken Mendenhall .25 .11
❑ 14 Sam Adams .25 .11
❑ 15 Charlie Waters 1.00 .45
❑ 16 Bill Stanfill .25 .11
❑ 17 John Holland .25 .11
❑ 18 Pat Haden RC 2.00 .90
❑ 19 Bob Young .25 .11
❑ 20 Wally Chambers .25 .11
❑ 21 Lawrence Gaines .25 .11
❑ 22 Larry McCarren .25 .11
❑ 23 Horst Muhlmann .25 .11
❑ 24 Phil Villapiano .50 .23
❑ 25 Greg Pruitt .50 .23
❑ 26 Ron Howard .25 .11
❑ 27 Craig Morton 1.00 .45
❑ 28 Rufus Mayes .25 .11
❑ 29 Lee Roy Selmon RC UER 12.00 5.50
Misspelled Leroy
❑ 30 Ed White .50 .23
❑ 31 Harold McLinton .25 .11
❑ 32 Glenn Doughty .25 .11
❑ 33 Bob Kuechenberg 1.00 .45
❑ 34 Duane Carrell .25 .11
❑ 35 Riley Odoms .25 .11
❑ 36 Bobby Scott .25 .11
❑ 37 Nick Mike-Mayer .25 .11
❑ 38 Bill Lenkaitis .25 .11
❑ 39 Roland Harper .50 .23
❑ 40 Tommy Hart .25 .11
❑ 41 Mike Sensibaugh .25 .11
❑ 42 Rusty Jackson .25 .11
❑ 43 Levi Johnson .25 .11
❑ 44 Mike McCoy .25 .11
❑ 45 Roger Staubach 20.00 9.00
❑ 46 Fred Cox .25 .11
❑ 47 Bob Babich .25 .11
❑ 48 Reggie McKenzie .50 .23
❑ 49 Dave Jennings .25 .11
❑ 50 Mike Haynes AP RC 10.00 4.50
❑ 51 Larry Brown .50 .23
❑ 52 Marvin Cobb .25 .11
❑ 53 Fred Cook .25 .11
❑ 54 Freddie Solomon .50 .23
❑ 55 John Riggins 2.50 1.10
❑ 56 John Bunting .50 .23
❑ 57 Ray Wersching .50 .23
❑ 58 Mike Livingston .25 .11
❑ 59 Billy Johnson .50 .23
❑ 60 Mike Wagner .25 .11
❑ 61 Waymond Bryant .25 .11
❑ 62 Jim Otis .50 .23
❑ 63 Ed Galigher .25 .11
❑ 64 Randy Vataha .25 .11
❑ 65 Jim Zorn RC 4.00 1.80
❑ 66 Jon Keyworth .25 .11
❑ 67 Checklist 1-132 2.00 .50
❑ 68 Henry Childs .25 .11
❑ 69 Thom Darden .25 .11
❑ 70 George Kunz .25 .11
❑ 71 Lenvil Elliott .25 .11
❑ 72 Curtis Johnson .25 .11
❑ 73 Doug Van Horn .25 .11
❑ 74 Joe Theismann 4.00 1.80
❑ 75 Dwight White .50 .23
❑ 76 Scott Laidlaw .25 .11
❑ 77 Monte Johnson .25 .11
❑ 78 Dave Beverly .25 .11
❑ 79 Jim Mitchell .25 .11
❑ 80 Jack Youngblood AP 1.00 .45
❑ 81 Mel Gray .50 .23
❑ 82 Dwight Harrison .25 .11
❑ 83 John Hadl .50 .23
❑ 84 Matt Blair RC 1.00 .45
❑ 85 Charlie Sanders .25 .11
❑ 86 Noah Jackson .25 .11
❑ 87 Ed Marinaro .50 .23
❑ 88 Bob Howard .25 .11
❑ 89 John McDaniel .25 .11
❑ 90 Dan Dierdorf AP 1.50 .70
❑ 91 Mark Moseley .50 .23
❑ 92 Cleo Miller .25 .11
❑ 93 Andre Tillman .25 .11
❑ 94 Bruce Taylor .25 .11
❑ 95 Bert Jones 1.00 .45
❑ 96 Anthony Davis RC 1.00 .45
❑ 97 Don Goode .25 .11
❑ 98 Ray Rhodes RC 6.00 2.70
❑ 99 Mike Webster RC 12.00 5.50
❑ 100 O.J. Simpson AP 6.00 2.70
❑ 101 Doug Plank RC .25 .11
❑ 102 Efren Herrera .50 .23
❑ 103 Charlie Smith .25 .11
❑ 104 Carlos Brown RC 1.00 .45
❑ 105 Jim Marshall 1.00 .45
❑ 106 Paul Naumoff .25 .11
❑ 107 Walter White .25 .11
❑ 108 John Cappelletti RC 3.00 1.35
❑ 109 Chip Myers .25 .11
❑ 110 Ken Stabler AP 10.00 4.50
❑ 111 Joe Ehrmann .25 .11
❑ 112 Rick Engles .25 .11
❑ 113 Jack Dolbin RC .25 .11
❑ 114 Ron Bolton .25 .11
❑ 115 Mike Thomas .25 .11
❑ 116 Mike Fuller .25 .11
❑ 117 John Hill .25 .11
❑ 118 Richard Todd RC 1.00 .45
❑ 119 Duriel Harris RC .50 .23
❑ 120 John James .25 .11
❑ 121 Lionel Antoine .25 .11
❑ 122 John Skorupan .25 .11
❑ 123 Skip Butler .25 .11
❑ 124 Bob Tucker .25 .11
❑ 125 Paul Krause 1.00 .45
❑ 126 Dave Hampton .25 .11
❑ 127 Tom Wittum .25 .11
❑ 128 Gary Huff .50 .23
❑ 129 Emmitt Thomas .25 .11
❑ 130 Drew Pearson AP 2.00 .90
❑ 131 Ron Saul .25 .11
❑ 132 Steve Niehaus .25 .11
❑ 133 Fred Carr 1.00 .45
❑ 134 Norm Bulaich .25 .11
❑ 135 Bob Trumpy .50 .23
❑ 136 Greg Landry .50 .23
❑ 137 George Buehler .25 .11
❑ 138 Reggie Rucker .50 .23
❑ 139 Julius Adams .25 .11
❑ 140 Jack Ham AP 2.50 1.10
❑ 141 Wayne Morris RC .25 .11
❑ 142 Marv Bateman .25 .11
❑ 143 Bobby Maples .25 .11
❑ 144 Harold Carmichael 1.00 .45
❑ 145 Bob Avellini .50 .23
❑ 146 Harry Carson RC 3.00 1.35
❑ 147 Lawrence Pillers .25 .11
❑ 148 Ed Williams RC .25 .11
❑ 149 Dan Pastorini .50 .23
❑ 150 Ron Yary 1.00 .45
❑ 151 Joe Lavender .25 .11
❑ 152 Pat McInally RC .50 .23
❑ 153 Lloyd Mumphord .25 .11
❑ 154 Cullen Bryant .50 .23
❑ 155 Willie Lanier 1.00 .45
❑ 156 Gene Washington 49er .50 .23
❑ 157 Scott Hunter .25 .11
❑ 158 Jim Merlo .25 .11
❑ 159 Randy Grossman .50 .23
❑ 160 Blaine Nye .25 .11
❑ 161 Ike Harris .25 .11
❑ 162 Doug Dieken .25 .11
❑ 163 Guy Morriss .25 .11
❑ 164 Bob Parsons .25 .11
❑ 165 Steve Grogan 1.00 .45
❑ 166 John Brockington .50 .23
❑ 167 Charlie Joiner 2.50 1.10
❑ 168 Ron Carpenter .25 .11
❑ 169 Jeff Wright .25 .11
❑ 170 Chris Hanburger .25 .11
❑ 171 Roosevelt Leaks RC .50 .23
❑ 172 Larry Little 1.00 .45
❑ 173 John Matuszak .50 .23
❑ 174 Joe Ferguson .50 .23
❑ 175 Brad Van Pelt .50 .23
❑ 176 Dexter Bussey RC .50 .23
❑ 177 Steve Largent RC 40.00 18.00
❑ 178 Dewey Selmon .50 .23
❑ 179 Randy Gradishar 1.00 .45
❑ 180 Mel Blount AP 3.00 1.35
❑ 181 Dan Neal .25 .11
❑ 182 Rich Szaro .25 .11
❑ 183 Mike Boryla .25 .11
❑ 184 Steve Jones .25 .11
❑ 185 Paul Warfield 2.50 1.10
❑ 186 Greg Buttle RC .25 .11
❑ 187 Rich McGeorge .25 .11
❑ 188 Leon Gray RC .50 .23
❑ 189 John Shinners .25 .11
❑ 190 Toni Linhart .25 .11
❑ 191 Robert Miller .25 .11
❑ 192 Jake Scott .25 .11
❑ 193 Jon Morris .25 .11
❑ 194 Randy Crowder .25 .11
❑ 195 Lynn Swann UER 18.00 8.00
(Interception Record
on card back)
❑ 196 Marsh White .25 .11
❑ 197 Rod Perry RC 1.00 .45
❑ 198 Willie Hall .25 .11
❑ 199 Mike Hartenstine .25 .11
❑ 200 Jim Bakken .25 .11
❑ 201 Atlanta Falcons UER 1.25 .30
Team Checklist
(79 Jim Mitchell
is not listed)
❑ 202 Baltimore Colts 1.25 .30
Team Checklist
❑ 203 Buffalo Bills 1.25 .30
Team Checklist
❑ 204 Chicago Bears 1.25 .30
Team Checklist
❑ 205 Cincinnati Bengals 1.25 .30

Team Checklist
❑ 206 Cleveland Browns 1.25 .30
Team Checklist
❑ 207 Dallas Cowboys 1.25 .30
Team Checklist
❑ 208 Denver Broncos 1.25 .30
Team Checklist
❑ 209 Detroit Lions 1.25 .30
Team Checklist
❑ 210 Green Bay Packers 1.25 .30
Team Checklist
❑ 211 Houston Oilers 1.25 .30
Team Checklist
❑ 212 Kansas City Chiefs 1.25 .30
Team Checklist
❑ 213 Los Angeles Rams 1.25 .30
Team Checklist
❑ 214 Miami Dolphins 1.25 .30
Team Checklist
❑ 215 Minnesota Vikings 1.25 .30
Team Checklist
❑ 216 New England Patriots 1.25 .30
Team Checklist
❑ 217 New Orleans Saints 1.25 .30
Team Checklist
❑ 218 New York Giants 1.25 .30
Team Checklist
❑ 219 New York Jets 1.25 .30
Team Checklist
❑ 220 Oakland Raiders 1.25 .30
Team Checklist
❑ 221 Philadelphia Eagles 1.25 .30
Team Checklist
❑ 222 Pittsburgh Steelers 1.25 .30
Team Checklist
❑ 223 St. Louis Cardinals 1.25 .30
Team Checklist
❑ 224 San Diego Chargers 1.25 .30
Team Checklist
❑ 225 San Francisco 49ers 1.25 .30
Team Checklist
❑ 226 Seattle Seahawks 1.25 .30
Team Checklist
❑ 227 Tampa Bay Buccaneers 1.25 .30
Team Checklist UER
(Lee Roy Selmon mis-
spelled as Leroy)
❑ 228 Washington Redskins 1.25 .30
Team Checklist
❑ 229 Sam Cunningham .50 .23
❑ 230 Alan Page AP 1.00 .45
❑ 231 Eddie Brown .25 .11
❑ 232 Stan White .25 .11
❑ 233 Vern Den Herder .25 .11
❑ 234 Clarence Davis .25 .11
❑ 235 Ken Anderson 1.00 .45
❑ 236 Karl Chandler .25 .11
❑ 237 Will Harrell .25 .11
❑ 238 Clarence Scott .25 .11
❑ 239 Bo Rather .25 .11
❑ 240 Robert Brazile AP .50 .23
❑ 241 Bob Bell .25 .11
❑ 242 Rolland Lawrence .25 .11
❑ 243 Tom Sullivan .25 .11
❑ 244 Larry Brunson .25 .11
❑ 245 Terry Bradshaw 20.00 9.00
❑ 246 Rich Saul .25 .11
❑ 247 Cleveland Elam .25 .11
❑ 248 Don Woods .25 .11
❑ 249 Bruce Laird .25 .11
❑ 250 Coy Bacon .50 .23
❑ 251 Russ Francis 1.00 .45
❑ 252 Jim Braxton .25 .11
❑ 253 Perry Smith .25 .11
❑ 254 Jerome Barkum .25 .11
❑ 255 Garo Yepremian .50 .23
❑ 256 Checklist 133-264 2.00 .50
❑ 257 Tony Galbreath RC .50 .23
❑ 258 Troy Archer .25 .11
❑ 259 Brian Sipe 1.00 .45
❑ 260 Billy Joe DuPree AP .50 .23
❑ 261 Bobby Walden .25 .11
❑ 262 Larry Marshall .25 .11
❑ 263 Ted Fritsch Jr. .25 .11
❑ 264 Larry Hand .25 .11
❑ 265 Tom Mack 1.00 .45
❑ 266 Ed Bradley .25 .11
❑ 267 Pat Leahy .50 .23
❑ 268 Louis Carter .25 .11
❑ 269 Archie Griffin RC 6.00 2.70
❑ 270 Art Shell AP 1.00 .45
❑ 271 Stu Voigt .25 .11
❑ 272 Prentice McCray .25 .11
❑ 273 MacArthur Lane .25 .11
❑ 274 Dan Fouts 6.00 2.70
❑ 275 Charle Young .50 .23
❑ 276 Wilbur Jackson RC .25 .11
❑ 277 John Hicks .25 .11
❑ 278 Nat Moore 1.00 .45
❑ 279 Virgil Livers .25 .11
❑ 280 Curley Culp .50 .23
❑ 281 Rocky Bleier 2.50 1.10
❑ 282 John Zook .25 .11
❑ 283 Tom DeLeone .25 .11
❑ 284 Danny White RC 10.00 4.50
❑ 285 Otis Armstrong .50 .23
❑ 286 Larry Walton .25 .11
❑ 287 Jim Carter .25 .11
❑ 288 Don McCauley .25 .11
❑ 289 Frank Grant .25 .11
❑ 290 Roger Wehrli .50 .23
❑ 291 Mick Tingelhoff .50 .23
❑ 292 Bernard Jackson .25 .11
❑ 293 Tom Owen RC .25 .11
❑ 294 Mike Esposito .25 .11
❑ 295 Fred Biletnikoff 2.50 1.10
❑ 296 Revie Sorey RC .25 .11
❑ 297 John McMakin .25 .11
❑ 298 Dan Ryczek .25 .11
❑ 299 Wayne Moore .25 .11
❑ 300 Franco Harris AP 4.00 1.80
❑ 301 Rick Upchurch RC 1.00 .45
❑ 302 Jim Stienke .25 .11
❑ 303 Charlie Davis .25 .11
❑ 304 Don Cockroft .25 .11
❑ 305 Ken Burrough .50 .23
❑ 306 Clark Gaines .25 .11
❑ 307 Bobby Douglass .25 .11
❑ 308 Ralph Perretta .25 .11
❑ 309 Wally Hilgenberg .25 .11
❑ 310 Monte Jackson AP RC .50 .23
❑ 311 Chris Bahr RC .50 .23
❑ 312 Jim Cheyunski .25 .11
❑ 313 Mike Patrick .25 .11
❑ 314 Ed Too Tall Jones 5.00 2.20
❑ 315 Bill Bradley .25 .11
❑ 316 Benny Malone .25 .11
❑ 317 Paul Seymour .25 .11
❑ 318 Jim Laslavic .25 .11
❑ 319 Frank Lewis .50 .23
❑ 320 Ray Guy AP 1.00 .45
❑ 321 Allan Ellis .25 .11
❑ 322 Conrad Dobler .50 .23
❑ 323 Chester Marcol .25 .11
❑ 324 Doug Kotar .25 .11
❑ 325 Lemar Parrish .50 .23
❑ 326 Steve Holden .25 .11
❑ 327 Jeff Van Note .50 .23
❑ 328 Howard Stevens .25 .11
❑ 329 Brad Dusek .50 .23
❑ 330 Joe DeLamielleure 1.00 .45
❑ 331 Jim Plunkett 1.00 .45
❑ 332 Checklist 265-396 2.00 .50
❑ 333 Lou Piccone .25 .11
❑ 334 Ray Hamilton .25 .11
❑ 335 Jan Stenerud 1.00 .45
❑ 336 Jeris White .25 .11
❑ 337 Sherman Smith RC .25 .11
❑ 338 Dave Green .25 .11
❑ 339 Terry Schmidt .25 .11
❑ 340 Sammie White AP RC 1.00 .45
❑ 341 Jon Kolb RC .25 .11
❑ 342 Randy White 8.00 3.60
❑ 343 Bob Klein .25 .11
❑ 344 Bob Kowalkowski .25 .11
❑ 345 Terry Metcalf .50 .23
❑ 346 Joe Danelo .25 .11
❑ 347 Ken Payne .25 .11
❑ 348 Neal Craig .25 .11
❑ 349 Dennis Johnson .25 .11
❑ 350 Bill Bergey AP .50 .23
❑ 351 Raymond Chester .25 .11
❑ 352 Bob Matheson .25 .11
❑ 353 Mike Kadish .25 .11
❑ 354 Mark Van Eeghen RC 1.00 .45
❑ 355 L.C. Greenwood 1.00 .45
❑ 356 Sam Hunt .25 .11
❑ 357 Darrell Austin .25 .11
❑ 358 Jim Turner .25 .11
❑ 359 Ahmad Rashad 2.00 .90
❑ 360 Walter Payton AP 40.00 18.00
❑ 361 Mark Arneson .25 .11
❑ 362 Jerrel Wilson .25 .11
❑ 363 Steve Bartkowski 1.00 .45
❑ 364 John Watson .25 .11
❑ 365 Ken Riley .50 .23
❑ 366 Gregg Bingham .25 .11
❑ 367 Golden Richards .50 .23
❑ 368 Clyde Powers .25 .11
❑ 369 Diron Talbert .25 .11
❑ 370 Lydell Mitchell .50 .23
❑ 371 Bob Jackson .25 .11
❑ 372 Jim Mandich .25 .11
❑ 373 Frank LeMaster .25 .11
❑ 374 Benny Ricardo .25 .11
❑ 375 Lawrence McCutcheon .50 .23
❑ 376 Lynn Dickey .50 .23
❑ 377 Phil Wise .25 .11
❑ 378 Tony McGee .25 .11
❑ 379 Norm Thompson .25 .11
❑ 380 Dave Casper AP RC 4.00 1.80
❑ 381 Glen Edwards .25 .11
❑ 382 Bob Thomas .25 .11
❑ 383 Bob Chandler .50 .23
❑ 384 Rickey Young .50 .23
❑ 385 Carl Eller 1.00 .45
❑ 386 Lyle Alzado 1.00 .45
❑ 387 John Leypoldt .25 .11
❑ 388 Gordon Bell .25 .11
❑ 389 Mike Bragg .25 .11
❑ 390 Jim Langer AP 1.00 .45
❑ 391 Vern Holland .25 .11
❑ 392 Nelson Munsey .25 .11
❑ 393 Mack Mitchell .25 .11
❑ 394 Tony Adams RC .25 .11
❑ 395 Preston Pearson .50 .23
❑ 396 Emanuel Zanders .25 .11
❑ 397 Vince Papale .25 .11
❑ 398 Joe Fields RC .50 .23
❑ 399 Craig Clemons .25 .11
❑ 400 Fran Tarkenton AP 5.00 2.20
❑ 401 Andy Johnson .25 .11
❑ 402 Willie Buchanon .25 .11
❑ 403 Pat Curran .25 .11
❑ 404 Ray Jarvis .25 .11
❑ 405 Joe Greene 2.50 1.10
❑ 406 Bill Simpson .25 .11
❑ 407 Ronnie Coleman .25 .11
❑ 408 J.K. McKay RC .50 .23
❑ 409 Pat Fischer .50 .23
❑ 410 John Dutton .50 .23
❑ 411 Boobie Clark .25 .11
❑ 412 Pat Tilley RC 1.00 .45
❑ 413 Don Strock .50 .23
❑ 414 Brian Kelley .25 .11
❑ 415 Gene Upshaw 1.00 .45
❑ 416 Mike Montler .25 .11
❑ 417 Checklist 397-528 2.00 .50
❑ 418 John Gilliam .25 .11
❑ 419 Brent McClanahan .25 .11
❑ 420 Jerry Sherk .25 .11
❑ 421 Roy Gerela .25 .11
❑ 422 Tim Fox .50 .23

❑ 423 John Ebersole .25 .11
❑ 424 James Scott RC .25 .11
❑ 425 Delvin Williams RC .50 .23
❑ 426 Spike Jones .25 .11
❑ 427 Harvey Martin 1.00 .45
❑ 428 Don Herrmann .25 .11
❑ 429 Calvin Hill .50 .23
❑ 430 Isiah Robertson .25 .11
❑ 431 Tony Greene .25 .11
❑ 432 Bob Johnson .25 .11
❑ 433 Lem Barney 1.00 .45
❑ 434 Eric Torkelson .25 .11
❑ 435 John Mendenhall .25 .11
❑ 436 Larry Seiple .50 .23
❑ 437 Art Kuehn .25 .11
❑ 438 John Vella .25 .11
❑ 439 Greg Latta .25 .11
❑ 440 Roger Carr .50 .23
❑ 441 Doug Sutherland .25 .11
❑ 442 Mike Kruczek .25 .11
❑ 443 Steve Zabel .25 .11
❑ 444 Mike Pruitt RC 1.00 .45
❑ 445 Harold Jackson .50 .23
❑ 446 George Jakowenko .25 .11
❑ 447 John Fitzgerald .25 .11
❑ 448 Carey Joyce .25 .11
❑ 449 Jim LeClair .25 .11
❑ 450 Ken Houston AP 1.00 .45
❑ 451 Steve Grogan RB Most TDs Rushing by QB in a Season .50 .23
❑ 452 Jim Marshall RB Most Games Played: Lifetime .50 .23
❑ 453 O.J. Simpson RB Most Yardage, Rushing: Game 2.50 1.10
❑ 454 Fran Tarkenton RB Most Yardage, Passing: Lifetime 3.00 1.35
❑ 455 Jim Zorn RB Most Passing Yards Season& Rookie .50 .23
❑ 456 Robert Pratt .25 .11
❑ 457 Walker Gillette .25 .11
❑ 458 Charlie Hall .25 .11
❑ 459 Robert Newhouse .50 .23
❑ 460 John Hannah AP 1.00 .45
❑ 461 Ken Reaves .25 .11
❑ 462 Herman Weaver .25 .11
❑ 463 James Harris .50 .23
❑ 464 Howard Twilley .50 .23
❑ 465 Jeff Siemon .50 .23
❑ 466 John Outlaw .25 .11
❑ 467 Chuck Muncie RC 1.00 .45
❑ 468 Bob Moore .25 .11
❑ 469 Robert Woods .25 .11
❑ 470 Cliff Branch AP 2.00 .90
❑ 471 Johnnie Gray .25 .11
❑ 472 Don Hardeman .25 .11
❑ 473 Steve Ramsey .25 .11
❑ 474 Steve Mike-Mayer .25 .11
❑ 475 Gary Garrison .25 .11
❑ 476 Walter Johnson .25 .11
❑ 477 Neil Clabo .25 .11
❑ 478 Len Hauss .25 .11
❑ 479 Darryl Stingley .50 .23
❑ 480 Jack Lambert AP 8.00 3.60
❑ 481 Mike Adamle .50 .23
❑ 482 David Lee .25 .11
❑ 483 Tom Mullen .25 .11
❑ 484 Claude Humphrey .25 .11
❑ 485 Jim Hart 1.00 .45
❑ 486 Bobby Thompson RB .25 .11
❑ 487 Jack Rudnay .25 .11
❑ 488 Rich Sowells .25 .11
❑ 489 Reuben Gant .25 .11
❑ 490 Cliff Harris AP 1.00 .45
❑ 491 Bob Brown DT .25 .11
❑ 492 Don Nottingham .25 .11
❑ 493 Ron Jessie .25 .11
❑ 494 Otis Sistrunk .50 .23
❑ 495 Billy Kilmer .50 .23
❑ 496 Oscar Roan .25 .11
❑ 497 Bill Van Heusen .25 .11
❑ 498 Randy Logan .25 .11
❑ 499 John Smith .25 .11
❑ 500 Chuck Foreman AP .50 .23
❑ 501 J.T. Thomas .25 .11
❑ 502 Steve Schubert .25 .11
❑ 503 Mike Barnes .25 .11
❑ 504 J.V. Cain .25 .11
❑ 505 Larry Csonka 3.00 1.35
❑ 506 Elvin Bethea 1.00 .45
❑ 507 Ray Easterling .25 .11
❑ 508 Joe Reed .25 .11
❑ 509 Steve Odom .25 .11
❑ 510 Tommy Casanova .25 .11
❑ 511 Dave Dalby .25 .11
❑ 512 Richard Caster .25 .11
❑ 513 Fred Dryer 1.00 .45
❑ 514 Jeff Kinney .25 .11
❑ 515 Bob Griese 3.00 1.35
❑ 516 Butch Johnson RC 1.00 .45
❑ 517 Gerald Irons .25 .11
❑ 518 Don Calhoun .25 .11
❑ 519 Jack Gregory .25 .11
❑ 520 Tom Banks .25 .11
❑ 521 Bobby Bryant .25 .11
❑ 522 Reggie Harrison .25 .11
❑ 523 Terry Hermeling .25 .11
❑ 524 David Taylor .25 .11
❑ 525 Brian Baschnagel RC .50 .23
❑ 526 AFC Championship Raiders 24; Steelers 7 (Ken Stabler) 1.00 .45
❑ 527 NFC Championship Vikings 24; Rams 13 .50 .23
❑ 528 Super Bowl XI Raiders 32; Vikings 14 (line play) 1.00 .25

1978 Topps

	Nm-Mt	Ex-Mt
COMPLETE SET (528)	150.00	70.00

❑ 1 Gary Huff HL Huff Leads Bucs to First Win 1.00 .25
❑ 2 Craig Morton HL Morton Passes Broncos to Super Bowl 1.00 .45
❑ 3 Walter Payton HL Rushes for 275 Yards 8.00 3.60
❑ 4 O.J. Simpson HL Reaches 10,000 Yards 2.00 .90
❑ 5 Fran Tarkenton HL Completes 17 of 18 2.00 .90
❑ 6 Bob Thomas HL Thomas' FG Sends Bears to Playoffs .20 .09
❑ 7 Joe Pisarcik .50 .23
❑ 8 Skip Thomas .20 .09
❑ 9 Roosevelt Leaks .20 .09
❑ 10 Ken Houston AP 1.00 .45
❑ 11 Tom Blanchard .20 .09
❑ 12 Jim Turner .20 .09
❑ 13 Tom DeLeone .20 .09
❑ 14 Jim LeClair .20 .09
❑ 15 Bob Avellini .50 .23
❑ 16 Tony McGee .20 .09
❑ 17 James Harris .50 .23
❑ 18 Terry Nelson .20 .09
❑ 19 Rocky Bleier 2.00 .90
❑ 20 Joe DeLamielleure 1.00 .45
❑ 21 Richard Caster .20 .09
❑ 22 A.J. Duhe RC 1.00 .45
❑ 23 John Outlaw .20 .09
❑ 24 Danny White 1.25 .55
❑ 25 Larry Csonka 2.50 1.10
❑ 26 David Hill RC .50 .23
❑ 27 Mark Arneson .20 .09
❑ 28 Jack Tatum .50 .23
❑ 29 Norm Thompson .20 .09
❑ 30 Sammie White .50 .23
❑ 31 Dennis Johnson .20 .09
❑ 32 Robin Earl .20 .09
❑ 33 Don Cockroft .20 .09
❑ 34 Bob Johnson .20 .09
❑ 35 John Hannah 1.00 .45
❑ 36 Scott Hunter .20 .09
❑ 37 Ken Burrough .50 .23
❑ 38 Wilbur Jackson .50 .23
❑ 39 Rich McGeorge .20 .09
❑ 40 Lyle Alzado AP 1.00 .45
❑ 41 John Ebersole .20 .09
❑ 42 Gary Green RC .20 .09
❑ 43 Art Kuehn .20 .09
❑ 44 Glen Edwards .50 .23
❑ 45 Lawrence McCutcheon .50 .23
❑ 46 Duriel Harris .20 .09
❑ 47 Rich Szaro .20 .09
❑ 48 Mike Washington .20 .09
❑ 49 Stan White .20 .09
❑ 50 Dave Casper AP 1.00 .45
❑ 51 Len Hauss .20 .09
❑ 52 James Scott .20 .09
❑ 53 Brian Sipe 1.00 .45
❑ 54 Gary Shirk .20 .09
❑ 55 Archie Griffin 1.00 .45
❑ 56 Mike Patrick .20 .09
❑ 57 Mario Clark .20 .09
❑ 58 Jeff Siemon .20 .09
❑ 59 Steve Mike-Mayer .20 .09
❑ 60 Randy White AP 4.00 1.80
❑ 61 Darrell Austin .20 .09
❑ 62 Tom Sullivan .20 .09
❑ 63 Johnny Rodgers RC 1.00 .45
❑ 64 Ken Reaves .20 .09
❑ 65 Terry Bradshaw 12.00 5.50
❑ 66 Fred Steinfort .20 .09
❑ 67 Curley Culp .50 .23
❑ 68 Ted Hendricks 1.00 .45
❑ 69 Raymond Chester .20 .09
❑ 70 Jim Langer AP 1.00 .45
❑ 71 Calvin Hill .50 .23
❑ 72 Mike Hartenstine .20 .09
❑ 73 Gerald Irons .20 .09
❑ 74 Billy Brooks .50 .23
❑ 75 John Mendenhall .20 .09
❑ 76 Andy Johnson .20 .09
❑ 77 Tom Wittum .20 .09
❑ 78 Lynn Dickey .50 .23
❑ 79 Carl Eller 1.00 .45
❑ 80 Tom Mack 1.00 .45
❑ 81 Clark Gaines .20 .09
❑ 82 Lem Barney 1.00 .45
❑ 83 Mike Montler .20 .09
❑ 84 Jon Kolb .20 .09
❑ 85 Bob Chandler .50 .23
❑ 86 Robert Newhouse .50 .23
❑ 87 Frank LeMaster .20 .09
❑ 88 Jeff West .20 .09
❑ 89 Lyle Blackwood .50 .23

❑	90 Gene Upshaw AP	1.00	.45
❑	91 Frank Grant	.20	.09
❑	92 Tom Hicks	.20	.09
❑	93 Mike Pruitt	.50	.23
❑	94 Chris Bahr	.20	.09
❑	95 Russ Francis	.50	.23
❑	96 Norris Thomas	.20	.09
❑	97 Gary Barbaro RC	.50	.23
❑	98 Jim Merlo	.20	.09
❑	99 Karl Chandler	.20	.09
❑	100 Fran Tarkenton	4.00	1.80
❑	101 Abdul Salaam	.20	.09
❑	102 Marv Kellum	.20	.09
❑	103 Herman Weaver	.20	.09
❑	104 Roy Gerela	.20	.09
❑	105 Harold Jackson	.50	.23
❑	106 Dewey Selmon	.50	.23
❑	107 Checklist 1-132	1.00	.25
❑	108 Clarence Davis	.20	.09
❑	109 Robert Pratt	.20	.09
❑	110 Harvey Martin AP	1.00	.45
❑	111 Brad Dusek	.20	.09
❑	112 Greg Latta	.20	.09
❑	113 Tony Peters	.20	.09
❑	114 Jim Braxton	.20	.09
❑	115 Ken Riley	.50	.23
❑	116 Steve Nelson	.20	.09
❑	117 Rick Upchurch	.50	.23
❑	118 Spike Jones	.20	.09
❑	119 Doug Kotar	.20	.09
❑	120 Bob Griese AP	2.50	1.10
❑	121 Burgess Owens	.20	.09
❑	122 Rolf Benirschke RC	.50	.23
❑	123 Haskel Stanback RC	.20	.09
❑	124 J.T. Thomas	.20	.09
❑	125 Ahmad Rashad	1.50	.70
❑	126 Rick Kane	.20	.09
❑	127 Elvin Bethea	1.00	.45
❑	128 Dave Dalby	.20	.09
❑	129 Mike Barnes	.20	.09
❑	130 Isiah Robertson	.20	.09
❑	131 Jim Plunkett	1.00	.45
❑	132 Allan Ellis	.20	.09
❑	133 Mike Bragg	.20	.09
❑	134 Bob Jackson	.20	.09
❑	135 Coy Bacon	.20	.09
❑	136 John Smith	.20	.09
❑	137 Chuck Muncie	.50	.23
❑	138 Johnnie Gray	.20	.09
❑	139 Jimmy Robinson	.20	.09
❑	140 Tom Banks	.20	.09
❑	141 Marvin Powell RC	.20	.09
❑	142 Jerrel Wilson	.20	.09
❑	143 Ron Howard	.20	.09
❑	144 Rob Lytle RC	.50	.23
❑	145 L.C. Greenwood	1.00	.45
❑	146 Morris Owens	.20	.09
❑	147 Joe Reed	.20	.09
❑	148 Mike Kadish	.20	.09
❑	149 Phil Villapiano	.50	.23
❑	150 Lydell Mitchell	.50	.23
❑	151 Randy Logan	.20	.09
❑	152 Mike Williams RC	.20	.09
❑	153 Jeff Van Note	.50	.23
❑	154 Steve Schubert	.20	.09
❑	155 Billy Kilmer	.50	.23
❑	156 Boobie Clark	.20	.09
❑	157 Charlie Hall	.20	.09
❑	158 Raymond Clayborn RC	1.00	.45
❑	159 Jack Gregory	.20	.09
❑	160 Cliff Harris AP	1.00	.45
❑	161 Joe Fields	.20	.09
❑	162 Don Nottingham	.20	.09
❑	163 Ed White	.50	.23
❑	164 Toni Fritsch	.20	.09
❑	165 Jack Lambert	4.00	1.80
❑	166 NFC Champions Cowboys 23; Vikings 6 (Roger Staubach)	1.50	.70
❑	167 AFC Champions Broncos 20; Raiders 17 (Lytle running)	.50	.23
❑	168 Super Bowl XII Cowboys 27; Broncos 10 (Tony Dorsett)	3.00	1.35
❑	169 Neal Colzie RC	.20	.09
❑	170 Cleveland Elam	.20	.09
❑	171 David Lee	.20	.09
❑	172 Jim Otis	.20	.09
❑	173 Archie Manning	1.00	.45
❑	174 Jim Carter	.20	.09
❑	175 Jean Fugett	.20	.09
❑	176 Willie Parker	.20	.09
❑	177 Haven Moses	.50	.23
❑	178 Horace King RC	.20	.09
❑	179 Bob Thomas	.20	.09
❑	180 Monte Jackson	.20	.09
❑	181 Steve Zabel	.20	.09
❑	182 John Fitzgerald	.20	.09
❑	183 Mike Livingston	.20	.09
❑	184 Larry Poole	.20	.09
❑	185 Isaac Curtis	.50	.23
❑	186 Chuck Ramsey	.20	.09
❑	187 Bob Klein	.20	.09
❑	188 Ray Rhodes	1.00	.45
❑	189 Otis Sistrunk	.50	.23
❑	190 Bill Bergey	.50	.23
❑	191 Sherman Smith	.50	.23
❑	192 Dave Green	.20	.09
❑	193 Carl Mauck	.20	.09
❑	194 Reggie Harrison	.20	.09
❑	195 Roger Carr	.50	.23
❑	196 Steve Bartkowski	1.00	.45
❑	197 Ray Wersching	.20	.09
❑	198 Willie Buchanon	.20	.09
❑	199 Neil Clabo	.20	.09
❑	200 Walter Payton AP UER (Born 7/5/54; should be 7/25/54)	25.00	11.00
❑	201 Sam Adams	.20	.09
❑	202 Larry Gordon	.20	.09
❑	203 Pat Tilley	.50	.23
❑	204 Mack Mitchell	.20	.09
❑	205 Ken Anderson	1.00	.45
❑	206 Scott Dierking	.20	.09
❑	207 Jack Rudnay	.20	.09
❑	208 Jim Stienke	.20	.09
❑	209 Bill Simpson	.20	.09
❑	210 Errol Mann	.20	.09
❑	211 Bucky Dilts	.20	.09
❑	212 Reuben Gant	.20	.09
❑	213 Thomas Henderson RC	1.50	.70
❑	214 Steve Furness	.50	.23
❑	215 John Riggins	2.00	.90
❑	216 Keith Krepfle RC	.20	.09
❑	217 Fred Dean RC	.50	.23
❑	218 Emanuel Zanders	.20	.09
❑	219 Don Testerman	.20	.09
❑	220 George Kunz	.20	.09
❑	221 Darryl Stingley	.50	.23
❑	222 Ken Sanders	.20	.09
❑	223 Gary Huff	.20	.09
❑	224 Gregg Bingham	.20	.09
❑	225 Jerry Sherk	.20	.09
❑	226 Doug Plank	.20	.09
❑	227 Ed Taylor	.20	.09
❑	228 Emery Moorehead	.20	.09
❑	229 Reggie Williams RC	1.00	.45
❑	230 Claude Humphrey	.20	.09
❑	231 Randy Cross RC	2.00	.90
❑	232 Jim Hart	1.00	.45
❑	233 Bobby Bryant	.20	.09
❑	234 Larry Brown	.20	.09
❑	235 Mark Van Eeghen	.50	.23
❑	236 Terry Hermeling	.20	.09
❑	237 Steve Odom	.20	.09
❑	238 Jan Stenerud	1.00	.45
❑	239 Andre Tillman	.20	.09
❑	240 Tom Jackson AP RC	5.00	2.20
❑	241 Ken Mendenhall	.20	.09
❑	242 Tim Fox	.20	.09
❑	243 Don Herrmann	.20	.09
❑	244 Eddie McMillan	.20	.09
❑	245 Greg Pruitt	.50	.23
❑	246 J.K. McKay	.20	.09
❑	247 Larry Keller	.20	.09
❑	248 Dave Jennings	.50	.23
❑	249 Bo Harris	.20	.09
❑	250 Revie Sorey	.20	.09
❑	251 Tony Greene	.20	.09
❑	252 Butch Johnson	.50	.23
❑	253 Paul Naumoff	.20	.09
❑	254 Rickey Young	.50	.23
❑	255 Dwight White	.50	.23
❑	256 Joe Lavender	.20	.09
❑	257 Checklist 133-264	1.00	.25
❑	258 Ronnie Coleman	.20	.09
❑	259 Charlie Smith	.20	.09
❑	260 Ray Guy AP	1.00	.45
❑	261 David Taylor	.20	.09
❑	262 Bill Lenkaitis	.20	.09
❑	263 Jim Mitchell	.20	.09
❑	264 Delvin Williams	.20	.09
❑	265 Jack Youngblood	1.00	.45
❑	266 Chuck Crist	.20	.09
❑	267 Richard Todd	.50	.23
❑	268 Dave Logan RC	1.00	.45
❑	269 Rufus Mayes	.20	.09
❑	270 Brad Van Pelt	.20	.09
❑	271 Chester Marcol	.20	.09
❑	272 J.V. Cain	.20	.09
❑	273 Larry Seiple	.20	.09
❑	274 Brent McClanahan	.20	.09
❑	275 Mike Wagner	.20	.09
❑	276 Diron Talbert	.20	.09
❑	277 Brian Baschnagel	.20	.09
❑	278 Ed Podolak	.20	.09
❑	279 Don Goode	.20	.09
❑	280 John Dutton	.50	.23
❑	281 Don Calhoun	.20	.09
❑	282 Monte Johnson	.20	.09
❑	283 Ron Jessie	.20	.09
❑	284 Jon Morris	.20	.09
❑	285 Riley Odoms	.20	.09
❑	286 Marv Bateman	.20	.09
❑	287 Joe Klecko RC	1.00	.45
❑	288 Oliver Davis	.20	.09
❑	289 John McDaniel	.20	.09
❑	290 Roger Staubach	12.00	5.50
❑	291 Brian Kelley	.20	.09
❑	292 Mike Hogan	.20	.09
❑	293 John Leypoldt	.20	.09
❑	294 Jack Novak	.20	.09
❑	295 Joe Greene	2.00	.90
❑	296 John Hill	.20	.09
❑	297 Danny Buggs	.20	.09
❑	298 Ted Albrecht	.20	.09
❑	299 Nelson Munsey	.20	.09
❑	300 Chuck Foreman	.50	.23
❑	301 Dan Pastorini	.50	.23
❑	302 Tommy Hart	.20	.09
❑	303 Dave Beverly	.20	.09
❑	304 Tony Reed RC	.50	.23
❑	305 Cliff Branch	1.50	.70
❑	306 Clarence Duren	.20	.09
❑	307 Randy Rasmussen	.20	.09
❑	308 Oscar Roan	.20	.09
❑	309 Lenvil Elliott	.20	.09
❑	310 Dan Dierdorf AP	1.00	.45
❑	311 Johnny Perkins	.20	.09
❑	312 Rafael Septien RC	.50	.23
❑	313 Terry Beeson	.20	.09
❑	314 Lee Roy Selmon	2.00	.90
❑	315 Tony Dorsett RC	40.00	18.00
❑	316 Greg Landry	.50	.23
❑	317 Jake Scott	.20	.09
❑	318 Dan Peiffer	.20	.09
❑	319 John Bunting	.50	.23
❑	320 John Stallworth RC	20.00	9.00
❑	321 Bob Howard	.20	.09

❑	322	Larry Little	1.00	.45
❑	323	Reggie McKenzie	.50	.23
❑	324	Duane Carrell	.20	.09
❑	325	Ed Simonini	.20	.09
❑	326	John Vella	.20	.09
❑	327	Wesley Walker RC	3.00	1.35
❑	328	Jon Keyworth	.20	.09
❑	329	Ron Bolton	.20	.09
❑	330	Tommy Casanova	.20	.09
❑	331	Passing Leaders	4.00	1.80
		Bob Griese		
		Roger Staubach		
❑	332	Receiving Leaders	1.00	.45
		Lydell Mitchell		
		Ahmad Rashad		
❑	333	Rushing Leaders	3.00	1.35
		Mark Van Eeghen		
		Walter Payton		
❑	334	Scoring Leaders	3.00	1.35
		Errol Mann		
		Walter Payton		
❑	335	Interception Leaders	.20	.09
		Lyle Blackwood		
		Rolland Lawrence		
❑	336	Punting Leaders	.50	.23
		Ray Guy		
		Tom Blanchard		
❑	337	Robert Brazile	.50	.23
❑	338	Charlie Joiner	1.50	.70
❑	339	Joe Ferguson	.50	.23
❑	340	Bill Thompson	.20	.09
❑	341	Sam Cunningham	.50	.23
❑	342	Curtis Johnson	.20	.09
❑	343	Jim Marshall	1.00	.45
❑	344	Charlie Sanders	.20	.09
❑	345	Willie Hall	.20	.09
❑	346	Pat Haden	1.00	.45
❑	347	Jim Bakken	.20	.09
❑	348	Bruce Taylor	.20	.09
❑	349	Barty Smith	.20	.09
❑	350	Drew Pearson AP	1.50	.70
❑	351	Mike Webster	2.50	1.10
❑	352	Bobby Hammond	.20	.09
❑	353	Dave Mays	.20	.09
❑	354	Pat McInally	.20	.09
❑	355	Toni Linhart	.20	.09
❑	356	Larry Hand	.20	.09
❑	357	Ted Fritsch Jr.	.20	.09
❑	358	Larry Marshall	.20	.09
❑	359	Waymond Bryant	.20	.09
❑	360	Louie Kelcher RC	.50	.23
❑	361	Stanley Morgan RC	2.00	.90
❑	362	Bruce Harper RC	.50	.23
❑	363	Bernard Jackson	.20	.09
❑	364	Walter White	.20	.09
❑	365	Ken Stabler	8.00	3.60
❑	366	Fred Dryer	1.00	.45
❑	367	Ike Harris	.20	.09
❑	368	Norm Bulaich	.20	.09
❑	369	Merv Krakau	.20	.09
❑	370	John James	.20	.09
❑	371	Bennie Cunningham RC	.20	.09
❑	372	Doug Van Horn	.20	.09
❑	373	Thom Darden	.20	.09
❑	374	Eddie Edwards RC	.20	.09
❑	375	Mike Thomas	.20	.09
❑	376	Fred Cook	.20	.09
❑	377	Mike Phipps	.50	.23
❑	378	Paul Krause	1.00	.45
❑	379	Harold Carmichael	1.00	.45
❑	380	Mike Haynes AP	1.00	.45
❑	381	Wayne Morris	.20	.09
❑	382	Greg Buttle	.20	.09
❑	383	Jim Zorn	1.00	.45
❑	384	Jack Dolbin	.20	.09
❑	385	Charlie Waters	.50	.23
❑	386	Dan Ryczek	.20	.09
❑	387	Joe Washington RC	1.00	.45
❑	388	Checklist 265-396	1.00	.25
❑	389	James Hunter	.20	.09
❑	390	Billy Johnson	.50	.23
❑	391	Jim Allen	.20	.09
❑	392	George Buehler	.20	.09
❑	393	Harry Carson	1.00	.45
❑	394	Cleo Miller	.20	.09
❑	395	Gary Burley	.20	.09
❑	396	Mark Moseley	.50	.23
❑	397	Virgil Livers	.20	.09
❑	398	Joe Ehrmann	.20	.09
❑	399	Freddie Solomon	.20	.09
❑	400	O.J. Simpson	4.00	1.80
❑	401	Julius Adams	.20	.09
❑	402	Artimus Parker	.20	.09
❑	403	Gene Washington 49er	.50	.23
❑	404	Herman Edwards	.20	.09
❑	405	Craig Morton	1.00	.45
❑	406	Alan Page	1.00	.45
❑	407	Larry McCarren	.20	.09
❑	408	Tony Galbreath	.50	.23
❑	409	Roman Gabriel	1.00	.45
❑	410	Efren Herrera	.20	.09
❑	411	Jim Smith RC	1.00	.45
❑	412	Bill Bryant	.20	.09
❑	413	Doug Dieken	.20	.09
❑	414	Marvin Cobb	.20	.09
❑	415	Fred Biletnikoff	2.00	.90
❑	416	Joe Theismann	2.50	1.10
❑	417	Roland Harper	.20	.09
❑	418	Derrel Luce	.20	.09
❑	419	Ralph Perretta	.20	.09
❑	420	Louis Wright RC	1.00	.45
❑	421	Prentice McCray	.20	.09
❑	422	Garry Puetz	.20	.09
❑	423	Alfred Jenkins RC	1.00	.45
❑	424	Paul Seymour	.20	.09
❑	425	Garo Yepremian	.50	.23
❑	426	Emmitt Thomas	.20	.09
❑	427	Dexter Bussey	.20	.09
❑	428	John Sanders	.20	.09
❑	429	Ed Too Tall Jones	2.00	.90
❑	430	Ron Yary	1.00	.45
❑	431	Frank Lewis	.50	.23
❑	432	Jerry Golsteyn	.20	.09
❑	433	Clarence Scott	.20	.09
❑	434	Pete Johnson RC	1.00	.45
❑	435	Charle Young	.50	.23
❑	436	Harold McLinton	.20	.09
❑	437	Noah Jackson	.20	.09
❑	438	Bruce Laird	.20	.09
❑	439	John Matuszak	.50	.23
❑	440	Nat Moore AP	.50	.23
❑	441	Leon Gray	.20	.09
❑	442	Jerome Barkum	.20	.09
❑	443	Steve Largent	12.00	5.50
❑	444	John Zook	.20	.09
❑	445	Preston Pearson	.50	.23
❑	446	Conrad Dobler	.50	.23
❑	447	Wilbur Summers	.20	.09
❑	448	Lou Piccone	.20	.09
❑	449	Ron Jaworski	1.00	.45
❑	450	Jack Ham AP	1.50	.70
❑	451	Mick Tingelhoff	.50	.23
❑	452	Clyde Powers	.20	.09
❑	453	John Cappelletti	1.00	.45
❑	454	Dick Ambrose	.20	.09
❑	455	Lemar Parrish	.20	.09
❑	456	Ron Saul	.20	.09
❑	457	Bob Parsons	.20	.09
❑	458	Glenn Doughty	.20	.09
❑	459	Don Woods	.20	.09
❑	460	Art Shell AP	1.00	.45
❑	461	Sam Hunt	.20	.09
❑	462	Lawrence Pillers	.20	.09
❑	463	Henry Childs	.20	.09
❑	464	Roger Wehrli	.20	.09
❑	465	Otis Armstrong	.50	.23
❑	466	Bob Baumhower RC	2.00	.90
❑	467	Ray Jarvis	.20	.09
❑	468	Guy Morriss	.20	.09
❑	469	Matt Blair	.50	.23
❑	470	Billy Joe DuPree	.50	.23
❑	471	Roland Hooks	.20	.09
❑	472	Joe Danelo	.20	.09
❑	473	Reggie Rucker	.50	.23
❑	474	Vern Holland	.20	.09
❑	475	Mel Blount	1.50	.70
❑	476	Eddie Brown	.20	.09
❑	477	Bo Rather	.20	.09
❑	478	Don McCauley	.20	.09
❑	479	Glen Walker	.20	.09
❑	480	Randy Gradishar AP	1.00	.45
❑	481	Dave Rowe	.20	.09
❑	482	Pat Leahy	.50	.23
❑	483	Mike Fuller	.20	.09
❑	484	David Lewis RC	.20	.09
❑	485	Steve Grogan	1.00	.45
❑	486	Mel Gray	.50	.23
❑	487	Eddie Payton RC	.50	.23
❑	488	Checklist 397-528	1.00	.25
❑	489	Stu Voigt	.20	.09
❑	490	Rolland Lawrence	.20	.09
❑	491	Nick Mike-Mayer	.20	.09
❑	492	Troy Archer	.20	.09
❑	493	Benny Malone	.20	.09
❑	494	Golden Richards	.50	.23
❑	495	Chris Hanburger	.20	.09
❑	496	Dwight Harrison	.20	.09
❑	497	Gary Fencik RC	1.00	.45
❑	498	Rich Saul	.20	.09
❑	499	Dan Fouts	4.00	1.80
❑	500	Franco Harris AP	4.00	1.80
❑	501	Atlanta Falcons TL	.75	.19
		Haskel Stanback		
		Alfred Jenkins		
		Claude Humphrey		
		Jeff Merrow		
		Rolland Lawrence		
		(checklist back)		
❑	502	Baltimore Colts TL	.75	.19
		Lydell Mitchell		
		Lydell Mitchell		
		Lyle Blackwood		
		Fred Cook		
		(checklist back)		
❑	503	Buffalo Bills TL	1.50	.35
		O.J. Simpson		
		Bob Chandler		
		Tony Greene		
		Sherman White		
		(checklist back)		
❑	504	Chicago Bears TL	2.00	.50
		Walter Payton		
		James Scott		
		Allan Ellis		
		Ron Rydalch		
		(checklist back)		
❑	505	Cincinnati Bengals TL	.75	.19
		Pete Johnson		
		Billy Brooks		
		Lemar Parrish		
		Reggie Williams		
		Gary Burley		
		(checklist back)		
❑	506	Cleveland Browns TL	.75	.19
		Greg Pruitt		
		Reggie Rucker		
		Thom Darden		
		Mack Mitchell		
		(checklist back)		
❑	507	Dallas Cowboys TL	2.50	.60
		Tony Dorsett		
		Drew Pearson		
		Cliff Harris		
		Harvey Martin		
		(checklist back)		
❑	508	Denver Broncos TL	1.00	.25
		Otis Armstrong		
		Haven Moses		
		Bill Thompson		
		Rick Upchurch		
		(checklist back)		
❑	509	Detroit Lions TL	.75	.19
		Horace King		

David Hill
James Hunter
Ken Sanders
(checklist back)

❑ 510 Green Bay Packers TL 1.00 .25
Barty Smith
Steve Odom
Steve Luke
Mike C. McCoy
Dave Pureifory
Dave Roller
(checklist back)

❑ 511 Houston Oilers TL .75 .19
Ronnie Coleman
Ken Burrough
Mike Reinfeldt
James Young
(checklist back)

❑ 512 Kansas City Chiefs TL .75 .19
Ed Podolak
Walter White
Gary Barbaro
Wilbur Young
(checklist back)

❑ 513 Los Angeles Rams TL .75 .19
Lawrence McCutcheon
Harold Jackson
Bill Simpson
Jack Youngblood
(checklist back)

❑ 514 Miami Dolphins TL 1.00 .25
Benny Malone
Nat Moore
Curtis Johnson
A.J. Duhe
(checklist back)

❑ 515 Minnesota Vikings TL .75 .19
Chuck Foreman
Sammie White
Bobby Bryant
Carl Eller
(checklist back)

❑ 516 New England Patriots TL .75 .19
Sam Cunningham
Darryl Stingley
Mike Haynes
Tony McGee
(checklist back)

❑ 517 New Orleans Saints TL .75 .19
Chuck Muncie
Don Herrmann
Chuck Crist
Elois Grooms
(checklist back)

❑ 518 New York Giants TL .75 .19
Bobby Hammond
Jimmy Robinson
Bill Bryant
John Mendenhall
(checklist back)

❑ 519 New York Jets TL .75 .19
Clark Gaines
Wesley Walker
Burgess Owens
Joe Klecko
(checklist back)

❑ 520 Oakland Raiders TL 1.00 .25
Mark Van Eeghen
Dave Casper
Jack Tatum
Neal Colzie
(checklist back)

❑ 521 Philadelphia Eagles TL .75 .19
Mike Hogan
Harold Carmichael
Herman Edwards
John Sanders
Lem Burnham
(checklist back)

❑ 522 Pittsburgh Steelers TL 1.00 .25
Franco Harris
Jim Smith
Mel Blount
Steve Furness
(checklist back)

❑ 523 St.Louis Cardinals TL .75 .19
Terry Metcalf
Mel Gray
Roger Wehrli
Mike Dawson
(checklist back)

❑ 524 San Diego Chargers TL 1.00 .25
Rickey Young
Charlie Joiner
Mike Fuller
Gary Johnson
(checklist back)

❑ 525 San Francisco 49ers TL .75 .19
Delvin Williams
Gene Washington
Mel Phillips
Dave Washington
Cleveland Elam
(checklist back)

❑ 526 Seattle Seahawks TL 1.50 .35
Sherman Smith
Steve Largent
Autry Beamon
Walter Packer
(checklist back)

❑ 527 Tampa Bay Bucs TL .75 .19
Morris Owens
Isaac Hagins
Mike Washington
Lee Roy Selmon
(checklist back)

❑ 528 Wash. Redskins TL 1.00 .25
Mike Thomas
Jean Fugett
Ken Houston
Dennis Johnson
(checklist back)

1979 Topps

	Nm-Mt	Ex-Mt
COMPLETE SET (528)	150.00	70.00
❑ 1 Passing Leaders Roger Staubach Terry Bradshaw	8.00	2.00
❑ 2 Receiving Leaders Rickey Young Steve Largent	1.00	.45
❑ 3 Rushing Leaders Walter Payton Earl Campbell	8.00	3.60
❑ 4 Scoring Leaders Frank Corral Pat Leahy	.20	.09
❑ 5 Interception Leaders Willie Buchanon Ken Stone Thom Darden	.20	.09
❑ 6 Punting Leaders Tom Skladany Pat McInally	.20	.09
❑ 7 Johnny Perkins	.20	.09
❑ 8 Charles Phillips	.20	.09
❑ 9 Derrel Luce	.20	.09
❑ 10 John Riggins	1.25	.55
❑ 11 Chester Marcol	.20	.09
❑ 12 Bernard Jackson	.20	.09
❑ 13 Dave Logan	.20	.09
❑ 14 Bo Harris	.20	.09
❑ 15 Alan Page	1.00	.45
❑ 16 John Smith	.20	.09
❑ 17 Dwight McDonald	.20	.09
❑ 18 John Cappelletti	.50	.23
❑ 19 Pittsburgh Steelers TL Franco Harris Larry Anderson Tony Dungy L.C. Greenwood (checklist back)	1.00	.45
❑ 20 Bill Bergey AP	.50	.23
❑ 21 Jerome Barkum	.20	.09
❑ 22 Larry Csonka	2.50	1.10
❑ 23 Joe Ferguson	.50	.23
❑ 24 Ed Too Tall Jones	1.25	.55
❑ 25 Dave Jennings	.50	.23
❑ 26 Horace King	.20	.09
❑ 27 Steve Little	.50	.23
❑ 28 Morris Bradshaw	.20	.09
❑ 29 Joe Ehrmann	.20	.09
❑ 30 Ahmad Rashad AP	1.00	.45
❑ 31 Joe Lavender	.20	.09
❑ 32 Dan Neal	.20	.09
❑ 33 Johnny Evans	.20	.09
❑ 34 Pete Johnson	.50	.23
❑ 35 Mike Haynes AP	1.00	.45
❑ 36 Tim Mazzetti	.20	.09
❑ 37 Mike Barber RC	.20	.09
❑ 38 San Francisco 49ers TL O.J. Simpson Freddie Solomon Chuck Crist Cedrick Hardman (checklist back)	1.50	.70
❑ 39 Bill Gregory	.20	.09
❑ 40 Randy Gradishar AP	1.00	.45
❑ 41 Richard Todd	.50	.23
❑ 42 Henry Marshall	.20	.09
❑ 43 John Hill	.20	.09
❑ 44 Sidney Thornton	.20	.09
❑ 45 Ron Jessie	.20	.09
❑ 46 Bob Baumhower	.50	.23
❑ 47 Johnnie Gray	.20	.09
❑ 48 Doug Williams RC	6.00	2.70
❑ 49 Don McCauley	.20	.09
❑ 50 Ray Guy AP	.50	.23
❑ 51 Bob Klein	.20	.09
❑ 52 Golden Richards	.20	.09
❑ 53 Mark Miller	.20	.09
❑ 54 John Sanders	.20	.09
❑ 55 Gary Burley	.20	.09
❑ 56 Steve Nelson	.20	.09
❑ 57 Buffalo Bills TL Terry Miller Frank Lewis Mario Clark Lucius Sanford (checklist back)	.75	.35
❑ 58 Bobby Bryant	.20	.09
❑ 59 Rick Kane	.20	.09
❑ 60 Larry Little	1.00	.45
❑ 61 Ted Fritsch Jr.	.20	.09
❑ 62 Larry Mallory	.20	.09
❑ 63 Marvin Powell	.20	.09
❑ 64 Jim Hart	1.00	.45
❑ 65 Joe Greene AP	1.50	.70
❑ 66 Walter White	.20	.09
❑ 67 Gregg Bingham	.20	.09
❑ 68 Errol Mann	.20	.09
❑ 69 Bruce Laird	.20	.09
❑ 70 Drew Pearson	1.00	.45
❑ 71 Steve Bartkowski	1.00	.45
❑ 72 Ted Albrecht	.20	.09

❑ 73 Charlie Hall .20 .09
❑ 74 Pat McInally .20 .09
❑ 75 Al(Bubba) Baker AP RC 1.00 .45
❑ 76 New England Pats TL .75 .35
Sam Cunningham
Stanley Morgan
Mike Haynes
Tony McGee
(checklist back)
❑ 77 Steve DeBerg RC 2.00 .90
❑ 78 John Yarno .20 .09
❑ 79 Stu Voigt .20 .09
❑ 80 Frank Corral AP .20 .09
❑ 81 Troy Archer .20 .09
❑ 82 Bruce Harper .20 .09
❑ 83 Tom Jackson 1.50 .70
❑ 84 Larry Brown .50 .23
❑ 85 Wilbert Montgomery AP RC 1.00 .45
❑ 86 Butch Johnson .50 .23
❑ 87 Mike Kadish .20 .09
❑ 88 Ralph Perretta .20 .09
❑ 89 David Lee .20 .09
❑ 90 Mark Van Eeghen .50 .23
❑ 91 John McDaniel .20 .09
❑ 92 Gary Fencik .50 .23
❑ 93 Mack Mitchell .20 .09
❑ 94 Cincinnati Bengals TL 1.00 .45
Pete Johnson
Isaac Curtis
Dick Jauron
Ross Browner
(checklist back)
❑ 95 Steve Grogan 1.00 .45
❑ 96 Garo Yepremian .50 .23
❑ 97 Barty Smith .20 .09
❑ 98 Frank Reed .20 .09
❑ 99 Jim Clack .20 .09
❑ 100 Chuck Foreman .50 .23
❑ 101 Joe Klecko 1.00 .45
❑ 102 Pat Tilley .50 .23
❑ 103 Conrad Dobler .50 .23
❑ 104 Craig Colquitt .20 .09
❑ 105 Dan Pastorini .50 .23
❑ 106 Rod Perry AP .20 .09
❑ 107 Nick Mike-Mayer .20 .09
❑ 108 John Matuszak .50 .23
❑ 109 David Taylor .20 .09
❑ 110 Billy Joe DuPree AP .50 .23
❑ 111 Harold McLinton .20 .09
❑ 112 Virgil Livers .20 .09
❑ 113 Cleveland Browns TL .75 .35
Greg Pruitt
Reggie Rucker
Thom Darden
Mack Mitchell
(checklist back)
❑ 114 Checklist 1-132 1.00 .25
❑ 115 Ken Anderson 1.00 .45
❑ 116 Bill Lenkaitis .20 .09
❑ 117 Bucky Dilts .20 .09
❑ 118 Tony Greene .20 .09
❑ 119 Bobby Hammond .20 .09
❑ 120 Nat Moore .50 .23
❑ 121 Pat Leahy AP .50 .23
❑ 122 James Harris .50 .23
❑ 123 Lee Roy Selmon 1.25 .55
❑ 124 Bennie Cunningham .50 .23
❑ 125 Matt Blair AP .50 .23
❑ 126 Jim Allen .20 .09
❑ 127 Alfred Jenkins .50 .23
❑ 128 Arthur Whittington .20 .09
❑ 129 Norm Thompson .20 .09
❑ 130 Pat Haden 1.00 .45
❑ 131 Freddie Solomon .20 .09
❑ 132 Chicago Bears TL 2.00 .90
Walter Payton
James Scott
Gary Fencik
Alan Page
(checklist back)
❑ 133 Mark Moseley .20 .09
❑ 134 Cleo Miller .20 .09
❑ 135 Ross Browner RC .50 .23
❑ 136 Don Calhoun .20 .09
❑ 137 David Whitehurst .20 .09
❑ 138 Terry Beeson .20 .09
❑ 139 Ken Stone .20 .09
❑ 140 Brad Van Pelt AP .20 .09
❑ 141 Wesley Walker AP 1.00 .45
❑ 142 Jan Stenerud 1.00 .45
❑ 143 Henry Childs .20 .09
❑ 144 Otis Armstrong 1.00 .45
❑ 145 Dwight White .50 .23
❑ 146 Steve Wilson .20 .09
❑ 147 Tom Skladany AP RC .20 .09
❑ 148 Lou Piccone .20 .09
❑ 149 Monte Johnson .20 .09
❑ 150 Joe Washington .50 .23
❑ 151 Philadelphia Eagles TL .75 .35
Wilbert Montgomery
Harold Carmichael
Herman Edwards
Dennis Harrison
(checklist back)
❑ 152 Fred Dean .20 .09
❑ 153 Rolland Lawrence .20 .09
❑ 154 Brian Baschnagel .20 .09
❑ 155 Joe Theismann 2.00 .90
❑ 156 Marvin Cobb .20 .09
❑ 157 Dick Ambrose .20 .09
❑ 158 Mike Patrick .20 .09
❑ 159 Gary Shirk .20 .09
❑ 160 Tony Dorsett 12.00 5.50
❑ 161 Greg Buttle .20 .09
❑ 162 A.J. Duhe .50 .23
❑ 163 Mick Tingelhoff .50 .23
❑ 164 Ken Burrough .50 .23
❑ 165 Mike Wagner .20 .09
❑ 166 AFC Championship 1.00 .45
Steelers 34;
Oilers 5
(Franco Harris)
❑ 167 NFC Championship .50 .23
Cowboys 28;
Rams 0
(line of scrimmage)
❑ 168 Super Bowl XIII 1.25 .55
Steelers 35;
Cowboys 31
(Franco Harris)
❑ 169 Oakland Raiders TL 1.00 .45
Mark Van Eeghen
Dave Casper
Charles Phillips
Ted Hendricks
(checklist back)
❑ 170 O.J. Simpson 4.00 1.80
❑ 171 Doug Nettles .20 .09
❑ 172 Dan Dierdorf AP 1.00 .45
❑ 173 Dave Beverly .20 .09
❑ 174 Jim Zorn 1.00 .45
❑ 175 Mike Thomas .20 .09
❑ 176 John Outlaw .20 .09
❑ 177 Jim Turner .20 .09
❑ 178 Freddie Scott .20 .09
❑ 179 Mike Phipps .50 .23
❑ 180 Jack Youngblood AP 1.00 .45
❑ 181 Sam Hunt .20 .09
❑ 182 Tony Hill RC 1.00 .45
❑ 183 Gary Barbaro .20 .09
❑ 184 Archie Griffin .50 .23
❑ 185 Jerry Sherk .20 .09
❑ 186 Bobby Jackson .20 .09
❑ 187 Don Woods .20 .09
❑ 188 New York Giants TL .75 .35
Doug Kotar
Jimmy Robinson
Terry Jackson
George Martin
(checklist back)
❑ 189 Raymond Chester .20 .09
❑ 190 Joe DeLamielleure AP 1.00 .45
❑ 191 Tony Galbreath .50 .23
❑ 192 Robert Brazile AP .50 .23
❑ 193 Neil O'Donoghue .20 .09
❑ 194 Mike Webster AP 1.00 .45
❑ 195 Ed Simonini .20 .09
❑ 196 Benny Malone .20 .09
❑ 197 Tom Wittum .20 .09
❑ 198 Steve Largent AP 8.00 3.60
❑ 199 Tommy Hart .20 .09
❑ 200 Fran Tarkenton 3.00 1.35
❑ 201 Leon Gray AP .20 .09
❑ 202 Leroy Harris .20 .09
❑ 203 Eric Williams .20 .09
❑ 204 Thom Darden AP .20 .09
❑ 205 Ken Riley .50 .23
❑ 206 Clark Gaines .20 .09
❑ 207 Kansas City Chiefs TL .75 .35
Tony Reed
Tony Reed
Tim Gray
Art Still
(checklist back)
❑ 208 Joe Danelo .20 .09
❑ 209 Glen Walker .20 .09
❑ 210 Art Shell 1.00 .45
❑ 211 Jon Keyworth .20 .09
❑ 212 Herman Edwards .20 .09
❑ 213 John Fitzgerald .20 .09
❑ 214 Jim Smith .50 .23
❑ 215 Coy Bacon .50 .23
❑ 216 Dennis Johnson RBK RC .20 .09
❑ 217 John Jefferson RC 3.00 1.35
(Charlie Joiner
in background)
❑ 218 Gary Weaver .20 .09
❑ 219 Tom Blanchard .20 .09
❑ 220 Bert Jones 1.00 .45
❑ 221 Stanley Morgan 1.00 .45
❑ 222 James Hunter .20 .09
❑ 223 Jim O'Bradovich .20 .09
❑ 224 Carl Mauck .20 .09
❑ 225 Chris Bahr .20 .09
❑ 226 New York Jets TL .75 .35
Kevin Long
Wesley Walker
Bobby Jackson
Burgess Owens
Joe Klecko
(checklist back)
❑ 227 Roland Harper .20 .09
❑ 228 Randy Dean .20 .09
❑ 229 Bob Jackson .20 .09
❑ 230 Sammie White .50 .23
❑ 231 Mike Dawson .20 .09
❑ 232 Checklist 133-264 1.00 .25
❑ 233 Ken MacAfee RC .20 .09
❑ 234 Jon Kolb AP .20 .09
❑ 235 Willie Hall .20 .09
❑ 236 Ron Saul AP .20 .09
❑ 237 Haskel Stanback .20 .09
❑ 238 Zenon Andrusyshyn .20 .09
❑ 239 Norris Thomas .20 .09
❑ 240 Rick Upchurch .50 .23
❑ 241 Robert Pratt .20 .09
❑ 242 Julius Adams .20 .09
❑ 243 Rich McGeorge .20 .09
❑ 244 Seattle Seahawks TL 1.25 .55
Sherman Smith
Steve Largent
Cornell Webster
Bill Gregory
(checklist back)
❑ 245 Blair Bush RC .20 .09
❑ 246 Billy Johnson .50 .23
❑ 247 Randy Rasmussen .20 .09
❑ 248 Brian Kelley .20 .09
❑ 249 Mike Pruitt .50 .23
❑ 250 Harold Carmichael AP 1.00 .45
❑ 251 Mike Hartenstine .20 .09
❑ 252 Robert Newhouse .50 .23
❑ 253 Gary Danielson RC 1.00 .45

❑ 254 Mike Fuller .20 .09
❑ 255 L.C. Greenwood AP 1.00 .45
❑ 256 Lemar Parrish .20 .09
❑ 257 Ike Harris .20 .09
❑ 258 Ricky Bell RC 1.00 .45
❑ 259 Willie Parker .20 .09
❑ 260 Gene Upshaw 1.00 .45
❑ 261 Glenn Doughty .20 .09
❑ 262 Steve Zabel .20 .09
❑ 263 Atlanta Falcons TL .75 .35
Bubba Bean
Wallace Francis
Rolland Lawrence
Greg Brezina
(checklist back)
❑ 264 Ray Wersching .20 .09
❑ 265 Lawrence McCutcheon .50 .23
❑ 266 Willie Buchanon AP .20 .09
❑ 267 Matt Robinson .20 .09
❑ 268 Reggie Rucker .50 .23
❑ 269 Doug Van Horn .20 .09
❑ 270 Lydell Mitchell .50 .23
❑ 271 Vern Holland .20 .09
❑ 272 Eason Ramson .20 .09
❑ 273 Steve Towle .20 .09
❑ 274 Jim Marshall 1.00 .45
❑ 275 Mel Blount 1.25 .55
❑ 276 Bob Kuziel .20 .09
❑ 277 James Scott .20 .09
❑ 278 Tony Reed .20 .09
❑ 279 Dave Green .20 .09
❑ 280 Toni Linhart .20 .09
❑ 281 Andy Johnson .20 .09
❑ 282 Los Angeles Rams TL .75 .35
Cullen Bryant
Willie Miller
Rod Perry
Pat Thomas
Larry Brooks
(checklist back)
❑ 283 Phil Villapiano .50 .23
❑ 284 Dexter Bussey .20 .09
❑ 285 Craig Morton 1.00 .45
❑ 286 Guy Morriss .20 .09
❑ 287 Lawrence Pillers .20 .09
❑ 288 Gerald Irons .20 .09
❑ 289 Scott Perry .20 .09
❑ 290 Randy White AP 2.00 .90
❑ 291 Jack Gregory .20 .09
❑ 292 Bob Chandler .20 .09
❑ 293 Rich Szaro .20 .09
❑ 294 Sherman Smith .20 .09
❑ 295 Tom Banks AP .20 .09
❑ 296 Revie Sorey AP .20 .09
❑ 297 Ricky Thompson .20 .09
❑ 298 Ron Yary 1.00 .45
❑ 299 Lyle Blackwood .20 .09
❑ 300 Franco Harris 2.50 1.10
❑ 301 Houston Oilers TL 3.00 1.35
Earl Campbell
Ken Burrough
Willie Alexander
Elvin Bethea
(checklist back)
❑ 302 Scott Bull .20 .09
❑ 303 Dewey Selmon .50 .23
❑ 304 Jack Rudnay .20 .09
❑ 305 Fred Biletnikoff 2.00 .90
❑ 306 Jeff West .20 .09
❑ 307 Shafer Suggs .20 .09
❑ 308 Ozzie Newsome RC 12.00 5.50
❑ 309 Boobie Clark .20 .09
❑ 310 James Lofton RC 12.00 5.50
❑ 311 Joe Pisarcik .20 .09
❑ 312 Bill Simpson AP .20 .09
❑ 313 Haven Moses .50 .23
❑ 314 Jim Merlo .20 .09
❑ 315 Preston Pearson .50 .23
❑ 316 Larry Tearry .20 .09
❑ 317 Tom Dempsey .20 .09
❑ 318 Greg Latta .20 .09
❑ 319 Wash. Redskins TL 1.50 .70
John Riggins
John McDaniel
Jake Scott
Coy Bacon
(checklist back)
❑ 320 Jack Ham AP 1.25 .55
❑ 321 Harold Jackson .50 .23
❑ 322 George Roberts .20 .09
❑ 323 Ron Jaworski 1.00 .45
❑ 324 Jim Otis .20 .09
❑ 325 Roger Carr .50 .23
❑ 326 Jack Tatum .50 .23
❑ 327 Derrick Gaffney .20 .09
❑ 328 Reggie Williams 1.00 .45
❑ 329 Doug Dieken .20 .09
❑ 330 Efren Herrera .20 .09
❑ 331 Earl Campbell RB 6.00 2.70
Most Yards
Rushing& Rookie
❑ 332 Tony Galbreath RB .20 .09
Most Receptions&
Running Back& Game
❑ 333 Bruce Harper RB .20 .09
Most Combined Kick
Return Yards& Season
❑ 334 John James RB .20 .09
Most Punts& Season
❑ 335 Walter Payton RB 4.00 1.80
Most Combined
Attempts& Season
❑ 336 Rickey Young RB .20 .09
Most Receptions&
Running Back& Season
❑ 337 Jeff Van Note .50 .23
❑ 338 San Diego Chargers TL 1.00 .45
Lydell Mitchell
John Jefferson
Mike Fuller
Fred Dean
(checklist back)
❑ 339 Stan Walters AP RC .20 .09
❑ 340 Louis Wright AP .50 .23
❑ 341 Horace Ivory .20 .09
❑ 342 Andre Tillman .20 .09
❑ 343 Greg Coleman RC .20 .09
❑ 344 Doug English AP RC 1.00 .45
❑ 345 Ted Hendricks 1.00 .45
❑ 346 Rich Saul .20 .09
❑ 347 Mel Gray .50 .23
❑ 348 Toni Fritsch .20 .09
❑ 349 Cornell Webster .20 .09
❑ 350 Ken Houston 1.00 .45
❑ 351 Ron Johnson DB RC .50 .23
❑ 352 Doug Kotar .20 .09
❑ 353 Brian Sipe 1.00 .45
❑ 354 Billy Brooks .20 .09
❑ 355 John Dutton .50 .23
❑ 356 Don Goode .20 .09
❑ 357 Detroit Lions TL .75 .35
Dexter Bussey
David Hill
Jim Allen
Al(Bubba) Baker
(checklist back)
❑ 358 Reuben Gant .20 .09
❑ 359 Bob Parsons .20 .09
❑ 360 Cliff Harris AP 1.00 .45
❑ 361 Raymond Clayborn .50 .23
❑ 362 Scott Dierking .20 .09
❑ 363 Bill Bryan .20 .09
❑ 364 Mike Livingston .20 .09
❑ 365 Otis Sistrunk .50 .23
❑ 366 Charle Young .50 .23
❑ 367 Keith Wortman .20 .09
❑ 368 Checklist 265-396 1.00 .25
❑ 369 Mike Michel .20 .09
❑ 370 Delvin Williams AP .20 .09
❑ 371 Steve Furness .50 .23
❑ 372 Emery Moorehead .20 .09
❑ 373 Clarence Scott .20 .09
❑ 374 Rufus Mayes .20 .09
❑ 375 Chris Hanburger .20 .09
❑ 376 Baltimore Colts TL .75 .35
Joe Washington
Roger Carr
Norm Thompson
John Dutton
(checklist back)
❑ 377 Bob Avellini .50 .23
❑ 378 Jeff Siemon .20 .09
❑ 379 Roland Hooks .20 .09
❑ 380 Russ Francis .50 .23
❑ 381 Roger Wehrli .20 .09
❑ 382 Joe Fields .20 .09
❑ 383 Archie Manning 1.00 .45
❑ 384 Rob Lytle .20 .09
❑ 385 Thomas Henderson .50 .23
❑ 386 Morris Owens .20 .09
❑ 387 Dan Fouts 3.00 1.35
❑ 388 Chuck Crist .20 .09
❑ 389 Ed O'Neil .20 .09
❑ 390 Earl Campbell AP RC 30.00 13.50
❑ 391 Randy Grossman .20 .09
❑ 392 Monte Jackson .20 .09
❑ 393 John Mendenhall .20 .09
❑ 394 Miami Dolphins TL 1.00 .45
Delvin Williams
Duriel Harris
Tim Foley
Vern Den Herder
(checklist back)
❑ 395 Isaac Curtis .50 .23
❑ 396 Mike Bragg .20 .09
❑ 397 Doug Plank .20 .09
❑ 398 Mike Barnes .20 .09
❑ 399 Calvin Hill .50 .23
❑ 400 Roger Staubach AP 10.00 4.50
❑ 401 Doug Beaudoin .20 .09
❑ 402 Chuck Ramsey .20 .09
❑ 403 Mike Hogan .20 .09
❑ 404 Mario Clark .20 .09
❑ 405 Riley Odoms .20 .09
❑ 406 Carl Eller 1.00 .45
❑ 407 Green Bay Packers TL 1.50 .70
Terdell Middleton
James Lofton
Willie Buchanon
Ezra Johnson
(checklist back)
❑ 408 Mark Arneson .20 .09
❑ 409 Vince Ferragamo RC 1.00 .45
❑ 410 Cleveland Elam .20 .09
❑ 411 Donnie Shell RC 4.00 1.80
❑ 412 Ray Rhodes 1.00 .45
❑ 413 Don Cockroft .20 .09
❑ 414 Don Bass .50 .23
❑ 415 Cliff Branch 1.00 .45
❑ 416 Diron Talbert .20 .09
❑ 417 Tom Hicks .20 .09
❑ 418 Roosevelt Leaks .20 .09
❑ 419 Charlie Joiner 1.00 .45
❑ 420 Lyle Alzado AP 1.00 .45
❑ 421 Sam Cunningham .50 .23
❑ 422 Larry Keller .20 .09
❑ 423 Jim Mitchell .20 .09
❑ 424 Randy Logan .20 .09
❑ 425 Jim Langer 1.00 .45
❑ 426 Gary Green .20 .09
❑ 427 Luther Blue .20 .09
❑ 428 Dennis Johnson .20 .09
❑ 429 Danny White 1.00 .45
❑ 430 Roy Gerela .20 .09
❑ 431 Jimmy Robinson .20 .09
❑ 432 Minnesota Vikings TL .75 .35
Chuck Foreman
Ahmad Rashad
Bobby Bryant
Mark Mullaney
(checklist back)
❑ 433 Oliver Davis .20 .09
❑ 434 Lenvil Elliott .20 .09

❑ 435 Willie Miller RC .20 .09
❑ 436 Brad Dusek .20 .09
❑ 437 Bob Thomas .20 .09
❑ 438 Ken Mendenhall .20 .09
❑ 439 Clarence Davis .20 .09
❑ 440 Bob Griese 2.50 1.10
❑ 441 Tony McGee .20 .09
❑ 442 Ed Taylor .20 .09
❑ 443 Ron Howard .20 .09
❑ 444 Wayne Morris .20 .09
❑ 445 Charlie Waters .50 .23
❑ 446 Rick Danmeier .20 .09
❑ 447 Paul Naumoff .20 .09
❑ 448 Keith Krepfle .20 .09
❑ 449 Rusty Jackson .20 .09
❑ 450 John Stallworth 4.00 1.80
❑ 451 New Orleans Saints TL .75 .35
Tony Galbreath
Henry Childs
Tom Myers
Elex Price
(checklist back)
❑ 452 Ron Mikolajczyk .20 .09
❑ 453 Fred Dryer 1.00 .45
❑ 454 Jim LeClair .20 .09
❑ 455 Greg Pruitt .50 .23
❑ 456 Jake Scott .20 .09
❑ 457 Steve Schubert .20 .09
❑ 458 George Kunz .20 .09
❑ 459 Mike Williams .20 .09
❑ 460 Dave Casper AP 1.00 .45
❑ 461 Sam Adams .20 .09
❑ 462 Abdul Salaam .20 .09
❑ 463 Terdell Middleton .50 .23
❑ 464 Mike Wood .20 .09
❑ 465 Bill Thompson AP .20 .09
❑ 466 Larry Gordon .20 .09
❑ 467 Benny Ricardo .20 .09
❑ 468 Reggie McKenzie .50 .23
❑ 469 Dallas Cowboys TL 1.50 .70
Tony Dorsett
Tony Hill
Benny Barnes
Harvey Martin
Randy White
(checklist back)
❑ 470 Rickey Young .50 .23
❑ 471 Charlie Smith .20 .09
❑ 472 Al Dixon .20 .09
❑ 473 Tom DeLeone .20 .09
❑ 474 Louis Breeden .50 .23
❑ 475 Jack Lambert 2.00 .90
❑ 476 Terry Hermeling .20 .09
❑ 477 J.K. McKay .20 .09
❑ 478 Stan White .20 .09
❑ 479 Terry Nelson .20 .09
❑ 480 Walter Payton AP 20.00 9.00
❑ 481 Dave Dalby .20 .09
❑ 482 Burgess Owens .20 .09
❑ 483 Rolf Benirschke .20 .09
❑ 484 Jack Dolbin .20 .09
❑ 485 John Hannah AP 1.00 .45
❑ 486 Checklist 397-528 1.00 .25
❑ 487 Greg Landry .50 .23
❑ 488 St. Louis Cardinals TL .75 .35
Jim Otis
Pat Tilley
Ken Stone
Mike Dawson
(checklist back)
❑ 489 Paul Krause 1.00 .45
❑ 490 John James .20 .09
❑ 491 Merv Krakau .20 .09
❑ 492 Dan Doornink .20 .09
❑ 493 Curtis Johnson .20 .09
❑ 494 Rafael Septien .20 .09
❑ 495 Jean Fugett .20 .09
❑ 496 Frank LeMaster .20 .09
❑ 497 Allan Ellis .20 .09
❑ 498 Billy Waddy RC .50 .23
❑ 499 Hank Bauer .20 .09
❑ 500 Terry Bradshaw AP UER 10.00 4.50
(Stat headers on back
are for a runner)
❑ 501 Larry McCarren .20 .09
❑ 502 Fred Cook .20 .09
❑ 503 Chuck Muncie .50 .23
❑ 504 Herman Weaver .20 .09
❑ 505 Eddie Edwards .20 .09
❑ 506 Tony Peters .20 .09
❑ 507 Denver Broncos TL .75 .35
Lonnie Perrin
Riley Odoms
Steve Foley
Bernard Jackson
Lyle Alzado
(checklist back)
❑ 508 Jimbo Elrod .20 .09
❑ 509 David Hill .20 .09
❑ 510 Harvey Martin .50 .23
❑ 511 Terry Miller .50 .23
❑ 512 June Jones RC .50 .23
❑ 513 Randy Cross 1.00 .45
❑ 514 Duriel Harris .20 .09
❑ 515 Harry Carson 1.00 .45
❑ 516 Tim Fox .20 .09
❑ 517 John Zook .20 .09
❑ 518 Bob Tucker .20 .09
❑ 519 Kevin Long RC .20 .09
❑ 520 Ken Stabler 6.00 2.70
❑ 521 John Bunting .50 .23
❑ 522 Rocky Bleier 1.25 .55
❑ 523 Noah Jackson .20 .09
❑ 524 Cliff Parsley .20 .09
❑ 525 Louie Kelcher AP .50 .23
❑ 526 Tampa Bay Bucs TL .75 .35
Ricky Bell
Morris Owens
Cedric Brown
Lee Roy Selmon
(checklist back)
❑ 527 Bob Brudzinski RC .20 .09
❑ 528 Danny Buggs .20 .09

1980 Topps

	Nm-Mt	Ex-Mt
COMPLETE SET (528)	60.00	27.00

❑ 1 Ottis Anderson RB 1.00 .45
Most Yardage
Rushing: Rookie
❑ 2 Harold Carmichael RB 1.00 .45
Most Consec. Games
One or More Receptions
❑ 3 Dan Fouts RB 1.00 .45
Most Yardage
Passing: Season
❑ 4 Paul Krause RB .50 .23
Most Interceptions
Lifetime
❑ 5 Rick Upchurch RB .50 .23
Most Punt Return
Yards: Lifetime
❑ 6 Garo Yepremian RB .15 .07
Most Consecutive
Field Goals
❑ 7 Harold Jackson .50 .23
❑ 8 Mike Williams .15 .07
❑ 9 Calvin Hill .50 .23
❑ 10 Jack Ham AP 1.00 .45
❑ 11 Dan Melville .15 .07
❑ 12 Matt Robinson .15 .07
❑ 13 Billy Campfield .15 .07
❑ 14 Phil Tabor .15 .07
❑ 15 Randy Hughes UER .15 .07
(Cowboys didn't play
in SB VII)
❑ 16 Andre Tillman .15 .07
❑ 17 Isaac Curtis .50 .23
❑ 18 Charley Hannah .15 .07
❑ 19 Wash. Redskins TL 1.00 .45
John Riggins
Danny Buggs
Joe Lavender
Coy Bacon
(checklist back)
❑ 20 Jim Zorn .50 .23
❑ 21 Brian Baschnagel .15 .07
❑ 22 Jon Keyworth .15 .07
❑ 23 Phil Villapiano .15 .07
❑ 24 Richard Osborne .15 .07
❑ 25 Rich Saul AP .15 .07
❑ 26 Doug Beaudoin .15 .07
❑ 27 Cleveland Elam .15 .07
❑ 28 Charlie Joiner 1.00 .45
❑ 29 Dick Ambrose .15 .07
❑ 30 Mike Reinfeldt AP RC .15 .07
❑ 31 Matt Bahr RC 1.00 .45
❑ 32 Keith Krepfle .15 .07
❑ 33 Herb Scott .15 .07
❑ 34 Doug Kotar .15 .07
❑ 35 Bob Griese 1.50 .70
❑ 36 Jerry Butler RC .15 .07
❑ 37 Rolland Lawrence .15 .07
❑ 38 Gary Weaver .15 .07
❑ 39 Kansas City Chiefs TL .50 .23
Ted McKnight
J.T. Smith
Gary Barbaro
Art Still
(checklist back)
❑ 40 Chuck Muncie .50 .23
❑ 41 Mike Hartenstine .15 .07
❑ 42 Sammie White .50 .23
❑ 43 Ken Clark .15 .07
❑ 44 Clarence Harmon .15 .07
❑ 45 Bert Jones 1.00 .45
❑ 46 Mike Washington .15 .07
❑ 47 Joe Fields .15 .07
❑ 48 Mike Wood .15 .07
❑ 49 Oliver Davis .15 .07
❑ 50 Stan Walters AP .15 .07
❑ 51 Riley Odoms .15 .07
❑ 52 Steve Pisarkiewicz .15 .07
❑ 53 Tony Hill 1.00 .45
❑ 54 Scott Perry .15 .07
❑ 55 George Martin RC .15 .07
❑ 56 George Roberts .15 .07
❑ 57 Seattle Seahawks TL 1.00 .45
Sherman Smith
Steve Largent
Dave Brown
Manu Tuiasosopo
(checklist back)
❑ 58 Billy Johnson .50 .23
❑ 59 Reuben Gant .15 .07
❑ 60 Dennis Harrah AP RC .15 .07
❑ 61 Rocky Bleier 1.00 .45
❑ 62 Sam Hunt .15 .07
❑ 63 Allan Ellis .15 .07
❑ 64 Ricky Thompson .15 .07
❑ 65 Ken Stabler 4.00 1.80
❑ 66 Dexter Bussey .15 .07
❑ 67 Ken Mendenhall .15 .07
❑ 68 Woodrow Lowe .15 .07
❑ 69 Thom Darden .15 .07
❑ 70 Randy White AP 1.50 .70

❑ 71 Ken MacAfee .15 .07
❑ 72 Ron Jaworski 1.00 .45
❑ 73 William Andrews RC 1.00 .45
❑ 74 Jimmy Robinson .15 .07
❑ 75 Roger Wehrli AP .15 .07
❑ 76 Miami Dolphins TL 1.00 .45
Larry Csonka
Nat Moore
Neal Colzie
Gerald Small
Vern Den Herder
(checklist back)
❑ 77 Jack Rudnay .15 .07
❑ 78 James Lofton 2.00 .90
❑ 79 Robert Brazile .50 .23
❑ 80 Russ Francis .50 .23
❑ 81 Ricky Bell 1.00 .45
❑ 82 Bob Avellini .50 .23
❑ 83 Bobby Jackson .15 .07
❑ 84 Mike Bragg .15 .07
❑ 85 Cliff Branch 1.00 .45
❑ 86 Blair Bush .15 .07
❑ 87 Sherman Smith .15 .07
❑ 88 Glen Edwards .15 .07
❑ 89 Don Cockroft .15 .07
❑ 90 Louis Wright AP .50 .23
❑ 91 Randy Grossman .15 .07
❑ 92 Carl Hairston RC 1.00 .45
❑ 93 Archie Manning 1.00 .45
❑ 94 New York Giants TL .50 .23
Billy Taylor
Earnest Gray
George Martin
(checklist back)
❑ 95 Preston Pearson .50 .23
❑ 96 Rusty Chambers .15 .07
❑ 97 Greg Coleman .15 .07
❑ 98 Charle Young .15 .07
❑ 99 Matt Cavanaugh RC .50 .23
❑ 100 Jesse Baker .15 .07
❑ 101 Doug Plank .15 .07
❑ 102 Checklist 1-132 .75 .19
❑ 103 Luther Bradley RC .15 .07
❑ 104 Bob Kuziel .15 .07
❑ 105 Craig Morton .50 .23
❑ 106 Sherman White .15 .07
❑ 107 Jim Breech RC .50 .23
❑ 108 Hank Bauer .15 .07
❑ 109 Tom Blanchard .15 .07
❑ 110 Ozzie Newsome AP 2.00 .90
❑ 111 Steve Furness .15 .07
❑ 112 Frank LeMaster .15 .07
❑ 113 Dallas Cowboys TL 1.00 .45
Tony Dorsett
Tony Hill
Harvey Martin
(checklist back)
❑ 114 Doug Van Horn .15 .07
❑ 115 Delvin Williams .15 .07
❑ 116 Lyle Blackwood .15 .07
❑ 117 Derrick Gaffney .15 .07
❑ 118 Cornell Webster .15 .07
❑ 119 Sam Cunningham .50 .23
❑ 120 Jim Youngblood AP .50 .23
❑ 121 Bob Thomas .15 .07
❑ 122 Jack Thompson RC .50 .23
❑ 123 Randy Cross 1.00 .45
❑ 124 Karl Lorch RC .15 .07
❑ 125 Mel Gray .15 .07
❑ 126 John James .15 .07
❑ 127 Terdell Middleton .15 .07
❑ 128 Leroy Jones .15 .07
❑ 129 Tom DeLeone .15 .07
❑ 130 John Stallworth AP 1.50 .70
❑ 131 Jimmie Giles RC .50 .23
❑ 132 Philadelphia Eagles TL 1.00 .45
Wilbert Montgomery
Harold Carmichael
Brenard Wilson
Carl Hairston
(checklist back)
❑ 133 Gary Green .15 .07
❑ 134 John Dutton .50 .23
❑ 135 Harry Carson AP 1.00 .45
❑ 136 Bob Kuechenberg .50 .23
❑ 137 Ike Harris .15 .07
❑ 138 Tommy Kramer RC 1.00 .45
❑ 139 Sam Adams .15 .07
❑ 140 Doug English AP .50 .23
❑ 141 Steve Schubert .15 .07
❑ 142 Rusty Jackson .15 .07
❑ 143 Reese McCall .15 .07
❑ 144 Scott Dierking .15 .07
❑ 145 Ken Houston AP 1.00 .45
❑ 146 Bob Martin .15 .07
❑ 147 Sam McCullum .15 .07
❑ 148 Tom Banks .15 .07
❑ 149 Willie Buchanon .15 .07
❑ 150 Greg Pruitt .50 .23
❑ 151 Denver Broncos TL 1.00 .45
Otis Armstrong
Rick Upchurch
Steve Foley
Brison Manor
(checklist back)
❑ 152 Don Smith RC .15 .07
❑ 153 Pete Johnson .50 .23
❑ 154 Charlie Smith .15 .07
❑ 155 Mel Blount 1.00 .45
❑ 156 John Mendenhall .15 .07
❑ 157 Danny White 1.00 .45
❑ 158 Jimmy Cefalo RC .50 .23
❑ 159 Richard Bishop AP .15 .07
❑ 160 Walter Payton AP 12.00 5.50
❑ 161 Dave Dalby .15 .07
❑ 162 Preston Dennard .15 .07
❑ 163 Johnnie Gray .15 .07
❑ 164 Russell Erxleben .15 .07
❑ 165 Toni Fritsch AP .15 .07
❑ 166 Terry Hermeling .15 .07
❑ 167 Roland Hooks .15 .07
❑ 168 Roger Carr .15 .07
❑ 169 San Diego Chargers TL 1.00 .45
Clarence Williams
John Jefferson
Woodrow Lowe
Ray Preston
Wilbur Young
(checklist back)
❑ 170 Ottis Anderson AP RC 4.00 1.80
❑ 171 Brian Sipe 1.00 .45
❑ 172 Leonard Thompson .15 .07
❑ 173 Tony Reed .15 .07
❑ 174 Bob Tucker .15 .07
❑ 175 Joe Greene 1.00 .45
❑ 176 Jack Dolbin .15 .07
❑ 177 Chuck Ramsey .15 .07
❑ 178 Paul Hofer .15 .07
❑ 179 Randy Logan .15 .07
❑ 180 David Lewis AP .15 .07
❑ 181 Duriel Harris .15 .07
❑ 182 June Jones .50 .23
❑ 183 Larry McCarren .15 .07
❑ 184 Ken Johnson .15 .07
❑ 185 Charlie Waters .50 .23
❑ 186 Noah Jackson .15 .07
❑ 187 Reggie Williams .50 .23
❑ 188 New England Patriots TL .50 .23
Sam Cunningham
Harold Jackson
Raymond Clayborn
Tony McGee
(checklist back)
❑ 189 Carl Eller 1.00 .45
❑ 190 Ed White AP .15 .07
❑ 191 Mario Clark .15 .07
❑ 192 Roosevelt Leaks .15 .07
❑ 193 Ted McKnight .15 .07
❑ 194 Danny Buggs .15 .07
❑ 195 Lester Hayes RC 2.00 .90
❑ 196 Clarence Scott .15 .07
❑ 197 New Orleans Saints TL .50 .23
Chuck Muncie
Wes Chandler
Tom Myers
Elois Grooms
Don Reese
(checklist back)
❑ 198 Richard Caster .15 .07
❑ 199 Louie Giammona .15 .07
❑ 200 Terry Bradshaw 8.00 3.60
❑ 201 Ed Newman .15 .07
❑ 202 Fred Dryer 1.00 .45
❑ 203 Dennis Franks .15 .07
❑ 204 Bob Breunig RC .50 .23
❑ 205 Alan Page 1.00 .45
❑ 206 Earnest Gray RC .15 .07
❑ 207 Minnesota Vikings TL 1.00 .45
Rickey Young
Ahmad Rashad
Tom Hannon
Nate Wright
Mark Mullaney
(checklist back)
❑ 208 Horace Ivory .15 .07
❑ 209 Isaac Hagins .15 .07
❑ 210 Gary Johnson AP .15 .07
❑ 211 Kevin Long .15 .07
❑ 212 Bill Thompson .15 .07
❑ 213 Don Bass .15 .07
❑ 214 George Starke RC .15 .07
❑ 215 Efren Herrera .15 .07
❑ 216 Theo Bell .15 .07
❑ 217 Monte Jackson .15 .07
❑ 218 Reggie McKenzie .15 .07
❑ 219 Bucky Dilts .15 .07
❑ 220 Lyle Alzado 1.00 .45
❑ 221 Tim Foley .15 .07
❑ 222 Mark Arneson .15 .07
❑ 223 Fred Quillan .15 .07
❑ 224 Benny Ricardo .15 .07
❑ 225 Phil Simms RC 12.00 5.50
❑ 226 Chicago Bears TL 1.25 .55
Walter Payton
Brian Baschnagel
Gary Fencik
Terry Schmidt
Jim Osborne
(checklist back)
❑ 227 Max Runager .15 .07
❑ 228 Barty Smith .15 .07
❑ 229 Jay Saldi .50 .23
❑ 230 John Hannah AP 1.00 .45
❑ 231 Tim Wilson .15 .07
❑ 232 Jeff Van Note .15 .07
❑ 233 Henry Marshall .15 .07
❑ 234 Diron Talbert .15 .07
❑ 235 Garo Yepremian .50 .23
❑ 236 Larry Brown .15 .07
❑ 237 Clarence Williams .15 .07
❑ 238 Burgess Owens .15 .07
❑ 239 Vince Ferragamo .50 .23
❑ 240 Rickey Young .15 .07
❑ 241 Dave Logan .15 .07
❑ 242 Larry Gordon .15 .07
❑ 243 Terry Miller .15 .07
❑ 244 Baltimore Colts TL 1.00 .45
Joe Washington
Joe Washington
Fred Cook
(checklist back)
❑ 245 Steve DeBerg 1.00 .45
❑ 246 Checklist 133-264 .75 .19
❑ 247 Greg Latta .15 .07
❑ 248 Raymond Clayborn .50 .23
❑ 249 Jim Clack .15 .07
❑ 250 Drew Pearson 1.00 .45
❑ 251 John Bunting .50 .23
❑ 252 Rob Lytle .15 .07
❑ 253 Jim Hart 1.00 .45
❑ 254 John McDaniel .15 .07
❑ 255 Dave Pear AP .15 .07
❑ 256 Donnie Shell 1.00 .45

❑ 257 Dan Doornink .15 .07
❑ 258 Wallace Francis RC 1.00 .45
❑ 259 Dave Beverly .15 .07
❑ 260 Lee Roy Selmon AP 1.00 .45
❑ 261 Doug Dieken .15 .07
❑ 262 Gary Davis .15 .07
❑ 263 Bob Rush .15 .07
❑ 264 Buffalo Bills TL .50 .23
Curtis Brown
Frank Lewis
Keith Moody
Sherman White
(checklist back)
❑ 265 Greg Landry .50 .23
❑ 266 Jan Stenerud 1.00 .45
❑ 267 Tom Hicks .15 .07
❑ 268 Pat McInally .15 .07
❑ 269 Tim Fox .15 .07
❑ 270 Harvey Martin .50 .23
❑ 271 Dan Lloyd .15 .07
❑ 272 Mike Barber .15 .07
❑ 273 Wendell Tyler RC 1.00 .45
❑ 274 Jeff Komlo .15 .07
❑ 275 Wes Chandler RC 1.00 .45
❑ 276 Brad Dusek .15 .07
❑ 277 Charlie Johnson .15 .07
❑ 278 Dennis Swilley .15 .07
❑ 279 Johnny Evans .15 .07
❑ 280 Jack Lambert AP 1.50 .70
❑ 281 Vern Den Herder .15 .07
❑ 282 Tampa Bay Bucs TL 1.00 .45
Ricky Bell
Isaac Hagins
Lee Roy Selmon
(checklist back)
❑ 283 Bob Klein .15 .07
❑ 284 Jim Turner .15 .07
❑ 285 Marvin Powell AP .50 .23
❑ 286 Aaron Kyle .15 .07
❑ 287 Dan Neal .15 .07
❑ 288 Wayne Morris .15 .07
❑ 289 Steve Bartkowski .50 .23
❑ 290 Dave Jennings AP .50 .23
❑ 291 John Smith .15 .07
❑ 292 Bill Gregory .15 .07
❑ 293 Frank Lewis .15 .07
❑ 294 Fred Cook .15 .07
❑ 295 David Hill AP .15 .07
❑ 296 Wade Key .15 .07
❑ 297 Sidney Thornton .15 .07
❑ 298 Charlie Hall .15 .07
❑ 299 Joe Lavender .15 .07
❑ 300 Tom Rafferty RC .15 .07
❑ 301 Mike Renfro RC .50 .23
❑ 302 Wilbur Jackson .50 .23
❑ 303 Green Bay Packers TL 1.00 .45
Terdell Middleton
James Lofton
Johnnie Gray
Robert Barber
Ezra Johnson
(checklist back)
❑ 304 Henry Childs .15 .07
❑ 305 Russ Washington AP .15 .07
❑ 306 Jim LeClair .15 .07
❑ 307 Tommy Hart .15 .07
❑ 308 Gary Barbaro .15 .07
❑ 309 Billy Taylor .15 .07
❑ 310 Ray Guy .50 .23
❑ 311 Don Hasselbeck RC .50 .23
❑ 312 Doug Williams 1.00 .45
❑ 313 Nick Mike-Mayer .15 .07
❑ 314 Don McCauley .15 .07
❑ 315 Wesley Walker 1.00 .45
❑ 316 Dan Dierdorf 1.00 .45
❑ 317 Dave Brown RC .50 .23
❑ 318 Leroy Harris .15 .07
❑ 319 Pittsburgh Steelers TL 1.00 .45
Franco Harris
John Stallworth
Jack Lambert
Steve Furness
L.C. Greenwood
(checklist back)
❑ 320 Mark Moseley AP UER .15 .07
(Bio on back refers
to him as Mike)
❑ 321 Mark Dennard .15 .07
❑ 322 Terry Nelson .15 .07
❑ 323 Tom Jackson 1.00 .45
❑ 324 Rick Kane .15 .07
❑ 325 Jerry Sherk .15 .07
❑ 326 Ray Preston .15 .07
❑ 327 Golden Richards .15 .07
❑ 328 Randy Dean .15 .07
❑ 329 Rick Danmeier .15 .07
❑ 330 Tony Dorsett 6.00 2.70
❑ 331 Passing Leaders 3.00 1.35
Dan Fouts
Roger Staubach
❑ 332 Receiving Leaders .50 .23
Joe Washington
Ahmad Rashad
❑ 333 Sacks Leaders 1.00 .45
Jesse Baker
Al(Bubba) Baker
Jack Youngblood
❑ 334 Scoring Leaders 1.00 .45
John Smith
Mark Moseley
❑ 335 Interception Leaders 1.00 .45
Mike Reinfeldt
Lemar Parrish
❑ 336 Punting Leaders 1.00 .45
Bob Grupp
Dave Jennings
❑ 337 Freddie Solomon .15 .07
❑ 338 Cincinnati Bengals TL 1.00 .45
Pete Johnson
Don Bass
Dick Jauron
Gary Burley
(checklist back)
❑ 339 Ken Stone .15 .07
❑ 340 Greg Buttle AP .15 .07
❑ 341 Bob Baumhower .50 .23
❑ 342 Billy Waddy .15 .07
❑ 343 Cliff Parsley .15 .07
❑ 344 Walter White .15 .07
❑ 345 Mike Thomas .15 .07
❑ 346 Neil O'Donoghue .15 .07
❑ 347 Freddie Scott .15 .07
❑ 348 Joe Ferguson .50 .23
❑ 349 Doug Nettles .15 .07
❑ 350 Mike Webster AP 1.00 .45
❑ 351 Ron Saul .15 .07
❑ 352 Julius Adams .15 .07
❑ 353 Rafael Septien .15 .07
❑ 354 Cleo Miller .15 .07
❑ 355 Keith Simpson AP .15 .07
❑ 356 Johnny Perkins .15 .07
❑ 357 Jerry Sisemore .15 .07
❑ 358 Arthur Whittington .15 .07
❑ 359 St. Louis Cardinals TL 1.00 .45
Ottis Anderson
Pat Tilley
Ken Stone
Bob Pollard
(checklist back)
❑ 360 Rick Upchurch .50 .23
❑ 361 Kim Bokamper RC .15 .07
❑ 362 Roland Harper .15 .07
❑ 363 Pat Leahy .15 .07
❑ 364 Louis Breeden .15 .07
❑ 365 John Jefferson 1.00 .45
❑ 366 Jerry Eckwood .15 .07
❑ 367 David Whitehurst .15 .07
❑ 368 Willie Parker .15 .07
❑ 369 Ed Simonini .15 .07
❑ 370 Jack Youngblood AP 1.00 .45
❑ 371 Don Warren RC 1.00 .45
❑ 372 Andy Johnson .15 .07
❑ 373 D.D. Lewis .50 .23
❑ 374A Beasley Reece RC ERR 1.00 .45
(No S in position
on front of card)
❑ 374B B.Reece COR RC .50 .23
❑ 375 L.C. Greenwood 1.00 .45
❑ 376 Cleveland Browns TL .50 .23
Mike Pruitt
Dave Logan
Thom Darden
Jerry Sherk
(checklist back)
❑ 377 Herman Edwards .15 .07
❑ 378 Rob Carpenter RC .15 .07
❑ 379 Herman Weaver .15 .07
❑ 380 Gary Fencik AP .15 .07
❑ 381 Don Strock .50 .23
❑ 382 Art Shell 1.00 .45
❑ 383 Tim Mazzetti .15 .07
❑ 384 Bruce Harper .15 .07
❑ 385 Al (Bubba) Baker .50 .23
❑ 386 Conrad Dobler .15 .07
❑ 387 Stu Voigt .15 .07
❑ 388 Ken Anderson 1.00 .45
❑ 389 Pat Tilley .15 .07
❑ 390 John Riggins 1.00 .45
❑ 391 Checklist 265-396 .75 .19
❑ 392 Fred Dean AP .15 .07
❑ 393 Benny Barnes RC .15 .07
❑ 394 Los Angeles Rams TL .50 .23
Wendell Tyler
Preston Dennard
Nolan Cromwell
Jim Youngblood
Jack Youngblood
(checklist back)
❑ 395 Brad Van Pelt .15 .07
❑ 396 Eddie Hare .15 .07
❑ 397 John Sciarra RC .15 .07
❑ 398 Bob Jackson .15 .07
❑ 399 John Yarno .15 .07
❑ 400 Franco Harris AP 2.00 .90
❑ 401 Ray Wersching .15 .07
❑ 402 Virgil Livers .15 .07
❑ 403 Raymond Chester .15 .07
❑ 404 Leon Gray .15 .07
❑ 405 Richard Todd .50 .23
❑ 406 Larry Little 1.00 .45
❑ 407 Ted Fritsch Jr. .15 .07
❑ 408 Larry Mucker .15 .07
❑ 409 Jim Allen .15 .07
❑ 410 Randy Gradishar 1.00 .45
❑ 411 Atlanta Falcons TL 1.00 .45
William Andrews
Wallace Francis
Rolland Lawrence
Don Smith
(checklist back)
❑ 412 Louie Kelcher .50 .23
❑ 413 Robert Newhouse .50 .23
❑ 414 Gary Shirk .15 .07
❑ 415 Mike Haynes AP 1.00 .45
❑ 416 Craig Colquitt .15 .07
❑ 417 Lou Piccone .15 .07
❑ 418 Clay Matthews RC 2.50 1.10
❑ 419 Marvin Cobb .15 .07
❑ 420 Harold Carmichael AP 1.00 .45
❑ 421 Uwe Von Schamann .50 .23
❑ 422 Mike Phipps .50 .23
❑ 423 Nolan Cromwell RC 1.00 .45
❑ 424 Glenn Doughty .15 .07
❑ 425 Bob Young AP .15 .07
❑ 426 Tony Galbreath .15 .07
❑ 427 Luke Prestridge RC .15 .07
❑ 428 Terry Beeson .15 .07
❑ 429 Jack Tatum .50 .23
❑ 430 Lemar Parrish AP .15 .07
❑ 431 Chester Marcol .15 .07
❑ 432 Houston Oilers TL 1.00 .45
Dan Pastorini
Ken Burrough

Mike Reinfeldt
Jesse Baker
(checklist back)
❑ 433 John Fitzgerald .15 .07
❑ 434 Gary Jeter RC .50 .23
❑ 435 Steve Grogan 1.00 .45
❑ 436 Jon Kolb UER .15 .07
John on front
❑ 437 Jim O'Bradovich UER .15 .07
(Neil O'Donoghue's bio)
❑ 438 Gerald Irons .15 .07
❑ 439 Jeff West .15 .07
❑ 440 Wilbert Montgomery .50 .23
❑ 441 Norris Thomas .15 .07
❑ 442 James Scott .15 .07
❑ 443 Curtis Brown .15 .07
❑ 444 Ken Fantetti .15 .07
❑ 445 Pat Haden 1.00 .45
❑ 446 Carl Mauck .15 .07
❑ 447 Bruce Laird .15 .07
❑ 448 Otis Armstrong .15 .07
❑ 449 Gene Upshaw 1.00 .45
❑ 450 Steve Largent AP 6.00 2.70
❑ 451 Benny Malone .15 .07
❑ 452 Steve Nelson .15 .07
❑ 453 Mark Cotney .15 .07
❑ 454 Joe Danelo .15 .07
❑ 455 Billy Joe DuPree .50 .23
❑ 456 Ron Johnson .15 .07
❑ 457 Archie Griffin .50 .23
❑ 458 Reggie Rucker .15 .07
❑ 459 Claude Humphrey .15 .07
❑ 460 Lydell Mitchell .50 .23
❑ 461 Steve Towle .15 .07
❑ 462 Revie Sorey .15 .07
❑ 463 Tom Skladany .15 .07
❑ 464 Clark Gaines .15 .07
❑ 465 Frank Corral .15 .07
❑ 466 Steve Fuller RC .50 .23
❑ 467 Ahmad Rashad AP 1.00 .45
❑ 468 Oakland Raiders TL 1.00 .45
Mark Van Eeghen
Cliff Branch
Lester Hayes
Willie Jones
(checklist back)
❑ 469 Brian Peets .15 .07
❑ 470 Pat Donovan AP RC .50 .23
❑ 471 Ken Burrough .15 .07
❑ 472 Don Calhoun .15 .07
❑ 473 Bill Bryan .15 .07
❑ 474 Terry Jackson .15 .07
❑ 475 Joe Theismann 1.25 .55
❑ 476 Jim Smith .50 .23
❑ 477 Joe DeLamielleure 1.00 .45
❑ 478 Mike Pruitt AP .50 .23
❑ 479 Steve Mike-Mayer .15 .07
❑ 480 Bill Bergey .50 .23
❑ 481 Mike Fuller .15 .07
❑ 482 Bob Parsons .15 .07
❑ 483 Billy Brooks .15 .07
❑ 484 Jerome Barkum .15 .07
❑ 485 Larry Csonka 1.50 .70
❑ 486 John Hill .15 .07
❑ 487 Mike Dawson .15 .07
❑ 488 Detroit Lions TL .50 .23
Dexter Bussey
Freddie Scott
Jim Allen
Luther Bradley
Al(Bubba) Baker
(checklist back)
❑ 489 Ted Hendricks 1.00 .45
❑ 490 Dan Pastorini .50 .23
❑ 491 Stanley Morgan 1.00 .45
❑ 492 AFC Championship 1.00 .45
Steelers 27,
Oilers 13
(Rocky Bleier running)
❑ 493 NFC Championship .50 .23
Rams 9,
Buccaneers 0
(Vince Ferragamo)
❑ 494 Super Bowl XIV 1.00 .45
Steelers 31,
Rams 19
(line play)
❑ 495 Dwight White .50 .23
❑ 496 Haven Moses .15 .07
❑ 497 Guy Morriss .15 .07
❑ 498 Dewey Selmon .50 .23
❑ 499 Dave Butz RC 1.00 .45
❑ 500 Chuck Foreman .50 .23
❑ 501 Chris Bahr .15 .07
❑ 502 Mark Miller .15 .07
❑ 503 Tony Greene .15 .07
❑ 504 Brian Kelley .15 .07
❑ 505 Joe Washington .50 .23
❑ 506 Butch Johnson .50 .23
❑ 507 New York Jets TL .50 .23
Clark Gaines
Wesley Walker
Burgess Owens
Joe Klecko
(checklist back0
❑ 508 Steve Little .15 .07
❑ 509 Checklist 397-528 .75 .19
❑ 510 Mark Van Eeghen .15 .07
❑ 511 Gary Danielson .50 .23
❑ 512 Manu Tuiasosopo .15 .07
❑ 513 Paul Coffman RC .50 .23
❑ 514 Cullen Bryant .15 .07
❑ 515 Nat Moore .50 .23
❑ 516 Bill Lenkaitis .15 .07
❑ 517 Lynn Cain RC .15 .07
❑ 518 Gregg Bingham .15 .07
❑ 519 Ted Albrecht .15 .07
❑ 520 Dan Fouts AP 2.00 .90
❑ 521 Bernard Jackson .15 .07
❑ 522 Coy Bacon .15 .07
❑ 523 Tony Franklin RC .50 .23
❑ 524 Bo Harris .15 .07
❑ 525 Bob Grupp AP .15 .07
❑ 526 San Francisco 49ers TL 1.00 .45
Paul Hofer
Freddie Solomon
James Owens
Dwaine Board
(checklist back)
❑ 527 Steve Wilson .15 .07
❑ 528 Bennie Cunningham .50 .23

1981 Topps

	Nm-Mt	Ex-Mt
COMPLETE SET (528)	200.00	90.00

❑ 1 Passing Leaders .75 .35
Ron Jaworski
Brian Sipe
❑ 2 Receiving Leaders .75 .35
Earl Cooper
Kellen Winslow
❑ 3 Sack Leaders .40 .18
Al(Bubba) Baker
Gary Johnson
❑ 4 Scoring Leaders .15 .07
Eddie Murray
John Smith
❑ 5 Interception Leaders .40 .18
Nolan Cromwell
Lester Hayes
❑ 6 Punting Leaders .15 .07
Dave Jennings
Luke Prestridge
❑ 7 Don Calhoun .15 .07
❑ 8 Jack Tatum .40 .18
❑ 9 Reggie Rucker .15 .07
❑ 10 Mike Webster AP .75 .35
❑ 11 Vince Evans RC .75 .35
❑ 12 Ottis Anderson SA .75 .35
❑ 13 Leroy Harris .15 .07
❑ 14 Gordon King .15 .07
❑ 15 Harvey Martin .40 .18
❑ 16 Johnny Lam Jones RC .40 .18
❑ 17 Ken Greene .15 .07
❑ 18 Frank Lewis .15 .07
❑ 19 Seattle Seahawks TL .75 .35
Jim Jodat
Dave Brown
John Harris
Steve Largent
Jacob Green
(checklist back)
❑ 20 Lester Hayes AP .75 .35
❑ 21 Uwe Von Schamann .15 .07
❑ 22 Joe Washington .15 .07
❑ 23 Louie Kelcher .15 .07
❑ 24 Willie Miller .15 .07
❑ 25 Steve Grogan .75 .35
❑ 26 John Hill .15 .07
❑ 27 Stan White .15 .07
❑ 28 William Andrews SA .40 .18
❑ 29 Clarence Scott .15 .07
❑ 30 Leon Gray AP .15 .07
❑ 31 Craig Colquitt .15 .07
❑ 32 Doug Williams .75 .35
❑ 33 Bob Breunig .40 .18
❑ 34 Billy Taylor .15 .07
❑ 35 Harold Carmichael .75 .35
❑ 36 Ray Wersching .15 .07
❑ 37 Dennis Johnson LB RC .15 .07
❑ 38 Archie Griffin .40 .18
❑ 39 Los Angeles Rams TL .40 .18
Cullen Bryant
Billy Waddy
Nolan Cromwell
Jack Youngblood
(checklist back)
❑ 40 Gary Fencik .40 .18
❑ 41 Lynn Dickey .15 .07
❑ 42 Steve Bartkowski SA .40 .18
❑ 43 Art Shell .75 .35
❑ 44 Wilbur Jackson .15 .07
❑ 45 Frank Corral .15 .07
❑ 46 Ted McKnight .15 .07
❑ 47 Joe Klecko .40 .18
❑ 48 Dan Doornink .15 .07
❑ 49 Doug Dieken .15 .07
❑ 50 Jerry Robinson AP RC .40 .18
❑ 51 Wallace Francis .15 .07
❑ 52 Dave Preston RC .15 .07
❑ 53 Jay Saldi .15 .07
❑ 54 Rush Brown .15 .07
❑ 55 Phil Simms 3.00 1.35
❑ 56 Nick Mike-Mayer .15 .07
❑ 57 Wash. Redskins TL 2.00 .90
Wilbur Jackson
Art Monk
Lemar Parrish
Coy Bacon
(checklist back)
❑ 58 Mike Renfro .15 .07
❑ 59 Ted Brown SA .15 .07
❑ 60 Steve Nelson .15 .07
❑ 61 Sidney Thornton .15 .07
❑ 62 Kent Hill .15 .07
❑ 63 Don Bessillieu .15 .07

- ❑ 64 Fred Cook .15 .07
- ❑ 65 Raymond Chester .15 .07
- ❑ 66 Rick Kane .15 .07
- ❑ 67 Mike Fuller .15 .07
- ❑ 68 Dewey Selmon .40 .18
- ❑ 69 Charles White RC .75 .35
- ❑ 70 Jeff Van Note .15 .07
- ❑ 71 Robert Newhouse .40 .18
- ❑ 72 Roynell Young RC .15 .07
- ❑ 73 Lynn Cain SA .15 .07
- ❑ 74 Mike Friede .15 .07
- ❑ 75 Earl Cooper RC .15 .07
- ❑ 76 New Orleans Saints TL .40 .18
  Jimmy Rogers
  Wes Chandler
  Tom Myers
  Elois Grooms
  Derland Moore
  (checklist back)
- ❑ 77 Rick Danmeier .15 .07
- ❑ 78 Darrol Ray .15 .07
- ❑ 79 Gregg Bingham .15 .07
- ❑ 80 John Hannah AP .75 .35
- ❑ 81 Jack Thompson .40 .18
- ❑ 82 Rick Upchurch .40 .18
- ❑ 83 Mike Butler .15 .07
- ❑ 84 Don Warren .15 .07
- ❑ 85 Mark Van Eeghen .15 .07
- ❑ 86 J.T. Smith RC .75 .35
- ❑ 87 Herman Weaver .15 .07
- ❑ 88 Terry Bradshaw SA 2.00 .90
- ❑ 89 Charlie Hall .15 .07
- ❑ 90 Donnie Shell .75 .35
- ❑ 91 Ike Harris .15 .07
- ❑ 92 Charlie Johnson .15 .07
- ❑ 93 Rickey Watts .15 .07
- ❑ 94 New England Patriots TL .75 .35
  Vagas Ferguson
  Stanley Morgan
  Raymond Clayborn
  Julius Adams
  (checklist back)
- ❑ 95 Drew Pearson .75 .35
- ❑ 96 Neil O'Donoghue .15 .07
- ❑ 97 Conrad Dobler .15 .07
- ❑ 98 Jewerl Thomas RC .15 .07
- ❑ 99 Mike Barber .15 .07
- ❑ 100 Billy Sims AP RC 3.00 1.35
- ❑ 101 Vern Den Herder .15 .07
- ❑ 102 Greg Landry .40 .18
- ❑ 103 Joe Cribbs SA .40 .18
- ❑ 104 Mark Murphy RC .15 .07
- ❑ 105 Chuck Muncie .40 .18
- ❑ 106 Alfred Jackson - .40 .18
- ❑ 107 Chris Bahr .15 .07
- ❑ 108 Gordon Jones .15 .07
- ❑ 109 Willie Harper RC .15 .07
- ❑ 110 Dave Jennings .15 .07
- ❑ 111 Bennie Cunningham .15 .07
- ❑ 112 Jerry Sisemore .15 .07
- ❑ 113 Cleveland Browns TL .75 .35
  Mike Pruitt
  Dave Logan
  Ron Bolton
  Lyle Alzado
  (checklist back)
- ❑ 114 Rickey Young .15 .07
- ❑ 115 Ken Anderson .75 .35
- ❑ 116 Randy Gradishar .75 .35
- ❑ 117 Eddie Lee Ivery RC .15 .07
- ❑ 118 Wesley Walker .75 .35
- ❑ 119 Chuck Foreman .40 .18
- ❑ 120 Nolan Cromwell AP .40 .18
  UER (Rushing TD's
  added wrong)
- ❑ 121 Curtis Dickey SA .15 .07
- ❑ 122 Wayne Morris .15 .07
- ❑ 123 Greg Stemrick .15 .07
- ❑ 124 Coy Bacon .15 .07
- ❑ 125 Jim Zorn .40 .18
  (Steve Largent
  in background)
- ❑ 126 Henry Childs .15 .07
- ❑ 127 Checklist 1-132 .75 .35
- ❑ 128 Len Walterscheid .15 .07
- ❑ 129 Johnny Evans .15 .07
- ❑ 130 Gary Barbaro .15 .07
- ❑ 131 Jim Smith .15 .07
- ❑ 132 New York Jets TL .40 .18
  Scott Dierking
  Bruce Harper
  Ken Schroy
  Mark Gastineau
  (checklist back)
- ❑ 133 Curtis Brown .15 .07
- ❑ 134 D.D. Lewis .15 .07
- ❑ 135 Jim Plunkett .75 .35
- ❑ 136 Nat Moore .40 .18
- ❑ 137 Don McCauley .15 .07
- ❑ 138 Tony Dorsett SA .75 .35
- ❑ 139 Julius Adams .15 .07
- ❑ 140 Ahmad Rashad AP .75 .35
- ❑ 141 Rich Saul .15 .07
- ❑ 142 Ken Fantetti .15 .07
- ❑ 143 Kenny Johnson .15 .07
- ❑ 144 Clark Gaines .15 .07
- ❑ 145 Mark Moseley .15 .07
- ❑ 146 Vernon Perry RC .15 .07
- ❑ 147 Jerry Eckwood .15 .07
- ❑ 148 Freddie Solomon .15 .07
- ❑ 149 Jerry Sherk .15 .07
- ❑ 150 Kellen Winslow AP RC 8.00 3.60
- ❑ 151 Green Bay Packers TL .75 .35
  Eddie Lee Ivery
  James Lofton
  Johnnie Gray
  Mike Butler
  (checklist back)
- ❑ 152 Ross Browner .15 .07
- ❑ 153 Dan Fouts SA .75 .35
- ❑ 154 Woody Peoples .15 .07
- ❑ 155 Jack Lambert 1.00 .45
- ❑ 156 Mike Dennis .15 .07
- ❑ 157 Rafael Septien .15 .07
- ❑ 158 Archie Manning .75 .35
- ❑ 159 Don Hasselbeck .15 .07
- ❑ 160 Alan Page AP .75 .35
- ❑ 161 Arthur Whittington .15 .07
- ❑ 162 Billy Waddy .15 .07
- ❑ 163 Horace Belton .15 .07
- ❑ 164 Luke Prestridge .15 .07
- ❑ 165 Joe Theismann .75 .35
- ❑ 166 Morris Towns .15 .07
- ❑ 167 Dave Brown .15 .07
- ❑ 168 Ezra Johnson .15 .07
- ❑ 169 Tampa Bay Bucs TL .15 .07
  Ricky Bell
  Gordon Jones
  Mike Washington
  Lee Roy Selmon
  (checklist back)
- ❑ 170 Joe DeLamielleure .75 .35
- ❑ 171 Earnest Gray SA .15 .07
- ❑ 172 Mike Thomas .15 .07
- ❑ 173 Jim Haslett RC 2.00 .90
- ❑ 174 David Woodley RC .40 .18
- ❑ 175 Al(Bubba) Baker .40 .18
- ❑ 176 Nesby Glasgow RC .15 .07
- ❑ 177 Pat Leahy .15 .07
- ❑ 178 Tom Brahaney .15 .07
- ❑ 179 Herman Edwards .15 .07
- ❑ 180 Junior Miller AP RC .15 .07
- ❑ 181 Richard Wood RC .15 .07
- ❑ 182 Lenvil Elliott .15 .07
- ❑ 183 Sammie White .40 .18
- ❑ 184 Russell Erxleben .15 .07
- ❑ 185 Ed Too Tall Jones .75 .35
- ❑ 186 Ray Guy SA .40 .18
- ❑ 187 Haven Moses .15 .07
- ❑ 188 New York Giants TL .40 .18
  Billy Taylor
  Earnest Gray
  Mike Dennis
  Gary Jeter
  (checklist back)
- ❑ 189 David Whitehurst .15 .07
- ❑ 190 John Jefferson AP .75 .35
- ❑ 191 Terry Beeson .15 .07
- ❑ 192 Dan Ross RC .40 .18
- ❑ 193 Dave Williams RB RC .15 .07
- ❑ 194 Art Monk RC 15.00 6.75
- ❑ 195 Roger Wehrli .15 .07
- ❑ 196 Ricky Feacher .15 .07
- ❑ 197 Miami Dolphins TL .75 .35
  Delvin Williams
  Tony Nathan
  Gerald Small
  Kim Bokamper
  A.J. Duhe
  (checklist back)
- ❑ 198 Carl Roaches RC .15 .07
- ❑ 199 Billy Campfield .15 .07
- ❑ 200 Ted Hendricks AP .75 .35
- ❑ 201 Fred Smerlas RC .75 .35
- ❑ 202 Walter Payton SA 3.00 1.35
- ❑ 203 Luther Bradley .15 .07
- ❑ 204 Herb Scott .15 .07
- ❑ 205 Jack Youngblood .75 .35
- ❑ 206 Danny Pittman .15 .07
- ❑ 207 Houston Oilers TL .40 .18
  Carl Roaches
  Mike Barber
  Jack Tatum
  Jesse Baker
  Robert Brazile
  (checklist back)
- ❑ 208 Vagas Ferguson RC .40 .18
- ❑ 209 Mark Dennard .15 .07
- ❑ 210 Lemar Parrish .15 .07
- ❑ 211 Bruce Harper .15 .07
- ❑ 212 Ed Simonini .15 .07
- ❑ 213 Nick Lowery RC .75 .35
- ❑ 214 Kevin House RC .40 .18
- ❑ 215 Mike Kenn RC .75 .35
- ❑ 216 Joe Montana RC 150.00 70.00
- ❑ 217 Joe Senser .15 .07
- ❑ 218 Lester Hayes SA .40 .18
- ❑ 219 Gene Upshaw .75 .35
- ❑ 220 Franco Harris 1.25 .55
- ❑ 221 Ron Bolton .15 .07
- ❑ 222 Charles Alexander RC .40 .18
- ❑ 223 Matt Robinson .15 .07
- ❑ 224 Ray Oldham .15 .07
- ❑ 225 George Martin .15 .07
- ❑ 226 Buffalo Bills TL .75 .35
  Joe Cribbs
  Jerry Butler
  Steve Freeman
  Ben Williams
  (checklist back)
- ❑ 227 Tony Franklin .15 .07
- ❑ 228 George Cumby .15 .07
- ❑ 229 Butch Johnson .40 .18
- ❑ 230 Mike Haynes .75 .35
- ❑ 231 Rob Carpenter .40 .18
- ❑ 232 Steve Fuller .40 .18
- ❑ 233 John Sawyer .15 .07
- ❑ 234 Kenny King SA .15 .07
- ❑ 235 Jack Ham .75 .35
- ❑ 236 Jimmy Rogers .15 .07
- ❑ 237 Bob Parsons .15 .07
- ❑ 238 Marty Lyons RC .75 .35
- ❑ 239 Pat Tilley .15 .07
- ❑ 240 Dennis Harrah .15 .07
- ❑ 241 Thom Darden .15 .07
- ❑ 242 Rolf Benirschke .15 .07
- ❑ 243 Gerald Small .15 .07
- ❑ 244 Atlanta Falcons TL .75 .35
  William Andrews
  Alfred Jenkins
  Al Richardson
  Joel Williams
  (checklist back)

❑ 245 Roger Carr .15 .07
❑ 246 Sherman White .15 .07
❑ 247 Ted Brown .15 .07
❑ 248 Matt Cavanaugh .40 .18
❑ 249 John Dutton .15 .07
❑ 250 Bill Bergey AP .40 .18
❑ 251 Jim Allen .15 .07
❑ 252 Mike Nelms SA .15 .07
❑ 253 Tom Blanchard .15 .07
❑ 254 Ricky Thompson .15 .07
❑ 255 John Matuszak .40 .18
❑ 256 Randy Grossman .15 .07
❑ 257 Ray Griffin .15 .07
❑ 258 Lynn Cain .15 .07
❑ 259 Checklist 133-264 .75 .35
❑ 260 Mike Pruitt .40 .18
❑ 261 Chris Ward .15 .07
❑ 262 Fred Steinfort .15 .07
❑ 263 James Owens .15 .07
❑ 264 Chicago Bears TL 1.50 .70
Walter Payton
James Scott
Len Walterscheid
Dan Hampton
(checklist back)
❑ 265 Dan Fouts 1.50 .70
❑ 266 Arnold Morgado .15 .07
❑ 267 John Jefferson SA .75 .35
❑ 268 Bill Lenkaitis .15 .07
❑ 269 James Jones .15 .07
❑ 270 Brad Van Pelt .15 .07
❑ 271 Steve Largent 2.50 1.10
❑ 272 Elvin Bethea .75 .35
❑ 273 Cullen Bryant .15 .07
❑ 274 Gary Danielson .40 .18
❑ 275 Tony Galbreath .15 .07
❑ 276 Dave Butz .15 .07
❑ 277 Steve Mike-Mayer .15 .07
❑ 278 Ron Johnson .15 .07
❑ 279 Tom DeLeone .15 .07
❑ 280 Ron Jaworski .75 .35
❑ 281 Mel Gray .15 .07
❑ 282 San Diego Chargers TL .75 .35
Chuck Muncie
John Jefferson
Glen Edwards
Gary Johnson
(checklist back)
❑ 283 Mark Brammer RC .15 .07
❑ 284 Alfred Jenkins SA .40 .18
❑ 285 Greg Buttle .15 .07
❑ 286 Randy Hughes .15 .07
❑ 287 Delvin Williams .15 .07
❑ 288 Brian Baschnagel .15 .07
❑ 289 Gary Jeter .15 .07
❑ 290 Stanley Morgan AP .75 .35
❑ 291 Gerry Ellis .15 .07
❑ 292 Al Richardson .15 .07
❑ 293 Jimmie Giles .40 .18
❑ 294 Dave Jennings SA .15 .07
❑ 295 Wilbert Montgomery .40 .18
❑ 296 Dave Pureifory .15 .07
❑ 297 Greg Hawthorne .15 .07
❑ 298 Dick Ambrose .15 .07
❑ 299 Terry Hermeling .15 .07
❑ 300 Danny White .75 .35
❑ 301 Ken Burrough .15 .07
❑ 302 Paul Hofer .15 .07
❑ 303 Denver Broncos TL .75 .35
Jim Jensen
Haven Moses
Steve Foley
Rulon Jones
(checklist back)
❑ 304 Eddie Payton .40 .18
❑ 305 Isaac Curtis .40 .18
❑ 306 Benny Ricardo .15 .07
❑ 307 Riley Odoms .15 .07
❑ 308 Bob Chandler .15 .07
❑ 309 Larry Heater .15 .07
❑ 310 Art Still AP RC .75 .35
❑ 311 Harold Jackson .40 .18
❑ 312 Charlie Joiner SA .75 .35
❑ 313 Jeff Nixon .15 .07
❑ 314 Aundra Thompson .15 .07
❑ 315 Richard Todd .40 .18
❑ 316 Dan Hampton RC 3.00 1.35
❑ 317 Doug Marsh .15 .07
❑ 318 Louie Giammona .15 .07
❑ 319 San Francisco 49ers TL .75 .35
Earl Cooper
Dwight Clark
Ricky Churchman
Dwight Hicks
Jim Stuckey
(checklist back)
❑ 320 Manu Tuiasosopo .15 .07
❑ 321 Rich Milot .15 .07
❑ 322 Mike Guman RC .15 .07
❑ 323 Bob Kuechenberg .40 .18
❑ 324 Tom Skladany .15 .07
❑ 325 Dave Logan .15 .07
❑ 326 Bruce Laird .15 .07
❑ 327 James Jones SA .15 .07
❑ 328 Joe Danelo .15 .07
❑ 329 Kenny King RC .40 .18
❑ 330 Pat Donovan .15 .07
❑ 331 Earl Cooper RB .40 .18
Most Receptions
Running Back;
Season: Rookie
❑ 332 John Jefferson RB .75 .35
Most Consec. Seasons,
1000 Yards Receiving,
Start of Career
❑ 333 Kenny King RB .40 .18
Longest Pass Caught,
Super Bowl History
❑ 334 Rod Martin RB .40 .18
Most Interceptions
Super Bowl Game
❑ 335 Jim Plunkett RB .75 .35
Longest Pass,
Super Bowl History
❑ 336 Bill Thompson RB .40 .18
Most Touchdowns,
Fumble Recoveries:
Lifetime
❑ 337 John Cappelletti .40 .18
❑ 338 Detroit Lions TL .75 .35
Billy Sims
Freddie Scott
Jim Allen
James Hunter
Al(Bubba) Baker
(checklist back)
❑ 339 Don Smith .15 .07
❑ 340 Rod Perry .15 .07
❑ 341 David Lewis .15 .07
❑ 342 Mark Gastineau RC 1.00 .45
❑ 343 Steve Largent SA .75 .35
❑ 344 Charle Young .15 .07
❑ 345 Toni Fritsch .15 .07
❑ 346 Matt Blair .40 .18
❑ 347 Don Bass .15 .07
❑ 348 Jim Jensen RC .40 .18
❑ 349 Karl Lorch .15 .07
❑ 350 Brian Sipe AP .40 .18
❑ 351 Theo Bell .15 .07
❑ 352 Sam Adams .15 .07
❑ 353 Paul Coffman .15 .07
❑ 354 Eric Harris .15 .07
❑ 355 Tony Hill .40 .18
❑ 356 J.T. Turner .15 .07
❑ 357 Frank LeMaster .15 .07
❑ 358 Jim Jodat .15 .07
❑ 359 Oakland Raiders TL .75 .35
Mark Van Eeghen
Cliff Branch
Lester Hayes
Cedrick Hardman
Ted Hendricks
(checklist back)
❑ 360 Joe Cribbs AP RC .75 .35
❑ 361 James Lofton SA .75 .35
❑ 362 Dexter Bussey .15 .07
❑ 363 Bobby Jackson .15 .07
❑ 364 Steve DeBerg .75 .35
❑ 365 Ottis Anderson 1.00 .45
❑ 366 Tom Myers .15 .07
❑ 367 John James .15 .07
❑ 368 Reese McCall .15 .07
❑ 369 Jack Reynolds .40 .18
❑ 370 Gary Johnson .15 .07
❑ 371 Jimmy Cefalo .15 .07
❑ 372 Horace Ivory .15 .07
❑ 373 Garo Yepremian .15 .07
❑ 374 Brian Kelley .15 .07
❑ 375 Terry Bradshaw 6.00 2.70
❑ 376 Dallas Cowboys TL .75 .35
Tony Dorsett
Tony Hill
Dennis Thurman
Charlie Waters
Harvey Martin
(checklist back)
❑ 377 Randy Logan .15 .07
❑ 378 Tim Wilson .15 .07
❑ 379 Archie Manning SA .75 .35
❑ 380 Revie Sorey .15 .07
❑ 381 Randy Holloway .15 .07
❑ 382 Henry Lawrence .15 .07
❑ 383 Pat McInally .15 .07
❑ 384 Kevin Long .15 .07
❑ 385 Louis Wright .40 .18
❑ 386 Leonard Thompson .15 .07
❑ 387 Jan Stenerud .40 .18
❑ 388 Raymond Butler RC .15 .07
❑ 389 Checklist 265-396 .75 .35
❑ 390 Steve Bartkowski AP .40 .18
❑ 391 Clarence Harmon .15 .07
❑ 392 Wilbert Montgomery SA .40 .18
❑ 393 Billy Joe DuPree .40 .18
❑ 394 Kansas City Chiefs TL .40 .18
Ted McKnight
Henry Marshall
Gary Barbaro
Art Still
(checklist back)
❑ 395 Earnest Gray .15 .07
❑ 396 Ray Hamilton .15 .07
❑ 397 Brenard Wilson .15 .07
❑ 398 Calvin Hill .75 .35
❑ 399 Robin Cole .15 .07
❑ 400 Walter Payton AP 10.00 4.50
❑ 401 Jim Hart .75 .35
❑ 402 Ron Yary .75 .35
❑ 403 Cliff Branch .75 .35
❑ 404 Roland Hooks .15 .07
❑ 405 Ken Stabler 3.00 1.35
❑ 406 Chuck Ramsey .15 .07
❑ 407 Mike Nelms RC .15 .07
❑ 408 Ron Jaworski SA .40 .18
❑ 409 James Hunter .15 .07
❑ 410 Lee Roy Selmon AP .75 .35
❑ 411 Baltimore Colts TL .40 .18
Curtis Dickey
Roger Carr
Bruce Laird
Mike Barnes
(checklist back)
❑ 412 Henry Marshall .15 .07
❑ 413 Preston Pearson .40 .18
❑ 414 Richard Bishop .15 .07
❑ 415 Greg Pruitt .40 .18
❑ 416 Matt Bahr .40 .18
❑ 417 Tom Mullady .15 .07
❑ 418 Glen Edwards .15 .07
❑ 419 Sam McCullum .15 .07
❑ 420 Stan Walters .15 .07
❑ 421 George Roberts .15 .07
❑ 422 Dwight Clark RC 5.00 2.20
❑ 423 Pat Thomas RC .15 .07

❑ 424 Bruce Harper SA	.15	.07
❑ 425 Craig Morton	.40	.18
❑ 426 Derrick Gaffney	.15	.07
❑ 427 Pete Johnson	.15	.07
❑ 428 Wes Chandler	.75	.35
❑ 429 Burgess Owens	.15	.07
❑ 430 James Lofton AP	2.00	.90
❑ 431 Tony Reed	.15	.07
❑ 432 Minnesota Vikings TL	.75	.35
Ted Brown		
Ahmad Rashad		
John Turner		
Doug Sutherland		
(checklist back)		
❑ 433 Ron Springs RC	.40	.18
❑ 434 Tim Fox	.15	.07
❑ 435 Ozzie Newsome	2.00	.90
❑ 436 Steve Furness	.15	.07
❑ 437 Will Lewis	.15	.07
❑ 438 Mike Hartenstine	.15	.07
❑ 439 John Bunting	.15	.07
❑ 440 Eddie Murray RC	.75	.35
❑ 441 Mike Pruitt SA	.40	.18
❑ 442 Larry Swider	.15	.07
❑ 443 Steve Freeman	.15	.07
❑ 444 Bruce Hardy RC	.15	.07
❑ 445 Pat Haden	.40	.18
❑ 446 Curtis Dickey RC	.15	.07
❑ 447 Doug Wilkerson	.15	.07
❑ 448 Alfred Jenkins	.40	.18
❑ 449 Dave Dalby	.15	.07
❑ 450 Robert Brazile	.15	.07
❑ 451 Bobby Hammond	.15	.07
❑ 452 Raymond Clayborn	.15	.07
❑ 453 Jim Miller P RC	.15	.07
❑ 454 Roy Simmons	.15	.07
❑ 455 Charlie Waters	.40	.18
❑ 456 Ricky Bell	.75	.35
❑ 457 Ahmad Rashad SA	.75	.35
❑ 458 Don Cockroft	.15	.07
❑ 459 Keith Krepfle	.15	.07
❑ 460 Marvin Powell	.15	.07
❑ 461 Tommy Kramer	.75	.35
❑ 462 Jim LeClair	.15	.07
❑ 463 Freddie Scott	.15	.07
❑ 464 Rob Lytle	.15	.07
❑ 465 Johnnie Gray	.15	.07
❑ 466 Doug France RC	.15	.07
❑ 467 Carlos Carson RC	.40	.18
❑ 468 St. Louis Cardinals TL	.75	.35
Ottis Anderson		
Pat Tilley		
Ken Stone		
Curtis Greer		
Steve Neils		
(checklist back)		
❑ 469 Efren Herrera	.15	.07
❑ 470 Randy White AP	1.00	.45
❑ 471 Richard Caster	.15	.07
❑ 472 Andy Johnson	.15	.07
❑ 473 Billy Sims SA	.75	.35
❑ 474 Joe Lavender	.15	.07
❑ 475 Harry Carson	.40	.18
❑ 476 John Stallworth	1.00	.45
❑ 477 Bob Thomas	.15	.07
❑ 478 Keith Wright RC	.15	.07
❑ 479 Ken Stone	.15	.07
❑ 480 Carl Hairston	.40	.18
❑ 481 Reggie McKenzie	.15	.07
❑ 482 Bob Griese	1.50	.70
❑ 483 Mike Bragg	.15	.07
❑ 484 Scott Dierking	.15	.07
❑ 485 David Hill	.15	.07
❑ 486 Brian Sipe SA	.40	.18
❑ 487 Rod Martin RC	.40	.18
❑ 488 Cincinnati Bengals TL	.40	.18
Pete Johnson		
Dan Ross		
Louis Breeden		
Eddie Edwards		
(checklist back)		
❑ 489 Preston Dennard	.15	.07
❑ 490 John Smith	.15	.07
❑ 491 Mike Reinfeldt	.15	.07
❑ 492 1980 NFC Champions	.75	.35
Eagles 20,		
Cowboys 7		
(Ron Jaworski)		
❑ 493 1980 AFC Champions	.75	.35
Raiders 34,		
Chargers 27		
(Jim Plunkett)		
❑ 494 Super Bowl XV	.75	.35
Raiders 27,		
Eagles 10		
(Plunkett handing		
off to Kenny King)		
❑ 495 Joe Greene	.75	.35
❑ 496 Charlie Joiner	.75	.35
❑ 497 Rolland Lawrence	.15	.07
❑ 498 Al(Bubba) Baker SA	.40	.18
❑ 499 Brad Dusek	.15	.07
❑ 500 Tony Dorsett	4.00	1.80
❑ 501 Robin Earl	.15	.07
❑ 502 Theotis Brown RC	.15	.07
❑ 503 Joe Ferguson	.40	.18
❑ 504 Beasley Reece	.15	.07
❑ 505 Lyle Alzado	.75	.35
❑ 506 Tony Nathan RC	.75	.35
❑ 507 Philadelphia Eagles TL	.40	.18
Wilbert Montgomery		
Charlie Smith		
Brenard Wilson		
Claude Humphrey		
(checklist back)		
❑ 508 Herb Orvis	.15	.07
❑ 509 Clarence Williams	.15	.07
❑ 510 Ray Guy AP	.40	.18
❑ 511 Jeff Komio	.15	.07
❑ 512 Freddie Solomon SA	.15	.07
❑ 513 Tim Mazzetti	.15	.07
❑ 514 Elvis Peacock RC	.15	.07
❑ 515 Russ Francis	.40	.18
❑ 516 Roland Harper	.15	.07
❑ 517 Checklist 397-528	.75	.35
❑ 518 Billy Johnson	.40	.18
❑ 519 Dan Dierdorf	.75	.35
❑ 520 Fred Dean	.15	.07
❑ 521 Jerry Butler	.15	.07
❑ 522 Ron Saul	.15	.07
❑ 523 Charlie Smith	.15	.07
❑ 524 Kellen Winslow SA	3.00	1.35
❑ 525 Bert Jones	.75	.35
❑ 526 Pittsburgh Steelers TL	.75	.35
Franco Harris		
Theo Bell		
Donnie Shell		
L.C. Greenwood		
(checklist back)		
❑ 527 Duriel Harris	.15	.07
❑ 528 William Andrews	.75	.35

1982 Topps

	Nm-Mt	Ex-Mt
COMPLETE SET (528)	80.00	36.00
❑ 1 Ken Anderson RB	.75	.35
Most Completions		
Super Bowl Game		
❑ 2 Dan Fouts RB	.75	.35
Most Passing Yards		
Playoff Game		
❑ 3 LeRoy Irvin RB	.15	.07
Most Punt Return		
Yardage: Game		
❑ 4 Stump Mitchell RB	.15	.07
Most Return		
Yardage: Season		
❑ 5 George Rogers RB	.75	.35
Most Rushing Yards:		
Rookie Season		
❑ 6 Dan Ross RB	.15	.07
Most Receptions:		
Super Bowl Game		
❑ 7 AFC Championship	.75	.35
Bengals 27,		
Chargers 7		
(Ken Anderson		
handing off to		
Pete Johnson)		
❑ 8 NFC Championship	.75	.35
49ers 28,		
Cowboys 27		
(Earl Cooper)		
❑ 9 Super Bowl XVI	.75	.35
49ers 26,		
Bengals 7		
(Anthony Munoz		
blocking)		
❑ 10 Baltimore Colts TL	.15	.07
Curtis Dickey		
Raymond Butler		
Larry Braziel		
Bruce Laird		
❑ 11 Raymond Butler	.15	.07
❑ 12 Roger Carr	.15	.07
❑ 13 Curtis Dickey	.40	.18
❑ 14 Zachary Dixon	.15	.07
❑ 15 Nesby Glasgow	.15	.07
❑ 16 Bert Jones	.75	.35
❑ 17 Bruce Laird	.15	.07
❑ 18 Reese McCall	.15	.07
❑ 19 Randy McMillan	.15	.07
❑ 20 Ed Simonini	.15	.07
❑ 21 Buffalo Bills TL	.40	.18
Joe Cribbs		
Frank Lewis		
Mario Clark		
Fred Smerlas		
❑ 22 Mark Brammer	.15	.07
❑ 23 Curtis Brown	.15	.07
❑ 24 Jerry Butler	.15	.07
❑ 25 Mario Clark	.15	.07
❑ 26 Joe Cribbs	.40	.18
❑ 27 Joe Cribbs IA	.40	.18
❑ 28 Joe Ferguson	.40	.18
❑ 29 Jim Haslett	.75	.35
❑ 30 Frank Lewis	.15	.07
❑ 31 Frank Lewis IA	.15	.07
❑ 32 Shane Nelson	.15	.07
❑ 33 Charles Romes	.15	.07
❑ 34 Bill Simpson	.15	.07
❑ 35 Fred Smerlas	.15	.07
❑ 36 Cincinnati Bengals TL	.40	.18
Pete Johnson		
Cris Collinsworth		
Ken Riley		
Reggie Williams		
❑ 37 Charles Alexander	.15	.07
❑ 38 Ken Anderson AP	.75	.35
❑ 39 Ken Anderson IA	.75	.35
❑ 40 Jim Breech	.15	.07
❑ 41 Jim Breech IA	.15	.07
❑ 42 Louis Breeden	.15	.07
❑ 43 Ross Browner	.15	.07
❑ 44 Cris Collinsworth RC	2.00	.90
❑ 45 Cris Collinsworth IA	.75	.35

❑ 46	Isaac Curtis	.15	.07
❑ 47	Pete Johnson	.15	.07
❑ 48	Pete Johnson IA	.15	.07
❑ 49	Steve Kreider	.15	.07
❑ 50	Pat McInally	.15	.07
❑ 51	Anthony Munoz AP RC	8.00	3.60
❑ 52	Dan Ross	.15	.07
❑ 53	David Verser RC	.15	.07
❑ 54	Reggie Williams	.40	.18
❑ 55	Cleveland Browns TL Mike Pruitt Ozzie Newsome Clarence Scott Lyle Alzado	.40	.18
❑ 56	Lyle Alzado	.75	.35
❑ 57	Dick Ambrose	.15	.07
❑ 58	Ron Bolton	.15	.07
❑ 59	Steve Cox	.15	.07
❑ 60	Joe DeLamielleure	.75	.35
❑ 61	Tom DeLeone	.15	.07
❑ 62	Doug Dieken	.15	.07
❑ 63	Ricky Feacher	.15	.07
❑ 64	Don Goode	.15	.07
❑ 65	Robert L. Jackson RC	.15	.07
❑ 66	Dave Logan	.15	.07
❑ 67	Ozzie Newsome	1.00	.45
❑ 68	Ozzie Newsome IA	.75	.35
❑ 69	Greg Pruitt	.40	.18
❑ 70	Mike Pruitt	.40	.18
❑ 71	Mike Pruitt IA	.40	.18
❑ 72	Reggie Rucker	.15	.07
❑ 73	Clarence Scott	.15	.07
❑ 74	Brian Sipe	.40	.18
❑ 75	Charles White	.40	.18
❑ 76	Denver Broncos TL Rick Parros Steve Watson Steve Foley Rulon Jones	.40	.18
❑ 77	Rubin Carter	.15	.07
❑ 78	Steve Foley	.15	.07
❑ 79	Randy Gradishar	.40	.18
❑ 80	Tom Jackson	.75	.35
❑ 81	Craig Morton	.40	.18
❑ 82	Craig Morton IA	.40	.18
❑ 83	Riley Odoms	.15	.07
❑ 84	Rick Parros	.15	.07
❑ 85	Dave Preston	.15	.07
❑ 86	Tony Reed	.15	.07
❑ 87	Bob Swenson RC	.15	.07
❑ 88	Bill Thompson	.15	.07
❑ 89	Rick Upchurch	.40	.18
❑ 90	Steve Watson AP RC	.40	.18
❑ 91	Steve Watson IA	.15	.07
❑ 92	Houston Oilers TL Carl Roaches Ken Burrough Carter Hartwig Greg Stemrick Jesse Baker	.15	.07
❑ 93	Mike Barber	.15	.07
❑ 94	Elvin Bethea	.75	.35
❑ 95	Gregg Bingham	.15	.07
❑ 96	Robert Brazile	.15	.07
❑ 97	Ken Burrough	.15	.07
❑ 98	Toni Fritsch	.15	.07
❑ 99	Leon Gray	.15	.07
❑ 100	Gifford Nielsen RC	.40	.18
❑ 101	Vernon Perry	.15	.07
❑ 102	Mike Reinfeldt	.15	.07
❑ 103	Mike Renfro	.15	.07
❑ 104	Carl Roaches	.15	.07
❑ 105	Ken Stabler	2.00	.90
❑ 106	Greg Stemrick	.15	.07
❑ 107	J.C. Wilson	.15	.07
❑ 108	Tim Wilson	.15	.07
❑ 109	Kansas City Chiefs TL Joe Delaney J.T. Smith Eric Harris Ken Kremer	.15	.07
❑ 110	Gary Barbaro	.15	.07
❑ 111	Brad Budde RC	.15	.07
❑ 112	Joe Delaney AP RC	.75	.35
❑ 113	Joe Delaney IA	.40	.18
❑ 114	Steve Fuller	.15	.07
❑ 115	Gary Green	.15	.07
❑ 116	James Hadnot	.15	.07
❑ 117	Eric Harris	.15	.07
❑ 118	Billy Jackson	.15	.07
❑ 119	Bill Kenney RC	.15	.07
❑ 120	Nick Lowery AP	.75	.35
❑ 121	Nick Lowery IA	.40	.18
❑ 122	Henry Marshall	.15	.07
❑ 123	J.T. Smith	.40	.18
❑ 124	Art Still	.15	.07
❑ 125	Miami Dolphins TL Tony Nathan Duriel Harris Glenn Blackwood Bob Baumhower	.40	.18
❑ 126	Bob Baumhower	.40	.18
❑ 127	Glenn Blackwood RC	.15	.07
❑ 128	Jimmy Cefalo	.15	.07
❑ 129	A.J. Duhe	.40	.18
❑ 130	Andra Franklin RC	.15	.07
❑ 131	Duriel Harris	.15	.07
❑ 132	Nat Moore	.40	.18
❑ 133	Tony Nathan	.40	.18
❑ 134	Ed Newman	.15	.07
❑ 135	Earnie Rhone	.15	.07
❑ 136	Don Strock	.15	.07
❑ 137	Tommy Vigorito	.15	.07
❑ 138	Uwe Von Schamann	.15	.07
❑ 139	Uwe Von Schamann IA	.15	.07
❑ 140	David Woodley	.40	.18
❑ 141	New England Pats TL Tony Collins Stanley Morgan Tim Fox Rick Sanford Tony McGee	.40	.18
❑ 142	Julius Adams	.15	.07
❑ 143	Richard Bishop	.15	.07
❑ 144	Matt Cavanaugh	.15	.07
❑ 145	Raymond Clayborn	.15	.07
❑ 146	Tony Collins RC	.15	.07
❑ 147	Vagas Ferguson	.15	.07
❑ 148	Tim Fox	.15	.07
❑ 149	Steve Grogan	.40	.18
❑ 150	John Hannah AP	.75	.35
❑ 151	John Hannah IA	.40	.18
❑ 152	Don Hasselbeck	.15	.07
❑ 153	Mike Haynes	.40	.18
❑ 154	Harold Jackson	.40	.18
❑ 155	Andy Johnson	.15	.07
❑ 156	Stanley Morgan	.40	.18
❑ 157	Stanley Morgan IA	.40	.18
❑ 158	Steve Nelson	.15	.07
❑ 159	Rod Shoate	.15	.07
❑ 160	New York Jets TL Freeman McNeil Wesley Walker Darrol Ray Joe Klecko	.40	.18
❑ 161	Dan Alexander RC	.15	.07
❑ 162	Mike Augustyniak	.15	.07
❑ 163	Jerome Barkum	.15	.07
❑ 164	Greg Buttle	.15	.07
❑ 165	Scott Dierking	.15	.07
❑ 166	Joe Fields	.15	.07
❑ 167	Mark Gastineau AP	.40	.18
❑ 168	Mark Gastineau IA	.40	.18
❑ 169	Bruce Harper	.15	.07
❑ 170	Johnny Lam Jones	.15	.07
❑ 171	Joe Klecko AP	.40	.18
❑ 172	Joe Klecko IA	.40	.18
❑ 173	Pat Leahy	.40	.18
❑ 174	Pat Leahy IA	.15	.07
❑ 175	Marty Lyons	.40	.18
❑ 176	Freeman McNeil RC	.75	.35
❑ 177	Marvin Powell	.15	.07
❑ 178	Chuck Ramsey	.15	.07
❑ 179	Darrol Ray	.15	.07
❑ 180	Abdul Salaam	.15	.07
❑ 181	Richard Todd	.40	.18
❑ 182	Richard Todd IA	.40	.18
❑ 183	Wesley Walker	.40	.18
❑ 184	Chris Ward	.15	.07
❑ 185	Oakland Raiders TL Kenny King Derrick Ramsey Lester Hayes Odis McKinney Rod Martin	.40	.18
❑ 186	Cliff Branch	.75	.35
❑ 187	Bob Chandler	.15	.07
❑ 188	Ray Guy	.40	.18
❑ 189	Lester Hayes	.40	.18
❑ 190	Ted Hendricks AP	.75	.35
❑ 191	Monte Jackson	.15	.07
❑ 192	Derrick Jensen	.15	.07
❑ 193	Kenny King	.15	.07
❑ 194	Rod Martin	.15	.07
❑ 195	John Matuszak	.40	.18
❑ 196	Matt Millen RC	1.50	.70
❑ 197	Derrick Ramsey	.15	.07
❑ 198	Art Shell	.75	.35
❑ 199	Mark Van Eeghen	.15	.07
❑ 200	Arthur Whittington	.15	.07
❑ 201	Marc Wilson RC	.40	.18
❑ 202	Pittsburgh Steelers TL Franco Harris John Stallworth Mel Blount Jack Lambert Gary Dunn	.75	.35
❑ 203	Mel Blount AP	.75	.35
❑ 204	Terry Bradshaw	5.00	2.20
❑ 205	Terry Bradshaw IA	1.25	.55
❑ 206	Craig Colquitt	.15	.07
❑ 207	Bennie Cunningham	.15	.07
❑ 208	Russell Davis RC	.15	.07
❑ 209	Gary Dunn	.15	.07
❑ 210	Jack Ham	.75	.35
❑ 211	Franco Harris	1.00	.45
❑ 212	Franco Harris IA	.75	.35
❑ 213	Jack Lambert AP	.75	.35
❑ 214	Jack Lambert IA	.75	.35
❑ 215	Mark Malone RC	.75	.35
❑ 216	Frank Pollard RC	.15	.07
❑ 217	Donnie Shell AP	.75	.35
❑ 218	Jim Smith	.15	.07
❑ 219	John Stallworth	.75	.35
❑ 220	John Stallworth IA	.75	.35
❑ 221	David Trout	.15	.07
❑ 222	Mike Webster AP	.75	.35
❑ 223	San Diego Chargers TL Chuck Muncie Charlie Joiner Willie Buchanon Gary Johnson	.75	.35
❑ 224	Rolf Benirschke	.15	.07
❑ 225	Rolf Benirschke IA	.15	.07
❑ 226	James Brooks RC	.75	.35
❑ 227	Willie Buchanon	.15	.07
❑ 228	Wes Chandler	.75	.35
❑ 229	Wes Chandler IA	.40	.18
❑ 230	Dan Fouts	1.00	.45
❑ 231	Dan Fouts IA	.75	.35
❑ 232	Gary Johnson	.15	.07
❑ 233	Charlie Joiner	.75	.35
❑ 234	Charlie Joiner IA	.75	.35
❑ 235	Louie Kelcher	.15	.07
❑ 236	Chuck Muncie	.40	.18
❑ 237	Chuck Muncie IA	.15	.07
❑ 238	George Roberts	.15	.07
❑ 239	Ed White	.15	.07
❑ 240	Doug Wilkerson	.15	.07
❑ 241	Kellen Winslow AP	2.00	.90
❑ 242	Kellen Winslow IA	.75	.35
❑ 243	Seattle Seahawks TL Theotis Brown	.75	.35

	Steve Largent		
	John Harris		
	Jacob Green		
244	Theotis Brown	.15	.07
245	Dan Doornink	.15	.07
246	John Harris	.15	.07
247	Efren Herrera	.15	.07
248	David Hughes	.15	.07
249	Steve Largent	2.00	.90
250	Steve Largent IA	.75	.35
251	Sam McCullum	.15	.07
252	Sherman Smith	.15	.07
253	Manu Tuiasosopo	.15	.07
254	John Yarno	.15	.07
255	Jim Zorn	.40	.18
	(Sitting with Dave Krieg)		
256	Jim Zorn IA	.40	.18
257	Passing Leaders	4.00	1.80
	Ken Anderson		
	Joe Montana		
258	Receiving Leaders	.75	.35
	Kellen Winslow		
	Dwight Clark		
259	QB Sack Leaders	.15	.07
	Joe Klecko		
	Curtis Greer		
260	Scoring Leaders	.40	.18
	Jim Breech		
	Nick Lowery		
	Eddie Murray		
	Rafael Septien		
261	Interception Leaders	.40	.18
	John Harris		
	Everson Walls		
262	Punting Leaders	.15	.07
	Pat McInally		
	Tom Skladany		
263	Brothers: Bahr	.15	.07
	Chris and Matt		
264	Brothers: Blackwood	.40	.18
	Lyle and Glenn		
265	Brothers: Brock	.15	.07
	Pete and Stan		
266	Brothers: Griffin	.40	.18
	Archie and Ray		
267	Brothers: Hannah	.75	.35
	John and Charley		
268	Brothers: Jackson	.15	.07
	Monte and Terry		
269	Brothers: Payton	1.00	.45
	Eddie and Walter		
270	Brothers: Selmon	.75	.35
	Dewey and Lee Roy		
271	Atlanta Falcons TL	.40	.18
	William Andrews		
	Alfred Jenkins		
	Tom Pridemore		
	Al Richardson		
272	William Andrews	.40	.18
273	William Andrews IA	.40	.18
274	Steve Bartkowski	.40	.18
275	Steve Bartkowski IA	.40	.18
276	Bobby Butler RC	.15	.07
277	Lynn Cain	.15	.07
278	Wallace Francis	.15	.07
279	Alfred Jackson	.15	.07
280	John James	.15	.07
281	Alfred Jenkins	.15	.07
282	Alfred Jenkins IA	.15	.07
283	Kenny Johnson	.15	.07
284	Mike Kenn AP	.75	.35
285	Fulton Kuykendall	.15	.07
286	Mick Luckhurst RC	.15	.07
287	Mick Luckhurst IA	.15	.07
288	Junior Miller	.15	.07
289	Al Richardson	.15	.07
290	R.C. Thielemann RC	.15	.07
291	Jeff Van Note	.15	.07
292	Chicago Bears TL	.75	.35
	Walter Payton		
	Ken Margerum		
	Gary Fencik		
	Dan Hampton		
	Alan Page		
293	Brian Baschnagel	.15	.07
294	Robin Earl	.15	.07
295	Vince Evans	.40	.18
296	Gary Fencik	.15	.07
297	Dan Hampton	.75	.35
298	Noah Jackson	.15	.07
299	Ken Margerum	.15	.07
300	Jim Osborne	.15	.07
301	Bob Parsons	.15	.07
302	Walter Payton	10.00	4.50
303	Walter Payton IA	3.00	1.35
304	Revie Sorey	.15	.07
305	Matt Suhey RC	.75	.35
	(Walter Payton		
	in background)		
306	Rickey Watts	.15	.07
307	Dallas Cowboys TL	.75	.35
	Tony Dorsett		
	Tony Hill		
	Everson Walls		
	Harvey Martin		
308	Bob Breunig	.15	.07
309	Doug Cosbie RC	.15	.07
310	Pat Donovan	.15	.07
311	Tony Dorsett AP	1.50	.70
312	Tony Dorsett IA	.75	.35
313	Michael Downs RC	.15	.07
314	Billy Joe DuPree	.40	.18
315	John Dutton	.15	.07
316	Tony Hill	.40	.18
317	Butch Johnson	.40	.18
318	Ed Too Tall Jones AP	.75	.35
319	James Jones	.15	.07
320	Harvey Martin	.40	.18
321	Drew Pearson	.75	.35
322	Herb Scott AP	.15	.07
323	Rafael Septien	.15	.07
324	Rafael Septien IA	.15	.07
325	Ron Springs	.40	.18
326	Dennis Thurman RC	.15	.07
327	Everson Walls RC	.75	.35
328	Everson Walls IA	.75	.35
329	Danny White	.75	.35
330	Danny White IA	.40	.18
331	Randy White AP	.75	.35
332	Randy White IA	.75	.35
333	Detroit Lions TL	.40	.18
	Billy Sims		
	Freddie Scott		
	Jim Allen		
	Dave Pureifory		
334	Jim Allen	.15	.07
335	Al(Bubba) Baker	.40	.18
336	Dexter Bussey	.15	.07
337	Doug English	.40	.18
338	Ken Fantetti	.15	.07
339	William Gay	.15	.07
340	David Hill	.15	.07
341	Eric Hipple RC	.15	.07
342	Rick Kane	.15	.07
343	Ed Murray	.75	.35
344	Ed Murray IA	.40	.18
345	Ray Oldham	.15	.07
346	Dave Pureifory	.15	.07
347	Freddie Scott	.15	.07
348	Freddie Scott IA	.15	.07
349	Billy Sims AP	.75	.35
350	Billy Sims IA	.75	.35
351	Tom Skladany	.15	.07
352	Leonard Thompson	.15	.07
353	Stan White	.15	.07
354	Green Bay Packers TL	.75	.35
	Gerry Ellis		
	James Lofton		
	Maurice Harvey		
	Mark Lee		
	Mike Butler		
355	Paul Coffman	.15	.07
356	George Cumby	.15	.07
357	Lynn Dickey	.15	.07
358	Lynn Dickey IA	.15	.07
359	Gerry Ellis	.15	.07
360	Maurice Harvey	.15	.07
361	Harlan Huckleby	.15	.07
362	John Jefferson	.75	.35
363	Mark Lee RC	.15	.07
364	James Lofton AP	1.00	.45
365	James Lofton IA	.75	.35
366	Jan Stenerud	.40	.18
367	Jan Stenerud IA	.40	.18
368	Rich Wingo	.15	.07
369	Los Angeles Rams TL	.40	.18
	Wendell Tyler		
	Preston Dennard		
	Nolan Cromwell		
	Jack Youngblood		
370	Frank Corral	.15	.07
371	Nolan Cromwell AP	.40	.18
372	Nolan Cromwell IA	.40	.18
373	Preston Dennard	.15	.07
374	Mike Fanning	.15	.07
375	Doug France	.15	.07
376	Mike Guman	.15	.07
377	Pat Haden	.40	.18
378	Dennis Harrah	.15	.07
379	Drew Hill RC	.75	.35
380	LeRoy Irvin RC	.15	.07
381	Cody Jones	.15	.07
382	Rod Perry	.15	.07
383	Rich Saul	.15	.07
384	Pat Thomas	.15	.07
385	Wendell Tyler	.40	.18
386	Wendell Tyler IA	.40	.18
387	Billy Waddy	.15	.07
388	Jack Youngblood	.75	.35
389	Minnesota Vikings TL	.15	.07
	Ted Brown		
	Joe Senser		
	Tom Hannon		
	Willie Teal		
	Matt Blair		
390	Matt Blair	.15	.07
391	Ted Brown	.15	.07
392	Ted Brown IA	.15	.07
393	Rick Danmeier	.15	.07
394	Tommy Kramer	.40	.18
395	Mark Mullaney	.15	.07
396	Eddie Payton	.15	.07
397	Ahmad Rashad	.75	.35
398	Joe Senser	.15	.07
399	Joe Senser IA	.15	.07
400	Sammie White	.40	.18
401	Sammie White IA	.15	.07
402	Ron Yary	.75	.35
403	Rickey Young	.15	.07
404	New Orleans Saints TL	.40	.18
	George Rogers		
	Guido Merkens		
	Dave Waymer		
	Rickey Jackson		
405	Russell Erxleben	.15	.07
406	Elois Grooms	.15	.07
407	Jack Holmes	.15	.07
408	Archie Manning	.75	.35
409	Derland Moore	.15	.07
410	George Rogers RC	.75	.35
411	George Rogers IA	.75	.35
412	Toussaint Tyler	.15	.07
413	Dave Waymer RC	.15	.07
414	Wayne Wilson	.15	.07
415	New York Giants TL	.15	.07
	Rob Carpenter		
	Johnny Perkins		
	Beasley Reece		
	George Martin		
416	Scott Brunner RC	.15	.07
417	Rob Carpenter	.15	.07
418	Harry Carson AP	.40	.18
419	Bill Currier	.15	.07

❑ 420 Joe Danelo .15 .07
❑ 421 Joe Danelo IA .15 .07
❑ 422 Mark Haynes RC .15 .07
❑ 423 Terry Jackson .15 .07
❑ 424 Dave Jennings .15 .07
❑ 425 Gary Jeter .15 .07
❑ 426 Brian Kelley .15 .07
❑ 427 George Martin .15 .07
❑ 428 Curtis McGriff .15 .07
❑ 429 Bill Neill .15 .07
❑ 430 Johnny Perkins .15 .07
❑ 431 Beasley Reece .15 .07
❑ 432 Gary Shirk .15 .07
❑ 433 Phil Simms 2.00 .90
❑ 434 Lawrence Taylor AP RC 20.00 9.00
❑ 435 Lawrence Taylor IA 10.00 4.50
❑ 436 Brad Van Pelt .15 .07
❑ 437 Philadelphia Eagles TL .40 .18
Wilbert Montgomery
Harold Carmichael
Brenard Wilson
Carl Hairston
❑ 438 John Bunting .15 .07
❑ 439 Billy Campfield .15 .07
❑ 440 Harold Carmichael .75 .35
❑ 441 Harold Carmichael IA .75 .35
❑ 442 Herman Edwards .15 .07
❑ 443 Tony Franklin .15 .07
❑ 444 Tony Franklin IA .15 .07
❑ 445 Carl Hairston .15 .07
❑ 446 Dennis Harrison .15 .07
❑ 447 Ron Jaworski .75 .35
❑ 448 Charlie Johnson .15 .07
❑ 449 Keith Krepfle .15 .07
❑ 450 Frank LeMaster .15 .07
❑ 451 Randy Logan .15 .07
❑ 452 Wilbert Montgomery .40 .18
❑ 453 Wilbert Montgomery IA .40 .18
❑ 454 Hubie Oliver .15 .07
❑ 455 Jerry Robinson .15 .07
❑ 456 Jerry Robinson IA .15 .07
❑ 457 Jerry Sisemore .15 .07
❑ 458 Charlie Smith .15 .07
❑ 459 Stan Walters .15 .07
❑ 460 Brenard Wilson .15 .07
❑ 461 Roynell Young .15 .07
❑ 462 St. Louis Cardinals TL .40 .18
Ottis Anderson
Pat Tilley
Ken Greene
Curtis Greer
❑ 463 Ottis Anderson .75 .35
❑ 464 Ottis Anderson IA .75 .35
❑ 465 Carl Birdsong .15 .07
❑ 466 Rush Brown .15 .07
❑ 467 Mel Gray .40 .18
❑ 468 Ken Greene .15 .07
❑ 469 Jim Hart .75 .35
❑ 470 E.J. Junior RC .40 .18
❑ 471 Neil Lomax RC .75 .35
❑ 472 Stump Mitchell RC .75 .35
❑ 473 Wayne Morris .15 .07
❑ 474 Neil O'Donoghue .15 .07
❑ 475 Pat Tilley .15 .07
❑ 476 Pat Tilley IA .15 .07
❑ 477 San Francisco 49ers TL .40 .18
Ricky Patton
Dwight Clark
Dwight Hicks
Fred Dean
❑ 478 Dwight Clark .75 .35
❑ 479 Dwight Clark IA .75 .35
❑ 480 Earl Cooper .15 .07
❑ 481 Randy Cross .40 .18
❑ 482 Johnny Davis RC .15 .07
❑ 483 Fred Dean .15 .07
❑ 484 Fred Dean IA .15 .07
❑ 485 Dwight Hicks RC .75 .35
❑ 486 Ronnie Lott AP RC 20.00 9.00
❑ 487 Ronnie Lott IA 6.00 2.70
❑ 488 Joe Montana AP 20.00 9.00
❑ 489 Joe Montana IA 12.00 5.50
❑ 490 Ricky Patton .15 .07
❑ 491 Jack Reynolds .40 .18
❑ 492 Freddie Solomon .15 .07
❑ 493 Ray Wersching .15 .07
❑ 494 Charle Young .15 .07
❑ 495 Tampa Bay Bucs TL .40 .18
Jerry Eckwood
Kevin House
Cedric Brown
Lee Roy Selmon
❑ 496 Cedric Brown .15 .07
❑ 497 Neal Colzie .15 .07
❑ 498 Jerry Eckwood .15 .07
❑ 499 Jimmie Giles .40 .18
❑ 500 Hugh Green RC .75 .35
❑ 501 Kevin House .15 .07
❑ 502 Kevin House IA .15 .07
❑ 503 Cecil Johnson .15 .07
❑ 504 James Owens .15 .07
❑ 505 Lee Roy Selmon AP .75 .35
❑ 506 Mike Washington .15 .07
❑ 507 James Wilder RC .40 .18
❑ 508 Doug Williams .40 .18
❑ 509 Wash. Redskins TL .75 .35
Joe Washington
Art Monk
Mark Murphy
Perry Brooks
❑ 510 Perry Brooks .15 .07
❑ 511 Dave Butz .40 .18
❑ 512 Wilbur Jackson .15 .07
❑ 513 Joe Lavender .15 .07
❑ 514 Terry Metcalf .40 .18
❑ 515 Art Monk 3.00 1.35
❑ 516 Mark Moseley .15 .07
❑ 517 Mark Murphy .15 .07
❑ 518 Mike Nelms .15 .07
❑ 519 Lemar Parrish .15 .07
❑ 520 John Riggins .75 .35
❑ 521 Joe Theismann .75 .35
❑ 522 Ricky Thompson .15 .07
❑ 523 Don Warren UER .15 .07
(photo actually
Ricky Thompson)
❑ 524 Joe Washington .40 .18
❑ 525 Checklist 1-132 .50 .23
❑ 526 Checklist 133-264 .50 .23
❑ 527 Checklist 265-396 .50 .23
❑ 528 Checklist 397-528 .50 .23

1983 Topps

	Nm-Mt	Ex-Mt
COMPLETE SET (396)	50.00	22.00

❑ 1 Ken Anderson RB .60 .25
20 Consecutive
Pass Completions
❑ 2 Tony Dorsett RB .60 .25
99 Yard Run
❑ 3 Dan Fouts RB .60 .25
30 Games Over
300 Yards Passing
❑ 4 Joe Montana RB 3.00 1.35
Five Straight
300 Yard Games
❑ 5 Mark Moseley RB .30 .14
21 Straight
Field Goals
❑ 6 Mike Nelms RB .10 .05
Most Yards
Punt Returns:
Super Bowl Game
❑ 7 Darrol Ray RB .10 .05
Longest Interception
Return: Playoff Game
❑ 8 John Riggins RB .60 .25
Most Yards Rushing:
Super Bowl Game
❑ 9 Fulton Walker RB .10 .05
Most Yards
Kickoff Returns:
Super Bowl Game
❑ 10 NFC Championship .60 .25
Redskins 31,
Cowboys 17
(John Riggins tackled)
❑ 11 AFC Championship .30 .14
Dolphins 14,
Jets 0
❑ 12 Super Bowl XVII .10 .05
Redskins 27,
Dolphins 17
(John Riggins running)
❑ 13 Atlanta Falcons TL .30 .14
William Andrews
❑ 14 William Andrews DP .30 .14
❑ 15 Steve Bartkowski .30 .14
❑ 16 Bobby Butler .10 .05
❑ 17 Buddy Curry .10 .05
❑ 18 Alfred Jackson DP .10 .05
❑ 19 Alfred Jenkins .10 .05
❑ 20 Kenny Johnson .10 .05
❑ 21 Mike Kenn .10 .05
❑ 22 Mick Luckhurst .10 .05
❑ 23 Junior Miller .10 .05
❑ 24 Al Richardson .10 .05
❑ 25 Gerald Riggs DP RC .30 .14
❑ 26 R.C. Thielemann .10 .05
❑ 27 Jeff Van Note .10 .05
❑ 28 Chicago Bears TL 1.00 .45
Walter Payton
❑ 29 Brian Baschnagel .10 .05
❑ 30 Dan Hampton PB .60 .25
❑ 31 Mike Hartenstine .10 .05
❑ 32 Noah Jackson .10 .05
❑ 33 Jim McMahon RC 8.00 3.60
❑ 34 Emery Moorehead DP .10 .05
❑ 35 Bob Parsons .10 .05
❑ 36 Walter Payton 6.00 2.70
❑ 37 Terry Schmidt .10 .05
❑ 38 Mike Singletary RC 8.00 3.60
❑ 39 Matt Suhey DP .30 .14
❑ 40 Rickey Watts DP .10 .05
❑ 41 Otis Wilson DP RC .30 .14
❑ 42 Dallas Cowboys TL .60 .25
Tony Dorsett
❑ 43 Bob Breunig .30 .14
❑ 44 Doug Cosbie .10 .05
❑ 45 Pat Donovan .10 .05
❑ 46 Tony Dorsett DP PB 1.00 .45
❑ 47 Tony Hill .30 .14
❑ 48 Butch Johnson DP .30 .14
❑ 49 Ed Jones DP PB .60 .25
❑ 50 Harvey Martin DP .30 .14
❑ 51 Drew Pearson .60 .25
❑ 52 Rafael Septien .10 .05
❑ 53 Ron Springs DP .10 .05
❑ 54 Dennis Thurman .10 .05
❑ 55 Everson Walls PB .30 .14
❑ 56 Danny White DP PB .60 .25
❑ 57 Randy White PB .60 .25
❑ 58 Detroit Lions TL .30 .14
Billy Sims
❑ 59 Al(Bubba) Baker DP .30 .14
❑ 60 Dexter Bussey DP .10 .05

❑ 61 Gary Danielson DP .10 .05
❑ 62 Keith Dorney DP .10 .05
❑ 63 Doug English .10 .05
❑ 64 Ken Fantetti DP .10 .05
❑ 65 Alvin Hall DP .10 .05
❑ 66 David Hill DP .10 .05
❑ 67 Eric Hipple .10 .05
❑ 68 Ed Murray DP .30 .14
❑ 69 Freddie Scott .10 .05
❑ 70 Billy Sims DP PB .30 .14
❑ 71 Tom Skladany DP .10 .05
❑ 72 Leonard Thompson DP .10 .05
❑ 73 Bobby Watkins .10 .05
❑ 74 Green Bay Packers TL .10 .05
Eddie Lee Ivery
❑ 75 John Anderson .10 .05
❑ 76 Paul Coffman .10 .05
❑ 77 Lynn Dickey .10 .05
❑ 78 Mike Douglass DP .10 .05
❑ 79 Eddie Lee Ivery .10 .05
❑ 80 John Jefferson DP PB .60 .25
❑ 81 Ezra Johnson .10 .05
❑ 82 Mark Lee .10 .05
❑ 83 James Lofton PB .60 .25
❑ 84 Larry McCarren .10 .05
❑ 85 Jan Stenerud DP .30 .14
❑ 86 Los Angeles Rams TL .10 .05
Wendell Tyler
❑ 87 Bill Bain DP .10 .05
❑ 88 Nolan Cromwell .30 .14
❑ 89 Preston Dennard .10 .05
❑ 90 Vince Ferragamo DP .30 .14
❑ 91 Mike Guman .10 .05
❑ 92 Kent Hill .10 .05
❑ 93 Mike Lansford DP RC .10 .05
❑ 94 Rod Perry .10 .05
❑ 95 Pat Thomas DP .10 .05
❑ 96 Jack Youngblood .60 .25
❑ 97 Minnesota Vikings TL .10 .05
Ted Brown
❑ 98 Matt Blair .10 .05
❑ 99 Ted Brown .10 .05
❑ 100 Greg Coleman .10 .05
❑ 101 Randy Holloway .10 .05
❑ 102 Tommy Kramer .30 .14
❑ 103 Doug Martin DP .10 .05
❑ 104 Mark Mullaney .10 .05
❑ 105 Joe Senser .10 .05
❑ 106 Willie Teal DP .10 .05
❑ 107 Sammie White .30 .14
❑ 108 Rickey Young .10 .05
❑ 109 New Orleans Saints TL .30 .14
George Rogers
❑ 110 Stan Brock RC .10 .05
❑ 111 Bruce Clark RC .10 .05
❑ 112 Russell Erxleben DP .10 .05
❑ 113 Russell Gary .10 .05
❑ 114 Jeff Groth DP .10 .05
❑ 115 John Hill DP .10 .05
❑ 116 Derland Moore .10 .05
❑ 117 George Rogers PB .30 .14
❑ 118 Ken Stabler 1.50 .70
❑ 119 Wayne Wilson .10 .05
❑ 120 New York Giants TL .10 .05
Butch Woolfolk
❑ 121 Scott Brunner .10 .05
❑ 122 Rob Carpenter .10 .05
❑ 123 Harry Carson PB .30 .14
❑ 124 Joe Danelo DP .10 .05
❑ 125 Earnest Gray .10 .05
❑ 126 Mark Haynes DP .30 .14
❑ 127 Terry Jackson .10 .05
❑ 128 Dave Jennings .10 .05
❑ 129 Brian Kelley .10 .05
❑ 130 George Martin .10 .05
❑ 131 Tom Mullady .10 .05
❑ 132 Johnny Perkins .10 .05
❑ 133 Lawrence Taylor PB 5.00 2.20
❑ 134 Brad Van Pelt .10 .05
❑ 135 Butch Woolfolk DP RC .10 .05
❑ 136 Philadelphia Eagles TL .30 .14
Wilbert Montgomery
❑ 137 Harold Carmichael .60 .25
❑ 138 Herman Edwards .10 .05
❑ 139 Tony Franklin DP .10 .05
❑ 140 Carl Hairston DP .10 .05
❑ 141 Dennis Harrison DP .10 .05
❑ 142 Ron Jaworski DP .30 .14
❑ 143 Frank LeMaster .10 .05
❑ 144 Wilbert Montgomery DP .30 .14
❑ 145 Guy Morriss .10 .05
❑ 146 Jerry Robinson .10 .05
(TD stats don't match)
❑ 147 Max Runager .10 .05
❑ 148 Ron Smith DP RC .10 .05
❑ 149 John Spagnola .10 .05
❑ 150 Stan Walters DP .10 .05
❑ 151 Roynell Young DP .10 .05
❑ 152 St. Louis Cardinals TL .30 .14
Ottis Anderson
❑ 153 Ottis Anderson .60 .25
❑ 154 Carl Birdsong .10 .05
❑ 155 Dan Dierdorf DP .60 .25
❑ 156 Roy Green RC .60 .25
❑ 157 Elois Grooms .10 .05
❑ 158 Neil Lomax DP .30 .14
❑ 159 Wayne Morris .10 .05
❑ 160 Tootie Robbins RC .10 .05
❑ 161 Luis Sharpe RC .10 .05
❑ 162 Pat Tilley .10 .05
❑ 163 San Francisco 49ers TL .10 .05
Jeff Moore
❑ 164 Dwight Clark PB .60 .25
❑ 165 Randy Cross .30 .14
❑ 166 Russ Francis .30 .14
❑ 167 Dwight Hicks .10 .05
❑ 168 Ronnie Lott PB 2.50 1.10
❑ 169 Joe Montana DP 10.00 4.50
❑ 170 Jeff Moore .10 .05
❑ 171 R.Nehemiah DP RC .60 .25
❑ 172 Freddie Solomon .10 .05
❑ 173 Ray Wersching DP .10 .05
❑ 174 Tampa Bay Bucs TL .10 .05
James Wilder
❑ 175 Cedric Brown .10 .05
❑ 176 Bill Capece .10 .05
❑ 177 Neal Colzie .10 .05
❑ 178 Jimmie Giles .10 .05
❑ 179 Hugh Green PB .30 .14
❑ 180 Kevin House DP .10 .05
❑ 181 James Owens .10 .05
❑ 182 Lee Roy Selmon PB .60 .25
❑ 183 Mike Washington .10 .05
❑ 184 James Wilder .10 .05
❑ 185 Doug Williams DP .30 .14
❑ 186 Wash. Redskins TL .60 .25
John Riggins
❑ 187 Jeff Bostic DP RC 1.00 .45
❑ 188 Charlie Brown PB RC .30 .14
❑ 189 Vernon Dean DP RC .10 .05
❑ 190 Joe Jacoby RC 1.00 .45
❑ 191 Dexter Manley RC .30 .14
❑ 192 Rich Milot .10 .05
❑ 193 Art Monk DP 1.00 .45
❑ 194 Mark Moseley DP .10 .05
❑ 195 Mike Nelms .10 .05
❑ 196 Neal Olkewicz DP .10 .05
❑ 197 Tony Peters .10 .05
❑ 198 John Riggins DP .60 .25
❑ 199 Joe Theismann PB .60 .25
❑ 200 Don Warren .10 .05
❑ 201 Jeris White DP .10 .05
❑ 202 Passing Leaders .60 .25
Joe Theismann
Ken Anderson
❑ 203 Receiving Leaders .30 .14
Dwight Clark
Kellen Winslow
❑ 204 Rushing Leaders .60 .25
Tony Dorsett
Freeman McNeil
❑ 205 Scoring Leaders 1.25 .55
Wendell Tyler
Marcus Allen
❑ 206 Interception Leaders .30 .14
Everson Walls
AFC Tie (Four)
❑ 207 Punting Leaders .10 .05
Carl Birdsong
Luke Prestridge
❑ 208 Baltimore Colts TL .10 .05
Randy McMillan
❑ 209 Matt Bouza .10 .05
❑ 210 Johnie Cooks DP RC .10 .05
❑ 211 Curtis Dickey .10 .05
❑ 212 Nesby Glasgow DP .10 .05
❑ 213 Derrick Hatchett .10 .05
❑ 214 Randy McMillan .10 .05
❑ 215 Mike Pagel RC .30 .14
❑ 216 Rohn Stark DP RC .30 .14
❑ 217 D.Thompson DP RC .10 .05
❑ 218 Leo Wisniewski DP .10 .05
❑ 219 Buffalo Bills TL .30 .14
Joe Cribbs
❑ 220 Curtis Brown .10 .05
❑ 221 Jerry Butler .10 .05
❑ 222 Greg Cater DP .10 .05
❑ 223 Joe Cribbs .30 .14
❑ 224 Joe Ferguson .30 .14
❑ 225 Roosevelt Leaks .10 .05
❑ 226 Frank Lewis .10 .05
❑ 227 Eugene Marve RC .10 .05
❑ 228 Fred Smerlas DP PB .10 .05
❑ 229 Ben Williams DP .10 .05
❑ 230 Cincinnati Bengals TL .10 .05
Pete Johnson
❑ 231 Charles Alexander .10 .05
❑ 232 Ken Anderson DP PB .60 .25
❑ 233 Jim Breech DP .10 .05
❑ 234 Ross Browner .10 .05
❑ 235 Cris Collinsworth .60 .25
DP PB
❑ 236 Isaac Curtis .10 .05
❑ 237 Pete Johnson .10 .05
❑ 238 Steve Kreider DP .10 .05
❑ 239 Max Montoya DP RC .10 .05
❑ 240 Anthony Munoz PB 1.00 .45
❑ 241 Ken Riley .10 .05
❑ 242 Dan Ross .10 .05
❑ 243 Reggie Williams .30 .14
❑ 244 Cleveland Browns TL .30 .14
Mike Pruitt
❑ 245 Chip Banks DP PB RC .30 .14
❑ 246 Tom Cousineau DP RC .30 .14
❑ 247 Joe DeLamielleure DP .30 .14
❑ 248 Doug Dieken DP .10 .05
❑ 249 Hanford Dixon RC .10 .05
❑ 250 Ricky Feacher DP .10 .05
❑ 251 Lawrence Johnson DP .10 .05
❑ 252 Dave Logan DP .10 .05
❑ 253 Paul McDonald DP .10 .05
❑ 254 Ozzie Newsome DP .60 .25
❑ 255 Mike Pruitt .30 .14
❑ 256 Clarence Scott DP .10 .05
❑ 257 Brian Sipe DP .30 .14
❑ 258 Dwight Walker DP .10 .05
❑ 259 Charles White .30 .14
❑ 260 Denver Broncos TL .10 .05
Gerald Willhite
❑ 261 Steve DeBerg DP .30 .14
❑ 262 Randy Gradishar DP PB .30 .14
❑ 263 Rulon Jones DP RC .10 .05
❑ 264 Rich Karlis DP .10 .05
❑ 265 Don Latimer .10 .05
❑ 266 Rick Parros DP .10 .05
❑ 267 Luke Prestridge .10 .05
❑ 268 Rick Upchurch .30 .14
❑ 269 Steve Watson DP .10 .05
❑ 270 Gerald Willhite DP .10 .05
❑ 271 Houston Oilers TL .10 .05
Gifford Nielsen
❑ 272 Harold Bailey .10 .05
❑ 273 Jesse Baker DP .10 .05

❑ 274 Gregg Bingham DP .10 .05
❑ 275 Robert Brazile DP .10 .05
❑ 276 Donnie Craft .10 .05
❑ 277 Daryl Hunt .10 .05
❑ 278 Archie Manning DP .30 .14
❑ 279 Gifford Nielsen .10 .05
❑ 280 Mike Renfro .10 .05
❑ 281 Carl Roaches DP .10 .05
❑ 282 Kansas City Chiefs TL .30 .14
Joe Delaney
❑ 283 Gary Barbaro .10 .05
❑ 284 Joe Delaney .10 .05
❑ 285 Jeff Gossett RC .60 .25
❑ 286 Gary Green DP .10 .05
❑ 287 Eric Harris DP .10 .05
❑ 288 Billy Jackson DP .10 .05
❑ 289 Bill Kenney DP .10 .05
❑ 290 Nick Lowery .60 .25
❑ 291 Henry Marshall .10 .05
❑ 292 Art Still DP .10 .05
❑ 293 Los Angeles Raiders TL 2.00 .90
Marcus Allen
❑ 294 Marcus Allen DP PB RC 15.00 6.75
❑ 295 Lyle Alzado .60 .25
❑ 296 Chris Bahr DP .10 .05
❑ 297 Cliff Branch .60 .25
❑ 298 Todd Christensen RC .75 .35
❑ 299 Ray Guy .30 .14
❑ 300 Frank Hawkins DP .10 .05
❑ 301 Lester Hayes DP .10 .05
❑ 302 Ted Hendricks DP PB .60 .25
❑ 303 Kenny King DP .10 .05
❑ 304 Rod Martin .10 .05
❑ 305 Matt Millen DP .60 .25
❑ 306 Burgess Owens .10 .05
❑ 307 Jim Plunkett .60 .25
❑ 308 Miami Dolphins TL .30 .14
Andra Franklin
❑ 309 Bob Baumhower .10 .05
❑ 310 Glenn Blackwood .10 .05
❑ 311 Lyle Blackwood DP .10 .05
❑ 312 A.J. Duhe .10 .05
❑ 313 Andra Franklin .10 .05
❑ 314 Duriel Harris .10 .05
❑ 315 Bob Kuechenberg DP .30 .14
❑ 316 Don McNeal .10 .05
❑ 317 Tony Nathan .30 .14
❑ 318 Ed Newman .10 .05
❑ 319 Earnie Rhone DP .10 .05
❑ 320 Joe Rose DP .10 .05
❑ 321 Don Strock DP .10 .05
❑ 322 Uwe Von Schamann .10 .05
❑ 323 David Woodley DP .30 .14
❑ 324 New England Pats TL .10 .05
Tony Collins
❑ 325 Julius Adams .10 .05
❑ 326 Pete Brock .10 .05
❑ 327 Rich Camarillo DP RC .10 .05
❑ 328 Tony Collins DP .10 .05
❑ 329 Steve Grogan .30 .14
❑ 330 John Hannah PB .60 .25
❑ 331 Don Hasselbeck .10 .05
❑ 332 Mike Haynes .30 .14
❑ 333 Roland James RC .10 .05
❑ 334A Stanley Morgan ERR .60 .25
("Inside Linebacker" is
printed upside down
on card back)
❑ 334B Stanley Morgan COR .30 .14
❑ 335 Steve Nelson .10 .05
❑ 336 Kenneth Sims DP .10 .05
❑ 337 Mark Van Eeghen .30 .14
❑ 338 New York Jets TL .30 .14
Freeman McNeil
❑ 339 Greg Buttle .10 .05
❑ 340 Joe Fields .10 .05
❑ 341 Mark Gastineau DP .30 .14
❑ 342 Bruce Harper .10 .05
❑ 343 Bobby Jackson .10 .05
❑ 344 Bobby Jones .10 .05
❑ 345 Johnny Lam Jones DP .10 .05
❑ 346 Joe Klecko .30 .14
❑ 347 Marty Lyons .10 .05
❑ 348 Freeman McNeil PB .60 .25
❑ 349 Lance Mehl RC .10 .05
❑ 350 Marvin Powell DP .10 .05
❑ 351 Darrol Ray DP .10 .05
❑ 352 Abdul Salaam .10 .05
❑ 353 Richard Todd .30 .14
❑ 354 Wesley Walker PB .30 .14
❑ 355 Pittsburgh Steelers TL .60 .25
Franco Harris
❑ 356 Gary Anderson K DP RC 6.00 2.70
❑ 357 Mel Blount DP .60 .25
❑ 358 Terry Bradshaw DP 1.50 .70
❑ 359 Larry Brown .10 .05
❑ 360 Bennie Cunningham .10 .05
❑ 361 Gary Dunn .10 .05
❑ 362 Franco Harris .75 .35
❑ 363 Jack Lambert PB .60 .25
❑ 364 Frank Pollard .10 .05
❑ 365 Donnie Shell .30 .14
❑ 366 John Stallworth PB .60 .25
❑ 367 Loren Toews .10 .05
❑ 368 Mike Webster DP PB .60 .25
❑ 369 Dwayne Woodruff RC .10 .05
❑ 370 San Diego Chargers TL .30 .14
Chuck Muncie
❑ 371 Rolf Benirschke DP .10 .05
❑ 372 James Brooks .60 .25
❑ 373 Wes Chandler .30 .14
❑ 374 Dan Fouts DP PB .60 .25
❑ 375 Tim Fox .10 .05
❑ 376 Gary Johnson .10 .05
❑ 377 Charlie Joiner DP .60 .25
❑ 378 Louie Kelcher .10 .05
❑ 379 Chuck Muncie .10 .05
❑ 380 Cliff Thrift .10 .05
❑ 381 Doug Wilkerson .10 .05
❑ 382 Kellen Winslow PB .75 .35
❑ 383 Seattle Seahawks TL .10 .05
Sherman Smith
❑ 384 Kenny Easley PB RC .60 .25
❑ 385 Jacob Green RC .30 .14
❑ 386 John Harris .10 .05
❑ 387 Michael Jackson .10 .05
❑ 388 Norm Johnson RC .10 .05
❑ 389 Steve Largent 1.25 .55
❑ 390 Keith Simpson .10 .05
❑ 391 Sherman Smith .10 .05
❑ 392 Jeff West DP .10 .05
❑ 393 Jim Zorn DP .30 .14
❑ 394 Checklist 1-132 .50 .23
❑ 395 Checklist 133-264 .50 .23
❑ 396 Checklist 265-396 .50 .23

1984 Topps

	Nm-Mt	Ex-Mt
COMPLETE SET (396)	200.00	90.00
COMP.FACT.SET (396)	250.00	110.00

❑ 1 Eric Dickerson RB .50 .23
Sets Rookie Mark
With 1808 Yards
❑ 2 Ali Haji-Sheikh RB .25 .11
Sets Field Goal
Mark as a Rookie
❑ 3 Franco Harris RB .50 .23
Records Eighth
1000 Yard Year
❑ 4 Mark Moseley RB .25 .11
161 Points Sets
Mark for Kickers
❑ 5 John Riggins RB .50 .23
24 Rushing TD's
❑ 6 Jan Stenerud RB .25 .11
338th Career FG
❑ 7 AFC Championship .50 .23
Raiders 30,
Seahawks 14
(Marcus Allen running)
❑ 8 NFC Championship .25 .11
Redskins 24,
49ers 21
(John Riggins running)
❑ 9 Super Bowl XVIII UER .50 .23
Raiders 38,
Redskins 9
(hand-off to Marcus
Allen; score wrong,
28-9 on card front)
❑ 10 Indianapolis Colts TL .10 .05
Curtis Dickey
❑ 11 Raul Allegre RC .10 .05
❑ 12 Curtis Dickey .25 .11
❑ 13 Ray Donaldson RC .25 .11
❑ 14 Nesby Glasgow .10 .05
❑ 15 Chris Hinton PB RC .50 .23
❑ 16 Vernon Maxwell RC .10 .05
❑ 17 Randy McMillan .10 .05
❑ 18 Mike Pagel .25 .11
❑ 19 Rohn Stark .25 .11
❑ 20 Leo Wisniewski .10 .05
❑ 21 Buffalo Bills TL .25 .11
Joe Cribbs
❑ 22 Jerry Butler .10 .05
❑ 23 Joe Danelo .10 .05
❑ 24 Joe Ferguson .25 .11
❑ 25 Steve Freeman .10 .05
❑ 26 Roosevelt Leaks .25 .11
❑ 27 Frank Lewis .10 .05
❑ 28 Eugene Marve .10 .05
❑ 29 Booker Moore .10 .05
❑ 30 Fred Smerlas .10 .05
❑ 31 Ben Williams .25 .11
❑ 32 Cincinnati Bengals TL .25 .11
Cris Collinsworth
❑ 33 Charles Alexander .10 .05
❑ 34 Ken Anderson .50 .23
❑ 35 Ken Anderson IR .50 .23
❑ 36 Jim Breech .10 .05
❑ 37 Cris Collinsworth PB .50 .23
❑ 38 Cris Collinsworth IR .50 .23
❑ 39 Isaac Curtis .25 .11
❑ 40 Eddie Edwards .10 .05
❑ 41 Ray Horton RC .10 .05
❑ 42 Pete Johnson .25 .11
❑ 43 Steve Kreider .10 .05
❑ 44 Max Montoya .10 .05
❑ 45 Anthony Munoz PB .50 .23
❑ 46 Reggie Williams .25 .11
❑ 47 Cleveland Browns TL .25 .11
Mike Pruitt
❑ 48 Matt Bahr .25 .11
❑ 49 Chip Banks PB .10 .05
❑ 50 Tom Cousineau .10 .05
❑ 51 Joe DeLamielleure .50 .23
❑ 52 Doug Dieken .10 .05
❑ 53 Bob Golic RC .50 .23
❑ 54 Bobby Jones .10 .05
❑ 55 Dave Logan .10 .05
❑ 56 Clay Matthews .50 .23
❑ 57 Paul McDonald .10 .05
❑ 58 Ozzie Newsome .50 .23
❑ 59 Ozzie Newsome IR .50 .23
❑ 60 Mike Pruitt .25 .11
❑ 61 Denver Broncos TL .25 .11

Steve Watson		
❑ 62 Barney Chavous RC	.10	.05
❑ 63 John Elway RC	80.00	36.00
❑ 64 Steve Foley	.10	.05
❑ 65 Tom Jackson	.50	.23
❑ 66 Rich Karlis	.10	.05
❑ 67 Luke Prestridge	.10	.05
❑ 68 Zach Thomas	.10	.05
❑ 69 Rick Upchurch	.25	.11
❑ 70 Steve Watson	.25	.11
❑ 71 Sammy Winder RC	.25	.11
❑ 72 Louis Wright	.25	.11
❑ 73 Houston Oilers TL	.10	.05
Tim Smith		
❑ 74 Jesse Baker	.10	.05
❑ 75 Gregg Bingham	.10	.05
❑ 76 Robert Brazile	.25	.11
❑ 77 Steve Brown RC	.10	.05
❑ 78 Chris Dressel	.10	.05
❑ 79 Doug France	.10	.05
❑ 80 Florian Kempf	.10	.05
❑ 81 Carl Roaches	.25	.11
❑ 82 Tim Smith RC	.25	.11
❑ 83 Willie Tullis	.10	.05
❑ 84 Kansas City Chiefs TL	.10	.05
Carlos Carson		
❑ 85 Mike Bell	.10	.05
❑ 86 Theotis Brown	.10	.05
❑ 87 Carlos Carson PB	.50	.23
❑ 88 Carlos Carson IR	.25	.11
❑ 89 Deron Cherry PB RC	.25	.11
❑ 90 Gary Green	.10	.05
❑ 91 Billy Jackson	.10	.05
❑ 92 Bill Kenney	.25	.11
❑ 93 Bill Kenney IR	.25	.11
❑ 94 Nick Lowery	.50	.23
❑ 95 Henry Marshall	.10	.05
❑ 96 Art Still	.10	.05
❑ 97 Los Angeles Raiders TL	.25	.11
Todd Christensen		
❑ 98 Marcus Allen	5.00	2.20
❑ 99 Marcus Allen IR	2.50	1.10
❑ 100 Lyle Alzado	.25	.11
❑ 101 Lyle Alzado IR	.25	.11
❑ 102 Chris Bahr	.10	.05
❑ 103 Malcolm Barnwell RC	.10	.05
❑ 104 Cliff Branch	.50	.23
❑ 105 Todd Christensen PB	.50	.23
❑ 106 Todd Christensen IR	.50	.23
❑ 107 Ray Guy	.50	.23
❑ 108 Frank Hawkins	.10	.05
❑ 109 Lester Hayes	.25	.11
❑ 110 Ted Hendricks PB	.50	.23
❑ 111 Howie Long PB RC	15.00	6.75
❑ 112 Rod Martin	.25	.11
❑ 113 Vann McElroy PB RC	.10	.05
❑ 114 Jim Plunkett	.50	.23
❑ 115 Greg Pruitt PB	.25	.11
❑ 116 Miami Dolphins TL	.50	.23
Mark Duper		
❑ 117 Bob Baumhower	.10	.05
❑ 118 Doug Betters PB RC	.10	.05
❑ 119 A.J. Duhe	.10	.05
❑ 120 Mark Duper PB RC	.50	.23
❑ 121 Andra Franklin	.10	.05
❑ 122 William Judson	.10	.05
❑ 123 Dan Marino PB RC UER	80.00	36.00
(Quaterback on back)		
❑ 124 Dan Marino IR	12.00	5.50
❑ 125 Nat Moore	.25	.11
❑ 126 Ed Newman	.10	.05
❑ 127 Reggie Roby RC	.25	.11
❑ 128 Gerald Small	.10	.05
❑ 129 Dwight Stephenson RC	3.00	1.35
❑ 130 Uwe Von Schamann	.10	.05
❑ 131 New England Pats TL	.10	.05
Tony Collins		
❑ 132 Rich Camarillo	.25	.11
❑ 133 Tony Collins	.25	.11
❑ 134 Tony Collins IR	.10	.05
❑ 135 Bob Cryder	.10	.05
❑ 136 Steve Grogan	.25	.11
❑ 137 John Hannah PB	.50	.23
❑ 138 Brian Holloway PB RC	.10	.05
❑ 139 Roland James	.10	.05
❑ 140 Stanley Morgan	.25	.11
❑ 141 Rick Sanford	.10	.05
❑ 142 Mosi Tatupu RC	.10	.05
❑ 143 Andre Tippett RC	.50	.23
❑ 144 New York Jets TL	.25	.11
Wesley Walker		
❑ 145 Jerome Barkum	.10	.05
❑ 146 Mark Gastineau	.25	.11
❑ 147 Mark Gastineau IR	.25	.11
❑ 148 Bruce Harper	.10	.05
❑ 149 Johnny Lam Jones	.10	.05
❑ 150 Joe Klecko	.25	.11
❑ 151 Pat Leahy	.10	.05
❑ 152 Freeman McNeil	.25	.11
❑ 153 Lance Mehl	.10	.05
❑ 154 Marvin Powell	.25	.11
❑ 155 Darrol Ray	.10	.05
❑ 156 Pat Ryan RC	.10	.05
❑ 157 Kirk Springs	.10	.05
❑ 158 Wesley Walker	.25	.11
❑ 159 Pittsburgh Steelers TL	.50	.23
Franco Harris		
❑ 160 Walter Abercrombie RC	.25	.11
❑ 161 Gary Anderson K	.50	.23
❑ 162 Terry Bradshaw	2.00	.90
❑ 163 Craig Colquitt	.10	.05
❑ 164 Bennie Cunningham	.10	.05
❑ 165 Franco Harris	.50	.23
❑ 166 Franco Harris IR	.50	.23
❑ 167 Jack Lambert PB	.50	.23
❑ 168 Jack Lambert IR	.50	.23
❑ 169 Frank Pollard	.10	.05
❑ 170 Donnie Shell	.25	.11
❑ 171 Mike Webster PB	.25	.11
❑ 172 Keith Willis RC	.10	.05
❑ 173 Rick Woods	.10	.05
❑ 174 San Diego Chargers TL	.50	.23
Kellen Winslow		
❑ 175 Rolf Benirschke	.10	.05
❑ 176 James Brooks	.25	.11
❑ 177 Maury Buford	.10	.05
❑ 178 Wes Chandler	.25	.11
❑ 179 Dan Fouts PB	.60	.25
❑ 180 Dan Fouts IR	.50	.23
❑ 181 Charlie Joiner	.50	.23
❑ 182 Linden King	.10	.05
❑ 183 Chuck Muncie	.25	.11
❑ 184 Billy Ray Smith RC	.50	.23
❑ 185 Danny Walters RC	.10	.05
❑ 186 Kellen Winslow PB	.60	.25
❑ 187 Kellen Winslow IR	.50	.23
❑ 188 Seattle Seahawks TL	.50	.23
Curt Warner		
❑ 189 Steve August	.10	.05
❑ 190 Dave Brown	.10	.05
❑ 191 Zachary Dixon	.10	.05
❑ 192 Kenny Easley	.25	.11
❑ 193 Jacob Green	.10	.05
❑ 194 Norm Johnson	.25	.11
❑ 195 Dave Krieg RC	1.50	.70
❑ 196 Steve Largent	1.00	.45
❑ 197 Steve Largent IR	.50	.23
❑ 198 Curt Warner PB RC	.50	.23
❑ 199 Curt Warner IR	.50	.23
❑ 200 Jeff West	.10	.05
❑ 201 Charle Young	.10	.05
❑ 202 Passing Leaders	6.00	2.70
Dan Marino		
Steve Bartkowski		
❑ 203 Receiving Leaders	.25	.11
Todd Christensen		
Charlie Brown		
Earnest Gray		
Roy Green		
❑ 204 Rushing Leaders	.50	.23
Curt Warner		
Eric Dickerson		
❑ 205 Scoring Leaders	.10	.05
Gary Anderson K		
Mark Moseley		
❑ 206 Interception Leaders	.10	.05
Vann McElroy		
Ken Riley		
Mark Murphy		
❑ 207 Punting Leaders	.10	.05
Rich Camarillo		
Greg Coleman		
❑ 208 Atlanta Falcons TL	.25	.11
William Andrews		
❑ 209 William Andrews	.25	.11
❑ 210 William Andrews IR	.25	.11
❑ 211 Stacey Bailey RC	.10	.05
❑ 212 Steve Bartkowski	.50	.23
❑ 213 Steve Bartkowski IR	.25	.11
❑ 214 Ralph Giacomarro	.10	.05
❑ 215 Billy Johnson	.25	.11
❑ 216 Mike Kenn	.25	.11
❑ 217 Mick Luckhurst	.10	.05
❑ 218 Gerald Riggs	.50	.23
❑ 219 R.C. Thielemann	.10	.05
❑ 220 Jeff Van Note	.25	.11
❑ 221 Chicago Bears TL	.75	.35
Walter Payton		
❑ 222 Jim Covert RC	.50	.23
❑ 223 Leslie Frazier	.10	.05
❑ 224 Willie Gault RC	.50	.23
❑ 225 Mike Hartenstine	.10	.05
❑ 226 Noah Jackson UER	.10	.05
(photo actually		
Jim Osborne)		
❑ 227 Jim McMahon	1.25	.55
❑ 228 Walter Payton PB	4.00	1.80
❑ 229 Walter Payton IR	1.25	.55
❑ 230 Mike Richardson RC	.10	.05
❑ 231 Terry Schmidt	.10	.05
❑ 232 Mike Singletary PB	1.25	.55
❑ 233 Matt Suhey	.25	.11
❑ 234 Bob Thomas	.10	.05
❑ 235 Dallas Cowboys TL	.50	.23
Tony Dorsett		
❑ 236 Bob Breunig	.10	.05
❑ 237 Doug Cosbie	.25	.11
❑ 238 Tony Dorsett PB	1.00	.45
❑ 239 Tony Dorsett IR	.50	.23
❑ 240 John Dutton	.10	.05
❑ 241 Tony Hill	.25	.11
❑ 242 Ed Jones PB	.50	.23
❑ 243 Drew Pearson	.50	.23
❑ 244 Rafael Septien	.10	.05
❑ 245 Ron Springs	.25	.11
❑ 246 Dennis Thurman	.10	.05
❑ 247 Everson Walls PB	.10	.05
❑ 248 Danny White	.50	.23
❑ 249 Randy White PB	.50	.23
❑ 250 Detroit Lions TL	.25	.11
Billy Sims		
❑ 251 Jeff Chadwick RC	.25	.11
❑ 252 Garry Cobb	.10	.05
❑ 253 Doug English	.25	.11
❑ 254 William Gay	.10	.05
❑ 255 Eric Hipple	.25	.11
❑ 256 James Jones RC	.25	.11
❑ 257 Bruce McNorton	.10	.05
❑ 258 Eddie Murray	.25	.11
❑ 259 Ulysses Norris	.10	.05
❑ 260 Billy Sims	.50	.23
❑ 261 Billy Sims IR	.25	.11
❑ 262 Leonard Thompson	.10	.05
❑ 263 Green Bay Packers TL	.50	.23
James Lofton		
❑ 264 John Anderson	.10	.05
❑ 265 Paul Coffman	.25	.11
❑ 266 Lynn Dickey	.25	.11
❑ 267 Gerry Ellis	.10	.05
❑ 268 John Jefferson	.50	.23
❑ 269 John Jefferson IR	.50	.23
❑ 270 Ezra Johnson	.10	.05
❑ 271 Tim Lewis	.10	.05

❑ 272 James Lofton PB .50 .23
❑ 273 James Lofton IR .50 .23
❑ 274 Larry McCarren .10 .05
❑ 275 Jan Stenerud .25 .11
❑ 276 Los Angeles Rams TL .50 .23
Eric Dickerson
❑ 277 Mike Barber .10 .05
❑ 278 Jim Collins .10 .05
❑ 279 Nolan Cromwell .25 .11
❑ 280 Eric Dickerson PB RC 10.00 4.50
❑ 281 Eric Dickerson IR 2.00 .90
❑ 282 George Farmer .10 .05
❑ 283 Vince Ferragamo .25 .11
❑ 284 Kent Hill .10 .05
❑ 285 John Misko .10 .05
❑ 286 Jackie Slater PB RC 4.00 1.80
❑ 287 Jack Youngblood .25 .11
❑ 288 Minnesota Vikings TL .10 .05
Darrin Nelson
❑ 289 Ted Brown .25 .11
❑ 290 Greg Coleman .10 .05
❑ 291 Steve Dils .10 .05
❑ 292 Tony Galbreath .10 .05
❑ 293 Tommy Kramer .25 .11
❑ 294 Doug Martin .10 .05
❑ 295 Darrin Nelson RC .25 .11
❑ 296 Benny Ricardo .10 .05
❑ 297 John Swain .10 .05
❑ 298 John Turner .10 .05
❑ 299 New Orleans Saints TL .25 .11
George Rogers
❑ 300 Morten Andersen RC 1.50 .70
❑ 301 Russell Erxleben .10 .05
❑ 302 Jeff Groth .10 .05
❑ 303 Rickey Jackson PB RC .50 .23
❑ 304 Johnnie Poe RC .10 .05
❑ 305 George Rogers .25 .11
❑ 306 Richard Todd .25 .11
❑ 307 Jim Wilks RC .10 .05
❑ 308 Dave Wilson RC .10 .05
❑ 309 Wayne Wilson .10 .05
❑ 310 New York Giants TL .10 .05
Earnest Gray
❑ 311 Leon Bright .10 .05
❑ 312 Scott Brunner .10 .05
❑ 313 Rob Carpenter .10 .05
❑ 314 Harry Carson PB .25 .11
❑ 315 Earnest Gray .10 .05
❑ 316 Ali Haji-Sheikh PB RC .10 .05
❑ 317 Mark Haynes .25 .11
❑ 318 Dave Jennings .10 .05
❑ 319 Brian Kelley .10 .05
❑ 320 Phil Simms .75 .35
❑ 321 Lawrence Taylor PB 3.00 1.35
❑ 322 Lawrence Taylor IR 1.50 .70
❑ 323 Brad Van Pelt .10 .05
❑ 324 Butch Woolfolk .10 .05
❑ 325 Philadelphia Eagles TL .25 .11
Mike Quick
❑ 326 Harold Carmichael .25 .11
❑ 327 Herman Edwards .10 .05
❑ 328 Michael Haddix RC .10 .05
❑ 329 Dennis Harrison .10 .05
❑ 330 Ron Jaworski .25 .11
❑ 331 Wilbert Montgomery .25 .11
❑ 332 Hubie Oliver .10 .05
❑ 333 Mike Quick PB RC .50 .23
❑ 334 Jerry Robinson .10 .05
❑ 335 Max Runager .10 .05
❑ 336 Michael Williams .10 .05
❑ 337 St. Louis Cardinals TL .25 .11
Ottis Anderson
❑ 338 Ottis Anderson .50 .23
❑ 339 Al(Bubba) Baker .25 .11
❑ 340 Carl Birdsong .10 .05
❑ 341 David Galloway .10 .05
❑ 342 Roy Green PB .25 .11
❑ 343 Roy Green IR .25 .11
❑ 344 Curtis Greer RC .10 .05
❑ 345 Neil Lomax .25 .11
❑ 346 Doug Marsh .10 .05
❑ 347 Stump Mitchell .25 .11
❑ 348 Lionel Washington RC .25 .11
❑ 349 San Francisco 49ers TL .25 .11
Dwight Clark
❑ 350 Dwaine Board .10 .05
❑ 351 Dwight Clark .50 .23
❑ 352 Dwight Clark IR .25 .11
❑ 353 Roger Craig RC 3.00 1.35
❑ 354 Fred Dean .25 .11
❑ 355 Fred Dean IR .50 .23
Marino in background
❑ 356 Dwight Hicks .25 .11
❑ 357 Ronnie Lott PB 1.50 .70
❑ 358 Joe Montana PB 10.00 4.50
❑ 359 Joe Montana IR 3.00 1.35
❑ 360 Freddie Solomon .10 .05
❑ 361 Wendell Tyler .10 .05
❑ 362 Ray Wersching .10 .05
❑ 363 Eric Wright RC .25 .11
❑ 364 Tampa Bay Bucs TL .10 .05
Kevin House
❑ 365 Gerald Carter .10 .05
❑ 366 Hugh Green .25 .11
❑ 367 Kevin House .25 .11
❑ 368 Michael Morton RC .10 .05
❑ 369 James Owens .10 .05
❑ 370 Booker Reese .10 .05
❑ 371 Lee Roy Selmon .50 .23
❑ 372 Jack Thompson .25 .11
❑ 373 James Wilder .25 .11
❑ 374 Steve Wilson .10 .05
❑ 375 Wash. Redskins TL .50 .23
John Riggins
❑ 376 Jeff Bostic .10 .05
❑ 377 Charlie Brown .50 .23
❑ 378 Charlie Brown IR .25 .11
❑ 379 Dave Butz .25 .11
❑ 380 Darrell Green RC 10.00 4.50
❑ 381 Russ Grimm PB RC 1.00 .45
❑ 382 Joe Jacoby PB .25 .11
❑ 383 Dexter Manley .25 .11
❑ 384 Art Monk 1.00 .45
❑ 385 Mark Moseley .25 .11
❑ 386 Mark Murphy .10 .05
❑ 387 Mike Nelms .10 .05
❑ 388 John Riggins .50 .23
❑ 389 John Riggins IR .50 .23
❑ 390 Joe Theismann PB .50 .23
❑ 391 Joe Theismann IR .50 .23
❑ 392 Don Warren .25 .11
❑ 393 Joe Washington .25 .11
❑ 394 Checklist 1-132 .30 .14
❑ 395 Checklist 133-264 .30 .14
❑ 396 Checklist 265-396 .30 .14

1984 Topps USFL

	Nm-Mt	Ex-Mt
COMP.FACT.SET (132)	250.00	110.00
COMPLETE SET (132)	250.00	110.00

❑ 1 Luther Bradley 2.00 .90
❑ 2 Frank Corral 2.00 .90
❑ 3 Trumaine Johnson 2.00 .90
❑ 4 Greg Landry 2.50 1.10
❑ 5 Kit Lathrop 2.00 .90
❑ 6 Kevin Long 2.00 .90
❑ 7 Tim Spencer 2.00 .90
❑ 8 Stan White 2.00 .90
❑ 9 Buddy Aydelette 2.00 .90
❑ 10 Tom Banks 2.00 .90
❑ 11 Fred Bohannon 2.00 .90
❑ 12 Joe Cribbs 4.00 1.80
❑ 13 Joey Jones 2.00 .90
❑ 14 Scott Norwood XRC 2.50 1.10
❑ 15 Jim Smith 2.50 1.10
❑ 16 Cliff Stoudt 4.00 1.80
❑ 17 Vince Evans 4.00 1.80
❑ 18 Vagas Ferguson 2.00 .90
❑ 19 John Gillen 2.00 .90
❑ 20 Kris Haines 2.00 .90
❑ 21 Glenn Hyde 2.00 .90
❑ 22 Mark Keel 2.00 .90
❑ 23 Gary Lewis XRC 2.00 .90
❑ 24 Doug Plank 2.00 .90
❑ 25 Neil Balholm 2.00 .90
❑ 26 David Dumars 2.00 .90
❑ 27 David Martin XRC 2.00 .90
❑ 28 Craig Penrose 2.00 .90
❑ 29 Dave Stalls 2.00 .90
❑ 30 Harry Sydney XRC 2.00 .90
❑ 31 Vincent White 2.00 .90
❑ 32 George Yarno 2.00 .90
❑ 33 Kiki DeAyala 2.00 .90
❑ 34 Sam Harrell 2.00 .90
❑ 35 Mike Hawkins 2.00 .90
❑ 36 Jim Kelly XRC 80.00 36.00
❑ 37 Mark Rush 2.00 .90
❑ 38 Ricky Sanders XRC 6.00 2.70
❑ 39 Paul Bergmann 2.00 .90
❑ 40 Tom Dinkel 2.00 .90
❑ 41 Wyatt Henderson 2.00 .90
❑ 42 Vaughan Johnson XRC 2.50 1.10
❑ 43 Willie McClendon 2.00 .90
❑ 44 Matt Robinson 2.00 .90
❑ 45 George Achica 2.00 .90
❑ 46 Mark Adickes 2.00 .90
❑ 47 Howard Carson 2.00 .90
❑ 48 Kevin Nelson 2.00 .90
❑ 49 Jeff Partridge 2.00 .90
❑ 50 Jo Jo Townsell 2.50 1.10
❑ 51 Eddie Weaver 2.00 .90
❑ 52 Steve Young XRC 120.00 55.00
❑ 53 Derrick Crawford 2.00 .90
❑ 54 Walter Lewis 2.00 .90
❑ 55 Phil McKinnely 2.00 .90
❑ 56 Vic Minore 2.00 .90
❑ 57 Gary Shirk 2.00 .90
❑ 58 Reggie White XRC 60.00 27.00
❑ 59 Anthony Carter XRC UER 12.00 5.50
College stats are wrong
❑ 60 John Corker 2.00 .90
❑ 61 David Greenwood 2.00 .90
❑ 62 Bobby Hebert XRC 4.00 1.80
❑ 63 Derek Holloway 2.00 .90
❑ 64 Ken Lacy 2.00 .90
❑ 65 Tyrone McGriff 2.00 .90
❑ 66 Ray Pinney 2.00 .90
❑ 67 Gary Barbaro 2.00 .90
❑ 68 Sam Bowers 2.00 .90
❑ 69 Clarence Collins 2.00 .90
❑ 70 Willie Harper 2.00 .90
❑ 71 Jim LeClair 2.00 .90
❑ 72 Bobby Leopold RC 2.00 .90
❑ 73 Brian Sipe 4.00 1.80
❑ 74 Herschel Walker XRC 25.00 11.00
❑ 75 Junior Ah You RC 2.00 .90
❑ 76 Marcus Dupree XRC 6.00 2.70
❑ 77 Marcus Marek 2.00 .90
❑ 78 Tim Mazzetti 2.00 .90
❑ 79 Mike Robinson RC 2.00 .90
❑ 80 Dan Ross 4.00 1.80
❑ 81 Mark Schellen 2.00 .90
❑ 82 Johnnie Walton 2.00 .90
❑ 83 Gordon Banks 2.00 .90
❑ 84 Fred Besana 2.00 .90
❑ 85 Dave Browning 2.00 .90

❑ 86 Eric Jordan	2.00	.90
❑ 87 Frank Manumaleuga	2.00	.90
❑ 88 Gary Plummer XRC	4.00	1.80
❑ 89 Stan Talley	2.00	.90
❑ 90 Arthur Whittington	2.00	.90
❑ 91 Terry Beeson	2.00	.90
❑ 92 Mel Gray	4.00	1.80
❑ 93 Mike Katolin	2.00	.90
❑ 94 Dewey McClain	2.00	.90
❑ 95 Sidney Thornton	2.00	.90
❑ 96 Doug Williams	4.00	1.80
❑ 97 Kelvin Bryant XRC	4.00	1.80
❑ 98 John Bunting	2.00	.90
❑ 99 Irv Eatman XRC	2.50	1.10
❑ 100 Scott Fitzkee	2.00	.90
❑ 101 Chuck Fusina	2.00	.90
❑ 102 Sean Landeta XRC	2.50	1.10
❑ 103 David Trout	2.00	.90
❑ 104 Scott Woerner	2.00	.90
❑ 105 Glenn Carano	2.00	.90
❑ 106 Ron Crosby	2.00	.90
❑ 107 Jerry Holmes	2.00	.90
❑ 108 Bruce Huther	2.00	.90
❑ 109 Mike Rozier XRC	4.00	1.80
❑ 110 Larry Swider	2.00	.90
❑ 111 Danny Buggs	2.00	.90
❑ 112 Putt Choate	2.00	.90
❑ 113 Rich Garza	2.00	.90
❑ 114 Joey Hackett	2.00	.90
❑ 115 Rick Neuheisel XRC	4.00	1.80
❑ 116 Mike St. Clair	2.00	.90
❑ 117 Gary Anderson XRC	4.00	1.80
❑ 118 Zenon Andrusyshyn	2.00	.90
❑ 119 Doug Beaudoin	2.00	.90
❑ 120 Mike Butler	2.00	.90
❑ 121 Willie Gillespie	2.00	.90
❑ 122 Fred Nordgren	2.00	.90
❑ 123 John Reaves	2.00	.90
❑ 124 Eric Truvillion	2.00	.90
❑ 125 Reggie Collier	2.00	.90
❑ 126 Mike Guess	2.00	.90
❑ 127 Mike Hohensee	2.00	.90
❑ 128 Craig James XRC	8.00	3.60
❑ 129 Eric Robinson	2.00	.90
❑ 130 Billy Taylor	2.00	.90
❑ 131 Joey Walters	2.00	.90
❑ 132 Checklist 1-132	2.50	1.10

1985 Topps

	Nm-Mt	Ex-Mt
COMPLETE SET (396)	60.00	27.00
COMP.FACT.SET (396)	75.00	34.00
❑ 1 Mark Clayton RB	.50	.23
Most Touchdown		
Receptions: Season		
❑ 2 Eric Dickerson RB	.50	.23
Most Yards		
Rushing: Season		
❑ 3 Charlie Joiner RB	.50	.23
Most Receptions:		
Career		
❑ 4 Dan Marino RB UER	6.00	2.70
Most Touchdown		
Passes: Season		
(Dolphins misspelled		
as Dophins)		
❑ 5 Art Monk RB	.50	.23
Most Receptions:		
Season		
❑ 6 Walter Payton RB	1.00	.45
Most Yards		
Rushing: Career		
❑ 7 NFC Championship	.25	.11
49ers 23, Bears 0		
(Matt Suhey tackled)		
❑ 8 AFC Championship	.25	.11
Dolphins 45,		
Steelers 28		
(Woody Bennett over)		
❑ 9 Super Bowl XIX	.25	.11
49ers 38,		
Dolphins 16		
(Wendell Tyler)		
❑ 10 Atlanta Falcons TL	.10	.05
Stretching For The		
First Down		
(Gerald Riggs)		
❑ 11 William Andrews	.25	.11
❑ 12 Stacey Bailey	.10	.05
❑ 13 Steve Bartkowski	.50	.23
❑ 14 Rick Bryan RC	.10	.05
❑ 15 Alfred Jackson	.10	.05
❑ 16 Kenny Johnson	.10	.05
❑ 17 Mike Kenn	.10	.05
❑ 18 Mike Pitts RC	.10	.05
❑ 19 Gerald Riggs	.25	.11
❑ 20 Sylvester Stamps	.10	.05
❑ 21 R.C. Thielemann	.10	.05
❑ 22 Chicago Bears TL	.75	.35
Sweetness Sets		
Record Straight		
(Walter Payton)		
❑ 23 Todd Bell AP RC	.10	.05
❑ 24 Richard Dent AP RC	4.00	1.80
❑ 25 Gary Fencik	.25	.11
❑ 26 Dave Finzer	.10	.05
❑ 27 Leslie Frazier	.10	.05
❑ 28 Steve Fuller	.25	.11
❑ 29 Willie Gault	.50	.23
❑ 30 Dan Hampton AP	.50	.23
❑ 31 Jim McMahon	.75	.35
❑ 32 Steve McMichael RC	.50	.23
❑ 33 Walter Payton AP	4.00	1.80
❑ 34 Mike Singletary	.75	.35
❑ 35 Matt Suhey	.10	.05
❑ 36 Bob Thomas	.10	.05
❑ 37 Dallas Cowboys TL	.50	.23
Busting Through		
The Defense		
(Tony Dorsett)		
❑ 38 Bill Bates RC	1.00	.45
❑ 39 Doug Cosbie	.25	.11
❑ 40 Tony Dorsett	.75	.35
❑ 41 Michael Downs	.10	.05
❑ 42 Mike Hegman RC UER	.10	.05
(reference to SB VIII,		
should be SB XIII)		
❑ 43 Tony Hill	.25	.11
❑ 44 Gary Hogeboom RC	.10	.05
❑ 45 Jim Jeffcoat RC	.50	.23
❑ 46 Ed Too Tall Jones	.50	.23
❑ 47 Mike Renfro	.10	.05
❑ 48 Rafael Septien	.10	.05
❑ 49 Dennis Thurman	.10	.05
❑ 50 Everson Walls	.25	.11
❑ 51 Danny White	.50	.23
❑ 52 Randy White	.50	.23
❑ 53 Detroit Lions TL	.10	.05
Popping One Loose		
(Lions' Defense)		
❑ 54 Jeff Chadwick	.10	.05
❑ 55 Mike Cofer RC	.10	.05
❑ 56 Gary Danielson	.10	.05
❑ 57 Keith Dorney	.10	.05
❑ 58 Doug English	.25	.11
❑ 59 William Gay	.10	.05
❑ 60 Ken Jenkins	.10	.05
❑ 61 James Jones	.25	.11
❑ 62 Eddie Murray	.25	.11
❑ 63 Billy Sims	.50	.23
❑ 64 Leonard Thompson	.10	.05
❑ 65 Bobby Watkins	.10	.05
❑ 66 Green Bay Packers TL	.25	.11
Spotting His		
Deep Receiver		
(Lynn Dickey)		
❑ 67 Paul Coffman	.10	.05
❑ 68 Lynn Dickey	.25	.11
❑ 69 Mike Douglass	.10	.05
❑ 70 Tom Flynn RC	.10	.05
❑ 71 Eddie Lee Ivery	.10	.05
❑ 72 Ezra Johnson	.10	.05
❑ 73 Mark Lee	.10	.05
❑ 74 Tim Lewis	.10	.05
❑ 75 James Lofton	.50	.23
❑ 76 Bucky Scribner	.10	.05
❑ 77 Los Angeles Rams TL	.50	.23
Record-Setting		
Ground Attack		
(Eric Dickerson)		
❑ 78 Nolan Cromwell	.25	.11
❑ 79 Eric Dickerson AP	1.25	.55
❑ 80 Henry Ellard RC	2.50	1.10
❑ 81 Kent Hill	.10	.05
❑ 82 LeRoy Irvin	.25	.11
❑ 83 Jeff Kemp RC	.25	.11
❑ 84 Mike Lansford	.10	.05
❑ 85 Barry Redden	.10	.05
❑ 86 Jackie Slater	.50	.23
❑ 87 Doug Smith C RC	.25	.11
❑ 88 Jack Youngblood	.25	.11
❑ 89 Minnesota Vikings TL	.10	.05
Smothering The		
Opposition		
(Vikings' Defense)		
❑ 90 Alfred Anderson RC	.10	.05
❑ 91 Ted Brown	.25	.11
❑ 92 Greg Coleman	.10	.05
❑ 93 Tommy Hannon	.10	.05
❑ 94 Tommy Kramer	.25	.11
❑ 95 Leo Lewis RC	.25	.11
❑ 96 Doug Martin	.10	.05
❑ 97 Darrin Nelson	.25	.11
❑ 98 Jan Stenerud AP	.25	.11
❑ 99 Sammie White	.25	.11
❑ 100 New Orleans Saints TL	.10	.05
Hurdling Over		
Front Line		
❑ 101 Morten Andersen	.50	.23
❑ 102 Hoby Brenner RC	.25	.11
❑ 103 Bruce Clark	.10	.05
❑ 104 Hokie Gajan	.10	.05
❑ 105 Brian Hansen RC	.10	.05
❑ 106 Rickey Jackson	.50	.23
❑ 107 George Rogers	.25	.11
❑ 108 Dave Wilson	.10	.05
❑ 109 Tyrone Young	.10	.05
❑ 110 New York Giants TL	.10	.05
Engulfing The		
Quarterback		
(Giants' Defense)		
❑ 111 Carl Banks RC	.50	.23
❑ 112 Jim Burt RC	.50	.23
❑ 113 Rob Carpenter	.10	.05
❑ 114 Harry Carson	.25	.11
❑ 115 Earnest Gray	.10	.05
❑ 116 Ali Haji-Sheikh	.10	.05
❑ 117 Mark Haynes	.25	.11
❑ 118 Bobby Johnson	.10	.05
❑ 119 Lionel Manuel RC	.25	.11
❑ 120 Joe Morris RC	.50	.23
❑ 121 Zeke Mowatt RC	.25	.11
❑ 122 Jeff Rutledge RC	.10	.05
❑ 123 Phil Simms	.50	.23
❑ 124 Lawrence Taylor AP	1.50	.70
❑ 125 Philadelphia Eagles TL	.10	.05

Finding The Wide
Open Spaces
(Wilbert Montgomery)
❑ 126 Greg Brown .10 .05
❑ 127 Ray Ellis .10 .05
❑ 128 Dennis Harrison .10 .05
❑ 129 Wes Hopkins RC .25 .11
❑ 130 Mike Horan RC .10 .05
❑ 131 Kenny Jackson RC .10 .05
❑ 132 Ron Jaworski .25 .11
❑ 133 Paul McFadden .10 .05
❑ 134 Wilbert Montgomery .25 .11
❑ 135 Mike Quick .50 .23
❑ 136 John Spagnola .10 .05
❑ 137 St.Louis Cardinals TL .10 .05
Exploiting The
Air Route
(Neil Lomax)
❑ 138 Ottis Anderson .50 .23
❑ 139 Al(Bubba) Baker .25 .11
❑ 140 Roy Green .25 .11
❑ 141 Curtis Greer .10 .05
❑ 142 E.J. Junior AP .10 .05
❑ 143 Neil Lomax .25 .11
❑ 144 Stump Mitchell .25 .11
❑ 145 Neil O'Donoghue .10 .05
❑ 146 Pat Tilley .10 .05
❑ 147 Lionel Washington .10 .05
❑ 148 San Francisco 49ers TL 1.25 .55
The Road To
Super Bowl XIX
(Joe Montana)
❑ 149 Dwaine Board .10 .05
❑ 150 Dwight Clark .50 .23
❑ 151 Roger Craig 1.00 .45
❑ 152 Randy Cross .25 .11
❑ 153 Fred Dean .25 .11
❑ 154 Keith Fahnhorst RC .10 .05
❑ 155 Dwight Hicks .10 .05
❑ 156 Ronnie Lott .50 .23
❑ 157 Joe Montana 10.00 4.50
❑ 158 Renaldo Nehemiah .25 .11
❑ 159 Fred Quillan .10 .05
❑ 160 Jack Reynolds .10 .05
❑ 161 Freddie Solomon .10 .05
❑ 162 Keena Turner RC .10 .05
❑ 163 Wendell Tyler .10 .05
❑ 164 Ray Wersching .10 .05
❑ 165 Carlton Williamson .10 .05
❑ 166 Tampa Bay Bucs TL .25 .11
Protecting The
Quarterback
(Steve DeBerg)
❑ 167 Gerald Carter .10 .05
❑ 168 Mark Cotney .10 .05
❑ 169 Steve DeBerg .50 .23
❑ 170 Sean Farrell RC .10 .05
❑ 171 Hugh Green .25 .11
❑ 172 Kevin House .25 .11
❑ 173 David Logan .10 .05
❑ 174 Michael Morton .10 .05
❑ 175 Lee Roy Selmon .50 .23
❑ 176 James Wilder .10 .05
❑ 177 Wash. Redskins TL .50 .23
Diesel Named Desire
(John Riggins)
❑ 178 Charlie Brown .10 .05
❑ 179 Monte Coleman RC .25 .11
❑ 180 Vernon Dean .10 .05
❑ 181 Darrell Green .50 .23
❑ 182 Russ Grimm .25 .11
❑ 183 Joe Jacoby .25 .11
❑ 184 Dexter Manley .25 .11
❑ 185 Art Monk AP .50 .23
❑ 186 Mark Moseley .25 .11
❑ 187 Calvin Muhammad .10 .05
❑ 188 Mike Nelms .10 .05
❑ 189 John Riggins .50 .23
❑ 190 Joe Theismann .50 .23
❑ 191 Joe Washington .25 .11
❑ 192 Passing Leaders 10.00 4.50
Dan Marino
Joe Montana
❑ 193 Receiving Leaders .25 .11
Ozzie Newsome
Art Monk
❑ 194 Rushing Leaders .50 .23
Earnest Jackson
Eric Dickerson
❑ 195 Scoring Leaders .10 .05
Gary Anderson K
Ray Wersching
❑ 196 Interception Leaders .10 .05
Kenny Easley
Tom Flynn
❑ 197 Punting Leaders .10 .05
Jim Arnold
Brian Hansen
❑ 198 Buffalo Bills TL .10 .05
Rushing Toward
Rookie Stardom
(Greg Bell)
❑ 199 Greg Bell RC .25 .11
❑ 200 Preston Dennard .10 .05
❑ 201 Joe Ferguson .25 .11
❑ 202 Byron Franklin .10 .05
❑ 203 Steve Freeman .10 .05
❑ 204 Jim Haslett .25 .11
❑ 205 Charles Romes .10 .05
❑ 206 Fred Smerlas .10 .05
❑ 207 Darryl Talley RC .50 .23
❑ 208 Van Williams .10 .05
❑ 209 Cincinnati Bengals TL .25 .11
Advancing The
Ball Downfield
(Ken Anderson and
Larry Kinnebrew)
❑ 210 Ken Anderson .50 .23
❑ 211 Jim Breech .10 .05
❑ 212 Louis Breeden .10 .05
❑ 213 James Brooks .25 .11
❑ 214 Ross Browner .25 .11
❑ 215 Eddie Edwards .10 .05
❑ 216 M.L. Harris .10 .05
❑ 217 Bobby Kemp .10 .05
❑ 218 Larry Kinnebrew RC .10 .05
❑ 219 Anthony Munoz AP .50 .23
❑ 220 Reggie Williams .25 .11
❑ 221 Cleveland Browns TL .10 .05
Evading The
Defensive Pursuit
(Boyce Green)
❑ 222 Matt Bahr .25 .11
❑ 223 Chip Banks .10 .05
❑ 224 Reggie Camp .10 .05
❑ 225 Tom Cousineau .10 .05
❑ 226 Joe DeLamielleure .50 .23
❑ 227 Ricky Feacher .10 .05
❑ 228 Boyce Green RC .10 .05
❑ 229 Al Gross .10 .05
❑ 230 Clay Matthews .50 .23
❑ 231 Paul McDonald .10 .05
❑ 232 Ozzie Newsome AP .50 .23
❑ 233 Mike Pruitt .25 .11
❑ 234 Don Rogers .10 .05
❑ 235 Denver Broncos TL 2.50 1.10
Thousand Yarder
Gets The Ball
(Sammy Winder and
John Elway)
❑ 236 Rubin Carter .10 .05
❑ 237 Barney Chavous .10 .05
❑ 238 John Elway 12.00 5.50
❑ 239 Steve Foley .10 .05
❑ 240 Mike Harden RC .10 .05
❑ 241 Tom Jackson .50 .23
❑ 242 Butch Johnson .10 .05
❑ 243 Rulon Jones .10 .05
❑ 244 Rich Karlis .10 .05
❑ 245 Steve Watson .25 .11
❑ 246 Gerald Willhite .10 .05
❑ 247 Sammy Winder .25 .11
❑ 248 Houston Oilers TL .10 .05
Eluding A
Traffic Jam
(Larry Moriarty)
❑ 249 Jesse Baker .10 .05
❑ 250 Carter Hartwig .10 .05
❑ 251 Warren Moon RC 15.00 6.75
❑ 252 Larry Moriarty RC .10 .05
❑ 253 Mike Munchak RC 1.50 .70
❑ 254 Carl Roaches .10 .05
❑ 255 Tim Smith .25 .11
❑ 256 Willie Tullis .10 .05
❑ 257 Jamie Williams RC .10 .05
❑ 258 Indianapolis Colts TL .10 .05
Start Of A
Long Gainer
(Art Schlichter)
❑ 259 Raymond Butler .10 .05
❑ 260 Johnie Cooks .10 .05
❑ 261 Eugene Daniel RC .10 .05
❑ 262 Curtis Dickey .25 .11
❑ 263 Chris Hinton .25 .11
❑ 264 Vernon Maxwell .10 .05
❑ 265 Randy McMillan .10 .05
❑ 266 Art Schlichter RC .50 .23
❑ 267 Rohn Stark .25 .11
❑ 268 Leo Wisniewski .10 .05
❑ 269 Kansas City Chiefs TL .10 .05
Pigskin About To
Soar Upward
(Bill Kenney)
❑ 270 Jim Arnold .10 .05
❑ 271 Mike Bell .10 .05
❑ 272 Todd Blackledge RC .25 .11
❑ 273 Carlos Carson .25 .11
❑ 274 Deron Cherry .25 .11
❑ 275 Herman Heard RC .10 .05
❑ 276 Bill Kenney .25 .11
❑ 277 Nick Lowery .50 .23
❑ 278 Bill Maas RC .10 .05
❑ 279 Henry Marshall .10 .05
❑ 280 Art Still .10 .05
❑ 281 Los Angeles Raiders TL .50 .23
Diving For The
Goal Line
(Marcus Allen)
❑ 282 Marcus Allen 2.50 1.10
❑ 283 Lyle Alzado .25 .11
❑ 284 Chris Bahr .10 .05
❑ 285 Malcolm Barnwell .10 .05
❑ 286 Cliff Branch .50 .23
❑ 287 Todd Christensen .50 .23
❑ 288 Ray Guy .50 .23
❑ 289 Lester Hayes .25 .11
❑ 290 Mike Haynes .25 .11
❑ 291 Henry Lawrence .10 .05
❑ 292 Howie Long 2.00 .90
❑ 293 Rod Martin .25 .11
❑ 294 Vann McElroy .10 .05
❑ 295 Matt Millen .25 .11
❑ 296 Bill Pickel RC .10 .05
❑ 297 Jim Plunkett .50 .23
❑ 298 Dokie Williams RC .10 .05
❑ 299 Marc Wilson .25 .11
❑ 300 Miami Dolphins TL .25 .11
Super Duper
Performance
(Mark Duper)
❑ 301 Bob Baumhower .10 .05
❑ 302 Doug Betters .10 .05
❑ 303 Glenn Blackwood .25 .11
❑ 304 Lyle Blackwood .25 .11
❑ 305 Kim Bokamper .10 .05
❑ 306 Charles Bowser RC .10 .05
❑ 307 Jimmy Cefalo .10 .05
❑ 308 Mark Clayton AP RC .75 .35
❑ 309 A.J. Duhe .10 .05
❑ 310 Mark Duper .50 .23
❑ 311 Andra Franklin .10 .05
❑ 312 Bruce Hardy .10 .05
❑ 313 Pete Johnson .25 .11

❑ 314 Dan Marino AP UER (Fouts 4802 yards in 1981, should be 4082)	12.00	5.50
❑ 315 Tony Nathan	.25	.11
❑ 316 Ed Newman	.10	.05
❑ 317 Reggie Roby AP	.50	.23
❑ 318 Dwight Stephenson	1.00	.45
❑ 319 Uwe Von Schamann	.10	.05
❑ 320 New England Pats TL Refusing To Be Denied (Tony Collins)	.10	.05
❑ 321 Raymond Clayborn	.25	.11
❑ 322 Tony Collins	.25	.11
❑ 323 Tony Eason RC	.50	.23
❑ 324 Tony Franklin	.10	.05
❑ 325 Irving Fryar RC	5.00	2.20
❑ 326 John Hannah AP	.50	.23
❑ 327 Brian Holloway	.10	.05
❑ 328 Craig James RC	.75	.35
❑ 329 Stanley Morgan	.25	.11
❑ 330 Steve Nelson	.10	.05
❑ 331 Derrick Ramsey	.10	.05
❑ 332 Stephen Starring RC	.25	.11
❑ 333 Mosi Tatupu	.10	.05
❑ 334 Andre Tippett	.50	.23
❑ 335 New York Jets TL Thwarting The Passing Game (Mark Gastineau and Joe Ferguson)	.25	.11
❑ 336 Russell Carter RC	.10	.05
❑ 337 Mark Gastineau	.25	.11
❑ 338 Bruce Harper	.10	.05
❑ 339 Bobby Humphery RC	.10	.05
❑ 340 Johnny Lam Jones	.10	.05
❑ 341 Joe Klecko	.25	.11
❑ 342 Pat Leahy	.10	.05
❑ 343 Marty Lyons	.25	.11
❑ 344 Freeman McNeil	.25	.11
❑ 345 Lance Mehl	.10	.05
❑ 346 Ken O'Brien RC	.50	.23
❑ 347 Marvin Powell	.10	.05
❑ 348 Pat Ryan	.10	.05
❑ 349 Mickey Shuler RC	.10	.05
❑ 350 Wesley Walker	.25	.11
❑ 351 Pittsburgh Steelers TL Testing Defensive Pass Coverage (Mark Malone)	.25	.11
❑ 352 Walter Abercrombie	.10	.05
❑ 353 Gary Anderson K	.25	.11
❑ 354 Robin Cole	.10	.05
❑ 355 Bennie Cunningham	.10	.05
❑ 356 Rich Erenberg	.10	.05
❑ 357 Jack Lambert	.50	.23
❑ 358 Louis Lipps RC	.50	.23
❑ 359 Mark Malone	.25	.11
❑ 360 Mike Merriweather RC	.10	.05
❑ 361 Frank Pollard	.10	.05
❑ 362 Donnie Shell	.25	.11
❑ 363 John Stallworth	.50	.23
❑ 364 Sam Washington	.10	.05
❑ 365 Mike Webster	.25	.11
❑ 366 Dwayne Woodruff	.10	.05
❑ 367 San Diego Chargers TL Jarring The Ball Loose (Chargers' Defense)	.10	.05
❑ 368 Rolf Benirschke	.10	.05
❑ 369 Gill Byrd RC	.50	.23
❑ 370 Wes Chandler	.25	.11
❑ 371 Bobby Duckworth	.10	.05
❑ 372 Dan Fouts	.50	.23
❑ 373 Mike Green	.10	.05
❑ 374 Pete Holohan RC	.10	.05
❑ 375 Earnest Jackson RC	.25	.11
❑ 376 Lionel James RC	.25	.11
❑ 377 Charlie Joiner	.50	.23
❑ 378 Billy Ray Smith	.25	.11
❑ 379 Kellen Winslow	.50	.23
❑ 380 Seattle Seahawks TL Setting Up For The Air Attack (Dave Krieg)	.25	.11
❑ 381 Dave Brown	.10	.05
❑ 382 Jeff Bryant	.10	.05
❑ 383 Dan Doornink	.10	.05
❑ 384 Kenny Easley	.25	.11
❑ 385 Jacob Green	.25	.11
❑ 386 David Hughes	.10	.05
❑ 387 Norm Johnson	.10	.05
❑ 388 Dave Krieg	.50	.23
❑ 389 Steve Largent	1.00	.45
❑ 390 Joe Nash RC	.10	.05
❑ 391 Daryl Turner RC	.10	.05
❑ 392 Curt Warner	.50	.23
❑ 393 Fredd Young RC	.25	.11
❑ 394 Checklist 1-132	.25	.11
❑ 395 Checklist 133-264	.25	.11
❑ 396 Checklist 265-396	.25	.11

1985 Topps USFL

	Nm-Mt	Ex-Mt
COMP.FACT.SET (132)	120.00	55.00
COMPLETE SET (132)	120.00	55.00
❑ 1 Case DeBruijn	.50	.23
❑ 2 Mike Katolin	.50	.23
❑ 3 Bruce Laird	.50	.23
❑ 4 Kit Lathrop	.50	.23
❑ 5 Kevin Long	.50	.23
❑ 6 Karl Lorch	.50	.23
❑ 7 Dave Tipton	.50	.23
❑ 8 Doug Williams	2.00	.90
❑ 9 Luis Zendejas XRC	.50	.23
❑ 10 Kelvin Bryant	1.00	.45
❑ 11 Willie Collier	.50	.23
❑ 12 Irv Eatman	.50	.23
❑ 13 Scott Fitzkee	.50	.23
❑ 14 William Fuller XRC	3.00	1.35
❑ 15 Chuck Fusina	.50	.23
❑ 16 Pete Kugler	.50	.23
❑ 17 Garcia Lane	.50	.23
❑ 18 Mike Lush	.50	.23
❑ 19 Sam Mills XRC	5.00	2.20
❑ 20 Buddy Aydelette	.50	.23
❑ 21 Joe Cribbs	2.00	.90
❑ 22 David Dumars	.50	.23
❑ 23 Robin Earl	.50	.23
❑ 24 Joey Jones	.50	.23
❑ 25 Leon Perry	.50	.23
❑ 26 Dave Pureifory	.50	.23
❑ 27 Bill Roe	.50	.23
❑ 28 Doug Smith DT XRC	2.00	.90
❑ 29 Cliff Stoudt	1.00	.45
❑ 30 Jeff Delaney	.50	.23
❑ 31 Vince Evans	1.00	.45
❑ 32 Leonard Harris XRC	.50	.23
❑ 33 Bill Johnson	.50	.23
❑ 34 Marc Lewis XRC	.50	.23
❑ 35 David Martin	.50	.23
❑ 36 Bruce Thornton	.50	.23
❑ 37 Craig Walls	.50	.23
❑ 38 Vincent White	.50	.23
❑ 39 Luther Bradley	.50	.23
❑ 40 Pete Catan	.50	.23
❑ 41 Kiki DeAyala	.50	.23
❑ 42 Toni Fritsch	.50	.23
❑ 43 Sam Harrell	.50	.23
❑ 44 Richard Johnson WR XRC	1.00	.45
❑ 45 Jim Kelly	20.00	9.00
❑ 46 Gerald McNeil XRC	.50	.23
❑ 47 Clarence Verdin XRC	2.00	.90
❑ 48 Dale Walters	.50	.23
❑ 49 Gary Clark XRC	6.00	2.70
❑ 50 Tom Dinkel	.50	.23
❑ 51 Mike Edwards	.50	.23
❑ 52 Brian Franco	.50	.23
❑ 53 Bob Gruber	.50	.23
❑ 54 Robbie Mahfouz	.50	.23
❑ 55 Mike Rozier	2.00	.90
❑ 56 Brian Sipe	1.00	.45
❑ 57 J.T. Turner	.50	.23
❑ 58 Howard Carson	.50	.23
❑ 59 Wymon Henderson XRC	.50	.23
❑ 60 Kevin Nelson	.50	.23
❑ 61 Jeff Partridge	.50	.23
❑ 62 Ben Rudolph	.50	.23
❑ 63 Jo Jo Townsell	1.00	.45
❑ 64 Eddie Weaver	.50	.23
❑ 65 Steve Young	30.00	13.50
❑ 66 Tony Zendejas XRC	1.00	.45
❑ 67 Mossy Cade	.50	.23
❑ 68 Leonard Coleman XRC	.50	.23
❑ 69 John Corker	.50	.23
❑ 70 Derrick Crawford	.50	.23
❑ 71 Art Kuehn	.50	.23
❑ 72 Walter Lewis	.50	.23
❑ 73 Tyrone McGriff	.50	.23
❑ 74 Tim Spencer	1.00	.45
❑ 75 Reggie White	25.00	11.00
❑ 76 Gizmo Williams XRC	2.00	.90
❑ 77 Sam Bowers	.50	.23
❑ 78 Maurice Carthon XRC	1.00	.45
❑ 79 Clarence Collins	.50	.23
❑ 80 Doug Flutie XRC	30.00	13.50
❑ 81 Freddie Gilbert	.50	.23
❑ 82 Kerry Justin	.50	.23
❑ 83 Dave Lapham	.50	.23
❑ 84 Rick Partridge	.50	.23
❑ 85 Roger Ruzek XRC	1.00	.45
❑ 86 Herschel Walker	8.00	3.60
❑ 87 Gordon Banks	.50	.23
❑ 88 Monte Bennett	.50	.23
❑ 89 Albert Bentley XRC	1.00	.45
❑ 90 Novo Bojovic	.50	.23
❑ 91 Dave Browning	.50	.23
❑ 92 Anthony Carter	2.00	.90
❑ 93 Bobby Hebert	2.00	.90
❑ 94 Ray Pinney	.50	.23
❑ 95 Stan Talley	.50	.23
❑ 96 Ruben Vaughan	.50	.23
❑ 97 Curtis Bledsoe	.50	.23
❑ 98 Reggie Collier	.50	.23
❑ 99 Jerry Doerger	.50	.23
❑ 100 Jerry Golsteyn	.50	.23
❑ 101 Bob Niziolek	.50	.23
❑ 102 Joel Patten	.50	.23
❑ 103 Ricky Simmons	.50	.23
❑ 104 Joey Walters	.50	.23
❑ 105 Marcus Dupree	1.00	.45
❑ 106 Jeff Gossett	1.00	.45
❑ 107 Frank Lockett	.50	.23
❑ 108 Marcus Marek	.50	.23
❑ 109 Kenny Neil	.50	.23
❑ 110 Robert Pennywell	.50	.23
❑ 111 Matt Robinson	.50	.23
❑ 112 Dan Ross	1.00	.45
❑ 113 Doug Woodward	.50	.23
❑ 114 Danny Buggs	.50	.23
❑ 115 Putt Choate	.50	.23
❑ 116 Greg Fields	.50	.23
❑ 117 Ken Hartley	.50	.23
❑ 118 Nick Mike-Mayer	.50	.23
❑ 119 Rick Neuheisel	2.00	.90
❑ 120 Peter Raeford	.50	.23

❑ 121 Gary Worthy .50 .23
❑ 122 Gary Anderson RB 1.00 .45
❑ 123 Zenon Andrusyshyn .50 .23
❑ 124 Greg Boone .50 .23
❑ 125 Mike Butler .50 .23
❑ 126 Mike Clark .50 .23
❑ 127 Willie Gillespie .50 .23
❑ 128 James Harrell .50 .23
❑ 129 Marvin Harvey .50 .23
❑ 130 John Reaves 1.00 .45
❑ 131 Eric Truvillion .50 .23
❑ 132 Checklist 1-132 1.00 .45

1986 Topps

	Nm-Mt	Ex-Mt
COMPLETE SET (396)	120.00	55.00
COMP.FACT.SET (396)	200.00	90.00

❑ 1 Marcus Allen RB .75 .35
Most Yards From Scrimmage: Season
❑ 2 Eric Dickerson RB .50 .23
Most Yards Rushing: Playoff Game
❑ 3 Lionel James RB .10 .05
Most All-Purpose Yards: Season
❑ 4 Steve Largent RB .50 .23
Most Seasons 50 or More Receptions
❑ 5 George Martin RB .10 .05
Most Touchdowns Defensive Lineman: Career
❑ 6 Stephone Paige RB .10 .05
Most Yards Receiving: Game
❑ 7 Walter Payton RB .75 .35
Most Consecutive Games 100 or More Yards Rushing
❑ 8 Super Bowl XX .25 .11
Bears 46, Patriots 10 (Jim McMahon handing off)
❑ 9 Bears TL .60 .25
(Walter Payton in Motion)
❑ 10 Jim McMahon .50 .23
❑ 11 Walter Payton AP 3.00 1.35
❑ 12 Matt Suhey .10 .05
❑ 13 Willie Gault .25 .11
❑ 14 Dennis McKinnon RC .10 .05
❑ 15 Emery Moorehead .10 .05
❑ 16 Jim Covert AP .25 .11
❑ 17 Jay Hilgenberg AP RC .50 .23
❑ 18 Kevin Butler RC .25 .11
❑ 19 Richard Dent AP .75 .35
❑ 20 William Perry RC .50 .23
❑ 21 Steve McMichael .50 .23
❑ 22 Dan Hampton .50 .23
❑ 23 Otis Wilson .10 .05
❑ 24 Mike Singletary .60 .25
❑ 25 Wilber Marshall RC .50 .23
❑ 26 Leslie Frazier .10 .05
❑ 27 Dave Duerson RC .10 .05
❑ 28 Gary Fencik .10 .05
❑ 29 Patriots TL .50 .23
(Craig James on the Run)
❑ 30 Tony Eason .10 .05
❑ 31 Steve Grogan .25 .11
❑ 32 Craig James .50 .23
❑ 33 Tony Collins .10 .05
❑ 34 Irving Fryar 1.25 .55
❑ 35 Brian Holloway .10 .05
❑ 36 John Hannah AP .50 .23
❑ 37 Tony Franklin .10 .05
❑ 38 Garin Veris RC .10 .05
❑ 39 Andre Tippett AP .25 .11
❑ 40 Steve Nelson .10 .05
❑ 41 Raymond Clayborn .10 .05
❑ 42 Fred Marion RC .10 .05
❑ 43 Rich Camarillo .10 .05
❑ 44 Dolphins TL 2.00 .90
(Dan Marino Sets Up)
❑ 45 Dan Marino AP 8.00 3.60
❑ 46 Tony Nathan .25 .11
❑ 47 Ron Davenport RC .10 .05
❑ 48 Mark Duper .50 .23
❑ 49 Mark Clayton .50 .23
❑ 50 Nat Moore .25 .11
❑ 51 Bruce Hardy .10 .05
❑ 52 Roy Foster .10 .05
❑ 53 Dwight Stephenson .75 .35
❑ 54 Fuad Reveiz RC .25 .11
❑ 55 Bob Baumhower .10 .05
❑ 56 Mike Charles .10 .05
❑ 57 Hugh Green .25 .11
❑ 58 Glenn Blackwood .10 .05
❑ 59 Reggie Roby .25 .11
❑ 60 Raiders TL .50 .23
(Marcus Allen Cuts Upfield)
❑ 61 Marc Wilson .10 .05
❑ 62 Marcus Allen AP 1.50 .70
❑ 63 Dokie Williams .10 .05
❑ 64 Todd Christensen .50 .23
❑ 65 Chris Bahr .10 .05
❑ 66 Fulton Walker .10 .05
❑ 67 Howie Long 1.25 .55
❑ 68 Bill Pickel .10 .05
❑ 69 Ray Guy .50 .23
❑ 70 Greg Townsend RC .50 .23
❑ 71 Rod Martin .25 .11
❑ 72 Matt Millen .25 .11
❑ 73 Mike Haynes .25 .11
❑ 74 Lester Hayes .25 .11
❑ 75 Vann McElroy .10 .05
❑ 76 Rams TL .50 .23
(Eric Dickerson Stiff-Arm)
❑ 77 Dieter Brock RC .25 .11
❑ 78 Eric Dickerson .75 .35
❑ 79 Henry Ellard 1.00 .45
❑ 80 Ron Brown RC .25 .11
❑ 81 Tony Hunter RC .10 .05
❑ 82 Kent Hill AP .10 .05
❑ 83 Doug Smith .10 .05
❑ 84 Dennis Harrah .10 .05
❑ 85 Jackie Slater .50 .23
❑ 86 Mike Lansford .10 .05
❑ 87 Gary Jeter .10 .05
❑ 88 Mike Wilcher .10 .05
❑ 89 Jim Collins .10 .05
❑ 90 LeRoy Irvin .25 .11
❑ 91 Gary Green .10 .05
❑ 92 Nolan Cromwell .25 .11
❑ 93 Dale Hatcher RC .10 .05
❑ 94 Jets TL .25 .11
(Freeman McNeil Powers)
❑ 95 Ken O'Brien .50 .23
❑ 96 Freeman McNeil .25 .11
❑ 97 Tony Paige RC .10 .05
❑ 98 Johnny Lam Jones .10 .05
❑ 99 Wesley Walker .25 .11
❑ 100 Kurt Sohn .10 .05
❑ 101 Al Toon RC .50 .23
❑ 102 Mickey Shuler .10 .05
❑ 103 Marvin Powell .10 .05
❑ 104 Pat Leahy .10 .05
❑ 105 Mark Gastineau .25 .11
❑ 106 Joe Klecko .25 .11
❑ 107 Marty Lyons .10 .05
❑ 108 Lance Mehl .10 .05
❑ 109 Bobby Jackson .10 .05
❑ 110 Dave Jennings .10 .05
❑ 111 Broncos TL .25 .11
(Sammy Winder Up Middle)
❑ 112 John Elway 8.00 3.60
❑ 113 Sammy Winder .25 .11
❑ 114 Gerald Willhite .10 .05
❑ 115 Steve Watson .10 .05
❑ 116 Vance Johnson RC .50 .23
❑ 117 Rich Karlis .10 .05
❑ 118 Rulon Jones .10 .05
❑ 119 Karl Mecklenburg AP RC .50 .23
❑ 120 Louis Wright .10 .05
❑ 121 Mike Harden .10 .05
❑ 122 Dennis Smith RC .50 .23
❑ 123 Steve Foley .10 .05
❑ 124 Cowboys TL .25 .11
(Tony Hill Evades Defender)
❑ 125 Danny White .50 .23
❑ 126 Tony Dorsett .60 .25
❑ 127 Timmy Newsome .10 .05
❑ 128 Mike Renfro .10 .05
❑ 129 Tony Hill .25 .11
❑ 130 Doug Cosbie .25 .11
❑ 131 Rafael Septien .10 .05
❑ 132 Ed Too Tall Jones .50 .23
❑ 133 Randy White .50 .23
❑ 134 Jim Jeffcoat .50 .23
❑ 135 Everson Walls .25 .11
❑ 136 Dennis Thurman .10 .05
❑ 137 Giants TL .25 .11
(Joe Morris Opening)
❑ 138 Phil Simms .50 .23
❑ 139 Joe Morris .50 .23
❑ 140 George Adams RC .10 .05
❑ 141 Lionel Manuel .25 .11
❑ 142 Bobby Johnson .10 .05
❑ 143 Phil McConkey RC .25 .11
❑ 144 Mark Bavaro RC .50 .23
❑ 145 Zeke Mowatt .10 .05
❑ 146 Brad Benson RC .10 .05
❑ 147 Bart Oates RC .25 .11
❑ 148 Leonard Marshall AP RC .50 .23
❑ 149 Jim Burt .25 .11
❑ 150 George Martin .10 .05
❑ 151 Lawrence Taylor AP 1.25 .55
❑ 152 Harry Carson AP .25 .11
❑ 153 Elvis Patterson RC .10 .05
❑ 154 Sean Landeta RC .25 .11
❑ 155 49ers TL .50 .23
(Roger Craig Scampers)
❑ 156 Joe Montana 8.00 3.60
❑ 157 Roger Craig .50 .23
❑ 158 Wendell Tyler .10 .05
❑ 159 Carl Monroe .10 .05
❑ 160 Dwight Clark .25 .11
❑ 161 Jerry Rice RC 80.00 36.00
❑ 162 Randy Cross .25 .11
❑ 163 Keith Fahnhorst .10 .05
❑ 164 Jeff Stover .10 .05
❑ 165 Michael Carter RC .10 .05
❑ 166 Dwaine Board .10 .05
❑ 167 Eric Wright .25 .11
❑ 168 Ronnie Lott .75 .35
❑ 169 Carlton Williamson .10 .05
❑ 170 Redskins TL .25 .11
(Dave Butz Gets His Man)
❑ 171 Joe Theismann .50 .23
❑ 172 Jay Schroeder RC .50 .23
❑ 173 George Rogers .25 .11
❑ 174 Ken Jenkins .10 .05
❑ 175 Art Monk AP .50 .23
❑ 176 Gary Clark RC 2.00 .90
❑ 177 Joe Jacoby .25 .11
❑ 178 Russ Grimm .25 .11
❑ 179 Mark Moseley .10 .05
❑ 180 Dexter Manley .25 .11

❑	181	Charles Mann RC	.50	.23
❑	182	Vernon Dean	.10	.05
❑	183	Raphel Cherry RC	.10	.05
❑	184	Curtis Jordan	.10	.05
❑	185	Browns TL	.50	.23
		(Bernie Kosar Fakes Handoff)		
❑	186	Gary Danielson	.25	.11
❑	187	Bernie Kosar RC	3.00	1.35
❑	188	Kevin Mack RC	.50	.23
❑	189	Earnest Byner RC	.75	.35
❑	190	Glen Young	.10	.05
❑	191	Ozzie Newsome	.50	.23
❑	192	Mike Baab	.10	.05
❑	193	Cody Risien	.25	.11
❑	194	Bob Golic	.25	.11
❑	195	Reggie Camp	.10	.05
❑	196	Chip Banks	.25	.11
❑	197	Tom Cousineau	.10	.05
❑	198	Frank Minnifield RC	.10	.05
❑	199	Al Gross	.10	.05
❑	200	Seahawks TL	.25	.11
		(Curt Warner Breaks Free)		
❑	201	Dave Krieg	.50	.23
❑	202	Curt Warner	.25	.11
❑	203	Steve Largent AP	.60	.25
❑	204	Norm Johnson	.10	.05
❑	205	Daryl Turner	.10	.05
❑	206	Jacob Green	.10	.05
❑	207	Joe Nash	.10	.05
❑	208	Jeff Bryant	.10	.05
❑	209	Randy Edwards	.10	.05
❑	210	Fredd Young	.10	.05
❑	211	Kenny Easley	.10	.05
❑	212	John Harris	.10	.05
❑	213	Packers TL	.10	.05
		(Paul Coffman Conquers)		
❑	214	Lynn Dickey	.25	.11
❑	215	Gerry Ellis	.10	.05
❑	216	Eddie Lee Ivery	.10	.05
❑	217	Jessie Clark	.10	.05
❑	218	James Lofton	.50	.23
❑	219	Paul Coffman	.10	.05
❑	220	Alphonso Carreker	.10	.05
❑	221	Ezra Johnson	.10	.05
❑	222	Mike Douglass	.10	.05
❑	223	Tim Lewis	.10	.05
❑	224	Mark Murphy RC	.10	.05
❑	225	Passing Leaders:	1.00	.45
		Ken O'Brien AFC		
		Joe Montana NFC		
❑	226	Receiving Leaders:	.25	.11
		Lionel James AFC		
		Roger Craig NFC		
❑	227	Rushing Leaders:	.50	.23
		Marcus Allen AFC		
		Gerald Riggs NFC		
❑	228	Scoring Leaders:	.25	.11
		Gary Anderson K AFC		
		Kevin Butler NFC		
❑	229	Interception Leaders:	.10	.05
		Eugene Daniel AFC		
		Albert Lewis AFC		
		Everson Walls NFC		
❑	230	Chargers TL	.50	.23
		(Dan Fouts Over Top)		
❑	231	Dan Fouts	.50	.23
❑	232	Lionel James	.10	.05
❑	233	Gary Anderson RB RC	.50	.23
❑	234	Tim Spencer RC	.25	.11
❑	235	Wes Chandler	.25	.11
❑	236	Charlie Joiner	.50	.23
❑	237	Kellen Winslow	.50	.23
❑	238	Jim Lachey RC	.50	.23
❑	239	Bob Thomas	.10	.05
❑	240	Jeffery Dale	.10	.05
❑	241	Ralf Mojsiejenko	.10	.05
❑	242	Lions TL	.10	.05
		(Eric Hipple Spots Receiver)		
❑	243	Eric Hipple	.10	.05
❑	244	Billy Sims	.25	.11
❑	245	James Jones	.10	.05
❑	246	Pete Mandley RC	.10	.05
❑	247	Leonard Thompson	.10	.05
❑	248	Lomas Brown RC	.25	.11
❑	249	Eddie Murray	.25	.11
❑	250	Curtis Green	.10	.05
❑	251	William Gay	.10	.05
❑	252	Jimmy Williams	.10	.05
❑	253	Bobby Watkins	.10	.05
❑	254	Bengals TL	.50	.23
		(Boomer Esiason Zeroes In)		
❑	255	Boomer Esiason RC	5.00	2.20
❑	256	James Brooks	.25	.11
❑	257	Larry Kinnebrew	.10	.05
❑	258	Cris Collinsworth	.25	.11
❑	259	Mike Martin	.10	.05
❑	260	Eddie Brown RC	.50	.23
❑	261	Anthony Munoz	.50	.23
❑	262	Jim Breech	.10	.05
❑	263	Ross Browner	.25	.11
❑	264	Carl Zander	.10	.05
❑	265	James Griffin	.10	.05
❑	266	Robert Jackson	.10	.05
❑	267	Pat McInally	.10	.05
❑	268	Eagles TL	.50	.23
		(Ron Jaworski Surveys)		
❑	269	Ron Jaworski	.25	.11
❑	270	Earnest Jackson	.25	.11
❑	271	Mike Quick	.25	.11
❑	272	John Spagnola	.10	.05
❑	273	Mark Dennard	.10	.05
❑	274	Paul McFadden	.10	.05
❑	275	Reggie White RC	20.00	9.00
❑	276	Greg Brown	.10	.05
❑	277	Herman Edwards	.10	.05
❑	278	Roynell Young	.10	.05
❑	279	Wes Hopkins	.10	.05
❑	280	Steelers TL	.25	.11
		(Walter Abercrombie Inches)		
❑	281	Mark Malone	.25	.11
❑	282	Frank Pollard	.10	.05
❑	283	Walter Abercrombie	.10	.05
❑	284	Louis Lipps	.50	.23
❑	285	John Stallworth	.50	.23
❑	286	Mike Webster	.25	.11
❑	287	Gary Anderson K	.25	.11
❑	288	Keith Willis	.10	.05
❑	289	Mike Merriweather	.10	.05
❑	290	Dwayne Woodruff	.10	.05
❑	291	Donnie Shell	.25	.11
❑	292	Vikings TL	.25	.11
		(Tommy Kramer Audible)		
❑	293	Tommy Kramer	.25	.11
❑	294	Darrin Nelson	.10	.05
❑	295	Ted Brown	.25	.11
❑	296	Buster Rhymes	.10	.05
❑	297	Anthony Carter RC	1.00	.45
❑	298	Steve Jordan RC	.50	.23
❑	299	Keith Millard RC	.50	.23
❑	300	Joey Browner RC	.50	.23
❑	301	John Turner	.10	.05
❑	302	Greg Coleman	.10	.05
❑	303	Chiefs TL	.10	.05
		(Todd Blackledge)		
❑	304	Bill Kenney	.10	.05
❑	305	Herman Heard	.10	.05
❑	306	Stephone Paige RC	.50	.23
❑	307	Carlos Carson	.25	.11
❑	308	Nick Lowery	.25	.11
❑	309	Mike Bell	.10	.05
❑	310	Bill Maas	.10	.05
❑	311	Art Still	.10	.05
❑	312	Albert Lewis RC	.50	.23
❑	313	Deron Cherry AP	.25	.11
❑	314	Colts TL	.10	.05
		(Rohn Stark Booms It)		
❑	315	Mike Pagel	.10	.05
❑	316	Randy McMillan	.10	.05
❑	317	Albert Bentley RC	.25	.11
❑	318	George Wonsley RC	.10	.05
❑	319	Robbie Martin	.10	.05
❑	320	Pat Beach	.10	.05
❑	321	Chris Hinton	.25	.11
❑	322	Duane Bickett RC	.50	.23
❑	323	Eugene Daniel	.10	.05
❑	324	Cliff Odom RC	.10	.05
❑	325	Rohn Stark	.25	.11
❑	326	Cardinals TL	.10	.05
		(Stump Mitchell Outside)		
❑	327	Neil Lomax	.25	.11
❑	328	Stump Mitchell	.25	.11
❑	329	Ottis Anderson	.50	.23
❑	330	J.T. Smith	.25	.11
❑	331	Pat Tilley	.10	.05
❑	332	Roy Green	.25	.11
❑	333	Lance Smith RC	.10	.05
❑	334	Curtis Greer	.10	.05
❑	335	Freddie Joe Nunn RC	.25	.11
❑	336	E.J. Junior	.25	.11
❑	337	Lonnie Young RC	.10	.05
❑	338	Saints TL	.10	.05
		(Wayne Wilson running)		
❑	339	Bobby Hebert RC	.50	.23
❑	340	Dave Wilson	.10	.05
❑	341	Wayne Wilson	.10	.05
❑	342	Hoby Brenner	.10	.05
❑	343	Stan Brock	.25	.11
❑	344	Morten Andersen	.50	.23
❑	345	Bruce Clark	.10	.05
❑	346	Rickey Jackson	.50	.23
❑	347	Dave Waymer	.10	.05
❑	348	Brian Hansen	.10	.05
❑	349	Oilers TL	.50	.23
		(Warren Moon Throws Bomb)		
❑	350	Warren Moon	3.00	1.35
❑	351	Mike Rozier RC	.50	.23
❑	352	Butch Woolfolk	.10	.05
❑	353	Drew Hill	.50	.23
❑	354	Willie Drewrey RC	.10	.05
❑	355	Tim Smith	.25	.11
❑	356	Mike Munchak	.50	.23
❑	357	Ray Childress RC	.50	.23
❑	358	Frank Bush	.10	.05
❑	359	Steve Brown	.10	.05
❑	360	Falcons TL	.10	.05
		(Gerald Riggs Around End)		
❑	361	David Archer RC	.50	.23
❑	362	Gerald Riggs	.25	.11
❑	363	William Andrews	.25	.11
❑	364	Billy Johnson	.25	.11
❑	365	Arthur Cox	.10	.05
❑	366	Mike Kenn	.10	.05
❑	367	Bill Fralic RC	.25	.11
❑	368	Mick Luckhurst	.10	.05
❑	369	Rick Bryan	.10	.05
❑	370	Bobby Butler	.10	.05
❑	371	Rick Donnelly RC	.10	.05
❑	372	Buccaneers TL	.10	.05
		(James Wilder Sweeps Left)		
❑	373	Steve DeBerg	.50	.23
❑	374	Steve Young RC	20.00	9.00
❑	375	James Wilder	.10	.05
❑	376	Kevin House	.10	.05
❑	377	Gerald Carter	.10	.05
❑	378	Jimmie Giles	.25	.11
❑	379	Sean Farrell	.10	.05
❑	380	Donald Igwebuike	.10	.05
❑	381	David Logan	.10	.05
❑	382	Jeremiah Castille RC	.10	.05
❑	383	Bills TL	.10	.05
		(Greg Bell Sees Daylight)		
❑	384	Bruce Mathison RC	.10	.05
❑	385	Joe Cribbs	.25	.11
❑	386	Greg Bell	.25	.11
❑	387	Jerry Butler	.10	.05
❑	388	Andre Reed RC	6.00	2.70
❑	389	Bruce Smith RC	5.00	2.20
❑	390	Fred Smerlas	.10	.05
❑	391	Darryl Talley	.50	.23
❑	392	Jim Haslett	.25	.11
❑	393	Charles Romes	.10	.05
❑	394	Checklist 1-132	.20	.09

❑ 395 Checklist 133-264 .20 .09
❑ 396 Checklist 265-396 .20 .09

1987 Topps

	Nm-Mt	Ex-Mt
COMPLETE SET (396)	30.00	13.50
COMP.FACT.SET (396)	40.00	18.00

❑ 1 Super Bowl XXI .50 .23
Giants 39,
Broncos 20
(Line play shown)
❑ 2 Todd Christensen RB .25 .11
Most Seasons
80 or More Receptions
❑ 3 Dave Jennings RB .10 .05
Most Punts: Career
❑ 4 Charlie Joiner RB .50 .23
Most Receiving
Yards: Career
❑ 5 Steve Largent RB .50 .23
Most Consec. Games
With a Reception
❑ 6 Dan Marino RB 2.00 .90
Most Consec. Seasons
30 or More TD Passes
❑ 7 Donnie Shell RB .25 .11
Most Interceptions&
Strong Safety: Career
❑ 8 Phil Simms RB .50 .23
Highest Completion
Percentage: Super Bowl
❑ 9 New York Giants TL .25 .11
(Mark Bavaro Pulls Free)
❑ 10 Phil Simms .50 .23
❑ 11 Joe Morris AP .25 .11
❑ 12 Maurice Carthon RC .10 .05
❑ 13 Lee Rouson .10 .05
❑ 14 Bobby Johnson .10 .05
❑ 15 Lionel Manuel .10 .05
❑ 16 Phil McConkey .10 .05
❑ 17 Mark Bavaro AP .50 .23
❑ 18 Zeke Mowatt .10 .05
❑ 19 Raul Allegre .10 .05
❑ 20 Sean Landeta .10 .05
❑ 21 Brad Benson .10 .05
❑ 22 Jim Burt .10 .05
❑ 23 Leonard Marshall .50 .23
❑ 24 Carl Banks .50 .23
❑ 25 Harry Carson .10 .05
❑ 26 Lawrence Taylor AP .75 .35
❑ 27 Terry Kinard RC .10 .05
❑ 28 Pepper Johnson RC .50 .23
❑ 29 Erik Howard RC .10 .05
❑ 30 Broncos TL .10 .05
(Gerald Willhite Dives)
❑ 31 John Elway 6.00 2.70
❑ 32 Gerald Willhite .10 .05
❑ 33 Sammy Winder .25 .11
❑ 34 Ken Bell .10 .05
❑ 35 Steve Watson .10 .05
❑ 36 Rich Karlis .10 .05
❑ 37 Keith Bishop .10 .05
❑ 38 Rulon Jones .10 .05
❑ 39 Karl Mecklenburg AP .50 .23
❑ 40 Louis Wright .10 .05
❑ 41 Mike Harden .10 .05
❑ 42 Dennis Smith .25 .11
❑ 43 Bears TL .50 .23
(Walter Payton Barrels)
❑ 44 Jim McMahon .50 .23
❑ 45 Doug Flutie RC 12.00 5.50
❑ 46 Walter Payton 2.00 .90
❑ 47 Matt Suhey .10 .05
❑ 48 Willie Gault .25 .11
❑ 49 Dennis Gentry RC .10 .05
❑ 50 Kevin Butler .10 .05
❑ 51 Jim Covert .10 .05
❑ 52 Jay Hilgenberg .25 .11
❑ 53 Dan Hampton .50 .23
❑ 54 Steve McMichael .50 .23
❑ 55 William Perry .50 .23
❑ 56 Richard Dent .50 .23
❑ 57 Otis Wilson .10 .05
❑ 58 Mike Singletary AP .50 .23
❑ 59 Wilber Marshall .50 .23
❑ 60 Mike Richardson .10 .05
❑ 61 Dave Duerson .10 .05
❑ 62 Gary Fencik .10 .05
❑ 63 Redskins TL .25 .11
(George Rogers Plunges)
❑ 64 Jay Schroeder .25 .11
❑ 65 George Rogers .25 .11
❑ 66 Kelvin Bryant RC .25 .11
❑ 67 Ken Jenkins .10 .05
❑ 68 Gary Clark .50 .23
❑ 69 Art Monk .50 .23
❑ 70 Clint Didier RC .10 .05
❑ 71 Steve Cox .10 .05
❑ 72 Joe Jacoby .10 .05
❑ 73 Russ Grimm .10 .05
❑ 74 Charles Mann .25 .11
❑ 75 Dave Butz .10 .05
❑ 76 Dexter Manley .25 .11
❑ 77 Darrell Green AP .50 .23
❑ 78 Curtis Jordan .10 .05
❑ 79 Browns TL .10 .05
(Harry Holt Sees Daylight)
❑ 80 Bernie Kosar .50 .23
❑ 81 Curtis Dickey .10 .05
❑ 82 Kevin Mack .25 .11
❑ 83 Herman Fontenot .10 .05
❑ 84 Brian Brennan RC .10 .05
❑ 85 Ozzie Newsome .50 .23
❑ 86 Jeff Gossett .25 .11
❑ 87 Cody Risien .10 .05
❑ 88 Reggie Camp .10 .05
❑ 89 Bob Golic .10 .05
❑ 90 Carl Hairston .10 .05
❑ 91 Chip Banks .10 .05
❑ 92 Frank Minnifield .10 .05
❑ 93 Hanford Dixon .10 .05
❑ 94 Gerald McNeil RC .10 .05
❑ 95 Dave Puzzuoli .10 .05
❑ 96 Patriots TL .10 .05
(Andre Tippett Gets
His Man (Marcus Allen))
❑ 97 Tony Eason .25 .11
❑ 98 Craig James .25 .11
❑ 99 Tony Collins .25 .11
❑ 100 Mosi Tatupu .10 .05
❑ 101 Stanley Morgan .25 .11
❑ 102 Irving Fryar .50 .23
❑ 103 Stephen Starring .10 .05
❑ 104 Tony Franklin .10 .05
❑ 105 Rich Camarillo .10 .05
❑ 106 Garin Veris .10 .05
❑ 107 Andre Tippett AP .25 .11
❑ 108 Don Blackmon .10 .05
❑ 109 Ronnie Lippett RC .10 .05
❑ 110 Raymond Clayborn .10 .05
❑ 111 49ers TL .25 .11
(Roger Craig Up the Middle)
❑ 112 Joe Montana 6.00 2.70
❑ 113 Roger Craig .50 .23
❑ 114 Joe Cribbs .25 .11
❑ 115 Jerry Rice AP 6.00 2.70
❑ 116 Dwight Clark .25 .11
❑ 117 Ray Wersching .10 .05
❑ 118 Max Runager .10 .05
❑ 119 Jeff Stover .10 .05
❑ 120 Dwaine Board .10 .05
❑ 121 Tim McKyer RC .25 .11
❑ 122 Don Griffin RC .25 .11
❑ 123 Ronnie Lott AP .50 .23
❑ 124 Tom Holmoe .10 .05
❑ 125 Charles Haley RC 1.25 .55
❑ 126 Jets TL .10 .05
(Mark Gastineau Seeks)
❑ 127 Ken O'Brien .25 .11
❑ 128 Pat Ryan .10 .05
❑ 129 Freeman McNeil .25 .11
❑ 130 Johnny Hector RC .10 .05
❑ 131 Al Toon AP .50 .23
❑ 132 Wesley Walker .25 .11
❑ 133 Mickey Shuler .10 .05
❑ 134 Pat Leahy .10 .05
❑ 135 Mark Gastineau .25 .11
❑ 136 Joe Klecko .25 .11
❑ 137 Marty Lyons .10 .05
❑ 138 Bob Crable .10 .05
❑ 139 Lance Mehl .10 .05
❑ 140 Dave Jennings .10 .05
❑ 141 Harry Hamilton RC .10 .05
❑ 142 Lester Lyles .10 .05
❑ 143 Bobby Humphery UER .10 .05
(Misspelled Humphrey
on card front)
❑ 144 Rams TL .50 .23
(Eric Dickerson
Through the Line)
❑ 145 Jim Everett RC 2.00 .90
❑ 146 Eric Dickerson AP .50 .23
❑ 147 Barry Redden .10 .05
❑ 148 Ron Brown .25 .11
❑ 149 Kevin House .10 .05
❑ 150 Henry Ellard .50 .23
❑ 151 Doug Smith .10 .05
❑ 152 Dennis Harrah .10 .05
❑ 153 Jackie Slater .25 .11
❑ 154 Gary Jeter .10 .05
❑ 155 Carl Ekern .10 .05
❑ 156 Mike Wilcher .10 .05
❑ 157 Jerry Gray RC .10 .05
❑ 158 LeRoy Irvin .10 .05
❑ 159 Nolan Cromwell .25 .11
❑ 160 Chiefs TL .10 .05
(Todd Blackledge Hands Off)
❑ 161 Bill Kenney .10 .05
❑ 162 Stephone Paige .25 .11
❑ 163 Henry Marshall .10 .05
❑ 164 Carlos Carson .10 .05
❑ 165 Nick Lowery .25 .11
❑ 166 Irv Eatman RC .10 .05
❑ 167 Brad Budde .10 .05
❑ 168 Art Still .10 .05
❑ 169 Bill Maas .10 .05
❑ 170 Lloyd Burruss RC .10 .05
❑ 171 Deron Cherry AP .10 .05
❑ 172 Seahawks TL .25 .11
(Curt Warner Finds Opening)
❑ 173 Dave Krieg .50 .23
❑ 174 Curt Warner .25 .11
❑ 175 John L. Williams RC .50 .23
❑ 176 Bobby Joe Edmonds RC .25 .11
❑ 177 Steve Largent .60 .25
❑ 178 Bruce Scholtz .10 .05
❑ 179 Norm Johnson .10 .05
❑ 180 Jacob Green .10 .05
❑ 181 Fredd Young .10 .05
❑ 182 Dave Brown .10 .05
❑ 183 Kenny Easley .10 .05
❑ 184 Bengals TL .25 .11
(James Brooks Stiff-Arm)
❑ 185 Boomer Esiason .50 .23
❑ 186 James Brooks .25 .11
❑ 187 Larry Kinnebrew .10 .05

❑ 188 Cris Collinsworth .25 .11
❑ 189 Eddie Brown .50 .23
❑ 190 Tim McGee RC .50 .23
❑ 191 Jim Breech .10 .05
❑ 192 Anthony Munoz .50 .23
❑ 193 Max Montoya .10 .05
❑ 194 Eddie Edwards .10 .05
❑ 195 Ross Browner .25 .11
❑ 196 Emanuel King .10 .05
❑ 197 Louis Breeden .10 .05
❑ 198 Vikings TL .10 .05
(Darrin Nelson In Motion)
❑ 199 Tommy Kramer .25 .11
❑ 200 Darrin Nelson .10 .05
❑ 201 Allen Rice .10 .05
❑ 202 Anthony Carter .50 .23
❑ 203 Leo Lewis .10 .05
❑ 204 Steve Jordan .50 .23
❑ 205 Chuck Nelson RC .10 .05
❑ 206 Greg Coleman .10 .05
❑ 207 Gary Zimmerman RC .50 .23
❑ 208 Doug Martin .10 .05
❑ 209 Keith Millard .10 .05
❑ 210 Issiac Holt RC .10 .05
❑ 211 Joey Browner .25 .11
❑ 212 Rufus Bess .10 .05
❑ 213 Raiders TL .50 .23
(Marcus Allen Quick Feet)
❑ 214 Jim Plunkett .50 .23
❑ 215 Marcus Allen 1.00 .45
❑ 216 Napoleon McCallum RC .25 .11
❑ 217 Dokie Williams .10 .05
❑ 218 Todd Christensen .50 .23
❑ 219 Chris Bahr .10 .05
❑ 220 Howie Long .60 .25
❑ 221 Bill Pickel .10 .05
❑ 222 Sean Jones RC .75 .35
❑ 223 Lester Hayes .25 .11
❑ 224 Mike Haynes .25 .11
❑ 225 Vann McElroy .10 .05
❑ 226 Fulton Walker .10 .05
❑ 227 Passing Leaders 1.25 .55
Tommy Kramer
Dan Marino
❑ 228 Receiving Leaders 1.25 .55
Jerry Rice
Todd Christensen
❑ 229 Rushing Leaders .50 .23
Eric Dickerson
Curt Warner
❑ 230 Scoring Leaders .10 .05
Kevin Butler
Tony Franklin
❑ 231 Interception Leaders .50 .23
Ronnie Lott
Deron Cherry
❑ 232 Dolphins TL .25 .11
(Reggie Roby Booms It)
❑ 233 Dan Marino AP 6.00 2.70
❑ 234 Lorenzo Hampton RC .10 .05
❑ 235 Tony Nathan .25 .11
❑ 236 Mark Duper .50 .23
❑ 237 Mark Clayton .50 .23
❑ 238 Nat Moore .25 .11
❑ 239 Bruce Hardy .10 .05
❑ 240 Reggie Roby .25 .11
❑ 241 Roy Foster .10 .05
❑ 242 Dwight Stephenson .50 .23
❑ 243 Hugh Green .10 .05
❑ 244 John Offerdahl RC .50 .23
❑ 245 Mark Brown .10 .05
❑ 246 Doug Betters .10 .05
❑ 247 Bob Baumhower .10 .05
❑ 248 Falcons TL .10 .05
(Gerald Riggs Uses Blockers)
❑ 249 David Archer .50 .23
❑ 250 Gerald Riggs .25 .11
❑ 251 William Andrews .25 .11
❑ 252 Charlie Brown .10 .05
❑ 253 Arthur Cox .10 .05
❑ 254 Rick Donnelly .10 .05
❑ 255 Bill Fralic AP .10 .05
❑ 256 Mike Gann RC .10 .05
❑ 257 Rick Bryan .10 .05
❑ 258 Bret Clark .10 .05
❑ 259 Mike Pitts .10 .05
❑ 260 Cowboys TL .50 .23
(Tony Dorsett Cuts)
❑ 261 Danny White .50 .23
❑ 262 Steve Pelluer RC .10 .05
❑ 263 Tony Dorsett .50 .23
❑ 264 Herschel Walker RC UER 2.50 1.10
(Stats show 12 TD's
in 1986, text says 14)
❑ 265 Timmy Newsome .10 .05
❑ 266 Tony Hill .25 .11
❑ 267 Mike Sherrard RC .50 .23
❑ 268 Jim Jeffcoat .50 .23
❑ 269 Ron Fellows .10 .05
❑ 270 Bill Bates .50 .23
❑ 271 Michael Downs .10 .05
❑ 272 Saints TL .25 .11
(Bobby Hebert Fakes)
❑ 273 Dave Wilson .10 .05
❑ 274 Rueben Mayes RC UER .10 .05
(Stats show 1353 comple-
tions, should be yards)
❑ 275 Hoby Brenner .10 .05
❑ 276 Eric Martin RC .50 .23
❑ 277 Morten Andersen .25 .11
❑ 278 Brian Hansen .10 .05
❑ 279 Rickey Jackson .50 .23
❑ 280 Dave Waymer .10 .05
❑ 281 Bruce Clark .10 .05
❑ 282 James Geathers RC .25 .11
❑ 283 Steelers TL .25 .11
(Walter Abercrombie Resists)
❑ 284 Mark Malone .25 .11
❑ 285 Earnest Jackson .10 .05
❑ 286 Walter Abercrombie .10 .05
❑ 287 Louis Lipps .25 .11
❑ 288 John Stallworth UER .50 .23
(Stats only go up
through 1981)
❑ 289 Gary Anderson K .10 .05
❑ 290 Keith Willis .10 .05
❑ 291 Mike Merriweather .10 .05
❑ 292 Lupe Sanchez .10 .05
❑ 293 Donnie Shell .25 .11
❑ 294 Eagles TL .50 .23
(Keith Byars Inches Ahead)
❑ 295 Mike Reichenbach .10 .05
❑ 296 R.Cunningham RC 6.00 2.70
❑ 297 Keith Byars RC .75 .35
❑ 298 Mike Quick .25 .11
❑ 299 Kenny Jackson .10 .05
❑ 300 John Teltschik RC .10 .05
❑ 301 Reggie White AP 3.00 1.35
❑ 302 Ken Clarke .10 .05
❑ 303 Greg Brown .10 .05
❑ 304 Roynell Young .10 .05
❑ 305 Andre Waters RC .50 .23
❑ 306 Oilers TL .50 .23
(Warren Moon Plots Play)
❑ 307 Warren Moon 1.50 .70
❑ 308 Mike Rozier .25 .11
❑ 309 Drew Hill .25 .11
❑ 310 Ernest Givins RC .50 .23
❑ 311 Lee Johnson RC .10 .05
❑ 312 Kent Hill .10 .05
❑ 313 Dean Steinkuhler RC .25 .11
❑ 314 Ray Childress .50 .23
❑ 315 John Grimsley RC .10 .05
❑ 316 Jesse Baker .10 .05
❑ 317 Lions TL .10 .05
(Eric Hipple Surveys)
❑ 318 Chuck Long RC .25 .11
❑ 319 James Jones .10 .05
❑ 320 Garry James .10 .05
❑ 321 Jeff Chadwick .10 .05
❑ 322 Leonard Thompson .10 .05
❑ 323 Pete Mandley .10 .05
❑ 324 Jimmie Giles .25 .11
❑ 325 Herman Hunter .10 .05
❑ 326 Keith Ferguson .10 .05
❑ 327 Devon Mitchell .10 .05
❑ 328 Cardinals TL .10 .05
(Neil Lomax Audible)
❑ 329 Neil Lomax .25 .11
❑ 330 Stump Mitchell .10 .05
❑ 331 Earl Ferrell .10 .05
❑ 332 Vai Sikahema RC .25 .11
❑ 333 Ron Wolfley RC .10 .05
❑ 334 J.T. Smith .25 .11
❑ 335 Roy Green .25 .11
❑ 336 Al(Bubba) Baker .10 .05
❑ 337 Freddie Joe Nunn .10 .05
❑ 338 Cedric Mack .10 .05
❑ 339 Chargers TL .25 .11
(Gary Anderson Evades)
❑ 340 Dan Fouts .50 .23
❑ 341 Gary Anderson UER .50 .23
(Two Topps logos
on card front)
❑ 342 Wes Chandler .25 .11
❑ 343 Kellen Winslow .50 .23
❑ 344 Ralf Mojsiejenko .10 .05
❑ 345 Rolf Benirschke .10 .05
❑ 346 Lee Williams RC .25 .11
❑ 347 Leslie O'Neal RC 1.00 .45
❑ 348 Billy Ray Smith .25 .11
❑ 349 Gill Byrd .25 .11
❑ 350 Packers TL .10 .05
(Paul Ott Carruth Around End)
❑ 351 Randy Wright .10 .05
❑ 352 Kenneth Davis RC .50 .23
❑ 353 Gerry Ellis .10 .05
❑ 354 James Lofton .50 .23
❑ 355 Phillip Epps RC .10 .05
❑ 356 Walter Stanley RC .10 .05
❑ 357 Eddie Lee Ivery .10 .05
❑ 358 Tim Harris RC .50 .23
❑ 359 Mark Lee UER .10 .05
(Red flag, rest of
Packers have yellow)
❑ 360 Mossy Cade .10 .05
❑ 361 Bills TL 1.00 .45
(Jim Kelly Works Ground)
❑ 362 Jim Kelly RC 10.00 4.50
❑ 363 Robb Riddick RC .10 .05
❑ 364 Greg Bell .10 .05
❑ 365 Andre Reed 1.25 .55
❑ 366 Pete Metzelaars RC .50 .23
❑ 367 Sean McNanie .10 .05
❑ 368 Fred Smerlas .10 .05
❑ 369 Bruce Smith 2.00 .90
❑ 370 Darryl Talley .25 .11
❑ 371 Charles Romes .10 .05
❑ 372 Colts TL .10 .05
(Rohn Stark High and Far)
❑ 373 Jack Trudeau RC .25 .11
❑ 374 Gary Hogeboom .10 .05
❑ 375 Randy McMillan .10 .05
❑ 376 Albert Bentley .10 .05
❑ 377 Matt Bouza .10 .05
❑ 378 Bill Brooks RC 1.00 .45
❑ 379 Rohn Stark .10 .05
❑ 380 Chris Hinton .10 .05
❑ 381 Ray Donaldson .10 .05
❑ 382 Jon Hand RC .10 .05
❑ 383 Buccaneers TL .10 .05
(James Wilder Braces)
❑ 384 Steve Young 5.00 2.20
❑ 385 James Wilder .10 .05
❑ 386 Frank Garcia .10 .05
❑ 387 Gerald Carter .10 .05
❑ 388 Phil Freeman .10 .05
❑ 389 Calvin Magee .10 .05
❑ 390 Donald Igwebuike .10 .05
❑ 391 David Logan .10 .05
❑ 392 Jeff Davis .10 .05
❑ 393 Chris Washington .10 .05
❑ 394 Checklist 1-132 .10 .05

Card	Nm-Mt	Ex-Mt
❑ 395 Checklist 133-264	.10	.05
❑ 396 Checklist 265-396	.10	.05

1988 Topps

	Nm-Mt	Ex-Mt
COMPLETE SET (396)	15.00	6.75
COMP.FACT.SET (396)	20.00	9.00
❑ 1 Super Bowl XXII Redskins 42, Broncos 10 (Redskins celebrating)	.20	.09
❑ 2 Vencie Glenn RB Longest Interception Return	.05	.02
❑ 3 Steve Largent RB Most Receptions: Career	.40	.18
❑ 4 Joe Montana RB Most Consecutive Pass Completions	.75	.35
❑ 5 Walter Payton RB Most Rushing Touchdowns: Career	.40	.18
❑ 6 Jerry Rice RB Most Touchdown Receptions: Season	.75	.35
❑ 7 Redskins TL (Kelvin Bryant Sees Daylight)	.20	.09
❑ 8 Doug Williams	.20	.09
❑ 9 George Rogers	.20	.09
❑ 10 Kelvin Bryant	.20	.09
❑ 11 Timmy Smith SR	.20	.09
❑ 12 Art Monk	.40	.18
❑ 13 Gary Clark	.40	.18
❑ 14 Ricky Sanders RC	.40	.18
❑ 15 Steve Cox	.05	.02
❑ 16 Joe Jacoby	.05	.02
❑ 17 Charles Mann	.20	.09
❑ 18 Dave Butz	.05	.02
❑ 19 Darrell Green AP	.20	.09
❑ 20 Dexter Manley	.05	.02
❑ 21 Barry Wilburn	.05	.02
❑ 22 Broncos TL (Sammy Winder Winds Through)	.05	.02
❑ 23 John Elway AP	2.00	.90
❑ 24 Sammy Winder	.05	.02
❑ 25 Vance Johnson	.20	.09
❑ 26 Mark Jackson RC	.40	.18
❑ 27 Ricky Nattiel SR RC	.05	.02
❑ 28 Clarence Kay	.05	.02
❑ 29 Rich Karlis	.05	.02
❑ 30 Keith Bishop	.05	.02
❑ 31 Mike Horan	.05	.02
❑ 32 Rulon Jones	.05	.02
❑ 33 Karl Mecklenburg	.20	.09
❑ 34 Jim Ryan	.05	.02
❑ 35 Mark Haynes	.20	.09
❑ 36 Mike Harden	.05	.02
❑ 37 49ers TL (Roger Craig Gallops For Yardage)	.40	.18
❑ 38 Joe Montana	2.00	.90
❑ 39 Steve Young	1.00	.45
❑ 40 Roger Craig	.20	.09
❑ 41 Tom Rathman RC	.40	.18
❑ 42 Joe Cribbs	.20	.09
❑ 43 Jerry Rice AP	2.00	.90
❑ 44 Mike Wilson RC	.05	.02
❑ 45 Ron Heller RC	.05	.02
❑ 46 Ray Wersching	.05	.02
❑ 47 Michael Carter	.05	.02
❑ 48 Dwaine Board	.05	.02
❑ 49 Michael Walter	.05	.02
❑ 50 Don Griffin	.05	.02
❑ 51 Ronnie Lott	.40	.18
❑ 52 Charles Haley	.40	.18
❑ 53 Dana McLemore	.05	.02
❑ 54 Saints TL (Bobby Hebert Hands Off)	.20	.09
❑ 55 Bobby Hebert	.20	.09
❑ 56 Rueben Mayes	.05	.02
❑ 57 Dalton Hilliard RC	.05	.02
❑ 58 Eric Martin	.20	.09
❑ 59 John Tice RC	.05	.02
❑ 60 Brad Edelman	.05	.02
❑ 61 Morten Andersen AP	.20	.09
❑ 62 Brian Hansen	.05	.02
❑ 63 Mel Gray RC	.40	.18
❑ 64 Rickey Jackson	.20	.09
❑ 65 Sam Mills RC	.75	.35
❑ 66 Pat Swilling RC	.40	.18
❑ 67 Dave Waymer	.05	.02
❑ 68 Bears TL (Willie Gault Powers Forward)	.20	.09
❑ 69 Jim McMahon	.40	.18
❑ 70 Mike Tomczak RC	.05	.02
❑ 71 Neal Anderson RC	.40	.18
❑ 72 Willie Gault	.20	.09
❑ 73 Dennis Gentry	.05	.02
❑ 74 Dennis McKinnon	.05	.02
❑ 75 Kevin Butler	.05	.02
❑ 76 Jim Covert	.05	.02
❑ 77 Jay Hilgenberg	.05	.02
❑ 78 Steve McMichael	.20	.09
❑ 79 William Perry	.20	.09
❑ 80 Richard Dent	.40	.18
❑ 81 Ron Rivera RC	.05	.02
❑ 82 Mike Singletary AP	.40	.18
❑ 83 Dan Hampton	.40	.18
❑ 84 Dave Duerson	.05	.02
❑ 85 Browns TL (Bernie Kosar Lets it Go)	.20	.09
❑ 86 Bernie Kosar	.40	.18
❑ 87 Earnest Byner	.40	.18
❑ 88 Kevin Mack	.20	.09
❑ 89 Webster Slaughter RC	.40	.18
❑ 90 Gerald McNeil	.05	.02
❑ 91 Brian Brennan	.05	.02
❑ 92 Ozzie Newsome	.40	.18
❑ 93 Cody Risien	.05	.02
❑ 94 Bob Golic	.05	.02
❑ 95 Carl Hairston	.05	.02
❑ 96 Mike Johnson RC	.05	.02
❑ 97 Clay Matthews	.20	.09
❑ 98 Frank Minnifield	.05	.02
❑ 99 Hanford Dixon	.05	.02
❑ 100 Dave Puzzuoli	.05	.02
❑ 101 Felix Wright RC	.05	.02
❑ 102 Oilers TL (Warren Moon Over The Top)	.40	.18
❑ 103 Warren Moon	.50	.23
❑ 104 Mike Rozier	.05	.02
❑ 105 Alonzo Highsmith SR RC	.20	.09
❑ 106 Drew Hill	.20	.09
❑ 107 Ernest Givins	.40	.18
❑ 108 Curtis Duncan RC	.40	.18
❑ 109 Tony Zendejas RC	.05	.02
❑ 110 Mike Munchak AP	.40	.18
❑ 111 Kent Hill	.05	.02
❑ 112 Ray Childress	.20	.09
❑ 113 Al Smith RC	.20	.09
❑ 114 Keith Bostic RC	.05	.02
❑ 115 Jeff Donaldson	.05	.02
❑ 116 Colts TL (Eric Dickerson Finds Opening)	.40	.18
❑ 117 Jack Trudeau	.05	.02
❑ 118 Eric Dickerson AP	.40	.18
❑ 119 Albert Bentley	.05	.02
❑ 120 Matt Bouza	.05	.02
❑ 121 Bill Brooks	.40	.18
❑ 122 Dean Biasucci RC	.05	.02
❑ 123 Chris Hinton	.05	.02
❑ 124 Ray Donaldson	.05	.02
❑ 125 Ron Solt RC	.05	.02
❑ 126 Donnell Thompson	.05	.02
❑ 127 Barry Krauss RC	.05	.02
❑ 128 Duane Bickett	.05	.02
❑ 129 Mike Prior RC	.05	.02
❑ 130 Seahawks TL (Curt Warner Follows Blocking)	.20	.09
❑ 131 Dave Krieg	.20	.09
❑ 132 Curt Warner	.20	.09
❑ 133 John L. Williams	.40	.18
❑ 134 Bobby Joe Edmonds	.05	.02
❑ 135 Steve Largent	.40	.18
❑ 136 Raymond Butler	.05	.02
❑ 137 Norm Johnson	.05	.02
❑ 138 Ruben Rodriguez	.05	.02
❑ 139 Blair Bush	.05	.02
❑ 140 Jacob Green	.05	.02
❑ 141 Joe Nash	.05	.02
❑ 142 Jeff Bryant	.05	.02
❑ 143 Fredd Young	.05	.02
❑ 144 Brian Bosworth SR RC	1.50	.70
❑ 145 Kenny Easley	.05	.02
❑ 146 Vikings TL (Tommy Kramer Spots His Man)	.20	.09
❑ 147 Wade Wilson RC	.40	.18
❑ 148 Tommy Kramer	.20	.09
❑ 149 Darrin Nelson	.05	.02
❑ 150 D.J. Dozier SR RC	.20	.09
❑ 151 Anthony Carter	.20	.09
❑ 152 Leo Lewis	.05	.02
❑ 153 Steve Jordan	.20	.09
❑ 154 Gary Zimmerman	.05	.02
❑ 155 Chuck Nelson	.05	.02
❑ 156 Henry Thomas SR RC	.40	.18
❑ 157 Chris Doleman RC	.40	.18
❑ 158 Scott Studwell RC	.05	.02
❑ 159 Jesse Solomon RC	.05	.02
❑ 160 Joey Browner AP	.05	.02
❑ 161 Neal Guggemos	.05	.02
❑ 162 Steelers TL (Louis Lipps In a Crowd)	.20	.09
❑ 163 Mark Malone	.05	.02
❑ 164 Walter Abercrombie	.05	.02
❑ 165 Earnest Jackson	.05	.02
❑ 166 Frank Pollard	.05	.02
❑ 167 Dwight Stone RC	.20	.09
❑ 168 Gary Anderson K	.05	.02
❑ 169 Harry Newsome RC	.05	.02
❑ 170 Keith Willis	.05	.02
❑ 171 Keith Gary	.05	.02
❑ 172 David Little RC	.20	.09
❑ 173 Mike Merriweather	.05	.02
❑ 174 Dwayne Woodruff	.05	.02
❑ 175 Patriots TL (Irving Fryar One on One)	.40	.18
❑ 176 Steve Grogan	.20	.09
❑ 177 Tony Eason	.20	.09
❑ 178 Tony Collins	.20	.09
❑ 179 Mosi Tatupu	.05	.02
❑ 180 Stanley Morgan	.20	.09
❑ 181 Irving Fryar	.40	.18
❑ 182 Stephen Starring	.05	.02
❑ 183 Tony Franklin	.05	.02
❑ 184 Rich Camarillo	.05	.02
❑ 185 Garin Veris	.05	.02
❑ 186 Andre Tippett	.20	.09
❑ 187 Ronnie Lippett	.05	.02
❑ 188 Fred Marion	.05	.02
❑ 189 Dolphins TL (Dan Marino Play-Action Pass)	.75	.35

❑ 190 Dan Marino 2.00 .90
❑ 191 Troy Stradford SR RC .20 .09
❑ 192 Lorenzo Hampton .05 .02
❑ 193 Mark Duper .20 .09
❑ 194 Mark Clayton .20 .09
❑ 195 Reggie Roby .20 .09
❑ 196 Dwight Stephenson .40 .18
❑ 197 T.J. Turner RC .05 .02
❑ 198 John Bosa RC .05 .02
❑ 199 Jackie Shipp .05 .02
❑ 200 John Offerdahl .20 .09
❑ 201 Mark Brown .05 .02
❑ 202 Paul Lankford .05 .02
❑ 203 Chargers TL .40 .18
(Kellen Winslow Sure Hands)
❑ 204 Tim Spencer .05 .02
❑ 205 Gary Anderson RB .20 .09
❑ 206 Curtis Adams .05 .02
❑ 207 Lionel James .05 .02
❑ 208 Chip Banks .05 .02
❑ 209 Kellen Winslow .40 .18
❑ 210 Ralf Mojsiejenko .05 .02
❑ 211 Jim Lachey .20 .09
❑ 212 Lee Williams .05 .02
❑ 213 Billy Ray Smith .05 .02
❑ 214 Vencie Glenn RC .20 .09
❑ 215 Passing Leaders .50 .23
Bernie Kosar
Joe Montana
❑ 216 Receiving Leaders .20 .09
Al Toon
J.T. Smith
❑ 217 Rushing Leaders .20 .09
Charles White
Eric Dickerson
❑ 218 Scoring Leaders .40 .18
Jim Breech
Jerry Rice
❑ 219 Interception Leaders .05 .02
Keith Bostic
Mark Kelso
Mike Prior
Barry Wilburn
❑ 220 Bills TL .40 .18
(Jim Kelly Plots His Course)
❑ 221 Jim Kelly .75 .35
❑ 222 Ronnie Harmon RC .40 .18
❑ 223 Robb Riddick .05 .02
❑ 224 Andre Reed .40 .18
❑ 225 Chris Burkett RC .05 .02
❑ 226 Pete Metzelaars .40 .18
❑ 227 Bruce Smith AP .50 .23
❑ 228 Darryl Talley .20 .09
❑ 229 Eugene Marve .05 .02
❑ 230 Cornelius Bennett SR RC .75 .35
❑ 231 Mark Kelso RC .05 .02
❑ 232 Shane Conlan SR RC .40 .18
❑ 233 Eagles TL .40 .18
(Randall Cunningham
QB Keeper)
❑ 234 Randall Cunningham 1.00 .45
❑ 235 Keith Byars .40 .18
❑ 236 Anthony Toney RC .05 .02
❑ 237 Mike Quick .20 .09
❑ 238 Kenny Jackson .05 .02
❑ 239 John Spagnola .05 .02
❑ 240 Paul McFadden .05 .02
❑ 241 Reggie White AP .60 .25
❑ 242 Ken Clarke .05 .02
❑ 243 Mike Pitts .05 .02
❑ 244 Clyde Simmons RC .40 .18
❑ 245 Seth Joyner RC .40 .18
❑ 246 Andre Waters .40 .18
❑ 247 Jerome Brown SR RC .40 .18
❑ 248 Cardinals TL .05 .02
(Stump Mitchell On the Run)
❑ 249 Neil Lomax .20 .09
❑ 250 Stump Mitchell .05 .02
❑ 251 Earl Ferrell .05 .02
❑ 252 Vai Sikahema .05 .02
❑ 253 J.T. Smith .20 .09
❑ 254 Roy Green .20 .09
❑ 255 Robert Awalt RC .20 .09
❑ 256 Freddie Joe Nunn .05 .02
❑ 257 Leonard Smith RC .05 .02
❑ 258 Travis Curtis .05 .02
❑ 259 Cowboys TL .40 .18
(Herschel Walker Around End)
❑ 260 Danny White .40 .18
❑ 261 Herschel Walker .40 .18
❑ 262 Tony Dorsett .40 .18
❑ 263 Doug Cosbie .05 .02
❑ 264 Roger Ruzek RC .20 .09
❑ 265 Darryl Clack .05 .02
❑ 266 Ed Too Tall Jones .40 .18
❑ 267 Jim Jeffcoat .05 .02
❑ 268 Everson Walls .05 .02
❑ 269 Bill Bates .20 .09
❑ 270 Michael Downs .05 .02
❑ 271 Giants TL .20 .09
(Mark Bavaro Drives Ahead)
❑ 272 Phil Simms .40 .18
❑ 273 Joe Morris .20 .09
❑ 274 Lee Rouson .05 .02
❑ 275 George Adams .05 .02
❑ 276 Lionel Manuel .05 .02
❑ 277 Mark Bavaro .20 .09
❑ 278 Raul Allegre .05 .02
❑ 279 Sean Landeta .05 .02
❑ 280 Erik Howard .05 .02
❑ 281 Leonard Marshall .20 .09
❑ 282 Carl Banks AP .20 .09
❑ 283 Pepper Johnson .20 .09
❑ 284 Harry Carson .20 .09
❑ 285 Lawrence Taylor .40 .18
❑ 286 Terry Kinard .05 .02
❑ 287 Rams TL .40 .18
(Jim Everett Races Downfield)
❑ 288 Jim Everett .40 .18
❑ 289 Charles White .20 .09
❑ 290 Ron Brown .20 .09
❑ 291 Henry Ellard .40 .18
❑ 292 Mike Lansford .05 .02
❑ 293 Dale Hatcher .05 .02
❑ 294 Doug Smith .05 .02
❑ 295 Jackie Slater .20 .09
❑ 296 Jim Collins .05 .02
❑ 297 Jerry Gray .05 .02
❑ 298 LeRoy Irvin .05 .02
❑ 299 Nolan Cromwell .20 .09
❑ 300 Kevin Greene RC 1.25 .55
❑ 301 Jets TL .20 .09
(Ken O'Brien Reads Defense)
❑ 302 Ken O'Brien .20 .09
❑ 303 Freeman McNeil .20 .09
❑ 304 Johnny Hector .05 .02
❑ 305 Al Toon .20 .09
❑ 306 Jo Jo Townsell RC .20 .09
❑ 307 Mickey Shuler .05 .02
❑ 308 Pat Leahy .05 .02
❑ 309 Roger Vick .05 .02
❑ 310 Alex Gordon RC .05 .02
❑ 311 Troy Benson .05 .02
❑ 312 Bob Crable .05 .02
❑ 313 Harry Hamilton .05 .02
❑ 314 Packers TL .05 .02
(Phillip Epps Ready
for Contact)
❑ 315 Randy Wright .05 .02
❑ 316 Kenneth Davis .20 .09
❑ 317 Phillip Epps .05 .02
❑ 318 Walter Stanley .05 .02
❑ 319 Frankie Neal .05 .02
❑ 320 Don Bracken .05 .02
❑ 321 Brian Noble RC .20 .09
❑ 322 Johnny Holland SR RC .20 .09
❑ 323 Tim Harris .20 .09
❑ 324 Mark Murphy .05 .02
❑ 325 Raiders TL .50 .23
(Bo Jackson All Alone)
❑ 326 Marc Wilson .05 .02
❑ 327 Bo Jackson SR RC 5.00 2.20
❑ 328 Marcus Allen .40 .18
❑ 329 James Lofton .40 .18
❑ 330 Todd Christensen .20 .09
❑ 331 Chris Bahr .05 .02
❑ 332 Stan Talley .05 .02
❑ 333 Howie Long .40 .18
❑ 334 Sean Jones .40 .18
❑ 335 Matt Millen .20 .09
❑ 336 Stacey Toran .05 .02
❑ 337 Vann McElroy .05 .02
❑ 338 Greg Townsend .20 .09
❑ 339 Bengals TL .40 .18
(Boomer Esiason Calls Signals)
❑ 340 Boomer Esiason .40 .18
❑ 341 Larry Kinnebrew .05 .02
❑ 342 Stanford Jennings RC .05 .02
❑ 343 Eddie Brown .20 .09
❑ 344 Jim Breech .05 .02
❑ 345 Anthony Munoz AP .40 .18
❑ 346 Scott Fulhage RC .05 .02
❑ 347 Tim Krumrie RC .05 .02
❑ 348 Reggie Williams .20 .09
❑ 349 David Fulcher RC .05 .02
❑ 350 Buccaneers TL .05 .02
(James Wilder Free
and Clear)
❑ 351 Frank Garcia .05 .02
❑ 352 Vinny Testaverde SR RC 4.00 1.80
❑ 353 James Wilder .05 .02
❑ 354 Jeff Smith .05 .02
❑ 355 Gerald Carter .05 .02
❑ 356 Calvin Magee .05 .02
❑ 357 Donald Igwebuike .05 .02
❑ 358 Ron Holmes RC .05 .02
❑ 359 Chris Washington .05 .02
❑ 360 Ervin Randle .05 .02
❑ 361 Chiefs TL .05 .02
(Bill Kenney Ground Attack)
❑ 362 Bill Kenney .05 .02
❑ 363 Christian Okoye SR RC .40 .18
❑ 364 Paul Palmer .05 .02
❑ 365 Stephone Paige .20 .09
❑ 366 Carlos Carson .05 .02
❑ 367 Kelly Goodburn RC .05 .02
❑ 368 Bill Maas .05 .02
❑ 369 Mike Bell .05 .02
❑ 370 Dino Hackett RC .05 .02
❑ 371 Deron Cherry .05 .02
❑ 372 Lions TL .05 .02
(James Jones Stretches
For More)
❑ 373 Chuck Long .20 .09
❑ 374 Garry James .05 .02
❑ 375 James Jones .05 .02
❑ 376 Pete Mandley .05 .02
❑ 377 Gary Lee RC .05 .02
❑ 378 Eddie Murray .05 .02
❑ 379 Jim Arnold .05 .02
❑ 380 Dennis Gibson SR RC .05 .02
❑ 381 Mike Cofer .05 .02
❑ 382 James Griffin .05 .02
❑ 383 Falcons TL .05 .02
(Gerald Riggs Carries
Heavy Load)
❑ 384 Scott Campbell .05 .02
❑ 385 Gerald Riggs .20 .09
❑ 386 Floyd Dixon RC .05 .02
❑ 387 Rick Donnelly .05 .02
❑ 388 Bill Fralic .20 .09
❑ 389 Major Everett .05 .02
❑ 390 Mike Gann .05 .02
❑ 391 Tony Casillas RC .20 .09
❑ 392 Rick Bryan .05 .02
❑ 393 John Rade RC .05 .02
❑ 394 Checklist 1-132 .05 .02
❑ 395 Checklist 133-264 .05 .02
❑ 396 Checklist 265-396 .05 .02

1989 Topps

	Nm-Mt	Ex-Mt
COMPLETE SET (396)	12.00	5.50
COMP.FACT.SET (396)	25.00	11.00
❑ 1 Super Bowl XXIII	.50	.23
(Joe Montana back		
to pass)		
❑ 2 Tim Brown RB	.50	.23
Most Combined Net		
Yards Gained:		
Rookie Season		
❑ 3 Eric Dickerson RB	.10	.05
Most Consecutive		
Seasons Start of		
Career: 1000 or More		
Yards Rushing		
❑ 4 Steve Largent RB	.25	.11
Most Yards Receiving:		
Career		
❑ 5 Dan Marino RB	.75	.35
Most Seasons 4000 or		
More Yards Passing		
❑ 6 49ers Team	.50	.23
Joe Montana On The Run		
❑ 7 Jerry Rice	1.50	.70
❑ 8 Roger Craig	.25	.11
❑ 9 Ronnie Lott	.10	.05
❑ 10 Michael Carter	.05	.02
❑ 11 Charles Haley	.25	.11
❑ 12 Joe Montana	2.00	.90
❑ 13 John Taylor RC	.10	.05
❑ 14 Michael Walter	.05	.02
❑ 15 Mike Cofer K RC	.05	.02
❑ 16 Tom Rathman	.05	.02
❑ 17 Daniel Stubbs RC	.05	.02
❑ 18 Keena Turner	.05	.02
❑ 19 Tim McKyer	.05	.02
❑ 20 Larry Roberts	.05	.02
❑ 21 Jeff Fuller	.05	.02
❑ 22 Bubba Paris	.05	.02
❑ 23 Bengals Team UER	.10	.05
Boomer Esiason Measures		
Up (Should be versus		
Steelers in week three)		
❑ 24 Eddie Brown	.05	.02
❑ 25 Boomer Esiason	.10	.05
❑ 26 Tim Krumrie	.05	.02
❑ 27 Ickey Woods RC	.10	.05
❑ 28 Anthony Munoz	.10	.05
❑ 29 Tim McGee	.05	.02
❑ 30 Max Montoya	.05	.02
❑ 31 David Grant	.05	.02
❑ 32 Rodney Holman RC	.05	.02
(Cincinnati Bengals on		
card front is subject to		
various printing errors)		
❑ 33 David Fulcher	.10	.05
❑ 34 Jim Skow	.05	.02
❑ 35 James Brooks	.10	.05
❑ 36 Reggie Williams	.05	.02
❑ 37 Eric Thomas RC	.05	.02
❑ 38 Stanford Jennings	.05	.02
❑ 39 Jim Breech	.05	.02
❑ 40 Bills Team	.25	.11
Jim Kelly Reads Defense		
❑ 41 Shane Conlan	.05	.02
❑ 42 Scott Norwood RC	.05	.02
❑ 43 Cornelius Bennett	.10	.05
❑ 44 Bruce Smith	.25	.11
❑ 45 Thurman Thomas RC	1.00	.45
❑ 46 Jim Kelly	.50	.23
❑ 47 John Kidd	.05	.02
❑ 48 Kent Hull RC	.05	.02
❑ 49 Art Still	.05	.02
❑ 50 Fred Smerlas	.05	.02
❑ 51A Derrick Burroughs	.05	.02
(White name plate)		
❑ 51B Derrick Burroughs	.05	.02
(Yellow name plate)		
❑ 52 Andre Reed	.25	.11
❑ 53 Robb Riddick	.05	.02
❑ 54 Chris Burkett	.05	.02
❑ 55 Ronnie Harmon	.10	.05
❑ 56 Mark Kelso UER	.05	.02
(team shown as "Buffalo Bill"		
❑ 57 Bears Team	.05	.02
Thomas Sanders		
Changes Pace		
❑ 58 Mike Singletary	.10	.05
❑ 59 Jay Hilgenberg UER	.05	.02
(letter "g" missing from Chicago)		
❑ 60 Richard Dent	.10	.05
❑ 61 Ron Rivera	.05	.02
❑ 62 Jim McMahon	.10	.05
❑ 63 Mike Tomczak	.10	.05
❑ 64 Neal Anderson	.10	.05
❑ 65 Dennis Gentry	.05	.02
❑ 66 Dan Hampton	.10	.05
❑ 67 David Tate	.05	.02
❑ 68 Thomas Sanders RC	.05	.02
❑ 69 Steve McMichael	.10	.05
❑ 70 Dennis McKinnon	.05	.02
❑ 71 Brad Muster RC	.05	.02
❑ 72 Vestee Jackson RC	.05	.02
❑ 73 Dave Duerson	.05	.02
❑ 74 Vikings Team	.05	.02
Millard Gets His Man		
❑ 75 Joey Browner	.05	.02
❑ 76 Carl Lee RC	.05	.02
❑ 77 Gary Zimmerman	.05	.02
❑ 78 Hassan Jones RC	.05	.02
❑ 79 Anthony Carter	.10	.05
❑ 80 Ray Berry	.05	.02
❑ 81 Steve Jordan	.05	.02
❑ 82 Issiac Holt	.05	.02
❑ 83 Wade Wilson	.10	.05
❑ 84 Chris Doleman	.10	.05
❑ 85 Alfred Anderson	.05	.02
❑ 86 Keith Millard	.05	.02
❑ 87 Darrin Nelson	.05	.02
❑ 88 D.J. Dozier	.05	.02
❑ 89 Scott Studwell	.05	.02
❑ 90 Oilers Team	.05	.02
Tony Zendejas Big Boot		
❑ 91 Bruce Matthews RC	.60	.25
❑ 92 Curtis Duncan	.05	.02
❑ 93 Warren Moon	.25	.11
❑ 94 Johnny Meads RC	.05	.02
❑ 95 Drew Hill	.05	.02
❑ 96 Alonzo Highsmith	.05	.02
❑ 97 Mike Munchak	.10	.05
❑ 98 Mike Rozier	.05	.02
❑ 99 Tony Zendejas	.05	.02
❑ 100 Jeff Donaldson	.05	.02
❑ 101 Ray Childress	.05	.02
❑ 102 Sean Jones	.10	.05
❑ 103 Ernest Givins	.10	.05
❑ 104 William Fuller RC	.25	.11
❑ 105 Allen Pinkett RC	.05	.02
❑ 106 Eagles Team	.10	.05
Randall Cunningham		
Fakes Field		
❑ 107 Keith Jackson RC	.25	.11
❑ 108 Reggie White	.25	.11
❑ 109 Clyde Simmons	.10	.05
❑ 110 John Teltschik	.05	.02
❑ 111 Wes Hopkins	.05	.02
❑ 112 Keith Byars	.10	.05
❑ 113 Jerome Brown	.10	.05
❑ 114 Mike Quick	.05	.02
❑ 115 Randall Cunningham	.40	.18
❑ 116 Anthony Toney	.05	.02
❑ 117 Ron Johnson	.05	.02
❑ 118 Terry Hoage	.05	.02
❑ 119 Seth Joyner	.10	.05
❑ 120 Eric Allen RC	.25	.11
❑ 121 Cris Carter RC	1.50	.70
❑ 122 Rams Team	.05	.02
Greg Bell Runs To Glory		
❑ 123 Tom Newberry RC	.05	.02
❑ 124 Pete Holohan	.05	.02
❑ 125 Robert Delpino RC UER	.05	.02
(Listed as Raider		
on card back)		
❑ 126 Carl Ekern	.05	.02
❑ 127 Greg Bell	.05	.02
❑ 128 Mike Lansford	.05	.02
❑ 129 Jim Everett	.10	.05
❑ 130 Mike Wilcher	.05	.02
❑ 131 Jerry Gray	.05	.02
❑ 132 Dale Hatcher	.05	.02
❑ 133 Doug Smith	.05	.02
❑ 134 Kevin Greene	.25	.11
❑ 135 Jackie Slater	.05	.02
❑ 136 Aaron Cox RC	.05	.02
❑ 137 Henry Ellard	.25	.11
❑ 138 Browns Team	.10	.05
Bernie Kosar Quick		
Release		
❑ 139 Frank Minnifield	.05	.02
❑ 140 Webster Slaughter	.10	.05
❑ 141 Bernie Kosar	.10	.05
❑ 142 Charles Buchanan	.05	.02
❑ 143 Clay Matthews	.10	.05
❑ 144 Reggie Langhorne RC	.05	.02
❑ 145 Hanford Dixon	.05	.02
❑ 146 Brian Brennan	.05	.02
❑ 147 Earnest Byner	.05	.02
❑ 148 Michael Dean Perry RC	.10	.05
❑ 149 Kevin Mack	.05	.02
❑ 150 Matt Bahr	.05	.02
❑ 151 Ozzie Newsome	.10	.05
❑ 152 Saints Team	.10	.05
Craig Heyward Motors		
Forward		
❑ 153 Morten Andersen	.05	.02
❑ 154 Pat Swilling	.10	.05
❑ 155 Sam Mills	.10	.05
❑ 156 Lonzell Hill	.05	.02
❑ 157 Dalton Hilliard	.05	.02
❑ 158 Craig Heyward RC	.10	.05
❑ 159 Vaughan Johnson RC	.05	.02
❑ 160 Rueben Mayes	.05	.02
❑ 161 Gene Atkins RC	.05	.02
❑ 162 Bobby Hebert	.10	.05
❑ 163 Rickey Jackson	.10	.05
❑ 164 Eric Martin	.05	.02
❑ 165 Giants Team	.05	.02
Joe Morris Up		
The Middle		
❑ 166 Lawrence Taylor	.25	.11
❑ 167 Bart Oates	.05	.02
❑ 168 Carl Banks	.05	.02
❑ 169 Eric Moore	.05	.02
❑ 170 Sheldon White RC	.05	.02
❑ 171 Mark Collins RC	.05	.02
❑ 172 Phil Simms	.10	.05
❑ 173 Jim Burt	.05	.02
❑ 174 Stephen Baker RC	.10	.05
❑ 175 Mark Bavaro	.10	.05
❑ 176 Pepper Johnson	.05	.02
❑ 177 Lionel Manuel	.05	.02
❑ 178 Joe Morris	.05	.02
❑ 179 John Elliott RC	.05	.02
❑ 180 Gary Reasons RC	.05	.02

❑	181 Seahawks Team Dave Krieg Winds Up	.10	.05
❑	182 Brian Blades RC	.25	.11
❑	183 Steve Largent	.25	.11
❑	184 Rufus Porter RC	.05	.02
❑	185 Ruben Rodriguez	.05	.02
❑	186 Curt Warner	.05	.02
❑	187 Paul Moyer	.05	.02
❑	188 Dave Krieg	.10	.05
❑	189 Jacob Green	.05	.02
❑	190 John L. Williams	.05	.02
❑	191 Eugene Robinson RC	.05	.02
❑	192 Brian Bosworth	.10	.05
❑	193 Patriots Team Tony Eason Behind Blocking	.05	.02
❑	194 John Stephens RC	.05	.02
❑	195 Robert Perryman RC	.05	.02
❑	196 Andre Tippett	.05	.02
❑	197 Fred Marion	.05	.02
❑	198 Doug Flutie	1.00	.45
❑	199 Stanley Morgan	.05	.02
❑	200 Johnny Rembert RC	.05	.02
❑	201 Tony Eason	.05	.02
❑	202 Marvin Allen	.05	.02
❑	203 Raymond Clayborn	.05	.02
❑	204 Irving Fryar	.25	.11
❑	205 Colts Team Chris Chandler All Alone	.05	.02
❑	206 Eric Dickerson	.10	.05
❑	207 Chris Hinton	.05	.02
❑	208 Duane Bickett	.05	.02
❑	209 Chris Chandler RC	1.00	.45
❑	210 Jon Hand	.05	.02
❑	211 Ray Donaldson	.05	.02
❑	212 Dean Biasucci	.05	.02
❑	213 Bill Brooks	.10	.05
❑	214 Chris Goode RC	.05	.02
❑	215 Clarence Verdin RC	.05	.02
❑	216 Albert Bentley	.05	.02
❑	217 Passing Leaders Wade Wilson Boomer Esiason	.10	.05
❑	218 Receiving Leaders Henry Ellard Al Toon	.10	.05
❑	219 Rushing Leaders Herschel Walker Eric Dickerson	.10	.05
❑	220 Scoring Leaders Mike Cofer Scott Norwood	.05	.02
❑	221 Intercept Leaders Scott Case Erik McMillan	.05	.02
❑	222 Jets Team Ken O'Brien Surveys Scene	.05	.02
❑	223 Erik McMillan RC	.05	.02
❑	224 James Hasty RC	.05	.02
❑	225 Al Toon	.10	.05
❑	226 John Booty RC	.05	.02
❑	227 Johnny Hector	.05	.02
❑	228 Ken O'Brien	.05	.02
❑	229 Marty Lyons	.05	.02
❑	230 Mickey Shuler	.05	.02
❑	231 Robin Cole	.05	.02
❑	232 Freeman McNeil	.05	.02
❑	233 Marion Barber RC	.05	.02
❑	234 Jo Jo Townsell	.05	.02
❑	235 Wesley Walker	.05	.02
❑	236 Roger Vick	.05	.02
❑	237 Pat Leahy	.05	.02
❑	238 Broncos Team UER John Elway Ground Attack (Score of week 15 says 42-21; should be 42-14)	.50	.23
❑	239 Mike Horan	.05	.02
❑	240 Tony Dorsett	.25	.11
❑	241 John Elway	2.00	.90
❑	242 Mark Jackson	.05	.02
❑	243 Sammy Winder	.05	.02
❑	244 Rich Karlis	.05	.02
❑	245 Vance Johnson	.10	.05
❑	246 Steve Sewell RC	.05	.02
❑	247 Karl Mecklenburg UER (Drafted 2, should be 12)	.05	.02
❑	248 Rulon Jones	.05	.02
❑	249 Simon Fletcher RC	.05	.02
❑	250 Redskins Team Doug Williams Sets Up	.10	.05
❑	251 Chip Lohmiller RC	.05	.02
❑	252 Jamie Morris	.05	.02
❑	253 Mark Rypien RC UER (14 1988 completions; should be 114)	.10	.05
❑	254 Barry Wilburn	.05	.02
❑	255 Mark May RC	.05	.02
❑	256 Wilber Marshall	.05	.02
❑	257 Charles Mann	.05	.02
❑	258 Gary Clark	.25	.11
❑	259 Doug Williams	.10	.05
❑	260 Art Monk	.10	.05
❑	261 Kelvin Bryant	.05	.02
❑	262 Dexter Manley	.05	.02
❑	263 Ricky Sanders	.05	.02
❑	264 Raiders Team Marcus Allen Through the Line	.25	.11
❑	265 Tim Brown RC	1.50	.70
❑	266 Jay Schroeder	.05	.02
❑	267 Marcus Allen	.25	.11
❑	268 Mike Haynes	.10	.05
❑	269 Bo Jackson	.30	.14
❑	270 Steve Beuerlein RC	.60	.25
❑	271 Vann McElroy	.05	.02
❑	272 Willie Gault	.10	.05
❑	273 Howie Long	.25	.11
❑	274 Greg Townsend	.05	.02
❑	275 Mike Wise	.05	.02
❑	276 Cardinals Team Neil Lomax Looks Long	.05	.02
❑	277 Luis Sharpe	.05	.02
❑	278 Scott Dill	.05	.02
❑	279 Vai Sikahema	.05	.02
❑	280 Ron Wolfley	.05	.02
❑	281 David Galloway	.05	.02
❑	282 Jay Novacek RC	.25	.11
❑	283 Neil Lomax	.05	.02
❑	284 Robert Awalt	.05	.02
❑	285 Cedric Mack	.05	.02
❑	286 Freddie Joe Nunn	.05	.02
❑	287 J.T. Smith	.05	.02
❑	288 Stump Mitchell	.05	.02
❑	289 Roy Green	.10	.05
❑	290 Dolphins Team Dan Marino High and Far	.50	.23
❑	291 Jarvis Williams RC	.05	.02
❑	292 Troy Stradford	.05	.02
❑	293 Dan Marino	2.00	.90
❑	294 T.J. Turner	.05	.02
❑	295 John Offerdahl	.05	.02
❑	296 Ferrell Edmunds RC	.05	.02
❑	297 Scott Schwedes	.05	.02
❑	298 Lorenzo Hampton	.05	.02
❑	299 Jim C.Jensen RC	.05	.02
❑	300 Brian Sochia	.05	.02
❑	301 Reggie Roby	.05	.02
❑	302 Mark Clayton	.10	.05
❑	303 Chargers Team Tim Spencer Leads the Way	.05	.02
❑	304 Lee Williams	.05	.02
❑	305 Gary Plummer RC	.05	.02
❑	306 Gary Anderson RB	.05	.02
❑	307 Gill Byrd	.05	.02
❑	308 Jamie Holland RC	.05	.02
❑	309 Billy Ray Smith	.05	.02
❑	310 Lionel James	.05	.02
❑	311 Mark Vlasic RC	.05	.02
❑	312 Curtis Adams	.05	.02
❑	313 Anthony Miller RC	.25	.11
❑	314 Steelers Team Frank Pollard Set for Action	.05	.02
❑	315 Bubby Brister RC	.25	.11
❑	316 David Little	.05	.02
❑	317 Tunch Ilkin RC	.05	.02
❑	318 Louis Lipps	.10	.05
❑	319 Warren Williams RC	.05	.02
❑	320 Dwight Stone	.10	.05
❑	321 Merril Hoge RC	.05	.02
❑	322 Thomas Everett RC	.05	.02
❑	323 Rod Woodson RC	.50	.23
❑	324 Gary Anderson K	.05	.02
❑	325 Buccaneers Team Ron Hall in Pursuit	.05	.02
❑	326 Donnie Elder	.05	.02
❑	327 Vinny Testaverde	.30	.14
❑	328 Harry Hamilton	.05	.02
❑	329 James Wilder	.05	.02
❑	330 Lars Tate	.05	.02
❑	331 Mark Carrier WR RC	.25	.11
❑	332 Bruce Hill RC	.05	.02
❑	333 Paul Gruber RC	.05	.02
❑	334 Ricky Reynolds	.05	.02
❑	335 Eugene Marve	.05	.02
❑	336 Falcons Team Joel Williams Holds On	.05	.02
❑	337 Aundray Bruce RC	.05	.02
❑	338 John Rade	.05	.02
❑	339 Scott Case RC	.05	.02
❑	340 Robert Moore	.05	.02
❑	341 Chris Miller RC	.25	.11
❑	342 Gerald Riggs	.10	.05
❑	343 Gene Lang	.05	.02
❑	344 Marcus Cotton	.05	.02
❑	345 Rick Donnelly	.05	.02
❑	346 John Settle RC	.05	.02
❑	347 Bill Fralic	.05	.02
❑	348 Chiefs Team Dino Hackett Zeros In	.05	.02
❑	349 Steve DeBerg	.05	.02
❑	350 Mike Stensrud	.05	.02
❑	351 Dino Hackett	.05	.02
❑	352 Deron Cherry	.10	.05
❑	353 Christian Okoye	.05	.02
❑	354 Bill Maas	.05	.02
❑	355 Carlos Carson	.05	.02
❑	356 Albert Lewis	.05	.02
❑	357 Paul Palmer	.05	.02
❑	358 Nick Lowery	.05	.02
❑	359 Stephone Paige	.05	.02
❑	360 Lions Team Chuck Long Gets the Snap	.05	.02
❑	361 Chris Spielman RC	.25	.11
❑	362 Jim Arnold	.05	.02
❑	363 Devon Mitchell	.05	.02
❑	364 Mike Cofer	.05	.02
❑	365 Bennie Blades RC	.05	.02
❑	366 James Jones	.05	.02
❑	367 Garry James	.05	.02
❑	368 Pete Mandley	.05	.02
❑	369 Keith Ferguson	.05	.02
❑	370 Dennis Gibson	.05	.02
❑	371 Packers Team UER Johnny Holland Over the Top (Week 16 has vs. Vikings but they played Bears)	.05	.02
❑	372 Brent Fullwood RC	.05	.02
❑	373 Don Majkowski RC UER (3 TD's in 1987; should be 5)	.10	.05
❑	374 Tim Harris	.05	.02
❑	375 Keith Woodside RC	.05	.02
❑	376 Mark Murphy	.05	.02
❑	377 Dave Brown DB	.05	.02
❑	378 Perry Kemp RC	.05	.02
❑	379 Sterling Sharpe RC	.75	.35
❑	380 Chuck Cecil RC	.05	.02

	Card	Nm-Mt	Ex-Mt
❑ 381	Walter Stanley	.05	.02
❑ 382	Cowboys Team Steve Pelluer Lets It Go	.05	.02
❑ 383	Michael Irvin RC	1.25	.55
❑ 384	Bill Bates	.10	.05
❑ 385	Herschel Walker	.25	.11
❑ 386	Darryl Clack	.05	.02
❑ 387	Danny Noonan	.05	.02
❑ 388	Eugene Lockhart RC	.05	.02
❑ 389	Ed Too Tall Jones	.10	.05
❑ 390	Steve Pelluer	.05	.02
❑ 391	Ray Alexander	.05	.02
❑ 392	Nate Newton RC	.10	.05
❑ 393	Garry Cobb	.05	.02
❑ 394	Checklist 1-132	.05	.02
❑ 395	Checklist 133-264	.05	.02
❑ 396	Checklist 265-396	.05	.02

1989 Topps Traded

	Card	Nm-Mt	Ex-Mt
	COMP.FACT.SET (132)	12.00	5.50
❑ 1T	Eric Ball RC	.05	.02
❑ 2T	Tony Mandarich RC	.05	.02
❑ 3T	Shawn Collins RC	.05	.02
❑ 4T	Ray Bentley RC	.05	.02
❑ 5T	Tony Casillas	.05	.02
❑ 6T	Al Del Greco RC	.05	.02
❑ 7T	Dan Saleaumua RC	.10	.05
❑ 8T	Keith Bishop	.05	.02
❑ 9T	Rodney Peete RC	.60	.25
❑ 10T	Lorenzo White RC	.25	.11
❑ 11T	Steve Smith RC	.10	.05
❑ 12T	Pete Mandley	.05	.02
❑ 13T	M.Fernandez RC**/C	.05	.02
❑ 14T	Flipper Anderson RC	.25	.11
❑ 15T	Louis Oliver RC	.10	.05
❑ 16T	Rick Fenney	.05	.02
❑ 17T	Gary Jeter	.05	.02
❑ 18T	Greg Cox	.05	.02
❑ 19T	Bubba McDowell RC	.10	.05
❑ 20T	Ron Heller	.05	.02
❑ 21T	Tim McDonald RC	.05	.02
❑ 22T	Jerrol Williams RC	.05	.02
❑ 23T	Marion Butts RC	.10	.05
❑ 24T	Steve Young	.75	.35
❑ 25T	Mike Merriweather	.05	.02
❑ 26T	Richard Johnson	.05	.02
❑ 27T	Gerald Riggs	.10	.05
❑ 28T	Dave Waymer	.05	.02
❑ 29T	Issiac Holt	.05	.02
❑ 30T	Deion Sanders RC	1.50	.70
❑ 31T	Todd Blackledge	.05	.02
❑ 32T	Jeff Cross RC	.05	.02
❑ 33T	Steve Wisniewski RC	.10	.05
❑ 34T	Ron Brown	.10	.05
❑ 35T	Rod Bernstine RC	.05	.02
❑ 36T	Jeff Uhlenhake RC	.05	.02
❑ 37T	Donnell Woolford RC	.25	.11
❑ 38T	Bob Gagliano RC	.05	.02
❑ 39T	Ezra Johnson	.05	.02
❑ 40T	Ron Jaworski	.05	.02
❑ 41T	Lawyer Tillman RC	.05	.02
❑ 42T	Lorenzo Lynch RC	.05	.02
❑ 43T	Mike Alexander	.05	.02
❑ 44T	Tim Worley RC	.05	.02
❑ 45T	Guy Bingham	.05	.02
❑ 46T	Cleveland Gary RC	.05	.02
❑ 47T	Danny Peebles	.05	.02
❑ 48T	Clarence Weathers RC	.05	.02
❑ 49T	Jeff Lageman RC	.25	.11
❑ 50T	Eric Metcalf RC	.25	.11
❑ 51T	Myron Guyton RC	.05	.02
❑ 52T	Steve Atwater RC	.05	.02
❑ 53T	John Fourcade RC	.05	.02
❑ 54T	Randall McDaniel RC	.25	.11
❑ 55T	Al Noga RC	.05	.02
❑ 56T	Sammie Smith RC	.10	.05
❑ 57T	Jesse Solomon	.05	.02
❑ 58T	Greg Kragen RC	.05	.02
❑ 59T	Don Beebe RC	.25	.11
❑ 60T	Hart Lee Dykes RC	.10	.05
❑ 61T	Trace Armstrong RC	.10	.05
❑ 62T	Steve Pelluer	.05	.02
❑ 63T	Barry Krauss	.05	.02
❑ 64T	Kevin Murphy RC	.05	.02
❑ 65T	Steve Tasker RC	.25	.11
❑ 66T	Jessie Small RC	.05	.02
❑ 67T	Dave Meggett RC	.25	.11
❑ 68T	Dean Hamel	.05	.02
❑ 69T	Jim Covert	.05	.02
❑ 70T	Troy Aikman RC	5.00	2.20
❑ 71T	Raul Allegre	.05	.02
❑ 72T	Chris Jacke RC	.10	.05
❑ 73T	Leslie O'Neal	.10	.05
❑ 74T	Keith Taylor RC	.05	.02
❑ 75T	Steve Walsh RC	.25	.11
❑ 76T	Tracy Rocker	.05	.02
❑ 77T	Robert Massey RC	.10	.05
❑ 78T	Bryan Wagner	.05	.02
❑ 79T	Steve DeOssie	.05	.02
❑ 80T	Carnell Lake RC	.25	.11
❑ 81T	Frank Reich RC	.25	.11
❑ 82T	Tyrone Braxton RC	.05	.02
❑ 83T	Barry Sanders RC	6.00	2.70
❑ 84T	Pete Stoyanovich RC	.10	.05
❑ 85T	Paul Palmer	.05	.02
❑ 86T	Billy Joe Tolliver RC	.05	.02
❑ 87T	Eric Hill RC	.10	.05
❑ 88T	Gerald McNeil	.05	.02
❑ 89T	Bill Hawkins RC	.05	.02
❑ 90T	Derrick Thomas RC	1.25	.55
❑ 91T	Jim Harbaugh RC	.75	.35
❑ 92T	Brian Williams OL RC	.05	.02
❑ 93T	Jack Trudeau	.05	.02
❑ 94T	Leonard Smith	.05	.02
❑ 95T	Gary Hogeboom	.05	.02
❑ 96T	A.J. Johnson RC	.05	.02
❑ 97T	Jim McMahon	.10	.05
❑ 98T	David Williams RC	.05	.02
❑ 99T	Rohn Stark	.05	.02
❑ 100T	Sean Landeta	.05	.02
❑ 101T	Tim Johnson RC	.05	.02
❑ 102T	Andre Rison RC	.75	.35
❑ 103T	Earnest Byner	.10	.05
❑ 104T	Don McPherson RC	.05	.02
❑ 105T	Zefross Moss RC	.05	.02
❑ 106T	Frank Stams RC	.05	.02
❑ 107T	Courtney Hall RC	.10	.05
❑ 108T	Marc Logan RC	.05	.02
❑ 109T	James Lofton	.25	.11
❑ 110T	Lewis Tillman RC	.10	.05
❑ 111T	Irv Pankey RC	.05	.02
❑ 112T	Ralf Mojsiejenko	.05	.02
❑ 113T	Bobby Humphrey RC	.05	.02
❑ 114T	Chris Burkett	.05	.02
❑ 115T	Greg Lloyd RC	.25	.11
❑ 116T	Matt Millen	.10	.05
❑ 117T	Carl Zander	.05	.02
❑ 118T	Wayne Martin RC	.25	.11
❑ 119T	Mike Saxon	.05	.02
❑ 120T	Herschel Walker	.10	.05
❑ 121T	Andy Heck RC	.05	.02
❑ 122T	Mark Robinson	.05	.02
❑ 123T	Keith Van Horne RC	.05	.02
❑ 124T	Ricky Hunley	.05	.02
❑ 125T	Timm Rosenbach RC	.10	.05
❑ 126T	Steve Grogan	.10	.05
❑ 127T	Stephen Braggs RC	.05	.02
❑ 128T	Terry Long	.05	.02
❑ 129T	Evan Cooper	.05	.02
❑ 130T	Robert Lyles	.05	.02
❑ 131T	Mike Webster	.10	.05
❑ 132T	Checklist 1-132	.05	.02

1990 Topps Traded

	Card	Nm-Mt	Ex-Mt
	COMP.FACT.SET (132)	15.00	6.75
❑ 1T	Gerald McNeil	.05	.02
❑ 2T	Andre Rison	.25	.11
❑ 3T	Steve Walsh	.25	.11
❑ 4T	Lorenzo White	.10	.05
❑ 5T	Max Montoya	.05	.02
❑ 6T	William Roberts RC	.05	.02
❑ 7T	Alonzo Highsmith	.05	.02
❑ 8T	Chris Hinton	.10	.05
❑ 9T	Stanley Morgan	.10	.05
❑ 10T	Mickey Shuler	.05	.02
❑ 11T	Bobby Humphery	.05	.02
❑ 12T	Gary Anderson RB	.05	.02
❑ 13T	Mike Tomczak	.10	.05
❑ 14T	Anthony Pleasant RC	.10	.05
❑ 15T	Walter Stanley	.05	.02
❑ 16T	Greg Bell	.05	.02
❑ 17T	Tony Martin RC	.75	.35
❑ 18T	Terry Kinard	.05	.02
❑ 19T	Cris Carter	.50	.23
❑ 20T	James Wilder	.05	.02
❑ 21T	Jerry Kauric	.05	.02
❑ 22T	Irving Fryar	.25	.11
❑ 23T	Ken Harvey RC	.25	.11
❑ 24T	James Williams DB RC	.05	.02
❑ 25T	Ron Cox RC	.05	.02
❑ 26T	Andre Ware	.25	.11
❑ 27T	Emmitt Smith RC	10.00	4.50
❑ 28T	Junior Seau	.75	.35
❑ 29T	Mark Carrier RC	.25	.11
❑ 30T	Rodney Hampton	.25	.11
❑ 31T	Rob Moore RC	.50	.23
❑ 32T	Bern Brostek RC	.05	.02
❑ 33T	Dexter Carter	.10	.05
❑ 34T	Blair Thomas	.10	.05
❑ 35T	Harold Green RC	.25	.11
❑ 36T	Darrell Thompson	.05	.02
❑ 37T	Eric Green RC	.25	.11
❑ 38T	Renaldo Turnbull RC	.25	.11
❑ 39T	Leroy Hoard RC	.25	.11
❑ 40T	Anthony Thompson RC	.10	.05
❑ 41T	Jeff George	.50	.23
❑ 42T	Alexander Wright RC	.05	.02
❑ 43T	Richmond Webb	.05	.02
❑ 44T	Cortez Kennedy	.25	.11
❑ 45T	Ray Agnew RC	.05	.02
❑ 46T	Percy Snow	.05	.02
❑ 47T	Chris Singleton	.05	.02
❑ 48T	James Francis RC	.10	.05
❑ 49T	Tony Bennett	.10	.05
❑ 50T	Reggie Cobb RC	.10	.05
❑ 51T	Barry Foster	.25	.11

❑ 52T Ben Smith	.05	.02
❑ 53T Anthony Smith RC	.25	.11
❑ 54T Steve Christie RC	.05	.02
❑ 55T Johnny Bailey RC	.10	.05
❑ 56T Alan Grant RC	.05	.02
❑ 57T Eric Floyd RC	.05	.02
❑ 58T Robert Blackmon RC	.05	.02
❑ 59T Brent Williams	.05	.02
❑ 60T Raymond Clayborn	.05	.02
❑ 61T Dave Duerson	.05	.02
❑ 62T Derrick Fenner RC	.10	.05
❑ 63T Ken Willis	.05	.02
❑ 64T Brad Baxter RC	.10	.05
❑ 65T Tony Paige	.05	.02
❑ 66T Jay Schroeder	.05	.02
❑ 67T Jim Breech	.05	.02
❑ 68T Barry Word RC	.10	.05
❑ 69T Anthony Dilweg	.05	.02
❑ 70T Rich Gannon RC	2.50	1.10
❑ 71T Stan Humphries RC	.25	.11
❑ 72T Jay Novacek	.25	.11
❑ 73T Tommy Kane RC	.05	.02
❑ 74T Everson Walls	.05	.02
❑ 75T Mike Rozier	.10	.05
❑ 76T Robb Thomas	.05	.02
❑ 77T Terance Mathis RC	1.25	.55
❑ 78T LeRoy Irvin	.05	.02
❑ 79T Jeff Donaldson	.05	.02
❑ 80T Ethan Horton RC	.10	.05
❑ 81T J.B. Brown RC	.05	.02
❑ 82T Joe Kelly	.05	.02
❑ 83T John Carney RC	.05	.02
❑ 84T Dan Stryzinski RC	.05	.02
❑ 85T John Kidd	.05	.02
❑ 86T Al Smith	.10	.05
❑ 87T Travis McNeal	.05	.02
❑ 88T Reyna Thompson RC	.05	.02
❑ 89T Rick Donnelly	.05	.02
❑ 90T Marv Cook RC	.10	.05
❑ 91T Mike Farr RC	.05	.02
❑ 92T Daniel Stubbs	.05	.02
❑ 93T Jeff Campbell RC	.05	.02
❑ 94T Tim McKyer	.05	.02
❑ 95T Ian Beckles RC	.05	.02
❑ 96T Lemuel Stinson	.05	.02
❑ 97T Frank Cornish	.05	.02
❑ 98T Riki Ellison	.05	.02
❑ 99T Jamie Mueller RC	.05	.02
❑ 100T Brian Hansen	.05	.02
❑ 101T Warren Powers RC	.05	.02
❑ 102T Howard Cross RC	.05	.02
❑ 103T Tim Grunhard RC	.05	.02
❑ 104T Johnny Johnson RC	.25	.11
❑ 105T Calvin Williams RC	.25	.11
❑ 106T Keith McCants	.05	.02
❑ 107T Lamar Lathon RC	.10	.05
❑ 108T Steve Broussard RC	.10	.05
❑ 109T Glenn Parker RC	.05	.02
❑ 110T Alton Montgomery RC	.05	.02
❑ 111T Jim McMahon	.10	.05
❑ 112T Aaron Wallace RC	.05	.02
❑ 113T Keith Sims RC	.05	.02
❑ 114T Ervin Randle	.05	.02
❑ 115T Walter Wilson	.05	.02
❑ 116T Terry Wooden RC	.05	.02
❑ 117T Bernard Clark	.05	.02
❑ 118T Tony Stargell RC	.05	.02
❑ 119T Jimmie Jones RC	.05	.02
❑ 120T Andre Collins RC	.10	.05
❑ 121T Ricky Proehl RC	.25	.11
❑ 122T Darion Conner RC	.10	.05
❑ 123T Jeff Rutledge	.05	.02
❑ 124T Heath Sherman RC	.10	.05
❑ 125T Tommie Agee RC	.05	.02
❑ 126T Tory Epps RC	.05	.02
❑ 127T Tommy Hodson RC	.05	.02
❑ 128T Jessie Hester RC	.05	.02
❑ 129T Alfred Oglesby RC	.05	.02
❑ 130T Chris Chandler	.25	.11
❑ 131T Fred Barnett RC	.25	.11
❑ 132T Checklist 1-132	.05	.02

1997 Topps Hall of Fame Class Autographs

	MINT	NRMT
COMPLETE SET (4)	200.00	90.00
HAYNES/WEBSTER ODDS 1:436H,1:120J		
MARA ODDS 1:872 HOB,1:240 JUM		
SHULA ODDS 1:290HOB,1:80 JUM		
❑ HF1 Mike Haynes (1989 Topps style)	60.00	27.00
❑ HF2 Don Shula (1972 Topps style)	80.00	36.00
❑ HF3 Wellington Mara (1986 Topps style)	100.00	45.00
❑ HF4 Mike Webster (1988 Topps style)	80.00	36.00

1998 Topps Autographs

	Nm-Mt	Ex-Mt
❑ A1 Randy Moss	135.00	60.00
❑ A2 Mike Alstott	30.00	13.50
❑ A3 Jake Plummer	30.00	13.50
❑ A4 Corey Dillon	30.00	13.50
❑ A5 Kordell Stewart	30.00	13.50
❑ A6 Eddie George	30.00	13.50
❑ A7 Jason Sehorn	30.00	13.50
❑ A8 Joey Galloway	20.00	9.00
❑ A9 Ryan Leaf	15.00	6.75
❑ A10B Peyton Manning Bronze	225.00	100.00
❑ A10G Peyton Manning Gold	225.00	70.00
❑ A11 Dwight Stephenson	30.00	13.50
❑ A12 Anthony Munoz	50.00	22.00
❑ A13 Mike Singletary	40.00	18.00
❑ A14 Tommy McDonald	30.00	13.50
❑ A15 Paul Krause	30.00	13.50

1999 Topps

	Nm-Mt	Ex-Mt
COMPLETE SET (357)	50.00	22.00
COMP.SET w/o SP's (330)	20.00	9.00
❑ 1 Terrell Davis	.60	.25
❑ 2 Adrian Murrell	.40	.18
❑ 3 Ernie Mills	.25	.11
❑ 4 Jimmy Hitchcock	.25	.11
❑ 5 Charlie Garner	.40	.18
❑ 6 Blaine Bishop	.25	.11
❑ 7 Junior Seau	.60	.25
❑ 8 Andre Rison	.40	.18
❑ 9 Jake Reed	.40	.18
❑ 10 Cris Carter	.60	.25
❑ 11 Torrance Small	.25	.11
❑ 12 Ronald McKinnon	.25	.11
❑ 13 Tyrone Davis	.25	.11
❑ 14 Warren Moon	.60	.25
❑ 15 Joe Johnson	.25	.11
❑ 16 Bert Emanuel	.40	.18
❑ 17 Brad Culpepper	.25	.11
❑ 18 Henry Jones	.25	.11
❑ 19 Jonathan Ogden	.25	.11
❑ 20 Terrell Owens	.60	.25
❑ 21 Derrick Mason	.40	.18
❑ 22 Jon Ritchie	.25	.11
❑ 23 Eric Metcalf	.25	.11
❑ 24 Kevin Carter	.25	.11
❑ 25 Fred Taylor	.60	.25
❑ 26 DeWayne Washington	.25	.11
❑ 27 William Thomas	.25	.11
❑ 28 Rocket Ismail	.40	.18
❑ 29 Jason Taylor	.25	.11
❑ 30 Doug Flutie	.60	.25
❑ 31 Michael Sinclair	.25	.11
❑ 32 Yancey Thigpen	.25	.11
❑ 33 Darnay Scott	.25	.11
❑ 34 Amani Toomer	.25	.11
❑ 35 Edgar Bennett	.25	.11
❑ 36 LeRoy Butler	.25	.11
❑ 37 Jessie Tuggle	.25	.11
❑ 38 Andrew Glover	.25	.11
❑ 39 Tim McDonald	.25	.11
❑ 40 Marshall Faulk	.75	.35
❑ 41 Ray Mickens	.25	.11
❑ 42 Kimble Anders	.40	.18
❑ 43 Trent Green	.60	.25
❑ 44 Dermontti Dawson	.25	.11
❑ 45 Greg Ellis	.25	.11
❑ 46 Hugh Douglas	.25	.11
❑ 47 Amp Lee	.25	.11
❑ 48 Lamar Thomas	.25	.11
❑ 49 Curtis Conway	.40	.18
❑ 50 Emmitt Smith	1.25	.55
❑ 51 Elvis Grbac	.40	.18
❑ 52 Tony Simmons	.25	.11
❑ 53 Darrin Smith	.25	.11
❑ 54 Donovin Darius	.25	.11
❑ 55 Corey Chavous	.25	.11
❑ 56 Phillippi Sparks	.25	.11
❑ 57 Luther Elliss	.25	.11
❑ 58 Tim Dwight	.60	.25
❑ 59 Andre Hastings	.25	.11

❑ 60 Dan Marino 2.00 .90
❑ 61 Micheal Barrow .25 .11
❑ 62 Corey Fuller .25 .11
❑ 63 Bill Romanowski .25 .11
❑ 64 Derrick Rodgers .40 .18
❑ 65 Natrone Means .40 .18
❑ 66 Peter Boulware .25 .11
❑ 67 Brian Mitchell .25 .11
❑ 68 Cornelius Bennett .25 .11
❑ 69 Dedric Ward .25 .11
❑ 70 Drew Bledsoe .75 .35
❑ 71 Freddie Jones .25 .11
❑ 72 Derrick Thomas .40 .18
❑ 73 Willie Davis .25 .11
❑ 74 Larry Centers .25 .11
❑ 75 Mark Brunell .60 .25
❑ 76 Chuck Smith .25 .11
❑ 77 Desmond Howard .40 .18
❑ 78 Sedrick Shaw .25 .11
❑ 79 Tiki Barber .40 .18
❑ 80 Curtis Martin .60 .25
❑ 81 Barry Minter .25 .11
❑ 82 Skip Hicks .25 .11
❑ 83 O.J. Santiago .25 .11
❑ 84 Ed McCaffrey .40 .18
❑ 85 Terrell Buckley .25 .11
❑ 86 Charlie Jones .25 .11
❑ 87 Pete Mitchell .25 .11
❑ 88 La'Roi Glover RC .60 .25
❑ 89 Eric Davis .25 .11
❑ 90 John Elway 2.00 .90
❑ 91 Kavika Pittman .25 .11
❑ 92 Fred Lane .25 .11
❑ 93 Warren Sapp .25 .11
❑ 94 Lorenzo Bromell RC .60 .25
❑ 95 Lawyer Milloy .40 .18
❑ 96 Aeneas Williams .25 .11
❑ 97 Michael McCrary .25 .11
❑ 98 Rickey Dudley .25 .11
❑ 99 Bryce Paup .25 .11
❑ 100 Jamal Anderson .60 .25
❑ 101 D'Marco Farr .25 .11
❑ 102 Johnnie Morton .40 .18
❑ 103 Jeff Graham .25 .11
❑ 104 Sam Cowart .25 .11
❑ 105 Bryant Young .25 .11
❑ 106 Jermaine Lewis .40 .18
❑ 107 Chad Bratzke .25 .11
❑ 108 Jeff Burris .25 .11
❑ 109 Roell Preston .25 .11
❑ 110 Vinny Testaverde .40 .18
❑ 111 Ruben Brown .25 .11
❑ 112 Darryll Lewis .25 .11
❑ 113 Billy Davis .25 .11
❑ 114 Bryant Westbrook .25 .11
❑ 115 Stephen Alexander .25 .11
❑ 116 Terrell Fletcher .25 .11
❑ 117 Terry Glenn .60 .25
❑ 118 Rod Smith .40 .18
❑ 119 Carl Pickens .40 .18
❑ 120 Tim Brown .60 .25
❑ 121 Mikhael Ricks .25 .11
❑ 122 Jason Gildon .25 .11
❑ 123 Charles Way .25 .11
❑ 124 Rob Moore .40 .18
❑ 125 Jerome Bettis .60 .25
❑ 126 Kerry Collins .40 .18
❑ 127 Bruce Smith .40 .18
❑ 128 James Hasty .25 .11
❑ 129 Ken Norton Jr. .25 .11
❑ 130 Charles Woodson .60 .25
❑ 131 Tony McGee .25 .11
❑ 132 Kevin Turner .25 .11
❑ 133 Jerome Pathon .25 .11
❑ 134 Garrison Hearst .40 .18
❑ 135 Craig Newsome .25 .11
❑ 136 Hardy Nickerson .25 .11
❑ 137 Ray Lewis .60 .25
❑ 138 Derrick Alexander .25 .11
❑ 139 Phil Hansen .25 .11
❑ 140 Joey Galloway .40 .18
❑ 141 Oronde Gadsden .40 .18
❑ 142 Herman Moore .40 .18
❑ 143 Bobby Taylor .25 .11
❑ 144 Mario Bates .25 .11
❑ 145 Kevin Dyson .40 .18
❑ 146 Aaron Glenn .25 .11
❑ 147 Ed McDaniel .25 .11
❑ 148 Terry Allen .40 .18
❑ 149 Ike Hilliard .25 .11
❑ 150 Steve Young .75 .35
❑ 151 Eugene Robinson .25 .11
❑ 152 John Mobley .25 .11
❑ 153 Kevin Hardy .25 .11
❑ 154 Lance Johnstone .25 .11
❑ 155 Willie McGinest .25 .11
❑ 156 Gary Anderson .25 .11
❑ 157 Dexter Coakley .25 .11
❑ 158 Mark Fields .25 .11
❑ 159 Steve McNair .60 .25
❑ 160 Corey Dillon .60 .25
❑ 161 Zach Thomas .60 .25
❑ 162 Kent Graham .25 .11
❑ 163 Tony Parrish .25 .11
❑ 164 Sam Gash .25 .11
❑ 165 Kyle Brady .25 .11
❑ 166 Donnell Bennett .25 .11
❑ 167 Tony Martin .40 .18
❑ 168 Michael Bates .25 .11
❑ 169 Bobby Engram .40 .18
❑ 170 Jimmy Smith .40 .18
❑ 171 Vonnie Holliday .25 .11
❑ 172 Simeon Rice .40 .18
❑ 173 Kevin Greene .25 .11
❑ 174 Mike Alstott .60 .25
❑ 175 Eddie George .60 .25
❑ 176 Michael Jackson .25 .11
❑ 177 Neil O'Donnell .40 .18
❑ 178 Sean Dawkins .25 .11
❑ 179 Courtney Hawkins .25 .11
❑ 180 Michael Irvin .40 .18
❑ 181 Thurman Thomas .40 .18
❑ 182 Cam Cleeland .25 .11
❑ 183 Ellis Johnson .25 .11
❑ 184 Will Blackwell .25 .11
❑ 185 Ty Law .40 .18
❑ 186 Merton Hanks .25 .11
❑ 187 Dan Wilkinson .25 .11
❑ 188 Andre Wadsworth .25 .11
❑ 189 Troy Vincent .25 .11
❑ 190 Frank Sanders .40 .18
❑ 191 Stephen Boyd .25 .11
❑ 192 Jason Elam .25 .11
❑ 193 Kordell Stewart .40 .18
❑ 194 Ted Johnson .25 .11
❑ 195 Glyn Milburn .25 .11
❑ 196 Gary Brown .25 .11
❑ 197 Travis Hall .25 .11
❑ 198 John Randle .40 .18
❑ 199 Jay Riemersma .25 .11
❑ 200 Barry Sanders 2.00 .90
❑ 201 Chris Spielman .25 .11
❑ 202 Rod Woodson .40 .18
❑ 203 Darrell Russell .25 .11
❑ 204 Tony Boselli .25 .11
❑ 205 Darren Woodson .25 .11
❑ 206 Muhsin Muhammad .40 .18
❑ 207 Jim Harbaugh .40 .18
❑ 208 Isaac Bruce .60 .25
❑ 209 Mo Lewis .25 .11
❑ 210 Dorsey Levens .60 .25
❑ 211 Frank Wycheck .25 .11
❑ 212 Napoleon Kaufman .60 .25
❑ 213 Walt Harris .25 .11
❑ 214 Leon Lett .25 .11
❑ 215 Karim Abdul-Jabbar .40 .18
❑ 216 Carnell Lake .25 .11
❑ 217 Byron Bam Morris .25 .11
❑ 218 John Avery .25 .11
❑ 219 Chris Slade .25 .11
❑ 220 Robert Smith .60 .25
❑ 221 Mike Pritchard .25 .11
❑ 222 Ty Detmer .40 .18
❑ 223 Randall Cunningham .60 .25
❑ 224 Alonzo Mayes .25 .11
❑ 225 Jake Plummer .40 .18
❑ 226 Derrick Mayes .25 .11
❑ 227 Jeff Brady .25 .11
❑ 228 John Lynch .40 .18
❑ 229 Steve Atwater .25 .11
❑ 230 Warrick Dunn .60 .25
❑ 231 Shawn Jefferson .25 .11
❑ 232 Erik Kramer .25 .11
❑ 233 Ken Dilger .25 .11
❑ 234 Ryan Leaf .60 .25
❑ 235 Ray Buchanan .25 .11
❑ 236 Kevin Williams .25 .11
❑ 237 Ricky Watters .40 .18
❑ 238 Dwayne Rudd .25 .11
❑ 239 Duce Staley .60 .25
❑ 240 Charlie Batch .60 .25
❑ 241 Tim Biakabutuka .40 .18
❑ 242 Tony Gonzalez .60 .25
❑ 243 Bryan Still .25 .11
❑ 244 Donnie Edwards .25 .11
❑ 245 Troy Aikman 1.25 .55
❑ 246 Tony Banks .40 .18
❑ 247 Curtis Enis .25 .11
❑ 248 Chris Chandler .40 .18
❑ 249 James Jett .40 .18
❑ 250 Brett Favre 2.00 .90
❑ 251 Keith Poole .25 .11
❑ 252 Ricky Proehl .25 .11
❑ 253 Shannon Sharpe .40 .18
❑ 254 Robert Jones .25 .11
❑ 255 Chad Brown .25 .11
❑ 256 Ben Coates .40 .18
❑ 257 Jacquez Green .25 .11
❑ 258 Jessie Armstead .25 .11
❑ 259 Dale Carter .25 .11
❑ 260 Antowain Smith .60 .25
❑ 261 Mark Chmura .25 .11
❑ 262 Michael Westbrook .40 .18
❑ 263 Marvin Harrison .60 .25
❑ 264 Darrien Gordon .25 .11
❑ 265 Rodney Harrison .25 .11
❑ 266 Charles Johnson .25 .11
❑ 267 Roman Phifer .25 .11
❑ 268 Reidel Anthony .40 .18
❑ 269 Jerry Rice 1.25 .55
❑ 270 Eric Moulds .60 .25
❑ 271 Robert Porcher .25 .11
❑ 272 Deion Sanders .60 .25
❑ 273 Germane Crowell .25 .11
❑ 274 Randy Moss 1.50 .70
❑ 275 Antonio Freeman .60 .25
❑ 276 Trent Dilfer .40 .18
❑ 277 Eric Turner .25 .11
❑ 278 Jeff George .40 .18
❑ 279 Levon Kirkland .25 .11
❑ 280 O.J. McDuffie .40 .18
❑ 281 Takeo Spikes .25 .11
❑ 282 Jim Flanigan .25 .11
❑ 283 Chris Warren .25 .11
❑ 284 J.J. Stokes .40 .18
❑ 285 Bryan Cox .25 .11
❑ 286 Sam Madison .25 .11
❑ 287 Priest Holmes 1.00 .45
❑ 288 Keenan McCardell .40 .18
❑ 289 Michael Strahan .40 .18
❑ 290 Robert Edwards .25 .11
❑ 291 Tommy Vardell .25 .11
❑ 292 Wayne Chrebet .40 .18
❑ 293 Chris Calloway .25 .11
❑ 294 Wesley Walls .40 .18
❑ 295 Derrick Brooks .60 .25
❑ 296 Trace Armstrong .25 .11
❑ 297 Brian Simmons .25 .11
❑ 298 Darrell Green .25 .11
❑ 299 Robert Brooks .40 .18
❑ 300 Peyton Manning 2.00 .90
❑ 301 Dana Stubblefield .25 .11
❑ 302 Shawn Springs .25 .11

❑ 303 Leslie Shepherd	.25	.11
❑ 304 Ken Harvey	.25	.11
❑ 305 Jon Kitna	.60	.25
❑ 306 Terance Mathis	.40	.18
❑ 307 Andre Reed	.40	.18
❑ 308 Jackie Harris	.25	.11
❑ 309 Rich Gannon	.60	.25
❑ 310 Keyshawn Johnson	.60	.25
❑ 311 Victor Green	.25	.11
❑ 312 Eric Allen	.25	.11
❑ 313 Terry Fair	.25	.11
❑ 314 Jason Elam SH	.25	.11
❑ 315 Garrison Hearst SH	.40	.18
❑ 316 Jake Plummer SH	.40	.18
❑ 317 Randall Cunningham SH	.60	.25
❑ 318 Randy Moss SH	.75	.35
❑ 319 Jamal Anderson SH	.60	.25
❑ 320 John Elway SH	1.00	.45
❑ 321 Doug Flutie SH	.40	.18
❑ 322 Emmitt Smith SH	.75	.35
❑ 323 Terrell Davis SH	.60	.25
❑ 324 Jerris McPhail	.25	.11
❑ 325 Damon Gibson	.25	.11
❑ 326 Jim Pyne	.25	.11
❑ 327 Antonio Langham	.25	.11
❑ 328 Freddie Solomon	.25	.11
❑ 329 Ricky Williams RC	4.00	1.80
❑ 330 Daunte Culpepper RC	8.00	3.60
❑ 331 Chris Claiborne RC	1.25	.55
❑ 332 Amos Zereoue RC	2.50	1.10
❑ 333 Chris McAlister RC	2.00	.90
❑ 334 Kevin Faulk RC	2.50	1.10
❑ 335 James Johnson RC	2.00	.90
❑ 336 Mike Cloud RC	2.00	.90
❑ 337 Jevon Kearse RC	4.00	1.80
❑ 338 Akili Smith RC	2.00	.90
❑ 339 Edgerrin James RC	8.00	3.60
❑ 340 Cecil Collins RC	1.25	.55
❑ 341 Donovan McNabb RC	10.00	4.50
❑ 342 Kevin Johnson RC	2.50	1.10
❑ 343 Torry Holt RC	5.00	2.20
❑ 344 Rob Konrad RC	1.25	.55
❑ 345 Tim Couch RC	2.50	1.10
❑ 346 David Boston RC	2.50	1.10
❑ 347 Karsten Bailey RC	2.00	.90
❑ 348 Troy Edwards RC	2.00	.90
❑ 349 Sedrick Irvin RC	1.25	.55
❑ 350 Shaun King RC	2.00	.90
❑ 351 Peerless Price RC	4.00	1.80
❑ 352 Brock Huard RC	2.50	1.10
❑ 353 Cade McNown RC	2.00	.90
❑ 354 Champ Bailey RC	3.00	1.35
❑ 355 D'Wayne Bates RC	2.00	.90
❑ 356 Checklist Card	.25	.11
❑ 357 Checklist Card	.25	.11

1999 Topps Autographs

	Nm-Mt	Ex-Mt
❑ A1 Randy Moss	60.00	27.00
❑ A2 Wayne Chrebet	20.00	9.00
❑ A3 Tim Couch	25.00	11.00
❑ A4 Joey Galloway	25.00	11.00
❑ A5 Ricky Williams	80.00	36.00
❑ A6 Doug Flutie	40.00	18.00
❑ A7 Terrell Owens	40.00	18.00
❑ A8 Marshall Faulk	40.00	18.00
❑ A9 Rod Smith	25.00	11.00
❑ A10 Dan Marino	120.00	55.00

1999 Topps Hall of Fame Autographs

	Nm-Mt	Ex-Mt
❑ HOF1 Eric Dickerson	50.00	22.00
❑ HOF2 Billy Shaw	50.00	22.00
❑ HOF3 Lawrence Taylor	80.00	36.00
❑ HOF4 Tom Mack	50.00	22.00
❑ HOF5 Ozzie Newsome	50.00	22.00

2000 Topps

	Nm-Mt	Ex-Mt
COMPLETE SET (400)	60.00	27.00
COMP.SET w/o SP's (360)	20.00	9.00
❑ 1 Kurt Warner	1.25	.55
❑ 2 Darrell Russell	.25	.11
❑ 3 Tai Streets	.25	.11
❑ 4 Bryant Young	.25	.11
❑ 5 Kent Graham	.25	.11
❑ 6 Shawn Jefferson	.25	.11
❑ 7 Wesley Walls	.25	.11
❑ 8 Jessie Armstead	.25	.11
❑ 9 Dedric Ward	.25	.11
❑ 10 Emmitt Smith	1.25	.55
❑ 11 James Stewart	.40	.18
❑ 12 Frank Sanders	.25	.11
❑ 13 Ray Buchanan	.25	.11
❑ 14 Olindo Mare	.25	.11
❑ 15 Andre Reed	.40	.18
❑ 16 Curtis Conway	.40	.18
❑ 17 Patrick Jeffers	.60	.25
❑ 18 Greg Hill	.25	.11
❑ 19 John Unitas	.60	.25
❑ 20 Brett Favre	2.00	.90
❑ 21 Jerome Pathon	.40	.18
❑ 22 Jason Tucker	.25	.11
❑ 23 Charles Johnson	.40	.18
❑ 24 Brian Mitchell	.25	.11
❑ 25 Billy Miller	.25	.11
❑ 26 Jay Fiedler	.60	.25
❑ 27 Marcus Pollard	.25	.11
❑ 28 De'Mond Parker	.25	.11
❑ 29 Leslie Shepherd	.25	.11
❑ 30 Fred Taylor	.60	.25
❑ 31 Michael Pittman	.25	.11
❑ 32 Ricky Watters	.40	.18
❑ 33 Derrick Brooks	.60	.25
❑ 34 Junior Seau	.60	.25
❑ 35 Troy Vincent	.25	.11
❑ 36 Eric Allen	.25	.11
❑ 37 Pete Mitchell	.25	.11
❑ 38 Tony Simmons	.25	.11
❑ 39 Az-Zahir Hakim	.40	.18
❑ 40 Dan Marino	2.00	.90
❑ 41 Mac Cody	.25	.11
❑ 42 Scott Dreisbach	.25	.11
❑ 43 Al Wilson	.25	.11
❑ 44 Luther Broughton RC	.40	.18
❑ 45 Wane McGarity	.25	.11
❑ 46 Stephen Boyd	.25	.11
❑ 47 Michael Strahan	.40	.18
❑ 48 Chris Chandler	.40	.18
❑ 49 Tony Martin	.40	.18
❑ 50 Edgerrin James	1.00	.45
❑ 51 John Randle	.40	.18
❑ 52 Warrick Dunn	.60	.25
❑ 53 Elvis Grbac	.40	.18
❑ 54 Champ Bailey	.40	.18
❑ 55 Kyle Brady	.25	.11
❑ 56 John Lynch	.40	.18
❑ 57 Kevin Carter	.25	.11
❑ 58 Mike Pritchard	.25	.11
❑ 59 Deon Mitchell RC	.40	.18
❑ 60 Randy Moss	1.25	.55
❑ 61 Jermaine Fazande	.25	.11
❑ 62 Donovan McNabb	1.00	.45
❑ 63 Richard Huntley	.25	.11
❑ 64 Rich Gannon	.60	.25
❑ 65 Aaron Glenn	.25	.11
❑ 66 Amani Toomer	.25	.11
❑ 67 Andre Hastings	.25	.11
❑ 68 Ricky Williams	.60	.25
❑ 69 Sam Madison	.25	.11
❑ 70 Drew Bledsoe	.75	.35
❑ 71 Eric Moulds	.60	.25
❑ 72 Justin Armour	.25	.11
❑ 73 Jamal Anderson	.60	.25
❑ 74 Mario Bates	.25	.11
❑ 75 Sam Gash	.25	.11
❑ 76 Macey Brooks	.25	.11
❑ 77 Tremain Mack	.25	.11
❑ 78 David LaFleur	.25	.11
❑ 79 Dexter Coakley	.25	.11
❑ 80 Cris Carter	.60	.25
❑ 81 Byron Chamberlain	.25	.11
❑ 82 David Sloan	.25	.11
❑ 83 Mike Devlin RC	.25	.11
❑ 84 Jimmy Smith	.40	.18
❑ 85 Derrick Alexander	.40	.18
❑ 86 Damon Huard	.60	.25
❑ 87 Jake Reed	.40	.18
❑ 88 Darrell Green	.25	.11
❑ 89 Derrick Mason	.40	.18
❑ 90 Curtis Martin	.60	.25
❑ 91 Donnie Abraham	.25	.11
❑ 92 D'Marco Farr	.25	.11
❑ 93 Ahman Green	.60	.25
❑ 94 Shane Matthews	.40	.18
❑ 95 Torrance Small	.25	.11
❑ 96 Duce Staley	.60	.25
❑ 97 Jon Ritchie	.25	.11
❑ 98 Victor Green	.25	.11
❑ 99 Kerry Collins	.40	.18
❑ 100 Peyton Manning	1.50	.70
❑ 101 Ben Coates	.25	.11
❑ 102 Thurman Thomas	.40	.18
❑ 103 Cornelius Bennett	.25	.11
❑ 104 Terance Mathis	.40	.18
❑ 105 Adrian Murrell	.40	.18
❑ 106 Donald Hayes	.25	.11
❑ 107 Terry Kirby	.25	.11
❑ 108 James Allen	.40	.18
❑ 109 Ty Law	.40	.18
❑ 110 Tim Brown	.60	.25

❑ 111 Chad Bratzke	.25	.11
❑ 112 Deion Sanders	.60	.25
❑ 113 James Johnson	.25	.11
❑ 114 Tony Richardson RC	.40	.18
❑ 115 Tony Brackens	.25	.11
❑ 116 Ken Dilger	.25	.11
❑ 117 Albert Connell	.25	.11
❑ 118 Neil O'Donnell	.25	.11
❑ 119 Selucio Sanford EP RC	.60	.25
❑ 120 Steve Young	.75	.35
❑ 121 Tony Horne	.25	.11
❑ 122 Charlie Rogers	.25	.11
❑ 123 J.J. Stokes	.40	.18
❑ 124 Kenny Bynum	.25	.11
❑ 125 Jeff Graham	.25	.11
❑ 126 Ike Hilliard	.40	.18
❑ 127 Ray Lucas	.40	.18
❑ 128 Terry Glenn	.40	.18
❑ 129 Rickey Dudley	.25	.11
❑ 130 Joey Galloway	.40	.18
❑ 131 Brian Dawkins	.25	.11
❑ 132 Rob Moore	.40	.18
❑ 133 Bob Christian	.25	.11
❑ 134 Anthony Wright RC	2.00	.90
❑ 135 Antowain Smith	.40	.18
❑ 136 Kevin Johnson	.60	.25
❑ 137 Scott Covington	.25	.11
❑ 138 D'Wayne Bates	.25	.11
❑ 139 Sam Cowart	.25	.11
❑ 140 Isaac Bruce	.60	.25
❑ 141 Tony McGee	.25	.11
❑ 142 Dale Carter	.25	.11
❑ 143 Matt Hasselbeck	.40	.18
❑ 144 Torry Holt	.60	.25
❑ 145 Daunte Culpepper	.75	.35
❑ 146 Yatil Green	.25	.11
❑ 147 Chris Howard	.25	.11
❑ 148 Irving Fryar	.40	.18
❑ 149 Derrick Mayes	.40	.18
❑ 150 Warren Sapp	.40	.18
❑ 151 Ricky Proehl	.25	.11
❑ 152 Eric Kresser EP	.50	.23
❑ 153 Jeff Garcia	.60	.25
❑ 154 Freddie Jones	.25	.11
❑ 155 Mike Cloud	.25	.11
❑ 156 Wayne Chrebet	.40	.18
❑ 157 Joe Montgomery	.25	.11
❑ 158 Shannon Sharpe	.40	.18
❑ 159 Eddie Kennison	.25	.11
❑ 160 Eddie George	.60	.25
❑ 161 Jay Riemersma	.25	.11
❑ 162 Peter Boulware	.25	.11
❑ 163 Aeneas Williams	.25	.11
❑ 164 Jim Miller	.25	.11
❑ 165 Jamir Miller	.25	.11
❑ 166 Tim Biakabutuka	.40	.18
❑ 167 Kordell Stewart	.40	.18
❑ 168 Charlie Garner	.40	.18
❑ 169 Germane Crowell	.25	.11
❑ 170 Stephen Davis	.60	.25
❑ 171 Jeff George	.40	.18
❑ 172 Mark Brunell	.60	.25
❑ 173 Stephen Alexander	.25	.11
❑ 174 Mike Alstott	.60	.25
❑ 175 Terry Allen	.40	.18
❑ 176 Ed McCaffrey	.60	.25
❑ 177 Bobby Engram	.25	.11
❑ 178 Andre Cooper	.25	.11
❑ 179 Kevin Faulk	.25	.11
❑ 180 Errict Rhett	.40	.18
❑ 181 Jammi German	.25	.11
❑ 182 Oronde Gadsden	.40	.18
❑ 183 Jevon Kearse	.60	.25
❑ 184 Herman Moore	.40	.18
❑ 185 Terrence Wilkins	.25	.11
❑ 186 Rocket Ismail	.40	.18
❑ 187 Patrick Johnson	.25	.11
❑ 188 Simeon Rice	.40	.18
❑ 189 Mo Lewis	.25	.11
❑ 190 Qadry Ismail	.40	.18
❑ 191 Terry Jackson	.25	.11
❑ 192 Rashaan Shehee	.25	.11
❑ 193 Charles Woodson	.40	.18
❑ 194 Akili Smith	.25	.11
❑ 195 Yancey Thigpen	.25	.11
❑ 196 Michael Westbrook	.40	.18
❑ 197 Donnell Bennett	.25	.11
❑ 198 Sedrick Irvin	.25	.11
❑ 199 Keenan McCardell	.40	.18
❑ 200 Marshall Faulk	.75	.35
❑ 201 Jeff Blake	.40	.18
❑ 202 Rob Johnson	.40	.18
❑ 203 Vinny Testaverde	.40	.18
❑ 204 Andy Katzenmoyer	.25	.11
❑ 205 Michael Basnight	.25	.11
❑ 206 Lance Schulters	.25	.11
❑ 207 Shaun King	.25	.11
❑ 208 Bill Schroeder	.40	.18
❑ 209 Skip Hicks	.25	.11
❑ 210 Jake Plummer	.40	.18
❑ 211 Leroy Hoard	.25	.11
❑ 212 Reggie Barlow	.25	.11
❑ 213 E.G. Green	.25	.11
❑ 214 Fred Lane	.25	.11
❑ 215 Antonio Freeman	.60	.25
❑ 216 Grant Wistrom	.25	.11
❑ 217 Kevin Dyson	.40	.18
❑ 218 Mikhael Ricks	.25	.11
❑ 219 Rod Woodson	.40	.18
❑ 220 Tim Dwight	.60	.25
❑ 221 Darnay Scott	.40	.18
❑ 222 Curtis Enis	.25	.11
❑ 223 Sean Bennett	.25	.11
❑ 224 Napoleon Kaufman	.40	.18
❑ 225 Jonathan Linton	.25	.11
❑ 226 Jim Harbaugh	.40	.18
❑ 227 Hardy Nickerson	.25	.11
❑ 228 Todd Lyght	.25	.11
❑ 229 Dorsey Levens	.40	.18
❑ 230 Steve Beuerlein	.40	.18
❑ 231 Marty Booker	.40	.18
❑ 232 Andre Wadsworth	.25	.11
❑ 233 James Hasty	.25	.11
❑ 234 Shawn Bryson	.25	.11
❑ 235 Larry Centers	.25	.11
❑ 236 Charlie Batch	.60	.25
❑ 237 Steve McNair	.60	.25
❑ 238 Darrin Chiaverini	.25	.11
❑ 239 Jerome Bettis	.60	.25
❑ 240 Muhsin Muhammad	.40	.18
❑ 241 Terrell Fletcher	.25	.11
❑ 242 Jon Kitna	.60	.25
❑ 243 Frank Wycheck	.25	.11
❑ 244 Tony Gonzalez	.40	.18
❑ 245 Ron Rivers	.25	.11
❑ 246 Olandis Gary	.60	.25
❑ 247 Jermaine Lewis	.25	.11
❑ 248 Joe Jurevicius	.25	.11
❑ 249 Richie Anderson	.40	.18
❑ 250 Marcus Robinson	.60	.25
❑ 251 Shawn Springs	.25	.11
❑ 252 William Floyd	.25	.11
❑ 253 Bobby Shaw RC	.60	.25
❑ 254 Glyn Milburn	.25	.11
❑ 255 Brian Griese	.60	.25
❑ 256 Donnie Edwards	.25	.11
❑ 257 Joe Horn	.40	.18
❑ 258 Cameron Cleeland	.25	.11
❑ 259 Glenn Foley	.25	.11
❑ 260 Corey Dillon	.60	.25
❑ 261 Troy Brown	.40	.18
❑ 262 Stoney Case	.25	.11
❑ 263 Kevin Williams	.25	.11
❑ 264 London Fletcher RC	.40	.18
❑ 265 O.J. McDuffie	.40	.18
❑ 266 Jonathan Quinn	.25	.11
❑ 267 Trent Dilfer	.40	.18
❑ 268 Dameyune Craig	.25	.11
❑ 269 Terrell Owens	.60	.25
❑ 270 Tim Couch	.40	.18
❑ 271 Dameane Douglas	.25	.11
❑ 272 Moses Moreno	.25	.11
❑ 273 Bruce Smith	.40	.18
❑ 274 Peerless Price	.60	.25
❑ 275 Sam Games	.25	.11
❑ 276 Natrone Means	.25	.11
❑ 277 Na Brown	.25	.11
❑ 278 Dave Moore	.25	.11
❑ 279 Chris Sanders	.25	.11
❑ 280 Troy Aikman	1.25	.55
❑ 281 Cecil Collins	.25	.11
❑ 282 Matthew Hatchette	.25	.11
❑ 283 Bill Romanowski	.25	.11
❑ 284 Basil Mitchell	.25	.11
❑ 285 Tony Banks	.40	.18
❑ 286 Jake Delhomme RC	2.50	1.10
❑ 287 Keyshawn Johnson	.60	.25
❑ 288 Dexter McCleon RC	.60	.25
❑ 289 Corey Bradford	.40	.18
❑ 290 Terrell Davis	.60	.25
❑ 291 Johnnie Morton	.40	.18
❑ 292 Kevin Lockett	.25	.11
❑ 293 Robert Smith	.60	.25
❑ 294 Jeff Lewis	.25	.11
❑ 295 Wali Rainer	.25	.11
❑ 296 Troy Edwards	.25	.11
❑ 297 Keith Poole	.25	.11
❑ 298 Priest Holmes	.75	.35
❑ 299 David Boston	.60	.25
❑ 300 Marvin Harrison	.60	.25
❑ 301 Levon Kirkland	.25	.11
❑ 302 Robert Holcombe	.25	.11
❑ 303 Autry Denson	.25	.11
❑ 304 Kevin Hardy	.25	.11
❑ 305 Rod Smith	.40	.18
❑ 306 Robert Porcher	.25	.11
❑ 307 Cade McNown	.25	.11
❑ 308 Craig Yeast	.25	.11
❑ 309 Doug Flutie	.60	.25
❑ 310 Jerry Rice	1.25	.55
❑ 311 Brad Johnson	.60	.25
❑ 312 Tiki Barber	.40	.18
❑ 313 Will Blackwell	.25	.11
❑ 314 Sean Dawkins	.25	.11
❑ 315 Jacquez Green	.25	.11
❑ 316 Zach Thomas	.60	.25
❑ 317 Gus Frerotte	.25	.11
❑ 318 Chris Warren	.25	.11
❑ 319 Carl Pickens	.40	.18
❑ 320 Tyrone Wheatley HL	.25	.11
❑ 321 Kurt Warner HL	.60	.25
❑ 322 Dan Marino HL	1.00	.45
❑ 323 Cris Carter HL	.40	.18
❑ 324 Brett Favre HL	1.00	.45
❑ 325 Marshall Faulk HL	.60	.25
❑ 326 Jevon Kearse HL	.40	.18
❑ 327 Edgerrin James HL	.60	.25
❑ 328 Emmitt Smith HL	.60	.25
❑ 329 Andre Reed HL	.25	.11
❑ 330 Kevin Dyson Frank Wycheck	.25	.11
❑ 331 Olindo Mare MM	.25	.11
❑ 332 Marcus Coleman MM	.25	.11
❑ 333 James Johnson MM	.25	.11
❑ 334 Ray Lucas MM	.40	.18
❑ 335 Dedric Ward MM	.25	.11
❑ 336 Richie Cunningham MM	.25	.11
❑ 337 James Hasty MM	.25	.11
❑ 338 Sedrick Shaw MM	.25	.11
❑ 339 Kurt Warner MM	.60	.25
❑ 340 Marshall Faulk MM	.60	.25
❑ 341 Brian Shay EP	.50	.23
❑ 342 L.C. Stevens EP	.50	.23
❑ 343 Corey Thomas EP	.50	.23
❑ 344 Scott Milanovich EP	.60	.25
❑ 345 Pat Barnes EP	.60	.25
❑ 346 Danny Wuerffel EP	.60	.25
❑ 347 Kevin Daft EP	.50	.23
❑ 348 Ron Powlus EP RC	1.00	.45
❑ 349 Tony Graziani EP	.60	.25
❑ 350 Norman Miller EP RC	.50	.23
❑ 351 Cory Sauter EP	.50	.23
❑ 352 Marcus Crandell EP RC	.60	.25

❑ 353 Sean Morey EP RC	.60	.25
❑ 354 Jeff Ogden EP	.60	.25
❑ 355 Ted White EP	.50	.23
❑ 356 Jim Kubiak EP RC	.60	.25
❑ 357 Aaron Stecker EP RC	1.00	.45
❑ 358 Ronnie Powell EP	.50	.23
❑ 359 Matt Lytle EP RC	.60	.25
❑ 360 Kendrick Nord EP RC	.50	.23
❑ 361 Tim Rattay RC	5.00	2.20
❑ 362 Rob Morris RC	2.50	1.10
❑ 363 Chris Samuels RC	2.00	.90
❑ 364 Todd Husak RC	2.50	1.10
❑ 365 Ahmed Plummer RC	2.50	1.10
❑ 366 Frank Murphy RC	2.00	.90
❑ 367 Michael Wiley RC	2.50	1.10
❑ 368 Giovanni Carmazzi RC	2.50	1.10
❑ 369 Anthony Becht RC	2.50	1.10
❑ 370 John Abraham RC	2.50	1.10
❑ 371 Shaun Alexander RC	6.00	2.70
❑ 372 Thomas Jones RC	4.00	1.80
❑ 373 Courtney Brown RC	1.00	.45
❑ 374 Curtis Keaton RC	2.00	.90
❑ 375 Jerry Porter RC	3.00	1.35
❑ 376 Corey Simon RC	1.00	.45
❑ 377 Dez White RC	2.50	1.10
❑ 378 Jamal Lewis RC	6.00	2.70
❑ 379 Ron Dayne RC	2.50	1.10
❑ 380 R.Jay Soward RC	2.50	1.10
❑ 381 Tee Martin RC	2.50	1.10
❑ 382 Shaun Ellis RC	2.50	1.10
❑ 383 Brian Urlacher RC	10.00	4.50
❑ 384 Reuben Droughns RC	4.00	1.80
❑ 385 Travis Taylor RC	1.00	.45
❑ 386 Plaxico Burress RC	5.00	2.20
❑ 387 Chad Pennington RC	10.00	4.50
❑ 388 Sylvester Morris RC	2.50	1.10
❑ 389 Ron Dugans RC	2.00	.90
❑ 390 Joe Hamilton RC	2.50	1.10
❑ 391 Chris Redman RC	.60	.25
❑ 392 Trung Canidate RC	2.50	1.10
❑ 393 J.R. Redmond RC	2.50	1.10
❑ 394 Danny Farmer RC	2.50	1.10
❑ 395 Todd Pinkston RC	2.50	1.10
❑ 396 Dennis Northcutt RC	2.50	1.10
❑ 397 Laveranues Coles RC	3.00	1.35
❑ 398 Bubba Franks RC	2.50	1.10
❑ 399 Travis Prentice RC	2.50	1.10
❑ 400 Peter Warrick RC	2.50	1.10
❑ SB1 Kurt Warner FB AUTO	120.00	55.00

2000 Topps Autographs

	Nm-Mt	Ex-Mt
❑ CP Chad Pennington	60.00	27.00
❑ EJ Edgerrin James	40.00	18.00
❑ JK Jon Kitna	20.00	9.00
❑ JS Jimmy Smith	15.00	6.75
❑ KC Kevin Carter	20.00	6.00
❑ KW Kurt Warner	30.00	13.50
❑ MF Marshall Faulk	30.00	13.50
❑ MH Marvin Harrison	30.00	13.50
❑ PM Peyton Manning	100.00	45.00
❑ PW Peter Warrick SP	40.00	18.00
❑ RD Ron Dayne	20.00	9.00
❑ SA Shaun Alexander	40.00	18.00
❑ SD Stephen Davis	20.00	9.00
❑ SM Sylvester Morris	15.00	6.75
❑ TJ Thomas Jones	30.00	13.50
❑ ZT Zach Thomas	30.00	13.50

2000 Topps Hall of Fame Autographs

	Nm-Mt	Ex-Mt
❑ HOF1 Joe Montana	200.00	90.00
❑ HOF2 Howie Long	100.00	45.00
❑ HOF3 Ronnie Lott	80.00	36.00
❑ HOF4 Dan Rooney	100.00	45.00
❑ HOF5 Dave Wilcox	60.00	27.00

2000 Topps Unitas Reprints Autographs

	Nm-Mt	Ex-Mt
COMMON CARD (R1-R18)	200.00	90.00

AUTO.ODDS 1:13,678 H, 1:3048 HTA

2000 Topps Rookie Premier Autographs

	Nm-Mt	Ex-Mt
❑ AB Anthony Becht	100.00	45.00
❑ BU Brian Urlacher	500.00	220.00
❑ CB Courtney Brown	120.00	55.00
❑ CK Curtis Keaton	60.00	27.00
❑ CP Chad Pennington	500.00	220.00
❑ CR Chris Redman	100.00	45.00
❑ CS Corey Simon	120.00	55.00
❑ DF Danny Farmer	100.00	45.00
❑ DN Dennis Northcutt	120.00	55.00
❑ DW Dez White	120.00	55.00
❑ JH Joe Hamilton	100.00	45.00
❑ JL Jamal Lewis	300.00	135.00
❑ JP Jerry Porter	150.00	70.00
❑ JR J.R. Redmond	100.00	45.00
❑ LC Laveranues Coles	150.00	70.00
❑ PB Plaxico Burress	200.00	90.00
❑ PW Peter Warrick	150.00	70.00
❑ RD Ron Dayne	120.00	55.00
❑ SA Shaun Alexander	300.00	135.00
❑ SM Sylvester Morris	100.00	45.00
❑ TC Trung Canidate	100.00	45.00
❑ TJ Thomas Jones	150.00	70.00
❑ TM Tee Martin	120.00	55.00
❑ TP Todd Pinkston	120.00	55.00
❑ TT Travis Taylor	120.00	55.00
❑ DFR Bubba Franks	120.00	55.00
❑ RDR Reuben Droughns	150.00	70.00
❑ RDU Ron Dugans	60.00	27.00
❑ TPR Travis Prentice	100.00	45.00

2001 Topps

	Nm-Mt	Ex-Mt
COMPLETE SET (385)	60.00	27.00
❑ 1 Marshall Faulk	.75	.35
❑ 2 Lawyer Milloy	.40	.18
❑ 3 Rich Gannon	.60	.25
❑ 4 Rod Smith	.40	.18
❑ 5 David Boston	.60	.25
❑ 6 Jeremy McDaniel	.25	.11
❑ 7 Joey Galloway	.40	.18
❑ 8 Ron Dixon	.25	.11
❑ 9 Terrell Fletcher	.25	.11
❑ 10 Deion Sanders	.60	.25
❑ 11 Jevon Kearse	.40	.18
❑ 12 Charles Woodson	.40	.18
❑ 13 Brian Walker	.25	.11
❑ 14 Mike Peterson	.25	.11
❑ 15 Marcus Robinson	.60	.25
❑ 16 Duane Starks	.25	.11
❑ 17 KaRon Coleman	.25	.11
❑ 18 Randy Moss	1.25	.55
❑ 19 Reggie Jones	.25	.11
❑ 20 Derrick Brooks	.60	.25
❑ 21 Eddie George	.60	.25
❑ 22 Wayne Chrebet	.40	.18
❑ 23 Kevin Hardy	.25	.11
❑ 24 Bill Schroeder	.40	.18
❑ 25 Doug Flutie	.60	.25
❑ 26 Tim Dwight	.60	.25
❑ 27 Eddie Kennison	.40	.18
❑ 28 Reggie Kelly	.25	.11
❑ 29 Ricky Watters	.40	.18
❑ 30 Stephen Alexander	.25	.11
❑ 31 Az-Zahir Hakim	.25	.11
❑ 32 Henri Crockett	.25	.11
❑ 33 Joe Horn	.40	.18
❑ 34 Danny Farmer	.25	.11
❑ 35 Shannon Sharpe	.40	.18
❑ 36 Brad Hoover	.25	.11
❑ 37 David Patten	.25	.11
❑ 38 Kevin Faulk	.40	.18
❑ 39 Freddie Jones	.25	.11
❑ 40 Michael Westbrook	.40	.18
❑ 41 Jacquez Green	.25	.11
❑ 42 Torrance Small	.25	.11
❑ 43 Terrence Wilkins	.25	.11
❑ 44 Brett Favre	2.00	.90
❑ 45 Tony Banks	.40	.18
❑ 46 Johnnie Morton	.40	.18
❑ 47 Jimmy Smith	.40	.18
❑ 48 Jerry Rice	1.25	.55
❑ 49 Jeff George	.40	.18
❑ 50 Ray Lewis	.60	.25
❑ 51 Joe Johnson	.25	.11
❑ 52 Rocket Ismail	.40	.18
❑ 53 Muhsin Muhammad	.40	.18
❑ 54 Ken Dilger	.25	.11

❑ 55 Ike Hilliard .40 .18
❑ 56 Joey Porter RC .60 .25
❑ 57 Shaun Alexander .75 .35
❑ 58 Jeff Garcia .60 .25
❑ 59 Jay Fiedler .60 .25
❑ 60 Wane McGarity .25 .11
❑ 61 Steve Beuerlein .25 .11
❑ 62 Tywan Mitchell .25 .11
❑ 63 Travis Prentice .25 .11
❑ 64 Robert Griffith .25 .11
❑ 65 Napoleon Kaufman .25 .11
❑ 66 Randall Godfrey .25 .11
❑ 67 Junior Seau .60 .25
❑ 68 Willie Jackson .25 .11
❑ 69 Larry Foster .25 .11
❑ 70 Brandon Stokley .40 .18
❑ 71 Hugh Douglas .25 .11
❑ 72 James Thrash .40 .18
❑ 73 Vinny Testaverde .40 .18
❑ 74 Leslie Shepherd .25 .11
❑ 75 Terrell Davis .60 .25
❑ 76 Jake Plummer .40 .18
❑ 77 Corey Dillon .60 .25
❑ 78 Ron Dayne .60 .25
❑ 79 Brock Huard .25 .11
❑ 80 Todd Husak .25 .11
❑ 81 Richard Huntley .25 .11
❑ 82 Shaun Ellis .25 .11
❑ 83 Kyle Brady .25 .11
❑ 84 Corey Bradford .25 .11
❑ 85 Eric Moulds .40 .18
❑ 86 Brian Finneran .25 .11
❑ 87 Antonio Freeman .60 .25
❑ 88 Terry Glenn .25 .11
❑ 89 Tai Streets .25 .11
❑ 90 Chris Sanders .25 .11
❑ 91 Sylvester Morris .25 .11
❑ 92 Peter Warrick .60 .25
❑ 93 Chris Greisen .25 .11
❑ 94 Cade McNown .25 .11
❑ 95 Jerome Pathon .40 .18
❑ 96 John Randle .25 .11
❑ 97 Curtis Conway .40 .18
❑ 98 Keyshawn Johnson .60 .25
❑ 99 Trent Green .60 .25
❑ 100 Mike Anderson .60 .25
❑ 101 Jeff Blake .40 .18
❑ 102 Tee Martin .40 .18
❑ 103 Darrell Jackson .60 .25
❑ 104 Mark Brunell .60 .25
❑ 105 Charlie Batch .60 .25
❑ 106 Wesley Walls .25 .11
❑ 107 Edgerrin James .75 .35
❑ 108 Robert Wilson .25 .11
❑ 109 Donovan McNabb .75 .35
❑ 110 Champ Bailey .40 .18
❑ 111 Isaac Bruce .60 .25
❑ 112 Michael Strahan .40 .18
❑ 113 Donnie Edwards .25 .11
❑ 114 Randall Cunningham .60 .25
❑ 115 Germane Crowell .25 .11
❑ 116 Jermaine Lewis .25 .11
❑ 117 Dennis McKinley .25 .11
❑ 118 Ryan Leaf .40 .18
❑ 119 Samari Rolle .25 .11
❑ 120 Daunte Culpepper .60 .25
❑ 121 Tim Couch .40 .18
❑ 122 Greg Biekert .25 .11
❑ 123 Warrick Dunn .60 .25
❑ 124 Richie Anderson .25 .11
❑ 125 Trace Armstrong .25 .11
❑ 126 Bernardo Harris .25 .11
❑ 127 Kwame Cavil .25 .11
❑ 128 James Allen .40 .18
❑ 129 Anthony Becht .25 .11
❑ 130 Tiki Barber .40 .18
❑ 131 Brad Johnson .60 .25
❑ 132 Tyrone Wheatley .40 .18
❑ 133 Kurt Warner 1.25 .55
❑ 134 Desmond Howard .25 .11
❑ 135 Thomas Jones .40 .18
❑ 136 Peyton Manning 1.50 .70
❑ 137 Tony Richardson .25 .11
❑ 138 Chris Chandler .40 .18
❑ 139 Plaxico Burress .60 .25
❑ 140 J.R. Redmond .25 .11
❑ 141 Fred Taylor .60 .25
❑ 142 Akili Smith .25 .11
❑ 143 Sammy Morris .25 .11
❑ 144 Jessie Armstead .25 .11
❑ 145 Charlie Garner .40 .18
❑ 146 Steve McNair .60 .25
❑ 147 Charles Johnson .25 .11
❑ 148 Troy Aikman 1.00 .45
❑ 149 Kevin Johnson .40 .18
❑ 150 Brian Urlacher 1.00 .45
❑ 151 Travis Taylor .40 .18
❑ 152 Aaron Shea .25 .11
❑ 153 Mike Cloud .25 .11
❑ 154 Donald Driver .40 .18
❑ 155 Chad Pennington 1.00 .45
❑ 156 Troy Edwards .25 .11
❑ 157 Reidel Anthony .25 .11
❑ 158 Michael Bishop .25 .11
❑ 159 Mo Lewis .25 .11
❑ 160 Damon Huard .25 .11
❑ 161 James McKnight .40 .18
❑ 162 Craig Yeast .25 .11
❑ 163 Michael Pittman .25 .11
❑ 164 Robert Smith .40 .18
❑ 165 Terrelle Smith .25 .11
❑ 166 Jeremiah Trotter .40 .18
❑ 167 Amani Toomer .25 .11
❑ 168 JaJuan Dawson .25 .11
❑ 169 Tim Biakabutuka .40 .18
❑ 170 Oronde Gadsden .40 .18
❑ 171 Ray Lucas .25 .11
❑ 172 Jermaine Fazande .25 .11
❑ 173 Todd Bouman .40 .18
❑ 174 Frank Wycheck .25 .11
❑ 175 Hines Ward .60 .25
❑ 176 Ahman Green .60 .25
❑ 177 Kaseem Sinceno .25 .11
❑ 178 Jamal Anderson .60 .25
❑ 179 Jay Riemersma .25 .11
❑ 180 Jarious Jackson .40 .18
❑ 181 Andre Rison .40 .18
❑ 182 Jerome Bettis .60 .25
❑ 183 Blaine Bishop .25 .11
❑ 184 Dorsey Levens .25 .11
❑ 185 James Stewart .40 .18
❑ 186 Chad Lewis .25 .11
❑ 187 Justin Watson .25 .11
❑ 188 Warren Sapp .40 .18
❑ 189 Rod Woodson .40 .18
❑ 190 Ricky Williams .60 .25
❑ 191 Marty Booker .25 .11
❑ 192 MarTay Jenkins .25 .11
❑ 193 Peerless Price .40 .18
❑ 194 Tony Gonzalez .40 .18
❑ 195 Jon Kitna .40 .18
❑ 196 Stephen Davis .60 .25
❑ 197 Curtis Martin .60 .25
❑ 198 Matt Hasselbeck .40 .18
❑ 199 Pat Johnson .25 .11
❑ 200 Emmitt Smith 1.25 .55
❑ 201 Doug Johnson .25 .11
❑ 202 Autry Denson .25 .11
❑ 203 Troy Brown .40 .18
❑ 204 Jeff Graham .25 .11
❑ 205 Corey Simon .40 .18
❑ 206 Jamel White .25 .11
❑ 207 Jeff Lewis .25 .11
❑ 208 Frank Sanders .25 .11
❑ 209 Al Wilson .25 .11
❑ 210 Jason Sehorn .25 .11
❑ 211 Shaun King .25 .11
❑ 212 Torry Holt .60 .25
❑ 213 Kordell Stewart .40 .18
❑ 214 Keenan McCardell .25 .11
❑ 215 Dedric Ward .25 .11
❑ 216 Michael Wiley .25 .11
❑ 217 Rob Johnson .40 .18
❑ 218 Jamal Lewis 1.00 .45
❑ 219 Herman Moore .40 .18
❑ 220 Ron Dugans .25 .11
❑ 221 Jason Taylor .25 .11
❑ 222 Charles Lee .25 .11
❑ 223 J.J. Stokes .40 .18
❑ 224 Albert Connell .25 .11
❑ 225 Keith Poole .25 .11
❑ 226 Elvis Grbac .40 .18
❑ 227 Shawn Jefferson .25 .11
❑ 228 Jackie Harris .25 .11
❑ 229 Derrick Alexander .40 .18
❑ 230 Darnell Autry .25 .11
❑ 231 Bobby Shaw .25 .11
❑ 232 Aaron Brooks .60 .25
❑ 233 Cris Carter .60 .25
❑ 234 Desmond Clark .25 .11
❑ 235 Spergon Wynn .25 .11
❑ 236 Qadry Ismail .40 .18
❑ 237 Sam Cowart .25 .11
❑ 238 Zach Thomas .60 .25
❑ 239 Drew Bledsoe .75 .35
❑ 240 Ronney Jenkins .25 .11
❑ 241 Keith Mitchell RC .25 .11
❑ 242 Laveranues Coles .60 .25
❑ 243 Marcus Pollard .25 .11
❑ 244 Darren Sharper .25 .11
❑ 245 Donald Hayes .25 .11
❑ 246 Brian Griese .60 .25
❑ 247 Frank Moreau .25 .11
❑ 248 Bruce Smith .25 .11
❑ 249 Fred Beasley .25 .11
❑ 250 Mike Alstott .60 .25
❑ 251 Trent Dilfer .40 .18
❑ 252 Terance Mathis .40 .18
❑ 253 Shawn Bryson .25 .11
❑ 254 Dennis Northcutt .40 .18
❑ 255 Brandon Bennett .25 .11
❑ 256 Stacey Mack .25 .11
❑ 257 Tim Brown .60 .25
❑ 258 Duce Staley .60 .25
❑ 259 Sean Dawkins .25 .11
❑ 260 Ricky Proehl .25 .11
❑ 261 Chris Fuamatu-ma'afala .25 .11
❑ 262 La'Roi Glover .25 .11
❑ 263 Bubba Franks .40 .18
❑ 264 Kevin Lockett .25 .11
❑ 265 Lamar Smith .40 .18
❑ 266 Priest Holmes .75 .35
❑ 267 Macey Brooks .25 .11
❑ 268 Anthony Wright .25 .11
❑ 269 Ed McCaffrey .60 .25
❑ 270 Joe Jurevicius .25 .11
❑ 271 Terrell Owens .60 .25
❑ 272 Tony Simmons .25 .11
❑ 273 Itula Mili .25 .11
❑ 274 Chad Morton .25 .11
❑ 275 Marvin Harrison .60 .25
❑ 276 Jason Gildon .25 .11
❑ 277 Derrick Mason .40 .18
❑ 278 Greg Clark .25 .11
❑ 279 Casey Crawford .25 .11
❑ 280 Kerry Collins .40 .18
❑ 281 Terrell Owens .60 .25
❑ 282 Marshall Faulk .60 .25
❑ 283 Mike Anderson .40 .18
❑ 284 Cris Carter .40 .18
❑ 285 Corey Dillon .40 .18
❑ 286 Daunte Culpepper .60 .25
❑ 287 Peyton Manning .75 .35
❑ 288 Torry Holt .60 .25
❑ 289 Marvin Harrison .40 .18
❑ 290 Edgerrin James .75 .35
❑ 291 Takeo Spikes .25 .07
❑ 292 John Lynch .40 .12
❑ 293 Sam Madison .25 .07
❑ 294 Stephen Boyd .25 .07
❑ 295 Tony Siragusa .25 .07
❑ 296 Robert Porcher .25 .07
❑ 297 Donnell Bennett .25 .07

❑ 298	Hardy Nickerson	.25	.07
❑ 299	Jonathan Quinn	.25	.07
❑ 300	Rob Morris	.25	.07
❑ 301	E.G. Green	.25	.07
❑ 302	David Sloan	.25	.07
❑ 303	Jason Tucker	.25	.07
❑ 304	Darrin Chiaverini	.25	.07
❑ 305	Wali Rainer	.25	.07
❑ 306	Jerry Azumah	.25	.07
❑ 307	Jonathan Linton	.25	.07
❑ 308	Dameyune Craig	.25	.07
❑ 309	Courtney Brown	.25	.07
❑ 310	Jammi German	.25	.07
❑ 311	Michael Vick RC	8.00	2.40
❑ 312	Jamar Fletcher RC	.75	.23
❑ 313	Will Allen RC	.75	.23
❑ 314	Jamal Reynolds RC	1.25	.35
❑ 315	Quincy Morgan RC	1.25	.35
❑ 316	Eric Kelly RC	.50	.15
❑ 317	Michael Stone RC	.50	.15
❑ 318	Rod Gardner RC	1.25	.35
❑ 319	Ken-Yon Rambo RC	.75	.23
❑ 320	Eric Westmoreland RC	.75	.23
❑ 321	Steve Smith RC	1.50	.45
❑ 322	George Layne RC	.75	.23
❑ 323	Justin McCareins RC	1.25	.35
❑ 324	Adam Archuleta RC	1.25	.35
❑ 325	Justin Smith RC	1.25	.35
❑ 326	David Terrell RC	1.25	.35
❑ 327	Correll Buckhalter RC	1.50	.45
❑ 328	Drew Brees RC	2.50	.75
❑ 329	Chris Barnes RC	.75	.23
❑ 330	Santana Moss RC	2.00	.60
❑ 331	Josh Heupel RC	1.25	.35
❑ 332	Cedrick Wilson RC	1.25	.35
❑ 333	Gerard Warren RC	1.25	.35
❑ 334	Jamie Henderson RC	.75	.23
❑ 335	Onomo Ojo RC	.75	.23
❑ 336	Marcus Stroud RC	1.25	.35
❑ 337	Quincy Carter RC	1.25	.35
❑ 338	Koren Robinson RC	1.50	.45
❑ 339	Ryan Pickett RC	.50	.15
❑ 340	Chad Johnson RC	2.50	.75
❑ 341	Nate Clements RC	1.25	.35
❑ 342	Jesse Palmer RC	1.25	.35
❑ 343	Snoop Minnis RC	.75	.23
❑ 344	Reggie Wayne RC	2.00	.60
❑ 345	Kevin Kasper RC	1.25	.35
❑ 346	Will Peterson RC	.75	.23
❑ 347	Marques Tuiasosopo RC	1.25	.35
❑ 348	Sage Rosenfels RC	1.25	.35
❑ 349	Dan Alexander RC	1.25	.35
❑ 350	LaDainian Tomlinson RC	4.00	1.20
❑ 351	Dan Morgan RC	1.25	.35
❑ 352	Scotty Anderson RC	.75	.23
❑ 353	Deuce McAllister RC	2.50	.75
❑ 354	Todd Heap RC	1.25	.35
❑ 355	Tony Dixon RC	.75	.23
❑ 356	Chris Chambers RC	1.50	.45
❑ 357	Eddie Berlin RC	.75	.23
❑ 358	Anthony Thomas RC	2.00	.60
❑ 359	James Jackson RC	1.25	.35
❑ 360	Richard Seymour RC	1.25	.35
❑ 361	Andre Carter RC	1.25	.35
❑ 362	Bobby Newcombe RC	.75	.23
❑ 363	Robert Ferguson RC	1.25	.35
❑ 364	Jonathan Carter RC	.75	.23
❑ 365	Damione Lewis RC	.75	.23
❑ 366	Damerien McCants RC	.75	.23
❑ 367	Tim Hasselbeck RC	1.25	.35
❑ 368	Derrick Gibson RC	.75	.23
❑ 369	Rudi Johnson RC	2.50	.75
❑ 370	Alge Crumpler RC	1.50	.45
❑ 371	Derrick Blaylock RC	1.25	.35
❑ 372	Moran Norris RC	.50	.15
❑ 373	Travis Minor RC	.75	.23
❑ 374	LaMont Jordan RC	1.50	.45
❑ 375	Kevan Barlow RC	1.25	.35
❑ 376	Freddie Mitchell RC	1.25	.35
❑ 377	Shaun Rogers RC	1.25	.35
❑ 378	Tay Cody RC	.50	.15
❑ 379	Travis Henry RC	1.50	.45
❑ 380	Chris Weinke RC	1.25	.35
❑ 381	Willie Middlebrooks RC	.75	.23
❑ 382	Rashard Casey RC	.75	.23
❑ 383	Mike McMahon RC	1.25	.35
❑ 384	Michael Bennett RC	2.50	.75
❑ 385	Jabari Holloway RC	.75	.23

2001 Topps Autographs

		Nm-Mt	Ex-Mt
❑ TABU	Brian Urlacher 4	50.00	22.00
❑ TACC	Chris Chambers 4	20.00	9.00
❑ TACJ	Chad Johnson 6	30.00	9.00
❑ TADB	Drew Brees 3	50.00	22.00
❑ TADC	Daunte Culpepper 1	120.00	55.00
❑ TADH	Donald Hayes 4	12.00	5.50
❑ TADJM	Deuce McAllister 1	60.00	27.00
❑ TADM	Derrick Mason 4	15.00	6.75
❑ TAEM	Eric Moulds 4	20.00	9.00
❑ TAES	Emmitt Smith 2	150.00	70.00
❑ TAJB	Josh Booty 5	15.00	4.50
❑ TAJH	Joe Horn 4	15.00	6.75
❑ TAJP	Jesse Palmer 5	15.00	4.50
❑ TAJS	Jimmy Smith 4	12.00	5.50
❑ TAJT	James Thrash 6	12.00	3.60
❑ TAKB	Kevan Barlow 6	20.00	6.00
❑ TAMF	Marshall Faulk 2 EXCH		
❑ TAMV	Michael Vick 1	150.00	70.00
❑ TASM	Santana Moss 3	30.00	13.50
❑ TATM	Travis Minor 5	12.00	3.60
❑ TATW	Terrence Wilkins 3	12.00	5.50

2001 Topps Hall of Fame Autographs

		Nm-Mt	Ex-Mt
❑ TADJ	Deacon Jones	125.00	38.00
❑ TAJS	Jackie Slater	100.00	45.00
❑ TAJY	Jack Youngblood	100.00	45.00
❑ TAML	Marv Levy	120.00	55.00
❑ TAMM	Mike Munchak EXCH		
❑ TANB	Nick Buoniconti		
❑ TARY	Ron Yary	100.00	45.00

2001 Topps King of Kings

		Nm-Mt	Ex-Mt
❑ KCD	Corey Dillon	20.00	9.00
❑ KDM	Dan Marino	80.00	36.00
❑ KES	Emmitt Smith	80.00	36.00
❑ KFT	Fred Taylor	20.00	9.00
❑ KJR	Jerry Rice	50.00	22.00
❑ KRM	Randy Moss	40.00	12.00
❑ KTO	Terrell Owens	20.00	9.00
❑ KWP	Walter Payton	100.00	45.00

2001 Topps King of Kings Golden Edition

		Nm-Mt	Ex-Mt
❑ KGDT	Corey Dillon Fred Taylor	60.00	27.00
❑ KGOR	Terrell Owens Jerry Rice	120.00	55.00
❑ KGSP	Emmitt Smith Walter Payton	250.00	110.00

2001 Topps Pro Bowl Jerseys

		Nm-Mt	Ex-Mt
❑ TPCG	Charlie Garner	15.00	6.75
❑ TPCL	Chad Lewis	15.00	6.75
❑ TPDM	Derrick Mason	15.00	6.75
❑ TPEM	Eric Moulds	30.00	13.50
❑ TPJG	Jeff Garcia	25.00	11.00
❑ TPJL	John Lynch	25.00	11.00
❑ TPJS	Junior Seau	25.00	11.00
❑ TPJT	Jason Taylor	15.00	6.75
❑ TPMA	Mike Alstott	25.00	11.00
❑ TPRG	Rich Gannon	25.00	11.00
❑ TPRL	Ray Lewis	30.00	13.50
❑ TPTH	Torry Holt	25.00	11.00

2001 Topps Pro Bowl Jerseys Autographs

	Nm-Mt	Ex-Mt
❑ TPADC Daunte Culpepper	150.00	70.00
❑ TPADM Derrick Mason	50.00	22.00
❑ TPAEJ Edgerrin James	150.00	70.00
❑ TPARL Ray Lewis EXCH		

2001 Topps Rookie Premier Autographs

	Nm-Mt	Ex-Mt
❑ RPAC Andre Carter	60.00	18.00
❑ RPAT Anthony Thomas	100.00	30.00
❑ RPCC Chris Chambers	100.00	30.00
❑ RPCJ Chad Johnson	150.00	45.00
❑ RPCW Chris Weinke	60.00	18.00
❑ RPDB Drew Brees	150.00	45.00
❑ RPDM Dan Morgan	50.00	15.00
❑ RPDMC Deuce McAllister	250.00	75.00
❑ RPDT David Terrell	100.00	30.00
❑ RPDTM David Terrell Santana Moss	150.00	45.00
❑ RPDVB Michael Vick Drew Brees	750.00	220.00
❑ RPFM Freddie Mitchell	80.00	24.00
❑ RPJH Josh Heupel	60.00	18.00
❑ RPJJ James Jackson	60.00	18.00
❑ RPJP Jesse Palmer	50.00	15.00
❑ RPJS Justin Smith	50.00	15.00
❑ RPKB Kevan Barlow	100.00	30.00
❑ RPKR Koren Robinson	80.00	24.00
❑ RPLD Leonard Davis	60.00	18.00
❑ RPLT LaDainian Tomlinson	300.00	90.00
❑ RPMB Michael Bennett	120.00	36.00
❑ RPMMC Mike McMahon	60.00	18.00
❑ RPMT Marques Tuiasosopo	80.00	24.00
❑ RPMV Michael Vick	600.00	180.00
❑ RPQC Quincy Carter	80.00	24.00
❑ RPQM Quincy Morgan	60.00	18.00
❑ RPRF Robert Ferguson	60.00	18.00
❑ RPRG Rod Gardner	100.00	30.00
❑ RPRJ Rudi Johnson	150.00	45.00
❑ RPRS Richard Seymour	80.00	24.00
❑ RPRW Reggie Wayne	120.00	36.00
❑ RPSM Santana Moss	150.00	45.00
❑ RPSM Snoop Minnis	50.00	15.00
❑ RPSR Sage Rosenfels	50.00	15.00
❑ RPTH Travis Henry	100.00	30.00
❑ RPTM Travis Minor	60.00	18.00

2001 Topps Rookie Reprint Jerseys

	Nm-Mt	Ex-Mt
❑ TODM Dan Marino	120.00	36.00
❑ TOES Emmitt Smith	80.00	24.00
❑ TOJR Jerry Rice	80.00	24.00
❑ TOWP Walter Payton	120.00	36.00

2001 Topps Team Topps Legends Autographs

	Nm-Mt	Ex-Mt
❑ TTF2 Dick Butkus EXCH		
❑ TTF4 Tommy McDonald 68T	12.00	3.60
❑ TTF5 John Hannah EXCH		
❑ TTF6 Terry Metcalf 82T	12.00	3.60
❑ TTF7 Art Donovan 59T	40.00	12.00
❑ TTF8 Frank Gifford		
❑ TTF9 Otis Sistrunk 79T	12.00	3.60
❑ TTF10 Chuck Foreman 81T	12.00	3.60
❑ TTF11 Sonny Jurgensen		
❑ TTF12 Don Maynard 73T	12.00	3.60
❑ TTF13 Joe Namath 73T	150.00	45.00
❑ TTF14 Charlie Joiner 87T	12.00	3.60
❑ TTF16 Cliff Branch 85T	12.00	3.60
❑ TTF18 Fred Biletnikoff		
❑ TTF19 Paul Hornung	50.00	15.00
❑ TTF20 Tom Dempsey 79T	12.00	3.60
❑ TTF21 Billy Kilmer 1978 Topps Reprint	12.00	3.60
❑ TTF22 Barry Sanders		
❑ TTF23 Len Dawson		
❑ TTR1 Jim Brown 58T	120.00	36.00
❑ TTR2 Dick Butkus 68T	60.00	18.00
❑ TTR3 John Riggins		
❑ TTR4 Tommy McDonald 57T	12.00	3.60
❑ TTR5 John Hannah 74T	12.00	3.60
❑ TTR6 Terry Metcalf 74T	12.00	3.60
❑ TTR7 Art Donovan 56T	40.00	18.00
❑ TTR8 Frank Gifford		
❑ TTR9 Otis Sistrunk 74T	12.00	3.60
❑ TTR10 Chuck Foreman	12.00	3.60
❑ TTR11 Sonny Jurgensen 58T	60.00	18.00
❑ TTR12 Don Maynard 61T	12.00	5.50
❑ TTR13 Joe Namath 65T	175.00	80.00
❑ TTR14 Charlie Joiner 72T	12.00	3.60
❑ TTR15 Mike Singletary 83T	30.00	13.50
❑ TTR16 Cliff Branch 75T	12.00	3.60
❑ TTR17 Johnny Unitas 57T	250.00	75.00
❑ TTR18 Fred Biletnikoff 65T	40.00	12.00
❑ TTR19 Paul Hornung EXCH		
❑ TTR20 Tom Dempsey 70T	12.00	5.50
❑ TTR21 Billy Kilmer 1962 Topps Reprint	12.00	5.50
❑ TTR22 Barry Sanders 89TT	125.00	38.00
❑ TTR23 Len Dawson 64T	30.00	9.00

2002 Topps

	Nm-Mt	Ex-Mt
COMPLETE SET (385)	50.00	15.00
❑ 1 Kurt Warner	.60	.18
❑ 2 Jeff Graham	.25	.07
❑ 3 Todd Bouman	.25	.07
❑ 4 Duce Staley	.60	.18
❑ 5 Jon Kitna	.40	.12
❑ 6 Shannon Sharpe	.40	.12
❑ 7 Darrell Jackson	.40	.12
❑ 8 Michael Pittman	.25	.07
❑ 9 Tony Gonzalez	.40	.12
❑ 10 Wayne Chrebet	.40	.12
❑ 11 Jevon Kearse	.40	.12
❑ 12 Bill Schroeder	.40	.12
❑ 13 Jeremy McDaniel	.25	.07
❑ 14 Todd Pinkston	.40	.12
❑ 15 Maurice Smith	.40	.12
❑ 16 Charlie Batch	.40	.12
❑ 17 Olandis Gary	.40	.12
❑ 18 Ron Dugans	.25	.07
❑ 19 Brian Urlacher	1.00	.30
❑ 20 Amani Toomer	.40	.12
❑ 21 Tim Couch	.40	.12
❑ 22 Derrick Brooks	.60	.18
❑ 23 Frank Sanders	.25	.07
❑ 24 James Williams	.25	.07
❑ 25 Lamar Smith	.40	.12
❑ 26 Darrick Vaughn	.25	.07
❑ 27 Cris Carter	.60	.18
❑ 28 Roland Williams	.25	.07
❑ 29 Bobby Shaw	.25	.07
❑ 30 Jerome Pathon	.40	.12
❑ 31 Rod Woodson	.40	.12
❑ 32 Ronney Jenkins	.25	.07
❑ 33 Chris Chandler	.40	.12
❑ 34 Dez White	.25	.07
❑ 35 Rod Smith	.40	.12
❑ 36 Troy Brown	.40	.12
❑ 37 JaJuan Dawson	.25	.07
❑ 38 Reidel Anthony	.25	.07
❑ 39 Mike Green	.25	.07
❑ 40 Steve Smith	.40	.12
❑ 41 Willie Jackson	.25	07
❑ 42 MarTay Jenkins	.25	.07
❑ 43 Reggie Germany	.25	.07
❑ 44 Desmond Howard	.25	.07
❑ 45 Fred Taylor	.60	.18
❑ 46 Scotty Anderson	.25	.07
❑ 47 John Lynch	.40	.12
❑ 48 Amos Zereoue	.60	.18
❑ 49 Darnay Scott	.25	.07
❑ 50 Anthony Thomas	.60	.18
❑ 51 Jeff Garcia	.60	.18
❑ 52 Charlie Garner	.40	.12
❑ 53 Drew Bledsoe	.60	.18
❑ 54 Donnie Edwards	.25	.07
❑ 55 Corey Bradford	.25	.07
❑ 56 Desmond Clark	.25	.07
❑ 57 Courtney Brown	.40	.12
❑ 58 Wesley Walls	.25	.07
❑ 59 Chad Brown	.25	.07
❑ 60 Shawn Jefferson	.25	.07
❑ 61 Corey Dillon	.40	.12
❑ 62 Johnnie Morton	.40	.12
❑ 63 Marcus Pollard	.25	.07
❑ 64 Jason Taylor	.25	.07
❑ 65 Kevin Faulk	.40	.12
❑ 66 Shane Matthews	.25	.07
❑ 67 Hines Ward	.60	.18
❑ 68 Garrison Hearst	.40	.12
❑ 69 Trung Canidate	.40	.12
❑ 70 Tony Banks	.25	.07
❑ 71 Matt Hasselbeck	.40	.12
❑ 72 Correll Buckhalter	.40	.12
❑ 73 Ron Dayne	.40	.12
❑ 74 Zach Thomas	.60	.18
❑ 75 Emmitt Smith	1.50	.45
❑ 76 Peter Warrick	.40	.12
❑ 77 Rob Johnson	.40	.12
❑ 78 Michael Strahan	.40	.12
❑ 79 Ray Lewis	.60	.18
❑ 80 Jamir Miller	.25	.07
❑ 81 Brian Griese	.60	.18
❑ 82 Stacey Mack	.25	.07
❑ 83 Michael Bennett	.40	.12
❑ 84 Ricky Williams	1.00	.30
❑ 85 Jamal Lewis	.60	.18
❑ 86 Doug Flutie	.60	.18
❑ 87 Jonathan Quinn	.25	.07
❑ 88 Mike Alstott	.60	.18
❑ 89 Samari Rolle	.25	.07
❑ 90 LaMont Jordan	.60	.18
❑ 91 Dominic Rhodes	.40	.12
❑ 92 Quincy Carter	.40	.12
❑ 93 Marcus Robinson	.40	.12

❑ 94 Travis Henry .60 .18
❑ 95 Jason Brookins .25 .07
❑ 96 Nick Goings .25 .07
❑ 97 Brian Finneran .25 .07
❑ 98 Dorsey Levens .40 .12
❑ 99 Reggie Swinton .25 .07
❑ 100 Chris Chambers .60 .18
❑ 101 Kordell Stewart .40 .12
❑ 102 Tai Streets .25 .07
❑ 103 Chris Redman .25 .07
❑ 104 Jacquez Green .25 .07
❑ 105 Rod Gardner .40 .12
❑ 106 Kevin Kasper .25 .07
❑ 107 Anthony Henry .25 .07
❑ 108 Dan Morgan .25 .07
❑ 109 Ronald McKinnon .25 .07
❑ 110 Qadry Ismail .40 .12
❑ 111 Chad Johnson .60 .18
❑ 112 James Stewart .40 .12
❑ 113 Terrence Wilkins .25 .07
❑ 114 Joey Galloway .40 .12
❑ 115 Deuce McAllister .75 .23
❑ 116 Joe Jurevicius .25 .07
❑ 117 Tyrone Wheatley .40 .12
❑ 118 Jason Gildon .25 .07
❑ 119 LaDainian Tomlinson 1.00 .30
❑ 120 Grant Wistrom .25 .07
❑ 121 Eddie George .60 .18
❑ 122 Laveranues Coles .40 .12
❑ 123 Antowain Smith .40 .12
❑ 124 Larry Parker .25 .07
❑ 125 Bubba Franks .40 .12
❑ 126 Troy Hambrick .25 .07
❑ 127 Jamal Reynolds .25 .07
❑ 128 Doug Chapman .25 .07
❑ 129 Freddie Mitchell .40 .12
❑ 130 Tim Dwight .40 .12
❑ 131 Erron Kinney .25 .07
❑ 132 James Allen .40 .12
❑ 133 Eric Moulds .40 .12
❑ 134 Keenan McCardell .25 .07
❑ 135 David Sloan .25 .07
❑ 136 Dennis Northcutt .40 .12
❑ 137 Kevan Barlow .40 .12
❑ 138 Bobby Engram .25 .07
❑ 139 Champ Bailey .40 .12
❑ 140 Donald Hayes .25 .07
❑ 141 Brandon Bennett .25 .07
❑ 142 Deltha O'Neal .25 .07
❑ 143 James Jackson .25 .07
❑ 144 Shaun Rogers .25 .07
❑ 145 Joe Johnson .25 .07
❑ 146 Ricky Watters .40 .12
❑ 147 Warrick Dunn .60 .18
❑ 148 Steve McNair .60 .18
❑ 149 Marvin Harrison .60 .18
❑ 150 Kendrell Bell .60 .18
❑ 151 Jim Miller .25 .07
❑ 152 Terry Allen .25 .07
❑ 153 Jake Plummer .40 .12
❑ 154 James McKnight .25 .07
❑ 155 Curtis Martin .60 .18
❑ 156 Keyshawn Johnson .60 .18
❑ 157 Kevin Lockett .25 .07
❑ 158 Jeremiah Trotter .25 .07
❑ 159 Derrick Alexander .40 .12
❑ 160 Brandon Stokley .40 .12
❑ 161 J.J. Stokes .40 .12
❑ 162 Drew Bennett .60 .18
❑ 163 Drew Brees .60 .18
❑ 164 Tim Brown .60 .18
❑ 165 Daunte Culpepper .60 .18
❑ 166 Rocket Ismail .40 .12
❑ 167 Alex Van Pelt .40 .12
❑ 168 Arnold Jackson .25 .07
❑ 169 Oronde Gadsden .40 .12
❑ 170 Isaac Bruce .60 .18
❑ 171 Warren Sapp .40 .12
❑ 172 Michael Westbrook .25 .07
❑ 173 John Abraham .40 .12
❑ 174 Jessie Armstead .25 .07
❑ 175 Brock Marion .25 .07
❑ 176 Brett Favre 1.50 .45
❑ 177 Benjamin Gay .40 .12
❑ 178 Muhsin Muhammad .40 .12
❑ 179 Reggie Wayne .40 .12
❑ 180 Kailee Wong .25 .07
❑ 181 Rich Gannon .60 .18
❑ 182 Chris Fuamatu-Ma'afala .25 .07
❑ 183 Shaun Alexander .60 .18
❑ 184 Kevin Dyson .40 .12
❑ 185 Kwamie Lassiter .25 .07
❑ 186 Elvis Joseph .25 .07
❑ 187 Trent Dilfer .40 .12
❑ 188 Marty Booker .25 .07
❑ 189 Travis Taylor .40 .12
❑ 190 Michael Vick 2.00 .60
❑ 191 Mike McMahon .60 .18
❑ 192 Jay Fiedler .40 .12
❑ 193 Zack Bronson .25 .07
❑ 194 Derrick Mason .40 .12
❑ 195 Anthony Becht .25 .07
❑ 196 Ahman Green .60 .18
❑ 197 Alge Crumpler .40 .12
❑ 198 Thomas Jones .40 .12
❑ 199 Tiki Barber .40 .12
❑ 200 Donovan McNabb .75 .23
❑ 201 Andre Carter .25 .07
❑ 202 Stephen Davis .40 .12
❑ 203 Troy Edwards .25 .07
❑ 204 Lawyer Milloy .40 .12
❑ 205 Peyton Manning 1.25 .35
❑ 206 James Farrior .25 .07
❑ 207 Gerard Warren .25 .07
❑ 208 Peerless Price .40 .12
❑ 209 Avion Black .25 .07
❑ 210 Marcellus Wiley .25 .07
❑ 211 Torry Holt .60 .18
❑ 212 A.J. Feeley .60 .18
❑ 213 Travis Minor .25 .07
❑ 214 Darren Sharper .25 .07
❑ 215 Jerry Porter .25 .07
❑ 216 Randall Cunningham .25 .07
❑ 217 Chris Weinke .40 .12
❑ 218 Mike Anderson .60 .18
❑ 219 Snoop Minnis .25 .07
❑ 220 David Martin .25 .07
❑ 221 Vinny Sutherland .25 .07
❑ 222 Ki-Jana Carter .25 .07
❑ 223 Kevin Swayne .25 .07
❑ 224 Mark Brunell .60 .18
❑ 225 Quincy Morgan .25 .07
❑ 226 David Terrell .60 .18
❑ 227 Terance Mathis .25 .07
❑ 228 Frank Wycheck .25 .07
❑ 229 Az-Zahir Hakim .25 .07
❑ 230 Freddie Jones .25 .07
❑ 231 Jerry Rice 1.25 .35
❑ 232 Ike Hilliard .40 .12
❑ 233 Terrell Davis .60 .18
❑ 234 Shawn Bryson .25 .07
❑ 235 David Boston .60 .18
❑ 236 Edgerrin James .75 .23
❑ 237 Trent Green .40 .12
❑ 238 Charlie Rogers .25 .07
❑ 239 Vinny Testaverde .40 .12
❑ 240 Koren Robinson .40 .12
❑ 241 Ronde Barber .25 .07
❑ 242 Dwayne Carswell .25 .07
❑ 243 Dedric Ward .25 .07
❑ 244 Richard Huntley .25 .07
❑ 245 Jamal Anderson .40 .12
❑ 246 Ryan Leaf .40 .12
❑ 247 Priest Holmes .75 .23
❑ 248 Tom Brady 1.50 .45
❑ 249 Charles Woodson .40 .12
❑ 250 Jerome Bettis .60 .18
❑ 251 Tommy Polley .25 .07
❑ 252 Anthony Wright .25 .07
❑ 253 Chad Pennington .75 .23
❑ 254 David Patten .25 .07
❑ 255 Antonio Freeman .60 .18
❑ 256 Jamel White .25 .07
❑ 257 Jermaine Lewis .25 .07
❑ 258 Aaron Brooks .60 .18
❑ 259 Ron Dixon .25 .07
❑ 260 James Thrash .40 .12
❑ 261 Junior Seau .60 .18
❑ 262 Byron Chamberlain .25 .07
❑ 263 Ed McCaffrey .60 .18
❑ 264 Nate Clements .25 .07
❑ 265 Tony Martin .40 .12
❑ 266 Germane Crowell .25 .07
❑ 267 Terrell Owens .60 .18
❑ 268 Marshall Faulk .60 .18
❑ 269 Dat Nguyen .25 .07
❑ 270 Elvis Grbac .40 .12
❑ 271 Dante Hall .60 .18
❑ 272 Sylvester Morris .25 .07
❑ 273 Mike Brown .60 .18
❑ 274 Kevin Johnson .40 .12
❑ 275 Jimmy Smith .40 .12
❑ 276 Randy Moss 1.25 .35
❑ 277 Kerry Collins .40 .12
❑ 278 Santana Moss .60 .18
❑ 279 Plaxico Burress .40 .12
❑ 280 Brad Johnson .40 .12
❑ 281 Curtis Conway .25 .07
❑ 282 Eric Johnson .40 .12
❑ 283 Joe Horn .40 .12
❑ 284 Peter Boulware .25 .07
❑ 285 Larry Foster .25 .07
❑ 286 Nate Jacquet .25 .07
❑ 287 Terry Glenn .40 .12
❑ 288 Jarious Jackson .25 .07
❑ 289 Hugh Douglas .25 .07
❑ 290 Chad Lewis .25 .07
❑ 291 Ahman Green WW .40 .12
❑ 292 Peyton Manning WW .60 .18
❑ 293 Kurt Warner WW .40 .12
❑ 294 Daunte Culpepper WW .60 .18
❑ 295 Tom Brady WW .75 .23
❑ 296 Rod Gardner WW .25 .07
❑ 297 Corey Dillon WW .40 .12
❑ 298 Priest Holmes WW .50 .15
❑ 299 Shaun Alexander WW .40 .12
❑ 300 Randy Moss WW .60 .18
❑ 301 Eric Moulds WW .25 .07
❑ 302 Brett Favre WW .75 .23
❑ 303 Todd Bouman WW .25 .07
❑ 304 Dominic Rhodes WW .40 .12
❑ 305 Marvin Harrison WW .40 .12
❑ 306 Torry Holt WW .60 .18
❑ 307 Derrick Mason WW .25 .07
❑ 308 Jerry Rice WW .60 .18
❑ 309 Donovan McNabb WW .40 .12
❑ 310 Marshall Faulk WW .40 .12
❑ 311 David Carr RC 4.00 1.20
❑ 312 Quentin Jammer RC 1.25 .35
❑ 313 Mike Williams RC 1.00 .30
❑ 314 Rocky Calmus RC 1.25 .35
❑ 315 Travis Fisher RC 1.25 .35
❑ 316 Dwight Freeney RC 1.50 .45
❑ 317 Jeremy Shockey RC 4.00 1.20
❑ 318 Marquise Walker RC 1.00 .30
❑ 319 Eric Crouch RC 2.00 .60
❑ 320 DeShaun Foster RC 1.25 .35
❑ 321 Roy Williams RC 3.00 .90
❑ 322 Andre Davis RC 1.25 .35
❑ 323 Alex Brown RC 1.25 .35
❑ 324 Michael Lewis RC 1.25 .35
❑ 325 Terry Charles RC 1.00 .30
❑ 326 Clinton Portis RC 4.00 1.20
❑ 327 Dennis Johnson RC .60 .18
❑ 328 Lito Sheppard RC 1.25 .35
❑ 329 Ryan Sims RC 1.25 .35
❑ 330 Raonall Smith RC 1.00 .30
❑ 331 Albert Haynesworth RC 1.00 .30
❑ 332 Eddie Freeman RC .60 .18
❑ 333 Levi Jones RC 1.00 .30
❑ 334 Josh McCown RC 1.50 .45
❑ 335 Cliff Russell RC 1.00 .30
❑ 336 Maurice Morris RC 1.25 .35
❑ 337 Antwaan Randle El RC 1.50 .45
❑ 338 Ladell Betts RC 1.25 .35
❑ 339 Daniel Graham RC 1.25 .35
❑ 340 David Garrard RC 1.25 .35
❑ 341 Antonio Bryant RC 1.25 .35
❑ 342 Patrick Ramsey RC 2.50 .75
❑ 343 Kelly Campbell RC 1.00 .30
❑ 344 Will Overstreet RC .60 .18
❑ 345 Ryan Denney RC .60 .18

❑ 346 John Henderson RC	1.25	.35
❑ 347 Freddie Milons RC	1.00	.30
❑ 348 Tim Carter RC	1.00	.30
❑ 349 Kurt Kittner RC	1.00	.30
❑ 350 Joey Harrington RC	4.00	1.20
❑ 351 Ricky Williams RC	1.25	.35
❑ 352 Bryant McKinnie RC	1.00	.30
❑ 353 Ed Reed RC	2.00	.60
❑ 354 Josh Reed RC	1.25	.35
❑ 355 Seth Burford RC	1.00	.30
❑ 356 Javon Walker RC	2.50	.75
❑ 357 Jamar Martin RC	1.00	.30
❑ 358 Leonard Henry RC	1.00	.30
❑ 359 Julius Peppers RC	2.50	.75
❑ 360 Jabar Gaffney RC	1.25	.35
❑ 361 Kalimba Edwards RC	1.25	.35
❑ 362 Napoleon Harris RC	1.25	.35
❑ 363 Ashley Lelie RC	2.50	.75
❑ 364 Anthony Weaver RC	1.00	.30
❑ 365 Bryan Thomas RC	1.00	.30
❑ 366 Wendell Bryant RC	1.25	.35
❑ 367 Damien Anderson RC	1.00	.30
❑ 368 Travis Stephens RC	1.00	.30
❑ 369 Rohan Davey RC	1.25	.35
❑ 370 Mike Pearson RC	.60	.18
❑ 371 Marc Colombo RC	.60	.18
❑ 372 Phillip Buchanon RC	1.25	.35
❑ 373 T.J. Duckett RC	2.00	.60
❑ 374 Ron Johnson RC	1.00	.30
❑ 375 Larry Tripplett RC	.60	.18
❑ 376 Randy Fasani RC	1.00	.30
❑ 377 Keyuo Craver RC	1.00	.30
❑ 378 Marquand Manuel RC	.60	.18
❑ 379 Jonathan Wells RC	1.25	.35
❑ 380 Reche Caldwell RC	1.25	.35
❑ 381 Luke Staley RC	1.00	.30
❑ 382 Donte Stallworth RC	2.50	.75
❑ 383 Levar Fisher RC	.60	.18
❑ 384 Lamar Gordon RC	1.25	.35
❑ 385 William Green RC	2.00	.60
❑ SBMVP Tom Brady FB AU/150	500.00	150.00

2002 Topps Autographs

	Nm-Mt	Ex-Mt
❑ TAAT Anthony Thomas	30.00	9.00
❑ TACC Chris Chambers		
❑ TADM Derrick Mason	12.00	3.60
❑ TALT LaDainian Tomlinson	30.00	9.00
❑ TARL Ray Lewis	30.00	9.00
❑ TAWJ Willie Jackson	12.00	3.60

2002 Topps King of Kings Super Bowl MVP's

	Nm-Mt	Ex-Mt
❑ KDA Terrell Davis Marcus Allen	60.00	18.00
❑ KME Joe Montana John Elway	200.00	60.00
❑ KMJ Joe Montana Jerry Rice	250.00	75.00
❑ KYR Steve Young Jerry Rice	100.00	30.00

2002 Topps Ring of Honor Autographs

	Nm-Mt	Ex-Mt
❑ RHBS Bart Starr	200.00	60.00
❑ RHBS2 Bart Starr	200.00	60.00
❑ RHCH Chuck Howley	60.00	18.00
❑ RHDH Desmond Howard	60.00	18.00
❑ RHDJ Dexter Jackson	80.00	24.00
❑ RHDW Doug Williams	80.00	24.00
❑ RHES Emmitt Smith	300.00	90.00
❑ RHFB Fred Biletnikoff	100.00	30.00
❑ RHFH Franco Harris	150.00	45.00
❑ RHJE John Elway	250.00	75.00
❑ RHJM Joe Montana	250.00	75.00
❑ RHJM2 Joe Montana	250.00	75.00
❑ RHJM3 Joe Montana	250.00	75.00
❑ RHJN Joe Namath	125.00	38.00
❑ RHJP Jim Plunkett	60.00	18.00
❑ RHJR Jerry Rice	300.00	90.00
❑ RHJRI John Riggins	100.00	30.00
❑ RHJS Jake Scott	60.00	18.00
❑ RHKW Kurt Warner	100.00	30.00
❑ RHLB Larry Brown	80.00	24.00
❑ RHLC Larry Csonka	100.00	30.00
❑ RHLD Len Dawson	120.00	36.00
❑ RHMA Marcus Allen	100.00	30.00
❑ RHMR Mark Rypien	80.00	24.00
❑ RHOA Ottis Anderson	60.00	18.00
❑ RHPS Phil Simms	100.00	30.00
❑ RHPS Phil Simms	100.00	30.00
❑ RHRD Richard Dent	80.00	24.00
❑ RHRL Ray Lewis	125.00	38.00
❑ RHRS Roger Staubach	150.00	45.00
❑ RHRW Randy White	80.00	24.00
❑ RHSY Steve Young	150.00	45.00
❑ RHTA Troy Aikman	150.00	45.00
❑ RHTB Terry Bradshaw	120.00	36.00
❑ RHTBR Tom Brady	250.00	75.00
❑ RHTB2 Terry Bradshaw	120.00	36.00
❑ RHTD Terrell Davis	80.00	24.00

2002 Topps Rookie Premier Autographs

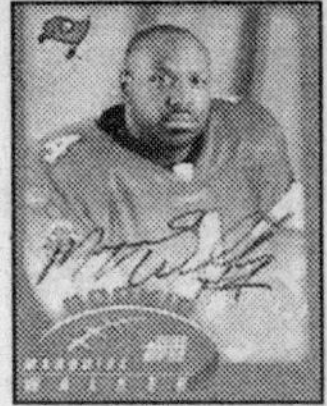

	Nm-Mt	Ex-Mt
❑ RPAB Antonio Bryant	50.00	15.00
❑ RPAD Andre Davis	50.00	15.00
❑ RPAL Ashley Lelie	100.00	30.00
❑ RPAR Antwaan Randle El	100.00	30.00
❑ RPCP Clinton Portis	200.00	60.00
❑ RPCR Cliff Russell	40.00	12.00
❑ RPDC David Carr		
❑ RPDCH David Carr Joey Harrington		
❑ RPDF DeShaun Foster	100.00	30.00
❑ RPDG Daniel Graham	50.00	15.00
❑ RPDGA David Garrard	50.00	15.00
❑ RPDGD William Green T.J. Duckett	150.00	45.00
❑ RPDS Donte Stallworth	80.00	24.00
❑ RPDSL Donte Stallworth Ashley Lelie	150.00	45.00
❑ RPEC Eric Crouch	80.00	24.00
❑ RPJG Jabar Gaffney	50.00	15.00
❑ RPJH Joey Harrington	150.00	45.00
❑ RPJM Josh McCown	80.00	24.00
❑ RPJP Julius Peppers	120.00	36.00
❑ RPJR Josh Reed	50.00	15.00
❑ RPJS Jeremy Shockey	150.00	45.00
❑ RPJW Javon Walker	100.00	30.00
❑ RPLB Ladell Betts	50.00	15.00
❑ RPMM Maurice Morris	50.00	15.00
❑ RPMW Marquise Walker	40.00	12.00
❑ RPMWI Mike Williams	50.00	15.00
❑ RPPR Patrick Ramsey	80.00	24.00
❑ RPQJ Quentin Jammer	50.00	15.00
❑ RPRC Reche Caldwell	50.00	15.00
❑ RPRD Rohan Davey	50.00	15.00
❑ RPRJ Ron Johnson	40.00	12.00
❑ RPRW Roy Williams	120.00	36.00
❑ RPTC Tim Carter	40.00	12.00
❑ RPTJD T.J. Duckett	80.00	24.00
❑ RPTS Travis Stephens	40.00	12.00
❑ RPWG William Green	80.00	24.00

2002 Topps Super Bowl Goal Posts

	Nm-Mt	Ex-Mt
❑ SBG1 Tom Brady	80.00	24.00
❑ SBG2 Kurt Warner	25.00	7.50
❑ SBG3 Antowain Smith	25.00	7.50
❑ SBG4 Marshall Faulk	30.00	9.00
❑ SBG5 Troy Brown	30.00	9.00
❑ SBG6 Adam Vinatieri	60.00	18.00
❑ SBG7 David Patten	30.00	9.00
❑ SBG8 Torry Holt	30.00	9.00
❑ SBG9 Ty Law	30.00	9.00
❑ SBG10 Isaac Bruce	30.00	9.00
❑ SBGAV Adam Vinatieri AUTO	225.00	70.00

2003 Topps

	MINT	NRMT
COMPLETE SET (385)	60.00	27.00
❑ 1 Michael Vick	1.50	.70
❑ 2 Wesley Walls	.25	.11
❑ 3 Josh Reed	.40	.18
❑ 4 Josh McCown	.40	.18
❑ 5 James Stewart	.40	.18
❑ 6 Deltha O'Neal	.25	.11
❑ 7 Quincy Morgan	.40	.18
❑ 8 Tony Fisher	.25	.11
❑ 9 Corey Bradford	.25	.11
❑ 10 Byron Chamberlain	.25	.11
❑ 11 James McKnight	.25	.11
❑ 12 Fred Taylor	.60	.25
❑ 13 David Patten	.25	.11
❑ 14 Jerome Bettis	.60	.25
❑ 15 Jerry Porter	.40	.18
❑ 16 Anthony Becht	.25	.11
❑ 17 Steve McNair	.60	.25
❑ 18 Stephen Davis	.40	.18
❑ 19 Terrence Wilkins	.25	.11
❑ 20 Jamie Martin	.25	.11
❑ 21 Tai Streets	.25	.11
❑ 22 Frank Wycheck	.25	.11
❑ 23 Sammy Knight	.25	.11
❑ 24 Marcus Pollard	.25	.11
❑ 25 Jamie Sharper	.25	.11
❑ 26 T.J. Houshmandzadeh	.25	.11
❑ 27 Javin Hunter	.25	.11
❑ 28 Alge Crumpler	.40	.18
❑ 29 Chris Weinke	.40	.18
❑ 30 David Terrell	.40	.18
❑ 31 Troy Hambrick	.25	.11
❑ 32 Bubba Franks	.40	.18
❑ 33 Todd Bouman	.25	.11
❑ 34 Trent Green	.40	.18
❑ 35 Mark Brunell	.40	.18
❑ 36 James Thrash	.25	.11
❑ 37 Donnie Edwards	.25	.11
❑ 38 Mike Alstott	.60	.25
❑ 39 Bobby Engram	.25	.11
❑ 40 Deuce McAllister	.60	.25
❑ 41 Santana Moss	.40	.18
❑ 42 Kordell Stewart	.40	.18
❑ 43 Jason Taylor	.25	.11
❑ 44 Corey Dillon	.40	.18
❑ 45 Damien Anderson	.25	.11
❑ 46 Rodney Peete	.25	.11
❑ 47 Jeff Blake	.25	.11
❑ 48 Mike McMahon	.40	.18
❑ 49 Ed McCaffrey	.60	.25
❑ 50 Priest Holmes	.75	.35
❑ 51 Moe Williams	.25	.11
❑ 52 Brian Dawkins	.25	.11
❑ 53 Tim Brown	.60	.25
❑ 54 Curtis Martin	.60	.25
❑ 55 Charles Stackhouse	.25	.11
❑ 56 Derrius Thompson	.25	.11
❑ 57 John Simon	.25	.11
❑ 58 Joe Jurevicius	.25	.11
❑ 59 Jonathan Wells	.25	.11
❑ 60 William Green	.40	.18
❑ 61 Ken-Yon Rambo	.25	.11
❑ 62 Frank Sanders	.25	.11
❑ 63 Chester Taylor	.25	.11
❑ 64 Keith Brooking	.25	.11
❑ 65 Bill Schroeder	.40	.18
❑ 66 Travis Minor	.25	.11
❑ 67 Eric Parker RC	.60	.25
❑ 68 Phillip Buchanon	.25	.11
❑ 69 Amos Zereoue	.40	.18
❑ 70 Warren Sapp	.40	.18
❑ 71 Ladell Betts	.40	.18
❑ 72 Lamar Gordon	.25	.11
❑ 73 Koren Robinson	.25	.11
❑ 74 Ron Dayne	.25	.11
❑ 75 Donovan McNabb	.75	.35
❑ 76 Edgerrin James	.60	.25
❑ 77 Stacey Mack	.25	.11
❑ 78 Justin Smith	.25	.11
❑ 79 Kelly Holcomb	.40	.18
❑ 80 Thomas Jones	.40	.18
❑ 81 Randy McMichael	.40	.18
❑ 82 Daunte Culpepper	.60	.25
❑ 83 Tommy Maddox	.60	.25
❑ 84 Tyrone Wheatley	.25	.11
❑ 85 Kevin Dyson	.40	.18
❑ 86 Rod Gardner	.40	.18
❑ 87 Wayne Chrebet	.40	.18
❑ 88 Marc Boerigter	.40	.18
❑ 89 Darnay Scott	.25	.11
❑ 90 T.J. Duckett	.40	.18
❑ 91 Marcel Shipp	.40	.18
❑ 92 Ross Tucker	.25	.11
❑ 93 Drew Bledsoe	.60	.25
❑ 94 Scotty Anderson	.25	.11
❑ 95 Rod Smith	.40	.18
❑ 96 Jim Kleinsasser	.25	.11
❑ 97 Peyton Manning	1.00	.45
❑ 98 Junior Seau	.60	.25
❑ 99 Darrell Jackson	.40	.18
❑ 100 Brett Favre	1.50	.70
❑ 101 Ashley Lelie	.60	.25
❑ 102 Jajuan Dawson	.25	.11
❑ 103 Kyle Brady	.25	.11
❑ 104 Kevin Faulk	.25	.11
❑ 105 Jeremy Shockey	1.00	.45
❑ 106 Hines Ward	.60	.25
❑ 107 Jeff Garcia	.60	.25
❑ 108 Shane Matthews	.25	.11
❑ 109 Jevon Kearse	.40	.18
❑ 110 Eddie Kennison	.25	.11
❑ 111 Quincy Carter	.40	.18
❑ 112 Brian Urlacher	1.00	.45
❑ 113 Charlie Rogers	.25	.11
❑ 114 Robert Ferguson	.25	.11
❑ 115 Christian Fauria	.25	.11
❑ 116 Brian Westbrook	.40	.18
❑ 117 Antwaan Randle El	.60	.25
❑ 118 Eddie George	.40	.18
❑ 119 Derrick Brooks	.40	.18
❑ 120 Isaac Bruce	.60	.25
❑ 121 Joe Horn	.40	.18
❑ 122 Jermaine Lewis	.25	.11
❑ 123 Jon Kitna	.40	.18
❑ 124 David Boston	.40	.18
❑ 125 Todd Heap	.40	.18
❑ 126 Lamar Smith	.25	.11
❑ 127 Marcus Robinson	.40	.18
❑ 128 Germane Crowell	.25	.11
❑ 129 Kevin Johnson	.40	.18
❑ 130 Cris Carter	.60	.25
❑ 131 Drew Brees	.60	.25
❑ 132 Champ Bailey	.40	.18
❑ 133 Brian Finneran	.25	.11
❑ 134 Mike Anderson	.60	.25
❑ 135 Derek Ross	.25	.11
❑ 136 Javon Walker	.40	.18
❑ 137 D'Wayne Bates	.25	.11
❑ 138 Chad Lewis	.25	.11
❑ 139 Charlie Garner	.40	.18
❑ 140 Laveranues Coles	.40	.18
❑ 141 Ron Dixon	.25	.11
❑ 142 Rob Johnson	.40	.18
❑ 143 Shaun Alexander	.60	.25
❑ 144 Kevan Barlow	.40	.18
❑ 145 Aaron Brooks	.60	.25
❑ 146 Jay Foreman	.25	.11
❑ 147 Mike Peterson	.25	.11
❑ 148 Brandon Bennett	.25	.11
❑ 149 Jake Plummer	.40	.18
❑ 150 Emmitt Smith	1.50	.70
❑ 151 Mikhael Ricks	.25	.11
❑ 152 Terry Glenn	.25	.11
❑ 153 Michael Bennett	.40	.18
❑ 154 Deion Branch	.60	.25
❑ 155 Justin McCareins	.25	.11
❑ 156 Keyshawn Johnson	.60	.25
❑ 157 Marc Bulger	.60	.25
❑ 158 Matt Hasselbeck	.40	.18
❑ 159 Garrison Hearst	.40	.18
❑ 160 Jamel White	.25	.11
❑ 161 Doug Johnson	.25	.11
❑ 162 Larry Centers	.25	.11
❑ 163 Dee Brown	.25	.11
❑ 164 Dez White	.25	.11
❑ 165 Brian Griese	.60	.25
❑ 166 Johnnie Morton	.40	.18
❑ 167 Oronde Gadsden	.25	.11
❑ 168 Chad Morton	.25	.11
❑ 169 Rod Woodson	.40	.18
❑ 170 Ricky Proehl	.25	.11
❑ 171 Tim Dwight	.40	.18
❑ 172 Patrick Ramsey	.60	.25
❑ 173 Donald Driver	.40	.18
❑ 174 Joey Harrington	1.00	.45
❑ 175 Ricky Williams	.60	.25
❑ 176 David Givens	.60	.25
❑ 177 Antonio Freeman	.40	.18
❑ 178 Dwight Freeney	.25	.11
❑ 179 Jabar Gaffney	.40	.18
❑ 180 Leon Johnson	.25	.11
❑ 181 Freddie Jones	.25	.11
❑ 182 Ron Johnson	.25	.11
❑ 183 Duce Staley	.40	.18
❑ 184 Charles Woodson	.40	.18
❑ 185 Trung Canidate	.40	.18
❑ 186 Jerome Pathon	.25	.11
❑ 187 Jimmy Smith	.40	.18
❑ 188 Reggie Wayne	.40	.18
❑ 189 Chad Johnson	.40	.18
❑ 190 Steve Beuerlein	.25	.11
❑ 191 Joey Galloway	.40	.18
❑ 192 Chris Walsh	.25	.11
❑ 193 Ty Law	.40	.18
❑ 194 Ike Hilliard	.25	.11
❑ 195 Curtis Conway	.25	.11
❑ 196 Kenny Watson	.25	.11
❑ 197 Brad Johnson	.40	.18
❑ 198 Shawn Jefferson	.25	.11
❑ 199 Jamal Lewis	.60	.25
❑ 200 Terrell Owens	.60	.25
❑ 201 Todd Pinkston	.40	.18
❑ 202 Maurice Morris	.25	.11
❑ 203 Dante Hall	.60	.25
❑ 204 Jeremiah Trotter UER Small pic features LaVar Arrington	.25	.11
❑ 205 Keenan McCardell	.25	.11
❑ 206 Antonio Bryant	.40	.18
❑ 207 Trevor Gaylor	.25	.11
❑ 208 Eric Moulds	.40	.18
❑ 209 Jim Miller	.25	.11
❑ 210 Kabeer Gbaja-Biamila	.40	.18
❑ 211 James Mungro	.25	.11
❑ 212 Troy Brown	.40	.18
❑ 213 J.J. Stokes	.40	.18
❑ 214 Rich Gannon	.40	.18
❑ 215 Chad Pennington	.75	.35
❑ 216 Michael Strahan	.40	.18
❑ 217 David Garrard	.25	.11
❑ 218 Chris Chambers	.60	.25
❑ 219 Antowain Smith	.40	.18
❑ 220 Olandis Gary	.40	.18
❑ 221 Jason McAddley	.25	.11
❑ 222 Brandon Stokley	.40	.18
❑ 223 Derrick Alexander	.25	.11
❑ 224 Hugh Douglas	.25	.11
❑ 225 Danny Wuerffel	.25	.11
❑ 226 Derrick Mason	.40	.18
❑ 227 Michael Pittman	.25	.11
❑ 228 Torry Holt	.60	.25
❑ 229 Bobby Shaw	.25	.11
❑ 230 Tony Gonzalez	.40	.18

❑ 231 Ed Hartwell	.25	.11
❑ 232 Kris Mangum RC	.40	.18
❑ 233 Martay Jenkins	.25	.11
❑ 234 Marty Booker	.40	.18
❑ 235 London Fletcher	.25	.11
❑ 236 Shannon Sharpe	.40	.18
❑ 237 Zach Thomas	.60	.25
❑ 238 Plaxico Burress	.60	.25
❑ 239 Trent Dilfer	.40	.18
❑ 240 Kurt Warner	.60	.25
❑ 241 Vinny Testaverde	.40	.18
❑ 242 Al Wilson	.25	.11
❑ 243 Chris Redman	.25	.11
❑ 244 Warrick Dunn	.40	.18
❑ 245 Jay Fiedler	.40	.18
❑ 246 A.J. Feeley	.25	.11
❑ 247 Lamont Jordan	.40	.18
❑ 248 Kerry Collins	.40	.18
❑ 249 Michael Lewis	.25	.11
❑ 250 Jerry Rice	1.25	.55
❑ 251 Simeon Rice	.40	.18
❑ 252 Reche Caldwell	.25	.11
❑ 253 Randy Moss	1.00	.45
❑ 254 Az-Zahir Hakim	.25	.11
❑ 255 Nate Wayne	.25	.11
❑ 256 James Allen	.40	.18
❑ 257 Qadry Ismail	.40	.18
❑ 258 Tom Brady	1.00	.45
❑ 259 Brian Kelly	.25	.11
❑ 260 Ray Lucas	.25	.11
❑ 261 Amani Toomer	.40	.18
❑ 262 Travis Henry	.40	.18
❑ 263 Chris Chandler	.25	.11
❑ 264 Peter Warrick	.40	.18
❑ 265 Ray Lewis	.60	.25
❑ 266 Sam Cowart	.25	.11
❑ 267 Donte Stallworth	.60	.25
❑ 268 David Carr	1.00	.45
❑ 269 Andre Davis	.25	.11
❑ 270 Jake Delhomme	.60	.25
❑ 271 Travis Taylor	.40	.18
❑ 272 Steve Smith	.25	.11
❑ 273 Tiki Barber	.40	.18
❑ 274 Chad Hutchinson	.40	.18
❑ 275 Marshall Faulk	.60	.25
❑ 276 Chris Claiborne	.25	.11
❑ 277 Billy Miller	.25	.11
❑ 278 Peerless Price	.40	.18
❑ 279 Ed Reed	.40	.18
❑ 280 Ahman Green	.60	.25
❑ 281 Roy Williams	.60	.25
❑ 282 Dennis Northcutt	.25	.11
❑ 283 Julius Peppers	.60	.25
❑ 284 John Davis	.25	.11
❑ 285 LaDainian Tomlinson	.60	.25
❑ 286 Muhsin Muhammad	.40	.18
❑ 287 Tim Couch	.25	.11
❑ 288 Clinton Portis	1.00	.45
❑ 289 Anthony Thomas	.60	.25
❑ 290 Marvin Harrison	.60	.25
❑ 291 Priest Holmes WW	.40	.18
❑ 292 Drew Bledsoe WW	.40	.18
❑ 293 Tom Brady WW	.40	.18
❑ 294 Shaun Alexander WW	.25	.11
❑ 295 Brett Favre WW	.75	.35
❑ 296 Travis Henry WW	.25	.11
❑ 297 Marshall Faulk WW	.40	.18
❑ 298 Terrell Owens WW	.25	.11
❑ 299 Jeff Garcia WW	.25	.11
❑ 300 Plaxico Burress WW	.25	.11
❑ 301 Donovan McNabb WW	.40	.18
❑ 302 Ricky Williams WW	.40	.18
❑ 303 Michael Vick WW	.75	.35
❑ 304 Steve Smith WW	.25	.11
❑ 305 Marvin Harrison WW	.25	.11
❑ 306 Chad Pennington WW	.40	.18
❑ 307 Jeremy Shockey WW	.60	.25
❑ 308 Tommy Maddox WW	.25	.11
❑ 309 Steve McNair WW	.25	.11
❑ 310 Rich Gannon WW	.25	.11
❑ 311 Carson Palmer RC	4.00	1.80
❑ 312 Keenan Howry RC	1.25	.55
❑ 313 Michael Haynes RC	1.25	.55
❑ 314 Terrell Suggs RC	2.00	.90
❑ 315 Rashean Mathis RC	1.00	.45
❑ 316 Chris Kelsay RC	1.25	.55
❑ 317 Brad Banks RC	1.00	.45
❑ 318 Jordan Gross RC	1.00	.45
❑ 319 Lee Suggs RC	2.50	1.10
❑ 320 Kliff Kingsbury RC	1.00	.45
❑ 321 William Joseph RC	1.25	.55
❑ 322 Kelley Washington RC	1.25	.55
❑ 323 Jerome McDougle RC	1.25	.55
❑ 324 Osi Umenyiora RC	1.25	.55
❑ 325 Chris Simms RC	2.50	1.10
❑ 326 Alonzo Jackson RC	1.00	.45
❑ 327 L.J. Smith RC	1.25	.55
❑ 328 Mike Doss RC	1.25	.55
❑ 329 Bobby Wade RC	1.25	.55
❑ 330 Ken Hamlin RC	1.25	.55
❑ 331 Brandon Lloyd RC	1.50	.70
❑ 332 Justin Fargas RC	1.25	.55
❑ 333 DeWayne Robertson RC	1.25	.55
❑ 334 Bryant Johnson RC	1.25	.55
❑ 335 Boss Bailey RC	1.50	.70
❑ 336 Onterrio Smith RC	1.50	.70
❑ 337 Doug Gabriel RC	1.25	.55
❑ 338 Jimmy Kennedy RC	1.25	.55
❑ 339 B.J. Askew RC	1.25	.55
❑ 340 Taylor Jacobs RC	1.25	.55
❑ 341 Dallas Clark RC	1.25	.55
❑ 342 DeWayne White RC	1.00	.45
❑ 343 Arnaz Battle RC	1.25	.55
❑ 344 Kareem Kelly RC	1.00	.45
❑ 345 Terry Pierce RC	1.00	.45
❑ 346 Billy McMullen RC	1.00	.45
❑ 347 Talman Gardner RC	1.25	.55
❑ 348 Anquan Boldin RC	3.00	1.35
❑ 349 Travis Anglin RC	.60	.25
❑ 350 Byron Leftwich RC	5.00	2.20
❑ 351 Marcus Trufant RC	1.25	.55
❑ 352 Sam Aiken RC	1.00	.45
❑ 353 LaBrandon Toefield RC	1.25	.55
❑ 354 J.R. Tolver RC	1.00	.45
❑ 355 Charles Rogers RC	1.50	.70
❑ 356 Chaun Thompson RC	.60	.25
❑ 357 Chris Brown RC	2.50	1.10
❑ 358 Justin Gage RC	1.25	.55
❑ 359 Kevin Williams RC	1.25	.55
❑ 360 Willis McGahee RC	3.00	1.35
❑ 361 Victor Hobson RC	1.25	.55
❑ 362 Brian St.Pierre RC	1.25	.55
❑ 363 Nate Burleson RC	2.50	1.10
❑ 364 Calvin Pace RC	1.00	.45
❑ 365 Larry Johnson RC	2.50	1.10
❑ 366 Andre Woolfolk RC	1.25	.55
❑ 367 Tyrone Calico RC	1.50	.70
❑ 368 Seneca Wallace RC	1.25	.55
❑ 369 Domanick Davis RC	2.50	1.10
❑ 370 Rex Grossman RC	3.00	1.35
❑ 371 Artose Pinner RC	1.25	.55
❑ 372 Jason Witten RC	2.00	.90
❑ 373 Bennie Joppru RC	1.25	.55
❑ 374 Bethel Johnson RC	2.00	.90
❑ 375 Kyle Boller RC	3.00	1.35
❑ 376 Shaun McDonald RC	1.25	.55
❑ 377 Musa Smith RC	1.25	.55
❑ 378 Ken Dorsey RC	2.00	.90
❑ 379 Johnathan Sullivan RC	1.00	.45
❑ 380 Andre Johnson RC	3.00	1.35
❑ 381 Nick Barnett RC	2.00	.90
❑ 382 Teyo Johnson RC	1.25	.55
❑ 383 Terence Newman RC	2.50	1.10
❑ 384 Kevin Curtis RC	1.25	.55
❑ 385 Dave Ragone RC	1.25	.55
❑ SBMVP Dexter Jackson/250 Autographed Super Bowl Football swatch	60.00	27.00

2003 Topps Black

MINT NRMT

*STARS: 6X TO 15X BASIC CARDS
*ROOKIES: 5X TO 12X

2003 Topps Collection

MINT NRMT

*STARS: .4X TO 1X BASIC TOPPS
*ROOKIES: .4X TO 1X

2003 Topps First Edition

MINT NRMT

*STARS: 1.5X TO 4X BASIC CARDS
*ROOKIES: 1.2X TO 3X

2003 Topps Gold

MINT NRMT

*STARS: 2X TO 5X BASIC CARDS
*ROOKIES: 1.5X TO 4X

2003 Topps Autographs

GROUP A ODDS 1:11,293HOB, 1:3256HTA
GROUP B ODDS 1:8266HOB, 1:2383HTA
GROUP C ODDS 1:4334HOB, 1:1376HTA
GROUP D ODDS 1:1814HOB, 1:645HTA
GROUP E ODDS 1:684HOB, 1:191HTA
GROUP F ODDS 1:384HOB, 1:95HTA

	MINT	NRMT
❑ TAD Andre Davis E EXCH	15.00	6.75
❑ TBL Byron Leftwich A	120.00	55.00
❑ TCR Charles Rogers B EXCH	50.00	22.00
❑ TDD Donald Driver F	25.00	11.00
❑ TDM0 Derrick Mason C	20.00	9.00
❑ TDN Dennis Northcutt F	15.00	6.75
❑ TJM James Mungro F	25.00	11.00
❑ TJP Jerry Porter E	25.00	11.00
❑ TJT Jason Taylor C	40.00	18.00
❑ TLC Laveranues Coles E	20.00	9.00
❑ TLJ Larry Johnson D	40.00	18.00
❑ TMS Marcel Shipp F	20.00	9.00
❑ TRL0 ReShard Lee E	25.00	11.00
❑ TSS Steve Smith F	25.00	11.00
❑ TTH Travis Henry D	25.00	11.00
❑ TTM Tommy Maddox B	100.00	45.00
❑ TCPA Carson Palmer A	80.00	36.00
❑ TJPE Julian Peterson D EXCH	25.00	11.00

2003 Topps Pro Bowl Jerseys

	MINT	NRMT
❑ APBF Bubba Franks	12.00	5.50
❑ APBU Brian Urlacher	25.00	11.00
❑ APHW Hines Ward	15.00	6.75
❑ APJG Jeff Garcia	15.00	6.75
❑ APJH Joe Horn	12.00	5.50
❑ APJP Joey Porter	20.00	9.00
❑ APJR Jerry Rice	25.00	11.00
❑ APLT LaDainian Tomlinson	15.00	6.75

	MINT	NRMT
❑ APMA Mike Alstott	15.00	6.75
❑ APMH Marvin Harrison	12.00	5.50
❑ APML Michael Lewis	12.00	5.50
❑ APMS Michael Strahan	12.00	5.50
❑ APRG Rich Gannon	15.00	6.75
❑ APRW Ricky Williams	15.00	6.75
❑ APTH Todd Heap	12.00	5.50

2003 Topps Record Breakers Autographs

GROUP A ODDS 1:13,590HOB, 1:3926HTA
GROUP B ODDS 1:4070HOB, 1:1112HTA
GROUP C ODDS 1:22,908HOB, 1:6357HTA
GROUP D ODDS 1:17,059HOB, 1:4603HTA

	MINT	NRMT
❑ RBBF Brett Favre A	250.00	110.00
❑ RBBS Barry Sanders A	150.00	70.00
❑ RBCP Clinton Portis C	80.00	36.00
❑ RBDM Dan Marino A	250.00	110.00
❑ RBDMA Derrick Mason B	30.00	13.50
❑ RBJE John Elway B	250.00	110.00
❑ RBJS Jimmy Smith B	25.00	11.00
❑ RBJT Jason Taylor B	40.00	18.00
❑ RBLTO LaDainian Tomlinson A	40.00	18.00
❑ RBMH Marvin Harrison B	40.00	18.00
❑ RBMS Michael Strahan A	25.00	11.00
❑ RBPH Priest Holmes D	50.00	22.00
❑ RBSY Steve Young B	100.00	45.00

2003 Topps Record Breakers Autographs Duals

	MINT	NRMT
❑ RBDEM John Elway	550.00	250.00
Dan Marino		
❑ RBDMS Derrick Mason	40.00	18.00
Jimmy Smith		
❑ RBDSS Barry Sanders	500.00	220.00
Emmitt Smith		
❑ RBDST Michael Strahan	40.00	18.00
Jason Taylor		
❑ RBDTP Ladainian Tomlinson EXCH	150.00	70.00
Clinton Portis		

2003 Topps Record Breakers Jerseys

	MINT	NRMT
❑ RBRBS Barry Sanders B	40.00	18.00
❑ RBRDM Dan Marino B	60.00	27.00
❑ RBRES Emmitt Smith B	50.00	22.00
❑ RBRJE John Elway B	50.00	22.00
❑ RBRJR Jerry Rice B	30.00	13.50
❑ RBRKW Kurt Warner B	25.00	11.00
❑ RBRLT LaDainian Tomlinson B	20.00	9.00
❑ RBRMF Marshall Faulk B	25.00	11.00
❑ RBRRW Ricky Williams B	25.00	11.00
❑ RBRSY Steve Young B	30.00	13.50
❑ RBRWP Walter Payton A	100.00	45.00

2003 Topps Record Breakers Jerseys Duals

	MINT	NRMT
❑ RDRDT Corey Dillon	40.00	18.00
LaDainian Tomlinson		
❑ RDRFW Marshall Faulk	50.00	22.00
Ricky Williams		
❑ RDRME Dan Marino	200.00	90.00
John Elway		
❑ RDRPS Walter Payton	250.00	110.00
Emmitt Smith		
❑ RDRSP Barry Sanders	200.00	90.00
Walter Payton		
❑ RDRSR Emmitt Smith	200.00	90.00
Jerry Rice		
❑ RDRSS Barry Sanders	120.00	55.00
Emmitt Smith		
❑ RDRYE Steve Young	100.00	45.00
John Elway		

2003 Topps Rookie Premiere Autographs

GROUP A ODDS 1:336,480 TOPPS CHROME
GROUP B ODDS 1:56,080 TOPPS CHROME
GROUP C ODDS 1:29,206 TOPPS CHROME
GROUP D ODDS 1:8628 TOPPS CHROME
GROUP E ODDS 1:1482 TOPPS CHROME

	MINT	NRMT
❑ RPAB Anquan Boldin E	200.00	90.00
❑ RPAJ Andre Johnson C	175.00	80.00
❑ RPAP Artose Pinner E	60.00	27.00
❑ RPBJ Bethel Johnson E	120.00	55.00
❑ RPBJ2 Bryant Johnson B		
❑ RPBL Byron Leftwich A	300.00	135.00
❑ RPBS Brian St.Pierre E	80.00	36.00
❑ RPCB Chris Brown E	175.00	80.00
❑ RPCP Carson Palmer A	250.00	110.00
❑ RPDC Dallas Clark E	80.00	36.00
❑ RPDMJ Willis McGahee	175.00	80.00
Larry Johnson		
❑ RPDPL Carson Palmer	350.00	160.00
Byron Leftwich		
❑ RPDR Dave Ragone E	60.00	27.00
❑ RPDRJ Andre Johnson	175.00	80.00
Bryant Johnson		
❑ RPDR2 DeWayne Robertson C	50.00	22.00
❑ RPJF Justin Fargas E	80.00	36.00
❑ RPKB Kyle Boller E	150.00	70.00
❑ RPKC Kevin Curtis E	50.00	22.00
❑ RPKK Kliff Kingsbury E	60.00	27.00
❑ RPKW Kelley Washington E	100.00	45.00
❑ RPLJ Larry Johnson B	125.00	55.00
❑ RPMS Musa Smith D	60.00	27.00
❑ RPMT Marcus Trufant E	60.00	27.00
❑ RPNB Nate Burleson E	125.00	55.00
❑ RPOS Onterrio Smith E	80.00	36.00
❑ RPRG Rex Grossman D	150.00	70.00
❑ RPSW Seneca Wallace E	60.00	27.00
❑ RPTC Tyrone Calico D	100.00	45.00
❑ RPTJ Taylor Jacobs E	80.00	36.00
❑ RPTJ2 Teyo Johnson E	60.00	27.00
❑ RPTN Terence Newman E	120.00	55.00
❑ RPTS Terrell Suggs D	80.00	36.00
❑ RPWM Willis McGahee A	125.00	55.00

2003 Topps Split the Uprights

	MINT	NRMT
❑ SU1 Martin Gramatica	50.00	22.00
❑ SU2 Sebastian Janikowski	40.00	18.00

2003 Topps Super Tix

	MINT	NRMT
❑ ST1 Brad Johnson	25.00	11.00
❑ ST2 Rich Gannon	25.00	11.00
❑ ST3 Keyshawn Johnson	20.00	9.00
❑ ST4 Jerry Rice	40.00	18.00
❑ ST5 Michael Pittman	15.00	6.75
❑ ST6 Charlie Garner	20.00	9.00
❑ ST7 Derrick Brooks	20.00	9.00
❑ ST8 Jerry Porter	25.00	11.00
❑ ST9 Warren Sapp	20.00	9.00
❑ ST10 Tim Brown	25.00	11.00

2004 Topps

	Nm-Mt	Ex-Mt
COMPLETE SET (385)	60.00	18.00
RH38 STATED ODDS 1:36 H/HTA/R		
RH38A ODDS 1:13,494H, 1:3895HTA		
SBMVP ODDS		
1:35,787H,1:10,710HTA,1:33,984R		
UNPRICED COACHES' CUTS #'d TO 1		
❑ 1 Peyton Manning	1.00	.30
❑ 2 Curtis Conway	.25	.07
❑ 3 Tim Brown	.60	.18
❑ 4 David Givens	.40	.12
❑ 5 Dorsey Levens	.25	.07
❑ 6 Jamal Robertson	.25	.07
❑ 7 Doug Flutie	.60	.18
❑ 8 Lamar Gordon	.25	.07
❑ 9 Leonard Little	.25	.07
❑ 10 Patrick Ramsey	.40	.12
❑ 11 Justin McCareins	.25	.07
❑ 12 Charles Lee	.25	.07
❑ 13 Matt Hasselbeck	.40	.12
❑ 14 Chris Chambers	.40	.12
❑ 15 Derrick Blaylock	.40	.12
❑ 16 Shannon Sharpe	.40	.12
❑ 17 Bubba Franks	.40	.12
❑ 18 London Fletcher	.25	.07
❑ 19 Eric Moulds	.40	.12
❑ 20 Anquan Boldin	.60	.18
❑ 21 Brian Urlacher	.75	.23
❑ 22 Stephen Davis	.40	.12
❑ 23 Mikhael Ricks	.25	.07
❑ 24 Jason Taylor	.25	.07
❑ 25 Michael Vick	1.25	.35
❑ 26 Dante Hall	.60	.18
❑ 27 Marcus Pollard	.25	.07
❑ 28 Rick Mirer	.25	.07
❑ 29 David Tyree	.25	.07
❑ 30 Chad Pennington	.75	.23
❑ 31 Kevan Barlow	.40	.12
❑ 32 James Farrior	.25	.07
❑ 33 James Thrash	.25	.07
❑ 34 Damerien McCants	.25	.07
❑ 35 L.J. Smith	.40	.12
❑ 36 Tommy Maddox	.40	.12
❑ 37 Tedy Bruschi	.40	.12
❑ 38 Moe Williams	.25	.07
❑ 39 Todd Bouman	.25	.07
❑ 40 Domanick Davis	.60	.18
❑ 41 Dwight Freeney	.25	.07
❑ 42 Kyle Brady	.25	.07
❑ 43 LaVar Arrington	1.25	.35
❑ 44 Troy Hambrick	.25	.07
❑ 45 Jake Plummer	.40	.12
❑ 46 Freddie Jones	.25	.07
❑ 47 Chester Taylor	.25	.07
❑ 48 Willis McGahee	.60	.18
❑ 49 Bobby Wade	.25	.07
❑ 50 Steve McNair	.60	.18
❑ 51 Joe Jurevicius	.25	.07
❑ 52 Ladell Betts	.25	.07
❑ 53 LaMont Jordan	.40	.12
❑ 54 Kerry Collins	.40	.12
❑ 55 Hines Ward	.60	.18
❑ 56 Scott Fujita	.25	.07
❑ 57 Kevin Johnson	.25	.07
❑ 58 Troy Brown	.40	.12
❑ 59 Jerome Pathon	.25	.07
❑ 60 Andre Johnson	.60	.18
❑ 61 DeShaun Foster	.40	.12
❑ 62 Terrell Suggs	.40	.12
❑ 63 Marcel Shipp	.40	.12
❑ 64 Allen Rossum	.25	.07
❑ 65 Kyle Boller	.60	.18
❑ 66 Terence Newman	.40	.12
❑ 67 Javon Walker	.40	.12
❑ 68 Shawn Bryson	.25	.07
❑ 69 Travis Minor	.25	.07
❑ 70 Terrell Owens	.60	.18
❑ 71 Kassim Osgood	.25	.07
❑ 72 Bobby Engram	.25	.07
❑ 73 Drew Bennett	.40	.12
❑ 74 Rock Cartwright	.25	.07
❑ 75 Ahman Green	.60	.18
❑ 76 Steve Beuerlein	.25	.07
❑ 77 Takeo Spikes	.25	.07
❑ 78 Dez White	.40	.12
❑ 79 Tim Couch	.25	.07
❑ 80 Travis Henry	.40	.12
❑ 81 T.J. Duckett	.40	.12
❑ 82 LaBrandon Toefield	.25	.07
❑ 83 Randy McMichael	.25	.07
❑ 84 Jonathan Carter	.25	.07
❑ 85 Jerry Rice	1.25	.35
❑ 86 Maurice Morris	.25	.07
❑ 87 Kurt Warner	.60	.18
❑ 88 Josh Scobey	.25	.07
❑ 89 Travis Taylor	.25	.07
❑ 90 Fred Taylor	.40	.12
❑ 91 Zach Thomas	.60	.18
❑ 92 Kelly Campbell	.25	.07
❑ 93 Tim Carter	.25	.07
❑ 94 Marques Tuiasosopo	.40	.12
❑ 95 Laveranues Coles	.40	.12
❑ 96 Chris Brown	.60	.18
❑ 97 Thomas Jones	.40	.12
❑ 98 Dane Looker	.40	.12
❑ 99 Ross Tucker	.25	.07
❑ 100 Priest Holmes	.75	.23
❑ 101 Troy Walters	.25	.07
❑ 102 Jamie Sharper	.25	.07
❑ 103 Quincy Morgan	.40	.12
❑ 104 Aveion Cason	.25	.07
❑ 105 Joey Galloway	.40	.12
❑ 106 Bill Schroeder	.25	.07
❑ 107 Tony Fisher	.25	.07
❑ 108 Adewale Ogunleye	.40	.12
❑ 109 Justin Fargas	.40	.12
❑ 110 Daunte Culpepper	.60	.18
❑ 111 Donnie Edwards	.25	.07
❑ 112 Jed Weaver	.25	.07
❑ 113 Arlen Harris	.25	.07
❑ 114 Keenan McCardell	.25	.07
❑ 115 Chad Johnson	.40	.12
❑ 116 Marty Booker	.40	.12
❑ 117 Anthony Wright	.25	.07
❑ 118 Brian Finneran	.25	.07
❑ 119 Robert Ferguson	.25	.07
❑ 120 Ricky Williams	.60	.18
❑ 121 Shaun Ellis	.25	.07
❑ 122 Brian Westbrook	.40	.12
❑ 123 Sam Cowart	.25	.07
❑ 124 Tim Rattay	.40	.12
❑ 125 LaDainian Tomlinson	.60	.18
❑ 126 Simeon Rice	.40	.12
❑ 127 Jason Witten	.40	.12
❑ 128 Lee Suggs	.60	.18
❑ 129 Keith Brooking	.25	.07
❑ 130 Rex Grossman	.60	.18
❑ 131 Kelley Washington	.25	.07
❑ 132 Antonio Bryant	.40	.12
❑ 133 Dallas Clark	.40	.12
❑ 134 Stacey Mack	.25	.07
❑ 135 Charles Rogers	.40	.12
❑ 136 Donte' Stallworth	.40	.12
❑ 137 Deion Branch	.60	.18
❑ 138 Nate Burleson	.60	.18
❑ 139 Ike Hilliard	.25	.07
❑ 140 Randy Moss	.75	.23
❑ 141 Michael Strahan	.40	.12
❑ 142 John Abraham	.25	.07
❑ 143 Tim Dwight	.40	.12
❑ 144 Isaac Bruce	.40	.12
❑ 145 Brad Johnson	.40	.12
❑ 146 Trung Canidate	.25	.07
❑ 147 Warrick Dunn	.40	.12
❑ 148 Josh McCown	.40	.12
❑ 149 Muhsin Muhammad	.40	.12
❑ 150 Donovan McNabb	.75	.23
❑ 151 Tai Streets	.25	.07
❑ 152 Antonio Gates	.60	.18
❑ 153 Antwaan Randle El	.40	.12
❑ 154 Doug Jolley	.25	.07
❑ 155 Shaun Alexander	.60	.18
❑ 156 William Green	.40	.12
❑ 157 Carson Palmer	.75	.23
❑ 158 Quentin Griffin	.60	.18
❑ 159 Az-Zahir Hakim	.25	.07
❑ 160 Edgerrin James	.60	.18
❑ 161 Gus Frerotte	.25	.07
❑ 162 Brandon Lloyd	.40	.12
❑ 163 Brian Griese	.40	.12
❑ 164 Boo Williams	.25	.07
❑ 165 Santana Moss	.40	.12
❑ 166 Tyrone Wheatley	.25	.07
❑ 167 Eric Parker	.25	.07
❑ 168 Amos Zereoue	.25	.07
❑ 169 Itula Mili	.25	.07
❑ 170 Marshall Faulk	.60	.18
❑ 171 Tyrone Calico	.40	.12
❑ 172 Tim Hasselbeck	.25	.07
❑ 173 Anthony Becht	.25	.07
❑ 174 Larry Johnson	.40	.12
❑ 175 Marvin Harrison	.60	.18
❑ 176 Tony Gonzalez	.40	.12
❑ 177 Wayne Chrebet	.40	.12
❑ 178 Mike Barrow	.25	.07
❑ 179 Bethel Johnson	.40	.12
❑ 180 Deuce McAllister	.60	.18
❑ 181 Drew Brees	.60	.18
❑ 182 Teyo Johnson	.25	.07
❑ 183 Garrison Hearst	.40	.12
❑ 184 Todd Pinkston	.25	.07
❑ 185 Jeff Garcia	.60	.18
❑ 186 Darrell Jackson	.40	.12
❑ 187 Billy Volek	.60	.18
❑ 188 Ray Lewis	.60	.18
❑ 189 Ricky Proehl	.25	.07
❑ 190 Rudi Johnson	.40	.12
❑ 191 Emmitt Smith	1.25	.35
❑ 192 Cedrick Wilson	.25	.07
❑ 193 Julius Peppers	.60	.18
❑ 194 Peter Warrick	.40	.12
❑ 195 Trent Green	.40	.12
❑ 196 Derrius Thompson	.25	.07
❑ 197 Onterrio Smith	.40	.12
❑ 198 Jerome Bettis	.60	.18
❑ 199 Keyshawn Johnson	.40	.12
❑ 200 Jamal Lewis	.60	.18
❑ 201 Alge Crumpler	.40	.12
❑ 202 Justin Gage	.40	.12
❑ 203 Mike Rucker	.25	.07
❑ 204 Michael Bennett	.40	.12
❑ 205 Jimmy Smith	.40	.12
❑ 206 Ricky Williams TT	.25	.07
❑ 207 Corey Bradford	.25	.07
❑ 208 Jerry Porter	.40	.12
❑ 209 Erron Kinney	.25	.07

❑ 210 Marc Bulger	.60	.18
❑ 211 Jeff Blake	.25	.07
❑ 212 Terry Jones	.25	.07
❑ 213 Kordell Stewart	.40	.12
❑ 214 Andra Davis	.25	.07
❑ 215 David Carr	.60	.18
❑ 216 Nick Barnett	.40	.12
❑ 217 Mark Brunell	.40	.12
❑ 218 Daniel Graham	.25	.07
❑ 219 Jim Kleinsasser	.25	.07
❑ 220 Aaron Brooks	.40	.12
❑ 221 Plaxico Burress	.40	.12
❑ 222 Correll Buckhalter	.40	.12
❑ 223 Jevon Kearse	.40	.12
❑ 224 Michael Pittman	.25	.07
❑ 225 Clinton Portis	.60	.18
❑ 226 Corey Dillon	.40	.12
❑ 227 Steve Smith	.40	.12
❑ 228 David Thornton	.25	.07
❑ 229 Eddie Kennison	.25	.07
❑ 230 Amani Toomer	.40	.12
❑ 231 Artose Pinner	.25	.07
❑ 232 Kelly Holcomb	.40	.12
❑ 233 Jay Fiedler	.25	.07
❑ 234 Ernie Conwell	.25	.07
❑ 235 Torry Holt	.60	.18
❑ 236 Eddie George	.40	.12
❑ 237 Jeremy Shockey	.60	.18
❑ 238 Troy Edwards	.25	.07
❑ 239 Antowain Smith	.40	.12
❑ 240 Jon Kitna	.40	.12
❑ 241 Bryant Johnson	.25	.07
❑ 242 Todd Heap	.40	.12
❑ 243 Doug Johnson	.25	.07
❑ 244 Ashley Lelie	.40	.12
❑ 245 Byron Leftwich	1.00	.30
❑ 246 Shawn Barber	.25	.07
❑ 247 Duce Staley	.40	.12
❑ 248 Rod Gardner	.40	.12
❑ 249 Warren Sapp	.40	.12
❑ 250 Brett Favre	1.50	.45
❑ 251 Olandis Gary	.25	.07
❑ 252 Reggie Wayne	.40	.12
❑ 253 Billy Miller	.25	.07
❑ 254 Johnnie Morton	.40	.12
❑ 255 Joe Horn	.40	.12
❑ 256 Curtis Martin	.60	.18
❑ 257 Freddie Mitchell	.40	.12
❑ 258 Charlie Garner	.40	.12
❑ 259 Marcus Robinson	.40	.12
❑ 260 Derrick Mason	.40	.12
❑ 261 Bobby Shaw	.25	.07
❑ 262 Desmond Clark	.25	.07
❑ 263 James Jackson	.25	.07
❑ 264 Josh Reed	.25	.07
❑ 265 David Boston	.40	.12
❑ 266 Drew Bledsoe	.60	.18
❑ 267 Brock Forsey	.25	.07
❑ 268 Dat Nguyen	.25	.07
❑ 269 Mike Anderson	.40	.12
❑ 270 Anthony Thomas	.40	.12
❑ 271 Najeh Davenport	.25	.07
❑ 272 Jabar Gaffney	.40	.12
❑ 273 Tiki Barber	.40	.12
❑ 274 Rich Gannon	.40	.12
❑ 275 Tom Brady	1.00	.30
❑ 276 Terry Glenn	.25	.07
❑ 277 Dennis Northcutt	.25	.07
❑ 278 A.J. Feeley	.60	.18
❑ 279 Peerless Price	.40	.12
❑ 280 Jake Delhomme	.60	.18
❑ 281 Kevin Faulk	.25	.07
❑ 282 Quincy Carter	.40	.12
❑ 283 Andre' Davis	.25	.07
❑ 284 Tony Hollings	.25	.07
❑ 285 Joey Harrington	.60	.18
❑ 286 Richie Anderson	.25	.07
❑ 287 Donald Driver	.40	.12
❑ 288 Koren Robinson	.40	.12
❑ 289 Tony Banks	.25	.07
❑ 290 Rod Smith	.40	.12
❑ 291 Anquan Boldin WW	.25	.07
❑ 292 Jamal Lewis WW	.40	.12
❑ 293 Priest Holmes WW	.60	.18
❑ 294 Peyton Manning WW	.60	.18
❑ 295 Marvin Harrison WW	.40	.12
❑ 296 Steve McNair WW	.40	.12
❑ 297 Travis Henry WW	.25	.07
❑ 298 Torry Holt WW	.40	.12
❑ 299 Tom Brady WW	.60	.18
❑ 300 Ahman Green WW	.40	.12
❑ 301 Donovan McNabb WW	.60	.18
❑ 302 Deuce McAllister WW	.40	.12
❑ 303 Domanick Davis WW	.40	.12
❑ 304 Clinton Portis WW	.60	.18
❑ 305 Rudi Johnson WW	.25	.07
❑ 306 Brett Favre WW	.75	.23
❑ 307 LaDainian Tomlinson WW	.40	.12
❑ 308 Steve Smith WW	.25	.07
❑ 309 Edgerrin James WW	.40	.12
❑ 310 Ty Law WW	.25	.07
❑ 311 Ben Roethlisberger RC	15.00	4.50
❑ 312 Ahmad Carroll RC	2.00	.60
❑ 313 Johnnie Morant RC	1.50	.45
❑ 314 Greg Jones RC	1.50	.45
❑ 315 Michael Clayton RC	4.00	1.20
❑ 316 Josh Harris RC	1.50	.45
❑ 317 Tatum Bell RC	2.50	.75
❑ 318 Robert Gallery RC	2.50	.75
❑ 319 B.J. Symons RC	1.50	.45
❑ 320 Roy Williams RC	5.00	1.50
❑ 321 DeAngelo Hall RC	2.00	.60
❑ 322 Jeff Smoker RC	2.50	.75
❑ 323 Lee Evans RC	2.50	.75
❑ 324 Michael Jenkins RC	1.50	.45
❑ 325 Steven Jackson RC	5.00	1.50
❑ 326 Will Smith RC	1.50	.45
❑ 327 Vince Wilfork RC	2.00	.60
❑ 328 Ben Troupe RC	1.50	.45
❑ 329 Chris Gamble RC	2.00	.60
❑ 330 Kevin Jones RC	5.00	1.50
❑ 331 Jonathan Vilma RC	1.50	.45
❑ 332 Dontarrious Thomas RC	1.50	.45
❑ 333 Michael Boulware RC	1.50	.45
❑ 334 Mewelde Moore RC	2.00	.60
❑ 335 Drew Henson RC	4.00	1.20
❑ 336 D.J. Williams RC	2.00	.60
❑ 337 Ernest Wilford RC	1.50	.45
❑ 338 John Navarre RC	1.50	.45
❑ 339 Jerricho Cotchery RC	1.50	.45
❑ 340 Derrick Hamilton RC	1.25	.35
❑ 341 Carlos Francis RC	1.25	.35
❑ 342 Ben Watson RC	1.50	.45
❑ 343 Reggie Williams RC	2.00	.60
❑ 344 Devard Darling RC	1.50	.45
❑ 345 Chris Perry RC	3.00	.90
❑ 346 Derrick Strait RC	1.50	.45
❑ 347 Sean Taylor RC	2.00	.60
❑ 348 Michael Turner RC	1.25	.35
❑ 349 Keary Colbert RC	2.00	.60
❑ 350 Eli Manning RC	8.00	2.40
❑ 351 Julius Jones RC	6.00	1.80
❑ 352 Jason Babin RC	1.50	.45
❑ 353 Cody Pickett RC	1.50	.45
❑ 354 Kenechi Udeze RC	1.50	.45
❑ 355 Rashaun Woods RC	2.00	.60
❑ 356 Matt Schaub RC	2.50	.75
❑ 357 Tommie Harris RC	2.00	.60
❑ 358 Dwan Edwards RC	.75	.23
❑ 359 Shawn Andrews RC	1.50	.45
❑ 360 Larry Fitzgerald RC	5.00	1.50
❑ 361 P.K. Sam RC	1.25	.35
❑ 362 Teddy Lehman RC	1.50	.45
❑ 363 Darius Watts RC	2.00	.60
❑ 364 D.J. Hackett RC	1.25	.35
❑ 365 Cedric Cobbs RC	1.50	.45
❑ 366 Antwan Odom RC	1.50	.45
❑ 367 Marquise Hill RC	1.25	.35
❑ 368 Luke McCown RC	1.50	.45
❑ 369 Triandos Luke RC	1.50	.45
❑ 370 Kellen Winslow RC	4.00	1.20
❑ 371 Derek Abney RC	1.50	.45
❑ 372 Chris Cooley RC	1.50	.45
❑ 373 Dunta Robinson RC	1.50	.45
❑ 374 Sean Jones RC	1.25	.35
❑ 375 Philip Rivers RC	5.00	1.50
❑ 376 Craig Krenzel RC	1.50	.45
❑ 377 Daryl Smith RC	1.50	.45
❑ 378 Samie Parker RC	1.50	.45
❑ 379 Ben Hartsock RC	1.50	.45
❑ 380 J.P. Losman RC	4.00	1.20
❑ 381 Karlos Dansby RC	1.50	.45
❑ 382 Ricardo Colclough RC	1.50	.45
❑ 383 Bernard Berrian RC	1.50	.45
❑ 384 Junior Siavii RC	1.50	.45
❑ 385 Devery Henderson RC	1.25	.35
❑ RH38 Tom Brady RH	6.00	1.80
❑ RH38A Tom Brady RH AU	350.00	105.00
❑ SBMVP Tom Brady FB AU/99	450.00	135.00

2004 Topps Black

	Nm-Mt	Ex-Mt

*VETERANS: 5X TO 12X BASIC CARDS
*ROOKIES: 3X TO 8X BASIC CARDS
STATED ODDS 1:25 H/R, 1:6 HTA
STATED PRINT RUN 150 SER.#'d SETS

2004 Topps Collection

	Nm-Mt	Ex-Mt
COMP.FACT SET (385)	60.00	18.00

*STARS: .4X TO 1X BASIC TOPPS
*ROOKIES: .4X TO 1X BASIC TOPPS

2004 Topps First Edition

	Nm-Mt	Ex-Mt
COMPLETE SET (385)	150.00	45.00

*FIRST EDIT.VETS: 1.2X TO 3X BASIC CARDS
*FIRST EDITION RCs: .8X TO 2X BASIC CARDS

2004 Topps Gold

	Nm-Mt	Ex-Mt

*VETERANS: 2X TO 5X BASIC CARDS
*ROOKIES: 1.5X TO 4X BASIC CARDS
STATED ODDS 1:18 H, 1:5 HTA, 1:15 R
STATED PRINT RUN 499 SER.#'d SETS

2004 Topps Autographs

	Nm-Mt	Ex-Mt

GROUP A ODDS 1:8664H, 1:2472HTA, 1:7313R
GROUP B ODDS 1:6750H, 1:1890HTA, 1:5811R
GROUP C ODDS 1:3200H, 1:1212HTA, 1:5644R
GROUP D ODDS 1:3360H, 1:952HTA, 1:2913R
GROUP E ODDS 1:2230H, 1:636HTA, 1:1937R
GROUP F ODDS 1:983H, 1:280HTA, 1:859R
GROUP G ODDS 1:3724H, 1:1062HTA, 1:3234R
GROUP H ODDS 1:3346H, 1:952HTA, 1:2913R
GROUP I ODDS 1:1112H, 1:317HTA, 1:978R

❑ TAG0 Ahman Green A	60.00	18.00
❑ TBR Ben Roethlisberger B	200.00	60.00
❑ TBS Brandon Stokley E	30.00	9.00
❑ TCP Chad Pennington B	50.00	15.00
❑ TDD Domanick Davis E	25.00	7.50
❑ TDH Dante Hall D EXCH	30.00	9.00
❑ TEM Eli Manning C	120.00	36.00
❑ TGJ Greg Jones F	25.00	7.50
❑ TKB Kevan Barlow D	25.00	7.50
❑ TKJ Kevin Jones F	60.00	18.00
❑ TLE Lee Evans G	30.00	9.00
❑ TMC Michael Clayton I	40.00	12.00

	Nm-Mt	Ex-Mt
❑ TMS Matt Schaub I	30.00	9.00
❑ TPM Peyton Manning A	100.00	30.00
❑ TRW Roy Williams WR F	50.00	15.00
❑ TSJ Steven Jackson A	80.00	24.00
❑ TCPE Chris Perry A	60.00	18.00
❑ TCPI Cody Pickett H	25.00	7.50
❑ TRWI Reggie Williams F EXCH	25.00	7.50
❑ TRWO Rashaun Woods C	25.00	7.50

2004 Topps Game Breakers Relics

STATED ODDS 1:7035H, 1:1977HTA, 1:5997R

	Nm-Mt	Ex-Mt
❑ GB1 Deion Branch	60.00	18.00
❑ GB2 Tom Brady	100.00	30.00
❑ GB3 Steve Smith	50.00	15.00
❑ GB4 Jake Delhomme	60.00	18.00
❑ GB5 David Givens	60.00	18.00
❑ GB6 Antowain Smith	50.00	15.00
❑ GB7 DeShaun Foster	60.00	18.00
❑ GB8 Muhsin Muhammad	50.00	15.00
❑ GB9 Mike Vrabel	60.00	18.00
❑ GB10 Ricky Proehl		

2004 Topps Hall of Fame Autographs

STATED ODDS 1:17,513H, 1:4943HTA, 1:14,625R

	Nm-Mt	Ex-Mt
❑ HOFBB Bob Brown	200.00	60.00
❑ HOFBS Barry Sanders	350.00	105.00
❑ HOFCE Carl Eller	200.00	60.00
❑ HOFJE John Elway	400.00	120.00

2004 Topps Hobby Masters

	Nm-Mt	Ex-Mt
COMPLETE SET (10)	25.00	7.50
STATED ODDS 1:18 H/R, 1:6 HTA		
❑ HM1 Peyton Manning	3.00	.90
❑ HM2 Michael Vick	4.00	1.20
❑ HM3 Steve McNair	2.00	.60
❑ HM4 Ricky Williams	2.00	.60
❑ HM5 Priest Holmes	2.50	.75
❑ HM6 Brett Favre	5.00	1.50
❑ HM7 Clinton Portis	2.00	.60
❑ HM8 Donovan McNabb	2.50	.75
❑ HM9 Randy Moss	2.50	.75
❑ HM10 LaDainian Tomlinson	2.00	.60

2004 Topps League Leaders Relics

STATED ODDS 1:538 H, 1:35 HTA

	Nm-Mt	Ex-Mt
❑ LLRJL Jamal Lewis	12.00	3.60
❑ LLRMS Michael Strahan	12.00	3.60
❑ LLRPM Peyton Manning	20.00	6.00
❑ LLRRL Ray Lewis	10.00	3.00
❑ LLRTH Torry Holt	12.00	3.60

2004 Topps Own the Game

	Nm-Mt	Ex-Mt
COMPLETE SET (30)	50.00	15.00
STATED ODDS 1:12 H/HTA/R		
❑ OTG1 Brett Favre	6.00	1.80
❑ OTG2 Donovan McNabb	3.00	.90
❑ OTG3 Trent Green	1.50	.45
❑ OTG4 Peyton Manning	4.00	1.20
❑ OTG5 Matt Hasselbeck	1.50	.45
❑ OTG6 Jon Kitna	1.50	.45
❑ OTG7 Steve McNair	2.50	.75
❑ OTG8 Tom Brady	4.00	1.20
❑ OTG9 Marc Bulger	2.50	.75
❑ OTG10 Jamal Lewis	2.50	.75
❑ OTG11 Deuce McAllister	2.50	.75
❑ OTG12 Ahman Green	2.50	.75
❑ OTG13 Stephen Davis	1.50	.45
❑ OTG14 Clinton Portis	2.50	.75
❑ OTG15 Priest Holmes	3.00	.90
❑ OTG16 LaDainian Tomlinson	2.50	.75
❑ OTG17 Fred Taylor	1.50	.45
❑ OTG18 Shaun Alexander	2.50	.75
❑ OTG19 Torry Holt	2.50	.75
❑ OTG20 Randy Moss	3.00	.90
❑ OTG21 Chad Johnson	1.50	.45
❑ OTG22 Anquan Boldin	2.50	.75
❑ OTG23 Laveranues Coles	1.50	.45
❑ OTG24 Derrick Mason	1.50	.45
❑ OTG25 Hines Ward	2.50	.75
❑ OTG26 Marvin Harrison	2.50	.75
❑ OTG27 Santana Moss	1.50	.45
❑ OTG28 Michael Strahan	1.50	.45
❑ OTG29 Ray Lewis	2.50	.75
❑ OTG30 Jamie Sharper	1.00	.30

2004 Topps Premiere Prospects

	Nm-Mt	Ex-Mt
COMPLETE SET (20)	30.00	9.00
STATED ODDS 1:6 H/HTA/R		
❑ PP1 Ben Roethlisberger	15.00	4.50
❑ PP2 Chris Perry	3.00	.90
❑ PP3 Darius Watts	2.00	.60
❑ PP4 Devery Henderson	1.25	.35
❑ PP5 Eli Manning	8.00	2.40
❑ PP6 Greg Jones	1.50	.45
❑ PP7 J.P. Losman	4.00	1.20
❑ PP8 Julius Jones	6.00	1.80
❑ PP9 Kellen Winslow	4.00	1.20
❑ PP10 Kevin Jones	5.00	1.50
❑ PP11 Larry Fitzgerald	5.00	1.50
❑ PP12 Lee Evans	2.50	.75
❑ PP13 Michael Clayton	4.00	1.20
❑ PP14 Michael Jenkins	1.50	.45
❑ PP15 Philip Rivers	5.00	1.50
❑ PP16 Rashaun Woods	2.00	.60
❑ PP17 Reggie Williams	2.00	.60
❑ PP18 Roy Williams WR	5.00	1.50
❑ PP19 Steven Jackson	5.00	1.50
❑ PP20 Tatum Bell	2.50	.75

2004 Topps Premiere Prospects Autographs

SINGLE AU ODDS 1:3473H,1:996HTA,1:2913R
SINGLE PRINT RUN 100 SER.#'d SETS
DUAL AU ODDS
1:13,951H,1:4016HTA,1:11,622R
DUAL PRINT RUN 50 SER.#'d SETS

	Nm-Mt	Ex-Mt
❑ PPBR Ben Roethlisberger	400.00	120.00
❑ PPCP Chris Perry	100.00	30.00
❑ PPDFW Larry Fitzgerald Roy Williams WR	250.00	75.00
❑ PPDJJ Steven Jackson Kevin Jones	250.00	75.00
❑ PPDMR Eli Manning Ben Roethlisberger	800.00	240.00
❑ PPDPJ Chris Perry Greg Jones	120.00	36.00
❑ PPDWW Reggie Williams Rashaun Woods	120.00	36.00
❑ PPEM Eli Manning	300.00	90.00
❑ PPGJ Greg Jones	60.00	18.00
❑ PPKJ Kevin Jones	125.00	38.00
❑ PPLE Lee Evans	80.00	24.00
❑ PPRW Roy Williams WR	120.00	36.00

❑ PPRWI Reggie Williams	80.00	24.00
❑ PPRWO Rashaun Woods	80.00	24.00
❑ PPSJ Steven Jackson	120.00	36.00

2004 Topps Pro Bowl Jerseys

	Nm-Mt	Ex-Mt
STATED ODDS 1:204 H, 1:34 HTA, 1:190 R		
❑ PBAG Ahman Green	15.00	4.50
❑ PBBU Brian Urlacher	20.00	6.00
❑ PBCB Champ Bailey	12.00	3.60
❑ PBCJ Chad Johnson	12.00	3.60
❑ PBHW Hines Ward	15.00	4.50
❑ PBKB Keith Brooking	10.00	3.00
❑ PBLA LaVar Arrington	40.00	12.00
❑ PBMH Marvin Harrison	15.00	4.50
❑ PBMS Michael Strahan	12.00	3.60
❑ PBPH Priest Holmes	20.00	6.00
❑ PBPM Peyton Manning	20.00	6.00
❑ PBSM Steve McNair	15.00	4.50
❑ PBTG Trent Green	15.00	4.50
❑ PBTGO Tony Gonzalez	15.00	4.50
❑ PBTH Torry Holt	15.00	4.50

2004 Topps Ring of Honor Coaches' Cuts

	Nm-Mt	Ex-Mt
STATED ODDS 1:102,888 H, 1:25,704 HTA		
UNPRICED COACHES' CUTS #'d TO 1		

2004 Topps Rookie Premiere Autographs

	Nm-Mt	Ex-Mt
SINGLE AUTO ODDS 1:890 H, 1:225 HTA		
DUAL AUTO ODDS 1:1977 HTA		
AUTO 1/1 STATED ODDS 1:4016 HTA		
❑ RPBB Bernard Berrian	80.00	24.00
❑ RPBR Ben Roethlisberger	800.00	240.00
❑ RPBT Ben Troupe	80.00	24.00
❑ RPBW Ben Watson	80.00	24.00
❑ RPCC Cedric Cobbs	80.00	24.00
❑ RPCP Chris Perry	100.00	30.00
❑ RPDD Devard Darling	80.00	24.00
❑ RPDEH DeAngelo Hall	100.00	30.00
❑ RPDFW Larry Fitzgerald Roy Williams WR	400.00	120.00
❑ RPDHA Derrick Hamilton	80.00	24.00
❑ RPDHE Devery Henderson	80.00	24.00
❑ RPDJJ Steven Jackson Kevin Jones	300.00	90.00
❑ RPDMR Eli Manning Philip Rivers	600.00	180.00
❑ RPDR Dunta Robinson	80.00	24.00
❑ RPDW Darius Watts	100.00	30.00
❑ RPEM Eli Manning	550.00	160.00
❑ RPGJ Greg Jones	80.00	24.00
❑ RPJJ Julius Jones	350.00	105.00
❑ RPJPL J.P. Losman	200.00	60.00
❑ RPKC Keary Colbert	150.00	45.00
❑ RPKJ Kevin Jones	250.00	75.00
❑ RPKW Kellen Winslow	200.00	60.00
❑ RPLE Lee Evans	135.00	40.00
❑ RPLF Larry Fitzgerald	250.00	75.00
❑ RPLM Luke McCown	80.00	24.00
❑ RPMC Michael Clayton	175.00	52.50
❑ RPMJ Michael Jenkins	80.00	24.00
❑ RPMM Mewelde Moore	120.00	36.00
❑ RPMS Matt Schaub	120.00	36.00
❑ RPPR Philip Rivers	250.00	75.00
❑ RPRG Robert Gallery	120.00	36.00
❑ RPRW Roy Williams WR	300.00	90.00
❑ RPRWI Reggie Williams	120.00	36.00
❑ RPRWO Rashaun Woods	120.00	36.00
❑ RPSJ Steven Jackson	250.00	75.00
❑ RPTB Tatum Bell	150.00	45.00

2004 Topps Super Tix

	Nm-Mt	Ex-Mt
STATED ODDS 1:696 H, 1:199 HTA, 1:580 R		
STATB ODDS		
1:74,827H,1:21,420HTA,1:65,856R		
❑ ST1 Tom Brady	50.00	15.00
❑ ST2 Jake Delhomme	30.00	9.00
❑ ST3 Antowain Smith	30.00	9.00
❑ ST4 Stephen Davis	25.00	7.50
❑ ST5 Deion Branch	30.00	9.00
❑ ST6 Steve Smith	25.00	7.50
❑ ST7 Troy Brown	30.00	9.00
❑ ST8 Muhsin Muhammad	25.00	7.50
❑ ST9 Ty Law	30.00	9.00
❑ ST10 Julius Peppers	25.00	7.50
❑ STATB Tom Brady AU	800.00	240.00

2003 Topps All American

	Nm-Mt	Ex-Mt
COMPLETE SET (150)	100.00	30.00
COMP.SET w/o SP's (100)	25.00	7.50
❑ 1 Marvin Harrison	1.25	.35
❑ 2 Tiki Barber	.75	.23
❑ 3 Jamal Lewis	1.25	.35
❑ 4 Tim Couch	.75	.23
❑ 5 Michael Bennett	.75	.23
❑ 6 Brad Johnson	.75	.23
❑ 7 Garrison Hearst	.75	.23
❑ 8 Plaxico Burress	.75	.23
❑ 9 Rod Gardner	.75	.23
❑ 10 Charlie Garner	.75	.23
❑ 11 Chad Pennington	1.50	.45
❑ 12 Brian Griese	1.25	.35
❑ 13 Julius Peppers	1.25	.35
❑ 14 David Boston	.75	.23
❑ 15 Anthony Thomas	1.25	.35
❑ 16 Ahman Green	1.25	.35
❑ 17 Fred Taylor	1.25	.35
❑ 18 Joe Horn	.75	.23
❑ 19 Joey Galloway	.75	.23
❑ 20 Eddie George	.75	.23
❑ 21 Jeff Garcia	1.25	.35
❑ 22 Hines Ward	1.25	.35
❑ 23 Kurt Warner	1.25	.35
❑ 24 Marty Booker	.75	.23
❑ 25 Joey Harrington	2.00	.60
❑ 26 Jay Fiedler	.75	.23
❑ 27 Troy Brown	.75	.23
❑ 28 David Carr	2.00	.60
❑ 29 Eric Moulds	.75	.23
❑ 30 Michael Vick	3.00	.90
❑ 31 Keyshawn Johnson	1.25	.35
❑ 32 Torry Holt	1.25	.35
❑ 33 LaDainian Tomlinson	1.25	.35
❑ 34 Duce Staley	.75	.23
❑ 35 Curtis Martin	1.25	.35
❑ 36 Stephen Davis	.75	.23
❑ 37 Jim Miller	.50	.15
❑ 38 Travis Taylor	.50	.15
❑ 39 Jimmy Smith	.75	.23
❑ 40 Trent Green	.75	.23
❑ 41 Tom Brady	2.00	.60
❑ 42 Randy Moss	2.00	.60
❑ 43 Clinton Portis	2.00	.60
❑ 44 Emmitt Smith	3.00	.90
❑ 45 Steve McNair	1.25	.35
❑ 46 Shaun Alexander	1.25	.35
❑ 47 Jerome Bettis	1.25	.35
❑ 48 Rich Gannon	.75	.23
❑ 49 William Green	.75	.23
❑ 50 Priest Holmes	1.50	.45
❑ 51 James Stewart	.75	.23
❑ 52 Warrick Dunn	.75	.23
❑ 53 Jake Plummer	.75	.23
❑ 54 Antowain Smith	.75	.23
❑ 55 Peyton Manning	2.00	.60
❑ 56 Deuce McAllister	1.25	.35
❑ 57 Jeremy Shockey	2.00	.60
❑ 58 Darrell Jackson	.75	.23
❑ 59 Derrick Mason	.75	.23
❑ 60 Terrell Owens	1.25	.35
❑ 61 Laveranues Coles	.75	.23
❑ 62 Amani Toomer	.75	.23
❑ 63 Tony Gonzalez	.75	.23
❑ 64 Corey Bradford	.50	.15
❑ 65 Donald Driver	.75	.23
❑ 66 Rod Smith	.75	.23
❑ 67 Chad Johnson	.75	.23
❑ 68 Travis Henry	.75	.23
❑ 69 Mark Brunell	.75	.23
❑ 70 Edgerrin James	1.25	.35
❑ 71 Jerry Rice	2.50	.75
❑ 72 Aaron Brooks	1.25	.35
❑ 73 Marshall Faulk	1.25	.35
❑ 74 Curtis Conway	.50	.15
❑ 75 Tommy Maddox	1.25	.35
❑ 76 Isaac Bruce	1.25	.35
❑ 77 Matt Hasselbeck	.75	.23
❑ 78 Muhsin Muhammad	.75	.23
❑ 79 Drew Bledsoe	1.25	.35
❑ 80 Ricky Williams	1.25	.35
❑ 81 Daunte Culpepper	1.25	.35
❑ 82 Chad Hutchinson	.75	.23
❑ 83 Brian Urlacher	2.00	.60
❑ 84 Drew Brees	1.25	.35

❑ 85 Corey Dillon	.75	.23
❑ 86 Chris Chambers	1.25	.35
❑ 87 Peerless Price	.75	.23
❑ 88 Kerry Collins	.75	.23
❑ 89 Donovan McNabb	1.50	.45
❑ 90 Brett Favre	3.00	.90
❑ 91 Patrick Ramsey	1.25	.35
❑ 92 T.J. Duckett	.75	.23
❑ 93 Derrick Brooks	.75	.23
❑ 94 Jon Kitna	.75	.23
❑ 95 Jerry Porter	.75	.23
❑ 96 Todd Pinkston	.75	.23
❑ 97 Tai Streets	.50	.15
❑ 98 Ray Lewis	1.25	.35
❑ 99 Michael Pittman	.50	.15
❑ 100 Brian Finneran	.50	.15
❑ 101 Carson Palmer RC	10.00	3.00
❑ 102 Terrell Suggs RC	5.00	1.50
❑ 103 Boss Bailey RC	4.00	1.20
❑ 104 Justin Gage RC	3.00	.90
❑ 105 Bobby Wade RC	3.00	.90
❑ 106 Larry Johnson RC	6.00	1.80
❑ 107 Ken Dorsey RC	5.00	1.50
❑ 108 Quentin Griffin RC	6.00	1.80
❑ 109 Musa Smith RC	3.00	.90
❑ 110 Chris Simms RC	6.00	1.80
❑ 111 Michael Haynes RC	3.00	.90
❑ 112 Charles Rogers RC	4.00	1.20
❑ 113 Kliff Kingsbury RC	2.50	.75
❑ 114 Jerome McDougle RC	3.00	.90
❑ 115 ReShard Lee RC	3.00	.90
❑ 116 Chris Brown RC	6.00	1.80
❑ 117 Bryant Johnson RC	3.00	.90
❑ 118 Teyo Johnson RC	3.00	.90
❑ 119 Talman Gardner RC	3.00	.90
❑ 120 Brian St.Pierre RC	3.00	.90
❑ 121 Onterrio Smith RC	4.00	1.20
❑ 122 Marcus Trufant RC	3.00	.90
❑ 123 Earnest Graham RC	2.50	.75
❑ 124 Kareem Kelly RC	2.50	.75
❑ 125 Jason Witten RC	5.00	1.50
❑ 126 Brandon Lloyd RC	4.00	1.20
❑ 127 Anquan Boldin RC	8.00	2.40
❑ 128 Lee Suggs RC	5.00	1.50
❑ 129 Terry Pierce RC	2.50	.75
❑ 130 Dallas Clark RC	3.00	.90
❑ 131 Kelley Washington RC	3.00	.90
❑ 132 Seneca Wallace RC	3.00	.90
❑ 133 Domanick Davis RC	6.00	1.80
❑ 134 Terrence Edwards RC	2.50	.75
❑ 135 Dave Ragone RC	3.00	.90
❑ 136 Andre Johnson RC	8.00	2.40
❑ 137 Taylor Jacobs RC	3.00	.90
❑ 138 Kyle Boller RC	8.00	2.40
❑ 139 Willis McGahee RC	8.00	2.40
❑ 140 Byron Leftwich RC	12.00	3.60
❑ 141 Sam Aiken RC	2.50	.75
❑ 142 Bennie Joppru RC	3.00	.90
❑ 143 Justin Fargas RC	3.00	.90
❑ 144 Avon Cobourne RC	2.50	.75
❑ 145 Rex Grossman RC	8.00	2.40
❑ 146 LaBrandon Toefield RC	3.00	.90
❑ 147 Tyrone Calico RC	4.00	1.20
❑ 148 Brad Banks RC	2.50	.75
❑ 149 Terence Newman RC	6.00	1.80
❑ 150 Jimmy Kennedy RC	3.00	.90

2003 Topps All American Foil

Nm-Mt Ex-Mt

*STARS: 1X TO 2.5X BASIC CARDS
*ROOKIES: .6X TO 1.5X

2003 Topps All American Foil Gold

Nm-Mt Ex-Mt

*STARS: 5X TO 12X BASIC CARDS
*ROOKIES: 3X TO 8X

2003 Topps All American Autographs

Nm-Mt Ex-Mt

GROUP A STATED ODDS 1:856
GROUP B STATED ODDS 1:2007
GROUP C STATED ODDS 1:997
GROUP D STATED ODDS 1:1198
GROUP E STATED ODDS 1:598
GROUP F STATED ODDS 1:460
GROUP G STATED ODDS 1:332
GROUP H STATED ODDS 1:315
GROUP I STATED ODDS 1:28

	Nm-Mt	Ex-Mt
❑ AAAC Avon Cobourne G	12.00	3.60
❑ AAAJ Andre Johnson C	60.00	18.00
❑ AABBE Brad Banks D	20.00	6.00
❑ AABJ Bryant Johnson A	25.00	7.50
❑ AABL Byron Leftwich C	80.00	24.00
❑ AABM0 Billy McMullen I	12.00	3.60
❑ AACB Chris Brown A	50.00	15.00
❑ AACP Carson Palmer A	80.00	24.00
❑ AACR Charles Rogers A EXCH	40.00	12.00
❑ AACS Chris Simms A	50.00	15.00
❑ AAEG Earnest Graham I	12.00	3.60
❑ AAJF Justin Fargas I	15.00	4.50
❑ AAJT Jason Thomas D	12.00	3.60
❑ AAKB0 Kyle Boller B	50.00	15.00
❑ AAKD Ken Dorsey A	50.00	15.00
❑ AAKKE Kareem Kelly I	12.00	3.60
❑ AAKW Kelley Washington E	15.00	4.50
❑ AALJ0 Larry Johnson C	50.00	15.00
❑ AALS Lee Suggs B EXCH	60.00	18.00
❑ AALT LaBrandon Toefield I	15.00	4.50
❑ AAOS Onterrio Smith I	30.00	9.00
❑ AAQG Quentin Griffin H	40.00	12.00
❑ AARG0 Rex Grossman A	50.00	15.00
❑ AASW Seneca Wallace I	15.00	4.50
❑ AATC0 Tyrone Calico I	20.00	6.00
❑ AATG Talman Gardner I	12.00	3.60
❑ AATJ Taylor Jacobs E	15.00	4.50
❑ AAWM Willis McGahee F	40.00	12.00

2003 Topps All American Campus Connection Autographs

	Nm-Mt	Ex-Mt
❑ CCHS Priest Holmes Chris Simms	100.00	30.00
❑ CCMD Ken Dorsey Santana Moss	80.00	24.00
❑ CCMR Derrick Mason Charles Rogers	60.00	18.00
❑ CCPD Clinton Portis Ken Dorsey	80.00	24.00
❑ CCZC Amos Zereoue Avon Cobourne	40.00	12.00

2003 Topps All American Conference Call Autographs

	Nm-Mt	Ex-Mt
❑ CCABP Carson Palmer Kyle Boller	120.00	36.00
❑ CCACM Willis McGahee Avon Cobourne	60.00	18.00
❑ CCAGB Chris Brown Quentin Griffin	100.00	30.00
❑ CCAJR Bryant Johnson EXCH Charles Rogers	30.00	9.00
❑ CCASM Willis McGahee EXCH Lee Suggs	80.00	24.00

2001 Topps Archives

	Nm-Mt	Ex-Mt
COMPLETE SET (178)	80.00	24.00
❑ 1 Warren Moon 85	2.00	.60
❑ 2 Alan Ameche 56	.75	.23
❑ 3 Art Donovan 56	1.25	.35
❑ 4 Jackie Slater 84	.75	.23
❑ 5 Bart Starr 57	5.00	1.50
❑ 6 Billy Howton 56	.75	.23
❑ 7 Jack Youngblood 73	.75	.23
❑ 8 Billy Kilmer 62	1.25	.35
❑ 9 Billy Sims 81	.75	.23
❑ 10 Bo Jackson 88	3.00	.90
❑ 11 Bob Griese 68	2.00	.60
❑ 12 Boomer Esiason 86	1.25	.35
❑ 13 Charley Conerly 56	1.25	.35
❑ 14 Charlie Joiner 72	.75	.23
❑ 15 Christian Okoye 88	.75	.23
❑ 16 Chuck Bednarik 56	1.25	.35
❑ 17 Cliff Branch 75	1.25	.35
❑ 18 Dan Fouts 75	2.00	.60
❑ 19 Dan Marino 84	6.00	1.80
❑ 20 Dave Casper 77	.75	.23
❑ 21 Deacon Jones 63	1.25	.35
❑ 22 Dick Lane 57	.75	.23
❑ 23 Don Maynard 61	1.25	.35
❑ 24 Doug Williams 79	.75	.23

Card	Nm-Mt	Ex-Mt
❑ 25 Barry Sanders 89	4.00	1.20
❑ 26 Bubba Smith 70	1.25	.35
❑ 27 Ed Too Tall Jones 76	.75	.23
❑ 28 Chuck Foreman 74	.75	.23
❑ 29 Elroy Hirsch 56	1.25	.35
❑ 30 Eric Dickerson 84	1.25	.35
❑ 31 Harold Carmichael 74	.75	.23
❑ 32 Frank Gifford 56	2.00	.60
❑ 33 Fred Biletnikoff 65	1.25	.35
❑ 34 Gale Sayers 68	3.00	.90
❑ 35 John Brodie 61	.75	.23
❑ 36 Henry Ellard 85	.75	.23
❑ 37 Jack Lambert 76	2.00	.60
❑ 38 Jim Brown 58	4.00	1.20
❑ 39 James Lofton 79	.75	.23
❑ 40 Joe Montana 81	8.00	2.40
❑ 41 Joe Namath 65	5.00	1.50
❑ 42 Joe Theismann 75	2.00	.60
❑ 43 Tommy McDonald 57	.75	.23
❑ 44 John Elway 84	6.00	1.80
❑ 45 John Riggins 72	1.25	.35
❑ 46 Johnny Unitas 57	4.00	1.20
❑ 47 Kellen Winslow 81	.75	.23
❑ 48 Ken Anderson 73	1.25	.35
❑ 49 Ken Stabler 73	3.00	.90
❑ 50 Drew Pearson 75	1.25	.35
❑ 51 Lawrence Taylor 82	2.00	.60
❑ 52 Len Dawson 64	2.00	.60
❑ 53 Lenny Moore 56	1.25	.35
❑ 54 Lester Hayes 80	.75	.23
❑ 55 Troy Aikman 89	3.00	.90
❑ 56 Mark Clayton 85	.75	.23
❑ 57 John Taylor 89	.75	.23
❑ 58 Norm Van Brocklin 56	1.25	.35
❑ 59 Gene Upshaw 72	.75	.23
❑ 60 Otis Sistrunk 74	.75	.23
❑ 61 Ottis Anderson 80	.75	.23
❑ 62 Ozzie Newsome 79	1.25	.35
❑ 63 Paul Hornung 57	2.50	.75
❑ 64 Phil Simms 80	1.25	.35
❑ 65 Raymond Berry 57	1.25	.35
❑ 66 Roger Staubach 72	5.00	1.50
❑ 67 Ronnie Lott 82	1.25	.35
❑ 68 Roosevelt Brown 56	.75	.23
❑ 69 Roosevelt Grier 56	.75	.23
❑ 70 Sonny Jurgensen 58	2.00	.60
❑ 71 Marcus Allen 83	2.00	.60
❑ 72 Steve Grogan 76	.75	.23
❑ 73 Roger Craig 84	1.25	.35
❑ 74 Ted Hendricks 72	.75	.23
❑ 75 Jim Plunkett 72	1.25	.35
❑ 76 Terry Metcalf 74	.75	.23
❑ 77 Tom Dempsey 70	.75	.23
❑ 78 Tom Fears 56	.75	.23
❑ 79 Tony Dorsett 78	2.00	.60
❑ 80 Walter Payton 76	6.00	1.80
❑ 81 Y.A. Tittle 56	2.00	.60
❑ 82 William Perry 86	.75	.23
❑ 83 Steve Young 86	3.00	.90
❑ 84 Rodney Hampton 90	.75	.23
❑ 85 Jim Kelly 87	2.00	.60
❑ 86 Gino Marchetti 57	.75	.23
❑ 87 Sid Luckman 55	1.00	.30
❑ 88 Sammy Baugh 55	2.50	.75
❑ 89 Red Grange 55	3.00	.90
❑ 90 Otto Graham 55	2.00	.60
❑ 91 Knute Rockne 55	3.00	.90
❑ 92 Jim Thorpe 55	3.00	.90
❑ 93 Don Maynard 73	.75	.23
❑ 94 Barry Sanders 99	2.50	.75
❑ 95 Joe Theismann 86	1.25	.35
❑ 96 John Riggins 85	.75	.23
❑ 97 William Perry 93	.50	.15
❑ 98 Jim Brown 62	2.50	.75
❑ 99 Chuck Bednarik 61	.75	.23
❑ 100 Warren Moon 99	1.25	.35
❑ 101 Frank Gifford 62	1.25	.35
❑ 102 Billy Sims 86	.50	.15
❑ 103 Doug Williams 89	.50	.15
❑ 104 Lester Hayes 87	.50	.15
❑ 105 Jim Plunkett 87	.75	.23
❑ 106 Dan Marino 00	4.00	1.20
❑ 107 Jack Youngblood 85	.50	.15
❑ 108 Tom Dempsey 79	.50	.15
❑ 109 Otis Sistrunk 79	.50	.15
❑ 110 Gale Sayers 72	2.00	.60
❑ 111 Billy Howton 62	.50	.15
❑ 112 Chuck Foreman 81	.50	.15
❑ 113 Jim Kelly 97	1.25	.35
❑ 114 Norm Van Brocklin 57	.75	.23
❑ 115 Tommy McDonald 68	.50	.15
❑ 116 John Brodie 73	.50	.15
❑ 117 Art Donovan 59	.75	.23
❑ 118 Ted Hendricks 84	.50	.15
❑ 119 Henry Ellard 98	.50	.15
❑ 120 Bart Starr 71	3.00	.90
❑ 121 Bo Jackson 91	2.00	.60
❑ 122 Tom Fears 58	.50	.15
❑ 123 Drew Pearson 84	.75	.23
❑ 124 Ronnie Lott 94	.75	.23
❑ 125 Terry Metcalf 82	.50	.15
❑ 126 Lenny Moore 63	.75	.23
❑ 127 Raymond Berry 63	.75	.23
❑ 128 John Elway 99	4.00	1.20
❑ 129 Steve Grogan 90	.50	.15
❑ 130 Roger Craig 93	.75	.23
❑ 131 Bob Griese 81	1.25	.35
❑ 132 Johnny Unitas 74	2.50	.75
❑ 133 Cliff Branch 85	.75	.23
❑ 134 Billy Kilmer 78	.75	.23
❑ 135 Boomer Esiason 97	.75	.23
❑ 136 Fred Biletnikoff 79	.75	.23
❑ 137 Marcus Allen 95	1.25	.35
❑ 138 Paul Hornung 62	1.50	.45
❑ 139 Kellen Winslow 88	.50	.15
❑ 140 Joe Namath 73	3.00	.90
❑ 141 Jackie Slater 94	.50	.15
❑ 142 John Taylor 95	.50	.15
❑ 143 Phil Simms 94	.75	.23
❑ 144 Ken Stabler 83	2.00	.60
❑ 145 Dave Casper 79	.50	.15
❑ 146 Dan Fouts 87	1.25	.35
❑ 147 Dick Lane 63	.50	.15
❑ 148 Alan Ameche 61	.50	.15
❑ 149 Sonny Jurgensen 72	1.25	.35
❑ 150 Harold Carmichael 84	.50	.15
❑ 151 Ed Too Tall Jones 89	.50	.15
❑ 152 Lawrence Taylor 93	1.25	.35
❑ 153 Ken Anderson 85	.75	.23
❑ 154 Deacon Jones 74	.75	.23
❑ 155 Ozzie Newsome 90	.75	.23
❑ 156 Steve Young 00	2.00	.60
❑ 157 Charlie Joiner 87	.50	.15
❑ 158 Tony Dorsett 89	1.25	.35
❑ 159 Christian Okoye 93	.50	.15
❑ 160 Charley Conerly 61	.75	.23
❑ 161 Elroy Hirsch 57	.75	.23
❑ 162 Len Dawson 76	1.25	.35
❑ 163 Jack Lambert 85	1.25	.35
❑ 164 Mark Clayton 93	.50	.15
❑ 165 Y.A. Tittle 63	1.25	.35
❑ 166 Troy Aikman 01	2.00	.60
❑ 167 Roger Staubach 79	3.00	.90
❑ 168 Roosevelt Grier 63	.50	.15
❑ 169 Gino Marchetti 63	.50	.15
❑ 170 Walter Payton 87	4.00	1.20
❑ 171 Rodney Hampton 97	.50	.15
❑ 172 Eric Dickerson 92	.75	.23
❑ 173 Ottis Anderson 91	.50	.15
❑ 174 James Lofton 93	.50	.15
❑ 175 Bubba Smith 76	.75	.23
❑ 176 Roosevelt Brown 61	.50	.15
❑ 177 Gene Upshaw 81	.50	.15
❑ 178 Joe Montana 95	5.00	1.50
❑ NNO Checklist	.20	.06

2001 Topps Archives Rookie Reprint Autographs

Card	Nm-Mt	Ex-Mt
❑ AABG Bob Griese C	80.00	24.00
❑ AABK Billy Kilmer	20.00	6.00
❑ AABS Barry Sanders C	150.00	45.00
❑ AABSI Billy Sims J	25.00	7.50
❑ AABSM Bubba Smith J	30.00	9.00
❑ AACB Cliff Branch	25.00	7.50
❑ AACBE Chuck Bednarik J	30.00	9.00
❑ AACO Christian Okoye K	20.00	6.00

Card	Nm-Mt	Ex-Mt
❑ AADB Dick Butkus D	80.00	24.00
❑ AADC Dave Casper J	25.00	7.50
❑ AADF Dan Fouts F	50.00	15.00
❑ AADJ Deacon Jones J	30.00	9.00
❑ AADMA Don Maynard L	20.00	6.00
❑ AADW Doug Williams I	30.00	9.00
❑ AAED Eric Dickerson F	30.00	9.00
❑ AAEJ Ed Too Tall Jones J	25.00	7.50
❑ AAFG Frank Gifford E	50.00	15.00
❑ AAGM Gino Marchetti I	30.00	9.00
❑ AAGS Gale Sayers F	60.00	18.00
❑ AAHE Henry Ellard I	20.00	6.00
❑ AAJB Jim Brown B		
❑ AAJH John Hannah	20.00	6.00
❑ AAJM Joe Montana B	300.00	90.00
❑ AAJN Joe Namath A	250.00	75.00
❑ AAJR John Riggins G	50.00	15.00
❑ AAJU Johnny Unitas H	250.00	75.00
❑ AAKA Ken Anderson J	25.00	7.50
❑ AAKW Kellen Winslow F	40.00	12.00
❑ AALD Len Dawson E	40.00	12.00
❑ AALH Lester Hayes J	30.00	9.00
❑ AALT Lawrence Taylor B	125.00	38.00
❑ AAMA Marcus Allen B	80.00	24.00
❑ AAMC Mark Clayton K	25.00	7.50
❑ AAOA Ottis Anderson J	20.00	6.00
❑ AAON Ozzie Newsome F	25.00	7.50
❑ AARB Roosevelt Brown J	30.00	9.00
❑ AARBE Raymond Berry I	30.00	9.00
❑ AARG Roosevelt Grier J	25.00	7.50
❑ AARH Rodney Hampton J	20.00	6.00
❑ AARS Roger Staubach F	150.00	45.00
❑ AASG Steve Grogan J	25.00	7.50
❑ AATD Tom Dempsey	20.00	6.00
❑ AATH Ted Hendricks K	20.00	6.00
❑ AAWP William Perry J	20.00	6.00
❑ AAYT Y.A. Tittle I	30.00	9.00

2001 Topps Archives Reserve Rookie Reprint Autographs

Card	Nm-Mt	Ex-Mt
❑ ARABK Billy Kilmer	15.00	4.50
❑ ARABS Barry Sanders	120.00	36.00
❑ ARACB Cliff Branch	20.00	6.00
❑ ARACF Chuck Foreman	15.00	4.50
❑ ARACJ Charlie Joiner	15.00	4.50
❑ ARADB Dick Butkus	100.00	30.00
❑ ARADC Dave Casper	20.00	6.00

❑ ARADJ Deacon Jones	20.00	6.00
❑ ARADM Don Maynard	15.00	4.50
❑ ARADW Doug Williams	25.00	7.50
❑ ARAED Eric Dickerson	30.00	9.00
❑ ARAEJ Ed Too Tall Jones	20.00	6.00
❑ ARAFG Frank Gifford	50.00	15.00
❑ ARAHE Henry Ellard	15.00	4.50
❑ ARAJH John Hannah	15.00	4.50
❑ ARAJM Joe Montana	275.00	80.00
❑ ARAJN Joe Namath	200.00	60.00
❑ ARAJR John Riggins	60.00	18.00
❑ ARAJU Johnny Unitas	200.00	60.00
❑ ARALD Len Dawson	40.00	12.00
❑ ARALH Lester Hayes	25.00	7.50
❑ ARALT Lawrence Taylor	80.00	24.00
❑ ARAMA Marcus Allen	50.00	15.00
❑ ARAMC Mark Clayton	15.00	4.50
❑ ARAON Ozzie Newsome	15.00	4.50
❑ ARARB Raymond Berry	25.00	7.50
❑ ARARH Rodney Hampton	15.00	4.50
❑ ARATD Tom Dempsey	15.00	4.50
❑ ARATH Ted Hendricks	15.00	4.50
❑ ARATM Terry Metcalf	15.00	4.50
❑ ARAWP William Perry	15.00	4.50

1996 Topps Chrome

	Nm-Mt	Ex-Mt
COMPLETE SET (165)	100.00	45.00
❑ 1 Troy Aikman	2.50	1.10
❑ 2 Kevin Greene	.50	.23
❑ 3 Robert Brooks	1.00	.45
❑ 4 Junior Seau	1.00	.45
❑ 5 Brett Perriman	.20	.09
❑ 6 Cortez Kennedy	.20	.09
❑ 7 Orlando Thomas	.20	.09
❑ 8 Anthony Miller	.50	.23
❑ 9 Jeff Blake	1.00	.45
❑ 10 Trent Dilfer	1.00	.45
❑ 11 Heath Shuler	.50	.23
❑ 12 Michael Jackson	.50	.23
❑ 13 Merton Hanks	.20	.09
❑ 14 Dale Carter	.20	.09
❑ 15 Eric Metcalf	.20	.09
❑ 16 Barry Sanders	4.00	1.80
❑ 17 Joey Galloway	1.00	.45
❑ 18 Bryan Cox	.20	.09
❑ 19 Harvey Williams	.20	.09
❑ 20 Terrell Davis	1.50	.70
❑ 21 Darnay Scott	.50	.23
❑ 22 Kerry Collins	1.00	.45
❑ 23 Warren Sapp	.20	.09
❑ 24 Michael Westbrook	1.00	.45
❑ 25 Mark Brunell	1.50	.70
❑ 26 Craig Heyward	.20	.09
❑ 27 Eric Allen	.20	.09
❑ 28 Dana Stubblefield	.50	.23
❑ 29 Steve Bono	.20	.09
❑ 30 Larry Brown	.20	.09
❑ 31 Warren Moon	.50	.23
❑ 32 Jim Kelly	1.00	.45
❑ 33 Terry McDaniel	.20	.09
❑ 34 Dan Wilkinson	.20	.09
❑ 35 Dave Brown	.20	.09
❑ 36 Todd Lyght	.20	.09
❑ 37 Aeneas Williams	.20	.09
❑ 38 Shannon Sharpe	.50	.23
❑ 39 Errict Rhett	.50	.23
❑ 40 Yancey Thigpen	.50	.23
❑ 41 J.J. Stokes	1.00	.45
❑ 42 Marshall Faulk	1.25	.55
❑ 43 Chester McGlockton	.20	.09
❑ 44 Darryll Lewis	.20	.09
❑ 45 Drew Bledsoe	1.50	.70
❑ 46 Tyrone Wheatley	.50	.23
❑ 47 Herman Moore	.50	.23
❑ 48 Darren Woodson	.50	.23
❑ 49 Ricky Watters	.50	.23
❑ 50 Emmitt Smith TYC	1.50	.70
❑ 51 Barry Sanders TYC	1.50	.70
❑ 52 Curtis Martin TYC	1.00	.45
❑ 53 Chris Warren TYC	.50	.23
❑ 54 Errict Rhett TYC	.50	.23
❑ 55 Rodney Hampton TYC	.20	.09
❑ 56 Terrell Davis TYC	1.00	.45
❑ 57 Marshall Faulk TYC	1.00	.45
❑ 58 Rashaan Salaam TYC	.50	.23
❑ 59 Curtis Conway	1.00	.45
❑ 60 Isaac Bruce	1.00	.45
❑ 61 Thurman Thomas	1.00	.45
❑ 62 Terry Allen	.50	.23
❑ 63 Lamar Lathon	.20	.09
❑ 64 Mark Chmura	.50	.23
❑ 65 Chris Warren	.50	.23
❑ 66 Jessie Tuggle	.20	.09
❑ 67 Erik Kramer	.20	.09
❑ 68 Tim Brown	1.00	.45
❑ 69 Derrick Thomas	.50	.23
❑ 70 Willie McGinest	.20	.09
❑ 71 Frank Sanders	.50	.23
❑ 72 Bernie Parmalee	.20	.09
❑ 73 Kordell Stewart	1.00	.45
❑ 74 Brent Jones	.20	.09
❑ 75 Edgar Bennett	.50	.23
❑ 76 Rashaan Salaam	.50	.23
❑ 77 Carl Pickens	.50	.23
❑ 78 Terance Mathis	.20	.09
❑ 79 Deion Sanders	1.25	.55
❑ 80 Glyn Milburn	.20	.09
❑ 81 Lee Woodall	.20	.09
❑ 82 Neil Smith	.50	.23
❑ 83 Stan Humphries	.50	.23
❑ 84 Rick Mirer	.50	.23
❑ 85 Troy Vincent	.20	.09
❑ 86 Sam Mills	.20	.09
❑ 87 Brian Mitchell	.20	.09
❑ 88 Hardy Nickerson	.20	.09
❑ 89 Tamarick Vanover	.50	.23
❑ 90 Steve McNair	1.50	.70
❑ 91 Jerry Rice TYC	1.00	.45
❑ 92 Isaac Bruce TYC	1.00	.45
❑ 93 Herman Moore TYC	.50	.23
❑ 94 Cris Carter TYC	1.00	.45
❑ 95 Tim Brown TYC	.50	.23
❑ 96 Carl Pickens TYC	.50	.23
❑ 97 Joey Galloway TYC	1.00	.45
❑ 98 Jerry Rice	2.50	1.10
❑ 99 Cris Carter	1.00	.45
❑ 100 Curtis Martin	1.50	.70
❑ 101 Scott Mitchell	.50	.23
❑ 102 Ken Harvey	.20	.09
❑ 103 Rodney Hampton	.50	.23
❑ 104 Reggie White	1.00	.45
❑ 105 Eddie Robinson	.20	.09
❑ 106 Greg Lloyd	.50	.23
❑ 107 Phillippi Sparks	.20	.09
❑ 108 Emmitt Smith	4.00	1.80
❑ 109 Tom Carter	.20	.09
❑ 110 Jim Everett	.20	.09
❑ 111 James O.Stewart	.50	.23
❑ 112 Kyle Brady	.20	.09
❑ 113 Irving Fryar	.50	.23
❑ 114 Vinny Testaverde	.50	.23
❑ 115 John Elway	5.00	2.20
❑ 116 Chris Spielman	.20	.09
❑ 117 Mike Mamula	.20	.09
❑ 118 Jim Harbaugh	.50	.23
❑ 119 Ken Norton	.20	.09
❑ 120 Bruce Smith	.50	.23
❑ 121 Daryl Johnston	.50	.23
❑ 122 Blaine Bishop	.20	.09
❑ 123 Jeff George	.50	.23
❑ 124 Jeff Hostetler	.20	.09
❑ 125 Jerome Bettis	1.00	.45
❑ 126 Jay Novacek	.20	.09
❑ 127 Bryce Paup	.20	.09
❑ 128 Neil O'Donnell	.50	.23
❑ 129 Marcus Allen	1.00	.45
❑ 130 Steve Young	1.50	.70
❑ 131 Brett Favre TYC	2.00	.90
❑ 132 Scott Mitchell TYC	.20	.09
❑ 133 John Elway TYC	2.00	.90
❑ 134 Jeff Blake TYC	.50	.23
❑ 135 Dan Marino TYC	2.00	.90
❑ 136 Drew Bledsoe TYC	1.00	.45
❑ 137 Troy Aikman TYC	1.00	.45
❑ 138 Steve Young TYC	1.00	.45
❑ 139 Jim Kelly TYC	1.00	.45
❑ 140 Jeff Graham	.20	.09
❑ 141 Hugh Douglas	.50	.23
❑ 142 Dan Marino	5.00	2.20
❑ 143 Darrell Green	.20	.09
❑ 144 Eric Zeier	.20	.09
❑ 145 Brett Favre	5.00	2.20
❑ 146 Carnell Lake	.20	.09
❑ 147 Ben Coates	.50	.23
❑ 148 Tony Martin	.50	.23
❑ 149 Michael Irvin	1.00	.45
❑ 150 Lawrence Phillips RC	1.00	.45
❑ 151 Alex Van Dyke RC	1.50	.70
❑ 152 Kevin Hardy RC	1.50	.70
❑ 153 Rickey Dudley RC	5.00	2.20
❑ 154 Eric Moulds RC	12.00	5.50
❑ 155 Simeon Rice RC	4.00	1.80
❑ 156 Marvin Harrison RC	25.00	11.00
❑ 157 Tim Biakabutuka RC	4.00	1.80
❑ 158 Duane Clemons RC	1.00	.45
❑ 159 Keyshawn Johnson RC	10.00	4.50
❑ 160 John Mobley RC	1.50	.70
❑ 161 Leeland McElroy RC	1.50	.70
❑ 162 Eddie George RC	15.00	6.75
❑ 163 Jonathan Ogden RC	2.00	.90
❑ 164 Eddie Kennison RC	5.00	2.20
❑ 165 Checklist	.20	.09

1996 Topps Chrome Refractors

	Nm-Mt	Ex-Mt
*REF.STARS: 2X TO 5X BASIC CARDS		
*UNLISTED REF.RCs: .8X TO 2X		
❑ 154 Eric Moulds	40.00	18.00
❑ 156 Marvin Harrison	100.00	45.00
❑ 159 Keyshawn Johnson	30.00	13.50
❑ 162 Eddie George	60.00	27.00

1997 Topps Chrome

	Nm-Mt	Ex-Mt
COMPLETE SET (165)	60.00	27.00
❑ 1 Brett Favre	6.00	2.70
❑ 2 Tim Biakabutuka	1.00	.45
❑ 3 Deion Sanders	1.50	.70
❑ 4 Marshall Faulk	2.00	.90
❑ 5 John Randle	1.00	.45
❑ 6 Stan Humphries	1.00	.45
❑ 7 Ki-Jana Carter	.60	.25
❑ 8 Rashaan Salaam	.60	.25
❑ 9 Rickey Dudley	1.00	.45
❑ 10 Isaac Bruce	1.50	.70

❑ 11 Keyshawn Johnson 1.50 .70
❑ 12 Ben Coates 1.00 .45
❑ 13 Ty Detmer 1.00 .45
❑ 14 Gus Frerotte .60 .25
❑ 15 Mario Bates .60 .25
❑ 16 Chris Calloway .60 .25
❑ 17 Frank Sanders 1.00 .45
❑ 18 Bruce Smith 1.00 .45
❑ 19 Jeff Graham .60 .25
❑ 20 Trent Dilfer 1.50 .70
❑ 21 Tyrone Wheatley 1.00 .45
❑ 22 Chris Warren 1.00 .45
❑ 23 Terry Kirby 1.00 .45
❑ 24 Tony Gonzalez RC 8.00 3.60
❑ 25 Ricky Watters 1.00 .45
❑ 26 Tamarick Vanover 1.00 .45
❑ 27 Kerry Collins 1.50 .70
❑ 28 Bobby Engram 1.00 .45
❑ 29 Derrick Alexander WR 1.00 .45
❑ 30 Hugh Douglas .60 .25
❑ 31 Thurman Thomas 1.50 .70
❑ 32 Drew Bledsoe 2.00 .90
❑ 33 LeShon Johnson .60 .25
❑ 34 Byron Bam Morris .60 .25
❑ 35 Herman Moore 1.00 .45
❑ 36 Troy Aikman 3.00 1.35
❑ 37 Mel Gray .60 .25
❑ 38 Adrian Murrell 1.00 .45
❑ 39 Carl Pickens 1.00 .45
❑ 40 Tony Brackens .60 .25
❑ 41 O.J. McDuffie 1.00 .45
❑ 42 Napoleon Kaufman 1.50 .70
❑ 43 Chris T. Jones .60 .25
❑ 44 Kordell Stewart 1.50 .70
❑ 45 Steve Young 2.00 .90
❑ 46 Shannon Sharpe 1.00 .45
❑ 47 Leeland McElroy .60 .25
❑ 48 Eric Moulds 1.50 .70
❑ 49 Eddie George 1.50 .70
❑ 50 Jamal Anderson 1.50 .70
❑ 51 Robert Smith 1.00 .45
❑ 52 Mike Alstott 1.50 .70
❑ 53 Darrell Green 1.00 .45
❑ 54 Irving Fryar 1.00 .45
❑ 55 Derrick Thomas 1.00 .45
❑ 56 Antonio Freeman 1.50 .70
❑ 57 Terrell Davis 2.00 .90
❑ 58 Henry Ellard .60 .25
❑ 59 Daryl Johnston 1.00 .45
❑ 60 Bryan Cox .60 .25
❑ 61 Vinny Testaverde 1.00 .45
❑ 62 Andre Reed 1.00 .45
❑ 63 Larry Centers 1.00 .45
❑ 64 Hardy Nickerson .60 .25
❑ 65 Tony Banks 1.00 .45
❑ 66 Dave Meggett .60 .25
❑ 67 Simeon Rice 1.00 .45
❑ 68 Warrick Dunn RC 6.00 2.70
❑ 69 Michael Irvin 1.50 .70
❑ 70 John Elway 6.00 2.70
❑ 71 Jake Reed 1.00 .45
❑ 72 Rodney Hampton 1.00 .45
❑ 73 Aaron Glenn .60 .25
❑ 74 Terry Allen 1.50 .70
❑ 75 Blaine Bishop .60 .25
❑ 76 Bert Emanuel 1.00 .45
❑ 77 Mark Carrier WR .60 .25
❑ 78 Jimmy Smith 1.00 .45
❑ 79 Jim Harbaugh 1.00 .45
❑ 80 Brent Jones 1.00 .45
❑ 81 Emmitt Smith 5.00 2.20
❑ 82 Fred Barnett .60 .25
❑ 83 Errict Rhett .60 .25
❑ 84 Michael Sinclair .60 .25
❑ 85 Jerome Bettis 1.50 .70
❑ 86 Chris Sanders .60 .25
❑ 87 Kent Graham .60 .25
❑ 88 Cris Carter 1.50 .70
❑ 89 Harvey Williams .60 .25
❑ 90 Eric Allen .60 .25
❑ 91 Bryant Young .60 .25
❑ 92 Marcus Allen 1.50 .70
❑ 93 Michael Jackson 1.00 .45
❑ 94 Mark Chmura 1.00 .45
❑ 95 Keenan McCardell 1.00 .45
❑ 96 Joey Galloway 1.00 .45
❑ 97 Eddie Kennison 1.00 .45
❑ 98 Steve Atwater .60 .25
❑ 99 Dorsey Levens 1.50 .70
❑ 100 Rob Moore 1.00 .45
❑ 101 Steve McNair 2.00 .90
❑ 102 Sean Dawkins .60 .25
❑ 103 Don Beebe .60 .25
❑ 104 Willie McGinest .60 .25
❑ 105 Tony Martin 1.00 .45
❑ 106 Mark Brunell 2.00 .90
❑ 107 Karim Abdul-Jabbar 1.50 .70
❑ 108 Michael Westbrook 1.00 .45
❑ 109 Lawrence Phillips .60 .25
❑ 110 Barry Sanders 5.00 2.20
❑ 111 Willie Davis .60 .25
❑ 112 Wesley Walls 1.00 .45
❑ 113 Todd Collins .60 .25
❑ 114 Jerry Rice 3.00 1.35
❑ 115 Scott Mitchell 1.00 .45
❑ 116 Terance Mathis 1.00 .45
❑ 117 Chris Spielman .60 .25
❑ 118 Curtis Conway 1.00 .45
❑ 119 Marvin Harrison 1.50 .70
❑ 120 Terry Glenn 1.50 .70
❑ 121 Dave Brown .60 .25
❑ 122 Neil O'Donnell 1.00 .45
❑ 123 Junior Seau 1.50 .70
❑ 124 Reggie White 1.50 .70
❑ 125 Lamar Lathon .60 .25
❑ 126 Natrone Means 1.00 .45
❑ 127 Tim Brown 1.50 .70
❑ 128 Eric Swann .60 .25
❑ 129 Dan Marino 6.00 2.70
❑ 130 Anthony Johnson .60 .25
❑ 131 Edgar Bennett 1.00 .45
❑ 132 Kevin Hardy .60 .25
❑ 133 Brian Blades .60 .25
❑ 134 Curtis Martin 2.00 .90
❑ 135 Zach Thomas 1.50 .70
❑ 136 Darnay Scott 1.00 .45
❑ 137 Desmond Howard 1.00 .45
❑ 138 Aeneas Williams .60 .25
❑ 139 Bryce Paup .60 .25
❑ 140 Brad Johnson 1.50 .70
❑ 141 Jeff Blake 1.00 .45
❑ 142 Wayne Chrebet 1.50 .70
❑ 143 Will Blackwell RC 1.25 .55
❑ 144 Tom Knight RC .60 .25
❑ 145 Darnell Autry RC 1.00 .45
❑ 146 Bryant Westbrook RC .60 .25
❑ 147 David LaFleur RC .75 .35
❑ 148 Antowain Smith RC 8.00 3.60
❑ 149 Rae Carruth RC .75 .35
❑ 150 Jim Druckenmiller RC 1.00 .45
❑ 151 Shawn Springs RC .75 .35
❑ 152 Troy Davis RC 1.25 .55
❑ 153 Orlando Pace RC 2.00 .90
❑ 154 Byron Hanspard RC 1.25 .55
❑ 155 Corey Dillon RC 20.00 9.00
❑ 156 Reidel Anthony RC 2.00 .90
❑ 157 Peter Boulware RC 2.00 .90
❑ 158 Reinard Wilson RC 1.25 .55
❑ 159 Pat Barnes RC 2.00 .90
❑ 160 Joey Kent RC 2.00 .90
❑ 161 Ike Hilliard RC 3.00 1.35
❑ 162 Jake Plummer RC 15.00 6.75
❑ 163 Darrell Russell RC .75 .35
❑ 164 Checklist Card .60 .25
❑ 165 Checklist Card .60 .25

1997 Topps Chrome Refractors

	Nm-Mt	Ex-Mt
COMPLETE SET (165)	800.00	350.00

*STARS: 2X TO 5X BASIC CARDS
*RC'S: 1.2X TO 3X BASIC CARDS

❑ 24 Tony Gonzalez 50.00 22.00
❑ 68 Warrick Dunn 40.00 18.00
❑ 148 Antowain Smith 50.00 22.00
❑ 155 Corey Dillon 100.00 45.00
❑ 162 Jake Plummer 80.00 36.00

1998 Topps Chrome

	Nm-Mt	Ex-Mt
COMPLETE SET (165)	120.00	55.00

❑ 1 Barry Sanders 4.00 1.80
❑ 2 Duane Starks RC 2.00 .90
❑ 3 J.J. Stokes .75 .35
❑ 4 Joey Galloway .75 .35
❑ 5 Deion Sanders 1.25 .55
❑ 6 Anthony Miller .50 .23
❑ 7 Jamal Anderson 1.25 .55
❑ 8 Shannon Sharpe .75 .35
❑ 9 Irving Fryar .75 .35
❑ 10 Curtis Martin 1.25 .55
❑ 11 Shawn Jefferson .50 .23
❑ 12 Charlie Garner .75 .35
❑ 13 Robert Edwards RC 3.00 1.35
❑ 14 Napoleon Kaufman 1.25 .55
❑ 15 Gus Frerotte .50 .23
❑ 16 John Elway 5.00 2.20
❑ 17 Jerome Pathon RC 4.00 1.80
❑ 18 Marshall Faulk 1.50 .70
❑ 19 Michael McCrary .50 .23
❑ 20 Marcus Allen 1.25 .55
❑ 21 Trent Dilfer 1.25 .55
❑ 22 Frank Wycheck .50 .23
❑ 23 Terrell Owens 1.25 .55
❑ 24 Herman Moore .75 .35
❑ 25 Neil O'Donnell .75 .35
❑ 26 Darnay Scott .75 .35
❑ 27 Keith Brooking RC 4.00 1.80
❑ 28 Eric Green .50 .23
❑ 29 Dan Marino 5.00 2.20
❑ 30 Antonio Freeman 1.25 .55
❑ 31 Tony Martin .75 .35
❑ 32 Isaac Bruce 1.25 .55
❑ 33 Rickey Dudley .50 .23
❑ 34 Scott Mitchell .75 .35
❑ 35 Randy Moss RC 20.00 9.00
❑ 36 Fred Lane .50 .23
❑ 37 Frank Sanders .75 .35
❑ 38 Jerry Rice 2.50 1.10
❑ 39 O.J. McDuffie .75 .35
❑ 40 Jessie Armstead .50 .23
❑ 41 Reidel Anthony .75 .35
❑ 42 Steve McNair 1.25 .55
❑ 43 Jake Reed .75 .35
❑ 44 Charles Woodson RC 5.00 2.20
❑ 45 Tiki Barber 1.25 .55
❑ 46 Mike Alstott 1.25 .55
❑ 47 Keyshawn Johnson 1.25 .55
❑ 48 Tony Banks .75 .35
❑ 49 Michael Westbrook .75 .35
❑ 50 Chris Slade .50 .23
❑ 51 Terry Allen 1.25 .55
❑ 52 Karim Abdul-Jabbar 1.25 .55
❑ 53 Brad Johnson 1.25 .55
❑ 54 Tony McGee .50 .23
❑ 55 Kevin Dyson RC 4.00 1.80
❑ 56 Warren Moon 1.25 .55
❑ 57 Byron Hanspard .50 .23
❑ 58 Jermaine Lewis .75 .35
❑ 59 Neil Smith .75 .35
❑ 60 Tamarick Vanover .50 .23
❑ 61 Terrell Davis 1.25 .55
❑ 62 Robert Smith 1.25 .55
❑ 63 Junior Seau 1.25 .55

❑ 64 Warren Sapp	.75	.35
❑ 65 Michael Sinclair	.50	.23
❑ 66 Ryan Leaf RC	4.00	1.80
❑ 67 Drew Bledsoe	2.00	.90
❑ 68 Jason Sehorn	.75	.35
❑ 69 Andre Hastings	.50	.23
❑ 70 Tony Gonzalez	1.25	.55
❑ 71 Dorsey Levens	1.25	.55
❑ 72 Ray Lewis	1.25	.55
❑ 73 Grant Wistrom RC	3.00	1.35
❑ 74 Elvis Grbac	.75	.35
❑ 75 Mark Chmura	.75	.35
❑ 76 Zach Thomas	1.25	.55
❑ 77 Ben Coates	.75	.35
❑ 78 Rod Smith WR	.75	.35
❑ 79 Andre Wadsworth RC	3.00	1.35
❑ 80 Garrison Hearst	1.25	.55
❑ 81 Will Blackwell	.50	.23
❑ 82 Cris Carter	1.25	.55
❑ 83 Mark Fields	.50	.23
❑ 84 Ken Dilger	.50	.23
❑ 85 Johnnie Morton	.75	.35
❑ 86 Michael Irvin	1.25	.55
❑ 87 Eddie George	1.25	.55
❑ 88 Rob Moore	.75	.35
❑ 89 Takeo Spikes RC	4.00	1.80
❑ 90 Wesley Walls	.75	.35
❑ 91 Andre Reed	.75	.35
❑ 92 Thurman Thomas	1.25	.55
❑ 93 Ed McCaffrey	.75	.35
❑ 94 Carl Pickens	.75	.35
❑ 95 Jason Taylor	.75	.35
❑ 96 Kordell Stewart	1.25	.55
❑ 97 Greg Ellis RC	2.00	.90
❑ 98 Aaron Glenn	.50	.23
❑ 99 Jake Plummer	1.25	.55
❑ 100 Checklist	.50	.23
❑ 101 Chris Sanders	.50	.23
❑ 102 Michael Jackson	.50	.23
❑ 103 Bobby Hoying	.75	.35
❑ 104 Wayne Chrebet	1.25	.55
❑ 105 Charles Way	.50	.23
❑ 106 Derrick Thomas	.75	.35
❑ 107 Troy Drayton	.50	.23
❑ 108 Robert Holcombe RC	3.00	1.35
❑ 109 Pete Mitchell	.50	.23
❑ 110 Bruce Smith	.75	.35
❑ 111 Terance Mathis	.75	.35
❑ 112 Lawrence Phillips	.50	.23
❑ 113 Brett Favre	5.00	2.20
❑ 114 Darrell Green	.75	.35
❑ 115 Charles Johnson	.50	.23
❑ 116 Jeff Blake	.75	.35
❑ 117 Mark Brunell	1.25	.55
❑ 118 Simeon Rice	.75	.35
❑ 119 Robert Brooks	.75	.35
❑ 120 Jacquez Green RC	3.00	1.35
❑ 121 Willie Davis	.50	.23
❑ 122 Jeff George	.75	.35
❑ 123 Andre Rison	.75	.35
❑ 124 Erik Kramer	.50	.23
❑ 125 Peter Boulware	.50	.23
❑ 126 Marcus Nash RC	2.00	.90
❑ 127 Troy Aikman	2.50	1.10
❑ 128 Keenan McCardell	.75	.35
❑ 129 Bryant Westbrook	.50	.23
❑ 130 Terry Glenn	1.25	.55
❑ 131 Blaine Bishop	.50	.23
❑ 132 Tim Brown	1.25	.55
❑ 133 Brian Griese RC	8.00	3.60
❑ 134 John Mobley	.50	.23
❑ 135 Larry Centers	.50	.23
❑ 136 Eric Bjornson	.50	.23
❑ 137 Kevin Hardy	.50	.23
❑ 138 John Randle	.75	.35
❑ 139 Michael Strahan	.75	.35
❑ 140 Jerome Bettis	1.25	.55
❑ 141 Rae Carruth	.50	.23
❑ 142 Reggie White	1.25	.55
❑ 143 Antowain Smith	1.25	.55
❑ 144 Aeneas Williams	.50	.23
❑ 145 Bobby Engram	.75	.35
❑ 146 Germane Crowell RC	3.00	1.35
❑ 147 Freddie Jones	.50	.23
❑ 148 Kimble Anders	.75	.35
❑ 149 Steve Young	1.50	.70
❑ 150 Willie McGinest	.50	.23
❑ 151 Emmitt Smith	4.00	1.80
❑ 152 Fred Taylor RC	6.00	2.70
❑ 153 Danny Kanell	.75	.35
❑ 154 Warrick Dunn	1.25	.55
❑ 155 Kerry Collins	.75	.35
❑ 156 Chris Chandler	.75	.35
❑ 157 Curtis Conway	.75	.35
❑ 158 Curtis Enis RC	2.00	.90
❑ 159 Corey Dillon	1.25	.55
❑ 160 Glenn Foley	.75	.35
❑ 161 Marvin Harrison	1.25	.55
❑ 162 Chad Brown	.50	.23
❑ 163 Derrick Rodgers	.50	.23
❑ 164 Levon Kirkland	.50	.23
❑ 165 Peyton Manning RC	40.00	18.00

1998 Topps Chrome Refractors

	Nm-Mt	Ex-Mt
*REFRACT.STARS: 4X TO 10X BASIC CARDS		
*UNLISTED REF.RCs: 1X TO 2.5X		
❑ 35 Randy Moss	80.00	36.00
❑ 133 Brian Griese	40.00	18.00
❑ 152 Fred Taylor	30.00	13.50
❑ 158 Curtis Enis	20.00	9.00
❑ 165 Peyton Manning	150.00	70.00

1999 Topps Chrome

	Nm-Mt	Ex-Mt
COMPLETE SET (165)	200.00	90.00
COMP.SET w/o SP's (135)	50.00	22.00
❑ 1 Randy Moss	3.00	1.35
❑ 2 Keyshawn Johnson	1.25	.55
❑ 3 Priest Holmes	2.00	.90
❑ 4 Warren Moon	1.25	.55
❑ 5 Joey Galloway	.75	.35
❑ 6 Zach Thomas	1.25	.55
❑ 7 Cam Cleeland	.50	.23
❑ 8 Jim Harbaugh	.75	.35
❑ 9 Napoleon Kaufman	1.25	.55
❑ 10 Fred Taylor	1.25	.55
❑ 11 Mark Brunell	1.25	.55
❑ 12 Shannon Sharpe	.75	.35
❑ 13 Jacquez Green	.50	.23
❑ 14 Adrian Murrell	.75	.35
❑ 15 Cris Carter	1.25	.55
❑ 16 Jerome Pathon	.50	.23
❑ 17 Drew Bledsoe	1.50	.70
❑ 18 Curtis Martin	1.25	.55
❑ 19 Johnnie Morton	.75	.35
❑ 20 Doug Flutie	1.25	.55
❑ 21 Carl Pickens	.75	.35
❑ 22 Jerome Bettis	1.25	.55
❑ 23 Derrick Alexander	.50	.23
❑ 24 Antowain Smith	1.25	.55
❑ 25 Barry Sanders	4.00	1.80
❑ 26 Reidel Anthony	.75	.35
❑ 27 Wayne Chrebet	.75	.35
❑ 28 Terance Mathis	.75	.35
❑ 29 Shawn Springs	.50	.23
❑ 30 Emmitt Smith	2.50	1.10
❑ 31 Robert Smith	1.25	.55
❑ 32 Charles Johnson	.50	.23
❑ 33 Mike Alstott	1.25	.55
❑ 34 Ike Hilliard	.50	.23
❑ 35 Ricky Watters	.75	.35
❑ 36 Charles Woodson	1.25	.55
❑ 37 Rod Smith	.75	.35
❑ 38 Pete Mitchell	.50	.23
❑ 39 Derrick Thomas	.75	.35
❑ 40 Dan Marino	4.00	1.80
❑ 41 Darnay Scott	.50	.23
❑ 42 Jake Reed	.75	.35
❑ 43 Chris Chandler	.75	.35
❑ 44 Dorsey Levens	1.25	.55
❑ 45 Kordell Stewart	.75	.35
❑ 46 Eddie George	1.25	.55
❑ 47 Corey Dillon	1.25	.55
❑ 48 Rich Gannon	1.25	.55
❑ 49 Chris Spielman	.50	.23
❑ 50 Jerry Rice	2.50	1.10
❑ 51 Trent Dilfer	.75	.35
❑ 52 Mark Chmura	.50	.23
❑ 53 Jimmy Smith	.75	.35
❑ 54 Isaac Bruce	1.25	.55
❑ 55 Karim Abdul-Jabbar	.75	.35
❑ 56 Sedrick Shaw	.50	.23
❑ 57 Jake Plummer	.75	.35
❑ 58 Tony Gonzalez	1.25	.55
❑ 59 Ben Coates	.75	.35
❑ 60 John Elway	4.00	1.80
❑ 61 Bruce Smith	.75	.35
❑ 62 Tim Brown	1.25	.55
❑ 63 Tim Dwight	1.25	.55
❑ 64 Yancey Thigpen	.50	.23
❑ 65 Terrell Owens	1.25	.55
❑ 66 Kyle Brady	.50	.23
❑ 67 Tony Martin	.75	.35
❑ 68 Michael Strahan	.75	.35
❑ 69 Deion Sanders	1.25	.55
❑ 70 Steve Young	1.50	.70
❑ 71 Dale Carter	.50	.23
❑ 72 Ty Law	.75	.35
❑ 73 Frank Wycheck	.50	.23
❑ 74 Marshall Faulk	1.50	.70
❑ 75 Vinny Testaverde	.75	.35
❑ 76 Chad Brown	.50	.23
❑ 77 Natrone Means	.75	.35
❑ 78 Bert Emanuel	.75	.35
❑ 79 Kerry Collins	.75	.35
❑ 80 Randall Cunningham	1.25	.55
❑ 81 Garrison Hearst	.75	.35
❑ 82 Curtis Enis	.50	.23
❑ 83 Steve Atwater	.50	.23
❑ 84 Kevin Greene	.50	.23
❑ 85 Steve McNair	1.25	.55
❑ 86 Andre Reed	.75	.35
❑ 87 J.J. Stokes	.75	.35
❑ 88 Eric Moulds	1.25	.55
❑ 89 Marvin Harrison	1.25	.55
❑ 90 Troy Aikman	2.50	1.10
❑ 91 Herman Moore	.75	.35
❑ 92 Michael Irvin	.75	.35
❑ 93 Frank Sanders	.75	.35
❑ 94 Duce Staley	1.25	.55
❑ 95 James Jett	.75	.35
❑ 96 Ricky Proehl	.50	.23
❑ 97 Andre Rison	.75	.35
❑ 98 Leslie Shepherd	.50	.23
❑ 99 Trent Green	1.25	.55
❑ 100 Terrell Davis	1.25	.55
❑ 101 Freddie Jones	.50	.23
❑ 102 Skip Hicks	.50	.23
❑ 103 Jeff Graham	.50	.23
❑ 104 Rob Moore	.75	.35
❑ 105 Torrance Small	.50	.23
❑ 106 Antonio Freeman	1.25	.55
❑ 107 Robert Brooks	.75	.35
❑ 108 Jon Kitna	1.25	.55
❑ 109 Curtis Conway	.75	.35
❑ 110 Brett Favre	4.00	1.80
❑ 111 Warrick Dunn	1.25	.55
❑ 112 Elvis Grbac	.75	.35
❑ 113 Corey Fuller	.50	.23
❑ 114 Rickey Dudley	.50	.23
❑ 115 Jamal Anderson	1.25	.55
❑ 116 Terry Glenn	1.25	.55

❑ 117 Rocket Ismail	.75	.35
❑ 118 John Randle	.75	.35
❑ 119 Chris Calloway	.50	.23
❑ 120 Peyton Manning	4.00	1.80
❑ 121 Keenan McCardell	.75	.35
❑ 122 O.J. McDuffie	.75	.35
❑ 123 Ed McCaffrey	.75	.35
❑ 124 Charlie Batch	1.25	.55
❑ 125 Jason Elam SH	.50	.23
❑ 126 Randy Moss SH	1.50	.70
❑ 127 John Elway SH	2.00	.90
❑ 128 Emmitt Smith SH	1.25	.55
❑ 129 Terrell Davis SH	1.25	.55
❑ 130 Jerris McPhail	.50	.23
❑ 131 Damon Gibson	.50	.23
❑ 132 Jim Pyne	.50	.23
❑ 133 Antonio Langham	.50	.23
❑ 134 Freddie Solomon	.50	.23
❑ 135 Ricky Williams RC	10.00	4.50
❑ 136 Daunte Culpepper RC	25.00	11.00
❑ 137 Chris Claiborne RC	2.00	.90
❑ 138 Amos Zereoue RC	5.00	2.20
❑ 139 Chris McAlister RC	4.00	1.80
❑ 140 Kevin Faulk RC	5.00	2.20
❑ 141 James Johnson RC	4.00	1.80
❑ 142 Mike Cloud RC	4.00	1.80
❑ 143 Jevon Kearse RC	10.00	4.50
❑ 144 Akili Smith RC	4.00	1.80
❑ 145 Edgerrin James RC	20.00	9.00
❑ 146 Cecil Collins RC	2.00	.90
❑ 147 Donovan McNabb RC	25.00	11.00
❑ 148 Kevin Johnson RC	5.00	2.20
❑ 149 Torry Holt RC	15.00	6.75
❑ 150 Rob Konrad RC	5.00	2.20
❑ 151 Tim Couch RC	5.00	2.20
❑ 152 David Boston RC	5.00	2.20
❑ 153 Karsten Bailey RC	4.00	1.80
❑ 154 Troy Edwards RC	4.00	1.80
❑ 155 Sedrick Irvin RC	2.00	.90
❑ 156 Shaun King RC	4.00	1.80
❑ 157 Peerless Price RC	10.00	4.50
❑ 158 Brock Huard RC	5.00	2.20
❑ 159 Cade McNown RC	4.00	1.80
❑ 160 Champ Bailey RC	8.00	3.60
❑ 161 D'Wayne Bates RC	4.00	1.80
❑ 162 Joe Germaine RC	4.00	1.80
❑ 163 Andy Katzenmoyer RC	4.00	1.80
❑ 164 Antoine Winfield RC	2.00	.90
❑ 165 Checklist Card	.50	.23

1999 Topps Chrome Refractors

	Nm-Mt	Ex-Mt
*REFRACTOR STARS: 2.5X TO 6X BASIC CARDS.		
❑ 135 Ricky Williams	25.00	11.00
❑ 136 Daunte Culpepper	50.00	22.00
❑ 137 Chris Claiborne	4.00	1.80
❑ 138 Amos Zereoue	10.00	4.50
❑ 139 Chris McAlister	8.00	3.60
❑ 140 Kevin Faulk	10.00	4.50
❑ 141 James Johnson	8.00	3.60
❑ 142 Mike Cloud	8.00	3.60
❑ 143 Jevon Kearse	20.00	9.00
❑ 144 Akili Smith	8.00	3.60
❑ 145 Edgerrin James	50.00	22.00
❑ 146 Cecil Collins	4.00	1.80
❑ 147 Donovan McNabb	60.00	27.00
❑ 148 Kevin Johnson	10.00	4.50
❑ 149 Torry Holt	40.00	18.00
❑ 150 Rob Konrad	10.00	4.50
❑ 151 Tim Couch	10.00	4.50
❑ 152 David Boston	10.00	4.50
❑ 153 Karsten Bailey	8.00	3.60
❑ 154 Troy Edwards	8.00	3.60
❑ 155 Sedrick Irvin	4.00	1.80
❑ 156 Shaun King	8.00	3.60
❑ 157 Peerless Price	20.00	9.00
❑ 158 Brock Huard	10.00	4.50
❑ 159 Cade McNown	8.00	3.60
❑ 160 Champ Bailey	15.00	6.75
❑ 161 D'Wayne Bates	8.00	3.60
❑ 162 Joe Germaine	8.00	3.60
❑ 163 Andy Katzenmoyer	8.00	3.60
❑ 164 Antoine Winfield	4.00	1.80

2000 Topps Chrome

	Nm-Mt	Ex-Mt
COMPLETE SET (270)	800.00	350.00
COMP.SET w/o SPs (180)	50.00	22.00
❑ 1 Daunte Culpepper	1.50	.70
❑ 2 Troy Edwards	.40	.18
❑ 3 Terrell Owens	1.25	.55
❑ 4 Ricky Proehl	.40	.18
❑ 5 Shaun King	.40	.18
❑ 6 Jeff George	.60	.25
❑ 7 Champ Bailey	.60	.25
❑ 8 Amani Toomer	.40	.18
❑ 9 Stephen Boyd	.40	.18
❑ 10 Thurman Thomas	.60	.25
❑ 11 Patrick Jeffers	1.25	.55
❑ 12 Jake Plummer	.60	.25
❑ 13 Peter Boulware	.40	.18
❑ 14 Darrin Chiaverini	.40	.18
❑ 15 Olandis Gary	1.25	.55
❑ 16 Peyton Manning	3.00	1.35
❑ 17 Joe Horn	.60	.25
❑ 18 Wayne Chrebet	.60	.25
❑ 19 Freddie Jones	.40	.18
❑ 20 Kurt Warner	2.50	1.10
❑ 21 Mike Alstott	1.25	.55
❑ 22 Stephen Davis	1.25	.55
❑ 23 Tim Brown	1.25	.55
❑ 24 Damon Huard	1.25	.55
❑ 25 Terry Glenn	.60	.25
❑ 26 Ricky Williams	1.25	.55
❑ 27 Tim Dwight	1.25	.55
❑ 28 Jay Riemersma	.40	.18
❑ 29 Carl Pickens	.60	.25
❑ 30 Brett Favre	4.00	1.80
❑ 31 Oronde Gadsden	.60	.25
❑ 32 Steve McNair	1.25	.55
❑ 33 Michael Pittman	.40	.18
❑ 34 Emmitt Smith	2.50	1.10
❑ 35 Mark Brunell	1.25	.55
❑ 36 Ed McCaffrey	1.25	.55
❑ 37 Tyrone Wheatley	.60	.25
❑ 38 Sean Dawkins	.40	.18
❑ 39 Jevon Kearse	1.25	.55
❑ 40 Tai Streets	.40	.18
❑ 41 Keyshawn Johnson	1.25	.55
❑ 42 Germane Crowell	.40	.18
❑ 43 Yatil Green	.40	.18
❑ 44 Anthony Wright RC	4.00	1.80
❑ 45 Jerry Rice	2.50	1.10
❑ 46 Az-Zahir Hakim	.60	.25
❑ 47 Stephen Alexander	.40	.18
❑ 48 Zach Thomas	1.25	.55
❑ 49 Tony Simmons	.40	.18
❑ 50 Jessie Armstead	.40	.18
❑ 51 Kordell Stewart	.60	.25
❑ 52 Cade McNown	.40	.18
❑ 53 Tony Gonzalez	.60	.25
❑ 54 John Randle	.60	.25
❑ 55 Donovan McNabb	2.00	.90
❑ 56 Warrick Dunn	1.25	.55
❑ 57 Dorsey Levens	.60	.25
❑ 58 Errict Rhett	.60	.25
❑ 59 Priest Holmes	1.50	.70
❑ 60 Terrell Davis	1.25	.55
❑ 61 Natrone Means	.40	.18
❑ 62 Brad Johnson	1.25	.55
❑ 63 Rickey Dudley	.40	.18
❑ 64 Moses Moreno	.40	.18
❑ 65 Randy Moss	2.50	1.10
❑ 66 Joe Montgomery	.40	.18
❑ 67 Johnnie Morton	.60	.25
❑ 68 Peerless Price	1.25	.55
❑ 69 Rocket Ismail	.60	.25
❑ 70 David Boston	1.25	.55
❑ 71 Fred Taylor	1.25	.55
❑ 72 Jermaine Fazande	.40	.18
❑ 73 Elvis Grbac	.60	.25
❑ 74 Derrick Mayes	.60	.25
❑ 75 Yancey Thigpen	.40	.18
❑ 76 Ike Hilliard	.60	.25
❑ 77 Muhsin Muhammad	.60	.25
❑ 78 Shawn Jefferson	.40	.18
❑ 79 Rod Smith	.60	.25
❑ 80 Darnay Scott	.60	.25
❑ 81 Cam Cleeland	.40	.18
❑ 82 Steve Young	1.50	.70
❑ 83 E.G. Green	.40	.18
❑ 84 Robert Smith	1.25	.55
❑ 85 Jermaine Lewis	.60	.25
❑ 86 Tim Biakabutuka	.60	.25
❑ 87 Jerome Pathon	.60	.25
❑ 88 Kent Graham	.40	.18
❑ 89 Bruce Smith	.60	.25
❑ 90 Isaac Bruce	1.25	.55
❑ 91 Curtis Enis	.40	.18
❑ 92 Bert Emanuel	.40	.18
❑ 93 Keith Poole	.40	.18
❑ 94 Troy Aikman	2.50	1.10
❑ 95 Rich Gannon	1.25	.55
❑ 96 Michael Westbrook	.60	.25
❑ 97 Albert Connell	.40	.18
❑ 98 James Johnson	.40	.18
❑ 99 Jeff Blake	.60	.25
❑ 100 Joey Galloway	.60	.25
❑ 101 Rob Moore	.60	.25
❑ 102 Chris Chandler	.60	.25
❑ 103 Fred Lane	.40	.18
❑ 104 Eddie Kennison	.60	.25
❑ 105 Kevin Hardy	.40	.18
❑ 106 Napoleon Kaufman	.60	.25
❑ 107 Kevin Dyson	.60	.25
❑ 108 Keenan McCardell	.60	.25
❑ 109 Drew Bledsoe	1.50	.70
❑ 110 Kevin Johnson	1.25	.55
❑ 111 Terance Mathis	.60	.25
❑ 112 Gus Frerotte	.40	.18
❑ 113 Matthew Hatchette	.40	.18
❑ 114 Herman Moore	.60	.25
❑ 115 Curtis Martin	1.25	.55
❑ 116 Jacquez Green	.40	.18
❑ 117 Jake Reed	.60	.25
❑ 118 Antonio Freeman	1.25	.55
❑ 119 Jim Miller	.40	.18
❑ 120 Frank Sanders	.60	.25
❑ 121 Brian Griese	1.25	.55
❑ 122 Troy Brown	.60	.25
❑ 123 Jeff Graham	.40	.18
❑ 124 Marshall Faulk	1.50	.70
❑ 125 Vinny Testaverde	.60	.25
❑ 126 Frank Wycheck	.40	.18
❑ 127 Kerry Collins	.60	.25
❑ 128 Jay Fiedler	1.25	.55
❑ 129 Cris Carter	1.25	.55
❑ 130 Jason Tucker	.40	.18
❑ 131 Antowain Smith	.60	.25
❑ 132 Tony Banks	.60	.25
❑ 133 Terrence Wilkins	.40	.18
❑ 134 Tony Martin	.60	.25
❑ 135 Richard Huntley	.40	.18
❑ 136 J.J. Stokes	.60	.25
❑ 137 Ricky Watters	.60	.25
❑ 138 Pete Mitchell	.40	.18
❑ 139 Jimmy Smith	.60	.25
❑ 140 Doug Flutie	1.25	.55
❑ 141 Corey Bradford	.60	.25
❑ 142 Curtis Conway	.60	.25
❑ 143 Pete Mitchell	.40	.18
❑ 144 Torry Holt	1.25	.55

❑ 145 Warren Sapp .60 .25
❑ 146 Duce Staley 1.25 .55
❑ 147 Mikhael Ricks .40 .18
❑ 148 Edgerrin James 2.00 .90
❑ 149 Charlie Batch 1.25 .55
❑ 150 Rob Johnson .60 .25
❑ 151 Jamal Anderson 1.25 .55
❑ 152 Tim Couch .60 .25
❑ 153 O.J. McDuffie .60 .25
❑ 154 Charles Woodson .60 .25
❑ 155 Jake Delhomme RC 10.00 4.50
❑ 156 Eddie George 1.25 .55
❑ 157 Jim Harbaugh .60 .25
❑ 158 Jon Kitna 1.25 .55
❑ 159 Derrick Alexander .60 .25
❑ 160 Marvin Harrison 1.25 .55
❑ 161 James Stewart .60 .25
❑ 162 Qadry Ismail .60 .25
❑ 163 Wesley Walls .40 .18
❑ 164 Steve Beuerlein .60 .25
❑ 165 Marcus Robinson 1.25 .55
❑ 166 Bill Schroeder .60 .25
❑ 167 Charles Johnson .60 .25
❑ 168 Charlie Garner .60 .25
❑ 169 Eric Moulds 1.25 .55
❑ 170 Jerome Bettis 1.25 .55
❑ 171 Tai Streets .40 .18
❑ 172 Akili Smith .40 .18
❑ 173 Jonathan Linton .40 .18
❑ 174 Corey Dillon 1.25 .55
❑ 175 Junior Seau 1.25 .55
❑ 176 Jonathan Quinn .40 .18
❑ 177 Bobby Engram .40 .18
❑ 178 Shannon Sharpe .60 .25
❑ 179 Michael Basnight .40 .18
❑ 180 Sedrick Irvin .40 .18
❑ 181 Sammy Morris RC 10.00 4.50
❑ 182 Ron Dixon RC 10.00 4.50
❑ 183 Trevor Gaylor RC 10.00 4.50
❑ 184 Chris Cole RC 8.00 3.60
❑ 185 Deltha O'Neal RC 15.00 6.75
❑ 186 Sebastian Janikowski RC 15.00 6.75
❑ 187 Kwame Cavil RC 8.00 3.60
❑ 188 Chad Morton RC 15.00 6.75
❑ 189 Terrelle Smith RC 10.00 4.50
❑ 190 Frank Moreau RC 10.00 4.50
❑ 191 Kurt Warner HL 1.50 .70
❑ 192 Dan Marino HL 2.50 1.10
❑ 193 Cris Carter HL .60 .25
❑ 194 Brett Favre HL 2.50 1.10
❑ 195 Marshall Faulk HL 1.25 .55
❑ 196 Jevon Kearse HL .60 .25
❑ 197 Edgerrin James HL 1.50 .70
❑ 198 Emmitt Smith HL 1.50 .70
❑ 199 Andre Reed HL .40 .18
❑ 200 Kevin Dyson HL .40 .18
Frank Wycheck HL
❑ 201 Olindo Mare MM .40 .18
❑ 202 Marcus Coleman MM .40 .18
❑ 203 James Johnson MM .40 .18
❑ 204 Ray Lucas MM .60 .25
❑ 205 Dedric Ward MM .40 .18
❑ 206 Richie Cunningham MM .40 .18
❑ 207 James Hasty MM .40 .18
❑ 208 Sedrick Shaw MM .40 .18
❑ 209 Kurt Warner MM 1.50 .70
❑ 210 Marshall Faulk MM 1.25 .55
❑ 211 Brian Shay EP 1.00 .45
❑ 212 L.C. Stevens EP 1.00 .45
❑ 213 Corey Thomas EP 1.00 .45
❑ 214 Scott Milanovich EP 1.50 .70
❑ 215 Pat Barnes EP 1.50 .70
❑ 216 Danny Wuerffel EP 1.50 .70
❑ 217 Kevin Daft EP 1.00 .45
❑ 218 Ron Powlus EP RC 2.00 .90
❑ 219 Eric Kresser EP 1.00 .45
❑ 220 Norman Miller EP RC 1.00 .45
❑ 221 Cory Sauter EP 1.00 .45
❑ 222 Marcus Crandell EP RC 1.50 .70
❑ 223 Sean Morey EP RC 1.50 .70
❑ 224 Jeff Ogden EP 1.50 .70
❑ 225 Ted White EP 1.00 .45
❑ 226 Jim Kubiak EP RC 1.50 .70
❑ 227 Aaron Stecker EP RC 2.00 .90
❑ 228 Ronnie Powell EP 1.00 .45
❑ 229 Matt Lytle EP RC 1.50 .70
❑ 230 Kendrick Nord EP RC 1.00 .45
❑ 231 Tim Rattay RC 30.00 13.50
❑ 232 Rob Morris RC 10.00 4.50
❑ 233 Chris Samuels RC 10.00 4.50
❑ 234 Todd Husak RC 15.00 6.75
❑ 235 Ahmed Plummer RC 15.00 6.75
❑ 236 Frank Murphy RC 8.00 3.60
❑ 237 Michael Wiley RC 10.00 4.50
❑ 238 Giovanni Carmazzi RC 10.00 4.50
❑ 239 Anthony Becht RC 15.00 6.75
❑ 240 John Abraham RC 20.00 9.00
❑ 241 Shaun Alexander RC 40.00 18.00
❑ 242 Thomas Jones RC 25.00 11.00
❑ 243 Courtney Brown RC 15.00 6.75
❑ 244 Curtis Keaton RC 10.00 4.50
❑ 245 Jerry Porter RC 25.00 11.00
❑ 246 Corey Simon RC 15.00 6.75
❑ 247 Dez White RC 15.00 6.75
❑ 248 Jamal Lewis RC 40.00 18.00
❑ 249 Ron Dayne RC 15.00 6.75
❑ 250 R.Jay Soward RC 10.00 4.50
❑ 251 Tee Martin RC 15.00 6.75
❑ 252 Shaun Ellis RC 15.00 6.75
❑ 253 Brian Urlacher RC 50.00 22.00
❑ 254 Reuben Droughns RC 15.00 6.75
❑ 255 Travis Taylor RC 15.00 6.75
❑ 256 Plaxico Burress RC 30.00 13.50
❑ 257 Chad Pennington RC 50.00 22.00
❑ 258 Sylvester Morris RC 10.00 4.50
❑ 259 Ron Dugans RC 8.00 3.60
❑ 260 Joe Hamilton RC 10.00 4.50
❑ 261 Chris Redman RC 10.00 4.50
❑ 262 Trung Canidate RC 10.00 4.50
❑ 263 J.R. Redmond RC 10.00 4.50
❑ 264 Danny Farmer RC 10.00 4.50
❑ 265 Todd Pinkston RC 15.00 6.75
❑ 266 Dennis Northcutt RC 15.00 6.75
❑ 267 Laveranues Coles RC 20.00 9.00
❑ 268 Bubba Franks RC 15.00 6.75
❑ 269 Travis Prentice RC 10.00 4.50
❑ 270 Peter Warrick RC 15.00 6.75

2000 Topps Chrome Refractors

Nm-Mt Ex-Mt
*REFRACTOR STARS: 2.5X TO 6X BASIC CARDS
*REFRACTOR RCs: .8X TO 2X BASIC CARDS

2001 Topps Chrome

Nm-Mt Ex-Mt
COMP.SET w/o SP's (210) 50.00 15.00
❑ 1 Randy Moss 2.50 .75
❑ 2 Desmond Howard .50 .15
❑ 3 Shawn Bryson .50 .15
❑ 4 Lamar Smith .75 .23
❑ 5 Peter Warrick 1.25 .35
❑ 6 Hines Ward 1.25 .35
❑ 7 J.R. Redmond .50 .15
❑ 8 Reidel Anthony .50 .15
❑ 9 Rich Gannon 1.25 .35
❑ 10 Ed McCaffrey 1.25 .35
❑ 11 Jamel White .50 .15
❑ 12 Michael Pittman .50 .15
❑ 13 Rob Johnson .75 .23
❑ 14 Tim Couch .75 .23
❑ 15 Stephen Alexander .50 .15
❑ 16 Ricky Watters .75 .23
❑ 17 Kerry Collins .75 .23
❑ 18 Ricky Williams 1.25 .35
❑ 19 Joey Galloway .75 .23
❑ 20 Chris Chandler .75 .23
❑ 21 Marty Booker .50 .15
❑ 22 Mark Brunell 1.25 .35
❑ 23 Antonio Freeman 1.25 .35
❑ 24 Richie Anderson .50 .15
❑ 25 Amani Toomer .75 .23
❑ 26 Trent Green 1.25 .35
❑ 27 Terrell Fletcher .50 .15
❑ 28 Kevin Lockett .50 .15
❑ 29 Ron Dixon .50 .15
❑ 30 Charlie Batch 1.25 .35
❑ 31 Oronde Gadsden .75 .23
❑ 32 Dorsey Levens .75 .23
❑ 33 Jamal Lewis 2.00 .60
❑ 34 Craig Yeast .50 .15
❑ 35 Muhsin Muhammad .75 .23
❑ 36 Willie Jackson .50 .15
❑ 37 Isaac Bruce 1.25 .35
❑ 38 Frank Wycheck .50 .15
❑ 39 Troy Brown .75 .23
❑ 40 Anthony Wright .50 .15
❑ 41 Zach Thomas 1.25 .35
❑ 42 Qadry Ismail .75 .23
❑ 43 Jake Plummer .75 .23
❑ 44 Keenan McCardell .50 .15
❑ 45 Charles Johnson .50 .15
❑ 46 Brett Favre 4.00 1.20
❑ 47 Jacquez Green .50 .15
❑ 48 Matt Hasselbeck .75 .23
❑ 49 Tiki Barber .75 .23
❑ 50 Jeff Garcia 1.25 .35
❑ 51 Shawn Jefferson .50 .15
❑ 52 Kevin Johnson .75 .23
❑ 53 Terrence Wilkins .50 .15
❑ 54 Mike Anderson 1.25 .35
❑ 55 Tim Brown 1.25 .35
❑ 56 Champ Bailey 1.25 .35
❑ 57 Jimmy Smith .75 .23
❑ 58 Trent Dilfer .75 .23
❑ 59 James Allen .75 .23
❑ 60 David Boston 1.25 .35
❑ 61 Jeremiah Trotter .75 .23
❑ 62 Freddie Jones .50 .15
❑ 63 Deion Sanders 1.25 .35
❑ 64 Darrell Jackson 1.25 .35
❑ 65 David Patten .50 .15
❑ 66 Jeremy McDaniel .50 .15
❑ 67 Jay Fiedler 1.25 .35
❑ 68 Chad Lewis .50 .15
❑ 69 Rocket Ismail .75 .23
❑ 70 Cade McNown .50 .15
❑ 71 Jevon Kearse .75 .23
❑ 72 Jermaine Fazande .50 .15
❑ 73 Junior Seau 1.25 .35
❑ 74 Rod Smith .75 .23
❑ 75 Jermaine Lewis .50 .15
❑ 76 Dennis Northcutt .75 .23
❑ 77 Charlie Garner .75 .23
❑ 78 Charles Woodson .75 .23
❑ 79 Wayne Chrebet .75 .23
❑ 80 Ahman Green 1.25 .35
❑ 81 Donald Hayes .50 .15
❑ 82 Terance Mathis .50 .15
❑ 83 Warrick Dunn 1.25 .35
❑ 84 Chris Sanders .50 .15
❑ 85 Albert Connell .50 .15
❑ 86 Robert Griffith .50 .15
❑ 87 Germane Crowell .50 .15
❑ 88 Tony Banks .75 .23
❑ 89 Travis Taylor .75 .23
❑ 90 Akili Smith .50 .15
❑ 91 Michael Westbrook .75 .23
❑ 92 Doug Flutie 1.25 .35
❑ 93 Ike Hilliard .75 .23
❑ 94 Terry Glenn .50 .15
❑ 95 Leslie Shepherd .50 .15
❑ 96 Az-Zahir Hakim .50 .15

❑ 97 La'Roi Glover .50 .15
❑ 98 Peyton Manning 3.00 .90
❑ 99 Jackie Harris .50 .15
❑ 100 Edgerrin James 1.50 .45
❑ 101 Peerless Price .75 .23
❑ 102 Jamal Anderson 1.25 .35
❑ 103 Keyshawn Johnson 1.25 .35
❑ 104 Derrick Mason .75 .23
❑ 105 J.J. Stokes .75 .23
❑ 106 Kevin Faulk .75 .23
❑ 107 Tony Richardson .50 .15
❑ 108 James Stewart .75 .23
❑ 109 Tim Biakabutuka .75 .23
❑ 110 Jon Kitna 1.25 .35
❑ 111 Thomas Jones .75 .23
❑ 112 Steve McNair 1.25 .35
❑ 113 Sean Dawkins .50 .15
❑ 114 Jerome Bettis 1.25 .35
❑ 115 Donovan McNabb 1.50 .45
❑ 116 Bill Schroeder .75 .23
❑ 117 Rod Woodson .75 .23
❑ 118 James McKnight .75 .23
❑ 119 Daunte Culpepper 1.25 .35
❑ 120 Todd Husak .50 .15
❑ 121 Shaun King .50 .15
❑ 122 Tyrone Wheatley .75 .23
❑ 123 Curtis Martin 1.25 .35
❑ 124 Terrell Davis 1.25 .35
❑ 125 Steve Beuerlein .75 .23
❑ 126 Brad Johnson 1.25 .35
❑ 127 Joe Horn .75 .23
❑ 128 Fred Taylor 1.25 .35
❑ 129 Brian Urlacher 2.00 .60
❑ 130 Ray Lewis 1.25 .35
❑ 131 Marshall Faulk 1.50 .45
❑ 132 Curtis Conway .75 .23
❑ 133 Jason Sehorn .50 .15
❑ 134 Jerome Pathon .75 .23
❑ 135 Derrick Alexander .75 .23
❑ 136 Jerry Rice 2.50 .75
❑ 137 Jeff George .75 .23
❑ 138 Johnnie Morton .75 .23
❑ 139 Eric Moulds .75 .23
❑ 140 Duce Staley 1.25 .35
❑ 141 Vinny Testaverde .75 .23
❑ 142 Eddie George 1.25 .35
❑ 143 Shaun Alexander 1.50 .45
❑ 144 Drew Bledsoe 1.50 .45
❑ 145 Emmitt Smith 2.50 .75
❑ 146 Marvin Harrison 1.25 .35
❑ 147 Frank Sanders .50 .15
❑ 148 Aaron Shea .50 .15
❑ 149 Cris Carter 1.25 .35
❑ 150 Tony Gonzalez .75 .23
❑ 151 Marcus Robinson 1.25 .35
❑ 152 Danny Farmer .50 .15
❑ 153 Warren Sapp .75 .23
❑ 154 Kurt Warner 2.50 .75
❑ 155 Jessie Armstead .50 .15
❑ 156 Lawyer Milloy .75 .23
❑ 157 Brian Griese 1.25 .35
❑ 158 Jason Taylor .50 .15
❑ 159 Jeff Lewis .50 .15
❑ 160 Travis Prentice .50 .15
❑ 161 Tim Dwight 1.25 .35
❑ 162 Kyle Brady .50 .15
❑ 163 Bubba Franks .75 .23
❑ 164 James Thrash .75 .23
❑ 165 Bobby Shaw .50 .15
❑ 166 Ron Dayne 1.25 .35
❑ 167 Mike Alstott 1.25 .35
❑ 168 Bruce Smith .50 .15
❑ 169 Jeff Graham .50 .15
❑ 170 Jeff Blake .75 .23
❑ 171 Laveranues Coles 1.25 .35
❑ 172 Herman Moore .75 .23
❑ 173 Shannon Sharpe .75 .23
❑ 174 Corey Dillon 1.25 .35
❑ 175 Ken Dilger .50 .15
❑ 176 Eddie Kennison .50 .15
❑ 177 Andre Rison .75 .23
❑ 178 Stephen Davis 1.25 .35
❑ 179 Torry Holt 1.25 .35
❑ 180 Samari Rolle .50 .15
❑ 181 Michael Strahan .75 .23
❑ 182 Plaxico Burress 1.25 .35
❑ 183 Darnell Autry .50 .15
❑ 184 Wesley Walls .50 .15
❑ 185 Elvis Grbac .75 .23
❑ 186 Marcus Pollard .50 .15
❑ 187 Keith Poole .50 .15
❑ 188 Ryan Leaf .75 .23
❑ 189 Terrell Owens 1.25 .35
❑ 190 Dedric Ward .50 .15
❑ 191 Donald Driver .75 .23
❑ 192 Larry Foster .50 .15
❑ 193 Priest Holmes 1.50 .45
❑ 194 Sammy Morris .50 .15
❑ 195 Reggie Jones .50 .15
❑ 196 Kordell Stewart .75 .23
❑ 197 Sylvester Morris .50 .15
❑ 198 Aaron Brooks 1.25 .35
❑ 199 Tai Streets .50 .15
❑ 200 Chad Pennington 2.00 .60
❑ 201 Terrell Owens SH 1.25 .35
❑ 202 Marshall Faulk SH 1.25 .35
❑ 203 Mike Anderson SH .75 .23
❑ 204 Cris Carter SH 1.25 .35
❑ 205 Corey Dillon SH 1.25 .35
❑ 206 Daunte Culpepper SH 1.25 .35
❑ 207 Peyton Manning SH 1.50 .45
❑ 208 Torry Holt SH 1.25 .35
❑ 209 Marvin Harrison SH 1.25 .35
❑ 210 Edgerrin James SH 1.25 .35
❑ 211 Sam Madison .50 .15
❑ 212 Jonathan Quinn .50 .15
❑ 213 Rob Morris .50 .15
❑ 214 E.G. Green .50 .15
❑ 215 David Sloan .50 .15
❑ 216 Jason Tucker .50 .15
❑ 217 Wali Rainer .50 .15
❑ 218 Jerry Azumah .50 .15
❑ 219 Dameyune Craig .50 .15
❑ 220 Jammi German .50 .15
❑ 221 LaDainian Tomlinson RC 100.00 30.00
❑ 222 Quincy Morgan RC 20.00 6.00
❑ 223 Steve Smith RC 25.00 7.50
❑ 224 Santana Moss RC 30.00 9.00
❑ 225 Koren Robinson RC 20.00 6.00
❑ 226 Kevin Kasper RC 20.00 6.00
❑ 227 Jamie Henderson RC 12.00 3.60
❑ 228 Adam Archuleta RC 20.00 6.00
❑ 229 Drew Brees RC 40.00 12.00
❑ 230 Michael Stone RC 8.00 2.40
❑ 231 Jamar Fletcher RC 12.00 3.60
❑ 232 Eric Westmoreland RC 12.00 3.60
❑ 233 Chris Barnes RC 12.00 3.60
❑ 234 Gerard Warren RC 20.00 6.00
❑ 235 Snoop Minnis RC 12.00 3.60
❑ 236 Chris Chambers RC 25.00 7.50
❑ 237 Damerien McCants RC 12.00 3.60
❑ 238 Kevan Barlow RC 20.00 6.00
❑ 239 Mike McMahon RC 20.00 6.00
❑ 240 Jabari Holloway RC 12.00 3.60
❑ 241 Travis Henry RC 25.00 7.50
❑ 242 Derrick Blaylock RC 25.00 7.50
❑ 243 Tim Hasselbeck RC 20.00 6.00
❑ 244 Andre Carter RC 20.00 6.00
❑ 245 Sage Rosenfels RC 20.00 6.00
❑ 246 Cedrick Wilson RC 20.00 6.00
❑ 247 Scotty Anderson RC 12.00 3.60
❑ 248 Ken-Yon Rambo RC 12.00 3.60
❑ 249 Marques Tuiasosopo RC 20.00 6.00
❑ 250 Reggie Wayne RC 30.00 9.00
❑ 251 Onomo Ojo RC 12.00 3.60
❑ 252 James Jackson RC 20.00 6.00
❑ 253 Moran Norris RC 8.00 2.40
❑ 254 Rashard Casey RC 12.00 3.60
❑ 255 Rudi Johnson RC 40.00 12.00
❑ 256 Willie Middlebrooks RC 12.00 3.60
❑ 257 Freddie Mitchell RC 20.00 6.00
❑ 258 Deuce McAllister RC 50.00 15.00
❑ 259 Chad Johnson RC 40.00 12.00
❑ 260 David Terrell RC 20.00 6.00
❑ 261 Jamal Reynolds RC 20.00 6.00
❑ 262 Michael Vick RC 200.00 60.00
❑ 263 Marcus Stroud RC 20.00 6.00
❑ 264 Dan Alexander RC 20.00 6.00
❑ 265 Jonathan Carter RC 12.00 3.60
❑ 266 Bobby Newcombe RC 12.00 3.60
❑ 267 Eddie Berlin RC 12.00 3.60
❑ 268 LaMont Jordan RC 25.00 7.50
❑ 269 Michael Bennett RC 40.00 12.00
❑ 270 Shaun Rogers RC 20.00 6.00
❑ 271 Travis Minor RC 12.00 3.60
❑ 272 Jesse Palmer RC 20.00 6.00
❑ 273 Derrick Gibson RC 12.00 3.60
❑ 274 Chris Weinke RC 20.00 6.00
❑ 275 Nate Clements RC 20.00 6.00
❑ 276 Eric Kelly RC 8.00 2.40
❑ 277 Justin Smith RC 20.00 6.00
❑ 278 Ryan Pickett RC 8.00 2.40
❑ 279 Anthony Thomas RC 30.00 9.00
❑ 280 Will Allen RC 12.00 3.60
❑ 281 Quincy Carter RC 20.00 6.00
❑ 282 Richard Seymour RC 20.00 6.00
❑ 283 Dan Morgan RC 20.00 6.00
❑ 284 Tay Cody RC 8.00 2.40
❑ 285 Alge Crumpler RC 25.00 7.50
❑ 286 Robert Ferguson RC 20.00 6.00
❑ 287 Will Peterson RC 12.00 3.60
❑ 288 Tony Dixon RC 12.00 3.60
❑ 289 Correll Buckhalter RC 25.00 7.50
❑ 290 Rod Gardner RC 20.00 6.00
❑ 291 Justin McCareins RC 20.00 6.00
❑ 292 Josh Heupel RC 20.00 6.00
❑ 293 Todd Heap RC 20.00 6.00
❑ 294 Damione Lewis RC 12.00 3.60
❑ 295 George Layne RC 12.00 3.60
❑ 296 Jamie Winborn RC 12.00 3.60
❑ 297 Billy Baber RC 8.00 2.40
❑ 298 T.J. Houshmandzadeh RC 20.00 6.00
❑ 299 Aaron Schobel RC 20.00 6.00
❑ 300 Gary Baxter RC 12.00 3.60
❑ 301 DeLawrence Grant RC 8.00 2.40
❑ 302 Morlon Greenwood RC 12.00 3.60
❑ 303 Shad Meier RC 12.00 3.60
❑ 304 Torrance Marshall RC 20.00 6.00
❑ 305 David Martin RC 12.00 3.60
❑ 306 Anthony Henry RC 20.00 6.00
❑ 307 Derrick Burgess RC 20.00 6.00
❑ 308 Andre Dyson RC 8.00 2.40
❑ 309 Ryan Helming RC 8.00 2.40
❑ 310 Fred Smoot RC 20.00 6.00
❑ 311 Arther Love RC 8.00 2.40
❑ 312 John Capel RC 12.00 3.60
❑ 313 Brandon Spoon RC 12.00 3.60
❑ 314 Karon Riley RC 8.00 2.40
❑ 315 Andre King RC 12.00 3.60
❑ 316 Quentin McCord RC 12.00 3.60
❑ 317 Zeke Moreno RC 20.00 6.00
❑ 318 Francis St. Paul RC 12.00 3.60
❑ 319 Richmond Flowers RC 12.00 3.60
❑ 320 Derek Combs RC 12.00 3.60

2001 Topps Chrome Refractors

Nm-Mt Ex-Mt

*STARS: 2X TO 5X BASIC CARDS
*ROOKIES: 1X TO 2.5X

2001 Topps Chrome King of Kings

	Nm-Mt	Ex-Mt
❑ KCD Corey Dillon/375	30.00	9.00
❑ KDM Dan Marino/125	120.00	36.00
❑ KES Emmitt Smith/150	120.00	36.00
❑ KFT Fred Taylor/250	40.00	12.00
❑ KJR Jerry Rice/125	100.00	30.00
❑ KRM Randy Moss EXCH		
❑ KTO Terrell Owens/275	40.00	12.00
❑ KWP Walter Payton/75	250.00	75.00

2001 Topps Chrome Rookie Reprint Jerseys

	Nm-Mt	Ex-Mt
❑ TODM Dan Marino/125	150.00	45.00
❑ TOES Emmitt Smith/150	120.00	36.00
❑ TOJR Jerry Rice/100	150.00	45.00
❑ TOWP Walter Payton/75	150.00	45.00

2002 Topps Chrome

	Nm-Mt	Ex-Mt
COMP.SET w/o SP's (165)	50.00	15.00
❑ 1 Anthony Thomas	1.25	.35
❑ 2 Jake Plummer	.75	.23
❑ 3 Maurice Smith	.75	.23
❑ 4 Jamal Lewis	1.25	.35
❑ 5 Ray Lewis	1.25	.35
❑ 6 Alex Van Pelt	.50	.15
❑ 7 Chris Weinke	.75	.23
❑ 8 Corey Dillon	.75	.23
❑ 9 Quincy Morgan	.50	.15
❑ 10 Rocket Ismail	.75	.23
❑ 11 Brian Griese	1.25	.35
❑ 12 Johnnie Morton	.75	.23
❑ 13 Edgerrin James	1.50	.45
❑ 14 Keenan McCardell	.50	.15
❑ 15 Travis Minor	.75	.23
❑ 16 Sylvester Morris	.50	.15
❑ 17 Randy Moss	2.50	.75
❑ 18 Drew Bledsoe	1.50	.45
❑ 19 Willie Jackson	.50	.15
❑ 20 Michael Strahan	.75	.23
❑ 21 Santana Moss	1.25	.35
❑ 22 Duce Staley	1.25	.35
❑ 23 Kendrell Bell	1.25	.35
❑ 24 LaDainian Tomlinson	2.00	.60
❑ 25 Terrell Owens	1.25	.35
❑ 26 Shaun Alexander	1.25	.35
❑ 27 Trung Canidate	.75	.23
❑ 28 Mike Alstott	1.25	.35
❑ 29 Kevin Dyson	.75	.23
❑ 30 Rod Gardner	.75	.23
❑ 31 David Boston	1.25	.35
❑ 32 Michael Vick	4.00	1.20
❑ 33 Qadry Ismail	.75	.23
❑ 34 Peerless Price	.75	.23
❑ 35 Rob Johnson	.75	.23
❑ 36 Marcus Robinson	.75	.23
❑ 37 Peter Warrick	.75	.23
❑ 38 Kevin Johnson	.75	.23
❑ 39 Ed McCaffrey	1.25	.35
❑ 40 Shaun Rogers	.50	.15
❑ 41 Marvin Harrison	1.25	.35
❑ 42 Priest Holmes	1.50	.45
❑ 43 Oronde Gadsden	.75	.23
❑ 44 Terry Glenn	.75	.23
❑ 45 Ike Hilliard	.75	.23
❑ 46 Charles Woodson	.75	.23
❑ 47 Freddie Mitchell	.75	.23
❑ 48 Drew Brees	1.25	.35
❑ 49 Jeff Garcia	1.25	.35
❑ 50 Kurt Warner	1.25	.35
❑ 51 Keyshawn Johnson	1.25	.35
❑ 52 Jevon Kearse	.75	.23
❑ 53 Stephen Davis	.75	.23
❑ 54 Shannon Sharpe	.75	.23
❑ 55 Eric Moulds	.75	.23
❑ 56 Muhsin Muhammad	.75	.23
❑ 57 Brian Urlacher	2.00	.60
❑ 58 Chad Johnson	1.25	.35
❑ 59 Tim Couch	.75	.23
❑ 60 Mike Anderson	1.25	.35
❑ 61 James Stewart	.75	.23
❑ 62 Corey Bradford	.50	.15
❑ 63 Reggie Wayne	.75	.23
❑ 64 Mark Brunell	1.25	.35
❑ 65 Trent Green	.75	.23
❑ 66 Zach Thomas	1.25	.35
❑ 67 Michael Bennett	.75	.23
❑ 68 Troy Brown	.75	.23
❑ 69 Amani Toomer	.75	.23
❑ 70 Curtis Martin	1.25	.35
❑ 71 Tim Brown	1.25	.35
❑ 72 Correll Buckhalter	.75	.23
❑ 73 Kordell Stewart	.75	.23
❑ 74 Junior Seau	1.25	.35
❑ 75 Kevan Barlow	.75	.23
❑ 76 Matt Hasselbeck	.75	.23
❑ 77 Marshall Faulk	1.25	.35
❑ 78 Warren Sapp	.75	.23
❑ 79 Frank Wycheck	.50	.15
❑ 80 Michael Westbrook	.50	.15
❑ 81 Travis Henry	1.25	.35
❑ 82 David Terrell	1.25	.35
❑ 83 Jon Kitna	.75	.23
❑ 84 James Jackson	.50	.15
❑ 85 Joey Galloway	.75	.23
❑ 86 Rod Smith	.75	.23
❑ 87 Germane Crowell	.50	.15
❑ 88 Bill Schroeder	.75	.23
❑ 89 Dominic Rhodes	.75	.23
❑ 90 Fred Taylor	1.25	.35
❑ 91 Snoop Minnis	.50	.15
❑ 92 Chris Chambers	1.25	.35
❑ 93 Daunte Culpepper	1.25	.35
❑ 94 Deuce McAllister	1.50	.45
❑ 95 Kerry Collins	.75	.23
❑ 96 John Abraham	.75	.23
❑ 97 Rich Gannon	1.25	.35
❑ 98 Tiki Barber	.75	.23
❑ 99 Hines Ward	1.25	.35
❑ 100 Tom Brady	3.00	.90
❑ 101 Tim Dwight	.75	.23
❑ 102 Garrison Hearst	.75	.23
❑ 103 Darrell Jackson	.75	.23
❑ 104 Isaac Bruce	1.25	.35
❑ 105 Brad Johnson	.75	.23
❑ 106 Steve McNair	1.25	.35
❑ 107 Champ Bailey	.75	.23
❑ 108 Emmitt Smith	3.00	.90
❑ 109 Mike McMahon	1.25	.35
❑ 110 Terrell Davis	1.25	.35
❑ 111 Antonio Freeman	1.25	.35
❑ 112 Jimmy Smith	.75	.23
❑ 113 Tony Gonzalez	.75	.23
❑ 114 Jay Fiedler	.75	.23
❑ 115 Cris Carter	1.25	.35
❑ 116 David Patten	.50	.15
❑ 117 Joe Horn	.75	.23
❑ 118 Laveranues Coles	.75	.23
❑ 119 Charlie Garner	.75	.23
❑ 120 Donovan McNabb	1.50	.45
❑ 121 Jerome Bettis	1.25	.35
❑ 122 Curtis Conway	.50	.15
❑ 123 Az-Zahir Hakim	.50	.15
❑ 124 Warrick Dunn	1.25	.35
❑ 125 Eddie George	1.25	.35
❑ 126 Quincy Carter	.75	.23
❑ 127 Ahman Green	1.25	.35
❑ 128 Peyton Manning	2.50	.75
❑ 129 James McKnight	.50	.15
❑ 130 Antowain Smith	.75	.23
❑ 131 Ricky Williams	8.00	2.40
❑ 132 Chad Pennington	1.50	.45
❑ 133 Jerry Rice	2.50	.75
❑ 134 Todd Pinkston	.75	.23
❑ 135 Plaxico Burress	.75	.23
❑ 136 Doug Flutie	1.25	.35
❑ 137 Koren Robinson	.75	.23
❑ 138 Torry Holt	1.25	.35
❑ 139 Aaron Brooks	1.25	.35
❑ 140 Ron Dayne	.75	.23
❑ 141 Vinny Testaverde	.75	.23
❑ 142 Brett Favre	3.00	.90
❑ 143 James Thrash	.75	.23
❑ 144 Wayne Chrebet	.75	.23
❑ 145 Derrick Mason	.75	.23
❑ 146 Ahman Green WWU	.75	.23
❑ 147 Peyton Manning WWU	1.25	.35
❑ 148 Kurt Warner WWU	.75	.23
❑ 149 Daunte Culpepper WWU	.75	.23
❑ 150 Tom Brady WWU	1.50	.45
❑ 151 Rod Gardner WWU	.75	.23
❑ 152 Corey Dillon WWU	.75	.23
❑ 153 Priest Holmes WWU	1.00	.30
❑ 154 Shaun Alexander WWU	.75	.23
❑ 155 Randy Moss WWU	1.25	.35
❑ 156 Eric Moulds WWU	.50	.15
❑ 157 Brett Favre WWU	1.50	.45
❑ 158 Todd Bouman WWU	.50	.15
❑ 159 Dominic Rhodes WWU	.50	.15
❑ 160 Marvin Harrison WWU	.75	.23
❑ 161 Torry Holt WWU	1.25	.35
❑ 162 Derrick Mason WWU	.50	.15
❑ 163 Jerry Rice WWU	1.25	.35
❑ 164 Donovan McNabb WWU	1.25	.35
❑ 165 Marshall Faulk WWU	1.25	.35
❑ 166 David Carr RC	40.00	12.00
❑ 167 Quentin Jammer RC	10.00	3.00
❑ 168 Mike Williams RC	8.00	2.40
❑ 169 Rocky Calmus RC	10.00	3.00
❑ 170 Travis Fisher RC	10.00	3.00
❑ 171 Dwight Freeney RC	12.00	3.60
❑ 172 Jeremy Shockey RC	40.00	12.00
❑ 173 Marquise Walker RC	8.00	2.40
❑ 174 Eric Crouch RC	15.00	4.50
❑ 175 DeShaun Foster RC	10.00	3.00
❑ 176 Roy Williams RC	25.00	7.50
❑ 177 Andre Davis RC	10.00	3.00
❑ 178 Alex Brown RC	10.00	3.00
❑ 179 Michael Lewis RC	10.00	3.00
❑ 180 Terry Charles RC	8.00	2.40
❑ 181 Clinton Portis RC	40.00	12.00
❑ 182 Dennis Johnson RC	5.00	1.50
❑ 183 Lito Sheppard RC	10.00	3.00
❑ 184 Ryan Sims RC	10.00	3.00
❑ 185 Raonall Smith RC	8.00	2.40
❑ 186 Albert Haynesworth RC	8.00	2.40
❑ 187 Eddie Freeman RC	5.00	1.50
❑ 188 Levi Jones RC	8.00	2.40
❑ 189 Josh McCown RC	12.00	3.60
❑ 190 Cliff Russell RC	8.00	2.40
❑ 191 Maurice Morris RC	10.00	3.00
❑ 192 Antwaan Randle El RC	12.00	3.60
❑ 193 Ladell Betts RC	10.00	3.00
❑ 194 Daniel Graham RC	10.00	3.00
❑ 195 David Garrard RC	10.00	3.00
❑ 196 Antonio Bryant RC	10.00	3.00

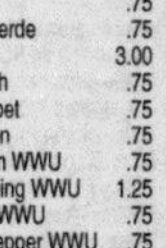

❑ 197	Patrick Ramsey RC	20.00	6.00
❑ 198	Kelly Campbell RC	8.00	2.40
❑ 199	Will Overstreet RC	5.00	1.50
❑ 200	Ryan Denney RC	5.00	1.50
❑ 201	John Henderson RC	10.00	3.00
❑ 202	Freddie Milons RC	8.00	2.40
❑ 203	Tim Carter RC	8.00	2.40
❑ 204	Kurt Kittner RC	8.00	2.40
❑ 205	Joey Harrington RC	40.00	12.00
❑ 206	Ricky Williams RC	8.00	2.40
❑ 207	Bryant McKinnie RC	8.00	2.40
❑ 208	Ed Reed RC	15.00	4.50
❑ 209	Josh Reed RC	10.00	3.00
❑ 210	Seth Burford RC	8.00	2.40
❑ 211	Javon Walker RC	20.00	6.00
❑ 212	Jamar Martin RC	8.00	2.40
❑ 213	Leonard Henry RC	8.00	2.40
❑ 214	Julius Peppers RC	20.00	6.00
❑ 215	Jabar Gaffney RC	10.00	3.00
❑ 216	Kalimba Edwards RC	10.00	3.00
❑ 217	Napoleon Harris RC	10.00	3.00
❑ 218	Ashley Lelie RC	20.00	6.00
❑ 219	Anthony Weaver RC	8.00	2.40
❑ 220	Bryan Thomas RC	8.00	2.40
❑ 221	Wendell Bryant RC	10.00	3.00
❑ 222	Damien Anderson RC	8.00	2.40
❑ 223	Travis Stephens RC	8.00	2.40
❑ 224	Rohan Davey RC	10.00	3.00
❑ 225	Mike Pearson RC	5.00	1.50
❑ 226	Marc Colombo RC	5.00	1.50
❑ 227	Phillip Buchanon RC	10.00	3.00
❑ 228	T.J. Duckett RC	15.00	4.50
❑ 229	Ron Johnson RC	8.00	2.40
❑ 230	Larry Tripplett RC	5.00	1.50
❑ 231	Randy Fasani RC	8.00	2.40
❑ 232	Keyuo Craver RC	8.00	2.40
❑ 233	Marquand Manuel RC	5.00	1.50
❑ 234	Jonathan Wells RC	10.00	3.00
❑ 235	Reche Caldwell RC	10.00	3.00
❑ 236	Luke Staley RC	8.00	2.40
❑ 237	Donte Stallworth RC	20.00	6.00
❑ 238	Levar Fisher RC	10.00	3.00
❑ 239	Lamar Gordon RC	10.00	3.00
❑ 240	William Green RC	15.00	4.50
❑ 241	Dusty Bonner RC	5.00	1.50
❑ 242	Craig Nall RC	10.00	3.00
❑ 243	Eric McCoo RC	5.00	1.50
❑ 244	David Thornton RC	5.00	1.50
❑ 245	Terry Jones RC	8.00	2.40
❑ 246	Lee Mays RC	10.00	3.00
❑ 247	Bryan Fletcher RC	5.00	1.50
❑ 248	Verron Haynes RC	10.00	3.00
❑ 249	Zak Kustok RC	10.00	3.00
❑ 250	Chad Hutchinson RC	10.00	3.00
❑ 251	Andra Davis RC	8.00	2.40
❑ 252	Wes Pate RC	5.00	1.50
❑ 253	Jon McGraw RC	5.00	1.50
❑ 254	Howard Green RC	5.00	1.50
❑ 255	Daryl Jones RC	8.00	2.40
❑ 256	David Priestley RC	8.00	2.40
❑ 257	Marques Anderson RC	10.00	3.00
❑ 258	Roosevelt Williams RC	5.00	1.50
❑ 259	Major Applewhite RC	10.00	3.00
❑ 260	Ronald Curry RC	10.00	3.00
❑ 261	Adrian Peterson RC	10.00	3.00
❑ 262	Tellis Redmon RC	8.00	2.40
❑ 263	Chester Taylor RC	10.00	3.00
❑ 264	Deion Branch RC	25.00	7.50
❑ 265	Tank Williams RC	5.00	1.50

2002 Topps Chrome Refractors

	Nm-Mt	Ex-Mt

*STARS: 3X TO 8X BASIC CARDS
*ROOKIES: 1.2X TO 3X

2002 Topps Chrome King of Kings Super Bowl MVP's

		Nm-Mt	Ex-Mt
❑ KDA	Terrell Davis Marcus Allen	60.00	18.00
❑ KME	Joe Montana John Elway	250.00	75.00
❑ KMR	Joe Montana Jerry Rice	350.00	105.00
❑ KYR	Steve Young Jerry Rice	120.00	36.00

2002 Topps Chrome Super Bowl Goal Posts

		Nm-Mt	Ex-Mt
❑ SBG1	Tom Brady	80.00	24.00
❑ SBG2	Kurt Warner	25.00	7.50
❑ SBG3	Antowain Smith	25.00	7.50
❑ SBG4	Marshall Faulk	30.00	9.00
❑ SBG5	Troy Brown	30.00	9.00
❑ SBG6	Adam Vinatieri	60.00	18.00
❑ SBG7	David Patten	30.00	9.00
❑ SBG8	Torry Holt	30.00	9.00
❑ SBG9	Ty Law	30.00	9.00
❑ SBG10	Isaac Bruce	30.00	9.00

2003 Topps Chrome

		MINT	NRMT
COMP.SET w/o SP's (165)		40.00	18.00
❑ 1	Michael Vick	3.00	1.35
❑ 2	Josh Reed	.75	.35
❑ 3	James Stewart	.75	.35
❑ 4	Quincy Morgan	.75	.35
❑ 5	Corey Bradford	.50	.23
❑ 6	Fred Taylor	1.25	.55
❑ 7	David Patten	.50	.23
❑ 8	Jerome Bettis	1.25	.55
❑ 9	Jerry Porter	.75	.35
❑ 10	Steve McNair	1.25	.55
❑ 11	Stephen Davis	.75	.35
❑ 12	Frank Wycheck	.50	.23
❑ 13	Marcus Pollard	.50	.23
❑ 14	David Terrell	.75	.35
❑ 15	Bubba Franks	.75	.35
❑ 16	Trent Green	.75	.35
❑ 17	Mark Brunell	.75	.35
❑ 18	James Thrash	.50	.23
❑ 19	Mike Alstott	1.25	.55
❑ 20	Deuce McAllister	1.25	.55
❑ 21	Santana Moss	.75	.35
❑ 22	Jason Taylor	.50	.23
❑ 23	Corey Dillon	.75	.35
❑ 24	Jeff Blake	.50	.23
❑ 25	Ed McCaffrey	1.25	.55
❑ 26	Priest Holmes	1.50	.70
❑ 27	Tim Brown	1.25	.55
❑ 28	Curtis Martin	1.25	.55
❑ 29	Derrius Thompson	.50	.23
❑ 30	Jonathan Wells	.50	.23
❑ 31	William Green	.75	.35
❑ 32	Bill Schroeder	.75	.35
❑ 33	Amos Zereoue	.75	.35
❑ 34	Warren Sapp	.75	.35
❑ 35	Koren Robinson	.75	.35
❑ 36	Donovan McNabb	1.50	.70
❑ 37	Edgerrin James	1.25	.55
❑ 38	Kelly Holcomb	.75	.35
❑ 39	Daunte Culpepper	1.25	.55
❑ 40	Tommy Maddox	1.25	.55
❑ 41	Rod Gardner	.75	.35
❑ 42	T.J. Duckett	.75	.35
❑ 43	Drew Bledsoe	1.25	.55
❑ 44	Rod Smith	.75	.35
❑ 45	Peyton Manning	2.00	.90
❑ 46	Darrell Jackson	.75	.35
❑ 47	Brett Favre	3.00	1.35
❑ 48	Ashley Lelie	1.25	.55
❑ 49	Jeremy Shockey	2.00	.90
❑ 50	Hines Ward	1.25	.55
❑ 51	Jeff Garcia	1.25	.55
❑ 52	Eddie Kennison	.50	.23
❑ 53	Brian Urlacher	2.00	.90
❑ 54	Antwaan Randle El	1.25	.55
❑ 55	Eddie George	.75	.35
❑ 56	Derrick Brooks	.75	.35
❑ 57	Isaac Bruce	1.25	.55
❑ 58	Joe Horn	.75	.35
❑ 59	Jon Kitna	.75	.35
❑ 60	David Boston	.75	.35
❑ 61	Todd Heap	.75	.35
❑ 62	Lamar Smith	.50	.23
❑ 63	Germane Crowell	.50	.23
❑ 64	Kevin Johnson	.75	.35
❑ 65	Drew Brees	1.25	.55
❑ 66	Chad Lewis	.50	.23
❑ 67	Charlie Garner	.75	.35
❑ 68	Laveranues Coles	.75	.35
❑ 69	Shaun Alexander	1.25	.55
❑ 70	Kevan Barlow	.75	.35
❑ 71	Aaron Brooks	1.25	.55
❑ 72	Jake Plummer	.75	.35
❑ 73	Emmitt Smith	3.00	1.35
❑ 74	Terry Glenn	.50	.23
❑ 75	Michael Bennett	.75	.35
❑ 76	Deion Branch	1.25	.55
❑ 77	Keyshawn Johnson	1.25	.55
❑ 78	Marc Bulger	1.25	.55
❑ 79	Matt Hasselbeck	.75	.35
❑ 80	Garrison Hearst	.75	.35
❑ 81	Brian Griese	1.25	.55
❑ 82	Johnnie Morton	.75	.35
❑ 83	Patrick Ramsey	1.25	.55
❑ 84	Donald Driver	.75	.35
❑ 85	Joey Harrington	2.00	.90
❑ 86	Ricky Williams	1.25	.55
❑ 87	Jabar Gaffney	.75	.35
❑ 88	Duce Staley	.75	.35
❑ 89	Jimmy Smith	.75	.35
❑ 90	Reggie Wayne	.75	.35
❑ 91	Chad Johnson	.75	.35
❑ 92	Steve Beuerlein	.50	.23
❑ 93	Joey Galloway	.75	.35

Card	MINT	NRMT
❑ 94 Curtis Conway	.50	.23
❑ 95 Brad Johnson	.75	.35
❑ 96 Jamal Lewis	1.25	.55
❑ 97 Terrell Owens	1.25	.55
❑ 98 Todd Pinkston	.75	.35
❑ 99 Keenan McCardell	.50	.23
❑ 100 Antonio Bryant	.75	.35
❑ 101 Eric Moulds	.75	.35
❑ 102 Jim Miller	.50	.23
❑ 103 Troy Brown	.75	.35
❑ 104 Rich Gannon	.75	.35
❑ 105 Chad Pennington	1.50	.70
❑ 106 Michael Strahan	.75	.35
❑ 107 Chris Chambers	1.25	.55
❑ 108 Antowain Smith	.75	.35
❑ 109 Derrick Mason	.75	.35
❑ 110 Michael Pittman	.50	.23
❑ 111 Torry Holt	1.25	.55
❑ 112 Tony Gonzalez	.75	.35
❑ 113 Marty Booker	.75	.35
❑ 114 Shannon Sharpe	.50	.23
❑ 115 Zach Thomas	1.25	.55
❑ 116 Plaxico Burress	.75	.35
❑ 117 Kurt Warner	1.25	.55
❑ 118 Warrick Dunn	.75	.35
❑ 119 Jay Fiedler	.75	.35
❑ 120 LaMont Jordan	.75	.35
❑ 121 Kerry Collins	.75	.35
❑ 122 Jerry Rice	2.50	1.10
❑ 123 Randy Moss	2.00	.90
❑ 124 Tom Brady	2.00	.90
❑ 125 Amani Toomer	.75	.35
❑ 126 Travis Henry	.75	.35
❑ 127 Chris Chandler	.50	.23
❑ 128 Ray Lewis	1.25	.55
❑ 129 Donte Stallworth	1.25	.55
❑ 130 David Carr	2.00	.90
❑ 131 Andre Davis	.50	.23
❑ 132 Travis Taylor	.75	.35
❑ 133 Steve Smith	.75	.35
❑ 134 Tiki Barber	.75	.35
❑ 135 Chad Hutchinson	.75	.35
❑ 136 Marshall Faulk	1.25	.55
❑ 137 Peerless Price	.75	.35
❑ 138 Ahman Green	1.25	.55
❑ 139 Julius Peppers	1.25	.55
❑ 140 LaDainian Tomlinson	1.25	.55
❑ 141 Muhsin Muhammad	.75	.35
❑ 142 Tim Couch	.50	.23
❑ 143 Clinton Portis	2.00	.90
❑ 144 Anthony Thomas	1.25	.55
❑ 145 Marvin Harrison	1.25	.55
❑ 146 Priest Holmes WW	.75	.35
❑ 147 Drew Bledsoe WW	.75	.35
❑ 148 Tom Brady WW	.75	.35
❑ 149 Shaun Alexander WW	.75	.35
❑ 150 Brett Favre WW	1.50	.70
❑ 151 Travis Henry WW	.50	.23
❑ 152 Marshall Faulk WW	.75	.35
❑ 153 Terrell Owens WW	.50	.23
❑ 154 Jeff Garcia WW	.50	.23
❑ 155 Plaxico Burress WW	.50	.23
❑ 156 Donovan McNabb WW	.75	.35
❑ 157 Ricky Williams WW	.75	.35
❑ 158 Michael Vick WW	1.50	.70
❑ 159 Steve Smith WW	.50	.23
❑ 160 Marvin Harrison WW	.50	.23
❑ 161 Chad Pennington WW	.75	.35
❑ 162 Jeremy Shockey WW	.75	.35
❑ 163 Tommy Maddox WW	.50	.23
❑ 164 Steve McNair WW	.50	.23
❑ 165 Rich Gannon WW	.50	.23
❑ 166 Carson Palmer RC	25.00	11.00
❑ 167 J.R. Tolver RC	6.00	2.70
❑ 168 Michael Haynes RC	8.00	3.60
❑ 169 Terrell Suggs RC	12.00	5.50
❑ 170 Rashean Mathis RC	6.00	2.70
❑ 171 Chris Kelsay RC	8.00	3.60
❑ 172 Brad Banks RC	6.00	2.70
❑ 173 Jordan Gross RC	6.00	2.70
❑ 174 Lee Suggs RC	15.00	6.75
❑ 175 Kliff Kingsbury RC	6.00	2.70
❑ 176 William Joseph RC	8.00	3.60
❑ 177 Kelley Washington RC	8.00	3.60
❑ 178 Jerome McDougle RC	8.00	3.60
❑ 179 Keenan Howry RC	8.00	3.60
❑ 180 Chris Simms RC	15.00	6.75
❑ 181 Alonzo Jackson RC	6.00	2.70
❑ 182 L.J. Smith RC	8.00	3.60
❑ 183 Mike Doss RC	8.00	3.60
❑ 184 Bobby Wade RC	8.00	3.60
❑ 185 Ken Hamlin RC	8.00	3.60
❑ 186 Brandon Lloyd RC	10.00	4.50
❑ 187 Justin Fargas RC	8.00	3.60
❑ 188 DeWayne Robertson RC	8.00	3.60
❑ 189 Bryant Johnson RC	8.00	3.60
❑ 190 Boss Bailey RC	10.00	4.50
❑ 191 Onterrio Smith RC	10.00	4.50
❑ 192 Doug Gabriel RC	8.00	3.60
❑ 193 Jimmy Kennedy RC	8.00	3.60
❑ 194 B.J. Askew RC	8.00	3.60
❑ 195 Taylor Jacobs RC	8.00	3.60
❑ 196 Dallas Clark RC	8.00	3.60
❑ 197 DeWayne White RC	6.00	2.70
❑ 198 Arnaz Battle RC	8.00	3.60
❑ 199 Kareem Kelly RC	6.00	2.70
❑ 200 Talman Gardner RC	8.00	3.60
❑ 201 Billy McMullen RC	6.00	2.70
❑ 202 Travis Anglin RC	4.00	1.80
❑ 203 Anquan Boldin RC	20.00	9.00
❑ 204 Osi Umenyiora RC	8.00	3.60
❑ 205 Byron Leftwich RC	30.00	13.50
❑ 206 Marcus Trufant RC	8.00	3.60
❑ 207 Sam Aiken RC	6.00	2.70
❑ 208 LaBrandon Toefield RC	8.00	3.60
❑ 209 Terry Pierce RC	6.00	2.70
❑ 210 Charles Rogers RC	10.00	4.50
❑ 211 Chaun Thompson RC	4.00	1.80
❑ 212 Chris Brown RC	15.00	6.75
❑ 213 Justin Gage RC	8.00	3.60
❑ 214 Kevin Williams RC	8.00	3.60
❑ 215 Willis McGahee RC	20.00	9.00
❑ 216 Victor Hobson RC	8.00	3.60
❑ 217 Brian St.Pierre RC	8.00	3.60
❑ 218 Nate Burleson RC	12.00	5.50
❑ 219 Calvin Pace RC	6.00	2.70
❑ 220 Larry Johnson RC	15.00	6.75
❑ 221 Andre Woolfolk RC	8.00	3.60
❑ 222 Tyrone Calico RC	10.00	4.50
❑ 223 Seneca Wallace RC	8.00	3.60
❑ 224 Domanick Davis RC	15.00	6.75
❑ 225 Rex Grossman RC	20.00	9.00
❑ 226 Artose Pinner RC	8.00	3.60
❑ 227 Jason Witten RC	12.00	5.50
❑ 228 Bennie Joppru RC	8.00	3.60
❑ 229 Bethel Johnson RC	12.00	5.50
❑ 230 Kyle Boller RC	20.00	9.00
❑ 231 Shaun McDonald RC	8.00	3.60
❑ 232 Musa Smith RC	8.00	3.60
❑ 233 Ken Dorsey RC	12.00	5.50
❑ 234 Johnathan Sullivan RC	6.00	2.70
❑ 235 Andre Johnson RC	20.00	9.00
❑ 236 Nick Barnett RC	12.00	5.50
❑ 237 Teyo Johnson RC	8.00	3.60
❑ 238 Terence Newman RC	15.00	6.75
❑ 239 Kevin Curtis RC	8.00	3.60
❑ 240 Dave Ragone RC	8.00	3.60
❑ 241 Ty Warren RC	8.00	3.60
❑ 242 Walter Young RC	4.00	1.80
❑ 243 Kevin Walter RC	6.00	2.70
❑ 244 Carl Ford RC	4.00	1.80
❑ 245 Cecil Sapp RC	6.00	2.70
❑ 246 Sultan McCullough RC	6.00	2.70
❑ 247 Eugene Wilson RC	6.00	2.70
❑ 248 Ricky Manning RC	8.00	3.60
❑ 249 Andrew Williams RC	6.00	2.70
❑ 250 Juston Wood RC	4.00	1.80
❑ 251 Cory Redding RC	6.00	2.70
❑ 252 Charles Tillman RC	12.00	5.50
❑ 253 Terrence Edwards RC	6.00	2.70
❑ 254 Adrian Madise RC	6.00	2.70
❑ 255 David Kircus RC	6.00	2.70
❑ 256 Zuriel Smith RC	4.00	1.80
❑ 257 Earnest Graham RC	6.00	2.70
❑ 258 Ronald Bellamy RC	6.00	2.70
❑ 259 John Anderson RC	4.00	1.80
❑ 260 David Tyree RC	6.00	2.70
❑ 261 Malaefou MacKenzie RC	4.00	1.80
❑ 262 Amhmad Galloway RC	6.00	2.70
❑ 263 Brooks Bollinger RC	8.00	3.60
❑ 264 Gibran Hamdan RC	4.00	1.80
❑ 265 Taco Wallace RC	6.00	2.70
❑ 266 LaTarence Dunbar RC	6.00	2.70
❑ 267 Justin Griffith RC	6.00	2.70
❑ 268 Bradie James RC	8.00	3.60
❑ 269 Danny Curley RC	4.00	1.80
❑ 270 Kenny Peterson RC	6.00	2.70
❑ 271 DeAndrew Rubin RC	4.00	1.80
❑ 272 Ryan Hoag RC	4.00	1.80
❑ 273 Rien Long RC	4.00	1.80
❑ 274 Troy Polamalu RC	8.00	3.60
❑ 275 Terrence Holt RC	6.00	2.70
❑ URB1 Emmitt Smith Walter Payton Barry Sanders		

2003 Topps Chrome Black Refractors

MINT NRMT

*STARS: 2.5X TO 6X BASIC CARDS
*ROOKIES: 1.5X TO 4X

2003 Topps Chrome Gold Xfractors

MINT NRMT

*STARS: 4X TO 10X BASIC CARDS
*ROOKIES: 1.2X TO 3X

2003 Topps Chrome Gridiron Badges

Card	MINT	NRMT
❑ GBBF Bubba Franks	25.00	11.00
❑ GBBU Brian Urlacher	40.00	18.00
❑ GBCB Champ Bailey	20.00	9.00
❑ GBCD Corey Dillon	25.00	11.00
❑ GBDB Drew Bledsoe	25.00	11.00
❑ GBEM Eric Moulds	20.00	9.00
❑ GBES Emmitt Smith	60.00	27.00
❑ GBHW Hines Ward	25.00	11.00
❑ GBJA John Abraham	15.00	6.75
❑ GBJG Jeff Garcia	20.00	9.00
❑ GBJH Joe Horn	15.00	6.75
❑ GBJL John Lynch	25.00	11.00
❑ GBJR Jerry Rice	50.00	22.00
❑ GBJS Jeremy Shockey	30.00	13.50
❑ GBJT Jason Taylor	20.00	9.00
❑ GBMF Marshall Faulk	25.00	11.00
❑ GBMH Marvin Harrison	25.00	11.00
❑ GBMS Michael Strahan	15.00	6.75
❑ GBPM Peyton Manning	50.00	22.00
❑ GBRG Rich Gannon	20.00	9.00
❑ GBRW Ricky Williams	25.00	11.00
❑ GBRWO Rod Woodson	15.00	6.75
❑ GBTD Todd Heap	15.00	6.75
❑ GBTO Terrell Owens	20.00	9.00

2003 Topps Chrome Pro Bowl Jerseys

Card	MINT	NRMT
❑ PBCB Champ Bailey	12.00	5.50
❑ PBDB Drew Bledsoe	12.00	5.50
❑ PBEM Eric Moulds	10.00	4.50

❑ PBJL	John Lynch	12.00	5.50
❑ PBJP	Julian Peterson	12.00	5.50
❑ PBJS	Jeremy Shockey	15.00	6.75
❑ PBJT	Jason Taylor	12.00	5.50
❑ PBLG	La'Roi Glover	10.00	4.50
❑ PBMF	Marshall Faulk	12.00	5.50
❑ PBPM	Peyton Manning	15.00	6.75
❑ PBRW	Rod Woodson	12.00	5.50
❑ PBTL	Ty Law	15.00	6.75

2003 Topps Chrome Record Breakers Jerseys

		MINT	NRMT
❑ RBRBS	Barry Sanders	50.00	22.00
❑ RBRDM	Dan Marino	120.00	55.00
❑ RBRES	Emmitt Smith	60.00	27.00
❑ RBRJE	John Elway	100.00	45.00
❑ RBRJR	Jerry Rice	50.00	22.00
❑ RBRKW	Kurt Warner	25.00	11.00
❑ RBRLT	LaDainian Tomlinson	20.00	9.00
❑ RBRMF	Marshall Faulk	25.00	11.00
❑ RBRRW	Ricky Williams	25.00	11.00
❑ RBRSY	Steve Young	40.00	18.00
❑ RBRWP	Walter Payton	120.00	55.00

2004 Topps Chrome

	Nm-Mt	Ex-Mt
COMP.SET w/o SP's (165)	30.00	9.00
ROOKIE STATED ODDS 1:2		
RH38 STATED ODDS 1:24 HOB/RET		

❑ 1	Peyton Manning	1.50	.45
❑ 2	Patrick Ramsey	.60	.18
❑ 3	Justin McCareins	.40	.12
❑ 4	Matt Hasselbeck	.60	.18
❑ 5	Chris Chambers	.60	.18
❑ 6	Bubba Franks	.60	.18
❑ 7	Eric Moulds	.60	.18
❑ 8	Anquan Boldin	1.00	.30
❑ 9	Brian Urlacher	1.25	.35
❑ 10	Stephen Davis	.60	.18
❑ 11	Michael Vick	2.00	.60
❑ 12	Dante Hall	1.00	.30
❑ 13	Chad Pennington	1.25	.35
❑ 14	Kevan Barlow	.60	.18
❑ 15	Tommy Maddox	.60	.18
❑ 16	Domanick Davis	1.00	.30
❑ 17	Dwight Freeney	.40	.12
❑ 18	LaVar Arrington	2.00	.60
❑ 19	Troy Hambrick	.40	.12
❑ 20	Jake Plummer	.60	.18
❑ 21	Willis McGahee	1.00	.30
❑ 22	Steve McNair	1.00	.30
❑ 23	Kerry Collins	.60	.18
❑ 24	Hines Ward	1.00	.30
❑ 25	Terrell Owens	1.00	.30
❑ 26	Jerome Pathon	.40	.12
❑ 27	Andre Johnson	1.00	.30
❑ 28	DeShaun Foster	.60	.18
❑ 29	Terrell Suggs	.60	.18
❑ 30	Marcel Shipp	.60	.18
❑ 31	Kyle Boller	1.00	.30
❑ 32	Javon Walker	.60	.18
❑ 33	Ahman Green	1.00	.30
❑ 34	Travis Henry	.60	.18
❑ 35	Randy McMichael	.40	.12
❑ 36	Jerry Rice	2.00	.60
❑ 37	Travis Taylor	.40	.12
❑ 38	Fred Taylor	.60	.18
❑ 39	Zach Thomas	1.00	.30
❑ 40	Marques Tuiasosopo	.60	.18
❑ 41	Laveranues Coles	.60	.18
❑ 42	Thomas Jones	.60	.18
❑ 43	Jamie Sharper	.40	.12
❑ 44	Quincy Morgan	.60	.18
❑ 45	Troy Brown	.60	.18
❑ 46	Joey Galloway	.60	.18
❑ 47	Justin Fargas	.60	.18
❑ 48	Daunte Culpepper	1.00	.30
❑ 49	Keenan McCardell	.40	.12
❑ 50	Priest Holmes	1.25	.35
❑ 51	Chad Johnson	.60	.18
❑ 52	Marty Booker	.60	.18
❑ 53	Tim Rattay	.60	.18
❑ 54	Brian Westbrook	.60	.18
❑ 55	Ricky Williams	1.00	.30
❑ 56	Lee Suggs	1.00	.30
❑ 57	Keith Brooking	.40	.12
❑ 58	Rex Grossman	1.00	.30
❑ 59	Dallas Clark	.60	.18
❑ 60	Charles Rogers	.60	.18
❑ 61	Donte' Stallworth	.60	.18
❑ 62	Deion Branch	1.00	.30
❑ 63	Ike Hilliard	.40	.12
❑ 64	Michael Strahan	.60	.18
❑ 65	Randy Moss	1.25	.35
❑ 66	Isaac Bruce	.60	.18
❑ 67	Brad Johnson	.60	.18
❑ 68	Warrick Dunn	.60	.18
❑ 69	Josh McCown	.60	.18
❑ 70	Donovan McNabb	1.25	.35
❑ 71	Shaun Alexander	1.00	.30
❑ 72	William Green	.60	.18
❑ 73	Carson Palmer	1.25	.35
❑ 74	Quentin Griffin	1.00	.30
❑ 75	LaDainian Tomlinson	1.00	.30
❑ 76	Edgerrin James	1.00	.30
❑ 77	Santana Moss	.60	.18
❑ 78	Marshall Faulk	1.00	.30
❑ 79	Tyrone Calico	.60	.18
❑ 80	Marvin Harrison	1.00	.30
❑ 81	Tony Gonzalez	.60	.18
❑ 82	Deuce McAllister	1.00	.30
❑ 83	Drew Brees	1.00	.30
❑ 84	Todd Pinkston	.40	.12
❑ 85	Jeff Garcia	1.00	.30
❑ 86	Darrell Jackson	.60	.18
❑ 87	Ray Lewis	1.00	.30
❑ 88	Billy Volek	1.00	.30
❑ 89	Rudi Johnson	.60	.18
❑ 90	Julius Peppers	1.00	.30
❑ 91	Peter Warrick	.60	.18
❑ 92	Trent Green	.60	.18
❑ 93	Onterrio Smith	.60	.18
❑ 94	Jerome Bettis	1.00	.30
❑ 95	Keyshawn Johnson	.60	.18
❑ 96	Jamal Lewis	1.00	.30
❑ 97	Alge Crumpler	.60	.18
❑ 98	Michael Bennett	.60	.18
❑ 99	Jimmy Smith	.60	.18
❑ 100	Brett Favre	2.50	.75
❑ 101	Jerry Porter	.60	.18
❑ 102	Marc Bulger	1.00	.30
❑ 103	David Carr	1.00	.30
❑ 104	Mark Brunell	.60	.18
❑ 105	Aaron Brooks	.60	.18
❑ 106	Plaxico Burress	.60	.18
❑ 107	Correll Buckhalter	.60	.18
❑ 108	Jevon Kearse	.60	.18
❑ 109	Michael Pittman	.40	.12
❑ 110	Clinton Portis	1.00	.30
❑ 111	Corey Dillon	.60	.18
❑ 112	Steve Smith	.60	.18
❑ 113	Eddie Kennison	.40	.12
❑ 114	Amani Toomer	.60	.18
❑ 115	Kelly Holcomb	.60	.18
❑ 116	Torry Holt	1.00	.30
❑ 117	Eddie George	.60	.18
❑ 118	Jeremy Shockey	1.00	.30
❑ 119	Jon Kitna	.60	.18
❑ 120	Todd Heap	.60	.18
❑ 121	Ashley Lelie	.60	.18
❑ 122	Byron Leftwich	1.50	.45
❑ 123	Duce Staley	.60	.18
❑ 124	Rod Gardner	.60	.18
❑ 125	Tom Brady	1.50	.45
❑ 126	Reggie Wayne	.60	.18
❑ 127	Joe Horn	.60	.18
❑ 128	Curtis Martin	1.00	.30
❑ 129	Charlie Garner	.60	.18
❑ 130	Derrick Mason	.60	.18
❑ 131	Marcus Robinson	.60	.18
❑ 132	David Boston	.60	.18
❑ 133	Drew Bledsoe	1.00	.30
❑ 134	Anthony Thomas	.60	.18
❑ 135	Tiki Barber	.60	.18
❑ 136	Terry Glenn	.40	.12
❑ 137	A.J. Feeley	1.00	.30
❑ 138	Peerless Price	.60	.18
❑ 139	Jake Delhomme	1.00	.30
❑ 140	Kevin Faulk	.40	.12
❑ 141	Quincy Carter	.60	.18
❑ 142	Joey Harrington	1.00	.30
❑ 143	Donald Driver	.60	.18
❑ 144	Koren Robinson	.60	.18
❑ 145	Rod Smith	.60	.18
❑ 146	Anquan Boldin WW	.40	.12
❑ 147	Jamal Lewis WW	.60	.18
❑ 148	Priest Holmes WW	1.00	.30
❑ 149	Peyton Manning WW	1.00	.30
❑ 150	Marvin Harrison WW	.60	.18
❑ 151	Steve McNair WW	.60	.18
❑ 152	Travis Henry WW	.40	.12
❑ 153	Torry Holt WW	.60	.18
❑ 154	Tom Brady WW	1.00	.30
❑ 155	Ahman Green WW	.60	.18
❑ 156	Donovan McNabb WW	1.00	.30
❑ 157	Deuce McAllister WW	.60	.18
❑ 158	Domanick Davis WW	.60	.18
❑ 159	Clinton Portis WW	1.00	.30
❑ 160	Rudi Johnson WW	.40	.12
❑ 161	Brett Favre WW	1.25	.35
❑ 162	LaDainian Tomlinson WW	.60	.18
❑ 163	Steve Smith WW	.40	.12
❑ 164	Edgerrin James WW	.60	.18
❑ 165	Ty Law WW	.40	.12
❑ 166	Ben Roethlisberger RC	60.00	18.00
❑ 167	Ahmad Carroll RC	6.00	1.80
❑ 168	Johnnie Morant RC	5.00	1.50
❑ 169	Greg Jones RC	5.00	1.50
❑ 170	Michael Clayton RC	12.00	3.60

	Nm-Mt	Ex-Mt
❑ 171 Josh Harris RC	5.00	1.50
❑ 172 Tatum Bell RC	8.00	2.40
❑ 173 Robert Gallery RC	8.00	2.40
❑ 174 B.J. Symons RC	5.00	1.50
❑ 175 Roy Williams RC	15.00	4.50
❑ 176 DeAngelo Hall RC	6.00	1.80
❑ 177 Jeff Smoker RC	8.00	2.40
❑ 178 Lee Evans RC	8.00	2.40
❑ 179 Michael Jenkins RC	5.00	1.50
❑ 180 Steven Jackson RC	15.00	4.50
❑ 181 Will Smith RC	5.00	1.50
❑ 182 Vince Wilfork RC	6.00	1.80
❑ 183 Ben Troupe RC	5.00	1.50
❑ 184 Chris Gamble RC	6.00	1.80
❑ 185 Kevin Jones RC	15.00	4.50
❑ 186 Jonathan Vilma RC	5.00	1.50
❑ 187 Dontarrious Thomas RC	5.00	1.50
❑ 188 Michael Boulware RC	5.00	1.50
❑ 189 Mewelde Moore RC	6.00	1.80
❑ 190 Drew Henson RC	12.00	3.60
❑ 191 D.J. Williams RC	6.00	1.80
❑ 192 Ernest Wilford RC	5.00	1.50
❑ 193 John Navarre RC	5.00	1.50
❑ 194 Jerricho Cotchery RC	5.00	1.50
❑ 195 Derrick Hamilton RC	4.00	1.20
❑ 196 Carlos Francis RC	4.00	1.20
❑ 197 Ben Watson RC	5.00	1.50
❑ 198 Reggie Williams RC	6.00	1.80
❑ 199 Devard Darling RC	5.00	1.50
❑ 200 Chris Perry RC	10.00	3.00
❑ 201 Derrick Strait RC	5.00	1.50
❑ 202 Sean Taylor RC	6.00	1.80
❑ 203 Michael Turner RC	4.00	1.20
❑ 204 Keary Colbert RC	6.00	1.80
❑ 205 Eli Manning RC	30.00	9.00
❑ 206 Julius Jones RC	20.00	6.00
❑ 207 Jason Babin RC	5.00	1.50
❑ 208 Cody Pickett RC	5.00	1.50
❑ 209 Kenechi Udeze RC	5.00	1.50
❑ 210 Rashaun Woods RC	6.00	1.80
❑ 211 Matt Schaub RC	8.00	2.40
❑ 212 Tommie Harris RC	6.00	1.80
❑ 213 Dwan Edwards RC	2.50	.75
❑ 214 Shawn Andrews RC	5.00	1.50
❑ 215 Larry Fitzgerald RC	15.00	4.50
❑ 216 P.K. Sam RC	4.00	1.20
❑ 217 Teddy Lehman RC	5.00	1.50
❑ 218 Darius Watts RC	6.00	1.80
❑ 219 D.J. Hackett RC	4.00	1.20
❑ 220 Cedric Cobbs RC	5.00	1.50
❑ 221 Antwan Odom RC	5.00	1.50
❑ 222 Marquise Hill RC	4.00	1.20
❑ 223 Luke McCown RC	5.00	1.50
❑ 224 Triandos Luke RC	5.00	1.50
❑ 225 Kellen Winslow RC	12.00	3.60
❑ 226 Derek Abney RC	5.00	1.50
❑ 227 Chris Cooley RC	5.00	1.50
❑ 228 Dunta Robinson RC	5.00	1.50
❑ 229 Sean Jones RC	4.00	1.20
❑ 230 Philip Rivers RC	15.00	4.50
❑ 231 Craig Krenzel RC	5.00	1.50
❑ 232 Daryl Smith RC	5.00	1.50
❑ 233 Samie Parker RC	5.00	1.50
❑ 234 Ben Hartsock RC	5.00	1.50
❑ 235 J.P. Losman RC	12.00	3.60
❑ 236 Karlos Dansby RC	5.00	1.50
❑ 237 Ricardo Colclough RC	5.00	1.50
❑ 238 Bernard Berrian RC	5.00	1.50
❑ 239 Junior Siavii RC	5.00	1.50
❑ 240 Devery Henderson RC	4.00	1.20
❑ 241 Adimchinobe Echemandu RC	4.00	1.20
❑ 242 Patrick Crayton RC	5.00	1.50
❑ 243 Marcus Tubbs RC	5.00	1.50
❑ 244 Jamaar Taylor RC	5.00	1.50
❑ 245 Andy Hall RC	4.00	1.20
❑ 246 Darnell Dockett RC	4.00	1.20
❑ 247 Darrion Scott RC	5.00	1.50
❑ 248 Jim Sorgi RC	5.00	1.50
❑ 249 Jeff Dugan RC	2.50	.75
❑ 250 Ryan Krause RC	4.00	1.20
❑ 251 Nate Lawrie RC	4.00	1.20
❑ 252 Casey Bramlet RC	4.00	1.20
❑ 253 Donnell Washington RC	5.00	1.50
❑ 254 Jonathan Smith RC	4.00	1.20
❑ 255 Tank Johnson RC	4.00	1.20
❑ 256 Keith Smith RC	4.00	1.20
❑ 257 Brandon Miree RC	4.00	1.20
❑ 258 Michael Gaines RC	4.00	1.20
❑ 259 Keiwan Ratliff RC	4.00	1.20
❑ 260 Stuart Schweigert RC	5.00	1.50
❑ 261 Derrick Ward RC	2.50	.75
❑ 262 Matt Ware RC	5.00	1.50
❑ 263 Tim Anderson RC	5.00	1.50
❑ 264 Bradlee Van Pelt RC	5.00	1.50
❑ 265 Shawntae Spencer RC	5.00	1.50
❑ 266 Joey Thomas RC	5.00	1.50
❑ 267 Maurice Mann RC	4.00	1.20
❑ 268 Tim Euhus RC	5.00	1.50
❑ 269 Matt Mauck RC	5.00	1.50
❑ 270 Sloan Thomas RC	4.00	1.20
❑ 271 Jeris McIntyre RC	4.00	1.20
❑ 272 Randy Starks RC	4.00	1.20
❑ 273 Clarence Moore RC	5.00	1.50
❑ 274 Drew Carter RC	5.00	1.50
❑ 275 Sean Ryan RC	4.00	1.20
❑ RH38 Tom Brady RH	5.00	1.50

2004 Topps Chrome Black Refractors

Nm-Mt Ex-Mt

*STARS: 5X TO 12X BASE CARD HI
*ROOKIES: 2.5X TO 6X BASE CARD HI
STATED ODDS 1:45 HOB, 1:46 RET
STATED PRINT RUN 100 SER.#'d SETS

2004 Topps Chrome Gold Xfractors

Nm-Mt Ex-Mt

*ROOKIES: 1.2X TO 3X BASE CARD HI
ONE PER HOBBY BOX
STATED PRINT RUN 279 SER.#'d SETS

2004 Topps Chrome Refractors

Nm-Mt Ex-Mt

*STARS: 2.5X TO 6X BASE CARD HI
*ROOKIES: .8X TO 2X BASE CARD HI
STATED ODDS 1:6 HOB/RET
RH38 STATED ODDS 1:12,581H, 1:13,248R

	Nm-Mt	Ex-Mt
❑ RH38 Tom Brady RH/100	40.00	12.00

2004 Topps Chrome Gridiron Badges

STATED ODDS 1:1707 HOB, 1:1816 RET
STATED PRINT RUN 50 SER.#'d SETS

	Nm-Mt	Ex-Mt
❑ GBAB Anquan Boldin	25.00	7.50
❑ GBAG Ahman Green	30.00	9.00
❑ GBBU Brian Urlacher	40.00	12.00
❑ GBCJ Chad Johnson	25.00	7.50
❑ GBHW Hines Ward	30.00	9.00
❑ GBJL Jamal Lewis	30.00	9.00
❑ GBLA LaVar Arrington	60.00	18.00
❑ GBMH Marvin Harrison	30.00	9.00
❑ GBPH Priest Holmes	40.00	12.00
❑ GBPM Peyton Manning	50.00	15.00
❑ GBRL Ray Lewis	30.00	9.00
❑ GBSM Steve McNair	30.00	9.00
❑ GBTH Torry Holt	30.00	9.00

2004 Topps Chrome Premiere Prospects

	Nm-Mt	Ex-Mt
COMPLETE SET (20)	40.00	12.00

STATED ODDS 1:6 HOB/RET
*REFRACTORS: 2.5X TO 6X BASIC INSERTS
REFRACTOR STATED ODDS 1:627H, 1:629R
REFRACTOR PRINT RUN 100 SER.#'d SETS

	Nm-Mt	Ex-Mt
❑ PP1 Ben Roethlisberger	25.00	7.50
❑ PP2 Chris Perry	4.00	1.20
❑ PP3 Darius Watts	2.50	.75
❑ PP4 Devery Henderson	1.50	.45
❑ PP5 Eli Manning	12.00	3.60
❑ PP6 Greg Jones	2.00	.60
❑ PP7 J.P. Losman	5.00	1.50
❑ PP8 Julius Jones	8.00	2.40
❑ PP9 Kellen Winslow	5.00	1.50
❑ PP10 Kevin Jones	6.00	1.80
❑ PP11 Larry Fitzgerald	6.00	1.80
❑ PP12 Lee Evans	3.00	.90
❑ PP13 Michael Clayton	5.00	1.50
❑ PP14 Michael Jenkins	2.00	.60
❑ PP15 Philip Rivers	6.00	1.80
❑ PP16 Rashaun Woods	2.50	.75
❑ PP17 Reggie Williams	2.50	.75
❑ PP18 Roy Williams WR	6.00	1.80
❑ PP19 Steven Jackson	6.00	1.80
❑ PP20 Tatum Bell	3.00	.90

2004 Topps Chrome Premium Performers Autographed Jerseys

Nm-Mt Ex-Mt

GROUP A/50 ODDS 1:25,611 H, 1:27,648 R
GROUP B/100 ODDS 1:3187 H, 1:3170 R
UNPRICED GOLD/10 ODDS 1:27,581H, 1:32,496R

	Nm-Mt	Ex-Mt
❑ PPCP Chad Pennington/50	120.00	36.00
❑ PPEM Eli Manning/100	300.00	90.00
❑ PPMV Michael Vick/100	120.00	36.00
❑ PPPM Peyton Manning/100	100.00	30.00
❑ PPRW Roy Williams WR/100	150.00	45.00

2004 Topps Chrome Pro Bowl Jerseys

	Nm-Mt	Ex-Mt
GROUP A STATED ODDS 1:1260H, 1:1273R		
GROUP B STATED ODDS 1:965 H, 1:984 R		
GROUP C STATED ODDS 1:89 H, 1:89 R		
❑ AB Anquan Boldin C	10.00	3.00
❑ AO Adewale Ogunleye C	8.00	2.40
❑ CB Champ Bailey B	12.00	3.60
❑ DF Dwight Freeney C	8.00	2.40
❑ DH Dante Hall C	12.00	3.60
❑ JL Jamal Lewis C	12.00	3.60
❑ KB Keith Brooking B	10.00	3.00
❑ LL Leonard Little B	10.00	3.00
❑ RL Ray Lewis C	12.00	3.60
❑ SD Stephen Davis C	10.00	3.00
❑ SE Shaun Ellis B	10.00	3.00
❑ TH Todd Heap C	10.00	3.00
❑ TL Ty Law A	10.00	3.00
❑ ZT Zach Thomas C	12.00	3.60

2001 Topps Debut

	Nm-Mt	Ex-Mt
COMP.SET w/o SP's (100)	20.00	6.00
❑ 1 Marshall Faulk	1.25	.55
❑ 2 Ricky Watters	.60	.25
❑ 3 Bill Schroeder	.60	.25
❑ 4 Muhsin Muhammad	.60	.25
❑ 5 Peter Warrick	1.00	.45
❑ 6 Marvin Harrison	1.00	.45
❑ 7 Stephen Davis	1.00	.45
❑ 8 Cris Carter	1.00	.45
❑ 9 Charlie Batch	1.00	.45
❑ 10 David Boston	1.00	.45
❑ 11 Ike Hilliard	.60	.25
❑ 12 Steve McNair	1.00	.45
❑ 13 Kordell Stewart	.60	.25
❑ 14 Travis Prentice	.40	.18
❑ 15 Sammy Morris	.40	.18
❑ 16 Vinny Testaverde	.60	.25
❑ 17 Tyrone Wheatley	.60	.25
❑ 18 Jeff Garcia	1.00	.45
❑ 19 Brett Favre	3.00	1.35
❑ 20 Jake Plummer	.60	.25
❑ 21 Cade McNown	.40	.18
❑ 22 Rob Johnson	.60	.25
❑ 23 Tim Couch	.60	.25
❑ 24 Jerome Bettis	1.00	.45
❑ 25 Ricky Williams	1.00	.45
❑ 26 Darrell Jackson	1.00	.45
❑ 27 Troy Brown	.60	.25
❑ 28 Jamal Lewis	1.50	.70
❑ 29 Isaac Bruce	1.00	.45
❑ 30 Lamar Smith	.60	.25
❑ 31 Qadry Ismail	.60	.25
❑ 32 Elvis Grbac	.60	.25
❑ 33 Shaun Alexander	1.25	.55
❑ 34 Peyton Manning	2.50	1.10
❑ 35 Curtis Martin	1.00	.45
❑ 36 Jamal Anderson	1.00	.45
❑ 37 Mark Brunell	1.00	.45
❑ 38 Emmitt Smith	2.00	.90
❑ 39 Chad Lewis	.40	.18
❑ 40 Randy Moss	2.00	.90
❑ 41 Kurt Warner	2.00	.90
❑ 42 Terrence Wilkins	.40	.18
❑ 43 Corey Dillon	1.00	.45
❑ 44 Brian Griese	1.00	.45
❑ 45 Jon Kitna	1.00	.45
❑ 46 Eric Moulds	.60	.25
❑ 47 Steve Beuerlein	.60	.25
❑ 48 James Allen	.60	.25
❑ 49 Amani Toomer	.40	.18
❑ 50 Daunte Culpepper	1.00	.45
❑ 51 Michael Pittman	.40	.18
❑ 52 Warrick Dunn	1.00	.45
❑ 53 Terrell Owens	1.00	.45
❑ 54 Donald Hayes	.40	.18
❑ 55 Keenan McCardell	.40	.18
❑ 56 Tony Gonzalez	.60	.25
❑ 57 Freddie Jones	.40	.18
❑ 58 Charlie Garner	.60	.25
❑ 59 Shawn Jefferson	.40	.18
❑ 60 Brian Urlacher	1.50	.70
❑ 61 Donovan McNabb	1.25	.55
❑ 62 Az-Zahir Hakim	.40	.18
❑ 63 James Thrash	.60	.25
❑ 64 Hines Ward	1.00	.45
❑ 65 Shawn Bryson	.40	.18
❑ 66 Wayne Chrebet	.60	.25
❑ 67 Kevin Johnson	.60	.25
❑ 68 Eddie George	1.00	.45
❑ 69 Derrick Alexander	.60	.25
❑ 70 Tim Brown	1.00	.45
❑ 71 Jay Fiedler	1.00	.45
❑ 72 Aaron Brooks	1.00	.45
❑ 73 Torry Holt	1.00	.45
❑ 74 Edgerrin James	1.25	.55
❑ 75 Shannon Sharpe	.60	.25
❑ 76 Oronde Gadsden	.60	.25
❑ 77 Rod Smith	.60	.25
❑ 78 Rich Gannon	1.00	.45
❑ 79 Fred Taylor	1.00	.45
❑ 80 Derrick Mason	.60	.25
❑ 81 Joe Horn	.60	.25
❑ 82 Robert Smith	.60	.25
❑ 83 James Stewart	.60	.25
❑ 84 Jeff George	.60	.25
❑ 85 Troy Aikman	1.50	.70
❑ 86 Charles Johnson	.40	.18
❑ 87 Ahman Green	1.00	.45
❑ 88 Shaun King	.40	.18
❑ 89 Ray Lewis	1.00	.45
❑ 90 Trent Dilfer	.60	.25
❑ 91 Drew Bledsoe	1.25	.55
❑ 92 Jimmy Smith	.60	.25
❑ 93 Ed McCaffrey	1.00	.45
❑ 94 Kerry Collins	.60	.25
❑ 95 Terry Glenn	.60	.25
❑ 96 Ron Dayne	1.00	.45
❑ 97 Keyshawn Johnson	1.00	.45
❑ 98 Antonio Freeman	1.00	.45
❑ 99 Tiki Barber	.60	.25
❑ 100 Mike Anderson	1.00	.45
❑ 101 Drew Brees AU RC	50.00	22.00
❑ 102 Chris Weinke AU RC	20.00	9.00
❑ 103 LaDainian Tomlinson AUTO RC	80.00	36.00
❑ 104 Michael Bennett AUTO RC	30.00	13.50
❑ 105 Anthony Thomas AUTO RC	50.00	22.00
❑ 106 LaMont Jordan AUTO RC	25.00	11.00
❑ 107 David Terrell AU RC	25.00	11.00
❑ 108 Michael Vick AU RC	300.00	135.00
❑ 109 Deuce McAllister AUTO RC	60.00	27.00
❑ 110 James Jackson AUTO RC	20.00	9.00
❑ 111 Mike McMahon JSY RC	15.00	6.75
❑ 112 Cedrick Wilson JSY RC	15.00	6.75
❑ 113 Ken Lucas JSY RC	15.00	6.75
❑ 114 Fred Smoot JSY RC	15.00	6.75
❑ 115 Alge Crumpler JSY RC	20.00	9.00
❑ 116 Sage Rosenfels JSY RC	15.00	6.75
❑ 117 Rashard Casey JSY RC	10.00	4.50
❑ 118 David Allen JSY RC	10.00	4.50
❑ 119 B.Newcombe JSY RC	10.00	4.50
❑ 120 Jesse Palmer JSY RC	15.00	6.75
❑ 121 Tommy Polley JSY RC	15.00	6.75
❑ 122 Kevan Barlow JSY RC	15.00	6.75
❑ 123 Scotty Anderson JSY RC	10.00	4.50
❑ 124 Travis Minor JSY RC	10.00	4.50
❑ 125 Snoop Minnis JSY RC	10.00	4.50
❑ 126 Moran Norris JSY RC	8.00	3.60
❑ 127 Alex Lincoln JSY RC	10.00	4.50
❑ 128 Chad Johnson JSY RC	30.00	13.50
❑ 129 Boo Williams JSY RC	10.00	4.50
❑ 130 Brian Natkin JSY RC	8.00	3.60
❑ 131 Orlando Huff JSY RC	8.00	3.60
❑ 132 Derrick Gibson JSY RC	10.00	4.50
❑ 133 Tony Driver JSY RC	15.00	6.75
❑ 134 T.Marshall JSY RC	15.00	6.75
❑ 135 Alex Bannister JSY RC	10.00	4.50
❑ 136 M.Greenwood JSY RC	8.00	3.60
❑ 137 Ennis Davis JSY RC	8.00	3.60
❑ 138 Mike Cerimele JSY RC	8.00	3.60
❑ 139 David Rivers JSY RC	10.00	4.50
❑ 140 D.McClintock JSY RC	10.00	4.50
❑ 141 Tay Cody JSY RC	8.00	3.60
❑ 142 Arther Love JSY RC	8.00	3.60
❑ 143 Sly Johnson JSY RC	10.00	4.50
❑ 144 Dan Alexander JSY RC	15.00	6.75
❑ 145 Will Allen JSY RC	10.00	4.50
❑ 146 Andre Dyson JSY RC	8.00	3.60
❑ 147 Margin Hooks JSY RC	8.00	3.60
❑ 148 Adam Archuleta JSY RC	15.00	6.75
❑ 149 Sedrick Hodge JSY RC	8.00	3.60
❑ 150 Kendrell Bell JSY RC	30.00	13.50
❑ 151 Reggie Wayne RC	10.00	4.50
❑ 152 Rod Gardner RC	6.00	2.70
❑ 153 Chris Chambers RC	8.00	3.60
❑ 154 Jamal Reynolds RC	6.00	2.70
❑ 155 Ben Hamilton RC	6.00	2.70
❑ 156 Dan Morgan RC	20.00	9.00
❑ 157 Quincy Morgan RC	6.00	2.70
❑ 158 Travis Henry RC	8.00	3.60
❑ 159 Ken-Yon Rambo RC	4.00	1.80
❑ 160 Josh Heupel RC	6.00	2.70
❑ 161 Marcus Stroud RC	6.00	2.70
❑ 162 Marques Tuiasosopo RC	6.00	2.70
❑ 163 Reggie Germany RC	4.00	1.80
❑ 164 R.Ferguson RC	6.00	2.70
❑ 165 Jabari Holloway RC	4.00	1.80
❑ 166 Ben Leard RC	6.00	2.70
❑ 167 Bhawoh Jue RC	8.00	3.60
❑ 168 Freddie Mitchell RC	6.00	2.70
❑ 169 Vinny Sutherland RC	4.00	1.80
❑ 170 Jeff Backus RC	4.00	1.80
❑ 171 Correll Buckhalter RC	8.00	3.60
❑ 172 Mario Fatefehi RC	4.00	1.80
❑ 173 Rudi Johnson RC	12.00	5.50
❑ 174 Koren Robinson RC	8.00	3.60
❑ 175 Santana Moss RC	10.00	4.50

2002 Topps Debut

	Nm-Mt	Ex-Mt
COMP.SET w/o SP's (150)	25.00	7.50
❑ 1 Kurt Warner	1.00	.30
❑ 2 James Thrash	.60	.18
❑ 3 Aaron Brooks	1.00	.30
❑ 4 Mark Brunell	1.00	.30
❑ 5 Mike Anderson	1.00	.30
❑ 6 Benjamin Gay	.60	.18

❑ 7 Marvin Harrison	1.00	.30
❑ 8 Randy Moss	2.00	.60
❑ 9 Ron Dayne	.60	.18
❑ 10 Tim Brown	1.00	.30
❑ 11 Vinny Testaverde	.60	.18
❑ 12 Mike Alstott	1.00	.30
❑ 13 Tony Banks	.40	.12
❑ 14 Plaxico Burress	.60	.18
❑ 15 Chris Chambers	1.00	.30
❑ 16 Brett Favre	2.50	.75
❑ 17 Quincy Carter	.60	.18
❑ 18 Brian Urlacher	1.50	.45
❑ 19 Byron Chamberlain	.40	.12
❑ 20 Tony Gonzalez	.60	.18
❑ 21 Troy Brown	.60	.18
❑ 22 Drew Brees	1.00	.30
❑ 23 Koren Robinson	.60	.18
❑ 24 Donald Hayes	.40	.12
❑ 25 Michael Vick	3.00	.90
❑ 26 Travis Taylor	.60	.18
❑ 27 Peerless Price	.60	.18
❑ 28 Chad Johnson	1.00	.30
❑ 29 Tim Couch	.60	.18
❑ 30 Edgerrin James	1.25	.35
❑ 31 Willie Jackson	.40	.12
❑ 32 Hines Ward	1.00	.30
❑ 33 Terrell Owens	1.00	.30
❑ 34 Eddie George	1.00	.30
❑ 35 Michael Westbrook	.40	.12
❑ 36 Kerry Collins	.60	.18
❑ 37 Terrell Davis	1.00	.30
❑ 38 Marcus Robinson	.60	.18
❑ 39 Charlie Batch	.60	.18
❑ 40 Jake Plummer	.60	.18
❑ 41 Qadry Ismail	.60	.18
❑ 42 Snoop Minnis	.40	.12
❑ 43 Jimmy Smith	.60	.18
❑ 44 Charlie Garner	.60	.18
❑ 45 Jeff Graham	.40	.12
❑ 46 Torry Holt	1.00	.30
❑ 47 Kevin Dyson	.60	.18
❑ 48 Maurice Smith	.60	.18
❑ 49 Muhsin Muhammad	.60	.18
❑ 50 Curtis Martin	1.00	.30
❑ 51 Todd Pinkston	.60	.18
❑ 52 Matt Hasselbeck	.60	.18
❑ 53 Corey Dillon	.60	.18
❑ 54 Michael Pittman	.40	.12
❑ 55 Antonio Freeman	1.00	.30
❑ 56 Oronde Gadsden	.60	.18
❑ 57 Tiki Barber	.60	.18
❑ 58 Isaac Bruce	1.00	.30
❑ 59 Rod Gardner	.60	.18
❑ 60 Derrick Mason	.60	.18
❑ 61 Joe Horn	.60	.18
❑ 62 Antowain Smith	.60	.18
❑ 63 Johnnie Morton	.60	.18
❑ 64 Kevin Johnson	.60	.18
❑ 65 Nick Goings	.40	.12
❑ 66 Jason Brookins	.40	.12
❑ 67 Travis Henry	1.00	.30
❑ 68 Brian Griese	1.00	.30
❑ 69 Priest Holmes	1.25	.35
❑ 70 Daunte Culpepper	1.00	.30
❑ 71 Amani Toomer	.60	.18
❑ 72 Rich Gannon	1.00	.30
❑ 73 Correll Buckhalter	.60	.18
❑ 74 Kevan Barlow	.60	.18
❑ 75 Stephen Davis	.60	.18
❑ 76 Keenan McCardell	.40	.12
❑ 77 Jon Kitna	.60	.18
❑ 78 Eric Moulds	.60	.18
❑ 79 Dez White	.40	.12
❑ 80 Rocket Ismail	.60	.18
❑ 81 Dominic Rhodes	.60	.18
❑ 82 Lamar Smith	.60	.18
❑ 83 David Patten	.40	.12
❑ 84 Duce Staley	1.00	.30
❑ 85 Curtis Conway	.40	.12
❑ 86 Kordell Stewart	.60	.18
❑ 87 Brad Johnson	.60	.18
❑ 88 Wayne Chrebet	.60	.18
❑ 89 Michael Bennett	.60	.18
❑ 90 Quincy Morgan	.40	.12
❑ 91 Steve Smith	.60	.18
❑ 92 David Boston	1.00	.30
❑ 93 Shannon Sharpe	.60	.18
❑ 94 Mike McMahon	1.00	.30
❑ 95 Stacey Mack	.40	.12
❑ 96 Santana Moss	1.00	.30
❑ 97 Jeff Garcia	1.00	.30
❑ 98 Keyshawn Johnson	1.00	.30
❑ 99 Rod Smith	.60	.18
❑ 100 Jerome Bettis	1.00	.30
❑ 101 LaDainian Tomlinson	1.50	.45
❑ 102 Warrick Dunn	1.00	.30
❑ 103 Ray Lewis	1.00	.30
❑ 104 Chris Chandler	.60	.18
❑ 105 Jim Miller	.40	.12
❑ 106 Ahman Green	1.00	.30
❑ 107 Jay Fiedler	.60	.18
❑ 108 Tom Brady	2.50	.75
❑ 109 Michael Strahan	.60	.18
❑ 110 James Jackson	.40	.12
❑ 111 Rob Johnson	.60	.18
❑ 112 Elvis Grbac	.60	.18
❑ 113 Troy Hambrick	.40	.12
❑ 114 Corey Bradford	.40	.12
❑ 115 Trent Green	.60	.18
❑ 116 Cris Carter	1.00	.30
❑ 117 Chris Fuamatu-Ma'afala	.40	.12
❑ 118 Chris Weinke	.60	.18
❑ 119 MarTay Jenkins	.40	.12
❑ 120 Laveranues Coles	.60	.18
❑ 121 Donovan McNabb	1.25	.35
❑ 122 Jerry Rice	2.00	.60
❑ 123 Garrison Hearst	.60	.18
❑ 124 Steve McNair	1.00	.30
❑ 125 Trung Canidate	.60	.18
❑ 126 Doug Flutie	1.00	.30
❑ 127 Ricky Williams		
❑ 128 Peyton Manning	2.00	.60
❑ 129 Kevin Kasper	.40	.12
❑ 130 Emmitt Smith	2.50	.75
❑ 131 Peter Warrick	.60	.18
❑ 132 Anthony Thomas	1.00	.30
❑ 133 Ike Hilliard	.40	.12
❑ 134 Kendrell Bell	1.00	.30
❑ 135 Shaun Alexander	1.00	.30
❑ 136 Wesley Walls	.40	.12
❑ 137 Gerard Warren	.40	.12
❑ 138 James Stewart	.60	.18
❑ 139 Drew Bledsoe	1.25	.35
❑ 140 Fred Taylor	1.00	.30
❑ 141 Marshall Faulk	1.00	.30
❑ 142 Marcus Pollard	.40	.12
❑ 143 Bill Schroeder	.60	.18
❑ 144 Marty Booker	.40	.12
❑ 145 Amos Zereoue	1.00	.30
❑ 146 Darrell Jackson	.60	.18
❑ 147 Brian Finneran	.40	.12
❑ 148 Alex Van Pelt	.60	.18
❑ 149 Andre Carter	.40	.12
❑ 150 Joey Galloway	.60	.18
❑ 151 Joey Harrington AU RC	60.00	18.00
❑ 152 Andre Davis AU RC	25.00	7.50
❑ 153 Eric Crouch AU RC	30.00	9.00
❑ 154 Kelly Campbell AU RC	15.00	4.50
❑ 155 Ron Johnson AU RC	15.00	4.50
❑ 156 David Carr JSY RC	40.00	12.00
❑ 157 Kurt Kittner JSY RC	12.00	3.60
❑ 158 Javon Walker JSY RC	30.00	9.00
❑ 159 DeShaun Foster JSY RC	12.00	3.60
❑ 160 Lamar Gordon JSY RC	15.00	4.50
❑ 161 Antwaan Randle El RC	4.00	1.20
❑ 162 Clinton Portis RC	12.00	3.60
❑ 163 Luke Staley RC	2.50	.75
❑ 164 Daniel Graham RC	3.00	.90
❑ 165 Ashley Lelie RC	6.00	1.80
❑ 166 Ladell Betts RC	3.00	.90
❑ 167 Rocky Calmus RC	3.00	.90
❑ 168 Ryan Sims RC	3.00	.90
❑ 169 Jeremy Shockey RC	12.00	3.60
❑ 170 Damien Anderson RC	3.00	.90
❑ 171 Bryant McKinnie RC	3.00	.90
❑ 172 Kahlil Hill RC	2.50	.75
❑ 173 John Henderson RC	3.00	.90
❑ 174 Donte Stallworth RC	6.00	1.80
❑ 175 Kalimba Edwards RC	3.00	.90
❑ 176 Freddie Milons RC	2.50	.75
❑ 177 Antonio Bryant RC	3.00	.90
❑ 178 Cliff Russell RC	2.50	.75
❑ 179 T.J. Duckett RC	5.00	1.50
❑ 180 Roy Williams RC	8.00	2.40
❑ 181 Patrick Ramsey RC	6.00	1.80
❑ 182 Josh Reed RC	3.00	.90
❑ 183 Wendell Bryant RC	3.00	.90
❑ 184 Jabar Gaffney RC	3.00	.90
❑ 185 Napoleon Harris RC	3.00	.90
❑ 186 Adrian Peterson RC	3.00	.90
❑ 187 David Garrard RC	3.00	.90
❑ 188 Levar Fisher RC	2.50	.75
❑ 189 Quentin Jammer RC	3.00	.90
❑ 190 Anthony Weaver RC	2.50	.75
❑ 191 Dwight Freeney RC	4.00	1.20
❑ 192 Reche Caldwell RC	3.00	.90
❑ 193 Larry Tripplett RC	2.50	.75
❑ 194 Rohan Davey RC	3.00	.90
❑ 195 Marquise Walker RC	2.50	.75
❑ 196 William Green RC	5.00	1.50
❑ 197 Tracey Wistrom RC	2.50	.75
❑ 198 Alan Harper RC	1.50	.45
❑ 199 Lito Sheppard RC	3.00	.90
❑ 200 Albert Haynesworth RC	3.00	.90

2002 Topps Debut Red

	Nm-Mt	Ex-Mt
*STARS: 3X TO 8X BASIC CARDS		
*151-155 ROOKIES: .6X TO 1.5X		
*156-160 ROOKIES: .6X TO 1.5X		
*161-200 ROOKIES: 1.2X TO 3X		
❑ 151 Joey Harrington AU	120.00	36.00
❑ 152 Andre Davis AU	40.00	12.00
❑ 153 Eric Crouch AU	60.00	18.00
❑ 154 Kelly Campbell AU	30.00	9.00
❑ 155 Ron Johnson AU	30.00	9.00
❑ 156 David Carr JSY	100.00	30.00
❑ 157 Kurt Kittner JSY	25.00	7.50
❑ 158 Javon Walker JSY	40.00	12.00
❑ 159 DeShaun Foster JSY	25.00	7.50
❑ 160 Lamar Gordon JSY	30.00	9.00

2003 Topps Draft Picks and Prospects

	Nm-Mt	Ex-Mt
COMPLETE SET (165)	50.00	15.00
❑ 1 Priest Holmes	1.25	.35

	Card	Nm-Mt	Ex-Mt
❑	2 Tommy Maddox	1.00	.30
❑	3 Donald Driver	.60	.18
❑	4 Drew Bledsoe	1.00	.30
❑	5 Tiki Barber	.60	.18
❑	6 Terrell Owens	1.00	.30
❑	7 Rich Gannon	.60	.18
❑	8 Isaac Bruce	1.00	.30
❑	9 Stephen Davis	.60	.18
❑	10 Peyton Manning	1.50	.45
❑	11 Tony Gonzalez	.60	.18
❑	12 Marty Booker	.60	.18
❑	13 Warrick Dunn	.60	.18
❑	14 Jimmy Smith	.60	.18
❑	15 Troy Brown	.60	.18
❑	16 Jerry Rice	2.00	.60
❑	17 Curtis Conway	.40	.12
❑	18 Kurt Warner	1.00	.30
❑	19 Steve McNair	1.00	.30
❑	20 Edgerrin James	1.00	.30
❑	21 Aaron Brooks	1.00	.30
❑	22 Joey Galloway	.60	.18
❑	23 Peerless Price	.60	.18
❑	24 Torry Holt	1.00	.30
❑	25 Derrick Mason	.60	.18
❑	26 Curtis Martin	1.00	.30
❑	27 Daunte Culpepper	1.00	.30
❑	28 Ahman Green	1.00	.30
❑	29 Tim Couch	.40	.12
❑	30 Ricky Williams	1.00	.30
❑	31 Darrell Jackson	.60	.18
❑	32 Keyshawn Johnson	1.00	.30
❑	33 Jeff Garcia	1.00	.30
❑	34 Charlie Garner	.60	.18
❑	35 Randy Moss	1.50	.45
❑	36 Rod Smith	.60	.18
❑	37 Jamal Lewis	1.00	.30
❑	38 Corey Dillon	.60	.18
❑	39 Marvin Harrison	1.00	.30
❑	40 Joe Horn	.60	.18
❑	41 Laveranues Coles	.60	.18
❑	42 Hines Ward	1.00	.30
❑	43 Brad Johnson	.60	.18
❑	44 Eddie George	.60	.18
❑	45 Donovan McNabb	1.25	.35
❑	46 Marshall Faulk	1.00	.30
❑	47 Amani Toomer	.60	.18
❑	48 Trent Green	.60	.18
❑	49 Emmitt Smith	2.50	.75
❑	50 Brett Favre	2.50	.75
❑	51 Brian Griese	1.00	.30
❑	52 Eric Moulds	.60	.18
❑	53 Plaxico Burress	.60	.18
❑	54 Fred Taylor	1.00	.30
❑	55 Tom Brady	1.50	.45
❑	56 Michael Vick	2.50	.75
❑	57 Andre Davis	.40	.12
❑	58 Chris Chambers	1.00	.30
❑	59 Javon Walker	.60	.18
❑	60 Marc Bulger	1.00	.30
❑	61 LaDainian Tomlinson	1.00	.30
❑	62 Chad Pennington	1.25	.35
❑	63 Marc Boerigter	.60	.18
❑	64 Rod Gardner	.60	.18
❑	65 DeShaun Foster	.40	.12
❑	66 Chris Redman	.40	.12
❑	67 Chad Hutchinson	.60	.18
❑	68 Deion Branch	1.00	.30
❑	69 Jeremy Shockey	1.50	.45
❑	70 Shaun Alexander	1.00	.30
❑	71 Derrius Thompson	.40	.12
❑	72 A.J. Feeley	.60	.18
❑	73 Reggie Wayne	.60	.18
❑	74 William Green	.60	.18
❑	75 Julius Peppers	1.00	.30
❑	76 Travis Henry	.60	.18
❑	77 Marcel Shipp	.60	.18
❑	78 Michael Bennett	.60	.18
❑	79 Maurice Morris	.40	.12
❑	80 Josh Reed	.60	.18
❑	81 David Terrell	.60	.18
❑	82 Drew Brees	1.00	.30
❑	83 Jonathan Wells	.40	.12
❑	84 Anthony Thomas	1.00	.30
❑	85 Quincy Morgan	.60	.18
❑	86 Jerry Porter	.60	.18
❑	87 Ron Johnson	.40	.12
❑	88 Najeh Davenport	.40	.12
❑	89 Lamar Gordon	.40	.12
❑	90 Joey Harrington	1.50	.45
❑	91 Donte Stallworth	1.00	.30
❑	92 Kenny Watson	.40	.12
❑	93 LaMont Jordan	.60	.18
❑	94 Antonio Bryant	.60	.18
❑	95 Steve Smith	.40	.12
❑	96 T.J. Duckett	.60	.18
❑	97 Patrick Ramsey	1.00	.30
❑	98 Santana Moss	.60	.18
❑	99 Chad Johnson	.60	.18
❑	100 Clinton Portis	1.50	.45
❑	101 Reche Caldwell	.40	.12
❑	102 Kevan Barlow	.60	.18
❑	103 Deuce McAllister	1.00	.30
❑	104 Koren Robinson	.40	.12
❑	105 Todd Heap	.60	.18
❑	106 Jabar Gaffney	.60	.18
❑	107 Randy McMichael	.60	.18
❑	108 Dwight Freeney	.40	.12
❑	109 Antwaan Randle El	1.00	.30
❑	110 David Carr	1.50	.45
❑	111 Carson Palmer RC	5.00	1.50
❑	112 Dahrran Diedrick RC	1.50	.45
❑	113 Kyle Boller RC	4.00	1.20
❑	114 Terrell Suggs RC	2.50	.75
❑	115 Rien Long RC	.75	.23
❑	116 Justin Gage RC	1.50	.45
❑	117 William Joseph RC	1.50	.45
❑	118 Chris Simms RC	3.00	.90
❑	119 Avon Cobourne RC	.75	.23
❑	120 Victor Hobson RC	1.50	.45
❑	121 Jason Gesser RC	1.50	.45
❑	122 Ronald Bellamy RC	1.25	.35
❑	123 Terence Newman RC	3.00	.90
❑	124 Terrence Edwards RC	1.25	.35
❑	125 Sultan McCullough RC	1.25	.35
❑	126 Kareem Kelly RC	1.25	.35
❑	127 Jason Witten RC	2.00	.60
❑	128 Mike Doss RC	1.50	.45
❑	129 Seneca Wallace RC	1.50	.45
❑	130 Chris Brown RC	3.00	.90
❑	131 Larry Johnson RC	3.00	.90
❑	132 Taylor Jacobs RC	1.50	.45
❑	133 Jerome McDougle RC	1.50	.45
❑	134 Kelley Washington RC	1.50	.45
❑	135 Brad Banks RC	1.25	.35
❑	136 DeWayne White RC	1.25	.35
❑	137 LaBrandon Toefield RC	1.50	.45
❑	138 Brian St.Pierre RC	1.50	.45
❑	139 Kindal Moorehead RC	1.25	.35
❑	140 Willis McGahee RC	4.00	1.20
❑	141 Jimmy Kennedy RC	1.50	.45
❑	142 Talman Gardner RC	1.50	.45
❑	143 Chris Kelsay RC	1.50	.45
❑	144 Cory Redding RC	1.25	.35
❑	145 Dave Ragone RC	1.50	.45
❑	146 Earnest Graham RC	1.25	.35
❑	147 Andre Johnson RC	4.00	1.20
❑	148 Boss Bailey RC	2.00	.60
❑	149 Sam Aiken RC	1.25	.35
❑	150 Byron Leftwich RC	6.00	1.80
❑	151 Teyo Johnson RC	1.50	.45
❑	152 Quentin Griffin RC	4.00	1.20
❑	153 Justin Fargas RC	1.50	.45
❑	154 Bradie James RC	1.50	.45
❑	155 Andre Woolfolk RC	1.50	.45
❑	156 Marcus Trufant RC	1.50	.45
❑	157 Ken Dorsey RC	2.50	.75
❑	158 Onterrio Smith RC	2.00	.60
❑	159 Bryant Johnson RC	1.50	.45
❑	160 Charles Rogers RC	2.00	.60
❑	161 Kliff Kingsbury RC	1.25	.35
❑	162 Michael Haynes RC	1.50	.45
❑	163 Bennie Joppru RC	1.50	.45
❑	164 Brandon Lloyd RC	2.00	.60
❑	165 Jarret Johnson RC	1.25	.35

2003 Topps Draft Picks and Prospects Chrome

Nm-Mt Ex-Mt

*STARS: .8X TO 2X BASIC CARDS
*ROOKIES: 1.2X TO 3X

2003 Topps Draft Picks and Prospects Chrome Gold Refractors

Nm-Mt Ex-Mt

*STARS: 2X TO 5X BASIC CARDS
*ROOKIES: 3X TO 8X

2003 Topps Draft Picks and Prospects Class Marks Autographs

Nm-Mt Ex-Mt

GROUP A STATED ODDS 1:7647
GROUP B STATED ODDS 1:826
GROUP C STATED ODDS 1:4904
GROUP D STATED ODDS 1:1825
GROUP E STATED ODDS 1:839
GROUP F STATED ODDS 1:559
GROUP G STATED ODDS 1:93
*FOIL: .6X TO 1.5X BASIC CARDS
FOIL STATED PRINT RUN 100 SER.#'d SETS

	Card	Nm-Mt	Ex-Mt
❑	CMAC Avon Cobourne G	12.00	3.60
❑	CMAJ Andre Johnson B	40.00	12.00
❑	CMBJ Bryant Johnson C	20.00	6.00
❑	CMBL Byron Leftwich A	120.00	36.00
❑	CMCB Chris Brown B	50.00	15.00
❑	CMCP Carson Palmer A	100.00	30.00
❑	CMCR Charles Rogers B EXCH	30.00	9.00
❑	CMJT Jason Thomas B	12.00	3.60
❑	CMKB Kyle Boller B	30.00	9.00
❑	CMKD Ken Dorsey B	30.00	9.00
❑	CMKKE Kareem Kelly G	12.00	3.60
❑	CMKW Kelley Washington D	20.00	6.00
❑	CMLJ Larry Johnson B	30.00	9.00
❑	CMLS Lee Suggs B EXCH	40.00	12.00
❑	CMLT LaBrandon Toefield G	15.00	4.50
❑	CMMB Marquel Blackwell B	12.00	3.60
❑	CMOS Onterrio Smith E	25.00	7.50
❑	CMQB Quentin Griffin G	30.00	9.00
❑	CMSW Seneca Wallace G	15.00	4.50
❑	CMTG Talman Gardner G	12.00	3.60
❑	CMTJ Taylor Jacobs D	20.00	6.00
❑	CMWM Willis McGahee F	30.00	9.00

2003 Topps Draft Picks and Prospects Classmate Cuts

Nm-Mt Ex-Mt

FOIL/25 NOT PRICED DUE TO SCARCITY
FOIL STATED ODDS 1:5854

	Card	Nm-Mt	Ex-Mt
❑	CCDCW Kevin Curtis Kelley Washington	15.00	4.50
❑	CCDDG Ken Dorsey Jason Gesser	50.00	15.00
❑	CCDFJ Justin Fargas Larry Johnson	30.00	9.00
❑	CCDJL Bryant Johnson Brandon Lloyd	50.00	15.00

❑ CCDRB Dave Ragone Kyle Boller	30.00	9.00

2003 Topps Draft Picks and Prospects Collegiate Cuts

	Nm-Mt	Ex-Mt
GROUP A STATED ODDS 1:811		
GROUP B STATED ODDS 1:135		
GROUP C STATED ODDS 1:487		
GROUP D STATED ODDS 1:90		
GROUP E STATED ODDS 1:192		
GROUP F STATED ODDS 1:98		
GROUP G STATED ODDS 1:90		
GROUP H STATED ODDS 1:292		
*FOIL: .6X TO 1.5X BASIC CARDS		
FOIL STATED ODDS 1:96		
*PATCHES: 1X TO 2.5X BASIC CARDS		
PATCHES STATED ODDS 1:427		
PATCHES PRINT RUN 75 SER.#'d SETS		
UNPRICED FOIL PATCHES #'d TO 25		
❑ CCAJ Andre Johnson B	30.00	9.00
❑ CCBJ Bryant Johnson C	10.00	3.00
❑ CCBLL Brandon Lloyd B	12.00	3.60
❑ CCDC Dallas Clark B	10.00	3.00
❑ CCDR Dave Ragone F	10.00	3.00
❑ CCJF Justin Fargas D	10.00	3.00
❑ CCJG Justin Gage D	10.00	3.00
❑ CCJGE Jason Gesser E	12.00	3.60
❑ CCJJ Jarret Johnson D	8.00	2.40
❑ CCJW Jason Witten G	20.00	6.00
❑ CCKB Kyle Boller H	20.00	6.00
❑ CCKC Kevin Curtis F	8.00	2.40
❑ CCKD Ken Dorsey B	20.00	6.00
❑ CCKK Kliff Kingsbury A	8.00	2.40
❑ CCKM Kindal Moorehead G	8.00	2.40
❑ CCKW Kelley Washington D	10.00	3.00
❑ CCLJ Larry Johnson F	12.00	3.60
❑ CCRL ReShard Lee D	10.00	3.00
❑ CCSW Seneca Wallace G	10.00	3.00
❑ CCTC Tyrone Calico F	20.00	6.00
❑ CCTE Terrence Edwards G	12.00	3.60
❑ CCTS Terrell Suggs E	20.00	6.00
❑ CCWM Willis McGahee B	25.00	7.50

2003 Topps Draft Picks and Prospects Pen Pals Autographs

	Nm-Mt	Ex-Mt
FOIL STATED ODDS 1:6180		
FOIL PRINT RUN 25 SER.#'d SETS		
FOIL NOT PRICED DUE TO SCARCITY		
❑ PPDS Ken Dorsey Chris Simms	150.00	45.00
❑ PPJM Larry Johnson Willis McGahee	60.00	18.00
❑ PPLP Byron Leftwich Carson Palmer	250.00	75.00
❑ PPRJ Charles Rogers Andre Johnson EXCH	100.00	30.00
❑ PPSS Lee Suggs Onterrio Smith	80.00	24.00

2004 Topps Draft Picks and Prospects

	Nm-Mt	Ex-Mt
COMPLETE SET (165)	80.00	24.00
❑ 1 Steve McNair	1.00	.30
❑ 2 Stephen Davis	.60	.18
❑ 3 Chris Chambers	.60	.18
❑ 4 Curtis Martin	1.00	.30
❑ 5 Shaun Alexander	1.00	.30
❑ 6 Jon Kitna	.60	.18
❑ 7 Jimmy Smith	.60	.18
❑ 8 Travis Henry	.60	.18
❑ 9 Torry Holt	1.00	.30
❑ 10 Jamal Lewis	1.00	.30
❑ 11 Clinton Portis	1.00	.30
❑ 12 Aaron Brooks	.60	.18
❑ 13 Plaxico Burress	.60	.18
❑ 14 Trent Green	.60	.18
❑ 15 Chad Johnson	.60	.18
❑ 16 Jake Delhomme	1.00	.30
❑ 17 David Boston	.60	.18
❑ 18 Joe Horn	.60	.18
❑ 19 Ahman Green	1.00	.30
❑ 20 Fred Taylor	.60	.18
❑ 21 Terrell Owens	1.00	.30
❑ 22 Brad Johnson	.60	.18
❑ 23 Laveranues Coles	.60	.18
❑ 24 Ricky Williams	1.00	.30
❑ 25 Peyton Manning	1.50	.45
❑ 26 Hines Ward	1.00	.30
❑ 27 Matt Hasselbeck	.60	.18
❑ 28 Marshall Faulk	1.00	.30
❑ 29 Tony Gonzalez	.60	.18
❑ 30 Marvin Harrison	1.00	.30
❑ 31 Eric Moulds	.60	.18
❑ 32 Chad Pennington	1.25	.35
❑ 33 Jerry Porter	.60	.18
❑ 34 Jeff Garcia	1.00	.30
❑ 35 Derrick Mason	.60	.18
❑ 36 Anthony Thomas	.60	.18
❑ 37 Drew Bledsoe	1.00	.30
❑ 38 Jake Plummer	.60	.18
❑ 39 Tiki Barber	.60	.18
❑ 40 Brett Favre	2.50	.75
❑ 41 Joey Harrington	1.00	.30
❑ 42 Daunte Culpepper	1.00	.30
❑ 43 LaVar Arrington	2.00	.60
❑ 44 Santana Moss	.60	.18
❑ 45 David Carr	1.00	.30
❑ 46 Randy Moss	1.25	.35
❑ 47 LaDainian Tomlinson	1.00	.30
❑ 48 Deuce McAllister	1.00	.30
❑ 49 Amani Toomer	.60	.18
❑ 50 Donovan McNabb	1.25	.35
❑ 51 Priest Holmes	1.25	.35
❑ 52 Corey Dillon	.60	.18
❑ 53 Tom Brady	1.50	.45
❑ 54 Edgerrin James	1.00	.30
❑ 55 Michael Vick	2.00	.60
❑ 56 Anquan Boldin	1.00	.30
❑ 57 Robert Ferguson	.40	.12
❑ 58 Onterrio Smith	.60	.18
❑ 59 Marques Tuiasosopo	.60	.18
❑ 60 Rudi Johnson	.60	.18
❑ 61 Alge Crumpler	.60	.18
❑ 62 Antonio Bryant	.60	.18
❑ 63 LaMont Jordan	.60	.18
❑ 64 Lamar Gordon	.40	.12
❑ 65 Tim Rattay	.60	.18
❑ 66 Antwaan Randle El	.60	.18
❑ 67 Ladell Betts	.40	.12
❑ 68 LaBrandon Toefield	.40	.12
❑ 69 Ashley Lelie	.60	.18
❑ 70 Marc Bulger	1.00	.30
❑ 71 Reggie Wayne	.60	.18
❑ 72 William Green	.60	.18
❑ 73 Josh Reed	.40	.12
❑ 74 T.J. Duckett	.60	.18
❑ 75 Andre Johnson	1.00	.30
❑ 76 Deion Branch	1.00	.30
❑ 77 Tyrone Calico	.60	.18
❑ 78 Jeremy Shockey	1.00	.30
❑ 79 Najeh Davenport	.40	.12
❑ 80 Byron Leftwich	1.50	.45
❑ 81 Correll Buckhalter	.60	.18
❑ 82 Justin McCareins	.40	.12
❑ 83 Carson Palmer	1.25	.35
❑ 84 Bryant Johnson	.40	.12
❑ 85 Patrick Ramsey	.60	.18
❑ 86 Justin Fargas	.60	.18
❑ 87 Dallas Clark	.60	.18
❑ 88 Kelly Campbell	.40	.12
❑ 89 DeShaun Foster	.60	.18
❑ 90 Charles Rogers	.60	.18
❑ 91 Donte' Stallworth	.60	.18
❑ 92 Dante Hall	1.00	.30
❑ 93 Randy McMichael	.40	.12
❑ 94 Marcel Shipp	.60	.18
❑ 95 Kyle Boller	1.00	.30
❑ 96 Steve Smith	.60	.18
❑ 97 Brian Westbrook	.60	.18
❑ 98 Kevan Barlow	.60	.18
❑ 99 Damerien McCants	.40	.12
❑ 100 Domanick Davis	1.00	.30
❑ 101 Andre' Davis	.40	.12
❑ 102 Nate Burleson	1.00	.30
❑ 103 Larry Johnson	.60	.18
❑ 104 Drew Brees	1.00	.30
❑ 105 Koren Robinson	.60	.18
❑ 106 Quincy Carter	.60	.18
❑ 107 Javon Walker	.60	.18
❑ 108 Willis McGahee	1.00	.30
❑ 109 Chris Simms	.60	.18

❑ 110 Rex Grossman 1.00 .30
❑ 111 Steven Jackson RC 6.00 1.80
❑ 112 Greg Jones RC 2.00 .60
❑ 113 Brandon Everage RC 1.50 .45
❑ 114 DeAngelo Hall RC 2.50 .75
❑ 115 Tatum Bell RC 3.00 .90
❑ 116 B.J. Symons RC 2.00 .60
❑ 117 Michael Clayton RC 5.00 1.50
❑ 118 Jared Lorenzen RC 1.50 .45
❑ 119 Josh Harris RC 2.00 .60
❑ 120 Roy Williams RC 6.00 1.80
❑ 121 Mewelde Moore RC 2.50 .75
❑ 122 Jeff Smoker RC 3.00 .90
❑ 123 Lee Evans RC 3.00 .90
❑ 124 Michael Jenkins RC 2.00 .60
❑ 125 Drew Henson RC 5.00 1.50
❑ 126 Ben Watson RC 2.00 .60
❑ 127 Jerricho Cotchery RC 2.00 .60
❑ 128 Ben Troupe RC 2.00 .60
❑ 129 Chris Gamble RC 2.50 .75
❑ 130 Kevin Jones RC 6.00 1.80
❑ 131 Cody Pickett RC 2.00 .60
❑ 132 J.P. Losman RC 5.00 1.50
❑ 133 Michael Boulware RC 2.00 .60
❑ 134 Julius Jones RC 8.00 2.40
❑ 135 Keary Colbert RC 2.50 .75
❑ 136 Vince Wilfork RC 2.50 .75
❑ 137 Ernest Wilford RC 2.00 .60
❑ 138 John Navarre RC 2.00 .60
❑ 139 D.J. Williams RC 2.50 .75
❑ 140 Larry Fitzgerald RC 6.00 1.80
❑ 141 Quincy Wilson RC 1.50 .45
❑ 142 James Newson RC 1.50 .45
❑ 143 Reggie Williams RC 2.50 .75
❑ 144 Devard Darling RC 2.00 .60
❑ 145 Chris Perry RC 4.00 1.20
❑ 146 Derrick Strait RC 2.00 .60
❑ 147 Teddy Lehman RC 2.00 .60
❑ 148 Michael Turner RC 1.50 .45
❑ 149 Will Smith RC 2.00 .60
❑ 150 Eli Manning RC 10.00 3.00
❑ 151 Cedric Cobbs RC 2.00 .60
❑ 152 Eli Roberson UER RC 2.00 .60
(name misspelled Eli)
❑ 153 Matt Schaub RC 3.00 .90
❑ 154 Derrick Knight RC 1.50 .45
❑ 155 Rashaun Woods RC 2.50 .75
❑ 156 Jonathan Vilma RC 2.00 .60
❑ 157 Tommie Harris RC 2.50 .75
❑ 158 Dwan Edwards RC 1.50 .45
❑ 159 Will Poole RC 2.00 .60
❑ 160 Mike Williams RC 20.00 6.00
❑ 161 Philip Rivers RC 6.00 1.80
❑ 162 Sean Taylor RC 2.50 .75
❑ 163 Darius Watts RC 2.50 .75
❑ 164 Casey Clausen RC 2.50 .75
❑ 165 Ben Roethlisberger RC 20.00 6.00

2004 Topps Draft Picks and Prospects Chrome

Nm-Mt Ex-Mt
COMPLETE SET (165) 150.00 45.00
*VETERANS: .8X TO 2X BASE CARD HI
*ROOKIES: .6X TO 1.5X BASE CARD HI
STATED ODDS 1:1

2004 Topps Draft Picks and Prospects Gold Chrome

Nm-Mt Ex-Mt
*VETERANS: 3X TO 8X BASE CARD HI
*ROOKIES: 2.5X TO 6X BASE CARD HI
STATED ODDS 1:12 H/R

2004 Topps Draft Picks and Prospects Big Dog Relics

Nm-Mt Ex-Mt
GROUP A STATED ODDS 1:207H, 1:204R
GROUP B STATED ODDS 1:275H, 1:272R
GROUP C STATED ODDS 1:158H, 1:155R
GROUP D STATED ODDS 1:259H, 1:239R
GROUP E STATED ODDS 1:242H, 1:236R
GROUP F STATED ODDS 1:68H, 1:49R

GROUP G STATED ODDS 1:161H,1:156R
GROUP H STATED ODDS 1:99H, 1:97R
*SILVER: .6X TO 1.5X BASIC INSERTS
SILVER STATED ODDS 1:245H, 1:175R
SILVER PRINT RUN 100 SER.#'d SETS
UNPRICED PATCHES ODDS 1:574H, 1:541R

❑ BDAS Antonio Smith F 10.00 3.00
❑ BDBE Brandon Everage G 10.00 3.00
❑ BDBH Bryan Hickman F 12.00 3.60
❑ BDBM Bobby McCray F 10.00 3.00
❑ BDBW Ben Watson E 12.00 3.60
❑ BDCC Cedric Cobbs C 10.00 3.00
❑ BDCCO Chris Cooley H 12.00 3.60
❑ BDCP Cody Pickett A 12.00 3.60
❑ BDCW Courtney Watson F 12.00 3.60
❑ BDDC Darrell Campbell G 8.00 2.40
❑ BDDE Dwan Edwards H 8.00 2.40
❑ BDDH Devery Henderson H 10.00 3.00
❑ BDDM DeMarco McNeil F 8.00 2.40
❑ BDDS Derrick Strait E 12.00 3.60
❑ BDDSM Daryl Smith F 12.00 3.60
❑ BDDT Dontarrious Thomas F 12.00 3.60
❑ BDDW Demorrio Williams F 12.00 3.60
❑ BDEW Ernest Wilford A 12.00 3.60
❑ BDGJ Greg Jones A 12.00 3.60
❑ BDJC Jerricho Cotchery D 12.00 3.60
❑ BDJH Josh Harris B 12.00 3.60
❑ BDJJ Julius Jones B 30.00 9.00
❑ BDJM Johnnie Morant F 12.00 3.60
❑ BDJN John Navarre D 12.00 3.60
❑ BDJNE James Newson E 10.00 3.00
❑ BDJPL J.P. Losman C 25.00 7.50
❑ BDKC Keary Colbert C 12.00 3.60
❑ BDKF Keyaron Fox F 10.00 3.00
❑ BDKW Kris Wilson F 12.00 3.60
❑ BDMB Michael Boulware G 12.00 3.60
❑ BDMBR Maurice Brown F 8.00 2.40
❑ BDMJ Michael Jenkins A 12.00 3.60
❑ BDMM Mewelde Moore C 15.00 4.50
❑ BDMS Matt Schaub C 20.00 6.00
❑ BDMT Michael Turner B 10.00 3.00
❑ BDNK Niko Koutouvides H 10.00 3.00
❑ BDPR Philip Rivers A 25.00 7.50
❑ BDRL Rodney Leisle H 8.00 2.40
❑ BDTB Tatum Bell D 20.00 6.00
❑ BDTL Teddy Lehman G 12.00 3.60
❑ BDTLU Triandos Luke H 12.00 3.60

2004 Topps Draft Picks and Prospects Class Marks Autographs

Nm-Mt Ex-Mt
GROUP A STATED ODDS 1:5702H, 1:5561R
GROUP B STATED ODDS 1:1026H, 1:1029R
GROUP C STATED ODDS 1:457H/R
GROUP D STATED ODDS 1:165H, 1:325R
GROUP E STATED ODDS 1:97H, 1:273R
GROUP F STATED ODDS 1:421H/R
EXCH EXPIRATION: 5/31/2006

❑ CMBR Ben Roethlisberger B 200.00 60.00
❑ CMCC Cedric Cobbs E 20.00 6.00
❑ CMCP Chris Perry C 25.00 7.50
❑ CMCPI Cody Pickett C 30.00 9.00
❑ CMEM Eli Manning A 175.00 52.50
❑ CMEW Ernest Wilford D 15.00 4.50

❑ CMGJ Greg Jones B 25.00 7.50
❑ CMJC Jerricho Cotchery D 15.00 4.50
❑ CMKJ Kevin Jones E 40.00 12.00
❑ CMLE Lee Evans D 25.00 7.50
❑ CMLF Larry Fitzgerald A 100.00 30.00
❑ CMMC Michael Clayton E 30.00 9.00
❑ CMMJ Michael Jenkins D 25.00 7.50
❑ CMMS Matt Schaub C 30.00 9.00
❑ CMPR Philip Rivers B 60.00 18.00
❑ CMRW Roy Williams WR C 50.00 15.00
❑ CMRWI Reggie Williams E 25.00 7.50
❑ CMRWO Rashaun Woods B 40.00 12.00
❑ CMSJ Steven Jackson A 60.00 18.00
❑ CMTB Tatum Bell F 25.00 7.50

2004 Topps Draft Picks and Prospects Class Marks Autographs Silver

Nm-Mt Ex-Mt
SILVER STATED ODDS 1:847H, 1:824R
SILVER PRINT RUN 50 SER.#'d SETS
EXCH EXPIRATION: 5/31/2006

❑ CMBR Ben Roethlisberger 300.00 90.00
❑ CMCC Cedric Cobbs 30.00 9.00
❑ CMCP Chris Perry 50.00 15.00
❑ CMCPI Cody Pickett 50.00 15.00
❑ CMEM Eli Manning 250.00 75.00
❑ CMEW Ernest Wilford 30.00 9.00
❑ CMGJ Greg Jones 30.00 9.00
❑ CMJC Jerricho Cotchery 30.00 9.00
❑ CMKJ Kevin Jones 80.00 24.00
❑ CMLE Lee Evans 50.00 15.00
❑ CMLF Larry Fitzgerald 150.00 45.00
❑ CMMC Michael Clayton 60.00 18.00
❑ CMMJ Michael Jenkins 30.00 9.00
❑ CMMS Matt Schaub 50.00 15.00
❑ CMPR Philip Rivers 100.00 30.00
❑ CMRW Roy Williams WR 100.00 30.00
❑ CMRWI Reggie Williams EXCH
❑ CMRWO Rashaun Woods 30.00 9.00
❑ CMSJ Steven Jackson 100.00 30.00
❑ CMTB Tatum Bell 50.00 15.00

2004 Topps Draft Picks and Prospects Old School Dual Relics

Nm-Mt Ex-Mt
STATED ODDS 1:846H, 1:820R

- ❑ OSBJ Anquan Boldin 25.00 7.50
  Greg Jones
- ❑ OSDP Corey Dillon 25.00 7.50
  Cody Pickett
- ❑ OSDW Andre Davis 15.00 4.50
  Ernest Wilford
- ❑ OSGJ Eddie George 20.00 6.00
  Michael Jenkins
- ❑ OSHR Torry Holt 50.00 15.00
  Philip Rivers

2004 Topps Draft Picks and Prospects Quarterback Legacy Autographs

Nm-Mt Ex-Mt

SINGLE AUTO ODDS 1:2753H, 1:2780R
TRIPLE SILVER ODDS 1:16,630H, 1:46,320R
TRIPLE GOLD 1/1 STATED ODDS 1:399,120

- ❑ QBG Archie Manning Gold/1
  Peyton Manning
  Eli Manning
- ❑ QBS Archie Manning Silver/50 500.00 150.00
  Peyton Manning
  Eli Manning
- ❑ QBAM Archie Manning/100 40.00 12.00
- ❑ QBEM Eli Manning/100 150.00 45.00
- ❑ QBPM Peyton Manning/100 80.00 24.00

2004 Topps Fan Favorites

	Nm-Mt	Ex-Mt
COMPLETE SET (85)	40.00	12.00
❑ 1 Alan Page	1.25	.35
❑ 2 Abdul Salaam	1.00	.30
❑ 3 Bob Baumhower	1.00	.30
❑ 4 Bob Brudzinski	1.00	.30
❑ 5 Billy Johnson	1.00	.30
❑ 6 Cliff Branch	1.25	.35
❑ 7 Carl Banks	1.00	.30
❑ 8 Charles Bowser	1.00	.30
❑ 9 Clint Didier	1.00	.30
❑ 10 Carl Eller	1.00	.30
❑ 11 Charlie Joiner	1.00	.30
❑ 12 Dick Anderson	1.00	.30
❑ 13 Doug Betters	1.00	.30
❑ 14 Dave Casper	1.00	.30
❑ 15 Dwight Clark	1.25	.35
❑ 16 Dan Fouts	1.50	.45
❑ 17 Dave Foley	1.00	.30
❑ 18 Donnie Green	1.00	.30
❑ 19 Deacon Jones	1.25	.35
❑ 20 Don Maynard	1.25	.35
❑ 21 Dan Pastorini	1.00	.30
❑ 22 Drew Pearson	1.25	.35
❑ 23 Dwight White	1.00	.30
❑ 24 Emerson Boozer	1.00	.30
❑ 25 Earl Campbell	1.50	.45
❑ 26 Ernie Holmes	1.25	.35
❑ 27 Fred Biletnikoff	1.50	.45
❑ 28 Glenn Blackwood	1.00	.30
❑ 29 Gary Larsen	1.00	.30
❑ 30 Greg Lloyd	1.25	.35
❑ 31 George Martin	1.00	.30
❑ 32 Gene Upshaw	1.00	.30
❑ 33 Harry Carson	1.00	.30
❑ 34 Harold Jackson	1.00	.30
❑ 35 Hugh McElhenny	1.00	.30
❑ 36 Jeff Bostic	1.00	.30
❑ 37 Jim Burt	1.00	.30
❑ 38 Joe Greene	1.50	.45
❑ 39 John Hannah	1.00	.30
❑ 40 John Henry Johnson	1.00	.30
❑ 41 Joe Jacoby	1.00	.30
❑ 42 Jim Kiick	1.00	.30
❑ 43 Joe Klecko	1.00	.30
❑ 44 Joe Delamielleure	1.00	.30
❑ 45 Joe Montana	5.00	1.50
❑ 46 Jim Marshall	1.00	.30
❑ 47 Joe Namath	3.00	.90
❑ 48 Jake Scott	1.00	.30
❑ 49 John Taylor	1.00	.30
❑ 50 Kim Bokamper	1.00	.30
❑ 51 Kevin Greene	1.25	.35
❑ 52 Karl Mecklenburg	1.00	.30
❑ 53 Ken Stabler	2.50	.75
❑ 54 Kellen Winslow	1.25	.35
❑ 55 Lyle Blackwood	1.00	.30
❑ 56 Larry Csonka	1.50	.45
❑ 57 L.C. Greenwood	1.25	.35
❑ 58 Lamar Lundy	1.00	.30
❑ 59 Leonard Marshall	1.00	.30
❑ 60 Lawrence Taylor	1.50	.45
❑ 61 Mark Clayton	1.00	.30
❑ 62 Mark Duper	1.00	.30
❑ 63 Manny Fernandez	1.00	.30
❑ 64 Mark Gastineau	1.00	.30
❑ 65 Marty Lyons	1.00	.30
❑ 66 Mark May	1.00	.30
❑ 67 Mike Montler	1.00	.30
❑ 68 Merlin Olsen	1.25	.35
❑ 69 Matt Snell	1.00	.30
❑ 70 Ozzie Newsome	1.25	.35
❑ 71 Otis Sistrunk	1.00	.30
❑ 72 Phil Villapiano UER (name spelled Villipiano)	1.00	.30
❑ 73 Roger Craig	1.25	.35
❑ 74 Richard Dent	1.00	.30
❑ 75 Randy Gradishar	1.00	.30
❑ 76 Russ Grimm	1.00	.30
❑ 77 Reggie McKenzie	1.00	.30
❑ 78 Roosevelt Grier	1.00	.30
❑ 79 Roger Staubach	3.00	.90
❑ 80 Steve Grogan	1.00	.30
❑ 81 Stanley Morgan	1.00	.30
❑ 82 Tony Dorsett	1.50	.45
❑ 83 Ted Hendricks	1.00	.30
❑ 84 Tony Hill	1.00	.30
❑ 85 Y.A. Tittle	1.50	.45

2004 Topps Fan Favorites Chrome

Nm-Mt Ex-Mt

*SINGLES: 3X TO 8X BASIC CARDS
STATED ODDS 1:14 H/R
STATED PRINT RUN 499 SER.#'d SETS

2004 Topps Fan Favorites Chrome Refractors

Nm-Mt Ex-Mt

*SINGLES: 5X TO 12X BASIC CARDS
STATED ODDS 1:74 HOB, 1:123 RET
STATED PRINT RUN 99 SER.#'d SETS

2004 Topps Fan Favorites Autographs

Nm-Mt Ex-Mt

GROUP A ODDS 1:5362 H, 1:6144 R
GROUP B ODDS 1:2289 H, 1:2458 R
GROUP C ODDS 1:1014 H, 1:1024 R
GROUP D ODDS 1:3754 H, 1:4096 R
GROUP E ODDS 1:3412 H, 1:3520 R
GROUP F ODDS 1:140 H, 1:141 R
GROUP G ODDS 1:2208 H, 1:2261 R
GROUP H ODDS 1:22 H, 1:193 R
GROUP I ODDS 1:168 H/R
GROUP J ODDS 1:1188 H, 1:1229 R
GROUP K ODDS 1:1031 H, 1:1039 R
GROUP L ODDS 1:500 H, 1:503 R
GROUP M ODDS 1:67 H, 1:66 R
EXCH EXPIRATION: 2/28/2007
ANNOUNCED PRINT RUNS BELOW
UNPRICED NOTATIONS PRINT RUN 10 SETS

	Nm-Mt	Ex-Mt
❑ AP Alan Page K	40.00	12.00
❑ AS Abdul Salaam M	20.00	6.00
❑ BB Bob Baumhower H	40.00	12.00
❑ BJ Billy Johnson M	20.00	6.00
❑ CB Cliff Branch H	20.00	6.00
❑ CD Clint Didier F	20.00	6.00
❑ CE Carl Eller L	30.00	9.00
❑ CJ Charlie Joiner M	20.00	6.00
❑ DA Dick Anderson F	30.00	9.00
❑ DB Doug Betters H	30.00	9.00
❑ DC Dave Casper/90 C	50.00	15.00
❑ DF Dan Fouts/190 E	50.00	15.00
❑ DG Donnie Green H	20.00	6.00
❑ DH Dan Hampton I	30.00	9.00
❑ DJ Deacon Jones/90 C	50.00	15.00
❑ DM Don Maynard/170 D	40.00	12.00
❑ DP Dan Pastorini H	20.00	6.00
❑ DW Dwight White H	80.00	24.00
❑ EB Emerson Boozer H	40.00	12.00
❑ EC Earl Campbell/90 C	100.00	30.00
❑ EH Ernie Holmes H	60.00	18.00
❑ FB Fred Biletnikoff/70 B	80.00	24.00
❑ GB Glenn Blackwood H	30.00	9.00
❑ GF Gary Fencik M	30.00	9.00
❑ GL Gary Larsen M	30.00	9.00
❑ GM George Martin H	30.00	9.00
❑ GU Gene Upshaw F	40.00	12.00
❑ HC Harry Carson F	40.00	12.00
❑ HJ Harold Jackson M	20.00	6.00

❑ HM Hugh McElhenny H 30.00 9.00
❑ JB Jeff Bostic H 30.00 9.00
❑ JG Joe Greene/70 B 150.00 45.00
❑ JH John Hannah I 20.00 6.00
❑ JJ Joe Jacoby H 30.00 9.00
❑ JL Joe Delamielleure H 30.00 9.00
❑ JM Joe Montana/90 C 250.00 75.00
❑ JN Joe Namath/40 A 200.00 60.00
❑ JS Jake Scott/90 C 100.00 30.00
❑ JT John Taylor F 30.00 9.00
❑ KB Kim Bokamper H 30.00 9.00
❑ KG Kevin Greene F 60.00 18.00
❑ KM Karl Mecklenburg H 30.00 9.00
❑ KS Ken Stabler F 50.00 15.00
❑ KW Kellen Winslow F EXCH 30.00 9.00
❑ LB Lyle Blackwood H 30.00 9.00
❑ LC Larry Csonka/70 B EXCH 100.00 30.00
❑ LL Lamar Lundy I 40.00 12.00
❑ LM Leonard Marshall H 30.00 9.00
❑ LT Lawrence Taylor/90 C 80.00 24.00
❑ MC Mark Clayton I 30.00 9.00
❑ MD Mark Duper I 30.00 9.00
❑ MF Manny Fernandez F 30.00 9.00
❑ MG Mark Gastineau H 40.00 12.00
❑ MJ Mark Jackson M 20.00 6.00
❑ ML Marty Lyons M 20.00 6.00
❑ MM Mark May F 30.00 9.00
❑ MO Merlin Olsen I 40.00 12.00
❑ MS Matt Snell H 30.00 9.00
❑ ON Ozzie Newsome/90 C 60.00 18.00
❑ OS Otis Sistrunk H 30.00 9.00
❑ PV Phil Villapiano H 30.00 9.00
❑ RC Roger Craig F 30.00 9.00
❑ RD Richard Dent I 30.00 9.00
❑ RG Randy Gradishar F 30.00 9.00
❑ RM Reggie McKenzie F 30.00 9.00
❑ RN Ricky Nattiel M 20.00 6.00
❑ RS Roger Staubach/40 A 200.00 60.00
❑ SG Steve Grogan J 30.00 9.00
❑ SM Stanley Morgan M 20.00 6.00
❑ TD Tony Dorsett/40 A EXCH 100.00 30.00
❑ TH Ted Hendricks F 30.00 9.00
❑ VJ Vance Johnson M 20.00 6.00
❑ WP William Perry M 30.00 9.00
❑ BBR Bob Brudzinski H 40.00 12.00
❑ CBA Carl Banks F 30.00 9.00
❑ CBO Charles Bowser H 30.00 9.00
❑ CBR Charlie Brown H 30.00 9.00
❑ DCL Dwight Clark F 30.00 9.00
❑ DFO Dave Foley F 30.00 9.00
❑ DPE Drew Pearson M 30.00 9.00
❑ GLL Greg Lloyd F 40.00 12.00
❑ JBU Jim Burt H 30.00 9.00
❑ JHJ John Henry Johnson H 40.00 12.00
❑ JKI Jim Kiick G 40.00 12.00
❑ JKL Joe Klecko L 30.00 9.00
❑ JMA Jim Marshall M 30.00 9.00
❑ LCG L.C. Greenwood H 50.00 15.00
❑ MMO Mike Montler F 30.00 9.00
❑ RGR Russ Grimm I EXCH 30.00 9.00
❑ ROG Roosevelt Grier H 30.00 9.00
❑ THI Tony Hill H 20.00 6.00
❑ YAT Y.A. Tittle/70 B 100.00 30.00

2004 Topps Fan Favorites Co-Signers

Nm-Mt Ex-Mt
STATED ODDS 1:2288 H, 1:2148 R
EXCH EXPIRATION: 2/28/2007
ANNOUNCED PRINT RUN 50 SETS

❑ CODC Mark Duper 100.00 30.00
Mark Clayton
❑ COFW Dan Fouts EXCH 100.00 30.00
Kellen Winslow
❑ COKG Joe Klecko 100.00 30.00
Mark Gastineau
❑ CONM Joe Namath 200.00 60.00
Don Maynard
❑ COPE Alan Page 100.00 30.00
Carl Eller
❑ COSD Roger Staubach EXCH 200.0060.00
Tony Dorsett

2004 Topps Fan Favorites Jumbos

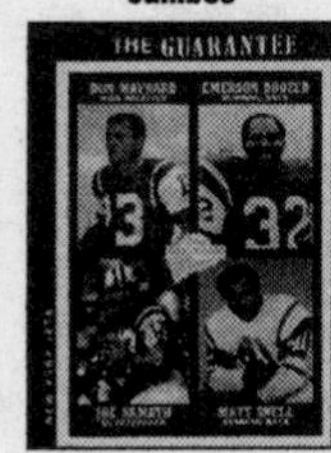

Nm-Mt Ex-Mt
ONE PER BOX

❑ 1 Charlie Joiner 8.00 2.40
Dan Fouts
Kellen Winslow
❑ 2 Drew Pearson 15.00 4.50
Roger Staubach
Tony Dorsett
Tony Hill
❑ 3 Deacon Jones 8.00 2.40
Lamar Lundy
Merlin Olsen
Roosevelt Grier
❑ 4 Mark Clayton 6.00 1.80
Mark Duper
❑ 5 Hugh McElhenny 8.00 2.40
John Henry Johnson
Y.A. Tittle
❑ 6 Abdul Salaam 6.00 1.80
Joe Klecko
Mark Gastineau
Marty Lyons
❑ 7 Alan Page 8.00 2.40
Carl Eller
Gary Larsen
Jim Marshall
❑ 8 Cliff Branch 12.00 3.60
Dave Casper
Fred Biletnikoff
Ken Stabler
❑ 9 Don Maynard 15.00 4.50
Emerson Boozer
Joe Namath
Matt Snell
❑ 10 Dwight White 10.00 3.00
Ernie Holmes
Joe Greene
L.C. Greenwood

2000 Topps Gallery

Nm-Mt Ex-Mt
COMPLETE SET (175) 50.00 22.00
COMP.SET w/o SP's (125) 20.00 9.00
UNPRICED PRESS PLATES EXIST

❑ 1 Marshall Faulk 1.00 .45
❑ 2 Kordell Stewart .50 .23
❑ 3 Priest Holmes 1.00 .45

❑ 4 James Johnson .30 .14
❑ 5 Charlie Garner .50 .23
❑ 6 Jeff Blake .50 .23
❑ 7 Joey Galloway .50 .23
❑ 8 Terrell Davis .75 .35
❑ 9 Jerome Bettis .75 .35
❑ 10 Bobby Engram .50 .23
❑ 11 Muhsin Muhammad .50 .23
❑ 12 Marcus Robinson .75 .35
❑ 13 Kerry Collins .50 .23
❑ 14 Jake Plummer .50 .23
❑ 15 J.J. Stokes .50 .23
❑ 16 Tim Couch .50 .23
❑ 17 Napoleon Kaufman .50 .23
❑ 18 Az-Zahir Hakim .50 .23
❑ 19 Jimmy Smith .50 .23
❑ 20 Eddie George .75 .35
❑ 21 Jacquez Green .30 .14
❑ 22 Champ Bailey .50 .23
❑ 23 Wesley Walls .30 .14
❑ 24 Eric Moulds .75 .35
❑ 25 Corey Dillon .75 .35
❑ 26 Freddie Jones .30 .14
❑ 27 Jevon Kearse .75 .35
❑ 28 Ray Lucas .50 .23
❑ 29 Germane Crowell .30 .14
❑ 30 Randy Moss 1.50 .70
❑ 31 Patrick Jeffers .75 .35
❑ 32 Zach Thomas .75 .35
❑ 33 Shannon Sharpe .50 .23
❑ 34 Derrick Mayes .50 .23
❑ 35 Antonio Freeman .75 .35
❑ 36 Terance Mathis .50 .23
❑ 37 Herman Moore .50 .23
❑ 38 Tony Banks .50 .23
❑ 39 Jerry Rice 1.50 .70
❑ 40 Troy Aikman 1.50 .70
❑ 41 Rickey Dudley .30 .14
❑ 42 Troy Edwards .30 .14
❑ 43 Curtis Martin .75 .35
❑ 44 Eddie Kennison .50 .23
❑ 45 Mark Brunell .75 .35
❑ 46 Shaun King .30 .14
❑ 47 Duce Staley .75 .35
❑ 48 Darnay Scott .50 .23
❑ 49 Sean Dawkins .30 .14
❑ 50 Edgerrin James 1.25 .55
❑ 51 Olandis Gary .75 .35
❑ 52 Peerless Price .75 .35
❑ 53 Akili Smith .30 .14
❑ 54 Charlie Batch .75 .35
❑ 55 Tim Biakabutuka .50 .23
❑ 56 Rob Moore .50 .23
❑ 57 Keenan McCardell .50 .23
❑ 58 Dan Marino 2.50 1.10
❑ 59 Tony Gonzalez .50 .23
❑ 60 Stephen Davis .75 .35
❑ 61 Ricky Watters .50 .23
❑ 62 Frank Wycheck .30 .14
❑ 63 Kevin Johnson .75 .35
❑ 64 Isaac Bruce .75 .35
❑ 65 Andre Reed .50 .23
❑ 66 Jamal Anderson .75 .35
❑ 67 Dorsey Levens .50 .23
❑ 68 Rocket Ismail .50 .23
❑ 69 Albert Connell .30 .14
❑ 70 Brett Favre 2.50 1.10

❑ 71 Wayne Chrebet	.50	.23
❑ 72 Jon Kitna	.75	.35
❑ 73 Brian Griese	.75	.35
❑ 74 Rob Johnson	.50	.23
❑ 75 Qadry Ismail	.50	.23
❑ 76 Derrick Alexander	.50	.23
❑ 77 Tim Dwight	.75	.35
❑ 78 Ike Hilliard	.50	.23
❑ 79 Frank Sanders	.50	.23
❑ 80 Fred Taylor	.75	.35
❑ 81 Robert Smith	.75	.35
❑ 82 Vinny Testaverde	.50	.23
❑ 83 Steve Young	1.00	.45
❑ 84 Tyrone Wheatley	.50	.23
❑ 85 Mikhael Ricks	.30	.14
❑ 86 Tony Martin	.50	.23
❑ 87 Carl Pickens	.50	.23
❑ 88 Warrick Dunn	.75	.35
❑ 89 Emmitt Smith	1.50	.70
❑ 90 Keyshawn Johnson	.75	.35
❑ 91 James Stewart	.50	.23
❑ 92 Doug Flutie	.75	.35
❑ 93 Torry Holt	.75	.35
❑ 94 Jeff Graham	.30	.14
❑ 95 Steve McNair	.75	.35
❑ 96 Errict Rhett	.50	.23
❑ 97 Terrell Owens	.75	.35
❑ 98 Terry Glenn	.50	.23
❑ 99 Steve Beuerlein	.50	.23
❑ 100 Kurt Warner	1.50	.70
❑ 101 Jeff George	.50	.23
❑ 102 Deion Sanders	.75	.35
❑ 103 Johnnie Morton	.50	.23
❑ 104 Antowain Smith	.50	.23
❑ 105 O.J. McDuffie	.50	.23
❑ 106 Rod Smith	.50	.23
❑ 107 Jim Harbaugh	.50	.23
❑ 108 Marvin Harrison	.75	.35
❑ 109 Curtis Enis	.30	.14
❑ 110 Drew Bledsoe	1.00	.45
❑ 111 Mike Alstott	.75	.35
❑ 112 Amani Toomer	.50	.23
❑ 113 Elvis Grbac	.50	.23
❑ 114 Tim Brown	.75	.35
❑ 115 Cris Carter	.75	.35
❑ 116 Donovan McNabb	1.25	.55
❑ 117 Chris Chandler	.50	.23
❑ 118 Kevin Dyson	.50	.23
❑ 119 Rich Gannon	.75	.35
❑ 120 Ricky Williams	.75	.35
❑ 121 Brad Johnson	.75	.35
❑ 122 Cade McNown	.30	.14
❑ 123 Ed McCaffrey	.75	.35
❑ 124 Michael Westbrook	.50	.23
❑ 125 Peyton Manning	2.00	.90
❑ 126 Brett Favre MAS	4.00	1.80
❑ 127 Emmitt Smith MAS	2.50	1.10
❑ 128 Tim Brown MAS	1.00	.45
❑ 129 Troy Aikman MAS	2.50	1.10
❑ 130 Jimmy Smith MAS	.75	.35
❑ 131 Dan Marino MAS	4.00	1.80
❑ 132 Cris Carter MAS	1.00	.45
❑ 133 Jerry Rice MAS	2.50	1.10
❑ 134 Steve Young MAS	1.50	.70
❑ 135 Marshall Faulk MAS	1.50	.70
❑ 136 Eddie George MAS	1.00	.45
❑ 137 Drew Bledsoe MAS	1.50	.70
❑ 138 Randy Moss ART	2.50	1.10
❑ 139 Germane Crowell ART	.75	.35
❑ 140 Akili Smith ART	.75	.35
❑ 141 Tim Couch ART	.75	.35
❑ 142 Marcus Robinson ART	1.00	.45
❑ 143 Daunte Culpepper ART	1.50	.70
❑ 144 Jevon Kearse ART	1.00	.45
❑ 145 Edgerrin James ART	2.00	.90
❑ 146 Tony Gonzalez ART	.75	.35
❑ 147 Cade McNown ART	.75	.35
❑ 148 Fred Taylor ART	1.00	.45
❑ 149 Donovan McNabb ART	2.00	.90
❑ 150 Ricky Williams ART	1.00	.45
❑ 151 Jamal Lewis RC	5.00	2.20
❑ 152 Tee Martin RC	2.00	.90
❑ 153 Plaxico Burress RC	4.00	1.80
❑ 154 Chad Pennington RC	8.00	3.60
❑ 155 Curtis Keaton RC	1.50	.70
❑ 156 Thomas Jones RC	3.00	1.35
❑ 157 Courtney Brown RC	1.00	.45
❑ 158 Ron Dayne RC	2.00	.90
❑ 159 Shaun Alexander RC	5.00	2.20
❑ 160 Travis Taylor RC	1.00	.45
❑ 161 Sylvester Morris RC	1.50	.70
❑ 162 Giovanni Carmazzi RC	1.50	.70
❑ 163 Laveranues Coles RC	2.50	1.10
❑ 164 Chris Redman RC	1.50	.70
❑ 165 Bubba Franks RC	2.00	.90
❑ 166 R.Jay Soward RC	1.50	.70
❑ 167 Reuben Droughns RC	2.50	1.10
❑ 168 Todd Pinkston RC	2.00	.90
❑ 169 Trung Canidate RC	1.50	.70
❑ 170 Danny Farmer RC	1.50	.70
❑ 171 Ron Dugans RC	1.50	.70
❑ 172 Dennis Northcutt RC	2.00	.90
❑ 173 J.R. Redmond RC	1.50	.70
❑ 174 Travis Prentice RC	1.50	.70
❑ 175 Peter Warrick RC	2.00	.90

2001 Topps Gallery

	Nm-Mt	Ex-Mt
COMP.SET w/o SP's (100)	25.00	7.50
❑ 1 Donovan McNabb	1.00	.30
❑ 2 Jamal Anderson	.75	.23
❑ 3 Steve McNair	.75	.23
❑ 4 Peyton Manning	2.00	.60
❑ 5 Curtis Martin	.75	.23
❑ 6 Joey Galloway	.50	.15
❑ 7 Daunte Culpepper	.75	.23
❑ 8 Corey Dillon	.75	.23
❑ 9 Brad Johnson	.75	.23
❑ 10 Doug Flutie	.75	.23
❑ 11 Jerome Bettis	.75	.23
❑ 12 Elvis Grbac	.50	.15
❑ 13 Aaron Brooks	.75	.23
❑ 14 Ray Lewis	.75	.23
❑ 15 Tim Dwight	.75	.23
❑ 16 Robert Smith	.30	.09
❑ 17 Jake Plummer	.50	.15
❑ 18 Jay Fiedler	.75	.23
❑ 19 Fred Taylor	.75	.23
❑ 20 Jerry Rice	1.50	.45
❑ 21 Shaun King	.30	.09
❑ 22 Cade McNown	.30	.09
❑ 23 Drew Bledsoe	1.00	.30
❑ 24 Ricky Watters	.50	.15
❑ 25 Muhsin Muhammad	.50	.15
❑ 26 Shawn Jefferson	.30	.09
❑ 27 Tiki Barber	.50	.15
❑ 28 Derrick Alexander	.50	.15
❑ 29 Stephen Davis	.75	.23
❑ 30 James Stewart	.50	.15
❑ 31 Terrell Owens	.75	.23
❑ 32 Ed McCaffrey	.75	.23
❑ 33 Jeff Graham	.30	.09
❑ 34 Jamal Lewis	1.25	.35
❑ 35 Edgerrin James	1.00	.30
❑ 36 Tim Couch	.50	.15
❑ 37 Marshall Faulk	1.00	.30
❑ 38 Ike Hilliard	.50	.15
❑ 39 Ahman Green	.75	.23
❑ 40 Tim Biakabutuka	.50	.15
❑ 41 Akili Smith	.30	.09
❑ 42 David Boston	.75	.23
❑ 43 Eddie George	.75	.23
❑ 44 Hines Ward	.75	.23
❑ 45 Chad Lewis	.30	.09
❑ 46 Brian Urlacher	1.25	.35
❑ 47 Eric Moulds	.50	.15
❑ 48 Ricky Williams	.75	.23
❑ 49 Warrick Dunn	.75	.23
❑ 50 Kerry Collins	.50	.15
❑ 51 Isaac Bruce	.75	.23
❑ 52 Jimmy Smith	.50	.15
❑ 53 Emmitt Smith	1.50	.45
❑ 54 Cris Carter	.75	.23
❑ 55 Jeff Garcia	.75	.23
❑ 56 Mike Anderson	.75	.23
❑ 57 Lamar Smith	.50	.15
❑ 58 Brett Favre	2.50	.75
❑ 59 Steve Beuerlein	.50	.15
❑ 60 Terry Glenn	.30	.09
❑ 61 Tyrone Wheatley	.50	.15
❑ 62 Charlie Batch	.75	.23
❑ 63 Chris Chandler	.50	.15
❑ 64 Sylvester Morris	.30	.09
❑ 65 Joe Horn	.50	.15
❑ 66 Kevin Johnson	.50	.15
❑ 67 Rob Johnson	.50	.15
❑ 68 Jeff George	.50	.15
❑ 69 Keyshawn Johnson	.75	.23
❑ 70 Wayne Chrebet	.50	.15
❑ 71 Randy Moss	1.50	.45
❑ 72 Marvin Harrison	.75	.23
❑ 73 Peter Warrick	.75	.23
❑ 74 Darrell Jackson	.75	.23
❑ 75 Derrick Mason	.50	.15
❑ 76 Oronde Gadsden	.50	.15
❑ 77 Charles Johnson	.30	.09
❑ 78 James Allen	.50	.15
❑ 79 Torry Holt	.75	.23
❑ 80 Troy Brown	.50	.15
❑ 81 Amani Toomer	.50	.15
❑ 82 Junior Seau	.75	.23
❑ 83 Troy Aikman	1.25	.35
❑ 84 Mark Brunell	.75	.23
❑ 85 Brian Griese	.75	.23
❑ 86 Charlie Garner	.50	.15
❑ 87 Rich Gannon	.75	.23
❑ 88 Jeff Blake	.50	.15
❑ 89 Donald Hayes	.30	.09
❑ 90 Germane Crowell	.30	.09
❑ 91 Tony Gonzalez	.50	.15
❑ 92 Jon Kitna	.75	.23
❑ 93 Vinny Testaverde	.50	.15
❑ 94 Kordell Stewart	.50	.15
❑ 95 Keenan McCardell	.30	.09
❑ 96 Kurt Warner	1.50	.45
❑ 97 Bill Schroeder	.50	.15
❑ 98 Rod Smith	.50	.15
❑ 99 Tim Brown	.75	.23
❑ 100 Trent Dilfer	.50	.15
❑ 101 Michael Vick RC	12.00	3.60
❑ 102 Koren Robinson RC	2.00	.60
❑ 103 LaDainian Tomlinson RC	5.00	1.50
❑ 104 Todd Heap RC	1.50	.45
❑ 105 Correll Buckhalter RC	2.00	.60
❑ 106 Freddie Mitchell RC	1.50	.45
❑ 107 Josh Booty RC	1.50	.45
❑ 108 Chris Chambers RC	2.00	.60
❑ 109 Chris Weinke RC	1.50	.45
❑ 110 Steve Smith RC	2.00	.60
❑ 111 Travis Minor RC	1.00	.30
❑ 112 Ken-Yon Rambo RC	1.00	.30
❑ 113 Marques Tuiasosopo RC	1.50	.45
❑ 114 Bobby Newcombe RC	1.00	.30
❑ 115 Drew Brees RC	3.00	.90
❑ 116 LaMont Jordan RC	2.00	.60
❑ 117 Dan Morgan RC	1.50	.45
❑ 118 Reggie Wayne RC	2.50	.75
❑ 119 Dan Alexander RC	1.50	.45
❑ 120 Alge Crumpler RC	2.00	.60
❑ 121 Robert Ferguson RC	1.50	.45
❑ 122 Rod Gardner RC	1.50	.45
❑ 123 Mike McMahon RC	1.50	.45
❑ 124 Kevan Barlow RC	1.50	.45
❑ 125 Snoop Minnis RC	1.00	.30
❑ 126 Sage Rosenfels RC	1.50	.45

❑ 127 Jesse Palmer RC	1.50	.45
❑ 128 Michael Bennett RC	3.00	.90
❑ 129 Rudi Johnson RC	3.00	.90
❑ 130 Deuce McAllister RC	3.00	.90
❑ 131 Santana Moss RC	2.50	.75
❑ 132 Josh Heupel RC	1.50	.45
❑ 133 Quincy Morgan RC	1.50	.45
❑ 134 Quincy Carter RC	1.50	.45
❑ 135 Anthony Thomas RC	2.50	.75
❑ 136 James Jackson RC	1.50	.45
❑ 137 Kevin Kasper RC	1.50	.45
❑ 138 Alex Bannister RC	1.00	.30
❑ 139 David Terrell RC	1.50	.45
❑ 140 Chad Johnson RC	3.00	.90
❑ 141 Walter Payton	5.00	1.50
❑ 142 Bart Starr	3.00	.90
❑ 143 Sonny Jurgensen	1.50	.45
❑ 144 Jim Brown	2.50	.75
❑ 145A Joe Namath HTA	10.00	3.00
❑ 145B Joe Namath RETAIL	15.00	4.50
❑ NNO Joe Namath Bucks	4.00	1.20

2001 Topps Gallery Autographs

	Nm-Mt	Ex-Mt
❑ AB Aaron Brooks E	20.00	6.00
❑ DC Daunte Culpepper A	50.00	15.00
❑ EG Eddie George A	40.00	12.00
❑ JG Jeff Garcia B	25.00	7.50
❑ JL Jamal Lewis B	20.00	6.00
❑ MA Mike Anderson C	20.00	6.00
❑ TB Tim Brown A	40.00	12.00
❑ TD Tim Dwight D	15.00	4.50
❑ WC Wayne Chrebet D	15.00	4.50

2001 Topps Gallery Originals Relics

	Nm-Mt	Ex-Mt
❑ GOCC Cris Carter	20.00	6.00
❑ GOCD Corey Dillon	20.00	6.00
❑ GOCJ Chad Johnson	50.00	15.00
❑ GODA Dan Alexander	20.00	6.00
❑ GOKB Kevan Barlow	20.00	6.00
❑ GOKW Kurt Warner	25.00	7.50
❑ GOPM Peyton Manning	40.00	12.00
❑ GORC Rashard Casey	20.00	6.00
❑ GORG Rod Gardner	20.00	6.00
❑ GOWS Warren Sapp	20.00	6.00

2002 Topps Gallery

	Nm-Mt	Ex-Mt
COMPLETE SET (200)	80.00	24.00
COMP.SET w/o SP's (150)	40.00	12.00

UNPRICED PRESS PLATES EXIST
FOUR DIFF.COLOR PP's MADE PER CARD
PRESS PLATE STATED ODDS 1:617

❑ 1 Marshall Faulk	.75	.23
❑ 2 Mark Brunell	.75	.23
❑ 3 Jeff Garcia	.75	.23
❑ 4 David Terrell	.75	.23
❑ 5 Curtis Martin	.75	.23
❑ 6 Terrell Davis	.75	.23
❑ 7 Jake Plummer	.50	.15
❑ 8 Eric Moulds	.50	.15
❑ 9 Peyton Manning	1.50	.45
❑ 10 Hines Ward	.75	.23
❑ 11 Koren Robinson	.50	.15
❑ 12 Eddie George	.75	.23
❑ 13 Shane Matthews	.30	.09
❑ 14 Trent Green	.50	.15
❑ 15 Marcus Robinson	.50	.15
❑ 16 Michael Vick	2.50	.75
❑ 17 Muhsin Muhammad	.50	.15
❑ 18 Rocket Ismail	.50	.15
❑ 19 Quincy Morgan	.30	.09
❑ 20 Mike McMahon	.75	.23
❑ 21 Randy Moss	1.50	.45
❑ 22 Willie Jackson	.30	.09
❑ 23 Freddie Mitchell	.50	.15
❑ 24 LaDainian Tomlinson	1.25	.35
❑ 25 Warrick Dunn	.75	.23
❑ 26 Zach Thomas	.75	.23
❑ 27 Bill Schroeder	.50	.15
❑ 28 Jon Kitna	.50	.15
❑ 29 Rob Johnson	.50	.15
❑ 30 Drew Bledsoe	1.00	.30
❑ 31 Ron Dayne	.50	.15
❑ 32 Tim Brown	.75	.23
❑ 33 Michael Westbrook	.30	.09
❑ 34 Terrell Owens	.75	.23
❑ 35 Santana Moss	.75	.23
❑ 36 Edgerrin James	1.00	.30
❑ 37 Ray Lewis	.75	.23
❑ 38 Chris Weinke	.50	.15
❑ 39 Brian Griese	.75	.23
❑ 40 Trent Dilfer	.50	.15
❑ 41 Jay Fiedler	.50	.15
❑ 42 Joe Horn	.50	.15
❑ 43 Chad Johnson	.75	.23
❑ 44 Plaxico Burress	.50	.15
❑ 45 Trung Canidate	.50	.15
❑ 46 Steve McNair	.75	.23
❑ 47 Curtis Conway	.30	.09
❑ 48 James Stewart	.50	.15
❑ 49 James Jackson	.30	.09
❑ 50 Tom Brady	2.00	.60
❑ 51 Emmitt Smith	2.00	.60
❑ 52 Michael Pittman	.30	.09
❑ 53 Tony Gonzalez	.50	.15
❑ 54 Daunte Culpepper	.75	.23
❑ 55 Michael Strahan	.50	.15
❑ 56 Keyshawn Johnson	.75	.23
❑ 57 Marvin Harrison	.75	.23
❑ 58 Brian Urlacher	1.25	.35
❑ 59 Jeff Blake	.30	.09
❑ 60 Chris Redman	.30	.09
❑ 61 James McKnight	.30	.09
❑ 62 Jerome Bettis	.75	.23
❑ 63 Shaun Alexander	.75	.23
❑ 64 Rod Gardner	.50	.15
❑ 65 Jimmy Smith	.50	.15
❑ 66 Thomas Jones	.50	.15
❑ 67 Peter Warrick	.50	.15
❑ 68 Mike Anderson	.75	.23
❑ 69 Ahman Green	.75	.23
❑ 70 Amani Toomer	.50	.15
❑ 71 Rich Gannon	.75	.23
❑ 72 Vinny Testaverde	.50	.15
❑ 73 Isaac Bruce	.75	.23
❑ 74 Derrick Mason	.50	.15
❑ 75 John Abraham	.50	.15
❑ 76 Shannon Sharpe	.50	.15
❑ 77 Quincy Carter	.50	.15
❑ 78 Todd Pinkston	.50	.15
❑ 79 Drew Brees	.75	.23
❑ 80 Brad Johnson	.50	.15
❑ 81 Garrison Hearst	.50	.15
❑ 82 Anthony Thomas	.75	.23
❑ 83 Brett Favre	2.00	.60
❑ 84 Troy Brown	.50	.15
❑ 85 Charlie Garner	.50	.15
❑ 86 Kendrell Bell	.75	.23
❑ 87 Darrell Jackson	.50	.15
❑ 88 Ricky Williams	1.50	.45
❑ 89 Duce Staley	.75	.23
❑ 90 Stephen Davis	.50	.15
❑ 91 Dominic Rhodes	.50	.15
❑ 92 Travis Henry	.75	.23
❑ 93 David Boston	.75	.23
❑ 94 Deuce McAllister	1.00	.30
❑ 95 Ike Hilliard	.50	.15
❑ 96 Doug Flutie	.75	.23
❑ 97 Torry Holt	.75	.23
❑ 98 Keenan McCardell	.30	.09
❑ 99 Rod Smith	.50	.15
❑ 100 Donovan McNabb	1.00	.30
❑ 101 Corey Bradford	.30	.09
❑ 102 Germane Crowell	.30	.09
❑ 103 Michael Bennett	.50	.15
❑ 104 Wayne Chrebet	.50	.15
❑ 105 Mike Alstott	.75	.23
❑ 106 Kevin Dyson	.50	.15
❑ 107 Tim Couch	.50	.15
❑ 108 Donald Hayes	.30	.09
❑ 109 Maurice Smith	.50	.15
❑ 110 Snoop Minnis	.30	.09
❑ 111 Antowain Smith	.50	.15
❑ 112 Kordell Stewart	.50	.15
❑ 113 Kurt Warner	.75	.23
❑ 114 Jerry Rice	1.50	.45
❑ 115 Aaron Brooks	.75	.23
❑ 116 Tiki Barber	.50	.15
❑ 117 Marty Booker	.30	.09
❑ 118 Qadry Ismail	.50	.15
❑ 119 Peerless Price	.50	.15
❑ 120 Marcus Pollard	.30	.09
❑ 121 James Allen	.50	.15
❑ 122 Junior Seau	.75	.23
❑ 123 Fred Taylor	.75	.23
❑ 124 Corey Dillon	.50	.15
❑ 125 Lamar Smith	.50	.15
❑ 126 Laveranues Coles	.50	.15
❑ 127 James Thrash	.50	.15
❑ 128 Kevan Barlow	.50	.15
❑ 129 Matt Hasselbeck	.50	.15
❑ 130 David Patten	.30	.09
❑ 131 Antonio Freeman	.75	.23
❑ 132 Johnnie Morton	.50	.15
❑ 133 Priest Holmes	1.00	.30
❑ 134 Cris Carter	.75	.23
❑ 135 Kevin Johnson	.50	.15
❑ 136 Jim Miller	.30	.09
❑ 137 Kerry Collins	.50	.15
❑ 138 Joey Galloway	.50	.15
❑ 139 Correll Buckhalter	.50	.15
❑ 140 Chris Chambers	.75	.23
❑ 141 Travis Taylor	.50	.15
❑ 142 Ed McCaffrey	.75	.23
❑ 143 J.J. Stokes	.50	.15

❑ 144 Reggie Wayne	.50	.15
❑ 145 Az-Zahir Hakim	.30	.09
❑ 146 Tim Dwight	.50	.15
❑ 147 Jevon Kearse	.50	.15
❑ 148 Jamal Lewis	.75	.23
❑ 149 Warren Sapp	.50	.15
❑ 150 Jermaine Lewis	.30	.09
❑ 151 William Green RC	3.00	.90
❑ 152 Roy Williams RC	5.00	1.50
❑ 153 Kurt Kittner RC	1.50	.45
❑ 154 Daniel Graham RC	2.00	.60
❑ 155 Andre Davis RC	2.00	.60
❑ 156 Donte Stallworth RC	4.00	1.20
❑ 157 Josh Reed RC	2.00	.60
❑ 158 Rohan Davey RC	2.00	.60
❑ 159 Wendell Bryant RC	2.00	.60
❑ 160 Lito Sheppard RC	2.00	.60
❑ 161 Najeh Davenport RC	2.00	.60
❑ 162 Freddie Milons RC	1.50	.45
❑ 163 Patrick Ramsey RC	4.00	1.20
❑ 164 Luke Staley RC	1.50	.45
❑ 165 Maurice Morris RC	2.00	.60
❑ 166 Dwight Freeney RC	2.50	.75
❑ 167 Jeremy Shockey RC	6.00	1.80
❑ 168 Jabar Gaffney RC	2.00	.60
❑ 169 DeShaun Foster RC	2.00	.60
❑ 170 Chad Hutchinson RC	2.00	.60
❑ 171 Tim Carter RC	1.50	.45
❑ 172 Napoleon Harris RC	2.00	.60
❑ 173 Kahlil Hill RC	1.50	.45
❑ 174 Josh McCown RC	3.00	.90
❑ 175 Ron Johnson RC	1.50	.45
❑ 176 Marquise Walker RC	1.50	.45
❑ 177 Joey Harrington RC	6.00	1.80
❑ 178 Travis Stephens RC	1.50	.45
❑ 179 Julius Peppers RC	4.00	1.20
❑ 180 Ryan Sims RC	2.00	.60
❑ 181 Albert Haynesworth RC	1.50	.45
❑ 182 Phillip Buchanon RC	2.00	.60
❑ 183 Jonathan Wells RC	2.00	.60
❑ 184 Chester Taylor RC	2.00	.60
❑ 185 Antonio Bryant RC	2.00	.60
❑ 186 Adrian Peterson RC	2.00	.60
❑ 187 Clinton Portis RC	6.00	1.80
❑ 188 Lamar Gordon RC	2.00	.60
❑ 189 Reche Caldwell RC	2.00	.60
❑ 190 Ashley Lelie RC	4.00	1.20
❑ 191 T.J. Duckett RC	3.00	.90
❑ 192 Eric Crouch RC	3.00	.90
❑ 193 David Garrard RC	2.00	.60
❑ 194 Quentin Jammer RC	2.00	.60
❑ 195 Ladell Betts RC	2.00	.60
❑ 196 Antwaan Randle El RC	2.50	.75
❑ 197 Cliff Russell RC	1.50	.45
❑ 198 Javon Walker RC	4.00	1.20
❑ 199 John Henderson RC	2.00	.60
❑ 200 David Carr RC	6.00	1.80

2002 Topps Gallery Autographs

	Nm-Mt	Ex-Mt
*ARTISTS PROOFS: 1X TO 2X BASIC CARDS		
❑ GAB Aaron Brooks B	25.00	7.50
❑ GAT Anthony Thomas B	25.00	7.50
❑ GCC Chris Chambers B	25.00	7.50
❑ GDS Duce Staley B	20.00	6.00
❑ GHW Hines Ward B	30.00	9.00
❑ GJA John Abraham B	25.00	7.50
❑ GKB Kendrell Bell B	25.00	7.50
❑ GMB Marty Booker B	20.00	6.00
❑ GTB Tom Brady A	125.00	38.00

1999 Topps Gold Label Class 1

	Nm-Mt	Ex-Mt
COMPLETE SET (100)	60.00	27.00
❑ 1 Terrell Davis	1.25	.55
❑ 2 Jake Plummer	.75	.35
❑ 3 Mike Cloud RC	1.50	.70
❑ 4 D'Wayne Bates RC	1.50	.70
❑ 5 Jamal Anderson	1.25	.55
❑ 6 Cecil Collins RC	1.00	.45
❑ 7 Keyshawn Johnson	1.25	.55
❑ 8 Jerome Bettis	1.25	.55
❑ 9 Ricky Watters	.75	.35
❑ 10 Brett Favre	4.00	1.80
❑ 11 Joe Germaine RC	1.50	.70
❑ 12 Eddie George	1.25	.55
❑ 13 Jevon Kearse RC	3.00	1.35
❑ 14 Skip Hicks	.50	.23
❑ 15 James Johnson RC	1.50	.70
❑ 16 Terry Glenn	1.25	.55
❑ 17 Troy Edwards RC	1.50	.70
❑ 18 Karsten Bailey RC	1.50	.70
❑ 19 Trent Dilfer	.75	.35
❑ 20 Barry Sanders	4.00	1.80
❑ 21 Vinny Testaverde	.75	.35
❑ 22 Ed McCaffrey	.75	.35
❑ 23 Shannon Sharpe	.75	.35
❑ 24 Robert Smith	1.25	.55
❑ 25 Emmitt Smith	2.50	1.10
❑ 26 Rob Moore	.75	.35
❑ 27 J.J. Stokes	.75	.35
❑ 28 Champ Bailey RC	2.50	1.10
❑ 29 Napoleon Kaufman	1.25	.55
❑ 30 Fred Taylor	1.25	.55
❑ 31 Corey Dillon	1.25	.55
❑ 32 Sedrick Irvin RC	1.00	.45
❑ 33 Chris McAlister RC	1.50	.70
❑ 34 Warrick Dunn	1.25	.55
❑ 35 Isaac Bruce	1.25	.55
❑ 36 Peerless Price RC	3.00	1.35
❑ 37 Dorsey Levens	1.25	.55
❑ 38 Wayne Chrebet	.75	.35
❑ 39 Randall Cunningham	1.25	.55
❑ 40 Dan Marino	4.00	1.80
❑ 41 Chris Chandler	.75	.35
❑ 42 Mark Brunell	1.25	.55
❑ 43 Kevin Johnson RC	2.00	.90
❑ 44 Natrone Means	.75	.35
❑ 45 Jerome Pathon	.50	.23
❑ 46 Daunte Culpepper RC	6.00	2.70
❑ 47 Akili Smith RC	1.50	.70
❑ 48 Keenan McCardell	.75	.35
❑ 49 Steve McNair	1.25	.55
❑ 50 Randy Moss	3.00	1.35
❑ 51 Terance Mathis	.75	.35
❑ 52 Eric Moulds	1.25	.55
❑ 53 Rocket Ismail	.75	.35
❑ 54 Cade McNown RC	1.50	.70
❑ 55 Kordell Stewart	.75	.35
❑ 56 Rob Konrad RC	2.00	.90
❑ 57 Andre Rison	.75	.35
❑ 58 Curtis Conway	.75	.35
❑ 59 Chris Claiborne RC	1.00	.45
❑ 60 Jerry Rice	2.50	1.10
❑ 61 Peyton Manning	4.00	1.80
❑ 62 Jimmy Smith	.75	.35
❑ 63 Doug Flutie	1.25	.55
❑ 64 Frank Sanders	.75	.35
❑ 65 Antowain Smith	1.25	.55
❑ 66 Curtis Enis	.50	.23
❑ 67 Charlie Batch	1.25	.55
❑ 68 Marvin Harrison	1.25	.55
❑ 69 Garrison Hearst	.75	.35
❑ 70 Ricky Williams RC	3.00	1.35
❑ 71 Torry Holt RC	4.00	1.80
❑ 72 Mike Alstott	1.25	.55
❑ 73 Drew Bledsoe	1.50	.70
❑ 74 O.J. McDuffie	.75	.35
❑ 75 Donovan McNabb RC	8.00	3.60
❑ 76 Curtis Martin	1.25	.55
❑ 77 Priest Holmes	2.00	.90
❑ 78 Antonio Freeman	1.25	.55
❑ 79 Herman Moore	.75	.35
❑ 80 Tim Couch RC	2.00	.90
❑ 81 Troy Aikman	2.50	1.10
❑ 82 David Boston RC	2.00	.90
❑ 83 Tim Brown	1.25	.55
❑ 84 Kevin Faulk RC	2.00	.90
❑ 85 Cris Carter	1.25	.55
❑ 86 Marshall Faulk	1.50	.70
❑ 87 Shaun King RC	1.50	.70
❑ 88 Terrell Owens	1.25	.55
❑ 89 Carl Pickens	.75	.35
❑ 90 Steve Young	1.50	.70
❑ 91 Rod Smith	.75	.35
❑ 92 Michael Irvin	.75	.35
❑ 93 Ike Hilliard	.50	.23
❑ 94 Jon Kitna	1.25	.55
❑ 95 Brock Huard RC	2.00	.90
❑ 96 Joey Galloway	.75	.35
❑ 97 Amos Zereoue RC	2.00	.90
❑ 98 Duce Staley	1.25	.55
❑ 99 John Elway	4.00	1.80
❑ 100 Edgerrin James RC	6.00	2.70

2000 Topps Gold Label Rookie Autographs

	Nm-Mt	Ex-Mt
❑ CP Chad Pennington	60.00	27.00
❑ CR Chris Redman	15.00	6.75
❑ DF Bubba Franks	15.00	6.75
❑ DN Dennis Northcutt	20.00	9.00
❑ JL Jamal Lewis	50.00	22.00
❑ JP Jerry Porter	20.00	9.00
❑ JR J.R. Redmond	15.00	6.75
❑ PB Plaxico Burress	40.00	18.00
❑ PW Peter Warrick	15.00	6.75
❑ RD Ron Dayne	20.00	9.00
❑ RS R.Jay Soward	15.00	6.75
❑ SA Shaun Alexander	40.00	18.00
❑ SM Sylvester Morris	15.00	6.75
❑ TC Trung Canidate	15.00	6.75
❑ TJ Thomas Jones	25.00	11.00
❑ TM Tee Martin	15.00	6.75
❑ TP Travis Prentice	15.00	6.75
❑ TT Travis Taylor	15.00	6.75
❑ RDU Ron Dugans	12.00	5.50

2001 Topps Heritage

	Nm-Mt	Ex-Mt
COMPLETE SET (146)	300.00	135.00
COMP.SET w/o SP's (110)	25.00	7.50
❑ 1 Ray Lewis	1.25	.55
❑ 2 Peter Warrick	1.25	.55
❑ 3 James Stewart	.75	.35
❑ 4 Junior Seau	1.25	.55
❑ 5 Jeff George	.75	.35
❑ 6 Amani Toomer	.50	.23
❑ 7 Elvis Grbac	.75	.35
❑ 8 David Boston	1.25	.55
❑ 9 Jimmy Smith	.75	.35
❑ 10 Warrick Dunn	1.25	.55
❑ 11 Hines Ward	1.25	.55
❑ 12 Joe Horn	.75	.35
❑ 13 Stephen Davis	1.25	.55
❑ 14 Tyrone Wheatley	.75	.35
❑ 15 Brian Urlacher	2.00	.90
❑ 16 Fred Taylor	1.25	.55
❑ 17 Jerry Rice	2.50	1.10
❑ 18 Keyshawn Johnson	1.25	.55
❑ 19 Jay Fiedler	1.25	.55
❑ 20 Jamal Anderson	1.25	.55
❑ 21 Emmitt Smith	2.50	1.10
❑ 22 Tiki Barber	.75	.35
❑ 23 Daunte Culpepper	1.25	.55
❑ 24 Torry Holt	1.25	.55
❑ 25 Peyton Manning	3.00	1.35
❑ 26 Eddie George	1.25	.55
❑ 27 Jamal Lewis	2.00	.90
❑ 28 Ricky Williams	1.25	.55
❑ 29 Ahman Green	1.25	.55
❑ 30 Ed McCaffrey	1.25	.55
❑ 31 Curtis Martin	1.25	.55
❑ 32 Isaac Bruce	1.25	.55
❑ 33 Doug Flutie	1.25	.55
❑ 34 Steve McNair	1.25	.55
❑ 35 Donovan McNabb	1.50	.70
❑ 36 Keenan McCardell	.50	.23
❑ 37 Charlie Batch	1.25	.55
❑ 38 Cade McNown	.50	.23
❑ 39 Terrell Owens	1.25	.55
❑ 40 Brad Johnson	1.25	.55
❑ 41 Robert Smith	1.25	.55
❑ 42 Muhsin Muhammad	.75	.35
❑ 43 Kurt Warner	2.50	1.10
❑ 44 Lamar Smith	.75	.35
❑ 45 Brian Griese	1.25	.55
❑ 46 Trent Dilfer	.75	.35
❑ 47 Jeff Garcia	1.25	.55
❑ 48 Derrick Mason	.75	.35
❑ 49 Drew Bledsoe	1.50	.70
❑ 50 Marshall Faulk	1.50	.70
❑ 51 Corey Dillon	1.25	.55
❑ 52 Tony Gonzalez	.75	.35
❑ 53 Chad Lewis	.50	.23
❑ 54 Shaun Alexander	1.50	.70
❑ 55 Edgerrin James	1.50	.70
❑ 56 Eric Moulds	.75	.35
❑ 57 Aaron Brooks	1.25	.55
❑ 58 Zach Thomas	1.25	.55
❑ 59 Jerome Bettis	1.25	.55
❑ 60 Shannon Sharpe	.75	.35
❑ 61 Kerry Collins	.75	.35
❑ 62 Ricky Watters	.75	.35
❑ 63 Tim Couch	.75	.35
❑ 64 Marvin Harrison	1.25	.55
❑ 65 Tim Brown	1.25	.55
❑ 66 Mark Brunell	1.25	.55
❑ 67 Wayne Chrebet	.75	.35
❑ 68 Terry Glenn	.75	.35
❑ 69 Mike Anderson	1.25	.55
❑ 70 Randy Moss	2.50	1.10
❑ 71 Freddie Jones	.50	.23
❑ 72 Ike Hilliard	.75	.35
❑ 73 Derrick Alexander	.75	.35
❑ 74 Travis Prentice	.50	.23
❑ 75 Brett Favre	4.00	1.80
❑ 76 Rod Smith	.75	.35
❑ 77 Troy Aikman	2.00	.90
❑ 78 Cris Carter	1.25	.55
❑ 79 Rich Gannon	1.25	.55
❑ 80 Charlie Garner	.75	.35
❑ 81 Michael Pittman	.50	.23
❑ 82 Jeff Graham	.50	.23
❑ 83 Albert Connell	.50	.23
❑ 84 Bill Schroeder	.75	.35
❑ 85 Jeff Blake	.75	.35
❑ 86 Jon Kitna	1.25	.55
❑ 87 Qadry Ismail	.75	.35
❑ 88 Joey Galloway	.75	.35
❑ 89 Charles Johnson	.50	.23
❑ 90 Troy Brown	.75	.35
❑ 91 Johnnie Morton	.75	.35
❑ 92 Chris Chandler	.75	.35
❑ 93 Donald Hayes	.50	.23
❑ 94 Shaun King	.50	.23
❑ 95 Vinny Testaverde	.75	.35
❑ 96 James Allen	.75	.35
❑ 97 Jake Plummer	.75	.35
❑ 98 Antonio Freeman	1.25	.55
❑ 99 Sean Dawkins	.50	.23
❑ 100 Ron Dayne	1.25	.55
❑ 101 Rob Johnson	.75	.35
❑ 102 Kordell Stewart	.75	.35
❑ 103 Akili Smith	.50	.23
❑ 104 Shawn Jefferson	.50	.23
❑ 105 Germane Crowell	.50	.23
❑ 106 Kevin Johnson	.75	.35
❑ 107 Steve Beuerlein	.75	.35
❑ 108 Marcus Robinson	1.25	.55
❑ 109 Peerless Price	.75	.35
❑ 110 Jerome Pathon	.75	.35
❑ 111 Sage Rosenfels RC	8.00	3.60
❑ 112 Quincy Morgan RC	8.00	3.60
❑ 113 Chad Johnson RC	15.00	6.75
❑ 114 Josh Heupel RC	8.00	3.60
❑ 115 Anthony Thomas RC	12.00	5.50
❑ 116 Drew Brees RC	15.00	6.75
❑ 117 Kevan Barlow RC	8.00	3.60
❑ 118 Chris Chambers RC	10.00	4.50
❑ 119 Mike McMahon RC	8.00	3.60
❑ 120 Todd Heap RC	8.00	3.60
❑ 121 Leonard Davis RC	5.00	2.20
❑ 122 Richard Seymour RC	8.00	3.60
❑ 123 Robert Ferguson RC	8.00	3.60
❑ 124 Andre Carter RC	8.00	3.60
❑ 125 Jesse Palmer RC	8.00	3.60
❑ 126 Travis Minor RC	5.00	2.20
❑ 127 Rudi Johnson RC	15.00	6.75
❑ 128 Rod Gardner RC	8.00	3.60
❑ 129 Snoop Minnis RC	5.00	2.20
❑ 130 Koren Robinson RC	10.00	4.50
❑ 131 Chris Weinke RC	8.00	3.60
❑ 132 James Jackson RC	8.00	3.60
❑ 133 Michael Vick RC	50.00	22.00
❑ 134 Marques Tuiasosopo RC		
❑ 135 Michael Bennett RC	15.00	6.75
❑ 136 LaDainian Tomlinson RC	25.00	11.00
❑ 137 Freddie Mitchell RC	8.00	3.60
❑ 138 Deuce McAllister RC	15.00	6.75
❑ 139 Quincy Carter RC		
❑ 140 Santana Moss RC	12.00	5.50
❑ 141 David Terrell RC	8.00	3.60
❑ 142 Reggie Wayne RC	12.00	5.50
❑ 143 Justin Smith RC	8.00	3.60
❑ 144 Gerard Warren RC	8.00	3.60
❑ 145 Travis Henry RC	10.00	4.50
❑ 146 Dan Morgan RC	8.00	3.60
❑ NNO Checklist CL	.50	.15

2001 Topps Heritage Retrofractor

	Nm-Mt	Ex-Mt

*STARS: 5X TO 12X BASIC CARDS
*ROOKIES: .6X TO 1.5X

2001 Topps Heritage Classic Renditions

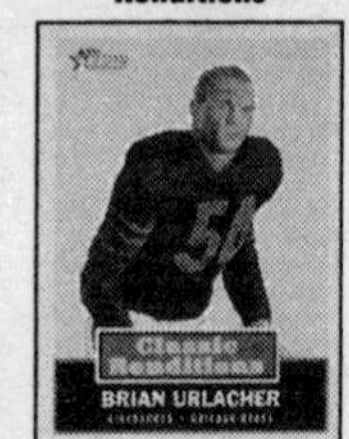

	Nm-Mt	Ex-Mt
COMPLETE SET (10)	15.00	6.75
❑ CR1 Donovan McNabb	2.00	.90
❑ CR2 Brett Favre	5.00	2.20
❑ CR3 Edgerrin James	2.00	.90
❑ CR4 Peyton Manning	4.00	1.80
❑ CR5 Marvin Harrison	1.50	.70
❑ CR6 Kurt Warner	3.00	1.35
❑ CR7 Marshall Faulk	2.00	.90
❑ CR8 Brian Urlacher	2.00	.90
❑ CR9 Jeff Garcia	1.50	.70
❑ CR10 Terrell Owens	1.50	.70
❑ CRABF Brett Favre AU	250.00	75.00
❑ CRABU Brian Urlacher AU	120.00	36.00
❑ CRAEJ Edgerrin James AU	200.00	60.00

2001 Topps Heritage Real One Autographs

	Nm-Mt	Ex-Mt

*RED INK SER.#'d: 1.5X TO 3X BASIC AUTOS
RED INK SER.#'d PRINT RUN 56 SETS

❑ THROAB Aaron Brooks	25.00	11.00
❑ THROBU Brian Urlacher	40.00	18.00
❑ THROCB Chuck Bednarik	30.00	13.50
❑ THRODC Daunte Culpepper	30.00	13.50
❑ THROEH Elroy Hirsch	80.00	36.00
❑ THROEJ Edgerrin James	40.00	18.00
❑ THROEM Eric Moulds	20.00	6.00
❑ THROJL Jamal Lewis	30.00	13.50
❑ THROJS Jimmy Smith	25.00	11.00
❑ THROLM Lenny Moore	40.00	18.00
❑ THROMA Mike Anderson	20.00	9.00
❑ THROMH Marvin Harrison	30.00	13.50
❑ THROOM Ollie Matson	40.00	12.00
❑ THRORB Roosevelt Brown	30.00	13.50
❑ THRORG Roosevelt Grier	25.00	11.00
❑ THRORW Ricky Williams	30.00	13.50

❑ THROSD Stephen Davis	25.00	11.00
❑ THROTO Terrell Owens	30.00	13.50
❑ THROWC Wayne Chrebet	25.00	11.00
❑ THROYT Y.A. Tittle	40.00	18.00
❑ THROJSC Joe Schmidt	30.00	9.00

2002 Topps Heritage

	Nm-Mt	Ex-Mt
COMPLETE SET (194)	250.00	75.00
❑ 1 Jerome Bettis	1.25	.35
❑ 2 Jeff Blake SP	1.00	.30
❑ 3 Rod Smith	.75	.23
❑ 4 Eric Moulds	.75	.23
❑ 5 Michael Vick	4.00	1.20
❑ 6 Randy Moss	2.50	.75
❑ 7 Todd Pinkston	.75	.23
❑ 8 Trung Canidate SP	1.50	.45
❑ 9 Steve McNair	1.25	.35
❑ 10 J.J. Stokes SP	1.50	.45
❑ 11 Ricky Williams	2.50	.75
❑ 12 Germane Crowell SP	1.00	.30
❑ 13 Muhsin Muhammad SP	1.50	.45
❑ 14 Michael Pittman SP	1.00	.30
❑ 15 James Jackson SP	1.00	.30
❑ 16 Dominic Rhodes	.75	.23
❑ 17 Jay Fiedler	.75	.23
❑ 18 Marcus Robinson	.75	.23
❑ 19 Qadry Ismail SP	1.50	.45
❑ 20 Michael Strahan	.75	.23
❑ 21 Koren Robinson	.75	.23
❑ 22 James Allen SP	1.50	.45
❑ 23 Chad Pennington	1.50	.45
❑ 24 Fred Taylor	1.25	.35
❑ 25 Corey Dillon	.75	.23
❑ 26 Thomas Jones SP	1.50	.45
❑ 27 Anthony Thomas	1.25	.35
❑ 28 Priest Holmes	1.50	.45
❑ 29 Troy Brown	.75	.23
❑ 30 Jerry Rice	2.50	.75
❑ 31 Correll Buckhalter	.75	.23
❑ 32 Drew Brees	1.25	.35
❑ 33 Isaac Bruce	1.25	.35
❑ 34 Warrick Dunn SP	2.50	.75
❑ 35 Chris Chambers	1.25	.35
❑ 36 Antonio Freeman	1.25	.35
❑ 37 Joey Galloway SP	1.50	.45
❑ 38 Rob Johnson SP	1.50	.45
❑ 39 Reggie Wayne	.75	.23
❑ 40 Santana Moss	1.25	.35
❑ 41 Plaxico Burress	.75	.23
❑ 42 Frank Wycheck SP	1.00	.30
❑ 43 Johnnie Morton	.75	.23
❑ 44 Chris Weinke	.75	.23
❑ 45 Rocket Ismail SP	1.50	.45
❑ 46 Daunte Culpepper	1.25	.35
❑ 47 Deuce McAllister SP	3.00	.90
❑ 48 Terrell Owens	1.25	.35
❑ 49 Michael Westbrook	.50	.15
❑ 50 Tom Brady	3.00	.90
❑ 51 Mike Anderson	1.25	.35
❑ 52 Jake Plummer	.75	.23
❑ 53 Travis Taylor SP	1.50	.45
❑ 54 Marcus Pollard SP	1.00	.30
❑ 55 Zach Thomas	1.25	.35
❑ 56 Duce Staley	1.25	.35
❑ 57 Trent Dilfer	.75	.23
❑ 58 Keyshawn Johnson	1.25	.35
❑ 59 Amani Toomer SP	1.50	.45
❑ 60 David Terrell	1.25	.35
❑ 61 Robert Ferguson SP	1.00	.30
❑ 62 Jeff Garcia	1.25	.35
❑ 63 Eddie George	1.25	.35
❑ 64 Marshall Faulk	1.25	.35
❑ 65 Travis Henry	1.25	.35
❑ 66 Tim Couch	.75	.23
❑ 67 Mike McMahon	1.25	.35
❑ 68 John Abraham SP	1.50	.45
❑ 69 James Thrash	.75	.23
❑ 70 Shaun Alexander	1.25	.35
❑ 71 Ike Hilliard SP	1.50	.45
❑ 72 Brian Griese	1.25	.35
❑ 73 Ray Lewis	1.25	.35
❑ 74 Jon Kitna	.75	.23
❑ 75 Az-Zahir Hakim SP	1.00	.30
❑ 76 Oronde Gadsden SP	1.50	.45
❑ 77 Joe Horn	.75	.23
❑ 78 Tim Brown	1.25	.35
❑ 79 Kendrell Bell	1.25	.35
❑ 80 LaDainian Tomlinson	2.00	.60
❑ 81 Brad Johnson	.75	.23
❑ 82 Tony Gonzalez	.75	.23
❑ 83 Bill Schroeder	.75	.23
❑ 84 Quincy Carter	.75	.23
❑ 85 Donald Hayes SP	1.00	.30
❑ 86 Peyton Manning	2.50	.75
❑ 87 Drew Bledsoe	1.25	.35
❑ 88 Darrell Jackson	.75	.23
❑ 89 Rod Gardner	.75	.23
❑ 90 Derrick Mason	.75	.23
❑ 91 Byron Chamberlain SP	1.00	.30
❑ 92 James Mcknight SP	1.00	.30
❑ 93 Kevin Johnson	.75	.23
❑ 94 Terry Glenn	.75	.23
❑ 95 Marty Booker SP	1.00	.30
❑ 96 Terrell Davis	1.25	.35
❑ 97 Vinny Testaverde	.75	.23
❑ 98 Hines Ward	1.25	.35
❑ 99 Chad Lewis SP	1.00	.30
❑ 100 Kurt Warner	1.25	.35
❑ 101 Michael Bennett	.75	.23
❑ 102 Edgerrin James	1.50	.45
❑ 103 Corey Bradford SP	1.00	.30
❑ 104 Chad Johnson SP	2.50	.75
❑ 105 Alex Van Pelt	.75	.23
❑ 106 Antowain Smith	.75	.23
❑ 107 Rich Gannon	1.25	.35
❑ 108 Kevan Barlow SP	1.50	.45
❑ 109 Mike Alstott SP	2.50	.75
❑ 110 Kerry Collins SP	1.50	.45
❑ 111 Jimmy Smith	.75	.23
❑ 112 Jermaine Lewis SP	1.00	.30
❑ 113 Quincy Morgan SP	1.00	.30
❑ 114 Maurice Smith SP	1.50	.45
❑ 115 Willie Jackson	.50	.15
❑ 116 Doug Flutie	1.25	.35
❑ 117 Matt Hasselbeck	.75	.23
❑ 118 Amos Zereoue SP	2.50	.75
❑ 119 Lamar Smith	.75	.23
❑ 120 Snoop Minnis	.50	.15
❑ 121 Troy Hambrick SP	1.00	.30
❑ 122 Shannon Sharpe SP	1.50	.45
❑ 123 Laveranues Coles	.75	.23
❑ 124 Freddie Mitchell	.75	.23
❑ 125 Kevin Dyson SP	1.50	.45
❑ 126 Torry Holt	1.25	.35
❑ 127 James Stewart SP	1.50	.45
❑ 128 Brian Urlacher	2.00	.60
❑ 129 David Boston	1.25	.35
❑ 130 Ron Dayne	.75	.23
❑ 131 Garrison Hearst	.75	.23
❑ 132 Stephen Davis	.75	.23
❑ 133 Donovan McNabb	1.50	.45
❑ 134 David Patten	.50	.15
❑ 135 Travis Minor SP	1.00	.30
❑ 136 Peerless Price SP	1.50	.45
❑ 137 Chris Redman SP	1.00	.30
❑ 138 Ahman Green	1.25	.35
❑ 139 Mark Brunell	1.25	.35
❑ 140 Charlie Garner	.75	.23
❑ 141 Curtis Conway	.50	.15
❑ 142 Wayne Chrebet	.75	.23
❑ 143 Kordell Stewart	.75	.23
❑ 144 Peter Warrick	.75	.23
❑ 145 Emmitt Smith	3.00	.90
❑ 146 Jim Miller SP	1.00	.30
❑ 147 Trent Green	.75	.23
❑ 148 Cris Carter	1.25	.35
❑ 149 Aaron Brooks	1.25	.35
❑ 150 Curtis Martin	1.25	.35
❑ 151 Tiki Barber SP	1.50	.45
❑ 152 Marvin Harrison	1.25	.35
❑ 153 Tyrone Wheatley SP	1.50	.45
❑ 154 Brett Favre	3.00	.90
❑ 155 David Carr RC	10.00	3.00
❑ 156 Quentin Jammer RC	3.00	.90
❑ 157 Julius Peppers RC	6.00	1.80
❑ 158 Mike Williams RC	2.50	.75
❑ 159 Antwaan Randle El RC	4.00	1.20
❑ 160 Joey Harrington RC	10.00	3.00
❑ 161 Ashley Lelie RC	6.00	1.80
❑ 162 Marquise Walker RC	2.50	.75
❑ 163 Rohan Davey RC	3.00	.90
❑ 164 Patrick Ramsey RC	6.00	1.80
❑ 165 T.J. Duckett RC	5.00	1.50
❑ 166 DeShaun Foster RC	3.00	.90
❑ 167 Donte Stallworth RC	6.00	1.80
❑ 168 William Green RC	5.00	1.50
❑ 169 Ron Johnson RC	2.50	.75
❑ 170 Maurice Morris RC	3.00	.90
❑ 171 Travis Stephens RC	2.50	.75
❑ 172 Eric Crouch RC	5.00	1.50
❑ 173 David Garrard RC	3.00	.90
❑ 174 Daniel Graham RC	3.00	.90
❑ 175 Roy Williams RC	8.00	2.40
❑ 176 Jeremy Shockey RC	10.00	3.00
❑ 177 Josh McCown RC	4.00	1.20
❑ 178 Josh Reed RC	3.00	.90
❑ 179 Andre Davis RC	3.00	.90
❑ 180 Antonio Bryant RC	3.00	.90
❑ 181 Clinton Portis RC	10.00	3.00
❑ 182 Javon Walker RC	6.00	1.80
❑ 183 Jabar Gaffney RC	3.00	.90
❑ 184 Ladell Betts RC	3.00	.90
❑ 185 Tim Carter RC	2.50	.75
❑ 186 Reche Caldwell RC	3.00	.90
❑ 187 Cliff Russell RC	2.50	.75
❑ 188 Brian Westbrook SP RC	6.00	1.80
❑ 189 Freddie Milons RC	2.50	.75
❑ 190 Phillip Buchanon RC	3.00	.90
❑ 191 Lamar Gordon RC	3.00	.90
❑ 192 Luke Staley RC	2.50	.75
❑ 193 Albert Haynesworth RC	2.50	.75
❑ 194 Kurt Kittner RC	2.50	.75

2002 Topps Heritage Hall of Fame Autographs

	Nm-Mt	Ex-Mt
❑ HOFDC Dave Casper	60.00	18.00
❑ HOFDH Dan Hampton	120.00	36.00
❑ HOFJK Jim Kelly	150.00	45.00
❑ HOFJS John Stallworth		

2002 Topps Heritage Real One Autographs

	Nm-Mt	Ex-Mt
*RED INK SER.#'d: 1X TO 2X BASIC AUTOS		
❑ HRAD Art Donovan	30.00	9.00

❑ HRAT Anthony Thomas	25.00	7.50
❑ HRBS Bart Starr	150.00	45.00
❑ HRCB Chuck Bednarik	30.00	9.00
❑ HRDB David Boston	25.00	7.50
❑ HRDR Dominic Rhodes	25.00	7.50
❑ HRGB George Blanda	50.00	15.00
❑ HRGH Garrison Hearst	25.00	7.50
❑ HRGM Gino Marchetti	30.00	9.00
❑ HRHW Hines Ward	30.00	9.00
❑ HRJA John Abraham	30.00	9.00
❑ HRKB Kendrell Bell	30.00	9.00
❑ HRMB Marty Booker	25.00	7.50
❑ HRPH Paul Hornung	60.00	18.00
❑ HRPHO Priest Holmes	40.00	12.00
❑ HRPS Pat Summerall	60.00	18.00
❑ HRRB Raymond Berry	25.00	7.50
❑ HRTB Tom Brady	125.00	38.00
❑ HRTM Tommy McDonald	25.00	7.50
❑ HRYT Y.A. Tittle	50.00	15.00
❑ HRZT Zach Thomas	30.00	9.00

2002 Topps Pristine

	Nm-Mt	Ex-Mt
COMP.SET w/o SP's (50)	50.00	15.00
❑ 1 Peyton Manning	5.00	1.50
❑ 2 Darrell Jackson	1.50	.45
❑ 3 Donovan McNabb	3.00	.90
❑ 4 Rod Smith	1.50	.45
❑ 5 Daunte Culpepper	2.50	.75
❑ 6 Drew Brees	2.50	.75
❑ 7 Stephen Davis	1.50	.45
❑ 8 Kurt Warner	2.50	.75
❑ 9 Eric Moulds	1.50	.45
❑ 10 Jake Plummer	1.50	.45
❑ 11 Chris Weinke	1.50	.45
❑ 12 Brian Griese	2.50	.75
❑ 13 Corey Bradford	1.00	.30
❑ 14 Trent Green	1.50	.45
❑ 15 Tom Brady	6.00	1.80
❑ 16 Jeff Garcia	2.50	.75
❑ 17 Tiki Barber	1.50	.45
❑ 18 Eddie George	2.50	.75
❑ 19 Jamal Lewis	2.50	.75
❑ 20 Troy Brown	1.50	.45
❑ 21 Priest Holmes	3.00	.90
❑ 22 Jimmy Smith	1.50	.45
❑ 23 Tim Brown	2.50	.75
❑ 24 Plaxico Burress	2.50	.75
❑ 25 Aaron Brooks	2.50	.75
❑ 26 Marshall Faulk	2.50	.75
❑ 27 Steve McNair	2.50	.75
❑ 28 Curtis Martin	2.50	.75
❑ 29 Corey Dillon	1.50	.45
❑ 30 Tim Couch	1.50	.45
❑ 31 Michael Vick	8.00	2.40
❑ 32 David Boston	2.50	.75
❑ 33 Kordell Stewart	1.50	.45
❑ 34 Jerome Bettis	2.50	.75
❑ 35 Keyshawn Johnson	2.50	.75
❑ 36 Torry Holt	2.50	.75
❑ 37 Shaun Alexander	2.50	.75
❑ 38 Brett Favre	6.00	1.80
❑ 39 Marvin Harrison	2.50	.75
❑ 40 Randy Moss	5.00	1.50
❑ 41 Jerry Rice	5.00	1.50
❑ 42 LaDainian Tomlinson	4.00	1.20
❑ 43 Terrell Owens	2.50	.75
❑ 44 Edgerrin James	3.00	.90
❑ 45 Anthony Thomas	2.50	.75
❑ 46 Drew Bledsoe	3.00	.90
❑ 47 Ahman Green	2.50	.75
❑ 48 Ricky Williams	2.50	.75
❑ 49 Tony Gonzalez	1.50	.45
❑ 50 Emmitt Smith	6.00	1.80
❑ 51 Joey Harrington C RC	10.00	3.00
❑ 52 Joey Harrington U	12.00	3.60
❑ 53 Joey Harrington R	20.00	6.00
❑ 54 Josh McCown C RC	4.00	1.20
❑ 55 Josh McCown U	5.00	1.50
❑ 56 Josh McCown R	8.00	2.40
❑ 57 Antwaan Randle El C RC	4.00	1.20
❑ 58 Antwaan Randle El U	5.00	1.50
❑ 59 Antwaan Randle El R	8.00	2.40
❑ 60 Reche Caldwell C RC	3.00	.90
❑ 61 Reche Caldwell U	4.00	1.20
❑ 62 Reche Caldwell R	6.00	1.80
❑ 63 Jason McAddley C RC	2.50	.75
❑ 64 Jason McAddley U	3.00	.90
❑ 65 Jason McAddley R	5.00	1.50
❑ 66 Ashley Lelie C RC	6.00	1.80
❑ 67 Ashley Lelie U	8.00	2.40
❑ 68 Ashley Lelie R	12.00	3.60
❑ 69 Travis Stephens C RC	2.50	.75
❑ 70 Travis Stephens U	3.00	.90
❑ 71 Travis Stephens R	5.00	1.50
❑ 72 Chad Hutchinson C RC	3.00	.90
❑ 73 Chad Hutchinson U	4.00	1.20
❑ 74 Chad Hutchinson R	6.00	1.80
❑ 75 Quentin Jammer C RC	3.00	.90
❑ 76 Quentin Jammer U	4.00	1.20
❑ 77 Quentin Jammer R	6.00	1.80
❑ 78 Tim Carter C RC	2.50	.75
❑ 79 Tim Carter U	3.00	.90
❑ 80 Tim Carter R	5.00	1.50
❑ 81 Antonio Bryant C RC	3.00	.90
❑ 82 Antonio Bryant U	4.00	1.20
❑ 83 Antonio Bryant R	6.00	1.80
❑ 84 Cliff Russell C RC	2.50	.75
❑ 85 Cliff Russell U	3.00	.90
❑ 86 Cliff Russell R	5.00	1.50
❑ 87 Rohan Davey C RC	3.00	.90
❑ 88 Rohan Davey U	4.00	1.20
❑ 89 Rohan Davey R	6.00	1.80
❑ 90 Javon Walker C RC	6.00	1.80
❑ 91 Javon Walker U	8.00	2.40
❑ 92 Javon Walker R	10.00	3.00
❑ 93 T.J. Duckett C RC	5.00	1.50
❑ 94 T.J. Duckett U	6.00	1.80
❑ 95 T.J. Duckett R	10.00	3.00
❑ 96 Donte Stallworth C RC	6.00	1.80
❑ 97 Donte Stallworth U	8.00	2.40
❑ 98 Donte Stallworth R	12.00	3.60
❑ 99 Andre Davis C RC	3.00	.90
❑ 100 Andre Davis U	4.00	1.20
❑ 101 Andre Davis R	6.00	1.80
❑ 102 Mike Williams C RC	2.50	.75
❑ 103 Mike Williams U	3.00	.90
❑ 104 Mike Williams R	5.00	1.50
❑ 105 Freddie Milons C RC	2.50	.75
❑ 106 Freddie Milons U	3.00	.90
❑ 107 Freddie Milons R	5.00	1.50
❑ 108 John Henderson C RC	3.00	.90
❑ 109 John Henderson U	3.00	.90
❑ 110 John Henderson R	6.00	1.80
❑ 111 Deshaun Foster C RC	3.00	.90
❑ 112 Deshaun Foster U	4.00	1.20
❑ 113 Deshaun Foster R	6.00	1.80
❑ 114 Josh Reed C RC	3.00	.90
❑ 115 Josh Reed U	4.00	1.20
❑ 116 Josh Reed R	6.00	1.80
❑ 117 Jabar Gaffney C RC	3.00	.90
❑ 118 Jabar Gaffney U	4.00	1.20
❑ 119 Jabar Gaffney R	6.00	1.80
❑ 120 Clinton Portis C RC	10.00	3.00
❑ 121 Clinton Portis U	12.00	3.60
❑ 122 Clinton Portis R	20.00	6.00
❑ 123 Jeremy Shockey C RC	10.00	3.00
❑ 124 Jeremy Shockey U	12.00	3.60
❑ 125 Jeremy Shockey R	20.00	6.00
❑ 126 Dwight Freeney C RC	4.00	1.20
❑ 127 Dwight Freeney U	5.00	1.50
❑ 128 Dwight Freeney R	8.00	2.40
❑ 129 Brian Westbrook C RC	5.00	1.50
❑ 130 Brian Westbrook U	6.00	1.80
❑ 131 Brian Westbrook R	10.00	3.00
❑ 132 Randy Fasani C RC	2.50	.75
❑ 133 Randy Fasani U	3.00	.90
❑ 134 Randy Fasani R	5.00	1.50
❑ 135 Julius Peppers C RC	6.00	1.80
❑ 136 Julius Peppers U	8.00	2.40
❑ 137 Julius Peppers R	12.00	3.60
❑ 138 Patrick Ramsey C RC	6.00	1.80
❑ 139 Patrick Ramsey U	8.00	2.40
❑ 140 Patrick Ramsey R	12.00	3.60
❑ 141 William Green C RC	5.00	1.50
❑ 142 William Green U	6.00	1.80
❑ 143 William Green R	10.00	3.00
❑ 144 Daniel Graham C RC	3.00	.90
❑ 145 Daniel Graham U	4.00	1.20
❑ 146 Daniel Graham R	6.00	1.80
❑ 147 Ron Johnson C RC	2.50	.75
❑ 148 Ron Johnson U	3.00	.90
❑ 149 Ron Johnson R	5.00	1.50
❑ 150 Maurice Morris C RC	3.00	.90
❑ 151 Maurice Morris U	4.00	1.20
❑ 152 Maurice Morris R	6.00	1.80
❑ 153 Eric Crouch C RC	5.00	1.50
❑ 154 Eric Crouch U	6.00	1.80
❑ 155 Eric Crouch R	10.00	3.00
❑ 156 Roy Williams C RC	8.00	2.40
❑ 157 Roy Williams U	10.00	3.00
❑ 158 Roy Williams R	15.00	4.50
❑ 159 Ladell Betts C RC	3.00	.90
❑ 160 Ladell Betts U	5.00	1.50
❑ 161 Ladell Betts R	8.00	2.40
❑ 162 David Garrard C RC	3.00	.90
❑ 163 David Garrard U	4.00	1.20
❑ 164 David Garrard R	6.00	1.80
❑ 165 Marquise Walker C RC	2.50	.75
❑ 166 Marquise Walker U	3.00	.90
❑ 167 Marquise Walker R	5.00	1.50
❑ 168 David Carr C RC	10.00	3.00
❑ 169 David Carr U	12.00	3.60
❑ 170 David Carr R	20.00	6.00
❑ ESA1 Emmitt Smith AU	275.00	80.00
❑ ESJ1 Emmitt Smith JSY	40.00	12.00

2002 Topps Pristine Gold Refractors

Nm-Mt Ex-Mt

*STARS: 3X TO 8X BASIC CARDS
*GOLD REF.C 51-170: 2.5X TO 6X
*GOLD REF.U 51-170: 2X TO 5X
*GOLD REF.R 51-170: 1.2X TO 3X

2002 Topps Pristine Refractors

Nm-Mt Ex-Mt

*STARS: 1.5X TO 4X BASIC CARDS
*REFRACTORS C 51-170: 1X TO 2.5X
*REFRACTORS U 51-170: 1X TO 2.5X
*REFRACTORS R 51-170: 1.2X TO 3X

2002 Topps Pristine Autographs

	Nm-Mt	Ex-Mt
❑ PAD Andre Davis B	15.00	4.50
❑ PAL Ashley Lelie D	30.00	9.00
❑ PBF Brett Favre C	175.00	52.50
❑ PBM Bryant McKinnie F	15.00	4.50
❑ PCR Cliff Russell G	10.00	3.00
❑ PDC David Carr B	60.00	18.00
❑ PDF Deshaun Foster B	25.00	7.50
❑ PDG David Garrard D	15.00	4.50
❑ PJH Joey Harrington A	60.00	18.00
❑ PJM Josh McCown D	25.00	7.50
❑ PJR Josh Reed D	15.00	4.50
❑ PJW Javon Walker B	30.00	9.00
❑ PKC Kelly Campbell B	10.00	3.00
❑ PKK Kurt Kittner B	10.00	3.00
❑ PPR Patrick Ramsey B	40.00	12.00
❑ PRD Rohan Davey F	15.00	4.50
❑ PRJ Ron Johnson B	10.00	3.00
❑ PTS Travis Stephens D	10.00	3.00
❑ PWG William Green C	25.00	7.50
❑ PDRC Reche Caldwell D	15.00	4.50
❑ PTJD T.J. Duckett B	25.00	7.50

2002 Topps Pristine Patches

	Nm-Mt	Ex-Mt
❑ PPAB Aaron Brooks	20.00	6.00
❑ PPAT Anthony Thomas	25.00	7.50
❑ PPBF Brett Favre	60.00	18.00
❑ PPBG Brian Griese	20.00	6.00
❑ PPCM Curtis Martin	25.00	7.50
❑ PPDF Doug Flutie	20.00	6.00
❑ PPDG Darrell Green	20.00	6.00
❑ PPDS Duce Staley	20.00	6.00
❑ PPEG Eddie George	20.00	6.00
❑ PPES Emmitt Smith	60.00	18.00
❑ PPJG Jeff Garcia	20.00	6.00
❑ PPJR Jerry Rice	30.00	9.00
❑ PPKJ Keyshawn Johnson	15.00	4.50
❑ PPKW Kurt Warner	20.00	6.00
❑ PPMB Mark Brunell	15.00	4.50
❑ PPMF Marshall Faulk	20.00	6.00
❑ PPTO Terrell Owens	20.00	6.00

2003 Topps Pristine

	MINT	NRMT
COMP.SET w/o SP's (50)	40.00	18.00

UNPRICED PRESS PLATES EXIST
FOUR DIFF.COLOR PP's MADE PER CARD
PRESS PLATES STATED ODDS 1:107

❑ 1 Brett Favre	6.00	2.70
❑ 2 Rich Gannon	1.50	.70
❑ 3 Randy Moss	4.00	1.80
❑ 4 Travis Henry	1.50	.70
❑ 5 Troy Brown	1.50	.70
❑ 6 Darrell Jackson	1.50	.70
❑ 7 Steve McNair	2.50	1.10
❑ 8 Plaxico Burress	1.50	.70
❑ 9 Jerry Rice	5.00	2.20
❑ 10 Donovan McNabb	3.00	1.35
❑ 11 Marty Booker	1.50	.70
❑ 12 Joey Galloway	1.50	.70
❑ 13 Peerless Price	1.50	.70
❑ 14 Emmitt Smith	6.00	2.70
❑ 15 David Carr	4.00	1.80
❑ 16 Priest Holmes	3.00	1.35
❑ 17 LaDainian Tomlinson	2.50	1.10
❑ 18 Hines Ward	2.50	1.10
❑ 19 Tiki Barber	1.50	.70
❑ 20 Fred Taylor	2.50	1.10
❑ 21 Marvin Harrison	2.50	1.10
❑ 22 Marshall Faulk	2.50	1.10
❑ 23 Terrell Owens	2.50	1.10
❑ 24 Patrick Ramsey	2.50	1.10
❑ 25 Michael Vick	6.00	2.70
❑ 26 Tom Brady	4.00	1.80
❑ 27 Shaun Alexander	2.50	1.10
❑ 28 Derrick Mason	1.50	.70
❑ 29 Keyshawn Johnson	2.50	1.10
❑ 30 Ricky Williams	2.50	1.10
❑ 31 Ahman Green	2.50	1.10
❑ 32 Joey Harrington	4.00	1.80
❑ 33 Corey Dillon	1.50	.70
❑ 34 Jamal Lewis	2.50	1.10
❑ 35 Drew Bledsoe	2.50	1.10
❑ 36 Tommy Maddox	2.50	1.10
❑ 37 Kurt Warner	2.50	1.10
❑ 38 Deuce McAllister	2.50	1.10
❑ 39 Curtis Martin	2.50	1.10
❑ 40 Chad Pennington	3.00	1.35
❑ 41 Trent Green	1.50	.70
❑ 42 Edgerrin James	2.50	1.10
❑ 43 Clinton Portis	4.00	1.80
❑ 44 Eric Moulds	1.50	.70
❑ 45 Peyton Manning	4.00	1.80
❑ 46 Jeff Garcia	2.50	1.10
❑ 47 Daunte Culpepper	2.50	1.10
❑ 48 Tim Couch	1.00	.45
❑ 49 Drew Brees	2.50	1.10
❑ 50 Aaron Brooks	2.50	1.10
❑ 51 Anquan Boldin C RC	8.00	3.60
❑ 52 Anquan Boldin U	10.00	4.50
❑ 53 Anquan Boldin R	15.00	6.75
❑ 54 Andre Johnson C RC	8.00	3.60
❑ 55 Andre Johnson U	10.00	4.50
❑ 56 Andre Johnson R	15.00	6.75
❑ 57 Artose Pinner C RC	3.00	1.35
❑ 58 Artose Pinner U	4.00	1.80
❑ 59 Artose Pinner R	6.00	2.70
❑ 60 Bryant Johnson C RC	3.00	1.35
❑ 61 Bryant Johnson U	4.00	1.80
❑ 62 Bryant Johnson R	6.00	2.70
❑ 63 Bethel Johnson C RC	5.00	2.20
❑ 64 Bethel Johnson U	6.00	2.70
❑ 65 Bethel Johnson R	10.00	4.50
❑ 66 Byron Leftwich C RC	12.00	5.50
❑ 67 Byron Leftwich U	15.00	6.75
❑ 68 Byron Leftwich R	25.00	11.00
❑ 69 Brian St.Pierre C RC	3.00	1.35
❑ 70 Brian St.Pierre U	4.00	1.80
❑ 71 Brian St.Pierre R	6.00	2.70
❑ 72 Chris Brown C RC	6.00	2.70
❑ 73 Chris Brown U	8.00	3.60
❑ 74 Chris Brown R	12.00	5.50
❑ 75 Carson Palmer C RC	10.00	4.50
❑ 76 Carson Palmer U	12.00	5.50
❑ 77 Carson Palmer R	20.00	9.00
❑ 78 Charles Rogers C RC	4.00	1.80
❑ 79 Charles Rogers U	5.00	2.20
❑ 80 Charles Rogers R	8.00	3.60
❑ 81 Chris Simms C RC	6.00	2.70
❑ 82 Chris Simms U	8.00	3.60
❑ 83 Chris Simms R	12.00	5.50
❑ 84 Dallas Clark C RC	3.00	1.35
❑ 85 Dallas Clark U	4.00	1.80
❑ 86 Dallas Clark R	6.00	2.70
❑ 87 Dave Ragone C RC	3.00	1.35
❑ 88 Dave Ragone U	4.00	1.80
❑ 89 Dave Ragone R	6.00	2.70
❑ 90 DeWayne Robertson C RC	3.00	1.35
❑ 91 DeWayne Robertson U	4.00	1.80
❑ 92 DeWayne Robertson R	6.00	2.70
❑ 93 Justin Fargas C RC	3.00	1.35
❑ 94 Justin Fargas U	4.00	1.80
❑ 95 Justin Fargas R	6.00	2.70
❑ 96 Kyle Boller C RC	8.00	3.60
❑ 97 Kyle Boller U	10.00	4.50
❑ 98 Kyle Boller R	15.00	6.75
❑ 99 Kevin Curtis C RC	3.00	1.35
❑ 100 Kevin Curtis U	4.00	1.80
❑ 101 Kevin Curtis R	6.00	2.70
❑ 102 Ken Dorsey C RC	5.00	2.20
❑ 103 Ken Dorsey U	6.00	2.70
❑ 104 Ken Dorsey R	10.00	4.50
❑ 105 Kelley Washington C RC	3.00	1.35
❑ 106 Kelley Washington U	4.00	1.80
❑ 107 Kelley Washington R	6.00	2.70
❑ 108 Kliff Kingsbury C RC	2.50	1.10
❑ 109 Kliff Kingsbury U	3.00	1.35
❑ 110 Kliff Kingsbury R	5.00	2.20
❑ 111 Larry Johnson C RC	6.00	2.70
❑ 112 Larry Johnson U	8.00	3.60
❑ 113 Larry Johnson R	12.00	5.50
❑ 114 Musa Smith C RC	3.00	1.35
❑ 115 Musa Smith U	4.00	1.80
❑ 116 Musa Smith R	6.00	2.70
❑ 117 Marcus Trufant C RC	3.00	1.35
❑ 118 Marcus Trufant U	4.00	1.80
❑ 119 Marcus Trufant R	6.00	2.70
❑ 120 Nate Burleson C RC	5.00	2.20
❑ 121 Nate Burleson U	6.00	2.70
❑ 122 Nate Burleson R	10.00	4.50
❑ 123 Onterrio Smith C RC	4.00	1.80
❑ 124 Onterrio Smith U	6.00	2.70
❑ 125 Onterrio Smith R	8.00	3.60
❑ 126 Rex Grossman C RC	8.00	3.60
❑ 127 Rex Grossman U	10.00	4.50
❑ 128 Rex Grossman R	15.00	6.75
❑ 129 Seneca Wallace C RC	3.00	1.35
❑ 130 Seneca Wallace U	4.00	1.80
❑ 131 Seneca Wallace R	6.00	2.70
❑ 132 Tyrone Calico C RC	4.00	1.80
❑ 133 Tyrone Calico U	5.00	2.20
❑ 134 Tyrone Calico R	8.00	3.60
❑ 135 Taylor Jacobs C RC	3.00	1.35
❑ 136 Taylor Jacobs U	4.00	1.80
❑ 137 Taylor Jacobs R	6.00	2.70
❑ 138 Teyo Johnson C RC	3.00	1.35
❑ 139 Teyo Johnson U	4.00	1.80
❑ 140 Teyo Johnson R	6.00	2.70
❑ 141 Terence Newman C RC	6.00	2.70
❑ 142 Terence Newman U	8.00	3.60
❑ 143 Terence Newman R	12.00	5.50
❑ 144 Terrell Suggs C RC	5.00	2.20
❑ 145 Terrell Suggs U	6.00	2.70
❑ 146 Terrell Suggs R	10.00	4.50
❑ 147 Willis McGahee C RC	8.00	3.60
❑ 148 Willis McGahee U	10.00	4.50
❑ 149 Willis McGahee R	15.00	6.75

2003 Topps Pristine Gold Refractors

MINT NRMT

*STARS: 2X TO 5X BASIC CARDS
*C ROOKIES 51-149: 1.5X TO 4X
*U ROOKIES 51-149: 1.5X TO 4X
*R ROOKIES 51-149: 1.5X TO 4X

2003 Topps Pristine Refractors

MINT NRMT

*STARS 1-50: 2.5X TO 6X BASIC CARDS
*C ROOKIES 51-149: .6X TO 1.5X
*U ROOKIES 51-149: .6X TO 1.5X
*R ROOKIES 51-149: .8X TO 2X

2003 Topps Pristine All-Star Jersey Autographs

Card	Player	MINT	NRMT
❑ ASEBY	Bryant Young B EXCH	15.00	6.75
❑ ASEDM	Deuce McAllister A	40.00	18.00
❑ ASEJO	Jonathon Ogden B EXCH	15.00	6.75
❑ ASELK	Lincoln Kennedy B	20.00	9.00
❑ ASEMB	Marty Booker B	20.00	9.00
❑ ASEOK	Olin Kreutz C	20.00	9.00
❑ ASETG	Tony Gonzalez A	25.00	11.00
❑ ASEWR	Willie Roaf C	15.00	6.75

2003 Topps Pristine Autographs

MINT NRMT

*GOLD: .8X TO 2X BASIC AUTOS
GOLD STATED ODDS 1:165

Card	Player	MINT	NRMT
❑ PEBJ	Bryant Johnson C	15.00	6.75
❑ PEBL	Byron Leftwich C	60.00	27.00
❑ PEBS	Barry Sanders B	100.00	45.00
❑ PECB	Chris Brown C	40.00	18.00
❑ PECS	Chris Simms F	25.00	11.00
❑ PEDM	Dan Marino A	300.00	135.00
❑ PEJF	Justin Fargas E	15.00	6.75
❑ PEJR	Jerry Rice B	150.00	70.00
❑ PEKB	Kyle Boller E	30.00	13.50
❑ PEKW	Kelly Washington C	15.00	6.75
❑ PELJ	Larry Johnson C	25.00	11.00
❑ PERG	Rex Grossman C	40.00	18.00
❑ PETC	Tyrone Calico D	20.00	9.00
❑ PETJ	Taylor Jacobs C	15.00	6.75
❑ PETJO	Teyo Johnson F	15.00	6.75
❑ PETS	Terrell Suggs F	20.00	9.00

2003 Topps Pristine Gems Relics

Card	Player	MINT	NRMT
❑ PGABU	Brian Urlacher C	20.00	9.00
❑ PGACP	Clinton Portis C	15.00	6.75
❑ PGADM	Deuce McAllister D	12.00	5.50
❑ PGADS	Duce Staley C	10.00	4.50
❑ PGAJK	Jevon Kearse D	10.00	4.50
❑ PGAJS	Jeremy Shockey B	15.00	6.75
❑ PGAJT	Jason Taylor D	10.00	4.50
❑ PGARW	Ricky Williams C	12.00	5.50
❑ PGAT	Amani Toomer B	10.00	4.50
❑ PGATH	Anthony Thomas B	12.00	5.50
❑ PGATO	Terrell Owens C	12.00	5.50
❑ PGAZT	Zach Thomas C	12.00	5.50
❑ PGCP	Chad Pennington A	15.00	6.75
❑ PGDC	David Carr A	15.00	6.75
❑ PGJH	Joey Harrington A	15.00	6.75

2003 Topps Pristine Igniters Relics

MINT NRMT

*REFRACTORS: 2.5X TO 6X BASIC INSERTS
REFR.STATED ODDS 1:634

Card	Player	MINT	NRMT
❑ PICP	Chad Pennington A	12.00	5.50
❑ PIJH	Joey Harrington B	12.00	5.50
❑ PIJS	Jeremy Shockey B	12.00	5.50
❑ PIJT	Jason Taylor B	8.00	3.60
❑ PITO	Terrell Owens A	10.00	4.50

2003 Topps Pristine Performance

MINT NRMT

*REFRACTORS: 2X TO 5X BASIC INSERTS
REFR.STATED ODDS 1:311

Card	Player	MINT	NRMT
❑ PPAT	Amani Toomer C	8.00	3.60
❑ PPATH	Anthony Thomas C	10.00	4.50
❑ PPBU	Brian Urlacher C	15.00	6.75
❑ PPCP	Clinton Portis C	12.00	5.50
❑ PPDC	David Carr A	12.00	5.50
❑ PPDM	Deuce McAllister C	10.00	4.50
❑ PPDS	Duce Staley C	8.00	3.60
❑ PPJK	Jevon Kearse C	8.00	3.60
❑ PPRW	Ricky Williams C	10.00	4.50
❑ PPZT	Zach Thomas B	10.00	4.50

2004 Topps Pristine

	Nm-Mt	Ex-Mt
COMP.SET w/o SP's (50)	40.00	12.00

U/999 STATED ODDS 1:2
R/499 STATED ODDS 1:4
UNPRICED PRESS PLATES #'d OF 1

Card	Player	Nm-Mt	Ex-Mt
❑ 1	Michael Vick	5.00	1.50
❑ 2	Tony Gonzalez	1.50	.45
❑ 3	Terrell Owens	2.50	.75
❑ 4	Brett Favre	6.00	1.80
❑ 5	Jamal Lewis	2.50	.75
❑ 6	Tim Rattay	1.50	.45
❑ 7	Ricky Williams	2.50	.75
❑ 8	Edgerrin James	2.50	.75
❑ 9	Torry Holt	2.50	.75
❑ 10	Randy Moss	3.00	.90
❑ 11	Derrick Mason	1.50	.45
❑ 12	Joe Horn	1.50	.45
❑ 13	Marvin Harrison	2.50	.75
❑ 14	Carson Palmer	3.00	.90
❑ 15	Anquan Boldin	2.50	.75
❑ 16	Quincy Carter	1.50	.45
❑ 17	Byron Leftwich	4.00	1.20
❑ 18	Eric Moulds	1.50	.45
❑ 19	Marc Bulger	2.50	.75
❑ 20	Ahman Green	2.50	.75
❑ 21	Jeff Garcia	2.50	.75
❑ 22	Laveranues Coles	1.50	.45
❑ 23	Hines Ward	2.50	.75
❑ 24	Santana Moss	1.50	.45
❑ 25	LaDainian Tomlinson	2.50	.75
❑ 26	Domanick Davis	2.50	.75
❑ 27	Stephen Davis	1.50	.45
❑ 28	Tiki Barber	1.50	.45
❑ 29	Chris Chambers	1.50	.45
❑ 30	Priest Holmes	3.00	.90
❑ 31	Chad Pennington	3.00	.90
❑ 32	Shaun Alexander	2.50	.75
❑ 33	Brad Johnson	1.50	.45
❑ 34	Marshall Faulk	2.50	.75
❑ 35	Peyton Manning	4.00	1.20
❑ 36	Jake Plummer	1.50	.45
❑ 37	Clinton Portis	2.50	.75
❑ 38	Matt Hasselbeck	1.50	.45
❑ 39	Amani Toomer	1.50	.45
❑ 40	Steve McNair	2.50	.75
❑ 41	Daunte Culpepper	2.50	.75
❑ 42	Fred Taylor	1.50	.45
❑ 43	Joey Harrington	2.50	.75
❑ 44	Jake Delhomme	2.50	.75
❑ 45	Deuce McAllister	2.50	.75
❑ 46	Chad Johnson	1.50	.45
❑ 47	Travis Henry	1.50	.45
❑ 48	Corey Dillon	1.50	.45

❑ 49	Tom Brady	4.00	1.20
❑ 50	Donovan McNabb	3.00	.90
❑ 51	Ben Roethlisberger C RC	30.00	9.00
❑ 52	Ben Roethlisberger U	40.00	12.00
❑ 53	Ben Roethlisberger R	50.00	15.00
❑ 54	Ben Troupe C RC	3.00	.90
❑ 55	Ben Troupe U	4.00	1.20
❑ 56	Ben Troupe R	5.00	1.50
❑ 57	Ben Watson C RC	3.00	.90
❑ 58	Ben Watson U	4.00	1.20
❑ 59	Ben Watson R	5.00	1.50
❑ 60	Bernard Berrian C RC	3.00	.90
❑ 61	Bernard Berrian U	4.00	1.20
❑ 62	Bernard Berrian R	5.00	1.50
❑ 63	Cedric Cobbs C RC	3.00	.90
❑ 64	Cedric Cobbs U	4.00	1.20
❑ 65	Cedric Cobbs R	5.00	1.50
❑ 66	Chris Perry C RC	6.00	1.80
❑ 67	Chris Perry U	8.00	2.40
❑ 68	Chris Perry R	10.00	3.00
❑ 69	Darius Watts C RC	4.00	1.20
❑ 70	Darius Watts U	5.00	1.50
❑ 71	Darius Watts R	6.00	1.80
❑ 72	DeAngelo Hall C RC	4.00	1.20
❑ 73	DeAngelo Hall U	5.00	1.50
❑ 74	DeAngelo Hall R	6.00	1.80
❑ 75	Derrick Hamilton C RC	2.50	.75
❑ 76	Derrick Hamilton U	3.00	.90
❑ 77	Derrick Hamilton R	5.00	1.50
❑ 78	Devard Darling C RC	3.00	.90
❑ 79	Devard Darling U	4.00	1.20
❑ 80	Devard Darling R	5.00	1.50
❑ 81	Devery Henderson C RC	2.50	.75
❑ 82	Devery Henderson U	3.00	.90
❑ 83	Devery Henderson R	4.00	1.20
❑ 84	Dunta Robinson C RC	3.00	.90
❑ 85	Dunta Robinson U	4.00	1.20
❑ 86	Dunta Robinson R	5.00	1.50
❑ 87	Eli Manning C RC	15.00	4.50
❑ 88	Eli Manning U	20.00	6.00
❑ 89	Eli Manning R	25.00	7.50
❑ 90	Greg Jones C RC	3.00	.90
❑ 91	Greg Jones U	4.00	1.20
❑ 92	Greg Jones R	5.00	1.50
❑ 93	J.P. Losman C RC	8.00	2.40
❑ 94	J.P. Losman U	10.00	3.00
❑ 95	J.P. Losman R	12.00	3.60
❑ 96	Julius Jones C RC	12.00	3.60
❑ 97	Julius Jones U	15.00	4.50
❑ 98	Julius Jones R	20.00	6.00
❑ 99	Keary Colbert C RC	4.00	1.20
❑ 100	Keary Colbert U	5.00	1.50
❑ 101	Keary Colbert R	6.00	1.80
❑ 102	Kellen Winslow C RC	8.00	2.40
❑ 103	Kellen Winslow U	10.00	3.00
❑ 104	Kellen Winslow R	12.00	3.60
❑ 105	Kevin Jones C RC	10.00	3.00
❑ 106	Kevin Jones U	12.00	3.60
❑ 107	Kevin Jones R	15.00	4.50
❑ 108	Larry Fitzgerald C RC	10.00	3.00
❑ 109	Larry Fitzgerald U	12.00	3.60
❑ 110	Larry Fitzgerald R	15.00	4.50
❑ 111	Lee Evans C RC	5.00	1.50
❑ 112	Lee Evans U	6.00	1.80
❑ 113	Lee Evans R	8.00	2.40
❑ 114	Luke McCown C RC	3.00	.90
❑ 115	Luke McCown U	4.00	1.20
❑ 116	Luke McCown R	5.00	1.50
❑ 117	Matt Schaub C RC	5.00	1.50
❑ 118	Matt Schaub U	6.00	1.80
❑ 119	Matt Schaub R	8.00	2.40
❑ 120	Mewelde Moore C RC	4.00	1.20
❑ 121	Mewelde Moore U	5.00	1.50
❑ 122	Mewelde Moore R	6.00	1.80
❑ 123	Michael Clayton C RC	8.00	2.40
❑ 124	Michael Clayton U	10.00	3.00
❑ 125	Michael Clayton R	12.00	3.60
❑ 126	Michael Jenkins C RC	3.00	.90
❑ 127	Michael Jenkins U	4.00	1.20
❑ 128	Michael Jenkins R	5.00	1.50
❑ 129	Philip Rivers C RC	10.00	3.00
❑ 130	Philip Rivers U	12.00	3.60
❑ 131	Philip Rivers R	15.00	4.50
❑ 132	Rashaun Woods C RC	4.00	1.20
❑ 133	Rashaun Woods U	5.00	1.50
❑ 134	Rashaun Woods R	6.00	1.80
❑ 135	Reggie Williams C RC	4.00	1.20
❑ 136	Reggie Williams U	5.00	1.50
❑ 137	Reggie Williams R	6.00	1.80
❑ 138	Robert Gallery C RC	5.00	1.50
❑ 139	Robert Gallery U	6.00	1.80
❑ 140	Robert Gallery R	8.00	2.40
❑ 141	Roy Williams C RC	10.00	3.00
❑ 142	Roy Williams U	12.00	3.60
❑ 143	Roy Williams R	15.00	4.50
❑ 144	Steven Jackson C RC	10.00	3.00
❑ 145	Steven Jackson U	12.00	3.60
❑ 146	Steven Jackson R	15.00	4.50
❑ 147	Tatum Bell C RC	5.00	1.50
❑ 148	Tatum Bell U	6.00	1.80
❑ 149	Tatum Bell R	8.00	2.40

2004 Topps Pristine Gold Refractors

Nm-Mt Ex-Mt

*STARS 1-50: 1.5X TO 4X BASE CARD HI
*C ROOKIES 51-149: 2X TO 5X BASE CARD
1-50/C ROOKIES #'d/99: ONE PER HOBBY BOX
*U ROOKIES 51-149: 3X TO 8X BASE CARD
U ROOKIES PRINT RUN 25 SER.#'d SETS
UNPRICED R ROOKIES PRINT RUN 10

2004 Topps Pristine Refractors

Nm-Mt Ex-Mt

*STARS 1-50: 1.5X TO 4X BASE CARD HI
1-50 VETERAN #'d/99 STATED ODDS 1:13
*C ROOKIES 51-149: .8X TO 2X BASE CARD
51-149 C PRINT RUN 1099 SER.#'d SETS
*U ROOKIES 51-149: 1X TO 2.5X BASE CARD
51-149 U #'d/499 STATED ODDS 1:4
*R ROOKIES 51-149: 1.2X TO 3X BASE CARD
51-149 R #'d/99 STATED ODDS 1:19
ONE REFRACTOR PER HOBBY PACK

2004 Topps Pristine All-Pro Endorsement Jersey Autographs

Nm-Mt Ex-Mt

GROUP A STATED ODDS 1:308
GROUP B STATED ODDS 1:202
GROUP C STATED ODDS 1:175
GROUP D STATED ODDS 1:86

❑ APEAC	Alge Crumpler D	20.00	6.00
❑ APEDF	Dwight Freeney B	20.00	6.00
❑ APEDH	Dante Hall C	20.00	6.00
❑ APEPM	Peyton Manning A	100.00	30.00
❑ APESE	Shaun Ellis A	15.00	4.50

2004 Topps Pristine Clutch Performers Jersey

Nm-Mt Ex-Mt

GROUP A STATED ODDS 1:20
GROUP B STATED ODDS 1:19
GROUP C STATED ODDS 1:31
*REFRACTORS: 2X TO 5X BASIC INSERTS
REFRACTORS #'d/25; STATED ODDS 1:510

❑ CPAB	Aaron Brooks A	8.00	2.40
❑ CPDB	Deion Branch B	10.00	3.00

❑ CPDH	Dante Hall A	8.00	2.40
❑ CPJH	Joey Harrington C	10.00	3.00
❑ CPTL	Ty Law B	10.00	3.00

2004 Topps Pristine Fantasy Favorites Jersey

Nm-Mt Ex-Mt

GROUP A STATED ODDS 1:121
GROUP B STATED ODDS 1:77
GROUP C STATED ODDS 1:67
GROUP D STATED ODDS 1:48
GROUP E STATED ODDS 1:42
GROUP F STATED ODDS 1:37
GROUP G STATED ODDS 1:18
GROUP H STATED ODDS 1:33
GROUP I STATED ODDS 1:28
*REFRACTORS: 2X TO 5X BASIC INSERTS
REFRACTORS #'d/25; STATED ODDS 1:254

❑ FFCM	Curtis Martin C	8.00	2.40
❑ FFDM	Donovan McNabb I	10.00	3.00
❑ FFJW	Javon Walker D	8.00	2.40
❑ FFMF	Marshall Faulk H	8.00	2.40
❑ FFMV	Michael Vick A	15.00	4.50
❑ FFPB	Plaxico Burress B	8.00	2.40
❑ FFPM	Peyton Manning G	12.00	3.60
❑ FFRJ	Rudi Johnson G	6.00	1.80
❑ FFRM	Randy Moss F	10.00	3.00
❑ FFSM	Santana Moss E	6.00	1.80

2004 Topps Pristine Minis

Nm-Mt Ex-Mt

STATED ODDS 1:6
VICK AUTO STATED ODDS 1:472

❑ PM1 Michael Vick 10.00 3.00
❑ PM2 Randy Moss 6.00 1.80
❑ PM3 Marshall Faulk 5.00 1.50
❑ PM4 Deuce McAllister 5.00 1.50
❑ PM5 Peyton Manning 8.00 2.40
❑ PM6 Donovan McNabb 6.00 1.80
❑ PM7 Jamal Lewis 5.00 1.50
❑ PM8 Tom Brady 8.00 2.40
❑ PM9 Torry Holt 5.00 1.50
❑ PM10 Priest Holmes 6.00 1.80
❑ PM11 Clinton Portis 5.00 1.50
❑ PM12 Terrell Owens 5.00 1.50
❑ PM13 Anquan Boldin 5.00 1.50
❑ PM14 Ahman Green 5.00 1.50
❑ PM15 Brett Favre 12.00 3.60
❑ PM16 Chris Perry 6.00 1.80
❑ PM17 Greg Jones 3.00 .90
❑ PM18 Derrick Hamilton 3.00 .90
❑ PM19 Keary Colbert 4.00 1.20
❑ PM20 Reggie Williams 4.00 1.20
❑ PM21 Philip Rivers 10.00 3.00
❑ PM22 Steven Jackson 10.00 3.00
❑ PM23 Luke McCown 5.00 1.50
❑ PM24 Kevin Jones 10.00 3.00
❑ PM25 Darius Watts 4.00 1.20
❑ PM26 Eli Manning 15.00 4.50
❑ PM27 Michael Jenkins 3.00 .90
❑ PM28 Lee Evans 5.00 1.50
❑ PM29 Julius Jones 12.00 3.60
❑ PM30 Matt Schaub 5.00 1.50
❑ PM31 Roy Williams WR 10.00 3.00
❑ PM32 Tatum Bell 5.00 1.50
❑ PM33 Rashaun Woods 4.00 1.20
❑ PM34 Michael Clayton 8.00 2.40
❑ PM35 Devery Henderson 3.00 .90
❑ PM36 Larry Fitzgerald 10.00 3.00
❑ PM37 J.P. Losman 8.00 2.40
❑ PM38 Kellen Winslow 8.00 2.40
❑ PM39 Ben Roethlisberger 30.00 9.00
❑ PMAMV Michael Vick AU 80.00 24.00

2004 Topps Pristine Minis Jersey

Nm-Mt Ex-Mt

JERSEY STATED ODDS 1:312

❑ PMRBR Ben Roethlisberger 250.00 75.00
❑ PMRDM Donovan McNabb 50.00 15.00
❑ PMREM Eli Manning 150.00 45.00
❑ PMRMF Marshall Faulk 30.00 9.00
❑ PMRMV Michael Vick 60.00 18.00
❑ PMRPM Peyton Manning
❑ PMRRM Randy Moss 50.00 15.00
❑ PMRRW Roy Williams WR 80.00 24.00
❑ PMRSJ Steven Jackson 80.00 24.00

2004 Topps Pristine Personal Endorsement Autographs

Nm-Mt Ex-Mt

GROUP A STATED ODDS 1:829
GROUP B STATED ODDS 1:734
GROUP C STATED ODDS 1:480
GROUP D STATED ODDS 1:412
GROUP E STATED ODDS 1:97
GROUP F STATED ODDS 1:167
GROUP G STATED ODDS 1:24
GROUP H STATED ODDS 1:8

❑ PEBB Bernard Berrian F EXCH 12.00 3.60
❑ PECPE Chris Perry D 20.00 6.00
❑ PEDF0 Dwight Freeney G EXCH 12.00 3.60
❑ PEDHA Derrick Hamilton H 12.00 3.60
❑ PEDHE Devery Henderson H 12.00 3.60
❑ PEDRH Drew Henson E 40.00 12.00
❑ PEEM Eli Manning E 120.00 36.00
❑ PEGJ Greg Jones G 15.00 4.50
❑ PEJC Jerricho Cotchery H 12.00 3.60
❑ PEJPL J.P. Losman G 35.00 10.50
❑ PEJV Jonathan Vilma G 20.00 6.00
❑ PEKJ0 Kevin Jones G 40.00 12.00
❑ PEMJ Michael Jenkins H 12.00 3.60
❑ PEMV Michael Vick C 80.00 24.00
❑ PEPKS P.K. Sam H 12.00 3.60
❑ PEPM Peyton Manning B 80.00 24.00
❑ PEPR Philip Rivers E 40.00 12.00
❑ PERW Roy Williams WR A 60.00 18.00
❑ PESE Shaun Ellis H 12.00 3.60
❑ PETB Tatum Bell H 20.00 6.00

2004 Topps Pristine Personal Endorsement Autographs Gold

Nm-Mt Ex-Mt

*GOLDS: 1.2X TO 3X BASIC INSERTS
GOLDS #'d TO 25; STATED ODDS 1:127

❑ PEEM Eli Manning 300.00 90.00

2004 Topps Pristine Pristine Gems Jersey

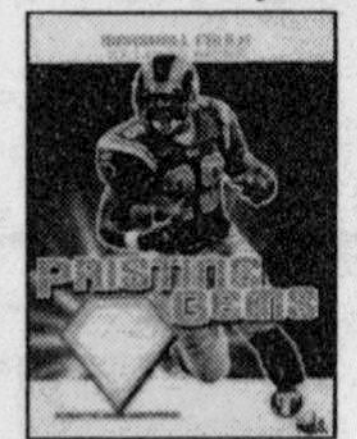

Nm-Mt Ex-Mt

GROUP A STATED ODDS 1:624
GROUP B STATED ODDS 1:87
GROUP C STATED ODDS 1:102

❑ PGAB Aaron Brooks C 8.00 2.40
❑ PGDM Donovan McNabb C 12.00 3.60
❑ PGJPL J.P. Losman B 15.00 4.50
❑ PGKJ Kevin Jones B 20.00 6.00
❑ PGLF Larry Fitzgerald B 20.00 6.00
❑ PGMF Marshall Faulk C 10.00 3.00
❑ PGMV Michael Vick A 20.00 6.00
❑ PGPM Peyton Manning B 20.00 6.00
❑ PGRJ Rudi Johnson B 10.00 3.00
❑ PGRM Randy Moss B 15.00 4.50
❑ PGRW Roy Williams WR B 20.00 6.00
❑ PGSM Santana Moss A 10.00 3.00

2004 Topps Pristine Real Deal Jersey

Nm-Mt Ex-Mt

GROUP A STATED ODDS 1:1263
GROUP B STATED ODDS 1:154
*REFRACTORS: 1.5X TO 4X BASIC INSERTS
REFRACTORS #'d TO 25; ODDS 1:510

❑ RDEL Eli Manning / J.P.Losman 25.00 7.50
❑ RDFW Larry Fitzgerald / Roy Williams WR 20.00 6.00
❑ RDMR Eli Manning / Ben Roethlisberger 60.00 18.00
❑ RDPJ Chris Perry / Kevin Jones 15.00 4.50
❑ RDRC Philip Rivers / Michael Clayton 20.00 6.00

2004 Topps Pristine Rookie Revolution Jersey

Nm-Mt Ex-Mt

GROUP A STATED ODDS 1:123
GROUP B STATED ODDS 1:30
GROUP C STATED ODDS 1:16
GROUP D STATED ODDS 1:23
GROUP E STATED ODDS 1:41
GROUP F STATED ODDS 1:19
GROUP G STATED ODDS 1:18
GROUP H STATED ODDS 1:6
GROUP I STATED ODDS 1:30
GROUP J STATED ODDS 1:10
*REFRACTORS: 2X TO 5X BASIC INSERTS
REFRACTORS #'d TO 25; ODDS 1:111

❑ RRBB Bernard Berrian E 5.00 1.50
❑ RRBR Ben Roethlisberger A 50.00 15.00
❑ RRBW Ben Watson G 5.00 1.50
❑ RRCC Cedric Cobbs E 5.00 1.50
❑ RRCP Chris Perry H 8.00 2.40
❑ RRDD Devard Darling G 5.00 1.50
❑ RRDHA Derrick Hamilton D 5.00 1.50
❑ RRDHE Devery Henderson G 5.00 1.50
❑ RRDR Dunta Robinson E 5.00 1.50
❑ RRDW Darius Watts F 6.00 1.80
❑ RREM Eli Manning B 25.00 7.50
❑ RRGJ Greg Jones F 5.00 1.50
❑ RRJJ Julius Jones I 20.00 6.00
❑ RRJPL J.P. Losman G 10.00 3.00
❑ RRKC Keary Colbert I 6.00 1.80
❑ RRKJ Kevin Jones D 12.00 3.60
❑ RRLF Larry Fitzgerald G 10.00 3.00
❑ RRMC Michael Clayton C 10.00 3.00
❑ RRMM Mewelde Moore I 6.00 1.80
❑ RRMS Matt Schaub B 6.00 1.80
❑ RRRG Robert Gallery C 6.00 1.80
❑ RRRW Roy Williams WR C 12.00 3.60
❑ RRRWO Rashaun Woods G 6.00 1.80

2001 Topps Reserve

Nm-Mt Ex-Mt

COMP.SET w/o SP's (100) 60.00 18.00

❑ 1 Jeff Garcia 1.50 .45
❑ 2 Joe Horn 1.00 .30
❑ 3 Jeff George 1.00 .30
❑ 4 Ed McCaffrey 1.50 .45
❑ 5 Keenan McCardell .60 .18
❑ 6 Jerome Bettis 1.50 .45
❑ 7 Jake Plummer 1.00 .30

8 Doug Flutie	1.50	.45
9 Wayne Chrebet	1.00	.30
10 Brett Favre	5.00	1.50
11 Emmitt Smith	3.00	.90
12 Derrick Mason	1.00	.30
13 Lamar Smith	1.00	.30
14 Brian Urlacher	2.50	.75
15 Kurt Warner	3.00	.90
16 Jerry Rice	3.00	.90
17 Tony Gonzalez	1.00	.30
18 Jeff Blake	1.00	.30
19 Warrick Dunn	1.50	.45
20 Vinny Testaverde	1.00	.30
21 Peyton Manning	4.00	1.20
22 Drew Bledsoe	2.00	.60
23 Tim Dwight	1.50	.45
24 Brad Johnson	1.50	.45
25 Peter Warrick	1.50	.45
26 Steve McNair	1.50	.45
27 James Thrash	1.00	.30
28 Kordell Stewart	1.00	.30
29 Randy Moss	3.00	.90
30 Brian Griese	1.50	.45
31 Curtis Martin	1.50	.45
32 Ike Hilliard	1.00	.30
33 Torry Holt	1.50	.45
34 James Allen	1.00	.30
35 Jay Fiedler	1.50	.45
36 Junior Seau	1.50	.45
37 Troy Brown	1.00	.30
38 Ricky Williams	1.50	.45
39 Charlie Garner	1.00	.30
40 Eddie George	1.50	.45
41 Stephen Davis	1.50	.45
42 Tim Couch	1.00	.30
43 Jimmy Smith	1.00	.30
44 Trent Green	1.50	.45
45 Rod Smith	1.00	.30
46 Isaac Bruce	1.50	.45
47 Oronde Gadsden	1.00	.30
48 Keyshawn Johnson	1.50	.45
49 Jeff Graham	.60	.18
50 Mark Brunell	1.50	.45
51 Cade McNown	.60	.18
52 Terry Glenn	.60	.18
53 Derrick Alexander	.60	.18
54 Ron Dayne	1.50	.45
55 Shaun Alexander	2.00	.60
56 Chris Chandler	1.00	.30
57 Rob Johnson	1.00	.30
58 Germane Crowell	.60	.18
59 Cris Carter	1.50	.45
60 Ahman Green	1.50	.45
61 Marshall Faulk	2.00	.60
62 Darrell Jackson	1.50	.45
63 Duce Staley	1.50	.45
64 Kevin Johnson	1.00	.30
65 Muhsin Muhammad	1.00	.30
66 Elvis Grbac	1.00	.30
67 Fred Taylor	1.50	.45
68 Marcus Robinson	1.50	.45
69 Edgerrin James	2.00	.60
70 Kerry Collins	1.00	.30
71 Daunte Culpepper	1.50	.45
72 Matt Hasselbeck	1.00	.30
73 Akili Smith	.60	.18
74 Aaron Brooks	1.50	.45
75 Tim Biakabutuka	1.00	.30
76 Ray Lewis	1.50	.45
77 David Boston	1.50	.45
78 Donovan Mcnabb	2.00	.60
79 Marvin Harrison	1.50	.45
80 Rich Gannon	1.50	.45
81 Tony Richardson	.60	.18
82 Peerless Price	1.00	.30
83 Jamal Anderson	1.50	.45
84 Mike Anderson	1.50	.45
85 Terrell Owens	1.50	.45
86 Antonio Freeman	1.50	.45
87 Charlie Batch	1.50	.45
88 Jamal Lewis	2.50	.75
89 Jon Kitna	1.00	.30
90 Joey Galloway	1.00	.30
91 Tyrone Wheatley	1.00	.30
92 Jeff Lewis	.60	.18
93 Eric Moulds	1.00	.30
94 Shawn Jefferson	.60	.18
95 Tiki Barber	1.00	.30
96 Tim Brown	1.50	.45
97 Corey Dillon	1.50	.45
98 Tony Banks	1.00	.30
99 James Stewart	1.00	.30
100 Amani Toomer	1.00	.30
101 Freddie Mitchell RC	6.00	1.80
102 James Jackson RC	6.00	1.80
103 Michael Bennett RC	12.00	3.60
104 LaDainian Tomlinson RC	20.00	6.00
105 Gerard Warren RC	6.00	1.80
106 Dan Morgan RC	6.00	1.80
107 Alge Crumpler RC	8.00	2.40
108 Mike McMahon RC	6.00	1.80
109 Justin Smith RC	6.00	1.80
110 Chris Weinke RC	6.00	1.80
111 Rudi Johnson RC	12.00	3.60
112 Rod Gardner RC	6.00	1.80
113 Koren Robinson RC	8.00	2.40
114 Andre Carter RC	6.00	1.80
115 Kevan Barlow RC	6.00	1.80
116 Jesse Palmer RC	6.00	1.80
117 Anthony Thomas RC	10.00	3.00
118 Michael Vick RC	40.00	12.00
119 Sage Rosenfels RC	6.00	1.80
120 Chad Johnson RC	12.00	3.60
121 Robert Ferguson RC	6.00	1.80
122 Quincy Carter RC	6.00	1.80
123 Travis Minor RC	4.00	1.20
124 Travis Henry RC	8.00	2.40
125 Reggie Wayne RC	10.00	3.00
126 David Terrell RC	6.00	1.80
127 Josh Heupel RC	6.00	1.80
128 Deuce McAllister RC	12.00	3.60
129 Todd Heap RC	6.00	1.80
130 Drew Brees RC	12.00	3.60
131 Snoop Minnis RC	4.00	1.20
132 Marques Tuiasosopo RC	6.00	1.80
133 Santana Moss RC	10.00	3.00
134 Quincy Morgan RC	6.00	1.80
135 Chris Chambers RC	8.00	2.40
136 Richard Seymour RC	6.00	1.80
137 LaMont Jordan RC	8.00	2.40
138 Eddie Berlin RC	4.00	1.20
139 Correll Buckhalter RC	8.00	2.40
140 Justin McCareins RC	6.00	1.80
141 Vinny Sutherland RC	4.00	1.20
142 Chris Taylor RC	4.00	1.20
143 Scotty Anderson RC	4.00	1.20
144 Nate Clements RC	6.00	1.80
145 Damerien McCants RC	4.00	1.20
146 Dan Alexander RC	6.00	1.80
147 A.J. Feeley RC	6.00	1.80
148 Chris Barnes RC	4.00	1.20
149 Dee Brown RC	6.00	1.80
150 Milton Wynn RC	4.00	1.20
NNO Checklist Card	.10	.03

2001 Topps Reserve Autographs

	Nm-Mt	Ex-Mt
TRAB Aaron Brooks	15.00	4.50
TRCC Chris Chambers	15.00	4.50
TRCJ Chad Johnson	30.00	9.00
TRCW Chris Weinke	15.00	4.50
TRDB Drew Brees	30.00	9.00
TRDC Daunte Culpepper	20.00	6.00
TRDM Derrick Mason	10.00	3.00
TRDMO Dan Morgan	15.00	4.50
TRDT David Terrell	20.00	6.00
TREM Eric Moulds	15.00	4.50
TRJB Josh Booty	10.00	3.00
TRJH Joe Horn	10.00	3.00
TRJJ James Jackson	15.00	4.50
TRJL Jamal Lewis	20.00	6.00
TRJP Jesse Palmer	15.00	4.50
TRJS Jimmy Smith	10.00	3.00
TRJT James Thrash	10.00	3.00
TRKB Kevan Barlow	15.00	4.50
TRKR Koren Robinson	15.00	4.50
TRLS Lamar Smith	10.00	3.00
TRLT LaDainian Tomlinson	100.00	30.00
TRMA Mike Anderson	15.00	4.50
TRMB Michael Bennett	25.00	7.50
TRMV Michael Vick	200.00	60.00
TRQM Quincy Morgan	15.00	4.50
TRRG Rod Gardner	15.00	4.50
TRRW Ricky Williams EXCH		
TRRWA Reggie Wayne EXCH	15.00	4.50
TRSM Santana Moss	20.00	6.00
TRSMO Sammy Morris	10.00	3.00
TRTH Travis Henry	15.00	4.50
TRWJ Willie Jackson	10.00	3.00

2002 Topps Reserve Autographs

	Nm-Mt	Ex-Mt
RAAT Anthony Thomas F	15.00	4.50
RABF Brett Favre B	200.00	60.00
RABS Bill Schroeder H	10.00	3.00
RABU Brian Urlacher C	40.00	12.00
RACC Chris Chambers G	12.00	3.60
RADM Derrick Mason J	10.00	3.00
RADT David Terrell C	12.00	3.60
RAJG Jeff Garcia C	30.00	9.00
RAJR Jerry Rice A	125.00	38.00
RALJ LaMont Jordan E	15.00	4.50
RALS Lamar Smith D	10.00	3.00
RALT LaDainian Tomlinson I	40.00	12.00
RAMR Marcus Robinson D	12.00	3.60
RARD Richard Dent E	20.00	6.00
RASM Sammy Morris F	10.00	3.00
RATS Tai Streets F	12.00	3.60
RAWJ Willie Jackson F	10.00	3.00

2002 Topps Reserve Jerseys

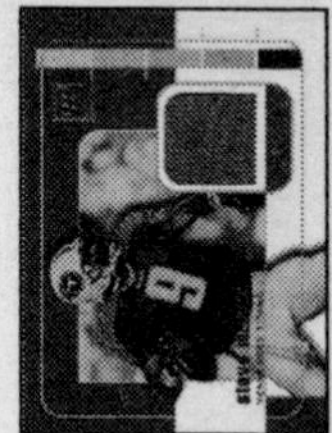

	Nm-Mt	Ex-Mt
❑ RRCD Corey Dillon C	8.00	2.40
❑ RRCG Charlie Garner B	8.00	2.40
❑ RRDB Drew Brees C	10.00	3.00
❑ RRDC Daunte Culpepper D	10.00	3.00
❑ RRDM Dan Marino F DP	25.00	7.50
❑ RRDS Duce Staley E DP	8.00	2.40
❑ RREG Eddie George A	10.00	3.00
❑ RREJ Edgerrin James D	12.00	3.60
❑ RREM Eric Moulds A	10.00	3.00
❑ RRFT Fred Taylor C	8.00	2.40
❑ RRJN Joe Namath C	40.00	12.00
❑ RRJS Jimmy Smith C	8.00	2.40
❑ RRKJ Keyshawn Johnson C	8.00	2.40
❑ RRMA Mike Alstott F	10.00	3.00
❑ RRMB Mark Brunell A	10.00	3.00
❑ RRPM Peyton Manning C	20.00	6.00
❑ RRRG Rich Gannon B	10.00	3.00
❑ RRSC Sam Cowart B	8.00	2.40
❑ RRSM Steve McNair C	10.00	3.00
❑ RRTG Tony Gonzalez D	8.00	2.40
❑ RRTM Travis Minor C	8.00	2.40
❑ RRTO Terrell Owens C	10.00	3.00

1999 Topps Season Opener

	Nm-Mt	Ex-Mt
COMPLETE SET (165)	40.00	18.00
❑ 1 Jerry Rice	1.00	.45
❑ 2 Emmitt Smith	1.00	.45
❑ 3 Curtis Martin	.50	.23
❑ 4 Ed McCaffrey	.30	.14
❑ 5 Oronde Gadsden	.30	.14
❑ 6 Byron Bam Morris	.20	.09
❑ 7 Michael Irvin	.30	.14
❑ 8 Shannon Sharpe	.30	.14
❑ 9 Levon Kirkland	.20	.09
❑ 10 Fred Taylor	.50	.23
❑ 11 Andre Reed	.30	.14
❑ 12 Chad Brown	.20	.09
❑ 13 Skip Hicks	.20	.09
❑ 14 Tim Dwight	.50	.23
❑ 15 Michael Sinclair	.20	.09
❑ 16 Carl Pickens	.30	.14
❑ 17 Derrick Alexander WR	.30	.14
❑ 18 Kevin Greene	.20	.09
❑ 19 Duce Staley	.50	.23
❑ 20 Dan Marino	1.50	.70
❑ 21 Frank Sanders	.30	.14
❑ 22 Ricky Proehl	.20	.09
❑ 23 Frank Wycheck	.20	.09
❑ 24 Andre Rison	.30	.14
❑ 25 Natrone Means	.30	.14
❑ 26 Steve McNair	.50	.23
❑ 27 Vonnie Holliday	.20	.09
❑ 28 Charles Woodson	.50	.23
❑ 29 Rob Moore	.30	.14
❑ 30 John Elway	1.50	.70
❑ 31 Derrick Thomas	.30	.14
❑ 32 Jake Plummer	.30	.14
❑ 33 Mike Alstott	.50	.23
❑ 34 Keenan McCardell	.30	.14
❑ 35 Mark Chmura	.20	.09
❑ 36 Keyshawn Johnson	.50	.23
❑ 37 Priest Holmes	.75	.35
❑ 38 Antonio Freeman	.50	.23
❑ 39 Ty Law	.30	.14
❑ 40 Jamal Anderson	.50	.23
❑ 41 Courtney Hawkins	.20	.09
❑ 42 James Jett	.30	.14
❑ 43 Aaron Glenn	.20	.09
❑ 44 Jimmy Smith	.30	.14
❑ 45 Michael McCrary	.20	.09
❑ 46 Junior Seau	.50	.23
❑ 47 Bill Romanowski	.20	.09
❑ 48 Mark Brunell	.50	.23
❑ 49 Yancey Thigpen	.20	.09
❑ 50 Steve Young	.60	.25
❑ 51 Cris Carter	.50	.23
❑ 52 Vinny Testaverde	.30	.14
❑ 53 Zach Thomas	.50	.23
❑ 54 Kordell Stewart	.30	.14
❑ 55 Tim Biakabutuka	.30	.14
❑ 56 J.J. Stokes	.30	.14
❑ 57 Jon Kitna	.50	.23
❑ 58 Jacquez Green	.20	.09
❑ 59 Marvin Harrison	.50	.23
❑ 60 Barry Sanders	1.50	.70
❑ 61 Darrell Green	.20	.09
❑ 62 Terance Mathis	.30	.14
❑ 63 Ricky Watters	.30	.14
❑ 64 Chris Chandler	.30	.14
❑ 65 Cameron Cleeland	.20	.09
❑ 66 Rod Smith	.30	.14
❑ 67 Freddie Jones	.20	.09
❑ 68 Adrian Murrell	.30	.14
❑ 69 Terrell Owens	.50	.23
❑ 70 Troy Aikman	1.00	.45
❑ 71 John Mobley	.20	.09
❑ 72 Corey Dillon	.50	.23
❑ 73 Rickey Dudley	.20	.09
❑ 74 Randall Cunningham	.50	.23
❑ 75 Muhsin Muhammad	.30	.14
❑ 76 Stephen Boyd	.20	.09
❑ 77 Tony Gonzalez	.50	.23
❑ 78 Deion Sanders	.50	.23
❑ 79 Ben Coates	.30	.14
❑ 80 Brett Favre	1.50	.70
❑ 81 Shawn Springs	.20	.09
❑ 82 Dorsey Levens	.50	.23
❑ 83 Ray Buchanan	.20	.09
❑ 84 Charlie Batch	.50	.23
❑ 85 John Randle	.30	.14
❑ 86 Eddie George	.50	.23
❑ 87 Ray Lewis	.50	.23
❑ 88 Johnnie Morton	.30	.14
❑ 89 Kevin Hardy	.20	.09
❑ 90 O.J. McDuffie	.30	.14
❑ 91 Herman Moore	.30	.14
❑ 92 Tim Brown	.50	.23
❑ 93 Bert Emanuel	.30	.14
❑ 94 Elvis Grbac	.30	.14
❑ 95 Peter Boulware	.20	.09
❑ 96 Curtis Conway	.30	.14
❑ 97 Doug Flutie	.50	.23
❑ 98 Jake Reed	.30	.14
❑ 99 Ike Hilliard	.20	.09
❑ 100 Randy Moss	1.25	.55
❑ 101 Warren Sapp	.20	.09
❑ 102 Bruce Smith	.30	.14
❑ 103 Joey Galloway	.30	.14
❑ 104 Napoleon Kaufman	.50	.23
❑ 105 Warrick Dunn	.50	.23
❑ 106 Wayne Chrebet	.30	.14
❑ 107 Robert Brooks	.30	.14
❑ 108 Antowain Smith	.50	.23
❑ 109 Trent Dilfer	.30	.14
❑ 110 Peyton Manning	1.50	.70
❑ 111 Isaac Bruce	.50	.23
❑ 112 John Lynch	.30	.14
❑ 113 Terry Glenn	.50	.23
❑ 114 Garrison Hearst	.30	.14
❑ 115 Jerome Bettis	.50	.23
❑ 116 Darnay Scott	.20	.09
❑ 117 Lamar Thomas	.20	.09
❑ 118 Chris Spielman	.20	.09
❑ 119 Robert Smith	.50	.23
❑ 120 Drew Bledsoe	.60	.25
❑ 121 Reidel Anthony	.30	.14
❑ 122 Wesley Walls	.30	.14
❑ 123 Eric Moulds	.50	.23
❑ 124 Terrell Davis	.50	.23
❑ 125 Dale Carter	.20	.09
❑ 126 Charles Johnson	.20	.09
❑ 127 Steve Atwater	.20	.09
❑ 128 Jim Harbaugh	.30	.14
❑ 129 Tony Martin	.30	.14
❑ 130 Kerry Collins	.30	.14
❑ 131 Trent Green	.50	.23
❑ 132 Marshall Faulk	.60	.25
❑ 133 Rocket Ismail	.30	.14
❑ 134 Warren Moon	.50	.23
❑ 135 Jerris McPhail	.20	.09
❑ 136 Damon Gibson	.20	.09
❑ 137 Jim Pyne	.20	.09
❑ 138 Antonio Langham	.20	.09
❑ 139 Freddie Solomon	.20	.09
❑ 140 Randy Moss SH	.60	.25
❑ 141 John Elway SH	.75	.35
❑ 142 Doug Flutie SH	.30	.14
❑ 143 Emmitt Smith SH	.50	.23
❑ 144 Terrell Davis SH	.30	.14
❑ 145 Troy Edwards RC	1.50	.70
❑ 146 Torry Holt RC	5.00	2.20
❑ 147 Tim Couch RC	2.00	.90
❑ 148 Sedrick Irvin RC	1.00	.45
❑ 149 Ricky Williams RC	4.00	1.80
❑ 150 Peerless Price RC	3.00	1.35
❑ 151 Mike Cloud RC	1.50	.70
❑ 152 Kevin Faulk RC	2.00	.90
❑ 153 Kevin Johnson RC	2.00	.90
❑ 154 James Johnson RC	1.50	.70
❑ 155 Edgerrin James RC	8.00	3.60
❑ 156 D'Wayne Bates RC	1.50	.70
❑ 157 Donovan McNabb RC	10.00	4.50
❑ 158 David Boston RC	2.00	.90
❑ 159 Daunte Culpepper RC	8.00	3.60
❑ 160 Champ Bailey RC	2.50	1.10
❑ 161 Cecil Collins RC	1.00	.45
❑ 162 Cade McNown RC	1.50	.70
❑ 163 Brock Huard RC	2.00	.90
❑ 164 Akili Smith RC	1.50	.70
❑ 165 Checklist Card	.20	.09

2000 Topps Season Opener

	Nm-Mt	Ex-Mt
COMPLETE SET (220)	40.00	18.00
❑ 1 Tyrone Wheatley	.25	.11
❑ 2 Carl Pickens	.25	.11
❑ 3 Zach Thomas	.40	.18
❑ 4 Jacquez Green	.15	.07
❑ 5 Sean Dawkins	.15	.07
❑ 6 Brad Johnson	.40	.18
❑ 7 Jerry Rice	.75	.35
❑ 8 Doug Flutie	.40	.18
❑ 9 Cade McNown	.15	.07
❑ 10 Rod Smith	.25	.11
❑ 11 Kevin Hardy	.15	.07
❑ 12 Marvin Harrison	.40	.18
❑ 13 David Boston	.40	.18
❑ 14 Priest Holmes	.50	.23
❑ 15 Keith Poole	.15	.07
❑ 16 Troy Edwards	.15	.07
❑ 17 Robert Smith	.40	.18
❑ 18 Kevin Lockett	.15	.07
❑ 19 Johnnie Morton	.25	.11
❑ 20 Terrell Davis	.40	.18
❑ 21 Corey Bradford	.25	.11
❑ 22 Keyshawn Johnson	.40	.18
❑ 23 Tony Banks	.25	.11
❑ 24 Matthew Hatchette	.15	.07
❑ 25 Troy Aikman	.75	.35

❑ 26	Natrone Means	.15	.07
❑ 27	Peerless Price	.40	.18
❑ 28	Bruce Smith	.25	.11
❑ 29	Tim Couch	.25	.11
❑ 30	Terrell Owens	.40	.18
❑ 31	O.J. McDuffie	.25	.11
❑ 32	Troy Brown	.25	.11
❑ 33	Corey Dillon	.40	.18
❑ 34	Cam Cleeland	.15	.07
❑ 35	Brian Griese	.40	.18
❑ 36	Shawn Springs	.15	.07
❑ 37	Marcus Robinson	.40	.18
❑ 38	Jermaine Lewis	.25	.11
❑ 39	Olandis Gary	.40	.18
❑ 40	Tony Gonzalez	.25	.11
❑ 41	Frank Wycheck	.15	.07
❑ 42	Jon Kitna	.40	.18
❑ 43	Muhsin Muhammad	.25	.11
❑ 44	Jerome Bettis	.40	.18
❑ 45	Darrin Chiaverini	.15	.07
❑ 46	Steve McNair	.40	.18
❑ 47	Charlie Batch	.40	.18
❑ 48	Steve Beuerlein	.25	.11
❑ 49	Dorsey Levens	.25	.11
❑ 50	Jim Harbaugh	.25	.11
❑ 51	Jonathan Linton	.15	.07
❑ 52	Napoleon Kaufman	.25	.11
❑ 53	Curtis Enis	.15	.07
❑ 54	Darnay Scott	.25	.11
❑ 55	Tim Dwight	.40	.18
❑ 56	Mikhael Ricks	.15	.07
❑ 57	Kevin Dyson	.25	.11
❑ 58	Antonio Freeman	.40	.18
❑ 59	E.G. Green	.15	.07
❑ 60	Jake Plummer	.25	.11
❑ 61	Bill Schroeder	.25	.11
❑ 62	Shaun King	.15	.07
❑ 63	Michael Basnight	.15	.07
❑ 64	Vinny Testaverde	.25	.11
❑ 65	Rob Johnson	.25	.11
❑ 66	Jeff Blake	.25	.11
❑ 67	Marshall Faulk	.50	.23
❑ 68	Keenan McCardell	.25	.11
❑ 69	Michael Westbrook	.25	.11
❑ 70	Yancey Thigpen	.15	.07
❑ 71	Akili Smith	.15	.07
❑ 72	Charles Woodson	.25	.11
❑ 73	Qadry Ismail	.25	.11
❑ 74	Pat Johnson	.15	.07
❑ 75	Rocket Ismail	.25	.11
❑ 76	Terrence Wilkins	.15	.07
❑ 77	Herman Moore	.25	.11
❑ 78	Jevon Kearse	.40	.18
❑ 79	Oronde Gadsden	.25	.11
❑ 80	Errict Rhett	.25	.11
❑ 81	Ed McCaffrey	.40	.18
❑ 82	Mike Alstott	.40	.18
❑ 83	Stephen Alexander	.15	.07
❑ 84	Mark Brunell	.40	.18
❑ 85	Jeff George	.25	.11
❑ 86	Stephen Davis	.40	.18
❑ 87	Germane Crowell	.15	.07
❑ 88	Charlie Garner	.25	.11
❑ 89	Kordell Stewart	.25	.11
❑ 90	Tim Biakabutuka	.25	.11
❑ 91	Jim Miller	.15	.07
❑ 92	Eddie George	.40	.18
❑ 93	Joe Montgomery	.15	.07
❑ 94	Wayne Chrebet	.25	.11
❑ 95	Freddie Jones	.15	.07
❑ 96	Ricky Proehl	.15	.07
❑ 97	Warren Sapp	.25	.11
❑ 98	Derrick Mayes	.25	.11
❑ 99	Daunte Culpepper	.50	.23
❑ 100	Torry Holt	.40	.18
❑ 101	Isaac Bruce	.40	.18
❑ 102	Kevin Johnson	.40	.18
❑ 103	Antowain Smith	.25	.11
❑ 104	Rob Moore	.25	.11
❑ 105	Joey Galloway	.25	.11
❑ 106	Rickey Dudley	.15	.07
❑ 107	Terry Glenn	.25	.11
❑ 108	Ike Hilliard	.25	.11
❑ 109	Jeff Graham	.15	.07
❑ 110	J.J. Stokes	.25	.11
❑ 111	Steve Young	.50	.23
❑ 112	Albert Connell	.15	.07
❑ 113	Tony Brackens	.15	.07
❑ 114	James Johnson	.15	.07
❑ 115	Tim Brown	.40	.18
❑ 116	Terance Mathis	.25	.11
❑ 117	Peyton Manning	1.00	.45
❑ 118	Kerry Collins	.25	.11
❑ 119	Duce Staley	.40	.18
❑ 120	Torrance Small	.15	.07
❑ 121	Curtis Martin	.40	.18
❑ 122	Damon Huard	.40	.18
❑ 123	Derrick Alexander	.25	.11
❑ 124	Jimmy Smith	.25	.11
❑ 125	Cris Carter	.40	.18
❑ 126	Jamal Anderson	.40	.18
❑ 127	Eric Moulds	.40	.18
❑ 128	Drew Bledsoe	.50	.23
❑ 129	Ricky Williams	.40	.18
❑ 130	Andre Hastings	.15	.07
❑ 131	Amani Toomer	.15	.07
❑ 132	Rich Gannon	.40	.18
❑ 133	Richard Huntley	.15	.07
❑ 134	Donovan McNabb	.60	.25
❑ 135	Jermaine Fazande	.15	.07
❑ 136	Randy Moss	.75	.35
❑ 137	Champ Bailey	.25	.11
❑ 138	Elvis Grbac	.25	.11
❑ 139	Warrick Dunn	.40	.18
❑ 140	John Randle	.25	.11
❑ 141	Edgerrin James	.60	.25
❑ 142	Tony Martin	.25	.11
❑ 143	Chris Chandler	.25	.11
❑ 144	Stephen Boyd	.15	.07
❑ 145	Az-Zahir Hakim	.25	.11
❑ 146	Tony Simmons	.15	.07
❑ 147	Pete Mitchell	.15	.07
❑ 148	Junior Seau	.40	.18
❑ 149	Ricky Watters	.25	.11
❑ 150	Michael Pittman	.15	.07
❑ 151	Fred Taylor	.40	.18
❑ 152	Charles Johnson	.25	.11
❑ 153	Jason Tucker	.15	.07
❑ 154	Brett Favre	1.25	.55
❑ 155	Patrick Jeffers	.40	.18
❑ 156	Curtis Conway	.25	.11
❑ 157	Frank Sanders	.25	.11
❑ 158	James Stewart	.25	.11
❑ 159	Emmitt Smith	.75	.35
❑ 161	Wesley Walls	.15	.07
❑ 162	Kent Graham	.15	.07
❑ 163	Kurt Warner	.75	.35
❑ 164	Shawn Jefferson	.15	.07
❑ 165	Jammi German	.15	.07
❑ 166	Jay Riemersma	.15	.07
❑ 167	Fred Lane	.15	.07
❑ 168	Jamir Miller	.15	.07
❑ 169	David LaFleur	.15	.07
❑ 170	David Sloan	.15	.07
❑ 171	Jerome Pathon	.25	.11
❑ 172	Sam Madison	.15	.07
❑ 173	Tiki Barber	.25	.11
❑ 174	Yatil Green	.15	.07
❑ 175	Checklist	.15	.07
❑ 176	Kurt Warner HL	.40	.18
❑ 177	Brett Favre HL	.60	.25
❑ 178	Marshall Faulk HL	.40	.18
❑ 179	Jevon Kearse HL	.25	.11
❑ 180	Edgerrin James CL	.40	.18
❑ 181	Troy Aikman CS	.40	.18
❑ 182	Terrell Davis CS	.40	.18
❑ 183	Steve Beuerlein CS	.15	.07
❑ 184	Tim Brown CS	.25	.11
❑ 185	Randy Moss CS	.40	.18
❑ 186	Drew Bledsoe CS	.40	.18
❑ 187	Curtis Martin CS	.25	.11
❑ 188	Shannon Sharpe CS	.15	.07
❑ 189	Brett Favre CS	.60	.25
❑ 190	Brad Johnson CS	.25	.11
❑ 191	Tony Gonzalez CS	.15	.07
❑ 192	Jon Kitna CS	.25	.11
❑ 193	Peyton Manning CS	.50	.23
❑ 194	Mark Brunell CS	.25	.11
❑ 195	Cade McNown CS	.15	.07
❑ 196	Jim Harbaugh CS	.15	.07
❑ 197	Shaun King CS	.15	.07
❑ 198	Kurt Warner CS	4.00	1.80
❑ 199	Eddie George CS	.25	.11
❑ 200	Ricky Williams CS	.40	.18
❑ 201	Curtis Keaton RC	.75	.35
❑ 202	Tee Martin RC	1.00	.45
❑ 203	Thomas Jones RC	1.50	.70
❑ 204	Giovanni Carmazzi RC	.75	.35
❑ 205	Courtney Brown RC	1.00	.45
❑ 206	Shaun Alexander RC	2.50	1.10
❑ 207	Travis Taylor RC	1.00	.45
❑ 208	Dennis Northcutt RC	1.00	.45
❑ 209	Trung Canidate RC	.75	.35
❑ 210	Jamal Lewis RC	2.50	1.10
❑ 211	R.Jay Soward RC	.75	.35
❑ 212	Sylvester Morris RC	.75	.35
❑ 213	Ron Dugans RC	.75	.35
❑ 214	Chris Redman RC	.75	.35
❑ 215	Plaxico Burress RC	2.00	.90
❑ 216	Peter Warrick RC	1.00	.45
❑ 217	Travis Prentice RC	.75	.35
❑ 218	Ron Dayne RC	1.00	.45
❑ 219	J.R. Redmond RC	.75	.35
❑ 220	Chad Pennington RC	4.00	1.80

2000 Topps Season Opener Autographs

		Nm-Mt	Ex-Mt
❑ A1	Kurt Warner/100	60.00	27.00
❑ A2	Marvin Harrison/300	25.00	11.00
❑ A3	Stephen Davis/300	25.00	11.00
❑ A4	Joe Montana/200	150.00	70.00

2004 Topps Signature

	Nm-Mt	Ex-Mt
COMP.SET w/o SP's (55)	40.00	12.00
56-75 ROOKIE/499 STATED ODDS 1:3		
ROOKIE AU/299 GROUP A ODDS 1:15		
ROOKIE AU/999 GROUP B ODDS 1:11		
ROOKIE AU/1099 GROUP C ODDS 1:4		
ROOKIE AU/1499 GROUP D ODDS 1:3		

❑ 1	Tom Brady	4.00	1.20
❑ 2	Chad Johnson	1.50	.45
❑ 3	Amani Toomer	1.50	.45
❑ 4	Shaun Alexander	2.50	.75
❑ 5	Terrell Owens	2.50	.75
❑ 6	Jake Delhomme	2.50	.75
❑ 7	Eric Moulds	1.50	.45
❑ 8	Fred Taylor	1.50	.45
❑ 9	Mark Brunell	1.50	.45

❑ 10 Priest Holmes 3.00 .90
❑ 11 Marvin Harrison 2.50 .75
❑ 12 Jeff Garcia 2.50 .75
❑ 13 Brad Johnson 1.50 .45
❑ 14 Laveranues Coles 1.50 .45
❑ 15 LaDainian Tomlinson 2.50 .75
❑ 16 Anquan Boldin 2.50 .75
❑ 17 Curtis Martin 2.50 .75
❑ 18 Joe Horn 1.50 .45
❑ 19 Domanick Davis 2.50 .75
❑ 20 Jamal Lewis 2.50 .75
❑ 21 Steve Smith 1.50 .45
❑ 22 Aaron Brooks 1.50 .45
❑ 23 Hines Ward 2.50 .75
❑ 24 Marc Bulger 2.50 .75
❑ 25 Randy Moss 3.00 .90
❑ 26 Jerry Rice 5.00 1.50
❑ 27 Tiki Barber 1.50 .45
❑ 28 Jake Plummer 1.50 .45
❑ 29 Travis Henry 1.50 .45
❑ 30 Michael Vick 5.00 1.50
❑ 31 Matt Hasselbeck 1.50 .45
❑ 32 Santana Moss 1.50 .45
❑ 33 Corey Dillon 1.50 .45
❑ 34 Byron Leftwich 4.00 1.20
❑ 35 Clinton Portis 2.50 .75
❑ 36 Derrick Mason 1.50 .45
❑ 37 Tim Rattay 1.50 .45
❑ 38 Chris Chambers 1.50 .45
❑ 39 Joey Harrington 2.50 .75
❑ 40 Deuce McAllister 2.50 .75
❑ 41 Tony Gonzalez 1.50 .45
❑ 42 Kurt Warner 2.50 .75
❑ 43 Carson Palmer 3.00 .90
❑ 44 Marshall Faulk 2.50 .75
❑ 45 Peyton Manning 4.00 1.20
❑ 46 Ahman Green 2.50 .75
❑ 47 Torry Holt 2.50 .75
❑ 48 Chad Pennington 3.00 .90
❑ 49 Trent Green 1.50 .45
❑ 50 Brett Favre 6.00 1.80
❑ 51 Stephen Davis 1.50 .45
❑ 52 Steve McNair 2.50 .75
❑ 53 Daunte Culpepper 2.50 .75
❑ 54 Edgerrin James 2.50 .75
❑ 55 Donovan McNabb 3.00 .90
❑ 56 Sean Taylor RC 8.00 2.40
❑ 57 Darius Watts RC 8.00 2.40
❑ 58 Ben Troupe RC 6.00 1.80
❑ 59 Josh Harris RC 6.00 1.80
❑ 60 Jeff Smoker RC 10.00 3.00
❑ 61 Mewelde Moore RC 8.00 2.40
❑ 62 Reggie Williams RC 8.00 2.40
❑ 63 Ben Watson RC 6.00 1.80
❑ 64 Rashaun Woods RC 8.00 2.40
❑ 65 Kellen Winslow RC 15.00 4.50
❑ 66 Robert Gallery RC 10.00 3.00
❑ 67 Steven Jackson RC 25.00 7.50
❑ 68 Craig Krenzel RC 6.00 1.80
❑ 69 DeAngelo Hall RC 8.00 2.40
❑ 70 Devard Darling RC 6.00 1.80
❑ 71 Julius Jones RC 25.00 7.50
❑ 72 Derrick Hamilton RC 5.00 1.50
❑ 73 Devery Henderson RC 5.00 1.50
❑ 74 Dunta Robinson RC 6.00 1.80
❑ 75 Larry Fitzgerald RC 20.00 6.00
❑ 76 Chris Perry AU/999 RC 30.00 9.00
❑ 77 J.P. Losman AU/1099 RC 50.00 15.00
❑ 78 Lee Evans AU/1099 RC 30.00 9.00
❑ 79 Cedric Cobbs AU/1499 RC 15.00 4.50
❑ 80 Philip Rivers AU/299 RC 80.00 24.00
❑ 81 Greg Jones AU/1499 RC 15.00 4.50
❑ 82 Michael Clayton AU/1099 RC 40.0012.00
❑ 83 Jonathan Vilma AU/1499 RC 20.00 6.00
❑ 84 Jerricho Cotchery AU/1499 RC 15.00 4.50
❑ 85 Roy Williams AU/299 RC 80.00 24.00
❑ 86 Keary Colbert AU/1499 RC 25.00 7.50
❑ 87 Luke McCown AU/1499 RC 15.00 4.50
❑ 88 Bernard Berrian AU/1499 RC 15.004.50
❑ 89 Michael Jenkins AU/1499 RC 20.006.00
❑ 90 Eli Manning AU/299 RC 200.00 60.00
❑ 91 Matt Schaub AU/1499 RC 25.00 7.50
❑ 92 Tatum Bell AU/1099 RC 40.00 12.00
❑ 93 Roethlisberger AU/299 RC 350.00105.00
❑ 94 Kevin Jones AU/1099 RC 50.00 15.00
❑ 95 Cody Pickett AU/999 RC 20.00 6.00
❑ 96 Drew Henson AU/299 RC 50.00 15.00

2004 Topps Signature Blue

Nm-Mt Ex-Mt

*BLUE STARS 1-55: 2.5X TO 6X BASE CARDS
*BLUE ROOKIES 56-75: .6X TO 1.5X
1-75 PRINT RUN 50; STATED ODDS 1:6
*ROOKIE AU: 1.2X TO 3X BASE AU/1499
*ROOKIE AU: 1X TO 2.5X BASE AU/1099/999
ROOKIE AU STATED ODDS 1:39
*ROOKIE JSY AU: X TO X BASE CARD HI
ROOKIE JSY AU STATED ODDS 1:43

2004 Topps Signature Autographs Green

Nm-Mt Ex-Mt

GROUP A STATED ODDS 1:72
GROUP B STATED ODDS 1:12
*BLUE GROUP A AUTOS: .5X TO 1.2X
*BLUE GROUP B AUTOS: .8X TO 2X
BLUE/50 STATED ODDS 1:62
UNPRICED GOLD/1 STATED ODDS 1:2903

❑ ACB Chris Brown A 25.00 7.50
❑ ADD Domanick Davis B 20.00 6.00
❑ AJE John Elway A 200.00 60.00
❑ AJM Justin McCareins B 15.00 4.50
❑ AKB Kevan Barlow B 15.00 4.50
❑ AMV Michael Vick A 100.00 30.00
❑ ASS Steve Smith B 20.00 6.00

2004 Topps Signature Buy Back Autographs

Nm-Mt Ex-Mt

STATED ODDS 1:813
EXCH EXPIRATION: 11/30/2006

❑ BS Bart Starr EXCH 200.00 60.00
❑ DF Dan Fouts EXCH 50.00 15.00
❑ JE1 John Elway 87T 200.00 60.00
❑ JE2 John Elway 88T 200.00 60.00
❑ JM Joe Montana EXCH 250.00 75.00
❑ JN Joe Namath EXCH
❑ RS Roger Staubach EXCH 150.00 45.00

2004 Topps Signature Canton Cuts Autographs

Nm-Mt Ex-Mt

STATED ODDS 1:451
UNPRICED CANTON CUTS PRINT RUN 1

❑ CCAD Art Donovan
❑ CCAR Art Rooney
❑ CCBB Buck Buchanan
❑ CCBBE Bert Bell
❑ CCBL Bobby Layne
❑ CCBN Bronko Nagurski
❑ CCCB Chuck Bednarik
❑ CCCBA Cliff Battles
❑ CCCL Curly Lambeau EXCH
❑ CCCT Bulldog Turner
❑ CCDH Don Hutson
❑ CCDL Dick Lane
❑ CCDW Doak Walker
❑ CCEH Elroy Hirsch
❑ CCEN Ernie Nevers
❑ CCENE Greasy Neale
❑ CCFG Frank Gifford
❑ CCGA George Allen
❑ CCGB George Blanda
❑ CCGH George Halas
❑ CCGM Gino Marchetti
❑ CCGS Gale Sayers
❑ CCHG Red Grange
❑ CCJB Jim Brown
❑ CCJC Jack Christiansen
❑ CCJM Johnny Blood McNally
❑ CCJN Joe Namath
❑ CCJU Johnny Unitas
❑ CCLA Lance Alworth
❑ CCLG Lou Groza
❑ CCMM Marion Motley
❑ CCNVB Norm Van Brocklin
❑ CCOG Otto Graham
❑ CCOJS O.J. Simpson
❑ CCPB Paul Brown
❑ CCPR Pete Rozelle
❑ CCRB Raymond Berry
❑ CCRN Ray Nitschke
❑ CCSB Sammy Baugh
❑ CCSL Sid Luckman
❑ CCSVB Steve Van Buren
❑ CCTF Tom Fears
❑ CCTL Tom Landry
❑ CCTS Tex Schramm
❑ CCVL Vince Lombardi
❑ CCWE Weeb Ewbank
❑ CCWP Walter Payton
❑ CCYAT Y.A. Tittle

1997 Topps Stars Rookie Reprints Autographs

	Nm-Mt	Ex-Mt
COMPLETE SET (10)	400.00	180.00
❑ 1 George Blanda	50.00	22.00
❑ 2 Dick Butkus	60.00	27.00
❑ 3 Len Dawson	50.00	22.00
❑ 4 Jack Ham	50.00	22.00
❑ 5 Sam Huff	50.00	22.00
❑ 6 Deacon Jones	50.00	22.00
❑ 7 Ray Nitschke	125.00	55.00
❑ 8 Gale Sayers	60.00	27.00
❑ 9 Randy White	50.00	22.00
❑ 10 Kellen Winslow	50.00	22.00

1998 Topps Stars Rookie Reprints Autographs

	Nm-Mt	Ex-Mt
❑ 1 Walter Payton	400.00	180.00
❑ 2 Don Maynard	20.00	9.00
❑ 3 Charlie Joiner	30.00	13.50
❑ 4 Fred Biletnikoff	60.00	27.00
❑ 5 Paul Hornung	50.00	22.00
❑ 6 Gale Sayers	60.00	27.00
❑ 7 John Hannah	40.00	18.00
❑ 8 Paul Warfield	40.00	18.00

1999 Topps Stars

	Nm-Mt	Ex-Mt
COMPLETE SET (140)	50.00	22.00
❑ 1 Champ Bailey RC	1.50	.70
❑ 2 Akili Smith RC	1.00	.45
❑ 3 Randy Moss	2.50	1.10
❑ 4 Cade McNown RC	1.00	.45
❑ 5 Torry Holt RC	3.00	1.35
❑ 6 Troy Edwards RC	1.00	.45
❑ 7 David Boston RC	1.25	.55
❑ 8 Edgerrin James RC	5.00	2.20
❑ 9 Daunte Culpepper RC	5.00	2.20
❑ 10 Tim Couch RC	1.25	.55
❑ 11 Ricky Williams RC	2.50	1.10
❑ 12 Fred Taylor	1.00	.45
❑ 13 Barry Sanders	3.00	1.35
❑ 14 Emmitt Smith	2.00	.90
❑ 15 Jerry Rice	2.00	.90
❑ 16 Jake Plummer	.60	.25
❑ 17 Terrell Owens	1.00	.45
❑ 18 Eric Moulds	1.00	.45
❑ 19 Dan Marino	3.00	1.35
❑ 20 Steve McNair	1.00	.45
❑ 21 Donovan McNabb RC	6.00	2.70
❑ 22 Curtis Martin	1.00	.45
❑ 23 Peyton Manning	3.00	1.35
❑ 24 Garrison Hearst	.60	.25
❑ 25 Eddie George	1.00	.45
❑ 26 Antonio Freeman	1.00	.45
❑ 27 Doug Flutie	1.00	.45
❑ 28 Kevin Faulk RC	1.25	.55
❑ 29 Brett Favre	3.00	1.35
❑ 30 Randall Cunningham	1.00	.45
❑ 31 Mark Brunell	1.00	.45
❑ 32 Keyshawn Johnson	1.00	.45
❑ 33 Terrell Davis	1.00	.45
❑ 34 Drew Bledsoe	1.25	.55
❑ 35 Jerome Bettis	1.00	.45
❑ 36 Charlie Batch	1.00	.45
❑ 37 Steve Young	1.25	.55
❑ 38 Jamal Anderson	1.00	.45
❑ 39 Troy Aikman	2.00	.90
❑ 40 John Elway	3.00	1.35
❑ 41 Amos Zereoue RC	1.25	.55
❑ 42 J.J. Stokes	.60	.25
❑ 43 Antowain Smith	1.00	.45
❑ 44 Jimmy Smith	.60	.25
❑ 45 Shaun King RC	1.00	.45
❑ 46 Jevon Kearse RC	2.00	.90
❑ 47 Sedrick Irvin RC	.60	.25
❑ 48 Rod Smith	.60	.25
❑ 49 Kevin Johnson RC	1.25	.55
❑ 50 Joey Galloway	.60	.25
❑ 51 Mike Cloud RC	1.00	.45
❑ 52 D'Wayne Bates RC	1.00	.45
❑ 53 Peerless Price RC	2.00	.90
❑ 54 Herman Moore	.60	.25
❑ 55 Rob Konrad RC	1.00	.45
❑ 56 James Johnson RC	1.00	.45
❑ 57 Cecil Collins RC	.60	.25
❑ 58 Wayne Chrebet	1.00	.45
❑ 59 Cris Carter	1.00	.45
❑ 60 Tim Brown	1.00	.45
❑ 61 Frank Wycheck	.60	.25
❑ 62 Charles Woodson	1.00	.45
❑ 63 Antoine Winfield RC	.60	.25
❑ 64 Ryan Leaf	1.00	.45
❑ 65 Ricky Watters	.60	.25
❑ 66 Yancey Thigpen	.40	.18
❑ 67 Michael Westbrook	.60	.25
❑ 68 Vinny Testaverde	.60	.25
❑ 69 Kordell Stewart	.60	.25
❑ 70 Duce Staley	1.00	.45
❑ 71 Shannon Sharpe	.60	.25
❑ 72 Junior Seau	1.00	.45
❑ 73 Bruce Smith	.60	.25
❑ 74 Frank Sanders	.60	.25
❑ 75 Lawrence Phillips	.60	.25
❑ 76 Robert Smith	1.00	.45
❑ 77 Andre Reed	.60	.25
❑ 78 Darnay Scott	.60	.25
❑ 79 Adrian Murrell	.60	.25
❑ 80 Ricky Proehl	.40	.18
❑ 81 Zach Thomas	1.00	.45
❑ 82 Deion Sanders	1.00	.45
❑ 83 Andre Rison	.60	.25
❑ 84 Jake Reed	.60	.25
❑ 85 Carl Pickens	.60	.25
❑ 86 John Randle	.60	.25
❑ 87 Jerome Pathon	.40	.18
❑ 88 Brock Huard RC	1.25	.55
❑ 89 Elvis Grbac	.60	.25
❑ 90 Curtis Enis	.40	.18
❑ 91 Rickey Dudley	.40	.18
❑ 92 Amani Toomer	.40	.18
❑ 93 Robert Brooks	.40	.18
❑ 94 Derrick Alexander	.60	.25
❑ 95 Reidel Anthony	.40	.18
❑ 96 Mark Chmura	.40	.18
❑ 97 Trent Dilfer	.60	.25
❑ 98 Ebenezer Ekuban RC	.60	.25
❑ 99 Tony Banks	.60	.25
❑ 100 Terry Glenn	1.00	.45
❑ 101 Andre Hastings	.40	.18
❑ 102 Ike Hilliard	.60	.25
❑ 103 Michael Irvin	.60	.25
❑ 104 Napoleon Kaufman	1.00	.45
❑ 105 Dorsey Levens	1.00	.45
❑ 106 Ed McCaffrey	.60	.25
❑ 107 Natrone Means	.60	.25
❑ 108 Skip Hicks	.40	.18
❑ 109 James Jett	.40	.18
❑ 110 Priest Holmes	1.50	.70
❑ 111 Tim Dwight	1.00	.45
❑ 112 Curtis Conway	.60	.25
❑ 113 Jeff Blake	.60	.25
❑ 114 Karim Abdul-Jabbar	.60	.25
❑ 115 Karsten Bailey RC	1.00	.45
❑ 116 Chris Chandler	.60	.25
❑ 117 Germane Crowell	.40	.18
❑ 118 Warrick Dunn	1.00	.45
❑ 119 Bert Emanuel	.60	.25
❑ 120 Jermaine Fazande RC	1.00	.45
❑ 121 Joe Germaine RC	1.00	.45
❑ 122 Tony Gonzalez	1.00	.45
❑ 123 Jacquez Green	.40	.18
❑ 124 Marvin Harrison	1.00	.45
❑ 125 Corey Dillon	1.00	.45
❑ 126 Ben Coates	.40	.18
❑ 127 Chris Claiborne RC	.60	.25
❑ 128 Isaac Bruce	1.00	.45
❑ 129 Mike Alstott	1.00	.45
❑ 130 Andy Katzenmoyer RC	1.00	.45
❑ 131 Jon Kitna	1.00	.45
❑ 132 Keenan McCardell	.60	.25
❑ 133 Johnnie Morton	.60	.25
❑ 134 O.J. McDuffie	.60	.25
❑ 135 Chris McAlister	.60	.25
❑ 136 Terance Mathis	.60	.25
❑ 137 Thurman Thomas	.60	.25
❑ 138 Jermaine Lewis	.60	.25
❑ 139 Rob Moore	.60	.25
❑ 140 Brad Johnson	1.00	.45
❑ P1 Pro Bowl Jersey EXCH	1.00	.45
❑ PP4 Terrell Davis PROMO	2.50	.75

1999 Topps Stars Rookie Reprints Autographs

	Nm-Mt	Ex-Mt
❑ RA1 Roger Staubach	120.00	55.00
❑ RA2 Terry Bradshaw	120.00	55.00

2000 Topps Stars

	Nm-Mt	Ex-Mt
COMPLETE SET (175)	40.00	18.00
❑ 1 Keyshawn Johnson	.75	.35
❑ 2 Marcus Robinson	.75	.35
❑ 3 Antonio Freeman	.75	.35
❑ 4 Jake Plummer	.50	.23
❑ 5 Zach Thomas	.75	.35

❑ 6 Kordell Stewart	.50	.23
❑ 7 Mike Alstott	.75	.35
❑ 8 Fred Taylor	.75	.35
❑ 9 J.J. Stokes	.50	.23
❑ 10 Emmitt Smith	1.50	.70
❑ 11 Derrick Mayes	.50	.23
❑ 12 Stephen Davis	.75	.35
❑ 13 Jamal Anderson	.75	.35
❑ 14 Antowain Smith	.50	.23
❑ 15 Steve Beuerlein	.50	.23
❑ 16 Olandis Gary	.75	.35
❑ 17 Rickey Dudley	.30	.14
❑ 18 Sean Dawkins	.30	.14
❑ 19 Mark Brunell	.75	.35
❑ 20 Brett Favre	2.50	1.10
❑ 21 Jim Harbaugh	.50	.23
❑ 22 Darnay Scott	.50	.23
❑ 23 Herman Moore	.50	.23
❑ 24 Drew Bledsoe	1.00	.45
❑ 25 Priest Holmes	1.00	.45
❑ 26 Albert Connell	.30	.14
❑ 27 Ike Hilliard	.50	.23
❑ 28 Charlie Garner	.50	.23
❑ 29 Jimmy Smith	.50	.23
❑ 30 Randy Moss	1.50	.70
❑ 31 Peerless Price	.75	.35
❑ 32 Terrell Davis	.75	.35
❑ 33 Troy Edwards	.30	.14
❑ 34 Kevin Dyson	.50	.23
❑ 35 O.J. McDuffie	.50	.23
❑ 36 Troy Aikman	1.50	.70
❑ 37 Frank Sanders	.50	.23
❑ 38 Bobby Engram	.30	.14
❑ 39 Tyrone Wheatley	.50	.23
❑ 40 Ricky Williams	.75	.35
❑ 41 Warrick Dunn	.75	.35
❑ 42 Elvis Grbac	.50	.23
❑ 43 Dorsey Levens	.50	.23
❑ 44 Curtis Conway	.50	.23
❑ 45 Johnnie Morton	.50	.23
❑ 46 Ed McCaffrey	.75	.35
❑ 47 Kevin Johnson	.75	.35
❑ 48 Muhsin Muhammad	.50	.23
❑ 49 Terance Mathis	.50	.23
❑ 50 Eddie George	.75	.35
❑ 51 Daunte Culpepper	1.00	.45
❑ 52 Jeff Graham	.30	.14
❑ 53 Jon Kitna	.75	.35
❑ 54 Marvin Harrison	.75	.35
❑ 55 Steve McNair	.75	.35
❑ 56 Jeff Blake	.50	.23
❑ 57 Carl Pickens	.50	.23
❑ 58 Germane Crowell	.30	.14
❑ 59 Rob Moore	.50	.23
❑ 60 Marshall Faulk	1.00	.45
❑ 61 Jerome Bettis	.75	.35
❑ 62 Michael Westbrook	.50	.23
❑ 63 Keenan McCardell	.50	.23
❑ 64 Shannon Sharpe	.50	.23
❑ 65 Rod Smith	.50	.23
❑ 66 Curtis Enis	.30	.14
❑ 67 Vinny Testaverde	.50	.23
❑ 68 Freddie Jones	.30	.14
❑ 69 Jevon Kearse	.75	.35
❑ 70 Jerry Rice	1.50	.70
❑ 71 Champ Bailey	.50	.23
❑ 72 Peyton Manning	2.00	.90
❑ 73 Rich Gannon	.75	.35
❑ 74 Cris Carter	.75	.35
❑ 75 Doug Flutie	.75	.35
❑ 76 Corey Dillon	.75	.35
❑ 77 Tony Gonzalez	.50	.23
❑ 78 Shaun King	.30	.14
❑ 79 Terrell Owens	.75	.35
❑ 80 Dan Marino	2.50	1.10
❑ 81 Curtis Martin	.75	.35
❑ 82 Patrick Jeffers	.75	.35
❑ 83 Brian Griese	.75	.35
❑ 84 Akili Smith	.30	.14
❑ 85 Charlie Batch	.75	.35
❑ 86 Tim Dwight	.75	.35
❑ 87 Robert Smith	.75	.35
❑ 88 Duce Staley	.75	.35
❑ 89 Jacquez Green	.30	.14
❑ 90 Steve Young	1.00	.45
❑ 91 Tony Martin	.50	.23
❑ 92 Az-Zahir Hakim	.50	.23
❑ 93 Tim Brown	.75	.35
❑ 94 Donovan McNabb	1.25	.55
❑ 95 Chris Chandler	.50	.23
❑ 96 Tim Couch	.50	.23
❑ 97 Tim Biakabutuka	.50	.23
❑ 98 Terry Glenn	.50	.23
❑ 99 Wayne Chrebet	.50	.23
❑ 100 Kurt Warner	1.50	.70
❑ 101 Qadry Ismail	.50	.23
❑ 102 Torry Holt	.75	.35
❑ 103 Ray Lucas	.50	.23
❑ 104 James Johnson	.30	.14
❑ 105 Errict Rhett	.50	.23
❑ 106 James Stewart	.50	.23
❑ 107 Tony Banks	.50	.23
❑ 108 Amani Toomer	.30	.14
❑ 109 Isaac Bruce	.75	.35
❑ 110 Brad Johnson	.75	.35
❑ 111 Kerry Collins	.50	.23
❑ 112 Eric Moulds	.75	.35
❑ 113 Rocket Ismail	.50	.23
❑ 114 Keith Poole	.30	.14
❑ 115 Rob Johnson	.50	.23
❑ 116 Deion Sanders	.75	.35
❑ 117 Ricky Watters	.50	.23
❑ 118 Cade McNown	.30	.14
❑ 119 Joey Galloway	.50	.23
❑ 120 Edgerrin James	1.25	.55
❑ 121 Franco Harris	1.00	.45
❑ 122 Steve Largent	1.00	.45
❑ 123 Joe Montana	4.00	1.80
❑ 124 Deacon Jones	.75	.35
❑ 125 Ronnie Lott	.75	.35
❑ 126 Mark Brunell HH	.50	.23
❑ 127 Rich Gannon HH	.50	.23
❑ 128 Tony Gonzalez HH	.30	.14
❑ 129 Randy Moss HH	1.00	.45
❑ 130 Kurt Warner HH	1.00	.45
❑ 131 Marvin Harrison HH	.50	.23
❑ 132 Jimmy Smith HH	.30	.14
❑ 133 Edgerrin James HH	1.25	.55
❑ 134 Corey Dillon HH	.50	.23
❑ 135 Peyton Manning HH	1.25	.55
❑ 136 Brad Johnson HH	.50	.23
❑ 137 Steve Beuerlein HH	.30	.14
❑ 138 Emmitt Smith HH	1.00	.45
❑ 139 Marshall Faulk HH	.75	.35
❑ 140 Mike Alstott HH	.50	.23
❑ 141 Deacon Jones HH	.50	.23
❑ 142 Joe Montana HH	3.00	1.35
❑ 143 Franco Harris HH	.75	.35
❑ 144 Steve Largent HH	.75	.35
❑ 145 Ronnie Lott HH	.50	.23
❑ 146 Chad Pennington HF	2.50	1.10
❑ 147 Peter Warrick HF	.75	.35
❑ 148 Plaxico Burress HF	1.25	.55
❑ 149 Thomas Jones HF	1.00	.45
❑ 150 Jamal Lewis HF	1.50	.70
❑ 151 Travis Taylor RC	.75	.35
❑ 152 Shaun Alexander RC	2.00	.90
❑ 153 Dez White RC	.75	.35
❑ 154 Thomas Jones RC	1.25	.55
❑ 155 Curtis Keaton RC	.50	.23
❑ 156 Courtney Brown RC	.75	.35
❑ 157 Danny Farmer RC	.60	.25
❑ 158 Trung Canidate RC	.60	.25
❑ 159 R.Jay Soward RC	.60	.25
❑ 160 Jamal Lewis RC	2.00	.90
❑ 161 Todd Pinkston RC	.75	.35
❑ 162 Reuben Droughns RC	1.00	.45
❑ 163 Ron Dugans RC	.50	.23
❑ 164 Ron Dayne RC	.75	.35
❑ 165 Laveranues Coles RC	1.00	.45
❑ 166 Sylvester Morris RC	.60	.25
❑ 167 Peter Warrick RC	.75	.35
❑ 168 Dennis Northcutt RC	.75	.35
❑ 169 Tee Martin RC	.75	.35
❑ 170 Brian Urlacher RC	4.00	1.80
❑ 171 Chris Redman RC	.60	.25
❑ 172 Chad Pennington RC	2.50	1.10
❑ 173 J.R. Redmond RC	.60	.25
❑ 174 Travis Prentice RC	.60	.25
❑ 175 Plaxico Burress RC	1.50	.70

2000 Topps Stars Autographs

	Nm-Mt	Ex-Mt
❑ CC Cris Carter	40.00	18.00
❑ CR Chris Redman	20.00	9.00
❑ DG Darrell Green	40.00	18.00
❑ DJ Deacon Jones	25.00	11.00
❑ EJ Edgerrin James	50.00	22.00
❑ JM Joe Montana	150.00	70.00
❑ KC Kevin Carter	20.00	9.00
❑ KW Kurt Warner	50.00	22.00
❑ RD Ron Dayne	20.00	9.00
❑ RL Ronnie Lott	40.00	18.00
❑ SL Steve Largent	50.00	22.00

2003 Topps Total

	MINT	NRMT
COMPLETE SET (550)	80.00	36.00
❑ 1 Rich Gannon	.50	.23
❑ 2 Travis Henry	.50	.23
❑ 3 Brian Finneran	.30	.14
❑ 4 Ed Hartwell	.30	.14
❑ 5 Az-Zahir Hakim	.30	.14
❑ 6 Rodney Peete	.30	.14
❑ 7 David Terrell	.50	.23
❑ 8 Matt Schobel	.30	.14
❑ 9 Andre Davis	.30	.14
❑ 10 Dexter Coakley	.30	.14
❑ 11 Rod Smith	.50	.23
❑ 12 Damerien McCants	.30	.14
❑ 13 Robert Ferguson	.30	.14
❑ 14 Kailee Wong	.30	.14
❑ 15 James Mungro	.30	.14
❑ 16 Fred Taylor	.75	.35
❑ 17 Tony Gonzalez	.50	.23
❑ 18 Randall Godfrey	.30	.14
❑ 19 Robert Thomas	.30	.14
❑ 20 Rohan Davey	.50	.23
❑ 21 Terrell Owens	.75	.35
❑ 22 Ron Dayne	.30	.14
❑ 23 Charlie Batch	.30	.14
❑ 24 Brian Westbrook	.50	.23
❑ 25 Plaxico Burress	.50	.23
❑ 26 Reche Caldwell	.30	.14
❑ 27 Fred Beasley	.30	.14
❑ 28 Anthony Simmons	.30	.14
❑ 29 Rod Woodson	.50	.23
❑ 30 Derrick Brooks	.50	.23
❑ 31 Shaun Ellis	.30	.14
❑ 32 Ladell Betts	.50	.23

❑ 33 Russell Davis	.30	.14
❑ 34 Warrick Dunn	.50	.23
❑ 35 Jeremy Shockey	1.25	.55
❑ 36 Alex Van Pelt	.30	.14
❑ 37 Todd Bouman	.30	.14
❑ 38 Kelly Campbell	.30	.14
❑ 39 Justin Smith	.30	.14
❑ 40 Jamel White	.30	.14
❑ 41 La'Roi Glover	.30	.14
❑ 42 Ian Gold	.30	.14
❑ 43 Robert Porcher	.30	.14
❑ 44 Jermaine Lewis	.30	.14
❑ 45 Marvin Harrison	.75	.35
❑ 46 Darren Sharper	.30	.14
❑ 47 Jamie Sharper	.30	.14
❑ 48 Tony Richardson	.30	.14
❑ 49 Moe Williams	.30	.14
❑ 50 Ricky Williams	.75	.35
❑ 51 Ty Law	.50	.23
❑ 52 Donte Stallworth	.75	.35
❑ 53 Shannon Sharpe	.50	.23
❑ 54 Santana Moss	.50	.23
❑ 55 Charlie Garner	.50	.23
❑ 56 Brian Dawkins	.30	.14
❑ 57 Dan Campbell	.30	.14
❑ 58 William Green	.50	.23
❑ 59 Ron Dugans	.30	.14
❑ 60 Darrell Jackson	.50	.23
❑ 61 Marc Bulger	.75	.35
❑ 62 Joe Jurevicius	.30	.14
❑ 63 Erron Kinney	.30	.14
❑ 64 Champ Bailey	.50	.23
❑ 65 Peerless Price	.50	.23
❑ 66 Gary Baxter	.30	.14
❑ 67 Chris Redman	.30	.14
❑ 68 London Fletcher	.30	.14
❑ 69 Dee Brown	.30	.14
❑ 70 Anthony Thomas	.75	.35
❑ 71 Jake Delhomme	.75	.35
❑ 72 Dorsey Levens	.30	.14
❑ 73 Roy Williams	.75	.35
❑ 74 Ashley Lelie	.75	.35
❑ 75 Joey Harrington	1.25	.55
❑ 76 William Henderson	.30	.14
❑ 77 Corey Bradford	.30	.14
❑ 78 Reggie Wayne	.50	.23
❑ 79 Kyle Brady	.30	.14
❑ 80 Trent Green	.50	.23
❑ 81 Bill Romanowski	.30	.14
❑ 82 Chike Okeafor RC	.75	.35
❑ 83 David Patten	.30	.14
❑ 84 Terrelle Smith	.30	.14
❑ 85 Kerry Collins	.50	.23
❑ 86 Derrick Mason	.50	.23
❑ 87 Trung Canidate	.50	.23
❑ 88 A.J. Feeley	.50	.23
❑ 89 Jason Gildon	.30	.14
❑ 90 Doug Flutie	.75	.35
❑ 91 Tai Streets	.30	.14
❑ 92 Keith Newman	.30	.14
❑ 93 Adam Archuleta	.30	.14
❑ 94 Simeon Rice	.50	.23
❑ 95 Eddie George	.50	.23
❑ 96 Frank Sanders	.30	.14
❑ 97 Freddie Jones	.30	.14
❑ 98 Charles Johnson	.30	.14
❑ 99 Keith Traylor	.30	.14
❑ 100 Drew Bledsoe	.75	.35
❑ 101 Muhsin Muhammad	.50	.23
❑ 102 Marques Anderson	.30	.14
❑ 103 Donald Hayes	.30	.14
❑ 104 Quincy Morgan	.50	.23
❑ 105 Chad Hutchinson	.50	.23
❑ 106 Mike Anderson	.50	.23
❑ 107 Randy McMichael	.50	.23
❑ 108 Vonnie Holliday	.30	.14
❑ 109 Marcus Coleman	.30	.14
❑ 110 Edgerrin James	.75	.35
❑ 111 Michael Lewis	.30	.14
❑ 112 Wayne Chrebet	.50	.23
❑ 113 Antwaan Randle El	.75	.35
❑ 114 Byron Chamberlain	.30	.14
❑ 115 Jeff Garcia	.75	.35
❑ 116 Kim Herring	.30	.14
❑ 117 Kenny Holmes	.30	.14
❑ 118 John Lynch	.50	.23
❑ 119 Doug Jolley	.30	.14
❑ 120 Duce Staley	.50	.23
❑ 121 Kordell Stewart	.50	.23
❑ 122 Stephen Alexander	.30	.14
❑ 123 Andre Carter	.30	.14
❑ 124 Bobby Engram	.30	.14
❑ 125 Marshall Faulk	.75	.35
❑ 126 Peter Sirmon RC	.50	.23
❑ 127 Alge Crumpler	.50	.23
❑ 128 Kenny Watson	.30	.14
❑ 129 Duane Starks	.30	.14
❑ 130 Jeff Blake	.30	.14
❑ 131 Todd Heap	.50	.23
❑ 132 Bobby Shaw	.30	.14
❑ 133 Ricky Proehl	.30	.14
❑ 134 John Abraham	.30	.14
❑ 135 T.J. Houshmandzadeh	.30	.14
❑ 136 Brian Urlacher	1.25	.55
❑ 137 Darren Woodson	.30	.14
❑ 138 Steve Beuerlein	.30	.14
❑ 139 Cory Schlesinger	.30	.14
❑ 140 Ahman Green	.75	.35
❑ 141 Jabar Gaffney	.50	.23
❑ 142 Eddie Drummond	.30	.14
❑ 143 Stacey Mack	.30	.14
❑ 144 Johnnie Morton	.50	.23
❑ 145 Chris Chambers	.75	.35
❑ 146 Jim Kleinsasser	.30	.14
❑ 147 Tebucky Jones	.30	.14
❑ 148 Marcus Pollard	.30	.14
❑ 149 Tony Brackens	.30	.14
❑ 150 Chad Pennington	1.00	.45
❑ 151 Kevin Faulk	.30	.14
❑ 152 Michael Lewis	.30	.14
❑ 153 Mark Bruener	.30	.14
❑ 154 Tim Dwight	.50	.23
❑ 155 Jerry Rice	1.50	.70
❑ 156 Trent Dilfer	.50	.23
❑ 157 Jon Ritchie	.30	.14
❑ 158 Michael Pittman	.30	.14
❑ 159 Lamar Gordon	.30	.14
❑ 160 Rod Gardner	.50	.23
❑ 161 Ken Dilger	.30	.14
❑ 162 Doug Johnson	.30	.14
❑ 163 Peter Boulware	.30	.14
❑ 164 Jevon Kearse	.50	.23
❑ 165 Julius Peppers	.75	.35
❑ 166 Chris Chandler	.30	.14
❑ 167 Lorenzo Neal	.30	.14
❑ 168 Kevin Johnson	.50	.23
❑ 169 Kevin Hardy	.30	.14
❑ 170 KaRon Coleman	.30	.14
❑ 171 James Stewart	.50	.23
❑ 172 Tony Fisher	.30	.14
❑ 173 Billy Miller	.30	.14
❑ 174 Phillip Crosby	.30	.14
❑ 175 Priest Holmes	1.00	.45
❑ 176 Elvis Joseph	.30	.14
❑ 177 Bryan Gilmore	.30	.14
❑ 178 D'Wayne Bates	.30	.14
❑ 179 Quincy Carter	.50	.23
❑ 180 Joe Horn	.50	.23
❑ 181 Anthony Henry	.30	.14
❑ 182 Anthony Becht	.30	.14
❑ 183 Mike Peterson	.30	.14
❑ 184 James Thrash	.30	.14
❑ 185 Jerome Bettis	.75	.35
❑ 186 Marcellus Wiley	.30	.14
❑ 187 Tim Rattay	.50	.23
❑ 188 Maurice Morris	.30	.14
❑ 189 Jason Taylor	.30	.14
❑ 190 Keyshawn Johnson	.75	.35
❑ 191 John Simon	.30	.14
❑ 192 Fred Smoot	.30	.14
❑ 193 Wendell Bryant	.30	.14
❑ 194 Brandon Stokley	.50	.23
❑ 195 Kurt Warner	.75	.35
❑ 196 Steve Smith	.30	.14
❑ 197 Dez White	.30	.14
❑ 198 Jim Miller	.30	.14
❑ 199 Robert Griffith	.30	.14
❑ 200 Michael Vick	2.00	.90
❑ 201 Antonio Bryant	.50	.23
❑ 202 Laveranues Coles	.50	.23
❑ 203 Kalimba Edwards	.30	.14
❑ 204 Bubba Franks	.50	.23
❑ 205 David Carr	1.25	.55
❑ 206 Dwight Freeney	.30	.14
❑ 207 Eric Johnson	.50	.23
❑ 208 Reggie Tongue	.30	.14
❑ 209 Cam Cleeland	.30	.14
❑ 210 Michael Bennett	.50	.23
❑ 211 Antowain Smith	.50	.23
❑ 212 Warren Sapp	.50	.23
❑ 213 Ike Hilliard	.30	.14
❑ 214 Olandis Gary	.50	.23
❑ 215 Tim Brown	.75	.35
❑ 216 Kevin Dyson	.50	.23
❑ 217 Eddie Kennison	.30	.14
❑ 218 Junior Seau	.75	.35
❑ 219 Donnie Edwards	.30	.14
❑ 220 Shaun Alexander	.75	.35
❑ 221 Terrence Wilkins	.30	.14
❑ 222 Garrison Hearst	.50	.23
❑ 223 Keith Bulluck	.30	.14
❑ 224 Zeron Flemister	.30	.14
❑ 225 Jake Plummer	.50	.23
❑ 226 Chad Johnson	.50	.23
❑ 227 Travis Taylor	.50	.23
❑ 228 Josh Reed	.50	.23
❑ 229 James Farrior	.30	.14
❑ 230 Marty Booker	.50	.23
❑ 231 Todd Pinkston	.50	.23
❑ 232 Dennis Northcutt	.50	.23
❑ 233 Troy Hambrick	.30	.14
❑ 234 Roland Williams	.30	.14
❑ 235 Bill Schroeder	.50	.23
❑ 236 Javon Walker	.50	.23
❑ 237 Kevin Swayne	.30	.14
❑ 238 Dominic Rhodes	.50	.23
❑ 239 David Garrard	.30	.14
❑ 240 Mike Maslowski RC	.50	.23
❑ 241 Travis Minor	.30	.14
❑ 242 Terry Glenn	.30	.14
❑ 243 Deion Branch	.75	.35
❑ 244 Adrian Peterson	.30	.14
❑ 245 Tiki Barber	.50	.23
❑ 246 Ray Lewis	.75	.35
❑ 247 Marques Tuiasosopo	.50	.23
❑ 248 Chad Lewis	.30	.14
❑ 249 Takeo Spikes	.30	.14
❑ 250 LaDainian Tomlinson	.75	.35
❑ 251 Stephen Davis	.50	.23
❑ 252 Koren Robinson	.50	.23
❑ 253 Daylon McCutcheon	.30	.14
❑ 254 Rob Johnson	.50	.23
❑ 255 Donovan McNabb	1.00	.45
❑ 256 Derrius Thompson	.30	.14
❑ 257 Marcel Shipp	.50	.23
❑ 258 Keith Brooking	.30	.14
❑ 259 Chris McAlister	.30	.14
❑ 260 Eric Moulds	.50	.23
❑ 261 Amos Zereoue	.50	.23
❑ 262 Drew Brees	.75	.35
❑ 263 Jon Kitna	.50	.23
❑ 264 Brad Johnson	.50	.23
❑ 265 Emmitt Smith	2.00	.90
❑ 266 Trevor Pryce	.30	.14
❑ 267 Mike McMahon	.50	.23
❑ 268 Patrick Ramsey	.75	.35
❑ 269 Jonathan Wells	.30	.14
❑ 270 Mark Brunell	.50	.23
❑ 271 Marc Boerigter	.50	.23
❑ 272 Rob Konrad	.30	.14
❑ 273 Derrick Alexander	.30	.14
❑ 274 Joey Galloway	.50	.23
❑ 275 Peyton Manning	1.25	.55
❑ 276 Najeh Davenport	.30	.14
❑ 277 Jesse Palmer	.30	.14
❑ 278 LaMont Jordan	.50	.23
❑ 279 Ernie Conwell	.30	.14
❑ 280 Hines Ward	.75	.35
❑ 281 Freddie Mitchell	.50	.23
❑ 282 Curtis Conway	.30	.14
❑ 283 Cedrick Wilson	.30	.14
❑ 284 Troy Brown	.50	.23
❑ 285 Torry Holt	.75	.35
❑ 286 Mike Alstott	.75	.35
❑ 287 Frank Wycheck	.30	.14

❑ 288 Jeremiah Trotter .30 .14
❑ 289 Tyrone Wheatley .30 .14
❑ 290 David Boston .50 .23
❑ 291 Jay Fiedler .50 .23
❑ 292 Troy Walters .30 .14
❑ 293 Warrick Holdman .30 .14
❑ 294 Peter Warrick .50 .23
❑ 295 Tim Couch .30 .14
❑ 296 Aaron Glenn .30 .14
❑ 297 Deuce McAllister .75 .35
❑ 298 Michael Strahan .50 .23
❑ 299 Tom Brady 1.25 .55
❑ 300 Brett Favre 2.00 .90
❑ 301 Isaac Bruce .75 .35
❑ 302 Jimmy Smith .50 .23
❑ 303 Dante Hall .75 .35
❑ 304 James McKnight .30 .14
❑ 305 Daunte Culpepper .75 .35
❑ 306 Lawyer Milloy .50 .23
❑ 307 Jerome Pathon .30 .14
❑ 308 Steve McNair .75 .35
❑ 309 Vinny Testaverde .50 .23
❑ 310 Tommy Maddox .75 .35
❑ 311 Amani Toomer .50 .23
❑ 312 Aaron Brooks .75 .35
❑ 313 Gus Frerotte .30 .14
❑ 314 Kevan Barlow .50 .23
❑ 315 Matt Hasselbeck .50 .23
❑ 316 Clinton Portis 1.25 .55
❑ 317 Keenan McCardell .30 .14
❑ 318 Zach Thomas .75 .35
❑ 319 Curtis Martin .75 .35
❑ 320 Jamal Lewis .75 .35
❑ 321 T.J. Duckett .50 .23
❑ 322 Jerry Porter .50 .23
❑ 323 Randy Moss 1.25 .55
❑ 324 Rosevelt Colvin .30 .14
❑ 325 Corey Dillon .50 .23
❑ 326 Kelly Holcomb .50 .23
❑ 327 Josh McCown .50 .23
❑ 328 Ed McCaffrey .75 .35
❑ 329 Mikhael Ricks .30 .14
❑ 330 Donald Driver .50 .23
❑ 331 James Darling .30 .14
Ray Thompson
Ronald McKinnon
❑ 332 Cory Hall .30 .14
Keion Carpenter
Ray Buchanon
❑ 333 Adalius Thomas .50 .23
Anthony Weaver
Kelly Gregg RC
❑ 334 Antoine Winfield .30 .14
Coy Wire
Nate Clements
❑ 335 Dan Morgan .50 .23
Mark Fields
Will Witherspoon
❑ 336 Alex Brown .50 .23
Bryan Robinson RC
Phillip Daniels
❑ 337 Carl Powell RC .50 .23
John Thornton
Tony Williams RC
❑ 338 Ben Taylor RC .50 .23
Earl Little
Kevin Bentley
❑ 339 Ebenezer Ekuban .30 .14
Greg Ellis
Michael Myers
❑ 340 Daryl Gardener .75 .35
Lional Dalton RC
Bert Berry RC
❑ 341 Barrett Green .50 .23
Donte Curry RC
Earl Holmes
❑ 342 Cletidus Hunt RC .75 .35
Kabeer Gbaja-Biamila
Rod Walker RC
❑ 343 Gary Walker .30 .14
Jerry Deloach RC
Seth Payne
❑ 344 Chad Bratzke .30 .14
Marcus Washington
Rob Morris
❑ 345 John Henderson .50 .23
Marco Coleman
Marcus Stroud
❑ 346 Eric Hicks .50 .23
John Browning RC
Ryan Sims
❑ 347 Adewale Ogunleye RC 1.25 .55
Larry Chester RC
Tim Bowens
❑ 348 Fred Robbins .30 .14
Kenny Mixon
Lance Johnstone
❑ 349 Roman Phifer .75 .35
Ted Johnson
Tedy Bruschi
❑ 350 Charles Grant .50 .23
Martin Chase RC
Darren Howard
❑ 351 Brandon Short .50 .23
Dhani Jones RC
Mike Barrow
❑ 352 Marvin Jones .30 .14
Mo Lewis
Sam Cowart
❑ 353 Eric Barton .30 .14
John Parrella
Napoleon Harris
❑ 354 Brandon Whiting .30 .14
Corey Simon
Darwin Walker
❑ 355 Aaron Smith RC .75 .35
Casey Hampton
Kimo von Oelhoffen
❑ 356 Jamal William RCs .50 .23
Jason Fisk
Raylee Johnson
❑ 357 Derek Smith .30 .14
Jeff Ulbrich
Julian Peterson
❑ 358 Antonio Cochran RC .50 .23
Chad Eaton
John Randle
❑ 359 Damione Lewis .30 .14
Grant Wistrom
Leonard Little
❑ 360 Dwayne Rudd .30 .14
Greg Spires
Shelton Quarles
❑ 361 Albert Haynesworth .30 .14
Kevin Carter
Robaire Smith
❑ 362 Bruce Smith .30 .14
Jessie Armstead
Regan Upshaw
❑ 363 Adrian Wilson .75 .35
Dexter Jackson RC
❑ 364 Fred Wakefield .30 .14
Kyle Vanden
❑ 365 Kevin Kasper .30 .14
Jason McAddley
❑ 366 Brady Smith .30 .14
Patrick Kerney
❑ 367 Martay Jenkins .30 .14
Trevor Gaylor
❑ 368 Chris Draft .30 .14
Matt Stewart
❑ 369 Javin Hunter .30 .14
Ron Johnson
❑ 370 Corey Fuller .50 .23
Ed Reed
❑ 371 Aaron Schobel .50 .23
Jeff Posey RC
❑ 372 Pat Williams .30 .14
Sam Adams
❑ 373 Deon Grant .30 .14
Mike Minter
❑ 374 Brentson Buckner .30 .14
Kris Jenkins
❑ 375 Reggie Howard RC .50 .23
Terry Cousin RC
❑ 376 Mike Brown .50 .23
Mike Green
❑ 377 Jerry Azumah .30 .14
R.W. McQuarters
❑ 378 Brian Simmons .30 .14
Steve Foley
❑ 379 Artrell Hawkins .30 .14
Jeff Burris
❑ 380 JoJuan Armour RC .30 .14
Marquand Manuel
❑ 381 Gerard Warren .30 .14
Orpheus Roye
❑ 382 Courtney Brown .30 .14
Kenard Lang
❑ 383 Derek Ross .30 .14
Mario Edwards
❑ 384 Al Singleton RC .50 .23
Dat Nguyen
❑ 385 Al Wilson .30 .14
John Mobley
❑ 386 Deltha O'Neal .30 .14
Kenoy Kennedy
❑ 387 Luther Elliss .30 .14
Shaun Rogers
❑ 388 Chris Cash .30 .14
Dre' Bly
❑ 389 Brian Walker .30 .14
Corey Harris
❑ 390 Hannibal Navies RC .30 .14
Na'il Diggs
❑ 391 Al Harris .30 .14
Mike McKenzie
❑ 392 Charlie Clemons .30 .14
Jay Foreman
❑ 393 Eric Brown .30 .14
Matt Stevens
❑ 394 Brad Scioli .30 .14
Larry Tripplett
❑ 395 David Macklin .30 .14
Walt Harris
❑ 396 Akin Ayodele .30 .14
Hugh Douglas
❑ 397 Fernando Bryant .30 .14
Jason Craft RC
❑ 398 Donovin Darius .30 .14
Marlon McCree
❑ 399 Scott Fujita .50 .23
Shawn Barber
❑ 400 Eric Warfield RC .75 .35
William Bartee
❑ 401 Greg Wesley .30 .14
Jerome Woods
❑ 402 Patrick Surtain .30 .14
Sam Madison
❑ 403 Brock Marion .30 .14
Sammy Knight
❑ 404 Greg Biekert .30 .14
Henri Crockett
❑ 405 Chris Claiborne .30 .14
Chris Hovan
❑ 406 Corey Chavous .30 .14
Ken Irvin
❑ 407 Christian Fauria .30 .14
Daniel Graham
❑ 408 Otis Smith .30 .14
Rodney Harrison
❑ 409 Anthony Pleasant .30 .14
Richard Seymour
❑ 410 Darrin Smith .30 .14
Sedrick Hodge
❑ 411 Ashley Ambrose .30 .14
Dale Carter
❑ 412 Mel Mitchell .30 .14
Derrick Rodgers
❑ 413 Will Allen .30 .14
William Peterson
❑ 414 Cornelius Griffin .30 .14
Keith Hamilton
❑ 415 Omar Stoutmire .30 .14
Shaun Williams
❑ 416 Aaron Beasley .30 .14
Donnie Abraham
❑ 417 Jon McGraw .30 .14
Sam Garnes
❑ 418 Charles Woodson .50 .23
Phillip Buchanon
❑ 419 Tony Bryant .30 .14
Trace Armstrong
❑ 420 Bobby Taylor .30 .14
Troy Vincent

❑	421 Carlos Emmons	.30	.14
	Nate Wayne		
❑	422 Brent Alexander	.30	.14
	Chris Hope		
❑	423 Joey Porter	.50	.23
	Kendrell Bell		
❑	424 Chad Scott	.30	.14
	Dewayne Washington		
❑	425 Ben Leber	.30	.14
	Ryan McNeil		
❑	426 Quentin Jammer	.30	.14
	Tay Cody		
❑	427 Ahmed Plummer	.30	.14
	Jason Webster		
❑	428 Tony Parrish	.30	.14
	Zack Bronson		
❑	429 Itula Mili	.30	.14
	Jerramy Stevens		
❑	430 Ken Lucas	.30	.14
	Shawn Springs		
❑	431 Chad Brown	.30	.14
	Orlando Huff		
❑	432 Jamie Duncan	.30	.14
	Tommy Polley		
❑	433 Aeneas Williams	.30	.14
	Travis Fisher		
❑	434 Brian Kelly	.30	.14
	Ronde Barber		
❑	435 Aaron Stecker	.30	.14
	Karl Williams		
❑	436 Drew Bennett	.50	.23
	Justin McCareins		
❑	437 Lance Schulters	.30	.14
	Tank Williams		
❑	438 Andre Dyson	.30	.14
	Samari Rolle		
❑	439 Ifeanyi Ohalete	.30	.14
	Matt Bowen		
❑	440 Brandon Noble	.30	.14
	Dan Wilkinson		
❑	441 Charles Rogers RC	1.50	.70
❑	442 Jimmy Kennedy RC	1.25	.55
❑	443 Kelley Washington RC	1.25	.55
❑	444 Trent Smith RC	1.00	.45
❑	445 Rashean Mathis RC	1.00	.45
❑	446 Brian St.Pierre RC	1.25	.55
❑	447 Bethel Johnson RC	2.00	.90
❑	448 Alonzo Jackson RC	1.00	.45
❑	449 Arnaz Battle RC	1.25	.55
❑	450 Carson Palmer RC	4.00	1.80
❑	451 Michael Haynes RC	1.25	.55
❑	452 LaBrandon Toefield RC	1.25	.55
❑	453 Earnest Graham RC	1.00	.45
❑	454 Walter Young RC	.60	.25
❑	455 Terry Pierce RC	1.00	.45
❑	456 Talman Gardner RC	1.25	.55
❑	457 J.T. Wall RC	.60	.25
❑	458 DeWayne Robertson RC	1.25	.55
❑	459 Bradie James RC	1.25	.55
❑	460 Andre Johnson RC	3.00	1.35
❑	461 Bobby Wade RC	1.25	.55
❑	462 Chris Davis RC	1.00	.45
❑	463 Kliff Kingsbury RC	1.00	.45
❑	464 Osi Umenyiora RC	1.25	.55
❑	465 Domanick Davis RC	2.50	1.10
❑	466 Sam Aiken RC	1.00	.45
❑	467 Ty Warren RC	1.25	.55
❑	468 Terence Newman RC	2.50	1.10
❑	469 Zuriel Smith RC	.60	.25
❑	470 Willis Mcgahee RC	3.00	1.35
❑	471 David Kircus RC	1.00	.45
❑	472 Billy McMullen RC	1.00	.45
❑	473 Antwoine Sanders RC	.60	.25
❑	474 Adrian Madise RC	1.00	.45
❑	475 Byron Leftwich RC	5.00	2.20
❑	476 Justin Gage RC	1.25	.55
❑	477 Jason Witten RC	2.00	.90
❑	478 Lee Suggs RC	2.50	1.10
❑	479 Kareem Kelly RC	1.00	.45
❑	480 Rex Grossman RC	3.00	1.35
❑	481 Nate Burleson RC	2.00	.90
❑	482 Chris Brown RC	2.50	1.10
❑	483 Julian Battle RC	1.00	.45
❑	484 Carl Ford RC	.60	.25
❑	485 Angelo Crowell RC	1.00	.45
❑	486 Bennie Joppru RC	1.25	.55
❑	487 Aaron Walker RC	1.00	.45
❑	488 Brandon Green RC	1.00	.45
❑	489 L.J. Smith RC	1.25	.55
❑	490 Ken Dorsey RC	2.00	.90
❑	491 Eugene Wilson RC	1.00	.45
❑	492 Chaun Thompson RC	.60	.25
❑	493 Kevin Curtis RC	1.25	.55
❑	494 Marcus Trufant RC	1.25	.55
❑	495 Andrew Williams RC	1.00	.45
❑	496 Visanthe Shiancoe RC	1.00	.45
❑	497 Terrence Edwards RC	1.00	.45
❑	498 Rien Long RC	1.00	.45
❑	499 Nick Barnett RC	2.00	.90
❑	500 Larry Johnson RC	2.50	1.10
❑	501 Ken Hamlin RC	1.25	.55
❑	502 Johnathan Sullivan RC	1.00	.45
❑	503 Jeremi Johnson RC	1.00	.45
❑	504 William Joseph RC	1.25	.55
❑	505 Boss Bailey RC	1.50	.70
❑	506 Anquan Boldin RC	3.00	1.35
❑	507 Dave Ragone RC	1.25	.55
❑	508 DeJuan Groce RC	1.25	.55
❑	509 Rashad Moore RC	1.00	.45
❑	510 Mike Doss RC	1.25	.55
❑	511 Kenny Peterson RC	1.00	.45
❑	512 Justin Griffith RC	1.00	.45
❑	513 Jordan Gross RC	1.00	.45
❑	514 Terrence Holt RC	1.00	.45
❑	515 Seneca Wallace RC	1.25	.55
❑	516 Ovie Mughelli RC	.60	.25
❑	517 Jerome McDougle RC	1.25	.55
❑	518 Kevin Williams RC	1.25	.55
❑	519 Musa Smith RC	1.25	.55
❑	520 Teyo Johnson RC	1.25	.55
❑	521 Victor Hobson RC	1.25	.55
❑	522 Cory Redding RC	1.00	.45
❑	523 Cecil Sapp RC	1.00	.45
❑	524 Brandon Lloyd RC	1.50	.70
❑	525 Chris Simms RC	2.50	1.10
❑	526 Artose Pinner RC	1.25	.55
❑	527 DeWayne White RC	1.00	.45
❑	528 Doug Gabriel RC	1.25	.55
❑	529 Calvin Pace RC	1.00	.45
❑	530 Onterrio Smith RC	1.50	.70
❑	531 Terrell Suggs RC	2.00	.90
❑	532 Ronald Bellamy RC	1.00	.45
❑	533 Jimmy Wilkerson RC	1.00	.45
❑	534 Travis Anglin RC	.60	.25
❑	535 Tyrone Calico RC	1.50	.70
❑	536 Keenan Howry RC	1.25	.55
❑	537 Gibran Hamdan RC	.60	.25
❑	538 Bryant Johnson RC	1.25	.55
❑	539 Brad Banks RC	1.00	.45
❑	540 Justin Fargas RC	1.25	.55
❑	541 B.J. Askew RC	1.25	.55
❑	542 J.R. Tolver RC	1.00	.45
❑	543 Tully Banta-Cain RC	1.00	.45
❑	544 Shaun McDonald RC	1.25	.55
❑	545 Taylor Jacobs RC	1.25	.55
❑	546 Ricky Manning RC	1.25	.55
❑	547 Dallas Clark RC	1.25	.55
❑	548 Juston Wood RC	.60	.25
❑	549 Andre Woolfolk RC	1.25	.55
❑	550 Kyle Boller RC	3.00	1.35
❑	CL1 Checklist Card 1	.10	.05
❑	CL2 Checklist Card 2	.10	.05
❑	CL3 Checklist Card 3	.10	.05
❑	CL4 Checklist Card 4	.10	.05

2003 Topps Total Silver

	MINT	NRMT
*SILVER: 1X TO 2.5X BASIC CARDS		
*ROOKIES: .8X TO 2X		

2003 Topps Total Signatures

		MINT	NRMT
❑	TSCJ Chad Johnson C	20.00	9.00
❑	TSDN Dennis Northcutt B	15.00	6.75
❑	TSJJ Joe Jurevicius A	40.00	18.00
❑	TSJT Jason Taylor A	40.00	18.00
❑	TSLB Ladell Betts D	15.00	6.75
❑	TSMB Marc Boerigter D	30.00	13.50
❑	TSTB Todd Bouman D	20.00	9.00

2004 Topps Total

		Nm-Mt	Ex-Mt
	COMPLETE SET (440)	80.00	24.00
❑	1 Donovan McNabb	1.00	.30
❑	2 Zach Thomas	.75	.23
❑	3 Randy Moss	1.00	.30
❑	4 Kerry Collins	.50	.15
❑	5 Hines Ward	.75	.23
❑	6 Tyrone Calico	.50	.15
❑	7 Patrick Ramsey	.50	.15
❑	8 Jeff Garcia	.75	.23
❑	9 Aveion Cason	.30	.09
❑	10 Stephen Davis	.50	.15
❑	11 Marcel Shipp	.50	.15
❑	12 T.J. Duckett	.50	.15
❑	13 Chris McAlister	.30	.09
❑	14 Peter Warrick	.50	.15
❑	15 Ahman Green	.75	.23
❑	16 Deion Branch	.75	.23
❑	17 David Boston	.50	.15
❑	18 Wayne Chrebet	.50	.15
❑	19 Michael Strahan	.50	.15
❑	20 Arnaz Battle	.50	.15
❑	21 Darrell Jackson	.50	.15
❑	22 Chris Chandler	.50	.15
❑	23 Charlie Garner	.50	.15
❑	24 James Thrash	.30	.09
❑	25 LaDainian Tomlinson	.75	.23
❑	26 Jerry Porter	.50	.15
❑	27 Jerome Pathon	.30	.09
❑	28 Jerome Bettis	.75	.23
❑	29 Eddie George	.50	.15
❑	30 Jamal Lewis	.75	.23
❑	31 Ricky Proehl	.30	.09
❑	32 Josh Reed	.30	.09
❑	33 David Terrell	.50	.15
❑	34 Antonio Bryant	.50	.15
❑	35 Domanick Davis	.75	.23
❑	36 Artose Pinner	.30	.09
❑	37 Jed Weaver	.30	.09
❑	38 Johnnie Morton	.50	.15
❑	39 Troy Edwards	.30	.09
❑	40 Marvin Harrison	.75	.23
❑	41 Chris Hovan	.30	.09
❑	42 Boo Williams	.30	.09
❑	43 Ike Hilliard	.30	.09
❑	44 Sam Cowart	.30	.09
❑	45 Shaun Alexander	.75	.23
❑	46 Freddie Mitchell	.50	.15
❑	47 Garrison Hearst	.50	.15

❑ 48 Joe Jurevicius .30 .09
❑ 49 Freddie Jones .30 .09
❑ 50 Michael Vick 1.50 .45
❑ 51 Mike Rucker .30 .09
❑ 52 Carson Palmer 1.00 .30
❑ 53 Az-Zahir Hakim .30 .09
❑ 54 Billy Miller .30 .09
❑ 55 Chad Pennington 1.00 .30
❑ 56 Charles Woodson .50 .15
❑ 57 Andre Carter .30 .09
❑ 58 Maurice Morris .30 .09
❑ 59 Leonard Little .30 .09
❑ 60 Travis Henry .50 .15
❑ 61 Thomas Jones .50 .15
❑ 62 Dennis Northcutt .30 .09
❑ 63 Quentin Griffin .75 .23
❑ 64 Joey Harrington .75 .23
❑ 65 Edgerrin James .75 .23
❑ 66 Cortez Hankton .30 .09
❑ 67 Jason Taylor .30 .09
❑ 68 Eddie Kennison .30 .09
❑ 69 Ty Law .50 .15
❑ 70 Aaron Brooks .50 .15
❑ 71 Antonio Gates .75 .23
❑ 72 Antwaan Randle El .50 .15
❑ 73 Kevan Barlow .50 .15
❑ 74 Chris Brown .75 .23
❑ 75 Clinton Portis .75 .23
❑ 76 Rod Gardner .50 .15
❑ 77 Isaac Bruce .50 .15
❑ 78 Mike Alstott .50 .15
❑ 79 Brian Westbrook .50 .15
❑ 80 Amani Toomer .50 .15
❑ 81 Justin Fargas .50 .15
❑ 82 Michael Bennett .50 .15
❑ 83 Dante Hall .75 .23
❑ 84 Marcus Pollard .30 .09
❑ 85 Fred Taylor .50 .15
❑ 86 Tai Streets .30 .09
❑ 87 Robert Ferguson .30 .09
❑ 88 Roy Williams S .50 .15
❑ 89 Lee Suggs .75 .23
❑ 90 Chad Johnson .50 .15
❑ 91 DeShaun Foster .50 .15
❑ 92 Alge Crumpler .50 .15
❑ 93 Travis Taylor .30 .09
❑ 94 London Fletcher .30 .09
❑ 95 Priest Holmes 1.00 .30
❑ 96 A.J. Feeley .75 .23
❑ 97 Kevin Faulk .30 .09
❑ 98 Shaun Ellis .30 .09
❑ 99 Tim Dwight .50 .15
❑ 100 Peyton Manning 1.25 .35
❑ 101 Dane Looker .50 .15
❑ 102 Mark Brunell .50 .15
❑ 103 Bryant Johnson .30 .09
❑ 104 Kelley Washington .30 .09
❑ 105 Rex Grossman .75 .23
❑ 106 William Green .50 .15
❑ 107 Keyshawn Johnson .50 .15
❑ 108 Trevor Pryce .30 .09
❑ 109 Donald Driver .50 .15
❑ 110 David Carr .75 .23
❑ 111 Marcus Robinson .50 .15
❑ 112 Justin McCareins .30 .09
❑ 113 Tim Brown .75 .23
❑ 114 James Farrior .30 .09
❑ 115 Deuce McAllister .75 .23
❑ 116 Simeon Rice .50 .15
❑ 117 Koren Robinson .50 .15
❑ 118 Kassim Osgood .30 .09
❑ 119 Tim Rattay .50 .15
❑ 120 Laveranues Coles .50 .15
❑ 121 Brian Finneran .30 .09
❑ 122 Todd Heap .50 .15
❑ 123 Bobby Shaw .30 .09
❑ 124 Anthony Thomas .50 .15
❑ 125 Brett Favre 2.00 .60
❑ 126 Dwight Freeney .30 .09
❑ 127 Randy McMichael .30 .09
❑ 128 David Givens .50 .15
❑ 129 Rich Gannon .50 .15
❑ 130 Tiki Barber .50 .15
❑ 131 Terrell Owens .75 .23
❑ 132 Drew Bennett .50 .15
❑ 133 Shawn Bryson .30 .09
❑ 134 Jabar Gaffney .50 .15
❑ 135 Jake Delhomme .75 .23
❑ 136 Warrick Dunn .50 .15
❑ 137 Brandon Lloyd .50 .15
❑ 138 Brad Johnson .50 .15
❑ 139 Jon Kitna .50 .15
❑ 140 Marshall Faulk .75 .23
❑ 141 Javon Walker .50 .15
❑ 142 Nate Burleson .75 .23
❑ 143 Jimmy Smith .50 .15
❑ 144 Adewale Ogunleye .50 .15
❑ 145 Trent Green .50 .15
❑ 146 Richard Seymour .30 .09
❑ 147 Donte' Stallworth .50 .15
❑ 148 Curtis Martin .75 .23
❑ 149 Todd Pinkston .30 .09
❑ 150 Steve McNair .75 .23
❑ 151 Josh McCown .50 .15
❑ 152 Ray Lewis .75 .23
❑ 153 Muhsin Muhammad .50 .15
❑ 154 Quincy Morgan .50 .15
❑ 155 Jake Plummer .50 .15
❑ 156 Jason Witten .50 .15
❑ 157 Dallas Clark .50 .15
❑ 158 Onterrio Smith .50 .15
❑ 159 Jeremy Shockey .75 .23
❑ 160 Ricky Williams .75 .23
❑ 161 Jevon Kearse .50 .15
❑ 162 Plaxico Burress .50 .15
❑ 163 Drew Brees .75 .23
❑ 164 Bobby Engram .30 .09
❑ 165 Torry Holt .75 .23
❑ 166 Ladell Betts .30 .09
❑ 167 Kelly Holcomb .50 .15
❑ 168 Vinny Testaverde .50 .15
❑ 169 Marty Booker .50 .15
❑ 170 Rudi Johnson .50 .15
❑ 171 Andra Davis .30 .09
❑ 172 Kurt Warner .75 .23
❑ 173 Troy Brown .50 .15
❑ 174 Jerry Rice 1.50 .45
❑ 175 Daunte Culpepper .75 .23
❑ 176 Darren Sharper .30 .09
❑ 177 Charles Rogers .50 .15
❑ 178 Ashley Lelie .50 .15
❑ 179 Correll Buckhalter .50 .15
❑ 180 Anquan Boldin .75 .23
❑ 181 Terrell Suggs .50 .15
❑ 182 Reggie Wayne .50 .15
❑ 183 Duce Staley .50 .15
❑ 184 Donnie Edwards .30 .09
❑ 185 Joe Horn .50 .15
❑ 186 LaVar Arrington 1.50 .45
❑ 187 Keenan McCardell .30 .09
❑ 188 Cedrick Wilson .30 .09
❑ 189 Bubba Franks .50 .15
❑ 190 Santana Moss .50 .15
❑ 191 Peerless Price .50 .15
❑ 192 Kyle Boller .75 .23
❑ 193 Julius Peppers .75 .23
❑ 194 Drew Bledsoe .75 .23
❑ 195 Marc Bulger .75 .23
❑ 196 Brian Urlacher 1.00 .30
❑ 197 Andre' Davis .30 .09
❑ 198 Terry Glenn .30 .09
❑ 199 Champ Bailey .50 .15
❑ 200 Tom Brady 1.25 .35
❑ 201 Chris Chambers .50 .15
❑ 202 Tommy Maddox .50 .15
❑ 203 Derrick Brooks .50 .15
❑ 204 Corey Dillon .50 .15
❑ 205 Matt Hasselbeck .50 .15
❑ 206 Keith Brooking .30 .09
❑ 207 Steve Smith .50 .15
❑ 208 Tony Gonzalez .50 .15
❑ 209 Joey Galloway .50 .15
❑ 210 Derrick Mason .50 .15
❑ 211 Quincy Carter .50 .15
❑ 212 Rod Smith .50 .15
❑ 213 Andre Johnson .75 .23
❑ 214 Rod Woodson .50 .15
❑ 215 Byron Leftwich 1.25 .35
❑ 216 Kevin Dyson .30 .09
❑ 217 Keith Bulluck .30 .09
❑ 218 Eric Moulds .50 .15
❑ 219 Jamie Sharper .30 .09
❑ 220 Takeo Spikes .30 .09
❑ 221 Calvin Pace .30 .09
Fred Wakefield
❑ 222 Brady Smith .30 .09
Patrick Kerney
❑ 223 Ed Reed .50 .15
Gary Baxter
❑ 224 Aaron Schobel .30 .09
Jeff Posey
❑ 225 Kris Jenkins .30 .09
Brentson Buckner
❑ 226 Justin Smith .30 .09
Duane Clemons
❑ 227 Michael Haynes .30 .09
Bryan Robinson
❑ 228 Courtney Brown .50 .15
Gerard Warren
❑ 229 Terence Newman .50 .15
Darren Woodson
❑ 230 Raylee Johnson .30 .09
Mario Fatafehi
❑ 231 Robert Porcher .75 .23
James Hall RC
❑ 232 Kabeer Gbaja-Biamila .50 .15
Cletidus Hunt
❑ 233 Aaron Glenn .30 .09
Marcus Coleman
❑ 234 Nick Harper RC .30 .09
Joseph Jefferson
❑ 235 Hugh Douglas .30 .09
Tony Brackens
❑ 236 Vonnie Holliday .30 .09
Eric Hicks
❑ 237 Sammy Knight .30 .09
Arturo Freeman
❑ 238 Steve Martin .30 .09
Nick Rogers
❑ 239 Rosevelt Colvin .30 .09
Willie McGinest
❑ 240 Omar Stoutmire .30 .09
Shaun Williams
❑ 241 Eric Barton .30 .09
Victor Hobson
❑ 242 Warren Sapp .50 .15
Ted Washington
❑ 243 Corey Simon .50 .15
Darwin Walker
❑ 244 Troy Polamalu .50 .15
Mike Logan
❑ 245 Jamal Williams .30 .09
Adrian Dingle RC
❑ 246 Bryant Young .30 .09
Brandon Whiting
❑ 247 Ken Hamlin .30 .09
Damien Robinson RC
❑ 248 Damione Lewis .30 .09
Ryan Pickett
❑ 249 Anthony McFarland .30 .09
Greg Spires
❑ 250 Albert Haynesworth .30 .09
Rien Long
❑ 251 Ifeanyi Ohalete .30 .09
Matt Bowen
❑ 252 Bertrand Berry .30 .09
Kenny King
❑ 253 Ellis Johnson .30 .09
Ed Jasper
❑ 254 Charles Tillman .30 .09
Jerry Azumah
❑ 255 Marcellus Wiley .30 .09
La'Roi Glover
❑ 256 Shaun Rogers .30 .09
Dan Wilkinson
❑ 257 Gary Walker .30 .09
Robaire Smith
❑ 258 Mike Doss .30 .09
Idrees Bashir
❑ 259 Marcus Stroud .50 .15
John Henderson
❑ 260 Ryan Sims .30 .09
John Browning
❑ 261 Junior Seau .75 .23
Morlon Greenwood

❑	262 Kevin Williams	.30	.09
	Kenny Mixon		
❑	263 Ty Warren	.30	.09
	Keith Traylor		
❑	264 Will Allen	.30	.09
	William Peterson		
❑	265 David Barrett	.30	.09
	Reggie Tongue		
❑	266 Phillip Buchanon	.30	.09
	Derrick Gibson		
❑	267 Lito Sheppard	.30	.09
	Sheldon Brown		
❑	268 Bobby Taylor	.50	.15
	Marcus Trufant		
❑	269 Marcus Washington	.30	.09
	Micheal Barrow		
❑	270 Chris Draft	.30	.09
	Matt Stewart		
❑	271 Mike Brown	.50	.15
	Mike Green		
❑	272 Eric Brown	.30	.09
	Marlon McCree		
❑	273 Patrick Surtain	.50	.15
	Sam Madison		
❑	274 Brian Dawkins	.30	.09
	Michael Lewis		
❑	275 Shawn Springs	.50	.15
	Fred Smoot		
❑	276 Ronald McKinnon	.30	.09
	Levar Fisher		
	Ray Thompson		
❑	277 Jason Webster	.30	.09
	Tod McBride RC		
	Bryan Scott		
❑	278 Peter Boulware	.50	.15
	Ed Hartwell		
	Adalius Thomas		
❑	279 Troy Vincent	.50	.15
	Lawyer Milloy		
	Nate Clements		
❑	280 Will Witherspoon	.50	.15
	Dan Morgan		
	Mark Fields		
❑	281 Brian Simmons	.30	.09
	Kevin Hardy		
	Nate Webster		
❑	282 Joe Odom RC	.75	.23
	Alex Brown		
	Lance Briggs		
❑	283 Warrick Holdman	.30	.09
	Chaun Thompson		
	Kenard Lang		
❑	284 Dat Nguyen	.30	.09
	Dexter Coakley		
	Al Singleton		
❑	285 Al Wilson	.30	.09
	Donnie Spragan RC		
	Darius Holland		
❑	286 Earl Holmes	.75	.23
	James Davis RC		
	Boss Bailey		
❑	287 Nick Barnett	.30	.09
	Na'il Diggs		
	Hannibal Navies		
❑	288 Jay Foreman	.30	.09
	Antwan Peek		
	Kailee Wong		
❑	289 Raheem Brock	.30	.09
	Montae Reagor		
	Larry Tripplett		
❑	290 Akin Ayodele	.50	.15
	Greg Favors		
	Mike Peterson		
❑	291 Shawn Barber	.50	.15
	Mike Maslowski		
	Scott Fujita		
❑	292 Chris Claiborne	.50	.15
	E.J. Henderson		
	Mike Nattiel		
❑	293 Tedy Bruschi	1.00	.30
	Roman Phifer		
	Mike Vrabel		
❑	294 Charles Grant	.30	.09
	Darren Howard		
	Johnathan Sullivan		
❑	295 Fred Robbins	.30	.09
	William Joseph		
	Osi Umenyiora		
❑	296 John Abraham	1.25	.35
	DeWayne Robertson		
	Jason Ferguson RC		
❑	297 Napoleon Harris	.50	.15
	Dwayne Rudd		
	Tyler Brayton		
❑	298 Mark Simoneau	.30	.09
	Nate Wayne		
	Dhani Jones		
❑	299 Joey Porter	.75	.23
	Kendrell Bell		
	Clark Haggans RC		
❑	300 Quentin Jammer	.50	.15
	Sammy Davis		
	Drayton Florence		
❑	301 Julian Peterson	.30	.09
	Jeff Ulbrich		
	Derek Smith		
❑	302 Anthony Simmons	.30	.09
	Orlando Huff		
	Chad Brown		
❑	303 Pisa Tinoisamoa	.30	.09
	Tommy Polley		
	Robert Thomas		
❑	304 Shelton Quarles	.30	.09
	Ellis Wyms		
	Ryan Nece		
❑	305 Kevin Carter	.50	.15
	Carlos Hall		
	Peter Sirmon		
❑	306 Cornelius Griffin	.30	.09
	Phillip Daniels		
	Renaldo Wynn		
❑	307 Dexter Jackson	.30	.09
	Adrian Wilson		
	David Macklin		
❑	308 Kelly Gregg	.30	.09
	Marques Douglas		
	Anthony Weaver		
❑	309 Pat Williams	.30	.09
	Ryan Denney		
	Sam Adams		
❑	310 Artrell Hawkins	.30	.09
	Mike Minter		
	Ricky Manning		
❑	311 Tory James	.30	.09
	Kim Herring		
	Rogers Beckett		
❑	312 Robert Griffith	.30	.09
	Earl Little		
	Anthony Henry		
❑	313 John Lynch	.75	.23
	Nick Ferguson RC		
	Kelly Herndon RC		
❑	314 Dre' Bly	.30	.09
	Brock Marion		
	Fernando Bryant		
❑	315 Al Harris	.30	.09
	Mark Roman		
	Mike McKenzie		
❑	316 David Thornton	.50	.15
	Rob Morris		
	Gary Brackett RC		
❑	317 Rashean Mathis	.50	.15
	Donovin Darius		
	Juran Bolden RC		
❑	318 Eric Warfield	.30	.09
	Greg Wesley		
	Jerome Woods		
❑	319 Antoine Winfield	.50	.15
	Brian Russell RC		
	Corey Chavous		
❑	320 Rodney Harrison	.30	.09
	Eugene Wilson		
	Tyrone Poole		
❑	321 Derrick Rodgers	.30	.09
	Orlando Ruff		
	Sedrick Hodge		
❑	322 Barrett Green	.30	.09
	Nick Greisen		
	Carlos Emmons		
❑	323 Kimo Von Oelhoffen	.50	.15
	Aaron Smith		
	Casey Hampton		
❑	324 Randall Godfrey	.30	.09
	Steve Foley		
	Ben Leber		
❑	325 Ahmed Plummer	.30	.09
	Tony Parrish		
	Mike Rumph		
❑	326 Chike Okeafor	.30	.09
	Grant Wistrom		
	Rashad Moore		
❑	327 Adam Archuleta	.30	.09
	Aeneas Williams		
	Jerametrius Butler		
❑	328 Ronde Barber	.50	.15
	Dwight Smith		
	Jermaine Phillips		
❑	329 Andre Dyson	.30	.09
	Lance Schulters		
	Tank Williams		
❑	330 Fred Thomas	.30	.09
	Jay Bellamy		
	Tebucky Jones		
❑	331 Philip Rivers RC	5.00	1.50
❑	332 Dwan Edwards RC	.75	.23
❑	333 Ben Watson RC	1.50	.45
❑	334 Karlos Dansby RC	1.50	.45
❑	335 Cedric Cobbs RC	1.50	.45
❑	336 Chris Perry RC	3.00	.90
❑	337 Darius Watts RC	2.00	.60
❑	338 Ricardo Colclough RC	1.50	.45
❑	339 Derrick Hamilton RC	1.25	.35
❑	340 Devard Darling RC	1.50	.45
❑	341 Daryl Smith RC	1.50	.45
❑	342 Luke McCown RC	1.50	.45
❑	343 Dunta Robinson RC	1.50	.45
❑	344 Keith Smith RC	1.25	.35
❑	345 Ben Hartsock RC	1.50	.45
❑	346 J.P. Losman RC	4.00	1.20
❑	347 Chris Cooley RC	1.50	.45
❑	348 Keary Colbert RC	2.00	.60
❑	349 Tommie Harris RC	2.00	.60
❑	350 Eli Manning RC	8.00	2.40
❑	351 Kevin Jones RC	5.00	1.50
❑	352 Lee Evans RC	2.50	.75
❑	353 D.J. Williams RC	2.00	.60
❑	354 Ben Troupe RC	1.50	.45
❑	355 Mewelde Moore RC	2.00	.60
❑	356 Michael Clayton RC	4.00	1.20
❑	357 Michael Jenkins RC	1.50	.45
❑	358 Adimchinobe Echemandu RC	1.25	.35
❑	359 Rashaun Woods RC	2.00	.60
❑	360 Bernard Berrian RC	1.50	.45
❑	361 Carlos Francis RC	1.25	.35
❑	362 Roy Williams RC	5.00	1.50
❑	363 Sean Taylor RC	2.00	.60
❑	364 Steven Jackson RC	5.00	1.50
❑	365 Tatum Bell RC	2.50	.75
❑	366 Jonathan Vilma RC	1.50	.45
❑	367 Derrick Strait RC	2.00	.60
❑	368 Andy Hall RC	1.25	.35
❑	369 Jason Babin RC	1.50	.45
❑	370 Will Smith RC	1.50	.45
❑	371 Kenechi Udeze RC	1.50	.45
❑	372 Vince Wilfork RC	2.00	.60
❑	373 Ahmad Carroll RC	2.00	.60
❑	374 Marquise Hill RC	1.25	.35
❑	375 Ben Roethlisberger RC	15.00	4.50
❑	376 Chris Gamble RC	2.00	.60
❑	377 Junior Siavii RC	1.50	.45
❑	378 Teddy Lehman RC	1.50	.45
❑	379 Antwan Odom RC	1.50	.45
❑	380 DeAngelo Hall RC	2.00	.60
❑	381 Nathan Vasher RC	1.50	.45
❑	382 B.J. Symons RC	1.50	.45
❑	383 Reggie Williams RC	2.00	.60
❑	384 Michael Boulware RC	1.50	.45
❑	385 Matt Schaub RC	2.50	.75
❑	386 Sean Jones RC	1.25	.35
❑	387 Courtney Watson RC	1.50	.45
❑	388 Nathaniel Adibi RC	1.50	.45
❑	389 Devery Henderson RC	1.25	.35
❑	390 Greg Jones RC	1.50	.45
❑	391 Joey Thomas RC	1.50	.45
❑	392 Drew Carter RC	1.50	.45

❑ 393 Julius Jones RC 6.00 1.80
❑ 394 Keyaron Fox RC 1.25 .35
❑ 395 Darrion Scott RC 1.50 .45
❑ 396 Rich Gardner RC 1.25 .35
❑ 397 Jeff Smoker RC 2.50 .75
❑ 398 Will Poole RC 1.50 .45
❑ 399 Samie Parker RC 1.50 .45
❑ 400 Larry Fitzgerald RC 5.00 1.50
❑ 401 Jerricho Cotchery RC 1.50 .45
❑ 402 Ernest Wilford RC 1.50 .45
❑ 403 Johnnie Morant RC 1.50 .45
❑ 404 Craig Krenzel RC 1.50 .45
❑ 405 Michael Turner RC 1.25 .35
❑ 406 D.J. Hackett RC 1.25 .35
❑ 407 P.K. Sam RC 1.25 .35
❑ 408 Triandos Luke RC 1.50 .45
❑ 409 Josh Harris RC 1.50 .45
❑ 410 Drew Henson RC 4.00 1.20
❑ 411 John Navarre RC 1.50 .45
❑ 412 Cody Pickett RC 1.50 .45
❑ 413 Clarence Moore RC 1.50 .45
❑ 414 Michael Gaines RC 1.25 .35
❑ 415 Derek Abney RC 1.50 .45
❑ 416 Dontarrious Thomas RC 1.50 .45
❑ 417 Reggie Torbor RC 1.25 .35
❑ 418 Ryan Krause RC 1.25 .35
❑ 419 Travis LaBoy RC 1.50 .45
❑ 420 Kellen Winslow RC 4.00 1.20
❑ 421 Keiwan Ratliff RC 1.25 .35
❑ 422 Gilbert Gardner RC 1.25 .35
❑ 423 Jamaar Taylor RC 1.50 .45
❑ 424 Matt Ware RC 1.50 .45
❑ 425 Stuart Schweigert RC 1.50 .45
❑ 426 Marcus Tubbs RC 1.50 .45
❑ 427 Brandon Chillar RC 1.25 .35
❑ 428 Shawntae Spencer RC 1.50 .45
❑ 429 Marquis Cooper RC 1.25 .35
❑ 430 Derrick Ward RC .75 .23
❑ 431 Tim Euhus RC 1.50 .45
❑ 432 Patrick Crayton RC 1.50 .45
❑ 433 Caleb Miller RC 1.25 .35
❑ 434 Donnell Washington RC 1.50 .45
❑ 435 Thomas Tapeh RC 1.25 .35
❑ 436 Randy Starks RC 1.25 .35
❑ 437 Sloan Thomas RC 1.25 .35
❑ 438 Maurice Mann RC 1.25 .35
❑ 439 Jim Sorgi RC 1.50 .45
❑ 440 Nate Lawrie RC 1.25 .35

2004 Topps Total First Edition

Nm-Mt Ex-Mt
COMPLETE SET (440) 150.00 45.00
*FIRST EDIT.VETS: 1X TO 2.5X BASE CARD HI
*FIRST EDITION RCs: .8X TO 2X BASE CARD HI

2004 Topps Total Silver

Nm-Mt Ex-Mt
*SILVER VETS: 1.2X TO 3X BASE CARD HI
*SILVER RCs: 1X TO 2.5X BASE CARD HI
ONE PER PACK

2004 Topps Total Award Winners

Nm-Mt Ex-Mt
COMPLETE SET (20) 25.00 7.50
STATED ODDS 1:9 HOB/RET
❑ AW1 Jamal Lewis 2.50 .75
❑ AW2 Ahman Green 2.50 .75
❑ AW3 Priest Holmes 3.00 .90
❑ AW4 Torry Holt 2.50 .75
❑ AW5 Randy Moss 3.00 .90
❑ AW6 Chris Chambers 1.50 .45
❑ AW7 LaDainian Tomlinson 2.50 .75
❑ AW8 Peyton Manning 4.00 1.20
❑ AW9 Marc Bulger 2.50 .75
❑ AW10 Brett Favre 6.00 1.80
❑ AW11 Steve McNair 2.50 .75
❑ AW12 Daunte Culpepper 2.50 .75
❑ AW13 Michael Strahan 1.50 .45
❑ AW14 Adewale Ogunleye 1.50 .45
❑ AW15 Jamie Sharper 1.00 .30
❑ AW16 Micheal Barrow 1.00 .30
❑ AW17 Mike Vanderjagt 1.00 .30
❑ AW18 Anquan Boldin 2.50 .75
❑ AW19 Terrell Suggs 1.50 .45
❑ AW20 Tom Brady 4.00 1.20

2004 Topps Total Signatures

Nm-Mt Ex-Mt
GROUP A ODDS 1:33,480 H, 1:17,383 R
GROUP B ODDS 1:11,160 H, 1:6773 R
GROUP C ODDS 1:427 HOB, 1:3369 RET
GROUP D ODDS 1:4058 HOB, 1:2173 RET
GROUP E ODDS 1:2829 HOB, 1:1644 RET
OVERALL AUTO ODDS 1:327 HOB, 1:605 RET
❑ TSBS Brandon Stokley D 30.00 9.00
❑ TSCC Cedric Cobbs C 30.00 9.00
❑ TSCP Chad Pennington A 80.00 24.00
❑ TSDD Domanick Davis B 40.00 12.00
❑ TSKC Keary Colbert C 30.00 9.00
❑ TSMCL Michael Clayton E 40.00 12.00
❑ TSNB Nate Burleson C 30.00 9.00

2004 Topps Total Team Checklists

Nm-Mt Ex-Mt
COMPLETE SET (32) 40.00 12.00
❑ TTC1 Anquan Boldin 1.25 .35
❑ TTC2 Michael Vick 2.50 .75
❑ TTC3 Jamal Lewis 1.25 .35
❑ TTC4 Travis Henry .75 .23
❑ TTC5 Jake Delhomme 1.25 .35
❑ TTC6 Brian Urlacher 1.50 .45
❑ TTC7 Chad Johnson .75 .23
❑ TTC8 Jeff Garcia 1.25 .35
❑ TTC9 Keyshawn Johnson .75 .23
❑ TTC10 Jake Plummer .75 .23
❑ TTC11 Joey Harrington 1.25 .35
❑ TTC12 Brett Favre 3.00 .90
❑ TTC13 Domanick Davis 1.25 .35
❑ TTC14 Peyton Manning 2.00 .60
❑ TTC15 Byron Leftwich 2.00 .60
❑ TTC16 Priest Holmes 1.50 .45
❑ TTC17 Ricky Williams 1.25 .35
❑ TTC18 Randy Moss 1.50 .45
❑ TTC19 Tom Brady 2.00 .60
❑ TTC20 Deuce McAllister 1.25 .35
❑ TTC21 Amani Toomer .75 .23
❑ TTC22 Chad Pennington 1.50 .45
❑ TTC23 Jerry Rice 2.50 .75
❑ TTC24 Donovan McNabb 1.50 .45
❑ TTC25 Hines Ward 1.25 .35
❑ TTC26 LaDainian Tomlinson 1.25 .35
❑ TTC27 Kevan Barlow .75 .23
❑ TTC28 Matt Hasselbeck .75 .23
❑ TTC29 Torry Holt 1.25 .35
❑ TTC30 Keenan McCardell .50 .15
❑ TTC31 Steve McNair 1.25 .35
❑ TTC32 Clinton Portis 1.25 .35

2004 Topps Total Total Production

Nm-Mt Ex-Mt
COMPLETE SET (10) 15.00 4.50
STATED ODDS 1:18 HOB/RET
❑ TP1 Brett Favre 6.00 1.80
❑ TP2 Peyton Manning 4.00 1.20
❑ TP3 Priest Holmes 3.00 .90
❑ TP4 Jon Kitna 1.50 .45
❑ TP5 Matt Hasselbeck 1.50 .45
❑ TP6 Daunte Culpepper 2.50 .75
❑ TP7 Ahman Green 2.50 .75
❑ TP8 LaDainian Tomlinson 2.50 .75
❑ TP9 Randy Moss 3.00 .90
❑ TP10 Shaun Alexander 2.50 .75

2004 Topps Total Total Topps

Nm-Mt Ex-Mt
COMPLETE SET (20) 25.00 7.50
STATED ODDS 1:9 HOB/RET
❑ TT1 Peyton Manning 4.00 1.20

❑ TT2 Steve McNair	2.50	.75
❑ TT3 Torry Holt	2.50	.75
❑ TT4 Brett Favre	6.00	1.80
❑ TT5 Jamal Lewis	2.50	.75
❑ TT6 Deuce McAllister	2.50	.75
❑ TT7 Randy Moss	3.00	.90
❑ TT8 Marvin Harrison	2.50	.75
❑ TT9 Ahman Green	2.50	.75
❑ TT10 Tom Brady	4.00	1.20
❑ TT11 Shaun Alexander	2.50	.75
❑ TT12 LaDainian Tomlinson	2.50	.75
❑ TT13 Daunte Culpepper	2.50	.75
❑ TT14 Hines Ward	2.50	.75
❑ TT15 Anquan Boldin	2.50	.75
❑ TT16 Priest Holmes	3.00	.90
❑ TT17 Derrick Mason	1.50	.45
❑ TT18 Donovan McNabb	3.00	.90
❑ TT19 Clinton Portis	2.50	.75
❑ TT20 Terrell Owens	2.50	.75

1997 UD3 Signature Performers

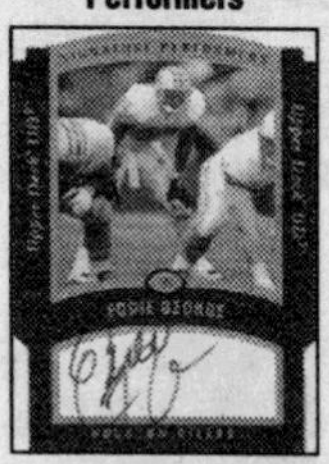

	Nm-Mt	Ex-Mt
COMPLETE SET (4)	200.00	90.00
❑ PF1 Curtis Martin (issued via redemption)	60.00	27.00
❑ PF2 Troy Aikman	120.00	55.00
❑ PF3 Marcus Allen	60.00	27.00
❑ PF4 Eddie George	40.00	18.00

2002 UD Authentics

	Nm-Mt	Ex-Mt
COMP.SET w/o SP's (90)	25.00	7.50
❑ 1 Jake Plummer	.60	.18
❑ 2 David Boston	1.00	.30
❑ 3 Thomas Jones	.60	.18
❑ 4 Michael Vick	3.00	.90
❑ 5 Warrick Dunn	1.00	.30
❑ 6 Jamal Lewis	1.00	.30
❑ 7 Chris Redman	.40	.12
❑ 8 Travis Taylor	.60	.18
❑ 9 Drew Bledsoe	1.25	.35
❑ 10 Eric Moulds	.60	.18
❑ 11 Travis Henry	1.00	.30
❑ 12 Chris Weinke	.60	.18
❑ 13 Muhsin Muhammad	.60	.18
❑ 14 Anthony Thomas	1.00	.30
❑ 15 Jim Miller	.40	.12
❑ 16 Marty Booker	.60	.18
❑ 17 Corey Dillon	.60	.18
❑ 18 Jon Kitna	.60	.18
❑ 19 Peter Warrick	.60	.18
❑ 20 Tim Couch	.60	.18
❑ 21 Emmitt Smith	2.50	.75
❑ 22 Joey Galloway	.60	.18
❑ 23 Quincy Carter	.60	.18
❑ 24 Brian Griese	1.00	.30
❑ 25 Terrell Davis	1.00	.30
❑ 26 Shannon Sharpe	.60	.18
❑ 27 Germane Crowell	.40	.12
❑ 28 James Stewart	.60	.18
❑ 29 Az-Zahir Hakim	.40	.12
❑ 30 Brett Favre	2.50	.75
❑ 31 Ahman Green	1.00	.30
❑ 32 Terry Glenn	.60	.18
❑ 33 Jermaine Lewis	.40	.12
❑ 34 James Allen	.60	.18
❑ 35 Corey Bradford	.40	.12
❑ 36 Edgerrin James	1.25	.35
❑ 37 Marvin Harrison	1.00	.30
❑ 38 Peyton Manning	2.00	.60
❑ 39 Jimmy Smith	.60	.18
❑ 40 Mark Brunell	1.00	.30
❑ 41 Trent Green	.60	.18
❑ 42 Johnnie Morton	.60	.18
❑ 43 Priest Holmes	1.25	.35
❑ 44 Ricky Williams	5.00	1.50
❑ 45 Chris Chambers	1.00	.30
❑ 46 Jay Fiedler	.60	.18
❑ 47 Daunte Culpepper	1.00	.30
❑ 48 Randy Moss	2.00	.60
❑ 49 Michael Bennett	.60	.18
❑ 50 Troy Brown	.60	.18
❑ 51 Antowain Smith	.60	.18
❑ 52 Tom Brady	2.50	.75
❑ 53 Aaron Brooks	1.00	.30
❑ 54 Deuce McAllister	1.25	.35
❑ 55 Joe Horn	.60	.18
❑ 56 Amani Toomer	.60	.18
❑ 57 Kerry Collins	.60	.18
❑ 58 Ron Dayne	.60	.18
❑ 59 Chad Pennington	1.25	.35
❑ 60 Curtis Martin	1.00	.30
❑ 61 Vinny Testaverde	.60	.18
❑ 62 Jerry Rice	2.00	.60
❑ 63 Rich Gannon	1.00	.30
❑ 64 Tim Brown	1.00	.30
❑ 65 Donovan McNabb	1.25	.35
❑ 66 Duce Staley	1.00	.30
❑ 67 James Thrash	.60	.18
❑ 68 Plaxico Burress	.60	.18
❑ 69 Jerome Bettis	1.00	.30
❑ 70 Kordell Stewart	.60	.18
❑ 71 Doug Flutie	1.00	.30
❑ 72 Drew Brees	1.00	.30
❑ 73 LaDainian Tomlinson	1.50	.45
❑ 74 Garrison Hearst	.60	.18
❑ 75 Jeff Garcia	1.00	.30
❑ 76 Terrell Owens	1.00	.30
❑ 77 Ricky Watters	.60	.18
❑ 78 Shaun Alexander	1.00	.30
❑ 79 Trent Dilfer	.60	.18
❑ 80 Isaac Bruce	1.00	.30
❑ 81 Kurt Warner	1.00	.30
❑ 82 Marshall Faulk	1.00	.30
❑ 83 Keyshawn Johnson	1.00	.30
❑ 84 Michael Pittman	.40	.12
❑ 85 Brad Johnson	.60	.18
❑ 86 Eddie George	1.00	.30
❑ 87 Jevon Kearse	.60	.18
❑ 88 Steve McNair	1.00	.30
❑ 89 Shane Matthews	.40	.12
❑ 90 Stephen Davis	.60	.18
❑ 91 Josh McCown RC	8.00	2.40
❑ 92 Kurt Kittner RC	5.00	1.50
❑ 93 T.J. Duckett RC	10.00	3.00
❑ 94 Wes Pate RC	3.00	.90
❑ 95 Chester Taylor RC	6.00	1.80
❑ 96 Ron Johnson RC	5.00	1.50
❑ 97 Lamont Brightful RC	3.00	.90
❑ 98 Josh Reed RC	6.00	1.80
❑ 99 Randy Fasani RC	5.00	1.50
❑ 100 DeShaun Foster RC	6.00	1.80
❑ 101 Julius Peppers RC	12.00	3.60
❑ 102 William Green RC	10.00	3.00
❑ 103 Andre Davis RC	6.00	1.80
❑ 104 Chad Hutchinson RC	6.00	1.80
❑ 105 Antonio Bryant RC	6.00	1.80
❑ 106 Roy Williams RC	15.00	4.50
❑ 107 Clinton Portis RC	20.00	6.00
❑ 108 Herb Haygood RC	3.00	.90
❑ 109 Ashley Lelie RC	12.00	3.60
❑ 110 Joey Harrington RC	20.00	6.00
❑ 111 Luke Staley RC	5.00	1.50
❑ 112 Javon Walker RC	12.00	3.60
❑ 113 David Carr RC	20.00	6.00
❑ 114 Jonathan Wells RC	6.00	1.80
❑ 115 Jabar Gaffney RC	6.00	1.80
❑ 116 Brian Allen RC	5.00	1.50
❑ 117 David Garrard RC	6.00	1.80
❑ 118 Leonard Henry RC	5.00	1.50
❑ 119 Rohan Davey RC	6.00	1.80
❑ 120 Deion Branch RC	12.00	3.60
❑ 121 J.T. O'Sullivan RC	5.00	1.50
❑ 122 Donte Stallworth RC	12.00	3.60
❑ 123 Tim Carter RC	5.00	1.50
❑ 124 Daryl Jones RC	5.00	1.50
❑ 125 Ronald Curry RC	6.00	1.80
❑ 126 Napoleon Harris RC	6.00	1.80
❑ 127 Brian Westbrook RC	10.00	3.00
❑ 128 Antwaan Randle El RC	8.00	2.40
❑ 129 Reche Caldwell RC	6.00	1.80
❑ 130 Quentin Jammer RC	6.00	1.80
❑ 131 Brandon Doman RC	6.00	1.80
❑ 132 Maurice Morris RC	6.00	1.80
❑ 133 Eric Crouch RC	10.00	3.00
❑ 134 Lamar Gordon RC	6.00	1.80
❑ 135 Travis Stephens RC	5.00	1.50
❑ 136 Marquise Walker RC	5.00	1.50
❑ 137 Jake Schifino RC	5.00	1.50
❑ 138 Patrick Ramsey RC	12.00	3.60
❑ 139 Ladell Betts RC	6.00	1.80
❑ 140 Cliff Russell RC	5.00	1.50
❑ 141 Chris Chandler/1989	3.00	.90
❑ 142 Tim Brown/1989	4.00	1.20
❑ 143 Wesley Walls/1989	2.00	.60
❑ 144 Rod Woodson/1989	4.00	1.20
❑ 145 Rich Gannon/1990	4.00	1.20
❑ 146 Emmitt Smith/1990	12.00	3.60
❑ 147 Junior Seau/1990	4.00	1.20
❑ 148 Shannon Sharpe/1990	3.00	.90

2002 UD Authentics Gold 25

Nm-Mt Ex-Mt

*STARS: 8X TO 20X BASIC CARDS
*ROOKIES: 2X TO 5X
*STARS 140-149: 1.5X TO 4X

2002 UD Authentics American Authentics Level 1

	Nm-Mt	Ex-Mt
UNPRICED GOLD SER.#'d OF 15		
UNPRICED LEVEL 2 SER.#'d OF 25		
UNPRICED LEVEL 2 GOLD SER.#'d OF 5		
❑ ST1AT Anthony Thomas	20.00	6.00
❑ ST1DC Daunte Culpepper/56	40.00	12.00
❑ ST1LT LaDainian Tomlinson SP	40.00	12.00
❑ ST1PM Peyton Manning	60.00	18.00
❑ ST1TG Tony Gonzalez/56	40.00	12.00

2004 UD Diamond All-Star

	Nm-Mt	Ex-Mt
COMP.SET w/o SP's (90)	20.00	6.00
ROOKIE STATED ODDS 1:6		
❑ 1 Michael Vick	1.00	.30
❑ 2 Julius Peppers	.50	.15
❑ 3 Roy Williams S	.30	.09
❑ 4 Ahman Green	.50	.15
❑ 5 Trent Green	.30	.09
❑ 6 Tom Brady	.75	.23
❑ 7 Rich Gannon	.30	.09
❑ 8 Drew Brees	.50	.15
❑ 9 Brad Johnson	.30	.09
❑ 10 Todd Heap	.30	.09
❑ 11 Chad Johnson	.30	.09
❑ 12 Ashley Lelie	.30	.09
❑ 13 Marvin Harrison	.50	.15
❑ 14 Daunte Culpepper	.50	.15
❑ 15 Amani Toomer	.30	.09
❑ 16 Terrell Owens	.50	.15
❑ 17 Shaun Alexander	.50	.15
❑ 18 Mark Brunell	.30	.09
❑ 19 Drew Bledsoe	.50	.15
❑ 20 Rudi Johnson	.30	.09
❑ 21 Charles Rogers	.30	.09
❑ 22 Edgerrin James	.50	.15
❑ 23 Randy Moss	.60	.18
❑ 24 Tiki Barber	.30	.09
❑ 25 Hines Ward	.50	.15
❑ 26 Koren Robinson	.30	.09
❑ 27 Laveranues Coles	.30	.09
❑ 28 Travis Henry	.30	.09
❑ 29 Carson Palmer	.60	.18
❑ 30 Joey Harrington	.50	.15
❑ 31 Byron Leftwich	.75	.23
❑ 32 Moe Williams	.20	.06
❑ 33 Chad Pennington	.60	.18
❑ 34 Duce Staley	.30	.09
❑ 35 Marshall Faulk	.50	.15
❑ 36 Clinton Portis	.50	.15
❑ 37 Marcel Shipp	.30	.09
❑ 38 Eric Moulds	.30	.09
❑ 39 Andre Davis	.20	.06
❑ 40 Brett Favre	1.25	.35
❑ 41 Fred Taylor	.30	.09
❑ 42 Ty Law	.30	.09
❑ 43 Santana Moss	.30	.09
❑ 44 Tommy Maddox	.30	.09
❑ 45 Torry Holt	.50	.15
❑ 46 Peerless Price	.30	.09
❑ 47 Stephen Davis	.30	.09
❑ 48 Quincy Carter	.30	.09
❑ 49 David Carr	.50	.15
❑ 50 Dante Hall	.50	.15
❑ 51 Deuce McAllister	.50	.15
❑ 52 Jerry Rice	1.00	.30
❑ 53 Tim Rattay	.30	.09
❑ 54 Derrick Brooks	.30	.09
❑ 55 Warrick Dunn	.30	.09
❑ 56 Anthony Thomas	.30	.09
❑ 57 Keyshawn Johnson	.30	.09
❑ 58 Domanick Davis	.50	.15
❑ 59 Ricky Williams	.50	.15
❑ 60 Aaron Brooks	.30	.09
❑ 61 Tim Brown	.50	.15
❑ 62 Brandon Lloyd	.30	.09
❑ 63 Steve McNair	.50	.15
❑ 64 Kyle Boller	.50	.15
❑ 65 Brian Urlacher	.60	.18
❑ 66 Jake Plummer	.30	.09
❑ 67 Peyton Manning	.75	.23
❑ 68 Chris Chambers	.30	.09
❑ 69 Jeremy Shockey	.50	.15
❑ 70 Brian Westbrook	.30	.09
❑ 71 Matt Hasselbeck	.30	.09
❑ 72 Derrick Mason	.30	.09
❑ 73 Anquan Boldin	.50	.15
❑ 74 Jake Delhomme	.50	.15
❑ 75 Jeff Garcia	.50	.15
❑ 76 Donald Driver	.30	.09
❑ 77 Priest Holmes	.60	.18
❑ 78 Corey Dillon	.30	.09
❑ 79 Curtis Martin	.50	.15
❑ 80 LaDainian Tomlinson	.50	.15
❑ 81 Marc Bulger	.50	.15
❑ 82 Jamal Lewis	.50	.15
❑ 83 Marty Booker	.30	.09
❑ 84 Quentin Griffin	.50	.15
❑ 85 Andre Johnson	.50	.15
❑ 86 Junior Seau	.50	.15
❑ 87 Joe Horn	.30	.09
❑ 88 Donovan McNabb	.60	.18
❑ 89 Kevan Barlow	.30	.09
❑ 90 Eddie George	.30	.09
❑ 91 Eli Manning RC	15.00	4.50
❑ 92 Larry Fitzgerald RC	10.00	3.00
❑ 93 Ben Roethlisberger RC	30.00	9.00
❑ 94 Roy Williams RC	10.00	3.00
❑ 95 Derrick Hamilton RC	2.50	.75
❑ 96 Kellen Winslow RC	8.00	2.40
❑ 97 Bernard Berrian RC	3.00	.90
❑ 98 Steven Jackson RC	10.00	3.00
❑ 99 DeAngelo Hall RC	4.00	1.20
❑ 100 Kevin Jones RC	10.00	3.00
❑ 101 Reggie Williams RC	4.00	1.20
❑ 102 Michael Clayton RC	8.00	2.40
❑ 103 Rashaun Woods RC	4.00	1.20
❑ 104 Devery Henderson RC	2.50	.75
❑ 105 Ben Troupe RC	3.00	.90
❑ 106 Cedric Cobbs RC	3.00	.90
❑ 107 Lee Evans RC	5.00	1.50
❑ 108 Luke McCown RC	3.00	.90
❑ 109 Chris Perry RC	6.00	1.80
❑ 110 J.P. Losman RC	8.00	2.40
❑ 111 Philip Rivers RC	10.00	3.00
❑ 112 Michael Jenkins RC	3.00	.90
❑ 113 Greg Jones RC	3.00	.90
❑ 114 Darius Watts RC	4.00	1.20
❑ 115 Tatum Bell RC	5.00	1.50
❑ 116 Ben Watson RC	3.00	.90
❑ 117 Drew Henson RC	8.00	2.40
❑ 118 Keary Colbert RC	4.00	1.20
❑ 119 Matt Schaub RC	5.00	1.50
❑ 120 Julius Jones RC	12.00	3.60

2004 UD Diamond All-Star Gold Honors

	Nm-Mt	Ex-Mt
*GOLD STARS: 10X TO 25X BASIC CARDS		
*GOLD ROOKIES: 2.5X TO 6X BASIC CARDS		
STATED PRINT RUN 50 SER.#'d SETS		

2004 UD Diamond All-Star Silver Honors

	Nm-Mt	Ex-Mt
*SILVER STARS: 2X TO 5X BASIC CARDS		
*SILVER ROOKIES: .6X TO 1.5X BASIC CARDS		
OVERALL GOLD/SILVER ODDS 1:6		

2004 UD Diamond All-Star Dean's List Jersey

	Nm-Mt	Ex-Mt
OVERALL INSERT ODDS 1:24		
❑ DLAG Ahman Green	10.00	3.00
❑ DLBF Brett Favre	30.00	9.00
❑ DLBU Brian Urlacher	15.00	4.50
❑ DLCP Clinton Portis SP	12.00	3.60
❑ DLDC Daunte Culpepper	10.00	3.00
❑ DLDM Donovan McNabb	12.00	3.60
❑ DLLT LaDainian Tomlinson	10.00	3.00
❑ DLMH Marvin Harrison	10.00	3.00
❑ DLMV Michael Vick SP	25.00	7.50
❑ DLPH Priest Holmes	12.00	3.60
❑ DLPM Peyton Manning	15.00	4.50
❑ DLRM Randy Moss	12.00	3.60
❑ DLRW Ricky Williams	10.00	3.00
❑ DLSM Steve McNair	8.00	2.40
❑ DLTB Tom Brady	20.00	6.00
❑ DLTH Torry Holt	10.00	3.00

2004 UD Diamond All-Star Future Gems Jersey

	Nm-Mt	Ex-Mt
OVERALL INSERT ODDS 1:24		
❑ FGAB Anquan Boldin SP	10.00	3.00
❑ FGAJ Andre Johnson SP	8.00	2.40
❑ FGBJ Bethel Johnson	8.00	2.40
❑ FGBL Byron Leftwich	15.00	4.50
❑ FGCB Chris Brown	10.00	3.00
❑ FGCP Carson Palmer	10.00	3.00
❑ FGCR Charles Rogers SP	8.00	2.40
❑ FGDC Dallas Clark	6.00	1.80
❑ FGDD Domanick Davis SP	10.00	3.00
❑ FGJF Justin Fargas	6.00	1.80
❑ FGKB Kyle Boller	8.00	2.40
❑ FGKW Kelley Washington	6.00	1.80
❑ FGLJ Larry Johnson	6.00	1.80
❑ FGLS Lee Suggs	8.00	2.40
❑ FGOS Onterrio Smith	8.00	2.40
❑ FGRG Rex Grossman	8.00	2.40
❑ FGTC Tyrone Calico	6.00	1.80
❑ FGTN Terence Newman	8.00	2.40
❑ FGTS Terrell Suggs	6.00	1.80
❑ FGWM Willis McGahee	10.00	3.00

2004 UD Diamond All-Star Premium Stars

	Nm-Mt	Ex-Mt
OVERALL INSERT ODDS 1:24		
❑ PS1 Michael Vick	6.00	1.80
❑ PS2 Brett Favre	8.00	2.40
❑ PS3 Peyton Manning	5.00	1.50
❑ PS4 Randy Moss	4.00	1.20
❑ PS5 Clinton Portis	3.00	.90
❑ PS6 Donovan McNabb	4.00	1.20
❑ PS7 LaDainian Tomlinson	3.00	.90
❑ PS8 Jerry Rice	6.00	1.80
❑ PS9 Ricky Williams	3.00	.90

❑ PS10 Chad Pennington	4.00	1.20
❑ PS11 Priest Holmes	4.00	1.20
❑ PS12 Tom Brady	5.00	1.50
❑ PS13 Deuce McAllister	3.00	.90
❑ PS14 Michael Strahan	2.00	.60
❑ PS15 Steve McNair	3.00	.90

2004 UD Diamond All-Star Promo

	Nm-Mt	Ex-Mt
ONE PER PACK		
❑ AS1 Eli Manning	8.00	2.40
❑ AS2 Larry Fitzgerald	5.00	1.50
❑ AS3 Ben Roethlisberger	15.00	4.50
❑ AS4 Philip Rivers	5.00	1.50
❑ AS5 Roy Williams WR	5.00	1.50
❑ AS6 Steven Jackson	5.00	1.50
❑ AS7 Kellen Winslow Jr.	4.00	1.20
❑ AS8 Reggie Williams	2.00	.60
❑ AS9 Sean Taylor	2.00	.60
❑ AS10 Chris Gamble	2.00	.60
❑ AS11 DeAngelo Hall	2.00	.60
❑ AS12 Kevin Jones	5.00	1.50
❑ AS13 Teddy Lehman	1.50	.45
❑ AS14 Michael Clayton	4.00	1.20
❑ AS15 Rashaun Woods	2.00	.60
❑ AS16 Karlos Dansby	1.50	.45
❑ AS17 Ben Troupe	1.50	.45
❑ AS18 Kenechi Udeze	1.50	.45
❑ AS19 Lee Evans	2.50	.75
❑ AS20 Jonathan Vilma	1.50	.45
❑ AS21 J.P. Losman	4.00	1.20
❑ AS22 Michael Jenkins	1.50	.45
❑ AS23 Greg Jones	1.50	.45
❑ AS24 Carlos Francis	1.25	.35
❑ AS25 Devery Henderson	1.25	.35
❑ AS26 Michael Turner	1.25	.35
❑ AS27 Chris Perry	3.00	.90
❑ AS28 Keary Colbert	2.00	.60
❑ AS29 Matt Schaub	2.50	.75
❑ AS30 Cody Pickett	1.50	.45
❑ AS31 Julius Jones	6.00	1.80
❑ AS32 Tommie Harris	2.00	.60
❑ AS33 Will Smith	1.50	.45
❑ AS34 Vince Wilfork	2.00	.60
❑ AS35 D.J. Williams	2.00	.60
❑ AS36 Joey Thomas	1.25	.35
❑ AS37 Antwan Odom	1.50	.45
❑ AS38 Dunta Robinson	1.50	.45
❑ AS39 Craig Krenzel	2.00	.60
❑ AS40 Cedric Cobbs	1.50	.45
❑ AS41 Tatum Bell	2.50	.75
❑ AS42 B.J. Symons	1.50	.45
❑ AS43 P.K. Sam	1.25	.35
❑ AS44 Jerricho Cotchery	1.50	.45
❑ AS45 John Navarre	1.50	.45
❑ AS46 Josh Harris	1.50	.45
❑ AS47 Will Poole	1.50	.45
❑ AS48 Matt Ware	1.50	.45
❑ AS49 Samie Parker	1.50	.45
❑ AS50 Drew Henson	4.00	1.20
❑ AS51 Michael Boulware	1.50	.45
❑ AS52 Jared Lorenzen	1.25	.35
❑ AS53 Derrick Strait	1.50	.45
❑ AS54 Ben Watson	1.50	.45
❑ AS55 Ernest Wilford	1.50	.45
❑ AS56 Darius Watts	2.00	.60
❑ AS57 Devard Darling	1.50	.45
❑ AS58 Bob Sanders	1.50	.45
❑ AS59 Stuart Schweigert	1.50	.45
❑ AS60 Robert Gallery	2.50	.75
❑ AS61 Mewelde Moore	2.00	.60
❑ AS62 Johnnie Morant	1.50	.45
❑ AS63 Bernard Berrian	1.50	.45
❑ AS64 Kris Wilson	1.50	.45
❑ AS65 Ben Hartsock	1.50	.45
❑ AS66 Jeff Smoker	2.50	.75
❑ AS67 Luke McCown	1.50	.45
❑ AS68 Derrick Hamilton	1.25	.35
❑ AS69 Wild Card	1.50	.45

2004 UD Diamond All-Star Stars of 2004 Autographs

	Nm-Mt	Ex-Mt
STATED PRINT RUN 100 SER.#'d SETS		
❑ BL Brandon Lloyd	40.00	12.00
❑ CC Chris Chambers		
❑ CJ Chad Johnson		
❑ DD Domanick Davis		
❑ DH Dante Hall		
❑ TG Tony Gonzalez	40.00	12.00

2004 UD Diamond Pro Sigs

	Nm-Mt	Ex-Mt
COMP.SET w/o SP's (90)	20.00	6.00
91-140 ROOKIE STATED ODDS 1:6		
❑ 1 Marcel Shipp	.40	.12
❑ 2 Anquan Boldin	.60	.18
❑ 3 Michael Vick	1.25	.35
❑ 4 Peerless Price	.40	.12
❑ 5 Warrick Dunn	.40	.12
❑ 6 Todd Heap	.40	.12
❑ 7 Kyle Boller	.60	.18
❑ 8 Jamal Lewis	.60	.18
❑ 9 Drew Bledsoe	.60	.18
❑ 10 Travis Henry	.40	.12
❑ 11 Eric Moulds	.40	.12
❑ 12 Julius Peppers	.60	.18
❑ 13 Stephen Davis	.40	.12
❑ 14 Jake Delhomme	.60	.18
❑ 15 Anthony Thomas	.40	.12
❑ 16 Brian Urlacher	.75	.23
❑ 17 Marty Booker	.40	.12
❑ 18 Chad Johnson	.40	.12
❑ 19 Rudi Johnson	.40	.12
❑ 20 Carson Palmer	.75	.23
❑ 21 Andre Davis	.25	.07
❑ 22 Jeff Garcia	.60	.18
❑ 23 Eddie George	.40	.12
❑ 24 Vinny Testaverde	.40	.12
❑ 25 Keyshawn Johnson	.40	.12
❑ 26 Ashley Lelie	.40	.12
❑ 27 Jake Plummer	.40	.12
❑ 28 Quentin Griffin	.60	.18
❑ 29 Charles Rogers	.40	.12
❑ 30 Joey Harrington	.60	.18
❑ 31 Ahman Green	.60	.18
❑ 32 Brett Favre	1.50	.45
❑ 33 Donald Driver	.40	.12
❑ 34 David Carr	.60	.18
❑ 35 Domanick Davis	.60	.18
❑ 36 Andre Johnson	.60	.18
❑ 37 Marvin Harrison	.60	.18
❑ 38 Edgerrin James	.60	.18
❑ 39 Peyton Manning	1.00	.30
❑ 40 Byron Leftwich	1.00	.30
❑ 41 Fred Taylor	.40	.12
❑ 42 Trent Green	.40	.12
❑ 43 Dante Hall	.60	.18
❑ 44 Priest Holmes	.75	.23
❑ 45 Ricky Williams	.60	.18
❑ 46 Chris Chambers	.40	.12
❑ 47 Junior Seau	.60	.18
❑ 48 Daunte Culpepper	.60	.18
❑ 49 Randy Moss	.75	.23
❑ 50 Moe Williams	.25	.07
❑ 51 Tom Brady	1.00	.30
❑ 52 Deion Branch	.60	.18
❑ 53 Corey Dillon	.40	.12
❑ 54 Deuce McAllister	.60	.18
❑ 55 Aaron Brooks	.40	.12
❑ 56 Joe Horn	.40	.12
❑ 57 Michael Strahan	.40	.12
❑ 58 Tiki Barber	.40	.12
❑ 59 Jeremy Shockey	.60	.18
❑ 60 Chad Pennington	.75	.23
❑ 61 Santana Moss	.40	.12
❑ 62 Curtis Martin	.60	.18
❑ 63 Rich Gannon	.40	.12
❑ 64 Jerry Rice	1.25	.35
❑ 65 Jerry Porter	.40	.12
❑ 66 Terrell Owens	.60	.18
❑ 67 Brian Westbrook	.40	.12
❑ 68 Donovan McNabb	.75	.23
❑ 69 Hines Ward	.60	.18
❑ 70 Duce Staley	.40	.12
❑ 71 Tommy Maddox	.40	.12
❑ 72 Drew Brees	.60	.18
❑ 73 LaDainian Tomlinson	.60	.18
❑ 74 Tim Rattay	.40	.12
❑ 75 Brandon Lloyd	.40	.12
❑ 76 Kevan Barlow	.40	.12
❑ 77 Shaun Alexander	.60	.18
❑ 78 Koren Robinson	.40	.12
❑ 79 Matt Hasselbeck	.40	.12
❑ 80 Marshall Faulk	.60	.18
❑ 81 Torry Holt	.60	.18
❑ 82 Marc Bulger	.60	.18
❑ 83 Brad Johnson	.40	.12
❑ 84 Derrick Brooks	.40	.12
❑ 85 Steve McNair	.60	.18
❑ 86 Derrick Mason	.40	.12
❑ 87 Chris Brown	.60	.18
❑ 88 Mark Brunell	.40	.12
❑ 89 Laveranues Coles	.40	.12
❑ 90 Clinton Portis	.60	.18
❑ 91 Eli Manning RC	15.00	4.50
❑ 92 Larry Fitzgerald RC	10.00	3.00
❑ 93 Ben Roethlisberger RC	30.00	9.00
❑ 94 Roy Williams RC	10.00	3.00
❑ 95 Sean Taylor RC	4.00	1.20
❑ 96 Kellen Winslow RC	8.00	2.40
❑ 97 Chris Gamble RC	4.00	1.20
❑ 98 Steven Jackson RC	10.00	3.00
❑ 99 DeAngelo Hall RC	4.00	1.20
❑ 100 Kevin Jones RC	10.00	3.00
❑ 101 Reggie Williams RC	4.00	1.20
❑ 102 Michael Clayton RC	8.00	2.40
❑ 103 Rashaun Woods RC	4.00	1.20
❑ 104 D.J. Williams RC	4.00	1.20
❑ 105 Ben Troupe RC	3.00	.90
❑ 106 Mewelde Moore RC	4.00	1.20

❑ 107 Lee Evans RC	5.00	1.50
❑ 108 Jonathan Vilma RC	3.00	.90
❑ 109 Chris Perry RC	6.00	1.80
❑ 110 J.P. Losman RC	8.00	2.40
❑ 111 Philip Rivers RC	10.00	3.00
❑ 112 Michael Jenkins RC	3.00	.90
❑ 113 Greg Jones RC	3.00	.90
❑ 114 John Navarre RC	3.00	.90
❑ 115 Jerricho Cotchery RC	3.00	.90
❑ 116 Michael Turner RC	2.50	.75
❑ 117 Drew Henson RC	8.00	2.40
❑ 118 Keary Colbert RC	4.00	1.20
❑ 119 Matt Schaub RC	5.00	1.50
❑ 120 Cody Pickett RC	3.00	.90
❑ 121 Luke McCown RC	3.00	.90
❑ 122 P.K. Sam RC	2.50	.75
❑ 123 Ernest Wilford RC	3.00	.90
❑ 124 Will Smith RC	3.00	.90
❑ 125 Bernard Berrian RC	3.00	.90
❑ 126 Robert Gallery RC	5.00	1.50
❑ 127 Ben Watson RC	3.00	.90
❑ 128 Devery Henderson RC	2.50	.75
❑ 129 Jeff Smoker RC	5.00	1.50
❑ 130 Josh Harris RC	3.00	.90
❑ 131 Julius Jones RC	12.00	3.60
❑ 132 Dunta Robinson RC	3.00	.90
❑ 133 Tatum Bell RC	5.00	1.50
❑ 134 Cedric Cobbs RC	3.00	.90
❑ 135 Devard Darling RC	3.00	.90
❑ 136 Johnnie Morant RC	3.00	.90
❑ 137 Derrick Hamilton RC	2.50	.75
❑ 138 Darius Watts RC	4.00	1.20
❑ 139 Tommie Harris RC	4.00	1.20
❑ 140 B.J. Symons RC	3.00	.90

2004 UD Diamond Pro Sigs Rookie Gold

Nm-Mt Ex-Mt

*ROOKIES: .8X TO 2X BASE CARD HI
STATED PRINT RUN 349 SER.#'d SETS

2004 UD Diamond Pro Sigs Signature Collection

	Nm-Mt	Ex-Mt
STATED ODDS 1:24		
*GOLDS: 1.2X TO 3X BASIC AUTOS		
GOLD PRINT RUN 25 SER.#'d SETS		
UNPRICED PLATINUM PRINT RUN 10 SETS		
EXCH EXPIRATION: 9/16/2007		
❑ SCAR Antwaan Randle El	15.00	4.50
❑ SCBB Bernard Berrian	20.00	6.00
❑ SCBC Brandon Chillar	10.00	3.00
❑ SCBF Brett Favre SP		
❑ SCBH Ben Hartsock SP	10.00	3.00
❑ SCBJ B.J. Symons	10.00	3.00
❑ SCBL Brandon Lloyd	10.00	3.00
❑ SCBR Ben Roethlisberger SP	300.00	90.00
❑ SCBT Ben Troupe	15.00	4.50
❑ SCBW Ben Watson	15.00	4.50
❑ SCCB Chris Brown SP	20.00	6.00
❑ SCCC Cedric Cobbs	20.00	6.00
❑ SCCF Clarence Farmer	10.00	3.00
❑ SCCJ Chad Johnson SP	20.00	6.00
❑ SCCL Casey Clausen	20.00	6.00
❑ SCCP Cody Pickett	20.00	6.00
❑ SCDA Dante Hall SP		
❑ SCDD Devard Darling	20.00	6.00
❑ SCDE Derrick Mason SP	20.00	6.00
❑ SCDH DeAngelo Hall	20.00	6.00
❑ SCDV Devery Henderson SP		
❑ SCDW Darius Watts SP	15.00	4.50
❑ SCEM Eli Manning	100.00	30.00
❑ SCEW Ernest Wilford	15.00	4.50
❑ SCGJ Greg Jones	15.00	4.50
❑ SCHE Todd Heap SP		
❑ SCJC Jerricho Cotchery	15.00	4.50
❑ SCJE Jesse Palmer SP	10.00	3.00
❑ SCJG Joey Galloway SP	15.00	4.50
❑ SCJM Johnnie Morant	10.00	3.00
❑ SCJN John Navarre	15.00	4.50
❑ SCJP J.P. Losman	50.00	15.00
❑ SCJS Jeff Smoker	20.00	6.00
❑ SCJV Jonathan Vilma	15.00	4.50
❑ SCJW Javon Walker EXCH	20.00	6.00
❑ SCKC Keary Colbert	20.00	6.00
❑ SCKJ Kevin Jones	50.00	15.00
❑ SCKU Kenechi Udeze	15.00	4.50
❑ SCLE Lee Evans SP	20.00	6.00
❑ SCLM Luke McCown	20.00	6.00
❑ SCMC Michael Clayton	40.00	12.00
❑ SCMJ Michael Jenkins	15.00	4.50
❑ SCMS Matt Schaub	25.00	7.50
❑ SCPE Chris Perry	25.00	7.50
❑ SCPM Peyton Manning SP	60.00	18.00
❑ SCQW Quincy Wilson	10.00	3.00
❑ SCRA Rashaun Woods	20.00	6.00
❑ SCRE Reggie Williams EXCH	20.00	6.00
❑ SCRG Robert Gallery	25.00	7.50
❑ SCRJ Rudi Johnson SP	15.00	4.50
❑ SCRW Roy Williams WR SP	60.00	18.00
❑ SCSJ Steven Jackson	50.00	15.00
❑ SCSP Samie Parker	20.00	6.00
❑ SCST Sean Taylor EXCH	25.00	7.50
❑ SCTH Tommie Harris	15.00	4.50
❑ SCTR Travis Henry	15.00	4.50
❑ SCVW Vince Wilfork	20.00	6.00
❑ SCWM Willis McGahee SP		
❑ SCWS Will Smith EXCH	10.00	3.00
❑ SCZT Zach Thomas SP		

2001 UD Game Gear

	Nm-Mt	Ex-Mt
COMP.SET w/o SP's (90)	30.00	9.00
❑ 1 Jake Plummer	.75	.23
❑ 2 David Boston	1.25	.35
❑ 3 Jamal Anderson	1.25	.35
❑ 4 Shawn Jefferson	.50	.15
❑ 5 Jamal Lewis	2.00	.60
❑ 6 Elvis Grbac	.75	.23
❑ 7 Ray Lewis	1.25	.35
❑ 8 Rob Johnson	.75	.23
❑ 9 Shawn Bryson	.50	.15
❑ 10 Muhsin Muhammad	.75	.23
❑ 11 Jeff Lewis	.50	.15
❑ 12 Marcus Robinson	1.25	.35
❑ 13 James Allen	.75	.23
❑ 14 Brian Urlacher	2.00	.60
❑ 15 Cade McNown	.50	.15
❑ 16 Peter Warrick	1.25	.35
❑ 17 Akili Smith	.50	.15
❑ 18 Corey Dillon	1.25	.35
❑ 19 Tim Couch	.75	.23
❑ 20 Kevin Johnson	.75	.23
❑ 21 Emmitt Smith	2.50	.75
❑ 22 Rocket Ismail	.75	.23
❑ 23 Joey Galloway	.75	.23
❑ 24 Terrell Davis	1.25	.35
❑ 25 Brian Griese	1.25	.35
❑ 26 Ed McCaffrey	1.25	.35
❑ 27 Mike Anderson	1.25	.35
❑ 28 Charlie Batch	1.25	.35
❑ 29 Germane Crowell	.50	.15
❑ 30 James Stewart	.75	.23
❑ 31 Brett Favre	4.00	1.20
❑ 32 Dorsey Levens	.75	.23
❑ 33 Ahman Green	1.25	.35
❑ 34 Peyton Manning	3.00	.90
❑ 35 Edgerrin James	1.50	.45
❑ 36 Marvin Harrison	1.25	.35
❑ 37 Mark Brunell	1.25	.35
❑ 38 Jimmy Smith	.75	.23
❑ 39 Fred Taylor	1.25	.35
❑ 40 Tony Gonzalez	.75	.23
❑ 41 Derrick Alexander	.75	.23
❑ 42 Trent Green	1.25	.35
❑ 43 Lamar Smith	.75	.23
❑ 44 Oronde Gadsden	.75	.23
❑ 45 Zach Thomas	1.25	.35
❑ 46 Randy Moss	2.50	.75
❑ 47 Daunte Culpepper	1.25	.35
❑ 48 Doug Chapman	.50	.15
❑ 49 Cris Carter	1.25	.35
❑ 50 Drew Bledsoe	1.50	.45
❑ 51 Terry Glenn	.75	.23
❑ 52 Troy Brown	.75	.23
❑ 53 Ricky Williams	1.25	.35
❑ 54 Jeff Blake	.75	.23
❑ 55 Aaron Brooks	1.25	.35
❑ 56 Joe Horn	.75	.23
❑ 57 Kerry Collins	.75	.23
❑ 58 Ron Dayne	1.25	.35
❑ 59 Amani Toomer	.75	.23
❑ 60 Tiki Barber	.75	.23
❑ 61 Vinny Testaverde	.75	.23
❑ 62 Curtis Martin	1.25	.35
❑ 63 Wayne Chrebet	.75	.23
❑ 64 Rich Gannon	1.25	.35
❑ 65 Jerry Rice	2.50	.75
❑ 66 Tim Brown	1.25	.35
❑ 67 Duce Staley	1.25	.35
❑ 68 Donovan McNabb	1.50	.45
❑ 69 Jerome Bettis	1.25	.35
❑ 70 Kordell Stewart	.75	.23
❑ 71 Marshall Faulk	1.50	.45
❑ 72 Kurt Warner	2.50	.75
❑ 73 Torry Holt	1.25	.35
❑ 74 Isaac Bruce	1.25	.35
❑ 75 Doug Flutie	1.25	.35
❑ 76 Junior Seau	1.25	.35
❑ 77 Jeff Garcia	1.25	.35
❑ 78 Terrell Owens	1.25	.35
❑ 79 Matt Hasselbeck	.75	.23
❑ 80 Shaun Alexander	1.50	.45
❑ 81 Ricky Watters	.75	.23
❑ 82 Keyshawn Johnson	1.25	.35
❑ 83 Brad Johnson	1.25	.35
❑ 84 Warrick Dunn	1.25	.35
❑ 85 Mike Alstott	1.25	.35
❑ 86 Eddie George	1.25	.35
❑ 87 Steve McNair	1.25	.35
❑ 88 Jeff George	.75	.23
❑ 89 Michael Westbrook	.75	.23
❑ 90 Stephen Davis	.75	.23
❑ 91 Mike McMahon RC	5.00	1.50
❑ 92 James Jackson RC	5.00	1.50
❑ 93 Quincy Morgan RC	5.00	1.50
❑ 94 Travis Minor RC	5.00	1.50
❑ 95 Chris Chambers RC	8.00	2.40
❑ 96 Jesse Palmer RC	5.00	1.50
❑ 97 Santana Moss RC	10.00	3.00
❑ 98 Marques Tuiasosopo RC	5.00	1.50
❑ 99 Freddie Mitchell RC	5.00	1.50
❑ 100 Kevan Barlow RC	5.00	1.50
❑ 101 Michael Vick RC	60.00	18.00
❑ 102 Chris Weinke RC	8.00	2.40
❑ 103 Reggie Wayne RC	15.00	4.50
❑ 104 Robert Ferguson RC	8.00	2.40
❑ 105 Michael Bennett RC	20.00	6.00
❑ 106 Deuce McAllister RC	20.00	6.00
❑ 107 Drew Brees RC	20.00	6.00

	Nm-Mt	Ex-Mt
❑ 108 LaDainian Tomlinson RC	30.00	9.00
❑ 109 Koren Robinson RC	12.00	3.60
❑ 110 Rod Gardner RC	8.00	2.40
❑ EJ Edgerrin James SAMPLE	2.50	.75

2001 UD Game Gear Rookie Jerseys

	Nm-Mt	Ex-Mt
❑ 91 Mike McMahon	15.00	4.50
❑ 92 James Jackson	12.00	3.60
❑ 93 Quincy Morgan	15.00	4.50
❑ 94 Travis Minor	15.00	4.50
❑ 95 Chris Chambers	20.00	6.00
❑ 96 Jesse Palmer	12.00	3.60
❑ 97 Santana Moss	25.00	7.50
❑ 98 Marques Tuiasosopo	15.00	4.50
❑ 99 Freddie Mitchell	15.00	4.50
❑ 100 Kevan Barlow	15.00	4.50
❑ 101 Michael Vick	80.00	24.00
❑ 102 Chris Weinke	15.00	4.50
❑ 103 Reggie Wayne	25.00	7.50
❑ 104 Robert Ferguson	15.00	4.50
❑ 105 Michael Bennett	30.00	9.00
❑ 106 Deuce McAllister	40.00	12.00
❑ 107 Drew Brees	30.00	9.00
❑ 108 LaDainian Tomlinson	50.00	15.00
❑ 109 Koren Robinson	15.00	4.50
❑ 110 Rod Gardner	15.00	4.50

2001 UD Game Gear Autographs

	Nm-Mt	Ex-Mt
❑ ATGS Anthony Thomas	25.00	7.50
❑ AZGS Az-Zahir Hakim	12.00	3.60
❑ CCGS Chris Chambers	15.00	4.50
❑ CJGS Chad Johnson	25.00	7.50
❑ CWGS Chris Weinke SP/390	15.00	4.50
❑ DBGS Drew Brees	30.00	9.00
❑ DMGS Dan Morgan	15.00	4.50
❑ DTGS David Terrell	25.00	7.50
❑ DUGS Deuce McAllister	40.00	12.00
❑ GAGS Rich Gannon SP/360	25.00	7.50
❑ GWGS Gerard Warren	15.00	4.50
❑ JBGS Jim Brown SP/295	80.00	24.00
❑ JGGS Jeff Garcia	25.00	7.50
❑ JLGS Jamal Lewis SP/295	25.00	7.50
❑ JNGS Joe Namath SP/295	100.00	30.00
❑ JRGS John Riggins SP/395	50.00	15.00
❑ KRGS Koren Robinson	15.00	4.50
❑ KYGS Ken-Yon Rambo	12.00	3.60
❑ LTGS LaDainian Tomlinson	60.00	18.00
❑ MBGS Michael Bennett	25.00	7.50
❑ MVGS Michael Vick SP/195	150.00	45.00
❑ PMGS Peyton Manning	80.00	24.00
❑ RDGS Ron Dayne	15.00	4.50
❑ RGGS Rod Gardner SP/150	50.00	15.00
❑ RMGS Randy Moss SP/95	150.00	45.00
❑ RWGS Reggie Wayne	25.00	7.50
❑ SMGS Santana Moss	25.00	7.50
❑ TGGS Tony Gonzalez	25.00	7.50

2000 UD Graded

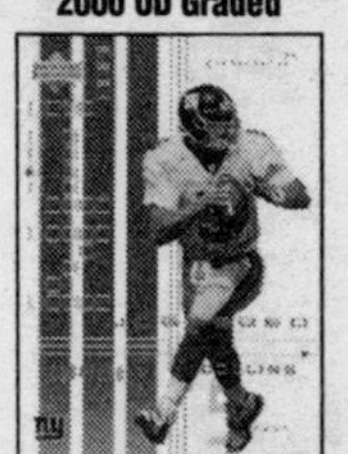

	Nm-Mt	Ex-Mt
COMP.SET w/o SP's (90)	100.00	45.00
❑ 1 Jake Plummer	2.50	1.10
❑ 2 David Boston	4.00	1.80
❑ 3 Jamal Anderson	4.00	1.80
❑ 4 Shawn Jefferson	1.50	.70
❑ 5 Qadry Ismail	2.50	1.10
❑ 6 Tony Banks	2.50	1.10
❑ 7 Priest Holmes	5.00	2.20
❑ 8 Rob Johnson	2.50	1.10
❑ 9 Eric Moulds	4.00	1.80
❑ 10 Steve Beuerlein	2.50	1.10
❑ 11 Muhsin Muhammad	2.50	1.10
❑ 12 Donald Hayes	1.50	.70
❑ 13 Tim Biakabutuka	2.50	1.10
❑ 14 Cade McNown	1.50	.70
❑ 15 Marcus Robinson	4.00	1.80
❑ 16 James Allen	1.50	.70
❑ 17 Akili Smith	1.50	.70
❑ 18 Corey Dillon	4.00	1.80
❑ 19 Tim Couch	2.50	1.10
❑ 20 Kevin Johnson	4.00	1.80
❑ 21 Troy Aikman	8.00	3.60
❑ 22 Emmitt Smith	8.00	3.60
❑ 23 Rocket Ismail	2.50	1.10
❑ 24 Terrell Davis	4.00	1.80
❑ 25 Rod Smith	2.50	1.10
❑ 26 Brian Griese	4.00	1.80
❑ 27 Charlie Batch	4.00	1.80
❑ 28 James Stewart	2.50	1.10
❑ 29 Germane Crowell	1.50	.70
❑ 30 Brett Favre	12.00	5.50
❑ 31 Antonio Freeman	4.00	1.80
❑ 32 Dorsey Levens	2.50	1.10
❑ 33 Peyton Manning	10.00	4.50
❑ 34 Edgerrin James	6.00	2.70
❑ 35 Marvin Harrison	4.00	1.80
❑ 36 Mark Brunell	4.00	1.80
❑ 37 Jimmy Smith	2.50	1.10
❑ 38 Fred Taylor	4.00	1.80
❑ 39 Elvis Grbac	2.50	1.10
❑ 40 Tony Gonzalez	2.50	1.10
❑ 41 Lamar Smith	2.50	1.10
❑ 42 Jay Fiedler	4.00	1.80
❑ 43 Randy Moss	8.00	3.60
❑ 44 Daunte Culpepper	5.00	2.20
❑ 45 Robert Smith	4.00	1.80
❑ 46 Cris Carter	4.00	1.80
❑ 47 Drew Bledsoe	5.00	2.20
❑ 48 Kevin Faulk	2.50	1.10
❑ 49 Terry Glenn	4.00	1.80
❑ 50 Ricky Williams	4.00	1.80
❑ 51 Jeff Blake	2.50	1.10
❑ 52 Joe Horn	2.50	1.10
❑ 53 Kerry Collins	2.50	1.10
❑ 54 Amani Toomer	2.50	1.10
❑ 55 Tiki Barber	2.50	1.10
❑ 56 Wayne Chrebet	2.50	1.10
❑ 57 Curtis Martin	4.00	1.80
❑ 58 Vinny Testaverde	2.50	1.10
❑ 59 Tyrone Wheatley	2.50	1.10
❑ 60 Tim Brown	4.00	1.80
❑ 61 Rich Gannon	4.00	1.80
❑ 62 Duce Staley	4.00	1.80
❑ 63 Charles Johnson	2.50	1.10
❑ 64 Donovan McNabb	6.00	2.70
❑ 65 Bobby Shaw RC	5.00	2.20
❑ 66 Kordell Stewart	2.50	1.10
❑ 67 Jerome Bettis	4.00	1.80
❑ 68 Marshall Faulk	5.00	2.20
❑ 69 Isaac Bruce	4.00	1.80
❑ 70 Torry Holt	4.00	1.80
❑ 71 Kurt Warner	8.00	3.60
❑ 72 Neil Smith	1.50	.70
❑ 73 Ryan Leaf	2.50	1.10
❑ 74 Curtis Conway	2.50	1.10
❑ 75 Jeff Garcia	4.00	1.80
❑ 76 Charlie Garner	2.50	1.10
❑ 77 Jerry Rice	8.00	3.60
❑ 78 Ricky Watters	2.50	1.10
❑ 79 Brock Huard	2.50	1.10
❑ 80 Jon Kitna	4.00	1.80
❑ 81 Keyshawn Johnson	4.00	1.80
❑ 82 Jacquez Green	1.50	.70
❑ 83 Mike Alstott	4.00	1.80
❑ 84 Shaun King	1.50	.70
❑ 85 Eddie George	4.00	1.80
❑ 86 Kevin Dyson	2.50	1.10
❑ 87 Steve McNair	4.00	1.80
❑ 88 Brad Johnson	4.00	1.80
❑ 89 Stephen Davis	4.00	1.80
❑ 90 Jeff George	2.50	1.10
❑ 91 Ron Dixon RC	8.00	3.60
❑ 92 Avion Black RC	8.00	3.60
❑ 93 Hank Poteat RC	8.00	3.60
❑ 94 Doug Chapman RC	8.00	3.60
❑ 95 Drew Haddad RC	6.00	2.70
❑ 96 Rondell Mealey RC	6.00	2.70
❑ 97 Spergon Wynn RC	8.00	3.60
❑ 98 Keith Bulluck RC	10.00	4.50
❑ 99 John Abraham RC	10.00	4.50
❑ 100 Rob Morris RC	8.00	3.60
❑ 101 Jerry Porter RC	12.00	5.50
❑ 102 Laveranues Coles RC	12.00	5.50
❑ 103 Jarious Jackson RC	8.00	3.60
❑ 104 Tom Brady RC	150.00	70.00
❑ 105 Jonas Lewis RC	6.00	2.70
❑ 106 Todd Husak RC	10.00	4.50
❑ 107 Shyrone Stith RC	8.00	3.60
❑ 108 Sammy Morris RC	8.00	3.60
❑ 109 Corey Simon RC	10.00	4.50
❑ 110 Chad Morton RC	10.00	4.50
❑ 111 Brian Urlacher RC	40.00	18.00
❑ 112 Anthony Becht RC	10.00	4.50
❑ 113 Chris Cole RC	8.00	3.60
❑ 114 Anthony Lucas RC	6.00	2.70
❑ 115 Charles Lee RC	6.00	2.70
❑ 116 JaJuan Dawson RC	6.00	2.70
❑ 117 Darrell Jackson RC	20.00	9.00
❑ 118 Gari Scott RC	6.00	2.70
❑ 119 Windrell Hayes RC	8.00	3.60
❑ 120 Paul Smith RC	8.00	3.60
❑ 121 Mareno Philyaw RC	6.00	2.70
❑ 122 Trevor Gaylor RC	8.00	3.60
❑ 123 Muneer Moore RC	6.00	2.70
❑ 124 Michael Wiley RC	8.00	3.60
❑ 125 Ronney Jenkins RC	8.00	3.60
❑ 126 Frank Moreau RC	8.00	3.60
❑ 127 Dante Hall RC	20.00	9.00
❑ 128 Darren Howard RC	8.00	3.60
❑ 129 Todd Pinkston RC	10.00	4.50
❑ 130 Mike Anderson RC	10.00	4.50
❑ 131 Doug Johnson RC	10.00	4.50
❑ 132 Shaun Ellis RC	10.00	4.50
❑ 133 James Williams RC	8.00	3.60
❑ 134 Ron Dugans RC	6.00	2.70
❑ 135 Frank Murphy RC	6.00	2.70
❑ 136 Dez White AU RC	30.00	13.50
❑ 137 Danny Farmer AU RC	25.00	11.00
❑ 140 Reuben Droughns AU RC	40.00	18.00
❑ 141 Jamal Lewis AU RC	80.00	36.00

Card	Nm-Mt	Ex-Mt
❑ 142 J.R. Redmond AU RC	25.00	11.00
❑ 143 Tee Martin AU RC	30.00	13.50
❑ 144 G.Carmazzi AU RC	25.00	11.00
❑ 145 Tim Rattay AU RC	60.00	27.00
❑ 146 Trung Canidate AU RC	25.00	11.00
❑ 149 Chris Coleman AU RC	20.00	9.00
❑ 150 Corey Moore AU RC	20.00	9.00
❑ 151 Troy Walters AU RC	30.00	13.50
❑ 152 Joe Hamilton AU RC	25.00	11.00
❑ 153 Kwame Cavil AU RC	20.00	9.00
❑ 154 Dennis Northcutt AU RC	30.00	13.50
❑ 155 Travis Taylor AU RC	30.00	13.50
❑ 156 Curtis Keaton AU RC	30.00	13.50
❑ 157 Shaun Alexander AU RC	150.00	70.00
❑ 158 Chad Pennington AU RC	325.00	145.00
❑ 159 Sylvester Morris AU RC	30.00	13.50
❑ 160 Plaxico Burress AU RC	80.00	36.00
❑ 161 Ron Dayne AU RC	40.00	18.00
❑ 162 Courtney Brown AU RC	30.00	13.50
❑ 164 Peter Warrick AU RC	30.00	13.50
❑ 165 Chris Redman AU RC	25.00	11.00

2000 UD Graded Jerseys

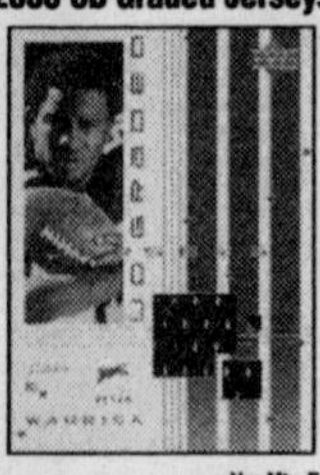

	Nm-Mt	Ex-Mt
❑ GBF Brett Favre	40.00	18.00
❑ GCC Cris Carter	20.00	9.00
❑ GDB Drew Bledsoe	30.00	13.50
❑ GDM Dan Marino	50.00	22.00
❑ GEJ Edgerrin James	40.00	18.00
❑ GES Emmitt Smith	60.00	27.00
❑ GIB Isaac Bruce	60.00	27.00
❑ GJR Jerry Rice	40.00	18.00
❑ GKJ Keyshawn Johnson	20.00	9.00
❑ GKW Kurt Warner	40.00	18.00
❑ GMB Mark Brunell	30.00	13.50
❑ GPM Peyton Manning	40.00	18.00
❑ GPW Peter Warrick	20.00	9.00
❑ GRD Ron Dayne	20.00	9.00
❑ GRJ Rob Johnson	15.00	6.75
❑ GRM Randy Moss	30.00	13.50
❑ GSK Shaun King	15.00	6.75
❑ GSM Steve McNair	20.00	9.00
❑ GTA Troy Aikman	30.00	13.50
❑ GTH Torry Holt	20.00	9.00
❑ GTJ Thomas Jones	20.00	9.00

2001 UD Graded

	Nm-Mt	Ex-Mt
COMP.SET w/o SP's (45)	60.00	18.00
❑ 1 Jake Plummer	1.50	.45
❑ 2 Jamal Anderson	2.50	.75
❑ 3 Jamal Lewis	4.00	1.20
❑ 4 Rob Johnson	1.50	.45
❑ 5 Muhsin Muhammad	1.50	.45
❑ 6 Marcus Robinson	2.50	.75
❑ 7 Peter Warrick	2.50	.75
❑ 8 Corey Dillon	2.50	.75
❑ 9 Tim Couch	1.50	.45
❑ 10 Emmitt Smith	5.00	1.50
❑ 11 Terrell Davis	2.50	.75
❑ 12 Brian Griese	2.50	.75
❑ 13 Charlie Batch	2.50	.75
❑ 14 Brett Favre	8.00	2.40
❑ 15 Peyton Manning	6.00	1.80
❑ 16 Edgerrin James	3.00	.90
❑ 17 Mark Brunell	2.50	.75
❑ 18 Fred Taylor	2.50	.75
❑ 19 Tony Gonzalez	1.50	.45
❑ 20 Trent Green	2.50	.75
❑ 21 Lamar Smith	1.50	.45
❑ 22 Randy Moss	5.00	1.50
❑ 23 Daunte Culpepper	2.50	.75
❑ 24 Drew Bledsoe	3.00	.90
❑ 25 Ricky Williams	2.50	.75
❑ 26 Kerry Collins	1.50	.45
❑ 27 Ron Dayne	2.50	.75
❑ 28 Vinny Testaverde	1.50	.45
❑ 29 Curtis Martin	2.50	.75
❑ 30 Rich Gannon	2.50	.75
❑ 31 Charlie Garner	1.50	.45
❑ 32 Duce Staley	2.50	.75
❑ 33 Donovan McNabb	3.00	.90
❑ 34 Jerome Bettis	2.50	.75
❑ 35 Marshall Faulk	3.00	.90
❑ 36 Kurt Warner	5.00	1.50
❑ 37 Doug Flutie	2.50	.75
❑ 38 Jeff Garcia	2.50	.75
❑ 39 Terrell Owens	2.50	.75
❑ 40 Matt Hasselbeck	1.50	.45
❑ 41 Keyshawn Johnson	2.50	.75
❑ 42 Mike Alstott	2.50	.75
❑ 43 Eddie George	2.50	.75
❑ 44 Steve McNair	2.50	.75
❑ 45 Stephen Davis	2.50	.75
❑ 46 Michael Bennett Action RC	25.00	7.50
❑ 46P Michael Bennett Portrait RC	25.00	7.50
❑ 47 Drew Brees Action RC	25.00	7.50
❑ 47P Drew Brees Portrait RC	25.00	7.50
❑ 48 Chad Johnson Action RC	25.00	7.50
❑ 48P Chad Johnson Portrait RC	25.00	7.50
❑ 49 Deuce McAllister Action RC	30.00	9.00
❑ 49P Deuce McAllister Portrait RC	30.00	9.00
❑ 50 Santana Moss Action RC	25.00	7.50
❑ 50P Santana Moss Portrait RC	25.00	7.50
❑ 51 Koren Robinson Action RC	10.00	3.00
❑ 51P Koren Robinson Portrait RC	10.00	3.00
❑ 52 David Terrell Action RC	10.00	3.00
❑ 52P David Terrell Portrait RC	10.00	3.00
❑ 53 LaDainian Tomlinson Action RC	50.00	15.00
❑ 53P LaDainian Tomlinson Portrait RC	50.00	15.00
❑ 54 Michael Vick Action RC	120.00	36.00
❑ 54P Michael Vick Portrait RC	120.00	36.00
❑ 55 Chris Weinke Action RC	10.00	3.00
❑ 55P Chris Weinke Portrait RC	20.00	6.00
❑ 56 Reggie Wayne Action RC	15.00	4.50
❑ 56P Reggie Wayne Portrait RC	15.00	4.50
❑ 57 Anthony Thomas Action RC	25.00	7.50
❑ 57P Anthony Thomas Portrait RC	25.00	7.50
❑ 58 Sage Rosenfels Action RC	10.00	3.00
❑ 58P Sage Rosenfels Portrait RC	10.00	3.00
❑ 59 Rod Gardner Action RC	10.00	3.00
❑ 59P Rod Gardner Portrait RC	10.00	3.00
❑ 60 Quincy Morgan Action RC	10.00	3.00
❑ 60P Quincy Morgan Portrait RC	10.00	3.00
❑ 61 Freddie Mitchell Action RC	10.00	3.00
❑ 61P Freddie Mitchell Portrait RC	10.00	3.00
❑ 62 Gerard Warren Action RC	10.00	3.00
❑ 62P Gerard Warren Portrait RC	10.00	3.00
❑ 63 James Jackson Action RC	10.00	3.00
❑ 63P James Jackson Portrait RC	10.00	3.00
❑ 64 Travis Henry Action RC	15.00	4.50
❑ 64P Travis Henry Portrait RC	15.00	4.50
❑ 65 Chris Chambers Action RC	15.00	4.50
❑ 65P Chris Chambers Portrait RC	15.00	4.50
❑ 66 Vinny Sutherland Action RC	6.00	1.80
❑ 66P Vinny Sutherland Portrait RC	6.00	1.80
❑ 67 Todd Heap Action RC	10.00	3.00
❑ 67P Todd Heap Portrait RC	10.00	3.00
❑ 68 Dan Morgan Action RC	10.00	3.00
❑ 68P Dan Morgan Portrait RC	10.00	3.00
❑ 69 Rudi Johnson Action RC	25.00	7.50
❑ 69P Rudi Johnson Portrait RC	25.00	7.50
❑ 70 Quincy Carter Action RC	10.00	3.00
❑ 70P Quincy Carter Portrait RC	10.00	3.00
❑ 71 Kevin Kasper Action RC	10.00	3.00
❑ 71P Kevin Kasper Portrait RC	10.00	3.00
❑ 72 Scotty Anderson Action RC	6.00	1.80
❑ 72P Scotty Anderson Portrait RC	6.00	1.80
❑ 73 Mike McMahon Action RC	10.00	3.00
❑ 73P Mike McMahon Portrait RC	10.00	3.00
❑ 74 Robert Ferguson Action RC	10.00	3.00
❑ 74P Robert Ferguson Portrait RC	10.00	3.00
❑ 75 Snoop Minnis Action RC	6.00	1.80
❑ 75P Snoop Minnis Portrait RC	10.00	3.00
❑ 76 Josh Heupel Action RC	10.00	3.00
❑ 76P Josh Heupel Portrait RC	10.00	3.00
❑ 77 Travis Minor Action RC	6.00	1.80
❑ 77P Travis Minor Portrait RC	6.00	1.80
❑ 78 Justin Smith Action RC	10.00	3.00
❑ 78P Justin Smith Portrait RC	10.00	3.00
❑ 79 Jesse Palmer Action RC	10.00	3.00
❑ 79P Jesse Palmer Portrait RC	10.00	3.00
❑ 80 Marques Tuiasosopo Action RC	10.00	3.00
❑ 80P Marques Tuiasosopo Portrait RC	10.00	3.00
❑ 81 A.J. Feeley Action RC	10.00	3.00
❑ 81P A.J. Feeley Portrait RC	10.00	3.00
❑ 82 Correll Buckhalter Action RC	12.00	3.60
❑ 82P Correll Buckhalter Portrait RC	12.00	3.60
❑ 83 Kevan Barlow Action RC	10.00	3.00
❑ 83P Kevan Barlow Portrait RC	10.00	3.00
❑ 84 Alex Bannister Action RC	6.00	1.80
❑ 84P Alex Bannister Portrait RC	6.00	1.80
❑ 85 Josh Booty Action RC	10.00	3.00
❑ 85P Josh Booty Portrait RC	10.00	3.00
❑ 86 Eddie Berlin Action RC	6.00	1.80
❑ 86P Eddie Berlin Portrait RC	6.00	1.80
❑ 87 Andre Carter Action RC	10.00	3.00
❑ 87P Andre Carter Portrait RC	10.00	3.00
❑ 88 LaMont Jordan Action RC	12.00	3.60
❑ 88P LaMont Jordan Portrait RC	12.00	3.60
❑ 89 Ken-Yon Rambo Action RC	6.00	1.80
❑ 89P Ken-Yon Rambo	6.00	1.80

	Nm-Mt	Ex-Mt
Portrait RC		
❑ 90 Alge Crumpler Action RC	12.00	3.60
❑ 90P Alge Crumpler Portrait RC	12.00	3.60

2001 UD Graded Rookie Autographs

	Nm-Mt	Ex-Mt
❑ 46 Michael Bennett	60.00	18.00
❑ 47 Drew Brees	60.00	18.00
❑ 48 Chad Johnson	50.00	15.00
❑ 49 Deuce McAllister	60.00	18.00
❑ 50 Santana Moss	50.00	15.00
❑ 51 Koren Robinson	25.00	7.50
❑ 52 David Terrell	30.00	9.00
❑ 53 LaDainian Tomlinson	80.00	24.00
❑ 54 Michael Vick	175.00	52.50
❑ 55 Chris Weinke	30.00	9.00
❑ 56 Reggie Wayne	30.00	9.00
❑ 57 Anthony Thomas	50.00	15.00
❑ 58 Sage Rosenfels	25.00	7.50
❑ 59 Rod Gardner	40.00	12.00
❑ 60 Quincy Morgan	25.00	7.50
❑ 61 Freddie Mitchell	20.00	6.00
❑ 62 Gerard Warren	20.00	6.00
❑ 63 James Jackson	20.00	6.00
❑ 64 Travis Henry	40.00	12.00
❑ 65 Chris Chambers	40.00	12.00

2001 UD Graded Rookie Jerseys

	Nm-Mt	Ex-Mt
❑ 46 Michael Bennett	30.00	9.00
❑ 47 Drew Brees	30.00	9.00
❑ 48 Chad Johnson	30.00	9.00
❑ 49 Deuce McAllister	40.00	12.00
❑ 50 Santana Moss	30.00	9.00
❑ 51 Koren Robinson	15.00	4.50
❑ 52 David Terrell	15.00	4.50
❑ 53 LaDainian Tomlinson	60.00	18.00
❑ 54 Michael Vick	120.00	36.00
❑ 55 Chris Weinke	15.00	4.50
❑ 56 Reggie Wayne	30.00	9.00
❑ 57 Anthony Thomas	30.00	9.00
❑ 58 Sage Rosenfels	15.00	4.50
❑ 59 Rod Gardner	15.00	4.50
❑ 60 Quincy Morgan	20.00	6.00
❑ 61 Freddie Mitchell	15.00	4.50
❑ 62 Gerard Warren	15.00	4.50
❑ 63 James Jackson	15.00	4.50
❑ 64 Travis Henry	25.00	7.50
❑ 65 Chris Chambers	25.00	7.50

2002 UD Graded

	Nm-Mt	Ex-Mt
COMP.SET w/o SP's (90)	50.00	15.00
❑ 1 David Boston	1.50	.45
❑ 2 Frank Sanders	.60	.18
❑ 3 Jake Plummer	1.00	.30
❑ 4 Shawn Jefferson	.60	.18
❑ 5 Michael Vick	5.00	1.50
❑ 6 Warrick Dunn	1.50	.45
❑ 7 Chris Redman	.60	.18
❑ 8 Ray Lewis	1.50	.45
❑ 9 Travis Taylor	1.00	.30
❑ 10 Drew Bledsoe	2.00	.60
❑ 11 Eric Moulds	1.00	.30
❑ 12 Travis Henry	1.50	.45
❑ 13 Chris Weinke	1.00	.30
❑ 14 Muhsin Muhammad	1.00	.30
❑ 15 Anthony Thomas	1.50	.45
❑ 16 Brian Urlacher	2.50	.75
❑ 17 Jim Miller	.60	.18
❑ 18 Corey Dillon	1.00	.30
❑ 19 Jon Kitna	1.00	.30
❑ 20 Peter Warrick	1.00	.30
❑ 21 James Jackson	.60	.18
❑ 22 Kevin Johnson	1.00	.30
❑ 23 Tim Couch	1.00	.30
❑ 24 Emmitt Smith	4.00	1.20
❑ 25 Joey Galloway	1.00	.30
❑ 26 Quincy Carter	1.00	.30
❑ 27 Brian Griese	1.50	.45
❑ 28 Shannon Sharpe	1.00	.30
❑ 29 Terrell Davis	1.50	.45
❑ 30 Az-Zahir Hakim	1.00	.30
❑ 31 Germane Crowell	.60	.18
❑ 32 Mike McMahon	1.50	.45
❑ 33 Ahman Green	1.50	.45
❑ 34 Brett Favre	4.00	1.20
❑ 35 Terry Glenn	1.00	.30
❑ 36 Jermaine Lewis	.60	.18
❑ 37 James Allen	1.00	.30
❑ 38 Edgerrin James	2.00	.60
❑ 39 Marvin Harrison	1.50	.45
❑ 40 Peyton Manning	3.00	.90
❑ 41 Fred Taylor	1.50	.45
❑ 42 Jimmy Smith	1.00	.30
❑ 43 Mark Brunell	1.50	.45
❑ 44 Priest Holmes	2.00	.60
❑ 45 Trent Green	1.00	.30
❑ 46 Chris Chambers	1.50	.45
❑ 47 Jay Fiedler	1.00	.30
❑ 48 Ricky Williams	5.00	1.50
❑ 49 Daunte Culpepper	1.50	.45
❑ 50 Michael Bennett	1.50	.45
❑ 51 Randy Moss	3.00	.90
❑ 52 Antowain Smith	1.00	.30
❑ 53 Tom Brady	4.00	1.20
❑ 54 Troy Brown	1.00	.30
❑ 55 Aaron Brooks	1.50	.45
❑ 56 Deuce McAllister	2.00	.60
❑ 57 Joe Horn	1.00	.30
❑ 58 Kerry Collins	1.00	.30
❑ 59 Ron Dayne	1.00	.30
❑ 60 Chad Pennington	2.00	.60
❑ 61 Curtis Martin	1.50	.45
❑ 62 Vinny Testaverde	1.00	.30
❑ 63 Jerry Rice	3.00	.90
❑ 64 Rich Gannon	1.50	.45
❑ 65 Tim Brown	1.50	.45
❑ 66 Donovan McNabb	2.00	.60
❑ 67 Duce Staley	1.50	.45
❑ 68 Freddie Mitchell	1.00	.30
❑ 69 Hines Ward	1.50	.45
❑ 70 Jerome Bettis	1.50	.45
❑ 71 Kordell Stewart	1.00	.30
❑ 72 Doug Flutie	1.50	.45
❑ 73 Drew Brees	1.50	.45
❑ 74 LaDainian Tomlinson	2.50	.75
❑ 75 Garrison Hearst	1.00	.30
❑ 76 Jeff Garcia	1.50	.45
❑ 77 Terrell Owens	1.50	.45
❑ 78 Koren Robinson	1.00	.30
❑ 79 Shaun Alexander	1.50	.45
❑ 80 Trent Dilfer	1.00	.30
❑ 81 Isaac Bruce	1.50	.45
❑ 82 Kurt Warner	1.50	.45
❑ 83 Marshall Faulk	1.50	.45
❑ 84 Brad Johnson	1.00	.30
❑ 85 Keyshawn Johnson	1.50	.45
❑ 86 Rob Johnson	1.00	.30
❑ 87 Eddie George	1.50	.45
❑ 88 Steve McNair	1.50	.45
❑ 89 Rod Gardner	1.00	.30
❑ 90 Stephen Davis	1.00	.30
❑ 91 Daniel Graham A RC	6.00	1.80
❑ 92 Josh McCown A RC	8.00	2.40
❑ 93 Josh Scobey A RC	6.00	1.80
❑ 94 T.J. Duckett A RC	10.00	3.00
❑ 95 Ronald Curry A RC	6.00	1.80
❑ 96 Kalimba Edwards A RC	6.00	1.80
❑ 97 Chester Taylor A RC	6.00	1.80
❑ 98 Randy Fasani A RC	5.00	1.50
❑ 99 Adrian Peterson A RC	6.00	1.80
❑ 100 Chad Hutchinson A RC	6.00	1.80
❑ 101 Javon Walker A RC	12.00	3.60
❑ 102 Jonathan Wells A RC	6.00	1.80
❑ 103 David Garrard A RC	6.00	1.80
❑ 104 Leonard Henry A RC	5.00	1.50
❑ 105 Dusty Bonner A RC	5.00	1.50
❑ 106 Donte Stallworth A RC	12.00	3.60
❑ 107 J.T. O'Sullivan A RC	5.00	1.50
❑ 108 Mike Williams A RC	6.00	1.80
❑ 109 Tim Carter A RC	5.00	1.50
❑ 110 Larry Ned A RC	5.00	1.50
❑ 111 Brian Westbrook A RC	10.00	3.00
❑ 112 Freddie Milons A RC	5.00	1.50
❑ 113 Ed Reed A RC	10.00	3.00
❑ 114 Antwaan Randle El A RC	8.00	2.40
❑ 115 Julius Peppers A RC	12.00	3.60
❑ 116 Quentin Jammer A RC	6.00	1.80
❑ 117 John Henderson A RC	6.00	1.80
❑ 118 Travis Stephens A RC	5.00	1.50
❑ 119 Ladell Betts A RC	6.00	1.80
❑ 120 Cliff Russell A RC	5.00	1.50
❑ 121 Daniel Graham P RC	6.00	1.80
❑ 122 Josh McCown P RC	8.00	2.40
❑ 123 Josh Scobey P RC	6.00	1.80
❑ 124 T.J. Duckett P RC	10.00	3.00
❑ 125 Ronald Curry P RC	6.00	1.80
❑ 126 Kalimba Edwards P RC	6.00	1.80
❑ 127 Chester Taylor P RC	6.00	1.80
❑ 128 Randy Fasani P RC	5.00	1.50
❑ 129 Adrian Peterson P RC	6.00	1.80
❑ 130 Chad Hutchinson P RC	6.00	1.80
❑ 131 Javon Walker P RC	12.00	3.60
❑ 132 Jonathan Wells P RC	6.00	1.80
❑ 133 David Garrard P RC	6.00	1.80
❑ 134 Leonard Henry P RC	5.00	1.50
❑ 135 Dusty Bonner P RC	5.00	1.50
❑ 136 Donte Stallworth P RC	12.00	3.60
❑ 137 J.T. O'Sullivan P RC	5.00	1.50
❑ 138 Mike Williams P RC	6.00	1.80
❑ 139 Tim Carter P RC	5.00	1.50
❑ 140 Larry Ned P RC	5.00	1.50
❑ 141 Brian Westbrook P RC	10.00	3.00
❑ 142 Freddie Milons P RC	5.00	1.50
❑ 143 Ed Reed P RC	10.00	3.00
❑ 144 Antwaan Randle El P RC	8.00	2.40
❑ 145 Julius Peppers P RC	12.00	3.60
❑ 146 Quentin Jammer P RC	6.00	1.80

Card	Nm-Mt	Ex-Mt
❑ 147 John Henderson P RC	6.00	1.80
❑ 148 Travis Stephens P RC	5.00	1.50
❑ 149 Ladell Betts P RC	8.00	2.40
❑ 150 Cliff Russell P RC	5.00	1.50
❑ 151 Ron Johnson A AU RC	15.00	4.50
❑ 152 Josh Reed A AU RC	20.00	6.00
❑ 153 DeShaun Foster A AU RC	25.00	7.50
❑ 154 Andre Davis A AU RC	20.00	6.00
❑ 155 Antonio Bryant A AU RC	20.00	6.00
❑ 156 Roy Williams A AU RC	50.00	15.00
❑ 157 Woody Dantzler A AU RC	20.00	6.00
❑ 158 Luke Staley A AU RC	15.00	4.50
❑ 159 Jabar Gaffney A AU RC	20.00	6.00
❑ 160 Rohan Davey A AU RC	20.00	6.00
❑ 161 Brandon Doman A AU RC	20.00	6.00
❑ 162 Napoleon Harris A AU RC	20.00	6.00
❑ 163 Reche Caldwell A AU RC	20.00	6.00
❑ 164 Kelly Campbell A AU RC	15.00	4.50
❑ 165 Eric Crouch A AU RC	30.00	9.00
❑ 166 Ron Johnson P AU RC	15.00	4.50
❑ 167 Josh Reed P AU RC	20.00	6.00
❑ 168 DeShaun Foster P AU RC	25.00	7.50
❑ 169 Andre Davis P AU RC	20.00	6.00
❑ 170 Antonio Bryant P AU RC	20.00	6.00
❑ 171 Roy Williams P AU RC	50.00	15.00
❑ 172 Woody Dantzler P AU RC	20.00	6.00
❑ 173 Luke Staley P AU RC	15.00	4.50
❑ 174 Jabar Gaffney P AU RC	20.00	6.00
❑ 175 Rohan Davey P AU RC	20.00	6.00
❑ 176 Brandon Doman P AU RC	20.00	6.00
❑ 177 Napoleon Harris P AU RC	20.00	6.00
❑ 178 Reche Caldwell P AU RC	20.00	6.00
❑ 179 Kelly Campbell P AU RC	15.00	4.50
❑ 180 Eric Crouch P AU RC	30.00	9.00
❑ 181 Kurt Kittner A AU RC	30.00	9.00
❑ 182 Jeremy Shockey A AU RC	80.00	24.00
❑ 183 William Green A AU RC	50.00	15.00
❑ 184 Clinton Portis A AU RC	80.00	24.00
❑ 185 Ashley Lelie A AU RC	50.00	15.00
❑ 186 Joey Harrington A AU RC	80.00	24.00
❑ 187 David Carr A AU RC	80.00	24.00
❑ 188 Maurice Morris A AU RC	25.00	7.50
❑ 189 Marquise Walker A AU RC	25.00	7.50
❑ 190 Patrick Ramsey A AU RC	60.00	18.00
❑ 191 Kurt Kittner P AU RC	30.00	9.00
❑ 192 Jeremy Shockey P AU RC	80.00	24.00
❑ 193 William Green P AU RC	50.00	15.00
❑ 194 Clinton Portis P AU RC	80.00	24.00
❑ 195 Ashley Lelie P AU RC	50.00	15.00
❑ 196 Joey Harrington P AU RC	80.00	24.00
❑ 197 David Carr P AU RC	80.00	24.00
❑ 198 Maurice Morris P AU RC	25.00	7.50
❑ 199 Marquise Walker P AU RC	25.00	7.50
❑ 200 Patrick Ramsey P AU RC	60.00	18.00

2002 UD Graded Gold

Nm-Mt Ex-Mt

*STARS: 5X TO 12X BASIC CARDS
*91-150 ROOKIES: 1X TO 2.5X
*151-180 ROOKIES: 1X TO 2.5X
*181-200 ROOKIES: .6X TO 1.5X

2002 UD Graded Dual Game Jerseys

Card	Nm-Mt	Ex-Mt
❑ BP100 Drew Bledsoe Peerless Price	30.00	9.00
❑ BS100 Mark Brunell Jimmy Smith	15.00	4.50
❑ BT100 Drew Brees LaDainian Tomlinson	30.00	9.00
❑ CM100 Daunte Culpepper Randy Moss	40.00	12.00
❑ FC100 Jay Fiedler Chris Chambers	20.00	6.00
❑ FS100 Junior Seau Doug Flutie	20.00	6.00
❑ GR100 Rich Gannon Jerry Rice	40.00	12.00
❑ JC100 Tim Couch Kevin Johnson	15.00	4.50
❑ JP100 Michael Pittman Keyshawn Johnson	15.00	4.50
❑ MJ100 Peyton Manning Edgerrin James	40.00	12.00
❑ MT100 Curtis Martin Vinny Testaverde	20.00	6.00
❑ PB100 Jake Plummer David Boston	15.00	4.50
❑ SB100 Kordell Stewart Kendrell Bell	20.00	6.00
❑ SS100 Corey Simon Duce Staley	20.00	6.00
❑ TB100 Anthony Thomas Marty Booker	25.00	7.50
❑ WF100 Brett Favre Kurt Warner	50.00	15.00
❑ WH100 Kurt Warner Torry Holt	20.00	6.00

2002 UD Graded Jerseys

Card	Nm-Mt	Ex-Mt
❑ G1AN Mike Anderson/200	12.00	3.60
❑ G1BA Brad Johnson/200	10.00	3.00
❑ G1BL Drew Bledsoe/200	20.00	6.00
❑ G1BO David Boston/200	12.00	3.60
❑ G1BR Drew Brees/200	15.00	4.50
❑ G1BU Brian Urlacher/200	25.00	7.50
❑ G1CM Curtis Martin/200	12.00	3.60
❑ G1CP Chad Pennington/200	25.00	7.50
❑ G1CW Chris Weinke/200	12.00	3.60
❑ G1DB Drew Bledsoe/200	20.00	6.00
❑ G1DF Doug Flutie/200	12.00	3.60
❑ G1EG Eddie George/200	12.00	3.60
❑ G1EJ Edgerrin James/200	15.00	4.50
❑ G1JJ J.J. Stokes/200	10.00	3.00
❑ G1JS Junior Seau/200	15.00	4.50
❑ G1KJ Keyshawn Johnson/200	10.00	3.00
❑ G1KW Kurt Warner/200	15.00	4.50
❑ G1LT LaDainian Tomlinson/200	20.00	6.00
❑ G1MA Mike Alstott/200	12.00	3.60
❑ G1MB Mark Brunell/200	12.00	3.60
❑ G1MF Marshall Faulk/200	15.00	4.50
❑ G1MN Peyton Manning/200	25.00	7.50
❑ G1MO Johnnie Morton/200	10.00	3.00
❑ G1MS Michael Strahan/200	12.00	3.60
❑ G1PH Priest Holmes/200	20.00	6.00
❑ G1PM Peyton Manning/200	25.00	7.50
❑ G1RA Ron Dayne/200	10.00	3.00
❑ G1RD Ron Dayne/200	10.00	3.00
❑ G1RG Rod Gardner/200	12.00	3.60
❑ G1RG Rich Gannon/200	15.00	4.50
❑ G1RM Randy Moss/200	25.00	7.50
❑ G1SD Stephen Davis/200	10.00	3.00
❑ G1SE Junior Seau/200	15.00	4.50
❑ G1SM Steve McNair/200	12.00	3.60
❑ G1TC Tim Couch/200	12.00	3.60
❑ G1TD Terrell Davis/200	12.00	3.60
❑ G1TG Trent Green/200	12.00	3.60
❑ G1TJ Thomas Jones/200	10.00	3.00
❑ G1TO Terrell Owens/200	15.00	4.50
❑ G1TT Travis Taylor/200	10.00	3.00
❑ G1VT Vinny Testaverde/200	10.00	3.00
❑ G1WE Chris Weinke/200	12.00	3.60
❑ G2DB Drew Bledsoe/100	25.00	7.50
❑ G2EJ Edgerrin James/100	15.00	4.50
❑ G2JP Jake Plummer/100	12.00	3.60
❑ G2JR Jerry Rice/100	30.00	9.00
❑ G2KW Kurt Warner/100	15.00	4.50
❑ G2RM Randy Moss/100	30.00	9.00
❑ G2SD Stephen Davis/100	15.00	4.50
❑ G2SM Steve McNair/100	15.00	4.50
❑ G2TC Tim Couch/100	12.00	3.60
❑ G2TO Terrell Owens/100	20.00	6.00
❑ G3BO David Boston/50	20.00	6.00
❑ G3CA David Carr/50	50.00	15.00
❑ G3CB Champ Bailey/50	20.00	6.00
❑ G3CM Curtis Martin/50	20.00	6.00
❑ G3CO Courtney Brown/50	20.00	6.00
❑ G3DS Duce Staley/50	20.00	6.00
❑ G3EG Eddie George/50	20.00	6.00
❑ G3EJ Edgerrin James/50	20.00	6.00
❑ G3IB Isaac Bruce/50	20.00	6.00
❑ G3KS Kordell Stewart/50	15.00	4.50
❑ G3KW Kurt Warner/50	30.00	9.00
❑ G3MB Mark Brunell/50	20.00	6.00
❑ G3MH Marvin Harrison/50	20.00	6.00
❑ G3PM Peyton Manning/50	50.00	15.00
❑ G3RD Ron Dayne/50	15.00	4.50
❑ G3RG Rich Gannon/50	20.00	6.00
❑ G3RM Randy Moss/50	60.00	18.00
❑ G3SM Steve McNair/50	20.00	6.00
❑ G3TB Tim Brown/50	20.00	6.00
❑ G3TC Tim Couch/50	15.00	4.50
❑ G3TD Terrell Davis/50	20.00	6.00
❑ G3TO Terrell Owens/50	20.00	6.00
❑ G4AT Anthony Thomas/75	15.00	4.50
❑ G4BF Brett Favre/75	60.00	18.00
❑ G4BO David Boston/75	15.00	4.50
❑ G4BR Drew Brees/75	15.00	4.50
❑ G4CM Curtis Martin/75	15.00	4.50
❑ G4DB Drew Bledsoe/75	25.00	7.50
❑ G4DC Daunte Culpepper/75	25.00	7.50
❑ G4DF Doug Flutie/75	20.00	6.00
❑ G4DM Dan Marino/75	80.00	24.00
❑ G4DS Duce Staley/75	15.00	4.50
❑ G4EJ Edgerrin James/75	20.00	6.00
❑ G4EM Eric Moulds/75	12.00	3.60
❑ G4FO DeShaun Foster/75	15.00	4.50
❑ G4IB Isaac Bruce/75	15.00	4.50
❑ G4JE John Elway/75	80.00	24.00
❑ G4JH Joey Harrington/75	50.00	15.00
❑ G4JP Jake Plummer/75	12.00	3.60
❑ G4JR Jerry Rice/75	30.00	9.00
❑ G4JS James Stewart/75	12.00	3.60
❑ G4KS Kordell Stewart/75	12.00	3.60
❑ G4KW Kurt Warner/75	15.00	4.50
❑ G4MB Mark Brunell/75	15.00	4.50
❑ G4MH Marvin Harrison/75	15.00	4.50
❑ G4PM Peyton Manning/75	40.00	12.00
❑ G4PR Patrick Ramsey/75	40.00	12.00
❑ G4RG Rich Gannon/75	15.00	4.50
❑ G4SD Stephen Davis/75	15.00	4.50
❑ G4SM Steve McNair/75	15.00	4.50
❑ G4TH Torry Holt/75	15.00	4.50
❑ G4WS Warren Sapp/75	15.00	4.50
❑ G5AT Anthony Thomas/75	15.00	4.50
❑ G5BF Brett Favre/75	60.00	18.00
❑ G5BO David Boston/75	15.00	4.50
❑ G5BU Brian Urlacher/75	40.00	12.00
❑ G5CA David Carr/75	50.00	15.00
❑ G5CM Curtis Martin/75	15.00	4.50
❑ G5CP Chad Pennington/75	30.00	9.00
❑ G5DC Daunte Culpepper/75	25.00	7.50
❑ G5DF Doug Flutie/75	20.00	6.00
❑ G5EM Eric Moulds/75	12.00	3.60
❑ G5JH Joey Harrington/75	50.00	15.00
❑ G5JL Jamal Lewis/75	15.00	4.50
❑ G5JP Jake Plummer/75	12.00	3.60
❑ G5JR Jerry Rice/75	30.00	9.00

❑ G5JS James Stewart/75	12.00	3.60
❑ G5KJ Keyshawn Johnson/75	15.00	4.50
❑ G5KW Kurt Warner/75	15.00	4.50
❑ G5LT LaDainian Tomlinson/75	15.00	4.50
❑ G5MB Mark Brunell/75	15.00	4.50
❑ G5PM Peyton Manning/75	40.00	12.00
❑ G5RL Ray Lewis/75	15.00	4.50
❑ G5WD Warrick Dunn/75	15.00	4.50
❑ G6AT Anthony Thomas/50	20.00	6.00
❑ G6BF Brett Favre/50	80.00	24.00
❑ G6BO David Boston/50	20.00	6.00
❑ G6CG Charlie Garner/50	20.00	6.00
❑ G6DC David Carr/50	50.00	15.00
❑ G6DF Doug Flutie/50	25.00	7.50
❑ G6JR Jerry Rice/50	40.00	12.00
❑ G6KW Kurt Warner/50	30.00	9.00
❑ G6LT LaDainian Tomlinson/50	25.00	7.50
❑ G6TJ Thomas Jones/50	15.00	4.50

2002 UD Graded Rookie Jerseys

	Nm-Mt	Ex-Mt
*GOLD/125: .5X TO 1.2X BASIC INSERTS		
GOLD #d/10 NOT PRICED DUE TO SCARCITY		
❑ AB500 Antonio Bryant	12.00	3.60
❑ AD500 Andre Davis	12.00	3.60
❑ AL500 Ashley Lelie	30.00	9.00
❑ CP500 Clinton Portis	40.00	12.00
❑ CR500 Cliff Russell	10.00	3.00
❑ DC500 David Carr	40.00	12.00
❑ DF500 DeShaun Foster	12.00	3.60
❑ DG500 Daniel Graham	12.00	3.60
❑ DS500 Donte Stallworth	20.00	6.00
❑ EC500 Eric Crouch	20.00	6.00
❑ EL500 Antwaan Randle El	15.00	4.50
❑ JG500 Jabar Gaffney	12.00	3.60
❑ JH500 Joey Harrington/50	60.00	18.00
❑ JM500 Josh McCown	20.00	6.00
❑ JP500 Julius Peppers	25.00	7.50
❑ JR500 Josh Reed	12.00	3.60
❑ JS500 Jeremy Shockey	30.00	9.00
❑ LB500 Ladell Betts	12.00	3.60
❑ MM500 Maurice Morris	12.00	3.60
❑ MW500 Marquise Walker	10.00	3.00
❑ PR500 Patrick Ramsey	25.00	7.50
❑ RC500 Reche Caldwell	12.00	3.60
❑ RD500 Rohan Davey	12.00	3.60
❑ RJ500 Ron Johnson	10.00	3.00
❑ RW500 Roy Williams	30.00	9.00
❑ TC500 Tim Carter	10.00	3.00
❑ TJ500 T.J. Duckett	20.00	6.00
❑ TS500 Travis Stephens	10.00	3.00
❑ WA500 Javon Walker	20.00	6.00
❑ WG500 William Green	25.00	7.50
❑ RGDC David Carr/50	60.00	18.00
❑ RGDS Donte Stallworth/50	40.00	12.00
❑ RGJP Julius Peppers/50	30.00	9.00
❑ RGWG William Green/50	30.00	9.00

1999 UD Ionix

	Nm-Mt	Ex-Mt
COMPLETE SET (90)	100.00	45.00
COMP.SET w/o SP's (60)	25.00	11.00
❑ 1 Jake Plummer	.75	.35
❑ 2 Adrian Murrell	.75	.35
❑ 3 Jamal Anderson	1.25	.55
❑ 4 Chris Chandler	.75	.35
❑ 5 Priest Holmes	2.00	.90
❑ 6 Michael Jackson	.50	.23
❑ 7 Antowain Smith	1.25	.55
❑ 8 Doug Flutie	1.25	.55
❑ 9 Tim Biakabutuka	.75	.35
❑ 10 Muhsin Muhammad	.75	.35
❑ 11 Erik Kramer	.50	.23
❑ 12 Curtis Enis	.50	.23
❑ 13 Corey Dillon	1.25	.55
❑ 14 Ty Detmer	.75	.35
❑ 15 Justin Armour	.50	.23
❑ 16 Troy Aikman	2.50	1.10
❑ 17 Emmitt Smith	2.50	1.10
❑ 18 John Elway	4.00	1.80
❑ 19 Terrell Davis	1.25	.55
❑ 20 Barry Sanders	4.00	1.80
❑ 21 Charlie Batch	1.25	.55
❑ 22 Brett Favre	4.00	1.80
❑ 23 Dorsey Levens	1.25	.55
❑ 24 Marshall Faulk	1.50	.70
❑ 25 Peyton Manning	4.00	1.80
❑ 26 Mark Brunell	1.25	.55
❑ 27 Fred Taylor	1.25	.55
❑ 28 Elvis Grbac	.75	.35
❑ 29 Andre Rison	.75	.35
❑ 30 Dan Marino	4.00	1.80
❑ 31 Karim Abdul-Jabbar	.75	.35
❑ 32 Randall Cunningham	1.25	.55
❑ 33 Randy Moss	3.00	1.35
❑ 34 Drew Bledsoe	1.50	.70
❑ 35 Terry Glenn	1.25	.55
❑ 36 Danny Wuerffel	.50	.23
❑ 37 Kent Graham	.50	.23
❑ 38 Gary Brown	.50	.23
❑ 39 Vinny Testaverde	.75	.35
❑ 40 Keyshawn Johnson	1.25	.55
❑ 41 Napoleon Kaufman	1.25	.55
❑ 42 Tim Brown	1.25	.55
❑ 43 Koy Detmer	.50	.23
❑ 44 Duce Staley	1.25	.55
❑ 45 Kordell Stewart	.75	.35
❑ 46 Jerome Bettis	1.25	.55
❑ 47 Isaac Bruce	1.25	.55
❑ 48 Robert Holcombe	.50	.23
❑ 49 Jim Harbaugh	.75	.35
❑ 50 Natrone Means	.75	.35
❑ 51 Steve Young	1.50	.70
❑ 52 Jerry Rice	2.50	1.10
❑ 53 Jon Kitna	1.25	.55
❑ 54 Joey Galloway	.75	.35
❑ 55 Warrick Dunn	1.25	.55
❑ 56 Trent Dilfer	.75	.35
❑ 57 Steve McNair	1.25	.55
❑ 58 Eddie George	1.25	.55
❑ 59 Skip Hicks	.50	.23
❑ 60 Michael Westbrook	.75	.35
❑ 61 Tim Couch RC	2.50	1.10
❑ 62 Ricky Williams RC	5.00	2.20
❑ 63 Daunte Culpepper RC	10.00	4.50
❑ 64 Akili Smith RC	2.00	.90
❑ 65 Donovan McNabb RC	12.00	5.50
❑ 66 Michael Bishop RC	2.50	1.10
❑ 67 Brock Huard RC	2.50	1.10
❑ 68 Torry Holt RC	6.00	2.70
❑ 69 Cade McNown RC	2.00	.90
❑ 70 Shaun King RC	2.00	.90
❑ 71 Champ Bailey RC	3.00	1.35
❑ 72 Chris Claiborne RC	1.25	.55
❑ 73 Jevon Kearse RC	4.00	1.80
❑ 74 D'Wayne Bates RC	2.00	.90
❑ 75 David Boston RC	2.50	1.10
❑ 76 Edgerrin James RC	10.00	4.50
❑ 77 Sedrick Irvin RC	1.25	.55
❑ 78 Dameane Douglas RC	1.25	.55
❑ 79 Troy Edwards RC	2.00	.90
❑ 80 Ebenezer Ekuban RC	1.25	.55
❑ 81 Kevin Faulk RC	2.50	1.10
❑ 82 Joe Germaine RC	2.00	.90
❑ 83 Kevin Johnson RC	2.50	1.10
❑ 84 Andy Katzenmoyer RC	2.00	.90
❑ 85 Rob Konrad RC	2.50	1.10
❑ 86 Chris McAlister RC	2.00	.90
❑ 87 Peerless Price RC	4.00	1.80
❑ 88 Tai Streets RC	2.50	1.10
❑ 89 Autry Denson RC	2.00	.90
❑ 90 Amos Zereoue RC	2.50	1.10

1999 UD Ionix UD Authentics

	Nm-Mt	Ex-Mt
❑ AS Akili Smith	50.00	22.00
❑ BH Brock Huard	50.00	22.00
❑ CM Cade McNown	50.00	22.00
❑ DC Daunte Culpepper	80.00	36.00
❑ DM Donovan McNabb	100.00	45.00
❑ MB Michael Bishop	50.00	22.00
❑ RW Ricky Williams	50.00	22.00
❑ SK Shaun King	50.00	22.00
❑ TC Tim Couch	50.00	22.00
❑ TH Torry Holt	60.00	27.00

2000 UD Ionix

	Nm-Mt	Ex-Mt
COMPLETE SET (120)	400.00	180.00
COMP.SET w/o SP's (60)	12.00	5.50
❑ 1 Jake Plummer	.30	.14
❑ 2 Jamal Anderson	.50	.23
❑ 3 Qadry Ismail	.30	.14
❑ 4 Rob Johnson	.30	.14
❑ 5 Eric Moulds	.50	.23
❑ 6 Muhsin Muhammad	.30	.14
❑ 7 Patrick Jeffers	.50	.23
❑ 8 Cade McNown	.20	.09
❑ 9 Marcus Robinson	.50	.23
❑ 10 Akili Smith	.20	.09
❑ 11 Corey Dillon	.50	.23
❑ 12 Tim Couch	.30	.14
❑ 13 Kevin Johnson	.50	.23
❑ 14 Troy Aikman	1.00	.45
❑ 15 Emmitt Smith	1.00	.45

❑ 16 Rocket Ismail	.30	.14
❑ 17 Terrell Davis	.50	.23
❑ 18 Olandis Gary	.50	.23
❑ 19 Charlie Batch	.50	.23
❑ 20 James Stewart	.30	.14
❑ 21 Brett Favre	1.50	.70
❑ 22 Antonio Freeman	.50	.23
❑ 23 Peyton Manning	1.25	.55
❑ 24 Edgerrin James	.75	.35
❑ 25 Marvin Harrison	.50	.23
❑ 26 Mark Brunell	.50	.23
❑ 27 Fred Taylor	.50	.23
❑ 28 Elvis Grbac	.30	.14
❑ 29 Tony Gonzalez	.30	.14
❑ 30 O.J. McDuffie	.30	.14
❑ 31 Damon Huard	.50	.23
❑ 32 Randy Moss	1.00	.45
❑ 33 Cris Carter	.50	.23
❑ 34 Drew Bledsoe	.60	.25
❑ 35 Terry Glenn	.30	.14
❑ 36 Ricky Williams	.50	.23
❑ 37 Kerry Collins	.30	.14
❑ 38 Amani Toomer	.30	.14
❑ 39 Keyshawn Johnson	.50	.23
❑ 40 Vinny Testaverde	.30	.14
❑ 41 Tim Brown	.50	.23
❑ 42 Rich Gannon	.50	.23
❑ 43 Duce Staley	.50	.23
❑ 44 Donovan McNabb	.75	.35
❑ 45 Troy Edwards	.20	.09
❑ 46 Jerome Bettis	.50	.23
❑ 47 Marshall Faulk	.60	.25
❑ 48 Kurt Warner	1.00	.45
❑ 49 Junior Seau	.50	.23
❑ 50 Jeff Graham	.20	.09
❑ 51 Charlie Garner	.30	.14
❑ 52 Jerry Rice	1.00	.45
❑ 53 Ricky Watters	.30	.14
❑ 54 Jon Kitna	.50	.23
❑ 55 Mike Alstott	.50	.23
❑ 56 Shaun King	.20	.09
❑ 57 Eddie George	.50	.23
❑ 58 Steve McNair	.50	.23
❑ 59 Brad Johnson	.50	.23
❑ 60 Stephen Davis	.50	.23
❑ 61 Ahmed Plummer RC	6.00	2.70
❑ 62 Courtney Brown RC	6.00	2.70
❑ 63 Deltha O'Neal RC	6.00	2.70
❑ 64 Chad Morton RC	6.00	2.70
❑ 65 Corey Simon RC	6.00	2.70
❑ 66 Hank Poteat RC	5.00	2.20
❑ 67 Raynoch Thompson RC	5.00	2.20
❑ 68 Darren Howard RC	5.00	2.20
❑ 69 Rondell Mealey RC	3.00	1.35
❑ 70 Marcus Knight RC	5.00	2.20
❑ 71 Keith Bulluck RC UER	6.00	2.70
Name spelled Bullock on card		
❑ 72 John Abraham RC	6.00	2.70
❑ 73 Rob Morris RC	6.00	2.70
❑ 74 Chris Redman RC	5.00	2.20
❑ 75 Joe Hamilton RC	5.00	2.20
❑ 76 Jarious Jackson RC	5.00	2.20
❑ 77 Tom Brady RC	60.00	27.00
❑ 78 Chad Pennington RC	25.00	11.00
❑ 79 Tee Martin RC	6.00	2.70
❑ 80 Giovanni Carmazzi RC	5.00	2.20
❑ 81 Tim Rattay RC	12.00	5.50
❑ 82 Marc Bulger RC	12.00	5.50
❑ 83 Todd Husak RC	6.00	2.70
❑ 84 Curtis Keaton RC	5.00	2.20
❑ 85 Ron Dayne RC	6.00	2.70
❑ 86 Shaun Alexander RC	15.00	6.75
❑ 87 Thomas Jones RC	10.00	4.50
❑ 88 Reuben Droughns RC	8.00	3.60
❑ 89 Jamal Lewis RC	15.00	6.75
❑ 90 J.R. Redmond RC	5.00	2.20
❑ 91 Travis Prentice RC	5.00	2.20
❑ 92 Shyrone Stith RC	5.00	2.20
❑ 93 Chris Hovan RC	5.00	2.20
❑ 94 Michael Wiley RC	5.00	2.20
❑ 95 Trung Canidate RC	5.00	2.20
❑ 96 Sebastian Janikowski RC	6.00	2.70
❑ 97 Brian Urlacher RC	25.00	11.00
❑ 98 Bubba Franks RC	6.00	2.70
❑ 99 Anthony Becht RC	6.00	2.70
❑ 100 Chris Cole RC	5.00	2.20
❑ 101 R.Jay Soward RC	5.00	2.20
❑ 102 Peter Warrick RC	6.00	2.70
❑ 103 Plaxico Burress RC	12.00	5.50
❑ 104 Sylvester Morris RC	5.00	2.20
❑ 105 Dez White RC	6.00	2.70
❑ 106 Travis Taylor RC	6.00	2.70
❑ 107 Trevor Gaylor RC	5.00	2.20
❑ 108 Anthony Lucas RC	3.00	1.35
❑ 109 Sherrod Gideon RC	3.00	1.35
❑ 110 Todd Pinkston RC	6.00	2.70
❑ 111 Dennis Northcutt RC	6.00	2.70
❑ 112 Jerry Porter RC	8.00	3.60
❑ 113 Ron Dugans RC	3.00	1.35
❑ 114 Laveranues Coles RC	8.00	3.60
❑ 115 Darrell Jackson RC	12.00	5.50
❑ 116 Danny Farmer RC	5.00	2.20
❑ 117 Gari Scott RC	3.00	1.35
❑ 118 JaJuan Dawson RC	3.00	1.35
❑ 119 Troy Walters RC	6.00	2.70
❑ 120 Quinton Spotwood RC	3.00	1.35

2000 UD Ionix UD Authentics

	Nm-Mt	Ex-Mt
❑ AF Antonio Freeman G	25.00	11.00
❑ BG Brian Griese B	12.00	5.50
❑ BJ Brad Johnson G	25.00	11.00
❑ BU Brian Urlacher B	50.00	22.00
❑ CA Champ Bailey B	20.00	9.00
❑ CB Charlie Batch B	10.00	4.50
❑ CC Cris Carter B	20.00	9.00
❑ CN Chris Coleman B	10.00	4.50
❑ CP Chad Pennington G	100.00	45.00
❑ CR Chris Redman G	25.00	11.00
❑ DA David Boston B	12.00	5.50
❑ DF Danny Farmer B	12.00	5.50
❑ DL Dorsey Levens G	20.00	9.00
❑ DN Dennis Northcutt B	10.00	4.50
❑ EJ Edgerrin James G	60.00	27.00
❑ EM Eric Moulds G	25.00	11.00
❑ FR Bubba Franks B	12.00	5.50
❑ IB Isaac Bruce B	20.00	9.00
❑ JH Joe Hamilton B	12.00	5.50
❑ JL Jamal Lewis G	60.00	27.00
❑ JP Jake Plummer G	30.00	13.50
❑ KJ Keyshawn Johnson G	25.00	11.00
❑ KW Kurt Warner G	50.00	22.00
❑ MB Mark Brunell G	30.00	13.50
❑ MC Cade McNown G	20.00	9.00
❑ MF Marshall Faulk G	30.00	13.50
❑ MH Marvin Harrison G	30.00	13.50
❑ MW Michael Wiley B	10.00	4.50
❑ OG Olandis Gary B	12.00	5.50
❑ PM Peyton Manning G	100.00	45.00
❑ PW Peter Warrick G	30.00	13.50
❑ RD Ron Dayne G	30.00	13.50
❑ RJ Rob Johnson B	12.00	5.50
❑ RL Ray Lucas B	10.00	4.50
❑ RM Randy Moss G	100.00	45.00
❑ RS R.Jay Soward B	10.00	4.50
❑ SA Shaun Alexander B	30.00	13.50
❑ SG Sherrod Gideon B	10.00	4.50
❑ SJ Seb.Janikowski B EXCH		
❑ SL Sylvester Morris G	20.00	9.00
❑ TA Troy Aikman G	60.00	27.00
❑ TB Tim Brown B	20.00	9.00
❑ TC Tim Couch G	25.00	11.00
❑ TD Terrell Davis G	30.00	13.50
❑ TH Torry Holt G	30.00	13.50
❑ TJ Thomas Jones G	30.00	13.50
❑ TM Tee Martin B	12.00	5.50
❑ TO Terrell Owens B	20.00	9.00
❑ TP Travis Prentice B	10.00	4.50
❑ TR Tim Rattay B	25.00	11.00
❑ TW Troy Walters B	12.00	5.50
❑ WC Wayne Chrebet B	12.00	5.50

2000 UD Ionix UD Authentics Green

Nm-Mt Ex-Mt

*BLUE CARDS: 1X TO 2.5X HI COL.
*GOLD CARDS: .6X TO 1.5X HI COL.

2003 UD Patch Collection

	MINT	NRMT
COMP.SET w/o SP's (90)	20.00	9.00
❑ 1 Peyton Manning	1.50	.70
❑ 2 Aaron Brooks	1.00	.45
❑ 3 Joey Harrington	1.50	.70
❑ 4 Brett Favre	2.50	1.10
❑ 5 Donovan McNabb	1.25	.55
❑ 6 Jeff Garcia	1.00	.45
❑ 7 Michael Vick	2.50	1.10
❑ 8 David Carr	1.50	.70
❑ 9 Drew Brees	1.00	.45
❑ 10 Chad Pennington	1.25	.55
❑ 11 Daunte Culpepper	1.00	.45
❑ 12 Tom Brady	1.50	.70
❑ 13 Kurt Warner	1.00	.45
❑ 14 Brad Johnson	.60	.25
❑ 15 Josh McCown	.60	.25
❑ 16 Drew Bledsoe	1.00	.45
❑ 17 Rich Gannon	.60	.25
❑ 18 Tim Couch	.40	.18
❑ 19 Keyshawn Johnson	1.00	.45
❑ 20 Travis Henry	.60	.25
❑ 21 LaDainian Tomlinson	1.00	.45
❑ 22 Emmitt Smith	2.50	1.10
❑ 23 Michael Bennett	.60	.25
❑ 24 Mark Brunell	.60	.25
❑ 25 Steve McNair	1.00	.45
❑ 26 Clinton Portis	1.50	.70
❑ 27 Eddie George	.60	.25
❑ 28 Marshall Faulk	1.00	.45
❑ 29 Curtis Martin	1.00	.45
❑ 30 Ahman Green	1.00	.45
❑ 31 Priest Holmes	1.25	.55
❑ 32 Edgerrin James	1.00	.45
❑ 33 Deuce McAllister	1.00	.45
❑ 34 Ricky Williams	1.00	.45
❑ 35 Anthony Thomas	1.00	.45
❑ 36 Jerome Bettis	1.00	.45
❑ 37 Shaun Alexander	1.00	.45
❑ 38 Jake Plummer	.60	.25
❑ 39 Patrick Ramsey	1.00	.45
❑ 40 Laveranues Coles	.60	.25
❑ 41 David Boston	.60	.25
❑ 42 Jay Fiedler	.60	.25
❑ 43 Garrison Hearst	.60	.25
❑ 44 Corey Dillon	.60	.25
❑ 45 Charlie Garner	.60	.25
❑ 46 Fred Taylor	1.00	.45
❑ 47 Chad Hutchinson	.60	.25
❑ 48 Quincy Carter	.60	.25
❑ 49 Kevan Barlow	.60	.25

❑ 50 Tommy Maddox 1.00 .45
❑ 51 Kordell Stewart .60 .25
❑ 52 Chris Redman .40 .18
❑ 53 Jamal Lewis 1.00 .45
❑ 54 Zach Thomas 1.00 .45
❑ 55 Junior Seau 1.00 .45
❑ 56 Chris Chambers 1.00 .45
❑ 57 Matt Hasselbeck .60 .25
❑ 58 Marc Bulger 1.00 .45
❑ 59 Isaac Bruce 1.00 .45
❑ 60 Torry Holt 1.00 .45
❑ 61 Kelly Holcomb .60 .25
❑ 62 Plaxico Burress .60 .25
❑ 63 Ray Lewis 1.00 .45
❑ 64 Brian Urlacher 1.50 .70
❑ 65 Tim Brown 1.00 .45
❑ 66 William Green .60 .25
❑ 67 Kevin Johnson .60 .25
❑ 68 Trent Green .60 .25
❑ 69 Santana Moss .60 .25
❑ 70 Tony Gonzalez .60 .25
❑ 71 Rod Smith .60 .25
❑ 72 Ashley Lelie 1.00 .45
❑ 73 Peerless Price .60 .25
❑ 74 Antonio Bryant .60 .25
❑ 75 Duce Staley .60 .25
❑ 76 Darrell Jackson .60 .25
❑ 77 Jeremy Shockey 1.50 .70
❑ 78 Kerry Collins .60 .25
❑ 79 Koren Robinson .60 .25
❑ 80 Jerry Rice 2.00 .90
❑ 81 Terrell Owens 1.00 .45
❑ 82 Antwaan Randle El 1.00 .45
❑ 83 Donte Stallworth 1.00 .45
❑ 84 Randy Moss 1.50 .70
❑ 85 Chad Johnson .60 .25
❑ 86 Hines Ward 1.00 .45
❑ 87 Rod Gardner .60 .25
❑ 88 Marvin Harrison 1.00 .45
❑ 89 Eric Moulds .60 .25
❑ 90 Julius Peppers 1.00 .45
❑ 91 Nate Hybl RC 3.00 1.35
❑ 92 Lon Sheriff RC 1.50 .70
❑ 93 Gerald Hayes RC 1.50 .70
❑ 94 B.J. Askew RC 3.00 1.35
❑ 95 Artose Pinner RC 3.00 1.35
❑ 96 Domanick Davis RC 6.00 2.70
❑ 97 LaBrandon Toefield RC 3.00 1.35
❑ 98 Lee Suggs RC 6.00 2.70
❑ 99 Cecil Sapp RC 2.50 1.10
❑ 100 Kelley Washington RC 3.00 1.35
❑ 101 Kevin Curtis RC 3.00 1.35
❑ 102 Zuriel Smith RC 1.50 .70
❑ 103 Carl Ford RC 1.50 .70
❑ 104 Travis Anglin RC 1.50 .70
❑ 105 Terrence Edwards RC 2.50 1.10
❑ 106 Troy Polamalu RC 3.00 1.35
❑ 107 Nate Burleson RC 5.00 2.20
❑ 108 Cecil Moore RC 1.50 .70
❑ 109 Kassim Osgood RC 3.00 1.35
❑ 110 Teyo Johnson RC 3.00 1.35
❑ 111 Jason Witten RC 5.00 2.20
❑ 112 Vishante Shiancoe RC 2.50 1.10
❑ 113 Kevin Ware RC 1.50 .70
❑ 114 Mike Pinkard RC 1.50 .70
❑ 115 Donald Lee RC 2.50 1.10
❑ 116 Justin Gage RC 3.00 1.35
❑ 117 Adrian Madise RC 2.50 1.10
❑ 118 Anthony Adams RC 2.50 1.10
❑ 119 Dan Curley RC 1.50 .70
❑ 120 Dallas Clark RC 3.00 1.35
❑ 121 Kyle Boller RI RC 12.00 5.50
❑ 122 Chris Simms RI RC 10.00 4.50
❑ 123 Dave Ragone RI RC 5.00 2.20
❑ 124 Kliff Kingsbury RI RC 5.00 2.20
❑ 125 Brad Banks RI RC 5.00 2.20
❑ 126 Gibran Hamdan RI RC 5.00 2.20
❑ 127 Ken Dorsey RI RC 8.00 3.60
❑ 128 Seneca Wallace RI RC 5.00 2.20
❑ 129 Brian St.Pierre RI RC 5.00 2.20
❑ 130 Rex Grossman RI RC 15.00 6.75
❑ 131 Brooks Bollinger RI RC 5.00 2.20
❑ 132 Jason Gesser RI RC 5.00 2.20
❑ 133 Carson Palmer RI RC 20.00 9.00
❑ 134 Byron Leftwich RI RC 25.00 11.00
❑ 135 Charles Rogers RI RC 8.00 3.60
❑ 136 Andre Johnson RI RC 15.00 6.75
❑ 137 Willis McGahee RI RC 15.00 6.75
❑ 138 Larry Johnson RI RC 12.00 5.50
❑ 139 Musa Smith RI RC 6.00 2.70
❑ 140 Chris Brown RI RC 12.00 5.50
❑ 141 Onterrio Smith RI RC 8.00 3.60
❑ 142 Justin Fargas RI RC 6.00 2.70
❑ 143 Bryant Johnson RI RC 6.00 2.70
❑ 144 Taylor Jacobs RI RC 6.00 2.70
❑ 145 Bethel Johnson RI RC 10.00 4.50
❑ 146 Tyrone Calico RI RC 8.00 3.60
❑ 147 Anquan Boldin RI RC 15.00 6.75
❑ 148 Michael Vick AP 15.00 6.75
❑ 149 Brett Favre AP 15.00 6.75
❑ 150 Chad Pennington AP 8.00 3.60
❑ 151 Kurt Warner AP 6.00 2.70
❑ 152 David Carr AP 10.00 4.50
❑ 153 Donovan McNabb AP 8.00 3.60
❑ 154 LaDainian Tomlinson AP 6.00 2.70
❑ 155 Marshall Faulk AP 6.00 2.70
❑ 156 Emmitt Smith AP 15.00 6.75
❑ 157 Jerry Rice AP 12.00 5.50
❑ 158 Terrell Owens AP 6.00 2.70
❑ 159 Brian Urlacher AP 10.00 4.50
❑ 160 Randy Moss AP 10.00 4.50
❑ 161 Ricky Williams AP 6.00 2.70
❑ 162 Peyton Manning AP 10.00 4.50
❑ P162 Peyton Manning AP 4.00 1.80
SAMPLE

2003 UD Patch Collection Gold Patches

MINT NRMT

*ROOKIES 121-132: 2X TO 5X BASE CARD HI
*ROOKIES 133-147: 1.5X TO 4X BASE CARD HI
*AP STARS 148-162: 2.5X TO 6X
STATED PRINT RUN 25 SERIAL #'d SETS

2003 UD Patch Collection Signature Patches

MINT NRMT

*GOLDS: .8X TO 2X BASIC AUTOS

❑ SPAB Aaron Brooks 20.00 9.00
❑ SPBL Byron Leftwich 120.00 55.00
❑ SPCH Chad Pennington 75.00 34.00
❑ SPCJ Chad Johnson 30.00 13.50
❑ SPCP Carson Palmer SP 100.00 45.00
❑ SPDB Drew Brees SP 40.00 18.00
❑ SPJG Jeff Garcia 30.00 13.50
❑ SPJJ James Jackson 15.00 6.75
❑ SPKB Kevan Barlow 20.00 9.00
❑ SPPM Peyton Manning 100.00 45.00
❑ SPRG Rod Gardner 20.00 9.00
❑ SPRJ Rudi Johnson 20.00 9.00
❑ SPRW Reggie Wayne 30.00 13.50
❑ SPTH Todd Heap 30.00 13.50
❑ SPWM Willis McGahee SP 60.00 27.00

2002 UD Piece of History

Nm-Mt Ex-Mt

COMP.SET w/o SP's (100) 25.00 7.50

❑ 1 David Boston 1.00 .30
❑ 2 Jake Plummer .60 .18
❑ 3 Chris Chandler .60 .18

❑ 4 Jamal Anderson 1.00 .30
❑ 5 Michael Vick 3.00 .90
❑ 6 Elvis Grbac .60 .18
❑ 7 Qadry Ismail .60 .18
❑ 8 Ray Lewis 1.00 .30
❑ 9 Eric Moulds .60 .18
❑ 10 Rob Johnson .60 .18
❑ 11 Travis Henry 1.00 .30
❑ 12 Chris Weinke .60 .18
❑ 13 Donald Hayes 1.00 .30
❑ 14 Muhsin Muhammad .60 .18
❑ 15 Anthony Thomas 1.00 .30
❑ 16 Brian Urlacher 1.50 .45
❑ 17 David Terrell 1.00 .30
❑ 18 Jim Miller .40 .12
❑ 19 Marty Booker .40 .12
❑ 20 Corey Dillon .60 .18
❑ 21 Jon Kitna .60 .18
❑ 22 Peter Warrick .60 .18
❑ 23 James Jackson .40 .12
❑ 24 Kevin Johnson .60 .18
❑ 25 Tim Couch .60 .18
❑ 26 Emmitt Smith 2.50 .75
❑ 27 Quincy Carter .60 .18
❑ 28 Rocket Ismail .60 .18
❑ 29 Brian Griese 1.00 .30
❑ 30 Ed McCaffrey 1.00 .30
❑ 31 Rod Smith .60 .18
❑ 32 Terrell Davis 1.00 .30
❑ 33 Charlie Batch .60 .18
❑ 34 James Stewart .60 .18
❑ 35 Mike McMahon 1.00 .30
❑ 36 Ahman Green 1.00 .30
❑ 37 Antonio Freeman 1.00 .30
❑ 38 Bill Schroeder .60 .18
❑ 39 Brett Favre 2.50 .75
❑ 40 Dominic Rhodes .60 .18
❑ 41 Edgerrin James 1.25 .35
❑ 42 Marvin Harrison 1.00 .30
❑ 43 Peyton Manning 2.00 .60
❑ 44 Jimmy Smith .60 .18
❑ 45 Mark Brunell 1.00 .30
❑ 46 Priest Holmes 1.25 .35
❑ 47 Tony Gonzalez .60 .18
❑ 48 Trent Green .60 .18
❑ 49 Chris Chambers 1.00 .30
❑ 50 Jay Fiedler .60 .18
❑ 51 Lamar Smith .60 .18
❑ 52 Oronde Gadsden .60 .18
❑ 53 Daunte Culpepper 1.00 .30
❑ 54 Michael Bennett .60 .18
❑ 55 Randy Moss 2.00 .60
❑ 56 Antowain Smith .60 .18
❑ 57 Drew Bledsoe 1.25 .35
❑ 58 Tom Brady 2.50 .75
❑ 59 Troy Brown .60 .18
❑ 60 Aaron Brooks 1.00 .30
❑ 61 Joe Horn .60 .18
❑ 62 Michael Strahan .60 .18
❑ 63 Kerry Collins .60 .18
❑ 64 Ron Dayne .60 .18
❑ 65 Tiki Barber .60 .18
❑ 66 Curtis Martin 1.00 .30
❑ 67 Laveranues Coles .60 .18
❑ 68 Santana Moss 1.00 .30
❑ 69 Vinny Testaverde .60 .18
❑ 70 Jerry Rice 2.00 .60
❑ 71 Rich Gannon 1.00 .30

❑ 72 Tim Brown	1.00	.30
❑ 73 Donovan McNabb	1.25	.35
❑ 74 Duce Staley	1.00	.30
❑ 75 Freddie Mitchell	.60	.18
❑ 76 James Thrash	.60	.18
❑ 77 Jerome Bettis	1.00	.30
❑ 78 Kendrell Bell	1.00	.30
❑ 79 Kordell Stewart	.60	.18
❑ 80 Doug Flutie	1.00	.30
❑ 81 Junior Seau	1.00	.30
❑ 82 LaDainian Tomlinson	1.50	.45
❑ 83 Garrison Hearst	.60	.18
❑ 84 Jeff Garcia	1.00	.30
❑ 85 Terrell Owens	1.00	.30
❑ 86 Matt Hasselbeck	.60	.18
❑ 87 Ricky Watters	.60	.18
❑ 88 Shaun Alexander	1.00	.30
❑ 89 Isaac Bruce	1.00	.30
❑ 90 Kurt Warner	1.00	.30
❑ 91 Marshall Faulk	1.00	.30
❑ 92 Torry Holt	1.00	.30
❑ 93 Brad Johnson	.60	.18
❑ 94 Keyshawn Johnson	1.00	.30
❑ 95 Mike Alstott	1.00	.30
❑ 96 Warrick Dunn	1.00	.30
❑ 97 Eddie George	1.00	.30
❑ 98 Steve McNair	1.00	.30
❑ 99 Stephen Davis	.60	.18
❑ 100 Tony Banks	.60	.18
❑ 101 Antonio Bryant RC	8.00	2.40
❑ 102 Adrian Peterson RC	8.00	2.40
❑ 103 Brian Poli-Dixon RC	6.00	1.80
❑ 104 Kyle Johnson RC	4.00	1.20
❑ 105 Clinton Portis RC	25.00	7.50
❑ 106 David Carr/500 RC	50.00	15.00
❑ 107 Rocky Calmus RC	8.00	2.40
❑ 108 Eric Crouch RC	12.00	3.60
❑ 109 Jeremy Shockey RC	25.00	7.50
❑ 110 Jabar Gaffney RC	8.00	2.40
❑ 111 Damien Anderson RC	6.00	1.80
❑ 112 Josh Reed RC	8.00	2.40
❑ 113 Lamar Gordon RC	8.00	2.40
❑ 114 Julius Peppers/500 RC	30.00	9.00
❑ 115 Kelly Campbell RC	6.00	1.80
❑ 116 Leonard Henry RC	6.00	1.80
❑ 117 Chad Hutchinson/500 RC	20.00	6.00
❑ 118 Luke Staley RC	6.00	1.80
❑ 119 Josh Scobey RC	8.00	2.40
❑ 120 Marquise Walker RC	6.00	1.80
❑ 121 Roy Williams RC	20.00	6.00
❑ 122 Patrick Ramsey RC	15.00	4.50
❑ 123 Ashley Lelie/500 RC	30.00	9.00
❑ 124 Rohan Davey RC	8.00	2.40
❑ 125 Ron Johnson RC	6.00	1.80
❑ 126 T.J. Duckett RC	12.00	3.60
❑ 127 Cliff Russell RC	6.00	1.80
❑ 128 William Green/500 RC	25.00	7.50
❑ 129 Reche Caldwell RC	8.00	2.40
❑ 130 Donte Stallworth RC	15.00	4.50
❑ 131 Javon Walker RC	15.00	4.50
❑ 132 David Garrard RC	8.00	2.40
❑ 133 Quentin Jammer RC	8.00	2.40
❑ 134 Ladell Betts RC	8.00	2.40
❑ 135 Freddie Milons RC	6.00	1.80
❑ 136 Brian Westbrook RC	12.00	3.60
❑ 137 John Henderson RC	8.00	2.40
❑ 138 Kalimba Edwards RC	8.00	2.40
❑ 139 Daniel Graham RC	8.00	2.40
❑ 140 Josh McCown RC	10.00	3.00
❑ 141 Joey Harrington JSY RC/500	50.00	15.00
❑ 142 Phillip Buchanon JSY/500 RC	20.00	6.00
❑ 143 Maurice Morris JSY/1500 RC	12.00	3.60
❑ 144 George Godsey/1500 JSY RC	8.00	2.40
❑ 145 J.T. O'Sullivan JSY/1500 RC	10.00	3.00
❑ 146 Kurt Kittner/500 JSY RC	15.00	4.50
❑ 147 DeShaun Foster JSY RC/500	20.00	6.00
❑ 148 Antwaan Randle El JSY RC/1500	15.00	4.50
❑ 149 Woody Dantzler JSY RC/1500	12.00	3.60
❑ 150 Randy Fasani JSY/1500 RC	10.00	3.00
❑ 151 Kahlil Hill/1500 JSY RC	10.00	3.00
❑ 152 Atrews Bell/1500 JSY RC	12.00	3.60
❑ 153 Eric McCoo/1500 JSY RC	8.00	2.40
❑ 154 Ricky Williams JSY/1500 RC	10.00	3.00
❑ 155 Albert Haynesworth 500 EXCH	15.00	4.50
❑ 156 Lamont Thompson JSY RC/1500	10.00	3.00
❑ 157 Andre Davis/1500 JSY RC	15.00	4.50
❑ 158 Travis Stephens JSY/500 RC	20.00	6.00
❑ 159 Delvon Flowers/1500 JSY RC	10.00	3.00
❑ 160 Robert Thomas/1500 JSY RC	12.00	3.60
❑ 161 Marques Anderson JSY RC/1500	15.00	4.50
❑ 162 Kenyon Coleman JSY RC/1500	10.00	3.00

2003 Ultimate Collection

	MINT	NRMT
❑ 1 Peyton Manning	8.00	3.60
❑ 2 Aaron Brooks	5.00	2.20
❑ 3 Joey Harrington	8.00	3.60
❑ 4 Brett Favre	12.00	5.50
❑ 5 Donovan McNabb	6.00	2.70
❑ 6 Jeff Garcia	5.00	2.20
❑ 7 Michael Vick	12.00	5.50
❑ 8 David Carr	8.00	3.60
❑ 9 Drew Brees	5.00	2.20
❑ 10 Chad Pennington	6.00	2.70
❑ 11 Drew Bledsoe	5.00	2.20
❑ 12 Tom Brady	8.00	3.60
❑ 13 Kurt Warner	5.00	2.20
❑ 14 Brad Johnson	3.00	1.35
❑ 15 Jay Fiedler	3.00	1.35
❑ 16 Tim Couch	2.00	.90
❑ 17 Trent Green	3.00	1.35
❑ 18 Daunte Culpepper	5.00	2.20
❑ 19 Keyshawn Johnson	5.00	2.20
❑ 20 Garrison Hearst	3.00	1.35
❑ 21 LaDainian Tomlinson	5.00	2.20
❑ 22 Emmitt Smith	12.00	5.50
❑ 23 Steve McNair	5.00	2.20
❑ 24 Chris Redman	2.00	.90
❑ 25 Chad Hutchinson	5.00	2.20
❑ 26 Deuce McAllister	5.00	2.20
❑ 27 Eddie George	3.00	1.35
❑ 28 Marshall Faulk	5.00	2.20
❑ 29 Ahman Green	5.00	2.20
❑ 30 Julius Peppers	5.00	2.20
❑ 31 Priest Holmes	6.00	2.70
❑ 32 Edgerrin James	5.00	2.20
❑ 33 Jerry Rice	10.00	4.50
❑ 34 Ricky Williams	5.00	2.20
❑ 35 Anthony Thomas	5.00	2.20
❑ 36 Jerome Bettis	5.00	2.20
❑ 37 Shaun Alexander	5.00	2.20
❑ 38 Randy Moss	8.00	3.60
❑ 39 Jeremy Shockey	8.00	3.60
❑ 40 Patrick Ramsey	5.00	2.20
❑ 41 Clinton Portis	8.00	3.60
❑ 42 Terrell Owens	5.00	2.20
❑ 43 Corey Dillon	3.00	1.35
❑ 44 Mark Brunell	3.00	1.35
❑ 45 Rich Gannon	3.00	1.35
❑ 46 Curtis Martin	5.00	2.20
❑ 47 Josh McCown	3.00	1.35
❑ 48 Kerry Collins	3.00	1.35
❑ 49 Peerless Price	3.00	1.35
❑ 50 David Boston	3.00	1.35
❑ 51 Plaxico Burress	3.00	1.35
❑ 52 Marvin Harrison	5.00	2.20
❑ 53 Travis Henry	3.00	1.35
❑ 54 Brian Urlacher	8.00	3.60
❑ 55 Jake Plummer	3.00	1.35
❑ 56 Dave Ragone/750 RC	10.00	4.50
❑ 57 Brian St.Pierre AU/250 RC	20.00	9.00
❑ 58 Tony Romo/750 RC	10.00	4.50
❑ 59 Dallas Clark/750 RC	10.00	4.50
❑ 60 Kirk Farmer/750 RC	8.00	3.60
❑ 61 Juston Wood/750 RC	8.00	3.60
❑ 62 Justin Gage/750 RC	10.00	4.50
❑ 63 Sam Aiken/750 RC	8.00	3.60
❑ 64 LaBrandon Toefield/750 RC	10.00	4.50
❑ 65 L.J. Smith/750 RC	10.00	4.50
❑ 66 Domanick Davis/750 RC	25.00	11.00
❑ 67 Artose Pinner/750 RC	10.00	4.50
❑ 68 Dahrran Diedrick/750 RC	10.00	4.50
❑ 69 Lee Suggs/750 RC	25.00	11.00
❑ 70 Bethel Johnson/750 RC	15.00	6.75
❑ 71 Tyrone Calico/750 RC	12.00	5.50
❑ 72 Kevin Curtis/750 RC	10.00	4.50
❑ 73 Bobby Wade/750 RC	10.00	4.50
❑ 74 Brandon Lloyd/750 RC	12.00	5.50
❑ 75 Bryant Johnson/750 RC	10.00	4.50
❑ 76 J.R. Tolver/750 RC	8.00	3.60
❑ 77 Billy McMullen/750 RC	8.00	3.60
❑ 78 Nate Burleson/750 RC	15.00	6.75
❑ 79 Jason Johnson AU/250 RC	20.00	9.00
❑ 80 Talman Gardner/250 RC	15.00	6.75
❑ 81 Anquan Boldin/250 RC	60.00	27.00
❑ 82 Musa Smith/250 RC	15.00	6.75
❑ 83 Teyo Johnson/250 RC	20.00	9.00
❑ 84 Kyle Boller AU/250 RC	80.00	36.00
❑ 85 Carson Palmer AU/250 RC	150.00	70.00
❑ 86 Byron Leftwich AU/250 RC	200.00	90.00
❑ 87 Earnest Graham AU/250 RC	30.00	13.50
❑ 88 Chris Brown AU/250 RC	100.00	45.00
❑ 89 Chris Simms AU/250 RC	100.00	45.00
❑ 90 Kliff Kingsbury AU/250 RC	30.00	13.50
❑ 91 Jason Gesser/750 RC	10.00	4.50
❑ 92 Brad Banks AU/250 RC	25.00	11.00
❑ 93 Ken Dorsey AU/250 RC	60.00	27.00
❑ 94 Rex Grossman AU/250 RC	100.00	45.00
❑ 95 Willis McGahee AU/250 RC	120.00	55.00
❑ 96 Larry Johnson AU/250 RC	80.00	36.00
❑ 97 Quentin Griffin AU/250 RC	60.00	27.00
❑ 98 Onterrio Smith AU/250 RC	60.00	27.00
❑ 99 Justin Fargas AU/250 RC	50.00	22.00
❑ 100 Kareem Kelly AU/250 RC	25.00	11.00
❑ 101 Arnaz Battle AU/250 RC	40.00	18.00
❑ 102 Kelley Washington/250 AU RC	40.00	18.00
❑ 103 Seneca Wallace AU/250 RC	25.00	11.00
❑ 104 Taylor Jacobs AU/250 RC	30.00	13.50
❑ 105 Andre Johnson/750 RC	30.00	13.50
❑ 106 Charles Rogers/250 RC	50.00	22.00
❑ 107 Terrell Suggs AU/250 RC	60.00	27.00

2003 Ultimate Collection Gold

MINT NRMT

*STARS: 1X TO 2.5X BASIC CARDS
*ROOKIES/75: .8X TO 2X
*ROOKIES/25: .8X TO 2X
*ROOKIE AUTO/25: .6X TO 1.5X

2003 Ultimate Collection Buy Back Autographs

	MINT	NRMT
❑ 1 S.Alexander 02SP/19	50.00	22.00
❑ 3 S.Alexander 02UDG/35	40.00	18.00
❑ 4 S.Alexander 02UDSS/36	40.00	18.00
❑ 13 A.Brooks 02UDG/20	40.00	18.00
❑ 15 A.Brooks 02UDSS/23	40.00	18.00
❑ 26 T.Couch 02SP/24	50.00	22.00
❑ 27 T.Couch 02UDA/19	50.00	22.00
❑ 28 T.Couch 02UDG/28	50.00	22.00
❑ 35 J.Garcia 01UDPPJsy/29	50.00	22.00
❑ 37 J.Garcia 02UDSS/24	50.00	22.00

❑ 38 R.Gardner 02SP/29 50.00 22.00
❑ 40 R.Gardner 02UDSS/24 50.00 22.00
❑ 43 P.Manning 01UDPPJsy/29 100.00 45.00
❑ 44 P.Manning 02SPLC/25 100.00 45.00
❑ 48 P.Manning 02UDSS/24 100.00 45.00
❑ 53 T.Owens 02 UDG/20 50.00 22.00
❑ 57 A.Thomas 02UDG/34 40.00 18.00
❑ 59 A.Thomas 02UDSS/35 40.00 18.00
❑ 61 L.Tomlinson 02UDG/20 80.00 36.00

2003 Ultimate Collection Game Jerseys

MINT NRMT
*GOLD/250: .8X TO 2X BASIC INSERTS
*GOLD/99: .6X TO 1.5X BASIC INSERTS
GOLDS PRINT RUN 25 SER.#'d SETS

❑ UJAB Aaron Brooks/250 10.00 4.50
❑ UJAG Ahman Green/250 12.00 5.50
❑ UJBA Tom Brady/250 25.00 11.00
❑ UJBF Brett Favre/250 40.00 18.00
❑ UJBR Drew Brees/250 12.00 5.50
❑ UJBS Barry Sanders/99 40.00 18.00
❑ UJBU Brian Urlacher/250 25.00 11.00
❑ UJCP1 Chad Pennington/250 15.00 6.75
❑ UJCP2 Clinton Portis/250 25.00 11.00
❑ UJDA Dan Marino/99 60.00 27.00
❑ UJDB Drew Bledsoe/250 12.00 5.50
❑ UJDC Daunte Culpepper/250 12.00 5.50
❑ UJDM Donovan McNabb/250 20.00 9.00
❑ UJEJ Edgerrin James/250 12.00 5.50
❑ UJFT Fran Tarkenton/99 30.00 13.50
❑ UJJE John Elway/99 60.00 27.00
❑ UJJG Jeff Garcia/250 12.00 5.50
❑ UJJK Jim Kelly/99 30.00 13.50
❑ UJJM Joe Montana/99 80.00 36.00
❑ UJJN Joe Namath/99 50.00 22.00
❑ UJJR Jerry Rice/250 25.00 11.00
❑ UJKJ Keyshawn Johnson/250 10.00 4.50
❑ UJKW Kurt Warner/250 12.00 5.50
❑ UJLT LaDainian Tomlinson/250 12.00 5.50
❑ UJMA Marcus Allen/99 25.00 11.00
❑ UJMC Deuce McAllister/250 12.00 5.50
❑ UJMF Marshall Faulk/250 12.00 5.50
❑ UJMV Michael Vick/250 30.00 13.50
❑ UJPH Priest Holmes/250 20.00 9.00
❑ UJPM Peyton Manning/250 25.00 11.00
❑ UJRM Randy Moss/250 20.00 9.00
❑ UJRW Ricky Williams/250 12.00 5.50
❑ UJST Bart Starr/99 50.00 22.00
❑ UJSY Steve Young/99 25.00 11.00
❑ UJTA Troy Aikman/99 25.00 11.00
❑ UJTC Tim Couch/250 10.00 4.50
❑ UJTO Terrell Owens/250 12.00 5.50
❑ UJWP Walter Payton/99 80.00 36.00

2003 Ultimate Collection Game Jersey Autographs

MINT NRMT
❑ UJSBS Bart Starr 200.00 90.00
❑ UJSDM Dan Marino 300.00 135.00
❑ UJSJM Joe Montana 300.00 135.00
❑ UJSJN Joe Namath 175.00 80.00
❑ UJSMV Michael Vick 250.00 110.00
❑ UJSPM Peyton Manning 200.00 90.00

2003 Ultimate Collection Game Jersey Duals

MINT NRMT
*GOLD/250: 1X TO 2.5X BASIC INSERTS
*GOLD/99: .8X TO 2X BASIC INSERTS
GOLD PRINT RUN 25 SER.#'d SETS

❑ UDJAM Troy Aikman 40.00 18.00
Peyton Manning/99
❑ UDJBC Aaron Brooks 12.00 5.50
Tim Couch/250
❑ UDJCB David Carr 40.00 18.00
Tom Brady/250
❑ UDJFM Marshall Faulk 15.00 6.75
Curtis Martin/250
❑ UDJFR Brett Favre 50.00 22.00
Jerry Rice/250
❑ UDJHB Joey Harrington 20.00 9.00
Drew Brees/250
❑ UDJHW Priest Holmes 30.00 13.50
Ricky Williams/250
❑ UDJKB Jim Kelly 50.00 22.00
Drew Bledsoe/250
❑ UDJMC Dan Marino 80.00 36.00
David Carr/99
❑ UDJMS Deuce McAllister 50.00 22.00
Barry Sanders/100
❑ UDJMV Donovan McNabb 30.00 13.50
Michael Vick/250
❑ UDJMG1 Donovan McNabb 20.00 9.00
Jeff Garcia/250
❑ UDJMG2 Joe Montana 80.00 36.00
Jeff Garcia/99
❑ UDJNP Joe Namath 50.00 22.00
Chad Pennington/99
❑ UDJPD Clinton Portis 30.00 13.50
Terrell Davis/250
❑ UDJPF Walter Payton 80.00 36.00
Marshall Faulk/99
❑ UDJPM Chad Pennington 30.00 13.50
Randy Moss/250
❑ UDJPT Walter Payton 50.00 22.00
Anthony Thomas/250
❑ UDJPW Walter Payton 80.00 36.00
Ricky Williams/99
❑ UDJRO Jerry Rice 30.00 13.50
Terrell Owens/250
❑ UDJSF Bart Starr 80.00 36.00
Brett Favre/99
❑ UDJST Barry Sanders 60.00 27.00
LaDainian Tomlinson/99
❑ UDJTC Fran Tarkenton 40.00 18.00
Daunte Culpepper/99
❑ UDJYV Steve Young 50.00 22.00
Michael Vick/99

2003 Ultimate Collection Game Jersey Duals Autographs

MINT NRMT
GOLD/10 NOT PRICED DUE TO SCARCITY

❑ DJSEM John Elway 400.00 180.00
Donovan McNabb
❑ DJSMM Dan Marino 500.00 220.00
Peyton Manning
❑ DJSNP Joe Namath 250.00 110.00
Chad Pennington
❑ DJSSF Bart Starr 550.00 250.00
Brett Favre
❑ DJSVM Michael Vick 400.00 180.00
Donovan McNabb
❑ DJSYV Steve Young 350.00 160.00
Michael Vick

2003 Ultimate Collection Game Jersey Patches

MINT NRMT
*GOLD/175/141: .8X TO 2X BASIC INSERTS
*GOLD/99: .8X TO 2X BASIC INSERTS
GOLDS #'d OF 10 NOT PRICED DUE

❑ GJPAB Aaron Brooks/175 20.00 9.00
❑ GJPAG Ahman Green/175 25.00 11.00
❑ GJPBA Barry Sanders/25 120.00 55.00
❑ GJPBF Brett Favre/99 60.00 27.00
❑ GJPBS Bart Starr/25 120.00 55.00
❑ GJPBU Brian Urlacher/175 40.00 18.00
❑ GJPCA David Carr/175 40.00 18.00
❑ GJPCP1 Chad Pennington/99 30.00 13.50
❑ GJPCP2 Clinton Portis/141 40.00 18.00
❑ GJPDC Daunte Culpepper/175 30.00 13.50
❑ GJPDB1 Drew Bledsoe/175 25.00 11.00
❑ GJPDB2 Drew Brees/99 25.00 11.00
❑ GJPDM1 Dan Marino/25 200.00 90.00
❑ GJPDM2 Deuce McAllister/175 25.00 11.00
❑ GJPDM3 Donovan McNabb/99 40.00 18.00
❑ GJPEG Eddie George/175 20.00 9.00
❑ GJPEJ Edgerrin James/99 25.00 11.00
❑ GJPES Emmitt Smith/175 50.00 22.00
❑ GJPFT Fran Tarkenton/99 40.00 18.00
❑ GJPJE John Elway/99 80.00 36.00
❑ GJPJG Jeff Garcia/175 25.00 11.00
❑ GJPJM Joe Montana/25 200.00 90.00

❑ GJPJN Joe Namath/25 100.00 45.00
❑ GJPJR Jerry Rice/175 40.00 18.00
❑ GJPKJ Keyshawn Johnson/175 20.00 9.00
❑ GJPKW Kurt Warner/99 40.00 18.00
❑ GJPLT LaDainian Tomlinson/175 25.00 11.00
❑ GJPMF Marshall Faulk/175 25.00 11.00
❑ GJPMV Michael Vick/99 50.00 22.00
❑ GJPPH Priest Holmes/175 40.00 18.00
❑ GJPPM Peyton Manning/175 40.00 18.00
❑ GJPRM Randy Moss/175 40.00 18.00
❑ GJPRW Ricky Williams/99 25.00 11.00
❑ GJPSY Steve Young/25 100.00 45.00
❑ GJPTA Troy Aikman/99 50.00 22.00
❑ GJPTC Tim Couch/175 20.00 9.00
❑ GJPTO Terrell Owens/175 25.00 11.00
❑ GJPTB1 Terry Bradshaw/25 120.00 55.00
❑ GJPTB2 Tom Brady/175 50.00 22.00
❑ GJPWP Walter Payton/25 250.00 110.00

2003 Ultimate Collection Ultimate Signatures

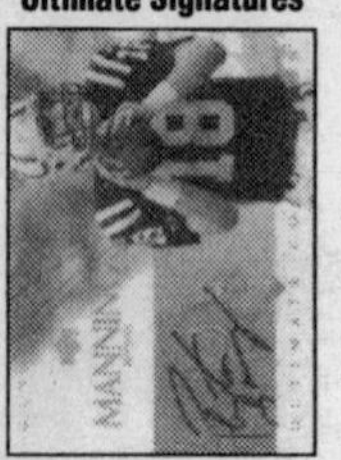

MINT NRMT
*GOLD/50: .6X TO 1.5X BASIC CARDS
GOLD/10 NOT PRICED DUE TO SCARCITY

❑ USAB Aaron Brooks 25.00 11.00
❑ USBA Barry Sanders 120.00 55.00
❑ USBB Brad Banks 25.00 11.00
❑ USBF Brett Favre/25 300.00 135.00
❑ USBL Byron Leftwich 100.00 45.00
❑ USBS Bart Starr/25 175.00 80.00
❑ USCH Chad Pennington 40.00 18.00
❑ USCP Carson Palmer 80.00 36.00
❑ USCS Chris Simms 50.00 22.00
❑ USDB Drew Brees 30.00 13.50
❑ USDC David Carr/25 100.00 45.00
❑ USDE Deuce McAllister 30.00 13.50
❑ USDM Dan Marino/25 300.00 135.00
❑ USFT Fran Tarkenton/25 60.00 27.00
❑ USJE John Elway/25 250.00 110.00
❑ USJF Justin Fargas 30.00 13.50
❑ USJK Jim Kelly 60.00 27.00
❑ USJM Joe Montana/25 300.00 135.00
❑ USJN Joe Namath/25 120.00 55.00
❑ USJR Jerry Rice/25 250.00 110.00
❑ USKK Kliff Kingsbury 25.00 11.00
❑ USKS Ken Stabler 50.00 22.00
❑ USLT LaDainian Tomlinson 30.00 13.50
❑ USMA Marcus Allen 40.00 18.00
❑ USPM Peyton Manning 80.00 36.00
❑ USRG Rex Grossman 50.00 22.00
❑ USRM0 Randy Moss EXCH 75.00 34.00
❑ USSU Donovan McNabb 50.00 22.00
❑ USSY Steve Young/25 120.00 55.00
❑ USTA Troy Aikman/25 120.00 55.00
❑ USTB Terry Bradshaw/25 150.00 70.00
❑ USTC Tim Couch 25.00 11.00

2003 Ultimate Collection Ultimate Signatures Duals

MINT NRMT
❑ DSBT Drew Brees 60.00 27.00
LaDainian Tomlinson/50
❑ DSGM Jeff Garcia 250.00 110.00
Joe Montana/25
❑ DSGY Jeff Garcia 150.00 70.00
Steve Young/25

❑ DSMF Dan Marino 250.00 110.00
Jay Fiedler/25
❑ DSMM Peyton Manning 175.00 80.00
Archie Manning/50
❑ DSMP Peyton Manning 200.00 90.00
Carson Palmer/50
❑ DSMY Joe Montana 400.00 180.00
Steve Young/25
❑ DSNP Joe Namath 250.00 110.00
Chad Pennington/25
❑ DSPL Carson Palmer 250.00 110.00
Byron Leftwich/50
❑ DSSF Bart Starr 450.00 200.00
Brett Favre/25
❑ DSSS Phil Simms 100.00 45.00
Chris Simms/50

2003 Ultimate Collection Ultimate Signatures Duals Gold

MINT NRMT
SER.#'d TO 10 NOT PRICED
❑ DSBT Drew Brees 100.00 45.00
LaDainian Tomlinson/25
❑ DSGM Jeff Garcia
Joe Montana/10
❑ DSGY Jeff Garcia
Steve Young/10
❑ DSMF Dan Marino
Jay Fiedler/10
❑ DSMM Peyton Manning 200.00 90.00
Archie Manning/25
❑ DSMP Peyton Manning 250.00 110.00
Carson Palmer/25
❑ DSMY Joe Montana
Steve Young/10
❑ DSNP Joe Namath
Chad Pennington/10
❑ DSPL Carson Palmer 300.00 135.00
Byron Leftwich/25
❑ DSSF Bart Starr
Brett Favre/10
❑ DSSS Phil Simms 150.00 70.00
Chris Simms/25

2004 Ultimate Collection

Nm-Mt Ex-Mt
COMP.SET w/o RC's (65)
COMP.SET w/o SP's (95)
1-65 PRINT RUN 750 SER.#'d SETS
66-91/99A/133-135 PRINT RUN 750 SETS
92-98 RC PRINT RUN 250 SER.#'d SETS
99B-124/131-132 AU RC PRINT RUN 250 SETS
125-130 AU RC PRINT RUN 150 SER.#'d SETS
UNPRICED PLATINUM PRINT RUN 10 SETS

❑ 1 Emmitt Smith 10.00 3.00
❑ 2 Anquan Boldin 5.00 1.50
❑ 3 Michael Vick 10.00 3.00
❑ 4 Peerless Price 3.00 .90
❑ 5 Kyle Boller 5.00 1.50
❑ 6 Jamal Lewis 5.00 1.50
❑ 7 Drew Bledsoe 5.00 1.50
❑ 8 Travis Henry 3.00 .90
❑ 9 Stephen Davis 3.00 .90
❑ 10 Jake Delhomme 5.00 1.50
❑ 11 Rex Grossman 5.00 1.50
❑ 12 Brian Urlacher 6.00 1.80
❑ 13 Carson Palmer 6.00 1.80
❑ 14 Chad Johnson 3.00 .90
❑ 15 Jeff Garcia 5.00 1.50
❑ 16 Keyshawn Johnson 3.00 .90
❑ 17 Roy Williams S 3.00 .90
❑ 18 Jake Plummer 3.00 .90
❑ 19 Joey Harrington 5.00 1.50
❑ 20 Charles Rogers 3.00 .90
❑ 21 Ahman Green 5.00 1.50
❑ 22 Brett Favre 12.00 3.60
❑ 23 David Carr 5.00 1.50
❑ 24 Domanick Davis 5.00 1.50
❑ 25 Andre Johnson 5.00 1.50
❑ 26 Edgerrin James 5.00 1.50
❑ 27 Peyton Manning 8.00 2.40
❑ 28 Marvin Harrison 5.00 1.50
❑ 29 Byron Leftwich 8.00 2.40
❑ 30 Fred Taylor 3.00 .90
❑ 31 Priest Holmes 6.00 1.80
❑ 32 Tony Gonzalez 3.00 .90
❑ 33 Trent Green 3.00 .90
❑ 34 Ricky Williams 5.00 1.50
❑ 35 Chris Chambers 3.00 .90
❑ 36 Jay Fiedler 2.00 .60
❑ 37 Randy Moss 6.00 1.80
❑ 38 Daunte Culpepper 5.00 1.50
❑ 39 Tom Brady 8.00 2.40
❑ 40 Corey Dillon 3.00 .90
❑ 41 Deuce McAllister 5.00 1.50
❑ 42 Aaron Brooks 3.00 .90
❑ 43 Tiki Barber 3.00 .90
❑ 44 Jeremy Shockey 5.00 1.50
❑ 45 Chad Pennington 6.00 1.80
❑ 46 Curtis Martin 5.00 1.50
❑ 47 Santana Moss 3.00 .90
❑ 48 Jerry Rice 10.00 3.00
❑ 49 Rich Gannon 3.00 .90
❑ 50 Donovan McNabb 6.00 1.80
❑ 51 Terrell Owens 5.00 1.50
❑ 52 Hines Ward 5.00 1.50
❑ 53 Plaxico Burress 3.00 .90
❑ 54 LaDainian Tomlinson 5.00 1.50
❑ 55 Tim Rattay 3.00 .90
❑ 56 Matt Hasselbeck 3.00 .90
❑ 57 Shaun Alexander 5.00 1.50
❑ 58 Marc Bulger 5.00 1.50
❑ 59 Marshall Faulk 5.00 1.50
❑ 60 Torry Holt 5.00 1.50
❑ 61 Brad Johnson 3.00 .90
❑ 62 Steve McNair 5.00 1.50
❑ 63 Chris Brown 5.00 1.50
❑ 64 Mark Brunell 3.00 .90
❑ 65 Clinton Portis 5.00 1.50
❑ 66 Michael Turner RC 8.00 2.40
❑ 67 Kris Wilson RC 10.00 3.00
❑ 68 Jeff Smoker RC 12.00 3.60
❑ 69 Adimchinobe Echemandu RC 8.00 2.40
❑ 71 Thomas Tapeh RC 8.00 2.40
❑ 72 Chris Cooley RC 10.00 3.00
❑ 73 Cody Pickett RC 10.00 3.00
❑ 74 P.K. Sam RC 8.00 2.40
❑ 75 Ben Hartsock RC 10.00 3.00
❑ 76 Tim Euhus RC 10.00 3.00
❑ 77 Jammal Lord RC 10.00 3.00
❑ 78 Ricardo Colclough RC 10.00 3.00
❑ 79 D.J. Hackett RC 8.00 2.40
❑ 80 Ahmad Carroll RC 12.00 3.60
❑ 81 Troy Fleming RC 8.00 2.40

- ❑ 82 John Navarre RC 10.00 3.00
- ❑ 83 Craig Krenzel RC 10.00 3.00
- ❑ 84 Johnnie Morant RC 10.00 3.00
- ❑ 85 D.J. Williams RC 12.00 3.60
- ❑ 86 Jarrett Payton RC 10.00 3.00
- ❑ 87 Quincy Wilson RC 8.00 2.40
- ❑ 88 B.J. Symons RC 10.00 3.00
- ❑ 89 Tommie Harris RC 12.00 3.60
- ❑ 90 Jonathan Vilma RC 10.00 3.00
- ❑ 91 Karlos Dansby RC 10.00 3.00
- ❑ 92 Jerricho Cotchery RC 12.00 3.60
- ❑ 93 Samie Parker RC 12.00 3.60
- ❑ 94 Carlos Francis RC 10.00 3.00
- ❑ 95 Jim Sorgi RC 12.00 3.60
- ❑ 96 Derrick Hamilton RC 10.00 3.00
- ❑ 97 Dunta Robinson RC 12.00 3.60
- ❑ 98 Chris Gamble RC 15.00 4.50
- ❑ 99A Josh Harris RC 10.00 3.00
- ❑ 99B Devery Henderson AU RC 25.00 7.50
- ❑ 100 Julius Jones AU RC 225.00 70.00
- ❑ 101 Cedric Cobbs AU RC 25.00 7.50
- ❑ 102 Greg Jones AU RC 25.00 7.50
- ❑ 103 Tatum Bell AU RC EXCH 80.00 24.00
- ❑ 104 Michael Jenkins AU RC EXCH 30.00 9.00
- ❑ 105 Devard Darling AU RC 25.00 7.50
- ❑ 106 Lee Evans AU RC 50.00 15.00
- ❑ 107 Keary Colbert AU RC 40.00 12.00
- ❑ 108 Bernard Berrian AU RC 25.00 7.50
- ❑ 109 Ben Watson AU RC 25.00 7.50
- ❑ 110 Matt Schaub AU RC 40.00 12.00
- ❑ 111 Darius Watts AU RC 30.00 9.00
- ❑ 112 Kevin Jones AU RC 150.00 45.00
- ❑ 113 Luke McCown AU RC 30.00 9.00
- ❑ 114 DeAngelo Hall AU RC 35.00 10.50
- ❑ 115 Rashaun Woods AU RC 30.00 9.00
- ❑ 116 Michael Clayton AU RC 100.00 30.00
- ❑ 117 Ben Troupe AU RC 25.00 7.50
- ❑ 118 B.J. Sams AU RC EXCH 25.00 7.50
- ❑ 119 Reggie Williams AU RC 30.00 9.00
- ❑ 120 Chris Perry AU RC 60.00 18.00
- ❑ 121 Roy Williams AU RC 120.00 36.00
- ❑ 122 Robert Gallery AU RC 30.00 9.00
- ❑ 123 J.P. Losman AU RC 120.00 36.00
- ❑ 124 Steven Jackson AU RC 150.00 45.00
- ❑ 125 Drew Henson AU RC 100.00 30.00
- ❑ 126 Kellen Winslow AU RC 80.00 24.00
- ❑ 127 Ben Roethlisberger AU RC 600.00 180.00
- ❑ 128 Philip Rivers AU RC 150.00 45.00
- ❑ 129 Larry Fitzgerald AU RC 120.00 36.00
- ❑ 130 Eli Manning AU RC 300.00 90.00
- ❑ 131 Ernest Wilford AU RC
- ❑ 132 Mewelde Moore AU RC 30.00 9.00
- ❑ 133 Will Smith RC 10.00 3.00
- ❑ 134 Kenechi Udeze RC 10.00 3.00
- ❑ 135 Matt Mauck RC 10.00 3.00

2004 Ultimate Collection Gold

Nm-Mt Ex-Mt

*GOLD STARS: .8X TO 2X BASIC CARDS
*GOLD ROOK/75: .8X TO 2X BASIC RC/750
1-91/99A/133-135 PRINT RUN 75 SETS
*GOLD ROOK/25: .8X TO 2X BASIC RC/250
92-98 STATED PRINT RUN 25 SETS

2004 Ultimate Collection HoloGold

Nm-Mt Ex-Mt

*GOLD STARS: 1.2X TO 3X BASIC CARDS
*GOLD ROOK/30: 1.2X TO 3X BASIC RC/750
1-91/99A/133-135 PRINT RUN 30 SETS
UNPRICED 92-98 PRINT RUN 5 SETS

2004 Ultimate Collection Buy Back Autographs

Nm-Mt Ex-Mt

SER.#'d UNDER 22 NOT PRICED
EXCH EXPIRATION: 12/20/2007

- ❑ BBAG A.Green 03UDMS/3
- ❑ BBAM2 A.Manning 01UDLPP/2
- ❑ BBAM3 A.Manning 03SPSIG/8
- ❑ BBBF1 B.Favre 01UDRLM/10

- ❑ BBBF2 B.Favre 01UDMS/11
- ❑ BBBF3 B.Favre 03SPGUFF/9
- ❑ BBBF4 B.Favre 03UDGJ/6
- ❑ BBBF5 B.Favre 03UDGJN/1
- ❑ BBBL2 B.Leftwich 03UDRFJ/15
- ❑ BBBO B.Lilly 02UDLLJ/5
- ❑ BBBS B.Sanders 03SPSIG/20
- ❑ BBCB C.Brown 03UDRFJ/14
- ❑ BBCC C.Chambers 01UDRT/25 40.00 12.00
- ❑ BBCJ1 C.Johnson 03SPA/26 40.00 12.00
- ❑ BBCJ2 C.Johnson 03SPSIG/42 30.00 9.00
- ❑ BBCJ3 C.Johnson 03SS/45 30.00 9.00
- ❑ BBCJ4 C.Johnson 03UDGJ/33 30.00 9.00
- ❑ BBCP1 C.Pennington 02UDMS/14
- ❑ BBCP2 C.Pennington 03SPA/10
- ❑ BBDA1 D.Carr 02UDRFJ/8
- ❑ BBDA2 D.Carr 03UDFJ/7
- ❑ BBDB1 D.Bledsoe 00UDGJ/21
- ❑ BBDB2 D.Bledsoe 03SPA/10
- ❑ BBDB3 D.Bledsoe 03UDGJN/2
- ❑ BBDE1 D.McAllister 01UDRT/5
- ❑ BBDE2 D.McAllister 03SPA/26 40.00 12.00
- ❑ BBDK D.Mason 03SPA/40 30.00 9.00
- ❑ BBDM1 D.McAllister 03SPGUP/7
- ❑ BBFM Brett Favre Donovan McNabb
- ❑ BBFT F.Tarkenton 03SPSIG/28 40.00 12.00
- ❑ BBHL H.Long 00UDLLJ/3
- ❑ BBJE1 J.Elway 01SPGUAF/4
- ❑ BBJE2 J.Elway 01UDLMM/7
- ❑ BBJE3 J.Elway 02UDOTTJ/19
- ❑ BBJE4 J.Elway 03SPSIG/9
- ❑ BBJM1 J.Montana 93SPSIG/5
- ❑ BBJN1 J.Namath 01UDLPP/3
- ❑ BBJN2 J.Namath 03SPSIG/6
- ❑ BBJO1 J.McCown 02SSRGJ/14
- ❑ BBJO2 J.McCown 02UDAGB/10
- ❑ BBJO3 J.McCown 03SPA/27 30.00 9.00
- ❑ BBJO4 J.McCown 03SPSIG/22 30.00 9.00
- ❑ BBJO5 J.McCown 03UDSOS/24 30.00 9.00
- ❑ BBJW J.Walker EXCH 60.00 18.00
- ❑ BBKB1 K.Boller 03UDRFJ/15
- ❑ BBKB2 K.Boller 03UDHRDL/14
- ❑ BBKS1 K.Stabler 00UDLJ/7
- ❑ BBKS2 K.Stabler 03SPSIG/26 40.00 12.00
- ❑ BBKW1 K.Washington 03SPAT/10
- ❑ BBKW2 K.Washington 03UDRFJ/12
- ❑ BBLT1 L.Tomlinson EXCH 60.00 18.00
- ❑ BBMA D.Marino 03SPSIG/7
- ❑ BBMB1 M.Brunell 00UDMGUS/14
- ❑ BBMB2 M.Brunell 01UDOTG/18
- ❑ BBMB3 M.Brunell 02UDU/12
- ❑ BBMB4 M.Brunell 03UDSOS/15
- ❑ BBMV1 M.Vick 01UDORG/11
- ❑ BBMV2 M.Vick 03SPA/10
- ❑ BBMV3 M.Vick 03SPSIG/6
- ❑ BBMV4 M.Vick 03UDGJ/5
- ❑ BBMV5 M.Vick 03UDHRDL/13
- ❑ BBMV6 M.Vick 03UDHRDLS/1
- ❑ BBPH P.Hornung 01UDPPGJ/3
- ❑ BBPM1 P.Manning 01UDRFLM/1
- ❑ BBPM2 P.Manning 01UDPPGJ/10
- ❑ BBPM3 P.Manning 02UDOJ/9
- ❑ BBPM4 P.Manning 02UDFQF/6
- ❑ BBPM5 P.Manning 03SPGUS/14
- ❑ BBPM6 P.Manning 03UDHRJsy/1
- ❑ BBRA R.White 02UDLTT/33 40.00 12.00
- ❑ BBRG R.Grossman 03UDRF/13
- ❑ BBRG1 R.Grossman 03UDHRDLJ/19
- ❑ BBRW1 R.Williams S 02SPLCRR/9
- ❑ BBRW2 R.Williams S 02UDAGB/10
- ❑ BBRW3 R.Williams S 03UDGJ/31 40.00 12.00
- ❑ BBSJ S.Jurgensen 01UDLPP/5
- ❑ BBSM1 S.McNair 01UDGGJ/2
- ❑ BBSM2 S.McNair 02UDAASA/4
- ❑ BBSM3 S.McNair 03UDMVPGB/3
- ❑ BBTA1 T.Aikman 00UDMGUS/12
- ❑ BBTA2 T.Aikman 01UDLPP/4
- ❑ BBTA3 T.Aikman 03SPSIG/8
- ❑ BBTB T.Brady EXCH 200.00 60.00
- ❑ BBTG1 T.Gonzalez 03SPGUFF/8
- ❑ BBTG2 T.Gonzalez 03SS/15
- ❑ BBTH1 T.Henry 01UDRT/14
- ❑ BBTH2 T.Henry 03SPA/36 25.00 7.50
- ❑ BBTH3 T.Henry 03SPSIG/46 25.00 7.50
- ❑ BBTH4 T.Henry 03SS/39 25.00 7.50
- ❑ BBTO T.Heap 03SS/30 25.00 7.50

2004 Ultimate Collection Game Jerseys

Nm-Mt Ex-Mt

STATED PRINT RUN 175 SER.#'d SETS
*GOLD: 1X TO 2.5X BASIC INSERTS
GOLD PRINT RUN 25 SER.#'d SETS

- ❑ UGJBF Brett Favre 25.00 7.50
- ❑ UGJBL Byron Leftwich 12.00 3.60
- ❑ UGJBS Barry Sanders 25.00 7.50
- ❑ UGJCA Carson Palmer 10.00 3.00
- ❑ UGJCL Clinton Portis 10.00 3.00
- ❑ UGJCP Chad Pennington 12.00 3.60
- ❑ UGJDA David Carr 10.00 3.00
- ❑ UGJDC Daunte Culpepper 10.00 3.00
- ❑ UGJDM Deuce McAllister 10.00 3.00
- ❑ UGJDO Donovan McNabb 12.00 3.60
- ❑ UGJED Eric Dickerson 15.00 4.50
- ❑ UGJES Emmitt Smith 20.00 6.00
- ❑ UGJFT Fran Tarkenton 15.00 4.50
- ❑ UGJJE John Elway 25.00 7.50
- ❑ UGJJM Joe Montana 40.00 12.00
- ❑ UGJJN Joe Namath 25.00 7.50
- ❑ UGJJR Jerry Rice 20.00 6.00
- ❑ UGJJS Jeremy Shockey 10.00 3.00
- ❑ UGJLS Lynn Swann 30.00 9.00
- ❑ UGJLT LaDainian Tomlinson 10.00 3.00
- ❑ UGJMA Dan Marino 30.00 9.00
- ❑ UGJMF Marshall Faulk 10.00 3.00
- ❑ UGJMH Marvin Harrison 10.00 3.00
- ❑ UGJMV Michael Vick 20.00 6.00
- ❑ UGJPH Priest Holmes 12.00 3.60
- ❑ UGJPM Peyton Manning 15.00 4.50
- ❑ UGJPS Phil Simms 10.00 3.00
- ❑ UGJRM Randy Moss 12.00 3.60
- ❑ UGJRS Roger Staubach 25.00 7.50
- ❑ UGJRW Ricky Williams 10.00 3.00
- ❑ UGJSM Steve McNair 8.00 2.40
- ❑ UGJSY Steve Young 20.00 6.00
- ❑ UGJTA Troy Aikman 20.00 6.00
- ❑ UGJTB Tom Brady 20.00 6.00
- ❑ UGJTE Terry Bradshaw 25.00 7.50
- ❑ UGJTO Terrell Owens 10.00 3.00
- ❑ UGJWP Walter Payton 40.00 12.00

2004 Ultimate Collection Game Jersey Autographs

	Nm-Mt	Ex-Mt
STATED PRINT RUN 25 SER.#'d SETS		
EXCH EXPIRATION: 12/20/2007		
❑ UGJSBF Brett Favre	350.00	105.00
❑ UGJSCP Chad Pennington	60.00	18.00
❑ UGJSDA Daunte Culpepper EXCH	60.00	18.00
❑ UGJSDC David Carr	50.00	15.00
❑ UGJSDM Deuce McAllister	50.00	15.00
❑ UGJSDO Donovan McNabb EXCH	120.00	36.00
❑ UGJSJE John Elway	300.00	90.00
❑ UGJSJM Joe Montana	350.00	105.00
❑ UGJSJN Joe Namath	175.00	52.50
❑ UGJSJT Joe Theismann	50.00	15.00
❑ UGJSLT LaDainian Tomlinson EXCH	60.00	18.00
❑ UGJSMV Michael Vick	200.00	60.00
❑ UGJSPM Peyton Manning	200.00	60.00
❑ UGJSSM Steve McNair	50.00	15.00
❑ UGJSTB Tom Brady	250.00	75.00

2004 Ultimate Collection Game Jersey Duals

	Nm-Mt	Ex-Mt
STATED PRINT RUN 99 SER.#'d SETS		
CARD NUMBERS HAVE UGJ2 PREFIX		
UNPRICED GOLD PRINT RUN 15 SETS		
UNPRICED DUAL AU PRINT RUN 15 SETS		
❑ BP Tom Brady / Chad Pennington	30.00	9.00
❑ CF David Carr / Brett Favre	40.00	12.00
❑ CM Daunte Culpepper / Steve McNair	20.00	6.00
❑ EM John Elway / Joe Montana	80.00	24.00
❑ EP Eli Manning / Philip Rivers	40.00	12.00
❑ FM Brett Favre / Peyton Manning	60.00	18.00
❑ HJ Priest Holmes / Edgerrin James	20.00	6.00
❑ LP Byron Leftwich / Carson Palmer	20.00	6.00
❑ LR Larry Fitzgerald / Randy Moss	25.00	7.50
❑ MB Joe Montana / Tom Brady	80.00	24.00
❑ MM Dan Marino / Joe Montana	80.00	24.00
❑ MO Randy Moss / Terrell Owens	25.00	7.50
❑ MR Randy Moss / Jerry Rice	30.00	9.00
❑ NU Joe Namath / Johnny Unitas	60.00	18.00
❑ OM Terrell Owens / Donovan McNabb	25.00	7.50
❑ PG Clinton Portis / Ahman Green	20.00	6.00
❑ PM Chad Pennington / Peyton Manning	30.00	9.00
❑ PS Walter Payton / Gale Sayers	80.00	24.00
❑ RO Jerry Rice / Terrell Owens	30.00	9.00
❑ SA Roger Staubach / Troy Aikman	30.00	9.00
❑ SF Emmitt Smith / Marshall Faulk	25.00	7.50
❑ SG Jeremy Shockey / Tony Gonzalez	20.00	6.00
❑ SP Barry Sanders / Walter Payton	100.00	30.00
❑ SW Jeremy Shockey / Kellen Winslow Jr.	25.00	7.50
❑ TL Lawrence Taylor / Ronnie Lott	25.00	7.50
❑ TM LaDainian Tomlinson / Deuce McAllister	20.00	6.00
❑ UT Brian Urlacher / Zach Thomas	25.00	7.50
❑ VB Michael Vick / Tom Brady	40.00	12.00
❑ VM Michael Vick / Mark Brunell	25.00	7.50
❑ WH Ricky Williams / Priest Holmes	20.00	6.00

2004 Ultimate Collection Game Jersey Dual Patches

	Nm-Mt	Ex-Mt
STATED PRINT RUN 25 SER.#'d SETS		
UNPRICED GOLD PRINT RUN 10 SETS		
UNPRICED AU PRINT RUN 5 SER.#'d SETS		
CARD NUMBERS HAVE UP2 PREFIX		
❑ AE Troy Aikman / John Elway	80.00	24.00
❑ BP Tom Brady / Chad Pennington	80.00	24.00
❑ FV Brett Favre / Michael Vick	120.00	36.00
❑ MC Randy Moss / Daunte Culpepper	60.00	18.00
❑ MM Dan Marino / Joe Montana	200.00	60.00
❑ NU Joe Namath / Johnny Unitas	120.00	36.00
❑ PS Peyton Manning / Steve McNair	80.00	24.00
❑ SM Barry Sanders / Deuce McAllister	80.00	24.00
❑ VM Michael Vick / Donovan McNabb	80.00	24.00
❑ WT Ricky Williams / LaDainian Tomlinson	50.00	15.00

2004 Ultimate Collection Game Jersey Patches

	Nm-Mt	Ex-Mt
STATED PRINT RUN 150 SER.#'d SETS		
*GOLD: .8X TO 2X BASIC INSERTS		
GOLD PRINT RUN 25 SER.#'d SETS		
❑ UPAG Ahman Green	25.00	7.50
❑ UPBF Brett Favre	60.00	18.00
❑ UPBL Byron Leftwich	30.00	9.00
❑ UPBS Barry Sanders	60.00	18.00
❑ UPBU Brian Urlacher	30.00	9.00
❑ UPCA Carson Palmer	25.00	7.50
❑ UPCC Cris Carter	25.00	7.50
❑ UPCL Clinton Portis	25.00	7.50
❑ UPCP Chad Pennington	30.00	9.00
❑ UPDA David Carr	25.00	7.50
❑ UPDB Drew Bledsoe	25.00	7.50
❑ UPDC Daunte Culpepper	25.00	7.50
❑ UPDE Deuce McAllister	25.00	7.50
❑ UPDM Donovan McNabb	30.00	9.00
❑ UPED Eric Dickerson	25.00	7.50
❑ UPEJ Edgerrin James	25.00	7.50
❑ UPES Emmitt Smith	40.00	12.00
❑ UPFT Fran Tarkenton	25.00	7.50
❑ UPGS Gale Sayers	50.00	15.00
❑ UPJE John Elway	50.00	15.00
❑ UPJM Joe Montana	80.00	24.00
❑ UPJN Joe Namath	40.00	12.00
❑ UPJR Jerry Rice	30.00	9.00
❑ UPJS Jeremy Shockey	25.00	7.50
❑ UPJU Johnny Unitas	50.00	15.00
❑ UPLT LaDainian Tomlinson	25.00	7.50
❑ UPMA Dan Marino	80.00	24.00
❑ UPMB Mark Brunell	20.00	6.00
❑ UPMF Marshall Faulk	25.00	7.50
❑ UPMH Marvin Harrison	25.00	7.50
❑ UPMV Michael Vick	30.00	9.00
❑ UPPH Priest Holmes	25.00	7.50
❑ UPPM Peyton Manning	40.00	12.00
❑ UPRM Randy Moss	30.00	9.00
❑ UPRS Roger Staubach	40.00	12.00
❑ UPRW Ricky Williams	25.00	7.50
❑ UPSM Steve McNair	20.00	6.00
❑ UPTA Troy Aikman	30.00	9.00
❑ UPTB Tom Brady	40.00	12.00
❑ UPTO Terrell Owens	25.00	7.50
❑ UPWP Walter Payton	80.00	24.00
❑ UPZT Zach Thomas	25.00	7.50

2004 Ultimate Collection Game Jersey Super Patches

	Nm-Mt	Ex-Mt
UNPRICED SUPER PRINT RUN 15 SETS		
❑ USPBF Brett Favre		
❑ USPCP Chad Pennington		
❑ USPDE Deuce McAllister		
❑ USPDM Donovan McNabb		
❑ USPES Emmitt Smith		
❑ USPJR Jerry Rice		
❑ USPMV Michael Vick		
❑ USPPM Peyton Manning		
❑ USPRM Randy Moss		
❑ USPTB Tom Brady		

2004 Ultimate Collection Rookie Jerseys

STATED PRINT RUN 199 SER.#'d SETS
*GOLD: .8X TO 2X BASIC INSERTS
GOLD PRINT RUN 25 SER.#'d SETS
UNPRICED AUTO PRINT RUN 1 SET

	Nm-Mt	Ex-Mt
❑ URJBR Ben Roethlisberger	80.00	24.00
❑ URJCC Cedric Cobbs	10.00	3.00
❑ URJCP Chris Perry	15.00	4.50
❑ URJDD Devard Darling	10.00	3.00
❑ URJDE Devery Henderson	10.00	3.00
❑ URJEM Eli Manning	40.00	12.00
❑ URJGJ Greg Jones	10.00	3.00
❑ URJJJ Julius Jones	30.00	9.00
❑ URJJP J.P. Losman	20.00	6.00
❑ URJKJ Kevin Jones	25.00	7.50
❑ URJKW Kellen Winslow Jr.	20.00	6.00
❑ URJLE Lee Evans	12.00	3.60
❑ URJLF Larry Fitzgerald	20.00	6.00
❑ URJMC Michael Clayton	15.00	4.50
❑ URJMJ Michael Jenkins	10.00	3.00
❑ URJPR Philip Rivers	20.00	6.00
❑ URJRA Rashaun Woods	12.00	3.60
❑ URJRO Roy Williams WR	25.00	7.50
❑ URJRW Reggie Williams	12.00	3.60
❑ URJSJ Steven Jackson	25.00	7.50
❑ URJTB Tatum Bell	15.00	4.50

2004 Ultimate Collection Ultimate Signatures

EXCH EXPIRATION: 12/20/2007
UNPRICED QUAD AU PRINT RUN 5 SETS

	Nm-Mt	Ex-Mt
❑ USAG0 Ahman Green/100	40.00	12.00
❑ USAR Andy Reid/100	30.00	9.00
❑ USBF Brett Favre/25	300.00	90.00
❑ USBL0 Byron Leftwich/275	30.00	9.00
❑ USBP Bill Parcells/25	50.00	15.00
❑ USBR Ben Roethlisberger/100	350.00	105.00
❑ USBS Barry Sanders/25	300.00	90.00
❑ USCC Chris Chambers/275	20.00	6.00
❑ USCJ Chad Johnson/275	20.00	6.00
❑ USDB Drew Bledsoe/275	30.00	9.00
❑ USEC Earl Campbell/275	40.00	12.00
❑ USEM Eli Manning/100	175.00	52.50
❑ USFT Fran Tarkenton/275	40.00	12.00
❑ USHL Howie Long/100	40.00	12.00
❑ USJE John Elway/25	250.00	75.00
❑ USJF John Fox/100	20.00	6.00
❑ USJG Jon Gruden/100	20.00	6.00
❑ USJJ Jimmy Johnson/100	30.00	9.00
❑ USJM Joe Montana/25	300.00	90.00
❑ USJN Joe Namath/25	200.00	60.00
❑ USJP J.P. Losman/275	80.00	24.00
❑ USJT Joe Theismann/275	30.00	9.00
❑ USKB Kyle Boller/275	20.00	6.00
❑ USKJ Kevin Jones/275	100.00	30.00
❑ USKW Kellen Winslow Jr./100	80.00	24.00
❑ USLD Len Dawson/275	30.00	9.00
❑ USMB Mark Brunell/275	20.00	6.00
❑ USMV Michael Vick/25	150.00	45.00
❑ USPH Paul Hornung/275	40.00	12.00
❑ USPM Peyton Manning/25	175.00	52.50
❑ USPR Philip Rivers/275	80.00	24.00
❑ USRG Rex Grossman/275	20.00	6.00
❑ USRW Roy Williams WR/275	100.00	30.00
❑ USTA Troy Aikman/25	120.00	36.00
❑ USTB Tom Brady/25	250.00	75.00
❑ USTH Travis Henry/275	20.00	6.00
❑ USTS Tony Siragusa/275	20.00	6.00
❑ USWI Kellen Winslow Sr./100	30.00	9.00

2004 Ultimate Collection Ultimate Signatures Duals

EXCH EXPIRATION: 12/20/2007
CARD NUMBERS HAVE US2 PREFIX

	Nm-Mt	Ex-Mt
❑ AS Troy Aikman/50 Roger Staubach	150.00	45.00
❑ BB Tom Brady/50 EXCH Drew Bledsoe	150.00	45.00
❑ CV Daunte Culpepper/25 EXCH Michael Vick	175.00	52.50
❑ EA John Elway/25 Troy Aikman	300.00	90.00
❑ FM Brett Favre/25 Peyton Manning	400.00	120.00
❑ JG Jimmy Johnson/25 Jon Gruden	50.00	15.00
❑ LV Byron Leftwich/50 Michael Vick	150.00	45.00
❑ MF Donovan McNabb/25 EXCH Brett Favre	300.00	90.00
❑ MG Deuce McAllister/50 Ahman Green	50.00	15.00
❑ MM Peyton Manning/50 Eli Manning	300.00	90.00
❑ MN Joe Montana/25 Joe Namath	350.00	105.00
❑ MT Deuce McAllister/50 LaDainian Tomlinson	50.00	15.00
❑ PF Chad Pennington/50 Brett Favre	250.00	75.00
❑ PR Bill Parcells/25 Andy Reid	60.00	18.00
❑ SP Steve McNair/25 Peyton Manning	175.00	52.50
❑ TB Joe Theismann/50 Mark Brunell	40.00	12.00
❑ TG LaDainian Tomlinson/50 Ahman Green	60.00	18.00
❑ TS Fran Tarkenton/25 Ken Stabler	80.00	24.00
❑ VB Michael Vick EXCH/25 Tom Brady	250.00	75.00
❑ WW Kellen Winslow Sr./50 Kellen Winslow Jr.	80.00	24.00

1991 Ultra

	Nm-Mt	Ex-Mt
COMPLETE SET (300)	20.00	9.00
❑ 1 Don Beebe	.05	.02
❑ 2 Shane Conlan	.05	.02
❑ 3 Pete Metzelaars	.05	.02
❑ 4 Jamie Mueller	.05	.02
❑ 5 Scott Norwood	.05	.02
❑ 6 Andre Reed	.10	.05
❑ 7 Leon Seals	.05	.02
❑ 8 Bruce Smith	.25	.11
❑ 9 Leonard Smith	.05	.02
❑ 10 Thurman Thomas	.25	.11
❑ 11 Lewis Billups	.05	.02
❑ 12 Jim Breech	.05	.02
❑ 13 James Brooks	.10	.05
❑ 14 Eddie Brown	.05	.02
❑ 15 Boomer Esiason	.10	.05
❑ 16 David Fulcher	.05	.02
❑ 17 Rodney Holman	.05	.02
❑ 18 Bruce Kozerski	.05	.02
❑ 19 Tim Krumrie	.05	.02
❑ 20 Tim McGee	.05	.02
❑ 21 Anthony Munoz	.10	.05
❑ 22 Leon White	.05	.02
❑ 23 Ickey Woods	.05	.02
❑ 24 Carl Zander	.05	.02
❑ 25 Brian Brennan	.05	.02
❑ 26 Thane Gash	.05	.02
❑ 27 Leroy Hoard	.10	.05
❑ 28 Mike Johnson	.05	.02
❑ 29 Reggie Langhorne	.05	.02
❑ 30 Kevin Mack	.05	.02
❑ 31 Clay Matthews	.10	.05
❑ 32 Eric Metcalf	.10	.05
❑ 33 Steve Atwater	.05	.02
❑ 34 Melvin Bratton	.05	.02
❑ 35 John Elway	1.25	.55
❑ 36 Bobby Humphrey	.05	.02
❑ 37 Mark Jackson	.05	.02
❑ 38 Vance Johnson	.05	.02
❑ 39 Ricky Nattiel	.05	.02
❑ 40 Steve Sewell	.05	.02
❑ 41 Dennis Smith	.05	.02
❑ 42 David Treadwell	.05	.02
❑ 43 Michael Young	.05	.02
❑ 44 Ray Childress	.05	.02

❑ 45	Cris Dishman RC	.05	.02
❑ 46	William Fuller	.10	.05
❑ 47	Ernest Givins	.10	.05
❑ 48	John Grimsley UER (Acquired line should be Trade '91, not Draft 6-'84)	.05	.02
❑ 49	Drew Hill	.05	.02
❑ 50	Haywood Jeffires	.10	.05
❑ 51	Sean Jones	.10	.05
❑ 52	Johnny Meads	.05	.02
❑ 53	Warren Moon	.25	.11
❑ 54	Al Smith	.05	.02
❑ 55	Lorenzo White	.05	.02
❑ 56	Albert Bentley	.05	.02
❑ 57	Duane Bickett	.05	.02
❑ 58	Bill Brooks	.05	.02
❑ 59	Jeff George	.25	.11
❑ 60	Mike Prior	.05	.02
❑ 61	Rohn Stark	.05	.02
❑ 62	Jack Trudeau	.05	.02
❑ 63	Clarence Verdin	.05	.02
❑ 64	Steve DeBerg	.05	.02
❑ 65	Emile Harry	.05	.02
❑ 66	Albert Lewis	.05	.02
❑ 67	Nick Lowery UER (NFL Exp. has 12 years, should be 13)	.05	.02
❑ 68	Todd McNair	.05	.02
❑ 69	Christian Okoye	.05	.02
❑ 70	Stephone Paige	.05	.02
❑ 71	Kevin Porter UER (Front has traded logo, but he has been a Chief all career)	.05	.02
❑ 72	Derrick Thomas	.25	.11
❑ 73	Robb Thomas	.05	.02
❑ 74	Barry Word	.05	.02
❑ 75	Marcus Allen	.25	.11
❑ 76	Eddie Anderson	.05	.02
❑ 77	Tim Brown	.25	.11
❑ 78	Mervyn Fernandez	.05	.02
❑ 79	Willie Gault	.10	.05
❑ 80	Ethan Horton	.05	.02
❑ 81	Howie Long	.25	.11
❑ 82	Vance Mueller	.05	.02
❑ 83	Jay Schroeder	.05	.02
❑ 84	Steve Smith	.05	.02
❑ 85	Greg Townsend	.05	.02
❑ 86	Mark Clayton	.10	.05
❑ 87	Jim C. Jensen	.05	.02
❑ 88	Dan Marino	1.25	.55
❑ 89	Tim McKyer UER (Acquired line should be Trade '91, not Trade '90)	.05	.02
❑ 90	John Offerdahl	.05	.02
❑ 91	Louis Oliver	.05	.02
❑ 92	Reggie Roby	.05	.02
❑ 93	Sammie Smith	.05	.02
❑ 94	Hart Lee Dykes	.05	.02
❑ 95	Irving Fryar	.10	.05
❑ 96	Tommy Hodson	.05	.02
❑ 97	Maurice Hurst	.05	.02
❑ 98	John Stephens	.05	.02
❑ 99	Andre Tippett	.05	.02
❑ 100	Mark Boyer	.05	.02
❑ 101	Kyle Clifton	.05	.02
❑ 102	James Hasty	.05	.02
❑ 103	Erik McMillan	.05	.02
❑ 104	Rob Moore	.25	.11
❑ 105	Joe Mott	.05	.02
❑ 106	Ken O'Brien	.05	.02
❑ 107	Ron Stallworth UER (Acquired line should be Trade '91, not Draft 4-'89)	.05	.02
❑ 108	Al Toon	.10	.05
❑ 109	Gary Anderson K	.05	.02
❑ 110	Bubby Brister	.05	.02
❑ 111	Thomas Everett	.05	.02
❑ 112	Merril Hoge	.05	.02
❑ 113	Louis Lipps	.05	.02
❑ 114	Greg Lloyd	.25	.11
❑ 115	Hardy Nickerson	.10	.05
❑ 116	Dwight Stone	.05	.02
❑ 117	Rod Woodson	.25	.11
❑ 118	Tim Worley	.05	.02
❑ 119	Rod Bernstine	.05	.02
❑ 120	Marion Butts	.10	.05
❑ 121	Gill Byrd	.05	.02
❑ 122	Arthur Cox	.05	.02
❑ 123	Burt Grossman	.05	.02
❑ 124	Ronnie Harmon	.05	.02
❑ 125	Anthony Miller	.10	.05
❑ 126	Leslie O'Neal	.10	.05
❑ 127	Gary Plummer	.05	.02
❑ 128	Sam Seale	.05	.02
❑ 129	Junior Seau	.25	.11
❑ 130	Broderick Thompson	.05	.02
❑ 131	Billy Joe Tolliver	.05	.02
❑ 132	Brian Blades	.10	.05
❑ 133	Jeff Bryant	.05	.02
❑ 134	Derrick Fenner	.05	.02
❑ 135	Jacob Green	.05	.02
❑ 136	Andy Heck	.05	.02
❑ 137	Patrick Hunter RC UER (Photos on back show 23 and 27)	.05	.02
❑ 138	Norm Johnson	.05	.02
❑ 139	Tommy Kane	.05	.02
❑ 140	Dave Krieg	.10	.05
❑ 141	John L. Williams	.05	.02
❑ 142	Terry Wooden	.05	.02
❑ 143	Steve Broussard	.05	.02
❑ 144	Keith Jones	.05	.02
❑ 145	Brian Jordan	.10	.05
❑ 146	Chris Miller	.10	.05
❑ 147	John Rade	.05	.02
❑ 148	Andre Rison	.10	.05
❑ 149	Mike Rozier	.05	.02
❑ 150	Deion Sanders	.40	.18
❑ 151	Neal Anderson	.10	.05
❑ 152	Trace Armstrong	.05	.02
❑ 153	Kevin Butler	.05	.02
❑ 154	Mark Carrier DB	.10	.05
❑ 155	Richard Dent	.10	.05
❑ 156	Dennis Gentry	.05	.02
❑ 157	Jim Harbaugh	.25	.11
❑ 158	Brad Muster	.05	.02
❑ 159	William Perry	.10	.05
❑ 160	Mike Singletary	.10	.05
❑ 161	Lemuel Stinson	.05	.02
❑ 162	Troy Aikman	.75	.35
❑ 163	Michael Irvin	.25	.11
❑ 164	Mike Saxon	.05	.02
❑ 165	Emmitt Smith	2.00	.90
❑ 166	Jerry Ball	.05	.02
❑ 167	Michael Cofer	.05	.02
❑ 168	Rodney Peete	.10	.05
❑ 169	Barry Sanders	1.25	.55
❑ 170	Robert Brown	.05	.02
❑ 171	Anthony Dilweg	.05	.02
❑ 172	Tim Harris	.05	.02
❑ 173	Johnny Holland	.05	.02
❑ 174	Perry Kemp	.05	.02
❑ 175	Don Majkowski	.05	.02
❑ 176	Brian Noble	.05	.02
❑ 177	Jeff Query	.05	.02
❑ 178	Sterling Sharpe	.25	.11
❑ 179	Charles Wilson	.05	.02
❑ 180	Keith Woodside	.05	.02
❑ 181	Flipper Anderson UER (Back photo not him)	.05	.02
❑ 182	Bern Brostek	.05	.02
❑ 183	Pat Carter RC	.05	.02
❑ 184	Aaron Cox	.05	.02
❑ 185	Henry Ellard	.10	.05
❑ 186	Jim Everett	.10	.05
❑ 187	Cleveland Gary	.05	.02
❑ 188	Jerry Gray	.05	.02
❑ 189	Kevin Greene	.10	.05
❑ 190	Mike Wilcher	.05	.02
❑ 191	Alfred Anderson	.05	.02
❑ 192	Joey Browner	.05	.02
❑ 193	Anthony Carter	.10	.05
❑ 194	Chris Doleman	.05	.02
❑ 195	Rick Fenney	.05	.02
❑ 196	Darrell Fullington	.05	.02
❑ 197	Rich Gannon	.25	.11
❑ 198	Hassan Jones	.05	.02
❑ 199	Steve Jordan	.05	.02
❑ 200	Mike Merriweather	.05	.02
❑ 201	Al Noga	.05	.02
❑ 202	Herschel Walker	.10	.05
❑ 203	Wade Wilson	.10	.05
❑ 204	Morten Andersen	.05	.02
❑ 205	Gene Atkins	.05	.02
❑ 206	Toi Cook RC	.05	.02
❑ 207	Craig Heyward	.10	.05
❑ 208	Dalton Hilliard	.05	.02
❑ 209	Vaughan Johnson	.05	.02
❑ 210	Eric Martin	.05	.02
❑ 211	Brett Perriman	.25	.11
❑ 212	Pat Swilling	.10	.05
❑ 213	Steve Walsh	.05	.02
❑ 214	Ottis Anderson	.10	.05
❑ 215	Carl Banks	.05	.02
❑ 216	Maurice Carthon	.05	.02
❑ 217	Mark Collins	.05	.02
❑ 218	Rodney Hampton	.25	.11
❑ 219	Erik Howard	.05	.02
❑ 220	Mark Ingram	.10	.05
❑ 221	Pepper Johnson	.05	.02
❑ 222	Dave Meggett	.10	.05
❑ 223	Phil Simms	.10	.05
❑ 224	Lawrence Taylor	.25	.11
❑ 225	Lewis Tillman	.05	.02
❑ 226	Everson Walls	.05	.02
❑ 227	Fred Barnett	.25	.11
❑ 228	Jerome Brown	.05	.02
❑ 229	Keith Byars	.05	.02
❑ 230	Randall Cunningham	.25	.11
❑ 231	Byron Evans	.05	.02
❑ 232	Wes Hopkins	.05	.02
❑ 233	Keith Jackson	.10	.05
❑ 234	Heath Sherman	.05	.02
❑ 235	Anthony Toney	.05	.02
❑ 236	Reggie White	.25	.11
❑ 237	Rich Camarillo	.05	.02
❑ 238	Ken Harvey	.10	.05
❑ 239	Eric Hill	.05	.02
❑ 240	Johnny Johnson	.05	.02
❑ 241	Ernie Jones	.05	.02
❑ 242	Tim McDonald	.05	.02
❑ 243	Timm Rosenbach	.05	.02
❑ 244	Jay Taylor	.05	.02
❑ 245	Dexter Carter	.05	.02
❑ 246	Mike Cofer	.05	.02
❑ 247	Kevin Fagan	.05	.02
❑ 248	Don Griffin	.05	.02
❑ 249	Charles Haley	.10	.05
❑ 250	Brent Jones	.25	.11
❑ 251	Joe Montana UER (Born: Monongahela, not New Eagle)	1.25	.55
❑ 252	Darryl Pollard	.05	.02
❑ 253	Tom Rathman	.05	.02
❑ 254	Jerry Rice	.75	.35
❑ 255	John Taylor	.10	.05
❑ 256	Steve Young	.75	.35
❑ 257	Gary Anderson RB	.05	.02
❑ 258	Mark Carrier WR	.25	.11
❑ 259	Chris Chandler	.25	.11
❑ 260	Reggie Cobb	.05	.02
❑ 261	Reuben Davis	.05	.02
❑ 262	Willie Drewrey	.05	.02
❑ 263	Ron Hall	.05	.02
❑ 264	Eugene Marve	.05	.02
❑ 265	Winston Moss UER (Acquired line should be Trade '91, not Draft 2-'87)	.05	.02
❑ 266	Vinny Testaverde	.10	.05
❑ 267	Broderick Thomas	.05	.02
❑ 268	Jeff Bostic	.05	.02
❑ 269	Earnest Byner	.05	.02
❑ 270	Gary Clark	.25	.11
❑ 271	Darrell Green	.05	.02
❑ 272	Jim Lachey	.05	.02
❑ 273	Wilber Marshall	.05	.02
❑ 274	Art Monk	.10	.05
❑ 275	Gerald Riggs	.05	.02
❑ 276	Mark Rypien	.10	.05
❑ 277	Ricky Sanders	.05	.02

❑ 278 Alvin Walton	.05	.02
❑ 279 Nick Bell RC	.05	.02
❑ 280 Eric Bieniemy RC	.05	.02
❑ 281 Jarrod Bunch RC	.05	.02
❑ 282 Mike Croel RC	.05	.02
❑ 283 Brett Favre RC	10.00	4.50
❑ 284 Moe Gardner RC	.05	.02
❑ 285 Pat Harlow RC	.05	.02
❑ 286 Randal Hill RC	.10	.05
❑ 287 Todd Marinovich RC	.05	.02
❑ 288 Russell Maryland RC	.25	.11
❑ 289 Dan McGwire RC	.05	.02
❑ 290 Ernie Mills RC UER (Patterns misspelled as pattersn in first sentence)	.10	.05
❑ 291 Herman Moore RC	.25	.11
❑ 292 Godfrey Myles RC	.05	.02
❑ 293 Browning Nagle RC	.05	.02
❑ 294 Mike Pritchard RC	.25	.11
❑ 295 Esera Tuaolo RC	.05	.02
❑ 296 Mark Vander Poel RC	.05	.02
❑ 297 Ricky Watters RC UER (Photo on back actually Ray Griggs)	1.50	.70
❑ 298 Chris Zorich RC	.25	.11
❑ 299 Checklist Card (Randall Cunningham and Emmitt Smith)	.10	.05
❑ 300 Checklist Card (Randall Cunningham and Emmitt Smith)	.10	.05

1991 Ultra Update

	Nm-Mt	Ex-Mt
COMP.FACT.SET (100)	25.00	11.00
❑ U1 Brett Favre	20.00	9.00
❑ U2 Moe Gardner	.10	.05
❑ U3 Tim McKyer	.10	.05
❑ U4 Bruce Pickens RC	.10	.05
❑ U5 Mike Pritchard	.40	.18
❑ U6 Cornelius Bennett	.20	.09
❑ U7 Phil Hansen RC	.10	.05
❑ U8 Henry Jones RC	.20	.09
❑ U9 Mark Kelso	.10	.05
❑ U10 James Lofton	.20	.09
❑ U11 Anthony Morgan RC	.10	.05
❑ U12 Stan Thomas	.10	.05
❑ U13 Chris Zorich	.20	.09
❑ U14 Reggie Rembert	.10	.05
❑ U15 Alfred Williams RC	.10	.05
❑ U16 Michael Jackson RC	.40	.18
❑ U17 Ed King RC	.10	.05
❑ U18 Joe Morris	.10	.05
❑ U19 Vince Newsome	.10	.05
❑ U20 Tony Casillas	.10	.05
❑ U21 Russell Maryland	.40	.18
❑ U22 Jay Novacek	.40	.18
❑ U23 Mike Croel	.10	.05
❑ U24 Gaston Green	.10	.05
❑ U25 Kenny Walker RC	.10	.05
❑ U26 Melvin Jenkins RC	.10	.05
❑ U27 Herman Moore	.40	.18
❑ U28 Kelvin Pritchett RC	.20	.09
❑ U29 Chris Spielman	.20	.09
❑ U30 Vinnie Clark RC	.10	.05
❑ U31 Allen Rice	.10	.05
❑ U32 Vai Sikahema	.10	.05
❑ U33 Esera Tuaolo	.10	.05
❑ U34 Mike Dumas RC	.10	.05
❑ U35 John Flannery RC	.10	.05
❑ U36 Allen Pinkett	.10	.05
❑ U37 Tim Barnett RC	.10	.05
❑ U38 Dan Saleaumua	.10	.05
❑ U39 Harvey Williams RC	.40	.18
❑ U40 Nick Bell	.10	.05
❑ U41 Roger Craig	.20	.09
❑ U42 Ronnie Lott	.20	.09
❑ U43 Todd Marinovich	.10	.05
❑ U44 Robert Delpino	.10	.05
❑ U45 Todd Lyght RC	.10	.05
❑ U46 Robert Young RC	.20	.09
❑ U47 Aaron Craver RC	.10	.05
❑ U48 Mark Higgs RC	.10	.05
❑ U49 Vestee Jackson	.10	.05
❑ U50 Carl Lee	.10	.05
❑ U51 Felix Wright	.10	.05
❑ U52 Darrell Fullington	.10	.05
❑ U53 Pat Harlow	.10	.05
❑ U54 Eugene Lockhart	.10	.05
❑ U55 Hugh Millen RC	.10	.05
❑ U56 Leonard Russell RC	.40	.18
❑ U57 Jon Vaughn RC	.10	.05
❑ U58 Quinn Early	.20	.09
❑ U59 Bobby Hebert	.10	.05
❑ U60 Rickey Jackson	.10	.05
❑ U61 Sam Mills	.20	.09
❑ U62 Jarrod Bunch	.10	.05
❑ U63 John Elliott	.10	.05
❑ U64 Jeff Hostetler	.20	.09
❑ U65 Ed McCaffrey RC	6.00	2.70
❑ U66 Kanavis McGhee RC	.10	.05
❑ U67 Mo Lewis RC	.20	.09
❑ U68 Browning Nagle	.10	.05
❑ U69 Blair Thomas	.10	.05
❑ U70 Antone Davis RC	.10	.05
❑ U71 Brad Goebel RC (See card U74)	.10	.05
❑ U72 Jim McMahon	.20	.09
❑ U73 Clyde Simmons	.10	.05
❑ U74 Randal Hill UER (Card number on back U71 instead of U74)	.20	.09
❑ U75 Eric Swann RC	.40	.18
❑ U76 Tom Tupa	.10	.05
❑ U77 Jeff Graham RC	.40	.18
❑ U78 Eric Green	.10	.05
❑ U79 Neil O'Donnell RC	.40	.18
❑ U80 Huey Richardson RC	.10	.05
❑ U81 Eric Bieniemy	.10	.05
❑ U82 John Friesz	.40	.18
❑ U83 Eric Moten RC	.10	.05
❑ U84 Stanley Richard RC	.10	.05
❑ U85 Todd Bowles	.10	.05
❑ U86 Merton Hanks RC	.40	.18
❑ U87 Tim Harris	.10	.05
❑ U88 Pierce Holt	.10	.05
❑ U89 Ted Washington RC	.10	.05
❑ U90 John Kasay RC	.20	.09
❑ U91 Dan McGwire	.10	.05
❑ U92 Lawrence Dawsey RC	.20	.09
❑ U93 Charles McRae RC	.10	.05
❑ U94 Jesse Solomon	.10	.05
❑ U95 Robert Wilson RC	.10	.05
❑ U96 Ricky Ervins RC	.20	.09
❑ U97 Charles Mann	.10	.05
❑ U98 Bobby Wilson RC	.10	.05
❑ U99 Jerry Rice Pro-Visions	1.50	.70
❑ U100 Checklist 1-100 (Nick Bell and Jim McMahon)	.10	.05

1997 Ultra

	Nm-Mt	Ex-Mt
COMPLETE SET (350)	80.00	36.00
COMP.SERIES 1 (200)	30.00	13.50
COMP.SERIES 2 (150)	50.00	22.00
❑ 1 Brett Favre	2.50	1.10
❑ 2 Ricky Watters	.40	.18
❑ 3 Dan Marino	2.50	1.10
❑ 4 Bryan Still	.25	.11
❑ 5 Chester McGlockton	.25	.11
❑ 6 Tim Biakabutuka	.40	.18
❑ 7 Dave Brown	.25	.11
❑ 8 Mike Alstott	.60	.25
❑ 9 O.J. McDuffie	.40	.18
❑ 10 Mark Brunell	.75	.35
❑ 11 Michael Bates	.25	.11
❑ 12 Tyrone Wheatley	.40	.18
❑ 13 Eddie George	.60	.25
❑ 14 Kevin Greene	.40	.18
❑ 15 Jerris McPhail	.25	.11
❑ 16 Harvey Williams	.25	.11
❑ 17 Eric Swann	.25	.11
❑ 18 Carl Pickens	.40	.18
❑ 19 Terrell Davis	.75	.35
❑ 20 Charles Way	.25	.11
❑ 21 Jamie Asher	.25	.11
❑ 22 Qadry Ismail	.40	.18
❑ 23 Lawrence Phillips	.25	.11
❑ 24 John Friesz	.25	.11
❑ 25 Dorsey Levens	.60	.25
❑ 26 Willie McGinest	.25	.11
❑ 27 Chris T. Jones	.25	.11
❑ 28 Cortez Kennedy	.25	.11
❑ 29 Raymont Harris	.25	.11
❑ 30 William Roaf	.25	.11
❑ 31 Ted Johnson	.25	.11
❑ 32 Tony Martin	.40	.18
❑ 33 Jim Everett	.25	.11
❑ 34 Ray Zellars	.25	.11
❑ 35 Derrick Alexander WR	.40	.18
❑ 36 Leonard Russell	.25	.11
❑ 37 William Thomas	.25	.11
❑ 38 Karim Abdul-Jabbar	.40	.18
❑ 39 Kevin Turner	.25	.11
❑ 40 Robert Brooks	.40	.18
❑ 41 Kent Graham	.25	.11
❑ 42 Tony Brackens	.25	.11
❑ 43 Rodney Hampton	.40	.18
❑ 44 Drew Bledsoe	.75	.35
❑ 45 Barry Sanders	2.00	.90
❑ 46 Tim Brown	.60	.25
❑ 47 Reggie White	.60	.25
❑ 48 Terry Allen	.60	.25
❑ 49 Jim Harbaugh	.40	.18
❑ 50 John Elway	2.50	1.10
❑ 51 William Floyd	.40	.18
❑ 52 Michael Jackson	.40	.18
❑ 53 Larry Centers	.40	.18
❑ 54 Emmitt Smith	2.00	.90
❑ 55 Bruce Smith	.40	.18
❑ 56 Terrell Owens	.75	.35
❑ 57 Deion Sanders	.60	.25
❑ 58 Neil O'Donnell	.40	.18
❑ 59 Kordell Stewart	.60	.25
❑ 60 Bobby Engram	.40	.18
❑ 61 Keenan McCardell	.40	.18
❑ 62 Ben Coates	.40	.18
❑ 63 Curtis Martin	.75	.35
❑ 64 Hugh Douglas	.25	.11
❑ 65 Eric Moulds	.60	.25
❑ 66 Derrick Thomas	.40	.18
❑ 67 Byron Bam Morris	.25	.11
❑ 68 Bryan Cox	.25	.11
❑ 69 Rob Moore	.40	.18
❑ 70 Michael Haynes	.25	.11
❑ 71 Brian Mitchell	.25	.11
❑ 72 Alex Molden	.25	.11
❑ 73 Steve Young	.75	.35

❏ 74	Andre Reed	.40	.18
❏ 75	Michael Westbrook	.40	.18
❏ 76	Eric Metcalf	.40	.18
❏ 77	Tony Banks	.40	.18
❏ 78	Ken Dilger	.25	.11
❏ 79	John Henry Mills RC	.25	.11
❏ 80	Ashley Ambrose	.25	.11
❏ 81	Jason Dunn	.25	.11
❏ 82	Trent Dilfer	.60	.25
❏ 83	Wayne Chrebet	.60	.25
❏ 84	Ty Detmer	.40	.18
❏ 85	Aeneas Williams	.25	.11
❏ 86	Frank Wycheck	.25	.11
❏ 87	Jessie Tuggle	.25	.11
❏ 88	Steve McNair	.75	.35
❏ 89	Chris Slade	.25	.11
❏ 90	Anthony Johnson	.25	.11
❏ 91	Simeon Rice	.40	.18
❏ 92	Mike Tomczak	.25	.11
❏ 93	Sean Jones	.25	.11
❏ 94	Wesley Walls	.40	.18
❏ 95	Thurman Thomas	.60	.25
❏ 96	Scott Mitchell	.40	.18
❏ 97	Desmond Howard	.40	.18
❏ 98	Chris Warren	.40	.18
❏ 99	Glyn Milburn	.25	.11
❏ 100	Vinny Testaverde	.40	.18
❏ 101	James O.Stewart	.40	.18
❏ 102	Iheanyi Uwaezuoke	.25	.11
❏ 103	Stan Humphries	.40	.18
❏ 104	Terance Mathis	.40	.18
❏ 105	Thomas Lewis	.25	.11
❏ 106	Eddie Kennison	.40	.18
❏ 107	Rashaan Salaam	.25	.11
❏ 108	Curtis Conway	.40	.18
❏ 109	Chris Sanders	.25	.11
❏ 110	Marcus Allen	.60	.25
❏ 111	Gilbert Brown	.40	.18
❏ 112	Jason Sehorn	.40	.18
❏ 113	Zach Thomas	.60	.25
❏ 114	Bobby Hebert	.25	.11
❏ 115	Herman Moore	.40	.18
❏ 116	Ray Lewis	1.00	.45
❏ 117	Darnay Scott	.40	.18
❏ 118	Jamal Anderson	.60	.25
❏ 119	Keyshawn Johnson	.60	.25
❏ 120	Adrian Murrell	.40	.18
❏ 121	Sam Mills	.25	.11
❏ 122	Irving Fryar	.40	.18
❏ 123	Ki-Jana Carter	.25	.11
❏ 124	Gus Frerotte	.25	.11
❏ 125	Terry Glenn	.60	.25
❏ 126	Quentin Coryatt	.25	.11
❏ 127	Robert Smith	.40	.18
❏ 128	Jeff Blake	.40	.18
❏ 129	Natrone Means	.40	.18
❏ 130	Isaac Bruce	.60	.25
❏ 131	Lamar Lathon	.25	.11
❏ 132	Johnnie Morton	.40	.18
❏ 133	Jerry Rice	1.25	.55
❏ 134	Errict Rhett	.25	.11
❏ 135	Junior Seau	.60	.25
❏ 136	Joey Galloway	.40	.18
❏ 137	Napoleon Kaufman	.60	.25
❏ 138	Troy Aikman	1.25	.55
❏ 139	Kevin Hardy	.25	.11
❏ 140	Jimmy Smith	.40	.18
❏ 141	Edgar Bennett	.40	.18
❏ 142	Hardy Nickerson	.25	.11
❏ 143	Greg Lloyd	.25	.11
❏ 144	Dale Carter	.25	.11
❏ 145	Jake Reed	.40	.18
❏ 146	Cris Carter	.60	.25
❏ 147	Todd Collins	.25	.11
❏ 148	Mel Gray	.25	.11
❏ 149	Lawyer Milloy	.40	.18
❏ 150	Kimble Anders	.40	.18
❏ 151	Darick Holmes	.25	.11
❏ 152	Bert Emanuel	.40	.18
❏ 153	Marshall Faulk	.75	.35
❏ 154	Frank Sanders	.40	.18
❏ 155	Leeland McElroy	.25	.11
❏ 156	Rickey Dudley	.40	.18
❏ 157	Tamarick Vanover	.40	.18
❏ 158	Kerry Collins	.60	.25
❏ 159	Jeff Graham	.25	.11
❏ 160	Jerome Bettis	.60	.25
❏ 161	Greg Hill	.25	.11
❏ 162	John Mobley	.25	.11
❏ 163	Michael Irvin	.60	.25
❏ 164	Marvin Harrison	.60	.25
❏ 165	Jim Schwantz RC	.25	.11
❏ 166	Jermaine Lewis	.60	.25
❏ 167	Levon Kirkland	.25	.11
❏ 168	Nilo Silvan	.25	.11
❏ 169	Ken Norton	.25	.11
❏ 170	Yancey Thigpen	.40	.18
❏ 171	Antonio Freeman	.60	.25
❏ 172	Terry Kirby	.40	.18
❏ 173	Brad Johnson	.60	.25
❏ 174	Reidel Anthony RC	.60	.25
❏ 175	Tiki Barber RC	3.00	1.35
❏ 176	Pat Barnes RC	.60	.25
❏ 177	Michael Booker RC	.25	.11
❏ 178	Peter Boulware RC	.60	.25
❏ 179	Rae Carruth RC	.25	.11
❏ 180	Troy Davis RC	.40	.18
❏ 181	Corey Dillon RC	5.00	2.20
❏ 182	Jim Druckenmiller RC	.40	.18
❏ 183	Warrick Dunn RC	2.00	.90
❏ 184	James Farrior RC	.60	.25
❏ 185	Yatil Green RC	.40	.18
❏ 186	Walter Jones RC	.60	.25
❏ 187	Tom Knight RC	.25	.11
❏ 188	Sam Madison RC	.60	.25
❏ 189	Tyrus McCloud RC	.25	.11
❏ 190	Orlando Pace RC	.60	.25
❏ 191	Jake Plummer RC	4.00	1.80
❏ 192	Dwayne Rudd RC	.60	.25
❏ 193	Darrell Russell RC	.25	.11
❏ 194	Sedrick Shaw RC	.40	.18
❏ 195	Shawn Springs RC	.40	.18
❏ 196	Bryant Westbrook RC	.25	.11
❏ 197	Danny Wuerffel RC	.60	.25
❏ 198	Reinard Wilson RC	.40	.18
❏ 199	Checklist Rodney Hampton	.25	.11
❏ 200	Checklist John Elway	.60	.25
❏ 201	Rick Mirer	.25	.11
❏ 202	Torrance Small	.25	.11
❏ 203	Ricky Proehl	.25	.11
❏ 204	Will Blackwell RC	.40	.18
❏ 205	Warrick Dunn	1.00	.45
❏ 206	Rob Johnson	.60	.25
❏ 207	Jim Schwantz	.25	.11
❏ 208	Ike Hilliard RC	1.25	.55
❏ 209	Chris Canty RC	.25	.11
❏ 210	Chris Boniol	.25	.11
❏ 211	Jim Druckenmiller	.25	.11
❏ 212	Tony Gonzalez RC	2.50	1.10
❏ 213	Scottie Graham	.25	.11
❏ 214	Byron Hanspard RC	.40	.18
❏ 215	Gary Brown	.25	.11
❏ 216	Darrell Russell	.25	.11
❏ 217	Sedrick Shaw	.40	.18
❏ 218	Boomer Esiason	.40	.18
❏ 219	Peter Boulware	.40	.18
❏ 220	Willie Green	.25	.11
❏ 221	Dietrich Jells	.25	.11
❏ 222	Freddie Jones RC	.40	.18
❏ 223	Eric Metcalf	.40	.18
❏ 224	John Henry Mills	.25	.11
❏ 225	Michael Timpson	.25	.11
❏ 226	Danny Wuerffel	.60	.25
❏ 227	Daimon Shelton RC	.25	.11
❏ 228	Henry Ellard	.25	.11
❏ 229	Flipper Anderson	.25	.11
❏ 230	Hunter Goodwin RC	.25	.11
❏ 231	Jay Graham RC	.40	.18
❏ 232	Duce Staley RC	6.00	2.70
❏ 233	Lamar Thomas	.25	.11
❏ 234	Rod Woodson	.40	.18
❏ 235	Zack Crockett	.25	.11
❏ 236	Ernie Mills	.25	.11
❏ 237	Kyle Brady	.25	.11
❏ 238	Jesse Campbell	.25	.11
❏ 239	Anthony Miller	.25	.11
❏ 240	Michael Haynes	.25	.11
❏ 241	Qadry Ismail	.40	.18
❏ 242	Tom Knight	.25	.11
❏ 243	Brian Manning RC	.25	.11
❏ 244	Derrick Mayes	.40	.18
❏ 245	Jamie Sharper RC	.40	.18
❏ 246	Sherman Williams	.25	.11
❏ 247	Yatil Green	.40	.18
❏ 248	Howard Griffith	.25	.11
❏ 249	Brian Blades	.25	.11
❏ 250	Mark Chmura	.40	.18
❏ 251	Chris Darkins	.25	.11
❏ 252	Willie Davis	.25	.11
❏ 253	Quinn Early	.25	.11
❏ 254	Marc Edwards RC	.25	.11
❏ 255	Charlie Jones	.25	.11
❏ 256	Jake Plummer	1.50	.70
❏ 257	Heath Shuler	.25	.11
❏ 258	Fred Barnett	.25	.11
❏ 259	William Henderson	.40	.18
❏ 260	Michael Booker	.25	.11
❏ 261	Chad Brown	.25	.11
❏ 262	Garrison Hearst	.40	.18
❏ 263	Leon Johnson RC	.40	.18
❏ 264	Antowain Smith RC	2.00	.90
❏ 265	Darnell Autry RC	.40	.18
❏ 266	Craig Heyward	.25	.11
❏ 267	Walter Jones	.25	.11
❏ 268	Dexter Coakley RC	.60	.25
❏ 269	Mercury Hayes	.25	.11
❏ 270	Brett Perriman	.25	.11
❏ 271	Chris Spielman	.25	.11
❏ 272	Kevin Greene	.40	.18
❏ 273	Kevin Lockett RC	.40	.18
❏ 274	Troy Davis	.40	.18
❏ 275	Brent Jones	.25	.11
❏ 276	Chris Chandler	.40	.18
❏ 277	Bryant Westbrook	.25	.11
❏ 278	Desmond Howard	.40	.18
❏ 279	Tyrone Hughes	.25	.11
❏ 280	Kez McCorvey	.25	.11
❏ 281	Stephen Davis	.60	.25
❏ 282	Steve Everitt	.25	.11
❏ 283	Andre Hastings	.25	.11
❏ 284	Marcus Robinson RC	5.00	2.20
❏ 285	Donnell Woolford	.25	.11
❏ 286	Mario Bates	.25	.11
❏ 287	Corey Dillon	2.00	.90
❏ 288	Jackie Harris	.25	.11
❏ 289	Lorenzo Neal	.25	.11
❏ 290	Anthony Pleasant	.25	.11
❏ 291	Andre Rison	.40	.18
❏ 292	Amani Toomer	.40	.18
❏ 293	Eric Turner	.25	.11
❏ 294	Elvis Grbac	.40	.18
❏ 295	Cris Dishman	.25	.11
❏ 296	Tom Carter	.25	.11
❏ 297	Mark Carrier DB	.25	.11
❏ 298	Orlando Pace	.40	.18
❏ 299	Jay Riemersma RC	.25	.11
❏ 300	Daryl Johnston	.40	.18
❏ 301	Joey Kent RC	.60	.25
❏ 302	Ronnie Harmon	.25	.11
❏ 303	Rocket Ismail	.40	.18
❏ 304	Terrell Davis	.75	.35
❏ 305	Sean Dawkins	.25	.11
❏ 306	Jeff George	.40	.18
❏ 307	David Palmer	.25	.11
❏ 308	Dwayne Rudd	.25	.11
❏ 309	J.J. Stokes	.40	.18
❏ 310	James Farrior	.40	.18
❏ 311	William Fuller	.25	.11
❏ 312	George Jones RC	.40	.18
❏ 313	John Allred RC	.25	.11
❏ 314	Tony Graziani RC	.60	.25
❏ 315	Jeff Hostetler	.25	.11
❏ 316	Keith Poole RC	.60	.25
❏ 317	Neil Smith	.40	.18
❏ 318	Steve Tasker	.25	.11
❏ 319	Mike Vrabel RC	10.00	4.50
❏ 320	Pat Barnes	.60	.25
❏ 321	James Hundon RC	.60	.25
❏ 322	O.J. Santiago RC	.40	.18
❏ 323	Billy Davis RC	.25	.11
❏ 324	Shawn Springs	.40	.18
❏ 325	Reinard Wilson	.25	.11
❏ 326	Charles Johnson	.40	.18

❑ 327 Micheal Barrow	.25	.11
❑ 328 Derrick Mason RC	3.00	1.35
❑ 329 Muhsin Muhammad	.40	.18
❑ 330 David LaFleur RC	.25	.11
❑ 331 Reidel Anthony	.40	.18
❑ 332 Tiki Barber	1.25	.55
❑ 333 Ray Buchanan	.25	.11
❑ 334 John Elway	2.50	1.10
❑ 335 Alvin Harper	.25	.11
❑ 336 Damon Jones RC	.25	.11
❑ 337 Dedric Ward RC	.40	.18
❑ 338 Jim Everett	.25	.11
❑ 339 Jon Harris	.25	.11
❑ 340 Warren Moon	.60	.25
❑ 341 Rae Carruth	.25	.11
❑ 342 John Mobley	.25	.11
❑ 343 Tyrone Poole	.25	.11
❑ 344 Mike Cherry RC	.25	.11
❑ 345 Horace Copeland	.25	.11
❑ 346 Deon Figures	.25	.11
❑ 347 Antwuan Wyatt RC	.25	.11
❑ 348 Tommy Vardell	.25	.11
❑ 349 Checklist (201-324)	.25	.11
❑ 350 Checklist 325-350/inserts	.25	.11
❑ S1A Terrell Davis (Sample Auto)	80.00	36.00
❑ AU3 Dan Marino AUTO (reportedly 100 were signed)	100.00	45.00
❑ S1 Terrell Davis Sample	3.00	1.35

1997 Ultra Gold Medallion

	Nm-Mt	Ex-Mt
COMPLETE SET (346)	400.00	180.00
COMP.SERIES 1 (198)	150.00	70.00
COMP.SERIES 2 (148)	250.00	110.00

*STARS: 1.5X TO 3X BASIC CARDS
*RCs: 1X TO 2X BASIC CARDS

1997 Ultra Platinum Medallion

Nm-Mt Ex-Mt

*STARS: 25X TO 50X BASIC CARDS
*RCs: 8X TO 20X BASIC CARDS

1998 Ultra

	Nm-Mt	Ex-Mt
COMPLETE SET (425)	120.00	55.00
COMP.SERIES 1 (225)	80.00	36.00
COMP.SERIES 2 (200)	50.00	22.00
❑ 1 Barry Sanders	2.50	1.10
❑ 2 Brett Favre	3.00	1.35
❑ 3 Napoleon Kaufman	.75	.35
❑ 4 Robert Smith	.75	.35
❑ 5 Terry Allen	.75	.35
❑ 6 Vinny Testaverde	.50	.23
❑ 7 William Floyd	.30	.14
❑ 8 Carl Pickens	.50	.23
❑ 9 Antonio Freeman	.75	.35
❑ 10 Ben Coates	.50	.23
❑ 11 Elvis Grbac	.50	.23
❑ 12 Kerry Collins	.50	.23
❑ 13 Orlando Pace	.30	.14
❑ 14 Steve Broussard	.30	.14
❑ 15 Terance Mathis	.50	.23
❑ 16 Tiki Barber	.75	.35
❑ 17 Cris Carter	.75	.35
❑ 18 Eric Green	.30	.14
❑ 19 Eric Metcalf	.30	.14
❑ 20 Jeff George	.50	.23
❑ 21 Leslie Shepherd	.30	.14
❑ 22 Natrone Means	.50	.23
❑ 23 Scott Mitchell	.50	.23
❑ 24 Adrian Murrell	.50	.23
❑ 25 Gilbert Brown	.30	.14
❑ 26 Jimmy Smith	.50	.23
❑ 27 Mark Bruener	.30	.14
❑ 28 Troy Aikman	1.50	.70
❑ 29 Warrick Dunn	.75	.35
❑ 30 Jay Graham	.30	.14
❑ 31 Craig Whelihan RC	.30	.14
❑ 32 Ed McCaffrey	.50	.23
❑ 33 Jamie Asher	.30	.14
❑ 34 John Randle	.50	.23
❑ 35 Michael Jackson	.30	.14
❑ 36 Rickey Dudley	.30	.14
❑ 37 Sean Dawkins	.30	.14
❑ 38 Andre Rison	.50	.23
❑ 39 Bert Emanuel	.50	.23
❑ 40 Jeff Blake	.50	.23
❑ 41 Curtis Conway	.50	.23
❑ 42 Eddie Kennison	.50	.23
❑ 43 James McKnight	.75	.35
❑ 44 Rae Carruth	.30	.14
❑ 45 Tito Wooten RC	.30	.14
❑ 46 Cris Dishman	.30	.14
❑ 47 Ernie Conwell	.30	.14
❑ 48 Fred Lane	.30	.14
❑ 49 Jamal Anderson	.75	.35
❑ 50 Lake Dawson	.30	.14
❑ 51 Michael Strahan	.50	.23
❑ 52 Reggie White	.75	.35
❑ 53 Trent Dilfer	.75	.35
❑ 54 Troy Brown	.50	.23
❑ 55 Wesley Walls	.50	.23
❑ 56 Chidi Ahanotu	.30	.14
❑ 57 Dwayne Rudd	.30	.14
❑ 58 Jerry Rice	1.50	.70
❑ 59 Johnnie Morton	.50	.23
❑ 60 Sherman Williams	.30	.14
❑ 61 Steve McNair	.75	.35
❑ 62 Will Blackwell	.30	.14
❑ 63 Chris Chandler	.50	.23
❑ 64 Dexter Coakley	.30	.14
❑ 65 Horace Copeland	.30	.14
❑ 66 Jerald Moore	.30	.14
❑ 67 Leon Johnson	.30	.14
❑ 68 Mark Chmura	.50	.23
❑ 69 Micheal Barrow	.30	.14
❑ 70 Muhsin Muhammad	.50	.23
❑ 71 Terry Glenn	.75	.35
❑ 72 Tony Brackens	.30	.14
❑ 73 Chad Scott	.30	.14
❑ 74 Glenn Foley	.50	.23
❑ 75 Keenan McCardell	.50	.23
❑ 76 Peter Boulware	.30	.14
❑ 77 Reidel Anthony	.50	.23
❑ 78 William Henderson	.50	.23
❑ 79 Tony Martin	.50	.23
❑ 80 Tony Gonzalez	.75	.35
❑ 81 Charlie Jones	.30	.14
❑ 82 Chris Gedney	.30	.14
❑ 83 Chris Calloway	.30	.14
❑ 84 Dale Carter	.30	.14
❑ 85 Ki-Jana Carter	.30	.14
❑ 86 Shawn Springs	.30	.14
❑ 87 Antowain Smith	.75	.35
❑ 88 Eric Turner	.30	.14
❑ 89 John Mobley	.30	.14
❑ 90 Ken Dilger	.30	.14
❑ 91 Bobby Hoying	.50	.23
❑ 92 Curtis Martin	.75	.35
❑ 93 Drew Bledsoe	1.25	.55
❑ 94 Gary Brown	.30	.14
❑ 95 Marvin Harrison	.75	.35
❑ 96 Todd Collins	.30	.14
❑ 97 Chris Warren	.50	.23
❑ 98 Danny Kanell	.50	.23
❑ 99 Tony McGee	.30	.14
❑ 100 Rod Smith	.50	.23
❑ 101 Frank Sanders	.50	.23
❑ 102 Irving Fryar	.50	.23
❑ 103 Marcus Allen	.75	.35
❑ 104 Marshall Faulk	1.00	.45
❑ 105 Bruce Smith	.50	.23
❑ 106 Charlie Garner	.50	.23
❑ 107 Paul Justin	.30	.14
❑ 108 Randal Hill	.30	.14
❑ 109 Erik Kramer	.30	.14
❑ 110 Rob Moore	.50	.23
❑ 111 Shannon Sharpe	.50	.23
❑ 112 Warren Moon	.75	.35
❑ 113 Zach Thomas	.75	.35
❑ 114 Dan Marino	3.00	1.35
❑ 115 Duce Staley	1.00	.45
❑ 116 Eric Swann	.30	.14
❑ 117 Kenny Holmes	.30	.14
❑ 118 Merton Hanks	.30	.14
❑ 119 Raymont Harris	.30	.14
❑ 120 Terrell Davis	.75	.35
❑ 121 Thurman Thomas	.75	.35
❑ 122 Wayne Martin	.30	.14
❑ 123 Charles Way	.30	.14
❑ 124 Chuck Smith	.30	.14
❑ 125 Corey Dillon	.75	.35
❑ 126 Darnell Autry	.30	.14
❑ 127 Isaac Bruce	.75	.35
❑ 128 Joey Galloway	.50	.23
❑ 129 Kimble Anders	.50	.23
❑ 130 Aeneas Williams	.30	.14
❑ 131 Andre Hastings	.30	.14
❑ 132 Chad Lewis	.50	.23
❑ 133 J.J. Stokes	.50	.23
❑ 134 John Elway	3.00	1.35
❑ 135 Karim Abdul-Jabbar	.75	.35
❑ 136 Ken Harvey	.30	.14
❑ 137 Robert Brooks	.50	.23
❑ 138 Rodney Thomas	.30	.14
❑ 139 James Stewart	.50	.23
❑ 140 Billy Joe Hobert	.30	.14
❑ 141 Frank Wycheck	.30	.14
❑ 142 Jake Plummer	.75	.35
❑ 143 Jerris McPhail	.30	.14
❑ 144 Kordell Stewart	.75	.35
❑ 145 Terrell Owens	.75	.35
❑ 146 Willie Green	.30	.14
❑ 147 Anthony Miller	.30	.14
❑ 148 Courtney Hawkins	.30	.14
❑ 149 Larry Centers	.30	.14
❑ 150 Gus Frerotte	.30	.14
❑ 151 O.J. McDuffie	.50	.23
❑ 152 Ray Zellars	.30	.14
❑ 153 Terry Kirby	.30	.14
❑ 154 Tommy Vardell	.30	.14
❑ 155 Willie Davis	.30	.14
❑ 156 Chris Canty	.30	.14
❑ 157 Byron Hanspard	.30	.14
❑ 158 Chris Penn	.30	.14
❑ 159 Damon Jones	.30	.14
❑ 160 Derrick Mayes	.50	.23
❑ 161 Emmitt Smith	2.50	1.10
❑ 162 Keyshawn Johnson	.75	.35
❑ 163 Mike Alstott	.75	.35
❑ 164 Tom Carter	.30	.14
❑ 165 Tony Banks	.50	.23
❑ 166 Bryant Westbrook	.30	.14
❑ 167 Chris Sanders	.30	.14
❑ 168 Deion Sanders	.75	.35
❑ 169 Garrison Hearst	.75	.35
❑ 170 Jason Taylor	.50	.23
❑ 171 Jerome Bettis	.75	.35
❑ 172 John Lynch	.50	.23
❑ 173 Troy Davis	.30	.14
❑ 174 Freddie Jones	.30	.14
❑ 175 Herman Moore	.50	.23
❑ 176 Jake Reed	.50	.23
❑ 177 Mark Brunell	.75	.35
❑ 178 Ray Lewis	.75	.35
❑ 179 Stephen Davis	.30	.14
❑ 180 Tim Brown	.75	.35
❑ 181 Willie McGinest	.30	.14
❑ 182 Andre Reed	.50	.23
❑ 183 Darrien Gordon	.30	.14
❑ 184 David Palmer	.30	.14
❑ 185 James Jett	.50	.23
❑ 186 Junior Seau	.75	.35
❑ 187 Zack Crockett	.30	.14

❑ 188 Brad Johnson .75 .35
❑ 189 Charles Johnson .30 .14
❑ 190 Eddie George .75 .35
❑ 191 Jermaine Lewis .50 .23
❑ 192 Michael Irvin .75 .35
❑ 193 Reggie Brown LB .30 .14
❑ 194 Steve Young 1.00 .45
❑ 195 Warren Sapp .50 .23
❑ 196 Wayne Chrebet .75 .35
❑ 197 David Dunn .30 .14
❑ 198 Dorsey Levens CL .50 .23
❑ 199 Troy Aikman CL .75 .35
❑ 200 John Elway CL .75 .35
❑ 201 Peyton Manning RC 30.00 13.50
❑ 202 Ryan Leaf RC 3.00 1.35
❑ 203 Charles Woodson RC 4.00 1.80
❑ 204 Andre Wadsworth RC 2.50 1.10
❑ 205 Brian Simmons RC 2.50 1.10
❑ 206 Curtis Enis RC 1.50 .70
❑ 207 Randy Moss RC 15.00 6.75
❑ 208 Germane Crowell RC 2.50 1.10
❑ 209 Greg Ellis RC 1.50 .70
❑ 210 Kevin Dyson RC 3.00 1.35
❑ 211 Skip Hicks RC 2.50 1.10
❑ 212 Alonzo Mayes RC 1.50 .70
❑ 213 Robert Edwards RC 2.50 1.10
❑ 214 Fred Taylor RC 5.00 2.20
❑ 215 Robert Holcombe RC 2.50 1.10
❑ 216 John Dutton RC 1.50 .70
❑ 217 Vonnie Holliday RC 2.50 1.10
❑ 218 Tim Dwight RC 3.00 1.35
❑ 219 Tavian Banks RC 2.50 1.10
❑ 220 Marcus Nash RC 1.50 .70
❑ 221 Jason Peter RC 1.50 .70
❑ 222 Michael Myers RC 1.50 .70
❑ 223 Takeo Spikes RC 3.00 1.35
❑ 224 Kivuusama Mays RC 1.50 .70
❑ 225 Jacquez Green RC 2.50 1.10
❑ 226 Doug Flutie .75 .35
❑ 227 Ike Hilliard .50 .23
❑ 228 Craig Heyward .30 .14
❑ 229 Kevin Hardy .30 .14
❑ 230 Jason Dunn .30 .14
❑ 231 Billy Davis .30 .14
❑ 232 Chester McGlockton .30 .14
❑ 233 Sean Gilbert .30 .14
❑ 234 Bert Emanuel .50 .23
❑ 235 Keith Byars .30 .14
❑ 236 Tyrone Wheatley .50 .23
❑ 237 Ricky Proehl .30 .14
❑ 238 Michael Bates .30 .14
❑ 239 Derrick Alexander .50 .23
❑ 240 Harvey Williams .30 .14
❑ 241 Mike Pritchard .30 .14
❑ 242 Paul Justin .30 .14
❑ 243 Jeff Hostetler .30 .14
❑ 244 Eric Moulds .75 .35
❑ 245 Jeff Burris .30 .14
❑ 246 Gary Brown .30 .14
❑ 247 Anthony Johnson .30 .14
❑ 248 Dan Wilkinson .30 .14
❑ 249 Chris Warren .50 .23
❑ 250 Chris Darkins .30 .14
❑ 251 Eric Metcalf .30 .14
❑ 252 Pat Swilling .30 .14
❑ 253 Lamar Smith .50 .23
❑ 254 Quinn Early .30 .14
❑ 255 Carlester Crumpler .30 .14
❑ 256 Eric Bieniemy .30 .14
❑ 257 Aaron Bailey .30 .14
❑ 258 Neil O'Donnell .50 .23
❑ 259 Rod Woodson .50 .23
❑ 260 Ricky Whittle .30 .14
❑ 261 Iheanyi Uwaezuoke .30 .14
❑ 262 Heath Shuler .30 .14
❑ 263 Darren Sharper .50 .23
❑ 264 John Henry Mills .30 .14
❑ 265 Marco Battaglia .30 .14
❑ 266 Yancey Thigpen .30 .14
❑ 267 Irv Smith .30 .14
❑ 268 Jamie Sharper .30 .14
❑ 269 Marcus Robinson 5.00 2.20
❑ 270 Dorsey Levens .75 .35
❑ 271 Qadry Ismail .50 .23
❑ 272 Desmond Howard .50 .23
❑ 273 Webster Slaughter .30 .14
❑ 274 Eugene Robinson .30 .14
❑ 275 Bill Romanowski .30 .14
❑ 276 Vincent Brisby .30 .14
❑ 277 Errict Rhett .50 .23
❑ 278 Albert Connell .30 .14
❑ 279 Thomas Lewis .30 .14
❑ 280 John Farquhar RC .30 .14
❑ 281 Marc Edwards .30 .14
❑ 282 Tyrone Davis .30 .14
❑ 283 Eric Allen .30 .14
❑ 284 Aaron Glenn .30 .14
❑ 285 Roosevelt Potts .30 .14
❑ 286 Kez McCorvey .30 .14
❑ 287 Joey Kent .50 .23
❑ 288 Jim Druckenmiller .30 .14
❑ 289 Sean Dawkins .30 .14
❑ 290 Edgar Bennett .30 .14
❑ 291 Vinny Testaverde .50 .23
❑ 292 Chris Slade .30 .14
❑ 293 Lamar Lathon .30 .14
❑ 294 Jackie Harris .30 .14
❑ 295 Jim Harbaugh .50 .23
❑ 296 Rob Fredrickson .30 .14
❑ 297 Ty Detmer .50 .23
❑ 298 Karl Williams .30 .14
❑ 299 Troy Drayton .30 .14
❑ 300 Curtis Martin .75 .35
❑ 301 Tamarick Vanover .30 .14
❑ 302 Lorenzo Neal .30 .14
❑ 303 John Hall .30 .14
❑ 304 Kevin Greene .50 .23
❑ 305 Bryan Still .30 .14
❑ 306 Neil Smith .50 .23
❑ 307 Greg Lloyd .30 .14
❑ 308 Shawn Jefferson .30 .14
❑ 309 Aaron Taylor .30 .14
❑ 310 Sedrick Shaw .30 .14
❑ 311 O.J. Santiago .30 .14
❑ 312 Kevin Abrams .30 .14
❑ 313 Dana Stubblefield .30 .14
❑ 314 Daryl Johnston .50 .23
❑ 315 Bryan Cox .30 .14
❑ 316 Jeff Graham .30 .14
❑ 317 Mario Bates .50 .23
❑ 318 Adrian Murrell .50 .23
❑ 319 Greg Hill .30 .14
❑ 320 Jahine Arnold .30 .14
❑ 321 Justin Armour .30 .14
❑ 322 Ricky Watters .50 .23
❑ 323 Lamont Warren .30 .14
❑ 324 Mack Strong .30 .14
❑ 325 Darnay Scott .50 .23
❑ 326 Brian Mitchell .30 .14
❑ 327 Rob Johnson .50 .23
❑ 328 Kent Graham .30 .14
❑ 329 Hugh Douglas .30 .14
❑ 330 Simeon Rice .50 .23
❑ 331 Rick Mirer .30 .14
❑ 332 Randall Cunningham .75 .35
❑ 333 Steve Atwater .30 .14
❑ 334 Latario Rachal .30 .14
❑ 335 Tony Martin .50 .23
❑ 336 Leroy Hoard .30 .14
❑ 337 Howard Griffith .30 .14
❑ 338 Kevin Lockett .30 .14
❑ 339 William Floyd .30 .14
❑ 340 Jerry Ellison .30 .14
❑ 341 Kyle Brady .30 .14
❑ 342 Michael Westbrook .50 .23
❑ 343 Kevin Turner .30 .14
❑ 344 David LaFleur .30 .14
❑ 345 Robert Jones .30 .14
❑ 346 Dave Brown .30 .14
❑ 347 Kevin Williams .30 .14
❑ 348 Amani Toomer .50 .23
❑ 349 Amp Lee .30 .14
❑ 350 Bryce Paup .30 .14
❑ 351 Dewayne Washington .30 .14
❑ 352 Mercury Hayes .30 .14
❑ 353 Tim Biakabutuka .50 .23
❑ 354 Ray Crockett .30 .14
❑ 355 Ted Washington .30 .14
❑ 356 Pete Mitchell .30 .14
❑ 357 Billy Jenkins RC .30 .14
❑ 358 Troy Aikman CL .75 .35
❑ 359 Drew Bledsoe CL .75 .35
❑ 360 Steve Young CL .75 .35
❑ 361 Antonio Freeman NG .50 .23
❑ 362 Antowain Smith NG .50 .23
❑ 363 Barry Sanders NG 1.50 .70
❑ 364 Bobby Hoying NG .30 .14
❑ 365 Brett Favre NG 2.00 .90
❑ 366 Corey Dillon NG .50 .23
❑ 367 Dan Marino NG 2.00 .90
❑ 368 Drew Bledsoe NG .75 .35
❑ 369 Eddie George NG .50 .23
❑ 370 Emmitt Smith NG 1.50 .70
❑ 371 Herman Moore NG .50 .23
❑ 372 Jake Plummer NG .50 .23
❑ 373 Jerome Bettis NG .50 .23
❑ 374 Jerry Rice NG 1.00 .45
❑ 375 Joey Galloway NG .50 .23
❑ 376 John Elway NG 2.00 .90
❑ 377 Kordell Stewart NG .50 .23
❑ 378 Mark Brunell NG .75 .35
❑ 379 Keyshawn Johnson NG .50 .23
❑ 380 Steve Young NG .75 .35
❑ 381 Steve McNair NG .50 .23
❑ 382 Terrell Davis NG .75 .35
❑ 383 Tim Brown NG .50 .23
❑ 384 Troy Aikman NG 1.00 .45
❑ 385 Warrick Dunn NG .75 .35
❑ 386 Ryan Leaf 3.00 1.35
❑ 387 Tony Simmons RC 2.00 .90
❑ 388 Rodney Williams RC 1.25 .55
❑ 389 John Avery RC 2.00 .90
❑ 390 Shaun Williams RC 2.00 .90
❑ 391 Anthony Simmons RC 2.00 .90
❑ 392 Rashaan Shehee RC 2.00 .90
❑ 393 Robert Holcombe 2.00 .90
❑ 394 Larry Shannon RC 1.25 .55
❑ 395 Skip Hicks 2.00 .90
❑ 396 Rod Rutledge RC 1.25 .55
❑ 397 Donald Hayes RC 2.00 .90
❑ 398 Curtis Enis 1.25 .55
❑ 399 Mikhael Ricks RC 2.00 .90
❑ 400 Brian Griese RC 6.00 2.70
❑ 401 Michael Pittman RC 4.00 1.80
❑ 402 Jacquez Green 2.00 .90
❑ 403 Jerome Pathon RC 3.00 1.35
❑ 404 Ahman Green RC 15.00 6.75
❑ 405 Marcus Nash 1.25 .55
❑ 406 Randy Moss 12.00 5.50
❑ 407 Terry Fair RC 2.00 .90
❑ 408 Jammi German RC 1.25 .55
❑ 409 Stephen Alexander RC 2.00 .90
❑ 410 Grant Wistrom RC 2.00 .90
❑ 411 Charlie Batch RC 3.00 1.35
❑ 412 Fred Taylor 4.00 1.80
❑ 413 Pat Johnson RC 2.00 .90
❑ 414 Robert Edwards 2.00 .90
❑ 415 Keith Brooking RC 3.00 1.35
❑ 416 Peyton Manning 25.00 11.00
❑ 417 Duane Starks RC 1.25 .55
❑ 418 Andre Wadsworth 2.00 .90
❑ 419 Brian Alford RC 1.25 .55
❑ 420 Brian Kelly RC 2.00 .90
❑ 421 Joe Jurevicius RC 3.00 1.35
❑ 422 Tebucky Jones RC 1.25 .55
❑ 423 R.W. McQuarters RC 2.00 .90
❑ 424 Kevin Dyson 2.50 1.10
❑ 425 Charles Woodson 3.00 1.35
❑ R1 Reggie White COMM .60 .25
❑ P20 Jeff George Promo .75 .35

1998 Ultra Gold Medallion

Nm-Mt Ex-Mt
COMPLETE SET (425) 1000.00 450.00
*GOLD MED.STARS: 1.2X TO 3X BASIC CARDS
*GOLD MED.RCs: .8X TO 2X BASIC CARDS
*GOLD MED.SER.2 DRAFT PICKS: 1.5X TO $$4X

1998 Ultra Platinum Medallion

Nm-Mt Ex-Mt
*PLAT.MED.STARS: 12X TO 30X
*PLAT.MED.SER.1 RCs: 5X TO 10X
*PLAT.MED.SER.2 DRAFT PICKS: 5X TO 10X

1999 Ultra

	Nm-Mt	Ex-Mt
COMPLETE SET (300)	120.00	55.00
COMP.SET w/o SP's (250)	20.00	9.00
❑ 1 Terrell Davis	.75	.35
❑ 2 Courtney Hawkins	.30	.14
❑ 3 Cris Carter	.75	.35
❑ 4 Darnay Scott	.30	.14
❑ 5 Darrell Green	.50	.23
❑ 6 Jimmy Smith	.50	.23
❑ 7 Doug Flutie	.75	.35
❑ 8 Michael Jackson	.30	.14
❑ 9 Warren Sapp	.50	.23
❑ 10 Greg Hill	.30	.14
❑ 11 Karim Abdul-Jabbar	.50	.23
❑ 12 Greg Ellis	.30	.14
❑ 13 Dan Marino	2.50	1.10
❑ 14 Napoleon Kaufman	.75	.35
❑ 15 Peyton Manning	2.50	1.10
❑ 16 Simeon Rice	.50	.23
❑ 17 Tony Simmons	.30	.14
❑ 18 Carlester Crumpler	.30	.14
❑ 19 Charles Johnson	.30	.14
❑ 20 Derrick Alexander	.30	.14
❑ 21 Kent Graham	.30	.14
❑ 22 Randall Cunningham	.75	.35
❑ 23 Trent Green	.75	.35
❑ 24 Chris Spielman	.30	.14
❑ 25 Carl Pickens	.50	.23
❑ 26 Bill Romanowski	.30	.14
❑ 27 Jermaine Lewis	.50	.23
❑ 28 Ahman Green	.75	.35
❑ 29 Bryan Still	.30	.14
❑ 30 Dorsey Levens	.75	.35
❑ 31 Frank Wycheck	.30	.14
❑ 32 Jerome Bettis	.75	.35
❑ 33 Reidel Anthony	.50	.23
❑ 34 Robert Jones	.30	.14
❑ 35 Terry Glenn	.75	.35
❑ 36 Tim Brown	.75	.35
❑ 37 Eric Metcalf	.30	.14
❑ 38 Kevin Greene	.50	.23
❑ 39 Takeo Spikes	.30	.14
❑ 40 Brian Mitchell	.30	.14
❑ 41 Duane Starks	.30	.14
❑ 42 Eddie George	.75	.35
❑ 43 Joe Jurevicius	.50	.23
❑ 44 Kimble Anders	.50	.23
❑ 45 Kordell Stewart	.50	.23
❑ 46 Leroy Hoard	.30	.14
❑ 47 Rod Smith	.50	.23
❑ 48 Terrell Owens	.75	.35
❑ 49 Ty Detmer	.50	.23
❑ 50 Charles Woodson	.75	.35
❑ 51 Andre Rison	.50	.23
❑ 52 Chris Slade	.30	.14
❑ 53 Frank Sanders	.50	.23
❑ 54 Michael Irvin	.50	.23
❑ 55 Jerome Pathon	.30	.14
❑ 56 Desmond Howard	.50	.23
❑ 57 Billy Davis	.30	.14
❑ 58 Anthony Simmons	.30	.14
❑ 59 James Jett	.50	.23
❑ 60 Jake Plummer	.50	.23
❑ 61 John Avery	.30	.14
❑ 62 Marvin Harrison	.75	.35
❑ 63 Merton Hanks	.30	.14
❑ 64 Ricky Proehl	.30	.14
❑ 65 Steve Beuerlein	.30	.14
❑ 66 Willie McGinest	.30	.14
❑ 67 Bryce Paup	.30	.14
❑ 68 Brett Favre	2.50	1.10
❑ 69 Brian Griese	.75	.35
❑ 70 Curtis Martin	.75	.35
❑ 71 Drew Bledsoe	1.00	.45
❑ 72 Jim Harbaugh	.50	.23
❑ 73 Joey Galloway	.50	.23
❑ 74 Natrone Means	.50	.23
❑ 75 O.J. McDuffie	.50	.23
❑ 76 Tiki Barber	.50	.23
❑ 77 Wesley Walls	.50	.23
❑ 78 Will Blackwell	.30	.14
❑ 79 Bert Emanuel	.50	.23
❑ 80 J.J. Stokes	.50	.23
❑ 81 Steve McNair	.75	.35
❑ 82 Adrian Murrell	.50	.23
❑ 83 Dexter Coakley	.30	.14
❑ 84 Jeff George	.50	.23
❑ 85 Marshall Faulk	1.00	.45
❑ 86 Tim Biakabutuka	.50	.23
❑ 87 Troy Drayton	.30	.14
❑ 88 Ty Law	.50	.23
❑ 89 Brian Simmons	.30	.14
❑ 90 Eric Allen	.30	.14
❑ 91 Jon Kitna	.75	.35
❑ 92 Junior Seau	.75	.35
❑ 93 Kevin Turner	.30	.14
❑ 94 Larry Centers	.30	.14
❑ 95 Robert Edwards	.30	.14
❑ 96 Rocket Ismail	.50	.23
❑ 97 Sam Madison	.30	.14
❑ 98 Stephen Alexander	.30	.14
❑ 99 Trent Dilfer	.50	.23
❑ 100 Vonnie Holliday	.30	.14
❑ 101 Charlie Garner	.50	.23
❑ 102 Deion Sanders	.75	.35
❑ 103 Jamal Anderson	.75	.35
❑ 104 Mike Vanderjagt	.30	.14
❑ 105 Aeneas Williams	.30	.14
❑ 106 Daryl Johnston	.50	.23
❑ 107 Hugh Douglas	.30	.14
❑ 108 Torrance Small	.30	.14
❑ 109 Amani Toomer	.30	.14
❑ 110 Amp Lee	.30	.14
❑ 111 Germane Crowell	.30	.14
❑ 112 Marco Battaglia	.30	.14
❑ 113 Michael Westbrook	.50	.23
❑ 114 Randy Moss	2.00	.90
❑ 115 Ricky Watters	.50	.23
❑ 116 Rob Johnson	.50	.23
❑ 117 Tony Gonzalez	.75	.35
❑ 118 Charles Way	.30	.14
❑ 119 Chris Penn	.30	.14
❑ 120 Eddie Kennison	.50	.23
❑ 121 Elvis Grbac	.50	.23
❑ 122 Eric Moulds	.75	.35
❑ 123 Terry Fair	.30	.14
❑ 124 Tony Banks	.50	.23
❑ 125 Chris Chandler	.50	.23
❑ 126 Emmitt Smith	1.50	.70
❑ 127 Herman Moore	.50	.23
❑ 128 Irv Smith	.30	.14
❑ 129 Kyle Brady	.30	.14
❑ 130 Lamont Warren	.30	.14
❑ 131 Troy Davis	.30	.14
❑ 132 Andre Reed	.50	.23
❑ 133 Justin Armour	.30	.14
❑ 134 James Hasty	.30	.14
❑ 135 Johnnie Morton	.50	.23
❑ 136 Reggie Barlow	.30	.14
❑ 137 Robert Holcombe	.30	.14
❑ 138 Sean Dawkins	.30	.14
❑ 139 Steve Atwater	.30	.14
❑ 140 Tim Dwight	.75	.35
❑ 141 Wayne Chrebet	.50	.23
❑ 142 Alonzo Mayes	.30	.14
❑ 143 Mark Brunell	.75	.35
❑ 144 Antowain Smith	.75	.35
❑ 145 Byron Bam Morris	.30	.14
❑ 146 Isaac Bruce	.75	.35
❑ 147 Bryan Cox	.30	.14
❑ 148 Bryant Westbrook	.30	.14
❑ 149 Duce Staley	.75	.35
❑ 150 Barry Sanders	2.50	1.10
❑ 151 La'Roi Glover RC	.75	.35
❑ 152 Ray Crockett	.30	.14
❑ 153 Tony Brackens	.30	.14
❑ 154 Roy Barker	.30	.14
❑ 155 Kerry Collins	.50	.23
❑ 156 Andre Wadsworth	.30	.14
❑ 157 Cameron Cleeland	.30	.14
❑ 158 Koy Detmer	.30	.14
❑ 159 Marcus Pollard	.30	.14
❑ 160 Patrick Jeffers RC	6.00	2.70
❑ 161 Aaron Glenn	.30	.14
❑ 162 Andre Hastings	.30	.14
❑ 163 Bruce Smith	.50	.23
❑ 164 David Palmer	.30	.14
❑ 165 Erik Kramer	.50	.23
❑ 166 Orlando Pace	.30	.14
❑ 167 Robert Brooks	.50	.23
❑ 168 Shawn Springs	.30	.14
❑ 169 Terance Mathis	.50	.23
❑ 170 Chris Calloway	.30	.14
❑ 171 Gilbert Brown	.30	.14
❑ 172 Charlie Jones	.30	.14
❑ 173 Curtis Enis	.30	.14
❑ 174 Eugene Robinson	.30	.14
❑ 175 Garrison Hearst	.50	.23
❑ 176 Jason Elam	.30	.14
❑ 177 John Randle	.50	.23
❑ 178 Keith Poole	.30	.14
❑ 179 Kevin Hardy	.30	.14
❑ 180 Keyshawn Johnson	.75	.35
❑ 181 O.J. Santiago	.30	.14
❑ 182 Jacquez Green	.30	.14
❑ 183 Bobby Engram	.50	.23
❑ 184 Damon Jones	.30	.14
❑ 185 Freddie Jones	.30	.14
❑ 186 Jake Reed	.50	.23
❑ 187 Jerry Rice	1.50	.70
❑ 188 Joey Kent	.30	.14
❑ 189 Lamar Smith	.50	.23
❑ 190 John Elway	2.50	1.10
❑ 191 Leon Johnson	.30	.14
❑ 192 Mark Chmura	.50	.23
❑ 193 Peter Boulware	.30	.14
❑ 194 Zach Thomas	.75	.35
❑ 195 Marc Edwards	.30	.14
❑ 196 Mike Alstott	.75	.35
❑ 197 Yancey Thigpen	.30	.14
❑ 198 Oronde Gadsden	.50	.23
❑ 199 Rae Carruth	.30	.14
❑ 200 Troy Aikman	1.50	.70
❑ 201 Shawn Jefferson	.30	.14
❑ 202 Rob Moore	.50	.23
❑ 203 Rickey Dudley	.30	.14
❑ 204 Jason Taylor	.30	.14
❑ 205 Curtis Conway	.50	.23
❑ 206 Darrien Gordon	.30	.14
❑ 207 Eric Green	.30	.14
❑ 208 Jessie Armstead	.30	.14
❑ 209 Keenan McCardell	.50	.23
❑ 210 Robert Smith	.75	.35
❑ 211 Mo Lewis	.30	.14
❑ 212 Ryan Leaf	.75	.35
❑ 213 Steve Young	1.00	.45
❑ 214 Tyrone Davis	.30	.14
❑ 215 Chad Brown	.30	.14
❑ 216 Ike Hilliard	.30	.14
❑ 217 Jimmy Hitchcock	.30	.14
❑ 218 Kevin Dyson	.50	.23
❑ 219 Levon Kirkland	.30	.14
❑ 220 Neil O'Donnell	.50	.23
❑ 221 Ray Lewis	.75	.35
❑ 222 Shannon Sharpe	.50	.23
❑ 223 Skip Hicks	.30	.14
❑ 224 Brad Johnson	.75	.35
❑ 225 Charlie Batch	.75	.35
❑ 226 Corey Dillon	.75	.35
❑ 227 Dale Carter	.30	.14
❑ 228 John Mobley	.30	.14
❑ 229 Hines Ward	.75	.35
❑ 230 Leslie Shepherd	.30	.14
❑ 231 Michael Strahan	.50	.23
❑ 232 R.W. McQuarters	.30	.14
❑ 233 Mike Pritchard	.30	.14

❑ 234	Antonio Freeman	.75	.35
❑ 235	Ben Coates	.50	.23
❑ 236	Michael Bates	.30	.14
❑ 237	Ed McCaffrey	.50	.23
❑ 238	Gary Brown	.30	.14
❑ 239	Mark Bruener	.30	.14
❑ 240	Mikhael Ricks	.30	.14
❑ 241	Muhsin Muhammad	.50	.23
❑ 242	Priest Holmes	1.25	.55
❑ 243	Stephen Davis	.75	.35
❑ 244	Vinny Testaverde	.50	.23
❑ 245	Warrick Dunn	.75	.35
❑ 246	Derrick Mayes	.30	.14
❑ 247	Fred Taylor	.75	.35
❑ 248	Drew Bledsoe CL	.50	.23
❑ 249	Eddie George CL	.50	.23
❑ 250	Steve Young CL	.50	.23
❑ 251	Jamal Anderson BB	.60	.25
❑ 252	Darrien Gordon BB Bill Romanowski BB	.30	.14
❑ 253	Shannon Sharpe BB	.30	.14
❑ 254	Terrell Davis BB	1.00	.45
❑ 255	Rod Smith BB	.30	.14
❑ 256	Rod Smith BB	.30	.14
❑ 257	John Elway BB	5.00	2.20
❑ 258	Tim Dwight BB	.60	.25
❑ 259	John Elway BB Ed McCaffrey BB Howard Griffith BB Terrell Davis BB	3.00	1.35
❑ 260	John Elway BB	5.00	2.20
❑ 261	Ricky Williams RC	6.00	2.70
❑ 262	Tim Couch RC	3.00	1.35
❑ 263	Chris Claiborne RC	1.50	.70
❑ 264	Champ Bailey RC	5.00	2.20
❑ 265	Torry Holt RC	8.00	3.60
❑ 266	Donovan McNabb RC	15.00	6.75
❑ 267	David Boston RC	3.00	1.35
❑ 268	Chris McAlister RC	2.50	1.10
❑ 269	Brock Huard RC	3.00	1.35
❑ 270	Daunte Culpepper RC	12.00	5.50
❑ 271	Matt Stinchcomb RC	1.50	.70
❑ 272	Edgerrin James RC	12.00	5.50
❑ 273	Jevon Kearse RC	6.00	2.70
❑ 274	Ebenezer Ekuban RC	2.50	1.10
❑ 275	Kris Farris RC	1.50	.70
❑ 276	Chris Terry RC	1.50	.70
❑ 277	Jerame Tuman RC	2.50	1.10
❑ 278	Akili Smith RC	2.50	1.10
❑ 279	Aaron Gibson RC	1.50	.70
❑ 280	Rahim Abdullah RC	2.50	1.10
❑ 281	Peerless Price RC	6.00	2.70
❑ 282	Antoine Winfield RC	2.50	1.10
❑ 283	Antuan Edwards RC	1.50	.70
❑ 284	Rob Konrad RC	3.00	1.35
❑ 285	Troy Edwards RC	2.50	1.10
❑ 286	John Thornton RC	1.50	.70
❑ 287	James Johnson RC	2.50	1.10
❑ 288	Gary Stills RC	1.50	.70
❑ 289	Mike Peterson RC	2.50	1.10
❑ 290	Kevin Faulk RC	3.00	1.35
❑ 291	Jared DeVries RC	1.50	.70
❑ 292	Martin Gramatica RC	1.50	.70
❑ 293	Montae Reagor RC	1.50	.70
❑ 294	Andy Katzenmoyer RC	2.50	1.10
❑ 295	Sedrick Irvin RC	1.50	.70
❑ 296	D'Wayne Bates RC	2.50	1.10
❑ 297	Amos Zereoue RC	3.00	1.35
❑ 298	Dre' Bly RC	3.00	1.35
❑ 299	Kevin Johnson RC	3.00	1.35
❑ 300	Cade McNown RC	2.50	1.10
❑ P247	Fred Taylor Promo	2.00	.90

2000 Ultra

		Nm-Mt	Ex-Mt
COMPLETE SET (249)		100.00	45.00
COMP.SET w/o SP's (220)		20.00	9.00
❑ 1	Kurt Warner	1.50	.70
❑ 2	Derrick Alexander	.50	.23
❑ 3	Aaron Craver	.30	.14
❑ 4	Kevin Faulk	.50	.23
❑ 5	Marcus Robinson	.75	.35
❑ 6	Tony Banks	.50	.23
❑ 7	Jon Ritchie	.30	.14
❑ 8	Torry Holt	.75	.35
❑ 9	Joe Horn	.50	.23
❑ 10	Eddie George	.75	.35
❑ 11	Michael Westbrook	.50	.23
❑ 12	Gus Frerotte	.30	.14
❑ 13	Tim Brown	.75	.35
❑ 14	Tamarick Vanover	.30	.14
❑ 15	David Sloan	.30	.14
❑ 16	Darnay Scott	.30	.14
❑ 17	Junior Seau	.75	.35
❑ 18	Warren Sapp	.50	.23
❑ 19	Priest Holmes	1.00	.45
❑ 20	Jerry Rice	1.50	.70
❑ 21	Cade McNown	.30	.14
❑ 22	Johnnie Morton	.50	.23
❑ 23	Vinny Testaverde	.50	.23
❑ 24	James Jett	.30	.14
❑ 25	Tony Gonzalez	.50	.23
❑ 26	Charlie Batch	.75	.35
❑ 27	Tony Simmons	.30	.14
❑ 28	James Stewart	.50	.23
❑ 29	Corey Dillon	.75	.35
❑ 30	Ricky Williams	.75	.35
❑ 31	Ryan Leaf	.50	.23
❑ 32	Terry Allen	.50	.23
❑ 33	Freddie Jones	.30	.14
❑ 34	Terry Kirby	.30	.14
❑ 35	Charles Johnson	.50	.23
❑ 36	William Henderson	.50	.23
❑ 37	Stephen Alexander	.30	.14
❑ 38	Moe Williams	.50	.23
❑ 39	David Boston	.75	.35
❑ 40	Emmitt Smith	1.50	.70
❑ 41	Ken Oxendine	.30	.14
❑ 42	Byron Hanspard	.30	.14
❑ 43	Dwight Stone	.30	.14
❑ 44	Jim Harbaugh	.50	.23
❑ 45	Curtis Enis	.30	.14
❑ 46	Peerless Price	.75	.35
❑ 47	Terance Mathis	.50	.23
❑ 48	Mike Alstott	.75	.35
❑ 49	Rod Smith	.50	.23
❑ 50	Marshall Faulk	1.00	.45
❑ 51	Derrick Mayes	.50	.23
❑ 52	Keenan McCardell	.50	.23
❑ 53	Curtis Martin	.75	.35
❑ 54	Bobby Engram	.30	.14
❑ 55	Carl Pickens	.50	.23
❑ 56	Robert Smith	.75	.35
❑ 57	Ike Hilliard	.50	.23
❑ 58	Reidel Anthony	.50	.23
❑ 59	Jeff Graham	.30	.14
❑ 60	Mark Brunell	.75	.35
❑ 61	Joe Montgomery	.30	.14
❑ 62	Ed McCaffrey	.75	.35
❑ 63	Kenny Bynum	.30	.14
❑ 64	Curtis Conway	.50	.23
❑ 65	Trent Dilfer	.50	.23
❑ 66	Jake Reed	.50	.23
❑ 67	Jake Plummer	.50	.23
❑ 68	Tony Martin	.50	.23
❑ 69	Yatil Green	.30	.14
❑ 70	Keyshawn Johnson	.75	.35
❑ 71	Leroy Hoard	.30	.14
❑ 72	Skip Hicks	.30	.14
❑ 73	Marvin Harrison	.75	.35
❑ 74	Steve Beuerlein	.50	.23
❑ 75	Will Blackwell	.30	.14
❑ 76	Derek Loville	.30	.14
❑ 77	Warrick Dunn	.75	.35
❑ 78	Amos Zereoue	.75	.35
❑ 79	Ray Lucas	.50	.23
❑ 80	Randy Moss	1.50	.70
❑ 81	Wesley Walls	.30	.14
❑ 82	Jimmy Smith	.50	.23
❑ 83	Kordell Stewart	.50	.23
❑ 84	Brian Griese	.75	.35
❑ 85	Martin Gramatica	.30	.14
❑ 86	Chris Chandler	.50	.23
❑ 87	Reggie Barlow	.30	.14
❑ 88	Jeff George	.50	.23
❑ 89	Tavian Banks	.30	.14
❑ 90	Mushin Muhammad	.50	.23
❑ 91	Steve McNair	.75	.35
❑ 92	Hines Ward	.75	.35
❑ 93	Brian Mitchell	.30	.14
❑ 94	Daunte Culpepper	1.00	.45
❑ 95	Tim Dwight	.75	.35
❑ 96	Terrence Wilkins	.30	.14
❑ 97	Fred Lane	.30	.14
❑ 98	Brett Favre	2.50	1.10
❑ 99	Richie Anderson	.50	.23
❑ 100	Jamal Anderson	.75	.35
❑ 101	Doug Flutie	.75	.35
❑ 102	Charles Woodson	.50	.23
❑ 103	Jacquez Green	.30	.14
❑ 104	Olandis Gary	.75	.35
❑ 105	Steve Young	1.00	.45
❑ 106	Wayne Chrebet	.50	.23
❑ 107	Karim Abdul-Jabbar	.50	.23
❑ 108	Andre Rison	.50	.23
❑ 109	Eddie Kennison	.30	.14
❑ 110	Jevon Kearse	.75	.35
❑ 111	Tony Richardson RC	.50	.23
❑ 112	Jake Delhomme RC	3.00	1.35
❑ 113	Errict Rhett	.50	.23
❑ 114	Akili Smith	.30	.14
❑ 115	Tyrone Wheatley	.50	.23
❑ 116	Corey Bradford	.50	.23
❑ 117	J.J. Stokes	.50	.23
❑ 118	Simeon Rice	.50	.23
❑ 119	Brad Johnson	.75	.35
❑ 120	Edgerrin James	1.25	.55
❑ 121	Amani Toomer	.30	.14
❑ 122	O.J. McDuffie	.50	.23
❑ 123	Az-Zahir Hakim	.50	.23
❑ 124	Troy Edwards	.30	.14
❑ 125	Tim Biakabutuka	.50	.23
❑ 126	Jason Tucker	.30	.14
❑ 127	Charles Way	.30	.14
❑ 128	Terrell Davis	.75	.35
❑ 129	Garrison Hearst	.50	.23
❑ 130	Fred Taylor	.75	.35
❑ 131	Robert Holcombe	.30	.14
❑ 132	Frank Sanders	.50	.23
❑ 133	Morten Andersen	.30	.14
❑ 134	Cris Carter	.75	.35
❑ 135	Patrick Jeffers	.75	.35
❑ 136	Antonio Freeman	.75	.35
❑ 137	Jonathan Linton	.30	.14
❑ 138	Rashaan Shehee	.30	.14
❑ 139	Luther Broughton RC	.50	.23
❑ 140	Tim Couch	.50	.23
❑ 141	Keith Poole	.30	.14
❑ 142	Champ Bailey	.50	.23
❑ 143	Yancey Thigpen	.30	.14
❑ 144	Joey Galloway	.50	.23
❑ 145	Mac Cody	.30	.14
❑ 146	Damon Huard	.75	.35
❑ 147	Dorsey Levens	.50	.23
❑ 148	Donovan McNabb	1.25	.55
❑ 149	Jamie Asher	.30	.14
❑ 150	Peyton Manning	2.00	.90
❑ 151	Leslie Shepherd	.30	.14
❑ 152	Charlie Rogers	.30	.14
❑ 153	Tony Horne	.30	.14
❑ 154	Jim Miller	.30	.14
❑ 155	Richard Huntley	.30	.14
❑ 156	Germane Crowell	.30	.14
❑ 157	Natrone Means	.30	.14
❑ 158	Justin Armour	.30	.14
❑ 159	Drew Bledsoe	1.00	.45
❑ 160	Dedric Ward	.30	.14
❑ 161	Allen Rossum	.30	.14

❑ 162 Ricky Watters	.50	.23
❑ 163 Kerry Collins	.50	.23
❑ 164 James Johnson	.30	.14
❑ 165 Elvis Grbac	.50	.23
❑ 166 Larry Centers	.30	.14
❑ 167 Rob Moore	.50	.23
❑ 168 Jay Riemersma	.30	.14
❑ 169 Bill Schroeder	.50	.23
❑ 170 Deion Sanders	.75	.35
❑ 171 Jerome Bettis	.75	.35
❑ 172 Dan Marino	2.50	1.10
❑ 173 Terrell Owens	.75	.35
❑ 174 Kevin Carter	.30	.14
❑ 175 Lamar Smith	.50	.23
❑ 176 Ken Dilger	.30	.14
❑ 177 Napoleon Kaufman	.50	.23
❑ 178 Kevin Williams	.30	.14
❑ 179 Tremain Mack	.30	.14
❑ 180 Troy Aikman	1.50	.70
❑ 181 Glyn Milburn	.30	.14
❑ 182 Pete Mitchell	.30	.14
❑ 183 Cameron Cleeland	.30	.14
❑ 184 Qadry Ismail	.50	.23
❑ 185 Michael Pittman	.30	.14
❑ 186 Kevin Dyson	.50	.23
❑ 187 Matt Hasselbeck	.50	.23
❑ 188 Kevin Johnson	.75	.35
❑ 189 Rich Gannon	.75	.35
❑ 190 Stephen Davis	.75	.35
❑ 191 Frank Wycheck	.30	.14
❑ 192 Eric Moulds	.75	.35
❑ 193 Jon Kitna	.75	.35
❑ 194 Mario Bates	.30	.14
❑ 195 Na Brown	.30	.14
❑ 196 Jeff Blake	.50	.23
❑ 197 Charles Evans	.30	.14
❑ 198 Oronde Gadsden	.50	.23
❑ 199 Donnell Bennett	.30	.14
❑ 200 Isaac Bruce	.75	.35
❑ 201 Olindo Mare	.30	.14
❑ 202 Damell McDonald	.30	.14
❑ 203 Charlie Gamer	.50	.23
❑ 204 Shawn Jefferson	.30	.14
❑ 205 Adrian Murrell	.50	.23
❑ 206 Peter Boulware	.30	.14
❑ 207 LeShon Johnson	.30	.14
❑ 208 Herman Moore	.50	.23
❑ 209 Duce Staley	.75	.35
❑ 210 Sean Dawkins	.30	.14
❑ 211 Antowain Smith	.50	.23
❑ 212 Albert Connell	.30	.14
❑ 213 Jeff Garcia	.75	.35
❑ 214 Kimble Anders	.30	.14
❑ 215 Shaun King	.30	.14
❑ 216 Rocket Ismail	.50	.23
❑ 217 Andrew Glover	.30	.14
❑ 218 Rickey Dudley	.30	.14
❑ 219 Michael Basnight	.30	.14
❑ 220 Terry Glenn	.50	.23
❑ 221 Peter Warrick RC	3.00	1.35
❑ 222 Ron Dayne RC	3.00	1.35
❑ 223 Thomas Jones RC	5.00	2.20
❑ 224 Joe Hamilton RC	2.50	1.10
❑ 225 Tim Rattay RC	6.00	2.70
❑ 226 Chad Pennington RC	12.00	5.50
❑ 227 Dennis Northcutt RC	3.00	1.35
❑ 228 Troy Walters RC	3.00	1.35
❑ 229 Travis Prentice RC	2.50	1.10
❑ 230 Shaun Alexander RC	8.00	3.60
❑ 231 J.R. Redmond RC	2.50	1.10
❑ 232 Chris Redman RC	2.50	1.10
❑ 233 Tee Martin RC	3.00	1.35
❑ 234 Tom Brady RC	30.00	13.50
❑ 235 Travis Taylor RC	3.00	1.35
❑ 236 R.Jay Soward RC	2.50	1.10
❑ 237 Jamal Lewis RC	8.00	3.60
❑ 238 Giovanni Carmazzi RC	2.50	1.10
❑ 239 Dez White RC	3.00	1.35
❑ 240 LaVar Arrington RC SP	200.00	90.00
❑ 241 Laveranues Coles RC	4.00	1.80
❑ 242 Sherrod Gideon RC	2.00	.90
❑ 243 Trung Canidate RC	2.50	1.10
❑ 244 Michael Wiley RC	2.50	1.10
❑ 245 Anthony Lucas RC	2.00	.90
❑ 246 Darrell Jackson RC	6.00	2.70
❑ 247 Plaxico Burress RC	6.00	2.70
❑ 248 Reuben Droughns RC	4.00	1.80
❑ 249 Marc Bulger RC	6.00	2.70
❑ 250 Danny Farmer RC	2.50	1.10

2000 Ultra Gold Medallion

	Nm-Mt	Ex-Mt
COMPLETE SET (249)	300.00	135.00

*GOLD MED.STARS: 1.2X TO 3X BASIC CARDS
*GOLD MED.RC's: .6X TO 1.5X

❑ 240 LaVar Arrington SP	350.00	160.00

2000 Ultra Platinum Medallion

Nm-Mt Ex-Mt

*PLAT.STARS: 20X TO 50X BASIC CARDS
*PLAT.RC's: 10X TO 25X

2001 Ultra

	Nm-Mt	Ex-Mt
COMP.SET w/o SP's (250)	25.00	7.50
❑ 1 Daunte Culpepper	.75	.23
❑ 2 Kurt Warner	1.50	.45
❑ 3 Emmitt Smith	1.50	.45
❑ 4 Eddie George	.75	.23
❑ 5 Ron Dayne	.75	.23
❑ 6 Zach Thomas	.75	.23
❑ 7 Itula Mili	.30	.09
❑ 8 Jake Reed	.50	.15
❑ 9 James Stewart	.50	.15
❑ 10 Terrence Wilkins	.30	.09
❑ 11 Jeff Blake	.50	.15
❑ 12 Kerry Collins	.50	.15
❑ 13 Christian Fauria	.30	.09
❑ 14 Jackie Harris	.30	.09
❑ 15 Kevin Johnson	.50	.15
❑ 16 Tony Martin	.30	.09
❑ 17 Joey Galloway	.50	.15
❑ 18 Junior Seau	.75	.23
❑ 19 Jason Tucker	.30	.09
❑ 20 Steve Beuerlein	.30	.09
❑ 21 Mike Cloud	.30	.09
❑ 22 Kevin Faulk	.50	.15
❑ 23 Az-Zahir Hakim	.30	.09
❑ 24 Charles Johnson	.30	.09
❑ 25 Curtis Martin	.75	.23
❑ 26 Eric Moulds	.50	.15
❑ 27 Bill Schroeder	.50	.15
❑ 28 Amani Toomer	.30	.09
❑ 29 Obafemi Ayanbadejo	.30	.09
❑ 30 Aaron Shea	.30	.09
❑ 31 Ken Dilger	.30	.09
❑ 32 Terry Glenn	.30	.09
❑ 33 Rocket Ismail	.50	.15
❑ 34 Dorsey Levens	.30	.09
❑ 35 Brian Mitchell	.30	.09
❑ 36 Tony Richardson	.30	.09
❑ 37 Sam Madison	.30	.09
❑ 38 Darren Sharper	.30	.09
❑ 39 Derrick Alexander	.50	.15
❑ 40 Aaron Brooks	.75	.23
❑ 41 Casey Crawford	.30	.09
❑ 42 Terrell Fletcher	.30	.09
❑ 43 William Henderson	.30	.09
❑ 44 Thomas Jones	.50	.15
❑ 45 Keenan McCardell	.30	.09
❑ 46 Chad Pennington	1.25	.35
❑ 47 Akili Smith	.30	.09
❑ 48 Hines Ward	.75	.23
❑ 49 Champ Bailey	.50	.15
❑ 50 Cris Carter	.75	.23
❑ 51 Corey Dillon	.75	.23
❑ 52 Tony Gonzalez	.50	.15
❑ 53 Darrell Jackson	.75	.23
❑ 54 Chad Lewis	.30	.09
❑ 55 Dave Moore	.30	.09
❑ 56 Jay Riemersma	.30	.09
❑ 57 J.J. Stokes	.50	.15
❑ 58 Frank Wycheck	.30	.09
❑ 59 Tiki Barber	.50	.15
❑ 60 Tony Carter	.30	.09
❑ 61 Rickey Dudley	.30	.09
❑ 62 John Lynch	.50	.15
❑ 63 Larry Foster	.30	.09
❑ 64 Willie Jackson	.30	.09
❑ 65 Jamal Lewis	1.25	.35
❑ 66 Herman Moore	.50	.15
❑ 67 Andre Rison	.50	.15
❑ 68 Michael Strahan	.50	.15
❑ 69 Charlie Batch	.75	.23
❑ 70 Larry Centers	.30	.09
❑ 71 Ron Dugans	.30	.09
❑ 72 Jeff Graham	.30	.09
❑ 73 Edgerrin James	1.00	.30
❑ 74 Jermaine Lewis	.30	.09
❑ 75 Charles Woodson	.50	.15
❑ 76 Chris Redman	.30	.09
❑ 77 Jon Ritchie	.30	.09
❑ 78 Fred Taylor	.75	.23
❑ 79 Jamal Anderson	.75	.23
❑ 80 Isaac Bruce	.75	.23
❑ 81 Terrell Davis	.75	.23
❑ 82 Rich Gannon	.75	.23
❑ 83 Joe Horn	.50	.15
❑ 84 Eddie Kennison	.50	.15
❑ 85 Steve McNair	.75	.23
❑ 86 Travis Prentice	.30	.09
❑ 87 Rod Smith	.50	.15
❑ 88 Ricky Watters	.50	.15
❑ 89 Michael Bates	.30	.09
❑ 90 Byron Chamberlain	.30	.09
❑ 91 Warrick Dunn	.75	.23
❑ 92 Elvis Grbac	.50	.15
❑ 93 Patrick Jeffers	.50	.15
❑ 94 Ray Lewis	.75	.23
❑ 95 Sammy Morris	.30	.09
❑ 96 Marcus Robinson	.75	.23
❑ 97 Travis Taylor	.50	.15
❑ 98 Fred Beasley	.30	.09
❑ 99 Chris Chandler	.50	.15
❑ 100 Tim Dwight	.75	.23
❑ 101 Ahman Green	.75	.23
❑ 102 Shawn Jefferson	.30	.09
❑ 103 Jeremy McDaniel	.30	.09
❑ 104 Sylvester Morris	.30	.09
❑ 105 John Randle	.30	.09
❑ 106 Vinny Testaverde	.50	.15
❑ 107 Anthony Becht	.30	.09
❑ 108 Wayne Chrebet	.50	.15
❑ 109 Stephen Boyd	.30	.09
❑ 110 Jacquez Green	.30	.09
❑ 111 MarTay Jenkins	.30	.09
❑ 112 Jason Gildon	.30	.09
❑ 113 Chad Morton	.30	.09
❑ 114 Deion Sanders	.75	.23
❑ 115 Yancey Thigpen	.30	.09
❑ 116 Marty Booker	.30	.09
❑ 117 Curtis Conway	.50	.15
❑ 118 Jermaine Fazande	.30	.09
❑ 119 Matthew Hatchette	.30	.09
❑ 120 Pat Johnson	.30	.09
❑ 121 Terance Mathis	.50	.15
❑ 122 Terrell Owens	.75	.23
❑ 123 Corey Simon	.50	.15
❑ 124 Darrick Vaughn	.30	.09
❑ 125 Drew Bledsoe	1.00	.30
❑ 126 Albert Connell	.30	.09
❑ 127 Brett Favre	2.50	.75
❑ 128 Marvin Harrison	.75	.23
❑ 129 Keyshawn Johnson	.75	.23
❑ 130 Derrick Mason	.50	.15

❑ 131 Dennis Northcutt	.50	.15
❑ 132 Shannon Sharpe	.50	.15
❑ 133 Brian Urlacher	1.25	.35
❑ 134 Mike Anderson	.75	.23
❑ 135 Mark Bruener	.30	.09
❑ 136 Sean Dawkins	.30	.09
❑ 137 Jeff Garcia	.75	.23
❑ 138 Tony Horne	.30	.09
❑ 139 Shaun King	.30	.09
❑ 140 Cade McNown	.30	.09
❑ 141 Peerless Price	.75	.23
❑ 142 R.Jay Soward	.30	.09
❑ 143 Tyrone Wheatley	.50	.15
❑ 144 Richie Anderson	.30	.09
❑ 145 Mark Brunell	.75	.23
❑ 146 JaJuan Dawson	.30	.09
❑ 147 Charlie Garner	.50	.15
❑ 148 Desmond Howard	.30	.09
❑ 149 Jon Kitna	.50	.15
❑ 150 Duane Starks	.30	.09
❑ 151 J.R. Redmond	.30	.09
❑ 152 Duce Staley	.75	.23
❑ 153 Dez White	.30	.09
❑ 154 David Boston	.75	.23
❑ 155 Tim Couch	.50	.15
❑ 156 Jay Fiedler	.75	.23
❑ 157 Jessie Armstead	.30	.09
❑ 158 Rob Johnson	.50	.15
❑ 159 Brad Johnson	.75	.23
❑ 160 Derrick Mayes	.30	.09
❑ 161 Jerome Pathon	.50	.15
❑ 162 David Sloan	.30	.09
❑ 163 Wesley Walls	.30	.09
❑ 164 Shaun Alexander	1.00	.30
❑ 165 Derrick Brooks	.75	.23
❑ 166 Germane Crowell	.30	.09
❑ 167 Doug Flutie	.75	.23
❑ 168 Ike Hilliard	.50	.15
❑ 169 Hugh Douglas	.30	.09
❑ 170 Wane McGarity	.30	.09
❑ 171 Michael Pittman	.30	.09
❑ 172 Shawn Bryson	.30	.09
❑ 173 Richard Huntley	.30	.09
❑ 174 Darnell Autry	.30	.09
❑ 175 Plaxico Burress	.75	.23
❑ 176 Trent Dilfer	.50	.15
❑ 177 Jeff George	.50	.15
❑ 178 Qadry Ismail	.50	.15
❑ 179 Ryan Leaf	.50	.15
❑ 180 Jim Miller	.30	.09
❑ 181 Jerry Rice	1.50	.45
❑ 182 Kordell Stewart	.50	.15
❑ 183 Ricky Williams	.75	.23
❑ 184 James Allen	.50	.15
❑ 185 Courtney Brown	.50	.15
❑ 186 Reidel Anthony	.30	.09
❑ 187 Bubba Franks	.50	.15
❑ 188 Priest Holmes	1.00	.30
❑ 189 Napoleon Kaufman	.30	.09
❑ 190 Trevor Pryce	.30	.09
❑ 191 Jake Plummer	.50	.15
❑ 192 Jimmy Smith	.50	.15
❑ 193 Michael Wiley	.30	.09
❑ 194 Brock Huard	.30	.09
❑ 195 Troy Brown	.50	.15
❑ 196 Stephen Davis	.75	.23
❑ 197 Oronde Gadsden	.50	.15
❑ 198 Brad Hoover	.30	.09
❑ 199 La'Roi Glover	.30	.09
❑ 200 Donovan McNabb	1.00	.30
❑ 201 Jerry Porter	.50	.15
❑ 202 Robert Smith	.50	.15
❑ 203 Justin Watson	.30	.09
❑ 204 Tim Biakabutuka	.50	.15
❑ 205 Laveranues Coles	.75	.23
❑ 206 Marshall Faulk	1.00	.30
❑ 207 Jim Harbaugh	.50	.15
❑ 208 Doug Johnson	.30	.09
❑ 209 Tee Martin	.50	.15
❑ 210 Muhsin Muhammad	.50	.15
❑ 211 Darnay Scott	.30	.09
❑ 212 Jeremiah Trotter	.50	.15
❑ 213 Troy Aikman	1.25	.35
❑ 214 Kyle Brady	.30	.09
❑ 215 Sam Cowart	.30	.09
❑ 216 Darren Howard	.30	.09
❑ 217 Donald Hayes	.30	.09
❑ 218 Freddie Jones	.30	.09
❑ 219 Ed McCaffrey	.75	.23
❑ 220 David Patten	.30	.09
❑ 221 Brian Griese	.75	.23
❑ 222 Dedric Ward	.30	.09
❑ 223 Jerome Bettis	.75	.23
❑ 224 Greg Clark	.30	.09
❑ 225 Bobby Engram	.30	.09
❑ 226 Matt Hasselbeck	.50	.15
❑ 227 James Jett	.30	.09
❑ 228 Peyton Manning	2.00	.60
❑ 229 Randy Moss	1.50	.45
❑ 230 Warren Sapp	.50	.15
❑ 231 James Thrash	.50	.15
❑ 232 Mike Alstott	.75	.23
❑ 233 Tim Brown	.75	.23
❑ 234 Randall Cunningham	.75	.23
❑ 235 Antonio Freeman	.75	.23
❑ 236 Torry Holt	.75	.23
❑ 237 Jevon Kearse	.50	.15
❑ 238 James McKnight	.50	.15
❑ 239 Marcus Pollard	.30	.09
❑ 240 Lamar Smith	.50	.15
❑ 241 Peter Warrick	.75	.23
❑ 242 Donnell Bennett	.30	.09
❑ 243 Joe Johnson	.30	.09
❑ 244 Troy Edwards	.30	.09
❑ 245 Trent Green	.75	.23
❑ 246 Jason Taylor	.30	.09
❑ 247 Aeneas Williams	.30	.09
❑ 248 Johnnie Morton	.50	.15
❑ 249 Frank Sanders	.30	.09
❑ 250 Jason Sehorn	.30	.09
❑ 251 Chris Weinke RC	6.00	1.80
❑ 252 Bobby Newcombe RC	4.00	1.20
❑ 253 LaDainian Tomlinson RC	20.00	6.00
❑ 254 Chad Johnson RC	12.00	3.60
❑ 255 Derrick Gibson RC	4.00	1.20
❑ 256 Sage Rosenfels RC	6.00	1.80
❑ 257 LaMont Jordan RC	8.00	2.40
❑ 258 Mike McMahon RC	6.00	1.80
❑ 259 Vinny Sutherland RC	4.00	1.20
❑ 260 Drew Brees RC	12.00	3.60
❑ 261 Deuce McAllister RC	12.00	3.60
❑ 262 Kevan Barlow RC	6.00	1.80
❑ 263 Jamar Fletcher RC	4.00	1.20
❑ 264 Gerard Warren RC	6.00	1.80
❑ 265 Todd Heap RC	6.00	1.80
❑ 266 Travis Henry RC	8.00	2.40
❑ 267 Quincy Morgan RC	6.00	1.80
❑ 268 Anthony Thomas RC	10.00	3.00
❑ 269 Andre Carter RC	6.00	1.80
❑ 270 Freddie Mitchell RC	6.00	1.80
❑ 271 Richard Seymour RC	6.00	1.80
❑ 272 Josh Booty RC	6.00	1.80
❑ 273 Robert Ferguson RC	6.00	1.80
❑ 274 Marques Tuiasosopo RC	6.00	1.80
❑ 275 Reggie Wayne RC	10.00	3.00
❑ 276 Jabari Holloway RC	4.00	1.20
❑ 277 Rudi Johnson RC	12.00	3.60
❑ 278 Michael Bennett RC	12.00	3.60
❑ 279 Snoop Minnis RC	4.00	1.20
❑ 280 Dan Morgan RC	6.00	1.80
❑ 281 Rod Gardner RC	6.00	1.80
❑ 282 Jesse Palmer RC	6.00	1.80
❑ 283 Michael Vick RC	40.00	12.00
❑ 284 Chris Chambers RC	8.00	2.40
❑ 285 James Jackson RC	6.00	1.80
❑ 286 David Terrell RC	6.00	1.80
❑ 287 Koren Robinson RC	8.00	2.40
❑ 288 Travis Minor RC	4.00	1.20
❑ 289 Santana Moss RC	10.00	3.00
❑ 290 Josh Heupel RC	6.00	1.80
❑ 291 Jamal Reynolds RC	6.00	1.80
❑ 292 Ken-Yon Rambo RC	4.00	1.20
❑ 293 Cedrick Wilson RC	6.00	1.80
❑ 294 Alge Crumpler RC	8.00	2.40
❑ 295 Fred Smoot RC	6.00	1.80
❑ 296 Dan Alexander RC	6.00	1.80
❑ 297 Tim Hasselbeck RC	6.00	1.80
❑ 298 Will Allen RC	4.00	1.20
❑ 299 Keith Adams RC	4.00	1.20
❑ 300 Heath Evans RC	4.00	1.20
❑ U301 Quincy Carter RC	6.00	1.80
❑ U302 Derrick Blaylock RC	6.00	1.80
❑ U303 Correll Buckhalter RC	8.00	2.40
❑ U304 A.J. Feeley RC	6.00	1.80
❑ U305 Milton Wynn RC	4.00	1.20
❑ U306 Kevin Kasper RC	6.00	1.80
❑ U307 Justin McCareins RC	6.00	1.80
❑ U308 Dave Dickenson RC	4.00	1.20
❑ U309 Steve Smith RC	4.00	1.20
❑ U310 Moran Norris RC	2.50	.75

2001 Ultra Gold Medallion

Nm-Mt Ex-Mt

*STARS: 4X TO 10X BASIC CARDS
*ROOKIES: 1.2X TO 3X

2001 Ultra Platinum Medallion

Nm-Mt Ex-Mt

*STARS: 15X TO 40X BASIC CARDS
*ROOKIES: 3X TO 8X

2001 Ultra College Greats Previews Autographs

	Nm-Mt	Ex-Mt
❑ 1 Marcus Allen	30.00	9.00
❑ 2 Drew Brees	30.00	9.00
❑ 3 Tim Brown	40.00	12.00
❑ 4 Earl Campbell	30.00	9.00
❑ 5 John Cappelletti	20.00	6.00
❑ 6 Ron Dayne	20.00	6.00
❑ 7 Tony Dorsett	30.00	9.00
❑ 8 Tim Dwight	20.00	6.00
❑ 9 Doug Flutie	25.00	7.50
❑ 10 Eddie George	25.00	7.50
❑ 12 Archie Griffin	25.00	7.50
❑ 13 Franco Harris	40.00	12.00
❑ 14 Bob Hayes	50.00	15.00
❑ 15 Josh Heupel	25.00	7.50
❑ 16 Paul Hornung	30.00	9.00
❑ 17 Bo Jackson	125.00	38.00
❑ 19 Jamal Lewis	25.00	7.50
❑ 20 Bob Lilly	25.00	7.50
❑ 22 Donovan McNabb	50.00	15.00
❑ 23 Santana Moss	20.00	6.00
❑ 24 Jim Plunkett	25.00	7.50
❑ 26 Roger Staubach	80.00	24.00
❑ 27 Pat Sullivan	20.00	6.00
❑ 28 David Terrell	25.00	7.50
❑ 29 LaDainian Tomlinson	60.00	18.00
❑ 30 Amani Toomer	15.00	4.50
❑ 31 Michael Vick	120.00	36.00
❑ 33 Chris Weinke	15.00	4.50

2002 Ultra

	Nm-Mt	Ex-Mt
COMP.SET w/o SP's (200)	25.00	7.50
❑ 1 Donovan McNabb	1.00	.30
❑ 2 Chad Pennington	1.00	.30
❑ 3 Shaun Alexander	.75	.23
❑ 4 Corey Dillon	.50	.15
❑ 5 Kurt Warner	.75	.23
❑ 6 Ed McCaffrey	.75	.23
❑ 7 Hugh Douglas	.30	.09
❑ 8 Tony Gonzalez	.50	.15
❑ 9 Travis Taylor	.50	.15

Card	Nm-Mt	Ex-Mt
❑ 10 Tony Boselli	.30	.09
❑ 11 Chad Scott	.30	.09
❑ 12 Ernie Conwell	.30	.09
❑ 13 Brad Johnson	.50	.15
❑ 14 Donald Hayes	.30	.09
❑ 15 Emmitt Smith	2.00	.60
❑ 16 Jimmy Smith	.50	.15
❑ 17 Anthony Becht	.30	.09
❑ 18 Rod Gardner	.50	.15
❑ 19 Muhsin Muhammad	.50	.15
❑ 20 Troy Hambrick	.30	.09
❑ 21 Keenan McCardell	.30	.09
❑ 22 Laveranues Coles	.50	.15
❑ 23 Kevin Dyson	.50	.15
❑ 24 Grant Wistrom	.30	.09
❑ 25 Eric Moulds	.50	.15
❑ 26 Nate Clements	.30	.09
❑ 27 Terrell Davis	.75	.23
❑ 28 Aaron Glenn	.30	.09
❑ 29 Eric Hicks	.30	.09
❑ 30 Tiki Barber	.50	.15
❑ 31 Jake Plummer	.50	.15
❑ 32 Junior Seau	.75	.23
❑ 33 Marshall Faulk	.75	.23
❑ 34 Warrick Dunn	.75	.23
❑ 35 Bill Gramatica	.30	.09
❑ 36 Tim Couch	.50	.15
❑ 37 Kabeer Gbaja-Biamila	.50	.15
❑ 38 Kailee Wong	.30	.09
❑ 39 David Patten	.30	.09
❑ 40 Correll Buckhalter	.50	.15
❑ 41 Troy Brown	.50	.15
❑ 42 Drew Bledsoe	1.00	.30
❑ 43 Travis Henry	.75	.23
❑ 44 Jim Miller	.30	.09
❑ 45 Rod Smith	.50	.15
❑ 46 Tai Streets	.30	.09
❑ 47 Snoop Minnis	.30	.09
❑ 48 Ron Dayne	.50	.15
❑ 49 Tyrone Wheatley	.50	.15
❑ 50 LaDainian Tomlinson	1.25	.35
❑ 51 Akili Smith	.30	.09
❑ 52 Warren Sapp	.50	.15
❑ 53 Adam Archuleta	.30	.09
❑ 54 Chris Fuamatu-Ma'afala	.30	.09
❑ 55 Marty Booker	.30	.09
❑ 56 Trevor Pryce	.30	.09
❑ 57 Peyton Manning	1.50	.45
❑ 58 Lamar Smith	.50	.15
❑ 59 Amani Toomer	.50	.15
❑ 60 Greg Biekert	.30	.09
❑ 61 Marcellus Wiley	.30	.09
❑ 62 Ahmed Plummer	.30	.09
❑ 63 Mike Alstott	.75	.23
❑ 64 Gary Walker	.30	.09
❑ 65 Champ Bailey	.50	.15
❑ 66 Chris Redman	.30	.09
❑ 67 David Terrell	.75	.23
❑ 68 Mike McMahon	.75	.23
❑ 69 Marvin Harrison	.75	.23
❑ 70 Jay Fiedler	.50	.15
❑ 71 JaJuan Dawson	.30	.09
❑ 72 Charlie Garner	.50	.15
❑ 73 Curtis Conway	.30	.09
❑ 74 J.J. Stokes	.50	.15
❑ 75 Ronde Barber	.30	.09
❑ 76 Alge Crumpler	.50	.15
❑ 77 Jamir Miller	.30	.09
❑ 78 Brett Favre	2.00	.60
❑ 79 Randy Moss	1.50	.45
❑ 80 Joe Horn	.50	.15
❑ 81 Hines Ward	.75	.23
❑ 82 Lawyer Milloy	.50	.15
❑ 83 Aeneas Williams	.30	.09
❑ 84 Chris McAlister	.30	.09
❑ 85 Anthony Thomas	.75	.23
❑ 86 Johnnie Morton	.50	.15
❑ 87 Edgerrin James	1.00	.30
❑ 88 Chris Chambers	.75	.23
❑ 89 Michael Strahan	.50	.15
❑ 90 Charles Woodson	.50	.15
❑ 91 Tim Dwight	.50	.15
❑ 92 Kevan Barlow	.50	.15
❑ 93 Donnie Abraham	.30	.09
❑ 94 Peter Boulware	.30	.09
❑ 95 Marcus Robinson	.50	.15
❑ 96 Shaun Rogers	.30	.09
❑ 97 Dominic Rhodes	.50	.15
❑ 98 Zach Thomas	.75	.23
❑ 99 Kerry Collins	.50	.15
❑ 100 Tim Brown	.75	.23
❑ 101 Garrison Hearst	.50	.15
❑ 102 Steve McNair	.75	.23
❑ 103 Fred Smoot	.30	.09
❑ 104 Isaac Bruce	.75	.23
❑ 105 Jamal Lewis	.75	.23
❑ 106 Brian Urlacher	1.25	.35
❑ 107 Takeo Spikes	.30	.09
❑ 108 Marcus Pollard	.30	.09
❑ 109 Jason Taylor	.30	.09
❑ 110 Deuce McAllister	1.00	.30
❑ 111 Jerry Rice	1.50	.45
❑ 112 Terrell Owens	.75	.23
❑ 113 Eddie George	.75	.23
❑ 114 Rob Morris	.30	.09
❑ 115 Mike Brown	.75	.23
❑ 116 Joey Galloway	.50	.15
❑ 117 Fred Taylor	.75	.23
❑ 118 Rich Gannon	.75	.23
❑ 119 Chris Chandler	.50	.15
❑ 120 Koren Robinson	.50	.15
❑ 121 Dan Morgan	.30	.09
❑ 122 Rocket Ismail	.50	.15
❑ 123 Mark Brunell	.75	.23
❑ 124 John Abraham	.50	.15
❑ 125 Stephen Davis	.50	.15
❑ 126 Patrick Kerney	.30	.09
❑ 127 Anthony Henry	.30	.09
❑ 128 Scotty Anderson	.30	.09
❑ 129 Oronde Gadsden	.30	.09
❑ 130 Willie Jackson	.30	.09
❑ 131 Kendrell Bell	.75	.23
❑ 132 Ray Lewis	.75	.23
❑ 133 Quincy Carter	.50	.15
❑ 134 James Stewart	.50	.15
❑ 135 Travis Minor	.30	.09
❑ 136 Kyle Turley	.30	.09
❑ 137 Jason Gildon	.30	.09
❑ 138 David Boston	.75	.23
❑ 139 Justin Smith	.30	.09
❑ 140 Jamie Sharper	.30	.09
❑ 141 Antowain Smith	.50	.15
❑ 142 Freddie Mitchell	.50	.15
❑ 143 Frank Sanders	.30	.09
❑ 144 Kevin Johnson	.50	.15
❑ 145 Darren Sharper	.30	.09
❑ 146 Eric Johnson	.30	.09
❑ 147 Ty Law	.50	.15
❑ 148 James Thrash	.50	.15
❑ 149 Matt Hasselbeck	.50	.15
❑ 150 Peerless Price	.50	.15
❑ 151 T.J. Houshmandzadeh	.50	.15
❑ 152 Mike Anderson	.75	.23
❑ 153 Jermaine Lewis	.30	.09
❑ 154 Trent Green	.50	.15
❑ 155 Ron Dixon	.30	.09
❑ 156 Duce Staley	.75	.23
❑ 157 Drew Brees	.75	.23
❑ 158 Torry Holt	.75	.23
❑ 159 Keyshawn Johnson	.75	.23
❑ 160 Michael Vick	2.50	.75
❑ 161 Benjamin Gay	.30	.09
❑ 162 Bill Schroeder	.50	.15
❑ 163 Byron Chamberlain	.30	.09
❑ 164 Tedy Bruschi	.75	.23
❑ 165 Kordell Stewart	.50	.15
❑ 166 Deltha O'Neal	.30	.09
❑ 167 Quincy Morgan	.30	.09
❑ 168 Bubba Franks	.50	.15
❑ 169 Daunte Culpepper	.75	.23
❑ 170 Ricky Williams	4.00	1.20
❑ 171 Plaxico Burress	.50	.15
❑ 172 Trent Dilfer	.50	.15
❑ 173 Steve Smith	.50	.15
❑ 174 Greg Ellis	.30	.09
❑ 175 Tony Brackens	.30	.09
❑ 176 Santana Moss	.75	.23
❑ 177 Frank Wycheck	.30	.09
❑ 178 Michael Pittman	.30	.09
❑ 179 Peter Warrick	.50	.15
❑ 180 Antonio Freeman	.75	.23
❑ 181 Tom Brady	2.00	.60
❑ 182 Bobby Taylor	.30	.09
❑ 183 Jeff Garcia	.75	.23
❑ 184 Darrell Jackson	.50	.15
❑ 185 Chris Weinke	.50	.15
❑ 186 Darren Woodson	.30	.09
❑ 187 Hardy Nickerson	.30	.09
❑ 188 Wayne Chrebet	.50	.15
❑ 189 Samari Rolle	.30	.09
❑ 190 Jamal Anderson	.50	.15
❑ 191 James Jackson	.30	.09
❑ 192 Ahman Green	.75	.23
❑ 193 Michael Bennett	.50	.15
❑ 194 Aaron Brooks	.75	.23
❑ 195 Jerome Bettis	.75	.23
❑ 196 Jay Riemersma	.30	.09
❑ 197 Brian Griese	.75	.23
❑ 198 Priest Holmes	1.00	.30
❑ 199 Curtis Martin	.75	.23
❑ 200 Derrick Mason	.50	.15
❑ 201 Antonio Bryant RC	5.00	1.50
❑ 202 David Carr RC	15.00	4.50
❑ 203 Eric Crouch RC	8.00	2.40
❑ 204 Freddie Milons RC	4.00	1.20
❑ 205 Najeh Davenport RC	5.00	1.50
❑ 206 Rohan Davey RC	5.00	1.50
❑ 207 T.J. Duckett RC	8.00	2.40
❑ 208 DeShaun Foster RC	5.00	1.50
❑ 209 Jabar Gaffney RC	5.00	1.50
❑ 210 William Green RC	8.00	2.40
❑ 211 Joey Harrington RC	15.00	4.50
❑ 212 Travis Stephens RC	4.00	1.20
❑ 213 Julius Peppers RC	10.00	3.00
❑ 214 Adrian Peterson RC	5.00	1.50
❑ 215 Josh Reed RC	5.00	1.50
❑ 216 Mike Williams RC	5.00	1.50
❑ 217 Javon Walker RC	10.00	3.00
❑ 218 Marquise Walker RC	4.00	1.20
❑ 219 Patrick Ramsey RC	10.00	3.00
❑ 220 Lamar Gordon RC	5.00	1.50
❑ 221 David Garrard RC	5.00	1.50
❑ 222 Major Applewhite RC	5.00	1.50
❑ 223 Andre Davis RC	5.00	1.50
❑ 224 Roy Williams RC	12.00	3.60
❑ 225 Tim Carter RC	4.00	1.20
❑ 226 Ron Johnson RC	4.00	1.20
❑ 227 Randy Fasani RC	4.00	1.20
❑ 228 Ashley Lelie RC	10.00	3.00
❑ 229 Ladell Betts RC	5.00	1.50
❑ 230 Antwaan Randle El RC	6.00	1.80
❑ 231 Jonathan Wells RC	5.00	1.50
❑ 232 Brian Westbrook RC	8.00	2.40
❑ 233 Clinton Portis RC	15.00	4.50
❑ 234 Luke Staley RC	4.00	1.20
❑ 235 Cliff Russell RC	4.00	1.20
❑ 236 Jeremy Shockey RC	15.00	4.50
❑ 237 Donte Stallworth RC	10.00	3.00
❑ 238 Daniel Graham RC	5.00	1.50
❑ 239 Reche Caldwell RC	5.00	1.50
❑ 240 Ryan Sims RC	5.00	1.50

2002 Ultra Gold Medallion

Nm-Mt Ex-Mt

*STARS: 1.5X TO 4X BASIC CARDS
*ROOKIES: 1.2X TO 3X
ROOKIE PRINT RUN 100 SER.#'d SETS

2003 Ultra

	Nm-Mt	Ex-Mt
COMP.SET w/o SP's (160)	30.00	9.00
❑ 1 Rich Gannon	.50	.15
❑ 2 Warren Sapp	.50	.15
❑ 3 Steve McNair	.75	.23
❑ 4 Donovan McNabb	1.00	.30
❑ 5 Chad Pennington	1.00	.30
❑ 6 Michael Vick	2.00	.60
❑ 7 Hines Ward	.75	.23
❑ 8 Terrell Owens	.75	.23
❑ 9 Brett Favre	2.00	.60
❑ 10 Jeremy Shockey	1.25	.35
❑ 11 William Green	.50	.15
❑ 12 Marvin Harrison	.75	.23
❑ 13 Mark Brunell	.50	.15
❑ 14 Todd Heap	.50	.15
❑ 15 Tim Couch	.30	.09
❑ 16 Javon Walker	.50	.15
❑ 17 Zach Thomas	.50	.15
❑ 18 Brian Westbrook	.50	.15
❑ 19 Matt Hasselbeck	.50	.15
❑ 20 Jevon Kearse	.50	.15
❑ 21 David Boston	.50	.15
❑ 22 Michael Bennett	.50	.15
❑ 23 James Mungro	.30	.09
❑ 24 Antowain Smith	.50	.15
❑ 25 Laveranues Coles	.50	.15
❑ 26 Curtis Conway	.30	.09
❑ 27 Peerless Price	.50	.15
❑ 28 Michael Strahan	.50	.15
❑ 29 Tommy Maddox	.75	.23
❑ 30 Dennis Northcutt	.50	.15
❑ 31 Rod Gardner	.50	.15
❑ 32 Marcel Shipp	.50	.15
❑ 33 Quincy Morgan	.50	.15
❑ 34 Reggie Wayne	.50	.15
❑ 35 Troy Brown	.50	.15
❑ 36 John Abraham	.30	.09
❑ 37 Tim Dwight	.50	.15
❑ 38 Jamal Lewis	.75	.23
❑ 39 Chad Hutchinson	.50	.15
❑ 40 Jerramy Stevens	.30	.09
❑ 41 Deion Branch	.75	.23
❑ 42 Jake Plummer	.50	.15
❑ 43 Junior Seau	.75	.23
❑ 44 T.J. Duckett	.50	.15
❑ 45 Emmitt Smith	2.00	.60
❑ 46 Edgerrin James	.75	.23
❑ 47 David Patten	.30	.09
❑ 48 Charlie Garner	.50	.15
❑ 49 Quentin Jammer	.30	.09
❑ 50 Corey Dillon	.50	.15
❑ 51 Rod Smith	.50	.15
❑ 52 Marc Boerigter	.50	.15
❑ 53 Michael Lewis	.30	.09
❑ 54 Kendrell Bell	.50	.15
❑ 55 Isaac Bruce	.75	.23
❑ 56 Warrick Dunn	.50	.15
❑ 57 Antonio Bryant	.50	.15
❑ 58 Peyton Manning	1.25	.35
❑ 59 Ty Law	.50	.15
❑ 60 Jerry Rice	1.50	.45
❑ 61 Jeff Garcia	.75	.23
❑ 62 Joey Galloway	.50	.15
❑ 63 Aaron Glenn	.30	.09
❑ 64 Aaron Brooks	.75	.23
❑ 65 Tim Brown	.75	.23
❑ 66 David Terrell	.50	.15
❑ 67 Fred Smoot	.30	.09
❑ 68 Brian Finneran	.30	.09
❑ 69 Roy Williams	.75	.23
❑ 70 Corey Bradford	.30	.09
❑ 71 Deuce McAllister	.75	.23
❑ 72 Jerry Porter	.50	.15
❑ 73 Kevan Barlow	.50	.15
❑ 74 Keith Brooking	.30	.09
❑ 75 Brian Urlacher	1.25	.35
❑ 76 Jabar Gaffney	.50	.15
❑ 77 Randy Moss	1.25	.35
❑ 78 Charles Woodson	.50	.15
❑ 79 Darrell Jackson	.50	.15
❑ 80 John Lynch	.50	.15
❑ 81 Chester Taylor	.30	.09
❑ 82 Anthony Thomas	.75	.23
❑ 83 Jonathan Wells	.30	.09
❑ 84 Daunte Culpepper	.75	.23
❑ 85 Phillip Buchanon	.30	.09
❑ 86 Koren Robinson	.30	.09
❑ 87 Ronde Barber	.30	.09
❑ 88 Julius Peppers	.75	.23
❑ 89 Clinton Portis	1.25	.35
❑ 90 Jay Fiedler	.50	.15
❑ 91 Donte Stallworth	.75	.23
❑ 92 Marc Bulger	.75	.23
❑ 93 Joe Jurevicius	.30	.09
❑ 94 Jon Kitna	.50	.15
❑ 95 Ricky Williams	.75	.23
❑ 96 Joe Horn	.50	.15
❑ 97 Jerome Bettis	.75	.23
❑ 98 Kurt Warner	.75	.23
❑ 99 Travis Henry	.50	.15
❑ 100 Ahman Green	.75	.23
❑ 101 Jimmy Smith	.50	.15
❑ 102 Curtis Martin	.75	.23
❑ 103 Simeon Rice	.50	.15
❑ 104 Patrick Ramsey	.75	.23
❑ 105 Josh Reed	.50	.15
❑ 106 James Stewart	.50	.15
❑ 107 Trent Green	.50	.15
❑ 108 Randy McMichael	.50	.15
❑ 109 Amos Zereoue	.50	.15
❑ 110 Keyshawn Johnson	.75	.23
❑ 111 DeShaun Foster	.30	.09
❑ 112 Kevin Johnson	.50	.15
❑ 113 Dwight Freeney	.30	.09
❑ 114 Tom Brady	1.25	.35
❑ 115 Santana Moss	.50	.15
❑ 116 LaDainian Tomlinson	.75	.23
❑ 117 Joey Harrington	1.25	.35
❑ 118 Priest Holmes	1.00	.30
❑ 119 Amani Toomer	.50	.15
❑ 120 Plaxico Burress	.50	.15
❑ 121 Brad Johnson	.50	.15
❑ 122 Champ Bailey	.50	.15
❑ 123 Muhsin Muhammad	.50	.15
❑ 124 Ashley Lelie	.75	.23
❑ 125 Tony Gonzalez	.50	.15
❑ 126 Kerry Collins	.50	.15
❑ 127 Antwaan Randle El	.75	.23
❑ 128 Torry Holt	.75	.23
❑ 129 Ladell Betts	.50	.15
❑ 130 Travis Taylor	.30	.09
❑ 131 Marty Booker	.50	.15
❑ 132 Patrick Surtain	.30	.09
❑ 133 Duce Staley	.50	.15
❑ 134 Shaun Alexander	.75	.23
❑ 135 Eddie George	.50	.15
❑ 136 Eric Moulds	.50	.15
❑ 137 David Carr	1.25	.35
❑ 138 Fred Taylor	.75	.23
❑ 139 Wayne Chrebet	.50	.15
❑ 140 Bobby Taylor	.30	.09
❑ 141 Derrick Brooks	.50	.15
❑ 142 Stephen Davis	.50	.15
❑ 143 Ray Lewis	.75	.23
❑ 144 Kelly Holcomb	.50	.15
❑ 145 Terry Glenn	.30	.09
❑ 146 Jason Taylor	.30	.09
❑ 147 Todd Pinkston	.50	.15
❑ 148 Derrick Mason	.50	.15
❑ 149 Chad Johnson	.50	.15
❑ 150 Ed McCaffrey	.50	.15
❑ 151 Tiki Barber	.50	.15
❑ 152 Drew Brees	.75	.23
❑ 153 Marshall Faulk	.75	.23
❑ 154 Drew Bledsoe	.75	.23
❑ 155 Andre Davis	.30	.09
❑ 156 Donald Driver	.50	.15
❑ 157 Chris Chambers	.75	.23
❑ 158 Brian Dawkins	.30	.09
❑ 159 Garrison Hearst	.50	.15
❑ 160 Frank Wycheck	.30	.09
❑ 161 Carson Palmer RC	12.00	3.60
❑ 162 Byron Leftwich RC	15.00	4.50
❑ 163 Charles Rogers RC	5.00	1.50
❑ 164 Andre Johnson RC	10.00	3.00
❑ 165 Chris Simms RC	8.00	2.40
❑ 166 Rex Grossman RC	10.00	3.00
❑ 167 Brandon Lloyd RC	5.00	1.50
❑ 168 Lee Suggs RC	8.00	2.40
❑ 169 Larry Johnson RC	8.00	2.40
❑ 170 Onterrio Smith RC	5.00	1.50
❑ 171 Dave Ragone RC	4.00	1.20
❑ 172 Taylor Jacobs RC	4.00	1.20
❑ 173 Kelley Washington RC	4.00	1.20
❑ 174 Bryant Johnson RC	4.00	1.20
❑ 175 Kyle Boller RC	10.00	3.00
❑ 176 Ken Dorsey RC	6.00	1.80
❑ 177 Kliff Kingsbury RC	3.00	.90
❑ 178 Jason Gesser RC	4.00	1.20
❑ 179 Brian St.Pierre RC	4.00	1.20
❑ 180 Brad Banks RC	3.00	.90
❑ 181 Seneca Wallace RC	4.00	1.20
❑ 182 Tony Romo RC	4.00	1.20
❑ 183 Terrell Suggs RC	6.00	1.80
❑ 184 Terence Newman RC	8.00	2.40
❑ 185 Willis McGahee RC	10.00	3.00
❑ 186 Justin Fargas RC	4.00	1.20
❑ 187 Musa Smith RC	4.00	1.20
❑ 188 Earnest Graham RC	3.00	.90
❑ 189 Chris Brown RC	8.00	2.40
❑ 190 LaBrandon Toefield RC	4.00	1.20
❑ 191 Bennie Joppru RC	4.00	1.20
❑ 192 Jason Witten RC	6.00	1.80
❑ 193 Anquan Boldin RC	10.00	3.00
❑ 194 Talman Gardner RC	4.00	1.20
❑ 195 Justin Gage RC	4.00	1.20
❑ 196 Sam Aiken RC	3.00	.90
❑ 197 Kevin Curtis RC	4.00	1.20
❑ 198 Terrence Edwards RC	3.00	.90
❑ U199 DeWayne Robertson RC	4.00	1.20
❑ U200 Kevin Williams RC	4.00	1.20
❑ U201 Marcus Trufant RC	4.00	1.20
❑ U202 Jimmy Kennedy RC	4.00	1.20
❑ U203 Ty Warren RC	4.00	1.20
❑ U204 Michael Haynes RC	4.00	1.20
❑ U205 Jerome McDougle RC	4.00	1.20
❑ U206 Dallas Clark RC	4.00	1.20
❑ U207 William Joseph RC	4.00	1.20
❑ U208 Andre Woolfolk RC	4.00	1.20
❑ U209 Bethel Johnson RC	6.00	1.80
❑ U210 Teyo Johnson RC	4.00	1.20
❑ U211 Tyrone Calico RC	5.00	1.50
❑ U212 L.J. Smith RC	4.00	1.20
❑ U213 Nate Burleson RC	6.00	1.80
❑ U214 B.J. Askew RC	4.00	1.20
❑ U215 Billy McMullen RC	4.00	1.20
❑ U216 Domanick Davis RC	8.00	2.40
❑ U217 Doug Gabriel RC	4.00	1.20
❑ U218 Quentin Griffin RC	10.00	3.00

2003 Ultra Gold Medallion

Nm-Mt Ex-Mt

*STARS: 1.5X TO 4X BASIC CARDS
*ROOKIES: .5X TO 1.2X

2003 Ultra Platinum Medallion

Nm-Mt Ex-Mt

*STARS: 6X TO 15X BASIC CARDS
*ROOKIES: 2X TO 5X

2003 Ultra Autographs

	Nm-Mt	Ex-Mt
❑ UAJ Andre Johnson/300	80.00	24.00
❑ UBL Byron Leftwich/300	100.00	30.00

	Nm-Mt	Ex-Mt
❑ UCP Carson Palmer/300	80.00	24.00
❑ ULJ Larry Johnson/350	40.00	12.00

2003 Ultra Award Winners Memorabilia

	Nm-Mt	Ex-Mt
❑ AWCP Clinton Portis	15.00	4.50
❑ AWCP2 Chad Pennington	12.00	3.60
❑ AWDB Derrick Brooks	10.00	3.00
❑ AWDM Deuce McAllister	12.00	3.60
❑ AWJS Jeremy Shockey	15.00	4.50
❑ AWLT LaDainian Tomlinson	12.00	3.60
❑ AWMF Marshall Faulk	12.00	3.60
❑ AWMH Marvin Harrison	12.00	3.60
❑ AWMV Michael Vick	25.00	7.50
❑ AWPH Priest Holmes	15.00	4.50
❑ AWRG Rich Gannon	10.00	3.00
❑ AWRW Ricky Williams	12.00	3.60
❑ AWTH Travis Henry	10.00	3.00
❑ AWTO Terrell Owens	12.00	3.60

2003 Ultra Award Winners Memorabilia UltraSwatch

	Nm-Mt	Ex-Mt
❑ AWCP Clinton Portis/26	50.00	15.00
❑ AWCP2 Chad Pennington/10		
❑ AWDB Derrick Brooks/55	25.00	7.50
❑ AWDM Deuce McAllister/26	40.00	12.00
❑ AWJS Jeremy Shockey/80	25.00	7.50
❑ AWLT LaDainain Tomlinson/21		
❑ AWMF Marshall Faulk/28	40.00	12.00
❑ AWMH Marvin Harrison/88	20.00	6.00
❑ AWMV Michael Vick/7		
❑ AWPH Priest Holmes/31	40.00	12.00
❑ AWRG Rich Gannon/12		
❑ AWRW Ricky Williams/34	50.00	15.00
❑ AWTH Travis Henry/20		
❑ AWTO Terrell Owens/81	25.00	7.50

2003 Ultra Touchdown Kings Memorabilia

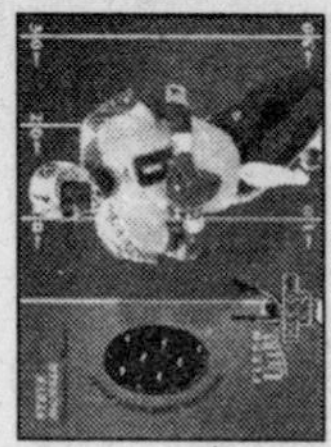

	Nm-Mt	Ex-Mt
❑ TKBF Brett Favre	30.00	9.00
❑ TKCP Clinton Portis	15.00	4.50
❑ TKCP2 Chad Pennington	15.00	4.50
❑ TKDB Drew Bledsoe	12.00	3.60
❑ TKDM Donovan McNabb	15.00	4.50
❑ TKES Emmitt Smith	30.00	9.00
❑ TKJR Jerry Rice	20.00	6.00
❑ TKMV Michael Vick	25.00	7.50
❑ TKPH Priest Holmes	15.00	4.50
❑ TKPM Peyton Manning	15.00	4.50
❑ TKRM Randy Moss	15.00	4.50
❑ TKRW Ricky Williams	12.00	3.60
❑ TKSA Shaun Alexander	12.00	3.60
❑ TKSM Steve McNair	12.00	3.60
❑ TKTB Tom Brady	20.00	6.00

2003 Ultra Touchdown Kings Memorabilia Career

	Nm-Mt	Ex-Mt
❑ TKBF Brett Favre/326	30.00	9.00
❑ TKCP Clinton Portis/17		
❑ TKCP2 Chad Pennington/26	50.00	15.00
❑ TKDB Drew Bledsoe/194	15.00	4.50
❑ TKDM Donovan McNabb/85	25.00	7.50
❑ TKES Emmitt Smith/164	50.00	15.00
❑ TKJR Jerry Rice/202	30.00	9.00
❑ TKMV Michael Vick/27	50.00	15.00
❑ TKPH Priest Holmes/45	25.00	7.50
❑ TKPM Peyton Manning/147	30.00	9.00
❑ TKRM Randy Moss/60	50.00	15.00
❑ TKRW Ricky Williams/35	30.00	9.00
❑ TKSA Shaun Alexander/36	20.00	6.00
❑ TKSM Steve McNair/103	15.00	4.50
❑ TKTB Tom Brady/47	25.00	7.50

2003 Ultra Touchdown Kings Memorabilia UltraSwatch

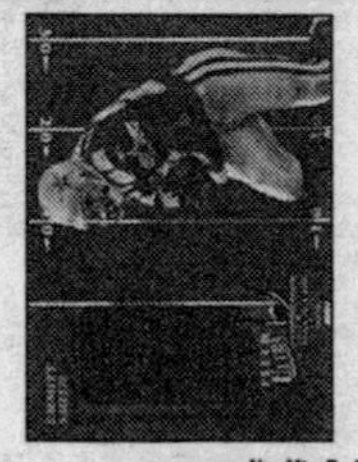

	Nm-Mt	Ex-Mt
CARDS #'d UNDER 25 NOT PRICED		
❑ TKCP Clinton Portis/26	60.00	18.00
❑ TKPH Priest Holmes/31	40.00	12.00
❑ TKRW Ricky Williams/34	40.00	12.00
❑ TKSA Shaun Alexander/37	30.00	9.00

2004 Ultra

	Nm-Mt	Ex-Mt
COMP.SET w/o L13's (218)	60.00	18.00
COMP.SET w/o SP's (200)	30.00	9.00
COMP.UPDATE SET (21)	40.00	12.00
L13 201-213 ROOKIE ODDS 1:100H,1:530R		
L13 ROOKIE PRINT RUN 500 SER.#'d SETS		
214-232 ROOKIE STATED ODDS 1:4H,1:6R		
U234-U254 ODDS 2:1 TRADITION HOT PACK		
❑ 1 Michael Vick	1.50	.45
❑ 2 Kelley Washington	.30	.09
❑ 3 Rex Grossman	.75	.23
❑ 4 Boss Bailey	.50	.15
❑ 5 Johnnie Morton	.50	.15
❑ 6 Michael Strahan	.50	.15
❑ 7 Joey Porter	.30	.09
❑ 8 Keenan McCardell	.30	.09
❑ 9 Quincy Carter	.50	.15
❑ 10 Travis Henry	.50	.15
❑ 11 Bert Berry	.30	.09
❑ 12 Marvin Harrison	.75	.23
❑ 13 Ty Law	.50	.15
❑ 14 Phillip Buchanon	.30	.09
❑ 15 Kevan Barlow	.50	.15
❑ 16 Eddie George	.50	.15
❑ 17 Drew Bledsoe	.75	.23
❑ 18 Antonio Bryant	.50	.15
❑ 19 Marcus Pollard	.30	.09
❑ 20 Brian Russell RC	.75	.23
❑ 21 Santana Moss	.50	.15
❑ 22 Julian Peterson	.30	.09
❑ 23 Justin McCareins	.30	.09
❑ 24 Ed Reed	.50	.15
❑ 25 Charles Tillman	.50	.15
❑ 26 Dat Nguyen	.30	.09
❑ 27 Ricky Manning	.30	.09
❑ 28 Dwight Freeney	.30	.09
❑ 29 Zach Thomas	.75	.23
❑ 30 Tiki Barber	.50	.15
❑ 31 Jay Riemersma	.30	.09
❑ 32 Joe Jurevicius	.30	.09
❑ 33 Marcel Shipp	.50	.15
❑ 34 Justin Gage	.50	.15
❑ 35 Charles Rogers	.50	.15
❑ 36 Eddie Kennison	.30	.09
❑ 37 Deion Branch	.75	.23
❑ 38 Matt Hasselbeck	.50	.15
❑ 39 L.J. Smith	.50	.15
❑ 40 Jamal Lewis	.75	.23
❑ 41 Muhsin Muhammad	.50	.15
❑ 42 Terence Newman	.50	.15
❑ 43 Jabar Gaffney	.50	.15
❑ 44 Junior Seau	.75	.23
❑ 45 Jeremy Shockey	.75	.23
❑ 46 Hines Ward	.75	.23
❑ 47 Brad Johnson	.50	.15
❑ 48 Kyle Boller	.75	.23
❑ 49 Steve Smith	.50	.15
❑ 50 Quincy Morgan	.50	.15
❑ 51 Corey Bradford	.30	.09
❑ 52 Ricky Williams	.75	.23
❑ 53 Amani Toomer	.50	.15
❑ 54 Plaxico Burress	.50	.15
❑ 55 Derrick Brooks	.50	.15
❑ 56 Dre Bly	.30	.09
❑ 57 Terrell Suggs	.50	.15
❑ 58 DeShaun Foster	.50	.15
❑ 59 Andre Davis	.30	.09
❑ 60 Rod Smith	.50	.15
❑ 61 Andre Johnson	.75	.23
❑ 62 Randy McMichael	.30	.09
❑ 63 Ike Hilliard	.30	.09
❑ 64 Antwaan Randle El	.50	.15
❑ 65 Warren Sapp	.50	.15
❑ 66 LaBrandon Toefield	.30	.09
❑ 67 Chad Johnson	.50	.15
❑ 68 Javon Walker	.50	.15
❑ 69 Jimmy Smith	.50	.15
❑ 70 Donte Stallworth	.50	.15
❑ 71 Brian Dawkins	.30	.09

❑ 72 Leonard Little .30 .09
❑ 73 Ladell Betts .30 .09
❑ 74 Ray Lewis .75 .23
❑ 75 Stephen Davis .50 .15
❑ 76 Dennis Northcutt .30 .09
❑ 77 Ashley Lelie .50 .15
❑ 78 Billy Miller .30 .09
❑ 79 Chris Chambers .50 .15
❑ 80 John Abraham .30 .09
❑ 81 Quentin Jammer .30 .09
❑ 82 Isaac Bruce .50 .15
❑ 83 Peerless Price .50 .15
❑ 84 Jake Delhomme .75 .23
❑ 85 Lee Suggs .75 .23
❑ 86 Shannon Sharpe .50 .15
❑ 87 Domanick Davis .75 .23
❑ 88 Daunte Culpepper .75 .23
❑ 89 Shaun Ellis .30 .09
❑ 90 Drew Brees .75 .23
❑ 91 Torry Holt .75 .23
❑ 92 Alge Crumpler .50 .15
❑ 93 Mike Rucker .50 .15
❑ 94 Tim Couch .30 .09
❑ 95 Quentin Griffin .75 .23
❑ 96 David Carr .75 .23
❑ 97 Moe Williams .30 .09
❑ 98 Chad Pennington 1.00 .30
❑ 99 LaDainian Tomlinson .75 .23
❑ 100 Adam Archuleta .30 .09
❑ 101 Julius Peppers .75 .23
❑ 102 Clinton Portis .75 .23
❑ 103 Marcus Stroud .30 .09
❑ 104 Tom Brady 1.25 .35
❑ 105 Teyo Johnson .30 .09
❑ 106 Terrell Owens .75 .23
❑ 107 Keith Bulluck .30 .09
❑ 108 Eric Moulds .50 .15
❑ 109 Jake Plummer .50 .15
❑ 110 Reggie Wayne .50 .15
❑ 111 Tedy Bruschi .50 .15
❑ 112 Rich Gannon .50 .15
❑ 113 Tony Parrish .30 .09
❑ 114 Steve McNair .75 .23
❑ 115 T.J. Duckett .50 .15
❑ 116 Peter Warrick .50 .15
❑ 117 Donald Driver .50 .15
❑ 118 Fred Taylor .50 .15
❑ 119 Joe Horn .50 .15
❑ 120 Jerry Porter .50 .15
❑ 121 Marc Bulger .75 .23
❑ 122 Trung Canidate .30 .09
❑ 123 Warrick Dunn .50 .15
❑ 124 Kelly Holcomb .50 .15
❑ 125 Robert Ferguson .30 .09
❑ 126 Byron Leftwich 1.25 .35
❑ 127 Michael Lewis .30 .09
❑ 128 Jerry Rice 1.50 .45
❑ 129 Marshall Faulk .75 .23
❑ 130 Patrick Ramsey .50 .15
❑ 131 Josh McCown .50 .15
❑ 132 Anthony Thomas .50 .15
❑ 133 Joey Harrington .75 .23
❑ 134 Dante Hall .75 .23
❑ 135 Daniel Graham .30 .09
❑ 136 Richard Seymour .30 .09
❑ 137 Brandon Lloyd .50 .15
❑ 138 Anquan Boldin .75 .23
❑ 139 Jon Kitna .50 .15
❑ 140 Nick Barnett .50 .15
❑ 141 Priest Holmes 1.00 .30
❑ 142 Bethel Johnson .50 .15
❑ 143 Shaun Alexander .75 .23
❑ 144 Todd Heap .50 .15
❑ 145 Brian Urlacher 1.00 .30
❑ 146 Peyton Manning 1.25 .35
❑ 147 Jason Taylor .30 .09
❑ 148 Kerry Collins .50 .15
❑ 149 Tommy Maddox .50 .15
❑ 150 Charles Lee .30 .09
❑ 151 Tim Rattay .50 .15
❑ 152 Carson Palmer 1.00 .30
❑ 153 Brett Favre 2.00 .60
❑ 154 Trent Green .50 .15
❑ 155 Aaron Brooks .50 .15
❑ 156 Brian Westbrook .50 .15
❑ 157 Itula Mili .30 .09
❑ 158 Keith Brooking .30 .09
❑ 159 Rudi Johnson .50 .15
❑ 160 Najeh Davenport .30 .09
❑ 161 Kevin Johnson .30 .09
❑ 162 Boo Williams .30 .09
❑ 163 Corey Simon .50 .15
❑ 164 Darrell Jackson .50 .15
❑ 165 Darnerien McCants .30 .09
❑ 166 Willis McGahee .75 .23
❑ 167 Terry Glenn .30 .09
❑ 168 Dallas Clark .50 .15
❑ 169 Randy Moss 1.00 .30
❑ 170 Charles Woodson .50 .15
❑ 171 Jeff Garcia .75 .23
❑ 172 Chris Brown .75 .23
❑ 173 Emmitt Smith 1.50 .45
❑ 174 Marty Booker .50 .15
❑ 175 Artose Pinner .30 .09
❑ 176 Tony Gonzalez .50 .15
❑ 177 Troy Brown .50 .15
❑ 178 Freddie Mitchell .50 .15
❑ 179 Marcus Trufant .30 .09
❑ 180 London Fletcher .30 .09
❑ 181 Roy Williams S .50 .15
❑ 182 Edgerrin James .75 .23
❑ 183 Michael Bennett .50 .15
❑ 184 Jerald Sowell .30 .09
❑ 185 David Boston .50 .15
❑ 186 Derrick Mason .50 .15
❑ 187 Bryant Johnson .30 .09
❑ 188 Corey Dillon .50 .15
❑ 189 Ahman Green .75 .23
❑ 190 Vonnie Holliday .30 .09
❑ 191 Deuce McAllister .75 .23
❑ 192 Donovan McNabb 1.00 .30
❑ 193 Koren Robinson .50 .15
❑ 194 Laveranues Coles .50 .15
❑ 195 Takeo Spikes .30 .09
❑ 196 Richie Anderson .30 .09
❑ 197 Onterrio Smith .50 .15
❑ 198 Curtis Martin .75 .23
❑ 199 Antonio Gates .75 .23
❑ 200 Champ Bailey .50 .15
❑ 201 Eli Manning L13 RC 80.00 24.00
❑ 202 Philip Rivers L13 RC 60.00 18.00
❑ 203 Roy Williams L13 RC 60.00 18.00
❑ 204 Drew Henson L13 RC 40.00 12.00
❑ 205 Chris Perry L13 RC 30.00 9.00
❑ 206 Larry Fitzgerald L13 RC 60.00 18.00
❑ 207 Rashaun Woods L13 RC 25.00 7.50
❑ 208 Reggie Williams L13 RC 30.00 9.00
❑ 209 Mike Williams L13 RC 125.00 38.00
❑ 210 Kellen Winslow L13 RC 50.00 15.00
❑ 211 Steven Jackson L13 RC 60.00 18.00
❑ 212 Kevin Jones L13 RC 60.00 18.00
❑ 213 Ben Roethlisberger L13 RC 120.00 36.00
❑ 214 Michael Turner RC 2.50 .75
❑ 215 Tatum Bell RC 6.00 1.80
❑ 216 Quincy Wilson RC 2.50 .75
❑ 217 Devery Henderson RC 2.50 .75
❑ 218 Ernest Wilford RC 4.00 1.20
❑ 219 Cody Pickett RC 4.00 1.20
❑ 220 Ryan Dinwiddie RC 2.50 .75
❑ 221 J.P. Losman RC 10.00 3.00
❑ 222 Derrick Knight RC 2.50 .75
❑ 223 Michael Jenkins RC 4.00 1.20
❑ 224 Greg Jones RC 4.00 1.20
❑ 225 Cedric Cobbs RC 4.00 1.20
❑ 226 Will Poole RC 4.00 1.20
❑ 227 Michael Clayton RC 10.00 3.00
❑ 228 Sean Taylor RC 6.00 1.80
❑ 229 Will Smith RC 4.00 1.20
❑ 230 Jonathan Vilma RC 4.00 1.20
❑ 231 Lee Evans RC 6.00 1.80
❑ 232 Julius Jones RC 15.00 4.50
❑ U234 D.J. Williams RC 6.00 1.80
❑ U235 Mewelde Moore RC 6.00 1.80
❑ U236 Ben Watson RC 5.00 1.50
❑ U237 Robert Gallery RC 8.00 2.40
❑ U238 DeAngelo Hall RC 6.00 1.80
❑ U239 Luke McCown RC 5.00 1.50
❑ U240 Ben Troupe RC 5.00 1.50
❑ U241 Keary Colbert RC 6.00 1.80
❑ U242 Matt Schaub RC 8.00 2.40
❑ U243 Kenechi Udeze RC 5.00 1.50
❑ U244 Jeff Smoker RC 8.00 2.40
❑ U245 Derrick Hamilton RC 4.00 1.20
❑ U246 Bernard Berrian RC 5.00 1.50
❑ U247 Devard Darling RC 5.00 1.50
❑ U248 Johnnie Morant RC 5.00 1.50
❑ U249 Vince Wilfork RC 6.00 1.80
❑ U250 Jerricho Cotchery RC 5.00 1.50
❑ U251 Darius Watts RC 6.00 1.80
❑ U252 Carlos Francis RC 4.00 1.20
❑ U253 P.K. Sam RC 4.00 1.20

2004 Ultra Gold Medallion

Nm-Mt Ex-Mt

*VETERANS: 1.5X TO 4X BASE CARD HI
*ROOKIES 201-213: .15X TO .3X BASE CARD HI
*ROOKIES 214-232: .4X TO 1X BASE CARD HI
OVERALL STATED ODDS 1:1H,1:3R
ROOKIE 201-232 ODDS 1:8H,1:12R

2004 Ultra Platinum Medallion

Nm-Mt Ex-Mt

*VETERANS: 10X TO 25X BASE CARD HI
*ROOKIES 214-232: 2X TO 5X
1-200/214-232 STATED ODDS 1:45 HOB
1-200/214-232 PRINT RUN 66 #'d SETS
L13 201-213 STATED ODDS 1:3650
UNPRICED L13 201-213 PRINT RUN 13 SETS

2004 Ultra Gridiron Producers

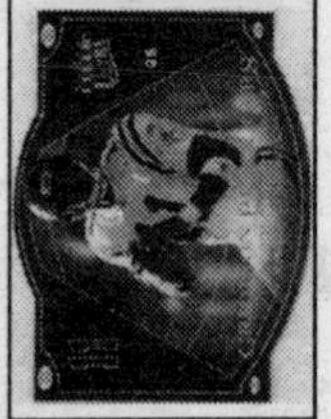

Nm-Mt Ex-Mt

STATED ODDS 1:144H,1:288R

❑ 1GP Donovan McNabb 8.00 4.00
❑ 2GP Charles Rogers 4.00 2.00
❑ 3GP Daunte Culpepper 6.00 3.00
❑ 4GP Matt Hasselbeck 4.00 2.00
❑ 5GP Jerry Rice 12.00 6.00
❑ 6GP Tom Brady 10.00 5.00
❑ 7GP Byron Leftwich 10.00 5.00
❑ 8GP Ahman Green 6.00 3.00
❑ 9GP Stephen Davis 4.00 2.00
❑ 10GP LaDainian Tomlinson 6.00 3.00

2004 Ultra Gridiron Producers Game Used Copper

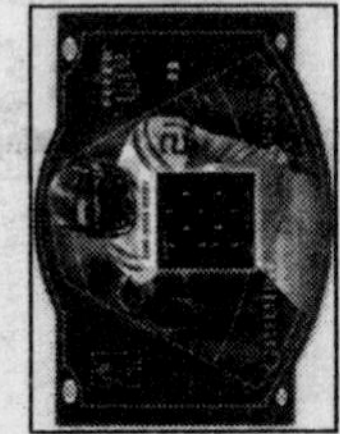

	Nm-Mt	Ex-Mt
OVERALL GAME USED/AUTO ODDS 1:12		
*GOLD: .6X TO 1.5X COPPER		
GOLD PRINT RUN 77 SER.#'d SETS		
UNPRICED PLATINUM PRINT RUN 9 SETS		
❑ GPAG Ahman Green	12.00	3.60
❑ GPBL Byron Leftwich	12.00	3.60
❑ GPCR Charles Rogers	10.00	3.00
❑ GPDC Daunte Culpepper	12.00	3.60
❑ GPDM Donovan McNabb	15.00	4.50
❑ GPJR Jerry Rice	20.00	6.00
❑ GPLT LaDainian Tomlinson	12.00	3.60
❑ GPMH Matt Hasselbeck	10.00	3.00
❑ GPSD Stephen Davis	10.00	3.00
❑ GPTB Tom Brady	15.00	4.50

2004 Ultra Gridiron Producers Game Used UltraSwatch

	Nm-Mt	Ex-Mt
ULTRASWATCH #'d TO PLAYER'S JERSEY		
❑ GPAG Ahman Green/30	30.00	9.00
❑ GPBL Byron Leftwich/7		
❑ GPCR Charles Rogers/80	25.00	7.50
❑ GPDC Daunte Culpepper/11		
❑ GPDM Donovan McNabb/5		
❑ GPJR Jerry Rice/80	40.00	12.00
❑ GPLT LaDainian Tomlinson/21	30.00	9.00
❑ GPMH Matt Hasselbeck/8		
❑ GPSD Stephen Davis/48	25.00	7.50
❑ GPTB Tom Brady/12		

2004 Ultra Hummer H2 In Package

	Nm-Mt	Ex-Mt
COMPLETE SET (6)		
*SINGLE CARDS: .4X TO 1X PACKAGE		
❑ 201 Eli Manning	10.00	3.00
❑ 202 Philip Rivers	6.00	1.80
❑ 204 Drew Henson	6.00	1.80
❑ 206 Larry Fitzgerald	6.00	1.80
❑ 210 Kellen Winslow	6.00	1.80
❑ 213 Ben Roethlisberger	20.00	6.00

2004 Ultra Passing Kings

	Nm-Mt	Ex-Mt
COMPLETE SET (10)	30.00	9.00
OVERALL KINGS ODDS 1:12H,1:24R		
*GOLDS: 1.5X TO 4X BASIC INSERTS		
GOLD PRINT RUN 50 SER.#'d SETS		
❑ 1PA Brett Favre	10.00	3.00
❑ 2PA Donovan McNabb	5.00	1.50
❑ 3PA Peyton Manning	6.00	1.80
❑ 4PA Steve McNair	4.00	1.20
❑ 5PA Daunte Culpepper	4.00	1.20
❑ 6PA Tom Brady	6.00	1.80
❑ 7PA Byron Leftwich	6.00	1.80
❑ 8PA Joey Harrington	4.00	1.20
❑ 9PA Matt Hasselbeck	2.50	.75
❑ 10PA Marc Bulger	4.00	1.20
❑ NNO Manning Family AU/50	600.00	180.00

2004 Ultra Performers

	Nm-Mt	Ex-Mt
STATED ODDS 1:6H,1:8R		
*GOLD DIE CUTS: .4X TO 1X BASIC INSERTS		
ONE GOLD PER RETAIL PACK		
❑ 1UP Tom Brady	4.00	1.20
❑ 2UP Clinton Portis	2.50	.75
❑ 3UP Priest Holmes	3.00	.90
❑ 4UP Marshall Faulk	2.50	.75
❑ 5UP Randy Moss	3.00	.90
❑ 6UP Marvin Harrison	2.50	.75
❑ 7UP Donovan McNabb	3.00	.90
❑ 8UP Ricky Williams	2.50	.75
❑ 9UP Brett Favre	6.00	1.80
❑ 10UP Steve McNair	2.50	.75
❑ 11UP Peyton Manning	4.00	1.20
❑ 12UP Shaun Alexander	2.50	.75
❑ 13UP Edgerrin James	2.50	.75
❑ 14UP Chad Johnson	1.50	.45
❑ 15UP Torry Holt	2.50	.75

2004 Ultra Performers Game Used Copper

	Nm-Mt	Ex-Mt
OVERALL GAME USED/AUTO ODDS 1:12		
*GOLD: .6X TO 1.5X COPPER		
GOLD PRINT RUN 88 SER.# SETS		
*PLATINUM: 1.5X TO 4X COPPER		
PLATINUM PRINT RUN 19 #'d SETS		
❑ UPBF Brett Favre	25.00	7.50
❑ UPCJ Chad Johnson	10.00	3.00
❑ UPCP Clinton Portis	12.00	3.60
❑ UPDM Donovan McNabb	15.00	4.50
❑ UPEJ Edgerrin James	12.00	3.60
❑ UPMF Marshall Faulk	12.00	3.60
❑ UPMH Marvin Harrison	10.00	3.00
❑ UPPH Priest Holmes	15.00	4.50
❑ UPPM Peyton Manning	15.00	4.50
❑ UPRM Randy Moss	15.00	4.50
❑ UPRW Ricky Williams	12.00	3.60
❑ UPSA Shaun Alexander	12.00	3.60
❑ UPSM Steve McNair	12.00	3.60
❑ UPTB Tom Brady	15.00	4.50
❑ UPTH Torry Holt	12.00	3.60

2004 Ultra Performers Game Used UltraSwatch

	Nm-Mt	Ex-Mt
ULTRASWATCH #'d TO PLAYER'S JERSEY		
❑ UPBF Brett Favre/4		
❑ UPCJ Chad Johnson/85	20.00	6.00
❑ UPCP Clinton Portis/26	40.00	12.00
❑ UPDM Donovan McNabb/34	40.00	12.00
❑ UPEJ Edgerrin James/32	30.00	9.00
❑ UPMF Marshall Faulk/28	30.00	9.00
❑ UPMH Marvin Harrison/88	20.00	6.00
❑ UPPH Priest Holmes/31	40.00	12.00
❑ UPPM Peyton Manning/18		
❑ UPRM Randy Moss/84	30.00	9.00
❑ UPRW Ricky Williams/34	30.00	9.00
❑ UPSA Shaun Alexander/37	30.00	9.00
❑ UPSM Steve McNair/27	30.00	9.00
❑ UPTB Tom Brady/12		
❑ UPTH Torry Holt/81	20.00	6.00

2004 Ultra Receiving Kings

	Nm-Mt	Ex-Mt
OVERALL KINGS ODDS 1:12H,1:24R		
*GOLDS: 2X TO 5X BASIC INSERTS		
GOLD PRINT RUN 50 SER.#'d SETS		
❑ 1RE Randy Moss	4.00	1.20
❑ 2RE Torry Holt	3.00	.90
❑ 3RE Anquan Boldin	3.00	.90
❑ 4RE Chad Johnson	2.00	.60
❑ 5RE Derrick Mason	2.00	.60
❑ 6RE Marvin Harrison	3.00	.90
❑ 7RE Laveranues Coles	2.00	.60
❑ 8RE Terrell Owens	3.00	.90
❑ 9RE Charles Rogers	2.00	.60
❑ 10RE Jerry Rice	6.00	1.80

2004 Ultra Rushing Kings

	Nm-Mt	Ex-Mt
OVERALL KINGS ODDS 1:12H,1:24R		
*GOLDS: 2X TO 5X BASIC INSERTS		
GOLD PRINT RUN 50 SER.#'d SETS		

❑ 1RU	Clinton Portis	3.00	.90
❑ 2RU	Priest Holmes	4.00	1.20
❑ 3RU	Stephen Davis	2.00	.60
❑ 4RU	Marshall Faulk	3.00	.90
❑ 5RU	LaDainian Tomlinson	3.00	.90
❑ 6RU	Shaun Alexander	3.00	.90
❑ 7RU	Deuce McAllister	3.00	.90
❑ 8RU	Ricky Williams	3.00	.90
❑ 9RU	Jamal Lewis	3.00	.90
❑ 10RU	Ahman Green	3.00	.90

2004 Ultra Season Crowns Autographs

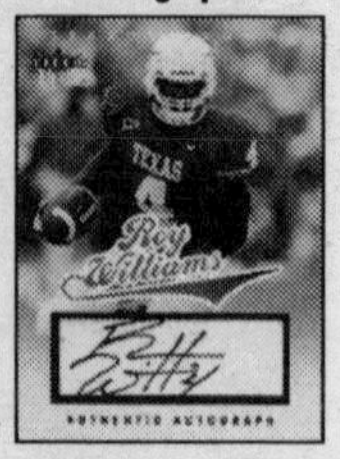

PRINT RUN 150 SETS UNLESS NOTED

		Nm-Mt	Ex-Mt
❑ 1	Kyle Boller EXCH	25.00	7.50
❑ 2	Plaxico Burress	20.00	6.00
❑ 3	David Carr	25.00	7.50
❑ 4	LaDainian Tomlinson	25.00	7.50
❑ 5	Chad Pennington EXCH	30.00	9.00
❑ 6	Donovan McNabb/25	100.00	30.00
❑ 7	Matt Hasselbeck/75 EXCH	40.00	12.00
❑ 8	Philip Rivers EXCH	60.00	18.00
❑ 9	Roy Williams WR	75.00	22.00
❑ 10	Eli Manning	150.00	45.00
❑ 11	Dante Hall EXCH	30.00	9.00
❑ 12	Brian Westbrook	20.00	6.00
❑ 13	Jake Delhomme	25.00	7.50
❑ 14	Kelley Washington	20.00	6.00
❑ 15	Joe Jurevicius EXCH	15.00	4.50
❑ 16	Byron Leftwich	40.00	12.00
❑ 17	Shaun Alexander	25.00	7.50
❑ 18	Drew Henson	60.00	18.00
❑ 19	Deuce McAllister	25.00	7.50
❑ 20	Mike Williams EXCH	200.00	60.00
❑ 21	Steven Jackson	50.00	15.00
❑ 22	Will Poole	25.00	7.50

2004 Ultra Season Crowns Autographs Gold

*GOLD VETS: 1X TO 2X BASIC AUTOS
*GOLD ROOKIES: 1.2X TO 2.5X BASIC AUTOS
GOLD STATED PRINT RUN 25 SETS

		Nm-Mt	Ex-Mt
❑ 6	Donovan McNabb	100.00	30.00
❑ 10	Eli Manning	350.00	105.00

2004 Ultra Season Crowns Game Used Copper

COPPER PRINT RUN 349 SER.#'d SETS
*GOLD: .6X TO 1.5X COPPER
GOLD PRINT RUN 99 SER.#'d SETS
*PLATINUM: 1X TO 2.5X COPPER
PLATINUM PRINT RUN 29 SER.#'d SETS
*SILVER: .5X TO 1.2X COPPER
SILVER PRINT RUN 149 SER.#'d SETS

		Nm-Mt	Ex-Mt
❑ 1	Rex Grossman	12.00	3.60
❑ 2	Julius Peppers	12.00	3.60
❑ 3	Antwaan Randle El	12.00	3.60
❑ 4	Charles Rogers	10.00	3.00
❑ 5	Brian Urlacher	15.00	4.50
❑ 6	Carson Palmer	15.00	4.50
❑ 7	Priest Holmes	15.00	4.50
❑ 8	Travis Henry	10.00	3.00
❑ 9	Andre Johnson	12.00	3.60
❑ 10	Marvin Harrison	12.00	3.60
❑ 11	Randy Moss	15.00	4.50
❑ 12	Corey Dillon	10.00	3.00
❑ 13	Ray Lewis	12.00	3.60
❑ 14	Ricky Williams	12.00	3.60
❑ 15	Peyton Manning Pants	15.00	4.50
❑ 16	Michael Bennett	10.00	3.00
❑ 17	Torry Holt	12.00	3.60
❑ 18	Deuce McAllister	12.00	3.60
❑ 19	Deion Branch	12.00	3.60
❑ 20	DeShaun Foster	8.00	2.40
❑ 21	Edgerrin James	12.00	3.60
❑ 22	Steve McNair	12.00	3.60
❑ 23	Brett Favre	25.00	7.50
❑ 24	Chad Pennington	15.00	4.50
❑ 25	Brad Johnson	10.00	3.00
❑ 26	Fred Taylor	8.00	2.40
❑ 27	Michael Vick	20.00	6.00
❑ 28	Derrick Brooks	10.00	3.00
❑ 29	LaDainian Tomlinson	12.00	3.60
❑ 30	Warren Sapp	12.00	3.60
❑ 31	Byron Leftwich	12.00	3.60
❑ 32	Donovan McNabb	15.00	4.50
❑ 33	Ahman Green	12.00	3.60
❑ 34	Emmitt Smith	20.00	6.00
❑ 35	Tommy Maddox	10.00	3.00
❑ 36	Shaun Alexander	12.00	3.60
❑ 37	Joey Harrington	12.00	3.60
❑ 38	Marshall Faulk	12.00	3.60
❑ 39	Jerry Rice	20.00	6.00
❑ 40	T.J. Duckett	8.00	2.40
❑ 41	Eric Moulds	10.00	3.00
❑ 42	Tom Brady	15.00	4.50
❑ 43	David Carr	12.00	3.60
❑ 44	Daunte Culpepper	12.00	3.60
❑ 45	Isaac Bruce	10.00	3.00
❑ 46	Chad Johnson	10.00	3.00
❑ 47	Jeremy Shockey	12.00	3.60
❑ 48	Eddie George	10.00	3.00
❑ 49	Quincy Carter	10.00	3.00
❑ 50	Aaron Brooks	10.00	3.00

2004 Ultra Three Kings Game Used

STATED PRINT RUN 33 SER.#'d SETS

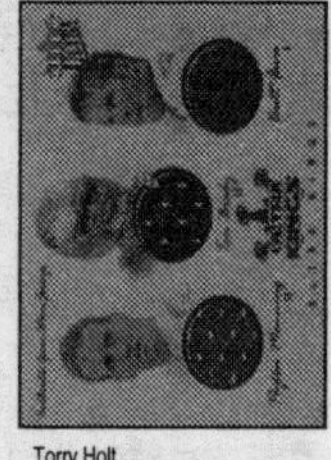

		Nm-Mt	Ex-Mt
❑ FHB	Marshall Faulk Torry Holt Marc Bulger	40.00	12.00
❑ GMT	Ahman Green Deuce McAllister LaDainian Tomlinson	40.00	12.00
❑ HHL	Matt Hasselbeck Joey Harrington Byron Leftwich	40.00	12.00
❑ HMR	Marvin Harrison Randy Moss Jerry Rice	80.00	24.00
❑ HWF	Priest Holmes Ricky Williams Marshall Faulk	60.00	18.00
❑ JRB	Chad Johnson Charles Rogers Anquan Boldin	40.00	12.00
❑ LAD	Jamal Lewis Shaun Alexander Stephen Davis	40.00	12.00
❑ MBF	Peyton Manning Tom Brady Brett Favre	150.00	45.00
❑ MMC	Steve McNair Donovan McNabb Daunte Culpepper	60.00	18.00
❑ ORM	Terrell Owens Jerry Rice Randy Moss	80.00	24.00

1991 Upper Deck

	Nm-Mt	Ex-Mt
COMPLETE SET (700)	15.00	6.75
COMP.FACT.SET (700)	25.00	11.00
COMP.SERIES 1 SET (500)	10.00	4.50
COMP.SERIES 2 SET (200)	5.00	2.20
COMP.FACT.SERIES 2 (200)	6.00	2.70
❑ 1 Star Rookie Checklist Dan McGwire	.05	.02
❑ 2 Eric Bieniemy RC	.05	.02
❑ 3 Mike Dumas RC	.05	.02
❑ 4 Mike Croel RC	.05	.02
❑ 5 Russell Maryland RC	.25	.11
❑ 6 Charles McRae RC	.05	.02
❑ 7 Dan McGwire RC	.05	.02
❑ 8 Mike Pritchard RC	.25	.11
❑ 9 Ricky Watters RC	1.50	.70
❑ 10 Chris Zorich RC	.25	.11
❑ 11 Browning Nagle RC	.05	.02
❑ 12 Wesley Carroll RC	.05	.02
❑ 13 Brett Favre RC	10.00	4.50

❑ 14 Rob Carpenter RC	.05	.02
❑ 15 Eric Swann RC	.25	.11
❑ 16 Stanley Richard RC	.05	.02
❑ 17 Herman Moore RC	.25	.11
❑ 18 Todd Marinovich RC	.05	.02
❑ 19 Aaron Craver RC	.05	.02
❑ 20 Chuck Webb RC	.05	.02
❑ 21 Todd Lyght RC	.05	.02
❑ 22 Greg Lewis RC	.05	.02
❑ 23 Eric Turner RC	.10	.05
❑ 24 Alvin Harper RC	.25	.11
❑ 25 Jarrod Bunch RC	.05	.02
❑ 26 Bruce Pickens RC	.05	.02
❑ 27 Harvey Williams RC	.25	.11
❑ 28 Randal Hill RC	.10	.05
❑ 29 Nick Bell RC	.05	.02
❑ 30 Jim Everett AT Henry Ellard	.10	.05
❑ 31 Randall Cunningham AT Keith Jackson	.05	.02
❑ 32 Steve DeBerg AT Stephone Paige	.05	.02
❑ 33 Warren Moon AT Drew Hill	.10	.05
❑ 34 Dan Marino AT Mark Clayton	.50	.23
❑ 35 Joe Montana AT Jerry Rice	.50	.23
❑ 36 Percy Snow	.05	.02
❑ 37 Kelvin Martin	.05	.02
❑ 38 Scott Case	.05	.02
❑ 39 John Gesek RC	.05	.02
❑ 40 Barry Word	.05	.02
❑ 41 Cornelius Bennett	.10	.05
❑ 42 Mike Kenn	.05	.02
❑ 43 Andre Reed	.10	.05
❑ 44 Bobby Hebert	.05	.02
❑ 45 William Perry	.10	.05
❑ 46 Dennis Byrd	.05	.02
❑ 47 Martin Mayhew	.05	.02
❑ 48 Issiac Holt	.05	.02
❑ 49 William White	.05	.02
❑ 50 JoJo Townsell	.05	.02
❑ 51 Jarvis Williams	.05	.02
❑ 52 Joey Browner	.05	.02
❑ 53 Pat Terrell	.05	.02
❑ 54 Joe Montana UER (Born Monongahela, not New Eagle)	1.25	.55
❑ 55 Jeff Herrod	.05	.02
❑ 56 Cris Carter	.50	.23
❑ 57 Jerry Rice	.75	.35
❑ 58 Brett Perriman	.25	.11
❑ 59 Kevin Fagan	.05	.02
❑ 60 Wayne Haddix	.05	.02
❑ 61 Tommy Kane	.05	.02
❑ 62 Pat Beach	.05	.02
❑ 63 Jeff Lageman	.05	.02
❑ 64 Hassan Jones	.05	.02
❑ 65 Bennie Blades	.05	.02
❑ 66 Tim McGee	.05	.02
❑ 67 Robert Blackmon	.05	.02
❑ 68 Fred Stokes RC	.05	.02
❑ 69 Barney Bussey RC	.05	.02
❑ 70 Eric Metcalf	.10	.05
❑ 71 Mark Kelso	.05	.02
❑ 72 Neal Anderson TC	.05	.02
❑ 73 Boomer Esiason TC	.05	.02
❑ 74 Thurman Thomas TC	.25	.11
❑ 75 John Elway TC	.50	.23
❑ 76 Eric Metcalf TC	.10	.05
❑ 77 Vinny Testaverde TC	.10	.05
❑ 78 Johnny Johnson TC	.05	.02
❑ 79 Anthony Miller TC	.10	.05
❑ 80 Derrick Thomas TC	.10	.05
❑ 81 Jeff George TC	.10	.05
❑ 82 Troy Aikman TC	.40	.18
❑ 83 Dan Marino TC	.50	.23
❑ 84 Randall Cunningham TC	.10	.05
❑ 85 Deion Sanders TC	.05	.02
❑ 86 Jerry Rice TC	.40	.18
❑ 87 Lawrence Taylor TC	.10	.05
❑ 88 Al Toon TC	.05	.02
❑ 89 Barry Sanders TC	.50	.23
❑ 90 Warren Moon TC	.10	.05
❑ 91 Don Majkowski TC	.05	.02
❑ 92 Andre Tippett TC	.05	.02
❑ 93 Bo Jackson TC	.30	.14
❑ 94 Jim Everett TC	.10	.05
❑ 95 Art Monk TC	.10	.05
❑ 96 Morten Andersen TC	.05	.02
❑ 97 John L. Williams TC	.05	.02
❑ 98 Rod Woodson TC	.10	.05
❑ 99 Herschel Walker TC	.10	.05
❑ 100 Checklist 1-100	.05	.02
❑ 101 Steve Young	.75	.35
❑ 102 Jim Lachey	.05	.02
❑ 103 Tom Rathman	.05	.02
❑ 104 Earnest Byner	.05	.02
❑ 105 Karl Mecklenburg	.05	.02
❑ 106 Wes Hopkins	.05	.02
❑ 107 Michael Irvin	.25	.11
❑ 108 Burt Grossman	.05	.02
❑ 109 Jay Novacek UER (Wearing 82, but card says he wears 84)	.25	.11
❑ 110 Ben Smith	.05	.02
❑ 111 Rod Woodson	.25	.11
❑ 112 Ernie Jones	.05	.02
❑ 113 Bryan Hinkle	.05	.02
❑ 114 Vai Sikahema	.05	.02
❑ 115 Bubby Brister	.05	.02
❑ 116 Brian Blades	.10	.05
❑ 117 Don Majkowski	.05	.02
❑ 118 Rod Bernstine	.05	.02
❑ 119 Brian Noble	.05	.02
❑ 120 Eugene Robinson	.05	.02
❑ 121 John Taylor	.10	.05
❑ 122 Vance Johnson	.05	.02
❑ 123 Art Monk	.10	.05
❑ 124 John Elway	1.25	.55
❑ 125 Dexter Carter	.05	.02
❑ 126 Anthony Miller	.10	.05
❑ 127 Keith Jackson	.10	.05
❑ 128 Albert Lewis	.05	.02
❑ 129 Billy Ray Smith	.05	.02
❑ 130 Clyde Simmons	.05	.02
❑ 131 Merril Hoge	.05	.02
❑ 132 Ricky Proehl	.05	.02
❑ 133 Tim McDonald	.05	.02
❑ 134 Louis Lipps	.05	.02
❑ 135 Ken Harvey	.10	.05
❑ 136 Sterling Sharpe	.10	.05
❑ 137 Gill Byrd	.05	.02
❑ 138 Tim Harris	.05	.02
❑ 139 Derrick Fenner	.05	.02
❑ 140 Johnny Holland	.05	.02
❑ 141 Ricky Sanders	.05	.02
❑ 142 Bobby Humphrey	.05	.02
❑ 143 Roger Craig	.10	.05
❑ 144 Steve Atwater	.05	.02
❑ 145 Ickey Woods	.05	.02
❑ 146 Randall Cunningham	.25	.11
❑ 147 Marion Butts	.10	.05
❑ 148 Reggie White	.25	.11
❑ 149 Ronnie Harmon	.05	.02
❑ 150 Mike Saxon	.05	.02
❑ 151 Greg Townsend	.05	.02
❑ 152 Troy Aikman	.75	.35
❑ 153 Shane Conlan	.05	.02
❑ 154 Deion Sanders	.40	.18
❑ 155 Bo Jackson	.30	.14
❑ 156 Jeff Hostetler	.10	.05
❑ 157 Albert Bentley	.05	.02
❑ 158 James Williams	.05	.02
❑ 159 Bill Brooks	.05	.02
❑ 160 Nick Lowery	.05	.02
❑ 161 Ottis Anderson	.10	.05
❑ 162 Kevin Greene	.10	.05
❑ 163 Neil Smith	.25	.11
❑ 164 Jim Everett	.10	.05
❑ 165 Derrick Thomas	.25	.11
❑ 166 John L. Williams	.05	.02
❑ 167 Timm Rosenbach	.05	.02
❑ 168 Leslie O'Neal	.10	.05
❑ 169 Clarence Verdin	.05	.02
❑ 170 Dave Krieg	.10	.05
❑ 171 Steve Broussard	.05	.02
❑ 172 Emmitt Smith	2.00	.90
❑ 173 Andre Rison	.10	.05
❑ 174 Bruce Smith	.25	.11
❑ 175 Mark Clayton	.10	.05
❑ 176 Christian Okoye	.05	.02
❑ 177 Duane Bickett	.05	.02
❑ 178 Stephone Paige	.05	.02
❑ 179 Fredd Young	.05	.02
❑ 180 Mervyn Fernandez	.05	.02
❑ 181 Phil Simms	.10	.05
❑ 182 Pete Holohan	.05	.02
❑ 183 Pepper Johnson	.05	.02
❑ 184 Jackie Slater	.05	.02
❑ 185 Stephen Baker	.05	.02
❑ 186 Frank Cornish	.05	.02
❑ 187 Dave Waymer	.05	.02
❑ 188 Terance Mathis	.10	.05
❑ 189 Darryl Talley	.05	.02
❑ 190 James Hasty	.05	.02
❑ 191 Jay Schroeder	.05	.02
❑ 192 Kenneth Davis	.05	.02
❑ 193 Chris Miller	.10	.05
❑ 194 Scott Davis	.05	.02
❑ 195 Tim Green	.05	.02
❑ 196 Dan Saleaumua	.05	.02
❑ 197 Rohn Stark	.05	.02
❑ 198 John Alt	.05	.02
❑ 199 Steve Tasker	.10	.05
❑ 200 Checklist 101-200	.05	.02
❑ 201 Freddie Joe Nunn	.05	.02
❑ 202 Jim Breech	.05	.02
❑ 203 Roy Green	.05	.02
❑ 204 Gary Anderson RB	.05	.02
❑ 205 Rich Camarillo	.05	.02
❑ 206 Mark Bortz	.05	.02
❑ 207 Eddie Brown	.05	.02
❑ 208 Brad Muster	.05	.02
❑ 209 Anthony Munoz	.10	.05
❑ 210 Dalton Hilliard	.05	.02
❑ 211 Erik McMillan	.05	.02
❑ 212 Perry Kemp	.05	.02
❑ 213 Jim Thornton	.05	.02
❑ 214 Anthony Dilweg	.05	.02
❑ 215 Cleveland Gary	.05	.02
❑ 216 Leo Goeas	.05	.02
❑ 217 Mike Merriweather	.05	.02
❑ 218 Courtney Hall	.05	.02
❑ 219 Wade Wilson	.10	.05
❑ 220 Billy Joe Tolliver	.05	.02
❑ 221 Harold Green	.10	.05
❑ 222 Al(Bubba) Baker	.10	.05
❑ 223 Carl Zander	.05	.02
❑ 224 Thane Gash	.05	.02
❑ 225 Kevin Mack	.05	.02
❑ 226 Morten Andersen	.05	.02
❑ 227 Dennis Gentry	.05	.02
❑ 228 Vince Buck	.05	.02
❑ 229 Mike Singletary	.10	.05
❑ 230 Rueben Mayes	.05	.02
❑ 231 Mark Carrier WR	.25	.11
❑ 232 Tony Mandarich	.05	.02
❑ 233 Al Toon	.10	.05
❑ 234 Renaldo Turnbull	.05	.02
❑ 235 Broderick Thomas	.05	.02
❑ 236 Anthony Carter	.10	.05
❑ 237 Flipper Anderson	.05	.02
❑ 238 Jerry Robinson	.05	.02
❑ 239 Vince Newsome	.05	.02
❑ 240 Keith Millard	.05	.02
❑ 241 Reggie Langhorne	.05	.02
❑ 242 James Francis	.05	.02
❑ 243 Felix Wright	.05	.02
❑ 244 Neal Anderson	.10	.05
❑ 245 Boomer Esiason	.10	.05
❑ 246 Pat Swilling	.10	.05
❑ 247 Richard Dent	.10	.05
❑ 248 Craig Heyward	.10	.05
❑ 249 Ron Morris	.05	.02
❑ 250 Eric Martin	.05	.02
❑ 251 Jim C. Jensen	.05	.02
❑ 252 Anthony Toney	.05	.02
❑ 253 Sammie Smith	.05	.02
❑ 254 Calvin Williams	.10	.05
❑ 255 Dan Marino	1.25	.55
❑ 256 Warren Moon	.25	.11
❑ 257 Tommie Agee	.05	.02
❑ 258 Haywood Jeffires	.10	.05

❑ 259 Eugene Lockhart .05 .02
❑ 260 Drew Hill .05 .02
❑ 261 Vinny Testaverde .10 .05
❑ 262 Jim Arnold .05 .02
❑ 263 Steve Christie .05 .02
❑ 264 Chris Spielman .10 .05
❑ 265 Reggie Cobb .05 .02
❑ 266 John Stephens .05 .02
❑ 267 Jay Hilgenberg .05 .02
❑ 268 Brent Williams .05 .02
❑ 269 Rodney Hampton .25 .11
❑ 270 Irving Fryar .10 .05
❑ 271 Terry McDaniel .05 .02
❑ 272 Reggie Roby .05 .02
❑ 273 Allen Pinkett .05 .02
❑ 274 Tim McKyer .05 .02
❑ 275 Bob Golic .05 .02
❑ 276 Wilber Marshall .05 .02
❑ 277 Ray Childress .05 .02
❑ 278 Charles Mann .05 .02
❑ 279 Cris Dishman RC .05 .02
❑ 280 Mark Rypien .10 .05
❑ 281 Michael Cofer .05 .02
❑ 282 Keith Byars .05 .02
❑ 283 Mike Rozier .05 .02
❑ 284 Seth Joyner .10 .05
❑ 285 Jessie Tuggle .05 .02
❑ 286 Mark Bavaro .05 .02
❑ 287 Eddie Anderson .05 .02
❑ 288 Sean Landeta .05 .02
❑ 289 Howie Long .25 .11
(With George Brett)
❑ 290 Reyna Thompson .05 .02
❑ 291 Ferrell Edmunds .05 .02
❑ 292 Willie Gault .10 .05
❑ 293 John Offerdahl .05 .02
❑ 294 Tim Brown .25 .11
❑ 295 Bruce Matthews .10 .05
❑ 296 Kevin Ross .05 .02
❑ 297 Lorenzo White .05 .02
❑ 298 Dino Hackett .05 .02
❑ 299 Curtis Duncan .05 .02
❑ 300 Checklist 201-300 .05 .02
❑ 301 Andre Ware .10 .05
❑ 302 David Little .05 .02
❑ 303 Jerry Ball .05 .02
❑ 304 Dwight Stone UER .05 .02
(He's a WR; not RB)
❑ 305 Rodney Peete .10 .05
❑ 306 Mike Baab .05 .02
❑ 307 Tim Worley .05 .02
❑ 308 Paul Farren .05 .02
❑ 309 Carnell Lake .05 .02
❑ 310 Clay Matthews .10 .05
❑ 311 Alton Montgomery .05 .02
❑ 312 Ernest Givins .10 .05
❑ 313 Mike Horan .05 .02
❑ 314 Sean Jones .10 .05
❑ 315 Leonard Smith .05 .02
❑ 316 Carl Banks .05 .02
❑ 317 Jerome Brown .05 .02
❑ 318 Everson Walls .05 .02
❑ 319 Ron Heller .05 .02
❑ 320 Mark Collins .05 .02
❑ 321 Eddie Murray .05 .02
❑ 322 Jim Harbaugh .25 .11
❑ 323 Mel Gray .10 .05
❑ 324 Keith Van Horne .05 .02
❑ 325 Lomas Brown .05 .02
❑ 326 Carl Lee .05 .02
❑ 327 Ken O'Brien .05 .02
❑ 328 Dermontti Dawson .05 .02
❑ 329 Brad Baxter .05 .02
❑ 330 Chris Doleman .05 .02
❑ 331 Louis Oliver .05 .02
❑ 332 Frank Stams .05 .02
❑ 333 Mike Munchak .10 .05
❑ 334 Fred Strickland .05 .02
❑ 335 Mark Duper .10 .05
❑ 336 Jacob Green .05 .02
❑ 337 Tony Paige .05 .02
❑ 338 Jeff Bryant .05 .02
❑ 339 Lemuel Stinson .05 .02
❑ 340 David Wyman .05 .02
❑ 341 Lee Williams .05 .02
❑ 342 Trace Armstrong .05 .02
❑ 343 Junior Seau .25 .11
❑ 344 John Roper .05 .02
❑ 345 Jeff George .25 .11
❑ 346 Herschel Walker .10 .05
❑ 347 Sam Clancy .05 .02
❑ 348 Steve Jordan .05 .02
❑ 349 Nate Odomes .05 .02
❑ 350 Martin Bayless .05 .02
❑ 351 Brent Jones .25 .11
❑ 352 Ray Agnew .05 .02
❑ 353 Charles Haley .10 .05
❑ 354 Andre Tippett .05 .02
❑ 355 Ronnie Lott .10 .05
❑ 356 Thurman Thomas .25 .11
❑ 357 Fred Barnett .25 .11
❑ 358 James Lofton .10 .05
❑ 359 William Frizzell RC .05 .02
❑ 360 Keith McKeller .05 .02
❑ 361 Rodney Holman .05 .02
❑ 362 Henry Ellard .10 .05
❑ 363 David Fulcher .05 .02
❑ 364 Jerry Gray .05 .02
❑ 365 James Brooks .10 .05
❑ 366 Tony Stargell .05 .02
❑ 367 Keith McCants .05 .02
❑ 368 Lewis Billups .05 .02
❑ 369 Ervin Randle .05 .02
❑ 370 Pat Leahy .05 .02
❑ 371 Bruce Armstrong .05 .02
❑ 372 Steve DeBerg .05 .02
❑ 373 Guy McIntyre .05 .02
❑ 374 Deron Cherry .05 .02
❑ 375 Fred Marion .05 .02
❑ 376 Michael Haddix .05 .02
❑ 377 Kent Hull .05 .02
❑ 378 Jerry Holmes .05 .02
❑ 379 Jim Ritcher .05 .02
❑ 380 Ed West .05 .02
❑ 381 Richmond Webb .05 .02
❑ 382 Mark Jackson .05 .02
❑ 383 Tom Newberry .05 .02
❑ 384 Ricky Nattiel .05 .02
❑ 385 Keith Sims .05 .02
❑ 386 Ron Hall .05 .02
❑ 387 Ken Norton .10 .05
❑ 388 Paul Gruber .05 .02
❑ 389 Daniel Stubbs .05 .02
❑ 390 Ian Beckles .05 .02
❑ 391 Hoby Brenner .05 .02
❑ 392 Tory Epps .05 .02
❑ 393 Sam Mills .05 .02
❑ 394 Chris Hinton .05 .02
❑ 395 Steve Walsh .05 .02
❑ 396 Simon Fletcher .05 .02
❑ 397 Tony Bennett .10 .05
❑ 398 Aundray Bruce .05 .02
❑ 399 Mark Murphy .05 .02
❑ 400 Checklist 301-400 .05 .02
❑ 401 Barry Sanders LL .50 .23
❑ 402 Jerry Rice LL .40 .18
❑ 403 Warren Moon LL .10 .05
❑ 404 Derrick Thomas LL .10 .05
❑ 405 Nick Lowery LL .05 .02
❑ 406 Mark Carrier DB LL .10 .05
❑ 407 Michael Carter .05 .02
❑ 408 Chris Singleton .05 .02
❑ 409 Matt Millen .10 .05
❑ 410 Ronnie Lippett .05 .02
❑ 411 E.J. Junior .05 .02
❑ 412 Ray Donaldson .05 .02
❑ 413 Keith Willis .05 .02
❑ 414 Jessie Hester .05 .02
❑ 415 Jeff Cross .05 .02
❑ 416 Greg Jackson RC .05 .02
❑ 417 Alvin Walton .05 .02
❑ 418 Bart Oates .05 .02
❑ 419 Chip Lohmiller .05 .02
❑ 420 John Elliott .05 .02
❑ 421 Randall McDaniel .05 .02
❑ 422 Richard Johnson RC .05 .02
❑ 423 Al Noga .05 .02
❑ 424 Lamar Lathon .05 .02
❑ 425 Rick Fenney .05 .02
❑ 426 Jack Del Rio .10 .05
❑ 427 Don Mosebar .05 .02
❑ 428 Luis Sharpe .05 .02
❑ 429 Steve Wisniewski .05 .02
❑ 430 Jimmie Jones .05 .02
❑ 431 Freeman McNeil .05 .02
❑ 432 Ron Rivera .05 .02
❑ 433 Hart Lee Dykes .05 .02
❑ 434 Mark Carrier DB .10 .05
❑ 435 Rob Moore .25 .11
❑ 436 Gary Clark .25 .11
❑ 437 Heath Sherman .05 .02
❑ 438 Darrell Green .05 .02
❑ 439 Jessie Small .05 .02
❑ 440 Monte Coleman .05 .02
❑ 441 Leonard Marshall .05 .02
❑ 442 Richard Johnson .05 .02
❑ 443 Dave Meggett .10 .05
❑ 444 Barry Sanders 1.25 .55
❑ 445 Lawrence Taylor .25 .11
❑ 446 Marcus Allen .25 .11
❑ 447 Johnny Johnson .05 .02
❑ 448 Aaron Wallace .05 .02
❑ 449 Anthony Thompson .05 .02
❑ 450 Steve DeBerg .40 .18
Dan Marino
Team MVP CL 453-473
❑ 451 Andre Rison MVP .10 .05
❑ 452 Thurman Thomas MVP .10 .05
❑ 453 Neal Anderson MVP .05 .02
❑ 454 Boomer Esiason MVP .05 .02
❑ 455 Eric Metcalf MVP .10 .05
❑ 456 Emmitt Smith MVP 1.00 .45
❑ 457 Bobby Humphrey MVP .05 .02
❑ 458 Barry Sanders MVP .50 .23
❑ 459 Sterling Sharpe MVP .10 .05
❑ 460 Warren Moon MVP .10 .05
❑ 461 Albert Bentley MVP .05 .02
❑ 462 Steve DeBerg MVP .05 .02
❑ 463 Greg Townsend MVP .05 .02
❑ 464 Henry Ellard MVP .10 .05
❑ 465 Dan Marino MVP .50 .23
❑ 466 Anthony Carter MVP .10 .05
❑ 467 John Stephens MVP .05 .02
❑ 468 Pat Swilling MVP .05 .02
❑ 469 Ottis Anderson MVP .10 .05
❑ 470 Dennis Byrd MVP .05 .02
❑ 471 Randall Cunningham .10 .05
MVP
❑ 472 Johnny Johnson MVP .05 .02
❑ 473 Rod Woodson MVP .10 .05
❑ 474 Anthony Miller MVP .10 .05
❑ 475 Jerry Rice MVP .40 .18
❑ 476 John L.Williams MVP .05 .02
❑ 477 Wayne Haddix MVP .05 .02
❑ 478 Earnest Byner MVP .05 .02
❑ 479 Doug Widell .05 .02
❑ 480 Tommy Hodson .05 .02
❑ 481 Shawn Collins .05 .02
❑ 482 Rickey Jackson .05 .02
❑ 483 Tony Casillas .05 .02
❑ 484 Vaughan Johnson .05 .02
❑ 485 Floyd Dixon .05 .02
❑ 486 Eric Green .05 .02
❑ 487 Harry Hamilton .05 .02
❑ 488 Gary Anderson K .05 .02
❑ 489 Bruce Hill .05 .02
❑ 490 Gerald Williams .05 .02
❑ 491 Cortez Kennedy .25 .11
❑ 492 Chet Brooks .05 .02
❑ 493 Dwayne Harper RC .05 .02
❑ 494 Don Griffin .05 .02
❑ 495 Andy Heck .05 .02
❑ 496 David Treadwell .05 .02
❑ 497 Irv Pankey .05 .02
❑ 498 Dennis Smith .05 .02
❑ 499 Marcus Dupree .05 .02
❑ 500 Checklist 401-500 .05 .02
❑ 501 Wendell Davis .05 .02
❑ 502 Matt Bahr .05 .02
❑ 503 Rob Burnett RC .10 .05
❑ 504 Maurice Carthon .05 .02
❑ 505 Donnell Woolford .05 .02
❑ 506 Howard Ballard .05 .02
❑ 507 Mark Boyer .05 .02
❑ 508 Eugene Marve .05 .02

❑ 509 Joe Kelly	.05	.02
❑ 510 Will Wolford	.05	.02
❑ 511 Robert Clark	.05	.02
❑ 512 Matt Brock RC	.05	.02
❑ 513 Chris Warren	.25	.11
❑ 514 Ken Willis	.05	.02
❑ 515 George Jamison RC	.05	.02
❑ 516 Rufus Porter	.05	.02
❑ 517 Mark Higgs RC	.05	.02
❑ 518 Thomas Everett	.05	.02
❑ 519 Robert Brown	.05	.02
❑ 520 Gene Atkins	.05	.02
❑ 521 Hardy Nickerson	.10	.05
❑ 522 Johnny Bailey	.05	.02
❑ 523 William Frizzell	.05	.02
❑ 524 Steve McMichael	.10	.05
❑ 525 Kevin Porter	.05	.02
❑ 526 Carwell Gardner	.05	.02
❑ 527 Eugene Daniel	.05	.02
❑ 528 Vestee Jackson	.05	.02
❑ 529 Chris Goode	.05	.02
❑ 530 Leon Seals	.05	.02
❑ 531 Darion Conner	.05	.02
❑ 532 Stan Brock	.05	.02
❑ 533 Kirby Jackson RC	.05	.02
❑ 534 Marv Cook	.05	.02
❑ 535 Bill Fralic	.05	.02
❑ 536 Keith Woodside	.05	.02
❑ 537 Hugh Green	.05	.02
❑ 538 Grant Feasel	.05	.02
❑ 539 Bubba McDowell	.05	.02
❑ 540 Vai Sikahema	.05	.02
❑ 541 Aaron Cox	.05	.02
❑ 542 Roger Craig	.10	.05
❑ 543 Robb Thomas	.05	.02
❑ 544 Ronnie Lott	.10	.05
❑ 545 Robert Delpino	.05	.02
❑ 546 Greg McMurtry	.05	.02
❑ 547 Jim Morrissey RC	.05	.02
❑ 548 Johnny Rembert	.05	.02
❑ 549 Markus Paul RC	.05	.02
❑ 550 Karl Wilson RC	.05	.02
❑ 551 Gaston Green	.05	.02
❑ 552 Willie Drewrey	.05	.02
❑ 553 Michael Young	.05	.02
❑ 554 Tom Tupa	.05	.02
❑ 555 John Friesz	.25	.11
❑ 556 Cody Carlson RC	.05	.02
❑ 557 Eric Allen	.05	.02
❑ 558 Thomas Benson	.05	.02
❑ 559 Scott Mersereau RC	.05	.02
❑ 560 Lionel Washington	.05	.02
❑ 561 Brian Brennan	.05	.02
❑ 562 Jim Jeffcoat	.05	.02
❑ 563 Jeff Jaeger	.05	.02
❑ 564 D.J. Johnson	.05	.02
❑ 565 Danny Villa	.05	.02
❑ 566 Don Beebe	.05	.02
❑ 567 Michael Haynes	.25	.11
❑ 568 Brett Faryniarz RC	.05	.02
❑ 569 Mike Prior	.05	.02
❑ 570 John Davis RC	.05	.02
❑ 571 Vernon Turner RC	.05	.02
❑ 572 Michael Brooks	.05	.02
❑ 573 Mike Gann	.05	.02
❑ 574 Ron Holmes	.05	.02
❑ 575 Gary Plummer	.05	.02
❑ 576 Bill Romanowski	.05	.02
❑ 577 Chris Jacke	.05	.02
❑ 578 Gary Reasons	.05	.02
❑ 579 Tim Jorden RC	.05	.02
❑ 580 Tim McKyer	.05	.02
❑ 581 Johnnie Jackson RC	.05	.02
❑ 582 Ethan Horton	.05	.02
❑ 583 Pete Stoyanovich	.05	.02
❑ 584 Jeff Query	.05	.02
❑ 585 Frank Reich	.10	.05
❑ 586 Riki Ellison	.05	.02
❑ 587 Eric Hill	.05	.02
❑ 588 Anthony Shelton RC	.05	.02
❑ 589 Steve Smith	.05	.02
❑ 590 Garth Jax RC	.05	.02
❑ 591 Greg Davis RC	.05	.02
❑ 592 Bill Maas	.05	.02
❑ 593 Henry Rolling RC	.05	.02
❑ 594 Keith Jones	.05	.02
❑ 595 Tootie Robbins	.05	.02
❑ 596 Brian Jordan	.10	.05
❑ 597 Derrick Walker RC	.05	.02
❑ 598 Jonathan Hayes	.05	.02
❑ 599 Nate Lewis RC	.05	.02
❑ 600 Checklist 501-600	.05	.02
❑ 601 AFC Checklist RF	.05	.02
Mike Croel		
Greg Lewis		
Keith Traylor		
Kenny Walker		
❑ 602 James Jones RF RC	.05	.02
❑ 603 Tim Barnett RF RC	.05	.02
❑ 604 Ed King RF RC	.05	.02
❑ 605 Shane Curry RF	.05	.02
❑ 606 Mike Croel RF	.05	.02
❑ 607 Bryan Cox RF RC	.25	.11
❑ 608 Shawn Jefferson RF RC	.10	.05
❑ 609 Kenny Walker RF RC	.05	.02
❑ 610 Michael Jackson RF RC	.25	.11
❑ 611 Jon Vaughn RF RC	.05	.02
❑ 612 Greg Lewis RF	.05	.02
❑ 613 Joe Valerio RF	.05	.02
❑ 614 Pat Harlow RF RC	.05	.02
❑ 615 Henry Jones RF RC	.10	.05
❑ 616 Jeff Graham RF RC	.25	.11
❑ 617 Darryll Lewis RF RC	.10	.05
❑ 618 Keith Traylor RF RC UER	.05	.02
(Bronchos on back)		
❑ 619 Scott Miller RF	.05	.02
❑ 620 Nick Bell RF	.05	.02
❑ 621 John Flannery RF RC	.05	.02
❑ 622 Leonard Russell RF RC	.10	.05
❑ 623 Alfred Williams RF RC	.05	.02
❑ 624 Browning Nagle RF	.05	.02
❑ 625 Harvey Williams RF	.10	.05
❑ 626 Dan McGwire RF	.05	.02
❑ 627 NFC Checklist RF	.50	.23
Brett Favre		
Moe Gardner		
Erric Pegram		
Bruce Pickens		
Mike Pritchard		
❑ 628 William Thomas RF RC	.05	.02
❑ 629 L.Dawsey RF RC	.10	.05
❑ 630 Aeneas Williams RF RC	.25	.11
❑ 631 Stan Thomas RF	.05	.02
❑ 632 Randal Hill RF	.05	.02
❑ 633 Moe Gardner RF RC	.05	.02
❑ 634 Alvin Harper RF	.10	.05
❑ 635 Esera Tuaolo RF RC	.05	.02
❑ 636 Russell Maryland RF	.10	.05
❑ 637 Anthony Morgan RF RC	.05	.02
❑ 638 Erric Pegram RF RC	.25	.11
❑ 639 Herman Moore RF	.25	.11
❑ 640 Ricky Ervins RF RC	.10	.05
❑ 641 Kelvin Pritchett RF RC	.10	.05
❑ 642 Roman Phifer RF RC	.05	.02
❑ 643 Antone Davis RF RC	.05	.02
❑ 644 Mike Pritchard RF	.10	.05
❑ 645 Vinnie Clark RF RC	.05	.02
❑ 646 Jake Reed RF RC	.50	.23
❑ 647 Brett Favre RF	4.00	1.80
❑ 648 Todd Lyght RF	.05	.02
❑ 649 Bruce Pickens RF	.05	.02
❑ 650 Darren Lewis RF RC	.05	.02
❑ 651 Wesley Carroll RF	.05	.02
❑ 652 James Joseph RF RC	.10	.05
❑ 653 Robert Delpino AR	.05	.02
Tim McDonald		
❑ 654 Vencie Glenn AR	.05	.02
Deion Sanders		
❑ 655 Jerry Rice AR	.30	.14
Terry McDaniel		
❑ 656 Barry Sanders AR	.50	.23
Derrick Thomas		
❑ 657 Ken Tippins AR	.05	.02
Lorenzo White		
❑ 658 Christian Okoye AR	.05	.02
Jacob Green		
❑ 659 Rich Gannon	.25	.11
❑ 660 Johnny Meads	.05	.02
❑ 661 J.J. Birden RC	.10	.05
❑ 662 Bruce Kozerski	.05	.02
❑ 663 Felix Wright	.05	.02
❑ 664 Al Smith	.05	.02
❑ 665 Stan Humphries	.25	.11
❑ 666 Alfred Anderson	.05	.02
❑ 667 Nate Newton	.10	.05
❑ 668 Vince Workman RC	.10	.05
❑ 669 Ricky Reynolds	.05	.02
❑ 670 Bryce Paup RC	.25	.11
❑ 671 Gill Fenerty	.05	.02
❑ 672 Darrell Thompson	.05	.02
❑ 673 Anthony Smith	.05	.02
❑ 674 Darryl Henley RC	.05	.02
❑ 675 Brett Maxie	.05	.02
❑ 676 Craig Taylor RC	.05	.02
❑ 677 Steve Wallace	.10	.05
❑ 678 Jeff Feagles RC	.05	.02
❑ 679 James Washington RC	.05	.02
❑ 680 Tim Harris	.05	.02
❑ 681 Dennis Gibson	.05	.02
❑ 682 Toi Cook RC	.05	.02
❑ 683 Lorenzo Lynch	.05	.02
❑ 684 Brad Edwards RC	.05	.02
❑ 685 Ray Crockett RC	.05	.02
❑ 686 Harris Barton	.05	.02
❑ 687 Byron Evans	.05	.02
❑ 688 Eric Thomas	.05	.02
❑ 689 Jeff Criswell	.05	.02
❑ 690 Eric Ball	.05	.02
❑ 691 Brian Mitchell	.10	.05
❑ 692 Quinn Early	.10	.05
❑ 693 Aaron Jones	.05	.02
❑ 694 Jim Dombrowski	.05	.02
❑ 695 Jeff Bostic	.05	.02
❑ 696 Tony Casillas	.05	.02
❑ 697 Ken Lanier	.05	.02
❑ 698 Henry Thomas	.05	.02
❑ 699 Steve Beuerlein	.10	.05
❑ 700 Checklist 601-700	.05	.02
❑ P1 Joe Montana Promo	2.50	1.10
Numbered 1		
❑ P2 Barry Sanders Promo	2.00	.90
Numbered 500		
❑ SP1 Darrell Green	.50	.23
NFL's Fastest Man		
❑ SP2 Don Shula CO	2.00	.90
300th Victory		

1991 Upper Deck Joe Montana Heroes

	Nm-Mt	Ex-Mt
COMPLETE SET (10)	10.00	4.50
COMMON MONTANA (1-9)	.75	.35
❑ AU Joe Montana AUTO (Certified Autograph)	150.00	70.00
❑ NNO Title/Header Card SP	8.00	3.60

1991 Upper Deck Joe Namath Heroes

	Nm-Mt	Ex-Mt
COMPLETE SET (10)	10.00	4.50
COMMON NAMATH (10-18)	.75	.35
❑ AU Joe Namath AUTO (Certified Autograph)	120.00	55.00
❑ NNO Title/Header Card SP	8.00	3.60

1992 Upper Deck Dan Marino Heroes

	Nm-Mt	Ex-Mt
COMPLETE SET (10)	25.00	11.00
COMMON MARINO (28-36)	3.00	1.35
MARINO HEADER (NNO)	5.00	2.20
❑ NNO Dan Marino AUTO Header Card UDA #'d of 2800	100.00	45.00

1992 Upper Deck Walter Payton Heroes

	Nm-Mt	Ex-Mt
COMPLETE SET (10)	25.00	11.00
COMMON PAYTON (19-27)	3.00	1.35
PAYTON HEADER (NNO)	5.00	2.20
❑ NNO Walter Payton AUTO Header Card UDA #'d of 2800	175.00	80.00

1996 Upper Deck Game Jerseys

	Nm-Mt	Ex-Mt
❑ GJ1 Dan Marino Teal	300.00	135.00
❑ GJ2 Jerry Rice Red	200.00	90.00
❑ GJ3 Joe Montana	300.00	135.00
❑ GJ4 Jerry Rice White	200.00	90.00
❑ GJ5 Rashaan Salaam	40.00	18.00
❑ GJ6 Marshall Faulk	100.00	45.00
❑ GJ7 Dan Marino White	300.00	135.00
❑ GJ8 Steve Young	120.00	55.00

❑ GJ9 Barry Sanders	250.00	110.00
❑ GJ10 Mark Brunell	60.00	27.00

1997 Upper Deck Game Jerseys

	Nm-Mt	Ex-Mt
❑ GJ1 Warren Moon	60.00	27.00
❑ GJ2 Joey Galloway	40.00	18.00
❑ GJ3 Terrell Davis	80.00	36.00
❑ GJ4 Brett Favre (green jersey)	200.00	90.00
❑ GJ5 Brett Favre (white jersey)	200.00	90.00
❑ GJ6 Reggie White	80.00	36.00
❑ GJ7 John Elway	200.00	90.00
❑ GJ8 Troy Aikman	100.00	45.00
❑ GJ9 Carl Pickens	40.00	18.00
❑ GJ10 Herman Moore	40.00	18.00

1998 Upper Deck

	Nm-Mt	Ex-Mt
COMPLETE SET (255)	200.00	90.00
COMP.SET w/o SP's (213)	25.00	11.00
❑ 1 Peyton Manning RC	50.00	22.00
❑ 2 Ryan Leaf RC	5.00	2.20
❑ 3 Andre Wadsworth RC	3.00	1.35
❑ 4 Charles Woodson RC	6.00	2.70
❑ 5 Curtis Enis RC	2.50	1.10
❑ 6 Grant Wistrom RC	3.00	1.35
❑ 7 Greg Ellis RC	2.50	1.10
❑ 8 Fred Taylor RC	8.00	3.60
❑ 9 Duane Starks RC	2.50	1.10
❑ 10 Keith Brooking RC	5.00	2.20
❑ 11 Takeo Spikes RC	5.00	2.20
❑ 12 Jason Peter RC	2.50	1.10
❑ 13 Anthony Simmons RC	3.00	1.35
❑ 14 Kevin Dyson RC	5.00	2.20
❑ 15 Brian Simmons RC	3.00	1.35
❑ 16 Robert Edwards RC	3.00	1.35
❑ 17 Randy Moss RC	25.00	11.00
❑ 18 John Avery RC	3.00	1.35
❑ 19 Marcus Nash RC	2.50	1.10
❑ 20 Jerome Pathon RC	5.00	2.20
❑ 21 Jacquez Green RC	3.00	1.35
❑ 22 Robert Holcombe RC	3.00	1.35
❑ 23 Pat Johnson RC	3.00	1.35
❑ 24 Germane Crowell RC	3.00	1.35
❑ 25 Joe Jurevicius RC	5.00	2.20
❑ 26 Skip Hicks RC	3.00	1.35
❑ 27 Ahman Green RC	25.00	11.00
❑ 28 Brian Griese RC	10.00	4.50
❑ 29 Hines Ward RC	12.00	5.50
❑ 30 Tavian Banks RC	3.00	1.35
❑ 31 Tony Simmons RC	3.00	1.35
❑ 32 Victor Riley RC	2.50	1.10
❑ 33 Rashaan Shehee RC	3.00	1.35
❑ 34 R.W. McQuarters RC	3.00	1.35
❑ 35 Flozell Adams RC	2.50	1.10
❑ 36 Tra Thomas RC	2.50	1.10
❑ 37 Greg Favors RC	3.00	1.35
❑ 38 Jon Ritchie RC	3.00	1.35
❑ 39 Jesse Haynes RC	2.50	1.10
❑ 40 Ryan Sutter RC	2.50	1.10
❑ 41 Mo Collins RC	2.50	1.10
❑ 42 Tim Dwight RC	5.00	2.20
❑ 43 Chris Chandler	.40	.18
❑ 44 Byron Hanspard	.25	.11
❑ 45 Jessie Tuggle	.25	.11
❑ 46 Jamal Anderson	.60	.25
❑ 47 Terance Mathis	.40	.18
❑ 48 Morten Andersen	.25	.11
❑ 49 Jake Plummer	.60	.25
❑ 50 Mario Bates	.40	.18
❑ 51 Frank Sanders	.40	.18
❑ 52 Adrian Murrell	.40	.18
❑ 53 Simeon Rice	.40	.18
❑ 54 Aeneas Williams	.25	.11
❑ 55 Eric Swann UER (number on back 98)	.25	.11
❑ 56 Jim Harbaugh	.40	.18
❑ 57 Michael Jackson	.25	.11
❑ 58 Peter Boulware	.25	.11
❑ 59 Errict Rhett	.40	.18
❑ 60 Jermaine Lewis	.40	.18
❑ 61 Eric Zeier	.40	.18
❑ 62 Rod Woodson	.40	.18
❑ 63 Rob Johnson	.60	.25
❑ 64 Antowain Smith	.60	.25
❑ 65 Bruce Smith	.40	.18
❑ 66 Eric Moulds	.60	.25
❑ 67 Andre Reed	.40	.18
❑ 68 Thurman Thomas	.60	.25
❑ 69 Lonnie Johnson	.25	.11
❑ 70 Kerry Collins	.40	.18
❑ 71 Kevin Greene	.40	.18
❑ 72 Fred Lane	.25	.11
❑ 73 Rae Carruth	.25	.11
❑ 74 Michael Bates	.25	.11
❑ 75 William Floyd	.25	.11
❑ 76 Sean Gilbert	.25	.11
❑ 77 Erik Kramer	.25	.11
❑ 78 Edgar Bennett	.25	.11
❑ 79 Curtis Conway	.40	.18
❑ 80 Darnell Autry	.25	.11
❑ 81 Ryan Wetnight RC	.25	.11
❑ 82 Walt Harris	.25	.11
❑ 83 Bobby Engram	.40	.18
❑ 84 Jeff Blake	.40	.18
❑ 85 Carl Pickens	.40	.18
❑ 86 Darnay Scott	.40	.18
❑ 87 Corey Dillon	.60	.25
❑ 88 Reinard Wilson	.25	.11
❑ 89 Ashley Ambrose	.25	.11
❑ 90 Troy Aikman	1.25	.55
❑ 91 Michael Irvin	.60	.25
❑ 92 Emmitt Smith	2.00	.90
❑ 93 Deion Sanders	.60	.25
❑ 94 David LaFleur	.25	.11

❑ 95 Chris Warren	.40	.18
❑ 96 Darren Woodson	.25	.11
❑ 97 John Elway	2.50	1.10
❑ 98 Terrell Davis	.60	.25
❑ 99 Rod Smith	.40	.18
❑ 100 Shannon Sharpe	.40	.18
❑ 101 Ed McCaffrey	.40	.18
❑ 102 Steve Atwater	.25	.11
❑ 103 John Mobley	.25	.11
❑ 104 Darrien Gordon	.25	.11
❑ 105 Barry Sanders	2.00	.90
❑ 106 Scott Mitchell	.40	.18
❑ 107 Herman Moore	.40	.18
❑ 108 Johnnie Morton	.40	.18
❑ 109 Robert Porcher	.25	.11
❑ 110 Bryant Westbrook	.25	.11
❑ 111 Tommy Vardell	.25	.11
❑ 112 Brett Favre	2.50	1.10
❑ 113 Dorsey Levens	.60	.25
❑ 114 Reggie White	.60	.25
❑ 115 Antonio Freeman	.60	.25
❑ 116 Robert Brooks	.40	.18
❑ 117 Mark Chmura	.40	.18
❑ 118 Derrick Mayes	.40	.18
❑ 119 Gilbert Brown	.25	.11
❑ 120 Marshall Faulk	.75	.35
❑ 121 Jeff Burris	.25	.11
❑ 122 Marvin Harrison	.60	.25
❑ 123 Quentin Coryatt	.25	.11
❑ 124 Ken Dilger	.25	.11
❑ 125 Zack Crockett	.25	.11
❑ 126 Mark Brunell	.60	.25
❑ 127 Bryce Paup	.25	.11
❑ 128 Tony Brackens	.25	.11
❑ 129 Renaldo Wynn	.25	.11
❑ 130 Keenan McCardell	.40	.18
❑ 131 Jimmy Smith	.40	.18
❑ 132 Kevin Hardy	.25	.11
❑ 133 Elvis Grbac	.40	.18
❑ 134 Tamarick Vanover	.25	.11
❑ 135 Chester McGlockton	.25	.11
❑ 136 Andre Rison	.40	.18
❑ 137 Derrick Alexander	.40	.18
❑ 138 Tony Gonzalez	.60	.25
❑ 139 Derrick Thomas	.40	.18
❑ 140 Dan Marino	2.50	1.10
❑ 141 Karim Abdul-Jabbar	.60	.25
❑ 142 O.J. McDuffie	.40	.18
❑ 143 Yatil Green	.25	.11
❑ 144 Charles Jordan	.25	.11
❑ 145 Brock Marion	.25	.11
❑ 146 Zach Thomas	.60	.25
❑ 147 Brad Johnson	.60	.25
❑ 148 Cris Carter	.60	.25
❑ 149 Jake Reed	.40	.18
❑ 150 Robert Smith	.60	.25
❑ 151 John Randle	.40	.18
❑ 152 Dwayne Rudd	.25	.11
❑ 153 Randall Cunningham	.60	.25
❑ 154 Drew Bledsoe	1.00	.45
❑ 155 Terry Glenn	.60	.25
❑ 156 Ben Coates	.40	.18
❑ 157 Willie Clay	.25	.11
❑ 158 Chris Slade	.25	.11
❑ 159 Derrick Cullors RC	.25	.11
❑ 160 Ty Law	.40	.18
❑ 161 Danny Wuerffel	.40	.18
❑ 162 Andre Hastings	.25	.11
❑ 163 Troy Davis	.25	.11
❑ 164 Billy Joe Hobert	.25	.11
❑ 165 Eric Guliford	.25	.11
❑ 166 Mark Fields	.25	.11
❑ 167 Alex Molden	.25	.11
❑ 168 Danny Kanell	.40	.18
❑ 169 Tiki Barber	.60	.25
❑ 170 Charles Way	.25	.11
❑ 171 Amani Toomer	.40	.18
❑ 172 Michael Strahan	.40	.18
❑ 173 Jessie Armstead	.25	.11
❑ 174 Jason Sehorn	.40	.18
❑ 175 Glenn Foley	.40	.18
❑ 176 Curtis Martin	.60	.25
❑ 177 Aaron Glenn	.25	.11
❑ 178 Keyshawn Johnson	.60	.25
❑ 179 James Farrior	.25	.11
❑ 180 Wayne Chrebet	.60	.25
❑ 181 Keith Byars	.25	.11
❑ 182 Jeff George	.40	.18
❑ 183 Napoleon Kaufman	.60	.25
❑ 184 Tim Brown	.60	.25
❑ 185 Darrell Russell	.25	.11
❑ 186 Rickey Dudley	.25	.11
❑ 187 James Jett	.40	.18
❑ 188 Desmond Howard	.40	.18
❑ 189 Bobby Hoying	.40	.18
❑ 190 Charlie Garner	.40	.18
❑ 191 Irving Fryar	.40	.18
❑ 192 Chris T. Jones	.25	.11
❑ 193 Mike Mamula	.25	.11
❑ 194 Troy Vincent	.25	.11
❑ 195 Kordell Stewart	.60	.25
❑ 196 Jerome Bettis	.60	.25
❑ 197 Will Blackwell	.25	.11
❑ 198 Levon Kirkland	.25	.11
❑ 199 Carnell Lake	.25	.11
❑ 200 Charles Johnson	.25	.11
❑ 201 Greg Lloyd	.25	.11
❑ 202 Donnell Woolford	.25	.11
❑ 203 Tony Banks	.40	.18
❑ 204 Amp Lee	.25	.11
❑ 205 Isaac Bruce	.60	.25
❑ 206 Eddie Kennison	.40	.18
❑ 207 Ryan McNeil	.25	.11
❑ 208 Mike Jones	.25	.11
❑ 209 Ernie Conwell	.25	.11
❑ 210 Natrone Means	.40	.18
❑ 211 Junior Seau	.60	.25
❑ 212 Tony Martin	.40	.18
❑ 213 Freddie Jones	.25	.11
❑ 214 Bryan Still	.25	.11
❑ 215 Rodney Harrison	.40	.18
❑ 216 Steve Young	.75	.35
❑ 217 Jerry Rice	1.25	.55
❑ 218 Garrison Hearst	.60	.25
❑ 219 J.J. Stokes	.40	.18
❑ 220 Ken Norton	.25	.11
❑ 221 Greg Clark	.25	.11
❑ 222 Terrell Owens	.60	.25
❑ 223 Bryant Young	.25	.11
❑ 224 Warren Moon	.60	.25
❑ 225 Jon Kitna	.60	.25
❑ 226 Ricky Watters	.40	.18
❑ 227 Chad Brown	.25	.11
❑ 228 Joey Galloway	.40	.18
❑ 229 Shawn Springs	.25	.11
❑ 230 Cortez Kennedy	.25	.11
❑ 231 Trent Dilfer	.60	.25
❑ 232 Warrick Dunn	.60	.25
❑ 233 Mike Alstott	.60	.25
❑ 234 Warren Sapp	.40	.18
❑ 235 Bert Emanuel	.40	.18
❑ 236 Reidel Anthony	.40	.18
❑ 237 Hardy Nickerson	.25	.11
❑ 238 Derrick Brooks	.60	.25
❑ 239 Steve McNair	.60	.25
❑ 240 Yancey Thigpen	.25	.11
❑ 241 Anthony Dorsett	.25	.11
❑ 242 Blaine Bishop	.25	.11
❑ 243 Kenny Holmes	.25	.11
❑ 244 Eddie George	.60	.25
❑ 245 Chris Sanders	.25	.11
❑ 246 Gus Frerotte	.25	.11
❑ 247 Terry Allen	.60	.25
❑ 248 Dana Stubblefield	.25	.11
❑ 249 Michael Westbrook	.40	.18
❑ 250 Darrell Green	.40	.18
❑ 251 Brian Mitchell	.25	.11
❑ 252 Ken Harvey	.25	.11
❑ CL1 Troy Aikman CL	.60	.25
❑ CL2 Dan Marino CL	.75	.35
❑ CL3 Herman Moore CL	.40	.18

1998 Upper Deck Bronze

	Nm-Mt	Ex-Mt
*BRONZE STARS: 25X TO 60X BASIC CARDS		
*BRONZE RCs: 2X TO 4X BASIC CARDS		

1998 Upper Deck Game Jerseys

	Nm-Mt	Ex-Mt
❑ GJ1 Brett Favre	120.00	55.00
❑ GJ2 Reggie White	100.00	45.00
❑ GJ3 Barry Sanders	100.00	45.00
❑ GJ4 John Elway	100.00	45.00
❑ GJ5 Mark Brunell	40.00	18.00
❑ GJ6 Mike Alstott	40.00	18.00
❑ GJ7 Ryan Leaf	30.00	13.50
❑ GJ8 Andre Wadsworth	30.00	13.50
❑ GJ9 Robert Edwards	30.00	13.50
❑ GJ10 Kevin Dyson	30.00	13.50
❑ GJ11 Dan Marino	120.00	55.00
❑ GJ11S Dan Marino AUTO/13		
❑ GJ12 Deion Sanders	30.00	13.50
❑ GJ13 Steve Young	50.00	22.00
❑ GJ14 Terrell Davis	30.00	13.50
❑ GJ15 Tim Brown	30.00	13.50
❑ GJ16 Peyton Manning	250.00	110.00
❑ GJ17 Takeo Spikes	25.00	11.00
❑ GJ18 Curtis Enis	20.00	9.00
❑ GJ19 Fred Taylor	30.00	13.50
❑ GJ20 John Avery	20.00	9.00

1999 Upper Deck

	Nm-Mt	Ex-Mt
COMPLETE SET (270)	100.00	45.00
COMP.SET w/o SP's (225)	25.00	11.00
❑ 1 Jake Plummer	.50	.23
❑ 2 Adrian Murrell	.50	.23
❑ 3 Rob Moore	.50	.23
❑ 4 Larry Centers	.30	.14
❑ 5 Simeon Rice	.50	.23
❑ 6 Andre Wadsworth	.30	.14
❑ 7 Frank Sanders	.50	.23
❑ 8 Tim Dwight	.75	.35
❑ 9 Ray Buchanan	.30	.14
❑ 10 Chris Chandler	.50	.23
❑ 11 Jamal Anderson	.75	.35
❑ 12 O.J. Santiago	.30	.14
❑ 13 Danny Kanell	.30	.14
❑ 14 Terance Mathis	.50	.23
❑ 15 Priest Holmes	1.25	.55
❑ 16 Tony Banks	.50	.23
❑ 17 Ray Lewis	.75	.35
❑ 18 Patrick Johnson	.30	.14
❑ 19 Michael Jackson	.30	.14

❑ 20 Michael McCrary	.30	.14
❑ 21 Jermaine Lewis	.50	.23
❑ 22 Eric Moulds	.75	.35
❑ 23 Doug Flutie	.75	.35
❑ 24 Antowain Smith	.75	.35
❑ 25 Rob Johnson	.50	.23
❑ 26 Bruce Smith	.50	.23
❑ 27 Andre Reed	.50	.23
❑ 28 Thurman Thomas	.50	.23
❑ 29 Fred Lane	.30	.14
❑ 30 Wesley Walls	.50	.23
❑ 31 Tim Biakabutuka	.50	.23
❑ 32 Kevin Greene	.30	.14
❑ 33 Steve Beuerlein	.30	.14
❑ 34 Muhsin Muhammad	.50	.23
❑ 35 Rae Carruth	.30	.14
❑ 36 Bobby Engram	.50	.23
❑ 37 Curtis Enis	.30	.14
❑ 38 Edgar Bennett	.30	.14
❑ 39 Erik Kramer	.30	.14
❑ 40 Steve Stenstrom	.30	.14
❑ 41 Alonzo Mayes	.30	.14
❑ 42 Curtis Conway	.50	.23
❑ 43 Tony McGee	.30	.14
❑ 44 Darnay Scott	.30	.14
❑ 45 Jeff Blake	.50	.23
❑ 46 Corey Dillon	.75	.35
❑ 47 Ki-Jana Carter	.30	.14
❑ 48 Takeo Spikes	.30	.14
❑ 49 Carl Pickens	.50	.23
❑ 50 Ty Detmer	.50	.23
❑ 51 Leslie Shepherd	.30	.14
❑ 52 Terry Kirby	.30	.14
❑ 53 Marquez Pope	.30	.14
❑ 54 Antonio Langham	.30	.14
❑ 55 Jamir Miller	.30	.14
❑ 56 Derrick Alexander DT	.30	.14
❑ 57 Troy Aikman	1.50	.70
❑ 58 Rocket Ismail	.50	.23
❑ 59 Emmitt Smith	1.50	.70
❑ 60 Michael Irvin	.50	.23
❑ 61 David LaFleur	.30	.14
❑ 62 Chris Warren	.30	.14
❑ 63 Deion Sanders	.75	.35
❑ 64 Greg Ellis	.30	.14
❑ 65 John Elway	2.50	1.10
❑ 66 Bubby Brister	.30	.14
❑ 67 Terrell Davis	.75	.35
❑ 68 Ed McCaffrey	.50	.23
❑ 69 John Mobley	.30	.14
❑ 70 Bill Romanowski	.30	.14
❑ 71 Rod Smith	.50	.23
❑ 72 Shannon Sharpe	.50	.23
❑ 73 Charlie Batch	.75	.35
❑ 74 Germane Crowell	.30	.14
❑ 75 Johnnie Morton	.30	.14
❑ 76 Barry Sanders	2.50	1.10
❑ 77 Robert Porcher	.30	.14
❑ 78 Stephen Boyd	.30	.14
❑ 79 Herman Moore	.50	.23
❑ 80 Brett Favre	2.50	1.10
❑ 81 Mark Chmura	.30	.14
❑ 82 Antonio Freeman	.75	.35
❑ 83 Robert Brooks	.50	.23
❑ 84 Vonnie Holliday	.30	.14
❑ 85 Bill Schroeder	.75	.35
❑ 86 Dorsey Levens	.75	.35
❑ 87 Santana Dotson	.30	.14
❑ 88 Peyton Manning	2.50	1.10
❑ 89 Jerome Pathon	.30	.14
❑ 90 Marvin Harrison	.75	.35
❑ 91 Ellis Johnson	.30	.14
❑ 92 Ken Dilger	.30	.14
❑ 93 E.G. Green	.30	.14
❑ 94 Jeff Burris	.30	.14
❑ 95 Mark Brunell	.75	.35
❑ 96 Fred Taylor	.75	.35
❑ 97 Jimmy Smith	.50	.23
❑ 98 James Stewart	.50	.23
❑ 99 Kyle Brady	.30	.14
❑ 100 Dave Thomas RC	.30	.14
❑ 101 Keenan McCardell	.50	.23
❑ 102 Elvis Grbac	.50	.23
❑ 103 Tony Gonzalez	.75	.35
❑ 104 Andre Rison	.50	.23
❑ 105 Donnell Bennett	.30	.14
❑ 106 Derrick Thomas	.50	.23
❑ 107 Warren Moon	.75	.35
❑ 108 Derrick Alexander WR	.50	.23
❑ 109 Dan Marino	2.50	1.10
❑ 110 O.J. McDuffie	.50	.23
❑ 111 Karim Abdul-Jabbar	.50	.23
❑ 112 John Avery	.30	.14
❑ 113 Sam Madison	.30	.14
❑ 114 Jason Taylor	.30	.14
❑ 115 Zach Thomas	.75	.35
❑ 116 Randall Cunningham	.75	.35
❑ 117 Randy Moss	2.00	.90
❑ 118 Cris Carter	.75	.35
❑ 119 Jake Reed	.50	.23
❑ 120 Matthew Hatchette	.30	.14
❑ 121 John Randle	.50	.23
❑ 122 Robert Smith	.75	.35
❑ 123 Drew Bledsoe	1.00	.45
❑ 124 Ben Coates	.50	.23
❑ 125 Terry Glenn	.75	.35
❑ 126 Ty Law	.50	.23
❑ 127 Tony Simmons	.30	.14
❑ 128 Ted Johnson	.30	.14
❑ 129 Tony Carter	.30	.14
❑ 130 Willie McGinest	.30	.14
❑ 131 Danny Wuerffel	.30	.14
❑ 132 Cameron Cleeland	.30	.14
❑ 133 Eddie Kennison	.50	.23
❑ 134 Joe Johnson	.30	.14
❑ 135 Andre Hastings	.30	.14
❑ 136 La'Roi Glover RC	.75	.35
❑ 137 Kent Graham	.30	.14
❑ 138 Tiki Barber	.50	.23
❑ 139 Gary Brown	.30	.14
❑ 140 Ike Hilliard	.30	.14
❑ 141 Jason Sehorn	.30	.14
❑ 142 Michael Strahan	.50	.23
❑ 143 Amani Toomer	.30	.14
❑ 144 Kerry Collins	.50	.23
❑ 145 Vinny Testaverde	.50	.23
❑ 146 Wayne Chrebet	.50	.23
❑ 147 Curtis Martin	.75	.35
❑ 148 Mo Lewis	.30	.14
❑ 149 Aaron Glenn	.30	.14
❑ 150 Steve Atwater	.30	.14
❑ 151 Keyshawn Johnson	.75	.35
❑ 152 James Farrior	.30	.14
❑ 153 Rich Gannon	.75	.35
❑ 154 Tim Brown	.75	.35
❑ 155 Darrell Russell	.30	.14
❑ 156 Rickey Dudley	.30	.14
❑ 157 Charles Woodson	.75	.35
❑ 158 James Jett	.50	.23
❑ 159 Napoleon Kaufman	.75	.35
❑ 160 Duce Staley	.75	.35
❑ 161 Doug Pederson	.30	.14
❑ 162 Bobby Hoying	.50	.23
❑ 163 Koy Detmer	.30	.14
❑ 164 Kevin Turner	.30	.14
❑ 165 Charles Johnson	.30	.14
❑ 166 Mike Mamula	.30	.14
❑ 167 Jerome Bettis	.75	.35
❑ 168 Courtney Hawkins	.30	.14
❑ 169 Will Blackwell	.30	.14
❑ 170 Kordell Stewart	.50	.23
❑ 171 Richard Huntley	.50	.23
❑ 172 Levon Kirkland	.30	.14
❑ 173 Hines Ward	.75	.35
❑ 174 Trent Green	.75	.35
❑ 175 Marshall Faulk	1.00	.45
❑ 176 Az-Zahir Hakim	.30	.14
❑ 177 Amp Lee	.30	.14
❑ 178 Robert Holcombe	.30	.14
❑ 179 Isaac Bruce	.75	.35
❑ 180 Kevin Carter	.30	.14
❑ 181 Jim Harbaugh	.50	.23
❑ 182 Junior Seau	.75	.35
❑ 183 Natrone Means	.50	.23
❑ 184 Ryan Leaf	.75	.35
❑ 185 Charlie Jones	.30	.14
❑ 186 Rodney Harrison	.30	.14
❑ 187 Mikhael Ricks	.30	.14
❑ 188 Steve Young	1.00	.45
❑ 189 Terrell Owens	.75	.35
❑ 190 Jerry Rice	1.50	.70
❑ 191 J.J. Stokes	.50	.23
❑ 192 Irv Smith	.30	.14
❑ 193 Bryant Young	.30	.14
❑ 194 Garrison Hearst	.50	.23
❑ 195 Jon Kitna	.75	.35
❑ 196 Ahman Green	.75	.35
❑ 197 Joey Galloway	.50	.23
❑ 198 Ricky Watters	.50	.23
❑ 199 Chad Brown	.30	.14
❑ 200 Shawn Springs	.30	.14
❑ 201 Mike Pritchard	.30	.14
❑ 202 Trent Dilfer	.50	.23
❑ 203 Reidel Anthony	.50	.23
❑ 204 Bert Emanuel	.50	.23
❑ 205 Warrick Dunn	.75	.35
❑ 206 Jacquez Green	.30	.14
❑ 207 Hardy Nickerson	.30	.14
❑ 208 Mike Alstott	.75	.35
❑ 209 Eddie George	.75	.35
❑ 210 Steve McNair	.75	.35
❑ 211 Kevin Dyson	.50	.23
❑ 212 Frank Wycheck	.30	.14
❑ 213 Jackie Harris	.30	.14
❑ 214 Blaine Bishop	.30	.14
❑ 215 Yancey Thigpen	.30	.14
❑ 216 Brad Johnson	.75	.35
❑ 217 Rodney Peete	.30	.14
❑ 218 Michael Westbrook	.50	.23
❑ 219 Skip Hicks	.30	.14
❑ 220 Brian Mitchell	.30	.14
❑ 221 Dan Wilkinson	.30	.14
❑ 222 Dana Stubblefield	.30	.14
❑ 223 Kordell Stewart CL	.50	.23
❑ 224 Fred Taylor CL	.75	.35
❑ 225 Warrick Dunn CL	.50	.23
❑ 226 Champ Bailey RC	3.00	1.35
❑ 227 Chris McAlister RC	1.50	.70
❑ 228 Jevon Kearse RC	4.00	1.80
❑ 229 Ebenezer Ekuban RC	1.50	.70
❑ 230 Chris Claiborne RC	1.00	.45
❑ 231 Andy Katzenmoyer RC	1.50	.70
❑ 232 Tim Couch RC	2.00	.90
❑ 233 Daunte Culpepper RC	10.00	4.50
❑ 234 Akili Smith RC	1.50	.70
❑ 235 Donovan McNabb RC	12.00	5.50
❑ 236 Sean Bennett RC	1.00	.45
❑ 237 Brock Huard RC	2.00	.90
❑ 238 Cade McNown RC	1.50	.70
❑ 239 Shaun King RC	1.50	.70
❑ 240 Joe Germaine RC	1.50	.70
❑ 241 Ricky Williams RC	5.00	2.20
❑ 242 Edgerrin James RC	10.00	4.50
❑ 243 Sedrick Irvin RC	1.00	.45
❑ 244 Kevin Faulk RC	2.00	.90
❑ 245 Rob Konrad RC	2.00	.90
❑ 246 James Johnson RC	1.50	.70
❑ 247 Amos Zereoue RC	2.00	.90
❑ 248 Torry Holt RC	6.00	2.70
❑ 249 D'Wayne Bates RC	1.50	.70
❑ 250 David Boston RC	2.00	.90
❑ 251 Dameane Douglas RC	2.00	.90
❑ 252 Troy Edwards RC	1.50	.70
❑ 253 Kevin Johnson RC	2.00	.90
❑ 254 Peerless Price RC	4.00	1.80
❑ 255 Antoine Winfield RC	1.50	.70
❑ 256 Mike Cloud RC	1.50	.70
❑ 257 Joe Montgomery RC	1.50	.70
❑ 258 Jermaine Fazande RC	1.50	.70
❑ 259 Scott Covington RC	2.00	.90
❑ 260 Aaron Brooks RC	8.00	3.60
❑ 261 Patrick Kerney RC	2.00	.90
❑ 262 Cecil Collins RC	1.00	.45
❑ 263 Chris Greisen RC	1.50	.70
❑ 264 Craig Yeast RC	1.50	.70
❑ 265 Karsten Bailey RC	1.50	.70
❑ 266 Reginald Kelly RC	1.00	.45
❑ 267 Al Wilson RC	1.50	.70
❑ 268 Jeff Paulk RC	1.00	.45
❑ 269 Jim Kleinsasser RC	2.00	.90
❑ 270 Darrin Chiaverini RC	1.50	.70

1999 Upper Deck Game Jersey

	Nm-Mt	Ex-Mt
❑ BH Brock Huard H	25.00	11.00
❑ BS Barry Sanders H	50.00	22.00
❑ CM Cade McNown H	25.00	11.00
❑ DB Drew Bledsoe H/R	60.00	27.00
❑ DC Daunte Culpepper H	50.00	22.00
❑ DF Doug Flutie H/R	40.00	18.00
❑ DM Dan Marino H/R	100.00	45.00
❑ DV David Boston H	25.00	11.00
❑ EJ Edgerrin James H/R	50.00	22.00
❑ EM Eric Moulds H	25.00	11.00
❑ JA Jamal Anderson H/R	30.00	13.50
❑ JE John Elway H	80.00	36.00
❑ JR Jerry Rice H	60.00	27.00
❑ KJ Keyshawn Johnson H/R	30.00	13.50
❑ MC Donovan McNabb H	60.00	27.00
❑ PM Peyton Manning H	60.00	27.00
❑ RM Randy Moss H/R	60.00	27.00
❑ SY Steve Young H/R	60.00	27.00
❑ TA Troy Aikman H	40.00	18.00
❑ TC Tim Couch H	30.00	13.50
❑ TD Terrell Davis H/R	50.00	22.00
❑ BH-A Brock Huard AUTO/5 H		
❑ CM-A Cade McNown AUTO/8 H		
❑ TC-A Tim Couch AUTO/2 H/R		
❑ TD-A T.Davis AUTO/30 H/R	300.00	135.00

1999 Upper Deck Game Jersey Patch

	Nm-Mt	Ex-Mt
❑ BHP Brock Huard	60.00	27.00
❑ BSP Barry Sanders	200.00	90.00
❑ CMP Cade McNown	60.00	27.00
❑ DBP Drew Bledsoe	120.00	55.00
❑ DCP Daunte Culpepper	100.00	45.00
❑ DFP Doug Flutie	120.00	55.00
❑ DMP Dan Marino	200.00	90.00
❑ DVP David Boston	60.00	27.00
❑ EJP Edgerrin James	100.00	45.00
❑ JAP Jamal Anderson	80.00	36.00
❑ JEP John Elway	200.00	90.00
❑ JRP Jerry Rice	150.00	70.00
❑ MCP Donovan McNabb	120.00	55.00
❑ PMP Peyton Manning	200.00	90.00
❑ RMP Randy Moss	150.00	70.00
❑ SYP Steve Young	120.00	55.00
❑ TAP Troy Aikman	120.00	55.00
❑ TCP Tim Couch	80.00	36.00
❑ TDP Terrell Davis	80.00	36.00

2000 Upper Deck

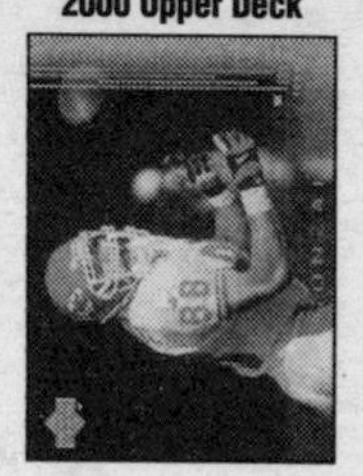

	Nm-Mt	Ex-Mt
COMPLETE SET (1-270)	120.00	55.00
COMP.SET w/o SPs (222)	30.00	13.50
❑ 1 Jake Plummer	.50	.23
❑ 2 Michael Pittman	.30	.14
❑ 3 Rob Moore	.50	.23
❑ 4 David Boston	.75	.35
❑ 5 Frank Sanders	.50	.23
❑ 6 Aeneas Williams	.30	.14
❑ 7 Kwamie Lassiter	.30	.14
❑ 8 Rob Fredrickson	.30	.14
❑ 9 Tim Dwight	.75	.35
❑ 10 Chris Chandler	.50	.23
❑ 11 Jamal Anderson	.75	.35
❑ 12 Shawn Jefferson	.30	.14
❑ 13 Ken Oxendine	.30	.14
❑ 14 Terance Mathis	.50	.23
❑ 15 Bob Christian	.30	.14
❑ 16 Qadry Ismail	.50	.23
❑ 17 Jermaine Lewis	.50	.23
❑ 18 Rod Woodson	.50	.23
❑ 19 Michael McCrary	.30	.14
❑ 20 Tony Banks	.50	.23
❑ 21 Peter Boulware	.30	.14
❑ 22 Shannon Sharpe	.50	.23
❑ 23 Peerless Price	.75	.35
❑ 24 Rob Johnson	.50	.23
❑ 25 Eric Moulds	.75	.35
❑ 26 Doug Flutie	.75	.35
❑ 27 Jay Riemersma	.30	.14
❑ 28 Antowain Smith	.50	.23
❑ 29 Jonathan Linton	.30	.14
❑ 30 Muhsin Muhammad	.50	.23
❑ 31 Patrick Jeffers	.75	.35
❑ 32 Steve Beuerlein	.50	.23
❑ 33 Natrone Means	.30	.14
❑ 34 Tim Biakabutuka	.50	.23
❑ 35 Michael Bates	.30	.14
❑ 36 Chuck Smith	.30	.14
❑ 37 Wesley Walls	.30	.14
❑ 38 Cade McNown	.30	.14
❑ 39 Curtis Enis	.30	.14
❑ 40 Marcus Robinson	.75	.35
❑ 41 Eddie Kennison	.50	.23
❑ 42 Bobby Engram	.50	.23
❑ 43 Glyn Milburn	.30	.14
❑ 44 Marty Booker	.50	.23
❑ 45 Akili Smith	.30	.14
❑ 46 Corey Dillon	.75	.35
❑ 47 Darnay Scott	.50	.23
❑ 48 Tremain Mack	.30	.14
❑ 49 Damon Griffin	.30	.14
❑ 50 Takeo Spikes	.30	.14
❑ 51 Tony McGee	.30	.14
❑ 52 Tim Couch	.50	.23
❑ 53 Kevin Johnson	.75	.35
❑ 54 Darrin Chiaverini	.30	.14
❑ 55 Jamir Miller	.30	.14
❑ 56 Errict Rhett	.50	.23
❑ 57 Terry Kirby	.30	.14
❑ 58 Marc Edwards	.30	.14
❑ 59 Troy Aikman	1.50	.70
❑ 60 Emmitt Smith	1.50	.70
❑ 61 Rocket Ismail	.50	.23
❑ 62 Jason Tucker	.30	.14
❑ 63 Dexter Coakley	.30	.14
❑ 64 Joey Galloway	.50	.23
❑ 65 Wane McGarity	.30	.14
❑ 66 Terrell Davis	.75	.35
❑ 67 Olandis Gary	.75	.35
❑ 68 Brian Griese	.75	.35
❑ 69 Gus Frerotte	.30	.14
❑ 70 Byron Chamberlain	.30	.14
❑ 71 Ed McCaffrey	.75	.35
❑ 72 Rod Smith	.50	.23
❑ 73 Al Wilson	.30	.14
❑ 74 Charlie Batch	.75	.35
❑ 75 Germane Crowell	.30	.14
❑ 76 Sedrick Irvin	.30	.14
❑ 77 Johnnie Morton	.50	.23
❑ 78 Robert Porcher	.30	.14
❑ 79 Herman Moore	.50	.23
❑ 80 James Stewart	.50	.23
❑ 81 Brett Favre	2.50	1.10
❑ 82 Antonio Freeman	.75	.35
❑ 83 Bill Schroeder	.50	.23
❑ 84 Dorsey Levens	.50	.23
❑ 85 Corey Bradford	.50	.23
❑ 86 De'Mond Parker	.30	.14
❑ 87 Vonnie Holliday	.30	.14
❑ 88 Peyton Manning	2.00	.90
❑ 89 Edgerrin James	1.25	.55
❑ 90 Marvin Harrison	.75	.35
❑ 91 Ken Dilger	.30	.14
❑ 92 Terrence Wilkins	.30	.14
❑ 93 Marcus Pollard	.30	.14
❑ 94 Fred Lane	.30	.14
❑ 95 Mark Brunell	.75	.35
❑ 96 Fred Taylor	.75	.35
❑ 97 Jimmy Smith	.50	.23
❑ 98 Keenan McCardell	.50	.23
❑ 99 Carnell Lake	.30	.14
❑ 100 Tavian Banks	.30	.14
❑ 101 Kyle Brady	.30	.14
❑ 102 Hardy Nickerson	.30	.14
❑ 103 Elvis Grbac	.50	.23
❑ 104 Tony Gonzalez	.50	.23
❑ 105 Derrick Alexander WR	.50	.23
❑ 106 Donnell Bennett	.30	.14
❑ 107 Mike Cloud	.30	.14
❑ 108 Donnie Edwards	.30	.14
❑ 109 Jay Fiedler	.75	.35
❑ 110 James Johnson	.30	.14
❑ 111 Tony Martin	.50	.23
❑ 112 Damon Huard	.75	.35
❑ 113 O.J. McDuffie	.50	.23
❑ 114 Thurman Thomas	.50	.23
❑ 115 Zach Thomas	.75	.35
❑ 116 Oronde Gadsden	.50	.23
❑ 117 Randy Moss	1.50	.70
❑ 118 Robert Smith	.75	.35
❑ 119 Cris Carter	.75	.35
❑ 120 Matthew Hatchette	.30	.14
❑ 121 Daunte Culpepper	1.00	.45
❑ 122 Leroy Hoard	.30	.14
❑ 123 Drew Bledsoe	1.00	.45
❑ 124 Terry Glenn	.50	.23
❑ 125 Troy Brown	.50	.23
❑ 126 Kevin Faulk	.30	.14
❑ 127 Lawyer Milloy	.50	.23
❑ 128 Ricky Williams	.75	.35
❑ 129 Keith Poole	.30	.14
❑ 130 Jake Reed	.50	.23
❑ 131 Cam Cleeland	.30	.14
❑ 132 Jeff Blake	.50	.23
❑ 133 Andrew Glover	.30	.14
❑ 134 Kerry Collins	.50	.23
❑ 135 Amani Toomer	.50	.23
❑ 136 Joe Montgomery	.30	.14
❑ 137 Ike Hilliard	.50	.23
❑ 138 Tiki Barber	.50	.23
❑ 139 Pete Mitchell	.30	.14
❑ 140 Ray Lucas	.50	.23
❑ 141 Mo Lewis	.30	.14
❑ 142 Curtis Martin	.75	.35
❑ 143 Vinny Testaverde	.50	.23
❑ 144 Wayne Chrebet	.50	.23
❑ 145 Dedric Ward	.30	.14
❑ 146 Tim Brown	.75	.35

147 Rich Gannon	.75	.35
148 Tyrone Wheatley	.50	.23
149 Napoleon Kaufman	.50	.23
150 Charles Woodson	.50	.23
151 Darrell Russell	.30	.14
152 James Jett	.30	.14
153 Rickey Dudley	.30	.14
154 Jon Ritchie	.30	.14
155 Duce Staley	.75	.35
156 Donovan McNabb	1.25	.55
157 Torrance Small	.30	.14
158 Allen Rossum	.30	.14
159 Mike Mamula	.30	.14
160 Na Brown	.30	.14
161 Charles Johnson	.50	.23
162 Kent Graham	.30	.14
163 Troy Edwards	.30	.14
164 Jerome Bettis	.75	.35
165 Hines Ward	.75	.35
166 Kordell Stewart	.50	.23
167 Levon Kirkland	.30	.14
168 Richard Huntley	.30	.14
169 Marshall Faulk	1.00	.45
170 Kurt Warner	1.50	.70
171 Torry Holt	.75	.35
172 Isaac Bruce	.75	.35
173 Kevin Carter	.30	.14
174 Az-Zahir Hakim	.50	.23
175 Ricky Proehl	.30	.14
176 Jermaine Fazande	.30	.14
177 Curtis Conway	.50	.23
178 Freddie Jones	.30	.14
179 Junior Seau	.75	.35
180 Jeff Graham	.30	.14
181 Jim Harbaugh	.50	.23
182 Rodney Harrison	.30	.14
183 Steve Young	1.00	.45
184 Jerry Rice	1.50	.70
185 Charlie Garner	.50	.23
186 Terrell Owens	.75	.35
187 Jeff Garcia	.75	.35
188 Fred Beasley	.30	.14
189 J.J. Stokes	.50	.23
190 Ricky Watters	.50	.23
191 Jon Kitna	.75	.35
192 Derrick Mayes	.50	.23
193 Sean Dawkins	.30	.14
194 Charlie Rogers	.30	.14
195 Mike Pritchard	.30	.14
196 Cortez Kennedy	.30	.14
197 Christian Fauria	.30	.14
198 Warrick Dunn	.75	.35
199 Shaun King	.30	.14
200 Mike Alstott	.75	.35
201 Warren Sapp	.50	.23
202 Jacquez Green	.30	.14
203 Reidel Anthony	.30	.14
204 Dave Moore	.30	.14
205 Keyshawn Johnson	.75	.35
206 Eddie George	.75	.35
207 Steve McNair	.75	.35
208 Kevin Dyson	.50	.23
209 Jevon Kearse	.75	.35
210 Yancey Thigpen	.30	.14
211 Frank Wycheck	.30	.14
212 Isaac Byrd	.30	.14
213 Neil O'Donnell	.30	.14
214 Brad Johnson	.75	.35
215 Stephen Davis	.75	.35
216 Michael Westbrook	.50	.23
217 Albert Connell	.30	.14
218 Brian Mitchell	.30	.14
219 Bruce Smith	.50	.23
220 Stephen Alexander	.30	.14
221 Jeff George	.50	.23
222 Adrian Murrell	.30	.14
223 Courtney Brown RC	4.00	1.80
224 John Engelberger RC	2.50	1.10
225 Deltha O'Neal RC	4.00	1.80
226 Corey Simon RC	4.00	1.80
227 R.Jay Soward RC	2.50	1.10
228 Marc Bulger RC	8.00	3.60
229 Raynoch Thompson RC	2.50	1.10
230 Deon Grant RC	2.50	1.10
231 Darrell Jackson RC	8.00	3.60
232 Chris Cole RC	2.50	1.10
233 Trevor Gaylor RC	2.50	1.10
234 John Abraham RC	4.00	1.80
235 Chris Redman RC	2.50	1.10
236 Joe Hamilton RC	2.50	1.10
237 Chad Pennington RC	15.00	6.75
238 Tee Martin RC	4.00	1.80
239 Giovanni Carmazzi RC	2.50	1.10
240 Tim Rattay RC	8.00	3.60
241 Ron Dayne RC	4.00	1.80
242 Shaun Alexander RC	10.00	4.50
243 Thomas Jones RC	6.00	2.70
244 Reuben Droughns RC	4.00	1.80
245 Jamal Lewis RC	10.00	4.50
246 Michael Wiley RC	2.50	1.10
247 J.R. Redmond RC	2.50	1.10
248 Travis Prentice RC	2.50	1.10
249 Todd Husak RC	4.00	1.80
250 Trung Canidate RC	2.50	1.10
251 Brian Urlacher RC	15.00	6.75
252 Anthony Becht RC	4.00	1.80
253 Bubba Franks RC	4.00	1.80
254 Tom Brady RC	50.00	22.00
255 Peter Warrick RC	4.00	1.80
256 Plaxico Burress RC	8.00	3.60
257 Sylvester Morris RC	2.50	1.10
258 Dez White RC	4.00	1.80
259 Travis Taylor RC	4.00	1.80
260 Todd Pinkston RC	4.00	1.80
261 Dennis Northcutt RC	4.00	1.80
262 Jerry Porter RC	5.00	2.20
263 Laveranues Coles RC	5.00	2.20
264 Danny Farmer RC	2.50	1.10
265 Curtis Keaton RC	2.50	1.10
266 Sherrod Gideon RC	2.00	.90
267 Ron Dugans RC	2.00	.90
268 Steve McNair CL	.50	.23
269 Jake Plummer CL	.50	.23
270 Antonio Freeman CL	.50	.23

2000 Upper Deck Exclusives Gold

Nm-Mt Ex-Mt

*EXCL.GOLD STARS: 20X TO 50X BASIC CARDS

*EXCL.GOLD ROOKIES: 4X TO 10X

2000 Upper Deck Exclusives Silver

Nm-Mt Ex-Mt

*EXCL.SILVER STARS: 8X TO 20X HI COL.

*EXCL.SILVER ROOKIES: 2X TO 5X

2000 Upper Deck Game Jersey

	Nm-Mt	Ex-Mt
AF Antonio Freeman	25.00	11.00
BF Brett Favre	50.00	22.00
BG Brian Griese	25.00	11.00
BO David Boston	25.00	11.00
CB Courtney Brown	25.00	11.00
CM Curtis Martin	25.00	11.00
CR Chris Redman	25.00	11.00
DA Daunte Culpepper	25.00	11.00
DL Dorsey Levens	25.00	11.00
DO Donovan McNabb	30.00	13.50
EM Eric Moulds	20.00	9.00
ES Emmitt Smith	60.00	27.00
FA Danny Farmer	25.00	11.00
FR Bubba Franks	20.00	9.00
HM Herman Moore	20.00	9.00
JA Jamal Anderson	25.00	11.00
JJ J.J. Stokes	20.00	9.00
JL Jamal Lewis	30.00	13.50
JR Jerry Rice	50.00	22.00
MA Mike Alstott	25.00	11.00
OG Olandis Gary	25.00	11.00
PB Plaxico Burress	30.00	13.50
RJ R.Jay Soward	25.00	11.00
RL Ray Lucas	25.00	11.00
RW Ricky Williams	25.00	11.00
SK Shaun King	20.00	9.00
SL Sylvester Morris	25.00	11.00
SM Steve McNair	25.00	11.00
SY Steve Young	30.00	13.50
TB Tim Brown	25.00	11.00
TH Torry Holt	25.00	11.00
TJ Thomas Jones	30.00	13.50
TM Tee Martin	25.00	11.00
TO Terrell Owens	25.00	11.00
TT Travis Taylor	25.00	11.00
KPGJ Brett Favre/60 Promo (produced for Krause)	200.00	90.00

2000 Upper Deck Game Jersey Autographs

	Nm-Mt	Ex-Mt
CPA Chad Pennington	200.00	90.00
DBA Drew Bledsoe	60.00	27.00
DMA Dan Marino	250.00	110.00
EGA Eddie George	50.00	22.00
EJA Edgerrin James	80.00	36.00
IBA Isaac Bruce	50.00	22.00
JOA Kevin Johnson	40.00	18.00
KJA Keyshawn Johnson	50.00	22.00
KWA Kurt Warner	80.00	36.00
MBA Mark Brunell	50.00	22.00
MCA Cade McNown	40.00	18.00
MFA Marshall Faulk	60.00	27.00
MHA Marvin Harrison	60.00	27.00
PMA Peyton Manning	150.00	70.00
PWA Peter Warrick	50.00	22.00
RDA Ron Dayne	50.00	22.00
RMA Randy Moss	120.00	55.00
SAA Shaun Alexander	80.00	36.00
TAA Troy Aikman	120.00	55.00
TCA Tim Couch	40.00	18.00
TDA Terrell Davis	60.00	27.00

2000 Upper Deck Game Jersey Autographs Numbered

	Nm-Mt	Ex-Mt
AFA Antonio Freeman/86		
BGA Brian Griese/14		
BOA David Boston/80	80.00	36.00
CBA Courtney Brown/92	60.00	27.00
CPA Chad Pennington/10		
DBA Drew Bledsoe/11		
DFA Danny Farmer/16		
DLA Dorsey Levens/25	100.00	45.00
DMA Dan Marino/13		
EGA Eddie George/27	150.00	70.00

❑ EJA Edgerrin James/32	400.00	180.00
❑ IBA Isaac Bruce/80	100.00	45.00
❑ JAA Jamal Anderson/32	100.00	45.00
❑ JOA Kevin Johnson/85	60.00	27.00
❑ KJA Keyshawn Johnson/19		
❑ KWA Kurt Warner/13		
❑ MBA Mark Brunell/8		
❑ MCA Cade McNown/8		
❑ MFA Marshall Faulk/28	250.00	110.00
❑ MHA Marvin Harrison/88	80.00	36.00
❑ PMA Peyton Manning/18		
❑ PWA Peter Warrick/80	100.00	45.00
❑ RDA Ron Dayne/27	100.00	45.00
❑ SAA Shaun Alexander/37	150.00	70.00
❑ SYA Steve Young/8		
❑ TBA Tim Brown/81	120.00	55.00
❑ TDA Terrell Davis/30	150.00	70.00

2000 Upper Deck Game Jersey Greats Autographs

	Nm-Mt	Ex-Mt
❑ GJGBS1 Bart Starr/200	250.00	110.00
❑ GJGBS2 Bart Starr/200	250.00	75.00
❑ GJGDM Dan Marino/375	300.00	135.00
❑ GJGJE John Elway/350	250.00	110.00
❑ GJGJM Joe Montana	300.00	135.00
❑ GJGJU Johnny Unitas/400	300.00	135.00
❑ GJGJN1 Joe Namath/175	225.00	100.00
❑ GJGJN2 Joe Namath/175	225.00	100.00
❑ GJGRS Roger Staubach/400	150.00	70.00
❑ GJGSY Steve Young/175	250.00	110.00
❑ GJGTB Terry Bradshaw/400	150.00	70.00

2000 Upper Deck Game Jersey Patch

	Nm-Mt	Ex-Mt
*SERIAL #'d: .5X TO 1.2X HI COL.		
SERIAL #'d STATED PRINT RUN 25 SETS		
❑ AFP Antonio Freeman	60.00	27.00
❑ BFP Brett Favre	250.00	110.00
❑ BGP Brian Griese	60.00	27.00
❑ BOP David Boston	60.00	27.00
❑ CMP Curtis Martin	60.00	27.00
❑ DAP Daunte Culpepper	100.00	45.00
❑ DBP Drew Bledsoe	120.00	55.00
❑ DLP Dorsey Levens	50.00	22.00
❑ DMP Dan Marino	250.00	110.00
❑ EGP Eddie George	60.00	27.00
❑ EJP Edgerrin James	120.00	55.00
❑ ESP Emmitt Smith	200.00	90.00
❑ FTP Fred Taylor	60.00	27.00
❑ JAP Jamal Anderson	50.00	22.00
❑ JOP Kevin Johnson	50.00	22.00
❑ KJP Keyshawn Johnson	50.00	22.00
❑ MBP Mark Brunell	60.00	27.00
❑ MCP Cade McNown	40.00	18.00
❑ MFP Marshall Faulk	120.00	55.00
❑ MHP Marvin Harrison	60.00	27.00
❑ OGP Olandis Gary	50.00	22.00
❑ PMP Peyton Manning	200.00	90.00
❑ RLP Ray Lucas	50.00	22.00
❑ RMP Randy Moss	150.00	70.00
❑ SKP Shaun King	40.00	18.00
❑ TBP Tim Brown	60.00	27.00
❑ TCP Tim Couch	50.00	22.00
❑ TDP Terrell Davis	60.00	27.00
❑ THP Torry Holt	60.00	27.00
❑ TOP Terrell Owens	60.00	27.00

2000 Upper Deck Game Jersey Patch Autographs

	Nm-Mt	Ex-Mt
❑ EGSP Eddie George	250.00	110.00
❑ EJSP Edgerrin James	250.00	110.00
❑ KWSP Kurt Warner	300.00	135.00
❑ MFSP Marshall Faulk	300.00	135.00
❑ RMSP Randy Moss EXCH	20.00	9.00
❑ TCSP Tim Couch		

2001 Upper Deck

	Nm-Mt	Ex-Mt
COMPLETE SET (280)	300.00	90.00
COMP.SET w/o SP's (180)	25.00	7.50
❑ 1 Jake Plummer	.50	.15
❑ 2 David Boston	.75	.23
❑ 3 Thomas Jones	.50	.15
❑ 4 Frank Sanders	.30	.09
❑ 5 Eric Zeier	.30	.09
❑ 6 Jamal Anderson	.75	.23
❑ 7 Chris Chandler	.50	.15
❑ 8 Shawn Jefferson	.30	.09
❑ 9 Darrick Vaughn	.30	.09
❑ 10 Terance Mathis	.50	.15
❑ 11 Jamal Lewis	1.25	.35
❑ 12 Shannon Sharpe	.50	.15
❑ 13 Elvis Grbac	.50	.15
❑ 14 Ray Lewis	.75	.23
❑ 15 Qadry Ismail	.50	.15
❑ 16 Chris Redman	.30	.09
❑ 17 Rob Johnson	.75	.23
❑ 18 Eric Moulds	.50	.15
❑ 19 Sammy Morris	.30	.09
❑ 20 Shawn Bryson	.30	.09
❑ 21 Jeremy McDaniel	.30	.09
❑ 22 Muhsin Muhammad	.50	.15
❑ 23 Brad Hoover	.30	.09
❑ 24 Tim Biakabutuka	.50	.15
❑ 25 Steve Beuerlein	.30	.09
❑ 26 Jeff Lewis	.30	.09
❑ 27 Wesley Walls	.30	.09
❑ 28 Cade McNown	.30	.09
❑ 29 James Allen	.50	.15
❑ 30 Marcus Robinson	.75	.23
❑ 31 Brian Urlacher	1.25	.35
❑ 32 Bobby Engram	.30	.09
❑ 33 Peter Warrick	.75	.23
❑ 34 Corey Dillon	.75	.23
❑ 35 Akili Smith	.30	.09
❑ 36 Danny Farmer	.30	.09
❑ 37 Ron Dugans	.30	.09
❑ 38 Jon Kitna	.75	.23
❑ 39 Tim Couch	.50	.15
❑ 40 Kevin Johnson	.50	.15
❑ 41 Travis Prentice	.30	.09
❑ 42 Spergon Wynn	.30	.09
❑ 43 Errict Rhett	.30	.09
❑ 44 Dennis Northcutt	.50	.15
❑ 45 Courtney Brown	.50	.15
❑ 46 Tony Banks	.30	.09
❑ 47 Emmitt Smith	1.50	.45
❑ 48 Joey Galloway	.50	.15
❑ 49 Rocket Ismail	.50	.15
❑ 50 Randall Cunningham	.75	.23
❑ 51 James McKnight	.50	.15
❑ 52 Terrell Davis	.75	.23
❑ 53 Mike Anderson	.75	.23
❑ 54 Brian Griese	.75	.23
❑ 55 Rod Smith	.50	.15
❑ 56 Ed McCaffrey	.75	.23
❑ 57 Eddie Kennison	.50	.15
❑ 58 Olandis Gary	.50	.15
❑ 59 Charlie Batch	.75	.23
❑ 60 Germane Crowell	.30	.09
❑ 61 James O. Stewart	.50	.15
❑ 62 Johnnie Morton	.50	.15
❑ 63 Brett Favre	2.50	.75
❑ 64 Antonio Freeman	.75	.23
❑ 65 Dorsey Levens	.50	.15
❑ 66 Ahman Green	.75	.23
❑ 67 Bill Schroeder	.50	.15
❑ 68 Peyton Manning	2.00	.60
❑ 69 Edgerrin James	1.00	.30
❑ 70 Marvin Harrison	.75	.23
❑ 71 Jerome Pathon	.50	.15
❑ 72 Ken Dilger	.30	.09
❑ 73 Mark Brunell	.75	.23
❑ 74 Fred Taylor	.75	.23
❑ 75 Jimmy Smith	.50	.15
❑ 76 Keenan McCardell	.30	.09
❑ 77 R.Jay Soward	.30	.09
❑ 78 Todd Collins	.30	.09
❑ 79 Tony Gonzalez	.50	.15
❑ 80 Derrick Alexander	.50	.15
❑ 81 Tony Richardson	.30	.09
❑ 82 Sylvester Morris	.30	.09
❑ 83 Oronde Gadsden	.50	.15
❑ 84 Lamar Smith	.50	.15
❑ 85 Jay Fiedler	.75	.23
❑ 86 Jason Taylor	.30	.09
❑ 87 Ray Lucas	.30	.09
❑ 88 O.J. McDuffie	.30	.09
❑ 89 Randy Moss	1.50	.45
❑ 90 Cris Carter	.75	.23
❑ 91 Daunte Culpepper	.75	.23
❑ 92 Moe Williams	.50	.15
❑ 93 Troy Walters	.30	.09
❑ 94 Drew Bledsoe	1.00	.30
❑ 95 Terry Glenn	.50	.15
❑ 96 Kevin Faulk	.50	.15
❑ 97 J.R. Redmond	.30	.09
❑ 98 Troy Brown	.50	.15
❑ 99 Ricky Williams	.75	.23
❑ 100 Jeff Blake	.50	.15
❑ 101 Joe Horn	.50	.15
❑ 102 Albert Connell	.30	.09

Card	Nm-Mt	Ex-Mt
❑ 103 Aaron Brooks	.75	.23
❑ 104 Chad Morton	.30	.09
❑ 105 Kerry Collins	.50	.15
❑ 106 Amani Toomer	.50	.15
❑ 107 Ron Dayne	.75	.23
❑ 108 Tiki Barber	.50	.15
❑ 109 Ike Hilliard	.50	.15
❑ 110 Ron Dixon	.30	.09
❑ 111 Jason Sehorn	.30	.09
❑ 112 Vinny Testaverde	.50	.15
❑ 113 Wayne Chrebet	.50	.15
❑ 114 Curtis Martin	.75	.23
❑ 115 Dedric Ward	.30	.09
❑ 116 Laveranues Coles	.75	.23
❑ 117 Windrell Hayes	.30	.09
❑ 118 Tim Brown	.75	.23
❑ 119 Rich Gannon	.75	.23
❑ 120 Tyrone Wheatley	.50	.15
❑ 121 Charlie Garner	.50	.15
❑ 122 Andre Rison	.50	.15
❑ 123 Charles Woodson	.50	.15
❑ 124 Trace Armstrong	.30	.09
❑ 125 Duce Staley	.75	.23
❑ 126 Donovan McNabb	1.00	.30
❑ 127 Darnell Autry	.30	.09
❑ 128 Charles Johnson	.30	.09
❑ 129 Torrance Small	.30	.09
❑ 130 Kordell Stewart	.50	.15
❑ 131 Jerome Bettis	.75	.23
❑ 132 Plaxico Burress	.75	.23
❑ 133 Bobby Shaw	.30	.09
❑ 134 Troy Edwards	.30	.09
❑ 135 Marshall Faulk	1.00	.30
❑ 136 Kurt Warner	1.50	.45
❑ 137 Isaac Bruce	.75	.23
❑ 138 Torry Holt	.75	.23
❑ 139 Trent Green	.75	.23
❑ 140 Az-Zahir Hakim	.30	.09
❑ 141 Junior Seau	.75	.23
❑ 142 Curtis Conway	.50	.15
❑ 143 Doug Flutie	.75	.23
❑ 144 Jeff Graham	.30	.09
❑ 145 Freddie Jones	.30	.09
❑ 146 Marcellus Wiley	.30	.09
❑ 147 Jeff Garcia	.75	.23
❑ 148 Jerry Rice	1.50	.45
❑ 149 Fred Beasley	.30	.09
❑ 150 Terrell Owens	.75	.23
❑ 151 J.J. Stokes	.50	.15
❑ 152 Garrison Hearst	.50	.15
❑ 153 Ricky Watters	.30	.09
❑ 154 Shaun Alexander	1.00	.30
❑ 155 Matt Hasselbeck	.50	.15
❑ 156 Brock Huard	.30	.09
❑ 157 Darrell Jackson	.75	.23
❑ 158 John Randle	.30	.09
❑ 159 Warrick Dunn	.75	.23
❑ 160 Shaun King	.30	.09
❑ 161 Ryan Leaf	.50	.15
❑ 162 Mike Alstott	.75	.23
❑ 163 Jacquez Green	.30	.09
❑ 164 Brad Johnson	.75	.23
❑ 165 Keyshawn Johnson	.75	.23
❑ 166 Eddie George	.75	.23
❑ 167 Steve McNair	.75	.23
❑ 168 Neil O'Donnell	.30	.09
❑ 169 Derrick Mason	.50	.15
❑ 170 Frank Wycheck	.30	.09
❑ 171 Kevin Dyson	.50	.15
❑ 172 Jevon Kearse	.50	.15
❑ 173 Jeff George	.50	.15
❑ 174 Stephen Davis	.75	.23
❑ 175 Larry Centers	.30	.09
❑ 176 Michael Westbrook	.50	.15
❑ 177 Stephen Alexander	.50	.15
❑ 178 Ron Dayne	.75	.23
❑ 179 Donovan McNabb	1.00	.30
❑ 180 Jimmy Smith	.50	.15
❑ 181 Adam Archuleta RC	5.00	1.50
❑ 182 A.J. Feeley RC	5.00	1.50
❑ 183 Alex Bannister RC	3.00	.90
❑ 184 Alge Crumpler RC	6.00	1.80
❑ 185 Andre Carter RC	5.00	1.50
❑ 186 Andre Dyson RC	2.00	.60
❑ 187 Anthony Thomas RC	8.00	2.40
❑ 188 Arther Love RC	2.00	.60
❑ 189 Bobby Newcombe RC	3.00	.90
❑ 190 Brandon Spoon RC	5.00	1.50
❑ 191 Carlos Polk RC	2.00	.60
❑ 192 Casey Hampton RC	3.00	.90
❑ 193 Cedrick Wilson RC	5.00	1.50
❑ 194 Chad Johnson RC	10.00	3.00
❑ 195 Chris Chambers RC	6.00	1.80
❑ 196 Chris Taylor RC	3.00	.90
❑ 197 Chris Weinke RC	5.00	1.50
❑ 198 Correll Buckhalter RC	6.00	1.80
❑ 199 Damione Lewis RC	3.00	.90
❑ 200 Dan Alexander RC	5.00	1.50
❑ 201 Dan Morgan RC	5.00	1.50
❑ 202 Willie Middlebrooks RC	3.00	.90
❑ 203 David Terrell RC	5.00	1.50
❑ 204 Derrick Gibson RC	3.00	.90
❑ 205 Deuce McAllister RC	10.00	3.00
❑ 206 Drew Brees RC	10.00	3.00
❑ 207 Edgerton Hartwell RC	2.00	.60
❑ 208 Fred Smoot RC	5.00	1.50
❑ 209 Freddie Mitchell RC	5.00	1.50
❑ 210 Gary Baxter RC	3.00	.90
❑ 211 Gerard Warren RC	5.00	1.50
❑ 212 Hakim Akbar RC	2.00	.60
❑ 213 Heath Evans RC	3.00	.90
❑ 214 Jabari Holloway RC	3.00	.90
❑ 215 Jamal Reynolds RC	5.00	1.50
❑ 216 Jamar Fletcher RC	3.00	.90
❑ 217 James Jackson RC	5.00	1.50
❑ 218 Jamie Winborn RC	3.00	.90
❑ 219 Jesse Palmer RC	5.00	1.50
❑ 220 Josh Booty RC	5.00	1.50
❑ 221 Josh Heupel RC	5.00	1.50
❑ 222 Justin Smith RC	5.00	1.50
❑ 223 Karon Riley RC	2.00	.60
❑ 224 Ken Lucas RC	3.00	.90
❑ 225 Kenyatta Walker RC	2.00	.60
❑ 226 Ken-Yon Rambo RC	3.00	.90
❑ 227 Kevan Barlow RC	5.00	1.50
❑ 228 Kevin Kasper RC	5.00	1.50
❑ 229 Koren Robinson RC	6.00	1.80
❑ 230 LaDainian Tomlinson RC	15.00	4.50
❑ 231 LaMont Jordan RC	6.00	1.80
❑ 232 Leonard Davis RC	3.00	.90
❑ 233 Marcus Stroud RC	5.00	1.50
❑ 234 Marques Tuiasosopo RC	5.00	1.50
❑ 235 Snoop Minnis RC	3.00	.90
❑ 236 Michael Bennett RC	10.00	3.00
❑ 237 Michael Stone RC	2.00	.60
❑ 238 Mike McMahon RC	5.00	1.50
❑ 239 Michael Vick RC	30.00	9.00
❑ 240 Moran Norris RC	2.00	.60
❑ 241 Morlon Greenwood RC	3.00	.90
❑ 242 Nate Clements RC	5.00	1.50
❑ 243 Orlando Huff RC	2.00	.60
❑ 244 Quincy Morgan RC	5.00	1.50
❑ 245 Reggie Wayne RC	8.00	2.40
❑ 246 Richard Seymour RC	5.00	1.50
❑ 247 Robert Ferguson RC	5.00	1.50
❑ 248 Rod Gardner RC	5.00	1.50
❑ 249 Rudi Johnson RC	10.00	3.00
❑ 250 Sage Rosenfels RC	5.00	1.50
❑ 251 Santana Moss RC	8.00	2.40
❑ 252 Scotty Anderson RC	3.00	.90
❑ 253 Sedrick Hodge RC	2.00	.60
❑ 254 Shaun Rogers RC	5.00	1.50
❑ 255 Steve Hutchinson RC	3.00	.90
❑ 256 T.J. Houshmandzadeh RC	5.00	1.50
❑ 257 Tay Cody RC	2.00	.60
❑ 258 George Layne RC	3.00	.90
❑ 259 Todd Heap RC	5.00	1.50
❑ 260 Tommy Polley RC	5.00	1.50
❑ 261 Tony Dixon RC	3.00	.90
❑ 262 Brian Allen RC	2.00	.60
❑ 263 Torrance Marshall RC	5.00	1.50
❑ 264 Travis Henry RC	6.00	1.80
❑ 265 Travis Minor RC	3.00	.90
❑ 266 Vinny Sutherland RC	3.00	.90
❑ 267 Will Allen RC	3.00	.90
❑ 268 Derrick Blaylock RC	5.00	1.50
❑ 269 Zeke Moreno RC	5.00	1.50
❑ 270 Chris Barnes RC	3.00	.90
❑ 271 Dee Brown RC	5.00	1.50
❑ 272 Reggie White RC	3.00	.90
❑ 273 Derek Combs RC	3.00	.90
❑ 274 Steve Smith RC	6.00	1.80
❑ 275 John Capel RC	3.00	.90
❑ 276 Justin McCareins RC	5.00	1.50
❑ 277 Damerien McCants RC	3.00	.90
❑ 278 Eddie Berlin RC	3.00	.90
❑ 279 Francis St. Paul RC	3.00	.90
❑ 280 Quincy Carter RC	5.00	1.50

2001 Upper Deck Gold

Nm-Mt Ex-Mt

*STARS: 4X TO 10X BASIC CARDS
*ROOKIES: 2.5X TO 6X

2001 Upper Deck e-Card Prizes

Card	Nm-Mt	Ex-Mt
❑ EACW Chris Weinke AU	40.00	12.00
❑ EADB Drew Brees AU	60.00	18.00
❑ EAFM Freddie Mitchell AU	25.00	7.50
❑ EALT LaDainian Tomlinson AU	80.00	24.00
❑ EAMB Michael Bennett AU	60.00	18.00
❑ EAMV Michael Vick AU	200.00	60.00
❑ EJCW Chris Weinke JSY	25.00	7.50
❑ EJDB Drew Brees JSY	40.00	12.00
❑ EJFM Freddie Mitchell JSY	20.00	6.00
❑ EJLT LaDainian Tomlinson JSY	50.00	15.00
❑ EJMB Michael Bennett JSY	40.00	12.00
❑ EJMV Michael Vick JSY	60.00	18.00

2001 Upper Deck Game Jersey Autographs

Card	Nm-Mt	Ex-Mt
❑ BJAJ Brad Johnson	40.00	12.00
❑ DCAJ Daunte Culpepper	50.00	15.00
❑ IBAJ Isaac Bruce	50.00	15.00
❑ JGAJ Jeff Garcia	50.00	15.00
❑ JLAJ Jamal Lewis	50.00	15.00
❑ JPAJ Jake Plummer	40.00	12.00
❑ MAAJ Mike Alstott	50.00	15.00
❑ PMAJ Peyton Manning	120.00	36.00
❑ RMAJ Randy Moss	120.00	36.00

2002 Upper Deck

Card	Nm-Mt	Ex-Mt
COMP.SET w/o SP's (180)	25.00	7.50
❑ 1 Jake Plummer	.50	.15
❑ 2 Marcel Shipp	.75	.23
❑ 3 David Boston	.75	.23

❑	4	Arnold Jackson	.30	.09
❑	5	Frank Sanders	.30	.09
❑	6	Freddie Jones	.30	.09
❑	7	Michael Vick	2.50	.75
❑	8	Jamal Anderson	.50	.15
❑	9	Warrick Dunn	.75	.23
❑	10	Maurice Smith	.30	.09
❑	11	Shawn Jefferson	.30	.09
❑	12	Chris Redman	.30	.09
❑	13	Jeff Blake	.30	.09
❑	14	Jamal Lewis	.75	.23
❑	15	Travis Taylor	.50	.15
❑	16	Ray Lewis	.75	.23
❑	17	Chris McAlister	.30	.09
❑	18	Drew Bledsoe	1.00	.30
❑	19	Travis Henry	.75	.23
❑	20	Larry Centers	.30	.09
❑	21	Eric Moulds	.50	.15
❑	22	Reggie Germany	.30	.09
❑	23	Peerless Price	.50	.15
❑	24	Chris Weinke	.50	.15
❑	25	Lamar Smith	.50	.15
❑	26	Nick Goings	.30	.09
❑	27	Muhsin Muhammad	.50	.15
❑	28	Isaac Byrd	.30	.09
❑	29	Wesley Walls	.30	.09
❑	30	Jim Miller	.30	.09
❑	31	Anthony Thomas	.75	.23
❑	32	Dez White	.30	.09
❑	33	David Terrell	.75	.23
❑	34	Marty Booker	.50	.15
❑	35	Brian Urlacher	1.25	.35
❑	36	Jon Kitna	.50	.15
❑	37	Corey Dillon	.50	.15
❑	38	Peter Warrick	.50	.15
❑	39	Darnay Scott	.30	.09
❑	40	Chad Johnson	.75	.23
❑	41	Tim Couch	.50	.15
❑	42	James Jackson	.30	.09
❑	43	JaJuan Dawson	.30	.09
❑	44	Kevin Johnson	.50	.15
❑	45	Quincy Morgan	.30	.09
❑	46	Courtney Brown	.50	.15
❑	47	Quincy Carter	.50	.15
❑	48	Emmitt Smith	2.00	.60
❑	49	Joey Galloway	.50	.15
❑	50	Rocket Ismail	.50	.15
❑	51	Ken-Yon Rambo	.30	.09
❑	52	Brian Griese	.75	.23
❑	53	Terrell Davis	.75	.23
❑	54	Mike Anderson	.75	.23
❑	55	Shannon Sharpe	.50	.15
❑	56	Ed McCaffrey	.75	.23
❑	57	Rod Smith	.50	.15
❑	58	Mike McMahon	.75	.23
❑	59	James Stewart	.50	.15
❑	60	Az-Zahir Hakim	.30	.09
❑	61	Desmond Howard	.30	.09
❑	62	Germane Crowell	.30	.09
❑	63	Brett Favre	2.00	.60
❑	64	Ahman Green	.75	.23
❑	65	Antonio Freeman	.75	.23
❑	66	Terry Glenn	.50	.15
❑	67	Kabeer Gbaja-Biamila	.30	.09
❑	68	Kent Graham	.30	.09
❑	69	James Allen	.50	.15
❑	70	Corey Bradford	.30	.09
❑	71	Jermaine Lewis	.30	.09
❑	72	Jamie Sharper	.30	.09
❑	73	Peyton Manning	1.50	.45
❑	74	Edgerrin James	1.00	.30
❑	75	Dominic Rhodes	.50	.15
❑	76	Marvin Harrison	.75	.23
❑	77	Qadry Ismail	.50	.15
❑	78	Mark Brunell	.75	.23
❑	79	Fred Taylor	.75	.23
❑	80	Stacey Mack	.30	.09
❑	81	Jimmy Smith	.50	.15
❑	82	Keenan McCardell	.30	.09
❑	83	Trent Green	.50	.15
❑	84	Priest Holmes	1.00	.30
❑	85	Derrick Alexander	.50	.15
❑	86	Johnnie Morton	.50	.15
❑	87	Snoop Minnis	.30	.09
❑	88	Tony Gonzalez	.50	.15
❑	89	Jay Fiedler	.50	.15
❑	90	Ricky Williams	2.50	.75
❑	91	Chris Chambers	.75	.23
❑	92	Oronde Gadsden	.30	.09
❑	93	Zach Thomas	.75	.23
❑	94	Daunte Culpepper	.75	.23
❑	95	Michael Bennett	.50	.15
❑	96	Randy Moss	1.50	.45
❑	97	Sean Dawkins	.30	.09
❑	98	Tom Brady	2.00	.60
❑	99	Antowain Smith	.50	.15
❑	100	David Patten	.30	.09
❑	101	Troy Brown	.50	.15
❑	102	Adam Vinatieri	.75	.23
❑	103	Aaron Brooks	.75	.23
❑	104	Deuce McAllister	1.00	.30
❑	105	Jake Reed	.50	.15
❑	106	Jerome Pathon	.50	.15
❑	107	Joe Horn	.50	.15
❑	108	Kyle Turley	.30	.09
❑	109	Kerry Collins	.50	.15
❑	110	Ron Dayne	.50	.15
❑	111	Tiki Barber	.50	.15
❑	112	Amani Toomer	.50	.15
❑	113	Ike Hilliard	.50	.15
❑	114	Michael Strahan	.50	.15
❑	115	Vinny Testaverde	.50	.15
❑	116	Chad Pennington	1.00	.30
❑	117	Curtis Martin	.75	.23
❑	118	Santana Moss	.75	.23
❑	119	Laveranues Coles	.50	.15
❑	120	Wayne Chrebet	.50	.15
❑	121	Rich Gannon	.75	.23
❑	122	Charlie Garner	.50	.15
❑	123	Jerry Rice	1.50	.45
❑	124	Tim Brown	.75	.23
❑	125	Charles Woodson	.50	.15
❑	126	Donovan McNabb	1.00	.30
❑	127	Duce Staley	.75	.23
❑	128	Correll Buckhalter	.50	.15
❑	129	Freddie Mitchell	.50	.15
❑	130	James Thrash	.50	.15
❑	131	Todd Pinkston	.50	.15
❑	132	Kordell Stewart	.50	.15
❑	133	Jerome Bettis	.75	.23
❑	134	Chris Fuamatu-Ma'afala	.30	.09
❑	135	Hines Ward	.75	.23
❑	136	Plaxico Burress	.50	.15
❑	137	Kendrell Bell	.75	.23
❑	138	Doug Flutie	.75	.23
❑	139	Drew Brees	.75	.23
❑	140	LaDainian Tomlinson	1.25	.35
❑	141	Curtis Conway	.30	.09
❑	142	Tim Dwight	.50	.15
❑	143	Junior Seau	.75	.23
❑	144	Jeff Garcia	.75	.23
❑	145	Garrison Hearst	.50	.15
❑	146	Kevan Barlow	.50	.15
❑	147	Terrell Owens	.75	.23
❑	148	J.J. Stokes	.50	.15
❑	149	Trent Dilfer	.50	.15
❑	150	Shaun Alexander	.75	.23
❑	151	Ricky Watters	.50	.15
❑	152	Bobby Engram	.30	.09
❑	153	Koren Robinson	.50	.15
❑	154	Kurt Warner	.75	.23
❑	155	Marshall Faulk	.75	.23
❑	156	Isaac Bruce	.75	.23
❑	157	Ricky Proehl	.30	.09
❑	158	Terrence Wilkins	.30	.09
❑	159	Torry Holt	.75	.23
❑	160	Brad Johnson	.50	.15
❑	161	Shaun King	.30	.09
❑	162	Rob Johnson	.50	.15
❑	163	Mike Alstott	.75	.23
❑	164	Michael Pittman	.30	.09
❑	165	Keyshawn Johnson	.75	.23
❑	166	Steve McNair	.75	.23
❑	167	Eddie George	.75	.23
❑	168	Derrick Mason	.50	.15
❑	169	Kevin Dyson	.50	.15
❑	170	Frank Wycheck	.30	.09
❑	171	Jevon Kearse	.50	.15
❑	172	Danny Wuerffel	.50	.15
❑	173	Stephen Davis	.50	.15
❑	174	Michael Westbrook	.30	.09
❑	175	Rod Gardner	.50	.15
❑	176	Champ Bailey	.50	.15
❑	177	Darrell Green	.30	.09
❑	178	Kurt Warner CL	.50	.15
❑	179	Brett Favre CL	1.00	.30
❑	180	Randy Moss CL	.75	.23
❑	181	David Boston SS	4.00	1.20
❑	182	Jake Plummer SS	2.50	.75
❑	183	Michael Vick SS	12.00	3.60
❑	184	Drew Bledsoe SS	5.00	1.50
❑	185	Anthony Thomas SS	4.00	1.20
❑	186	Tim Couch SS	2.50	.75
❑	187	Emmitt Smith SS	10.00	3.00
❑	188	Ahman Green SS	4.00	1.20
❑	189	Brett Favre SS	10.00	3.00
❑	190	Edgerrin James SS	5.00	1.50
❑	191	Peyton Manning SS	8.00	2.40
❑	192	Mark Brunell SS	4.00	1.20
❑	193	Daunte Culpepper SS	4.00	1.20
❑	194	Randy Moss SS	8.00	2.40
❑	195	Tom Brady SS	10.00	3.00
❑	196	Aaron Brooks SS	4.00	1.20
❑	197	Ricky Williams SS	4.00	1.20
❑	198	Curtis Martin SS	4.00	1.20
❑	199	Jerry Rice SS	8.00	2.40
❑	200	Donovan McNabb SS	5.00	1.50
❑	201	Jerome Bettis SS	4.00	1.20
❑	202	Kordell Stewart SS	2.50	.75
❑	203	LaDainian Tomlinson SS	6.00	1.80
❑	204	Jeff Garcia SS	4.00	1.20
❑	205	Terrell Owens SS	4.00	1.20
❑	206	Shaun Alexander SS	4.00	1.20
❑	207	Kurt Warner SS	4.00	1.20
❑	208	Marshall Faulk SS	4.00	1.20
❑	209	Keyshawn Johnson SS	4.00	1.20
❑	210	Steve McNair SS	4.00	1.20
❑	211	Damien Anderson RC	5.00	1.50
❑	212	Jason McAddley RC	5.00	1.50
❑	213	Josh McCown RC	8.00	2.40
❑	214	Josh Scobey RC	4.00	1.20
❑	215	Preston Parsons RC	3.00	.90
❑	216	Dusty Bonner RC	3.00	.90
❑	217	Kahlil Hill RC	5.00	1.50
❑	218	Kurt Kittner RC	5.00	1.50
❑	219	T.J. Duckett RC	10.00	3.00
❑	220	Chester Taylor RC	6.00	1.80
❑	221	Kalimba Edwards RC	6.00	1.80
❑	223	Ron Johnson RC	5.00	1.50
❑	224	Tellis Redmon RC	5.00	1.50
❑	225	Wes Pate RC	3.00	.90
❑	226	David Priestley RC	5.00	1.50
❑	227	Josh Reed RC	6.00	1.80
❑	228	Mike Williams RC	5.00	1.50
❑	229	Ryan Denney RC	3.00	.90
❑	230	DeShaun Foster RC	6.00	1.80
❑	231	Julius Peppers RC	12.00	3.60
❑	232	Randy Fasani RC	5.00	1.50
❑	233	Adrian Peterson RC	6.00	1.80
❑	234	Alex Brown RC	6.00	1.80
❑	235	Gavin Hoffman RC	3.00	.90
❑	236	Levi Jones RC	5.00	1.50
❑	237	Andra Davis RC	5.00	1.50
❑	238	Andre Davis RC	6.00	1.80
❑	239	William Green RC	10.00	3.00
❑	240	Antonio Bryant RC	6.00	1.80
❑	241	Chad Hutchinson RC	6.00	1.80
❑	242	Roy Williams RC	15.00	4.50

❑ 243 Woody Dantzler RC	6.00	1.80
❑ 244 Ashley Lelie RC	12.00	3.60
❑ 245 Clinton Portis RC	20.00	6.00
❑ 246 Lamont Thompson RC	5.00	1.50
❑ 247 James Mungro RC	6.00	1.80
❑ 248 Joey Harrington RC	20.00	6.00
❑ 249 Luke Staley RC	5.00	1.50
❑ 250 Craig Nall RC	6.00	1.80
❑ 251 Javon Walker RC	12.00	3.60
❑ 252 Najeh Davenport RC	6.00	1.80
❑ 253 David Carr RC	20.00	6.00
❑ 254 Saleem Rasheed RC	6.00	1.80
❑ 255 Mike Rumph RC	6.00	1.80
❑ 256 Jabar Gaffney RC	6.00	1.80
❑ 257 Jonathan Wells RC	6.00	1.80
❑ 258 Dwight Freeney RC	8.00	2.40
❑ 259 Larry Tripplett RC	3.00	.90
❑ 260 David Garrard RC	6.00	1.80
❑ 261 John Henderson RC	6.00	1.80
❑ 262 Ryan Sims RC	6.00	1.80
❑ 263 Leonard Henry RC	5.00	1.50
❑ 264 Brian Allen RC	5.00	1.50
❑ 265 Atrews Bell RC	3.00	.90
❑ 266 Bryant McKinnie RC	5.00	1.50
❑ 267 Kelly Campbell RC	5.00	1.50
❑ 268 Raonall Smith RC	5.00	1.50
❑ 269 Antwoine Womack RC	5.00	1.50
❑ 270 Daniel Graham RC	6.00	1.80
❑ 271 Deion Branch RC	12.00	3.60
❑ 272 Sam Simmons RC	3.00	.90
❑ 273 Rohan Davey RC	6.00	1.80
❑ 274 Charles Grant RC	6.00	1.80
❑ 275 Derrick Lewis RC	3.00	.90
❑ 276 Donte Stallworth RC	12.00	3.60
❑ 277 J.T. O'Sullivan RC	5.00	1.50
❑ 278 Keyuo Craver RC	5.00	1.50
❑ 279 Ricky Williams RC	5.00	1.50
❑ 280 Bryan Thomas RC	5.00	1.50
❑ 281 Jeremy Shockey RC	20.00	6.00
❑ 282 Tim Carter RC	5.00	1.50
❑ 283 Larry Ned RC	2.50	.75
❑ 284 Napoleon Harris RC	4.00	1.20
❑ 285 Phillip Buchanon RC	6.00	1.80
❑ 286 Ronald Curry RC	6.00	1.80
❑ 287 Brian Westbrook RC	10.00	3.00
❑ 288 Freddie Milons RC	5.00	1.50
❑ 289 Lito Sheppard RC	6.00	1.80
❑ 290 Antwaan Randle El RC	8.00	2.40
❑ 291 Lee Mays RC	2.50	.75
❑ 292 Daryl Jones RC	5.00	1.50
❑ 293 Justin Peelle RC	3.00	.90
❑ 294 Quentin Jammer RC	4.00	1.20
❑ 295 Reche Caldwell RC	6.00	1.80
❑ 296 Seth Burford RC	5.00	1.50
❑ 297 Terry Charles RC	5.00	1.50
❑ 298 Brandon Doman RC	6.00	1.80
❑ 299 Maurice Morris RC	6.00	1.80
❑ 300 Eric Crouch RC	10.00	3.00
❑ 301 Lamar Gordon RC	6.00	1.80
❑ 302 Marquise Walker RC	5.00	1.50
❑ 303 Tracey Wistrom RC	5.00	1.50
❑ 304 Travis Stephens RC	5.00	1.50
❑ 305 Herb Haygood RC	3.00	.90
❑ 306 Albert Haynesworth RC	5.00	1.50
❑ 307 Rocky Calmus RC	6.00	1.80
❑ 308 Cliff Russell RC	5.00	1.50
❑ 309 Ladell Betts RC	6.00	1.80
❑ 310A Patrick Ramsey RC	12.00	3.60
❑ 310B Ed Reed RC	10.00	3.00

2003 Upper Deck

	MINT	NRMT
COMP.SET w/o SP's (180)	25.00	11.00
❑ 1 Brad Johnson	.50	.23
❑ 2 Derrick Brooks	.50	.23
❑ 3 Simeon Rice	.50	.23
❑ 4 Warren Sapp	.50	.23
❑ 5 Thomas Jones	.50	.23
❑ 6 Mike Alstott	.75	.35
❑ 7 Michael Pittman	.30	.14
❑ 8 Tim Brown	.75	.35
❑ 9 Rich Gannon	.50	.23
❑ 10 Charlie Garner	.50	.23
❑ 11 Jerry Porter	.50	.23
❑ 12 Phillip Buchanon	.30	.14

❑ 13 Charles Woodson	.50	.23
❑ 14 James Thrash	.30	.14
❑ 15 Duce Staley	.50	.23
❑ 16 Brian Westbrook	.50	.23
❑ 17 Correll Buckhalter	.50	.23
❑ 18 Koy Detmer	.30	.14
❑ 19 Brian Dawkins	.30	.14
❑ 20 Jon Ritchie	.30	.14
❑ 21 Ahman Green	.75	.35
❑ 22 Donald Driver	.50	.23
❑ 23 Bubba Franks	.50	.23
❑ 24 Javon Walker	.50	.23
❑ 25 Kabeer Gbaja-Biamila	.50	.23
❑ 26 Robert Ferguson	.30	.14
❑ 27 Eddie George	.50	.23
❑ 28 Jevon Kearse	.50	.23
❑ 29 Billy Volek	.75	.35
❑ 30 Frank Wycheck	.30	.14
❑ 31 Derrick Mason	.50	.23
❑ 32 Tommy Maddox	.75	.35
❑ 33 Jerome Bettis	.75	.35
❑ 34 Antwaan Randle El	.75	.35
❑ 35 Amos Zereoue	.50	.23
❑ 36 Hines Ward	.75	.35
❑ 37 Jeff Garcia	.75	.35
❑ 38 Terrell Owens	.75	.35
❑ 39 Tim Rattay	.50	.23
❑ 40 Brandon Doman	.30	.14
❑ 41 Tai Streets	.30	.14
❑ 42 Garrison Hearst	.50	.23
❑ 43 Kerry Collins	.50	.23
❑ 44 Tiki Barber	.50	.23
❑ 45 Amani Toomer	.50	.23
❑ 46 Jesse Palmer	.30	.14
❑ 47 Tim Carter	.30	.14
❑ 48 Michael Strahan	.50	.23
❑ 49 Ike Hilliard	.30	.14
❑ 50 Marvin Harrison	.75	.35
❑ 51 Peyton Manning	1.25	.55
❑ 52 Marcus Pollard	.30	.14
❑ 53 James Mungro	.30	.14
❑ 54 Reggie Wayne	.50	.23
❑ 55 Peerless Price	.50	.23
❑ 56 Warrick Dunn	.50	.23
❑ 57 T.J. Duckett	.50	.23
❑ 58 Keith Brooking	.30	.14
❑ 59 Doug Johnson	.30	.14
❑ 60 Brian Finneran	.30	.14
❑ 61 Chad Pennington	1.00	.45
❑ 62 Curtis Martin	.75	.35
❑ 63 Marvin Jones	.30	.14
❑ 64 Wayne Chrebet	.50	.23
❑ 65 LaMont Jordan	.50	.23
❑ 66 Curtis Conway	.30	.14
❑ 67 Vinny Testaverde	.50	.23
❑ 68 Tim Couch	.30	.14
❑ 69 William Green	.50	.23
❑ 70 Andre Davis	.30	.14
❑ 71 Quincy Morgan	.50	.23
❑ 72 Dennis Northcutt	.50	.23
❑ 73 Kelly Holcomb	.50	.23
❑ 74 Jake Plummer	.50	.23
❑ 75 Mike Anderson	.75	.35
❑ 76 Ashley Lelie	.75	.35
❑ 77 Ed McCaffrey	.75	.35
❑ 78 Shannon Sharpe	.30	.14
❑ 79 Rod Smith	.50	.23
❑ 80 Terrell Davis	.75	.35
❑ 81 Antowain Smith	.50	.23
❑ 82 Kevin Faulk	.30	.14
❑ 83 David Patten	.30	.14
❑ 84 Deion Branch	.75	.35
❑ 85 Troy Brown	.50	.23
❑ 86 Rohan Davey	.50	.23
❑ 87 Jay Fiedler	.50	.23
❑ 88 Randy McMichael	.50	.23
❑ 89 Derrius Thompson	.30	.14
❑ 90 Jason Taylor	.30	.14
❑ 91 Zach Thomas	.75	.35
❑ 92 Ricky Williams	.75	.35
❑ 93 Deuce McAllister	.75	.35
❑ 94 Donte Stallworth	.75	.35
❑ 95 Jerome Pathon	.30	.14
❑ 96 Michael Lewis	.30	.14
❑ 97 Joe Horn	.50	.23
❑ 98 Priest Holmes	1.00	.45
❑ 99 Johnnie Morton	.50	.23
❑ 100 Eddie Kennison	.30	.14
❑ 101 Dante Hall	.75	.35
❑ 102 Tony Gonzalez	.50	.23
❑ 103 Marc Boerigter	.50	.23
❑ 104 Drew Brees	.75	.35
❑ 105 David Boston	.50	.23
❑ 106 Reche Caldwell	.30	.14
❑ 107 Tim Dwight	.50	.23
❑ 108 Doug Flutie	.75	.35
❑ 109 Drew Bledsoe	.75	.35
❑ 110 Eric Moulds	.50	.23
❑ 111 Alex Van Pelt	.30	.14
❑ 112 Charles Johnson	.30	.14
❑ 113 Takeo Spikes	.30	.14
❑ 114 Josh Reed	.50	.23
❑ 115 Ladell Betts	.50	.23
❑ 116 Laveranues Coles	.50	.23
❑ 117 Champ Bailey	.50	.23
❑ 118 Trung Canidate	.50	.23
❑ 119 Kenny Watson	.30	.14
❑ 120 Rod Gardner	.50	.23
❑ 121 Kurt Warner	.75	.35
❑ 122 Lamar Gordon	.30	.14
❑ 123 Shaun McDonald RC	.75	.35
❑ 124 Marc Bulger	.75	.35
❑ 125 Isaac Bruce	.75	.35
❑ 126 Torry Holt	.75	.35
❑ 127 Matt Hasselbeck	.50	.23
❑ 128 Maurice Morris	.30	.14
❑ 129 Bobby Engram	.30	.14
❑ 130 Darrell Jackson	.50	.23
❑ 131 Koren Robinson	.50	.23
❑ 132 Chris Redman	.30	.14
❑ 133 Todd Heap	.50	.23
❑ 134 Travis Taylor	.50	.23
❑ 135 Ron Johnson	.30	.14
❑ 136 Ray Lewis	.75	.35
❑ 137 Jake Delhomme	.75	.35
❑ 138 Muhsin Muhammad	.50	.23
❑ 139 Stephen Davis	.50	.23
❑ 140 Julius Peppers	.75	.35
❑ 141 Rodney Peete	.30	.14
❑ 142 Mark Brunell	.50	.23
❑ 143 Jimmy Smith	.50	.23
❑ 144 Kyle Brady	.30	.14
❑ 145 Kevin Lockett	.30	.14
❑ 146 David Garrard	.30	.14
❑ 147 Fred Taylor	.75	.35
❑ 148 Michael Bennett	.50	.23
❑ 149 Ronald Bellamy RC	1.00	.45
❑ 150 Randy Moss	1.25	.55
❑ 151 D'Wayne Bates	.30	.14
❑ 152 Josh McCown	.50	.23
❑ 153 Marquise Walker	.30	.14
❑ 154 Jeff Blake	.30	.14
❑ 155 Freddie Jones	.30	.14
❑ 156 Marcel Shipp	.50	.23
❑ 157 Troy Hambrick	.30	.14
❑ 158 Joey Galloway	.50	.23
❑ 159 Terry Glenn	.30	.14
❑ 160 Roy Williams	.75	.35
❑ 161 Antonio Bryant	.50	.23
❑ 162 Quincy Carter	.50	.23
❑ 163 Anthony Thomas	.75	.35
❑ 164 Marty Booker	.50	.23
❑ 165 Dez White	.30	.14

❑ 166 Adrian Peterson .30 .14
❑ 167 Kordell Stewart .50 .23
❑ 168 David Terrell .50 .23
❑ 169 Jabar Gaffney .50 .23
❑ 170 Bennie Joppru RC 1.00 .45
❑ 171 Corey Bradford .30 .14
❑ 172 David Carr 1.25 .55
❑ 173 James Stewart .50 .23
❑ 174 Ty Detmer .30 .14
❑ 175 Az-Zahir Hakim .30 .14
❑ 176 Bill Schroeder .50 .23
❑ 177 Jon Kitna .50 .23
❑ 178 Chad Johnson .50 .23
❑ 179 Ron Dugans .30 .14
❑ 180 Peter Warrick .50 .23
❑ 181 Brett Favre SS 12.00 5.50
❑ 182 Emmitt Smith SS 12.00 5.50
❑ 183 LaDainian Tomlinson SS 5.00 2.20
❑ 184 Joey Harrington SS 8.00 3.60
❑ 185 Brian Urlacher SS 8.00 3.60
❑ 186 Daunte Culpepper SS 5.00 2.20
❑ 187 Jamal Lewis SS 5.00 2.20
❑ 188 Shaun Alexander SS 5.00 2.20
❑ 189 Marshall Faulk SS 5.00 2.20
❑ 190 Travis Henry SS 4.00 1.80
❑ 191 Trent Green SS 4.00 1.80
❑ 192 Aaron Brooks SS 5.00 2.20
❑ 193 Chris Chambers SS 5.00 2.20
❑ 194 Tom Brady SS 6.00 2.70
❑ 195 Clinton Portis SS 8.00 3.60
❑ 196 Kevin Johnson SS 4.00 1.80
❑ 197 Santana Moss SS 4.00 1.80
❑ 198 Michael Vick SS 12.00 5.50
❑ 199 Edgerrin James SS .75 .35
❑ 200 Jeremy Shockey SS 8.00 3.60
❑ 201 Kevan Barlow SS 4.00 1.80
❑ 202 Plaxico Burress SS 4.00 1.80
❑ 203 Steve McNair SS 5.00 2.20
❑ 204 Donovan McNabb SS 6.00 2.70
❑ 205 Jerry Rice SS 10.00 4.50
❑ 206 Keyshawn Johnson SS 5.00 2.20
❑ 207 Patrick Ramsey SS 5.00 2.20
❑ 208 Stephen Davis SS 4.00 1.80
❑ 209 Corey Dillon SS 4.00 1.80
❑ 210 Chad Hutchinson SS 4.00 1.80
❑ 211 Brad Banks RC 4.00 1.80
❑ 212 Kliff Kingsbury RC 4.00 1.80
❑ 213 Jason Gesser RC 5.00 2.20
❑ 214 Jason Johnson RC 3.00 1.35
❑ 215 Brian St.Pierre RC 5.00 2.20
❑ 216 Ken Dorsey RC 8.00 3.60
❑ 217 Seneca Wallace RC 5.00 2.20
❑ 218 Brooks Bollinger RC 5.00 2.20
❑ 219 Chris Brown RC 10.00 4.50
❑ 220 B.J Askew RC 5.00 2.20
❑ 221 Earnest Graham RC 4.00 1.80
❑ 222 Quentin Griffin RC 15.00 6.75
❑ 223 Musa Smith RC 5.00 2.20
❑ 224 Artose Pinner RC 5.00 2.20
❑ 225 Domanick Davis RC 10.00 4.50
❑ 226 Anquan Boldin RC 12.00 5.50
❑ 227 Talman Gardner RC 5.00 2.20
❑ 228 Brandon Lloyd RC 6.00 2.70
❑ 229 Bryant Johnson RC 5.00 2.20
❑ 230 Kareem Kelly RC 4.00 1.80
❑ 231 Arnaz Battle RC 5.00 2.20
❑ 232 Keenan Howry RC 5.00 2.20
❑ 233 Justin Gage RC 5.00 2.20
❑ 234 Tyrone Calico RC 8.00 3.60
❑ 235 Teyo Johnson RC 5.00 2.20
❑ 236 Malaefou MacKenzie RC 3.00 1.35
❑ 237 Terence Newman RC 10.00 4.50
❑ 238 Marcus Trufant RC 5.00 2.20
❑ 239 Mike Doss RC 5.00 2.20
❑ 240 Terrell Suggs RC 8.00 3.60
❑ 241 Carson Palmer RC 25.00 11.00
❑ 242 Byron Leftwich RC 30.00 13.50
❑ 243 Rex Grossman RC 20.00 9.00
❑ 244 Kyle Boller RC 20.00 9.00
❑ 245 Dave Ragone RC 8.00 3.60
❑ 246 Chris Simms RC 15.00 6.75
❑ 247 Larry Johnson RC 15.00 6.75
❑ 248 Lee Suggs RC 15.00 6.75
❑ 249 Justin Fargas RC 8.00 3.60
❑ 250 Onterrio Smith RC 8.00 3.60
❑ 251 Willis McGahee RC 20.00 9.00
❑ 252 Charles Rogers RC 8.00 3.60
❑ 253 Andre Johnson RC 20.00 9.00
❑ 254 Taylor Jacobs RC 8.00 3.60
❑ 255 Kelley Washington RC 8.00 3.60
❑ 256 Tony Romo RC 6.00 2.70
❑ 257 Jerel Myers RC 4.00 1.80
❑ 258 Kirk Farmer RC 4.00 1.80
❑ 259 Kevin Walter RC 5.00 2.20
❑ 260 Gibran Hamdan RC 4.00 1.80
❑ 261 Juston Wood RC 4.00 1.80
❑ 262 Travis Anglin RC 4.00 1.80
❑ 263 Marquel Blackwell RC 4.00 1.80
❑ 264 Jason Thomas RC 5.00 2.20
❑ 265 Carl Ford RC 4.00 1.80
❑ 266 Walter Young RC 4.00 1.80
❑ 267 Sultan McCullough RC 5.00 2.20
❑ 268 Dahrran Diedrick RC 6.00 2.70
❑ 269 Cecil Sapp RC 5.00 2.20
❑ 270 Doug Gabriel RC 6.00 2.70
❑ 271 LaBrandon Toefield RC 6.00 2.70
❑ 272 Adrian Madise RC 5.00 2.20
❑ 273 J.R. Tolver RC 5.00 2.20
❑ 274 Kevin Curtis RC 6.00 2.70
❑ 275 Bobby Wade RC 6.00 2.70
❑ 276 Sam Aiken RC 5.00 2.20
❑ 277 Mike Bush RC 4.00 1.80
❑ 278 Billy McMullen RC 5.00 2.20
❑ 279 Bethel Johnson RC 10.00 4.50
❑ 280 David Kircus RC 5.00 2.20
❑ 281 Zuriel Smith RC 4.00 1.80
❑ 282 LaTarence Dunbar RC 5.00 2.20
❑ 283 Nate Burleson RC 10.00 4.50
❑ 284 Antwone Savage RC 4.00 1.80
❑ 285 Terrence Edwards RC 5.00 2.20

2003 Upper Deck Gold

MINT NRMT

*STARS: 8X TO 20X BASIC CARDS
*SS 181-210: 1.2X TO 3X
*ROOKIES 211-240: 1.2X TO 3X
*ROOKIES 241-255: .8X TO 2X
*ROOKIES 256-285: 1X TO 2.5X

2003 Upper Deck Game Jerseys

MINT NRMT

*GOLD: .8X TO 2X BASIC CARDS

❑ GJAB Aaron Brooks 2 12.00 5.50
❑ GJAL Ashley Lelie 1 12.00 5.50
❑ GJAT Amani Toomer 1 10.00 4.50
❑ GJBF Brett Favre 2 30.00 13.50
❑ GJBG Brian Griese 1 12.00 5.50
❑ GJBJ Brad Johnson 1 10.00 4.50
❑ GJBR Antonio Bryant 2 10.00 4.50
❑ GJCB1 Champ Bailey 1 10.00 4.50
❑ GJCB2 Correll Buckhalter 1 10.00 4.50
❑ GJCJ Chad Johnson 1 10.00 4.50
❑ GJCP Clinton Portis 2 15.00 6.75
❑ GJCW Charles Woodson 1 10.00 4.50
❑ GJDC David Carr 2 15.00 6.75
❑ GJDS Duce Staley 1 10.00 4.50
❑ GJEM Eric Moulds 1 10.00 4.50
❑ GJJB Jerome Bettis 2 12.00 5.50
❑ GJJK Jevon Kearse 1 10.00 4.50
❑ GJJL Jamal Lewis 2 15.00 6.75
❑ GJJS Jeremy Shockey 2 12.00 5.50
❑ GJKJ Kevin Johnson 2 10.00 4.50
❑ GJKS Kordell Stewart 1 10.00 4.50
❑ GJKW Kurt Warner 2 15.00 6.75
❑ GJMA Mike Alstott 1 12.00 5.50
❑ GJMB Mark Brunell 2 10.00 4.50
❑ GJMF Marshall Faulk 2 12.00 5.50
❑ GJMS Michael Strahan 1 12.00 5.50
❑ GJMV Michael Vick 2 25.00 11.00
❑ GJOG Olandis Gary 1 10.00 4.50
❑ GJPM Peyton Manning 2 15.00 6.75
❑ GJPW Peter Warrick 1 10.00 4.50
❑ GJQJ Quentin Jammer 1 10.00 4.50
❑ GJRG Rich Gannon 2 12.00 5.50
❑ GJRL Ray Lewis 1 12.00 5.50
❑ GJRM Randy Moss 2 15.00 6.75
❑ GJRW Roy Williams 1 12.00 5.50
❑ GJSE Junior Seau 2 10.00 4.50
❑ GJSM Steve McNair 2 12.00 5.50
❑ GJTH Torry Holt 2 12.00 5.50
❑ GJWC Wayne Chrebet 1 10.00 4.50
❑ GJWS Warren Sapp 1 12.00 5.50
❑ GJZT Zach Thomas 1 12.00 5.50

2003 Upper Deck Game Jerseys Autographs

MINT NRMT

❑ GJAAB Antonio Bryant/99 30.00 13.50
❑ GJAAL Ashley Lelie/99 80.00 36.00
❑ GJACP Clinton Portis/26 175.00 80.00
❑ GJADC David Carr/99 120.00 55.00
❑ GJADF DeShaun Foster/99 40.00 18.00
❑ GJADM Donovan McNabb/5
❑ GJAJS Jeremy Shockey/99 120.00 55.00
❑ GJAKK Kurt Kittner/45 30.00 13.50
❑ GJAMV Michael Vick/7
❑ GJAPM Peyton Manning/18
❑ GJARW Roy Williams/99 80.00 36.00
❑ GJAWD Woody Dantzler/99 40.00 18.00

2003 Upper Deck Game Jerseys Duals

MINT NRMT

*GOLD: .6X TO 1.5X BASIC CARDS
GOLD STATED PRINT RUN 99 SER.#'d SETS

❑ DGJBM Drew Bledsoe 30.00 13.50
Willis McGahee
❑ DGJBS Nate Burleson 20.00 9.00
Onterrio Smith
❑ DGJBT Drew Brees 15.00 6.75
LaDainian Tomlinson

❑ DGJCJ Tim Couch 15.00 6.75
Kevin Johnson
❑ DGJCR David Carr 20.00 9.00
Dave Ragone
❑ DGJCS Kerry Collins 15.00 6.75
Jeremy Shockey
❑ DGJCW Carson Palmer 20.00 9.00
Kelley Washington
❑ DGJDM Daunte Culpepper 30.00 13.50
Randy Moss
❑ DGJFC Jay Fiedler 15.00 6.75
Chris Chambers
❑ DGJFG Brett Favre 40.00 18.00
Ahman Green
❑ DGJGR Rich Gannon 25.00 11.00
Jerry Rice
❑ DGJJB Bryant Johnson 30.00 13.50
Anquan Boldin
❑ DGJJG Taylor Jacobs 15.00 6.75
Rod Gardner
❑ DGJKJ Keyshawn Johnson 15.00 6.75
Dual swatches
❑ DGJMC Peyton Manning 25.00 11.00
Dallas Clark
❑ DGJPC Chad Pennington 20.00 9.00
Wayne Chrebet
❑ DGJWH Kurt Warner 15.00 6.75
Torry Holt

2003 Upper Deck Rookie Future Jerseys

MINT NRMT
*GOLD: .8X TO 2X BASIC CARDS
GOLD STATED PRINT RUN 99 SER.#'d SETS

❑ RFAB Anquan Boldin 20.00 9.00
❑ RFAJ Andre Johnson 15.00 6.75
❑ RFAP Artose Pinner 8.00 3.60
❑ RFBE Bethel Johnson 15.00 6.75
❑ RFBJ Bryant Johnson 10.00 4.50
❑ RFBL Byron Leftwich 25.00 11.00
❑ RFBS Brian St.Pierre 10.00 4.50
❑ RFCB Chris Brown 20.00 9.00
❑ RFCP Carson Palmer 20.00 9.00
❑ RFDC Dallas Clark 10.00 4.50
❑ RFDR Dave Ragone 10.00 4.50
❑ RFJF Justin Fargas 10.00 4.50
❑ RFKB Kyle Boller 20.00 9.00
❑ RFKC Kevin Curtis 10.00 4.50
❑ RFKK Kliff Kingsbury 8.00 3.60
❑ RFKW Kelley Washington 10.00 4.50
❑ RFLJ Larry Johnson 12.00 5.50
❑ RFMS Musa Smith 10.00 4.50
❑ RFMT Marcus Trufant 10.00 4.50
❑ RFNB Nate Burleson 15.00 6.75
❑ RFOS Onterrio Smith 12.00 5.50
❑ RFRG Rex Grossman 15.00 6.75
❑ RFRM Ricky Manning 10.00 4.50
❑ RFRO DeWayne Robertson EXCH 10.00 4.50
❑ RFSW Seneca Wallace 10.00 4.50
❑ RFTE Teyo Johnson 10.00 4.50
❑ RFTG Tyrone Calico 12.00 5.50
❑ RFTJ Taylor Jacobs 10.00 4.50
❑ RFTN Terence Newman 15.00 6.75
❑ RFTS Terrell Suggs 12.00 5.50
❑ RFWM Willis McGahee 15.00 6.75
❑ RFWP Willie Pile 10.00 4.50

2003 Upper Deck Rookie Future Jerseys Autographs

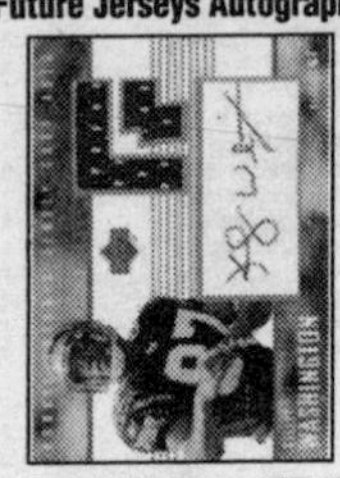

MINT NRMT
SERIAL #'d UNDER 21 NOT PRICED

❑ RFABL Byron Leftwich/7
❑ RFACP Carson Palmer/9
❑ RFADR Dave Ragone/4
❑ RFAJF Justin Fargas/20
❑ RFAKB Kyle Boller/8
❑ RFAKK Kliff Kingsbury/15
❑ RFAKW Kelley Washington/87 30.00 13.50
❑ RFALJ Larry Johnson/34 60.00 27.00
❑ RFARG Rex Grossman/8
❑ RFARO DeWayne Robertson/63 40.00 18.00

2004 Upper Deck

Nm-Mt Ex-Mt
COMP.SET w/o SP's (250) 60.00 18.00
COMP.SET w/o RC's (200) 25.00 7.50
201-225 ROOKIE STATED ODDS 1:8
226-275 ROOKIE STATED ODDS 1:1
UNPRICED PRINT PLATE PRINT RUN 1 SET

❑ 1 Anquan Boldin .75 .23
❑ 2 Josh McCown .50 .15
❑ 3 Emmitt Smith 1.50 .45
❑ 4 Freddie Jones .30 .09
❑ 5 Marcel Shipp .50 .15
❑ 6 Shaun King .30 .09
❑ 7 Michael Vick 1.50 .45
❑ 8 T.J. Duckett .50 .15
❑ 9 Peerless Price .50 .15
❑ 10 Warrick Dunn .50 .15
❑ 11 Keith Brooking .30 .09
❑ 12 Brian Finneran .30 .09
❑ 13 Anthony Wright .30 .09
❑ 14 Kyle Boller .75 .23
❑ 15 Jamal Lewis .75 .23
❑ 16 Todd Heap .50 .15
❑ 17 Ray Lewis .75 .23
❑ 18 Terrell Suggs .50 .15
❑ 19 Travis Taylor .30 .09
❑ 20 Drew Bledsoe .75 .23
❑ 21 Willis McGahee .75 .23
❑ 22 Eric Moulds .50 .15
❑ 23 Travis Henry .50 .15
❑ 24 Takeo Spikes .30 .09
❑ 25 Josh Reed .30 .09
❑ 26 Lawyer Milloy .50 .15
❑ 27 Stephen Davis .50 .15
❑ 28 Jake Delhomme .75 .23
❑ 29 Steve Smith .50 .15
❑ 30 DeShaun Foster .50 .15
❑ 31 Dan Morgan .30 .09
❑ 32 Julius Peppers .75 .23
❑ 33 Rod Smart .30 .09
❑ 34 Rex Grossman .75 .23
❑ 35 Thomas Jones .50 .15
❑ 36 Marty Booker .50 .15
❑ 37 Anthony Thomas .50 .15
❑ 38 Brian Urlacher 1.00 .30
❑ 39 Justin Gage .50 .15
❑ 40 Chad Johnson .50 .15
❑ 41 Carson Palmer 1.00 .30
❑ 42 Peter Warrick .50 .15
❑ 43 Jon Kitna .50 .15
❑ 44 Kelley Washington .30 .09
❑ 45 Rudi Johnson .50 .15
❑ 46 Jeff Garcia .75 .23
❑ 47 Dennis Northcutt .30 .09
❑ 48 Lee Suggs .75 .23
❑ 49 Andre Davis .30 .09
❑ 50 Quincy Morgan .50 .15
❑ 51 Kelly Holcomb .50 .15
❑ 52 Keyshawn Johnson .50 .15
❑ 53 Quincy Carter .50 .15
❑ 54 Antonio Bryant .50 .15
❑ 55 Terry Glenn .30 .09
❑ 56 Terence Newman .50 .15
❑ 57 Roy Williams S .50 .15
❑ 58 Champ Bailey .50 .15
❑ 59 Jake Plummer .50 .15
❑ 60 Quentin Griffin .75 .23
❑ 61 John Lynch .50 .15
❑ 62 Rod Smith .50 .15
❑ 63 Ashley Lelie .50 .15
❑ 64 Joey Harrington .75 .23
❑ 65 Az-Zahir Hakim .30 .09
❑ 66 Charles Rogers .50 .15
❑ 67 Tai Streets .30 .09
❑ 68 Shawn Bryson .30 .09
❑ 69 Artose Pinner .30 .09
❑ 70 Brett Favre 2.00 .60
❑ 71 Nick Barnett .50 .15
❑ 72 Ahman Green .75 .23
❑ 73 Kabeer Gbaja-Biamila .50 .15
❑ 74 Javon Walker .50 .15
❑ 75 Donald Driver .50 .15
❑ 76 Tim Couch .30 .09
❑ 77 David Carr .75 .23
❑ 78 Corey Bradford .30 .09
❑ 79 J.J. Moses .30 .09
❑ 80 Domanick Davis .75 .23
❑ 81 Jabar Gaffney .50 .15
❑ 82 Andre Johnson .75 .23
❑ 83 Marvin Harrison .75 .23
❑ 84 Peyton Manning 1.25 .35
❑ 85 Dallas Clark .50 .15
❑ 86 Edgerrin James .75 .23
❑ 87 Reggie Wayne .50 .15
❑ 88 Dwight Freeney .30 .09
❑ 89 Byron Leftwich 1.25 .35
❑ 90 LaBrandon Toefield .30 .09
❑ 91 Fred Taylor .50 .15
❑ 92 Troy Edwards .30 .09
❑ 93 Jimmy Smith .50 .15
❑ 94 Kyle Brady .30 .09
❑ 95 Trent Green .50 .15
❑ 96 Tony Gonzalez .50 .15
❑ 97 Dante Hall .75 .23
❑ 98 Priest Holmes 1.00 .30
❑ 99 Eddie Kennison .30 .09
❑ 100 Johnnie Morton .50 .15
❑ 101 Jay Fiedler .30 .09
❑ 102 Junior Seau .75 .23
❑ 103 Ricky Williams .75 .23
❑ 104 Chris Chambers .50 .15
❑ 105 Zach Thomas .75 .23
❑ 106 David Boston .50 .15
❑ 107 A.J. Feeley .75 .23
❑ 108 Daunte Culpepper .75 .23
❑ 109 Onterrio Smith .50 .15
❑ 110 Randy Moss 1.00 .30
❑ 111 Moe Williams .30 .09
❑ 112 Michael Bennett .50 .15

❑ 113 Jim Kleinsasser	.30	.09
❑ 114 Tom Brady	1.25	.35
❑ 115 Kevin Faulk	.30	.09
❑ 116 Deion Branch	.75	.23
❑ 117 Corey Dillon	.50	.15
❑ 118 Troy Brown	.50	.15
❑ 119 Adam Vinatieri	.75	.23
❑ 120 Tedy Bruschi	.50	.15
❑ 121 Aaron Brooks	.50	.15
❑ 122 Deuce McAllister	.75	.23
❑ 123 Donte' Stallworth	.50	.15
❑ 124 Joe Horn	.50	.15
❑ 125 Jerome Pathon	.30	.09
❑ 126 Boo Williams	.30	.09
❑ 127 Jeremy Shockey	.75	.23
❑ 128 Kurt Warner	.75	.23
❑ 129 Amani Toomer	.50	.15
❑ 130 Tiki Barber	.50	.15
❑ 131 Ike Hilliard	.30	.09
❑ 132 Michael Strahan	.50	.15
❑ 133 Chad Pennington	1.00	.30
❑ 134 Santana Moss	.50	.15
❑ 135 Wayne Chrebet	.50	.15
❑ 136 Curtis Martin	.75	.23
❑ 137 LaMont Jordan	.50	.15
❑ 138 Justin McCareins	.30	.09
❑ 139 Jerry Rice	1.50	.45
❑ 140 Rich Gannon	.50	.15
❑ 141 Tim Brown	.75	.23
❑ 142 Jerry Porter	.50	.15
❑ 143 Warren Sapp	.50	.15
❑ 144 Charles Woodson	.50	.15
❑ 145 Donovan McNabb	1.00	.30
❑ 146 Brian Westbrook	.50	.15
❑ 147 Todd Pinkston	.30	.09
❑ 148 Jevon Kearse	.50	.15
❑ 149 Freddie Mitchell	.50	.15
❑ 150 Correll Buckhalter	.50	.15
❑ 151 Terrell Owens	.75	.23
❑ 152 Tommy Maddox	.50	.15
❑ 153 Duce Staley	.50	.15
❑ 154 Plaxico Burress	.50	.15
❑ 155 Hines Ward	.75	.23
❑ 156 Antwaan Randle El	.50	.15
❑ 157 Jerome Bettis	.75	.23
❑ 158 Kendrell Bell	.50	.15
❑ 159 LaDainian Tomlinson	.75	.23
❑ 160 Doug Flutie	.75	.23
❑ 161 Quentin Jammer	.30	.09
❑ 162 Drew Brees	.75	.23
❑ 163 Reche Caldwell	.30	.09
❑ 164 Tim Dwight	.50	.15
❑ 165 Tim Rattay	.50	.15
❑ 166 Kevan Barlow	.50	.15
❑ 167 Brandon Lloyd	.50	.15
❑ 168 Cedrick Wilson	.30	.09
❑ 169 Julian Peterson	.30	.09
❑ 170 Ahmed Plummer	.30	.09
❑ 171 Matt Hasselbeck	.50	.15
❑ 172 Koren Robinson	.50	.15
❑ 173 Shaun Alexander	.75	.23
❑ 174 Darrell Jackson	.50	.15
❑ 175 Marcus Trufant	.30	.09
❑ 176 Bobby Engram	.30	.09
❑ 177 Marc Bulger	.75	.23
❑ 178 Torry Holt	.75	.23
❑ 179 Marshall Faulk	.75	.23
❑ 180 Orlando Pace	.30	.09
❑ 181 Isaac Bruce	.50	.15
❑ 182 Kyle Turley	.30	.09
❑ 183 Brad Johnson	.50	.15
❑ 184 Charlie Garner	.50	.15
❑ 185 Keenan McCardell	.30	.09
❑ 186 Mike Alstott	.50	.15
❑ 187 Derrick Brooks	.50	.15
❑ 188 Brian Griese	.50	.15
❑ 189 Steve McNair	.75	.23
❑ 190 Chris Brown	.75	.23
❑ 191 Eddie George	.50	.15
❑ 192 Tyrone Calico	.50	.15
❑ 193 Derrick Mason	.50	.15
❑ 194 Drew Bennett	.50	.15
❑ 195 Mark Brunell	.50	.15
❑ 196 LaVar Arrington	1.50	.45
❑ 197 Clinton Portis	.75	.23
❑ 198 Laveranues Coles	.50	.15
❑ 199 Patrick Ramsey	.50	.15
❑ 200 Rod Gardner	.50	.15
❑ 201 Eli Manning RC	30.00	9.00
❑ 202 Larry Fitzgerald RC	15.00	4.50
❑ 203 Michael Jenkins RC	5.00	1.50
❑ 204 Ben Roethlisberger RC	50.00	15.00
❑ 205 Philip Rivers RC	15.00	4.50
❑ 206 Kellen Winslow RC	12.00	3.60
❑ 207 Kevin Jones RC	15.00	4.50
❑ 208 Steven Jackson RC	15.00	4.50
❑ 209 Reggie Williams RC	6.00	1.80
❑ 210 Chris Perry RC	10.00	3.00
❑ 211 Roy Williams RC	15.00	4.50
❑ 212 Rashaun Woods RC	6.00	1.80
❑ 213 Chris Gamble RC	6.00	1.80
❑ 214 Sean Taylor RC	6.00	1.80
❑ 215 Robert Gallery RC	8.00	2.40
❑ 216 Ben Troupe RC	5.00	1.50
❑ 217 Lee Evans RC	8.00	2.40
❑ 218 Michael Clayton RC	12.00	3.60
❑ 219 J.P. Losman RC	12.00	3.60
❑ 220 Devery Henderson RC	4.00	1.20
❑ 221 Drew Henson RC	12.00	3.60
❑ 222 DeAngelo Hall RC	6.00	1.80
❑ 223 Julius Jones RC	20.00	6.00
❑ 224 Ben Watson RC	5.00	1.50
❑ 225 Greg Jones RC	5.00	1.50
❑ 226 D.J. Williams RC	2.50	.75
❑ 227 Tommie Harris RC	2.50	.75
❑ 228 Shawn Andrews RC	1.50	.45
❑ 229 Vince Wilfork RC	2.50	.75
❑ 230 Dunta Robinson RC	1.50	.45
❑ 231 Will Smith RC	1.50	.45
❑ 232 Jonathan Vilma RC	1.50	.45
❑ 233 Ricardo Colclough RC	1.50	.45
❑ 234 Ahmad Carroll RC	2.50	.75
❑ 235 Karlos Dansby RC	1.50	.45
❑ 236 Matt Ware RC	1.50	.45
❑ 237 Jim Sorgi RC	1.50	.45
❑ 238 Will Poole RC	1.50	.45
❑ 239 Derrick Strait RC	1.50	.45
❑ 240 Andy Hall RC	1.25	.35
❑ 241 Nathan Vasher RC	1.50	.45
❑ 242 D.J. Hackett RC	1.25	.35
❑ 243 Jason Babin RC	1.50	.45
❑ 244 Derrick Hamilton RC	1.25	.35
❑ 245 Michael Boulware RC	1.50	.45
❑ 246 Michael Turner RC	1.25	.35
❑ 247 Sean Jones RC	1.25	.35
❑ 248 Ernest Wilford RC	1.50	.45
❑ 249 Cedric Cobbs RC	1.50	.45
❑ 250 Tatum Bell RC	3.00	.90
❑ 251 Bernard Berrian RC	1.50	.45
❑ 252 Vernon Carey RC	1.25	.35
❑ 253 Kenechi Udeze RC	1.50	.45
❑ 254 P.K. Sam RC	1.25	.35
❑ 255 Ben Hartsock RC	1.50	.45
❑ 256 Chris Cooley RC	1.50	.45
❑ 257 Josh Harris RC	1.50	.45
❑ 258 Cody Pickett RC	1.50	.45
❑ 259 Carlos Francis RC	1.25	.35
❑ 260 Devard Darling RC	1.50	.45
❑ 261 Johnnie Morant RC	1.50	.45
❑ 262 John Navarre RC	1.50	.45
❑ 263 Kris Wilson RC	1.50	.45
❑ 264 Jerricho Cotchery RC	1.50	.45
❑ 265 Darius Watts RC	2.50	.75
❑ 266 Quincy Wilson RC	1.25	.35
❑ 267 Maurice Mann RC	1.25	.35
❑ 268 Samie Parker RC	1.50	.45
❑ 269 B.J. Symons RC	1.50	.45
❑ 270 Matt Schaub RC	3.00	.90
❑ 271 Jeff Smoker RC	3.00	.90
❑ 272 Craig Krenzel RC	1.50	.45
❑ 273 Luke McCown RC	1.50	.45
❑ 274 Mewelde Moore RC	2.00	.60
❑ 275 Keary Colbert RC	2.50	.75

2004 Upper Deck UD Exclusive

Nm-Mt Ex-Mt

*STARS: 6X TO 15X BASE CARD HI
*ROOKIES 201-225: 1.2X TO 3X BASE CARD HI
*ROOKIES 226-275: 3X TO 8X BASE CARD HI
STATED PRINT RUN 50 SER.#'d SETS

2004 Upper Deck Game Jersey Duals

STATED ODDS 1:480

	Nm-Mt	Ex-Mt
❑ BD2J Tom Brady / Jake Delhomme	25.00	7.50
❑ FM2J Brett Favre / Peyton Manning	40.00	12.00
❑ HF2J Priest Holmes / Marshall Faulk	20.00	6.00
❑ MH2J Randy Moss / Marvin Harrison	25.00	7.50
❑ SR2J Emmitt Smith / Jerry Rice	30.00	9.00
❑ TP2J LaDainian Tomlinson / Clinton Portis	20.00	6.00
❑ US2J Brian Urlacher / Junior Seau	20.00	6.00
❑ VM2J Michael Vick / Donovan McNabb	25.00	7.50

2004 Upper Deck Game Jersey Patch Logos

LOGOS STATED ODDS 1:2500

	Nm-Mt	Ex-Mt
❑ PLOAG Ahman Green	30.00	9.00
❑ PLOBL Byron Leftwich		
❑ PLOBU Brian Urlacher	40.00	12.00
❑ PLOCL Clinton Portis	30.00	9.00
❑ PLOCP Chad Pennington	40.00	12.00
❑ PLODC David Carr		
❑ PLOHW Hines Ward	30.00	9.00
❑ PLOJH Joe Horn	25.00	7.50
❑ PLOMF Marshall Faulk		
❑ PLOMH Marvin Harrison		
❑ PLOMV Michael Vick	50.00	15.00
❑ PLOPH Priest Holmes	40.00	12.00
❑ PLORM Randy Moss		
❑ PLOTH Todd Heap	30.00	9.00

2004 Upper Deck Game Jersey Patch Names

NAMES STATED ODDS 1:5000

	Nm-Mt	Ex-Mt
❑ PNAAB Anquan Boldin		
❑ PNADD Domanick Davis		
❑ PNADM Donovan McNabb		
❑ PNAEJ Edgerrin James SP	60.00	18.00
❑ PNAGO Tony Gonzalez		
❑ PNALT LaDainian Tomlinson	50.00	15.00
❑ PNAMS Michael Strahan	40.00	12.00
❑ PNARW Ricky Williams		
❑ PNASA Santana Moss		
❑ PNASM Steve McNair	40.00	12.00
❑ PNATB Tom Brady	80.00	24.00
❑ PNATG Trent Green		
❑ PNATH Torry Holt	50.00	15.00
❑ PNATO Terrell Owens	50.00	15.00

2004 Upper Deck Game Jersey Patch Numbers

	Nm-Mt	Ex-Mt
NUMBERS STATED ODDS 1:1500		
❑ PNUBF Brett Favre	60.00	18.00
❑ PNUCC Chris Chambers	20.00	6.00
❑ PNUCJ Chad Johnson	20.00	6.00
❑ PNUCP Clinton Portis	25.00	7.50
❑ PNUDC Daunte Culpepper	25.00	7.50
❑ PNUDH Dante Hall	25.00	7.50
❑ PNUDM Deuce McAllister	25.00	7.50
❑ PNUJK Jevon Kearse		
❑ PNUJL Jamal Lewis	25.00	7.50
❑ PNUJR Jerry Rice	50.00	15.00
❑ PNUJS Jeremy Shockey		
❑ PNUMB Marc Bulger	25.00	7.50
❑ PNUPM Peyton Manning	40.00	12.00
❑ PNURG Rex Grossman	25.00	7.50

2004 Upper Deck Game Jerseys

	Nm-Mt	Ex-Mt
STATED ODDS 1:32 HOB, 1:28 RET		
❑ ABGJ Anquan Boldin	6.00	1.80
❑ AJGJ Andre Johnson	6.00	1.80
❑ BFGJ Brett Favre	20.00	6.00
❑ CDGJ Corey Dillon	8.00	2.40
❑ CJGJ Chad Johnson	6.00	1.80
❑ CPGJ Clinton Portis	8.00	2.40
❑ DCGJ Daunte Culpepper	8.00	2.40
❑ DDGJ Domanick Davis	8.00	2.40
❑ DMGJ Deuce McAllister	8.00	2.40
❑ DOGJ Donovan McNabb	10.00	3.00
❑ JDGJ Jake Delhomme	8.00	2.40
❑ KBGJ Kyle Boller SP	10.00	3.00
❑ LTGJ LaDainian Tomlinson	8.00	2.40
❑ MVGJ Michael Vick	12.00	3.60
❑ PHGJ Priest Holmes	10.00	3.00
❑ PMGJ Peyton Manning	12.00	3.60
❑ RMGJ Randy Moss	10.00	3.00
❑ SAGJ Shaun Alexander	8.00	2.40
❑ SMGJ Steve McNair	8.00	2.40
❑ TBGJ Tom Brady	15.00	4.50
❑ TSGJ Terrell Suggs SP	10.00	3.00

2004 Upper Deck Rewind to 1997 Jerseys

	Nm-Mt	Ex-Mt
STATED ODDS 1:480		
❑ 97BF Brett Favre	30.00	9.00
❑ 97CD Corey Dillon	12.00	3.60
❑ 97CM Curtis Martin	12.00	3.60
❑ 97DF Doug Flutie	12.00	3.60
❑ 97EM Eric Moulds	10.00	3.00
❑ 97ES Emmitt Smith SP	30.00	9.00
❑ 97JB Jerome Bettis	12.00	3.60
❑ 97JP Jake Plummer	10.00	3.00
❑ 97JR Jerry Rice SP	30.00	9.00
❑ 97JS Junior Seau	12.00	3.60
❑ 97MF Marshall Faulk	12.00	3.60
❑ 97TB Tim Brown SP	15.00	4.50
❑ 97TG Tony Gonzalez	10.00	3.00
❑ 97WD Warrick Dunn	10.00	3.00

2004 Upper Deck Rookie Futures Jerseys

	Nm-Mt	Ex-Mt
STATED ODDS 1:24		
❑ RFBB Bernard Berrian	8.00	2.40
❑ RFBR Ben Roethlisberger	60.00	18.00
❑ RFBT Ben Troupe	10.00	3.00
❑ RFBW Ben Watson	6.00	1.80
❑ RFCC Cedric Cobbs	8.00	2.40
❑ RFCP Chris Perry	12.00	3.60
❑ RFDD Devard Darling	6.00	1.80
❑ RFDE Devery Henderson	6.00	1.80
❑ RFDK Derrick Hamilton	6.00	1.80
❑ RFDR Dunta Robinson	6.00	1.80
❑ RFDW Darius Watts	8.00	2.40
❑ RFEM Eli Manning	30.00	9.00
❑ RFGJ Greg Jones	8.00	2.40
❑ RFHA DeAngelo Hall	10.00	3.00
❑ RFJJ Julius Jones	25.00	7.50
❑ RFJP J.P. Losman	15.00	4.50
❑ RFKC Keary Colbert	8.00	2.40
❑ RFKJ Kevin Jones	20.00	6.00
❑ RFKW Kellen Winslow Jr.	15.00	4.50
❑ RFLE Lee Evans	10.00	3.00
❑ RFLF Larry Fitzgerald	20.00	6.00
❑ RFLM Luke McCown	10.00	3.00
❑ RFMI Michael Clayton	15.00	4.50
❑ RFMJ Michael Jenkins	8.00	2.40
❑ RFMM Mewelde Moore	10.00	3.00
❑ RFMS Matt Schaub	10.00	3.00
❑ RFPR Philip Rivers	20.00	6.00
❑ RFRA Rashaun Woods	10.00	3.00
❑ RFRG Robert Gallery	10.00	3.00
❑ RFRO Roy Williams WR	20.00	6.00
❑ RFRW Reggie Williams	10.00	3.00
❑ RFSJ Steven Jackson	20.00	6.00
❑ RFTB Tatum Bell	12.00	3.60

2004 Upper Deck Rookie Prospects

	Nm-Mt	Ex-Mt
COMPLETE SET (30)	40.00	12.00
ONE PER RETAIL PACK		
❑ RPBR Ben Roethlisberger	12.00	3.60
❑ RPBT Ben Troupe	1.25	.35
❑ RPBW Ben Watson	1.25	.35
❑ RPCC Cedric Cobbs	1.00	.30
❑ RPCP Chris Perry	2.50	.75
❑ RPDD Devard Darling	1.00	.30
❑ RPDE Devery Henderson	1.00	.30
❑ RPDH Derrick Hamilton	.75	.23
❑ RPDR Drew Henson	3.00	.90
❑ RPDW Darius Watts	1.50	.45
❑ RPEM Eli Manning	8.00	2.40
❑ RPGJ Greg Jones	1.25	.35
❑ RPJJ Julius Jones	5.00	1.50
❑ RPJP J.P. Losman	3.00	.90
❑ RPKC Keary Colbert	1.50	.45
❑ RPKJ Kevin Jones	4.00	1.20
❑ RPKW Kellen Winslow Jr.	3.00	.90
❑ RPLE Lee Evans	2.00	.60
❑ RPLF Larry Fitzgerald	4.00	1.20
❑ RPLM Luke McCown	1.00	.30
❑ RPMI Michael Clayton	3.00	.90
❑ RPMJ Michael Jenkins	1.25	.35
❑ RPMM Mewelde Moore	1.25	.35
❑ RPMS Matt Schaub	2.00	.60
❑ RPPR Philip Rivers	4.00	1.20
❑ RPRA Rashaun Woods	1.50	.45
❑ RPRO Roy Williams WR	4.00	1.20
❑ RPRW Reggie Williams	1.50	.45
❑ RPSJ Steven Jackson	4.00	1.20
❑ RPTB Tatum Bell	2.00	.60

2004 Upper Deck Rookie Review Jerseys

	Nm-Mt	Ex-Mt
STATED ODDS 1:480		
❑ RRAB Anquan Boldin	8.00	2.40
❑ RRAJ Andre Johnson	8.00	2.40
❑ RRAP Artose Pinner	6.00	1.80
❑ RRBJ Bethel Johnson	8.00	2.40
❑ RRBL Byron Leftwich	12.00	3.60
❑ RRCB Chris Brown	10.00	3.00
❑ RRCP Carson Palmer	12.00	3.60
❑ RRDC Dallas Clark		
❑ RRJF Justin Fargas	8.00	2.40
❑ RRKB Kyle Boller	10.00	3.00
❑ RRKW Kelley Washington	6.00	1.80
❑ RRLJ Larry Johnson	8.00	2.40
❑ RRMT Marcus Trufant	6.00	1.80
❑ RROS Onterrio Smith	8.00	2.40
❑ RRRG Rex Grossman	10.00	3.00
❑ RRTC Tyrone Calico	8.00	2.40
❑ RRTJ Teyo Johnson	8.00	2.40
❑ RRTN Terence Newman	8.00	2.40
❑ RRTS Terrell Suggs	8.00	2.40
❑ RRWM Willis McGahee		

2004 Upper Deck Signature Sensations

	Nm-Mt	Ex-Mt
RANDOM INSERTS IN PACKS		
CARDS SER.#'d UNDER 25 NOT PRICED		
❑ SSBE Ben Watson/84	30.00	9.00
❑ SSBF Brett Favre/4		
❑ SSBL Brandon Lloyd/85	25.00	7.50
❑ SSBP Bill Parcells/10		
❑ SSBR Ben Roethlisberger/7		
❑ SSBS Barry Sanders/20		
❑ SSBT Ben Troupe/86	40.00	12.00
❑ SSBW Brian Westbrook/36		
❑ SSCC Cedric Cobbs/34	40.00	12.00
❑ SSCP Chris Perry/26	60.00	18.00
❑ SSDA Daunte Culpepper/11		
❑ SSDC David Carr/8		
❑ SSDD Domanick Davis/37		
❑ SSDE Devard Darling/11		
❑ SSDH DeAngelo Hall/21		
❑ SSDM Deuce McAllister/26	40.00	12.00
❑ SSDR Drew Henson/11		
❑ SSDV Devery Henderson/19		
❑ SSEM Eli Manning/10		
❑ SSFT Fran Tarkenton/10		
❑ SSGJ Greg Jones/33	40.00	12.00
❑ SSHA Dante Hall/82	30.00	9.00
❑ SSHE0 Todd Heap/86 EXCH	30.00	9.00
❑ SSJE John Elway/7		
❑ SSJG Jon Gruden/60	30.00	9.00
❑ SSJH Joe Horn/87	25.00	7.50
❑ SSJJ Jimmy Johnson/60	40.00	12.00
❑ SSJM Josh McCown/12		
❑ SSJN John Navarre/16		
❑ SSJO Joe Montana/16		
❑ SSJP J.P. Losman/7		
❑ SSJT Joe Theismann/7		
❑ SSJU Julius Jones/21		
❑ SSKB Kyle Boller/8		
❑ SSKC Keary Colbert/85	30.00	9.00
❑ SSKJ Kevin Jones/34	100.00	30.00
❑ SSKW Kellen Winslow Jr./81	80.00	24.00
❑ SSLE Lee Evans/83	30.00	9.00
❑ SSLF Larry Fitzgerald/11		
❑ SSLM Luke McCown/12		
❑ SSLT LaDainian Tomlinson/21		
❑ SSMI Michael Clayton/80	60.00	18.00
❑ SSMJ Michael Jenkins/12		
❑ SSMS Matt Schaub/8		
❑ SSMV Michael Vick/7		
❑ SSPM Peyton Manning/18		
❑ SSPR Philip Rivers/17		
❑ SSRA Rashaun Woods/81	40.00	12.00
❑ SSRG Robert Gallery/74	40.00	12.00
❑ SSRJ Rudi Johnson/32	30.00	9.00
❑ SSRO Roy Williams WR/11		
❑ SSRW Roy Williams S/31		
❑ SSSJ Steven Jackson/39	100.00	30.00
❑ SSST Sean Taylor/36		
❑ SSTA Tatum Bell/26	60.00	18.00
❑ SSTB Tom Brady/12		
❑ SSTG Tony Gonzalez/88	25.00	7.50
❑ SSTH Travis Henry/20		
❑ SSWI Kellen Winslow Sr./80	25.00	7.50
❑ SSWM Willis McGahee/21		

2004 Upper Deck Rookie Premiere

	Nm-Mt	Ex-Mt
COMPLETE SET (30)	30.00	9.00
❑ 1 Eli Manning	8.00	2.40
❑ 2 Ben Roethlisberger	15.00	4.50
❑ 3 Philip Rivers	3.00	.90
❑ 4 Roy Williams WR	2.50	.75
❑ 5 Larry Fitzgerald	3.00	.90
❑ 6 Tatum Bell	2.00	.60
❑ 7 J.P. Losman	2.50	.75
❑ 8 Steven Jackson	3.00	.90
❑ 9 Ben Watson	1.00	.30
❑ 10 Devery Henderson	.75	.23
❑ 11 Kevin Jones	3.00	.90
❑ 12 Chris Perry	2.00	.60
❑ 13 Kellen Winslow Jr.	2.50	.75
❑ 14 Lee Evans	1.50	.45
❑ 15 Reggie Williams	1.25	.35
❑ 16 Ben Troupe	1.00	.30
❑ 17 Michael Clayton	2.50	.75
❑ 18 Michael Jenkins	1.00	.30
❑ 19 Rashaun Woods	1.25	.35
❑ 20 DeAngelo Hall	1.25	.35
❑ 21 Cedric Cobbs	1.00	.30
❑ 22 Luke McCown	1.00	.30
❑ 23 Robert Gallery	1.50	.45
❑ 24 Julius Jones	4.00	1.20
❑ 25 Matt Schaub	1.00	.30
❑ 26 Keary Colbert	1.25	.35
❑ 27 Bernard Berrian	1.00	.30
❑ 28 Greg Jones	1.25	.35
❑ 29 Darius Watts	1.00	.30
❑ 30 Checklist Card	1.00	.30

2004 Upper Deck Rookie Premiere Gold

	Nm-Mt	Ex-Mt
COMPLETE SET (30)	50.00	15.00
*GOLD: 1X TO 2.5X BASE CARD HI		
ONE GOLD PER FACTORY SET		

2004 Upper Deck Rookie Premiere Autographs

	Nm-Mt	Ex-Mt
❑ BB Bernard Berrian	40.00	12.00
❑ BR Ben Roethlisberger	350.00	105.00
❑ BT Ben Troupe	40.00	12.00
❑ BW Ben Watson	40.00	12.00
❑ CC Cedric Cobbs	40.00	12.00
❑ CP Chris Perry	60.00	18.00
❑ DD Devard Darling	40.00	12.00
❑ DH DeAngelo Hall	50.00	15.00
❑ DH2 Devery Henderson	30.00	9.00
❑ DW Darius Watts	40.00	12.00
❑ EM Eli Manning	250.00	75.00
❑ GJ Greg Jones	50.00	15.00
❑ JJ Julius Jones	150.00	45.00
❑ KC Keary Colbert	50.00	15.00
❑ KJ Kevin Jones	120.00	36.00
❑ LE Lee Evans	60.00	18.00
❑ LF Larry Fitzgerald	120.00	36.00
❑ LM Luke McCown	40.00	12.00
❑ MC Michael Clayton	80.00	24.00
❑ MJ Michael Jenkins	40.00	12.00
❑ MS Matt Schaub	40.00	12.00
❑ PR Philip Rivers	120.00	36.00
❑ RG Robert Gallery	80.00	24.00
❑ RW Rashaun Woods	50.00	15.00
❑ RW2 Reggie Williams	50.00	15.00
❑ RW3 Roy Williams WR	120.00	36.00

2005 Upper Deck AFL

	Nm-Mt	Ex-Mt
COMPLETE SET (90)	50.00	15.00
❑ 1 Hunkie Cooper	1.00	.30
❑ 2 Siaha Burley	1.00	.30
❑ 3 Sherdrick Bonner	1.00	.30
❑ 4 Bo Kelly	.75	.23
❑ 5 Evan Hlavacek	.75	.23
❑ 6 Tacoma Fontaine	.75	.23
❑ 7 Troy Bergeron	1.50	.45
❑ 8 Darrin Chiaverini	1.00	.30
❑ 9 Bobby Pesavento	.75	.23
❑ 10 Tom Pace	.75	.23
❑ 11 Raymond Philyaw	1.00	.30
❑ 12 Bob McMillen	1.00	.30
❑ 13 Etu Molden	1.00	.30
❑ 14 Jeremy McDaniel	1.00	.30
❑ 15 Todd Hammel	1.00	.30
❑ 16 John Dutton	1.00	.30
❑ 17 Damian Harrell	1.50	.45
❑ 18 Kevin McKenzie	.75	.23
❑ 19 Willis Marshall	.75	.23
❑ 20 Rashad Floyd	.75	.23
❑ 21 Andy McCullough	.75	.23
❑ 22 Damien Groce	1.00	.30
❑ 23 Chad Salisbury	.75	.23
❑ 24 Sedrick Robinson	.75	.23
❑ 25 Cornelius White	.75	.23
❑ 26 Wilmont Perry	.75	.23
❑ 27 Clint Stoerner	3.00	.90
❑ 28 Will Pettis	1.00	.30
❑ 29 Bobby Sippio	1.00	.30
❑ 30 Jason Shelley	.75	.23
❑ 31 Duke Pettijohn	.75	.23
❑ 32 Robert Thomas	.75	.23
❑ 33 Jim Kubiak	1.00	.30
❑ 34 Dialleo Burks	1.00	.30
❑ 35 Matt Nagy	2.50	.75
❑ 36 Kevin Gaines	.75	.23
❑ 37 Josh Bush	.75	.23
❑ 38 Michael Bishop	1.50	.45
❑ 39 Anthony Hines	.75	.23
❑ 40 Chris Jackson	1.00	.30
❑ 41 Jerome Riley	.75	.23

Card	Player	Nm-Mt	Ex-Mt
❑ 42	Josh Jeffries	.75	.23
❑ 43	Clint Dolezel	1.00	.30
❑ 44	Marcus Nash	1.50	.45
❑ 45	Coco Blalock	1.00	.30
❑ 46	Cornelius Bonner	.75	.23
❑ 47	Frank Carter	.75	.23
❑ 48	John Kaleo	1.00	.30
❑ 49	Kevin Ingram	.75	.23
❑ 50	Greg Hopkins	1.00	.30
❑ 51	Lonnie Ford	.75	.23
❑ 52	Brian Sump	.75	.23
❑ 53	Leon Murray	.75	.23
❑ 54	Darryl Hammond	.75	.23
❑ 55	Fred Coleman	.75	.23
❑ 56	Ahmad Hawkins	.75	.23
❑ 57	Gabe Amey	.75	.23
❑ 58	Andy Kelly	1.00	.30
❑ 59	Chris Pointer	.75	.23
❑ 60	Aaron Bailey	1.00	.30
❑ 61	Dan Curran	.75	.23
❑ 62	Lamont Moore	.75	.23
❑ 63	Thabiti Davis	1.00	.30
❑ 64	Aaron Garcia	1.50	.45
❑ 65	Lincoln DuPree	.75	.23
❑ 66	William Holder	.75	.23
❑ 67	Chris Anthony	.75	.23
❑ 68	Markeith Cooper	.75	.23
❑ 69	Cory Fleming	1.00	.30
❑ 70	Kenny McEntyre	1.00	.30
❑ 71	Bret Cooper	.75	.23
❑ 72	Travis McGriff	1.00	.30
❑ 73	Joe Hamilton	1.00	.30
❑ 74	Tony Graziani	1.50	.45
❑ 75	Takuya Furutani	.75	.23
❑ 76	Chris Ryan	.75	.23
❑ 77	Joseph Todd	.75	.23
❑ 78	Sean Scott	1.00	.30
❑ 79	Mark Grieb	1.50	.45
❑ 80	James Hundon	1.00	.30
❑ 81	James Roe	1.00	.30
❑ 82	Omarr Smith	1.00	.30
❑ 83	Rashied Davis	1.00	.30
❑ 84	Calvin Schexnayder	.75	.23
❑ 85	Shane Stafford	1.00	.30
❑ 86	Lawrence Samuels	1.00	.30
❑ 87	T.T. Toliver	.75	.23
❑ 88	Freddie Solomon	1.00	.30
❑ 89	Cliff Dell	.75	.23
❑ 90	Rich Young	.75	.23

2005 Upper Deck AFL Gold

Nm-Mt Ex-Mt

*SINGLES: 4X TO 10X BASIC CARDS
STATED PRINT RUN 100 SER.#'d SETS

2005 Upper Deck AFL Arena Action

STATED ODDS 1:10

Card	Player	Nm-Mt	Ex-Mt
❑ AA1	Kenny McEntyre	5.00	1.50
❑ AA2	Cory Fleming	5.00	1.50
❑ AA3	Marcus Nash	8.00	2.40
❑ AA4	Hunkie Cooper	5.00	1.50
❑ AA5	Tony Graziani	8.00	2.40
❑ AA6	Kevin Ingram	4.00	1.20
❑ AA7	Dan Curran	4.00	1.20
❑ AA8	Mark Grieb	8.00	2.40
❑ AA9	Joe Hamilton	5.00	1.50
❑ AA10	Will Pettis	5.00	1.50
❑ AA11	Damian Harrell	8.00	2.40
❑ AA12	Rashad Floyd	4.00	1.20
❑ AA13	Etu Molden	5.00	1.50
❑ AA14	Lincoln DuPree	4.00	1.20
❑ AA15	Kevin McKenzie	4.00	1.20
❑ AA16	James Roe	5.00	1.50
❑ AA17	T.T. Toliver	4.00	1.20
❑ AA18	Sedrick Robinson	4.00	1.20
❑ AA19	Rashied Davis	5.00	1.50
❑ AA20	Clint Dolezel	5.00	1.50
❑ AA21	Chris Jackson	5.00	1.50
❑ AA22	Thabiti Davis	5.00	1.50
❑ AA23	Aaron Bailey	5.00	1.50
❑ AA24	Freddie Solomon	5.00	1.50
❑ AA25	Bobby Sippio	5.00	1.50
❑ AA26	Lawrence Samuels	5.00	1.50
❑ AA27	Siaha Burley	5.00	1.50
❑ AA28	Markeith Cooper	4.00	1.20
❑ AA29	Aaron Garcia	8.00	2.40
❑ AA30	Cornelius White	4.00	1.20

2005 Upper Deck AFL ArenaBowl Archives

Card	Name	Nm-Mt	Ex-Mt
COMPLETE SET (18)		25.00	7.50
STATED ODDS 1:20			
❑ AB1	Arena Bowl I	2.00	.60
❑ AB2	Arena Bowl II	2.00	.60
❑ AB3	Arena Bowl III	2.00	.60
❑ AB4	Arena Bowl IV	2.00	.60
❑ AB5	Arena Bowl V	2.00	.60
❑ AB6	Arena Bowl VI	2.00	.60
❑ AB7	Arena Bowl VII	2.00	.60
❑ AB8	Arena Bowl VIII	2.00	.60
❑ AB9	Arena Bowl IX	2.00	.60
❑ AB10	Arena Bowl X	2.00	.60
❑ AB11	Arena Bowl XI	2.00	.60
❑ AB12	Arena Bowl XII	2.00	.60
❑ AB13	Arena Bowl XIII	2.00	.60
❑ AB14	Arena Bowl XIV	2.00	.60
❑ AB15	Arena Bowl XV	2.00	.60
❑ AB16	Arena Bowl XVI	2.00	.60
❑ AB17	Arena Bowl XVII	2.00	.60
❑ AB18	Arena Bowl XVIII	2.00	.60

2005 Upper Deck AFL Arenagraphs

STATED ODDS 1:24 HOB, 1:48 RET

Card	Player	Nm-Mt	Ex-Mt
❑ ABA	Aaron Bailey	20.00	6.00
❑ AGA	Aaron Garcia	25.00	7.50
❑ AMA	Adrian McPherson	60.00	18.00
❑ BMA	Bob McMillen	20.00	6.00
❑ CDA	Clint Dolezel		
❑ CFA	Cory Fleming		
❑ CJA	Chris Jackson	20.00	6.00
❑ DBA	David Baker	15.00	4.50
❑ DHA	Damian Harrell	25.00	7.50
❑ EMA	Etu Molden	20.00	6.00
❑ HCA	Hunkie Cooper	20.00	6.00
❑ JEA	John Elway		
❑ JHA	James Hundon		
❑ JJA	Jerry Jones		
❑ KEA	Kevin McKenzie	15.00	4.50
❑ KIA	Kevin Ingram	15.00	4.50
❑ KMA	Kenny McEntyre		
❑ LSA	Lawrence Samuels	20.00	6.00
❑ MDA	Mike Ditka		
❑ MGA	Mark Grieb	25.00	7.50
❑ MNA	Marcus Nash		
❑ OSA	Omarr Smith	20.00	6.00
❑ RDA	Rashied Davis	20.00	6.00
❑ SBA	Siaha Burley		
❑ SRA	Sedrick Robinson	15.00	4.50
❑ TFA	Tacoma Fontaine	15.00	4.50
❑ TGA	Tony Graziani	25.00	7.50
❑ TMA	Tim McGraw	100.00	30.00
❑ TTA	T.T. Toliver		
❑ WPA	Will Pettis	20.00	6.00

2005 Upper Deck AFL Arenagraphs Duals

STATED PRINT RUN 50 SER.#'d SETS

Card	Players	Nm-Mt	Ex-Mt
❑ BBA2	Aaron Bailey Coco Blalock		
❑ BFA2	Siaha Burley Tacoma Fontaine		
❑ DNA2	Clint Dolezel Marcus Nash	50.00	15.00
❑ EHA2	John Elway/25 Damian Harrell	175.00	52.50
❑ FMA2	Cory Fleming Kenny McEntyre	40.00	12.00
❑ GGA2	Tony Graziani Aaron Garcia		
❑ GHA2	Mark Grieb James Hundon		
❑ GIA2	Tony Graziani Kevin Ingram	50.00	15.00
❑ HMA2	Damian Harrell Kevin McKenzie	40.00	12.00
❑ MBA2	Tim McGraw/25 David Baker	175.00	52.50
❑ MMA2	Bob McMillen Etu Molden	40.00	12.00
❑ RPA2	Sedrick Robinson Will Pettis		
❑ SDA2	Omarr Smith Rashied Davis	40.00	12.00
❑ STA2	Lawrence Samuels T.T. Toliver		
❑ TCA2	Robert Thomas Hunkie Cooper		

2005 Upper Deck AFL Dance Team Stars

Card	Name	Nm-Mt	Ex-Mt
COMPLETE SET (10)		40.00	12.00
STATED ODDS 1:36			
❑ DTS1	Crystal	5.00	1.50
❑ DTS2	Gina	5.00	1.50
❑ DTS3	Katie	5.00	1.50
❑ DTS4	Christina	5.00	1.50
❑ DTS5	Heather	5.00	1.50
❑ DTS6	Lisa	5.00	1.50
❑ DTS7	Gloria	5.00	1.50
❑ DTS8	Kelli	5.00	1.50
❑ DTS9	Bridget	5.00	1.50
❑ DTS10	Katie	5.00	1.50

2005 Upper Deck AFL Jerseys

STATED ODDS 1:12

Card	Nm-Mt	Ex-Mt
❑ AGJ Aaron Garcia	20.00	6.00
❑ BSJ Bobby Sippio	12.00	3.60
❑ CAJ Chris Anthony	10.00	3.00
❑ CDJ Clint Dolezel	12.00	3.60
❑ CJJ Chris Jackson	12.00	3.60
❑ CRJ Chris Ryan	10.00	3.00
❑ CSJ Corey Sawyer		
❑ DHJ Damian Harrell	20.00	6.00
❑ HCJ Hunkie Cooper	12.00	3.60
❑ JHJ James Hundon	20.00	6.00
❑ JRJ James Roe	12.00	3.60
❑ KEJ Kevin McKenzie	10.00	3.00
❑ KIJ Kevin Ingram	10.00	3.00
❑ LSJ Lawrence Samuels	12.00	3.60
❑ MGJ Mark Grieb	20.00	6.00
❑ MNJ Marcus Nash	20.00	6.00
❑ MRJ Mark Ricks		
❑ OSJ Omarr Smith	12.00	3.60
❑ RDJ Rashied Davis	12.00	3.60
❑ RRJ Ricky Ross	10.00	3.00
❑ SBJ Siaha Burley	12.00	3.60
❑ SRJ Sedrick Robinson	10.00	3.00
❑ TFJ Tacoma Fontaine	10.00	3.00
❑ TGJ Tony Graziani	20.00	6.00
❑ THJ Todd Hammel	12.00	3.60
❑ TTJ T.T. Toliver	10.00	3.00
❑ WPJ Will Pettis	12.00	3.60

2005 Upper Deck AFL League Luminaries

STATED ODDS 1:24

Card	Nm-Mt	Ex-Mt
❑ LL1 Tommy Maddox	6.00	1.80
❑ LL2 David Baker	5.00	1.50
❑ LL3 Kurt Warner	6.00	1.80
❑ LL4 John Elway OWN	12.00	3.60
❑ LL5 Danny White CO	6.00	1.80
❑ LL6 Tim McGraw OWN	10.00	3.00
❑ LL7 Adrian McPherson	20.00	6.00
❑ LL8 Marcus Nash	6.00	1.80
❑ LL9 Tony Graziani	8.00	2.40
❑ LL10 Cory Fleming	6.00	1.80
❑ LL11 Mike Ditka OWN	12.00	3.60
❑ LL12 Jay Gruden	5.00	1.50
❑ LL13 Tim Marcum CO	5.00	1.50
❑ LL14 Kevin Swayne	5.00	1.50
❑ LL15 Barry Wagner	5.00	1.50

2005 Upper Deck AFL Timeline

STATED ODDS 1:30

Card	Nm-Mt	Ex-Mt
❑ AFL1 Barry Wagner	5.00	1.50
❑ AFL2 Sherdrick Bonner	5.00	1.50
❑ AFL3 Jerry Jones OWN	6.00	1.80
❑ AFL4 Tim McGraw OWN	10.00	3.00
❑ AFL5 John Elway OWN	12.00	3.60
❑ AFL6 Jay Gruden	5.00	1.50
❑ AFL7 Tim Marcum	5.00	1.50
❑ AFL8 Mike Ditka OWN	12.00	3.60
❑ AFL9 Jim Kubiak	6.00	1.80
❑ AFL10 David Baker COM	5.00	1.50
❑ AFL11 Aaron Garcia	6.00	1.80
❑ AFL12 2004 Attendance Record	5.00	1.50

1999 Upper Deck Century Legends Epic Signatures

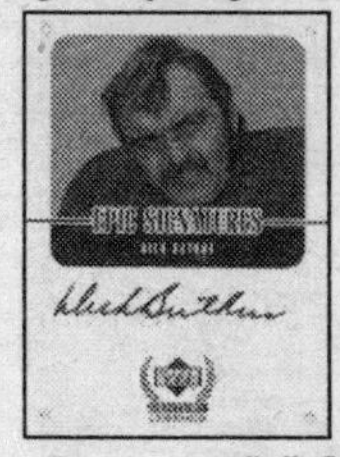

Card	Nm-Mt	Ex-Mt
❑ AM Art Monk	30.00	13.50
❑ CC Cris Carter	30.00	13.50
❑ CJ Charlie Joiner	20.00	9.00
❑ DB Dick Butkus	50.00	22.00
❑ DF Dan Fouts	30.00	13.50
❑ DM Dan Marino	200.00	90.00
❑ DR Dan Reeves	20.00	9.00
❑ DW Doug Williams	20.00	9.00
❑ EC Earl Campbell	30.00	13.50
❑ FL Floyd Little	12.00	5.50
❑ FT Fran Tarkenton	50.00	22.00
❑ GS Gale Sayers	40.00	18.00
❑ HC Harold Carmichael	12.00	5.50
❑ JM Joe Montana	200.00	90.00
❑ JN Joe Namath	150.00	70.00
❑ JR Jerry Rice	250.00	110.00
❑ JU Johnny Unitas	200.00	90.00
❑ JY Jack Youngblood	20.00	9.00
❑ LD Len Dawson	30.00	13.50
❑ MS Mike Singletary	30.00	13.50
❑ MY Don Maynard	12.00	5.50
❑ ON Ozzie Newsome	12.00	5.50
❑ PW Paul Warfield	20.00	9.00
❑ RB Raymond Berry	20.00	9.00
❑ RM Randy Moss	120.00	55.00
❑ RS Roger Staubach	80.00	36.00
❑ SL Steve Largent	30.00	13.50
❑ TA Troy Aikman	80.00	36.00
❑ TB Terry Bradshaw	80.00	36.00
❑ TD Terrell Davis	30.00	13.50

1999 Upper Deck Century Legends Epic Signatures Century Gold

*GOLDS: .8X TO 2X BASIC INSERTS

Card	Nm-Mt	Ex-Mt
❑ JRC Jerry Rice	200.00	90.00

1999 Upper Deck Century Legends Jerseys of the Century

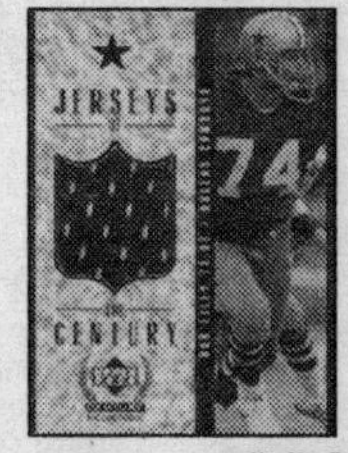

*MULTI-COLORED SWATCHES: .6X TO 1.2X

Card	Nm-Mt	Ex-Mt
❑ GJ1 Jerry Rice	120.00	55.00
❑ GJ2 Roger Staubach	80.00	36.00
❑ GJ3 Warren Moon	40.00	18.00
❑ GJ4 Ken Stabler	80.00	36.00
❑ GJ5 Reggie White	80.00	36.00
❑ GJ6 Dan Marino	250.00	110.00
❑ GJ7 Doug Flutie	80.00	36.00
❑ GJ8 Bob Lilly	40.00	18.00
❑ GJ10 Jim Brown	100.00	45.00

1998 Upper Deck Encore UD Authentics

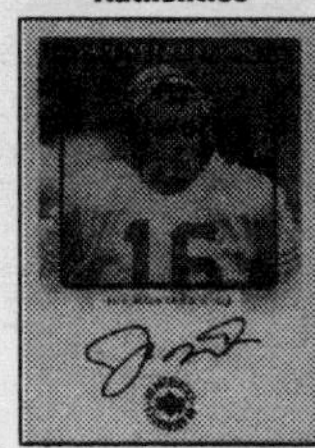

Card	Nm-Mt	Ex-Mt
❑ DM2 Dan Marino	120.00	55.00
❑ JM2 Joe Montana (49ers photo)	100.00	45.00

		Nm-Mt	Ex-Mt
❑ MB2	Mark Brunell	40.00	18.00
❑ RM	Randy Moss	120.00	55.00
❑ TD	Terrell Davis	40.00	18.00

1999 Upper Deck Encore

	Nm-Mt	Ex-Mt
COMPLETE SET (225)	200.00	90.00
COMP.SET w/o SP's (180)	40.00	18.00
❑ 1 Jake Plummer	.60	.25
❑ 2 Adrian Murrell	.60	.25
❑ 3 Rob Moore	.60	.25
❑ 4 Simeon Rice	.60	.25
❑ 5 Andre Wadsworth	.40	.18
❑ 6 Frank Sanders	.60	.25
❑ 7 Tim Dwight	1.00	.45
❑ 8 Chris Chandler	.60	.25
❑ 9 Jamal Anderson	1.00	.45
❑ 10 O.J. Santiago	.60	.25
❑ 11 Tony Graziani	.40	.18
❑ 12 Terance Mathis	.60	.25
❑ 13 Priest Holmes	1.50	.70
❑ 14 Stoney Case	.40	.18
❑ 15 Ray Lewis	1.00	.45
❑ 16 Peter Boulware	.40	.18
❑ 17 Errict Rhett	.60	.25
❑ 18 Jermaine Lewis	.60	.25
❑ 19 Eric Moulds	1.00	.45
❑ 20 Doug Flutie	1.00	.45
❑ 21 Antowain Smith	1.00	.45
❑ 22 Rob Johnson	.60	.25
❑ 23 Bruce Smith	.60	.25
❑ 24 Andre Reed	.60	.25
❑ 25 Wesley Walls	.60	.25
❑ 26 Tim Biakabutuka	.60	.25
❑ 27 Fred Lane	.40	.18
❑ 28 Steve Beuerlein	.60	.25
❑ 29 Muhsin Muhammad	.60	.25
❑ 30 Rae Carruth	.40	.18
❑ 31 Bobby Engram	.60	.25
❑ 32 Curtis Enis	.40	.18
❑ 33 Edgar Bennett	.40	.18
❑ 34 Curtis Conway	.60	.25
❑ 35 Shane Matthews	1.00	.45
❑ 36 Tony McGee	.40	.18
❑ 37 Darnay Scott	.60	.25
❑ 38 Jeff Blake	.60	.25
❑ 39 Corey Dillon	1.00	.45
❑ 40 Ki-Jana Carter	.40	.18
❑ 41 Ty Detmer	.60	.25
❑ 42 Leslie Shepherd	.40	.18
❑ 43 Terry Kirby	.60	.25
❑ 44 Antonio Langham	.40	.18
❑ 45 Jamir Miller	.40	.18
❑ 46 Marc Edwards	.40	.18
❑ 47 Troy Aikman	2.00	.90
❑ 48 Rocket Ismail	.60	.25
❑ 49 Emmitt Smith	2.00	.90
❑ 50 Michael Irvin	.60	.25
❑ 51 Deion Sanders	1.00	.45
❑ 52 Greg Ellis	.40	.18
❑ 53 Bubby Brister	.60	.25
❑ 54 Terrell Davis	1.00	.45
❑ 55 Ed McCaffrey	.60	.25
❑ 56 Rod Smith	.60	.25
❑ 57 Shannon Sharpe	.60	.25
❑ 58 Brian Griese	1.00	.45
❑ 59 Charlie Batch	1.00	.45
❑ 60 Germane Crowell	.40	.18
❑ 61 Johnnie Morton	.60	.25
❑ 62 Robert Porcher	.40	.18
❑ 63 Ron Rivers	.40	.18
❑ 64 Herman Moore	.60	.25
❑ 65 Brett Favre	3.00	1.35
❑ 66 Bill Schroeder	1.00	.45
❑ 67 Antonio Freeman	1.00	.45
❑ 68 Dorsey Levens	1.00	.45
❑ 69 Desmond Howard	.60	.25
❑ 70 Vonnie Holliday	.60	.25
❑ 71 Peyton Manning	2.50	1.10
❑ 72 Jerome Pathon	.60	.25
❑ 73 Marvin Harrison	1.00	.45
❑ 74 Ken Dilger	.60	.25
❑ 75 E.G. Green	.40	.18
❑ 76 Cornelius Bennett	.40	.18
❑ 77 Mark Brunell	1.00	.45
❑ 78 Fred Taylor	1.00	.45
❑ 79 Jimmy Smith	.60	.25
❑ 80 James Stewart	.60	.25
❑ 81 Keenan McCardell	.60	.25
❑ 82 Carnell Lake	.40	.18
❑ 83 Elvis Grbac	.60	.25
❑ 84 Tony Gonzalez	1.00	.45
❑ 85 Andre Rison	.60	.25
❑ 86 Derrick Thomas	.60	.25
❑ 87 Warren Moon	1.00	.45
❑ 88 Derrick Alexander WR	.60	.25
❑ 89 Dan Marino	3.00	1.35
❑ 90 O.J. McDuffie	.60	.25
❑ 91 Karim Abdul-Jabbar	.60	.25
❑ 92 Sam Madison	.40	.18
❑ 93 Zach Thomas	1.00	.45
❑ 94 Tony Martin	.60	.25
❑ 95 Randall Cunningham	1.00	.45
❑ 96 Randy Moss	2.00	.90
❑ 97 Cris Carter	1.00	.45
❑ 98 Jake Reed	.60	.25
❑ 99 John Randle	.60	.25
❑ 100 Robert Smith	1.00	.45
❑ 101 Drew Bledsoe	1.25	.55
❑ 102 Ben Coates	.60	.25
❑ 103 Terry Glenn	.60	.25
❑ 104 Tony Simmons	.40	.18
❑ 105 Terry Allen	.60	.25
❑ 106 Danny Wuerffel	.40	.18
❑ 107 Cameron Cleeland	.40	.18
❑ 108 Eddie Kennison	.60	.25
❑ 109 Billy Joe Hobert	.40	.18
❑ 110 Andre Hastings	.40	.18
❑ 111 Kent Graham	.40	.18
❑ 112 Tiki Barber	.60	.25
❑ 113 Gary Brown	.40	.18
❑ 114 Ike Hilliard	.60	.25
❑ 115 Jason Sehorn	.40	.18
❑ 116 Kerry Collins	.60	.25
❑ 117 Vinny Testaverde	.60	.25
❑ 118 Wayne Chrebet	1.00	.45
❑ 119 Curtis Martin	1.00	.45
❑ 120 Rick Mirer	.40	.18
❑ 121 Aaron Glenn	.40	.18
❑ 122 Keyshawn Johnson	1.00	.45
❑ 123 Rich Gannon	1.00	.45
❑ 124 Tim Brown	1.00	.45
❑ 125 Darrell Russell	.40	.18
❑ 126 Tyrone Wheatley	1.00	.45
❑ 127 Charles Woodson	1.00	.45
❑ 128 Napoleon Kaufman	1.00	.45
❑ 129 Duce Staley	1.00	.45
❑ 130 Doug Pederson	.40	.18
❑ 131 Kevin Turner	.40	.18
❑ 132 Charles Johnson	.40	.18
❑ 133 Jerome Bettis	1.00	.45
❑ 134 Courtney Hawkins	.40	.18
❑ 135 Kordell Stewart	.60	.25
❑ 136 Richard Huntley	.60	.25
❑ 137 Levon Kirkland	.40	.18
❑ 138 Hines Ward	1.00	.45
❑ 139 Kurt Warner RC	12.00	5.50
❑ 140 Marshall Faulk	1.25	.55
❑ 141 Az-Zahir Hakim	.60	.25
❑ 142 Amp Lee	.40	.18
❑ 143 Isaac Bruce	1.00	.45
❑ 144 Kevin Carter	.40	.18
❑ 145 Jim Harbaugh	.60	.25
❑ 146 Junior Seau	1.00	.45
❑ 147 Natrone Means	.60	.25
❑ 148 Rodney Harrison	.40	.18
❑ 149 Mikhael Ricks	.40	.18
❑ 150 Erik Kramer	.40	.18
❑ 151 Steve Young	1.25	.55
❑ 152 Terrell Owens	1.00	.45
❑ 153 Jerry Rice	2.00	.90
❑ 154 J.J. Stokes	.60	.25
❑ 155 Jeff Garcia RC	12.00	5.50
❑ 156 Lawrence Phillips	.60	.25
❑ 157 Jon Kitna	1.00	.45
❑ 158 Derrick Mayes	.60	.25
❑ 159 Ricky Watters	.60	.25
❑ 160 Chad Brown	.40	.18
❑ 161 Shawn Springs	.40	.18
❑ 162 Sean Dawkins	.40	.18
❑ 163 Trent Dilfer	.60	.25
❑ 164 Reidel Anthony	.60	.25
❑ 165 Bert Emanuel	.60	.25
❑ 166 Warrick Dunn	1.00	.45
❑ 167 Jacquez Green	.40	.18
❑ 168 Mike Alstott	1.00	.45
❑ 169 Eddie George	1.00	.45
❑ 170 Steve McNair	1.00	.45
❑ 171 Kevin Dyson	.60	.25
❑ 172 Frank Wycheck	.40	.18
❑ 173 Blaine Bishop	.40	.18
❑ 174 Yancey Thigpen	.60	.25
❑ 175 Brad Johnson	1.00	.45
❑ 176 Michael Westbrook	.60	.25
❑ 177 Skip Hicks	.40	.18
❑ 178 Brian Mitchell	.40	.18
❑ 179 Dana Stubblefield	.40	.18
❑ 180 Stephen Davis	1.00	.45
❑ 181 Champ Bailey RC	5.00	2.20
❑ 182 Chris McAlister RC	3.00	1.35
❑ 183 Jevon Kearse RC	6.00	2.70
❑ 184 Ebenezer Ekuban RC	3.00	1.35
❑ 185 Chris Claiborne RC	2.00	.90
❑ 186 Andy Katzenmoyer RC	3.00	1.35
❑ 187 Tim Couch RC	4.00	1.80
❑ 188 Daunte Culpepper RC	12.00	5.50
❑ 189 Akili Smith RC	3.00	1.35
❑ 190 Donovan McNabb RC	15.00	6.75
❑ 191 Sean Bennett RC	2.00	.90
❑ 192 Brock Huard RC	4.00	1.80
❑ 193 Cade McNown RC	3.00	1.35
❑ 194 Shaun King RC	3.00	1.35
❑ 195 Joe Germaine RC	3.00	1.35
❑ 196 Ricky Williams RC	6.00	2.70
❑ 197 Edgerrin James RC	12.00	5.50
❑ 198 Sedrick Irvin RC	2.00	.90
❑ 199 Kevin Faulk RC	4.00	1.80
❑ 200 Rob Konrad RC	4.00	1.80
❑ 201 James Johnson RC	3.00	1.35
❑ 202 Amos Zereoue RC	4.00	1.80
❑ 203 Torry Holt RC	8.00	3.60
❑ 204 D'Wayne Bates RC	3.00	1.35
❑ 205 David Boston RC	4.00	1.80
❑ 206 Dameane Douglas RC	3.00	1.35
❑ 207 Troy Edwards RC	3.00	1.35
❑ 208 Kevin Johnson RC	4.00	1.80
❑ 209 Peerless Price RC	6.00	2.70
❑ 210 Antoine Winfield RC	3.00	1.35
❑ 211 Mike Cloud RC	3.00	1.35
❑ 212 Joe Montgomery RC	3.00	1.35
❑ 213 Jermaine Fazande RC	3.00	1.35
❑ 214 Scott Covington RC	4.00	1.80
❑ 215 Aaron Brooks RC	10.00	4.50
❑ 216 Terry Jackson RC	3.00	1.35
❑ 217 Cecil Collins RC	2.00	.90
❑ 218 Olandis Gary RC	4.00	1.80
❑ 219 Craig Yeast RC	3.00	1.35
❑ 220 Karsten Bailey RC	3.00	1.35
❑ 221 Reginald Kelly RC	2.00	.90
❑ 222 Travis McGriff RC	2.00	.90
❑ 223 Jeff Paulk RC	2.00	.90
❑ 224 Jim Kleinsasser RC	4.00	1.80
❑ 225 Jason Tucker RC	3.00	1.35
❑ WPE Walter Payton Jersey AUTO/34	1000.00	450.00

1999 Upper Deck Encore Game Used Helmets

	Nm-Mt	Ex-Mt
COMPLETE SET (20)	600.00	275.00
❑ H-AS Akili Smith	25.00	11.00
❑ H-BF Brett Favre	100.00	45.00
❑ H-BH Brock Huard	25.00	11.00

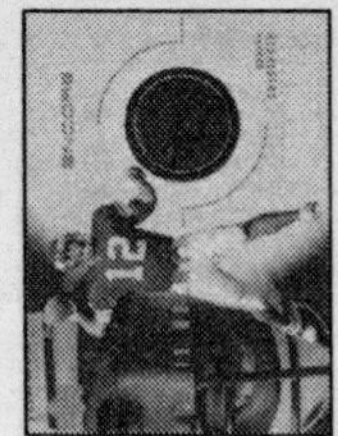

❑ H-CB Champ Bailey	30.00	13.50
❑ H-CC Cecil Collins	25.00	11.00
❑ H-CM Cade McNown	25.00	11.00
❑ H-DB David Boston	25.00	11.00
❑ H-DC Daunte Culpepper	80.00	36.00
❑ H-DM Dan Marino	100.00	45.00
❑ H-DW D'Wayne Bates	25.00	11.00
❑ H-EJ Edgerrin James	60.00	27.00
❑ H-JR Jerry Rice	60.00	27.00
❑ H-KF Kevin Faulk	25.00	11.00
❑ H-KJ Kevin Johnson	25.00	11.00
❑ H-MB Mark Brunell	25.00	11.00
❑ H-MC Donovan McNabb	80.00	36.00
❑ H-TC Tim Couch	25.00	11.00
❑ H-TD Terrell Davis	25.00	11.00
❑ H-TE Troy Edwards	25.00	11.00
❑ H-TH Torry Holt	50.00	22.00

1999 Upper Deck Encore UD Authentics

	Nm-Mt	Ex-Mt
❑ BH Brock Huard	20.00	9.00
❑ CM Cade McNown	20.00	9.00
❑ DB David Boston	25.00	11.00
❑ EJ Edgerrin James	60.00	27.00
❑ JN Joe Namath	120.00	55.00
❑ KF Kevin Faulk	25.00	11.00
❑ KW Kurt Warner	60.00	27.00
❑ MB Mark Brunell	25.00	11.00
❑ PM Peyton Manning	120.00	55.00
❑ RM Randy Moss	100.00	45.00
❑ SK Shaun King EXCH	3.00	1.35
❑ TA Troy Aikman	80.00	36.00
❑ TC Tim Couch	25.00	11.00
❑ TE Troy Edwards	20.00	9.00
❑ TH Torry Holt	30.00	13.50

2000 Upper Deck Encore

	Nm-Mt	Ex-Mt
COMPLETE SET (270)	120.00	55.00
COMP.SET w/o SP's (225)	15.00	6.75
❑ 1 Jake Plummer	.40	.18
❑ 2 Michael Pittman	.25	.11
❑ 3 Rob Moore	.40	.18
❑ 4 David Boston	.40	.18
❑ 5 Frank Sanders	.40	.18
❑ 6 Aeneas Williams	.25	.11
❑ 7 Kwamie Lassiter	.25	.11
❑ 8 Rob Fredrickson	.25	.11
❑ 9 Tim Dwight	.60	.25
❑ 10 Chris Chandler	.40	.18
❑ 11 Jamal Anderson	.60	.25
❑ 12 Shawn Jefferson	.25	.11
❑ 13 Brian Finneran RC	.60	.25
❑ 14 Terance Mathis	.40	.18
❑ 15 Bob Christian	.25	.11
❑ 16 Qadry Ismail	.40	.18
❑ 17 Jermaine Lewis	.40	.18
❑ 18 Rod Woodson	.40	.18
❑ 19 Michael McCrary	.25	.11
❑ 20 Tony Banks	.40	.18
❑ 21 Peter Boulware	.25	.11
❑ 22 Shannon Sharpe	.40	.18
❑ 23 Peerless Price	.60	.25
❑ 24 Rob Johnson	.40	.18
❑ 25 Eric Moulds	.60	.25
❑ 26 Doug Flutie	.60	.25
❑ 27 Jeremy McDaniel	.40	.18
❑ 28 Antowain Smith	.40	.18
❑ 29 Shawn Bryson	.25	.11
❑ 30 Muhsin Muhammad	.40	.18
❑ 31 Donald Hayes	.25	.11
❑ 32 Steve Beuerlein	.40	.18
❑ 33 Reggie White	.60	.25
❑ 34 Tim Biakabutuka	.40	.18
❑ 35 Michael Bates	.25	.11
❑ 36 Chuck Smith	.25	.11
❑ 37 Wesley Walls	.25	.11
❑ 38 Cade McNown	.25	.11
❑ 39 Curtis Enis	.25	.11
❑ 40 Marcus Robinson	.60	.25
❑ 41 Eddie Kennison	.40	.18
❑ 42 Bobby Engram	.25	.11
❑ 43 Glyn Milburn	.25	.11
❑ 44 Marty Booker	.40	.18
❑ 45 Akili Smith	.25	.11
❑ 46 Corey Dillon	.60	.25
❑ 47 James Allen	.40	.18
❑ 48 Tremain Mack	.25	.11
❑ 49 Damon Griffin	.25	.11
❑ 50 Takeo Spikes	.25	.11
❑ 51 Tony McGee	.25	.11
❑ 52 Tim Couch	.40	.18
❑ 53 Kevin Johnson	.60	.25
❑ 54 Darrin Chiaverini	.25	.11
❑ 55 Jamir Miller	.25	.11
❑ 56 Errict Rhett	.25	.11
❑ 57 Aaron Shea RC	2.50	1.10
❑ 58 Kevin Thompson RC	.25	.11
❑ 59 Troy Aikman	1.25	.55
❑ 60 Emmitt Smith	1.25	.55
❑ 61 Rocket Ismail	.40	.18
❑ 62 Jason Tucker	.25	.11
❑ 63 Chris Brazzell RC	.40	.18
❑ 64 Joey Galloway	.40	.18
❑ 65 Wane McGarity	.25	.11
❑ 66 Terrell Davis	.60	.25
❑ 67 Olandis Gary	.60	.25
❑ 68 Brian Griese	.60	.25
❑ 69 Gus Frerotte	.40	.18
❑ 70 Byron Chamberlain	.25	.11
❑ 71 Ed McCaffrey	.60	.25
❑ 72 Rod Smith	.40	.18
❑ 73 Al Wilson	.25	.11
❑ 74 Charlie Batch	.60	.25
❑ 75 Germane Crowell	.25	.11
❑ 76 Sedrick Irvin	.25	.11
❑ 77 Johnnie Morton	.40	.18
❑ 78 Robert Porcher	.25	.11
❑ 79 Herman Moore	.40	.18
❑ 80 James Stewart	.40	.18
❑ 81 Brett Favre	2.00	.90
❑ 82 Antonio Freeman	.60	.25
❑ 83 Bill Schroeder	.40	.18
❑ 84 Dorsey Levens	.40	.18
❑ 85 Herbert Goodman RC	.40	.18
❑ 86 Ahman Green	.60	.25
❑ 87 Matt Hasselbeck	.40	.18
❑ 88 Peyton Manning	1.50	.70
❑ 89 Edgerrin James	1.00	.45
❑ 90 Marvin Harrison	.60	.25
❑ 91 Basil Mitchell	.25	.11
❑ 92 Terrence Wilkins	.25	.11
❑ 93 Karim Abdul-Jabbar	.40	.18
❑ 94 Ken Dilger	.25	.11
❑ 95 Mark Brunell	.60	.25
❑ 96 Fred Taylor	.60	.25
❑ 97 Jimmy Smith	.40	.18
❑ 98 Keenan McCardell	.40	.18
❑ 99 Stacey Mack	.25	.11
❑ 100 Jonathan Quinn	.25	.11
❑ 101 Kyle Brady	.25	.11
❑ 102 Hardy Nickerson	.25	.11
❑ 103 Elvis Grbac	.40	.18
❑ 104 Tony Gonzalez	.40	.18
❑ 105 Derrick Alexander WR	.40	.18
❑ 106 Tony Richardson RC	.25	.11
❑ 107 Michael Cloud	.25	.11
❑ 108 Donnie Edwards	.25	.11
❑ 109 Jay Fiedler	.60	.25
❑ 110 James Johnson	.25	.11
❑ 111 Tony Martin	.40	.18
❑ 112 Damon Huard	.60	.25
❑ 113 Lamar Smith	.40	.18
❑ 114 Thurman Thomas	.40	.18
❑ 115 Mike Quinn	.25	.11
❑ 116 Oronde Gadsden	.40	.18
❑ 117 Randy Moss	1.25	.55
❑ 118 Robert Smith	.60	.25
❑ 119 Cris Carter	.60	.25
❑ 120 Matthew Hatchette	.25	.11
❑ 121 Daunte Culpepper	.75	.35
❑ 122 Moe Williams	.40	.18
❑ 123 Drew Bledsoe	.75	.35
❑ 124 Terry Glenn	.40	.18
❑ 125 Troy Brown	.40	.18
❑ 126 Kevin Faulk	.40	.18
❑ 127 Lawyer Milloy	.40	.18
❑ 128 Ricky Williams	.60	.25
❑ 129 Keith Poole	.25	.11
❑ 130 Jake Reed	.40	.18
❑ 131 Jake Delhomme RC	2.50	1.10
❑ 132 Jeff Blake	.40	.18
❑ 133 Andrew Glover	.25	.11
❑ 134 Kerry Collins	.40	.18
❑ 135 Amani Toomer	.25	.11
❑ 136 Joe Montgomery	.25	.11
❑ 137 Ike Hilliard	.40	.18
❑ 138 Tiki Barber	.40	.18
❑ 139 Pete Mitchell	.25	.11
❑ 140 Ray Lucas	.40	.18
❑ 141 Mo Lewis	.25	.11
❑ 142 Curtis Martin	.60	.25
❑ 143 Vinny Testaverde	.40	.18
❑ 144 Wayne Chrebet	.40	.18
❑ 145 Dedric Ward	.25	.11
❑ 146 Tim Brown	.60	.25
❑ 147 Rich Gannon	.60	.25
❑ 148 Tyrone Wheatley	.40	.18
❑ 149 Napoleon Kaufman	.40	.18
❑ 150 Charles Woodson	.40	.18
❑ 151 Darrell Russell	.25	.11
❑ 152 James Jett	.25	.11
❑ 153 Rickey Dudley	.25	.11
❑ 154 Jon Ritchie	.25	.11
❑ 155 Duce Staley	.60	.25
❑ 156 Donovan McNabb	1.00	.45
❑ 157 Torrance Small	.25	.11
❑ 158 Ron Powlus RC	3.00	1.35
❑ 159 Mike Mamula	.25	.11
❑ 160 Dameane Douglas	.25	.11
❑ 161 Charles Johnson	.40	.18
❑ 162 Kent Graham	.25	.11
❑ 163 Troy Edwards	.25	.11
❑ 164 Jerome Bettis	.60	.25
❑ 165 Hines Ward	.60	.25
❑ 166 Kordell Stewart	.40	.18
❑ 167 Levon Kirkland	.25	.11

❑ 168 Bobby Shaw RC	.75	.35
❑ 169 Marshall Faulk	.75	.35
❑ 170 Kurt Warner	1.25	.55
❑ 171 Torry Holt	.60	.25
❑ 172 Isaac Bruce	.60	.25
❑ 173 Kevin Carter	.25	.11
❑ 174 Az-Zahir Hakim	.25	.11
❑ 175 Ricky Proehl	.25	.11
❑ 176 Robert Chancey	.25	.11
❑ 177 Curtis Conway	.40	.18
❑ 178 Freddie Jones	.25	.11
❑ 179 Junior Seau	.60	.25
❑ 180 Jeff Graham	.25	.11
❑ 181 Reggie Jones RC	.25	.11
❑ 182 Rodney Harrison	.25	.11
❑ 183 Rick Mirer	.25	.11
❑ 184 Jerry Rice	1.25	.55
❑ 185 Charlie Garner	.40	.18
❑ 186 Terrell Owens	.60	.25
❑ 187 Jeff Garcia	.60	.25
❑ 188 Fred Beasley	.25	.11
❑ 189 J.J. Stokes	.40	.18
❑ 190 Ricky Watters	.40	.18
❑ 191 Jon Kitna	.60	.25
❑ 192 Derrick Mayes	.40	.18
❑ 193 Sean Dawkins	.25	.11
❑ 194 Charlie Rogers	.25	.11
❑ 195 Brock Huard	.40	.18
❑ 196 Cortez Kennedy	.25	.11
❑ 197 Christian Fauria	.25	.11
❑ 198 Warrick Dunn	.60	.25
❑ 199 Shaun King	.25	.11
❑ 200 Mike Alstott	.60	.25
❑ 201 Warren Sapp	.40	.18
❑ 202 Jacquez Green	.25	.11
❑ 203 Reidel Anthony	.25	.11
❑ 204 Dave Moore	.25	.11
❑ 205 Keyshawn Johnson	.60	.25
❑ 206 Eddie George	.60	.25
❑ 207 Steve McNair	.60	.25
❑ 208 Billy Volek RC	1.25	.55
❑ 209 Jevon Kearse	.60	.25
❑ 210 Yancey Thigpen	.25	.11
❑ 211 Frank Wycheck	.25	.11
❑ 212 Carl Pickens	.40	.18
❑ 213 Neil O'Donnell	.25	.11
❑ 214 Brad Johnson	.60	.25
❑ 215 Stephen Davis	.60	.25
❑ 216 Michael Westbrook	.40	.18
❑ 217 Albert Connell	.25	.11
❑ 218 Aaron Stecker RC	3.00	1.35
❑ 219 Bruce Smith	.40	.18
❑ 220 Stephen Alexander	.25	.11
❑ 221 Jeff George	.40	.18
❑ 222 Adrian Murrell	.25	.11
❑ 223 Courtney Brown RC	3.00	1.35
❑ 224 John Engelberger RC	2.50	1.10
❑ 225 Deltha O'Neal RC	3.00	1.35
❑ 226 Corey Simon RC	3.00	1.35
❑ 227 R.Jay Soward RC	2.50	1.10
❑ 228 Chris Samuels RC	2.50	1.10
❑ 229 Avion Black RC	2.50	1.10
❑ 230 Doug Chapman RC	2.50	1.10
❑ 231 Darrell Jackson RC	6.00	2.70
❑ 232 Chris Cole RC	2.50	1.10
❑ 233 Trevor Gaylor RC	3.00	1.35
❑ 234 Chad Morton RC	3.00	1.35
❑ 235 Chris Redman RC	2.50	1.10
❑ 236 Joe Hamilton RC	2.50	1.10
❑ 237 Chad Pennington RC	12.00	5.50
❑ 238 Tee Martin RC	3.00	1.35
❑ 239 Giovanni Carmazzi RC	2.50	1.10
❑ 240 Tim Rattay RC	6.00	2.70
❑ 241 Ron Dayne RC	3.00	1.35
❑ 242 Shaun Alexander RC	8.00	3.60
❑ 243 Thomas Jones RC	5.00	2.20
❑ 244 Reuben Droughns RC	4.00	1.80
❑ 245 Jamal Lewis RC	8.00	3.60
❑ 246 Michael Wiley RC	2.50	1.10
❑ 247 J.R. Redmond RC	2.50	1.10
❑ 248 Travis Prentice RC	2.50	1.10
❑ 249 Todd Husak RC	3.00	1.35
❑ 250 Trung Canidate RC	2.50	1.10
❑ 251 Brian Urlacher RC	12.00	5.50
❑ 252 Anthony Becht RC	3.00	1.35
❑ 253 Bubba Franks RC	3.00	1.35
❑ 254 Tom Brady RC	30.00	13.50
❑ 255 Peter Warrick RC	3.00	1.35
❑ 256 Plaxico Burress RC	6.00	2.70
❑ 257 Sylvester Morris RC	2.50	1.10
❑ 258 Dez White RC	3.00	1.35
❑ 259 Travis Taylor RC	3.00	1.35
❑ 260 Todd Pinkston RC	3.00	1.35
❑ 261 Dennis Northcutt RC	3.00	1.35
❑ 262 Jerry Porter RC	4.00	1.80
❑ 263 Laveranues Coles RC	4.00	1.80
❑ 264 Danny Farmer RC	2.50	1.10
❑ 265 Curtis Keaton RC	2.50	1.10
❑ 266 Windrell Hayes RC	2.50	1.10
❑ 267 Ron Dugans RC	1.50	.70
❑ 268 Steve McNair CL	.40	.18
❑ 269 Jake Plummer CL	.40	.18
❑ 270 Antonio Freeman CL	.40	.18
❑ 271 Brad Hoover RC	2.50	1.10
❑ 272 Charles Lee RC	2.50	1.10
❑ 273 Deon Dyer RC	2.50	1.10
❑ 274 Doug Johnson RC	3.00	1.35
❑ 275 JaJuan Dawson RC	1.50	.70
❑ 276 Jarious Jackson RC	2.50	1.10
❑ 277 Larry Foster RC	2.50	1.10
❑ 278 Mike Anderson RC	3.00	1.35
❑ 279 Ron Dixon RC	2.50	1.10
❑ 280 Sammy Morris RC	2.50	1.10
❑ 281 Shyrone Stith RC	2.50	1.10
❑ 282 Spergon Wynn RC	2.50	1.10
❑ 283 Troy Walters RC	3.00	1.35

2000 Upper Deck Encore UD Authentics

	Nm-Mt	Ex-Mt
❑ BU Brian Urlacher	60.00	27.00
❑ CB Courtney Brown	20.00	9.00
❑ CC Chris Coleman	8.00	3.60
❑ CM Corey Moore	8.00	3.60
❑ CP Chad Pennington	60.00	27.00
❑ CR Chris Redman	12.00	5.50
❑ DF Danny Farmer	12.00	5.50
❑ DJ Darrell Jackson	20.00	9.00
❑ DN Dennis Northcutt	8.00	3.60
❑ DU Ron Dugans	8.00	3.60
❑ DW Dez White	12.00	5.50
❑ DX Ron Dixon	8.00	3.60
❑ JO Doug Johnson	8.00	3.60
❑ KC Kwame Cavil	8.00	3.60
❑ LC Laveranues Coles	20.00	9.00
❑ MA Mike Anderson	12.00	5.50
❑ MW Michael Wiley	8.00	3.60
❑ PB Plaxico Burress	30.00	13.50
❑ RD Ron Dayne	20.00	9.00
❑ SA Shaun Alexander	40.00	18.00
❑ SG Sherrod Gideon	8.00	3.60
❑ SM Sylvester Morris	8.00	3.60
❑ TC Trung Canidate	8.00	3.60
❑ TG Trevor Gaylor	8.00	3.60
❑ TM Tee Martin	20.00	9.00
❑ TP Travis Prentice	12.00	5.50
❑ TR Tim Rattay	25.00	11.00
❑ TW Troy Walters	12.00	5.50

2003 Upper Deck Finite

	MINT	NRMT
COMP.SET w/o SP's (100)	60.00	27.00
❑ 1 Peyton Manning	3.00	1.35
❑ 2 Aaron Brooks	2.00	.90
❑ 3 Joey Harrington	3.00	1.35
❑ 4 Brett Favre	5.00	2.20
❑ 5 Donovan McNabb	2.50	1.10
❑ 6 Steve McNair	2.00	.90
❑ 7 Michael Vick	5.00	2.20
❑ 8 David Carr	3.00	1.35
❑ 9 Drew Brees	2.00	.90
❑ 10 Chad Pennington	2.50	1.10
❑ 11 Daunte Culpepper	2.00	.90
❑ 12 Tom Brady	3.00	1.35
❑ 13 Kurt Warner	2.00	.90
❑ 14 Brad Johnson	1.25	.55
❑ 15 Drew Bledsoe	2.00	.90
❑ 16 Jake Plummer	1.25	.55
❑ 17 Jeff Garcia	2.00	.90
❑ 18 Mark Brunell	1.25	.55
❑ 19 Josh McCown	1.25	.55
❑ 20 Travis Henry	1.25	.55
❑ 21 LaDainian Tomlinson	2.00	.90
❑ 22 Emmitt Smith	5.00	2.20
❑ 23 Michael Bennett	1.25	.55
❑ 24 Brian Westbrook	1.25	.55
❑ 25 Curtis Martin	2.00	.90
❑ 26 Clinton Portis	3.00	1.35
❑ 27 Eddie George	1.25	.55
❑ 28 Marshall Faulk	2.00	.90
❑ 29 Deuce McAllister	2.00	.90
❑ 30 Ahman Green	2.00	.90
❑ 31 Lamont Jordan	1.25	.55
❑ 32 Edgerrin James	2.00	.90
❑ 33 Jamel White	.75	.35
❑ 34 Ricky Williams	2.00	.90
❑ 35 Anthony Thomas	2.00	.90
❑ 36 Amos Zereoue	1.25	.55
❑ 37 Ladell Betts	1.25	.55
❑ 38 Stephen Davis	1.25	.55
❑ 39 T.J. Duckett	1.25	.55
❑ 40 Troy Hambrick	.75	.35
❑ 41 Maurice Morris	.75	.35
❑ 42 James Jackson	.75	.35
❑ 43 Correll Buckhalter	1.25	.55
❑ 44 Keith Brooking	.75	.35
❑ 45 Michael Strahan	1.25	.55
❑ 46 Jason Taylor	.75	.35
❑ 47 Kendrell Bell	1.25	.55
❑ 48 Jevon Kearse	1.25	.55
❑ 49 Chris Horn RC	1.25	.55
❑ 50 Quentin Jammer	.75	.35
❑ 51 Phillip Buchanon	.75	.35
❑ 52 Charles Woodson	1.25	.55
❑ 53 Rod Woodson	1.25	.55
❑ 54 Simeon Rice	1.25	.55
❑ 55 Derrick Brooks	1.25	.55
❑ 56 Warren Sapp	1.25	.55
❑ 57 John Lynch	1.25	.55
❑ 58 Champ Bailey	1.25	.55
❑ 59 Reggie Wayne	1.25	.55
❑ 60 Darrell Jackson	1.25	.55
❑ 61 Derrick Mason	1.25	.55
❑ 62 Travis Minor	1.25	.55
❑ 63 Eric Parker RC	2.00	.90
❑ 64 Ron Johnson	.75	.35
❑ 65 Dante Hall	2.00	.90
❑ 66 David Terrell	1.25	.55
❑ 67 Daniel Graham	.75	.35
❑ 68 Randy McMichael	1.25	.55
❑ 69 Jeremy Shockey	3.00	1.35
❑ 70 J.J. Stokes	1.25	.55
❑ 71 Johnnie Morton	1.25	.55
❑ 72 Dennis Northcutt	1.25	.55
❑ 73 Peter Warrick	1.25	.55
❑ 74 Rod Smith	1.25	.55

❑ 75 Javon Walker 1.25 .55
❑ 76 Tim Carter .75 .35
❑ 77 Wayne Chrebet 1.25 .55
❑ 78 Corey Bradford .75 .35
❑ 79 Deion Branch 2.00 .90
❑ 80 Jerry Rice 4.00 1.80
❑ 81 Terrell Owens 2.00 .90
❑ 82 Josh Reed 1.25 .55
❑ 83 Ed McCaffrey 2.00 .90
❑ 84 Randy Moss 3.00 1.35
❑ 85 Chad Johnson 1.25 .55
❑ 86 Hines Ward 2.00 .90
❑ 87 Rod Gardner 1.25 .55
❑ 88 Tony Gonzalez 1.25 .55
❑ 89 David Boston 1.25 .55
❑ 90 Jerry Porter 1.25 .55
❑ 91 Kevin Johnson 1.25 .55
❑ 92 Rohan Davey 1.25 .55
❑ 93 Tim Rattay 1.25 .55
❑ 94 Jon Kitna 1.25 .55
❑ 95 Jay Fiedler 1.25 .55
❑ 96 Doug Flutie 2.00 .90
❑ 97 Quincy Carter 1.25 .55
❑ 98 Vinny Testaverde 1.25 .55
❑ 99 Kelly Holcomb 1.25 .55
❑ 100 Marc Bulger 2.00 .90
❑ 101 Patrick Ramsey MF 4.00 1.80
❑ 102 Tim Couch MF 1.50 .70
❑ 103 Tommy Maddox MF 4.00 1.80
❑ 104 Chad Hutchinson MF 2.50 1.10
❑ 105 Trent Green MF 2.50 1.10
❑ 106 Kerry Collins MF 2.50 1.10
❑ 107 Will Heller MF RC 4.00 1.80
❑ 108 Brian Griese MF 4.00 1.80
❑ 109 Kordell Stewart MF 2.50 1.10
❑ 110 Jake Delhomme MF 4.00 1.80
❑ 111 Chris Redman MF 1.50 .70
❑ 112 Mike Anderson MF 2.50 1.10
❑ 113 Olandis Gary MF 2.50 1.10
❑ 114 Antonio Gates MF RC 40.00 18.00
❑ 115 Garrison Hearst MF 2.50 1.10
❑ 116 Fred Taylor MF 4.00 1.80
❑ 117 Casey Fitzsimmons MF RC 5.00 2.20
❑ 118 Tiki Barber MF 2.50 1.10
❑ 119 Mike Alstott MF 4.00 1.80
❑ 120 Kevan Barlow MF 2.50 1.10
❑ 121 Jamal Lewis MF 4.00 1.80
❑ 122 Mike Banks MF RC 2.50 1.10
❑ 123 Jimmy Farris MF RC 4.00 1.80
❑ 124 Warrick Dunn MF 2.50 1.10
❑ 125 Jerome Bettis MF 4.00 1.80
❑ 126 Antonio Chatman MF RC 5.00 2.20
❑ 127 Bubba Franks MF 2.50 1.10
❑ 128 Todd Heap MF 2.50 1.10
❑ 129 Shannon Sharpe MF 2.50 1.10
❑ 130 Donald Driver MF 2.50 1.10
❑ 131 Antonio Freeman MF 2.50 1.10
❑ 132 Joey Galloway MF 2.50 1.10
❑ 133 Marc Boerigter MF 2.50 1.10
❑ 134 Torry Holt MF 4.00 1.80
❑ 135 Amani Toomer MF 2.50 1.10
❑ 136 Marty Booker MF 2.50 1.10
❑ 137 Santana Moss MF 2.50 1.10
❑ 138 Jimmy Smith MF 2.50 1.10
❑ 139 Jabar Gaffney MF 2.50 1.10
❑ 140 Isaac Bruce MF 4.00 1.80
❑ 141 Laveranues Coles MF 2.50 1.10
❑ 142 Quincy Morgan MF 2.50 1.10
❑ 143 Peerless Price MF 2.50 1.10
❑ 144 Eric Moulds MF 2.50 1.10
❑ 145 Troy Brown MF 2.50 1.10
❑ 146 Plaxico Burress MF 2.50 1.10
❑ 147 Chris Chambers MF 4.00 1.80
❑ 148 Tim Brown MF 4.00 1.80
❑ 149 Antonio Brown MF RC 2.50 1.10
❑ 150 Koren Robinson MF 2.50 1.10
❑ 151 David Boston MF 2.50 1.10
❑ 152 C.J. Jones MF RC 2.50 1.10
❑ 153 Marvin Harrison MF 4.00 1.80
❑ 154 Keyshawn Johnson MF 4.00 1.80
❑ 155 J.J. Moses MF RC 4.00 1.80
❑ 156 Antwaan Randle El MF 4.00 1.80
❑ 157 Ashley Lelie MF 4.00 1.80
❑ 158 Andre Davis MF 1.50 .70
❑ 159 Donte Stallworth MF 4.00 1.80
❑ 160 Antonio Bryant MF 2.50 1.10
❑ 161 Tom Brady PP 8.00 3.60
❑ 162 Drew Bledsoe PP 5.00 2.20
❑ 163 Rich Gannon PP 3.00 1.35
❑ 164 David Carr PP 8.00 3.60
❑ 165 Drew Brees PP 5.00 2.20
❑ 166 Aaron Brooks PP 5.00 2.20
❑ 167 Joey Harrington PP 8.00 3.60
❑ 168 Matt Hasselbeck PP 3.00 1.35
❑ 169 Jake Plummer PP 3.00 1.35
❑ 170 Edgerrin James PP 5.00 2.20
❑ 171 Ahman Green PP 5.00 2.20
❑ 172 Deuce McAllister PP 5.00 2.20
❑ 173 Priest Holmes PP 6.00 2.70
❑ 174 Travis Henry PP 3.00 1.35
❑ 175 William Green PP 3.00 1.35
❑ 176 Corey Dillon PP 3.00 1.35
❑ 177 Shaun Alexander PP 5.00 2.20
❑ 178 Jeremy Shockey PP 8.00 3.60
❑ 179 Brian Dawkins PP 2.00 .90
❑ 180 Roy Williams PP 5.00 2.20
❑ 181 Julius Peppers PP 5.00 2.20
❑ 182 Ray Lewis PP 5.00 2.20
❑ 183 Junior Seau PP 5.00 2.20
❑ 184 Zach Thomas PP 5.00 2.20
❑ 185 Brian Urlacher PP 8.00 3.60
❑ 186 Michael Vick FCF 20.00 9.00
❑ 187 Jeff Garcia FCF 8.00 3.60
❑ 188 Daunte Culpepper FCF 8.00 3.60
❑ 189 Steve McNair FCF 8.00 3.60
❑ 190 Chad Pennington FCF 10.00 4.50
❑ 191 LaDainian Tomlinson FCF 8.00 3.60
❑ 192 Clinton Portis FCF 12.00 5.50
❑ 193 Ricky Williams FCF 8.00 3.60
❑ 194 Donovan McNabb FCF 10.00 4.50
❑ 195 Peyton Manning FCF 12.00 5.50
❑ 196 Marshall Faulk FCF 8.00 3.60
❑ 197 Kurt Warner FCF 8.00 3.60
❑ 198 Emmitt Smith FCF 20.00 9.00
❑ 199 Jerry Rice FCF 15.00 6.75
❑ 200 Brett Favre FCF 20.00 9.00
❑ 201 Carson Palmer RC 15.00 6.75
❑ 202 Kyle Boller RC 12.00 5.50
❑ 203 Kliff Kingsbury RC 4.00 1.80
❑ 204 Brooks Bollinger RC 5.00 2.20
❑ 205 Mike Doss RC 5.00 2.20
❑ 206 Dewayne White RC 4.00 1.80
❑ 207 Roderick Babers RC 4.00 1.80
❑ 208 Seneca Wallace RC 5.00 2.20
❑ 209 Nate Hybl RC 5.00 2.20
❑ 210 Jason Gesser RC 5.00 2.20
❑ 211 Willis McGahee RC 12.00 5.50
❑ 212 George Wrighster RC 4.00 1.80
❑ 213 Drayton Florence RC 2.50 1.10
❑ 214 L.J. Smith RC 5.00 2.20
❑ 215 B.J. Askew RC 5.00 2.20
❑ 216 Adewale Ogunleye RC 5.00 2.20
❑ 217 Ahmaad Galloway RC 4.00 1.80
❑ 218 Dwone Hicks RC 2.50 1.10
❑ 219 Travaris Robinson RC 2.50 1.10
❑ 220 William Joseph RC 5.00 2.20
❑ 221 Terrence Kiel RC 5.00 2.20
❑ 222 Marcus Trufant RC 5.00 2.20
❑ 223 Terence Newman RC 10.00 4.50
❑ 224 Nnamdi Asomugha RC 4.00 1.80
❑ 225 Troy Polamalu RC 5.00 2.20
❑ 226 Terrell Suggs RC 8.00 3.60
❑ 227 Boss Bailey RC 6.00 2.70
❑ 228 Dan Klecko RC 6.00 2.70
❑ 229 Jerome McDougle RC 5.00 2.20
❑ 230 Johnathan Sullivan RC 4.00 1.80
❑ 231 Mike Seidman RC 2.50 1.10
❑ 232 Dallas Clark RC 5.00 2.20
❑ 233 Tony Romo RC 5.00 2.20
❑ 234 Reggie Newhouse RC 4.00 1.80
❑ 235 David Tyree RC 4.00 1.80
❑ 236 Andre Woolfolk RC 5.00 2.20
❑ 237 Domanick Davis RC 10.00 4.50
❑ 238 Zuriel Smith RC 2.50 1.10
❑ 239 Tommy Jones RC 2.50 1.10
❑ 240 Arnaz Battle RC 5.00 2.20
❑ 241 Kassim Osgood RC 5.00 2.20
❑ 242 Gerald Hayes RC 2.50 1.10
❑ 243 Keenan Howry RC 5.00 2.20
❑ 244 Bobby Wade RC 5.00 2.20
❑ 245 Brock Forsey RC 6.00 2.70
❑ 246 Walter Young RC 2.50 1.10
❑ 247 Shaun McDonald RC 5.00 2.20
❑ 248 Nate Burleson RC 8.00 3.60
❑ 249 Anquan Boldin RC 12.00 5.50
❑ 250 Taylor Jacobs RC 5.00 2.20
❑ 251 Chris Simms RC 12.00 5.50
❑ 252 Rex Grossman RC 20.00 9.00
❑ 253 Arlen Harris RC 6.00 2.70
❑ 254 Dave Ragone RC 6.00 2.70
❑ 255 Chris Brown RC 10.00 4.50
❑ 256 Musa Smith RC 6.00 2.70
❑ 257 Artose Pinner RC 6.00 2.70
❑ 258 Sammy Davis RC 6.00 2.70
❑ 259 Dewayne Robertson RC 6.00 2.70
❑ 260 Tony Hollings RC 6.00 2.70
❑ 261 LaBrandon Toefield RC 6.00 2.70
❑ 262 Cortez Hankton RC 5.00 2.20
❑ 263 Justin Griffith RC 5.00 2.20
❑ 264 Jeremi Johnson RC 5.00 2.20
❑ 265 E.J. Henderson RC 6.00 2.70
❑ 266 Casey Moore RC 5.00 2.20
❑ 267 Ken Hamlin RC 6.00 2.70
❑ 268 Nick Barnett RC 10.00 4.50
❑ 269 Vishante Shiancoe RC 5.00 2.20
❑ 270 Aaron Walker RC 5.00 2.20
❑ 271 Bennie Joppru RC 6.00 2.70
❑ 272 Terrence Edwards RC 5.00 2.20
❑ 273 Willie Ponder RC 3.00 1.35
❑ 274 Pisa Tinoisamoa RC 10.00 4.50
❑ 275 Doug Gabriel RC 6.00 2.70
❑ 276 Kerry Carter RC 5.00 2.20
❑ 277 Avon Cobourne RC 3.00 1.35
❑ 278 Sam Aiken RC 5.00 2.20
❑ 279 Brandon Lloyd RC 8.00 3.60
❑ 280 LaTarence Dunbar RC 5.00 2.20
❑ 281 J.R. Tolver RC 5.00 2.20
❑ 282 Kevin Curtis RC 6.00 2.70
❑ 283 Tyrone Calico RC 8.00 3.60
❑ 284 Bryant Johnson RC 6.00 2.70
❑ 285 Charles Rogers RC 8.00 3.60
❑ 286 Teyo Johnson RC 20.00 9.00
❑ 287 Jason Witten RC 30.00 13.50
❑ 288 Kelley Washington RC 20.00 9.00
❑ 289 Billy McMullen RC 15.00 6.75
❑ 290 Adrian Madise RC 15.00 6.75
❑ 291 Justin Gage RC 20.00 9.00
❑ 292 Andre Johnson RC 50.00 22.00
❑ 293 Bethel Johnson RC 30.00 13.50
❑ 294 Lee Suggs RC 40.00 18.00
❑ 295 Larry Johnson RC 50.00 22.00
❑ 296 Justin Fargas RC 20.00 9.00
❑ 297 Onterrio Smith RC 25.00 11.00
❑ 298 Ken Dorsey RC 30.00 13.50
❑ 299 Brian St.Pierre RC 20.00 9.00
❑ 300 Byron Leftwich RC 80.00 36.00

2003 Upper Deck Finite Gold

MINT NRMT
*STARS 1-100: 2.5X TO 6X BASIC CARDS
*STARS 101-160: 1.2X TO 3X
*ROOKIES 101-160: 1.2X TO 3X
*STARS 161-185: 1X TO 2.5X
*STARS 186-200: .6X TO 1.5X
*ROOKIES 201-250: 1.2X TO 3X
*ROOKIES 251-285: 1X TO 2.5X
*ROOKIES 286-300: .5X TO 1.2X

2003 Upper Deck Finite Autographs

MINT NRMT
OVERALL AUTO STATED ODDS 1:10
❑ AB Antonio Bryant/100 20.00 9.00

❑ AD Andre Davis/263	12.00	5.50
❑ AL Mike Alstott/175	40.00	18.00
❑ AP Artose Pinner/396	20.00	9.00
❑ AQ Anquan Boldin/396	40.00	18.00
❑ AZ Az-Zahir Hakim/186	12.00	5.50
❑ BB Brad Banks/1000	12.00	5.50
❑ BD Brandon Doman/262	12.00	5.50
❑ BR Bryant Johnson/396	12.00	5.50
❑ BS Brian St.Pierre/720	12.00	5.50
❑ CB Chris Brown/396	40.00	18.00
❑ CJ Chad Johnson/815	20.00	9.00
❑ CP Clinton Portis/70	100.00	45.00
❑ CS Chris Simms/80	50.00	22.00
❑ DC Dallas Clark/396	20.00	9.00
❑ DF DeShaun Foster/207	25.00	11.00
❑ DF2 DeShaun Foster/651	20.00	9.00
❑ DR Dewayne Robertson/20 EXCH		
❑ EC Eric Crouch/263	20.00	9.00
❑ EG Earnest Graham/800	12.00	5.50
❑ JA Jason Johnson/205	12.00	5.50
❑ JB Jeff Blake/35	20.00	9.00
❑ JF Justin Fargas/396	20.00	9.00
❑ JG Jabar Gaffney/260	12.00	5.50
❑ JJ James Jackson/300	12.00	5.50
❑ JS Jeremy Shockey/93	50.00	22.00
❑ KA Kareem Kelly/1300	12.00	5.50
❑ KB Kevan Barlow/107	25.00	11.00
❑ KC Kelly Campbell/262	12.00	5.50
❑ KC Kevin Curtis/396	12.00	5.50
❑ KK Kurt Kittner/55	30.00	13.50
❑ KL Kliff Kingsbury/396	12.00	5.50
❑ KM Keenan McCardell/30	20.00	9.00
❑ KW Kelley Washington/1058	12.00	5.50
❑ LJ Larry Johnson/396	30.00	13.50
❑ LS Luke Staley/263	12.00	5.50
❑ MB Marc Bulger/35	50.00	22.00
❑ MS Musa Smith/396	12.00	5.50
❑ MT Marcus Trufant/396	12.00	5.50
❑ NB Nate Burleson/396	30.00	13.50
❑ NH Napoleon Harris/262	12.00	5.50
❑ PM1 Peyton Manning/1280	50.00	22.00
❑ PM2 Peyton Manning/1254	50.00	22.00
❑ PR Patrick Ramsey/190	25.00	11.00
❑ QG Quentin Griffin/447	30.00	13.50
❑ RC Reche Caldwell/261	12.00	5.50
❑ RD Rohan Davey/262	25.00	11.00
❑ RJ Ron Johnson/263	12.00	5.50
❑ RW Roy Williams/151	50.00	22.00
❑ SU Lee Suggs/30	120.00	55.00
❑ SW Seneca Wallace/414	12.00	5.50
❑ TA Taylor Jacobs/409	20.00	9.00
❑ TG Tony Gonzalez/46	40.00	18.00
❑ TH Todd Heap/63	30.00	13.50
❑ TM Travis Minor/364	12.00	5.50
❑ TS Terrell Suggs/950	20.00	9.00
❑ VT Vinny Testaverde/212	20.00	9.00
❑ WD0 Woody Dantzler/207	20.00	9.00

2003 Upper Deck Finite Autographs Gold

	MINT	NRMT
❑ AB Antonio Bryant	30.00	13.50
❑ AD Andre Davis	50.00	22.00
❑ AL Mike Alstott	60.00	27.00
❑ AL Ashley Lelie	60.00	27.00
❑ AP Artose Pinner	30.00	13.50
❑ AQ Anquan Boldin	100.00	45.00
❑ AZ Az-Zahir Hakim	30.00	13.50
❑ BB Brad Banks		
❑ BD Brandon Doman	30.00	13.50
❑ BR Bryant Johnson		
❑ BS Brian St.Pierre	30.00	13.50
❑ CB Chris Brown	50.00	22.00
❑ CJ Chad Johnson	50.00	22.00
❑ CP Clinton Portis	60.00	27.00
❑ CS Chris Simms		
❑ DC David Carr	80.00	36.00
❑ DC Dallas Clark	50.00	22.00
❑ DF DeShaun Foster	50.00	22.00
❑ DF2 DeShaun Foster	50.00	22.00
❑ EC Eric Crouch	50.00	22.00
❑ EG Earnest Graham	30.00	13.50
❑ JA Jason Johnson		
❑ JB Jeff Blake		
❑ JF Justin Fargas		
❑ JG Jabar Gaffney	30.00	13.50
❑ JJ James Jackson		
❑ JS Jeremy Shockey	60.00	27.00
❑ KA Kareem Kelly		
❑ KB Kevan Barlow		
❑ KC Kelly Campbell		
❑ KC Kevin Curtis		
❑ KK Kurt Kittner	30.00	13.50
❑ KL Kliff Kingsbury	30.00	13.50
❑ KM Keenan McCardell	50.00	22.00
❑ KW Kelley Washington		
❑ LJ Larry Johnson	60.00	27.00
❑ LS Luke Staley	30.00	13.50
❑ MB Marc Bulger		
❑ MM Maurice Morris	50.00	22.00
❑ MS Musa Smith		
❑ MT Marcus Trufant	30.00	13.50
❑ NB Nate Burleson	60.00	27.00
❑ NH Napoleon Harris	30.00	13.50
❑ PM1 Peyton Manning	120.00	55.00
❑ PM2 Peyton Manning	120.00	55.00
❑ PR Patrick Ramsey	50.00	22.00
❑ QG Quentin Griffin	80.00	36.00
❑ RC Reche Caldwell	30.00	13.50
❑ RD Rohan Davey	30.00	13.50
❑ RJ Ron Johnson		
❑ RW Roy Williams	60.00	27.00
❑ SU Lee Suggs	80.00	36.00
❑ SW Seneca Wallace	30.00	13.50
❑ TA Taylor Jacobs	30.00	13.50
❑ TG Tony Gonzalez	50.00	22.00
❑ TH Todd Heap	30.00	13.50
❑ TM Travis Minor	30.00	13.50
❑ TS Terrell Suggs	50.00	22.00
❑ VT Vinny Testaverde	50.00	22.00
❑ WD Woody Dantzler		

2004 Upper Deck Finite HG

	Nm-Mt	Ex-Mt
COMP.SET w/o SP's (100)	30.00	9.00
101-265 RC PRINT RUN 275 SER.#'d SETS		
266-278 RC PRINT RUN 99 SER.#'d SETS		
❑ 1 Emmitt Smith	2.50	.75
❑ 2 Anquan Boldin	1.25	.35
❑ 3 Josh McCown	.75	.23
❑ 4 Michael Vick	2.50	.75
❑ 5 Peerless Price	.75	.23
❑ 6 Warrick Dunn	.75	.23
❑ 7 Todd Heap	.75	.23
❑ 8 Jamal Lewis	1.25	.35
❑ 9 Kyle Boller	1.25	.35
❑ 10 Drew Bledsoe	1.25	.35
❑ 11 Travis Henry	.75	.23
❑ 12 Eric Moulds	.75	.23
❑ 13 Jake Delhomme	1.25	.35
❑ 14 Steve Smith	.75	.23
❑ 15 Stephen Davis	.75	.23
❑ 16 Rex Grossman	1.25	.35
❑ 17 Brian Urlacher	1.50	.45
❑ 18 Thomas Jones	.75	.23
❑ 19 Rudi Johnson	.75	.23
❑ 20 Carson Palmer	1.50	.45
❑ 21 Chad Johnson	.75	.23
❑ 22 Jeff Garcia	1.25	.35
❑ 23 Andre Davis	.50	.15
❑ 24 Lee Suggs	1.25	.35
❑ 25 Keyshawn Johnson	.75	.23
❑ 26 Eddie George	.75	.23
❑ 27 Vinny Testaverde	.75	.23
❑ 28 Quentin Griffin	1.25	.35
❑ 29 Champ Bailey	.75	.23
❑ 30 Jake Plummer	.75	.23
❑ 31 Az-Zahir Hakim	.50	.15
❑ 32 Joey Harrington	1.25	.35
❑ 33 Charles Rogers	.75	.23
❑ 34 Javon Walker	.75	.23
❑ 35 Ahman Green	1.25	.35
❑ 36 Brett Favre	3.00	.90
❑ 37 Domanick Davis	1.25	.35
❑ 38 David Carr	1.25	.35
❑ 39 Andre Johnson	1.25	.35
❑ 40 Edgerrin James	1.25	.35
❑ 41 Marvin Harrison	1.25	.35
❑ 42 Reggie Wayne	.75	.23
❑ 43 Peyton Manning	2.00	.60
❑ 44 Fred Taylor	.75	.23
❑ 45 Jimmy Smith	.75	.23
❑ 46 Byron Leftwich	2.00	.60
❑ 47 Dante Hall	1.25	.35
❑ 48 Tony Gonzalez	.75	.23
❑ 49 Trent Green	.75	.23
❑ 50 Priest Holmes	1.50	.45
❑ 51 Zach Thomas	1.25	.35
❑ 52 A.J. Feeley	1.25	.35
❑ 53 Chris Chambers	.75	.23
❑ 54 Randy McMichael	.50	.15
❑ 55 Randy Moss	1.50	.45
❑ 56 Onterrio Smith	.75	.23
❑ 57 Daunte Culpepper	1.25	.35
❑ 58 Tom Brady	2.00	.60
❑ 59 Deion Branch	1.25	.35
❑ 60 Corey Dillon	.75	.23
❑ 61 Donte' Stallworth	.75	.23
❑ 62 Deuce McAllister	1.25	.35
❑ 63 Aaron Brooks	.75	.23
❑ 64 Amani Toomer	.75	.23
❑ 65 Jeremy Shockey	1.25	.35
❑ 66 Kurt Warner	1.25	.35
❑ 67 Curtis Martin	1.25	.35
❑ 68 Chad Pennington	1.50	.45
❑ 69 Santana Moss	.75	.23
❑ 70 Jerry Porter	.75	.23
❑ 71 Jerry Rice	2.50	.75
❑ 72 Rich Gannon	.75	.23
❑ 73 Justin Fargas	.75	.23
❑ 74 Terrell Owens	1.25	.35
❑ 75 Brian Westbrook	.75	.23
❑ 76 Donovan McNabb	1.50	.45
❑ 77 Tommy Maddox	.75	.23
❑ 78 Hines Ward	1.25	.35
❑ 79 Plaxico Burress	.75	.23
❑ 80 Antonio Gates	1.25	.35
❑ 81 LaDainian Tomlinson	1.25	.35
❑ 82 Drew Brees	1.25	.35
❑ 83 Brandon Lloyd	.75	.23
❑ 84 Tim Rattay	.75	.23
❑ 85 Kevan Barlow	.75	.23
❑ 86 Koren Robinson	.75	.23
❑ 87 Shaun Alexander	1.25	.35
❑ 88 Matt Hasselbeck	.75	.23
❑ 89 Torry Holt	1.25	.35
❑ 90 Marc Bulger	1.25	.35
❑ 91 Marshall Faulk	1.25	.35
❑ 92 Chris Simms	.75	.23
❑ 93 Keenan McCardell	.50	.15
❑ 94 Derrick Brooks	.75	.23
❑ 95 Steve McNair	1.25	.35
❑ 96 Chris Brown	1.25	.35
❑ 97 Derrick Mason	.75	.23
❑ 98 Mark Brunell	.75	.23
❑ 99 Laveranues Coles	.75	.23
❑ 100 Clinton Portis	1.25	.35
❑ 101 Michael Jenkins RC	12.00	3.60
❑ 102 Ryan Krause RC	10.00	3.00
❑ 103 Darnell Dockett RC	10.00	3.00
❑ 104 Quincy Wilson RC	10.00	3.00
❑ 105 Nate Lawrie RC	10.00	3.00
❑ 106 Joey Thomas RC	12.00	3.60
❑ 107 Junior Siavii RC	12.00	3.60
❑ 108 Landon Johnson RC	10.00	3.00
❑ 109 Michael Waddell RC	6.00	1.80
❑ 110 Lee Evans RC	20.00	6.00
❑ 111 Jason David RC	12.00	3.60
❑ 112 Chris Collins RC	10.00	3.00
❑ 113 Troy Fleming RC	10.00	3.00
❑ 114 Tim Euhus RC	12.00	3.60
❑ 115 Sean Jones RC	10.00	3.00

❑ 116 Jason Babin RC 12.00 3.60
❑ 117 Jorge Cordova RC 6.00 1.80
❑ 118 Josh Scobee RC 6.00 1.80
❑ 119 Luke McCown RC 12.00 3.60
❑ 120 Darius Watts RC 15.00 4.50
❑ 121 Clarence Moore RC 12.00 3.60
❑ 122 Randy Starks RC 10.00 3.00
❑ 123 Brandon Miree RC 10.00 3.00
❑ 124 Gibril Wilson RC 12.00 3.60
❑ 125 Jeremy LeSueur RC 10.00 3.00
❑ 126 Dwan Edwards RC 6.00 1.80
❑ 127 Richard Seigler RC 10.00 3.00
❑ 128 Stanford Samuels RC 10.00 3.00
❑ 129 Casey Clausen RC 15.00 4.50
❑ 130 Erik Coleman RC 12.00 3.60
❑ 131 Donnell Washington RC 12.00 3.60
❑ 132 Jammal Lord RC 12.00 3.60
❑ 133 Chris Cooley RC 12.00 3.60
❑ 134 Shawntae Spencer RC 12.00 3.60
❑ 135 Marcus Tubbs RC 12.00 3.60
❑ 136 Caleb Miller RC 10.00 3.00
❑ 137 Jeff Shoate RC 6.00 1.80
❑ 138 Bradlee Van Pelt RC 12.00 3.60
❑ 139 D.J. Hackett RC 10.00 3.00
❑ 140 Greg Brooks RC 6.00 1.80
❑ 141 Thomas Tapeh RC 10.00 3.00
❑ 142 Ben Hartsock RC 12.00 3.60
❑ 143 Madieu Williams RC 10.00 3.00
❑ 144 Vince Wilfork RC 15.00 4.50
❑ 145 Marquis Cooper RC 10.00 3.00
❑ 146 Nate Kaeding RC 12.00 3.60
❑ 147 B.J. Symons RC 12.00 3.60
❑ 148 Maurice Mann RC 10.00 3.00
❑ 149 Tim Anderson RC 12.00 3.60
❑ 150 Michael Turner RC 10.00 3.00
❑ 151 Kris Wilson RC 12.00 3.60
❑ 152 Keiwan Ratliff RC 10.00 3.00
❑ 153 Kenechi Udeze RC 12.00 3.60
❑ 154 Courtney Watson RC 12.00 3.60
❑ 155 Stacy Andrews RC 10.00 3.00
❑ 156 Jeff Smoker RC 20.00 6.00
❑ 157 Carlos Francis RC 10.00 3.00
❑ 158 Derek Abney RC 12.00 3.60
❑ 159 Dexter Wynn RC 10.00 3.00
❑ 160 Jason Wright RC 10.00 3.00
❑ 161 Dunta Robinson RC 12.00 3.60
❑ 162 Nathan Vasher RC 12.00 3.60
❑ 163 Karlos Dansby RC 12.00 3.60
❑ 164 Jake Grove RC 6.00 1.80
❑ 165 Matt Mauck RC 12.00 3.60
❑ 166 Johnnie Morant RC 12.00 3.60
❑ 167 Justin Jenkins RC 10.00 3.00
❑ 168 Cedric Cobbs RC 12.00 3.60
❑ 169 Ben Troupe RC 12.00 3.60
❑ 170 Bob Sanders RC 12.00 3.60
❑ 171 Will Smith RC 12.00 3.60
❑ 172 Michael Boulware RC 12.00 3.60
❑ 173 Nat Dorsey RC 6.00 1.80
❑ 174 Casey Bramlet RC 10.00 3.00
❑ 175 Ernest Wilford RC 12.00 3.60
❑ 176 Kendrick Starling RC 6.00 1.80
❑ 177 Mewelde Moore RC 15.00 4.50
❑ 178 Ben Watson RC 12.00 3.60
❑ 179 Ricardo Colclough RC 12.00 3.60
❑ 180 Tommie Harris RC 15.00 4.50
❑ 181 Dontarrious Thomas RC 12.00 3.60
❑ 182 Keith Lewis RC 6.00 1.80
❑ 183 John Navarre RC 12.00 3.60
❑ 184 Samie Parker RC 12.00 3.60
❑ 185 B.J. Johnson RC 10.00 3.00
❑ 186 Tatum Bell RC 20.00 6.00
❑ 187 Mike Karney RC 10.00 3.00
❑ 188 Ahmad Carroll RC 15.00 4.50
❑ 189 Will Allen RC 12.00 3.60
❑ 190 Teddy Lehman RC 12.00 3.60
❑ 191 Justin Smiley RC 12.00 3.60
❑ 192 Cody Pickett RC 12.00 3.60
❑ 193 Jerricho Cotchery RC 12.00 3.60
❑ 194 Tramon Douglas RC 6.00 1.80
❑ 195 Greg Jones RC 12.00 3.60
❑ 196 Kellen Winslow RC 40.00 12.00
❑ 197 Chris Gamble RC 15.00 4.50
❑ 198 Dexter Reid RC 6.00 1.80
❑ 199 Daryl Smith RC 12.00 3.60
❑ 200 Max Starks RC 10.00 3.00
❑ 201 J.P. Losman RC 30.00 9.00
❑ 202 Rashaun Woods RC 15.00 4.50
❑ 203 Triandos Luke RC 12.00 3.60
❑ 204 Rashad Washington RC 10.00 3.00
❑ 205 Derrick Ward RC 6.00 1.80
❑ 206 Matt Kranchick RC 12.00 3.60
❑ 207 Keith Smith RC 10.00 3.00
❑ 208 Travis LaBoy RC 12.00 3.60
❑ 209 Demorrio Williams RC 12.00 3.60
❑ 210 Jason Shivers RC 6.00 1.80
❑ 211 Craig Krenzel RC 12.00 3.60
❑ 212 Keary Colbert RC 15.00 4.50
❑ 213 Mark Jones RC 10.00 3.00
❑ 214 Shawn Johnson RC 10.00 3.00
❑ 215 Jarrett Payton RC 12.00 3.60
❑ 216 Michael Gaines RC 10.00 3.00
❑ 217 Matt Ware RC 12.00 3.60
❑ 218 Antwan Odom RC 12.00 3.60
❑ 219 Brandon Chillar RC 10.00 3.00
❑ 220 Michael Clayton RC 30.00 9.00
❑ 221 Jamaar Taylor RC 12.00 3.60
❑ 222 George Wilson RC 10.00 3.00
❑ 223 Tony Hargrove RC 10.00 3.00
❑ 224 Sean Ryan RC 10.00 3.00
❑ 225 Stuart Schweigert RC 12.00 3.60
❑ 226 Igor Olshansky RC 12.00 3.60
❑ 227 Keyaron Fox RC 10.00 3.00
❑ 228 Glenn Earl RC 10.00 3.00
❑ 229 Bruce Thornton RC 6.00 1.80
❑ 230 Derrick Hamilton RC 10.00 3.00
❑ 231 Sloan Thomas RC 10.00 3.00
❑ 232 Matthias Askew RC 10.00 3.00
❑ 233 Ran Carthon RC 10.00 3.00
❑ 234 Ben Utecht RC 6.00 1.80
❑ 235 Kendyll Pope RC 10.00 3.00
❑ 236 Marquise Hill RC 10.00 3.00
❑ 237 Shawn Andrews RC 12.00 3.60
❑ 238 Jim Sorgi RC 12.00 3.60
❑ 239 Devard Darling RC 12.00 3.60
❑ 240 Patrick Crayton RC 12.00 3.60
❑ 241 Ryan McGuffey RC 6.00 1.80
❑ 242 Darrion Scott RC 12.00 3.60
❑ 243 DeAngelo Hall RC 15.00 4.50
❑ 244 Alex Lewis RC 12.00 3.60
❑ 245 D.J. Williams RC 15.00 4.50
❑ 246 Chris Snee RC 10.00 3.00
❑ 247 Matt Schaub RC 20.00 6.00
❑ 248 Devery Henderson RC 10.00 3.00
❑ 249 Jeris McIntyre RC 10.00 3.00
❑ 250 Wes Welker RC 12.00 3.60
❑ 251 Bruce Perry RC 10.00 3.00
❑ 252 Jeff Dugan RC 6.00 1.80
❑ 253 Derrick Strait RC 12.00 3.60
❑ 254 Terry Johnson RC 10.00 3.00
❑ 255 Niko Koutouvides RC 10.00 3.00
❑ 256 Von Hutchins RC 10.00 3.00
❑ 257 Josh Harris RC 12.00 3.60
❑ 258 Bernard Berrian RC 12.00 3.60
❑ 259 Roderick Green RC 10.00 3.00
❑ 260 Romar Crenshaw RC 6.00 1.80
❑ 261 Jacob Rogers RC 40.00 12.00
❑ 262 Sean Taylor RC 15.00 4.50
❑ 263 J.R. Reed RC 10.00 3.00
❑ 264 Jonathan Vilma RC 12.00 3.60
❑ 265 Stephen Peterman RC 40.00 12.00
❑ 266 Eli Manning RC 80.00 24.00
❑ 267 Philip Rivers RC 40.00 12.00
❑ 268 Larry Fitzgerald RC 50.00 15.00
❑ 269 Ben Roethlisberger RC 150.00 45.00
❑ 270 Kevin Jones RC 50.00 15.00
❑ 271 Steven Jackson RC 50.00 15.00
❑ 272 Roy Williams RC 50.00 15.00
❑ 273 Julius Jones RC 60.00 18.00
❑ 274 Reggie Williams RC 20.00 6.00
❑ 275 Chris Perry RC 30.00 9.00
❑ 276 Robert Gallery RC 25.00 7.50
❑ 277 Kellen Winslow RC 40.00 12.00
❑ 278 Drew Henson RC 40.00 12.00

2004 Upper Deck Finite HG Fabrics

Nm-Mt Ex-Mt

STATED ODDS 1:10
*ACTIVE PLAYER RADIANCE: 1.2X TO 3X
*RETIRED PLAYER RADIANCE: 1X TO 2.5X
RADIANCE PRINT RUN 25 SER.#'d SETS

❑ FFBA Barry Sanders SP 40.00 12.00
❑ FFBF Brett Favre 25.00 7.50

❑ FFBU Brian Urlacher 10.00 3.00
❑ FFCP Clinton Portis 10.00 3.00
❑ FFCR Charles Rogers 8.00 2.40
❑ FFCW Charles Woodson 8.00 2.40
❑ FFDA David Boston 8.00 2.40
❑ FFDB Drew Bledsoe 10.00 3.00
❑ FFDC Daunte Culpepper 10.00 3.00
❑ FFDE Deuce McAllister 10.00 3.00
❑ FFDM Dan Marino SP 50.00 15.00
❑ FFEM Eric Moulds 8.00 2.40
❑ FFES Emmitt Smith 20.00 6.00
❑ FFFT Fred Taylor 8.00 2.40
❑ FFIB Isaac Bruce 8.00 2.40
❑ FFJB Jerome Bettis 10.00 3.00
❑ FFJE John Elway 25.00 7.50
❑ FFJK Jevon Kearse 8.00 2.40
❑ FFJM Joe Montana SP 60.00 18.00
❑ FFJP Jake Plummer 8.00 2.40
❑ FFJU Johnny Unitas 30.00 9.00
❑ FFKC Kerry Collins 8.00 2.40
❑ FFKE Kellen Winslow Sr. SP 15.00 4.50
❑ FFKW Kurt Warner 10.00 3.00
❑ FFLA LaVar Arrington 15.00 4.50
❑ FFLD Len Dawson SP 25.00 7.50
❑ FFLT LaDainian Tomlinson 10.00 3.00
❑ FFMA Mark Brunell 8.00 2.40
❑ FFMB Marc Bulger 8.00 2.40
❑ FFMV Michael Vick 15.00 4.50
❑ FFPM Peyton Manning 15.00 4.50
❑ FFRM Randy Moss 12.00 3.60
❑ FFRS Roger Staubach SP 25.00 7.50
❑ FFSM Santana Moss 8.00 2.40
❑ FFST Steve McNair 10.00 3.00
❑ FFTA Troy Aikman SP 20.00 6.00
❑ FFTB Tom Brady 15.00 4.50
❑ FFTG Tony Gonzalez 10.00 3.00
❑ FFTM Tommy Maddox 8.00 2.40
❑ FFTO Terrell Owens 10.00 3.00
❑ FFWS Warren Sapp 8.00 2.40
❑ FFZT Zach Thomas 10.00 3.00

2004 Upper Deck Finite HG Fabrics Duals

Nm-Mt Ex-Mt

STATED ODDS 1:30
CARD NUMBERS HAVE FF2 PREFIX

❑ AS Troy Aikman SP 40.00 12.00
Roger Staubach
❑ BB Marc Bulger 15.00 4.50
Isaac Bruce
❑ BM David Boston 12.00 3.60

		Nm-Mt	Ex-Mt
	Eric Moulds		
❑ BP	Mark Brunell Clinton Portis	15.00	4.50
❑ BW	Tom Brady Kurt Warner	20.00	6.00
❑ EM	John Elway SP Dan Marino	80.00	24.00
❑ FW	Larry Fitzgerald Roy Williams WR	20.00	6.00
❑ JJ	Julius Jones Kevin Jones	30.00	9.00
❑ LR	J.P. Losman Ben Roethlisberger	50.00	15.00
❑ MB	Tommy Maddox Jerome Bettis	15.00	4.50
❑ MM	Peyton Manning Steve McNair	20.00	6.00
❑ PA	Clinton Portis LaVar Arrington	20.00	6.00
❑ RM	Philip Rivers Eli Manning	40.00	12.00
❑ UD	Johnny Unitas SP Len Dawson	50.00	15.00
❑ WS	Charles Woodson Warren Sapp	15.00	4.50

2004 Upper Deck Finite HG Fabrics Triples

STATED ODDS 1:40
CARD NUMBERS HAVE FF3 PREFIX

		Nm-Mt	Ex-Mt
❑ BRB	Isaac Bruce Charles Rogers David Boston	20.00	6.00
❑ BVB	Marc Bulger Michael Vick Mark Brunell	25.00	7.50
❑ JJJ	Julius Jones Greg Jones Kevin Jones	40.00	12.00
❑ MMF	Eli Manning Joe Montana Brett Favre	80.00	24.00
❑ MRR	Eli Manning Philip Rivers Ben Roethlisberger	80.00	24.00
❑ NAM	Joe Namath SP Troy Aikman Dan Marino	60.00	18.00
❑ OMM	Terrell Owens SP Randy Moss Santana Moss	25.00	7.50
❑ PBM	Jake Plummer Drew Bledsoe Steve McNair	20.00	6.00
❑ PST	Clinton Portis Emmitt Smith LaDainian Tomlinson	30.00	9.00
❑ SPT	Barry Sanders Chris Perry LaDainian Tomlinson	40.00	12.00
❑ UAT	Brian Urlacher LaVar Arrington Zach Thomas	25.00	7.50
❑ USE	Johnny Unitas SP Roger Staubach John Elway	80.00	24.00
❑ WFW	Roy Williams WR Larry Fitzgerald Kellen Winslow Jr.	30.00	9.00
❑ WMF	Reggie Williams Randy Moss Larry Fitzgerald	25.00	7.50
❑ WWG	Kellen Winslow Jr. Kellen Winslow Sr. Tony Gonzalez	20.00	6.00

2004 Upper Deck Finite HG Rookie Fabrics

STATED ODDS 1:10

		Nm-Mt	Ex-Mt
❑ BB	Bernard Berrian	8.00	2.40
❑ BR	Ben Roethlisberger	50.00	15.00
❑ BT	Ben Troupe	8.00	2.40
❑ CP	Chris Perry	12.00	3.60
❑ DH	Devery Henderson	6.00	1.80
❑ DW	Darius Watts	8.00	2.40
❑ EM	Eli Manning	25.00	7.50
❑ GJ	Greg Jones	8.00	2.40
❑ JJ	Julius Jones	20.00	6.00
❑ JP	J.P. Losman	12.00	3.60
❑ KC	Keary Colbert	8.00	2.40
❑ KJ	Kevin Jones	15.00	4.50
❑ KW	Kellen Winslow Jr.	15.00	4.50
❑ LE	Lee Evans	10.00	3.00
❑ LF	Larry Fitzgerald	15.00	4.50
❑ LM	Luke McCown	10.00	3.00
❑ MC	Michael Clayton	12.00	3.60
❑ MJ	Michael Jenkins	8.00	2.40
❑ PR	Philip Rivers	15.00	4.50
❑ RA	Rashaun Woods	10.00	3.00
❑ RE	Reggie Williams	10.00	3.00
❑ RG	Robert Gallery	10.00	3.00
❑ RW	Roy Williams WR	20.00	6.00
❑ SJ	Steven Jackson	15.00	4.50
❑ TB	Tatum Bell	12.00	3.60

2004 Upper Deck Finite HG Signatures

STATED ODDS 1:10
EXCH EXPIRATON: 11/18/2007

		Nm-Mt	Ex-Mt
❑ FSAN	Andy Reid SP		
❑ FSAR	Antwaan Randle El	20.00	6.00
❑ FSBC	Brandon Chillar	10.00	3.00
❑ FSBE	Ben Watson	15.00	4.50
❑ FSBH	Ben Hartsock	10.00	3.00
❑ FSBL	Brandon Lloyd	15.00	4.50
❑ FSBR	Ben Roethlisberger SP	250.00	75.00
❑ FSBS	Barry Sanders SP	150.00	45.00
❑ FSBT	Ben Troupe	15.00	4.50
❑ FSBW	Brian Westbrook	20.00	6.00
❑ FSCC	Casey Clausen	15.00	4.50
❑ FSCE	Cedric Cobbs	20.00	6.00
❑ FSCF	Clarence Farmer	10.00	3.00
❑ FSCO	Cody Pickett	15.00	4.50
❑ FSCP	Chad Pennington	40.00	12.00
❑ FSDB	Drew Bledsoe SP		
❑ FSDD	Devard Darling	15.00	4.50
❑ FSDE	Deuce McAllister	20.00	6.00
❑ FSDH	Devery Henderson	10.00	3.00
❑ FSDR	Drew Henson SP	40.00	12.00
❑ FSDW	Darius Watts	15.00	4.50
❑ FSEM	Eli Manning	100.00	30.00
❑ FSGA	Robert Gallery	20.00	6.00
❑ FSGR	Jon Gruden SP		
❑ FSHA	DeAngelo Hall	20.00	6.00
❑ FSJC	Jerricho Cotchery	10.00	3.00
❑ FSJF	John Fox SP	15.00	4.50
❑ FSJG	Joey Galloway	15.00	4.50
❑ FSJJ	Julius Jones	80.00	24.00
❑ FSJM	Johnnie Morant	10.00	3.00
❑ FSJN	John Navarre	15.00	4.50
❑ FSJO	Joe Montana SP	200.00	60.00
❑ FSJP	J.P. Losman	40.00	12.00
❑ FSJS	Josh McCown	15.00	4.50
❑ FSJT	Joe Theismann SP	25.00	7.50
❑ FSJU	Justin Fargas		
❑ FSJV	Jonathan Vilma	25.00	7.50
❑ FSJW	Javon Walker		
❑ FSKC	Keary Colbert	20.00	6.00
❑ FSKE	Kelley Washington	10.00	3.00
❑ FSKJ	Kevin Jones	60.00	18.00
❑ FSLE	Lee Evans	20.00	6.00
❑ FSMJ	Michael Jenkins EXCH	20.00	6.00
❑ FSMS	Matt Schaub	20.00	6.00
❑ FSMV	Michael Vick SP	100.00	30.00
❑ FSNA	Joe Namath	100.00	30.00
❑ FSPM	Peyton Manning SP	100.00	30.00
❑ FSPR	Philip Rivers	50.00	15.00
❑ FSQW	Quincy Wilson	10.00	3.00
❑ FSRE	Reggie Williams	20.00	6.00
❑ FSRG	Rex Grossman	20.00	6.00
❑ FSRJ	Rudi Johnson	20.00	6.00
❑ FSRW	Roy Williams WR	60.00	18.00
❑ FSSJ	Steven Jackson	50.00	15.00
❑ FSSP	Samie Parker	15.00	4.50
❑ FSTB	Tatum Bell	25.00	7.50
❑ FSTH	Tommie Harris	20.00	6.00
❑ FSTR	Travis Henry	10.00	3.00
❑ FSWM	Willis McGahee	20.00	6.00

2004 Upper Deck Finite HG Signatures Radiance

*RADIANCE: .8X TO 2X BASIC SIGS
RADIANCE PRINT RUN 25 SER.#'d SETS
EXCH EXPIRATON: 11/18/2007

		Nm-Mt	Ex-Mt
❑ FSBR	Ben Roethlisberger	300.00	90.00

2004 Upper Deck Foundations

	Nm-Mt	Ex-Mt
COMP.SET w/o SP's (100)	20.00	6.00

101-240 RC PRINT RUN 350 SER.#'d SETS
241-257 RC JSY PRINT RUN 1299 SER.#'d SETS
258-263 RC JSY PRINT RUN 499 SER.#'d SETS

❑ 1 Josh McCown .50 .15
❑ 2 Emmitt Smith 1.50 .45
❑ 3 Anquan Boldin .75 .23
❑ 4 T.J. Duckett .50 .15
❑ 5 Peerless Price .50 .15
❑ 6 Michael Vick 1.50 .45
❑ 7 Todd Heap .50 .15
❑ 8 Kyle Boller .75 .23
❑ 9 Jamal Lewis .75 .23
❑ 10 Travis Henry .50 .15
❑ 11 Eric Moulds .50 .15
❑ 12 Drew Bledsoe .75 .23
❑ 13 Steve Smith .50 .15
❑ 14 Stephen Davis .50 .15
❑ 15 Jake Delhomme .75 .23
❑ 16 Rex Grossman .75 .23
❑ 17 Brian Urlacher 1.00 .30
❑ 18 Anthony Thomas .50 .15
❑ 19 Rudi Johnson .50 .15
❑ 20 Chad Johnson .50 .15
❑ 21 Carson Palmer 1.00 .30
❑ 22 Quincy Morgan .50 .15
❑ 23 Jeff Garcia .75 .23
❑ 24 Andre Davis .30 .09
❑ 25 Roy Williams S .50 .15
❑ 26 Eddie George .50 .15
❑ 27 Keyshawn Johnson .50 .15
❑ 28 Jake Plummer .50 .15
❑ 29 Champ Bailey .50 .15
❑ 30 Ashley Lelie .50 .15
❑ 31 Joey Harrington .75 .23
❑ 32 Charles Rogers .50 .15
❑ 33 Az-Zahir Hakim .30 .09
❑ 34 Javon Walker .50 .15
❑ 35 Brett Favre 2.00 .60
❑ 36 Ahman Green .75 .23
❑ 37 Domanick Davis .75 .23
❑ 38 David Carr .75 .23
❑ 39 Andre Johnson .75 .23
❑ 40 Peyton Manning 1.25 .35
❑ 41 Marvin Harrison .75 .23
❑ 42 Edgerrin James .75 .23
❑ 43 Jimmy Smith .50 .15
❑ 44 Fred Taylor .50 .15
❑ 45 Byron Leftwich 1.25 .35
❑ 46 Trent Green .50 .15
❑ 47 Tony Gonzalez .50 .15
❑ 48 Priest Holmes 1.00 .30
❑ 49 Dante Hall .75 .23
❑ 50 Ricky Williams .75 .23
❑ 51 David Boston .50 .15
❑ 52 Chris Chambers .50 .15
❑ 53 A.J. Feeley .75 .23
❑ 54 Randy Moss 1.00 .30
❑ 55 Michael Bennett .50 .15
❑ 56 Daunte Culpepper .75 .23
❑ 57 Troy Brown .50 .15
❑ 58 Tom Brady 1.25 .35
❑ 59 Corey Dillon .50 .15
❑ 60 Donte' Stallworth .50 .15
❑ 61 Deuce McAllister .75 .23
❑ 62 Aaron Brooks .50 .15
❑ 63 Kurt Warner .75 .23
❑ 64 Jeremy Shockey .75 .23
❑ 65 Santana Moss .50 .15
❑ 66 Curtis Martin .75 .23
❑ 67 Chad Pennington 1.00 .30
❑ 68 Amani Toomer .50 .15
❑ 69 Tim Brown .75 .23
❑ 70 Rich Gannon .50 .15
❑ 71 Jerry Rice 1.50 .45
❑ 72 Jerry Porter .50 .15
❑ 73 Terrell Owens .75 .23
❑ 74 Jevon Kearse .50 .15
❑ 75 Donovan McNabb 1.00 .30
❑ 76 Tommy Maddox .50 .15
❑ 77 Plaxico Burress .50 .15
❑ 78 Hines Ward .75 .23
❑ 79 Duce Staley .50 .15
❑ 80 LaDainian Tomlinson .75 .23
❑ 81 Drew Brees .75 .23
❑ 82 Donnie Edwards .30 .09
❑ 83 Tim Rattay .50 .15
❑ 84 Kevan Barlow .50 .15
❑ 85 Brandon Lloyd .50 .15
❑ 86 Shaun Alexander .75 .23
❑ 87 Matt Hasselbeck .50 .15
❑ 88 Koren Robinson .50 .15
❑ 89 Torry Holt .75 .23
❑ 90 Marshall Faulk .75 .23
❑ 91 Marc Bulger .75 .23
❑ 92 Keenan McCardell .30 .09
❑ 93 Derrick Brooks .50 .15
❑ 94 Brad Johnson .50 .15
❑ 95 Steve McNair .75 .23
❑ 96 Derrick Mason .50 .15
❑ 97 Chris Brown .75 .23
❑ 98 Mark Brunell .50 .15
❑ 99 LaVar Arrington 1.50 .45
❑ 100 Clinton Portis .75 .23
❑ 101 Brandon Chillar RC 8.00 2.40
❑ 102 Mike Karney RC 8.00 2.40
❑ 103 Jamaar Taylor RC 10.00 3.00
❑ 104 Casey Clausen RC 12.00 3.60
❑ 105 Drew Carter RC 10.00 3.00
❑ 106 Travis LaBoy RC 10.00 3.00
❑ 107 Jonathan Vilma RC 10.00 3.00
❑ 108 Tramon Douglas RC 5.00 1.50
❑ 109 Bob Sanders RC 10.00 3.00
❑ 110 Mewelde Moore RC 12.00 3.60
❑ 111 Randy Starks RC 8.00 2.40
❑ 112 Tank Johnson RC 8.00 2.40
❑ 113 Triandos Luke RC 10.00 3.00
❑ 114 Dexter Reid RC 5.00 1.50
❑ 115 Cedric Cobbs RC 10.00 3.00
❑ 116 Darius Watts RC 12.00 3.60
❑ 117 Ryan Krause RC 8.00 2.40
❑ 118 Igor Olshansky RC 10.00 3.00
❑ 119 Adimchinobe Echemandu RC 8.00 2.40
❑ 120 Jason Fife RC 8.00 2.40
❑ 121 Justin Smiley RC 10.00 3.00
❑ 122 Marcus Tubbs RC 10.00 3.00
❑ 123 Nathan Vasher RC 10.00 3.00
❑ 124 Troy Fleming RC 8.00 2.40
❑ 125 Ben Troupe RC 10.00 3.00
❑ 126 Jammal Lord RC 10.00 3.00
❑ 127 Jared Lorenzen RC 8.00 2.40
❑ 128 Shawntae Spencer RC 10.00 3.00
❑ 129 Darnell Dockett RC 8.00 2.40
❑ 130 Derrick Strait RC 10.00 3.00
❑ 131 Clarence Moore RC 10.00 3.00
❑ 132 Jason Babin RC 10.00 3.00
❑ 133 Jerricho Cotchery RC 10.00 3.00
❑ 134 Karlos Dansby RC 10.00 3.00
❑ 135 Marquise Hill RC 8.00 2.40
❑ 136 Niko Koutouvides RC 8.00 2.40
❑ 137 Andy Hall RC 8.00 2.40
❑ 138 Teddy Lehman RC 10.00 3.00
❑ 139 Will Smith RC 10.00 3.00
❑ 140 Bernard Berrian RC 10.00 3.00
❑ 141 Chris Cooley RC 10.00 3.00
❑ 142 Landon Johnson RC 8.00 2.40
❑ 143 Devard Darling RC 10.00 3.00
❑ 144 Mark Jones RC 8.00 2.40
❑ 145 Jake Grove RC 5.00 1.50
❑ 146 John Navarre RC 10.00 3.00
❑ 147 Keary Colbert RC 12.00 3.60
❑ 148 Gilbert Gardner RC 8.00 2.40
❑ 149 P.K. Sam RC 8.00 2.40
❑ 150 Richard Seigler RC 8.00 2.40
❑ 151 Marquis Cooper RC 8.00 2.40
❑ 152 Tommie Harris RC 12.00 3.60
❑ 153 Thomas Tapeh RC 8.00 2.40
❑ 154 Ben Utecht RC 5.00 1.50
❑ 155 Chris Gamble RC 12.00 3.60
❑ 156 Daryl Smith RC 10.00 3.00
❑ 157 Sean Taylor RC 12.00 3.60
❑ 158 Caleb Miller RC 8.00 2.40
❑ 159 Johnnie Morant RC 10.00 3.00
❑ 160 Keith Smith RC 8.00 2.40
❑ 161 Matt Mauck RC 10.00 3.00
❑ 162 Matt Ware RC 10.00 3.00
❑ 163 Quincy Wilson RC 8.00 2.40
❑ 164 Samie Parker RC 10.00 3.00
❑ 165 Kendrick Starling RC 5.00 1.50
❑ 166 Antwan Odom RC 10.00 3.00
❑ 167 Brandon Miree RC 8.00 2.40
❑ 168 Casey Bramlet RC 8.00 2.40
❑ 169 Cody Pickett RC 10.00 3.00
❑ 170 Demorrio Williams RC 10.00 3.00
❑ 171 Dunta Robinson RC 10.00 3.00
❑ 172 D.J. Hackett RC 8.00 2.40
❑ 173 Josh Harris RC 10.00 3.00
❑ 174 Kenechi Udeze RC 10.00 3.00
❑ 175 Michael Boulware RC 10.00 3.00
❑ 176 Ricardo Colclough RC 10.00 3.00
❑ 177 Shawn Andrews RC 10.00 3.00
❑ 178 Jeris McIntyre RC 8.00 2.40
❑ 179 Jim Sorgi RC 10.00 3.00
❑ 180 Clarence Farmer RC 8.00 2.40
❑ 181 Courtney Watson RC 10.00 3.00
❑ 182 Derek Abney RC 10.00 3.00
❑ 183 Dwan Edwards RC 5.00 1.50
❑ 184 Ryan Dinwiddie RC 8.00 2.40
❑ 185 B.J. Johnson RC 8.00 2.40
❑ 186 Ben Watson RC 10.00 3.00
❑ 187 Kris Wilson RC 10.00 3.00
❑ 188 Michael Turner RC 8.00 2.40
❑ 189 Derrick Ward RC 5.00 1.50
❑ 190 Jonathan Smith RC 8.00 2.40
❑ 191 Vernon Carey RC 8.00 2.40
❑ 192 Ben Hartsock RC 10.00 3.00
❑ 193 Rich Gardner RC 8.00 2.40
❑ 194 D.J. Williams RC 12.00 3.60
❑ 195 Derrick Hamilton RC 8.00 2.40
❑ 196 Drew Henson RC 25.00 7.50
❑ 197 Jeff Smoker RC 15.00 4.50
❑ 198 Joey Thomas RC 10.00 3.00
❑ 199 Keyaron Fox RC 8.00 2.40
❑ 200 Nate Lawrie RC 8.00 2.40
❑ 201 Sloan Thomas RC 8.00 2.40
❑ 202 Justin Jenkins RC 8.00 2.40
❑ 203 Stuart Schweigert RC 10.00 3.00
❑ 204 Ran Carthon RC 8.00 2.40
❑ 205 Ahmad Carroll RC 12.00 3.60
❑ 206 Bradlee Van Pelt RC 10.00 3.00
❑ 207 Patrick Crayton RC 10.00 3.00
❑ 208 Chris Snee RC 8.00 2.40
❑ 209 Fred Russell RC 10.00 3.00
❑ 210 Dontarrious Thomas RC 10.00 3.00
❑ 211 Will Poole RC 10.00 3.00
❑ 212 Jarrett Payton RC 10.00 3.00
❑ 213 Keiwan Ratliff RC 8.00 2.40
❑ 214 Nate Kaeding RC 10.00 3.00
❑ 215 Tim Euhus RC 10.00 3.00
❑ 216 Sean Jones RC 8.00 2.40
❑ 217 Will Allen RC 10.00 3.00
❑ 218 B.J. Symons RC 10.00 3.00
❑ 219 Carlos Francis RC 8.00 2.40
❑ 220 Craig Krenzel RC 10.00 3.00
❑ 221 Andrae Thurman RC 5.00 1.50
❑ 222 Ernest Wilford RC 10.00 3.00
❑ 223 Glenn Earl RC 8.00 2.40
❑ 224 Jeremy LeSueur RC 8.00 2.40
❑ 225 Junior Siavii RC 10.00 3.00
❑ 226 Maurice Mann RC 8.00 2.40
❑ 227 Michael Waddell RC 5.00 1.50
❑ 228 Jason Wright RC 8.00 2.40
❑ 229 Sean Ryan RC 8.00 2.40
❑ 230 Vince Wilfork RC 12.00 3.60
❑ 231 Matt Kegel RC 10.00 3.00
❑ 232 Chris Collins RC 8.00 2.40
❑ 233 Jonathan Smith RC 8.00 2.40
❑ 234 Renaldo Works RC 10.00 3.00
❑ 235 Matt Kranchick RC 10.00 3.00
❑ 236 J.R. Reed RC 8.00 2.40
❑ 237 Jason Shivers RC 8.00 2.40
❑ 238 Donnell Washington RC 10.00 3.00
❑ 239 Jorge Cordova RC 5.00 1.50
❑ 240 Wes Welker RC 10.00 3.00
❑ 241 Robert Gallery JSY RC 10.00 3.00
❑ 242 Luke McCown JSY RC 6.00 1.80
❑ 243 Roy Williams JSY RC 20.00 6.00
❑ 244 Julius Jones JSY RC 25.00 7.50
❑ 245 Tatum Bell JSY RC 10.00 3.00
❑ 246 Steven Jackson JSY RC 20.00 6.00
❑ 247 Reggie Williams JSY RC 8.00 2.40
❑ 248 Devery Henderson JSY RC 5.00 1.50
❑ 249 DeAngelo Hall JSY RC 8.00 2.40
❑ 250 Rashaun Woods JSY RC 8.00 2.40
❑ 251 Chris Perry JSY RC 12.00 3.60
❑ 252 Matt Schaub JSY RC 10.00 3.00
❑ 253 Lee Evans JSY RC 10.00 3.00
❑ 254 Michael Jenkins JSY RC 6.00 1.80
❑ 255 J.P. Losman JSY RC 15.00 4.50
❑ 256 Kevin Jones JSY RC 20.00 6.00
❑ 257 Michael Clayton JSY RC 15.00 4.50
❑ 258 Eli Manning JSY RC 30.00 9.00
❑ 259 Ben Roethlisberger JSY RC 60.00 18.00
❑ 260 Larry Fitzgerald JSY RC 20.00 6.00
❑ 261 Philip Rivers JSY RC 20.00 6.00

❑ 262 Greg Jones JSY RC 10.00 3.00
❑ 263 Kellen Winslow JSY RC 15.00 4.50

2004 Upper Deck Foundations Exclusive Gold

Nm-Mt Ex-Mt

*STARS: 4X TO 10X BASE CARD HI
*ROOKIES 101-240: .5X TO 1.2X BASE CARD HI
STATED PRINT RUN 100 SER.#'d SETS

2004 Upper Deck Foundations Dual Endorsements

Nm-Mt Ex-Mt

STATED ODDS 1:96

❑ DEBH Tom Brady SP 120.00 36.00
Drew Henson
❑ DEBL Drew Bledsoe
J.P. Losman
❑ DEBR Kyle Boller 100.00 30.00
Philip Rivers
❑ DEBW Tatum Bell 40.00 12.00
Darius Watts
❑ DECH Michael Clayton 40.00 12.00
Devery Henderson
❑ DEEW Lee Evans 80.00 24.00
J.P. Losman
❑ DEFW Reggie Williams 80.00 24.00
Roy Williams WR
❑ DEHJ DeAngelo Hall 50.00 15.00
Michael Jenkins
❑ DEHW Joe Horn 60.00 18.00
Roy Williams WR
❑ DEJH Julius Jones/50 * 100.00 30.00
Drew Henson
❑ DEJJ Kevin Jones 100.00 30.00
Steven Jackson
❑ DEJW Greg Jones EXCH 30.00 9.00
Reggie Williams
❑ DEMM Peyton Manning 250.00 75.00
Eli Manning
❑ DEMP Deuce McAllister SP 40.00 12.00
Chris Perry
❑ DEMR Eli Manning 500.00 150.00
Ben Roethlisberger
❑ DERR Ben Roethlisberger 300.00 90.00
Philip Rivers
❑ DERS Roy Williams S
Sean Taylor
❑ DEVM Michael Vick SP 250.00 75.00
Eli Manning
❑ DEWJ Roy Williams WR 120.00 36.00
Kevin Jones
❑ DEWW Kellen Winslow Sr. SP 80.00 24.00
Kellen Winslow Jr.

2004 Upper Deck Foundations Patches

Nm-Mt Ex-Mt

STATED PRINT RUN 50 SER.#'d SETS

❑ FPAB Antonio Bryant 20.00 6.00
❑ FPAL Ashley Lelie 25.00 7.50
❑ FPAN Anthony Thomas 25.00 7.50
❑ FPAT Amani Toomer 25.00 7.50
❑ FPBF Brett Favre 60.00 18.00
❑ FPBL Byron Leftwich 40.00 12.00

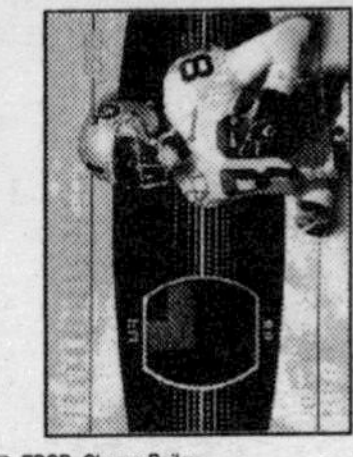

❑ FPCB Champ Bailey
❑ FPCC Chris Chambers
❑ FPCD Corey Dillon 25.00 7.50
❑ FPCJ Chad Johnson 25.00 7.50
❑ FPCM Curtis Martin 30.00 9.00
❑ FPCW Charles Woodson 25.00 7.50
❑ FPDB David Boston 20.00 6.00
❑ FPDC Daunte Culpepper
❑ FPDS Duce Staley 30.00 9.00
❑ FPEM Eric Moulds 25.00 7.50
❑ FPFT Fred Taylor 25.00 7.50
❑ FPIB Isaac Bruce 30.00 9.00
❑ FPJG Jeff Garcia 25.00 7.50
❑ FPJH Joey Harrington 30.00 9.00
❑ FPJK Jevon Kearse 25.00 7.50
❑ FPJL Jamal Lewis 30.00 9.00
❑ FPJR Jerry Rice 50.00 15.00
❑ FPJS Junior Seau 30.00 9.00
❑ FPKB Kyle Boller 25.00 7.50
❑ FPKJ Keyshawn Johnson 25.00 7.50
❑ FPKM Keenan McCardell 25.00 7.50
❑ FPLT LaDainian Tomlinson
❑ FPMB Mark Brunell 25.00 7.50
❑ FPMF Marshall Faulk 30.00 9.00
❑ FPMH Marvin Harrison 30.00 9.00
❑ FPPP Peerless Price 25.00. 7.50
❑ FPRL Ray Lewis 30.00 9.00
❑ FPRM Randy Moss 40.00 12.00
❑ FPRW Ricky Williams 30.00 9.00
❑ FPTB Tiki Barber 25.00 7.50
❑ FPTH Travis Henry 25.00 7.50
❑ FPTI Tim Brown 30.00 9.00
❑ FPTO Terrell Owens 30.00 9.00
❑ FPWD Warrick Dunn 25.00 7.50
❑ FPWS Warren Sapp 30.00 9.00
❑ FPZT Zach Thomas 30.00 9.00

2004 Upper Deck Foundations Rookie Foundations Patch

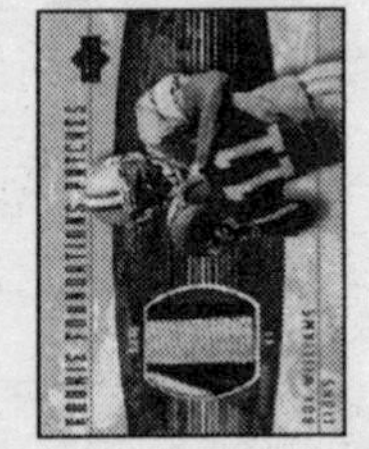

Nm-Mt Ex-Mt

STATED PRINT RUN 25 SER.#'d SETS
UNPRICED PATCH AUs PRINT RUN 25 SETS

❑ 241P Robert Gallery 30.00 9.00
❑ 242P Luke McCown 20.00 6.00
❑ 243P Roy Williams WR 60.00 18.00
❑ 244P Julius Jones
❑ 245P Tatum Bell
❑ 246P Steven Jackson 60.00 18.00
❑ 247P Reggie Williams 25.00 7.50
❑ 248P Devery Henderson 15.00 4.50
❑ 249P DeAngelo Hall 25.00 7.50
❑ 250P Rashaun Woods 25.00 7.50
❑ 251P Chris Perry
❑ 252P Matt Schaub 30.00 9.00
❑ 253P Lee Evans 30.00 9.00
❑ 254P Michael Jenkins 20.00 6.00
❑ 255P J.P. Losman 50.00 15.00
❑ 256P Kevin Jones 60.00 18.00
❑ 257P Michael Clayton
❑ 258P Eli Manning 100.00 30.00
❑ 259P Ben Roethlisberger 200.00 60.00
❑ 260P Larry Fitzgerald 60.00 18.00
❑ 261P Philip Rivers
❑ 262P Greg Jones 30.00 9.00
❑ 263P Kellen Winslow Jr. 50.00 15.00

2004 Upper Deck Foundations Signature Foundations

Nm-Mt Ex-Mt

STATED ODDS 1:12
EXCH EXPIRATION: 11/15/2007

❑ SFBB Bernard Berrian 15.00 4.50
❑ SFBC Brandon Chillar 12.00 3.60
❑ SFBH Ben Hartsock SP 15.00 4.50
❑ SFBJ B.J. Symons 12.00 3.60
❑ SFBR Ben Roethlisberger SP 300.00 90.00
❑ SFBW Ben Watson 20.00 6.00
❑ SFCC Casey Clausen 20.00 6.00
❑ SFCO Cody Pickett 15.00 4.50
❑ SFCP Chris Perry SP 30.00 9.00
❑ SFDA Devard Darling 15.00 4.50
❑ SFDE DeAngelo Hall 20.00 6.00
❑ SFDH Dante Hall SP 25.00 7.50
❑ SFDR Drew Henson SP 40.00 12.00
❑ SFDV Devery Henderson EXCH 12.00 3.60
❑ SFDW Darius Watts 20.00 6.00
❑ SFEM Eli Manning SP 120.00 36.00
❑ SFEW Ernest Wilford 15.00 4.50
❑ SFGJ Greg Jones 15.00 4.50
❑ SFJC Jericho Cotchery 15.00 4.50
❑ SFJJ Julius Jones SP EXCH 75.00 22.00
❑ SFJN John Navarre 15.00 4.50
❑ SFJO Johnnie Morant 15.00 4.50
❑ SFJP J.P. Losman SP 50.00 15.00
❑ SFJS Jeff Smoker 20.00 6.00
❑ SFJV Jonathan Vilma 20.00 6.00
❑ SFKC Keary Colbert 20.00 6.00
❑ SFKE Kellen Winslow Jr. SP 40.00 12.00
❑ SFKJ Kevin Jones SP 50.00 15.00
❑ SFKU Kenechi Udeze 15.00 4.50
❑ SFLE Lee Evans SP 25.00 7.50
❑ SFLM Luke McCown 15.00 4.50
❑ SFLT LaDainian Tomlinson SP 30.00 9.00
❑ SFMI Michael Clayton 30.00 9.00
❑ SFMJ Michael Jenkins 15.00 4.50
❑ SFMS Matt Schaub 20.00 6.00
❑ SFMV Michael Vick/100 * EXCH 80.00 24.00
❑ SFPM Peyton Manning SP 80.00 24.00
❑ SFPR Philip Rivers SP 50.00 15.00
❑ SFQW Quincy Wilson EXCH 12.00 3.60
❑ SFRE Reggie Williams EXCH 20.00 6.00
❑ SFRG Robert Gallery 25.00 7.50
❑ SFRO Roy Williams WR 50.00 15.00
❑ SFRW Rashaun Woods SP 30.00 9.00
❑ SFSJ Steven Jackson SP 50.00 15.00
❑ SFST Sean Taylor EXCH 25.00 7.50
❑ SFTB Tatum Bell SP 30.00 9.00

❑ SFTH Todd Heap SP	12.00	3.60
❑ SFTO Tommie Harris	15.00	4.50
❑ SFVW Vince Wilfork	15.00	4.50
❑ SFWS Will Smith EXCH	12.00	3.60

2000 Upper Deck Gold Reserve UD Authentics

	Nm-Mt	Ex-Mt
*GOLD CARDS: 1.5X TO 4X BASIC AUTOS		
GOLD STATED PRINT RUN 25 SER.#'d SETS		
❑ CC Chris Coleman EXCH	.75	.35
❑ CP Chad Pennington	50.00	22.00
❑ CR Chris Redman	12.00	5.50
❑ DF Doug Flutie	20.00	9.00
❑ DU Ron Dugans EXCH	1.00	.45
❑ DW Dez White	15.00	6.75
❑ FA Danny Farmer EXCH	1.00	.45
❑ JH Joe Hamilton EXCH	1.25	.55
❑ KC Kwame Cavil	10.00	4.50
❑ MW Michael Wiley	12.00	5.50
❑ RD Ron Dayne	25.00	11.00
❑ SA Shaun Alexander	40.00	18.00
❑ SG Sherrod Gideon	10.00	4.50
❑ SJ Sebastian Janikowski EXCH	1.00	.30
❑ SK Shaun King EXCH	1.00	.30
❑ TA Troy Aikman	60.00	27.00
❑ TJ Thomas Jones EXCH	1.00	.30
❑ TM Tee Martin	12.00	3.60
❑ TR Tim Rattay	25.00	7.50
❑ TW Troy Walters	12.00	5.50

1999 Upper Deck HoloGrFX

	Nm-Mt	Ex-Mt
COMPLETE SET (89)	30.00	13.50
❑ 1 Jake Plummer	.40	.18
❑ 2 Jamal Anderson	.60	.25
❑ 3 Priest Holmes	1.00	.45
❑ 4 Antowain Smith	.60	.25
❑ 5 Doug Flutie	.60	.25
❑ 6 Tim Biakabutuka	.40	.18
❑ 7 Curtis Enis	.25	.11
❑ 8 Corey Dillon	.60	.25
❑ 9 Darnay Scott	.25	.11
❑ 10 Leslie Shepherd	.25	.11
❑ 11 Troy Aikman	2.00	.90
❑ 12 Emmitt Smith	2.00	.90
❑ 13 Michael Irvin	.40	.18
❑ 14 Terrell Davis	.60	.25
❑ 15 Shannon Sharpe	.40	.18
❑ 16 Rod Smith	.40	.18
❑ 17 Barry Sanders	3.00	1.35
❑ 18 Charlie Batch	.60	.25
❑ 19 Herman Moore	.40	.18
❑ 20 Brett Favre	3.00	1.35
❑ 21 Dorsey Levens	.60	.25
❑ 22 Antonio Freeman	.60	.25
❑ 23 Peyton Manning	3.00	1.35
❑ 24 Mark Brunell	.60	.25
❑ 25 Fred Taylor	.60	.25
❑ 26 Jimmy Smith	.40	.18
❑ 27 Andre Rison	.40	.18
❑ 28 Tony Gonzalez	.60	.25
❑ 29 Dan Marino	3.00	1.35
❑ 30 Karim Abdul-Jabbar	.40	.18
❑ 31 Randy Moss	2.50	1.10
❑ 32 Randall Cunningham	.60	.25
❑ 33 Drew Bledsoe	1.25	.55
❑ 34 Terry Glenn	.60	.25
❑ 35 Cameron Cleeland	.25	.11
❑ 36 Andre Hastings	.25	.11
❑ 37 Amani Toomer	.25	.11
❑ 38 Kent Graham	.25	.11
❑ 39 Curtis Martin	.60	.25
❑ 40 Keyshawn Johnson	.60	.25
❑ 41 Vinny Testaverde	.40	.18
❑ 42 Napoleon Kaufman	.60	.25
❑ 43 Tim Brown	.60	.25
❑ 44 Duce Staley	.60	.25
❑ 45 Kordell Stewart	.40	.18
❑ 46 Jerome Bettis	.60	.25
❑ 47 Marshall Faulk	.75	.35
❑ 48 Natrone Means	.40	.18
❑ 49 Ryan Leaf	.25	.11
❑ 50 Steve Young	1.25	.55
❑ 51 Jerry Rice	2.00	.90
❑ 52 Terrell Owens	.60	.25
❑ 53 Joey Galloway	.40	.18
❑ 54 Ricky Watters	.40	.18
❑ 55 Jon Kitna	.60	.25
❑ 56 Warrick Dunn	.60	.25
❑ 57 Trent Dilfer	.40	.18
❑ 58 Steve McNair	.60	.25
❑ 59 Eddie George	.60	.25
❑ 60 Brad Johnson	.60	.25
❑ 61 Tim Couch RC	1.25	.55
❑ 62 Donovan McNabb RC	8.00	3.60
❑ 63 Akili Smith RC	1.00	.45
❑ 64 Edgerrin James RC	6.00	2.70
❑ 65 Ricky Williams RC	3.00	1.35
❑ 66 Torry Holt RC	4.00	1.80
❑ 67 Champ Bailey RC	1.50	.70
❑ 68 David Boston RC	1.25	.55
❑ 69 Daunte Culpepper RC	6.00	2.70
❑ 70 Cade McNown RC	1.00	.45
❑ 71 Troy Edwards RC	1.00	.45
❑ 72 Kevin Johnson RC	1.25	.55
❑ 73 James Johnson RC	1.00	.45
❑ 74 Rob Konrad RC	1.25	.55
❑ 75 Kevin Faulk RC	1.25	.55
❑ 76 Shaun King RC	1.00	.45
❑ 77 Peerless Price RC	2.50	1.10
❑ 78 Mike Cloud RC	1.00	.45
❑ 79 Jermaine Fazande RC	1.00	.45
❑ 80 D'Wayne Bates RC	1.00	.45
❑ 81 Brock Huard RC	1.25	.55
❑ 82 Marty Booker RC	1.25	.55
❑ 83 Karsten Bailey RC	1.00	.45
❑ 84 Al Wilson RC	1.25	.55
❑ 85 Joe Germaine RC	1.00	.45
❑ 86 Dameane Douglas RC	.60	.25
❑ 87 Sedrick Irvin RC	.60	.25
❑ 88 Aaron Brooks RC	5.00	2.20
❑ 89 Cecil Collins RC	.60	.25

1999 Upper Deck HoloGrFX UD Authentics

	Nm-Mt	Ex-Mt
❑ AS Akili Smith	25.00	11.00
❑ BH Brock Huard	30.00	13.50
❑ CM Cade McNown	25.00	11.00
❑ DC Daunte Culpepper	50.00	22.00
❑ DM Donovan McNabb	60.00	27.00
❑ EG Eddie George	40.00	18.00
❑ EJ Edgerrin James	50.00	22.00
❑ EM Eric Moulds	30.00	13.50
❑ JA Jamal Anderson	30.00	13.50
❑ JP Jake Plummer	40.00	18.00

❑ JR Jerry Rice	120.00	55.00
❑ PM Peyton Manning	100.00	45.00
❑ RW Ricky Williams	40.00	18.00
❑ SK Shaun King	25.00	11.00
❑ SY Steve Young	80.00	36.00
❑ TA Troy Aikman	100.00	45.00
❑ TC Tim Couch	40.00	18.00
❑ TH Torry Holt	40.00	18.00

2002 Upper Deck Honor Roll

	Nm-Mt	Ex-Mt
COMP.SET w/o SP's (90)	25.00	7.50
❑ 1 Jake Plummer	.40	.12
❑ 2 David Boston	.60	.18
❑ 3 Michael Vick	2.00	.60
❑ 4 Warrick Dunn	.60	.18
❑ 5 Jamal Lewis	.60	.18
❑ 6 Chris Redman	.25	.07
❑ 7 Drew Bledsoe	.75	.23
❑ 8 Travis Henry	.60	.18
❑ 9 Chris Weinke	.40	.12
❑ 10 Anthony Thomas	.60	.18
❑ 11 Marty Booker	.40	.12
❑ 12 Corey Dillon	.40	.12
❑ 13 Michael Westbrook	.25	.07
❑ 14 Tim Couch	.40	.12
❑ 15 Emmitt Smith	1.50	.45
❑ 16 Quincy Carter	.40	.12
❑ 17 Brian Griese	.60	.18
❑ 18 Terrell Davis	.60	.18
❑ 19 Az-Zahir Hakim	.25	.07
❑ 20 Brett Favre	1.50	.45
❑ 21 Ahman Green	.60	.18
❑ 22 Corey Bradford	.25	.07
❑ 23 Edgerrin James	.75	.23
❑ 24 Peyton Manning	1.25	.35
❑ 25 Stacey Mack	.25	.07
❑ 26 Mark Brunell	.60	.18
❑ 27 Trent Green	.40	.12
❑ 28 Priest Holmes	.75	.23
❑ 29 Ricky Williams	4.00	1.20
❑ 30 Jay Fiedler	.40	.12
❑ 31 Daunte Culpepper	.60	.18
❑ 32 Randy Moss	1.25	.35
❑ 33 Antowain Smith	.40	.12
❑ 34 Tom Brady	1.50	.45
❑ 35 Aaron Brooks	.60	.18
❑ 36 Deuce McAllister	.75	.23
❑ 37 Kerry Collins	.40	.12
❑ 38 Ron Dayne	.40	.12
❑ 39 Curtis Martin	.60	.18

❏ 40 Vinny Testaverde .40 .12
❏ 41 Jerry Rice 1.25 .35
❏ 42 Rich Gannon .60 .18
❏ 43 Donovan McNabb .75 .23
❏ 44 Duce Staley .60 .18
❏ 45 Jerome Bettis .60 .18
❏ 46 Kordell Stewart .40 .12
❏ 47 Doug Flutie .60 .18
❏ 48 LaDainian Tomlinson 1.00 .30
❏ 49 Jeff Garcia .60 .18
❏ 50 Terrell Owens .60 .18
❏ 51 Darrell Jackson .40 .12
❏ 52 Shaun Alexander .60 .18
❏ 53 Kurt Warner .60 .18
❏ 54 Marshall Faulk .60 .18
❏ 55 Keyshawn Johnson .60 .18
❏ 56 Brad Johnson .40 .12
❏ 57 Eddie George .60 .18
❏ 58 Steve McNair .60 .18
❏ 59 Stephen Davis .40 .12
❏ 60 Rod Gardner .40 .12
❏ 61 Jake Plummer .40 .12
Thomas Jones
David Boston
❏ 62 Michael Vick 1.00 .30
Warrick Dunn
Shawn Jefferson
❏ 63 Chris Redman .40 .12
Jamal Lewis
Travis Taylor
❏ 64 Drew Bledsoe .60 .18
Travis Henry
Peerless Price
❏ 65 Jim Miller .60 .18
Anthony Thomas
Marty Booker
❏ 66 Jon Kitna .40 .12
Corey Dillon
Peter Warrick
❏ 67 Tim Couch .60 .18
Jamel White
Kevin Johnson
❏ 68 Quincy Carter .75 .23
Emmitt Smith
Rocket Ismail
❏ 69 Brian Griese .60 .18
Terrell Davis
Rod Smith
❏ 70 Mike McMahon .60 .18
James Stewart
Az-Zahir Hakim
❏ 71 Brett Favre .75 .23
Ahman Green
Terry Glenn
❏ 72 Peyton Manning .60 .18
Edgerrin James
Marvin Harrison
❏ 73 Mark Brunell .40 .12
Fred Taylor
Jimmy Smith
❏ 74 Trent Green .60 .18
Priest Holmes
Johnnie Morton
❏ 75 Jay Fiedler .60 .18
Ricky Williams
Chris Chambers
❏ 76 Daunte Culpepper .60 .18
Michael Bennett
Randy Moss
❏ 77 Tom Brady .75 .23
Antowain Smith
Troy Brown
❏ 78 Aaron Brooks .75 .23
Deuce McAllister
Joe Horn
❏ 79 Kerry Collins .40 .12
Ron Dayne
Amani Toomer
❏ 80 Vinny Testaverde .40 .12
Curtis Martin
Laveranues Coles
❏ 81 Rich Gannon .60 .18
Tim Brown
Jerry Rice
❏ 82 Donovan McNabb .60 .18
Duce Staley
James Thrash
❏ 83 Kordell Stewart .60 .18
Jerome Bettis
Hines Ward
❏ 84 Ddrew Brees .60 .18
LaDainian Tomlinson
Curtis Conway
❏ 85 Jeff Garcia .60 .18
Garrison Hearst
Terrell Owens
❏ 86 Trent Dilfer .60 .18
Shaun Alexander
Darrell Jackson
❏ 87 Kurt Warner .60 .18
Marshall Faulk
Isaac Bruce
❏ 88 Brad Johnson .40 .12
Michael Pittman
Keyshawn Johnson
❏ 89 Steve McNair .60 .18
Eddie George
Derrick Mason
❏ 90 Shane Matthews .40 .12
Stephen Davis
Rod Gardner
❏ 91 Adrian Peterson RC 5.00 1.50
❏ 92 Albert Haynesworth RC 4.00 1.20
❏ 93 Alex Brown RC 5.00 1.50
❏ 94 Andre Davis RC 5.00 1.50
❏ 95 Antwoine Womack RC 4.00 1.20
❏ 96 Antonio Bryant RC 5.00 1.50
❏ 97 Antwaan Randle El RC 6.00 1.80
❏ 98 Ashley Lelie RC 10.00 3.00
❏ 99 Ed Reed RC 8.00 2.40
❏ 100 Brandon Doman RC 5.00 1.50
❏ 101 Brian Allen RC 4.00 1.20
❏ 102 Najeh Davenport RC 5.00 1.50
❏ 103 Brian Westbrook RC 8.00 2.40
❏ 104 Chad Hutchinson RC 5.00 1.50
❏ 105 Chester Taylor RC 5.00 1.50
❏ 106 Cliff Russell RC 4.00 1.20
❏ 107 Clinton Portis RC 15.00 4.50
❏ 108 Craig Nall RC 5.00 1.50
❏ 109 Javin Hunter RC 3.00 .90
❏ 110 Bryan Thomas RC 4.00 1.20
❏ 111 Daniel Graham RC 5.00 1.50
❏ 112 Daryl Jones RC 4.00 1.20
❏ 113 David Carr RC 15.00 4.50
❏ 114 David Garrard RC 5.00 1.50
❏ 115 Shaun Hill RC 5.00 1.50
❏ 116 Deion Branch RC 10.00 3.00
❏ 117 Derrick Lewis RC 3.00 .90
❏ 118 DeShaun Foster RC 5.00 1.50
❏ 119 Jeff Kelly RC 4.00 1.20
❏ 120 Donte Stallworth RC 10.00 3.00
❏ 121 Levi Jones RC 4.00 1.20
❏ 122 Dwight Freeney RC 6.00 1.80
❏ 123 Eric Crouch RC 8.00 2.40
❏ 124 Freddie Milons RC 4.00 1.20
❏ 125 Jamin Elliott RC 3.00 .90
❏ 126 Herb Haygood RC 3.00 .90
❏ 127 J.T. O'Sullivan RC 4.00 1.20
❏ 128 Jabar Gaffney RC 5.00 1.50
❏ 129 Jake Schifino RC 4.00 1.20
❏ 130 Jason McAddley RC 4.00 1.20
❏ 131 Javon Walker RC 10.00 3.00
❏ 132 Jeremy Shockey RC 15.00 4.50
❏ 133 Jerramy Stevens RC 5.00 1.50
❏ 134 Joey Harrington RC 15.00 4.50
❏ 135 John Henderson RC 5.00 1.50
❏ 136 Jonathan Wells RC 5.00 1.50
❏ 137 Josh McCown RC 6.00 1.80
❏ 138 Josh Reed RC 5.00 1.50
❏ 139 Josh Scobey RC 5.00 1.50
❏ 140 Julius Peppers RC 10.00 3.00
❏ 141 Kalimba Edwards RC 5.00 1.50
❏ 142 Kelly Campbell RC 4.00 1.20
❏ 143 Keyuo Craver RC 4.00 1.20
❏ 144 Kurt Kittner RC 4.00 1.20
❏ 145 Ladell Betts RC 5.00 1.50
❏ 146 Lamar Gordon RC 5.00 1.50
❏ 147 Larry Ned RC 4.00 1.20
❏ 148 Lee Mays RC 4.00 1.20
❏ 149 Leonard Henry RC 4.00 1.20
❏ 150 Lito Sheppard RC 5.00 1.50
❏ 151 Luke Staley RC 4.00 1.20
❏ 152 Marquise Walker RC 4.00 1.20
❏ 153 Maurice Morris RC 5.00 1.50
❏ 154 Darrell Hill RC 4.00 1.20
❏ 155 Napoleon Harris RC 5.00 1.50
❏ 156 Patrick Ramsey RC 10.00 3.00
❏ 157 Kevin Curtis RC 3.00 .90
❏ 158 Phillip Buchanon RC 5.00 1.50
❏ 159 Kendall Newson RC 3.00 .90
❏ 160 Quentin Jammer RC 5.00 1.50
❏ 161 Randy Fasani RC 4.00 1.20
❏ 162 Reche Caldwell RC 5.00 1.50
❏ 163 Ricky Williams RC 5.00 1.50
❏ 164 Rocky Calmus RC 5.00 1.50
❏ 165 Rohan Davey RC 5.00 1.50
❏ 166 Ron Johnson RC 4.00 1.20
❏ 167 Ronald Curry RC 5.00 1.50
❏ 168 Roy Williams RC 12.00 3.60
❏ 169 Ryan Sims RC 5.00 1.50
❏ 170 Sam Simmons RC 3.00 .90
❏ 171 Seth Burford RC 4.00 1.20
❏ 172 T.J. Duckett RC 8.00 2.40
❏ 173 Tellis Redmon RC 4.00 1.20
❏ 174 Tim Carter RC 4.00 1.20
❏ 175 Travis Stephens RC 4.00 1.20
❏ 176 Wendell Bryant RC 5.00 1.50
❏ 177 Lamont Thompson RC 4.00 1.20
❏ 178 William Green RC 8.00 2.40
❏ 179 Dennis Johnson RC 3.00 .90
❏ 180 Michael Lewis RC 5.00 1.50

2002 Upper Deck Honor Roll Letterman Autographs

	Nm-Mt	Ex-Mt
❏ HRLAT Anthony Thomas	30.00	9.00
❏ HRLBR Drew Brees	40.00	12.00
❏ HRLCW Chris Weinke	30.00	9.00
❏ HRLLT LaDainian Tomlinson	60.00	18.00
❏ HRLLP Luke Petitgout	30.00	9.00
❏ HRLMV Michael Vick	120.00	36.00
❏ HRLPM Peyton Manning	60.00	18.00
❏ HRLRC Rosevelt Colvin	30.00	9.00
❏ HRLRW Roy Williams	50.00	15.00

2003 Upper Deck Honor Roll

	MINT	NRMT
COMP.SET w/o SP's (100)	25.00	11.00
❏ 1 Corey Dillon	.40	.18
❏ 2 Kelley Washington RC	2.00	.90

❑ 3 Peter Warrick	.40	.18
❑ 4 Joey Harrington	1.00	.45
❑ 5 Az-Zahir Hakim	.25	.11
❑ 6 David Kircus RC	1.50	.70
❑ 7 Jabar Gaffney	.40	.18
❑ 8 Domanick Davis RC	4.00	1.80
❑ 9 Dave Ragone RC	2.00	.90
❑ 10 Kordell Stewart	.40	.18
❑ 11 Justin Gage RC	2.00	.90
❑ 12 Bobby Wade RC	2.00	.90
❑ 13 Anthony Thomas	.60	.25
❑ 14 Chad Hutchinson	.40	.18
❑ 15 Antonio Bryant	.40	.18
❑ 16 Bradie James RC	2.00	.90
❑ 17 Josh McCown	.40	.18
❑ 18 Jeff Blake	.25	.11
❑ 19 Kenny King RC	1.50	.70
❑ 20 Daunte Culpepper	.60	.25
❑ 21 Michael Bennett	.40	.18
❑ 22 Randy Moss	1.00	.45
❑ 23 Onterrio Smith RC	2.50	1.10
❑ 24 Mark Brunell	.40	.18
❑ 25 George Wrighster RC	1.50	.70
❑ 26 Fred Taylor	.60	.25
❑ 27 Jake Delhomme	.60	.25
❑ 28 Mike Seidman RC	1.00	.45
❑ 29 Walter Young RC	1.00	.45
❑ 30 Chris Redman	.25	.11
❑ 31 Jamal Lewis	.60	.25
❑ 32 Ovie Mughelli RC	1.00	.45
❑ 33 Koren Robinson	.40	.18
❑ 34 Shaun Alexander	.60	.25
❑ 35 Taco Wallace RC	1.50	.70
❑ 36 Kurt Warner	.60	.25
❑ 37 Kevin Curtis RC	2.00	.90
❑ 38 Torry Holt	.60	.25
❑ 39 Patrick Ramsey	.60	.25
❑ 40 Laveranues Coles	.40	.18
❑ 41 Gibran Hamdan RC	1.00	.45
❑ 42 Drew Bledsoe	.60	.25
❑ 43 Jerel Myers RC	1.00	.45
❑ 44 Eric Moulds	.40	.18
❑ 45 Drew Brees	.60	.25
❑ 46 David Boston	.40	.18
❑ 47 LaDainian Tomlinson	.60	.25
❑ 48 Reche Caldwell	.25	.11
❑ 49 Priest Holmes	.75	.35
❑ 50 Tony Gonzalez	.40	.18
❑ 51 Mike Pinkard RC	1.00	.45
❑ 52 Aaron Brooks	.60	.25
❑ 53 Deuce McAllister	.60	.25
❑ 54 Montrae Holland RC	1.00	.45
❑ 55 Jay Fiedler	.40	.18
❑ 56 Junior Seau	.60	.25
❑ 57 Chris Chambers	.60	.25
❑ 58 Ricky Williams	.60	.25
❑ 59 Tom Brady	1.00	.45
❑ 60 Troy Brown	.40	.18
❑ 61 Antowain Smith	.40	.18
❑ 62 Jake Plummer	.40	.18
❑ 63 Cecil Sapp RC	1.50	.70
❑ 64 Adrian Madise RC	1.50	.70
❑ 65 Tim Couch	.25	.11
❑ 66 William Green	.40	.18
❑ 67 Kelly Holcomb	.40	.18
❑ 68 Chad Pennington	.75	.35
❑ 69 Santana Moss	.40	.18
❑ 70 Curtis Martin	.60	.25
❑ 71 Michael Vick	1.50	.70
❑ 72 LaTarence Dunbar RC	1.50	.70
❑ 73 Peerless Price	.40	.18
❑ 74 Marvin Harrison	.60	.25
❑ 75 Peyton Manning	1.00	.45
❑ 76 Edgerrin James	.60	.25
❑ 77 Jeremy Shockey	1.00	.45
❑ 78 Tiki Barber	.40	.18
❑ 79 Kevin Walter RC	1.50	.70
❑ 80 Jeff Garcia	.60	.25
❑ 81 Terrell Owens	.60	.25
❑ 82 Andrew Williams RC	1.50	.70
❑ 83 Tommy Maddox	.60	.25
❑ 84 Plaxico Burress	.40	.18
❑ 85 Brian St.Pierre RC	2.00	.90
❑ 86 Steve McNair	.60	.25
❑ 87 Eddie George	.40	.18
❑ 88 Derrick Mason	.40	.18
❑ 89 Brett Favre	1.50	.70
❑ 90 Ahman Green	.60	.25
❑ 91 Donald Driver	.40	.18
❑ 92 Donovan McNabb	.75	.35
❑ 93 Brian Dawkins	.25	.11
❑ 94 Norman LeJeune RC	1.00	.45
❑ 95 Jerry Rice	1.25	.55
❑ 96 Rich Gannon	.40	.18
❑ 97 Siddeeq Shabazz RC	1.00	.45
❑ 98 DeWayne White RC	1.50	.70
❑ 99 Brad Johnson	.40	.18
❑ 100 Keyshawn Johnson	.60	.25
❑ 101 Chad Johnson SP	2.00	.90
❑ 102 Artose Pinner SP RC	4.00	1.80
❑ 103 David Carr SP	5.00	2.20
❑ 104 Brian Urlacher SP	5.00	2.20
❑ 105 Jason Witten SP RC	6.00	2.70
❑ 106 Emmitt Smith SP	8.00	3.60
❑ 107 Nate Burleson SP RC	6.00	2.70
❑ 108 LaBrandon Toefield SP RC	4.00	1.80
❑ 109 Julius Peppers SP	3.00	1.35
❑ 110 Musa Smith SP RC	4.00	1.80
❑ 111 Seneca Wallace SP RC	4.00	1.80
❑ 112 Marshall Faulk SP	3.00	1.35
❑ 113 Brad Banks SP RC	3.00	1.35
❑ 114 Travis Henry SP	2.00	.90
❑ 115 Mike Scifres SP RC	2.00	.90
❑ 116 J.R. Tolver SP RC	3.00	1.35
❑ 117 Kliff Kingsbury SP RC	3.00	1.35
❑ 118 Clinton Portis SP	5.00	2.20
❑ 119 Kevin Johnson SP	2.00	.90
❑ 120 Brooks Bollinger SP RC	4.00	1.80
❑ 121 Terrence Edwards SP RC	3.00	1.35
❑ 122 Steve Sciullo SP RC	2.00	.90
❑ 123 Ken Dorsey SP RC	6.00	2.70
❑ 124 Jerome Bettis SP	3.00	1.35
❑ 125 Chris Brown SP RC	8.00	3.60
❑ 126 Carl Ford SP RC	2.00	.90
❑ 127 Billy McMullen SP RC	3.00	1.35
❑ 128 Doug Gabriel SP RC	4.00	1.80
❑ 129 Earnest Graham SP RC	3.00	1.35
❑ 130 Chris Simms SP RC	8.00	3.60
❑ 131 Carson Palmer RC	15.00	6.75
❑ 132 Charles Rogers RC	6.00	2.70
❑ 133 Andre Johnson RC	12.00	5.50
❑ 134 DeWayne Robertson RC	5.00	2.20
❑ 135 Terence Newman RC	10.00	4.50
❑ 136 Johnathan Sullivan RC	4.00	1.80
❑ 137 Byron Leftwich RC	20.00	9.00
❑ 138 Jordan Gross RC	4.00	1.80
❑ 139 Kevin Williams RC	5.00	2.20
❑ 140 Terrell Suggs RC	8.00	3.60
❑ 141 Marcus Trufant RC	5.00	2.20
❑ 142 Jimmy Kennedy RC	5.00	2.20
❑ 143 Ty Warren RC	5.00	2.20
❑ 144 Michael Haynes RC	5.00	2.20
❑ 145 Jerome McDougle RC	5.00	2.20
❑ 146 J.T. Wall RC	2.50	1.10
❑ 147 Bryant Johnson RC	5.00	2.20
❑ 148 Calvin Pace RC	4.00	1.80
❑ 149 Kyle Boller RC	12.00	5.50
❑ 150 Quentin Griffin RC	12.00	5.50
❑ 151 Lee Suggs RC	10.00	4.50
❑ 152 Rex Grossman RC	12.00	5.50
❑ 153 Willis McGahee RC	12.00	5.50
❑ 154 Dallas Clark RC	5.00	2.20
❑ 155 William Joseph RC	5.00	2.20
❑ 156 Kwame Harris RC	4.00	1.80
❑ 157 Larry Johnson RC	10.00	4.50
❑ 158 Andre Woolfolk RC	5.00	2.20
❑ 159 Nick Barnett RC	8.00	3.60
❑ 160 Dahrran Diedrick RC	5.00	2.20
❑ 161 Teyo Johnson RC	5.00	2.20
❑ 162 Justin Fargas RC	5.00	2.20
❑ 163 Eric Steinbach RC	4.00	1.80
❑ 164 Boss Bailey RC	6.00	2.70
❑ 165 Charles Tillman RC	8.00	3.60
❑ 166 Eugene Wilson RC	4.00	1.80
❑ 167 Jonathan Stinchcomb RC	2.50	1.10
❑ 168 Al Johnson RC	5.00	2.20
❑ 169 Rashean Mathis RC	4.00	1.80
❑ 170 Keenan Howry RC	5.00	2.20
❑ 171 Ben Joppru RC	5.00	2.20
❑ 172 Rashad Moore RC	4.00	1.80
❑ 173 Shaun McDonald RC	5.00	2.20
❑ 174 Taylor Jacobs RC	5.00	2.20
❑ 175 Bethel Johnson RC	8.00	3.60
❑ 176 Matt Wilhelm RC	5.00	2.20
❑ 177 Kawika Mitchell RC	4.00	1.80
❑ 178 Chris Kelsay RC	5.00	2.20
❑ 179 Lon Sheriff RC	2.50	1.10
❑ 180 Ricky Manning RC	5.00	2.20
❑ 181 Terry Pierce RC	4.00	1.80
❑ 182 Chaun Thompson RC	2.50	1.10
❑ 183 Victor Hobson RC	5.00	2.20
❑ 184 Anquan Boldin RC	12.00	5.50
❑ 185 Justin Griffith RC	4.00	1.80
❑ 186 Osi Umenyiora RC	5.00	2.20
❑ 187 Brandon Lloyd RC	6.00	2.70
❑ 188 Michael Doss RC	5.00	2.20
❑ 189 Alonzo Jackson RC	4.00	1.80
❑ 190 Tyrone Calico RC	6.00	2.70

2003 Upper Deck Honor Roll Silver

	MINT	NRMT

*SILVER 1-100: 3X TO 8X BASE CARD HI
*SILVER ROOKIES 1-100: 1.5X TO 4X
*SILVER 101-130: .6X TO 1.5X BASE CARD HI
*SILVER ROOKIES 101-130: .8X TO 2X
*SILVER ROOKIES 131-190: .6X TO 1.5X

2003 Upper Deck Honor Roll Dean's List

*SILVERS: .6X TO 1.5X BASIC INSERTS
SILVER PRINT RUN 200 SER.#'d SETS

	MINT	NRMT
❑ DLAN Mike Anderson	8.00	3.60
❑ DLBL Byron Leftwich	25.00	11.00
❑ DLBO Kyle Boller	15.00	6.75
❑ DLBS Brandon Stokley	8.00	3.60
❑ DLCB Champ Bailey SP	10.00	4.50
❑ DLCJ Chad Johnson	8.00	3.60
❑ DLCM Chris McAlister	6.00	2.70
❑ DLCS Chris Samuels	6.00	2.70
❑ DLCU Curtis Martin	10.00	4.50
❑ DLDC Dallas Clark	10.00	4.50
❑ DLDM Damerian McCants	6.00	2.70
❑ DLDR Dave Ragone	10.00	4.50
❑ DLDW Dez White SP	10.00	4.50
❑ DLJB Josh Booty	8.00	3.60
❑ DLJK Jevon Kearse SP	10.00	4.50
❑ DLKB Kendrell Bell	12.00	5.50
❑ DLKC Kerry Collins	10.00	4.50

❑ DLKW Kevin Ware	6.00	2.70
❑ DLMA Mike Alstott	10.00	4.50
❑ DLMB Marty Booker	8.00	3.60
❑ DLMC Donovan McNabb SP	15.00	6.75
❑ DLMM Michael McCrary	6.00	2.70
❑ DLMR Marcus Robinson	8.00	3.60
❑ DLMV Michael Vick SP	25.00	11.00
❑ DLOG Olandis Gary	8.00	3.60
❑ DLOP Orlando Pace	6.00	2.70
❑ DLPB Plaxico Burress SP	10.00	4.50
❑ DLPM Peyton Manning SP	20.00	9.00
❑ DLQJ Quentin Jammer	6.00	2.70
❑ DLRG Rex Grossman	15.00	6.75
❑ DLRO DeWayne Robertson	8.00	3.60
❑ DLRW Reggie Wayne	8.00	3.60
❑ DLSA Shaun Alexander	10.00	4.50
❑ DLSC Carson Palmer	20.00	9.00
❑ DLSH Jeremy Shockey	15.00	6.75
❑ DLSI Corey Simon	8.00	3.60
❑ DLSM Sammy Morris	6.00	2.70
❑ DLTB Tiki Barber	10.00	4.50
❑ DLTH Torry Holt	10.00	4.50
❑ DLZT Zach Thomas	10.00	4.50

2003 Upper Deck Honor Roll Letterman Autographs

	MINT	NRMT
❑ HRLCJ Chad Johnson	25.00	11.00
❑ HRLDM Deuce McAllister		
❑ HRLHE Travis Henry	25.00	11.00
❑ HRLJJ James Jackson EXCH	20.00	9.00
❑ HRLKB Kevan Barlow	25.00	11.00
❑ HRLMM Snoop Minnis	15.00	6.75
❑ HRLPM Peyton Manning	50.00	22.00
❑ HRLRJ Rudi Johnson	20.00	9.00
❑ HRLTH Todd Heap	25.00	11.00
❑ HRLTM Travis Minor	25.00	11.00

1997 Upper Deck Legends Autographs

	Nm-Mt	Ex-Mt
❑ AL1 Bart Starr SP	700.00	325.00
❑ AL2 Jim Brown SP	850.00	375.00
❑ AL3 Joe Namath SP	800.00	350.00
❑ AL4 Walter Payton SP	850.00	375.00
❑ AL5 Terry Bradshaw SP	700.00	325.00
❑ AL6 Franco Harris SP	700.00	325.00
❑ AL7 Dan Fouts	40.00	18.00
❑ AL8 Steve Largent	40.00	18.00
❑ AL9 Johnny Unitas SP	800.00	350.00
❑ AL10 Gale Sayers	50.00	22.00
❑ AL11 Roger Staubach	150.00	70.00
❑ AL12 Tony Dorsett SP	350.00	160.00
❑ AL13 Fran Tarkenton	60.00	27.00
❑ AL14 Charley Taylor	20.00	9.00
❑ AL15 Ray Nitschke	120.00	55.00
❑ AL16 Jim Ringo	30.00	13.50
❑ AL17 Dick Butkus SP	750.00	350.00
❑ AL18 Fred Biletnikoff	40.00	18.00
❑ AL19 Lenny Moore	30.00	13.50
❑ AL20 Len Dawson	50.00	22.00
❑ AL21 Lance Alworth	80.00	36.00
❑ AL22 Chuck Bednarik	40.00	18.00
❑ AL23 Raymond Berry	30.00	13.50
❑ AL24 Donnie Shell	30.00	13.50
❑ AL25 Mel Blount	30.00	13.50
❑ AL26 Willie Brown	30.00	13.50
❑ AL27 Ken Houston	20.00	9.00
❑ AL28 Larry Csonka SP	250.00	110.00
❑ AL29 Mike Ditka	50.00	22.00
❑ AL30 Art Donovan	60.00	27.00
❑ AL31 Sam Huff	40.00	18.00
❑ AL32 Lem Barney	30.00	13.50
❑ AL33 Hugh McElhenny	30.00	13.50
❑ AL34 Otto Graham	50.00	22.00
❑ AL35 Joe Greene SP	150.00	70.00
❑ AL36 Mike Rozier	50.00	22.00
❑ AL37 Lou Groza	40.00	18.00
❑ AL38 Ted Hendricks	25.00	11.00
❑ AL39 Elroy Hirsch	60.00	27.00
❑ AL40 Paul Hornung	50.00	22.00
❑ AL41 Charlie Joiner	25.00	11.00
❑ AL42 Deacon Jones	30.00	13.50
❑ AL43 Bill Bradley	20.00	9.00
❑ AL44 Floyd Little	25.00	11.00
❑ AL45 Willie Lanier	30.00	13.50
❑ AL46 Bob Lilly	30.00	13.50
❑ AL47 Sid Luckman EXCH never signed	3.00	1.35
❑ AL48 John Mackey	25.00	11.00
❑ AL49 Don Maynard	30.00	13.50
❑ AL50 Mike McCormack	30.00	13.50
❑ AL51 Bobby Mitchell	20.00	9.00
❑ AL52 Ron Mix	30.00	13.50
❑ AL53 Marion Motley	50.00	22.00
❑ AL54 Leo Nomellini	40.00	18.00
❑ AL55 Mark Duper	50.00	22.00
❑ AL56 Mel Renfro	30.00	13.50
❑ AL57 Jim Otto	30.00	13.50
❑ AL58 Alan Page	30.00	13.50
❑ AL59 Joe Perry	50.00	22.00
❑ AL60 Andy Robustelli	30.00	13.50
❑ AL61 Lee Roy Selmon	30.00	13.50
❑ AL62 Jackie Smith	25.00	11.00
❑ AL63 Art Shell SP	120.00	55.00
❑ AL64 Jan Stenerud	30.00	13.50
❑ AL65 Gene Upshaw	40.00	18.00
❑ AL66 Y.A. Tittle	30.00	13.50
❑ AL67 Paul Warfield	30.00	13.50
❑ AL68 Kellen Winslow	50.00	22.00
❑ AL69 Randy White	40.00	18.00
❑ AL70 Larry Wilson	30.00	13.50
❑ AL71 Willie Wood EXCH never signed	3.00	1.35
❑ AL72 Jack Ham	60.00	27.00
❑ AL73 Jack Youngblood	30.00	13.50
❑ AL74 Danny Abramowicz	20.00	9.00
❑ AL75 Dick Anderson	30.00	13.50
❑ AL76 Ken Anderson	25.00	11.00
❑ AL77 Steve Bartkowski	30.00	13.50
❑ AL78 Bill Bergey	20.00	9.00
❑ AL79 Rocky Bleier	40.00	18.00
❑ AL80 Cliff Branch	30.00	13.50
❑ AL81 John Brodie	40.00	18.00
❑ AL82 Bobby Bell	25.00	11.00
❑ AL83 Billy Cannon SP	120.00	55.00
❑ AL84 Gino Cappelletti	20.00	9.00
❑ AL85 Harold Carmichael	20.00	9.00
❑ AL86 Dave Casper	40.00	18.00
❑ AL87 Wes Chandler	30.00	13.50
❑ AL88 Todd Christensen	25.00	11.00
❑ AL89 Dwight Clark	30.00	13.50
❑ AL90 Mark Clayton	30.00	13.50
❑ AL91 Cris Collinsworth	25.00	11.00
❑ AL92 Roger Craig	30.00	13.50
❑ AL93 Randy Cross	30.00	13.50
❑ AL94 Isaac Curtis	25.00	11.00
❑ AL95 Mike Curtis	30.00	13.50
❑ AL96 Ben Davidson	25.00	11.00
❑ AL97 Fred Dean EXCH never signed	3.00	1.35
❑ AL98 Tom Dempsey	20.00	9.00
❑ AL99 Eric Dickerson	30.00	13.50
❑ AL100 Lynn Dickey	30.00	13.50
❑ AL102 Carl Eller	50.00	22.00
❑ AL103 Chuck Foreman	25.00	11.00
❑ AL104 Russ Francis		
❑ AL104X Russ Francis EXCH never signed	3.00	1.35
❑ AL106 Gary Garrison	20.00	9.00
❑ AL107 Randy Gradishar	25.00	11.00
❑ AL108 L.C. Greenwood	40.00	18.00
❑ AL109 Rosey Grier	40.00	18.00
❑ AL110 Steve Grogan	30.00	13.50
❑ AL111 Ray Guy	30.00	13.50
❑ AL112 John Hadl	30.00	13.50
❑ AL113 Jim Hart	20.00	9.00
❑ AL115 Mike Haynes	30.00	13.50
❑ AL116 Charlie Hennigan	20.00	9.00
❑ AL117 Chuck Howley	30.00	13.50
❑ AL118 Harold Jackson	20.00	9.00
❑ AL119 Tom Jackson	30.00	13.50
❑ AL120 Ron Jaworski	25.00	11.00
❑ AL121 John Jefferson	30.00	13.50
❑ AL122 Billy Johnson EXCH never signed	3.00	1.35
❑ AL123 Ed Too Tall Jones	40.00	18.00
❑ AL124 Jack Kemp	60.00	27.00
❑ AL125 Jim Kiick	30.00	13.50
❑ AL126 Billy Kilmer	20.00	9.00
❑ AL127 Jerry Kramer	40.00	18.00
❑ AL128 Paul Krause	30.00	13.50
❑ AL129 Daryle Lamonica	40.00	18.00
❑ AL131 James Lofton	30.00	13.50
❑ AL133 Archie Manning	40.00	18.00
❑ AL134 Jim Marshall	80.00	36.00
❑ AL135 Harvey Martin	40.00	18.00
❑ AL136 Tommy McDonald	30.00	13.50
❑ AL137 Max McGee	30.00	13.50
❑ AL138 Reggie McKenzie	25.00	11.00
❑ AL139 Karl Mecklenburg	25.00	11.00
❑ AL141 Terry Metcalf	30.00	13.50
❑ AL142 Matt Millen SP	100.00	45.00
❑ AL143 Earl Morrall	30.00	13.50
❑ AL144 Mercury Morris	30.00	13.50
❑ AL146 Joe Morris	30.00	13.50
❑ AL147 Mark Moseley	20.00	9.00
❑ AL148 Haven Moses	25.00	11.00
❑ AL149 Chuck Muncie	20.00	9.00
❑ AL150 Anthony Munoz	30.00	13.50
❑ AL151 Tommy Nobis	20.00	9.00
❑ AL152 Babe Parilli	20.00	9.00
❑ AL153 Drew Pearson	30.00	13.50
❑ AL154 Ozzie Newsome	30.00	13.50
❑ AL155 Jim Plunkett	30.00	13.50
❑ AL156 William Perry	30.00	13.50
❑ AL157 Johnny Robinson	20.00	9.00
❑ AL158 Ahmad Rashad	30.00	13.50
❑ AL159 George Rogers	50.00	22.00
❑ AL160 Sterling Sharpe	30.00	13.50
❑ AL161 Billy Sims	30.00	13.50
❑ AL163 Mike Singletary	30.00	13.50
❑ AL164 Charlie Sanders	20.00	9.00
❑ AL165 Bubba Smith SP	150.00	70.00
❑ AL166 Ken Stabler	75.00	34.00
❑ AL167 Freddie Solomon	25.00	11.00
❑ AL168 John Stallworth	40.00	18.00
❑ AL169 Dwight Stephenson	25.00	11.00
❑ AL172 Lionel Taylor	25.00	11.00
❑ AL173 Otis Taylor SP	100.00	45.00
❑ AL174 Joe Theismann	30.00	13.50
❑ AL175 Bob Trumpy EXCH never signed	3.00	1.35
❑ AL176 Mike Webster SP	100.00	45.00
❑ AL177 Jim Zorn	20.00	9.00
❑ AL178 Joe Montana	250.00	110.00

1997 Upper Deck Legends Sign of the Times

	Nm-Mt	Ex-Mt
❑ ST1 Joe Montana	400.00	180.00
❑ ST2 Fran Tarkenton	150.00	70.00
❑ ST3 Johnny Unitas	200.00	90.00
❑ ST3X Johnny Unitas EXCH	10.00	3.00
❑ ST4 Joe Namath	200.00	90.00
❑ ST5 Terry Bradshaw	200.00	90.00
❑ ST6 Jim Brown	200.00	90.00
❑ ST7 Franco Harris	125.00	55.00
❑ ST8 Walter Payton	400.00	180.00
❑ ST9 Steve Largent	120.00	55.00
❑ ST10 Bart Starr	200.00	90.00

2000 Upper Deck Legends

	Nm-Mt	Ex-Mt
COMPLETE SET (132)	400.00	180.00
COMP.SET w/o SP's (90)	20.00	9.00
❑ 1 Jake Plummer	.30	.14
❑ 2 Jamal Anderson	.50	.23
❑ 3 Doug Flutie	.50	.23
❑ 4 Jim Kelly	.60	.25
❑ 5 Dick Butkus	1.00	.45
❑ 6 Mike Singletary	.50	.23
❑ 7 Gale Sayers	1.00	.45
❑ 8 Boomer Esiason	.30	.14
❑ 9 Anthony Munoz	.30	.14
❑ 10 Otto Graham	.30	.14
❑ 11 Jim Brown	1.25	.55
❑ 12 Ozzie Newsome	.20	.09
❑ 13 Bob Lilly	.30	.14
❑ 14 Troy Aikman	1.25	.55
❑ 15 Emmitt Smith	1.25	.55
❑ 16 Roger Staubach	1.25	.55
❑ 17 Deion Sanders	.50	.23
❑ 18 Tony Dorsett	.50	.23
❑ 19 Terrell Davis	.50	.23
❑ 20 John Elway	2.00	.90
❑ 21 Charlie Batch	.50	.23
❑ 22 Brett Favre	2.00	.90
❑ 23 Bart Starr	1.50	.70
❑ 24 Reggie White	.50	.23
❑ 25 Earl Campbell	.50	.23
❑ 26 Peyton Manning	1.50	.70
❑ 27 Edgerrin James	1.00	.45
❑ 28 Johnny Unitas	1.25	.55
❑ 29 Marvin Harrison	.50	.23
❑ 30 Mark Brunell	.50	.23
❑ 31 Fred Taylor	.50	.23
❑ 32 Len Dawson	.50	.23
❑ 33 Dan Marino	2.00	.90
❑ 34 Bob Griese	.50	.23
❑ 35 Mark Duper	.20	.09
❑ 36 Thurman Thomas	.30	.14
❑ 37 Fran Tarkenton	1.00	.45
❑ 38 Randy Moss	1.25	.55
❑ 39 Cris Carter	.50	.23
❑ 40 Gary Anderson	.20	.09
❑ 41 John Randle	.30	.14
❑ 42 Drew Bledsoe	.75	.35
❑ 43 Archie Manning	.30	.14
❑ 44 Ricky Williams	.50	.23
❑ 45 Frank Gifford	.50	.23
❑ 46 Kerry Collins	.30	.14
❑ 47 Phil Simms	.30	.14
❑ 48 Vinny Testaverde	.30	.14
❑ 49 Curtis Martin	.50	.23
❑ 50 Keyshawn Johnson	.50	.23
❑ 51 Joe Namath	1.25	.55
❑ 52 Marcus Allen	.60	.25
❑ 53 Bruce Smith	.30	.14
❑ 54 Ken Stabler	1.25	.55
❑ 55 Fred Biletnikoff	.50	.23
❑ 56 Howie Long	.60	.25
❑ 57 Ron Jaworski	.20	.09
❑ 58 Harold Carmichael	.20	.09
❑ 59 Kordell Stewart	.30	.14
❑ 60 Levon Kirkland	.20	.09
❑ 61 Mel Blount	.30	.14
❑ 62 Jerome Bettis	.50	.23
❑ 63 John Stallworth	.30	.14
❑ 64 Franco Harris	.60	.25
❑ 65 Jim Harbaugh	.30	.14
❑ 66 Kellen Winslow	.30	.14
❑ 67 Charlie Joiner	.20	.09
❑ 68 Junior Seau	.50	.23
❑ 69 Jerry Rice	1.25	.55
❑ 70 Steve Young	1.00	.45
❑ 71 Joe Montana	2.50	1.10
❑ 72 Roger Craig	.30	.14
❑ 73 Ronnie Lott	.30	.14
❑ 74 Jon Kitna	.50	.23
❑ 75 Steve Largent	.50	.23
❑ 76 Ricky Watters	.30	.14
❑ 77 Kurt Warner	1.25	.55
❑ 78 Marshall Faulk	.75	.35
❑ 79 Isaac Bruce	.50	.23
❑ 80 Merlin Olsen	.30	.14
❑ 81 Lee Roy Selmon	.20	.09
❑ 82 Tim Brown	.50	.23
❑ 83 Tim Couch	.30	.14
❑ 84 Mike Alstott	.50	.23
❑ 85 Eddie George	.50	.23
❑ 86 Steve McNair	.50	.23
❑ 87 Brad Johnson	.50	.23
❑ 88 Sonny Jurgensen	.50	.23
❑ 89 Art Monk	.30	.14
❑ 90 Joe Theismann	.50	.23
❑ 91 Ray Nitschke TCL	10.00	4.50
❑ 92 Doak Walker TCL	10.00	4.50
❑ 93 Thurman Thomas TCL	10.00	4.50
❑ 94 Jim Brown TCL	12.00	5.50
❑ 95 Sammy Baugh TCL	15.00	6.75
❑ 96 Reggie White TCL	10.00	4.50
❑ 97 Eric Dickerson TCL	10.00	4.50
❑ 98 Paul Hornung TCL	10.00	4.50
❑ 99 Deion Sanders TCL	12.00	5.50
❑ 100 Bronko Nagurski TCL	10.00	4.50
❑ 101 Walter Payton TCL	25.00	11.00
❑ 102 Jim Thorpe TCL	12.00	5.50
❑ 103 Ron Dayne RC	6.00	2.70
❑ 104 Tim Rattay RC	12.00	5.50
❑ 105 Brian Urlacher RC	25.00	11.00
❑ 106 Bubba Franks RC	6.00	2.70
❑ 107 Chad Pennington RC	25.00	11.00
❑ 108 Chris Cole RC	5.00	2.20
❑ 109 Chris Redman RC	5.00	2.20
❑ 110 Courtney Brown RC	6.00	2.70
❑ 111 Curtis Keaton RC	5.00	2.20
❑ 112 Dennis Northcutt RC	10.00	4.50
❑ 113 Dez White RC	6.00	2.70
❑ 114 Giovanni Carmazzi RC	10.00	4.50
❑ 115 J.R. Redmond RC	5.00	2.20
❑ 116 JaJuan Dawson RC	10.00	4.50
❑ 117 Jamal Lewis RC	15.00	6.75
❑ 118 Jerry Porter RC	8.00	3.60
❑ 119 Laveranues Coles RC	8.00	3.60
❑ 120 Peter Warrick RC	6.00	2.70
❑ 121 Plaxico Burress RC	12.00	5.50
❑ 122 R.Jay Soward RC	5.00	2.20
❑ 123 Reuben Droughns RC	8.00	3.60
❑ 124 Ron Dixon RC	5.00	2.20
❑ 125 Ron Dugans RC	10.00	4.50
❑ 126 Shaun Alexander RC	15.00	6.75
❑ 127 Sylvester Morris RC	5.00	2.20
❑ 128 Thomas Jones RC	10.00	4.50
❑ 129 Todd Pinkston RC	6.00	2.70
❑ 130 Travis Prentice RC	5.00	2.20
❑ 131 Travis Taylor RC	10.00	4.50
❑ 132 Trung Canidate RC	5.00	2.20

2000 Upper Deck Legends Autographs

	Nm-Mt	Ex-Mt
*GOLD CARDS: 1X TO 2X BASIC INSERTS		
❑ AM Archie Manning	40.00	18.00
❑ AZ Anthony Munoz	30.00	13.50
❑ BE Boomer Esiason	30.00	13.50
❑ BG Bob Griese	40.00	18.00
❑ BJ Brad Johnson	20.00	9.00
❑ BL Drew Bledsoe	50.00	22.00
❑ BL2 Bob Lilly	30.00	13.50
❑ BR Mark Brunell	20.00	9.00
❑ BS Bart Starr	135.00	60.00
❑ CC Cris Carter	30.00	13.50
❑ CJ Charlie Joiner	20.00	9.00
❑ DA Terrell Davis	30.00	13.50
❑ DB Dick Butkus	60.00	27.00
❑ DF Doug Flutie	30.00	13.50
❑ DM Dan Marino	175.00	80.00
❑ EC Earl Campbell	50.00	22.00
❑ EG Eddie George	30.00	13.50
❑ EJ Edgerrin James	40.00	18.00
❑ FB Fred Biletnikoff	40.00	18.00
❑ FG Frank Gifford	60.00	27.00
❑ FH Franco Harris	50.00	22.00
❑ FT Fran Tarkenton	50.00	22.00
❑ GS Gale Sayers	50.00	22.00
❑ HC Harold Carmichael	20.00	9.00
❑ HL Howie Long	50.00	22.00
❑ IB Isaac Bruce	30.00	13.50
❑ JA Jamal Anderson	20.00	9.00
❑ JB Jerome Bettis	40.00	18.00
❑ JB2 Jim Brown	80.00	36.00
❑ JK Jim Kelly	80.00	36.00
❑ JM Joe Montana	120.00	55.00
❑ JN Joe Namath	100.00	45.00
❑ JP Jake Plummer	30.00	13.50
❑ JS John Stallworth	40.00	18.00
❑ JT Joe Theismann	40.00	18.00
❑ JU Johnny Unitas	200.00	90.00
❑ KI Jon Kitna	20.00	9.00
❑ KJ Keyshawn Johnson	30.00	13.50
❑ KS Ken Stabler	50.00	22.00
❑ KW Kellen Winslow	30.00	13.50
❑ LD Len Dawson	40.00	18.00
❑ LS Lee Roy Selmon	20.00	9.00
❑ MA Marcus Allen	40.00	18.00
❑ MB Mel Blount	40.00	18.00
❑ MD Mark Duper	20.00	9.00
❑ MH Marvin Harrison	40.00	18.00

	Nm-Mt	Ex-Mt
❑ MK Art Monk	30.00	13.50
❑ MS Mike Singletary	40.00	18.00
❑ OG Otto Graham	50.00	22.00
❑ ON Ozzie Newsome	20.00	9.00
❑ PM Peyton Manning	100.00	45.00
❑ PS Phil Simms	40.00	18.00
❑ RC Roger Craig	20.00	9.00
❑ RI Ricky Watters	20.00	9.00
❑ RJ Ron Jaworski	20.00	9.00
❑ RL Ronnie Lott SP		
❑ RM Randy Moss	100.00	45.00
❑ RS Roger Staubach	80.00	36.00
❑ RW Ricky Williams EXCH	4.00	1.80
❑ SJ Sonny Jurgensen	30.00	13.50
❑ SL Steve Largent	40.00	18.00
❑ SY Steve Young	50.00	22.00
❑ TA Troy Aikman	60.00	27.00
❑ TB Tim Brown	40.00	18.00
❑ TC Tim Couch	20.00	9.00
❑ TD Tony Dorsett	60.00	27.00
❑ VT Vinny Testaverde	20.00	9.00
❑ WA Kurt Warner	40.00	18.00

2000 Upper Deck Legends Legendary Jerseys

	Nm-Mt	Ex-Mt
❑ LJBF Brett Favre	50.00	22.00
❑ LJBL Bob Lilly	30.00	13.50
❑ LJCB Cliff Branch	25.00	11.00
❑ LJCH Charles Haley	25.00	11.00
❑ LJDB Drew Bledsoe	30.00	13.50
❑ LJDF Doug Flutie	30.00	13.50
❑ LJDJ Daryl Johnston	30.00	13.50
❑ LJDM Dan Marino	50.00	22.00
❑ LJDS Deion Sanders	30.00	13.50
❑ LJED Eric Dickerson	30.00	13.50
❑ LJEM John Elway Dan Marino	300.00	135.00
❑ LJES Emmitt Smith	40.00	18.00
❑ LJFB Fred Biletnikoff	30.00	13.50
❑ LJFT Fran Tarkenton	30.00	13.50
❑ LJGU Gene Upshaw	20.00	9.00
❑ LJHL Howie Long	40.00	18.00
❑ LJHW Herschel Walker	30.00	13.50
❑ LJJA Jamal Anderson	20.00	9.00
❑ LJJB John Brodie	30.00	13.50
❑ LJJE John Elway	40.00	18.00
❑ LJJM Joe Montana	60.00	27.00
❑ LJJN Joe Namath	40.00	18.00
❑ LJJP Jim Plunkett	25.00	11.00
❑ LJJR Jerry Rice	40.00	18.00
❑ LJKN Ken Norton Jr.	20.00	9.00
❑ LJKS Ken Stabler	30.00	13.50
❑ LJKW Kurt Warner	30.00	13.50
❑ LJMA1 Marcus Allen	25.00	11.00
❑ LJMA2 Marcus Allen SE	30.00	9.00
❑ LJMB Mark Brunell	30.00	13.50
❑ LJMF Marshall Faulk	30.00	13.50
❑ LJMI Michael Irvin	30.00	13.50
❑ LJNO Jay Novacek	30.00	13.50
❑ LJOS Otis Sistrunk	20.00	9.00
❑ LJPM Peyton Manning	40.00	18.00
❑ LJRL Ronnie Lott	25.00	11.00
❑ LJRM Randy Moss	30.00	13.50
❑ LJRS Roger Staubach	40.00	18.00
❑ LJRW Reggie White	30.00	13.50
❑ LJSM Bruce Smith	25.00	11.00
❑ LJSY Steve Young	40.00	18.00
❑ LJTA Troy Aikman	40.00	18.00
❑ LJTC Todd Christensen	20.00	9.00
❑ LJTD Terrell Davis	30.00	13.50
❑ LJTH1 Ted Hendricks	20.00	9.00
❑ LJTH2 Ted Hendricks SE	25.00	7.50
❑ LJVE Mark Van Eghen	20.00	9.00
❑ LJWM Warren Moon	30.00	13.50
❑ LJWP Walter Payton	80.00	36.00

2001 Upper Deck Legends

	Nm-Mt	Ex-Mt
COMP.SET w/o SP's (90)	30.00	9.00
❑ 1 Jake Plummer	.50	.15
❑ 2 Jamal Anderson	.75	.23
❑ 3 Ray Lewis	.75	.23
❑ 4 Johnny Unitas	1.50	.45
❑ 5 Jamal Lewis	1.50	.45
❑ 6 Andre Reed	.50	.15
❑ 7 Jim Kelly	1.25	.35
❑ 8 Thurman Thomas	.50	.15
❑ 9 Rob Johnson	.50	.15
❑ 10 Brian Urlacher	1.50	.45
❑ 11 Dick Butkus	1.50	.45
❑ 12 Gale Sayers	1.50	.45
❑ 13 James Allen	.50	.15
❑ 14 Corey Dillon	.75	.23
❑ 15 Jim Brown	1.50	.45
❑ 16 Tim Couch	.50	.15
❑ 17 Joey Galloway	.50	.15
❑ 18 Emmitt Smith	2.00	.60
❑ 19 Randy White	.50	.15
❑ 20 Roger Staubach	1.50	.45
❑ 21 Troy Aikman	1.50	.45
❑ 22 Tony Dorsett	.75	.23
❑ 23 Brian Griese	.75	.23
❑ 24 Floyd Little	.30	.09
❑ 25 John Elway	3.00	.90
❑ 26 Mike Anderson	.75	.23
❑ 27 Terrell Davis	.75	.23
❑ 28 Barry Sanders	2.00	.60
❑ 29 Charlie Batch	.75	.23
❑ 30 Bart Starr	2.00	.60
❑ 31 Paul Hornung	.75	.23
❑ 32 Reggie White	.75	.23
❑ 33 Warren Moon	.75	.23
❑ 34 Edgerrin James	1.25	.35
❑ 35 Peyton Manning	2.50	.75
❑ 36 Mark Brunell	.75	.23
❑ 37 Tony Gonzalez	.50	.15
❑ 38 Eric Dickerson	.50	.15
❑ 39 Jack Youngblood	.30	.09
❑ 40 Jay Fiedler	.75	.23
❑ 41 Lamar Smith	.50	.15
❑ 42 Dan Marino	3.00	.90
❑ 43 Oronde Gadsden	.50	.15
❑ 44 Cris Carter	.75	.23
❑ 45 Fran Tarkenton	1.25	.35
❑ 46 Daunte Culpepper	.75	.23
❑ 47 Randy Moss	2.00	.60
❑ 48 Robert Smith	.30	.09
❑ 49 Drew Bledsoe	1.25	.35
❑ 50 Archie Manning	.50	.15
❑ 51 Jeff Blake	.50	.15
❑ 52 Ricky Williams	.75	.23
❑ 53 Kerry Collins	.50	.15
❑ 54 Ron Dayne	.75	.23
❑ 55 Lawrence Taylor	.75	.23
❑ 56 Wayne Chrebet	.50	.15
❑ 57 Vinny Testaverde	.50	.15
❑ 58 Joe Namath	1.50	.45
❑ 59 Jim Plunkett	.50	.15
❑ 60 George Blanda	.75	.23
❑ 61 Tim Brown	.75	.23
❑ 62 Jerry Rice	2.00	.60
❑ 63 Ken Stabler	1.50	.45
❑ 64 Marcus Allen	1.25	.35
❑ 65 Donovan McNabb	1.25	.35
❑ 66 Harold Carmichael	.30	.09
❑ 67 Franco Harris	1.25	.35
❑ 68 Jerome Bettis	.75	.23
❑ 69 Terry Bradshaw	1.50	.45
❑ 70 Doug Flutie	.75	.23
❑ 71 Lance Alworth	.50	.15
❑ 72 Junior Seau	.75	.23
❑ 73 Kellen Winslow	.50	.15
❑ 74 Dan Fouts	.75	.23
❑ 75 Joe Montana	5.00	1.50
❑ 76 Terrell Owens	.75	.23
❑ 77 Jeff Garcia	.75	.23
❑ 78 Steve Young	1.25	.35
❑ 79 Matt Hasselbeck	.50	.15
❑ 80 Kurt Warner	2.00	.60
❑ 81 Marshall Faulk	1.25	.35
❑ 82 Brad Johnson	.75	.23
❑ 83 Eddie George	.75	.23
❑ 84 Charley Taylor	.50	.15
❑ 85 Stephen Davis	.75	.23
❑ 86 Jeff George	.50	.15
❑ 87 John Riggins	1.25	.35
❑ 88 Joe Theismann	.75	.23
❑ 89 Michael Westbrook	.50	.15
❑ 90 Sonny Jurgensen	.75	.23
❑ 91 Andre Carter RC	8.00	2.40
❑ 92 Cedrick Wilson RC	8.00	2.40
❑ 93 Kevan Barlow RC	8.00	2.40
❑ 94 Anthony Thomas RC	12.00	3.60
❑ 95 David Terrell RC	8.00	2.40
❑ 96 Chad Johnson RC	15.00	4.50
❑ 97 Justin Smith RC	8.00	2.40
❑ 98 Rudi Johnson RC	15.00	4.50
❑ 99 T.J. Houshmandzadeh RC	8.00	2.40
❑ 100 Brandon Spoon RC	8.00	2.40
❑ 101 Nate Clements RC	8.00	2.40
❑ 102 Travis Henry RC	10.00	3.00
❑ 103 Kevin Kasper RC	8.00	2.40
❑ 104 Willie Middlebrooks RC	5.00	1.50
❑ 105 Gerard Warren RC	8.00	2.40
❑ 106 James Jackson RC	8.00	2.40
❑ 107 Quincy Morgan RC	8.00	2.40
❑ 108 Bobby Newcombe RC	5.00	1.50
❑ 109 Arnold Jackson RC	5.00	1.50
❑ 110 Carlos Polk RC	3.00	.90
❑ 111 Drew Brees RC	15.00	4.50
❑ 112 LaDainian Tomlinson RC	25.00	7.50
❑ 113 Tay Cody RC	3.00	.90
❑ 114 Zeke Moreno RC	8.00	2.40
❑ 115 Snoop Minnis RC	5.00	1.50
❑ 116 George Layne RC	5.00	1.50
❑ 117 Derrick Blaylock RC	8.00	2.40
❑ 118 Reggie Wayne RC	12.00	3.60
❑ 119 Tony Dixon RC	5.00	1.50
❑ 120 Quincy Carter RC	8.00	2.40
❑ 121 Chris Chambers RC	10.00	3.00
❑ 122 Jamar Fletcher RC	5.00	1.50
❑ 123 Josh Heupel RC	8.00	2.40
❑ 124 Travis Minor RC	5.00	1.50
❑ 125 A.J. Feeley RC	8.00	2.40
❑ 126 Correll Buckhalter RC	10.00	3.00
❑ 127 Freddie Mitchell RC	8.00	2.40
❑ 128 Alge Crumpler RC	10.00	3.00
❑ 129 Michael Vick RC	50.00	15.00
❑ 130 Vinny Sutherland RC	5.00	1.50
❑ 131 Marcus Stroud RC	8.00	2.40
❑ 132 Mike McMahon RC	8.00	2.40
❑ 133 Scotty Anderson RC	5.00	1.50
❑ 134 Shaun Rogers RC	8.00	2.40
❑ 135 Jesse Palmer RC	8.00	2.40
❑ 136 Will Allen RC	5.00	1.50
❑ 137 LaMont Jordan RC	10.00	3.00
❑ 138 Santana Moss RC	12.00	3.60
❑ 139 Reggie White RC	5.00	1.50
❑ 140 Jamal Reynolds RC	8.00	2.40
❑ 141 Robert Ferguson RC	8.00	2.40

❑ 142 Torrance Marshall RC 8.00 2.40
❑ 143 Chris Weinke RC 8.00 2.40
❑ 144 Dan Morgan RC 8.00 2.40
❑ 145 Steve Smith RC 10.00 3.00
❑ 146 Dee Brown RC 8.00 2.40
❑ 147 Arther Love RC 3.00 .90
❑ 148 Hakim Akbar RC 3.00 .90
❑ 149 Jabari Holloway RC 5.00 1.50
❑ 150 Derek Combs RC 5.00 1.50
❑ 151 Derrick Gibson RC 5.00 1.50
❑ 152 Ken-Yon Rambo RC 5.00 1.50
❑ 153 Marques Tuiasosopo RC 8.00 2.40
❑ 154 Adam Archuleta RC 8.00 2.40
❑ 155 Tommy Polley RC 8.00 2.40
❑ 156 Brian Allen RC 3.00 .90
❑ 157 Milton Wynn RC 5.00 1.50
❑ 158 Francis St.Paul RC 5.00 1.50
❑ 159 Edgerton Hartwell RC 3.00 .90
❑ 160 Gary Baxter RC 5.00 1.50
❑ 161 Todd Heap RC 8.00 2.40
❑ 162 Chris Barnes RC 5.00 1.50
❑ 163 Fred Smoot RC 8.00 2.40
❑ 164 Rod Gardner RC 8.00 2.40
❑ 165 Sage Rosenfels RC 8.00 2.40
❑ 166 Damerien McCants RC 5.00 1.50
❑ 167 Deuce McAllister RC 15.00 4.50
❑ 168 Moran Norris RC 3.00 .90
❑ 169 Sedrick Hodge RC 3.00 .90
❑ 170 Alex Bannister RC 5.00 1.50
❑ 171 Heath Evans RC 5.00 1.50
❑ 172 Josh Booty RC 8.00 2.40
❑ 173 Ken Lucas RC 5.00 1.50
❑ 174 Koren Robinson RC 10.00 3.00
❑ 175 Chris Taylor RC 5.00 1.50
❑ 176 Andre Dyson RC 3.00 .90
❑ 177 Dan Alexander RC 8.00 2.40
❑ 178 Justin McCareins RC 8.00 2.40
❑ 179 Eddie Berlin RC 5.00 1.50
❑ 180 Michael Bennett RC 15.00 4.50

2001 Upper Deck Legends Autographs

	Nm-Mt	Ex-Mt
❑ AM Archie Manning	40.00	12.00
❑ AR Andre Reed	15.00	4.50
❑ BS1 Barry Sanders	100.00	30.00
❑ BS2 Bart Starr	120.00	36.00
❑ BU Brian Urlacher	50.00	15.00
❑ CM Cade McNown SP/50		
❑ CT Charley Taylor	25.00	7.50
❑ DB Dick Butkus	60.00	18.00
❑ DC Daunte Culpepper SP/50	150.00	45.00
❑ DF1 Dan Fouts	40.00	12.00
❑ DF2 Doug Flutie SP/50	40.00	12.00
❑ DM Dan Marino	175.00	52.50
❑ ED Eric Dickerson	40.00	12.00
❑ EJ Ed Too Tall Jones		
❑ FH Franco Harris	50.00	15.00
❑ FT Fran Tarkenton	50.00	15.00
❑ GS Gale Sayers	50.00	15.00
❑ HC Harold Carmichael	15.00	4.50
❑ JB1 Jeff Blake	15.00	4.50
❑ JB2 Jim Brown SP/50	175.00	52.50
❑ JE John Elway	120.00	36.00
❑ JG1 Jeff Garcia SP/50	60.00	18.00
❑ JG2 Jeff George SP/50	40.00	12.00
❑ JK Jim Kelly SP/100 EXCH		
❑ JM Joe Montana	120.00	36.00
❑ JN Joe Namath	100.00	30.00
❑ JP1 Jake Plummer SP/50	40.00	12.00
❑ JP2 Jim Plunkett	25.00	7.50
❑ JR John Riggins	50.00	15.00
❑ JT Joe Theismann	50.00	15.00
❑ JU Johnny Unitas	200.00	60.00
❑ JY Jack Youngblood	25.00	7.50
❑ KS Ken Stabler	60.00	18.00
❑ KW1 Kellen Winslow	40.00	12.00
❑ KW2 Kurt Warner	40.00	12.00
❑ LA Lance Alworth SP/100	60.00	18.00
❑ LT Lawrence Taylor SP/100	100.00	30.00
❑ MA Marcus Allen	40.00	12.00
❑ PH Paul Hornung	50.00	15.00
❑ PM Peyton Manning	120.00	36.00
❑ RM Randy Moss SP/50	120.00	36.00
❑ RS Roger Staubach	80.00	24.00
❑ RW Ricky Williams SP/50	100.00	30.00
❑ SY Steve Young SP/100 EXCH	100.00	30.00
❑ TA Troy Aikman	80.00	24.00
❑ TB1 Terry Bradshaw	80.00	24.00
❑ TB2 Tim Brown	40.00	12.00
❑ TD Tony Dorsett SP/100	50.00	15.00
❑ TT Thurman Thomas	40.00	12.00
❑ VT Vinny Testaverde SP/50 EXCH		
❑ WC Wayne Chrebet	15.00	4.50
❑ WM Warren Moon	40.00	12.00

2001 Upper Deck Legends Legendary Cuts

	Nm-Mt	Ex-Mt
CARDS SER.#'d UNDER 11 NOT PRICED		
❑ LCBL Bobby Layne/10		
❑ LCBN Bronko Nagurski/28	400.00	120.00
❑ LCEN Ernie Nevers/63	200.00	60.00
❑ LCET Emlen Tunnell/22	200.00	60.00
❑ LCGH George Halas/113	450.00	135.00
❑ LCJT Jim Thorpe/1		
❑ LCMM Marion Motley/6		
❑ LCPR Pete Rozelle/3		
❑ LCRB Red Badgro		
❑ LCRG Red Grange/10		
❑ LCRN Ray Nitschke/10		
❑ LCSL Sid Luckman/9		
❑ LCTF Tom Fears/6		
❑ LCTL Tom Landry/8		
❑ LCVB Norm Van Brocklin/3		
❑ LCVL Vince Lombardi/5		
❑ LCWE Weeb Ewbank/10		

2001 Upper Deck Legends Memorable Materials

	Nm-Mt	Ex-Mt
❑ MMBS Barry Sanders	30.00	9.00
❑ MMCB Charlie Batch	10.00	3.00
❑ MMDB Drew Bledsoe	20.00	6.00
❑ MMDF Doug Flutie	15.00	4.50
❑ MMDM Dan Marino	40.00	12.00
❑ MMED Eric Dickerson SP/150	15.00	4.50
❑ MMIB Isaac Bruce	15.00	4.50
❑ MMJE John Elway	40.00	12.00
❑ MMMB Mark Brunell	15.00	4.50
❑ MMMF Marshall Faulk	30.00	9.00
❑ MMSM Steve McNair	15.00	4.50
❑ MMWP Walter Payton SP/150	100.00	30.00

2004 Upper Deck Legends

	Nm-Mt	Ex-Mt
COMP.SET w/o SP's (90)	20.00	6.00
91-110 LEGENDS/1250 ODDS 1:24		
111-190 ROOKIE/650 ODDS 1:12		
❑ 1 Josh McCown	.50	.15
❑ 2 Emmitt Smith	1.50	.45
❑ 3 Michael Vick	1.50	.45
❑ 4 Peerless Price	.50	.15
❑ 5 Ray Lewis	.75	.23
❑ 6 Kyle Boller	.75	.23
❑ 7 Deion Sanders	.75	.23
❑ 8 Drew Bledsoe	.75	.23
❑ 9 Travis Henry	.50	.15
❑ 10 Eric Moulds	.50	.15
❑ 11 Steve Smith	.50	.15
❑ 12 Stephen Davis	.50	.15
❑ 13 Jake Delhomme	.75	.23
❑ 14 Rex Grossman	.75	.23
❑ 15 Brian Urlacher	1.00	.30
❑ 16 Thomas Jones	.50	.15
❑ 17 Chad Johnson	.50	.15
❑ 18 Rudi Johnson	.50	.15
❑ 19 Carson Palmer	1.00	.30
❑ 20 William Green	.50	.15
❑ 21 Andre Davis	.30	.09
❑ 22 Jeff Garcia	.75	.23
❑ 23 Roy Williams S	.50	.15
❑ 24 Eddie George	.50	.15
❑ 25 Keyshawn Johnson	.50	.15
❑ 26 Reuben Droughns	.50	.15
❑ 27 Jake Plummer	.50	.15
❑ 28 Champ Bailey	.50	.15
❑ 29 Charles Rogers	.50	.15
❑ 30 Joey Harrington	.75	.23
❑ 31 Ahman Green	.75	.23
❑ 32 Brett Favre	2.00	.60
❑ 33 Javon Walker	.50	.15
❑ 34 David Carr	.75	.23
❑ 35 Domanick Davis	.75	.23
❑ 36 Andre Johnson	.75	.23
❑ 37 Marvin Harrison	.75	.23
❑ 38 Edgerrin James	.75	.23
❑ 39 Peyton Manning	1.25	.35
❑ 40 Byron Leftwich	1.25	.35
❑ 41 Fred Taylor	.50	.15
❑ 42 Trent Green	.50	.15
❑ 43 Tony Gonzalez	.50	.15
❑ 44 Priest Holmes	1.00	.30
❑ 45 Zach Thomas	.75	.23

❑ 46 Chris Chambers .50 .15
❑ 47 Jay Fiedler .30 .09
❑ 48 Daunte Culpepper .75 .23
❑ 49 Randy Moss 1.00 .30
❑ 50 Onterrio Smith .50 .15
❑ 51 Tom Brady 1.25 .35
❑ 52 Deion Branch .75 .23
❑ 53 Corey Dillon .50 .15
❑ 54 Deuce McAllister .75 .23
❑ 55 Aaron Brooks .50 .15
❑ 56 Joe Horn .50 .15
❑ 57 Tiki Barber .50 .15
❑ 58 Kurt Warner .75 .23
❑ 59 Jeremy Shockey .75 .23
❑ 60 Chad Pennington 1.00 .30
❑ 61 Santana Moss .50 .15
❑ 62 Curtis Martin .75 .23
❑ 63 Kerry Collins .50 .15
❑ 64 Jerry Rice 1.50 .45
❑ 65 Jerry Porter .50 .15
❑ 66 Terrell Owens .75 .23
❑ 67 Jevon Kearse .50 .15
❑ 68 Donovan McNabb 1.00 .30
❑ 69 Hines Ward .75 .23
❑ 70 Plaxico Burress .50 .15
❑ 71 Duce Staley .50 .15
❑ 72 Drew Brees .75 .23
❑ 73 LaDainian Tomlinson .75 .23
❑ 74 Tim Rattay .50 .15
❑ 75 Brandon Lloyd .50 .15
❑ 76 Kevan Barlow .50 .15
❑ 77 Shaun Alexander .75 .23
❑ 78 Koren Robinson .50 .15
❑ 79 Matt Hasselbeck .50 .15
❑ 80 Marshall Faulk .75 .23
❑ 81 Torry Holt .75 .23
❑ 82 Marc Bulger .75 .23
❑ 83 Brian Griese .50 .15
❑ 84 Derrick Brooks .50 .15
❑ 85 Steve McNair .75 .23
❑ 86 Derrick Mason .50 .15
❑ 87 Chris Brown .75 .23
❑ 88 Mark Brunell .50 .15
❑ 89 Laveranues Coles .50 .15
❑ 90 Clinton Portis .75 .23
❑ 91 Dick Butkus 8.00 2.40
❑ 92 Gale Sayers 6.00 1.80
❑ 93 Mike Ditka 5.00 1.50
❑ 94 Jim Brown 8.00 2.40
❑ 95 Roger Staubach 8.00 2.40
❑ 96 Troy Aikman 6.00 1.80
❑ 97 John Elway 8.00 2.40
❑ 98 Barry Sanders 8.00 2.40
❑ 99 Bart Starr 10.00 3.00
❑ 100 Paul Hornung 5.00 1.50
❑ 101 Len Dawson 5.00 1.50
❑ 102 Dan Marino 10.00 3.00
❑ 103 Fran Tarkenton 6.00 1.80
❑ 104 Archie Manning 5.00 1.50
❑ 105 Joe Namath 8.00 2.40
❑ 106 Ken Stabler 6.00 1.80
❑ 107 Lynn Swann 6.00 1.80
❑ 108 Terry Bradshaw 8.00 2.40
❑ 109 Joe Montana 12.00 3.60
❑ 110 Joe Theismann 5.00 1.50
❑ 111 Bernard Berrian RC 5.00 1.50
❑ 112 Ben Hartsock RC 5.00 1.50
❑ 113 Karlos Dansby RC 5.00 1.50
❑ 114 Thomas Tapeh RC 4.00 1.20
❑ 115 Keary Colbert RC 6.00 1.80
❑ 116 Ben Troupe RC 5.00 1.50
❑ 117 Jonathan Vilma RC 5.00 1.50
❑ 118 Jamaar Taylor RC 5.00 1.50
❑ 119 Ben Roethlisberger RC 50.00 15.00
❑ 120 Samie Parker RC 5.00 1.50
❑ 121 Dunta Robinson RC 5.00 1.50
❑ 122 Dontarrious Thomas RC 5.00 1.50
❑ 123 Adimchinobe Echemandu RC 4.001.20
❑ 124 Darius Watts RC 6.00 1.80
❑ 125 Ben Watson RC 5.00 1.50
❑ 126 Terry Johnson RC 4.00 1.20
❑ 127 D.J. Hackett RC 4.00 1.20
❑ 128 Devery Henderson RC 4.00 1.20
❑ 129 Kellen Winslow Jr. RC 12.00 3.60
❑ 130 Travis LaBoy RC 5.00 1.50
❑ 131 Maurice Mann RC 4.00 1.20
❑ 132 Rashaun Woods RC 6.00 1.80
❑ 133 Michael Turner RC 4.00 1.20
❑ 134 Junior Siavii RC 5.00 1.50
❑ 135 Johnnie Morant RC 5.00 1.50
❑ 136 Larry Fitzgerald RC 15.00 4.50
❑ 137 Kevin Jones RC 15.00 4.50
❑ 138 Will Smith RC 5.00 1.50
❑ 139 Robert Gallery RC 8.00 2.40
❑ 140 Michael Jenkins RC 5.00 1.50
❑ 141 Cedric Cobbs RC 5.00 1.50
❑ 142 Igor Olshansky RC 5.00 1.50
❑ 143 Josh Harris RC 5.00 1.50
❑ 144 Michael Clayton RC 12.00 3.60
❑ 145 Mewelde Moore RC 6.00 1.80
❑ 146 Jason Babin RC 5.00 1.50
❑ 147 Cody Pickett RC 5.00 1.50
❑ 148 Lee Evans RC 8.00 2.40
❑ 149 Greg Jones RC 5.00 1.50
❑ 150 Marcus Tubbs RC 5.00 1.50
❑ 151 Craig Krenzel RC 5.00 1.50
❑ 152 Roy Williams RC 15.00 4.50
❑ 153 Tatum Bell RC 8.00 2.40
❑ 154 Kenechi Udeze RC 5.00 1.50
❑ 155 Shawn Andrews RC 5.00 1.50
❑ 156 Reggie Williams RC 6.00 1.80
❑ 157 Julius Jones RC 20.00 6.00
❑ 158 Vince Wilfork RC 6.00 1.80
❑ 159 Vernon Carey RC 4.00 1.20
❑ 160 Eli Manning RC 25.00 7.50
❑ 161 Devard Darling RC 5.00 1.50
❑ 162 Sean Taylor RC 6.00 1.80
❑ 163 Teddy Lehman RC 5.00 1.50
❑ 164 Jammal Lord RC 5.00 1.50
❑ 165 J.P. Losman RC 12.00 3.60
❑ 166 Jerricho Cotchery RC 5.00 1.50
❑ 167 Ahmad Carroll RC 6.00 1.80
❑ 168 Michael Boulware RC 5.00 1.50
❑ 169 Quincy Wilson RC 4.00 1.20
❑ 170 Derrick Hamilton RC 4.00 1.20
❑ 171 Kris Wilson RC 5.00 1.50
❑ 172 D.J. Williams RC 6.00 1.80
❑ 173 P.K. Sam RC 4.00 1.20
❑ 174 Matt Schaub RC 8.00 2.40
❑ 175 Ernest Wilford RC 5.00 1.50
❑ 176 Chris Gamble RC 6.00 1.80
❑ 177 Courtney Watson RC 5.00 1.50
❑ 178 Drew Henson RC 12.00 3.60
❑ 179 Chris Perry RC 10.00 3.00
❑ 180 Tommie Harris RC 6.00 1.80
❑ 181 Marquis Cooper RC 4.00 1.20
❑ 182 Philip Rivers RC 15.00 4.50
❑ 183 Carlos Francis RC 4.00 1.20
❑ 184 DeAngelo Hall RC 6.00 1.80
❑ 185 Daryl Smith RC 5.00 1.50
❑ 186 Troy Fleming RC 4.00 1.20
❑ 187 Luke McCown RC 5.00 1.50
❑ 188 Steven Jackson RC 15.00 4.50
❑ 189 Ricardo Colclough RC 5.00 1.50
❑ 190 Gilbert Gardner RC 4.00 1.20

2004 Upper Deck Legends Gold

Nm-Mt Ex-Mt

*GOLD STARS: 8X TO 20X BASE CARD HI
*GOLD LEGENDS: 1.5X TO 4X
*GOLD ROOKIES: 1.5X TO 4X
GOLD/25 STATED ODDS 1:192

2004 Upper Deck Legends Future Legends Jersey

Nm-Mt Ex-Mt

STATED ODDS 1:24

❑ FLBR Ben Roethlisberger 50.00 15.00
❑ FLCP Chris Perry 10.00 3.00
❑ FLEM Eli Manning 25.00 7.50
❑ FLGJ Greg Jones 6.00 1.80
❑ FLJJ Julius Jones 20.00 6.00
❑ FLJP J.P. Losman 12.00 3.60
❑ FLKJ Kevin Jones 15.00 4.50
❑ FLKW Kellen Winslow Jr. 12.00 3.60
❑ FLLE Lee Evans 8.00 2.40
❑ FLLF Larry Fitzgerald 15.00 4.50
❑ FLMC Michael Clayton 12.00 3.60

❑ FLMJ Michael Jenkins 8.00 2.40
❑ FLPR Philip Rivers 15.00 4.50
❑ FLRE Reggie Williams 8.00 2.40
❑ FLRG Robert Gallery 8.00 2.40
❑ FLRW Roy Williams WR 15.00 4.50
❑ FLSJ Steven Jackson 15.00 4.50
❑ FLTB Tatum Bell 8.00 2.40

2004 Upper Deck Legends Future Legends Throwback Jersey

Nm-Mt Ex-Mt

STATED ODDS 1:192

❑ FLTBB Bernard Berrian 12.00 3.60
❑ FLTBR Ben Roethlisberger 100.00 30.00
❑ FLTBT Ben Troupe 12.00 3.60
❑ FLTBW Ben Watson 10.00 3.00
❑ FLTCC Cedric Cobbs 12.00 3.60
❑ FLTCP Chris Perry 20.00 6.00
❑ FLTDE Devery Henderson 10.00 3.00
❑ FLTDH DeAngelo Hall 12.00 3.60
❑ FLTDW Darius Watts 12.00 3.60
❑ FLTEM Eli Manning 50.00 15.00
❑ FLTGJ Greg Jones 10.00 3.00
❑ FLTHA Derrick Hamilton 10.00 3.00
❑ FLTJJ Julius Jones 40.00 12.00
❑ FLTJP J.P. Losman 25.00 7.50
❑ FLTKC Keary Colbert 12.00 3.60
❑ FLTKJ Kevin Jones 30.00 9.00
❑ FLTKW Kellen Winslow Jr. 25.00 7.50
❑ FLTLE Lee Evans 15.00 4.50
❑ FLTLF Larry Fitzgerald 30.00 9.00
❑ FLTLM Luke McCown 12.00 3.60
❑ FLTMC Michael Clayton 25.00 7.50
❑ FLTMJ Michael Jenkins 12.00 3.60
❑ FLTMS Matt Schaub 15.00 4.50
❑ FLTPR Philip Rivers 30.00 9.00
❑ FLTRA Rashaun Woods 15.00 4.50
❑ FLTRE Reggie Williams 15.00 4.50
❑ FLTRG Robert Gallery 12.00 3.60
❑ FLTRW Roy Williams WR 30.00 9.00
❑ FLTSJ Steven Jackson 30.00 9.00
❑ FLTTB Tatum Bell 15.00 4.50

2004 Upper Deck Legends Immortal Inscriptions

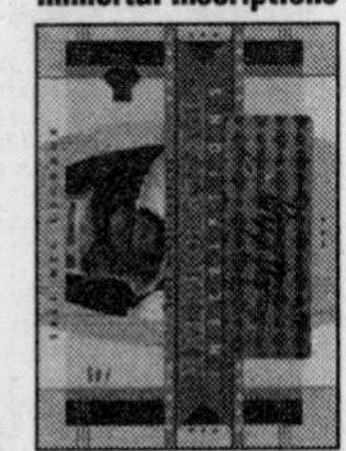

Nm-Mt Ex-Mt

STATED PRINT RUN 45 SER.#'d SETS

❑ IIAM Archie Manning 50.00 15.00

Card	Nm-Mt	Ex-Mt
❑ IIBS Barry Sanders	175.00	52.50
❑ IIDB Dick Butkus EXCH	100.00	30.00
❑ IIDM Dan Marino	200.00	60.00
❑ IIFH Franco Harris	60.00	18.00
❑ IIFT Fran Tarkenton	60.00	18.00
❑ IIGS Gale Sayers	100.00	30.00
❑ IIHL Howie Long	100.00	30.00
❑ IIJB Jim Brown EXCH	100.00	30.00
❑ IIJE John Elway	200.00	60.00
❑ IIJM Joe Montana	250.00	75.00
❑ IIJN Joe Namath	120.00	36.00
❑ IIJT Joe Theismann	50.00	15.00
❑ IIKS Ken Stabler	80.00	24.00
❑ IIKW Kellen Winslow Sr.	40.00	12.00
❑ IIPH Paul Hornung	60.00	18.00
❑ IIRS Roger Staubach	100.00	30.00
❑ IITA Troy Aikman	100.00	30.00
❑ IITB Terry Bradshaw EXCH	120.00	36.00

2004 Upper Deck Legends Legendary Jerseys

STATED PRINT RUN 99; ODDS 1:384

Card	Nm-Mt	Ex-Mt
❑ LJAM Archie Manning	25.00	7.50
❑ LJBS Barry Sanders	50.00	15.00
❑ LJDM Dan Marino	80.00	24.00
❑ LJFT Fran Tarkenton	30.00	9.00
❑ LJGS Gale Sayers	30.00	9.00
❑ LJHL Howie Long	40.00	12.00
❑ LJJE John Elway	50.00	15.00
❑ LJJM Joe Montana	80.00	24.00
❑ LJJN Joe Namath	50.00	15.00
❑ LJJT Joe Theismann	25.00	7.50
❑ LJJU Johnny Unitas	60.00	18.00
❑ LJKS Ken Stabler	30.00	9.00
❑ LJKW Kellen Winslow Sr.	20.00	6.00
❑ LJLD Len Dawson	25.00	7.50
❑ LJLS Lynn Swann	40.00	12.00
❑ LJON Ozzie Newsome	25.00	7.50
❑ LJRS Roger Staubach	40.00	12.00
❑ LJTA Troy Aikman	30.00	9.00
❑ LJTB Terry Bradshaw	40.00	12.00
❑ LJWP Walter Payton	80.00	24.00

2004 Upper Deck Legends Legendary Lines of Defense

STATED PRINT RUN 75 SER.#'d SETS
CARD NUMBERS HAVE LLD PREFIX

Card	Nm-Mt	Ex-Mt
❑ HGL Jack Ham	250.00	75.00
Joe Greene		
Jack Lambert		
❑ JGW Tom Jackson	60.00	18.00
Randy Gradishar		
Louis Wright		
❑ PEM Alan Page	150.00	45.00
Carl Eller		
Jim Marshall		
❑ SHD Mike Singletary	200.00	60.00
Dan Hampton		
Richard Dent		
❑ YYJ Jim Youngblood	80.00	24.00
Jack Youngblood		
Deacon Jones		

2004 Upper Deck Legends Legendary Signatures

STATED ODDS 1:8
EXCH EXPIRATION: 12/20/2007

Card	Nm-Mt	Ex-Mt
❑ LSAK Alex Karras	25.00	7.50
❑ LSAM Archie Manning SP	200.00	60.00
❑ LSAN Andy Russell	25.00	7.50
❑ LSAP Alan Page	25.00	7.50
❑ LSBB Bill Bergey	20.00	6.00
❑ LSBE Raymond Berry	25.00	7.50
❑ LSBG Bob Griese	30.00	9.00
❑ LSBI Billy Sims	20.00	6.00
❑ LSBJ Bert Jones	20.00	6.00
❑ LSBK Billy Kilmer	25.00	7.50
❑ LSBL Bob Lilly	25.00	7.50
❑ LSBS Barry Sanders SP	450.00	135.00
❑ LSBY Billy Johnson	15.00	4.50
❑ LSCB Cliff Branch	20.00	6.00
❑ LSCE Carl Eller	25.00	7.50
❑ LSCF Chuck Foreman	20.00	6.00
❑ LSCJ Charlie Joiner	15.00	4.50
❑ LSCM Craig Morton	20.00	6.00
❑ LSCT Charley Taylor	15.00	4.50
❑ LSDA Doug Atkins	20.00	6.00
❑ LSDB Dick Butkus SP EXCH	300.00	90.00
❑ LSDC Dave Casper	25.00	7.50
❑ LSDF Dan Fouts SP	80.00	24.00
❑ LSDH Dan Hampton	40.00	12.00
❑ LSDI0 Dick Anderson SP	30.00	9.00
❑ LSDJ Deacon Jones SP	50.00	15.00
❑ LSDL Daryle Lamonica	20.00	6.00
❑ LSDM Dan Marino SP	400.00	120.00
❑ LSDO Don Maynard	20.00	6.00
❑ LSDP Drew Pearson	25.00	7.50
❑ LSEC Earl Campbell SP	100.00	30.00
❑ LSED Eric Dickerson SP	40.00	12.00
❑ LSEJ Ed Too Tall Jones	30.00	9.00
❑ LSFG Frank Gifford SP	80.00	24.00
❑ LSFH Franco Harris SP		
❑ LSFT Fran Tarkenton SP	80.00	24.00
❑ LSGA Roman Gabriel	30.00	9.00
❑ LSGS Gale Sayers SP	300.00	90.00
❑ LSHA Chris Hanburger	20.00	6.00
❑ LSHC Harold Carmichael	20.00	6.00
❑ LSHL Howie Long SP	200.00	60.00
❑ LSHN John Hannah	20.00	6.00
❑ LSHT Jim Hart	15.00	4.50
❑ LSIC Isaac Curtis	15.00	4.50
❑ LSJB Jim Brown SP	250.00	75.00
❑ LSJE John Elway SP	600.00	180.00
❑ LSJG Joe Greene SP	300.00	90.00
❑ LSJH Jack Ham SP	200.00	60.00
❑ LSJI Jim Marshall	25.00	7.50
❑ LSJK Jerry Kramer	40.00	12.00
❑ LSJL Jack Lambert SP	80.00	24.00
❑ LSJM Joe Montana SP	350.00	105.00
❑ LSJN Joe Namath SP		
❑ LSJO John Taylor	20.00	6.00
❑ LSJP Jim Plunkett	25.00	7.50
❑ LSJT Joe Theismann SP	75.00	22.00
❑ LSJY Jim Youngblood	15.00	4.50
❑ LSKA Ken Anderson	25.00	7.50
❑ LSKI Jim Kiick	20.00	6.00
❑ LSKS Ken Stabler SP	200.00	60.00
❑ LSKW Kellen Winslow Sr. SP	50.00	15.00
❑ LSLC L.C. Greenwood SP	60.00	18.00
❑ LSLD Len Dawson SP	75.00	22.00
❑ LSLT Lawrence Taylor SP		
❑ LSLW Louis Wright	15.00	4.50
❑ LSMA Mark Duper	20.00	6.00
❑ LSMC Mark Clayton	20.00	6.00
❑ LSMD Mike Ditka SP EXCH	200.00	60.00
❑ LSMF Manny Fernandez	15.00	4.50
❑ LSMI Mike Curtis	15.00	4.50
❑ LSMM Mercury Morris	15.00	4.50
❑ LSMR Mel Renfro	20.00	6.00
❑ LSMS Mike Singletary SP	125.00	38.00
❑ LSMU Anthony Munoz	20.00	6.00
❑ LSOM Ollie Matson EXCH	75.00	22.00
❑ LSON Ozzie Newsome	25.00	7.50
❑ LSPH Paul Hornung SP	100.00	30.00
❑ LSPK Paul Krause	20.00	6.00
❑ LSRA Ray Guy	25.00	7.50
❑ LSRB Robert Brazile	15.00	4.50
❑ LSRC Roger Craig	20.00	6.00
❑ LSRD Richard Dent	30.00	9.00
❑ LSRG Randy Gradishar	15.00	4.50
❑ LSRJ Ron Jaworski	25.00	7.50
❑ LSRO Roger Wehrli	15.00	4.50
❑ LSRS Roger Staubach SP		
❑ LSRW Randy White	30.00	9.00
❑ LSSB Steve Bartkowski	15.00	4.50
❑ LSSH Sam Huff	25.00	7.50
❑ LSSJ Sonny Jurgensen SP	40.00	12.00
❑ LSSS Steve Spurrier SP	50.00	15.00
❑ LSTA Troy Aikman SP	150.00	45.00
❑ LSTB Terry Bradshaw/20 * EXCH		
❑ LSTD Tony Dorsett/45 * EXCH	150.00	45.00
❑ LSVG Vencie Glenn	15.00	4.50
❑ LSWB Willie Brown	20.00	6.00
❑ LSWM Wilbert Montgomery	25.00	7.50
❑ LSYO Jack Youngblood	20.00	6.00

2004 Upper Deck Legends Link to the Future

EXCH EXPIRATION: 12/21/2007

Card	Nm-Mt	Ex-Mt
❑ LFBL Drew Bledsoe/50	80.00	24.00
J.P. Losman		
❑ LFBM Kyle Boller/50	30.00	9.00
Luke McCown		
❑ LFBR Drew Bledsoe/25	100.00	30.00
Philip Rivers		
❑ LFCC Chris Chambers/25	50.00	15.00
Keary Colbert		
❑ LFDK Deuce McAllister/25	100.00	30.00
Kevin Jones		

❑ LFGB Ahman Green/50 50.00 15.00
Tatum Bell
❑ LFGC Joey Galloway/50 40.00 12.00
Michael Clayton
❑ LFGW Tony Gonzalez/50 50.00 15.00
Kellen Winslow Jr.
❑ LFHE Dante Hall/50 40.00 12.00
Lee Evans
❑ LFHH Joe Horn/50 EXCH 30.00 9.00
Devery Henderson
❑ LFHT Todd Heap/50 30.00 9.00
Ben Troupe
❑ LFJP Rudi Johnson/50
Chris Perry
❑ LFJW Chad Johnson/50 40.00 12.00
Reggie Williams
❑ LFMJ Deuce McAllister/25 100.00 30.00
Steven Jackson
❑ LFMM Peyton Manning/25 300.00 90.00
Eli Manning
❑ LFMW Derrick Mason/50 60.00 18.00
Roy Williams WR
❑ LFPS Chad Pennington/50 50.00 15.00
Matt Schaub
❑ LFRJ Roy Williams S/50 125.00 38.00
Julius Jones
❑ LFTE Tom Brady/25 300.00 90.00
Eli Manning
❑ LFTJ LaDainian Tomlinson/25 175.0052.50
Julius Jones
❑ LFTV Zach Thomas/50
Jonathan Vilma
❑ LFVR Michael Vick/25 400.00 120.00
Ben Roethlisberger
❑ LFWJ Brian Westbrook/50 40.00 12.00
Greg Jones

2004 Upper Deck Legends Link to the Past

	Nm-Mt	Ex-Mt

EXCH EXPIRATION: 12/21/2007
❑ LPBM Tom Brady/25 350.00 105.00
Joe Montana
❑ LPBS Mark Brunell/50 60.00 18.00
Ken Stabler
❑ LPCC Chris Chambers/50 50.00 15.00
Mark Clayton
❑ LPCT Daunte Culpepper/50 EXCH 80.00 24.00
Fran Tarkenton
❑ LPDC Domanick Davis/50 50.00 15.00
Earl Campbell
❑ LPDP Dan Marino/25 400.00 120.00
Peyton Manning
❑ LPFT Larry Fitzgerald/25 60.00 18.00
Charley Taylor
❑ LPGT Rex Grossman/50 50.00 15.00
Joe Theismann
❑ LPHH Tommie Harris/50 50.00 15.00
Dan Hampton
❑ LPHS Drew Henson/25 120.00 36.00
Roger Staubach
❑ LPJD Julius Jones/50 120.00 36.00
Tony Dorsett
❑ LPJE Steven Jackson/50 80.00 24.00
Eric Dickerson
❑ LPJH Greg Jones/50 50.00 15.00
Franco Harris
❑ LPJS Kevin Jones/25 300.00 90.00
Barry Sanders
❑ LPMJ Donovan McNabb/50 100.00 30.00
Ron Jaworski
❑ LPMM Eli Manning/50 175.00 52.50
Archie Manning
❑ LPPA Peyton Manning/25 300.00 90.00
Archie Manning
❑ LPPN Chad Pennington/25 120.00 36.00
Joe Namath
❑ LPRB Ben Roethlisberger/25 EXCH 350.00 105.00
Terry Bradshaw
❑ LPRF Philip Rivers/50 80.00 24.00
Dan Fouts
❑ LPUE Kenechi Udeze/50 40.00 12.00
Carl Eller
❑ LPVA Michael Vick/50 175.00 52.50
Troy Aikman
❑ LPWW Kellen Winslow Jr./50 60.00 18.00
Kellen Winslow Sr.

1999 Upper Deck MVP

	Nm-Mt	Ex-Mt
COMPLETE SET (220)	25.00	11.00
❑ 1 Jake Plummer	.30	.14
❑ 2 Adrian Murrell	.30	.14
❑ 3 Larry Centers	.20	.09
❑ 4 Frank Sanders	.30	.14
❑ 5 Andre Wadsworth	.20	.09
❑ 6 Rob Moore	.30	.14
❑ 7 Simeon Rice	.30	.14
❑ 8 Jamal Anderson	.50	.23
❑ 9 Chris Chandler	.30	.14
❑ 10 Chuck Smith	.20	.09
❑ 11 Terance Mathis	.30	.14
❑ 12 Tim Dwight	.50	.23
❑ 13 Ray Buchanan	.20	.09
❑ 14 O.J. Santiago	.20	.09
❑ 15 Eric Zeier	.30	.14
❑ 16 Priest Holmes	.75	.35
❑ 17 Michael Jackson	.20	.09
❑ 18 Jermaine Lewis	.30	.14
❑ 19 Michael McCrary	.20	.09
❑ 20 Rob Johnson	.30	.14
❑ 21 Antowain Smith	.50	.23
❑ 22 Thurman Thomas	.30	.14
❑ 23 Doug Flutie	.50	.23
❑ 24 Eric Moulds	.50	.23
❑ 25 Bruce Smith	.30	.14
❑ 26 Andre Reed	.30	.14
❑ 27 Fred Lane	.20	.09
❑ 28 Tim Biakabutuka	.30	.14
❑ 29 Rae Carruth	.20	.09
❑ 30 Wesley Walls	.30	.14
❑ 31 Steve Beuerlein	.20	.09
❑ 32 Muhsin Muhammad	.30	.14
❑ 33 Erik Kramer	.20	.09
❑ 34 Edgar Bennett	.20	.09
❑ 35 Curtis Conway	.30	.14
❑ 36 Curtis Enis	.20	.09
❑ 37 Bobby Engram	.30	.14
❑ 38 Alonzo Mayes	.20	.09
❑ 39 Corey Dillon	.50	.23
❑ 40 Jeff Blake	.30	.14
❑ 41 Carl Pickens	.30	.14
❑ 42 Darnay Scott	.20	.09
❑ 43 Tony McGee	.20	.09
❑ 44 Ki-Jana Carter	.20	.09
❑ 45 Ty Detmer	.30	.14
❑ 46 Terry Kirby	.20	.09
❑ 47 Justin Armour	.20	.09
❑ 48 Freddie Solomon	.20	.09
❑ 49 Marquez Pope	.20	.09
❑ 50 Antonio Langham	.20	.09
❑ 51 Troy Aikman	1.00	.45
❑ 52 Emmitt Smith	1.00	.45
❑ 53 Deion Sanders	.50	.23
❑ 54 Rocket Ismail	.30	.14
❑ 55 Michael Irvin	.30	.14
❑ 56 Chris Warren	.20	.09
❑ 57 Greg Ellis	.20	.09
❑ 58 John Elway	1.50	.70
❑ 59 Terrell Davis	.50	.23
❑ 60 Rod Smith	.30	.14
❑ 61 Shannon Sharpe	.30	.14
❑ 62 Ed McCaffrey	.30	.14
❑ 63 John Mobley	.20	.09
❑ 64 Bill Romanowski	.20	.09
❑ 65 Barry Sanders	1.50	.70
❑ 66 Johnnie Morton	.30	.14
❑ 67 Herman Moore	.30	.14
❑ 68 Charlie Batch	.50	.23
❑ 69 Germane Crowell	.20	.09
❑ 70 Robert Porcher	.20	.09
❑ 71 Brett Favre	1.50	.70
❑ 72 Antonio Freeman	.50	.23
❑ 73 Dorsey Levens	.50	.23
❑ 74 Mark Chmura	.30	.14
❑ 75 Vonnie Holliday	.20	.09
❑ 76 Bill Schroeder	.50	.23
❑ 77 Marshall Faulk	.60	.25
❑ 78 Marvin Harrison	.50	.23
❑ 79 Peyton Manning	1.50	.70
❑ 80 Jerome Pathon	.20	.09
❑ 81 E.G. Green	.20	.09
❑ 82 Ellis Johnson	.20	.09
❑ 83 Mark Brunell	.50	.23
❑ 84 Jimmy Smith	.30	.14
❑ 85 Keenan McCardell	.30	.14
❑ 86 Fred Taylor	.50	.23
❑ 87 James Stewart	.30	.14
❑ 88 Kevin Hardy	.20	.09
❑ 89 Elvis Grbac	.30	.14
❑ 90 Andre Rison	.30	.14
❑ 91 Derrick Alexander WR	.30	.14
❑ 92 Tony Gonzalez	.50	.23
❑ 93 Donnell Bennett	.20	.09
❑ 94 Derrick Thomas	.30	.14
❑ 95 Tamarick Vanover	.20	.09
❑ 96 Dan Marino	1.50	.70
❑ 97 Karim Abdul-Jabbar	.30	.14
❑ 98 Zach Thomas	.50	.23
❑ 99 O.J. McDuffie	.30	.14
❑ 100 John Avery	.20	.09
❑ 101 Sam Madison	.20	.09
❑ 102 Randall Cunningham	.50	.23
❑ 103 Cris Carter	.50	.23
❑ 104 Robert Smith	.50	.23
❑ 105 Randy Moss	1.25	.55
❑ 106 Jake Reed	.30	.14
❑ 107 Matthew Hatchette	.20	.09
❑ 108 John Randle	.30	.14
❑ 109 Drew Bledsoe	.60	.25
❑ 110 Terry Glenn	.50	.23
❑ 111 Ben Coates	.30	.14
❑ 112 Ty Law	.30	.14
❑ 113 Tony Simmons	.20	.09
❑ 114 Ted Johnson	.20	.09
❑ 115 Danny Wuerffel	.20	.09
❑ 116 Lamar Smith	.30	.14
❑ 117 Sean Dawkins	.20	.09
❑ 118 Cameron Cleeland	.20	.09
❑ 119 Joe Johnson	.20	.09
❑ 120 Andre Hastings	.20	.09
❑ 121 Kent Graham	.20	.09
❑ 122 Gary Brown	.20	.09
❑ 123 Amani Toomer	.20	.09
❑ 124 Tiki Barber	.30	.14
❑ 125 Ike Hilliard	.20	.09
❑ 126 Jason Sehorn	.20	.09
❑ 127 Vinny Testaverde	.30	.14

128 Curtis Martin	.50	.23
129 Keyshawn Johnson	.50	.23
130 Wayne Chrebet	.30	.14
131 Mo Lewis	.20	.09
132 Steve Atwater	.20	.09
133 Donald Hollas	.20	.09
134 Napoleon Kaufman	.50	.23
135 Tim Brown	.50	.23
136 Darrell Russell	.20	.09
137 Rickey Dudley	.20	.09
138 Charles Woodson	.50	.23
139 Koy Detmer	.20	.09
140 Duce Staley	.50	.23
141 Charlie Garner	.30	.14
142 Doug Pederson	.20	.09
143 Jeff Graham	.20	.09
144 Charles Johnson	.20	.09
145 Kordell Stewart	.30	.14
146 Jerome Bettis	.50	.23
147 Hines Ward	.50	.23
148 Courtney Hawkins	.20	.09
149 Will Blackwell	.20	.09
150 Richard Huntley	.30	.14
151 Levon Kirkland	.20	.09
152 Trent Green	.50	.23
153 Tony Banks	.30	.14
154 Isaac Bruce	.50	.23
155 Eddie Kennison	.30	.14
156 Az-Zahir Hakim	.20	.09
157 Amp Lee	.20	.09
158 Robert Holcombe	.20	.09
159 Ryan Leaf	.50	.23
160 Natrone Means	.30	.14
161 Jim Harbaugh	.30	.14
162 Junior Seau	.50	.23
163 Charlie Jones	.20	.09
164 Rodney Harrison	.20	.09
165 Steve Young	.60	.25
166 Jerry Rice	1.00	.45
167 Garrison Hearst	.30	.14
168 Terrell Owens	.50	.23
169 J.J. Stokes	.30	.14
170 Bryant Young	.20	.09
171 Ricky Watters	.30	.14
172 Joey Galloway	.30	.14
173 Jon Kitna	.50	.23
174 Ahman Green	.50	.23
175 Mike Pritchard	.20	.09
176 Chad Brown	.20	.09
177 Warrick Dunn	.50	.23
178 Trent Dilfer	.30	.14
179 Mike Alstott	.50	.23
180 Reidel Anthony	.30	.14
181 Bert Emanuel	.30	.14
182 Jacquez Green	.20	.09
183 Hardy Nickerson	.20	.09
184 Steve McNair	.50	.23
185 Eddie George	.50	.23
186 Yancey Thigpen	.20	.09
187 Frank Wycheck	.20	.09
188 Kevin Dyson	.30	.14
189 Jackie Harris	.20	.09
190 Blaine Bishop	.20	.09
191 Skip Hicks	.20	.09
192 Michael Westbrook	.30	.14
193 Stephen Alexander	.20	.09
194 Leslie Shepherd	.20	.09
195 Jeff Hostetler	.20	.09
196 Brian Mitchell	.20	.09
197 Dan Wilkinson	.20	.09
198 Terrell Davis CL	.50	.23
199 Troy Aikman CL	.50	.23
200 Tim Couch CL	.50	.23
201 Ricky Williams RC	2.50	1.10
202 Tim Couch RC	1.00	.45
203 Akili Smith RC	.75	.35
204 Daunte Culpepper RC	5.00	2.20
205 Torry Holt RC	3.00	1.35
206 Edgerrin James RC	5.00	2.20
207 David Boston RC	1.00	.45
208 Peerless Price RC	1.50	.70
209 Chris Claiborne RC	.50	.23
210 Champ Bailey RC	1.25	.55
211 Cade McNown RC	.75	.35
212 Jevon Kearse RC	1.50	.70
213 Joe Germaine RC	.75	.35
214 D'Wayne Bates RC	.75	.35
215 Dameane Douglas RC	.50	.23
216 Troy Edwards RC	.75	.35
217 Sedrick Irvin RC	.50	.23
218 Brock Huard RC	1.00	.45
219 Amos Zereoue RC	1.00	.45
220 Donovan McNabb RC	6.00	2.70

1999 Upper Deck MVP ProSign

	Nm-Mt	Ex-Mt
AG Ahman Green	30.00	13.50
AM Adrian Murrell	12.00	5.50
AS Akili Smith	12.00	5.50
AS Antowain Smith	30.00	13.50
BH Brock Huard	20.00	9.00
CB Charlie Batch	12.00	5.50
CC Curtis Conway	20.00	9.00
CM Cade McNown SP	40.00	18.00
DC Daunte Culpepper SP		
DM Donovan McNabb	60.00	27.00
EM Ed McCaffrey	20.00	9.00
EM Eric Moulds	20.00	9.00
FT Fred Taylor	50.00	22.00
GH Greg Hill	12.00	5.50
JA Jamal Anderson	20.00	9.00
JM John Mobley	12.00	5.50
JS Jimmy Smith	20.00	9.00
MB Michael Bishop	20.00	9.00
MF Marshall Faulk	40.00	18.00
MM Muhsin Muhammad	30.00	13.50
PH Priest Holmes	50.00	22.00
RE Robert Edwards	12.00	5.50
RL Ray Lewis	40.00	18.00
RM Randy Moss SP	350.00	160.00
RW Ricky Williams SP	250.00	110.00
RW Ricky Watters	20.00	9.00
SK Shaun King	12.00	5.50
SS Shannon Sharpe	30.00	13.50
TC Tim Couch	20.00	9.00
TD Terrell Davis	40.00	18.00
TG Trent Green	30.00	13.50
TH Torry Holt SP	40.00	18.00
TR Troy Drayton	12.00	5.50
KAJ Karim Abdul-Jabbar	12.00	5.50

2000 Upper Deck MVP

	Nm-Mt	Ex-Mt
COMPLETE SET (218)	25.00	11.00
1 Jake Plummer	.30	.14
2 Michael Pittman	.20	.09
3 Rob Moore	.30	.14
4 David Boston	.50	.23
5 Frank Sanders	.30	.14
6 Aeneas Williams	.20	.09
7 Kwamie Lassiter	.20	.09
8 Tim Dwight	.50	.23
9 Chris Chandler	.30	.14
10 Jamal Anderson	.50	.23
11 Shawn Jefferson	.20	.09
12 Qadry Ismail	.30	.14
13 Jermaine Lewis	.20	.09
14 Rod Woodson	.30	.14
15 Michael McCrary	.20	.09
16 Tony Banks	.30	.14
17 Peter Boulware	.20	.09
18 Shannon Sharpe	.30	.14
19 Peerless Price	.50	.23
20 Rob Johnson	.30	.14
21 Eric Moulds	.50	.23
22 Doug Flutie	.50	.23
23 Muhsin Muhammad	.30	.14
24 Patrick Jeffers	.50	.23
25 Steve Beuerlein	.30	.14
26 Tim Biakabutuka	.30	.14
27 Michael Bates	.20	.09
28 Cade McNown	.20	.09
29 Curtis Enis	.20	.09
30 Marcus Robinson	.50	.23
31 Shane Matthews	.30	.14
32 Bobby Engram	.30	.14
33 Glyn Milburn	.20	.09
34 Akili Smith	.20	.09
35 Corey Dillon	.50	.23
36 Darnay Scott	.30	.14
37 Tremain Mack	.20	.09
38 Tim Couch	.30	.14
39 Kevin Johnson	.50	.23
40 Darrin Chiaverini	.20	.09
41 Jamir Miller	.20	.09
42 Errict Rhett	.30	.14
43 Troy Aikman	1.00	.45
44 Emmitt Smith	1.00	.45
45 Rocket Ismail	.30	.14
46 Jason Tucker	.20	.09
47 Dexter Coakley	.20	.09
48 Joey Galloway	.30	.14
49 Greg Ellis	.20	.09
50 Terrell Davis	.50	.23
51 Olandis Gary	.50	.23
52 Brian Griese	.50	.23
53 Ed McCaffrey	.50	.23
54 Rod Smith	.30	.14
55 Trevor Pryce	.20	.09
56 Charlie Batch	.50	.23
57 Germane Crowell	.20	.09
58 Johnnie Morton	.30	.14
59 Robert Porcher	.20	.09
60 Luther Elliss	.20	.09
61 James Stewart	.30	.14
62 Brett Favre	1.50	.70
63 Antonio Freeman	.50	.23
64 Bill Schroeder	.30	.14
65 Dorsey Levens	.30	.14
66 Peyton Manning	1.25	.55
67 Edgerrin James	.75	.35
68 Marvin Harrison	.50	.23
69 Ken Dilger	.20	.09
70 Terrence Wilkins	.20	.09
71 Mark Brunell	.50	.23
72 Fred Taylor	.50	.23
73 Jimmy Smith	.30	.14
74 Keenan McCardell	.30	.14
75 Carnell Lake	.20	.09
76 Tony Brackens	.20	.09
77 Kevin Hardy	.20	.09
78 Hardy Nickerson	.20	.09
79 Elvis Grbac	.30	.14
80 Tony Gonzalez	.30	.14
81 Derrick Alexander	.30	.14
82 Donnell Bennett	.20	.09
83 James Hasty	.20	.09
84 Jay Fiedler	.50	.23
85 James Johnson	.20	.09

❑ 86 Tony Martin .30 .14
❑ 87 Damon Huard .50 .23
❑ 88 O.J. McDuffie .30 .14
❑ 89 Oronde Gadsden .30 .14
❑ 90 Zach Thomas .50 .23
❑ 91 Sam Madison .20 .09
❑ 92 Jeff George .30 .14
❑ 93 Randy Moss 1.00 .45
❑ 94 Robert Smith .50 .23
❑ 95 Cris Carter .50 .23
❑ 96 Matthew Hatchette .20 .09
❑ 97 Drew Bledsoe .60 .25
❑ 98 Terry Glenn .30 .14
❑ 99 Troy Brown .30 .14
❑ 100 Kevin Faulk .30 .14
❑ 101 Lawyer Milloy .30 .14
❑ 102 Ricky Williams .50 .23
❑ 103 Keith Poole .20 .09
❑ 104 Jake Reed .30 .14
❑ 105 Cam Cleeland .20 .09
❑ 106 Jeff Blake .30 .14
❑ 107 Andrew Glover .20 .09
❑ 108 Kerry Collins .30 .14
❑ 109 Amani Toomer .20 .09
❑ 110 Joe Montgomery .20 .09
❑ 111 Ike Hilliard .30 .14
❑ 112 Michael Strahan .30 .14
❑ 113 Jessie Armstead .20 .09
❑ 114 Ray Lucas .30 .14
❑ 115 Keyshawn Johnson .50 .23
❑ 116 Curtis Martin .50 .23
❑ 117 Vinny Testaverde .30 .14
❑ 118 Wayne Chrebet .30 .14
❑ 119 Dedric Ward .20 .09
❑ 120 Tim Brown .50 .23
❑ 121 Rich Gannon .50 .23
❑ 122 Tyrone Wheatley .30 .14
❑ 123 Napoleon Kaufman .30 .14
❑ 124 Charles Woodson .30 .14
❑ 125 Darrell Russell .20 .09
❑ 126 Duce Staley .50 .23
❑ 127 Donovan McNabb .75 .35
❑ 128 Torrance Small .20 .09
❑ 129 Allen Rossum .20 .09
❑ 130 Brian Dawkins .20 .09
❑ 131 Troy Vincent .20 .09
❑ 132 Troy Edwards .20 .09
❑ 133 Jerome Bettis .50 .23
❑ 134 Hines Ward .50 .23
❑ 135 Kordell Stewart .30 .14
❑ 136 Levon Kirkland .20 .09
❑ 137 Kent Graham .20 .09
❑ 138 Marshall Faulk .60 .25
❑ 139 Kurt Warner 1.00 .45
❑ 140 Torry Holt .50 .23
❑ 141 Isaac Bruce .50 .23
❑ 142 Kevin Carter .20 .09
❑ 143 Az-Zahir Hakim .30 .14
❑ 144 Todd Lyght .20 .09
❑ 145 Jermaine Fazande .20 .09
❑ 146 Curtis Conway .30 .14
❑ 147 Freddie Jones .20 .09
❑ 148 Junior Seau .50 .23
❑ 149 Jeff Graham .20 .09
❑ 150 Ryan Leaf .30 .14
❑ 151 Rodney Harrison .20 .09
❑ 152 Steve Young .60 .25
❑ 153 Jerry Rice 1.00 .45
❑ 154 Charlie Garner .30 .14
❑ 155 Terrell Owens .50 .23
❑ 156 Jeff Garcia .50 .23
❑ 157 Bryant Young .20 .09
❑ 158 Lance Schulters .20 .09
❑ 159 Ricky Watters .30 .14
❑ 160 Jon Kitna .50 .23
❑ 161 Derrick Mayes .30 .14
❑ 162 Sean Dawkins .20 .09
❑ 163 Cortez Kennedy .20 .09
❑ 164 Chad Brown .20 .09
❑ 165 Warrick Dunn .50 .23
❑ 166 Shaun King .20 .09
❑ 167 Mike Alstott .50 .23
❑ 168 Warren Sapp .30 .14
❑ 169 Jacquez Green .20 .09
❑ 170 Derrick Brooks .50 .23
❑ 171 John Lynch .30 .14
❑ 172 Donnie Abraham .20 .09
❑ 173 Eddie George .50 .23
❑ 174 Steve McNair .50 .23
❑ 175 Kevin Dyson .30 .14
❑ 176 Jevon Kearse .50 .23
❑ 177 Yancey Thigpen .20 .09
❑ 178 Frank Wycheck .20 .09
❑ 179 Eddie Robinson .20 .09
❑ 180 Samari Rolle .20 .09
❑ 181 Brad Johnson .50 .23
❑ 182 Stephen Davis .50 .23
❑ 183 Michael Westbrook .30 .14
❑ 184 Albert Connell .20 .09
❑ 185 Brian Mitchell .20 .09
❑ 186 Bruce Smith .30 .14
❑ 187 Stephen Alexander .20 .09
❑ 188 Peter Warrick RC .60 .25
❑ 189C Cutout Card/Arrington 15.00 6.75
❑ 190 Chris Redman RC .50 .23
❑ 191 Courtney Brown RC .60 .25
❑ 192 Brian Urlacher RC 2.50 1.10
❑ 193 Plaxico Burress RC 1.25 .55
❑ 194 Corey Simon RC .60 .25
❑ 195 Bubba Franks RC .60 .25
❑ 196 Deon Grant RC .50 .23
❑ 197 Michael Wiley RC .50 .23
❑ 198 Tim Rattay RC 1.25 .55
❑ 199 Ron Dayne RC .60 .25
❑ 200 Sylvester Morris RC .50 .23
❑ 201 Shaun Alexander RC 1.50 .70
❑ 202 Dez White RC .60 .25
❑ 203 Thomas Jones RC 1.00 .45
❑ 204 Reuben Droughns RC .75 .35
❑ 205 Travis Taylor RC .60 .25
❑ 206 Trevor Gaylor RC .40 .18
❑ 207 Jamal Lewis RC 1.50 .70
❑ 208 Chad Pennington RC 2.50 1.10
❑ 209 J.R. Redmond RC .50 .23
❑ 210 Laveranues Coles RC .75 .35
❑ 211 Travis Prentice RC .50 .23
❑ 212 R.Jay Soward RC .50 .23
❑ 213 Todd Pinkston RC .60 .25
❑ 214 Dennis Northcutt RC .60 .25
❑ 215 Shyrone Stith RC .40 .18
❑ 216 Tee Martin RC .60 .25
❑ 217 Giovanni Carmazzi RC .50 .23
❑ 218 Drew Bledsoe CL .30 .14
❑ 219 Steve Young CL .30 .14
❑ 220A Donovan McNabb CL SP 30.00 13.50
❑ 220B Donovan McNabb CL 30.00 9.00
(SP, embossed on front)

2000 Upper Deck MVP Game Used Souvenirs Autographs

	Nm-Mt	Ex-Mt
❑ ASA Akili Smith	50.00	22.00
❑ BGA Brian Griese	60.00	27.00
❑ BJA Brad Johnson	60.00	27.00
❑ CBA Charlie Batch	50.00	22.00
❑ CCA Cris Carter	100.00	45.00
❑ DFA Doug Flutie	100.00	45.00
❑ DMA Dan Marino	400.00	180.00
❑ EJA Edgerrin James	150.00	70.00
❑ JKA Jon Kitna	60.00	27.00
❑ JPA Jake Plummer	100.00	45.00
❑ KEA Keyshawn Johnson	60.00	27.00
❑ KWA Kurt Warner	120.00	55.00
❑ MBA Mark Brunell	60.00	27.00
❑ MFA Marshall Faulk	120.00	55.00
❑ PMA Peyton Manning	250.00	110.00
❑ RMA Randy Moss	200.00	90.00
❑ SDA Stephen Davis	60.00	27.00
❑ TAA Troy Aikman	250.00	110.00
❑ TCA Tim Couch	50.00	22.00
❑ TDA Terrell Davis	100.00	45.00

2000 Upper Deck MVP ProSign

	Nm-Mt	Ex-Mt
❑ BG Brian Griese	20.00	9.00
❑ CB Charlie Batch	20.00	9.00
❑ CP Chad Pennington	60.00	27.00
❑ CR Chris Redman	20.00	9.00
❑ DW Dez White	20.00	9.00
❑ EJ Edgerrin James	50.00	22.00
❑ HT Ron Dayne	20.00	9.00
❑ IB Isaac Bruce	30.00	13.50
❑ JK Jon Kitna	20.00	9.00
❑ JL Jamal Lewis	40.00	18.00
❑ JP Jake Plummer	30.00	13.50
❑ KC Kwame Cavil	20.00	9.00
❑ KJ Keyshawn Johnson	20.00	9.00
❑ KW Kurt Warner	60.00	27.00
❑ MB Mark Brunell	30.00	13.50
❑ MF Marshall Faulk	30.00	13.50
❑ PM Peyton Manning	80.00	36.00
❑ PW Peter Warrick EXCH	2.50	1.10
❑ RD Ron Dugans	20.00	9.00
❑ RM Randy Moss	80.00	36.00
❑ RW Ricky Williams		
❑ SA Shaun Alexander	40.00	18.00
❑ TC Tim Couch	20.00	9.00
❑ TH Torry Holt	30.00	13.50
❑ TJ Thomas Jones	30.00	13.50
❑ TM Tee Martin	20.00	9.00
❑ TT Travis Taylor	20.00	9.00

2000 Upper Deck MVP ProSign Gold

	Nm-Mt	Ex-Mt
*GOLD CARDS: 1X TO 2.5X BASIC INSERTS		
❑ DM Dan Marino	300.00	135.00

2001 Upper Deck MVP

	Nm-Mt	Ex-Mt
COMPLETE SET (330)	50.00	15.00

❑ 1 Jake Plummer .30 .09
❑ 2 David Boston .50 .15
❑ 3 Thomas Jones .30 .09
❑ 4 Michael Pittman .20 .06
❑ 5 Frank Sanders .20 .06
❑ 6 MarTay Jenkins .20 .06
❑ 7 Pat Tillman RC 20.00 6.00
❑ 8 Tywan Mitchell .20 .06
❑ 9 Jamal Anderson .50 .15
❑ 10 Doug Johnson .20 .06
❑ 11 Ephraim Salaam RC .50 .15
❑ 12 Chris Chandler .30 .09
❑ 13 Shawn Jefferson .20 .06
❑ 14 Tim Dwight .50 .15
❑ 15 Terance Mathis .30 .09
❑ 16 Jamal Lewis .75 .23
❑ 17 Shannon Sharpe .30 .09
❑ 18 Trent Dilfer .30 .09
❑ 19 Ray Lewis .50 .15
❑ 20 Qadry Ismail .30 .09
❑ 21 Travis Taylor .30 .09
❑ 22 Chris Redman .20 .06
❑ 23 Priest Holmes .60 .18
❑ 24 Rod Woodson .30 .09
❑ 25 Jamie Sharper .20 .06
❑ 26 Doug Flutie .50 .15
❑ 27 Rob Johnson .30 .09
❑ 28 Eric Moulds .30 .09
❑ 29 Sammy Morris .20 .06
❑ 30 Shawn Bryson .20 .06
❑ 31 Antowain Smith .30 .09
❑ 32 Jeremy McDaniel .20 .06
❑ 33 Sam Cowart .20 .06
❑ 34 Muhsin Muhammad .30 .09
❑ 35 Brad Hoover .20 .06
❑ 36 Tim Biakabutuka .30 .09
❑ 37 Steve Beuerlein .20 .06
❑ 38 Donald Hayes .20 .06
❑ 39 Jeff Lewis .20 .06
❑ 40 Dameyune Craig .20 .06
❑ 41 Wesley Walls .20 .06
❑ 42 Isaac Byrd .20 .06
❑ 43 Cade McNown .20 .06
❑ 44 James Allen .30 .09
❑ 45 Marcus Robinson .50 .15
❑ 46 Brian Urlacher .75 .23
❑ 47 Jim Miller .20 .06
❑ 48 Curtis Enis .20 .06
❑ 49 Eddie Kennison .30 .09
❑ 50 Marty Booker .20 .06
❑ 51 Bobby Engram .20 .06
❑ 52 Peter Warrick .50 .15
❑ 53 Corey Dillon .50 .15
❑ 54 Akili Smith .20 .06
❑ 55 Danny Farmer .20 .06
❑ 56 Brandon Bennett .20 .06
❑ 57 Curtis Keaton .20 .06
❑ 58 Ron Dugans .20 .06
❑ 59 Takeo Spikes .20 .06
❑ 60 Scott Mitchell .20 .06
❑ 61 Tim Couch .30 .09
❑ 62 Kevin Johnson .30 .09
❑ 63 Travis Prentice .20 .06
❑ 64 Spergon Wynn .20 .06
❑ 65 Errict Rhett .20 .06
❑ 66 David Patten .20 .06
❑ 67 Dennis Northcutt .30 .09
❑ 68 Aaron Shea .20 .06
❑ 69 Courtney Brown .30 .09
❑ 70 Troy Aikman .75 .23
❑ 71 Emmitt Smith 1.00 .30
❑ 72 Joey Galloway .30 .09
❑ 73 Rocket Ismail .30 .09
❑ 74 Randall Cunningham .50 .15
❑ 75 Anthony Wright .20 .06
❑ 76 James McKnight .30 .09
❑ 77 Dexter Coakley .20 .06
❑ 78 Terrell Davis .50 .15
❑ 79 Mike Anderson .50 .15
❑ 80 Brian Griese .50 .15
❑ 81 Rod Smith .30 .09
❑ 82 Ed McCaffrey .50 .15
❑ 83 Olandis Gary .30 .09
❑ 84 Trevor Pryce .20 .06
❑ 85 John Mobley .20 .06
❑ 86 Charlie Batch .50 .15
❑ 87 Germane Crowell .20 .06
❑ 88 James O. Stewart .30 .09
❑ 89 Johnnie Morton .30 .09
❑ 90 Herman Moore .30 .09
❑ 91 Mario Bates .20 .06
❑ 92 Desmond Howard .20 .06
❑ 93 Stephen Boyd .20 .06
❑ 94 Chris Claiborne .30 .09
❑ 95 Kurt Schulz .20 .06
❑ 96 Brett Favre 1.50 .45
❑ 97 Antonio Freeman .50 .15
❑ 98 Dorsey Levens .20 .06
❑ 99 Ahman Green .50 .15
❑ 100 Matt Hasselbeck .30 .09
❑ 101 De'Mond Parker .20 .06
❑ 102 Bill Schroeder .30 .09
❑ 103 Bubba Franks .30 .09
❑ 104 Donald Driver .30 .09
❑ 105 Darren Sharper .20 .06
❑ 106 Peyton Manning 1.25 .35
❑ 107 Edgerrin James .60 .18
❑ 108 Marvin Harrison .50 .15
❑ 109 Jerome Pathon .30 .09
❑ 110 Terrence Wilkins .20 .06
❑ 111 Ken Dilger .20 .06
❑ 112 Marcus Pollard .20 .06
❑ 113 Brad Scioli RC .50 .15
❑ 114 Mark Brunell .50 .15
❑ 115 Fred Taylor .50 .15
❑ 116 Jimmy Smith .30 .09
❑ 117 Jamie Martin .30 .09
❑ 118 Keenan McCardell .20 .06
❑ 119 Kyle Brady .20 .06
❑ 120 R.Jay Soward .20 .06
❑ 121 Alvis Whitted .20 .06
❑ 122 Brant Boyer RC .20 .06
❑ 123 Elvis Grbac .30 .09
❑ 124 Tony Gonzalez .30 .09
❑ 125 Derrick Alexander .30 .09
❑ 126 Tony Richardson .20 .06
❑ 127 Frank Moreau .20 .06
❑ 128 Sylvester Morris .20 .06
❑ 129 Kevin Lockett .20 .06
❑ 130 Donnie Edwards .20 .06
❑ 131 Oronde Gadsden .30 .09
❑ 132 Lamar Smith .30 .09
❑ 133 Jay Fiedler .50 .15
❑ 134 James Johnson .20 .06
❑ 135 Thurman Thomas .20 .06
❑ 136 Leslie Shepherd .20 .06
❑ 137 Tony Martin .20 .06
❑ 138 O.J. McDuffie .20 .06
❑ 139 Zach Thomas .50 .15
❑ 140 Randy Moss 1.00 .30
❑ 141 Bubby Brister .20 .06
❑ 142 Cris Carter .50 .15
❑ 143 Daunte Culpepper .50 .15
❑ 144 Moe Williams .30 .09
❑ 145 Troy Walters .20 .06
❑ 146 Chris Walsh RC .20 .06
❑ 147 Matthew Hatchette .20 .06
❑ 148 Kailee Wong .20 .06
❑ 149 Robert Griffith .20 .06
❑ 150 Drew Bledsoe .60 .18
❑ 151 Terry Glenn .20 .06
❑ 152 Kevin Faulk .30 .09
❑ 153 J.R. Redmond .20 .06
❑ 154 Tony Carter .20 .06
❑ 155 Patrick Pass .20 .06
❑ 156 Troy Brown .30 .09
❑ 157 Tony Simmons .20 .06
❑ 158 Michael Bishop .20 .06
❑ 159 Lawyer Milloy .30 .09
❑ 160 Ricky Williams .50 .15
❑ 161 Jeff Blake .30 .09
❑ 162 Joe Horn .30 .09
❑ 163 Aaron Brooks .50 .15
❑ 164 La'Roi Glover .20 .06
❑ 165 Chad Morton .20 .06
❑ 166 Keith Mitchell RC .30 .09
❑ 167 Willie Jackson .20 .06
❑ 168 Robert Wilson .20 .06
❑ 169 Jake Reed .30 .09
❑ 170 Kerry Collins .30 .09
❑ 171 Amani Toomer .20 .06
❑ 172 Ron Dayne .50 .15
❑ 173 Tiki Barber .30 .09
❑ 174 Greg Comella .20 .06
❑ 175 Ike Hilliard .30 .09
❑ 176 Joe Jurevicius .20 .06
❑ 177 Ron Dixon .20 .06
❑ 178 Jason Sehorn .20 .06
❑ 179 Michael Strahan .30 .09
❑ 180 Vinny Testaverde .30 .09
❑ 181 Wayne Chrebet .30 .09
❑ 182 Curtis Martin .50 .15
❑ 183 Richie Anderson .20 .06
❑ 184 Dedric Ward .20 .06
❑ 185 Laveranues Coles .50 .15
❑ 186 Windrell Hayes .20 .06
❑ 187 Chad Pennington .75 .23
❑ 188 Tim Brown .50 .15
❑ 189 Rich Gannon .50 .15
❑ 190 Tyrone Wheatley .30 .09
❑ 191 Napoleon Kaufman .20 .06
❑ 192 Jon Ritchie .20 .06
❑ 193 James Jett .20 .06
❑ 194 Rickey Dudley .20 .06
❑ 195 Andre Rison .30 .09
❑ 196 Eric Allen .20 .06
❑ 197 Charles Woodson .30 .09
❑ 198 Duce Staley .50 .15
❑ 199 Donovan McNabb .60 .18
❑ 200 Darnell Autry .20 .06
❑ 201 Chad Lewis .20 .06
❑ 202 Charles Johnson .20 .06
❑ 203 Torrance Small .20 .06
❑ 204 Todd Pinkston .20 .06
❑ 205 Brian Mitchell .20 .06
❑ 206 Hugh Douglas .20 .06
❑ 207 David Akers RC .30 .09
❑ 208 Kordell Stewart .30 .09
❑ 209 Jerome Bettis .50 .15
❑ 210 Bobby Shaw .20 .06
❑ 211 Hines Ward .50 .15
❑ 212 Plaxico Burress .50 .15
❑ 213 Courtney Hawkins .20 .06
❑ 214 Troy Edwards .20 .06
❑ 215 Earl Holmes .20 .06
❑ 216 Richard Huntley .20 .06
❑ 217 Marshall Faulk .60 .18
❑ 218 Kurt Warner 1.00 .30
❑ 219 Isaac Bruce .50 .15
❑ 220 Torry Holt .50 .15
❑ 221 Trent Green .50 .15
❑ 222 Justin Watson .20 .06
❑ 223 Trung Canidate .30 .09
❑ 224 Az-Zahir Hakim .20 .06
❑ 225 Ricky Proehl .20 .06
❑ 226 Dexter McCleon .20 .06
❑ 227 London Fletcher .20 .06
❑ 228 Junior Seau .50 .15
❑ 229 Curtis Conway .30 .09
❑ 230 Rodney Harrison .20 .06
❑ 231 Jeff Graham .20 .06
❑ 232 Freddie Jones .20 .06
❑ 233 Reggie Jones .20 .06
❑ 234 Ronney Jenkins .20 .06
❑ 235 Trevor Gaylor .20 .06
❑ 236 Jeff Garcia .50 .15
❑ 237 Jerry Rice 1.00 .30
❑ 238 Charlie Garner .30 .09
❑ 239 Terrell Owens .50 .15
❑ 240 J.J. Stokes .30 .09
❑ 241 Fred Beasley .20 .06
❑ 242 Tim Rattay .30 .09
❑ 243 Garrison Hearst .20 .06
❑ 244 Ricky Watters .30 .09
❑ 245 Shaun Alexander .60 .18
❑ 246 Jon Kitna .30 .09
❑ 247 Brock Huard .20 .06
❑ 248 Darrell Jackson .50 .15
❑ 249 James Williams WR .20 .06
❑ 250 Sean Dawkins .20 .06
❑ 251 John Hilliard RC .20 .06
❑ 252 Warrick Dunn .50 .15
❑ 253 Shaun King .20 .06
❑ 254 Ryan Leaf .30 .09
❑ 255 Mike Alstott .50 .15

❑ 256 Jacquez Green	.20	.06
❑ 257 Reidel Anthony	.20	.06
❑ 258 Derrick Brooks	.50	.15
❑ 259 John Lynch	.30	.09
❑ 260 Warren Sapp	.30	.09
❑ 261 Eddie George	.50	.15
❑ 262 Steve McNair	.50	.15
❑ 263 Rodney Thomas	.20	.06
❑ 264 Derrick Mason	.30	.09
❑ 265 Yancey Thigpen	.20	.06
❑ 266 Frank Wycheck	.20	.06
❑ 267 Chris Sanders	.20	.06
❑ 268 Carl Pickens	.20	.06
❑ 269 Kevin Dyson	.20	.06
❑ 270 Jevon Kearse	.30	.09
❑ 271 Jeff George	.30	.09
❑ 272 Stephen Davis	.50	.15
❑ 273 Brad Johnson	.50	.15
❑ 274 Albert Connell	.20	.06
❑ 275 James Thrash	.30	.09
❑ 276 Michael Westbrook	.30	.09
❑ 277 Stephen Alexander	.20	.06
❑ 278 Deion Sanders	.50	.15
❑ 279 Champ Bailey	.30	.09
❑ 280 Todd Husak	.20	.06
❑ 281 Dan Morgan RC	1.00	.30
❑ 282 Josh Booty RC	1.00	.30
❑ 283 Michael Vick RC	8.00	2.40
❑ 284 Mike McMahon RC	1.00	.30
❑ 285 Reggie White RC	.60	.18
❑ 286 Chris Weinke RC	1.00	.30
❑ 287 Drew Brees RC	2.00	.60
❑ 288 Sage Rosenfels RC	1.00	.30
❑ 289 Marques Tuiasosopo RC	1.00	.30
❑ 290 Josh Heupel RC	1.00	.30
❑ 291 David Rivers RC	.60	.18
❑ 292 Kevin Kasper RC	1.00	.30
❑ 293 Jesse Palmer RC	1.00	.30
❑ 294 LaDainian Tomlinson RC	3.00	.90
❑ 295 Deuce McAllister RC	2.00	.60
❑ 296 Kevan Barlow RC	1.00	.30
❑ 297 LaMont Jordan RC	1.25	.35
❑ 298 James Jackson RC	1.00	.30
❑ 299 Anthony Thomas RC	1.50	.45
❑ 300 Correll Buckhalter RC	1.25	.35
❑ 301 Travis Henry RC	1.25	.35
❑ 302 Dan Alexander RC	1.00	.30
❑ 303 Travis Minor RC	.60	.18
❑ 304 Derrick Gibson RC	.60	.18
❑ 305 Rudi Johnson RC	2.00	.60
❑ 306 Michael Bennett RC	2.00	.60
❑ 307 Alge Crumpler RC	1.25	.35
❑ 308 Todd Heap RC	1.00	.30
❑ 309 Snoop Minnis RC	.60	.18
❑ 310 Santana Moss RC	1.50	.45
❑ 311 Reggie Wayne RC	1.50	.45
❑ 312 Koren Robinson RC	1.25	.35
❑ 313 Chris Chambers RC	1.25	.35
❑ 314 David Terrell RC	1.00	.30
❑ 315 Rod Gardner RC	1.00	.30
❑ 316 Quincy Morgan RC	1.00	.30
❑ 317 Ken-Yon Rambo RC	.60	.18
❑ 318 Vinny Sutherland RC	.60	.18
❑ 319 David Allen RC	.60	.18
❑ 320 Bobby Newcombe RC	.60	.18
❑ 321 Ronney Daniels RC	.40	.12
❑ 322 T.J. Houshmandzadeh RC	1.00	.30
❑ 323 Chad Johnson RC	2.00	.60
❑ 324 Freddie Mitchell RC	1.00	.30
❑ 325 Moran Norris RC	.40	.12
❑ 326 Ron Dayne CL	.30	.09
❑ 327 Mike Anderson CL	.20	.06
❑ 328 Jamal Lewis CL	.40	.12
❑ 329 Brian Urlacher CL	.40	.12
❑ 330 Darren Howard CL	.20	.06

2001 Upper Deck MVP Campus Classics Game Jersey Autographs

	Nm-Mt	Ex-Mt
❑ CCSAT Anthony Thomas	120.00	36.00
❑ CCSCM Cade McNown	60.00	18.00
❑ CCSCW Chris Weinke	80.00	24.00
❑ CCSDB Drew Brees	250.00	75.00
❑ CCSDM Deuce McAllister	200.00	60.00
❑ CCSFM Freddie Mitchell	60.00	18.00
❑ CCSJF Jamar Fletcher	50.00	15.00
❑ CCSLT LaDainian Tomlinson	300.00	90.00
❑ CCSMB Michael Bennett	150.00	45.00
❑ CCSMF Marshall Faulk	100.00	30.00
❑ CCSMT Marques Tuiasosopo	80.00	24.00
❑ CCSMV Michael Vick	400.00	120.00
❑ CCSPM Peyton Manning	200.00	60.00
❑ CCSRD Ron Dayne	60.00	18.00
❑ CCSTA Troy Aikman	150.00	45.00

2002 Upper Deck MVP

	Nm-Mt	Ex-Mt
COMPLETE SET (300)	50.00	15.00
❑ 1 Arnold Jackson	.20	.06
❑ 2 Dave Brown	.20	.06
❑ 3 David Boston	.50	.15
❑ 4 Frank Sanders	.20	.06
❑ 5 Jake Plummer	.30	.09
❑ 6 MarTay Jenkins	.20	.06
❑ 7 Freddie Jones	.20	.06
❑ 8 Jamal Anderson	.30	.09
❑ 9 Keith Brooking	.20	.06
❑ 10 Michael Vick	1.50	.45
❑ 11 Rodney Thomas	.20	.06
❑ 12 Shawn Jefferson	.20	.06
❑ 13 Tony Martin	.20	.06
❑ 14 Warrick Dunn	.50	.15
❑ 15 Brandon Stokley	.30	.09
❑ 16 Chris McAlister	.20	.06
❑ 17 Chris Redman	.20	.06
❑ 18 Ray Lewis	.50	.15
❑ 19 Sam Gash	.20	.06
❑ 20 Travis Taylor	.30	.09
❑ 21 Terry Allen	.20	.06
❑ 22 Drew Bledsoe	.60	.18
❑ 23 Alex Van Pelt	.20	.06
❑ 24 Eric Moulds	.30	.09
❑ 25 Kenyatta Wright	.20	.06
❑ 26 Larry Centers	.20	.06
❑ 27 Peerless Price	.30	.09
❑ 28 Shawn Bryson	.20	.06
❑ 29 Travis Henry	.50	.15
❑ 30 Chris Weinke	.30	.09
❑ 31 Lamar Smith	.30	.09
❑ 32 Isaac Byrd	.50	.15
❑ 33 Muhsin Muhammad	.30	.09
❑ 34 Nick Goings	.20	.06
❑ 35 Richard Huntley	.20	.06
❑ 36 Tim Biakabutuka	.20	.06
❑ 37 Wesley Walls	.20	.06
❑ 38 Anthony Thomas	.50	.15
❑ 39 Brian Urlacher	.75	.23
❑ 40 David Terrell	.50	.15
❑ 41 Dez White	.20	.06
❑ 42 Jim Miller	.20	.06
❑ 43 Larry Whigham	.20	.06
❑ 44 Marty Booker	.20	.06
❑ 45 Chris Chandler	.30	.09
❑ 46 Corey Dillon	.30	.09
❑ 47 Darnay Scott	.20	.06
❑ 48 Jon Kitna	.30	.09
❑ 49 Peter Warrick	.30	.09
❑ 50 Ron Dugans	.20	.06
❑ 51 Scott Mitchell	.20	.06
❑ 52 Chad Johnson	.50	.15
❑ 53 Courtney Brown	.30	.09
❑ 54 JaJuan Dawson	.20	.06
❑ 55 James Jackson	.20	.06
❑ 56 Kevin Johnson	.30	.09
❑ 57 Quincy Morgan	.20	.06
❑ 58 Rickey Dudley	.20	.06
❑ 59 Tim Couch	.30	.09
❑ 60 Chris Sanders	.20	.06
❑ 61 Emmitt Smith	1.25	.35
❑ 62 Joey Galloway	.30	.09
❑ 63 Ken-Yon Rambo	.20	.06
❑ 64 La'Roi Glover	.20	.06
❑ 65 Quincy Carter	.30	.09
❑ 66 Rocket Ismail	.30	.09
❑ 67 Darren Woodson	.20	.06
❑ 68 Ryan Leaf	.30	.09
❑ 69 Chester McGlockton	.20	.06
❑ 70 Brian Griese	.50	.15
❑ 71 Shannon Sharpe	.30	.09
❑ 72 Kevin Kasper	.20	.06
❑ 73 Mike Anderson	.50	.15
❑ 74 Olandis Gary	.30	.09
❑ 75 Rod Smith	.30	.09
❑ 76 Terrell Davis	.50	.15
❑ 77 Anthony Carter	.20	.06
❑ 78 Az-Zahir Hakim	.20	.06
❑ 79 Charlie Batch	.30	.09
❑ 80 Chris Claiborne	.20	.06
❑ 81 Cory Schlesinger	.20	.06
❑ 82 Desmond Howard	.20	.06
❑ 83 Germane Crowell	.20	.06
❑ 84 James Stewart	.30	.09
❑ 85 Mike McMahon	.50	.15
❑ 86 Bill Schroeder	.30	.09
❑ 87 Ahman Green	.50	.15
❑ 88 Brett Favre	1.25	.35
❑ 89 Bubba Franks	.30	.09
❑ 90 Antonio Freeman	.50	.15
❑ 91 Donald Driver	.30	.09
❑ 92 Kabeer Gbaja-Biamila	.20	.06
❑ 93 William Henderson	.20	.06
❑ 94 Corey Bradford	.20	.06
❑ 95 Jamie Sharper	.20	.06
❑ 96 Jermaine Lewis	.20	.06
❑ 97 Kailee Wong	.20	.06
❑ 98 Matt Stevens	.20	.06
❑ 99 Tony Boselli	.20	.06
❑ 100 James Allen	.30	.09
❑ 101 Aaron Glenn	.20	.06
❑ 102 Edgerrin James	.60	.18
❑ 103 Dominic Rhodes	.30	.09
❑ 104 Marcus Pollard	.20	.06
❑ 105 Marvin Harrison	.50	.15
❑ 106 Peyton Manning	1.00	.30
❑ 107 Qadry Ismail	.30	.09
❑ 108 Reggie Wayne	.30	.09
❑ 109 Stacey Mack	.20	.06
❑ 110 Elvis Joseph	.20	.06
❑ 111 Fred Taylor	.50	.15
❑ 112 Jimmy Smith	.30	.09
❑ 113 Jonathan Quinn	.20	.06
❑ 114 Keenan McCardell	.20	.06
❑ 115 Mark Brunell	.50	.15
❑ 116 Trent Green	.30	.09
❑ 117 Derrick Alexander	.30	.09
❑ 118 Johnnie Morton	.30	.09
❑ 119 Snoop Minnis	.20	.06
❑ 120 Mike Cloud	.20	.06
❑ 121 Priest Holmes	.60	.18
❑ 122 Tony Gonzalez	.30	.09
❑ 123 Tony Richardson	.20	.06
❑ 124 Ricky Williams	1.00	.30
❑ 125 Chris Chambers	.50	.15
❑ 126 James McKnight	.20	.06
❑ 127 Jay Fiedler	.30	.09
❑ 128 Zach Thomas	.50	.15
❑ 129 Oronde Gadsden	.30	.09
❑ 130 Ray Lucas	.20	.06
❑ 131 Randy Moss	1.00	.30
❑ 132 Spergon Wynn	.20	.06
❑ 133 Cris Carter	.50	.15
❑ 134 Daunte Culpepper	.50	.15
❑ 135 Doug Chapman	.20	.06
❑ 136 Michael Bennett	.30	.09
❑ 137 Tom Brady	1.25	.35
❑ 138 Troy Brown	.30	.09

❑ 139 Adam Vinatieri .50 .15
❑ 140 Antowain Smith .30 .09
❑ 141 David Patten .20 .06
❑ 142 Donald Hayes .20 .06
❑ 143 J.R. Redmond .20 .06
❑ 144 Willie Jackson .20 .06
❑ 145 Jerome Pathon .30 .09
❑ 146 Jake Reed .30 .09
❑ 147 Aaron Brooks .50 .15
❑ 148 John Carney .20 .06
❑ 149 Deuce McAllister .60 .18
❑ 150 Joe Horn .30 .09
❑ 151 Kyle Turley .20 .06
❑ 152 Robert Wilson .20 .06
❑ 153 Tiki Barber .30 .09
❑ 154 Amani Toomer .30 .09
❑ 155 Ike Hilliard .30 .09
❑ 156 Jason Sehorn .20 .06
❑ 157 Joe Jurevicius .20 .06
❑ 158 Kerry Collins .30 .09
❑ 159 Michael Strahan .30 .09
❑ 160 Ron Dayne .30 .09
❑ 161 Wayne Chrebet .30 .09
❑ 162 Chad Pennington .60 .18
❑ 163 Curtis Martin .50 .15
❑ 164 LaMont Jordan .50 .15
❑ 165 Laveranues Coles .30 .09
❑ 166 Marvin Jones .20 .06
❑ 167 Santana Moss .50 .15
❑ 168 Vinny Testaverde .30 .09
❑ 169 Tyrone Wheatley .30 .09
❑ 170 Charles Woodson .30 .09
❑ 171 Charlie Garner .30 .09
❑ 172 Jerry Rice 1.00 .30
❑ 173 John Parrella .20 .06
❑ 174 Jon Ritchie .20 .06
❑ 175 Rich Gannon .50 .15
❑ 176 Tim Brown .50 .15
❑ 177 Todd Pinkston .30 .09
❑ 178 Correll Buckhalter .30 .09
❑ 179 Donovan McNabb .60 .18
❑ 180 Duce Staley .50 .15
❑ 181 Freddie Mitchell .30 .09
❑ 182 Hugh Douglas .20 .06
❑ 183 James Thrash .30 .09
❑ 184 Koy Detmer .20 .06
❑ 185 Troy Edwards .20 .06
❑ 186 Chris Fuamatu-Ma'afala .20 .06
❑ 187 Hines Ward .50 .15
❑ 188 Jerome Bettis .50 .15
❑ 189 Kendrell Bell .50 .15
❑ 190 Kordell Stewart .30 .09
❑ 191 Mark Bruener .20 .06
❑ 192 Plaxico Burress .30 .09
❑ 193 Tim Dwight .30 .09
❑ 194 Curtis Conway .20 .06
❑ 195 Doug Flutie .50 .15
❑ 196 Drew Brees .50 .15
❑ 197 Junior Seau .50 .15
❑ 198 LaDainian Tomlinson .75 .23
❑ 199 Marcellus Wiley .20 .06
❑ 200 Rodney Harrison .20 .06
❑ 201 Stephen Alexander .20 .06
❑ 202 Terrell Owens .50 .15
❑ 203 Andre Carter .20 .06
❑ 204 Cedrick Wilson .20 .06
❑ 205 Fred Beasley .20 .06
❑ 206 Garrison Hearst .30 .09
❑ 207 J.J. Stokes .30 .09
❑ 208 Jeff Garcia .50 .15
❑ 209 Kevan Barlow .30 .09
❑ 210 Tai Streets .20 .06
❑ 211 Doug Evans .20 .06
❑ 212 Bobby Engram .20 .06
❑ 213 Darrell Jackson .30 .09
❑ 214 James Williams .20 .06
❑ 215 John Randle .20 .06
❑ 216 Koren Robinson .30 .09
❑ 217 Matt Hasselbeck .30 .09
❑ 218 Shaun Alexander .50 .15
❑ 219 Trent Dilfer .30 .09
❑ 220 Aeneas Williams .20 .06
❑ 221 Isaac Bruce .50 .15
❑ 222 Kurt Warner .50 .15
❑ 223 Marshall Faulk .50 .15
❑ 224 Ricky Proehl .20 .06
❑ 225 Torry Holt .50 .15
❑ 226 Trung Canidate .30 .09
❑ 227 Terrence Wilkins .20 .06
❑ 228 John Lynch .30 .09
❑ 229 Keyshawn Johnson .50 .15
❑ 230 Michael Pittman .20 .06
❑ 231 Mike Alstott .50 .15
❑ 232 Rob Johnson .30 .09
❑ 233 Shaun King .20 .06
❑ 234 Warren Sapp .30 .09
❑ 235 Brad Johnson .30 .09
❑ 236 Derrick Mason .30 .09
❑ 237 Eddie George .50 .15
❑ 238 Frank Wycheck .20 .06
❑ 239 Jevon Kearse .30 .09
❑ 240 Kevin Dyson .30 .09
❑ 241 Steve McNair .50 .15
❑ 242 Chris Coleman .20 .06
❑ 243 Darrell Green .20 .06
❑ 244 Jacquez Green .20 .06
❑ 245 Ki-Jana Carter .20 .06
❑ 246 Michael Westbrook .20 .06
❑ 247 Rod Gardner .30 .09
❑ 248 Stephen Davis .30 .09
❑ 249 Tony Banks .20 .06
❑ 250 Champ Bailey .30 .09
❑ 251 David Carr RC 4.00 1.20
❑ 252 DeShaun Foster RC 1.25 .35
❑ 253 Antonio Bryant RC 1.25 .35
❑ 254 Joey Harrington RC 4.00 1.20
❑ 255 William Green RC 2.00 .60
❑ 256 Josh Reed RC 1.25 .35
❑ 257 Patrick Ramsey RC 2.50 .75
❑ 258 Clinton Portis RC 4.00 1.20
❑ 259 Jabar Gaffney RC 1.25 .35
❑ 260 Rohan Davey RC 1.25 .35
❑ 261 T.J. Duckett RC 2.00 .60
❑ 262 Ashley Lelie RC 2.50 .75
❑ 263 Kurt Kittner RC 1.00 .30
❑ 264 Luke Staley RC 1.00 .30
❑ 265 Ron Johnson RC 1.00 .30
❑ 266 Antwaan Randle El RC 1.50 .45
❑ 267 Travis Stephens RC 1.00 .30
❑ 268 Marquise Walker RC 1.00 .30
❑ 269 Julius Peppers RC 2.50 .75
❑ 270 Chad Hutchinson RC 1.25 .35
❑ 271 Maurice Morris RC 1.25 .35
❑ 272 Reche Caldwell RC 1.25 .35
❑ 273 Randy Fasani RC 1.00 .30
❑ 274 Lamar Gordon RC 1.25 .35
❑ 275 Donte Stallworth RC 2.50 .75
❑ 276 Brandon Doman RC 1.25 .35
❑ 277 Damien Anderson RC 1.00 .30
❑ 278 Roy Williams RC 3.00 .90
❑ 279 J.T. O'Sullivan RC 1.00 .30
❑ 280 Leonard Henry RC 1.00 .30
❑ 281 Javon Walker RC 2.50 .75
❑ 282 David Garrard RC 1.25 .35
❑ 283 Chester Taylor RC 1.25 .35
❑ 284 Andre Davis RC 1.25 .35
❑ 285 Josh McCown RC 1.50 .45
❑ 286 Adrian Peterson RC 1.25 .35
❑ 287 Seth Burford RC 1.00 .30
❑ 288 Deion Branch RC 2.50 .75
❑ 289 Jonathan Wells RC 1.25 .35
❑ 290 Ladell Betts RC 1.25 .35
❑ 291 Cliff Russell RC 1.00 .30
❑ 292 Eric Crouch RC 2.00 .60
❑ 293 Dusty Bonner RC .60 .18
❑ 294 Tim Carter RC 1.00 .30
❑ 295 Brian Westbrook RC 2.00 .60
❑ 296 Quentin Jammer RC 1.25 .35
❑ 297 Brian Poli-Dixon RC 1.00 .30
❑ 298 Donovan McNabb CL .30 .09
❑ 299 Curtis Martin CL .20 .06
❑ 300 Tom Brady CL .60 .18

2002 Upper Deck MVP ProSign

	Nm-Mt	Ex-Mt
❑ PSAT Anthony Thomas	40.00	12.00
❑ PSCC Chris Chambers	40.00	12.00
❑ PSCW Chris Weinke	30.00	9.00
❑ PSDB Drew Brees	40.00	12.00

❑ PSEC Eric Crouch	50.00	15.00
❑ PSFM Freddie Mitchell	25.00	7.50
❑ PSJR Josh Reed	30.00	9.00
❑ PSMMC Mike McMahon	40.00	12.00
❑ PSMW Marquise Walker	30.00	9.00
❑ PSPM Peyton Manning	80.00	24.00
❑ PSQM Quincy Morgan		
❑ PSRJ Ron Johnson	30.00	9.00
❑ PSWG William Green	40.00	12.00

2003 Upper Deck MVP

	MINT	NRMT
COMPLETE SET (440)	60.00	27.00
❑ 1 Brad Johnson	.30	.14
❑ 2 Dexter Jackson RC	.50	.23
❑ 3 Derrick Brooks	.30	.14
❑ 4 Simeon Rice	.30	.14
❑ 5 Warren Sapp	.30	.14
❑ 6 John Lynch	.30	.14
❑ 7 Joe Jurevicius	.20	.09
❑ 8 Ronde Barber	.20	.09
❑ 9 Mike Alstott	.50	.23
❑ 10 Michael Pittman	.20	.09
❑ 11 Keyshawn Johnson	.50	.23
❑ 12 Jerry Rice	1.00	.45
❑ 13 Tim Brown	.50	.23
❑ 14 Rich Gannon	.30	.14
❑ 15 Charlie Garner	.30	.14
❑ 16 Jerry Porter	.30	.14
❑ 17 Sebastian Janikowski	.20	.09
❑ 18 Zack Crockett	.20	.09
❑ 19 Tyrone Wheatley	.20	.09
❑ 20 Bill Romanowski	.20	.09
❑ 21 Charles Woodson	.30	.14
❑ 22 Rod Woodson	.30	.14
❑ 23 Donovan McNabb	.60	.25
❑ 24 James Thrash	.20	.09
❑ 25 Duce Staley	.30	.14
❑ 26 Brian Westbrook	.30	.14
❑ 27 A.J. Feeley	.30	.14
❑ 28 Koy Detmer	.20	.09
❑ 29 Brian Dawkins	.20	.09
❑ 30 Dorsey Levens	.20	.09
❑ 31 Jon Ritchie	.20	.09
❑ 32 Todd Pinkston	.30	.14
❑ 33 Chad Lewis	.20	.09
❑ 34 Brett Favre	1.25	.55
❑ 35 Ahman Green	.50	.23
❑ 36 Donald Driver	.30	.14
❑ 37 Bubba Franks	.30	.14
❑ 38 Javon Walker	.20	.09

❑ 39 Kabeer Gbaja-Biamila .20 .09
❑ 40 Robert Ferguson .20 .09
❑ 41 Tony Fisher .20 .09
❑ 42 Marques Anderson .20 .09
❑ 43 Ryan Longwell .20 .09
❑ 44 Craig Nall .20 .09
❑ 45 Steve McNair .50 .23
❑ 46 Eddie George .30 .14
❑ 47 Jevon Kearse .30 .14
❑ 48 Kevin Carter .20 .09
❑ 49 Samari Rolle .20 .09
❑ 50 Keith Bulluck .20 .09
❑ 51 Joe Nedney .20 .09
❑ 52 Robert Holcombe .20 .09
❑ 53 Drew Bennett .30 .14
❑ 54 Frank Wycheck .20 .09
❑ 55 Derrick Mason .30 .14
❑ 56 Tommy Maddox .50 .23
❑ 57 Jerome Bettis .50 .23
❑ 58 Plaxico Burress .30 .14
❑ 59 Antwaan Randle El .50 .23
❑ 60 Amos Zereoue .30 .14
❑ 61 Chris Fuamatu-Ma'afala .20 .09
❑ 62 Jason Gildon .20 .09
❑ 63 Kendrell Bell .30 .14
❑ 64 Dewayne Washington .20 .09
❑ 65 Jeff Reed .20 .09
❑ 66 Hines Ward .50 .23
❑ 67 Jeff Garcia .50 .23
❑ 68 Terrell Owens .50 .23
❑ 69 Andre Carter .20 .09
❑ 70 Tai Streets .20 .09
❑ 71 Tim Rattay .30 .14
❑ 72 Eric Johnson .30 .14
❑ 73 Cedrick Wilson .20 .09
❑ 74 Brandon Doman .20 .09
❑ 75 Kevan Barlow .30 .14
❑ 76 Bryant Young .20 .09
❑ 77 Garrison Hearst .30 .14
❑ 78 Kerry Collins .30 .14
❑ 79 Daryl Jones .20 .09
❑ 80 Tiki Barber .30 .14
❑ 81 Amani Toomer .30 .14
❑ 82 Tim Carter .20 .09
❑ 83 Michael Strahan .30 .14
❑ 84 Ike Hilliard .20 .09
❑ 85 Brian Mitchell .20 .09
❑ 86 Ron Dixon .20 .09
❑ 87 Jeremy Shockey .75 .35
❑ 88 Marvin Harrison .50 .23
❑ 89 Peyton Manning .75 .35
❑ 90 Edgerrin James .50 .23
❑ 91 Dominic Rhodes .30 .14
❑ 92 Brock Huard .20 .09
❑ 93 Marcus Pollard .20 .09
❑ 94 James Mungro .20 .09
❑ 95 Dwight Freeney .20 .09
❑ 96 Reggie Wayne .30 .14
❑ 97 Rob Morris .20 .09
❑ 98 Michael Vick 1.25 .55
❑ 99 Warrick Dunn .30 .14
❑ 100 T.J. Duckett .30 .14
❑ 101 Keith Brooking .20 .09
❑ 102 Ray Buchanan .20 .09
❑ 103 Alge Crumpler .30 .14
❑ 104 Quentin McCord .20 .09
❑ 105 Doug Johnson .20 .09
❑ 106 Brian Finneran .20 .09
❑ 107 Peerless Price .30 .14
❑ 108 Chad Pennington .60 .25
❑ 109 Curtis Martin .50 .23
❑ 110 Laveranues Coles .30 .14
❑ 111 Wayne Chrebet .30 .14
❑ 112 LaMont Jordan .30 .14
❑ 113 Anthony Becht .20 .09
❑ 114 Marvin Jones .20 .09
❑ 115 Mo Lewis .20 .09
❑ 116 Sam Cowart .20 .09
❑ 117 Vinnie Testaverde .30 .14
❑ 118 Santana Moss .30 .14
❑ 119 Tim Couch .20 .09
❑ 120 William Green .30 .14
❑ 121 Andre Davis .20 .09
❑ 122 Quincy Morgan .30 .14
❑ 123 Kevin Johnson .30 .14
❑ 124 James Jackson .20 .09
❑ 125 Jamel White .20 .09
❑ 126 Robert Griffith .20 .09
❑ 127 Dennis Northcutt .30 .14
❑ 128 Josh Booty .20 .09
❑ 129 Kelly Holcomb .30 .14
❑ 130 Jake Plummer .30 .14
❑ 131 Olandis Gary .30 .14
❑ 132 Clinton Portis .75 .35
❑ 133 Mike Anderson .50 .23
❑ 134 Ashley Lelie .50 .23
❑ 135 Ed McCaffrey .50 .23
❑ 136 Shannon Sharpe .30 .14
❑ 137 Rod Smith .30 .14
❑ 138 John Mobley .20 .09
❑ 139 Jason Elam .20 .09
❑ 140 Terrell Davis .50 .23
❑ 141 Tom Brady .75 .35
❑ 142 Christian Fauria .20 .09
❑ 143 Antowain Smith .30 .14
❑ 144 Kevin Faulk .20 .09
❑ 145 Ty Law .30 .14
❑ 146 Lawyer Milloy .30 .14
❑ 147 David Patten .20 .09
❑ 148 Deion Branch .50 .23
❑ 149 Troy Brown .30 .14
❑ 150 Rohan Davey .30 .14
❑ 151 Adam Vinatieri .50 .23
❑ 152 Jay Fiedler .30 .14
❑ 153 Chris Chambers .50 .23
❑ 154 Randy McMichael .30 .14
❑ 155 Rob Konrad .20 .09
❑ 156 Morlon Greenwood .20 .09
❑ 157 Derrius Thompson .20 .09
❑ 158 Travis Minor .20 .09
❑ 159 Olindo Mare .20 .09
❑ 160 Jason Taylor .20 .09
❑ 161 Zach Thomas .50 .23
❑ 162 Ricky Williams .50 .23
❑ 163 Aaron Brooks .50 .23
❑ 164 Deuce McAllister .50 .23
❑ 165 Donte Stallworth .50 .23
❑ 166 Jerome Pathon .20 .09
❑ 167 J.T. O'Sullivan .20 .09
❑ 168 Darrin Smith .20 .09
❑ 169 Michael Lewis .20 .09
❑ 170 John Carney .20 .09
❑ 171 Kyle Turley .20 .09
❑ 172 Joe Horn .30 .14
❑ 173 Trent Green .30 .14
❑ 174 Priest Holmes .60 .25
❑ 175 Johnnie Morton .30 .14
❑ 176 Eddie Kennison .20 .09
❑ 177 Marvcus Patton .20 .09
❑ 178 Omar Easy .20 .09
❑ 179 Derrick Blaylock .30 .14
❑ 180 Snoop Minnis .20 .09
❑ 181 Dante Hall .50 .23
❑ 182 Tony Gonzalez .30 .14
❑ 183 Marc Boerigter .30 .14
❑ 184 Drew Brees .50 .23
❑ 185 David Boston .30 .14
❑ 186 Stephen Alexander .20 .09
❑ 187 Quentin Jammer .20 .09
❑ 188 Donnie Edwards .20 .09
❑ 189 LaDainian Tomlinson .50 .23
❑ 190 Junior Seau .50 .23
❑ 191 Reche Caldwell .20 .09
❑ 192 Lorenzo Neal .20 .09
❑ 193 Tim Dwight .30 .14
❑ 194 Doug Flutie .30 .14
❑ 195 Drew Bledsoe .50 .23
❑ 196 Travis Henry .30 .14
❑ 197 Eric Moulds .30 .14
❑ 198 Alex Van Pelt .20 .09
❑ 199 Charles Johnson .20 .09
❑ 200 Nate Clements .20 .09
❑ 201 Takeo Spikes .20 .09
❑ 202 Bobby Shaw .20 .09
❑ 203 London Fletcher .20 .09
❑ 204 Sammy Morris .20 .09
❑ 205 Josh Reed .30 .14
❑ 206 Patrick Ramsey .50 .23
❑ 207 Ladell Betts .30 .14
❑ 208 Chad Morton .20 .09
❑ 209 Trung Canidate .30 .14
❑ 210 Kenny Watson .20 .09
❑ 211 Jessie Armstead .20 .09
❑ 212 Fred Smoot .20 .09
❑ 213 Champ Bailey .30 .14
❑ 214 Bruce Smith .20 .09
❑ 215 Rod Gardner .30 .14
❑ 216 Kurt Warner .50 .23
❑ 217 Troy Edwards .20 .09
❑ 218 Adam Archuleta .20 .09
❑ 219 Grant Wistrom .20 .09
❑ 220 Marshall Faulk .50 .23
❑ 221 Jeff Wilkins .20 .09
❑ 222 Aeneas Williams .20 .09
❑ 223 Lamar Gordon .20 .09
❑ 224 Marc Bulger .50 .23
❑ 225 Isaac Bruce .50 .23
❑ 226 Torry Holt .50 .23
❑ 227 Matt Hasselbeck .30 .14
❑ 228 Maurice Morris .20 .09
❑ 229 Bobby Engram .20 .09
❑ 230 Darrell Jackson .30 .14
❑ 231 James Williams .20 .09
❑ 232 Chad Brown .20 .09
❑ 233 Anthony Simmons .20 .09
❑ 234 Shaun Alexander .20 .09
❑ 235 Koren Robinson .30 .14
❑ 236 Chris Redman .20 .09
❑ 237 Jamal Lewis .50 .23
❑ 238 Brandon Stokley .30 .14
❑ 239 Peter Boulware .20 .09
❑ 240 Randy Hymes RC .30 .14
❑ 241 Todd Heap .30 .14
❑ 242 Travis Taylor .30 .14
❑ 243 Ron Johnson .20 .09
❑ 244 Ray Lewis .50 .23
❑ 245 Jake Delhomme .50 .23
❑ 246 DeShaun Foster .20 .09
❑ 247 Dee Brown .20 .09
❑ 248 Steve Smith .20 .09
❑ 249 Kevin Dyson .30 .14
❑ 250 Muhsin Muhammad .30 .14
❑ 251 Stephen Davis .30 .14
❑ 252 Julius Peppers .50 .23
❑ 253 Rodney Peete .20 .09
❑ 254 Mark Brunell .30 .14
❑ 255 Jimmy Smith .30 .14
❑ 256 Kyle Brady .20 .09
❑ 257 Kevin Lockett .20 .09
❑ 258 Quinn Gray .20 .09
❑ 259 Tony Brackens .20 .09
❑ 260 Marco Coleman .20 .09
❑ 261 David Garrard .20 .09
❑ 262 Fred Taylor .50 .23
❑ 263 Daunte Culpepper .50 .23
❑ 264 Michael Bennett .30 .14
❑ 265 D'Wayne Bates .20 .09
❑ 266 Cedric James .20 .09
❑ 267 Kelly Campbell .20 .09
❑ 268 Derrick Alexander .20 .09
❑ 269 Byron Chamberlain .20 .09
❑ 270 Shaun Hill .20 .09
❑ 271 Randy Moss .75 .35
❑ 272 Josh McCown .30 .14
❑ 273 Thomas Jones .30 .14
❑ 274 Wendell Bryant .20 .09
❑ 275 Kevin Kasper .20 .09
❑ 276 Jason McAddley .20 .09
❑ 277 Emmitt Smith 1.25 .55
❑ 278 Preston Parsons .20 .09
❑ 279 Freddie Jones .20 .09
❑ 280 Marcel Shipp .30 .14
❑ 281 Chad Hutchinson .30 .14
❑ 282 Troy Hambrick .20 .09
❑ 283 Dat Nguyen .20 .09
❑ 284 Michael Wiley .20 .09
❑ 285 Joey Galloway .30 .14
❑ 286 Terry Glenn .20 .09
❑ 287 La'Roi Glover .20 .09
❑ 288 Roy Williams .50 .23
❑ 289 Antonio Bryant .50 .23
❑ 290 Quincy Carter .30 .14
❑ 291 Anthony Thomas .50 .23
❑ 292 Marty Booker .30 .14
❑ 293 Dez White .20 .09

❑ 294 Marcus Robinson .30 .14
❑ 295 Kordell Stewart .30 .14
❑ 296 David Terrell .30 .14
❑ 297 John Davis .20 .09
❑ 298 Mike Brown .30 .14
❑ 299 Brian Urlacher .75 .35
❑ 300 Jabar Gaffney .30 .14
❑ 301 Jonathan Wells .20 .09
❑ 302 JaJuan Dawson .20 .09
❑ 303 Corey Bradford .20 .09
❑ 304 Frank Murphy .20 .09
❑ 305 Billy Miller .20 .09
❑ 306 Aaron Glenn .20 .09
❑ 307 Avion Black .20 .09
❑ 308 David Carr .75 .35
❑ 309 Joey Harrington .75 .35
❑ 310 James Stewart .30 .14
❑ 311 Ty Detmer .20 .09
❑ 312 Jason Hanson .20 .09
❑ 313 Bill Schroeder .30 .14
❑ 314 Mikhael Ricks .20 .09
❑ 315 Scotty Anderson .20 .09
❑ 316 Robert Porcher .20 .09
❑ 317 Az-Zahir Hakim .20 .09
❑ 318 Jon Kitna .30 .14
❑ 319 Ron Dugans .20 .09
❑ 320 Chad Johnson .30 .14
❑ 321 Brandon Bennett .20 .09
❑ 322 T.J. Houshmandzadeh .20 .09
❑ 323 Rudi Johnson .50 .23
❑ 324 Kevin Hardy .20 .09
❑ 325 Corey Dillon .30 .14
❑ 326 Peter Warrick .30 .14
❑ 327 Carson Palmer RC 4.00 1.80
❑ 328 Byron Leftwich RC 5.00 2.20
❑ 329 Rex Grossman RC 3.00 1.35
❑ 330 Kyle Boller RC 3.00 1.35
❑ 331 Dave Ragone RC 1.25 .55
❑ 332 Chris Simms RC 2.50 1.10
❑ 333 Brad Banks RC 1.00 .45
❑ 334 Kliff Kingsbury RC 1.00 .45
❑ 335 Jason Gesser RC 1.25 .55
❑ 336 Jason Johnson RC .60 .25
❑ 337 Brian St.Pierre RC 1.25 .55
❑ 338 Ken Dorsey RC 2.00 .90
❑ 339 Seneca Wallace RC 1.25 .55
❑ 340 Seth Marler RC 1.00 .45
❑ 341 Tony Romo RC 1.25 .55
❑ 342 J.T. Wall RC .60 .25
❑ 343 Kirk Farmer RC .60 .25
❑ 344 Ricky Manning RC 1.25 .55
❑ 345 B.J. Askew RC 1.25 .55
❑ 346 Juston Wood RC .60 .25
❑ 347 Jeremi Johnson RC 1.00 .45
❑ 348 Tom Lopienski RC 1.00 .45
❑ 349 Justin Griffith RC 1.00 .45
❑ 350 Ovie Mughelli RC .60 .25
❑ 351 Bradie James RC 1.25 .55
❑ 352 Larry Johnson RC 2.50 1.10
❑ 353 Lee Suggs RC 2.50 1.10
❑ 354 Justin Fargas RC 1.25 .55
❑ 355 Chris Brown RC 2.50 1.10
❑ 356 Onterrio Smith RC 1.50 .70
❑ 357 Willis McGahee RC 3.00 1.35
❑ 358 Claude Diggs RC .60 .25
❑ 359 Lance Briggs RC 1.25 .55
❑ 360 Earnest Graham RC 1.00 .45
❑ 361 Quentin Griffin RC 3.00 1.35
❑ 362 Michael Haynes RC 1.25 .55
❑ 363 Musa Smith RC 1.25 .55
❑ 364 Artose Pinner RC 1.25 .55
❑ 365 Domanick Davis RC 2.50 1.10
❑ 366 LaBrandon Toefield RC 1.25 .55
❑ 367 Bethel Johnson RC 2.00 .90
❑ 368 Sultan McCullough RC 1.00 .45
❑ 369 Dahrran Diedrick RC 1.25 .55
❑ 370 Soloman Bates RC .60 .25
❑ 371 Andrew Pinnock RC 1.00 .45
❑ 372 Charles Rogers RC 1.50 .70
❑ 373 Andre Johnson RC 3.00 1.35
❑ 374 Taylor Jacobs RC 1.25 .55
❑ 375 Anquan Boldin RC 3.00 1.35
❑ 376 Talman Gardner RC 1.25 .55
❑ 377 Brandon Lloyd RC 1.50 .70
❑ 378 Bryant Johnson RC 1.25 .55
❑ 379 Kelley Washington RC 1.25 .55
❑ 380 Kareem Kelly RC 1.00 .45
❑ 381 Arnaz Battle RC 1.25 .55
❑ 382 Billy McMullen RC 1.00 .45
❑ 383 Kennan Howry RC 1.25 .55
❑ 384 Nate Burleson RC 2.00 .90
❑ 385 Doug Gabriel RC 1.25 .55
❑ 386 J.R. Tolver RC 1.00 .45
❑ 387 Wayne Hunter RC .60 .25
❑ 388 Teyo Johnson RC 1.25 .55
❑ 389 Eric Steinbach RC 1.00 .45
❑ 390 Kevin Curtis RC 1.25 .55
❑ 391 Bobby Wade RC 1.25 .55
❑ 392 Sam Aiken RC 1.00 .45
❑ 393 Willie Pile RC 1.25 .55
❑ 394 Jerel Myers RC .60 .25
❑ 395 Tyrone Calico RC 1.50 .70
❑ 396 Terrence Edwards RC 1.00 .45
❑ 397 Travis Anglin RC .60 .25
❑ 398 Antwone Savage RC .60 .25
❑ 399 Cato June RC 1.00 .45
❑ 400 Charles Drake RC .60 .25
❑ 401 Ronald Bellamy RC 1.00 .45
❑ 402 Justin Gage RC 1.25 .55
❑ 403 Mat McBriar RC .60 .25
❑ 404 Kevin Garrett RC .60 .25
❑ 405 Kenny Peterson RC 1.00 .45
❑ 406 L.J. Smith RC 1.25 .55
❑ 407 Jason Witten RC 2.00 .90
❑ 408 Dallas Clark RC 1.25 .55
❑ 409 DeWayne White RC 1.00 .45
❑ 410 Mike Seidman RC .60 .25
❑ 411 Aaron Walker RC 1.00 .45
❑ 412 Bennie Joppru RC 1.25 .55
❑ 413 Mike Pinkard RC .60 .25
❑ 414 Danny Curley RC .60 .25
❑ 415 Trent Smith RC 1.00 .45
❑ 416 George Wrighster RC 1.00 .45
❑ 417 Terrell Suggs RC 2.00 .90
❑ 418 Tully Banta-Cain RC 1.00 .45
❑ 419 Jerome McDougle RC 1.25 .55
❑ 420 William Joseph RC 1.25 .55
❑ 421 DeWayne Robertson RC 1.25 .55
❑ 422 Jimmy Kennedy RC 1.25 .55
❑ 423 Chris Kelsay RC 1.25 .55
❑ 424 Kevin Williams RC 1.25 .55
❑ 425 Boss Bailey RC 1.50 .70
❑ 426 Terry Pierce RC 1.00 .45
❑ 427 Terence Newman RC 2.50 1.10
❑ 428 Marcus Trufant RC 1.25 .55
❑ 429 Mike Doss RC 1.25 .55
❑ 430 Dennis Weathersby RC .60 .25
❑ 431 Matt Wilhelm RC 1.25 .55
❑ 432 Andre Woolfolk RC 1.25 .55
❑ 433 Shane Walton RC .60 .25
❑ 434 DeJuan Groce RC 1.25 .55
❑ 435 Antwoine Sanders RC .60 .25
❑ 436 Julian Battle RC 1.00 .45
❑ 437 Brett Favre CL .60 .25
❑ 438 Chad Pennington CL .30 .14
❑ 439 David Carr CL .50 .23
❑ 440 Drew Brees CL .30 .14

2003 Upper Deck MVP Silver

MINT NRMT

*STARS: 3X TO 8X BASIC CARDS
*ROOKIES: 1.5X TO 4X

2003 Upper Deck MVP ProSign

MINT NRMT

❑ PSBL Byron Leftwich SP EXCH 150.00 70.00
❑ PSCP0 Carson Palmer SP 135.00 60.00
❑ PSCS0 Chris Simms SP 60.00 27.00
❑ PSEL Elvis Grbac 15.00 6.75
❑ PSJM Jim Miller 15.00 6.75
❑ PSJT J.T. O'Sullivan 15.00 6.75
❑ PSKB Kyle Boller SP EXCH
❑ PSKD Ken Dorsey SP
❑ PSKK Kurt Kittner 15.00 6.75
❑ PSKL Kliff Kingsbury SP
❑ PSLJ Larry Johnson SP EXCH
❑ PSLP Luke Petitgout 15.00 6.75
❑ PSPM Peyton Manning 60.00 27.00
❑ PSQM Quincy Morgan 20.00 9.00
❑ PSRC Reche Caldwell 15.00 6.75
❑ PSRF Randy Fasani 15.00 6.75
❑ PSRG0 Rex Grossman SP 120.00 55.00
❑ PSRJ Ron Johnson 15.00 6.75
❑ PSWM Willis McGahee SP 80.00 36.00

1999 Upper Deck Ovation

Nm-Mt Ex-Mt

COMPLETE SET (90) 120.00 55.00
COMP.SET w/o SP's (60) 20.00 9.00
❑ 1 Jake Plummer .60 .25
❑ 2 Adrian Murrell .60 .25
❑ 3 Jamal Anderson 1.00 .45
❑ 4 Chris Chandler .60 .25
❑ 5 Tony Banks .60 .25
❑ 6 Antowain Smith 1.00 .45
❑ 7 Doug Flutie 1.00 .45
❑ 8 Tim Biakabutuka .60 .25
❑ 9 Steve Beuerlein .40 .18
❑ 10 Curtis Conway .60 .25
❑ 11 Curtis Enis .40 .18
❑ 12 Corey Dillon 1.00 .45
❑ 13 Jeff Blake .60 .25
❑ 14 Ty Detmer .60 .25
❑ 15 Troy Aikman 2.00 .90
❑ 16 Emmitt Smith 2.00 .90
❑ 17 Terrell Davis 1.00 .45
❑ 18 Bubby Brister .40 .18
❑ 19 Barry Sanders 3.00 1.35
❑ 20 Charlie Batch 1.00 .45
❑ 21 Brett Favre 3.00 1.35
❑ 22 Dorsey Levens 1.00 .45
❑ 23 Peyton Manning 3.00 1.35
❑ 24 Marvin Harrison 1.00 .45
❑ 25 Mark Brunell 1.00 .45
❑ 26 Fred Taylor 1.00 .45
❑ 27 Elvis Grbac .60 .25
❑ 28 Andre Rison .60 .25
❑ 29 Dan Marino 3.00 1.35
❑ 30 Karim Abdul-Jabbar .60 .25
❑ 31 Randall Cunningham 1.00 .45
❑ 32 Randy Moss 2.50 1.10
❑ 33 Drew Bledsoe 1.25 .55
❑ 34 Terry Glenn 1.00 .45
❑ 35 Danny Wuerffel .40 .18
❑ 36 Cam Cleeland .40 .18
❑ 37 Kerry Collins .60 .25
❑ 38 Amani Toomer .40 .18
❑ 39 Curtis Martin 1.00 .45
❑ 40 Keyshawn Johnson 1.00 .45

Card	Nm-Mt	Ex-Mt
❑ 41 Napoleon Kaufman	1.00	.45
❑ 42 Tim Brown	1.00	.45
❑ 43 Doug Pederson	.40	.18
❑ 44 Charles Johnson	.40	.18
❑ 45 Kordell Stewart	.60	.25
❑ 46 Jerome Bettis	1.00	.45
❑ 47 Trent Green	1.00	.45
❑ 48 Marshall Faulk	1.25	.55
❑ 49 Natrone Means	.60	.25
❑ 50 Jim Harbaugh	.60	.25
❑ 51 Steve Young	1.25	.55
❑ 52 Jerry Rice	2.00	.90
❑ 53 Joey Galloway	.60	.25
❑ 54 Jon Kitna	1.00	.45
❑ 55 Warrick Dunn	1.00	.45
❑ 56 Trent Dilfer	.60	.25
❑ 57 Steve McNair	1.00	.45
❑ 58 Eddie George	1.00	.45
❑ 59 Brad Johnson	1.00	.45
❑ 60 Skip Hicks	.40	.18
❑ 61 Tim Couch RC	2.50	1.10
❑ 62 Donovan McNabb RC	12.00	5.50
❑ 63 Akili Smith RC	2.00	.90
❑ 64 Edgerrin James RC	10.00	4.50
❑ 65 Ricky Williams RC	5.00	2.20
❑ 66 Torry Holt RC	6.00	2.70
❑ 67 Champ Bailey RC	3.00	1.35
❑ 68 David Boston RC	2.50	1.10
❑ 69 Daunte Culpepper RC	10.00	4.50
❑ 70 Cade McNown RC	2.00	.90
❑ 71 Troy Edwards RC	2.00	.90
❑ 72 Kevin Johnson RC	2.50	1.10
❑ 73 James Johnson RC	2.00	.90
❑ 74 Rob Konrad RC	2.00	.90
❑ 75 Kevin Faulk RC	2.50	1.10
❑ 76 Shaun King RC	2.00	.90
❑ 77 Peerless Price RC	4.00	1.80
❑ 78 Mike Cloud RC	2.00	.90
❑ 79 Jermaine Fazande RC	2.00	.90
❑ 80 D'Wayne Bates RC	2.00	.90
❑ 81 Brock Huard RC	2.50	1.10
❑ 82 Marty Booker RC	2.50	1.10
❑ 83 Karsten Bailey RC	2.00	.90
❑ 84 Al Wilson RC	2.00	.90
❑ 85 Joe Germaine RC	2.00	.90
❑ 86 Dameane Douglas RC	1.25	.55
❑ 87 Sedrick Irvin RC	1.25	.55
❑ 88 Amos Zereoue RC	2.50	1.10
❑ 89 Cecil Collins RC	1.25	.55
❑ 90 Ebenezer Ekuban RC	1.25	.55
❑ WPO Walter Payton Jersey AUTO/34	1000.00	450.00

1999 Upper Deck Ovation Super Signatures Silver

	Nm-Mt	Ex-Mt
*GOLDS: .75X TO 1.5X SILVERS		
❑ JM Joe Montana	150.00	70.00
❑ JN Joe Namath	120.00	55.00
❑ WP Walter Payton	350.00	160.00

2000 Upper Deck Ovation

	Nm-Mt	Ex-Mt
COMPLETE SET (90)	250.00	110.00
COMP.SET w/o SP's (60)	20.00	9.00
❑ 1 Jake Plummer	.40	.18
❑ 2 Frank Sanders	.40	.18

Card	Nm-Mt	Ex-Mt
❑ 3 Chris Chandler	.40	.18
❑ 4 Jamal Anderson	.60	.25
❑ 5 Qadry Ismail	.40	.18
❑ 6 Eric Moulds	.60	.25
❑ 7 Muhsin Muhammad	.40	.18
❑ 8 Steve Beuerlein	.40	.18
❑ 9 Cade McNown	.25	.11
❑ 10 Marcus Robinson	.60	.25
❑ 11 Akili Smith	.25	.11
❑ 12 Corey Dillon	.60	.25
❑ 13 Tim Couch	.40	.18
❑ 14 Kevin Johnson	.60	.25
❑ 15 Troy Aikman	1.25	.55
❑ 16 Emmitt Smith	1.25	.55
❑ 17 Terrell Davis	.60	.25
❑ 18 Olandis Gary	.60	.25
❑ 19 Charlie Batch	.60	.25
❑ 20 Germane Crowell	.25	.11
❑ 21 Brett Favre	2.00	.90
❑ 22 Antonio Freeman	.60	.25
❑ 23 Peyton Manning	1.50	.70
❑ 24 Edgerrin James	1.00	.45
❑ 25 Mark Brunell	.60	.25
❑ 26 Fred Taylor	.60	.25
❑ 27 Elvis Grbac	.40	.18
❑ 28 Tony Gonzalez	.40	.18
❑ 29 Tony Martin	.40	.18
❑ 30 Damon Huard	.60	.25
❑ 31 Randy Moss	1.25	.55
❑ 32 Daunte Culpepper	.75	.35
❑ 33 Drew Bledsoe	.75	.35
❑ 34 Terry Glenn	.40	.18
❑ 35 Ricky Williams	.60	.25
❑ 36 Jeff Blake	.40	.18
❑ 37 Kerry Collins	.40	.18
❑ 38 Amani Toomer	.40	.18
❑ 39 Curtis Martin	.60	.25
❑ 40 Vinny Testaverde	.40	.18
❑ 41 Tim Brown	.60	.25
❑ 42 Rickey Dudley	.25	.11
❑ 43 Duce Staley	.60	.25
❑ 44 Donovan McNabb	1.00	.45
❑ 45 Troy Edwards	.25	.11
❑ 46 Jerome Bettis	.60	.25
❑ 47 Marshall Faulk	.75	.35
❑ 48 Kurt Warner	1.25	.55
❑ 49 Freddie Jones	.25	.11
❑ 50 Junior Seau	.60	.25
❑ 51 Jerry Rice	1.25	.55
❑ 52 Steve Young	.75	.35
❑ 53 Ricky Watters	.40	.18
❑ 54 Jon Kitna	.60	.25
❑ 55 Shaun King	.25	.11
❑ 56 Keyshawn Johnson	.60	.25
❑ 57 Eddie George	.60	.25
❑ 58 Steve McNair	.60	.25
❑ 59 Brad Johnson	.60	.25
❑ 60 Stephen Davis	.60	.25
❑ 61 Courtney Brown RC	5.00	2.20
❑ 62 Corey Simon RC	5.00	2.20
❑ 63 R.Jay Soward RC	4.00	1.80
❑ 64 Anthony Becht RC	5.00	2.20
❑ 65 Chris Redman RC	4.00	1.80
❑ 66 Chad Pennington RC	20.00	9.00
❑ 67 Tee Martin RC	5.00	2.20
❑ 68 Giovanni Carmazzi RC	4.00	1.80
❑ 69 Ron Dayne RC	5.00	2.20
❑ 70 Shaun Alexander RC	12.00	5.50
❑ 71 Thomas Jones RC	8.00	3.60
❑ 72 Reuben Droughns RC	6.00	2.70
❑ 73 Jamal Lewis RC	12.00	5.50
❑ 74 J.R. Redmond RC	4.00	1.80
❑ 75 Travis Prentice RC	4.00	1.80
❑ 76 Trung Canidate RC	4.00	1.80
❑ 77 Brian Urlacher RC	20.00	9.00
❑ 78 Bubba Franks RC	5.00	2.20
❑ 79 Peter Warrick RC	5.00	2.20
❑ 80 Plaxico Burress RC	10.00	4.50
❑ 81 Sylvester Morris RC	4.00	1.80
❑ 82 Dez White RC	5.00	2.20
❑ 83 Travis Taylor RC	5.00	2.20
❑ 84 Todd Pinkston RC	5.00	2.20
❑ 85 Dennis Northcutt RC	5.00	2.20
❑ 86 Jerry Porter RC	6.00	2.70
❑ 87 Laveranues Coles RC	6.00	2.70
❑ 88 Danny Farmer RC	4.00	1.80
❑ 89 Curtis Keaton RC	4.00	1.80
❑ 90 Ron Dugans RC	4.00	1.80

2000 Upper Deck Ovation Super Signatures Silver

	Nm-Mt	Ex-Mt
*GOLD CARDS: .6X TO 1.5X BASIC INSERTS		
❑ BJ Brad Johnson		
❑ DF Doug Flutie		
❑ EG Eddie George	50.00	22.00
❑ JB Jim Brown	120.00	55.00
❑ JN Joe Namath	120.00	55.00
❑ MB Mark Brunell	60.00	27.00
❑ MF Marshall Faulk	60.00	27.00
❑ PM Peyton Manning	120.00	55.00
❑ RM Randy Moss	120.00	55.00
❑ TD Terrell Davis	60.00	27.00

2001 Upper Deck Ovation

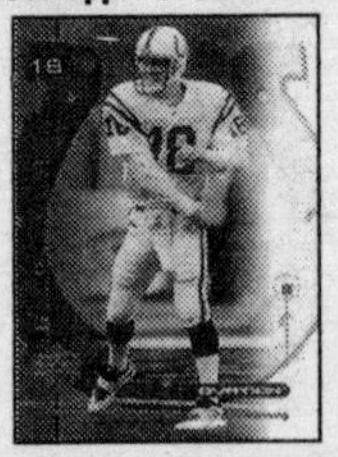

	Nm-Mt	Ex-Mt
COMP.SET w/o SP's (90)	25.00	7.50
❑ 1 Jake Plummer	.40	.12
❑ 2 Thomas Jones	.40	.12
❑ 3 Frank Sanders	.25	.07
❑ 4 Jamal Anderson	.60	.18
❑ 5 Chris Chandler	.40	.12
❑ 6 Terance Mathis	.25	.07
❑ 7 Jamal Lewis	1.00	.30
❑ 8 Elvis Grbac	.40	.12
❑ 9 Travis Taylor	.40	.12
❑ 10 Shawn Bryson	.25	.07
❑ 11 Rob Johnson	.40	.12

❑ 12 Eric Moulds	.40	.12
❑ 13 Muhsin Muhammad	.40	.12
❑ 14 Donald Hayes	.25	.07
❑ 15 Tim Biakabutuka	.40	.12
❑ 16 Cade McNown	.25	.07
❑ 17 Marcus Robinson	.60	.18
❑ 18 Brian Urlacher	1.00	.30
❑ 19 Akili Smith	.25	.07
❑ 20 Peter Warrick	.60	.18
❑ 21 Corey Dillon	.60	.18
❑ 22 Kevin Johnson	.40	.12
❑ 23 Spergon Wynn	.25	.07
❑ 24 Tim Couch	.40	.12
❑ 25 Tony Banks	.40	.12
❑ 26 Emmitt Smith	1.25	.35
❑ 27 Anthony Wright	.25	.07
❑ 28 Terrell Davis	.60	.18
❑ 29 Mike Anderson	.60	.18
❑ 30 Brian Griese	.60	.18
❑ 31 Ed McCaffrey	.60	.18
❑ 32 Charlie Batch	.60	.18
❑ 33 Germane Crowell	.25	.07
❑ 34 Johnnie Morton	.40	.12
❑ 35 Brett Favre	2.00	.60
❑ 36 Antonio Freeman	.60	.18
❑ 37 Dorsey Levens	.40	.12
❑ 38 Ahman Green	.60	.18
❑ 39 Peyton Manning	1.50	.45
❑ 40 Edgerrin James	.75	.23
❑ 41 Marvin Harrison	.60	.18
❑ 42 Mark Brunell	.60	.18
❑ 43 Fred Taylor	.60	.18
❑ 44 Jimmy Smith	.40	.12
❑ 45 Tony Gonzalez	.40	.12
❑ 46 Trent Green	.60	.18
❑ 47 Derrick Alexander	.40	.12
❑ 48 Oronde Gadsden	.40	.12
❑ 49 Tony Martin	.40	.12
❑ 50 Lamar Smith	.40	.12
❑ 51 Randy Moss	1.25	.35
❑ 52 Cris Carter	.60	.18
❑ 53 Daunte Culpepper	.60	.18
❑ 54 Drew Bledsoe	.75	.23
❑ 55 Terry Glenn	.40	.12
❑ 56 Ricky Williams	.60	.18
❑ 57 Jeff Blake	.40	.12
❑ 58 Aaron Brooks	.60	.18
❑ 59 Kerry Collins	.40	.12
❑ 60 Tiki Barber	.40	.12
❑ 61 Ron Dayne	.60	.18
❑ 62 Vinny Testaverde	.40	.12
❑ 63 Wayne Chrebet	.40	.12
❑ 64 Curtis Martin	.60	.18
❑ 65 Tim Brown	.60	.18
❑ 66 Rich Gannon	.60	.18
❑ 67 Jerry Rice	1.25	.35
❑ 68 Duce Staley	.60	.18
❑ 69 Donovan McNabb	.75	.23
❑ 70 Kordell Stewart	.40	.12
❑ 71 Jerome Bettis	.60	.18
❑ 72 Marshall Faulk	.75	.23
❑ 73 Kurt Warner	1.25	.35
❑ 74 Isaac Bruce	.60	.18
❑ 75 Doug Flutie	.60	.18
❑ 76 Junior Seau	.60	.18
❑ 77 Jeff Garcia	.60	.18
❑ 78 Garrison Hearst	.40	.12
❑ 79 Terrell Owens	.60	.18
❑ 80 Ricky Watters	.40	.12
❑ 81 Matt Hasselbeck	.40	.12
❑ 82 Keyshawn Johnson	.60	.18
❑ 83 Warrick Dunn	.60	.18
❑ 84 Mike Alstott	.60	.18
❑ 85 Kevin Dyson	.40	.12
❑ 86 Eddie George	.60	.18
❑ 87 Steve McNair	.60	.18
❑ 88 Jeff George	.40	.12
❑ 89 Michael Westbrook	.40	.12
❑ 90 Stephen Davis	.60	.18
❑ 91 Milton Wynn RC	5.00	1.50
❑ 92 Dan Alexander RC	8.00	2.40
❑ 93 Rudi Johnson RC	15.00	4.50
❑ 94 Ken-Yon Rambo RC	5.00	1.50
❑ 95 Alex Bannister RC	5.00	1.50
❑ 96 Adam Archuleta RC	8.00	2.40
❑ 97 Andre Dyson RC	3.00	.90
❑ 98 Cedrick Wilson RC	8.00	2.40
❑ 99 Chris Taylor RC	5.00	1.50
❑ 100 Eddie Berlin RC	5.00	1.50
❑ 101 Gary Baxter RC	5.00	1.50
❑ 102 Heath Evans RC	5.00	1.50
❑ 103 Jabari Holloway RC	5.00	1.50
❑ 104 Jamal Reynolds RC	8.00	2.40
❑ 105 Jamar Fletcher RC	5.00	1.50
❑ 106 Justin Smith RC	8.00	2.40
❑ 107 Kevin Kasper RC	8.00	2.40
❑ 108 Moran Norris RC	3.00	.90
❑ 109 Nate Clements RC	8.00	2.40
❑ 110 Scotty Anderson RC	5.00	1.50
❑ 111 T.J. Houshmandzadeh RC	8.00	2.40
❑ 112 Travis Minor RC	5.00	1.50
❑ 113 Vinny Sutherland RC	5.00	1.50
❑ 114 Will Allen RC	5.00	1.50
❑ 115 Derrick Gibson RC	5.00	1.50
❑ 116 Kevan Barlow RC	10.00	3.00
❑ 117 LaMont Jordan RC	12.00	3.60
❑ 118 Todd Heap RC	8.00	2.40
❑ 119 Quincy Morgan RC	8.00	2.40
❑ 120 Dan Morgan RC	10.00	3.00
❑ 121 Gerard Warren RC	10.00	3.00
❑ 122 Mike McMahon RC	10.00	3.00
❑ 123 Sage Rosenfels RC	8.00	2.40
❑ 124 Marques Tuiasosopo RC	10.00	3.00
❑ 125 Josh Heupel RC	8.00	2.40
❑ 126 Jesse Palmer RC	10.00	3.00
❑ 127 Quincy Carter RC	10.00	3.00
❑ 128 Josh Booty RC	10.00	3.00
❑ 129 Correll Buckhalter RC	12.00	3.60
❑ 130 Travis Henry RC	12.00	3.60
❑ 131 Alge Crumpler RC	12.00	3.60
❑ 132 Snoop Minnis RC	6.00	1.80
❑ 133 Bobby Newcombe RC	6.00	1.80
❑ 134 Robert Ferguson RC	10.00	3.00
❑ 135 James Jackson RC	8.00	2.40
❑ 136 Michael Bennett RC	25.00	7.50
❑ 137 Drew Brees RC	25.00	7.50
❑ 138 Chris Chambers RC	15.00	4.50
❑ 139 Rod Gardner RC	10.00	3.00
❑ 140 Chad Johnson RC	25.00	7.50
❑ 141 Freddie Mitchell RC	10.00	3.00
❑ 142 Deuce McAllister RC	30.00	9.00
❑ 143 Santana Moss RC	25.00	7.50
❑ 144 Koren Robinson RC	12.00	3.60
❑ 145 David Terrell RC	8.00	2.40
❑ 146 LaDainian Tomlinson RC	40.00	12.00
❑ 147 Anthony Thomas RC	20.00	6.00
❑ 148 Reggie Wayne RC	20.00	6.00
❑ 149 Michael Vick RC	80.00	24.00
❑ 150 Chris Weinke RC	10.00	3.00

2001 Upper Deck Ovation Rookie Autographs

	Nm-Mt	Ex-Mt
❑ 136 Michael Bennett	50.00	15.00
❑ 137 Drew Brees	60.00	18.00
❑ 138 Chris Chambers	30.00	9.00
❑ 139 Rod Gardner	25.00	7.50
❑ 140 Chad Johnson	60.00	18.00
❑ 141 Freddie Mitchell	25.00	7.50
❑ 142 Deuce McAllister	80.00	24.00
❑ 143 Santana Moss	40.00	12.00
❑ 144 Koren Robinson EXCH		
❑ 145 David Terrell	30.00	9.00
❑ 146 LaDainian Tomlinson	120.00	36.00
❑ 147 Anthony Thomas	40.00	12.00
❑ 148 Reggie Wayne	40.00	12.00
❑ 149 Michael Vick	200.00	60.00
❑ 150 Chris Weinke	25.00	7.50

2004 Upper Deck Power Up

	Nm-Mt	Ex-Mt
COMPLETE SET (100)	25.00	7.50
❑ 1 Emmitt Smith	1.25	.35
❑ 2 Anquan Boldin	.60	.18
❑ 3 Josh McCown	.40	.12
❑ 4 Michael Vick	1.25	.35
❑ 5 Peerless Price	.40	.12
❑ 6 Warrick Dunn	.40	.12
❑ 7 Jamal Lewis	.60	.18
❑ 8 Kyle Boller	.60	.18
❑ 9 Ray Lewis	.60	.18
❑ 10 Drew Bledsoe	.60	.18
❑ 11 Travis Henry	.40	.12
❑ 12 Eric Moulds	.40	.12
❑ 13 Jake Delhomme	.60	.18
❑ 14 Steve Smith	.40	.12
❑ 15 Stephen Davis	.40	.12
❑ 16 Anthony Thomas	.40	.12
❑ 17 Marty Booker	.40	.12
❑ 18 Rex Grossman	.60	.18
❑ 19 Chad Johnson	.40	.12
❑ 20 Rudi Johnson	.40	.12
❑ 21 Jon Kitna	.40	.12
❑ 22 Andre Davis	.25	.07
❑ 23 Jeff Garcia	.60	.18
❑ 24 William Green	.40	.12
❑ 25 Antonio Bryant	.40	.12
❑ 26 Quincy Carter	.40	.12
❑ 27 Keyshawn Johnson	.40	.12
❑ 28 Champ Bailey	.40	.12
❑ 29 Jake Plummer	.40	.12
❑ 30 Ashley Lelie	.40	.12
❑ 31 Charles Rogers	.40	.12
❑ 32 Joey Harrington	.60	.18
❑ 33 Az-Zahir Hakim	.25	.07
❑ 34 Brett Favre	1.50	.45
❑ 35 Javon Walker	.40	.12
❑ 36 Ahman Green	.60	.18
❑ 37 David Carr	.60	.18
❑ 38 Domanick Davis	.60	.18
❑ 39 Andre Johnson	.60	.18
❑ 40 Peyton Manning	1.00	.30
❑ 41 Marvin Harrison	.60	.18
❑ 42 Edgerrin James	.60	.18
❑ 43 Byron Leftwich	1.00	.30
❑ 44 Fred Taylor	.40	.12
❑ 45 Jimmy Smith	.40	.12
❑ 46 Priest Holmes	.75	.23
❑ 47 Trent Green	.40	.12
❑ 48 Dante Hall	.60	.18
❑ 49 Tony Gonzalez	.40	.12
❑ 50 Ricky Williams	.60	.18
❑ 51 Jay Fiedler	.25	.07
❑ 52 Chris Chambers	.40	.12
❑ 53 Daunte Culpepper	.60	.18
❑ 54 Randy Moss	.75	.23
❑ 55 Onterrio Smith	.40	.12
❑ 56 Troy Brown	.40	.12
❑ 57 Deion Branch	.60	.18
❑ 58 Tom Brady	1.00	.30
❑ 59 Deuce McAllister	.60	.18
❑ 60 Aaron Brooks	.40	.12
❑ 61 Joe Horn	.40	.12
❑ 62 Jeremy Shockey	.60	.18
❑ 63 Amani Toomer	.40	.12
❑ 64 Tiki Barber	.40	.12
❑ 65 Chad Pennington	.75	.23
❑ 66 Santana Moss	.40	.12
❑ 67 Curtis Martin	.60	.18
❑ 68 Rich Gannon	.40	.12
❑ 69 Jerry Rice	1.25	.35
❑ 70 Tim Brown	.60	.18
❑ 71 Jerry Porter	.40	.12
❑ 72 Donovan McNabb	.75	.23
❑ 73 Terrell Owens	.60	.18
❑ 74 Jevon Kearse	.40	.12
❑ 75 Hines Ward	.60	.18

Card	Nm-Mt	Ex-Mt
❑ 76 Jerome Bettis	.60	.18
❑ 77 Tommy Maddox	.40	.12
❑ 78 Plaxico Burress	.40	.12
❑ 79 LaDainian Tomlinson	.60	.18
❑ 80 Antonio Gates	.60	.18
❑ 81 Drew Brees	.60	.18
❑ 82 Tim Rattay	.40	.12
❑ 83 Brandon Lloyd	.40	.12
❑ 84 Kevan Barlow	.40	.12
❑ 85 Matt Hasselbeck	.40	.12
❑ 86 Shaun Alexander	.60	.18
❑ 87 Koren Robinson	.40	.12
❑ 88 Marshall Faulk	.60	.18
❑ 89 Torry Holt	.60	.18
❑ 90 Marc Bulger	.60	.18
❑ 91 Isaac Bruce	.40	.12
❑ 92 Brad Johnson	.40	.12
❑ 93 Charlie Garner	.40	.12
❑ 94 Keenan McCardell	.25	.07
❑ 95 Steve McNair	.60	.18
❑ 96 Eddie George	.40	.12
❑ 97 Derrick Mason	.40	.12
❑ 98 Mark Brunell	.40	.12
❑ 99 Laveranues Coles	.40	.12
❑ 100 Clinton Portis	.60	.18

2004 Upper Deck Power Up Blue

Nm-Mt Ex-Mt

*BLUE: 8X TO 20X BASE CARD HI
OVERALL PARALLEL STATED ODDS 1:4
BLUE WORTH 1000 POINTS EACH

2004 Upper Deck Power Up Green

Nm-Mt Ex-Mt

*GREENS: 2X TO 5X BASE CARD HI
OVERALL PARALLEL STATED ODDS 1:4
GREEN WORTH 100 POINTS EACH

2004 Upper Deck Power Up Orange

Nm-Mt Ex-Mt

*ORANGE: 3X TO 8X BASE CARD HI
OVERALL PARALLEL STATED ODDS 1:4
ORANGE WORTH 250 POINTS EACH

2004 Upper Deck Power Up Red

Nm-Mt Ex-Mt

*REDS: 5X TO 12X BASE CARD HI
OVERALL PARALLEL STATED ODDS 1:4
RED WORTH 500 POINTS EACH

2004 Upper Deck Power Up Shining Through

	Nm-Mt	Ex-Mt
COMPLETE SET (30)	20.00	6.00
STATED ODDS 1:1		
❑ ST1 Anquan Boldin	1.00	.30
❑ ST2 Michael Vick	2.00	.60
❑ ST3 Jamal Lewis	1.00	.30
❑ ST4 Aaron Brooks	.60	.18
❑ ST5 DeShaun Foster	.60	.18
❑ ST6 Rex Grossman	1.00	.30
❑ ST7 Rudi Johnson	.60	.18
❑ ST8 Andre Davis	.40	.12
❑ ST9 Antonio Bryant	.60	.18
❑ ST10 Clinton Portis	1.00	.30
❑ ST11 Brett Favre	2.50	.75
❑ ST12 David Carr	1.00	.30
❑ ST13 Marvin Harrison	1.00	.30
❑ ST14 Byron Leftwich	1.50	.45
❑ ST15 Priest Holmes	1.25	.35
❑ ST16 Dante Hall	1.00	.30
❑ ST17 Chris Chambers	.60	.18
❑ ST18 Daunte Culpepper	1.00	.30
❑ ST19 Tom Brady	1.50	.45
❑ ST20 Deuce McAllister	1.00	.30
❑ ST21 Jeremy Shockey	1.00	.30
❑ ST22 Santana Moss	.60	.18
❑ ST23 Jerry Rice	2.00	.60
❑ ST24 Donovan McNabb	1.25	.35
❑ ST25 Plaxico Burress	.60	.18
❑ ST26 LaDainian Tomlinson	1.00	.30
❑ ST27 Koren Robinson	.60	.18
❑ ST28 Ahman Green	1.00	.30
❑ ST29 Steve McNair	1.00	.30
❑ ST30 Laveranues Coles	.60	.18

2004 Upper Deck Power Up Stickers

	Nm-Mt	Ex-Mt
COMPLETE SET (30)	50.00	15.00
STATED ODDS 1:6		
❑ PU1 Emmitt Smith	4.00	1.20
❑ PU2 Michael Vick	4.00	1.20
❑ PU3 Kyle Boller	2.00	.60
❑ PU4 Drew Bledsoe	2.00	.60
❑ PU5 Jake Delhomme	2.00	.60
❑ PU6 Brian Urlacher	2.50	.75
❑ PU7 Carson Palmer	2.50	.75
❑ PU8 Quincy Carter	1.25	.35
❑ PU9 Jake Plummer	1.25	.35
❑ PU10 Joey Harrington	2.00	.60
❑ PU11 Brett Favre	5.00	1.50
❑ PU12 David Carr	2.00	.60
❑ PU13 Peyton Manning	3.00	.90
❑ PU14 Byron Leftwich	3.00	.90
❑ PU15 Priest Holmes	2.50	.75
❑ PU16 Ricky Williams	2.00	.60
❑ PU17 Randy Moss	2.50	.75
❑ PU18 Tom Brady	3.00	.90
❑ PU19 Deuce McAllister	2.00	.60
❑ PU20 Chad Pennington	2.50	.75
❑ PU21 Jeremy Shockey	2.00	.60
❑ PU22 Jerry Rice	4.00	1.20
❑ PU23 Donovan McNabb	2.50	.75
❑ PU24 Hines Ward	2.00	.60
❑ PU25 LaDainian Tomlinson	2.00	.60
❑ PU26 Kevan Barlow	1.25	.35
❑ PU27 Matt Hasselbeck	1.25	.35
❑ PU28 Marshall Faulk	2.00	.60
❑ PU29 Steve McNair	2.00	.60
❑ PU30 Clinton Portis	2.00	.60

2000 Upper Deck Pros and Prospects

	Nm-Mt	Ex-Mt
COMPLETE SET (126)	600.00	275.00
COMP.SET w/o SP's (84)	20.00	9.00
❑ 1 Jake Plummer	.30	.14
❑ 2 Michael Pittman	.20	.09
❑ 3 Tim Dwight	.50	.23
❑ 4 Chris Chandler	.30	.14
❑ 5 Qadry Ismail	.30	.14
❑ 6 Shannon Sharpe	.30	.14
❑ 7 Peerless Price	.50	.23
❑ 8 Rob Johnson	.30	.14
❑ 9 Eric Moulds	.50	.23
❑ 10 Muhsin Muhammad	.30	.14
❑ 11 Patrick Jeffers	.50	.23
❑ 12 Steve Beuerlein	.30	.14
❑ 13 Cade McNown	.20	.09
❑ 14 Curtis Enis	.20	.09
❑ 15 Marcus Robinson	.50	.23
❑ 16 Akili Smith	.20	.09
❑ 17 Corey Dillon	.50	.23
❑ 18 Tim Couch	.30	.14
❑ 19 Kevin Johnson	.50	.23
❑ 20 Errict Rhett	.30	.14
❑ 21 Troy Aikman	1.00	.45
❑ 22 Emmitt Smith	1.00	.45
❑ 23 Rocket Ismail	.30	.14
❑ 24 Terrell Davis	.50	.23
❑ 25 Olandis Gary	.50	.23
❑ 26 Brian Griese	.50	.23
❑ 27 Ed McCaffrey	.50	.23
❑ 28 Charlie Batch	.50	.23
❑ 29 Germane Crowell	.20	.09
❑ 30 James O. Stewart	.30	.14
❑ 31 Brett Favre	1.50	.70
❑ 32 Antonio Freeman	.50	.23
❑ 33 Dorsey Levens	.30	.14
❑ 34 Peyton Manning	1.25	.55
❑ 35 Edgerrin James	.75	.35
❑ 36 Marvin Harrison	.50	.23
❑ 37 Mark Brunell	.50	.23
❑ 38 Fred Taylor	.50	.23
❑ 39 Jimmy Smith	.30	.14
❑ 40 Elvis Grbac	.30	.14
❑ 41 Tony Gonzalez	.30	.14
❑ 42 Damon Huard	.50	.23
❑ 43 James Johnson	.20	.09
❑ 44 Jay Fiedler	.50	.23
❑ 45 Randy Moss	1.00	.45
❑ 46 Robert Smith	.50	.23
❑ 47 Cris Carter	.50	.23
❑ 48 Drew Bledsoe	.60	.25
❑ 49 Terry Glenn	.30	.14
❑ 50 Ricky Williams	.50	.23
❑ 51 Jeff Blake	.30	.14
❑ 52 Keith Poole	.20	.09
❑ 53 Kerry Collins	.30	.14
❑ 54 Amani Toomer	.20	.09
❑ 55 Vinny Testaverde	.30	.14
❑ 56 Keyshawn Johnson	.50	.23
❑ 57 Curtis Martin	.50	.23
❑ 58 Tim Brown	.50	.23
❑ 59 Rich Gannon	.50	.23
❑ 60 Tyrone Wheatley	.30	.14
❑ 61 Duce Staley	.50	.23
❑ 62 Donovan McNabb	.75	.35
❑ 63 Troy Edwards	.20	.09
❑ 64 Jerome Bettis	.50	.23
❑ 65 Marshall Faulk	.60	.25
❑ 66 Kurt Warner	1.00	.45
❑ 67 Torry Holt	.50	.23
❑ 68 Isaac Bruce	.50	.23
❑ 69 Junior Seau	.50	.23

❑ 70 Jeff Graham .20 .09
❑ 71 Steve Young .60 .25
❑ 72 Jerry Rice 1.00 .45
❑ 73 Charlie Garner .30 .14
❑ 74 Ricky Watters .30 .14
❑ 75 Jon Kitna .50 .23
❑ 76 Warrick Dunn .50 .23
❑ 77 Shaun King .20 .09
❑ 78 Mike Alstott .50 .23
❑ 79 Eddie George .50 .23
❑ 80 Steve McNair .50 .23
❑ 81 Kevin Dyson .30 .14
❑ 82 Brad Johnson .50 .23
❑ 83 Stephen Davis .50 .23
❑ 84 Michael Westbrook .30 .14
❑ 85 Peter Warrick RC 12.00 5.50
❑ 86 LaVar Arrington RC 60.00 27.00
❑ 87 Chris Redman RC 10.00 4.50
❑ 88 Courtney Brown RC 12.00 5.50
❑ 89 Plaxico Burress RC 25.00 11.00
❑ 90 Corey Simon RC 12.00 5.50
❑ 91 Bubba Franks RC 12.00 5.50
❑ 92 Deon Grant RC 10.00 4.50
❑ 93 Brian Urlacher RC 40.00 18.00
❑ 94 Ron Dayne RC 12.00 5.50
❑ 95 Sylvester Morris RC 10.00 4.50
❑ 96 Shaun Alexander RC 30.00 13.50
❑ 97 Dez White RC 12.00 5.50
❑ 98 Thomas Jones RC 20.00 9.00
❑ 99 Travis Taylor RC 12.00 5.50
❑ 100 Kwame Cavil RC 6.00 2.70
❑ 101 Jamal Lewis RC 30.00 13.50
❑ 102 Chad Pennington RC 40.00 18.00
❑ 103 J.R. Redmond RC 10.00 4.50
❑ 104 Sebastian Janikowski RC 12.00 5.50
❑ 105 Anthony Lucas RC 6.00 2.70
❑ 106 Travis Prentice RC 10.00 4.50
❑ 107 Danny Farmer RC 10.00 4.50
❑ 108 Sherrod Gideon RC 6.00 2.70
❑ 109 Todd Pinkston RC 12.00 5.50
❑ 110 Dennis Northcutt RC 12.00 5.50
❑ 111 Tim Rattay RC 25.00 11.00
❑ 112 Troy Walters RC 12.00 5.50
❑ 113 Michael Wiley RC 10.00 4.50
❑ 114 R.Jay Soward RC 10.00 4.50
❑ 115 Trung Canidate RC 10.00 4.50
❑ 116 Reuben Droughns RC 15.00 6.75
❑ 117 Rondell Mealey RC 6.00 2.70
❑ 118 Chris Coleman RC 12.00 5.50
❑ 119 Giovanni Carmazzi RC 10.00 4.50
❑ 120 Trevor Insley RC 10.00 4.50
❑ 121 Shyrone Stith RC 10.00 4.50
❑ 122 Gari Scott RC 6.00 2.70
❑ 123 Tee Martin RC 12.00 5.50
❑ 124 Tom Brady RC 135.00 60.00
❑ 125 Marcus Knight RC 10.00 4.50
❑ 126 Jerry Porter RC 25.00 11.00
❑ 127 Brad Hoover RC 5.00 2.20
❑ 128 Chad Morton RC 8.00 3.60
❑ 129 Charles Lee RC 5.00 2.20
❑ 130 Damon Hodge RC 5.00 2.20
❑ 131 Darrell Jackson RC 15.00 6.75
❑ 132 Doug Johnson RC 8.00 3.60
❑ 133 Frank Moreau RC 5.00 2.20
❑ 134 JaJuan Dawson RC 5.00 2.20
❑ 135 Jake Delhomme RC 30.00 13.50
❑ 136 Jarious Jackson RC 5.00 2.20
❑ 137 Joe Hamilton RC 5.00 2.20
❑ 138 Larry Foster RC 5.00 2.20
❑ 139 Laveranues Coles RC 10.00 4.50
❑ 140 Aaron Shea RC 8.00 3.60
❑ 141 Matt Lytle RC 5.00 2.20
❑ 142 Mike Anderson RC 12.00 5.50
❑ 143 Ron Dixon RC 5.00 2.20
❑ 144 Ronney Jenkins RC 5.00 2.20
❑ 145 Sammy Morris RC 5.00 2.20
❑ 146 Shockmain Davis RC 5.00 2.20
❑ 147 Spergon Wynn RC 5.00 2.20
❑ 148 Todd Husak RC 8.00 3.60
❑ 149 Trevor Gaylor RC 5.00 2.20
❑ 150 Tywan Mitchell RC 5.00 2.20
❑ 151 Windrell Hayes RC 5.00 2.20
❑ 152 Bobby Shaw RC 5.00 2.20

2000 Upper Deck Pros and Prospects Signature Piece 1

	Nm-Mt	Ex-Mt
❑ SPBG Brian Griese	40.00	18.00
❑ SPCB Champ Bailey	50.00	22.00
❑ SPCC Chris Claiborne	30.00	13.50
❑ SPDB Drew Bledsoe	80.00	36.00
❑ SPDF Danny Farmer	30.00	13.50
❑ SPDL Dorsey Levens	40.00	18.00
❑ SPDM Dan Marino	250.00	110.00
❑ SPEG Edgerrin James	80.00	36.00
❑ SPIB Isaac Bruce	50.00	22.00
❑ SPKJ Kevin Johnson	30.00	13.50
❑ SPKW Kurt Warner	80.00	36.00
❑ SPMB Mark Brunell	40.00	18.00
❑ SPMF Marshall Faulk	60.00	27.00
❑ SPMH Marvin Harrison	50.00	22.00
❑ SPOG Olandis Gary	40.00	18.00
❑ SPPM Peyton Manning	100.00	45.00
❑ SPRD Ron Dayne	30.00	13.50
❑ SPRL Ray Lucas	30.00	13.50
❑ SPRM Randy Moss	100.00	45.00
❑ SPTA Troy Aikman	100.00	45.00
❑ SPTH Torry Holt	50.00	22.00
❑ SPTO Terrell Owens	50.00	22.00
❑ SPWR Key. Johnson	40.00	18.00

2000 Upper Deck Pros and Prospects Signature Piece 2

	Nm-Mt	Ex-Mt
❑ SPBG Brian Griese/14		
❑ SPCB Champ Bailey/24		
❑ SPCC Chris Claiborne/50	100.00	45.00
❑ SPDB Drew Bledsoe/11		
❑ SPDF Danny Farmer/87	100.00	45.00
❑ SPDL Dorsey Levens/25	120.00	55.00
❑ SPDM Dan Marino/13		
❑ SPED Edgerrin James/32	300.00	135.00
❑ SPIB Isaac Bruce/80	100.00	45.00
❑ SPKJ Kevin Johnson/86	100.00	45.00
❑ SPKW Kurt Warner/13		
❑ SPMB Mark Brunell/8		
❑ SPMF Marshall Faulk/28	200.00	90.00
❑ SPMH Marvin Harrison/88	100.00	45.00
❑ SPOG Olandis Gary/22		
❑ SPPM Peyton Manning/18		
❑ SPRD Ron Dayne/33	150.00	70.00
❑ SPRL Ray Lucas/6		
❑ SPRM Randy Moss/84	200.00	90.00
❑ SPTA Troy Aikman/8		
❑ SPTH Torry Holt/88	150.00	70.00
❑ SPTO Terrell Owens/81	150.00	70.00
❑ SPWR Keyshawn Johnson/19		

2001 Upper Deck Pros and Prospects

	Nm-Mt	Ex-Mt
COMP.SET w/o SP's (90)	15.00	4.50
❑ 1 Jake Plummer	.30	.14
❑ 2 David Boston	.50	.23
❑ 3 Jamal Anderson	.50	.23
❑ 4 Doug Johnson	.20	.09
❑ 5 Maurice Smith	.30	.14
❑ 6 Jamal Lewis	.75	.35
❑ 7 Shannon Sharpe	.30	.14
❑ 8 Trent Dilfer	.30	.14
❑ 9 Doug Flutie	.50	.23
❑ 10 Rob Johnson	.30	.14
❑ 11 Eric Moulds	.50	.23
❑ 12 Muhsin Muhammad	.30	.14
❑ 13 Brad Hoover	.20	.09
❑ 14 Tim Biakabutuka	.30	.14
❑ 15 Cade McNown	.20	.09
❑ 16 James Allen	.30	.14
❑ 17 Marcus Robinson	.50	.23
❑ 18 Brian Urlacher	.75	.35
❑ 19 Peter Warrick	.50	.23
❑ 20 Corey Dillon	.50	.23
❑ 21 Tim Couch	.30	.14
❑ 22 Kevin Johnson	.30	.14
❑ 23 Travis Prentice	.20	.09
❑ 24 Troy Aikman	.75	.35
❑ 25 Emmitt Smith	1.00	.45
❑ 26 Terrell Davis	.50	.23
❑ 27 Mike Anderson	.50	.23
❑ 28 Brian Griese	.50	.23
❑ 29 Charlie Batch	.50	.23
❑ 30 Germane Crowell	.20	.09
❑ 31 James Stewart	.30	.14
❑ 32 Brett Favre	1.50	.70
❑ 33 Antonio Freeman	.50	.23
❑ 34 Dorsey Levens	.30	.14
❑ 35 Ahman Green	.50	.23
❑ 36 Peyton Manning	1.25	.55
❑ 37 Edgerrin James	.60	.25
❑ 38 Marvin Harrison	.50	.23
❑ 39 Mark Brunell	.50	.23
❑ 40 Fred Taylor	.50	.23
❑ 41 Jimmy Smith	.30	.14
❑ 42 Elvis Grbac	.30	.14
❑ 43 Tony Gonzalez	.30	.14
❑ 44 Derrick Alexander	.30	.14
❑ 45 Oronde Gadsden	.30	.14
❑ 46 Lamar Smith	.30	.14
❑ 47 Jay Fiedler	.50	.23
❑ 48 Randy Moss	1.00	.45
❑ 49 Moe Williams	.30	.14
❑ 50 Cris Carter	.50	.23
❑ 51 Daunte Culpepper	.50	.23
❑ 52 Drew Bledsoe	.60	.25
❑ 53 Terry Glenn	.30	.14
❑ 54 Ricky Williams	.50	.23
❑ 55 Jeff Blake	.30	.14
❑ 56 Joe Horn	.30	.14
❑ 57 Aaron Brooks	.50	.23
❑ 58 La'Roi Glover	.20	.09

❑ 59 Kerry Collins	.30	.14
❑ 60 Amani Toomer	.30	.14
❑ 61 Ron Dayne	.50	.23
❑ 62 Vinny Testaverde	.30	.14
❑ 63 Wayne Chrebet	.30	.14
❑ 64 Curtis Martin	.50	.23
❑ 65 Tim Brown	.50	.23
❑ 66 Rich Gannon	.50	.23
❑ 67 Tyrone Wheatley	.30	.14
❑ 68 Duce Staley	.50	.23
❑ 69 Donovan McNabb	.60	.25
❑ 70 Kordell Stewart	.30	.14
❑ 71 Jerome Bettis	.50	.23
❑ 72 Marshall Faulk	.60	.25
❑ 73 Kurt Warner	1.00	.45
❑ 74 Isaac Bruce	.50	.23
❑ 75 Junior Seau	.50	.23
❑ 76 Curtis Conway	.30	.14
❑ 77 Jeff Garcia	.50	.23
❑ 78 Jerry Rice	1.00	.45
❑ 79 Charlie Garner	.30	.14
❑ 80 Terrell Owens	.50	.23
❑ 81 Ricky Watters	.20	.09
❑ 82 Shaun Alexander	.60	.25
❑ 83 Warrick Dunn	.50	.23
❑ 84 Shaun King	.20	.09
❑ 85 Derrick Brooks	.50	.23
❑ 86 Eddie George	.50	.23
❑ 87 Steve McNair	.50	.23
❑ 88 Brad Johnson	.50	.23
❑ 89 Jeff George	.30	.14
❑ 90 Stephen Davis	.50	.23
❑ 91 Jamal Reynolds RC	12.00	5.50
❑ 92 Justin Smith RC	12.00	5.50
❑ 93 Dan Morgan RC	12.00	5.50
❑ 94 Deuce McAllister RC	40.00	18.00
❑ 95 Drew Brees RC	30.00	13.50
❑ 96 Josh Booty RC	12.00	5.50
❑ 97 Mike McMahon RC	12.00	5.50
❑ 98 Sage Rosenfels RC	12.00	5.50
❑ 99 Marques Tuiasosopo RC	12.00	5.50
❑ 100 Josh Heupel RC	12.00	5.50
❑ 101 Heath Evans RC	8.00	3.60
❑ 102 Reggie White RC	8.00	3.60
❑ 103 Tim Hasselbeck RC	12.00	5.50
❑ 104 LaDainian Tomlinson RC	60.00	27.00
❑ 105 Kevan Barlow RC	12.00	5.50
❑ 106 LaMont Jordan RC	15.00	6.75
❑ 107 James Jackson RC	12.00	5.50
❑ 108 Anthony Thomas RC	25.00	11.00
❑ 109 Correll Buckhalter RC	15.00	6.75
❑ 110 Travis Henry RC	12.00	5.50
❑ 111 Dan Alexander RC	12.00	5.50
❑ 112 Travis Minor RC	8.00	3.60
❑ 113 Rudi Johnson RC	30.00	13.50
❑ 114 Michael Bennett RC	25.00	11.00
❑ 115 Todd Heap RC	12.00	5.50
❑ 116 Snoop Minnis RC	8.00	3.60
❑ 117 Santana Moss RC	25.00	11.00
❑ 118 Reggie Wayne RC	25.00	11.00
❑ 119 Koren Robinson RC	15.00	6.75
❑ 120 Chris Chambers RC	15.00	6.75
❑ 121 David Terrell RC	12.00	5.50
❑ 122 Rod Gardner RC	12.00	5.50
❑ 123 Quincy Morgan RC	12.00	5.50
❑ 124 Ken-Yon Rambo RC	8.00	3.60
❑ 125 Ronney Daniels RC	5.00	2.20
❑ 126 Ja'Mar Toombs RC	8.00	3.60
❑ 127 Bobby Newcombe RC	8.00	3.60
❑ 128 Cedrick Wilson RC	12.00	5.50
❑ 129 Chad Johnson RC	30.00	13.50
❑ 130 Shaun Rogers RC	12.00	5.50
❑ 131 Robert Ferguson RC	12.00	5.50
❑ 132 Kevin Kasper RC	12.00	5.50
❑ 133 Chris Weinke JSY RC	25.00	11.00
❑ 134 Freddie Mitchell JSY RC	15.00	6.75
❑ 135 Michael Vick JSY RC	100.00	45.00
❑ 136 Chris Taylor RC	8.00	3.60
❑ 137 Vinny Sutherland RC	8.00	3.60
❑ 138 Gerard Warren RC	12.00	5.50
❑ 139 Torrance Marshall RC	12.00	5.50
❑ 140 Jesse Palmer RC	12.00	5.50

2001 Upper Deck Pros and Prospects A Piece of History Autographs

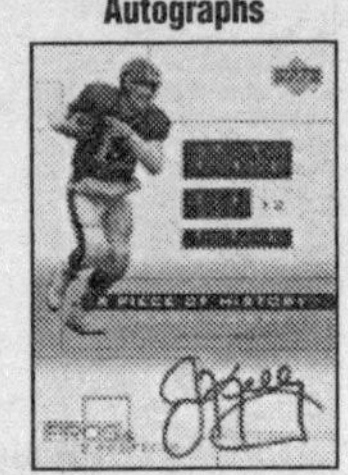

	Nm-Mt	Ex-Mt
*SERIAL #'d: 1X TO 2X BASIC INSERTS		
❑ BSAJ Bart Starr	135.00	60.00
❑ CTAJ Charley Taylor	30.00	13.50
❑ FTAJ Fran Tarkenton	60.00	27.00
❑ JKAJ Jim Kelly	100.00	45.00
❑ JTAJ Joe Theismann	50.00	22.00
❑ JUAJ Johnny Unitas	250.00	110.00
❑ JYAJ Jack Youngblood	25.00	11.00
❑ RSAJ Roger Staubach	100.00	45.00
❑ SYAJ Steve Young	100.00	45.00

2003 Upper Deck Pros and Prospects

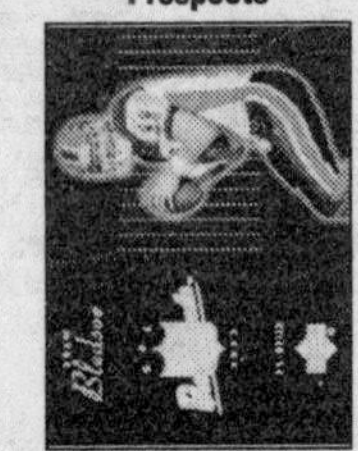

	Nm-Mt	Ex-Mt
COMP.SET w/o SP's (90)	20.00	6.00
❑ 1 Jake Plummer	.60	.18
❑ 2 David Boston	.60	.18
❑ 3 Warrick Dunn	.60	.18
❑ 4 T.J. Duckett	.60	.18
❑ 5 Chris Redman	.40	.12
❑ 6 Jamal Lewis	1.00	.30
❑ 7 Drew Bledsoe	1.00	.30
❑ 8 Travis Henry	.60	.18
❑ 9 Eric Moulds	.60	.18
❑ 10 Peerless Price	.60	.18
❑ 11 Rodney Peete	.60	.18
❑ 12 Julius Peppers	1.00	.30
❑ 13 Anthony Thomas	1.00	.30
❑ 14 Brian Urlacher	1.50	.45
❑ 15 Marty Booker	.60	.18
❑ 16 David Terrell	.60	.18
❑ 17 Corey Dillon	.60	.18
❑ 18 Peter Warrick	.60	.18
❑ 19 Jon Kitna	.60	.18
❑ 20 Tim Couch	.40	.12
❑ 21 Andre Davis	.40	.12
❑ 22 Quincy Morgan	.60	.18
❑ 23 Dennis Northcutt	.60	.18
❑ 24 Roy Williams	1.00	.30
❑ 25 Emmitt Smith	2.50	.75
❑ 26 Joey Galloway	.60	.18
❑ 27 Antonio Bryant	.60	.18
❑ 28 Brian Griese	1.00	.30
❑ 29 Clinton Portis	1.50	.45
❑ 30 Shannon Sharpe	.60	.18
❑ 31 Joey Harrington	1.50	.45
❑ 32 Az-Zahir Hakim	.40	.12
❑ 33 Brett Favre	2.50	.75
❑ 34 Robert Ferguson	.40	.12
❑ 35 Donald Driver	.60	.18
❑ 36 David Carr	1.50	.45
❑ 37 Jabar Gaffney	.60	.18
❑ 38 Edgerrin James	1.00	.30
❑ 39 Marvin Harrison	1.00	.30
❑ 40 Reggie Wayne	.60	.18
❑ 41 Mark Brunell	.60	.18
❑ 42 Fred Taylor	1.00	.30
❑ 43 Priest Holmes	1.25	.35
❑ 44 Trent Green	.60	.18
❑ 45 Marc Boerigter	.60	.18
❑ 46 Jay Fiedler	.60	.18
❑ 47 Chris Chambers	1.00	.30
❑ 48 Randy McMichael	.60	.18
❑ 49 Randy Moss	1.50	.45
❑ 50 Daunte Culpepper	1.00	.30
❑ 51 Michael Bennett	.60	.18
❑ 52 Antowain Smith	.60	.18
❑ 53 David Patten	.40	.12
❑ 54 Troy Brown	.60	.18
❑ 55 Aaron Brooks	1.00	.30
❑ 56 Joe Horn	.60	.18
❑ 57 Donte Stallworth	1.00	.30
❑ 58 Amani Toomer	.60	.18
❑ 59 Kerry Collins	.60	.18
❑ 60 Tiki Barber	.60	.18
❑ 61 Santana Moss	.60	.18
❑ 62 Curtis Martin	1.00	.30
❑ 63 Wayne Chrebet	.60	.18
❑ 64 Rich Gannon	.60	.18
❑ 65 Charlie Garner	.60	.18
❑ 66 Tim Brown	1.00	.30
❑ 67 Donovan McNabb	1.25	.35
❑ 68 Duce Staley	.60	.18
❑ 69 Hines Ward	1.00	.30
❑ 70 Antwaan Randle El	1.00	.30
❑ 71 Plaxico Burress	.60	.18
❑ 72 Jerome Bettis	1.00	.30
❑ 73 Junior Seau	1.00	.30
❑ 74 LaDainian Tomlinson	1.00	.30
❑ 75 Tai Streets	.40	.12
❑ 76 Kevan Barlow	.60	.18
❑ 77 Garrison Hearst	.60	.18
❑ 78 Jeff Garcia	1.00	.30
❑ 79 Shaun Alexander	1.00	.30
❑ 80 Matt Hasselbeck	.60	.18
❑ 81 Marshall Faulk	1.00	.30
❑ 82 Marc Bulger	1.00	.30
❑ 83 Torry Holt	1.00	.30
❑ 84 Isaac Bruce	1.00	.30
❑ 85 Brad Johnson	.60	.18
❑ 86 Keyshawn Johnson	1.00	.30
❑ 87 Steve McNair	1.00	.30
❑ 88 Kevin Dyson	.60	.18
❑ 89 Patrick Ramsey	1.00	.30
❑ 90 Ladell Betts	.60	.18
❑ 91 Marcel Shipp SP	2.50	.75
❑ 92 Michael Vick SP	8.00	2.40
❑ 93 Ray Lewis SP	3.00	.90
❑ 94 Josh Reed SP	2.50	.75
❑ 95 Josh McCown SP	2.50	.75
❑ 96 Kelly Holcomb SP	2.50	.75
❑ 97 William Green SP	2.50	.75
❑ 98 Chad Hutchinson SP	2.50	.75
❑ 99 Rod Smith SP	2.50	.75
❑ 100 James Stewart SP	2.50	.75
❑ 101 Ahman Green SP	3.00	.90
❑ 102 Peyton Manning SP	5.00	1.50
❑ 103 Jimmy Smith SP	2.50	.75
❑ 104 Tony Gonzalez SP	2.50	.75
❑ 105 Ricky Williams SP	3.00	.90
❑ 106 Jason Taylor SP	1.50	.45
❑ 107 Tom Brady SP	5.00	1.50
❑ 108 Deuce McAllister SP	3.00	.90
❑ 109 Jeremy Shockey SP	5.00	1.50
❑ 110 Chad Pennington SP	4.00	1.20
❑ 111 Jerry Rice SP	6.00	1.80
❑ 112 A.J. Feeley SP	2.50	.75
❑ 113 Tommy Maddox SP	3.00	.90
❑ 114 Drew Brees SP	3.00	.90

❑ 115 Terrell Owens SP	3.00	.90
❑ 116 Maurice Morris SP	1.50	.45
❑ 117 Kurt Warner SP	3.00	.90
❑ 118 Derrick Brooks SP	2.50	.75
❑ 119 Eddie George SP	2.50	.75
❑ 120 Rod Gardner SP	2.50	.75
❑ 121 Byron Leftwich AU RC	200.00	60.00
Chad Pennington AU/250		
❑ 122 Ken Dorsey AU RC	25.00	7.50
Vinny Testaverde/2000		
❑ 123 Carson Palmer AU RC	150.00	45.00
Peyton Manning AU/250		
❑ 124 Chris Simms AU RC	80.00	24.00
Mark Brunell AU/250		
❑ 125 Andre Johnson RC	20.00	6.00
Santana Moss		
❑ 126 Brad Banks AU RC	40.00	12.00
Aaron Brooks AU/250		
❑ 127 J.R. Tolver RC	4.00	1.20
Az-Zahir Hakim		
❑ 128 Jerel Myers RC	2.50	.75
Josh Reed		
❑ 129 Ronald Bellamy RC	4.00	1.20
Amani Toomer		
❑ 130 Jason Gesser RC	5.00	1.50
Drew Bledsoe		
❑ 131 Kliff Kingsbury AU RC	20.00	6.00
Sammy Baugh/2000		
❑ 132 Kyle Boller RC	50.00	15.00
Drew Brees AU/500		
❑ 133 Larry Johnson RC	25.00	7.50
Anthony Thomas AU		
❑ 134 Kareem Kelly AU RC	20.00	6.00
Johnnie Morton/2000		
❑ 135 Bryant Johnson RC	20.00	6.00
Rod Gardner AU/500		
❑ 136 Jason Johnson RC	25.00	7.50
Tim Couch AU/500		
❑ 137 Terrell Suggs AU RC	20.00	6.00
Leo Nomellini/2000		
❑ 138 Dave Ragone RC	40.00	12.00
Mark Brunell AU/500		
❑ 139 Musa Smith RC	5.00	1.50
Charley Trippi		
❑ 140 Juston Wood RC	4.00	1.20
Joey Harrington		
❑ 141 Jason Thomas RC	5.00	1.50
Michael Vick		
❑ 142 Earnest Graham AU RC	30.00	9.00
Emmitt Smith/2000		
❑ 143 Willis McGahee AU RC	50.00	15.00
Edgerrin James/2000		
❑ 144 ReShard Lee RC	15.00	4.50
Shaun Alexander AU/500		
❑ 145 Anquan Boldin RC	12.00	3.60
Javon Walker		
❑ 146 Taylor Jacobs AU RC	30.00	9.00
Reche Caldwell AU/250		
❑ 147 Talman Gardner RC	5.00	1.50
Laveranues Coles		
❑ 148 Bobby Wade RC	5.00	1.50
Dennis Northcutt		
❑ 149 Billy McMullen RC	20.00	6.00
Isaac Bruce AU/500		
❑ 150 Avon Cobourne RC	2.50	.75
Amos Zereoue		
❑ 151 Bradie James RC	5.00	1.50
Frank Kinard RC		
❑ 152 Kelley Washington AU RC	25.00	7.50
Peerless Price/2000		
❑ 153 Eric Steinbach RC	4.00	1.20
Jim Parker		
❑ 154 Jimmy Kennedy RC	5.00	1.50
Ernie Stautner		
❑ 155 Rien Long RC	2.50	.75
Arnie Weinmeister		
❑ 156 Chris Brown AU RC	25.00	7.50
Mike Anderson/2000		
❑ 157 Teyo Johnson RC	5.00	1.50
Tony Gonzalez		
❑ 158 Onterrio Smith RC	8.00	2.40
Maurice Morris		
❑ 159 Justin Fargas AU RC	30.00	9.00
Clinton Portis/2000		
❑ 160 Seneca Wallace RC	5.00	1.50
Antwaan Randle El		
❑ 161 Brian St.Pierre RC	50.00	15.00
Peyton Manning AU/500		
❑ 162 LaBrandon Toefield RC	25.00	7.50
LaDainian Tomlinson AU/500		
❑ 163 Marquel Blackwell RC	2.50	.75
Daunte Culpepper		
❑ 164 Keenan Howry RC	5.00	1.50
A.J. Feeley		
❑ 165 Justin Gage RC	5.00	1.50
Kirk Farmer RC		
❑ 166 Shawn Witten RC	2.50	.75
Andre Davis		
❑ 167 Dennis Weathersby RC	2.50	.75
Aeneas Williams		
❑ 168 Boss Bailey RC	8.00	2.40
Champ Bailey		
❑ 169 Brandon Lloyd RC	6.00	1.80
Kurt Kittner		
❑ 170 Doug Gabriel RC	5.00	1.50
Chris Chambers		
❑ 171 Akbar Gbaja-Biamila RC	5.00	1.50
K.Gbaja-Biamila		
❑ 172 Dahrran Diedrick RC	5.00	1.50
Ahman Green		
❑ 173 Kevin Curtis RC	5.00	1.50
Kevin Dyson		
❑ 174 Sultan McCullough RC	25.00	7.50
Deuce McAllister AU EXCH		
❑ 175 Mike Bush RC	5.00	1.50
Marcus Trufant RC		
❑ 176 Zach Hilton RC	4.00	1.20
Sam Aiken RC		
❑ 177 Terence Newman RC	12.00	3.60
Andre Woolfolk RC		
❑ 178 Tyrone Calico RC	8.00	2.40
Kelly Holcomb		
❑ 179 J.T. Wall RC	8.00	2.40
Terrence Edwards RC		
❑ 180 Cory Paus RC	8.00	2.40
Mike Seidman RC		
❑ 181 L.J. Smith RC	5.00	1.50
Marco Battaglia		
❑ 182 Quentin Griffin AU RC	40.00	12.00
Antwone Savage RC/2000		
❑ 183 Lee Suggs RC	15.00	4.50
Michael Vick		
❑ 184 B.J. Askew RC	5.00	1.50
Ben Joppru RC		
❑ 185 Mike Pinkard RC	2.50	.75
Todd Heap		
❑ 186 Arnaz Battle RC	5.00	1.50
Tim Brown		
❑ 187 Charles Rogers RC	8.00	2.40
Plaxico Burress		
❑ 188 Andrew Pinnock RC	4.00	1.20
Duce Staley		
❑ 189 Rex Grossman RC	50.00	15.00
Peyton Manning AU/500		
❑ 190 George Wrighster RC	4.00	1.20
Justin Peelle		
❑ KBBF Kyle Boller	200.00	60.00
Brett Favre AU/25		
❑ RGBF Rex Grossman	150.00	45.00
Brett Favre AU/25		

2003 Upper Deck Pros and Prospects Game Day Jerseys

	Nm-Mt	Ex-Mt
*GOLD/50: .8X TO 2X BASIC CARDS		
GOLD/50 RANDOM INSERT IN PACKS		
*BRONZE/75: .6X TO 1.5X BASIC CARDS		
BRONZE/75 RANDOM INSERT IN PACKS		
❑ JCAC Avon Cobourne	10.00	3.00
❑ JCAG Antonio Gilbert	12.00	3.60
❑ JCAP Andrew Pinnock	12.00	3.60
❑ JCBL Byron Leftwich	50.00	15.00
❑ JCBS Brian St.Pierre	12.00	3.60
❑ JCCP Carson Palmer	40.00	12.00
❑ JCDR Dave Ragone	12.00	3.60
❑ JCGA Justin Gage	12.00	3.60
❑ JCJG Jason Gesser	15.00	4.50
❑ JCJJ Jason Johnson	10.00	3.00
❑ JCJS Jeremy Shockey	15.00	4.50
❑ JCJT J.R. Tolver	10.00	3.00
❑ JCJW Juston Wood	10.00	3.00
❑ JCKD Ken Dorsey	25.00	7.50
❑ JCKH Keenan Howry	12.00	3.60
❑ JCKI Kliff Kingsbury	10.00	3.00
❑ JCKJ Keyshawn Johnson	12.00	3.60
❑ JCKK Kareem Kelly	12.00	3.60
❑ JCLS Lee Suggs	25.00	7.50
❑ JCMD Mike Doss	15.00	4.50
❑ JCMF Marshall Faulk	12.00	3.60
❑ JCPM Peyton Manning	20.00	6.00
❑ JCRB Ronald Bellamy	10.00	3.00
❑ JCSM Sultan McCullough	15.00	4.50
❑ JCST J.J. Stokes	10.00	3.00
❑ JCSW Seneca Wallace	12.00	3.60
❑ JCTI Jason Thomas	10.00	3.00
❑ JCTS Terrell Suggs	20.00	6.00
❑ JCZH Zach Hilton	10.00	3.00

2003 Upper Deck Pros and Prospects Game Day Jersey Duals

	Nm-Mt	Ex-Mt
*GOLD/50: .8X TO 2X BASIC CARDS		
GOLD/50 RANDOM INSERT IN PACKS		
*BRONZE/75: .6X TO 1.5X BASIC CARDS		
BRONZE/75 RANDOM INSERT IN PACKS		
❑ DJCBT Ronald Bellamy	12.00	3.60
Anthony Thomas		
❑ DJCCD Carson Palmer	50.00	15.00
Ken Dorsey		
❑ DJCDS Ken Dorsey	25.00	7.50
Jeremy Shockey		
❑ DJCDT Ken Dorsey	30.00	9.00
Vinny Testaverde		
❑ DJCGB Jason Gesser	30.00	9.00
Drew Bledsoe		
❑ DJCHH Keenan Howry	20.00	6.00
Joey Harrington		
❑ DJCJF J.J. Stokes	15.00	4.50
DeShaun Foster		
❑ DJCJT Jason Johnson	15.00	4.50
Jason Thomas		
❑ DJCKG Ken Dorsey	20.00	6.00
Jason Gesser		
❑ DJCKM Kareem Kelly	12.00	3.60
Sultan McCullough		
❑ DJCLD Byron Leftwich	60.00	18.00
Ken Dorsey		
❑ DJCLP Byron Leftwich	60.00	18.00
Chad Pennington		

Card	Nm-Mt	Ex-Mt
❑ DJCPJ Carson Palmer / Keyshawn Johnson	30.00	9.00
❑ DJCPK Carson Palmer / Kareem Kelly	30.00	9.00
❑ DJCPL Carson Palmer / Byron Leftwich/255	100.00	30.00
❑ DJCPW Brian St.Pierre / Juston Wood	15.00	4.50
❑ DJCRK Dave Ragone / Kliff Kingsbury	15.00	4.50
❑ DJCRU Dave Ragone / Johnny Unitas	50.00	15.00
❑ DJCSB Terrell Suggs / Wendell Bryant	30.00	9.00
❑ DJCSF Brian St.Pierre / Doug Flutie	15.00	4.50
❑ DJCSS Terrell Suggs / Warren Sapp	15.00	4.50
❑ DJCSV Lee Suggs / Michael Vick	60.00	18.00
❑ DJCTD Marcus Trufant / Mike Doss	15.00	4.50
❑ DJCTF J.R. Tolver / Marshall Faulk	15.00	4.50
❑ DJCWJ Juston Wood / Jason Johnson	12.00	3.60
❑ DJCWR Seneca Wallace / Antwaan Randle El	15.00	4.50

1999 Upper Deck Retro

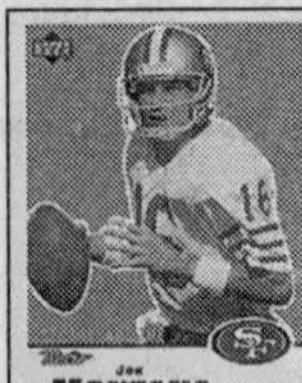

Card	Nm-Mt	Ex-Mt
COMPLETE SET (165)	40.00	18.00
❑ 1 Jake Plummer	.50	.23
❑ 2 Adrian Murrell	.50	.23
❑ 3 Rob Moore	.50	.23
❑ 4 Frank Sanders	.50	.23
❑ 5 David Boston RC	1.25	.55
❑ 6 Tim Dwight	.75	.35
❑ 7 Chris Chandler	.50	.23
❑ 8 Jamal Anderson	.75	.35
❑ 9 O.J. Santiago	.30	.14
❑ 10 Terance Mathis	.50	.23
❑ 11 Priest Holmes	1.25	.55
❑ 12 Tony Banks	.50	.23
❑ 13 Patrick Johnson	.30	.14
❑ 14 Scott Mitchell	.30	.14
❑ 15 Jermaine Lewis	.50	.23
❑ 16 Eric Moulds	.75	.35
❑ 17 Doug Flutie	.75	.35
❑ 18 Antowain Smith	.75	.35
❑ 19 Thurman Thomas	.50	.23
❑ 20 Peerless Price RC	2.00	.90
❑ 21 Fred Lane	.30	.14
❑ 22 Tim Biakabutuka	.50	.23
❑ 23 Steve Beuerlein	.30	.14
❑ 24 Muhsin Muhammad	.50	.23
❑ 25 Rae Carruth	.30	.14
❑ 26 Curtis Enis	.30	.14
❑ 27 Walter Payton	5.00	2.20
❑ 28 Bobby Engram	.50	.23
❑ 29 Cade McNown RC	1.00	.45
❑ 30 Curtis Conway	.50	.23
❑ 31 Darnay Scott	.30	.14
❑ 32 Jeff Blake	.50	.23
❑ 33 Corey Dillon	.75	.35
❑ 34 Akili Smith RC	1.00	.45
❑ 35 Carl Pickens	.50	.23
❑ 36 Tim Couch RC	1.25	.55
❑ 37 Ty Detmer	.50	.23
❑ 38 Jim Brown UER (photo is Terry Kirby)	2.50	1.10
❑ 39 Kevin Johnson RC	1.25	.55
❑ 40 Ozzie Newsome	.30	.14
❑ 41 Troy Aikman	1.50	.70
❑ 42 Rocket Ismail	.50	.23
❑ 43 Emmitt Smith	1.50	.70
❑ 44 Michael Irvin	.50	.23
❑ 45 Deion Sanders	.75	.35
❑ 46 Roger Staubach	2.00	.90
❑ 47 John Elway	2.50	1.10
❑ 48 Bubby Brister	.30	.14
❑ 49 Terrell Davis	.75	.35
❑ 50 Ed McCaffrey	.50	.23
❑ 51 Rod Smith	.50	.23
❑ 52 Shannon Sharpe	.50	.23
❑ 53 Charlie Batch	.75	.35
❑ 54 Johnnie Morton	.50	.23
❑ 55 Barry Sanders	2.50	1.10
❑ 56 Sedrick Irvin RC	.60	.25
❑ 57 Herman Moore	.50	.23
❑ 58 Brett Favre	2.50	1.10
❑ 59 Mark Chmura	.30	.14
❑ 60 Antonio Freeman	.75	.35
❑ 61 Robert Brooks	.50	.23
❑ 62 Dorsey Levens	.75	.35
❑ 63 Peyton Manning	2.50	1.10
❑ 64 Jerome Pathon	.30	.14
❑ 65 Marvin Harrison	.75	.35
❑ 66 Edgerrin James RC	5.00	2.20
❑ 67 Ken Dilger	.30	.14
❑ 68 Mark Brunell	.75	.35
❑ 69 Fred Taylor	.75	.35
❑ 70 Jimmy Smith	.50	.23
❑ 71 James Stewart	.50	.23
❑ 72 Keenan McCardell	.50	.23
❑ 73 Elvis Grbac	.50	.23
❑ 74 Mike Cloud RC	1.00	.45
❑ 75 Andre Rison	.50	.23
❑ 76 Tony Gonzalez	.75	.35
❑ 77 Warren Moon	.75	.35
❑ 78 Derrick Alexander WR	.50	.23
❑ 79 Dan Marino	2.50	1.10
❑ 80 O.J. McDuffie	.50	.23
❑ 81 James Johnson RC	1.00	.45
❑ 82 Paul Warfield	.30	.14
❑ 83 Cecil Collins RC	.60	.25
❑ 84 Randall Cunningham	.75	.35
❑ 85 Randy Moss	2.00	.90
❑ 86 Cris Carter	.75	.35
❑ 87 Fran Tarkenton	1.00	.45
❑ 88 Daunte Culpepper RC	5.00	2.20
❑ 89 Robert Smith	.75	.35
❑ 90 Drew Bledsoe	1.00	.45
❑ 91 Terry Glenn	.75	.35
❑ 92 Kevin Faulk RC	1.25	.55
❑ 93 Tony Simmons	.30	.14
❑ 94 Ben Coates	.50	.23
❑ 95 Billy Joe Hobert	.30	.14
❑ 96 Cameron Cleeland	.30	.14
❑ 97 Eddie Kennison	.50	.23
❑ 98 Andre Hastings	.30	.14
❑ 99 Ricky Williams RC	2.50	1.10
❑ 100 Kerry Collins	.50	.23
❑ 101 Joe Montgomery RC	1.00	.45
❑ 102 Gary Brown	.30	.14
❑ 103 Ike Hilliard	.30	.14
❑ 104 Amani Toomer	.30	.14
❑ 105 Vinny Testaverde	.50	.23
❑ 106 Wayne Chrebet	.50	.23
❑ 107 Curtis Martin	.75	.35
❑ 108 Joe Namath	2.50	1.10
❑ 109 Keyshawn Johnson	.75	.35
❑ 110 Don Maynard	.30	.14
❑ 111 Rich Gannon	.75	.35
❑ 112 Tim Brown	.75	.35
❑ 113 Charles Woodson	.75	.35
❑ 114 Rickey Dudley	.30	.14
❑ 115 Darrell Russell	.30	.14
❑ 116 Napoleon Kaufman	.75	.35
❑ 117 Donovan McNabb RC	6.00	2.70
❑ 118 Doug Pederson	.30	.14
❑ 119 Duce Staley	.75	.35
❑ 120 Torrance Small	.30	.14
❑ 121 Charles Johnson	.30	.14
❑ 122 Jerome Bettis	.75	.35
❑ 123 Courtney Hawkins	.30	.14
❑ 124 Kordell Stewart	.50	.23
❑ 125 Troy Edwards RC	1.00	.45
❑ 126 Amos Zereoue RC	1.25	.55
❑ 127 Trent Green	.75	.35
❑ 128 Marshall Faulk	1.00	.45
❑ 129 Az-Zahir Hakim	.30	.14
❑ 130 Joe Germaine RC	1.00	.45
❑ 131 Torry Holt RC	3.00	1.35
❑ 132 Isaac Bruce	.75	.35
❑ 133 Jim Harbaugh	.50	.23
❑ 134 Junior Seau	.75	.35
❑ 135 Natrone Means	.50	.23
❑ 136 Ryan Leaf	.75	.35
❑ 137 Dan Fouts	.75	.35
❑ 138 Mikhael Ricks	.30	.14
❑ 139 Steve Young	1.00	.45
❑ 140 Terrell Owens	.75	.35
❑ 141 Jerry Rice	1.50	.70
❑ 142 J.J. Stokes	.50	.23
❑ 143 Lawrence Phillips	.50	.23
❑ 144 Joe Montana	4.00	1.80
❑ 145 Jon Kitna	.75	.35
❑ 146 Ahman Green	.75	.35
❑ 147 Joey Galloway	.50	.23
❑ 148 Ricky Watters	.50	.23
❑ 149 Brock Huard RC	1.25	.55
❑ 150 Steve Largent	.75	.35
❑ 151 Trent Dilfer	.50	.23
❑ 152 Reidel Anthony	.50	.23
❑ 153 Warrick Dunn	.75	.35
❑ 154 Mike Alstott	.75	.35
❑ 155 Shaun King RC	1.00	.45
❑ 156 Eddie George	.75	.35
❑ 157 Steve McNair	.75	.35
❑ 158 Kevin Dyson	.50	.23
❑ 159 Frank Wycheck	.30	.14
❑ 160 Yancey Thigpen	.30	.14
❑ 161 Brad Johnson	.75	.35
❑ 162 Rodney Peete	.30	.14
❑ 163 Michael Westbrook	.50	.23
❑ 164 Skip Hicks	.30	.14
❑ 165 Champ Bailey RC	1.50	.70
❑ WP1 Walter Payton AU	300.00	135.00
❑ WPR Walter Payton Jersey AUTO/34	1000.00	450.00

1999 Upper Deck Retro Inkredible

Card	Nm-Mt	Ex-Mt
❑ AK Akili Smith	12.00	5.50
❑ AM Adrian Murrell	12.00	5.50
❑ AS Antowain Smith	15.00	6.75
❑ BH Brock Huard	12.00	5.50
❑ CC Cris Carter	25.00	11.00
❑ CM Cade McNown	12.00	5.50
❑ DB David Boston	12.00	5.50
❑ DC Daunte Culpepper	60.00	27.00
❑ DF Dan Fouts	25.00	11.00
❑ DL Dorsey Levens	20.00	9.00
❑ FT Fran Tarkenton	40.00	18.00
❑ GH Garrison Hearst	15.00	6.75
❑ JK Jon Kitna	20.00	9.00
❑ JM Joe Montana	120.00	55.00
❑ JN Joe Namath	100.00	45.00
❑ MC Donovan McNabb	60.00	27.00

❑ OZ Ozzie Newsome	20.00	9.00
❑ PW Paul Warfield	20.00	9.00
❑ RG Roger Staubach	60.00	27.00
❑ RM Randy Moss	100.00	45.00
❑ RS Rod Smith	15.00	6.75
❑ RW Ricky Williams	30.00	13.50
❑ SK Shaun King	12.00	5.50
❑ SL Steve Largent	25.00	11.00
❑ TC Tim Couch	15.00	6.75
❑ TD Terrell Davis	25.00	11.00
❑ TH Torry Holt	40.00	18.00
❑ TO Terrell Owens	25.00	11.00
❑ WC Wayne Chrebet	20.00	9.00
❑ WP Walter Payton	350.00	160.00

1999 Upper Deck Retro Inkredible Gold

	Nm-Mt	Ex-Mt
❑ AK Akili Smith/11		
❑ AM Adrian Murrell/29	50.00	22.00
❑ AS Antowain Smith/23	80.00	36.00
❑ BH Brock Huard/5		
❑ CC Cris Carter/80	60.00	27.00
❑ CM Cade McNown/8		
❑ DB David Boston/89	30.00	13.50
❑ DC Daunte Culpepper/12		
❑ DF Dan Fouts/14		
❑ DL Dorsey Levens/25	80.00	36.00
❑ FT Fran Tarkenton/10		
❑ GH Garrison Hearst/20	60.00	27.00
❑ JK Jon Kitna/7		
❑ JM Joe Montana/16		
❑ JN Joe Namath/12		
❑ MC Donovan McNabb/5		
❑ OZ Ozzie Newsome/82	30.00	13.50
❑ PW Paul Warfield/42	80.00	36.00
❑ RG Roger Staubach/12		
❑ RM Randy Moss/84	250.00	110.00
❑ RS Rod Smith/80	30.00	13.50
❑ RW Ricky Williams/34	200.00	90.00
❑ SK Shaun King/10		
❑ SL Steve Largent/80	80.00	36.00
❑ TC Tim Couch/2		
❑ TD Terrell Davis/30	120.00	55.00
❑ TH Torry Holt/88	80.00	36.00
❑ TO Terrell Owens/81	60.00	27.00
❑ WC Wayne Chrebet/80	30.00	13.50
❑ WP Walter Payton/34	800.00	350.00

2001 Upper Deck Rookie F/X

	Nm-Mt	Ex-Mt
COMP.SET w/o SP's (225)	40.00	12.00
❑ 1 Jake Plummer	.50	.15
❑ 2 Thomas Jones	.50	.15
❑ 3 David Boston	.75	.23
❑ 4 Jamal Anderson	.75	.23
❑ 5 Chris Chandler	.50	.15
❑ 6 Tony Martin	.50	.15
❑ 7 Jamal Lewis	1.25	.35
❑ 8 Elvis Grbac	.50	.15
❑ 9 Ray Lewis	.75	.23
❑ 10 Rob Johnson	.50	.15
❑ 11 Eric Moulds	.50	.15
❑ 12 Muhsin Muhammad	.50	.15
❑ 13 Tim Biakabutuka	.50	.15
❑ 14 James Allen	.50	.15
❑ 15 Marcus Robinson	.75	.23
❑ 16 Brian Urlacher	1.25	.35
❑ 17 Jon Kitna	.50	.15
❑ 18 Peter Warrick	.75	.23
❑ 19 Corey Dillon	.75	.23
❑ 20 Kevin Johnson	.50	.15
❑ 21 Dennis Northcutt	.50	.15
❑ 22 Tim Couch	.50	.15
❑ 23 Rocket Ismail	.50	.15
❑ 24 Emmitt Smith	1.50	.45
❑ 25 Joey Galloway	.50	.15
❑ 26 Terrell Davis	.75	.23
❑ 27 Rod Smith	.50	.15
❑ 28 Brian Griese	.75	.23
❑ 29 Mike Anderson	.75	.23
❑ 30 Charlie Batch	.75	.23
❑ 31 James O. Stewart	.50	.15
❑ 32 Germane Crowell	.30	.09
❑ 33 Brett Favre	2.50	.75
❑ 34 Antonio Freeman	.75	.23
❑ 35 Ahman Green	.75	.23
❑ 36 Peyton Manning	2.00	.60
❑ 37 Edgerrin James	1.00	.30
❑ 38 Marvin Harrison	.75	.23
❑ 39 Jerome Pathon	.50	.15
❑ 40 Mark Brunell	.75	.23
❑ 41 Fred Taylor	.75	.23
❑ 42 Jimmy Smith	.50	.15
❑ 43 Tony Gonzalez	.50	.15
❑ 44 Priest Holmes	1.00	.30
❑ 45 Trent Green	.75	.23
❑ 46 Oronde Gadsden	.50	.15
❑ 47 Jay Fiedler	.75	.23
❑ 48 Lamar Smith	.50	.15
❑ 49 Randy Moss	1.50	.45
❑ 50 Cris Carter	.75	.23
❑ 51 Daunte Culpepper	.75	.23
❑ 52 Drew Bledsoe	1.00	.30
❑ 53 Antowain Smith	.50	.15
❑ 54 Tom Brady	8.00	2.40
❑ 55 Ricky Williams	.75	.23
❑ 56 Joe Horn	.50	.15
❑ 57 Aaron Brooks	.75	.23
❑ 58 Kerry Collins	.50	.15
❑ 59 Tiki Barber	.50	.15
❑ 60 Ron Dayne	.75	.23
❑ 61 Vinny Testaverde	.50	.15
❑ 62 Wayne Chrebet	.75	.23
❑ 63 Curtis Martin	.75	.23
❑ 64 Tyrone Wheatley	.50	.15
❑ 65 Rich Gannon	.75	.23
❑ 66 Jerry Rice	1.50	.45
❑ 67 Duce Staley	.75	.23
❑ 68 Donovan McNabb	1.00	.30
❑ 69 Kordell Stewart	.75	.23
❑ 70 Jerome Bettis	.75	.23
❑ 71 Marshall Faulk	1.00	.30
❑ 72 Kurt Warner	1.50	.45
❑ 73 Torry Holt	.75	.23
❑ 74 Doug Flutie	.75	.23
❑ 75 Freddie Jones	.30	.09
❑ 76 Jeff Garcia	.75	.23
❑ 77 Garrison Hearst	.50	.15
❑ 78 Terrell Owens	.75	.23
❑ 79 Tai Streets	.30	.09
❑ 80 Ricky Watters	.50	.15
❑ 81 Matt Hasselbeck	.50	.15
❑ 82 Darrell Jackson	.75	.23
❑ 83 Brad Johnson	.75	.23
❑ 84 Warrick Dunn	.75	.23
❑ 85 Keyshawn Johnson	.75	.23
❑ 86 Eddie George	.75	.23
❑ 87 Steve McNair	.75	.23
❑ 88 Tony Banks	.50	.15
❑ 89 Michael Westbrook	.50	.15
❑ 90 Stephen Davis	.75	.23
❑ 91 Bob Christian	.30	.09
❑ 92 Brian Finneran	.30	.09
❑ 93 Brandon Stokley	.50	.15
❑ 94 Jeremy McDaniel	.30	.09
❑ 95 Brad Hoover	.30	.09
❑ 96 Donald Hayes	.30	.09
❑ 97 Jim Miller	.30	.09
❑ 98 Danny Farmer	.30	.09
❑ 99 Anthony Wright	.30	.09
❑ 100 Jackie Harris	.30	.09
❑ 101 Howard Griffith	.30	.09
❑ 102 Desmond Howard	.30	.09
❑ 103 Bill Schroeder	.50	.15
❑ 104 Terrence Wilkins	.30	.09
❑ 105 Todd Collins	.30	.09
❑ 106 Sylvester Morris	.30	.09
❑ 107 Zach Thomas	.75	.23
❑ 108 Robert Griffith	.30	.09
❑ 109 Kevin Faulk	.50	.15
❑ 110 Willie Jackson	.30	.09
❑ 111 Ron Dixon	.30	.09
❑ 112 Michael Strahan	.50	.15
❑ 113 Richie Anderson	.30	.09
❑ 114 Chad Pennington	1.25	.35
❑ 115 Charles Woodson	.50	.15
❑ 116 Chad Lewis	.30	.09
❑ 117 Az-Zahir Hakim	.30	.09
❑ 118 Rodney Harrison	.30	.09
❑ 119 Mike Alstott	.75	.23
❑ 120 Jevon Kearse	.50	.15
❑ 121 Martay Jenkins	.30	.09
❑ 122 Pat Tillman RC	20.00	6.00
❑ 123 Rod Woodson	.50	.15
❑ 124 Marty Booker	.50	.15
❑ 125 Scott Mitchell	.30	.09
❑ 126 John Mobley	.30	.09
❑ 127 Stephen Boyd	.30	.09
❑ 128 Kurt Schulz	.30	.09
❑ 129 Kyle Brady	.30	.09
❑ 130 Donnie Edwards	.30	.09
❑ 131 J.J. Johnson	.30	.09
❑ 132 Chris Walsh RC	.30	.09
❑ 133 J.R. Redmond	.30	.09
❑ 134 Keith Mitchell	.30	.09
❑ 135 Joe Jurevicius	.30	.09
❑ 136 Eric Allen	.30	.09
❑ 137 Todd Pinkston	.50	.15
❑ 138 Bobby Shaw	.30	.09
❑ 139 Hines Ward	.75	.23
❑ 140 Ricky Proehl	.30	.09
❑ 141 London Fletcher	.30	.09
❑ 142 Jeff Graham	.30	.09
❑ 143 Tim Rattay	.50	.15
❑ 144 Fred Beasley	.30	.09
❑ 145 James Williams	.30	.09
❑ 146 Derrick Brooks	.75	.23
❑ 147 Warren Sapp	.50	.15
❑ 148 Derrick Mason	.50	.15
❑ 149 Kevin Dyson	.50	.15
❑ 150 Champ Bailey	.50	.15
❑ 151 Michael Pittman	.30	.09
❑ 152 Kwamie Lassiter	.30	.09
❑ 153 Maurice Smith	.30	.09
❑ 154 Keith Brooking	.30	.09
❑ 155 Travis Taylor	.50	.15
❑ 156 Tony Siragusa	.30	.09
❑ 157 Alex Van Pelt	.30	.09
❑ 158 Shane Matthews	.30	.09
❑ 159 Darnay Scott	.30	.09
❑ 160 Aaron Shea	.30	.09
❑ 161 JaJuan Dawson	.30	.09
❑ 162 Clint Stoerner	.30	.09
❑ 163 Dat Nguyen	.30	.09
❑ 164 Bill Romanowski	.30	.09
❑ 165 Robert Porcher	.30	.09
❑ 166 Bubba Franks	.50	.15
❑ 167 Rob Morris	.30	.09
❑ 168 Stacey Mack	.30	.09
❑ 169 Chris Hovan	.30	.09
❑ 170 Lawyer Milloy	.50	.15
❑ 171 La'Roi Glover	.30	.09
❑ 172 Jessie Armstead	.30	.09
❑ 173 Mo Lewis	.30	.09
❑ 174 Jon Ritchie	.30	.09
❑ 175 James Thrash	.50	.15
❑ 176 Trung Canidate	.50	.15
❑ 177 Grant Wistrom	.30	.09
❑ 178 Curtis Conway	.30	.09
❑ 179 Ronney Jenkins	.30	.09
❑ 180 John Lynch	.50	.15
❑ 181 Frank Sanders	.30	.09
❑ 182 Shawn Jefferson	.30	.09
❑ 183 Darrick Vaughn	.30	.09
❑ 184 Terance Mathis	.30	.09
❑ 185 Shannon Sharpe	.50	.15

❑ 186 Qadry Ismail .50 .15
❑ 187 Sammy Morris .30 .09
❑ 188 Shawn Bryson .30 .09
❑ 189 Wesley Walls .30 .09
❑ 190 Akili Smith .30 .09
❑ 191 Ron Dugans .30 .09
❑ 192 Travis Prentice .30 .09
❑ 193 Courtney Brown .50 .15
❑ 194 Ed McCaffrey .75 .23
❑ 195 Olandis Gary .50 .15
❑ 196 Johnnie Morton .50 .15
❑ 197 Dorsey Levens .50 .15
❑ 198 Ken Dilger .30 .09
❑ 199 Keenan McCardell .30 .09
❑ 200 Derrick Alexander .50 .15
❑ 201 Tony Richardson .30 .09
❑ 202 Jason Taylor .30 .09
❑ 203 O.J. McDuffie .30 .09
❑ 204 Troy Walters .30 .09
❑ 205 Troy Brown .50 .15
❑ 206 Jeff Blake .50 .15
❑ 207 Albert Connell .30 .09
❑ 208 Amani Toomer .50 .15
❑ 209 Ike Hilliard .50 .15
❑ 210 Jason Sehorn .30 .09
❑ 211 Laveranues Coles .30 .09
❑ 212 Tim Brown .75 .23
❑ 213 Charlie Garner .50 .15
❑ 214 Plaxico Burress .75 .23
❑ 215 Troy Edwards .30 .09
❑ 216 Isaac Bruce .75 .23
❑ 217 Junior Seau .75 .23
❑ 218 Marcellus Wiley .30 .09
❑ 219 J.J. Stokes .50 .15
❑ 220 Shaun Alexander 1.00 .30
❑ 221 John Randle .30 .09
❑ 222 Jacquez Green .30 .09
❑ 223 Neil O'Donnell .30 .09
❑ 224 Frank Wycheck .30 .09
❑ 225 Stephen Alexander .30 .09
❑ 226F A.J. Feeley F/X RC 3.00 .90
❑ 226U A.J. Feeley UD 2.50 .75
❑ 226VN A.J. Feeley VINT 2.50 .75
❑ 227U Adam Archuleta UD 2.50 .75
❑ 227VC Adam Archuleta VICT 2.50 .75
❑ 227VN Adam Archuleta VINT 2.50 .75
❑ 228U Willie Middlebrooks UD 2.00 .60
❑ 228VN Willie Middlebrooks VINT 2.00 .60
❑ 229U Alex Bannister UD 2.00 .60
❑ 229VC Alex Bannister VICT 2.00 .60
❑ 230M Alge Crumpler MVP 3.00 .90
❑ 230U Alge Crumpler UD 3.00 .90
❑ 230VC Alge Crumpler VICT 3.00 .90
❑ 230VN Alge Crumpler VINT 3.00 .90
❑ 231U Andre Carter UD 2.50 .75
❑ 231VN Andre Carter VINT 2.50 .75
❑ 232U Andre Dyson UD 1.25 .35
❑ 233F Anthony Thomas F/X RC 6.00 1.80
❑ 233M Anthony Thomas MVP 5.00 1.50
❑ 233U Anthony Thomas UD 5.00 1.50
❑ 233VC Anthony Thomas VICT 5.00 1.50
❑ 233VN Anthony Thomas VINT 5.00 1.50
❑ 234U Arther Love UD 1.25 .35
❑ 235M Bobby Newcombe MVP 2.00 .60
❑ 235U Bobby Newcombe UD 2.00 .60
❑ 235VC Bobby Newcombe VICT 2.00 .60
❑ 235VN Bobby Newcombe VINT 2.00 .60
❑ 236U Zeke Moreno UD .75 .23
❑ 237U Brandon Spoon UD 2.50 .75
❑ 238U Brian Allen UD 1.25 .35
❑ 239U Carlos Polk UD 1.25 .35
❑ 240U Casey Hampton UD 2.00 .60
❑ 241F Cedrick Wilson F/X RC 3.00 .90
❑ 241U Cedrick Wilson UD 2.50 .75
❑ 241VC Cedrick Wilson VICT 2.50 .75
❑ 242F Chad Johnson F/X RC 8.00 2.40
❑ 242M Chad Johnson MVP 6.00 1.80
❑ 242U Chad Johnson UD 6.00 1.80
❑ 242VC Chad Johnson VICT 6.00 1.80
❑ 242VN Chad Johnson VINT 6.00 1.80
❑ 243U Chris Barnes UD 2.00 .60
❑ 243VC Chris Barnes VICT 2.00 .60
❑ 243VN Chris Barnes VINT 2.00 .60
❑ 244F Chris Chambers F/X RC 5.00 1.50
❑ 244M Chris Chambers MVP 4.00 1.20
❑ 244U Chris Chambers UD 4.00 1.20
❑ 244VC Chris Chambers VICT 4.00 1.20
❑ 244VN Chris Chambers VINT 4.00 1.20
❑ 245U Chris Taylor UD 2.00 .60
❑ 246F Chris Weinke F/X RC 3.00 .90
❑ 246M Chris Weinke MVP 2.50 .75
❑ 246U Chris Weinke UD 2.50 .75
❑ 246VC Chris Weinke VICT 2.50 .75
❑ 246VN Chris Weinke VINT 2.50 .75
❑ 247F Correll Buckhalter F/X RC 5.00 1.50
❑ 247M Correll Buckhalter MVP 4.00 1.20
❑ 247U Correll Buckhalter UD 4.00 1.20
❑ 247VC Correll Buckhalter VICT 4.00 1.20
❑ 247VN Correll Buckhalter VINT 4.00 1.20
❑ 248U Damione Lewis UD 2.00 .60
❑ 249M Dan Alexander MVP 2.50 .75
❑ 249U Dan Alexander UD 2.50 .75
❑ 249VC Dan Alexander VICT 2.50 .75
❑ 250F Dan Morgan F/X RC 3.00 .90
❑ 250M Dan Morgan MVP 2.50 .75
❑ 250U Dan Morgan UD 2.50 .75
❑ 250VC Dan Morgan VICT 2.50 .75
❑ 250VN Dan Morgan VINT 2.50 .75
❑ 251U Damerien McCants UD 2.00 .60
❑ 252VN Dave Dickenson VINT 2.00 .60
❑ 253M David Allen MVP 2.00 .60
❑ 253VN David Allen VINT 2.00 .60
❑ 254M David Rivers MVP 2.00 .60
❑ 255F David Terrell F/X RC 3.00 .90
❑ 255M David Terrell MVP 3.00 .90
❑ 255U David Terrell UD 3.00 .90
❑ 255VC David Terrell VICT 3.00 .90
❑ 255VN David Terrell VINT 3.00 .90
❑ 256U Dee Brown UD 2.50 .75
❑ 257U Derek Combs UD 2.00 .60
❑ 258U Derrick Blaylock UD 2.50 .75
❑ 259M Derrick Gibson MVP 2.00 .60
❑ 259U Derrick Gibson UD 2.00 .60
❑ 259VC Derrick Gibson VICT 2.00 .60
❑ 260F Deuce McAllister F/X RC 8.00 2.40
❑ 260M Deuce McAllister MVP 6.00 1.80
❑ 260U Deuce McAllister UD 6.00 1.80
❑ 260VC Deuce McAllister VICT 6.00 1.80
❑ 260VN Deuce McAllister VINT 6.00 1.80
❑ 261F Dominic Rhodes F/X RC 5.00 1.50
❑ 262F Drew Bennett F/X RC 12.00 3.60
❑ 263F Drew Brees F/X RC 8.00 2.40
❑ 263M Drew Brees MVP 6.00 1.80
❑ 263U Drew Brees UD 6.00 1.80
❑ 263VC Drew Brees VICT 6.00 1.80
❑ 263VN Drew Brees VINT 6.00 1.80
❑ 264VN Dustin McClintock VINT 2.00 .60
❑ 265U Eddie Berlin UD 2.00 .60
❑ 265VC Eddie Berlin VICT 2.00 .60
❑ 266U Edgerton Hartwell UD 1.25 .35
❑ 267U Francis St.Paul UD 2.00 .60
❑ 268U Fred Smoot UD 2.50 .75
❑ 269F Freddie Mitchell F/X RC 3.00 .90
❑ 269M Freddie Mitchell MVP 2.50 .75
❑ 269U Freddie Mitchell UD 2.50 .75
❑ 269VC Freddie Mitchell VICT 2.50 .75
❑ 269VN Freddie Mitchell VINT 2.50 .75
❑ 270U Gary Baxter UD 2.00 .60
❑ 270VC Gary Baxter VICT 2.00 .60
❑ 271U George Layne UD 2.00 .60
❑ 272U Gerard Warren UD 2.50 .75
❑ 272VC Gerard Warren VICT 2.50 .75
❑ 272VN Gerard Warren VINT 2.50 .75
❑ 273U Hakim Akbar UD 1.25 .35
❑ 273VN Hakim Akbar VINT 1.25 .35
❑ 274U Heath Evans UD 2.00 .60
❑ 274VC Heath Evans VICT 2.00 .60
❑ 275U Jabari Holloway UD 2.00 .60
❑ 275VC Jabari Holloway VICT 2.00 .60
❑ 276U Jamal Reynolds UD 2.50 .75
❑ 276VC Jamal Reynolds VICT 2.50 .75
❑ 276VN Jamal Reynolds VINT 2.50 .75
❑ 277U Jamar Fletcher UD 2.00 .60
❑ 277VC Jamar Fletcher VICT 2.00 .60
❑ 278F James Jackson F/X RC 2.50 .75
❑ 278M James Jackson MVP 2.50 .75
❑ 278U James Jackson UD 2.50 .75
❑ 278VC James Jackson VICT 2.50 .75
❑ 278VN James Jackson VINT 2.50 .75
❑ 279U Jamie Winborn UD 2.00 .60
❑ 280F Jesse Palmer F/X RC 3.00 .90
❑ 280M Jesse Palmer MVP 2.50 .75
❑ 280U Jesse Palmer UD 2.50 .75
❑ 280VC Jesse Palmer VICT 2.50 .75
❑ 280VN Jesse Palmer VINT 2.50 .75
❑ 281U John Capel UD 2.00 .60
❑ 282F Josh Booty F/X RC 3.00 .90
❑ 282M Josh Booty MVP 2.50 .75
❑ 282U Josh Booty UD 2.50 .75
❑ 282VC Josh Booty VICT 2.50 .75
❑ 282VN Josh Booty VINT 2.50 .75
❑ 283M Josh Heupel MVP 3.00 .90
❑ 283U Josh Heupel UD 3.00 .90
❑ 283VC Josh Heupel VICT 3.00 .90
❑ 283VN Josh Heupel VINT 3.00 .90
❑ 284F Justin McCareins F/X RC 3.00 .90
❑ 284U Justin McCareins UD 3.00 .90
❑ 285U Justin Smith UD 2.50 .75
❑ 285VC Justin Smith VICT 2.50 .75
❑ 285VN Justin Smith VINT 2.50 .75
❑ 286U Karon Riley UD 1.25 .35
❑ 287U Ken Lucas UD 2.00 .60
❑ 288M Ken-Yon Rambo MVP 2.00 .60
❑ 288U Ken-Yon Rambo UD 2.00 .60
❑ 288VC Ken-Yon Rambo VICT 2.00 .60
❑ 289U Kenyatta Walker UD 1.25 .35
❑ 290F Kevan Barlow F/X RC 3.00 .90
❑ 290M Kevan Barlow MVP 2.50 .75
❑ 290U Kevan Barlow UD 2.50 .75
❑ 290VC Kevan Barlow VICT 2.50 .75
❑ 290VN Kevan Barlow VINT 2.50 .75
❑ 291F Kevin Kasper F/X RC 2.50 .75
❑ 291M Kevin Kasper MVP 2.50 .75
❑ 291U Kevin Kasper UD 2.50 .75
❑ 291VC Kevin Kasper VICT 2.50 .75
❑ 291VN Kevin Kasper VINT 2.50 .75
❑ 292F Koren Robinson F/X RC 5.00 1.50
❑ 292M Koren Robinson MVP 4.00 1.20
❑ 292U Koren Robinson UD 4.00 1.20
❑ 292VC Koren Robinson VICT 4.00 1.20
❑ 292VN Koren Robinson VINT 4.00 1.20
❑ 293F LaDainian Tomlinson F/X RC 12.00 3.60
❑ 293M LaDainian Tomlinson MVP 10.00 3.00
❑ 293U LaDainian Tomlinson UD 10.00 3.00
❑ 293VC LaDainian Tomlinson VICT 10.00 3.00
❑ 293VN LaDainian Tomlinson VINT 10.00 3.00
❑ 294F LaMont Jordan F/X RC 4.00 1.20
❑ 294M LaMont Jordan MVP 3.00 .90
❑ 294U LaMont Jordan UD 3.00 .90
❑ 294VC LaMont Jordan VICT 3.00 .90
❑ 294VN LaMont Jordan VINT 3.00 .90
❑ 295U Leonard Davis UD 2.00 .60
❑ 295VN Leonard Davis VINT 2.00 .60
❑ 296U Marcus Stroud UD 2.50 .75
❑ 296VN Marcus Stroud VINT 2.50 .75
❑ 297F Marques Tuiasosopo F/X RC 3.00 .90
❑ 297M Marques Tuiasosopo MVP 2.50 .75
❑ 297U Marques Tuiasosopo UD 2.50 .75
❑ 297VC Marques Tuiasosopo VICT 2.50 .75
❑ 297VN Marques Tuiasosopo VINT 2.50 .75
❑ 298F Snoop Minnis F/X RC 2.50 .75

❑ 298M Snoop Minnis MVP	2.00	.60
❑ 298U Snoop Minnis UD	2.00	.60
❑ 298VC Snoop Minnis VICT	2.00	.60
❑ 298VN Snoop Minnis VINT	2.00	.60
❑ 299F Michael Bennett F/X RC	8.00	2.40
❑ 299M Michael Bennett MVP	6.00	1.80
❑ 299U Michael Bennett UD	6.00	1.80
❑ 299VC Michael Bennett VICT	6.00	1.80
❑ 299VN Michael Bennett VINT	6.00	1.80
❑ 300U Michael Stone UD	1.25	.35
❑ 301F Michael Vick F/X RC	25.00	7.50
❑ 301M Michael Vick MVP	20.00	6.00
❑ 301U Michael Vick UD	20.00	6.00
❑ 301VN Michael Vick VINT	20.00	6.00
❑ 302F Mike McMahon F/X RC	3.00	.90
❑ 302M Mike McMahon MVP	2.50	.75
❑ 302U Mike McMahon UD	2.50	.75
❑ 302VC Mike McMahon VICT	2.50	.75
❑ 302VN Mike McMahon VINT	2.50	.75
❑ 303M Moran Norris MVP	1.25	.35
❑ 303U Moran Norris UD	1.25	.35
❑ 303VC Moran Norris VICT	1.25	.35
❑ 303VN Moran Norris VINT	1.25	.35
❑ 304U Morlon Greenwood UD	2.00	.60
❑ 305U Nate Clements UD	2.50	.75
❑ 305VC Nate Clements VICT	2.50	.75
❑ 305VN Nate Clements VINT	2.50	.75
❑ 306F Nick Goings F/X RC	3.00	.90
❑ 307U Orlando Huff UD	1.25	.35
❑ 308F Quincy Carter F/X RC	3.00	.90
❑ 308U Quincy Carter UD	2.50	.75
❑ 308VC Quincy Carter VICT	2.50	.75
❑ 308VN Quincy Carter VINT	2.50	.75
❑ 309F Quincy Morgan F/X RC	3.00	.90
❑ 309M Quincy Morgan MVP	3.00	.90
❑ 309U Quincy Morgan UD	3.00	.90
❑ 309VC Quincy Morgan VICT	3.00	.90
❑ 309VN Quincy Morgan VINT	3.00	.90
❑ 310F Reggie Wayne F/X RC	6.00	1.80
❑ 310M Reggie Wayne MVP	5.00	1.50
❑ 310U Reggie Wayne UD	5.00	1.50
❑ 310VC Reggie Wayne VICT	5.00	1.50
❑ 310VN Reggie Wayne VINT	5.00	1.50
❑ 311M Reggie White MVP	2.00	.60
❑ 311U Reggie White UD	2.00	.60
❑ 312U Richard Seymour UD	2.50	.75
❑ 312VN Richard Seymour VINT	2.50	.75
❑ 313F Robert Ferguson F/X RC	3.00	.90
❑ 313U Robert Ferguson UD	2.50	.75
❑ 313VC Robert Ferguson VICT	2.50	.75
❑ 313VN Robert Ferguson VINT	2.50	.75
❑ 314F Rod Gardner F/X RC	3.00	.90
❑ 314M Rod Gardner MVP	2.50	.75
❑ 314U Rod Gardner UD	2.50	.75
❑ 314VC Rod Gardner VICT	2.50	.75
❑ 314VN Rod Gardner VINT	2.50	.75
❑ 315M Ronney Daniels MVP	2.00	.60
❑ 316F Rudi Johnson F/X RC	8.00	2.40
❑ 316M Rudi Johnson MVP	6.00	1.80
❑ 316U Rudi Johnson UD	6.00	1.80
❑ 316VC Rudi Johnson VICT	6.00	1.80
❑ 316VN Rudi Johnson VINT	6.00	1.80
❑ 317M Sage Rosenfels MVP	2.50	.75
❑ 317U Sage Rosenfels UD	2.50	.75
❑ 317VC Sage Rosenfels VICT	2.50	.75
❑ 317VN Sage Rosenfels VINT	2.50	.75
❑ 318F Santana Moss F/X RC	6.00	1.80
❑ 318M Santana Moss MVP	5.00	1.50
❑ 318U Santana Moss UD	5.00	1.50
❑ 318VC Santana Moss VICT	5.00	1.50
❑ 318VN Santana Moss VINT	5.00	1.50
❑ 319U Scotty Anderson UD	2.00	.60
❑ 319VC Scotty Anderson VICT	2.00	.60
❑ 320U Sedrick Hodge UD	1.25	.35
❑ 321U Shaun Rogers UD	2.50	.75
❑ 321VN Shaun Rogers VINT	2.50	.75
❑ 322U Steve Hutchinson UD	2.00	.60
❑ 323F Steve Smith F/X RC	5.00	1.50
❑ 323U Steve Smith UD	4.00	1.20
❑ 323VC Steve Smith VICT	4.00	1.20
❑ 324M T.J. Houshmandzadeh MVP	2.50	.75
❑ 324U T.J. Houshmandzadeh UD	2.50	.75
❑ 324VC T.J. Houshmandzadeh VICT	2.50	.75
❑ 324VN T.J. Houshmandzadeh VINT	2.50	.75
❑ 325U Tay Cody UD	1.25	.35
❑ 326VC Tim Hasselbeck VICT	2.50	.75
❑ 326VN Tim Hasselbeck VINT	2.50	.75
❑ 327F Todd Heap F/X RC	3.00	.90
❑ 327M Todd Heap MVP	3.00	.90
❑ 327U Todd Heap UD	3.00	.90
❑ 327VC Todd Heap VICT	3.00	.90
❑ 327VN Todd Heap VINT	3.00	.90
❑ 328U Tommy Polley UD	2.50	.75
❑ 329U Tony Dixon UD	2.00	.60
❑ 329VN Tony Dixon VINT	2.00	.60
❑ 330U Torrance Marshall UD	2.50	.75
❑ 331F Travis Henry F/X RC	5.00	1.50
❑ 331M Travis Henry MVP	4.00	1.20
❑ 331U Travis Henry UD	4.00	1.20
❑ 331VC Travis Henry VICT	4.00	1.20
❑ 331VN Travis Henry VINT	4.00	1.20
❑ 332F Travis Minor F/X RC	2.50	.75
❑ 332M Travis Minor MVP	2.00	.60
❑ 332U Travis Minor UD	2.00	.60
❑ 332VC Travis Minor VICT	2.00	.60
❑ 332VN Travis Minor VINT	2.00	.60
❑ 333M Vinny Sutherland MVP	2.00	.60
❑ 333U Vinny Sutherland UD	2.00	.60
❑ 333VC Vinny Sutherland VICT	2.00	.60
❑ 333VN Vinny Sutherland VINT	2.00	.60
❑ 334U Will Allen UD	2.00	.60
❑ 334VC Will Allen VICT	2.00	.60
❑ 334VN Will Allen VINT	2.00	.60
❑ 335VN Jason Brookins VINT RC	2.50	.75
❑ 336VN Dominic Rhodes VINT RC	5.00	1.50
❑ 337VN Ben Gay VINT RC	2.50	.75
❑ 338VC Troy Hambrick VICT RC	10.00	3.00
❑ 338VN Troy Hambrick VINT RC	10.00	3.00

2001 Upper Deck Rookie F/X Legendary Cuts

	Nm-Mt	Ex-Mt
❑ LCAS Alonzo Stagg/3		
❑ LCBL Bobby Layne/5		
❑ LCBN Bronko Nagurski/50	300.00	90.00
❑ LCDT Derrick Thomas/37		
❑ LCEN Ernie Nevers/13		
❑ LCGH George Halas/2		
❑ LCGN Earle Neale/5		
❑ LCJC Jim Conzelman/9		
❑ LCJT Jim Thorpe/1		
❑ LCLG Lou Groza/15		
❑ LCMM Marion Motley/3		
❑ LCPR Pete Rozelle/9		
❑ LCRB Red Badgro/65	100.00	30.00
❑ LCRF Ray Flaherty/7		
❑ LCRG Red Grange/6		
❑ LCRN Ray Nitschke/5		
❑ LCTL Tom Landry/1		
❑ LCVL Vince Lombardi/221	400.00	120.00
❑ LCWE Weeb Ewbank/38	200.00	60.00

2003 Upper Deck Standing O Signatures

	MINT	NRMT
❑ SIAB Antonio Bryant/164	25.00	11.00
❑ SIAD Andre Davis/141	30.00	13.50
❑ SIAL Ashley Lelie/86	25.00	11.00
❑ SIAM Archie Manning/95	30.00	13.50
❑ SIBD Brandon Doman/141	20.00	9.00
❑ SIDC David Carr/86	60.00	27.00
❑ SIDF DeShaun Foster/95	30.00	13.50
❑ SIEC Eric Crouch/141	30.00	13.50
❑ SIJG Jabar Gaffney/141	20.00	9.00
❑ SIKC Kelly Campbell/141	20.00	9.00
❑ SIKK Kurt Kittner/86	20.00	9.00
❑ SILS Luke Staley/85	20.00	9.00
❑ SIMM Maurice Morris/86		
❑ SIMW Marquise Walker/109		
❑ SINH Napoleon Harris/141	20.00	9.00
❑ SIPM Peyton Manning/95	100.00	45.00
❑ SIRC Reche Caldwell/141	20.00	9.00
❑ SIRD Rohan Davey/141	20.00	9.00
❑ SIRJ Ron Johnson/141	20.00	9.00
❑ SIRW Roy Williams/149	50.00	22.00
❑ SIWD0 Woody Dantzler/95		

2001 Upper Deck Top Tier

	Nm-Mt	Ex-Mt
COMP.SET w/o SP's (180)	40.00	12.00
❑ 1 Jake Plummer	.60	.18
❑ 2 David Boston	1.00	.30
❑ 3 Thomas Jones	.60	.18
❑ 4 Frank Sanders	.40	.12
❑ 5 Tony Martin	.40	.12
❑ 6 Jamal Anderson	1.00	.30
❑ 7 Chris Chandler	.60	.18
❑ 8 Shawn Jefferson	.40	.12
❑ 9 Jammi German	.40	.12
❑ 10 Terance Mathis	.40	.12
❑ 11 Jamal Lewis	1.50	.45
❑ 12 Shannon Sharpe	.60	.18
❑ 13 Elvis Grbac	.60	.18
❑ 14 Ray Lewis	1.00	.30
❑ 15 Qadry Ismail	.60	.18
❑ 16 Sam Gash	.40	.12
❑ 17 Rob Johnson	.60	.18
❑ 18 Eric Moulds	.60	.18
❑ 19 Sammy Morris	.40	.12
❑ 20 Shawn Bryson	.40	.12
❑ 21 Jeremy McDaniel	.40	.12
❑ 22 Muhsin Muhammad	.60	.18

23	Brad Hoover	.40	.12
24	Tim Biakabutuka	.60	.18
25	Donald Hayes	.40	.12
26	Dameyune Craig	.40	.12
27	Wesley Walls	.40	.12
28	Cade McNown	.40	.12
29	James Allen	.60	.18
30	Marcus Robinson	1.00	.30
31	Brian Urlacher	1.50	.45
32	Bobby Engram	.40	.12
33	Shane Matthews	.40	.12
34	Peter Warrick	1.00	.30
35	Corey Dillon	1.00	.30
36	Akili Smith	.40	.12
37	Scott Mitchell	.40	.12
38	Jon Kitna	.60	.18
39	Tim Couch	.60	.18
40	Kevin Johnson	.60	.18
41	Travis Prentice	.40	.12
42	Spergon Wynn	.40	.12
43	Jamel White	.40	.12
44	JaJuan Dawson	.40	.12
45	Courtney Brown	.60	.18
46	Tony Banks	.60	.18
47	Emmitt Smith	2.00	.60
48	Joey Galloway	.60	.18
49	Rocket Ismail	.60	.18
50	Anthony Wright	.40	.12
51	Darren Woodson	.40	.12
52	Terrell Davis	1.00	.30
53	Mike Anderson	1.00	.30
54	Brian Griese	1.00	.30
55	Rod Smith	.60	.18
56	Ed McCaffrey	1.00	.30
57	Eddie Kennison	.60	.18
58	Olandis Gary	.60	.18
59	Charlie Batch	1.00	.30
60	Germane Crowell	.40	.12
61	James O. Stewart	.60	.18
62	Johnnie Morton	.60	.18
63	Desmond Howard	.40	.12
64	Brett Favre	3.00	.90
65	Antonio Freeman	1.00	.30
66	Dorsey Levens	.60	.18
67	Ahman Green	.60	.18
68	Bill Schroeder	.60	.18
69	Bubba Franks	.60	.18
70	Peyton Manning	2.50	.75
71	Edgerrin James	1.25	.35
72	Marvin Harrison	1.00	.30
73	Jerome Pathon	.60	.18
74	Lennox Gordon	.40	.12
75	Terrence Wilkins	.40	.12
76	Mark Brunell	1.00	.30
77	Fred Taylor	1.00	.30
78	Jimmy Smith	.60	.18
79	Keenan McCardell	.40	.12
80	Kevin Hardy	.40	.12
81	Stacey Mack	.40	.12
82	Tony Gonzalez	.60	.18
83	Derrick Alexander	.60	.18
84	Priest Holmes	1.25	.35
85	Trent Green	1.00	.30
86	Tony Horne	.40	.12
87	Oronde Gadsden	.60	.18
88	Lamar Smith	.60	.18
89	Jay Fiedler	1.00	.30
90	Zach Thomas	1.00	.30
91	Ray Lucas	.40	.12
92	O.J. McDuffie	.40	.12
93	Randy Moss	2.00	.60
94	Cris Carter	1.00	.30
95	Daunte Culpepper	1.00	.30
96	Robert Griffith	.40	.12
97	Jake Reed	.60	.18
98	Drew Bledsoe	1.25	.35
99	Terry Glenn	.60	.18
100	Kevin Faulk	.60	.18
101	Michael Bishop	.40	.12
102	Troy Brown	.60	.18
103	Ricky Williams	1.00	.30
104	Jeff Blake	.60	.18
105	Joe Horn	.60	.18
106	Willie Jackson	.40	.12
107	Aaron Brooks	1.00	.30
108	Albert Connell	.40	.12
109	Kerry Collins	.60	.18
110	Amani Toomer	.60	.18
111	Ron Dayne	1.00	.30
112	Tiki Barber	.60	.18
113	Ike Hilliard	.60	.18
114	Ron Dixon	.40	.12
115	Michael Strahan	.60	.18
116	Vinny Testaverde	.60	.18
117	Wayne Chrebet	.60	.18
118	Curtis Martin	1.00	.30
119	Richie Anderson	.40	.12
120	Laveranues Coles	1.00	.30
121	Chad Pennington	1.50	.45
122	Tim Brown	1.00	.30
123	Rich Gannon	1.00	.30
124	Tyrone Wheatley	.60	.18
125	Charlie Garner	.60	.18
126	Jerry Rice	2.00	.60
127	Charles Woodson	.60	.18
128	Duce Staley	1.00	.30
129	Donovan McNabb	1.25	.35
130	Todd Pinkston	.60	.18
131	Chad Lewis	.40	.12
132	Brian Mitchell	.40	.12
133	Kordell Stewart	.60	.18
134	Jerome Bettis	1.00	.30
135	Plaxico Burress	1.00	.30
136	Bobby Shaw	.40	.12
137	Hines Ward	1.00	.30
138	Marshall Faulk	1.25	.35
139	Kurt Warner	2.00	.60
140	Isaac Bruce	1.00	.30
141	Torry Holt	1.00	.30
142	Justin Watson	.40	.12
143	Az-Zahir Hakim	.40	.12
144	Junior Seau	1.00	.30
145	Curtis Conway	.60	.18
146	Doug Flutie	1.00	.30
147	Jeff Graham	.40	.12
148	Freddie Jones	.40	.12
149	Rodney Harrison	.40	.12
150	Jeff Garcia	1.00	.30
151	Tai Streets	.40	.12
152	Terrell Owens	1.00	.30
153	J.J. Stokes	.60	.18
154	Garrison Hearst	.60	.18
155	Paul Smith	.40	.12
156	Ricky Watters	.60	.18
157	Shaun Alexander	1.25	.35
158	Matt Hasselbeck	.60	.18
159	Brock Huard	.40	.12
160	Darrell Jackson	1.00	.30
161	Karsten Bailey	.40	.12
162	Warrick Dunn	1.00	.30
163	Shaun King	.40	.12
164	Reidel Anthony	.40	.12
165	Mike Alstott	1.00	.30
166	Jacquez Green	.40	.12
167	Brad Johnson	1.00	.30
168	Keyshawn Johnson	1.00	.30
169	Eddie George	1.00	.30
170	Steve McNair	1.00	.30
171	Neil O'Donnell	.40	.12
172	Derrick Mason	.60	.18
173	Frank Wycheck	.40	.12
174	Chris Sanders	.40	.12
175	Jevon Kearse	.60	.18
176	Jeff George	.60	.18
177	Stephen Davis	1.00	.30
178	Kevin Lockett	.40	.12
179	Michael Westbrook	.60	.18
180	Stephen Alexander	.40	.12
181	Arnold Jackson/2000 RC	4.00	1.20
182	B.Newcombe RC/2000	6.00	1.80
183	V.Sutherland RC/2000	4.00	1.20
184	Michael Vick/1500 RC	50.00	15.00
185	Quentin McCord/2500 RC	3.00	.90
186	Todd Heap/1500 RC	8.00	2.40
187	Chris Barnes/2000 RC	4.00	1.20
188	Travis Henry/1500 RC	10.00	3.00
189	R.Germany RC/2500	3.00	.90
190	Tim Hasselbeck/2000 RC	6.00	1.80
191	Dan Morgan/2500 RC	4.00	1.20
192	Dee Brown/2000 RC	6.00	1.80
193	Chris Weinke/2000 RC	6.00	1.80
194	David Terrell/1500 RC	8.00	2.40
195	A.Thomas RC/1500	12.00	3.60
196	Rudi Johnson/2500 RC	10.00	3.00
197	Chad Johnson/1500 RC	15.00	4.50
198	Quincy Morgan/2500 RC	4.00	1.20
199	James Jackson/1500 RC	8.00	2.40
200	Quincy Carter/2000 RC	6.00	1.80
201	Kevin Kasper/2500 RC	4.00	1.20
202	Scotty Anderson/2000 RC	4.00	1.20
203	Mike McMahon/1500 RC	8.00	2.40
204	R.Ferguson RC/1500	8.00	2.40
205	David Martin/2000 RC	4.00	1.20
206	Reggie Wayne/2000 RC	10.00	3.00
207	K.Gbaja-Biamila/2500 RC	8.00	2.40
208	Snoop Minnis/2000 RC	4.00	1.20
209	Derrick Blaylock/1500 RC	8.00	2.40
210	Josh Heupel/2500 RC	4.00	1.20
211	Travis Minor/2000 RC	4.00	1.20
212	Chris Chambers/2000 RC	8.00	2.40
213	Michael Bennett/1500 RC	15.00	4.50
214	Justin Smith/1500 RC	8.00	2.40
215	D.McAllister RC/2000	15.00	4.50
216	Moran Norris/2500 RC	2.00	.60
217	Onome Ojo/2500 RC	3.00	.90
218	Jesse Palmer/1500 RC	8.00	2.40
219	Santana Moss/2000 RC	10.00	3.00
220	LaMont Jordan/2000 RC	8.00	2.40
221	M.Tuiasosopo RC/2000	6.00	1.80
222	A.J. Feeley/1500 RC	8.00	2.40
223	C.Buckhalter RC/1500	10.00	3.00
224	Freddie Mitchell/2000 RC	6.00	1.80
225	Chris Taylor/2500 RC	3.00	.90
226	Drew Brees/1500 RC	15.00	4.50
227	L.Tomlinson RC/1500	25.00	7.50
228	Dave Dickenson/2000 RC	4.00	1.20
229	Kevan Barlow/2000 RC	6.00	1.80
230	Andre Carter/2000 RC	6.00	1.80
231	Cedrick Wilson/2000 RC	6.00	1.80
232	David Allen/2500 RC	3.00	.90
233	Alex Bannister/1500 RC	5.00	1.50
234	Josh Booty/2000 RC	6.00	1.80
235	Koren Robinson/2500 RC	6.00	1.80
236	Damione Lewis/2000 RC	4.00	1.20
237	Eddie Berlin/2500 RC	3.00	.90
238	D.McCants RC/1500	5.00	1.50
239	Sage Rosenfels/2500 RC	4.00	1.20
240	Rod Gardner/1500 RC	8.00	2.40
241	Billy Baber/2500 RC	2.00	.60
242	Dan Alexander/2000 RC	6.00	1.80
243	Reggie White/2500 RC	3.00	.90
244	Adam Archuleta/2000 RC	6.00	1.80
245	Derrick Gibson/2500 RC	3.00	.90
246	Hakim Akbar/2000 RC	2.50	.75
247	B.Manumaleuna RC/2500	3.00	.90
248	Andre King/2500 RC	3.00	.90
249	Corey Alston/2500 RC	2.00	.60
250	Fred Smoot/1500 RC	8.00	2.40
251	K.Vanden Bosch RC/2500	4.00	1.20
252	R.Seymour RC/1500	8.00	2.40
253	Derek Combs/2000 RC	4.00	1.20
254	K.Rambo RC/2500	3.00	.90
255	Joey Getherall/2000 RC	4.00	1.20
256	Jonathan Carter/1500 RC	5.00	1.50
257	Gerard Warren/1500 RC	8.00	2.40
258	Carlos Polk/2000 RC	2.50	.75
259	Milton Wynn/2500 RC	3.00	.90
260	Ronney Daniels/2000 RC	2.50	.75
261	E.Hartwell RC/1500	5.00	1.50
262	Steve Smith/2000 RC	8.00	2.40
263	T.J. Houshmanza/1500 RC	8.00	2.40
264	Alge Crumpler/2000 RC	8.00	2.40
265	T.Marshall RC/1500	8.00	2.40
266	Tommy Polley/2000 RC	6.00	1.80
267	Sedrick Hodge/2000 RC	2.50	.75
268	Kendrell Bell/2500 RC	12.00	3.60
269	Jamie Winborn/1500 RC	5.00	1.50
270	Brian Allen/2000 RC	2.50	.75
271	Brandon Spoon/1500 RC	8.00	2.40
272	Paul Toviessa/2000 RC	2.50	.75
273	Aaron Schobel/2500 RC	4.00	1.20
274	Will Allen/2500 RC	3.00	.90
275	Jamar Fletcher/1500 RC	5.00	1.50
276	Andre Dyson/2000 RC	2.50	.75
277	Nate Clements/2500 RC	4.00	1.20

❑ 278 W.Middlebrooks RC/2500	3.00	.90
❑ 279 Ken Lucas/2500 RC	3.00	.90
❑ 280 Jamal Reynolds/2000 RC	6.00	1.80

2000 Upper Deck Ultimate Victory

	Nm-Mt	Ex-Mt
COMPLETE SET (150)	300.00	135.00
COMP.SET w/o SP's (90)	15.00	6.75
❑ 1 Jake Plummer	.30	.14
❑ 2 David Boston	.50	.23
❑ 3 Frank Sanders	.30	.14
❑ 4 Chris Chandler	.30	.14
❑ 5 Jamal Anderson	.50	.23
❑ 6 Shawn Jefferson	.20	.09
❑ 7 Qadry Ismail	.30	.14
❑ 8 Tony Banks	.30	.14
❑ 9 Shannon Sharpe	.30	.14
❑ 10 Peerless Price	.50	.23
❑ 11 Rob Johnson	.30	.14
❑ 12 Eric Moulds	.50	.23
❑ 13 Muhsin Muhammad	.30	.14
❑ 14 Steve Beuerlein	.30	.14
❑ 15 Tim Biakabutuka	.30	.14
❑ 16 Cade McNown	.20	.09
❑ 17 Curtis Enis	.20	.09
❑ 18 Marcus Robinson	.50	.23
❑ 19 Akili Smith	.20	.09
❑ 20 Corey Dillon	.50	.23
❑ 21 Darnay Scott	.30	.14
❑ 22 Tim Couch	.30	.14
❑ 23 Kevin Johnson	.50	.23
❑ 24 Errict Rhett	.30	.14
❑ 25 Troy Aikman	1.00	.45
❑ 26 Emmitt Smith	1.00	.45
❑ 27 Rocket Ismail	.30	.14
❑ 28 Joey Galloway	.30	.14
❑ 29 Terrell Davis	.50	.23
❑ 30 Olandis Gary	.50	.23
❑ 31 Ed McCaffrey	.50	.23
❑ 32 Charlie Batch	.50	.23
❑ 33 Germane Crowell	.20	.09
❑ 34 James Stewart	.30	.14
❑ 35 Brett Favre	1.50	.70
❑ 36 Antonio Freeman	.50	.23
❑ 37 Dorsey Levens	.30	.14
❑ 38 Peyton Manning	1.25	.55
❑ 39 Edgerrin James	.75	.35
❑ 40 Marvin Harrison	.50	.23
❑ 41 Mark Brunell	.50	.23
❑ 42 Fred Taylor	.50	.23
❑ 43 Jimmy Smith	.30	.14
❑ 44 Elvis Grbac	.30	.14
❑ 45 Tony Gonzalez	.30	.14
❑ 46 Derrick Alexander	.30	.14
❑ 47 Tony Martin	.30	.14
❑ 48 Damon Huard	.50	.23
❑ 49 O.J. McDuffie	.30	.14
❑ 50 Randy Moss	1.00	.45
❑ 51 Robert Smith	.50	.23
❑ 52 Daunte Culpepper	.60	.25
❑ 53 Drew Bledsoe	.60	.25
❑ 54 Terry Glenn	.30	.14
❑ 55 Ricky Williams	.50	.23
❑ 56 Jake Reed	.30	.14
❑ 57 Jeff Blake	.30	.14
❑ 58 Kerry Collins	.30	.14
❑ 59 Amani Toomer	.30	.14
❑ 60 Ike Hilliard	.30	.14
❑ 61 Ray Lucas	.30	.14
❑ 62 Curtis Martin	.50	.23
❑ 63 Vinny Testaverde	.30	.14
❑ 64 Tim Brown	.50	.23
❑ 65 Rich Gannon	.50	.23
❑ 66 Tyrone Wheatley	.30	.14
❑ 67 Duce Staley	.50	.23
❑ 68 Donovan McNabb	.75	.35
❑ 69 Troy Edwards	.20	.09
❑ 70 Jerome Bettis	.50	.23
❑ 71 Marshall Faulk	.60	.25
❑ 72 Kurt Warner	1.00	.45
❑ 73 Isaac Bruce	.50	.23
❑ 74 Curtis Conway	.30	.14
❑ 75 Freddie Jones	.20	.09
❑ 76 Jeff Graham	.20	.09
❑ 77 Jeff Garcia	.50	.23
❑ 78 Jerry Rice	1.00	.45
❑ 79 Ricky Watters	.30	.14
❑ 80 Jon Kitna	.50	.23
❑ 81 Derrick Mayes	.30	.14
❑ 82 Keyshawn Johnson	.50	.23
❑ 83 Shaun King	.20	.09
❑ 84 Mike Alstott	.50	.23
❑ 85 Eddie George	.50	.23
❑ 86 Steve McNair	.50	.23
❑ 87 Jevon Kearse	.50	.23
❑ 88 Brad Johnson	.50	.23
❑ 89 Stephen Davis	.50	.23
❑ 90 Michael Westbrook	.30	.14
❑ 91 Anthony Becht RC	5.00	2.20
❑ 92 Anthony Lucas RC	2.50	1.10
❑ 93 Bashir Yamini RC	2.50	1.10
❑ 94 Brian Urlacher RC	20.00	9.00
❑ 95 Chad Morton RC	5.00	2.20
❑ 96 Chad Pennington RC	20.00	9.00
❑ 97 Chris Cole RC	4.00	1.80
❑ 98 Chris Hovan RC	4.00	1.80
❑ 99 Tim Rattay RC	10.00	4.50
❑ 100 Chris Redman RC	4.00	1.80
❑ 101 Chris Samuels RC	4.00	1.80
❑ 102 Corey Simon RC	5.00	2.20
❑ 103 Courtney Brown RC	5.00	2.20
❑ 104 Curtis Keaton RC	4.00	1.80
❑ 105 Danny Farmer RC	4.00	1.80
❑ 106 Erron Kinney RC	5.00	2.20
❑ 107 Darren Howard RC	4.00	1.80
❑ 108 Deltha O'Neal RC	5.00	2.20
❑ 109 Dennis Northcutt RC	5.00	2.20
❑ 110 Demario Brown RC	2.50	1.10
❑ 111 Dez White RC	5.00	2.20
❑ 112 Frank Murphy RC	2.50	1.10
❑ 113 Gari Scott RC	2.50	1.10
❑ 114 Giovanni Carmazzi RC	4.00	1.80
❑ 115 J.R. Redmond RC	4.00	1.80
❑ 116 JaJuan Dawson RC	2.50	1.10
❑ 117 Jamal Lewis RC	12.00	5.50
❑ 118 Leon Murray RC	2.50	1.10
❑ 119 Jerry Porter RC	6.00	2.70
❑ 120 Joe Hamilton RC	4.00	1.80
❑ 121 John Abraham RC	5.00	2.20
❑ 122 John Engelberger RC	4.00	1.80
❑ 123 Keith Bulluck RC	5.00	2.20
❑ 124 Kwame Cavil RC	2.50	1.10
❑ 125 Laveranues Coles RC	6.00	2.70
❑ 126 Marc Bulger RC	10.00	4.50
❑ 127 Marcus Knight RC	4.00	1.80
❑ 128 Mareno Philyaw RC	2.50	1.10
❑ 129 Michael Wiley RC	4.00	1.80
❑ 130 Na'il Diggs RC	4.00	1.80
❑ 131 Peter Warrick RC	5.00	2.20
❑ 132 Plaxico Burress RC	10.00	4.50
❑ 133 Raynoch Thompson RC	4.00	1.80
❑ 134 Reuben Droughns RC	6.00	2.70
❑ 135 Rob Morris RC	4.00	1.80
❑ 136 Ron Dayne RC	5.00	2.20
❑ 137 Ron Dugans RC	2.50	1.10
❑ 138 Sebastian Janikowski RC	5.00	2.20
❑ 139 Shaun Alexander RC	12.00	5.50
❑ 140 Sherrod Gideon RC	2.50	1.10
❑ 141 Sylvester Morris RC	4.00	1.80
❑ 142 Tee Martin RC	5.00	2.20
❑ 143 Thomas Jones RC	8.00	3.60
❑ 144 Todd Husak RC	5.00	2.20
❑ 145 Todd Pinkston RC	5.00	2.20
❑ 146 Tom Brady RC	50.00	22.00
❑ 147 Travis Prentice RC	4.00	1.80
❑ 148 Travis Taylor RC	5.00	2.20
❑ 149 Trevor Gaylor RC	4.00	1.80
❑ 150 Trung Canidate RC	4.00	1.80

1999 Upper Deck Victory

	Nm-Mt	Ex-Mt
COMPLETE SET (440)	60.00	27.00
COMP. SET w/o SP's (380)	10.00	4.50
❑ 1 Checklist Card	.20	.09
❑ 2 Jake Plummer	.30	.14
❑ 3 Adrian Murrell	.30	.14
❑ 4 Michael Pittman	.20	.09
❑ 5 Frank Sanders	.30	.14
❑ 6 Andre Wadsworth	.20	.09
❑ 7 Rob Moore	.30	.14
❑ 8 Simeon Rice	.30	.14
❑ 9 Kwamie Lassiter RC	.50	.23
❑ 10 Mario Bates	.20	.09
❑ 11 Checklist Card	.20	.09
❑ 12 Jamal Anderson	.50	.23
❑ 13 Chris Chandler	.30	.14
❑ 14 Chuck Smith	.20	.09
❑ 15 Terance Mathis	.30	.14
❑ 16 Tim Dwight	.50	.23
❑ 17 Ray Buchanan	.20	.09
❑ 18 O.J. Santiago	.20	.09
❑ 19 Lester Archambeau	.20	.09
❑ 20 Checklist Card	.20	.09
❑ 21 Tony Banks	.30	.14
❑ 22 Priest Holmes	.75	.35
❑ 23 Michael Jackson	.20	.09
❑ 24 Jermaine Lewis	.30	.14
❑ 25 Michael McCrary	.20	.09
❑ 26 Rod Woodson	.30	.14
❑ 27 Checklist Card	.20	.09
❑ 28 Rob Johnson	.30	.14
❑ 29 Antowain Smith	.50	.23
❑ 30 Thurman Thomas	.30	.14
❑ 31 Doug Flutie	.50	.23
❑ 32 Eric Moulds	.50	.23
❑ 33 Bruce Smith	.30	.14
❑ 34 Andre Reed	.30	.14
❑ 35 Phil Hansen	.20	.09
❑ 36 Checklist Card	.20	.09
❑ 37 Fred Lane	.20	.09
❑ 38 Tim Biakabutuka	.30	.14
❑ 39 Rae Carruth	.20	.09
❑ 40 Wesley Walls	.30	.14
❑ 41 Steve Beuerlein	.20	.09
❑ 42 Muhsin Muhammad	.30	.14
❑ 43 Kevin Greene	.20	.09
❑ 44 Checklist Card	.20	.09
❑ 45 Erik Kramer	.20	.09
❑ 46 Edgar Bennett	.20	.09
❑ 47 Curtis Conway	.30	.14
❑ 48 Curtis Enis	.20	.09
❑ 49 Bobby Engram	.30	.14
❑ 50 Alonzo Mayes	.20	.09
❑ 51 Tony Parrish	.20	.09
❑ 52 Glyn Milburn	.20	.09
❑ 53 Checklist Card	.20	.09
❑ 54 Corey Dillon	.50	.23
❑ 55 Jeff Blake	.30	.14
❑ 56 Carl Pickens	.30	.14

❑ 57 Darnay Scott	.20	.09
❑ 58 Tony McGee	.20	.09
❑ 59 Ki-Jana Carter	.20	.09
❑ 60 Takeo Spikes	.20	.09
❑ 61 Checklist Card	.20	.09
❑ 62 Ty Detmer	.30	.14
❑ 63 Terry Kirby	.20	.09
❑ 64 Derrick Alexander DT	.20	.09
❑ 65 Leslie Shepherd	.20	.09
❑ 66 Marquez Pope	.20	.09
❑ 67 Antonio Langham	.20	.09
❑ 68 Marc Edwards	.20	.09
❑ 69 Checklist Card	.20	.09
❑ 70 Troy Aikman	1.00	.45
❑ 71 Emmitt Smith	1.00	.45
❑ 72 Deion Sanders	.50	.23
❑ 73 Rocket Ismail	.30	.14
❑ 74 Michael Irvin	.30	.14
❑ 75 Chris Warren	.20	.09
❑ 76 Greg Ellis	.20	.09
❑ 77 Kavika Pittman	.20	.09
❑ 78 David LaFleur	.20	.09
❑ 79 Checklist Card	.20	.09
❑ 80 John Elway	1.50	.70
❑ 81 Terrell Davis	.50	.23
❑ 82 Rod Smith	.30	.14
❑ 83 Shannon Sharpe	.30	.14
❑ 84 Ed McCaffrey	.30	.14
❑ 85 John Mobley	.20	.09
❑ 86 Bill Romanowski	.20	.09
❑ 87 Jason Elam	.20	.09
❑ 88 Howard Griffith	.20	.09
❑ 89 Checklist Card	.20	.09
❑ 90 Barry Sanders	1.50	.70
❑ 91 Johnnie Morton	.30	.14
❑ 92 Herman Moore	.30	.14
❑ 93 Charlie Batch	.50	.23
❑ 94 Germane Crowell	.20	.09
❑ 95 Robert Porcher	.20	.09
❑ 96 Stephen Boyd	.20	.09
❑ 97 Checklist Card	.20	.09
❑ 98 Brett Favre	1.50	.70
❑ 99 Antonio Freeman	.50	.23
❑ 100 Dorsey Levens	.50	.23
❑ 101 Mark Chmura	.20	.09
❑ 102 Vonnie Holliday	.20	.09
❑ 103 Bill Schroeder	.50	.23
❑ 104 LeRoy Butler	.20	.09
❑ 105 William Henderson	.30	.14
❑ 106 Checklist Card	.20	.09
❑ 107 Peyton Manning	1.50	.70
❑ 108 Marvin Harrison	.50	.23
❑ 109 Ken Dilger	.20	.09
❑ 110 Jerome Pathon	.20	.09
❑ 111 E.G. Green	.20	.09
❑ 112 Ellis Johnson	.20	.09
❑ 113 Jeff Burris	.20	.09
❑ 114 Checklist Card	.20	.09
❑ 115 Mark Brunell	.50	.23
❑ 116 Jimmy Smith	.30	.14
❑ 117 Keenan McCardell	.30	.14
❑ 118 Fred Taylor	.50	.23
❑ 119 James Stewart	.30	.14
❑ 120 Dave Thomas	.20	.09
❑ 121 Kyle Brady	.20	.09
❑ 122 Bryce Paup	.20	.09
❑ 123 Checklist Card	.20	.09
❑ 124 Elvis Grbac	.30	.14
❑ 125 Andre Rison	.30	.14
❑ 126 Derrick Alexander WR	.30	.14
❑ 127 Tony Gonzalez	.50	.23
❑ 128 Donnell Bennett	.20	.09
❑ 129 Derrick Thomas	.30	.14
❑ 130 Tamarick Vanover	.20	.09
❑ 131 Donnie Edwards	.20	.09
❑ 132 Checklist Card	.20	.09
❑ 133 Dan Marino	1.50	.70
❑ 134 Karim Abdul-Jabbar	.30	.14
❑ 135 Zach Thomas	.50	.23
❑ 136 O.J. McDuffie	.30	.14
❑ 137 John Avery	.20	.09
❑ 138 Sam Madison	.20	.09
❑ 139 Terrell Buckley	.20	.09
❑ 140 Jason Taylor	.20	.09
❑ 141 Oronde Gadsden	.30	.14
❑ 142 Checklist Card	.20	.09
❑ 143 Randall Cunningham	.50	.23
❑ 144 Cris Carter	.50	.23
❑ 145 Robert Smith	.50	.23
❑ 146 Randy Moss	1.25	.55
❑ 147 Jake Reed	.30	.14
❑ 148 Leroy Hoard	.20	.09
❑ 149 Matthew Hatchette	.20	.09
❑ 150 John Randle	.30	.14
❑ 151 Gary Anderson	.20	.09
❑ 152 Checklist Card	.20	.09
❑ 153 Drew Bledsoe	.60	.25
❑ 154 Terry Glenn	.50	.23
❑ 155 Ben Coates	.30	.14
❑ 156 Ty Law	.30	.14
❑ 157 Tony Simmons	.20	.09
❑ 158 Ted Johnson	.20	.09
❑ 159 Willie McGinest	.20	.09
❑ 160 Tony Carter	.20	.09
❑ 161 Shawn Jefferson	.20	.09
❑ 162 Checklist Card	.20	.09
❑ 163 Danny Wuerffel	.20	.09
❑ 164 Lamar Smith	.30	.14
❑ 165 Keith Poole	.20	.09
❑ 166 Cameron Cleeland	.20	.09
❑ 167 Joe Johnson	.20	.09
❑ 168 Andre Hastings	.20	.09
❑ 169 La'Roi Glover RC	.50	.23
❑ 170 Aaron Craver	.20	.09
❑ 171 Checklist Card	.20	.09
❑ 172 Kent Graham	.20	.09
❑ 173 Gary Brown	.20	.09
❑ 174 Amani Toomer	.20	.09
❑ 175 Tiki Barber	.30	.14
❑ 176 Ike Hilliard	.20	.09
❑ 177 Jason Sehorn	.20	.09
❑ 178 Michael Strahan	.30	.14
❑ 179 Charles Way	.20	.09
❑ 180 Checklist Card	.20	.09
❑ 181 Vinny Testaverde	.30	.14
❑ 182 Curtis Martin	.50	.23
❑ 183 Keyshawn Johnson	.50	.23
❑ 184 Wayne Chrebet	.30	.14
❑ 185 Mo Lewis	.20	.09
❑ 186 Steve Atwater	.20	.09
❑ 187 Leon Johnson	.20	.09
❑ 188 Bryan Cox	.20	.09
❑ 189 Checklist Card	.20	.09
❑ 190 Rich Gannon	.50	.23
❑ 191 Napoleon Kaufman	.50	.23
❑ 192 Tim Brown	.50	.23
❑ 193 Darrell Russell	.20	.09
❑ 194 Rickey Dudley	.20	.09
❑ 195 Charles Woodson	.50	.23
❑ 196 Harvey Williams	.20	.09
❑ 197 James Jett	.30	.14
❑ 198 Checklist Card	.20	.09
❑ 199 Koy Detmer	.20	.09
❑ 200 Duce Staley	.50	.23
❑ 201 Bobby Taylor	.20	.09
❑ 202 Doug Pederson	.20	.09
❑ 203 Karl Hankton	.20	.09
❑ 204 Charles Johnson	.20	.09
❑ 205 Kevin Turner	.20	.09
❑ 206 Hugh Douglas	.20	.09
❑ 207 Checklist Card	.20	.09
❑ 208 Kordell Stewart	.30	.14
❑ 209 Jerome Bettis	.50	.23
❑ 210 Hines Ward	.50	.23
❑ 211 Courtney Hawkins	.20	.09
❑ 212 Will Blackwell	.20	.09
❑ 213 Richard Huntley	.30	.14
❑ 214 Levon Kirkland	.20	.09
❑ 215 Jason Gildon	.20	.09
❑ 216 Checklist Card	.20	.09
❑ 217 Trent Green	.50	.23
❑ 218 Isaac Bruce	.50	.23
❑ 219 Az-Zahir Hakim	.20	.09
❑ 220 Amp Lee	.20	.09
❑ 221 Robert Holcombe	.20	.09
❑ 222 Ricky Proehl	.20	.09
❑ 223 Kevin Carter	.20	.09
❑ 224 Marshall Faulk	.60	.25
❑ 225 Checklist Card	.20	.09
❑ 226 Ryan Leaf	.50	.23
❑ 227 Natrone Means	.30	.14
❑ 228 Jim Harbaugh	.30	.14
❑ 229 Junior Seau	.50	.23
❑ 230 Charlie Jones	.20	.09
❑ 231 Rodney Harrison	.20	.09
❑ 232 Terrell Fletcher	.20	.09
❑ 233 Tremayne Stephens	.20	.09
❑ 234 Checklist Card	.20	.09
❑ 235 Steve Young	.60	.25
❑ 236 Jerry Rice	1.00	.45
❑ 237 Garrison Hearst	.30	.14
❑ 238 Terrell Owens	.50	.23
❑ 239 J.J. Stokes	.30	.14
❑ 240 Bryant Young	.20	.09
❑ 241 Tim McDonald	.20	.09
❑ 242 Merton Hanks	.20	.09
❑ 243 Travis Jervey	.20	.09
❑ 244 Checklist Card	.20	.09
❑ 245 Ricky Watters	.30	.14
❑ 246 Joey Galloway	.30	.14
❑ 247 Jon Kitna	.50	.23
❑ 248 Ahman Green	.50	.23
❑ 249 Mike Pritchard	.20	.09
❑ 250 Chad Brown	.20	.09
❑ 251 Christian Fauria	.20	.09
❑ 252 Michael Sinclair	.20	.09
❑ 253 Checklist Card	.20	.09
❑ 254 Warrick Dunn	.50	.23
❑ 255 Trent Dilfer	.30	.14
❑ 256 Mike Alstott	.50	.23
❑ 257 Reidel Anthony	.30	.14
❑ 258 Bert Emanuel	.30	.14
❑ 259 Jacquez Green	.20	.09
❑ 260 Hardy Nickerson	.20	.09
❑ 261 Derrick Brooks	.50	.23
❑ 262 Dave Moore	.20	.09
❑ 263 Checklist Card	.20	.09
❑ 264 Steve McNair	.50	.23
❑ 265 Eddie George	.50	.23
❑ 266 Yancey Thigpen	.20	.09
❑ 267 Frank Wycheck	.20	.09
❑ 268 Kevin Dyson	.30	.14
❑ 269 Jackie Harris	.20	.09
❑ 270 Blaine Bishop	.20	.09
❑ 271 Willie Davis	.20	.09
❑ 272 Checklist Card	.20	.09
❑ 273 Skip Hicks	.20	.09
❑ 274 Michael Westbrook	.30	.14
❑ 275 Stephen Alexander	.20	.09
❑ 276 Dana Stubblefield	.20	.09
❑ 277 Brad Johnson	.50	.23
❑ 278 Brian Mitchell	.20	.09
❑ 279 Dan Wilkinson	.20	.09
❑ 280 Stephen Davis	.50	.23
❑ 281 John Elway AV	.60	.25
❑ 282 Dan Marino AV	.60	.25
❑ 283 Troy Aikman AV	.50	.23
❑ 284 Vinny Testaverde AV	.30	.14
❑ 285 Corey Dillon AV	.50	.23
❑ 286 Steve Young AV	.30	.14
❑ 287 Randy Moss AV	.50	.23
❑ 288 Drew Bledsoe AV	.30	.14
❑ 289 Jerome Bettis AV	.50	.23
❑ 290 Antonio Freeman AV	.50	.23
❑ 291 Fred Taylor AV	.50	.23
❑ 292 Doug Flutie AV	.30	.14
❑ 293 Jerry Rice AV	.50	.23
❑ 294 Peyton Manning AV	.60	.25
❑ 295 Brett Favre AV	.60	.25
❑ 296 Barry Sanders AV	.60	.25
❑ 297 Keyshawn Johnson AV	.50	.23
❑ 298 Mark Brunell AV	.30	.14
❑ 299 Jamal Anderson AV	.50	.23
❑ 300 Terrell Davis AV	.50	.23
❑ 301 Randall Cunningham AV	.50	.23
❑ 302 Kordell Stewart AV	.30	.14
❑ 303 Warrick Dunn AV	.50	.23
❑ 304 Jake Plummer AV	.30	.14
❑ 305 Junior Seau AV	.50	.23
❑ 306 Antowain Smith AV	.50	.23
❑ 307 Charlie Batch AV	.30	.14
❑ 308 Eddie George AV	.30	.14
❑ 309 Michael Irvin AV	.30	.14
❑ 310 Joey Galloway AV	.30	.14
❑ 311 Randall Cunningham SL	.50	.23

❑ 312 Vinny Testaverde SL	.30	.14
❑ 313 Steve Young SL	.30	.14
❑ 314 Chris Chandler SL	.30	.14
❑ 315 John Elway SL	.60	.25
❑ 316 Steve Young SL	.30	.14
❑ 317 Randall Cunningham SL	.50	.23
❑ 318 Brett Favre SL	.60	.25
❑ 319 Vinny Testaverde SL	.30	.14
❑ 320 Peyton Manning SL	.60	.25
❑ 321 Terrell Davis SL	.50	.23
❑ 322 Jamal Anderson SL	.50	.23
❑ 323 Garrison Hearst SL	.30	.14
❑ 324 Barry Sanders SL	.60	.25
❑ 325 Emmitt Smith SL	.50	.23
❑ 326 Terrell Davis SL	.50	.23
❑ 327 Fred Taylor SL	.50	.23
❑ 328 Jamal Anderson SL	.50	.23
❑ 329 Emmitt Smith SL	.50	.23
❑ 330 Ricky Watters SL	.30	.14
❑ 331 O.J. McDuffie SL	.30	.14
❑ 332 Frank Sanders SL	.30	.14
❑ 333 Rod Smith SL	.30	.14
❑ 334 Marshall Faulk SL	.60	.25
❑ 335 Antonio Freeman SL	.50	.23
❑ 336 Randy Moss SL	.60	.25
❑ 337 Antonio Freeman SL	.50	.23
❑ 338 Terrell Owens SL	.50	.23
❑ 339 Cris Carter SL	.50	.23
❑ 340 Terance Mathis SL	.30	.14
❑ 341 Jake Plummer VP	.30	.14
❑ 342 Steve McNair VP	.50	.23
❑ 343 Randy Moss VP	.50	.23
❑ 344 Peyton Manning VP	.60	.25
❑ 345 Mark Brunell VP	.30	.14
❑ 346 Terrell Owens VP	.50	.23
❑ 347 Antowain Smith VP	.50	.23
❑ 348 Jerry Rice VP	.50	.23
❑ 349 Troy Aikman VP	.50	.23
❑ 350 Fred Taylor VP	.50	.23
❑ 351 Charlie Batch VP	.30	.14
❑ 352 Dan Marino VP	.60	.25
❑ 353 Eddie George VP	.30	.14
❑ 354 Drew Bledsoe VP	.30	.14
❑ 355 Kordell Stewart VP	.30	.14
❑ 356 Doug Flutie VP	.30	.14
❑ 357 Deion Sanders VP	.50	.23
❑ 358 Keyshawn Johnson VP	.50	.23
❑ 359 Jerome Bettis VP	.50	.23
❑ 360 Warrick Dunn VP	.50	.23
❑ 361 John Elway RF	.60	.25
❑ 362 Dan Marino RF	.60	.25
❑ 363 Brett Favre RF	.60	.25
❑ 364 Andre Rison RF	.30	.14
❑ 365 Rod Woodson RF	.30	.14
❑ 366 Jerry Rice RF	.50	.23
❑ 367 Barry Sanders RF	.60	.25
❑ 368 Thurman Thomas RF	.30	.14
❑ 369 Troy Aikman RF	.50	.23
❑ 370 Ricky Watters RF	.30	.14
❑ 371 Jerome Bettis RF	.50	.23
❑ 372 Reggie White RF	.20	.09
❑ 373 Junior Seau RF	.50	.23
❑ 374 Deion Sanders RF	.50	.23
❑ 375 Chris Chandler RF	.30	.14
❑ 376 Curtis Martin RF	.50	.23
❑ 377 Kordell Stewart RF	.30	.14
❑ 378 Mark Brunell RF	.30	.14
❑ 379 Cris Carter RF	.50	.23
❑ 380 Emmitt Smith RF	.50	.23
❑ 381 Tim Couch RC	1.50	.70
❑ 382 Donovan McNabb RC	8.00	3.60
❑ 383 Akili Smith RC	1.00	.45
❑ 384 Edgerrin James RC	6.00	2.70
❑ 385 Ricky Williams RC	3.00	1.35
❑ 386 Torry Holt RC	4.00	1.80
❑ 387 Champ Bailey RC	2.00	.90
❑ 388 David Boston RC	1.50	.70
❑ 389 Chris Claiborne RC	.50	.23
❑ 390 Chris McAlister RC	1.00	.45
❑ 391 Daunte Culpepper RC	6.00	2.70
❑ 392 Cade McNown RC	1.00	.45
❑ 393 Troy Edwards RC	1.00	.45
❑ 394 John Tait RC	.50	.23
❑ 395 Anthony McFarland RC	1.50	.70
❑ 396 Jevon Kearse RC	2.50	1.10
❑ 397 Damien Woody RC	.50	.23
❑ 398 Matt Stinchcomb RC	.50	.23
❑ 399 Luke Petitgout RC	.50	.23
❑ 400 Ebenezer Ekuban RC	1.00	.45
❑ 401 L.J. Shelton RC	.50	.23
❑ 402 Daylon McCutcheon RC	.50	.23
❑ 403 Antoine Winfield RC	1.00	.45
❑ 404 Scott Covington RC	1.50	.70
❑ 405 Antuan Edwards RC	.50	.23
❑ 406 Fernando Bryant RC	1.00	.45
❑ 407 Aaron Gibson RC	.50	.23
❑ 408 Andy Katzenmoyer RC	1.00	.45
❑ 409 Dimitrius Underwood RC	1.00	.45
❑ 410 Patrick Kerney RC	1.50	.70
❑ 411 Al Wilson RC	1.50	.70
❑ 412 Kevin Johnson RC	1.50	.70
❑ 413 Joel Makovicka RC	1.50	.70
❑ 414 Reginald Kelly RC UER Card has the wrong birthdate	.50	.23
❑ 415 Jeff Paulk RC	.50	.23
❑ 416 Brandon Stokley RC	2.00	.90
❑ 417 Peerless Price RC	2.50	1.10
❑ 418 D'Wayne Bates RC	1.00	.45
❑ 419 Travis McGriff RC	.50	.23
❑ 420 Sedrick Irvin RC	.50	.23
❑ 421 Aaron Brooks RC	5.00	2.20
❑ 422 Mike Cloud RC	1.00	.45
❑ 423 Joe Montgomery RC	1.00	.45
❑ 424 Shaun King RC	1.00	.45
❑ 425 Dameane Douglas RC	1.50	.70
❑ 426 Joe Germaine RC	1.00	.45
❑ 427 James Johnson RC	1.00	.45
❑ 428 Michael Bishop RC	1.50	.70
❑ 429 Karsten Bailey RC	1.00	.45
❑ 430 Craig Yeast RC	1.00	.45
❑ 431 Jim Kleinsasser RC	1.50	.70
❑ 432 Martin Gramatica RC	.50	.23
❑ 433 Jermaine Fazande RC	1.00	.45
❑ 434 Dre'Bly RC	1.50	.70
❑ 435 Brock Huard RC	1.50	.70
❑ 436 Rob Konrad RC	1.50	.70
❑ 437 Tony Bryant RC	1.00	.45
❑ 438 Sean Bennett RC	.50	.23
❑ 439 Kevin Faulk RC	1.50	.70
❑ 440 Amos Zereoue RC	1.50	.70

2000 Upper Deck Victory

	Nm-Mt	Ex-Mt
COMPLETE SET (330)	50.00	22.00
❑ 1 Jake Plummer	.25	.11
❑ 2 Michael Pittman	.15	.07
❑ 3 Rob Moore	.25	.11
❑ 4 David Boston	.40	.18
❑ 5 Frank Sanders	.25	.11
❑ 6 Aeneas Williams	.15	.07
❑ 7 Tim Dwight	.40	.18
❑ 8 Chris Chandler	.25	.11
❑ 9 Jamal Anderson	.40	.18
❑ 10 Shawn Jefferson	.15	.07
❑ 11 Ken Oxendine	.15	.07
❑ 12 Terance Mathis	.25	.11
❑ 13 Qadry Ismail	.25	.11
❑ 14 Jermaine Lewis	.25	.11
❑ 15 Rod Woodson	.25	.11
❑ 16 Michael McCrary	.15	.07
❑ 17 Tony Banks	.25	.11
❑ 18 Peter Boulware	.15	.07
❑ 19 Shannon Sharpe	.25	.11
❑ 20 Peerless Price	.40	.18
❑ 21 Rob Johnson	.25	.11
❑ 22 Eric Moulds	.40	.18
❑ 23 Doug Flutie	.40	.18
❑ 24 Jay Riemersma	.15	.07
❑ 25 Antowain Smith	.25	.11
❑ 26 Sam Cowart	.15	.07
❑ 27 Muhsin Muhammad	.25	.11
❑ 28 Patrick Jeffers	.40	.18
❑ 29 Steve Beuerlein	.25	.11
❑ 30 Natrone Means	.15	.07
❑ 31 Tim Biakabutuka	.25	.11
❑ 32 Michael Bates	.15	.07
❑ 33 Wesley Walls	.15	.07
❑ 34 Cade McNown	.15	.07
❑ 35 Curtis Enis	.15	.07
❑ 36 Marcus Robinson	.40	.18
❑ 37 Bobby Engram	.15	.07
❑ 38 Glyn Milburn	.15	.07
❑ 39 Marty Booker	.25	.11
❑ 40 Akili Smith	.15	.07
❑ 41 Corey Dillon	.40	.18
❑ 42 Darnay Scott	.25	.11
❑ 43 Tremain Mack	.15	.07
❑ 44 Michael Bankston	.15	.07
❑ 45 Tony McGee	.15	.07
❑ 46 Tim Couch	.25	.11
❑ 47 Kevin Johnson	.40	.18
❑ 48 Darrin Chiaverini	.15	.07
❑ 49 Jamir Miller	.15	.07
❑ 50 Errict Rhett	.25	.11
❑ 51 Ty Detmer	.15	.07
❑ 52 Terry Kirby	.15	.07
❑ 53 Troy Aikman	.75	.35
❑ 54 Emmitt Smith	.75	.35
❑ 55 Rocket Ismail	.25	.11
❑ 56 Chris Warren	.15	.07
❑ 57 Joey Galloway	.25	.11
❑ 58 Terrell Davis	.40	.18
❑ 59 Olandis Gary	.40	.18
❑ 60 Brian Griese	.40	.18
❑ 61 Gus Frerotte	.15	.07
❑ 62 Glenn Cadrez	.15	.07
❑ 63 Ed McCaffrey	.40	.18
❑ 64 Rod Smith	.25	.11
❑ 65 Charlie Batch	.40	.18
❑ 66 Germane Crowell	.15	.07
❑ 67 Stephen Boyd	.15	.07
❑ 68 Johnnie Morton	.25	.11
❑ 69 Robert Porcher	.15	.07
❑ 70 James Stewart	.25	.11
❑ 71 Brett Favre	1.25	.55
❑ 72 Antonio Freeman	.40	.18
❑ 73 Bill Schroeder	.25	.11
❑ 74 Dorsey Levens	.25	.11
❑ 75 Darren Sharper	.15	.07
❑ 76 Peyton Manning	1.00	.45
❑ 77 Edgerrin James	.60	.25
❑ 78 Marvin Harrison	.40	.18
❑ 79 Ken Dilger	.15	.07
❑ 80 Terrence Wilkins	.15	.07
❑ 81 Cornelius Bennett	.15	.07
❑ 82 E.G. Green	.15	.07
❑ 83 Mark Brunell	.40	.18
❑ 84 Fred Taylor	.40	.18
❑ 85 Jimmy Smith	.25	.11
❑ 86 Keenan McCardell	.25	.11
❑ 87 Carnell Lake	.15	.07
❑ 88 Kevin Hardy	.15	.07
❑ 89 Elvis Grbac	.25	.11
❑ 90 Tony Gonzalez	.25	.11
❑ 91 Derrick Alexander	.25	.11
❑ 92 Donnell Bennett	.15	.07
❑ 93 James Hasty	.15	.07
❑ 94 Kevin Lockett	.15	.07
❑ 95 Trace Armstrong	.15	.07
❑ 96 Terrell Buckley	.15	.07
❑ 97 Tony Martin	.25	.11
❑ 98 Damon Huard	.40	.18
❑ 99 O.J. McDuffie	.25	.11
❑ 100 Brock Marion	.15	.07
❑ 101 Zach Thomas	.40	.18
❑ 102 Randy Moss	.75	.35
❑ 103 Robert Smith	.40	.18
❑ 104 Cris Carter	.40	.18

❑ 105 Bubby Brister .15 .07
❑ 106 Daunte Culpepper .50 .23
❑ 107 John Randle .25 .11
❑ 108 Drew Bledsoe .50 .23
❑ 109 Terry Glenn .25 .11
❑ 110 Willie McGinest .15 .07
❑ 111 Kevin Faulk .25 .11
❑ 112 Tedy Bruschi .40 .18
❑ 113 Ricky Williams .40 .18
❑ 114 Keith Poole .15 .07
❑ 115 Jake Reed .25 .11
❑ 116 Mark Fields .15 .07
❑ 117 Jeff Blake .25 .11
❑ 118 Andrew Glover .15 .07
❑ 119 Kerry Collins .25 .11
❑ 120 Amani Toomer .15 .07
❑ 121 Jessie Armstead .15 .07
❑ 122 Ike Hilliard .25 .11
❑ 123 Ray Lucas .25 .11
❑ 124 Curtis Martin .40 .18
❑ 125 Vinny Testaverde .25 .11
❑ 126 Wayne Chrebet .25 .11
❑ 127 Dedric Ward .15 .07
❑ 128 Tim Brown .40 .18
❑ 129 Rich Gannon .40 .18
❑ 130 Tyrone Wheatley .25 .11
❑ 131 Napoleon Kaufman .25 .11
❑ 132 Charles Woodson .25 .11
❑ 133 Greg Biekert .15 .07
❑ 134 Rickey Dudley .15 .07
❑ 135 Duce Staley .40 .18
❑ 136 Donovan McNabb .60 .25
❑ 137 Torrance Small .15 .07
❑ 138 Mike Mamula .15 .07
❑ 139 Brian Dawkins .15 .07
❑ 140 Troy Vincent .15 .07
❑ 141 Kent Graham .15 .07
❑ 142 Troy Edwards .15 .07
❑ 143 Jerome Bettis .40 .18
❑ 144 Hines Ward .40 .18
❑ 145 Kordell Stewart .25 .11
❑ 146 Levon Kirkland .15 .07
❑ 147 Richard Huntley .15 .07
❑ 148 Marshall Faulk .50 .23
❑ 149 Kurt Warner .75 .35
❑ 150 Torry Holt .40 .18
❑ 151 Isaac Bruce .40 .18
❑ 152 Kevin Carter .15 .07
❑ 153 Az-Zahir Hakim .25 .11
❑ 154 Todd Lyght .15 .07
❑ 155 Jermaine Fazande .15 .07
❑ 156 Curtis Conway .25 .11
❑ 157 Freddie Jones .15 .07
❑ 158 Junior Seau .40 .18
❑ 159 Jeff Graham .15 .07
❑ 160 Moses Moreno .15 .07
❑ 161 Rodney Harrison .15 .07
❑ 162 Steve Young .50 .23
❑ 163 Jerry Rice .75 .35
❑ 164 Ken Norton .15 .07
❑ 165 Terrell Owens .40 .18
❑ 166 Jeff Garcia .40 .18
❑ 167 Ricky Watters .25 .11
❑ 168 Jon Kitna .40 .18
❑ 169 Derrick Mayes .25 .11
❑ 170 Sean Dawkins .15 .07
❑ 171 Chad Brown .15 .07
❑ 172 Warrick Dunn .40 .18
❑ 173 Keyshawn Johnson .40 .18
❑ 174 Shaun King .15 .07
❑ 175 Mike Alstott .40 .18
❑ 176 Warren Sapp .25 .11
❑ 177 Jacquez Green .15 .07
❑ 178 Derrick Brooks .40 .18
❑ 179 John Lynch .25 .11
❑ 180 Eddie George .40 .18
❑ 181 Steve McNair .40 .18
❑ 182 Kevin Dyson .25 .11
❑ 183 Jevon Kearse .40 .18
❑ 184 Yancey Thigpen .15 .07
❑ 185 Frank Wycheck .15 .07
❑ 186 Eddie Robinson .25 .11
❑ 187 Jeff George .25 .11
❑ 188 Brad Johnson .40 .18
❑ 189 Stephen Davis .40 .18
❑ 190 Michael Westbrook .25 .11
❑ 191 Albert Connell .15 .07
❑ 192 Brian Mitchell .15 .07
❑ 193 Bruce Smith .25 .11
❑ 194 Champ Bailey .25 .11
❑ 195 Sam Shade .15 .07
❑ 196 Marvin Harrison SL .25 .11
❑ 197 Jimmy Smith SL .15 .07
❑ 198 Randy Moss SL .40 .18
❑ 199 Marcus Robinson SL .15 .07
❑ 200 Tim Brown SL .25 .11
❑ 201 Jimmy Smith SL .15 .07
❑ 202 Marvin Harrison SL .25 .11
❑ 203 Muhsin Muhammad SL .15 .07
❑ 204 Tim Brown SL .25 .11
❑ 205 Cris Carter SL .25 .11
❑ 206 Edgerrin James SL .40 .18
❑ 207 Curtis Martin SL .25 .11
❑ 208 Stephen Davis SL .25 .11
❑ 209 Emmitt Smith SL .40 .18
❑ 210 Marshall Faulk SL .40 .18
❑ 211 Kurt Warner SL .40 .18
❑ 212 Steve Beuerlein SL .15 .07
❑ 213 Jeff George SL .15 .07
❑ 214 Peyton Manning SL .50 .23
❑ 215 Brad Johnson SL .25 .11
❑ 216 Kurt Warner CL .40 .18
❑ 217 Peyton Manning CL .50 .23
❑ 218 Edgerrin James CL .40 .18
❑ 219 Marshall Faulk CL .25 .11
❑ 220 Randy Moss CL .40 .18
❑ 221 Jimmy Smith CL .15 .07
❑ 222 Tony Gonzalez CL .15 .07
❑ 223 Tony Boselli CL .15 .07
❑ 224 Orlando Pace CL .15 .07
❑ 225 Larry Allen CL .15 .07
❑ 226 Randall McDaniel CL .15 .07
❑ 227 Tom Nalen CL .15 .07
❑ 228 Kevin Carter CL .15 .07
❑ 229 Jevon Kearse CL .15 .07
❑ 230 Warren Sapp CL .15 .07
❑ 231 Darrell Russell CL .15 .07
❑ 232 Derrick Brooks CL .40 .18
❑ 233 Peter Boulware CL .15 .07
❑ 234 Junior Seau CL .25 .11
❑ 235 Sam Madison CL .15 .07
❑ 236 Charles Woodson CL .15 .07
❑ 237 John Lynch CL .15 .07
❑ 238 Carnell Lake CL .15 .07
❑ 239 Mitch Berger CL .15 .07
❑ 240 Jason Hanson CL .15 .07
❑ 241 Randy Moss PM .40 .18
❑ 242 Kurt Warner PM .40 .18
❑ 243 Peyton Manning PM .50 .23
❑ 244 Marshall Faulk PM .40 .18
❑ 245 Edgerrin James PM .40 .18
❑ 246 Eddie George PM .25 .11
❑ 247 Stephen Davis PM .25 .11
❑ 248 Keyshawn Johnson PM .25 .11
❑ 249 Brad Johnson PM .25 .11
❑ 250 Ricky Williams PM .40 .18
❑ 251 Jimmy Smith PM .15 .07
❑ 252 Isaac Bruce PM .25 .11
❑ 253 Muhsin Muhammad PM .15 .07
❑ 254 Marcus Robinson PM .15 .07
❑ 255 Kevin Johnson PM .25 .11
❑ 256 Tim Couch PM .25 .11
❑ 257 Curtis Martin PM .25 .11
❑ 258 Charlie Batch PM .25 .11
❑ 259 Tim Brown PM .25 .11
❑ 260 Jerry Rice PM .40 .18
❑ 261 Drew Bledsoe PM .40 .18
❑ 262 Brett Favre PM .60 .25
❑ 263 Mark Brunell PM .25 .11
❑ 264 Fred Taylor PM .25 .11
❑ 265 Troy Edwards PM .15 .07
❑ 266 Marvin Harrison PM .25 .11
❑ 267 Germane Crowell PM .15 .07
❑ 268 Terry Glenn PM .25 .11
❑ 269 Qadry Ismail PM .15 .07
❑ 270 Jake Plummer PM .25 .11
❑ 271 Anthony Becht RC .75 .35
❑ 272 Anthony Lucas RC .75 .35
❑ 273 Bashir Yamini RC .40 .18
❑ 274 Brian Urlacher RC 3.00 1.35
❑ 275 Chad Morton RC .75 .35
❑ 276 Chad Pennington RC 3.00 1.35
❑ 277 Chris Cole RC .60 .25
❑ 278 Chris Hovan RC .60 .25
❑ 279 Tim Rattay RC 1.50 .70
❑ 280 Chris Redman RC .60 .25
❑ 281 Chris Samuels RC .60 .25
❑ 282 Corey Simon RC .75 .35
❑ 283 Courtney Brown RC .75 .35
❑ 284 Curtis Keaton RC .60 .25
❑ 285 Danny Farmer RC .60 .25
❑ 286 Erron Kinney RC .75 .35
❑ 287 Darren Howard RC .60 .25
❑ 288 Deltha O'Neal RC .75 .35
❑ 289 Dennis Northcutt RC .75 .35
❑ 290 Demario Brown RC .40 .18
❑ 291 Dez White RC .75 .35
❑ 292 Frank Murphy RC .40 .18
❑ 293 Gari Scott RC .40 .18
❑ 294 Giovanni Carmazzi RC .60 .25
❑ 295 J.R. Redmond RC .60 .25
❑ 296 JaJuan Dawson RC .40 .18
❑ 297 Jamal Lewis RC 2.00 .90
❑ 298 Leon Murray RC .40 .18
❑ 299 Jerry Porter RC 1.00 .45
❑ 300 Joe Hamilton RC .60 .25
❑ 301 John Abraham RC .75 .35
❑ 302 John Engelberger RC .60 .25
❑ 303 Keith Bulluck RC .75 .35
❑ 304 Kwame Cavil RC .40 .18
❑ 305 Laveranues Coles RC 1.00 .45
❑ 306 Marc Bulger RC 1.50 .70
❑ 307 Marcus Knight RC .60 .25
❑ 308 Mareno Philyaw RC .60 .25
❑ 309 Michael Wiley RC .60 .25
❑ 310 Na'il Diggs RC .60 .25
❑ 311 Peter Warrick RC .75 .35
❑ 312 Plaxico Burress RC 1.50 .70
❑ 313 Raynoch Thompson RC .60 .25
❑ 314 Reuben Droughns RC 1.00 .45
❑ 315 Rob Morris RC .75 .35
❑ 316 Ron Dayne RC .75 .35
❑ 317 Ron Dugans RC .40 .18
❑ 318 Sebastian Janikowski RC .75 .35
❑ 319 Shaun Alexander RC 2.00 .90
❑ 320 Sherrod Gideon RC .60 .25
❑ 321 Sylvester Morris RC .60 .25
❑ 322 Tee Martin RC .75 .35
❑ 323 Thomas Jones RC 1.25 .55
❑ 324 Todd Husak RC .75 .35
❑ 325 Todd Pinkston RC .75 .35
❑ 326 Tom Brady RC 20.00 9.00
❑ 327 Travis Prentice RC .60 .25
❑ 328 Travis Taylor RC .75 .35
❑ 329 Trevor Gaylor RC .60 .25
❑ 330 Trung Canidate RC .60 .25

2001 Upper Deck Victory

	Nm-Mt	Ex-Mt
COMPLETE SET (440)	60.00	18.00
❑ 1 Jake Plummer	.30	.09
❑ 2 David Boston	.50	.15
❑ 3 Thomas Jones	.30	.09
❑ 4 Michael Pittman	.20	.06
❑ 5 Frank Sanders	.20	.06
❑ 6 Joel Makovicka	.20	.06
❑ 7 Corey Chavous	.20	.06
❑ 8 Kwamie Lassiter	.20	.06

	Card	Price 1	Price 2
❑	9 Rob Moore	.30	.09
❑	10 Jamal Anderson	.50	.15
❑	11 Tony Martin	.30	.09
❑	12 Travis Jervey	.20	.06
❑	13 Chris Chandler	.30	.09
❑	14 Shawn Jefferson	.20	.06
❑	15 Rodney Thomas	.20	.06
❑	16 Terance Mathis	.20	.06
❑	17 Jessie Tuggle	.20	.06
❑	18 Ashley Ambrose	.20	.06
❑	19 Brian Finneran	.20	.06
❑	20 Maurice Smith	.30	.09
❑	21 Keith Brooking	.20	.06
❑	22 Jamal Lewis	.75	.23
❑	23 Shannon Sharpe	.30	.09
❑	24 Brandon Stokley	.30	.09
❑	25 Ray Lewis	.50	.15
❑	26 Qadry Ismail	.30	.09
❑	27 Travis Taylor	.30	.09
❑	28 Chris Redman	.20	.06
❑	29 Rod Woodson	.30	.09
❑	30 Pat Johnson	.20	.06
❑	31 Jermaine Lewis	.20	.06
❑	32 Elvis Grbac	.30	.09
❑	33 Tony Siragusa	.20	.06
❑	34 Larry Centers	.20	.06
❑	35 Rob Johnson	.20	.06
❑	36 Eric Moulds	.30	.09
❑	37 Sammy Morris	.20	.06
❑	38 Shawn Bryson	.20	.06
❑	39 Alex Van Pelt	.20	.06
❑	40 Jeremy McDaniel	.20	.06
❑	41 Sam Cowart	.20	.06
❑	42 Peerless Price	.30	.09
❑	43 Avion Black	.20	.06
❑	44 Phil Hansen	.20	.06
❑	45 Muhsin Muhammad	.30	.09
❑	46 Brad Hoover	.20	.06
❑	47 Tim Biakabutuka	.30	.09
❑	48 Wesley Walls	.20	.06
❑	49 Donald Hayes	.20	.06
❑	50 Jeff Lewis	.20	.06
❑	51 Dameyune Craig	.20	.06
❑	52 Mike Minter RC	.30	.09
❑	53 Isaac Byrd	.20	.06
❑	54 Patrick Jeffers	.30	.09
❑	55 Cade McNown	.20	.06
❑	56 James Allen	.30	.09
❑	57 Marcus Robinson	.50	.15
❑	58 Brian Urlacher	.75	.23
❑	59 Shane Matthews	.20	.06
❑	60 Glyn Milburn	.20	.06
❑	61 Scott Dragos RC	.50	.15
❑	62 Marty Booker	.20	.06
❑	63 Bobby Engram	.20	.06
❑	64 Kaseem Sinceno	.20	.06
❑	65 Ted Washington	.20	.06
❑	66 Peter Warrick	.50	.15
❑	67 Corey Dillon	.50	.15
❑	68 Akili Smith UER (stats line is for receivers)	.20	.06
❑	69 Danny Farmer	.20	.06
❑	70 Scott Mitchell	.20	.06
❑	71 Darryl Williams	.20	.06
❑	72 Ron Dugans	.20	.06
❑	73 Takeo Spikes	.20	.06
❑	74 Jon Kitna	.30	.09
❑	75 Darnay Scott	.30	.09
❑	76 Tony McGee	.20	.06
❑	77 Tim Couch	.30	.09
❑	78 Kevin Johnson	.30	.09
❑	79 Travis Prentice	.20	.06
❑	80 Spergon Wynn	.20	.06
❑	81 Errict Rhett	.20	.06
❑	82 Ty Detmer	.20	.06
❑	83 Dennis Northcutt	.30	.09
❑	84 Aaron Shea	.20	.06
❑	85 Courtney Brown	.30	.09
❑	86 JaJuan Dawson	.20	.06
❑	87 Rickey Dudley	.20	.06
❑	88 Jamir Miller	.20	.06
❑	89 Clint Stoerner	.20	.06
❑	90 Emmitt Smith	1.00	.30
❑	91 Joey Galloway	.30	.09
❑	92 Rocket Ismail	.30	.09
❑	93 Ebenezer Ekuban	.20	.06
❑	94 Anthony Wright	.20	.06
❑	95 David LaFleur	.20	.06
❑	96 Dexter Coakley	.20	.06
❑	97 Jackie Harris	.20	.06
❑	98 Michael Wiley	.20	.06
❑	99 Wane McGarity	.20	.06
❑	100 Dat Nguyen	.20	.06
❑	101 Terrell Davis	.50	.15
❑	102 Mike Anderson	.50	.15
❑	103 Brian Griese	.50	.15
❑	104 Rod Smith	.30	.09
❑	105 Ed McCaffrey	.50	.15
❑	106 Olandis Gary	.30	.09
❑	107 Kavika Pittman	.20	.06
❑	108 Bill Romanowski	.20	.06
❑	109 Gus Frerotte	.20	.06
❑	110 Howard Griffith	.20	.06
❑	111 Eddie Kennison	.30	.09
❑	112 Charlie Batch	.50	.15
❑	113 Germane Crowell	.20	.06
❑	114 James O. Stewart	.30	.09
❑	115 Johnnie Morton	.30	.09
❑	116 Herman Moore	.30	.09
❑	117 Larry Foster	.20	.06
❑	118 Desmond Howard	.20	.06
❑	119 Cory Schlesinger	.20	.06
❑	120 Robert Porcher	.20	.06
❑	121 Sedrick Irvin	.20	.06
❑	122 David Sloan	.20	.06
❑	123 Jim Harbaugh	.30	.09
❑	124 Brett Favre	1.50	.45
❑	125 Antonio Freeman	.50	.15
❑	126 Dorsey Levens	.30	.09
❑	127 Ahman Green	.50	.15
❑	128 LeRoy Butler	.20	.06
❑	129 De'Mond Parker	.20	.06
❑	130 Bill Schroeder	.30	.09
❑	131 Bubba Franks	.30	.09
❑	132 Donald Driver	.30	.09
❑	133 Darren Sharper	.20	.06
❑	134 Corey Bradford	.20	.06
❑	135 Charles Lee	.20	.06
❑	136 Peyton Manning	1.25	.35
❑	137 Edgerrin James	.60	.18
❑	138 Marvin Harrison	.50	.15
❑	139 E.G. Green	.20	.06
❑	140 Terrence Wilkins	.20	.06
❑	141 Ken Dilger	.20	.06
❑	142 Jerome Pathon	.30	.09
❑	143 Rob Morris	.20	.06
❑	144 Lennox Gordon	.20	.06
❑	145 Chad Bratzke	.20	.06
❑	146 Mark Brunell	.50	.15
❑	147 Fred Taylor	.50	.15
❑	148 Jimmy Smith	.30	.09
❑	149 Jamie Martin	.30	.09
❑	150 Keenan McCardell	.20	.06
❑	151 Kyle Brady	.20	.06
❑	152 R.Jay Soward	.20	.06
❑	153 Alvis Whitted	.20	.06
❑	154 Stacey Mack	.20	.06
❑	155 Damon Jones	.20	.06
❑	156 Carnell Lake	.20	.06
❑	157 Kevin Hardy	.20	.06
❑	158 Trent Green	.50	.15
❑	159 Tony Gonzalez	.30	.09
❑	160 Derrick Alexander	.30	.09
❑	161 Tony Richardson	.20	.06
❑	162 Frank Moreau	.20	.06
❑	163 Sylvester Morris	.20	.06
❑	164 Priest Holmes	.60	.18
❑	165 Donnie Edwards	.20	.06
❑	166 Marvcus Patton	.20	.06
❑	167 Larry Parker	.20	.06
❑	168 Tony Horne	.20	.06
❑	169 Bubby Brister	.20	.06
❑	170 Oronde Gadsden	.30	.09
❑	171 Lamar Smith	.30	.09
❑	172 Jay Fiedler	.50	.15
❑	173 James Johnson	.20	.06
❑	174 Rob Konrad	.20	.06
❑	175 James McKnight	.30	.09
❑	176 Dedric Ward	.20	.06
❑	177 O.J. McDuffie	.20	.06
❑	178 Zach Thomas	.50	.15
❑	179 Ray Lucas	.20	.06
❑	180 Sam Madison	.20	.06
❑	181 Randy Moss	1.00	.30
❑	182 Jake Reed	.30	.09
❑	183 Cris Carter	.50	.15
❑	184 Daunte Culpepper	.50	.15
❑	185 Moe Williams	.30	.09
❑	186 Troy Walters	.20	.06
❑	187 Todd Bouman	.30	.09
❑	188 Jim Kleinsasser	.20	.06
❑	189 Ed McDaniel	.20	.06
❑	190 Robert Griffith	.20	.06
❑	191 Byron Chamberlain	.20	.06
❑	192 Chris Hovan	.20	.06
❑	193 Drew Bledsoe	.60	.18
❑	194 Terry Glenn	.30	.09
❑	195 Kevin Faulk	.30	.09
❑	196 J.R. Redmond	.20	.06
❑	197 Antowain Smith	.30	.09
❑	198 Bert Emanuel	.30	.09
❑	199 Troy Brown	.30	.09
❑	200 Tony Simmons	.20	.06
❑	201 Michael Bishop	.20	.06
❑	202 Lawyer Milloy	.30	.09
❑	203 Torrance Small	.20	.06
❑	204 Ty Law	.30	.09
❑	205 Charles Johnson	.20	.06
❑	206 Willie McGinest	.20	.06
❑	207 Ricky Williams	.50	.15
❑	208 Jeff Blake	.30	.09
❑	209 Joe Horn	.30	.09
❑	210 Aaron Brooks	.50	.15
❑	211 La'Roi Glover	.20	.06
❑	212 Chad Morton	.20	.06
❑	213 Keith Mitchell	.20	.06
❑	214 Willie Jackson	.20	.06
❑	215 Robert Wilson	.20	.06
❑	216 Norman Hand	.20	.06
❑	217 Albert Connell	.20	.06
❑	218 Joe Johnson	.20	.06
❑	219 Kerry Collins	.30	.09
❑	220 Amani Toomer	.30	.09
❑	221 Ron Dayne	.50	.15
❑	222 Tiki Barber	.30	.09
❑	223 Greg Comella	.20	.06
❑	224 Ike Hilliard	.30	.09
❑	225 Joe Jurevicius	.20	.06
❑	226 Ron Dixon	.20	.06
❑	227 Jason Sehorn	.20	.06
❑	228 Michael Strahan	.30	.09
❑	229 Jessie Armstead	.20	.06
❑	230 Michael Barrow	.20	.06
❑	231 Jason Garrett	.20	.06
❑	232 Vinny Testaverde	.30	.09
❑	233 Wayne Chrebet	.30	.09
❑	234 Curtis Martin	.50	.15
❑	235 Richie Anderson	.20	.06
❑	236 Mo Lewis	.20	.06
❑	237 Laveranues Coles	.50	.15
❑	238 Windrell Hayes	.20	.06
❑	239 Chad Pennington	.75	.23
❑	240 Matthew Hatchette	.20	.06
❑	241 Anthony Becht	.20	.06
❑	242 Marvin Jones	.20	.06
❑	243 Tim Brown	.50	.15
❑	244 Rich Gannon	.50	.15
❑	245 Tyrone Wheatley	.30	.09
❑	246 Charlie Garner	.30	.09
❑	247 Jon Ritchie	.20	.06
❑	248 James Jett	.20	.06
❑	249 Roland Williams	.20	.06
❑	250 Jerry Porter	.30	.09
❑	251 Darrell Russell	.20	.06
❑	252 Charles Woodson	.30	.09
❑	253 Jerry Rice	1.00	.30
❑	254 Greg Biekert	.20	.06
❑	255 Duce Staley	.50	.15
❑	256 Donovan McNabb	.60	.18
❑	257 Darnell Autry	.20	.06
❑	258 Chad Lewis	.20	.06
❑	259 Na Brown	.20	.06
❑	260 Koy Detmer	.20	.06
❑	261 Todd Pinkston	.30	.09
❑	262 Brian Mitchell	.20	.06

❑ 263 Hugh Douglas	.20	.06
❑ 264 James Thrash	.30	.09
❑ 265 Ron Powlus	.20	.06
❑ 266 Corey Simon	.30	.09
❑ 267 Kordell Stewart	.30	.09
❑ 268 Jerome Bettis	.50	.15
❑ 269 Bobby Shaw	.20	.06
❑ 270 Hines Ward	.50	.15
❑ 271 Plaxico Burress	.50	.15
❑ 272 Courtney Hawkins	.20	.06
❑ 273 Troy Edwards	.20	.06
❑ 274 Earl Holmes	.20	.06
❑ 275 Richard Huntley	.20	.06
❑ 276 Kent Graham	.20	.06
❑ 277 Tee Martin	.30	.09
❑ 278 Jon Witman	.20	.06
❑ 279 Marshall Faulk	.60	.18
❑ 280 Kurt Warner	1.00	.30
❑ 281 Isaac Bruce	.50	.15
❑ 282 Torry Holt	.50	.15
❑ 283 Joe Germaine	.20	.06
❑ 284 Ernie Conwell	.20	.06
❑ 285 Trung Canidate	.30	.09
❑ 286 Az-Zahir Hakim	.20	.06
❑ 287 Ricky Proehl	.20	.06
❑ 288 Grant Wistrom	.20	.06
❑ 289 London Fletcher	.20	.06
❑ 290 Paul Justin	.20	.06
❑ 291 Robert Holcombe	.20	.06
❑ 292 Junior Seau	.50	.15
❑ 293 Curtis Conway	.30	.09
❑ 294 Rodney Harrison	.20	.06
❑ 295 Jeff Graham	.20	.06
❑ 296 Freddie Jones	.20	.06
❑ 297 Reggie Jones	.20	.06
❑ 298 Ronney Jenkins	.20	.06
❑ 299 Trevor Gaylor	.20	.06
❑ 300 Tim Dwight	.50	.15
❑ 301 Fred McCrary	.20	.06
❑ 302 Terrell Fletcher	.20	.06
❑ 303 Doug Flutie	.50	.15
❑ 304 Dave Dickenson RC	.30	.09
❑ 305 Marcellus Wiley	.20	.06
❑ 306 Jeff Garcia	.50	.15
❑ 307 Jonas Lewis	.20	.06
❑ 308 Tai Streets	.20	.06
❑ 309 Terrell Owens	.50	.15
❑ 310 J.J. Stokes	.30	.09
❑ 311 Fred Beasley	.20	.06
❑ 312 Tim Rattay	.30	.09
❑ 313 Garrison Hearst	.30	.09
❑ 314 Giovanni Carmazzi	.20	.06
❑ 315 Bryant Young	.20	.06
❑ 316 Ricky Watters	.30	.09
❑ 317 Shaun Alexander	.60	.18
❑ 318 Matt Hasselbeck	.30	.09
❑ 319 Brock Huard	.20	.06
❑ 320 Darrell Jackson	.50	.15
❑ 321 James Williams	.20	.06
❑ 322 Charlie Rogers UER (name misspelled on back Rodgers)	.20	.06
❑ 323 Christian Fauria	.20	.06
❑ 324 Karsten Bailey	.20	.06
❑ 325 Travis Brown	.50	.15
❑ 326 Chad Brown	.20	.06
❑ 327 John Randle	.30	.09
❑ 328 Warrick Dunn	.50	.15
❑ 329 Shaun King	.20	.06
❑ 330 Rabih Abdullah	.20	.06
❑ 331 Mike Alstott	.50	.15
❑ 332 Jacquez Green	.20	.06
❑ 333 Reidel Anthony	.20	.06
❑ 334 Derrick Brooks	.50	.15
❑ 335 John Lynch	.30	.09
❑ 336 Warren Sapp	.30	.09
❑ 337 Brad Johnson	.50	.15
❑ 338 Keyshawn Johnson	.50	.15
❑ 339 Mark Royals	.20	.06
❑ 340 Dave Moore	.20	.06
❑ 341 Simeon Rice	.30	.09
❑ 342 Ronde Barber	.20	.06
❑ 343 Eddie George	.50	.15
❑ 344 Steve McNair	.50	.15
❑ 345 Samari Rolle	.20	.06
❑ 346 Derrick Mason	.30	.09
❑ 347 Randall Godfrey	.20	.06
❑ 348 Frank Wycheck	.20	.06
❑ 349 Chris Sanders	.20	.06
❑ 350 Neil O'Donnell	.20	.06
❑ 351 Kevin Dyson	.30	.09
❑ 352 Jevon Kearse	.30	.09
❑ 353 Chris Coleman	.20	.06
❑ 354 Mike Green	.20	.06
❑ 355 Blaine Bishop	.20	.06
❑ 356 Eddie Robinson	.20	.06
❑ 357 Jeff George	.30	.09
❑ 358 Stephen Davis	.50	.15
❑ 359 Donnell Bennett	.20	.06
❑ 360 Kevin Lockett	.20	.06
❑ 361 Derrius Thompson	.20	.06
❑ 362 Michael Westbrook	.30	.09
❑ 363 Stephen Alexander	.20	.06
❑ 364 Ki-Jana Carter	.20	.06
❑ 365 Champ Bailey	.30	.09
❑ 366 Todd Husak	.20	.06
❑ 367 Dan Wilkinson	.20	.06
❑ 368 Darrell Green	.20	.06
❑ 369 Sam Shade	.20	.06
❑ 370 Bruce Smith	.20	.06
❑ 371 Bobby Newcombe RC	.50	.15
❑ 372 Vinny Sutherland RC	.50	.15
❑ 373 Alge Crumpler RC	1.00	.30
❑ 374 Michael Vick RC	5.00	1.50
❑ 375 Gary Baxter RC	.50	.15
❑ 376 Todd Heap RC	.75	.23
❑ 377 Nate Clements RC	.75	.23
❑ 378 Travis Henry RC	1.00	.30
❑ 379 Dan Morgan RC	.75	.23
❑ 380 Chris Weinke RC	.75	.23
❑ 381 David Terrell RC	.75	.23
❑ 382 Anthony Thomas RC	1.25	.35
❑ 383 Rudi Johnson RC	1.50	.45
❑ 384 Justin Smith RC	.75	.23
❑ 385 T.J. Houshmandzadeh RC	.75	.23
❑ 386 Chad Johnson RC	1.50	.45
❑ 387 Quincy Morgan RC	.75	.23
❑ 388 Gerard Warren RC	.75	.23
❑ 389 James Jackson RC	.75	.23
❑ 390 Quincy Carter RC	.75	.23
❑ 391 Kevin Kasper RC	.75	.23
❑ 392 Scotty Anderson RC	.50	.15
❑ 393 Mike McMahon RC	.75	.23
❑ 394 Jamal Reynolds RC	.75	.23
❑ 395 Robert Ferguson RC	.75	.23
❑ 396 Reggie Wayne RC	1.25	.35
❑ 397 Snoop Minnis RC	.50	.15
❑ 398 Chris Chambers RC	1.00	.30
❑ 399 Jamar Fletcher RC	.50	.15
❑ 400 Travis Minor RC	.50	.15
❑ 401 Josh Heupel RC	.75	.23
❑ 402 Michael Bennett RC	1.50	.45
❑ 403 Jabari Holloway RC	.50	.15
❑ 404 Moran Norris RC	.30	.09
❑ 405 Deuce McAllister RC	1.50	.45
❑ 406 Will Allen RC	.50	.15
❑ 407 Jesse Palmer RC	.75	.23
❑ 408 LaMont Jordan RC	1.00	.30
❑ 409 Santana Moss RC	1.25	.35
❑ 410 Ken-Yon Rambo RC	.50	.15
❑ 411 Derrick Gibson RC	.50	.15
❑ 412 Marques Tuiasosopo RC	.75	.23
❑ 413 Correll Buckhalter RC	1.00	.30
❑ 414 Freddie Mitchell RC	.75	.23
❑ 415 Drew Brees RC	1.50	.45
❑ 416 LaDainian Tomlinson RC	2.50	.75
❑ 417 Cedrick Wilson RC	.75	.23
❑ 418 Kevan Barlow RC	.75	.23
❑ 419 Alex Bannister RC	.50	.15
❑ 420 Heath Evans RC	.50	.15
❑ 421 Josh Booty RC	.75	.23
❑ 422 Koren Robinson RC	1.00	.30
❑ 423 Adam Archuleta RC	.75	.23
❑ 424 Dan Alexander RC	.75	.23
❑ 425 Eddie Berlin RC	.50	.15
❑ 426 Rod Gardner RC	.75	.23
❑ 427 Sage Rosenfels RC	.75	.23
❑ 428 Steve Smith RC	1.00	.30
❑ 429 Chris Barnes RC	.50	.15
❑ 430 Tim Hasselbeck RC	.75	.23
❑ 431 Peyton Manning CL	.60	.18
❑ 432 Mike Anderson CL	.20	.06
❑ 433 Jamal Lewis CL	.40	.12
❑ 434 Randy Moss CL	.50	.15
❑ 435 Donovan McNabb CL		
❑ 436 Daunte Culpepper CL	.30	.09
❑ 437 Kurt Warner CL	.50	.15
❑ 438 Eddie George CL	.20	.06
❑ 439 Marshall Faulk CL	.50	.15
❑ 440 Brett Favre CL	.75	.23

2001 Upper Deck Vintage

	Nm-Mt	Ex-Mt
COMPLETE SET (290)	40.00	12.00
❑ 1 Jake Plummer	.30	.09
❑ 2 David Boston	.50	.15
❑ 3 Thomas Jones	.30	.09
❑ 4 Frank Sanders	.20	.06
❑ 5 Bob Christian	.20	.06
❑ 6 Jamal Anderson	.50	.15
❑ 7 Chris Chandler	.30	.09
❑ 8 Shawn Jefferson	.20	.06
❑ 9 Brian Finneran	.20	.06
❑ 10 Terance Mathis	.30	.09
❑ 11 Jamal Lewis	.75	.23
❑ 12 Shannon Sharpe	.30	.09
❑ 13 Elvis Grbac	.30	.09
❑ 14 Ray Lewis	.50	.15
❑ 15 Qadry Ismail	.30	.09
❑ 16 Brandon Stokley	.30	.09
❑ 17 Rob Johnson	.30	.09
❑ 18 Eric Moulds	.30	.09
❑ 19 Sammy Morris	.20	.06
❑ 20 Shawn Bryson	.20	.06
❑ 21 Jeremy McDaniel	.20	.06
❑ 22 Muhsin Muhammad	.30	.09
❑ 23 Brad Hoover	.20	.06
❑ 24 Tim Biakabutuka	.30	.09
❑ 25 Donald Hayes	.20	.06
❑ 26 Jeff Lewis	.20	.06
❑ 27 Wesley Walls	.20	.06
❑ 28 Cade McNown	.20	.06
❑ 29 James Allen	.30	.09
❑ 30 Marcus Robinson	.50	.15
❑ 31 Brian Urlacher	.75	.23
❑ 32 Jim Miller	.20	.06
❑ 33 Peter Warrick	.50	.15
❑ 34 Corey Dillon	.50	.15
❑ 35 Akili Smith	.20	.06
❑ 36 Danny Farmer	.20	.06
❑ 37 Ron Dugans	.20	.06
❑ 38 Jon Kitna	.50	.15
❑ 39 Tim Couch	.30	.09
❑ 40 Kevin Johnson	.30	.09
❑ 41 Travis Prentice	.20	.06
❑ 42 Spergon Wynn	.20	.06
❑ 43 Errict Rhett	.20	.06
❑ 44 Dennis Northcutt	.30	.09
❑ 45 Courtney Brown	.30	.09
❑ 46 Tony Banks	.30	.09
❑ 47 Emmitt Smith	1.00	.30
❑ 48 Joey Galloway	.30	.09
❑ 49 Rocket Ismail	.30	.09
❑ 50 Anthony Wright	.20	.06
❑ 51 Jackie Harris	.20	.06
❑ 52 Terrell Davis	.50	.15
❑ 53 Mike Anderson	.50	.15
❑ 54 Brian Griese	.50	.15
❑ 55 Rod Smith	.30	.09

❑ 56 Ed McCaffrey .50 .15
❑ 57 Howard Griffith .20 .06
❑ 58 Olandis Gary .30 .09
❑ 59 Charlie Batch .50 .15
❑ 60 Germane Crowell .20 .06
❑ 61 James O. Stewart .30 .09
❑ 62 Johnnie Morton .30 .09
❑ 63 Desmond Howard .20 .06
❑ 64 Brett Favre 1.50 .45
❑ 65 Antonio Freeman .50 .15
❑ 66 Dorsey Levens .30 .09
❑ 67 Ahman Green .50 .15
❑ 68 Bill Schroeder .30 .09
❑ 69 Bubba Franks .30 .09
❑ 70 Peyton Manning 1.25 .35
❑ 71 Edgerrin James .60 .18
❑ 72 Marvin Harrison .50 .15
❑ 73 Jerome Pathon .30 .09
❑ 74 Ken Dilger .20 .06
❑ 75 Terrence Wilkins .20 .06
❑ 76 Mark Brunell .50 .15
❑ 77 Fred Taylor .50 .15
❑ 78 Jimmy Smith .30 .09
❑ 79 Keenan McCardell .20 .06
❑ 80 R. Jay Soward .20 .06
❑ 81 Todd Collins .20 .06
❑ 82 Tony Gonzalez .30 .09
❑ 83 Derrick Alexander .30 .09
❑ 84 Trent Green .50 .15
❑ 85 Sylvester Morris .20 .06
❑ 86 Oronde Gadsden .30 .09
❑ 87 Lamar Smith .30 .09
❑ 88 Jay Fiedler .50 .15
❑ 89 Zach Thomas .50 .15
❑ 90 Ray Lucas .20 .06
❑ 91 O.J. McDuffie .20 .06
❑ 92 Randy Moss 1.00 .30
❑ 93 Cris Carter .50 .15
❑ 94 Daunte Culpepper .50 .15
❑ 95 Robert Griffith .20 .06
❑ 96 Jake Reed .30 .09
❑ 97 Drew Bledsoe .60 .18
❑ 98 Terry Glenn .20 .06
❑ 99 Kevin Faulk .30 .09
❑ 100 Michael Bishop .20 .06
❑ 101 Troy Brown .30 .09
❑ 102 Ricky Williams .50 .15
❑ 103 Jeff Blake .30 .09
❑ 104 Joe Horn .30 .09
❑ 105 Willie Jackson .20 .06
❑ 106 Aaron Brooks .50 .15
❑ 107 Keith Poole .20 .06
❑ 108 Kerry Collins .30 .09
❑ 109 Amani Toomer .30 .09
❑ 110 Ron Dayne .50 .15
❑ 111 Tiki Barber .30 .09
❑ 112 Ike Hilliard .30 .09
❑ 113 Ron Dixon .20 .06
❑ 114 Michael Strahan .30 .09
❑ 115 Vinny Testaverde .30 .09
❑ 116 Wayne Chrebet .30 .09
❑ 117 Curtis Martin .50 .15
❑ 118 Richie Anderson .20 .06
❑ 119 Laveranues Coles .50 .15
❑ 120 Chad Pennington .75 .23
❑ 121 Tim Brown .50 .15
❑ 122 Rich Gannon .50 .15
❑ 123 Tyrone Wheatley .30 .09
❑ 124 Charlie Garner .30 .09
❑ 125 Andre Rison .30 .09
❑ 126 Charles Woodson .30 .09
❑ 127 Jon Ritchie .20 .06
❑ 128 Duce Staley .50 .15
❑ 129 Donovan McNabb .60 .18
❑ 130 Darnell Autry .20 .06
❑ 131 Chad Lewis .20 .06
❑ 132 Brian Mitchell .20 .06
❑ 133 Kordell Stewart .30 .09
❑ 134 Jerome Bettis .50 .15
❑ 135 Plaxico Burress .50 .15
❑ 136 Bobby Shaw .20 .06
❑ 137 Hines Ward .50 .15
❑ 138 Marshall Faulk .60 .18
❑ 139 Kurt Warner 1.00 .30
❑ 140 Isaac Bruce .50 .15
❑ 141 Torry Holt .50 .15
❑ 142 Justin Watson .20 .06
❑ 143 Az-ZahirHakim .20 .06
❑ 144 Junior Seau .50 .15
❑ 145 Curtis Conway .30 .09
❑ 146 Doug Flutie .50 .15
❑ 147 Jeff Graham .20 .06
❑ 148 Freddie Jones .20 .06
❑ 149 Rodney Harrison .20 .06
❑ 150 Jeff Garcia .50 .15
❑ 151 Jerry Rice 1.00 .30
❑ 152 Jonas Lewis .20 .06
❑ 153 Terrell Owens .50 .15
❑ 154 J.J. Stokes .30 .09
❑ 155 Garrison Hearst .20 .06
❑ 156 Ricky Watters .30 .09
❑ 157 Shaun Alexander .60 .18
❑ 158 Matt Hasselbeck .30 .09
❑ 159 Brock Huard .20 .06
❑ 160 Darrell Jackson .50 .15
❑ 161 Itula Mili .20 .06
❑ 162 Warrick Dunn .50 .15
❑ 163 Shaun King .20 .06
❑ 164 Reidel Anthony .20 .06
❑ 165 Mike Alstott .50 .15
❑ 166 Jacquez Green .20 .06
❑ 167 Brad Johnson .50 .15
❑ 168 Keyshawn Johnson .50 .15
❑ 169 Eddie George .50 .15
❑ 170 Steve McNair .50 .15
❑ 171 Neil O'Donnell .20 .06
❑ 172 Derrick Mason .30 .09
❑ 173 Frank Wycheck .20 .06
❑ 174 Chris Sanders .20 .06
❑ 175 Jevon Kearse .30 .09
❑ 176 Jeff George .30 .09
❑ 177 Stephen Davis .50 .15
❑ 178 Skip Hicks .20 .06
❑ 179 Michael Westbrook .30 .09
❑ 180 Stephen Alexander .20 .06
❑ 181 Vinny Testaverde SH .30 .09
❑ 182 Trent Green SH .50 .15
❑ 183 Brian Griese SH .50 .15
❑ 184 Kerry Collins SH .30 .09
❑ 185 Aaron Brooks SH .50 .15
❑ 186 Jamal Lewis SH .40 .12
❑ 187 Jeff Garcia SH .50 .15
❑ 188 Warrick Dunn SH .50 .15
❑ 189 Mike Anderson SH .20 .06
❑ 190 Lamar Smith SH .30 .09
❑ 191 Daunte Culpepper SL .50 .15
❑ 192 Darren Sharper SL .20 .06
❑ 193 Marvin Harrison SL .50 .15
❑ 194 Torry Holt SL .50 .15
❑ 195 Trent Green SL .50 .15
❑ 196 Peyton Manning SL .60 .18
❑ 197 Muhsin Muhammad SL .30 .09
❑ 198 La'Roi Glover SL .20 .06
❑ 199 Brian Griese SL .20 .06
❑ 200 Darrick Vaughn SL .20 .06
❑ 201 Bobby Newcombe RC .75 .23
❑ 202 Leonard Davis RC .75 .23
❑ 203 Alge Crumpler RC 1.50 .45
❑ 204 Michael Vick RC 8.00 2.40
❑ 205 Vinny Sutherland RC .75 .23
❑ 206 Chris Barnes RC .75 .23
❑ 207 Todd Heap RC 1.25 .35
❑ 208 Travis Henry RC 1.50 .45
❑ 209 Tim Hasselbeck RC 1.25 .35
❑ 210 Nate Clements RC 1.25 .35
❑ 211 Chris Weinke RC 1.25 .35
❑ 212 Dan Morgan RC 1.25 .35
❑ 213 Anthony Thomas RC 2.00 .60
❑ 214 David Terrell RC 1.25 .35
❑ 215 Chad Johnson RC 2.50 .75
❑ 216 Justin Smith RC 1.25 .35
❑ 217 Rudi Johnson RC 2.50 .75
❑ 218 T.J. Houshmandzadeh RC 1.25 .35
❑ 219 Gerard Warren RC 1.25 .35
❑ 220 James Jackson RC 1.25 .35
❑ 221 Quincy Morgan RC 1.25 .35
❑ 222 Quincy Carter RC 1.25 .35
❑ 223 Tony Dixon RC .75 .23
❑ 224 Kevin Kasper RC 1.25 .35
❑ 225 Willie Middlebrooks RC .75 .23
❑ 226 Mike McMahon RC 1.25 .35
❑ 227 Shaun Rogers RC 1.25 .35
❑ 228 Jamal Reynolds RC 1.25 .35
❑ 229 Robert Ferguson RC 1.25 .35
❑ 230 Reggie Wayne RC 2.00 .60
❑ 231 Marcus Stroud RC 1.25 .35
❑ 232 Dustin McClintock RC .75 .23
❑ 233 Snoop Minnis RC .75 .23
❑ 234 Chris Chambers RC 1.50 .45
❑ 235 Josh Heupel RC 1.25 .35
❑ 236 Travis Minor RC .75 .23
❑ 237 Michael Bennett RC 2.50 .75
❑ 238 Richard Seymour RC 1.25 .35
❑ 239 Hakim Akbar RC .50 .15
❑ 240 Deuce McAllister RC 2.50 .75
❑ 241 Moran Norris RC .50 .15
❑ 242 Jesse Palmer RC 1.25 .35
❑ 243 Will Allen RC .75 .23
❑ 244 LaMont Jordan RC 1.50 .45
❑ 245 Santana Moss RC 2.00 .60
❑ 246 Marques Tuiasosopo RC 1.25 .35
❑ 247 Correll Buckhalter RC 1.50 .45
❑ 248 Freddie Mitchell RC 1.25 .35
❑ 249 A.J. Feeley RC 1.25 .35
❑ 250 Dave Dickenson RC .75 .23
❑ 251 Drew Brees RC 2.50 .75
❑ 252 LaDainian Tomlinson RC 4.00 1.20
❑ 253 David Allen RC .75 .23
❑ 254 Andre Carter RC 1.25 .35
❑ 255 Kevan Barlow RC 1.25 .35
❑ 256 Josh Booty RC 1.25 .35
❑ 257 Koren Robinson RC 1.50 .45
❑ 258 Adam Archuleta RC 1.25 .35
❑ 259 Rod Gardner RC 1.25 .35
❑ 260 Sage Rosenfels RC 1.25 .35
❑ 261 Reggie Germany .75 .23
Ken-Yon Rambo
❑ 262 Edgerton Hartwell .75 .23
Gary Baxter
❑ 263 Aaron Schobel 1.25 .35
Brandon Spoon
❑ 264 John Capel .75 .23
Karon Riley
❑ 265 Billy Baber 1.25 .35
Derrick Blaylock
❑ 266 Jamar Fletcher .75 .23
Morlon Greenwood
❑ 267 Andre King .75 .23
Ronney Daniels
❑ 268 Arther Love .75 .23
Jabari Holloway
❑ 269 Jonas Jennings .50 .15
Kenyatta Walker
❑ 270 Ben Hamilton .50 .15
Paul Toviessa
❑ 271 Chris Taylor .75 .23
Joey Getherall
❑ 272 Casey Hampton 3.00 .90
Kendrell Bell
❑ 273 Cedrick Wilson 1.25 .35
Jamie Winborn
❑ 274 Alex Bannister .75 .23
Heath Evans
❑ 275 Damione Lewis .75 .23
Ryan Pickett
❑ 276 Tommy Polley 1.25 .35
Brian Allen
❑ 277 Jamie Henderson .75 .23
Reggie White
❑ 278 Eddie Berlin 1.25 .35
Justin McCareins
❑ 279 Andre Dyson 1.25 .35
Dan Alexander
❑ 280 Quentin McCord .75 .23
Robert Garza
❑ 281 Scotty Anderson .75 .23
Eric Kelly
Willie Howard
❑ 282 Bhawoh Jue 1.25 .35
David Martin
Torrance Marshall
❑ 283 Stevonne Smith 1.50 .45
Dee Brown
Jarrod Cooper
❑ 284 DeLawrence Grant .75 .23

Derek Combs		
Derrick Gibson		
❑ 285 Carlos Polk	1.25	.35
Tay Cody		
Zeke Moreno		
❑ 286 David Rivers	.75	.23
Francis St. Paul		
Milton Wynn		
❑ 287 Ennis Davis	.75	.23
Kenny Smith		
Sedrick Hodge		
❑ 288 Ken Lucas	.75	.23
Orlando Huff		
Steve Hutchinson		
❑ 289 Marcellus Rivers	1.25	.35
Derrick Burgess		
Tony Driver		
❑ 290 Damerien McCants	1.25	.35
Fred Smoot		
Mike Cerimele		

2001 Upper Deck Vintage Signatures

	Nm-Mt	Ex-Mt
❑ ABVS Aaron Brooks	25.00	7.50
❑ CBVS Charlie Batch	15.00	4.50
❑ CDVS Corey Dillon	25.00	7.50
❑ DFVS Doug Flutie	25.00	7.50
❑ DIVS Trent Dilfer	15.00	4.50
❑ EJVS Edgerrin James	30.00	9.00
❑ IBVS Isaac Bruce	25.00	7.50
❑ JBVS Jim Brown	150.00	45.00
❑ JNVS Joe Namath	120.00	36.00
❑ JRVS John Riggins	250.00	75.00
❑ JSVS Junior Seau	25.00	7.50
❑ MAVS Mike Anderson	25.00	7.50
❑ MBVS Mark Brunell	25.00	7.50
❑ MFVS Marshall Faulk	30.00	9.00
❑ MRVS Marcus Robinson	15.00	4.50
❑ NOVS Jeff Blake EXCH	15.00	4.50
❑ PHVS Paul Hornung	30.00	9.00
❑ PMVS Peyton Manning	60.00	18.00
❑ TBVS Terry Bradshaw	120.00	36.00
❑ TCVS Tim Couch	15.00	4.50
❑ TDVS Terrell Davis	25.00	7.50
❑ TGVS Tony Gonzalez	25.00	7.50
❑ TOVS Terrell Owens	25.00	7.50
❑ VTVS Vinny Testaverde	15.00	4.50
❑ WCVS Wayne Chrebet	15.00	4.50

2001 Upper Deck Vintage Threads Autographs

	Nm-Mt	Ex-Mt
❑ CDSVT Corey Dillon	50.00	15.00
❑ DBSVT Drew Bledsoe	60.00	18.00
❑ DCSVT Daunte Culpepper	60.00	18.00
❑ JGSVT Jeff Garcia	50.00	15.00
❑ JMSVT Joe Montana	300.00	90.00
❑ JRSVT Jerry Rice	120.00	36.00
❑ KWSVT Kurt Warner	100.00	30.00
❑ MASVT Mike Alstott	50.00	15.00
❑ MBSVT Mark Brunell	50.00	15.00
❑ PMSVT Peyton Manning	120.00	36.00
❑ RMSVT Randy Moss	100.00	30.00
❑ SDSVT Stephen Davis	50.00	15.00
❑ TASVT Troy Aikman	100.00	30.00
❑ TCSVT Tim Couch	50.00	15.00

2001 Upper Deck Vintage Threads Combos

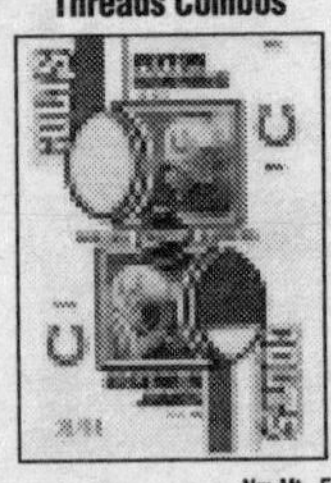

	Nm-Mt	Ex-Mt
❑ AMVTC Troy Aikman	60.00	18.00
Cade McNown		
❑ BDVTC Tiki Barber		
Ron Dayne		
❑ BFVTC Mark Brunell	100.00	30.00
Brett Favre		
❑ DBVTC Ron Dayne	50.00	15.00
Michael Bennett		
❑ FJVTC Marshall Faulk	80.00	24.00
Edgerrin James		
❑ FMVTC Marshall Faulk	50.00	15.00
Deuce McAllister		
❑ GSVTC Darrel Green	100.00	30.00
Deion Sanders		
❑ MCVTC Donovan McNabb	80.00	24.00
Daunte Culpepper		
❑ MJVTC Peyton Manning	120.00	36.00
Edgerrin James		
❑ MRVTC Randy Moss	150.00	45.00
Jerry Rice		
❑ WHVTC Kurt Warner	60.00	18.00
Torry Holt		

2002 Upper Deck XL

	Nm-Mt	Ex-Mt
COMPLETE SET (600)	150.00	45.00
COMP.SET w/o SP's (500)	60.00	18.00
❑ 1 David Boston	.60	.18
❑ 2 Dave Brown	.25	.07
❑ 3 Frank Sanders	.25	.07
❑ 4 Jake Plummer	.40	.12
❑ 5 Joel Makovicka	.25	.07
❑ 6 Kwamie Lassiter	.25	.07
❑ 7 MarTay Jenkins	.25	.07
❑ 8 Michael Pittman	.25	.07
❑ 9 Raynoch Thompson	.25	.07
❑ 10 Rob Fredrickson	.25	.07
❑ 11 Ronald McKinnon	.25	.07
❑ 12 Steve Bush	.25	.07
❑ 13 Thomas Jones	.40	.12
❑ 14 Tywan Mitchell	.25	.07
❑ 15 Alvis Whitted	.25	.07
❑ 16 Ashley Ambrose	.25	.07
❑ 17 Bob Christian	.25	.07
❑ 18 Brady Smith	.25	.07
❑ 19 Brian Finneran	.25	.07
❑ 20 Chris Chandler	.40	.12
❑ 21 Chris Draft RC	.40	.12
❑ 22 Darrien Gordon	.25	.07
❑ 23 Doug Johnson	.25	.07
❑ 24 Ephraim Salaam	.25	.07
❑ 25 Jamal Anderson	.40	.12
❑ 26 Keith Brooking	.25	.07
❑ 27 Maurice Smith	.25	.07
❑ 28 Michael Vick	2.00	.60
❑ 29 Ray Buchanan	.25	.07
❑ 30 Shawn Jefferson	.25	.07
❑ 31 Terance Mathis	.25	.07
❑ 32 Tony Martin	.25	.07
❑ 33 Brandon Stokley	.40	.12
❑ 34 Chris McAlister	.25	.07
❑ 35 Chris Redman	.25	.07
❑ 36 Elvis Grbac	.40	.12
❑ 37 Jonathan Ogden	.25	.07
❑ 38 Moe Williams	.25	.07
❑ 39 Obafemi Ayanbadejo	.25	.07
❑ 40 Peter Boulware	.25	.07
❑ 41 Qadry Ismail	.40	.12
❑ 42 Randall Cunningham	.60	.18
❑ 43 Ray Lewis	.60	.18
❑ 44 Rod Woodson	.40	.12
❑ 45 Sam Adams	.25	.07
❑ 46 Shannon Sharpe	.40	.12
❑ 47 Terry Allen	.25	.07
❑ 48 Todd Heap	.25	.07
❑ 49 Tony Siragusa	.25	.07
❑ 50 Travis Taylor	.40	.12
❑ 51 Alex Van Pelt	.25	.07
❑ 52 Antoine Winfield	.25	.07
❑ 53 Eric Moulds	.40	.12
❑ 54 Jay Foreman RC	.40	.12
❑ 55 Jay Riemersma	.25	.07
❑ 56 Jeremy McDaniel	.25	.07
❑ 57 Keith Newman	.25	.07
❑ 58 Kenyatta Wright	.25	.07
❑ 59 Larry Centers	.25	.07
❑ 60 Peerless Price	.40	.12
❑ 61 Rob Johnson	.40	.12
❑ 62 Ruben Brown	.25	.07
❑ 63 Shawn Bryson	.25	.07
❑ 64 Travis Brown	.25	.07
❑ 65 Travis Henry	.60	.18
❑ 66 Brad Hoover	.25	.07
❑ 67 Brentson Buckner	.25	.07
❑ 68 Chris Weinke	.40	.12
❑ 69 Dameyune Craig	.25	.07
❑ 70 Deon Grant	.25	.07
❑ 71 Donald Hayes	.25	.07
❑ 72 Doug Evans	.25	.07
❑ 73 Isaac Byrd	.25	.07
❑ 74 Jay Williams RC	.40	.12
❑ 75 Lester Towns	.25	.07
❑ 76 Muhsin Muhammad	.40	.12
❑ 77 Richard Huntley	.25	.07
❑ 78 Steve Smith	.40	.12
❑ 79 Tim Biakabutuka	.25	.07
❑ 80 Todd Sauerbrun	.25	.07
❑ 81 Wesley Walls	.25	.07
❑ 82 Anthony Thomas	.60	.18
❑ 83 Brian Urlacher	1.00	.30
❑ 84 Daimon Shelton	.25	.07
❑ 85 David Terrell	.60	.18
❑ 86 Dez White	.25	.07
❑ 87 Fred Baxter	.25	.07

❑ 88 James Allen .40 .12
❑ 89 James Williams .25 .07
❑ 90 Jim Miller .25 .07
❑ 91 Keith Traylor .25 .07
❑ 92 Larry Whigham .25 .07
❑ 93 Marcus Robinson .40 .12
❑ 94 Marty Booker .25 .07
❑ 95 Mike Brown .60 .18
❑ 96 Olin Kreutz RC .60 .18
❑ 97 R.W. McQuarters .25 .07
❑ 98 Rosevelt Colvin RC 1.00 .30
❑ 99 Shane Matthews .25 .07
❑ 100 Ted Washington .25 .07
❑ 101 Akili Smith .25 .07
❑ 102 Brandon Bennett .25 .07
❑ 103 Brian Simmons .25 .07
❑ 104 Chad Johnson .60 .18
❑ 105 Corey Dillon .40 .12
❑ 106 Darnay Scott .25 .07
❑ 107 Jon Kitna .40 .12
❑ 108 Lorenzo Neal .25 .07
❑ 109 Peter Warrick .40 .12
❑ 110 Ron Dugans .25 .07
❑ 111 Scott Mitchell .25 .07
❑ 112 Takeo Spikes .25 .07
❑ 113 Tony McGee .25 .07
❑ 114 Brant Boyer .25 .07
❑ 115 Corey Fuller .25 .07
❑ 116 Courtney Brown .40 .12
❑ 117 Dwayne Rudd .25 .07
❑ 118 JaJuan Dawson .25 .07
❑ 119 Jamel White .25 .07
❑ 120 James Jackson .25 .07
❑ 121 Jamir Miller .25 .07
❑ 122 Josh Booty .25 .07
❑ 123 Kelly Holcomb .60 .18
❑ 124 Kevin Johnson .40 .12
❑ 125 Lenoy Jones RC .40 .12
❑ 126 Quincy Morgan .25 .07
❑ 127 Raymond Jackson RC .40 .12
❑ 128 Rickey Dudley .25 .07
❑ 129 Tim Couch .40 .12
❑ 130 Darren Woodson .25 .07
❑ 131 Dat Nguyen .25 .07
❑ 132 Dexter Coakley .25 .07
❑ 133 Duane Hawthorne .25 .07
❑ 134 Emmitt Smith 1.50 .45
❑ 135 Jackie Harris .25 .07
❑ 136 Joey Galloway .40 .12
❑ 137 Ken-Yon Rambo .25 .07
❑ 138 Larry Allen .25 .07
❑ 139 Mike Lucky .25 .07
❑ 140 Quincy Carter .40 .12
❑ 141 Rocket Ismail .40 .12
❑ 142 Reggie Swinton .25 .07
❑ 143 Robert Thomas .25 .07
❑ 144 Ryan Leaf .40 .12
❑ 145 Troy Hambrick .25 .07
❑ 146 Al Wilson .25 .07
❑ 147 Bill Romanowski .25 .07
❑ 148 Brian Griese .60 .18
❑ 149 Chester McGlockton .25 .07
❑ 150 Chris Cole .25 .07
❑ 151 Deltha O'Neal .25 .07
❑ 152 Desmond Clark .25 .07
❑ 153 Dwayne Carswell .25 .07
❑ 154 Ian Gold .25 .07
❑ 155 Jarious Jackson .25 .07
❑ 156 Jason Elam .25 .07
❑ 157 Keith Burns .25 .07
❑ 158 Mike Anderson .60 .18
❑ 159 Olandis Gary .25 .07
❑ 160 Rod Smith .40 .12
❑ 161 Scottie Montgomery .25 .07
❑ 162 Terrell Davis .60 .18
❑ 163 Trevor Pryce .25 .07
❑ 164 Charlie Batch .40 .12
❑ 165 Chris Claiborne .25 .07
❑ 166 Cory Schlesinger .25 .07
❑ 167 David Sloan .25 .07
❑ 168 Desmond Howard .25 .07
❑ 169 Germane Crowell .25 .07
❑ 170 James Stewart .40 .12
❑ 171 Johnnie Morton .40 .12
❑ 172 Lamont Warren .25 .07
❑ 173 Larry Foster .25 .07
❑ 174 Mike McMahon .60 .18
❑ 175 Robert Porcher .25 .07
❑ 176 Shaun Rogers .25 .07
❑ 177 Todd Lyght .25 .07
❑ 178 Ty Detmer .25 .07
❑ 179 Ahman Green .60 .18
❑ 180 Antonio Freeman .60 .18
❑ 181 Bhawoh Jue .25 .07
❑ 182 Bill Schroeder .25 .07
❑ 183 Brett Favre 1.50 .45
❑ 184 Bubba Franks .40 .12
❑ 185 Corey Bradford .25 .07
❑ 186 Darren Sharper .25 .07
❑ 187 Donald Driver .40 .12
❑ 188 Dorsey Levens .25 .07
❑ 189 Doug Pederson .25 .07
❑ 190 Kabeer Gbaja-Biamila .40 .12
❑ 191 William Henderson .25 .07
❑ 192 Aaron Glenn .25 .07
❑ 193 Danny Wuerffel .25 .07
❑ 194 Gary Walker .25 .07
❑ 195 Jamie Sharper .25 .07
❑ 196 Jermaine Lewis .25 .07
❑ 197 Matt Stevens .25 .07
❑ 198 Seth Payne RC .40 .12
❑ 199 Tony Boselli .25 .07
❑ 200 Dominic Rhodes .40 .12
❑ 201 Edgerrin James .75 .23
❑ 202 Jerome Pathon .40 .12
❑ 203 Ken Dilger .25 .07
❑ 204 Kevin McDougal .25 .07
❑ 205 Marcus Pollard .25 .07
❑ 206 Mark Rypien .25 .07
❑ 207 Marvin Harrison .60 .18
❑ 208 Peyton Manning 1.25 .35
❑ 209 Reggie Wayne .40 .12
❑ 210 Terrence Wilkins .25 .07
❑ 211 Donovin Darius .25 .07
❑ 212 Elvis Joseph .25 .07
❑ 213 Fred Taylor .60 .18
❑ 214 Hardy Nickerson .25 .07
❑ 215 Jimmy Smith .40 .12
❑ 216 Jonathan Quinn .25 .07
❑ 217 Keenan McCardell .25 .07
❑ 218 Kevin Hardy .25 .07
❑ 219 Kyle Brady .25 .07
❑ 220 Mark Brunell .60 .18
❑ 221 Patrick Washington .25 .07
❑ 222 Sean Dawkins .25 .07
❑ 223 Stacey Mack .25 .07
❑ 224 Tony Brackens .25 .07
❑ 225 Derrick Alexander .40 .12
❑ 226 Donnie Edwards .25 .07
❑ 227 Eric Hicks .25 .07
❑ 228 Kendall Gammon RC .40 .12
❑ 229 Snoop Minnis .25 .07
❑ 230 Mike Cloud .25 .07
❑ 231 Priest Holmes .75 .23
❑ 232 Todd Collins .25 .07
❑ 233 Tony Gonzalez .40 .12
❑ 234 Tony Richardson .25 .07
❑ 235 Trent Green .40 .12
❑ 236 Will Shields .25 .07
❑ 237 Brock Marion .25 .07
❑ 238 Chris Chambers .60 .18
❑ 239 Dedric Ward .25 .07
❑ 240 Hunter Goodwin .25 .07
❑ 241 James McKnight .25 .07
❑ 242 Jay Fiedler .40 .12
❑ 243 Kenny Mixon .25 .07
❑ 244 Lamar Smith .25 .07
❑ 245 Oronde Gadsden .40 .12
❑ 246 Patrick Surtain .25 .07
❑ 247 Ray Lucas .25 .07
❑ 248 Sam Madison .25 .07
❑ 249 Travis Minor .25 .07
❑ 250 Zach Thomas .60 .18
❑ 251 Byron Chamberlain .25 .07
❑ 252 Chris Walsh .25 .07
❑ 253 Cris Carter .60 .18
❑ 254 Daunte Culpepper .60 .18
❑ 255 Doug Chapman .25 .07
❑ 256 Gary Anderson .25 .07
❑ 257 Jake Reed .40 .12
❑ 258 Jim Kleinsasser .25 .07
❑ 259 Kailee Wong .25 .07
❑ 260 Matt Birk .25 .07
❑ 261 Michael Bennett .40 .12
❑ 262 Randy Moss 1.25 .35
❑ 263 Robert Tate .25 .07
❑ 264 Spergon Wynn .25 .07
❑ 265 Antowain Smith .40 .12
❑ 266 Bryan Cox .25 .07
❑ 267 David Patten .25 .07
❑ 268 Drew Bledsoe .60 .18
❑ 269 Adam Vinatieri .60 .18
❑ 270 J.R. Redmond .25 .07
❑ 271 Jermaine Wiggins .25 .07
❑ 272 Kevin Faulk .40 .12
❑ 273 Lawyer Milloy .40 .12
❑ 274 Marc Edwards .25 .07
❑ 275 Tedy Bruschi .60 .18
❑ 276 Tom Brady 1.50 .45
❑ 277 Troy Brown .40 .12
❑ 278 Ty Law .40 .12
❑ 279 Willie McGinest .25 .07
❑ 280 Aaron Brooks .60 .18
❑ 281 Albert Connell .25 .07
❑ 282 Boo Williams .25 .07
❑ 283 Charlie Clemons RC .40 .12
❑ 284 Deuce McAllister .75 .23
❑ 285 Jay Bellamy .25 .07
❑ 286 Jeff Blake .25 .07
❑ 287 Joe Horn .40 .12
❑ 288 John Carney .25 .07
❑ 289 Kyle Turley .25 .07
❑ 290 La'Roi Glover .25 .07
❑ 291 Norman Hand .25 .07
❑ 292 Ricky Williams 2.50 .75
❑ 293 Robert Wilson .25 .07
❑ 294 Sammy Knight .25 .07
❑ 295 Terrelle Smith .25 .07
❑ 296 Willie Jackson .25 .07
❑ 297 Amani Toomer .40 .12
❑ 298 Anthony Becht .25 .07
❑ 299 Chad Pennington .75 .23
❑ 300 Curtis Martin .60 .18
❑ 301 Dan Campbell .25 .07
❑ 302 Dave Thomas .25 .07
❑ 303 Greg Comella .25 .07
❑ 304 Ike Hilliard .40 .12
❑ 305 James Farrior .25 .07
❑ 306 Jason Garrett .25 .07
❑ 307 Jason Sehorn .25 .07
❑ 308 Jessie Armstead .25 .07
❑ 309 Joe Jurevicius .25 .07
❑ 310 John Abraham .40 .12
❑ 311 Kerry Collins .40 .12
❑ 312 Kevin Mawae .25 .07
❑ 313 LaMont Jordan .60 .18
❑ 314 Laveranues Coles .40 .12
❑ 315 Marvin Jones .25 .07
❑ 316 Matthew Hatchette .25 .07
❑ 317 Michael Strahan .40 .12
❑ 318 Michael Barrow .25 .07
❑ 319 Morten Andersen .25 .07
❑ 320 Richie Anderson .25 .07
❑ 321 Ron Dayne .40 .12
❑ 322 Ron Dixon .25 .07
❑ 323 Ron Stone RC .25 .07
❑ 324 Santana Moss .60 .18
❑ 325 Tiki Barber .40 .12
❑ 326 Vinny Testaverde .40 .12
❑ 327 Wayne Chrebet .40 .12
❑ 328 Anthony Dorsett .25 .07
❑ 329 Charles Woodson .40 .12
❑ 330 Charlie Garner .40 .12
❑ 331 Regan Upshaw .25 .07
❑ 332 Jerry Porter .25 .07
❑ 333 Jerry Rice 1.25 .35
❑ 334 Jon Ritchie .25 .07
❑ 335 Lincoln Kennedy .25 .07
❑ 336 Marques Tuiasosopo .40 .12
❑ 337 Rich Gannon .60 .18
❑ 338 Roland Williams .25 .07
❑ 339 Sebastian Janikowski .25 .07
❑ 340 Barry Sims .25 .07
❑ 341 Terry Kirby .25 .07
❑ 342 Tim Brown .60 .18

❑ 343 Tyrone Wheatley .40 .12
❑ 344 Zack Crockett .25 .07
❑ 345 A.J. Feeley .60 .18
❑ 346 Brian Dawkins .25 .07
❑ 347 Cecil Martin .25 .07
❑ 348 Chad Lewis .25 .07
❑ 349 Corey Simon .25 .07
❑ 350 Correll Buckhalter .40 .12
❑ 351 David Akers .25 .07
❑ 352 Donovan McNabb .75 .23
❑ 353 Duce Staley .60 .18
❑ 354 Freddie Mitchell .40 .12
❑ 355 Hugh Douglas .25 .07
❑ 356 James Thrash .40 .12
❑ 357 Brian Mitchell .25 .07
❑ 358 Koy Detmer .25 .07
❑ 359 Todd Pinkston .40 .12
❑ 360 Tra Thomas .25 .07
❑ 361 Troy Vincent .25 .07
❑ 362 Alan Faneca RC .60 .18
❑ 363 Amos Zereoue .60 .18
❑ 364 Bobby Shaw .25 .07
❑ 365 Chris Fuamatu-Ma'afala .25 .07
❑ 366 Dan Kreider RC .60 .18
❑ 367 Hines Ward .60 .18
❑ 368 Jason Gildon .25 .07
❑ 369 Jerome Bettis .60 .18
❑ 370 Jon Witman .25 .07
❑ 371 Kendrell Bell .60 .18
❑ 372 Kordell Stewart .40 .12
❑ 373 Mark Bruener .25 .07
❑ 374 Plaxico Burress .40 .12
❑ 375 Tommy Maddox 1.50 .45
❑ 376 Troy Edwards .25 .07
❑ 377 Curtis Conway .25 .07
❑ 378 Darren Bennett .25 .07
❑ 379 Doug Flutie .60 .18
❑ 380 Drew Brees .60 .18
❑ 381 Fred McCrary .25 .07
❑ 382 Freddie Jones .25 .07
❑ 383 Jeff Graham .25 .07
❑ 384 John Parrella .25 .07
❑ 385 Junior Seau .60 .18
❑ 386 LaDainian Tomlinson 1.00 .30
❑ 387 Marcellus Wiley .25 .07
❑ 388 Tay Cody .25 .07
❑ 389 Raylee Johnson .25 .07
❑ 390 Rodney Harrison .25 .07
❑ 391 Ronney Jenkins .25 .07
❑ 392 Ryan McNeil .25 .07
❑ 393 Orlando Ruff .25 .07
❑ 394 Terrell Fletcher .25 .07
❑ 395 Tim Dwight .40 .12
❑ 396 Ahmed Plummer .25 .07
❑ 397 Andre Carter .25 .07
❑ 398 Bryant Young .25 .07
❑ 399 Dana Stubblefield .25 .07
❑ 400 Eric Johnson .40 .12
❑ 401 Fred Beasley .25 .07
❑ 402 Garrison Hearst .40 .12
❑ 403 J.J. Stokes .40 .12
❑ 404 Jeff Garcia .60 .18
❑ 405 Jeremy Newberry RC .40 .12
❑ 406 Junior Bryant .25 .07
❑ 407 Justin Swift .25 .07
❑ 408 Kevan Barlow .40 .12
❑ 409 Ray Brown .25 .07
❑ 410 Tai Streets .25 .07
❑ 411 Terrell Owens .60 .18
❑ 412 Terry Jackson .25 .07
❑ 413 Tim Rattay .40 .12
❑ 414 Bobby Engram .25 .07
❑ 415 Chad Brown .25 .07
❑ 416 Christian Fauria .25 .07
❑ 417 Darrell Jackson .40 .12
❑ 418 James Williams .25 .07
❑ 419 John Randle .25 .07
❑ 420 Koren Robinson .40 .12
❑ 421 Levon Kirkland .25 .07
❑ 422 Mack Strong .25 .07
❑ 423 Matt Hasselbeck .40 .12
❑ 424 Ricky Watters .40 .12
❑ 425 Shaun Alexander .60 .18
❑ 426 Shawn Springs .25 .07
❑ 427 Trent Dilfer .40 .12
❑ 428 Walter Jones .25 .07
❑ 429 Adam Timmerman .25 .07
❑ 430 Aeneas Williams .25 .07
❑ 431 Az-Zahir Hakim .25 .07
❑ 432 Dre' Bly .25 .07
❑ 433 Ernie Conwell .25 .07
❑ 434 Isaac Bruce .60 .18
❑ 435 James Hodgins .25 .07
❑ 436 Jamie Martin .40 .12
❑ 437 Kurt Warner .60 .18
❑ 438 Leonard Little .25 .07
❑ 439 London Fletcher .25 .07
❑ 440 Marshall Faulk .60 .18
❑ 441 O.J. Brigance .25 .07
❑ 442 Orlando Pace .25 .07
❑ 443 Ricky Proehl .25 .07
❑ 444 Torry Holt .60 .18
❑ 445 Trung Canidate .40 .12
❑ 446 Aaron Stecker .25 .07
❑ 447 Brad Johnson .25 .07
❑ 448 Dave Moore .25 .07
❑ 449 Derrick Brooks .60 .18
❑ 450 Jacquez Green .25 .07
❑ 451 John Lynch .40 .12
❑ 452 Karl Williams .25 .07
❑ 453 Kenyatta Walker .25 .07
❑ 454 Keyshawn Johnson .60 .18
❑ 455 Mark Royals .25 .07
❑ 456 Mike Alstott .60 .18
❑ 457 Rabih Abdullah .25 .07
❑ 458 Reidel Anthony .25 .07
❑ 459 Ronde Barber .25 .07
❑ 460 Shaun King .25 .07
❑ 461 Simeon Rice .40 .12
❑ 462 Warren Sapp .40 .12
❑ 463 Warrick Dunn .60 .18
❑ 464 Bruce Matthews .25 .07
❑ 465 Chris Sanders .25 .07
❑ 466 Derrick Mason .40 .12
❑ 467 Eddie George .60 .18
❑ 468 Erron Kinney .25 .07
❑ 469 Frank Wycheck .25 .07
❑ 470 Jevon Kearse .40 .12
❑ 471 Kevin Dyson .40 .12
❑ 472 Mike Green .25 .07
❑ 473 Neil O'Donnell .40 .12
❑ 474 Perry Phenix RC .40 .12
❑ 475 Skip Hicks .25 .07
❑ 476 Steve McNair .60 .18
❑ 477 Champ Bailey .40 .12
❑ 478 Chris Samuels .25 .07
❑ 479 Dan Wilkinson .25 .07
❑ 480 Darrell Green .25 .07
❑ 481 Donnell Bennett .25 .07
❑ 482 Donovan Greer RC .40 .12
❑ 483 Ethan Albright RC .40 .12
❑ 484 Fred Smoot .25 .07
❑ 485 Kent Graham .25 .07
❑ 486 Kevin Lockett .25 .07
❑ 487 Ki-Jana Carter .25 .07
❑ 488 Michael Bates .25 .07
❑ 489 Michael Westbrook .25 .07
❑ 490 Rod Gardner .40 .12
❑ 491 Shawn Barber .25 .07
❑ 492 Stephen Alexander .25 .07
❑ 493 Stephen Davis .40 .12
❑ 494 Tony Banks .25 .07
❑ 495 Jeremiah Trotter .25 .07
❑ 496 Jerome Bettis .60 .18
❑ 497 Kurt Warner .60 .18
❑ 498 Marshall Faulk .60 .18
❑ 499 Randy Moss 1.25 .35
❑ 500 Tom Brady 1.50 .45
❑ 501 Joey Harrington RC 10.00 3.00
❑ 502 David Carr RC 10.00 3.00
❑ 503 Rohan Davey RC 3.00 .90
❑ 504 Brandon Doman RC 3.00 .90
❑ 505 Woody Dantzler RC 3.00 .90
❑ 506 Kurt Kittner RC 2.50 .75
❑ 507 Donte Stallworth RC 6.00 1.80
❑ 508 Major Applewhite RC 3.00 .90
❑ 509 Eric Crouch RC 5.00 1.50
❑ 510 Justin Peelle RC 1.50 .45
❑ 511 J.T. O'Sullivan RC 2.50 .75
❑ 512 Jason McAddley RC 2.50 .75
❑ 513 Patrick Ramsey RC 6.00 1.80
❑ 514 Randy Fasani RC 2.50 .75
❑ 515 Antwaan Randle El RC 4.00 1.20
❑ 516 DeShaun Foster RC 3.00 .90
❑ 517 T.J. Duckett RC 5.00 1.50
❑ 518 William Green RC 5.00 1.50
❑ 519 Travis Stephens RC 2.50 .75
❑ 520 Luke Staley RC 2.50 .75
❑ 521 Leonard Henry RC 2.50 .75
❑ 522 Najeh Davenport RC 3.00 .90
❑ 523 Ricky Williams RC 2.50 .75
❑ 524 Maurice Morris RC 3.00 .90
❑ 525 Anthony Weaver RC 2.50 .75
❑ 526 Jeremy Allen RC 3.00 .90
❑ 527 Chester Taylor RC 3.00 .90
❑ 528 Clinton Portis RC 10.00 3.00
❑ 529 Damien Anderson RC 2.50 .75
❑ 530 Larry Ned RC 2.50 .75
❑ 531 Jonathan Wells RC 3.00 .90
❑ 532 Antwoine Womack RC 2.50 .75
❑ 533 Adrian Peterson RC 3.00 .90
❑ 534 Lamar Gordon RC 3.00 .90
❑ 535 Chad Hutchinson RC 3.00 .90
❑ 536 Antonio Bryant RC 3.00 .90
❑ 537 Josh Reed RC 3.00 .90
❑ 538 Jabar Gaffney RC 3.00 .90
❑ 539 Ashley Lelie RC 6.00 1.80
❑ 540 Ron Johnson RC 2.50 .75
❑ 541 Marquise Walker RC 2.50 .75
❑ 542 Kelly Campbell RC 2.50 .75
❑ 543 Andre Davis RC 3.00 .90
❑ 544 Deion Branch RC 6.00 1.80
❑ 545 James Mungro RC 3.00 .90
❑ 546 Brian Poli-Dixon RC 2.50 .75
❑ 547 Kahlil Hill RC 2.50 .75
❑ 548 Reche Caldwell RC 3.00 .90
❑ 549 Jeremy Shockey RC 10.00 3.00
❑ 550 Julius Peppers RC 6.00 1.80
❑ 551 Wendell Bryant RC 3.00 .90
❑ 552 John Henderson RC 3.00 .90
❑ 553 Quentin Jammer RC 3.00 .90
❑ 554 Roy Williams RC 8.00 2.40
❑ 555 Daniel Graham RC 3.00 .90
❑ 556 Charles Grant RC 2.50 .75
❑ 557 Verron Haynes RC 3.00 .90
❑ 558 Ed Reed RC 5.00 1.50
❑ 559 Pete Rebstock RC 1.50 .45
❑ 560 Tellis Redmon RC 2.50 .75
❑ 561 Javon Walker RC 6.00 1.80
❑ 562 Larry Tripplett RC 1.50 .45
❑ 563 Cliff Russell RC 2.50 .75
❑ 564 Rocky Calmus RC 3.00 .90
❑ 565 Tim Carter RC 2.50 .75
❑ 566 Josh Scobey RC 3.00 .90
❑ 567 Kyle Johnson RC 1.50 .45
❑ 568 Brian Westbrook RC 5.00 1.50
❑ 569 Zak Kustok RC 3.00 .90
❑ 570 Ronald Curry RC 3.00 .90
❑ 571 Atrews Bell RC 1.50 .45
❑ 572 Levar Fisher RC 1.50 .45
❑ 573 Dicenzo Miller RC 1.50 .45
❑ 574 Phillip Buchanon RC 3.00 .90
❑ 575 Freddie Milons RC 2.50 .75
❑ 576 Kalimba Edwards RC 3.00 .90
❑ 577 Raonall Smith RC 2.50 .75
❑ 578 Dameon Hunter RC 1.50 .45
❑ 579 Lee Mays RC 2.50 .75
❑ 580 Mike Rumph RC 3.00 .90
❑ 581 Josh McCown RC 4.00 1.20
❑ 582 Napoleon Harris RC 3.00 .90
❑ 583 David Garrard RC 3.00 .90
❑ 584 Wes Pate RC 1.50 .45
❑ 585 Lito Sheppard RC 3.00 .90
❑ 586 Gavin Hoffman RC 1.50 .45
❑ 587 David Priestley RC 2.50 .75
❑ 588 Dwight Freeney RC 4.00 1.20
❑ 589 Dusty Bonner RC 1.50 .45
❑ 590 Eric McCoo RC 1.50 .45
❑ 591 Robert Thomas RC 3.00 .90
❑ 592 Delvon Flowers RC 2.50 .75
❑ 593 LaDell Betts RC 3.00 .90
❑ 594 Jamar Martin RC 2.50 .75
❑ 595 Seth Burford RC 2.50 .75
❑ 596 Mike Williams RC 2.50 .75
❑ 597 Bryant McKinnie RC 2.50 .75

❑ 598 Ryan Sims RC	3.00	.90
❑ 599 Albert Haynesworth RC	2.50	.75
❑ 600 Craig Nall RC	3.00	.90

2001 Vanguard

	Nm-Mt	Ex-Mt
COMP.SET w/o SP's (100)	30.00	9.00
❑ 1 David Boston	1.00	.30
❑ 2 Thomas Jones	.60	.18
❑ 3 Jake Plummer	.60	.18
❑ 4 Jamal Anderson	1.00	.30
❑ 5 Chris Chandler	.60	.18
❑ 6 Elvis Grbac	.60	.18
❑ 7 Jamal Lewis	1.50	.45
❑ 8 Shannon Sharpe	.60	.18
❑ 9 Rob Johnson	.60	.18
❑ 10 Eric Moulds	.60	.18
❑ 11 Peerless Price	.60	.18
❑ 12 Tim Biakabutuka	.60	.18
❑ 13 Muhsin Muhammad	.60	.18
❑ 14 James Allen	.60	.18
❑ 15 Cade McNown	.40	.12
❑ 16 Marcus Robinson	1.00	.30
❑ 17 Corey Dillon	1.00	.30
❑ 18 Akili Smith	.40	.12
❑ 19 Peter Warrick	1.00	.30
❑ 20 Tim Couch	.60	.18
❑ 21 Kevin Johnson	.60	.18
❑ 22 Travis Prentice	.40	.12
❑ 23 Rocket Ismail	.60	.18
❑ 24 Emmitt Smith	2.00	.60
❑ 25 Mike Anderson	1.00	.30
❑ 26 Terrell Davis	1.00	.30
❑ 27 Brian Griese	1.00	.30
❑ 28 Ed McCaffrey	1.00	.30
❑ 29 Rod Smith	.60	.18
❑ 30 Charlie Batch	1.00	.30
❑ 31 Johnnie Morton	.60	.18
❑ 32 James Stewart	.60	.18
❑ 33 Brett Favre	3.00	.90
❑ 34 Antonio Freeman	1.00	.30
❑ 35 Ahman Green	1.00	.30
❑ 36 Bill Schroeder	.60	.18
❑ 37 Marvin Harrison	1.00	.30
❑ 38 Edgerrin James	1.25	.35
❑ 39 Peyton Manning	2.50	.75
❑ 40 Terrence Wilkins	.40	.12
❑ 41 Mark Brunell	1.00	.30
❑ 42 Keenan McCardell	.40	.12
❑ 43 Jimmy Smith	.60	.18
❑ 44 Fred Taylor	1.00	.30
❑ 45 Derrick Alexander	.60	.18
❑ 46 Tony Gonzalez	.60	.18
❑ 47 Sylvester Morris	.40	.12
❑ 48 Jay Fiedler	1.00	.30
❑ 49 Oronde Gadsden	.60	.18
❑ 50 Lamar Smith	.60	.18
❑ 51 Cris Carter	1.00	.30
❑ 52 Daunte Culpepper	1.00	.30
❑ 53 Randy Moss	2.00	.60
❑ 54 Drew Bledsoe	1.25	.35
❑ 55 Terry Glenn	.40	.12
❑ 56 Charles Johnson	.40	.12
❑ 57 J.R. Redmond	.40	.12
❑ 58 Jeff Blake	.60	.18
❑ 59 Joe Horn	.60	.18
❑ 60 Ricky Williams	1.00	.30
❑ 61 Tiki Barber	.60	.18
❑ 62 Kerry Collins	.60	.18
❑ 63 Ron Dayne	1.00	.30
❑ 64 Amani Toomer	.60	.18
❑ 65 Wayne Chrebet	.60	.18
❑ 66 Curtis Martin	1.00	.30
❑ 67 Vinny Testaverde	.60	.18
❑ 68 Tim Brown	1.00	.30
❑ 69 Rich Gannon	1.00	.30
❑ 70 Jerry Rice	2.00	.60
❑ 71 Tyrone Wheatley	.60	.18
❑ 72 Donovan McNabb	1.25	.35
❑ 73 Duce Staley	1.00	.30
❑ 74 Jerome Bettis	1.00	.30
❑ 75 Kordell Stewart	.60	.18
❑ 76 Hines Ward	1.00	.30
❑ 77 Isaac Bruce	1.00	.30
❑ 78 Marshall Faulk	1.25	.35
❑ 79 Torry Holt	1.00	.30
❑ 80 Kurt Warner	2.00	.60
❑ 81 Curtis Conway	.60	.18
❑ 82 Tim Dwight	1.00	.30
❑ 83 Doug Flutie	1.00	.30
❑ 84 Junior Seau	1.00	.30
❑ 85 Jeff Garcia	1.00	.30
❑ 86 Terrell Owens	1.00	.30
❑ 87 Shaun Alexander	1.25	.35
❑ 88 Matt Hasselbeck	.60	.18
❑ 89 Darrell Jackson	1.00	.30
❑ 90 Mike Alstott	1.00	.30
❑ 91 Warrick Dunn	1.00	.30
❑ 92 Keyshawn Johnson	1.00	.30
❑ 93 Brad Johnson	1.00	.30
❑ 94 Kevin Dyson	.40	.12
❑ 95 Eddie George	1.00	.30
❑ 96 Derrick Mason	.60	.18
❑ 97 Steve McNair	1.00	.30
❑ 98 Stephen Davis	1.00	.30
❑ 99 Jeff George	.60	.18
❑ 100 Michael Westbrook	.60	.18
❑ 101 Bobby Newcombe RC	12.00	3.60
❑ 102 Alge Crumpler RC	15.00	4.50
❑ 103 Vinny Sutherland RC	8.00	2.40
❑ 104 Michael Vick RC	50.00	15.00
❑ 105 Todd Heap RC	12.00	3.60
❑ 106 Nate Clements RC	12.00	3.60
❑ 107 Travis Henry RC	15.00	4.50
❑ 108 Dan Morgan RC	12.00	3.60
❑ 109 Chris Weinke RC	12.00	3.60
❑ 110 David Terrell RC	12.00	3.60
❑ 111 Anthony Thomas RC	20.00	6.00
❑ 112 T.J. Houshmandzadeh RC	12.00	3.60
❑ 113 Chad Johnson RC	25.00	7.50
❑ 114 Rudi Johnson RC	25.00	7.50
❑ 115 James Jackson RC	12.00	3.60
❑ 116 Quincy Morgan RC	12.00	3.60
❑ 117 Quincy Carter RC	12.00	3.60
❑ 118 Scotty Anderson RC	8.00	2.40
❑ 119 Mike McMahon RC	12.00	3.60
❑ 120 Robert Ferguson RC	12.00	3.60
❑ 121 Reggie Wayne RC	20.00	6.00
❑ 122 Snoop Minnis RC	8.00	2.40
❑ 123 Chris Chambers RC	15.00	4.50
❑ 124 Jamar Fletcher RC	8.00	2.40
❑ 125 Josh Heupel RC	12.00	3.60
❑ 126 Travis Minor RC	8.00	2.40
❑ 127 Michael Bennett RC	25.00	7.50
❑ 128 Deuce McAllister RC	25.00	7.50
❑ 129 Will Allen RC	8.00	2.40
❑ 130 Jesse Palmer RC	12.00	3.60
❑ 131 LaMont Jordan RC	15.00	4.50
❑ 132 Santana Moss RC	20.00	6.00
❑ 133 Ken-Yon Rambo RC	8.00	2.40
❑ 134 Marques Tuiasosopo RC	12.00	3.60
❑ 135 Correll Buckhalter RC	15.00	4.50
❑ 136 A.J. Feeley RC	12.00	3.60
❑ 137 Freddie Mitchell RC	12.00	3.60
❑ 138 Chris Taylor RC	8.00	2.40
❑ 139 Adam Archuleta RC	12.00	3.60
❑ 140 Drew Brees RC	25.00	7.50
❑ 141 LaDainian Tomlinson RC	30.00	9.00
❑ 142 Kevan Barlow RC	12.00	3.60
❑ 143 Cedrick Wilson RC	12.00	3.60
❑ 144 Alex Bannister RC	8.00	2.40
❑ 145 Josh Booty RC	12.00	3.60
❑ 146 Heath Evans RC	8.00	2.40
❑ 147 Koren Robinson RC	15.00	4.50
❑ 148 Dan Alexander RC	12.00	3.60
❑ 149 Rod Gardner RC	12.00	3.60
❑ 150 Sage Rosenfels RC	12.00	3.60

1992 Wild Card

	Nm-Mt	Ex-Mt
COMPLETE SET (460)	15.00	6.75
COMP.SERIES 1 (250)	5.00	2.20
COMP.SERIES 2 (210)	12.00	5.50

*5 STRIPES: 1X TO 2.5X BASIC CARDS
*10 STRIPES: 1.5X TO 3.5X BASIC CARDS
*20 STRIPE VETS: 2X TO 5X BASIC CARDS
*20 STRIPE RCs: 1.2X TO 3X BASIC CARDS
*50 STRIPE VETS: 5X TO 12X BASIC CARDS
*50 STRIPE RCs: 2.5X TO 6X BASIC CARDS
*100 STRIPE VETS: 12.5X TO 25X BASIC CARDS

❑ 1 Surprise Card	.05	.02
❑ 2 Marcus Dupree	.05	.02
❑ 3 Jackie Slater	.05	.02
❑ 4 Robert Delpino	.05	.02
❑ 5 Jerry Gray	.05	.02
❑ 6 Jim Everett	.10	.05
❑ 7 Roman Phifer	.05	.02
❑ 8 Alvin Wright	.05	.02
❑ 9 Todd Lyght	.05	.02
❑ 10 Reggie White	.25	.11
❑ 11 Randal Hill	.05	.02
❑ 12 Keith Byars	.05	.02
❑ 13 Clyde Simmons	.05	.02
❑ 14 Keith Jackson	.10	.05
❑ 15 Seth Joyner	.05	.02
❑ 16 James Joseph	.05	.02
❑ 17 Eric Allen	.05	.02
❑ 18 Sammie Smith	.05	.02
❑ 19 Mark Clayton	.05	.02
❑ 20 Aaron Craver	.05	.02
❑ 21 Hugh Green	.05	.02
❑ 22 John Offerdahl	.05	.02
❑ 23 Jeff Cross	.05	.02
❑ 24 Ferrell Edmunds	.05	.02
❑ 25 Mark Duper	.05	.02
❑ 26 Ronnie Harmon	.05	.02
❑ 27 Derrick Walker	.05	.02
❑ 28 Gary Plummer	.05	.02
❑ 29 Rod Bernstine	.05	.02
❑ 30 Burt Grossman	.05	.02
❑ 31 Donnie Elder	.05	.02
❑ 32 John Friesz	.10	.05
❑ 33 Billy Ray Smith	.05	.02
❑ 34 Luis Sharpe	.05	.02
❑ 35 Aeneas Williams	.10	.05
❑ 36 Ken Harvey	.05	.02
❑ 37 Johnny Johnson UER (1990 rushing stats are wrong)	.05	.02
❑ 38 Eric Swann	.10	.05
❑ 39 Tom Tupa	.05	.02
❑ 40 Anthony Thompson	.05	.02
❑ 41 Broderick Thomas	.05	.02
❑ 42 Vinny Testaverde	.10	.05
❑ 43 Mark Carrier WR	.10	.05
❑ 44 Gary Anderson RB	.05	.02
❑ 45 Keith McCants	.05	.02
❑ 46 Reggie Cobb	.05	.02
❑ 47 Lawrence Dawsey	.05	.02
❑ 48 Kevin Murphy	.05	.02

❑ 49 Keith Woodside	.05	.02
❑ 50 Darrell Thompson	.05	.02
❑ 51 Vinnie Clark	.05	.02
❑ 52 Sterling Sharpe	.25	.11
❑ 53 Mike Tomczak	.05	.02
❑ 54A Don Majkowski ERR (Listed as Dan)	.10	.05
❑ 54B Don Majikowski COR	.10	.05
❑ 55 Tony Mandarich	.05	.02
❑ 56 Mark Murphy	.05	.02
❑ 57 Dexter McNabb RC	.05	.02
❑ 58 Rick Fenney	.05	.02
❑ 59 Cris Carter	.25	.11
❑ 60 Wade Wilson	.05	.02
❑ 61 Mike Merriweather	.05	.02
❑ 62 Rich Gannon	.25	.11
❑ 63 Herschel Walker	.10	.05
❑ 64 Chris Doleman	.10	.05
❑ 65 Al Noga UER (On front, he's a DE; on back, he's a DT)	.05	.02
❑ 66 Chris Mims RC	.05	.02
❑ 67 Ed Cunningham RC	.05	.02
❑ 68 Marcus Allen	.25	.11
❑ 69 Kevin Turner RC	.05	.02
❑ 70 Howie Long	.25	.11
❑ 71 Tim Brown	.25	.11
❑ 72 Nick Bell	.05	.02
❑ 73 Todd Marinovich	.05	.02
❑ 74 Jay Schroeder	.05	.02
❑ 75 Mervyn Fernandez	.05	.02
❑ 76 Tony Smith RC	.05	.02
❑ 77 John Alt	.05	.02
❑ 78 Christian Okoye	.05	.02
❑ 79 Nick Lowery	.05	.02
❑ 80 Derrick Thomas	.10	.05
❑ 81 Bill Maas	.05	.02
❑ 82 Dino Hackett	.05	.02
❑ 83 Deron Cherry	.05	.02
❑ 84 Barry Word	.05	.02
❑ 85 Mike Mooney RC	.05	.02
❑ 86 Cris Dishman	.05	.02
❑ 87 Bruce Matthews	.05	.02
❑ 88 Tony Jones	.05	.02
❑ 89 William Fuller	.05	.02
❑ 90 Ray Childress	.05	.02
❑ 91 Warren Moon	.25	.11
❑ 92 Lorenzo White	.05	.02
❑ 93 Joe Bowden RC	.05	.02
❑ 94 Tom Rathman	.05	.02
❑ 95 Keith Henderson	.05	.02
❑ 96 Jesse Sapolu	.05	.02
❑ 97 Charles Haley	.10	.05
❑ 98 Steve Young	.60	.25
❑ 99 John Taylor	.10	.05
❑ 100 Tim Harris	.05	.02
❑ 101 Scott Davis	.05	.02
❑ 102 Steve Bono RC	.25	.11
❑ 103 Mike Kenn	.05	.02
❑ 104 Mike Farr	.05	.02
❑ 105 Rodney Peete	.10	.05
❑ 106 Jerry Ball	.05	.02
❑ 107 Chris Spielman	.10	.05
❑ 108 Barry Sanders	1.25	.55
❑ 109 Bennie Blades	.05	.02
❑ 110 Herman Moore	.25	.11
❑ 111 Erik Kramer	.10	.05
❑ 112 Vance Johnson	.05	.02
❑ 113 Mike Croel	.05	.02
❑ 114 Mark Jackson	.05	.02
❑ 115 Steve Atwater	.05	.02
❑ 116 Gaston Green	.05	.02
❑ 117 John Elway	1.25	.55
❑ 118 Simon Fletcher	.05	.02
❑ 119 Karl Mecklenburg	.05	.02
❑ 120 Hart Lee Dykes	.05	.02
❑ 121 Jerome Henderson	.05	.02
❑ 122 Chris Singleton	.05	.02
❑ 123 Marv Cook	.05	.02
❑ 124 Leonard Russell	.05	.02
❑ 125 Hugh Millen	.05	.02
❑ 126 Pat Harlow	.05	.02
❑ 127 Andre Tippett	.05	.02
❑ 128 Bruce Armstrong	.05	.02
❑ 129 Gary Clark	.10	.05
❑ 130 Art Monk	.10	.05
❑ 131 Darrell Green	.05	.02
❑ 132 Wilber Marshall	.05	.02
❑ 133 Jim Lachey	.05	.02
❑ 134 Earnest Byner	.05	.02
❑ 135 Chip Lohmiller	.05	.02
❑ 136 Mark Rypien	.05	.02
❑ 137 Ricky Sanders	.05	.02
❑ 138 Stan Thomas	.05	.02
❑ 139 Neal Anderson	.05	.02
❑ 140 Trace Armstrong	.05	.02
❑ 141 Kevin Butler	.05	.02
❑ 142 Mark Carrier DB	.05	.02
❑ 143 Dennis Gentry	.05	.02
❑ 144 Jim Harbaugh	.10	.05
❑ 145 Richard Dent	.10	.05
❑ 146 Andre Rison	.10	.05
❑ 147 Bruce Pickens	.05	.02
❑ 148 Chris Hinton UER (Dealt to Falcons in 1990, not 1989)	.05	.02
❑ 149 Brian Jordan	.10	.05
❑ 150 Chris Miller	.05	.02
❑ 151 Moe Gardner	.05	.02
❑ 152 Bill Fralic	.05	.02
❑ 153 Michael Haynes	.10	.05
❑ 154 Mike Pritchard	.10	.05
❑ 155 Dean Biasucci	.05	.02
❑ 156 Clarence Verdin	.05	.02
❑ 157 Donnell Thompson	.05	.02
❑ 158 Duane Bickett	.05	.02
❑ 159 Jon Hand	.05	.02
❑ 160 Sam Graddy RC	.05	.02
❑ 161 Emmitt Smith	1.50	.70
❑ 162 Michael Irvin	.25	.11
❑ 163 Danny Noonan	.05	.02
❑ 164 Jack Del Rio	.05	.02
❑ 165 Jim Jeffcoat	.05	.02
❑ 166 Alexander Wright	.05	.02
❑ 167 Frank Minnifield	.05	.02
❑ 168 Ed King	.05	.02
❑ 169 Reggie Langhorne	.05	.02
❑ 170 Mike Baab	.05	.02
❑ 171 Eric Metcalf	.10	.05
❑ 172 Clay Matthews	.05	.02
❑ 173 Kevin Mack	.05	.02
❑ 174 Mike Johnson	.05	.02
❑ 175 Jeff Lageman	.05	.02
❑ 176 Freeman McNeil	.10	.05
❑ 177 Erik McMillan	.05	.02
❑ 178 James Hasty	.05	.02
❑ 179 Kyle Clifton	.05	.02
❑ 180 Joe Kelly	.05	.02
❑ 181 Phil Simms	.10	.05
❑ 182 Everson Walls	.05	.02
❑ 183 Jeff Hostetler	.10	.05
❑ 184 Dave Meggett	.10	.05
❑ 185 Matt Bahr	.05	.02
❑ 186 Mark Ingram	.05	.02
❑ 187 Rodney Hampton	.10	.05
❑ 188 Kanavis McGhee	.05	.02
❑ 189 Tim McGee	.05	.02
❑ 190 Eddie Brown	.05	.02
❑ 191 Rodney Holman	.05	.02
❑ 192 Harold Green	.05	.02
❑ 193 James Francis	.05	.02
❑ 194 Anthony Munoz	.10	.05
❑ 195 David Fulcher	.05	.02
❑ 196 Tim Krumrie	.05	.02
❑ 197 Bubby Brister	.10	.05
❑ 198 Rod Woodson	.25	.11
❑ 199 Louis Lipps	.05	.02
❑ 200 Carnell Lake	.05	.02
❑ 201 Don Beebe	.05	.02
❑ 202 Thurman Thomas	.25	.11
❑ 203 Cornelius Bennett	.10	.05
❑ 204 Mark Kelso	.05	.02
❑ 205 James Lofton	.10	.05
❑ 206 Darryl Talley	.05	.02
❑ 207 Morten Andersen	.05	.02
❑ 208 Vince Buck	.05	.02
❑ 209 Wesley Carroll	.05	.02
❑ 210 Bobby Hebert	.05	.02
❑ 211 Craig Heyward	.10	.05
❑ 212 Dalton Hilliard	.05	.02
❑ 213 Rickey Jackson	.05	.02
❑ 214 Eric Martin	.05	.02
❑ 215 Pat Swilling	.05	.02
❑ 216 Steve Walsh	.05	.02
❑ 217 Torrance Small RC	.10	.05
❑ 218 Jacob Green	.05	.02
❑ 219 Cortez Kennedy	.10	.05
❑ 220 John L. Williams	.05	.02
❑ 221 Terry Wooden	.05	.02
❑ 222 Grant Feasel	.05	.02
❑ 223 Siran Stacy RC	.05	.02
❑ 224 Chris Hakel RC	.05	.02
❑ 225 Todd Harrison RC	.05	.02
❑ 226 Bob Whitfield RC	.05	.02
❑ 227 Eddie Blake RC	.05	.02
❑ 228 Keith Hamilton RC	.10	.05
❑ 229 Darryl Williams RC	.05	.02
❑ 230 Ricardo McDonald RC	.05	.02
❑ 231 Alan Haller RC	.05	.02
❑ 232 Leon Searcy RC	.05	.02
❑ 233 Patrick Rowe RC	.05	.02
❑ 234 Edgar Bennett RC	.25	.11
❑ 235 Terrell Buckley RC	.05	.02
❑ 236 Will Furrer RC	.05	.02
❑ 237 Amp Lee RC UER (Front photo actually Edgar Bennett)	.05	.02
❑ 238 Jimmy Smith RC	3.00	1.35
❑ 239 Tommy Vardell RC	.05	.02
❑ 240 Leonard Russell '91 Offensive ROY	.05	.02
❑ 241 Mike Croel '91 Defensive ROY	.05	.02
❑ 242 Warren Moon '91 AFC Passing Leader	.10	.05
❑ 243 Mark Rypien '91 NFC Passing Leader	.05	.02
❑ 244 Thurman Thomas '91 AFC Rushing Leader	.10	.05
❑ 245 Emmitt Smith '91 NFC Rushing Leader	.75	.35
❑ 246 Checklist 1-50	.05	.02
❑ 247 Checklist 51-100	.05	.02
❑ 248 Checklist 101-150	.05	.02
❑ 249 Checklist 151-200	.05	.02
❑ 250 Checklist 201-250	.05	.02
❑ 251 Surprise Card	.05	.02
❑ 252 Eric Pegram	.10	.05
❑ 253 Anthony Carter	.10	.05
❑ 254 Roger Craig	.10	.05
❑ 255 Hassan Jones	.05	.02
❑ 256 Steve Jordan	.05	.02
❑ 257 Randall McDaniel	.05	.02
❑ 258 Henry Thomas	.05	.02
❑ 259 Carl Lee	.05	.02
❑ 260 Ray Agnew	.05	.02
❑ 261 Irving Fryar	.10	.05
❑ 262 Tom Waddle	.05	.02
❑ 263 Greg McMurtry	.05	.02
❑ 264 Stephen Baker	.05	.02
❑ 265 Mark Collins	.05	.02
❑ 266 Howard Cross	.05	.02
❑ 267 Pepper Johnson	.05	.02
❑ 268 Fred Barnett	.10	.05
❑ 269 Heath Sherman	.05	.02
❑ 270 William Thomas	.05	.02
❑ 271 Bill Bates	.10	.05
❑ 272 Issiac Holt	.05	.02
❑ 273 Emmitt Smith	1.50	.70
❑ 274 Eric Bieniemy	.05	.02
❑ 275 Marion Butts	.05	.02
❑ 276 Gill Byrd	.05	.02
❑ 277 Robert Blackmon	.05	.02
❑ 278 Brian Blades	.10	.05
❑ 279 Joe Nash	.05	.02
❑ 280 Bill Brooks	.05	.02
❑ 281 Mel Gray	.05	.02
❑ 282 Andre Ware	.10	.05
❑ 283 Steve McMichael	.05	.02
❑ 284 Brad Muster	.05	.02
❑ 285 Ron Rivera	.05	.02
❑ 286 Chris Zorich	.10	.05
❑ 287 Chris Burkett	.05	.02
❑ 288 Irv Eatman	.05	.02
❑ 289 Rob Moore	.10	.05

❑ 290 Joe Mott .05 .02
❑ 291 Brian Washington .05 .02
❑ 292 Michael Carter .05 .02
❑ 293 Dexter Carter .05 .02
❑ 294 Don Griffin .05 .02
❑ 295 John Taylor .10 .05
❑ 296 Ted Washington .05 .02
❑ 297 Monte Coleman .05 .02
❑ 298 Andre Collins .05 .02
❑ 299 Charles Mann .05 .02
❑ 300 Shane Conlan .05 .02
❑ 301 Keith McKeller .05 .02
❑ 302 Nate Odomes .05 .02
❑ 303 Riki Ellison .05 .02
❑ 304 Willie Gault .10 .05
❑ 305 Bob Golic .05 .02
❑ 306 Ethan Horton .05 .02
❑ 307 Ronnie Lott .10 .05
❑ 308 Don Mosebar .05 .02
❑ 309 Aaron Wallace .05 .02
❑ 310 Wymon Henderson .05 .02
❑ 311 Vance Johnson .05 .02
❑ 312 Ken Lanier .05 .02
❑ 313 Steve Sewell .05 .02
❑ 314 Dennis Smith .05 .02
❑ 315 Kenny Walker .05 .02
❑ 316 Chris Martin .05 .02
❑ 317 Albert Lewis .05 .02
❑ 318 Todd McNair .05 .02
❑ 319 Tracy Simien RC .05 .02
❑ 320 Percy Snow .05 .02
❑ 321 Mark Rypien .05 .02
❑ 322 Bryan Hinkle .05 .02
❑ 323 David Little .05 .02
❑ 324 Dwight Stone .05 .02
❑ 325 Van Waiters RC .05 .02
❑ 326 Pio Sagapolutele RC .05 .02
❑ 327 Michael Jackson .10 .05
❑ 328 Vestee Jackson .05 .02
❑ 329 Tony Paige .05 .02
❑ 330 Reggie Roby .05 .02
❑ 331 Haywood Jeffires .10 .05
❑ 332 Lamar Lathon .05 .02
❑ 333 Bubba McDowell .05 .02
❑ 334 Doug Smith .05 .02
❑ 335 Dean Steinkuhler .05 .02
❑ 336 Jessie Tuggle .05 .02
❑ 337 Freddie Joe Nunn .05 .02
❑ 338 Pat Terrell .05 .02
❑ 339 Tom McHale RC .05 .02
❑ 340 Sam Mills .05 .02
❑ 341 John Tice .05 .02
❑ 342 Brent Jones .10 .05
❑ 343 Robert Porcher RC .25 .11
❑ 344 Mark D'Onofrio RC .05 .02
❑ 345 David Tate .05 .02
❑ 346 Courtney Hawkins RC .10 .05
❑ 347 Ricky Watters .25 .11
❑ 348 Amp Lee .05 .02
❑ 349 Steve Young .60 .25
❑ 350 Natu Tuatagaloa RC .05 .02
❑ 351 Alfred Williams .05 .02
❑ 352 Derek Brown TE RC .05 .02
❑ 353 Marco Coleman RC UER .05 .02
(Back photo actually a Denver Bronco)
❑ 354 Tommy Maddox RC 2.00 .90
❑ 355 Siran Stacy .05 .02
❑ 356 Greg Lewis .05 .02
❑ 357 Paul Gruber .05 .02
❑ 358 Troy Vincent RC .05 .02
❑ 359 Robert Wilson .05 .02
❑ 360 Jessie Hester .05 .02
❑ 361 Shaun Gayle .05 .02
❑ 362 Deron Cherry .05 .02
❑ 363 Wendell Davis .05 .02
❑ 364 David Klingler RC UER .05 .02
(Bio misspells his name as Klinger)
❑ 365 Jason Hanson RC .10 .05
❑ 366 Marquez Pope RC .05 .02
❑ 367 Robert Williams RC .05 .02
❑ 368 Kelvin Pritchett .05 .02
❑ 369 Dana Hall RC .05 .02
❑ 370 David Brandon RC .05 .02
❑ 371 Tim McKyer .05 .02
❑ 372 Darion Conner .05 .02
❑ 373 Derrick Fenner .05 .02
❑ 374 Hugh Millen .05 .02
❑ 375 Bill Jones RC .05 .02
❑ 376 J.J. Birden .05 .02
❑ 377 Ty Detmer .25 .11
❑ 378 Alonzo Spellman RC .10 .05
❑ 379 Sammie Smith .05 .02
❑ 380 Al Smith .05 .02
❑ 381 Louis Clark RC .05 .02
❑ 382 Vernice Smith RC .05 .02
❑ 383 Tony Martin .10 .05
❑ 384 Willie Green .05 .02
❑ 385 Sean Gilbert RC .10 .05
❑ 386 Eugene Chung RC .05 .02
❑ 387 Tol Cook .05 .02
❑ 388 Brett Maxie .05 .02
❑ 389 Steve Israel RC .05 .02
❑ 390 Mike Mularkey .05 .02
❑ 391 Barry Foster .10 .05
❑ 392 Hardy Nickerson .10 .05
❑ 393 Johnny Mitchell RC .05 .02
❑ 394 Thurman Thomas .25 .11
❑ 395 Tony Smith RC .05 .02
❑ 396 Keith Goganious RC .05 .02
❑ 397 Matt Darby RC .05 .02
❑ 398 Nate Turner RC .05 .02
❑ 399 Keith Jennings RC .05 .02
❑ 400 Mitchell Benson RC .05 .02
❑ 401 Kurt Barber RC .05 .02
❑ 402 Tony Sacca RC .05 .02
❑ 403 Steve Hendrickson RC .05 .02
❑ 404 Johnny Johnson .05 .02
❑ 405 Lorenzo Lynch .05 .02
❑ 406 Luis Sharpe .05 .02
❑ 407 Jim Everett .10 .05
❑ 408 Neal Anderson .05 .02
❑ 409 Ashley Ambrose RC .25 .11
❑ 410 George Williams RC .05 .02
❑ 411 Clarence Kay .05 .02
❑ 412 Dave Krieg .10 .05
❑ 413 Terrell Buckley .05 .02
❑ 414 Ricardo McDonald .05 .02
❑ 415 Kelly Stouffer .05 .02
❑ 416 Barney Bussey .05 .02
❑ 417 Ray Roberts RC .05 .02
❑ 418 Fred McAfee RC .05 .02
❑ 419 Fred Banks .05 .02
❑ 420 Tim McDonald .05 .02
❑ 421 Darryl Williams .05 .02
❑ 422 Bobby Abrams RC .05 .02
❑ 423 Tommy Vardell .05 .02
❑ 424 William White .05 .02
❑ 425 Billy Ray Smith .05 .02
❑ 426 Lemuel Stinson .05 .02
❑ 427 Brad Johnson RC 10.00 4.50
❑ 428 Herschel Walker .10 .05
❑ 429 Eric Thomas .05 .02
❑ 430 Anthony Thompson .05 .02
❑ 431 Ed West .05 .02
❑ 432 Edgar Bennett .25 .11
❑ 433 Warren Powers .05 .02
❑ 434 Byron Evans .05 .02
❑ 435 Rodney Culver RC .05 .02
❑ 436 Ray Horton .05 .02
❑ 437 Richmond Webb .05 .02
❑ 438 Mark McMillian RC .05 .02
❑ 439 Subset Checklist .05 .02
❑ 440 Lawrence Pete RC .05 .02
❑ 441 Rod Smith DB RC .05 .02
❑ 442 Mark Rodenhauser RC .05 .02
❑ 443 Scott Lockwood RC .05 .02
❑ 444 Charles Davenport RC .05 .02
❑ 445 Terry McDaniel .05 .02
❑ 446 Darren Perry RC .05 .02
❑ 447 Darrick Owens RC .05 .02
❑ 448 Alvin Wright .05 .02
❑ 449 Frank Stams .05 .02
❑ 450 Santana Dotson RC .10 .05
❑ 451 Mark Carrier DB .05 .02
❑ 452 Kevin Murphy .05 .02
❑ 453 Jeff Bryant .05 .02
❑ 454 Eric Allen .05 .02
❑ 455 Brian Bollinger RC .05 .02
❑ 456 Elston Ridgle RC .05 .02
❑ 457 Jim Riggs RC .05 .02
❑ 458 Checklist 251-320 .05 .02
❑ 459 Checklist 321-391 .05 .02
❑ 460 Checklist 392-460 .05 .02
❑ P1 Barry Sanders National Promo 1.00 .45
❑ P2 Barry Sanders (5-card National Promo sheet) 2.00 .90

1992 Wild Card 1000 Stripe

Nm-Mt Ex-Mt

*1000 STRIPE VETS: 50X TO 120X BASIC CARDS
*1000 STRIPE RCs: 15X TO 40X

❑ 238 Jimmy Smith 60.00 27.00
❑ 427 Brad Johnson 150.00 70.00

1996 Press Pass Autographs

	Nm-Mt	Ex-Mt
COMPLETE SET (12)	200.00	90.00
❑ 1 Karim Abdul-Jabbar	25.00	11.00
❑ 2 Tony Banks	25.00	11.00
❑ 3 Tim Biakabutuka	25.00	11.00
❑ 4 Duane Clemons	8.00	3.60
❑ 5 Stephen Davis	30.00	13.50
❑ 6 Chris Doering	8.00	3.60
❑ 7 Bobby Hoying	15.00	6.75
❑ 8 Keyshawn Johnson	40.00	18.00
❑ 9 Danny Kanell	15.00	6.75
❑ 10 Leeland McElroy	15.00	6.75
❑ 11 Jonathan Ogden	25.00	11.00
❑ 12 Steve Taneyhill	8.00	3.60

1996 Press Pass Paydirt Autographs

	Nm-Mt	Ex-Mt
COMPLETE SET (16)	200.00	90.00
❑ 1 Karim Abdul-Jabbar	20.00	9.00
❑ 2 Tony Banks	20.00	9.00
❑ 3 Tim Biakabutuka	20.00	9.00
❑ 4 Duane Clemons	8.00	3.60
❑ 5 Stephen Davis	40.00	18.00
❑ 6 Chris Doering	8.00	3.60
❑ 7 Bobby Hoying	20.00	9.00
❑ 8 Keyshawn Johnson	40.00	18.00
❑ 9 Danny Kanell	15.00	6.75
❑ 10 Derrick Mayes	15.00	6.75
❑ 11 Leeland McElroy	8.00	3.60

		Nm-Mt	Ex-Mt
❑ 12	Lawyer Milloy	20.00	9.00
❑ 13	Eric Moulds	40.00	18.00
❑ 14	Jonathan Ogden	20.00	9.00
❑ 15	Steve Taneyhill	8.00	3.60
❑ 16	Alex Van Dyke	8.00	3.60

1997 Press Pass Autographs

		Nm-Mt	Ex-Mt
COMPLETE SET (31)		400.00	180.00
❑ 1	Reidel Anthony	20.00	9.00
❑ 2	Michael Booker	8.00	3.60
❑ 3	Peter Boulware	20.00	9.00
❑ 4	Bobby Bowden CO	30.00	13.50
❑ 5	Chris Canty	8.00	3.60
❑ 6	Rae Carruth	12.00	5.50
❑ 7	Troy Davis	12.00	5.50
❑ 8	Koy Detmer	20.00	9.00
❑ 9	Corey Dillon	40.00	18.00
❑ 10	Jim Druckenmiller	12.00	5.50
❑ 11	Warrick Dunn	40.00	18.00
❑ 12	James Farrior	12.00	5.50
❑ 13	Tony Gonzalez	30.00	13.50
❑ 14	Yatil Green	12.00	5.50
❑ 15	Byron Hanspard	12.00	5.50
❑ 16	Ike Hilliard	25.00	11.00
❑ 17	Greg Jones	8.00	3.60
❑ 18	David LaFleur	8.00	3.60
❑ 19	Kevin Lockett	8.00	3.60
❑ 20	Tom Osborne CO	60.00	27.00
❑ 21	Orlando Pace	20.00	9.00
❑ 22	Keith Poole	8.00	3.60
❑ 23	Darrell Russell	8.00	3.60
❑ 24	Matt Russell	8.00	3.60
❑ 25	Bob Sapp	8.00	3.60
❑ 26	Steve Spurrier CO	30.00	13.50
❑ 27	Gene Stallings CO	25.00	11.00
❑ 28	Mike Vrabel	40.00	18.00
❑ 29	Bryant Westbrook	8.00	3.60
❑ 30	Reinard Wilson	8.00	3.60
❑ 31	Danny Wuerffel	20.00	9.00

1998 Press Pass Autographs

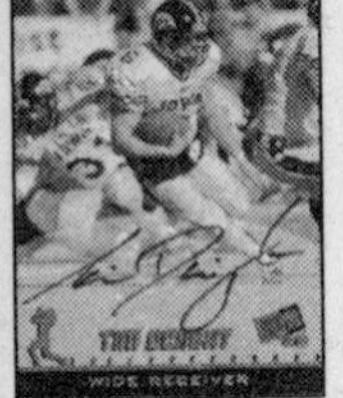

		Nm-Mt	Ex-Mt
COMPLETE SET (38)		600.00	275.00
❑ 1	Peyton Manning	100.00	45.00
❑ 2	Ryan Leaf	15.00	6.75
❑ 4	Andre Wadsworth	10.00	4.50
❑ 5	Randy Moss	60.00	27.00
❑ 6	Curtis Enis	8.00	3.60
❑ 9	Jason Peter	8.00	3.60
❑ 10	Brian Simmons	10.00	4.50
❑ 11	Takeo Spikes	15.00	6.75
❑ 12	Michael Myers	8.00	3.60
❑ 13	Kevin Dyson	15.00	6.75
❑ 14	Grant Wistrom	15.00	6.75
❑ 15	Fred Taylor	40.00	18.00
❑ 16	Germane Crowell	10.00	4.50
❑ 18	Anthony Simmons LB	10.00	4.50
❑ 19	Robert Edwards	10.00	4.50
❑ 20	Shaun Williams	15.00	6.75
❑ 21	Phil Savoy	8.00	3.60
❑ 25	John Avery	10.00	4.50
❑ 26	Vonnie Holliday	15.00	6.75
❑ 27	Tim Dwight	15.00	6.75
❑ 28	Donovin Darius	10.00	4.50
❑ 29	Alonzo Mayes	8.00	3.60
❑ 31	Brian Kelly	10.00	4.50
❑ 32	Hines Ward	40.00	18.00
❑ 33	Jacquez Green	10.00	4.50
❑ 34	Marcus Nash	8.00	3.60
❑ 35	Ahman Green	50.00	22.00
❑ 36	Joe Jurevicius	15.00	6.75
❑ 37	Tavian Banks	10.00	4.50
❑ 38	Donald Hayes	10.00	4.50
❑ 39	Robert Holcombe	10.00	4.50
❑ 42	Skip Hicks	10.00	4.50
❑ 43	Pat Johnson	10.00	4.50
❑ 45	Alan Faneca	20.00	9.00
❑ 46	Steve Spurrier CO	30.00	13.50
❑ 47	Mike Price CO	8.00	3.60
❑ 48	Bobby Bowden CO	40.00	18.00
❑ 49	Tom Osborne CO	30.00	13.50
❑ NNO	P.Manning SportsFest	80.00	36.00

1998 Press Pass Game Jerseys

		Nm-Mt	Ex-Mt
COMPLETE SET (4)		250.00	110.00
❑ JC1	Peyton Manning	150.00	70.00
❑ JC2	Ryan Leaf	25.00	11.00
❑ JC3	Kevin Dyson	25.00	11.00
❑ JC4	Tavian Banks	20.00	9.00
❑ JCTB	Tavian Banks Promo	10.00	4.50

1999 Press Pass

		Nm-Mt	Ex-Mt
COMPLETE SET (45)		15.00	6.75
❑ 1	Ricky Williams	1.25	.55
❑ 2	Tim Couch	.60	.25
❑ 3	Champ Bailey	1.00	.45
❑ 4	Chris Claiborne	.20	.09
❑ 5	Donovan McNabb	3.00	1.35
❑ 6	Edgerrin James	2.50	1.10
❑ 7	Akili Smith	1.00	.45
❑ 8	John Tait	.20	.09
❑ 9	Jevon Kearse	1.50	.70
❑ 10	Torry Holt	1.50	.70
❑ 11	Troy Edwards	.30	.14
❑ 12	Chris McAlister	.30	.14
❑ 13	Daunte Culpepper	2.50	1.10
❑ 14	Andy Katzenmoyer	.30	.14
❑ 15	David Boston	.60	.25
❑ 16	Ebenezer Ekuban	.30	.14
❑ 17	Peerless Price	1.25	.55
❑ 18	Shaun King	.30	.14
❑ 19	Joe Germaine	.30	.14
❑ 20	Brock Huard	.60	.25
❑ 21	Michael Bishop	.60	.25
❑ 22	Amos Zereoue	.60	.25
❑ 23	Sedrick Irvin	.20	.09
❑ 24	Autry Denson	.30	.14
❑ 25	Kevin Faulk	.60	.25
❑ 26	James Johnson	.30	.14
❑ 27	D'Wayne Bates	.30	.14
❑ 28	Kevin Johnson	1.00	.45
❑ 29	Tai Streets	.60	.25
❑ 30	Craig Yeast	.30	.14
❑ 31	Dre' Bly	.60	.25
❑ 32	Anthony Poindexter	.20	.09
❑ 33	Jared DeVries	.20	.09
❑ 34	Rob Konrad	.60	.25
❑ 35	Dat Nguyen	.60	.25
❑ 36	Cade McNown	.30	.14
❑ 37	Scott Covington	.60	.25
❑ 38	Jon Jansen	.20	.09
❑ 39	Rufus French	.20	.09
❑ 40	Mike Rucker	.60	.25
❑ 41	Aaron Gibson	.20	.09
❑ 42	Kris Farris	.20	.09
❑ 43	Anthony McFarland	.20	.09
❑ 44	Matt Stinchcomb	.30	.14
❑ 45	Dee Miller CL	.20	.09

1999 Press Pass Autographs

		Nm-Mt	Ex-Mt
COMPLETE SET (50)		600.00	275.00
❑ 1	Ricky Williams	20.00	9.00
❑ 2	Tim Couch	15.00	6.75
❑ 3	Champ Bailey	20.00	9.00
❑ 4	Chris Claiborne	10.00	4.50
❑ 5	Donovan McNabb	50.00	22.00
❑ 6	Edgerrin James	40.00	18.00
❑ 7	Akili Smith	20.00	9.00
❑ 8	John Tait	10.00	4.50
❑ 9	Jevon Kearse	25.00	11.00
❑ 10	Torry Holt	30.00	13.50
❑ 11	Troy Edwards	12.00	5.50
❑ 12	Chris McAlister	12.00	5.50
❑ 13	Daunte Culpepper	40.00	18.00
❑ 14	Andy Katzenmoyer	12.00	5.50
❑ 15	David Boston	15.00	6.75
❑ 16	Ebenezer Ekuban	12.00	5.50
❑ 17	Peerless Price	20.00	9.00
❑ 18	Shaun King	12.00	5.50
❑ 19	Joe Germaine	12.00	5.50
❑ 20	Brock Huard	15.00	6.75
❑ 21	Michael Bishop	15.00	6.75
❑ 22	Amos Zereoue	15.00	6.75

23 Sedrick Irvin	10.00	4.50
24 Autry Denson	12.00	5.50
25 Kevin Faulk	12.00	5.50
26 James Johnson	12.00	5.50
27 D'Wayne Bates	10.00	4.50
28 Kevin Johnson	15.00	6.75
29 Tai Streets	15.00	6.75
30 Craig Yeast	12.00	5.50
31 Dre Bly	15.00	6.75
32 Anthony Poindexter	10.00	4.50
33 Jared DeVries	10.00	4.50
34 Rob Konrad	15.00	6.75
35 Dat Nguyen	15.00	6.75
36 Cade McNown	12.00	5.50
37 Scott Covington	15.00	6.75
38 Jon Jansen	10.00	4.50
39 Rufus French	10.00	4.50
40 Mike Rucker	15.00	6.75
41 Aaron Gibson	10.00	4.50
42 Kris Farris	10.00	4.50
43 Anthony McFarland	10.00	4.50
44 Matt Stinchcomb	12.00	5.50
45 Dee Miller CL	10.00	4.50
46 Antuan Edwards	12.00	5.50
47 Mike Peterson	12.00	5.50
48 Mike Cloud	12.00	5.50
49 Darnell McDonald	12.00	5.50
50 Jerame Tuman	12.00	5.50

1999 Press Pass Game Jerseys

	Nm-Mt	Ex-Mt
COMPLETE SET (6)	250.00	110.00
JCAS Akili Smith	25.00	11.00
JCCM Cade McNown	25.00	11.00
JCDC Daunte Culpepper	80.00	36.00
JCPP Peerless Price	40.00	18.00
JCTC Tim Couch	40.00	18.00
JCTH Torry Holt	50.00	22.00

2000 Press Pass

	Nm-Mt	Ex-Mt
COMPLETE SET (45)	20.00	9.00
1 Peter Warrick	.50	.23
2 Travis Claridge	.25	.11
3 Courtney Brown	.60	.25
4 Plaxico Burress	1.00	.45
5 Chad Pennington	2.00	.90
6 Thomas Jones	.75	.35
7 Ron Dayne	.50	.23
8 Brian Urlacher	2.00	.90
9 Corey Simon	.60	.25
10 Chris Samuels	.40	.18
11 Stockar McDougle	.25	.11
12 Deon Grant	.40	.18
13 Cosey Coleman	.25	.11
14 Sylvester Morris	.40	.18
15 Shyrone Stith	.40	.18
16 Shaun Alexander	1.50	.70
17 Dez White	.50	.23
18 John Engelberger	.40	.18
19 Tim Rattay	1.00	.45
20 Todd Pinkston	.50	.23
21 John Abraham	.50	.23
22 R.Jay Soward	.40	.18
23 Shaun Ellis	.50	.23
24 Keith Bulluck	.50	.23
25 Jerry Porter	.60	.25
26 Darren Howard	.40	.18
27 Joe Hamilton	.40	.18
28 Deltha O'Neal	.50	.23
29 Chris Redman	.40	.18
30 Deon Dyer	.40	.18
31 Jamal Lewis	1.00	.45
32 Chris Hovan	.40	.18
33 Raynoch Thompson	.40	.18
34 Travis Taylor	.50	.23
35 Sebastian Janikowski	.50	.23
36 Travis Prentice	.40	.18
37 Tom Brady	12.00	5.50
38 Tee Martin	.50	.23
39 J.R. Redmond	.40	.18
40 Dennis Northcutt	.50	.23
41 Laveranues Coles	.60	.25
42 Danny Farmer	.40	.18
43 Darrell Jackson	1.00	.45
44 Chris McIntosh	.25	.11
45 Peter Warrick CL	.40	.18
P1 Peter Warrick Promo	2.00	.90

2000 Press Pass Autographs

	Nm-Mt	Ex-Mt
COMPLETE SET (51)	500.00	220.00
*HOLOFOILS: .8X TO 2X BASIC INSERTS		
1 John Abraham	15.00	6.75
2 Shaun Alexander	25.00	11.00
3 Tom Brady	150.00	70.00
4 Courtney Brown	12.00	5.50
5 Keith Bulluck	12.00	5.50
6 Plaxico Burress	20.00	9.00
7 Giovanni Carmazzi	6.00	2.70
8 Kwame Cavil	6.00	2.70
9 Travis Claridge	6.00	2.70
10 Cosey Coleman	6.00	2.70
11 Laveranues Coles	12.00	5.50
12 Ron Dayne	12.00	5.50
13 Na'il Diggs	8.00	3.60
14 Ron Dugans	6.00	2.70
15 Deon Dyer	6.00	2.70
16 Shaun Ellis	8.00	3.60
17 John Engelberger	6.00	2.70
18 Danny Farmer	8.00	3.60
19 Deon Grant	8.00	3.60
20 Joe Hamilton	6.00	2.70
21 Darren Howard	8.00	3.60
22 Chris Hovan	8.00	3.60
23 Darrell Jackson	20.00	9.00
24 Sebastian Janikowski	12.00	5.50
25 Thomas Jones	15.00	6.75
26 Jamal Lewis	25.00	11.00
27 Tee Martin	12.00	5.50
28 Stockar McDougle	6.00	2.70
29 Chris McIntosh	6.00	2.70
30 Corey Moore	6.00	2.70
31 Rob Morris	6.00	2.70
32 Sylvester Morris	8.00	3.60
33 Dennis Northcutt	8.00	3.60
34 Deltha O'Neal	8.00	3.60
35 Chad Pennington	40.00	18.00
36 Todd Pinkston	8.00	3.60
37 Jerry Porter	15.00	6.75
38 Travis Prentice	8.00	3.60
39 Tim Rattay	20.00	9.00
40 Chris Redman	8.00	3.60
41 J.R. Redmond	6.00	2.70
42 Chris Samuels	6.00	2.70
43 Corey Simon	12.00	5.50
44 Marvel Smith	12.00	5.50
45 Shyrone Stith	6.00	2.70
46 Travis Taylor	12.00	5.50
47 Raynoch Thompson	8.00	3.60
48 Brian Urlacher	40.00	18.00
49 Todd Wade	6.00	2.70
50 Peter Warrick	12.00	5.50
50C Peter Warrick Clear/50	60.00	18.00
51 Dez White	12.00	5.50

2001 Press Pass

	Nm-Mt	Ex-Mt
COMPLETE SET (50)	25.00	11.00
COMP.FACTORY SET (46)	25.00	7.50
COMP.SET w/o SP's (45)	20.00	6.00
1 Michael Vick CL	2.50	1.10
2 Drew Brees	1.50	.70
3 Michael Vick	6.00	2.70
4 Chris Weinke	.75	.35
5 Marques Tuiasosopo	.75	.35
6 Josh Booty	.75	.35
7 Josh Heupel	.75	.35
8 Sage Rosenfels	1.00	.45
9 Mike McMahon	.75	.35
10 Deuce McAllister	2.00	.90
11 LaDainian Tomlinson	3.00	1.35
12 LaMont Jordan	1.00	.45
13 James Jackson	.75	.35
14 Travis Henry	1.25	.55
15 Anthony Thomas	1.50	.70
16 Travis Minor	.60	.25
17 Michael Bennett	1.50	.70
18 Kevan Barlow	.75	.35
19 Rudi Johnson	1.50	.70
20 Santana Moss	1.50	.70
21 Quincy Morgan	.75	.35
22 Rod Gardner	.75	.35
23 David Terrell	.75	.35
24 Chris Chambers	1.25	.55
25 Reggie Wayne	1.50	.70
26 Ken-Yon Rambo	.60	.25
27 Chad Johnson	1.50	.70
28 Snoop Minnis	.60	.25
29 Freddie Mitchell	.75	.35
30 Koren Robinson	1.25	.55
31 Bobby Newcombe	.60	.25
32 Robert Ferguson	.75	.35
33 Todd Heap	.75	.35
34 Steve Hutchinson	.60	.25

35 Leonard Davis	.60	.25
36 Kenyatta Walker	.40	.18
37 Justin Smith	.75	.35
38 Jamal Reynolds	.75	.35
39 Richard Seymour	.75	.35
40 Shaun Rogers	.75	.35
41 Gerard Warren	.75	.35
42 Jamar Fletcher	.60	.25
43 Gary Baxter	.60	.25
44 Nate Clements	.75	.35
45 Derrick Gibson	.60	.25
46 Drew Brees PP	4.00	1.80
47 Michael Vick PP	10.00	4.50
48 Deuce McAllister PP	4.00	1.80
49 LaDainian Tomlinson PP	5.00	2.20
50 David Terrell PP	1.25	.55

2001 Press Pass Autographs

	Nm-Mt	Ex-Mt
1 Dan Alexander	15.00	4.50
2 Brian Allen	10.00	3.00
3 Jeff Backus	10.00	3.00
4 Kevan Barlow	20.00	6.00
5 Michael Bennett	25.00	7.50
6 Drew Brees	25.00	7.50
7 Josh Booty	12.00	3.60
8 Chris Chambers	20.00	6.00
9 Nate Clements	12.00	3.60
10 Ennis Davis	8.00	2.40
11 Robert Ferguson	12.00	3.60
12 Jamar Fletcher	12.00	3.60
13 Rod Gardner	12.00	3.60
14 Casey Hampton	12.00	3.60
15 Todd Heap	20.00	6.00
16 Travis Henry	20.00	6.00
17 Jabari Holloway	10.00	3.00
18 Steve Hutchinson	10.00	3.00
19 James Jackson	12.00	3.60
20 Chad Johnson	25.00	7.50
21 Rudi Johnson	25.00	7.50
22 LaMont Jordan	15.00	4.50
23 Ben Leard	20.00	6.00
24 Torrance Marshall	20.00	9.00
25 Deuce McAllister	30.00	9.00
26 Mike McMahon	12.00	3.60
27 Snoop Minnis	10.00	3.00
28 Quincy Morgan	15.00	4.50
29 Santana Moss	25.00	7.50
30 Bobby Newcombe	20.00	6.00
31 Moran Norris	8.00	2.40
32 Jesse Palmer	12.00	3.60
33 Tommy Polley	12.00	3.60
34 Dominic Raiola	12.00	3.60
35 Ken-Yon Rambo	10.00	3.00
36 Jamal Reynolds	20.00	6.00
37 Koren Robinson	15.00	4.50
38 Sage Rosenfels	20.00	6.00
39 Justin Smith	15.00	4.50
40 David Terrell	15.00	4.50
41 Anthony Thomas	25.00	7.50
42 LaDainian Tomlinson	50.00	15.00
43 Marques Tuiasosopo	12.00	3.60
44 Michael Vick	125.00	38.00
45 Kenyatta Walker	8.00	2.40
46 Chad Ward	8.00	2.40
47 Gerard Warren	12.00	3.60
48 Reggie Wayne	25.00	7.50
49 Chris Weinke	12.00	3.60

2001 Press Pass Autograph Power Picks

	Nm-Mt	Ex-Mt
1 Michael Vick/100	150.00	70.00
2 LaDainian Tomlinson	60.00	27.00
3 David Terrell	20.00	9.00
4 Koren Robinson	15.00	4.50
5 Santana Moss	25.00	7.50
7 Michael Bennett	30.00	9.00
8 Drew Brees	40.00	18.00
9 Chris Weinke	20.00	6.00

2002 Press Pass

	Nm-Mt	Ex-Mt
COMPLETE SET (50)	40.00	12.00
COMP.SET w/o SP's (45)	25.00	7.50
1 David Carr	4.00	1.20
2 Eric Crouch	1.50	.45
3 Rohan Davey	1.00	.30
4 David Garrard	1.00	.30
5 Joey Harrington	4.00	1.20
6 Kurt Kittner	.75	.23
7 David Neill	.75	.23
8 Patrick Ramsey	2.00	.60
9 Antwaan Randle El	1.25	.35
10 Damien Anderson	.75	.23
11 T.J. Duckett	2.00	.60
12 DeShaun Foster	1.00	.30
13 Lamar Gordon	1.00	.30
14 William Green	2.00	.60
15 Leonard Henry	.75	.23
16 Adrian Peterson	1.00	.30
17 Clinton Portis	4.00	1.20
18 Jonathan Wells	1.00	.30
19 Brian Westbrook	2.00	.60
20 Antonio Bryant	1.00	.30
21 Reche Caldwell	1.00	.30
22 Kelly Campbell	.75	.23
23 Andre Davis	1.00	.30
24 Jabar Gaffney	1.00	.30
25 Ron Johnson	.75	.23
26 Ashley Lelie	2.00	.60
27 Josh Reed	1.00	.30
28 Cliff Russell	.75	.23
29 Donte Stallworth	2.00	.60
30 Javon Walker	2.00	.60
31 Marquise Walker	.75	.23
32 Daniel Graham	1.00	.30
33 Jeremy Shockey	4.00	1.20
34 Bryant McKinnie	.75	.23
35 Mike Pearson	.50	.15
36 Mike Williams	.75	.23
37 Phillip Buchanon	1.00	.30
38 Quentin Jammer	1.00	.30
39 Kalimba Edwards	1.00	.30
40 Julius Peppers	2.00	.60
41 Wendell Bryant	1.00	.30
42 John Henderson	1.00	.30
43 Ryan Sims	1.00	.30
44 Roy Williams	2.50	.75
45 David Carr CL	1.50	.45
46 David Carr PP	8.00	2.40
47 Joey Harrington PP	8.00	2.40
48 T.J. Duckett PP	4.00	1.20
49 Donte Stallworth PP	4.00	1.20
50 William Green PP	4.00	1.20

2002 Press Pass Autographs

	Nm-Mt	Ex-Mt
1 Damien Anderson	12.00	3.60
2 Antonio Bryant	15.00	4.50
3 Phillip Buchanon	15.00	4.50
4 Reche Caldwell	15.00	4.50
5 Rocky Calmus	15.00	4.50
6 Kelly Campbell	12.00	3.60
7 David Carr	50.00	15.00
8 Eric Crouch	25.00	7.50
9 Rohan Davey	15.00	4.50
10 Andre Davis	15.00	4.50
11 T.J. Duckett	25.00	7.50
12 Kalimba Edwards	15.00	4.50
13 Jabar Gaffney	15.00	4.50
14 David Garrard	15.00	4.50
15 Lamar Gordon	15.00	4.50
16 Daniel Graham	15.00	4.50
17 William Green	25.00	7.50
18 Joey Harrington	50.00	15.00
19 John Henderson	15.00	4.50
20 Leonard Henry	12.00	3.60
21 Kyle Johnson	10.00	3.00
22 Ron Johnson	12.00	3.60
23 Levi Jones	12.00	3.60
24 Kurt Kittner	12.00	3.60
25 Ashley Lelie	25.00	7.50
26 Josh McCown	20.00	6.00
27 Freddie Milons	12.00	3.60
28 Maurice Morris	15.00	4.50
29 David Neill	12.00	3.60
30 Mike Pearson	10.00	3.00
31 Adrian Peterson	15.00	4.50
32 Patrick Ramsey	25.00	7.50
33 Antwaan Randle El	20.00	6.00
34 Josh Reed	15.00	4.50
35 Cliff Russell	12.00	3.60
36 Ryan Sims	15.00	4.50
37 Luke Staley	12.00	3.60
38 Donte Stallworth	20.00	6.00
39 Javon Walker	20.00	6.00
40 Marquise Walker	12.00	3.60
41 Anthony Weaver	12.00	3.60
42 Jonathan Wells	15.00	4.50
43 Brian Westbrook	25.00	7.50
44 Roy Williams	40.00	12.00

2002 Press Pass Autograph Power Picks

	Nm-Mt	Ex-Mt
❑ 1 Antonio Bryant	20.00	6.00
❑ 2 David Carr	50.00	15.00
❑ 3 Eric Crouch	40.00	12.00
❑ 4 Andre Davis	20.00	6.00
❑ 5 T.J. Duckett	30.00	9.00
❑ 6 DeShaun Foster	25.00	7.50
❑ 7 William Green	30.00	9.00
❑ 8 Joey Harrington	50.00	15.00
❑ 9 Kurt Kittner	15.00	4.50
❑ 10 Ashley Lelie	25.00	7.50
❑ 11 Josh Reed	20.00	6.00
❑ 12 Marquise Walker	20.00	6.00

2003 Press Pass

	Nm-Mt	Ex-Mt
COMPLETE SET (50)	50.00	15.00
COMP.SET w/o SP's (45)	25.00	7.50
❑ 1 Brad Banks	.75	.23
❑ 2 Kyle Boller	2.50	.75
❑ 3 Ken Dorsey	1.50	.45
❑ 4 Jason Gesser	1.00	.30
❑ 5 Rex Grossman	2.50	.75
❑ 6 Kliff Kingsbury	.75	.23
❑ 7 Byron Leftwich	4.00	1.20
❑ 8 Carson Palmer	3.00	.90
❑ 9 Dave Ragone	1.00	.30
❑ 10 Chris Simms	2.00	.60
❑ 11 Brian St.Pierre	1.00	.30
❑ 12 Chris Brown	2.00	.60
❑ 13 Avon Cobourne	.50	.15
❑ 14 Dahrran Diedrick	1.00	.30
❑ 15 Justin Fargas	1.00	.30
❑ 16 Earnest Graham	.75	.23
❑ 17 Larry Johnson	1.50	.45
❑ 18 Willis McGahee	2.50	.75
❑ 19 Musa Smith	1.00	.30
❑ 20 Onterrio Smith	1.25	.35
❑ 21 Lee Suggs	2.00	.60
❑ 22 Anquan Boldin	2.50	.75
❑ 23 Talman Gardner	1.00	.30
❑ 24 Taylor Jacobs	1.00	.30
❑ 25 Andre Johnson	2.50	.75
❑ 26 Bryant Johnson	1.00	.30
❑ 27 Brandon Lloyd	1.25	.35
❑ 28 Charles Rogers	1.25	.35
❑ 29 Kelley Washington	1.00	.30
❑ 30 Teyo Johnson	1.00	.30
❑ 31 Bennie Joppru	1.00	.30
❑ 32 Jason Witten	1.50	.45
❑ 33 Andrew Pinnock	.75	.23
❑ 34 Jordan Gross	.75	.23
❑ 35 Kwame Harris	.75	.23
❑ 36 Eric Steinbach	.75	.23
❑ 37 Brett Williams	.50	.15
❑ 38 Terence Newman	2.00	.60
❑ 39 Marcus Trufant	1.00	.30
❑ 40 Andre Woolfolk	1.00	.30
❑ 41 Terrell Suggs	1.50	.45
❑ 42 Jimmy Kennedy	1.00	.30
❑ 43 Boss Bailey	1.25	.35
❑ 44 Mike Doss	1.00	.30
❑ 45 Carson Palmer CL	1.50	.45
❑ 46 Carson Palmer PP	6.00	1.80
❑ 47 Byron Leftwich PP	8.00	2.40
❑ 48 Charles Rogers PP	2.50	.75
❑ 49 Kyle Boller PP	5.00	1.50
❑ 50 Andre Johnson PP	5.00	1.50

2003 Press Pass Gold Zone

	Nm-Mt	Ex-Mt
COMPLETE SET (45)	30.00	9.00

*SINGLES: .6X TO 1.5X BASIC CARDS

2003 Press Pass Reflectors

	Nm-Mt	Ex-Mt

*SINGLES: 2.5X TO 6X BASIC CARDS
*PROOFS: 5X TO 12X BASIC CARDS

2003 Press Pass Autographs Bronze

	Nm-Mt	Ex-Mt

*GOLDS: .6X TO 1.5X BRONZE AUTOS
GOLD PRINT RUN 100 SER.#'d SETS
*SILVERS: .5X TO 1.2X BRONZE
SILVER PRINT RUN 200 SER.#'d SETS

	Nm-Mt	Ex-Mt
❑ 1 Boss Bailey	20.00	6.00
❑ 2 Brad Banks	12.00	3.60
❑ 3 Anquan Boldin	40.00	12.00
❑ 4 Kyle Boller	50.00	15.00
❑ 5 Chris Brown	30.00	9.00
❑ 6 Mike Bush	8.00	2.40
❑ 7 Tyrone Calico	25.00	7.50
❑ 8 Avon Cobourne	8.00	2.40
❑ 9 Angelo Crowell	12.00	3.60
❑ 10 Chris Davis	12.00	3.60
❑ 11 Domanick Davis	25.00	7.50
❑ 12 Dahrran Diedrick	15.00	4.50
❑ 13 Ken Dorsey	25.00	7.50
❑ 14 Mike Doss	15.00	4.50
❑ 15 Justin Fargas	15.00	4.50
❑ 16 Talman Gardner	15.00	4.50
❑ 17 Jason Gesser	15.00	4.50
❑ 18 Earnest Graham	12.00	3.60
❑ 19 Justin Griffith	12.00	3.60
❑ 20 DeJuan Groce	15.00	4.50
❑ 21 Jordan Gross	12.00	3.60
❑ 22 Kwame Harris	12.00	3.60
❑ 23 Michael Haynes	15.00	4.50
❑ 24 Wayne Hunter	8.00	2.40
❑ 25 Taylor Jacobs	15.00	4.50
❑ 26 Larry Johnson	30.00	9.00
❑ 27 Teyo Johnson	15.00	4.50
❑ 28 Ben Johnson	8.00	2.40
❑ 29 Bryant Johnson	15.00	4.50
❑ 30 Bennie Joppru	20.00	6.00
❑ 31 Kareem Kelly	12.00	3.60
❑ 32 Chris Kelsay	15.00	4.50
❑ 33 Jimmy Kennedy	15.00	4.50
❑ 34 Kliff Kingsbury	12.00	3.60
❑ 35 Byron Leftwich	70.00	21.00
❑ 36 Brandon Lloyd	20.00	6.00
❑ 37 Vincent Manuwai	8.00	2.40
❑ 38 Rashean Mathis	12.00	3.60
❑ 39 Sultan McCullough	12.00	3.60
❑ 40 Jerome McDougle	15.00	4.50
❑ 41 Willis McGahee	40.00	12.00
❑ 42 Terence Newman	25.00	7.50
❑ 43 Tony Pashos	8.00	2.40
❑ 44 Carson Palmer	50.00	15.00
❑ 45 Andrew Pinnock	12.00	3.60
❑ 46 Dave Ragone	15.00	4.50
❑ 47 DeWayne Robertson	15.00	4.50
❑ 48 Steve Sciullo	8.00	2.40
❑ 49 Musa Smith	15.00	4.50
❑ 50 Brian St.Pierre	12.00	3.60
❑ 51 Eric Steinbach	12.00	3.60
❑ 52 Jon Stinchcomb	15.00	4.50
❑ 53 Terrell Suggs	20.00	6.00
❑ 54 LaBrandon Toefield	15.00	4.50
❑ 55 Marcus Trufant	15.00	4.50
❑ 56 Bobby Wade	15.00	4.50
❑ 57 Seneca Wallace	15.00	4.50
❑ 58 Shane Walton	8.00	2.40
❑ 59 Kelley Washington	15.00	4.50
❑ 60 Dennis Weathersby	12.00	3.60
❑ 61 DeWayne White	12.00	3.60
❑ 62 Brett Williams	8.00	2.40
❑ 63 Juston Wood	8.00	2.40
❑ 64 Andre Woolfolk	15.00	4.50

2003 Press Pass Autograph Power Picks

	Nm-Mt	Ex-Mt
❑ 1 Brad Banks	15.00	4.50
❑ 2 Anquan Boldin	40.00	12.00
❑ 3 Kyle Boller	50.00	15.00
❑ 4 Taylor Jacobs	15.00	4.50
❑ 5 Larry Johnson	30.00	9.00
❑ 6 Byron Leftwich	80.00	24.00
❑ 7 Brandon Lloyd	15.00	4.50
❑ 8 Carson Palmer	60.00	18.00
❑ 9 Dave Ragone	15.00	4.50

2003 Press Pass Game Used Jerseys Gold

	Nm-Mt	Ex-Mt
*HOLOFOILS: .6X TO 1.5X GOLD JERSEYS		
*SILVERS: .5X TO 1.2X GOLD JERSEYS		
❑ JCBJ Bennie Joppru	15.00	4.50
❑ JCBL Byron Leftwich	50.00	15.00
❑ JCCP Carson Palmer	40.00	12.00
❑ JCEG Earnest Graham	15.00	4.50
❑ JCKD Ken Dorsey	30.00	9.00
❑ JCKK Kareem Kelly	15.00	4.50
❑ JCSW Seneca Wallace	15.00	4.50
❑ JCTJ Teyo Johnson	15.00	4.50

2004 Press Pass

	Nm-Mt	Ex-Mt
COMPLETE SET (50)	50.00	15.00
COMP.SET w/o SP's (45)	30.00	9.00
❑ 1 Casey Clausen	1.25	.35
❑ 2 Craig Krenzel	1.00	.30
❑ 3 J.P. Losman	2.50	.75
❑ 4 Eli Manning	5.00	1.50
❑ 5 Luke McCown	1.00	.30
❑ 6 John Navarre	1.00	.30
❑ 7 Cody Pickett	1.00	.30
❑ 8 Philip Rivers	3.00	.90
❑ 9 Ben Roethlisberger	8.00	2.40
❑ 10 Matt Schaub	1.50	.45
❑ 11 Cedric Cobbs	1.00	.30
❑ 12 Steven Jackson	3.00	.90
❑ 13 Kevin Jones	3.00	.90
❑ 14 Greg Jones	1.00	.30
❑ 15 Julius Jones	4.00	1.20
❑ 16 Jarrett Payton	1.00	.30
❑ 17 Chris Perry	2.00	.60
❑ 18 Michael Turner	.75	.23
❑ 19 Quincy Wilson	.75	.23
❑ 20 Jason Wright	.50	.15
❑ 21 Bernard Berrian	1.00	.30
❑ 22 Michael Clayton	2.50	.75
❑ 23 Devard Darling	1.00	.30
❑ 24 Lee Evans	1.50	.45
❑ 25 Larry Fitzgerald	3.00	.90
❑ 26 Devery Henderson	.75	.23
❑ 27 Michael Jenkins	1.00	.30
❑ 28 Darius Watts	1.25	.35
❑ 29 Mike Williams	6.00	1.80
❑ 30 Roy Williams WR	3.00	.90
❑ 31 Rashaun Woods	1.25	.35
❑ 32 Ben Troupe	1.00	.30
❑ 33 Shawn Andrews	1.00	.30
❑ 34 Robert Gallery	1.50	.45
❑ 35 Tommie Harris	1.25	.35
❑ 36 Vince Wilfork	1.25	.35
❑ 37 Will Smith	1.00	.30
❑ 38 Teddy Lehman	1.00	.30
❑ 39 Jonathan Vilma	1.00	.30
❑ 40 D.J. Williams	1.25	.35
❑ 41 DeAngelo Hall	1.25	.35
❑ 42 Dunta Robinson	1.00	.30
❑ 43 Derrick Strait	1.00	.30
❑ 44 Keith Smith	.75	.23
❑ 45 Eli Manning CL	3.00	.90
❑ 46 Eli Manning PP	10.00	3.00
❑ 47 Ben Roethlisberger PP	15.00	4.50
❑ 48 Larry Fitzgerald PP	6.00	1.80
❑ 49 Roy Williams PP	6.00	1.80
❑ 50 Philip Rivers PP	6.00	1.80

2004 Press Pass Blue

Nm-Mt Ex-Mt

*BLUES: .8X TO 2X BASIC CARDS
ONE PER RETAIL PACK

2004 Press Pass Gold

Nm-Mt Ex-Mt

*GOLDS: .6X TO 1.5X BASIC CARDS
ONE GOLD PER HOBBY PACK

2004 Press Pass Reflectors

Nm-Mt Ex-Mt

*REFLECTORS: 2.5X TO 6X BASIC CARDS
STATED PRINT RUN 500 SER.#'d SETS

2004 Press Pass Reflectors Proof

Nm-Mt Ex-Mt

*REF.PROOFS: 5X TO 12X BASIC CARDS
STATED PRINT RUN 100 SER.#'d SETS

2004 Press Pass Autographs Bronze

	Nm-Mt	Ex-Mt
❑ 1 Bernard Berrian	15.00	4.50
❑ 2 Casey Clausen	20.00	6.00
❑ 2R Casey Clausen Red	25.00	7.50
❑ 3 Michael Clayton	30.00	9.00
❑ 3R Michael Clayton Red	40.00	12.00
❑ 4 Cedric Cobbs	15.00	4.50
❑ 5 Ricardo Colclough	15.00	4.50
❑ 6 Devard Darling	15.00	4.50
❑ 6R Devard Darling Red	20.00	6.00
❑ 7 Dwan Edwards	8.00	2.40
❑ 7R Dwan Edwards Red	15.00	4.50
❑ 8 Lee Evans	25.00	7.50
❑ 9 Larry Fitzgerald	60.00	18.00
❑ 10 Robert Gallery	25.00	7.50
❑ 10R Robert Gallery Red	30.00	9.00
❑ 11 Jermaine Green	12.00	3.60
❑ 12 DeAngelo Hall	20.00	6.00
❑ 13 Tommie Harris	20.00	6.00
❑ 14 Ben Hartsock	15.00	4.50
❑ 15 Devery Henderson	12.00	3.60
❑ 16 Steven Jackson SP	60.00	18.00
❑ 17 Michael Jenkins	15.00	4.50
❑ 17R Michael Jenkins Red	25.00	7.50
❑ 18 Greg Jones	15.00	4.50
❑ 18R Greg Jones Red	20.00	6.00
❑ 19 Julius Jones	60.00	18.00
❑ 21 Sean Jones	12.00	3.60
❑ 22 Nate Kaeding	15.00	4.50
❑ 22R Nate Kaeding Red	20.00	6.00
❑ 23 Robert Kent	8.00	2.40
❑ 23R Robert Kent Red	10.00	3.00
❑ 24 Teddy Lehman	15.00	4.50
❑ 24R Teddy Lehman Red	20.00	6.00
❑ 25 Jared Lorenzen	12.00	3.60
❑ 25R Jared Lorenzen Red	20.00	6.00
❑ 26 Eli Manning	80.00	24.00
❑ 27 Luke McCown	15.00	4.50
❑ 28 Mewelde Moore	20.00	6.00
❑ 29 John Navarre	15.00	4.50
❑ 29R John Navarre Red	20.00	6.00
❑ 30 James Newson	12.00	3.60
❑ 31 Tony Pape	12.00	3.60
❑ 31R Tony Pape Red	15.00	4.50
❑ 32 Jarrett Payton	15.00	4.50
❑ 33 Chris Perry	25.00	7.50
❑ 34 Cody Pickett	15.00	4.50
❑ 35 Philip Rivers	50.00	15.00
❑ 35R Philip Rivers Red	60.00	18.00
❑ 36 Ben Roethlisberger SP	150.00	45.00
❑ 37 P.K. Sam	12.00	3.60
❑ 38 Matt Schaub	25.00	7.50
❑ 38R Matt Schaub Red	30.00	9.00
❑ 39 Justin Smiley	15.00	4.50
❑ 40 Keith Smith	12.00	3.60
❑ 40R Keith Smith Red	15.00	4.50
❑ 41 Will Smith	15.00	4.50
❑ 41R Will Smith Red	20.00	6.00
❑ 42 Jeff Smoker	20.00	6.00
❑ 42R Jeff Smoker Red	25.00	7.50
❑ 43 Derrick Strait	15.00	4.50
❑ 44 Andrae Thurman	8.00	2.40
❑ 44R Andrae Thurman Red	10.00	3.00
❑ 45 Ben Troupe	15.00	4.50
❑ 45R Ben Troupe Red	15.00	4.50
❑ 46 Michael Turner	12.00	3.60
❑ 47 Jonathan Vilma	15.00	4.50
❑ 47R Jonathan Vilma Red	20.00	6.00
❑ 48 Ben Watson	15.00	4.50
❑ 49 Darius Watts	20.00	6.00
❑ 49R Darius Watts Red	25.00	7.50
❑ 50 Vince Wilfork	20.00	6.00
❑ 51 D.J. Williams	20.00	6.00
❑ 51R D.J. Williams Red	20.00	6.00
❑ 52 Mike Williams	150.00	45.00
❑ 53 Quincy Wilson	12.00	3.60
❑ 53R Quincy Wilson Red	20.00	6.00
❑ 54 Kellen Winslow	50.00	15.00
❑ 54R Kellen Winslow Red	60.00	18.00
❑ 55 Rashaun Woods	20.00	6.00
❑ 56 Jason Wright	8.00	2.40

2004 Press Pass Autographs Blue

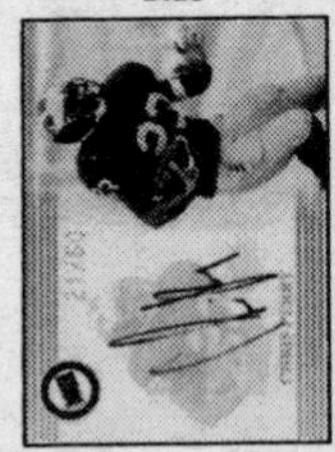

	Nm-Mt	Ex-Mt
*BLUES: .6X TO 1.5X BRONZE AUTOS		
STATED PRINT RUN 50 SER.#'d SETS		
BLUES WERE INSERTED IN PRESS PASS SE		
❑ 2R Casey Clausen Red	50.00	15.00
❑ 4R Cedric Cobbs Red	50.00	15.00

❑ 5R Ricardo Colclough Red	40.00	12.00
❑ 9 Larry Fitzgerald/25	120.00	36.00
❑ 12R DeAngelo Hall Red	50.00	15.00
❑ 19R Julius Jones Red	120.00	36.00
❑ 20 Kevin Jones	100.00	30.00
❑ 27R Luke McCown Red	40.00	12.00
❑ 34R Cody Pickett Red	40.00	12.00
❑ 36R Ben Roethlisberger Red	300.00	90.00
❑ 41R Will Smith Red	40.00	12.00
❑ 49R Darius Watts Red	50.00	15.00

2004 Press Pass Autographs Gold

	Nm-Mt	Ex-Mt
*GOLDS: .6X TO 1.5X BRONZE AUTOS		
STATED PRINT RUN 100 SER.#'d SETS		
❑ 2R Casey Clausen Red	40.00	12.00
❑ 4R Cedric Cobbs Red	40.00	12.00
❑ 9 Larry Fitzgerald/50		
❑ 12R DeAngelo Hall Red	40.00	12.00
❑ 16 Steven Jackson	60.00	18.00
❑ 19R Julius Jones Red	120.00	36.00
❑ 20 Kevin Jones	60.00	18.00
❑ 26 Eli Manning	120.00	36.00
❑ 26R Eli Manning Red	150.00	45.00
❑ 33R Chris Perry Red	50.00	15.00
❑ 35 Philip Rivers	80.00	24.00
❑ 36 Ben Roethlisberger	200.00	60.00
❑ 36R Ben Roethlisberger Red	225.00	70.00
❑ 40R Keith Smith Red	25.00	7.50
❑ 46R Michael Turner Red	25.00	7.50
❑ 47 Jonathan Vilma	25.00	7.50
❑ 49R Darius Watts Red	40.00	12.00
❑ 50R Vince Wilfork Red	40.00	12.00
❑ 51R D.J. Williams Red	30.00	9.00

2004 Press Pass Autographs Silver

	Nm-Mt	Ex-Mt
*SILVERS: .5X TO 1.2X BRONZE AUTOS		
STATED PRINT RUN 200 SER.#'d SETS		
❑ 2R Casey Clausen Red	30.00	9.00
❑ 5R Ricardo Colclough Red	25.00	7.50
❑ 9 Larry Fitzgerald/75	80.00	24.00
❑ 12R DeAngelo Hall Red	30.00	9.00
❑ 13R Tommie Harris Red	30.00	9.00
❑ 16 Steven Jackson/100	60.00	18.00
❑ 16R Steven Jackson/100 Red	80.00	24.00
❑ 20 Kevin Jones	50.00	15.00
❑ 26 Eli Manning	100.00	30.00
❑ 27R Luke McCown Red	25.00	7.50
❑ 34R Cody Pickett Red	25.00	7.50
❑ 35 Philip Rivers	60.00	18.00
❑ 36 Ben Roethlisberger	150.00	45.00
❑ 38R Matt Schaub Red	40.00	12.00
❑ 47 Jonathan Vilma	20.00	6.00
❑ 53R Quincy Wilson Red	25.00	7.50

2004 Press Pass Big Numbers

	Nm-Mt	Ex-Mt
COMPLETE SET (33)	30.00	9.00
ONE PER PACK		
*COLLECTOR SERIES: .3X TO .8X BASIC INSERTS		
❑ BN1 Casey Clausen	1.50	.45
❑ BN2 Michael Clayton	3.00	.90
❑ BN3 Cedric Cobbs	1.25	.35
❑ BN4 Devard Darling	1.25	.35
❑ BN5 Lee Evans	2.00	.60
❑ BN6 Larry Fitzgerald	4.00	1.20
❑ BN7 Robert Gallery	2.00	.60
❑ BN8 DeAngelo Hall	1.50	.45
❑ BN9 Steven Jackson	4.00	1.20
❑ BN10 Michael Jenkins	1.25	.35
❑ BN11 Greg Jones	1.25	.35
❑ BN12 Kevin Jones	4.00	1.20
❑ BN13 Craig Krenzel	1.25	.35
❑ BN14 J.P. Losman	3.00	.90
❑ BN15 Eli Manning	6.00	1.80
❑ BN16 John Navarre	1.25	.35
❑ BN17 Jarrett Payton	1.25	.35
❑ BN18 Chris Perry	2.50	.75
❑ BN19 Cody Pickett	1.25	.35
❑ BN20 Philip Rivers	4.00	1.20
❑ BN21 Ben Roethlisberger	10.00	3.00
❑ BN22 Matt Schaub	2.00	.60
❑ BN23 Will Smith	1.25	.35
❑ BN24 Ben Troupe	1.25	.35
❑ BN25 Michael Turner	1.00	.30
❑ BN26 Jonathan Vilma	1.25	.35
❑ BN27 Vince Wilfork	1.50	.45
❑ BN28 Quincy Wilson	1.00	.30
❑ BN29 D.J. Williams	1.50	.45
❑ BN30 Mike Williams	8.00	2.40
❑ BN31 Roy Williams WR	4.00	1.20
❑ BN32 Rashaun Woods	1.50	.45
❑ BN33 Eli Manning CL	4.00	1.20

2004 Press Pass Game Used Jerseys Silver

	Nm-Mt	Ex-Mt
SILVER PRINT RUN 300 SER.#'d SETS		
*GOLDS: .6X TO 1.5X SILVER JERSEYS		

GOLD PRINT RUN 100 SER.#'d SETS		
*HOLOFOILS: 1X TO 2.5X SILVER JERSEYS		
HOLOFOIL PRINT RUN 50 SER.#'d SETS		
OVERALL JERSEY ODDS 1:72 H		
❑ JCBR Ben Roethlisberger	60.00	18.00
❑ JCCP Cody Pickett	15.00	4.50
❑ JCDD Devard Darling	15.00	4.50
❑ JCDW Darius Watts	20.00	6.00
❑ JCEM Eli Manning	40.00	12.00
❑ JCJG Jermaine Green	12.00	3.60
❑ JCJL Jared Lorenzen	12.00	3.60
❑ JCJP Jarrett Payton	15.00	4.50
❑ JCLM Luke McCown	15.00	4.50
❑ JCMM Mewelde Moore	20.00	6.00
❑ JCMS Matt Schaub	25.00	7.50
❑ JCSJ Steven Jackson	30.00	9.00

2004 Press Pass Paydirt

	Nm-Mt	Ex-Mt
COMPLETE SET (12)	30.00	9.00
STATED ODDS 1:6		
❑ PD1 Eli Manning	8.00	2.40
❑ PD2 Roy Williams WR	5.00	1.50
❑ PD3 Kevin Jones	5.00	1.50
❑ PD4 Philip Rivers	5.00	1.50
❑ PD5 Rashaun Woods	2.00	.60
❑ PD6 Ben Roethlisberger	12.00	3.60
❑ PD7 Ben Troupe	1.50	.45
❑ PD8 Steven Jackson	5.00	1.50
❑ PD9 Michael Clayton	4.00	1.20
❑ PD10 Chris Perry	3.00	.90
❑ PD11 Larry Fitzgerald	5.00	1.50
❑ PD12 Greg Jones	1.50	.45

2004 Press Pass Showbound

	Nm-Mt	Ex-Mt
COMPLETE SET (9)	30.00	9.00
STATED ODDS 1:12		
❑ SB1 Steven Jackson	6.00	1.80
❑ SB2 Larry Fitzgerald	6.00	1.80
❑ SB3 Eli Manning	10.00	3.00
❑ SB4 Kevin Jones	6.00	1.80
❑ SB5 Roy Williams WR	6.00	1.80
❑ SB6 Ben Roethlisberger	15.00	4.50
❑ SB7 Philip Rivers	6.00	1.80
❑ SB8 Chris Perry	4.00	1.20
❑ SB9 J.P. Losman	5.00	1.50

2005 Press Pass

	Nm-Mt	Ex-Mt
COMPLETE SET (50)	50.00	15.00
COMP.SET w/o PP'S (45)	30.00	9.00

POWER PICK STATED ODDS 1:14 H/R
UNPRICED HOBBY SOLO PRINT RUN 1 SET

Card	Nm-Mt	Ex-Mt
❑ 1 Derek Anderson	1.00	.30
❑ 2 Brock Berlin	1.00	.30
❑ 3 Charlie Frye	1.50	.45
❑ 4 Gino Guidugli	.75	.23
❑ 5 David Greene	1.25	.35
❑ 6 Stefan LeFors	1.25	.35
❑ 7 Dan Orlovsky	1.25	.35
❑ 8 Kyle Orton	1.50	.45
❑ 9 Aaron Rodgers	4.00	1.20
❑ 10 Alex Smith QB	5.00	1.50
❑ 11 Andrew Walter	1.50	.45
❑ 12 Jason White	1.50	.45
❑ 13 J.J. Arrington	1.25	.35
❑ 14 Ronnie Brown	3.00	.90
❑ 15 Anthony Davis	1.00	.30
❑ 16 Kay-Jay Harris	.75	.23
❑ 17 T.A. McLendon	.75	.23
❑ 18 Ryan Moats	1.00	.30
❑ 19 Vernand Morency	1.00	.30
❑ 20 Carnell Williams	3.00	.90
❑ 21 Mark Bradley	1.25	.35
❑ 22 Reggie Brown	1.25	.35
❑ 23 Mark Clayton	1.50	.45
❑ 24 Braylon Edwards	3.00	.90
❑ 25 Fred Gibson	1.25	.35
❑ 26 Terrence Murphy	1.00	.30
❑ 27 J.R. Russell	.75	.23
❑ 28 Craphonso Thorpe	1.00	.30
❑ 29 Roddy White	1.00	.30
❑ 30 Mike Williams	3.00	.90
❑ 31 Troy Williamson	2.00	.60
❑ 32 Heath Miller	1.50	.45
❑ 33 Alex Smith TE	1.00	.30
❑ 34 Khalif Barnes	.75	.23
❑ 35 Jammal Brown	1.00	.30
❑ 36 Brandon Browner	.50	.15
❑ 37 Marlin Jackson	1.00	.30
❑ 38 Carlos Rogers	1.25	.35
❑ 39 Antrel Rolle	1.25	.35
❑ 40 Dan Cody	1.25	.35
❑ 41 Erasmus James	1.25	.35
❑ 42 David Pollack	1.50	.45
❑ 43 Anttaj Hawthorne	.75	.23
❑ 44 Derrick Johnson	1.50	.45
❑ 45 Ronnie Brown CL	1.50	.45
❑ 46 Carnell Williams PP	6.00	1.80
❑ 47 Aaron Rodgers PP	8.00	2.40
❑ 48 Alex Smith QB PP	10.00	3.00
❑ 49 Braylon Edwards PP	6.00	1.80
❑ 50 Mike Williams PP	6.00	1.80

2005 Press Pass Blue

	Nm-Mt	Ex-Mt
COMPLETE SET (45)	60.00	18.00

*SINGLES: .8X TO 2X BASIC CARDS
ONE PER RETAIL PACK

2005 Press Pass Reflectors

	Nm-Mt	Ex-Mt

*SINGLES: 2.5X TO 6X BASIC CARDS
STATED PRINT RUN 500 SER.#'d SETS

2005 Press Pass Reflectors Proof

	Nm-Mt	Ex-Mt

*SINGLES: 5X TO 12X BASIC CARDS
REFLECTORS/100 INSERTS IN HOBBY ONLY

2005 Press Pass Autograph Power Picks

Card	Nm-Mt	Ex-Mt
❑ 1 Ronnie Brown/100	100.00	30.00
❑ 1R Ronnie Brown/24* Red	150.00	45.00
❑ 2 Braylon Edwards/50		
❑ 2R Braylon Edwards/10* Red		
❑ 3 Charlie Frye/250	30.00	9.00
❑ 3R Charlie Frye/10* Red		
❑ 4 Heath Miller/50	100.00	30.00
❑ 4R Heath Miller/10* Red		
❑ 5 Aaron Rodgers/250	80.00	24.00
❑ 5R Aaron Rodgers/4* Red		
❑ 6 Andrew Walter/250	30.00	9.00
❑ 6R Andrew Walter/10* Red		
❑ 7 Mike Williams/100	100.00	30.00
❑ 7R Mike Williams/41* Red	120.00	36.00
❑ 8 Troy Williamson/250	40.00	12.00

2005 Press Pass Autographs Bronze

	Nm-Mt	Ex-Mt

AUTO OVERALL ODDS 1:7
*RED INK: .5X TO 1.2X

Card	Nm-Mt	Ex-Mt
❑ 1 Derek Anderson	15.00	4.50
❑ 1R Derek Anderson/50* Red	20.00	6.00
❑ 2 J.J. Arrington	20.00	6.00
❑ 3 Marion Barber	15.00	4.50
❑ 3R Marion Barber/20* Red		
❑ 4 Khalif Barnes	12.00	3.60
❑ 5 Brock Berlin	15.00	4.50
❑ 5R Brock Berlin/50* Red		
❑ 6 Mark Bradley	20.00	6.00
❑ 6R Mark Bradley/11* Red		
❑ 7 Elton Brown	10.00	3.00
❑ 7R Elton Brown/17* Red		
❑ 8 Jammal Brown	15.00	4.50
❑ 8R Jammal Brown/43* Red		
❑ 9 Reggie Brown	20.00	6.00
❑ 9R Reggie Brown/50* Red	25.00	7.50
❑ 10 Ronnie Brown SP	60.00	18.00
❑ 10R Ronnie Brown/10* Red		
❑ 11 Brandon Browner	10.00	3.00
❑ 11R Brandon Browner/25* Red		
❑ 12 Luis Castillo	12.00	3.60
❑ 12R Luis Castillo/9* Red		
❑ 13 Mark Clayton	25.00	7.50
❑ 13R Mark Clayton/50* Red		
❑ 14 Dan Cody	20.00	6.00
❑ 14R Dan Cody/55* Red	25.00	7.50
❑ 15 Jerome Collins	12.00	3.60
❑ 15R Jerome Collins/49* Red		
❑ 16 Sean Considine	12.00	3.60
❑ 16R Sean Considine/45* Red		
❑ 17 Anthony Davis	15.00	4.50
❑ 17R Anthony Davis/7* Red		
❑ 18 Thomas Davis	15.00	4.50
❑ 18R Thomas Davis/277* Red	15.00	4.50
❑ 19 Braylon Edwards SP	125.00	38.00
❑ 20 Ciatrick Fason	20.00	6.00
❑ 20R Ciatrick Fason/12* Red		
❑ 21 Diamond Ferri	10.00	3.00
❑ 21R Diamond Ferri/65* Red	12.00	3.60
❑ 22 Charlie Frye SP	25.00	7.50
❑ 22R Charlie Frye/9* Red		
❑ 23 Fred Gibson	20.00	6.00
❑ 23R Fred Gibson/50* Red		
❑ 24 David Greene	20.00	6.00
❑ 24R David Greene/50* Red	25.00	7.50
❑ 25 Gino Guidugli	12.00	3.60
❑ 25R Gino Guidugli/199* Red	15.00	4.50
❑ 26 Kay-Jay Harris	12.00	3.60
❑ 27 Anttaj Hawthorne	12.00	3.60
❑ 27R Anttaj Hawthorne/25* Red	20.00	6.00
❑ 28 Chris Henry	20.00	6.00

❑ 28R Chris Henry/50* Red 25.00 7.50
❑ 29 Keron Henry 10.00 3.00
❑ 29R Keron Henry/33* Red
❑ 30 Noah Herron 12.00 3.60
❑ 30R Noah Herron/49* Red
❑ 31 Marlin Jackson 15.00 4.50
❑ 31R Marlin Jackson/50* Red 20.00 6.00
❑ 32 Erasmus James 20.00 6.00
❑ 32R Erasmus James/34* Red 30.00 9.00
❑ 33 Derrick Johnson 25.00 7.50
❑ 33R Derrick Johnson/50* Red 30.00 9.00
❑ 34 Stefan LeFors 20.00 6.00
❑ 34R Stefan LeFors/50* Red 25.00 7.50
❑ 35 T.A. McLendon 12.00 3.60
❑ 35R T.A. McLendon/2* Red
❑ 36 Heath Miller 35.00 10.50
❑ 36R Heath Miller/10* Red
❑ 37 Ryan Moats 15.00 4.50
❑ 37R Ryan Moats/194* Red 20.00 6.00
❑ 38 Vernand Morency 15.00 4.50
❑ 38R Vernand Morency/29* Red 25.00 7.50
❑ 39 Terrence Murphy 15.00 4.50
❑ 39R Terrence Murphy/27* Red
❑ 40 Dan Orlovsky 20.00 6.00
❑ 40R Dan Orlovsky/130* Red 25.00 7.50
❑ 41 Kyle Orton 25.00 7.50
❑ 41R Kyle Orton/50* Red 30.00 9.00
❑ 42 David Pollack 25.00 7.50
❑ 42R David Pollack/25* Red
❑ 43 Walter Reyes 12.00 3.60
❑ 43R Walter Reyes/50* Red 15.00 4.50
❑ 44 Aaron Rodgers SP 80.00 24.00
❑ 44R Aaron Rodgers/14* Red
❑ 45 Carlos Rogers 20.00 6.00
❑ 45R Carlos Rogers/45* Red
❑ 46 Antrel Rolle 20.00 6.00
❑ 46R Antrel Rolle/50* Red
❑ 47 J.R. Russell 10.00 3.00
❑ 47R J.R. Russell/34* Red
❑ 48 Barrett Ruud 20.00 6.00
❑ 48R Barrett Ruud/290* Red 25.00 7.50
❑ 49 Eric Shelton 15.00 4.50
❑ 49R Eric Shelton/50* Red 20.00 6.00
❑ 50 Alex Smith TE 15.00 4.50
❑ 50R Alex Smith TE/112* Red 20.00 6.00
❑ 51 Craphonso Thorpe 15.00 4.50
❑ 51R Craphonso Thorpe/100* Red
❑ 52 Andrew Walter 25.00 7.50
❑ 52R Andrew Walter/10* Red
❑ 53 Jason White 25.00 7.50
❑ 53R Jason White/266* Red 30.00 9.00
❑ 54 Roddy White 15.00 4.50
❑ 54R Roddy White/138* Red 20.00 6.00
❑ 55 Carnell Williams SP 60.00 18.00
❑ 55R Carnell Williams/10* Red
❑ 56 Mike Williams SP 100.00 30.00
❑ 57 Troy Williamson 30.00 9.00
❑ 57R Troy Williamson Red 40.00 12.00
❑ 58 Stanley Wilson 10.00 3.00
❑ 58R Stanley Wilson/49* Red

2005 Press Pass Autographs Blue

Nm-Mt Ex-Mt
*BLUE: .8X TO 2X BRONZE AUTOS
*BLUE: .6X TO 1.5X BRONZE SP AUTOS
BLUES WERE INSERTED IN PRESS PASS SE
BLUE PRINT RUN 50 SER.#'d SETS
*RED INK: .5X TO 1.2X

❑ 3R Marion Barber/25* Red
❑ 6R Mark Bradley/17* Red
❑ 7R Elton Brown/6* Red
❑ 10 Ronnie Brown/25 150.00 45.00
❑ 12R Luis Castillo/10* Red
❑ 19 Braylon Edwards/25 150.00 45.00
❑ 19R Braylon Edwards/5* Red
❑ 20R Ciatrick Fason/13* Red
❑ 22R Charlie Frye/10* Red
❑ 24R David Greene/1* Red
❑ 35R T.A. McLendon/17* Red
❑ 36R Heath Miller/6* Red
❑ 37R Ryan Moats/21* Red
❑ 44 Aaron Rodgers 120.00 36.00
❑ 47R J.R. Russell/5* Red
❑ 50R Alex Smith TE/12* Red

❑ 55 Carnell Williams/25 200.00 60.00
❑ 55R Carnell Williams/10* Red
❑ 56 Mike Williams/25 150.00 45.00
❑ 58R Stanley Wilson/5* Red

2005 Press Pass Autographs Gold

Nm-Mt Ex-Mt
*GOLD: .6X TO 1.5X BRONZE AUTOS
*GOLD: .5X TO 1.2X BRONZE SP AUTOS
GOLD HOBBY PRINT RUN 100 SER.#'d SETS
*RED INK: .5X TO 1.2X

❑ 2R J.J. Arrington/50* Red
❑ 3R Marion Barber/19* Red
❑ 7R Elton Brown/7* Red
❑ 10 Ronnie Brown/50 100.00 30.00
❑ 12R Luis Castillo/10* Red
❑ 14R Dan Cody/5* Red
❑ 19 Braylon Edwards/50 125.00 38.00
❑ 19R Braylon Edwards/10* Red
❑ 22R Charlie Frye/10* Red
❑ 24R David Greene/1* Red
❑ 27R Anttaj Hawthorne/11* Red
❑ 35R T.A. McLendon/12* Red
❑ 36R Heath Miller/8* Red
❑ 37R Ryan Moats/28* Red
❑ 44 Aaron Rodgers 100.00 30.00
❑ 44R Aaron Rodgers/5* Red
❑ 47R J.R. Russell/5* Red
❑ 55 Carnell Williams/50 120.00 36.00
❑ 55R Carnell Williams/10* Red
❑ 56 Mike Williams/50 120.00 36.00

2005 Press Pass Autographs Silver

Nm-Mt Ex-Mt
*SILVER: .5X TO 1.2X BRONZE AUTOS
SILVER PRINT RUN 200 SER.#'d SETS
*RED INK: .5X TO 1.2X

❑ 4R Khalif Barnes/50* Red
❑ 6R Mark Bradley/4* Red
❑ 8 Jammal Brown 20.00 6.00
❑ 10 Ronnie Brown/75 80.00 24.00
❑ 11 Brandon Browner 12.00 3.60
❑ 12R Luis Castillo/15* Red
❑ 13 Mark Clayton 30.00 9.00
❑ 14R Dan Cody/10* Red
❑ 17R Anthony Davis/6* Red
❑ 19 Braylon Edwards/100 100.00 30.00
❑ 19R Braylon Edwards/19* Red
❑ 20R Ciatrick Fason/11* Red
❑ 21R Diamond Ferri/22* Red
❑ 22 Charlie Frye 25.00 7.50
❑ 22R Charlie Frye/10* Red
❑ 24R David Greene/4* Red
❑ 27R Anttaj Hawthorne/15* Red
❑ 32 Erasmus James 25.00 7.50
❑ 35R T.A. McLendon/19* Red
❑ 36R Heath Miller/10* Red
❑ 37R Ryan Moats/22* Red
❑ 44 Aaron Rodgers 80.00 24.00
❑ 44R Aaron Rodgers/14* Red
❑ 45 Carlos Rogers 25.00 7.50
❑ 47R J.R. Russell/5* Red
❑ 50R Alex Smith TE/13* Red
❑ 52R Andrew Walter/10* Red

❑ 55 Carnell Williams/100 100.00 30.00
❑ 55R Carnell Williams/10* Red
❑ 56 Mike Williams/75 125.00 38.00

2005 Press Pass Big Numbers

Nm-Mt Ex-Mt
COMPLETE SET (25) 30.00 9.00
ONE PER PACK

❑ BN1 Reggie Brown 1.50 .45
❑ BN2 Ronnie Brown 4.00 1.20
❑ BN3 Mark Clayton 2.00 .60
❑ BN4 Dan Cody 1.50 .45
❑ BN5 Anthony Davis 1.25 .35
❑ BN6 Braylon Edwards 4.00 1.20
❑ BN7 Charlie Frye 2.00 .60
❑ BN8 Fred Gibson 1.50 .45
❑ BN9 David Greene 1.50 .45
❑ BN10 Gino Guidugli 1.00 .30
❑ BN11 Derrick Johnson 2.00 .60
❑ BN12 T.A. McLendon 1.00 .30
❑ BN13 Heath Miller 2.00 .60
❑ BN14 Vernand Morency 1.25 .35
❑ BN15 Dan Orlovsky 1.50 .45
❑ BN16 Kyle Orton 2.00 .60
❑ BN17 Aaron Rodgers 5.00 1.50
❑ BN18 J.R. Russell 1.00 .30
❑ BN19 Alex Smith QB 6.00 1.80
❑ BN20 Andrew Walter 2.00 .60
❑ BN21 Jason White 2.00 .60
❑ BN22 Carnell Williams 4.00 1.20
❑ BN23 Mike Williams 4.00 1.20
❑ BN24 Troy Williamson 2.50 .75
❑ BN25 Aaron Rodgers CL 2.50 .75

2005 Press Pass Game Used Jerseys Silver

Nm-Mt Ex-Mt
OVERALL JERSEY ODDS 1:72H, 1:280R
SILVER PRINT RUN 300 SER.#'d SETS
*GOLD: .5X TO 1.2X SILVER JSYs
GOLD PRINT RUN 125 SER.#'d SETS
*HOLOFOIL: .8X TO 2X SILVER JSYs
HOLOFOIL PRINT RUN 50 SER.#'d SETS

❑ JCAS Alex Smith TE 12.00 3.60
❑ JCCT Craphonso Thorpe 12.00 3.60
❑ JCDO Dan Orlovsky 15.00 4.50
❑ JCJC Jerome Collins 12.00 3.60
❑ JCJW Jason White 20.00 6.00

❑ JCKO Kyle Orton	20.00	6.00
❑ JCMB Mark Bradley	15.00	4.50
❑ JCMJ Marlin Jackson	15.00	4.50
❑ JCRW Roddy White	15.00	4.50
❑ JCSL Stefan LeFors	20.00	6.00
❑ JCTM Terrence Murphy	12.00	3.60

2005 Press Pass Paydirt

	Nm-Mt	Ex-Mt
COMPLETE SET (12)	30.00	9.00
STATED ODDS 1:6 H/R		
❑ PD1 Carnell Williams	6.00	1.80
❑ PD2 Charlie Frye	3.00	.90
❑ PD3 Mike Williams	6.00	1.80
❑ PD4 Braylon Edwards	6.00	1.80
❑ PD5 Alex Smith QB	10.00	3.00
❑ PD6 Dan Orlovsky	2.50	.75
❑ PD7 Andrew Walter	3.00	.90
❑ PD8 Ronnie Brown	6.00	1.80
❑ PD9 Heath Miller	3.00	.90
❑ PD10 Troy Williamson	4.00	1.20
❑ PD11 Aaron Rodgers	8.00	2.40
❑ PD12 Mark Clayton	3.00	.90

2005 Press Pass Showbound

	Nm-Mt	Ex-Mt
COMPLETE SET (9)	30.00	9.00
STATED ODDS 1:12 H/R		
❑ SB1 Alex Smith QB	10.00	3.00
❑ SB2 Ronnie Brown	6.00	1.80
❑ SB3 Aaron Rodgers	8.00	2.40
❑ SB4 Carnell Williams	6.00	1.80
❑ SB5 Heath Miller	3.00	.90
❑ SB6 Braylon Edwards	6.00	1.80
❑ SB7 Mark Clayton	3.00	.90
❑ SB8 Mike Williams	6.00	1.80
❑ SB9 Troy Williamson	4.00	1.20

2002 Press Pass JE

	Nm-Mt	Ex-Mt
COMPLETE SET (45)	25.00	7.50
❑ 1 David Carr	4.00	1.20
❑ 2 Julius Peppers	2.00	.60
❑ 3 Joey Harrington	4.00	1.20
❑ 4 Mike Williams	.75	.23
❑ 5 Quentin Jammer	1.00	.30
❑ 6 Ryan Sims	1.00	.30
❑ 7 Bryant McKinnie	.75	.23
❑ 8 Roy Williams	2.50	.75

❑ 9 John Henderson	1.00	.30
❑ 10 Wendell Bryant	1.00	.30
❑ 11 Donte Stallworth	2.00	.60
❑ 12 Jeremy Shockey	4.00	1.20
❑ 13 William Green	2.00	.60
❑ 14 Phillip Buchanon	1.00	.30
❑ 15 T.J. Duckett	2.00	.60
❑ 16 Ashley Lelie	2.00	.60
❑ 17 Javon Walker	2.00	.60
❑ 18 Daniel Graham	1.00	.30
❑ 19 Jerramy Stevens	1.00	.30
❑ 20 Patrick Ramsey	2.00	.60
❑ 21 Jabar Gaffney	1.00	.30
❑ 22 DeShaun Foster	1.00	.30
❑ 23 Kalimba Edwards	1.00	.30
❑ 24 Josh Reed	1.00	.30
❑ 25 Mike Pearson	.50	.15
❑ 26 Andre Davis	1.00	.30
❑ 27 Reche Caldwell	1.00	.30
❑ 28 Clinton Portis	4.00	1.20
❑ 29 Maurice Morris	1.00	.30
❑ 30 Ladell Betts	1.00	.30
❑ 31 Antwaan Randle El	1.25	.35
❑ 32 Antonio Bryant	1.00	.30
❑ 33 Josh McCown	1.25	.35
❑ 34 Lamar Gordon	1.00	.30
❑ 35 Marquise Walker	.75	.23
❑ 36 Cliff Russell	.75	.23
❑ 37 Brian Westbrook	2.00	.60
❑ 38 Eric Crouch	1.50	.45
❑ 39 Jonathan Wells	1.00	.30
❑ 40 David Garrard	1.00	.30
❑ 41 Rohan Davey	1.00	.30
❑ 42 Ron Johnson	.75	.23
❑ 43 Kurt Kittner	.75	.23
❑ 44 Adrian Peterson	1.00	.30
❑ 45 David Carr CL	1.50	.45

2002 Press Pass JE Autographs

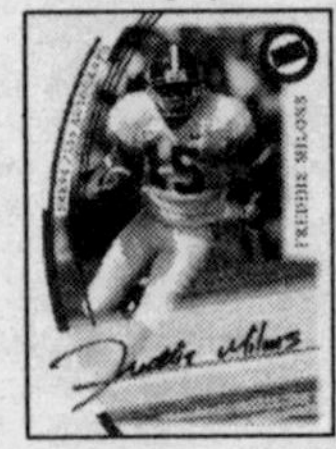

	Nm-Mt	Ex-Mt
*SILVER AU's: .8X TO 2X BASIC AUTOS		
❑ 1 Damien Anderson	8.00	2.40
❑ 2 Antonio Bryant	12.00	3.60
❑ 3 Phillip Buchanon	12.00	3.60
❑ 4 Reche Caldwell	12.00	3.60
❑ 5 Rocky Calmus	12.00	3.60
❑ 6 David Carr	50.00	15.00
❑ 7 Terry Charles	8.00	2.40
❑ 8 Eric Crouch	20.00	6.00
❑ 9 Najeh Davenport	12.00	3.60
❑ 10 Rohan Davey	12.00	3.60
❑ 11 Andre Davis	12.00	3.60
❑ 12 Kalimba Edwards	10.00	3.00
❑ 13 Jabar Gaffney	12.00	3.60
❑ 14 David Garrard	12.00	3.60
❑ 15 Lamar Gordon	12.00	3.60
❑ 16 Daniel Graham	12.00	3.60
❑ 17 William Green	20.00	6.00
❑ 18 Joey Harrington	50.00	15.00
❑ 19 John Henderson	12.00	3.60
❑ 20 Leonard Henry	10.00	3.00
❑ 21 Quentin Jammer	12.00	3.60
❑ 22 Ron Johnson	10.00	3.00
❑ 23 Kyle Johnson	8.00	2.40
❑ 24 Levi Jones	8.00	2.40
❑ 25 Kurt Kittner	10.00	3.00
❑ 26 Josh McCown	15.00	4.50
❑ 27 Freddie Milons	10.00	3.00
❑ 28 Maurice Morris	12.00	3.60
❑ 29 Mike Pearson	8.00	2.40
❑ 30 Adrian Peterson	12.00	3.60
❑ 31 Patrick Ramsey	20.00	6.00
❑ 32 Antwaan Randle El	15.00	4.50
❑ 33 Josh Reed	12.00	3.60
❑ 34 Cliff Russell	10.00	3.00
❑ 35 Josh Scobey	12.00	3.60
❑ 36 Ryan Sims	12.00	3.60
❑ 37 Luke Staley	10.00	3.00
❑ 38 Donte Stallworth	20.00	6.00
❑ 39 Marquise Walker	10.00	3.00
❑ 40 Anthony Weaver	10.00	3.00
❑ 41 Jonathan Wells	12.00	3.60
❑ 42 Brian Westbrook	20.00	6.00
❑ 43 Roy Williams	30.00	9.00

2002 Press Pass JE Class of 2002 Autographs

	Nm-Mt	Ex-Mt
❑ AB Antonio Bryant		
❑ AD Andre Davis	12.00	3.60
❑ DC David Carr	50.00	15.00
❑ DS Donte Stallworth	25.00	7.50
❑ JH Joey Harrington	50.00	15.00
❑ JR Josh Reed	12.00	3.60
❑ KK Kurt Kittner	12.00	3.60
❑ WG William Green	20.00	6.00

2003 Press Pass JE

	Nm-Mt	Ex-Mt
COMPLETE SET (45)	25.00	7.50
❑ 1 Boss Bailey	1.25	.35
❑ 2 Brad Banks	.75	.23
❑ 3 Anquan Boldin	2.50	.75
❑ 4 Kyle Boller	2.50	.75
❑ 5 Chris Brown	2.00	.60
❑ 6 Avon Cobourne	.50	.15
❑ 7 Ken Dorsey	1.50	.45
❑ 8 Justin Fargas	1.00	.30
❑ 9 Talman Gardner	1.00	.30
❑ 10 Jason Gesser	1.00	.30
❑ 11 Earnest Graham	.75	.23
❑ 12 Jordon Gross	.75	.23
❑ 13 Rex Grossman	2.50	.75
❑ 14 Kwame Harris	.75	.23

❑ 15 Taylor Jacobs	1.00	.30
❑ 16 Larry Johnson	1.50	.45
❑ 17 Bryant Johnson	1.00	.30
❑ 18 Andre Johnson	2.50	.75
❑ 19 Teyo Johnson	1.00	.30
❑ 20 William Joseph	1.00	.30
❑ 21 Bennie Joppru	1.00	.30
❑ 22 Jimmy Kennedy	1.00	.30
❑ 23 Kliff Kingsbury	.75	.23
❑ 24 Byron Leftwich	4.00	1.20
❑ 25 Brandon Lloyd	1.25	.35
❑ 26 Jerome McDougle	1.00	.30
❑ 27 Willis McGahee	2.50	.75
❑ 28 Terence Newman	2.00	.60
❑ 29 Carson Palmer	3.00	.90
❑ 30 Terry Pierce	.75	.23
❑ 31 Dave Ragone	1.00	.30
❑ 32 DeWayne Robertson	1.00	.30
❑ 33 Charles Rogers	1.25	.35
❑ 34 Chris Simms	2.00	.60
❑ 35 Musa Smith	1.00	.30
❑ 36 Onterrio Smith	1.25	.35
❑ 37 Brian St.Pierre	1.00	.30
❑ 38 Lee Suggs	2.00	.60
❑ 39 Terrell Suggs	1.50	.45
❑ 40 Marcus Trufant	1.00	.30
❑ 41 Seneca Wallace	1.00	.30
❑ 42 Kelley Washington	1.00	.30
❑ 43 Jason Witten	1.50	.45
❑ 44 Andre Woolfolk	1.00	.30
❑ 45 Byron Leftwich CL	2.00	.60

2003 Press Pass JE Class of 2003 Autographs

	Nm-Mt	Ex-Mt
❑ 1 Brad Banks	12.00	3.60
❑ 2 Anquan Boldin	40.00	12.00
❑ 3 Kyle Boller	50.00	15.00
❑ 4 Chris Brown	30.00	9.00
❑ 5 Justin Fargas	20.00	6.00
❑ 6 Taylor Jacobs	15.00	4.50
❑ 7 Byron Leftwich	60.00	18.00
❑ 8 Carson Palmer	50.00	15.00
❑ 9 Dave Ragone	20.00	6.00

2003 Press Pass JE Game Used Jerseys Autographs

	Nm-Mt	Ex-Mt
❑ AJCAW Andre Woolfolk		
❑ AJCBJ Bennie Joppru		
❑ AJCBL Byron Leftwich	150.00	45.00
❑ AJCCP Carson Palmer	150.00	45.00
❑ AJCTJ Teyo Johnson		

2003 Press Pass JE Game Used Jerseys Gold

	Nm-Mt	Ex-Mt
❑ JCAC Avon Cobourne/575	15.00	4.50
❑ JCAW Andre Woolfolk/575	20.00	6.00
❑ JCBL1 Brandon Lloyd/575	12.00	3.60
❑ JCDD Dahrran Diedrick/575	15.00	4.50
❑ JCJM Jerome McDougle/575	20.00	6.00
❑ JCJW Jason Witten/450	30.00	9.00

2003 Press Pass JE Game Used Jerseys Holofoil

*NAMES: .8X TO 2X HOLOFOILS
NAMES PRINT RUN 25 SER.#'d SETS

	Nm-Mt	Ex-Mt
❑ JCAC Avon Cobourne/150	25.00	7.50
❑ JCAW Andre Woolfolk/150	30.00	9.00
❑ JCBJ Bennie Joppru/125	25.00	7.50
❑ JCBL Byron Leftwich/100	100.00	30.00
❑ JCBL1 Brandon Lloyd/150	20.00	6.00
❑ JCCP Carson Palmer/100	60.00	18.00
❑ JCDD Dahrran Diedrick/150	25.00	7.50
❑ JCEG Earnest Graham/100	30.00	9.00
❑ JCJM Jerome McDougle/150	20.00	6.00
❑ JCJW Jason Witten/150	50.00	15.00
❑ JCKD Ken Dorsey/125	40.00	12.00
❑ JCKK Kareem Kelly/125	20.00	6.00
❑ JCSW Seneca Wallace/125	15.00	4.50
❑ JCTJ Teyo Johnson/100	25.00	7.50

2003 Press Pass JE Game Used Jerseys Silver

	Nm-Mt	Ex-Mt
❑ JCAC Avon Cobourne/375	20.00	6.00
❑ JCAW Andre Woolfolk/375	25.00	7.50
❑ JCBJ Bennie Joppru/250	20.00	6.00
❑ JCBL Byron Leftwich/250	50.00	15.00
❑ JCBL1 Brandon Lloyd/375	15.00	4.50
❑ JCCP Carson Palmer/200	30.00	9.00
❑ JCDD Dahrran Diedrick/375	20.00	6.00
❑ JCEG Earnest Graham/250	25.00	7.50
❑ JCJM Jerome McDougle/375	25.00	7.50
❑ JCJW Jason Witten/375	40.00	12.00

❑ JCKD Ken Dorsey/250	30.00	9.00
❑ JCKK Kareem Kelly/250	15.00	4.50
❑ JCSW Seneca Wallace/250	12.00	3.60
❑ JCTJ Teyo Johnson/250	20.00	6.00

2001 Press Pass SE

	Nm-Mt	Ex-Mt
COMPLETE SET (45)	40.00	18.00
❑ 1 Michael Vick	6.00	2.70
❑ 2 Drew Brees	1.50	.70
❑ 3 Quincy Carter	.75	.35
❑ 4 Marques Tuiasosopo	.75	.35
❑ 5 Chris Weinke	.75	.35
❑ 6 Sage Rosenfels	1.00	.45
❑ 7 Jesse Palmer	.75	.35
❑ 8 Mike McMahon	.75	.35
❑ 9 Josh Booty	.75	.35
❑ 10 Josh Heupel	.75	.35
❑ 11 LaDainian Tomlinson	3.00	1.35
❑ 12 Deuce McAllister	2.00	.90
❑ 13 Michael Bennett	1.50	.70
❑ 14 Anthony Thomas	1.50	.70
❑ 15 LaMont Jordan	1.00	.45
❑ 16 Travis Henry	1.25	.55
❑ 17 James Jackson	.75	.35
❑ 18 Kevan Barlow	.75	.35
❑ 19 Travis Minor	.60	.25
❑ 20 Rudi Johnson	1.50	.70
❑ 21 David Terrell	.75	.35
❑ 22 Koren Robinson	1.25	.55
❑ 23 Rod Gardner	.75	.35
❑ 24 Santana Moss	1.50	.70
❑ 25 Freddie Mitchell	.75	.35
❑ 26 Reggie Wayne	1.50	.70
❑ 27 Quincy Morgan	.75	.35
❑ 28 Chris Chambers	1.25	.55
❑ 29 Robert Ferguson	.75	.35
❑ 30 Chad Johnson	1.50	.70
❑ 31 Snoop Minnis	.60	.25
❑ 32 Todd Heap	.75	.35
❑ 33 Steve Hutchinson	.60	.25
❑ 34 Leonard Davis	.60	.25
❑ 35 Kenyatta Walker	.40	.18
❑ 36 Justin Smith	.75	.35
❑ 37 Andre Carter	.75	.35
❑ 38 Jamal Reynolds	.75	.35
❑ 39 Gerard Warren	.75	.35
❑ 40 Richard Seymour	.75	.35
❑ 41 Damione Lewis	.60	.25
❑ 42 Jamar Fletcher	.60	.25

❑ 43 Nate Clements	.75	.35
❑ 44 Derrick Gibson	.60	.25
❑ 45 David Terrell CL	.60	.25

2001 Press Pass SE Autographs Bronze

	Nm-Mt	Ex-Mt

*SILVERS: .6X TO 1.5X BRONZE AUTOS
SILVER STATED PRINT RUN 250 SER.#'d SETS

❑ 1 Dan Alexander	8.00	2.40
❑ 2 Brian Allen	5.00	1.50
❑ 3 Jeff Backus	6.00	1.80
❑ 4 Kevan Barlow	8.00	3.60
❑ 5 Michael Bennett	20.00	9.00
❑ 6 Josh Booty	8.00	3.60
❑ 7 Drew Brees	20.00	9.00
❑ 8 Chris Chambers	12.00	5.50
❑ 9 Ennis Davis	5.00	1.50
❑ 10 Rod Gardner	8.00	3.60
❑ 11 Todd Heap	8.00	3.60
❑ 12 Travis Henry	12.00	5.50
❑ 13 Josh Heupel	8.00	3.60
❑ 14 Jabari Holloway	6.00	2.70
❑ 15 Willie Howard	6.00	1.80
❑ 16 Steve Hutchinson	6.00	2.70
❑ 17 James Jackson	8.00	3.60
❑ 18 Chad Johnson	20.00	9.00
❑ 19 Rudi Johnson	20.00	9.00
❑ 20 LaMont Jordan	15.00	6.75
❑ 21 Ben Leard	6.00	1.80
❑ 22 Deuce McAllister	20.00	9.00
❑ 23 Mike McMahon	8.00	3.60
❑ 24 Snoop Minnis	6.00	2.70
❑ 25 Travis Minor	6.00	2.70
❑ 26 Freddie Mitchell	8.00	3.60
❑ 27 Quincy Morgan	8.00	3.60
❑ 28 Santana Moss	15.00	6.75
❑ 29 Bobby Newcombe	6.00	2.70
❑ 30 Moran Norris	5.00	1.50
❑ 31 Jesse Palmer	8.00	2.40
❑ 32 Tommy Polley	8.00	2.40
❑ 33 Dominic Raiola	6.00	1.80
❑ 34 Ken-Yon Rambo	6.00	2.70
❑ 35 Jamal Reynolds	8.00	3.60
❑ 36 Koren Robinson	10.00	4.50
❑ 37 Shaun Rogers	8.00	2.40
❑ 38 Sage Rosenfels	8.00	3.60
❑ 39 Richard Seymour	20.00	9.00
❑ 40 Justin Smith	8.00	3.60
❑ 41 David Terrell	12.00	5.50
❑ 42 Anthony Thomas	15.00	6.75
❑ 43 LaDainian Tomlinson	30.00	13.50
❑ 44 Marques Tuiasosopo	8.00	3.60
❑ 46 Kenyatta Walker	5.00	2.20
❑ 47 Chad Ward	5.00	2.20
❑ 48 Gerard Warren	8.00	3.60
❑ 49 Reggie Wayne	15.00	6.75
❑ 50 Chris Weinke	8.00	3.60
❑ 51 Maurice Williams	5.00	1.50
❑ 52 Jamie Winborn	6.00	1.80

2001 Press Pass SE Autographs Silver

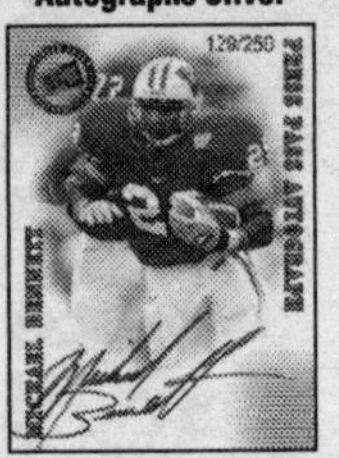

	Nm-Mt	Ex-Mt

*SILVERS: .6X TO 1.5X BRONZE AUTOS
STATED PRINT RUN 250 SERIAL #'d SETS
*BLUES: .8X TO 2X SILVER AUTOS
BLUE PRINT RUN 25 SER.#'d SETS

❑ 45 Michael Vick	100.00	45.00

2001 Press Pass SE Class of 2001 Autographs

	Nm-Mt	Ex-Mt
❑ 1 Michael Bennett	25.00	11.00
❑ 2 Drew Brees	30.00	13.50
❑ 3 Chris Chambers	30.00	9.00
❑ 4 Chad Johnson	25.00	7.50
❑ 5 Deuce McAllister EXCH		
❑ 6 Freddie Mitchell	15.00	6.75
❑ 7 Santana Moss	30.00	13.50
❑ 8 Koren Robinson	20.00	9.00
❑ 9 Justin Smith	15.00	4.50
❑ 10 David Terrell	20.00	9.00
❑ 11 LaDainian Tomlinson	50.00	22.00
❑ 12 Michael Vick	100.00	45.00
❑ 13 Chris Weinke	20.00	6.00

2001 Press Pass SE Game Jersey Autographs

	Nm-Mt	Ex-Mt
❑ AJCW Chris Weinke	50.00	22.00
❑ AJDB Drew Brees	120.00	55.00
❑ AJJS Justin Smith	50.00	15.00
❑ AJLT LaDainian Tomlinson	175.00	52.50
❑ AJMB Michael Bennett	80.00	36.00
❑ AJMV Michael Vick/15 EXCH		

2004 Press Pass SE

	Nm-Mt	Ex-Mt
COMPLETE SET (40)	30.00	9.00

MANN.MINI EXCH EXPIRATION 6/1/2005

❑ 1 Shawn Andrews	1.00	.30
❑ 2 Casey Clausen	1.25	.35
❑ 3 Michael Clayton	2.50	.75
❑ 4 Cedric Cobbs	1.00	.30
❑ 5 Devard Darling	1.00	.30
❑ 6 Lee Evans	1.50	.45
❑ 7 Larry Fitzgerald	3.00	.90
❑ 8 Robert Gallery	1.50	.45
❑ 9 DeAngelo Hall	1.25	.35
❑ 10 Tommie Harris	1.25	.35
❑ 11 Ben Hartsock	1.00	.30
❑ 12 Devery Henderson	.75	.23
❑ 13 Steven Jackson	3.00	.90
❑ 14 Michael Jenkins	1.00	.30
❑ 15 Greg Jones	1.00	.30
❑ 16 Kevin Jones	3.00	.90
❑ 17 Teddy Lehman	1.00	.30
❑ 18 J.P. Losman	2.50	.75
❑ 19 Eli Manning	5.00	1.50
❑ 20 Mewelde Moore	1.25	.35
❑ 21 John Navarre	1.00	.30
❑ 22 Jarrett Payton	1.00	.30
❑ 23 Chris Perry	2.00	.60
❑ 24 Cody Pickett	1.00	.30
❑ 25 Philip Rivers	3.00	.90
❑ 26 Ben Roethlisberger	8.00	2.40
❑ 27 Matt Schaub	1.50	.45
❑ 28 Will Smith	1.00	.30
❑ 29 Ben Troupe	1.00	.30
❑ 30 Michael Turner	.75	.23
❑ 31 Ben Watson	1.00	.30
❑ 32 Darius Watts	1.25	.35
❑ 33 Vince Wilfork	1.25	.35
❑ 34 Mike Williams	6.00	1.80
❑ 35 Reggie Williams	1.25	.35
❑ 36 Roy Williams WR	3.00	.90
❑ 37 Quincy Wilson	.75	.23
❑ 38 Rashaun Woods	1.25	.35
❑ 39 Jason Wright	.75	.23
❑ 40 Eli Manning CL	3.00	.90
❑ NNO Eli Manning Mini EXCH	120.00	36.00

2004 Press Pass SE First Down Gold

	Nm-Mt	Ex-Mt
COMPLETE SET (40)	60.00	18.00

*SINGLES: .8X TO 2X BASE CARD HI
ONE PER RETAIL PACK

2004 Press Pass SE Class of 2004

	Nm-Mt	Ex-Mt
COMPLETE SET (9)	25.00	7.50

STATED ODDS 1:3 H, 1:6 R

❑ CL1 Eli Manning	8.00	2.40
❑ CL2 Ben Roethlisberger	12.00	3.60
❑ CL3 Philip Rivers	5.00	1.50
❑ CL4 Mike Williams	10.00	3.00
❑ CL5 Kevin Jones	5.00	1.50
❑ CL6 Rashaun Woods	2.00	.60
❑ CL7 Steven Jackson	5.00	1.50
❑ CL8 Larry Fitzgerald	5.00	1.50
❑ CL9 Roy Williams WR	5.00	1.50

2004 Press Pass SE Class of 2004 Autographs

	Nm-Mt	Ex-Mt
❑ 1 Steven Jackson/50	100.00	30.00
❑ 2 Kevin Jones/50	100.00	30.00
❑ 3 Eli Manning/200	100.00	30.00
❑ 4 Chris Perry/200	30.00	9.00
❑ 5 Philip Rivers/200	60.00	18.00
❑ 6 Ben Roethlisberger/25	200.00	60.00
❑ 7 Ben Troupe/200	20.00	6.00
❑ 8 Mike Williams/200	175.00	52.50
❑ 9 Rashaun Woods/200	25.00	7.50

2004 Press Pass SE Game Used Jerseys Autographs

	Nm-Mt	Ex-Mt
STATED PRINT RUN 25 SERIAL #'d SETS		
❑ 1 Eli Manning	250.00	75.00
❑ 2 Ben Roethlisberger	300.00	90.00

2004 Press Pass SE Game Used Jerseys Bronze

	Nm-Mt	Ex-Mt
BRONZE PRINT RUN 700 UNLESS NOTED		
*GOLDS: .6X TO 1.5X BRONZE JERSEYS		
GOLD STATED PRINT RUN 100 SETS		
*NUMBERS: 2X TO 5X BRONZE JERSEYS		
NUMBERS STATED PRINT RUN 25 SETS		
UNPRICED PATCHES SER.#'d OF 10		
*SILVERS: .5X TO 1.2X BRONZE JERSEYS		
SILVER STATED PRINT RUN 400 SETS		
OVERALL JERSEY ODDS 1:3H, 1:280R		
❑ JCBB Bernard Berrian	10.00	3.00
❑ JCBH Ben Hartsock	10.00	3.00
❑ JCBR Ben Roethlisberger	40.00	12.00
❑ JCCC Casey Clausen	12.00	3.60
❑ JCCP Cody Pickett	10.00	3.00
❑ JCDD Devard Darling	10.00	3.00
❑ JCDW Darius Watts/675	12.00	3.60
❑ JCEM Eli Manning	30.00	9.00
❑ JCJG Jermaine Green	8.00	2.40
❑ JCJL Jared Lorenzen	8.00	2.40
❑ JCJP Jarrett Payton/625	10.00	3.00
❑ JCLM Luke McCown	10.00	3.00
❑ JCMM Mewelde Moore	12.00	3.60
❑ JCMS Matt Schaub	15.00	4.50
❑ JCPR Philip Rivers	20.00	6.00
❑ JCSJ Steven Jackson	20.00	6.00

2004 Press Pass SE Old School

	Nm-Mt	Ex-Mt
STATED ODDS 1:1 H, 1:2 R		
❑ OS1 Casey Clausen	1.50	.45
❑ OS2 J.P. Losman	3.00	.90
❑ OS3 Eli Manning	6.00	1.80
❑ OS4 John Navarre	1.25	.35
❑ OS5 Cody Pickett	1.25	.35
❑ OS6 Philip Rivers	4.00	1.20
❑ OS7 Ben Roethlisberger	10.00	3.00
❑ OS8 Matt Schaub	2.00	.60
❑ OS9 Steven Jackson	4.00	1.20
❑ OS10 Greg Jones	1.25	.35
❑ OS11 Kevin Jones	4.00	1.20
❑ OS12 Chris Perry	2.50	.75
❑ OS13 Michael Clayton	3.00	.90
❑ OS14 Lee Evans	2.00	.60
❑ OS15 Larry Fitzgerald	4.00	1.20
❑ OS16 Michael Jenkins	1.25	.35
❑ OS17 Mike Williams	8.00	2.40
❑ OS18 Roy Williams WR	4.00	1.20
❑ OS19 Rashaun Woods	1.50	.45
❑ OS20 Ben Troupe	1.25	.35
❑ OS21 Ben Watson	1.25	.35
❑ OS22 Kellen Winslow	3.00	.90
❑ OS23 Robert Gallery	2.00	.60
❑ OS24 Tommie Harris	1.50	.45
❑ OS25 Will Smith	1.25	.35
❑ OS26 Vince Wilfork	1.50	.45
❑ OS27 Eli Manning CL	4.00	1.20

2004 Press Pass SE Up Close

	Nm-Mt	Ex-Mt
STATED ODDS 1:4 H, 1:12 R		
❑ UC1 Eli Manning	8.00	2.40
❑ UC2 Larry Fitzgerald	5.00	1.50
❑ UC3 Roy Williams WR	5.00	1.50
❑ UC4 Ben Roethlisberger	12.00	3.60
❑ UC5 Philip Rivers	5.00	1.50
❑ UC6 Kevin Jones	5.00	1.50

2005 Press Pass SE

	Nm-Mt	Ex-Mt
COMPLETE SET (40)	30.00	9.00
❑ 1 Charlie Frye	1.50	.45
❑ 2 David Greene	1.25	.35
❑ 3 Gino Guidugli	.75	.23
❑ 4 Stefan LeFors	1.25	.35
❑ 5 Dan Orlovsky	1.25	.35
❑ 6 Kyle Orton	1.50	.45
❑ 7 Aaron Rodgers	4.00	1.20
❑ 8 Alex Smith QB	5.00	1.50
❑ 9 Andrew Walter	1.50	.45
❑ 10 Jason White	1.50	.45
❑ 11 J.J. Arrington	1.25	.35
❑ 12 Marion Barber	1.00	.30
❑ 13 Ronnie Brown	3.00	.90
❑ 14 Anthony Davis	1.00	.30
❑ 15 Ciatrick Fason	1.25	.35
❑ 16 T.A. McLendon	.75	.23
❑ 17 Vernand Morency	1.00	.30
❑ 18 Walter Reyes	.75	.23
❑ 19 Carnell Williams	3.00	.90
❑ 20 Mark Bradley	1.25	.35
❑ 21 Reggie Brown	1.25	.35
❑ 22 Mark Clayton	1.50	.45
❑ 23 Braylon Edwards	3.00	.90
❑ 24 Fred Gibson	1.25	.35
❑ 25 Chris Henry	1.00	.30
❑ 26 Terrence Murphy	1.00	.30
❑ 27 J.R. Russell	.75	.23
❑ 28 Craphonso Thorpe	1.00	.30
❑ 29 Roddy White	1.00	.30
❑ 30 Mike Williams	3.00	.90
❑ 31 Troy Williamson	2.00	.60
❑ 32 Heath Miller	1.50	.45
❑ 33 Alex Smith TE	1.00	.30
❑ 34 Jammal Brown	1.00	.30
❑ 35 Marlin Jackson	1.00	.30
❑ 36 Antrel Rolle	1.25	.35
❑ 37 Dan Cody	1.25	.35
❑ 38 Derrick Johnson	1.50	.45
❑ 39 Thomas Davis	1.00	.30
❑ 40 Aaron Rodgers CL	2.00	.60

2005 Press Pass SE Class of 2005

	Nm-Mt	Ex-Mt
COMPLETE SET (9)	25.00	7.50
STATED ODDS 1:3		
❑ CL1 Aaron Rodgers	6.00	1.80
❑ CL2 Braylon Edwards	5.00	1.50
❑ CL3 Charlie Frye	2.50	.75
❑ CL4 Heath Miller	2.50	.75
❑ CL5 Troy Williamson	3.00	.90
❑ CL6 Alex Smith QB	8.00	2.40
❑ CL7 Ronnie Brown	5.00	1.50
❑ CL8 Andrew Walter	2.50	.75
❑ CL9 Carnell Williams	5.00	1.50

2005 Press Pass SE Class of 2005 Autographs

	Nm-Mt	Ex-Mt
❑ AR1 Aaron Rodgers/200	80.00	24.00
❑ AR2 Aaron Rodgers/10* Red		
❑ BE1 Braylon Edwards/50	120.00	36.00
❑ BE2 Braylon Edwards/5* Red		
❑ CW Carnell Williams/200	60.00	18.00
❑ DO Dan Orlovsky/200	30.00	9.00
❑ HM Heath Miller/200	40.00	12.00
❑ HM2 Heath Miller/9* Red		
❑ RB1 Ronnie Brown/23		
❑ RB2 Ronnie Brown/20* Red		
❑ TW Troy Williamson/200	40.00	12.00

2005 Press Pass SE Game Used Jerseys Silver

	Nm-Mt	Ex-Mt
SILVER PRINT RUN 450-700 SER.#'d SETS		
*GOLD: .5X TO 1.2X SILVER JERSEYS		
GOLD PRINT RUN 450-550 SER.#'d SETS		
*HOLOFOIL: .6X TO 1.5X SILVER JERSEYS		
HOLOFOIL PRINT RUN 100 SER.#'d SETS		
*NAMES: 1.2X TO 3X SILVER JERSEYS		
NAMES PRINT RUN 25 SER.#'d SETS		
UNPRICED PATCH PRINT RUN 1-10 SETS		
❑ JCAS1 Alex Smith TE/700	10.00	3.00
❑ JCAS2 Alex Smith TE/300	10.00	3.00
❑ JCAW Andrew Walter/700	12.00	3.60
❑ JCBB Brock Berlin/700	10.00	3.00
❑ JCCT Craphonso Thorpe/700	10.00	3.00
❑ JCDA Derek Anderson/700	10.00	3.00
❑ JCDG David Greene/700	10.00	3.00
❑ JCDO Dan Orlovsky/700	12.00	3.60
❑ JCJC Jerome Collins/700	10.00	3.00
❑ JCJW Jason White/700	15.00	4.50
❑ JCKO Kyle Orton/700	15.00	4.50
❑ JCMB Mark Bradley/700	12.00	3.60
❑ JCMJ Marlin Jackson/700	12.00	3.60
❑ JCRB Reggie Brown/700	12.00	3.60
❑ JCRW Roddy White/700	12.00	3.60
❑ JCSL Stefan LeFors/700	12.00	3.60
❑ JCTM Terrence Murphy/450	10.00	3.00
❑ JCVM Vernand Morency/700	10.00	3.00

2005 Press Pass SE Game Used Jerseys Autographs

	Nm-Mt	Ex-Mt
STATED PRINT RUN 25 SER.#'d SETS		
❑ JCAW Andrew Walter		
❑ JCDG David Greene	60.00	18.00
❑ JCDO Dan Orlovsky	60.00	18.00
❑ JCJW Jason White	100.00	30.00
❑ JCKO Kyle Orton	80.00	24.00
❑ JCRB Reggie Brown	80.00	24.00

2005 Press Pass SE Old School

	Nm-Mt	Ex-Mt
COMPLETE SET (27)	40.00	12.00
STATED ODDS 1:1		
❑ OS1 Marion Barber	1.50	.45
❑ OS2 Reggie Brown	2.00	.60
❑ OS3 Ronnie Brown	5.00	1.50
❑ OS4 Mark Clayton	2.50	.75
❑ OS5 Dan Cody	2.00	.60
❑ OS6 Anthony Davis	1.50	.45
❑ OS7 Braylon Edwards	5.00	1.50
❑ OS8 Ciatrick Fason	2.00	.60
❑ OS9 Charlie Frye	2.50	.75
❑ OS10 David Greene	2.00	.60
❑ OS11 Gino Guidugli	1.25	.35
❑ OS12 Derrick Johnson	2.50	.75
❑ OS13 Heath Miller	2.50	.75
❑ OS14 Vernand Morency	1.50	.45
❑ OS15 Dan Orlovsky	2.00	.60
❑ OS16 Kyle Orton	2.50	.75
❑ OS17 Aaron Rodgers	6.00	1.80
❑ OS18 Antrel Rolle	2.00	.60
❑ OS19 Eric Shelton	1.50	.45
❑ OS20 Alex Smith QB	8.00	2.40
❑ OS21 Andrew Walter	2.50	.75
❑ OS22 Jason White	2.50	.75
❑ OS23 Roddy White	1.50	.45
❑ OS24 Carnell Williams	5.00	1.50
❑ OS25 Mike Williams	5.00	1.50
❑ OS26 Troy Williamson	3.00	.90
❑ OS27 Braylon Edwards CL	2.50	.75

2005 Press Pass SE Up Close

	Nm-Mt	Ex-Mt
COMPLETE SET (6)	20.00	6.00
STATED ODDS 1:4		
❑ UC1 Carnell Williams	5.00	1.50
❑ UC2 Aaron Rodgers	6.00	1.80
❑ UC3 Mike Williams	5.00	1.50
❑ UC4 Ronnie Brown	5.00	1.50
❑ UC5 Braylon Edwards	5.00	1.50
❑ UC6 Dan Orlovsky	2.00	.60

1999 SAGE

	Nm-Mt	Ex-Mt
COMPLETE SET (50)	30.00	13.50
❑ 1 Rahim Abdullah	.60	.25
❑ 2 Jerry Azumah	.60	.25
❑ 3 Champ Bailey	1.25	.55
❑ 4 D'Wayne Bates	.60	.25
❑ 5 Michael Bishop	1.00	.45
❑ 6 David Boston	1.00	.45
❑ 7 Fernando Bryant	.60	.25
❑ 8 Tony Bryant	.60	.25
❑ 9 Chris Claiborne	.40	.18
❑ 10 Mike Cloud	.60	.25
❑ 11 Cecil Collins	.40	.18
❑ 12 Tim Couch	1.00	.45
❑ 13 Daunte Culpepper	4.00	1.80
❑ 14 Jared DeVries	.60	.25
❑ 15 Adrian Dingle	.60	.25
❑ 16 Antuan Edwards	.60	.25
❑ 17 Troy Edwards	.60	.25
❑ 18 Kevin Faulk	1.00	.45
❑ 19 Rufus French	.40	.18
❑ 20 Martin Gramatica	.40	.18
❑ 21 Torry Holt	2.50	1.10
❑ 22 Sedrick Irvin	.40	.18
❑ 23 Edgerrin James	4.00	1.80
❑ 24 Jon Jansen	.40	.18
❑ 25 Andy Katzenmoyer	.60	.25
❑ 26 Jevon Kearse	2.50	1.10
❑ 27 Patrick Kerney	1.00	.45
❑ 28 Lamar King	.60	.25
❑ 29 Shaun King	.60	.25
❑ 30 Jim Kleinsasser	1.00	.45
❑ 31 Rob Konrad	1.00	.45
❑ 32 Brian Kuklick	.60	.25
❑ 33 Chris McAlister	.60	.25
❑ 34 Darnell McDonald	.60	.25
❑ 35 Reggie McGrew	.60	.25

Card	Nm-Mt	Ex-Mt
❑ 36 Donovan McNabb	5.00	2.20
❑ 37 Cade McNown	.60	.25
❑ 38 Dat Nguyen	1.00	.45
❑ 39 Solomon Page	.40	.18
❑ 40 Mike Peterson	1.00	.45
❑ 41 Anthony Poindexter	.60	.25
❑ 42 Peerless Price	1.25	.55
❑ 43 Mike Rucker	1.00	.45
❑ 44 L.J. Shelton	.40	.18
❑ 45 Akili Smith	1.50	.70
❑ 46 John Tait	.40	.18
❑ 47 Fred Vinson	.60	.25
❑ 48 Al Wilson	1.00	.45
❑ 49 Antoine Winfield	.60	.25
❑ 50 Damien Woody	.60	.25

1999 SAGE Autographs Red

	Nm-Mt	Ex-Mt
COMPLETE SET (50)	500.00	220.00

*BRONZE AUTOS: .5X TO 1.2X HI COL.
*SILVER AUTOS: .6X TO 1.5X HI COL.
*GOLD AUTOS: .8X TO 2X HI COL.
*PLATINUM AUTOS: 1.5X TO 3X HI COL.

Card	Nm-Mt	Ex-Mt
❑ A1 Rahim Abdullah/999	8.00	3.60
❑ A2 Jerry Azumah/999	8.00	3.60
❑ A3 Champ Bailey/999	20.00	9.00
❑ A4 D'Wayne Bates/999	8.00	3.60
❑ A5 Michael Bishop/999	12.00	5.50
❑ A6 David Boston/869	12.00	5.50
❑ A7 Fernando Bryant/999	8.00	3.60
❑ A8 Tony Bryant/999	8.00	3.60
❑ A9 Chris Claiborne/999	6.00	2.70
❑ A10 Mike Cloud/434	8.00	3.60
❑ A11 Cecil Collins/999	6.00	2.70
❑ A12 Tim Couch/999	12.00	5.50
❑ A13 Daunte Culpepper/419	50.00	22.00
❑ A14 Jared DeVries/887	8.00	3.60
❑ A15 Adrian Dingle/999	6.00	2.70
❑ A16 Antuan Edwards/999	8.00	3.60
❑ A17 Troy Edwards/999	8.00	3.60
❑ A18 Kevin Faulk/999	12.00	5.50
❑ A19 Rufus French/999	6.00	2.70
❑ A20 Martin Gramatica/999	6.00	2.70
❑ A21 Torry Holt/999	25.00	11.00
❑ A22 Sedrick Irvin/999	6.00	2.70
❑ A23 Edgerrin James/859	40.00	18.00
❑ A24 Jon Jansen/999	6.00	2.70
❑ A25 Andy Katzenmoyer/209	20.00	9.00
❑ A26 Jevon Kearse/999	20.00	9.00
❑ A27 Patrick Kerney/879	12.00	5.50
❑ A28 Lamar King/999	6.00	2.70
❑ A29 Shaun King/999	8.00	3.60
❑ A30 Jim Kleinsasser/999	12.00	5.50
❑ A31 Rob Konrad/999	12.00	5.50
❑ A32 Brian Kuklick/999	8.00	3.60
❑ A33 Chris McAlister/999	8.00	3.60
❑ A34 Darnell McDonald/999	8.00	3.60
❑ A35 Reggie McGrew/999	8.00	3.60
❑ A36 Donovan McNabb/999	50.00	22.00
❑ A37 Cade McNown/209	20.00	9.00
❑ A38 Dat Nguyen/999	12.00	5.50
❑ A39 Solomon Page/999	6.00	2.70
❑ A40 Mike Peterson/999	12.00	5.50
❑ A41 Anthony Poindexter/999	6.00	2.70
❑ A42 Peerless Price/232	30.00	13.50
❑ A43 Mike Rucker/999	12.00	5.50
❑ A44 L.J. Shelton/999	6.00	2.70
❑ A45 Akili Smith/419	20.00	9.00
❑ A46 John Tait/999	6.00	2.70
❑ A47 Fred Vinson/999	8.00	3.60
❑ A48 Al Wilson/999	12.00	5.50
❑ A49 Antoine Winfield/999	8.00	3.60
❑ A50 Damien Woody/999	6.00	2.70

2000 SAGE

	Nm-Mt	Ex-Mt
COMPLETE SET (50)	15.00	6.75
❑ 1 John Abraham	.75	.35
❑ 2 Shaun Alexander	2.50	1.10
❑ 3 LaVar Arrington	3.00	1.35
❑ 4 Courtney Brown	1.00	.45
❑ 5 Keith Bulluck	.75	.35
❑ 6 Plaxico Burress	1.50	.70
❑ 7 Giovanni Carmazzi	.60	.25
❑ 8 Kwame Cavil	.40	.18
❑ 9 Cosey Coleman	.40	.18
❑ 10 Laveranues Coles	1.00	.45
❑ 11 Tim Couch	.75	.35
❑ 12 Ron Dayne	.75	.35
❑ 13 Reuben Droughns	1.00	.45
❑ 14 Shaun Ellis	.75	.35
❑ 15 John Engelberger	.60	.25
❑ 16 Danny Farmer	.60	.25
❑ 17 Dwayne Goodrich	.75	.35
❑ 18 Deon Grant	.60	.25
❑ 19 Chris Hovan	.60	.25
❑ 20 Darren Howard	.60	.25
❑ 21 Todd Husak	.75	.35
❑ 22 Thomas Jones	1.25	.55
❑ 23 Curtis Keaton	.60	.25
❑ 24 Jamal Lewis	1.50	.70
❑ 25 Anthony Lucas	.40	.18
❑ 26 Tee Martin	.75	.35
❑ 27 Stockar McDougle	.40	.18
❑ 28 Corey Moore	.40	.18
❑ 29 Rob Morris	.60	.25
❑ 30 Sammy Morris	.60	.25
❑ 31 Sylvester Morris	.60	.25
❑ 32 Chad Pennington	3.00	1.35
❑ 33 Todd Pinkston	.75	.35
❑ 34 Ahmed Plummer	.75	.35
❑ 35 Jerry Porter	1.00	.45
❑ 36 Travis Prentice	.60	.25
❑ 37 Tim Rattay	1.50	.70
❑ 38 Chris Redman	.60	.25
❑ 39 J.R. Redmond	.60	.25
❑ 40 Chris Samuels	.60	.25
❑ 41 Brandon Short	.60	.25
❑ 42 Corey Simon	1.00	.45
❑ 43 R.Jay Soward	.60	.25
❑ 44 Shyrone Stith	.60	.25
❑ 45 Raynoch Thompson	.60	.25
❑ 46 Brian Urlacher	3.00	1.35
❑ 47 Todd Wade	.40	.18
❑ 48 Troy Walters	.75	.35
❑ 49 Dez White	.75	.35
❑ 50 Michael Wiley	.60	.25

2000 SAGE Autographs Red

	Nm-Mt	Ex-Mt
COMPLETE SET (50)	450.00	200.00

*BRONZE AUTOS: .5X TO 1.2X BASIC INSERTS
*GOLD AUTOS: 1X TO 2.5X BASIC INSERTS
*PLATINUM AUTOS: 1.5X TO 3X BASIC INSERTS
*SILVER AUTOS: .6X TO 1.5X BASIC INSERTS

Card	Nm-Mt	Ex-Mt
❑ 1 John Abraham/999	10.00	4.50
❑ 2 Shaun Alexander/999	20.00	9.00
❑ 3 LaVar Arrington/534	75.00	34.00
❑ 4 Courtney Brown/554	15.00	6.75
❑ 5 Keith Bulluck/999	8.00	3.60
❑ 6 Plaxico Burress/999	20.00	9.00
❑ 7 Giovanni Carmazzi/999	6.00	2.70
❑ 8 Kwame Cavil/999	4.00	1.80
❑ 9 Cosey Coleman/999	4.00	1.80
❑ 10 Laveranues Coles/999	12.00	5.50
❑ 11 Tim Couch/354	10.00	4.50
❑ 12 Ron Dayne/334	15.00	6.75
❑ 13 Reuben Droughns/999	10.00	4.50
❑ 14 Shaun Ellis/999	8.00	3.60
❑ 15 John Engelberger/999	6.00	2.70
❑ 16 Danny Farmer/999	6.00	2.70
❑ 17 Dwayne Goodrich/999	4.00	1.80
❑ 18 Deon Grant/999	6.00	2.70
❑ 19 Chris Hovan/999	6.00	2.70
❑ 20 Darren Howard/999	6.00	2.70
❑ 21 Todd Husak/999	8.00	3.60
❑ 22 Thomas Jones/999	12.00	5.50
❑ 23 Curtis Keaton/999	6.00	2.70
❑ 24 Jamal Lewis/999	20.00	9.00
❑ 25 Anthony Lucas/999	4.00	1.80
❑ 26 Tee Martin/999	8.00	3.60
❑ 27 Stockar McDougle/999	4.00	1.80
❑ 28 Corey Moore/999	4.00	1.80
❑ 29 Rob Morris/999	6.00	2.70
❑ 30 Sammy Morris/999	6.00	2.70
❑ 31 Sylvester Morris/999	6.00	2.70
❑ 32 Chad Pennington/749	30.00	13.50
❑ 33 Todd Pinkston/999	8.00	3.60
❑ 34 Ahmed Plummer/999	6.00	2.70
❑ 35 Jerry Porter/999	12.00	5.50
❑ 36 Travis Prentice/999	6.00	2.70
❑ 37 Tim Rattay/999	15.00	6.75
❑ 38 Chris Redman/999	6.00	2.70
❑ 39 J.R. Redmond/999	6.00	2.70
❑ 40 Chris Samuels/999	6.00	2.70
❑ 41 Brandon Short/999	6.00	2.70
❑ 42 Corey Simon/999	8.00	3.60
❑ 43 R.Jay Soward/999	6.00	2.70
❑ 44 Shyrone Stith/999	6.00	2.70
❑ 45 Raynoch Thompson/999	6.00	2.70
❑ 46 Brian Urlacher/999	30.00	13.50
❑ 47 Todd Wade/999	4.00	1.80
❑ 48 Troy Walters/999	6.00	2.70
❑ 49 Dez White/999	8.00	3.60
❑ 50 Michael Wiley/999	6.00	2.70

2001 SAGE

	Nm-Mt	Ex-Mt
COMPLETE SET (50)	20.00	9.00
❑ 1 Will Allen	.60	.25
❑ 2 Adam Archuleta	.75	.35
❑ 3 Jeff Backus	.60	.25
❑ 4 Alex Bannister	.60	.25
❑ 5 Gary Baxter	.60	.25
❑ 6 Michael Bennett	1.50	.70
❑ 7 Josh Booty	.75	.35
❑ 8 Drew Brees	1.50	.70
❑ 9 Correll Buckhalter	1.25	.55
❑ 10 Quincy Carter	.75	.35
❑ 11 Chris Chambers	1.25	.55
❑ 12 Alge Crumpler	1.00	.45
❑ 13 Andre Dyson	.40	.18
❑ 14 Robert Ferguson	.75	.35
❑ 15 Jamar Fletcher	.60	.25
❑ 16 Rod Gardner	.75	.35
❑ 17 Reggie Germany	.60	.25
❑ 18 Derrick Gibson	.60	.25
❑ 19 Casey Hampton	.60	.25
❑ 20 Tim Hasselbeck	.75	.35
❑ 21 Todd Heap	.75	.35
❑ 22 Travis Henry	1.25	.55
❑ 23 Josh Heupel	.75	.35
❑ 24 Willie Howard	.60	.25
❑ 25 Steve Hutchinson	.60	.25
❑ 26 James Jackson	.75	.35
❑ 27 Rudi Johnson	1.50	.70
❑ 28 LaMont Jordan	1.00	.45
❑ 29 Torrance Marshall	.75	.35
❑ 30 Deuce McAllister	2.00	.90
❑ 31 Willie Middlebrooks	.60	.25
❑ 32 Quincy Morgan	.75	.35
❑ 33 Santana Moss	1.50	.70
❑ 34 Jesse Palmer	.75	.35
❑ 35 Carlos Polk	.40	.18
❑ 36 Ken-Yon Rambo	.60	.25
❑ 37 Jamal Reynolds	.75	.35
❑ 38 Koren Robinson	1.25	.55
❑ 39 Richard Seymour	.75	.35
❑ 40 Justin Smith	.75	.35
❑ 41 Fred Smoot	.75	.35
❑ 42 Marcus Stroud	.75	.35
❑ 43 David Terrell	.75	.35
❑ 44 LaDainian Tomlinson	3.00	1.35
❑ 45 Ja'Mar Toombs	.60	.25
❑ 46 Michael Vick	6.00	2.70
❑ 47 Kenyatta Walker	.40	.18
❑ 48 Gerard Warren	.75	.35
❑ 49 Reggie Wayne	1.50	.70
❑ 50 Jamie Winborn	.60	.25

2001 SAGE Autographs Red

Nm-Mt Ex-Mt

RED PRINT RUN 999 UNLESS NOTED BELOW
*BRONZE AUTOS: .5X TO 1.2X REDS
BRONZE PRINT RUN 325-650 SER. #'d CARDS
BRONZE STATED ODDS 1:4
*GOLD AUTOS: .8X TO 2X REDS
GOLD PRINT RUN 100-200 SER.#'d CARDS
GOLD STATED ODDS 1:12
UNPRICED MASTER EDIT.PRINT RUN 1
*PLATINUM AUTOS: 1.5X TO 4X REDS
PLATINUM PRINT RUN 25-50 SER.#'d CARDS
PLATINUM STATED ODDS 1:46
*SILVER AUTOS: .6X TO 1.5X REDS
SILVER PRINT RUN 200-400 SER.#'d CARDS
SILVER STATED ODDS 1:6

	Nm-Mt	Ex-Mt
❑ A1 Will Allen	5.00	2.20
❑ A2 Adam Archuleta	8.00	3.60
❑ A3 Jeff Backus/900	10.00	4.50
❑ A4 Alex Bannister	5.00	2.20
❑ A5 Gary Baxter	5.00	2.20
❑ A6 Michael Bennett	15.00	6.75
❑ A7 Josh Booty/900	8.00	3.60
❑ A8 Drew Brees/749	20.00	9.00
❑ A9 Correll Buckhalter	12.00	5.50
❑ A10 Quincy Carter	8.00	3.60
❑ A11 Chris Chambers	12.00	5.50
❑ A12 Alge Crumpler	8.00	3.60
❑ A13 Andre Dyson	4.00	1.80
❑ A14 Robert Ferguson	8.00	3.60
❑ A16 Rod Gardner	8.00	3.60
❑ A17 Reggie Germany	5.00	2.20
❑ A18 Derrick Gibson	5.00	2.20
❑ A19 Casey Hampton	5.00	2.20
❑ A20 Tim Hasselbeck/900	8.00	3.60
❑ A21 Todd Heap	8.00	3.60
❑ A22 Travis Henry/800	12.00	5.50
❑ A23 Josh Heupel	8.00	3.60
❑ A24 Willie Howard/900	5.00	2.20
❑ A25 Steve Hutchinson	5.00	2.20
❑ A26 James Jackson	8.00	3.60
❑ A27 Rudi Johnson	15.00	6.75
❑ A28 LaMont Jordan	10.00	4.50
❑ A29 Torrance Marshall	8.00	3.60
❑ A30 Deuce McAllister/749	30.00	13.50
❑ A31 Willie Middlebrooks	5.00	2.20
❑ A32 Quincy Morgan	8.00	3.60
❑ A33 Santana Moss	12.00	5.50
❑ A34 Jesse Palmer	8.00	3.60
❑ A35 Carlos Polk	4.00	1.80
❑ A36 Ken-Yon Rambo/749	5.00	2.20
❑ A37 Jamal Reynolds	8.00	3.60
❑ A38 Koren Robinson	10.00	4.50
❑ A39 Richard Seymour	15.00	6.75
❑ A40 Justin Smith	8.00	3.60
❑ A41 Fred Smoot	8.00	3.60
❑ A42 Marcus Stroud	8.00	3.60
❑ A43 David Terrell/649	12.00	5.50
❑ A44 LaDainian Tomlinson	40.00	18.00
❑ A45 Ja'Mar Toombs	5.00	2.20
❑ A46 Michael Vick/499	80.00	36.00
❑ A47 Kenyatta Walker		
❑ A49 Reggie Wayne	12.00	5.50
❑ A50 Jamie Winborn	5.00	2.20

2002 SAGE

	Nm-Mt	Ex-Mt
COMPLETE SET (45)	40.00	12.00
❑ 1 Ladell Betts	1.50	.45
❑ 2 Antonio Bryant	1.50	.45
❑ 3 Reche Caldwell	1.50	.45
❑ 4 Kelly Campbell	1.25	.35
❑ 5 David Carr	6.00	1.80
❑ 6 Tim Carter	1.25	.35
❑ 7 Eric Crouch	2.50	.75
❑ 8 Ronald Curr	1.50	.45
❑ 9 Rohan Davey	1.50	.45
❑ 10 Andre Davis	1.50	.45
❑ 11 T.J. Duckett	3.00	.90
❑ 12 Randy Fasani	1.25	.35
❑ 13 DeShaun Foster	1.50	.45
❑ 14 Dwight Freeney	2.00	.60
❑ 15 Jabar Gaffney	1.50	.45
❑ 16 Lamar Gordon	1.50	.45
❑ 17 Daniel Graham	1.50	.45
❑ 18 Joey Harrington	6.00	1.80
❑ 19 Napoleon Harri	1.50	.45
❑ 20 Albert Haynesworth	1.25	.35
❑ 21 John Henderson	5.00	1.50
❑ 22 Chad Hutchinson	4.00	1.20
❑ 23 Quentin Jammer	1.50	.45
❑ 24 Ron Johnson	1.25	.35
❑ 25 Kurt Kittner	1.25	.35
❑ 26 Ashley Lelie	3.00	.90
❑ 27 Bryant McKinnie	1.25	.35
❑ 28 Maurice Morris	1.50	.45
❑ 29 David Neill	1.25	.35
❑ 30 J.T. O'Sullivan	1.25	.35
❑ 31 Brian Poli-Dixon	1.25	.35
❑ 32 Clinton Portis	6.00	1.80
❑ 33 Patrick Ramsey	3.00	.90
❑ 34 Josh Reed	1.50	.45
❑ 35 Cliff Russell	1.25	.35
❑ 36 Lito Sheppard	1.50	.45
❑ 37 Jeremy Shockey	6.00	1.80
❑ 38 Luke Staley	1.25	.35
❑ 39 Donte Stallworth	3.00	.90
❑ 40 Travis Stephens	1.25	.35
❑ 41 Chester Taylor	1.50	.45
❑ 42 Larry Tripplett	.75	.23
❑ 43 Javon Walker	3.00	.90
❑ 44 Marquise Walker	1.25	.35
❑ 45 Jonathan Wells	1.50	.45

2002 SAGE Autographs Red

Nm-Mt Ex-Mt

RED STATED ODDS 1:2
*BRONZE AUTOS: .5X TO 1.2X REDS
BRONZE STATED ODDS 1:4
*GOLD AUTOS: .8X TO 2X REDS
GOLD STATED ODDS 1:12

*PLATINUM 20-50: 1.5X TO 4X REDS
PLATINUM STATED ODDS 1:48
*SILVER AUTOS: .6X TO 1.5X REDS
SILVER STATED ODDS 1:6

❑ A1 Ladell Betts/40		
❑ A2 Antonio Bryant/740	10.00	3.00
❑ A3 Reche Caldwell/630	10.00	3.00
❑ A4 Kelly Campbell/750	8.00	2.40
❑ A5 David Carr/220	50.00	15.00
❑ A6 Tim Carter/720	6.00	1.80
❑ A7 Eric Crouch/220	25.00	7.50
❑ A8 Ronald Curry/800	10.00	3.00
❑ A9 Rohan Davey/650	10.00	3.00
❑ A10 Andre Davis/650	10.00	3.00
❑ A11 T.J. Duckett/860	15.00	4.50
❑ A12 Randy Fasani/700	8.00	2.40
❑ A13 DeShaun Foster/500	10.00	3.00
❑ A14 Dwight Freeney/800	12.00	3.60
❑ A15 Jabar Gaffney/700	10.00	3.00
❑ A16 Lamar Gordon/700	10.00	3.00
❑ A17 Daniel Graham/750	10.00	3.00
❑ A18 Joey Harrington/220	50.00	15.00
❑ A19 Napoleon Harris/770	10.00	3.00
❑ A20 Albert Haynesworth/125	20.00	6.00
❑ A21 John Henderson/625	10.00	3.00
❑ A22 Chad Hutchinson/500	20.00	6.00
❑ A23 Quentin Jammer/300	15.00	4.50
❑ A24 Ron Johnson/720	8.00	2.40
❑ A25 Kurt Kittner/500	8.00	2.40
❑ A26 Ashley Lelie/700	20.00	6.00
❑ A27 Bryant McKinnie/720	8.00	2.40
❑ A28 Maurice Morris/720	10.00	3.00
❑ A29 David Neill/770	8.00	2.40
❑ A30 J.T. O'Sullivan/660	8.00	2.40
❑ A31 Brian Poli-Dixon/700	8.00	2.40
❑ A32 Clinton Portis/70	80.00	24.00
❑ A33 Patrick Ramsey/720	20.00	6.00
❑ A34 Josh Reed/720	10.00	3.00
❑ A35 Cliff Russell/720	8.00	2.40
❑ A36 Lito Sheppard/670	10.00	3.00
❑ A37 Jeremy Shockey/700	40.00	12.00
❑ A38 Luke Staley/750	8.00	2.40
❑ A39 Donte Stallworth/800	20.00	6.00
❑ A40 Travis Stephens/660	8.00	2.40
❑ A41 Chester Taylor/700	10.00	3.00
❑ A42 Larry Tripplett/650	10.00	3.00
❑ A43 Javon Walker/650	15.00	4.50
❑ A44 Marquise Walker/600	8.00	2.40
❑ A45 Jonathan Wells/680	10.00	3.00
❑ VS1 Michael Vick/110	80.00	24.00

2003 SAGE

	Nm-Mt	Ex-Mt
COMPLETE SET (45)	25.00	7.50
❑ 1 Sam Aiken	1.25	.35
❑ 2 Boss Bailey	2.00	.60
❑ 3 Brad Banks	2.00	.60
❑ 4 Tully Banta-Cain	1.25	.35
❑ 5 Arnaz Battle	1.50	.45
❑ 6 Ronald Bellamy	1.25	.35
❑ 7 Kyle Boller	4.00	1.20
❑ 8 Chris Brown	3.00	.90
❑ 9 Tyrone Calico	2.00	.60
❑ 10 Dallas Clark	1.50	.45
❑ 11 Kevin Curtis	1.50	.45
❑ 12 Sammy Davis	1.50	.45
❑ 13 Dahrran Diedrick	1.50	.45
❑ 14 Ken Dorsey	2.50	.75
❑ 15 Justin Fargas	1.50	.45
❑ 16 Justin Gage	1.50	.45
❑ 17 Jason Gesser	1.50	.45
❑ 18 Cie Grant	1.50	.45
❑ 19 Rex Grossman	4.00	1.20
❑ 20 E.J. Henderson	1.50	.45
❑ 21 Taylor Jacobs	1.50	.45
❑ 22 Bryant Johnson	1.50	.45
❑ 23 Larry Johnson	3.00	.90
❑ 24 Teyo Johnson	1.50	.45
❑ 25 Kliff Kingsbury	1.25	.35
❑ 26 Brandon Lloyd	2.00	.60
❑ 27 Rashean Mathis	1.25	.35
❑ 28 Jerome McDougle	1.50	.45
❑ 29 Willis McGahee	4.00	1.20
❑ 30 Billy McMullen	1.25	.35
❑ 31 Terence Newman	3.00	.90
❑ 32 Donnie Nickey	1.25	.35
❑ 33 Terry Pierce	1.25	.35
❑ 34 Dave Ragone	1.50	.45
❑ 35 Charles Rogers	2.00	.60
❑ 36 Chris Simms	3.00	.90
❑ 37 Musa Smith	1.50	.45
❑ 38 Lee Suggs	3.00	.90
❑ 39 Terrell Suggs	2.50	.75
❑ 40 Marcus Trufant	1.50	.45
❑ 41 Seneca Wallace	1.50	.45
❑ 42 Kelley Washington	1.50	.45
❑ 43 Matt Wilhelm	1.50	.45
❑ 44 Jason Witten	2.50	.75
❑ 45 George Wrighster	1.25	.35

2003 SAGE Autographs Red

*BRONZE: .5X TO 1.2X REDS
BRONZE STATED ODDS 1:4
*GOLD: .8X TO 2X REDS
GOLD STATED ODDS 1:12
MASTER EDITION 1/1 STATED ODDS 1:1050
M.E. NOT PRICED DUE TO SCARCITY
PLAYERS PROOFS PRINT RUN 20 SER.#'d SETS
P.P. STATED ODDS 1:105
*SILVER: .6X TO 1.5X REDS
SILVER STATED ODDS 1:6

	Nm-Mt	Ex-Mt
❑ A1 Sam Aiken/379	8.00	2.40
❑ A2 Boss Bailey/370	12.00	3.60
❑ A3 Brad Banks/540	8.00	2.40
❑ A4 Tully Banta-Cain/620	8.00	2.40
❑ A5 Arnaz Battle/910	10.00	3.00
❑ A6 Ronald Bellamy/810	8.00	2.40
❑ A7 Kyle Boller/750	15.00	4.50
❑ A8 Chris Brown/920	25.00	7.50
❑ A9 Tyrone Calico/670	12.00	3.60
❑ A10 Dallas Clark/670	10.00	3.00
❑ A11 Kevin Curtis/930	8.00	2.40
❑ A12 Sammy Davis/799	10.00	3.00
❑ A13 Dahrran Diedrick/250	10.00	3.00
❑ A14 Ken Dorsey/335	15.00	4.50
❑ A15 Justin Fargas/999	10.00	3.00
❑ A16 Justin Gage/690	10.00	3.00
❑ A17 Jason Gesser/799	10.00	3.00
❑ A19 Rex Grossman/395	25.00	7.50
❑ A20 E.J. Henderson/640	10.00	3.00
❑ A21 Taylor Jacobs/700	10.00	3.00
❑ A22 Bryant Johnson/360	10.00	3.00
❑ A23 Larry Johnson/360	25.00	7.50
❑ A24 Teyo Johnson/679	10.00	3.00
❑ A25 Kliff Kingsbury/675	8.00	2.40
❑ A26 Brandon Lloyd/779	10.00	3.00
❑ A27 Rashean Mathis/500	8.00	2.40
❑ A28 Jerome McDougle/930	8.00	2.40
❑ A29 Willis McGahee/360	25.00	7.50
❑ A30 Billy McMullen/690	8.00	2.40
❑ A31 Terence Newman/640	20.00	6.00
❑ A32 Donnie Nickey/290	10.00	3.00
❑ A33 Terry Pierce/930	8.00	2.40
❑ A34 Dave Ragone/210	10.00	3.00
❑ A35 Charles Rogers/220	20.00	6.00
❑ A36 Chris Simms/350	20.00	6.00
❑ A37 Musa Smith/360	10.00	3.00
❑ A38 Lee Suggs/355	20.00	6.00
❑ A39 Terrell Suggs/350	20.00	6.00
❑ A40 Marcus Trufant/930	10.00	3.00
❑ A41 Seneca Wallace/799	10.00	3.00
❑ A42 Kelley Washington/75	50.00	15.00
❑ A43 Matt Wilhelm/650	10.00	3.00
❑ A44 Jason Witten/950	15.00	4.50
❑ A45 George Wrighster/670	8.00	2.40

2003 SAGE Jerseys Red

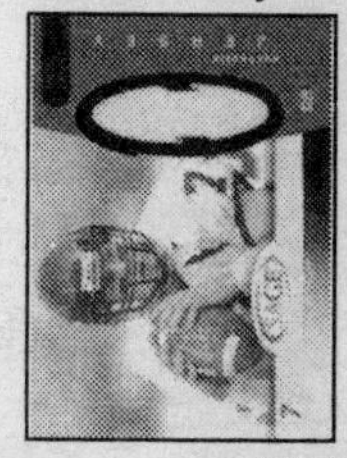

*BRONZE: .5X TO 1.2 BASIC JERSEYS
BRONZE PRINT RUN 75 SER.#'d SETS
BRONZE STATED ODDS 1:53
*GOLD: 1.2X TO 3X BASIC JERSEYS
GOLD PRINT RUN 25 SER.#'d SETS
GOLD STATED ODDS 1:160
*SILVER: .6X TO 1.5X BASIC JERSEYS
SILVER PRINT RUN 50 SER.#'d SETS
SILVER STATED ODDS 1:80
MASTER EDITION 1/1 STATED ODDS 1:3950
PLATINUM/10 STATED ODDS 1:395
PLAY.PROOFS/20 STATED ODDS 1:395

	Nm-Mt	Ex-Mt
❑ SJ1 Brad Banks	12.00	3.60
❑ SJ2 Arnaz Battle	25.00	7.50
❑ SJ3 Kyle Boller	40.00	12.00
❑ SJ4 Chris Brown	25.00	7.50
❑ SJ5 David Carr	25.00	7.50
❑ SJ6 Ken Dorsey	20.00	6.00
❑ SJ7 Rex Grossman	30.00	9.00
❑ SJ8 Taylor Jacobs	15.00	4.50
❑ SJ9 Bryant Johnson	15.00	4.50
❑ SJ10 Larry Johnson	20.00	6.00
❑ SJ11 Willis McGahee	30.00	9.00
❑ SJ12 Dave Ragone	15.00	4.50
❑ SJ13 Charles Rogers	20.00	6.00
❑ SJ14 Chris Simms	20.00	6.00
❑ SJ15 Musa Smith	15.00	4.50
❑ SJ16 Lee Suggs	30.00	9.00
❑ SJ17 Seneca Wallace	15.00	4.50
❑ SJ18 Kelley Washington	15.00	4.50

2004 SAGE

	Nm-Mt	Ex-Mt
COMPLETE SET (46)	30.00	9.00
STATED PRINT RUN 3200 SETS		
❑ 1 Tatum Bell	2.00	.60
❑ 2 Bernard Berrian	1.25	.35
❑ 3 Michael Boulware	1.25	.35
❑ 4 Drew Carter	1.25	.35
❑ 5 Maurice Clarett	4.00	1.20
❑ 6 Casey Clausen	1.50	.45
❑ 7 Michael Clayton	3.00	.90
❑ 8 Chris Collins	1.00	.30
❑ 9 Karlos Dansby	1.25	.35
❑ 10 Devard Darling	1.25	.35
❑ 11 Lee Evans	2.00	.60
❑ 12 Clarence Farmer	1.00	.30
❑ 13 Chris Gamble	1.50	.45
❑ 14 Jake Grove	1.00	.30
❑ 15 DeAngelo Hall	1.50	.45
❑ 16 Josh Harris	1.25	.35
❑ 17 Tommie Harris	1.50	.45
❑ 18 Devery Henderson	1.00	.30
❑ 19 Steven Jackson	4.00	1.20
❑ 20 Michael Jenkins	1.25	.35
❑ 21 Greg Jones	1.25	.35
❑ 22 Kevin Jones	4.00	1.20
❑ 23 Sean Jones	1.00	.30
❑ 24 Derrick Knight	1.00	.30
❑ 25 Craig Krenzel	1.25	.35
❑ 26 Jared Lorenzen	1.00	.30
❑ 27 Eli Manning	6.00	1.80
❑ 28 John Navarre	1.25	.35
❑ 29 Chris Perry	2.50	.75
❑ 30 Cody Pickett	1.25	.35
❑ 31 Will Poole	1.25	.35
❑ 32 Philip Rivers	4.00	1.20
❑ 33 Ell Roberson	1.25	.35
❑ 34 Dunta Robinson	1.25	.35
❑ 35 Ben Roethlisberger	10.00	3.00
❑ 36 Rod Rutherford	1.00	.30
❑ 37 P.K. Sam	1.00	.30
❑ 38 Matt Schaub	2.00	.60
❑ 39 Will Smith	1.25	.35
❑ 40 Jeff Smoker	2.00	.60
❑ 41 Ben Troupe	1.25	.35
❑ 42 Ernest Wilford	1.25	.35
❑ 43 Reggie Williams	1.50	.45
❑ 44 Roy Williams WR	4.00	1.20
❑ 45 Quincy Wilson	1.00	.30
❑ 46 Rashaun Woods	1.50	.45

2004 SAGE Autographs Red

	Nm-Mt	Ex-Mt
RED PRINT RUN 300-999		
*BRONZE: .5X TO 1.2X REDS		
BRONZE PRINT RUN 200-650		
*GOLD: .8X TO 2X REDS		
GOLD PRINT RUN 60-200		
*PLATINUM: 1.5X TO 4X REDS		
PLATINUM PRINT RUN 15-50		
UNPRICED PLAYER PROOFS #'d OF 20		
*SILVER: .6X TO 1.5X REDS		
SILVER PRINT RUN 120-400		
UNPRICED MASTER EDITION #'d OF 1		
CARDS #A12, A19, A25 NOT RELEASED		
❑ A1 Tatum Bell/500	20.00	6.00
❑ A2 Bernard Berrian/850	10.00	3.00
❑ A3 Michael Boulware/600	10.00	3.00
❑ A4 Drew Carter/700	10.00	3.00
❑ A5 Maurice Clarett/350	40.00	12.00
❑ A6 Casey Clausen/999	12.00	3.60
❑ A7 Michael Clayton/970	20.00	6.00
❑ A8 Chris Collins/300	8.00	2.40
❑ A9 Karlos Dansby/770	10.00	3.00
❑ A10 Devard Darling/550	10.00	3.00
❑ A11 Lee Evans/770	15.00	4.50
❑ A13 Chris Gamble/750	12.00	3.60
❑ A14 Jake Grove/650	8.00	2.40
❑ A15 DeAngelo Hall/470	15.00	4.50
❑ A16 Josh Harris/770	10.00	3.00
❑ A17 Tommie Harris/500	12.00	3.60
❑ A18 Devery Henderson/700	8.00	2.40
❑ A20 Michael Jenkins/850	10.00	3.00
❑ A21 Greg Jones/750	10.00	3.00
❑ A22 Kevin Jones/750	20.00	6.00
❑ A23 Sean Jones/999	8.00	2.40
❑ A24 Derrick Knight/550	8.00	2.40
❑ A26 Jared Lorenzen/800	8.00	2.40
❑ A27 Eli Manning/400	50.00	15.00
❑ A28 John Navarre/440	10.00	3.00
❑ A29 Chris Perry/750	20.00	6.00
❑ A30 Cody Pickett/600	10.00	3.00
❑ A31 Will Poole/420	10.00	3.00
❑ A32 Philip Rivers/500	25.00	7.50
❑ A33 Ell Roberson/999	10.00	3.00
❑ A34 Dunta Robinson/720	10.00	3.00
❑ A35 Ben Roethlisberger/300	80.00	24.00
❑ A36 Rod Rutherford/500	8.00	2.40
❑ A37 P.K. Sam/850	8.00	2.40
❑ A38 Matt Schaub/600	15.00	4.50
❑ A39 Will Smith/770	10.00	3.00
❑ A40 Jeff Smoker/500	15.00	4.50
❑ A41 Ben Troupe/999	10.00	3.00
❑ A42 Ernest Wilford/350	10.00	3.00
❑ A43 Reggie Williams/600	15.00	4.50
❑ A44 Roy Williams WR/350	30.00	9.00
❑ A45 Quincy Wilson/850	8.00	2.40
❑ A46 Rashaun Woods/777	15.00	4.50

2004 SAGE Jerseys Red

	Nm-Mt	Ex-Mt
RED PRINT RUN 99 SER.#'d SETS		
*BRONZE: .5X TO 1.2X REDS		
BRONZE PRINT RUN 75 SER.#'d SETS		
*GOLD: 1X TO 2.5X REDS		
GOLD PRINT RUN 25 SER.#'d SETS		
UNPRICED PLATINUM PRINT RUN 10		
*PLAYER PROOF: 1.2X TO 3X REDS		
PLAYER PROOF PRINT RUN 20 SER.#'d SETS		
*SILVER: .6X TO 1.5X REDS		
SILVER PRINT RUN 50 SER.#'d SETS		
UNPRICED MASTER EDITION #'d OF 1		
UNPRICED AUTOS PRINT RUN 10 SETS		
❑ J1 Tatum Bell	20.00	6.00
❑ J2 Maurice Clarett	30.00	9.00
❑ J3 Casey Clausen	15.00	4.50
❑ J4 Lee Evans	20.00	6.00
❑ J5 Josh Harris	12.00	3.60
❑ J6 Devery Henderson	10.00	3.00
❑ J7 Michael Jenkins	12.00	3.60
❑ J8 Greg Jones	12.00	3.60
❑ J9 Kevin Jones	25.00	7.50
❑ J10 Jared Lorenzen	10.00	3.00
❑ J11 Eli Manning	40.00	12.00
❑ J12 John Navarre	12.00	3.60
❑ J13 Chris Perry	20.00	6.00
❑ J14 Cody Pickett	12.00	3.60
❑ J15 Philip Rivers	25.00	7.50
❑ J16 Ell Roberson	12.00	3.60
❑ J17 Ben Roethlisberger	60.00	18.00
❑ J18 Rod Rutherford	10.00	3.00
❑ J19 Matt Schaub	20.00	6.00
❑ J20 Jeff Smoker	20.00	6.00
❑ J21 Reggie Williams	15.00	4.50
❑ J22 Roy Williams WR	30.00	9.00
❑ J23 Quincy Wilson	10.00	3.00
❑ J24 Rashaun Woods	15.00	4.50

2000 SAGE HIT

	Nm-Mt	Ex-Mt
COMPLETE SET (50)	25.00	11.00
❑ 1 Jerry Porter	1.00	.45
❑ 2 Tim Couch	.75	.35
❑ 3 Chris Samuels	.60	.25
❑ 4 Plaxico Burress	1.50	.70
❑ 5 Michael Wiley	.60	.25
❑ 6 Thomas Jones	1.25	.55
❑ 7 Chris Redman	.60	.25
❑ 8 Anthony Lucas	.40	.18
❑ 9 Kwame Cavil	.40	.18
❑ 10 Chad Pennington	3.00	1.35
❑ 11 LaVar Arrington	4.00	1.80
❑ 12 Giovanni Carmazzi	.60	.25
❑ 13 Tim Rattay	1.50	.70
❑ 14 Laveranues Coles	1.00	.45
❑ 15 Mario Edwards	.60	.25
❑ 16 John Engelberger	.60	.25
❑ 17 Tee Martin	.75	.35
❑ 18 R.Jay Soward	.60	.25
❑ 19 Ahmed Plummer	.75	.35
❑ 20 Na'il Diggs	.60	.25
❑ 21 J.R. Redmond	.60	.25
❑ 22 Dez White	.75	.35
❑ 23 Reuben Droughns	1.00	.45
❑ 24 Sylvester Morris	.60	.25
❑ 25 Cosey Coleman	.40	.18

❑ 26 Corey Moore	.40	.18
❑ 27 Curtis Keaton	.60	.25
❑ 28 Danny Farmer	.60	.25
❑ 29 Travis Claridge	.40	.18
❑ 30 Troy Walters	.75	.35
❑ 31 Jamal Lewis	1.50	.70
❑ 32 Shaun King	.40	.18
❑ 33 Ron Dayne	.75	.35
❑ 34 Keith Bulluck	.75	.35
❑ 35 Corey Simon	1.00	.45
❑ 36 Deon Dyer	.60	.25
❑ 37 Shaun Alexander	2.50	1.10
❑ 38 Shyrone Stith	.60	.25
❑ 39 Shaun Ellis	.75	.35
❑ 40 Todd Pinkston	.75	.35
❑ 41 Travis Prentice	.60	.25
❑ 42 Chris Hovan	.60	.25
❑ 43 Brandon Short	.60	.25
❑ 44 Brian Urlacher	3.00	1.35
❑ 45 Rob Morris	.75	.35
❑ 46 Raynoch Thompson	.60	.25
❑ 47 Deon Grant	.60	.25
❑ 48 Stockar McDougle	.40	.18
❑ 49 Darren Howard	.60	.25
❑ 50 Courtney Brown	1.00	.45

2000 SAGE HIT Autographs Emerald

	Nm-Mt	Ex-Mt
COMPLETE SET (49)	600.00	275.00

*EMERALD DIE CUTS: .6X TO 1.5X EMERALDS
*DIAMOND CARDS: .5X TO 1.2X EMERALDS
*DIAMOND DIE CUTS: 1X TO 2.5X EMERALDS

❑ 1 Jerry Porter	12.00	5.50
❑ 2 Tim Couch	12.00	5.50
❑ 3 Chris Samuels	8.00	3.60
❑ 4 Plaxico Burress	25.00	11.00
❑ 5 Michael Wiley	8.00	3.60
❑ 6 Thomas Jones	15.00	6.75
❑ 7 Chris Redman	8.00	3.60
❑ 8 Anthony Lucas	5.00	2.20
❑ 9 Kwame Cavil	5.00	2.20
❑ 10 Chad Pennington	40.00	18.00
❑ 11 LaVar Arrington	60.00	27.00
❑ 12 Giovanni Carmazzi	8.00	3.60
❑ 13 Tim Rattay	25.00	11.00
❑ 14 Laveranues Coles	12.00	5.50
❑ 15 Mario Edwards	8.00	3.60
❑ 16 John Engelberger	8.00	3.60
❑ 17 Tee Martin	10.00	4.50
❑ 18 R.Jay Soward	8.00	3.60
❑ 19 Ahmed Plummer	10.00	4.50
❑ 20 Na'il Diggs	8.00	3.60
❑ 21 J.R. Redmond	8.00	3.60
❑ 22 Dez White	10.00	4.50
❑ 23 Reuben Droughns	15.00	6.75
❑ 24 Sylvester Morris	8.00	3.60
❑ 25 Cosey Coleman	8.00	3.60
❑ 26 Corey Moore	5.00	2.20
❑ 27 Curtis Keaton	10.00	4.50
❑ 28 Danny Farmer	8.00	3.60
❑ 29 Travis Claridge	5.00	2.20
❑ 30 Troy Walters	10.00	4.50
❑ 31 Jamal Lewis	30.00	13.50
❑ 32 Shaun King	5.00	2.20
❑ 33 Ron Dayne	20.00	9.00
❑ 35 Corey Simon	12.00	5.50
❑ 36 Deon Dyer	8.00	3.60
❑ 37 Shaun Alexander	30.00	13.50
❑ 38 Shyrone Stith	8.00	3.60
❑ 39 Shaun Ellis	10.00	4.50
❑ 40 Todd Pinkston	10.00	4.50
❑ 41 Travis Prentice	8.00	3.60
❑ 42 Chris Hovan	8.00	3.60
❑ 43 Brandon Short	10.00	4.50
❑ 44 Brian Urlacher	40.00	18.00
❑ 45 Rob Morris	10.00	4.50
❑ 46 Raynoch Thompson	8.00	3.60
❑ 47 Deon Grant	8.00	3.60
❑ 48 Stockar McDougle	5.00	2.20
❑ 49 Darren Howard	8.00	3.60
❑ 50 Courtney Brown	25.00	11.00

2001 SAGE HIT

	Nm-Mt	Ex-Mt
COMPLETE SET (50)	25.00	11.00
❑ 1 David Terrell	.75	.35
❑ 2 Jamar Fletcher	.60	.25
❑ 3 Koren Robinson	1.25	.55
❑ 4 Ken-Yon Rambo	.60	.25
❑ 5 LaDainian Tomlinson	3.00	1.35
❑ 6 Santana Moss	1.50	.70
❑ 7 Michael Vick	6.00	2.70
❑ 8 Steve Hutchinson	.60	.25
❑ 9 Robert Ferguson	.75	.35
❑ 10 Torrance Marshall	.75	.35
❑ 11 Scotty Anderson	.75	.35
❑ 12 Derrick Gibson	.60	.25
❑ 13 Marcus Stroud	.75	.35
❑ 14 Josh Heupel	.75	.35
❑ 15 Drew Brees	1.50	.70
❑ 16 Gerard Warren	.75	.35
❑ 17 Quincy Carter	.75	.35
❑ 18 Gary Baxter	.60	.25
❑ 19 Alex Bannister	.60	.25
❑ 20 Travis Henry	1.25	.55
❑ 21 Andre Dyson	.40	.18
❑ 22 Deuce McAllister	2.00	.90
❑ 23 Rod Gardner	.75	.35
❑ 24 Jamie Winborn	.60	.25
❑ 25 Will Allen	.60	.25
❑ 26 Kenyatta Walker	.40	.18
❑ 27 Tim Hasselbeck	.75	.35
❑ 28 Alge Crumpler	1.00	.45
❑ 29 Michael Bennett	1.50	.70
❑ 30 LaMont Jordan	1.00	.45
❑ 31 Jeff Backus	.60	.25
❑ 32 Rudi Johnson	1.50	.70
❑ 33 Willie Howard	.60	.25
❑ 34 Josh Booty	.75	.35
❑ 35 Todd Heap	.75	.35
❑ 36 Correll Buckhalter	1.25	.55
❑ 37 Jesse Palmer	.75	.35
❑ 38 Carlos Polk	.40	.18
❑ 39 Richard Seymour	.75	.35
❑ 40 Adam Archuleta	.75	.35
❑ 41 James Jackson	.75	.35
❑ 42 Willie Middlebrooks	.60	.25
❑ 43 Ja'Mar Toombs	.60	.25
❑ 44 Chris Chambers	1.25	.55
❑ 45 Reggie Germany	.60	.25
❑ 46 Casey Hampton	.60	.25
❑ 47 Reggie Wayne	1.50	.70
❑ 48 Jamal Reynolds	.75	.35
❑ 49 Justin Smith	.75	.35
❑ 50 Quincy Morgan	.75	.35

2001 SAGE HIT Autographs

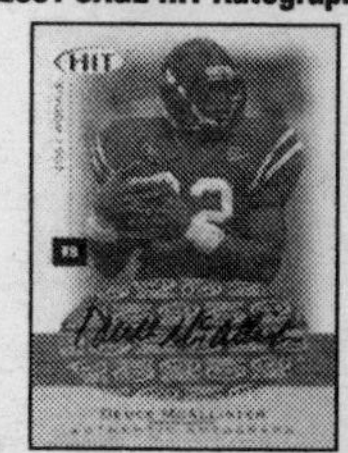

Nm-Mt Ex-Mt

*DIE CUTS: .6X TO 1.5X BASIC INSERTS
DIE CUT PRINT RUN 250 SER.#'d SETS
DIE CUT STATED ODDS 1:26
*FOILBOARD: .5X TO 1.2X BASIC INSERTS
FOILBOARD STATED ODDS 1:13
*FOILBOARD DCs: 1X TO 2.5X BASIC INSERTS
FOILBOARD DC PRINT RUN 100 #'d SETS
FOILBOARD DIE CUT STATED ODDS 1:64

	Nm-Mt	Ex-Mt
❑ A1 David Terrell	15.00	6.75
❑ A3 Koren Robinson	15.00	6.75
❑ A4 Ken-Yon Rambo	10.00	4.50
❑ A5 LaDainian Tomlinson	30.00	13.50
❑ A6 Santana Moss	20.00	9.00
❑ A7 Michael Vick	60.00	27.00
❑ A8 Steve Hutchinson	8.00	3.60
❑ A9 Robert Ferguson	12.00	5.50
❑ A10 Torrance Marshall	15.00	6.75
❑ A11 Scotty Anderson	8.00	3.60
❑ A12 Derrick Gibson	12.00	5.50
❑ A13 Marcus Stroud	8.00	3.60
❑ A14 Josh Heupel	12.00	5.50
❑ A15 Drew Brees	20.00	9.00
❑ A17 Quincy Carter	12.00	5.50
❑ A18 Gary Baxter	8.00	3.60
❑ A19 Alex Bannister	10.00	4.50
❑ A20 Travis Henry	15.00	6.75
❑ A21 Andre Dyson	8.00	3.60
❑ A22 Deuce McAllister	20.00	9.00
❑ A23 Rod Gardner	12.00	5.50
❑ A24 Jamie Winborn	8.00	3.60
❑ A25 Will Allen	10.00	4.50
❑ A26 Kenyatta Walker	8.00	3.60
❑ A27 Tim Hasselbeck	12.00	5.50
❑ A28 Alge Crumpler	15.00	6.75
❑ A29 Michael Bennett	15.00	6.75
❑ A30 LaMont Jordan	15.00	6.75
❑ A31 Jeff Backus	8.00	3.60
❑ A32 Rudi Johnson	20.00	9.00
❑ A33 Willie Howard	8.00	3.60
❑ A34 Josh Booty	12.00	5.50
❑ A35 Todd Heap	12.00	5.50
❑ A36 Correll Buckhalter	15.00	6.75
❑ A37 Jesse Palmer	12.00	5.50
❑ A38 Carlos Polk	8.00	3.60
❑ A39 Richard Seymour	15.00	6.75
❑ A40 Adam Archuleta	12.00	5.50
❑ A41 James Jackson	12.00	5.50

		Nm-Mt	Ex-Mt
❑ A42	Willie Middlebrooks	8.00	3.60
❑ A43	Ja'Mar Toombs	10.00	4.50
❑ A44	Chris Chambers	15.00	6.75
❑ A45	Reggie Germany	10.00	4.50
❑ A46	Casey Hampton	10.00	4.50
❑ A47	Reggie Wayne	20.00	9.00
❑ A48	Jamal Reynolds	10.00	4.50
❑ A49	Justin Smith	12.00	5.50
❑ A50	Quincy Morgan	12.00	5.50
❑ A51	Fred Smoot	15.00	4.50

2002 SAGE HIT

		Nm-Mt	Ex-Mt
COMPLETE SET (48)		30.00	9.00
❑ 1	John Henderson	1.25	.35
❑ 2	Tim Carter	1.00	.30
❑ 3	Joey Harrington	5.00	1.50
❑ 4	Marquise Walker	1.00	.30
❑ 5	Quentin Jammer	1.25	.35
❑ 6	Rohan Davey	1.25	.35
❑ 7A	Eric Crouch QB	2.00	.60
❑ 7B	Eric Crouch RB	2.00	.60
❑ 8	David Carr	5.00	1.50
❑ 9	Maurice Morris	1.25	.35
❑ 10	Jabar Gaffney	1.25	.35
❑ 11	David Neill	1.00	.30
❑ 12	Randy Fasani	1.00	.30
❑ 13	Alex Brown	1.25	.35
❑ 14	J.T. O'Sullivan	1.00	.30
❑ 15	Kurt Kittner	1.00	.30
❑ 16	Ashley Lelie	2.50	.75
❑ 17	Reche Caldwell	1.25	.35
❑ 18	T.J. Duckett	2.50	.75
❑ 19	Chester Taylor	1.25	.35
❑ 20	Jonathan Wells	1.25	.35
❑ 21	Kelly Campbell	1.00	.30
❑ 22	Bryant McKinnie	1.00	.30
❑ 23	Lito Sheppard	1.25	.35
❑ 24	Donte Stallworth	2.50	.75
❑ 25	Josh Reed	1.25	.35
❑ 26	DeShaun Foster	1.25	.35
❑ 27	Patrick Ramsey	2.50	.75
❑ 28	Clinton Portis	5.00	1.50
❑ 29	Albert Haynesworth	1.00	.30
❑ 31	Cliff Russell	1.00	.30
❑ 32	Luke Staley	1.00	.30
❑ 33	Ron Johnson	1.00	.30
❑ 34	Travis Stephens	1.00	.30
❑ 35	Chad Hutchinson	3.00	.90
❑ 36	Lamar Gordon	1.25	.35
❑ 37	Larry Tripplett	.60	.18
❑ 38	Napoleon Harris	1.25	.35
❑ 39	Daniel Graham	1.25	.35
❑ 40	Antonio Bryant	1.25	.35
❑ 41	Javon Walker	2.50	.75
❑ 42	Brian Poli-Dixon	1.00	.30
❑ 43	Jeremy Shockey	5.00	1.50
❑ 44	Andre Davis	1.25	.35
❑ 45	Ladell Betts	1.25	.35
❑ 46	Michael Vick	2.00	.60
❑ NNO	David Carr CL	2.00	.60

2002 SAGE HIT Autographs Emerald

*SILVER AUTOS: .5X TO 1.2X BASIC AUTOS
SILVER AUTOS STATED ODDS 1:16
*GOLD AUTOS: .6X TO 1.5X BASIC AUTOS
GOLD AUTOS STATED ODDS 1:22
GOLD AUTOS PRINT RUN 250 SER.#'d SETS
*RAREFIED GOLD AU'S: 1X TO 2.5X BASIC AU'S
RAREFIED GOLD PRINT RUN 100 SER.#'d SETS

		Nm-Mt	Ex-Mt
❑ H1	John Henderson	12.00	3.60
❑ H2	Tim Carter	8.00	2.40
❑ H3	Joey Harrington	40.00	12.00
❑ H4	Marquise Walker	8.00	2.40
❑ H5	Quentin Jammer	12.00	3.60
❑ H6	Rohan Davey	12.00	3.60
❑ H7A	Eric Crouch QB	15.00	4.50
❑ H7B	Eric Crouch RB	15.00	4.50
❑ H8	David Carr	40.00	12.00
❑ H9	Maurice Morris	12.00	3.60
❑ H10	Jabar Gaffney	12.00	3.60
❑ H11	David Neill	8.00	2.40
❑ H12	Randy Fasani	8.00	2.40
❑ H14	J.T. O'Sullivan	8.00	2.40
❑ H15	Kurt Kittner	8.00	2.40
❑ H16	Ashley Lelie	20.00	6.00
❑ H17	Reche Caldwell	12.00	3.60
❑ H18	T.J. Duckett	20.00	6.00
❑ H19	Chester Taylor	12.00	3.60
❑ H20	Jonathan Wells	12.00	3.60
❑ H21	Kelly Campbell	8.00	2.40
❑ H22	Bryant McKinnie	12.00	3.60
❑ H23	Lito Sheppard	12.00	3.60
❑ H25	Josh Reed	12.00	3.60
❑ H26	DeShaun Foster	12.00	3.60
❑ H27	Patrick Ramsey	20.00	6.00
❑ H28	Clinton Portis	30.00	9.00
❑ H29	Albert Haynesworth	12.00	3.60
❑ H30	Ronald Curry	12.00	3.60
❑ H31	Cliff Russell	8.00	2.40
❑ H32	Luke Staley	8.00	2.40
❑ H33	Ron Johnson	8.00	2.40
❑ H34	Travis Stephens	8.00	2.40
❑ H35	Chad Hutchinson	30.00	9.00
❑ H36	Lamar Gordon	12.00	3.60
❑ H37	Larry Tripplett	6.00	1.80
❑ H38	Napoleon Harris	12.00	3.60
❑ H39	Daniel Graham	12.00	3.60
❑ H40	Antonio Bryant	12.00	3.60
❑ H41	Javon Walker	15.00	4.50
❑ H42	Brian Poli-Dixon	8.00	2.40
❑ H43	Jeremy Shockey	30.00	9.00
❑ H44	Andre Davis	12.00	3.60
❑ H45	Ladell Betts	12.00	3.60

2003 SAGE HIT

		Nm-Mt	Ex-Mt
COMPLETE SET (48)		25.00	7.50
❑ 1	Charles Rogers	1.25	.35
❑ 2	Willis McGahee	2.50	.75
❑ 3	Arnaz Battle	1.00	.30
❑ 4	Terence Newman	2.00	.60
❑ 5	Larry Johnson	1.50	.45
❑ 6	Taylor Jacobs	1.00	.30
❑ 7	Kyle Boller	2.50	.75
❑ 8	Rex Grossman	2.50	.75
❑ 9	Jerome McDougle	1.00	.30
❑ 10	Jason Witten	1.50	.45
❑ 11	Ken Dorsey	1.50	.45
❑ 12	Justin Gage	1.00	.30
❑ 13	Andy Groom	.75	.23
❑ 14	Seneca Wallace	1.00	.30
❑ 15	Dave Ragone	1.00	.30
❑ 16	Kliff Kingsbury	.75	.23
❑ 17	Jason Gesser	1.00	.30
❑ 18	George Wrighster	.75	.23
❑ 19	Ronald Bellamy	.75	.23
❑ 20	Donnie Nickey	.75	.23
❑ 21	Billy McMullen	.75	.23
❑ 22	Lee Suggs	2.00	.60
❑ 23	Chris Brown	2.00	.60
❑ 24	Bryant Johnson	1.00	.30
❑ 25	Justin Fargas	1.00	.30
❑ 26	Brandon Lloyd	1.25	.35
❑ 27	Tyrone Calico	1.25	.35
❑ 28	Sam Aiken	.75	.23
❑ 29	Cie Grant	1.00	.30
❑ 30	Dahrran Diedrick	1.00	.30
❑ 31	Kelley Washington	1.00	.30
❑ 32	Musa Smith	1.00	.30
❑ 33	Kevin Curtis	1.00	.30
❑ 34	Terry Pierce	.75	.23
❑ 35	Matt Wilhelm	1.00	.30
❑ 36	Rashean Mathis	.75	.23
❑ 37	Brad Banks	.75	.23
❑ 38	Tully Banta-Cain	.75	.23
❑ 39	Sammy Davis	1.00	.30
❑ 40	Teyo Johnson	1.00	.30
❑ 41	Chris Simms	2.00	.60
❑ 42	E.J. Henderson	1.00	.30
❑ 43	Terrell Suggs	1.50	.45
❑ 44	Dallas Clark	1.00	.30
❑ 45	Marcus Trufant	1.00	.30
❑ 46	Boss Bailey	1.25	.35
❑ 47	David Carr	1.50	.45
❑ NNO	Charles Rogers CL	1.00	.30

2003 SAGE HIT Autographs Emerald

*GOLDS: .6X TO 1.5X EMERALD AUTOS
GOLD PRINT RUN 250 SER.#'d SETS
GOLD STATED ODDS 1:25
*SILVERS: .5X TO 1.2X EMERALD AUTOS
SILVER STATED ODDS 1:9

		Nm-Mt	Ex-Mt
❑ A1	Charles Rogers	12.00	3.60
❑ A2	Willis McGahee	25.00	7.50
❑ A3	Arnaz Battle	10.00	3.00
❑ A4	Terence Newman	20.00	6.00

❑ A5 Larry Johnson	20.00	6.00
❑ A6 Taylor Jacobs	10.00	3.00
❑ A7 Kyle Boller	25.00	7.50
❑ A8 Rex Grossman	25.00	7.50
❑ A9 Jerome McDougle	10.00	3.00
❑ A10 Jason Witten	20.00	6.00
❑ A11 Ken Dorsey	15.00	4.50
❑ A12 Justin Gage	10.00	3.00
❑ A13 Andy Groom	8.00	2.40
❑ A14 Seneca Wallace	10.00	3.00
❑ A15 Dave Ragone	10.00	3.00
❑ A16 Kliff Kingsbury	8.00	2.40
❑ A17 Jason Gesser	12.00	3.60
❑ A18 George Wrighster	8.00	2.40
❑ A19 Ronald Bellamy	8.00	2.40
❑ A20 Donnie Nickey	8.00	2.40
❑ A21 Billy McMullen	8.00	2.40
❑ A22 Lee Suggs	20.00	6.00
❑ A23 Chris Brown	20.00	6.00
❑ A24 Bryant Johnson	10.00	3.00
❑ A25 Justin Fargas	10.00	3.00
❑ A26 Brandon Lloyd	12.00	3.60
❑ A27 Tyrone Calico	12.00	3.60
❑ A28 Sam Aiken	8.00	2.40
❑ A29 Cie Grant	12.00	3.60
❑ A30 Dahrran Diedrick	12.00	3.60
❑ A32 Musa Smith	10.00	3.00
❑ A33 Kevin Curtis	10.00	3.00
❑ A34 Terry Pierce	8.00	2.40
❑ A35 Matt Wilhelm	10.00	3.00
❑ A36 Rashean Mathis	8.00	2.40
❑ A37 Brad Banks	8.00	2.40
❑ A38 Tully Banta-Cain	8.00	2.40
❑ A39 Sammy Davis	10.00	3.00
❑ A40 Teyo Johnson	10.00	3.00
❑ A41 Chris Simms	20.00	6.00
❑ A42 E.J. Henderson	12.00	3.60
❑ A43 Terrell Suggs	15.00	4.50
❑ A44 Dallas Clark	10.00	3.00
❑ A45 Marcus Trufant	10.00	3.00
❑ A46 Boss Bailey	12.00	3.60

2003 SAGE HIT Class of 2003 Autographs

	Nm-Mt	Ex-Mt
*SINGLES: 1X TO 2.5X EMERALD AUTOS		
❑ A31 Kelley Washington	40.00	12.00
❑ A47 David Carr		

2003 SAGE HIT Jerseys

	Nm-Mt	Ex-Mt
*PREMIUM SWATCHES: 1X TO 2X		
PREM.SWATCH PRINT RUN 50 SER.#'d SETS		
PREM.SWATCH STATED ODDS 1:460		
❑ HJ1 Brad Banks	12.00	3.60
❑ HJ2 Kyle Boller	30.00	9.00
❑ HJ3 Ken Dorsey	25.00	7.50
❑ HJ4 Rex Grossman	25.00	7.50
❑ HJ5 Taylor Jacobs	15.00	4.50
❑ HJ6 Larry Johnson	20.00	6.00
❑ HJ7 Willis McGahee	25.00	7.50
❑ HJ8 Dave Ragone	15.00	4.50
❑ HJ9 Charles Rogers	20.00	6.00
❑ HJ10 Chris Simms	25.00	7.50
❑ HJ11 Lee Suggs	25.00	7.50
❑ HJ12 Kelley Washington	25.00	7.50

2003 SAGE HIT Write Stuff Autographs

	Nm-Mt	Ex-Mt
❑ WSA1 Charles Rogers	60.00	18.00
❑ WSA2 Willis McGahee	100.00	30.00
❑ WSA3 Justin Fargas	50.00	15.00
❑ WSA4 Lee Suggs	80.00	24.00
❑ WSA5 Larry Johnson	80.00	24.00
❑ WSA6 Kliff Kingsbury	50.00	15.00
❑ WSA7 Kyle Boller	100.00	30.00
❑ WSA8 Rex Grossman	120.00	36.00
❑ WSA9 Seneca Wallace	50.00	15.00
❑ WSA10 Chris Simms	100.00	30.00
❑ WSA11 Ken Dorsey	80.00	24.00
❑ WSA12 Chris Brown	100.00	30.00
❑ WSA13 Musa Smith	50.00	15.00
❑ WSA14 Brad Banks	50.00	15.00
❑ WSA15 Dave Ragone	50.00	15.00
❑ WSA16 David Carr	120.00	36.00

2004 SAGE HIT

	Nm-Mt	Ex-Mt
COMPLETE SET (46)	30.00	9.00
❑ 1 Reggie Williams	1.25	.35
❑ 2 Bernard Berrian	1.00	.30
❑ 3 Lee Evans	1.50	.45
❑ 4 Roy Williams WR	3.00	.90
❑ 5 Josh Harris	1.00	.30
❑ 6 Greg Jones	1.00	.30
❑ 7 Ben Roethlisberger	8.00	2.40
❑ 8 Drew Carter	1.00	.30
❑ 9 Devery Henderson	.75	.23
❑ 10 Eli Manning	5.00	1.50
❑ 11 Karlos Dansby	1.00	.30
❑ 12 Michael Jenkins	1.00	.30
❑ 13 Maurice Clarett	3.00	.90
❑ 14 Michael Clayton	2.50	.75
❑ 15 Casey Clausen	1.25	.35
❑ 16 John Navarre	1.00	.30
❑ 17 Philip Rivers	3.00	.90
❑ 18 Jeff Smoker	1.50	.45
❑ 19 Ernest Wilford	1.00	.30
❑ 20 Derrick Knight	.75	.23
❑ 21 Chris Gamble	1.25	.35
❑ 22 Jared Lorenzen	.75	.23
❑ 23 Chris Perry	2.00	.60
❑ 24 Rod Rutherford	.75	.23
❑ 25 Kevin Jones	3.00	.90
❑ 26 Michael Boulware	1.00	.30
❑ 27 Tatum Bell	1.50	.45
❑ 28 Will Poole	1.00	.30
❑ 29 Jake Grove	.75	.23
❑ 30 Ell Roberson	1.00	.30
❑ 31 Devard Darling	1.00	.30
❑ 32 Dunta Robinson	1.00	.30
❑ 33 Cody Pickett	1.00	.30
❑ 34 Steven Jackson	3.00	.90
❑ 35 Matt Schaub	1.50	.45
❑ 36 Sean Jones	.75	.23
❑ 37 Tommie Harris	1.25	.35
❑ 38 Chris Collins	.75	.23
❑ 39 Will Smith	1.00	.30
❑ 40 DeAngelo Hall	1.25	.35
❑ 41 Rashaun Woods	1.25	.35
❑ 42 Ben Troupe	1.00	.30
❑ 43 Quincy Wilson	.75	.23
❑ 44 P.K. Sam	.75	.23
❑ 45 Clarence Farmer	.75	.23
❑ NNO Eli Manning CL	3.00	.90
❑ EM Eli Manning SEC/30	50.00	15.00

2004 SAGE HIT Autographs Emerald

	Nm-Mt	Ex-Mt
STATED ODDS 1:10		
❑ A1 Reggie Williams	15.00	4.50
❑ A2 Bernard Berrian	12.00	3.60

	Nm-Mt	Ex-Mt
❑ A3 Lee Evans	20.00	6.00
❑ A4 Roy Williams WR SP	50.00	15.00
❑ A5 Josh Harris	12.00	3.60
❑ A6 Greg Jones	12.00	3.60
❑ A7 Ben Roethlisberger	100.00	30.00
❑ A8 Drew Carter	12.00	3.60
❑ A9 Devery Henderson	10.00	3.00
❑ A10 Eli Manning	60.00	18.00
❑ A11 Karlos Dansby	12.00	3.60
❑ A12 Michael Jenkins	12.00	3.60
❑ A13 Maurice Clarett SP	60.00	18.00
❑ A14 Michael Clayton	25.00	7.50
❑ A15 Casey Clausen	15.00	4.50
❑ A16 John Navarre	12.00	3.60
❑ A17 Philip Rivers	30.00	9.00
❑ A18 Jeff Smoker	20.00	6.00
❑ A19 Ernest Wilford	12.00	3.60
❑ A20 Derrick Knight	10.00	3.00
❑ A21 Chris Gamble	15.00	4.50
❑ A22 Jared Lorenzen	10.00	3.00
❑ A23 Chris Perry	25.00	7.50
❑ A24 Rod Rutherford	10.00	3.00
❑ A25 Kevin Jones	30.00	9.00
❑ A26 Michael Boulware	12.00	3.60
❑ A27 Tatum Bell	20.00	6.00
❑ A28 Will Poole	12.00	3.60
❑ A29 Jake Grove	8.00	2.40
❑ A30 Ell Roberson SP		
❑ A31 Devard Darling	12.00	3.60
❑ A32 Dunta Robinson	12.00	3.60
❑ A33 Cody Pickett	12.00	3.60
❑ A35 Matt Schaub	20.00	6.00
❑ A36 Sean Jones	10.00	3.00
❑ A37 Tommie Harris	20.00	6.00
❑ A38 Chris Collins	10.00	3.00
❑ A39 Will Smith	12.00	3.60
❑ A40 DeAngelo Hall	15.00	4.50
❑ A41 Rashaun Woods	15.00	4.50
❑ A42 Ben Troupe	12.00	3.60
❑ A43 Quincy Wilson	10.00	3.00
❑ A44 P.K. Sam	10.00	3.00
❑ A46 Craig Krenzel SP		
❑ A47 Rex Grossman	20.00	6.00

2004 SAGE HIT Autographs Gold

*GOLD: .6X TO 1.5X EMERALD AUTOS
GOLD STATED ODDS 1:30
GOLD PRINT RUN 250 SER.#'d SETS

	Nm-Mt	Ex-Mt
❑ A30 Ell Roberson SP	25.00	7.50

2004 SAGE HIT Autographs Silver

*SILVERS: .5X TO 1.2X EMERALD AUTOS
SILVER AUTOGRAPH STATED ODDS 1:18

	Nm-Mt	Ex-Mt
❑ A30 Ell Roberson SP		
❑ A46 Craig Krenzel SP	40.00	12.00

2004 SAGE HIT Inside the Numbers

	Nm-Mt	Ex-Mt
❑ 1 Pittsburgh Wide Receiver (Larry Fitzgerald)	3.00	.90
❑ 2 USC Wide Receiver (Mike Williams)	5.00	1.50
❑ 3 Mississippi Quarterback (Eli Manning)	6.00	1.80
❑ 4 USC Quarterback (Matt Leinart)	6.00	1.80
❑ 5 Ohio St. Running Back (Maurice Clarett)	3.00	.90
❑ 6 Oklahoma Quarterback (Jason White)	5.00	1.50
❑ 7 Auburn Running Back (Carnell Williams)	4.00	1.20
❑ 8 Texas Running Back (Cedric Benson)	4.00	1.20
❑ 9 Kansas St. Running Back (Darren Sproles)	3.00	.90

2004 SAGE HIT Jerseys

STATED ODDS 1:31
*PREM.SWATCH: 1X TO 2.5X BASIC INSERTS
PREMUIM SWATCH PRINT RUN 50 SETS

	Nm-Mt	Ex-Mt
❑ JBR Ben Roethlisberger	50.00	15.00
❑ JCC Casey Clausen	15.00	4.50
❑ JCP Chris Perry	20.00	6.00

❑ JEM Eli Manning	30.00	9.00
❑ JER Ell Roberson	12.00	3.60
❑ JGJ Greg Jones	12.00	3.60
❑ JJL Jared Lorenzen	12.00	3.60
❑ JJN John Navarre	12.00	3.60
❑ JKJ Kevin Jones	25.00	7.50
❑ JLE Lee Evans	20.00	6.00
❑ JMC Maurice Clarett	30.00	9.00
❑ JMJ Michael Jenkins	12.00	3.60
❑ JPR Philip Rivers	25.00	7.50
❑ JRE Reggie Williams	15.00	4.50
❑ JRO Roy Williams WR	30.00	9.00
❑ JRW Rashaun Woods	15.00	4.50
❑ JTB Tatum Bell	20.00	6.00

2004 SAGE HIT Ohio State Autographs

INSERTS IN SPECIAL OHIO STATE BOXES
STATED PRINT RUN 50 SER.#'d SETS

	Nm-Mt	Ex-Mt
❑ OA1 Drew Carter	40.00	12.00
❑ OA2 Maurice Clarett	100.00	30.00
❑ OA3 Chris Gamble	40.00	12.00
❑ OA4 Michael Jenkins	50.00	15.00
❑ OA5 Craig Krenzel	50.00	15.00
❑ OA6 Will Smith	40.00	12.00

2004 SAGE HIT Q&A Autographs

	Nm-Mt	Ex-Mt
STATED ODDS 1:70		
STATED PRINT RUN 100 SER.#'d SETS		
CARDS QA34 AND QA45 NOT ISSUED		
❑ QA1 Reggie Williams	30.00	9.00
❑ QA2 Bernard Berrian	25.00	7.50
❑ QA3 Lee Evans	40.00	12.00
❑ QA4 Roy Williams WR	80.00	24.00
❑ QA5 Josh Harris	25.00	7.50
❑ QA6 Greg Jones	25.00	7.50
❑ QA7 Ben Roethlisberger	150.00	45.00
❑ QA8 Drew Carter	25.00	7.50
❑ QA9 Devery Henderson	20.00	6.00
❑ QA10 Eli Manning	120.00	36.00
❑ QA11 Karlos Dansby	25.00	7.50
❑ QA12 Michael Jenkins	25.00	7.50
❑ QA13 Maurice Clarett	60.00	18.00
❑ QA14 Michael Clayton	50.00	15.00
❑ QA15 Casey Clausen	30.00	9.00
❑ QA16 John Navarre	25.00	7.50
❑ QA17 Philip Rivers	60.00	18.00
❑ QA18 Jeff Smoker	40.00	12.00
❑ QA19 Ernest Wilford	25.00	7.50
❑ QA20 Derrick Knight	20.00	6.00
❑ QA21 Chris Gamble	30.00	9.00
❑ QA22 Jared Lorenzen	20.00	6.00
❑ QA23 Chris Perry	50.00	15.00
❑ QA24 Rod Rutherford	20.00	6.00
❑ QA25 Kevin Jones	60.00	18.00
❑ QA26 Michael Boulware	25.00	7.50
❑ QA27 Tatum Bell	40.00	12.00
❑ QA28 Will Poole	25.00	7.50
❑ QA29 Jake Grove	20.00	6.00
❑ QA30 Ell Roberson SP	25.00	7.50
❑ QA31 Devard Darling	25.00	7.50
❑ QA32 Dunta Robinson	25.00	7.50
❑ QA33 Cody Pickett	25.00	7.50
❑ QA35 Matt Schaub	40.00	12.00
❑ QA36 Sean Jones	20.00	6.00
❑ QA37 Tommie Harris	40.00	12.00
❑ QA38 Chris Collins	20.00	6.00
❑ QA39 Will Smith	25.00	7.50
❑ QA40 DeAngelo Hall	30.00	9.00
❑ QA41 Rashaun Woods	30.00	9.00
❑ QA42 Ben Troupe	25.00	7.50
❑ QA43 Quincy Wilson	20.00	6.00
❑ QA44 P.K. Sam	20.00	6.00
❑ QA46 Craig Krenzel	30.00	9.00

2004 SAGE HIT Q&A Emerald

	Nm-Mt	Ex-Mt
COMPLETE SET (46)	50.00	15.00
STATED ODDS 1:2		
*SILVERS: .5X TO 1.2X EMERALDS		
SILVER STATED ODDS 1:5		
❑ Q1 Reggie Williams	1.50	.45
❑ Q2 Bernard Berrian	1.25	.35
❑ Q3 Lee Evans	2.00	.60
❑ Q4 Roy Williams WR	4.00	1.20
❑ Q5 Josh Harris	1.25	.35
❑ Q6 Greg Jones	1.25	.35
❑ Q7 Ben Roethlisberger	10.00	3.00
❑ Q8 Drew Carter	1.25	.35
❑ Q9 Devery Henderson	1.00	.30
❑ Q10 Eli Manning	6.00	1.80
❑ Q11 Karlos Dansby	1.25	.35
❑ Q12 Michael Jenkins	1.25	.35
❑ Q13 Maurice Clarett	4.00	1.20
❑ Q14 Michael Clayton	3.00	.90
❑ Q15 Casey Clausen	1.50	.45
❑ Q16 John Navarre	1.25	.35
❑ Q17 Philip Rivers	4.00	1.20
❑ Q18 Jeff Smoker	2.00	.60
❑ Q19 Ernest Wilford	1.25	.35
❑ Q20 Derrick Knight	1.00	.30
❑ Q21 Chris Gamble	1.50	.45
❑ Q22 Jared Lorenzen	1.00	.30
❑ Q23 Chris Perry	2.50	.75
❑ Q24 Rod Rutherford	1.00	.30
❑ Q25 Kevin Jones	4.00	1.20
❑ Q26 Michael Boulware	1.25	.35
❑ Q27 Tatum Bell	2.00	.60
❑ Q28 Will Poole	1.25	.35
❑ Q29 Jake Grove	1.00	.30
❑ Q30 Ell Roberson	1.25	.35
❑ Q31 Devard Darling	1.25	.35
❑ Q32 Dunta Robinson	1.25	.35
❑ Q33 Cody Pickett	1.25	.35
❑ Q34 Steven Jackson	4.00	1.20
❑ Q35 Matt Schaub	2.00	.60
❑ Q36 Sean Jones	1.00	.30
❑ Q37 Tommie Harris	1.50	.45
❑ Q38 Chris Collins	1.00	.30
❑ Q39 Will Smith	1.25	.35
❑ Q40 DeAngelo Hall	1.50	.45
❑ Q41 Rashaun Woods	1.50	.45
❑ Q42 Ben Troupe	1.25	.35
❑ Q43 Quincy Wilson	1.00	.30
❑ Q44 P.K. Sam	1.00	.30
❑ Q45 Clarence Farmer	1.00	.30
❑ Q46 Craig Krenzel	1.25	.35

2004 SAGE HIT SEC Autographs

	Nm-Mt	Ex-Mt
INSERTS IN SPECIAL SEC BOXES		
STATED PRINT RUN 50 SER.#'d SETS		
❑ S1 Karlos Dansby	40.00	12.00
❑ S2 Ben Troupe	40.00	12.00
❑ S3 Sean Jones	30.00	9.00
❑ S4 Michael Clayton UER (listed as Mark on front)	60.00	18.00
❑ S5 Devery Henderson	30.00	9.00
❑ S6 Jared Lorenzen	30.00	9.00
❑ S7 Chris Collins	30.00	9.00
❑ S8 Eli Manning	150.00	45.00
❑ S9 Dunta Robinson	30.00	9.00
❑ S10 Casey Clausen	40.00	12.00

2004 SAGE HIT Write Stuff

	Nm-Mt	Ex-Mt
COMPLETE SET (15)	40.00	12.00
STATED ODDS 1:15		
❑ 1 Eli Manning	10.00	3.00
❑ 2 Ben Roethlisberger	15.00	4.50
❑ 3 Philip Rivers	6.00	1.80
❑ 4 Matt Schaub	3.00	.90
❑ 5 John Navarre	2.00	.60
❑ 6 Cody Pickett	2.00	.60
❑ 7 Roy Williams WR	6.00	1.80
❑ 8 Reggie Williams	2.50	.75
❑ 9 Lee Evans	3.00	.90
❑ 10 Rashaun Woods	2.50	.75
❑ 11 Michael Clayton	5.00	1.50
❑ 12 Greg Jones	2.00	.60
❑ 13 Maurice Clarett	6.00	1.80
❑ 14 Chris Perry	4.00	1.20
❑ 15 Kevin Jones	6.00	1.80

2004 SAGE HIT Write Stuff Autographs

	Nm-Mt	Ex-Mt
STATED ODDS 1:845		
STATED PRINT RUN 25 SER.#'d SETS		
❑ WSA1 Eli Manning	200.00	60.00
❑ WSA2 Ben Roethlisberger	350.00	105.00
❑ WSA3 Philip Rivers	120.00	36.00
❑ WSA4 Matt Schaub	60.00	18.00
❑ WSA5 John Navarre	50.00	15.00
❑ WSA6 Cody Pickett	50.00	15.00
❑ WSA7 Roy Williams WR	150.00	45.00
❑ WSA8 Reggie Williams	60.00	18.00
❑ WSA9 Lee Evans	80.00	24.00
❑ WSA10 Rashaun Woods	60.00	18.00
❑ WSA11 Michael Clayton	100.00	30.00
❑ WSA12 Greg Jones	50.00	15.00
❑ WSA13 Maurice Clarett	120.00	36.00
❑ WSA14 Chris Perry	100.00	30.00
❑ WSA15 Kevin Jones	120.00	36.00

2004 SAGE Jersey Update

	Nm-Mt	Ex-Mt
PREMIUM SWATCH/10 NOT PRICED		
❑ 1 Tatum Bell	15.00	4.50
❑ 2 Maurice Clarett	25.00	7.50
❑ 3 Casey Clausen	12.00	3.60
❑ 4 Lee Evans	15.00	4.50
❑ 5 Josh Harris	10.00	3.00
❑ 6 Devery Henderson	8.00	2.40
❑ 7 Michael Jenkins	12.00	3.60
❑ 8 Greg Jones	10.00	3.00
❑ 9 Kevin Jones	20.00	6.00
❑ 10 Jared Lorenzen	8.00	2.40
❑ 11 Eli Manning	30.00	9.00
❑ 12 John Navarre	10.00	3.00
❑ 13 Chris Perry	15.00	4.50
❑ 14 Cody Pickett	12.00	3.60
❑ 15 Philip Rivers	20.00	6.00
❑ 16 Eli Roberson	10.00	3.00
❑ 17 Ben Roethlisberger	50.00	15.00
❑ 18 Rod Rutherford	8.00	2.40
❑ 19 Matt Schaub	15.00	4.50
❑ 20 Jeff Smoker	15.00	4.50
❑ 21 Reggie Williams	15.00	4.50
❑ 22 Roy Williams WR	25.00	7.50
❑ 23 Quincy Wilson	8.00	2.40
❑ 24 Rashaun Woods	12.00	3.60

2004 SAGE Jersey Update Roethlisberger

	Nm-Mt	Ex-Mt
❑ 1B Ben Roethlisberger/70	80.00	24.00
❑ 1W Ben Roethlisberger/140	60.00	18.00
❑ BR1 Ben Roethlisberger/210	50.00	15.00

2005 SAGE HIT

	Nm-Mt	Ex-Mt
COMPLETE SET (50)	25.00	7.50
❑ 1 Craphonso Thorpe	1.00	.30
❑ 2 Derrick Johnson	1.50	.45
❑ 3 Frank Gore SP	1.50	.45
❑ 4 Ciatrick Fason	1.25	.35
❑ 5 Charlie Frye	1.50	.45
❑ 6 Antrel Rolle	1.25	.35
❑ 7 Dan Orlovsky	1.25	.35
❑ 8 Aaron Rodgers	4.00	1.20
❑ 9 Mark Clayton	1.50	.45
❑ 10 Thomas Davis	1.00	.30
❑ 11 Alex Smith QB	5.00	1.50
❑ 12 Fred Gibson SP	1.50	.45
❑ 13 Maurice Clarett SP	2.50	.75
❑ 14 David Greene	1.25	.35
❑ 15 Carlos Rogers	1.25	.35
❑ 16 Andrew Walter	1.50	.45
❑ 17 Jason Campbell	2.00	.60
❑ 18 Jason White	1.50	.45
❑ 19 Matt Jones	2.50	.75
❑ 20 Marion Barber SP	1.25	.35
❑ 21 Taylor Stubblefield	.75	.23
❑ 22 Jammal Brown SP	1.25	.35
❑ 23 Ronnie Brown	3.00	.90
❑ 24 Carnell Williams	3.00	.90
❑ 25 Kay-Jay Harris	.75	.23
❑ 26 Reggie Brown	1.25	.35
❑ 27 Troy Williamson	2.00	.60
❑ 28 Anthony Davis	1.00	.30
❑ 29 Josh Davis SP	1.00	.30
❑ 30 J.J. Arrington	1.25	.35
❑ 31 Alex Smith TE	1.00	.30
❑ 32 Corey Webster SP	1.25	.35
❑ 33 Vernand Morency	1.00	.30
❑ 34 Derek Anderson	1.00	.30
❑ 35 Demarcus Ware SP	1.50	.45
❑ 36 Kyle Orton	1.50	.45
❑ 37 Brock Berlin	1.00	.30
❑ 38 Marlin Jackson	1.00	.30
❑ 39 Channing Crowder	1.00	.30
❑ 40 Roddy White	1.00	.30
❑ 41 Roscoe Parrish	1.25	.35
❑ 42 Adrian McPherson	1.25	.35
❑ 43 Brodney Pool	1.00	.30
❑ 44 T.A. McLendon	.75	.23
❑ 45 Terrence Murphy	1.00	.30
❑ 46 Chris Rix	1.00	.30
❑ 47 Ben Roethlisberger SP	4.00	1.20
❑ 48 Dante Ridgeway SP	1.00	.30
❑ 49 Justin Miller	1.00	.30
❑ 50 Jonathan Goddard SP	1.00	.30
❑ BRJ Roethlisberger MAC JSY/7		
❑ EMJ Eli Manning SEC JSY/10		
❑ PRJ Philip Rivers AAC JSY/17		
❑ ROY Roethlisberger ROY/100	20.00	6.00

2005 SAGE HIT ACC Autographs

	Nm-Mt	Ex-Mt
STATED PRINT RUN 50 SER.#'d SETS		
❑ ACC1 Philip Rivers/7		
❑ ACC2 T.A. McLendon	25.00	7.50
❑ ACC3 Frank Gore	40.00	12.00
❑ ACC4 Roscoe Parrish	40.00	12.00
❑ ACC5 Brock Berlin	30.00	9.00
❑ ACC6 Justin Miller	30.00	9.00
❑ ACC7 Chris Rix	30.00	9.00
❑ ACC8 Craphonso Thorpe	25.00	7.50
❑ ACC9 Adrian McPherson	40.00	12.00

2005 SAGE HIT Autographs Blue

	Nm-Mt	Ex-Mt
BLUE AUTO STATED ODDS 1:10		
*GOLD: .6X TO 1.5X BLUE AUTO		
*GOLD: .5X TO 1.2X BLUE SP AUTO		
GOLD PRINT RUN 250 SER.#'d SETS		
GOLD AUTO STATED ODDS 1:30		
*SILVER: .5X TO 1.2X BLUE AUTO		
*SILVER: .4X TO 1X BLUE SP AUTO		
SILVER AUTO STATED ODDS 1:18		
❑ 1 Craphonso Thorpe	10.00	3.00
❑ 2 Derrick Johnson	20.00	6.00
❑ 3 Frank Gore	15.00	4.50
❑ 4 Ciatrick Fason	15.00	4.50
❑ 5 Charlie Frye	20.00	6.00
❑ 7 Dan Orlovsky	15.00	4.50
❑ 8 Aaron Rodgers SP	60.00	18.00
❑ 9 Mark Clayton	20.00	6.00
❑ 10 Thomas Davis	12.00	3.60
❑ 11 Alex Smith QB SP	80.00	24.00
❑ 12 Fred Gibson	15.00	4.50
❑ 14 David Greene	15.00	4.50
❑ 15 Carlos Rogers	15.00	4.50
❑ 16 Andrew Walter	20.00	6.00
❑ 17 Jason Campbell	20.00	6.00
❑ 18 Jason White	20.00	6.00
❑ 19 Matt Jones	30.00	9.00
❑ 20 Marion Barber	12.00	3.60
❑ 21 Taylor Stubblefield	10.00	3.00
❑ 22 Jammal Brown	12.00	3.60
❑ 23 Ronnie Brown	30.00	9.00
❑ 24 Carnell Williams	30.00	9.00
❑ 25 Kay-Jay Harris	10.00	3.00
❑ 26 Reggie Brown	15.00	4.50
❑ 27 Troy Williamson	25.00	7.50
❑ 28 Anthony Davis	12.00	3.60
❑ 29 Josh Davis	10.00	3.00
❑ 30 J.J. Arrington	15.00	4.50
❑ 31 Alex Smith TE	12.00	3.60
❑ 32 Corey Webster	12.00	3.60
❑ 33 Vernand Morency	12.00	3.60
❑ 34 Derek Anderson SP	12.00	3.60
❑ 35 Demarcus Ware	15.00	4.50
❑ 36 Kyle Orton	20.00	6.00
❑ 37 Brock Berlin SP	12.00	3.60
❑ 38 Marlin Jackson	12.00	3.60
❑ 39 Channing Crowder	12.00	3.60
❑ 41 Roscoe Parrish	15.00	4.50
❑ 42 Adrian McPherson	15.00	4.50
❑ 43 Brodney Pool	12.00	3.60
❑ 44 T.A. McLendon	10.00	3.00
❑ 45 Terrence Murphy	12.00	3.60
❑ 46 Chris Rix SP	12.00	3.60
❑ 48 Dante Ridgeway	10.00	3.00
❑ 49 Justin Miller	12.00	3.60
❑ 50 Jonathan Goddard	10.00	3.00

2005 SAGE HIT Ben Roethlisberger

	Nm-Mt	Ex-Mt
COMPLETE SET (36)	50.00	15.00
COMMON CARD (1-36)	2.50	.75
ONE PER MAC SPECIAL PACK		

2005 SAGE HIT Jerseys

	Nm-Mt	Ex-Mt
STATED ODDS 1:31		
*PREMIUM SWATCH: 1X TO 2.5X BASIC JSY		
*PREMIUM SWATCH: .5X TO 1.2X SP JSY		
PREMIUM SWATCH STATED ODDS 1:540		
PREMIUM SWATCH PRINT RUN 50 SETS		
❑ AD Anthony Davis	12.00	3.60
❑ AM Adrian McPherson	15.00	4.50
❑ AR Aaron Rodgers	25.00	7.50
❑ AS Alex Smith QB	30.00	9.00
❑ AW Andrew Walter	12.00	3.60
❑ BR Ben Roethlisberger SP	40.00	12.00
❑ CF Ciatrick Fason	12.00	3.60
❑ CR Chris Rix	12.00	3.60
❑ CW Carnell Williams	20.00	6.00
❑ DG David Greene	15.00	4.50
❑ DO Dan Orlovsky	12.00	3.60
❑ JA J.J. Arrington	12.00	3.60
❑ JC Jason Campbell	15.00	4.50
❑ JW Jason White	15.00	4.50
❑ KO Kyle Orton	15.00	4.50
❑ MC Mark Clayton	15.00	4.50
❑ MO Maurice Clarett SP	30.00	9.00
❑ RB Ronnie Brown	20.00	6.00
❑ RP Roscoe Parrish	15.00	4.50
❑ VM Vernand Morency	12.00	3.60

2005 SAGE HIT MAC Autographs

	Nm-Mt	Ex-Mt
STATED PRINT RUN 50 SER.#'d SETS		
❑ MAC1 Ben Roethlisberger/7		
❑ MAC2 Charlie Frye	50.00	15.00
❑ MAC3 Jonathan Goddard	25.00	7.50
❑ MAC4 Josh Davis	25.00	7.50
❑ MAC5 Dante Ridgeway	25.00	7.50

2005 SAGE HIT Reflect Blue

	Nm-Mt	Ex-Mt
COMPLETE SET (55)	50.00	15.00
*REFLECT BLUE: .6X TO 1.5X BASIC CARDS		
*REFLECT BLUE: .5X TO 1.2X BASIC SP's		
*REFLECT BLUE SP's: .8X TO 2X BASIC CARDS		
OVERALL REFLECT ODDS 1:1.5		
❑ R51 Michigan RB #20 SP (Michael Hart)	6.00	1.80
❑ R52 Oklahoma RB #28 SP (Adrian Peterson)	6.00	1.80
❑ R53 Texas QB #10 UER SP (Vince Young) (Longhorns misspelled on front)	4.00	1.20
❑ R54 USC RB #5 SP (Reggie Bush)	6.00	1.80
❑ R55 USC QB #11 SP (Matt Leinart)	8.00	2.40

2005 SAGE HIT Reflect Silver

	Nm-Mt	Ex-Mt
COMPLETE SET (55)	50.00	15.00
*REFLECT SILVER: .6X TO 1.5X BASIC CARDS		
*REFLECT SILVER: .5X TO 1.2X BASIC SP's		
*REFLECT SILV.SP's: .8X TO 2X BASIC CARDS		
OVERALL REFLECT ODDS 1:1.5		
❑ R51 Michigan RB #20 SP (Michael Hart)	6.00	1.80
❑ R52 Oklahoma RB #28 SP (Adrian Peterson)	6.00	1.80
❑ R53 Texas QB #10 SP (Vince Young)	4.00	1.20
❑ R54 USC RB #5 SP (Reggie Bush)	6.00	1.80
❑ R55 USC QB #11 SP (Matt Leinart)	8.00	2.40

2005 SAGE HIT Reflect Gold Autographs

	Nm-Mt	Ex-Mt
STATED ODDS 1:70		
STATED PRINT RUN 100 SER.#'d SETS		
❑ RA1 Craphonso Thorpe	20.00	6.00
❑ RA2 Derrick Johnson	40.00	12.00
❑ RA3 Frank Gore	30.00	9.00
❑ RA4 Ciatrick Fason	30.00	9.00
❑ RA5 Charlie Frye	40.00	12.00
❑ RA7 Dan Orlovsky	30.00	9.00
❑ RA8 Aaron Rodgers	100.00	30.00
❑ RA9 Mark Clayton	40.00	12.00
❑ RA10 Thomas Davis	25.00	7.50
❑ RA11 Alex Smith QB	120.00	36.00
❑ RA12 Fred Gibson	30.00	9.00
❑ RA14 David Greene	30.00	9.00
❑ RA15 Carlos Rogers	30.00	9.00
❑ RA16 Andrew Walter	40.00	12.00
❑ RA17 Jason Campbell	40.00	12.00
❑ RA18 Jason White	40.00	12.00
❑ RA19 Matt Jones	60.00	18.00
❑ RA20 Marion Barber	25.00	7.50
❑ RA21 Taylor Stubblefield	20.00	6.00
❑ RA22 Jammal Brown	25.00	7.50
❑ RA23 Ronnie Brown	60.00	18.00
❑ RA24 Carnell Williams	60.00	18.00
❑ RA25 Kay-Jay Harris	20.00	6.00
❑ RA26 Reggie Brown	30.00	9.00
❑ RA27 Troy Williamson	50.00	15.00
❑ RA28 Anthony Davis	25.00	7.50
❑ RA29 Josh Davis	20.00	6.00
❑ RA30 J.J. Arrington	30.00	9.00
❑ RA31 Alex Smith TE	25.00	7.50
❑ RA32 Corey Webster	25.00	7.50
❑ RA33 Vernand Morency	25.00	7.50
❑ RA34 Derek Anderson	25.00	7.50
❑ RA35 Demarcus Ware	30.00	9.00
❑ RA36 Kyle Orton	40.00	12.00
❑ RA37 Brock Berlin	25.00	7.50
❑ RA38 Marlin Jackson	25.00	7.50
❑ RA39 Channing Crowder	25.00	7.50
❑ RA41 Roscoe Parrish	30.00	9.00
❑ RA42 Adrian McPherson	30.00	9.00
❑ RA43 Brodney Pool	25.00	7.50
❑ RA44 T.A. McLendon	20.00	6.00
❑ RA45 Terrence Murphy	25.00	7.50
❑ RA46 Chris Rix	25.00	7.50
❑ RA48 Dante Ridgeway	20.00	6.00
❑ RA49 Justin Miller	25.00	7.50
❑ RA50 Jonathan Goddard	20.00	6.00

2005 SAGE HIT SEC Autographs

	Nm-Mt	Ex-Mt
STATED PRINT RUN 50 SER.#'d SETS		
❑ SEC1 Eli Manning/10		
❑ SEC2 Carnell Williams	80.00	24.00
❑ SEC3 Ronnie Brown	80.00	24.00
❑ SEC4 Jason Campbell	50.00	15.00
❑ SEC5 Carlos Rogers	40.00	12.00
❑ SEC6 David Greene	40.00	12.00
❑ SEC7 Reggie Brown	40.00	12.00
❑ SEC8 Fred Gibson	40.00	12.00
❑ SEC9 Thomas Davis	30.00	9.00
❑ SEC10 Troy Williamson	60.00	18.00
❑ SEC11 Matt Jones	100.00	30.00
❑ SEC12 Corey Webster	30.00	9.00
❑ SEC13 Ciatrick Fason	40.00	12.00
❑ SEC14 Channing Crowder	30.00	9.00

2005 SAGE HIT Write Stuff

	Nm-Mt	Ex-Mt
COMPLETE SET (15)	40.00	12.00
STATED ODDS 1:15		
❑ 1 Ronnie Brown	6.00	1.80
❑ 2 Jason Campbell	4.00	1.20
❑ 3 Mark Clayton	3.00	.90
❑ 4 Ciatrick Fason	2.50	.75
❑ 5 Charlie Frye	3.00	.90
❑ 6 David Greene	2.50	.75
❑ 7 Derrick Johnson	3.00	.90
❑ 8 Dan Orlovsky	2.50	.75
❑ 9 Kyle Orton	3.00	.90
❑ 10 Aaron Rodgers	8.00	2.40
❑ 11 Alex Smith QB	10.00	3.00
❑ 12 Andrew Walter	3.00	.90
❑ 13 Jason White	3.00	.90
❑ 14 Carnell Williams	6.00	1.80
❑ 15 Troy Williamson	4.00	1.20

2005 SAGE HIT Write Stuff Autographs

	Nm-Mt	Ex-Mt
STATED ODDS 1:845		
STATED PRINT RUN 25 SER.#'d SETS		
❑ WSA1 Ronnie Brown	120.00	36.00
❑ WSA2 Jason Campbell	100.00	30.00
❑ WSA3 Mark Clayton	80.00	24.00
❑ WSA4 Ciatrick Fason	60.00	18.00
❑ WSA5 Charlie Frye	80.00	24.00
❑ WSA6 David Greene	60.00	18.00
❑ WSA7 Derrick Johnson	80.00	24.00
❑ WSA8 Dan Orlovsky	60.00	18.00
❑ WSA9 Kyle Orton	80.00	24.00
❑ WSA10 Aaron Rodgers	250.00	75.00
❑ WSA11 Alex Smith QB	300.00	90.00
❑ WSA12 Andrew Walter	80.00	24.00
❑ WSA13 Jason White	80.00	24.00
❑ WSA14 Carnell Williams	120.00	36.00
❑ WSA15 Troy Williamson	100.00	30.00

Acknowledgments

Every year we make active solicitations for expert input. We are particularly appreciative of the help (however extensive or cursory) provided for this volume. We receive many inquiries, comments, and questions regarding material within this book. In fact, each and every one is read and digested. Time constraints, however, prevent us from personally replying. But keep sharing your knowledge. Even though we cannot respond to each letter, you are making significant contributions to the hobby through your interest and comments.

The effort to continually refine and improve our books also involves a growing number of people and types of expertise on our home team. Our company boasts a substantial Sports Data Publishing team, which strengthens our ability to provide comprehensive analysis of the marketplace.

Our football analysts played a major part in compiling this year s book, traveling thousands of miles during the past year to attend sports card shows and visit card shops around the United States and Canada. The Beckett Football specialists are Brian Fleischer and Dan Hitt (Senior Manager of SDP).

Bill Sutherland s coordination of input as BFCM editor this past year helped immeasurably; Rich Klein as research analyst and primary proofer also added many hours of painstaking work.

The effort was ably assisted by the rest of the SDP Team: Clint Hall, Gabe Haro, Keith Hower, Beverly Mills, Grant Sandground (Senior Price Guide Editor), and Tim Trout.

The price-gathering and analytical talents of this fine group of hobbyists have helped make our Beckett team stronger, while making this guide and its companion monthly Price Guide more widely recognized as the hobby s most reliable and relied-upon source of pricing information.

In addition, Andrew Taylor contributed many programming improvements to make this process smoother. Also this book could not produced without the fine work of our prepress team. Under the leadership of Pete Adauto, Gean Paul Figari was responsible for the layout and general presentation of this book.